PEARSON EDUCATION SECONDARY GROUP

1 Lake Street
Upper Saddle River, NJ 07458
201-236-5401...781-455-1309
Fax: 201-236-5553...781-433-8425
E-Mail: marty.smith@phschool.com

Martha G. Smith
President
Pearson Education
Secondary Group

To the Teacher:

As a former social studies teacher, I cannot imagine a more important time to be a social studies educator.

Since the terrorist attacks on New York City and Washington, D.C., on September 11, 2001, you have served at the front line of efforts to understand the causes and effects of those momentous events. In the social studies classroom, you have helped your students understand our nation's heritage of unity and determination in times of crisis. You have had the opportunity to instill in your students the core values of democracy, free enterprise, and the rule of law. Your students have probably explored concepts of freedom and justice, through primary sources from the Declaration of Independence to the "I Have a Dream" speech, and the rights and responsibilities of citizenship, through the Constitution of the United States. They may be learning and applying critical thinking skills as well—debating, for example, the benefits and challenges of living in an open and tolerant society.

As a social studies educator, you can help your students master the fundamentals of history, geography, civics, and economics, providing a context within which to analyze current events. With your guidance, this knowledge can inform and encourage young people's participation in the democratic process.

Today more than ever, you play a crucial role in the maturing of responsible citizens. You help create tomorrow's leaders—the future defenders of America's freedoms, as defined by one President during another time of great crisis:

> "In the future days which we seek to make secure, we look forward to a world founded upon four essential human freedoms. The first is freedom of speech and expression—everywhere in the world. The second is freedom of every person to worship God in his own way—everywhere in the world. The third is freedom from want . . . everywhere in the world. The fourth is freedom from fear . . . anywhere in the world."
>
> —President Franklin Delano Roosevelt
> State of the Union Address, January 6, 1941

Sincerely,

Martha G. Smith

TEACHER'S EDITION

PRENTICE HALL

IN ASSOCIATION WITH
American Heritage®

AMERICA

PATHWAYS TO THE PRESENT

Andrew Cayton

Elisabeth Israels Perry

Linda Reed

Allan M. Winkler

Prentice
Hall

Needham, Massachusetts
Upper Saddle River, New Jersey
Glenview, Illinois

American Heritage® *American Heritage*® magazine was founded in 1954, and it quickly rose to the position it occupies today: the country's preeminent magazine of history and culture. Dedicated to presenting the past in incisive, entertaining narratives underpinned by scrupulous scholarship, American Heritage today goes to more than 300,000 subscribers and counts the country's very best writers and historians among its contributors. Its innovative use of historical illustration and its wide variety of subject matter have gained the publication scores of honors across more than forty years, among them National Magazine Awards.

Prentice Hall

ISBN 0-13-062918-9
1 2 3 4 5 6 7 8 9 10   06 05 04 03 02

Visions of America

Contents

Teacher's Edition

Student Edition

Inspire students with the rich story of America.

Survey Edition

Student Edition
Teacher's Edition

Modern American History Edition

Student Edition
Teacher's Edition

Classroom Resources

Teaching Resources
  Program Overview
  Pacing Charts
  Learning Styles Lesson Plans
  Unit Books
    Section Quizzes
    Chapter Tests
    Chapter Summaries
    American Pathways Activities
    History's Lasting Impact
    Answer Key
  American Pathways Posters (10)
  Skills for Life
  Guided Reading and Review
  Learning with Documents
  Great Debates in American History

Biography, Literature, and Comparing Primary Sources
Geography and History
Constitution Study Guide
Constitution Study Guide Teacher's Guide
Guide to the Essentials (English)
Guide to the Essentials (Spanish)
Guide to the Essentials (Teacher's Edition)
Nystrom Atlas of Our Country
Guided Reading and Review Workbook (English)
Guided Reading and Review Workbook (Spanish)
Guided Reading and Review Workbook
  Teacher's Edition (English)
Guided Reading and Review Workbook
  Teacher's Edition (Spanish)
Color Transparencies with Lesson Suggestions
  American Photos
  Fine Art
  Time Lines
  Cause-and-Effect
  The Way it Works
  American Diversity
  Political Cartoons
  Historical Maps

Section Reading Support Transparency System
Perspectives: Readings in American History
Classroom Literature Library
American History Block Scheduling Support File
American History Historical Outline Map
Brief Review in U.S. History and Government
Brief Review in U.S. History and Government Answer Key
Humanities Pack

Assessment

Prentice Hall Assessment System
  <u>Program Assessment</u>
    Chapter Tests with ExamView® Test Bank CD-ROM
    Document-Based Assessment
    Alternative Assessment Handbook
  <u>Test Prep</u>
    Diagnose and Prescribe
      Diagnostic Tests for High School
        Social Studies Skills
    Review and Reteach
      Review Book for United States History
    Practice and Assess
      Test Prep Book for United States History
      Test-taking Strategies with
        Transparencies for High School
      Test-taking Strategies Posters
ExamView® Test Bank CD-ROM

Technology

Prentice Hall Presentation Pro CD-ROM (Survey)
Prentice Hall Presentation Pro CD-ROM
  (Modern American History)
Resource Pro® CD-ROM (Survey)
Resource Pro® CD-ROM (Modern American History)
Guided Reading Audiotapes (English/Spanish)
Survey Student Edition on Audio CD
Modern American History Edition on Audio CD
Sounds of an Era Audio CD
Exploring Primary Sources in U.S. History CD-ROM
Interactive Constitution CD-ROM
Social Studies Skills Tutor CD-ROM
American Heritage® My Brush with History™
  Video Program
    Videotapes (4) with Teacher's Guide
United States History Video Collection
  Videotapes with Teacher's Guide
iText®
Companion Web site

PH Success*Net*

Program Highlights:

- In-depth, balanced content makes history accessible for all students.

- Built-in reading strategies help students master content.

- Special features and technology develop social studies skills.

- Ongoing, embedded assessment prepare students for high-stakes exit exams.

- Association with **American Heritage**® brings the excitement of the nation's premier American history magazine right into the classroom.

Teach history in exciting new ways through our exclusive association with **American Heritage**®.

American Heritage® magazine was founded in 1954, and it quickly rose to the position it occupies today: the country's preeminent magazine of history and culture. Dedicated to presenting the past in entertaining narratives underpinned by scrupulous scholarship, *American Heritage* today goes to more than 300,000 subscribers and counts the country's very best writers and historians among its contributors. We have partnered to combine the best of their content with ours so you can teach history in exciting new ways.

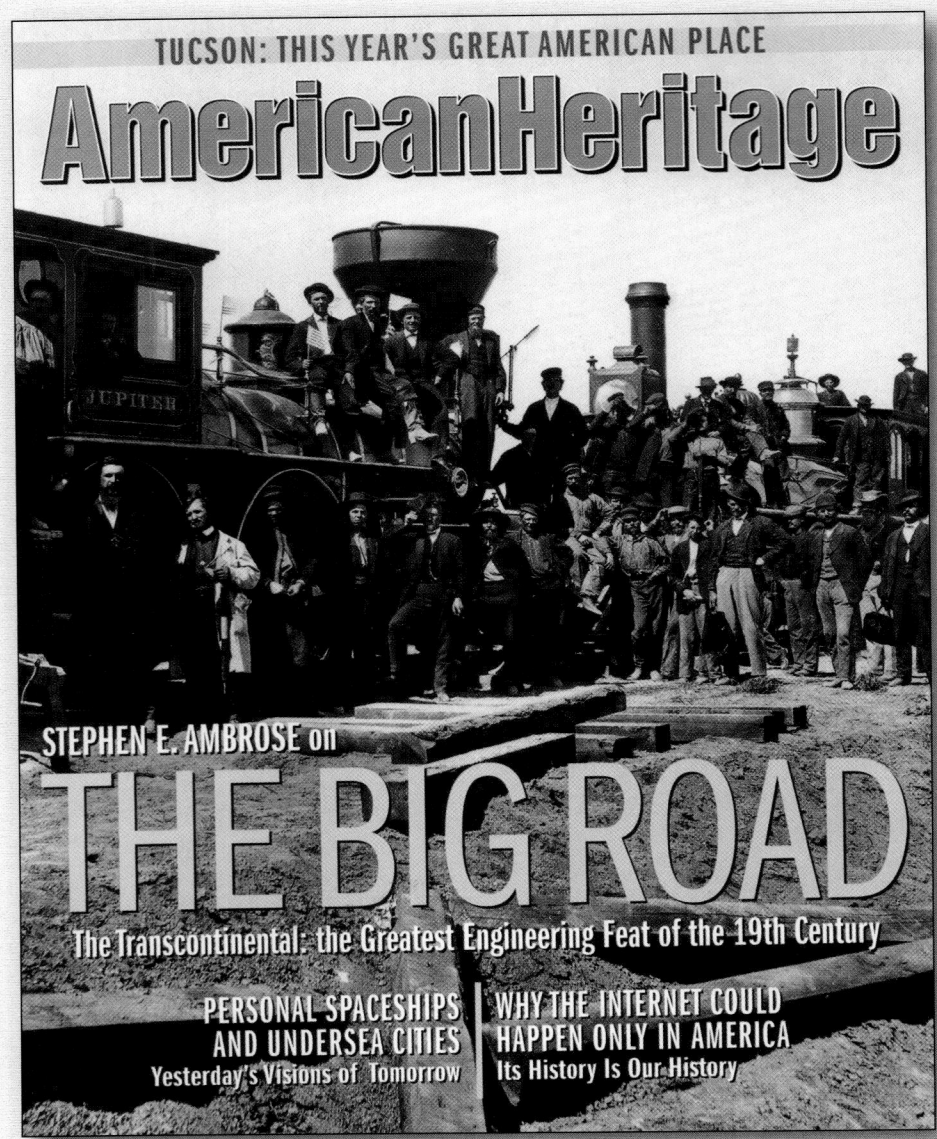

TUCSON: THIS YEAR'S GREAT AMERICAN PLACE

AmericanHeritage

STEPHEN E. AMBROSE on

THE BIG ROAD

The Transcontinental: the Greatest Engineering Feat of the 19th Century

PERSONAL SPACESHIPS AND UNDERSEA CITIES
Yesterday's Visions of Tomorrow

WHY THE INTERNET COULD HAPPEN ONLY IN AMERICA
Its History Is Our History

American Heritage magazine features compelling accounts and historical scholarship that add a whole new dimension to the way your students perceive their American history studies.

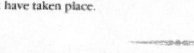

American Heritage

MY BRUSH WITH HISTORY
by DAVID CONYNGHAM

A Civil War Soldier's Story

One day soldiers from North and South are shooting at each other engaged in a life and death struggle, the next they're trading coffee and conversation. Though it sounds too strange to be true, the following eyewitness account, selected by the editors of *American Heritage* magazine, describes just such a scene. The account is written by David Conynham, an officer in the army of William T. Sherman and a journalist. As you read the following excerpt, think about why such "private truces" might have taken place.

It was no unusual thing to see our pickets and skirmishers enjoying themselves very comfortably with the rebels, drinking bad whiskey, smoking and chewing worse tobacco, and trading coffee and other little articles. The rebels had no coffee, and our men plenty, while the rebels had plenty of whiskey; so they very soon came to an understanding. It was strange to see these men, who had been just pitted in deadly conflict, trading, and bantering, and chatting, as if they were the best friends in the world. They discussed a battle with the same gusto they would a cockfight, or horse-race, and made inquiries about their friends, as to who was killed, and who not, in the friends that have been separated for years have often met in this way. Brothers who parted to try their fortune have often met on the picket line, or on the battle-field.

In those improvised truces, the best possible faith was observed by the men. These truces were brought about chiefly in the following manner. A rebel, who was heartily tired of his crippled position in his pit, would call out, "I say, Yank!"

"Well, Johnny Reb," would echo from another hole or tree.

"I'm going to put out my head; don't shoot."

"Well, I won't."

The reb would pop up his head; the Yank would do the same.

"Hain't you got any coffee, Johnny?"

"Na'r a bit, but plenty of rot-gut."

"All right; we'll have a trade."

They would meet, while several others would

402

My Brush with History™

Based on the popular *American Heritage* magazine feature, this engaging student edition feature presents eyewitness accounts of ordinary Americans and extraordinary events.

From the Archives of
American Heritage®

Ending the War to End All Wars

In 1921, three years after the end of the Great War, Americans dealt with some unfinished business from that conflict. On November 8, President Warren Harding signed a joint resolution to end the war. Then, three days later on November 11, the remains of an unknown American soldier, exhumed from a French grave, were buried in Washington, D.C. Military men from all nations paid tribute with medals, ribbons, and decorations, including a Native American who laid a coup stick and war bonnet on the bier. In a moving address, Harding asked the American people to give of their influence and strength "...to put mankind on a little higher plane, exulting and exalting, with war's distressing and depressing tragedies barred from the state of righteous civilization." Source: Frederic D. Schwarz, "The Time Machine," *American Heritage* magazine, November 1996.

READING CHECK
The Allies were vehemently opposed to some aspects of Wilson's program, and lacked enthusiasm for the Fourteen Points as a whole. Clemenceau, Lloyd George, and Orlando were determined to extract reparations and territory from the defeated nations. The Allies also defied Wilson by insisting that Germany accept guilt for starting the war.

Point-of-Use Teaching Notes

Point-of-use teaching notes from *American Heritage* magazines and books are woven throughout the Teacher's Edition to give you background information for vitalizing classroom lectures and discussions.

American Heritage®
My Brush with History™ Video Program

This brand-new video program extends the My Brush with History™ feature in the student edition. In-depth, first-person accounts, historical overviews, and interviews with well-known historians, provide a dramatic context for understanding larger events in American history.

But I'm Not a Reading Teacher!

*F*ew people choose to be social studies teachers in order to focus on reading. Yet a significant number of today's students lack reading proficiency. Without it, they cannot access the wealth of social studies content they need to absorb from textbooks, primary sources, literature, and more. When students can't read well, they don't read and won't read.

Lack of reading skills is a nationwide problem. The National Assessment of Educational Progress (NAEP) Reading Report Card in 1998 revealed that only 33 percent of eighth-grade students and 40 percent of twelfth-grade students were proficient readers, the standard that all students should reach. NAEP findings also indicated that 60 percent of twelfth-graders will not be able to function effectively in college or in the workplace of the future.

How can a social studies teacher build students' reading skills and still cover all of the content required in the curriculum? Begin by looking for reading difficulties in the classroom. Watch for these student behaviors that signal reading problems.

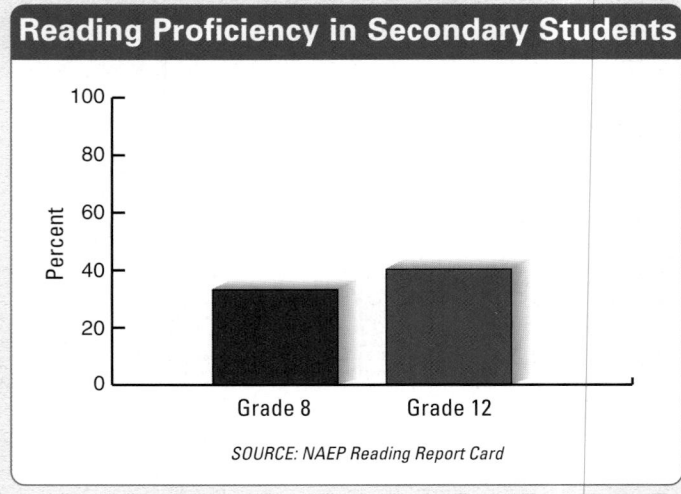

Reading Proficiency in Secondary Students

SOURCE: NAEP Reading Report Card

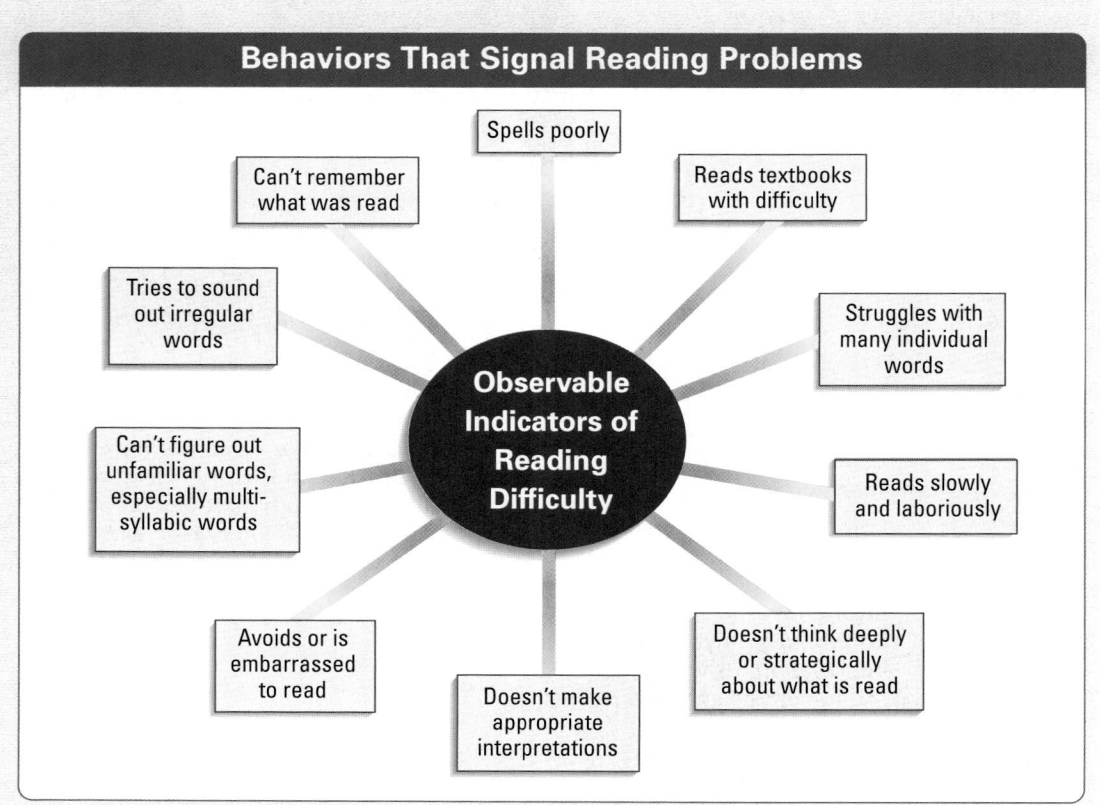

Behaviors That Signal Reading Problems

Observable Indicators of Reading Difficulty

- Spells poorly
- Can't remember what was read
- Reads textbooks with difficulty
- Tries to sound out irregular words
- Struggles with many individual words
- Can't figure out unfamiliar words, especially multi-syllabic words
- Reads slowly and laboriously
- Avoids or is embarrassed to read
- Doesn't make appropriate interpretations
- Doesn't think deeply or strategically about what is read

Best Practices in Reading

Instead of plunging in and plodding through a section, students need a plan of action, a strategy. Best practices for teaching reading in social studies focus on **comprehension strategies**—teaching students what to do *before reading, during reading,* and *after reading.*

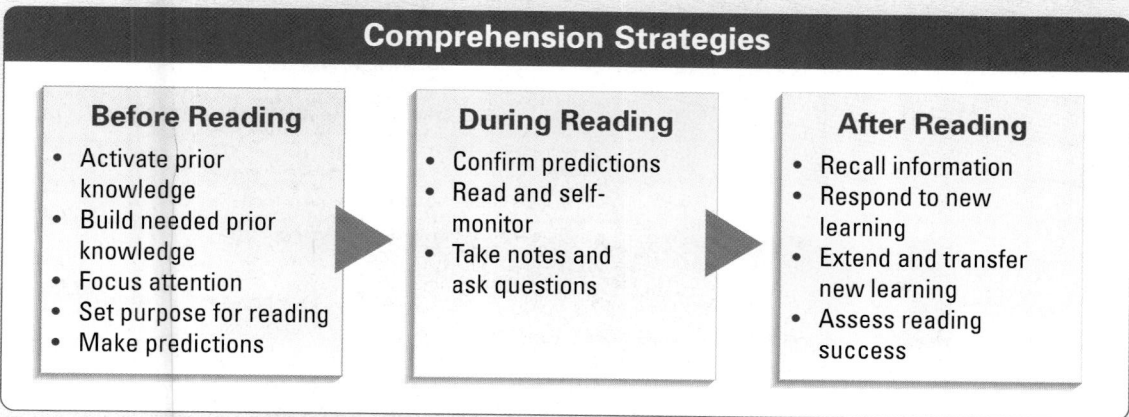

Comprehension Strategies

Before Reading
- Activate prior knowledge
- Build needed prior knowledge
- Focus attention
- Set purpose for reading
- Make predictions

During Reading
- Confirm predictions
- Read and self-monitor
- Take notes and ask questions

After Reading
- Recall information
- Respond to new learning
- Extend and transfer new learning
- Assess reading success

Here are some ways to implement these strategies with struggling readers:

Before Reading   Both teacher and student preparations precede reading.

- Use an anecdote, photo, artifact, or audio to set the scene.
- Display a map or other visual aid to encourage students to identify what they already know and to make predictions by applying this knowledge to new situations.
- Model for students how to look at pictures, captions, and headings in order to predict what they will be learning.

During Reading   Student-directed, individual activities take place during reading. Providing guided practice will help students develop these habits.

- Show students how to take notes, using graphic organizers that match the type of information they are reading. For example, use a Venn diagram for comparing and contrasting, a flowchart for sequencing, and a concept web for finding main idea and supporting details.
- Teach students to ask themselves questions as they read.
- Demonstrate for students how to make connections between what they read and what they already know.

After Reading   Both student-directed and teacher-directed activities can follow reading.

- Conduct a sample self-check for students—"What have I learned?"
- Teach students to ask themselves, "How does this relate to what I already know?"
- Demonstrate both formal and informal assessments that students will encounter.

Reading success happens when students can construct meaning from information.

Prentice Hall Reading Support in the Student Edition

The structure of each Prentice Hall program embeds the development of solid reading skills in the Student Edition. Each section of the text starts with suggestions to the student for *before reading* and *during reading*.

Notice that the *Reading Focus* questions align with the subheadings in the section.

Notice how the *READING CHECK* annotations ask students to think critically about the text.

Causes of World War I

The assassination of Archduke Francis Ferdinand ignited what was then called the Great War, later known as World War I. However, the main causes of the war existed well before 1914. Those causes included imperialism, militarism, nationalism, and a tangled system of alliances.

Imperialism A great scramble for colonies took place in the late 1800s. European powers rushed to claim the remaining uncolonized areas of the world, particularly in Africa, Asia, and the Pacific. Japan joined the roster of colonial powers when it won the Sino-Japanese War in 1895 and moved to

Section 1 **The Road to War**

READING FOCUS

- What were the main causes of World War I?
- How did the conflict expand to draw in much of Europe?
- In what ways did the United States respond to the war in Europe?

KEY TERMS

militarism
mobilization
Central Powers
Allies
stalemate
autocrat
propaganda

TAKING NOTES

As you read, complete the following cause-and-effect diagram that shows why World War I began.

CAUSES
- Assassination of Archduke Francis Ferdinand in Sarajevo
- Competition for colonies in Africa, Asia, and the Pacific

WORLD WAR I

MAIN IDEA

As World War I began and then spread to much of Europe, the United States tried to remain neutral as long as possible.

Setting the Scene On June 28, 1914, Archduke Francis Ferdinand and his wife made a state visit to Sarajevo, the capital of Bosnia. Bosnia was a new province within the Austro-Hungarian Empire, and Francis Ferdinand was heir to the empire.

READING CHECK How did competition for colonies help lead to war?

MAP SKILLS Before the war, Europe was a land of empires and alliances. When Austria-Hungary declared war on Serbia, much of the continent was drawn into the conflict. **Location** *Based on this map, which side, if any, had a geographical advantage in the war? Explain.*

Chapter 12 • Section 1 415

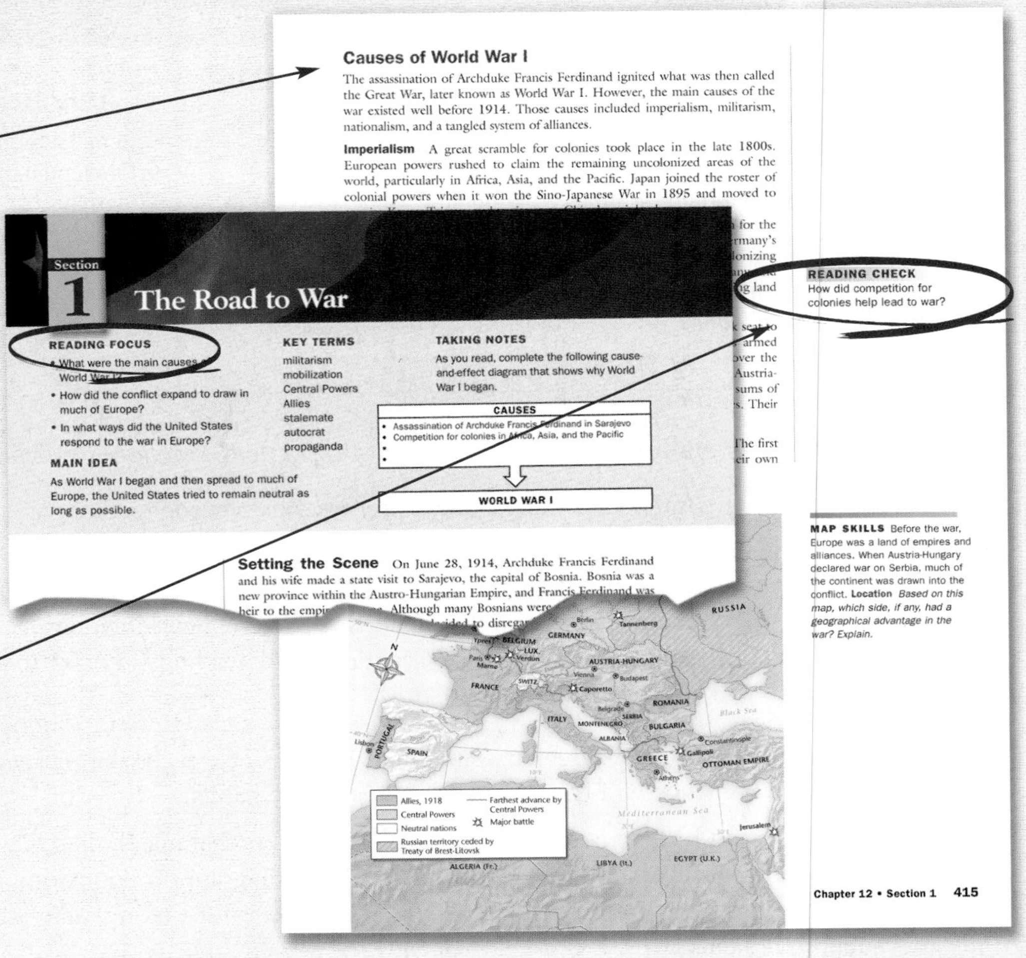

At the end of each section, students will find opportunities to recall and apply information and construct meaning from it.

Notice how the Section Assessment questions relate back to the focus questions and section subheadings.

Section 1 Assessment

READING COMPREHENSION

1. How did nationalism contribute to the start of World War I?
2. Which countries were known as the **Allies?** Which countries were known as the **Central Powers?**
3. What were two causes of the **stalemate** in the West?
4. What was the main reason that the United States stayed neutral at the start of World War I?

CRITICAL THINKING AND WRITING

5. **Checking Consistency** The alliance system in Europe was designed to maintain peace. Yet it seemed to make the conflict worse once the fighting began. Explain the apparent inconsistency.
6. **Writing to Persuade** Write an essay in which you express your support for the preparedness movement. Persuade your readers that the United States had no choice but to be ready to go to war.

Take It to the NET

Activity: Interpreting a Poem
Read a poem about World War I and write a short essay about the meaning of the poem. Discuss how the writer felt about the war. What symbols does the writer use? Use the links provided in the *America: Pathways to the Present* area of the following Web site for help in completing this activity.
www.phschool.com

Chapter 12 • Section 1 419

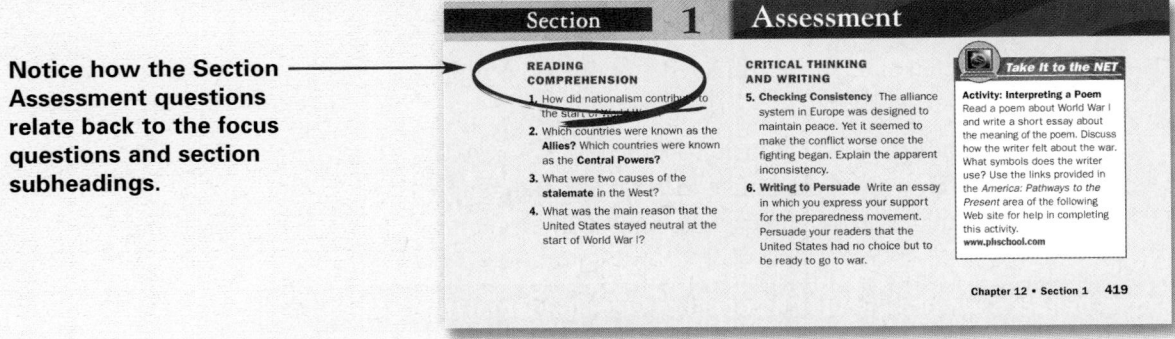

Prentice Hall Reading Support Beyond the Student Edition

Look for additional support for building reading skills in the Teacher's Edition, Teaching Resources box, and technology components.

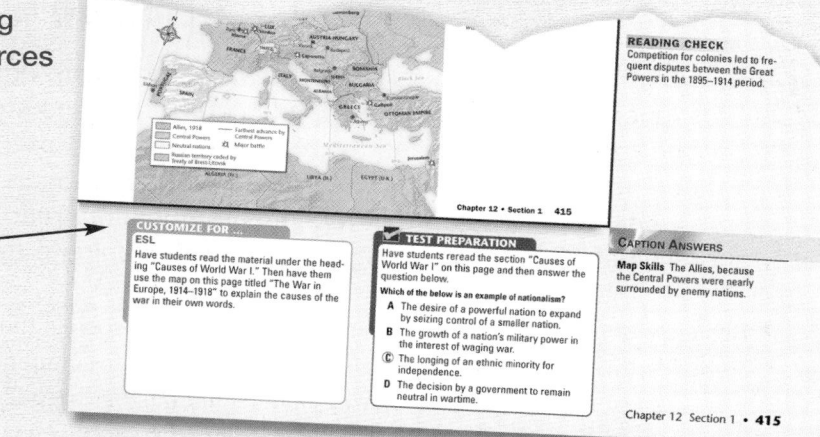

Teacher's Edition

Additional reading strategies as well as ways to customize instruction for less proficient readers and English language learners give you focused strategies to improve students' comprehension.

Section Reading Support Transparency System

Every section of the text has a companion reading support transparency that delivers the main points through a graphic organizer.

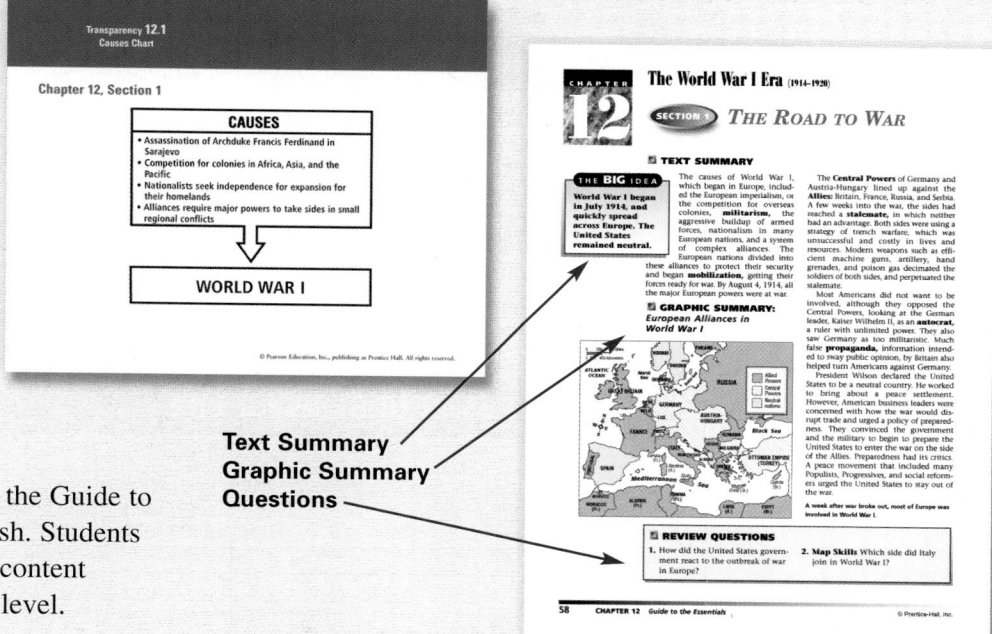

Text Summary
Graphic Summary
Questions

Guide to the Essentials

Look in the Teaching Resources box for the Guide to the Essentials in both English and Spanish. Students use this book to review and master new content through summaries written below grade level.

Student Edition on Audio

Auditory learners, less proficient readers, and English language learners can benefit from listening to the book on CD as they read the text.

Why Should I Teach Skills?

> "Give a man a fish, and he eats for a day. Teach a man to fish and he eats for a lifetime."
>
> — Anonymous

Following this advice, if we present our students with only content, we are, in essence, giving them the fish. If we are to prepare students for life, we need to teach the skills needed to make sense out of the increasing volume of information in the world. To help students become lifelong learners, we need to develop their abilities to question, read, analyze, interpret, and evaluate information, as well as to communicate their ideas to others.

Because these skills lie at the heart of understanding social studies, they need to be embedded in content instruction. Think of social studies content as having three levels: facts, concepts, and enduring understandings or "big ideas." Skills development is essential for comprehension at each level, as in this example.

Topic: Colonization		
	Example	**Skill**
Facts	Location of colonies	Map reading
Concepts	Migration	Cause and effect
Big Ideas	People make choices to meet needs	Problem-solving

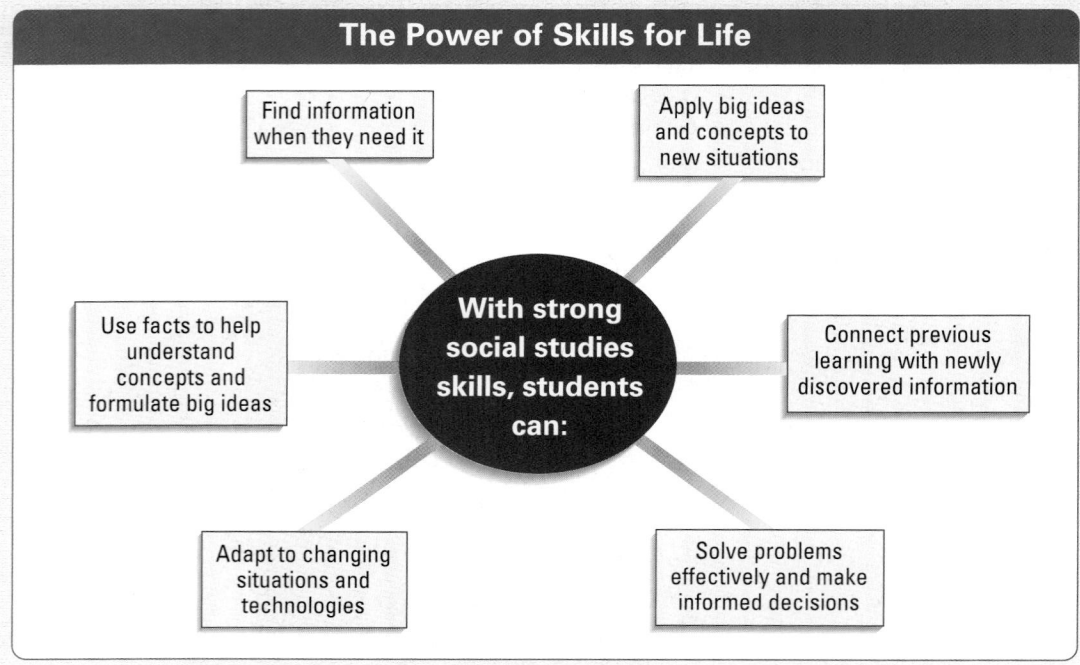

The Power of Skills for Life

With strong social studies skills, students can:
- Find information when they need it
- Apply big ideas and concepts to new situations
- Use facts to help understand concepts and formulate big ideas
- Connect previous learning with newly discovered information
- Adapt to changing situations and technologies
- Solve problems effectively and make informed decisions

Best Practices in Skills Integration

These guidelines will help you to embed skills development within content instruction.

1. **Plan each unit around an enduring understanding or big idea.** For example, if the unit you are about to teach is The Early Republic, 1789–1825, the big idea might be "new institutions face many challenges to their existence."

2. **Develop each lesson around the facts, concepts, the big idea, and the skills students need to be able to connect the content to the big idea.** For part of a lesson on foreign relations, you might want to focus on the Embargo Act and its impact.

Topic: Foreign Relations		
	Example	**Skill**
Facts	Economic impact of Embargo Act	Graph reading
Concepts	Supply and demand	Cause and effect
Big Ideas	New institutions face many challenges to their existence	Synthesizing information

3. **Teach skills that are new or that add another level of complexity to a previously mastered skill.** Follow the elements of good skill instruction:

   - Set a purpose for using the skill.
   - Present the steps to follow.
   - Model the process for using the skill.
   - Guide practice and provide feedback.
   - Apply to a prompt such as a picture, map, or reading passage.

4. **Reinforce skills whenever possible.** Ask critical thinking questions about maps, photos, graphs, charts, and primary sources.

5. **Assess both content and skills mastery regularly.** It is important to determine whether students are remembering important information, but equally important to determine whether they are internalizing skills as lifelong learners.

6. **Include skills in big projects.** Give students opportunities to combine their thinking and research abilities at least several times a year.

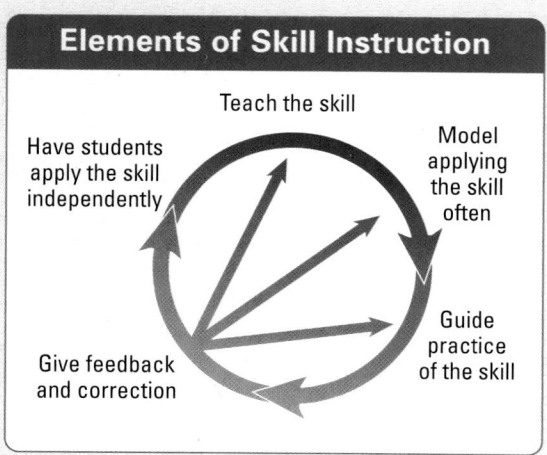

Elements of Skill Instruction

Teach the skill

Model applying the skill often

Guide practice of the skill

Give feedback and correction

Have students apply the skill independently

Prentice Hall Support for Skills

Skills mastery means developing habits of mind that enable us to turn information into meaning. To achieve mastery, students need both instruction and continuous rein-forcement— many, many opportunities to practice and apply skills in new situations. Every Prentice Hall social studies program contains a wealth of resources to build skills for life.

Skills pages in the Student Edition provide three-step instruction strategy.

Learn

Practice

Teaching suggestions accompany skills lessons and reinforcement activities.

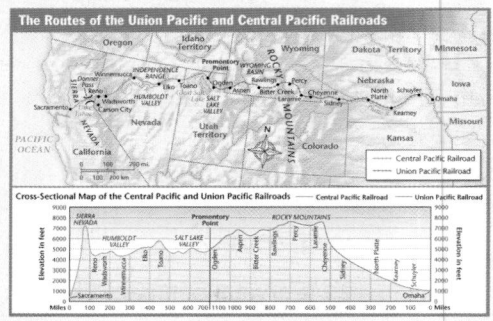

USING CROSS-SECTIONAL MAPS

Focus Students compare the data provided in a cross-sectional map with that in a physical-political map.

Instruct To be sure students understand the information presented in the cross-sectional map, ask them to identify the locations on the map at elevation 1,000 feet and 7,000 feet. Have them indicate the elevation at Bitter Creek. Ask students to think about some other useful subjects for cross-sectional maps. *(The ocean floor, rivers, and other waterways.)*

Extend See the Skills for Life activity in the Resource Directory below.

Apply

Skills reinforcement appears in all caption questions.

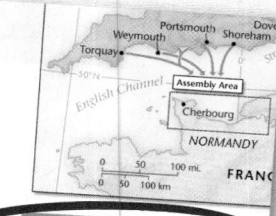

Social Studies Skills Tutor CD-ROM provides two levels of interactive instruction and practice in 20 core social studies skills.

The Prentice Hall Vertical Alignment System

Mastery also requires that students learn skills at increasing levels of complexity as they progress through school. Prentice Hall takes the guesswork out of aligning skills instruction by developing 20 core social studies skills with increasing difficulty from grade to grade in every Prentice Hall program.

Here you see how three Prentice Hall programs build and elaborate the skill of analyzing graphic data.

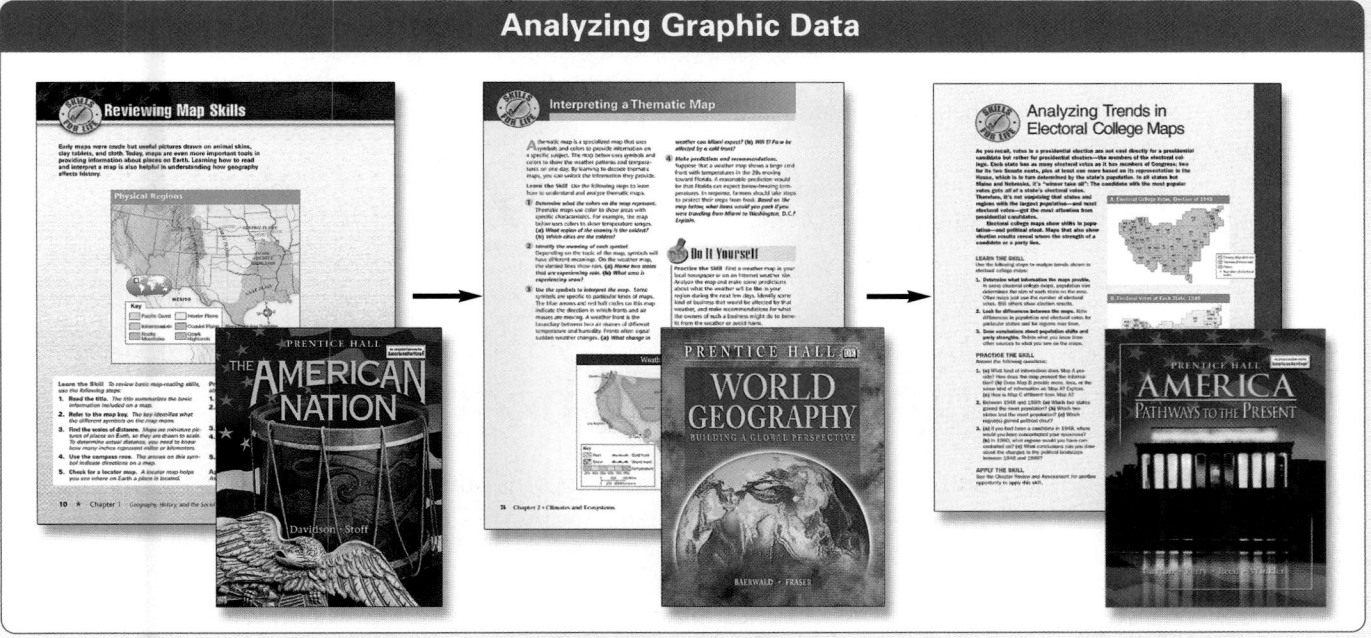

The 20 Core Social Studies Skills

1. Using the Cartographer's Tools
2. Using Special Purpose Maps
3. Analyzing Graphic Data
4. Analyzing Images
5. Identifying Main Ideas/Summarizing
6. Sequencing
7. Identifying Cause & Effect/ Making Predictions
8. Drawing Inferences and Conclusions
9. Making Valid Generalizations
10. Distinguishing Fact & Opinion

11. Comparing and Contrasting
12. Analyzing Primary Sources
13. Recognizing Bias and Propaganda
14. Identifying Frame of Reference and Point of View
15. Decision-making
16. Problem-solving
17. Using Reliable Information
18. Transferring Information from One Medium to Another
19. Synthesizing Information
20. Supporting a Position

Should I Teach to the Test?

*T*he increasing importance of state standards and student accountability leads many teachers to wonder whether they must limit their classes to the content of high-stakes exams. While based on state standards and student needs, a truly effective social studies program requires **alignment of curriculum, instruction,** and **assessment.** When each of these elements dovetails with the others, *all* instruction prepares students for assessment based on curriculum objectives.

In an aligned system, both teacher and student know what is expected. There are no secrets or surprises. To ensure alignment:

- Teach the objectives in your standards to the specified level of understanding.
- Make sure that students know what they should learn before you teach.
- Test those same objectives as precisely as possible to the same depth of understanding that the standards require.

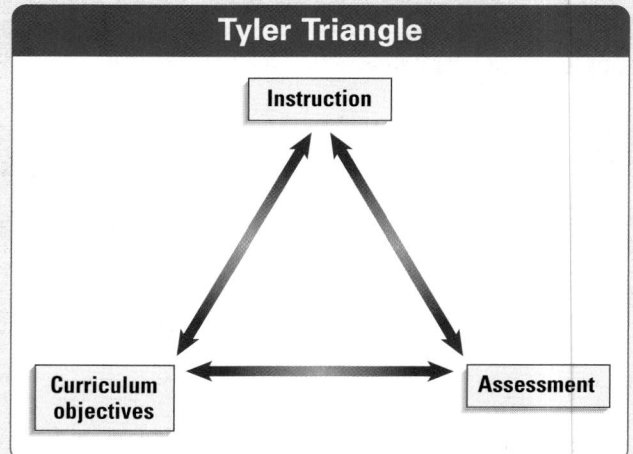

Tyler Triangle

Instruction

Curriculum objectives

Assessment

Constructing Aligned Assessments

The principle of aligning assessment questions to curriculum objectives and instruction needs to be applied for both standardized tests and teacher-created exams.

At the state level

To create assessments based on state standards, test writers dissect the objectives for the pieces of appropriate content and the thinking level required of the student. Test questions are written, reviewed, piloted, reviewed once again, and placed in testing banks.

At the classroom level

While state tests occur perhaps once a year, teachers must use an ongoing system of testing to measure student learning throughout the year. Teachers need to plan instruction and assessment simultaneously, with both of them based on the state curriculum objectives.

Best Practices in Assessment

Good assessment is part of an integrated cycle that is repeated throughout the school year. Following the principle of alignment, good assessment grows out of preparation that begins long before any test is administered and leads to improvements in teaching and learning long after the test. Here are some ways to integrate ongoing assessment into instruction:

Assessment Techniques	
Diagnose and Prescribe Evaluate student abilities at the beginning of the year.	The best way to know whether students are ready for the difficulty level you intend to use is to give a diagnostic test when school opens. Students will not know the content you are about to teach them, but they should bring with them a number of social studies skills that they will apply to new content. Evaluate student facility in these areas: • Map and globe skills • Critical thinking and reading • Graph and chart skills • Communications
Plan and Align Plan instruction to align with assessment.	• Examine objectives carefully. • Choose learning activities that require more than a knowledge level (or memorized level) from students. • Test students on all of the objectives, omitting none. Do not test information not contained in an objective. • Test skill development at the same time you assess content. • Integrate skill and content questions so that students must use what they know and combine it with new information that they gather. • Test students' understanding of the objectives on many levels of thinking.
Review and Reteach Weave ongoing review into aligned instruction and assessment.	One quick and easy way to check how much students remember from one unit to the next is to include some review questions on each of your tests. • Find ways to connect new learning to previous learning as you put your lessons together. This previous learning could come from units previously studied during the same year or from content studied in other courses. • Choose review questions that are aligned to your current lessons.
Practice and Assess Apply assessment results to improve teaching and learning.	• Use individual student information for tutoring and devising individualized plans for improvement. • Use whole-class data to determine if your teaching was aligned to the assessment. If many students missed an item, it was probably not aligned to your instruction and intent. Make changes when you teach this unit again. • Use review data on both individuals and the whole class to make a list of those objectives with which students may have difficulty on an end-of-year test.

Prentice Hall Assessment System

The Prentice Hall Assessment System provides comprehensive support for both program content assessment and preparation for high-stakes standardized tests.

Program Assessment

Use the Chapter Tests to assess core content for every chapter.

Develop your own customized tests and practice worksheets with the ExamView® Test Bank CD-ROM, selecting from hundreds of test questions and using the word-processing and editing capabilities. Create online tests and study guides and receive instant feedback on student progress.

Prepare students for document-based questions by evaluating, analyzing, and interpreting primary and secondary sources.

Use a variety of assessment options to evaluate students' performance, such as activity-based assessment or portfolio assessment.

Give students clear expectations and a means of self-assessment through a variety of rubrics, which include criteria, indicators, and standards.

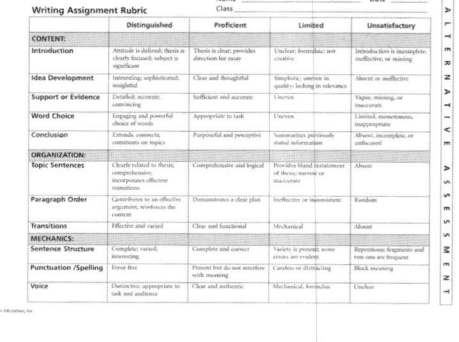

Standardized Test Preparation

Prentice Hall Assessment System gives you the tools to help your students succeed on standardized tests, from the beginning of the year to the culminating high-stakes exam.

Diagnose and Prescribe

📖 Profile student skills with Diagnostic Tests A & B.

📖 Address student needs with program resources correlated to diagnostic test questions.

Review and Reteach

📖 Provide cumulative content review with unit-level questions and study sheets.

Practice and Assess

📺 Build assessment skills using Test-Taking Strategies With Transparencies.

Reinforce assessment skills with Test-Taking Posters.

📖 Develop students' test-taking skills and improve their scores on standardized tests with the Test Preparation Workbook.

How Am I Doing?

*P*aired with the demand for high student achievement has come the drive for greater teacher accountability. More and more states and districts are establishing standards for teaching and new systems of teacher evaluation.

In the past, professional appraisals focused on teacher behaviors. Nationwide, the focus of teacher evaluation is now shifting to what students are able to do. Student success emerges as the most critical measure of teaching—the teacher has not taught if students have not learned. The goal is becoming the learner-centered class, alive with critical thinking, problem-solving activities, collaborative learning, projects, and investigations. Evaluation criteria now measure how well teachers promote this kind of learning.

Prentice Hall social studies programs provide a variety of ways to support learner-centered instruction. Below you will find a guide to program resources to help you address criteria commonly found in teacher evaluations.

Common Criteria	Where to Look for Support
Active, successful student participation in the learning process	• Structured reading support • Activities at section and chapter levels • Group and individual activities
Learner-centered instruction	• Critical-thinking questions in every caption • Strategies for different learner needs • Technology for students: Social Studies Skills Tutor CD-ROM, Interactive Constitution CD-ROM, Exploring Primary Sources in U.S. History CD-ROM, Companion Web Site
Evaluation and feedback on student progress	• Section and chapter assessments in student edition • ExamView® Test Bank CD-ROM
Classroom management of students, time, and materials	• Pacing charts • Chapter interleaf • Resource Pro® CD-ROM
Professional communications	• Letters to families • Resource Pro® lesson plans for supervisors
Improvement of student performance	• Prentice Hall Assessment System
Professional development	• eTeach • Skylight • PHSuccessNet.com

PRENTICE HALL

IN ASSOCIATION WITH
American Heritage®

AMERICA
PATHWAYS TO THE PRESENT

Andrew Cayton

Elisabeth Israels Perry

Linda Reed

Allan M. Winkler

Prentice
Hall

Needham, Massachusetts
Upper Saddle River, New Jersey
Glenview, Illinois

About the Authors

Andrew Cayton, Ph.D. Andrew Cayton is Distinguished Professor of History at Miami University in Oxford, Ohio. He received his B.A. in history from the University of Virginia and his M.A. and Ph.D. in American history from Brown University. A specialist in the history of the early republic and the Midwest, Dr. Cayton is the author of several books and articles, including *Frontier Indiana, Contact Points: American Frontiers From the Mohawk Valley to the Mississippi, The American Midwest: Essays in Regional History,* and *So Many Possibilities: A History of Ohio.* In 1999, Cayton was the John Adams Visiting Professor of American Studies at Leiden University in the Netherlands.

Elisabeth Israels Perry, Ph.D. Elisabeth Israels Perry holds the John Francis Bannon Endowed Chair in History at Saint Louis University in St. Louis, Missouri. She received her Ph.D. in history from the University of California at Los Angeles. Dr. Perry's period of specialization is the late nineteenth and early twentieth centuries. Her greatest scholarly interests are in women's political history and issues of citizenship and identity in U.S. history. She is the author of *Belle Moskowitz: Feminine Politics and the Exercise of Power in the Age of Alfred E. Smith* and *Women in Action: Rebels and Reformers, 1920–1980.* Since 1987, she has directed five NEH Summer Seminars for Secondary School Teachers.

Linda Reed, Ph.D. Linda Reed is Associate Professor of History at the University of Houston. For nine years she directed the African American Studies Program. She received her B.S. from Alabama A & M University, her M.A. from the University of Alabama, and her Ph.D. from Indiana University. Dr. Reed's specialization is twentieth-century African American history, particularly the modern-day civil rights era. She is the author of *Simple Decency and Common Sense: The Conference Movement, 1938–1963* and co-editor of *"We Specialize in the Wholly Impossible": A Reader in Black Women's History.*

Allan M. Winkler, Ph.D. Allan M. Winkler is Distinguished Professor of History at Miami University in Ohio. He has also taught at Yale University and the University of Oregon and, for one year each, at the University of Helsinki in Finland, the University of Amsterdam in the Netherlands, and the University of Nairobi in Kenya. A prize-winning teacher, he is the author of seven books, including *The Politics of Propaganda: The Office of War Information, 1942–1945; Home Front U.S.A.: America During World War II;* and *Life Under a Cloud: American Anxiety About the Atom.*

American Heritage® *American Heritage*® magazine was founded in 1954, and it quickly rose to the position it occupies today: the country's preeminent magazine of history and culture. Dedicated to presenting the past in incisive, entertaining narratives underpinned by scrupulous scholarship, *American Heritage* today has more than 300,000 subscribers and counts the country's very best writers and historians among its contributors. Its innovative use of historical illustration and its wide variety of subject matter have gained the publication scores of honors across more than 40 years, among them National Magazine Awards.

Prentice Hall

ISBN 0-13-052849-8
1 2 3 4 5 6 7 8 9 10   06 05 04 03 02

Program Reviewers

HISTORIAN REVIEWERS

William Childs
Department of History
Ohio State University
Columbus, Ohio

Donald L. Fixico
Department of History
Western Michigan
 University
Kalamazoo, Michigan

George Forgie
Department of History
University of Texas
 at Austin
Austin, Texas

Mario Garcia
Department of History
University of California at
 Santa Barbara
Santa Barbara, California

Gerald Gill
Department of History
Tufts University
Medford, Massachusetts

Huping Ling
Division of Social Science
Truman State University
Kirksville, Missouri

Roy Rosenzweig
Department of History
George Mason University
Fairfax, Virginia

Susan Smulyan
Department of
 American Civilization
Brown University
Providence, Rhode Island

TEACHER REVIEWERS

Suzanne P. Brock
Vestavia Hills High School
Birmingham, Alabama

Debra Brown
Eisenhower High School
Houston, Texas

Stephen Bullick
Mt. Lebanon
 School District
Pittsburgh, Pennsylvania

Alfred B. Cate, Jr.
Central High School
Memphis City Schools
Memphis, Tennessee

Janet K. Chandler
Hamilton Southeastern
 High School
Fishers, Indiana

Lee Chase
Chesterfield County
 Public Schools
Chesterfield County, Virginia

Vern Cobb
Okemos High School
Okemos, Michigan

Joyce Dixon Cooper
Sunset High School
Dallas I.S.D.
Dallas, Texas

Michael Jerry DaDurka
David Starr Jordan
 High School (LBUSD)
Long Beach, California

Mike Ferguson
Hebron High School
Lewisville, Texas

Robert Hasty
Lawrence Central
 High School
Indianapolis, Indiana

Robert C. McAdams
East Burke High School
Icard, North Carolina

Lawrence Moaton
Memphis City Schools
Memphis, Tennessee

Dr. Brent Muirhead
South Forsyth High School
Cumming, Georgia

Keith Denny Olmsted
Amon Carter Riverside
 High School
Fort Worth I.S.D.
Fort Worth, Texas

Debbie W. Powers
Fulton County
Atlanta, Georgia

Betsy Schmidt
Round Rock I.S.D.
Round Rock, Texas

Walter T. Thurnau
Southwestern Central
 High School
Jamestown, New York

Kevin Wheeler
Lamar High School
Houston, Texas

Barry Wilmoth
Lamar High School
Arlington, Texas

Judy Heckendorf Wood
Parkway West High School
Ballwin, Missouri

Program Reviewers

CONTENT CONSULTANTS

Senior Consultant
T. R. Fehrenbach
San Antonio, Texas
author, *Lone Star*

Senior Consultant
Herman Viola
Falls Church, Virginia
Curator emeritus
Smithsonian Institution

Curriculum and Assessment Specialist
Jan Moberley
Dallas, Texas

Reading Consultant
Dr. Bonnie Armbruster
Professor of Education
University of Illinois at Urbana-Champaign
Urbana, Illinois

Constitution Consultant
William A. McClenaghan
Department of Political Science
Oregon State University
Beaverton, Oregon
author, *Magruder's American Government*

Internet Consultant
Brent Muirhead
Teacher, Social Studies Department
South Forsyth High School
Cumming, Georgia

Holocaust Consultant
Marjorie B. Green
Director, Educational Policy & Programs
Anti-Defamation League
Los Angeles, California

PROGRAM ADVISORS

Pat Easterbrook
Social Studies Consultant
Cary, North Carolina

Michal Howden
Social Studies Consultant
Zionsville, Indiana

Kathy Lewis
Social Studies Consultant
Fort Worth, Texas

Rick Moulden
Social Studies Consultant
Federal Way, Washington

Sharon Pope
Social Studies Consultant
Houston, Texas

Joe Wieczorek
Social Studies Consultant
Baltimore, Maryland

Table of Contents

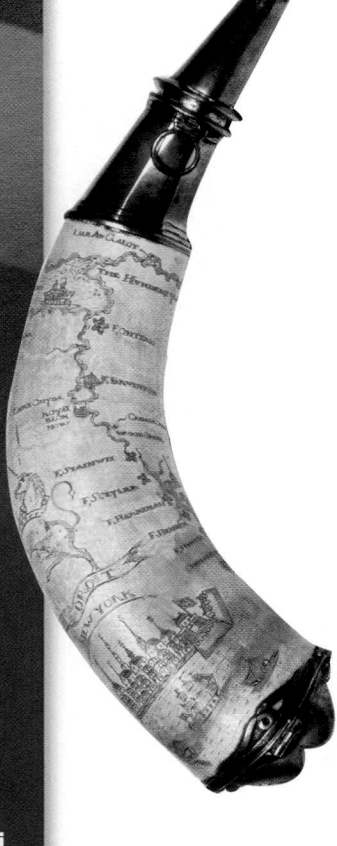

SENSATIONAL AND STARTLING "HOLD UP" OF THE "GOLD EXPRESS" BY FAMOUS WESTERN OUTLAWS

Reference Section

![] American Pathways

Thematic time tables clarify connections between events across time

AmericanHeritage®
MY BRUSH WITH **HISTORY**™

Eyewitness accounts from *American Heritage* magazine of ordinary Americans and extraordinary events

![] Geography & History

An in-depth look at the links between geography and history

Step-by-step lessons to learn and practice important skills

Focus on ...

■ CITIZENSHIP

■ CULTURE

■ DAILY LIFE

Fast Forward to Today

Links between events of the chapter and present-day issues

American BIOGRAPHIES

Profiles describing the lives and accomplishments of prominent Americans

NOTABLE PRESIDENTS

1st President 1789–1797

Biographies of some of the most highly respected Presidents

COMPARING PRIMARY SOURCES

Primary source quotations on controversial issues of the period

COMPARING HISTORIANS' VIEWPOINTS

Respected historians debate events in our nation's history

TEST PREPARATION

Practice questions to help prepare for classroom exams and standardized assessment

Key Documents

Primary Sources

Maps

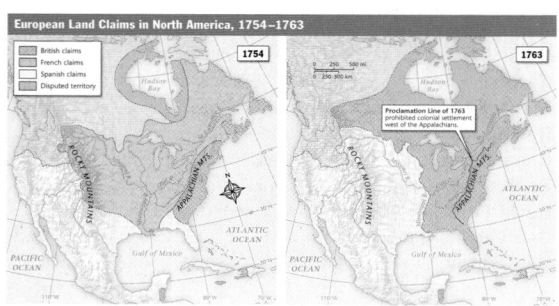

Charts, Graphs, and Tables

American Pathways

Much of what you learn about American history can be better understood if you view events as part of a larger pattern. The themes described below and the American Pathways features throughout this book can help you identify the larger patterns and see the connections between events across time.

Take It to the NET: **Creating a Study Guide** As you complete your course in American History, you can use the American Pathways features and the printable worksheets available at **www.phschool.com** to create your own thematic study guides.

▶ History

Fighting for Freedom and Democracy

Throughout the nation's history, Americans have risked their lives to protect their freedoms and fight for democracy both at home and abroad. Use the American Pathways feature on pages 642–643 to help you trace specific events in the struggle to protect and defend these cherished ideals.

A cannon used in the Battle of Gettysburg

▶ Geography

The Expansion of the United States

Through a series of treaties, purchases, and warfare, the United States has grown from a small country bordering the Atlantic Ocean to one that stretches from the Atlantic to the Pacific, as well as north to Alaska and west to Hawaii. This vast territory has provided American citizens with many natural resources. Use the American Pathways feature on pages 96–97 to help you trace specific events in the expansion of the United States.

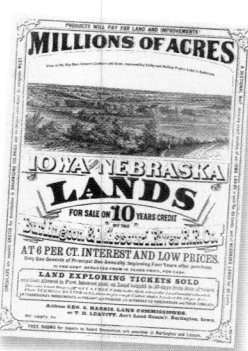

Advertisement for land in Iowa and Nebraska

Immigrants in Search of the American Dream

People from many nations, representing an extraordinary range of ethnic, racial, national, and religious groups, have come to the United States in search of better lives. Use the American Pathways feature on pages 548–549 to help you trace the patterns of immigration in our nation's history.

▶ Economics

Free Enterprise and the American Economy

The combination of abundant natural resources, an economic system that encourages individual initiative, and a political system that ensures private property rights has allowed hard-working Americans to build a strong and prosperous American economy. Use the American Pathways feature on pages 1152–1153 to help you trace specific events in the unfolding of our nation's economy.

▶ Government

Checks and Balances in the Federal Government

The Constitution not only limits the power of government, it also separates the federal government into three branches—executive, legislative, and judicial—to prevent the misuse of power by any one branch. Use the American Pathways feature on pages 232–233 to trace the shifting balance of power among the branches throughout American history.

Currency from the Free Banking Era, 1837–1863

Federalism and States' Rights

The Framers of the Constitution based the American system of government on federalism, the sharing of power between the national, or federal, government and state governments. Throughout the nation's history, Americans have debated exactly which powers belong to the federal government and which to the states. Use the American Pathways feature on pages 448–449 to help you trace specific events in this ongoing debate.

The United States Supreme Court

The power of the courts to rule on the constitutionality of executive and legislative acts makes the Supreme Court the final authority on the meaning of the Constitution. Use the American Pathways feature on pages 306–307 to help identify major trends in the rulings of the Supreme Court.

Thurgood Marshall (center) outside the U.S. Supreme Court

▶ Citizenship

Expanding Civil Rights

The United States was founded on such ideals as equality and democratic representation. Throughout American history many groups, including women and African Americans, have fought for and won important civil rights. Use the American Pathways feature on pages 964–965 to trace the events surrounding various groups' struggles for civil rights.

An American Suffragette

Dr. Martin Luther King, Jr.

▶ Culture

The Arts in America

In every period of their history, Americans have expressed their views in forms such as art, literature, films, and music. Use the American Pathways feature on pages 708–709 to help identify major contributions to the arts throughout American history.

Louis Armstrong's Hot Five jazz band and record labels from the 1920s

►Science and Technology

American Innovation in Technology

Innovations in science and technology have had an enormous impact on our nation's economy, standard of living, and quality of life. Use the American Pathways feature on pages 896–897 to identify important American inventions from the telephone to the microchip.

A textile mill label from Lowell, Massachusetts

Boeing B-17 bomber production during the 1940s

An implantable replacement heart

The Five Geographic Themes

*L*ike history, geography can be divided into themes. Geographers use five themes, described below, to organize their study of the world. You will find these themes in the captions that accompany the maps in this textbook. In addition, a Geography and History feature in each unit explores one of the themes in greater depth.

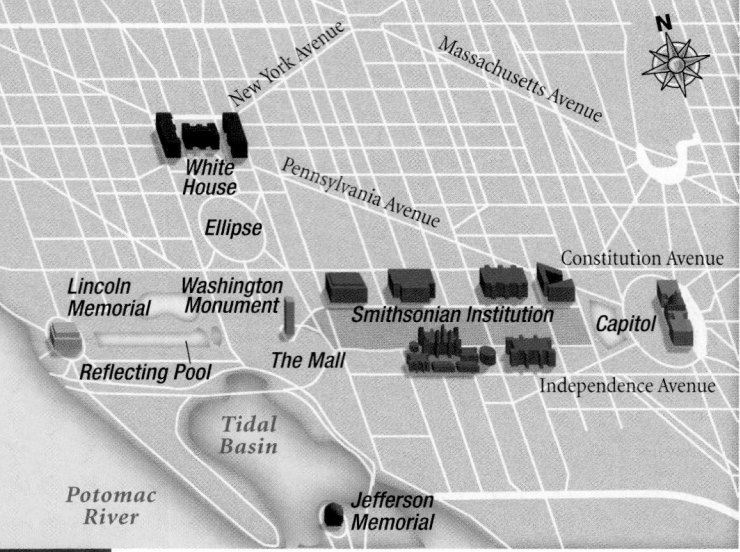

Location

The most basic of the geographic themes, location tells where a place is. Location can be expressed in two ways. Absolute location describes a place's position on the globe as determined by latitude and longitude. Relative location describes a place's position in relation to other places. While each place can have only one absolute location, its relative location can be expressed in a number of ways. For example, the relative location of the Smithsonian Institution can be described as "west of the Capitol," "at the Mall," or "east of the Washington Monument."

Place

Place describes the characteristics that make a location distinctive. There are two kinds of characteristics. Physical characteristics include landforms, vegetation, and climate. Human characteristics include the culture, economy, and government of the people who live in a place. Each place in the United States—indeed, on Earth—has a unique combination of physical and human characteristics.

Movement

People, goods, and ideas regularly travel from one place to another. Examples from American history include the continuing immigration of new Americans, the westward migration of Americans through the 1800s, and the spread of American ideals of individual liberty through the world following the American Revolution. Today's advances in communication and transportation make movement easier and more common than ever.

Regions

A region is any group of places with at least one common characteristic. Regions can be any size, and a single place can belong to several different regions. The city of San Diego, for example, is part of California (a political region), the Sunbelt (a demographic region), and the Pacific Rim (an economic region).

Human-Environment Interaction

Human-environment interaction explores the ways in which people use and modify their environment. The Brooklyn Bridge, the coal mines of West Virginia, the wheat fields of the Plains states, Hoover Dam—all are examples of Americans modifying their environment in order to produce or extract needed resources or to make movement more efficient.

You can use this book as a tool to master United States history. Spend a few minutes to become familiar with the way the book is set up and learn how it can help you succeed in understanding the rich story of America.

Read for Content Mastery

Before You Read The sections in this book begin with Reading Focus questions. These questions point out important ideas in the section. Another helpful aid is the Taking Notes exercise at the beginning of each section. It will help you take notes as you read.

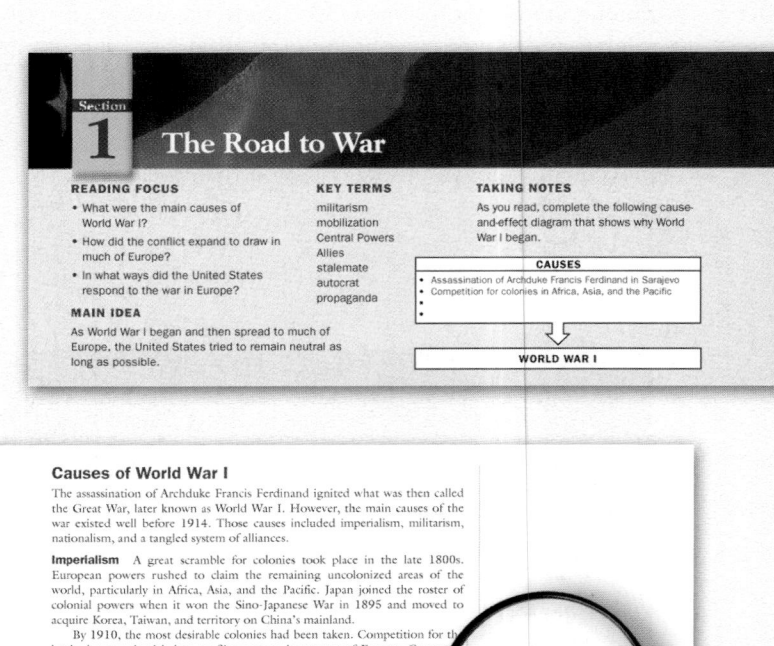

As You Read Asking questions will help you gather evidence and gain knowledge. Suppose you are reading about World War I. Here are some questions you might ask: What events led up to the start of the war? What effect would improved weapons have upon the war? Questions like these can be found in the margins of this book and are labeled "Reading Check." Use these questions to strengthen your understanding of new material.

After You Read The questions in the Section Assessment will help you understand what you read. Use these questions to assess yourself. Were your predictions on target? Did you find answers to your questions? Demonstrate your understanding by completing the activity.

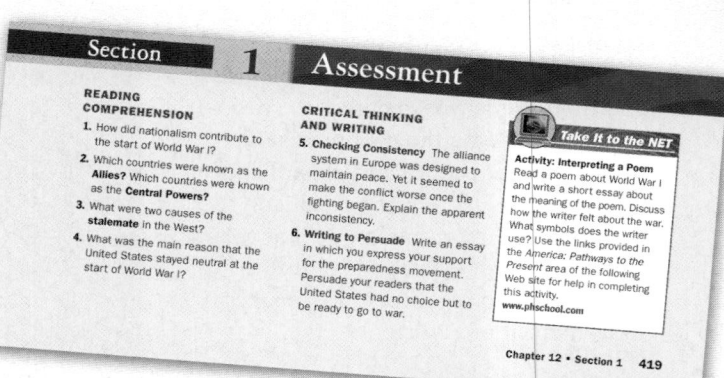

Develop Your Skills

Each chapter has a Skills for Life exercise. Use these exercises to learn and practice Social Studies skills. These skills will help you be successful in studying United States history. Complete the Skills Assessment at the end of every chapter to apply the skills you have learned.

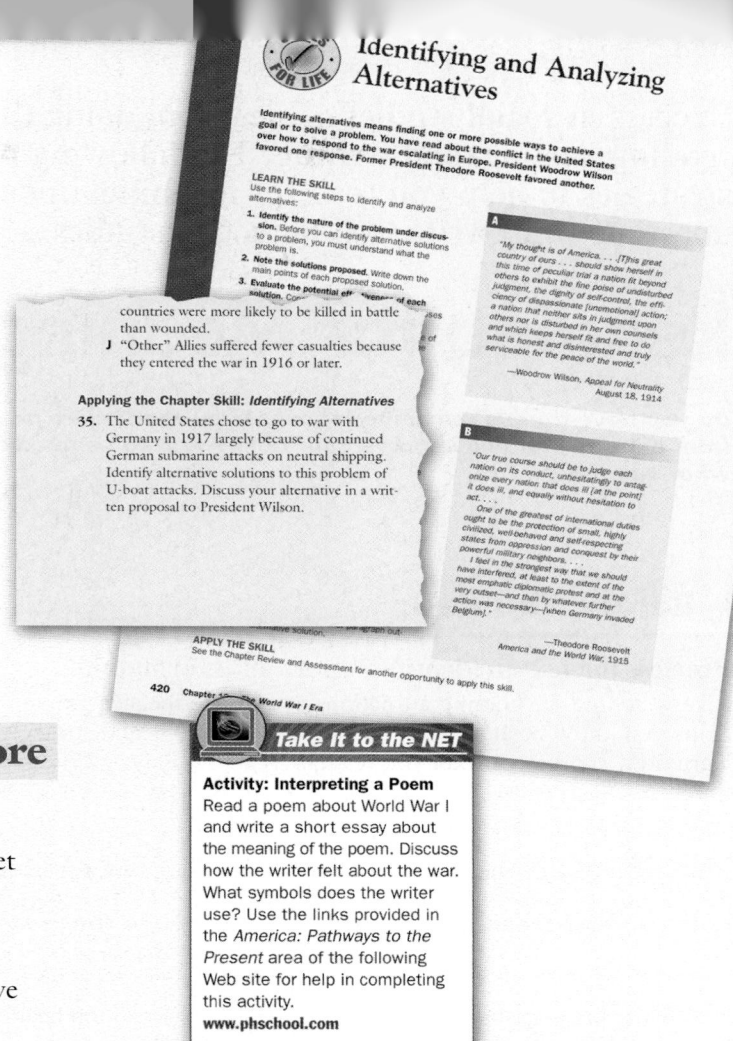

Use the Internet to Explore

At the click of a mouse, the Internet offers you access to a wealth of United States history resources. Use the Take It to the Net activities to research and learn more about key events and themes in United States History. At the Pathways Companion Web site you will find virtual field trips, interactive self-tests, and dozens of links to historical sites online.

Prepare for Tests

This book helps you prepare for tests. Start by answering the questions at the end of every section and chapter. Go to **www.phschool.com** at the end of each chapter to take the practice Self-Test. Then, use the Test Preparation pages at the end of the unit to check yourself further.

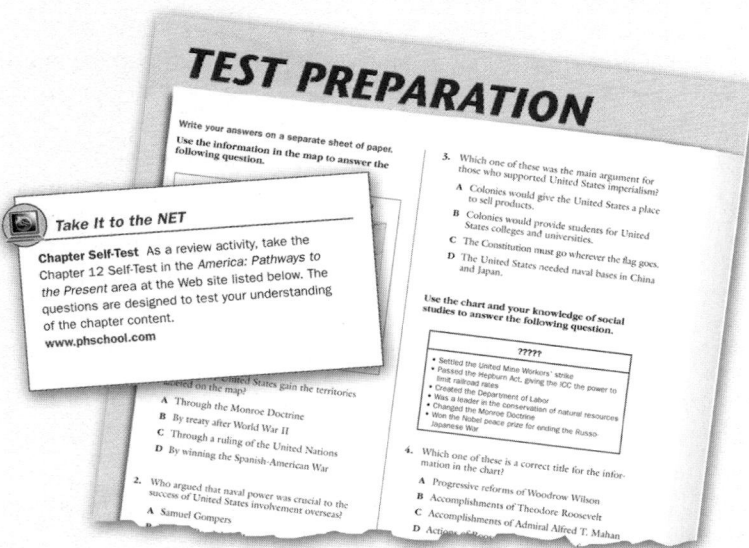

Success in social studies comes from doing three things well—reading, testing, and writing. The following pages present strategies to help you read for meaning, understand test questions, and write well for social studies.

Reading for Meaning

Do you have trouble remembering what you read? Here are some tips from experts that will improve your ability to recall and understand what you read:

▶ Before You Read

Preview the text to identify important information.
Like watching the coming attractions at a movie theater, previewing the text helps you know what to expect. Study the questions and strategies below to learn how to preview what you read.

Ask yourself these questions:	Use these strategies to find the answers:
• What is the text about?	Read the headings, subheadings, and captions. Study the photos, maps, tables, or graphs.
• What do I already know about the topic?	Read the questions at the end of the text to see if you can answer any of them.
• What is the purpose of the text?	Turn the headings into *who, what, when, where, why,* or *how* questions. This will help you decide if the text compares things, tells a chain of events, or explains causes and effects.

▶ As You Read

Organize information in a way that helps you see meaningful connections or relationships.

Taking notes as you read will improve your understanding. Use graphic organizers like the ones below to record the information you read. Study these descriptions and examples to learn how to create each type of organizer.

Sequencing

A **flowchart** helps you see how one event led to another. It can also display the steps in a process.

Use a flowchart if the text—
- tells about a chain of events.
- explains a method of doing something.

TIP▶ List the events or steps in order.

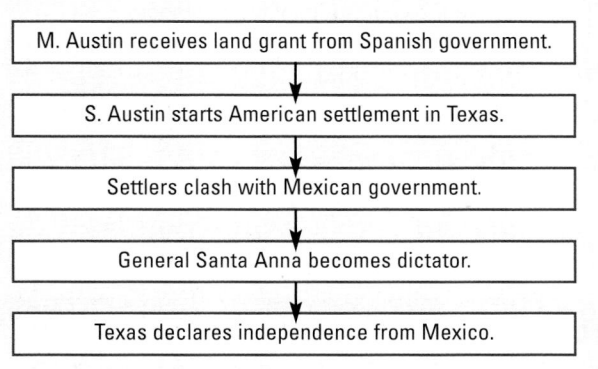

M. Austin receives land grant from Spanish government.

S. Austin starts American settlement in Texas.

Settlers clash with Mexican government.

General Santa Anna becomes dictator.

Texas declares independence from Mexico.

Comparing and Contrasting

A **Venn diagram** displays similarities and differences.

Use a Venn diagram if the text—
- compares and contrasts two individuals, groups, places, things, or events.

TIP▶ Label the outside section of each circle and list differences.

Label the shared section and list similarities.

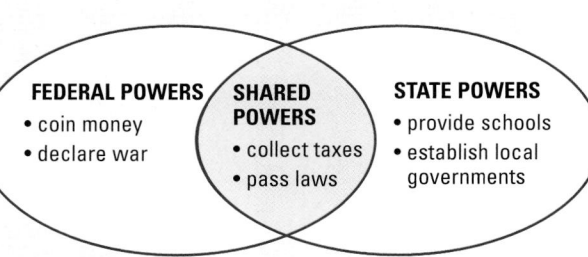

FEDERAL POWERS
- coin money
- declare war

SHARED POWERS
- collect taxes
- pass laws

STATE POWERS
- provide schools
- establish local governments

▶ As You Read (continued)

Categorizing Information

A **chart** organizes information in categories.

Use a chart if the text—
- lists similar facts about several places or things.
- presents characteristics of different groups.

TIP▶ Write an appropriate heading for each column in the chart to identify its category.

COLONY	FOUNDED	LEADERS
Massachusetts	1620	William Bradford John Winthrop
New Hampshire	1623	John Wentworth
Connecticut	1636	Thomas Hooker
Rhode Island	1636	Roger Williams

Identifying Main Ideas and Details

A **concept web** helps you understand relationships among ideas.

Use a concept web if the text—
- provides examples to support a main idea.
- links several ideas to a main topic.

TIP▶ Write the main idea in the largest circle.
Write details in smaller circles and draw lines to show relationships.

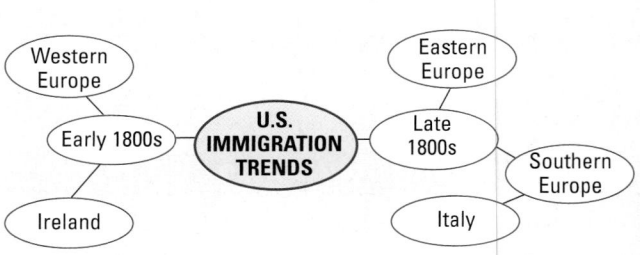

Organizing Information

An **outline** provides an overview, or a kind of blueprint for reading.

Use an outline to organize ideas—
- according to their importance.
- according to the order in which they are presented.

TIP▶ Use Roman numerals for main ideas, capital letters for secondary ideas, and Arabic numerals for supporting details.

I. Differences Between the North and the South
  A. Views on slavery
    1. Northern abolitionists
    2. Southern slave owners
  B. Economies
    1. Northern manufacturing
    2. Southern agriculture

Identifying Cause and Effect

A **cause-and-effect** diagram shows the relationship between what happened (effect) and the reason why it happened (cause).

Use a cause-and-effect diagram if the text—
- lists one or more causes for an event.
- lists one or more results of an event.

TIP▶ Label causes and effects. Draw arrows to indicate how ideas are related.

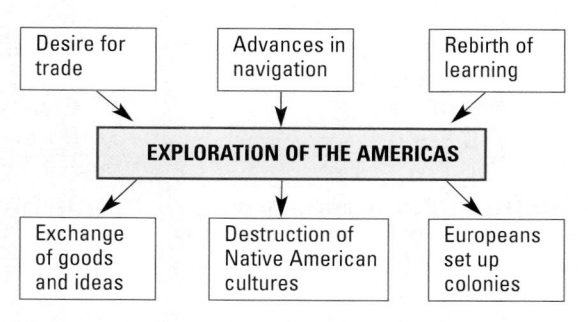

▶ After You Read

Test yourself to find out what you learned from reading the text.

Go back to the questions you asked yourself before you read the text. You should be able to give more complete answers to these questions:
- What is the text about?
- What is the purpose of the text?

You should also be able to make connections between the new information you learned from the text and what you already knew about the topic.

Study your graphic organizer. Use this information for the *answers*. Make up a meaningful *question* about each piece of information.

Taking Tests

Do you panic at the thought of taking a standardized test? Here are some tips that most test developers recommend to help you achieve good scores.

▶ Multiple-Choice Questions

Read each part of a multiple-choice question to make sure you understand what is being asked.

Many tests are made up of multiple-choice questions. Some multiple-choice items are **direct questions.** They are complete sentences followed by possible answers, called distractors.

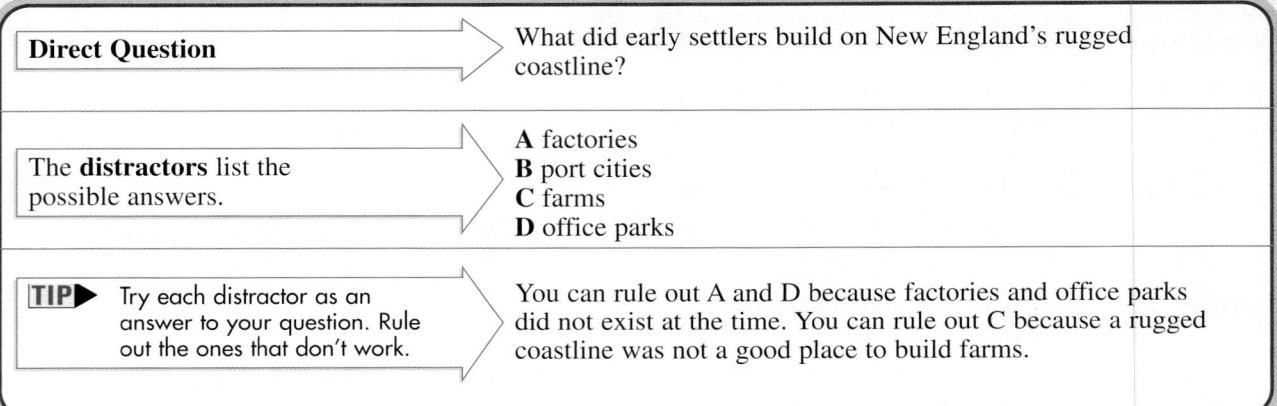

Direct Question	What did early settlers build on New England's rugged coastline?
The **distractors** list the possible answers.	A factories B port cities C farms D office parks
TIP▶ Try each distractor as an answer to your question. Rule out the ones that don't work.	You can rule out A and D because factories and office parks did not exist at the time. You can rule out C because a rugged coastline was not a good place to build farms.

Other multiple-choice questions are **incomplete sentences** that you are to finish. They are followed by possible answers.

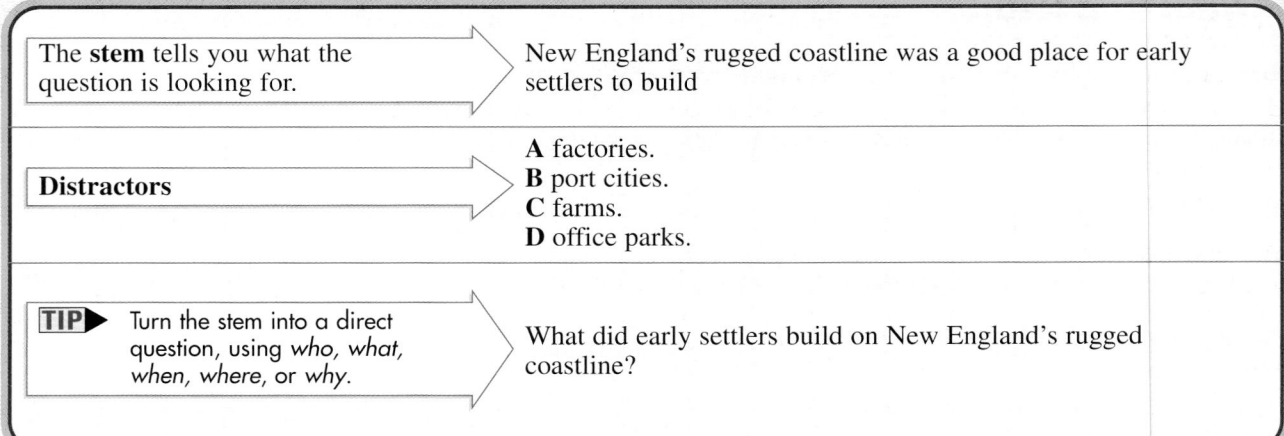

The **stem** tells you what the question is looking for.	New England's rugged coastline was a good place for early settlers to build
Distractors	A factories. B port cities. C farms. D office parks.
TIP▶ Turn the stem into a direct question, using *who, what, when, where,* or *why.*	What did early settlers build on New England's rugged coastline?

► What's Being Tested?

Identify the type of question you are being asked.

Social studies tests often ask questions that involve reading comprehension. Other questions may require you to gather or interpret information from a map, graph, or chart. The following strategies will help you answer different kinds of questions.

Reading Comprehension Questions

What to do:

How to do it:

1. Determine the content and organization of the selection.

Read the **title.** Skim the selection. Look for key words that indicate time, cause-and-effect, or comparison.

2. Analyze the questions.
Do they ask you to *recall facts?*

Look for **key words** in the stem:
<u>According to</u> the selection . . .
The selection <u>states</u> that . . .

Do they ask you to *make judgments?*

The <u>main idea</u> of the selection is . . .
The author <u>would likely</u> agree that . . .

3. Read the selection.

Read quickly. Keep the questions in mind.

4. Answer the questions.

Try out each distractor and choose the best answer. Refer back to the selection if necessary.

Example:

The Dust Bowl During the 1930s, an area of the southern Great Plains became known as the "Dust Bowl." Climate and farming methods combined to cause one of the worst environmental disasters in United States history. As a result of a severe drought, the soil was dry. When farmers plowed the land, they removed the prairie grasses that held the soil in place. When strong winds swept the region, the soil was easily eroded and carried hundreds of miles away. A series of destructive duststorms brought economic ruin to farmers.

What caused the soil to become dry?
A strong winds
B plowing
C drought
D high temperatures

TIP► The key words <u>as a result</u> tell why the soil was dry.

(The correct answer is C.)

▶ What's Being Tested? *(continued)*

Map Questions

What to do:	How to do it:

1. Determine what kind of information is presented on the map.

Read the map **title.** It will indicate the purpose of the map.
Study the **map key.** It will explain the symbols used on the map.
Look at the **scale.** It will help you calculate distance between places on the map.

2. Read the question. Determine which component on the map will help you find the answer.

Look for **key words** in the stem.
About <u>how far</u> . . . [use the scale]
<u>What crops</u> were grown in . . . [use the map key]

3. Look at the map and answer the question in your own words.

Do not read the distractors yet.

4. Choose the best answer.

Decide which distractor agrees with the answer you determined from the map.

Example

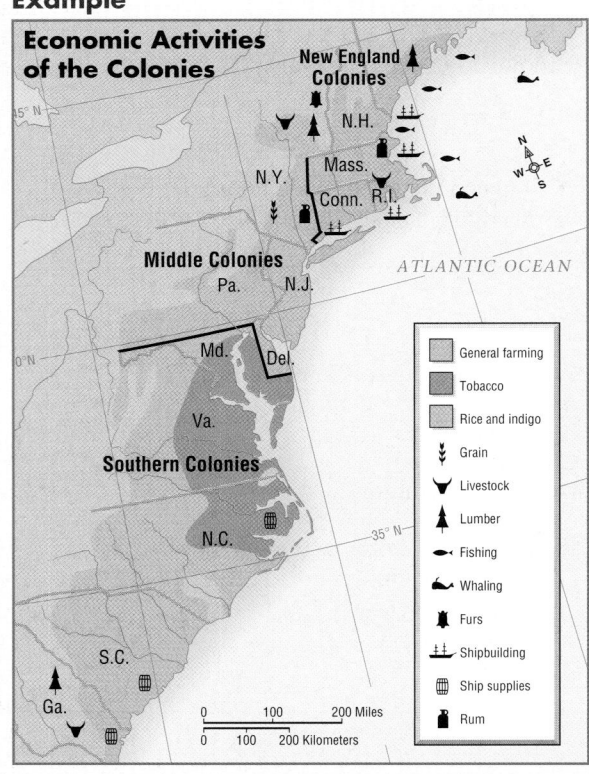

Which of the southern colonies produced ship supplies, tobacco, rice, and indigo?

A New Jersey
B North Carolina
C Virginia
D South Carolina

TIP▶ Read the labels and the key to understand the map.

(The correct answer is B.)

Graph Questions

What to do:

1. Determine the purpose of the graph.

2. Determine what information on the graph will help you find the answer.

3. Choose the best answer.

How to do it:

Read the graph **title.** It indicates what the graph represents.

Read the **labels** on the graph or on the key. They tell the units of measurement used by the graph.

Decide which distractor agrees with the answer you determined from the graph.

Example

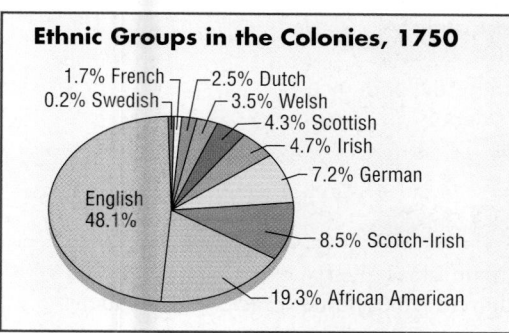

Ethnic Groups in the Colonies, 1750

1.7% French — 2.5% Dutch
0.2% Swedish — 3.5% Welsh
— 4.3% Scottish
— 4.7% Irish
— 7.2% German
English 48.1%
— 8.5% Scotch-Irish
— 19.3% African American

A **circle graph** shows the relationship of parts to the whole in terms of percentages.

After the English, the next largest ethnic group in the colonies was
A French.   **C** German.
B Irish.   **D** African American.

TIP ▶ Compare the percentages listed in the labels.
(The correct answer is D.)

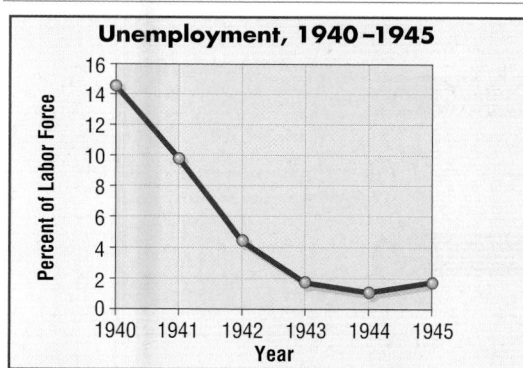

Unemployment, 1940–1945

Percent of Labor Force

Year

A **line graph** shows a pattern or change over time by the direction of the line.

Between 1940 and 1943, unemployment
A decreased a little.   **C** stayed about the same.
B decreased greatly.   **D** increased a little.

TIP ▶ Compare the vertical distance between the two points on the line graph.
(The correct answer is B.)

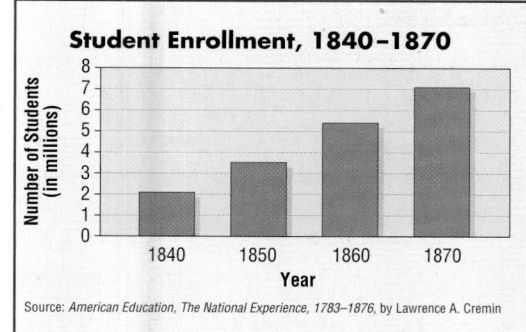

Student Enrollment, 1840–1870

Number of Students (in millions)

Year

Source: *American Education, The National Experience, 1783–1876,* by Lawrence A. Cremin

A **bar graph** compares differences in quantity by showing bars of different lengths.

Between 1850 and 1860, school enrollment increased by about
A 1 million.   **C** 3 million.
B 2 million.   **D** 4 million.

TIP ▶ Compare the heights of the bars to find the difference.
(The correct answer is B.)

Writing for Social Studies

When you face a writing assignment, do you think, "How will I ever get through this?" Here are some tips to guide you through any writing project from start to finish.

▶ The Writing Process

Follow each step of the writing process to communicate effectively.

Step 1. Prewrite

- Establish the purpose.
- Define the topic.
- Determine the audience.
- Gather details.

Step 2. Draft

- Organize information logically in an outline or graphic organizer.
- Write an introduction, body, and conclusion.
- State main ideas clearly.
- Include relevant details to support your ideas.

Step 3. Revise

- Edit for clarity of ideas and elaboration.

Step 4. Proofread

- Correct any errors in spelling, grammar, and punctuation.

Step 5. Publish and Present

- Copy text neatly by hand, or use a typewriter or word processor.
- Illustrate as needed.
- Create a cover if appropriate.

► Types of Writing for Social Studies

Identify the purpose for your writing.

Each type of writing assignment has a specific purpose, and each purpose needs a different plan for development. The following descriptions and examples will help you identify the three purposes for social studies writing. The lists of steps will help you plan your writing.

Writing to Inform

Purpose: to present facts or ideas

Example

During the 1960s, research indicated the dangers of the insecticide DDT. It killed insects but also had long-term effects. When birds and fish ate poisoned insects, DDT built up in their fatty tissue. The poison also showed up in human beings who ate birds and fish contaminated by DDT.

TIP▶ Look for these **key terms** in the assignment: explain, describe, report, narrate.

How to get started:
- Determine the topic you will write about.
- Write a topic sentence that tells the main idea.
- List all the ideas you can think of that are related to the topic.
- Arrange the ideas in logical order.

Writing to Persuade

Purpose: to influence someone

Example

Teaching computer skills in the classroom uses time that could be spent teaching students how to think for themselves or how to interact with others. Students who can reason well, express themselves clearly, and get along with other people will be better prepared for life than those who can use a computer.

TIP▶ Look for these **key terms** in the assignment: convince, argue, request.

How to get started:
- Make sure you understand the problem or issue clearly.
- Determine your position.
- List evidence to support your arguments.
- Predict opposing views.
- List evidence you can use to overcome the opposing arguments.

Writing to Provide Historical Interpretation

Purpose: to present the perspective of someone in a different era

Example

The crossing took a week, but the steamship voyage was hard. We were cramped in steerage with hundreds of others. At last we saw the huge statue of the lady with the torch. In the reception center, my mother held my hand while the doctor examined me. Then, my father showed our papers to the official, and we collected our bags. I was scared as we headed off to find a home in our new country.

TIP▶ Look for these **key terms** in the assignment: go back in time, create, suppose that, if you were.

How to get started:
- Study the events or issues of the time period you will write about.
- Consider how these events or issues might have affected different people at the time.
- Choose a person whose views you would like to present.
- Identify the thoughts and feelings this person might have experienced.

▶ Research for Writing

Follow each step of the writing process to communicate effectively.

After you have identified the purpose for your writing, you may need to do research. The following steps will help you plan, gather, organize, and present information.

Step 1. Ask Questions

Ask yourself questions to help guide your research.	What do I already know about the topic? What do I want to find out about the topic?

Step 2. Acquire Information

Locate and use appropriate sources of information about the topic.	Library Internet search Interviews
Take notes.	Follow accepted format for listing sources.

Step 3. Analyze Information

Evaluate the information you find.	Is it relevant to the topic? Is it up-to-date? Is it accurate? Is the writer an authority on the topic? Is there any bias?

Step 4. Use Information

Answer your research questions with the information you have found. (You may find that you need to do more research.)	Do I have all the information I need?
Organize your information into the main points you want to make. Identify supporting details.	Arrange ideas in outline form or in a graphic organizer.

Step 5. Communicate What You've Learned

Review the purpose for your writing and choose an appropriate way to present the information.	**Purpose**	**Presentation**
	inform	formal paper, documentary, multimedia
	persuade	essay, letter to the editor, speech
	interpret	journal, newspaper account, drama
Draft and revise your writing, and then evaluate it.	Use a rubric for self-evaluation.	

▶ Evaluating Your Writing

Use the following rubric to help you evaluate your writing.

	Excellent	Good	Acceptable	Unacceptable
Purpose	Achieves purpose—to inform, persuade, or provide historical interpretation—very well	Informs, persuades, or provides historical interpretation reasonably well	Reader cannot easily tell if the purpose is to inform, persuade, or provide historical interpretation	Lacks purpose
Organization	Develops ideas in a very clear and logical way	Presents ideas in a reasonably well-organized way	Reader has difficulty following the organization	Lacks organization
Elaboration	Explains all ideas with facts and details	Explains most ideas with facts and details	Includes some supporting facts and details	Lacks supporting details
Use of Language	Uses excellent vocabulary and sentence structure with no errors in spelling, grammar, or punctuation	Uses good vocabulary and sentence structure with very few errors in spelling, grammar, or punctuation	Includes some errors in grammar, punctuation, and spelling	Includes many errors in grammar, punctuation, and spelling

Unit 1

Origins of a New Society (to 1754)

INTRODUCING THE UNIT

Origins of a New Society (to 1754)
Five hundred years ago, frequent contact began among Native Americans, Europeans, and West Africans on the shores of North America. This contact grew as more and more European explorers established settlements on the continent. Later, colonies were established that eventually destroyed most Native American settlements and established a new way of life in North America.

USING HISTORICAL EVIDENCE

Direct students' attention to the painting on these pages. It depicts explorer Jacques Cartier discovering the St. Lawrence River in 1535. Discuss with students Cartier's several exploratory voyages of the St. Lawrence River between 1534 and 1542.

On Cartier's first journey, he explored the Gulf of St. Lawrence. On his second journey, with Indians as guides, Cartier discovered the island later known as Montreal, and he also learned about the vast natural resources that were to be found to the west.

Cartier returned to France and was prevented by war from revisiting this new land until 1541. When he did make one last trip to the St. Lawrence, he gathered what he believed were gold and diamonds. In direct disobedience to an order from a nobleman who was appointed by the King as ruler of the territory, Cartier returned to France, leaving behind severely damaged relations with the Iroquois. His booty turned out to be worthless, and he was eventually discredited, in spite of his early accomplishments.

eTeach

Be sure to check out this month's online discussion with a Master Teacher. Go to **www.phschool.com**.

> **“**I have come to believe that this is a mighty continent which was hitherto unknown. . . . Your Highnesses have an Other World here.**”**
>
> Christopher Columbus, 1498

Theodore Gudin painted this scene titled *Jacques Cartier discovers the St. Lawrence River in 1535.* ▶

xlvi

RESOURCE DIRECTORY

Teaching Resources
Units 1/2 booklet
- American Pathways Activity, pp. 36–37
- History's Lasting Impact, pp. 38–39
Geography and History booklet, pp. 2–3

Other Print Resources
Prentice Hall Assessment System
- Document-Based Assessment

Chapter 1 The Atlantic World, to 1600
Chapter 2 European Colonization of the Americas, 1492–1752
Chapter 3 Growth of the American Colonies, 1689–1754

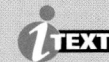

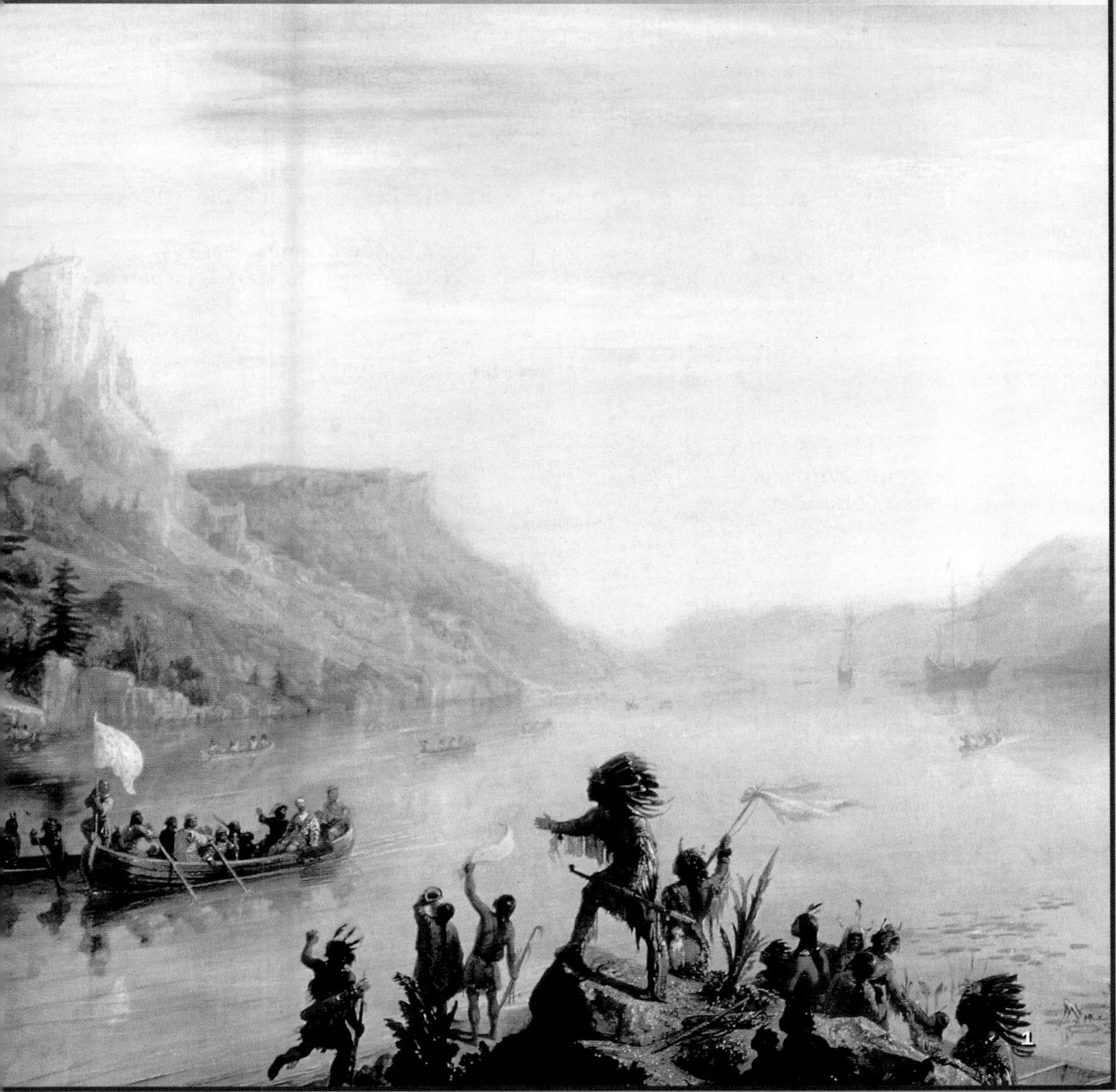

RESOURCE DIRECTORY

Technology

Color Transparencies *Historical Maps,* A1, A2, A3, A4, A5, A56; *Political Cartoons,* B1; *Time Lines,* C1; *Cause-and-Effect Charts,* D1; *Fine Art,* E1, E2, E3; *American Photo,* F1; *American Diversity,* G1, G2; *The Way It Works,* H1, H2, H3, H4

Section Reading Support Transparencies

Prentice Hall United States History Video Collection™ Volume 1, *Three Worlds Meet;* Volume 2, *The Era of Colonization (1585–1763);* Volume 3, *Slavery and Freedom*

Companion Web site, www.phschool.com

TECHNOLOGY CENTER

Take It to the NET

Prentice Hall School Web site offers student-appropriate Internet activities and links that extend core content. Visit us at the Social Studies area. **www.phschool.com**

AmericanHeritage®

My Brush with History™ Video Program This new video series lets your students learn history from the people who lived it.

RESOURCE PRO®

Teaching Resources on CD-ROM offer lesson-planning flexibility, test-generation capability, and resource manageability.

- **Presentation Pro CD-ROM** Provides you with multimedia lecture notes for each chapter.
- **Social Studies Skills Tutor CD-ROM** Provides interactive practice in Geographic Literacy, Critical Thinking and Reading, Visual Analysis, and Communications.
- **Interactive Constitution CD-ROM** Exploring active citizenship and civic responsibilities, this CD-ROM shows students how the Constitution affects their lives today.
- **Exploring Primary Sources in U.S. History CD-ROM** This interactive exploration of primary sources allows students to analyze and evaluate writing and images from American history.
- **Guided Reading Audiotapes**
- **Student Edition on Audio CD**
- **Sounds of an Era Audio CD** Bring the sounds of American history to life in the classroom with music, speeches, poetry, interviews, and news reports.

iTEXT

Don't miss the exclusive interactive version of this textbook on the Web and on CD-ROM.

Chapter 1 Planning Guide
Resource Manager

	CORE INSTRUCTION	READING/SKILLS
Chapter-Level Resources	Teaching Resources • Pacing Charts booklet • Block Scheduling booklet **Resource Pro® CD-ROM**, Ch. 1 **Prentice Hall Presentation Pro CD-ROM**, Ch. 1 **www.phschool.com** • eTeach	**Guided Reading Audiotapes (English/Spanish)** **Student Edition on Audio CD**, Ch. 1 **Social Studies Skills Tutor CD-ROM** **Color Transparencies**, A1, C1, E1, E2, G1
1 The Native American World 1. Find out how the Americas were settled and how the settlers adapted to the environment of North America. 2. Learn about the customs and beliefs shared by early Native Americans. 3. Discover how trade and beliefs about land affected Native American economies.	Teaching Resources **Units 1/2 booklet** • Section 1 Quiz, p. 4 **Learning Styles Lesson Plans booklet**, p. 4	**Guided Reading and Review booklet**, p. 3 **Guide to the Essentials**, p. 5 **Section Reading Support Transparencies**
2 The European World 1. Find out what life was like in Europe during the Early Middle Ages. 2. See what changes took place during the Late Middle Ages. 3. Read to find out about the Renaissance.	Teaching Resources **Units 1/2 booklet** • Section 2 Quiz, p. 5	**Guided Reading and Review booklet**, p. 4 **Guide to the Essentials**, p. 6 **Learning with Documents booklet**, pp. 40, 79 **Section Reading Support Transparencies**
3 The World of the West Africans 1. Learn how West Africans and Europeans first met. 2. Find out some key features of early West African cultures. 3. See how a trading relationship developed between Europe and the kingdoms of West Africa. 4. Discover the role of slavery in African society.	Teaching Resources **Units 1/2 booklet** • Section 3 Quiz, p. 6	**Guided Reading and Review booklet**, p. 5 **Guide to the Essentials**, p. 7 **Section Reading Support Transparencies**
4 The Atlantic World is Born 1. See what is known about the early life of Christopher Columbus. 2. Find out about events that occurred on Columbus's expeditions. 3. Learn about the debate concerning the impact of Columbus's voyages.	Teaching Resources **Units 1/2 booklet** • Section 4 Quiz, p. 7 **Learning Styles Lesson Plans booklet**, p. 5	**Guided Reading and Review booklet**, p. 6 **Guide to the Essentials**, p. 8 **Learning with Documents booklet**, p. 6 **Skills for Life booklet**, p. 3 **Section Reading Support Transparencies**

ENRICHMENT/PRE-AP

Prentice Hall United States History Video Collection™
www.phschool.com
  • Section Activities, Virtual Field Trip, Chapter Activities, Current Events Online

Nystrom *Atlas of Our Country,* pp. 10–11
Historical Outline Map Book, pp. 1, 2, 3, 4
Sounds of an Era Audio CD

Biography, Literature, and Comparing Primary Sources booklet, p. 40
Nystrom *Atlas of Our Country,* pp. 12–13
Exploring Primary Sources in U.S. History CD-ROM

Historical Outline Map Book, p. 71
Sounds of an Era Audio CD

Biography, Literature, and Comparing Primary Sources booklet, pp. 6, 97–98
Historical Outline Map Book, pp. 6, 7
Sounds of an Era Audio CD
Exploring Primary Sources in U.S. History CD-ROM
American Pathways Thematic Posters

ASSESSMENT

PRENTICE HALL ASSESSMENT SYSTEM

Core Assessment
  ExamView® Test Bank, Ch. 1
  ExamView® Test Bank CD-ROM, Ch. 1

Standardized Test Preparation
Diagnose and Prescribe
  Diagnostic Tests for High School Social Studies Skills

Review and Reteach
  Review Book for U.S. History

Practice and Assess
  Test-taking Strategies With Transparencies
  Test-taking Strategies Posters
  Test Prep Book for U.S. History
  Alternative Assessment Handbook
  Document-Based Assessment

Teaching Resources
Units 1/2 booklet
  • Section Quizzes, pp. 4–7
  • Chapter Tests, pp. 8, 11
www.phschool.com Ch. 1 Self-Test

AmericanHeritage RESOURCES

From the Archives of American Heritage®, p. 24
AmericanHeritage ® My Brush with History™ Videotapes
www.americanheritage.com

Don't miss the exclusive interactive version of this textbook on the Web and on CD-ROM.

Chapter 1 Planning Guide
In Your Classroom

CUSTOMIZE FOR INDIVIDUAL NEEDS

Gifted and Talented
Teacher's Edition
• Customize for Gifted and Talented, p. 5

Teaching Resources
• Biography, Literature, and Comparing Primary Sources booklet, pp. 6, 40, 97–98

Technology
• Exploring Primary Sources in U.S. History CD-ROM *Magna Carta; The Log of Christopher Columbus*

ESL
Teacher's Edition
• Customize for ESL, p. 11

Teaching Resources
• Guided Reading and Review booklet, pp. 3–6
• Guide to the Essentials (English/Spanish), Chapter 1

Technology
• Student Edition on Audio CD, Chapter 1
• Guided Reading Audiotapes (English/Spanish), Chapter 1
• Section Reading Support Transparencies

Less Proficient Readers
Teacher's Edition
• Customize for Less Proficient Readers, pp. 15, 23

Teaching Resources
• Guided Reading and Review booklet, pp. 3–6
• Guide to the Essentials (English/Spanish), Chapter 1

Technology
• Student Edition on Audio CD, Chapter 1
• Guided Reading Audiotapes (English/Spanish), Chapter 1
• Section Reading Support Transparencies

Less Proficient Writers
Teacher's Edition
• Customize for Less Proficient Writers, p. 19

Teaching Resources
• Guided Reading and Review booklet, pp. 3–6
• Guide to the Essentials (English/Spanish), Chapter 1

Technology
• Student Edition on Audio CD, Chapter 1
• Guided Reading Audiotapes (English/Spanish), Chapter 1
• Section Reading Support Transparencies

TEACHER'S EDITION INDEX

CHAPTER 1 – PACING SUGGESTIONS

For 90-minute Blocks
• Teach section 1 using Transparencies A1, C1, E1, E2, and G1, and the Recent Scholarship note on page 6 for class discussions.

Running Out of Time?
If you are running short on time to cover this chapter, consider the following options:

• Use the Prentice Hall Presentation Pro CD-ROM to create an outline for this chapter.

• Use the Section Summaries for Chapter 1, from **Guide to the Essentials (English/Spanish).**

ADDITIONAL ACTIVITIES

1	**The Native American World**	**Connnecting with Geography** Have students imagine what the area where their community now stands looked like before the coming of the Europeans. Then have them create a piece of artwork to depict it. **(Visual/Spatial)**
2	**The European World**	**Connecting with Culture** Invite musically inclined students to perform a piece of medieval music for the class. Additionally, you may wish to play recordings of Gregorian chants or other medieval music. **(Musical/Rhythmic)**
3	**The World of the West Africans**	**Connecting with Economics** Challenge students to arrange the classroom in the semblance of a map of West Africa (using chalk on the floor, desks to represent cities, and so forth). Assign students the roles of various nations, and have them use appropriate props to represent trade goods. Then have the class move in ways to simulate the thriving trade of the West African kingdoms. **(Bodily/Kinesthetic)**
4	**The Atlantic World is Born**	**Connecting with Culture** Have a group of students create a graphic organizer called a consequence wheel. The center cell should be labeled "Columbus Arrives in America." From this cell, radiant lines should go to other cells that identify the consequences of Columbus's first voyage. From these cells should radiate further lines and cells, identifying secondary consequences. Challenge the class to extend the consequence wheel as far as they can. **(Logical/Mathematical)**

INTRODUCING THE CHAPTER

Five hundred years ago, frequent contact began among Native Americans, Europeans, and West Africans on the shores of North America. The resulting conflicts and interactions among these different cultures had far-reaching effects, sometimes tragic and destructive, for the people of these three worlds.

TIME LINE ACTIVITY

To provide students with practice in using the time line, ask questions such as these.

1. Around when did the Mississippian culture form? *(around 800)*
2. Which event occurred first, the prophet Mohammed's journey from Mecca to Medina, or Leif Erickson's exploration of North America? *(Mohammed's journey to Medina)*
3. In what year did the name *America* first appear on a map? *(in 1507)*

Chapter 1

The Atlantic World, to 1600

SECTION 1 The Native American World
SECTION 2 The European World
SECTION 3 The World of the West Africans
SECTION 4 The Atlantic World Is Born

An embossed copper portrait, most likely of a prominent member of the Mississippian culture

An aerial view shows Serpent Mound in present-day Ohio. Recent findings indicate that the mound may have been built A.D. 1000–1140.

American Events

1000 B.C.
Mound-building groups arise around this time. Huge earthen mounds are used for burials and other purposes.

800
Mississippian culture forms around this time.

1000
Leif Ericson explores sites along the North American coast at or around this time.

1000 B.C.	B.C.	A.D.	500	·	·	1000	·

World Events

Europe's Early Middle Ages begin around this time.
500

The prophet Muhammad journeys from Mecca to Medina, marking the rise of Islam.
622

The Crusades for the city of Jerusalem begin.
1096

eTeach

Be sure to check out this month's online discussion with a Master Teacher. Go to **www.phschool.com**.

RESOURCE DIRECTORY

Teaching Resources
Pacing Charts booklet
Block Scheduling booklet, p. 13
Units 1/2 booklet
• Chapter Summary, p. 3

Technology
Guided Reading Audiotapes (English/Spanish), Ch. 1
Student Edition on Audio CD, Ch. 1
Prentice Hall United States History Video Collection™ Volume 1, *Three Worlds Meet*
Prentice Hall Presentation Pro CD-ROM, Ch. 1
Resource Pro® CD-ROM
Social Studies Skills Tutor CD-ROM
Companion Web site, www.phschool.com

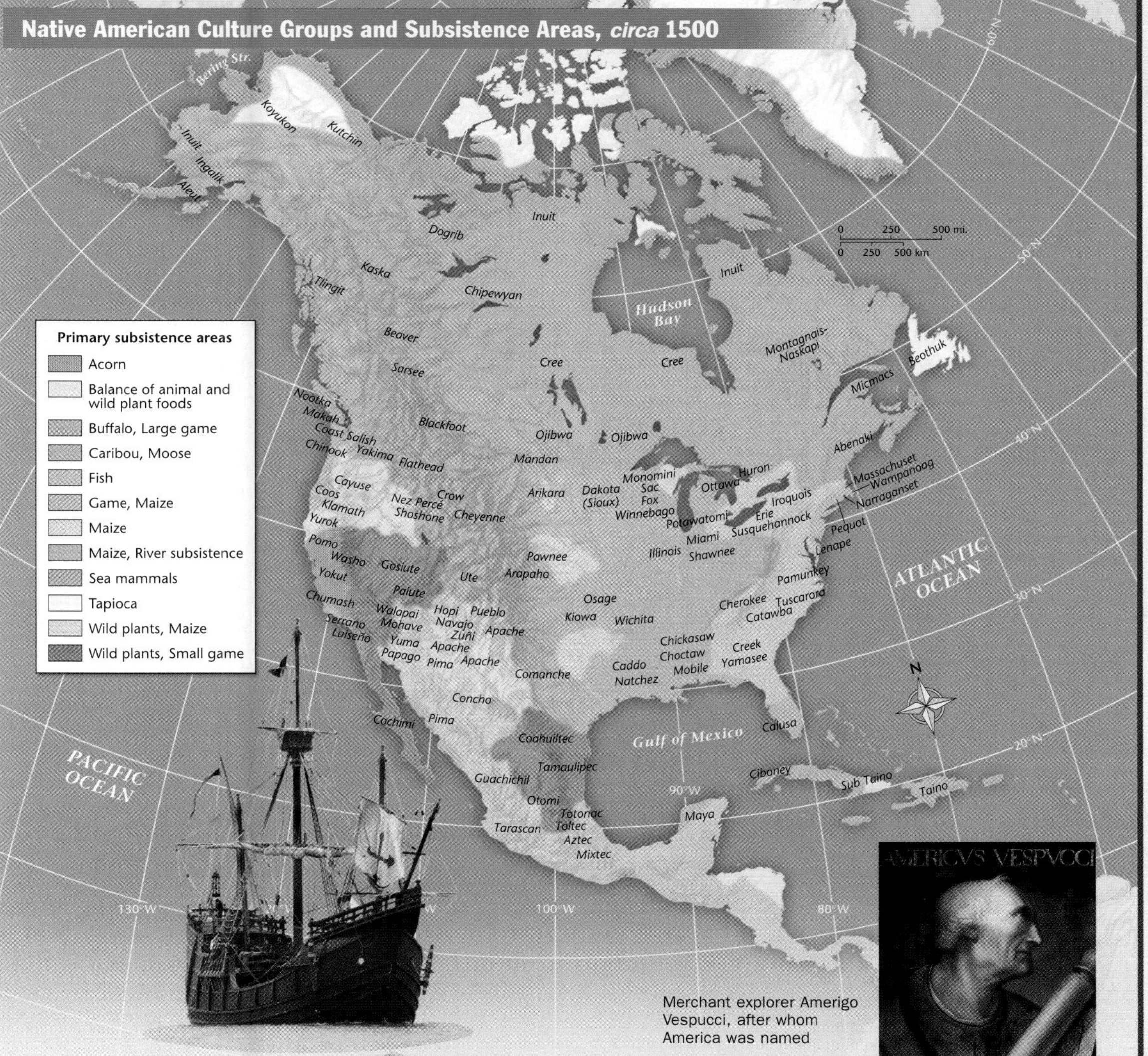

Map: Native American Culture Groups and Subsistence Areas, circa 1500

Primary subsistence areas
- Acorn
- Balance of animal and wild plant foods
- Buffalo, Large game
- Caribou, Moose
- Fish
- Game, Maize
- Maize
- Maize, River subsistence
- Sea mammals
- Tapioca
- Wild plants, Maize
- Wild plants, Small game

A modern replica of one of Columbus's ships

Merchant explorer Amerigo Vespucci, after whom America was named

1492 Columbus sails to the Americas.

1507 The name *America* first appears on a map.

1570–1600 The Iroquois League, a confederation of Native American nations, is formed.

1500

1550

1600

The Songhai empire of West Africa expands. **1464**

European slave raids begin in Africa. **1500**

Martin Luther leads the Protestant Reformation in Germany. **1517**

Chapter 1   3

Native American Culture Groups and Subsistence Areas, *circa* 1500

Activating Prior Knowledge What was the primary subsistence of the Cochimi? *(Wild plants and small game)*

Previewing Ask the students to examine the map and determine whether the Hopi were farmers or nomads. *(Because maize was their primary subsistence, it is obvious they were farmers.)*

BACKGROUND
About the Pictures

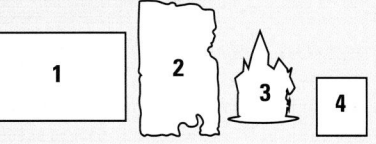

1. The mound stretches 405 meters in length and is about 1 to 2 meters high.
2. The Mississippian culture subsisted on farming corn, beans, and other crops.
3. Though there is still dispute over the exact location of where Columbus first landed, he never actually set foot on North American soil, and to his dying day he never admitted to discovering new land.
4. It was a man named Martin Waldseemüller who, in his printing of a pamphlet about Vespucci's voyages, suggested the New World be named America.

i TEXT

Don't miss the exclusive interactive version of this textbook on the Web and on CD-ROM.

BIBLIOGRAPHY

For the Teacher

Johnson, Paul. **The Renaissance: A Short History.** Modern Library, 2000. (A brief but insightful glimpse into trends in aspects of this pivotal era.)

Rouse, Irving. **The Tainos: Rise and Decline of the People Who Greeted Columbus.** Yale University Press, 1993. (Details the story of this lost people from their time in South America to their rapid disappearance.)

Thornton, John. **Africa and Africans in the Making of the Atlantic World, 1400–1680.** Cambridge University Press, 1998. (A careful analysis of this aspect of Western history.)

For the Student

Barter, James, ed. **Artists of the Renaissance.** Lucent Books, 1999. (Offers a general overview of the Renaissance and a discussion of six of its greatest artists.)

Pollard, Michael and Anna Sproule. **Johann Gutenberg: Master of Modern Printing.** Blackbirch Marketing, 2001. (Biography of the inventor of the printing press.)

Schwartz, Gary. **Hieronymus Bosch.** Harry N. Abrams, 1997. (Biography that combines historical information with beautiful artwork.)

The Native American World

SECTION OBJECTIVES

1. Find out how the Americas were settled and how the settlers adapted to the environment of North America.
2. Learn about customs and beliefs shared by early Native Americans.
3. Discover how trade and beliefs about land affected Native American economies.

BELLRINGER

Warm-Up Activity Ask students to name any Native American groups that are familiar to them from movies, television, reading, or local influences (such as geographical names). Ask them to recall any facts they know about the group, such as its location or way of life.

Activating Prior Knowledge Are there any geographical places in your area with Native American names? If students do not know of any such names, have them research names they find on a state map or a local map of your area.

READING STRATEGY

Have students create a two-column table comparing and contrasting Native American culture groups. In the first column, have them list similarities among the groups. In the second column, have them list differences.

CAPTION ANSWERS

Viewing History Sample answer: People and animals.

READING FOCUS

- How did people settle the Americas and adapt to the environment of North America?
- What customs and beliefs did the early Native Americans share?
- How did trade and beliefs about land affect the Native American economies?

MAIN IDEA

Early Native American societies, which populated North America for thousands of years, had different ways of life but held shared beliefs and participated in a wide trading network.

KEY TERMS

migration
nomad
kinship
clan
oral history
barter

TAKING NOTES

Copy the outline below. As you read, add details about the early Native American world.

> **The Native American World**
> I. Settlement of the Americas
>   A. Land bridge forms.
>   1. People migrate to the Americas.
>   2. _____
> II. North American Life

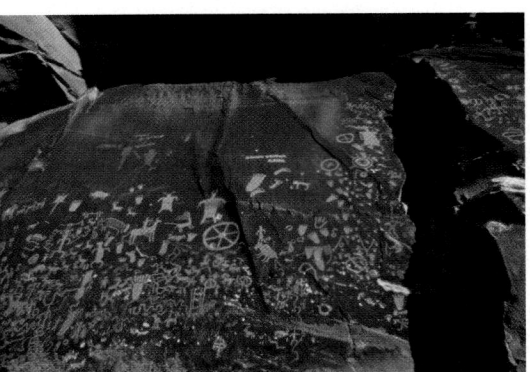

VIEWING HISTORY Early Native North Americans made petroglyphs—pictures and symbols carved into rocks—to express ideas and to serve as memory aids. The petroglyphs above are from Newspaper Rock State Historical Monument in Utah. **Analyzing Visual Information** *What recognizable images appear on the rock?*

Setting the Scene North America's landscape has not always looked the way it does today. During the last major ice age, areas of the continent that are now desert were cooler and green with vegetation. Animals still seen today, such as wolves, bison, and reindeer, roamed North America with species now extinct, including mastadons, saber-toothed cats, and ground sloths the size of oxen. Musk oxen that today are confined to the Arctic ranged as far south as Mexico. It was some time during this last ice age—and into this environment—that people first came to North America.

No one knows exactly when people first came to the Americas. Many experts date the arrival of these first Americans anywhere from 30,000 to 15,000 years ago, and as new findings emerge, estimates continue to change.

Studies suggest the climate and environment of southeastern Alaska was at least fit for humans to live in 40,000 years ago, at the very height of the last ice age. Plant remains found at one site in present-day Chile show possible human settlement to have occurred there some 12,500 years ago. Other findings in South America suggest humans may have arrived there even earlier, perhaps 30,000 years ago. In New Mexico, a stone point found with the remains of a now-extinct species of bison indicates that the animal was killed by humans at least 10,000 years ago.

Settlement of the Americas

We know that the earliest Americans came from the continent of Asia, and that geographical changes helped them to make their way here. Today, North America and Asia are separated by the Bering Strait, a waterway off Alaska's west coast. During the last ice age, glaciers trapped much of Earth's ocean water, causing global sea levels to drop. This exposed a "land bridge," making possible **migration,** or movement of people for the purpose of settling in a new place. (Some birds and animals also migrate, moving from place to place in large groups with the changing seasons.) Most experts believe that Asians,

---

RESOURCE DIRECTORY

Teaching Resources
Learning Styles Lesson Plans booklet, p. 4
Guided Reading and Review booklet, p. 3

Other Print Resources
Historical Outline Map Book *Hunters Reach America,* p. 1; *Physical Regions of the United States,* p. 2; *Climates of the United States,* p. 3; *Native American Cultures,* p. 4

Technology
Section Reading Support Transparencies
Guided Reading Audiotapes (English/Spanish), Ch. 1
Student Edition on Audio CD, Ch. 1
Color Transparencies *Historical Maps,* A1; *Time Lines,* C1
Prentice Hall Presentation Pro CD-ROM, Ch. 1
Companion Web site, www.phschool.com

perhaps following migrating herds of big game animals, walked across this bridge to North America. Some experts, however, point to evidence suggesting some people may have migrated to North America about 3,000 to 5,000 years before the land bridge was even exposed. In that case, the first arrivals may have entered from more than one point.

Gradually the human population spread out across the Western Hemisphere, from the Arctic Circle to the southernmost tip of South America. These ancient Americans and their descendants are called Native Americans, or Indians. Over thousands of years, Native American societies settling in different regions developed a variety of distinct languages and customs. These lifestyles were forever changed when Native Americans, Europeans, and Africans came into contact with one another just 500 years ago.

By the late 1400s, when this transatlantic encounter began, some 8 to 10 million people may have lived in what is now the United States. Some scholars say the figure is closer to 700,000 to 800,000.

North American Life

The North American environment varies greatly from region to region. It includes the surf-swept beaches of the West Coast, the windy plains of the Midwest and Canada, and the rocky New England Coast. The people who first inhabited this land adapted their ways of life to fit their local environments.

Many early Americans were **nomads.** That is, they moved their homes regularly in search of food. Nomads survived by hunting game, fishing, and gathering wild plants to eat and use as medicine. Although many groups found their plant foods in the wild, some societies also began to farm. In the Americas, farming practices that began in Mexico spread to the Southwest region of North America, enabling some groups to grow corn, squash, peppers, and beans. Methods of survival varied from group to group, depending on the resources available.

The North On the coastal edges of North America lived two northern peoples, the Inuit and Aleut. They were skilled at hunting on ice and snow, on shores and plains, in mild summers and bitter winters. Other northern groups such as the Koyukon and Ingalik were nomadic. These groups hunted, fished, and

VIEWING HISTORY This 1784 engraving shows a multifamily dwelling typical of the Nootka, a culture group of the Northwest Coast. **Drawing Conclusions** *How does the engraving show the importance of fish in the Nootka diet?*

The Lenape Longhouse

The **Oval Floor** shape represented the back of the turtle that was believed to form the earth.

The **Central Post** was a symbolic link to the sky, home of the Creator.

Carvings represented 12 sky spirits.

The **East Entry** symbolized birth.

Drummers

Circle of Men

Circle of Women

The **West Exit** symbolized death.

INTERPRETING DIAGRAMS
The design of the longhouse, and everything in it, reflected the Lenape view of relationships in the universe. For example, in this thanksgiving ceremony, men sat within a circle of women, who headed the clans. **Analyzing Visual Information** *Describe other symbolism evident in the longhouse.*

READING CHECK
How might the first people have arrived in North America?

gathered their food in huge forests and off the shores of lakes and waterways of present-day Canada and Alaska.

The Northwest Coast Waterways were also the primary source of food for Native Americans of the Northwest Pacific Coast. Here, rivers fed by heavy rainfall poured into a rich ocean fishing ground. The Coos, Coast Salish, Makah, and other peoples in the Northwest relied heavily on salmon, and developed remarkable fishing and food-storage technologies. Native Americans of the Northwest Coast made such good use of their abundant resources that the area was more densely populated than many other places in North America.

California Farther south along the Pacific Coast lies the present-day state of California. During the 1400s, about 300,000 people lived in its mountains and valleys, including the Chumash, Yurok, and other groups. They spoke more than 100 variations of 20 basic languages, and they generally lived in small bands. Depending on their location, their diets included deep-sea fish, flour from the acorns of mountain oaks, or beans from the desert mesquite plant. A few groups living along the Colorado River also practiced farming.

The Plateau Inland from the Northwest Coast, between the Cascade Mountains and the Rocky Mountains, stretches a plateau of dry plains crisscrossed by rivers. More than two dozen groups in this area, including the Chinook and Cayuse, fished the rivers for salmon and dug in the plains for edible roots. They often built villages that looked down from high riverbanks and dominated the waters below.

The Great Basin The Great Basin is a region that lies between the Rockies and another mountain range, the Sierra Nevada. In this mostly dry land, food was hard to find. Because of this, most people in the Great Basin, including the

Paiute, Ute, and Shoshone, lived in small local groups. Members of a group worked together hunting and gathering food, including roots, pine nuts, rabbits, and insects.

The Southwest As little as four inches of rain falls annually in some parts of the Southwest. Groups such as the Hopi and Zuñi lived settled lives and developed farming techniques to suit the dry environment. Others, such as the Apache, were nomadic. The Navaho moved to this region from the North, adapting their way of life as they did so.

The Anasazi, whose name is Navaho for "Ancient Ones," built their chambered cliff homes starting in about A.D. 900. In the late 1200s, they abandoned these dwellings, possibly, in part, because of a long drought in the region. The Anasazi's descendants are the Pueblo people.

The Plains In villages along the rivers that drain the central area of the continent, the Mandans, Wichita, Pawnee, and other groups planted corn, beans, and squash. They used dogs as pack animals and traveled great distances on foot, hunting the vast herds of buffalo that grazed on the Plains. The buffalo fulfilled many of their needs, from supplying food to providing materials for clothing and shelter.

The Northeast Vast woodlands and ample rainfall influenced the way of life of the Native Americans in the Northeast. People gathered wild plants, hunted, and grew corn and other crops. They fished in fresh water and salt water. In groups such as the Seneca and the Lenape, women managed the dwellings and the gardens around them. Men hunted deer, bear, moose, and other game in the woods.

The Iroquois people lived in the northeastern woodlands from the Atlantic Coast to the Great Lakes. Iroquois groups frequently waged war on one another. In the late 1500s, however, five Iroquois groups with similar cultures and languages (the Mohawk, Oneida, Onandaga, Cayuga, and Seneca) formed a spiritual alliance: the Iroquois League. Also called the Iroquois Confederacy or the Five Nations, the Iroquois League was centered in present-day New York State. (When the Tuscarora joined in 1722, it became known as the Six Nations.)

According to tradition, the League was formed to put an end to constant warfare among the tribes and to provide a united force to withstand invasion. The League was governed by a council made up of family leaders and village chiefs. Council members voted by tribe, and a unanimous vote was required to declare war. The Iroquois were extremely successful in war and subdued many of the neighboring tribes. The League survived for more than 200 years.

The Southeast Vegetation ranged from swamp to seacoast in the Southeast, but the region was mostly wooded. Its inhabitants depended on hunting and growing corn. They knew what plants to use to make rope, medicine, clothing, and even poison to catch fish.

Native North American Languages

Early Native Americans used spoken language, rather than the written word, to communicate ideas and to pass their histories on to the next generation. Before the arrival of the Europeans, about 300 distinct languages had been spoken among native peoples living north of Mexico.

Today Many of those languages are extinct, either because the groups that spoke them no longer exist, or their descendants never learned the language. In the photo above, first-graders in a Pueblo school in New Mexico learn their native language and help to keep it alive.

Many of the remaining native languages are in danger of extinction and have very few speakers. Some native languages, however, have a relatively large number of speakers; Navajo is spoken by about 100,000 people in Arizona and New Mexico. Ojibwa, Cherokee, Dakota-Assiniboin, and Inuit are also among the more widely spoken languages.

English borrows many words from Native American tongues. Some are place-names, such as *Minnesota*, which comes from the Sioux words for "water" *(mni)* and "clear" *(sota)*. Common nouns such as *chipmunk, moose, squash,* and *kayak* are also Native American in origin.

? **How did some Native American languages become extinct?**

ACTIVITY
Connecting with Geography

Provide students with physical outline maps of North America and have them shade and label the areas discussed in the text and annotate them. **(Visual/Spatial)**

BACKGROUND
Navajo Language

Changes in the language of the Navajo people dramatically demonstrate how culture and environment interact. The Navajos once lived in eastern Alaska, where they adapted to snow and cold by gathering wild food and hunting. Later they migrated to the more temperate Southwest, where they grew corn as a basic food. The Navajos chose the corn plant as a symbol of life and incorporated it into their religious beliefs and creation stories. Because they needed a word for seed, they adapted their old word for snowflake.

CAPTION ANSWERS

Fast Forward to Today In some cases the people who spoke the language have died, while their descendants have not learned the language.

✓ TEST PREPARATION

Have students read the material on this page under the heading *The Plains* and then answer the question below.

How did Indians of the Plains get food?

A Through agriculture

B Through hunting

C Through foraging

Ⓓ Through a combination of agriculture and hunting

ANALYZING VISUAL INFORMATION Recent evidence links Serpent Mound (top) to a group that lived in the Ohio River valley, A.D. 900–1650. Located in southwestern Ohio, the mound is nearly one-quarter of a mile long. **Drawing Inferences** *What can structures like Serpent Mound tell us about the ancient Americans?*

As early as 1000 B.C., Native American cultures were emerging in the Ohio and Mississippi River valleys. One group, the Hopewell, built huge earthen monuments—sometimes 30 feet high and more than 100 feet across, in various shapes. Hence, the Hopewell and similar groups are sometimes called the "mound builders." Some of the mounds were cone-shaped and used as burial sites, such as those found at Mound City of present-day Ohio. Other groups built animal-shaped mounds that experts believe may have served some symbolic purpose.

After about A.D. 800, the Mississippian culture developed. It included a variety of groups from Louisiana to Wisconsin with a shared a way of life. The Mississippians built towns of increasing size, the largest of which was Cahokia, in present-day Illinois. By the year 1200, Cahokia had a population of about 40,000 and more than 60 mounds.

The Natchez people settled the lower Mississippi River. Several thousand people lived in each Natchez town. Townspeople built magnificent temples on raised mounds of earth. East of the Natchez, other Mississippian cultures, such as the Creek and Cherokee, built similar towns. In the Cherokee town of Etowah (in present-day Georgia) stood a pyramid more than 60 feet high.

Shared Customs and Beliefs

Despite their different lifestyles, early Native American peoples held to traditions handed down to them through generations. This shared culture included a common social structure and religion.

Social Structure Native American societies of that time were not organized according to social classes, location, wealth, or age, as many cultures are today. Instead, family relationships, called **kinship,** determined the social structure. Individuals relied on their kin, or family, to fulfill many of their social needs. Kinship groups provided many of the services we expect today from governments, churches, and private organizations. Such services included medical care, child care, settlement of disputes, and education.

Native American kinship groups were organized by **clans.** A clan is made up of groups of families who are all descended from a common ancestor. In some groups, children belonged to the clan on the mother's side of the family, and in other groups, children belonged to the father's clan. The Lenape people, who lived along the mid-Atlantic Coast, included at least three clans. From time to time, the various Lenape clans would gather for social and religious ceremonies, as did other Indian clans across the continent.

Religion Early Native Americans shared the belief that the most powerful forces in the world are spiritual. They performed religious ceremonies that recognized the power of those spiritual forces.

Whether they were planting crops, choosing a mate, or burying their dead, Native Americans strictly followed traditional religious practices, or rituals. They believed that failure to perform their rituals led to disasters such as invasions, disease, or bad harvests.

Preserving Culture To keep their beliefs and customs alive, early Native Americans relied on **oral history**—traditions passed from generation to generation by word of mouth. Elders told young people stories, songs, and instructions for ceremonies, which they passed on to their own children.

Native American Trade

Large or small, all Native American groups traded food or goods both within their group and outside it. They traded not only for items they needed or wanted, but also to show hospitality and friendliness. Sharing was seen as a sign of respect.

Native American trading routes crisscrossed North America. The Inuit traded copper from the Copper River in southern Alaska for sharks' teeth collected by people living at the mouth of the Columbia River in Washington. Shells harvested by the Northwest Coast groups found their way to central California and North Dakota.

This Etowah neck ornament is made of shell, most likely a trade item from a distant seacoast.

The Mohave of the Great Basin carried out **barter,** or trade, with people on the California coast, and then traded the coastal goods to the Pueblo in what is now Arizona. Rocky Mountain groups took obsidian, a volcanic glass, eastward into Ohio. The Iroquois east of the Great Lakes bartered with groups from Minnesota to get stone for tobacco pipes. In the Southeast, Native Americans traded salt and copper from the Appalachian Mountains.

Although Native Americans used natural trade routes such as the Mississippi River and the Great Lakes, they also built a network of trading paths. These routes often led to centers where Native Americans held trade gatherings during the summer.

Native Americans and Land

One item that Native Americans never traded was land. In their view, the land could not be owned. They believed that people had a right to use land and could grant others the right to use it, too. To buy and sell land, as other peoples have done throughout history, was unthinkable to them. Land, like all of nature, deserved respect.

By contrast, the Europeans who arrived on North American soil in the 1400s had quite a different idea about land ownership. They frequently did not understand Indian attitudes and interpreted references to land use as meaning land ownership. Such fundamental differences would prove to have lasting consequences for both Native Americans and European settlers.

Section 1 Assessment

READING COMPREHENSION

1. What are **nomads?** Give some examples of nomadic groups.

2. How were **kinship** and **clan** membership important to the structure of Native American societies?

3. Why did Native Americans keep an **oral history?**

4. What types of items did various Native American groups use for **barter?**

CRITICAL THINKING AND WRITING

5. **Drawing Conclusions** Did cultural and environmental diversity among various Native American groups encourage or discourage trade? Explain.

6. **Writing a List** How does oral history differ from written history? List the advantages and disadvantages of each method of remembering history.

Take It to the NET

Virtual Field Trip Conduct an online exploration of ruins left by pre-Columbian Native Americans. Record your impressions in a brief essay. What do these ruins tell us about the people who used to live there? Use the links provided in the *America: Pathways to the Present* area of the following Web site for help in completing this activity.
www.phschool.com

Section 1 Assessment

Reading Comprehension

1. Nomadic peoples, such as the Koyukon and the Ingalik, moved their homes regularly in search of food.

2. Native American societies were based on familial structure and ancestry rather than on social classes, location, wealth, or age. Kinship and clan membership were integral parts of societal structure.

3. To keep their beliefs and customs alive, they passed traditions from generation to generation by word of mouth.

4. Possible answers: Food, copper, sharks' teeth, shells, obsidian, and salt.

Critical Thinking and Writing

5. Encouraged, because groups were able to barter for foods and materials that were not otherwise available to them due to geographic limitations or cultural differences.

6. Sample answer: Oral history advantages: preserves more of the sentiment and dynamic nature of events passed; Disadvantages: has a greater potential to change over time, is more dependant on individuals' memories. Written history advantages: may be less subjective since information does not change as easily as it may in memory once it is recorded, is potentially more accurate; Disadvantages: less effective in capturing the spirit of history.

Take It to the NET

Invite students to take a Virtual Field Trip at **www.phschool.com**

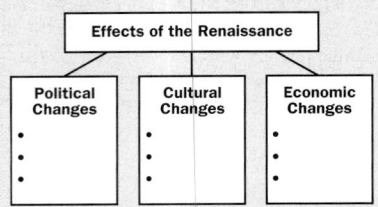

The European World

SECTION OBJECTIVES

1. Find out what life was like in Europe during the Early Middle Ages.
2. See what changes took place during the Late Middle Ages.
3. Read to find out about the Renaissance.

BELLRINGER

Warm-Up Activity Have students list the major nations of Western Europe today. Which do they think were important in the 1400s? Then ask them to underline the names of nations they believe made contact with Native American cultures in North America. Have them revise their lists as they read the chapter.

Activating Prior Knowledge Ask students to state what they believe to have been priorities among the nations of Europe at the time covered in this section. At what point did exploration become an important priority? What changes in society and in technology made exploration both desirable and feasible?

READING STRATEGY

As students read the section, have them write down details that support this statement: Europe experienced political, social, economic, and cultural change when it moved from the Middle Ages to the Renaissance.

ACTIVITY
Connecting with Culture

Ask students to choose one person important in European history at this time and prepare his or her biography. They may choose either a person mentioned in the chapter, such as Marco Polo or Queen Isabella, or another influential figure. **(Verbal/Linguistic)**

READING FOCUS
- What was life like in Europe during the Early Middle Ages?
- What changes took place during the Late Middle Ages?
- What was the Renaissance?

MAIN IDEA
The Middle Ages, a period when Europe was isolated from the rest of the world, was followed by the Renaissance, a period when Europeans sought knowledge of the world and began to explore it.

KEY TERMS
Middle Ages
feudalism
Crusades
middle class
monarch
Magna Carta
Renaissance
Reformation

TAKING NOTES
Copy the chart below. Under each heading, note changes brought about by the Renaissance.

Effects of the Renaissance

Political Changes	Cultural Changes	Economic Changes
•	•	•
•	•	•
•	•	•

Setting the Scene   Driven by curiosity, a desire for wealth, and a sense of duty to spread their religion, European explorers in the 1400s set sail for foreign lands. Since ancient Roman times, Europeans had known of continents beyond their own. Trade routes connecting Europe with Asia and Africa allowed for the exchange of goods and, through commerce, knowledge of life in other lands. Roman women draped themselves in Chinese silk. Wheat from Egypt fed the Roman Empire. Italian merchants traded salt for African gold.

When the Roman Empire collapsed in the 400s, life changed for Europeans, and they turned away from their foreign contacts. Internal problems, both political and economic, distracted Europeans from their trade with Asians and Africans. It would not be until after A.D. 1000 that this situation would begin to change.

The Early Middle Ages

The era in European history from about A.D. 500 to 1300 is known as the **Middle Ages,** or the medieval period. It is the historical era that came after ancient times and before the modern era. The period from 500 to 1000 is often called the Early Middle Ages.

European Invasions   The Early Middle Ages was a time of instability in Europe. Germanic tribes such as the Franks surged across the borders of the former Roman Empire and settled across much of Europe. From the north, fierce Viking warriors caused great destruction and disruption to areas of Europe, looting and burning the villages they passed through.

Out of Arabia, a powerful empire arose in the A.D. 600s. It was based on a new religion: Islam, inspired by the teachings of the prophet Muhammad. The followers of Islam, called Muslims, sought to spread their religion. Within 200 years, the Muslim empire spread across North Africa and into what is

In the Late Middle Ages, European merchants traveled in camel caravans along the ancient Silk Road that extended from the Mediterranean Sea into China. This detail is from the Catalan Atlas of 1375.

10   Chapter 1 • *The Atlantic World*

RESOURCE DIRECTORY

Teaching Resources
Guided Reading and Review booklet, p. 4
Biography, Literature, and Comparing Primary Sources booklet (Literature) *The Koran,* p. 40

Technology
Section Reading Support Transparencies
Guided Reading Audiotapes (English/Spanish), Ch. 1
Student Edition on Audio CD, Ch. 1
Prentice Hall Presentation Pro CD-ROM, Ch. 1
Companion Web site, www.phschool.com

present-day Spain, bringing the highly advanced Arab civilization to these regions.

Feudalism To protect themselves against these threats, Europeans created a political and economic system known as **feudalism.** Under feudalism, a powerful noble, or lord, divided his large landholdings among lesser lords, who in return owed him military service and other favors.

The basis of feudal society in Europe was the manor, the large estate of a lord. Peasants called serfs farmed the land and gave their lord a portion of the harvest in exchange for his shelter and protection. Born into lifelong servitude, serfs received no education. They knew little about the world outside the manor, which they were forbidden to leave.

The manor system produced everything a feudal society needed for survival. As a result, Europe's trade ties to foreign lands largely died out during the Middle Ages, and even the use of money declined.

Medieval Religion The Roman Catholic Church governed the spiritual life and daily life of medieval Christians, both rich and poor. The head of the Church, the pope, claimed authority over emperors and kings, and often appointed them. The clergy, or Church officials who were authorized to perform religious ceremonies, often owned large tracts of land and were lords of their own manors.

Much of the clergy's power came from the fact that they were virtually the only educated people in medieval Europe. They alone could read and study the Bible and other holy writings of Christianity, so they controlled how the faith was interpreted and communicated to the people. Every Christian was expected to show unquestioning obedience to Church authority.

The Late Middle Ages

Around the year 1000, Europe's economy entered a period of new growth that produced social changes. New farming methods increased food supplies. More food led to population growth and competition for land.

At the same time, new trade ties to Asia promoted interest in the world outside Europe's borders. In time, trade also led to the growth of cities and a weakening of the feudal system.

The Crusades Church power grew, and so did the might of the Muslim empire. In about the year 1077, Muslims from Turkey seized Jerusalem, a city holy to Christians and Muslims that previously had been shared by both groups. From 1096 to 1291, the Church organized a series of military campaigns to take Jerusalem from the Turks. These holy wars were called the **Crusades.**

Ultimately, the Christians failed to oust the Turks from Jerusalem. The Crusades' real impact on Europe was that they increased Europeans' awareness of the world beyond their borders and accelerated economic change. Returning to their homes in Europe, Crusaders brought back spices, perfumes, fabrics, and other Asian goods looted in war. Europeans quickly developed a taste for such goods. The growing demand for Asian products revived Europe's trade with the outside world, which had nearly ceased during the Early Middle Ages.

VIEWING HISTORY
Europeans loved the Asian spices—such as cinnamon, pepper, and cloves—that the Crusaders brought back to Europe. Merchants sold the spices in marketplaces like this one. **Predicting Consequences** *What were the consequences of European demand for Asian products?*

READING CHECK
How did the manor system lead to a period of European isolation in the Early Middle Ages?

LESSON PLAN

Focus Explain that Europeans in the 1400s were ready to expand and explore. Have students think about what factors in European society influenced and motivated this desire.

Instruct Discuss how the European worldview changed during the Renaissance. Ask students whether they think all levels of European society shared this changing point of view. Have them consider why the growth of a middle class was significant.

Have students locate England, France, Portugal, and Castille (Spain) on a European map. Ask why these nations were likely to lead in developing a transatlantic trade.

Assess/Reteach Ask students to list some of the most important changes that took place in Europe during the transition between the Middle Ages and the Renaissance.

READING CHECK
People were placed in certain roles for life according to birth in a system dominated by a noble lord. Serfs received no education and knew little about the outside world. The feudal manor system was self-sufficient. As a result, Europe moved away from a monetary economy as foreign trade largely ceased during the Middle Ages.

CAPTION ANSWERS

Viewing History Merchants began to set up trade routes to Asia so they could buy Asian products and then sell them at a profit to European consumers.

Norman knights charge the English in the above section of the Bayeux Tapestry, a 231-foot length of embroidered linen that tells the story of the Norman Conquest. Scenes from medieval fables are shown along parts of the border.

In 1271, a group of merchants from the Italian city of Venice set off on a journey to China, reaching its capital in 1275. Upon their return, one member of the group, Marco Polo, wrote an account of his experiences that sent European merchants scrambling to set up trading missions to the East.

The Growth of Cities Merchants sold their foreign goods at fairs set up along water routes and trade routes. These centers of trade grew into bustling towns and cities, particularly in northern Italy and in northern France. Growing cities needed men and women with skills in trades such as weaving, baking, and metalworking. Many places attracted workers by allowing runaway serfs to exercise some of the privileges of free men.

The growth of cities and trade in Europe had three major effects:
1. It created a new **middle class,** a social class between the very wealthy and the poor, made up of merchants, traders, and artisans who made goods and sold them to the manors.
2. It revived a money economy.
3. It contributed to the eventual breakdown of the feudal system.

The Rise of Monarchs Europe's growing wealth increased the power of **monarchs**—those who rule over a state or territory—to expand their control. Monarchs attracted the loyalty of the new middle class by protecting trade routes and keeping the peace.

Strong monarchs sometimes clashed with one another. In 1066, the Duke of Normandy (a region in present-day France) conquered England. This event, called the Norman Conquest, led to a gradual combination of French and Anglo-Saxon cultures that became part of the English and American heritage.

Monarchs also clashed with their own nobles. Disputes often arose from a king's attempts to impose heavy taxes in order to fund Crusades or simply to get richer. In 1215, England's King John, a weak leader insensitive to his subjects' needs, was forced by his nobles to sign a document granting them various legal rights. That document, the **Magna Carta,** or "Great Charter," not only shaped British law and government but became the foundation for future American ideals of liberty and justice. One important clause declared:

> *" No freeman shall be arrested or imprisoned or dis-
> possessed or . . . in any way harmed . . . except by
> the lawful judgment of his peers or by the law of
> the land. "*
>
> —Magna Carta, 1215

Ambitious rulers such as King John also came into conflict with the Church. For a time, certain popes prevailed in these struggles, but by the 1200s, monarchies grew stronger as papal supremacy declined.

The Rise of Universities As monarchies grew, so did the need for educated people to run these governments. A small number of young noble and wealthy men began to enroll in the universities that arose in the 1100s. Graduates hoped to get high posts in governments or the Church.

At the same time, new sources of knowledge became available in Europe. Ancient writings of the Greeks and Romans, preserved for centuries by both Catholic monks and Muslim scholars, began to be translated into Latin, the language of Christian scholars. Arab knowledge of science and mathematics ignited Europeans' interest. Latin literature was being translated into languages that were more commonly understood. A revival of Roman architecture could be seen in the new grand cathedrals of Europe. These were the beginnings of a cultural revolution soon to sweep the continent.

The "Black Death" In the 1300s, however, European growth was cut down by a new, invisible enemy. It was a plague, and it brought rapid and ugly death to one third of Europe's entire population. Europeans called the plague the "Black Death."

Carried by fleas on the rats that infested nearly every home, a global epidemic of bubonic plague ravaged China, India, and the Middle East before arriving in an Italian port in 1347. In just a few years, the plague seized all of Europe, turning entire cities into graveyards and causing starvation, riots, and economic collapse. The disease struck nobles and serfs alike. It spared no one, not even the priests to whom people turned to stop the horror. From this devastation came a loss of religious faith, and some people began to doubt the teachings of the Church.

The Renaissance

The final, fertile centuries of the Middle Ages gave birth to a new period. The **Renaissance,** a French word meaning "rebirth," was an era of enormous creativity and rapid change that began in Italy in the 1300s. From there, the movement spread throughout western Europe, reaching its height in the 1500s.

The Pursuit of Learning The Renaissance was a quest for knowledge in nearly every field of study: art, literature, science, philosophy, economics, and political thought. The period produced many of the giant figures of Western civilization, such as Michelangelo, Leonardo da Vinci, and Shakespeare.

Key Events in Europe, *circa* 500–1600

circa 500–1000	Breakup of the Roman Empire opens Europe to invasions
600s	Rise of the Muslim empire
700s	Feudal system evolves; trade and money economy dissolve
1066	Norman Conquest leads to blending of Anglo-Saxon and French cultures
1096–1291	Crusades draw Europe from isolation and help revive trade
1100s	Rise of universities
1215	King John signs the Magna Carta
1275	Merchants including Marco Polo arrive in China
1347	Bubonic plague reaches Europe
1300s	Renaissance begins in Italy
1418	Prince Henry of Portugal starts navigation school
1455	Gutenberg prints Bible text using movable type
1469	Marriage of Isabella and Ferdinand unites kingdoms in Spain
1488	Portugal's Bartolomeu Dias sails around the tip of Africa
1492	Muslims and Jews driven from Spain
1500s	Northern Renaissance begins
1517	Reformation begins

INTERPRETING TIME LINES
Europe experienced enormous changes during the medieval era. **Analyzing Information** *Compare life in Europe both before and after the Crusades. How did it change?*

ACTIVITY
Connecting with History and Conflict

To give students who are unfamiliar with world history a better grasp of the events covered in this section, you may wish to reproduce portions of the time line on page 13. Have students suggest other events discussed in this section to add to the time line (for example, the voyages of Diaz and da Gama). Encourage students to discuss the cause-effect relationships among events. **(Visual/Spatial)**

BACKGROUND
Geography in History

During the Middle Ages, spices from Southeast Asia traveled overland to the Mediterranean, where Italian merchants monopolized sales to Europe. Wealth from trade allowed Italian cities to sponsor the great artists and architects of the Renaissance. When the Portuguese rounded the Cape of Good Hope in 1488, they challenged the Italian monopoly. Lost income contributed to Italy's decline, and the great Renaissance centers of the 1500s, such as the Netherlands, were regions that profited from new trade routes.

☑ TEST PREPARATION

Have students read the quotation from the Magna Carta on this page and then complete the sentence below.

The word *dispossessed* means—

A placed in authority.
B deprived of a home or possessions.
C deceased.
D repealed.

CAPTION ANSWERS

Interpreting Time Lines Sample answer: Before the crusades, Europe saw invasions and empires form and break up; the feudal system served to organize society. Despite catastrophes such as the Black Death, advances were made after the Crusades. These included people demanding more rights, the formation of nation-states, and people expressing interest in the world beyond Europe.

Focus on CULTURE

The Renaissance Man The idea of the Renaissance is embodied in what we now call the Renaissance man, the person who is skilled and knowledgeable in all the arts and sciences. This concept came from Leon Battista Alberti (1404–1472), who said that "a man can do all things if he will."

Today, Leonardo da Vinci (1452–1519) is regarded as the ultimate Renaissance man. He was a painter, sculptor, architect, and musician. His *Mona Lisa* (above) still fascinates viewers. In addition, Leonardo was a scientist and engineer; some of his inventions, such as a type of helicopter (below) were centuries ahead of their time. In his notebooks, Leonardo combined a spirit of scientific inquiry with extraordinary powers of observation and artistic skill. He studied anatomy in order to be a better sculptor—even dissecting corpses to view the muscles, skeleton, and organs—thus making contributions to both art and science.

Compared to the chaos of the medieval period, the Renaissance brought order and unity in Europe. Yet it also was a rebellion against the rigid thinking of the past. Following the models of the Greeks, Romans, and Muslims, European thinkers began using reason and experimentation to understand the physical world.

Cultural Change in Italy The Renaissance flourished in the cities of northern Italy, where ancient buildings, bridges, and monuments recalled the cultural achievements of the once-powerful Roman Empire. Fascinated by their glorious past, Italians were also increasingly interested in their future. In Milan, Venice, Genoa, and Florence, a wealthy merchant class dominated local political and economic life. These nobles valued individual achievement and a well-rounded education. They studied the arts and became generous supporters of them.

Renaissance artists gained work by attracting the support of such a rich patron—a noble, a king, or even a pope. Sculptors, poets, and architects all worked in the service of their patrons, creating whatever was desired. In the city of Florence, the rich and powerful Medici family became the most famous Renaissance patrons. They made possible the work of Leonardo da Vinci, the legendary sculptor, painter, poet, inventor, and scientist.

A Golden Age Many of the most respected artists of all time lived and worked in Italy during the Renaissance. The 1400s and 1500s became a golden age in the arts. Although the movement drew inspiration from ancient models, it also produced new artistic forms and ideas. Renaissance art explored the physical world and the individual's role in it. This core philosophy of the period is called humanism.

Artistic subjects in the humanist world were heroic and full of emotion, and their physical features were presented more realistically than they had been in the past. Michelangelo's famous *Pietà* is a massive sculpture of the biblical Mary, serene and sorrowful, cradling the body of her dead son Jesus. Leonardo da Vinci studied the anatomy of the human body in order to sculpt it accurately. He even dissected corpses to view the muscles, skeleton, and organs. Among writers, the poet Petrarch is closely associated with the beginnings of humanism. Petrarch is best known for his poems about romantic love.

The Northern Renaissance As the plague died out and the rest of Europe began to prosper again, the Renaissance spread northward. By the late 1500s, the Renaissance was in bloom in the Netherlands, Belgium, France, Spain, England, and Germany.

This cultural period is called the Northern Renaissance. It produced its own geniuses, including several Dutch painters who warmly depicted everyday peasant life.

The period also produced the English playwright and poet William Shakespeare, generally regarded as the most gifted writer in the English language. His subjects ranged from a Danish prince, Hamlet, to the Roman emperor Julius Caesar. His characters included soldiers, innkeepers, and British monarchs.

The Printing Press In medieval times, books were rare, and most dealt with religious topics. Christian monks carefully copied each one by hand. Then, as Renaissance writers were putting new ideas onto paper, German Johann

14   Chapter 1 • *The Atlantic World*

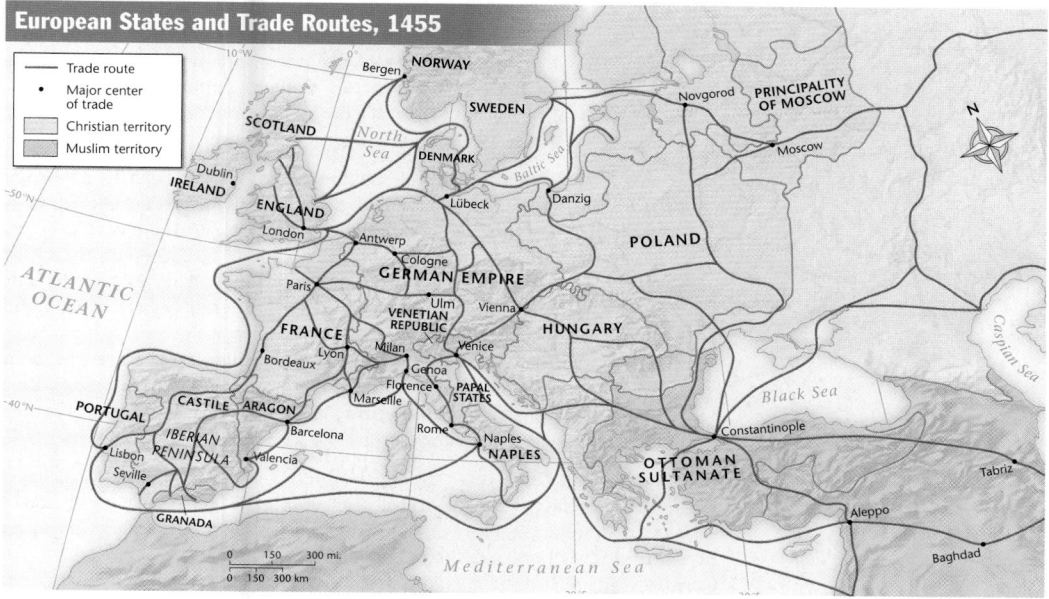

European States and Trade Routes, 1455

Legend:
- Trade route
- • Major center of trade
- Christian territory
- Muslim territory

Gutenberg figured out how to put them into print. In 1455, Gutenberg produced a Bible made on a printing press. The words were set in movable metal type. Books could then be printed over and over. The invention set off a communications revolution over the next century, as some 200 million books came off European printing presses.

The Reformation New ideas now traveled rapidly in print. The Bible circulated among a widening audience. The printing revolution occurred at a time when critics, angry at corruption among the clergy, were calling for reform of the Church. In 1517, criticism flared into a revolt known as the **Reformation.** It was led by Martin Luther, a German monk who declared that the Bible, not the Church, was the true authority. His followers called themselves Protestants because they protested Church authority. From northern Germany, the Reformation spread to England, where it became an official movement under a popular Protestant queen, Elizabeth I.

The Rise of Nations During the Renaissance, government by local nobles and the Church gradually declined. Instead, monarchs began to combine smaller areas into the larger nation-states of Europe that we know today. Now, for the first time, Europeans thought of themselves not in terms of community or region but as members of nations, such as France, England, or Portugal.

Seafaring Technology The young nations soon started to compete with one another for the highly profitable Asian trade. In 1400, the only way to reach Asia was still by land. Europeans did not have the technology to explore the faster sea route. Sailors who ventured out of sight of land often disappeared. They had no way to calculate their position at sea.

With the help of instruments developed by Renaissance scientists, however, long-range sea travel finally became possible. Sailors could use a compass to determine direction when neither the coastline nor the sun was visible. The

MAP SKILLS Europe at this time was divided into numerous states, which competed for control of the limited trade and land available on the continent.
Place *Describe a trade route that could be used to travel from Constantinople to Paris. Include the major trade centers along the way.*

ACTIVITY
Connecting with Science and Technology
Have students research the role of the cog (a kind of ship) and the lateen sail in the development of the full-rigged ship, with which Europeans took to the oceans. Have students fashion models, present them to the class, highlighting the attributes that made them so seaworthy. **(Bodily/Kinesthetic)**

BACKGROUND
Biography
Martin Luther is arguably one of the most important, or at least influential, people who have ever lived. It is difficult to overstate his influence. First, and foremost, he spearheaded the Reformation. The course of Western Civilization was marked and altered for centuries by conflict between Protestants and Catholics. His translation of the Bible into German obviated the need for the Church to interpret it, making it accessible to any literate person. In this and in other actions, Luther opened the door to freedom of religious thought, which paved the way for free thinking in other areas. Today, there are more Protestants than there are members of many entire religions. Thus, Luther's influence was both far-reaching and long-lasting.

CAPTION ANSWERS

Map Skills Sample answer: Sail from Constantinople to Venice via the Mediterranean, then travel over land, passing through Ulm before reaching Paris.

Reading Comprehension

1. The era in European history from about A.D. 500 to 1300, also known as the medieval period.

2. Political and economic system of medieval Europe in which lesser lords received lands from powerful nobles in exchange for service. Feudal society was based on the manor system, a rigid social structure in which socioeconomic status was determined by birth.

3. The middle class grew as a result of the growth of cities, increased trade, and a return to a money economy. Europe's growing wealth increased the power of monarchs, expanding their control. Monarchs attracted the loyalty of the new middle class by protecting trade routes and keeping the peace.

4. It granted various legal rights to nobles, no longer leaving power exclusively in the hands of the monarchy to shape British law and government, and it became the foundation for future American ideals of liberty and justice.

5. Gutenberg's invention of the printing press allowed information to become more widespread, beginning with the circulation of the Christian Bible. Luther declared that the Bible, not the Roman Catholic Church, was the supreme authority. His criticism grew into the Protestant Reformation, a revolt against the Church.

Critical Thinking and Writing

6. The Crusades contributed to the growth of foreign trade. Fairs set up to market foreign goods developed along water routes and trade routes that grew into busy towns and cities, particularly in northern Italy and northern France.

7. Outlines will vary, but should be supported with facts from the section. Students might mention that the Renaissance was a period in which the pursuit of both learning and artistic accomplishment flourished.

Take It to the NET

Summaries will vary, but should present information clearly and accurately and should include specific facts.

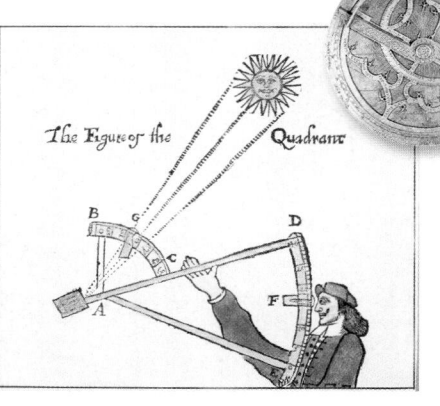

Early sailors sighted the North Star and used an astrolabe (top) to calculate their latitude. A quadrant (bottom) was used to read the position of the sun.

astrolabe and the quadrant now allowed ship captains to find their approximate location far from visible land, taking some of the guesswork out of marine navigation. Long ocean voyages continued to have their perils and discomforts, but the new technology widened their range of possibility.

Portugal Takes to the Seas In addition to navigation problems, sailors also had difficulty sailing against the wind. In 1418, Prince Henry of Portugal, later called Prince Henry the Navigator, established a mariners' school at Sagres, on the southwestern tip of Portugal. There, his seamen developed the final tool necessary for long-range voyages: the caravel, a ship that could sail against the wind as well as with it. In 1488, a Sagres-trained navigator, Bartolomeu Dias, sailed around the southernmost cape of Africa, the Cape of Good Hope. Nine years later, another Portuguese mariner, Vasco da Gama, sailed from Portugal to India. The first sea route from Europe to Asia was open.

Competition on the Seas About this time, a new power arose to challenge Portugal on the high seas. In 1469, Isabella of Castile and Ferdinand of Aragon were married, uniting their two powerful kingdoms in what is present-day Spain. At this time, the diversity of Spain's population—made up of Muslims, Jews, and Christians—made it distinct from other western European populations. Although Spain's unique mix of race and religion had been essential to the region's economic and cultural development, anti-Jewish and anti-Muslim fervor was widespread. In 1478, with permission from the Church, Isabella and Ferdinand launched a campaign based on racial prejudice known as the Inquisition. The goal of the Inquisition was to discover and punish Jews—and later Muslims—who were passing as Christians. In 1492, all Jews who refused to be baptized were expelled from Spain. In that same year, Ferdinand and Isabella succeeded in conquering Granada, the last independent Muslim kingdom in Spain.

Isabella was not content with military victory, however. She had two other goals: to surpass Portugal in the race to explore new sea routes and to bring Christianity to new lands. So, as her ships dropped anchor along the West Coast of Africa, they carried not only trade goods but Christian missionaries as well.

Section 2 Assessment

READING COMPREHENSION

1. What were the **Middle Ages?**
2. What was **feudalism?**
3. What is the relationship between the rise of the **middle class** and the increased power of **monarchs?**
4. What was the importance of the **Magna Carta?**
5. What events led to the **Reformation?**

CRITICAL THINKING AND WRITING

6. **Determining Cause and Effect** What effect, if any, did the Crusades have on the growth of cities in the Middle Ages?

7. **Writing an Outline** Form an outline for an essay that explains why the Renaissance is considered the beginning of the modern era.

Take It to the NET

Activity: Analyzing Primary Sources Examine writing and artwork from the Renaissance era to gain insight into the past. Summarize your research in a brief report. Use the links provided in the *America: Pathways to the Present* area of the following Web site for help in completing this activity.
www.phschool.com

RESOURCE DIRECTORY

Teaching Resources
Units 1/2 booklet
• Section 2 Quiz, p. 5
Guide to the Essentials
• Section 2 Summary, p. 6

The World of the West Africans

Section **3**
The World of the West Africans

READING FOCUS

- How did West Africans and Europeans first meet?
- What are some key features of early West African cultures?
- How did a trading relationship develop between Europe and the kingdoms of West Africa?
- What was the role of slavery in African society?

MAIN IDEA

At the time of their first contact with Europeans, West Africans had wealthy kingdoms with strong governments, unique cultures, and traditional religious beliefs.

KEY TERMS

savanna
lineage
scarce

TAKING NOTES

Copy the Venn diagram below. As you read, fill in the two circles with information about West African and European customs. Place details that are similar to both cultures in the area where the two circles overlap.

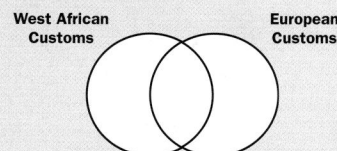

West African Customs   European Customs

SECTION OBJECTIVES

1. Learn how West Africans and Europeans first met.
2. Find out some key features of early West African cultures.
3. See how a trading relationship developed between Europe and the kingdoms of West Africa.
4. Discover the role of slavery in African society.

BELLRINGER

Warm-Up Activity Ask students to list as many facts as they can about the continent of Africa. You may want to display a map of Africa and point out both the places they name and those mentioned in this section.

Activating Prior Knowledge Ask students to list facts they know about West Africa prior to the time of encounters with Europeans.

READING STRATEGY

Before students read the section, have them make a list of questions they might have asked about the contact between Europe and West Africa. As they read the section, have them fill in the answers to their questions.

Setting the Scene The Atlantic Ocean that washed against the Americas and Europe broke also on the shores of Africa. Once long-range travel by ship became possible, traffic on the seas increased. By the 1400s, the Atlantic was already a highway over which Europeans traveled to reach Africa and the ancient, wealthy kingdoms that lay beyond its coast.

West Africans and Europeans Meet

Europeans and Africans first met in ancient times, when a wide trading network of land and sea routes thrived throughout the Mediterranean region. As you have read, much of this contact ceased during the Middle Ages but resumed during the Renaissance. Europeans traded cloth, metal goods made of iron and copper, and jewelry for gold from North African middlemen, who in turn obtained the gold from their trading partners in the interior of West Africa.

Europeans wanted to get around the middlemen and go directly to these sources of gold. This was the prize for which Spain and Portugal competed in the 1400s as their ships explored Africa's Atlantic Coast.

Early relations between the two cultures were mostly peaceful. Portugal established trade ties with wealthy coastal kingdoms, which produced much of the gold. The Portuguese built a string of forts along the coast for their ships to load and unload trade goods. Africans ran the trading operations and set their own prices. The Netherlands, France, and England soon launched expeditions to the region to set up similar trade arrangements.

West African Cultures

At the time of European contact, West Africa was home to a great variety of peoples and ways of life. As with all societies, Africans adapted their culture to their geographic surroundings.

Geography and Livelihoods In West Africa, three main types of vegetation regions influenced how people made a living, raised families, and worshipped.

Gold from the forest regions of West Africa was traded to other parts of Africa and to Europeans. This gold pendant was made by the Baule people.

RESOURCE DIRECTORY

Teaching Resources
Guided Reading and Review booklet, p. 5

Technology
Section Reading Support Transparencies
Guided Reading Audiotapes (English/Spanish), Ch. 1
Student Edition on Audio CD, Ch. 1
Sounds of an Era Audio CD *Olaudah Equiano on West Africa* (time: 45 seconds)
Prentice Hall Presentation Pro CD-ROM, Ch. 1
Companion Web site, www.phschool.com

Focus Explain that the first interactions between European and African cultures came in the 1400s along the coast of West Africa, where great kingdoms had prosperous, complex cultures. Have students think about what those cultures were like and what factors influenced their contact with European cultures.

Instruct Have students locate Songhai and Benin on the map on page 19 and notice trading posts and routes. How far did West African trade routes extend?

Point out that trade often brings new ideas and technology as well as goods to buy and sell. Discuss ways that Islam set Songhai apart from other cultures in West Africa at the time.

Assess/Reteach Ask students to reflect on the prosperity of West African kingdoms at the time they first made contact with Europeans. Can students imagine what might have happened to those kingdoms and those countries if Europeans had not made contact with them in the Age of Exploration?

ACTIVITY
Connecting with Economics

To help students better understand trade in West Africa, have them trace the route of a trader going from Benin to Songhai to North Africa. Have them use the map on page 19 to answer these questions: What direction will the trader travel from Benin to Songhai? About how far is it from the city of Benin to Timbuktu? From Timbuktu to Fez in North Africa? What kind of terrain will the trader have to cross? **(Visual/Spatial)**

This pair of leopards from the sixteenth century are among the many beautiful works of art created in Benin.

Rain forests supporting a wide variety of plant and animal life covered a large band of coastal land along the southern part of the region. Africans had migrated there from central Africa over hundreds of years. Some of the continent's earliest societies and cities evolved in the resource-rich region, where people hunted, fished, mined, and farmed the land.

Farther north lay a wide expanse of **savanna,** a region near the equator with tropical grasslands and scattered trees. The savanna has a dry season and a wet season, rather than hot and cold seasons. The wet season supported limited farming. Year round, nomadic peoples hunted and raised livestock in the savannah. Merchants did a brisk business obtaining gold and other goods from the forest regions and trading them to merchants farther north. From the busy cities of Gao and Timbuktu, trading expeditions crossed the desert to reach the northern markets.

Desert is the third major vegetation region in West Africa. The world's largest desert, the Sahara, remained largely uninhabited. Scattered towns arose at major watering holes, where camel caravans loaded with trade goods stopped to rest.

Family Life As in the Americas, societies throughout West Africa were organized according to kinship groups. Often, all the residents of a town or city belonged to kinship groups that traced their line of origin to a common ancestor. This type of organization is called a **lineage.** African lineage groups provided the types of support that modern governments and churches do in the United States. West Africa's ruling classes generally came from powerful lineage groups.

Religion From ancient times, a great variety of religious customs and ceremonies existed in Africa. Yet traditional cultures generally shared certain religious beliefs. People worshipped a Supreme Being as well as many lesser gods and goddesses, or spirits. As in most early religions, these spirits were thought to inhabit everything in the natural world, from animals to trees to stones. Humans also were thought to be living spirits both before and after death. Africans appealed to the spirits of their ancestors for help.

Information concerning religious beliefs, family stories, and laws was handed down from generation to generation through oral tradition. As in the Americas, oral histories gave kinship groups a distinct sense of identity and unity.

Focus on
GEOGRAPHY

The Savanna Geographically, savannas form transition areas between deserts and tropical rain forests. The African savanna, shown below, fits this description. It stretches from coast to coast just south of the Sahara desert, and curves around the rain forests of West and Central Africa. The savanna offers environmental transitions as well, with dry seasons similar to the climate of desert areas, and wet seasons that support lush plant growth, more typical of a rainforest environment. Not confined to Africa, savannas can be found in parts of Australia, South Asia, and South America.

Kingdoms and Trade

Africans also left a historical record in exquisite works of art. These treasures tell the story of governments that ruled for centuries.

Benin One such government ruled Benin, a coastal forest kingdom that arose in the late 1200s. There, artists left a record of their society in a series of bronze plaques that once decorated the palace of the king, or Oba. From the capital city, also called Benin, the Oba ruled surrounding lands. Through a network of administrators, Benin's rulers waged war, directed agriculture, and regulated trade.

A European traveler who had visited the capital several times made this observation: "This city is about a league [three miles] long from gate to gate; it has no wall but is surrounded by a large moat, very wide and deep, which suffices for its defense. . . . Its houses are made of mud walls covered with palm leaves." The streets of Benin were wide and clean, and they led to a grand palace.

Benin's wealth came from trade. The kingdom produced goods such as palm oil, ivory, and beautiful woods. Each group of artisans, such as those who worked in bronze or brass or ivory, had its own organization.

The kingdom produced some of the finest artwork of the time, especially sculptures of human heads created in a unique artistic style. In time, sculptors started creating figures with beards and helmets. These figures represented the Portuguese. A strong Oba had come to the throne in 1481 and had established friendly and profitable trade relations with the Portuguese.

Songhai In the 1400s, as European monarchs began to make plans for building empires, one of the largest empires in the world was expanding in the West African savanna. The Songhai empire, located between the coastal rain forest region and the dry Sahara, stretched across much of West Africa. The Songhai empire would exist until 1591.

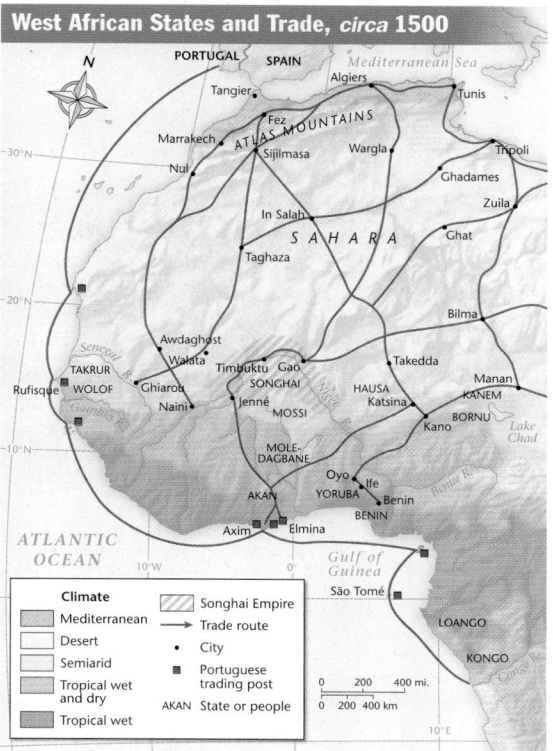

West African States and Trade, circa 1500

Climate
- Mediterranean
- Desert
- Semiarid
- Tropical wet and dry
- Tropical wet

- Songhai Empire
- → Trade route
- • City
- ■ Portuguese trading post
- AKAN State or people

MAP SKILLS By 1500, extensive trade routes crisscrossed West Africa. **Movement** *Why do you think the Portuguese established their trading posts along Africa's west coast?*

Chapter 1 • Section 3   **19**

ARRIVAL AT TIMBUKTU.

ACTIVITY

Connecting with Geography

Ask students to trace an outline map of the world and draw lines to represent the major interactions among the three cultures of the Atlantic World. Have them use symbols or icons to show the major items that were interchanged: foods and crops, animals, diseases, slaves, and gold and silver. **(Visual/Spatial)**

BACKGROUND

Art History

For centuries, West African craftsmen have fashioned evocative masks out of materials like wood and gold. Scary, cheerful, or impassive, these masks are not only decorative, but serve a variety of purposes such as worship and the warding off of dangerous spirits. See Hugh Honour and John Fleming, *The Visual Arts: A History*, Prentice Hall, 1986.

READING CHECK

Songhai's location made it an ideal trading region for goods traveling between the resource-rich coastal forests and inland North African traders. Songhai's government successfully controlled defense, banking, and farming. The empire negotiated peace with other nations, which helped Songhai gain educational resources.

VIEWING HISTORY In this engraving from the 1800s, a caravan arrives at the city of Timbuktu. Trade routes were used not only to transport goods but to spread and exchange ideas among cultures. **Drawing Conclusions** *How did Timbuktu's role as a trade center help lead to its development into a center of learning?*

READING CHECK
Which characteristics of the Songhai empire contributed to its success?

Songhai's most famed monarch, Askia Muhammad, created a complex government with separate departments for defense, banking, and farming. A bureaucracy of paid officials enforced laws, collected taxes, negotiated with other nations, and kept the peace.

Peace and prosperity supported the growth of education in Songhai. The capital city, Timbuktu, was a center of learning, with about 150 schools for a population of 100,000. An Arab traveler and writer of the time, Leo Africanus, wrote of Timbuktu:

> 66 *A great store of doctors, judges, priests, and other learned men . . . are bountifully maintained at the King's cost and charges. And hither [here] are brought various manuscripts of books from North Africa, which are sold for more money than any other merchandise.* 99
> —Leo Africanus, *The History and Description of Africa, circa* 1526

As in medieval Europe, most scholars studied religion. Islam had reached West Africa in about the year 1050 through trade and by invasion from the north. Askia Muhammad, a devout Muslim, had made Songhai a Muslim empire. Yet most people, especially outside the cities, still followed traditional African beliefs.

Songhai's location made it a major player in the growing trade with North Africa and Europe. From forest kingdoms such as Benin, Songhai traders obtained gold, ivory, and kola nuts (used to flavor drinks). They also bought pepper, a rare and much-desired spice in those days. Traders paid heavy fees to move their goods northward across Songhai. In caravans of as many as 12,000 camels, the groups continued north across the Sahara. On their return trip, they brought books, paper, weapons, cloth, horses, and salt.

Slavery in Africa

Africans, like Europeans, believed in the private ownership of goods and property. Yet Africans differed from Europeans in their attitudes toward land and

CAPTION ANSWERS

Viewing History Islamic scholars who settled there helped turn Timbuktu into a center of learning.

RESOURCE DIRECTORY

Teaching Resources
Units 1/2 booklet
• Section 3 Quiz, p. 6
Guide to the Essentials
• Section 3 Summary, p. 7

Other Print Resources
Historical Outline Map Book *The World,* p. 71

Technology
RESOURCE**PRO**® **Biography** *Askia Muhammad,* found on Resource Pro, profiles

the brilliant ruler of the West African kingdom of Songhai.

RESOURCE**PRO**® **Visual Learning Activity**
Slave Factories, found on Resource Pro, helps students understand slavery through illustration.

RESOURCE**PRO**® **Primary Source Activity**
The Portuguese in West Africa, found on Resource Pro, uses a chronicle written in the mid-1400s to present the reasons Portugal explored West Africa.

people. In Europe, land was **scarce**—in short supply—and thus was very valuable. Europeans' wealth, in fact, was determined by the amount of land they possessed. In Africa, land was plentiful, so no one could become wealthy and powerful by claiming a large area of land. Africans, therefore, tended to value labor more than land. Leaders' power rested on the number of people they ruled rather than the amount of land they controlled. Growing kingdoms such as Benin and Songhai needed increasing numbers of workers. As in many other societies, slaves provided the labor. They made or grew much of what was traded. In addition, slaves themselves had value as items of trade.

People cut off from their lineage were the most likely to be enslaved in Africa. Most slaves probably had been captured in war. The slave population also included orphans, criminals, and other people rejected by society. Many people were kidnapped in slave raids carried out by rival ethnic groups.

Africans' concept of slavery differed from slavery as it developed in the Americas. In Africa, for example, slaves became adopted members of the kinship group that enslaved them. Frequently they married into a lineage, sometimes even into the high ranks of society. Slaves also could move up in society and out of their slave role. Children of slaves were not presumed to be born into slavery. Finally, enslaved people carried out a variety of roles not limited to tough physical labor. While most women and many men labored in the fields, some men became soldiers or administrators.

In the 1500s, Europeans—mainly the Portuguese and Spanish, followed by the Dutch and the English—began to exchange valuable goods, such as guns, for slaves sold by coastal societies such as Benin. Both sides profited greatly. The Africans obtained advanced technology, and the Europeans obtained labor for use in large farming operations in the Americas and elsewhere.

As time wore on, the Europeans demanded more and more slaves. Those who resisted dealing in the human cargo became themselves the victims of bloody slave raids.

In the plaque above, an Oba, attended by servants, is offered merchandise by Portuguese traders.

Reading Comprehension

1. Long-range travel by ship enabled Mediterranean trade begun in ancient times to be resumed during the Renaissance. Cloth, metal goods made of iron and copper, and gold were traded.

2. Savanna: near the Equator; wet and dry seasons; year-round hunting and raising of livestock. Rain forests: wide variety of plant and animal life; located in the southern part of the region. Desert: largely uninhabited; scattered towns at major watering holes.

3. Lineage provides the type of support provided by modern governments and churches in the United States; the ruling classes generally came from powerful lineage lines.

4. In short supply.

5. A variety of religious customs and ceremonies existed. Traditional cultures shared certain religious beliefs; people worshipped a supreme being as well as many lesser gods, goddesses, or spirits.

6. Benin: From the capital city, the king ruled surrounding lands; through administrators, Benin's rulers waged war, directed agriculture, and regulated trade. Songhai: Complex monarchical government had separate departments for defense, banking, and farming; paid officials enforced laws, collected taxes, negotiated with other nations, and kept the peace.

Critical Thinking and Writing

7. In Africa, labor was valued more than land. Slaves became a valued trade item. Slaves were adopted by the kinship group that enslaved them. Some slaves were eventually freed.

8. Essays will vary, but should be persuasive and supported by facts from the section.

Section **3** Assessment

READING COMPREHENSION

1. How did trade develop between the West Africans and the Europeans? What items were traded?

2. Describe the **savanna** and other vegetation regions of West Africa.

3. What is the importance of **lineage** in West African society?

4. What does **scarce** mean?

5. What were the religious traditions of West Africa?

6. What were some characteristics of the Benin and Songhai governments?

CRITICAL THINKING AND WRITING

7. **Recognizing Cause and Effect** Describe the early Africans' attitudes toward the ownership of land and of slaves. How did such attitudes affect their society?

8. **Writing a Conclusion** Should African monarchs have established trade with the Europeans? Write a conclusion for a convincing essay that weighs the benefits and risks of such trade.

 Take It to the NET

Activity: Writing an Essay Investigate the history of West African kingdoms. Write an essay on the art, history, or some aspect of daily life in a West African kingdom. Use the links provided in the *America: Pathways to the Present* area of the following Web site for help in completing this activity.
www.phschool.com

✓ TEST PREPARATION

Have students read the section "Slavery in Africa" and then answer the question below.

Which of the following statements about African and European attitudes is correct?

A Land was valued as a possession in Europe but not in Africa.

B In both Europe and Africa, land ownership determined wealth.

C Africans believed in private ownership of goods, but Europeans did not.

D Europeans believed in private ownership of goods, but Africans did not.

 **Take It to the NET**

Essays will vary, but should demonstrate a thorough investigation of the chosen topic.

The Atlantic World Is Born

READING FOCUS
- What is known about the early life of Christopher Columbus?
- What events occurred on Columbus's expeditions?
- Describe the debate concerning the impact of Columbus's voyages.

MAIN IDEA
Columbus's voyages to the Americas permanently reshaped American, European, and African history.

KEY TERMS
Columbian Exchange
Treaty of Tordesillas
plantation
cash crop

TAKING NOTES
Copy the cause-and-effect diagram below. As you read, write down the reasons Columbus and other Europeans explored the Americas, and the effects of their exploration.

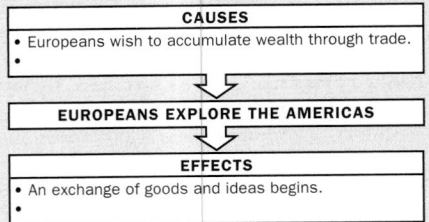

CAUSES
• Europeans wish to accumulate wealth through trade. •

⬇

EUROPEANS EXPLORE THE AMERICAS

⬇

EFFECTS
• An exchange of goods and ideas begins. •

Born into modest circumstances, Christopher Columbus had to seek the help of kings and queens to realize his ambitions.

Setting the Scene Throughout the years, many stories have been told about Christopher Columbus's voyage to America. According to one recently popular legend, Columbus believed that Earth was round, while everyone else thought it was flat. As he sailed west across the Atlantic Ocean, his crew nearly mutinied, thinking that they would fall off the edge of Earth. Just then, the story goes, the crew spotted land. Columbus had discovered America, the old histories claimed. He was said to be the first European to set foot on American soil.

This story steers from the truth at several points. First, Renaissance scholars of Columbus's time studied the work of ancient Greek and Arab scientists, who had shown that Earth is a sphere—shaped like a ball. Second, Native Americans had already been living in the Western Hemisphere for thousands of years before the arrival of Columbus. So, the "discovery" for Columbus and his fellow Europeans was a land already known to a great many people. Third, about 500 years before Columbus's famous journey, other Europeans had ventured to North America. Norsemen led by Leif Ericson most likely sailed along the North American coast and probably stopped occasionally in present-day Maine and Newfoundland, Canada.

The truth itself is amazing enough. Columbus was an experienced navigator who undertook a highly dangerous voyage into unknown waters. Aside from Leif Ericson and his fellow Norsemen, other mariners who had attempted the trip across the Atlantic never returned. Columbus did, and his accomplishment changed the course of history.

Christopher Columbus

Columbus wrote volumes about his journeys to the Americas, yet we know very little about his early life. Columbus, or Cristoforo Colombo in Italian, was born in 1451 in the bustling merchant city of Genoa, Italy. His father, Domenico, did a modest business as a merchant and worked in the wool industry. His mother, Susanna Fontanarossa, was the daughter of a wool weaver.

Columbus grew up determined to make his fortune and join the ranks of the wealthy nobility. Young Columbus had a variety of interests, spending some time as a mapmaker and a trader. His love, however, was the ocean. So he went where any aspiring mariner of that time would go: to Portugal, for navigator's training.

Much of the rest of Columbus's life was spent at sea. In 1476, at age 25, he survived a shipwreck off the coast of Portugal. With a fearlessness that would serve him well later on, he went right back to the sea. He joined Portuguese crews that sailed to Iceland and Ireland in 1477. After spending some time in Madeira as a sugar buyer for an Italian company, the restless sailor traveled to West Africa to trade along the forested coast. On these voyages Columbus developed a genius for navigation. He also learned much about the geography and wind currents of the eastern Atlantic Ocean.

Columbus was a complex man, moody and distant from others, ambitious and stubborn. He was also highly religious and well-schooled in the Bible. Columbus believed absolutely that he could succeed where others had failed and that God had given him a heroic mission.

A Daring Expedition

As his skills matured, Columbus became more eager to seek a westward sea route to the "Indies," meaning China, India, and other Asian lands. He did not only *think* of attempting it—he *knew* he would do it. But he did not have the personal wealth to fund such an undertaking. For years he petitioned various European monarchs to sponsor his risky project.

Columbus's pleas were answered in January 1492, when he appeared before the Spanish court of Queen Isabella and King Ferdinand. They authorized Columbus to make contact with the people of "the lands of India." Much to his pleasure, they granted him the title of a noble and made him "High Admiral of the Ocean Sea and . . . Governor of the islands and continent which I should discover," as Columbus wrote later. His sons and grandsons would inherit his title and the conquered lands, he said.

Reasons for the Voyage Spanish nobles and clergy strongly supported Columbus's voyage. All had reasons for wanting the mission to succeed:

1. Columbus hoped to enrich his family and to gain honor, fortune, and fame. Yet Columbus also planned to conquer non-Catholic lands and convert their peoples to Catholicism. He held the belief, widespread at that time, that other cultures were inferior to his own. In the very year of his voyage, Columbus witnessed the final battle of Queen Isabella's crusade to reconquer Spain from the Muslims. This he saw as proof that God wanted him to bring Christianity to other lands.
2. Columbus's royal patrons shared his desire to spread Catholicism, but they had economic motives as well. The Crusades had failed to retake Jerusalem, and Muslims still controlled the overland trade routes connecting Europe and Asia. Europeans wanted to bypass the Muslims and find a way to trade directly for the eastern spices and herbs that Europeans wanted for cooking and for medicine.

BIOGRAPHY

Leif Ericson

Most of what is known of explorer Leif Ericson comes from Norse legend and Viking tales. Leif Ericson lived during the late tenth century and early eleventh century and was one of three sons of Eric the Red, the first European colonizer of Greenland.

According to a Greenland legend, Leif Ericson first heard of a place called Vinland—so named for its grapes or berries—from an Icelandic explorer who had spotted its shores in 986. The story tells how Leif and a crew of 35 sailed to Vinland, and also spent time in places called Helluland ("Flat-Stone Land"), and Markland ("Wood Land"). Legend tells how other Norsemen made subsequent journeys to Vinland. Leif's brother Thorvald traveled there, followed by Thorfinn Karlsefni, who with a number of others spent three years attempting to colonize Vinland before returning to Greenland.

Actual physical evidence to support this account is difficult to come by, though some does exist. Features of a housing site in northern Newfoundland, and the date it is estimated to have been built—around 1000—suggest that the area might have been the Vinland of Norse legend.

READING CHECK
What motivated Columbus to set sail for the "Indies"?

Connecting with Science and Technology

Assign students the research task of determining the basic dimensions (length and beam) of one of Columbus's ships. Then, using those figures, trace a rough outline of the ship with sidewalk chalk outside of your school. To emphasize the small dimensions of the ship, have all the students stand inside the outline. **(Bodily/Kinesthetic)**

From the Archives of
AmericanHeritage®

Cabot Drops By

On June 24, 1497, the Genoa-born English mariner John Cabot became the first European since Viking days to set foot in North America, when he landed on what is now called Newfoundland. At least, that's the story. In actuality, an event resembling Cabot's voyage did take place in 1497, but virtually every detail is subject to question. Cabot left no written record of his journey, and the few surviving secondhand sources contradict one another. Even the basic biographical facts are skimpy. Cabot's point of disembarkation elicits the most controversy. Based on a few scraps of maddeningly vague description, historians have located the site everywhere from Labrador down to Maine, with Newfoundland the most popular choice. Source: Frederic D. Schwarz, "The Time Machine," *American Heritage*® magazine, May/June 1997.

Jean Leon Gerome Ferris's *The Eve of Discovery, 1492* offers a dramatic view of Columbus's voyage.

3. Spain's rivalry with Portugal gave the Spanish another reason for backing the voyage. Portuguese sailors had found an eastern route to India by sailing around Africa. If Spain could find an easier, western route to Asia, it might gain an advantage over Portuguese traders.

Destination: Asia Early in the morning on Friday, August 3, 1492, three ships under Columbus's command set sail from the seaport of Palos, in the Spanish kingdom of Castile. They bore Spanish names: *Niña, Pinta,* and *Santa Maria.* Before them stretched the blue curve of the horizon. Awaiting them were dangers such as ocean storms, starvation, and the sailor's enemies: rickets and scurvy, painful diseases resulting from a lack of vitamins found in fresh fruits and vegetables.

Columbus showed his navigational skills by first heading south, then west, avoiding the Atlantic storms that had blown other ships to pieces. The voyage was on a course for disaster, however, because Columbus had underestimated the size of the planet. By Columbus's measurements, for example, China would have been roughly where the city of San Diego, California, is today. He figured Japan to be on the same line of longitude as the present-day Virgin Islands. His ships had not brought enough food or water for a voyage all the way to Asia. Columbus's journals of the voyage suggest that as the tense weeks passed, the admiral did not reveal to his crews how far they had actually traveled, in order to ward off fears about the journey home.

On October 12, the crew of the *Pinta* finally spotted land. The explorers' actual landing place is disputed, but it certainly was not China. Columbus later wrote that the island was called Guanahani by its native inhabitants. Many scholars believe it was the island of San Salvador, in the Bahamas.

A Historic Meeting Fortunately for Columbus and his crew, they received a warm welcome from the first Native Americans they met, the Tainos. The Tainos greeted the newcomers and offered them such items as parrots, balls of cotton thread, and javelins tipped with fish

Focus on
DAILY LIFE

Life at Sea Little is known about daily life at sea during the late 1400s, but the work of a sailor was surely difficult. Sailing crews faced any number of problems, including malnutrition, disease, and at times, boredom. A list of provisions for one of Columbus's voyages offers some details on life at sea: Food stores included wheat, sea biscuit (an unleavened bread), barrels of wine and water, olive oil, sardines, raisins, and garlic. Sailors ate salt pork—pieces of pork that had been washed with hot lye, and then coated with a crust of clay and bran to protect the meat from spoilage. Some sailors dined in the dark so they would not have to look at the maggots that crawled on their bread. Infrequent hot meals were cooked over an open fire built inside of a sandbox on deck.

Among the crew, only the captain and the ship's pilot kept regular sleeping quarters—all other crew members slept wherever they could find a spot, either up on deck or below.

RESOURCE DIRECTORY

Technology
Sounds of an Era Audio CD *Letter to the Spanish Crown, Christopher Columbus* (time: 30 seconds)
Exploring Primary Sources in U.S. History CD-ROM *The Log of Christopher Columbus*

teeth (rather than the iron weapons Europeans commonly used). This astonished Columbus, who was not familiar with the Native American view of trade as an exchange of gifts. Columbus later wrote about his encounter with the Tainos to Isabella and Ferdinand:

> 66 They are so ingenuous [innocent] and free with all they have, that no one would believe it who has not seen it; of anything that they possess, if it be asked of them, they never say no; on the contrary, they invite you to share it and show as much love as if their hearts went with it, and they are content with whatever trifle be given them, whether it be a thing of value or of petty worth. I forbade that they be given things so worthless of broken crockery and of green glass and lace-points, although when they could get them, they thought they had the best jewel in the world. 99
>
> —Letter from Columbus to Queen Isabella and King Ferdinand of Spain, 1493

Continuing on to other islands, Columbus and his crew collected—often by force—other gifts to give to the queen. These "gifts" included some Native Americans, whom Columbus brought back to Spain to present to the Spanish monarchs. Columbus called these people "Indians," because he believed that he had reached the Indies. The term is still sometimes used today.

Heading Home   When the return trip to Spain began, on January 16, 1493, only two ships set sail. The *Santa Maria* had accidentally run aground. The crew used the ship's battered planks to help build a small fort, where they stored what treasure they couldn't carry. Columbus left part of the crew behind to guard the stockade until he could return.

Numerous disasters followed the voyagers home. Upon his return, Columbus received the honors he had sought, including the governorship of the present-day island of Hispaniola in the Caribbean. He did not stay long to enjoy his fame. After only six months, he was on his way back to the Americas.

Later Voyages   Columbus led a total of four trips to the Americas. Not all were profitable. In addition, Columbus proved to be a far better admiral than governor. The Spanish settlers on Hispaniola, where Columbus and his two brothers ruled, complained to the Spanish government of harsh and unfair treatment. Columbus lost his governorship, as well as his prestige at court. Furthermore, despite increasing evidence that he had found a new continent, Columbus clung to his claim that he had reached the "Indies."

The aging explorer returned from his fourth and last voyage in 1504, the same year Isabella died. Columbus asked Ferdinand to restore his governorship, but the king refused. Columbus died a disappointed man in 1506, never knowing how much he had changed the course of history.

Sounds of an Era

Listen to a reading of a letter written by Christopher Columbus, and sounds from other cultures that made up the Atlantic World.

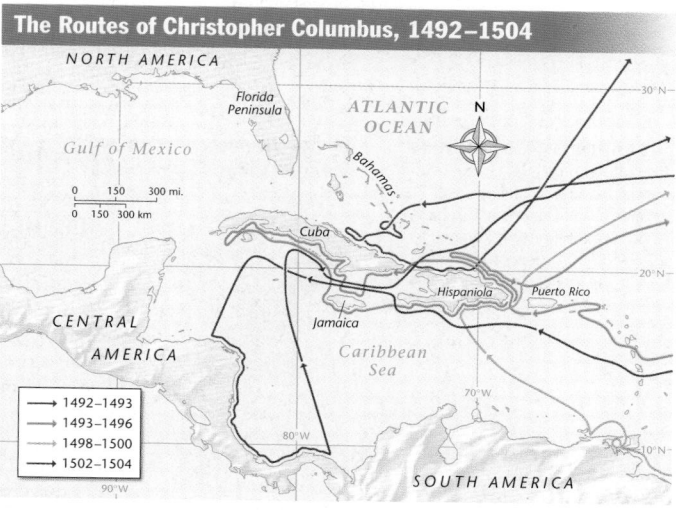
The Routes of Christopher Columbus, 1492–1504

NORTH AMERICA
Florida Peninsula
ATLANTIC OCEAN
N
Gulf of Mexico
Bahamas
0   150   300 mi.
0   150   300 km
Cuba
Hispaniola   Puerto Rico
CENTRAL   Jamaica
AMERICA   Caribbean Sea
SOUTH AMERICA

→ 1492–1493
→ 1493–1496
→ 1498–1500
→ 1502–1504

MAP SKILLS This map shows the routes traveled by Columbus on each of his four voyages. **Place** Which of the four voyages took Columbus along the coast of Central America?

A New Continent Others, however, realized the importance of Columbus's findings. In 1499, a merchant from Italy named Amerigo Vespucci made the first of two voyages to the Caribbean Sea. After sailing along the coast of South America, Vespucci suggested that these lands might be a continent previously unknown to Europeans, "what we may rightly call a New World." A German mapmaker named Waldseemüller read Vespucci's account and took it to heart. In 1507, he printed the first map showing the "New World" to be separate from Asia. He named the unfamiliar lands "America," after Amerigo Vespucci.

Columbus's Impact

In recent years, considerable public debate has arisen over the long-term impact of Columbus's voyages to the Americas. Most historians agree that the effects were both good and bad.

The Columbian Exchange Columbus's journeys launched a new era of transatlantic trade known as the **Columbian Exchange.** European ships returned with exciting new foods from the Americas, including peanuts, pineapples, and tomatoes. One new item, cocoa, set off a craze in Europe. Another food, the potato, quickly became the new food of Europe's poor, helping to save them from famines.

Europeans brought to the Americas crops such as wheat, and domesticated animals such as the cow and the horse. They brought firearms and the wheel and axle, technologies that Native Americans did not have. Finally, Europeans introduced their culture to the Americas, including European laws, languages, and customs.

Native Americans Devastated Any benefits the Native Americans received, however, were far outweighed by the misery brought upon them. The greatest source of this misery was disease. The Columbian Exchange brought together

INTERPRETING DIAGRAMS
Agricultural products, domesticated animals, and diseases crossed the Atlantic in the Columbian Exchange. **Analyzing Information** *What geographic barrier prevented these goods from being exchanged earlier?*

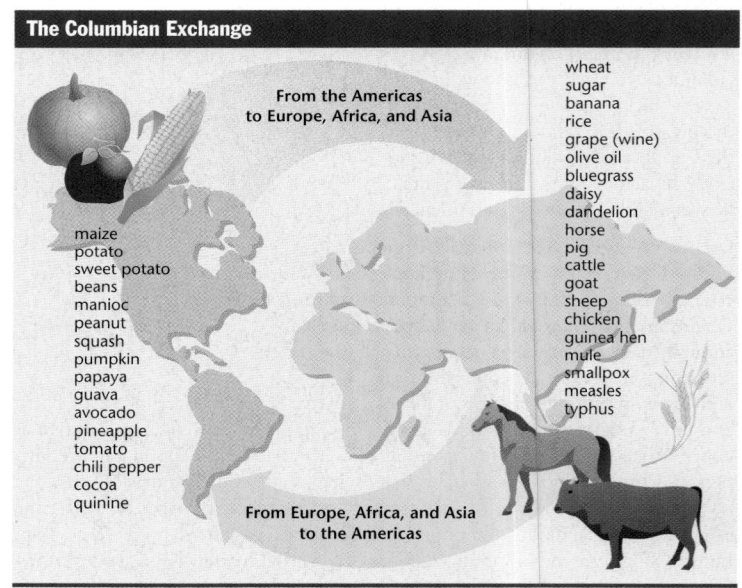

The Columbian Exchange

From the Americas to Europe, Africa, and Asia

maize
potato
sweet potato
beans
manioc
peanut
squash
pumpkin
papaya
guava
avocado
pineapple
tomato
chili pepper
cocoa
quinine

wheat
sugar
banana
rice
grape (wine)
olive oil
bluegrass
daisy
dandelion
horse
pig
cattle
goat
sheep
chicken
guinea hen
mule
smallpox
measles
typhus

From Europe, Africa, and Asia to the Americas

people who had been isolated from one another and thus had no resistance to one another's diseases.

Europeans had already experienced a severe decline in their population due to plague and other diseases. Now Europeans brought similar disasters to the Americas. Passing germs through even the most casual contact, explorers and soldiers infected Native Americans with smallpox, typhus, measles, and other deadly diseases.

The diseases spread rapidly along the extensive Native American trade network. One man, the son of a Native American woman and a Spanish captain, described what explorers found in 1540 when they first reached the Native American town of Talomeco, possibly located in present-day South Carolina:

> ❝ The Castilians found the town of Talomeco without any people at all, because [of] the recent pestilence [disease] . . . [Near] the rich temple, it is said they found four longhouses filled with bodies from the plague.❞
>
> —Garcilaso de la Vega (the Inca)

VIEWING HISTORY A Native American in Mexico drew this picture of a smallpox victim being comforted by a healer. The mark near the healer's mouth symbolizes spoken words. **Analyzing Information** How did European diseases such as smallpox travel throughout the Americas?

Europeans Gain Wealth At first, Europeans were unaware that they were passing on disease to the Native Americans. Many Europeans believed that the "pestilence" that ravaged the Native American population was a sign that God favored Europeans over Native Americans. God, these Europeans believed, had sent Europeans to conquer the Americas.

The rival nations of Europe all wanted a part of this sudden opportunity to gain land and wealth. The Portuguese, whose navigational technology made Columbus's voyage possible, resented Spain's claim to the Western Hemisphere. Portugal, therefore, sent a complaint to the pope.

European Catholics believed that the pope had the authority to divide up any newly conquered non-Christian lands. In 1494, at the urging of Pope Alexander, Portugal and Spain signed the **Treaty of Tordesillas.** Under the treaty, the two countries divided all lands on Earth not already claimed by other Christians. They did this by drawing an imaginary line around the world called the Line of Demarcation. Spain was to rule over lands west of the line, including most of the Americas. Portugal would control the rest, including Brazil and the sea route around Africa. The effects of this 500-year-old treaty can be seen today. People in most of South America, the part given to Spain, speak Spanish. In Brazil, the area set aside for Portugal, most people speak Portuguese.

At first, Spain and Portugal were able to control much of the regions they claimed. In the 1500s, however, France, England, and the Netherlands began to move into North America. In the first century after Columbus's voyage, the amount of gold and silver in Europe's economy increased eight times over, much of it made out of ore from mines in the Americas.

Africans Enslaved To supply the American foods that Europeans demanded, Portugal and Spain established **plantations,** the large farming operations that produced crops not for their own use but for sale. Such products are called **cash crops.** Plantation farming of tropical cash crops such as sugar and pineapple required huge numbers of workers who labored long hours in hot climates.

At first, soldiers kidnapped Native Americans and forced them to work on the plantations. Unaccustomed to that type of work and weakened by disease,

ACTIVITY
Student Portfolio

Have students reflect in journal entries on the implications of the Line of Demarcation. Students should consider such questions as whether the Europeans had the right to establish such a line, what it said about their view of the rest of the world and the peoples who lived there, and so on. **(Verbal/Linguistic)**

BACKGROUND
Global Connections

No one knows for certain how many Native Americans died from the diseases Europeans brought to the Americas, but the numbers are certainly staggering. Moreover, historians and scientists have continually increased their estimations of the death toll. The estimates range widely, but an idea of the scope of the devastation can be gleaned from just this one: the population of what is now Mexico was about 25 million when the Europeans arrived. Within one hundred years, the population had shrunk to just about 1.6 million. This pattern was repeated throughout the Americas.

CAPTION ANSWERS

Viewing History Disease spread from Europeans along the trade routes of the Columbian Exchange.

Reading Comprehension

1. To bring Christianity to other lands; economic advantage; direct trade route; the upper hand in the rivalry with Portugal.

2. The transatlantic trade of crops, technology, and culture between the Americas and Europe, Africa, and Asia that began in 1492 with Columbus's first voyage to the Americas.

3. Portugal and Spain agreed to divide all lands on Earth not previously claimed by other Christians; Spain would rule lands to the west of the Line of Demarcation, and Portugal would rule the rest, including Brazil, and the sea route around Africa.

4. In order to supply the American foods that Europeans demanded, large farming operations were established to produce these crops for sale, requiring huge numbers of workers and depending on the slave trade as a labor source.

Critical Thinking and Writing

5. That other cultures were inferior; that Europeans must convert non-Christians. These beliefs motivated the conquests of Spain and Portugal.

6. Arguments may include: the potential for increased wealth; glory for Spain; conversion of non-Christians; being first to find a route to Asia.

Take It to the NET

Tables should clearly and accurately compare information about the New and Old Worlds.

This engraving shows the trading post Sao Jorge da Mina on the coast of West Africa. Built by the Portuguese in 1482, the fort oversaw the traffic of gold, ivory, sugar, wax, pepper, and hides, as well as the growing export of slaves.

these slaves did not provide a reliable labor force. Europeans then turned to West Africa.

As you read in the previous section, a West African slave trade began to emerge in the 1400s. In 1517, the first enslaved Africans arrived in the Americas. The need for labor in the Western Hemisphere turned the slave trade into an industry.

From Benin and dozens of other thriving cultures and kingdoms, Europeans began trading for slaves. The West Africans who were forced into slavery generally included the healthiest people, those who would be well suited for conditions on American plantations and in other enterprises.

Historians continue to debate just how many Africans became enslaved. Some estimate that during the 1500s, about 275,000 West Africans were taken against their will across the Atlantic Ocean. That number grew to about 6 million in the 1700s, these historians say. Estimates of the total number of West Africans abducted from their homeland and taken to North and South America range from roughly 9 million to more than 11 million.

Mere numbers, however, cannot portray the full horror of slavery for West Africans. Europeans constructed a uniquely cruel system to supply slaves to the Americas. They regarded slaves as property and treated them as such. Slavery was a lifetime sentence—often a death sentence—from which there was no escape.

A New Culture Explorers and settlers from other European nations soon followed the Spanish. The Europeans would adopt ideas and customs from the Native Americans and from one another as well. While the United States derives its basic constitutional and legal institutions from Europeans, particularly the English, American culture today reflects the impact of centuries of exchange among many people.

Section 4 Assessment

READING COMPREHENSION

1. What did the Spanish hope to gain from Columbus's voyage?

2. What was the **Columbian Exchange?**

3. What did the **Treaty of Tordesillas** accomplish?

4. How were **plantations** and **cash crops** connected to the slave trade?

CRITICAL THINKING AND WRITING

5. **Recognizing Bias** What specific beliefs influenced Europeans' views of themselves and other cultures. How did their beliefs affect their actions?

6. **Writing to Persuade** From the point of view of Columbus, write an essay to try to persuade Queen Isabella and King Ferdinand to fund your voyage to the "Indies."

Take It to the NET

Activity: Creating a Table Learn more about the impact of Columbus's voyages to America. Create a table to compare resources, food, ideas, and culture of the New World with those of the Old World. Use the links provided in the *America: Pathways to the Present* area of the following Web site for help in completing this activity. **www.phschool.com**

RESOURCE DIRECTORY

Teaching Resources
Units 1/2 booklet
- Section 4 Quiz, p. 7
- Chapter 1 Test, pp. 8, 11

Guide to the Essentials
- Section 4 Summary, p. 8
- Chapter 1 Test, p. 9

Other Print Resources
Chapter Tests with ExamView® Test Bank
CD-ROM, Ch. 1

Technology
ExamView® Test Bank CD-ROM, Ch. 1
Social Studies Skills Tutor CD-ROM

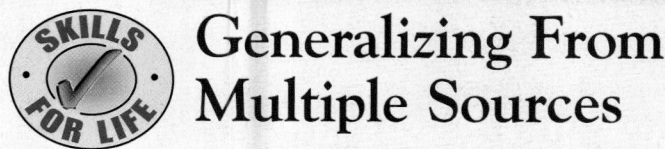

Generalizing From Multiple Sources

A generalization is a broad statement based on multiple examples or facts, often from various sources. Valid generalizations are useful for summing up information, but "sweeping generalizations"—those that are too broad and do not allow for exceptions—can be misleading. For example, you might generalize from your experience that *most* dogs like to be petted. But believing that *all* dogs *always* like to be petted could get you into serious trouble.

The time line and the quotation below relate to Christopher Columbus's effort to find financial backing for his first voyage. Friar Marchena, mentioned in the letter, was a priest whom Columbus had met in Spain.

1484 Columbus presents his proposal to King John II of Portugal.

1486 Columbus is summoned to the court of Ferdinand and Isabella of Spain.

1490–1491 Columbus and his brother request backing from the Italians, English, and French. All their requests are rejected.

| 1480 | • | 1485 | • | • | 1490 | • | 1495 |

1485 After a panel of experts reviews Columbus's calculations about the size of the earth and the ocean, they advise King John against supporting the venture.

1487 or 1488 Isabella's advisors recommend rejection of Columbus's proposal, again based on his calculations.

1492 Columbus again appears before Queen Isabella; again, her advisors reject his proposal, this time based on financial considerations. Before he reaches home, however, Columbus is overtaken by a messenger from the queen. She has reconsidered and agrees to finance the voyage.

LEARN THE SKILL

Use the following steps to make generalizations:

1. **Identify the main ideas of each source.** Consider both the information and the time period.
2. **List relevant facts.** Determine which facts in the sources support each main idea. You may find that some facts are not relevant to your topic.
3. **Find a common element.** Look for general trends, or a common thread, in the ideas stated in the sources. Also look for patterns or trends in the details and facts.
4. **Make a generalization.** "Add up" the facts and ideas in your sources to make a general statement. Be sure that you can support your generalization with facts and that it is not too broad. Valid generalizations often include words such as *many, most, often, usually, some, few,* and *sometimes.* Faulty generalizations may include words such as *all, none, always, never,* and *every.*

PRACTICE THE SKILL

Answer the following questions:

1. **(a)** What is the main idea of the time line? How do you know? **(b)** What time period does it cover? **(c)** What is the main idea of the excerpt? **(d)** What time period does the excerpt refer to?
2. **(a)** How many facts does the time line present to support its main idea? **(b)** What are two of those

Letter to the Spanish Monarchs

"Your majesties know that I spent seven years in the court pestering you for this; never in the whole time was there found a pilot, nor a sailor, nor a mariner, nor a philosopher, nor an expert in any other science who did not state that my enterprise was false, so I never found support from anyone, save father Friar Antonio de Marchena, beyond that of eternal God."

—Christopher Columbus, *circa* 1501

facts? **(c)** Describe how Columbus supports his main idea. **(d)** Is this support reliable? Explain.

3. **(a)** What main idea do both sources share? **(b)** How does the time line support the quotation and vice versa? In other words, what is the benefit of having these two kinds of sources?
4. What valid generalizations can you make about **(a)** Columbus, **(b)** his contemporaries, and **(c)** monarchs in the late 1400s?

APPLY THE SKILL

See the Chapter Review and Assessment for another opportunity to apply this skill.

GENERALIZING FROM MULTIPLE SOURCES

Focus Students learn to draw conclusions by identifying the main ideas of various sources, listing relevant facts, and finding a common element that enables them to make a generalization.

Instruct Ask students what type of evidence they would need to create a general statement about an event in history. How much evidence is necessary? What would they do if the evidence is contradictory? *(Research each source's reliability; find evidence that corroborates a point of view.)* Ask students to use the material on this page to write a brief essay on all of Columbus's efforts to get funded. Ask them to include quotes from Columbus.

Extend See the Skills for Life activity in the Resource Directory below.

ANSWERS

PRACTICE THE SKILL

1. **(a)** That Columbus persisted in trying to get backing for his first voyage even though, until 1492, each petition he made was rejected. **(b)** The years 1480–1495. **(c)** That Columbus persisted in his effort to gain backing, despite years of disappointment. **(d)** The period 1485–1492.

2. **(a)** Eight. **(b)** Students should name two of the following: presenting proposal to King John; King John's rejection; appearance at Spanish court; rejection by Spanish monarchs (1487 or 1488); requests to Italians, English, and French rejected; another rejection by Queen Isabella's advisers; Isabella's final agreement to finance voyage. **(c)** By noting all of the types of people who did not support it. **(d)** Students may note that this support would be hard to verify.

3. **(a)** Columbus's petition was rejected many times over several years. **(b)** Both show that Columbus appealed for backing over a seven-year period. The time line provides specific times and places.

4. **(a)** Columbus was persistent. **(b)** His contemporaries were cautious. **(c)** They relied on experts but were capable of independent decisions, as well.

Chapter 1

Review and Assessment

REVIEWING KEY TERMS

Students should refer to the definitions of key terms in the chapter to write sentences that show an understanding of the key aspects of the Atlantic prior to 1600.

REVIEWING MAIN IDEAS

11. (a) Determined social structure; helped meet individuals' needs by widening their familial circle. (b) Organized kinship groups by common ancestry. (c) Word-of-mouth to keep beliefs and customs alive over time. (d) Exchange of goods between groups without the use of money.
12. That the most powerful forces in the world are spiritual; their ceremonies reflected the power of spiritual forces.
13. Manor life was protected but isolated; rigid social structure was determined entirely by birth; each person owed loyalty and service to another. The Church was all-powerful in medieval life.
14. Military campaigns by European Christians from 1096 to 1291 to win Jerusalem from the Turks; exposed Europeans to ideas and goods from abroad.
15. Possible answers: contacts with the outside world; Church authority; the role of monarchs; culture.
16. Coastal rain forests: rich in resources; Savanna: suited to livestock and some farming; Desert: the populated areas clustered at watering holes.
17. Yes. Powerful monarchs ruled in kingdoms such as Benin and Songhai.
18. Spain wanted to convert non-Christians, acquire new lands and wealth, and compete for power with Portugal.
19. Positive effects: new products and wealth for Europeans; new products for Native Americans. Negative effects: disease spread; enslavement and conquest of Native Americans; enslavement of Africans.
20. Family and village life severely disrupted as Europeans forced Africans into slavery to provide labor for plantations producing cash crops in the Americas.

creating a CHAPTER SUMMARY

Copy this chart (right) and complete it by adding information about Native American, European, and African Cultures.

For additional review and enrichment activities, see the interactive version of *America: Pathways to the Present*, available on the Web and on CD-ROM.

	Native Americans	Europeans	Africans
Organization of Society			
Beliefs About Land			
Religion			
Trade Goods			

★ Reviewing Key Terms

For each of the terms below, write a sentence explaining how it relates to the early Americas or the cultures that shaped them.

1. migration
2. nomad
3. feudalism
4. middle class
5. monarch
6. Magna Carta
7. savanna
8. lineage
9. Columbian Exchange
10. Treaty of Tordesillas

★ Reviewing Main Ideas

11. Describe Native American society in terms of (a) kinship, (b) clan, (c) oral history, and (d) barter. (Section 1)
12. What were some religious beliefs held by Native Americans? (Section 1)
13. Describe how the manor system and the Church affected medieval life. (Section 2)
14. Where were the Crusades, and how did they affect life in Europe? (Section 2)
15. Compare and contrast the Middle Ages and the Renaissance. (Section 2)
16. What effects did geography have on the development of West African cultures? (Section 3)
17. Did West African cultures have organized governments at the time that they came into contact with Europeans? Explain. (Section 3)

18. Why did Spain finally agree to sponsor Columbus's voyage? (Section 4)
19. What long-term positive and negative effects did Columbus's voyages have? (Section 4)
20. How was Africa changed by the introduction of cash crops in the Americas? (Section 4)

★ Critical Thinking

21. **Making Comparisons** Explain how geography contributed to (a) the diversity of Native American peoples, (b) the rivalry between Spain and Portugal, and (c) the wealth of Songhai.
22. **Determining Relevance** Identify changes that occurred during the Middle Ages that helped bring about the Renaissance. In what way did each of these changes influence the Renaissance? Explain.
23. **Identifying Central Issues** What issues were at the heart of the Reformation?
24. **Recognizing Cause and Effect** In the early days of trade between West Africans and Europeans, the Africans controlled the exchange of goods. Within a century they had become victims of European slave raiders. What caused this change?
25. **Predicting Consequences** Explain how values, beliefs, and customs differed among the three Atlantic cultures. Choose one way in which the three cultures differed, and explain how this difference could have led to conflict.

30 Chapter 1 • *The Atlantic World*

CREATING A CHAPTER SUMMARY

	Native Americans	Europeans	Africans
Organization of Society	Kinship clans	Roman Catholic Church controlled Europe; feudal structures replaced by monarchies	Kinship groups, based on lineage
Beliefs About Land	Believed that land could not be owned; believed people had right to use land and could grant others right to use it, too	Believed land may be bought and sold; believed landowners have more rights and privileges than others	Different types of societies developed according to different land types: savannah, rain forest, and desert.
Religion	Believed that most powerful forces (i.e., those in nature) are spiritual	Predominantly Roman Catholic until the Reformation in the early 1500s	Many different religions, generally sharing a belief in a Supreme Being and lesser deities; believed in ancestor worship
Trade Goods	Tribes traded food and goods within their group and outside it. Trade was based on necessity and also to show hospitality and friendliness.	People traveled great distances to find trading partners and to find goods to trade.	Benin and Songhai were very active in trade; Songhai was a major player in trade with North Africa and Europe.

★ Skills Assessment

Analyzing Political Cartoons ▶

26. The topic of this modern-day cartoon is the current debate over whether the United States should place new restrictions on immigration.
    (a) Whom does the man in the center represent?
    (b) Whom do the people on the left represent?
    (c) Whom does the man on the right represent?

27. What point is the cartoonist making? Do you agree with the cartoonist's view? Explain your reasoning.

Analyzing Documents

Turn to the excerpt from Columbus's letter to Queen Isabella and King Ferdinand on page 25, and then answer the questions that follow.

28. Which statement best represents the meaning of the quotation?

    A The Tainos are innocent, generous, and obedient.
    B The Tainos love the Europeans.
    C The Tainos are loving but possessive.
    D The Tainos demand to be free.

29. What conclusion do you think the king and queen might have drawn from Columbus's description of the Tainos?

    F The Tainos should be treated with the respect that they showed Columbus.
    G The Tainos have nothing of use to the Spanish.
    H The Tainos must be wiped out.
    J The Tainos would provide no resistance to Spanish conquest.

Applying the Chapter Skill: *Generalizing From Multiple Sources*

30. What generalizations can you make about the people of the Native American world, the European world, or the West African world that you have read about in this chapter? Use the maps, text, charts, illustrations, and diagrams from the relevant sections as your sources.

ACTIVITIES

 Writing to LEARN

Writing to Inform
The voyages of exploration described in this chapter were an early step in the creation of today's global economy. Two of the main links in that economy are foreign trade and investment. Write an essay that describes the various types of trade among Native Americans, Europeans, and West Africans up until 1600. What types of contributions did each group make that would affect the economy of the Americas?

 Primary Source CD-ROM

Working With Primary Sources Find additional information on the cultures of the Atlantic World on the *Exploring Primary Sources in U.S. History CD-ROM* and use the selection(s) provided to complete the Chapter 1 primary source activity located in the *America: Pathways to the Present* area at the following Web site. **www.phschool.com**

Take It to the NET

Chapter Self-Test As a review activity, take the Chapter 1 Self-Test in the *America: Pathways to the Present* area at the Web site listed below. The questions are designed to test your understanding of the chapter content. **www.phschool.com**

Chapter 1 Assessment **31**

Writing to LEARN

Answers will vary.

Primary Source CD-ROM

Direct students to the additional primary sources that can be found on the *Exploring Primary Sources in U.S. History CD-ROM*.

 Take It to the NET

Additional support materials and activities for Chapter 1 of *America: Pathways to the Present* can be found in the Social Studies area at the Prentice Hall School Web site. **www.phschool.com**

---

21. (a) Native Americans in the north and northwest subsisted by hunting and fishing; others learned how to grow food in the semi-arid southwest. The vast woodlands in the northeast had an abundance of resources that enabled the alliance of Iroquois nations to establish a powerful confederation. (b) As rival powers on the Iberian Peninsula, Portugal resented Spain's claim to the Western Hemisphere. (c) Location made Songhai an ideal trading region for goods traveling between the resource-rich coastal forests and inland North African traders.

22. Sample answers: The Crusades, which made Europe less insular; Marco Polo's travels and his accounts thereof spurred trading missions to the East; cities grew along trade routes; a middle class developed, a money economy was revived, and the feudal system began to break down.

23. Anger at the amount of control the Church had within society, criticism about corruption among the clergy, and the rise of nationalism.

24. Possible answers: the Europeans' superior weaponry; the high demand in the Americas for slaves; and the Europeans' ability to transport large numbers of Africans overseas.

25. Students might choose examples such as views on gift-giving, attitudes about slavery, religious differences, attitudes about land, or economic values.

26. (a) A white male Anglo-Saxon American. (b) An immigrant family, perhaps Hispanic. (c) A Native American.

27. Everyone immigrated to America at some point in history. Answers should show an understanding of the issues raised in the cartoon, such as the hypocrisy of the man in the middle.

28. A

29. J

30. Sample answer: Different Native American groups had vastly different lifestyles, in part due to geographic differences; European interaction with Native Americans and African Americans was highly exploitative; some West African cultures were highly developed, and West Africans held very different views from Europeans in regard to slavery.

THE SEARCH FOR RICHES IN NORTH AMERICA

Focus Have students find the meaning of each of these words in a dictionary before they begin to read: *encounter, perforated, dejected, hastened, fertile, penetrated, apprehend, retaliation.* Explain that Cabeza de Vaca was one of a group of explorers who were shipwrecked on Florida's Gulf Coast, and who then wandered the area for eight years before being rescued. He was one of only four, from an original party of 600, to survive. Ask students to consider the impact that fact might have had on his attitude and approach.

Instruct Ask students to consider the descriptions of Cabeza de Vaca's experiences in light of what they read in Chapter 2 about the Spanish exploration of the New World. Discuss details that make this firsthand account believable. Ask volunteers for words or phrases describing the point of view of the account. Have students explain how this account enhances their understanding of the Spanish exploration of the New World.

Analyzing the Document Use this additional question to generate class discussion:

Critical Thinking: Making Inferences What does Cabeza de Vaca think about the actions of some of the Spanish explorers who visited native villages before he did? Give evidence from the document to support your answer. *(He was very unhappy that previous explorers had treated Native Americans with brutality; this went against his beliefs and made travel in the area very dangerous for him. He said: ". . . we began to apprehend [fear] that the Indians who were in arms against the Christians might ill-treat us in retaliation for what the Christians did to them.")*

The Search for Riches in North America

Cabeza de Vaca accompanied Panfilo de Narvaez on a voyage from Spain to North America in 1528 to claim riches and territory for the king. When Cabeza de Vaca returned to Spain eight years later, he was one of only four known survivors of about 600 who had arrived in Florida. In the following excerpt, selected by the editors of *American Heritage*, Cabeza de Vaca describes some of the events that occurred during his eight years of wandering from Florida into present-day Texas and Mexico.

AN ENCOUNTER WITH NATIVE AMERICANS In the afternoon we crossed a big river, the water being more than waist-deep. It may have been as wide as the one of Sevilla, and had a swift current. At sunset we reached a hundred Indian huts and, as we approached, the people came out to receive us, shouting frightfully, and slapping their thighs. They carried perforated gourds filled with pebbles, which are ceremonial objects of great importance. They only use them at dances, or as medicine, to cure, and nobody dares touch them but themselves. They claim that those gourds have healing virtues, and that they come from Heaven, not being found in that country; nor do they know where they come from, except that the rivers carry them down when they rise and overflow the land.

Fifteenth-century Spanish sword

So great was their excitement and eagerness to touch us that, every one wanting to be first, they nearly squeezed us to death, and, without suffering our feet to touch the ground, carried us to their abodes. So many crowded down upon us that we took refuge in the lodges they had prepared for our accommodation, and in no manner consented to be feasted by them on that night. The whole night they spent in celebration and dancing, and the next morning they brought us every living soul of that village to be touched by us and to have the cross made over them, as with the others. Then they gave to the women of the other village who had come with their own a great many arrows. The next day we went on, and all the people of that village with us, and when we came to other Indians were as well received as anywhere in the past; they also gave us of what they had and the deer they had killed during the day. Among these we saw a new custom. Those

32

RESOURCE DIRECTORY
Technology
AmericanHeritage® My Brush with History™
Videotapes *The Search for Riches in North America*

✓ TEST PREPARATION
Have students use the excerpt on these pages to answer the following question.

What point of view does this document provide on the Spanish conquest of Mexico?

A That of a slave trader.

B That of a historian.

C That of a missionary.

Ⓓ That of an explorer.

Spanish explorer Cabeza de Vaca and his men trek American terrain.

who were with us took away from those people who came to get cured their bows and arrows, their shoes and beads, if they wore any, and placed them before us to induce us to cure the sick. As soon as these had been treated they went away contented and saying they felt well. . . .

SIGNS OF EARLIER EXPLORERS During this time Castillo saw, on the neck of an Indian, a little buckle from a swordbelt, and in it was sewed a horseshoe nail. He took it from the Indian, and we asked what it was; they said it had come from Heaven. We further asked who had brought it, and they answered that some men, with beards like ours, had come from Heaven to that river; that they had horses, lances and swords, and had lanced two of them. . . .

We gave God our Lord many thanks for what we had heard, for we were despairing to ever hear of Christians again. On the other hand, we were in great sorrow and much dejected, lest those people had come by sea for the sake of discovery only. Finally, having such positive notice of them, we hastened onward, always finding more traces of the Christians, and we told the Indians that we were now sure to find the Christians, and would tell them not to kill Indians or make them slaves, nor take them out of their country, or do any other harm, and of that they were very glad.

We travelled over a great part of the country, and found it all deserted, as the people had fled to the mountains, leaving houses and fields out of fear of the Christians. This filled our hearts with sorrow, seeing the land so fertile and beautiful, so full of water and streams, but abandoned and the places burned down, and the people, so thin and wan, fleeing and hiding; and as they did not raise any crops their destitution had become so great that they ate tree-bark and roots. . . .

They brought us blankets, which they had been concealing from the Christians, and gave them to us, and told us how the Christians had penetrated into the country before, and had destroyed and burnt the villages, taking with them half of the men and all the women and children, and how

those who could escaped by flight. Seeing them in this plight, afraid to stay anywhere, and that they neither would nor could cultivate the soil, preferring to die rather than suffer such cruelties, while they showed the greatest pleasure at being with us, we began to apprehend [fear] that the Indians who were in arms against the Christians might ill-treat us in retaliation for what the Christians did to them. But when it pleased God our Lord to take us to those Indians, they respected and held us precious, as the former had done, and even a little more, at which we were not a little astonished, while it clearly shows how, in order to bring those people to Christianity and obedience unto Your Imperial Majesty, they should be well treated, and not otherwise. . . .

Source: *The Journey of Alvar Nuñez Cabeza de Vaca,* Ad. F. Bandelier, ed., A. S. Barnes, 1905.

Understanding Primary Sources

1. How were Cabeza de Vaca and his companions received by the Native Americans who had been mistreated by the previous explorers?

2. What does this tell you about the character of the native people?

American Heritage®
MY BRUSH WITH **HISTORY**™
 Videotapes

For more information about encounters between Native Americans and European explorers, view "The Search for Riches in North America."

33

Chapter 2 Planning Guide
Resource Manager

	CORE INSTRUCTION	READING/SKILLS
Chapter-Level Resources	**Teaching Resources** • Pacing Charts booklet • Block Scheduling booklet **Resource Pro® CD-ROM**, Ch. 2 **Prentice Hall Presentation Pro CD-ROM**, Ch. 2 **www.phschool.com** • eTeach	**Guided Reading Audiotapes** **(English/Spanish)** **Student Edition on Audio CD**, Ch. 2 **Social Studies Skills Tutor CD-ROM** **Color Transparencies**, A2, A3, B1, D1, F1
1 Spanish Explorers and Colonies 1. Find out how the Spanish built an empire in the Americas. 2. See why the Spanish pushed for settlement in regions of North America. 3. Learn how Native Americans resisted the Spanish.	**Teaching Resources** **Units 1/2 booklet** • Section 1 Quiz, p. 15	**Guided Reading and Review booklet,** p. 7 **Guide to the Essentials,** p. 10 **Section Reading Support Transparencies**
2 Jamestown 1. Discover the goals of England's explorers. 2. Learn about the challenges faced by Jamestown's early settlers. 3. Discover the role of tobacco in Virginia and find out how it contributed to Bacon's Rebellion. 4. See why relations were uneasy between English settlers and Native Americans.	**Teaching Resources** **Units 1/2 booklet** • Section 2 Quiz, p. 16 **Learning Styles Lesson Plans booklet,** p. 6	**Guided Reading and Review booklet,** p. 8 **Guide to the Essentials,** p. 11 **Learning with Documents booklet,** p. 7 **Section Reading Support Transparencies**
3 The New England Colonies 1. Learn about the pattern of French settlement in North America. 2. Discover the goals of the Plymouth and Massachusetts Bay colonies. 3. Understand why there was dissent within the Puritan community. 4. See why war broke out between the Indians and the English settlers.	**Teaching Resources** **Units 1/2 booklet** • Section 3 Quiz, p. 17 **Learning Styles Lesson Plans booklet,** p. 7	**Guided Reading and Review booklet,** p. 9 **Guide to the Essentials,** p. 12 **Learning with Documents booklet,** pp. 41, 75 **Skills for Life booklet,** p. 4 **Section Reading Support Transparencies**
4 The Middle and Southern Colonies 1. Discover the early history of the Dutch in New York. 2. Find out about characteristics of the other Middle Colonies. 3. See why people settled in the Southern Colonies.	**Teaching Resources** **Units 1/2 booklet** • Section 4 Quiz, p. 18	**Guided Reading and Review booklet,** p. 10 **Guide to the Essentials,** p. 13 **Section Reading Support Transparencies**

ENRICHMENT/PRE-AP

Prentice Hall United States History Video Collection™
www.phschool.com
- Section Activities, Virtual Field Trip, Chapter Activities, Current Events Online

Biography, Literature, and Comparing Primary Sources booklet, p. 7
Historical Outline Map Book, pp. 9, 11

Biography, Literature, and Comparing Primary Sources booklet, pp. 41, 99–100
Historical Outline Map Book, pp. 14, 15
Sounds of an Era Audio CD

Nystrom *Atlas of Our Country,* pp. 14–15
Historical Outline Map Book, pp. 10, 12, 16
Sounds of an Era Audio CD
Exploring Primary Sources in U.S. History CD-ROM

Historical Outline Map Book, pp. 13, 17, 18
American Pathways Thematic Posters

ASSESSMENT

Core Assessment
ExamView® Test Bank, Ch. 2
ExamView® Test Bank CD-ROM, Ch. 2

Standardized Test Preparation
Diagnose and Prescribe
Diagnostic Tests for High School Social Studies Skills

Review and Reteach
Review Book for U.S. History

Practice and Assess
Test-taking Strategies With Transparencies
Test-taking Strategies Posters
Test Prep Book for U.S. History
Alternative Assessment Handbook
Document-Based Assessment

Teaching Resources
Units 1/2 booklet
- Section Quizzes, pp. 15–18
- Chapter Tests, pp. 19, 22
www.phschool.com Ch. 2 Self-Test

AmericanHeritage RESOURCES

From the Archives of American Heritage®, p. 47
AmericanHeritage ® My Brush with History™ Videotapes
www.americanheritage.com

Don't miss the exclusive interactive version of this textbook on the Web and on CD-ROM.

Chapter 2 Planning Guide
In Your Classroom

CUSTOMIZE FOR INDIVIDUAL NEEDS

Gifted and Talented

Teacher's Edition
- Customize for Gifted and Talented, p. 47

Teaching Resources
- Biography, Literature, and Comparing Primary Sources booklet, pp. 7, 41, 99–100

Technology
- Exploring Primary Sources in U.S. History CD-ROM *Mayflower Compact; Fundamental Orders of 1693*

ESL

Teacher's Edition
- Customize for ESL, pp. 37, 51

Teaching Resources
- Guided Reading and Review booklet, pp. 7–10
- Guide to the Essentials (English/Spanish), Chapter 2

Technology
- Student Edition on Audio CD, Chapter 2
- Guided Reading Audiotapes (English/Spanish), Chapter 2
- Section Reading Support Transparencies

Less Proficient Readers

Teacher's Edition
- Customize for Less Proficient Readers, pp. 43, 45, 55

Teaching Resources
- Guided Reading and Review booklet, pp. 7–10
- Guide to the Essentials (English/Spanish), Chapter 2

Technology
- Student Edition on Audio CD, Chapter 2
- Guided Reading Audiotapes (English/Spanish), Chapter 2
- Section Reading Support Transparencies

Less Proficient Writers

Teacher's Edition
- Customize for Less Proficient Writers, p. 61

Teaching Resources
- Guided Reading and Review booklet, pp. 7–10
- Guide to the Essentials (English/Spanish), Chapter 2

Technology
- Student Edition on Audio CD, Chapter 2
- Guided Reading Audiotapes (English/Spanish), Chapter 2
- Section Reading Support Transparencies

TEACHER'S EDITION INDEX

Activities Connecting with Citizenship, 44, 53; Connecting with Culture, 45; Connecting with Economics, 52; Connecting with Geography, 36, 38, 39, 40, 43, 61; Connecting with Government, 51, 62; Connecting with History and Conflict, 46, 47, 54, 55, 56; Student Portfolio, 59; Time Line, 34

American Heritage 47

Assessment 41, 48, 57, 63, 64–65

Background Notes About the Pictures, 35; Art History, 45; Biography, 50, 62; Connections to Today, 39, 40, 55, 56; A Diverse Nation, 38; An Early Description of the Use of Tobacco, 46; Geography in History, 51; Interdisciplinary, 52; Recent Scholarship, 44, 54, 61; The Salem Witch Trials, 53

Bellringer 36, 42, 49, 59

Customize For . . . ESL, 37, 51; Gifted and Talented, 47; Less Proficient Readers, 43, 45, 55; Less Proficient Writers, 61

Disease, 43, 44 , 45, 55

King Philip's War, 50, 55, 56

Maryland Toleration Act, 62

Mayflower Compact, 35, 51

Powhatan Indians, 47

Pueblos, 35, 39, 41

Reading Strategy 36, 42, 49, 59

Roanoke, 43, 44, 46

Skills for Life 58

Slaves, 43, 47, 52

Test Preparation 39, 47, 53, 61

Tobacco, 42, 43, 46, 61

Wampanoags, 55, 56

CHAPTER 2 – PACING SUGGESTIONS

 For 90-minute Blocks
- Teach sections 1 and 3 using Transparencies A2, A3, B1, D1, and F1, and the Recent Scholarship notes on pages 44, 54, and 61 for class discussions.

 Running Out of Time?

If you are running short on time to cover this chapter, consider the following options:

- Use the Prentice Hall Presentation Pro CD-ROM to create an outline for this chapter.
- Use the Section Summaries for Chapter 2, from **Guide to the Essentials (English/Spanish).**

1 **Spanish Explorers and Colonies**	**Connecting with Culture** Tell students to discuss some of the cultural differences that led to clashes between the Spanish colonists and the Native Americans. Ask students to consider not only religious beliefs but also customs relating to food, family structure, language, and clothing. Encourage students to see how the complex differences between these people led to misunderstanding. **(Verbal/Linguistic)**
2 **Jamestown**	**Connecting with Citizenship** Have groups of students write and present a skit showing one of the conflicts that occurred in Jamestown. Students might choose to focus on the conflict between Native Americans and the English, indentured servants and landowners, or King James and the Virginia Company. Tell students to show how this conflict affected the development of the colony. **(Bodily/Kinesthetic)**
3 **The New England Colonies**	**Connecting with History and Conflict** Have groups of students collaborate on a chart showing the successes and failures of the Puritan community. Tell students to include such factors as economic well-being, health, farming, religion, and adapting to their new environment. When students are finished, have each group present its chart and explain why they placed certain items in the "success" column and others in the "failure" column. **(Visual/Spatial)**
4 **The Middle and Southern Colonies**	**Connecting with Government** Tell students to write an essay on the effect of religious tolerance on the development of colonies such as New Amsterdam and Pennsylvania. Have students consider why business flourished in colonies that practiced religious tolerance. Encourage students to think about the effect of religious tolerance not only on the economy but also on the overall growth of the colony. Why did religious tolerance have such a wide-reaching effect? **(Verbal/Linguistic)**

Chapter 2

European Colonization of the Americas

(1492–1752)

INTRODUCING THE CHAPTER

Between the first voyage of Christopher Columbus in 1492 and the mid-1700s, Europeans explored, conquered, and settled areas of the Americas. The influx of Europeans was marked by violence with the native people already living in the Americas and between the Europeans themselves as they competed for land and wealth. The Spanish colonization was heaviest in Mexico and Central and South America. The French settled mostly in what is now Canada, while the English established settlement along the North American Atlantic coast. By the mid-1700s, European nations were firmly established in the Americas, but further conflict was ahead.

TIME LINE ACTIVITY

To provide students with practice in using the time line, ask questions such as these.

1. Who explored and named Florida, and what was he actually looking for? *(Juan Ponce de León; looking for the "fountain of youth")*

2. What European settled Quebec, and in what year was it settled? *(French explorer Samuel de Champlain; in 1608)*

3. What event in England produced a bill of rights, and in what year did it take place? *(The Glorious Revolution; in 1689)*

eTeach

Be sure to check out this month's online discussion with a Master Teacher. Go to **www.phschool.com**.

Chapter 2

European Colonization of the Americas

(1492–1752)

The signing of the Mayflower Compact

American Events

1513
During his search for the "fountain of youth," Spanish explorer Juan Ponce de León explores and names Florida.

1565
The Spanish establish the settlement of St. Augustine in Florida to defend Spanish claims in North America.

1607
The Virginia Company sends colonists to Virginia, where they set up a colony at Jamestown, the first permanent English settlement in North America.

1500 · · ·   1550   ·   · 1600 · ·

World Events

Spanish conquistador Hernán Cortés conquers the Aztec Empire.
1521

England defeats the Spanish Armada.
1588

French explorer Samuel de Champlain establishes Quebec.
1608

34   Chapter 2 • *European Colonization of the Americas*

RESOURCE DIRECTORY

Teaching Resources
Pacing Charts booklet
Block Scheduling booklet, p. 14
Units 1/2 booklet
• Chapter Summary, p. 14

Technology
Guided Reading Audiotapes (English/Spanish), Ch. 2
Student Edition on Audio CD, Ch. 2
Prentice Hall United States History Video Collection™ Volume 2, *The Era of Colonization (1585–1763)*
Prentice Hall Presentation Pro CD-ROM, Ch. 2
Resource Pro® CD-ROM
Social Studies Skills Tutor CD-ROM
Companion Web site, www.phschool.com

The Thirteen Colonies, circa 1750

British possessions

- New England Colony
- Middle Colony
- Southern Colony
- British possession outside the 13 colonies
- French possession
- Spanish possession

1620 Founding date as an English colony

*North and South Carolina originally formed a single colony, Carolina, founded in 1663.

Lake Superior
Missouri River
Mississippi River
Lake Michigan
Lake Huron
St. Lawrence River
L. Ontario
Lake Erie
Ohio River
Mississippi River

N.H. 1679
Massachusetts 1691
Mass. Bay 1629
Plymouth 1620
New York 1664
Rhode Island
Connecticut 1636
Pennsylvania 1681
New Jersey 1664
Delaware 1704
Maryland 1632
Virginia 1607
North Carolina 1712*
South Carolina 1712*
Georgia 1732

APPALACHIAN MOUNTAINS

ATLANTIC OCEAN

Gulf of Mexico

40°N
70°W
30°N
80°W
90°W

0   150   300 mi.
0   150   300 km

A bell from a Spanish mission

1630
Puritans establish a "city upon a hill" when they settle the Massachusetts Bay Colony in New England.

1676
Nathaniel Bacon leads a rebellion against the colonial government of Jamestown, in which the settlement is attacked and burned.

1732
James Oglethorpe receives the charter for the Georgia colony, intended to be a haven for English debtors.

· 1650 · · 1700 · · 1750

England's Glorious Revolution produces a bill of rights.
1689

The Act of Union unites England and Scotland.
1707

Chapter 2   35

BIBLIOGRAPHY

For the Teacher

Boorstin, Daniel. *The Americans, The Colonial Experience (A Caravelle Edition).* Random House, 1964. (Examines how the habits of colonial America shaped American life today.)

Bradford, William and Samuel Eliot Morison. *Of Plymouth Plantation, 1620–1647.* Random House, 1952. (A firsthand account of the Pilgrims.)

Hill, Frances. *The Salem Witch Trials Reader.* Da Capo Press, 2000. (A collection of firsthand accounts about the Salem Witch Trials.)

For the Student

Bradford, William, and Margaret Wise Brown, eds. *Homes in the Wilderness: A Pilgrim's Journal of Plymouth Plantation in 1620.* Linnet Books, 1988. (Bradford's fascinating diary.)

Deetz, James. *In Small Things Forgotten: An Archaeology of Early American Life.* Anchor, 1996. (Early American history through an examination of a wide variety of artifacts.)

Hawthorne, Nathaniel. *The Scarlet Letter.* Silver Burdett Classics, 1985. (A famous novel that examines sin and guilt in Puritan New England.)

The Thirteen Colonies, circa 1750

Activating Prior Knowledge Of the thirteen original colonies, which was the last to become an English colony? *(Georgia)*

Previewing Ask students to list reasons why colonizing the New World became so attractive. *(Possible answers: religious freedom, entrepreneurial notions, resource exploitation)*

BACKGROUND
About the Pictures

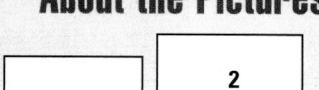
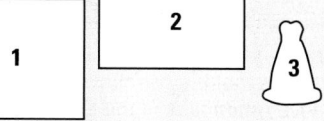

1. St. Augustine was settled by Spaniards under the command of Pedro Menéndez de Avilés. The site was chosen in part because there was an existing French settlement nearby, which the Spanish intended to attack.

2. Painting by E. Morgan of the signing of the Mayflower Compact. The document was created to prevent the passengers from leaving the group to begin their own settlement and was signed by 41 of the male passengers.

3. After the Pueblo Revolt, the Pueblo leader, Popé, tried to rid his tribes of anything related to Christianity or the Spanish culture.

iTEXT

Don't miss the exclusive interactive version of this textbook on the Web and on CD-ROM.

Section 1
Spanish Explorers and Colonies

SECTION OBJECTIVES

1. Find out how the Spanish built an empire in the Americas.
2. See why the Spanish pushed for settlement in regions of North America.
3. Learn how Native Americans resisted the Spanish.

BELLRINGER

Warm-Up Activity Ask students to list facts that they already know about Native Americans of the Southwest and about Spanish conquest of the Americas. Students may add to and revise their lists as they read the section.

Activating Prior Knowledge Ask students to state some goals of the Spanish exploration in the New World.

READING STRATEGY

Before students read the section, have them sketch maps of North, Central, and South America. Have them shade in the regions explored by the Spanish. Have them record key events, people, and places on their maps.

ACTIVITY
Connecting with Geography

Ask students to look at the map of European exploration of the Americas on this page. What nations sponsored explorations? *(Spain, Portugal, England, and France)* In what areas were the Spanish explorations focused? *(In Central and South America and the Southwest and Southeast regions of North America)* **(Visual/Spatial)**

CAPTION ANSWERS

Viewing History Workers are laying out the settlement according to a written plan held by someone in charge. There are many workers for labor, ships for supplies and protection, a fire with food cooking, and a structure for shelter.

36 • Chapter 2 Section 1

Spanish Explorers and Colonies

READING FOCUS

- How did the Spanish build an empire in the Americas?
- Why did the Spanish push for settlement in regions of North America?
- How did Native Americans resist the Spanish?

MAIN IDEA

Between 1492 and 1650, the Spanish built an empire in Central and South America, as well as the Southeast and Southwest regions of North America.

KEY TERMS

colony
hidalgo
isthmus
conquistador
encomienda system
mestizo
presidio
mission
congregación
Pueblo Revolt of 1680

TAKING NOTES

Copy this flowchart. As you read, fill in the boxes showing reasons why Spain encouraged settlement in different regions of North America.

Spanish Settlement in North America			
Southeast	Southwest	West	Missionaries
To build forts for protection			

VIEWING HISTORY This wood engraving shows the founding of St. Augustine. **Determining Relevance** *Why are the tasks shown here important to the founding of a colony?*

Setting the Scene In the summer of 1565, a Spanish force of 11 ships and roughly 2,000 men under the command of Pedro Menéndez de Avilés sailed into a bay in northeastern Florida that he would name St. Augustine. He also gave that name to a **colony** he established there. A colony is an area settled by immigrants who continue to be ruled by their parent country.

A year earlier, France had built Fort Caroline to the north of St. Augustine. In fact, Menéndez de Avilés had been sent not just to build a Spanish colony but to eliminate the French one, which Spain's King Philip II saw as a threat to Spanish control of the region. With the help of two Native American guides, a force of Spanish soldiers marched to Fort Caroline. They destroyed the fort and killed its inhabitants. Many of the French were Protestants, and the Spanish hung the French bodies on trees with a sign saying "Not as Frenchmen, but as heretics." (A heretic is someone who holds religious beliefs opposed to those of the established church or religion.) While Fort Caroline had lasted only a year, St. Augustine has lasted to this day.

The founding of St. Augustine illustrates several elements of Europe's colonization of the Americas. First, the competition among European powers for land in the Americas was sometimes violent. Second, Europeans were motivated not only by a desire for power and wealth, but by religious reasons as well. In addition, Native Americans were drawn into the conflicts among the Europeans. Later, they would also fight the Europeans over land. Finally, like the city of St. Augustine, the European presence in the Americas was there to stay.

Building a Spanish Empire

Spain was the first of the European powers to take major steps in the exploration and colonization of the Americas. Christopher Columbus made four voyages to the Americas between 1492 and 1504. His reports of lands and peoples, as well as his stories of pearls and other hints of wealth, soon drew other explorers after him. While Columbus had once been mocked as a dreamer, now he had many imitators.

RESOURCE DIRECTORY

Teaching Resources
Guided Reading and Review booklet, p. 7

Other Print Resources
Historical Outline Map Book *Spanish Explorers in North America,* p. 9; *Spain and Portugal in the Americas,* p. 11

Technology
Section Reading Support Transparencies
Guided Reading Audiotapes (English/Spanish), Ch. 2
Student Edition on Audio CD, Ch. 2
Color Transparencies *Historical Maps,* A2; *Cause-and-Effect Charts,* D1
Prentice Hall Presentation Pro CD-ROM, Ch. 2
Companion Web site, www.phschool.com

Spain's Major Explorers In the 50 years after Columbus's death, Spanish explorers expanded European knowledge of lands from Florida in the East to the shores of the Pacific Ocean in the West. Some of Spain's most important explorers are described below.

Juan Ponce de León One of the earliest explorers, Ponce de León was a typical **hidalgo,** or young Spanish gentleman. He was born into an upper-class family in Spain and fought against the Muslims. Ponce de León then took his military skills to the Americas, perhaps as early as 1493. In the early 1500s, he heard tales of a spring with amazing powers somewhere in the Caribbean. Anyone who drank the waters from this spring would become young again. While searching in vain for this "fountain of youth," Ponce de León explored and named Florida in 1513.

Vasco Núñez de Balboa Balboa was born to an upper-class family in the Estremadura, a poor region of Spain with a harsh climate. Seeking better opportunities for wealth in the Americas, he eventually arrived on the Isthmus of Panama. An **isthmus** is a narrow strip of land that joins two larger land areas, in this case North and South America. In 1513, Balboa led a group of Spaniards and Native Americans across the narrowest part of the isthmus. After crossing rivers, slashing their way through thick forests, and scaling rugged mountains, Balboa and his Spanish companions became the first known Europeans to see the Pacific Ocean from the American continent.

Ferdinand Magellan While Balboa may have been the first European explorer to see the mysterious "South Sea," the first to cross it starting from the Americas was Magellan. Though Portuguese, not Spanish, Magellan explored in Spanish ships on behalf of the Spanish king. Starting from Spain in September 1519, Magellan and his crew sailed to Brazil, then south and through the channel known today as the Strait of Magellan. Magellan and his fleet of ships boldly navigated west from the coast of South America on a course that would take them across the Pacific Ocean on a 99-day journey without fresh food or water. As the voyage wore on, his starving men were forced to eat the leather on the rigging of their ships. Finally, having crossed the Pacific Ocean, Magellan spotted the island of Guam. Though he later was killed in a fight with the people of the Philippine Islands, some of his crew continued on. After a three-year voyage, they became the first people known to have circumnavigated, or sailed around, the entire Earth.

The Spanish Pattern of Conquest The methods used by the Spanish to colonize the Americas were based on their long experience with violent conquest in their own land. Christians in Spain fought Muslims for 700 years in the *reconquista*—an effort to expel followers of Islam from the Iberian peninsula. The *reconquista* determined how the Spanish would treat the people it encountered in the Americas. In other words, it created a pattern of conquest.

European Exploration of the Americas, 1492–1682

MAP SKILLS For more than a century after Columbus's voyages, explorers sailed on behalf of any power that would sponsor them. Cabot and Verrazano were Italian, and Hudson was English. Estevanico was originally an African slave who was later freed to explore the Southwest. **Movement** *What nations sponsored Cabot, Verrazano, Hudson, and Estevanico?*

Focus Explain that the Spanish were the first Europeans to build an empire in the Americas. It included the Southwest and Southeast regions of North America. Ask students if they can think of any place names that reflect a Spanish heritage. *(Florida, Santa Fe, El Paso, San Antonio)*

Instruct Remind students that European Christians thought it was their duty to spread their religion throughout the world. Discuss how this belief affected their dealings with Native Americans. Ask students to compare the pattern of conquest in other parts of the Spanish empire with the pattern that emerged in New Mexico in the 1700s.

Assess/Reteach Ask students to speculate on what might have happened if the Spanish had not set out to establish a colony in the New World. Do they think other European countries would have found their way to these areas? How many years do students think this might have taken?

CAPTION ANSWERS

Map Skills Cabot: England; Verrazano: France; Hudson: England; and Estevanico: Spain.

CUSTOMIZE FOR ...

ESL

Ask students to turn each of the section's headings and subheadings into questions. Then have them skim the text to answer these questions before reading the section.

Connecting with Geography

Have students create a fact file on each of the following explorers: Ponce de León, Balboa, Magellan, Cortés, Pizarro, Cabeza de Vaca, Estevanico, Coronado, and de Soto. Fact files should include the explorer's nationality and a summary of what he accomplished. **(Verbal/ Linguistic)**

A Diverse Nation

Europeans adopted many Native American words to describe the animals and plants they found in the Americas, including *caribou, skunk, maize, avocado,* and *tapioca.* The English colonists had already picked up several Native American words that had entered English via Spanish, such as the Mayan *cigar* and the Taino *potato.*

READING CHECK
The Spanish modeled their patterns of conquest in the Americas after their experiences gained during the conquest of Muslims in the Iberian Peninsula.

READING CHECK
How did the *reconquista* create a pattern of conquest?

VIEWING HISTORY The Aztec ruler Montezuma greeted Cortés with gifts of gold, precious stones, and other valuable objects. Montezuma and the Aztecs at first believed Cortés to be a god and savior. **Analyzing Visual Information** *What important differences can you see between the Spanish and the Aztecs from this illustration?*

After the Spanish conquest, Spanish Christians gradually moved into Muslim lands on the Iberian peninsula. Over the centuries, Christians and Muslims began to live next to each other. The two groups traded with one another, intermarried, and borrowed from one another's cultures. For this reason, the Spanish expected the outcome of conquest to be a culture that had elements of both their own culture and the conquered culture. In their minds, the Spanish elements of this new culture would be superior.

The *reconquista* established three reasons for conquest. For centuries, hidalgos had led expeditions against Muslims in order to spread the Christian religion, to loot Muslim cities for wealth, and to win fame for their exploits—in short for "God, gold, and glory." The **conquistadors,** or Spanish conquerors of the Americas, were continuing that tradition.

Cortés and Pizarro Hernán Cortés was one such conquistador who left his harsh homeland in Spain for the opportunities of the Americas. He was especially eager for wealth. "I and my companions," he once remarked, "suffer from a disease of the heart which can be cured only by gold." In 1519, Cortés was sent by the Spanish governor of Cuba to conquer the vast empire ruled by the Aztec people in Mexico.

Cortés's plan was so bold as to seem impossible. The Aztec capital, Tenochtitlán (located on the site of present-day Mexico City), had 150,000 to 300,000 inhabitants (perhaps more) and was one of the world's largest urban centers. From this splendid city in the mountains of Mexico, the Aztecs governed some 10 to 12 million people. All Cortés could gather for his effort was a force of about 600 soldiers.

After landing in Mexico, Cortés quickly learned that many Native Americans in the area hated the Aztecs. Not only had the Aztecs conquered their neighbors, they had sacrificed untold numbers of them in religious ceremonies. With the help of a Native American princess known as Malinche or Doña Marina, Cortés used the divisions among Native Americans to rally thousands of them to his side. By 1521, Cortés and his soldiers had destroyed Tenochtitlán, and Cortés became the conqueror of one of the largest empires in the world.

Like Cortés, the conquistador Francisco Pizarro set out to conquer an empire—that of the Incas, centered in present-day Peru in South America. The Incas continued to resist as the Spanish attempted to take control of more and more of their empire. Neither Cortés nor Pizarro could have won without the help of Native American allies. They were also aided by smallpox and measles epidemics brought over by Europeans that killed millions of Native Americans.

Controlling the Spanish Empire As the conquistadors explored and conquered, they started settlements in favorable locations. By the 1550s, the Spanish colonies consisted of a large empire in Mexico, Central America, South America, and some of the islands of the Caribbean Sea.

The economic activity that took place in the colonies made the Spanish wealthy. Using the labor of enslaved Native Americans and Africans, the Spanish mined vast amounts of silver and gold from the mountains of Mexico and Peru. They also established farms and ranches that produced a variety of goods.

The success of this economic system required the Spanish to control the local population. They dealt with Native Americans differently than did other European conquerors in the Americas. They did not try to drive Indians out of

Viewing History The Spanish are dressed in steel armor, the Aztecs in cotton cloths; Cortés has come on horseback; the Aztecs possess many valuables that entice the Spanish.

RESOURCE DIRECTORY

Teaching Resources
Biography, Literature, and Comparing Primary Sources booklet (Biography) *Bartolomé de Las Casas,* p. 7

Technology
RESOURCE PRO® **Critical Thinking Activity** *Determining Relevance: Native American Words,* found on Resource Pro, helps students apply this skill by making a chart of Native American words.

their lands. Instead, they forced them to become a part of the colonial economy. One method they used was known as the ***encomienda* system.** Under this system, Native Americans were required to farm, ranch, or mine for the profit of an individual Spaniard. In return, the Spaniard was supposed to ensure the well-being of the workers.

Because the Spanish and Native Americans lived together on the same land, in time a population arose that was a mixture of both peoples. These people of mixed descent are called **mestizos,** which is Spanish for "mixed."

The Spanish Push North

Cortés and Pizarro strengthened Spain's grip on Mexico and Peru. Other conquistadors explored the southern parts of what would become the United States.

Alvar Núñez Cabeza de Vaca and Estevanico Cabeza de Vaca and Estevanico were part of a group of explorers who were shipwrecked in 1528 near present-day Galveston, Texas. Cabeza de Vaca was yet another hidalgo from Spain's Estremadura; Estevanico was an enslaved African. They wandered through the Gulf Coast region of Texas for eight years with two other survivors. After enduring extreme hunger and difficulty, they were rescued by Spanish raiders in northern Mexico. From the Native Americans with whom they had lived, they had heard stories of the Seven Cities of Cibola, rumored to be filled with gold somewhere to the north. As these stories spread among the Spanish in the area, other explorers were inspired to press northward. Estevanico himself later traveled into the present-day southwestern United States in search of the seven cities. Some Spaniards finally realized that the stories of the seven golden cities were most likely exaggerated stories about Pueblo villages to the north.

MAP SKILLS An advisor to the Spanish king in the 1500s remarked: "It is towards the south, not towards the frozen north, that those who seek their fortune should bend their way; for everything at the Equator is rich." **Location** *Cite evidence from the map to show that Spanish settlers followed this policy.*

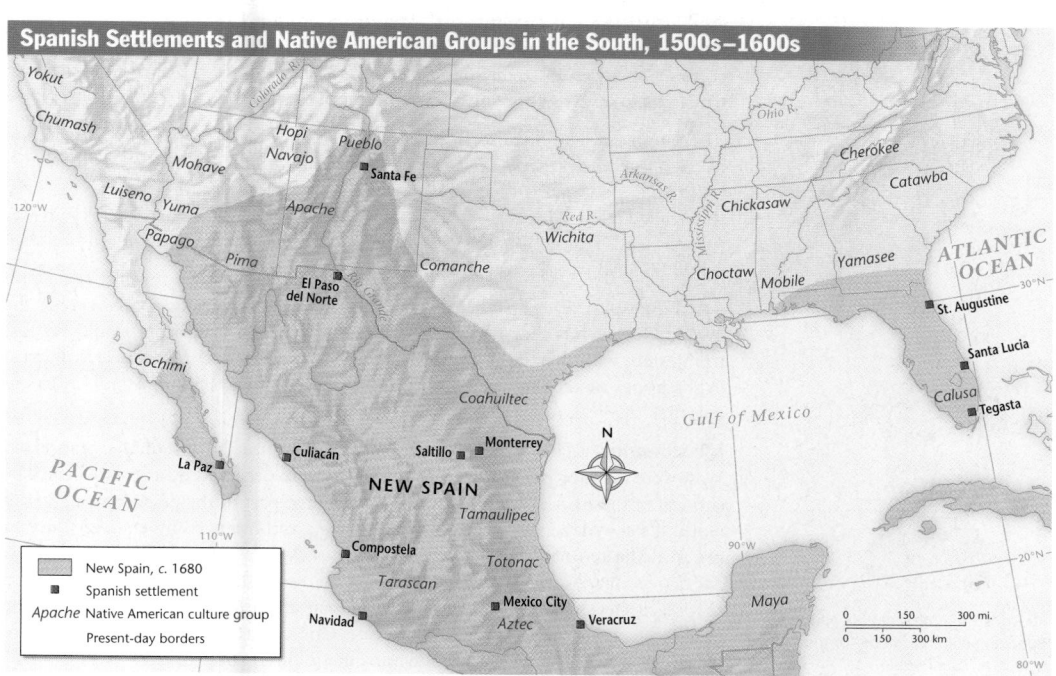

Spanish Settlements and Native American Groups in the South, 1500s–1600s

New Spain, c. 1680
■ Spanish settlement
Apache Native American culture group
Present-day borders

Connecting with Geography

This activity may take place over several class periods. Divide the class into groups of four to six students. Each group will produce a guidebook that describes a site in present-day New Mexico and provides an understanding of the interaction between Spanish and Native American cultures there. An example is the village of Isleta, a surviving Native American village rebuilt after its destruction in the 1680 Pueblo revolt. Groups should consult travel guides, atlases, and historical maps such as those produced by the National Geographic Society. **(Visual/Spatial; Verbal/Linguistic)**

BACKGROUND
Connections to Today

Nearly a decade before the English established any permanent settlement in North America, Don Juan de Oñate led a group of colonists from Mexico across the Rio Grande and into the land he called *Nuevo Mexico*. These settlers founded the towns, missions, and ranches that their descendants eventually spread throughout the American Southwest. New Mexico recently celebrated the 400th anniversary of Oñate's 1598 crossing of the Rio Grande.

CAPTION ANSWERS

Map Skills Most of their settlements were south of 30° N.

✔ TEST PREPARATION

Have students read the section "Controlling the Spanish Empire" and then complete the sentence below.

Under the *encomienda* system Native Americans were—

A freed from labor.

Ⓑ forced to work for an individual Spaniard.

C rounded up to work for Spanish cooperatives.

D sent to Spain.

Connecting with Geography

Tell students to choose one of the regions that the Spanish settled—the Southeast Coast, the Southwest, or the West Coast. Then have students research to learn more about the early settlement of the area. As they read, tell students to consider some of the following questions: What other groups settled the region? Who were some of the region's early leaders? What were some of the conflicts between the groups that settled the area? When students complete their research, have them write a short report summarizing what they have learned. **(Verbal/Linguistic)**

BACKGROUND

Connections to Today

The Third Order of Saint Francis of Assisi currently has more than 400,000 members around the world. The Franciscans pattern their lives after St. Francis of Assisi, who believed in living a simple life of poverty. This thirteenth-century saint devoted his life to prayer and is known for his love of birds. There are many paintings depicting St. Francis among a flock of birds. Following in the tradition of St. Francis, thousands of Franciscans continue to live a life of poverty as they renounce their ties to earthly possessions and live in sparse and sometimes remote environments.

Focus on ECONOMICS

Riches From America The Spanish came to the Americas seeking gold, and they found it in staggering amounts. They found vast silver resources as well. The average value of precious metal that was shipped back to Spain each year jumped from about one million pesos in the period 1526–1530 to more than 35 million pesos during 1591–1595.

The flow of so much American gold and silver into Spain, however, helped cause inflation. Since precious metal was used as money, an increase in the precious metal supply caused an increase in the money supply as well. That, in turn, led to inflation, or higher prices: More pesos in circulation meant each peso was worth less, so each peso could buy fewer goods than previously. Prices in Spain increased approximately three- to five-fold during the 1500s.

Above is the Archangel Michael, a Spanish sculpture made for the church at Zuni Pueblo.

Francisco Vásquez de Coronado Coronado, too, searched the present-day southwestern United States for the fabled golden cities. Between 1540 and 1542, he traveled through present-day Texas and pushed north as far as Kansas. Though he expected to come upon a rich city called Quivira at journey's end, instead he found only the camp of some nomadic Native Americans.

Hernán de Soto De Soto, another hidalgo from the Estremadura, landed near present-day Tampa Bay, Florida, in 1539. He had with him about 600 soldiers. Over the next few years, he traveled through much of what was the northern part of the Spanish empire. His route included parts of present-day Florida, Alabama, Tennessee, Mississippi, Arkansas, and Oklahoma. He and his men were probably the first Spaniards to cross the Mississippi River. Yet by the time de Soto died of fever in Louisiana in 1542, he still had not found the golden cities he had been seeking.

Forts for Defense The regions explored by Cabeza de Vaca, Estevanico, de Soto, and others did not seem to offer much in riches or farming possibilities. For this reason, few of the 450,000 Spanish immigrants to the Americas before 1650 settled in the lands that are now the United States. As a result, the Spanish government felt the need to encourage settlement in three neglected areas, each for a particular reason:

The Southeast Coast Fleets loaded with silver and gold from the Americas sailed from Cuba to Spain along the Gulf Stream, a powerful current that crosses the Atlantic Ocean. The Spanish government wanted to safeguard these fleets by building defensive bases, particularly in Florida. As you read at the start of this section, in 1565, Pedro Menéndez de Avilés established the settlement of St. Augustine in Florida for this purpose. In the next few years, he built a half-dozen other outposts. But the Spanish did not commit themselves to maintaining these forts. Only St. Augustine survived from this first wave of Spanish settlement in Florida.

The Southwest The Spanish hoped to stretch the profitable mining industry of Mexico into the present-day southwestern United States. In 1598, the conquistador Juan de Oñate and about 400 men, women, and children claimed an area they called New Mexico. (Spanish New Mexico included parts of present-day Arizona and Texas.) Oñate's New Mexican colony grew to include more than 2,000 Spanish people over the next 80 years.

The West Coast The Spanish also wanted to establish trade routes across the Pacific Ocean, but they realized that anyone living in California would be able to interfere with this trade. Thus they began to consider settlements in California in the hopes of keeping their European rivals out of the region. Major efforts to colonize this region, however, did not begin until the 1700s.

Missionaries The Spanish settlements that eventually dotted the South and West were forts, or **presidios,** most of which were occupied by a few soldiers. The survival of these Spanish outposts was due in large part to the persistence and hard work of a few dozen Franciscans. These priests and nuns, members of a Catholic group dedicated to the work of St. Francis of Assisi, settled in Florida and New Mexico as missionaries. Missionaries are people who are sent out by their church to preach, teach, and convert others to their religion. In North America, the Franciscans converted Native Americans to Christianity and established dozens of **missions**—headquarters where the missionaries lived and worked.

40   Chapter 2 • *European Colonization of the Americas*

RESOURCE DIRECTORY

Teaching Resources
Units 1/2 booklet
• Section 1 Quiz, p. 15
Guide to the Essentials
• Section 1 Summary, p. 10

Technology
Color Transparencies *Political Cartoons,* B1

In addition to converting Native Americans, the Spanish also wanted to make them follow European customs. With the help of soldiers, the Spanish forced the Native Americans into settled villages, or *congregaciones,* where they would farm and worship like Catholic Europeans.

In 1634, one missionary, Fray Alonso de Benavides, reported the following:

> 66 *[Many Native Americans] are now converted, baptized, and very well ministered to. . . . The whole land is dotted with churches, convents, and crosses along the roads. The people are so well taught that they now live like perfect Christians.* 99
>
> —Fray Alonso de Benavides

Native American Resistance to the Spanish

While missionaries such as Benavides might sometimes have felt that they were achieving their goals, overall they were not as successful as they wanted to be. Some Native Americans, particularly nomadic groups like the Apache of the Southwest, refused to cooperate with the Spanish. Even those who sometimes cooperated fiercely resisted at other times. Such resistance broke out as early as 1597 and continued occasionally throughout the 1600s.

Native American fighting against the Spanish was generally disorganized. In New Mexico, however, following years of drought that weakened Spanish power, the Pueblo people united in what is called the **Pueblo Revolt of 1680.** By the 1670s, widespread sickness and drought had reduced the Pueblo population to about 17,000 people. Seeking to reverse this decline, the Pueblo began to turn back to their traditional religious practices, which the Spanish denounced as witchcraft and tried to stamp out. In August of 1680, the Pueblo people in New Mexico under the leadership of a man named Popé rose up and drove the Spanish out of Santa Fe. During the fighting, the Pueblo destroyed all signs of Christianity and European culture. They killed priests, colonists, and soldiers, and destroyed the Spanish missions. Years passed before the Spanish were able to return and rebuild. Similar Native American rebellions also occurred in Florida.

VIEWING HISTORY This painting of a missionary pierced by a lance depicts the Revolt of 1680, which drove the Spanish out of New Mexico for 12 years.
Recognizing Cause and Effect
What caused the Pueblo Revolt?

Reading Comprehension

1. God, gold, and glory.

2. Cortés used the hatred of many Native Americans for the Aztecs to his advantage, and with the help of a princess known as Malinche, he rallied thousands of Native Americans to the cause of overthrowing the Aztecs.

3. It involved a system of paternal serfdom in which Native Americans provided labor to a Spanish master, who in turn looked after the basic needs of the workers.

4. For the defense and promotion of Spanish settlements.

5. Causes: The Spanish wanted to convert Native Americans to Christianity and get them to adopt a European lifestyle; Effects: The Pueblo people, under Popé's leadership, drove the Spanish out of Santa Fe, to which the Spanish were only able to return after many years.

Critical Thinking and Writing

6. Legends of a "fountain of youth" led Ponce de Léon to explore Florida; rumors of gold led Cortés to conquer the Aztecs and inspired later explorers to press north.

7. Spanish missionaries wished to spread the Christian religion and convert Native Americans. This was a driving force behind European conquests and a motivation, though to a lesser degree, in the conquest of the Americas.

8. Paragraphs will vary, but should be supported with facts from the section.

Section 1 Assessment

READING COMPREHENSION

1. Why did the **conquistadors** come to the Americas?

2. Explain how Cortés conquered the Aztecs.

3. How did the *encomienda* **system** fit into the pattern of economic activity in the new Spanish colonies?

4. Why did the Spanish build **presidios** in North America?

5. What were the causes and effects of Native American resistance in New Mexico and Florida?

CRITICAL THINKING AND WRITING

6. **Recognizing Cause and Effect** How did legends and rumors affect European knowledge of the Americas?

7. **Synthesizing Information** What role did religion play in the Spanish pattern of conquest—both in Europe and in the Americas?

8. **Writing to Describe** Write two paragraphs in which you comment on the following motto printed in a Spanish book in 1599: "By the sword and the compass, more and more and more and more."

 Take It to the NET

Activity: Writing History
Research accounts of Spanish explorers in North America. Then, write your own brief history of one of the explorers or events you studied. Use the links provided in the *America: Pathways to the Present* area of the following Web site for help in completing this activity.
www.phschool.com

 **Take It to the NET**

Essays should clearly and concisely describe a significant event or explorer discussed in the section.

CAPTION ANSWERS

Viewing History The Pueblo were dying in large numbers. In seeking to return to their traditional religious ways, they were resisting Spanish attempts to convert them to Christianity and a European way of life.

Section
2 Jamestown

SECTION OBJECTIVES

1. Discover the goals of England's explorers.
2. Learn about the challenges faced by Jamestown's early settlers.
3. Discover the role of tobacco in Virginia and find out how it contributed to Bacon's Rebellion.
4. See why relations were uneasy between English settlers and Native Americans.

BELLRINGER

Warm-Up Activity Ask students to think about why people want to own things such as land and other forms of property. What image does ownership convey?

Activating Prior Knowledge Ask students to imagine what it must be like to be a member of a group establishing a settlement in a new land. What would some of the greatest challenges be socially, economically, politically, and personally? Develop a classroom list of these challenges, and refer to them as students read the section.

READING STRATEGY

Before students read the section, have them write down the names of the headings. Have them write a question based on each heading and answer the question as they read that portion of the chapter.

READING FOCUS

- What were the goals of England's explorers?
- What challenges did Jamestown's early settlers face?
- What was the role of tobacco in Virginia and how did it contribute to Bacon's Rebellion?
- Why were relations uneasy between English settlers and Native Americans?

MAIN IDEA

Hunger, disease, and Native American resistance all contributed to the near failure of the English colony in Virginia. The discovery of tobacco as a cash crop, however, saved the colony.

KEY TERMS

privateer
charter
joint-stock company
royal colony
legislature
House of Burgesses
indentured servant
Bacon's Rebellion

TAKING NOTES

As you read, complete this chart listing reasons why the English settled in Virginia and the challenges they faced in doing so.

English Settlement in Virginia	
Reasons for Settling	**Challenges Settlers Faced**
• Privateers wanted a naval base in the Americas. •	• Colonists were unaccustomed to manual labor and lacked other necessary skills.

Setting the Scene In the summer of 1590, two ships from England arrived on American shores carrying supplies for a colony on Roanoke Island that had been established three years earlier. One of the men on this journey recalled what happened next:

John White discovers the mysterious message carved on a tree in what was once the colony of Roanoke.

" . . . We found no man or sign that any had been there lately. . . . [We] sounded with a trumpet a call, and afterwards many familiar English tunes of songs, and called to them friendly; but we had no answer. . . . In all this way we saw in the sand the print of the savages' feet of two or three sorts trodden at night, and as we entered up the sandy bank, upon a tree, in the very brow thereof, were curiously carved these fair Roman letters C R O. . . . We [then] passed toward the place where they were left in sundry houses, but we found the houses taken down, and the place very strongly enclosed with a high palisade of great trees. . . .and one of the chief trees or posts at the right side of the entrance had the bark taken off, and five foot from the ground in fair capital letters was graven CROATOAN without any cross or sign of distress. . . "

—John White, 1590

John White and the other men on this voyage never found the original settlers. What happened at Roanoke Island remains one of the greatest mysteries in American history. Historians now know that the word White found on the doorpost, "Croatoan," is an early form of the name of a nearby Native American group. Whether the settlers joined the Indians, or fought and were defeated by them, is not known.

42 Chapter 2 • *European Colonization of the Americas*

RESOURCE DIRECTORY

Teaching Resources
Learning Styles Lesson Plans booklet, p. 6
Guided Reading and Review booklet, p. 8

Other Print Resources
Historical Outline Map Book *The First English Settlements*, p. 14

Technology
Section Reading Support Transparencies
Guided Reading Audiotapes (English/Spanish), Ch. 2
Student Edition on Audio CD, Ch. 2
Sounds of an Era Audio CD *The First Voyage Made to the Coasts of America, Roger Barlowe* (time: one minute, 30 seconds)
Prentice Hall Presentation Pro CD-ROM, Ch. 2
Companion Web site, www.phschool.com

English Explorers

England's attempt to colonize Roanoke Island marked their entry into the race to take advantage of the opportunities of the Atlantic World. Roanoke's failure foreshadowed the difficulties the British would face colonizing this region of the Americas (the present-day Southeast Coast of the United States). However, they remained determined to continue their exploration of North America with the hope of establishing colonies there.

Several explorers sailed to the Americas for England before the 1600s. Although none discovered fabulous riches as the Spanish had, they did greatly expand England's knowledge of the North American Coast.

John Cabot An Italian whose original name was Giovanni Caboto, Cabot was the first known explorer sailing for the English to cross the Atlantic. Historians do not agree exactly where he landed, but he may have reached present-day Newfoundland, Canada, in 1497. Although the English were excited by his success, Cabot never returned from his second voyage to the Americas, and many years passed before England sponsored another American voyage.

Sir Martin Frobisher Frobisher sailed three voyages across the Atlantic Ocean—in 1576, 1577, and 1578. Like Cabot, he was searching for a trade route to Asia that went past or through the continent of North America. This route, called the Northwest Passage, does exist north of Canada. It is extremely hazardous, however, and was not successfully navigated until 1906.

John Davis Davis, too, made three voyages to North America in search of a Northwest Passage, in 1585, 1586, and 1587. Davis's voyages took him along the west coast of Greenland and the east coasts of Baffin Island and Labrador.

Henry Hudson Hudson explored for both the English and the Dutch. On his third voyage, in 1609, he reached the river now known as the Hudson, in present-day New York. He sailed 150 miles (240 km) upstream but finally realized that the river was not the Northwest Passage and turned back.

Sir Francis Drake While English explorers were looking for a shortcut to Asia through the Northwest Passage, English adventurers were taking their own shortcut to wealth. Sailing as **privateers,** they raided Spanish treasure ships and cities in the Americas. Privateers are privately owned ships hired by a government to attack foreign ships. Elizabeth I, the Protestant queen of England from 1558 to 1603, had authorized these raids against Catholic Spain.

The most famous of Queen Elizabeth's "sea dogs," as the English privateers were called, was Sir Francis Drake. On one expedition in 1586, Drake raided St. Augustine in Florida and several other Spanish port cities in the Americas. His thefts severely weakened the finances of the Spanish empire. Drake was more than a pirate, however. As an explorer between 1577 and 1580, he became the first English captain to sail around the world. On his voyage, he sailed into San Francisco Bay and continued as far north as the Pacific Coast of present-day Canada.

An English Interest in Colonization By Drake's time, England had decided that it should establish a

Sir Francis Drake became the first English sea captain to sail his own ship around the globe.

MAP SKILLS England struggled to establish colonies on the Atlantic Coast of North America. **Place** *Examine the map. (a) What features of the region do you think attracted settlers? (b) What is one drawback of the region?*

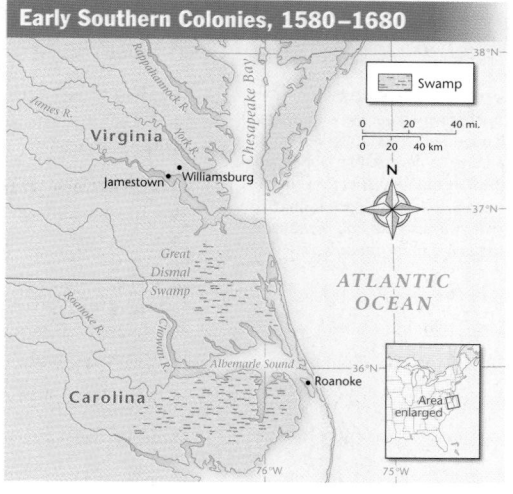

Early Southern Colonies, 1580–1680

Swamp

Rappahannock R.
James R.
York
Chesapeake Bay
38°N
Virginia
Jamestown • Williamsburg
0   20   40 mi.
0   20   40 km
N
37°N
Great Dismal Swamp
ATLANTIC OCEAN
Roanoke R.
Albemarle Sound
36°N • Roanoke
Carolina
Area enlarged
76°W   75°W

---

colony in the Americas. There were several reasons for England's interest in permanent settlements.

1. Privateers were sailing far from England in search of riches. They wanted a base in the Americas from which they could attack Spanish ships and cities.
2. Europeans were still convinced that they could find a Northwest Passage through the American continents to the Indies beyond. When they did find such a passage, they reasoned, they would need supply stations in North America for trading ships.
3. English merchants also wanted new markets. Some thought that Native Americans would buy their goods. Others hoped that a growing population in the colonies would someday become buyers of English cloth and other products.
4. Some of the English believed that their homeland was becoming too crowded. The Americas would be a good place to send those who could not find work or homes in England.

With these reasons in mind, a sea dog named Sir Walter Raleigh tried twice to start a colony on Roanoke Island in the 1580s. Roanoke is one of a chain of islands called the Outer Banks that runs along the coast of present-day North Carolina. Raleigh's first attempt, in 1585, ended when the starving settlers abandoned the colony and returned home. As you read at the start of this section, the second attempt, made two years later, ended mysteriously when its settlers seemingly vanished.

VIEWING HISTORY
Jamestown began as a heavily palisaded settlement huddled on a peninsula deep within Chesapeake Bay. The James River flowed nearby. **Synthesizing Information** *What advantages and disadvantages did the location have?*

The Jamestown Settlement

After the Roanoke disaster, years passed before the English tried again to settle on the Atlantic Coast of North America. Finally, in 1606, several Englishmen made plans to establish another colony. To do so, these businessmen first had to get a **charter,** or certificate of permission, from the king. The charter allowed them to form what is now called a **joint-stock company**—a company funded and run by a group of investors who share the company's profits and losses. The English investors called their company the Virginia Company and started plans to build a colony in the Americas.

In early 1607, the Virginia Company sent about 100 colonists to Virginia, a region discovered and named by Raleigh two decades earlier. The colonists started a settlement about 60 miles from the mouth of the James River, in the Chesapeake Bay region. The settlers called the new village Jamestown in honor of their king, James I.

The Settlers' Hardships Although the Virginia Company had high hopes for the Jamestown settlement, the colony nearly failed. There were several reasons for this.

Conflict with Native Americans Shortly after the arrival of the English settlers, about 200 Native Americans attacked them. Only an English cannon forced the Native Americans to retreat. About 14,000 Native Americans lived in the Chesapeake region. Most of them recognized the authority of one powerful group, the Powhatan people, formed by and named for the powerful chief, Powhatan. The English particularly honored Powhatan, paying him tribute—a kind of regular tax—in skins, beads, and food. Within weeks of the first attack on the English, several Englishmen traveled to neighboring Native American villages to offer tributes of their own and to persuade the Native Americans that their intentions in settling in the area were good. Powhatan did not easily trust those intentions, and the Indians remained suspicious of the English settlers. The efforts made by both sides to keep peace between them resulted in a tense, uneasy truce.

Unrealistic expectations The near failure of Jamestown also resulted from the unrealistic expectations of many of its early settlers. Most of the settlers were not used to doing the hard work required to start a settlement. Many had come to get rich quickly. For instance, some were goldsmiths who expected to find gold they could work into jewelry for quick sale back home. Others had been born into aristocratic families and had no experience with manual labor, such as growing crops or building houses. For these reasons, many of the settlers ignored the daily tasks necessary for their survival and instead searched feverishly for gold. John Smith, a colonist who had emerged as a strong leader in Jamestown by 1608, warned the settlers:

> 66 You must obey this now for a law, that he that will not work shall not eat . . . for the labors of thirty or forty honest and industrious men shall not be consumed to maintain a hundred and fifty idle loiterers. 99
> —John Smith, 1608

Location The site chosen for the settlement was a third factor in Jamestown's near failure. Because they lived near (and drew their water from) swamps and pools of standing water where disease-carrying mosquitos bred, the colonists suffered from dysentery, typhus, and malaria.

Starvation Despite the continued backing of the Virginia Company back in London, the colonists suffered from starvation and sickness during the first ten years of settlement. One particularly difficult period from October 1609 to March 1610 was remembered as the Starving Time. If Native Americans had not given the English help in the form of food and water, the settlement surely would have died out.

Poor leadership Lastly, leadership in the Jamestown settlement was poor. The settlers squabbled about minor matters even when they were in danger of starving. John Smith, a brave and experienced soldier, became the strong leader the colonists needed. Unfortunately for the colonists, however, Smith soon left the Virginia colony because of an injury and sailed back to England.

Meanwhile, back in England, writers were publishing pamphlets calling Virginia a paradise. Ministers gave sermons praising the colony. As a result, by 1623, approximately 5,500 English and other Europeans had migrated to Virginia. Yet life in this new "paradise" was so hard that about 4,000 of these settlers died within a short time of arriving in the colony.

COMPARING PRIMARY SOURCES
Life in Jamestown

Many English settlers were lured to the Americas by descriptions of an easy life. The realities of settlement life were very different, however.

Analyzing Viewpoints What motivated some of the English in London to describe America in such positive terms?

Dreams of Riches

"I tell thee, Golde is more plentifull there than Copper is with us. . . . Why man all their dripping Pans and their Chamber pottes are pure Golde; . . . and for Rubies and Diamonds, they goe forth on holy-dayes and gather them by the Sea-shore to hang on their childrens Coates and sticke in their Cappes."
—*Description of Virginia from* Eastward Ho!, *a popular London play, 1605*

Realities of Jamestown

"Of five hundred within six moneths after Captain Smith's departure, there remained not past sixtie men, women and children, most miserable and poore creatures. . . . [S]o great was our famine, that a Savage [Native American] we slew and buried, the poorer sort tooke him up againe and eat him. . . . [I]t were too vile to say, and scarce to be beleeved, what we endured."
—*A survivor's record of the Starving Time in Jamestown, October 1609 to March 1610*

Connecting with Culture

Ask students to write an advertisement designed to attract young English men and women to migrate to the Virginia Colony. Students should review the selections in Comparing Primary Sources before deciding how best to "sell" Virginia to the English. **(Verbal/Linguistic)**

BACKGROUND
Art History

The painting on the previous page shows that the Jamestown settlement was built at the water's edge. This location offered easy access for ships in England. But this access was a disadvantage when enemies made use of it. The location was also too wet, promoting illness among the colonists.

CUSTOMIZE FOR ...
Less Proficient Readers

Have students reread the quote from John Smith on this page. Then have students rewrite Smith's warning in their own words.

List with students three problems faced by settlers of the Jamestown colony in its early days. Ask students to review the section to find a cause and the ultimate resolution for each problem. (**Verbal/Linguistic; Logical/Mathematical**)

BACKGROUND

An Early Description of the Use of Tobacco

Thomas Hariot's *Briefe and True Report of the New Found Land of Virginia* was published in two parts in 1588 and 1590, probably at the request of Sir Walter Raleigh, who wanted to revive interest in exploration of the New World. Hariot spent time on Roanoke Island in 1585 and 1586 as part of a mission of exploration led by Sir Richard Grenville. Hariot's task was to create a detailed survey of the area's natural resources and native inhabitants. In the *Report,* he offers this description of tobacco: "There is an herbe which is sowed a part by it selfe & is called by the inhabitants Vppówoc: In the West Indies it hast divers names, according to the severall places & countries where it groweth and is used: The Spaniardes generally call it Tobacco. The leaves thereof being dried and brought into powder: they use to take the fume or smoke thereof by sucking it through pipes made of clai [clay] into their stomacke and heade; from whence it purgeth superfluous fleame [phlegm] & other grosse humors, openeth all the pores & passages of the body: by which meanse the use thereof, not only preserveth the body from obstructions . . . whereby their bodies are notably preserved in health & know not many greevous diseases wherewithal wee in England are oftentimes afflicted."

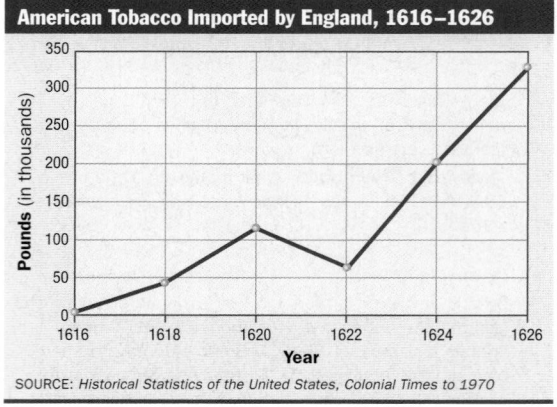

American Tobacco Imported by England, 1616–1626

SOURCE: *Historical Statistics of the United States, Colonial Times to 1970*

INTERPRETING GRAPHS
When John Rolfe introduced a mild tobacco to England, he saved the struggling Virginia colony. **Analyzing Information** *How much more tobacco did England import from America in 1626 than in 1616?*

The labor of indentured servants included bundling and packing dried tobacco leaves.

Governing the Colony As the colony struggled, the Virginia Company tried to improve its governing system. In 1609, the company received a new charter, under which it could appoint a governor who would actually live in the colony. When the Virginia Company proved unable to turn a steady profit, King James took away the company's charter and shut it down in 1624. Instead of a corporate colony, Virginia became a **royal colony,** with a governor appointed by the king.

In addition to its royal governor, Virginia also had a **legislature,** or lawmaking assembly, beginning in 1619. The legislature was made up of representatives from the colony. Because the representatives were called burgesses, the assembly itself came to be called the **House of Burgesses.** Though no one understood it in these terms at the time, this legislature was the first instance of limited self-government in the English colonies.

Growing Tobacco

During the early years of their settlement, one thing saved the Virginia colonists from failing completely: tobacco, a plant native to the Western Hemisphere. In 1613, colonist John Rolfe shipped some tobacco to Europe, where it quickly became popular. Soon, tobacco was the basis of the colony's economy. In 1616, Virginians sent 2,500 pounds of the plant to England. By 1618, this amount had increased to nearly 50,000 pounds. By 1640, Virginia and its neighbor colony, Maryland, were sending home 3 million pounds a year.

In order to cash in on the tobacco boom, settlers moved out from Jamestown. They carved out plantations on the banks of the James, York, Rappahannock, and Potomac rivers, and along the shores of Chesapeake Bay. Settlers established their plantations close to waterways, so that they could transport their tobacco more easily.

The Promise of Land To produce large crops of tobacco, planters needed laborers to work the fields. One way of persuading people to come to Virginia was to promise them land when they arrived. Over time, the custom developed of giving each "head," or person who came to the colony, the right to fifty acres of land. This system became known as the headright system.

The promise of land helped attract new colonists from England. So did changes that were taking place in England at the time. English landowners had found that they could make more money from raising livestock than they could from renting land to farmers. The landowners therefore forced the farmers off the land and turned their fields into animal pastures by enclosing them with fences. Many farmers lost their homes as a result of this enclosure movement. England was swarming with young people in search of food and work. They were called "masterless" men and women because they did not have a master, or patron.

Indentured Servants One of the few choices open to the masterless people was to sail to Virginia. Many, however, did not have the money for the voyage. To pay for the crossing, they became

46 Chapter 2 • *European Colonization of the Americas*

indentured servants. These were people who had to work for a master for a period of time, usually seven years, under a contract called an indenture. In return for their work, their master paid the cost of their voyage to Virginia and gave them food and shelter. Some indentures promised a piece of land to the servant at the end of the indenture period.

Historians estimate that between 100,000 and 150,000 men and women came as servants to work in the fields of Virginia and neighboring Maryland during the 1600s. Most of them were 18 to 22 years of age, unmarried, and poor. Few indentured servants lived long enough to claim their land at the end of their service. The hot climate and diseases of the Chesapeake Bay area killed them in large numbers.

Among Virginia's indentured servants were some Africans, the first to settle in the present-day United States. The first group of about 20 Africans arrived in 1619. Their numbers remained small, however.

Conflict With Native Americans

Although the Native Americans did help the English through the difficult times, tensions persisted. Incidents of violence occurred side by side with regular trade. Exchanges begun on both sides with good intentions could become angry confrontations in a matter of minutes through simple misunderstandings. Indeed, the failure of each group to understand the culture of the other prevented any permanent cooperation between the English and Native Americans.

The English Pattern of Conquest   English attitudes toward the Native Americans stemmed from events in Europe that had begun years earlier. Like the Spanish, the English, too, had a pattern of conquest, although one quite different. The English pattern grew out of their experiences in Ireland, the island nation off their western coast. For centuries, English rulers had been trying to assert control in this neighboring land, and the Irish people had steadfastly resisted.

Meanwhile, after Protestantism developed out of the Reformation in the early 1500s as a protest against the Catholic Church, European nations rapidly took sides as Catholic or Protestant. Because the English were Protestant and the Irish were Catholic, conflict between the two nations intensified. During the 1500s and 1600s, England made Ireland its first overseas colony, and English settlers poured onto the island. The English put down Irish resistance to this invasion with stern measures, repeatedly taking land away from the native Irish people.

During this colonizing effort, the English developed a harsh attitude toward conquered peoples. In their experience, it was best to remake completely any culture they conquered. They did not practice the forced blending of European and Native American societies that was taking place in the colonies of the Spanish. For the English, conquest would be all—or nothing.

Native Americans React   In March 1622, relations between Native Americans and the English broke down altogether. The new leader of the Native Americans, Opechancanough, Powhatan's younger brother, carefully planned and carried out a surprise attack on Jamestown with the intention of wiping out the English. Although the attack failed, he and his men did kill about 350 of the colonists, more than 25 percent of the population at that time.

Focus on CULTURE

Pocahontas When she was about 12 years old, the Indian princess Pocahontas, the daughter of powerful chief Powhatan, met the first settlers to arrive in Jamestown in 1607. It was then that the legendary and questionable story involving Pocahontas and John Smith took place. According to the story, the young girl saved Smith's life after he was taken captive by a group of Indians. As a result, the two became friends, and the settlers and Indians in the region remained on generally peaceful terms.

Pocahontas frequently visited Jamestown and became a favorite of the settlers there. In 1613, however, after relations between the settlers and Indians had grown worse, an English captain kidnapped Pocahontas and held her for ransom. While being held captive, she converted to Christianity and married John Rolfe, the successful tobacco planter. Both her father and Virginia Governor Sir Thomas Dale gave their consent to this marriage, which led to a period of peace between the English and the Indians. In 1617, Pocahontas contracted a fatal disease and died before returning to America after a trip to England. She was 22 years old. John Smith wrote, in 1617, that Pocahontas was "the instrument to preserve this colony from death, famine, and utter confusion."

Within days, the settlers struck back, killing as many or more Native Americans. Again, the English and the Native Americans patched up an uneasy truce.

Opechancanough's people made their last major attack on the English in the Chesapeake Bay area in 1644. Opechancanough took part again, still active and defiant at more than 70 years of age. This attack also failed, and Opechancanough was shot in the streets of Jamestown.

Bacon's Rebellion

As the population of Virginia increased, settlers pushed farther west in search of new farmland. Many were former indentured servants who lacked the money to buy farmland and so tried to take it from the Indians instead. Clashes between settlers and Native Americans took place along Virginia's western frontier.

Meanwhile, some wealthier men thrived as planters. They grew huge amounts of tobacco and used the profits to buy more land and more servants. A governor appointed by the English king served the interests of this new class of rich planters. Neither the rich planters nor the government responded to the needs of the less powerful members of Virginia society.

Governor William Berkeley refused to raise troops to defend the settlers against Indian raids. Although he was Berkeley's cousin, a planter, and a member of the governor's council, Nathaniel Bacon sympathized with the frontiersmen. In 1676, Bacon raised a private army to fight the Native Americans and take their land. Governor Berkeley, angry that Bacon was acting without his permission, declared him a rebel and gathered an army to stop him.

Suddenly, however, Bacon turned his army around. Complaining that Berkeley had failed to protect the western settlers, and charging that those western settlers had too little voice in colonial government, Bacon and his supporters attacked and burned Jamestown. For a time, Bacon controlled nearly all of Virginia. He died suddenly, probably from illness, and with his death **Bacon's Rebellion** crumbled.

Bacon's Rebellion is important for two reasons. First, it showed that the frontier settlers were frustrated with a government concerned only about the interests of a small group of wealthy planters. Second, it showed that the poorer colonists were unwilling to tolerate such a government.

VIEWING HISTORY Nathaniel Bacon, shown above, declared that he meant "not only to ruin . . . all Indians in General but all Manner of Trade and Commerce with them." **Drawing Inferences** *Why do you think Bacon felt this way?*

Section 2 Assessment

READING COMPREHENSION

1. What did early English explorers hope to find by sailing across the Atlantic?
2. Why did Virginia change from a corporate colony to a **royal colony?**
3. What was significant about the **House of Burgesses?**
4. Describe how tobacco influenced the economic system of Jamestown.
5. How did the English pattern of conquest affect their relations with Native Americans?

CRITICAL THINKING AND WRITING

6. **Identifying Central Issues** North America was a difficult, dangerous place for both the Spanish and the English. Why did they want to settle there?
7. **Writing to Persuade** Write an essay from the point of view of Nathaniel Bacon, arguing that the government in Virginia should protect the western planters from Native American attacks.

Take It to the NET

Activity: Writing an Advertisement Further investigate the history of the Jamestown settlement, focusing on what brought colonists to the area. Then, create an advertisement to appear in a British newspaper that would have been used to lure people to Virginia. Use the links provided in the *America: Pathways to the Present* area of the following Web site for help in completing this activity.
www.phschool.com

The New England Colonies

READING FOCUS

- What was the pattern of French settlement in North America?
- What were the goals of the Plymouth and Massachusetts Bay colonies?
- Why was there dissent within the Puritan community?
- Why did war break out between the Indians and the English settlers?

MAIN IDEA

With both help and resistance from Native Americans, English colonists succeeded in establishing permanent settlements in New England.

KEY TERMS

New England Colonies
Puritan
persecute
Pilgrim
Mayflower Compact
Great Migration
religious tolerance
Salem witch trials
sachem
Pequot War
King Philip's War

TAKING NOTES

As you read, complete this chart comparing the main characteristics of the following colonies: New France, Plymouth, and Massachusetts Bay.

Characteristics of New England Colonies	
Colony	Characteristics
New France	Based on fur trade, located along the St. Lawrence River and the Great Lakes
Plymouth	
Massachusetts Bay	

SECTION OBJECTIVES

1. Learn about the pattern of French settlement in North America.
2. Discover the goals of the Plymouth and Massachusetts Bay colonies.
3. Understand why there was dissent within the Puritan community.
4. See why war broke out between the Indians and the English settlers.

BELLRINGER

Warm-Up Activity Ask students to suppose that an unfamiliar group suddenly took over their classrooms. How would they react?

Activating Prior Knowledge Have students list some reasons for expanded colonial settlement in America by the English. What do students think would draw French explorers and colonists to North America at this time?

READING STRATEGY

As students read the section, have them write three questions about each of the following colonies: New France, Plymouth, and Massachusetts Bay. Have them look for answers to their questions as they read the section.

Setting the Scene The English were not the only Europeans interested in the East Coast of North America. The French, too, had been exploring the region for decades, looking for trading opportunities. These voyages would lead to the creation of a French North American colony. Eventually they would also lead to conflict between France and England for control of eastern North America.

The French in North America

Like their longtime rivals the English, the French sponsored several voyages of exploration to North America. As French explorers searched for the Northwest Passage, they came upon what is now known as the St. Lawrence River in Canada.

Giovanni da Verrazano Verrazano was an Italian who sailed for the French in 1523–1524. Searching for the Northwest Passage, he explored the coast of North America from present-day North Carolina to Newfoundland. Verrazano also entered New York harbor.

Jacques Cartier Cartier made three voyages to Canada: in 1534, 1535, and again in 1541–1542. On the basis of Cartier's explorations, the French king claimed a region called New France for his nation. New France included not only land covered by present-day Canada, but also parts of the present-day northern United States. Although he explored the St. Lawrence River as far as the modern-day city of Montreal, he did not succeed in establishing a permanent colony in North America.

Samuel de Champlain Champlain founded the first successful French colony in North America in 1608. The site he chose was at Quebec, on high ground above a narrow stretch of the St. Lawrence River in present-day Canada.

VIEWING HISTORY The French explorers Louis Joliet and Jacques Marquette, along with a crew and Native American guides, canoe on the Mississippi River. **Identifying Central Issues** *What did they hope to find?*

CAPTION ANSWERS

Viewing History Like most other explorers, they were looking for the Northwest Passage to the Pacific Ocean.

Chapter 2 • Section 3 **49**

RESOURCE DIRECTORY

Teaching Resources
Learning Styles Lesson Plans booklet, p. 7
Guided Reading and Review booklet, p. 9

Other Print Resources
Historical Outline Map Book *Search for a Northwest Passage,* p. 10; *The French Explore North America,* p. 12; *The New England Colonies,* p. 16

Technology
Section Reading Support Transparencies
Guided Reading Audiotapes (English/Spanish), Ch. 2
Student Edition on Audio CD, Ch. 2
Color Transparencies *Historical Maps,* A3; *American Photo,* F1
Exploring Primary Sources in U.S. History CD-ROM *Mayflower Compact*
Prentice Hall Presentation Pro CD-ROM, Ch. 2
Companion Web site, www.phschool.com

Focus Ask students how the French and English interacted with Native Americans. Explain that in 1675, Native Americans in New England fought back against English settlers in King Philip's War. Discuss the impact of the war on settlers and Native Americans.

Instruct Ask why the French had good relations with Native Americans, while the Puritans provoked resentment. Discuss the difficulty of a life such as Metacom's, moving between two societies that were at odds. Ask why Metacom gave up trying to maintain peace. What were the long-term causes of King Philip's War?

Assess/Reteach Discuss with students ways in which the Puritan settlers might have maintained good relations with Native Americans. Was the conflict between the two groups inevitable, or could it have been avoided?

BACKGROUND
Biography

Jacques Marquette (1637–1675) was sent to the French colonies in North America by the Jesuits. He befriended the Native Americans with whom he lived and quickly learned several of their languages. In 1672 Marquette joined fur trader Louis Joliet and five other traders in mapping a route down the Wisconsin River into the Mississippi River. Marquette and Joliet sought precious metals as well as a water passage to the Pacific Ocean. When Native Americans told them that the Mississippi emptied into the Gulf of Mexico, they returned north. Marquette and Joliet are believed to have been the first Europeans to explore the upper Mississippi.

Louis Joliet (bronze portrait above) befriended Native Americans, who aided the French on their journey down the Mississippi. Wampum belts, like this one made of shell beads, served as currency in the trade between Native Americans and Europeans. This one belonged to an Iroquois.

Champlain also mapped the Atlantic shores as far south as Massachusetts, and traveled inland to the lakes now known as Lake Huron and Lake Champlain.

Louis Joliet and Jacques Marquette Explorers Joliet and Marquette traveled together from the Great Lakes to the Mississippi River in 1673. Hoping that the Mississippi emptied into the Pacific Ocean, they traveled by canoe south along the waterway to present-day Arkansas. There they learned from Native Americans that the river flowed into the Gulf of Mexico. Realizing they had not found the Northwest Passage, they returned to New France.

The Fur Trade The French did not need the Northwest Passage to grow rich from New France. They discovered that a local product, fur, could be sold for great gain in Europe. Clothing made from the skins of deer, beaver, and other animals became highly fashionable in France and elsewhere in Europe in the 1600s. Native Americans trapped these animals, collected their furs, and traded them to the French.

The fur trade determined the shape of New France. By the late 1600s, New France was a long, narrow colony stretching far into the interior of Canada, along the St. Lawrence and the Great Lakes. New France stuck close to the waterways because, as in Virginia, water was vital for transporting goods.

The Iroquois The fur trade linked the Native Americans of northeastern North America with the trade of the Atlantic World. Native Americans gathered furs for European markets and became eager consumers of European goods, including guns, cloth, and jewelry. Many Native Americans learned of the Christian religion from Catholic missionaries, adopting and adapting Catholic rituals as they saw fit.

Along with new ways of trading and worshipping, the Europeans also brought the ravages of disease to the Native Americans. Because it was a Native American custom in the Northeast to capture members of other groups to adopt into shrinking lineages, wars grew more common as disease took its toll. Native American groups also fought one another over hunting grounds, since the number of furs they took determined how much of the new trade they could control. One group, the Iroquois, was particularly successful at both war and trade. They lived in present-day New York State between the Hudson River and Lake Erie. Having ended warfare among themselves, the Iroquois nations fought a series of wars against other Native American tribes in the middle and late 1600s. In the end, the Iroquois pushed their rivals out of their homelands, forcing them to migrate west of the Great Lakes.

Plymouth Colony

While the French were building the fur trade in New France, the English were beginning new colonies along the Atlantic Coast in the present-day northeastern region of the United States. Known as New England, this region included land that became the states of Connecticut, Rhode Island, Massachusetts, Vermont, New Hampshire, and Maine. The colonies in this region were called the **New England Colonies.**

Puritans and Separatists The first successful colony in New England was founded as a result of religious conflicts in England. In 1534, England's King Henry VIII had broken with the Catholic Church and had founded the Anglican

Other Print Resources
Historical Outline Map Book *The Thirteen Colonies,* p. 15

Technology
RESOURCE PRO® **Literature Activity**
Puritan Poetry, found on Resource Pro, enhances students' understanding of Puritan beliefs by contrasting the poetry of Anne Bradstreet and Edward Taylor.

Church, England's national Protestant church. Some of the English, however, complained that the Anglican Church continued too many Catholic practices and traditions. Because they wanted what they considered a "purer" kind of church, they were called **Puritans.** Some of the Puritans started separate churches of their own and were called Separatists. Both Puritans and Separatists were **persecuted,** or attacked because of their beliefs.

The Voyage of the *Mayflower* One group of Separatists, those who came to be called the **Pilgrims,** decided to make a new home in North America, where they hoped they would be free to worship as they wanted. In 1620, a group of roughly 100 Pilgrims sailed to New England on the *Mayflower.*

About two thirds of those aboard the *Mayflower* were non-Separatists, and as the ship neared shore, these settlers threatened to go off and live by themselves. Afraid that the group would break up, the Pilgrims made a compact, or agreement, called the **Mayflower Compact.** In the agreement, the settlers agreed to obey all of their government's laws. As they put it:

> **KEY DOCUMENTS** ❝ We . . . do . . . combine ourselves together into a civil body politic, for our better ordering and preservation . . . [and to] frame such just and equal laws . . . as shall be thought most [fitting] and convenient for the general good of the colony, unto which we promise all due . . . obedience.❞
>
> —The Mayflower Compact

The compact succeeded in keeping the Pilgrims together. It also showed that the Pilgrims expected to decide for themselves how they would be governed. Later this belief in self-government would become one of the founding principles of the United States.

One of the men who drew up the Mayflower Compact was William Bradford, who went on to be elected governor of the colony 30 times between 1621 and 1656. Bradford helped create a form of government in which the people guided their own affairs. Bradford later wrote a moving history of the colony

VIEWING FINE ART Although an idealized and imaginative portrait of English settlers reaching American shores, *Landing of the Pilgrims* shows the imminent meeting of two cultures. **Determining Relevance** *The Pilgrims signed the Mayflower Compact while still aboard ship. How do you think this agreement helped them survive their initial hardships and eventually prosper?*

ACTIVITY
Connecting with Government

Engage students in a discussion about William Bradford's idea of self-government. How does Bradford's idea differ from the European monarchies that were in place at the time? Why would a self-governing system appeal to the Puritans? Why would such a system not be attractive? How is this concept reflected in our current government? **(Verbal/Linguistic)**

BACKGROUND
Geography in History

The journey taken by Pilgrims from England to the coast of North America was much longer than we sometimes remember. Members of the English Separatists Church, some of whom would later be the first English settlers of Massachusetts, first left Great Britain in 1609 and sailed to the Netherlands. They stayed for a decade before they began to formulate a plan for founding a colony in the New World. It is worth noting, too, that they were not the only persecuted religious minority to seek refuge in the Netherlands. Among others were Jews whose ancestors had been persecuted in, and exiled from, Spain.

READING CHECK
They felt the Anglican Church continued too many Catholic practices and traditions, and they sought a "purer" church.

CUSTOMIZE FOR ...

ESL

Work with students to restate the quote from the Mayflower Compact on this page in their own words.

CAPTION **A**NSWERS

Viewing Fine Art The compact helped the Pilgrims stick together and help each other through tough times. In addition, it demonstrated that they were capable of some level of self-government and could guide their own affairs.

Fast Forward to Today

Blue Laws

Among the aspects of colonial society that can still be felt today are "blue laws," or laws which through various means restrict certain activities and businesses on Sunday. The first blue laws in the colonies developed in New Haven, Connecticut, as an attempt to regulate moral behavior on the Sabbath, or day of worship. Examples of early blue laws included the regulation of the sale or consumption of alcohol, mandatory church attendance, and a ban on the playing of games such as cards or dice in public. The penalties for breaking these laws were often harsh. Offenders could be fined, beaten, whipped, and in some cases put to death.

After the American Revolution, the influence of strict religious communities dwindled. As a result, blue laws slowly faded from the law books, or were generally not enforced. A revival of support for these types of laws came about with the temperance and purity crusader movements of the late 1800s, in which activists sought to ban alcohol altogether and rid communities of unwholesome activities.

By the end of the twentieth century, many blue laws had been abolished, but some remained throughout the country. The types of blue laws in effect today vary from state to state and even within states. Some states still prohibit the sale of alcohol in liquor stores on Sundays, but do allow bars to remain open. Many people object to the blue laws in their community or state because they feel that the laws are too closely tied to religion. Advocates of Sunday closure laws claim that, today, the laws serve more as a protection for workers by giving them a forced day off and are not intended to impose religious standards.

? **What purpose do you think blue laws served in colonial communities? What purpose do they serve today? Explain.**

---

titled *History of Plymouth Plantation*, in which he described the many difficulties faced by the early settlers.

Early Difficulties The Pilgrims started their colony at a harbor they called New Plymouth, or simply Plymouth, after the English port from which they had sailed. Like the Jamestown settlers in Virginia, the Pilgrims at Plymouth Colony endured tremendous hardships. Half of them died in the first winter alone. The next summer the colonists had the help of a Native American named Squanto who taught them how to plant corn. They harvested plenty of corn and held a great feast of thanksgiving in the fall of 1621.

The Massachusetts Bay Colony

In 1630, a thousand English settlers braved a voyage across the Atlantic to found the Massachusetts Bay Colony, located north of the Plymouth Colony in New England. These were the first of a flood of colonists who came to New England in a movement called the **Great Migration.** By 1643, the Massachusetts Bay Colony had grown to roughly 20,000 people living in 20 towns, including its capital, Boston.

Reasons for Migrating Many of these new settlers were Puritans hoping to live where they could worship as they wanted. However, they did not believe in **religious tolerance**—the idea that people of different religions should live in peace together. They had no desire to live among people who held beliefs different from their own. By law, everyone in the Massachusetts Bay Colony had to attend the Puritan church and pay taxes to support it.

For the Puritans, the Massachusetts Bay Colony was more than an opportunity to make a living on new farmland. They wanted to reform, or purify, the Protestant church from within. They disliked the Church of England's reliance on a hierarchy of bishops, highly decorated churches, and elaborate worship ceremonies. They preferred to study the Bible, listen to sermons, and closely examine their lives and their world for clues to God's will.

Transforming New England To accomplish their goals, some Puritans migrated to New England and transformed its landscape. They replaced forests with fields, cultivated wheat, barley, and corn, and raised domestic animals like cows and pigs rather than relying on wild deer or beaver.

Not only did the Puritans try to transform the land, they also attempted to remake Native Americans in their own image. They convinced about 1,000 Native Americans to adopt Puritan religious beliefs and customs and live in "praying towns." These English versions of *congregaciones* demanded radical changes by Native Americans. In the praying towns, for example, Native American men were forced to farm—a task that in their society was defined as belonging to women.

A City Upon a Hill   The term *Puritan* has come to be associated with joyless-ness and hypocritical morality. Contrary to this inaccurate image, Puritans were capable of affection and enjoyment as well as religious devotion. They did, however, insist that social order begins with personal order. In addition to laws requiring them to support and attend the Puritan church, Puritans generally frowned on people who wanted to live alone.

As a result of their shared goals, the Puritans were united and strong. When Puritan settlers established a new town, they left a large area of open land as a "common" to be used by all. Facing the common was the church or meeting-house, and nearby was the house for the minister, as well as a schoolhouse. The rest of the land near the common was divided into house lots. Outside the town, each family had a strip of farmland. The Puritan plan was to have well-ordered families in well-ordered towns in a well-ordered colony.

John Winthrop, a founder of the colony and later its governor, summarized the colonists' goals in a sermon he delivered on board the ship *Arbella* in 1630. To succeed, he said:

> **"** We must be knit together in this work, as one man. We must entertain each other in brotherly affection. . . . We must delight in each other; make others' condition our own; rejoice together, mourn together, labor and suffer together. . . . For we must consider that we shall be as a city upon a hill. The eyes of all people are upon us. **"**
>
> —John Winthrop, "A Model of Christian Charity"

Winthrop's sermon voiced a belief that America would be an example to people throughout the world. Many on board the ship, and many Americans since that time, have shared this belief.

In general it was a successful plan. The Puritans worked hard, took care of themselves and one another, and enjoyed relatively good health. Children born in the colony could be expected to live at least twice as long as children born in early Virginia. By 1700, New England was home to more than 93,000 people living fairly comfortable lives.

The Salem Witch Trials   Yet life in the Puritans' ideal community had its dark moments. In 1692, several girls and young women in Salem, Massachusetts,

VIEWING HISTORY This engraving of an English hanging is representative of the scene in Salem on September 22, 1692, when seven women and one man were hanged as witches. **Recognizing Ideologies** *How did the Salem witch trials reflect the Puritans' passion for social order?*

🔘 *Sounds of an Era*

Listen to a reading from John Winthrop's "A Model of Christian Charity" and other sounds from the period of European colonization.

ACTIVITY
Connecting with Citizenship

Have students conduct a debate on whether John Winthrop's image of a "city on a hill" is still relevant today. Do other countries perceive the U.S. to be a model of good citizenship? What recent actions and events prove that we are still that city on a hill? What actions or events disprove the notion? Have each team gather to draw up a list of key points to prove its position. After the debate, invite nonparticipants to discuss which team was more per-suasive, and why. **(Verbal/Linguistic)**

BACKGROUND
The Salem Witch Trials

Accusations of witchcraft in the town of Salem were used to punish people who deviated from the established social norms. Historian John Demos, in a study of witchcraft in colonial New England, found that women accused of being witches were most likely to be middle-aged (40 to 60), married but without children, of low social status, and involved in medical care such as midwifery.

☑ TEST PREPARATION

Have students read the first paragraph under the heading *The Salem Witch Trials* and then answer the question below.

Which is a fact from the passage?

A The devil took control of several girls and young women in Salem.

Ⓑ Accused townspeople were put on trial to determine if they were witches.

C The Puritans formed an ideal community in Salem.

D In 1692 three townspeople in Salem per-formed witchcraft.

CAPTION ANSWERS

Viewing History The Salem witch tri-als may have been influenced by the fear engendered in the colony by news of the changes ushered in by the Glor-ious Revolution in England. These changes included the merger of the Massachusetts Bay and Plymouth colonies.

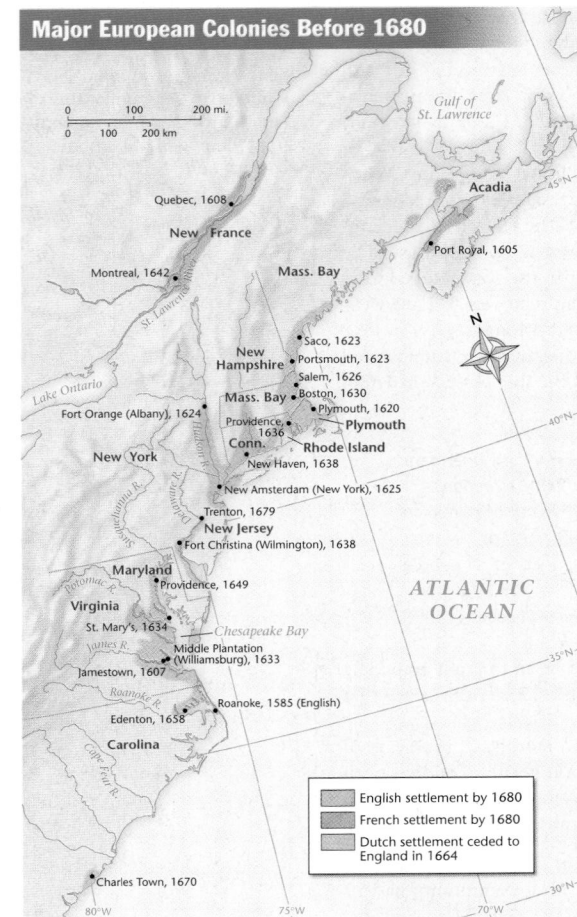

Major European Colonies Before 1680

MAP SKILLS Both the French and the Dutch were more interested in the fur trade than they were in the establishment of permanent settlements. The English were a strong presence along the mid-Atlantic Coast by 1680. **Location** *(a) How did the resulting settlement pattern of the French and Dutch differ from that of England? (b) Why do you think the English avoided settling farther inland?*

claimed that the devil had taken control of them. They also accused three townspeople of being witches. In the public uproar that followed, neighbors fearfully accused one another of dealing with the devil. Trials were held to determine if the accused townspeople really were witches. As a result of these **Salem witch trials,** the Massachusetts authorities ordered 20 men and women to be executed. However, after a few months the community regained its balance, and the trials and hangings came to a stop.

Some historians believe that the witch trials reflected colonists' fears about political changes taking place at the time. As you will read in the next chapter, a revolution known as the Glorious Revolution had recently occurred in England. The year before the trials, England's new monarchs, William and Mary, had joined the Massachusetts Bay Colony and the Plymouth Colony into one. They were now a single royal colony, known as Massachusetts.

Other Puritan Colonies As the population of New England increased, farmland in Massachusetts grew scarce. Some Puritans were given permission to search for better farmland and to establish new communities in New England.

Connecticut Puritan minister Thomas Hooker led a group of settlers from Massachusetts to Connecticut in the mid-1630s. In 1639, representatives from several Connecticut towns wrote a new plan of government for their colony. They called it the Fundamental Orders.

New Hampshire and Maine Similarly, settlements in Maine and New Hampshire were populated by Puritans from both England and Massachusetts. New Hampshire became a separate colony in 1680. Maine was a part of Massachusetts until it became a separate state in 1820.

Dissent in the Puritan Community

Not all of the people leaving the Massachusetts Bay Colony left simply to find new farmland. Some left because of religious conflicts with the colony's Puritan leaders.

Roger Williams Founds Providence In 1635, Roger Williams, a Separatist minister, was banished from Massachusetts after quarreling with Puritan authorities. One issue he debated concerned land rights. Williams insisted that a patent from the king did not give English settlers a just title to land in North America. Land could only rightly be owned, Williams claimed, through a direct purchase from the Native Americans living there. Another issue leading to his banishment was religious tolerance. Williams believed that the government should not interfere or punish settlers over matters of religion.

He started a settlement called Providence on Narragansett Bay, which is south of Massachusetts. In 1644, Providence joined with several other Separatist communities to become the self-governing colony of Rhode Island. Roger Williams's colony was remarkable because it guaranteed religious tolerance to all settlers.

Other Separatist Colonies   In 1638, a new group of Separatists came from England and founded New Haven, in present-day Connecticut. In 1662, New Haven and the Connecticut colony were combined into a single royal colony.

Also in 1638, John Wheelwright founded the settlement of Exeter, in present-day New Hampshire. He, too, had disagreed with Puritans on religious matters. Exeter soon became a part of the New Hampshire colony. Wheelwright was the brother-in-law of an even more famous opponent of the Puritan authorities in Massachusetts—a deeply religious woman by the name of Anne Hutchinson.

The Banishment of Anne Hutchinson   Anne Hutchinson did not accept Puritan authority. She believed that it was wrong to obey the church if by doing so a person felt he or she was disobeying God. Her home in Boston soon became a center for those in the colony who wanted to think for themselves. Critics of John Winthrop and the Massachusetts government gathered there, as did women interested in studying the Bible.

The Puritan authorities called Hutchinson to trial in November 1637 to explain her actions. At the trial, Hutchinson skillfully defended herself with references to law and the Bible. She proved to be more than a match for her chief accuser and judge, the learned Governor Winthrop. Still, the judges rejected her claim that her own beliefs about God could override the authority of Puritan laws and leaders. The court declared Hutchinson "unfit for our society" and banished her from the colony.

War With the Indians

Several wars erupted between English settlers and Indians in the 1600s. The cause of these wars was simple: English settlers were pushing Native Americans out of their homelands. As one **sachem,** or Native American leader, explained in 1642:

> 66 Our fathers had plenty of deer and skins, our plains were full of deer, as also our woods, and of turkies [sic], and our coves full of fish and fowl. But these English having gotten our land, they with scythes cut down the grass, and with axes fell the trees; their cows and horse eat the grass, and their hogs spoil our clam banks, and we shall be starved. 99
> —Miantonomo

The Pequot War   The Pequot people of Connecticut were among the first to strike back against the English settlers. In 1637, the Massachusetts Bay Colony responded to several violent incidents by sending an army to attack the Pequot in what is known as the **Pequot War.** The Puritans burned down a Pequot fort near Mystic, Connecticut, killing more than 500 people inside. The Puritans then went on to hunt down and kill or capture the rest of the Pequot. Although a handful of the Pequot did survive, their strength as a people had been shattered. About 35 years later, another major confrontation took place

BIOGRAPHY

Anne Hutchinson
1591–1643

Born in England in 1591, Anne Marbury married a wealthy merchant named William Hutchinson in 1612. Over the next 30 years she bore 14 children, of whom 12 survived. In 1634, the Hutchinsons left England to escape religious persecution and to join other Puritans living in Boston. Before she left England, Hutchinson had become a devout follower of the Reverend John Cotton, who preached that a church should be controlled by its congregation, not by leaders appointed by the king and the church hierarchy.

After being banished from Massachusetts, the Hutchinsons left for land on Narragansett Bay in present-day Rhode Island. There, Hutchinson and her followers formed a settlement in present-day Portsmouth. In 1642, after the death of her husband, Hutchinson and her family moved to Pelham Bay, now a part of New York City. The following year, Indians engaged in a war against the Europeans killed Hutchinson and her family.

Chapter 2   Section 3 • **55**

ACTIVITY
Connecting with History and Conflict

Use of land and the fundamental question of whether or not land can be owned were at the heart of the wars between Native Americans and English settlers in the mid- to late 1600s. Have students research the differing perspectives of the two groups on this issue. Hold a classroom debate in which students represent each perspective. Can the class as a whole find some equitable way to resolve the differences between Native Americans and colonial settlers? (**Verbal/Linguistic; Logical/ Mathematical**)

BACKGROUND
Connections to Today

By 1675, tuberculosis and smallpox had reduced the southern New England population of Native Americans to about 20,000—against the approximately 50,000 settlers who had displaced them. This put the Native Americans at a disadvantage before King Philip's War had even begun. In fact, one present-day writer regards King Philip's defeat as "America's first war of ethnic cleansing." Today, there are approximately 4,000 Wampanoags living in Massachusetts—many on Cape Cod and on the Gay Head reservation on Martha's Vineyard island.

CUSTOMIZE FOR ...
Less Proficient Readers

Have students copy the following headings: *The French in North America, Plymouth Colony, The Massachusetts Bay Colony,* and *War With the Indians.* Ask them to write five facts from the section under each heading.

King Philip's War, 1675–1676

Legend:
- • English settlement
- ■ Native American village
- *Pequot* Native American culture groups
- ✷ Attack on settlement
- ✸ Battle

MAP SKILLS The exact locations of Native American villages attacked by English settlers during King Philip's War are in many cases unclear. The illustration below reflects the violent nature of the struggle. **Location** *According to the map, which area saw the least amount of fighting?*

between Native Americans and English settlers. This one would turn out to be more violent and more devastating for both sides.

King Philip's War Thursday, June 24, 1675, was a day of prayer for the people of Swansea, in Plymouth Colony. They had gathered in the Baptist church in the center of their village, hoping that prayer would prevent a war between the English settlers and their Native American neighbors, the Wampanoags. But even while they prayed, war was beginning not far away.

On one of the Swansea farms, an old man and a boy had discovered some Wampanoags of the Pokanoket group killing the cows in their pasture. The boy took up a musket and fired on the Pokanokets, fatally wounding one. The death of this man, although it must have been tragic to his people, was also a good omen to them. The shamans, or wise ones, of the Wampanoags had stated that the Native Americans could succeed in a war against the English only if their enemy fired the first shot.

Why had relations between English settlers and Native Americans broken into open hostilities? Many of the settlers at the time blamed one man. His Native American name was Metacom, but he has been known in American history by the name the settlers gave him, King Philip. Metacom alone did not cause the war, although he bore some responsibility for the fighting.

Like many Native Americans of the 1600s, Metacom had spent much of his life moving between Native American and white society. He was the son of Massasoit, the leader of the Pokanokets, who had helped the Pilgrims of Plymouth Colony survive in the first years of settlement. In the years that followed, trade developed between the Indians and the English. But trade could not erase the basic tension between the two groups.

By 1670, some 45,000 English people were living in about 90 towns in New England. They were cutting down forests, putting up fences, and creating pasture. All of these actions threatened the livelihood of Native Americans. Metacom himself expressed his people's dilemma in a speech he was reported to have made in 1675, at a peace conference held in Rhode Island:

> " The English who came first to this country were but a handful of people, forlorn, poor, and distressed. My father was then sachem, he relieved their distresses in the most kind and hospitable manner. He gave them land to plant and build upon. . . . They flourished and increased. By various means they got possession of a great part of his territory. But he still remained their friend till he died. My elder brother became sachem. . . . He was seized and confined and thereby thrown into illness and died. Soon after I became sachem they disarmed all my people. . . their land was taken. But [only] a small part of the dominion [territory] of my ancestors remains. I am determined not to live [that is, not to simply keep on living] until I have no country. "

—Metacom, 1675

One week later, Metacom united Indian groups from Rhode Island to present-day Maine in a determined effort to drive out the English once and for all. In what became known as **King Philip's War,** he and his warriors destroyed more than 20 English towns, attacked dozens of others, and killed close to 2,000 settlers. In addition, they ruined fields, slaughtered cattle, and kidnapped dozens of people.

The English struck back, killing or wounding about 4,000 Native Americans. As time went on, the English began to gain the upper ground, in part because of their strength in numbers. While the English settlers were united by common language and customs, Metacom was having difficulty keeping his loose alliance of Native American groups together. Furthermore, in a twist that was typical of the shifting alliances of the time, the English were able to enlist other Native Americans on their side.

In August 1676, soldiers caught Metacom sleeping in his hideout near Mount Hope, Rhode Island. As he jumped up and tried to escape, he was shot through the heart. Even without Metacom, the war raged on for nearly a year and devastated the economy of northern New England. When it was over, the English conquest of the region was nearly complete and tribal Native American life in southern New England was virtually extinct.

Focus on ECONOMICS

New England's Postwar Economy
After King Philip's War, Native Americans were no longer as important to New England society and commerce as they had been before 1675. Instead, the colonists became dominant. Their control of the region came at great cost, however.

So staggering were the population loss and displacement in New England that even 20 years after the war, all the towns burned by Philip and his allies had still not been reoccupied. Fewer people also meant fewer laborers and a failure of economic growth. In fact, as a result of New England's war losses, income per person in the region did not surpass the prewar level for more than a century.

As New England's economy grew weaker, it soon became dependent on the support of its mother country. As New Englanders looked to England for leadership and financial assistance, the strains began that would contribute to the onset of the American Revolution.

Section 3 Assessment

READING COMPREHENSION

1. Why did the French depend heavily on rivers in New France?

2. How did John Winthrop's "city upon a hill" demonstrate **Puritan** beliefs?

3. What was the **Mayflower Compact** and why was it important?

4. Why did the Puritans in Massachusetts Bay Colony see Roger Williams and Anne Hutchinson as threats?

5. What were the results of **King Philip's War?**

CRITICAL THINKING AND WRITING

6. **Making Comparisons** (a) How did the French pattern of interacting with Native Americans differ from the English pattern? (b) How were they similar? Explain.

7. **Writing a Conclusion** Metacom and English settlers tried to settle their differences at a peace conference before the war. If they had succeeded in doing so, how might history have been changed? Write two paragraphs explaining your conclusion.

 Take It to the NET

Activity: Writing a Newspaper Article Research the events of King Philip's War. Then, using your research, write a newspaper article on the events of the war, including perspectives from both sides of the conflict. Use the links provided in the *America: Pathways to the Present* area of the following Web site for help in completing this activity.
www.phschool.com

Reading Comprehension

1. Rivers were vital for transporting goods, especially in the increasingly lucrative fur trade.

2. It represented order, community, and cooperation. Puritan communities in Massachusetts provided ready models of such beliefs for others.

3. The Mayflower Compact was an agreement in which the Pilgrims agreed to obey their government's laws. It shows that the Pilgrims decided early on that responsible self-government would be necessary in a new land.

4. Each supported religious tolerance and individuality rather than strict adherence to Puritan ways of life.

5. The economy of northern New England was devastated, and, after both sides had sustained great losses, the English conquest of the area was well advanced and Native Americans had been largely driven from southern New England.

Critical Thinking and Writing

6. (a) The French settled in the Americas in small numbers and were involved in the fur trade, which depended on maintaining ties with the Native Americans and did not interfere with Native Americans' traditional use of land. The English settled in large numbers and took over much Native American land; they did not see Native Americans as partners but rather as a hindrance to their goal of establishing agricultural colonies, and discord and conflict between the two sides ensued. (b) The French and the British both needed something from the Native Americans. The British needed their land, and the French depended upon Native Americans as partners in the fur trade.

7. Answers will vary, but students should consider the effects of King Philip's War, and suppositions should be based on facts from the section.

 **Take It to the NET**

Articles should chronicle the events of the war and should fairly represent the views of both sides of the conflict.

ANALYZING TIME LINES

Focus Tell students that a time line, either standard or condensed, can illustrate the significance of a date or period relative to other events.

Instruct Have students work through the exercise on time lines. Invite them to work in pairs to explore the relationship between events on the time line on this page and the time line at the beginning of the chapter. How many years passed between the settlement of Plymouth Colony and the settlement of the Massachusetts Bay Company? *(Ten)*

Extend See the Skills for Life activity in the Resource Directory below.

ANSWERS
PRACTICE THE SKILL

1. **(a)** 1565 and 1715. **(b)** 150. **(c)** 1608 and 1616. **(d)** 8.

2. **(a)** 25-year intervals. **(b)** 2-year intervals.

3. **(a)** Champlain's efforts to settle Quebec and develop a fur trade with the Native Americans. **(b)** 1609–1610, over control of the fur trade; the lower time line. **(c)** The Iroquois became allies of the English and Dutch following the battles they fought against Champlain and his allies, the Algonquin and Huron. **(d)** Approximately 90 years.

Analyzing Time Lines

A time line is a visual representation of events shown in the order in which they happened. Time lines can help you understand historical events and their relationships to each other.

By the early 1600s, Europe's major powers were scrambling to establish colonies in North America and fighting to secure their claims against rivals—both European and Native American. The two time lines below set out in chronological order a number of events relating to this struggle. The upper time line is a standard time line: it covers major events within a broad time frame. The lower time line is similar to the inset on a map and works something like a microscope. It magnifies a short time segment from the standard time line and reveals more details of a series of related events.

LEARN THE SKILL
Use the following steps to analyze time lines:

1. **Identify the time period covered by each time line.** Study the time lines to discover the span of history each covers.

2. **Determine how each time line has been divided.** Time lines are divided into equal periods of time, such as 10-year, 25-year, or 100-year intervals.

3. **Study the time lines to see how events in one are related to events in the other.** Note which time span is magnified by the lower time line. Explore the possible relationship between events on the two time lines.

PRACTICE THE SKILL
Answer the following questions:

1. **(a)** What are the earliest and the latest dates shown on the upper time line? **(b)** How many years

does it cover? **(c)** What are the earliest and the latest dates on the lower time line? **(d)** How many years does it cover?

2. **(a)** Into what intervals is the upper time line divided? **(b)** Into what intervals is the lower time line divided?

3. **(a)** What general topic does the lower time line examine in detail? **(b)** When and why did hostilities between the French and the Iroquois begin? Which time line shows this? **(c)** How does the lower time line help explain the 1649 entry on the standard time line? **(d)** How long did hostilities between the French and the Iroquois last?

APPLY THE SKILL
See the Chapter Review and Assessment for another opportunity to apply this skill.

58   Chapter 2 • *European Colonization of the Americas*

RESOURCE DIRECTORY

Teaching Resources
Skills for Life booklet, p. 4

Technology
Social Studies Skills Tutor CD-ROM
Interactive Practice in
- Geographic Literacy
- Critical Thinking and Reading
- Visual Analysis
- Communications

The Middle and Southern Colonies

READING FOCUS

- What was the early history of the Dutch in New York?
- What were the characteristics of the other Middle Colonies?
- Why did people settle in the Southern Colonies?

MAIN IDEA

The Middle and Southern Colonies were settled for a variety of political, economic, and religious reasons.

KEY TERMS

Middle Colonies
diversity
synagogue
proprietary colony
Quaker
haven
Southern Colonies
trustee

TAKING NOTES

As you read, complete this chart comparing important facts about each of the Middle and Southern Colonies.

Middle and Southern Colonies	
Colony	Important Facts
New York	Acquired by the English from the Dutch in 1664; practiced religious tolerance...
Pennsylvania	
Maryland	
Georgia	

SECTION OBJECTIVES

1. Discover the early history of the Dutch in New York.
2. Find out about characteristics of the other Middle Colonies.
3. See why people settled in the Southern Colonies.

BELLRINGER

Warm-Up Activity Have students examine a present-day map of the mid-Atlantic states. How do place names still reflect the Dutch, Swedes, Germans, and other groups who settled there?

Activating Prior Knowledge Ask students to list some of the reasons Dutch, Swedes, and Germans may have had for settling in the United States in the Colonial Era.

READING STRATEGY

As students read the section, have them take notes on the settlement of the Middle and Southern colonies. Encourage them to list at least three facts for every section.

ACTIVITY
Student Portfolio

You may wish to have students add the following to their portfolios: Ask students to prepare an illustrated report about the different styles of housing that developed in each of the three different regions. Reports should include information about the houses of the wealthy as well as those of ordinary citizens. Students may want to include information on the effect of climate on architecture in each of the regions. (Verbal/Linguistic)

Setting the Scene The colonies to the south of New England developed differently for a variety of reasons. The settlers of the **Middle Colonies,** for example, came from several countries. These colonies included New York, New Jersey, Pennsylvania, and Delaware. They are called the Middle Colonies because they are in the middle of the Atlantic Coast of North America. New York in particular had a great **diversity,** or variety, of people.

The Dutch in New York

The first Europeans to settle in the area that is now New York were the Dutch. They came from Holland, also called the Netherlands. In 1621, Dutch investors formed the Dutch West India Company to develop trade in the Americas. The company started a colony, New Netherland, in the Hudson and Delaware river valleys.

A Thriving Colony In 1625, the Dutch began building a trading station they called New Amsterdam, located at the mouth of the Hudson River. They quickly realized that the best spot for their homes was the beautiful island of Manhattan. The director of the colony, Peter Minuit, traded goods with the local Native Americans for the right to use the island. Meanwhile, the company also built Fort Orange upstream from the mouth of the Hudson and not far from the site of Albany, the modern capital of New York State.

The Dutch established connections with Native American trade in much the same way the Europeans linked up with existing trade in West Africa. The Dutch were less interested in conquering or transforming the countryside than in simply obtaining furs by trade. The settlers soon built up a prosperous trade in furs and other goods with Europe. In 1655, the Dutchman Adriaen Van der Donck gave three reasons for Dutch trading success in New Netherland:

This hand-carved trunk, with its tulip motif, was probably brought from Holland or made by a Dutch artisan in America.

66 First, it is a fine fruitful country. Secondly, it has fine navigable rivers extending far inland, by which the productions of the country can be brought to places of [sale]. [Thirdly,] the Indians, without our labor or trouble, bring to us their fur trade, worth tons of gold, which may be increased, and is like goods found. 99

—Adriaen Van der Donck

Focus Tell students that the colonies to the south of New England were not settled by the Puritans. The Middle and Southern Colonies developed differently because of the beliefs of the people who settled there. Unlike the Puritan colonies, many of these colonies showed religious tolerance.

Instruct Explain that most colonies that developed in the South and mid-Atlantic region were proprietary, which meant that an individual or group "owned" the colony and could make all its laws. An example was the Dutch colony of New Netherland, renamed New York by the Duke of York after he decided to take over the colony.

Assess/Reteach Remind students that people from Sweden settled in Delaware and that Pennsylvania grew out of William Penn's philosophy of religious tolerance. All the Southern Colonies, like Virginia, began as proprietary colonies. Discuss how settlers shaped the land they claimed.

READING CHECK

Its location, the vast amounts of trade that took place there, and the tolerant nature of its inhabitants.

READING CHECK
Why was New Netherland a diverse colony?

Farmers also grew wheat and rye on their Manhattan lands, and increased production of more crops as their holdings expanded along the Hudson and Delaware rivers. The settlers shipped most of these products to other colonies.

New Amsterdam became a port where Dutch, Swedish, French, German, English, and many other people carried on peaceful business together. Some 18 different languages were spoken in its streets. Religious tolerance was a firm rule. The town even boasted the first **synagogue**, or house of Jewish worship, on the North American continent.

Although Dutch rule was generally mild, the last governor, Peter Stuyvesant, was often at odds with the colonists. They wanted more self-government, and the hot-tempered Stuyvesant yielded little.

England Takes Over The English looked on the prosperity of the Dutch colony with envious eyes. In 1664, the English king, Charles II, decided to make a move. He declared that the entire region of the Dutch colonies belonged to his brother, the Duke of York.

The Duke of York sent a fleet of four ships and several hundred soldiers to New Amsterdam. The town had no fort or other defenses, and the Dutch realized at once that they could do nothing to stop the English. Although Stuyvesant stormed and raged, the Dutch would not fight, and in the end he was forced to give up the town. New Amsterdam was immediately renamed New York and became an English colony. Soon the rest of New Netherland surrendered to the English.

The Other Middle Colonies

The colony of New York was a **proprietary colony**—a colony granted by a king or queen to an individual or group who had full governing rights. *(Proprietor* means "owner.")* The colony of New York was owned by the Duke of York, who could make laws and rule it as he wished. The other Middle Colonies were also proprietary.

New Jersey The Duke of York's charter included land in present-day Maine, New York, New Jersey, and Delaware. He signed some of it over to two English noblemen. This land was divided into East Jersey and West Jersey. East Jersey was closely linked to New York, while West Jersey developed close ties to Pennsylvania. In 1702, both East and West Jersey became a single royal colony called New Jersey.

William Penn in Pennsylvania In 1681, a young Englishman named William Penn received a huge land grant from King Charles II of England. The king, who had owed debts to Penn's father, repaid the debts in the form of a land grant to Penn after the elder Penn had died. Penn called this land Pennsylvania, which means "Penn's woods." Like the Puritans, he saw his colony as a "holy experiment," but unlike the Puritans, he wanted his colonists to practice religious tolerance. Penn made agreements with the Native Americans about land use and then brought over the first of many settlers from England.

Penn made it a point to establish good relations with Indians in his colony. He managed to coordinate a series of treaties with the Lenni Lenape Indians in the area, which were based on mutual respect and trust. Like Roger Williams, Penn believed that the English should compensate Native Americans for their land—that the English could not simply take this land. For many years, almost no major conflicts occurred between Indians and European settlers in Pennsylvania.

Most of these settlers, like Penn, were **Quakers**, members of a Protestant group that had suffered persecution in England. Quakers believed firmly that all

William Penn rejected his Anglican upbringing and joined the Quakers, or Society of Friends, in 1666 at the age of 22. Penn was jailed several times for publicly expressing his views.

60　Chapter 2 • *European Colonization of the Americas*

The Colonies in America, 1607–1776

Colony	European Settlement	Reason for Settlement	Leaders	Charter[1]	Economic Activities
NEW ENGLAND COLONIES					
Massachusetts Plymouth (1620–1691) Massachusetts Bay Colony (1629–1691)	1620	Escape religious persecution Establish a Puritan commonwealth	William Bradford John Winthrop	Mayflower Compact 1620–1621; joint-stock 1621–1691; Joint-stock 1629–1684; royal 1684–1691 Two colonies merged in 1691; royal 1691–1776	Fishing, lumber, shipbuilding, triangular trade, rum, whaling
New Hampshire Exeter (1638)	1623	Profit from trade and fishing Escape religious persecution	Benning Wentworth; John Wentworth John Wheelwright	Proprietary 1622–1641; joint-stock (part of Massachusetts Bay) 1641–1679; royal 1679–1776	Trade, fishing
Connecticut	1634	Establish a Puritan settlement; establish a fur trade route	Thomas Hooker	Self-governing 1636–1662; corporate 1662–1776	Triangular trade
Rhode Island[2]	1636	Escape religious intolerance of Massachusetts Bay	Roger Williams	Self-governing 1636–1644; joint-stock 1644–1663; corporate 1663–1776	Shipping, livestock, agriculture
MIDDLE COLONIES					
New York[3]	1624	Expansion	Peter Stuyvesant; James, Duke of York; Richard Nicolls; Thomas Dongan	Colony of Dutch West Indian Co. 1624–1664; proprietary (English) 1664–1685; royal 1685–1776	Wheat, milling, lumber, furs, sugar refining, distilling, shipbuilding, trade
Delaware[4]	1638	Trade	Johan Pritz; Johan Rising; William Penn	Proprietary (Swedish) 1638–1655; Colony of Dutch West Indian Co. 1655–1664; proprietary 1664–1704 (part of Penn. after 1682); royal 1704–1776	Trade, farming
New Jersey	1630	Expansion; trading post; refuge for Quakers from England	John Berkeley; John Carteret	Colony of Dutch West Indian Co. 1630–1664; proprietary 1664–1702; royal 1702–1776	Trade, farming
Pennsylvania	1644	Swedish expansion; establish a Quaker colony, religious tolerance	William Penn	Part of neighboring Swedish, Dutch, and English colonies until 1681; proprietary 1681–1692; royal 1692–1694; proprietary 1694–1776	Trade, farming
SOUTHERN COLONIES					
Virginia	1607	Search for gold; English outpost against Spain	John Smith; John Rolfe; Thomas Dale	Joint-stock 1607–1624; royal 1625–1776	Tobacco
Maryland	1632	Establish a Catholic settlement; escape religious persecution	Cecilius Calvert (Lord Baltimore)	Proprietary 1632–1691; royal 1691–1716; proprietary 1716–1776	Tobacco
Carolina[5] North Carolina South Carolina	1655 1670	Land wealth, refuge for small farmers; strengthen English possessions in the Americas	William Berkeley; Anthony Ashley-Cooper; John Locke	Proprietary 1663–1712 Proprietary 1712–1729; royal 1729–1776 Proprietary 1712–1719; royal 1719–1776	Ship supplies, rice, indigo, tobacco
Georgia[6]	1732	Settlement for debtors; buffer Carolinas from Spanish Florida	James Oglethorpe	Proprietary 1732–1752; royal 1752–1776	Rice, indigo, ship supplies

[1] Corporate colonies were organized by a joint-stock company, or corporation, for the benefit of shareholders. Such colonies could only be formed when the English king issued a charter, or certificate of his approval. In a royal colony, a governor appointed by the king served as its chief official, though a colonial assembly approved laws before they could go into effect. Self-governing colonies were independent of the king or a corporation. Proprietary colonies were granted by the king to a proprietor, or owner, whether one person or a small group of people.
[2] The four original settlements of Providence, Portsmouth, Warwick, and Newport created a united government in 1647 under the name "Providence Plantations."
[3] Called New Netherland until 1664 when the English took it over from the Dutch.
[4] Settled in 1638 by the Swedes and called New Sweden. Seized by the Dutch in 1655 and became part of New Netherland. Conquered by English in 1664.
[5] North and South Carolina formed a single colony, Carolina, until they were separated in 1712.
[6] Originally part of South Carolina.

INTERPRETING CHARTS The thirteen colonies developed different characteristics for a variety of reasons.
Synthesizing Information *What regional patterns can you find in the chart?*

ACTIVITY
Connecting with Geography

Tell students to choose one colony listed in the chart on this page. Then have students research the colony's natural resources—waterways, arable land, and weather conditions. Tell students to imagine that they are writers working for the colony's public relations department. Have students write a profile designed to attract new residents to the colony. **(Verbal/Linguistic)**

BACKGROUND
Recent Scholarship

The traditional view of the Puritans is of a joyless people who did their best to repress their human instincts. Nathaniel Hawthorne's famous book *The Scarlet Letter* perpetuated this notion by depicting the Puritans as people who resisted happiness, leisure, and recreation. In *Puritans at Play,* Bruce C. Daniels offers an alternative viewpoint, presenting evidence that these supposedly stern people did participate in leisure activities. He shows that although the Puritans were religious, they also were capable of enjoying pleasurable pursuits.

CUSTOMIZE FOR ...
Less Proficient Writers

Ask students to turn each of the sections' headings and subheadings into questions. After they have read each portion of the text, have them write answers to the questions they posed.

☑ TEST PREPARATION

Have students review the chart on this page and then answer the question below.

What was the predominant reason for settlement of the Middle Colonies?

A trade

B religious freedom

Ⓒ expansion

D land wealth

CAPTION ANSWERS

Interpreting Charts Sample answer: The New England Colonies were largely religious-based settlements. The economy of the Middle Colonies was based on trade and farming. The economy of the Southern Colonies was based on farming, especially tobacco.

ACTIVITY

Connecting with Government

Tell students to debate the Maryland Toleration Act from the point of view of the colony's settlers. Have one team argue in favor of the act by showing its fairness. Have the other team argue against the act by pointing out its failure to protect non-Christians. Tell students who are not participating in the debate to prepare questions for the debaters. When the debate is over, engage students in a discussion about the strengths and weaknesses of each team's defense. **(Verbal/Linguistic)**

BACKGROUND

Biography

Paul Cuffe (1759–1817), the son of an ex-slave father and a Native American mother, went to sea at age 16. He became a successful ship owner, hiring only African American crews. Cuffe, who joined the Quakers in 1798, became convinced that African Americans should resettle in Africa. In 1811 he took the first African American recruits to Africa.

Focus on CULTURE

Women in Chesapeake Bay Unlike the Puritans who went to New England to recreate a close-knit, well-ordered society, those who set sail for Chesapeake Bay were driven more by economic motives. Most of these settlers were young men going over to grow tobacco. Therefore, whole family units were less likely to settle in the Chesapeake Bay region. As a result, males outnumbered females by a ratio of three to one. Another major difference between the two regions was environmental. Those living in the Chesapeake Bay region faced an environment filled with disease. Early deaths were common in colonies such as Maryland. In New England, by contrast, mortality rates were low.

Higher death rates and an imbalanced sex ratio meant that women were more likely to be on their own for longer periods of time in Chesapeake Bay. However, historians point out that this was not necessarily desirable for women at the time. Because a woman's primary role was as mistress of a household, she could take on more significance and wield more power while in a family unit.

The royal charter of North Carolina, 1663, includes the likeness of King Charles II.

people should be treated as equals, not only in church but also in society and government. Along with Delaware and West New Jersey, which Penn also owned at that time, Pennsylvania became a **haven,** or safe place, for people of every faith.

Soon Pennsylvania was drawing Quakers from other American colonies, as well as from Wales, Germany, and other lands. The colony also invited non-Quakers. Protestant groups such as German Lutherans, Scotch-Irish Presbyterians, and Swiss Mennonites built large settlements in Pennsylvania. So many Germans settled in the colony that they came to be known as the Pennsylvania Dutch, after the German word *Deutsch,* which means "German."

Delaware In 1638, settlers from Sweden started the first permanent colony in present-day Delaware. They built Fort Christina on the site of modern-day Wilmington. The Dutch, under Peter Stuyvesant, captured this trading village from the Swedes, and the Duke of York captured it from the Dutch. In 1682, he turned it over to William Penn, who allowed Delaware to become a separate colony in 1704.

The Southern Colonies

Virginia was the first of the **Southern Colonies** to be settled. The other Southern Colonies were Maryland, the Carolinas, and Georgia. All of these settlements began as proprietary colonies.

Maryland Maryland started as the idea of George Calvert, an English lord who had become a Roman Catholic after growing up in the Anglican Church. He saw Roman Catholics being persecuted in England and wanted to establish a safe place for them to live. He had also been a member of the Virginia Company, and was convinced that well-run colonies could be profitable. In the early 1630s, Calvert asked the king for a charter to establish a colony in the Chesapeake Bay area. The king approved his plan, but Calvert died before the charter could be written up. Thus it was issued in the name of his son, Lord Baltimore.

The first settlers arrived in Maryland in 1634. Although Maryland was supposed to be a haven for Roman Catholics, Puritans also moved to the colony. In fact, they outnumbered the Catholics from the very beginning. Therefore, Lord Baltimore ordered the adoption of a law that would protect Catholics from persecution in the colony. This Maryland Toleration Act was important as part of a general trend toward religious tolerance in the English colonies. The law said that no one who believed in Jesus would be "any ways troubled," that is, persecuted. The act was severely limited, however, in that it did not provide protection for non-Christians. In fact, Puritans in Maryland's assembly changed the law to state that non-Christians would be put to death.

The planters of Maryland, like those in Virginia, became prosperous during the 1600s by growing tobacco. Like the Virginians, as time went on they began to use enslaved Africans to work their fields. The Africans were brought to the colonies by slave traders. By 1704, roughly 15,000 of the 90,000 people in the two colonies were African slaves. Planters considered the Africans as property, and both colonies (as well as others) passed laws aimed at protecting the planters' "property"

RESOURCE DIRECTORY

Teaching Resources
Units 1/2 booklet
 • Section 4 Quiz, p. 18
 • Chapter 2 Test, pp. 19, 22
Guide to the Essentials
 • Section 4 Summary, p. 13
 • Chapter 2 Test, p. 14

Other Print Resources
Chapter Tests with ExamView® Test Bank CD-ROM, Ch. 2

Technology
ExamView® Test Bank CD-ROM, Ch. 2
Social Studies Skills Tutor CD-ROM

rights. For example, a Virginia law passed in 1642 punished people for hiding runaway slaves or indentured servants. A 1664 Maryland law specified that all black people imported to the colony were to be given the status of slaves.

The Carolinas South of Maryland and Virginia was a region known as Carolina. Although there had been earlier claims on the land, King Charles II granted its ownership to a group of English noblemen in 1663.

The large area called Carolina was first split into North and South Carolina in 1712, when two different governors were appointed. In 1719, South Carolina became a royal colony. North Carolina became a royal colony in 1729. Despite threats from the Spanish and Native Americans, both colonies thrived on tobacco profits and trade with Native Americans.

Georgia Although Georgia was set up like a proprietary colony in 1732, it was actually managed not by owners but by **trustees.** A trustee is someone entrusted to look after a business.

The trustees, led by James Oglethorpe, wanted to make a haven for people who had been in jail in England because they could not pay their debts. They also accepted another duty the English government had insisted upon: helping to protect the Southern Colonies against attack from Spanish raiders based in Florida.

Oglethorpe and the trustees ruled Georgia strictly. No one was allowed to own enslaved workers or drink hard liquor. Although the trustees did not allow Catholics to live in Georgia, all types of Protestants were permitted. Thanks to Oglethorpe's careful negotiations, the settlers lived at peace with the Native Americans.

Gradually, however, the colonists forced the trustees to change their rules. Settlers were allowed to use and sell liquor, and enslaved Africans were brought in to work the land. After 20 years, the trustees gave their charter back to the king, and Georgia became a royal colony in 1752.

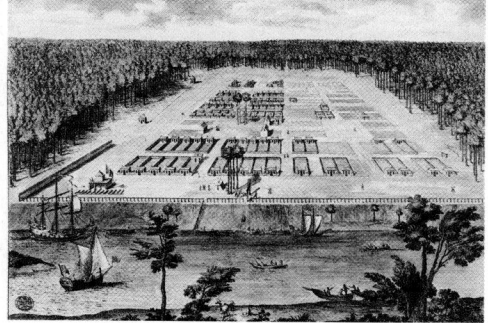

VIEWING HISTORY James Oglethorpe, a general as well as a member of Parliament, carefully planned the city of Savannah, Georgia, as a series of squares. He intended the colony to be a haven for debtors, but also realized its strategic value. **Drawing Conclusions** What was the strategic value of the Georgia colony?

Section 4 Assessment

READING COMPREHENSION

1. Why were the Dutch successful in New Netherland?

2. (a) What were some beliefs of the **Quakers?** (b) How did these beliefs influence William Penn's "holy experiment"?

3. (a) Why was the Maryland Toleration Act significant? (b) What were its limitations?

4. What plans did Georgia's **trustees** have for the colony?

CRITICAL THINKING AND WRITING

5. Predicting Consequences Proprietors were able to make their own laws in the colonies. What do you think might be the consequences of this fact?

6. Writing to Persuade Write two paragraphs in which you try to persuade a relative in Germany to join you in Pennsylvania as a settler in 1740.

 Take It to the NET

Activity: Analyzing Primary Sources Select one state from this section and research its founding charter or grant. Prepare a summary of how and why the colony was founded, noting any special provisions or other interesting aspects you find. Use the links provided in the *America: Pathways to the Present* area of the following Web site for help in completing this activity.
www.phschool.com

Section 4 Assessment

Reading Comprehension

1. They traded with local Native Americans, establishing a peaceful coexistence; they maintained a prosperous trade in fur and other goods with Europe; the area had navigable rivers; the land was conducive for growing wheat and rye.

2. (a) All people should be treated as equals, in church as well as in society and in government. (b) As he developed a colony, Quaker beliefs led Penn to want his colonists to practice religious tolerance and to cooperate with Native Americans.

3. (a) It was part of a general trend toward religious tolerance in the colonies. (b) It was limited in that it did not provide protection for non-Christians.

4. The trustees wanted to create a haven for people who had been jailed in England because they could not pay their debts, establish a southern bulwark against Spanish Florida, and enforce a strict code of behavior.

Critical Thinking and Writing

5. The fact that so many colonies began as proprietary colonies cemented the precedent for self-rule in North America. The American Revolution was, in part, a consequence of this precedent.

6. Answers will vary, and could include some of the following points: religious tolerance, good farmland, good trade, and peaceful relationships with Native Americans.

 **Take It to the NET**

Summaries should be comprehensive, highlighting the details of the founding of the colony and anything unique in its charter or grant.

CAPTION ANSWERS

Viewing History It served as a buffer between the Spanish in Florida and the Southern Colonies.

REVIEWING KEY TERMS

Students should refer to the definitions of key terms in the chapter to write sentences that show an understanding of the key aspects of the early colonization of America.

REVIEWING MAIN IDEAS

17. Southeast: to build forts to defend Spanish shipping; Southwest: to make money from mining; West Coast: to prepare to build trade routes across the Pacific and to keep other European nations away.

18. The Spanish were driven out of Santa Fe by the Pueblo, who resented forced conversion to Christianity and were experiencing widespread illness.

19. (a) Neglect of farming and other tasks necessary for survival; swampy site with disease-bearing mosquitoes; delay in finding good leadership; Native American resistance. (b) The development of the tobacco industry; discipline imposed on the settlers by John Smith.

20. Conflicts such as Bacon's Rebellion and (especially) Opechancanough's revolt centered on issues of Native American resistance to European settlers and the idea that Governor William Berkeley was concerned only with the wealthy.

21. The fur trade demanded that New France follow the course of the St. Lawrence River. Such a shape provided for easy transportation.

22. Largely to escape religious persecution. However, the Puritans in New England did not tolerate non-Puritans.

23. The Puritans wanted to create farmland and pastures, but Native Americans depended on pristine wilderness for hunting.

24. New Amsterdam was a thriving commercial center.

25. Quakers, members of a Protestant group that had suffered persecution in England, as well as Quakers from other American colonies and foreign lands; Protestant groups such as German Lutherans and other Germans, who became known as the Pennsylvania Dutch; Scotch-Irish Presbyterians; and Swiss Mennonites.

creating a CHAPTER SUMMARY

Copy this flowchart (right). As you review the chapter, fill in the locations of major settlements for each of the following countries.

i TEXT

For additional review and enrichment activities, see the interactive version of *America: Pathways to the Present*, available on the Web and on CD-ROM.

Locations of Major Settlements

Spain	England	France
• Southeast (Florida) • Southwest • West Coast	• • •	• • •

★ Reviewing Key Terms

For each of the terms below, write a sentence explaining how it relates to the European colonization of the Americas.

1. conquistador
2. *encomienda* system
3. mission
4. joint-stock company
5. royal colony
6. legislature
7. House of Burgesses
8. indentured servant
9. Bacon's Rebellion
10. Puritan
11. religious tolerance
12. sachem
13. diversity
14. Quaker
15. haven
16. trustee

★ Reviewing Main Ideas

17. Why did the Spanish encourage settlement in the Southeast, Southwest, and West Coast regions of North America? (Section 1)

18. Describe the Pueblo Revolt of 1680. (Section 1)

19. Explain the reasons for (a) Jamestown's near failure and (b) Jamestown's eventual success. (Section 2)

20. Explain the conflicts and issues faced by Jamestown's settlers once the settlement had become successful. (Section 2)

21. Why was New France shaped the way it was? (Section 3)

22. Why was there a Great Migration to New England in the 1630s? (Section 3)

23. Why did conflicts such as King Philip's War develop between Native Americans and English settlers in New England? (Section 3)

24. Why did the British want to take over New Amsterdam? (Section 4)

25. Describe the groups that settled in Pennsylvania. (Section 4)

★ Critical Thinking

26. Making Comparisons Compare the ways that religion contributed to colonies founded by (a) Spain, (b) the Virginia Company, (c) English Pilgrims, (d) Puritans, (e) the Dutch, and (f) Quakers.

27. Drawing Inferences Review the excerpt from "A Model of Christian Charity" on page 53. How might the ideals expressed in this sermon have contributed to the success of the New England settlers?

28. Demonstrating Reasoned Judgment Review the excerpt from the Mayflower Compact on page 51. How might the ideas in this document have contributed to the colonists' eventual fight for independence from England?

29. Recognizing Ideologies (a) How did relations between European settlers and Native Americans differ from colony to colony? (b) What factors do you think accounted for these differences (or similarities) in relations?

CREATING A CHAPTER SUMMARY

Locations of Major Settlements

Spain	England	France
• Southeast (Florida) • Southwest • West Coast	• South • Northeast (New England) • Middle Atlantic Coastal Region	• St. Lawrence River Valley • Part of Nova Scotia • Part of Newfoundland

★ Skills Assessment

Analyzing Political Cartoons ▶

30. This Puritan cartoon expresses sentiments about behavior in Massachusetts in the early colonial period. (a) What does the labeling in the two panels suggest? (b) What does the book in the top panel represent? (c) What do the dice, cards, cup, and pipe in the lower panel represent?

31. What is the message of this cartoon?

32. Given what you know about Puritans, what is the cartoonist's view of the situation?

Interpreting Data

Turn to the graph of tobacco exports in Section 2.

33. Which statement best summarizes the information on the graph?

    A England imported very little tobacco between 1622 and 1624.

    B English tobacco imports increased steadily after 1622.

    C English tobacco imports decreased steadily after 1622.

    D English tobacco imports reached their highest levels in 1620.

34. The amount of American tobacco imported by England in 1622

    F nearly equaled the amount imported in 1618.

    G was double the amount imported in 1618.

    H was half the amount imported in 1624.

    J nearly equaled the amount imported in 1626.

Applying the Chapter Skill: *Analyzing Time Lines*

35. Create a time line for the chapter that includes key dates for the Spanish, English, French, and Dutch settlement of North America. How are the key dates of each nation related to the others?

ACTIVITIES

Writing to LEARN

Writing to Inform
In the United States, the First Amendment to the Constitution guarantees people the right to practice their religion as they wish. Which early American colonies set precedents for such a law? Which did not? Write a brief essay explaining your answer.

Primary Source CD-ROM

Working With Primary Sources Find additional information on the European colonization of the Americas on the *Exploring Primary Sources in U.S. History CD-ROM* and use the selection(s) provided to complete the Chapter 2 primary source activity located in the *America: Pathways to the Present* area of the following Web site.
www.phschool.com

Take It to the NET

Chapter Self-Test As a review activity, take the Chapter 2 Self-Test in the *America: Pathways to the Present* area at the Web site listed below. The questions are designed to test your understanding of the chapter content.
www.phschool.com

Chapter 2 Assessment   **65**

---

seeking to convert Native Americans. (b) Not overly interested in religion, Jamestown was an economic venture. (c) One purpose of the Mayflower Compact was to ensure that religious differences would not ruin the political and economic cohesion of the group. (d) Conformity to Puritan tenets was of paramount importance. Intense hostility shown toward non-Puritans. (e) Tolerant people, more interested in fur trade and economic developments than in conquering or transforming the countryside or the Native Americans. (f) Very tolerant, created a haven for people of every faith.

27. The excerpt reflects the idea that the colonists must work together in order to be successful.

28. The excerpt reveals that the colonists at Plymouth intended to make their own laws. This set an early precedent for the idea of local self-government in the British colonies. Ideas similar to these fueled the American Revolution.

29. Sample answers: (a) In New France, white settlers worked together with Native Americans, resulting in peaceful relations. In Jamestown, however, neither group trusted the other. In New England, the religious beliefs of Puritan settlers and their desire to transform the landscape resulted in a radical transformation of the lifestyles of Native Americans who fell under Puritan influence. (b) Geography of the various colonies, religious and economic motivations of the European settlers, and their desires for conquest (or lack thereof).

SKILLS ASSESSMENT

30. (a) Change over time. (b) The Christian Bible. (c) Immoral behavior.

31. Society has abandoned religious principles and has adopted social vices.

32. Disapproval.

33. B

34. F

35. Accept reasonable variations of time lines. Students might mention such parallels as that the first permanent British and French colonies in North America, Jamestown, and Quebec were founded almost contemporaneously (in 1607 and 1608, respectively).

ANSWERS TO ACTIVITIES

Writing to LEARN

Colonies setting precedents for religious freedom include Rhode Island, New York, Pennsylvania, Maryland (partial), and Georgia (partial). Colonies setting precedents for religious intolerance include Massachusetts.

Primary Source CD-ROM

Direct students to the additional primary sources that can be found on the *Exploring Primary Sources in U.S. History CD-ROM*.

Take It to the NET

Additional support materials and activities for Chapter 2 of *America: Pathways to the Present* can be found in the Social Studies area at the Prentice Hall School Web site. **www.phschool.com**

Chapter 2 • **65**

Geography & History

COLONIAL SETTLEMENTS

Focus Review with students the priorities that were in the minds of colonial people when they established their settlements. What factors were foremost in the settlers' minds? How does the basic layout of a town like Sudbury reflect colonial priorities?

Instruct Explain to students that settlers in the new world of America brought ideas with them from their original countries. Among the most important was the notion of how a settlement should be set up. Yet, each new settlement also needed to take into consideration geographical factors, such as landforms, access to available water, proximity to established roads, and other factors. Ask students to list the general factors that would influence the establishment of a settlement in colonial New England. Then have them do library research to see how those factors were taken into consideration in the settlements of towns such as Andover, Dedham, and Watertown, Massachusetts.

Extend Have students do library research to find out about the dwellings of Wampanoag Indians, the native neighbors of Pilgrim settlers at Plymouth. How were they similar to the Pilgrims' houses? How were they different? In what ways were the Wampanoag houses more suited to the elements than the Pilgrim houses? In what ways did both types of structures draw upon available materials for their construction?

Colonial Settlements

Most early colonial settlements, particularly those in New England, consisted of tight clusters of houses, usually centered on a single church, or meetinghouse. Settlements often shared a mill where grain was ground. Near the center of many New England towns were commons, or commonly owned pastures, that were open to all townspeople. These shared spaces and institutions reflected the close-knit community spirit found in many early settlements.

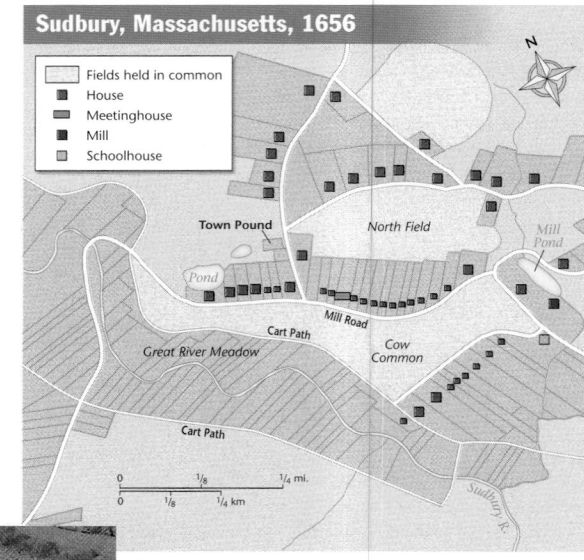

Sudbury, Massachusetts, 1656

Fields held in common
House
Meetinghouse
Mill
Schoolhouse

Town Pound
North Field
Pond
Mill Pond
Great River Meadow
Mill Road
Cart Path
Cow Common
Cart Path
Sudbury R.

0   1/8   1/4 mi.
0   1/8   1/4 km

Geographic Connection How did the layout of colonial Sudbury, Massachusetts, reflect its physical geography and cultural values?

A Familiar Pattern
In many ways, these early settlements resembled villages where the settlers might have lived in England. This modern view of an English village shows a striking similarity in layout to colonial Sudbury.

Geographic Connection How is the geography of this English village similar to the geography of colonial Sudbury?

Reminders of Home
Colonial settlers not only patterned their settlements after villages in their homeland, they also brought treasured possessions with them. This chest was carried from England to Plymouth, Massachusetts, on the *Mayflower*.

66

ANSWERS

1. The Sudbury settlement occupied a site between rich bottomlands along the Sudbury River and a smaller stream that could be harnessed to power a mill. It appears that the residents of colonial Sudbury were expected to farm large plots of land as a communal group, rather than as individuals farming their own land.

RESOURCE DIRECTORY

Teaching Resources
Geography and History booklet, pp. 2–3

Other Print Resources
Nystrom *Atlas of Our Country* *Colonies in the North and East,* pp. 14–15

Technology
Prentice Hall United States History Video Collection™ Volume 2, *The Era of Colonization*

Early Homes

In their first years in North America, settlers had to make do with small houses made of local wood with thatched (straw) roofs. These houses at Plimoth Plantation in Plymouth, Massachusetts, are part of a modern reconstruction of the first permanent English settlement in New England.

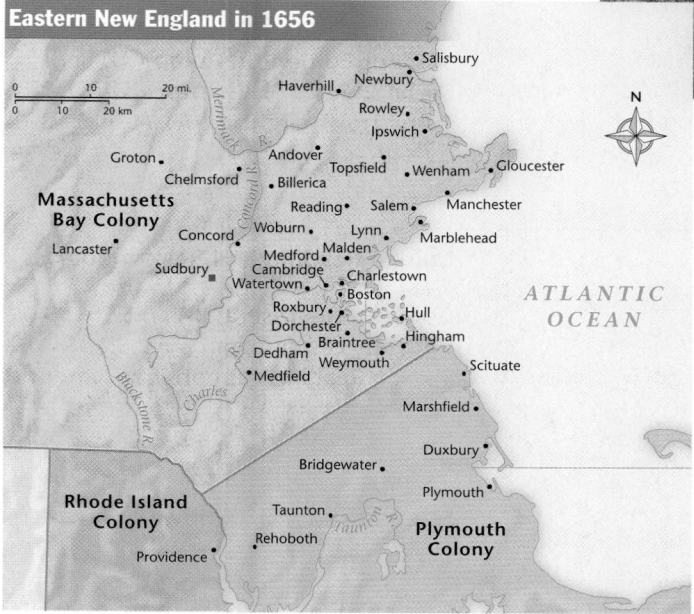

Eastern New England in 1656

- Salisbury
- Haverhill
- Newbury
- Rowley
- Ipswich
- Groton
- Andover
- Topsfield
- Wenham
- Gloucester
- Chelmsford
- Billerica
- Massachusetts Bay Colony
- Reading
- Salem
- Manchester
- Lancaster
- Woburn
- Lynn
- Marblehead
- Concord
- Medford
- Malden
- Sudbury
- Cambridge
- Charlestown
- Watertown
- Boston
- Roxbury
- Hull
- Dorchester
- Hingham
- Dedham
- Braintree
- Medfield
- Weymouth
- Scituate
- Marshfield
- Duxbury
- Bridgewater
- Plymouth
- Rhode Island Colony
- Taunton
- Plymouth Colony
- Rehoboth
- Providence

ATLANTIC OCEAN

Merrimack R.
Blackstone R.
Charles R.
Taunton R.

N

0 10 20 mi.
0 10 20 km

The Colonial Frontier

This map shows the towns that existed near Sudbury when it was first settled. As you can see, Sudbury was near the edge of the area already settled by the English. Tightly clustered villages may have given English settlers a sense of security at the edge of a vast wilderness inhabited by peoples with different customs.

Geographic Connection Where were most of the settlements in eastern New England located in 1656?

A Culture Takes Root

As a new generation came of age, colonists abandoned some of the traditions of the old country to develop their own new regional cultures. This meetinghouse shows the elegant building style that gradually replaced the crude structures of the first settlers across New England. An increasingly self-confident population gathered in meetinghouses like this one to hear native-born preachers such as Cotton Mather, pictured here.

67

Chapter-Level Resources	Teaching Resources	Guided Reading Audiotapes (English/Spanish)
	• Pacing Charts booklet	Student Edition on Audio CD, Ch. 3
	• Block Scheduling booklet	Social Studies Skills Tutor CD-ROM
	Resource Pro® CD-ROM, Ch. 3	**Color Transparencies**, A4, A5, A56, E3, G2, H2, H3, H4
	Prentice Hall Presentation Pro CD-ROM, Ch. 3	
	www.phschool.com	
	• eTeach	

1 An Empire and Its Colonies

1. Find out how the English Civil War affected the development of the colonies.
2. See how mercantilism influenced England's colonial laws and foreign policy.
3. Learn about Britain's colonial policy in the early 1700s.
4. Discover which farming, trade, and settlement patterns defined the diverse economies of the colonies.

Teaching Resources
Units 1/2 booklet
 • Section 1 Quiz, p. 26

Guided Reading and Review booklet, p. 11
Guide to the Essentials, p. 15
Skills for Life booklet, p. 5
Section Reading Support Transparencies

2 Life in Colonial America

1. Learn how colonial society was organized.
2. Find out why wealth in land was important.
3. Discover some of the common trades and occupations in the colonies.
4. Read to know more about the rights and responsibilities of colonial women.
5. Understand the nature of work and education in the colonies.

Teaching Resources
Units 1/2 booklet
 • Section 2 Quiz, p. 27

Guided Reading and Review booklet, p. 12
Guide to the Essentials, p. 16
Learning with Documents booklet, pp. 8, 42
Section Reading Support Transparencies

3 African Americans in the Colonies

1. Learn about the Middle Passage.
2. Find out how the experience of slavery differed from colony to colony.
3. See the restrictions faced by free blacks.
4. Discover how laws attempted to control slaves and prevent revolts.

Teaching Resources
Units 1/2 booklet
 • Section 3 Quiz, p. 28
Learning Styles Lesson Plans booklet, p. 8

Guided Reading and Review booklet, p. 13
Guide to the Essentials, p. 17
Section Reading Support Transparencies

4 Emerging Tensions

1. Find out what drove the western expansion of colonial settlement.
2. Learn how Native Americans and the French reacted to the expansion of the colonies.
3. Discover why the Great Awakening both resolved and contributed to religious tensions.

Teaching Resources
Units 1/2 booklet
 • Section 4 Quiz, p. 29
Learning Styles Lesson Plans booklet, p. 9

Guided Reading and Review booklet, p. 14
Guide to the Essentials, p. 18
Section Reading Support Transparencies

ENRICHMENT/PRE-AP

Prentice Hall United States History Video Collection™
www.phschool.com
- Section Activities, Virtual Field Trip, Chapter Activities, Current Events Online

Nystrom *Atlas of Our Country,* pp. 14–15
Historical Outline Map Book, pp. 16, 17, 18, 19
Sounds of an Era Audio CD
Exploring Primary Sources in U.S. History CD-ROM

Biography, Literature, and Comparing Primary Sources booklet, p. 42
Sounds of an Era Audio CD

Nystrom *Atlas of Our Country,* pp. 16–17
Sounds of an Era Audio CD
Exploring Primary Sources in U.S. History CD-ROM

Biography, Literature, and Comparing Primary Sources booklet, pp. 8, 101–102
American History Block Scheduling Support
Nystrom *Atlas of Our Country,* pp. 20–21
Historical Outline Map Book, p. 20
Sounds of an Era Audio CD
American Pathways Thematic Posters

ASSESSMENT

PRENTICE HALL
ASSESSMENT SYSTEM

Core Assessment
ExamView® Test Bank, Ch. 3
ExamView® Test Bank CD-ROM, Ch. 3

Standardized Test Preparation
Diagnose and Prescribe
Diagnostic Tests for High School Social Studies Skills

Review and Reteach
Review Book for U.S. History

Practice and Assess
Test-taking Strategies With Transparencies
Test-taking Strategies Posters
Test Prep Book for U.S. History
Alternative Assessment Handbook
Document-Based Assessment

Teaching Resources
Units 1/2 booklet
- Section Quizzes, pp. 26–29
- Chapter Tests, pp. 30, 33
www.phschool.com Ch. 3 Self-Test

AmericanHeritage RESOURCES

From the Archives of American Heritage®, p. 92
AmericanHeritage® My Brush with History™ Videotapes
www.americanheritage.com

Don't miss the exclusive interactive version of this textbook on the Web and on CD-ROM.

Chapter 3 Planning Guide
In Your Classroom

CUSTOMIZE FOR INDIVIDUAL NEEDS

Gifted and Talented

Teacher's Edition
• Customize for Gifted and Talented, p. 73

Teaching Resources
• Biography, Literature, and Comparing Primary Sources booklet, pp. 8, 42, 101–102

Technology
• Exploring Primary Sources in U.S. History CD-ROM *"Swing Low, Sweet Chariot," Spiritual*

ESL

Teacher's Edition
• Customize for ESL, pp. 71, 93

Teaching Resources
• Guided Reading and Review booklet, pp. 11–14
• Guide to the Essentials (English/Spanish), Chapter 3

Technology
• Student Edition on Audio CD, Chapter 3
• Guided Reading Audiotapes (English/Spanish), Chapter 3
• Section Reading Support Transparencies

Less Proficient Readers

Teacher's Edition
• Customize for Less Proficient Readers, p. 79

Teaching Resources
• Guided Reading and Review booklet, pp. 11–14
• Guide to the Essentials (English/Spanish), Chapter 3

Technology
• Student Edition on Audio CD, Chapter 3
• Guided Reading Audiotapes (English/Spanish), Chapter 3
• Section Reading Support Transparencies
• Exploring Primary Sources in U.S. History CD-ROM

Less Proficient Writers

Teacher's Edition
• Customize for Less Proficient Writers, p. 85

Teaching Resources
• Guided Reading and Review booklet, pp. 11–14
• Guide to the Essentials (English/Spanish), Chapter 3

Technology
• Student Edition on Audio CD, Chapter 3
• Guided Reading Audiotapes (English/Spanish), Chapter 3
• Section Reading Support Transparencies
• Exploring Primary Sources in U.S. History CD-ROM

TEACHER'S EDITION INDEX

CHAPTER 3 – PACING SUGGESTIONS

 ### For 90-minute Blocks

• Teach sections 1, 2, and 4 using Transparencies A4, A5, A56, E3, G2, H2, H3, and H4, and the Recent Scholarship note on page 85 for class discussions.

 ### Running Out of Time?

If you are running short on time to cover this chapter, consider the following options:

• Use the Prentice Hall Presentation Pro CD-ROM to create an outline for this chapter.

• Use the Section Summaries for Chapter 3, from **Guide to the Essentials (English/Spanish).**

ADDITIONAL ACTIVITIES

1 An Empire and Its Colonies	**Connnecting with Geography** Tell students to choose one region—the Southern Colonies, the Middle Colonies, or the New England Colonies. Then have students write a diary entry from the point of view of a young man or woman their own age living in the early 1700s. Tell students that their entry should accurately reflect their environment. They might include references to the weather, the crops, their meals, and their chores. **(Verbal/Linguistic)**	
2 Life in Colonial America	**Connecting with Culture** Tell students to create an artistic depiction of a colonial village. Students might make a drawing of a typical town, or they might create a three-dimensional model. Encourage students to include as many details as possible, including buildings, people, and animals. **(Visual/Spatial)**	
3 African Americans in the Colonies	**Connecting with History and Conflict** Have students make a map showing the route of the Middle Passage. Tell them to include the Caribbean islands mentioned in the text as places where Africans were sold at auction. Suggest that students include information telling the number of slaves living in the various colonies in 1750. **(Visual/Spatial)**	
4 Emerging Tensions	**Connecting with Government** Have students hold a peace conference aimed at resolving some of the differences among the inhabitants of colonial America. Students might address the tensions between Native Americans and colonists, or they might discuss the problems between the French settlers and the colonists in western Pennsylvania. Suggest that students prepare for the conference by reading more about the group that they are representing. **(Verbal/Linguistic)**	

Chapter 3

Growth of the American Colonies (1689–1754)

INTRODUCING THE CHAPTER

The years up to 1754 were a defining period for the American colonies. Varied landforms and climate, a steady stream of immigrants from different regions of the world, and England's policy of salutary neglect gave rise to a future hallmark of America: diversity of belief, economy, and people. A spirit of independence also spread among the colonists during this period; not just independence from England, but also from each other.

TIME LINE ACTIVITY

To provide students with practice in using the time line, ask questions such as these:

1. In 1700, enslaved Africans made up what percentage of Virginia's population? *(28 percent)*
2. In what year did Scotland and England join to form the United Kingdom? *(1707)*
3. What was the year in which Benjamin Franklin published the first issue of *Poor Richard's Almanac*? *(1732)*

Chapter 3

Growth of the American Colonies

(1689–1754)

Wren building at College of William and Mary

TO BE SOLD on board the Ship *Bance-Island*, on tuesday the 6th of *May* next, at *Ashley-Ferry*; a choice cargo of about 250 fine healthy

NEGROES,

just arrived from the Windward & Rice Coast. —The utmost care has already been taken, and shall be continued, to keep them free from the least danger of being infected with the SMALL-POX, no boat having been on board, and all other communication with people from *Charles-Town* prevented.

Austin, Laurens, & Appleby.

N. B. Full one Half of the above Negroes have had the SMALL-POX in their own Country.

American Events	**1689** Britain dissolves the Dominion of New England.	**1699** French colonists settle in present-day Louisiana and Mississippi.	**1700** Enslaved Africans make up 28 percent of the population of Virginia.

1680 · · · · **1700** ·

World Events	India's Mughal empire reaches its greatest geographic extent. **1690s**	Portuguese settlers discover gold in southern Brazil. **1695**	England and Scotland join to form the United Kingdom. **1707**

68   Chapter 3 • *Growth of the American Colonies*

---

eTeach

Be sure to check out this month's online discussion with a Master Teacher. Go to **www.phschool.com**.

RESOURCE DIRECTORY

Teaching Resources
Pacing Charts booklet
Block Scheduling booklet, p. 14
Units 1/2 booklet
• Chapter Summary, p. 25

Technology
Guided Reading Audiotapes (English/Spanish), Ch. 3
Student Edition on Audio CD, Ch. 3
Prentice Hall Presentation Pro CD-ROM, Ch. 3
Resource Pro® CD-ROM
Social Studies Skills Tutor CD-ROM
Companion Web site, www.phschool.com

Atlantic Trade in the 1700s

ASIA
EUROPE
London
Liverpool
Bristol
NORTH AMERICA
Boston
New York
Philadelphia
FISH, RICE, TAR, TIMBER, TOBACCO
AXES, CLOTH, FURNITURE, MUSKETS, TOOLS
BUTTER, GRAIN, MEAT
COFFEE, SUGAR, MOLASSES
IRON, MUSKETS, SILVER, TEXTILES
RUM, MUSKETS
SLAVES
N
ATLANTIC OCEAN
AFRICA
Cuba
Jamaica
Hispaniola
Puerto Rico
Windward Islands
Gulf of Guinea
SOUTH AMERICA
60°N
30°N
0°
120°W
60°W
30°W
0 500 1000 mi.
0 500 1000 km

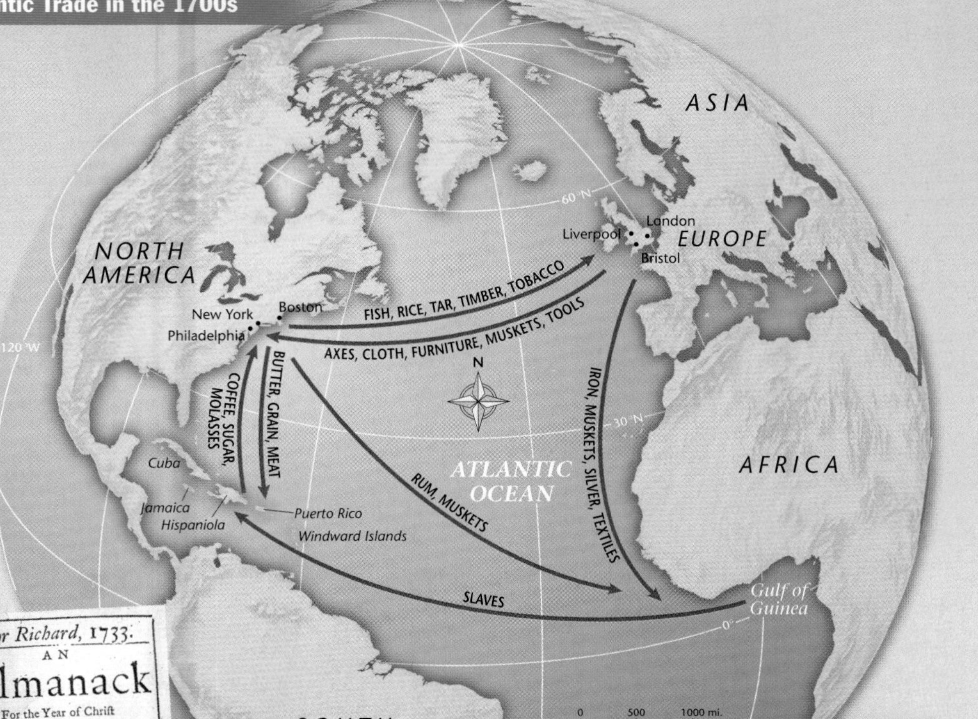

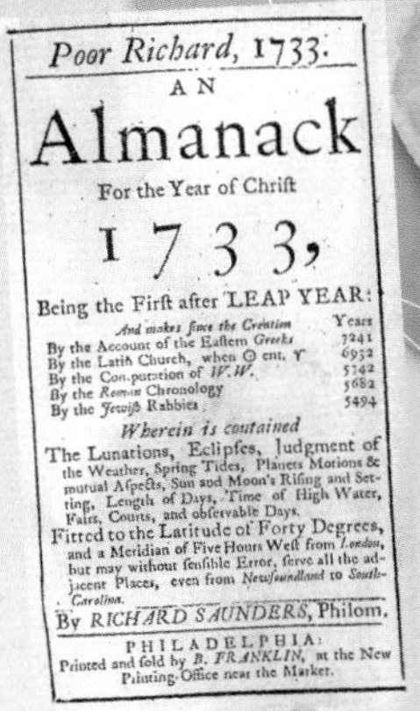

Poor Richard, 1733.

AN

Almanack

For the Year of Chrift

1733,

Being the Firft after LEAP YEAR:

Wherein is contained

The Lunations, Eclipfes, Judgment of the Weather, Spring Tides, Planets Motions & mutual Afpects, Sun and Moon's Rifing and Setting, Length of Days, Time of High Water, Fairs, Courts, and obfervable Days. Fitted to the Latitude of Forty Degrees, and a Meridian of Five Hours Weft from London, but may without fenfible Error, ferve all the adjacent Places, even from Newfoundland to South-Carolina.

By RICHARD SAUNDERS, Philom.

PHILADELPHIA: Printed and fold by B. FRANKLIN, at the New Printing-Office near the Market.

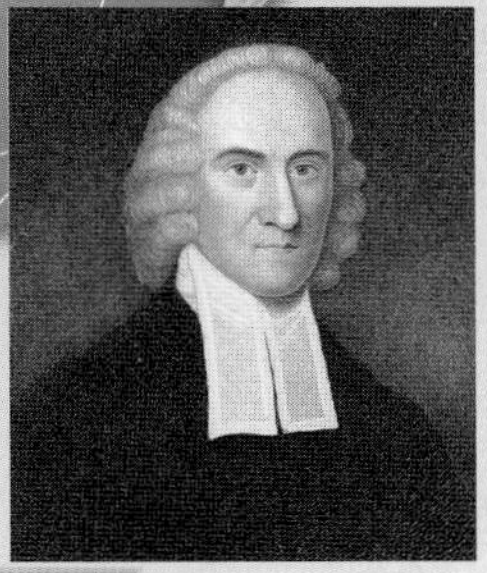

1732 For the year 1733, Benjamin Franklin prints the first issue of *Poor Richard's Almanac.*

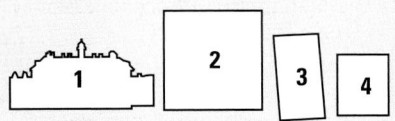

1739 In South Carolina, slaves rise up in the Stono Rebellion.

1741 Jonathan Edwards preaches "Sinners in the Hands of an Angry God."

1720 • **1740**

1713 France surrenders Newfoundland and Nova Scotia to Britain.

1722 Czar Peter the Great brings western reforms to Russia.

1739 John Wesley, the founder of Methodism, leads revivals in England.

Atlantic Trade in the 1700s

Activating Prior Knowledge What goods were imported from Cuba to North America? *(Coffee, sugar, and molasses)*

Previewing According to this map, which country has the smallest variety of exports? *(Africa: it only exports slaves)*

BACKGROUND
About the Pictures

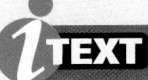

1
2
3
4

1. Chartered in 1693, William and Mary began as a college to educate clergymen and civil servants, and includes among its alumni seven signers of the Declaration of Independence.
2. Slaves typically arrived in Brazil or the Caribbean Islands, where they were auctioned to the highest bidders.
3. Poor Richard, characterized as pious, hardworking, and prudent, was the pen name used by Benjamin Franklin.
4. Edwards was part of a movement called the Great Awakening, which was intended to revive the colonists' faith, both in God and their ministers.

BIBLIOGRAPHY

For the Teacher

Boorstin, Daniel. ***The Americans, The Colonial Experience*** (A Caravelle Edition). Random House, 1964. (First book in a trilogy. An interpretation of how the habits of colonial America shaped American life today.)

Taylor, Alan and Eric Foner, eds. ***American Colonies, vol. 2, The Penguin History of the United States.*** Viking Press, 2001. (First in a new five-volume series, this book presents colonial history from a multicultural perspective.)

For the Student

Colonial America. C.A.I. Software. Video. (Narrated by eminent historian Henry Steele Commager. Focuses on the Pilgrims' search for freedom of religion.)

Hawthorne, Nathaniel. ***The Scarlet Letter.*** Silver Burdett Classics, 1985. (A famous novel that draws on the themes of sin and guilt in Puritan New England.)

iTEXT

Don't miss the exclusive interactive version of this textbook on the Web and on CD-ROM.

Section 1
An Empire and Its Colonies

READING FOCUS

- How did the English Civil War affect the development of the colonies?
- How did mercantilism influence England's colonial laws and foreign policy?
- What was Britain's colonial policy in the early 1700s?
- What farming, trade, and settlement patterns defined the diverse economies of the colonies?

MAIN IDEA

The English colonies grew and prospered with little direct interference from the English government from the mid-1600s to the early 1700s.

KEY TERMS

mercantilism
balance of trade
duty
salutary neglect
staple crop
triangular trade

TAKING NOTES

Copy the web diagram. As you read, fill in each blank circle with important events that affected colonial development from the mid-1600s to the early 1700s.

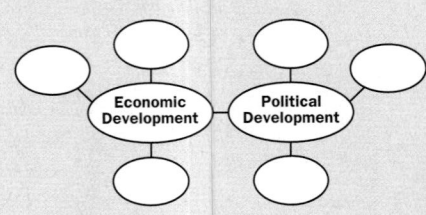

Setting the Scene In the late 1600s and early 1700s, England prized its cluster of colonies on the Atlantic Coast of North America for two reasons. The colonies supplied food and raw materials, and they bought large amounts of English goods.

Governing the colonies was a different matter, however. As early as the mid-1600s, English authorities complained about the rapid spread of settlements along the shores and rivers of Chesapeake Bay:

> 66 *For how is it possible to govern a people so dispersed; especially such as for the most part are sent over? . . . How can we raise soldiers to go upon the enemy or workmen for public employments, without weakening them too much, or undoing them by drawing them from their labors? Whereas if we had planted [settled] together we could have borne out one another's labors and given both strength and beauty to the colony.* 99
>
> —Anonymous

And yet the distances separating plantations in Virginia or towns in New England were small compared to the thousands of miles dividing the colonies from England itself.

Despite the freedom gained from isolation, the colonists were, in general, loyal to their parent country. Thus England got what it wanted from its colonies—raw materials and a place to sell its goods—by leaving them alone.

The English Civil War

From 1640 to 1660, England had another reason for ignoring the colonies. In the 1640s, tensions that had long simmered in England boiled over in a civil war. While England had never paid much attention to its North American colonies in the past, the nation became so preoccupied with conflicts within its own borders in those years that it neglected these colonies even more.

A 1710 map shows the extent of English settlement along the Atlantic coast of North America.

Two opponents faced off in the clash: King Charles I and Parliament. Made up of representatives of the people, Parliament had the power to make laws and approve new taxes. Charles upset Parliamentary leaders by demanding money from towns and cities without Parliament's consent. Many members of Parliament believed that Charles was attempting to limit the powers of Parliament and the rights of English property owners.

After troops loyal to Parliament defeated the king's army in a series of battles, Parliament ordered the execution of Charles in January 1649. Oliver Cromwell, a strict Puritan who had commanded the armies of Parliament, then governed England until his death in 1658. After two decades of upheaval, Parliament recognized the need for stability. In 1660, it restored the monarchy by placing Charles II, the son of the executed king, on the throne.

Mercantilism

As the political situation in England settled down, England's focus shifted to economic matters. England's government wanted the North American colonies to contribute to the parent country's economic health.

The Theory of Mercantilism By 1650, many nations in western Europe were working to improve their economies, spurred on by a new theory called **mercantilism.** Mercantilism held that a country should try to get and keep as much bullion, or gold and silver, as possible. The more gold and silver a country had, argued mercantilists, the wealthier and more powerful it would be.

For countries without the rich mines that Spain controlled in the Americas, the only way to obtain more bullion was through trade. If a country sold more goods to other countries than it bought from them, it would end up with more bullion. In other words, a country's **balance of trade,** or the difference in value between imports and exports, should show more exports than imports.

Mercantilists believed a nation should have colonies where it could harvest raw materials and sell products. By purchasing raw materials from its colonists, the parent country did not have to use its bullion to buy raw materials from its competitors. Any gold that flowed to the colonies in exchange for lumber, furs, or tobacco would soon return to the parent country as payment for expensive manufactured goods. According to mercantilist theory, the right to make goods for sale should usually be reserved for the parent country, since manufacturing was a major source of profit.

To ensure that colonists would buy manufactured goods from the parent country, the colonies would not be allowed to trade with other nations or even to manufacture goods. To maintain control over trade and to increase profits, the parent country would usually require the colonies to use its ships for transporting their raw materials.

Effects on Trade Laws Mercantilism appealed to English rulers. They came to realize that colonies could provide raw materials such as tobacco, furs, and perhaps gold for England to sell to other countries. Furthermore, the colonies would have to buy England's manufactured goods. This exchange would greatly improve England's balance of trade. English leaders therefore decided that it was necessary to have as many colonies as possible and to control colonial trade to provide the maximum profit to England.

In 1660, Charles II approved a stronger version of a previous law called the Navigation Act. Together with other legislation, the Navigation

Focus on ECONOMICS

Balance of Trade The balance of trade is the difference between the value of a country's exports and the value of its imports.

The Historical Context The theory of mercantilism argued that a nation would prosper by maintaining a positive balance of trade—that is, by consistently exporting more than it imported. The American colonies aided Britain's mercantilist policies by acting as a market for British exports.

The Concept Today In recent years the United States has maintained a negative balance of trade, importing much more than it exports. Experts disagree on whether this "trade deficit" harms the American economy. Some have argued that the United States should limit imports in order to balance its trade, while others believe the negative effects of the trade deficit are balanced out by other, positive factors including lower prices and access to imported goods.

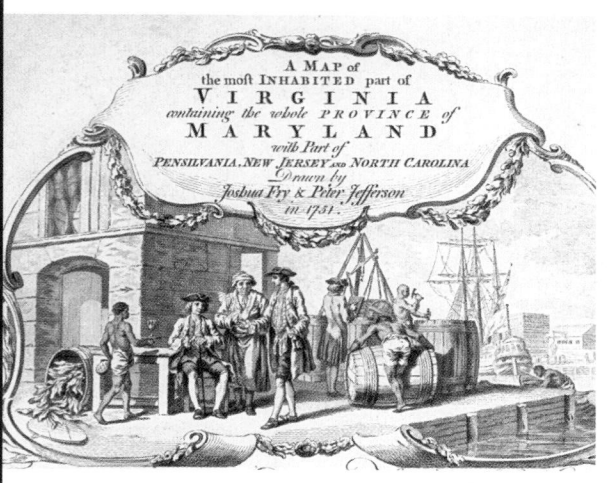

VIEWING HISTORY The colonies supplied England with food and raw materials. This detail from a map of 1751 shows tobacco being loaded at a southern dock for shipment to England. **Recognizing Ideologies** *Why did England require the colonies to supply it with raw materials?*

READING CHECK
Why were colonists unhappy with James II?

Act tightened English control over colonial trade. The new laws required the colonies to sell certain goods, including sugar, tobacco, and cotton, only to England. Moreover, if colonists wanted to sell anything to people in other parts of the world, they had to take the crop or product to England first and pay a **duty**, or tax, on it. They also had to use English ships for all their trade. The Navigation Act therefore discouraged trade between the American colonies and other European nations by increasing costs and funneling most profits to England.

Effects on War and Politics As European countries adopted mercantilism, the relations between them began to change. More and more, European countries fought each other over territory and trade routes rather than religion.

In the 1500s, for example, Protestant England's major enemy had been Catholic Spain. But from 1652 to 1654, and again from 1665 to 1667, the English fought wars against the Protestant Dutch over control of trade and land in North America. To eliminate the Dutch as a major trade rival in North America, the English conquered the Dutch colony of New Netherland in 1664, renaming it New York in honor of James, Duke of York and brother of King Charles II.

During the next two decades, Charles II and James tried in several ways to tighten their control over the colonies. Their actions reached a peak in 1686 when James, now King James II, attempted to take direct control over New York and the New England Colonies by creating the Dominion of New England. This action abolished colonial legislatures within the Dominion and replaced them with a governor and a council appointed by James II.

Anger in the Colonies Colonists up and down the Atlantic seaboard deeply resented James's grab for power. Edmund Andros, whom James II had appointed governor of the Dominion, made matters worse. From his headquarters in Boston, he collected taxes without the approval of either the king or the colonists and demanded payment of an annual land tax. He also declared a policy of religious tolerance, or respect for different religious beliefs. The Puritans felt these heavy-handed actions were a blow both to their freedom from English influence and to their tight control over religious affairs in their own colony.

Meanwhile, James II was making enemies in England. Members of Parliament worried that the king, as a Catholic, would undermine the Church of England, which was Protestant. News reached North America in the spring of 1689 that Parliament had replaced James II with his Protestant daughter Mary and her husband William of Orange, a change of rulers known as the Glorious Revolution. New England citizens promptly held their own mini-rebellion against the Andros government, imprisoning Governor Andros and his associates.

In response to this protest, William and Mary dissolved the Dominion of New England and reestablished the colonies that James had abolished. When they restored the charter of Massachusetts, however, they revised the organization of the government. The new charter allowed the king to appoint a royal governor of the colony.

Britain's Colonial Policy in the Early 1700s

England united with Scotland in 1707 to form the nation of Great Britain. In the early 1700s, the British government rarely interfered directly in the affairs of its North American colonies. By not interfering, Britain allowed colonial legislatures such as the House of Burgesses in Virginia to gain extensive power over local affairs.

Origins of Self-Government As you read earlier, England had established three different types of colonies in North America: royal, proprietary, and charter. Over time, England transformed several of the charter and proprietary colonies into royal colonies and appointed royal governors for them.

By the early 1700s, therefore, the colonies shared a similar pattern of government. In most colonies, a governor, appointed by the king, acted as the chief executive. A colonial legislature served under the governor. Most colonial assemblies consisted of an advisory council, or upper house of prominent colonists appointed by the king, and a lower house elected by qualified voters. Only male landowners were allowed to vote. Most adult white males did own land, however, and thus could vote.

In theory, the royal governor had a great amount of power. He decided when to call the legislature together and when to end its sessions. He could veto any laws that the legislature passed. The governor also appointed local officials, such as the treasurer and colonial judges.

In reality, it was the colonial legislatures, not the governors, that came to dominate the colonial governments. The legislatures created and passed laws regarding defense and taxation. Later they took over the job of setting salaries for royal officials. Colonial assemblies also influenced local appointments of judges and other officials because the governor usually accepted their recommendations. Even the governor's council came to be dominated by prominent local leaders who served the interests of the legislature rather than those of the royal government.

Salutary Neglect Why did the British government allow its colonies freedom in governing themselves—far more than was allowed in Spanish or French colonies? One reason is that England had a long tradition of strong local government and weak central power. Another reason is that the British government lacked the resources and the bureaucracy to enforce its wishes. Then, too, colonists recognized the authority of the king and Parliament without being forced to. Most were proud to be British subjects.

Finally, Britain allowed its colonies a large degree of freedom because the existing economy and politics of the colonists already served British interests. The British realized that the most salutary, or beneficial, policy was to neglect their colonies. Thus later historians would call British colonial policy during the early 1700s *salutary neglect.* In the early 1700s, Great Britain rarely enforced its trade regulations, such as the Navigation Act, because neglect served British economic interests better than strict enforcement. As a result, the colonies prospered, as did their trade with Britain, without much government interference.

VIEWING HISTORY The lawmaking assemblies of the colonies—such as the Virginia House of Burgesses shown here—continued the English tradition of strong local authority. **Drawing Conclusions** *What were some powers held by colonial assemblies?*

Connecting with Government

Have students make a chart showing the structure of colonial government during the 1700s. Tell students to include all of the key players: the king of England, the governor, the colonial legislature, male landowners, and so forth. (**Visual/Spatial**)

B**ACKGROUND**

Colonial Officeholders

Who could hold office in colonial America? Women and nonwhites could not hold office. Therefore, officeholders were white males, and most were landowners. The amount of land required to hold office varied from one colony to the next. Membership in the Church of England was often another requirement. Fewer than 5 percent of the population could actually vote. If a candidate ran against an opponent, he would meet voters at church, balls, picnics, and other public events. Some candidates "treated" their supporters after an election by offering them punch, apple cider, and food. Some candidates held balls after an election.

CUSTOMIZE FOR ...

Gifted and Talented

Have students analyze the role of the Middle Colonies as a region of tolerance and neutrality between the Anglican plantation colonies of the South and the Puritan colonies of New England. How did the Middle Colonies also take a middle ground in matters of religion and immigration?

☑ **TEST PREPARATION**

Have students read the section on this page called "Origins of Self-Government" and then answer the following question.

According to laws in the early 1700s, which of the following groups were allowed to vote?

A All men in the colonies.

B All men who owned land.

C All men who owned land and signed a document declaring their loyalty to the King.

D All colonial residents who owned land.

CAPTION ANSWERS

Viewing History The power to impose taxes, to set salaries for royal officials, to pass laws regarding defense, and to make recommendations regarding the appointment of local judges and officials.

Using physical and climate maps, discuss the geographical features that helped the colonies grow into distinct regions. Have students trace the long rivers of the Southern Colonies and compare them to those of New England. Point out the sea islands and coastal marshes of South Carolina and Georgia, where rice grew well. Compare the regions' climates. **(Visual/Spatial)**

BACKGROUND

Virginia's Tobacco Economy

By the 1700s it was said that "the Establishment [of Virginia] is indeed Tobacco." This staple was the crop around which much of the colony's economy revolved. Clergymen, for example, were paid in tobacco. In 1695 the annual salary of a clergyman was legally fixed at 16,600 pounds of tobacco. In addition, the money value of a minister's salary depended on the quality of the local crop. Ministers, often from England, were most easily lured to the colony by offers from regions growing the higher-priced "Sweet Scented" tobacco.

Diverse Colonial Economies

By the early 1700s, the economic foundations of Britain's American colonies were in place. While the Spanish colonies focused on mining silver and growing sugar, and New France focused on the fur trade, the British regions of eastern North America developed diverse economies. Each region's geography affected its economy.

For the most part, English-speaking settlements continued to hug the Atlantic Ocean and the deep rivers that empty into it. Most commerce took place on water. It was simply too expensive and too difficult to carry crops and goods long distances over land. Even water traffic on rivers, however, was blocked at the waterfalls and rapids of the fall line, where the inland hills meet the coastal plain. Roads were little more than footpaths or rutted trails. The Atlantic Ocean remained so vital to travel that there was more contact between Boston and London than between Boston and Virginia.

VIEWING HISTORY Thomas Coram painted this picture of slave huts on Mulberry Plantation in colonial South Carolina. **Making Comparisons** *How are the slave homes different from the plantation house in the background?*

The Southern Colonies In the Southern Colonies of Virginia, Maryland, South Carolina, North Carolina, and Georgia, the economy was based on growing **staple crops**—crops that are in constant demand. In Virginia and North Carolina, the staple crop was tobacco. In the warm and wet coastal regions of South Carolina and Georgia, it was rice. In the early 1730s, these two colonies were exporting 16.9 million pounds of rice per year; by 1770, the amount was 83.8 million pounds. Meanwhile, the number of pounds of tobacco exported per year by Virginia, Maryland, and Delaware rose from 32 million in 1700 to 88.3 million in 1770.

Growing and harvesting these crops was extremely difficult work that most free laborers were unwilling to do. Throughout the Southern Colonies, African slaves supplied most of the labor on tobacco and rice plantations. Virginia planters began to purchase large numbers of Africans in the mid-1600s. In 1650, Africans in Virginia numbered only about 400, which accounted for 2 percent of the colony's population. By 1700, enslaved Africans totaled 16,000, or 28 percent of the colony. Around 1750, the figure was 40 percent. In South Carolina, Africans outnumbered Europeans throughout the 1700s.

To produce staple crops, planters needed huge amounts of land and labor but very little else. As a result, the Southern Colonies remained a region of plantations strung out along rivers and coastlines. Except for the cities of Charles Town (later renamed Charleston), South Carolina, and Williamsburg, Virginia, the South had few towns and only a small group of people who could be called merchants.

The Middle Colonies From Maryland north to New York, the economy of the Middle Colonies was a mixture of farming and commerce. The long stretch of the Delaware and Hudson rivers and their tributaries allowed colonists to move into the interior and establish farms on rich, fertile soil. There they specialized in growing grains, including wheat, barley, and rye. This kind of farming was very profitable.

Commerce, however, was just as important as agriculture in the Middle Colonies. New York and Philadelphia were already among the largest cities in North America. Home to growing numbers of merchants, traders, and

CAPTION ANSWERS

Viewing History The slave huts are smaller and built with fewer windows and of somewhat rough materials. The slave homes are also very close together, while the plantation house stands alone.

RESOURCE DIRECTORY

Teaching Resources
Units 1/2 booklet
• Section 1 Quiz, p. 26
Guide to the Essentials
• Section 1 Summary, p. 15

Other Print Resources
Historical Outline Map Book *The New England Colonies,* p. 16; *The Middle Colonies,* p. 17; *The Southern Colonies,* p. 18; *Major Trade Routes,* p. 19

craftspeople, these cities teemed with people in the business of buying and selling goods. Ships from all over the Atlantic World arrived regularly in their ports. Philadelphia became the major port of entry for Germans and Scotch-Irish people coming to North America as indentured servants.

The populations of both New York and Pennsylvania were ethnically diverse. They included English, Dutch, French, Scots, Irish, Scotch-Irish, Germans, Swedes, Portuguese Jews, Welsh, Africans, and Native Americans. No wonder a traveler in the late 1750s believed he would never identify "any precise or determinate character" in the population of New York—it was made up of "different nations, different languages, and different religions."

The New England Colonies   In the 1700s, the New England Colonies were composed of small farms and towns dependent on long-distance trade. Unlike the merchants of Philadelphia and New York, those in Boston and Salem, Massachusetts, and Newport, Rhode Island, did not rely heavily on local crops for their commerce.

Instead, they carried crops and goods from one place to another—a "carrying trade." New England traders hauled china, books, and cloth from England to the West Indies in the Caribbean Sea. From the Caribbean they would transport sugar back to New England, where it was usually distilled into rum. They traded the rum and firearms for slaves in West Africa and then carried slaves to the West Indies for more sugar. This trade between three points in the Atlantic World—the Americas, Europe, and Africa—was called **triangular trade.**

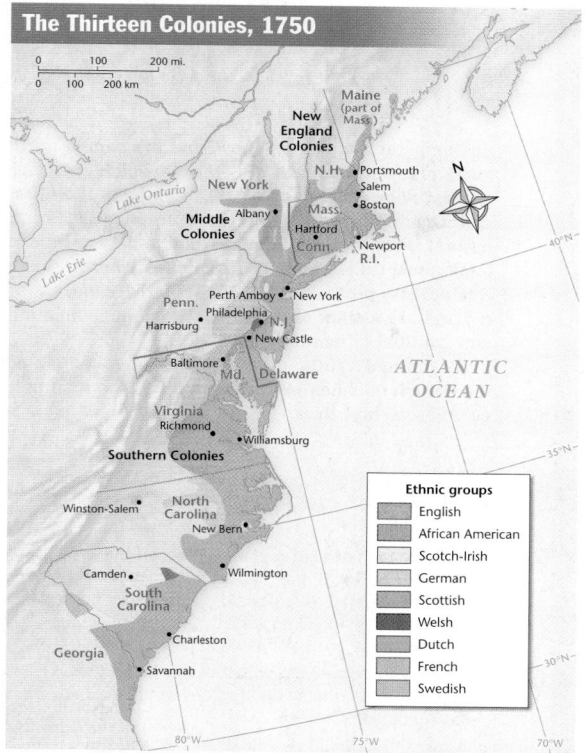

The Thirteen Colonies, 1750

Ethnic groups
- English
- African American
- Scotch-Irish
- German
- Scottish
- Welsh
- Dutch
- French
- Swedish

MAP SKILLS This map shows areas of major settlement by nationality. **Location** *Where did most Germans settle?*

Reading Comprehension

1. To acquire more gold and silver, countries relied upon favorable trade relations, the ideal being a home country trading with its colonies rather than with independent nations.

2. Possible answers: the Civil War that raged within Great Britain's borders; England got what it wanted from its colonies by leaving them alone (in the early 1700s); Great Britain lacked the power to exercise close control over the colonies.

3. Staple crops required a large amount of land and hard labor. The acute shortage of labor in the Southern Colonies resulted in the importation of large numbers of African slaves. The Southern Colonies became a region of plantations along rivers and coastlines, with only a few towns, and a small group of merchants.

4. The Middle Colonies, in particular New York and Pennsylvania.

Critical Thinking and Writing

5. Similar: All were located near the Atlantic coast. All relied primarily upon river and/or ocean travel for their transportation needs. The citizens in all the colonies cherished the idea of local government. Different: The Southern Colonies depended almost entirely upon agriculture; the Middle Colonies were engaged in commerce and agriculture. The New England Colonies relied primarily upon the carrying trade.

6. Time lines should include: 1660—stronger Navigation Act; 1686—Dominion of New England established; 1689—Glorious Revolution; early 1700s—salutory neglect.

Tables should clearly present the similarities and differences between the early systems of government described in the chosen documents.

CAPTION ANSWERS

Map Skills Pennsylvania, Maryland, central Virginia, and central and western North Carolina.

Section 1 Assessment

READING COMPREHENSION

1. Why were colonies important to an economy based on **mercantilism?**

2. List two reasons why England paid little attention to its colonies from the mid-1600s to the mid-1700s.

3. How did **staple crops** affect the growth and settlement of the Southern Colonies?

4. Which colonies had the most ethnic diversity?

CRITICAL THINKING AND WRITING

5. **Making Comparisons** How were the economies of the Southern, Middle, and New England Colonies similar? How did they differ?

6. **Creating a Time Line** Use the information in this section to create a time line of events in English and British colonial policy from 1660 to 1750.

 Take It to the NET

Activity: Analyzing Primary Sources Read early state constitutions and other governing documents. Take notes on the systems of government outlined by these documents and create a table comparing at least two of the documents you researched. Use the links provided in the *America: Pathways to the Present* area of the following Web site for help in completing this activity.
www.phschool.com

Interpreting an Economic Activity Map

Economic activity maps show how the land in particular regions is used. These maps also demonstrate the ways in which geography can influence historical events. For example, colonists often build their first settlements near waterways and natural harbors, giving these areas a headstart on development. A region's natural resources and climate also influence its economic development. Clearly, mining will take place only in regions where there are enough minerals to make this activity profitable. Economic activity maps also illustrate ways in which regions are similar or different. These economic differences often lead to social and political differences as well.

By the mid-1700s, clear patterns of economic activity were emerging among the British colonies in North America. The map below shows land use in the colonies at that time.

LEARN THE SKILL
Use the following steps to interpret an economic activity map:

1. **Identify the different regions shown on the map.** Look at the title of the map and at place names. Note the location of political boundaries, or borders. Often you can make regional distinctions, such as coastal areas or mountain regions, yourself.

2. **Identify the economic activities shown on the map.** Use the symbols and colors on the map key as your guide.

3. **Look for relationships or patterns among the regions and their economic activities.** Note how geography contributes to particular economic activities. Consider how different regions might interact with each other.

PRACTICE THE SKILL
Answer the following questions:

1. **(a)** According to the title, what regions are shown on the map? **(b)** What regions are distinguished by labels on the map?

2. **(a)** On this map, which activities are shown by colors? Name three activities shown by symbols. **(b)** According to the map, what was the major economic activity in Maryland? **(c)** What were the major economic activities north of Massachusetts? **(d)** Which colony produced tobacco, rice, and indigo? **(e)** What economic activity supported residents of Pennsylvania and New Jersey?

3. **(a)** As shown on the map, was farmland more extensive in the Southern or New England Colonies? **(b)** What other economic activities in New England encouraged shipbuilding? **(c)** How do you think shipbuilding in New England might have been related to economic activity in the Southern Colonies?

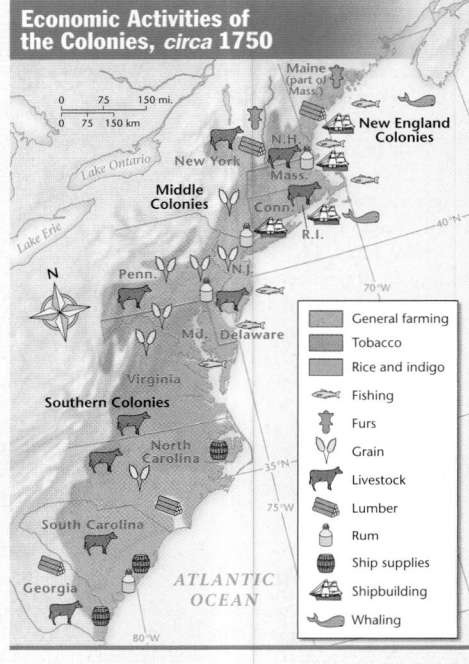

APPLY THE SKILL
See the Chapter Review and Assessment for another opportunity to apply this skill.

INTERPRETING AN ECONOMIC ACTIVITY MAP

Focus Identify the purpose of an economic activity map, interpret its symbols, and analyze the relationships indicated by the information displayed.

Instruct Ask students to define the term *region* as it is used by geographers and historians. *(A group of places bound together by one or more similar characteristics.)* Ask students what on the map justifies classifying the colonies into three regions. *(The symbols and color-coded key indicate the distinct economic activities of each region.)*

Ask students to find current economic activity maps in a geography textbook or encyclopedia showing the same regions. Have them compare the maps and name at least three things in each area that have changed.

Extend See the Skills for Life activity in the Resource Directory below.

ANSWERS
PRACTICE THE SKILL

1. **(a)** The Colonies, *ca.* 1750. **(b)** New England Colonies, Middle Colonies, Southern Colonies; more specifically, New Hampshire, Massachusetts, Connecticut, New York, New Jersey, Pennsylvania, Delaware, Maryland, Virginia, North Carolina, South Carolina, and Georgia.

2. **(a)** General farming; tobacco; rice and indigo. Students should choose three of the following: fishing, furs, grain, livestock, lumber, rum, ship supplies, shipbuilding, and whaling. **(b)** Growing tobacco. **(c)** General farming, raising livestock, logging, and the fur trade. **(d)** North Carolina. **(e)** General farming.

3. **(a)** It was more extensive in the Southern Colonies. **(b)** Fishing, whaling, and logging. **(c)** The Southern Colonies needed ships to export rum, tobacco, and indigo.

RESOURCE DIRECTORY

Teaching Resources
Skills for Life booklet, p. 5

Technology
Social Studies Skills Tutor CD-ROM
Interactive Practice in
• Geographic Literacy
• Critical Thinking and Reading
• Visual Analysis
• Communications

READING FOCUS

- How was colonial society organized?
- Why was wealth in land important?
- What were some common trades and occupations in the colonies?
- What rights and responsibilities did colonial women have?
- What was the nature of work and education in the colonies?

MAIN IDEA

The social groups that made up colonial society had different roles and ways of living.

KEY TERMS

gentry
apprentice
almanac
indigo
self-sufficient

TAKING NOTES

As you read, prepare an outline of this section. Use Roman numerals to indicate the major headings of this section, capital letters for the subheadings, and numbers for the supporting details. The sample below will help you get started.

> I. Colonial Society
>   A. Gender and race determined place in society.
>   B. Wealthy individuals were called gentry.
> II. Wealth in Land
>   A. Land ownership brought status and power.
>   1. _____
>   2. _____

Setting the Scene

Not quite 18 years old, Benjamin Franklin arrived in the city of Philadelphia in October 1723, after a journey of several days. He had $1 in his pocket. Franklin had quarreled with his brother (who was also his boss) and had left his home city of Boston to seek his fortune. He was determined to get ahead by improving himself. Franklin began by assembling a list of 13 virtues, including such qualities as temperance, frugality, and industry. He then set out to live by them. Each week, he decided, he would try to make one of the virtues part of his daily life. At the end of 13 weeks, he would repeat the cycle.

Although he did not succeed in mastering his virtues, Franklin did become the nation's best-known promoter of them. "Time is money"; "God helps them that helps themselves"; "Early to bed, early to rise, makes a man healthy, wealthy, and wise"—these and other famous sayings came from Franklin's pen.

Sayings like Franklin's helped convince American colonists of the economic opportunity available to them. According to Franklin, through hard work and clean living, a person from a humble background could prosper, maybe even become rich. In reality, this opportunity did not extend to all; enslaved African Americans in particular were excluded. Still, thanks to the labor of the colonists and the abundant resources of North America, England's American colonies grew in wealth, power, and self-confidence.

Benjamin Franklin first achieved success as a printer in Philadelphia (below) in the 1730s.

Colonial Society

It is common to speak of what "the American colonists" said or thought or did. Yet colonial society, like any society, consisted of a variety of groups with widely

77

RESOURCE DIRECTORY

Teaching Resources
Guided Reading and Review booklet, p. 12

Technology
Section Reading Support Transparencies
Guided Reading Audiotapes (English/Spanish), Ch. 3
Student Edition on Audio CD, Ch. 3
Color Transparencies Historical Maps, A5, A56; The Way It Works, H4
Prentice Hall Presentation Pro CD-ROM, Ch. 3
Companion Web site, www.phschool.com

Section 2
Life in Colonial America

SECTION OBJECTIVES

1. Learn how colonial society was organized.
2. Find out why wealth in land was important.
3. Discover some of the common trades and occupations in the colonies.
4. Read to know more about the rights and responsibilities of colonial women.
5. Understand the nature of work and education in the colonies.

BELLRINGER

Warm-Up Activity Write the words *Ladies and Gentlemen* on the chalkboard. Ask students what associations come to mind when they hear this phrase. How do the images of ladies and gentlemen during colonial times compare with those of today?

Activating Prior Knowledge Ask students if they can name United States' colleges or universities that trace their establishment back to the Colonial era.

READING STRATEGY

As students read the section, have them make a list of examples of what life was like in America in the colonial era.

ACTIVITY
Connecting with Culture

Tell students to write a position paper on one of the following topics: attending school or being home-schooled during the colonial era. Suggest that before they begin writing, students should consider the pros and cons of each form of education. They might also address the fact that schools were predominant in New England, while home schooling was more prevalent in the South. (**Verbal/Linguistic**)

Focus Point out that the colonists created a hierarchical society of many levels. Ask students who held power. What aspect of daily life governed the lives of most people?

Instruct Explain that colonial society was unequal. Ask students to describe the gentry and to identify the symbols of their class. Recall the Bellringer and compare colonial society with society today. Discuss the lives, rights, and duties of women, including rights single women had that married women and underage daughters with living fathers did not. How did work in colonial times differ from work today?

Assess/Reteach Have students summarize the different ways in which various sectors of colonial society lived.

VIEWING FINE ART Elizabeth Paddy Wensley lived in Boston with her husband, a successful merchant, in the late 1600s. Her lifestyle reflected the wealth some colonists enjoyed only 50 years after the settlement of Plymouth. **Drawing Inferences** *How does this painting indicate the wealth of the Wensley family?*

varying lives. A person's wealth, gender, or race went a long way toward determining his or her place in society.

American colonists brought many ideas and customs from Europe. Among these concepts was the belief that people are not equal. Most colonists accepted the notion that the wealthy were superior to the poor, that men were superior to women, and that whites were superior to blacks. They accepted too the idea that society was made up of different ranks or levels, with some groups having more wealth and power than others. In the words of one New Englander, "ranks and degrees" were as much a part of this world as "Mountains and Plains, Hills and Vallies."

The differences between social ranks could easily be seen in colonial clothes, houses, and manners. **Gentry,** or men and women wealthy enough to hire others to work for them, set themselves apart by their clothing: wigs, silk stockings, lace cuffs, and the latest fashions in suits, dresses, and hats. Ordinary people wore plain pants and shirts or dresses. Wigs were an unmistakable sign of status, power, and wealth.

"Gentle folk," a colonial term for the gentry class, were the most important members of colonial society. To be considered "gentle," one had to be wealthy.

Wealth in Land

For English colonists the foundation of real wealth was land. Land was plentiful and most white men owned some land. Although adult, single women and free African Americans could legally own land, very few did. The majority of landowners were white men.

In each colony a small group of elite, landowning men dominated politics. Lawyers, planters, and merchants held most of the seats in the colonial assemblies, or lawmaking bodies.

In the early 1700s, gentry devoted much of their time to displaying their status. The gentry socialized most with people of a similar class, especially in the Southern Colonies. In many cases they were related to one another by blood or marriage. To impress others, they had mansions and townhouses built for themselves and filled their homes with fine furniture, silver, and porcelain. To refine their manners, the gentry eagerly read newspapers and books from England. They sent their sons

Members of the gentry demonstrated their status by serving meals on fine porcelain imported from Europe.

Viewing Fine Art Possible answers: her elaborate dress, the large ring on her finger, and the ability to pay to have her portrait painted.

to expensive schools and taught their daughters how to manage a household. Rather than perform physical labor, they supervised others who did it.

We know from *The Diary, and Life, of William Byrd II of Virginia, 1674–1744* that gentlemen tried to live their lives according to a refined, well-mannered routine. William Byrd owned several plantations in the colony of Virginia. In his diary, Byrd relates that every day he read Greek or Latin, said his prayers, and "danced his dance" (performed a series of exercises) in the garden of his home.

Byrd rarely varied from these regular habits. Although he did have to keep an eye on his plantations, such labor was not the focus of his life. Like many other colonial gentlemen, Byrd wished to demonstrate to the world his refinement and self-control and to prove that he deserved the respect of others.

Trades and Occupations

Everyone recognized, however, that the colonies needed people from all walks of life, not just gentlemen. Those who were not gentry had the opportunity to develop specialized skills and trades.

Artisans At a very early age, boys from most families became **apprentices,** or persons placed under a legal contract to work for another person in exchange for learning a trade. Silversmith Paul Revere and artisans like him prospered by creating some of the items that the gentry desired. Cabinetmakers, such as John Goddard of Newport, Rhode Island, produced high-quality furniture with a distinctive colonial style. Other tradespeople provided equally important goods, such as tinware, pottery, and glassware.

Printers Colonial printers, who were respected members of colonial society, gathered and circulated local news and information. Printers, however, had to be cautious when deciding which stories to report. In 1734, authorities arrested John Peter Zenger, printer and publisher of the *New York Weekly Journal,* for printing libelous (false) stories critical of the governor of New York. Zenger's lawyer argued that if the stories were true then they could not be considered libel. Zenger won his case, a landmark victory for freedom of the press in America.

Benjamin Franklin was one of America's most famous printers in the 1700s. Among his best-known works is *Poor Richard's Almanac,* which was printed annually from 1732 to 1757. An **almanac** is a book containing information such as calendars, weather predictions, wise sayings, and advice. Franklin also published several newspapers and magazines.

Franklin retired from a successful career as a printer when he was only in his early forties. In retirement, Franklin dabbled in science and politics and spent much of his time in Europe. He is perhaps most famous for his experiments and inventions. Through his scientific work, Franklin invented the lightning rod, the Franklin stove, and bifocal eyeglasses. He also wrote his *Autobiography,* which set forth a number of rules for controlling oneself and behaving in a respectable manner.

Farmers and Fishermen Farms in the colonies varied in size from large cash-crop plantations in the Southern Colonies to small self-supporting farms in

VIEWING HISTORY A young man interested in becoming a potter (above) in the colonies had to work as an apprentice in an older potter's shop. Many colonists worked as silversmiths, producing silver goods (left) for the gentry. **Making Comparisons** What did an apprentice gain in exchange for his work?

 Sounds of an Era

Listen to Benjamin Franklin's *The Autobiography* and other sounds from the colonial era.

Connecting with Culture

Ask students to prepare a report about the lives of children in colonial times, answering questions such as the following: What types of schools were there for children? What was the apprentice system, and how did it work? Who went to school, and what subjects did they learn? What games and toys did children play with? How did they dress? How were children expected to behave? **(Verbal/Linguistic)**

BACKGROUND

Women Inventors

In the early 1700s, women were not allowed to hold patents for scientific inventions. Sybilla Masters, a Quaker mother of four children, invented a way to make cornmeal by stamping rather than grinding corn. In June 1712, she journeyed to London to get a patent for her invention. Three years later, a government patent was granted to Master's husband for "the sole use and benefit of 'a new invention . . . by Sybilla, his wife, for cleaning and curing the Indian Corn growing in the several colonies in America.'" Sybilla Masters later returned to Philadelphia and sold her cornmeal, which she called "Tuscarora Rice."

VIEWING HISTORY In most of colonial American society all members of the household worked, even children (above). Women of lesser means in colonial society also spent many hours at their spinning wheels (below). **Drawing Conclusions** *What was the economic goal of a typical colonial household?*

the New England and Middle Colonies. New England farmers who worked the thin, rocky soil gained a reputation for being tough, thrifty, and conservative.

Many coastal settlers turned their backs on the poor soil and earned their living from the sea. North America's shores abounded with haddock, bass, clams, mussels, and crabs. Colonists ate some of the bounty, but most was dried, salted, and shipped out from busy harbor cities. Fishing quickly became a main industry and promoted growth in the related industry of shipbuilding.

Indentured Servants   Many immigrants, both male and female, came to the colonies as indentured servants. As discussed in the previous chapter, indentured servants agreed to work for a master for a set amount of time, up to seven years. In exchange, the master agreed to pay for their travel costs to the colonies. Masters had total authority over indentured servants and sometimes treated them as if they were slaves. Those servants who served out their time were granted their freedom and in some cases a piece of land.

Colonial Women

The status of colonial women was determined by the men in their lives. Most women were legally the dependents of men and had no legal or political standing. Married women could not own property, for example. Laws prevented women from voting or holding office or serving on a jury. Even a widowed woman did not have any political rights, although she could inherit her husband's property and conduct business.

Women and the Law   Under English common law, a woman was under her husband's control. According to the English writer William Blackstone in his influential *Commentaries on the Laws of England*, published in the 1760s:

❝ *By marriage, the husband and wife are one person in law; that is, the very being or legal existence of the woman is suspended during the marriage, or at least is incorporated and consolidated into that of the husband.* ❞

—William Blackstone

Men held nearly unlimited power in colonial households. English law, for example, allowed husbands to beat their wives without fear of prosecution. Divorces, although legal, were rare. Surprisingly, the easiest place to obtain a divorce was Puritan New England. The Puritans were so concerned about order and stability that they preferred to allow a bad marriage to end rather than let it continue to create discord among them.

Women's Duties   In practice, however, men and women depended heavily on one another. In colonial America, women juggled a number of duties that contributed to the well-being of both the household and the community. Women managed the tasks that kept a household operating, such as cooking, gardening, washing, cleaning, weaving cloth, and sewing. They supported one another by helping in childbirth and sharing equipment and tools. They also trained their daughters in the traditional duties of women.

Women sometimes took on many tasks before marriage. One example is Eliza Lucas Pinckney of South Carolina, who as a teenager managed her father's

CAPTION ANSWERS

Viewing History   To survive; to be as self-sufficient as possible; and to earn a profit, if possible.

RESOURCE DIRECTORY

Teaching Resources

Biography, Literature, and Comparing Primary Sources booklet (Literature)   *As Poor Richard Says*, p. 42

Learning with Documents booklet (Visual Learning Activity)   *The First American Schoolbook*, p. 42

Learning with Documents booklet (Primary Source Activity)   *A Marriage Agreement*, p. 8

Technology

Color Transparencies   *The Way It Works*, H2, H3

RESOURCE PRO® Critical Thinking Activity *Identifying Central Issues: The Status of Colonial Women,* found on Resource Pro, enhances students' understanding of complex issues through summarizing excerpts from colonial authors.

plantations in the late 1730s and early 1740s. This duty fell to Pinckney because, as she wrote to a friend, "Mama's bad state of health prevents her going thro' any fatigue," and her father, the governor of the Caribbean island of Antigua, was usually absent. As she wrote to her friend:

> 66 I have the business of 3 plantations to transact, which requires much writing and more business and fatigue of other sorts than you can imagine, but lest you should imagine it too burdensome to a girl at my early time of life, give me leave to assure you I think myself happy that I can be useful to so good a father. 99

—Eliza Lucas Pinckney

Pinckney was more than just a stand-in for her father. She was one of the people responsible for promoting the growing of **indigo,** a type of plant used in making a blue dye for cloth. Indigo became a major staple crop in South Carolina.

READING CHECK
What were some responsibilities of colonial women?

The Nature of Work

By the mid-1700s, life was better for most white colonists than it would have been in Europe. They ate better, lived longer, and had more children to help them with their work. They also had many more opportunities to advance in wealth and status than average Europeans did. Still, whether they were skilled artisans in cities or small farmers in the countryside, colonists had to work very hard to keep themselves and their families alive.

Everyone in a household, including children and servants, worked to maintain the household by producing food and goods. In fact, the basic goal of the

Going to College

In 1650, the requirements for attending the English colonies' first and only college were simple. The earliest applicants to Harvard had to demonstrate that they understood Greek and knew Latin well enough to speak, write, and translate a passage by the Roman statesman Cicero. Some had never attended school before and prepared by training with a local minister.

There were no scholarships or student loans; Harvard did not even accept money in its first years. Students, of which there were about 50 at any given time, could pay in the form of wheat, milk, eggs, apples, horseshoes, or even a saddle. They were taught individually and the college determined what subjects they studied.

Today There are more than 3,500 colleges and universities in the United States today with an enrollment of about 15 million

students. Students can choose what they wish to study, and they have access to libraries and facilities far beyond those of the 1600s.

Costs have increased with opportunities, however. The annual cost of tuition, room, and board at four-year public universities averaged $8,100 a year in 2000, and most private universities are even more expensive. In 2002, tuition alone at Harvard College was about $23,500—the equivalent of about 55 tons of apples, 16,500 gallons of milk, or 450,000 eggs.

  **How did Harvard's financial needs reflect the realities of colonial life in 1650? Explain.**

Chapter 3 Section 2 • **81**

Sidebar (right column)

ACTIVITY
Connecting with Culture

Ask students to correct any of the following incorrect statements.
- The most powerful people in the English colonies were bankers, because they controlled the money supply.
- Any woman could own land in the colonies, but only unmarried women without fathers could vote.
- Most colonists did not work hard.
- Colonial women had few rights.
- Any colonists could become one of the gentry. **(Verbal/Linguistic)**

BACKGROUND
A Diverse Nation

Of the many jobs held by colonists, three were of prime importance: blacksmiths, shoemakers, and coopers. Unlike cobblers, who made simple repairs, shoemakers made shoes and other leather products. Some shoemakers made saddles and harnesses, a skill that required special training. Blacksmiths worked with iron to make or repair a variety of products, including axes, plows, hoes, gun parts, and carriage fittings. Coopers used wood to make barrels for storing and shipping goods. They also made buckets, butter churns, and laundry tubs.

CAPTION ANSWERS

Fast Forward to Today That the tuition payments in Harvard's early years consisted of items that were bartered in exchange for an education demonstrates that necessities of life, such as food, were more important than money in the colonial world of 1650.

Bottom left box

TEST PREPARATION

Have students read the quotation on this page by Eliza Lucas Pinckney and then complete the sentence below.

Based on the passage, you can tell that the author felt that running her father's plantations was—

A too burdensome.

B an easy task.

C a challenging but satisfying task.

D a way to earn money.

Reading Comprehension

1. (a) The ability to hire others to work for them. (b) Fine clothing and material possessions; status as the most important members of colonial society.

2. Apprentices contributed to the expansion of the economy because their training involved assisting artisans in the manufacture of fine glassware, furniture, and other high-quality items for purchase by the gentry.

3. Some children were educated by their parents at home. In the New England colonies, boys could attend public schools, while girls were educated at home by their mothers. In the Southern Colonies, plantation owners often hired private instructors to teach their children.

Critical Thinking and Writing

4. Everyone in the colonial family worked because a great deal of labor was usually required to maintain the household by producing food and goods.

5. Paragraphs should emphasize that although legally women lacked power and personal identity, in reality men and women depended on each other to maintain household and community.

Invite students to take a Virtual Field Trip at www.phschool.com

---

VIEWING HISTORY The first, second, and third colleges founded in the colonies were Harvard (top), William and Mary (center), and Yale (bottom). **Recognizing Cause and Effect** *Why did colonists in New England need to establish colleges in America?*

---

household was to be **self-sufficient,** or able to make everything needed to maintain itself.

While men grew crops or made goods such as shoes, guns, or candles, the rest of the household was equally busy. Wives often assisted in whatever work their husbands did, from planting crops to managing the business affairs of the family. Children helped both parents from an early age. Almost all work was performed in or around the home. Even artisans worked out of shops in the front of their houses.

Colonial Education

During the colonial period, attendance at school was not required by law, and most children received very little formal education. The New England Colonies, however, became early leaders in the development of public education, primarily because Puritan settlers believed everyone should be able to read the Bible. As a result, literacy rates were higher in New England than anywhere else in British North America.

In 1647, Massachusetts passed a law requiring every town with at least 50 families to hire a schoolmaster to teach basic reading, writing, and arithmetic. Towns with 100 or more families were expected to establish a grammar school that offered instruction in Greek and Latin. Boys attended the grammar school to prepare for college. Girls did not go to school. They were expected to learn everything they needed to know from their mothers at home.

Public schools did not develop as quickly outside New England. If there were no schools in the area, parents taught their children at home. In the Southern Colonies, plantation owners often hired private instructors to teach their children.

Colonial colleges were primarily training grounds for ministers and lawyers, and generally only the very wealthy attended. Up until the 1740s, there were only three colleges in the colonies: Harvard in Massachusetts (established in 1636), William and Mary in Virginia (1693), and Yale in Connecticut (1701). By 1769, five more colleges had been founded in the Middle and New England Colonies.

Section 2 Assessment

READING COMPREHENSION

1. (a) What made a colonist a member of the **gentry?** (b) What privileges did the gentry enjoy?

2. What role did **apprentices** play in the colonial economy?

3. How were children educated in the colonies?

CRITICAL THINKING AND WRITING

4. Drawing Conclusions Why did everyone in the average colonial household have to work?

5. Writing to Compare and Contrast Write a paragraph explaining how the legal status of women differed from their actual importance in colonial society.

Take It to the NET

Activity: Virtual Field Trip Take an online trek through the Christopher Wren building at William and Mary and write an essay on college life in the 1700s. Use the links provided in the *America: Pathways to the Present* area of the following Web site for help in completing this activity.
www.phschool.com

CAPTION ANSWERS

Viewing History To train ministers and lawyers.

RESOURCE DIRECTORY

Teaching Resources
Units 1/2 booklet
• Section 2 Quiz, p. 27
Guide to the Essentials
• Section 2 Summary, p. 16

Technology
Color Transparencies *Fine Art,* E3

African Americans in the Colonies

READING FOCUS

- What was the Middle Passage?
- How did the experience of slavery differ from colony to colony?
- What restrictions did free blacks face?
- How did laws attempt to control slaves and prevent revolts?

MAIN IDEA

Africans, brought across the Atlantic Ocean as slaves, helped build England's American colonies while enduring harsh and brutal treatment.

KEY TERMS

Middle Passage
mutiny
Stono Rebellion

TAKING NOTES

As you read, fill in the chart below with details about the lives of slaves in each region of the colonies.

Region	Experiences of African Americans
South Carolina and Georgia	• Harvested rice and indigo • Worked in brutal conditions •
Virginia and Maryland	
Middle Colonies and New England	

Setting the Scene Not counting Native Americans, about one out of every five people living in British North America by the middle of the 1700s was of African descent. As in the case of all immigrants, the experiences of African Americans in the colonies varied depending on where they lived. Yet the stories of Africans, uprooted from their homeland and sold into slavery, had many elements in common.

One African who later told his story was Olaudah Equiano. Equiano was born around 1745 in the country of Benin. He wrote in his autobiography decades later that the land of his youth was "uncommonly rich and fruitful" and "a nation of dancers, musicians and poets." As a child, he learned "the art of war" and proudly wore "the emblems of a warrior" made by his mother.

When Equiano was 10 years old, his world was shattered. Two men and a woman kidnapped him and one of his sisters while their parents were working. Separated from his sister, Equiano was enslaved to a series of African masters. About six months after he was kidnapped, Equiano was sold and put aboard a British slave ship bound for the Americas. In his autobiography, he wrote:

> 66 The first object which saluted my eyes when I arrived on the coast was the sea, and a slave ship which was then riding at anchor and waiting for its cargo. These filled me with astonishment, which was soon converted into terror when I was carried on board. 99
>
> —*Equiano's Travels*, 1789

Europeans built slave forts like Cape Coast Castle (below) in modern-day Ghana all along the coast of West Africa. Enslaved Africans were imprisoned here before boarding ships for the Middle Passage to the Americas.

Chapter 3 • Section 3   83

RESOURCE DIRECTORY

Teaching Resources
Learning Styles Lesson Plans booklet, p. 8
Guided Reading and Review booklet, p. 13

Technology
Section Reading Support Transparencies
Guided Reading Audiotapes (English/Spanish), Ch. 3
Student Edition on Audio CD, Ch. 3
Prentice Hall Presentation Pro CD-ROM, Ch. 3
Companion Web site, www.phschool.com

Section 3
African Americans in the Colonies

SECTION OBJECTIVES

1. Learn about the Middle Passage.
2. Find out how the experience of slavery differed from colony to colony.
3. See the restrictions faced by free blacks.
4. Discover how laws attempted to control slaves and prevent revolts.

BELLRINGER

Warm-Up Activity Ask students what makes up a family. What needs do families fill in people's lives?

Activating Prior Knowledge Ask students to state what they know about the policies of the various English colonies towards slave-holding in the 1700s.

READING STRATEGY

As students read this section, have them rewrite each of this section's main headings in the form of a question. Have them look for answers to the questions as they read.

*A*CTIVITY
Connecting with Culture

Tell students to research some aspect of the experience of Africans forced into slavery. Students might focus on what life had been like in Africa in the eighteenth century. They might read about how the African culture differed from American culture. Or students might look into the conditions on the boats that brought Africans to North America. Once students have completed their reading, have them write a short report on their findings. (**Verbal/Linguistic**)

Focus Point out that about 20 percent of the colonists were Africans or of African descent. Ask students what their lives were like. What contributions did they make to colonial society?

Instruct Discuss why slave traders treated Africans so poorly. Compare the lives of enslaved Africans and their descendants in the southern coastal colonies with the lives of those in the New England and Middle colonies. Ask whether plantation owners consciously allowed enslaved Africans to maintain some of their traditions. What factors enabled them to maintain a language with roots in Africa, for example? Why were their lives more varied in the New England and Middle colonies? Why were the revolts of enslaved African Americans unsuccessful?

Assess/Reteach Have students list the ways in which slaves helped build and strengthen the colonies, despite the cruel way in which they were treated, and the injustice to which they were subjected.

VIEWING HISTORY "No eye pities; no hand helps," said a slave trader describing the condition of his human cargo. An eyewitness painted this scene aboard a slave ship in 1846. **Drawing Conclusions** *What were conditions aboard slave ships like for enslaved Africans?*

For Equiano, and millions of other Africans captured and sold into slavery, much worse was to come.

The Middle Passage

The British ship carried Equiano across the Atlantic on a route known as the **Middle Passage.** The Middle Passage was one leg of the triangular trade between the Americas, Europe, and Africa. The term is also used to refer to the forced transport of slaves from Africa to the Americas. Although historians differ on the actual figures, from 10 to 40 percent of the Africans on a slave ship typically died in the crossing. Sick and frightened by what might lay ahead, they were forced to endure chains, heat, disease, and the overpowering odor caused by the lack of sanitation and their cramped, stuffy quarters.

During the Middle Passage, Equiano witnessed many scenes of brutality. He wrote, "Many a time we were near suffocation from the want [absence] of fresh air, which we were often without for whole days together." Conditions were so grim on Equiano's voyage that two people committed suicide. A third was prevented from doing so and was then whipped.

Occasionally, enslaved Africans physically resisted during the middle passage by staging a **mutiny,** or revolt. The slave traders lived in continual fear of mutinies, and crews were heavily armed. Statistics about the British slave trade show that a rebellion occurred every two years on the average. Many of these were successful.

Equiano's ship finally arrived at a port on the island of Barbados in the West Indies, where the Africans were sold at a public auction. Most went to work and die on the sugar plantations of the West Indies. Equiano noted that the sale separated families, leaving people grief-stricken and alone.

❝ *In this manner, without scruple [concern], are relations and friends separated, most of them never to see each other again. I remember in the vessel in which I was brought over, in the men's*

BIOGRAPHY

Olaudah Equiano 1745?–1797

As a young man, Olaudah Equiano was captured and brought to the West Indies from the African country of Benin. Unlike most enslaved Africans, he received an education and traveled widely with his British master. He was sold to an American in 1763 and later purchased his freedom in Virginia. Migrating to Great Britain, he found work as a barber and a personal servant and became active in the antislavery movement. His vivid account of his enslavement, *The Interesting Narrative of the Life of Olaudah Equiano,* was widely read in Britain and published for American, Dutch, German, and Russian audiences.

CAPTION ANSWERS

Viewing History Conditions were appalling. Chained below decks, slaves suffered from terrible crowding, heat, disease, and poor sanitation.

RESOURCE DIRECTORY

Other Print Resources
Nystrom *Atlas of Our Country* Unwilling *Immigrants and Native Americans,* pp. 16–17

Technology
Sounds of an Era Audio CD *Gullah Storyteller Janie Hunter* (time: 30 seconds)

apartment there were several brothers who, in the sale, were sold in different lots; and it was very moving on this occasion to see and hear their cries at parting. O, ye nominal Christians [Christians in name only]! might not an African ask you, Learned you this from your God, who says unto you, Do unto all men as you would men should do unto you? **99**

—Olaudah Equiano

Slavery in the Colonies

The experiences of Africans varied greatly in colonial times. Slavery was legal everywhere, but the number of slaves and the kind of labor they performed differed widely from region to region. In the northeast, where the population of blacks was small and mainly urban, blacks worked and talked regularly with whites. In Virginia and Maryland, blacks and whites lived close to each other on plantations and farms. But in South Carolina and Georgia, blacks enjoyed more freedom over their daily existence than elsewhere, although working conditions were extremely difficult.

South Carolina and Georgia   Much of the seaboard region of South Carolina and Georgia is formed by a coastal plain called the low country. Planters found the low country ideal for growing rice and indigo. Slaves there labored under especially brutal conditions. High temperatures and diseases made life particularly difficult. Charles Ball, an African American whose account was published in 1837, described the situation as it had existed for well over a century:

> **66** *The general features of slavery are the same every where; but the utmost rigor [strictness] of the system, is only to be met with on the cotton plantations of Carolina and Georgia, or in the rice fields which skirt the deep swamps and morasses of the southern rivers.* **99**
>
> —Charles Ball

African Americans made up the majority of the population in South Carolina and more than one third of the population in Georgia. Because rice was grown most efficiently on large tracts of land, this region had a greater number of plantations with more than 100 slaves than anywhere else in the colonies. Since wealthy planters often chose to spend most of their time away from their isolated estates, slaves generally had regular contact with only a handful of white colonists.

The lack of interaction allowed slaves in South Carolina and Georgia to preserve some of their cultural traditions. Many had come to the region directly from Africa. They continued to make the crafts of their homeland, such as baskets and pottery. They played the music they loved and told the stories their parents and grandparents had passed down to them. In some cases, they kept their culture alive in their speech. The most well-known example of this is the Gullah language, a combination of English and African languages. As late as the 1940s, speakers of Gullah were using 4,000 words from the languages of more than 21 separate groups in West Africa.

The skills that African Americans brought with them to South Carolina and Georgia also deeply affected the lives of their masters. African Americans often had superior knowledge of cattle herding and fishing. Because many had

Focus on CULTURE

The Gullah Language In the 1700s, owners of rice plantations in the Sea Islands off the South Carolina and Georgia coasts imported slaves from West African rice-growing regions, including present-day Sierra Leone. The Sea Islands could be reached only by boat, and white planters did not want to live there. Thus, these isolated enslaved Africans were able to preserve their distinctive culture.

The Gullah language that developed among these slaves and their descendants is a mixture of English and West African languages. For example, the Gullah "Dey fa go shum," translates to "They went to see her" in English.

When new roads linked the islands to the mainland in the 1960s, it was feared that the Gullah culture would die out. Today, however, there is renewed interest in preserving the Gullah language, and festivals celebrate Gullah storytelling, crafts (below), and cuisine.

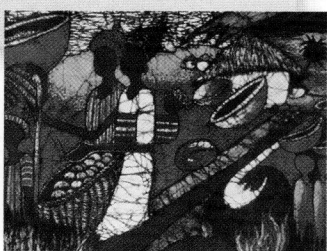

Estimated African American Population, 1690–1750			
Year	New England Colonies	Middle Colonies	Southern Colonies
1690	950	2,472	13,307
1700	1,680	3,661	22,476
1710	2,585	6,218	36,063
1720	3,956	10,825	54,058
1730	6,118	11,683	73,220
1740	8,541	16,452	125,031
1750	10,982	20,736	204,702

SOURCE: *Historical Statistics of the United States, Colonial Times to 1970*

INTERPRETING TABLES The growth in the number of African Americans, although relatively small in the 1600s, jumped considerably in the early 1700s. **Analyzing Information** *In which group of colonies did the number of African Americans increase most sharply?*

grown rice in their homelands, they had practical know-how about its cultivation.

Strong African kinship networks also helped people survive slavery and preserve their traditions. Africans highly valued the bonds between family members. When separated from their blood relatives, slaves created new relationships with one another by acting as substitute kin. In these relationships, people filled the roles of each other's brothers or sisters or aunts or uncles, though in fact they were not related.

In these and many other ways, the slaves in South Carolina and Georgia made the best of a horrible situation. Forced to come to North America, they found strength in each other's company and in the memory of their African origins.

Virginia and Maryland Colonists from England had begun to settle Virginia and Maryland in the early 1600s, decades before South Carolina and Georgia were founded. The longer history of European and African settlement in these colonies was one of several reasons why the lives of slaves in Virginia and Maryland differed from those of African Americans in South Carolina and parts of Georgia:

1. Slaves in Virginia and Maryland made up a minority rather than a majority of the population.
2. Relatively few slaves came to Virginia and Maryland directly from Africa. Slaves in Virginia were more likely to have been born in the American colonies.
3. Slaves performed different work. Cultivating tobacco, the major crop, did not take as much time as growing rice, so slave owners put enslaved African Americans to work at a variety of other tasks.
4. African Americans in Virginia and Maryland had more regular contact with European Americans. The result was greater integration of European American and African American cultures than in South Carolina and Georgia. In the

This watercolor painted on a South Carolina plantation in the late 1700s documents a dance form and musical instruments that have been linked to the Yoruba people of West Africa.

latter half of the 1700s, slaves in Virginia and Maryland blended customs of African and European origin. They mingled the African and the European in everything from food and clothes to religion.

The high costs of importing slaves from Africa led some Virginia and Maryland planters to encourage their slaves to raise families. It was in their economic interest to allow African Americans a fuller family and community life. Over time, therefore, some slaves were able to form fairly stable family lives, though they still lived in constant fear of being sold and separated from their families.

New England and the Middle Colonies   About 400,000 African Americans lived in the Southern Colonies by the late 1700s. In contrast, there were only about 50,000 African Americans in the New England and Middle Colonies combined. These colonies north of Maryland had a more diverse economy than that of the Southern Colonies. As a result, African Americans in the New England and Middle Colonies had more freedom to choose their occupations than did African Americans in the Southern Colonies.

Throughout the 1700s, farms in the New England and Middle Colonies were much smaller than those in the Southern Colonies and did not require as many slaves for field work. It was more common to find slaves in this region working in the cities as cooks, housekeepers, or personal servants. Male slaves often worked in manufacturing and trading or as skilled artisans. They also worked in the forests as lumberjacks. Because shipbuilding and shipping were major economic activities, some African American men worked along the sea-coast. As dockworkers, merchant sailors, fishermen, whalers, and privateers, they contributed to the growth of the Atlantic economy.

Free Blacks

Most African Americans in the colonies were enslaved. It was not until after the American Revolution that the free black population in the Northern and Southern Colonies grew significantly. Some slave laws discouraged people from freeing slaves. In some colonies, owners had to get permission from the legislature before freeing any of their slaves. Other laws demanded that freed slaves leave a colony within six months of gaining freedom. Despite the obstacles, those slaves who earned money as artisans or laborers had the possibility of saving enough to purchase their freedom.

Free African Americans did much of the same kind of work as enslaved African Americans. They were, however, probably worse off economically. Free blacks endured poorer living conditions and more severe discrimination than slaves who were identified with specific white households. Free blacks also faced limited rights compared to whites. They could not vote, testify in court against whites, or marry whites.

In Virginia and Maryland, some enslaved Africans worked in urban areas as artisans, laborers, or servants. Rather than let their slaves do very little work on their farms during winter or slow months, owners would encourage them to work in cities such as Richmond, Virginia, or Baltimore, Maryland. Slaves had to send a portion of their income to their owners and their living conditions were often

READING CHECK
What were conditions like for slaves in Virginia and Maryland?

VIEWING HISTORY   Some African Americans in South Carolina and Georgia escaped to freedom in Spanish Florida. Fort Mosé, established in St. Augustine in 1738, was home to many free blacks from the British colonies. **Drawing Inferences** *Why did many enslaved people risk their lives to escape to places like Fort Mosé?*

ACTIVITY
Connecting with Culture

This activity may take place over several class periods. Divide the class into groups of four students. Students will create a quilt based on the lives of African Americans. Each quilt should have at least eight pieces of colored paper or fabric. On the pieces, students may represent scenes such as passage to the colonies, life in different regions of the colonies, and attempts to revolt. **(Visual/Spatial)**

BACKGROUND
Connections to Today

Enslaved Africans brought with them to the United States the ancient tradition of storytelling. Alex Haley, who grew up listening to his grandmother's stories about an African ancestor, Kunta Kinte, journeyed to West Africa to research his family's origins. The trip led Haley to write his best-selling book *Roots,* which was viewed by a record 130 million people when it was dramatized for television in 1977. *Roots* awakened a popular interest in African American history and culture and, by the 1980s, in fiction written by African Americans. In 1993, Toni Morrison, whose works include the Pulitzer Prize-winning novel *Beloved,* was awarded the Nobel Prize in Literature, becoming the first African American to be so honored.

CAPTION ANSWERS

Viewing History To escape harsh working and living conditions; to win freedom for themselves and their families. Although living conditions for free blacks in the colonies were also very difficult, the desire to live as an independent person rather than as the property of another was a very powerful motivation.

Reading Comprehension

1. Slaves were chained below deck for the entire voyage. They experienced intense heat, disease, and a lack of fresh air and sanitation. Slave mortality rates on these voyages were quite high.

2. As students have already read, these areas were almost entirely given over to the farming of cash crops, which required an enormous amount of labor. Also, slaves were often skilled in cattle herding and fishing.

3. Laws restricting the movement of slaves made it difficult to organize rebellions. Denied the right to move freely, it was difficult for slaves to have the contact with slaves from other areas that would be necessary in order to plan a large revolt.

Critical Thinking and Writing

4. (a) He was kidnapped and separated from his family; he was forced to endure the Middle Passage; he lived through unspeakable hardship. (b) He received an education, traveled with his British master, and was later able to purchase his freedom and become active in the antislavery movement.

5. Sample answer: agricultural labor, cattle herding, fishing, cooking, housekeeping, manufacturing, and trading. Some worked as skilled artisans, dockworkers, privateers, and merchant sailors.

Essays should concisely describe the pivotal events and experiences in the life of Olaudah Equiano.

---

poor. They were still subject to harsh laws that controlled where they could go and what they could do. In addition, since they were not free, their children were born enslaved. But many welcomed the freedom they enjoyed away from daily supervision.

Laws and Revolts

Laws controlling the lives of slaves varied from region to region. Every colony passed its own slave laws, and colonies revised these laws over time. Settlers in Georgia, for example, barred slavery from the colony in 1735 but lifted the ban in 1750. Virginia enacted its first slave code in 1661. South Carolina passed fairly weak regulations in 1690 and then revised its laws in 1696, 1712, and 1740, each time strengthening the restrictions placed on slaves.

Generally, slaves could not go aboard ships or ferries or leave the town limits without a written pass. Slaves could be accused of crimes ranging from owning hogs or carrying canes to disturbing the peace or striking a white person. Punishments included whipping, banishment to the West Indies, and death. Many of these laws also applied to free African Americans and to Native Americans.

Laws restricting the movement of slaves made organizing slave rebellions extremely difficult. Because slaves could not travel or meet freely, they had only limited contact with slaves in other areas. A few early documented cases of slave revolts do stand out. In 1739, several dozen slaves near Charleston, South Carolina, killed more than 20 whites in what is known as the **Stono Rebellion.** The slaves burned an armory and began to march toward Spanish Florida, where a small colony of runaway slaves lived. Armed planters captured and killed the rebels. In New York City, brutal laws that had been passed to control African Americans led to rebellions in 1708, 1712, and 1741. After the 1741 revolt, 13 African Americans were burned alive as punishment. African Americans undertook almost 50 documented revolts between 1740 and 1800.

More commonly, African Americans opposed slavery through acts of indirect resistance, such as pretending to misunderstand orders or faking illness. While these actions could not give them freedom, they did grant the slaves a small degree of control over their own lives.

Treating humans as property led to unspeakable cruelties. This branding iron was used to mark an owner's initials on enslaved Africans.

Section 3 Assessment

READING COMPREHENSION

1. Describe the experiences of African Americans during the **Middle Passage.**

2. Why was slavery so important to the economies of South Carolina and Georgia in the 1700s?

3. How did colonial governments and planters try to prevent slave revolts like the **Stono Rebellion?**

CRITICAL THINKING AND WRITING

4. Making Comparisons (a) In what ways was Olaudah Equiano's experience similar to that of other enslaved Africans? (b) In what ways was his experience different?

5. Writing a List Use your reading in this section to prepare a list of jobs held by African Americans, enslaved and free, in the colonies.

Take It to the NET

Activity: Writing a Biography
Investigate the life and times of Olaudah Equiano. Use the information you gather to write a one-page biography outlining his experiences. Use the links provided in the *America: Pathways to the Present* area of the following Web site for help in completing this activity.
www.phschool.com

88 Chapter 3 • *Growth of the American Colonies*

RESOURCE DIRECTORY

Teaching Resources
Units 1/2 booklet
• Section 3 Quiz, p. 28
Guide to the Essentials
• Section 3 Summary, p. 17

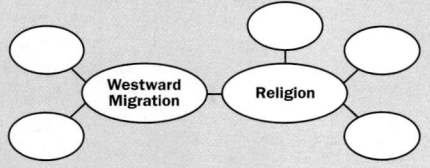

READING FOCUS

- What drove the western expansion of colonial settlement?
- How did Native Americans and the French react to the expansion of the colonies?
- Why did the Great Awakening both resolve and contribute to religious tensions?

MAIN IDEA

In the mid-1700s, the American colonies experienced a population boom and a powerful religious revival.

KEY TERMS

immigrant
migration
Great Awakening
itinerant
dissent

TAKING NOTES

Copy the web diagram below. As you read, fill in each blank circle with important trends relating to emerging tensions in the colonies.

[web diagram: Westward Migration — Religion with blank circles]

Setting the Scene By the mid-1700s, there were 13 prosperous British colonies hugging the Atlantic Coast. Colonial settlers had transformed the Atlantic Colonies into a world of thriving farms, towns, and plantations. Many people lived much better in the colonies than their ancestors had in England. In England, poverty discouraged people from having large families they could not easily support. In the American colonies, in contrast, land was abundant and people could marry and raise children earlier in life. One observer noted the extremely large families he found in rural Pennsylvania:

> 66 In the year 1739, May 30, the children, grandchildren, and great grandchildren of Mr Richard Buttington in the parish of Chester in Pennsylvania were assembled in his house; and they made together one hundred and fifteen persons. The parent of these children, Richard Buttington, who was born in England, was then entering his eighty-fifth year; . . . His eldest son, then sixty years old, was the first Englishman born in Pennsylvania. . . . 99
> —Peter Kalm

Kalm believed large families like the Buttingtons were the beneficiaries of inexpensive land and low taxes that enabled families to prosper. The success of the colonies came at a price, however, as the swelling population of young colonists and newcomers sought opportunities of their own. The growth of the colonies, both in population and territory, raised new issues in colonial life.

VIEWING FINE ART Charles Wilson Peale painted this portrait of a large colonial family. **Recognizing Cause and Effect** Why did colonists have more children on average than people in England?

Western Expansion

In the mid-1700s, the colonial population increased rapidly, almost doubling every 25 years. In addition to a rising birth rate, the colonies experienced a growth in the number of **immigrants,** or people who enter a new country to

Chapter 3 • Section 4 89

SECTION OBJECTIVES

1. Find out what drove the western expansion of colonial settlement.
2. Learn how Native Americans and the French reacted to the expansion of the colonies.
3. Discover why the Great Awakening both resolved and contributed to religious tensions.

BELLRINGER

Warm-Up Activity Ask students to think about what land ownership signifies. What are the reasons for wanting land today? What were they in colonial times?

Activating Prior Knowledge Have students speculate on the ways in which expansion of the colonies would impact others, such as Native Americans and settlers from other European countries.

READING STRATEGY

Have students reread the Main Idea shown on this page. Then, have them rewrite it as a question. As they read the section, have them take notes to help answer the question.

ACTIVITY
Connecting with Geography

Have students make maps showing the growth that occurred during the mid-1700s. Tell students to label the colonies, and indicate which ones experienced large growth. Also have students locate various immigrant groups in the appropriate colonies. **(Visual/Spatial)**

CAPTION ANSWERS

Viewing Fine Art The easy availability of land in America enabled farmers to support more children than could the average person in Great Britain.

Focus Explain that by the mid-1700s, conflicts emerged in colonial society. Ask what tensions arose from the desire of colonists to move westward. How did a revival of religious feeling challenge colonial society and British government?

Instruct Review why the French and Native Americans did not welcome English settlers. How did settlers disrupt Native Americans' lives? How did British settlement affect the French fur trade? Explain how religion both maintained order and threatened it. How did Great Awakening preachers stress each person's importance?

Assess/Reteach Ask students to speculate on what British settlers might have done to minimize friction with Native Americans.

settle. While colonists continued to come from England, they also began to arrive from Ireland and Germany. Those people immigrating from Ireland were often called Scotch-Irish, for their ancestors had originally traveled from Scotland across the Irish Sea to settle in Ireland before moving on to the North American colonies. As the population grew, the colonists began to feel crowded, especially in the smaller colonies of New England.

According to English custom, a father's land was divided up among all of his sons when he died. New Englanders now found it increasingly difficult to continue splitting their land from generation to generation. Maintaining a family required about 45 acres, and since colonists were having many children, there was simply not enough fertile land to go around. Benjamin Franklin and others feared a land shortage would make it more difficult for American men to secure their independence by owning property.

READING CHECK
What regions were first settled by Europeans in the mid-1700s?

Clearly the colonies could not continue to flourish if they were confined to the land along the Atlantic Ocean. By the mid-1700s, European settlers were moving into the interior of North America. Scotch-Irish and Germans settled central Pennsylvania and the Shenandoah Valley of Virginia. Farther to the north, colonists spread into the Mohawk River valley in New York and the Connecticut River valley in present-day Vermont and New Hampshire. In southern Pennsylvania and the Carolinas, settlements sprang up as far west as the Appalachian Mountains. In a few cases, settlers pushed through the Appalachians and began cultivating land in Indian territory. They were part of a **migration,** or movement, in search of land on which they could build independent lives and maintain their households.

Native American and French Reaction

The colonists' desire for more land raised tensions between the settlers and those groups who already lived on the land—French settlers and Native Americans. Contact between the groups was rare at first, but interactions continued to increase as greater numbers of colonists looked for new places to settle.

MAP SKILLS As English colonists pushed west, they came into conflict with both the French and the Indians. **Location** Which British forts are in disputed territory?

Native American Response Just ahead of the westward-moving English migrants were Native Americans. In the Ohio and Susquehanna River valleys lived a number of groups, including the Delaware, the Shawnee, and the Huron. They were moving west, too. As white settlers migrated into Native American territory, they forced the Indians to relocate into lands already occupied by other Native American groups.

By the mid-1700s, disease and wars over trade had taken a toll on Native Americans, especially in New England. The Iroquois, for example, were no longer as strong militarily as they had been in the 1600s. The southern frontier, however, remained a stronghold for Native Americans. There the Cherokees, Creeks, Chickasaws, and Choctaws created a powerful barrier to westward colonial expansion. In addition, Native Americans remained skilled at playing on the rivalry between the

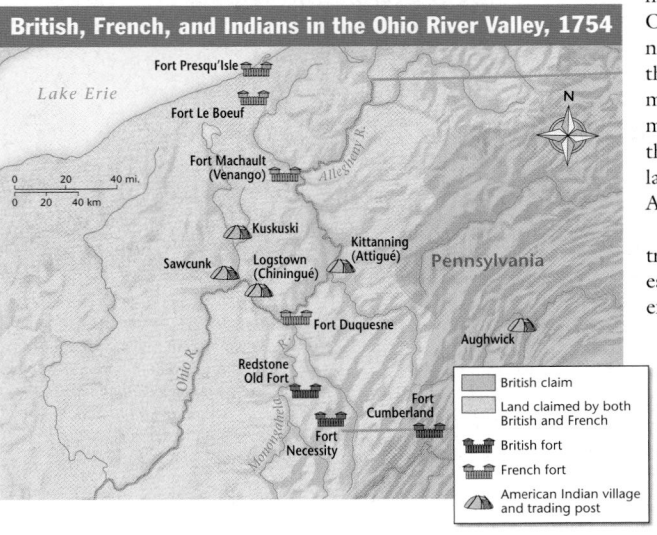

British, French, and Indians in the Ohio River Valley, 1754

Lake Erie
Fort Presqu'Isle
Fort Le Boeuf
Fort Machault (Venango)
Allegheny R.
0   20   40 mi.
0   20   40 km
Kuskuski
Kittanning (Attigué)
Sawcunk
Logstown (Chiningué)
Pennsylvania
Fort Duquesne
Aughwick
Ohio R.
Redstone Old Fort
Fort Cumberland
Monongahela R.
Fort Necessity

British claim
Land claimed by both British and French
British fort
French fort
American Indian village and trading post

RESOURCE DIRECTORY

Teaching Resources
Biography, Literature, and Comparing Primary Sources booklet (Comparing Primary Sources) *On Expansion into Native American Lands,* pp. 101–102

Other Print Resources
■ **American History Block Scheduling Support** *Reviving Religion: The Great Awakening,* found in the Forging a New Nation folder, includes interdisciplinary lesson suggestions and activities for Geography and History, Primary Sources, Biography, and Literature.

Nystrom *Atlas of Our Country* *Early Expansion of the United States,* pp. 20–21

Technology
RESOURCE PRO® **Primary Source Activity** *The Great Awakening,* found on Resource Pro, uses an account by Benjamin Franklin and the text of a sermon by Jonathan Edwards to help students understand the phenomenon of the Great Awakening.

Expansion Into Native American Lands

Colonial efforts to purchase Native American lands in Pennsylvania created a difference of opinion.
Analyzing Viewpoints How does each of the speakers below describe the value of the land?

Opposed to Expansion

"We know our Lands are now become more valuable. The white People think we do not know their Value; but we are sensible [aware] that the Land is everlasting, and the few Goods we receive for it are soon worn out and gone. . . . Besides, we are not well used [treated] with respect to the lands still unsold by us. Your people daily settle on these lands, and spoil our hunting. . . . Your horses and cows have eaten the grass our deer used to feed on."

—*Canassatego, Iroquois leader, July 7, 1742*

In Favor of Expansion

"It is very true that lands are of late becoming more valuable; but what rises their value? Is it not entirely owning to the industry and labor used by the white people in their cultivation and improvement? Had not they come among you, these lands would have been of no use to you, any further than to maintain you. . . . The value of the land is no more than it is worth in money."

—*Governor of Pennsylvania, July 7, 1742*

French in Canada and the British in New York and Pennsylvania. Chief Hendrick of the Mohawks, a member of the Iroquois Confederation, warned the British to treat the Iroquois fairly and invoked the name of their competitors:

> “ You have . . . thrown us behind your back, and disregarded us, whereas the French are a subtle and vigilant people, ever using the utmost endeavours to seduce and bring our people over to them. ”
>
> —Chief Hendrick, 1754

French Actions The steady migration of the English settlers alarmed the French as well as the Native Americans. In 1749, disturbed by the expansion of British trading posts in the Ohio Valley, the French sent defenders to strengthen the settlement of Detroit and to seize the Ohio Valley. Tensions continued to rise in the summer of 1752 when the French built Fort Presque Isle (in present-day Erie, Pennsylvania) and attacked and killed the men defending an English trading post in the Ohio Valley.

By the early 1750s, it was clear that some kind of explosion was rapidly approaching. The most likely setting was western Pennsylvania. There the interests of the colonies of Pennsylvania and Virginia conflicted with the Native Americans and the French. Whoever controlled the forks of the Ohio River, the place where the Allegheny and Monongahela rivers meet to form the Ohio, could dominate the entire region. This was, in other words, an area worth fighting for.

Religious Tensions

While tensions built along the outer edges of the British colonies, unrest was also increasing within them. Nowhere was this more obvious than in colonial religious life.

While the British colonies were overwhelmingly Protestant (aside from a small number of Jews in cities and some Catholics in Maryland), no single group of Protestants was more powerful than any other. Southern planters, northern merchants, and northern professionals tended to belong to the Church of England, while most New Englanders were either Congregationalists

Chapter 3 • Section 4   91

ACTIVITY

Connecting with Culture

Tell students to write a short report detailing the religious history of your state. As students do their research, they should consider the following questions. When your state was first settled, which religious group or groups were predominant? What kind of conflicts emerged between different religious groups? How has the religious makeup of your state changed over the years? What is the religious makeup of your state now? **(Verbal/Linguistic)**

BACKGROUND

A Diverse Nation

Small but stable Jewish communities emerged during the 1690s. There were almost 100 Jews living in New York by 1695. By 1770 there were about 250 Jewish families in the colonies, most living in Newport, New York City, Philadelphia, and Charleston. While most Jews were merchants and shopkeepers, a small number were artisans. Colonial Jews chose to stay in cities in order to keep their small communities intact. Although Jews faced discrimination from town officials, they managed to build a small synagogue in New York City in 1728. In Newport in 1763, the small Jewish community built what is now the nation's oldest synagogue.

✓ TEST PREPARATION

Have students read the quote by Chief Hendrick on this page, and then answer the question below.

Which of the following statements best summarizes the main point of the quotation from Chief Hendrick?

A He wished that French settlers would behave more like British settlers.

B He did not like to interact with either French or British settlers.

C The British did not respect the Native Americans.

(D) The British did not try as hard as the French to appeal to Native Americans.

Connecting with Citizenship

Have small groups of students work together to write an original sermon designed to inspire others to act on an issue of current importance. Tell students to try to imbue their sermon with the same kind of fervor used by the revivalist ministers. Have one student from each group deliver the group's sermon to the rest of the class. (**Verbal/Linguistic**)

From the Archives of AmericanHeritage®

The Inoculation Controversy

About three o'clock on the morning of November 4, 1721, a crude grenade made of black powder and turpentine sailed through a window of Cotton Mather's house in Boston. It failed to explode, but the attempted bombing was the most lurid episode in a campaign of intimidation aimed at Mather and his ally Dr. Zabdiel Boylston, whom mobs had threatened to hang. What offenses had these two men committed to enrage the masses so violently? They had inoculated their fellow citizens against smallpox. Mather heard of the African practice of inoculation from his slave Onesimus. When smallpox struck Boston in 1721, Mather and Boylston began an aggressive inoculation campaign. Instead of being hailed as saviors, the two were reviled by many Bostonians for interfering with God's will and spreading disease. Factors unrelated to medicine were at work in the dispute. Bostonians were losing their customary reverence for the clergy. Class-based resentment accounted for some anticlerical feeling, and Mather had recently made enemies by taking sides in a fight over the establishment of a new church. Source: Frederic D. Schwarz, "The Time Machine," *American Heritage®* magazine, November 1996.

or Presbyterians. Quakers were strong in Pennsylvania, as were Lutherans and Mennonites, and the Dutch Reformed Church thrived in the colonies of New York and New Jersey.

The Great Awakening In the early 1700s, many ministers, especially Congregationalists, believed that the colonists had fallen away from the faith of their Puritan ancestors. In the 1730s and 1740s, they led a series of revivals designed to renew religious enthusiasm and commitment. Their preaching especially touched women of all ages and young men. This revival of religious feeling is now known as the **Great Awakening.**

The Great Awakening was not a single event that began or ended all at one time. It did not even take place in every colony. Revivals had begun in scattered New England towns as early as the 1720s and continued through the 1760s. Most historians, however, date the beginning of the Great Awakening to the great explosion of religious feeling that arose in the 1730s in response to the preaching of Jonathan Edwards, a minister in Northampton, Massachusetts.

News of Edwards's success spread throughout the colonies and even to Britain. It encouraged other ministers to increase their efforts to energize their followers. These ministers sought to remind people of the power of God and, at least in the beginning, to remind them of the authority of their ministers as well. In a well-known fiery sermon, "Sinners in the Hands of an Angry God," Edwards gave his congregation a terrifying picture of their situation:

> ❝ O sinner! Consider the fearful danger you are in: it is a great furnace of wrath, a wide and bottomless pit, full of the fire of wrath, that you are held over in the hand of that God, whose wrath is provoked and incensed as much against you, as against many of the damned in hell. You hang by a slender thread. ❞
> —Jonathan Edwards

VIEWING HISTORY Preachers such as Jonathan Edwards (top) were known for their "pathetical," or emotional, style. They used their powerful speaking skills to encourage ordinary people to believe that they, too, could reach out to God. **Recognizing Ideologies** *What prompted the religious revivals of the Great Awakening?*

Edwards would eventually be overtaken in popularity by George Whitefield, a young English minister who toured the colonies seven times between 1738 and 1770. Whitefield's tour of New England in 1740 was a great triumph. In Boston, he preached to vast crowds packed into churches. Later he held open-air meetings at which thousands of listeners at a time could hear his ringing sermons.

As time went on, however, the Great Awakening did more than revive people's religious convictions. It energized them to speak for themselves and to rely less on the traditional authority of ministers and books. As George Whitefield said,

> ❝ The Generality of Preachers talk of an unknown, unfelt Christ. And the Reason why Congregations have been so dead, is because dead Men preach to them. ❞
> —George Whitefield

Sounds of an Era

Listen to "Sinners in the Hands of an Angry God" and other sounds from the colonial era.

In some areas the Great Awakening was led by ministers in established congregations. Many people, though, flocked to revival leaders, such as Whitefield, who were **itinerant,** or traveling, preachers. If welcomed by the local minister, the itinerants would preach inside the church as a "visiting minister." If unwelcome, they preached in fields and barns to anyone who would come to hear their sermons.

RESOURCE DIRECTORY

Teaching Resources
Units 1/2 booklet
- Section 4 Quiz, p. 29
- Chapter 3 Test, pp. 30, 33

Guide to the Essentials
- Section 4 Summary
- Chapter 3 Test, p. 18

Biography, Literature, and Comparing Primary Sources booklet (Biography) *Jonathan Edwards*, p. 8

Other Print Resources
Chapter Tests with ExamView® Test Bank CD-ROM, Ch. 3

Technology
Sounds of an Era Audio CD *"Sinners in the Hands of an Angry God,"* Jonathan Edwards (time: one minute, 50 seconds)
ExamView® Test Bank CD-ROM, Ch. 3
Social Studies Skills Tutor CD-ROM

These ministers, some of whom had had little formal education, preached that any Christian could have a personal relationship with Jesus Christ. The infinitely great power of God did not put Him beyond the reach of ordinary people, they argued. Faith and sincerity, rather than wealth or education, were the major requirements needed to understand the Gospel.

Churches Reorganize One sign of the new religious independence brought about by the Great Awakening was the shift of many New Englanders to the Baptist faith in the 1740s and 1750s. In the South, both the Baptist and, later, the Methodist churches drew new followers. Evangelical Baptists attracted followers among the common people who settled in the southern backcountry. The appeal of these two particular churches lay in their powerful, emotional ceremonies and their celebration of ordinary people. Both churches tended to draw people at the middle or bottom of colonial society.

Though it was a religious movement, the Great Awakening had long-term social and political effects as well. When Methodists and Baptists claimed that individuals could act on their own faith, without relying on a minister or other authority, they were indirectly attacking the idea that some people are better than others. Such talk of equality would, in time, have revolutionary consequences.

While the Methodist and Baptist churches grew, other denominations split. Revivals caused several churches to break apart as some church members embraced, while others rejected, the new emotionalism. Yet some of these splinter groups were more tolerant of **dissent,** or difference of opinion, than the organizations from which they had split. This helped make religion in the colonies more democratic.

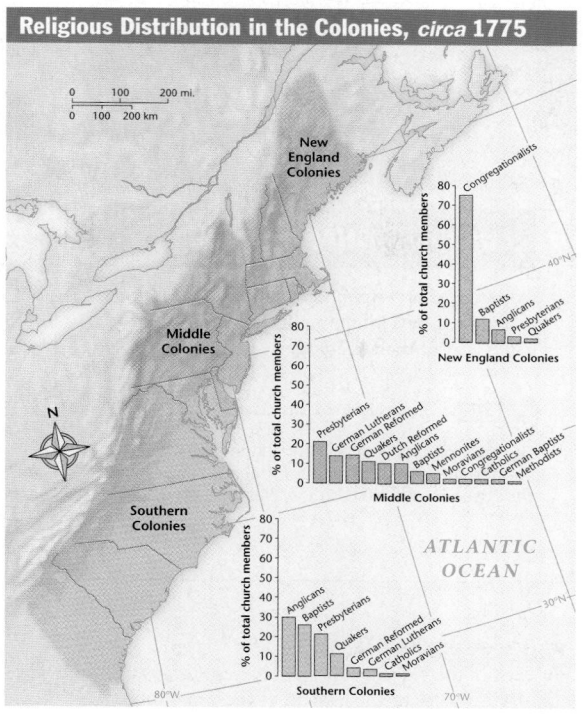

Religious Distribution in the Colonies, circa 1775

MAP SKILLS The colonies were home to members of several Protestant denominations, as well as small populations of Catholics and Jews. **Region** *In which region did a majority of colonists belong to the same Christian denomination?*

Section 4 Assessment

READING COMPREHENSION

1. What conditions in the colonies encouraged settlers to have large families and prompted **immigrants** to come to America?

2. How did the **Great Awakening** affect colonial churches?

3. Why was the Great Awakening an indirect challenge to the social order of the colonies?

CRITICAL THINKING AND WRITING

4. **Drawing Conclusions** Why was western Pennsylvania a likely hot spot for confrontation among the French, English, and Native Americans?

5. **Writing to Persuade** In your view, was it necessary for British colonists to expand westward in the mid-1700s? Write a short essay explaining your opinion. Support your ideas with specific examples.

Take It to the NET

Activity: Mapping History View historic maps from the 1600s and the 1700s online. Write a brief essay describing what the maps you have studied illustrate about this period of American history. Use the links provided in the *America: Pathways to the Present* area of the following Web site for help in completing this activity.
www.phschool.com

Section 4 Assessment

Reading Comprehension

1. Land was abundant, taxes were low, and people could marry and raise children earlier in life, in contrast to the poverty and overcrowding in England.

2. It brought about religious shifts, leading to the growth of the Methodist and Baptist churches, and the split of other denominations.

3. Ordinary people wondered: if they could question the authority of the ministers, could they not also question the stratified class structure in which they lived, or question the very authority exerted over them by the British government?

Critical Thinking and Writing

4. Because of the desire of settlers from the coastal colonies to move into the area around the strategically important forks of the Ohio River.

5. Answers will vary, but might expand on topics such as: In support of expansion—more land needed due to high birth rate and immigration; need to deter French. Against expansion—land already occupied by Native Americans and French; conflict thus inevitable.

Take It to the NET

Essays will vary, but should present observations of geographic shifts, such as those due to religion or westward expansion, and explain these changes using facts from the section.

CAPTION ANSWERS

Map Skills New England.

REVIEWING KEY TERMS

Students should refer to the definitions of key terms in the chapter to write sentences that show an understanding of the key aspects of the era characterized by the rapid growth of the American colonies.

REVIEWING MAIN IDEAS

13. Possible answers: Tradition of strong local government and weak central power; Great Britain lacked the resources to enforce its wishes overseas; most colonists recognized British authority without force; economy and politics of the colonies served Great Britain without needing much maintenance.

14. (a) agriculture. (b) commerce and agriculture. (c) long-distance carrying trade.

15. New Englanders shipped goods from England to the West Indies; transported sugar from the West Indies to New England to distill into rum; traded rum and firearms for slaves in West Africa; then carried the slaves to the West Indies for more sugar.

16. Cooking, gardening, washing, cleaning, weaving, and sewing; helping each other in childbirth; assisting in their respective husbands' work; training daughters in the traditional responsibilities of women.

17. Work was the central focus in most people's lives.

18. Slaves were forced to endure chains, oppressive heat, disease, and a lack of fresh air and sanitation.

19. Possible answers: They formed the majority of the population; most of them came directly from Africa; they had little contact with colonists; they created new kinship networks.

20. A rising birth rate and immigration caused population growth.

21. It encouraged them to speak for themselves and question the traditional authority of ministers, books, and ultimately of the existing political and social order.

creating a CHAPTER SUMMARY

Copy this chart (right) on a piece of paper and complete it by adding important events and issues that fit each heading.

 TEXT

For additional review and enrichment activities, see the interactive version of *America: Pathways to the Present*, available on the Web and on CD-ROM.

Section	Important Events
An Empire and Its Colonies	• During the English Civil War, the English government neglects the colonies. • After 1660, English mercantilist policies attempt to restrict colonial economies. •
Life in Colonial America	
African Americans in the Colonies	
Emerging Tensions	

★ Reviewing Key Terms

For each of the terms below, write a sentence explaining how it relates to the growth of the American colonies.

1. mercantilism
2. balance of trade
3. duty
4. salutary neglect
5. staple crop
6. triangular trade
7. gentry
8. indigo
9. Middle Passage
10. Stono Rebellion
11. Great Awakening
12. itinerant

★ Reviewing Main Ideas

13. Give three reasons why the British were able to neglect their colonies in the 1700s. (Section 1)

14. (a) What was the main economic activity in the Southern Colonies? (b) In the Middle Colonies? (c) In New England? (Section 1)

15. Describe the system of triangular trade used by New Englanders in the 1700s. (Section 1)

16. What duties did women perform in colonial America? (Section 2)

17. Describe the importance of work in colonial America. (Section 2)

18. Describe the conditions of the Middle Passage. (Section 3)

19. Give three reasons why slaves in South Carolina and Georgia were able to preserve many of their cultural traditions. (Section 3)

20. Why did the colonists feel pressure to expand westward in the mid-1700s? (Section 4)

21. Besides energizing religious feeling, what effect did the Great Awakening have on colonial people and society? (Section 4)

★ Critical Thinking

22. **Recognizing Ideologies**   Today many people consider it wrong for a nation to have colonies. How does this view of colonies contrast with the view held by the British in the late 1600s and early 1700s?

23. **Drawing Inferences**   Why was it necessary for colonial families to be mostly self-sufficient?

24. **Making Comparisons**   (a) Why was education viewed differently in New England and the Southern Colonies? (b) List four ways that education in the colonies differed from education today.

25. **Drawing Conclusions**   Why did the life of a slave differ in New England, the Middle Colonies, and the Southern Colonies?

26. **Distinguishing False From Accurate Images**   Would it be correct to state that colonial society was dominated by men? Explain your answer.

CREATING A CHAPTER SUMMARY

Section	Important Events
An Empire and Its Colonies	• During the English Civil War, the English goverment neglects the colonies. • After 1660, English mercantilist policies attempt to restrict colonial economies. • Attempts to assert royal control over the New England colonies angered the colonists. • Farming, trade, and settlement patterns defined the colonial economy.
Life in Colonial America	• Colonial society was established. • Gentry established themselves. • Specialized trades developed. • Colleges and universities were established.
African Americans in the Colonies	• Africans were kidnapped and sold into slavery. • African slaves contributed to the development of the colonial economy. • Free blacks were extremely poor.
Emerging Tensions	• As colonies grew in population, the movement to expand their area grew as well. • Native Americans and French fur trappers alike had strong reactions to the expansion of British colonies. • The Great Awakening resolved some and contributed to other religious tensions.

Severall young men playing at foote-ball on the Jce upon the LORDS-DAY are all Drownd

★ Skills Assessment

Analyzing Political Cartoons ▶

27. Examine this Puritan cartoon. (a) Describe the scene shown in the drawing. (b) What information does the caption add?

28. What is the message of the cartoon?

29. How is the message of the cartoon consistent with Puritan culture?

Analyzing Primary Sources

Turn to the quotation from Eliza Pinckney on p. 81.

30. How did Eliza Pinckney feel about her work on the plantations?

   A She thought it was too great a burden.

   B She was overwhelmed by the amount of writing involved.

   C She was happy and proud to be able to help her father.

   D She did not seem to like the work.

31. Why might Eliza Pinckney's friend have thought that the workload was too much for Eliza?

   F Eliza was in poor health.

   G It was rare for a girl to carry so much responsibility.

   H Most girls only managed one plantation at a time.

   J Eliza's letter complains about the amount of work.

32. **Writing** Write a brief letter responding to Eliza. You may want to comment on the amount of work she has taken on or ask about plantation life.

Applying the Chapter Skill:
Reviewing an Economic Activity Map

33. Review the economic activity map on page 76. Based on the crops you see listed, where do you think large-scale slavery existed?

ACTIVITIES

Writing to LEARN

Writing to Compare
Reread the section on diverse colonial economies that begins on page 74. Research and write an essay that describes the important economic activities in your region of the country today. What changes have there been in your region's economy in recent years?

Primary Source CD-ROM

Working With Primary Sources Find additional information on the growth of the American colonies on the *Exploring Primary Sources in U.S. History CD-ROM* and use the selection(s) provided to complete the Chapter 3 primary source activity located in the *America: Pathways to the Present* area of the following Web site. **www.phschool.com**

Take It to the NET

Chapter Self-Test As a review activity, take the Chapter 3 Self-Test in the *America: Pathways to the Present* area at the Web site listed below. The questions are designed to test your understanding of the chapter content. **www.phschool.com**

Chapter 3 Assessment 95

ANSWERS TO ACTIVITIES

Writing to LEARN

Answers will vary but should demonstrate an understanding of students' regional economy.

Primary Source CD-ROM

Direct students to the additional primary sources that can be found on the *Exploring Primary Sources in U.S. History CD-ROM.*

Take It to the NET

Additional support materials and activities for Chapter 3 of *America: Pathways to the Present* can be found in the Social Studies area at the Prentice Hall School Web site. **www.phschool.com**

CRITICAL THINKING

22. It is a direct contradiction. During the period 1650–1750, the British believed that nations should have colonies and should exploit them for wealth.

23. Families had to work very hard just to stay alive. In that context, being self-sufficient was very helpful in reducing expenses.

24. (a) Puritan settlers in New England established public schools primarily because they believed that everyone should be able to read the Bible. Residents of the Southern Colonies did not feel the same urgency, and wealthy southerners often hired private instructors to teach their children. (b) Lists may include: Girls did not attend school; grammar schools offered Greek and Latin; attendance was not required by law; colleges existed primarily to train ministers and lawyers; college tuition payments were more likely to be "in kind" rather than cash.

25. New England and the Middle Colonies had more diverse economies than did the Southern Colonies, creating different labor needs. Slaves in New England and the Middle Colonies worked on small farms or as domestic help; male slaves often worked in manufacturing or trading, or as skilled artisans. Slaves in the South worked as field hands on vast plantations.

26. Students who agree that men dominated society should provide examples from colonial laws and politics. Students who disagree should support their stance with examples of women's vital roles on the farm and in the community.

SKILLS ASSESSMENT

27. (a) Men are falling through ice into the frigid water of a pond while playing a game. (b) That the scene takes place on a Sunday.

28. The men are "treading on the thin ice" by playing a game on Sunday instead of going to church.

29. It shows how Puritan culture emphasized rules, punishment, and strict religious observation.

30. C

31. G

32. Possible answer: A letter reminding Eliza to be sure she gets enough rest, enquires after Eliza's ill mother, asks about the types of crops Eliza is growing; and asks Eliza whether she treats her slaves well.

33. Virginia, the Carolinas, and Georgia.

American Pathways
GEOGRAPHY

The Expansion of the United States

From its start as 13 former British colonies along the Atlantic Coast, the United States expanded steadily westward. Explorers, trappers, and settlers pushed across the Appalachian Mountains, the Great Plains, and the Rocky Mountains all the way to the Pacific Coast and beyond. Through more than a century of treaties, purchases, and warfare, the nation grew to its present size.

1 Establishing the Original States

1607–1776   In the 1600s and 1700s, a mix of English, Dutch, Swedes, Germans, enslaved Africans, and others settled in colonies along the Atlantic Coast. These colonies later united to seek their independence from Great Britain and establish a new nation.

E pluribus unum—"from many, one"—was chosen as the nation's motto in 1776 (right).

2 Crossing the Appalachians

1775–1830   As the population along the Atlantic Coast grew, Americans moved west to settle in the region between the Appalachian Mountains and the Mississippi River.

Covered wagons (left) carried settlers westward.

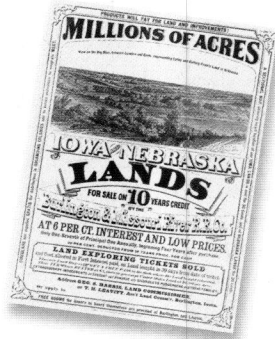

3 Moving Beyond the Mississippi

1803–1846   The Louisiana Purchase nearly doubled the size of the United States and gave Americans full control of the Mississippi River. Several groups explored the region in the early 1800s, but new settlements there remained sparse for many years. Most migrants who crossed the Mississippi in the mid-1800s had one goal in mind—reaching Oregon.

An advertisement for land in Iowa and Nebraska (above)

96

Map Legend:

- Proclamation of 1763
- Treaty of Paris, 1783
- Louisiana Purchase, 1803
- West Florida annexation, 1810, 1813
- East Florida ceded by Spain, 1819
- Ceded by Britain, 1818, 1842
- Texas annexation, 1845
- Oregon Country, 1846
- Ceded by Mexico, 1848
- Gadsden Purchase, 1853
- Purchased from Russia, 1867
- Annexed, 1898

Present-day state borders

American Pathways

Capturing Mexican Territory

1821–1853   During this period, Americans obtained Mexico's northern territories mainly through warfare. By 1853, they had established the boundaries of the continental United States as we now know them, fulfilling what many called the nation's "manifest destiny."

Acquiring Alaska and Hawaii

1867–1898   The United States expanded beyond its continental borders in the period following the Civil War, first with the purchase of Alaska in 1867 and later with the annexation of Hawaii in 1898.

A Hawaiian landscape (right)

Remaining a Mobile Society

1890–Present   Streams of settlers moving west reflected the mobility of American society. Even after the nation's frontier ceased to exist, Americans continued to migrate, usually in search of a better life.

Continuity and Change

1. What circumstances drove Americans to leave their homes and settle in new places?
2. **Map Skills** What lands were included in the Gadsden Purchase in 1853?

 Take It to the NET: Creating a Study Guide
Print and complete the study guide for this topic found in the *America: Pathways to the Present* area of the following Web site. **www.phschool.com**

97

Take It to the NET

Students can print the American Pathways thematic study guide for this topic at the Prentice Hall School Web site, or you can provide students with copies of the study guide, which is found in the Units 1/2 booklet, the American Pathways Activity, pages 36–37. Students should use their texts to fill in a one-sentence description for each event on the study guide. When completed for each of the American Pathways topics, the thematic study guides will aid students in preparing for an end-of-course exam.

ANSWERS

1. Answers will vary. Students may suggest that Americans left their homes in order to take advantage of new lands that became available as the nation expanded in size or to find jobs and a better quality of life.

2. The Gadsden Purchase included lands in southern New Mexico and southern Arizona.

Use this sample exam to help your students prepare for standardized tests.

TIPS FOR TEST TAKING

You might want to remind your students of the following:

1. Read the directions carefully.
2. Read each question carefully.
3. For multiple choice questions, try to answer the question before you look at the choices. Read all the choices. Then, eliminate those that are absolutely incorrect.
4. For short answer questions, be sure to answer the question completely if there is more than one part.
5. Answer the easy questions first. Then, go back to the ones that will take more time.
6. Pace yourself. Be sure to set aside enough time for the writing questions.

Write your answers on a separate sheet of paper.

1. How were Native Americans able to preserve their history, customs, and beliefs over long periods of time?

   A By writing on paper made from tree bark

   B By carving on stone pillars and cliffs

   C Through word of mouth from generation to generation

   D Through an elaborate archiving network

2. Which one of the following events led to an increase in European demand for goods from Asia?

   A The Crusades

   B The Norman Conquest

   C The Renaissance

   D The Reformation

3. Prince Henry the Navigator of Portugal is known for

   A having invented the compass.

   B having established a school for mariners.

   C having claimed all of South America for his country.

   D having been the first European to sail to India.

4. Which one of the following explorers conquered the Aztec empire?

   A Magellan

   B Balboa

   C Pizarro

   D Cortés

5. The economic success of the Jamestown colony was the result of the colonists' learning to grow

   A tobacco.

   B rice.

   C cotton.

   D indigo.

6. The economy of the French colony in North America was based on

   A gold.

   B furs.

   C ivory.

   D sugar.

> "For we must consider that we shall be as a city upon a hill."
>
> —John Winthrop

7. What is the meaning of the quotation?

   A The Puritans in Massachusetts were to be an example for the rest of the world.

   B All forts in Connecticut had to be built on high ground above the rivers.

   C Every colony should practice religious tolerance.

   D Puritan farmers were not permitted to live by themselves on their farms.

PRENTICE HALL
ASSESSMENT
SYSTEM

Diagnose and Prescribe
- Profile student skills with Diagnostic Tests A&B.
- Address student needs with program materials correlated to test questions.

Review and Reteach
- Provide cumulative content review with the Review Book.

Practice and Assess
- Build test-taking skills with Test-taking Strategies With Transparencies.

Use the chart and your knowledge of social studies to answer the following question.

Early American Colonies

- Connecticut
- Maryland
- Massachusetts Bay
- Plymouth
- Rhode Island

8. What common experience did all of these colonies share?

   A All had farming on plantations.

   B All had economies based on tobacco.

   C All were established for religious reasons.

   D All were created to block Spanish expansion.

9. The Middle Passage was

   A the northern water route from the Atlantic Ocean to the Pacific Ocean.

   B the all-weather road from Pennsylvania to New York.

   C the forced transport of slaves from Africa to North America.

   D the trade pattern between North America and Europe.

Use the information in the chart and your knowledge of social studies to answer the following question.

Population of Massachusetts Colony, Selected Years

Year	Population
1630	506
1650	14,037
1670	30,000
1690	49,504
1710	62,390
1730	114,116

SOURCE: *Historical Statistics of the United States*

10. Which one of the following is the reason for the trend shown in the table?

   A Immigration from Europe

   B Improved healthcare

   C Fewer wars and conflicts

   D Migration from Canada

11. Which religious group grew the most during the First Great Awakening?

   A The Quakers

   B The Episcopalians

   C The Baptists

   D The Catholics

Writing Practice

12. Explain the importance of lineage groups in West African societies.

13. Explain how the Columbian Exchange affected people in the Americas and in Europe.

14. Describe the Spanish system of *encomienda*.

1. C
2. A
3. B
4. D
5. A
6. B
7. A
8. C
9. C
10. A
11. C
12. Lineage groups in West Africa provided social organization and structure similar to that provided by modern governments and churches in the United States.
13. The Columbian Exchange brought European customs and technology to the Native Americans. It also brought devastating disease. To the Europeans, it brought new foods and great wealth from gold and silver mined in the Americas.
14. The *encomienda* system required Native Americans to work for the profit of a Spaniard, who was supposed to ensure their well-being in return.

Unit 2

Balancing Liberty and Order

(1753–1820)

INTRODUCING THE UNIT

Balancing Liberty and Order (1753–1820) The American Revolution was more than a war for independence. The struggle reflected the development of a unique American identity. After the war, a group of powerful men succeeded in writing and winning approval of the federal Constitution and established a strong central government. In the years following, leaders fought passionately over the shape of the new government.

USING HISTORICAL EVIDENCE

Direct students' attention to the painting on these pages. It depicts George Washington presiding over the Constitutional Convention held in Philadelphia, Pennsylvania, between May and September 1787. Discuss with students the fact that in the chaotic years following the American Revolution, the establishment of the United States was by no means certain. In 1783 Washington declared, "something must be done, or the fabric must fall, for it is certainly tottering." He urged a meeting to review and revise the country's original Articles of Confederation.

Though he sought a way to retire from public life, Washington was unanimously declared the leader of the meeting. He barely spoke during the meetings, but his conviction and his courage spoke more than his words. Shortly after the convention, he was chosen to be the first President of the United States, an honor he never sought, but a responsibility that he discharged with his customary sense of duty. Discuss with students Washington's urgent desire to see the establishment of a stable, unified country and his desire to return to a private life.

eTeach

Be sure to check out this month's online discussion with a Master Teacher. Go to **www.phschool.com**.

"We hold these truths to be self-evident, that all men are created equal, that they are endowed by their creator with certain unalienable rights, that among these are life, liberty, and the pursuit of happiness."

Declaration of Independence
July 4, 1776

This painting by Howard Chandler Christy shows George Washington presiding over the Constitutional Convention in Philadelphia, Pennsylvania, in 1787. ▶

100

RESOURCE DIRECTORY

Teaching Resources
Units 1/2 booklet
- American Pathways Activity, pp. 75–76
- History's Lasting Impact, pp. 77–78
Geography and History booklet, pp. 4–5

Other Print Resources
Prentice Hall Assessment System
- Document-Based Assessment

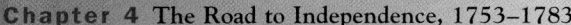

101

RESOURCE DIRECTORY

Technology

Color Transparencies *Historical Maps,* A6, A7, A8, A9, A10, A11, A12, A55, A60; *Political Cartoons,* B2, B3; *Time Lines,* C2; *Cause-and-Effect Charts,* D2; *Fine Art,* E4, E5

Section Reading Support Transparencies

Prentice Hall United States History Video Collection™ Volume 4, *The American Revolution;* Volume 5, *A New Nation (1776–1815);* Volume 6, *Expansionism*

Companion Web site, www.phschool.com

TECHNOLOGY CENTER

Take It to the NET

Prentice Hall School Web site offers student-appropriate Internet activities and links that extend core content. Visit us at the Social Studies area. **www.phschool.com**

AmericanHeritage®

My Brush with History™ Video Program This new video series lets your students learn history from the people who lived it.

RESOURCE●PRO®

Teaching Resources on CD-ROM offer lesson-planning flexibility, test-generation capability, and resource manageability.

- **PRESENTATION PRO CD-ROM** Provides you with multimedia lecture notes for each chapter.

- **SOCIAL STUDIES SKILLS TUTOR CD-ROM** Provides interactive practice in Geographic Literacy, Critical Thinking and Reading, Visual Analysis, and Communications.

- **Interactive Constitution CD-ROM** Exploring active citizenship and civic responsibilities, this CD-ROM shows students how the Constitution affects their lives today.

- **EXPLORING PRIMARY SOURCES IN U.S. HISTORY CD-ROM** This interactive exploration of primary sources allows students to analyze and evaluate writing and images from American history.

- **GUIDED READING AUDIOTAPES**

- **STUDENT EDITION ON AUDIO CD**

- **SOUNDS OF AN ERA AUDIO CD** Bring the sounds of American history to life in the classroom with music, speeches, poetry, interviews, and news reports.

iTEXT

Don't miss the exclusive interactive version of this textbook on the Web and on CD-ROM.

Chapter 4 Planning Guide
Resource Manager

	CORE INSTRUCTION	READING/SKILLS
Chapter-Level Resources	**Teaching Resources** • Pacing Charts booklet • Block Scheduling booklet **Resource Pro® CD-ROM**, Ch. 4 **Prentice Hall Presentation Pro CD-ROM**, Ch. 4 **www.phschool.com** • eTeach	**Guided Reading Audiotapes (English/Spanish)** **Student Edition on Audio CD**, Ch. 4 **Social Studies Skills Tutor CD-ROM** **Color Transparencies**, A6, A7, A60, C2, D2, E4, E5
1 The French and Indian War 1. Learn about the causes of the French and Indian War. 2. Find out how the British won the French and Indian War. 3. See how war weakened the colonists' loyalty to Britain.	**Teaching Resources** **Units 1/2 booklet** • Section 1 Quiz, p. 41	**Guided Reading and Review booklet,** p. 15 **Guide to the Essentials**, p. 20 **Learning with Documents booklet,** p. 9 **Section Reading Support Transparencies**
2 Issues Behind the Revolution 1. See how and why British policies in the colonies changed after 1763. 2. Learn about the causes and effects of the Stamp Act. 3. Discover how rising tensions in the colonies led to fighting at Lexington and Concord.	**Teaching Resources** **Units 1/2 booklet** • Section 2 Quiz, p. 42	**Guided Reading and Review booklet,** p. 16 **Guide to the Essentials**, p. 21 **Learning with Documents booklet,** p. 43 **Skills for Life booklet**, p. 6 **Section Reading Support Transparencies**
3 Ideas Behind the Revolution 1. Find out about the importance of Thomas Paine's *Common Sense*. 2. See what ideas and arguments are presented in the Declaration of Independence. 3. Learn more about the advice Abigail Adams gave her husband regarding the Declaration.	**Teaching Resources** **Units 1/2 booklet** • Section 3 Quiz, p. 43 **Learning Styles Lesson Plans booklet,** p. 10	**Guided Reading and Review booklet,** p. 17 **Guide to the Essentials**, p. 22 **Learning with Documents booklet,** p. 76 **Section Reading Support Transparencies**
4 Fighting for Independence 1. Discover what happened during the siege of Boston. 2. Find out about the strengths and weaknesses of the British and American forces. 3. See why the Battle of Saratoga was considered a turning point of the war.	**Teaching Resources** **Units 1/2 booklet** • Section 4 Quiz, p. 44 **Learning Styles Lesson Plans booklet,** p. 11	**Guided Reading and Review booklet,** p. 18 **Guide to the Essentials**, p. 23 **Section Reading Support Transparencies**
5 Winning Independence 1. Learn about hardships endured by Americans during the war. 2. See how American victories in the West and South led to an end of the war. 3. Discover the impact of the American Revolution.	**Teaching Resources** **Units 1/2 booklet** • Section 5 Quiz, p. 45	**Guided Reading and Review booklet,** p. 19 **Guide to the Essentials**, p. 24 **Section Reading Support Transparencies**

ENRICHMENT/PRE-AP

Prentice Hall United States History Video Collection™
www.phschool.com
• Section Activities, Virtual Field Trip, Chapter Activities, Current Events Online

Biography, Literature, and Comparing Primary Sources booklet, p. 43
Nystrom *Atlas of Our Country,* pp. 14–15
Historical Outline Map Book, p. 21

American History Block Scheduling Support
Historical Outline Map Book, pp. 22, 23, 24
Sounds of an Era Audio CD
Exploring Primary Sources in U.S. History CD-ROM

Biography, Literature, and Comparing Primary Sources booklet, p. 103
Sounds of an Era Audio CD
Exploring Primary Sources in U.S. History CD-ROM

Historical Outline Map Book, p. 25
Sounds of an Era Audio CD

Biography, Literature, and Comparing Primary Sources booklet, p. 9
Historical Outline Map Book, pp. 26, 27, 28
Sounds of an Era Audio CD
American Pathways Thematic Posters

ASSESSMENT

PRENTICE HALL
ASSESSMENT
SYSTEM

Core Assessment
ExamView® Test Bank, Ch. 4
ExamView® Test Bank CD-ROM, Ch. 4

Standardized Test Preparation
Diagnose and Prescribe
Diagnostic Tests for High School Social Studies Skills

Review and Reteach
Review Book for U.S. History

Practice and Assess
Test-taking Strategies With Transparencies
Test-taking Strategies Posters
Test Prep Book for U.S. History
Alternative Assessment Handbook
Document-Based Assessment

Teaching Resources
Units 1/2 booklet
• Section Quizzes, pp. 41–45
• Chapter Tests, pp. 46, 49
www.phschool.com Ch. 4 Self-Test

AmericanHeritage RESOURCES

From the Archives of American Heritage®, p. 47
AmericanHeritage® My Brush with History™ Videotapes
www.americanheritage.com

Don't miss the exclusive interactive version of this textbook on the Web and on CD-ROM.

Chapter 4 Planning Guide
In Your Classroom

CUSTOMIZE FOR INDIVIDUAL NEEDS

Gifted and Talented

Teacher's Edition
- Customize for Gifted and Talented, pp. 115, 124, 129

Teaching Resources
- Biography, Literature, and Comparing Primary Sources booklet, pp. 9, 43, 103

Technology
- Exploring Primary Sources in U.S. History CD-ROM *The Bloody Massacre, 1770; War is Inevitable—and Let it Come! Patrick Henry; Common Sense, Thomas Paine; The New American Man, Michel-Guillaume Jean de Crevecoeur; Correspondence on the Progress of the Revolution, Abigail and John Adams; Join, or Die; Declaration of Independence*

ESL

Teacher's Edition
- Customize for ESL, pp. 105, 124, 135

Teaching Resources
- Guided Reading and Review booklet, pp. 15–19
- Guide to the Essentials (English/Spanish), Chapter 4

Technology
- Student Edition on Audio CD, Chapter 4
- Guided Reading Audiotapes (English/Spanish), Chapter 4
- Section Reading Support Transparencies

Less Proficient Readers

Teacher's Edition
- Customize for Less Proficient Readers, pp. 111, 124

Teaching Resources
- Guided Reading and Review booklet, pp. 15–19
- Guide to the Essentials (English/Spanish), Chapter 4

Technology
- Student Edition on Audio CD, Chapter 4
- Guided Reading Audiotapes (English/Spanish), Chapter 4
- Section Reading Support Transparencies

Less Proficient Writers

Teacher's Edition
- Customize for Less Proficient Writers, pp. 121, 124

Teaching Resources
- Guided Reading and Review booklet, pp. 15–19
- Guide to the Essentials (English/Spanish), Chapter 4

Technology
- Student Edition on Audio CD, Chapter 4
- Guided Reading Audiotapes (English/Spanish), Chapter 4
- Section Reading Support Transparencies

TEACHER'S EDITION INDEX

CHAPTER 4 – PACING SUGGESTIONS

 For 90-minute Blocks
- Teach sections 2 and 4 using Transparencies A6, A7, A60, C2, D2, E4, and E5, and the Recent Scholarship note on page 121 for class discussions.

 Running Out of Time?

If you are running short on time to cover this chapter, consider the following options:

- Use the Prentice Hall Presentation Pro CD-ROM to create an outline for this chapter.

- Use the Section Summaries for Chapter 4, from **Guide to the Essentials (English/Spanish).**

1 **The French and Indian War**	**Connecting with History and Conflict** Have students construct annotated time lines of the major developments and results of the French and Indian War. **(Visual/Spatial)**	
2 **Issues Behind the Revolution**	**Connecting with History and Conflict** Direct students to list the major issues that lay behind the American Revolution. Then challenge them to rank those issues in order of importance, using their own criteria and explaining the reasons behind their rankings. **(Logical/Mathematical)**	
3 **Ideas Behind the Revolution**	**Connecting with Culture** Assign students the roles of spokespeople that represent the sources of ideas behind the American Revolution (*Common Sense,* Ancient Greek democracy, various English documents, and so on). Students should prepare brief speeches (about one minute) that summarize the ideas they represent. Have these students plan and present a brief panel or play-like presentation for the rest of the class. **(Bodily/Kinesthetic)**	
4 **Fighting for Independence**	**Connecting with Culture** Invite students to present a brief program, "Music of the Revolutionary Period," for the class. The program can include vocal and instrumental performances. Songs to consider include "Yankee Doodle" and "The World Turned Upside Down." Students should introduce each song with an explanation of its historical importance. **(Rhythmic/Musical)**	
5 **Winning Independence**	**Connecting with History and Conflict** Have students write summaries of the section using the major headings in their textbooks as the basis for paragraph topic sentences. **(Verbal/Linguistic)**	

Chapter 4

The Road to Independence

(1753–1783)

INTRODUCING THE CHAPTER

The American Revolution was more than a war for independence. The struggle reflected the development of a unique American identity that was fueled by colonists' personal definition of democracy and equality. This new consciousness inspired a war that led to independence from Great Britain and the creation of a radically new society.

TIME LINE ACTIVITY

To provide students with practice in using the time line, ask questions such as these:

1. What 1763 action led to the end of French Power in America? *(The Treaty of Paris)*

2. When did Catherine the Great become empress of Russia? *(1762)*

3. In what year did France and the United States sign a treaty of alliance? *(1778)*

Chapter 4

The Road to Independence
(1753–1783)

SECTION 1   The French and Indian War
SECTION 2   Issues Behind the Revolution
SECTION 3   Ideas Behind the Revolution
SECTION 4   Fighting for Independence
SECTION 5   Winning Independence

The Battle of Rogers Rock by Jean Leon Gerome Ferris

1754
The French and Indian War begins.

1763
The Treaty of Paris (1763) ends French power in North America. Britain's Proclamation of 1763 prohibits colonists from settling west of the Appalachian Mountains.

1765
The Stamp Act Congress sends the Declaration of Rights and Grievances to the king.

American Events

Presidential Terms:

| 1750 | • | 1760 | • • | 1770 |

World Events

George III becomes king of England.
1760

Catherine the Great becomes empress of Russia.
1762

eTeach

Be sure to check out this month's online discussion with a Master Teacher. Go to **www.phschool.com**.

RESOURCE DIRECTORY

Teaching Resources
Pacing Charts booklet
Block Scheduling booklet, p. 15
Units 1/2 booklet
 • Chapter Summary, p. 40

Technology
Guided Reading Audiotapes (English/Spanish), Ch. 4
Student Edition on Audio CD, Ch. 4
Prentice Hall United States History Video Collection™ Volume 4, *The American Revolution*
Color Transparencies *Historical Maps*, A6
Prentice Hall Presentation Pro CD-ROM, Ch. 4
Resource Pro® CD-ROM
Social Studies Skills Tutor CD-ROM
Companion Web site, www.phschool.com

British North America, 1763

Ojibwa
Menominee
Winnebago
Ottawa
Wyandot
Iroquois
Ohio Country
Illinois
Delaware
Miami
Shawnee
Watauga Settlements
Cherokee
Chickasaw
Creek
Choctaw

British Colonies

Mississippi River
Missouri River
Ohio River
St. Lawrence River

ATLANTIC OCEAN
Gulf of Mexico

N

40°N
70°W
30°N
90°W
80°
150
300 mi.
0
150
300 km

- British North America after 1763
- Areas settled by 1775
- Spanish territory
- Proclamation Line of 1763
- *Creek* Native American tribe

On their way to the Battle of Trenton, George Washington and his troops crossed the icy Delaware River.

A bronze relief commemorates the signing of the Treaty of Paris (1783).

1775
Battles at Lexington and Concord, Massachusetts, mark the beginning of the American Revolution.

1776
The Second Continental Congress issues the Declaration of Independence.

1781
The British surrender to the Americans at Yorktown.

1783
The Treaty of Paris (1783) formally ends the war and recognizes the United States as an independent nation.

George Washington 1789–1797

1780 • 1790

France and the United States sign a treaty of alliance.
1778

Emperor Joseph II of Austria initiates reforms based on Enlightenment ideas.
1781

Chapter 4   103

British North America, 1763

Activating Prior Knowledge
Explain the lack of French territories in North America after 1763. *(Because the French lost the French and Indian War, North American land east of the Mississippi River fell completely under British control.)*

Previewing Ask students what they think were the results of the proclamation of 1763. *(Though the Proclamation of 1763 was meant to prevent the colonists from settling west of the Appalachian Mountains, they continued to move into the land designated for the Native Americans, undermining the authority of the British government.)*

BACKGROUND
About the Pictures

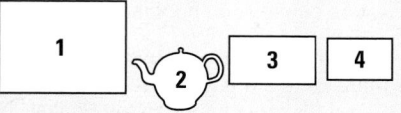

1. The French and Indian War began as a dispute between France and Great Britain over who would control the upper Ohio River valley.

2. Disgruntled colonists illustrated their outrage by rioting, burning stamps, threatening stamp distributors, and ignoring the stamps altogether.

3. Washington and about 2,400 of his men crossed the Delaware to surprise British troops on Christmas night of 1776.

4. The Treaty of Paris was an agreement made between Great Britain, France, Spain, and the United States. Attending representatives for the United States were John Adams, Benjamin Franklin, John Jay, and Henry Laurens.

Don't miss the exclusive interactive version of this textbook on the Web and on CD-ROM.

BIBLIOGRAPHY

For the Teacher

McCullough, David. *John Adams.* Simon & Schuster, 2001. (The definitive biography.)

Paine, Thomas. *Collected Writings: Common Sense/The Crisis/Rights of Man/The Age of Reason/Pamphlets, Articles, and Letters.* Library of America, 1995. (Some of the most important writings on the Revolutionary Era.)

Raphael, Ray. *A People's History of the American Revolution: How Common People Shaped the Fight for Independence (New Press People's History Series).* New Press, 2001. (A collection of the experiences of ordinary people.)

For the Student

Legguth, A. J. *Patriots: The Men Who Started the American Revolution.* Touchstone Books, 1989. (Well-illustrated biographical sketches.)

Meltzer, Milton. *The American Revolutionaries: A History in Their Own Words.* HarperTrophy, 1993. (Includes an exchange of letters between Abigail and John Adams.)

Washington, George. *George Washington's Rules of Civility and Decent Behavior in Company and Conversation (Little Books of Wisdom).* Applewood, 1994. (A compilation of sayings, many surprisingly timeless.)

Section 1

The French and Indian War

1. Learn about the causes of the French and Indian War.
2. Find out how the British won the French and Indian War.
3. See how war weakened the colonists' loyalty to Britain.

BELLRINGER

Warm-Up Activity Ask students to explain why relationships between teenagers and their parents are often difficult. Tell students this is similar to the colonies and Britain. What types of issues cause such conflict?

Activating Prior Knowledge Ask students to state what they know about the relationship between the English colonists and the Native Americans, and the relationship between French colonists and Native Americans, prior to the French and Indian War.

READING STRATEGY

As students read the section, have them create a graphic organizer showing the causes and effects of the French and Indian War.

ACTIVITY
Connecting with History and Conflict

This activity may take place over several class periods. Divide the class into groups of six to eight students. In order to show how the French and Indian War brought the British and the colonists into contact with one another, have students enact a discussion in a tavern on a given topic from the viewpoint of either British soldiers or colonists. Possible topics include life in the colonies, British mercantile policy, or the French and Indian War. **(Verbal/Linguistic)**

READING FOCUS

- What were the causes of the French and Indian War?
- How did the British win the French and Indian War?
- How did the war weaken the colonists' loyalty to Britain?

MAIN IDEA

The war that the colonists fought against the French and Indians caused them to rethink their relationship with Britain.

KEY TERMS

French and Indian War
Albany Plan of Union
militia
prime minister
siege
Treaty of Paris (1763)

TAKING NOTES

Copy the diagram below. As you read, fill in the causes and effects of the French and Indian War.

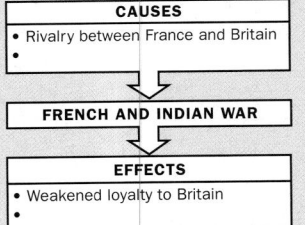

CAUSES
• Rivalry between France and Britain
•

⬇

FRENCH AND INDIAN WAR

⬇

EFFECTS
• Weakened loyalty to Britain
•

Setting the Scene In May 1754, a small force of British colonists ambushed a French scouting party in western Pennsylvania. Their 22-year-old commander, George Washington, described the incident:

> 66 *I fortunately escaped without wound, for the right wing, where I stood, was exposed to and received all the enemy's fire. . . . I heard the bullets whistle, and, believe me there is something charming in the sound.* 99
> —George Washington

Washington and his troops built a stronghold in the region and named it Fort Necessity. There they waited for the French to try to retake the Ohio Valley, which both Britain and France claimed. The French, who far outnumbered the British, soon surrounded the fort and forced a surrender. The colonists returned to Virginia defeated and disgraced. It was not a good start for their young commander. One day, however, his leadership both on and off the battlefield would make him a hero.

Causes of War

George Washington's unsuccessful expedition into western Pennsylvania was the first minor battle of a war that lasted until 1763. It was called the **French and Indian War** because the British and their American colonists waged it against the French and their Indian allies. This nine-year conflict was the final chapter in a long struggle among the French, the British, and various groups of Native Americans for control of eastern North America.

Rivalry Between Britain and France The rivalry among European nations for control of North America arose soon after they began to explore and colonize the continent. While English colonists built their settlements along the eastern seacoast during the 1600s, the French explored farther inland: along the St. Lawrence River, the Great Lakes, and the Mississippi River. As a result of these explorations, the French claimed a vast region stretching from the Appalachian Mountains in the east to the Rocky Mountains in the west. Conflict

This horn, used in the French and Indian War, served both as a container for gunpowder and as a map of wilderness forts.

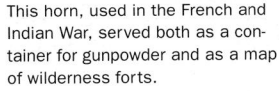

RESOURCE DIRECTORY

Teaching Resources
Guided Reading and Review booklet, p. 15

Other Print Resources
Historical Outline Map Book *The French and Indian War,* p. 21

Technology
Section Reading Support Transparencies
Guided Reading Audiotapes (English/Spanish), Ch. 4
Student Edition on Audio CD, Ch. 4
Prentice Hall Presentation Pro CD-ROM, Ch. 4
Social Studies Skills Tutor CD-ROM
Companion Web site, www.phschool.com

arose because the English claimed some of this territory as well—that of the upper Ohio River valley.

British and French colonization of North America followed different patterns. British settlers founded towns and cleared land for planting crops, while French colonists established forts to protect their land claims. The French forts also served as centers for trade with Native Americans. Because of these differences, the French fared better in their interactions with Native Americans than did the British. In 1718, the lieutenant governor of Virginia noted the French threat in a report to his superiors in England:

> 66 By . . . the forts [the French] have already built, the British Plantations [settlements] are in a manner Surrounded by [French] Commerce with the numerous Nations of Indians. . . . [The French] may, when they please, send out such Bodys of Indians on the back [outskirts] of these Plantations as may greatly distress [threaten] his Majesty's Subjects here. 99
>
> —Alexander Spotswood, lieutenant governor of Virginia

Beginning in the late 1600s, Great Britain and France were frequently at war with each other. It was often the case that when the English and French battled in Europe, their colonists would also fight in America. Increasingly, however, these conflicts focused on the rivalry in North America. The last of them, the French and Indian War, actually started in the colonies and spread to Europe, where it was called the Seven Years' War.

The Albany Plan of Union   In June 1754, while George Washington and his small force were holding out at Fort Necessity, a meeting of delegates from seven northern colonies convened in Albany, New York. The delegates hoped to strengthen ties with the Iroquois League, a Native American alliance you read of in an earlier chapter. British officials saw the powerful Iroquois as important potential allies.

Another reason for the Albany meeting was to work out a unified war effort in the northern colonies. With this in mind Benjamin Franklin, a Pennsylvania delegate, offered an ambitious plan for a permanent union of the colonies. Named the **Albany Plan of Union,** it called for a grand council of delegates from each colony, all elected by their colonial legislatures. Heading the council would be a president general, appointed by the British crown. Franklin believed that just as the Iroquois nation had strengthened itself by forming the Iroquois League, the British colonies would benefit from greater unity.

Although the delegates approved Franklin's plan, the colonial legislatures rejected it. They were unwilling to surrender that much power to a central government. The Albany Plan of Union is important, however, because it provided a model for the later government of the United States.

Early British Defeats   At first, the French and Indian War went poorly for the British. Although badly outnumbered, the French and their Native American allies won important victories. The most impressive of these victories—such as the one at Fort Necessity—took place in the forests of western Pennsylvania. On July 9, 1755, about 900 French and Native Americans surprised a force of nearly 1,500 British troops and 450 colonial **militia,** armed citizens who serve as soldiers during an emergency.

The British, more often than the French, tended to fight in the open and in straight lines, as was common in Europe. They were no match for an enemy

In 1754, Benjamin Franklin proposed a plan that he hoped would unite and strengthen the colonies.

106 • Chapter 4   Section 1

Connecting with History and Conflict

Ask students to research one of the major battles of the French and Indian War, such as those at Fort Duquesne, Fort Niagara, Fort Necessity, or Fort Ticonderoga. Have students diagram the battle they study. **(Visual/Spatial)**

BACKGROUND

Art History

The 1759 capture of Quebec inspired Benjamin West's 1771 painting *The Death of General Wolfe.* While European soldiers were usually painted in Roman togas and armor, West's subjects wore contemporary British uniforms, and the artist included a pensive Indian crouching at Wolfe's feet. King George III complained, but West replied that modern clothing was an appropriate choice "in a region of the world unknown to the Greeks and Romans."

READING CHECK

The French, the British, and various groups of Native Americans engaged in the struggle for control of eastern North America.

READING CHECK

Who was involved in the French and Indian War, and what was the conflict about?

MAP SKILLS The three main thrusts of British strategy are shown here. In 1758, British forces struck in two directions— at French strongholds in the west and against Louisbourg in the east. Finally, in 1759, they attacked Quebec and Montreal. **Movement** *Why was it necessary to capture Louisbourg before attacking Quebec?*

---

who hid behind rocks and trees, as did the Native Americans, and in this case, the French. In the fierce three-hour battle, about a third of the British force were killed or wounded. Among those killed was the British commander, General Edward Braddock. "We shall better know how to deal with them another time," Braddock is reported to have said of the French as he died.

Among the colonists who survived was wagon driver Daniel Boone, who later became known for his exploits on the Kentucky frontier. Another survivor was Braddock's aide, George Washington, who had had two horses killed under him and ended the battle with four bullet holes in his coat. Washington, who organized the British retreat, later reported that the colonists had shown "a great deal of Bravery" in the battle. He complained, though, that the colonists had been "exposed to almost certain death" during the fighting because of the "dastardly behavior" of the British soldiers, who ran away like "Sheep pursued by dogs."

The British Win the War

In 1756, Great Britain formally declared war on France. Fighting spread to Europe and Asia, but the British suffered defeats there, too, as they had in America.

In 1757, William Pitt became Britain's **prime minister,** the highest official of a parliamentary government. Believing that the entire British Empire could be at stake, Pitt persuaded Parliament to raise taxes and borrow large sums of money to fight the war.

The Tide of War Turns   Pitt's efforts soon paid off. In 1758, better-prepared and better-led British troops began to overwhelm French and Indian forces in western Pennsylvania and New France, or present-day Canada. They first attacked the long line of forts and settlements that the French had built. British forces seized Louisbourg, an important, strategically located French fortress on the Gulf

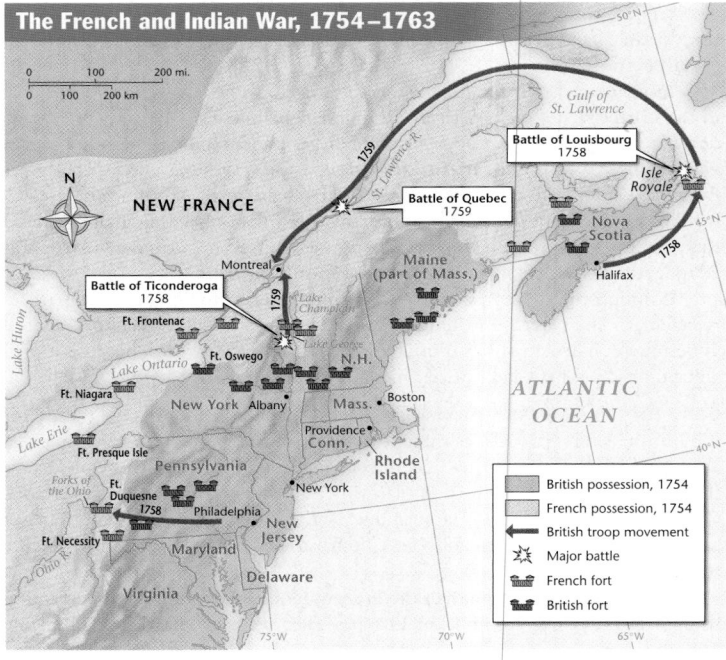

The French and Indian War, 1754–1763

CAPTION ANSWERS

Map Skills To gain access to the St. Lawrence River.

RESOURCE DIRECTORY

Teaching Resources
Learning with Documents booklet (Primary Source Activity) *Braddock's Defeat,* p. 9
Biography, Literature, and Comparing Primary Sources booklet (Literature) *Laying Siege to Quebec,* p. 43

Other Print Resources
Nystrom *Atlas of Our Country* *Colonies in the North and East,* pp. 14–15

VIEWING FINE ART *The Death of General Wolfe* by American painter Benjamin West dramatically portrays the British leader's last moments in the battle for Quebec. **Analyzing Information** *Why was Quebec so difficult and so important to capture?*

of St. Lawrence. Later in 1758, they captured Fort Duquesne in Pennsylvania. In 1759, British troops took Fort Niagara.

The British victories put the French on the defensive. They abandoned their forts in New York and retreated into New France. The Iroquois, who had cleverly been playing each side against the other, now decided that the French cause was hopeless. They began to support the British actively.

The Fall of Quebec   In the late spring of 1759, the British began a campaign to invade New France and capture Quebec, the capital of New France. The city sits high on the cliffs overlooking the St. Lawrence River. General James Wolfe commanded an attacking force of about 9,000 British troops. Some 7,500 French troops, led by the Marquis de Montcalm, successfully defended Quebec.

After suffering heavy losses in a direct attack in July 1759, Wolfe settled down to a **siege** of the city. During a siege, an enemy force is surrounded; trapped and without access to fresh supplies, the enemy is starved into surrendering. Wolfe had only limited time for the siege to work, however. The British warships that supported his army needed to withdraw from the river as winter approached. By September, he was ready to try a daring tactic.

On the night of September 12, Wolfe began moving his troops up a narrow, undefended path on the side of Quebec's cliffs. By dawn about 4,500 British troops were in position to threaten the French defenders of the city. Without waiting for some 3,000 reinforcements to arrive, Montcalm moved roughly 4,500 troops out of the city to battle the enemy. The British turned back his attack, inflicting heavy losses on the French. Both Wolfe and Montcalm were killed in the fighting. A few days later, the city surrendered.

With the fall of Quebec, the war was nearly over. The following September, British forces took the city of Montreal, giving Great Britain control over all of New France. By 1761, the British had seized Fort Detroit and other French posts along the Great Lakes.

The Treaty of Paris   In 1763, representatives of Great Britain, France, and France's ally Spain signed a

This engraving shows celebrations following the signing of the Treaty of Paris (1763).

Reading Comprehension

1. Conflict between France and Britain over territory in North America; British fears of the relationship between the French and Native Americans. The Albany Plan of Union was intended to assist the colonists in the French and Indian War by creating an alliance with the powerful Iroquois and by fostering a greater unity among British colonies.

2. Armed citizens who served as soldiers during an emergency.

3. The highest official of a parliamentary government.

4. British troops led by General James Wolfe carried out a daring and strategic siege of Quebec. Wolfe's forces inflicted heavy losses on the French, forcing the French to surrender the city.

Critical Thinking and Writing

5. The treaty that ended the French and Indian War. As a result of this treaty, France turned Canada over to the British and surrendered its claim to all lands east of the Mississippi River. New Orleans became a Spanish possession. The British returned Cuba to Spain in exchange for Florida.

6. Students' essays will vary, but should point out that Pitt believed the future of the British Empire was at stake and that drastic measures were necessary in order to retrieve the situation.

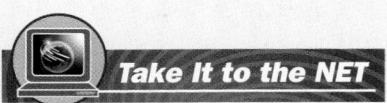
Take It to the NET

Essays should clearly and concisely analyze the primary source examined.

CAPTION ANSWERS

Viewing History Colonists lost respect for British military power and thought their military tactics to be weak. Also, they felt the British did not share the same values as Americans and that the British had not treated the colonists with respect.

VIEWING HISTORY British soldiers and colonial militia stormed Fort Ticonderoga and captured it from the French. **Drawing Conclusions** *What general impressions did the Americans have of the British after the French and Indian War?*

treaty in Paris, France. The **Treaty of Paris (1763)** ended the French and Indian War in America and the Seven Years' War in Europe. In the treaty, France turned present-day Canada over to Britain and surrendered its claim to all lands east of the Mississippi River. The only exception was the city of New Orleans, which France had given to Spain in a secret treaty the year before. The British returned Cuba, which they had captured during the war, to Spain in exchange for Florida.

Weakened Loyalty to Britain

Despite the victory, the French and Indian War seriously strained relations between the British and the American colonists. The British thought the colonists had not provided enough support for the long and costly war that Britain had fought to protect them.

For their part, the Americans had been shocked by the weakness of British military tactics. The Americans had demanded to be led by colonial officers, something the British viewed as treason. One militiaman expressed amazement at the orders of his British commander during the battle for Fort Ticonderoga:

> 66 The . . . roar of [muskets] terrified me. . . . Our regiment formed among the trees, behind which the men kept stepping from their ranks for shelter. Colonel Preble . . . swore he would knock the first man down who should step out of his ranks, which greatly surprised me, to think that I must stand still to be shot at. 99
>
> —Massachusetts militiaman

The end of the war left many colonists with two strong impressions. First, they felt a loss of respect for British military power. And second, they believed that the British did not treat them with the proper respect, and that they did not hold the same values as the colonists. Now that the French no longer controlled Canada or the region west of the Appalachian Mountains, the colonists saw no reason why they should not expand and prosper on their own, without British help. These feelings would soon combine with events to expand the rift between Britain and its colonies.

Section 1 Assessment

READING COMPREHENSION

1. What led to the **French and Indian War?** How was the **Albany Plan of Union** meant to assist the colonists in that war?

2. What are **militia?**

3. What is a **prime minister?**

4. Describe the **siege** of Quebec in 1759.

CRITICAL THINKING AND WRITING

5. **Drawing Conclusions** What was the Treaty of Paris (1763)? Why was it significant?

6. **Writing to Persuade** Write an outline for a speech by William Pitt persuading Parliament to raise taxes and borrow money to fight a war in North America.

Take It to the NET

Activity: Analyzing Primary Sources Examine documents from the French and Indian War. Summarize your research in an essay describing one of the documents you've studied. Use the links provided in the *America: Pathways to the Present* area of the following Web site for help in completing this activity.
www.phschool.com

RESOURCE DIRECTORY

Teaching Resources
Units 1/2 booklet
• Section 1 Quiz, p. 41
Guide to the Essentials
• Section 1 Summary, p. 20

Issues Behind the Revolution

READING FOCUS

- How and why did British policies in the colonies change after 1763?
- What were the causes and effects of the Stamp Act?
- How did rising tensions in the colonies lead to fighting at Lexington and Concord?

MAIN IDEA

The colonists, believing they should not be taxed without representation, protested new British laws.

KEY TERMS

Pontiac's Rebellion
Proclamation of 1763
Stamp Act
boycott
Boston Massacre
First Continental Congress
Battles of Lexington and Concord
Revolutionary War

TAKING NOTES

Copy the outline below. As you read, fill the outline with details from the chapter.

> I. Issues Behind the Revolution
>   A. Changing British policy
>   1. Proclamation of 1763
>   2. _____
>   B. Stamp Act crisis
>   1. _____
>   2. _____

Setting the Scene George III became king of England in 1760 upon the death of his grandfather, King George II. At age 22, George III was very young to assume the leadership of an empire. The new king had promised a quick end to the long and expensive war with France, which was accomplished in the Treaty of Paris of 1763. The British government's problems in North America were far from over, however.

Britain's attempts to control the colonies through laws and to exploit them through taxes caused growing resentment among colonists. Although most colonists viewed themselves as loyal British subjects, attitudes toward Britain began to change. Pennsylvania lawyer John Dickinson warned that Britain's policies presented a threat to the colonists:

> 66 *[M]y dear countrymen, ROUSE yourselves, and behold the ruin hanging over your heads. . . . If Great Britain can order us to come to her for necessaries we want, and can order us to pay what taxes she pleases before we take them away, or when we land them here, we are abject [miserable] slaves . . .* 99
>
> —John Dickinson

King George III of England ascended the throne at a difficult time in his nation's history.

Changing British Policy

As the end of the French and Indian War approached, British traders and land speculators showed more interest in the Great Lakes region and the Ohio River valley. Native Americans in these regions became alarmed. These British colonists were not hunters and traders like the French. As farmers, they represented a much greater threat to Indian lands and resources.

The Proclamation of 1763 When Native Americans approached British government officials with their concerns, they discovered another difference between the British and the French. General Jeffrey Amherst, the British military commander in North America, despised the Indians. Not only did Amherst ignore Indian protests, he ended the flow of trade goods on which the Indians had come to depend under French rule.

Chapter 4 • Section 2 **109**

Section 2

Issues Behind the Revolution

SECTION OBJECTIVES

1. See how and why British policies in the colonies changed after 1763.
2. Learn about the causes and effects of the Stamp Act.
3. Discover how rising tensions in the colonies led to fighting at Lexington and Concord.

BELLRINGER

Warm-Up Activity Ask students to jot down a list of items that the state and/or federal government single out for taxation. Ask students if they think these taxes are fair or unfair and whether they feel that they restrict individual freedom in any way.

Activating Prior Knowledge Ask students to list ways in which the government uses tax money. What do they think are the top five areas of government spending today?

READING STRATEGY

As students read this section, ask them to list and briefly describe the issues behind the Revolution.

ACTIVITY
Connecting with Government

Ask students to conduct research on George III's early life (prior to his becoming king) and write a brief biographical sketch. **(Verbal/Linguistic)**

RESOURCE DIRECTORY

Teaching Resources
Guided Reading and Review booklet, p. 16

Other Print Resources
Historical Outline Map Book *The North America in 1763*, p. 22

Technology
Section Reading Support Transparencies
Guided Reading Audiotapes (English/Spanish), Ch. 4
Student Edition on Audio CD, Ch. 4
Prentice Hall Presentation Pro CD-ROM, Ch. 4
Social Studies Skills Tutor CD-ROM
Companion Web site, www.phschool.com

Focus Tell students that the French and Indian War left Great Britain in debt. In order to increase tax revenues, it tried to tighten its control over the colonies. The colonists resisted fiercely.

Instruct Review British policy toward the colonies up until the 1760s. Ask why Great Britain felt justified in exerting more control over the colonies after the French and Indian War. Why did the colonists react so strongly? Ask why the passage of the Sugar Act was significant. What led Americans to believe that the British were going to take away their freedom?

Assess/Reteach What do students think about the protests launched by colonists against British laws? In students' opinions, were the colonists justified in their discontent?

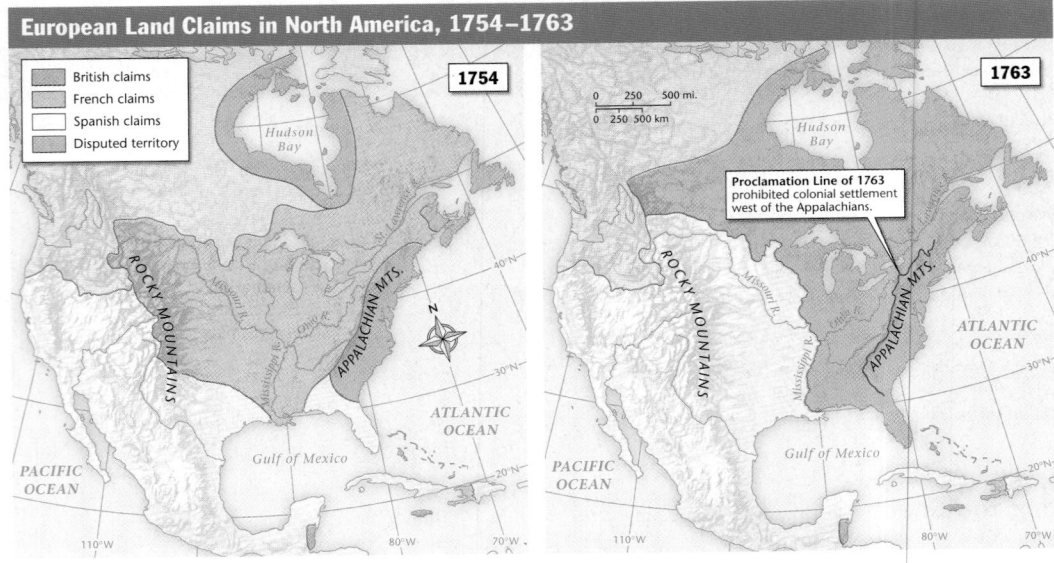

European Land Claims in North America, 1754–1763

Legend:
- British claims
- French claims
- Spanish claims
- Disputed territory

1754

1763

Proclamation Line of 1763 prohibited colonial settlement west of the Appalachians.

MAP SKILLS The Proclamation of 1763 prohibited settlement west of a line through the Appalachian Mountains. **Regions** *What European countries claimed land in North America in 1754?*

In response, the Ottawa, Huron, Potawatomi, and other Indians in the Great Lakes region rebelled against the British in the spring of 1763. Europeans named the uprising **Pontiac's Rebellion**, after one of the Ottawa leaders. By the end of the year, Native Americans had destroyed every British fort in the area west of the Appalachians except Fort Pitt and Fort Detroit. Some 2,000 colonists had been killed or captured. Thousands more hurried back east to safer areas.

As its army in America reeled from these setbacks, the British government acted to restore peace. In October, King George issued the **Proclamation of 1763.** This order closed the region west of the Appalachian Mountains to all settlement by colonists. The area, which had just been given up by the French, was placed under the control of the British military.

Between 1764 and 1766, Britain signed peace treaties with the Indian groups that had taken part in Pontiac's Rebellion. Yet despite the Proclamation of 1763, colonists continued to move west into the forbidden territory. Britain's lack of success in halting the colonists' migration further undermined its authority in America.

Britain's Financial Problems By 1763, the British were among the most heavily taxed people in the world. The costs of governing and defending Britain's vast empire contributed greatly to this burden. These costs had skyrocketed during the French and Indian War.

While Britain struggled with its heavy debts and taxes, its colonies in America were prospering. In April 1763, finance minister George Grenville became the prime minister. Although he was a brilliant money manager, Grenville ignored the interests of the colonists. With British citizens so burdened, Grenville asked, why shouldn't these colonists begin to pay some of the costs of their own government and defense?

In early 1764, Richard Jackson, a member of Parliament, wrote to his old friend Benjamin Franklin in Philadelphia. He advised Franklin that Grenville

Map Skills Britain, France, and Spain.

RESOURCE DIRECTORY

Technology
Color Transparencies *Historical Maps,* A60; *Time Lines,* C2

RESOURCE **PRO**® **Biography** *Pontiac,* found on Resource Pro, profiles the chief of the Ottawa who headed a Native American confederation to stop the spread of the British colonies.

RESOURCE **PRO**® **Visual Learning Activity** *The American Rattlesnake,* found on Resource Pro, uses a cartoon depicting the rebellious colonies as a rattlesnake to emphasize the seriousness and strength of the colonists' position.

planned to raise money in the colonies with some new form of taxation. This would be in addition to enforcing the duties, or taxes on imports, which had been in place for years.

The Sugar and Quartering Acts
The passage of the Sugar Act in 1764 marked the start of a new British policy designed to raise more income from the colonies. The law actually cut the duty on foreign molasses in half. Grenville predicted that the lower tax would encourage Americans to buy imported molasses and pay the tax rather than risk smuggling (illegally importing) molasses, as they had been doing. The result, he hoped, would be increased tax collections.

VIEWING HISTORY This detail from an engraving by Paul Revere shows a heavy British military presence in Boston. **Drawing Inferences** *Why were port cities such as Boston of particular importance to the British?*

To enforce this tax and others, Grenville issued a flurry of regulations. Ship owners were told that their ships would be seized if they "forgot" to pay their duties. The British navy was ordered to patrol the American coast to further discourage smuggling.

Most upsetting to colonists was Grenville's requirement that smuggling cases be tried in British rather than colonial courts. Under British law, such cases were decided by a judge alone, not by a jury. In addition, the judge received a 5 percent commission on all illegal cargoes and fines, a practice that encouraged judges to find accused smugglers guilty.

Another of Grenville's new policies was the Quartering Act, which Parliament passed in early 1765. This law required the colonies to provide housing and supplies for the British troops who remained in America after the French and Indian War.

Colonists complained about these changes, which violated their rights as British subjects, but most went along with them. Opposition to the next step in Grenville's program was much stronger, however.

The Stamp Act Crisis

In March 1765, the British Parliament passed the **Stamp Act.** This law placed a tax on newspapers, pamphlets, legal documents, and most other printed materials. It required that an official government stamp be printed on or attached to these materials to show that the tax had been paid. Grenville estimated that this tax would raise enough money to pay the cost of keeping British troops in America.

The Stamp Act marked the first time that the British government taxed the colonists for the stated purpose of raising money. Of course, the Sugar Act was really a way to raise money, too. It, however, had been presented to the American colonists as a way to regulate trade rather than to raise money.

People in England had been paying a stamp tax since 1694. Yet, because the law represented such a radical change for the colonists, Grenville was cautious about introducing the tax. Before putting the law into effect, he talked with agents of the colonies and gave them time to suggest alternatives. He also allowed the colonists to distribute the stamps themselves. Having taken these careful steps, Grenville was unprepared for the firestorm of protest that followed.

READING CHECK
What was the direct purpose of the Stamp Act?

Colonists in Boston burn stamped paper to protest the Stamp Act in 1764 in the above engraving (caption in German).

Above are shown some of the stamps attached to British goods entering the American colonies.

The Stamp Act Congress For a number of reasons, the reaction in the colonies against the Stamp Act was widespread and extreme. Most important, this measure touched almost all Americans in every colony. It was not like a trade measure, for example, which might apply only to New England shippers or to southern tobacco growers. The new law also directly affected some of the most powerful people in the colonies—printers, merchants, and lawyers.

In October 1765, delegates from nine colonies met in New York to hold a meeting that became known as the Stamp Act Congress. The main organizer of the meeting was James Otis, a lawyer from Massachusetts. In 1761, Otis had challenged in court Britain's authority to issue writs of assistance—general warrants used by custom house officials to enter any colonist's home to search for smuggled goods. At the same time, Otis had argued that Britain had no right to force laws on the colonies, because the colonists had no representatives in the British Parliament. In 1764, he had used the same "no taxation without representation" argument to protest the Sugar Act.

Otis and other delegates now made this argument again in petitions, or letters, they sent to the king and Parliament. In a series of resolutions, they claimed that colonists should have the same rights and liberties that the people of Great Britain enjoyed. Some of the resolutions of the Stamp Act Congress read, in part, as follows:

KEY DOCUMENTS

> *II. That His Majesty's . . . subjects in these colonies are [entitled] to all the inherent rights and liberties of his natural born subjects within the kingdom of Great Britain.*
> *III. That it is inseparably essential to the freedom of a people, and the undoubted right of Englishmen, that no taxes be imposed on them but with their own consent, given personally or by their representatives.*
> *V. That the only representatives of the people of these colonies are persons chosen therein by themselves, and that no taxes ever have been, or can be constitutionally imposed on them, but by their respective legislatures.*

—Declaration of Rights and Grievances

The Sons of Liberty Americans did not protest the Stamp Act with words alone. Merchants and others organized a **boycott** of British goods. A boycott is a refusal to buy certain products or use certain services as an act of protest. Groups sprang up throughout the colonies to enforce the boycott and to organize other ways of resisting British policies. The groups were known as the Sons of Liberty and the Daughters of Liberty.

Among the most active of these groups was the Boston Sons of Liberty. One of its founders was Samuel Adams. In August 1765, members of the Sons of Liberty visited the person who distributed stamps in Boston. They warned him that unless he resigned, "his House would be immediately Destroyed and his Life in Continual Danger." Several nights later a mob attacked the home of his brother-in-law, Thomas Hutchinson, who was lieutenant governor of the colony. After telling Hutchinson and his family to leave the house or be killed, the mob destroyed or carried off everything that was inside.

By November 1765, when the Stamp Act was to take effect, most stamp distributors had resigned or fled, leaving no one to sell the stamps. In Britain, merchants also howled in protest as the colonists' boycott threatened their profitable trade with America. Grenville was forced from power in 1765. In 1766, Parliament repealed the Stamp Act.

112 Chapter 4 • *The Road to Independence*

Rising Tensions in the Colonies

The colonists celebrated wildly when news arrived that the Stamp Act had been repealed. However, the larger issue had not gone away. Could Parliament tax the colonists without their representation in that body? Few colonists paid much attention to the fact that Parliament had also addressed this issue. On the very day the Stamp Act was repealed, Parliament had passed the Declaratory Act. This measure stated that Parliament had the authority to make laws that applied to the colonists "in all cases whatsoever."

The Townshend Acts In 1767, Parliament reasserted its power by placing duties on certain imported goods, including glass and tea. These laws were named after the British government's chief financial officer, Charles Townshend. After the Stamp Act disaster, Townshend hoped to satisfy the colonists by raising money through duties rather than direct taxes. The Townshend Acts, however, clearly stated that the money would be used for "the support of civil government" in the colonies.

The protests and violence began again. It made little difference, Americans said, whether Britain raised money through trade duties or direct taxes. Either way, the colonists were being taxed without their consent. Furthermore, Britain would use this money to pay the salaries of royal governors in America, who then would not have to turn to the colonial legislatures for their pay. This change would weaken the legislatures and undermine self-government in the colonies.

Colonists who poured their tea from this pot bolstered their resistance to the Stamp Act.

INTERPRETING CHARTS The years between 1764 and 1774 were beset with unrest in the American colonies. **Drawing Conclusions** *Why did England continue to pass controversial acts in the face of colonial protest?*

British Policies in the Colonies, 1764–1774

Date	British Action	Colonial Action
1764	**Sugar Act** Although it reduced the tax on imported foreign molasses, the Sugar Act, unlike its predecessor the Molasses Act, was strictly enforced.	Colonists responded with written protests, occasional boycotts, and cries of "No taxation without representation!"
1765	**Stamp Act** The first direct taxation of colonists, the Stamp Act taxed legal and commercial documents and printed matter, such as newspapers.	Colonists protested violently. The Stamp Act Congress met and a boycott of British goods began.
	Quartering Act Following the French and Indian War, England maintained a standing army in the colonies. The Quartering Act required colonial assemblies to house and provision the British soldiers.	Most colonial legislatures refused to pay for supplies as required by the Quartering Act.
1766	**Declaratory Act** England repealed the Stamp Act in the face of colonial protest. To reassert its authority over the colonies, it passed the Declaratory Act—a statement of England's right to rule the colonies in any way it saw fit.	Colonists were pleased with the repeal of the Stamp Act but continued to protest other British-imposed laws, such as the Quartering Act.
1767	**Townshend Acts** Import taxes on lead, paper, tea, paint, and glass were collected at port. Revenue from the Townshend duties were used to support British troops, royal governors, and royal judges, taking the power of the purse away from colonial assemblies. The Townshend Acts also created a customs commission and suspended the New York assembly for failing to comply with the act.	"Letters from a farmer in Pennsylvania," a widely read series of letters protesting the act, were published in nine colonial newspapers. Colonists resumed boycotting British goods, cutting trade in half.
1773	**Tea Act** The Tea Act was created to save the ailing East India Company. It allowed the company to sell its surplus tea in the American colonies. The act retained the import tax on tea—the only remaining tax of the nearly defunct Townshend Acts.	A group of Boston patriots destroyed a shipment of tea in a protest known as the Boston Tea Party.
1774	**Intolerable Acts** Also called the Coercive Acts, this series of punitive acts targeted Massachusetts. The Port Bill closed Boston harbor until Boston paid for the tea destroyed at the Boston Tea Party. Other acts nearly eliminated self-government in Massachusetts. New provisions to the Quartering Act required colonists to house British soldiers in private homes as necessary.	Delegates from 12 colonies met as the First Continental Congress. They created the Continental Association to boycott British goods. They also sent a petition to the king, outlining what they considered the rights of the colonists and their assemblies.

VIEWING FINE ART Paul Revere's engraving of the Boston Massacre shows British troops firing on citizens, but omits the events leading up to the shooting. **Drawing Inferences** Why would Revere illustrate this particular portion of the massacre?

INTERPRETING GRAPHS Compare the data in this graph with the table on the previous page. **Drawing Conclusions** How might this data reflect the success of colonial boycotts?

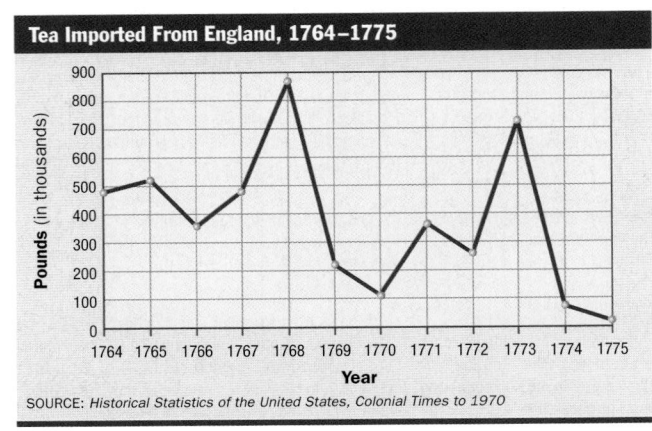

Tea Imported From England, 1764–1775

Pounds (in thousands) / Year

SOURCE: *Historical Statistics of the United States, Colonial Times to 1970*

Since the boycott had proved so successful against the Stamp Act, Congress again agreed to stop importing all British goods. Colonial women pledged to weave their own cloth rather than buy cloth made in England. Many also boycotted British tea.

The Boston Massacre   To put down violent resistance to the Townshend Acts, Britain sent troops to Boston, where officials feared a rebellion was at hand. A series of minor clashes occurred as the Sons of Liberty openly opposed the presence of the troops.

On the evening of March 5, 1770, a small but unruly crowd threatened a squad of British soldiers. The soldiers opened fire on the crowd, leaving five colonists dead or dying in the snow. Among the victims, African American Crispus Attucks fell first. The shooting added to an already tense situation. The incident became known as the **Boston Massacre.**

The next day, authorities arrested a British officer and eight soldiers and charged them with murder. Samuel Adams's cousin John Adams and another Boston lawyer agreed to defend them. John Adams was also a harsh critic of British policy. However, he believed the soldiers had a right to a fair trial. Seven of the accused were found not guilty, while two were convicted of lesser crimes. Their thumbs were branded as punishment and they were released.

Soon after the Boston Massacre, Parliament canceled the Townshend taxes. It kept only the duty on tea as a reminder of its authority over the colonies. With this move, the general boycott of British goods collapsed. Only the boycott of tea continued.

The colonies now entered a quiet period. Most Americans hoped the crisis had passed. Yet Samuel Adams and other Boston leaders continued to remind the colonists of British offenses. In 1772, Adams, James Otis, and other Bostonians formed a Committee of Correspondence to coordinate resistance throughout the colonies. By 1774, nearly all the colonies had such committees.

The Boston Tea Party   The Committees of Correspondence were soon put into action. In May 1773, in a move to help the struggling British East India Company, Parliament passed the Tea Act. The law gave that company the right to sell its tea in America without paying the normal taxes. Colonists had been smuggling tea in order to avoid paying these taxes. Now, however, the Tea Act would make the East India Company's tea even less expensive than smuggled tea, thereby driving the American tea merchants out of business.

Colonists, especially tea merchants, protested. The East India Company's sales agents in America were pressured to resign. When the company's tea began to arrive in November 1773, several colonial port cities refused to let the ships dock. On the night of December 16, 1773, colonists disguised as Indians boarded three tea ships in Boston. As a large crowd watched, they broke open every crate on board and dumped the tea into the harbor.

The Intolerable Acts To punish Boston and all of Massachusetts, in the spring of 1774, Parliament passed a series of laws known as the Coercive Acts. One of the laws limited town meetings to once a year; another suspended the Massachusetts general court. Because the measures seemed so harsh, the colonists labeled them the Intolerable Acts.

One "intolerable" new law, though it was not part of the Coercive Acts, extended Canada's boundary south to the Ohio River. This action stripped Massachusetts, Connecticut, and Virginia of their claims to western lands. In addition, General Thomas Gage, the commander of British forces in America, was named the new governor of Massachusetts.

Committees of Correspondence in several colonies called for a meeting to plan a united response to these developments. This gathering became known as the **First Continental Congress.**

The First Continental Congress On September 5, 1774, a gathering of 56 delegates met at Carpenter's Hall in Philadelphia. Delegates came from every colony but Georgia, and they had a wide range of viewpoints. George Washington from Virginia was a leading figure, as were Patrick Henry and Richard Henry Lee. Samuel Adams was the most rebellious of the delegates. Among those with moderate points of view were John Dickinson of Pennsylvania and New York's John Jay.

The First Continental Congress adopted a number of measures. Among these were a renewed boycott of British goods and a call to the people of all the English colonies to arm themselves and form militias. At the same time, the delegates made a direct appeal to the king, outlining their grievances and asking for understanding:

KEY DOCUMENTS
> *The foundation of English liberty, and of all free government, is a right of the people to participate in their legislative council: and as the English colonists are not represented, and . . . cannot properly be represented in the British parliament, they are entitled to a free and exclusive power of legislation in their several provincial legislatures, where their right of representation can alone be preserved.*
>
> —Declaration and Resolves of the First Continental Congress, 1774

On October 26, the Congress ended, though its members vowed to meet again in the spring if the crisis had not been resolved. George III remained stubborn and firm. On November 18, he wrote, "The New England governments are in a state of rebellion, blows must decide."

Fighting at Lexington and Concord

The Americans whom King George had labeled "rebels"—they preferred *Patriots*—followed the call of the First Continental Congress. Massachusetts Patriots formed militias and began to gather guns and ammunition. A major stockpile of weapons was stored in Concord, a town about 20 miles from Boston. Late at night on April 18, 1775, a force of about 800 British troops moved out of Boston and marched toward Concord with orders to seize these supplies. The plan was supposed to be secret.

Tea chests were lined with lead to make them watertight. Patriots at the Boston Tea Party (above) hacked open each chest to make sure every last tea leaf was destroyed.

Focus on TECHNOLOGY

Muskets The main weapon of the time was the musket, which fired a lead ball rather than the pointed bullet fired by later rifles. Muskets had short range and poor accuracy. "As to firing at a man at 200 yards with a common musket," said a British soldier, "you may just as well fire at the moon and have the same hopes of hitting your object." Therefore, aiming at a specific target was less important than firing and reloading quickly in order to fill the air with deadly lead.

Reading Comprehension

1. **Pontiac's Rebellion:** The 1763 rebellion by Native Americans in the Great Lakes region. **Proclamation of 1763:** The order by King George III closing the region west of the Appalachian Mountains to all settlement by colonists.

2. To raise money to pay the costs of maintaining British troops in the colonies. Colonists did not believe they should be taxed without representation in the British Parliament. They organized the Stamp Act Congress, petitioned the King, boycotted British goods, and harassed the distributors of the stamps.

3. British soldiers in Boston killed five colonists during a street confrontation on March 5, 1770.

4. The passing of the Intolerable Acts and the extension of Canada's boundary south to the Ohio River. Received colonists' agreement to boycott English goods, called on the people of all the English colonies to form militias, and made a direct appeal to the king.

Critical Thinking and Writing

5. The battles occurred when the British tried to seize the weapons that the colonists had stored in Concord. These events signified the beginning of the Revolutionary War.

6. British actions such as the Sugar Act of 1764, the Stamp Act of 1765, and the Intolerable Acts of 1774 were sources of rising frustration for the colonists, who eventually saw no peaceful means of redress. This situation led inevitably to war.

7. Students' letters will vary, but should be supported with facts from the section.

Minutemen had to respond to the call for arms at a moment's notice. This statue at the Old North Bridge in Concord, Massachusetts, commemorates the minutemen who stood their ground against the British on April 19, 1775.

However, Boston Patriots learned of it and sent Paul Revere, William Dawes, and Dr. Samuel Prescott on horseback through the countryside to alert Patriot leaders. Revere arrived in Lexington, about five miles from Concord, near midnight. Samuel Adams and John Hancock were there, and Revere warned them that the British soldiers were coming.

The main British force reached Lexington at about dawn on April 19. There they encountered 70 armed militia, known as minutemen, blocking their path on the village green. "Throw down your arms and you shall come to no harm," the British commander ordered. The colonists began to obey. Then someone fired a shot, though to this day no one knows for sure who it was. The troops fired a volley into the militia. Within minutes eight Americans lay dead on the green and another ten were wounded.

The British marched on to Concord, where they destroyed some of the militia's supplies (though the Patriots had hidden much of their stockpile). As the troops returned to Boston, some 4,000 Patriots gathered along the road to shoot at them from behind trees and stone walls. When the **Battles of Lexington and Concord** were over, what had seemed an easy British victory at dawn had turned into an exhausting and costly defeat. More than 70 British soldiers had been killed and more than 170 wounded before the force reached the safety of Boston. The Americans counted more than 90 Patriots as either killed, wounded, or missing. The **Revolutionary War,** which became a war for American independence from Britain, had begun.

Just days before this fateful clash, Patrick Henry had warned his fellow Virginians to prepare for what was soon to come:

> ❝ Gentlemen may cry, 'Peace! Peace!'—but there is no peace. . . . The next gale that sweeps from the north will bring to our ears the clash of resounding arms! . . . Is life so dear, or peace so sweet, as to be purchased at the price of chains and slavery? Forbid it, Almighty God! I know not what course others may take; but as for me, give me liberty or give me death! ❞
>
> —Patrick Henry

Section 2 Assessment

READING COMPREHENSION

1. What were **Pontiac's Rebellion** and the **Proclamation of 1763?**

2. Why did Parliament pass the **Stamp Act?** How did the colonists respond to it?

3 What happened during the **Boston Massacre?**

4. What events led to the **First Continental Congress?** What measures did the Congress adopt?

CRITICAL THINKING AND WRITING

5. **Determining Relevance** What happened at the Battles of Lexington and Concord? What is the significance of these battles in the Revolutionary War?

6. **Recognizing Cause and Effect** How did British rule in the Colonies finally lead to the Revolutionary War?

7. **Writing a Letter to the Editor** Write a letter a colonist might have written to support the boycott of English tea.

Take It to the NET

Activity: Recreating History
Examine the broadsides, petitions, and documents used to spread news throughout the colonies. Create a pamphlet declaring your stance on one of the issues you have read about in this section. Use the links provided in the *America: Pathways to the Present* area of the following Web site for help in completing this activity.
www.phschool.com

Take It to the NET

Pamphlets should clearly and effectively present the student's viewpoint on an issue such as the Stamp Act, the Boston Massacre, or the Proclamation of 1763.

RESOURCE DIRECTORY

Teaching Resources
Units 1/2 booklet
• Section 2 Quiz, p. 42
Guide to the Essentials
• Section 2 Summary, p. 21

Technology
Color Transparencies *Historical Maps,* A7; *Cause-and-Effect Charts,* D2
Sounds of an Era Audio CD *Newspaper Account of the Battle of Lexington and Concord* (time: 40 seconds); *Give Me Liberty or Give Me Death, Patrick Henry* (time: 20 seconds)

Exploring Primary Sources in U.S. History
CD-ROM *War Is Inevitable—and Let It Come! Patrick Henry*

Reading Biographies and Autobiographies

Biographies and autobiographies are two major sources of evidence about a historical period. A biography is an account of a person's life written by someone else; it is a secondary source. An autobiography, an account of a person's life written by that person, is a primary source. Both offer clues as to what society was like at the time the person lived; they reveal living conditions, people's reactions to those conditions and to events, and prevailing attitudes and values. While both must be evaluated for reliability and bias, autobiographies are especially likely to show the subject in a good light.

The excerpt below is from the first American autobiography to become a best-seller. In this passage, Benjamin Franklin describes his entry into government, beginning in the year 1748.

LEARN THE SKILL

Use the following steps when you read biographies and autobiographies:

1. **Identify the kind of account and the subject of the profile.** Determine not only who the subject is but also whether the profile covers all or part of the subject's life. If it is a biography, is it by someone who knew or interviewed the subject, or by someone relying on other sources?

2. **Analyze the account's reliability as historical evidence.** Evaluate these accounts as you would other sources: What is the writer's purpose? How objective is the writer? Does the account reveal only certain facts, or does it present some facts in a misleading way?

3. **Search for clues that tell what the historical period was like.** Look for facts about the period, but also for indications of how the subject's or writer's values and assumptions differ from current views.

PRACTICE THE SKILL

Answer the following questions:

1. **(a)** Is the excerpt from an autobiography or a biography? How can you tell? **(b)** What events are Franklin's focus in this part of his book?

2. **(a)** How well acquainted is the writer with the facts he describes? **(b)** How objective do you think he is about his achievements? About others' opinions of him? Explain. **(c)** Are there other historical sources that could support or challenge his description and interpretation of these events? Explain.

3. **(a)** What do you learn about Franklin from this excerpt? **(b)** What can you learn about the time period from Franklin's writing style? **(c)** What can you learn about how scientific experiments were done at that time? **(d)** What can you learn about colonial government? **(e)** What does Franklin's rise from rags to riches (implied in the excerpt) suggest about colonial life?

"When I disengag'd myself . . . from private Business, I flatter'd myself that, by the sufficient tho' moderate Fortune I had acquir'd, I had secur'd Leisure during the rest of my Life, for Philosophical Studies and Amusements; I purchas'd all Dr. Spencer's Apparatus, who had come from England to lecture here; and I proceeded in my Electrical Experiments with great Alacrity; but the Public now considering me as a Man of Leisure, laid hold of me for their Purposes; every Part of our Civil Government, and almost at the same time, imposing some Duty upon me. The Governor put me into the Commission of the Peace; the Corporation of the City chose me of the Common Council, and soon after an Alderman; and the Citizens at large chose me a Burgess to represent them in Assembly. This latter Station was the more agreeable to me, as I was at length tired with sitting there to hear Debates in which as Clerk I could take no part, and which were often so unentertaining, that I was induc'd to amuse myself with making magic Squares, or Circles, or anything to avoid Weariness. And I conceiv'd my becoming a Member would enlarge my Power of doing Good. I would not however insinuate that my Ambition was not flatter'd by all these Promotions. It certainly was. For considering my low Beginning they were great Things to me. And they were still more pleasing, as being so many spontaneous Testimonies of the public's good Opinion, and by me entirely unsolicited."

—Benjamin Franklin, *Autobiography*, 1793

APPLY THE SKILL

See the Chapter Review and Assessment for another opportunity to apply this skill.

READING BIOGRAPHIES AND AUTOBIOGRAPHIES

Focus Use biography and autobiography as sources of clues about society at a given time.

Instruct Ask students to work through the questions and discuss their responses. Then have groups use the library to choose a biography and an autobiography of an important figure in American history. Suggest that they focus on important events in the person's life. Ask them to use the questions in the feature as a guide to decide which source is more reliable.

Extend See the Skills for Life activity in the Resource Directory below.

ANSWERS

PRACTICE THE SKILL

1. **(a)** An autobiography. You can tell because he writes in the first person, and the title of the book is *Autobiography.* **(b)** He writes of political activities he engaged in following his retirement from business.

2. **(a)** He is well acquainted with the facts since he is describing his own life and experiences. **(b)** He is not completely objective about his accomplishments. He seems to engage in false modesty, especially regarding others' opinions of him. He says that he had risen high from low beginnings and that he "flatter'd" himself; but he does admit his pride in the public's good opinion of him. **(c)** Other first-hand contemporary accounts that describe Franklin's transition from private to public life could help verify his opinions.

3. **(a)** That he is an able, humorous, and curious man. **(b)** Spelling and capitalization rules were different and the style was more formal and flowery. **(c)** They were often conducted by amateurs in their homes or personal laboratories. **(d)** There were many opportunities for service; the colonies had a considerable degree of self-government. **(e)** That in colonial times there were many opportunities for a clever, ambitious man.

Section 3 Ideas Behind the Revolution

Setting the Scene On one level, the American Revolution was a struggle for power between the American colonists and Great Britain. The winner of this struggle was to be decided on the battlefield.

On another level, though, the Revolution was about ideas. The colonists were rethinking the relationship between people and government. It was during the revolution, and the years leading up to it, that Americans began to think of themselves as independent citizens rather than as subjects of a king.

Common Sense

One important document that expressed both levels of the Revolution was **Common Sense,** a pamphlet written by Thomas Paine. *Common Sense* first appeared in Philadelphia in January 1776. Paine was an artisan with little formal education. He avoided the references to Greek and Latin literature that were common in writing at that time. Instead, he wrote in a simple, direct style, suggesting that anyone could understand the conflict between Great Britain and the colonies:

KEY DOCUMENTS 66 [T]he period of debate is closed. Arms, as the last resource, decide the contest . . . Every thing that is right or natural pleads for separation. The blood of the slain, the weeping voice of nature cries, 'TIS TIME TO PART. 99

—*Common Sense*, 1776

VIEWING HISTORY Many colonists supported a separation from England after reading *Common Sense* (right), written by Thomas Paine (above). **Drawing Conclusions** *Why was* Common Sense *such a persuasive document?*

Within a year, 25 editions of *Common Sense* had been printed. The pamphlet persuaded many readers, including many who had favored a peaceful settlement of differences with the British government, to support a complete—and likely violent—break with Britain instead.

118   Chapter 4 • *The Road to Independence*

The Declaration of Independence

Common Sense appeared at a time when the **Second Continental Congress** was meeting in Philadelphia. This Congress had first gathered in May 1775, less than a month after British troops and colonial militia had clashed at Lexington and Concord, and it continued to meet throughout the Revolution.

The Delegates   Most of the delegates to the First Continental Congress returned for the second meeting. However, there were some important newcomers. Among the new faces were Benjamin Franklin of Pennsylvania and John Hancock of Massachusetts. In June, another new delegate, Thomas Jefferson, arrived from Virginia.

At first the delegates, like the American people, were deeply divided. Members such as Samuel Adams, John Adams, Patrick Henry, and Richard Henry Lee leaned toward independence. Moderates, led by John Dickinson, favored seeking some compromise with Britain that would increase colonial self-rule.

In November 1775, the Congress learned that George III had refused its **Olive Branch Petition.** Written by Dickinson, the document had expressed the colonists' continued loyalty to the monarch and their desire for peace. It begged the king to halt the fighting until a solution could be found.

In June 1776, after more than a year of war, the Congress decided it was time for the colonies to cut their ties with Britain. The Congress appointed a committee to prepare a statement of the reasons for the separation—a **Declaration of Independence.** (See the full text of the Declaration on the pages following this section.) Members of the committee were lawyer and plantation owner Thomas Jefferson; Boston lawyer John Adams; Roger Sherman, a judge from Connecticut; Robert Livingston, a lawyer from a wealthy New York family; and the well-known Benjamin Franklin. The committee chose Jefferson to draft the statement.

Drafting a Declaration   Jefferson's political ideas were influenced by the **Enlightenment,** an eighteenth-century European movement that emphasized science and reason as keys to improving society. He also drew ideas from earlier

A draft of the Declaration of Independence (above) shows some changes and corrections that Thomas Jefferson made during the writing process.

LESSON PLAN

Focus Tell students that the War for Independence was fueled by more than British actions. Powerful new ideas inspired Americans to challenge authority in hopes of creating a different kind of society. Ask students what these new ideas were.

Instruct Have students discuss the war in terms of the ideas of Thomas Paine and Thomas Jefferson. Why might these men be considered idealists? You might want to refer to the attributes students listed in the Bellringer activity. Discuss how the ideas that fueled the War for Independence also helped create a new society. Ask why *Common Sense* was important to the development of democracy.

Assess/Reteach Ask students to list and discuss how new ideas about equality and self-government contributed to the outbreak of the American Revolution.

COMPARING HISTORIANS' VIEWPOINTS
Rule by the People

In trying to decide whether or not to declare independence, colonists debated whether people were capable of ruling themselves.

Analyzing Viewpoints   Compare the main arguments made by the two writers.

For Rule by the People

"The American Congress derives all its power, wisdom, and justice, not from scrolls of parchment signed by kings but from the people. A more August [respectable] and a more equitable [fair] legislative body never existed in any quarter of the globe. It is founded upon the principles of the most perfect liberty. A free man, in honoring and obeying the Congress, honors and obeys himself."
—*Anonymous newspaper editorial, November 14, 1774*

Against Rule by the People

"Suppose we were to revolt from Great Britain, declare ourselves independent, and set up a republic of our own—what would be the consequence? I stand aghast at the prospect; my blood runs chill when I think of the calamities [disasters], the complicated evils that must ensue [result], and may be clearly seen—it is impossible for any man to foresee them all."
—*Rev. Charles Inglis, The True Interest of America, 1776*

Chapter 4 • Section 3   119

political thinkers, such as English philosopher John Locke. In Locke's writing, Jefferson found support for revolution. Locke had written:

 " [G]overnments are dissolved . . . when such a single person or prince sets up his own arbitrary will in place of the laws. . . . Secondly, when the prince hinders the legislative [legislature] from . . . acting freely. . . . Thirdly, when by the arbitrary power of the prince, the electors, or ways of election are altered, without the consent, and contrary to the common interest of the people. "

—John Locke, *Second Treatise of Government*, 1690

The Parts of the Declaration Jefferson divided the Declaration into four sections: a **preamble,** or introduction; a declaration of rights; a list of complaints against the king; and a resolution of independence.

Preamble Jefferson explained the purpose of the Declaration in its preamble:

 " When in the course of human events, it becomes necessary for one people to dissolve the political bands which have connected them with another, and to assume among the Powers of the earth, the separate and equal station to which the Laws of Nature and of Nature's God entitle them, a decent respect to the opinions of mankind requires that they should declare the causes which impel them to the separation. "

—Thomas Jefferson, Declaration of Independence

The Foundations of Democracy

Ancient Greece (*circa* 500 B.C.)	Democratic government in ancient Greek city-states 2,500 years ago. The word *democracy* comes from the Greek word *demos*, "the people," and *kratein*, "to rule."
Magna Carta (1215)	In 1215, English barons forced King John to sign a charter guaranteeing certain civil and political freedoms. Over time, these protections became the rights of all English people.
The Petition of Right (1626)	In 1626, the English Parliament forced Charles I to sign the Petition of Right, a document that limited the power of the monarchy. It included protections against (1) imprisonment without jury trial, (2) the institution of martial law during peacetime, (3) the mandatory quartering of troops, and (4) taxation without the permission of Parliament.
English Bill of Rights (1689)	This document forbade the monarchy from suspending or passing laws and from raising taxes without Parliament's consent, guaranteed the right to a fair and speedy trial, and forbade cruel and unusual punishment.
Social Contract Theory (1651)	Philosopher Thomas Hobbes described the relationship between the state and the governed as a social contract. Individuals surrendered their will to the state, which saved the people from anarchy.
Natural Rights (1690)	Political philosopher John Locke put forth an opposing view of the social contract. Locke maintained that the state exists to preserve the natural rights of its citizens—the right to life, liberty, and property. If the government fails in its duty to the citizens, the citizens then have the right to resist or rebel against that government.

INTERPRETING CHARTS
Democracy has evolved into a delicate balance between the rights of individuals and the need for social order. **Analyzing Information** *How are limits on government power a part of that balancing act?*

Declaration of rights In the second section, Jefferson explained the political ideas on which the document was based. Here is where he drew most heavily on the writings of John Locke. Locke believed that people have **natural rights**—rights that belong to them simply because they are human, not because kings or governments have granted them these rights. Jefferson used the expression "unalienable rights," meaning rights that could not be taken away.

According to Locke's view of the social contract (see the chart on page 120), people form governments to protect their natural rights, but they do not surrender control over their government. If a government fails to act in the best interests of the people it governs, then the people have the right to revolt and replace the government with a new one. Likewise, Jefferson took care to explain that governments derive their power from "the consent of the governed" and that people retain the right "to alter or to abolish" their government.

Complaints Jefferson followed the statement on rights with a third section that laid out a long list of wrongs the colonists believed the British king had committed. "The history of the present King of Great Britain is a history of repeated injuries . . . ," Jefferson wrote, "all having in direct object the establishment of an absolute Tyranny over these States."

In a government based on a **rule of law,** public officials must make decisions based on the law, not on their own personal wishes. Colonists were tired of what they saw as self-interested decisions made by the English king and his ministers.

Resolution Jefferson concluded the Declaration with a fourth section, a resolution. In it he wrote, "these United Colonies are, and of Right ought to be Free and Independent States. . . . "

The Declaration Is Adopted On July 4, the date now celebrated as Independence Day, delegates joined in voting to approve the Declaration. Jefferson's document did much more than declare a nation's independence, however. It also defined the basic principles on which American government and society would rest. The United States would be a nation in which ordinary citizens would have a strong voice in their own government.

"Remember the Ladies"

In the 1770s, as John Adams became one of the leaders of the opposition to British rule, his wife Abigail remained shut off from public debate because she was a woman. However, she did not hesitate to express her opinions to her husband. Several weeks before John was named to the committee to write the Declaration of Independence, Abigail sent him a letter in Philadelphia, where he was attending the Continental Congress:

> 66 I long to hear that you have declared an independency—and by the way in the new Code of Laws which I suppose it will be necessary for you to make I desire you would Remember the Ladies, and be more generous and favourable to them than your ancestors. Do not put such unlimited power into the hands of the Husbands. Remember all Men would be tyrants if they could. 99
>
> —Abigail Adams, March 31, 1776

BIOGRAPHY

Abigail Adams 1744–1818

Abigail Smith grew up in Massachusetts. Shortly before her twentieth birthday, Abigail married 29-year-old John Adams. The two had an affectionate relationship and truly respected each other. The humor and friendship that can be seen in their letters remained a part of their marriage through bad times and good. Together they weathered the Revolution—she ran the family farm while her husband was away working for American independence. They later became the first presidential couple to live in the White House. The Adamses had five children, including John Quincy Adams, who became the sixth President of the United States.

Reading Comprehension

1. The Declaration of Independence was written and accepted.

2. To express the colonists' continued loyalty to the monarchy, as well as their desire for peace.

3. Its primary purpose was to proclaim the complete independence of the former colonies from Great Britain. The Declaration of Independence was adopted by the Second Continental Congress on July 4, 1776.

4. The social contract theory; an emphasis upon natural rights; and that the purpose of government should be to benefit the population being governed, not hold it in bondage.

5. Natural rights: rights that belong to people simply because they are human; rule of law: a type of government in which decisions must be based on the law, not on the personal whim of a ruler.

Critical Thinking and Writing

6. *Common Sense* was written to help the colonists understand the issues behind the conflict with Britain. The Declaration of Independence was a more formal document explaining the colonists' actions. Both included ideas about natural rights and the proper relationship between citizens and government.

7. He refused it, convincing many colonists to adopt a more radical view of the war with Britain.

8. Answers will vary, but should demonstrate a complete understanding of the text.

Take It to the NET

Biographies should chronicle the important events that shaped the life and political views of one of the signers of the Declaration of Independence.

CAPTION ANSWERS

Viewing History So that different ideas and opinions would go into making the document. The job was too important to leave to just one person.

VIEWING HISTORY Committee members Thomas Jefferson, Roger Sherman, Benjamin Franklin, Robert Livingston, and John Adams gathered to prepare the Declaration of Independence. **Drawing Inferences** *Why did the Congress appoint a committee, rather than an individual, to create the Declaration of Independence?*

Some of Abigail's comments were intended to tease John. Her letter continues: "If particular care and attention is not paid to the Ladies we are determined to foment [stir up] a Rebellion, and will not hold ourselves bound by any Laws in which we have no voice, or Representation." Abigail Adams was serious, however, in her complaints about the status of women in American society. She employed the very ideas that men were using in their fight against Great Britain to suggest that it was time to rethink the relationship between men and women.

Earlier in that same letter, Abigail raised the issue of slavery, and suggested that it, too, should be addressed by the Congress. She felt it contradictory that delegates should speak of liberty for themselves, but not for others: "I have sometimes been ready to think that the passion for Liberty cannot be Equally Strong in the Breasts of those who have been accustomed to deprive their fellow Creature of theirs."

John did not attempt to follow through on any of Abigail's requests. The question of slavery was one that would surely divide the delegates at a time when unity was highly prized. And although Abigail Adams was no radical, the idea of civil rights for women was far too outrageous at the time to raise before the Congress.

The questions that Abigail Adams raised on the existing order was part of the revolution begun by men such as Jefferson and Paine when they attacked the sovereignty of kings, denounced tyranny, and declared the basic equality of men. But before any Americans could enjoy the fruits of that revolution, they had a difficult war to win.

Section 3 Assessment

READING COMPREHENSION

1. What did the **Second Continental Congress** accomplish?

2. What was the purpose of the **Olive Branch Petition?**

3. What was the purpose of the **Declaration of Independence,** and when was it adopted?

4. What political ideas from the **Enlightenment** influenced Thomas Jefferson?

5. Explain the ideas of **natural rights** and **rule of law.**

CRITICAL THINKING AND WRITING

6. **Making Comparisons** Compare and contrast Thomas Paine's *Common Sense* with the Declaration of Independence.

7. **Recognizing Cause and Effect** What was the king's reaction to the Olive Branch Petition? How did it lead to the Declaration of Independence?

8. **Writing to Inform** Rewrite the preamble to the Declaration of Independence, explaining the purpose of the document in your own words.

Take It to the NET

Activity: Writing a Biography Examine the lives of the men who signed the Declaration of Independence. Write a one-page biography of one of the signers. Use the links provided in the *America: Pathways to the Present* area of the following Web site for help in completing this activity.
www.phschool.com

RESOURCE DIRECTORY

Teaching Resources
Units 1/2 booklet
• Section 3 Quiz, p. 43
Guide to the Essentials
• Section 3 Summary, p. 22

The Declaration of INDEPENDENCE

In Congress, July 4, 1776

THE UNANIMOUS DECLARATION OF THE THIRTEEN UNITED STATES OF AMERICA,

When in the Course of human events, it becomes necessary for one people to dissolve the political bands which have connected them with another, and to assume among the Powers of the earth, the separate and equal station to which the Laws of Nature and of Nature's God entitle them, a decent respect to the opinions of mankind requires that they should declare the causes which impel them to the separation.

We hold these truths to be self-evident, that all men are created equal, that they are endowed by their Creator with certain unalienable Rights, that among these are Life, Liberty and the pursuit of Happiness. That to secure these rights, Governments are instituted among Men, deriving their just powers from the consent of the governed, That whenever any Form of Government becomes destructive of these ends, it is the Right of the People to alter or to abolish it, and to institute new Government, laying its foundation on such principles and organizing its powers in such form, as to them shall seem most likely to effect their Safety and Happiness. Prudence, indeed, will dictate that Governments long established should not be changed for light and transient causes; and accordingly all experience hath shown, that mankind are more disposed to suffer, while evils are sufferable, than to right themselves by abolishing the forms to which they are accustomed. But when a long train of abuses and usurpations, pursuing invariably the same Object evinces a design to reduce them under absolute Despotism, it is their right, it is their duty, to throw off such Government, and to provide new Guards for their future security.—Such has been the patient sufferance of these Colonies; and such is now the necessity which constrains them to alter their former Systems of Government. The history of the present King of Great Britain is a history of repeated injuries and usurpations, all having in direct object the establishment of an absolute Tyranny over these States. To prove this, let Facts be submitted to a candid world.

He has refused his Assent to Laws, the most wholesome and necessary for the public good.

He has forbidden his Governors to pass Laws of immediate and pressing importance, unless suspended in their operation till his Assent should be obtained; and when so suspended, he has utterly neglected to attend to them.

He has refused to pass other Laws for the accommodation of large districts of people, unless those people would relinquish the right of Representation in the Legislature, a right inestimable to them and formidable to tyrants only.

He has called together legislative bodies at places unusual, uncomfortable, and distant from the depository of their Public Records, for the sole purpose of fatiguing them into compliance with his measures.

Focus Write the following quotation on the chalkboard: "We must all hang together, or assuredly we will all hang separately." Explain that Benjamin Franklin spoke these words at the signing of the Declaration of Independence. Ask students what they think Franklin meant.

Instruct Explain how the ideals that inspired the American Revolution are embodied in the Declaration of Independence. Have students read the first paragraph of the Declaration and explain its purpose. Why was the Declaration such a revolutionary document in its time? How does it define basic principles upon which American society is based? Ask a volunteer to read from "We hold these truths to be self-evident" to ". . . effect their safety and happiness." Discuss why this section forms the heart of the Declaration.

Close The Declaration describes the basic rights on which the nation was founded, the wrongs committed by Britain, and the colonists' intentions to cut ties with Britain. The men who signed it made a brave commitment to pursue revolutionary ideals regarding human rights.

RESOURCE DIRECTORY

Teaching Resources
Biography, Literature and Comparing Primary Sources booklet (Comparing Primary Sources) *On Rule by the People,* p. 103

Technology
Prentice Hall United States History Video Collection™ Volume 4, *The American Revolution*

The Declaration of INDEPENDENCE

CUSTOMIZE FOR ...

Gifted and Talented

Have students research the ideas of John Locke and the English tradition of government. Then ask students to correlate these ideas with specific ideas in the Declaration. They may present the results of their project in essay or chart form.

CUSTOMIZE FOR ...

ESL

Ask students to make a list of sentences from the Declaration that they find challenging. Have them work together to restate the sentences in their own words.

CUSTOMIZE FOR ...

Less Proficient Readers

Have students draw cartoons that represent main ideas from the Declaration. Have them share their cartoons with the class and explain their meaning. You may want to collect their cartoons in a class political cartoon booklet.

CUSTOMIZE FOR ...

Less Proficient Writers

Ask students to select a passage from the Declaration and have them write the passage in their own words.

He has dissolved Representative Houses repeatedly, for opposing with manly firmness his invasions on the rights of the people.

He has refused for a long time, after such dissolutions, to cause others to be elected; whereby the Legislative powers, incapable of Annihilation, have returned to the People at large for their exercise; the State remaining in the mean time exposed to all the dangers of invasions from without, and convulsions within.

He has endeavored to prevent the population of these States; for that purpose obstructing the Laws for Naturalization of Foreigners; refusing to pass others to encourage their migration hither, and raising the conditions of new Appropriations of Lands.

He has obstructed the Administration of Justice, by refusing his Assent to Laws for establishing Judiciary powers.

He has made Judges dependent on his Will alone for the tenure of their offices, and the amount and payment of their salaries.

He has erected a multitude of New Offices, and sent hither swarms of Officers to harass our people and eat out their substance.

He has kept among us in time of peace, Standing Armies, without the Consent of our legislature.

He has affected to render the Military independent of and superior to the Civil power.

He has combined with others to subject us to a jurisdiction foreign to our constitutions, and unacknowledged by our laws; giving his Assent to their Acts of pretended Legislation:

For Quartering large bodies of armed troops among us:

For protecting them, by a mock Trial, from Punishment for any Murders which they should commit on the Inhabitants of these States:

For cutting off our Trade with all parts of the world:

For imposing Taxes on us without our Consent:

For depriving us in many cases, of the benefits of Trial by Jury:

For transporting us beyond Seas to be tried for pretended offenses:

For abolishing the free System of English Laws in a neighbouring Province, establishing therein an Arbitrary government, and enlarging its Boundaries so as to render it at once an example and fit instrument for introducing the same absolute rule into these Colonies:

For taking away our Charters, abolishing our most valuable Laws, and altering fundamentally the Forms of our Governments;

For suspending our own Legislature, and declaring themselves invested with Power to legislate for us in all cases whatsoever.

He has abdicated Government here, by declaring us out of his Protection, and waging War against us.

He has plundered our seas, ravaged our Coasts, burned our towns, and destroyed the lives of our people.

He is at this time transporting large Armies of foreign mercenaries to compleat the works of death, desolation and tyranny, already begun with circumstances of Cruelty and perfidy scarcely paralleled in the most barbarous ages, and totally unworthy the Head of a civilized nation.

He has constrained our fellow Citizens taken Captive on the high Seas to bear Arms against their Country, to become the executioners of their friends and Brethren, or to fall themselves by their Hands.

He has excited domestic insurrections amongst us, and has endeavored to bring on the inhabitants of our frontiers the merciless Indian Savages, whose known rule of warfare, is an undistinguished destruction of all ages, sexes, and conditions.

In every stage of these Oppressions We have Petitioned for Redress in the most humble terms. Our repeated Petitions have been answered only by repeated injury. A Prince, whose character is thus marked by every act which may define a Tyrant, is unfit to be the ruler of a free People.

Nor have We been wanting in attentions to our British brethren. We have warned them from time to time of attempts by their legislature to extend an unwarrantable jurisdiction over us. We have reminded them of the circumstances of our emigration and settlement here. We have appealed to their native justice and magnanimity, and we have conjured them by the ties of our common kindred to disavow these usurpations, which, would inevitably interrupt our connections and correspondence. They too have been deaf to the voice of Justice and of consanguinity. We must, therefore, acquiesce in the necessity, which denounces our Separation, and hold them, as we hold the rest of mankind, Enemies in War, in Peace Friends.

We, therefore, the Representatives of the United States of America, in General Congress, Assembled, appealing to the Supreme Judge of the world for the rectitude of our intentions, do, in the Name, and by the Authority of the good People of these Colonies, solemnly publish and declare, That these United Colonies are, and of Right ought to be Free and Independent States; that they are Absolved from all Allegiance to the British Crown, and that all political connection between them and the State of Great Britain, is and ought to be totally dissolved, and that as Free and Independent States, they have full Power to levy War, conclude Peace, contract Alliances, establish Commerce, and to do all other Acts and Things which Independent States may of right do. And for the support of this Declaration, with a firm reliance on the protection of Divine Providence, we mutually pledge to each other our Lives, our Fortunes and our sacred Honor.

JOHN HANCOCK
President of the Continental Congress 1775–1777

NEW HAMPSHIRE
Josiah Bartlett
William Whipple
Matthew Thornton
MASSACHUSETTS BAY
Samuel Adams
John Adams
Robert Treat Paine
Elbridge Gerry
RHODE ISLAND
Stephen Hopkins
William Ellery
CONNECTICUT
Roger Sherman
Samuel Huntington
William Williams
Oliver Wolcott
NEW YORK
William Floyd
Philip Livingston
Francis Lewis
Lewis Morris

NEW JERSEY
Richard Stockton
John Witherspoon
Francis Hopkinson
John Hart
Abraham Clark
DELAWARE
Caesar Rodney
George Read
Thomas McKean
MARYLAND
Samuel Chase
William Paca
Thomas Stone
Charles Carroll
of Carrollton
VIRGINIA
George Wythe
Richard Henry Lee
Thomas Jefferson
Benjamin Harrison
Thomas Nelson, Jr.
Francis Lightfoot Lee
Carter Braxton

PENNSYLVANIA
Robert Morris
Benjamin Rush
Benjamin Franklin
John Morton
George Clymer
James Smith
George Taylor
James Wilson
George Ross
NORTH CAROLINA
William Hooper
Joseph Hewes
John Penn
SOUTH CAROLINA
Edward Rutledge
Thomas Heyward, Jr.
Thomas Lynch, Jr.
Arthur Middleton
GEORGIA
Button Gwinnett
Lyman Hall
George Walton

The Declaration of Independence 125

Vocabulary Answers should reflect an understanding of the words selected.

Comprehension

1. That all men are created equal, and all are endowed by their Creator with certain rights.
2. Life, liberty, and the pursuit of happiness.
3. The consent of the governed.
4. The people may change or abolish the government.
5. King George III.
6. "imposing taxes on us without our consent."
7. Powers to declare war, conclude peace, contract alliances, and establish commerce.
8. New Hampshire, Massachusetts Bay, Rhode Island, Connecticut, New York, New Jersey, Delaware, Maryland, Virginia, Pennsylvania, North Carolina, South Carolina, and Georgia.

Critical Thinking

1. Judges were likely to favor the king over the colonists in court.
2. "When in the Course of human events"; "We hold these truths to be self-evident"; "The history of the present King of Great Britain is a history of repeated injuries and usurpations"; "We, therefore, the Representatives of the United States of America."
3. No. Many of the signers, including Thomas Jefferson, owned slaves and were unwilling to extend these basic rights to African Americans. Laws limited the rights of women and Native Americans, who were denied the right to live and govern themselves on their own land.
4. The Declaration accuses King George of encouraging "merciless Indian Savages" to attack colonists on the frontier. Colonists considered Native Americans to be barbarians who attacked indiscriminately.
5. The Declaration claims that the colonists had petitioned the king many times.

Issues Past and Present

1. Answers will vary. Women may discuss the use of "men" in the quote. An African American might read "all men are created equal" and hope that American independence would bring freedom.

2. It asserts that the right to life, liberty, and the pursuit of happiness comes from God. The signatories put their trust in "the protection of Divine Providence."

3. Answers may mention current issues such as censorship, children's rights, religion, gun control, abortion, or the death penalty.

Analyzing Political Cartoons

1. (a) America. (b) King George. (c) Britain was America's master, and the rider is dressed like King George.

2. (a) A whip made of swords, bayonets and axes. (b) The British Army.

3. Because Britain used force to control the colonies, Americans became angry and tried to throw off British control.

DECLARATION OF INDEPENDENCE

Reviewing the Declaration

Vocabulary

Choose ten words in the Declaration with which you are unfamiliar. Look them up in the dictionary. Then, on a piece of paper, copy the sentence in the Declaration in which each unfamiliar word is used, and after the sentence write the definition of the unfamiliar word.

Comprehension

1. Which truths in the second paragraph are "self-evident"?

2. Name the three unalienable rights listed in the Declaration.

3. From what source do governments derive their "just powers"?

4. What right do people have when their government becomes destructive?

5. In the series of paragraphs beginning, "He has refused his Assent," to whom does the word "He" refer?

6. Which phrase in the Declaration expresses the colonists' opposition to taxation without representation?

7. According to the Declaration, what powers does the United States have "as Free and Independent States"?

8. List the colonies that the signers of the Declaration represented.

Critical Thinking

1. **Cause and Effect** Why do you think the colonists were unhappy with the fact that their judges' salaries were paid by the king?

2. **Drawing Conclusions** As Section 3 of this chapter explains, the Declaration was divided into four parts. Write down the first phrase of each of those four parts.

3. **Identifying Assumptions** Do you think that the statement "all men are created equal" was intended to apply to all human beings? Explain your reasoning.

4. **Recognizing Bias** What reference do you see to Native Americans? What attitudes toward Native Americans does this express?

5. **Drawing Conclusions** What evidence is there that the colonists had already unsuccessfully voiced concerns to the King?

Issues Past and Present

1. Write a letter to the Continental Congress from the perspective of a woman or an African American who has just read the Declaration in 1776. In your letter, comment on the Declaration's statement that "all men are created equal" and also express your attitude toward American independence.

2. What evidence in the Declaration is there of religious faith? How do you think this religious faith influenced the ideals expressed in the Declaration?

3. Examine the unalienable rights of individuals as stated in the Declaration. Do you think these rights are upheld today? Give examples to support your answer.

Analyzing Political Cartoons

1. This cartoon was published in 1779. (a) Read the caption and identify the horse. (b) Who is the master being thrown? (c) How do you know?

2. Examine the figure on the horse. (a) What is he holding? (b) What does it represent?

3. What is the cartoonist's overall message?

THE HORSE AMERICA, *throwing his Master.*

READING FOCUS

- What happened during the Siege of Boston? What was its outcome?
- What were the strengths and weaknesses of the British and American forces?
- Why was the Battle of Saratoga considered a turning point of the war?

KEY TERMS

Battle of Bunker Hill
casualty
Loyalist
mercenary
Battle of Trenton
Battle of Saratoga

TAKING NOTES

Copy the chart below. As you read, fill in the major American victories and the reasons for these victories.

American Victories	Reason
Boston	From Dorchester Heights, Washington shelled British forces in the city and British ships in Boston harbor.

MAIN IDEA

Despite their considerable weaknesses, the Americans won important battles against the British between 1775 and 1777.

Setting the Scene

Although the Declaration of Independence was not approved until July 4, 1776, Britain and the American colonists had been fighting since the Battles of Lexington and Concord in April 1775. King George III had not expected a war, much less a long one. "Once these rebels have felt a smart blow, they will submit," he had vowed after Lexington and Concord. After all, the nation he ruled was the most powerful on Earth.

Yet the fighting continued, and even intensified. Its outcome would have long-lasting and far-reaching results, as American poet Ralph Waldo Emerson wrote:

❝ By the rude bridge that arched the flood,
Their flag to April's breeze unfurled,
Here once the embattled farmers stood,
And fired the shot heard round the world. ❞

—Ralph Waldo Emerson, "Concord Hymn," 1837

This engraving shows the retreat of the British from the Battle of Concord. The Siege of Boston followed this battle.

The Siege of Boston

Following the clashes at Lexington and Concord in April 1775, as many as 20,000 armed Patriots surrounded Boston. Although the Patriots were disorganized, their presence prevented the 6,000 British troops under General Thomas Gage from quickly crushing the rebellion.

With the main British force bottled up in Boston, the Patriots turned their attention to gathering badly needed military equipment. In May 1775, a group of Vermont militia under Colonel Ethan Allen crossed Lake Champlain and surprised the British troops at Fort Ticonderoga in northern New York. The capture of the fort provided the Patriots with cannons and other supplies.

The Battle of Bunker Hill In June 1775, the Americans occupied two hills north of Boston. General Gage decided that the rebels must be driven from

RESOURCE DIRECTORY

Teaching Resources
Learning Styles Lesson Plans booklet, p. 11
Guided Reading and Review booklet, p. 18

Other Print Resources
Historical Outline Map Book *The Revolutionary War in the Northeast*, p. 25

Technology
Section Reading Support Transparencies
Guided Reading Audiotapes (English/Spanish), Ch. 4
Student Edition on Audio CD, Ch. 4
Prentice Hall Presentation Pro CD-ROM, Ch. 4
Companion Web site, www.phschool.com

SECTION OBJECTIVES

1. Discover what happened during the siege of Boston.
2. Find out about the strengths and weaknesses of the British and American forces.
3. See why the Battle of Saratoga was considered a turning point of the war.

BELLRINGER

Warm-Up Activity Read students this quote by Thomas Paine: "These are the times that try men's souls." What is Paine referring to? What conditions created such anguish?

Activating Prior Knowledge Can students list countries that have experienced revolutionary wars in recent times?

READING STRATEGY

Before students read the section, have them write down several questions they might have about the Revolutionary War. As they read, have them note the answers to their questions.

ACTIVITY
Connecting with History and Conflict

Tell students to debate the positions taken by Colonists during the Revolutionary War. Assign one third of the class to represent the Patriots, one third to represent the Loyalists, and one third to remain neutral. Have students present their arguments clearly, stating why they maintain their position. **(Verbal/Linguistic)**

Focus Explain that in the fight for independence, both the British and American forces had strengths and weaknesses.

Instruct Tell students that not all the colonists supported the Revolution. In general, colonists were split in their loyalties. Some were Patriots, others were Loyalists or Tories, and the rest were neutral. Discuss the fact that more African Americans served in the Patriot cause than supported the British. Explain that important battles took place in the North, including the British victory at Bunker Hill and the American victory at Saratoga.

Assess/Reteach Have students make a chart of British and American strengths and weaknesses in the years between 1775 and 1777.

READING CHECK
The large cannons brought to Boston from Fort Ticonderoga by Colonel Knox were placed, by order of George Washington, on the Dorchester Heights. This American firepower on high ground rendered the British position in Boston completely untenable, forcing the British to evacuate Boston.

VIEWING HISTORY In a costly attempt to intimidate American forces, waves of British troops climb Breed's Hill toward the waiting enemy. **Drawing Inferences** *Why did the British decide to attack Breed's Hill?*

READING CHECK
Describe the Siege of Boston and its outcome.

these strategic high grounds. On June 17, 1775, the British army attacked. In an awesome display of power, the tightly packed lines of red-coated troops marched up Breed's Hill with battle flags flying and drummers tapping out the beat. As the British neared the American position, though, 1,600 Patriots poured musket fire into their ranks. The advancing troops slowed, stopped, and then fell back.

The British launched another assault. Again, heavy Patriot fire from the top of the hill drove them back. Determined, the British commander General William Howe ordered yet a third attack. This time, picking their way over the bodies of their fallen comrades, the troops succeeded in taking Breed's Hill. The Patriots, having used all of their ammunition, were forced to retreat. British forces then quickly overran the second, weaker Patriot position on nearby Bunker Hill.

The British won the **Battle of Bunker Hill,** but victory came at a tremendous cost. Nearly 1,100 of 2,400 British soldiers there had been killed or wounded. Patriot **casualties**—that is, persons killed, wounded, or missing— amounted to fewer than 400. "You can never conquer us," wrote a defiant Patriot after the battle. "All America will revenge our cause."

The British Leave Boston Warning that the Americans "are now spirited up by a rage and enthusiasm as great as ever people were possessed of," General Gage asked for permission to march on Rhode Island or New York. General Howe, still confident of an easy victory, advised against it. For the next nine months Gage's small army remained pinned down in Boston.

In July 1775, George Washington arrived from Philadelphia, where the Congress had named him commanding general of the Patriot forces. While Gage's troops remained in Boston, Washington worked to transform the Patriot militia groups into the Continental Army.

In January 1776, Colonel Henry Knox arrived outside Boston. He brought with him the cannons his Patriot troops had hauled through the snowy forests from Fort Ticonderoga. Washington placed these big guns on Dorchester Heights, south of Boston. From there he could shell the British forces in the city and the British ships in Boston Harbor.

Realizing that they could no longer defend their position, the British abandoned Boston in March 1776. The British fleet moved the army to the Canadian city of Halifax, taking along some 1,000 **Loyalists,** or people who remained loyal to Great Britain. These particular Loyalists had no desire to be left behind with no one to protect them from the rebels. During the Revolution, some Loyalists fled to England or the West Indies, as well as to Canada. Many others, though, remained behind during the conflict.

Strengths and Weaknesses

According to John Adams, about one third of the colonists were Patriots. He also believed another third were Loyalists, or Tories as the Patriots called them, though in all likelihood, the number of active Loyalists was probably less than 20 percent of the population. Adams believed that the remaining third of Americans were neutral in the war. Among these were the undecided and those who lacked the commitment or the conviction to join one side or the other.

128 Chapter 4 • *The Road to Independence*

Viewing History In June 1775 Americans occupied two hills north of Boston. British generals Gage and Howe were determined to drive the Americans off these hills due to their strategic value. The British acted in order to attempt to safeguard British forces on lower ground in and around Boston as well as British ships in the harbor.

RESOURCE DIRECTORY
Technology
Color Transparencies *Fine Art,* E4

RESOURCE PRO® **Critical Thinking Activity**
Checking Consistency: Lexington and Concord, found on Resource Pro, helps students apply this skill by comparing accounts of the battles.

RESOURCE PRO® **Primary Source Activity**
War Diary of Margaret Hill Morris, found on Resource Pro, profiles a colonial woman's reactions to the advances of British troops toward her Pennsylvania town.

The British Britain's main strength was its well-equipped, disciplined, and trained army. In addition, the British navy was the world's finest. It provided military support by transporting and landing troops and protecting supply lines at sea.

The British also received help from a number of sources. Roughly 50,000 Loyalists fought with the British army. Some African Americans, largely in the South, also helped Great Britain. The British promised freedom to all slaves who served their cause.

Additional help came from Native Americans. Most Indian nations believed an American victory would be harmful to their interests. As you read earlier, the American colonists were intent on moving into forbidden Indian territory despite Britain's Proclamation of 1763. Should the colonists gain independence, their westward advancement would surely continue. In the South and the West, the Creeks, Cherokees, and Shawnees fought alongside British and Loyalist forces. In the North the Mohawks, led by Joseph Brant, and most other Iroquois nations sided with the British.

The British also hired about 30,000 **mercenaries,** foreign soldiers who fight for pay. The colonists called these troops "Hessians" because most of their officers came from the German province of Hesse.

On the other hand, the British also had problems. The war was not popular in Great Britain. Many British citizens resented paying taxes to fight the war and sympathized with the Americans. British troops had to fight in hostile territory, and British commanders resisted adapting their tactics to conditions in America.

The Americans The very things that were British weaknesses were American strengths. Patriot forces were fighting on their own territory. Many of their officers were familiar with the fighting tactics that had worked in the French and Indian War. George Washington, in particular, proved to be an exceptional commander.

Focus on DAILY LIFE

Women in the Revolution Many soldiers' wives traveled with their husbands during the Revolutionary War. These women did cooking, washing, and sewing for the troops. Some women also distinguished themselves in battle.

When Margaret Corbin's husband was killed in battle, she took his place and continued to fight until she suffered wounds that left her disabled. After the war, Corbin became one of the first women to whom Congress awarded a military pension.

During the Battle of Monmouth, Mary Hays earned the nickname Molly Pitcher by carrying water to the soldiers. According to folklore, Mary helped fire her husband's cannon after he suffered heatstroke. The Pennsylvania legislature later awarded her a pension.

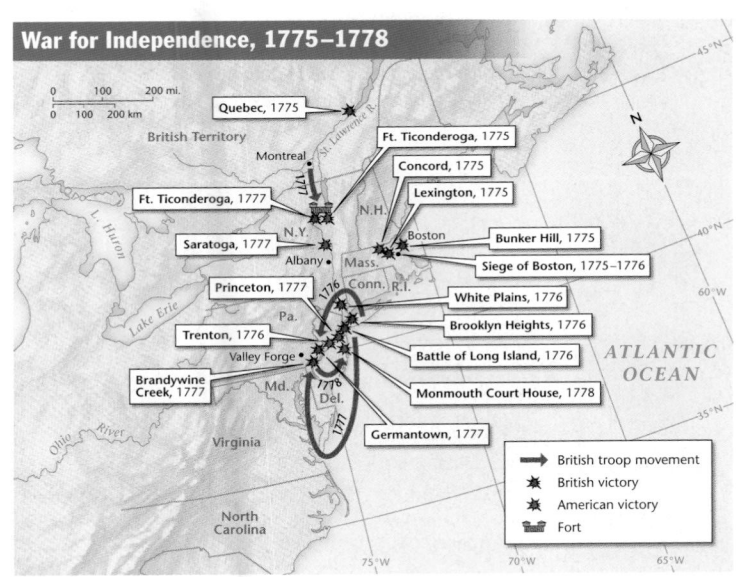

War for Independence, 1775–1778

Quebec, 1775
British Territory
Montreal
Ft. Ticonderoga, 1775
Ft. Ticonderoga, 1777
Concord, 1775
Lexington, 1775
Saratoga, 1777
Bunker Hill, 1775
N.Y.
Albany
Boston
Mass.
Siege of Boston, 1775–1776
Princeton, 1777
Conn. R.I.
White Plains, 1776
Trenton, 1776
Brooklyn Heights, 1776
Valley Forge
Battle of Long Island, 1776
Brandywine Creek, 1777
Md. Del.
Monmouth Court House, 1778
Virginia
Germantown, 1777
North Carolina
ATLANTIC OCEAN

0   100   200 mi.
0   100   200 km

→ British troop movement
✷ British victory
✷ American victory
⛉ Fort

MAP SKILLS The major battles of the early part of the war took place in the North. **Location** *Where were most of these battles fought? Be specific.*

Chapter 4   Section 4 • **129**

ACTIVITY
Connecting with Citizenship

Tell students that while the men were away fighting, many women took over the responsibility of running the family farm. Have students research information about these women and write a diary entry. **(Verbal/Linguistic)**

BACKGROUND
A Diverse Nation

In 1767 a Caribbean landowner traveled to London with his slave, Jonathan Strong, and, in a fit of rage, he beat Strong viciously. Strong was found and befriended by a white Englishman, Granville Sharp, who helped him to escape. In 1772 Sharp took the issue of slavery before the British Lord Chief Justice, who ruled, "Is not a Negro a Man? . . . As soon as any slave sets foot on English soil he shall be free." Sharp also helped organize the British Anti-Slavery Movement. In 1807 Parliament voted to halt Britain's slave trade, but it did not end slavery in British colonies.

CAPTION ANSWERS

Map Skills Massachusetts: Boston, Lexington, Concord; New York: in and around New York City, as well as upstate in the Hudson River valley; New Jersey: eastern; Pennsylvania: eastern; and Canada: St. Lawrence River valley and Quebec.

CUSTOMIZE FOR ...
Gifted and Talented

Have students analyze why the Revolution can be considered "a people's war." Why did so many different kinds of people become involved? What might African Americans have hoped to gain by participating in it? Why do you suppose many Americans sided with the British?

Patriot Nathan Hale disguised himself to gather information behind enemy lines.

For much of the war, however, the Americans lacked a well-supplied, stable, and effective fighting force. New recruits were constantly arriving while experienced soldiers, their time of service up, were heading home. As he tried to plan strategy, Washington never could be sure how many troops he would have.

More African Americans served in the Patriot cause than supported the British. Washington's army had some all-black units, but more often, African Americans served in white units.

Fighting in the North

In the summer of 1776, General Howe and a large British army appeared off the New York coast. The British had decided to concentrate on the Middle Colonies, where many Loyalists lived. In a series of battles, including the Battle of Long Island, some 32,000 British and German troops battered Washington's poorly trained and poorly equipped army.

Washington asked for a volunteer to cross enemy lines and obtain information on the British position. A young officer named Nathan Hale agreed to undertake the dangerous mission. Hale, disguised as a Dutch schoolmaster, succeeded in obtaining the information Washington needed. But as he returned to the American lines on September 21, 1776, he was captured by the British and condemned to hang. Before Hale died, he is reported to have said, "I only regret that I have but one life to lose for my country."

Retreat From New York By October, the British had captured New York City and driven the Continental Army into Pennsylvania. Many troops deserted General Washington. By the winter of 1776, the entire Patriot cause seemed on the point of collapse. Fearing for their safety, members of the Continental Congress fled Philadelphia.

In December 1776, Thomas Paine produced another pamphlet to inspire Americans once again to the cause of freedom. He called this work *The Crisis*. It began with this eloquent statement:

KEY DOCUMENTS ❝ *These are the times that try men's souls. The summer soldier and the sunshine patriot will, in this crisis, shrink from the service of their country; but he that stands it NOW,*

VIEWING FINE ART
Washington Crossing the Delaware by Emanuel Gottlieb Leutze is a famous American painting.
Analyzing Visual Information
(a) How does the artist show the hardships of the crossing? (b) How does he indicate heroism?

deserves the love and thanks of man and woman. Tyranny, like hell, is not easily conquered; yet we have this consolation with us, that the harder the conflict, the more glorious the triumph. "

—Thomas Paine, *The Crisis*

Trenton and Princeton Desperate times called for heroic measures. Lacking adequate financial support, supplies, and experienced troops, Washington had to be innovative. He and his troops met the challenge. Abandoning the tradition of armies not fighting during winter, Washington's army left their Pennsylvania camp on Christmas night of 1776 and went on the attack. Some 2,400 troops were ferried across the ice-choked Delaware River in small boats. Early the next morning they surprised about 1,400 Hessians stationed in Trenton, New Jersey. Nearly the entire Hessian force was captured, while the Americans suffered only five casualties in the **Battle of Trenton.**

A few days later, Washington made a similar attack on nearby Princeton. Leaving fires burning so the local Tories would think his army was still in camp, he led some 5,000 troops on a difficult nighttime march. One of the soldiers later described the ordeal:

" *The horses attached to our cannon were without shoes, and when passing over the ice they would slide in every direction. . . . Our men, too, were without shoes or other comfortable clothing; and as traces of our march towards Princeton, the ground was literally marked with the blood of the soldiers' feet.* "

—Soldier at the Battle of Princeton

The next morning, British troops under General Charles Cornwallis spotted Washington's army and attacked. The Americans drove them back, however, inflicting heavy losses on the British and capturing the town.

The victories in December 1776 and January 1777 greatly boosted Patriot morale and convinced more Americans to support the Patriot cause. "Volunteer companies are collecting in every county," a British traveler observed after the battles. "In a few months the rascals will be stronger than ever."

These silver pistols belonged to British Major John Pitcairn, who was killed in the Revolutionary War.

Victory at Saratoga

Despite the increasing Patriot numbers, the months that followed were difficult ones for the Continental Army. In July 1777, British General Howe moved his 15,000-member army from New York to attack the capital at Philadelphia. Washington's 10,500 defenders were defeated at Brandywine Creek, on the outskirts of the city, in early September. Later that month, the British occupied Philadelphia, as the Congress once again fled. In early October, Washington counterattacked to drive the British from the city, but lost again at the Battle of Germantown.

A British Attack From the North While Howe was advancing to capture Philadelphia, another British army was on the move in northern New York. Led by General John Burgoyne, its objective was to cut New England off from the rest of the colonies. In June, Burgoyne had moved out of Canada with a mixed force of about 8,000 British and German troops, Loyalists, Canadians, and Native Americans. The force quickly recaptured Fort Ticonderoga and then moved south through the dense New York forest toward Albany.

Sounds of an Era

Listen to descriptions of Revolutionary War battles, and other accounts from the journey toward independence.

ACTIVITY

Connecting with History and Conflict

Have students conduct research in order to sketch a map of troop movements surrounding the Battles of Trenton and Princeton and then present their map to the class. **(Visual/Spatial)**

BACKGROUND

Art History

Gottlieb Leutze's painting, *George Washington Crossing the Delaware,* is world famous and a heroic image. Yet it is historically inaccurate. The crossing was made at night, and in a storm. George Washington would doubtlessly not have struck the heroic pose. The flag shown did not yet exist. The boat, even, is of the wrong type. Yet the painting, though filled with artistic liberties, does in fact capture the feeling and spirit of the times.

☑ **TEST PREPARATION**

Have students read the quotation from Thomas Paine on these pages and then complete the sentence below.

"Summer soldiers" and "sunshine patriots" are those who—

A are eternally optimistic about the outcome.

B agree to fight only during the summer months.

Ⓒ are prepared to fight only when circumstances are favorable.

D join the battle eagerly at any time.

Reading Comprehension

1. The British attacked two hills occupied by the Americans near Boston Harbor. While the British were victorious, the cost was high. There were roughly 1,100 British casualties. The Patriot losses were lower by more than half (there were some 400 American casualties).

2. Great Britain.

3. Foreign soldiers who fight for pay.

4. Washington staged an innovative winter attack and successfully captured nearly the entire Hessian force, while the Americans suffered only five casualties.

5. It marked the turning point of the war, convincing the French government to aid the American cause.

Critical Thinking and Writing

6. These Patriot victories boosted morale and convinced more Americans to support the American cause.

7. Answers will vary, but might include: innovative fighting tactics, such as felling trees in order to slow Burgoyne's advance in upstate New York; General Washington's prestige and strength of character; and fighting on home ground with which the Patriots were already familiar and from where support could often be drawn from the local populace.

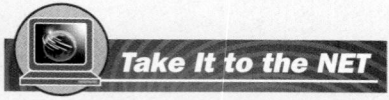
Take It to the NET

Students' representation of the material they researched should be clearly based on historical facts while also being creatively and dramatically presented.

Benjamin Franklin (above center) successfully courted the French in 1788 for an open alliance in America's fight for independence.

As the Americans retreated in Burgoyne's path, they destroyed bridges and felled trees across the road to slow his advance. Burgoyne's slow progress caused his army to run low on supplies. Meanwhile, the colonial force continued to grow, as the Continental Army and Patriot militias assembled to confront the invaders.

In mid-September, the Americans, led by General Horatio Gates, attacked Burgoyne's forces. This series of American victories, which took place around Saratoga, New York, is called the **Battle of Saratoga.** Finally, on October 17, 1777, surrounded by a force now much larger than his own, Burgoyne surrendered his army. It was the biggest American victory yet, and it marked the turning point of the war, bringing a major foreign power to aid in the American cause.

Help From Abroad A few months after the Continental Congress declared independence, it sent Benjamin Franklin on a mission to Paris. Although France had secretly been aiding the Americans in their struggle against its longtime enemy, Franklin pushed for an open alliance. The British defeat at Saratoga convinced the French that the Americans had a real chance of winning the war. On February 6, 1778, France and the United States signed a treaty of alliance.

The alliance with France helped the Americans tremendously. It meant not only more supplies but loans of money, French troops, and a navy. In addition, Britain now had to defend itself in Europe. A year later, Spain joined the war as France's ally, followed by the Netherlands in 1780. From Louisiana, Spanish governor Bernardo de Gálvez, who also had secretly been aiding the Patriots, attacked British outposts in Florida and along the Mississippi River.

Even before France and Spain entered the war, a number of Europeans volunteered to help the American cause against the British. Among them were the Marquis de Lafayette from France and Johann de Kalb from Germany. Both became generals in the Americans' Continental Army. Polish military engineer Thaddeus Kosciusko helped American forces build effective defenses. German Baron Friedrich von Steuben was largely responsible for training the Continental Army and transforming it into an effective fighting force.

Section 4 Assessment

READING COMPREHENSION

1. What happened during the **Battle of Bunker Hill,** and what were the **casualties** from both sides?

2. On whose side were the **Loyalists?**

3. What are **mercenaries?**

4. What happened during the **Battle of Trenton?**

5. Why was the American victory in the **Battle of Saratoga** important?

CRITICAL THINKING AND WRITING

6. **Drawing Conclusions** How did Patriot victories at Trenton and Princeton contribute to the victory at Saratoga?

7. **Writing an Opinion** What do you think were the Americans' greatest strengths in the early years of the war? Support your opinion with facts and details.

Take It to the NET

Activity: Drama Writing Investigate the role of intelligence, such as the use of spies, during the American Revolution. Then, write a one-act play or a series of monologues having to do with the subject. Use the links provided in the *America: Pathways to the Present* area of the following Web site for help in completing this activity.
www.phschool.com

RESOURCE DIRECTORY

Teaching Resources
Units 1/2 booklet
• Section 4 Quiz, p. 44
Guide to the Essentials
• Section 4 Summary, p. 23

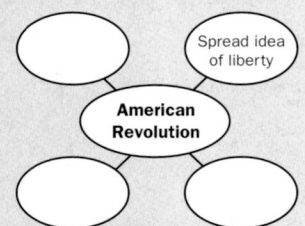

READING FOCUS

- What hardships did the Americans endure during the war?
- How did American victories in the West and the South lead to an end to the war?
- What was the impact of the American Revolution?

MAIN IDEA

Americans won their independence by outlasting the British in a long and costly war.

KEY TERMS

blockade
profiteering
inflation
Battle of Yorktown
Treaty of Paris (1783)
patriotism

TAKING NOTES

Copy the web diagram below. As you read, fill in each blank circle with information about the impact of the Revolution.

American Revolution — Spread idea of liberty

Setting the Scene There may be no better example of Americans' determination to be free than the Continental soldiers who spent the winter of 1777–1778 at Valley Forge in Pennsylvania. While British troops remained warm and well fed in Philadelphia, about 20 miles away, Patriot soldiers huddled in huts with few blankets, ragged clothing, and almost no food. Washington reported to Congress that nearly one third of his 10,000 soldiers were unfit for duty because they lacked coats or shoes:

> 66 I am now convinced, beyond a doubt that unless some great and capital change suddenly takes place. . . this Army must inevitably be reduced to one or the other of these three things. Starve, dissolve, or disperse in order to obtain subsistence in the best manner they can. 99
> —George Washington, Valley Forge, December 23, 1777

Americans Endure Hardships

The British lost their colonies in the end because Americans had the determination to outlast their rulers. George Washington understood this better than anyone. Although Britain seized New York, Philadelphia, and almost every other important colonial city, Washington knew the secret to winning the war. The British might capture territory, he said, but they could never win the war as long as Americans continued to fight them. Americans proved during the long war that they were both able and willing to make the sacrifices necessary for victory.

George Washington and his troops faced harsh winter conditions at Valley Forge.

Financing the War For Washington's army, a major source of hardship was a lack of support from the Continental Congress. Congress, in fact, had little real power. It asked the states to provide troops, money, and supplies, but without taxation power, it could not force them to do so.

Chapter 4 • Section 5 **133**

SECTION OBJECTIVES

1. Learn about hardships endured by Americans during the war.
2. See how American victories in the West and South led to the end of the war.
3. Discover the impact of the American Revolution.

BELLRINGER

Warm-Up Activity Ask students if they can recall a time in their life when they felt hopelessly defeated but kept going in spite of their feelings and were eventually successful. What techniques did they use to boost their morale?

Activating Prior Knowledge What do students think propelled the Americans to persevere in spite of the many disadvantages they faced in the Revolutionary War?

READING STRATEGY

As students read this section, have them create an outline by filling in the main ideas for each of the headings and subheadings.

ACTIVITY
Connecting with Citizenship

Have students create unique graphic organizers that indicate the hardships faced by Americans during the American Revolution. **(Visual/Spatial)**

RESOURCE DIRECTORY

Teaching Resources
Guided Reading and Review booklet, p. 19

Technology
Section Reading Support Transparencies
Guided Reading Audiotapes (English/Spanish), Ch. 4
Student Edition on Audio CD, Ch. 4
Sounds of an Era Audio CD *Champ Clark on Valley Forge* (time: one minute, 15 seconds)
Prentice Hall Presentation Pro CD-ROM, Ch. 4
Companion Web site, www.phschool.com

Focus Explain that the War for Independence was a long and costly war that caused people great hardship. In the end, Americans won their independence from Great Britain.

Instruct Tell students that Americans made great sacrifices during the war. Why were they willing to sacrifice so much? What kinds of hardships did Americans suffer during the war? Discuss the course of the war, and ask why it took the colonists so long to win.

Assess/Reteach Ask students to imagine what might have happened if the Americans had not defeated the British in the Revolutionary War. Discuss.

The above Georgia-issued bank note was worth four dollars in Continental currency in 1777.

Congress did issue paper money that the army could use to purchase supplies. Yet these bills were not backed by gold or silver, and if Britain were to win the war they would become worthless. So while Washington's army starved at Valley Forge, nearby farmers sold their crops in Philadelphia to the British army, who paid in gold.

Disruptions of Trade Civilians suffered hardships, too. During the war the British navy would **blockade,** or cut off from outside contact, the Atlantic Coast, which severely disrupted American trade. Measured in the British monetary unit of pounds sterling, the combined value of American imports and exports fell from about £2,700,000 in 1775 to £110,000 in 1777.

Nearly everyone felt the pinch of shortages during the war. Often even necessities were scarce. A few colonists took advantage of these shortages by **profiteering,** or selling scarce items at unreasonably high prices. Washington suggested that profiteers should be hanged. "No punishment in my opinion is too great for the man who can build his greatness upon his country's ruin," he said.

Even when goods were available, it was not always possible to buy them. **Inflation,** a steady increase in prices over time, reduced people's ability to buy goods. In Massachusetts, for example, the price of a bushel of corn rose from less than $1 in 1777 to almost $80 in 1779.

Victories in the West and the South

In June 1778, hearing that a French fleet was sailing for America, the British abandoned Philadelphia and moved north to reinforce New York defenses. Although they failed to stop the British from reaching New York, Washington's forces fought the British at Monmouth, New Jersey, and inflicted more casualties than they suffered.

Fighting in the West In the spring of 1778, Patriot militia under Colonel George Rogers Clark began fighting the British. By late summer, with the help of French settlers, Clark and his 175 soldiers had captured all the British posts in present-day Indiana and Illinois.

A few months later, a British force of roughly 500, about half of them Native Americans, advanced and retook the fort at Vincennes, Indiana. Clark then gathered nearly 200 French and American colonists and left his winter quarters near the Mississippi River. Marching through mud and icy water, the group reached Vincennes in late February 1779. After persuading most of the Indians to abandon their British allies, Clark recaptured the fort. This success strengthened the Patriots' claim to the Ohio River valley.

The War in the South In 1779, the focus of the war shifted to the South, where the British hoped to draw on Loyalist sympathies. Supported by the Royal navy, British forces from New York seized Savannah, Georgia, in December 1778 and Charleston, South Carolina, in May 1780.

The southern phase of the Revolution was especially vicious. It pitted Americans against Americans, because Loyalists did much of the fighting for the British. Although many battles in the South were fought on a smaller scale than those in the North, they proved just as important to the war's outcome.

In August 1780, some 2,400 British troops defeated Patriot militia and Continental Army troops at Camden, South Carolina.

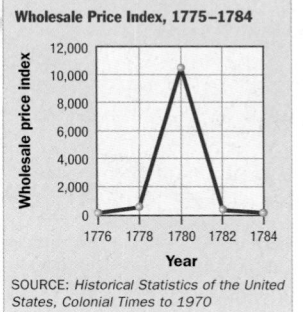

Focus on **ECONOMICS**

Inflation and Deflation *Inflation is a steady rise in prices; deflation is a steady drop in prices.*

The Historical Context Inflation, which has been described as "too much money chasing too few goods," plagued the American economy during the Revolutionary War. As Congress printed more and more Continental dollars, and the war limited the supply of goods available to consumers, the prices of goods rose.

The Concept Today Economists use a price index (below) to demonstrate inflation over a period of time. The federal government has several methods of fighting inflation, such as reducing the supply of money and limiting government spending.

Wholesale Price Index, 1775–1784

(Chart: Wholesale price index vs. Year, with values from 0 to 12,000; peak around 10,000+ near 1780)

SOURCE: *Historical Statistics of the United States, Colonial Times to 1970*

134 Chapter 4 • *The Road to Independence*

RESOURCE DIRECTORY

Teaching Resources
Biography, Literature, and Comparing Primary Resources booklet (Biography) *Deborah Sampson Gannett,* p. 9

Other Print Resources
Historical Outline Map Book *The Revolutionary War in the West,* p. 26; *The Revolutionary War in the South,* p. 27

British general Lord Cornwallis then began a campaign to invade North Carolina. At the Battle of Kings Mountain on the Carolina border that October, the Patriots defeated an army made up entirely of Loyalists. About 1,000 Patriots stopped Cornwallis' men again at the Battle of Cowpens in the same area in January 1781.

Despite the defeat, Cornwallis continued into North Carolina and defeated the Patriots at the Battle of Guilford Court House in March 1781. After stopping in Wilmington, North Carolina, to be resupplied by sea, Cornwallis advanced north into Virginia. His army was now much larger than the Patriot forces commanded by the Marquis de Lafayette.

Patriot reinforcements soon arrived, however, and Cornwallis marched his army to the coast, where it, too, could be reinforced with additional troops arriving by sea. In August, Cornwallis set up camp at Yorktown, on a peninsula between the York and James rivers, and waited for the Royal navy to arrive. Lafayette positioned his troops to block an overland escape from the peninsula.

Victory at Yorktown   To the north, Washington at once saw the opportunity to deal the British a fatal blow. A French army had just joined the Continental Army in New York. Washington quickly moved the combined American-French force south, while the French fleet set up a blockade off the Virginia coast. When the British navy arrived in early September, the French ships drove it off.

A few days later, Washington's troops arrived to reinforce Lafayette's force, and the **Battle of Yorktown** began. In early October, the American and French artillery began to pound Yorktown. Cornwallis now faced an army more than twice the size of his own, blocking his escape from the peninsula. The French fleet prevented him from being reinforced or removed by sea. He realized that escape was impossible. On October 19, 1781, Cornwallis surrendered to Washington.

In the illustration above, American colonists are pulling down a statue of King George III.

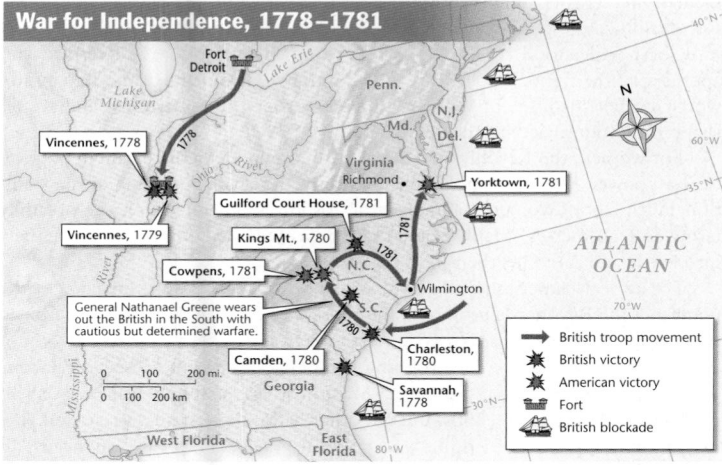

War for Independence, 1778–1781

General Nathanael Greene wears out the British in the South with cautious but determined warfare.

British troop movement
British victory
American victory
Fort
British blockade

MAP SKILLS Fighting shifted south during the latter part of the war. **Movement** *How was General Washington able to trap the British at Yorktown?*

ACTIVITY
Connecting with Culture

Tradition holds that, after their surrender at Yorktown, the British played a tune with an appropriate title: "The World Turned Upside Down." (Historians debate whether this really did occur.) Have students locate the lyrics to the song and write a brief essay about it. **(Verbal/Linguistic)**

BACKGROUND
Geography in History

From the beginning of the war, geography helped the American cause by making it impossible for Britain to control the American seacoast. Blockade-running colonists needed to go no farther than the Caribbean to beat the blockade and find a market. Since the trade winds from Europe led directly to the Caribbean islands, many other countries found them an ideal location for trading with America. The neutral port of the Dutch-held island of St. Eustasius was especially crowded with American ships, where traders could buy anything from tea to gunpowder, guns to sugar. In 1780 the Admiral of the British fleet wrote, "This rock of only six miles in length and three in breadth has done more harm than all the arms of her most potent enemies, and alone supported the infamous American rebellion."

CUSTOMIZE FOR ...

ESL

Have students read the material in this section. Then have them use the map on this page to explain the latter part of the Revolutionary War in their own words.

CAPTION ANSWERS

Map Skills The British were located on a peninsula. American and French troops under Washington's command attacked from the landward side while the French Navy defeated the British fleet off the coast, preventing British reinforcements from arriving by sea.

Fast Forward to Today

Having a Voice in Government

Lack of representation in Parliament fueled the conflicts that caused the American colonists to take up arms. Representation remains a fundamental right of Americans—a right that is exercised by voting.

"No taxation without representation!" So strong was American colonists' demand for a voice in government that they fought to secure it. Representation means that we choose our public officials and expect them to express our needs and wishes.

The Patriots' victory did not bring representation to all Americans. Only white men who owned a certain amount of property could vote. Women, African Americans, Native Americans, and many white men had little voice in government. Expansion of voting rights to include all adult citizens would occur only after a long and painful struggle.

The percentage of Americans who are eligible to vote has increased tremendously since our nation's founding, yet the percentage of Americans who actually exercise their voting rights has declined. In the late 1800s, voter participation averaged more than 70 percent. By the 1960s, it had fallen to around 60 percent. In the presidential election of 2000, only 51 percent of those eligible voted. This figure was up slightly from 49 percent in 1996. The United States continues to have one of the lowest voter turnouts of all democratic nations.

? Do you think Americans today are as interested in having a voice in government as they were at the time of the Revolution? Explain.

The Treaty of Paris Nearly two years passed between the surrender of Cornwallis and the signing of the peace treaty that formally ended the war. Because four nations (Great Britain, France, Spain, and the United States) were involved in the peace process, negotiations were long and complex. The **Treaty of Paris (1783)** contained these major provisions:

1. Great Britain recognized the independence of the United States of America.
2. The northern border between the United States and British Canada was set from New England to the Mississippi River, primarily along the Great Lakes.
3. The Mississippi River was established as the boundary between the new United States and Spanish territory to the west. Navigation on the river was to be forever open to American and British citizens.
4. Florida, which Britain had gained from the Spanish after the French and Indian War, was returned to Spain. The border between Florida and the United States was set.
5. Great Britain agreed to withdraw its remaining troops from United States territory.
6. Congress pledged to recommend to the states that the rights and property of American Loyalists be restored and that no future action be taken against them. Persecution of Loyalists continued after the war, however.

The Impact of the Revolution

In 1776, the American people declared their independence to the world, and in 1783, Great Britain accepted American independence. The Revolution did more than establish American independence. It also helped inspire Americans' **patriotism,** or love of their country. Patriotism is the passion that inspires a person to serve his or her country, either in defending it from invasion or protecting its rights and maintaining its laws and institutions. People who had made sacrifices during the Revolution, and especially people whose friends or relatives had given their lives in it, best understood the value of the freedom their country had earned, and appreciated the rights for which they had fought. The effects of the Revolution would be felt in different ways by different groups of Americans, and would shape American society to the present day.

For women, the Revolution did not produce any immediate gain in political or legal power. Yet experiences during the war did challenge some of the traditional ideas about women. As men set off for war, women took charge of family farms and businesses. Many women also followed their husbands and fathers into battle and cared for them.

For African Americans, the results of the Revolution were mixed. On the one hand, the Revolution promoted the antislavery cause in the North. As Abigail Adams put it, "It always appeared a most iniquitous [evil] scheme to me to fight ourselves for what we are daily robbing and plundering from those who have as good a right to freedom as we have." Most northern states abolished slavery in the late 1700s and early 1800s. On the other hand, these states also passed laws severely limiting the legal rights and political power of African Americans. In the South, if the Revolution brought about any change in slavery at all, that change was to make it more restrictive. At the same time, the Revolution opened a way for African Americans to become more conscious of the possibilities of freedom. Many free African Americans in Philadelphia and elsewhere named their children after George Washington and Thomas Jefferson, men who came to symbolize liberty and the Revolution, but who also held slaves. As blacks attempted to share in the benefits of the victory, they were faced with the limitations of what liberty could mean for them.

For Native Americans, the war's outcome was a disaster. The power of the Iroquois League was destroyed, and the nations were essentially pushed out of New York. For decades after the Revolution, Americans justified their attacks on Cherokees, Shawnees, and other southern and western Indians by pointing to these nations' support for the British.

Perhaps the greatest effect of the Revolution was to spread the idea of liberty, both at home and abroad. In 1776, the Congress had used Thomas Jefferson's assertion that "all men are created equal" to help justify a revolution. This was a radical concept in a world that had long accepted the idea of human inequality.

Jefferson, like most members of the Continental Congress, probably had no thought of applying the principle of liberty to people other than white men. However, he had set in motion a powerful force that no one could long control. Over the next two centuries and beyond, many groups in the United States, such as women and African Americans, would demand and win greater equality. At the same time, the principles for which the Patriots fought would inspire people around the world. Indeed, in the United States and many other parts of the world, people today are still discovering the full meaning of those principles.

VIEWING FINE ART Archibald Willard painted *The Spirit of '76* in 1875 for Pennsylvania's centennial celebration. He originally called the painting *Yankee Doodle*. **Identifying Central Issues** *What was this "spirit" that led the American colonists to rebel against England and win the war?*

Section 5 Assessment

READING COMPREHENSION

1. How did **blockades** and **profiteering** contribute to economic hardship for American soldiers?

2. What problems did **inflation** cause during the Revolution?

3. What happened during the **Battle of Yorktown?**

4. What were the terms of the **Treaty of Paris (1783)?**

5. How did the Revolutionary War inspire American **patriotism?**

CRITICAL THINKING AND WRITING

6. **Determining Relevance** Explain why the Continental Congress had difficulty financing the war. What impact did funding issues have on Washington's army?

7. **Drawing Conclusions** Which of the battles discussed in this section were most important in the American Revolution? Why?

8. **Writing to Describe** Make a list of George Washington's leadership qualitites. Use the list to write a description of his role in the American Revolution.

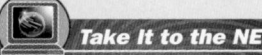
Take It to the NET

Activity: Writing a News Article
Learn more about the final battles of the Revolutionary War. Write a news article about the events leading to the British surrender at Yorktown, as if you were trying to explain it to American readers in 1781. Use the links provided in the *America: Pathways to the Present* area of the following Web site for help in completing this activity.
www.phschool.com

Section 5 Assessment

Reading Comprehension

1. Blockades led to shortages, which promoted profiteering and meant that military supplies and other necessities were harder to obtain.

2. It drastically reduced people's ability to buy goods.

3. General Washington trapped the British by land while the French Navy prevented reinforcements from landing. As a result, Cornwallis was forced to surrender.

4. Great Britain recognized U.S. independence; U.S. northern and western borders were decided; Mississippi River navigation was opened to American and British citizens; Florida was returned to Spain, and the border between Florida and the U.S. was set; Great Britain withdrew its remaining troops from U.S. territory.

5. In defending their country, people began to have a different kind of feeling toward their country. Through sacrifices people began to truly understand the value of the freedom their country had earned.

Critical Thinking and Writing

6. The Congress did not have taxation power; the army was starving and was often without proper clothing.

7. Answers will vary, but should be supported with facts from the section.

8. Lists might include Washington's daring and innovative ability and his willingness to share hardships. Descriptions will vary.

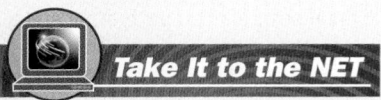
Take It to the NET

Students' articles should chronicle the events leading to the British surrender clearly and objectively, within the context of the time.

CAPTION ANSWERS

Viewing Fine Art The "spirit" was in part a growing confidence among the Patriots in their capacity for self-government.

REVIEWING KEY TERMS

Students should refer to the definitions of key terms in the chapter to write sentences that show an understanding of the key aspects of the era.

REVIEWING MAIN IDEAS

11. It proposed a grand council of representatives from the colonies. It provided a model for the future government of the United States.

12. British Prime Minister William Pitt persuaded Parliament to raise taxes and borrow money, enabling the British to fight a major campaign in North America. Americans lost respect for the British after witnessing British military blunders and believed that the British did not respect them.

13. The British had incurred heavy debts fighting the war, and so increased taxes on the colonists.

14. It caused widespread protests and a boycott.

15. It helped colonists to understand the issues behind the conflict and persuaded many to support a complete break with Britain.

16. It marked a radical change in the nature of the conflict. It made clear that the Revolution was a war of national liberation.

17. The British attacked two hills near Boston Harbor. The British were eventually successful, but suffered heavy casualties. The stubborn fight put up by the Americans strengthened the Patriot cause.

18. British strengths: superb army and navy; help from Loyalists, African Americans, Native Americans, and mercenaries. British weaknesses: The war was unpopular in Great Britain; troops had to fight in hostile territory at the end of extremely long supply lines; British commanders failed to adapt their tactics. American strengths: fighting on familiar territory; appropriate tactics; support from the majority of African Americans; leadership of George Washington. American weaknesses: lack of a well-supplied, effective fighting force; and for over two years the Americans had to fight alone, without European allies.

creating a CHAPTER SUMMARY

Copy this flowchart (right) on a piece of paper and complete it by adding information about the events that led to American victory in the Revolution.

iTEXT

For additional review and enrichment activities, see the interactive version of *America: Pathways to the Present*, available on the Web and on CD-ROM.

French and Indian War
↓
New British Policies
↓
↓
↓

★ Reviewing Key Terms

For each of the terms below, write a sentence explaining how it relates to the American Revolution.

1. siege
2. boycott
3. Boston Massacre
4. Enlightenment
5. natural rights
6. Loyalist
7. mercenary
8. inflation
9. Battle of Yorktown
10. Treaty of Paris (1783)

★ Reviewing Main Ideas

11. Describe the proposed Albany Plan of Union and its outcome. What was its long-term impact? (Section 1)

12. How did the British win the French and Indian War? How did the war weaken the colonists' loyalty to Britain? (Section 1)

13. Why did British policies in the colonies change after 1763? (Section 2)

14. What were the effects of the Stamp Act? (Section 2)

15. How did Thomas Paine's *Common Sense* influence colonists? (Section 3)

16. Explain the importance of the Declaration of Independence. (Section 3)

17. Describe the Battle of Bunker Hill. What was its importance in the American Revolution? (Section 4)

18. What were the strengths and weaknesses of the British and the Americans at the start of the war? (Section 4)

19. How did the fighting affect trade and the economy throughout the revolution? (Section 5)

20. What problems did the British army face at Yorktown? (Section 5)

★ Critical Thinking

21. Analyzing Information   The Iroquois League took sides against the British in the French and Indian War, but then fought with the British against the colonists during the Revolution. Were these alliances in the Indians' best interests? Explain.

22. Identifying Assumptions   What assumptions did the British make in deciding to enforce new taxes in the colonies?

23. Identifying Central Issues   Review the excerpt on page 115. Are the colonists demanding independence from Britain? Explain.

24. Predicting Consequences   Could the Americans have won the Revolutionary War without help from Europe? Explain your reasoning.

25. Making Comparisons   Evaluate the impact of the American Revolution from the point of view of (a) women, (b) African Americans, (c) Native Americans, and (d) people around the world.

CREATING A CHAPTER SUMMARY

French and Indian War
↓
New British Policies
↓
Declaration of Independence
↓
Fighting for Independence
↓
The War Is Won

JOIN, or DIE.

★ Skills Assessment

Analyzing Political Cartoons ▶

26. Several versions of this cartoon by Benjamin Franklin were printed during the American Revolution. (a) What do the segments of the snake represent? (b) How do you know?

27. What is the message of the cartoon?

28. What makes this an effective cartoon?

Analyzing Primary Sources

Read this excerpt that appeared in Section 3, and then answer the questions that follow.

> ❝ [G]overnments are dissolved . . . when such a single person or prince sets up his own arbitrary will in place of the laws. . . . Secondly, when the prince hinders the legislative [legislature] from . . . acting freely. . . . Thirdly, when by the arbitrary power of the prince, the electors, or ways of election are altered, without the consent, and contrary to the common interest of the people. ❞
> —John Locke, *Second Treatise of Government*, 1690

29. What does the word *arbitrary* in this passage mean?

    A weakened
    B unkind
    C absolute and based on one's own preference
    D careful

30. Which statement best summarizes the excerpt?

    F People can dissolve a government when the ruler ignores the laws.
    G Government by an arbitrary ruler interferes with elections.
    H The common people must not act against the elected ruler.
    J Rulers will often interfere with the legislature.

Applying the Chapter Skill: *Reading Biographies and Autobiographies*

31. Reread the excerpt about the soldier in the Battle of Princeton on page 131. Does the account appear to be biographical or autobiographical? Why? Analyze the account's reliability as historical evidence.

ACTIVITIES

Writing to LEARN

Writing an Opinion
What were the colonists' grievances against the British? How did the British respond to the colonists' complaints? Consider all the factors that contributed to the unrest in the colonies, then state your opinion as to whether or not revolution was necessary for the colonists to gain liberty. Support your opinion with facts and details from the chapter.

Primary Source CD-ROM

Working With Primary Sources Find additional information on the American Revolution on the *Exploring Primary Sources in U.S. History CD-ROM* and use the selection(s) provided to complete the Chapter 4 primary source activity located in the *America: Pathways to the Present* area of the following Web site. **www.phschool.com**

Take It to the NET

Chapter Self-Test As a review activity, take the Chapter 4 Self-Test in the *America: Pathways to the Present* area at the Web site listed below. The questions are designed to test your understanding of the chapter content. **www.phschool.com**

Chapter 4 Assessment **139**

---

19. Trade was interrupted due to the British blockade; profiteering and inflation made necessary goods unavailable to most Americans.

20. Blockade by the French and twice their number in American and French troops.

CRITICAL THINKING

21. The lifestyle and trading practices of the French were compatible with the Native American way of life, so they made natural allies. Conversely, Native Americans came to Britain's aid during the Revolution as they feared a Patriot victory would mean more westward migration.

22. The British government assumed the colonists would not object to the Sugar Act and other taxes.

23. No. They were outlining their grievances, looking for understanding and a way to resolve the crisis.

24. Answers will vary, but should discuss the assistance lent by France, Spain, and the Netherlands, as well as the contributions of individual foreign figures.

25. (a) While the Revolution did not produce any immediate gain in political or legal power for women, it did begin to challenge some of women's traditional roles. (b) The war created an awareness of the possibilities of freedom for African Americans. (c) The Iroquois nations were pushed off their land, and Native American support for the British was used as justification for future persecution. (d) It set an example for other nations of the triumph of liberty and popular sovereignty.

SKILLS ASSESSMENT

26. (a) The thirteen colonies. (b) Each segment is labeled with the initial of either a state or a region.

27. The colonies must unite to survive.

28. The imagery is easy to understand and makes a powerful impression.

29. C

30. F

31. Autobiographical, because the author is describing his own experiences and observations. This account seems to be reliable because it reflects what is known about the conditions Washington's army faced.

ANSWERS TO ACTIVITIES

Writing to LEARN

Answers will vary, but should be supported with facts and details from the chapter.

Primary Source CD-ROM

Direct students to the additional primary sources that can be found on the *Exploring Primary Sources in U.S. History CD-ROM.*

 ### Take It to the NET

Additional support materials and activities for Chapter 4 of *America: Pathways to the Present* can be found in the Social Studies area at the Prentice Hall School Web site. **www.phschool.com**

DIARY OF A WARTIME WINTER

Focus Have students find the meaning of each of these words in a dictionary before they begin to read: *acquaintance, conjectured, prophesy, procure.* Explain that Israel Putnam was an American general from Connecticut. Ask them to think, as they read, about the advantages of fighting on one's home soil.

Instruct Review the account of the battles at Trenton and Princeton in the textbook. Discuss details that make this a factual, objective account of the battle. Then discuss how the information provided in the diary entries differs from the description in the chapter. Ask volunteers for words and phrases describing the point of view of the diary entries. *(Personal, emotional)*

Analyzing the Document Have students explain how the diary entries enhance their understanding of the Revolution.

Use this additional question to generate class discussion:

Critical Thinking: Making Inferences How does Margaret Hill Morris regard Count Donop? Give evidence from the document to support your answer. *(At first, Morris resents Donop for ignoring her town's request to remain neutral, but later she comes to respect him. After his death, Morris observes that the Hessians "have lost a brave and humane commander.")*

AmericanHeritage®
MY BRUSH WITH HISTORY™
by MARGARET HILL MORRIS

Diary of a Wartime Winter

Fought in the towns and farms of the American colonies, the battles of the American Revolution dominated the lives not only of soldiers but of the unlucky civilians who lived nearby. The editors of *American Heritage* magazine have selected entries from the diary of Margaret Hill Morris. Morris lived in New Jersey, site of the Battle of Princeton and other battles.

DECEMBER 22, 1776: It is said Putnam with 1,000 men [600 New Jersey militia and Virginia artillerymen] are at Mount Holly. All the women removed from the town, except one widow of our acquaintance. This evening we hear the sound of much hammering at Bristol, and it is conjectured that a fortification is carrying on there. More cannon are said to be planted on the island. We hear this afternoon that the gentlemen who went last to the Count Donop [Col. Carl von Donop, Hessian]

The Death of General Mercer at the Battle of Princeton, January 3, 1777, *by John Trumbull*

140

with a request that our town might be allowed to remain a neutral one, are returned, and report that he had too many affairs of greater consequence in hand to attend to them, or give an answer. I think we don't like the Count quite so well today as we did yesterday. . . .

We hear this afternoon that our officers are afraid their men will not fight and wish they may all run home again. A peaceable man ventured to prophesy today that if the war is continued through the winter, the British troops will be scared at the sight of our men, for as they never fought with naked men, the novelty of it will terrify them and make them retreat faster than they advanced to meet them; for he says, from the present appearance of our ragged troops, he thinks it probable they will not have clothes to cover them a month or two hence. . . .

DEC. 29: This morning the soldiers at the next house prepared to depart, and as they passed my door, they stopped to bless and thank me for the food I sent them, which I received, not as my due, but as belonging to my Master who had reached a morsel to them by my hands. A great number of soldiers are in town today. Another company took possession of the next house when the first left it. The inhabitants are

---

RESOURCE DIRECTORY

Technology
AmericanHeritage® My Brush with History™
Videotapes *Diary of a Wartime Winter*

☑ **TEST PREPARATION**

Have students use the excerpt on these pages to answer the following question.

From what you have read, which statement best describes Margaret Hill Morris?

A She hates the enemy soldiers who were captured.

Ⓑ She is deeply compassionate.

C She despairs at humankind.

D She is prejudiced against soldiers.

much straitened for bread to supply the soldiers and firewood to keep them warm. This seems to be only one of the many calamities of war.

DEC. 30: A number of poor soldiers sick and wounded brought into town today, and lodged in the court-house; some of them in private houses. Today I hear several of our town's men have agreed to procure wood for the soldiers; but they found it was attended with considerable difficulty, as most of the wagons usually employed to bring in wood were pressed to take the soldiers' baggage.

DEC. 31: We have been told of an engagement between the two armies, in which it was said the English had 400 taken prisoners, and 300 killed and wounded. The report of the evening contradicts the above intelligence, and there is no certain account of a battle.

THE START OF A NEW YEAR

JANUARY 1, 1777: This New Year's day has not been ushered in with the usual ceremonies and rejoicing; indeed, I believe it will be the beginning of a sorrowful year to very many people. Yet the flatterer—hope—bids me look forward with confidence and trust in Him who can bring order out of this great confusion. I do not hear that any messengers have been in town from the camp.

JAN. 3: This morning between 8 and 9 o'clock we heard very distinctly a heavy firing of cannon. The sound came from toward Trenton. About noon a number of [American] soldiers, upwards of 1,000, came into town in great confusion with baggage and some cannon. From these soldiers we learn there was a smart engagement yesterday at Trenton, and that they left them engaged near Trenton Mill, but were not able to say which side was victorious. . . .

Several of those who lodged in Col. Cox's house last week returned tonight, and asked for the key, which I gave them. At about bedtime I went into the next house to see if the fires were safe, and my heart was melted with compassion to see such a number of my fellow creatures lying like swine on the floor, fast asleep, and many of

them without even a blanket to cover them. It seems very strange to me that such a number should be allowed to come from the camp at the very time of the engagements, and I shrewdly suspect they have run away—for they can give no account why they came, nor where they are to march next.

JAN. 4: The accounts hourly coming in are so contradictory and various that we know not which to give credit to. We have heard our people have gained another victory [Battle of Princeton], that the English are fleeing before them, some at Brunswick, some at Princeton. We hear today that Sharp Delany, Anthony Morris, and others of the Philadelphia militia are killed, and that the Count Donop is numbered with the dead; if so, the Hessians have lost a brave and humane commander. The prisoners taken by our troops are sent to Lancaster jail. A number of sick and wounded were brought into town—calls upon us to extend a hand of charity towards them. Several of my soldiers left the next house, and returned to the place from whence they came. Upon my questioning them pretty close, I brought several to confess they had run away, being scared at the heavy firing on the 3rd. There were several innocent looking lads among them, and I sympathised with their mothers when I saw them preparing to return to the army.

Source: *Weathering the Storm: Women of the American Revolution* by Elizabeth Evan, Scribner's, 1975.

Understanding Primary Sources

1. What is a "flatterer"?
2. Why, given her situation, does Morris refer to hope as a "flatterer"?

American Heritage®
MY BRUSH WITH **HISTORY**™
Videotapes

For more information about the Revolutionary War, view "Diary of a Wartime Winter."

141

Chapter 5 Planning Guide
Resource Manager

	CORE INSTRUCTION	READING/SKILLS
Chapter-Level Resources	**Teaching Resources** • Pacing Charts booklet • Block Scheduling booklet **Resource Pro® CD-ROM**, Ch. 5 **Prentice Hall Presentation Pro CD-ROM**, Ch. 5 **www.phschool.com** • eTeach	**Guided Reading Audiotapes (English/Spanish)** **Student Edition on Audio CD**, Ch. 5 **Social Studies Skills Tutor CD-ROM** **Color Transparencies**, A8, A55, B2, B3
1 Government by the States 1. Describe the early government of the United States. 2. State some reasons for opposition to the Articles of Confederation. 3. Learn about the causes and effect of Shays' Rebellion.	**Teaching Resources** **Units 1/2 booklet** • Section 1 Quiz, p. 53	**Guided Reading and Review booklet**, p. 20 **Guide to the Essentials**, p. 26 **Section Reading Support Transparencies**
2 The Constitutional Convention 1. Find out what the Founding Fathers hoped to achieve as they assembled for the Constitutional Convention. 2. Learn about issues that divided the convention. 3. See what the convention did to reach agreement. 4. Discover qualities that have made the Constitution a lasting document. 5. Realize how the structure of the government under the Constitution divides power.	**Teaching Resources** **Units 1/2 booklet** • Section 2 Quiz, p. 54 **Learning Styles Lesson Plans booklet**, p. 12	**Guided Reading and Review booklet**, p. 21 **Guide to the Essentials**, p. 27 **Learning with Documents booklet**, p. 10 **Section Reading Support Transparencies**
3 Ratifying the Constitution 1. Learn how the position of the Federalists differed from that of the anti-Federalists. 2. See how the Federalists won approval of the Constitution. 3. Find out about arguments for and against a Bill of Rights.	**Teaching Resources** **Units 1/2 booklet** • Section 3 Quiz, p. 55 **Learning Styles Lesson Plans booklet**, p. 13	**Guided Reading and Review booklet**, p. 22 **Guide to the Essentials**, p. 28 **Learning with Documents booklet**, p. 77 **Skills for Life booklet**, p. 7 **Section Reading Support Transparencies**
4 The New Government 1. Learn about the new leaders selected by President Washington. 2. Discover the challenges faced by Washington's government. 3. See the kinds of details that were involved in planning the capital city.	**Teaching Resources** **Units 1/2 booklet** • Section 4 Quiz, p. 56	**Guided Reading and Review booklet**, p. 23 **Guide to the Essentials**, p. 29 **Section Reading Support Transparencies**

142 A ★ Chapter 5 *Planning Guide*

ENRICHMENT/PRE-AP

Prentice Hall United States History Video Collection™
www.phschool.com
- Section Activities, Virtual Field Trip, Chapter Activities, Current Events Online

Biography, Literature, and Comparing Primary Sources booklet, pp. 105–106
Nystrom *Atlas of Our Country,* pp. 20–21
Exploring Primary Sources in U.S. History CD-ROM

Biography, Literature, and Comparing Primary Sources booklet, p. 44
American History Block Scheduling Support
Sounds of an Era Audio CD

American History Block Scheduling Support
Sounds of an Era Audio CD
Exploring Primary Sources in U.S. History CD-ROM

Biography, Literature, and Comparing Primary Sources booklet, p. 10
American Pathways Thematic Posters

ASSESSMENT

Core Assessment
ExamView® Test Bank, Ch. 5
ExamView® Test Bank CD-ROM, Ch. 5

Standardized Test Preparation
Diagnose and Prescribe
Diagnostic Tests for High School Social Studies Skills

Review and Reteach
Review Book for U.S. History

Practice and Assess
Test-taking Strategies With Transparencies
Test-taking Strategies Posters
Test Prep Book for U.S. History
Alternative Assessment Handbook
Document-Based Assessment

Teaching Resources
Units 1/2 booklet
- Section Quizzes, pp. 53–56
- Chapter Tests, pp. 57, 60

www.phschool.com Ch. 5 Self-Test

AmericanHeritage RESOURCES

From the Archives of American Heritage®, p. 166
AmericanHeritage® My Brush with History™ Videotapes
www.americanheritage.com

Don't miss the exclusive interactive version of this textbook on the Web and on CD-ROM.

Chapter 5 Planning Guide
In Your Classroom

CUSTOMIZE FOR INDIVIDUAL NEEDS

Gifted and Talented

Teacher's Edition
- Customize for Gifted and Talented, pp. 149, 157, 161

Teaching Resources
- Biography, Literature, and Comparing Primary Sources booklet, pp. 10, 44, 105–106

Technology
- Exploring Primary Sources in U.S. History CD-ROM *Articles of Confederation; New York State Constitution of 1777; The Federalist Papers, No. 1, Alexander Hamilton; Objections to the Constitution, George Madison; U.S. Constitution: The Bill of Rights; English Bill of Rights*

ESL

Teacher's Edition
- Customize for ESL, pp. 153, 169

Teaching Resources
- Guided Reading and Review booklet, pp. 20–23
- Guide to the Essentials (English/Spanish), Chapter 5

Technology
- Student Edition on Audio CD, Chapter 5
- Guided Reading Audiotapes (English/Spanish), Chapter 5
- Section Reading Support Transparencies

Less Proficient Readers

Teacher's Edition
- Customize for Less Proficient Readers, p. 145

Teaching Resources
- Guided Reading and Review booklet, pp. 20–23
- Guide to the Essentials (English/Spanish), Chapter 5

Technology
- Student Edition on Audio CD, Chapter 5
- Guided Reading Audiotapes (English/Spanish), Chapter 5
- Section Reading Support Transparencies

Less Proficient Writers

Teacher's Edition
- Customize for Less Proficient Writers, p. 167

Teaching Resources
- Guided Reading and Review booklet, pp. 20–23
- Guide to the Essentials (English/Spanish), Chapter 5

Technology
- Student Edition on Audio CD, Chapter 5
- Guided Reading Audiotapes (English/Spanish), Chapter 5
- Section Reading Support Transparencies

TEACHER'S EDITION INDEX

CHAPTER 5 – PACING SUGGESTIONS

For 90-minute Blocks

- Teach sections 1, 2, and 3 using Transparencies A8, A55, B2, and B3, and the Recent Scholarship note on page 162 for class discussions.

Running Out of Time?

If you are running short on time to cover this chapter, consider the following options:

- Use the Prentice Hall Presentation Pro CD-ROM to create an outline for this chapter.

- Use the Section Summaries for Chapter 5, from **Guide to the Essentials (English/Spanish).**

1 **Government by the States**	**Connecting with History and Government** Have students construct graphic organizers that detail the weaknesses of the Articles of Confederation. **(Visual/Spatial)**	
2 **The Constitutional Convention**	**Connecting with Citizenship** Direct students to review the Preamble to the Constitution and list the goals of the government it establishes. For each goal, have students identify at least two constitutional provisions, laws, or government actions that further that goal. **(Logical/Mathematical)**	
3 **Ratifying the Constitution**	**Connecting with History and Government** Assign students to one of two groups: Federalists or anti-Federalists. Each group will be responsible for creating and presenting a rap or other spoken mnemonic that summarizes their group's position toward the new Constitution and the arguments that support that position. **(Musical/Rhythmic)**	
4 **The New Government**	**Connecting with Citizenship** Assign selected students the roles of new leaders of the United States under the Constitution (Washington, Jefferson, Hamilton, etc.). Students should prepare brief, autobiographical speeches that summarize their characters' beliefs about and roles in the new government. Have these students plan and present a brief panel or play-like presentation for the rest of the class. **(Bodily/Kinesthetic)**	

INTRODUCING THE CHAPTER

A group of powerful men succeeded in writing and winning approval of the federal Constitution and in establishing a strong central government. The conflict generated by their efforts resulted in safeguards in the form of the Bill of Rights to protect Americans' liberty from government infringement.

TIME LINE ACTIVITY

To provide students with practice in using the time line, ask questions such as these:

1. In what year did George Washington retire from the Continental Army? *(1783)*

2. On which countries did France declare war in 1793? *(Britain and Spain)*

3. From where did the federal government move to Washington, D.C., and in what year did it move? *(The government moved from Philadelphia in 1800.)*

eTeach

Be sure to check out this month's online discussion with a Master Teacher. Go to **www.phschool.com**.

Chapter 5
The Constitution of the United States
(1776–1800)

SECTION 1   Government by the States
SECTION 2   The Constitutional Convention
SECTION 3   Ratifying the Constitution
SECTION 4   The New Government

E pluribus unum—"from many, one" was chosen as the nation's motto in 1776.

American Events

1777
The Continental Congress adopts the Articles of Confederation, which established a limited national government.

1783
George Washington retires from the Continental Army.

1786
Shays' Rebellion breaks out, convincing many Americans of the need for a stronger national government.

1787
The Constitutional Convention creates a new plan of government, the Constitution of the United States.

Presidential Terms:

1775   •   1780   •   •   1785   •   •

World Events

Pitt's India Act brings the East India Company under British government control.

1784

RESOURCE DIRECTORY

Teaching Resources
Pacing Charts booklet
Block Scheduling booklet, p. 15
Units 1/2 booklet
• Chapter Summary, p. 52

Other Print Resources
Constitution Study Guide

Technology
Guided Reading Audiotapes (English/Spanish), Ch. 5
Student Edition on Audio CD, Ch. 5
Prentice Hall United States History Video Collection™ Volume 5, *A New Nation*
Prentice Hall Presentation Pro CD-ROM, Ch. 5
Resource Pro® CD-ROM
Social Studies Skills Tutor CD-ROM
Companion Web site, www.phschool.com

Original States and Ratification of the Constitution

BRITISH NORTH AMERICA

NEW SPAIN

Northwest Territory

Territory South of the Ohio River

New Hampshire June 21, 1788

Vermont

Mass.

New York July 26, 1788

Mass., Feb. 6, 1788

R.I., May 29, 1790

Connecticut, Jan. 9, 1788

Pennsylvania Dec. 12, 1787

New Jersey, Dec. 19, 1787

Delaware, Dec. 7, 1787

Maryland, April 28, 1788

Virginia June 25, 1788

North Carolina Nov. 21, 1789

South Carolina May 23, 1788

Georgia Jan. 2, 1788

ATLANTIC OCEAN

Gulf of Mexico

Mississippi River

Missouri River

Ohio River

Red River

N

70° W

40° N

30° N

80° W

	Original 13 states
	United States territory
	United States claim
June 25, 1788	Date of ratification
	1790 borders

0   150   300 mi.
0   150   300 km

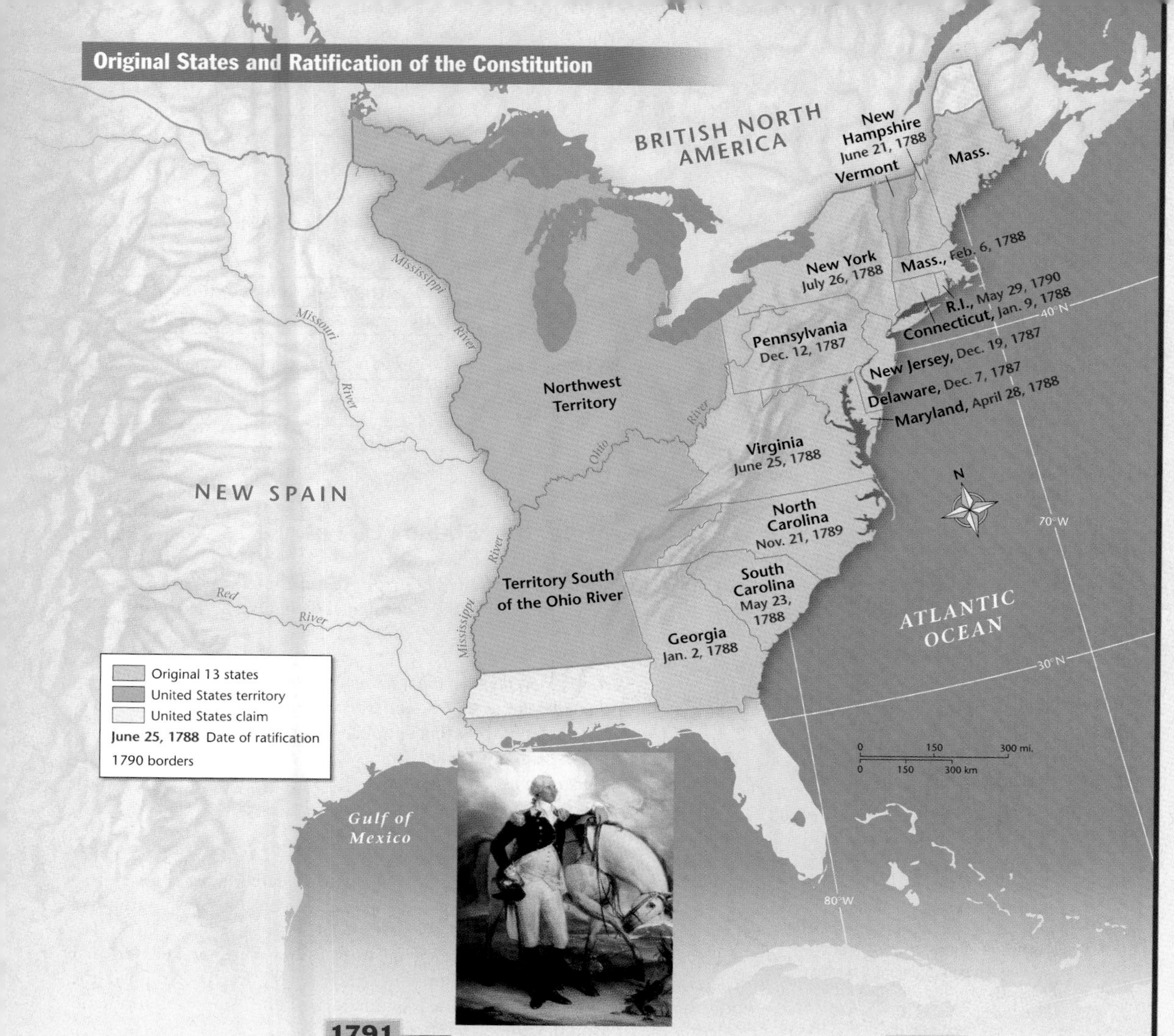

1788
The required number of states ratify the Constitution.

1791
Ten amendments are added to the Constitution and will become known as the Bill of Rights.

1792
President Washington unanimously wins reelection.

1800
The federal government moves from Philadelphia to the new capital, Washington, D.C.

George Washington 1789–1797   John Adams 1797–1801

1790 • • • 1795 • 1800

Citizens storm the Paris Bastille during the French Revolution.
1789

France declares war on Britain and Spain.
1793

Russia, Prussia, and Austria divide Poland.
1795

Napoleon seizes control of France.
1799

Original States and Ratification of the Constitution

Activating Prior Knowledge
Which of the original states was the last to ratify the Constitution? *(Rhode Island)*

Previewing Ask students why they think some states ratified the Constitution later than others did. *(Many people feared that the Constitution granted the President king-like powers and wished to prevent the government from becoming a monarchy by prolonging the ratification process.)*

BACKGROUND
About the Pictures

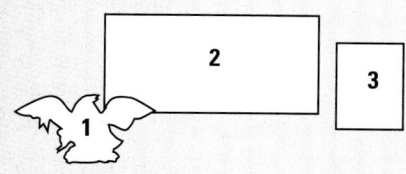

1. Pierre du Simitierre, a consultant and artist, recommended this motto at the first Great Seal Committee.

2. The Constitution was signed by 39 delegates, including George Washington, James Madison, and Benjamin Franklin.

3. Washington's inaugural ceremony was performed on Wall Street in New York.

TEXT

Don't miss the exclusive interactive version of this textbook on the Web and on CD-ROM.

BIBLIOGRAPHY

For the Teacher

Boorstin, D. **The Lost World of Thomas Jefferson.** University of Chicago Press, 1993. (An acclaimed re-creation of the Jeffersonian world view.)

Brookheiser, Richard. **Alexander Hamilton, American.** Touchstone, 2000. (Biography of the man some think of as "the most overlooked Founding Father.")

Grant, Linda. **Founding Mothers: Women in America in the Revolutionary Era.** Houghton Mifflin, 1975. (Narrative accounts of women's contributions during the revolutionary period.)

For the Student

Jefferson, Thomas. **The Portable Thomas Jefferson.** Viking, 1997. (Essential documents penned by one of this country's most influential leaders.)

Legguth, A. J. **Patriots: The Men Who Started the American Revolution.** Simon & Schuster, 1988. (Well-illustrated biographical sketches of some of the most important figures of the Revolution.)

Hamilton, Alexander (Freeman, Joanne B., editor). **Writings.** Library of America, 2001. (A compendium of Hamilton's writings.)

Section

1

Government by the States

SECTION OBJECTIVES

1. Describe the early government of the United States.

2. State some reasons for opposition to the Articles of Confederation.

3. Learn about the causes and effects of Shays' Rebellion.

BELLRINGER

Warm-Up Activity Remind students that federalism ensures that state governments will not usurp the powers of the federal government and vice versa. Ask students on what occasions, or for what reasons, people nowadays turn to the federal government. Why do people expect the federal government to help after disasters? Why are individual states prohibited (under Article 1 of the Constitution) from coining money?

Activating Prior Knowledge Ask students if they can describe the role and importance of the Constitution in the establishment of the United States government.

READING STRATEGY

As students read the section, ask them to list the arguments for and against the Articles of Confederation.

READING FOCUS

- Describe the early government of the United States.
- What were some reasons for opposition to the Articles of Confederation?
- What were the causes and effects of Shays' Rebellion?

MAIN IDEA

The national government under the Articles of Confederation was weak, and political power rested mostly with the states.

KEY TERMS

Articles of Confederation
legislative branch
executive branch
judicial branch
constitution
democracy
republic
Shays' Rebellion
specie

TAKING NOTES

Copy the chart below. As you read, fill in arguments for and against the Articles of Confederation.

The Articles of Confederation	
Arguments For	**Arguments Against**
Most political power belonged to the states.	Congress could not collect taxes.

VIEWING HISTORY This painting shows George Washington saying farewell to his officers after resigning his commission. **Drawing Inferences** Why did Washington's resignation come as a surprise?

Setting the Scene On December 23, 1783, a month after watching the British army leave New York, George Washington performed perhaps the most important act of his life. In an address before the Continental Congress, he voluntarily gave up power:

❝ Having now finished the work assigned me, I retire from the great theatre of Action—and bidding an Affectionate farewell to this August body under whose orders I have long acted, I here offer my Commission, and take my leave of all the employments of public life.❞

—George Washington

The triumphant general was easily the country's most popular and best-known figure. Many people expected him to move into a new role as head of the new nation, maybe even as its king. But Washington had other plans.

Having helped Americans win their freedom from a king, he believed that the nation did not need another supreme ruler. In an act that stunned the world, he gave up his commission as commander of the American army and headed home to Mount Vernon to retire.

Early Government

Americans now faced a new challenge. Could they enjoy their hard-won freedoms without a strong, unified national government? Could they keep their new liberty and maintain order at the same time? In short, what kind of government should a free people have?

The Continental Congress that had approved the Declaration of Independence in 1776 was simply a loose collection of delegates from 13 separate states. Almost no one wanted a powerful national government. Most people regarded the Congress as only a wartime necessity.

Americans at that time generally thought of themselves as citizens of individual states, not of a nation. In fact, when referring to the United States, most

CAPTION ANSWERS

Viewing History With command of the military, Washington had the means to take control of the country. Washington could have become a king. People were surprised that he refused to seize power.

RESOURCE DIRECTORY

Teaching Resources
Guided Reading and Review booklet, p. 20

Technology
Section Reading Support Transparencies
Guided Reading Audiotapes (English/Spanish), Ch. 5
Student Edition on Audio CD, Ch. 5
Color Transparencies *Political Cartoons,* B2
Exploring Primary Sources in U.S. History CD-ROM *Articles of Confederation; New York State Constitution of 1777*

Prentice Hall Presentation Pro CD-ROM, Ch. 5
Companion Web site, www.phschool.com

Americans wrote "the United States *are*" (plural) rather than "the United States *is*" (singular), as people do today. They believed that the country as a whole was less important than its 13 parts. It was not a nation as much as it was a confederation, an alliance of separate governments that work together.

The Articles of Confederation In 1777, the Continental Congress adopted a set of laws to govern the United States. These laws were called the **Articles of Confederation.** Approved in 1781, the Articles established a limited national government. Most of the political power lay with the states:

> **KEY DOCUMENTS** " The said States hereby severally enter into a firm league of friendship with each other, for their common defense, the security of their liberties, and their mutual and general welfare, binding themselves to assist each other, against all force offered to, or attacks made upon them, or any of them, on account of religion, sovereignty, trade, or any other pretense [reason] whatever."
>
> —Article III, Articles of Confederation

The Articles of Confederation established a limited national government.

The national government created by the Articles had only one branch: a legislature, or Congress, made up of delegates from the states. Today, Congress is one of the three separate branches of the American government. The **legislative branch,** or Congress, is the part of the government that is responsible for making laws. The **executive branch,** headed by the President, executes, or puts into action, the laws passed by the Congress. The third part of the government is the **judicial branch,** made up of the courts and judges who interpret and apply the laws in cases brought before them.

By contrast, under the Articles of Confederation, the Congress carried out the duties of both the legislative and executive branches. The Articles did not create a judicial branch. Each state maintained its own court system.

The Congress set up by the Articles differed in several ways from today's Congress. For example, although it could declare war and borrow money, it lacked the power to tax. To carry out its tasks, Congress had to petition the states for money. It had no power to force the states to provide money.

The Articles of Confederation allowed states to send as many representatives to Congress as they wished. However, each of the 13 states had only one vote in Congress. Passage of any measure involving money required 9 votes out of the 13, not just a simple majority of 7. Changes in the Articles themselves could be made only if all 13 states agreed. These provisions made it difficult for the national government to get things done. However, some legislative progress was made under the Articles, notably by establishing a way for settled lands in the West to achieve statehood.

State Constitutions Far more important in the country's early years were the individual state **constitutions.** A constitution is a plan of government that describes the different parts of the government and their duties and powers. During the Revolution and immediately afterward, state governments had more power than the national government of the United States. The individual state constitutions, which created and described the

---

Focus on GOVERNMENT

Three Branches of Government The legislative branch makes the laws; the executive branch enacts the laws; and the judicial branch interprets the laws.

The Historical Context The national government created by the Articles of Confederation did not include an executive or a judicial branch. This omission, which reflected Americans' fear of a strong central government, made it difficult for the national government to operate effectively.

The Concept Today The Constitution of the United States, which replaced the Articles, did provide for three separate branches of government. All three branches remain strong and vital parts of the federal government.

LESSON PLAN

Focus Explain that the years after the American Revolution were difficult ones for the United States, which was disorganized and suffered from economic and political problems. Some Americans, known as Nationalists, demanded a stronger national government. Ask why Nationalists saw this as beneficial.

Instruct Review the ideas that fueled the American Revolution. Have students explain how the United States government before 1788 reflected these ideas. Ask why many Americans were happy with a weak national government.

Assess/Reteach Ask students whether they agree with the Nationalists about the importance of the strongest possible national government. Ask students who agree with this viewpoint to state some of their reasons. Ask those who disagree with this viewpoint to state their reasons, as well.

BACKGROUND
Global Connections

After the success of the American Revolution, many British people blamed King George III, whose irascible nature and inability to compromise, they felt, provoked the American colonies to rebel. Also, the aftermath of the war with America left the British economy severely strained. Within a few years, however, the British economy greatly improved, as trade with the United States became a more lucrative enterprise than it had ever been with the American colonies.

CUSTOMIZE FOR ...

Less Proficient Readers
Have students list the headings in this section. Then ask them to write a brief sentence that summarizes the material under each heading.

Criticisms of the Articles of Confederation

- One vote for each state, regardless of size
- Congress cannot collect taxes to raise money
- Congress powerless to regulate foreign and interstate commerce
- No separate executive branch to enforce acts of Congress
- No national court system to interpret laws
- Amendment only with consent of all the states
- A 9/13 majority required to pass laws
- Articles only a "firm league of friendship"

INTERPRETING CHARTS The confederation entered into by the 13 states gave little real power to the national government. **Drawing Conclusions** How did the Articles limit the power of Congress?

READING CHECK

Why was the economy in trouble after the American Revolution?

Many states printed money during and after the War for Independence.

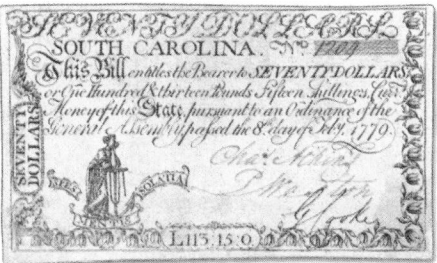

state governments, were thus the primary forms of government in the new nation. Most of these constitutions were established during the Revolution, well before the United States adopted the federal Constitution. State constitutions were also important as models and inspiration for the later national documents.

In its constitution, the state of Pennsylvania introduced bold new ideas about government. Written in 1776, the Pennsylvania constitution gave voting rights to all white men 21 years of age or older who paid taxes. Thus, that state became the first to open the voting process to ordinary people, not just wealthy gentlemen.

The Pennsylvania constitution also created a state legislature that was unicameral. That is, it had just one house, or body of representatives. Today, most state legislatures, as well as the United States Congress, are bicameral, having two houses. Congress, for example, has a House of Representatives and a Senate. Nebraska is currently the only state whose legislature is unicameral.

Finally, representatives in Pennsylvania's legislature had to run for election every year. This provision made state lawmakers very responsive to the people's wishes.

Opposition to the Articles

After fighting a war to gain independence from what they regarded as a tyrannical king and Parliament, Americans generally agreed that their new nation should be a **democracy,** or a government by the people. Specifically, they favored the creation of a **republic,** a government run by the people through their elected representatives. Yet people held widely differing views on how much influence ordinary citizens should have in the governing of the republic. This division became clear as objections to the Articles began to surface.

Economic Problems Wealthy, educated men worried that the Articles had given too much power to ordinary citizens, who were generally less educated. These educated men were more interested in preserving order than expanding freedom, and they had a great deal of disorder to be concerned about.

By 1786, three years after the American Revolution, the nation still had a debt of about $50 million, an unthinkably large sum at that time. State governments and the national government had borrowed money from foreign countries and from their own citizens to pay for the war.

Public and private debt was such a problem that some state governments, lacking gold or silver, printed cheap paper money to help their citizens pay off their loans. This created economic chaos. Desperate for money, states with good seaports put heavy taxes on goods destined for neighboring states, stirring up hostilities and upsetting interstate commerce.

Upper-class critics of the Articles believed that these troubles had arisen because citizens had too much power in their state legislatures. They feared that this was not the best way to run a government.

Concerns About Weak Government By the early 1780s, a group called the Nationalists sought to strengthen the national government. They wanted to restrain what they saw as the unpredictable behavior of the states. The Nationalists included several former military officers, many members of Congress, merchants, planters, and lawyers, and some whose names are now familiar: George Washington, James Madison, and Alexander Hamilton.

In newspaper articles and private letters, Nationalists expressed their views about the dangers of a weak national government. They pointed out that Congress sometimes was unable to act because so many lawmakers failed to attend the sessions. They predicted that the lack of a national court system and national economic policies would create chaos. They feared that the United States would not command respect from the rest of the world.

Most of all, they worried that Americans' fondness for challenging authority and for demanding individual rights was getting out of hand. Nationalists saw this period, from 1781 to 1787, as a dangerous time of indecision about how to govern the new nation.

> ❝ Every man of sense must be convinced that our disturbances have arisen more from the want [lack] of [government] power than the abuse of it. ❞
>
> —Fisher Ames, a Nationalist from Massachusetts

Most Americans did not agree with this view. They reasoned that the state constitutions and the Articles of Confederation were doing exactly what they were supposed to do: maintain a democratic republic. If the resulting government was disorderly and more likely to make mistakes, then so be it. Most Americans thought it was better to have mistakes under a government of the people than to have order under the rule of tyrants. They argued that the government established by the Articles had won independence from Britain. This feat alone showed that the government was strong enough.

Learning From History The Nationalists were well educated in European history. They knew that in Europe, attempts to establish republican governments had failed, dissolving into chaos and then tyranny. Nationalists pointed out that this had happened to the Roman republic more than 1,800 years earlier, and it could happen to the United States as well.

The Nationalists said that history had shown that people were not naturally wise enough to have so much power over their own affairs. George Washington expressed it this way: "We have . . . had too good an opinion of human nature in forming our confederation."

America as a Model Finally, the Nationalists agreed with Thomas Paine that America was a model for the world. It would be irresponsible, they believed, to allow the nation to fall into political violence. One Englishman commented that if this happened:

> ❝ The fairest experiment ever tried in human affairs will miscarry; and . . . a REVOLUTION which had revived the hopes of good men and promised an opening to better times, will become a discouragement to all future efforts in favor of liberty, and prove only an opening to a new scene of human degeneracy and misery. ❞
>
> —Richard Price, 1785

In fact, it was General Washington's understanding of history and his respect for this greater cause that had led him to give up his command to the

Focus on GEOGRAPHY

Who Owns the West? Although the Articles of Confederation were signed in 1777, they were not ratified until 1781 because of a disagreement among the states over western lands. Seven of the 13 states had claims to land west of the Appalachian Mountains. Most of these claims rested on states' colonial charters, some of which had granted states ownership of lands westward to the "South Sea."

The six states without western land claims argued that all such lands should become the property of the entire nation. The states with claims wrote their response into the Articles of Confederation, which declared that no state should be deprived of territory for the benefit of the United States. Furious, one state without a claim—Maryland—refused to ratify the Articles until 1781. Finally, though, the states with western claims gave them up, and the Articles were ratified.

The drawing shows the Great Seal of the United States, adopted by the Continental Congress in 1782.

Chapter 5 Section 1 • **147**

ACTIVITY
Connecting with Citizenship

Point out to students the heading *Learning From History,* and invite a volunteer to summarize the information presented. Then challenge the class to explain how the learning they are doing now is similar, and necessary in a democracy. **(Verbal/Linguistic)**

BACKGROUND
Articles of Confederation

One scholar has said that the Articles of Confederation formed not a government, since it could not govern people directly, "but rather the central agency of an alliance." The cohesiveness of this alliance was tested by foreign powers after 1783 and found wanting. Since the American states could not agree on a unified program of foreign affairs, England and Spain were able to pursue aggressive policies that cut deeply into American interests, especially in trade. Weakened overseas commerce was part of a general deterioration of the economy under the Articles of Confederation.

✓ TEST PREPARATION

Have students read the section "Learning from History" and then answer the question below.

Which of the following is the best restatement of George Washington's quote about the new country?

A It doesn't need a strong central government.

B It needs a strong central government to be able to resolve differences among individual factions.

C It must put the rights of states before the power of the federal government.

D It must study failed democracies.

Connecting with History and Conflict

Assign students the task of writing a one-page in-class essay on "Taxes and Conflict." Students should refer to pre-Revolutionary British taxes, Shays' Rebellion, and political issues today, and address the issue of why taxes are such a volatile issue. **(Verbal/Linguistic)**

BACKGROUND

Shays' Rebellion

About Shays' Rebellion George Washington said to James Madison, "If there exists not a power to check them, what security has a man for life, liberty, or property?" Thomas Jefferson, on the other hand, saw it differently: "A little revolution now and then is a good thing; the tree of liberty must be refreshed from time to time with the blood of patriots and tyrants."

COMPARING PRIMARY SOURCES

The Strength of a New Nation

Amid the social and political upheaval of the 1770s and 1780s, observers differed on whether the United States would survive as a nation.

Analyzing Viewpoints Compare the main arguments made by the two writers. Is there any way in which both writers could be considered correct? Explain your answer.

Unfavorable Opinion

"America is formed for happiness, but not for empire. . . . I [see] insurmountable causes for weakness that will prevent America from being a powerful state. . . . In short, such is the difference of character, manners, religion and interest of the different colonies that if they were left to themselves, there would soon be a civil war from one end of the continent to another."
—British clergyman Andrew Burnaby, Burnaby's Travels Through North America, 1775

Favorable Opinion

"Let us view [America] as it now is—an independent state that has taken an equal station amid the nations of the earth. . . . It is a vitality [living thing], liable, indeed, to many disorders, many dangerous diseases; but it is young and strong, and will struggle . . . against those evils and surmount them. . . . Its strength will grow with its years."
—Former Massachusetts Governor Thomas Pownall, A Memorial Most Humbly Addressed to the Sovereigns of Europe on the Present State of Affairs, Between the Old and New World, 1780

civilian government so promptly. He did not want to play the role of Julius Caesar of ancient Rome, a general who became a symbol of tyranny by replacing a republican government with a dictatorship.

The Annapolis Convention In 1786, Nationalists held a convention in Annapolis, Maryland, to discuss economic problems that could not be solved under the limits of the Articles. The Annapolis Convention grew out of a previous convention that had been held at Washington's home at Mount Vernon. There, Maryland and Virginia had met to resolve their trade disputes. In Annapolis, a federal plan for regulating interstate and foreign trade was sought. However, the convention failed to rally interest in dealing with the weaknesses in the Articles. Only 12 delegates from five states attended the convention. Those who came took only one step, but it would be an important one: they agreed to call another convention in Philadelphia in 1787 to try to fix the government.

Shays' Rebellion

Meanwhile, a crisis occurred in Massachusetts that would boost support for the Nationalists' cause: **Shays' Rebellion.**

The Causes of the Rebellion In the years following the war, merchants and wealthy people who had loaned money to the states started to demand their money back. They pressed the impoverished states to pass high taxes in order to collect the money to pay off the debts.

In Massachusetts, legislators passed the heaviest direct tax ever. The tax was to be paid in **specie**—gold or silver coin—rather than in paper money. Compared to paper money, specie was far more scarce, and worth much more.

The lawmakers and merchants who supported the tax generally lived in eastern coastal regions of the state. Opposition came from farmers in the western part of the state, the area most hard-hit by the new tax. To these citizens the situation brought back memories of the British taxes that had helped spark the American Revolution.

Liberty and order clashed in Shays' Rebellion, as protesters—shown here blocking a courthouse—refused to pay taxes, and the government insisted that laws be obeyed.

RESOURCE DIRECTORY

Teaching Resources

Units 1/2 booklet
• Section 1 Quiz, p. 53

Guide to the Essentials
• Section 1 Summary, p. 26

Other Print Resources

Nystrom *Atlas of Our Country* Early Expansion of the United States, pp. 20–21

Technology

RESOURCE PRO® **Literature Activity** *The Contrast,* found on Resource Pro, helps students understand some contemporary views of Shays' Rebellion.

RESOURCE PRO® **Biography** *Captain Daniel Shays,* found on Resource Pro, profiles the leader of the influential Shays' Rebellion against the Massachusetts state government.

Farmers complained bitterly to the state legislature to take back the tax. The state refused. Overloaded with debt, farmers grew desperate as the courts seized their possessions.

Like many farmers in the region, Daniel Shays was a war veteran who now found himself facing the possibility of being jailed for his debts. In 1786, he led a rebellion that quickly spread through the local area. Citizens drove off tax collectors and protested the new taxes with petitions and public meetings. When the state courts rejected their petitions, the rebels forced the courts to close.

Angry crowds rioted. Shays and a small army marched to the city of Springfield, where guns were stored at an arsenal. As open conflict raged, Congress could only look on helplessly. It had no money to raise an army and no way to force states to pay for one. Finally, the state government gathered an army and sent it to the western part of Massachusetts, where it quieted the rebellion in January 1787.

Many rebels and their families left Massachusetts for Vermont or New York, states with lower taxes. Shays and a few others were arrested and sentenced to death. Shays appealed the sentence and eventually regained his freedom.

Effects of the Rebellion For the rebels themselves, Shays' Rebellion demonstrated their determination to defy the authority of any government when it acted against the people's wishes. Far more important, the rebellion demonstrated to many prominent Americans that steps had to be taken to strengthen the national government and avoid civil unrest.

In May 1787, the convention called by the delegates at Annapolis opened in the city of Philadelphia. This time, convinced of the urgent need for government reform, 12 states (all but Rhode Island) sent delegates. The business at hand, wrote key delegate James Madison, was to "decide forever the fate of republican government."

VIEWING HISTORY Though the Revolution was over, many Americans were still challenging authority. In this engraving, an angry crowd puts an end to a county meeting by throwing a government official into a brook. **Drawing Conclusions** How did incidents such as this one bolster the arguments of the Nationalists?

Reading Comprehension

1. To create a limited national government, to create a set of laws to govern the United States, and to leave most of the political power with the states.

2. Legislative branch: makes the laws; executive branch: puts the laws passed by Congress into action; judicial branch: interprets and applies the laws.

3. White male suffrage granted, regardless of wealth; unicameral state legislature; representatives in Pennsylvania's legislature had to run for election every year.

4. A democracy is a government by the people. A republic is a government run by the people through their elected representatives.

5. Compared to paper money, specie was far more scarce and thus worth a great deal more.

Critical Thinking and Writing

6. Sample answers: causes—high taxes to be paid in specie, farmers drowning in debt, war veterans felt they should be treated better; effects—showed the resolve of citizens to fight heavy-handed government, supported Nationalists' claim that stronger government was needed to avoid chaos.

7. Lists will vary, but should be supported with facts from the section.

Articles should chronicle events leading up to either Shays' Rebellion or the Annapolis Convention, describe the event itself, and demonstrate an understanding of its historical significance.

Section **1** Assessment

READING COMPREHENSION

1. What was the purpose of the **Articles of Confederation?**

2. What are the responsibilities of the **legislative branch,** the **executive branch,** and the **judicial branch?**

3. What were some provisions of the Pennsylvania **constitution?**

4. What is a **democracy?** What is a **republic?**

5. Why did Massachusetts require taxes be paid in **specie?**

CRITICAL THINKING AND WRITING

6. **Recognizing Cause and Effect** Create a chart listing the causes and effects of Shays' Rebellion.

7. **Writing an Opinion** If you had lived at the time of Shays' Rebellion, would you have supported it or opposed it? Write a list of reasons you would use as the basis for an essay that might appear in a newspaper of the time.

 Take It to the NET

Activity: Writing a Newspaper Article Research either Shays' Rebellion or the Annapolis Convention. Write a newspaper article on the event you selected. Use the links provided in the *America: Pathways to the Present* area of the following Web site for help in completing this activity.
www.phschool.com

Chapter 5 • Section 1   149

CUSTOMIZE FOR ...

Gifted and Talented

Have students analyze the Nationalists' desire for a strong central government. Why do they think well-educated and prominent American gentlemen were generally in favor of a more powerful national government, while less privileged Americans were content with the highly democratic way the new nation was governed? Why did the Nationalists, who were themselves revolutionaries, feel so threatened by Shays' Rebellion?

CAPTION ANSWERS

Viewing History They could be used as evidence that a weak central government was allowing the country to descend into chaos and disorder.

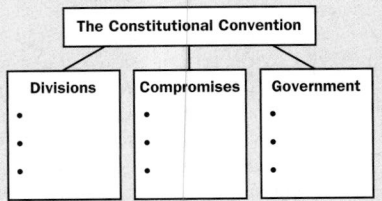

The Constitutional Convention

SECTION OBJECTIVES

1. Find out what the Founding Fathers hoped to achieve as they assembled for the Constitutional Convention.
2. Learn about issues that divided the convention.
3. See what the convention did to reach agreement.
4. Discover qualities that have made the Constitution a lasting document.
5. Realize how the structure of the government under the Constitution divides power.

BELLRINGER

Warm-Up Activity Ask students to define the word *compromise* and recall a time in their life when they compromised about an important issue.

Activating Prior Knowledge Why do students think it was necessary to hold a Constitutional Convention? Can they think of any other way to achieve the necessary consensus?

READING STRATEGY

As students read the section, ask them to list ways that the Constitutional Convention addressed the weaknesses of the Articles of Confederation.

ACTIVITY
Connecting with Government

Have groups of students research one of the 55 delegates to the Constitutional Convention. Tell students to find out where the delegate came from, how old he was at the time of the convention, and what stances he took during the meetings. Encourage students to think about how the interests of his home state influenced a delegate's positions. Once groups complete their research, have them present their findings to the class in an oral presentation. **(Verbal/Linguistic)**

READING FOCUS

- What did the Founding Fathers hope to achieve as they assembled for the Constitutional Convention?
- What issues divided the convention?
- What did the convention do to reach agreement?
- What qualities have made the Constitution a lasting document?
- How does the structure of the government under the Constitution divide power?

MAIN IDEA

In 1787, delegates to a convention in Philadelphia created a new plan of government, the Constitution of the United States.

KEY TERMS

Constitutional Convention
United States Constitution
amend
veto
Great Compromise
Three-Fifths Compromise
federal system of government
separation of powers
checks and balances
electoral college

TAKING NOTES

Copy the chart below. As you read, fill in details on divisions at the Constitutional Convention, compromises made at the Convention, and government structure under the Constitution.

The Constitutional Convention
- Divisions
  - •
  - •
  - •
- Compromises
  - •
  - •
  - •
- Government
  - •
  - •
  - •

Setting the Scene The air outside the Pennsylvania State House was hot and sticky, smelling of animals and rotten garbage. Around the modest brick building, which is now called Independence Hall, soldiers kept curious onlookers at a distance. Despite the heat, the windows of one room were closed so that no one could overhear the voices within. James Madison, recognizing the importance of this meeting, compiled a report of the proceedings, which was published as *Journal of the Federal Convention* after his death. In his will, Madison noted the following:

As they signed the Constitution at Philadelphia's Independence Hall on September 17, 1787, the delegates finally agreed on a framework for the nation's government.

❝ Considering the peculiarity and magnitude of the occasion which produced the Convention at Philadelphia, in 1787, the characters who composed it, the Constitution which resulted from their deliberations, . . . and the interest it has inspired among the friends of free government, it is not an unreasonable inference that a careful and extended report of the proceedings . . . will be particularly gratifying to the people of the United States, and to all who take an interest in the progress of political science and the cause of true liberty. ❞
—James Madison

The Convention Assembles

This historic meeting is known as the **Constitutional Convention.** In only four months, the Philadelphia convention produced the document that has governed the United States for more than 200 years, the **United States Constitution.** (See the complete text of the Constitution following this chapter.)

The Constitutional Convention grew out of an unsuccessful meeting in Annapolis, Maryland, in 1786. Having failed to stir up support for addressing the problems of the Articles of Confederation, the Annapolis delegates had decided to

150 Chapter 5 • *The Constitution of the United States*

RESOURCE DIRECTORY

Teaching Resources
Guided Reading and Review booklet, p. 21
Learning Styles Lesson Plans booklet, p. 12

Technology
Section Reading Support Transparencies
Guided Reading Audiotapes (English/Spanish), Ch. 5
Student Edition on Audio CD, Ch. 5
Prentice Hall Presentation Pro CD-ROM, Ch. 5
Companion Web site, www.phschool.com

tackle the issue again the next year. They called for a convention in Philadelphia to begin in May 1787 and invited states to send delegates.

During the passing months, disputes among states and violent outbreaks such as Shays' Rebellion raised fears that the fragile nation might collapse. This time, states responded to the call to fix the national government.

The Constitutional Convention drew 55 delegates from all the states except Rhode Island, which chose not to attend. The youngest delegate of all was 27, and the oldest was 81; the majority of delegates, however, were in their 30s and 40s. A few were very rich, but some had no more than a comfortable living. Many were well educated and familiar with the political theories of European philosophers of the Enlightenment which you read about in the previous chapter.

"The Father of the Constitution"

One delegate made it his business to attend every meeting of the convention. During these sessions, he could be seen busily taking the notes that later would become our best record of the proceedings. His name was James Madison. Later generations would call him "the father of the Constitution."

Madison was a quiet 36-year-old bachelor when he arrived in Philadelphia to help rescue the struggling government. Yet few men came better prepared for the task. In his home at the foot of the Blue Ridge Mountains of Virginia, Madison had spent evenings poring over books of history, government, and law. By the time of the Constitutional Convention, he had invested a year thinking specifically about how to craft a new government.

Despite his shyness and dislike for public speaking, Madison had been an early leader in the independence movement. He had served in the Continental Congress in 1780, and in the Virginia legislature, where he was influential in bringing about the Annapolis Convention.

Madison's studies of philosophy had led him to believe that people are naturally selfish creatures driven by powerful emotions and personal interests. That did not mean there was no hope for order in society, however. Madison drew from the writings of Enlightenment philosophers who argued that, through proper government, humans could take control of themselves and their world and improve the condition of both.

Madison believed that constitutions could establish political institutions that encouraged the best in people while restraining the worst. A dream of devising just such a constitution was exactly what brought James Madison to the Philadelphia convention. The business at hand, wrote Madison, was to "decide forever the fate of republican government."

Divisions at the Convention

The first act of the Constitutional Convention in 1787 was to elect George Washington as its president in a unanimous vote, that is, a vote in which everyone agrees. Other business proved far more difficult.

The major division was between those who wanted to **amend,** or revise, the Articles of Confederation and those who wanted to abandon them altogether. Nearly everyone agreed on the need for a stronger national government, but some saw no need to start from scratch. In fact, the Philadelphia convention had been empowered only to amend the Articles. In order to replace them, the convention would have to overstep its authority. That is what it did.

ACTIVITY

Connecting with Government

Ask students to suppose that they have found a spot where they can observe the proceedings at the Constitutional Convention unnoticed. Have them write a description of the event. **(Verbal/Linguistic)**

BACKGROUND

The Writers of the Constitution

The men who wrote and supported the Constitution are often thought of as wise old men. But the nine leading Federalists were, on average, 10 to 12 years younger than the anti-Federalists. George Washington, at 55, was the oldest of the leading Federalists in 1787. James Madison—"father of the Constitution"—was only 36, and Alexander Hamilton was 30. Anti-Federalist leaders reflected the generational split among the founders. Samuel Adams, for example, was 67 in 1787.

INTERPRETING CHARTS The Constitution borrows ideas about state representation from both the Virginia Plan and the New Jersey Plan. **Making Comparisons** *Evaluate the impact of both plans on the Constitution's provisions for determining representation.*

Comparing Plans for State Representation

	Virginia Plan	New Jersey Plan	Constitution's Provisions
Number of houses in legislature	2 Bicameral	1 Unicameral	2 Bicameral
How representation is determined	By each state's population OR by the financial support each state gives to the central government	Equal representation for each state	Equal representation for each state in the upper house; representation by each state's population in the lower house
How representatives are chosen	Elected by popular vote for the lower house; for the upper house, state legislators nominate representatives, who are then chosen by the lower house	Elected by state legislatures	Elected to the lower house by popular vote in each state; representatives are chosen by state legislatures for the upper house*

* 17th Amendment provided for popular election of senators

In the end, Madison and others who wanted a new government managed to dominate the meetings by bringing a plan with them. Their Virginia Plan became the focus of discussion against which all other ideas were weighed.

The Virginia Plan Submitted by Edmund Randolph of Virginia, the Virginia Plan called for the creation of a bicameral, or two-house, national legislature. Each state would send representatives in proportion to the number of its citizens. A state with a large population thus would have more representatives, and greater voting power, than a state with a small population.

The Virginia Plan addressed the shortcomings of the Articles in several ways:
1. The new legislature would have added powers, including the right to tax and to regulate foreign and interstate commerce.
2. The national legislature would have the power to **veto,** or prohibit from becoming law, any act of a state legislature. Should a state defy national authority, the national government would have the power to use force against the state. Such proposals frightened some people because they would give the national government greater power than the states.
3. In addition to the legislative branch, the proposed government would have an executive branch and a judicial branch.

States with large populations stood to benefit from the Virginia Plan because they would gain the most representatives in the legislature. Thus the larger states championed the Virginia Plan.

The New Jersey Plan Opposition to the Virginia Plan came from small states, which feared they would have little power in the new government. They proposed an alternative, the New Jersey Plan. Proposed by New Jersey's William Paterson, the New Jersey Plan had these key features:
1. It would give Congress the power to tax and to regulate foreign and interstate commerce.
2. It would create executive and judicial branches.
3. It would give every state an equal vote in a unicameral Congress. Smaller states thus would have the same voting power as larger states.

Like the Articles of Confederation, the New Jersey Plan aimed to keep state governments more powerful than the national government. The plan also ensured that heavily populated states would not overpower the smaller states.

CAPTION ANSWERS

Interpreting Charts The Constitution provides equal representation for each state in the upper house, which is part of the New Jersey Plan. Representation in the lower house is by state population, which is part of the Virginia Plan.

RESOURCE DIRECTORY

Technology
Color Transparencies *Historical Maps,* A55

Reaching Agreements

A central difference between the Virginia and New Jersey plans was representation in the legislature. To put it simply, should states with more people have more representatives in Congress? On July 2, the convention voted on this issue. The vote was split and the convention deadlocked. For a while, matters seemed hopeless.

The Great Compromise Within several days, a solution—introduced by Connecticut delegates Roger Sherman and Oliver Ellsworth—finally emerged. It is called the **Great Compromise.** It created a legislative branch made up of two houses, as called for in the Virginia Plan. In one house—the Senate—each state, regardless of its size, would have the same number of representatives. (That number is now two per state.) This pleased the small states. However, in the House of Representatives, the number of seats allowed per state would be based on each state's population. This won the support of the large states. The Great Compromise was approved on July 16, 1787.

The Three-Fifths Compromise Another difficult issue remained: When calculating a state's population, should enslaved people be included? Many of the Framers (creators) of the Constitution, including James Madison, owned slaves. Madison and others considered slavery immoral. Yet they were unable to bring themselves to do anything about this contradiction.

If slaves were to be included in a state's population count, the southern states, with their many slaves, would gain great power in the House of Representatives. If slaves were not counted, southern states would be weak in the House. Once again the delegates compromised, adopting a formula that became known as the **Three-Fifths Compromise.** Under this plan, three fifths of a state's slave population would be counted when determining representation.

The Three-Fifths Compromise did not mean that enslaved African Americans would be allowed to vote or that their interests would be represented in Congress. They, like Native Americans, were excluded from participating in the government, although in this early period certain free African Americans in some states could vote.

Although many features of Madison's Virginia Plan survived these compromises, the delegates never went as far in strengthening the national government

Connecticut delegate Roger Sherman helped introduce the Great Compromise at the Constitutional Convention.

The most important words of the Constitution, "We the People," are also the most visible on the document.

Chapter 5 • Section 2   153

Connecting with Geography

Tell students to choose one state that was represented at the Constitutional Convention. Have students find out the approximate population of this state at that time. Then tell them to learn how many representatives were allotted to this state at the time that the new Congress first convened in 1789. What is the current population of that state? How many representatives in the House of Representatives does the state now have? **(Logical/Mathematical)**

Interdisciplinary

The Founding Fathers all had a strong understanding of science. Thomas Jefferson was an inventor, as was Benjamin Franklin. John Adams and James Madison were also well versed in the sciences. These men applied their understanding of science to the framing of the Constitution. Some historians have maintained that the beliefs and discoveries of Sir Isaac Newton were a major influence on the Framers of the Constitution. They point to the separation of powers and the system of checks and balances as two areas of the Constitution that reflect the Newtonian system of the world.

 Sounds of an Era

Listen to a reading of a speech written by Benjamin Franklin, and other readings from the Constitutional era.

INTERPRETING DIAGRAMS
The federal system divides government powers into three categories.
Analyzing Information *Which powers are shared by both the federal and state governments? Name two of these powers.*

Federal System of Government

NATIONAL GOVERNMENT	CONCURRENT POWERS	STATE GOVERNMENTS
Powers delegated to the national government by the Constitution	Powers held and exercised by both the national and state governments	Powers not granted to the national government or denied to the states

---

as Madison would have liked. For example, they refused to give Congress the right to veto laws passed by the states. Yet the plan did create a stronger central government.

A Lasting Document

After further debate over the various provisions, the convention approved the final draft of the United States Constitution on September 17, 1787. Remarkably, this written plan of government has remained basically the same for over two hundred years.

The Constitution has many strengths that have helped it to endure. On certain issues it is specific enough not to be misinterpreted by later generations. Yet it has been flexible enough to adapt to social, economic, political, and technological changes that its creators could scarcely have imagined. Perhaps the best proof of this flexibility is the fact that the Constitution has been amended just 27 times in this nation's history.

The United States Constitution continues to inspire people around the world. Many nations have modeled their own governments after it, borrowing ideas not only about the structure of government but also about its goals. The Constitution's goals are set forth in its introduction, called the Preamble:

KEY DOCUMENTS 66 *We the People of the United States, in Order to form a more perfect Union, establish Justice, insure domestic Tranquility, provide for the common defense, promote the general Welfare, and secure the Blessings of Liberty to ourselves and our Posterity, do ordain and establish this Constitution for the United States of America.* 99

—Preamble to the Constitution, 1787

Over the years, Americans have come to see the first three words of the Constitution, "We the People," as the most important. Everything else in the document follows the basic idea that in the United States it is the people who govern.

Government Structure

The Framers of the Constitution knew that while government needed power in order to be effective, too much power could lead to abuses. So they kept government under control by dividing power, in two ways.

Federal and State Powers The Constitution created what some leaders began to call a **federal system of government,** a system in which power is shared among state and national authorities. Some powers, such as establishing an educational system, are called reserved powers because they are reserved for the states. Others, such as declaring war, are called delegated powers because they are delegated to the federal government. Still other powers, such as collecting taxes, borrowing money, and establishing courts, are called concurrent powers because the federal and state governments hold them at the same time, or concurrently.

Separation of Federal Powers To keep power under control within the national government, the

---

Interpreting Diagrams Concurrent powers. Sample answer: Collecting taxes and borrowing money.

RESOURCE DIRECTORY

Teaching Resources
Learning with Documents (Primary Source Activity) *Hamilton and Jefferson,* p. 10

Other Print Resources
American History Block Scheduling Support *The Birth of the Constitution: The Philadelphia Convention* and *Checks and Balances: The Rise of the American Judiciary,* found in the Forging a New Nation folder, include interdisciplinary lesson suggestions and activities for Geography and History, Primary Sources, Biography, and Literature.

Technology
Sounds of an Era Audio CD *Benjamin Franklin's Constitutional Convention Speech* (time: about one minute)

The American System of Checks and Balances

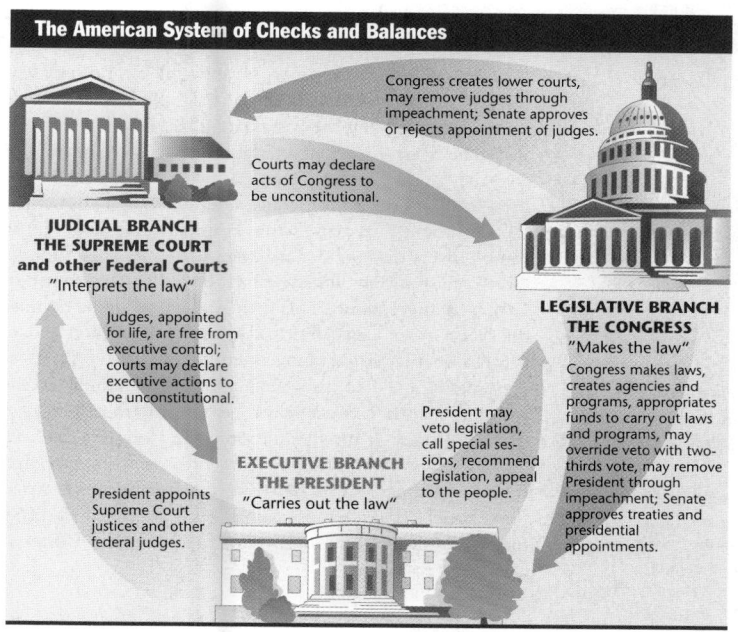

JUDICIAL BRANCH
THE SUPREME COURT
and other Federal Courts
"Interprets the law"

Judges, appointed for life, are free from executive control; courts may declare executive actions to be unconstitutional.

President appoints Supreme Court justices and other federal judges.

Courts may declare acts of Congress to be unconstitutional.

Congress creates lower courts, may remove judges through impeachment; Senate approves or rejects appointment of judges.

LEGISLATIVE BRANCH
THE CONGRESS
"Makes the law"

Congress makes laws, creates agencies and programs, appropriates funds to carry out laws and programs, may override veto with two-thirds vote, may remove President through impeachment; Senate approves treaties and presidential appointments.

President may veto legislation, call special sessions, recommend legislation, appeal to the people.

EXECUTIVE BRANCH
THE PRESIDENT
"Carries out the law"

INTERPRETING DIAGRAMS
"You must first enable the government to control the governed," wrote Madison, "and in the next place, oblige it to control itself." This control is found in the Constitution's system of checks and balances. **Analyzing Information** *How does the legislature check the executive branch?*

Constitution created what is called a **separation of powers** among the three branches of government—the legislative, executive, and judicial branches. That is, each branch has its own area of authority, but no one branch has complete power over the government.

In addition, the Constitution set up a system of **checks and balances.** This system gives each branch the power to check, or stop, the other branches in certain ways. For instance, the President, as the head of the executive branch, can veto acts of Congress. This executive power is balanced, however, by Congress's power to overturn the veto with a two-thirds vote of each house. (See the chart above.) The federal system of checks and balances prevents tyranny, or misuse of power, by any one branch of government.

Congress By creating a federal system with a separation of powers, the Framers both preserved and limited the people's control over the government. A comparison of the House of Representatives and the Senate demonstrates this effort at balance.

According to the Constitution, population size determines the number of seats that each state receives in the House of Representatives. This provision makes the House directly responsible to the people. Its members serve two-year terms so that voters have the opportunity to change the membership of the House relatively quickly if they wish to.

Members of the Senate were originally elected by the state legislatures, not by the voters. (In 1913, the Seventeenth Amendment changed this procedure, establishing direct election of senators by the people.) Furthermore, unlike representatives in the House, senators serve six-year terms. Every two years, only one third of the Senate comes up for reelection. Thus it is harder for voters to have a direct and sudden impact on the membership of the Senate.

READING CHECK
What are some differences between the House of Representatives and the Senate?

Fast Forward to Today

Presidential Electors

The Framers of the Constitution provided that presidential electors were to be chosen in whatever manner each state legislature directed. In several states, the legislatures themselves chose the electors in the first several elections. By 1832, however, electors were chosen by popular election in most states. Because the Framers did not anticipate political parties nominating a "ticket" for President and Vice President, their plan also provided that every elector would cast two votes—each for a different candidate for President. The candidate with the majority of votes would become President; the second-place candidate would become Vice President.

Today Presidential electors are now chosen by popular vote in all states. Except in Maine and Nebraska, the presidential candidate with the largest popular vote in the state wins all of the state's electoral votes. Electors now cast one vote for President and one for Vice President, as required by the Twelfth Amendment. Chosen by the parties, electors are expected—but usually not required by law—to vote for their party's candidates.

? From time to time throughout the nation's history, there have been calls to eliminate the electoral college and to choose the President by direct, popular vote. Do you favor this position? Why or why not?

The Framers made the Senate more removed from the people so that it would be less likely to follow the whims of popular opinion. For instance, since no bill can become federal law without the Senate's approval, voters are less likely to succeed in forcing the passage of a bad law. The Framers also granted to the Senate certain powers that they did not give the House, such as giving advice and consent to the President with regard to treaties and judicial appointments.

On the other hand, the Framers gave the House some powers that the Senate does not have. For example, bills to raise money must be introduced in the House of Representatives alone. This provision came about because the large states were afraid of losing their influence over tax matters that could affect them greatly.

The House and the Senate, when combined as the Congress of the United States, became the most powerful legislative body in the nation. Only the Congress can coin money, declare war, raise an army, provide for a navy, and regulate commerce. In a sweeping statement now known as the Elastic Clause because it has been stretched to fit so many situations, the Constitution declares that Congress can do the following:

> **KEY DOCUMENTS** 66 [M]ake all Laws which shall be necessary and proper for carrying into Execution the foregoing Powers, and all other Powers vested by this Constitution in the Government of the United States, or in any Department or Officer thereof. 99
> —United States Constitution, Article 1, Section 8, Clause 18, 1787

In other words, Congress has the authority to pass any laws reasonably necessary to carry out its duties. The Elastic Clause gives Congress great power, especially compared to its earlier role under the Articles of Confederation.

The President The Constitution created a strong executive officer, the President of the United States. The President's term was set at four years, but Presidents could be reelected as many times as the people wished. (Today the President is limited to two terms in office, a change made by the Twenty-second Amendment in 1951.)

Once again, the Framers placed a shield between the government and the people by making the election of the President indirect. The President is chosen by a vote of electors from each state. Each state gets as many electors as it has members of Congress. The candidate with the majority of the votes in the **electoral college,** or group of electors, becomes President.

The Framers knew that George Washington was likely to be the nation's first President. Washington, however, was unique in having support across the country. Later candidates for President, the Framers believed, would have difficulty winning the required majority of electoral votes.

Thus the Constitution provided for the House of Representatives to be the final decision maker in the presidential election. If the electoral college fails to produce a clear majority for one candidate, the election moves to the House. In

156   Chapter 5 • *The Constitution of the United States*

the House of Representatives, each state has one vote, and the representatives continue voting until one of the candidates receives a majority. As it has turned out, only twice in American history has the House needed to vote to break a deadlock of the electors, in the elections of 1800 and 1824.

The Constitution gives the President enormous powers. It assigns to the President the role of commander in chief of the armed forces, thus establishing the important principle of civilian control of the military. In the system of checks and balances, the President also has the power to veto acts of Congress. And, with the advice and consent of the Senate, the President chooses judges for the national courts.

Federal Courts The Constitution calls for a national court system. Because the Framers wanted to ensure an independent judiciary, they made the choice of judges two steps removed from the people—the President, indirectly chosen by the people, chooses the judges, but only with consent of the Senate. In addition, the Constitution makes the removal of judges difficult so that the people cannot directly control them. Federal judges hold office for life, as long as they do not act dishonorably.

Although the Constitution calls for one Supreme Court and several lesser ones, the details of the federal court system were left intentionally vague. Congress later developed the federal court system to fit the needs of the growing nation.

The Road Ahead This, then, was the outline of the new government as set forth in the Constitution, completed by the delegates in months of intense work during the summer of 1787. In order to take effect, however, the Constitution required the approval of 9 of the 13 states. Supporters of the new Constitution knew that winning approval for it would not be easy.

Focus on GOVERNMENT

Behind the Scenes at the Convention The delegates assembled at the convention had many ideas on how the new nation should be governed. Several ideas were discussed that never made their way into the United States Constitution. For instance, Gouverneur Morris of Pennsylvania thought that Presidents should have the power to appoint senators for office, and that the President should hold office for life. John Rutledge of South Carolina recommended that society be divided into classes for legislative representation. Alexander Hamilton favored a strong national government with unlimited power over the states. And Benjamin Franklin supported an executive governing committee in place of a President. Above is a detail from the chair Washington used at the convention. Franklin wondered if the decoration represented a sun setting or rising on America.

Section 2 Assessment

READING COMPREHENSION

1. What was produced at the **Constitutional Convention?**

2. What does it mean to **amend?** What does it mean to **veto?**

3. How did the **Great Compromise** and the **Three-Fifths Compromise** help the convention reach agreements?

4. How is the power within the **federal system of government** divided under the **separation of powers?** What **checks and balances** are provided by the Constitution?

5. What is the **electoral college,** and why was it established?

CRITICAL THINKING AND WRITING

6. **Synthesizing Information** How did the Constitutional Convention address the weaknesses of the Articles of Confederation?

7. **Distinguishing Fact From Opinion** Write two major facts about the kind of government set up by the Constitution. Then write an opinion about each of those facts.

8. **Writing to Describe** Explain the meaning of the Preamble to the Constitution by rewriting it in your own words. Feel free to use a writing style less formal than the original.

Take It to the NET

Activity: Writing a Diary Entry Research the lives of the delegates at the Constitutional Convention. Based on what you have learned, write a diary entry for one of the delegates that describes a day at the convention. Use the links provided in the *America: Pathways to the Present* area of the following Web site for help in completing this activity.
www.phschool.com

Section 2 Assessment

Reading Comprehension

1. The United States Constitution.

2. Amend: to revise; veto: to prohibit a bill, an appointment, or a treaty from being enacted.

3. Great Compromise: Both the small and large states were satisfied with the decision to have the same number of representatives from each state in the Senate and to have the number of seats per state in the House of Representatives determined by the size of each state's population; Three-Fifths Compromise: was accepted because in counting three fifths of a state's slave population when computing representation in the House, the compromise gave extra leverage to southern states, but not enough to antagonize northern states.

4. Each branch has its own area of authority, but no one branch has complete power over the entire government. Examples of checks and balances: Courts may declare acts of Congress and actions by the executive to be unconstitutional; the President may veto legislation.

5. The electoral college is a group of presidential electors from each state, established by the Framers of the Constitution to create a shield between the government and the people by making the election of the President indirect.

Critical Thinking and Writing

6. It created a new plan to replace them.

7. Sample answer: Fact: The Constitution created a system in which power is shared among state and national authorities. Opinion: The Constitution takes too much power away from the people. Fact: The Constitution created a strong executive officer. Opinion: The President has too much authority.

8. Answers will vary, but should demonstrate a thorough understanding of the meaning and intention of the Preamble.

Take It to the NET

Sample answer: James Madison might have written a diary entry detailing the debate between the Virginia and New Jersey Plans, which ended in the Great Compromise.

SECTION OBJECTIVES

1. Learn how the position of the Federalists differed from that of the anti-Federalists.
2. See how the Federalists won approval of the Constitution.
3. Find out about arguments for and against a Bill of Rights.

BELLRINGER

Warm-Up Activity Ask students if they think the United States government infringes too much on individual liberty. Possible examples include taxes or military services.

Activating Prior Knowledge Ask students to share their impressions of the process that caused the Constitution to come to life. In what ways did the Constitutional Convention further the ambitions of the Patriots who fought in the American Revolution? In what ways did the Constitution seek to serve different ambitions?

READING STRATEGY

As students read the section, have them make a list of questions they would want to ask the Federalists and anti-Federalists if they were trying to decide how to vote on the Constitution.

ACTIVITY
Connecting with History and Conflict

Assign volunteers one of the following roles: a farmer from western Pennsylvania, a French revolutionary, a Dutch banker, John Adams, John Marshall, the wife of a Virginia tobacco planter, a wealthy Boston merchant, or a tavern keeper from upper New York State. Ask students to state their point of view (Federalist or Jeffersonian), giving two reasons in support of their chosen party. **(Verbal/Linguistic; Logical/Mathematical)**

Ratifying the Constitution

READING FOCUS

- How did the position of the Federalists differ from that of the anti-Federalists?
- Why did the Federalists win approval of the Constitution?
- What were the arguments for and against a Bill of Rights?

MAIN IDEA

The states debated and then approved the new Constitution, and a Bill of Rights soon was added to protect individual liberties.

KEY TERMS

ratify
Federalist
faction
anti-Federalist
Bill of Rights

TAKING NOTES

Copy the chart below. As you read, list information about the Federalists and anti-Federalists.

The Constitution	
Federalists	**Anti-Federalists**
In favor of the Constitution	Opposed to the Constitution
In favor of a strong national government	

Setting the Scene As the ink was still drying on the final draft of the new Constitution, its proponents and opponents were busy trying to line up support for their positions. After all, the Constitution had yet to be accepted by the American people.

Thomas Jefferson had not been a delegate at the Constitutional Convention. He was in Paris, serving as United States ambassador to France. In a letter to Madison, Jefferson expressed his view of the proposed Constitution:

66 *After all, it is my principle that the will of the Majority should prevail. If they approve the proposed Convention [Constitution] in all its parts, I shall concur in it chearfully, in hopes that they will amend it whenever they shall find it work[s] wrong.* 99

—Thomas Jefferson, in a letter to James Madison, December 20, 1787

The Federalist View

For the Constitution to become law, 9 of the 13 states had to **ratify**, or approve, it. Ratification votes would be cast not by state legislatures but by special conventions called in each state. The Framers of the Constitution bypassed the state legislatures because they feared the legislatures would never approve a document that reduced their powers.

Those who favored the Constitution were called **Federalists.** They wanted the strong national government the Constitution provided. The Federalists included many Nationalists, such as George Washington, James Madison, and Alexander Hamilton. They argued that even if there were problems with the document, it had to be approved. To make their case for the Constitution, several supporters wrote a series of 85 essays, or papers, called *The Federalist.* These articles appeared in New York City newspapers between October 1787 and August 1788. The authors were Hamilton, Madison, and John Jay, a Nationalist from New York. (See the feature on page 159.)

John Jay (top), Alexander Hamilton (bottom), and James Madison made their case for approval of the Constitution in a collection of essays entitled *The Federalist.*

THE
FEDERALIST:
A COLLECTION
OF
ESSAYS,
WRITTEN IN FAVOUR OF THE
NEW CONSTITUTION,
AS AGREED UPON BY THE FEDERAL CONVENTION,
SEPTEMBER 17, 1787.
IN TWO VOLUMES.
VOL. I.

158   Chapter 5 • *The Constitution of the United States*

RESOURCE DIRECTORY

Teaching Resources
Learning Styles Lesson Plans booklet, p. 13
Guided Reading and Review booklet, p. 22

Technology
Section Reading Support Transparencies
Sounds of an Era Audio CD *"Federalist No. 51,"* *James Madison* (time: one minute, 15 seconds)
Exploring Primary Sources in U.S. History CD-ROM *The Federalist Papers, No. 1, Alexander Hamilton; Objections to the Constitution, George Madison*

Written to win approval of the Constitution in New York, the *Federalist* essays are today recognized as perhaps the most sophisticated explanation of the new American political system ever written. Hamilton and Madison offered a defense of the Constitution that was also a commentary on human nature and the role of government.

For example, in *The Federalist*, No. 10, Madison answered those who feared that a federal government could come under the control of one powerful **faction,** a group that is concerned only with its own interests. Because the United States was so large, Madison wrote, no single faction would be able to control the government. Factions based on regional or economic or other interests would struggle with each other within the federal government, but no single faction would be able to dominate the others for long. As Madison reasoned:

> **KEY DOCUMENTS** ❝ Extend the sphere [that is, enlarge the territory of the nation], and you take in a greater variety of parties and interests; you make it less probable that a majority of a whole will have a common motive to invade the rights of other citizens; or if such a common motive exists, it will be more difficult for all who feel it to discover their own strength, and to act in unison with each other. ❞
>
> —*The Federalist*, No. 10

Madison and Hamilton also answered those who feared the power of the federal government over the states. They agreed that the federal government was supreme over the states only in the exercise of its exclusively delegated powers. The states were supreme over the federal government in exercise of their constitutionally reserved powers.

The Anti-Federalist View

Those who opposed the Constitution were called the **anti-Federalists.** They believed that the Federalists' plan posed a threat to state governments and to the rights of individuals. The anti-Federalists rallied behind the leadership of older Revolutionary figures, such as Patrick Henry of Virginia. This group gained support in more isolated regions where protecting commerce was not a major concern. People in these areas had less need for the leadership and laws of a strong national government. The anti-Federalists also included some former Nationalists who still wanted a national government but were unhappy with the Constitution as written.

Most anti-Federalists saw the Constitution as a betrayal of the American Revolution. A President would be nothing but a king, they warned. Had American patriots fought and died to create yet another government to tax them and tell them what to do?

While the Federalists feared the people more than government, the anti-Federalists feared government more than the people. Many anti-Federalists objected not only to the presidency but to the new federal court system. They also worried that those governments closest to the people, the local and state authorities, would be crushed by this new federal monster. Finally, they feared

Chapter 5 • Section 3 159

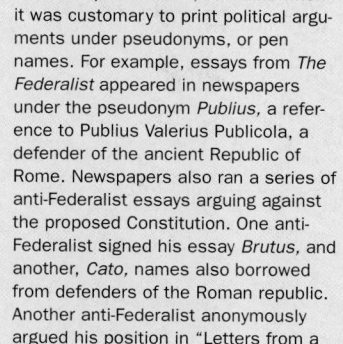

Focus on CITIZENSHIP

Public Debate Much debate over the proposed Constitution took place in New York publications, at a time when it was customary to print political arguments under pseudonyms, or pen names. For example, essays from *The Federalist* appeared in newspapers under the pseudonym *Publius*, a reference to Publius Valerius Publicola, a defender of the ancient Republic of Rome. Newspapers also ran a series of anti-Federalist essays arguing against the proposed Constitution. One anti-Federalist signed his essay *Brutus*, and another, *Cato*, names also borrowed from defenders of the Roman republic. Another anti-Federalist anonymously argued his position in "Letters from a Federal Farmer."

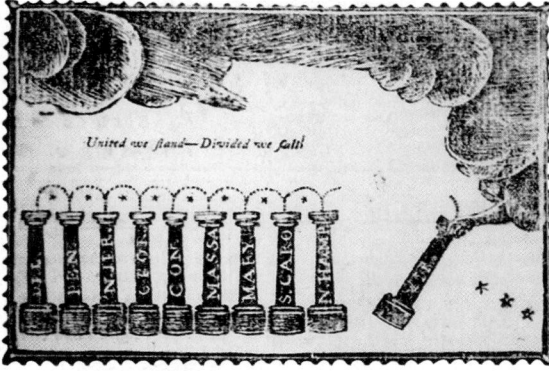

INTERPRETING POLITICAL CARTOONS This cartoon shows the states as pillars. Nine states had to approve the new Constitution before it became law. **Synthesizing Information** *What is the meaning of the statement that appears above the pillars?*

From Colonies to United States

1765	Stamp Act Congress
1770s	Committees of Correspondence
1774	First Continental Congress
1775–81	Second Continental Congress
1776	Declaration of Independence
1781	Articles of Confederation adopted
1783	Treaty of Paris
1785	Mount Vernon Convention
1786	Annapolis Convention
1787	Constitutional Convention
1788	Ninth State (New Hampshire) ratifies the Constitution
1789	Constitution goes into effect
1790	Thirteenth state (Rhode Island) ratifies the Constitution

1775–1783 War for Independence

INTERPRETING TIME LINES Important milestones mark the colonies' transformation into a new nation. **Drawing Inferences** *Why did the fight for ratification of the Constitution continue after the necessary number of states approved the document?*

for Americans' individual liberties. Two New York anti-Federalists argued:

KEY DOCUMENTS " *A general government, however guarded by declarations of rights, . . . must unavoidably, in a short time, be productive of the destruction of the civil liberty of such citizens who could be effectively coerced [dominated] by it.* "
—Robert Yates and John Lansing, in a letter to the governor of New York, 1787

Why the Federalists Won

The Constitution was officially submitted to the states for approval on September 28, 1787. From the start, the Federalists had several advantages in their campaign to promote it.

1. The Federalists drew on the widespread feeling that the Articles of Confederation had serious flaws. The young nation's economic problems and Shays' Rebellion convinced many Americans that something had to be done.
2. The Federalists were united around a specific plan—the Constitution. The anti-Federalists, in contrast, were united only in their opposition to the Constitution. They had no constructive plan of their own to offer.
3. The Federalists were a well-organized national group in regular contact with one another. The anti-Federalists tended to consist of local and state politicians who did not coordinate their activities on the national level.
4. Finally, the Federalists had George Washington's support. In 1786, Washington had foreseen the type of chaos that would erupt from Shays' Rebellion. "Something must be done," he warned his countrymen, "or the fabric [the Union] must fall, for it is certainly tottering." The following year, 1787, Washington had served as head of the Constitutional Convention. Federalists could point out that the Constitution had been crafted under the leadership of the nation's greatest hero and most respected public figure.

Washington's support was crucial for another reason. Everyone expected Washington to be the first President. That made people more willing to accept the idea of a stronger government and a powerful executive. During the war, Washington had proved his ability to lead in spite of defeat and discouragement. More significant, instead of using the military to secure his position as ruler of the new nation, he had voluntarily given up his power over the army at the end of the war. Washington's conduct was seen as a sign of his commitment to act within the law.

Delaware, New Jersey, and Connecticut ratified quickly. They were relatively small states whose citizens could benefit from being part of a large federal structure. Georgia ratified quickly as well. Georgians feared a war with Native

160 Chapter 5 • *The Constitution of the United States*

Americans and wanted a national government for support. In Pennsylvania, Federalists had come to power, and they readily agreed to the new Constitution. All these states acted in December 1787 and January 1788.

Then Massachusetts narrowly voted to ratify. Maryland and South Carolina soon fell into line. New Hampshire Federalists managed to delay the vote in their state until they had a majority. In June 1788, New Hampshire had the honor of being the ninth and final state needed to ratify the Constitution.

Yet everyone knew the new nation would not succeed without the backing of the highly populated states of Virginia and New York. Loud debates and quiet maneuvers during the summer of 1788 produced narrow Federalist victories in both of these states. North Carolina at first rejected the Constitution but reversed its decision and voted in favor in November 1789. In May 1790, Rhode Island similarly reversed its position and became the last of the original thirteen states to approve the new government.

The Bill of Rights

The states did adopt the Constitution. Yet the voting was close, and they might easily have rejected it. What turned the tide in close states like Massachusetts, Virginia, and New York? The skills of men such as Madison and Hamilton certainly had an impact. The most important factor, however, was the Federalists' offer to support several amendments to the Constitution.

Protecting Individual Rights Many Americans believed that a constitution should include a clear declaration of the rights of the people. Most state constitutions included such declarations. The Virginia Declaration of Rights, written by George Mason, was adopted by the Virginia Constitutional Convention in 1776. This document contained many of the rights that were added to the United States Constitution. It declared that all men are free and independent, possessing inherent rights, such as the right to enjoy life and liberty, the right

The Bill of Rights	
1st Amendment	Guarantees freedom of religion, speech, press, assembly, and petition
2nd Amendment	Guarantees the right to bear arms
3rd Amendment	Restricts the manner in which the federal government may house troops in the homes of citizens
4th Amendment	Protects individuals against unreasonable searches and seizures
5th Amendment	Provides that a person must be accused by a grand jury before being tried for a serious federal crime; protects individuals against self-incrimination and against being tried twice for the same crime; prohibits unfair actions by the federal government; prohibits the government from taking private property for public use without paying a fair price for it
6th Amendment	Guarantees persons accused of a crime the right to a swift and fair trial
7th Amendment	Guarantees the right to a jury trial in civil cases tried in federal courts
8th Amendment	Protects against cruel and unusual punishment and excessive bail
9th Amendment	Establishes that the people have rights beyond those stated in the Constitution
10th Amendment	Establishes that all powers not guaranteed to the federal government and not withheld from the state are held by each of the states, or their citizens

INTERPRETING CHARTS
The Bill of Rights was intended to protect Americans from the strong national government the Constitution created. **Synthesizing Information** *Which amendment protects people's right to express their views?*

ACTIVITY
Connecting with Citizenship

Have students keep "Rights Logs" for one week, in which they record the instances of their enjoyment of specific rights found in the Bill of Rights, and in which they identify which amendment guarantees each right. **(Verbal/Linguistic)**

BACKGROUND
Biography

As a 29-year-old adviser to General George Washington, Alexander Hamilton (1755–1804) saw the need for a strong central government to unify the thirteen states. He insisted that the states convene at a larger meeting to discuss the matter—the successful Constitutional Convention of 1787. As an army captain who helped turn back British General Cornwallis at Yorktown, a prominent attorney, and a political theorist who wrote most of the influential essays called *The Federalist,* Hamilton was one of the founders of the Republic. He died in 1804 as the result of a dramatic duel with political rival Aaron Burr.

READING CHECK
The Federalists capitalized on the following: the nearly unanimous sentiment that the Articles were inadequate; the Federalists had a specific plan—the Constitution—to offer; they were well organized on a national level; and they had George Washington's support.

CAPTION ANSWERS

Interpreting Charts The First Amendment, which guarantees freedom of speech.

to Today

The Bill of Rights Protects You

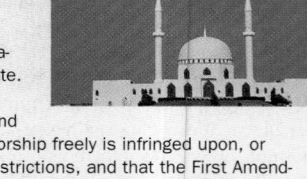

The Bill of Rights has endured for more than 200 years, guaranteeing individual freedoms to Americans. It speaks mainly in general principles. For example, the Eighth Amendment forbids but does not define "cruel and unusual punishment."

Because the Bill of Rights is open to interpretation, Americans sometimes disagree about what the amendments mean. In recent years, for example, controversy has arisen over religious freedom, particularly on the matter of school prayer. The Supreme Court has ruled that students cannot be compelled to participate in prayer. Those who support the rulings claim they uphold what Thomas Jefferson saw as the high wall needed to separate church and state. On the other hand, some people contend that their right to worship freely is infringed upon, or violated, by such restrictions, and that the First Amendment protects students' right to pray individually or in groups, on a voluntary basis. As provided by the First Amendment, freedom of religion—exercised in the Michigan mosque above—includes religious choice.

? The general language sometimes used in the Bill of Rights has left it open to interpretation. Is this an advantage or a disadvantage? Explain.

to own property, and the right to pursue and obtain happiness and safety. It also detailed the rights of the criminally accused:

> **KEY DOCUMENTS** 66 *That in all capital or criminal prosecutions a man has a right to demand the cause and nature of his accusation, to be confronted with the accusers and witnesses, to call for evidence in his favor, and to a speedy trial by an impartial jury of twelve men of his vicinage [vicinity], without whose unanimous consent he cannot be found guilty; nor can he be compelled to give evidence against himself. . . .* 99
>
> —The Virginia Declaration of Rights, Section 8

The Virginia Statute for Religious Liberty, drafted by Thomas Jefferson and adopted in 1786, also influenced changes to the Constitution:

> **KEY DOCUMENTS** 66 *That no man shall be compelled to frequent [attend] or support any religious worship, place, or ministry whatsoever . . . but that all men shall be free to profess, and by argument to maintain, their opinion in matters of religion, and that the same shall in no wise [way] diminish, enlarge, or affect their civil capacities.* 99
>
> —Virginia Statute for Religious Liberty

READING CHECK
Why was the Bill of Rights added to the Constitution?

In September 1789, Congress proposed twelve constitutional amendments, largely drafted by James Madison and designed to protect citizens' rights. The states ratified ten of the amendments, and they took effect on December 15, 1791. These first ten amendments to the Constitution are known today as the **Bill of Rights.** (See the chart on page 161.)

Against the Bill of Rights   Most Federalists saw no need for these amendments. Members of the Constitutional Convention had talked about protecting freedom of speech, the press, and religion. But they decided such measures were unnecessary. They were building a government of, for, and by the people. Under the Constitution, the people and the government were the same. Why, then, did the people need to protect their rights from themselves?

In *The Federalist*, No. 84, Hamilton quoted the Preamble of the Constitution to claim that "the people surrender nothing" under the new system. That is, they keep all the power. "Here is a better recognition of popular rights" than any added list of rights, he argued.

For the Bill of Rights Many Americans did not accept Hamilton's reasoning. Anti-Federalists warned that if the rights of the people were not spelled out in the Constitution, these rights would be considered unenumerated powers of government. They believed that the Constitution needed a bill of rights to restrain the federal government.

Thomas Jefferson favored the Constitution but insisted that it include a bill of rights. He wanted the "unalienable rights" he wrote of in the Declaration of Independence to be guaranteed in the Constitution. In a letter to Madison, he urged him to agree to specific protections for freedom of religion and of the press as well as protections from armies and unjust courts. "A bill of rights is what the people are entitled to against every government on earth," the ambassador wrote.

Jefferson unsuccessfully pushed for clearer, more detailed language in the Bill of Rights. For instance, he wanted it to specify the number of days a person could be held under arrest without a trial. He also believed it was important to ensure that the army would disband immediately after its service. Yet, upon returning home from France at the end of 1789, he threw his full support behind the Bill of Rights as written.

Facing overwhelming pressure for the Bill of Rights, the Federalists gave in. This compromise with the anti-Federalists led them to victory.

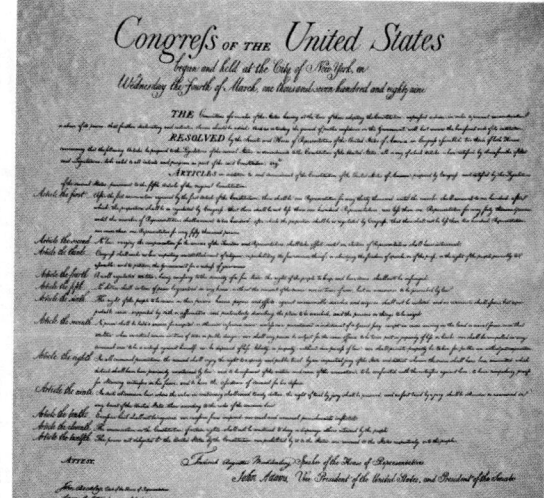

The Bill of Rights helps to ensure the protection of individual freedoms.

Section 3 Assessment

READING COMPREHENSION

1. Why were special conventions, and not state legislatures, called upon to **ratify** the Constitution?

2. How were the **Federalists** able to win ratification of the Constitution?

3. How did James Madison address fears that any **faction** might be able to control the government?

4. Why did the **anti-Federalists** oppose the Constitution?

5. Why did many Americans want a **Bill of Rights?**

CRITICAL THINKING AND WRITING

6. Predicting Consequences Would the Federalists have won approval for the Constitution if George Washington had not supported it? Explain your answer.

7. Writing an Interview Make a list of questions you would want to ask the Federalists and anti-Federalists if you were trying to decide how to vote on the Constitution.

Take It to the NET

Activity: Writing an Editorial
Craft a newspaper article that argues either for or against the proposed Constitution; try to write it in the style of the time. Find primary sources on the ratification process and quote them in your editorial. Use the links provided in the *America: Pathways to the Present* area of the following Web site for help in completing this activity.
www.phschool.com

Section 3 Assessment

Reading Comprehension

1. To prevent the state legislatures from disapproving of the Constitution because it reduced their powers.

2. The Federalists carried out an organized campaign that tapped people's fears of disunion, benefited from the brilliantly written Federalist papers, and emphasized George Washington's role in the Constitutional Convention.

3. The size of the United States precluded the notion that a single faction would be able to control the government.

4. Anti-Federalists saw the Constitution as a betrayal of the American Revolution, felt that a President would be just like a king, objected to the lack of a bill of rights in the new Constitution, and believed that the government would tax them and regulate their affairs even more than the British had proposed to do.

5. They believed that the Federal Constitution should contain a clear statement to protect the rights of the citizens, as many state constitutions already did.

Critical Thinking and Writing

6. Answers will vary, but should be supported with facts from the section.

7. Lists may include: Federalists: Why do the people not elect the President directly? What guarantee do the people have that the legislature will not pass laws that restrict their liberties, such as freedom of the press and freedom of religion? Anti-Federalists: Why do you see no difference between a presidency and a monarchy? Why do you oppose the new federal court system, and what would you propose in its place?

Take It to the NET

Students should persuasively oppose or support the proposed Constitution, supporting their opinions with evidence gathered from primary sources.

BUILDING FLOWCHARTS

Focus Use the flowcharting technique to sequentially break down the steps in a complex process.

Instruct Ask students to read the passage about the process of the election of the President and Vice President. Have them write each step in the process on a piece of paper, allowing a separate line for each step. How many steps are there altogether? Ask students to discuss the ways in which breaking a task down using a flowchart can help make it easier to understand.

Extend See the Skills for Life activity in the Resource Directory below.

ANSWERS

PRACTICE THE SKILL

1. **(a)** Electing a President and Vice President. **(b)** How the number of electors per state is determined. **(c)** (1) Electors are chosen in the states. (2) Electors, meeting in their states, each vote for two of the candidates running for President. (3) Electors total results and send them to the President of the Senate, who has them counted. (4) The person with the most electoral votes becomes the President. The person with the next largest number of votes becomes the Vice President. (5) If there is a tie, or if no candidate has a majority, the House of Representatives chooses the President and the Senate chooses the Vice President.

2. **(a)** Electors vote for two presidential candidates. **(b)** In case of a tie for Vice President, the Senate chooses.

3. **(a)** No. The first step is choosing the electors. **(b)** "After," "then," "However." **(c)** The process described includes some variables; one chart might show what happens when there's a tie for President, and another chart would show a tie for Vice President.

4. **(a)** Flowcharts should show all the steps in the correct order. **(b)** Five. **(c)** Flowcharts should show the appropriate steps. **(d)** Yes. That way, the whole process would be shown at a glance.

 # Building Flowcharts

A flowchart is a useful way to show steps in a sequence. It can help you understand a process, or how one event or action leads to another. In one kind of flowchart, each step in the sequence is shown in a box. An arrow pointing from one box to the next leads you from step to step in the sequence. These kinds of flowcharts may be horizontal (flowing from left to right) or vertical (flowing from top to bottom). When you need to fit many steps in a small space, you can connect one row of boxes to another, as in the example below.

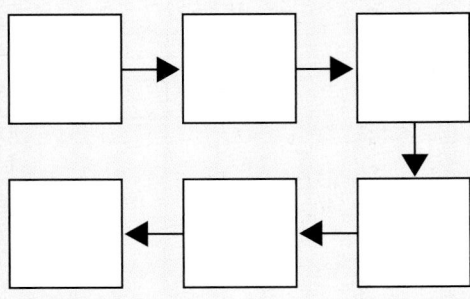

LEARN THE SKILL
Use the following steps to build a flowchart:

1. **Give the topic a title and identify the main steps.** Your title will help you pick out the most important pieces of information, which will become your main steps.

2. **Reword each main step so that it is brief enough to fit in a flowchart box.** This makes it easy to see the process at a glance. You can delete words like *the* and *a* to save space.

3. **Place the steps in time order.** Look for time words in your source, such as *first*, *second*, *next*, *then*, *later*, and *after*, but do not use these words in your flowchart. The arrows take the place of these transitional words.

4. **Create and fill in the flowchart.** Choose the kind of flowchart that is best for your topic, draw the boxes and arrows, and write the steps in the boxes.

PRACTICE THE SKILL
Answer the following questions:

1. Suppose you are using a flowchart to show the original Constitutional provision for the election of the President and Vice President. **(a)** What would be a good title for your flowchart? **(b)** What facts in the source (top of next column) do not need to be in the flowchart? **(c)** If you limited your flowchart to five main steps, what would they be?

The Constitution originally provided this process for the election of President and Vice President:

The electors meet in their states, and each elector votes for two of the candidates running for President. (The electors have already been chosen in their states, with each state having a number of electors equal to the sum of its senators and representatives. The Constitution allows state legislatures to decide how their electors are chosen.) After totaling up the votes, the electors send the results to the president of the Senate, and then the votes from all the states are counted. The person with the majority of electoral votes becomes President, and the runner-up (with the next highest number of votes) becomes Vice President. However, if there is a tie vote for President, or if no candidate has a majority, the House of Representatives chooses the President by ballot, with each state having one vote. If there is a tie for Vice President, the Senate chooses the Vice President.

2. **(a)** How would you reword the first step described in the source? **(b)** How would you reword the final step in the process?

3. **(a)** Should the first event mentioned in the source be the first step in the flowchart? Explain. **(b)** What transitional words in the source help you understand the order of the steps? **(c)** In this case, why might you need more than one flowchart to explain the process?

4. **(a)** Create a flowchart that shows the process when there is no tie for either President or Vice President. **(b)** To explain the process when there is a tie for Vice President, how many boxes would you need? **(c)** Create that flowchart. **(d)** Would a variation of a flowchart that shows all possibilities be useful? Explain.

APPLY THE SKILL
See the Chapter Review and Assessment for another opportunity to apply this skill.

RESOURCE DIRECTORY

Teaching Resources
Skills for Life booklet, p. 7

Technology
Social Studies Skills Tutor CD-ROM
Interactive Practice in
- Geographic Literacy
- Critical Thinking and Reading
- Visual Analysis
- Communications

READING FOCUS

- Who were the new leaders selected by President Washington?
- What challenges did Washington's government face?
- What details were involved in planning the capital city?

MAIN IDEA

President Washington led the effort to create an effective federal government that would earn the respect of the American people and of other nations.

KEY TERMS

inauguration
Cabinet
domestic affairs
administration
precedent

TAKING NOTES

Copy the outline below. As you read, add facts and details from this section. Use Roman numerals to indicate the major headings of this section, capital letters for the subheadings, and numbers for the supporting details.

> **The New Government**
> I. New Leaders
>   A. John Adams, Vice President
>   1. Federalist
>   2. _____
>   B. _____

Setting the Scene

On April 30, 1789, a crowd of thousands surrounded Federal Hall, an elegant building on New York City's Wall Street that served as the temporary home of the new government. From windows and rooftops, people strained to catch a glimpse of the tall figure with freshly powdered hair who now appeared on the front balcony of the building.

Those within earshot listened as George Washington repeated the oath of office of President of the United States and then kissed a Bible. The crowd roared its approval. In attendance for the proceedings was a minister from France, who later reported to his government:

> 66 *Never has [a] sovereign [a ruler] reigned more completely in the hearts of his subjects than did Washington in those of his fellow-citizens. . . . He has the soul, look and figure of a hero united in him.* 99
> —Le Comte de Moustier

The New Leaders

Washington took his oath as part of the official swearing-in ceremony, or **inauguration.** He also delivered a speech, in which he described the importance of the new government:

> 66 *. . . the preservation of the sacred fire of liberty and the destiny of the republican model of government are justly considered, perhaps, as deeply, as finally, staked on the experiment entrusted to the hands of the American people.* 99
> —George Washington, First Inaugural Address, April 30, 1789

Washington had been elected President in early 1789 by the new electoral college in a unanimous vote. Massachusetts patriot John Adams, a leading Federalist, became Vice President. As the nation celebrated this peaceful inauguration of leaders, difficult tasks lay ahead. The infant nation had a huge war debt. It lacked a

This inauguration souvenir proclaims, in part, "dumbness [silence] to the tongue that will utter a calumny [insult] against the immortal Washington."

RESOURCE DIRECTORY

Teaching Resources
Guided Reading and Review booklet, p. 23

Technology
Section Reading Support Transparencies
Guided Reading Audiotapes (English/Spanish), Ch. 5
Student Edition on Audio CD, Ch. 5
Prentice Hall Presentation Pro CD-ROM, Ch. 5
Companion Web site, www.phschool.com

The New Government

SECTION OBJECTIVES

1. Learn about the new leaders selected by President Washington.
2. Discover the challenges faced by Washington's government.
3. See the kinds of details that were involved in planning the capital city.

BELLRINGER

Warm-Up Activity Ask students to recall magazine, newspaper, or television pictures of Washington, D.C. What are their impressions of the capital?

Activating Prior Knowledge Ask students to think about the capital city of your own state. Do they know how it was chosen? How does the capitol building in your state compare to the Capitol in Washington, D.C.?

READING STRATEGY

As students read the section, have them write down facts that will help them define the new government of the United States. Then, have them use their notes to write a one-sentence definition.

*A*CTIVITY
Connecting with Citizenship

Have students conduct research to locate the complete text of Washington's First Inaugural Address. Ask volunteers to take turns reading portions of it for the class. **(Verbal/Linguistic; Bodily/ Kinesthetic)**

Focus Explain that ratification of the Constitution meant that a blueprint for the strengthening of the central government now existed. Americans now had to make the new government work.

Instruct Explain that although the Constitution provided a framework for the new government, it was untested. Washington and Congress were charting new territory. Ask students about the challenges they faced. How did Washington choose his Cabinet members? Was there provision for a Cabinet in the Constitution? What impression did officials hope to give the people?

Assess/Reteach Discuss with students George Washington's achievements as the first President. In students' opinion, what were some of his greatest challenges?

From the Archives of
AmericanHeritage®

About the Presidents

George Washington (1789–1797) was keenly aware of his powerful influence in setting precedents. "It is devoutly wished on my part," he said, "that these precedents may be fixed on true principles." In most matters Washington was guided by the Constitution. Nevertheless, he was not timid about asserting presidential authority. The Constitution does not mention the President's right to declare neutrality. But Washington did so during the Franco-British war. It does not mention a Cabinet of appointed officers. But Washington set up a strong Cabinet with men of talent and character. He also considered national unity and geographic balance in making his choices. Later Presidents followed respectfully in Washington's footsteps. Source: William Sullivan, "George Washington," *The American Heritage® Pictorial History of the Presidents of the United States,* vol. 1, 1968.

READING CHECK

Jefferson was a skilled diplomat, lawyer, legislator, and patriot. He was the chief author of the Declaration of Independence, a former governor of Virginia, and had served as a delegate to the Continental Congress and an ambassador to France.

This illustration shows the first Cabinet: (left to right) Henry Knox, Thomas Jefferson, Edmund Randolph (whose back is turned), and Alexander Hamilton, with George Washington (far right).

READING CHECK
What were Thomas Jefferson's qualifications for Secretary of State?

permanent capital. It had no federal officers beyond Washington, Adams, and the newly elected Congress.

Immediately, President Washington began selecting officials to head the major departments of the executive branch. This group of federal leaders is called the **Cabinet.** Besides running their own agencies, Cabinet officers advise the President.

President Washington selected prominent Americans to fill these new posts. Edmund Randolph of Virginia was named Attorney General, the nation's chief law officer and legal advisor. Henry Knox, who had been Secretary of War under the Articles of Confederation, continued in this position under Washington.

Washington called on two of the nation's most respected patriots to fill his most crucial Cabinet posts. Thomas Jefferson was named to head the Department of State, which handles relations with foreign countries. Alexander Hamilton accepted the job of Secretary of the Treasury.

Secretary of State Jefferson Despite his role as chief author of the Declaration of Independence, Thomas Jefferson had not yet achieved great fame when he became Secretary of State. He had been elected governor of Virginia in 1779, and served as a delegate to the Continental Congress a few years later. Since then, however, he had spent several years out of the spotlight, serving as ambassador to France. While ambassador, Jefferson was able to keep in touch with events in the United States only through correspondence with friends like James Madison.

Upon his return from France in 1789, Jefferson quickly became involved again in **domestic affairs**—that is, the country's internal matters, as opposed to foreign issues. He eventually supported the Federalists' efforts to ratify the Constitution. Yet Jefferson was not a strict Federalist. His passionate concern for individuals' rights led him to press for the Bill of Rights.

Jefferson, later to become the nation's third President, was one of this nation's most gifted public figures. Besides being a planter, lawyer, and diplomat, Jefferson was a writer, inventor, and violinist. He made contributions to philosophy, mathematics, agricultural science, linguistics, and archaeology. Jefferson's love of learning led him to found the University of Virginia. Interested in architecture, Jefferson built several homes for himself. The most famous is Monticello, a gracious house near Charlottesville, Virginia.

A sense of duty made Jefferson a politician, but he much preferred the life of a gentleman farmer. Like many other southern planters of his day, Jefferson relied on slave labor. He knew that slavery was wrong, and he wrote eloquently about it as a moral evil. Yet he could never bring himself to free more than a few of his slaves.

President Washington chose Jefferson to head the Department of State because of his experience in dealing with France, the closest ally of the United States. However, the President also chose a man who never fully trusted the new government. Jefferson later would become one of Washington's harshest critics.

Treasury Secretary Hamilton Alexander Hamilton, the new head of the Department of the Treasury, was an intellectually brilliant man. He had attended King's College (now Columbia University) in New York City. He had quickly become involved in politics, supporting the Patriot cause. As an officer in the Continental Army during the Revolution, Hamilton had served as private secretary to General Washington. He carried out important military missions, and led a battalion during the battle at Yorktown.

Now Hamilton headed the government's largest department. In contrast to Jefferson, who never really trusted government, Hamilton believed that governmental power, properly used, could accomplish great things.

Despite the strong contrasts between Jefferson and Hamilton, the first months, even years, of the new government went fairly smoothly. The economic problems brought on by the war eased, and the adoption of the Constitution gave the nation much-needed stability.

Washington's Government

The largest problems and the smallest details came to Washington's attention during his first **administration,** or term of office. (*Administration* may also refer to the members and agencies of the executive branch as a whole.) With every decision, every action, every inaction, Washington and his officials were establishing **precedents** for how to govern. A precedent is an act or statement that becomes an example, rule, or tradition to be followed.

Many precedents were needed to answer important questions on how the new nation was to be governed. How should Congress and the President interact with each other? What was the role of the Cabinet? Nobody yet knew.

Typical of this experimental period was the debate in the Senate over what, if anything, to call the President. "His Excellency" was rejected early in the discussion. A Senate committee later suggested "His Highness the President of the United States of America and Protector of their Liberties." But the House of Representatives rejected that title, and the issue was set aside. (Today we simply use "Mr. President.")

NOTABLE PRESIDENTS
George Washington

1st President
1789–1797

"The basis of our political systems is the right of the people to make and to alter their Constitutions of Government."

—Farewell Address, 1796

George Washington was not only the nation's first President, he was also the person for whom the office was created. A former Virginia planter and surveyor, he had fought the French and Indian War and had led the Continental Army during the Revolution. His leadership in the fight for independence made him the nation's leading public figure.

Washington was famous, too, for his honesty, dignity, and self-control. In 1787, the Framers of the Constitution were confident that he could be trusted with the enormous powers of the presidency. Washington actively supported ratification of the Constitution, and his dignity and restraint as President eased many people's fears about the new government.

Washington could not, however, make the new government universally popular. Many Americans distrusted strong government, Alexander Hamilton's economic plans, and Washington's pro-British foreign policy. Convinced that Washington was leading the nation away from the ideals of the Revolution, they rallied behind Thomas Jefferson. Saddened that he could not prevent factions, Washington refused to run for a third term in 1796.

When Washington died, however, Americans joined together to honor his steadfast service to the nation, first as a general fighting a difficult war and later as a President seeking a workable balance between order and liberty.

Connecting to Today

Do you believe that dignity and restraint are as important for American Presidents today as they were in Washington's era? Explain your answer.

Take It to the NET **Biography** To read more about George Washington, visit the links provided in the *America: Pathways to the Present* area of the following Web site. **www.phschool.com**

Connecting with Government

This activity may take place over several class periods. Divide the class into groups of four to six students. Remind them that the Federalists commissioned French architect Pierre L'Enfant to design Washington, D.C., as a city that would symbolize a strong republic with noble roots. His magnificent city plan had classical buildings and broad boulevards radiating outward from the center of government. Have students design a capital that reflects the anti-Federalist view of government. **(Visual/Spatial)**

BACKGROUND

Connections to Today

In 1800, when the federal government moved to Washington, only about 8,000 people lived in the new city and the surrounding area. Today, more than four million people live in Washington and its suburbs.

Focus on CITIZENSHIP

Charitable Cause In her role as the first President's wife, Martha Washington (below) set precedents of her own during her husband's administration. Famous for her support of the American cause in the Revolution, Mrs. Washington—or Lady Washington, as she was often called—rallied behind the veterans of the Revolutionary War and made it her mission to see to their well-being. If veterans came into any trouble with the law, she was known to plead to the President for their pardons. She organized relief drives for veterans, and regularly received them as visitors, handing out small gifts of money to those in need. Martha Washington's goodwill gestures set a precedent for future Presidents' wives to follow: to serve the public need through a particular cause and, by example, encourage other citizens to do the same.

Meanwhile, President Washington, aware of the precedents he was setting, worked to establish a tone of dignity in his administration. His own appearance and personality helped. More than 6 feet tall, Washington cut an impressive figure. By nature he was solemn, reserved, and very formal.

Washington was also intensely private. A man named Gouverneur Morris had found this out the hard way: During the Constitutional Convention, some of Morris's fellow delegates had dared him to put his hand on Washington's shoulder. According to one account of the incident, "Washington withdrew his hand, stepped suddenly back, [and] fixed his eye on Morris for several minutes with an angry frown, until the latter retreated abashed, and sought refuge in the crowd."

Throughout his first term, Washington remained a popular figure, and in 1792 he won unanimous reelection. Reluctantly, he accepted. As you will read in the next chapter, his second administration would prove to be more difficult, marked by criticism and controversy.

During his eight years in the capital, Washington lived in grand style. Soldiers escorted his carriage, which was pulled by a team of six horses. The President and his wife, Martha, held regular Friday receptions to entertain government officials and ambassadors. Every year, government officials celebrated the President's birthday with elaborate ceremonies.

Washington believed that such pomp was necessary to command the respect of the American public and the rest of the world. To some people, however, such activities made Washington seem like a king with a lavish court.

The need to make the government appear both powerful and democratic at the same time presented quite a challenge. Yet such issues were important because they would set precedents for generations to come.

Planning a Capital City

A new nation needed a new capital, one that could equal the beauty and stature of Europe's grand capital cities. New York City was home to the government during Washington's first year. In 1790, the capital was moved to Philadelphia. There it would remain for a decade, while a brand-new capital could be planned and built.

That effort began with the Residence Act of 1790. It specified that the capital would be a 10-square-mile stretch of land on the Potomac River near Washington's home at Mount Vernon. The city would be located along the Maryland-Virginia border, but it would be governed by federal authorities, not by either state. The new capital was called the District of Columbia, although after President Washington's death in 1799, the city was renamed Washington, District of Columbia.

At the suggestion of Thomas Jefferson, Washington appointed Benjamin Banneker, an African American mathematician and inventor, to the commission formed to survey the city. Pierre-Charles L'Enfant, a French artist and architect who had fought for the United States during the Revolution, developed the city plan.

L'Enfant designed a spacious capital with broad streets laid out in an elegant, European-style pattern. Though the capital would initially serve a nation of only 13 states, L'Enfant planned an expansive city that later proved fit to

RESOURCE DIRECTORY

Teaching Resources
Units 1/2 booklet
• Section 4 Quiz, p. 56
• Chapter 5 Test, pp. 57, 60
Guide to the Essentials
• Section 4 Summary, p. 29
• Chapter 5 Test, p. 30
**Biography, Literature, and Comparing Primary
Sources booklet** (Biography) *Pierre-Charles
L'Enfant,* p. 10

Technology
ExamView® Test Bank CD-ROM, Ch. 5
Social Studies Skills Tutor CD-ROM

VIEWING HISTORY This 1792 engraved map is based on Pierre-Charles L'Enfant's plan for Washington, D.C. **Drawing Conclusions** *What impressions were the Federalists hoping to make with L'Enfant's design for the new capital?*

administer to 50 states. He created plans for the official residence of the President, a mansion now called the White House, as well as Congress's new home, the Capitol building. The federal government moved to the new District of Columbia in 1800, decades before the plan was fully realized.

Today, Washington, D.C., with its great boulevards, marble buildings in the Roman style, and public monuments, is the most visible legacy of the Federalists' grand plans for the United States. It was meant to display the power and dignity of the new federal government that they had fought to build. Washington, D.C. was the symbol of the strong national government they had lobbied for throughout the 1780s and outlined in the Constitution.

Section 4 Assessment

READING COMPREHENSION

1. What points did Washington make in his **inauguration** speech?

2. Who were the first **Cabinet** officers and what were their jobs?

3. What are **domestic affairs?**

4. What issues did Washington's first **administration** face? What kinds of **precedents** did Washington set?

5. Why did Washington promote formality in his administration?

CRITICAL THINKING AND WRITING

6. **Making Comparisons** Compare and contrast Thomas Jefferson's views of government with those of Alexander Hamilton.

7. **Testing Conclusions** Cite evidence to show how Washington succeeded in his effort to create a federal government respected by other nations.

8. **Writing to Inform** Explain how precedents set by George Washington during his presidency still influence our government today.

 Take It to the NET

Activity: Writing a Progress Report Read the first four annual messages delivered by George Washington to Congress. Create a list of the topics raised in each message, and then use the list to write a report on the progress Washington made during his first term in office. Use the links provided in the *America: Pathways to the Present* area of the following Web site for help in completing this activity.
www.phschool.com

Reading Comprehension

1. That the American people were responsible for the preservation of liberty and for determining the future of the republican model of government.

2. Edmund Randolph: Attorney General, the nation's chief law officer and legal adviser; Henry Knox: Secretary of War; Thomas Jefferson: head of the Department of State, handling foreign relations; Alexander Hamilton: Secretary of the Treasury.

3. A country's internal matters.

4. The role of the Cabinet and how Congress and the President should interact. Washington set precedents by creating a Cabinet and establishing traditions within the White House.

5. To command the respect of Americans and of other nations.

Critical Thinking and Writing

6. Jefferson: concerned for individual rights, supported the Bill of Rights; Hamilton: a strong Nationalist, strongly supported governmental power as a force for good.

7. He actively supported ratification of the Constitution, established important precedents that could be followed by future Presidents, and helped to establish a capital that would reflect the power and dignity of the new federal government; his dignity and restraint inspired confidence in the new government.

8. Sample answer: There is still much formality and ceremony invested in the office of the President of the United States. Washington set the precedent that a President should serve no more than two terms, which is now the Twenty-Second Amendment to the Constitution.

 Take It to the NET

Answers should demonstrate students' abilities to extract the important topics addressed in Washington's speeches to Congress and chronicle his progress throughout his first term.

CAPTION ANSWERS

Viewing History They wanted the capital to show the power and majesty of the national government.

REVIEWING KEY TERMS

Students should refer to the definitions of key terms in the chapter to write sentences that show an understanding of the key aspects of the era in which the Constitution was written and adopted.

REVIEWING MAIN IDEAS

15. The Articles of Confederation combined the legislative and executive functions in a unicameral legislature and did not create a national judicial branch.

16. The rebellion took place because merchants and the wealthy people who had loaned money to the states began demanding their money back and pressed for high taxes. In Massachusetts the tax met with opposition. Shays' Rebellion demonstrated the resolve of citizens to fight a heavy-handed government and supported Nationalists' claims that stronger government was needed to avoid chaos.

17. Madison is known as "the father of the Constitution." He helped draft the Virginia Plan, which was the basis for the Constitution.

18. The Constitution established a government with three branches; gave them separate powers and checks and balances; and created a process for selecting the President, Congress, and federal judges. The federal government is granted delegated powers, the state governments have reserved powers, and some powers are shared between the two entities.

19. They drew on Washington's endorsement of the Constitution and people's fear that the Union would dissolve unless the government was strengthened.

20. Under the Constitution, the people and the government were the same. The people, therefore, would not need to protect their rights from themselves.

21. Possible answer: Thomas Jefferson believed that a strong national government would infringe on the rights of the people unless those rights were spelled out in the Constitution.

22. Jefferson became Secretary of State. Hamilton became Secretary of the Treasury.

creating a CHAPTER SUMMARY

Copy this chart (right) on a piece of paper and complete it by adding key ideas about the documents listed.

For additional review and enrichment activities, see the interactive version of *America: Pathways to the Present*, available on the Web and on CD-ROM.

Document	Arguments For	Arguments Against
Articles of Confederation		
Constitution		
Bill of Rights		

★ Reviewing Key Terms

For each of the terms below, write a sentence explaining how it relates to the Constitution of the United States.

1. legislative branch
2. executive branch
3. judicial branch
4. democracy
5. republic
6. amend
7. veto
8. federal system of government
9. separation of powers
10. checks and balances
11. electoral college
12. ratify
13. Bill of Rights
14. Cabinet

★ Reviewing Main Ideas

15. Evaluate the structure of the government under the Articles of Confederation. (Section 1)

16. Describe Shays' Rebellion. Identify the reasons the rebellion occurred, and evaluate its impact. (Section 1)

17. Who was James Madison, and what was his role at the Constitutional Convention? (Section 2)

18. What was the structure of the government created by the Constitution? (Section 2)

19. What arguments did the Federalists make to gain approval of the Constitution? (Section 3)

20. Why did Federalists think the Bill of Rights was unnecessary? (Section 3)

21. Name one supporter of the Bill of Rights. What was his argument for supporting it? (Section 3)

22. What roles did Jefferson and Hamilton have in Washington's administration? (Section 4)

23. Analyze the importance of setting precedents during Washington's presidency. (Section 4)

★ Critical Thinking

24. Distinguishing Fact From Opinion Write two facts and two opinions about the Articles of Confederation.

25. Demonstrating Reasoned Judgment Do you think that Shays' Rebellion was a sign that the nation was slipping into disorder? Explain your answer.

26. Drawing Conclusions Why was the year 1787 a turning point in American history?

27. Identifying Assumptions What did the Three-Fifths Compromise suggest about how the Framers of the Constitution viewed enslaved African Americans?

28. Making Comparisons Evaluate the Constitution from the differing viewpoints of a Federalist and an anti-Federalist.

29. Testing Conclusions Many Americans believed that a Bill of Rights was absolutely crucial to the protection of liberty. Do you think this conclusion has proven to be correct? Use examples from history or from the present to show your reasoning.

CREATING A CHAPTER SUMMARY

Document	Arguments For	Arguments Against
Articles of Confederation	By dividing power between federal and state governments, democracy is ensured. Better to have mistakes under a government for the people than be ruled by tyrants.	Too much power given to ordinary citizens Too much power in state legislatures Central government not strong enough to maintain unity
Constitution	Strong central government Bicameral legislature, representative government System of checks and balances among divisions of the government President is a strong leader with authority over military. Powerful federal legislature and judiciary help maintain unity.	Modify plan to have a Senate, with each state having two representatives, and a House of Representatives based on population. Federal government threatens rights of individuals. A betrayal of the American Revolution
Bill of Rights	Anti-Federalists believed Constitution should include provisions to preserve the rights of the people. Bill of Rights necessary to restrain power of Federal Government	Measures to protect freedom of speech, press, and religion unnecessary

★ Skills Assessment

Analyzing Political Cartoons ▶

30. This engraving shows the celebration of New York's ratification of the Constitution. (a) What does the ship represent? (b) How do you know? (c) In this engraving, who is identified with the success of ratification? (d) How do you know?

31. Was the cartoonist a Federalist or an anti-Federalist? Explain your answer.

Analyzing Primary Sources

Read this excerpt, and then answer the questions that follow.

> ❝ We the People of the United States, in Order to form a more perfect Union, establish Justice, insure domestic Tranquility, provide for the common defense, promote the general Welfare, and secure the Blessings of Liberty to ourselves and our Posterity, do ordain and establish this Constitution for the United States of America. ❞
>
> —Preamble to the Constitution, 1787

32. Which document was designed to "secure the Blessings of Liberty"?

 A the Constitution
 B *The Federalist*, No. 10
 C the Cabinet
 D the Eighth Amendment

33. Why were the Framers attempting to "form a more perfect Union"?

 F Under the Articles of Confederation, the national government had little power to resolve problems among states.
 G Smaller states threatened to leave the Union because they feared a strong national government.
 H Shays' Rebellion had shown Americans that their national government was too powerful.
 J The Articles of Confederation did not give people enough say in their government.

Applying the Chapter Skill: *Building Flowcharts*

34. Construct a flowchart to show the steps taken from the assembling of the Constitutional Convention to the ratification of the Constitution.

ACTIVITIES

Writing to LEARN

Writing to Persuade
The Constitution is often referred to as "The Living Constitution." Write an essay that shows how the Constitution is alive today. Include answers to these questions: (a) What features of the Constitution make it flexible enough to apply to the nation's needs today? (b) What freedoms do you enjoy because of the Constitution?

Primary Source CD-ROM

Working With Primary Sources Find additional information on the Constitution of the United States on the *Exploring Primary Sources in U.S. History CD-ROM* and use the selection(s) provided to complete the Chapter 5 primary source activity located in the *America: Pathways to the Present* area of the following Web site. **www.phschool.com**

Take It to the NET

Chapter Self-Test As a review activity, take the Chapter 5 Self-Test in the *America: Pathways to the Present* area at the Web site listed below. The questions are designed to test your understanding of the chapter content. **www.phschool.com**

---

23. Precedents set during this initial administration were of crucial importance because they would shape the American presidency.

CRITICAL THINKING

24. Sample facts: created limited national government, gave most powers to the states. Sample opinions: the Articles were too weak, but they could have been simply amended rather than replaced.

25. Possible answer: Yes. The exact powers of state governments and the federal government needed to be much more sharply defined in order to maintain order. In particular, Shays' Rebellion demonstrated that a much stronger national government was needed in order to stabilize the nation.

26. The historic debate over the structure and powers of the American government was resolved.

27. The Three-Fifths Compromise suggested that the Framers thought African American slaves counted for less than did white residents.

28. Federalist: argued that the new government based on the Constitution would have more success in dealing with the difficulties facing the nation; emphasized the separation of powers and the system of checks and balances. Anti-Federalist: saw the Constitution as a betrayal of the American Revolution; felt that a President would be just like a king; objected to the lack of a bill of rights.

29. Conclusions should be clearly stated and supported with examples.

SKILLS ASSESSMENT

30. (a) The Federalists, specifically Alexander Hamilton. (b) It is named *Hamilton,* after a leading Federalist. (c) Hamilton. (d) The ship is named for him.

31. The cartoonist was a Federalist, because the people in the cartoon are celebrating ratification.

32. A

33. F

34. Flowcharts might vary slightly, but should take into account major milestones such as acceptance of the Virginia Plan, the Great Compromise, the Three-Fifths Compromise, Washington's support for ratification, and the writing and impact of *The Federalist.*

The Constitution of the United States

Focus Ask students to describe their student government. Is there a constitution? If so, what is its purpose? What is the procedure for making changes? If there is no constitution, would the student government benefit from one? Why or why not? Explain that student governments and other organizations often use the Constitution of the United States as a model.

Instruct Review the issues that divided Federalists and anti-Federalists. Discuss how the Constitution preserves popular sovereignty and limits the powers of government while avoiding the weaknesses of the Articles of Confederation. On the chalkboard, write the Six Basic Principles of the Constitution that are listed on this page. Ask students to explain each one in their own words. Then ask them to find examples of each principle within the Constitution.

Discuss how the Bill of Rights protects Americans' basic rights. Ask students to make a list of examples of the rights that are protected in their own lives.

Close The Constitution provides a broad explanation of the limits of government, based on six basic principles. It has protected the rights of Americans for more than 200 years.

THE SIX BASIC PRINCIPLES

The classic textbook *Magruder's American Government* outlines the six basic principles of the Constitution. Below is a description of these principles:

1 Popular Sovereignty

The Preamble to the Constitution begins with the bold phrase, "We the people . . ." These words announce that in the United States, the people are sovereign. The government receives its power from the people and can govern only with their consent.

2 Limited Government

Because the people are the ultimate source of all government power, the government has only as much authority as the people give it. Government's power is thus limited. Much of the Constitution, in fact, consists of specific limitations on government power.

3 Separation of Powers

Government power is not only limited, but also divided. The Constitution assigns certain powers to each of the three branches: the legislative (Congress), executive (President), and judicial (federal courts). This separation of government's powers was intended to prevent the misuse of power.

4 Checks and Balances

The system of checks and balances gives each of the three branches of government the ability to restrain the other two. Such a system makes government less efficient but also less likely to trample on the rights of citizens.

5 Judicial Review

Who decides whether an act of government violates the Constitution? Historically, the courts have filled this function. The principle of judicial review means that federal courts have the power to review acts of the federal government and to cancel any acts that are unconstitutional, or violate a provision in the Constitution.

6 Federalism

A federal system of government is one in which power is divided between a central government and smaller governments. This sharing of powers is intended to ensure that the central government is powerful enough to be effective, yet not so powerful as to threaten states or individuals.

RESOURCE DIRECTORY

Teaching Resources
Constitution Study Guide

Other Print Resources
American History Block Scheduling Support Checks and Balances: The Rise of the American Judiciary, found in the Forging a New Nation folder, includes interdisciplinary lesson suggestions and activities for Geography and History, Primary Sources, Biography, and Literature.

Technology
Prentice Hall United States History Video Collection™ Volume 5, *A New Nation*
Interactive Constitution CD-ROM

PARTS OF THE CONSTITUTION

A Note on the Text of the Constitution

The complete text of the Constitution, including amendments, appears on the pages that follow. Portions of the Constitution altered by later amendments or that no longer apply have been crossed out. Commentary appears in the outside column of each page.

UNITED STATES CONSTITUTION

CUSTOMIZE FOR ...

Gifted and Talented

Have students research one amendment to the Constitution and give a report to the class on the importance of the amendment and its impact on American society.

CUSTOMIZE FOR ...

ESL

Ask a volunteer to read the Preamble to the Constitution aloud. Then have students paraphrase the Preamble in their own words.

CUSTOMIZE FOR ...

Less Proficient Readers

Help students to begin reading the Constitution by having volunteers read the first several sections and clauses aloud, then read the appropriate paraphrase found in the Commentary. Point out that students can look to the Commentary to help them understand the reading.

CUSTOMIZE FOR ...

Less Proficient Writers

Invite students to choose an amendment to the Constitution that is meaningful to them, and invite them to write a few paragraphs about why they feel that amendment is important.

The Preamble states the broad purposes the Constitution is intended to serve—to establish a government that provides for greater cooperation among the States, ensures justice and peace, provides for defense against foreign enemies, promotes the general well-being of the people, and secures liberty now and in the future. The phrase *We the People* emphasizes the twin concepts of popular sovereignty and of representative government.

LEGISLATIVE BRANCH

Section 1. Legislative Power; Congress

Congress, the nation's lawmaking body, is bicameral in form; that is, it is composed of two houses: the Senate and the House of Representatives. The Framers of the Constitution purposely separated the lawmaking power from the power to enforce the laws (Article II, the Executive Branch) and the power to interpret them (Article III, the Judicial Branch). This system of separation of powers is supplemented by a system of checks and balances; that is, in several provisions the Constitution gives to each of the three branches various powers with which it may restrain the actions of the other two branches.

Section 2. House of Representatives

Clause 1. Election Electors means voters. Members of the House of Representatives are elected every two years. Each State must permit the same persons to vote for United States representatives as it permits to vote for the members of the larger house of its own legislature. The 17th Amendment (1913) extends this requirement to the qualification of voters for United States senators.

Clause 2. Qualifications A member of the House of Representatives must be at least 25 years old, an American citizen for seven years, and a resident of the State he or she represents. In addition, political custom requires that a representative also reside in the district from which he or she is elected.

Clause 3. Apportionment The number of representatives each State is entitled to is based on its population, which is counted every 10 years in the census. Congress reapportions the seats among the States after each census. In the Reapportionment Act of 1929, Congress fixed the permanent size of the House at 435 members with each State having at least one representative. Today there is one House seat for approximately every 650,000 persons in the population.

The words "three-fifths of all other persons" referred to slaves and reflected the Three-Fifths Compromise reached by the Framers at Philadelphia in 1787; the phrase was made obsolete, was in effect repealed, by the 13th Amendment in 1865.

PREAMBLE

We the People of the United States, in Order to form a more perfect Union, establish Justice, insure domestic Tranquility, provide for the common defence, promote the general Welfare, and secure the Blessings of Liberty to ourselves and our Posterity, do ordain and establish this Constitution for the United States of America.

Article I.

Section 1.

All legislative Powers herein granted shall be vested in a Congress of the United States, which shall consist of a Senate and House of Representatives.

Section 2.

1. The House of Representatives shall be composed of Members chosen every second Year by the People of the several States, and the Electors in each State shall have the Qualifications requisite for Electors of the most numerous Branch of the State Legislature.

2. No Person shall be a Representative who shall not have attained to the age of twenty-five Years, and been seven Years a Citizen of the United States, and who shall not, when elected, be an Inhabitant of that State in which he shall be chosen.

3. Representatives ~~and direct Taxes~~* shall be apportioned among the several States which may be included within this Union, according to their respective Numbers, ~~which shall be determined by adding to the whole Number of free Persons, including those bound to Service for a Term of Years and excluding Indians not taxed, three fifths of all other Persons.~~ The actual Enumeration shall be made within three Years after the first Meeting of the Congress of the United States, and within every subsequent term of ten Years, in such Manner as they shall by Law direct. The Number of Representatives shall not exceed one for every thirty Thousand, but each State shall have at Least one Representative; and, until such enumeration shall be made, the State of New Hampshire shall be entitled to choose three, Massachusetts eight, Rhode Island and Providence Plantations one, Connecticut five, New York

*The black lines indicate portions of the Constitution altered by subsequent amendments to the document.

six, New Jersey four, Pennsylvania eight, Delaware one, Maryland six, Virginia ten, North Carolina five, South Carolina five, and Georgia three.

4. When vacancies happen in the Representation from any State, the Executive Authority thereof shall issue Writs of Election to fill such Vacancies.

5. The House of Representatives shall choose their Speaker and other Officers; and shall have the sole Power of Impeachment.

Section 3.

1. The Senate of the United States shall be composed of two Senators from each State ~~chosen by the Legislature thereof~~ for six Years; and each Senator shall have one Vote.

2. Immediately after they shall be assembled in Consequences of the first Election, they shall be divided, as equally as may be, into three Classes. The Seats of the Senators of the first Class shall be vacated at the Expiration of the second Year; of the second Class, at the Expiration of the fourth Year; and of the third Class, at the Expiration of the sixth Year; so that one-third may be chosen every second Year; ~~and if Vacancies happen by Resignation, or otherwise, during the Recess of the Legislature of any State, the Executive thereof may make temporary Appointments until the next Meeting of the Legislature, which shall then fill such Vacancies.~~

3. No Person shall be a Senator who shall not have attained to the Age of thirty Years, and been nine Years a Citizen of the United States, and who shall not, when elected, be an Inhabitant of that State for which he shall be chosen.

4. The Vice President of the United States shall be President of the Senate but shall have no Vote, unless they be equally divided.

5. The Senate shall choose their other Officers, and also a President pro tempore, in the Absence of the Vice President, or when he shall exercise the Office of President of the United States.

6. The Senate shall have the sole Power to try all Impeachments. When sitting for that Purpose, they shall be on Oath or Affirmation. When the President of the United States is tried, the Chief Justice shall preside: And no Person shall be convicted without the Concurrence of two thirds of the Members present.

Clause 4. Vacancies The executive authority refers to the governor of a State. If a member leaves office or dies before the expiration of his or her term, the governor is to call a special election to fill the vacancy.

Clause 5. Officers; impeachment The House elects a Speaker, customarily chosen from the majority party in the House. Impeachment means accusation. The House has the exclusive power to impeach, or accuse, civil officers; the Senate (Article I, Section 3, Clause 6) has the exclusive power to try those impeached by the House.

Section 3. Senate

Clause 1. Composition, election, term Each State has two senators. Each serves for six years and has one vote. Originally, senators were not elected directly by the people, but by each State's legislature. The 17th Amendment, added in 1913, provides for the popular election of senators.

Clause 2. Classification The senators elected in 1788 were divided into three groups so that the Senate could become a "continuing body." One-third of the Senate's seats are up for election every two years.

The 17th Amendment provides that a Senate vacancy is to be filled at a special election called by the governor; State law may also permit the governor to appoint a successor to serve until that election is held.

Clause 3. Qualifications A senator must be at least 30 years old, a citizen for at least nine years, and a resident of the State from which elected.

Clause 4. Presiding officer The Vice President presides over the Senate, but may vote only to break a tie.

Clause 5. Other officers The Senate chooses its own officers, including a president pro tempore to preside when the Vice President is not there.

Clause 6. Impeachment trials The Senate conducts the trials of those officials impeached by the House. The Vice President presides unless the President is on trial, in which case the Chief Justice of the United States does so. A conviction requires the votes of two-thirds of the senators present.

No President has ever been convicted. In 1868 the House voted eleven articles of impeachment against

President Andrew Johnson, but the Senate fell one vote short of convicting him. In 1974 President Richard M. Nixon resigned the presidency in the face of almost certain impeachment by the House. The House brought two articles of impeachment against President Bill Clinton in late 1998. Neither charge was supported by even a simple majority vote in the Senate, on February 12, 1999.

Clause 7. Penalty on conviction The punishment of an official convicted in an impeachment case has always been removal from office. The Senate can also bar a convicted person from ever holding any federal office, but it is not required to do so. A convicted person can also be tried and punished in a regular court for any crime involved in the impeachment case.

Section 4. Elections and Meetings

Clause 1. Election In 1842 Congress required that representatives be elected from districts within each State with more than one seat in the House. The districts in each State are drawn by that State's legislature. Seven States now have only one seat in the House: Alaska, Delaware, Montana, North Dakota, South Dakota, Vermont, and Wyoming. The 1842 law also directed that representatives be elected in each State on the same day: the Tuesday after the first Monday in November of every even-numbered year. In 1914 Congress also set that same date for the election of senators.

Clause 2. Sessions Congress must meet at least once a year. The 20th Amendment (1933) changed the opening date to January 3.

Section 5. Legislative Proceedings

Clause 1. Admission of members; quorum In 1969 the Supreme Court held that the House cannot exclude any member-elect who satisfies the qualifications set out in Article I, Section 2, Clause 2.

A majority in the House (218 members) or Senate (51) constitutes a quorum. In practice, both houses often proceed with less than a quorum present. However, any member may raise a point of order (demand a "quorum call"). If a roll call then reveals less than a majority of the members present, that chamber must either adjourn or the sergeant at arms must be ordered to round up absent members.

Clause 2. Rules Each house has adopted detailed rules to guide its proceedings. Each house may discipline members for unacceptable conduct; expulsion requires a two-thirds vote.

Clause 3. Record Each house must keep and publish a record of its meetings. The *Congressional Record* is published for every day that either house of Congress is in session, and provides a written record of all that is said and done on the floor of each house each session.

Clause 4. Adjournment Once in session, neither house may suspend (recess) its work for more than three days without the approval of the other house. Both houses must always meet in the same location.

7. Judgment in Cases of Impeachment shall not extend further than to removal from Office, and disqualification to hold and enjoy any Office of honor, Trust, or Profit under the United States: but the Party convicted shall nevertheless be liable and subject to Indictment, Trial, Judgment and Punishment, according to Law.

Section 4.

1. The Times, Places and Manner of holding Elections for Senators and Representatives, shall be prescribed in each State by the Legislature thereof; but the Congress may at any time by law make or alter such Regulations, except as to the Places of choosing Senators.

2. The Congress shall assemble at least once in every Year, and such Meeting shall be on the first Monday in December, unless they shall by Law appoint a different Day.

Section 5.

1. Each House shall be the Judge of the Elections, Returns and Qualifications of its own Members, and a Majority of each shall constitute a Quorum to do Business; but a smaller Number may adjourn from day to day, and may be authorized to compel the Attendance of absent Members, in such Manner, and under such Penalties, as each House may provide.

2. Each House may determine the Rules of its Proceedings, punish its Members for disorderly Behavior, and, with the Concurrence of two thirds, expel a Member.

3. Each House shall keep a Journal of its Proceedings, and from time to time publish the same, excepting such Parts as may in their Judgment require Secrecy; and the Yeas and Nays of the Members of either House on any question shall, at the Desire of one fifth of those Present, be entered on the Journal.

4. Neither House, during the Session of Congress, shall, without the Consent of the other, adjourn for more than three days, nor to any other Place than that in which the two Houses shall be sitting.

Section 6.

1. The Senators and Representatives shall receive a Compensation for their Services, to be ascertained by Law, and paid out of the Treasury of the United States. They shall in all Cases, except Treason, Felony, and Breach of the Peace, be privileged from Arrest during their Attendance at the Session of their respective Houses, and in going to and returning from the same; and for any Speech or Debate in either House, they shall not be questioned in any other Place.

2. No Senator or Representative shall, during the Time for which he was elected, be appointed to any civil Office under the Authority of the United States, which shall have been created, or the Emoluments whereof shall have been increased during such time; and no Person holding any Office under the United States, shall be a Member of either House during his Continuance in Office.

Section 7.

1. All Bills for raising Revenue shall originate in the House of Representatives; but the Senate may propose or concur with amendments as on other Bills.

2. Every Bill which shall have passed the House of Representatives and the Senate, shall, before it become a law, be presented to the President of the United States: If he approve, he shall sign it, but if not he shall return it, with his Objections to that House in which it shall have originated, who shall enter the Objections at large on their Journal, and proceed to reconsider it. If after such Reconsideration two thirds of the House shall agree to pass the Bill, it shall be sent, together with the Objections, to the other House, by which it shall likewise be reconsidered, and if approved by two thirds of that House, it shall become a Law. But in all such Cases the Votes of both Houses shall be deter-mined by Yeas and Nays, and the Names of the Persons voting for and against the Bill shall be entered on the Journal of each House respectively. If any Bill shall not be returned by the President within ten Days (Sunday excepted) after it shall have been presented to him, the Same shall be a law, in like Manner as if he had signed it, unless the Congress by their Adjournment, prevent its Return, in which Case it shall not be a Law.

3. Every Order, Resolution, or Vote to which the Concurrence of the Senate and House of Representatives may be necessary (except on a ques-tion of adjournment) shall be presented to the President of the United States; and before the Same shall take Effect, shall be approved by him, or, being disapproved by him, shall be repassed by two thirds of

Section 6. Compensation, Immunities, and Disabilities of Members

Clause 1. Salaries; immunities Each house sets its members' salaries, paid by the United States; the 27th Amendment (1992) modified this pay-setting power. This provision establishes "legislative immunity." The purpose of this immunity is to allow members to speak and debate freely in Congress itself. Treason is strictly defined in Article III, Section 3. A felony is any serious crime. A breach of the peace is any indictable offense less than treason or a felony; this exemption from arrest is of little real importance today.

Clause 2. Restrictions on office holding No sitting member of either house may be appointed to an office in the executive or in the judicial branch if that position was created or its salary was increased during that member's current elected term. The second part of this clause—forbidding any person serving in either the executive or the judicial branch from also serving in Congress—reinforces the principle of separation of powers.

Section 7. Revenue Bills, President's Veto

Clause 1. Revenue bills All bills that raise money must originate in the House. However, the Senate has the power to amend any revenue bill sent to it from the lower house.

Clause 2. Enactment of laws; veto Once both houses have passed a bill, it must be sent to the President. The President may (1) sign the bill, thus making it law; (2) veto the bill, whereupon it must be returned to the house in which it originated; or (3) allow the bill to become law with-out signature, by not acting upon it within 10 days of its receipt from Congress, not counting Sundays. The President has a fourth option at the end of a congressional session: If he does not act on a measure within 10 days, and Congress adjourns during that period, the bill dies; the "pocket veto" has been applied to it. A presidential veto may be overridden by a two-thirds vote in each house.

Clause 3. Other measures This clause refers to joint reso-lutions, measures Congress often passes to deal with unusual, temporary, or ceremonial matters. A joint resolu-tion passed by Congress and signed by the President has the force of law, just as a bill does. As a matter of custom, a joint resolution proposing an amendment to the Constitution is not submitted to the President for signature

UNITED STATES CONSTITUTION

or veto. Concurrent and simple resolutions do not have the force of law and, therefore, are not submitted to the President.

Section 8. Powers of Congress

Clause 1. The 18 separate clauses in this section set out 27 of the many expressed powers the Constitution grants to Congress. In this clause Congress is given the power to levy and provide for the collection of various kinds of taxes, in order to finance the operations of the government. All federal taxes must be levied at the same rates throughout the country.

Clause 2. Congress has power to borrow money to help finance the government. Federal borrowing is most often done through the sale of bonds on which interest is paid. The Constitution does not limit the amount the government may borrow.

Clause 3. This clause, the Commerce Clause, gives Congress the power to regulate both foreign and interstate trade. Much of what Congress does, it does on the basis of its commerce power.

Clause 4. Congress has the exclusive power to determine how aliens may become citizens of the United States. Congress may also pass laws relating to bankruptcy.

Clause 5. Congress has the power to establish and require the use of uniform gauges of time, distance, weight, volume, area, and the like.

Clause 6. Congress has the power to make it a federal crime to falsify the coins, paper money, bonds, stamps, and the like of the United States.

Clause 7. Congress has the power to provide for and regulate the transportation and delivery of mail; "post offices" are those buildings and other places where mail is deposited for dispatch; "post roads" include all routes over or upon which mail is carried.

Clause 8. Congress has the power to provide for copyrights and patents. A copyright gives an author or composer the exclusive right to control the reproduction, publication, and sale of literary, musical, or other creative work. A patent gives a person the exclusive right to control the manufacture or sale of his or her invention.

Clause 9. Congress has the power to create the lower federal courts, all of the several federal courts that function beneath the Supreme Court.

Clause 10. Congress has the power to prohibit, as a federal crime: (1) certain acts committed outside the territorial jurisdiction of the United States, and (2) the commission within the United States of any wrong against any nation with which we are at peace.

Clause 11. Only Congress can declare war. However, the President, as commander in chief of the armed forces (Article II, Section 2, Clause 1), can make war without such

178 **United States Constitution**

the Senate and House of Representatives, according to the Rules and Limitations prescribed in the Case of a Bill.

Section 8.

The Congress shall have Power

1. To lay and collect Taxes, Duties, Imposts and Excises to pay the Debts and provide for the common Defence and general Welfare of the United States; but all Duties, Imposts and Excises, shall be uniform throughout the United States;

2. To borrow Money on the credit of the United States;

3. To regulate Commerce with foreign Nations, and among the several States, and with the Indian Tribes;

4. To establish an uniform Rule of Naturalization, and uniform Laws on the subject of Bankruptcies throughout the United States;

5. To coin Money, regulate the Value thereof, and of foreign Coin, and fix the Standard of Weights and Measures;

6. To provide for the Punishment of counterfeiting the Securities and current Coin of the United States;

7. To establish Post Offices and post Roads;

8. To promote the Progress of Science and useful Arts, by securing, for limited Times to Authors and Inventors the exclusive Right to their respective Writings and Discoveries;

9. To constitute Tribunals inferior to the supreme Court;

10. To define and punish Piracies and Felonies committed on the high Seas, and Offences against the Law of nations;

11. To declare War, grant Letters of Marque and Reprisal, and make Rules concerning Captures on Land and Water;

12. To raise and support Armies; but no Appropriation of Money to that Use shall be for a longer Term than two Years;

13. To provide and maintain a Navy;

14. To make Rules for the Government and Regulation of the land and naval Forces;

15. To provide for calling forth the Militia to execute the Laws of the Union, suppress Insurrections and repel Invasions;

16. To provide for organizing, arming, and disciplining the Militia, and for governing such Part of them as may be employed in the Service of the United States, reserving to the States respectively the Appointment of the Officers, and the Authority of training the Militia according to the discipline prescribed by Congress;

17. To exercise exclusive Legislation in all Cases whatsoever, over such District (not exceeding ten Miles square) as may, by Cession of Particular States, and the Acceptance of Congress, become the Seat of the Government of the United States, and to exercise like Authority over all Places purchased by the Consent of the Legislature of the State in which the Same shall be, for the Erection of Forts, Magazines, Arsenals, Dockyards and other needful Buildings;—And

18. To make all Laws which shall be necessary and proper for carrying into Execution the foregoing Powers and all other Powers vested by this Constitution in the Government of the United States, or in any Department or Officer thereof.

Section 9.

1. The Migration or Importation of such Persons as any of the States now existing shall think proper to admit, shall not be prohibited by the Congress prior to the Year one thousand eight hundred and eight, but a Tax or duty may be imposed on such Importation, not exceeding ten dollars for each Person.

2. The Privilege of the Writ of Habeas Corpus shall not be suspended, unless when in Cases of Rebellion or Invasion the public safety may require it.

3. No Bill of Attainder or ex post facto Law shall be passed.

---

a formal declaration. Letters of marque and reprisal are commissions authorizing private persons to outfit vessels (privateers) to capture and destroy enemy ships in time of war; they were forbidden in international law by the Declaration of Paris of 1856, and the United States has honored the ban since the Civil War.

Clauses 12 and 13. Congress has the power to provide for and maintain the nation's armed forces. It established the air force as an independent element of the armed forces in 1947, an exercise of its inherent powers in foreign relations and national defense. The two-year limit on spending for the army insures civilian control of the military.

Clause 14. Today these rules are set out in a lengthy, oft-amended law, the Uniform Code of Military Justice, passed by Congress in 1950.

Clauses 15 and 16. In the National Defense Act of 1916, Congress made each State's militia (volunteer army) a part of the National Guard. Today, Congress and the States cooperate in its maintenance. Ordinarily, each State's National Guard is under the command of that State's governor; but Congress has given the President the power to call any or all of those units into federal service when necessary.

Clause 17. In 1791 Congress accepted land grants from Maryland and Virginia and established the District of Columbia for the nation's capital. Assuming Virginia's grant would never be needed, Congress returned it in 1846. Today, the elected government of the District's 69 square miles operates under the authority of Congress. Congress also has the power to acquire other lands from the States for various federal purposes.

Clause 18. This is the Necessary and Proper Clause, also often called the Elastic Clause. It is the constitutional basis for the many and far-reaching implied powers of the Federal Government.

Section 9. Powers Denied to Congress

Clause 1. The phrase "such persons" referred to slaves. This provision was part of the Commerce Compromise, one of the bargains struck in the writing of the Constitution. Congress outlawed the slave trade in 1808.

Clause 2. A writ of habeas corpus, the "great writ of liberty," is a court order directing a sheriff, warden, or other public officer, or a private person, who is detaining another to "produce the body" of the one being held in order that the legality of the detention may be determined by the court.

Clause 3. A bill of attainder is a legislative act that inflicts punishment without a judicial trial. See Article I, Section 10, and Article III, Section 3, Clause 2. An *ex post facto* law is

UNITED STATES CONSTITUTION

United States Constitution 179

any criminal law that operates retroactively to the disadvantage of the accused. See Article I, Section 10.

Clause 4. A capitation tax is literally a "head tax," a tax levied on each person in the population. A direct tax is one paid directly to the government by the taxpayer—for example, an income or a property tax; an indirect tax is one paid to another private party who then pays it to the government—for example, a sales tax. This provision was modified by the 16th Amendment (1913), giving Congress the power to levy "taxes on incomes, from whatever source derived."

Clause 5. This provision was a part of the Commerce Compromise made by the Framers in 1787. Congress has the power to tax imported goods, however.

Clause 6. All ports within the United States must be treated alike by Congress as it exercises its taxing and commerce powers. Congress cannot tax goods sent by water from one State to another, nor may it give the ports of one State any legal advantage over those of another.

Clause 7. This clause gives Congress its vastly important "power of the purse," a major check on presidential power. Federal money can be spent only in those amounts and for those purposes expressly authorized by an act of Congress. All federal income and spending must be accounted for, regularly and publicly.

Clause 8. This provision, preventing the establishment of a nobility, reflects the principle that "all men are created equal." It was also intended to discourage foreign attempts to bribe or otherwise corrupt officers of the government.

Section 10. Powers Denied to the States

Clause 1. The States are not sovereign governments and so cannot make agreements or otherwise negotiate with foreign states; the power to conduct foreign relations is an exclusive power of the National Government. The power to coin money is also an exclusive power of the National Government. Several powers forbidden to the National Government are here also forbidden to the States.

Clause 2. This provision relates to foreign, not interstate, commerce. Only Congress, not the States, can tax imports; and the States are, like Congress, forbidden the power to tax exports.

Clause 3. A duty of tonnage is a tax laid on ships according to their cargo capacity. Each State has a constitutional right to provide for and maintain a militia; but no State may keep a standing army or navy. The several restrictions here prevent the States from assuming powers that the Constitution elsewhere grants to the National Government.

4. No Capitation, ~~or other direct, Tax~~ shall be laid, unless in Proportion to the Census of Enumeration hereinbefore directed to be taken.

5. No Tax or Duty shall be laid on Articles exported from any State.

6. No Preference shall be given by any Regulation of Commerce or Revenue to the Ports of one State over those of another: nor shall Vessels bound to, or from, one State, be obliged to enter, clear or pay Duties in another.

7. No Money shall be drawn from the Treasury, but in Consequence of Appropriations made by Law; and a regular Statement and Account of the Receipts and Expenditures of all public Money shall be published from time to time.

8. No Title of Nobility shall be granted by the United States: And no Person holding any Office of Profit or Trust under them, shall, without the Consent of the Congress, accept of any present, Emolument, Office, or Title, of any kind whatever, from any King, Prince, or foreign State.

Section 10.

1. No State shall enter into any Treaty, Alliance, or Confederation; grant Letters of Marque and Reprisal; coin Money; emit Bills of Credit; make any Thing but gold and silver Coin a Tender in Payment of Debts; pass any Bill of Attainder, ex post facto Law, or Law impairing the Obligation of Contracts, or grant any Title of Nobility.

2. No State shall, without the Consent of the Congress, lay any Imposts or Duties on Imports or Exports, except what may be absolutely necessary for executing its inspection Laws; and the net Produce of all Duties and Imposts, laid by any State on Imports or Exports, shall be for the Use of the Treasury of the United States; and all such Laws shall be subject to the Revision and Control of the Congress.

3. No State shall, without the Consent of Congress, lay any Duty of Tonnage, keep Troops, or Ships of War in time of Peace, enter into any Agreement or Compact with another State, or with a foreign Power, or engage in War, unless actually invaded, or in such imminent Danger as will not admit of delay.

Article II

Section 1.

1. The executive Power shall be vested in a President of the United States of America. He shall hold his Office during the Term of four Years, and, together with the Vice President, chosen for the same Term, be elected as follows:

2. Each State shall appoint, in such Manner as the Legislature thereof may direct, a Number of Electors, equal to the whole Number of Senators and Representatives to which the State may be entitled in the Congress: but no Senator or Representative, or Person holding an Office of Trust or Profit, under the United States, shall be appointed an Elector.

3. ~~The Electors shall meet in their respective States, and vote by Ballot for two Persons, of whom one at least shall not be an Inhabitant of the same State with themselves. And they shall make a List of all the Persons voted for, and of the Number of Votes for each; which List they shall sign and certify, and transmit sealed to the Seat of the Government of the United States, directed to the President of the Senate. The President of the Senate shall, in the Presence of the Senate and House of Representatives, open all the Certificates, and the Votes shall then be counted. The Person having the greatest Number of Votes shall be the President, if such Number be a majority of the whole Number of Electors appointed; and if there be more than one who have such Majority, and have an equal Number of Votes, then, the House of Representatives shall immediately choose by Ballot one of them for President; and if no Person have a Majority, then from the five highest on the List the said House shall in like Manner choose the President. But in choosing the President, the Votes shall be taken by States, the Representatives from each State having one Vote; a quorum for this Purpose shall consist of a Member or Members from two thirds of the States, and a Majority of all the States shall be necessary to a Choice. In every Case, after the Choice of the President, the Person having the greatest Number of Votes of the Electors shall be the Vice President. But if there should remain two or more who have equal Votes, the Senate shall choose from them by Ballot the Vice President.~~

4. The Congress may determine the Time of choosing the Electors, and the Day on which they shall give their Votes; which Day shall be the same throughout the United States.

5. No Person except a natural born Citizen, or a Citizen of the United States, at the time of the Adoption of this

EXECUTIVE BRANCH

Section 1. President and Vice President

Clause 1. Executive power, term This clause gives to the President the very broad "executive power," the power to enforce the laws and otherwise administer the public policies of the United States. It also sets the length of the presidential (and vice-presidential) term of office; see the 22nd Amendment (1951), which places a limit on presidential (but not vice-presidential) tenure.

Clause 2. Electoral college This clause establishes the "electoral college," although the Constitution does not use that term. It is a body of presidential electors chosen in each State, and it selects the President and Vice President every four years. The number of electors chosen in each State equals the number of senators and representatives that State has in Congress.

Clause 3. Election of President and Vice President This clause was replaced by the 12th Amendment in 1804.

Clause 4. Date Congress has set the date for the choosing of electors as the Tuesday after the first Monday in November every fourth year, and for the casting of electoral votes as the Monday after the second Wednesday in December of that year.

Clause 5. Qualifications The President must have been born a citizen of the United States, be at least 35 years old, and have been a resident of the United States for at least 14 years.

Constitution, shall be eligible to the Office of President; neither shall any person be eligible to that Office who shall not have attained to the Age of thirty-five Years, and been fourteen Years a Resident within the United States.

Clause 6. Vacancy This clause was modified by the 25th Amendment (1967), which provides expressly for the succession of the Vice President, for the filling of a vacancy in the Vice Presidency, and for the determination of presidential inability.

6. In Case of the Removal of the President from Office, or of his Death, Resignation, or Inability to discharge the Powers and Duties of the said Office, the Same shall devolve on the Vice President, and the Congress may by Law provide for the Case of Removal, Death, Resignation or Inability, both of the President and Vice President, declaring what Officer shall then act as President, and such Officer shall act accordingly, until the Disability be removed, or a President shall be elected.

Clause 7. Compensation The President now receives a salary of $400,000 and a taxable expense account of $50,000 a year. Those amounts cannot be changed during a presidential term; thus, Congress cannot use the President's compensation as a bargaining tool to influence executive decisions. The phrase "any other emolument" means, in effect, any valuable gift; it does not mean that the President cannot be provided with such benefits of office as the White House, extensive staff assistance, and much else.

7. The President shall, at stated Times, receive for his Services, a Compensation, which shall neither be increased nor diminished during the Period for which he shall have been elected, and he shall not receive within that Period any other Emolument from the United States, or any of them.

Clause 8. Oath of office The chief justice of the United States regularly administers this oath or affirmation, but any judicial officer may do so. Thus, Calvin Coolidge was sworn into office in 1923 by his father, a justice of the peace in Vermont.

8. Before he enter on the Execution of his Office, he shall take the following Oath or Affirmation:
"I do solemnly swear (or affirm) that I will faithfully execute the Office of President of the United States, and will to the best of my Ability, preserve, protect and defend the Constitution of the United States."

Section 2. President's Powers and Duties

Clause 1. Military, civil powers The President, a civilian, heads the nation's armed forces, a key element in the Constitution's insistence on civilian control of the military. The President's power to "require the opinion, in writing" provides the constitutional basis for the cabinet. The President's power to grant reprieves and pardons, the power of clemency, extends only to federal cases.

Section 2.

1. The President shall be Commander in Chief of the Army and Navy of the United States, and of the Militia of the several States, when called into the actual Service of the United States; he may require the Opinion, in writing, of the principal Officer in each of the executive Departments, upon any Subject relating to the Duties of their respective Offices, and he shall have Power to Grant Reprieves and Pardons for Offences against the United States, except in Cases of Impeachment.

Clause 2. Treaties, appointments The President has the sole power to make treaties; to become effective, a treaty must be approved by a two-thirds vote in the Senate. In practice, the President can also make executive agreements with foreign governments; these pacts, which are frequently made and usually deal with routine matters, do not require Senate consent. The President appoints the principal officers of the executive branch and all federal judges; the "inferior officers" are those who hold lesser posts.

2. He shall have Power, by and with the Advice and Consent of the Senate, to make Treaties, provided two thirds of the Senators present concur; and he shall nominate, and by and with the Advice and Consent of the Senate, shall appoint Ambassadors, other public Ministers and Consuls, Judges of the supreme Court, and all other Officers of the United States, whose Appointments are not herein otherwise provided for, and which shall be established by Law: but the Congress may by Law vest the Appointment of such

UNITED STATES CONSTITUTION

inferior Officers, as they think proper, in the President alone, in the Courts of Law, or in the Heads of Departments.

3. The President shall have Power to fill up all Vacancies that may happen during the Recess of the Senate, by granting Commissions which shall expire at the End of their next Session.

Section 3.

He shall from time to time give to the Congress Information of the State of the Union, and recommend to their Consideration such Measures as he shall judge necessary and expedient; he may, on extraordinary Occasions, convene both Houses, or either of them, and in Case of Disagreement between them, with Respect to the Time of Adjournment, he may adjourn them to such Time as he shall think proper; he shall receive Ambassadors and other public Ministers; he shall take Care that the Laws be faithfully executed, and shall Commission all the Officers of the United States.

Section 4.

The President, Vice President and all Civil Officers of the United States, shall be removed from Office on Impeachment for and Conviction of, Treason, Bribery, or other high Crimes and Misdemeanors.

Article III

Section 1.

The judicial Power of the United States, shall be vested in one supreme Court, and in such inferior Courts as the Congress may from time to time ordain and establish. The Judges, both of the supreme and inferior Courts, shall hold their Offices during good Behavior, and shall, at stated Times, receive for their Services, a Compensation, which shall not be diminished during their Continuance in Office.

Section 2.

1. The judicial Power shall extend to all Cases, in Law and Equity, arising under this Constitution, the Laws of the United States, and Treaties made, or which shall be made, under their Authority;— to all Cases affecting Ambassadors, other public ministers, and Consuls;— to all Cases of Admiralty and maritime Jurisdiction;— to Controversies to which the United States shall be a Party;— to Controversies between two or more States;— between a State and Citizens of another State;— between Citizens of different States;—

Clause 3. Recess appointments When the Senate is not in session, appointments that require Senate consent can be made by the President on a temporary basis, as "recess appointments."

Section 3. President's Powers and Duties

The President delivers a State of the Union Message to Congress soon after that body convenes each year. That message is delivered to the nation's lawmakers and, importantly, to the American people, as well. It is shortly followed by the proposed federal budget and an economic report; and the President may send special messages to Congress at any time. In all of these communications, Congress is urged to take those actions the Chief Executive finds to be in the national interest. The President also has the power: to call special sessions of Congress; to adjourn Congress if its two houses cannot agree for that purpose; to receive the diplomatic representatives of other governments; to insure the proper execution of all federal laws; and to empower federal officers to hold their posts and perform their duties.

Section 4. Impeachment

The Constitution outlines the impeachment process in Article I, Section 2, Clause 5 and in Section 3, Clauses 6 and 7.

JUDICIAL BRANCH

Section 1. Courts, Terms of Office

The judicial power conferred here is the power of federal courts to hear and decide cases, disputes between the government and individuals and between private persons (parties). The Constitution creates only the Supreme Court of the United States; it gives to Congress the power to establish other, lower federal courts (Article I, Section 8, Clause 9) and to fix the size of the Supreme Court. The words "during good behavior" mean, in effect, for life.

Section 2. Jurisdiction

Clause 1. Cases to be heard This clause sets out the jurisdiction of the federal courts; that is, it identifies those cases that may be tried in those courts. The federal courts can hear and decide—have jurisdiction over—a case depending on either the subject matter or the parties involved in that case. The jurisdiction of the federal courts in cases involving States was substantially restricted by the 11th Amendment in 1795.

Clause 2. Supreme Court jurisdiction Original jurisdiction refers to the power of a court to hear a case in the first instance, not on appeal from a lower court. Appellate jurisdiction refers to a court's power to hear a case on appeal from a lower court, from the court in which the case was originally tried. This clause gives the Supreme Court both original and appellate jurisdiction. However, nearly all of the cases the High Court hears are brought to it on appeal from the lower federal courts and the highest State courts.

Clause 3. Jury trial in criminal cases A person accused of a federal crime is guaranteed the right to trial by jury in a federal court in the State where the crime was committed; see the 5th and 6th amendments. The right to trial by jury in serious criminal cases in the State courts is guaranteed by the 6th and 14th amendments.

Section 3. Treason

Clause 1. Definition Treason is the only crime defined in the Constitution. The Framers intended the very specific definition here to prevent the loose use of the charge of treason—for example, against persons who criticize the government. Treason can be committed only in time of war and only by a citizen or a resident alien.

Clause 2. Punishment Congress has provided that the punishment that a federal court may impose on a convicted traitor may range from a minimum of five years in prison and/or a $10,000 fine to a maximum of death; no person convicted of treason has ever been executed by the United States. No legal punishment can be imposed on the family or descendants of a convicted traitor. Congress has also made it a crime for any person (in either peace or wartime) to commit espionage or sabotage, to attempt to overthrow the government by force, or to conspire to do any of these things.

RELATIONS AMONG THE STATES

Section 1. Full Faith and Credit

Each State must recognize the validity of the laws, public records, and court decisions of every other State.

Section 2. Privileges and Immunities of Citizens

Clause 1. Residents of other States In effect, this clause means that no State may discriminate against the residents of other States; that is, a State's laws cannot draw unreasonable distinctions between its own residents and those of any of the other States. See Section 1 of the 14th Amendment.

between Citizens of the same State claiming Lands under Grants of different States, ~~and between a State, or the Citizens thereof, and foreign States, Citizens, or Subjects.~~

2. In all Cases affecting Ambassadors, other public Ministers and Consuls, and those in which a State shall be a Party, the supreme Court shall have original Jurisdiction. In all the other Cases before mentioned, the supreme Court shall have appellate Jurisdiction, both as to Law and Fact, with such Exceptions, and under such Regulations as the Congress shall make.

3. The trial of all Crimes, except in Cases of Impeachment, shall be by Jury; and such Trial shall be held in the State where the said Crimes shall have been committed; but when not committed within any State, the Trial shall be at such Place or Places as the Congress may by Law have directed.

Section 3.

1. Treason against the United States shall consist only in levying War against them, or in adhering to their Enemies, giving them Aid and Comfort. No Person shall be convicted of Treason unless on the Testimony of two Witnesses to the same overt Act, or on Confession in open Court.

2. The Congress shall have Power to declare the Punishment of Treason, but no Attainder of Treason shall work Corruption of Blood, or Forfeiture except during the Life of the Person attainted.

Article IV

Section 1.

Full Faith and Credit shall be given in each State to the public Acts, Records, and judicial Proceedings of every other State. And the Congress may by general Laws prescribe the Manner in which such Acts, Records and Proceedings shall be proved, and the Effect thereof.

Section 2.

1. The Citizens of each State shall be entitled to all Privileges and Immunities of Citizens in the several States.

UNITED STATES CONSTITUTION

2. A Person charged in any State with Treason, Felony, or other Crime, who shall flee from justice, and be found in another State, shall on Demand of the executive Authority of the State from which he fled, be delivered up, to be removed to the State having Jurisdiction of the Crime.

3. No Person held to Service or Labor in one State, under the Laws thereof, escaping into another, shall, in Consequence of any Law or Regulation therein, be discharged from Service or Labor, but shall be delivered up on Claim of the Party to whom such Service or Labor may be due.

Section 3.

1. New States may be admitted by the Congress into this Union; but no new State shall be formed or erected within the Jurisdiction of any other State; nor any State be formed by the Junction of two or more States, or Parts of States, without the Consent of the Legislatures of the States concerned as well as of the Congress.

2. The Congress shall have Power to dispose of and make all needful Rules and Regulations respecting the Territory or other Property belonging to the United States; and nothing in this Constitution shall be so construed as to Prejudice any Claims of the United States, or of any particular State.

Section 4.

The United States shall guarantee to every State in this Union a Republican Form of Government, and shall protect each of them against Invasion; and on Application of the Legislature, or of the Executive (when the Legislature cannot be convened) against domestic Violence.

Article V

The Congress, whenever two thirds of both Houses shall deem it necessary, shall propose Amendments to this Constitution, or, on the Application of the Legislatures of two thirds of the several States, shall call a Convention for proposing Amendments, which, in either Case, shall be valid to all Intents and Purposes, as Part of this Constitution, when ratified by the Legislatures of three fourths of the several States, or by Conventions in three fourths thereof, as the one or the other Mode of Ratification may be proposed by the Congress; Provided

Clause 2. Extradition The process of returning a fugitive to another State is known as "interstate rendition" or, more commonly, "extradition." Usually, that process works routinely; some extradition requests are contested however—especially in cases with racial or political overtones. A governor may refuse to extradite a fugitive; but the federal courts can compel an unwilling governor to obey this constitutional command.

Clause 3. Fugitive slaves This clause was nullified by the 13th Amendment, which abolished slavery in 1865.

Section 3. New States; Territories

Clause 1. New States Only Congress can admit new States to the Union. A new State may not be created by taking territory from an existing State without the consent of that State's legislature. Congress has admitted 37 States since the original 13 formed the Union. Five States—Vermont, Kentucky, Tennessee, Maine, and West Virginia—were created from parts of existing States. Texas was an independent republic before admission. California was admitted after being ceded to the United States by Mexico. Each of the other 30 States entered the Union only after a period of time as an organized territory of the United States.

Clause 2. Territory, property Congress has the power to make laws concerning the territories, other public lands, and all other property of the United States.

Section 4. Protection Afforded to States by the Nation

The Constitution does not define "a republican form of government," but the phrase is generally understood to mean a representative government. The Federal Government must also defend each State against attacks from outside its border and, at the request of a State's legislature or its governor, aid its efforts to put down internal disorders.

PROVISIONS FOR AMENDMENT

This section provides for the methods by which formal changes can be made in the Constitution. An amendment may be proposed in one of two ways: by a two-thirds vote in each house of Congress, or by a national convention called by Congress at the request of two-thirds of the State legislatures. A proposed amendment may be ratified in one of two ways: by three-fourths of the State legislatures, or by three-fourths of the States in conventions called for that purpose. Congress has the power to determine the method by which a proposed amendment may be ratified. The amendment process cannot be used to deny any State its equal representation in the

UNITED STATES CONSTITUTION

United States Constitution 185

United States Senate. To this point, 27 amendments have been adopted. To date, all of the amendments except the 21st Amendment were proposed by Congress and ratified by the State legislatures. Only the 21st Amendment was ratified by the convention method.

NATIONAL DEBTS, SUPREMACY OF NATIONAL LAW, OATH

Section 1. Validity of Debts

Congress had borrowed large sums of money during the Revolution and later during the Critical Period of the 1780s. This provision, a pledge that the new government would honor those debts, did much to create confidence in that government.

Section 2. Supremacy of National Law

This section sets out the Supremacy Clause, a specific declaration of the supremacy of federal law over any and all forms of State law. No State, including its local governments, may make or enforce any law that conflicts with any provision in the Constitution, an act of Congress, a treaty, or an order, rule, or regulation properly issued by the President or his subordinates in the executive branch.

Section 3. Oaths of Office

This provision reinforces the Supremacy Clause; all public officers, at every level in the United States, owe their first allegiance to the Constitution of the United States. No religious qualification can be imposed as a condition for holding any public office.

RATIFICATION OF CONSTITUTION

The proposed Constitution was signed by George Washington and 37 of his fellow Framers on September 17, 1787. (George Read of Delaware signed for himself and also for his absent colleague, John Dickinson.)

---

that no Amendment which may be made prior to the Year One thousand eight hundred and eight shall in any Manner affect the first and fourth Clauses in the Ninth section of the first Article; and that no State, without its Consent, shall be deprived of its equal Suffrage in the Senate.

Article VI

Section 1.

All Debts contracted and Engagements entered into, before the Adoption of this Constitution, shall be as valid against the United States under this Constitution, as under the Confederation.

Section 2.

This Constitution, and the Laws of the United States which shall be made in Pursuance thereof; and all Treaties made, or which shall be made, under the Authority of the United States, shall be the supreme Law of the Land; and the Judges in every State shall be bound thereby, anything in the constitution or Laws of any State to the Contrary notwithstanding.

Section 3.

The Senators and Representatives before mentioned, and the Members of the several State legislatures, and all executive and judicial Officers, both of the United States and of the several States, shall be bound by Oath or Affirmation, to support this Constitution; but no religious Test shall ever be required as a Qualification to any Office or public Trust under the the United States.

Article VII

The ratification of the Conventions of nine States, shall be sufficient for the Establishment of this Constitution between the States so ratifying the same.

Done in Convention by the Unanimous Consent of the States present the Seventeenth Day of September in the Year of our Lord one thousand seven hundred and Eighty-seven and of the Independence of the United States of America the twelfth. In witness whereof We have hereunto subscribed our Names.

Attest: William Jackson,
  SECRETARY
George Washington,
  PRESIDENT AND DEPUTY
  FROM VIRGINIA

NEW HAMPSHIRE
  John Langdon
  Nicholas Gilman
MASSACHUSETTS
  Nathaniel Gorham
  Rufus King
CONNECTICUT
  William Samuel Johnson
  Roger Sherman

NEW YORK
  Alexander Hamilton
NEW JERSEY
  William Livingston
  David Brearley
  William Paterson
  Jonathan Dayton
PENNSYLVANIA
  Benjamin Franklin
  Thomas Mifflin
  Robert Morris
  George Clymer
  Thomas Fitzsimons
  Jared Ingersoll
  James Wilson
  Gouverneur Morris

DELAWARE
  George Read
  Gunning Bedford, Jr.
  John Dickinson
  Richard Bassett
  Jacob Broom
MARYLAND
  James McHenry
  Dan of St. Thomas
    Jennifer
  Daniel Carroll
VIRGINIA
  John Blair
  James Madison, Jr.

NORTH CAROLINA
  William Blount
  Richard Dobbs Spaight
  Hugh Williamson
SOUTH CAROLINA
  John Rutledge
  Charles Cotesworth
    Pinckney
  Charles Pinckney
  Pierce Butler
GEORGIA
  William Few
  Abraham Baldwin

AMENDMENTS

The first 10 amendments, the Bill of Rights, were each proposed by Congress on September 25, 1789, and ratified by the necessary three-fourths of the States on December 15, 1791. These amendments were originally intended to restrict the National Government—not the States. However, the Supreme Court has several times held that most of their provisions also apply to the States, through the 14th Amendment's Due Process Clause.

1st Amendment.

Congress shall make no law respecting an establishment of religion, or prohibiting the free exercise thereof, or abridging the freedom of speech, or of the press; or the right of the people peaceably to assemble, and to petition the Government for a redress of grievances.

1st Amendment. Freedom of Religion, Speech, Press, Assembly, and Petition

The 1st Amendment sets out five basic liberties: The guarantee of freedom of religion is both a protection of religious thought and practice and a command of separation of church and state. The guarantees of freedom of speech and press assure to all persons a right to speak, publish, and otherwise express their views. The guarantees of the rights of assembly and petition protect the right to join with others in public meetings, political parties, interest groups, and other associations to discuss public affairs and influence public policy. None of these rights is guaranteed in absolute terms, however; like all other civil rights guarantees, each of them may be exercised only with regard to the rights of all other persons.

2nd Amendment.

A well-regulated Militia being necessary to the security of a free State, the right of the people to keep and bear Arms, shall not be infringed.

2nd Amendment. Bearing Arms

Each State has the right to maintain a militia, an armed force for its own protection—today, the National Guard. The National Government and the States can and do regulate the private possession and use of firearms.

3rd Amendment.

No Soldier shall, in time of peace be quartered in any house, without the consent of the Owner, nor, in time of war, but in a manner to be prescribed by law.

3rd Amendment. Quartering of Troops

This amendment was intended to prevent what had been common British practice in the colonial period; see the Declaration of Independence. This provision is of virtually no importance today.

4th Amendment.

The right of the people to be secure in their persons, houses, papers, and effects, against unreasonable

4th Amendment. Searches and Seizures

The basic rule laid down by the 4th Amendment is this: Police officers have no general right to search for or seize evidence or seize (arrest) persons. Except in particular circumstances, they

United States Constitution 187

must have a proper warrant (a court order) obtained with probable cause (on reasonable grounds). This guarantee is reinforced by the exclusionary rule, developed by the Supreme Court: Evidence gained as the result of an unlawful search or seizure cannot be used at the court trial of the person from whom it was seized.

5th Amendment. Criminal Proceedings; Due Process; Eminent Domain

A person can be tried for a serious federal crime only if he or she has been indicted (charged, accused of that crime) by a grand jury. No one may be subjected to double jeopardy—that is, tried twice for the same crime. All persons are protected against self-incrimination; no person can be legally compelled to answer any question in any governmental proceeding if that answer could lead to that person's prosecution. The 5th Amendment's Due Process Clause prohibits unfair, arbitrary actions by the Federal Government; a like prohibition is set out against the States in the 14th Amendment. Government may take private property for a legitimate public purpose; but when it exercises that power of eminent domain, it must pay a fair price for the property seized.

6th Amendment. Criminal Proceedings

A person accused of crime has the right to be tried in court without undue delay and by an impartial jury; see Article III, Section 2, Clause 3. The defendant must be informed of the charge upon which he or she is to be tried, has the right to cross-examine hostile witnesses, and has the right to require the testimony of favorable witnesses. The defendant also has the right to be represented by an attorney at every stage in the criminal process.

7th Amendment. Civil Trials

This amendment applies only to civil cases heard in federal courts. A civil case does not involve criminal matters; it is a dispute between private parties or between the government and a private party. The right to trial by jury is guaranteed in any civil case in a federal court if the amount of money involved in that case exceeds $20 (most cases today involve a much larger sum); that right may be waived (relinquished, put aside) if both parties agree to a bench trial (a trial by a judge, without a jury).

8th Amendment. Punishment for Crimes

Bail is the sum of money that a person accused of crime may be required to post (deposit with the court) as a guarantee that he or she will appear in court at the proper time. The amount of bail required and/or a fine imposed as punishment must bear a reasonable relationship to the seriousness of the crime involved in the case. The prohibition of cruel and unusual punishment forbids any punishment judged to be too harsh, too severe for the crime for which it is imposed.

9th Amendment. Unenumerated Rights

The fact that the Constitution sets out many civil rights guarantees, expressly provides for many protections against government, does not mean that there are not other rights also held by the people.

---

searches and seizures, shall not be violated, and no Warrants shall issue, but upon probable cause, supported by Oath or affirmation, and particularly describing the place to be searched, and the persons or things to be seized.

5th Amendment.

No person shall be held to answer for a capital, or otherwise infamous crime, unless on a presentment or indictment of a Grand Jury, except in cases arising in the land or naval forces, or in the Militia, when in actual service in time of War, or public danger; nor shall any person be subject for the same offence to be twice put in jeopardy of life or limb; nor shall be compelled in any criminal case to be a witness against himself, nor be deprived of life, liberty, or property, without due process of law; nor shall private property be taken for public use, without just compensation.

6th Amendment.

In all criminal prosecutions, the accused shall enjoy the right to a speedy and public trial, by an impartial jury of the State and district wherein the crime shall have been committed, which district shall have been previously ascertained by law, and to be informed of the nature and cause of the accusation; to be confronted with the witnesses against him; to have compulsory process for obtaining witnesses in his favor, and to have the Assistance of Counsel for his defence.

7th Amendment.

In Suits at common law, where the value in controversy shall exceed twenty dollars, the right of trial by jury shall be preserved, and no fact tried by a jury, shall be otherwise re-examined in any Court of the United States, than according to the rules of the common law.

8th Amendment.

Excessive bail shall not be required, nor excessive fines imposed, nor cruel and unusual punishment inflicted.

9th Amendment.

The enumeration in the Constitution, of certain rights, shall not be construed to deny or disparage others retained by the people.

10th Amendment.

The powers not delegated to the United States by the Constitution, nor prohibited by it to the States, are reserved to the States respectively, or to the people.

11th Amendment.

The Judicial power of the United States shall not be construed to extend to any suit in law or equity, commenced or prosecuted against one of the United States by Citizens of another State, or by Citizens or Subjects of any Foreign State.

12th Amendment.

The Electors shall meet in their respective States and vote by ballot for President and Vice President, one of whom, at least, shall not be an inhabitant of the same State with themselves; they shall name in their ballots the person voted for as President, and in distinct ballots the person voted for as Vice President, and they shall make distinct lists of all persons voted for as President, and of all persons voted for as Vice President, and of the number of votes for each, which lists they shall sign and certify, and transmit sealed to the seat of the government of the United States, directed to the President of the Senate;— The President of the Senate shall, in the presence of the Senate and the House of Representatives, open all the certificates and the votes shall then be counted;— the person having the greatest Number of votes for President shall be the President, if such number be a majority of the whole number of Electors appointed; and if no person have such a majority, then, from the persons having the highest numbers not exceeding three on the list of those voted for as President, the House of Representatives shall choose immediately, by ballot, the President. But in choosing the President, the votes shall be taken by States, the representation from each State having one vote; a quorum for this purpose shall consist of a member or members from two thirds of the States, and a majority of all the States shall be necessary to a choice. And if the House of Representatives shall not choose a President whenever the right of choice shall devolve upon them, before the fourth day of March next following, then the Vice President shall act as President, as in case of death or other constitutional disability of the President. The person having the greatest number of votes as Vice President, shall be the Vice President, if such number be a majority of the whole number of Electors appointed, and if no person have a majority, then from the two highest numbers on the list, the Senate shall choose the Vice President; a quorum for

10th Amendment. Powers Reserved to the States

This amendment identifies the area of power that may be exercised by the States. All of those powers the Constitution does not grant to the National Government, and at the same time does not forbid to the States, belong to each of the States, or to the people of each State.

11th Amendment. Suits Against States

Proposed by Congress March 4, 1794; ratified February 7, 1795, but official announcement of the ratification was delayed until January 8, 1798. This amendment repealed part of Article III, Section 2, Clause 1. No State may be sued in a federal court by a resident of another State or of a foreign country; the Supreme Court has long held that this provision also means that a State cannot be sued in a federal court by a foreign country or, more importantly, even by one of its own residents.

12th Amendment. Election of President and Vice President

Proposed by Congress December 9, 1803; ratified June 15, 1804. This amendment replaced Article II, Section 1, Clause 3. Originally, each elector cast two ballots, each for a different person for President. The person with the largest number of electoral votes, provided that number was a majority of the electors, was to become President; the person with the second highest number was to become Vice President. This arrangement produced an electoral vote tie between Thomas Jefferson and Aaron Burr in 1800; the House finally chose Jefferson as President in 1801. The 12th Amendment separated the balloting for President and Vice President; each elector now casts one ballot for someone as President and a second ballot for another person as Vice President. Note that the 20th Amendment changed the date set here (March 4) to January 20, and that the 23rd Amendment (1961) provides for electors from the District of Columbia. This amendment also provides that the Vice President must meet the same qualifications as those set out for the President in Article II, Section 1, Clause 5.

13th Amendment. Slavery and Involuntary Servitude

Proposed by Congress January 31, 1865; ratified December 6, 1865. This amendment forbids slavery in the United States and in any area under its control. It also forbids other forms of forced labor, except punishments for crime; but some forms of compulsory service are not prohibited—for example, service on juries or in the armed forces. Section 2 gives to Congress the power to carry out the provisions of Section 1 of this amendment.

14th Amendment. Rights of Citizens

Proposed by Congress June 13, 1866; ratified July 9, 1868. Section 1 defines citizenship. It provides for the acquisition of United States citizenship by birth or by naturalization. Citizenship at birth is determined according to the principle of *jus soli*—"the law of the soil," where born; naturalization is the legal process by which one acquires a new citizenship at some time after birth. Under certain circumstances, citizenship can also be gained at birth abroad, according to the principle of *jus sanguinis*—"the law of the blood," to whom born. This section also contains two major civil rights provisions: the Due Process Clause forbids a State (and its local governments) to act in any unfair or arbitrary way; the Equal Protection Clause forbids a State (and its local governments) to discriminate against, draw unreasonable distinctions between, persons.

Most of the rights set out against the National Government in the first eight amendments have been extended against the States (and their local governments) through Supreme Court decisions involving the 14th Amendment's Due Process Clause.

The first sentence here replaced Article I, Section 2, Clause 3, the Three-Fifths Compromise provision. Essentially, all persons in the United States are counted in each decennial census, the basis for the distribution of House seats. The balance of this section has never been enforced and is generally thought to be obsolete.

This section limited the President's power to pardon those persons who had led the Confederacy during the Civil War. Congress finally removed this disability in 1898.

---

the purpose shall consist of two thirds of the whole number of Senators, a majority of the whole number shall be necessary to a choice. But no person constitutionally ineligible to the office of President shall be eligible to that of Vice-President of the United States.

13th Amendment.

Section 1. Neither slavery nor involuntary servitude, except as a punishment for crime whereof the party shall have been duly convicted, shall exist within the United States, or any place subject to their jurisdiction.

Section 2. Congress shall have power to enforce this article by appropriate legislation.

14th Amendment.

Section 1. All persons born or naturalized in the United States and subject to the jurisdiction thereof, are citizens of the United States and of the State wherein they reside. No State shall make or enforce any law which shall abridge the privileges or immunities of citizens of the United States; nor shall any State deprive any person of life, liberty, or property, without due process of law; nor deny to any person within its jurisdiction the equal protection of the laws.

Section 2. Representatives shall be apportioned among the several States according to their respective numbers, counting the whole number of persons in each State, excluding Indians not taxed. But when the right to vote at any election for the choice of electors for President and Vice President of the United States, Representatives in Congress, the Executive and Judicial officers of a State, or the members of the Legislature thereof, is denied to any of the male inhabitants of such State, being twenty-one years of age and citizens of the United States, or in any way abridged, except for participation in rebellion, or other crime, the basis of representation therein shall be reduced in the proportion which the number of such male citizens shall bear to the whole number of male citizens twenty-one years of age in such State.

Section 3. No person shall be a Senator or Representative in Congress, or elector of President and

Vice President, or hold any office, civil or military, under the United States, or under any State, who, having previously taken an oath, as a member of Congress, or as an officer of the United States, or as a member of any State legislature, or as an executive or judicial officer of any State, to support the Constitution of the United States, shall have engaged in insurrection or rebellion against the same, or given aid or comfort to the enemies thereof. But Congress may, by a vote of two thirds of each House, remove such disability.

Section 4. The validity of the public debt of the United States, authorized by law, including debts incurred for payment of pensions and bounties for services in suppressing insurrection or rebellion, shall not be questioned. But neither the United States nor any State shall assume or pay any debt or obligation incurred in aid of insurrection or rebellion against the United States, or any claim for the loss or emancipation of any slave; but all such debts, obligations and claims shall be held illegal and void.

Section 5. The Congress shall have power to enforce, by appropriate legislation, the provisions of this article.

15th Amendment.

Section 1. The right of citizens of the United States to vote shall not be denied or abridged by the United States or by any State on account of race, color, or previous condition of servitude.

Section 2. The Congress shall have power to enforce this article by appropriate legislation.

16th Amendment.

The Congress shall have power to lay and collect taxes on incomes, from whatever source derived, without apportionment among the several States, and without regard to any census or enumeration.

17th Amendment.

The Senate of the United States shall be composed of two Senators from each State, elected by the people thereof, for six years; and each Senator shall have one vote. The electors in each State shall have the qualifications requisite for electors of the most numerous branch of the State legislatures.

When vacancies happen in the representation of any State in the Senate, the executive authority of such State shall issue writs of election to fill such vacancies: *Provided,* That the legislature of any State may empower the executive thereof to make temporary appointments until the people fill the vacancies by election as the legislature may direct.

This amendment shall not be so construed as to

Section 4 also dealt with matters directly related to the Civil War. It reaffirmed the public debt of the United States; but it invalidated, prohibited payment of, any debt contracted by the Confederate States and also prohibited any compensation of former slave owners.

15th Amendment. Right to Vote— Race, Color, Servitude

Proposed by Congress February 26, 1869; ratified February 3, 1870. The phrase "previous condition of servitude" refers to slavery. Note that this amendment does not guarantee the right to vote to African Americans, or to anyone else. Instead, it forbids the States from discriminating against any person on the grounds of his "race, color, or previous condition of servitude" in the setting of suffrage qualifications.

16th Amendment. Income Tax

Proposed by Congress July 12, 1909; ratified February 3, 1913. This amendment modified two provisions in Article I, Section 2, Clause 3, and Section 9, Clause 4. It gives to Congress the power to levy an income tax, a direct tax, without regard to the populations of any of the States.

17th Amendment. Popular Election of Senators

Proposed by Congress May 13, 1912; ratified April 8, 1913. This amendment repealed those portions of Article I, Section 3, Clauses 1 and 2 relating to the election of senators. Senators are now elected by the voters in each State. If a vacancy occurs, the governor of the State involved must call an election to fill the seat; the governor may appoint a senator to serve until the next election, if the State's legislature has authorized that step.

UNITED STATES CONSTITUTION

18th Amendment. Prohibition of Intoxicating Liquors

Proposed by Congress December 18, 1917; ratified January 16, 1919. This amendment outlawed the making, selling, transporting, importing, or exporting of alcoholic beverages in the United States. It was repealed in its entirety by the 21st Amendment in 1933.

19th Amendment. Equal Suffrage—Sex

Proposed by Congress June 4, 1919; ratified August 18, 1920. No person can be denied the right to vote in any election in the United States on account of his or her sex.

20th Amendment. Commencement of Terms; Sessions of Congress; Death or Disqualification of President-Elect

Proposed by Congress March 2, 1932; ratified January 23, 1933. The provisions of Sections 1 and 2 relating to Congress modified Article I, Section 4, Clause 2, and those provisions relating to the President, the 12th Amendment. The date on which the President and Vice President now take office was moved from March 4 to January 20. Similarly, the members of Congress now begin their terms on January 3. The 20th Amendment is sometimes called the "Lame Duck Amendment" because it shortened the period of time a member of Congress who was defeated for reelection (a "lame duck") remains in office.

This section deals with certain possibilities that were not covered by the presidential selection provisions of either Article II or the 12th Amendment. To this point, none of these situations has occurred. Note that there is neither a President-elect nor a Vice President-elect until the electoral votes have been counted by Congress, or, if the electoral college cannot decide the matter, the House has chosen a President or the Senate has chosen a Vice President.

---

affect the election or term of any Senator chosen before it becomes valid as part of the Constitution.

18th Amendment.

Section 1. After one year from the ratification of this article the manufacture, sale, or transportation of intoxicating liquors within, the importation thereof into, or the exportation thereof from the United States and all territory subject to the jurisdiction thereof for beverage purposes is hereby prohibited.

Section 2. The Congress and the several States shall have concurrent power to enforce this article by appropriate legislation.

Section 3. This article shall be inoperative unless it shall have been ratified as an amendment to the Constitution by the legislatures of the several States, as provided in the Constitution, within seven years of the date of the submission hereof to the States by Congress.

19th Amendment.

The right of citizens of the United States to vote shall not be denied or abridged by the United States or by any State on account of sex.

Congress shall have power to enforce this article by appropriate legislation.

20th Amendment.

Section 1. The terms of the President and Vice President shall end at noon on the 20th day of January, and the terms of Senators and Representatives at noon on the 3d day of January, of the years in which such terms would have ended if this article had not been ratified; and the terms of their successors shall then begin.

Section 2. The Congress shall assemble at least once in every year, and such meeting shall begin at noon on the 3d day of January, unless they shall by law appoint a different day.

Section 3. If, at the time fixed for the beginning of the term of the President, the President elect shall have died, the Vice President elect shall become President. If a President shall not have been chosen before the time fixed for the beginning of his term, or if the President-elect shall have failed to qualify, then the Vice President elect shall act as President until a President shall have qualified; and the Congress may by law provide for the case wherein neither a President elect nor a Vice President elect shall have qualified, declaring who shall then act as President, or the manner in which one who is to act shall be selected, and such person shall act accordingly until a President or Vice President shall have qualified.

Section 4. The Congress may by law provide for the case of the death of any of the persons from whom the House of Representatives may choose a President whenever the right of choice shall have devolved upon them, and for the case of the death of any of the persons from whom the Senate may choose a Vice President whenever the right of choice shall have devolved upon them.

Congress has not in fact ever passed such a law. See Section 2 of the 25th Amendment, regarding a vacancy in the vice presidency; that provision could some day have an impact here.

Section 5. Sections 1 and 2 shall take effect on the 15th day of October following the ratification of this article.

Section 5 set the date on which this amendment came into force.

Section 6. This article shall be inoperative unless it shall have been ratified as an amendment to the Constitution by the legislatures of three fourths of the several States within seven years from the date of its submission.

Section 6 placed a time limit on the ratification process; note that a similar provision was written into the 18th, 21st, and 22nd amendments.

21st Amendment.

Section 1. The eighteenth article of amendment to the Constitution of the United States is hereby repealed.

21st Amendment. Repeal of 18th Amendment

Proposed by Congress February 20, 1933; ratified December 5, 1933. This amendment repealed all of the 18th Amendment. Section 2 modifies the scope of the Federal Government's commerce power set out in Article I, Section 8, Clause 3; it gives to each State the power to regulate the transportation or importation and the distribution or use of intoxicating liquors in ways that would be unconstitutional in the case of any other commodity. The 21st Amendment is the only amendment Congress has thus far submitted to the States for ratification by conventions.

Section 2. The transportation or importation into any State, Territory, or possession of the United States for delivery or use therein of intoxicating liquors, in violation of the laws thereof, is hereby prohibited.

Section 3. This article shall be inoperative unless it shall have been ratified as an amendment to the Constitution by conventions in the several States, as provided in the Constitution, within seven years from the date of the submission hereof to the States by the Congress.

22nd Amendment.

Section 1. No person shall be elected to the office of the President more than twice, and no person who has held the office of President, or acted as President, for more than two years of a term to which some other person was elected President shall be elected to the office of the President more than once. But this Article shall not apply to any person holding the office of President, when this Article was proposed by the Congress, and shall not prevent any person who may be holding the office of President, or acting as President, during the term within which this Article becomes operative from holding the office of President or acting as President during the remainder of such term.

22nd Amendment. Presidential Tenure

Proposed by Congress March 24, 1947; ratified February 27, 1951. This amendment modified Article II, Section I, Clause 1. It stipulates that no President may serve more than two elected terms. But a President who has succeeded to the office beyond the midpoint in a term to which another President was originally elected may serve for more than eight years. In any case, however, a President may not serve more than 10 years. Prior to Franklin Roosevelt, who was elected to four terms, no President had served more than two full terms in office.

Section 2. This article shall be inoperative unless it shall have been ratified as an amendment to the Constitution by the legislatures of three fourths of the

UNITED STATES CONSTITUTION

23rd Amendment. Presidential Electors for the District of Columbia

Proposed by Congress June 16, 1960; ratified March 29, 1961. This amendment modified Article II, Section I, Clause 2 and the 12th Amendment. It included the voters of the District of Columbia in the presidential electorate; and provides that the District is to have the same number of electors as the least populous State—three electors—but no more than that number.

24th Amendment. Right to Vote in Federal Elections—Tax Payment

Proposed by Congress September 14, 1962; ratified January 23, 1964. This amendment outlawed the payment of any tax as a condition for taking part in the nomination or election of any federal officeholder.

25th Amendment. Presidential Succession, Vice Presidential Vacancy, Presidential Inability

Proposed by Congress July 6, 1965; ratified February 10, 1967. Section 1 revised the imprecise provision on presidential succession in Article II, Section 1, Clause 6. It wrote into the Constitution the precedent set by Vice President John Tyler, who became President on the death of William Henry Harrison in 1841.

Section 2 provides for the filling of a vacancy in the office of Vice President. Prior to its adoption, the office had been vacant on 16 occasions and had remained unfilled for the remainder of each term involved. When Spiro Agnew resigned the office in 1973, President Nixon selected Gerald Ford in accord with this provision; and, when President Nixon resigned in 1974, Gerald Ford became President and then chose Nelson Rockefeller as Vice President.

This section created a procedure for determining if a President is so incapacitated that he cannot perform the powers and duties of his office.

several states within seven years from the date of its submission to the States by the Congress.

23rd Amendment.

Section 1. The District constituting the seat of Government of the United States shall appoint in such manner as the Congress may direct:

A number of electors of President and Vice President equal to the whole number of Senators and Representatives in Congress to which the District would be entitled if it were a State, but in no event more than the least populous State; they shall be in addition to those appointed by the States, they shall be considered, for the purposes of the election of President and Vice President, to be electors appointed by a State; and they shall meet in the District and perform such duties as provided by the twelfth article of amendment.

Section 2. The Congress shall have power to enforce this article by appropriate legislation.

24th Amendment.

Section 1. The right of citizens of the United States to vote in any primary or other election for President or Vice President, for electors for President or Vice President, or for Senator or Representative in Congress, shall not be denied or abridged by the United States or any State by reason of failure to pay any poll tax or other tax.

Section 2. The Congress shall have power to enforce this article by appropriate legislation.

25th Amendment.

Section 1. In case of the removal of the President from office or of his death or resignation, the Vice President shall become President.

Section 2. Whenever there is a vacancy in the office of the Vice President, the President shall nominate a Vice President who shall take office upon confirmation by a majority vote of both Houses of Congress.

Section 3. Whenever the President transmits to the President *pro tempore* of the Senate and the Speaker of the House of Representatives his written declaration that he is unable to discharge the powers and duties of his office, and until he transmits to them a written declaration to the contrary, such powers and duties shall be discharged by the Vice President as Acting President.

Section 4. Whenever the Vice President and a majority of either the principal officers of the executive departments or of such other body as Congress may by law provide, transmit to the President *pro tempore* of the Senate and the Speaker of the House of Representatives their written declaration that the President is unable to discharge the powers and duties of his office, the Vice President shall immediately assume the powers and duties of the office as Acting President.

 Thereafter, when the President transmits to the President *pro tempore* of the Senate and the Speaker of the House of Representatives his written declaration that no inability exists, he shall resume the powers and duties of his office unless the Vice President and a majority of either the principal officers of the executive department or of such other body as Congress may by law provide, transmit within four days to the President *pro tempore* of the Senate and the Speaker of the House of Representatives their written declaration that the President is unable to discharge the powers and duties of his office. Thereupon Congress shall decide the issue, assembling within forty-eight hours for that purpose if not in session. If the Congress, within twenty-one days after receipt of the latter written declaration, or, if Congress is not in session, within twenty-one days after Congress is required to assemble, determines by two-thirds vote of both Houses that the President is unable to discharge the powers and duties of his office, the Vice President shall continue to discharge the same as Acting President; otherwise, the President shall resume the powers and duties of his office.

26th Amendment.

Section 1. The right of citizens of the United States, who are eighteen years of age or older, to vote shall not be denied or abridged by the United States or by any State on account of age.

Section 2. The Congress shall have the power to enforce this article by appropriate legislation.

27th Amendment.

No law varying the compensation for the services of the Senators and Representatives, shall take effect, until an election of Representatives shall have intervened.

Section 4 deals with the circumstance in which a President will not be able to determine the fact of incapacity. To this point, Congress has not established the "such other body" referred to here. This section contains the only typographical error in the Constitution; in its second paragraph, the word "department" should in fact read "departments."

26th Amendment. Right to Vote—Age

Proposed by Congress March 23, 1971; ratified July 1, 1971. This amendment provides that the minimum age for voting in any election in the United States cannot be more than 18 years. (A State may set a minimum voting age of less than 18, however.)

27th Amendment. Congressional Pay

Proposed by Congress September 25, 1789; ratified May 7, 1992. This amendment modified Article I, Section 6, Clause 1. It limits Congress's power to fix the salaries of its members—by delaying the effectiveness of any increase in that pay until after the next regular congressional election.

UNITED STATES CONSTITUTION

United States Constitution 195

SETTLING THE NORTHWEST TERRITORY

Focus Point out that the ordinance system established the process of determining township borders in the Northwest Territory by using an orderly grid system. Aspects of this system can still be seen in towns and cities of the Midwest. Have students use a United States atlas to compare a map of downtown Boston, which has short, curving streets, with a map of a midwestern city, such as Chicago, that follows a straight-line grid.

Instruct Ask students if any of them have lived in another part of the country. Discuss the differences between their former and present communities. What might account for such differences? What differences exist today between New England and the Midwest?

Ask students to find place names in Ohio that seem to be based on place names in New England. What places in their own region might have been named by immigrants or by people migrating from other parts of the country?

Extend Explain that new settlers formed covenants that resembled those made by their ancestors upon first reaching Massachusetts. The New England settlers of Oberlin, Ohio, for example, pledged themselves to "a life of simplicity, to special devotion to church and school, and to earnest labor in the missionary cause."

Ask students to suppose that a small group of settlers from their community is emigrating to an undeveloped, isolated section of Alaska. Ask each student to list at least five institutions that they would expect to see in the new settlement. On what principles would they hope to see the community based?

Settling the Northwest Territory

By the end of the Revolutionary War, the United States had acquired a vast territory west of the Appalachians that had few white settlers. A series of laws known as the Northwest Ordinances soon cleared the way for white settlement and statehood in the Northwest Territory. The territory later formed the Midwestern states of Ohio, Indiana, Illinois, Michigan, Wisconsin, and part of Minnesota.

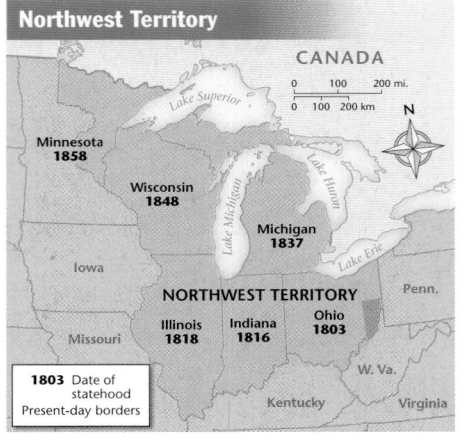

Northwest Territory

CANADA

Minnesota 1858

Wisconsin 1848

Michigan 1837

Iowa

NORTHWEST TERRITORY

Penn.

Illinois 1818　Indiana 1816　Ohio 1803

Missouri

W. Va.

Kentucky　Virginia

1803 Date of statehood
Present-day borders

The Land Ordinance System

The Land Ordinance of 1785 established a system for dividing the land into areas of uniform size that could be sold at standardized prices. This system replaced older surveying methods, which used natural features to mark off parcels of varying shapes and sizes. The new system was so successful that it was later extended across the central and western United States.

Carving Up the Land

Surveyors laid out a grid of lines spaced six miles apart. These lines marked off areas known as townships, which would form a basis for local government. Each township was divided into 36 equal sections, and sections could be subdivided for sale into smaller units. At the center of every township was Section 16, which the ordinance reserved for public education. Lands were reserved for school buildings like the one-room schoolhouse shown here, and the rest of the section was sold off to provide funding for the school.

Township and Range Lines

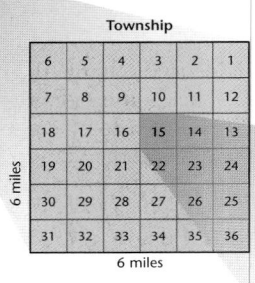

Township

6	5	4	3	2	1
7	8	9	10	11	12
18	17	16	15	14	13
19	20	21	22	23	24
30	29	28	27	26	25
31	32	33	34	35	36

6 miles

6 miles

Section

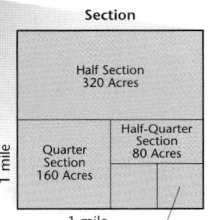

Half Section 320 Acres

Quarter Section 160 Acres

Half-Quarter Section 80 Acres

1 mile

1 mile

Quarter-Quarter Section 40 Acres

Surveyors at Work

Nineteenth-century surveyors used instruments such as this level and transit to draw survey lines in the Northwest Territory.

196

RESOURCE DIRECTORY

Teaching Resources
Geography and History booklet, pp. 4–5

Other Print Resources
Nystrom *Atlas of Our Country* *Early Expansion of the United States,* pp. 20–21

Technology
Prentice Hall United States History Video Collection™ Volume 5, *A New Nation*

Migrants Stream In

Many settlers from the East piled their belongings into covered wagons for the long journey to the Northwest Territory. Others traveled by ship to Great Lakes ports or by riverboat along the Ohio River or the Mississippi River.

Migration Patterns

This map shows the routes that many settlers followed into the territories and states formed from the Northwest Territory in the early 1800s.

Geographic Connection

What parts of the Northwest Territory attracted settlers from New England or New York? Where did most Virginians settle?

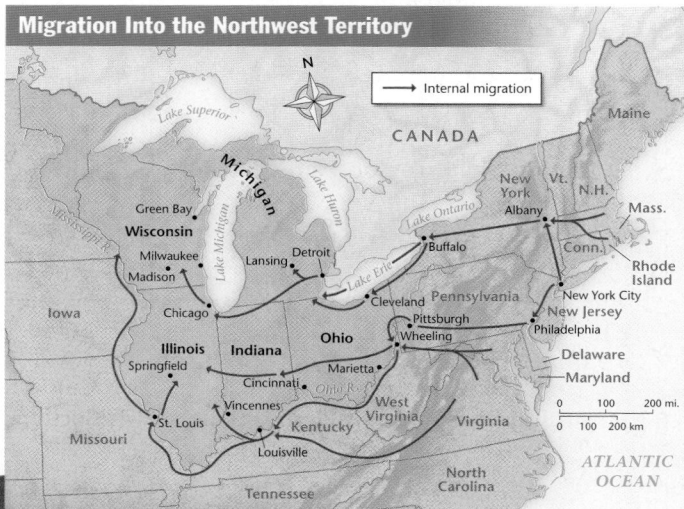

Migration Into the Northwest Territory

→ Internal migration

N

CANADA

Lake Superior

Maine

Michigan

Lake Huron

Green Bay

Wisconsin

Milwaukee
Lansing • Detroit
Madison

Lake Michigan

Lake Ontario

New York
Albany

Vt.
N.H.

Mass.

Buffalo

Conn.

Rhode Island

Iowa

Chicago

Lake Erie

Cleveland

Pennsylvania

Pittsburgh

New York City
New Jersey
Philadelphia

Illinois
Springfield

Indiana

Ohio

Wheeling

Delaware

Cincinnati

Marietta •

Maryland

Vincennes

Ohio R.

West Virginia

Virginia

0   100   200 mi.
0 100 200 km

Missouri

St. Louis

Kentucky

Louisville

ATLANTIC OCEAN

Tennessee

North Carolina

An Enduring Landscape

The grid established more than 200 years ago remains the basis for land division across the Midwest. Many roads and property lines still follow the straight lines and right angles the original surveyors laid out.

Geographic Connection

How does the modern landscape of the Midwest reflect the pattern set by the Land Ordinance of 1785?

197

Chapter 6 Planning Guide
Resource Manager

	CORE INSTRUCTION	READING/SKILLS
Chapter-Level Resources	**Teaching Resources** • Pacing Charts booklet • Block Scheduling booklet **Resource Pro® CD-ROM,** Ch. 6 **Prentice Hall Presentation Pro CD-ROM,** Ch. 6 **www.phschool.com** • eTeach	**Guided Reading Audiotapes (English/Spanish)** **Student Edition on Audio CD,** Ch. 6 **Social Studies Skills Tutor CD-ROM** **Color Transparencies,** A9, A11, A12, A60
1 Liberty Versus Order in the 1790s 1. Learn about Alexander Hamilton's program for dealing with national and state debt. 2. Find out how foreign policy issues divided Americans. 3. See what issues led to the emergence of political parties.	**Teaching Resources** **Units 1/2 booklet** • Section 1 Quiz, p. 64 **Learning Styles Lesson Plans booklet,** p. 14	**Guided Reading and Review booklet,** p. 24 **Guide to the Essentials,** p. 31 **Section Reading Support Transparencies**
2 The Election of 1800 1. Find out what actions John Adams took as President. 2. See why the election of 1800 was a turning point. 3. Discover what was significant about the transfer of power between parties in 1801.	**Teaching Resources** **Units 1/2 booklet** • Section 2 Quiz, p. 65 **Learning Styles Lesson Plans booklet,** p. 15	**Guided Reading and Review booklet,** p. 25 **Guide to the Essentials,** p. 32 **Section Reading Support Transparencies**
3 The Jefferson Administration 1. Discover how Jefferson reduced the power of the national government. 2. See what problem Jefferson had with the federal courts. 3. Find out how Jefferson achieved his program in the West. 4. Learn why Jefferson easily won reelection in 1804. 5. Understand how Jefferson responded to increasing tensions with Europe.	**Teaching Resources** **Units 1/2 booklet** • Section 3 Quiz, p. 66	**Guided Reading and Review booklet,** p. 26 **Guide to the Essentials,** p. 33 **Skills for Life,** p. 8 **Section Reading Support Transparencies**
4 Native American Resistance 1. Find out what led to war between the United States and Native Americans in the Old Northwest. 2. See the different ways in which Native American leaders reacted to United States expansion.	**Teaching Resources** **Units 1/2 booklet** • Section 4 Quiz, p. 67	**Guided Reading and Review booklet,** p. 27 **Guide to the Essentials,** p. 34 **Learning with Documents booklet,** p. 11 **Section Reading Support Transparencies**
5 The War of 1812 1. Find out why war broke out with Britain in 1812. 2. See how the war's end affected the United States. 3. Understand events that led to the economic panic of 1819. 4. Learn about issues that led to the Missouri Compromise.	**Teaching Resources** **Units 1/2 booklet** • Section 5 Quiz, p. 68	**Guided Reading and Review booklet,** p. 28 **Guide to the Essentials,** p. 35 **Learning with Documents booklet,** pp. 45, 78 **Section Reading Support Transparencies**

ENRICHMENT/PRE-AP

Prentice Hall United States History Video Collection™
www.phschool.com
- Section Activities, Virtual Field Trip, Chapter Activities, Current Events Online

Sounds of an Era Audio CD
Exploring Primary Sources in U.S. History CD-ROM

American History Block Scheduling Support

American History Block Scheduling Support
Nystrom *Atlas of Our Country,* pp. 20–21
Historical Map Outline Book, pp. 30, 82

Biography, Literature, and Comparing Primary Sources booklet, p. 11
American Pathways Thematic Posters

Biography, Literature, and Comparing Primary Sources booklet, pp. 45–46, 107–108
American History Block Scheduling Support
Historical Map Outline Book, pp. 32, 45
Sounds of an Era Audio CD
Exploring Primary Sources in U.S. History CD-ROM
American Pathways Thematic Posters

ASSESSMENT

Core Assessment
ExamView® Test Bank, Ch. 6
ExamView® Test Bank CD-ROM, Ch. 6

Standardized Test Preparation
Diagnose and Prescribe
Diagnostic Tests for High School Social Studies Skills

Review and Reteach
Review Book for U.S. History

Practice and Assess
Test-taking Strategies With Transparencies
Test-taking Strategies Posters
Test Prep Book for U.S. History
Alternative Assessment Handbook
Document-Based Assessment

Teaching Resources
Units 1/2 booklet
- Section Quizzes, pp. 64–68
- Chapter Tests, pp. 69, 72
www.phschool.com Ch. 6 Self-Test

AmericanHeritage RESOURCES

From the Archives of American Heritage®, pp. 205, 209, 215, 227, and 228
AmericanHeritage® My Brush with History™ Videotapes
www.americanheritage.com

Don't miss the exclusive interactive version of this textbook on the Web and on CD-ROM.

Chapter 6 Planning Guide
In Your Classroom

Gifted and Talented

Teacher's Edition
- Customize for Gifted and Talented, p. 203

Teaching Resources
- Biography, Literature, and Comparing Primary Sources booklet, pp. 11, 45–46, 107–108

Technology
- Exploring Primary Sources in U.S. History CD-ROM *Farewell Address, George Washington; The Journals of Lewis and Clark; Sell a Country? Why Not Sell the Air? Tecumseh; On the Burning of Washington, D.C., Dolley Madison; The Star-Spangled Banner, Francis Scott Key*

ESL

Teacher's Edition
- Customize for ESL, p. 211

Teaching Resources
- Guided Reading and Review booklet, pp. 24–28
- Guide to the Essentials (English/Spanish), Chapter 6

Technology
- Student Edition on Audio CD, Chapter 6
- Guided Reading Audiotapes (English/Spanish), Chapter 6
- Section Reading Support Transparencies

Less Proficient Readers

Teacher's Edition
- Customize for Less Proficient Readers, pp. 201, 215, 225

Teaching Resources
- Guided Reading and Review booklet, pp. 24–28
- Guide to the Essentials (English/Spanish), Chapter 6

Technology
- Student Edition on Audio CD, Chapter 6
- Guided Reading Audiotapes (English/Spanish), Chapter 6
- Section Reading Support Transparencies

Less Proficient Writers

Teacher's Edition
- Customize for Less Proficient Writers, pp. 217, 223

Teaching Resources
- Guided Reading and Review booklet, pp. 24–28
- Guide to the Essentials (English/Spanish), Chapter 6

Technology
- Student Edition on Audio CD, Chapter 6
- Guided Reading Audiotapes (English/Spanish), Chapter 6
- Section Reading Support Transparencies

CHAPTER 6 – PACING SUGGESTIONS

For 90-minute Blocks

- Teach sections 3 and 5 using Transparencies A9, A11, A12, and A60, and the Recent Scholarship notes on pages 205, 210, and 216 for class discussions.

Running Out of Time?

If you are running short on time to cover this chapter, consider the following options:

- Use the Prentice Hall Presentation Pro CD-ROM to create an outline for this chapter.

- Use the Section Summaries for Chapter 6, from **Guide to the Essentials (English/Spanish)**.

1	**Liberty Versus Order in the 1790s**	**Connecting with History and Conflict** Have students construct Venn diagrams that elaborate on the section title "Liberty Versus Order in the 1790s." Students should label one circle of their diagrams "Liberty" and the other "Order." In each circle, students should record appropriate examples that they gather from their reading of the section. Make sure students fill in the overlapping area with events or conditions of the time that were common to both. **(Visual/Spatial)**
2	**The Election of 1800**	**Connecting with Citizenship** Have students write summaries of the section using the major headings in their textbooks as the basis for paragraph topic sentences. **(Verbal/Linguistic)**
3	**The Jefferson Administration**	**Connecting with History and Conflict** Work with the class to construct a two-column table on the board. Title the left-hand column "President Jefferson's Beliefs" and the right-hand column "President Jefferson's Actions." Elicit from students appropriate entries for each column, and record them. Then challenge the class to link each belief with one or more actions, and each action with one or more beliefs. Indicate the connections with lines and arrows. **(Logical/Mathematical)**
4	**Native American Resistance**	**Connecting with Culture** Invite selected students to compose poems or lyrics about Native American resistance during the early years of the United States, expressed from a Native American point of view. **(Rhythmic/Musical; Verbal/Linguistic)**
5	**The War of 1812**	**Connecting with Science and Technology** The War of 1812 took place largely at sea. Have students make drawings or models typical of specific British or American warships of the period, and share them with the class. **(Visual/Spatial)**

Chapter 6
The Origins of American Politics
(1789–1820)

INTRODUCING THE CHAPTER

In the years following the ratification of the Constitution, American leaders fought passionately over the formation of the new government. Some groups that were not represented in the legislatures, including Native Americans and African Americans, tried to acquire or maintain liberty by other means. The new nation enjoyed prosperity and political harmony for only a brief period following the War of 1812.

TIME LINE ACTIVITY

To provide students with practice in using the time line, ask questions such as these.

1. What was of most symbolic importance in the inauguration of Thomas Jefferson in 1801? *(His inauguration represented a peaceful transition of power.)*

2. What was the impact of the Embargo Act? *(It outlawed most foreign trade and angered New England merchants.)*

3. In what year was the French leader Napoleon finally defeated, and where did this defeat take place? *(in 1815, at Waterloo)*

Chapter 6

The Origins of American Politics

(1789–1820)

SECTION 1   Liberty Versus Order in the 1790s
SECTION 2   The Election of 1800
SECTION 3   The Jefferson Administration
SECTION 4   Native American Resistance
SECTION 5   The War of 1812

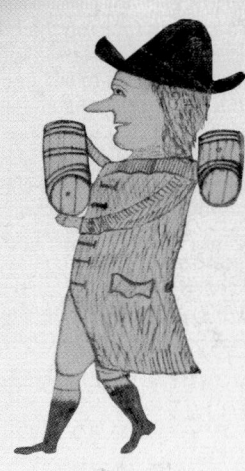

Lewis and Clark explore the West.

American Events

1794
The federal government uses the threat of military force to end the Whiskey Rebellion.

1795
The Treaty of Greenville forces Native Americans to give up land in the Old Northwest.

1801
The inauguration of Thomas Jefferson represents a peaceful transfer of power between parties.

Presidential Terms: George Washington 1789–1797   J. Adams 1797–1801   Thomas Jefferson 1801–1809

1790   •   • **1795**   **1800** •   • **1805**

World Events

The Reign of Terror begins in France.
1793

The United Kingdom of Great Britain and Ireland is established.
1801

Haiti declares independence from France.
1804

198   Chapter 6 • *The Origins of American Politics*

eTeach

Be sure to check out this month's online discussion with a Master Teacher. Go to **www.phschool.com**.

RESOURCE DIRECTORY

Teaching Resources
Pacing Charts booklet
Block Scheduling booklet, p. 16
Units 1/2 booklet
• Chapter Summary, p. 63

Technology
Guided Reading Audiotapes (English/Spanish), Ch. 6
Student Edition on Audio CD, Ch. 6
Prentice Hall United States History Video Collection™ Volume 5, *A New Nation (1776–1815)*
Prentice Hall Presentation Pro CD-ROM, Ch. 6
Resource Pro® CD-ROM
Social Studies Skills Tutor CD-ROM
Companion Web site, www.phschool.com

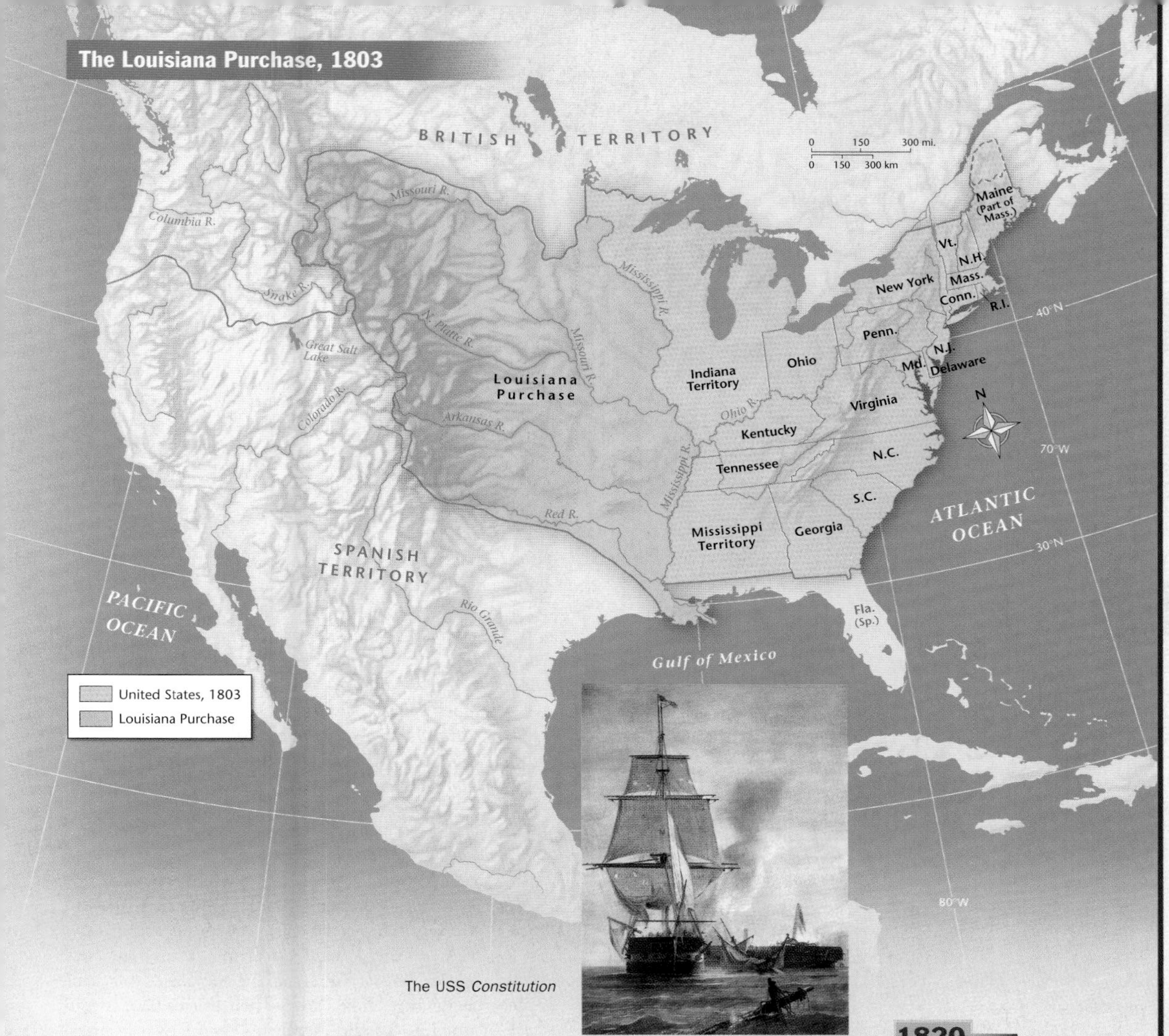

The Louisiana Purchase, 1803

BRITISH TERRITORY

0   150   300 mi.
0   150   300 km

Columbia R.

Snake R.

Missouri R.

Great Salt Lake

N. Platte R.

Colorado R.

Arkansas R.

Red R.

Rio Grande

PACIFIC OCEAN

SPANISH TERRITORY

Louisiana Purchase

Mississippi R.

Ohio R.

Indiana Territory

Ohio

Kentucky

Tennessee

Mississippi Territory

Georgia

ATLANTIC OCEAN

Maine (Part of Mass.)

Vt.

N.H.

New York

Mass.

Conn.

R.I.

Penn.

N.J.

Md.

Delaware

Virginia

N.C.

S.C.

Fla. (Sp.)

40° N

70° W

30° N

80° W

N

Gulf of Mexico

- United States, 1803
- Louisiana Purchase

The USS *Constitution*

Timeline

1807 The Embargo Act outlaws most foreign trade and angers New England merchants.

1814 The Treaty of Ghent ends the War of 1812.

1820 The Missouri Compromise maintains the balance in the Senate between slave states and free states.

James Madison 1809–1817

James Monroe 1817–1825

1810   •   1815   •   1820

1815 The French leader Napoleon is defeated at Waterloo.

1819 Simón Bolívar frees Colombia from Spanish rule.

Chapter 6   199

BIBLIOGRAPHY

For the Teacher

Adams, Henry. *The War of 1812.* Cooper Square Publishing, 1999. (A detailed look at this unpopular war.)

Adams, Henry. *History of the United States of America During the Administrations of Thomas Jefferson.* Library of America, 1986. (A comprehensive history of Jefferson's presidency.)

McCullough, David. *John Adams.* Simon & Schuster, 2001. (Definitive biography of the second President of the United States.)

For the Student

Bober, Natalie S. *Abigail Adams: Witness to a Revolution.* Aladdin Paperbacks, 1998. (An engaging, well-researched account.)

Bober, Natalie S. *Thomas Jefferson: Man on a Mountain.* Aladdin Paperbacks, 1997. (Critically acclaimed young adult biography.)

Cappon, Lester J., ed. *The Adams-Jefferson Letters: The Complete Correspondence Between Thomas Jefferson and Abigail and John Adams.* University of North Carolina Press, 1988. (A half-century of letters between pivotal figures.)

 **The Louisiana Purchase, 1803**

Activating Prior Knowledge What makes up the eastern border of the Louisiana Purchase? *(The Mississippi River)*

Previewing Ask the students why they think Thomas Jefferson hired Meriwether Lewis and William Clark. *(They were hired to explore the newly acquired resources of the Louisiana Purchase area, to search for passageways to the West, and to begin communicating with the regional Native Americans.)*

BACKGROUND
About the Pictures

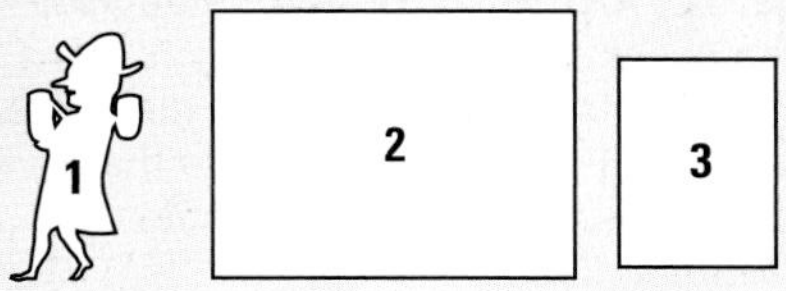

1. Pennsylvanian farmers rebelled against a federal tax levied on liquor.

2. Though Meriwether Lewis and William Clark are widely acknowledged for their exploits in the West, it is estimated that the expedition included about 40 people.

3. Paul Revere, a silversmith, made some of the bolts that were used on the USS *Constitution*.

 **TEXT**

Don't miss the exclusive interactive version of this textbook on the Web and on CD-ROM.

SECTION OBJECTIVES

1. Learn about Alexander Hamilton's program for dealing with national and state debt.
2. Find out how foreign policy issues divided Americans.
3. See what issues led to the emergence of political parties.

BELLRINGER

Warm-Up Activity Ask students if they consider themselves Republicans, Democrats, Independents, or members of a minor political party. Have them define the different political goals of these parties.

Activating Prior Knowledge Ask students to state what they perceive to be the role of political parties in a democracy. How do they think political parties come into being? What causes a political party to endure and grow strong?

READING STRATEGY

As students read, have them list some of the specific actions of the federal government that angered Jefferson and many Americans.

ACTIVITY
Connecting with Culture

Introduce the section by holding a brief, informal debate about whether "liberty" or "order" is more important in American society. Ask students to explain how the two concepts may come into conflict and why having both requires a balance. **(Logical/Mathematical)**

CAPTION ANSWERS

Viewing History That there was so much consent among Americans on major issues faced during the government's formation.

READING FOCUS

- What was Alexander Hamilton's program for dealing with national and state debt?
- How did foreign policy issues divide Americans?
- What issues led to the emergence of political parties?

MAIN IDEA

Americans became sharply divided in the 1790s over whether order or liberty was more important.

KEY TERMS

tariff
interest
strict construction
loose construction
neutral
Jay's Treaty
Whiskey Rebellion
political party

TAKING NOTES

Copy this incomplete Venn diagram. As you read, write key facts about Jefferson and Hamilton in the appropriate sections. Write common characteristics in the overlapping section.

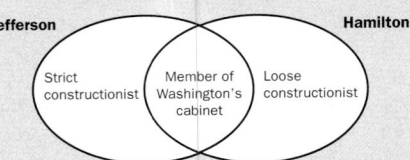

Jefferson — Strict constructionist | Member of Washington's cabinet | Loose constructionist — Hamilton

Setting the Scene In a letter written early in 1790, President George Washington expressed confidence in the new government:

“ *That the government, though not absolutely perfect, is one of the best in the world, I have little doubt. . . . It was indeed next to a miracle that there should have been so much unanimity [agreement], in points of such importance, among such a number of Citizens, so widely scattered, and so different in their habits in many respects as the Americans were.* ”

—George Washington, letter to Catharine Macaulay Graham, January 9, 1790

Although Americans quickly embraced the system of government created by the Constitution of 1787, they argued about the proper role of the federal government in their new nation. Most Americans, Federalists and anti-Federalists alike, hoped that this debate would not lead to the establishment of rival political groups. Struggles between such groups elsewhere in the world had often led to civil war.

Hamilton's Program

One of the biggest issues facing the new nation dealt with the huge debts it owed to other nations and its own citizens following the Revolutionary War. As Secretary of the Treasury, Alexander Hamilton had the responsibility of organizing an economic policy that could help the nation pay off its debts and become economically stable.

Hamilton used this opportunity to push for the kind of national government that he wanted. As he developed and proposed his policies, it became clear that two very different views of the new government were taking shape.

VIEWING HISTORY George Washington leaves for New York, waving his tricorn hat as he sails from Virginia. **Drawing Conclusions** *What impressed Washington about the new American government?*

RESOURCE DIRECTORY

Teaching Resources
Learning Styles Lesson Plans booklet, p. 14
Guided Reading and Review booklet, p. 24

Technology
Section Reading Support Transparencies
Guided Reading Audiotapes (English/Spanish), Ch. 6
Student Edition on Audio CD, Ch. 6
Sounds of an Era Audio CD *Farewell Address, George Washington* (time: one minute, 15 seconds)
Prentice Hall Presentation Pro CD-ROM, Ch. 6
Companion Web site, www.phschool.com

Hamilton, a Federalist, was a keen supporter of strong national power. He had little faith in the people. The Constitution, he believed, was not enough in itself to preserve the new nation. In his view, the government had to expand its role and actively direct the development of the American economy. To this end, Hamilton proposed a complicated plan designed to help the economy and strengthen the national government.

A Deal With the South   In 1790, after months of debate, Congress approved Hamilton's plan for the national government to assume (or take responsibility for) the debts acquired by the states during the Revolution. Congress's vote was a controversial one. Southern states did not want to help pay back the loans owed by northern states. Yet Hamilton managed to win the support of the southern states through a deal: If southern states would back Hamilton's debt plan, Hamilton would gain northern support for a plan to locate the nation's capital in the South. Thus, in 1790, Congress approved both the debt plan and a plan to locate the capital on the banks of the Potomac River.

Assuming State Debts   Gaining southern support was only one obstacle Hamilton's debt plan faced. His plan raised controversy for another reason as well. As critics pointed out, the federal government already had a huge debt of about $75 million. Why would the government want to add to this burden?

The answer is simpler than one might think—with this plan, the central government would be strengthened. Most of the state and national debt was owed to European banks and to American merchants and speculators, or people who take a financial risk in the hope of future profit. Hamilton knew that these lenders, or creditors, did not want any government that owed them money to collapse. If the states owed creditors money, Hamilton reasoned, creditors would care mostly about the states. If, on the other hand, the United States owed creditors money, creditors would care mostly about the nation as a whole. This idea appealed to Federalists, who believed in a strong central government.

Hamilton's Strategy   Why would creditors go along with this plan? To satisfy their concerns, Hamilton outlined a specific budget and set up a regular payment plan. Two measures would help raise money to pay off the debts. In 1789, Congress had created a **tariff**—a tax on imported goods. In 1791, Congress placed a tax on distilled liquors that was called the whiskey tax.

Most of the money raised by these two taxes went to pay the expenses of the government, such as the salaries of officials. Hamilton, however, also put some of it into a special fund used to pay creditors a little money every year. He did not intend to pay them off right away; if he did, they would have no reason to care about what happened to the United States. Instead, the government paid them **interest**—an extra sum of money that borrowers pay creditors in return for the loan. To handle these complicated financial matters, Congress established the Bank of the United States in 1791.

Hamilton thus transformed the debts of the state governments into what amounted to a long-term investment in the United States government. The country's creditors now held an interest in the stable functioning of the government.

Hamilton's Opponents   Many Americans did not like Hamilton's plan. They did not want the federal government to interfere in local and state affairs. They also disliked Hamilton's new taxes.

Focus on ECONOMICS

National Debt *The total amount of money owed by the federal government to citizens or other nations who have invested in the United States.*

The Historical Context In 1791, the national debt was about $75 million, and the population was roughly 4 million. Thus, each person's share of the national debt was about $18.75.

The Concept Today In 2001, the national debt was approximately $5.6 trillion, and the population was about 284 million. That means each person's share of the national debt was almost $20,000. (Keep in mind, though, that because of inflation a dollar buys much less today than it did in 1791!) Like anyone who borrows money, the federal government must pay interest on this debt. Reducing the national debt would lower the government's annual interest payments, allowing the government to spend more money in other areas, such as defense, education, or social security.

Alexander Hamilton participated in framing the Constitution and favored a strong central government.

Focus As the Federalists tried to institute their vision of government, their opponents created a new political party to stop them. What were the major differences between the Federalist Party and the Jeffersonian Republicans?

Instruct Explain that although the Federalists had a majority in both houses of Congress during its first session, there were strong regional differences within the party. Ask students how much of Hamilton's and Jefferson's respective policies can be deduced from the following information: Hamilton favored Great Britain and industry, while Jefferson favored France and rural life.

Assess/Reteach Ask students to think of rival politicians, either in your local area or on the national scene, who are active today. What are some ways in which the two opponents differ? How do their differences compare with those of Hamilton and Jefferson?

CUSTOMIZE FOR ...

Less Proficient Readers

Have students read the sections "Assuming State Debts" and "Hamilton's Strategy." Then have them explain orally in their own words what Hamilton wanted to do to pay off debts and how his plan would work.

Connecting with Government

Ask students to mark with the letter H each statement that correctly identifies one of Alexander Hamilton's beliefs or policies.

- Hamilton believed that national government should have strong powers.
- Hamilton had little faith in the people's ability to make good decisions.
- Hamilton wanted the individual states to pay their debts.
- Hamilton did not want the government to impose taxes on its citizens.
- Hamilton thought that the national debt could be a source of strength.

(Logical/Mathematical)

BACKGROUND

Biography

Alexander Hamilton was so enamored of a strong national government that at one point he argued that individual states should be eliminated. If he had prevailed, the country would have become, "The United State of America"!

Interpreting Charts They favored strict interpretation of the constitutional powers of the federal government. They trusted the people more than the federal government.

Federalists vs. Jeffersonian Republicans

Federalists (Alexander Hamilton)	Jeffersonian Republicans (Thomas Jefferson)
Typical view of Constitution: • Loose • Favored strong central government • Favored a national bank	Typical view of Constitution: • Strict • Favored weak central government • Opposed a national bank
Favored using national debt to establish credit	Favored paying off the national debt
Pro-business	Pro-agriculture
For strong standing armies and navies	Against large standing armies and navies
Believed political power should rest with wealthy, educated men	Believed that common men should hold political power
Pro-British	Pro-French
Generally businessmen from the commercial northeast, but also included professionals, artisans, congregational ministers, and rural people satisfied with the status quo	Tended to be more diverse, including southern slaveholders, urban artisans, tradespeople, and commercial farmers

INTERPRETING CHARTS The Federalists thought the Constitution should be considered a loose framework on which to build the nation. Thus they felt Congress could create a national bank, even though the Constitution does not explicitly give Congress the power to do so. **Identifying Central Issues** Why did Jeffersonian Republicans oppose the national bank?

Opponents of the Washington administration regarded Hamilton's policy of taxation and regulation as similar to the one the British had proposed in the 1760s. Combined with the elegant style of Washington's presidency, the Federalist program suggested to opponents a return to aristocracy and monarchy. Critics saw it as an all-out assault on the hard-won liberty of the American people.

Hamilton vs. Jefferson Secretary of State Jefferson was particularly opposed to Hamilton's plans. President Washington usually sided with Hamilton, and Jefferson increasingly found he held a minority opinion in the President's Cabinet. At the end of 1793, Jefferson, eager to spend more time at his home in Virginia and tired of political squabbles, resigned as Secretary of State.

One way to contrast Jefferson and Hamilton is in terms of their construction, or view, of the Constitution. Jefferson favored a **strict construction.** That is, he believed that the government should not do anything—such as start a national bank—that the Constitution did not specifically say it could do. Hamilton preferred a **loose construction.** He thought the Constitution was only a loose framework of laws on which the government could build the nation as it saw fit. The government, in other words, could do anything that the Constitution did not forbid.

The differences between the two men went deeper than their interpretation of the Constitution, however. Jefferson believed that Hamilton and his Federalist allies were betraying the American Revolution. They were, he told Thomas Paine in 1792, "a sect preaching up and pouting after an English constitution of king, lords, & commons." Jefferson had more faith in the people than in their government. He took pride in *not* preferring "the calm of despotism [tyranny] to the boisterous sea of liberty."

Foreign Policy Issues

That "boisterous sea" threw a tidal wave over France in 1789, when the people of that nation started the French Revolution. According to a public declaration, the revolution was committed to "liberty, fraternity, and equality." By the early 1790s, though, disagreement over how to make these ideals reality led not to fraternity (or brotherhood) but to a prolonged period of violence called the Reign of Terror. During this time, the revolutionary government executed thousands of people, including King Louis XVI and Queen Marie Antoinette.

Americans Split Over the French Revolution The French Revolution sharply divided Americans. Federalists tended to oppose it, seeing it as an example of a democratic revolution gone wrong. Jefferson's supporters, on the other hand, generally viewed the French Revolution as an extension of the American Revolution. Though upset by its violence, they applauded its rejection of government by kings and its acceptance of republican government. Even during the Reign of Terror, Jefferson said that he "would have seen half the earth desolated [ruined] rather than see the French Revolution fail."

Citizen Genêt The political split over the French Revolution grew more intense in 1793, when the French minister to the United States, "Citizen"

Edmond Genêt, arrived in South Carolina. France and Britain were now at war, and Genêt's mission was to win Americans' support for the French in that war.

In the process, Genêt overstepped the bounds of diplomacy. Without the permission of United States officials, he tried to convince private Americans to serve as soldiers and privateers against the British. Eventually, Genêt's actions forced Washington to ask that France recall him. Even Jefferson agreed that Genêt had to go. By this time, though, political power had again shifted in France, and Genêt feared he would face the guillotine if he returned home. To avoid being executed, Genêt married a governor's daughter and became a U.S. citizen.

Proclaiming American Neutrality   While Americans debated the French Revolution, the war between Britain and France created more immediate practical problems. Which side should the United States take? The nation could not afford to offend the British, whose navy dominated the oceans. Few people, however, wanted to abandon the French, who had helped Americans during the War for Independence.

The most sensible strategy was to remain **neutral,** or not to take either side. In April 1793, after being reelected for a second term as President, Washington issued a proclamation of neutrality. The United States would not take sides in the struggle.

Despite this proclamation, the United States found it very difficult to avoid getting involved in the war. In 1793, the British began to seize neutral U.S. trading ships headed for the French West Indies. At the same time, Americans were increasingly frustrated by British support for Indians in the Northwest Territory who wanted to keep settlers south of the Ohio River. With anti-British sentiment on the rise, by 1794, the debate over whether the United States should remain neutral in the conflict between Great Britain and France rose to a fever pitch.

Jay's Treaty   Washington and Hamilton believed that the long-term interests of the United States would be served best by avoiding war with Britain. In 1794, therefore, Washington sent Chief Justice John Jay to London to negotiate an agreement with the British. Jay wrote, "My objects are, to prevent a war, if justice can be obtained."

READING CHECK
Why did President Washington issue a proclamation of neutrality?

INTERPRETING POLITICAL CARTOONS The British Prime Minister William Pitt and French Emperor Napoleon Bonaparte sit down to a dinner in which they carve up the world. **Determining Relevance** *How does this cartoon express the world politics affecting the United States at the time?*

In the resulting agreement, called **Jay's Treaty**, Britain agreed to leave the forts it occupied in the Northwest Territory. Other provisions were aimed at expanding trade between the two nations. Jay was unable, however, to convince the British to end their practice of stopping American ships on the high seas and searching them for British subjects.

Jay's Treaty unleashed a storm of controversy throughout the United States. Critics complained that it contained no protection for American shipping. More broadly, many Americans saw the treaty as a betrayal of revolutionary ideals, a sellout to the hated British. Despite the anger, however, Congress ratified the treaty in 1795.

Political Parties Emerge

Meanwhile, within the United States, resistance to Hamilton's economic program grew. One aspect of his plan in particular, the tax on whiskey, led some citizens to challenge the new government.

The Whiskey Rebellion In western Pennsylvania and other frontier areas, many people refused to pay the tax on whiskey. Whiskey was of critical importance to the frontier economy. It was not just a traditional beverage—it was one of the only products that farmers could make out of corn that could be transported to market without spoiling. Whiskey was even used as a kind of currency, as tobacco leaves were in colonial Virginia. In 1794, opposition to the whiskey tax was so strong that western Pennsylvania appeared to be in a state of rebellion against the authority of the federal government.

The **Whiskey Rebellion** followed the tradition of Shays' Rebellion and the protests brought on by the Stamp Act. Rebels closed courts and attacked tax collectors. President Washington and Secretary Hamilton, though, were determined to end the rebellion. They saw it as an opportunity to demonstrate the power of the United States government. Hamilton himself declared that a government can never be said to be established until it has proved itself by exerting its military force.

In the summer of 1794, Washington gathered an army of close to 13,000 men. General "Light Horse Harry" Lee, accompanied by Hamilton, led the army to the Pittsburgh area. The rebellion soon dissolved. Washington's tough response had demonstrated to American citizens and the world that the young American government was committed to enforcing its laws.

VIEWING HISTORY This drawing shows a government agent collecting taxes—in the form of two kegs of whiskey. He is being followed by angry farmers wishing to tar and feather him. **Predicting Consequences** *What might have happened if the federal government had not responded forcefully to the Whiskey Rebellion?*

The Jeffersonian Republicans The Federalists had established their economic program, suppressed the Whiskey Rebellion, and ensured peace with Great Britain. Yet in so doing, they had lost the support of a great many Americans.

As early as 1793, artisans and professional men were forming what they called Democratic Societies to oppose the Federalists. Meanwhile, Jefferson and various state leaders were furiously promoting resistance to the Federalists in letters to one another. Some leaders also encouraged newspaper attacks on the Washington administration.

Originally these critics of the Federalists were called Republicans or Democratic-Republicans because they stood for a more democratic republic. To avoid confusing them with the modern Republican Party, historians call them Jeffersonian Republicans. They, along with the Federalists, were the first political

---

parties in the United States, although both groups denied that they were permanent organizations. A **political party** is a group of people who seek to win elections and hold public office in order to shape government policy and programs.

Alexander Hamilton summarized the differences between Federalists and Jeffersonian Republicans in 1792:

> 66 One side [the Jeffersonians] appears to believe that there is a serious plot to overturn the State governments and substitute a monarchy to the present republican system. The other side [the Federalists] firmly believes there is a serious plot to overturn the general government and elevate the separate powers of the States upon its ruins. 99
>
> —Alexander Hamilton, 1792

To this statement Hamilton added, "Both sides may be equally wrong." Only a few Federalists—and they did not include Washington or Hamilton—wanted to install a monarchy in the United States; most were deeply committed to the new republic. Similarly, virtually all of the Jeffersonian Republicans accepted the national government created by the Constitution.

The Election of 1796 President Washington had thought about retiring in 1792. However, Jefferson and Hamilton convinced him that the country needed his leadership for another term. By the end of his second term, in the midst of criticism from the Jeffersonian Republicans, Washington chose not to run for a third term. He thus set a precedent followed in later times.

With Washington out of the race and the nation politically divided, the election of 1796 was sure to be close. Washington's Vice President, John Adams, ran as the Federalist candidate for President, while Thomas Pinckney ran for Vice President. Thomas Jefferson and Aaron Burr ran on the Republican side. The Federalists won a narrow victory, as Adams captured 71 electoral votes to Jefferson's 68. Because Jefferson finished second in the electoral vote race, he became the new Vice President under the election system originally established by the Constitution.

Washington Says Farewell Washington had made the announcement that he would not seek a third term in his Farewell Address of 1796. In the address, he drew on his years of experience and offered much advice to the young nation for the years ahead.

Many people had labeled Washington a Federalist because he generally agreed with Hamilton on policy issues and because he was the head and symbol of the central government, which the Jeffersonians distrusted. Throughout both of his terms, however, Washington generally remained above the political bickering between Federalists and Jeffersonian Republicans. He did not believe political parties were good for the nation. In his farewell address he warned against competing political parties:

> **KEY DOCUMENTS** 66 [A system of political parties] agitates the community with ill-founded jealousies and false alarms; kindles the animosity of one part against another, [and] foments [stirs up] occasionally riot and insurrection. 99
>
> —George Washington, Farewell Address, 1796

Washington also called for a foreign policy of neutrality. He warned against "antipathies [hatreds] against particular nations and passionate attachments for

VIEWING HISTORY John Adams (top) and Thomas Jefferson (bottom) squared off in both the 1796 and 1800 presidential elections. **Synthesizing Information** (a) How did Jefferson become Adams's Vice President in 1796? (b) How might this have been a problem? (c) How are vice presidents chosen today?

Reading Comprehension

1. The goal of Hamilton's financial program was to strengthen international support for the national government by having the federal government assume the states' war debts, thus transforming that debt into a long-term foreign investment in the well-being of the United States. Hamilton's plan was controversial because it strengthened the national government, an idea to which many Americans were opposed.

2. Federalists generally opposed the French Revolution and saw it as an example of a democratic revolution failing. Jefferson's supporters generally viewed events in France as an extension of the American Revolution and supported its rejection of a government by kings and the acceptance of a republican government.

3. Many Americans opposed the treaty because they felt it contained no protection for American shipping, and they saw it as a betrayal of revolutionary ideals.

4. Federalists believed in a strong central government to maintain order in the country and build up its strength. Jeffersonian Republicans favored a weaker central government, stronger state governments, and more power for citizens.

5. He warned against competing political parties and called for a foreign policy of neutrality.

Critical Thinking and Writing

6. Answers will vary, but students may discuss the effects of the Information Age, globalization, and rapid transportation as factors that have decreased geographic barriers.

7. Speeches should include grievances against Federalist actions prior to 1796.

Take It to the NET

Students should describe Washington's quick and forceful reaction to the Whiskey Rebellion.

CAPTION ANSWERS

Viewing History Washington thought that political parties created disagreement and social disorder.

VIEWING HISTORY George Washington, shown here reviewing troops gathered to put down the Whiskey Rebellion, declined to run for a third term of office. **Analyzing Information** Why did Washington warn against the formation of political parties?

others." In Washington's view, the United States, because of its geographic location, had a unique opportunity to remain outside of the complicated entanglements of European nations:

 66 *The great rule of conduct for us in regard to foreign nations is, in extending our commercial relations to have with them as little political connection as possible. . . . Our detached and distant situation invites and enables us to pursue a different course. . . . Why forego the advantages of so peculiar a situation?* 99

—George Washington, Farewell Address, 1796

The events of the next several years would show that Washington's advice about the dangers of political parties and European conflicts was wise indeed.

Section 1 Assessment

READING COMPREHENSION

1. Why was Hamilton's debt plan controversial?

2. How did the French Revolution highlight political differences within the United States?

3. Why did many Americans oppose **Jay's Treaty?**

4. Summarize the differences between the first two **political parties** in the United States.

5. What advice did Washington give Americans in his farewell address?

CRITICAL THINKING AND WRITING

6. Making Comparisons Washington believed the United States had a unique opportunity to remain neutral in foreign affairs. (a) Do you think this is true in today's world? (b) Why might it be more difficult for the United States to remain neutral in the twenty-first century?

7. Writing to Persuade Prepare a campaign speech for a Jeffersonian Republican in 1796. List reasons why voters should elect Jefferson over Adams.

Take It to the NET

Activity: Analyzing Primary Sources Examine George Washington's response to the Whiskey Rebellion in 1794. How did our first President react to the insurrection? Write a brief report summarizing your findings. Use the links provided in the *America: Pathways to the Present* area of the following Web site for help in completing this activity.
www.phschool.com

206 Chapter 6 • *The Origins of American Politics*

RESOURCE DIRECTORY

Teaching Resources
Units 1/2 booklet
• Section 1 Quiz, p. 64
Guide to the Essentials
• Section 1 Summary, p. 31

READING FOCUS

- What actions did John Adams take as President?
- Why was the election of 1800 a turning point?
- What was significant about the transfer of power between parties in 1801?

MAIN IDEA

With the election of 1800, Americans peacefully accomplished the nation's first transfer of power from one party to another.

KEY TERMS

XYZ affair
Alien and Sedition Acts
Virginia and Kentucky Resolutions

TAKING NOTES

Copy the flowchart below. As you read, fill in the boxes with events during Adams's presidency that influenced the election of 1800.

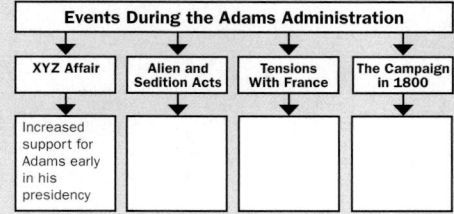

Events During the Adams Administration

XYZ Affair	Alien and Sedition Acts	Tensions With France	The Campaign in 1800
Increased support for Adams early in his presidency			

SECTION OBJECTIVES

1. Find out what actions John Adams took as President.
2. See why the election of 1800 was a turning point.
3. Discover what was significant about the transfer of power between parties in 1801.

BELLRINGER

Warm-Up Activity Ask students to rate (on a scale of 1 to 5, with 1 being the lowest possible score) the importance of the following conditions to presidential campaigns: length of the campaign, honesty of the campaign, relevance of issues raised during the campaign.

Activating Prior Knowledge Ask students to consider what it must have been like to follow George Washington as President. Have them state their opinion of the following statement: "George Washington—A Hard Act to Follow."

READING STRATEGY

As students read this section, have them create an outline of the major headings, and write main idea statements for each heading.

Setting the Scene Despite having served as one of the most important leaders of the Revolution and as the nation's first Vice President, John Adams lacked the prestige of George Washington. In his Inaugural Address, Adams expressed his determination to follow the example of his predecessor:

" [George Washington's] name may still be a rampart, and the knowledge that he lives a bulwark, against all open or secret enemies of his country's peace. This example has been recommended to the imitation of his successors by both Houses of Congress and by the voice of the legislatures and the people throughout the nation."

—John Adams, Inaugural Address, 1797

As President, Adams faced the threat of war from abroad. He also faced the difficult task of trying to govern a young country in which party differences were growing wider and wider.

John Adams as President

From the beginning of the Adams administration, the United States began to drift toward war with France. The French were angry about Jay's Treaty with the British and began seizing American ships in French harbors. Trying to avoid war, Adams sent officials to Paris to negotiate with the revolutionary government.

The XYZ Affair and Trouble With France Once in Paris, the American officials were met by secret agents sent by the French foreign minister. These agents were later identified only as X, Y, and Z. The French agents demanded a bribe of $250,000 and a loan to the French of $10 million before the Americans would even be allowed to see the French foreign minister. Although such a request was common practice in European diplomacy, it outraged Americans and became known as the **XYZ affair.**

VIEWING HISTORY John Adams, an outspoken and decisive Federalist President, was driven out of office after only one term when the Federalists and Jeffersonian Republicans clashed in the election of 1800. **Synthesizing Information** What were Adams's strengths and weaknesses as President?

RESOURCE DIRECTORY

Teaching Resources
Learning Styles Lesson Plans booklet, p. 15
Guided Reading and Review booklet, p. 25

Technology
Section Reading Support Transparencies
Guided Reading Audiotapes (English/Spanish), Ch. 6
Student Edition on Audio CD, Ch. 6
Prentice Hall Presentation Pro CD-ROM, Ch. 6
Companion Web site, www.phschool.com

CAPTION ANSWERS

Viewing History Strengths: kept the young United States out of war with France despite the popular cry for war; decisive; long experience in government service. Weaknesses: unable to keep the support of some in his party; unable to quell animosity between political parties; generally unpopular with the public; supported unpopular Alien and Sedition Acts.

Focus Although the election of 1800 was bitter and raucous, power was peacefully transferred from the Federalists to the Jeffersonians. Ask students to describe how this was accomplished.

Instruct Explain that Jefferson called the election of 1800 "as real a revolution in the principles of our government as that of 1776 was in its form."

Ask students to summarize the reasons behind the Alien and Sedition Acts and the effects of those laws. Then have them describe the Jeffersonian response to the acts. Discuss the reasons for Prosser's rebellion. Ask students to list reasons why Prosser failed.

Assess/Reteach Ask students to summarize some ways in which Jefferson's presidency differed from his Federalist predecessors, Washington and Adams. Can they define what "Jeffersonian Democracy" means?

ACTIVITY

Connecting with Government

Draw students' attention to the discussion of the XYZ affair. Point out that their textbook indicates that requesting such payments "was common practice in European diplomacy," but that it "outraged" Americans. Have students address this conflict by writing paragraphs on this question: "Were Americans correct to protest the demand for payment, or should they have gone along with the established practice?" **(Verbal/Linguistic)**

READING CHECK

The Spirit of 1776 was the idea of liberty found in the Declaration of Independence, whereas the Spirit of 1787 emphasized order as it was stated in the Constitution.

CAPTION ANSWERS

Interpreting Political Cartoons (a) The American diplomats sent to Paris. (b) This man, who represents France, is seen as evil. His several heads indicate that the Americans cannot trust him; they may also be an allusion to the countless heads cut off by guillotine during the French Revolution. (c) France is portrayed in a very dark light. Americans should not trust the French, because the French nation was highly unstable at that time.

CIVIC FEAST

INTERPRETING POLITICAL CARTOONS American diplomats refused to pay bribes to the French agents X, Y, and Z. **Analyzing Visual Information** (a) Who are the three men on the left? (b) Why does the man they are talking to have several heads? (c) What is the overall message of the cartoon?

READING CHECK
What was the difference between the Spirit of 1776 and the Spirit of 1787?

Refusing to pay the bribe, the American diplomats quickly returned home. They were met with public cries of patriotism, war, and defiance against the French. The slogan "Millions for defense, but not one cent for tribute [bribery]" rang out in the United States. Unable to resolve their differences, by 1798, France and the United States were involved in what amounted to an undeclared naval war. Both sides fired on and seized each other's ships.

The Alien and Sedition Acts The Federalists took advantage of the war crisis and Adams's popularity to push important new measures through Congress. These measures included an increase in the size of the army, higher taxes to support the army and navy, and the **Alien and Sedition Acts** of 1798. Under the Alien Act, the President gained the right to imprison or deport citizens of other countries living in the United States. Under the Sedition Act, persons who wrote, published, or said anything "false, scandalous, and malicious" against the American government or its officials could be fined or jailed. In other words, it was against the law to criticize government officials unless you could prove everything you said. The Federalists used the Sedition Act to silence Republican opposition. Under the act, ten Republicans were convicted and many others were put on trial.

The Virginia and Kentucky Resolutions Jefferson, James Madison, and other Republicans believed that the Sedition Act violated the constitutional protection of freedom of speech. Yet the Constitution did not spell out who had the authority to judge whether an act of Congress went beyond the powers stated in the Constitution.

Jefferson and Madison believed that the states should make that judgment. They responded to the Alien and Sedition Acts with the **Virginia and Kentucky Resolutions.** These resolutions, adopted by the legislatures of those two states, argued that the states had the right to judge whether federal laws agreed with the Constitution. If a state decided that a law was unconstitutional, it could declare that law "null and void" within the state.

For the time being, this principle of nullification remained untested. Neither Virginia nor Kentucky tried to enforce the resolutions. Still, their defiance of federal power was clear.

Increasing Tensions Tensions between Federalists and Jeffersonian Republicans continued to grow during the late 1790s. Members of Congress attacked each other in the House of Representatives. Crowds taunted President Adams, at times forcing him to enter the presidential residence in Philadelphia through the back door.

As the presidential election of 1800 loomed, many people believed that the future of the nation was at stake. Would the nation tilt toward what Jefferson called the Spirit of 1776 and the idea of liberty found in the Declaration of Independence, or would it choose the Spirit of 1787, with an emphasis on order as stated in the Constitution?

RESOURCE DIRECTORY

Other Print Resources

American History Block Scheduling Support *Taking Sides: The Creation of American Political Parties,* found in the Forging a New Nation folder, includes interdisciplinary lesson suggestions and activities for Geography and History, Primary Sources, Biography, and Literature.

Gabriel Prosser's Rebellion Although barred from any participation in the emerging political system, enslaved African Americans embraced the discussion of liberty all around them. In the summer before the election of 1800, an event took place that demonstrated the conflict surrounding the unresolved issue of slavery. A blacksmith named Gabriel Prosser and several other slaves planned a rebellion in the area around Richmond, Virginia. In meetings at night, Prosser encouraged his followers to adopt the ideas about liberty that sparked the American Revolution. The leaders intended to take over Richmond and win their freedom.

Prosser's small-scale rebellion failed before it could get underway. The rebels were caught and tried, and at least 30 of them, including Prosser, were executed. At the trial, one defendant said, "I have adventured my life in endeavoring [trying] to obtain the liberty of my countrymen, and am a willing sacrifice to their cause."

The Election of 1800

With the election of 1800, the nation turned from the Federalist interest in order to the Jeffersonian focus on liberty. In later years, Jefferson said that the election of 1800 was "as real a revolution in the principles of our government as that of 1776 was in its form." This complex and competitive election left its mark in several other areas of American politics as well.

Adams Loses Federalist Support President Adams reached the height of his popularity with the American people for his tough stand against France during the XYZ affair. Adams knew, however, that the undeclared naval war with France needed to stop. In seeking a peaceful resolution with France, Adams angered many Federalists, including Alexander Hamilton. These Federalist hardliners were in favor of a harsher policy toward France, one that included a formal declaration of war.

Rising above Federalist hostility to France, Adams sent a second diplomatic mission to that country in 1799. This mission cooled tensions between the United States and France considerably. Strangely, this triumphant moment for Adams hurt him in the coming election of 1800 for several reasons.

First, he lost a lot of support from the more aggressive Federalists in his party. Second, because the United States had made peace with France, the Jeffersonian Republicans' support for France became less of a rallying point for the Federalists and a non-issue for the Jeffersonians. Third, the highly unpopular Alien and Sedition Acts seemed to be even less justified now that the threat of war had faded. Thus, Adams entered the 1800 election without the support of much of his party and without the momentum he had picked up in 1798.

Adams could not win without Federalist backing. Yet Alexander Hamilton and his supporters rallied support

Political Parties

Political parties play a leading role in the American political system—a much greater role than the founders of the nation ever intended. The nation's early leaders initially opposed political parties. Yet during Washington's presidency, these same men actively encouraged their growth.

Today, as in most of our history, two major parties dominate American politics. The modern Democratic Party descended from the Jeffersonian Republicans. It is the oldest continuous political party in the United States. The modern Republican Party formed in the 1850s. From time to time, however, an independent candidate or third party challenges the two-party system.

Many other nations have multiparty systems—with as many as two dozen or more parties. Some people believe that having more than two parties would allow more views to be represented. With only two strong parties, they say, voters have less of a choice. Other people argue that multiple parties create confusion. They point out that reaching agreement is already difficult in Congress, which is dominated by only two parties.

? Can you think of a time when a third party played a major role in the outcome of a presidential election? What are the benefits and drawbacks of such an influence?

against Adams, urging Federalists to support their vice presidential nominee, Charles Pinckney, instead.

Adams's bid for reelection received another severe blow when the Jeffersonian Republican nominee for Vice President, Aaron Burr, obtained a copy of a privately distributed pamphlet written by Hamilton called "The Public Conduct and Character of John Adams, Esq., President of the United States," in which Hamilton had written:

> **❝** I should be deficient in candor were I to conceal the conviction, that he [Adams] does not possess the talents adapted to the Administration of Government, and that there are great and intrinsic [deep-seated] defects in his character which unfit him for the office of Chief Magistrate. **❞**
>
> —Alexander Hamilton, 1800

Without Hamilton's approval, Burr printed excerpts such as this in Republican newspapers during the campaign. Hamilton's plotting and the lack of unity within the Federalist Party would be major reasons for Adams's defeat in the upcoming election.

In a way, John Adams's defeat was an unfair judgment of his abilities. Some historians believe that Adams was more devoted to public service and more honest than most Presidents. Like most decisive Presidents, however, Adams failed to quiet his critics and angered many of his supporters.

The Jeffersonian Republicans   The Jeffersonians had reached a low point in the 1798 midterm congressional elections. Their support for France had damaged their popularity during the naval war and the XYZ affair.

NOTABLE PRESIDENTS
Thomas Jefferson

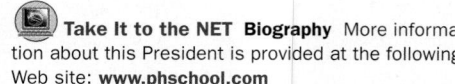

3rd President 1801–1809

"We hold these truths to be self-evident; that all men are created equal."

—Declaration of Independence

Thomas Jefferson had impressive qualifications for the presidency. The Virginia-born planter and lawyer had not only drafted the Declaration of Independence but had served as ambassador to France, Secretary of State, and Vice President. Jefferson promised a more democratic government, one that would leave most decisions in the hands of the people.

During his first term (1801–1805), Jefferson had considerable success. He trimmed the federal government's size and cost and acted as President in a simple, democratic manner. In addition, his approval of the purchase of the Louisiana Territory from France in 1803 considerably increased the country's size.

Jefferson's second term (1805–1809), though, was far less successful than his first. His Embargo Act of 1807, which halted trade with European nations until they promised to stop harassing American ships on the high seas, was a disaster.

Jefferson died on July 4, 1826, the fiftieth anniversary of the Declaration of Independence. Today, Jefferson remains a puzzle for historians, for the author of some of the most eloquent words ever written about human freedom was himself an owner of slaves.

Connecting to Today

Do you think the famous phrase from the Declaration of Independence, "all men are created equal," affects political issues today? Use examples from the news to support your answer.

 **Take It to the NET Biography** More information about this President is provided at the following Web site: **www.phschool.com**

However, they were able to use the conflicts within the Federalist Party to their advantage.

By 1800, Thomas Jefferson was the clear leader of those who preferred local to national government. Jefferson and his followers believed it was better to risk too much liberty than suffer from too much government. Jefferson always denied that he was a politician. He never saw himself as working to build a permanent political party. Nevertheless, that is exactly what he did.

The Campaign In 1800, there were no campaign speeches and no statements from the candidates. Candidates were expected to remain behind the scenes, preparing for the term of service they hoped to win. The campaigns for the candidates were instead conducted through newspapers, pamphlets, and other sources.

This did not mean, however, that the personal attacks and negative campaigning found in elections today did not exist two centuries ago. The election of 1800 was a truly nasty campaign. Jeffersonian newspapers accused Adams of being a monarchist, which was a terrible insult at the time. The Jeffersonians appealed to "the common man" and portrayed Adams as an enemy of the people. They linked Adams with the hard-line Federalists who had pushed for the Alien and Sedition Acts. In so doing, they also attempted to separate him in the public's mind from George Washington, who remained the nation's greatest hero.

Federalists, on the other hand, asserted that Jefferson was a godless man who would lead the United States into chaos. They claimed that he was an agent of the French Revolution and feared that the United States would become weak and disorganized under his leadership. Most American voters, however, did not share these fears.

Jefferson's Victory Jefferson won the popular vote in December 1800 but did not win a majority in the electoral college. His main rival there was not Adams but his own vice presidential running mate, Aaron Burr. Jefferson and Burr each received 73 electoral votes. Adams had won 65, and his running mate Pinckney won 64.

Under Article II of the Constitution, if two candidates tied for the same number of electoral votes, the House of Representatives had to choose the new President. Each delegation from the 16 states would get one vote. Though Jeffersonians had won most of the seats in the congressional elections of 1800, these new members had not yet entered office. Thus the vote for President would be taken by the old House, which the Federalists controlled.

Even before the voting began in the House on February 11, 1801, it was clear that no candidate could gain a majority immediately. The Republicans knew they could count on the votes from eight states, which meant that the Federalists would also have eight states. Some Federalists tried to gain votes for Burr, whom they viewed as less of a threat than Jefferson. However, Jefferson received support from an unlikely source—Alexander Hamilton, who preferred Jefferson over Burr. For several days the House remained deadlocked, unable to choose a President. Finally, on February 17, only a few days before the end of Adams's term, the House of Representatives elected Jefferson the third President of the United States on the thirty-sixth ballot.

Focus on GOVERNMENT

The Twelfth Amendment The elections of 1796 and 1800 demonstrated that there was an unexpected problem with the existing constitutional process for electing a President. According to Article II of the Constitution, which outlined election procedures, electors did not have to specify whether their vote was for President or Vice President. The candidate with the most votes became President and the runner-up became Vice President. In 1796, Jefferson, a Republican, became the Vice President under Adams, a Federalist. Clearly, this would be a difficult situation. Four years later, the controversy surrounding the election of 1800 would be enough for lawmakers to take a second look at the Constitution.

The goal of the Twelfth Amendment, which went into effect just before the 1804 election, was to avoid these problems in the future. The most major change instituted by the Twelfth Amendment thus required electors to cast separate votes for President and Vice President.

One reason why the framers of the Constitution did not foresee these issues had to do with the unexpected development of political parties. Without political parties, it made sense for the candidate with the most votes to become President and the runner-up to become Vice President. In a political party system, however, each party selects its own presidential and vice presidential candidates. Today, voters vote for electors who are morally bound to choose the candidates of their particular party.

Reading Comprehension

1. The XYZ affair increased suspicions of foreign espionage, inspired increased patriotism, and set the stage for the Federalists to take advantage of the war fever to push the Alien and Sedition Acts through Congress.

2. By giving the states the right to judge the constitutionality of federal laws, these resolutions were an effort to give more power to the states, rather than leaving ultimate control in the hands of the federal government.

3. It was a strong example of African Americans challenging their societal role: rebelling against slavery, seeking a voice in the emerging political system, and trying to adopt the ideas of liberty that sparked the American Revolution.

4. General disunity and rivalry among the Federalists; loss of support for Adams; improved relations with France; growing support for Jefferson's politics, which emphasized liberty over order.

Critical Thinking and Writing

5. The Sedition Act made it illegal to criticize government officials, thereby silencing the opposition. It therefore greatly limited an individual's freedom of expression in the interest of increasing the power and stability of the government.

6. Students' outlines may include the following points: Jeffersonian Republicans feared the growing power of the government in people's lives in the form of taxes and limits on freedom; Federalists feared a loss of order and the end of the rule of law if government did not become more powerful.

Take It to the NET

Articles should focus on an event such as the Alien and Sedition Acts, the Election of 1800, or Prosser's rebellion, and they should chronicle the chosen event using a style of writing appropriate for the time.

CAPTION ANSWERS

Map Skills The Democratic-Republicans received the most votes from people in the South, while people in the Northeast voted for the Federalists.

Presidential Election of 1800

Candidate/Party	Electoral Vote
Thomas Jefferson (Democratic-Republican)	73
Aaron Burr (Democratic-Republican)	73
John Adams (Federalist)	65
Charles C. Pinckney (Federalist)	64
John Jay (Federalist)	1

% Electoral Vote   47.1   52.9

MAP SKILLS The political divisions within the country were made clear by the election of 1800. **Place** *How does this map show the regional differences in the nation in 1800?*

A Peaceful Transfer of Power

Washington, D.C., in 1801 seemed very much like the Federalists' plans in general: grand but unfinished. The new capital, designed by Pierre L'Enfant to feature broad boulevards and Roman buildings, was little more than a swamp with muddy, rutted roads and half-completed structures. Here, on March 4, 1801, Thomas Jefferson took the oath of office administered by one of Adams's appointees, Chief Justice John Marshall.

With this inauguration, the Federalist leaders of the young country proved that they could do what so many leaders in other times and places had refused to do. Although few on either side could forget their bitter disagreements, the Federalists stepped down and let the Jeffersonian Republicans take over. Whether they stood for individual liberty or a strong, central government, Americans had proved that they could transfer power from one party to another—and do it peacefully.

Jefferson recognized the significance of this peaceful transfer of power. He also understood that his administration would not succeed, nor the nation survive, unless Americans were able to disagree peacefully. As he stated in his First Inaugural Address:

KEY DOCUMENTS
> *Every difference of opinion is not a difference of principle. We have called by different names brethren of the same principle. We are all republicans—we are all federalists. If there be any among us who would wish to dissolve this Union or to change its republican form, let them stand undisturbed as monuments of the safety with which error of opinion may be tolerated where reason is left free to combat it.*
>
> —Thomas Jefferson, First Inaugural Address, 1801

Section **2** Assessment

READING COMPREHENSION

1. How did the **XYZ affair** help lead to the **Alien and Sedition Acts?**

2. Explain how the **Virginia and Kentucky Resolutions** reflected the Jeffersonian philosophy of government.

3. What was the significance of Gabriel Prosser's rebellion?

4. What factors led to Jefferson's victory in the election of 1800?

CRITICAL THINKING AND WRITING

5. **Recognizing Ideologies** How did the Sedition Act reflect the Federalists' position in the controversy between those who favored liberty and those who favored order?

6. **Writing an Outline** Write an outline for a response to the following essay question: "What did Federalists and Jeffersonian Republicans fear most about each other's ideas before the election of 1800?"

Take It to the NET

Activity: Writing a Newspaper Article Use the Internet to learn more about one of the events mentioned in this section. Then, write a newspaper article on that event in the style of the time. Be sure not to mention any modern conveniences. Use the links provided in the *America: Pathways to the Present* area of the following Web site for help in completing this activity. **www.phschool.com**

RESOURCE DIRECTORY

Teaching Resources
Units 1/2 booklet
• Section 2 Quiz, p. 65
Guide to the Essentials
• Section 2 Summary, p. 32

The Jefferson Administration

READING FOCUS

- How did Jefferson reduce the power of the national government?
- What problem did Jefferson have with the federal courts?
- How did Jefferson achieve his program in the West?
- Why did Jefferson easily win reelection in 1804?
- How did Jefferson respond to increasing tensions with Europe?

MAIN IDEA

President Jefferson sought to reduce the power of the federal government, but he also demonstrated the government's power when he bought new lands and restricted foreign trade.

KEY TERMS

agenda
bureaucracy
midnight judge
Marbury v. *Madison*
judicial review
Louisiana Purchase
Lewis and Clark
  expedition
embargo

TAKING NOTES

Copy the web diagram below. As you read, fill in each circle with important facts about Jefferson's administration. You may add more circles as needed.

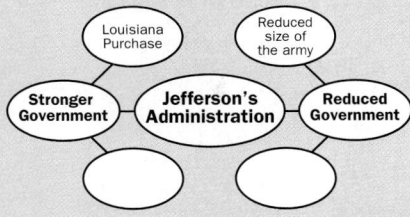

Setting the Scene

Thomas Jefferson entered office with a straightforward **agenda,** or list of things that he wanted to accomplish. His goal was to reduce the influence of the national government in the lives of the American people. Jefferson called the sum of a good government:

> ❝ *a wise and frugal Government, which shall restrain men from injuring one another, shall leave them otherwise free to regulate their own pursuits of industry and improvement, and shall not take from the mouth of labor the bread it has earned.* ❞
>
> —Thomas Jefferson, 1801

Reducing Government

To accomplish his goals, Jefferson reversed much of what the Federalists had done, starting with matters of presidential style. He refused to deliver speeches to Congress, claiming that to do so would seem too much like the act of a king. He also resolved a question that had troubled Congress for many years—what to call the President. Jefferson asked to be addressed simply as "Mr. President."

Of course, Jefferson's effect on government went beyond style. Together with Congress, he reduced the amount of taxes paid by the American people and severely cut the size of the federal **bureaucracy**—the departments and workers that make up the federal government. The Attorney General, for instance, was not even allowed a clerk. Jefferson also slashed the size of the army to just over 3,000 men. Jefferson's goal was to limit the national government's presence in people's lives.

Jefferson, however, did not intend to destroy the government created by the Constitution, or even to undo all the acts of the Federalists. For example, he

Jefferson's informal presidential style extended to his clothing, which was casual by the standards of the day.

Chapter 6 • Section 3   **213**

SECTION OBJECTIVES

1. Discover how Jefferson reduced the power of the national government.
2. See what problem Jefferson had with the federal courts.
3. Find out how Jefferson achieved his program in the West.
4. Learn why Jefferson easily won reelection in 1804.
5. Understand how Jefferson responded to increasing tensions with Europe.

BELLRINGER

Warm-Up Activity Have students consider the following question: Under what circumstances might reversing one's opinion be a sign of flexibility and strength? When might sticking to an opinion be a sign of weakness?

Activating Prior Knowledge What were Jefferson's goals on entering office? With students, list those goals on the chalkboard. At the end of the section, review the list with students. How successful was he in accomplishing his goals?

READING STRATEGY

Have students write two questions for each of the headings in this section. Have them look for answers to these questions as they read.

ACTIVITY

Connecting with Culture

Point out Jefferson's use of the word "men" in the quotation on this page. Ask students if they think Jefferson meant "people" or men exclusively. If they think the former, challenge them to explain why he used the word "men." If they think the latter, challenge them to explain what that implies. **(Verbal/Linguistic)**

Focus Although Jefferson was able to carry out much of his agenda to limit the national government, he was also willing to use and even expand his powers as President. Ask for what purposes Jefferson used the powers of government.

Instruct Discuss the steps Jefferson took to limit the role of government and why they were almost guaranteed to make him popular with voters. Now ask students to list the ways in which Jefferson used and expanded the power of the national government. Ask students to state in their own words Jefferson's dilemma concerning the Louisiana Purchase.

Assess/Reteach Ask students to consider how different the United States might be if Jefferson had never pursued the Louisiana Purchase and the expedition of Lewis and Clark.

BACKGROUND
Biography

Chief Justice John Marshall (1755–1835) was licensed to practice law by his cousin Thomas Jefferson. But Marshall, stating a firm belief in "a more efficient and better organized general government," embarked upon a lifelong crusade against the Jeffersonian cause of states' rights. One hundred years after his death, a scholar said that Marshall "embodied in his career clear proof that ours is a government of men, not laws."

READING CHECK
The Court declared a portion of the Judiciary Act of 1789 unconstitutional, thereby declaring the Court's power to find acts of Congress unconstitutional.

AMERICAN BIOGRAPHY

John Marshall
1755–1835

Born in a log cabin near Germantown, Virginia, John Marshall grew up on the family farm. He had little formal schooling and spent much of his time helping to raise his 14 siblings.

After serving in the Continental Army during the Revolutionary War, Marshall studied law at the College of William and Mary. He served in the Virginia legislature and helped win ratification of the Constitution. Marshall also served in the federal government as U.S. minister to France, in the U.S. House of Representatives, and as Secretary of State before his appointment to the Supreme Court.

In his 34 years as Chief Justice, John Marshall helped establish a strong judiciary. In addition to *Marbury* v. *Madison*, Marshall's landmark cases included the following: *Fletcher* v. *Peck* (1810), in which the Court declared a state law unconstitutional for the first time; *McCulloch* v. *Maryland* (1819), which established the superiority of federal power over state power; and *Gibbons* v. *Ogden* (1824), in which Marshall's opinion defined national power over interstate commerce.

READING CHECK
How did *Marbury* v. *Madison* establish the power of judicial review?

let the Bank of the United States continue to function, knowing that its 20-year term would run out in 1811.

Jefferson and the Courts

The most controversial part of Jefferson's first term was his relationship with the judicial branch, particularly the Supreme Court. The Constitution had not fully explained either the organization or the role of this branch of government.

The Judiciary Acts With the Judiciary Act of 1789, Congress had filled in the missing details. The act created a national court system with three circuit courts and thirteen district courts, all headed by the Supreme Court. The act also stated that the Supreme Court would settle differences between state and federal laws.

Not long before Jefferson took office, Congress passed the Judiciary Act of 1801. This act decreased the number of Supreme Court justices and increased the number of federal judges. Outgoing members of Congress, in cooperation with President Adams, were trying to limit Jefferson's opportunity to appoint judges to the Supreme Court. They were also working to leave behind a powerful group of Federalist judges who would hold their jobs for life. Adams quickly filled the new judicial posts just before leaving office. These last-minute appointments, known as the **midnight judges,** angered Jefferson, who believed that he had the right to appoint judges from his own party.

One of Adams's judicial appointments was John Marshall, a longtime Federalist leader and cousin of Thomas Jefferson. At the time of his appointment, Marshall was serving as Secretary of State. Marshall was sworn in as Chief Justice (the leading judge of the Supreme Court) on February 4, 1801. He held that post for 34 years, until his death in 1835. While on the Supreme Court, Marshall helped establish many important principles of constitutional law. Marshall also helped build the prestige and authority of the Supreme Court in such cases as the historic **Marbury v. Madison** (1803).

Marbury v. Madison The case of *Marbury* v. *Madison* arose when President Jefferson tried to deny the appointments of Federalist judges. Just before he left office, President Adams had appointed William Marbury as justice of the peace for the District of Columbia. Yet Secretary of State James Madison, under orders from President Jefferson, never delivered the official papers giving Marbury his authority. Marbury sued Madison, demanding that the Supreme Court order the Secretary of State to let him take his office. According to the Judiciary Act of 1789, the Court had the power to give such an order.

Judicial Review Chief Justice John Marshall ruled against Marbury, declaring that it was against the Constitution for the Supreme Court to give this order to the executive branch. In other words, Marshall declared part of the Judiciary Act of 1789 unconstitutional—the first time a federal court had been so bold.

The Court's ruling was a victory for the Jefferson administration. Yet in a much larger sense it was a victory for the Supreme Court, for the case established the power of **judicial review.** The power of judicial review enables courts to decide whether laws passed by Congress are constitutional. It also

---

RESOURCE DIRECTORY

Other Print Resources

American History Block Scheduling Support *Checks and Balances: The Rise of the American Judiciary,* found in the Forging a New Nation folder, includes interdisciplinary lesson suggestions and activities for Geography and History, Primary Sources, Biography, and Literature.

Nystrom *Atlas of Our Country* *Early Expansion of the United States,* pp. 20–21

Historical Outline Map Book *Political United States,* p. 82

Technology

Color Transparencies *Historical Maps,* A9, A60

RESOURCE PRO® **Visual Learning Activity** *Honoring Thomas Jefferson,* found on Resource Pro, features a picture of Jefferson's burial monument, which shows the achievements for which he wanted to be remembered.

allows federal courts to review state laws and state court decisions to determine if they are in keeping with the federal Constitution. In this way, the Court plays an important role in preserving the federal union. Marshall, a Federalist, wanted to establish the supremacy of the national government over the states.

Judicial review is not clearly stated anywhere in the Constitution. Yet thanks in part to *Marbury v. Madison*, it remains a vital power of the judicial branch today.

Jefferson's Program in the West

As a strict constructionist, Jefferson opposed the development of a strong central government. In issues concerning American expansion west of the Appalachians, however, Jefferson and his supporters used the power and money of the national government as boldly as the Federalists had ever dared.

The Land Act of 1800 The Northwest Ordinance of 1787 had established a process by which territories, as lands in the West were called, could become states. The Jeffersonians encouraged the development of the frontier—which now extended only as far west as the Mississippi River—through a new federal land policy. Under the Land Act of 1800, adopted before Jefferson became President, Americans were able to buy land in small parcels and on credit. Federal land offices appeared across the West, making the transfer of land easier from the government to private citizens.

Napoleon and the French American farmers in the West depended on the Mississippi River to transport their crops to foreign markets. When the French ruler Napoleon took over much of the Spanish land in the West, he gained control of the mouth of the Mississippi at New Orleans. The French used this control to extract large sums of money from American traders who had no choice but to travel the Mississippi.

Fearing this French control and Napoleon's ambitions, Jefferson appointed James Monroe envoy extraordinary to France and sent him to Paris in 1803 to buy the city of New Orleans. Congress instructed Monroe, along with Robert Livingston, the American minister in Paris, that they could pay up to $10 million for the land. What happened next was one of the most fateful events in American history.

The Louisiana Purchase Napoleon did in fact have ambitions to create a new French Empire in the Americas. When his attempt to crush a rebellion on the French island of Haiti failed, however, he quickly changed his mind. Rather than sell only New Orleans to the United States, Napoleon wanted to sell all of the French claims known as Louisiana. Not daring to ask him to wait for weeks or months for an answer, Monroe and Livingston offered Napoleon $15 million for the **Louisiana Purchase.** They desperately hoped that Congress and the President would support their decision.

When Jefferson heard of the agreement with the French, he was troubled. The Constitution did not mention the purchase of foreign lands. He was also wary of spending large amounts of public money. Jefferson overcame his doubts, however, and urged Congress to approve the sale. With the stroke of a

VIEWING HISTORY Above are pages from the official treaty of the Louisiana Purchase. **Identifying Central Issues** (a) Why did Jefferson want to buy New Orleans from Napoleon? (b) How did the United States end up acquiring much more than New Orleans?

ACTIVITY
Connecting with Geography

Have students consult atlases to create a list of all of the current U.S. states whose territory was part of the Louisiana Purchase. They will need to compare a map of the Louisiana Purchase with a current political map of the United States to complete the task. **(Visual/Spatial)**

From the Archives of
AmericanHeritage®

About the Presidents

Thomas Jefferson (1801–1809) had a definite understanding with Aaron Burr during the election of 1800: Jefferson was running for President, Burr for Vice President. Nevertheless, Burr stayed in the competition when they both received the same number of electoral votes for President. Hamilton swung the vote in Jefferson's favor—only because he hated Jefferson less than Burr. Jefferson never trusted Burr again. In his second term, Jefferson chose New York governor George Clinton as running mate. Still blinded by dreams of glory, Burr led an unsuccessful revolt of western states in 1807. He was tried for treason. Before the verdict, Jefferson made it clear he thought Burr should be found guilty. But Burr was acquitted under the anti-Jefferson Chief Justice John Marshall. Source: Wilson Sullivan, "Thomas Jefferson," *The American Heritage® Pictorial History of the Presidents of the United States,* vol. 1, 1968.

CUSTOMIZE FOR …

Less Proficient Readers

Have students reread the text on judicial review and answer the following questions: Why is the power of the Supreme Court to judge a law's constitutionality important to the United States system of government? How does this power help the Supreme Court check the power of Congress? What would happen without the power of judicial review?

✓ **TEST PREPARATION**

Have students read the section about the Louisiana Purchase on this page and then answer the question below.

What was the original goal of the expedition of Lewis and Clark?

A To discover new Indian tribes in western lands.

B To find the shortest route to the Pacific Ocean.

Ⓒ To explore the land included in the Louisiana Purchase.

D To claim more territory for the United States.

CAPTION ANSWERS

Viewing History (a) To protect American interests in the region. Traders who needed to ship goods via the Mississippi had to go through New Orleans, which the French controlled. The French demanded that the Americans pay for the right to pass through. (b) Napoleon, whose strategic plans in the Americas fell apart, preferred to sell the entire Louisiana region to the United States.

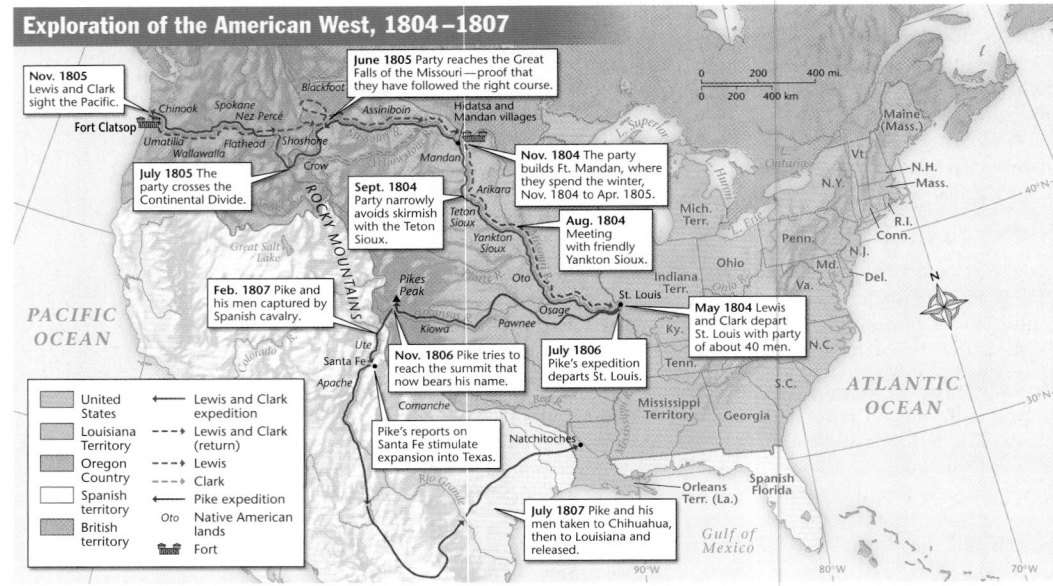
Exploration of the American West, 1804–1807

MAP SKILLS In their two-year expedition, Lewis and Clark explored thousands of miles and collected information on the lands, peoples, and plant and animal species they encountered. Their crossing of the Continental Divide proved once and for all that a water route to the Pacific did not exist. **Movement** Study the map above. What difficulties did the exploring parties face?

pen, the Louisiana Purchase dramatically increased both the national debt and the size of the United States. The Louisiana Purchase was to have an enormous impact on the history of the United States.

The Lewis and Clark Expedition Congress agreed to finance Jefferson's call for an expedition to explore the area included in the Louisiana Purchase. Jefferson chose Meriwether Lewis, his private secretary, to lead the expedition. Lewis in turn chose William Clark as his companion officer.

The **Lewis and Clark expedition** began in the spring of 1804. The expedition's goals were to search for river routes to the western ocean, make contact with the Native Americans living in the territory, and gather information about the region's natural resources. To help in this task, a year after setting out, the expedition hired a French-Canadian fur trapper and his wife Sacajawea, a Shoshone Indian, as interpreters.

The expedition reached the Pacific Ocean late in 1805 and returned east by September 1806. The journey, which had lasted two years and four months, succeeded in filling in many of the details of the vast lands to the west. Additional information about the West was gathered by Zebulon Pike, who traveled as far west as the Rockies and then south into Spanish-held territory between 1806 and 1807.

The Election of 1804

Jefferson's policies made him an extremely popular President during his first term. He succeeded in lowering taxes, acquiring vast new territory in the West, and allowing the unpopular Alien and Sedition Acts to expire. In addition to these domestic successes, he kept the nation at peace.

The Federalist Dilemma What had happened to the bitter rivalry between Federalists and Jeffersonian Republicans? The Federalists remained a strong force in national politics. However, the Louisiana Purchase, which they fiercely opposed, struck a great blow to their base of popular support. As the nation expanded into the new lands in the South and the West, the population of farmers, who tended to support the Jeffersonians, began to grow. The only real support for the Federalists came from the industrial centers of the Northeast. Even there, many people were happy with Jefferson's presidency. Jefferson, after all, had not dissolved the government or led the nation to ruin and tyranny, as some Federalists had feared.

Hamilton and Burr Meanwhile, Jefferson and his Vice President, Aaron Burr, had not worked very closely during Jefferson's first term. In fact, Burr, who had the support of the Federalists when the 1800 election was thrown to the House, decided to seek the governorship of New York in 1804. This time, Burr ran as a Federalist and not as a Jeffersonian Republican.

Alexander Hamilton, still a leading Federalist and patriot, strongly opposed Burr's bid for the governorship. Hamilton viewed Burr as an unprincipled man, concerned only with "interest and ambition." Determined to prevent Burr from the governorship, Hamilton urged his friends and followers in New York not to throw their support to Burr. Hamilton's efforts were successful. Burr did not even receive the Federalist nomination for governor of New York.

Burr was furious with Hamilton, for this was not the first time Hamilton had prevented Burr from scoring a political victory. In the 1800 election, Hamilton had urged Federalists to support Jefferson over Burr when the two candidates were tied in the electoral college. This time, Burr believed, Hamilton had gone too far. In the summer of 1804, Burr wrote to Hamilton and challenged him to a duel. Hamilton opposed duels, but he accepted the challenge so that he could prove his courage to a nation he might one day have to lead.

The two met on the morning of July 11, 1804, in northern New Jersey. They each fired a shot, and Hamilton fell, mortally wounded from a bullet below the chest. With one shot, Burr removed the leader of the Federalists and ruined his own political future. Usually, a duelist who had killed an opponent was not charged with murder. But this was not the case with Burr. In order to avoid prosecution, he fled New York, leaving behind his home and possessions. Burr's career following the duel went sharply downhill. He even attempted to invade Mexico and was tried for treason in 1807.

Jefferson Wins a Second Term The enormous success of Jefferson's first term, combined with a weakened Federalist Party, led to a landslide victory for Jefferson in 1804. Capturing all but two states, Jefferson defeated the Federalist candidate Charles Pinckney with 162 electoral votes to Pinckney's 14. Even the electoral votes from Massachusetts, a state dominated by Federalists, went to Jefferson.

Increasing Tensions With Europe

During Jefferson's first term, a brief peace had settled on European nations. When the European wars resumed, so too did troubles between Europe and the United States.

Focus on CULTURE

Dueling in America Dueling was a relatively common part of American culture in the early nineteenth century. The fateful duel between Hamilton and Burr in 1804 was not out of the ordinary. Duels were carefully planned out, provoked, and designed to restore or defend one's honor. After Hamilton foiled Burr's run for governor of New York in 1804, Burr, whose reputation was essentially ruined, needed a way to restore his honor.

According to the custom, the challenger needed specific evidence that their character had in fact been attacked. Once the evidence was gathered, the challenger could initiate a duel. Burr came across a newspaper in which it appeared Hamilton had attacked Burr's character. He quickly wrote a letter to Hamilton asking him to either deny or accept responsibility for these comments. Upon receiving the letter, Hamilton recognized immediately that Burr was looking for a duel. Not wanting to risk public ridicule and even the end of his political career, Hamilton did not back away from the challenge. Several letters passed between the two before the official duel was challenged, accepted, and arranged. Above, Hamilton's grave stands outside Trinity Church in New York City.

Chapter 6 • Section 3   **217**

Reading Comprehension

1. Refused to deliver speeches to Congress because doing so seemed too "kingly"; reduced taxes and severely cut the size of the federal bureaucracy.

2. Strengthened and helped define the role of the federal courts by allowing federal courts to determine the constitutionality of acts of Congress.

3. (a) Jefferson, a strict constructionalist, broke out of his role by purchasing foreign lands, an action not specifically outlined by the Constitution. (b) It increased the nation's debt.

4. Jefferson's desire to avoid the use of force in foreign policy led to an economic action: the passing of the Embargo Act of 1807. Many Americans objected to the embargo, despising the direct interference of the national government in the economy. Jefferson lost popularity and support.

Critical Thinking and Writing

5. Since they favored a weaker central government, stronger state governments, and protection of individual rights and freedoms, Jeffersonian Republicans might have felt that judicial review gave too much power to the federal government.

6. Possible answer: Both were examples of the people disobeying federal law and of the federal government using force to demand compliance.

7. Letters could include the following points: The embargo infringed upon the rights of ordinary citizens to make a living through trade. Also, it would not be effective because the foreign trade of both Britain and France was too strong and diverse to be severely injured.

Take It to the NET

Invite students to take a Virtual Field Trip at **www.phschool.com**

CAPTION ANSWERS

Interpreting Graphs (a) 1807: Approximately $105 million. (b) 1808: Approximately $20 million. (c) Not quite, although it did rebound to approximately $90 million in 1818.

United States Exports, 1800–1820

SOURCE: *Historical Statistics of the United States, Colonial Times to 1970*

INTERPRETING GRAPHS
The Embargo of 1807 sharply cut U.S. export trade. **Analyzing Information** *(a) What was the level of trade before the embargo? (b) After the embargo? (c) Did export trade return to its pre-embargo high during the period covered by the graph?*

The *Chesapeake* Jay's Treaty, under which the United States had remained at peace with Great Britain, expired in 1805. By then, Europeans were back at war with each other. French warships began harassing American ships trading with Britain, and British ships interfered with American ships trading with France. The British also kidnapped American sailors to serve in their navy. In 1807, a British ship, the *Leopard*, attacked the USS *Chesapeake*, inflicted 21 casualties, and boarded it to search for deserters from His Majesty's navy.

The Embargo of 1807 Like other Americans, Jefferson was outraged by these acts and believed that they should not go unpunished. Yet he rejected the use of force, in part because of the small size of the American navy. Instead, Jefferson chose an economic weapon against the British and French. At his insistence, Congress passed the Embargo Act of 1807, which outlawed almost all trade with foreign countries. An **embargo** is a restriction on trade. Britain's trade, however, had grown too strong to be severely injured by the embargo. The French, too, were largely unaffected.

Many Americans, on the other hand, hated the embargo—particularly New Englanders who made their living through trade. They now smuggled goods to Great Britain and other countries in defiance of the President and Congress. With the authority of the national government at stake, Jefferson had no alternative but to use his small navy and federal agents to enforce the law.

The embargo ruined Jefferson's second term. Many Americans despised the direct interference of the national government in the economy. Federalists exploited this anger, and the party enjoyed a revival. At the end of his second term, Jefferson retired to his home at Monticello, with his popularity shaken. Despite this loss of support for Jefferson and a Federalist revival, voters elected Jeffersonian Republican candidate James Madison President in 1808.

Section 3 Assessment

READING COMPREHENSION

1. What changes did Jefferson try to make in the relationship between government and the people?

2. Explain how **judicial review** shaped the role of the federal courts.

3. What effects did the **Louisiana Purchase** have on (a) national politics and (b) the national economy?

4. Why did Jefferson's foreign policy cause him to lose popularity in the United States?

CRITICAL THINKING AND WRITING

5. **Analyzing Information** Explain the position Jeffersonian Republicans would be likely to take on the principle of judicial review.

6. **Making Comparisons** How was the enforcement of the Embargo Act of 1807 like the suppression of the Whiskey Rebellion in 1794?

7. **Writing to Persuade** Write a letter to Thomas Jefferson from a Northeast merchant explaining why the Embargo Act should be lifted.

Take It to the NET

Activity: Virtual Field Trip Visit an online museum that focuses on the Lewis and Clark expedition. Write a brief essay describing an artifact or section of the trail that you were able to see. Be sure to describe the artifact or site in detail. Use the links provided in the *America: Pathways to the Present* area of the following Web site for help in completing this activity.
www.phschool.com

218 Chapter 6 • *The Origins of American Politics*

RESOURCE DIRECTORY

Teaching Resources
Units 1/2 booklet
• Section 3 Quiz, p. 66
Guide to the Essentials
• Section 3 Summary, p. 33

Creating an Oral or Visual Presentation

How can you make a historical event come alive for an audience? One way is to synthesize several kinds of sources to create an oral or visual presentation. Suppose your topic is the burning of Washington, D.C., by the British in 1814. Although there are no photographs or recordings of the event, you can show maps, diagrams, paintings, and drawings, or you can read aloud from primary sources such as newspaper accounts, letters, and journals. The author of Source A below was a captain in a British regiment that burned the White House. Source B was written in the White House by the First Lady.

LEARN THE SKILL
Use the following steps to create an oral or visual presentation:

1. **Explore a variety of sources.** Use a reliable secondary source for general information. Consider the topic: Are there likely to be letters or diaries? What visual depictions might be useful?

2. **Select and evaluate your sources.** Knowing the background of a writer or the source of a map helps you evaluate the information. For balance, try to select sources representing different points of view. Also vary the types of sources.

3. **Draw conclusions.** Determine the main points of each source. Combine different pieces of information to present and support your conclusions.

4. **Give life to your presentation.** Read excerpts from primary sources aloud as though you were the historical person who wrote them, show a variety of illustrations depicting the event, or combine oral and visual presentations for a more dramatic effect.

PRACTICE THE SKILL
Answer the following questions:

1. **(a)** Are Sources A and B primary or secondary sources? **(b)** How can you tell? **(c)** Taken together, do your sources represent one side of the War of 1812, or both sides?

2. **(a)** What information do you get from Source A that you would not get from the American side? **(b)** Do you think that this information is reliable? Explain. **(c)** What information do you get from Source B that you could not get from a newspaper account? **(d)** Evaluate Dolley Madison's reaction to the event.

3. **(a)** What is the main point of each excerpt? **(b)** Use what you already know and these sources to draw one or more conclusions about this event.

4. **(a)** What parts of each excerpt might make a good dramatic reading? **(b)** How might you use visuals in your presentation?

APPLY THE SKILL
See the Chapter Review and Assessment for another opportunity to apply this skill.

A

"[W]e entered Washington for the barbarous purpose of destroying the city. Admiral Cockburn would have burnt the whole, but [General] Ross would only consent to the burning of the public buildings. I had no objection to burn arsenals, dockyards . . . etc., but well do I recollect that . . . we were horrified at the order to burn the elegant Houses of Parliament [the Capitol] and the President's house. . . . I shall never forget the destructive majesty of the flames as the torches were applied to beds, curtains, etc."

—Harry Smith, *Various Anecdotes and Events of My Life*, 1846 (published 1901)

B

"Dear Sister—
My husband left me yesterday morning to join General Winder. . . .
    Three o'clock.—Will you believe it, my sister? We have had a battle, or skirmish, near Bladensburg, and here I am still, within sound of the cannon! Mr. Madison comes not. May God protect us! . . . Our kind friend, Mr. Carroll, has come to hasten my departure, and in a very bad humor [mood] with me, because I insist on waiting until the large picture of General Washington is secured, and it requires to be unscrewed from the wall. This process was found too tedious for these perilous moments; I have ordered the frame to be broken, and the canvas taken out. It is done! and the precious portrait placed in the hands of two gentlemen from New York, for safe keeping. And now, dear sister, I must leave this house, or the retreating army will make me a prisoner in it. . . . When I shall again write to you, or where I shall be tomorrow, I cannot tell!"

—Dolley Madison, August 23–24, 1814

CREATING AN ORAL OR VISUAL PRESENTATION

Focus Students learn how to use a variety of elements, including maps and primary sources, to build a presentation re-creating a historical event.

Instruct Ask students how they would re-create a historical event that took place in an era before photography or television. Remind them that in a situation such as a war, it might be necessary to use primary source documents and eyewitness accounts.

Have volunteers read the excerpts on the page. Then hold a class discussion on words or phrases that indicate the perspective of Dolley Madison and Harry Smith.

Extend See the Skills for Life activity in the Resource Directory below.

ANSWERS
PRACTICE THE SKILL

1. **(a)** They are primary sources. **(b)** Each is in the first person, describing events as they occurred. **(c)** Both sides.

2. **(a)** The British soldier was horrified at being asked to burn the Capitol and the White House. **(b)** Possible answer: It is reliable, insofar as it represents one person's perspective, written many years later. **(c)** Possible answer: Dolley Madison's feelings. **(d)** She seems to have remained calm and resourceful in the face of danger.

3. **(a)** Excerpt A: That some British soldiers in the War of 1812 were reluctant to destroy Washington, D.C. Excerpt B: That Dolley Madison gave less thought to her own safety than to preserving an important painting. **(b)** Possible answer: The destruction of Washington, D.C., by British forces was a terrifying event, and the First Lady came close to being captured by the British.

4. **(a)** Excerpt A: The description of flames engulfing the house. Excerpt B: Madison ordering the portrait to be taken. **(b)** Answers will vary, but students should include the portrait of George Washington.

Native American Resistance

SECTION OBJECTIVES

1. Find out what led to war between the United States and Native Americans in the Old Northwest.
2. See the different ways in which Native American leaders reacted to United States expansion.

BELLRINGER

Warm-Up Activity Ask students to define *accommodation* and *assimilation*. Ask whether they have ever accommodated to the wishes of a stronger power, such as an institution, or tried to become assimilated into a new group.

Activating Prior Knowledge Ask students to imagine the point of view of Native Americans in the Old Northwest. Have them consider the perspectives both of Native Americans who had not already been displaced from their native lands and of those who were newly experiencing this disruption and dislocation in the early 1800s.

READING STRATEGY

Have students write down the main headings in this section. As they read the section, have them make notes about the content that follows each heading.

CAPTION ANSWERS

Viewing History Sample answer: Tecumseh had to convince the various Native American groups to disregard their cultural differences and forget any existing conflicts. Many Indian groups had already been severely weakened by events such as the Revolution. Also, Tecumseh had to convince all groups to agree with his chosen approach to dealing with U.S. expansion.

RESOURCE DIRECTORY

Teaching Resources
Guided Reading and Review booklet, p. 27

Technology
Section Reading Support Transparencies
Guided Reading Audiotapes (English/Spanish), Ch. 6
Student Edition on Audio CD, Ch. 6
Prentice Hall Presentation Pro CD-ROM, Ch. 6
Companion Web site, www.phschool.com

READING FOCUS

* What led to war between the United States and Native Americans in the Old Northwest?
* In what different ways did Native American leaders react to United States expansion?

MAIN IDEA

As the United States continued to expand onto Native American lands, Indians responded in various ways, ranging from acceptance to war.

KEY TERMS

Battle of Fallen Timbers
Treaty of Greenville
reservation
assimilation
Battle of Tippecanoe

TAKING NOTES

Copy the chart below. As you read, fill in information about the views of the Native American leaders listed.

Native American Views

Leader	Strategy for Dealing With U.S. Expansion
Little Turtle	Accepted white culture; lived peacefully with white settlers; adopted some of their ways
Handsome Lake	
Tenskwatawa	
Tecumseh	

Setting the Scene Before the American colonies gained independence from Britain, relations between Native Americans and colonists often had been marked by violence. If anything, the creation of the United States had worsened the situation, as large numbers of European settlers had then moved westward onto Indian lands. A Shawnee chief declared:

VIEWING HISTORY William Henry Harrison reported that Tecumseh (above with a British general) wished to "form a combination of all the Indian Tribes . . . to put a stop to the encroachments of the white people." **Expressing Problems Clearly** *What difficulties did Tecumseh face in trying to unite Native American nations?*

66 *The being within, communing [communicating] with past ages, tells me that once, nor until lately, there was no white man on this continent; that it then all belonged to red men, children of the same parents, placed on it by the Great Spirit that made them, to keep it, to traverse [travel across] it, to enjoy its productions, and to fill it with the same race, once a happy race, since made miserable by the white people who are never contented but always encroaching [invading].* 99
—Tecumseh, 1810

War in the Old Northwest

The American Revolution had broken the power of the Iroquois nations in the North and beaten back the Cherokee in the South. In the early 1790s, however, the Miami, Delaware, Shawnee, and other Native American groups came together to fight American expansion. Assisted by the British in Canada and led by warriors such as Little Turtle and Blue Jacket, they defeated a United States army at Miamitown (present-day Fort Wayne, Indiana) in 1790. Then they defeated an expedition commanded by Northwest Territory Governor Arthur St. Clair, inflicting one of the biggest defeats ever suffered by a United States army in Indian warfare.

The British soon deserted the Native Americans, however. To add to their woes, Native Americans now faced a new national army known as the Legion of the United States. Realizing the skills and tools of this army, Little Turtle tried to persuade the other chiefs to seek a peace settlement rather than face military defeat.

The chiefs unwisely chose not to listen to Little Turtle's advice. In 1794, General "Mad Anthony" Wayne led the Legion to victory over the Native Americans at the **Battle of Fallen Timbers** in present-day northwestern Ohio. As a result of this battle, the Miami, Delaware, Shawnee, and other Native Americans were forced, in 1795, to accept the **Treaty of Greenville,** in which they relinquished the southern two thirds of Ohio. The treaty also forced them to accept that the Ohio River was no longer a permanent boundary between their lands and those of the white settlers. From New York to Indiana to Mississippi, Native Americans ended the 1700s in a greatly weakened condition.

Native American Reactions

In the early 1800s, several Native American leaders proposed different ways to deal with the United States. The options they suggested included four broad strategies: accepting white culture, blending Indian and white cultures, returning to Indian religious traditions, and taking military action.

Accepting White Culture Some Native Americans followed the path of Little Turtle, a leader of the Miami people. Though Little Turtle was a brilliant military leader who had engineered the great victories of the early 1790s, he later made peace with white settlers and lived in northern Indiana on annual payments from the government. Over time, Little Turtle adopted some of the settlers' customs. After devoting much of his life to fighting the white settlers, Little Turtle tried to live peacefully with them.

Blending Indian and White Cultures In western New York, a Seneca named Handsome Lake followed a different course. Handsome Lake had fought with the British against the Americans during the Revolutionary War. Later, he had been forced to live on a **reservation,** an area that the federal government set aside for Native Americans who had lost their homelands. In 1799, Handsome Lake called for a rebirth of Seneca culture that would blend Native American customs with those of the white Americans.

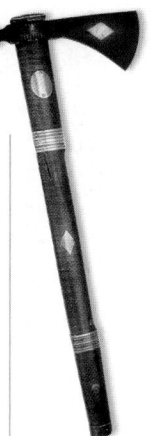

In 1807, Tecumseh presented this pipe tomahawk to Thomas Worthington, then senator and later governor of Ohio.

Chapter 6 • Section 4 **221**

Connecting with History and Conflict

Direct students to locate the texts of Tecumseh's speeches. Have them perform dramatic readings of selected portions for the class. **(Bodily/Kinesthetic)**

A Diverse Nation

More than two centuries before the Articles of Confederation, the Iroquois nation forged the first viable confederate government in North America. The Iroquois Confederacy (or League) united five Native American groups in the area of today's New York State into a defensive alliance, much as the Articles united the newly created states.

READING CHECK

To protest the methods by which Harrison and others were acquiring Native American lands, and to warn against the consequences of future acquisitions.

Handsome Lake urged Native Americans to abandon war and instead to give more attention to traditional Indian rituals. While holding on to age-old beliefs, Handsome Lake and his followers adopted white American notions about land, agriculture, and family life. While Little Turtle's way was acceptance, Handsome Lake's was acceptance on Native American terms. As he told President Jefferson:

> 66 Our lands are decaying because we do not think on [about] the Great Spirit, but we are now going to renew our Minds and think on the great Being who made us all. . . . Dear Brother, the Lord has confidence in your people as well as ours, provided we can settle all our Business. 99
> —Handsome Lake

VIEWING HISTORY The Shawnee prophet, Tenskwatawa, called on his followers to return to their ancient ways and obey the Master of Life. He said the Master of Life had told him: "If you Indians will do everything which I have told you, I will overturn the land, so that all the white people will be covered and you alone shall inhabit the land." **Recognizing Ideologies** *According to Tenskwatawa, how did assimilation threaten Native Americans?*

READING CHECK
Why did Tecumseh meet with Governor Harrison in 1810?

Returning to Indian Traditions In Indiana, another leader arose among the Shawnee, Delaware, and Miami. Tenskwatawa, also known simply as "the Prophet," called for a return to traditional Native American ways and a total rejection of European values. He strongly opposed **assimilation**, the process by which people of one culture merge into and become part of another culture.

In 1808, Tenskwatawa established Prophetstown on the Wabash River (near present-day Lafayette, Indiana). There, he offered his followers a sense of dignity and the promise of a stable life together. He also adopted an increasingly warlike attitude toward the United States. In this he was aided by his older brother, Tecumseh.

Taking Military Action Born in 1768, Tecumseh had fought against the United States in the 1780s and 1790s and had earned a reputation as a talented war chief. In 1795, he refused to participate in the talks that led to the Treaty of Greenville.

Tecumseh believed that the Indians' only hope of resisting U.S. expansion was to unite by overcoming local and group differences. He and Tenskwatawa acted on this belief by rallying opposition to the Treaty of Fort Wayne. In this treaty, negotiated in 1809 by Governor William Henry Harrison of the Indiana Territory, Native Americans had given up much of south-central Indiana. Like many treaties with Native Americans, this settlement made use of a legal trick. Because Native Americans held their land in common, they all had to agree before the status of the land could change. United States government officials would first persuade a few individuals to sign away their people's land, and then ignore protests from the rest of the group.

In August 1810, Tecumseh and several dozen warriors met with Governor Harrison to protest such a trick. Tecumseh warned that if the government continued to purchase lands, "it will produce war among the different tribes and at last I do not know what will be the consequence to the white people." Governor Harrison heeded the warning and moved first. While Tecumseh was in Alabama and Mississippi trying to get the Choctaw and the Creek to join in the resistance, Harrison marched north from Vincennes to Prophetstown with roughly 1,000 militia and soldiers.

Just before sunrise on November 7, 1811, Tenskwatawa sent his warriors to attack Harrison and his men. The **Battle of Tippecanoe** lasted about two hours. Neither side won, but the battle shattered Native American morale and eroded confidence in Tenskwatawa's leadership. Within a few days, Harrison burned an abandoned Prophetstown to the ground.

222 Chapter 6 • *The Origins of American Politics*

CAPTION ANSWERS

Viewing History Because assimilation into the culture of European settlers would make Native Americans forget their own traditions.

RESOURCE DIRECTORY

Teaching Resources
Units 1/2 booklet
  • Section 4 Quiz, p. 67
Guide to the Essentials
  • Section 4 Summary, p. 34
Learning with Documents booklet (Primary Source Activity) *Native American Politics,* p. 11
Biography, Literature, and Comparing Primary Sources booklet (Biography) *William Henry Harrison,* p. 11

Technology
RESOURCE PRO® **Primary Source Activity** *Native American Politics,* found on Resource Pro, uses excerpts from journals, letters, and speeches of both Native American and United States leaders to illustrate the pros and cons of westward expansion.
Exploring Primary Sources in U.S. History CD-ROM *Sell a Country! Why Not Sell the Air? Tecumseh*

VIEWING HISTORY Native Americans suffered great losses in the Battle of Tippecanoe. **Drawing Inferences** Why was this a turning point for Native American resistance?

Native American military resistance was not over, however. During the War of 1812 between the United States and Britain, Tecumseh rallied warriors to join the British in Canada. (See the next section.) When a British officer began to talk of retreat, Tecumseh responded:

 If you have an idea of going away, give [your weapons] to us, and you may go and welcome. As for us, our lives are in the hands of the Great Spirit. We are determined to defend our lands, and if it be his will we wish to leave our bones upon them. **"**

—Tecumseh

A few weeks later, on October 5, 1813, Tecumseh died in the Battle of the Thames in Ontario, Canada. Although Tecumseh and his brother did not accomplish their objectives, they left a vital legacy of defiance and respect for their people and their culture.

4 Assessment

READING COMPREHENSION

1. What were the causes of conflict between the United States and Native Americans in the Old Northwest?

2. How did the **Treaty of Greenville** affect Native Americans?

3. How did Tenskwatawa differ from Handsome Lake on the issue of accepting white American ideas and beliefs?

4. What was the outcome of the **Battle of Tippecanoe?**

CRITICAL THINKING AND WRITING

5. **Drawing Conclusions** Which of the Native American ways of dealing with United States expansion do you think was most successful? Explain your answer.

6. **Writing to Inform** Write an outline for an essay about the basic sources of conflict between Native Americans and Americans of European descent.

Activity: Writing an Editorial
Review the Treaty of Greenville between Native American tribes and the federal government. Create a newspaper editorial voicing your opinion in favor of or against the stipulations of this historic agreement. Use the links provided in the *America: Pathways to the Present* area of the following Web site for help in completing this activity.
www.phschool.com

Chapter 6 • Section 4   223

Section 4 Assessment

Reading Comprehension

1. Many Native Americans were not interested in becoming assimilated into the culture of white settlers. The most inflammatory issue was the tendency of white Americans to expand into Native American lands. Several Native American groups came together to forcibly resist further territorial expansion by white settlers.

2. Native Americans were forced to relinquish the southern two thirds of Ohio and to recognize that the Ohio River was no longer a permanent boundary between their lands and those of the white settlers, leaving the Native Americans in a greatly weakened condition.

3. Tenskwatawa strongly opposed assimilation by Native Americans into European culture, whereas Handsome Lake supported a blending of Native American customs with those of white Americans.

4. Neither side won, but the battle dissolved Native American morale and shattered confidence in Tenskwatawa's leadership.

Critical Thinking and Writing

5. Answers will vary, but should be supported with facts from the section.

6. Students' outlines should include the following points: White Americans wanted to transform the land into European-style farms. These settlers also kept demanding more and more land on which to grow crops. Native Americans were being pushed off their lands and tricked into unfair treaties. Some Native American cultures required large amounts of forest and untouched grassland to support their way of life.

Take It to the NET

Editorials should clearly and strongly support the student's position, using facts found in the online sources.

CAPTION ANSWERS

Viewing History The battle shattered Native American morale and eroded confidence in Tenskwatawa's leadership.

CUSTOMIZE FOR ...

Less Proficient Writers

What are other ways in which the United States might have dealt with Native Americans? Have students create a web graphic organizer that shows their responses.

SECTION OBJECTIVES

1. Find out why war broke out with Britain in 1812.
2. See how the war's end affected the United States.
3. Understand events that led to the economic panic of 1819.
4. Learn about issues that led to the Missouri Compromise.

BELLRINGER

Warm-Up Activity Ask students to think of times when they have had to compromise. When is compromise necessary? What elements are required for a compromise to work?

Activating Prior Knowledge Have students state their impressions of the relationship between Britain and the United States at the beginning of the nineteenth century.

READING STRATEGY

Have students make an outline using the headings in this section. As they read, have them fill in the main idea statements under each heading.

ACTIVITY
Connecting with History and Conflict

Tell students to research some of the underlying causes of the War of 1812, such as the conflict between Napoleon and Great Britain. Have students learn about the reasons for this conflict. Ask students to find out why the U.S. was caught in the conflict and how we became entangled in the war. **(Verbal/Linguistic)**

READING FOCUS

- Why did war break out with Britain in 1812?
- How did the war's end affect the United States?
- What events led to the economic panic of 1819?
- What issues led to the Missouri Compromise?

MAIN IDEA

Americans emerged from the War of 1812 with a new sense of national pride, but economic and moral conflicts continued to trouble the country.

KEY TERMS

impressment
War of 1812
Treaty of Ghent
Battle of New Orleans
depression
Missouri Compromise

TAKING NOTES

As you read, fill in the diagram below with the causes and effects of the War of 1812.

CAUSES
• Britain interferes with American trade overseas (impressment).

THE WAR OF 1812

EFFECTS
• The Treaty of Ghent restores the original boundaries between Britain and the United States.   •

The USS *Constitution* gained fame during the War of 1812. After an impressive victory against the British ship *Guerrière*, the warship became known as "Old Ironsides" because of its resilience to British shots. The *Constitution* remains to this day the oldest commissioned warship in the world still afloat.

Setting the Scene Following the Battle of Tippecanoe in November 1811, Native Americans increased their attacks against settlers who were moving onto their lands. Most Americans believed that the Indians were being encouraged and armed by the British:

❝ *In reviewing the conduct of Great Britain toward the United States our attention is necessarily drawn to the warfare just renewed by the [Native Americans] on one of our extensive frontiers. . . . It is difficult to account for the activity and combinations which have for some time been developing themselves among tribes in constant [dealings] with British traders and garrisons without connecting their hostility with that influence. . . .* ❞
—James Madison, message to Congress, 1812

War Breaks Out

Among those who blamed the British for the frontier violence were some members of Congress. Congress in 1812 included many new members from the South and West who represented the interests of farmers moving west onto Indian lands. The new members included Henry Clay of Kentucky and John C. Calhoun of South Carolina. The leaders of this new group were known as the War Hawks. They favored a war with Britain to push the British out of North America and thereby put a stop to Native American attacks in the West.

Anger Toward Britain In June 1812, President Madison sent a message urging Congress to declare war against the British. Madison argued that the British had not only encouraged the Indians to attack American settlers but had also interfered with United States shipping. For years, the American government had tried without success to stop the British practice of **impressment.** Impressment is the act of forcing people into military service. British ships

224   Chapter 6 • *The Origins of American Politics*

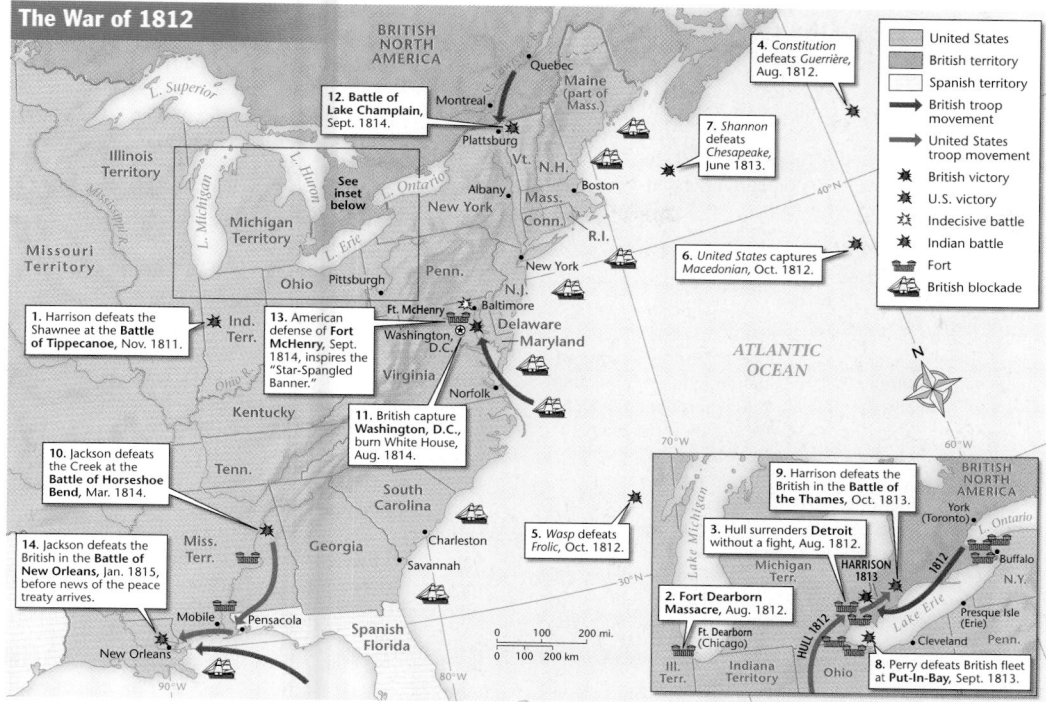

The War of 1812

12. Battle of Lake Champlain, Sept. 1814.

4. *Constitution* defeats *Guerrière,* Aug. 1812.

7. *Shannon* defeats *Chesapeake,* June 1813.

6. *United States* captures *Macedonian,* Oct. 1812.

1. Harrison defeats the Shawnee at the **Battle of Tippecanoe,** Nov. 1811.

13. American defense of **Fort McHenry,** Sept. 1814, inspires the "Star-Spangled Banner."

11. British capture **Washington, D.C.,** burn White House, Aug. 1814.

10. Jackson defeats the Creek at the **Battle of Horseshoe Bend,** Mar. 1814.

14. Jackson defeats the British in the **Battle of New Orleans,** Jan. 1815, before news of the peace treaty arrives.

5. *Wasp* defeats *Frolic,* Oct. 1812.

9. Harrison defeats the British in the **Battle of the Thames,** Oct. 1813.

3. Hull surrenders **Detroit** without a fight, Aug. 1812.

2. Fort Dearborn Massacre, Aug. 1812.

8. Perry defeats British fleet at **Put-In-Bay,** Sept. 1813.

Legend:
- United States
- British territory
- Spanish territory
- British troop movement
- United States troop movement
- British victory
- U.S. victory
- Indecisive battle
- Indian battle
- Fort
- British blockade

regularly stopped American ships at sea and removed men, including American citizens, to serve in the British navy. Congress approved Madison's call for war. The war that followed became known as the **War of 1812.**

In many ways, the declaration of war was a foolish action. The United States had only a small army and navy, and no offers of help from foreign countries. The nation would have to deal not only with the powerful British, but also with Native Americans to the north and south who were angered by western expansion.

The Land War Despite these disadvantages, Americans believed that the United States could strike swiftly and effectively at Britain by invading British-held Canada. To their surprise, American troops—poorly equipped and led—were beaten by the British in the summer of 1812.

The United States did manage *some* victories on land. William Henry Harrison defeated the British and Native Americans, including Tecumseh's forces, at the Battle of the Thames in October 1813. Andrew Jackson, a general who (like Harrison) would later be President, defeated the Creek Indians, who were British allies, at Horseshoe Bend in Alabama in March 1814. Jackson's army of 3,000 men and his superior weapons easily destroyed the Creeks, who tried to defend their land with about 1,000 men. The Americans massacred more than 800 warriors and imprisoned some 500 women and children. On August 9, 1814, the Creeks were forced to sign the Treaty of Fort Jackson by which they ceded 23 million acres of land, which made up most of present-day Alabama and southern Georgia. Victories such as these, however, were not enough to convince a great power like Britain to give up.

MAP SKILLS Although the United States considered the War of 1812 a victory over England, in the end neither side gained nor lost any territory. **Movement** *Why was the British naval blockade such a threat?*

LESSON PLAN

Focus Discuss the reasons that Congress declared war on Great Britain in 1812. Ask students to identify what the United States hoped to gain and what it actually accomplished.

Instruct Ask students to create a time line of major events in the War of 1812. Then have them write newspaper headlines on why the Battle of New Orleans united the country and restored patriotism.

Have students review Jefferson's comment at the end of the section about the Missouri Compromise. Ask students what they think Jefferson meant.

Assess/Reteach Ask students to describe various outcomes of the War of 1812. *(Some of the outcomes were concrete—such as the economic panic of 1819. Others were more subtle and abstract—such as an increased sense of national pride.)*

CUSTOMIZE FOR ...

Less Proficient Readers

Have students review the map on this page and make a list of the first five significant events in the War of 1812.

CAPTION ANSWERS

Map Skills It not only threatened the American economy, but it also allowed British troops access to the United States capital.

Connecting with Economics

War can take its toll—both emotionally and economically. But while the War of 1812 weakened the nation's economy, some wars, such as World War II, actually provide economic stimulus. Discuss with students ways in which war can mobilize the country. Suggest they consider the boost to war-related industries and the resulting jobs, both for civilians and those in combat. Encourage students to consider some of the other economic effects of war. **(Verbal/Linguistic)**

Biography

Francis Scott Key (1779–1843) was a successful lawyer in Washington, D.C., who wrote verse as a hobby. After the British burned Washington, Key went to the Chesapeake Bay to make sure that the British navy released a friend. Key stayed aboard a ship on the night of September 13, 1814, when the British attacked Fort McHenry. The following morning, after seeing the U.S. flag still flying, Key wrote a poem called "The Star-Spangled Banner." Although the Army and Navy adopted the song as the national anthem, it wasn't until 1931 that Congress officially voted "The Star-Spangled Banner" as our national anthem.

COMPARING PRIMARY SOURCES
For and Against the War of 1812

The War of 1812 was promoted by the War Hawks, mostly from the South and West, and opposed by leaders from New England and the Middle Atlantic states.

Analyzing Viewpoints Compare the main arguments made by the two writers.

For War With Britain

"We shall drive the British from our continent—they will no longer have an opportunity of intriguing [conspiring] with our Indian neighbors, and setting on the ruthless savage to tomahawk our women and children."

—Representative Felix Grundy of Kentucky, December 1811

Against War With Britain

"It was our own thirst for territory, our own want [lack] of moderation that had driven these sons of nature [Native Americans] to desperation, of which we felt the effects. . . . Go! March to Canada! . . . The coast is to be left defenseless, while men of the interior are reveling in conquest and spoil."

—Representative John Randolph of Virginia, December 1811

British troops burn government buildings as they storm through Washington, D.C., in 1814.

The Naval War Despite the fact that British ships outnumbered American vessels by about twenty to one, Americans at first won a number of victories at sea. The United States had a half-dozen frigates, or medium-sized sailing warships, that won several battles against the British. American victories fought by the crews of the *Constitution* ("Old Ironsides"), the *Wasp*, and the *United States* raised the country's morale. In addition, American privateers captured more than 1,000 British ships.

The Americans suffered a number of naval defeats, however. In 1813, a British warship fought and captured the American warship *Chesapeake* off the coast of Massachusetts. The dying order of *Chesapeake* captain James Lawrence, "Don't give up the ship," became the battle cry of the United States Navy.

The war's most important naval victory took place in the summer of 1813. Master Commandant Oliver Hazard Perry defeated a small British fleet on Lake Erie, enabling the United States to control that lake and protect a vital stretch of its northern border. "We have met the enemy, and they are ours," Perry reported after more than three hours of the war's bloodiest naval battle.

In time, the superiority of the British navy began to have an effect. The British blockaded the United States coast, strangling trade and putting a stop to the attacks made by American frigates.

The Burning of Washington, D.C. In 1814, the British ended a difficult and dangerous war they had been fighting against the French emperor, Napoleon Bonaparte, in Europe. They then turned their attention to the war in the United States. Some 14,000 British troops tried to invade the United States from Canada in the late summer of 1814. To the surprise of the British, however, a much smaller American force drove them back across the border.

By contrast, a fleet of British ships that arrived in Chesapeake Bay at about the same time scored a major success. About 4,000 British troops left the ships and descended on Washington, D.C., meeting little serious opposition. On August 24, President James Madison and his wife, Dolley Madison, were warned of the approach of the British and fled. Toward evening, the British entered the capital and started fires that consumed the city. Even the Capitol and the White House were gutted by flames.

From Washington, the British troops moved on toward Baltimore. Lawyer Francis Scott Key witnessed an all-night British bombardment of Fort McHenry, at the entrance to Baltimore harbor. Key wrote the following words as a testimony to the Americans' determination to stand strong against an overwhelming enemy:

226 Chapter 6 • *The Origins of American Politics*

RESOURCE DIRECTORY

Teaching Resources

Learning with Documents booklet (Key Documents) *The Star-Spangled Banner,* p. 78

Biography, Literature, and Comparing Primary Sources booklet (Literature) *An Illustrious Career,* pp. 45–46

Biography, Literature, and Comparing Primary Sources booklet (Comparing Primary Sources) *For and Against the War of 1812,* pp. 107–108

Technology

Sounds of an Era Audio CD *The Star-Spangled Banner*

Exploring Primary Sources in U.S. History CD-ROM *On the Burning of Washington, D.C., Dolley Madison; The Star-Spangled Banner, Francis Scott Key*

❝ *And the rocket's red glare,*
the bombs bursting in air
Gave proof through the night
that our flag was still there.
O say, does that Star-Spangled Banner yet wave
O'er the land of the free
and the home of the brave? ❞

—Francis Scott Key, "The Star-Spangled Banner"

Sounds of an Era

Listen to the "Star-Spangled Banner" and other sounds from our nation's early years.

The "star-spangled banner" did indeed still wave over the fort. The citizens of Baltimore had been strengthening their defenses, and American forces were able to turn back the enemy.

The War Ends

The British retreat from Baltimore lifted American spirits, but not all Americans felt as patriotic about the War of 1812 as did Francis Scott Key. Critics bitterly called it "Mr. Madison's War," while pointing to the harm it had done to the country. The national treasury was empty, the Capitol lay in ruins, and the British blockade had brought trade to a standstill.

The Hartford Convention New Englanders had suffered tremendous losses in trade during the war. In December 1814, they sent delegates to a meeting in Hartford, Connecticut, to consider the possibility of leaving the nation. In the end, however, the Hartford Convention called only for constitutional amendments to increase New England's political power.

The Treaty of Ghent Meanwhile, both the British and the Americans had recognized that this was a war no one wanted, and one the British realized they could not win. On December 24, 1814, representatives of the two nations met in Belgium and signed the **Treaty of Ghent,** ending the war. The treaty did not resolve the issues for which the United States declared war—the British practice of impressment and respect for the neutral rights of the United States. However, all the old boundaries between the United States and British territory in North America were restored.

Despite the questionable terms of the treaty, many in the United States seemed happy with the treaty and the end of the war. Some Americans called the war the "Second War of Independence," for now the United States had fully established itself as an independent nation in the eyes of the European powers.

The Battle of New Orleans Although the Treaty of Ghent had officially ended the war, the greatest victory for the United States came two weeks after the treaty was signed. This final twist to a strange war was the result of the slow communication of the times. News of the Treaty of Ghent did not reach the United States until mid-February 1815.

On December 23, 1814, a British force of more than 5,000 men tried to take New Orleans from the south. General Andrew Jackson and 5,000 soldiers and volunteers from all over the Mississippi Valley, including two battalions of free African Americans, defended the city.

On January 8, the overconfident British, fresh from victories over the French in Europe, foolishly threw their troops against the Americans' well-protected positions. Without cover, the advancing British were easy targets for

Focus on ECONOMICS

Wartime Manufacturing When the British blockaded the American coast during the War of 1812, they unintentionally did New England a big favor. Before the war, New England had developed a small manufacturing sector, but it had difficulty competing with imports from Britain, where factories operated on a larger scale with more advanced technologies. New Englanders generally preferred to invest in overseas trade, where they could make a better profit.

The British blockade ruined New England shipping, but it also cut the United States off from British imports. New Englanders rushed to invest in manufacturing. As a result, New England's manufacturing sector expanded. In addition, because the British blockade meant that British imports could not get into the United States, New England manufacturers were able to capture a growing share of the American market. By the end of the war, New England had developed larger and more advanced textile mills and machine shops that could compete effectively with British producers. Little did the British know that their blockade would help create such a strong economic competitor!

ACTIVITY
Connecting with History and Conflict

Assign students the task of learning more about the Hartford Convention (who participated, what their motives were, and so forth), including the constitutional amendments the convention proposed. Have students write brief essays about their findings. **(Verbal/Linguistic)**

BACKGROUND
Connections to Today

An intense spirit of nationalism ensued after both the American Revolution and the War of 1812. This unifying spirit, which usually accompanies times of conflict, was conspicuously absent during the Vietnam War in the 1960s and 1970s. Many citizens protested openly against the war on a grand scale, and many refused to join the armed forces.

From the Archives of
American Heritage®

About the Presidents

James Madison (1809–1817) understood clearly that Americans were divided about waging a war with Britain. But he had already tried diplomacy, embargo, and threats. American ships and seamen were still being harassed. The war vote in Congress reflected the nation's disunity—79 to 49 in the House, 19 to 13 in the Senate. Not surprisingly, Congress was slow to approve funds for fighting the war. And though the frontier states were united in the war effort, the New England states refused to be involved. In fact, the Treaty of Ghent settled few of the issues that started the war. But the President's prestige was enhanced for standing up to the world's strongest empire. Source: Vincent Buranelli, "James Madison," *The American Heritage® Pictorial History of the Presidents of the United States,* vol. 1, 1968.

✓ TEST PREPARATION

Have students read the section "The War Ends" and then complete the sentence below.

The Treaty of Ghent set the boundaries of the United States—

A on all four sides.

B where they are today.

Ⓒ back where they were before the war.

D with French territories.

VIEWING HISTORY This exaggerated painting highlights the new hero that the Battle of New Orleans gave to the United States: Andrew Jackson, shown riding a white horse. **Analyzing Visual Information** *How does this painting both contribute to and reflect the American reaction to the Battle of New Orleans?*

American riflemen. The battle was finished in just over an hour; in fact, most of the shooting took place in about 20 minutes. The British suffered more than 2,000 casualties; the Americans, a little more than 20.

The **Battle of New Orleans** was a remarkable victory for the United States. The battle allowed Americans to end an unhappy war on a powerful, positive note. The battle unified the country, restored patriotism, and made Andrew Jackson a national hero.

Postwar Boom and Panic

In 1815, the United States entered a period of growth and prosperity. Republican James Monroe, the former governor of Virginia, easily won election as the fifth President of the United States in 1816. Monroe and the Republican Party dominated American politics, as the Federalists faded out of existence.

The First Bank of the United States had dissolved in 1811, leaving the country with no central financing for the war. Congress, in an attempt to deal with financial problems resulting from the war, created the Second Bank of the United States in 1816. Encouraged by abundant credit from this bank and others, as well as by federal land laws, Americans began moving westward at an incredible rate. Meanwhile, American ships were busy carrying farm products and other goods to Europe.

Then, in 1819, the United States experienced the first **depression,** or severe economic downturn, in its history. Known as the Panic of 1819, it began across the Atlantic when London banks demanded that banks in the United States pay money owed to them. American banks, in turn, demanded the money that they had loaned to the American public. Many of the Americans who had borrowed too much in the days of easy loans after 1815 were financially ruined.

The Missouri Compromise

The economy would eventually rebound from the depression, but another problem that year posed a far greater long-term danger to the nation. In 1819, Congress began debating the admission of the state of Missouri to the United States. The basic issue at stake was slavery.

The Northwest Ordinance of 1787 had established that no state northwest of the Ohio River could be a slave state (that is, a state in which slavery was legal). Because Missouri was not northwest of the Ohio River, however, it was not covered by this definition. Several members of Congress from the North

READING CHECK
Why did some members of Congress from the North object to admitting Missouri as a slave state?

objected to admitting Missouri as a slave state. They were not simply concerned about the liberty of African Americans; they worried that another slave state would increase the power of the southern states in the Senate. At that time, there existed 11 free states and 11 slave states. Representative James Tallmadge of New York attached an amendment to the Missouri statehood bill, calling for a gradual end to slavery in Missouri. The bill passed the House but failed in the Senate.

Southern members of Congress believed that the federal government had no business telling states what they could and could not do. If the federal government could forbid slavery in Missouri, they feared, it could do so elsewhere.

After months of bitter debate, Congress, under the leadership of Henry Clay, reached what is now called the **Missouri Compromise.** It was signed into law in 1820. The Missouri Compromise had two main points: (1) Slavery would be permitted in Missouri; at the same time, Maine was carved out of what had been northern Massachusetts and admitted to the Union as a free, or nonslave, state. This arrangement kept the balance in the Senate between slave and free states at 12 each. (2) Furthermore, Congress agreed that as the United States expanded westward, states north of 36° 30' N latitude (the southern border of the Missouri state line) would be free states, as the map on this page shows.

By the mid-1820s, both the Panic of 1819 and the Missouri controversy had faded from public attention. The economy had recovered and politicians agreed to avoid the difficult issue of slavery. However, the economic and moral questions raised by these events were not going to go away.

To Thomas Jefferson, still a keen observer of the national scene, the Missouri controversy sounded "like a fire bell in the night" and "filled [him] with terror." Could compromises enable the United States to avoid confronting the issue of slavery indefinitely? As Jefferson had written earlier about the existence of slavery in a democratic republic: "I tremble for my country when I reflect that God is just, that His justice cannot sleep forever."

The Missouri Compromise, 1820

Legend:
- States formed by Missouri Compromise
- Free states and territories closed to slavery
- Slave states and territories open to slavery

MAP SKILLS Under the terms of the Missouri Compromise, Maine was admitted as a free state, Missouri was admitted as a slave state, and slavery was prohibited north of 36°30'N latitude. **Region** Which would cover more land under the compromise, new free states or new slave states?

Reading Comprehension

1. White farmers residing in western Indian lands. The War Hawks sought war in order to push the British out of North America and thereby stop Native American attacks against western settlers.
2. The Treaty of Ghent restored old boundaries between United States and British territory in North America. It did not resolve the British practices of impressment and scorn for the neutral rights of the United States.
3. It greatly boosted the morale and patriotism of the country; Andrew Jackson became a national hero.
4. London banks demanded money owed by the United States. American banks in turn demanded the money they had loaned to the American people, many of whom were unable to repay it.
5. It allowed Missouri to be admitted as a slave state, prohibited further slavery north of 36°30' N latitude, and brought Maine into the Union as a free state.

Critical Thinking and Writing

6. The motives for fighting the war seemed to benefit some more than others. For example, those on the frontier needed protection against Native Americans, while New Englanders, who were less involved geographically, suffered a trade disruption.
7. Weaknesses: small army and navy, no foreign assistance, no central bank to finance war, two adversaries (Native Americans and British) to fight simultaneously, regional opposition to the war; Strengths: fighting on home ground, making supply easier; high quality of the (very small) American Navy.
8. Lists should include some of the following points. For war: drive out British, who are (it seems) encouraging Native American attacks on western settlers; stop impressment. Against war: will leave East Coast unprotected, will disrupt trade with Britain, American army and navy too small to win.

READING COMPREHENSION

1. Whom did the War Hawks represent, and why did they want war against Britain?
2. What were the results of the **War of 1812?**
3. How did the Battle of New Orleans affect Americans' attitudes toward the War of 1812 and their country?
4. Why did the United States experience a **depression** in 1819?
5. How did the **Missouri Compromise** deal with the issue of slavery?

CRITICAL THINKING AND WRITING

6. **Synthesizing Information** Why did different sections of the country have different attitudes toward the War of 1812?
7. **Making Comparisons** Compare the strengths and weaknesses of the American military during the War of 1812.
8. **Writing to Persuade** List reasons you would use in an essay persuading members of Congress to vote for or against war with Britain in 1812.

Take It to the NET

Activity: Writing a Diary Entry Read firsthand accounts from the War of 1812. How is the conflict described? Based on what you've read, create a diary entry as if you were a citizen during the period. Use the links provided in the *America: Pathways to the Present* area of the following Web site for help in completing this activity. **www.phschool.com**

Chapter 6 • Section 5   229

Take It to the NET

Diary entries should reflect the mood and spirit of the people who witnessed or participated in the War of 1812.

CAPTION ANSWERS

Map Skills New free states.

REVIEWING KEY TERMS

Students should refer to the definitions of key terms in the chapter to write sentences that show an understanding of the key aspects of the origins of American politics.

REVIEWING MAIN IDEAS

16. Hamilton did this by having the federal government take on the states' debts. Hamilton thus transformed the debts of all the states into a long-term investment in the United States government by the country's foreign creditors.

17. George Washington and his administration knew that federal laws would not mean anything to people unless they were enforced by the federal government.

18. Sample answer: Federalists believed in a strong central government to maintain order in the country, favored a national bank, were pro-business, and believed political power should rest with the wealthy and educated. Jeffersonian Republicans favored a weakened central government and strong state governments, opposed a national bank, were pro-agriculture, and believed that the common man should hold political power.

19. The goals of the rebellion were to attain freedom from slavery and give a voice to African Americans in the developing government, reflecting the idea of liberty.

20. In 1776 the Declaration of Independence announced to the world the complete break of the American states with Britain. With the election of 1800, the government began to focus on encouraging liberty over order, marking a significant shift in principles as well as new ideas and attitudes about the role and philosophy of government.

21. The Constitution did not address the purchase of foreign lands, and Jefferson was wary of spending large amounts of public money.

22. To search for river routes to the western ocean, make contact with the Native Americans living in the territory, and gather information about the region's natural resources.

---

creating a CHAPTER SUMMARY

Copy the flowchart (right) on a piece of paper and complete it by adding information about the choices or actions taken by the group identified in each heading.

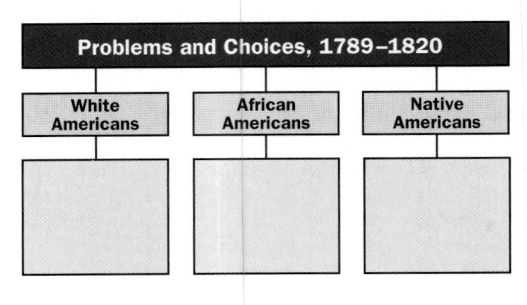

For additional review and enrichment activities, see the interactive version of *America: Pathways to the Present*, available on the Web and on CD-ROM.

Problems and Choices, 1789–1820

White Americans	African Americans	Native Americans

★ Reviewing Key Terms

For each of the terms below, write a sentence explaining how it relates to the period following ratification of the Constitution.

1. tariff
2. strict construction
3. Jay's Treaty
4. political party
5. XYZ affair
6. Alien and Sedition Acts
7. Virgina and Kentucky Resolutions
8. judicial review
9. Louisiana Purchase
10. embargo
11. Treaty of Greenville
12. assimilation
13. impressment
14. Treaty of Ghent
15. Missouri Compromise

★ Reviewing Main Ideas

16. How was Alexander Hamilton able to change the national debt from a weakness to a strength? (Section 1)
17. Why was the federal government determined to crush the Whiskey Rebellion? (Section 1)
18. Compare the views of Federalists and Jeffersonian Republicans in the 1790s. (Sections 1 and 2)
19. How did Gabriel Prosser's Rebellion reflect the political ideas of the time? (Section 2)
20. Explain why Jefferson called the election of 1800 "as real a revolution in the principles of our government as that of 1776 was in its form." (Section 2)

21. Why was the decision to approve the purchase of Louisiana from Napoleon a difficult one for Jefferson? (Section 3)
22. What was the purpose of the Lewis and Clark expedition? (Section 3)
23. What were Tenskwatawa and Tecumseh's beliefs about the path that Native Americans should follow? (Section 4)
24. What were the causes of the War of 1812? (Section 5)

★ Critical Thinking

25. **Identifying Assumptions** Today we expect a peaceful transfer of power when Americans vote to change political parties in a presidential election. Why were people unable to make this assumption in the election of 1800?
26. **Drawing Conclusions** How did John Marshall help establish the authority of the Supreme Court?
27. **Drawing Inferences** Why do you think Tecumseh had difficulty uniting Native Americans to resist the expansion of white people onto their lands?
28. **Predicting Consequences** Thomas Jefferson said that the Missouri Compromise "filled [him] with terror." Why might Jefferson have viewed the compromise with such fear?

CREATING A CHAPTER SUMMARY

Problems and Choices, 1789–1820

White Americans	African Americans	Native Americans
• Whiskey Rebellion	• Northwest Ordinance	• Forming allegiances to fight United States incursions
• Trouble with France	• Missouri Compromise	• Stress of blending Indian and white cultures
• Conflict over Alien and Sedition Acts; Virginia and Kentucky Resolutions		• Struggle to retain Indian traditions
• Tensions between Federalists and Jeffersonian Republicans		• Military actions
• Prosser's rebellion		• Battle of Tippecanoe
• XYZ affair		

★ Skills Assessment

Analyzing Political Cartoons ▶

29. During the Embargo of 1807, smuggling increased dramatically. (a) How do you know the man with the barrel is a smuggler? (b) What is *Ograbme* spelled backwards? (c) What does the turtle represent?

30. How does Ograbme depict the embargo's effect on traders?

31. What is the cartoonist's view of the Embargo of 1807?

Interpreting Data

Look at the graph of United States exports in Section 3.

32. In which year was the value of United States exports the highest?

A 1801
B 1807
C 1810
D 1818

33. Which of the following events explains the drop in trade between 1810 and 1814?

F the Embargo of 1807
G the Missouri Compromise
H the War of 1812
J the Louisiana Purchase

34. Before the embargo, what was the general trend in exports during the Jefferson administration?

A Exports were sharply decreasing.
B Exports generally remained at the same level.
C A general trend cannot be determined from the information given.
D Exports generally increased.

Applying the Chapter Skill:
Creating an Oral or Visual Presentation

35. Review the steps needed to create a presentation. Then, research and prepare an oral presentation about either George Washington or Thomas Jefferson. Use visual aids to add interest to your presentation.

ACTIVITIES

 Writing to LEARN

Writing a Letter to the Editor
The election of 1800 is rapidly approaching. Write a letter to the editor of your local newspaper explaining why you plan to vote for Thomas Jefferson or John Adams. List reasons why you support your candidate and oppose the other candidate. Note the direction you would like to see the nation take during the next presidential term, and explain why your candidate is the best person to lead the country in that direction.

💿 **Primary Source CD-ROM**

Working With Primary Sources Find additional information on the origins of American politics on the *Exploring Primary Sources in U.S. History CD-ROM* and use the selection(s) provided to complete the Chapter 6 primary source activity located in the *America: Pathways to the Present* area of the following Web site.
www.phschool.com

🖥 **Take It to the NET**

Chapter Self-Test As a review activity, take the Chapter 6 Self-Test in the *America: Pathways to the Present* area at the Web site listed below. The questions are designed to test your understanding of the chapter content.
www.phschool.com

Chapter 6 Assessment   **231**

---

23. Tenskwatawa strongly opposed assimilation by Native Americans into European culture. He called for a return to traditional Native American ways. Tecumseh favored united military action against American settlers.

24. Many members of Congress believed that the British were inciting and arming Native Americans in the west to attack American settlers. Americans were also offended by Britain's ongoing practice of impressment.

CRITICAL THINKING

25. Because that election campaign was exceedingly bitter, the electoral vote was tied between Burr and Jefferson, and Jefferson was only able to prevail after 36 ballots had been taken in the House of Representatives.

26. Marshall helped establish many important principles of constitutional law, used judicial review to establish a better check against the other branches of government, and generally helped build the prestige and authority of the Supreme Court.

27. Possible answer: Because not all Native Americans realized that the treaties made with white Americans contained "legal tricks" that robbed Native Americans of large tracts of land.

28. The compromise failed to resolve the important question of slavery, leaving the issue as a simmering problem ready to boil over at any time. Jefferson undoubtedly feared that the unresolved issue of slavery could lead to war or to the dissolution of the country. It also appears that Jefferson had moral qualms about allowing slavery to continue.

SKILLS ASSESSMENT

29. (a) Because he is carrying goods to a British ship (seen in the harbor). (b) Embargo. (c) The Embargo of 1807.

30. It indicates that the embargo is hurting the tradesman (smuggler) by restraining him from conducting business.

31. The cartoonist is opposed to the embargo because it hurts trade.

32. B
33. H
34. C
35. Students' presentations should be informative and well researched.

Checks and Balances in the Federal Government

The Constitution separates the federal government into three branches—executive, legislative, and judicial—each with its own powers. Each branch acts as a check, or restraint, on the other branches. Over the years, one branch or another has sometimes gained a momentary advantage through powers such as the veto, impeachment, and judicial review.

 A New Government Is Formed

1777–1789 To strengthen the national government, the Constitutional Convention replaced the Articles of Confederation with a new Constitution. The Framers hoped the checks and balances they built into the Constitution would prevent the new government from abusing its power.

Independence Hall, Philadelphia, Pennsylvania (right)

The Court Takes a Bold Step

1789–1824 Congress breathed life into the Supreme Court through its Judiciary Acts. Under the leadership of Chief Justice John Marshall, the Court then flexed its muscles by asserting its right to judge the constitutionality of actions taken by the other two branches and by the states.

 The Age of Jackson

1828–1836 President Andrew Jackson, a popular war hero and a man of forceful opinions, strengthened the executive branch. His administration instituted democratic reforms that influenced American politics for many years.

Portrait of Andrew Jackson (left)

232

Reconstruction

1863–1877 The President and Congress fought over which branch would control the process of Reconstruction. During this fight, President Andrew Johnson became the first President to be impeached by the U.S. House of Representatives. In the end, Congress won the power struggle, and their more radical plan for Reconstruction became law.

A ticket for the impeachment trial of Andrew Johnson (left)

The New Deal and Presidential Term Limits

1932–1951 In response to Franklin Roosevelt's election four times as President, and in an effort to place limits on executive power, Congress proposed and the states ratified the Twenty-second Amendment, which says that no President may serve more than two elected terms.

The inauguration of Franklin D. Roosevelt (above)

The Cold War and Watergate

1950–Present In fighting communism after World War II, Presidents assumed greater power by deploying American military forces without a formal declaration of war by Congress. Congress regained some power after Watergate and with the passage of the War Powers Act in 1973. However, critics of executive branch power still speak of the "imperial presidency."

President John F. Kennedy and Soviet Premier Nikita Khrushchev on June 4, 1961 (above left) and the Senate Watergate hearings (above right)

Continuity and Change

1. Name a power that each branch of the United States government can use to keep each of the other branches in check.
2. In which era did the balance of power seem to shift to Congress? In which era did it seem to shift to the President? In which era did it seem to shift to the Supreme Court?

 Take It to the NET: Creating a Study Guide
Print and complete the study guide for this topic found in the *America: Pathways to the Present* area of the following Web site. **www.phschool.com**

233

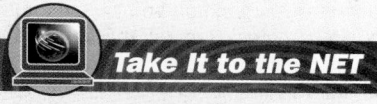

Take It to the NET

Students can print the American Pathways thematic study guide for this topic at the Prentice Hall School Web site, or you can provide students with copies of the study guide, which is found in the Units 1/2 booklet, the American Pathways Activity, pages 75–76. Students should use their texts to fill in a one-sentence description for each event on the study guide. When completed for each of the American Pathways topics, the thematic study guides will aid students in preparing for an end-of-course exam.

ANSWERS

1. Possible answers: The executive can veto acts of the legislature and appoint members of the federal judiciary. The legislature can impeach the President or any federal judge and can refuse to confirm presidential appointments of judges or other high officials. The judicial restrains the executive and the legislature through the power to declare the acts of either unconstitutional.

2. Power shifted toward Congress during Reconstruction and again with the passage of the War Powers Act in 1973. Power shifted toward the President during the Age of Jackson, the New Deal, and the Cold War. Power shifted toward the Supreme Court during the late 1700s and the early 1800s with the Judiciary Acts and the case of *Marbury* v. *Madison*, the latter of which affirmed the Court's right of judicial review.

TEST PREPARATION

Use this sample exam to help your students prepare for standardized tests.

TIPS FOR TEST TAKING

You might want to remind your students of the following:

1. Read the directions carefully.

2. Read each question carefully.

3. For multiple choice questions, try to answer the question before you look at the choices. Read all the choices. Then, eliminate those that are absolutely incorrect.

4. For short answer questions, be sure to answer the question completely if there is more than one part.

5. Answer the easy questions first. Then, go back to the ones that will take more time.

6. Pace yourself. Be sure to set aside enough time for the writing questions.

Write your answers on a separate sheet of paper.

1. Benjamin Franklin wanted the colonists to accept the Albany Plan of Union because

  A the colonies would be stronger if they were united.

  B it would make cooperation with France easier.

  C the British government wanted a single colonial government.

  D it would unite the Iroquois and the British colonists.

2. Which one of the following was used in the colonies to protest the Stamp Act?

  A A strike of workers in the cities

  B A march of colonists on Philadelphia

  C A boycott of British goods

  D A treaty with France

> "The period of debate is closed. Arms as the last resource decide the contest ... Every thing that is right or reasonable pleads for separation ... 'TIS TIME TO PART."
>
> —*Thomas Paine*, Common Sense

3. In this quotation, Thomas Paine is arguing for

  A the separation of church and state.

  B the return of colonial envoys in London to report to the Continental Congress.

  C a reasonable debate with Britain about colonial rights.

  D a war for independence.

4. According to the social contract theory, a government gets its power from

  A the power of the monarch.

  B the consent of the governed.

  C written constitutions.

  D traditions and customs.

5. The Battle of Saratoga was a turning point in the Revolutionary War because

  A it led the French to form an alliance with the Patriots.

  B the entire British army surrendered.

  C the British navy lost nine major ships.

  D it caused many Native Americans to join the Patriot cause.

6. The system of government set up by the Articles of Confederation included

  A a congress to make the laws.

  B an agency to collect a national income tax.

  C national judges to apply the laws.

  D an executive to carry out the laws.

PRENTICE HALL
ASSESSMENT
SYSTEM

Diagnose and Prescribe
- Profile student skills with Diagnostic Tests A&B.
- Address student needs with program materials correlated to test questions.

Review and Reteach
- Provide cumulative content review with the Review Book.

Practice and Assess
- Build test-taking skills with Test-taking Strategies With Transparencies.

Use the diagram and your knowledge of social studies to answer the following question.

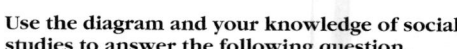
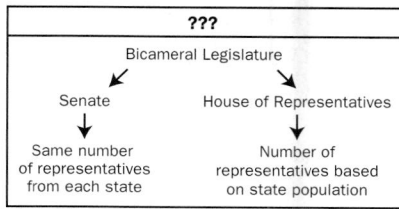

```
┌──────────────────────────────────────────────┐
│                     ???                        │
│                                                │
│             Bicameral Legislature              │
│            ↙                    ↘              │
│       Senate              House of Representatives │
│          ↓                        ↓            │
│    Same number              Number of          │
│    of representatives       representatives based │
│    from each state          on state population │
└──────────────────────────────────────────────┘
```

7. A correct title for this diagram is

A Government Under the Articles of Confederation

B The Consent of the Governed

C The Pennsylvania Plan

D The Great Compromise at Philadelphia

8. Which one of the following was an important factor in persuading the states to ratify the Constitution?

A The Federalists promised to support a bill of rights.

B Slaves would be counted as three fifths of the population.

C The national government would have the power to tax imported goods.

D The anti-Federalists promised to create a strong executive branch.

9. Under the system of checks and balances,

A two thirds of the states can veto an act of Congress.

B the President can veto a law passed by Congress.

C a state can decide not to follow a federal law.

D the United States has to support other revolutions.

10. The case of *Marbury* v. *Madison* (1803) established the power of

A the President to make laws.

B Congress to make treaties.

C federal courts to determine if a law is constitutional.

D states over the federal government.

11. Which one of the following was a cause of the War of 1812?

A The Treaty of Ghent

B American forces invading Canada

C Taxation without representation

D Impressment of American sailors

Writing Practice

12. Describe two of the strengths of the Patriots in the Revolutionary War.

13. How did the Federalists differ from the anti-Federalists?

14. What was the importance of the Louisiana Purchase?

1. A
2. C
3. D
4. B
5. A
6. A
7. D
8. A
9. C
10. C
11. D
12. Possible answer: The Patriots were fighting on their own territory, had familiarity with fighting tactics from the French and Indian War, and had a strong leader in George Washington.
13. Federalists supported ratifying the constitution and wanted strong national government. Anti-Federalists opposed the new constitution on the grounds that it posed a threat to state governments and the rights of individuals.
14. It vastly increased the size of the country (and its national debt).

235

Unit 3
An Emerging New Nation
(1783–1850)

INTRODUCING THE UNIT

An Emerging New Nation (1783–1850) Nineteenth-century America was characterized by movement and change. It was a time of dramatic population growth and new technology and a period of migration and settlement. Americans responded to the changes in society by putting greater reliance on material progress and religious salvation. Yet the fierce divisions between North and South were causing a growing alienation.

USING HISTORICAL EVIDENCE

Direct students' attention to the painting on these pages. It shows the hustle and bustle of Broadway in New York City in 1834. The city had a great spurt of growth following the opening of the Erie Canal in 1825. The Canal, which connected the Hudson River and the Great Lakes, hastened the expansion of the west. As a well-located port city, New York City was a major beneficiary.

Though the island of Manhattan is crowded and densely populated from one end to the other today, in the 1800s it was only the downtown area, starting with the Battery and moving northward for about a mile, that was crowded with commerce and activity. Areas of the island even a mile or two farther north were still rural farmland at that time.

New York City's rapid growth was temporarily derailed by a terrible fire in 1835, which destroyed its wooden downtown. It was thought at the time that the city's economy was destroyed. But resilience has always been a hallmark of New York City, and it soon rebounded from this catastrophe, as it has at many other times throughout its history.

eTeach

Be sure to check out this month's online discussion with a Master Teacher. Go to **www.phschool.com**.

"America is a land of wonders, in which everything is in constant motion and every change seems an improvement."

Alexis de Tocqueville
Democracy in America, 1835

The bustle of city life is shown in this 1834 print of Broadway, New York City. ▶

236

RESOURCE DIRECTORY

Teaching Resources
Units 3/4 booklet
• American Pathways Activity, pp. 36–37
• History's Lasting Impact, pp. 38–39
Geography and History booklet, pp. 6–7

Other Print Resources
Prentice Hall Assessment System
• Document-Based Assessment

237

Chapter 7 Planning Guide
Resource Manager

	CORE INSTRUCTION	READING/SKILLS
Chapter-Level Resources	**Teaching Resources** • Pacing Charts booklet • Block Scheduling booklet **Resource Pro® CD-ROM**, Ch. 7 **Prentice Hall Presentation Pro CD-ROM**, Ch. 7 **www.phschool.com** • eTeach	**Guided Reading Audiotapes (English/Spanish)** **Student Edition on Audio CD**, Ch. 7 **Social Studies Skills Tutor CD-ROM** **Color Transparencies**, A13, A14, A15, A16, A60, D3, E6, E7, F2, G3
1 Cultural, Social, and Religious Life 1. Find out how Americans tried to advance the culture of the new nation. 2. Learn about some important social changes of the early 1800s. 3. See how a renewal of religious faith affected Protestant churches.	**Teaching Resources** **Units 3/4 booklet** • Section 1 Quiz, p. 4 **Learning Styles Lesson Plans booklet**, p. 16	**Guided Reading and Review booklet**, p. 29 **Guide to the Essentials**, p. 37 **Learning with Documents booklet**, pp. 12, 46 **Section Reading Support Transparencies**
2 Trails to the West 1. Discover how and why settlers crossed the Appalachians. 2. See how the United States expanded into Florida. 3. Find out about factors that motivated American migrants bound for the Pacific.	**Teaching Resources** **Units 3/4 booklet** • Section 2 Quiz, p. 5 **Learning Styles Lesson Plans booklet**, p. 17	**Guided Reading and Review booklet**, p. 30 **Guide to the Essentials**, p. 38 **Skills for Life booklet**, p. 9 **Section Reading Support Transparencies**
3 The Great Plains and the Southwest 1. Learn how the lives of Plains Indians changed from the 1500s to the 1800s. 2. Discover how Spain integrated California and the Rio Grande valley into Hispanic North America. 3. Find out why Texas fought to win its independence from Mexico.	**Teaching Resources** **Units 3/4 booklet** • Section 3 Quiz, p. 6	**Guided Reading and Review booklet**, p. 31 **Guide to the Essentials**, p. 39 **Section Reading Support Transparencies**

ENRICHMENT/PRE-AP

Prentice Hall United States History Video Collection™
www.phschool.com
- Section Activities, Virtual Field Trip, Chapter Activities, Current Events Online

Sounds of an Era Audio CD

Biography, Literature, and Comparing Primary Sources booklet, pp. 12, 47–48, 109–110
American History Block Scheduling Support
Nystrom *Atlas of Our Country*, pp. 20–21
Historical Outline Map Book, pp. 29, 31, 32, 38, 40
Sounds of an Era Audio CD

Nystrom *Atlas of Our Country*, pp. 20–21, 24–25
Historical Outline Map Book, p. 39
Exploring Primary Sources in U.S. History CD-ROM
American Pathways Thematic Posters

ASSESSMENT

PRENTICE HALL ASSESSMENT SYSTEM

Core Assessment
- ExamView® Test Bank, Ch. 7
- ExamView® Test Bank CD-ROM, Ch. 7

Standardized Test Preparation

Diagnose and Prescribe
- Diagnostic Tests for High School Social Studies Skills

Review and Reteach
- Review Book for U.S. History

Practice and Assess
- Test-taking Strategies With Transparencies
- Test-taking Strategies Posters
- Test Prep Book for U.S. History
- Alternative Assessment Handbook
- Document-Based Assessment

Teaching Resources
Units 3/4 booklet
- Section Quizzes, pp. 4–6
- Chapter Tests, pp. 7, 10
www.phschool.com Ch. 7 Self-Test

AmericanHeritage RESOURCES

From the Archives of American Heritage®, p. 255
AmericanHeritage® My Brush with History™ Videotapes
www.americanheritage.com

TEXT

Don't miss the exclusive interactive version of this textbook on the Web and on CD-ROM.

Chapter 7 Planning Guide
In Your Classroom

CUSTOMIZE FOR INDIVIDUAL NEEDS

Gifted and Talented

Teacher's Edition
- Customize for Gifted and Talented, p. 259

Teaching Resources
- Biography, Literature, and Comparing Primary Sources booklet, pp. 12, 47–48, 109–110

Technology
- Exploring Primary Sources in U.S. History CD-ROM *Letter from the Alamo, Lt. Col. Comd't. William Barrett Travis*

ESL

Teacher's Edition
- Customize for ESL, pp. 243, 253, 265

Teaching Resources
- Guided Reading and Review booklet, pp. 28–30
- Guide to the Essentials (English/Spanish), Chapter 7

Technology
- Student Edition on Audio CD, Chapter 7
- Guided Reading Audiotapes (English/Spanish), Chapter 7
- Section Reading Support Transparencies

Less Proficient Readers

Teacher's Edition
- Customize for Less Proficient Readers, pp. 241, 245

Teaching Resources
- Guided Reading and Review booklet, pp. 28–30
- Guide to the Essentials (English/Spanish), Chapter 7

Technology
- Student Edition on Audio CD, Chapter 7
- Guided Reading Audiotapes (English/Spanish), Chapter 7
- Section Reading Support Transparencies

Less Proficient Writers

Teacher's Edition
- Customize for Less Proficient Writers, p. 255

Teaching Resources
- Guided Reading and Review booklet, pp. 28–30
- Guide to the Essentials (English/Spanish), Chapter 7

Technology
- Student Edition on Audio CD, Chapter 7
- Guided Reading Audiotapes (English/Spanish), Chapter 7
- Section Reading Support Transparencies

TEACHER'S EDITION INDEX

CHAPTER 7 – PACING SUGGESTIONS

 For 90-minute Blocks
- Teach sections 2 and 3 using Transparencies A13, A14, A15, A16, A60, D3, E6, E7, F2, and G3, and the Recent Scholarship notes on pages 251 and 262 for class discussions.

 Running Out of Time?

If you are running short on time to cover this chapter, consider the following options:

- Use the Prentice Hall Presentation Pro CD-ROM to create an outline for this chapter.
- Use the Section Summaries for Chapter 7, from **Guide to the Essentials (English/Spanish)**.

1 **Cultural, Social, and Religious Life**	**Connecting with Culture** Have students work in pairs to design posters that promote an urban or rural revival meeting in the early 1800s. Tell pairs that their posters should combine text and graphics to either entice the locals to attend or convince them of their need to take part. You may wish to have students create posters of full size or render reduced versions on standard-size copy paper. **(Visual/Spatial)**
2 **Trails to the West**	**Connecting with Geography** Organize students into groups to develop pamphlets to encourage American settlement in Oregon. Each group's pamphlet should be directed toward attracting a specific type of settler, such as merchants, farmers, missionaries, or trappers. Pamphlets should combine text, maps, and original drawings—and stress geographic factors—that are appropriate to their target group. **(Visual/Spatial; Verbal/Linguistic)**
3 **The Great Plains and the Southwest**	**Connecting with History and Conflict** Invite students to imagine that they are living in Texas at the time of the Texas War for Independence. Tell them to write letters to friends or family in the United States or Mexico, explaining which side they support in the war and why. Ask for volunteers to share their letters with the class. **(Verbal/Linguistic)**

Chapter 7

Life in the New Nation

(1783–1850)

INTRODUCING THE CHAPTER

Dramatic population growth and movement brought both opportunities and uncertainties to people of the new republic. Americans responded to the changes with growing confidence in religious salvation. They pushed westward into Texas, New Mexico, California, and Oregon in search of new opportunities, and as their numbers grew, tensions developed between the new settlers and the people who had already claimed these lands as home.

TIME LINE ACTIVITY

To provide students with practice in using the time line, ask questions such as these:

1. What was the first state west of the Appalachians, and in what year was it established? *(Kentucky, 1792)*

2. In what year was slavery abolished in the British Empire? *(1833)*

3. When did organized wagon trains begin traveling the Oregon Trail? *(1843)*

Chapter 7

Life in the New Nation
(1783–1850)

SECTION 1   Cultural, Social, and Religious Life
SECTION 2   Trails to the West
SECTION 3   The Great Plains and the Southwest

Revival meeting

American Events

1786	1792	1816
Charles Wilson Peale founds Peale's Museum in Philadelphia.	Kentucky becomes the first state west of the Appalachians.	Sixteen congregations form the African Methodist Episcopal Church.

Presidential Terms: George Washington 1789–1797   J. Adams 1797–1801   Thomas Jefferson 1801–1809   James Madison 1809–1817

1780	•1790•	•1800	1810

World Events

The French Revolution begins. — **1789**

Slaves in Haiti rise up against French authorities. — **1791**

The discovery of the Rosetta Stone leads to the translation of Egyptian hieroglyphics. — **1799**

238   Chapter 7 • *Life in the New Nation*

eTeach

Be sure to check out this month's online discussion with a Master Teacher. Go to **www.phschool.com**.

RESOURCE DIRECTORY

Teaching Resources
Pacing Charts booklet
Block Scheduling booklet, p. 16
Units 3/4 booklet
  • Chapter Summary, p. 3

Technology
Guided Reading Audiotapes (English/Spanish), Ch. 7
Student Edition on Audio CD, Ch. 7
Prentice Hall United States History Video Collection™, Volume 6, *Expansionism*
Prentice Hall Presentation Pro CD-ROM, Ch. 7
Resource Pro® CD-ROM
Social Studies Skills Tutor CD-ROM
Companion Web site, www.phschool.com

Growth of the United States, 1790–1830

Map: Growth of the United States, 1790–1830

BRITISH NORTH AMERICA

Maine 1820
Vt. 1791
N.H.
New York
Mass.
Conn.
R.I.
Pennsylvania
Md.
N.J.
Delaware
Virginia
North Carolina
South Carolina
Georgia

Unorganized Territory

Michigan Territory

Illinois 1818
Indiana 1816
Ohio 1803
Kentucky 1792
Tennessee 1796

Missouri 1821

Arkansas Territory

Mississippi 1817
Alabama 1819

Louisiana 1812

MEXICO

Lake Superior
Lake Michigan
Lake Huron
Lake Erie
L. Ontario
St. Lawrence River
Mississippi River
Missouri River
Red River

ATLANTIC OCEAN

Gulf of Mexico

Florida Terr.

Two or more persons per square mile
- 1790
- 1810
- 1830
- 1812 Year entered Union
- 1830 borders

0   150   300 mi.
0   150   300 km

40°N
70°W
30°N
80°W

Timeline

1819 Spain cedes Florida to the United States under the Adams-Onís Treaty.

1828 Noah Webster publishes the *American Dictionary of the English Language.*

1836 American settlers declare an independent Republic of Texas and successfully defend their country against Mexican forces.

1843 Organized wagon trains begin traveling the Oregon Trail.

1848 The discovery of gold draws thousands of migrants to California.

James Monroe 1817–1825 | John Q. Adams 1825–1829 | Andrew Jackson 1829–1837 | M. Van Buren 1837–1841 | W. Harrison 1841 | John Tyler 1841–45 | J. Polk 1845–49 | Z. Taylor 1849–50

• 1820 •   • 1830 •   • 1840 •   • 1850 •

Mexico wins independence from Spain.
1821

Slavery is abolished in the British Empire.
1833

Revolutions erupt in Paris, Berlin, Vienna, and Rome.
1848

Chapter 7   239

BIBLIOGRAPHY

For the Teacher

Ambrose, Stephen E. *Undaunted Courage: Meriwether Lewis, Thomas Jefferson, and the Opening of the American West.* Touchstone, 1997. (Biography of Meriwether Lewis combined with the author's own journey.)

Draper, Lyman Copeland and Ted Franklin Belue, eds. *The Life of Daniel Boone.* Stackpole Books, 1998. (The first in-depth study of his life.)

Groneman, Bill. *Eyewitness to the Alamo.* Republic of Texas Press, 1996. (Descriptions of the Battle of the Alamo by witnesses.)

For the Student

Parkman, Francis Jr. *The Oregon Trail.* Oxford University Press, 2000. (Eyewitness account of Parkman's 1846 journey.)

Petite, Mary Deborah. *1836 Facts About the Alamo and the Texas War for Independence.* Da Capo Press, 1999. (Provides detailed information about the battle from both perspectives.)

Schmidt, Thomas. *National Geographic's Guide to the Lewis and Clark Trail.* National Geographic Society, 1998. (Filled with maps, photographs, and insightful information.)

Growth of the United States, 1790–1830

Activating Prior Knowledge Of the states shown on this map, which was the last to enter the Union? *(Missouri)*

Previewing Ask students to explain some of the characteristics of growth that occurred during this 40-year period. *(Possible answers: the westward expansion of the United States; the growth around the Mississippi and Missouri rivers)*

BACKGROUND
About the Pictures

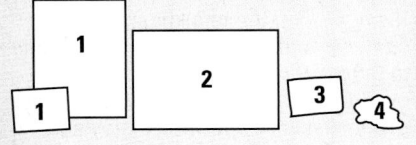

1. Peale was a painter, renowned for his portraits of prominent figures from the American Revolution.

2. Revival meetings were intended to bring people closer to their religion.

3. The chosen leader of the New Republic of Texas was David G. Burnet, and his military commander was Sam Houston.

4. Sutter's Mill was the location of the first major gold discovery in North America.

iTEXT

Don't miss the exclusive interactive version of this textbook on the Web and on CD-ROM.

Section 1
Cultural, Social, and Religious Life

SECTION OBJECTIVES

1. Find out how Americans tried to advance the culture of the new nation.
2. Learn about some important social changes of the early 1800s.
3. See how a renewal of religious faith affected Protestant churches.

BELLRINGER

Warm-Up Activity Write the word *evangelist* on the chalkboard and ask students to define it. Then ask students to think about what draws people to evangelism. Ask who some of today's evangelists are and where they can be seen.

Activating Prior Knowledge Review with students the reasons some early settlers, such as the Pilgrims, came to America. Ask students to discuss the ways in which later evangelist movements are similar to, and different from, the early religious movements in America.

READING STRATEGY

Have students skim the section, noting the headings and subheadings. Then ask them to rewrite the headings as questions and answer the questions as they read.

CAPTION ANSWERS

Viewing Fine Art The eagle represented freedom, beauty, independence, and raw energy.

Section 1

Cultural, Social, and Religious Life

READING FOCUS

- How did Americans try to advance the culture of the new nation?
- What were some important social changes of the early 1800s?
- How did a renewal of religious faith affect Protestant churches?

MAIN IDEA

In the early 1800s, the culture, religion, and social practices of Americans adapted to meet the challenges of a new and growing nation.

KEY TERMS

republican virtues
mobile society
Second Great Awakening
evangelical
congregation
revival
denomination

TAKING NOTES

Complete the chart below. Fill in the chart with examples of cultural, religious, and social changes of the early 1800s.

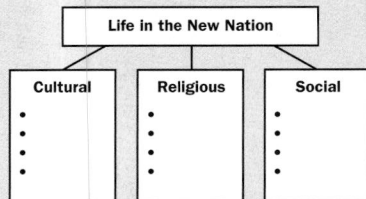

Life in the New Nation

Cultural	Religious	Social
•	•	•
•	•	•
•	•	•
•	•	•

VIEWING FINE ART In the early 1800s, John James Audubon studied the birds of the new nation and published his illustrations in *The Birds of America*. His book included a scientific look at the bald eagle. **Drawing Conclusions** *Why did the Continental Congress choose the bald eagle as a symbol of the nation?*

Setting the Scene With independence from Great Britain, Americans gained the right to determine their own destiny. What kind of country would they create? While politicians worked to fashion a new, American form of government, others began to think about a new, American way of life.

In 1782, the Continental Congress helped shape the image of the new nation by choosing the bald eagle as the symbol of the United States. Soaring fearlessly through the sky, the eagle represented freedom and independence, as well as raw energy. These characteristics were prized by many Americans, including Noah Webster, a respected teacher and author. In 1790, he called for the new nation to stride boldly into the future:

> 66 *Americans, unshackle your minds, and act like independent beings.*
> *. . . You have an empire to raise and support by your exertions, and a national character to establish and extend by your wisdom and virtues.* 99
>
> —Noah Webster

Cultural Advancement

Webster and others worked diligently to establish the country's "national character." They promoted education and the arts as well as virtuous behavior. Their goal was to improve the lives of all Americans. In this spirit of improvement, the nation began to focus on the importance of learning.

American Scholars and Artists As a result of increased prosperity, a growing number of people, like Noah Webster, had the time to devote themselves to scholarship and the arts. Many of these well-educated men and women contributed to the development of American learning.

Mercy Otis Warren Believing that she had a duty to participate in the Revolution, Warren hosted political meetings at her home in Plymouth, Massachusetts. She wrote several patriotic plays encouraging the cause of independence, and in 1805 she wrote a book titled *History of the American Revolution*. Warren actively

240   Chapter 7 • Life in the New Nation

RESOURCE DIRECTORY

Teaching Resources
Learning Styles Lesson Plans booklet, p. 16
Guided Reading and Review booklet, p. 29

Technology
Section Reading Support Transparencies
Guided Reading Audiotapes (English/Spanish), Ch. 7
Student Edition on Audio CD, Ch. 7
Prentice Hall Presentation Pro CD-ROM, Ch. 7
Companion Web site, www.phschool.com

encouraged other women to take up scholarly interests, but she cautioned them to balance their intellectual pursuits with responsibilities in the home.

Benjamin Rush A doctor, scientist, and revolutionary, Rush signed the Declaration of Independence and represented Pennsylvania in the Continental Congress. He published numerous books on chemistry and medicine. In a time when many believed that mental illness was caused by the devil, Rush suggested that it often resulted from physical disease. His medical lectures in Philadelphia attracted large audiences when they began in 1790.

Benjamin Banneker Born in Maryland to free parents of mixed African American and white ancestry, Banneker worked as a writer, inventor, mathematician, and astronomer. Largely self-educated, Banneker used his skills in many tasks, including surveying (mapping out) the site of the nation's new capital of Washington, D.C. In 1791, he published the first issue of an almanac detailing the motions of the moon, sun, planets, and stars. He presented a copy to Thomas Jefferson, along with a letter calling for better treatment of enslaved African Americans.

Charles Willson Peale A skilled artist, Peale painted more than 1,000 portraits in his long life. Yet he also served as a soldier in the Revolution, a representative in the Pennsylvania legislature, a scientist, and an inventor. He was the father of 17 children. In 1786, he founded the first major museum in the new nation. Peale's Museum, as it was called, soon housed about 100,000 objects, including a series of Peale's own paintings of heroes of the Revolution. Before Peale's time, people had thought of art and science as luxuries for the wealthy. Peale's Museum proved that these fields could be a source of enjoyment and education for ordinary citizens of the new republic.

Phillis Wheatley In 1761, the Wheatley family of Boston bought a young enslaved woman from Senegal, West Africa, and named her Phillis. They recognized her intelligence when she was still a child and allowed her to learn to read and write. Phillis Wheatley published her first poem in 1770, and her fame spread to Europe in 1773 when her collection *Poems on Various Subjects, Religious and Moral* was published in England. Wheatley gained further recognition and acclaim when a poem she wrote and dedicated to George Washington was published in 1776.

Education Some Americans began to see children's education as a means of developing a rich and uniquely American culture. In pursuit of this goal, Webster wrote *The American Spelling Book,* which first appeared in 1783. Webster also called for establishing standards for a national language. He backed up this call by compiling the first major dictionary of American English, the *American Dictionary of the English Language.* The growing republic offered a good market for Webster's books. Many state constitutions required free public education for all children. Even though few state governments actually provided free education in those early years, academies, or private high schools, often filled the gap.

American schools had a profound responsibility. In 1789, the Massachusetts legislature called on the state's schoolteachers to teach students "the principles of piety, justice, and a sacred regard to truth, love to their country, . . . chastity, moderation and temperance, and those other virtues which are the ornaments of human society, and the basis upon which the Republican Constitution is structured."

Republican Virtues Like the Massachusetts legislature, many Americans hoped to develop character by promoting certain virtues. The virtues that the

Benjamin Rush (top) pioneered the study and teaching of medicine in Philadelphia. Phillis Wheatley (bottom) won international recognition for her poetry.

American people would need to govern themselves in the new republic were called **republican virtues.** They included self-reliance, hard work, frugality, harmony, and sacrificing individual needs for the good of the community.

In the early 1800s, Americans began to look to women to set the standard for republican virtues. Women were mothers, wives, and sometimes teachers, they reasoned, and thus had a powerful influence on the men who would vote in, and lead, the republic. If women had such virtues as honesty, self-restraint, and discipline, they could teach these qualities to men.

To serve as examples of these virtues, however, women had to learn them first. In the late 1700s, the vast majority of schools accepted boys only. As people began to recognize the value of educating girls, many academies added "female departments" to help girls become "republican women." A republican woman was one who had the virtues that would help her contribute to the success of the republic.

Americans in the early 1800s believed that women should play only a supporting role in the new nation. Still, that represented a significant change from colonial times, when women had few rights and little, if any, power. People were now beginning to think about the importance of women in the life of the republic.

Social Changes

Americans in the early republic knew that they were living in a time of rapid change. The pressures created by change presented them with many challenges to resolve.

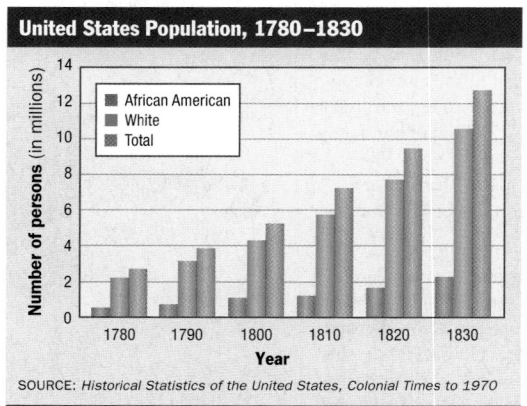

United States Population, 1780–1830

SOURCE: *Historical Statistics of the United States, Colonial Times to 1970*

INTERPRETING GRAPHS
The census, a national head count taken every ten years, recorded the startling population growth of the United States. **Analyzing Information** *Which group grew more rapidly, whites or African Americans? About how much did the total population increase between 1780 and 1830?*

Population Growth The young nation faced the problem of a mushrooming population. About 2.7 million people lived in the original 13 states in 1780. By 1830, the population had grown to an estimated 12 million people in 24 states. The graph on this page shows this explosive increase in population. From 1780 to 1830, the population doubled about every 20 years. In fact, in the first half of the 1800s, the American population grew more than twice as fast as that of any other nation.

Immigration played only a minor role in this growth. As you will read later, the great rise in the number of immigrants from Germany and Ireland did not begin until the 1830s and 1840s. In addition, fewer Africans came to the United States after a law banning the import of slaves took effect in 1808. Although some slave traders continued to smuggle Africans into the United States, by the early 1800s the slave trade primarily involved enslaved people sold within the United States.

About 90 percent of the American population growth came from an astonishing increase in the number of children born to each family. In the first half of the 1800s, the average American woman had nearly five children in her lifetime. By comparison, this figure declined to about three children by the 1870s. The huge growth of the population is all the more amazing in view of the high infant mortality rate at the time. The infant mortality rate is the rate at which infants (babies less than 1 year old) die. During the early 1800s, about 130 of every 1,000 children died before their first birthday. Today, the rate is only 7 deaths per 1,000 births.

242 Chapter 7 • *Life in the New Nation*

The large number of children meant that most of the population was young. The median age of Americans in 1820 was about 17. That is, half of the population was under the age of 17. Today, the median age is about 35, and fewer than one fourth of all Americans are younger than 17 years old.

Mobility The expanding population led to crowding, especially along the Atlantic Coast. Americans solved this problem by moving away from crowded areas. They could do this because the United States was (and remains) a **mobile society**—one in which people continually move from place to place. This ease of movement meant that Americans could readily change not only their location but also their position in society. The new mobility had two major effects:

1. Americans had great opportunities to improve their lives. Unlike Europeans, they were not tied to the land, but could pack up their belongings and leave. After the Revolution many Americans decided to move west, to the frontier beyond the Appalachian Mountains. They carved out new lives in Kentucky, Tennessee, Ohio, and other wilderness regions, where land was available and society placed no limits on their success. For example, the son of a poor farmhand in Vermont could become a successful store owner in frontier Ohio. Of course, not everyone had an equal chance to get ahead, and opportunity did not guarantee success. Enslaved Americans, especially, did not benefit from the mobile society.

2. People who moved often found themselves living among strangers. As a result, they felt lonely. Previously, people had enjoyed the company of family and friends in the villages where they had lived all their lives. Now they had to develop friendships with people whom they had never known before. Thus they had to learn new skills and make up new rules for getting along with others.

One social skill that became more important was the ability to judge strangers. This involved knowing what role a stranger played in society. Yet because people moved so often, their places in society were not clear. As a result, people were more likely to question one another's social position. On the frontier, questioning another's social position could lead to violence, sometimes in the form of a duel. In the early American republic, men of all social classes took up this tradition of formal one-on-one fights to defend one's honor, using weapons such as swords or pistols.

New Rules for Courtship and Marriage Women, too, had to deal with uncertainty about others in the changing world of the early republic. One of the few decisions in life that a young woman had some control over was her choice of a marriage partner. It was vital that she learn how to judge a potential mate. Many women looking for this kind of guidance found it in books. Some read advice manuals, but many more turned to moralizing novels.

By far the most popular of these works was the 1794 novel *Charlotte Temple* by Susanna Haswell Rowson. Rowson's novel tells the sad story of a 15-year-old girl who is carried off by a handsome man in a splendid military

VIEWING HISTORY Starting a new home in Ohio was tough work for most of the nearly one million people who settled there by 1830. **Drawing Conclusions** *What tasks are shown in the picture?*

READING CHECK

Why were new social skills important on the frontier?

Student Portfolio

You may wish to have students add the following to their portfolios: Have students choose either marriage or defending one's honor as the topic of a short paper in which they compare and contrast customs in Colonial days with customs today. **(Verbal/Linguistic)**

BACKGROUND

A Diverse Nation

Dueling was quite distinct from the gun and knife fights common on the frontier. Duels were governed by a strict code of rules. The offended party sent a note to the offender through a friend, called a "second," challenging him to a duel. The offender chose a second, and the two seconds met to try to work things out. If no settlement was reached, the duel took place. Chances of dying in a gun duel were fairly slim. Pistols of the time were highly inaccurate, and taking aim for longer than three seconds was considered dishonorable. However, the real purpose of dueling was not to kill one's adversary but to prove one's courage and honor. Often in the South, those who refused a challenge to a duel were often "posted"—that is, a notice of their cowardice was published in the newspaper or displayed in a public place.

READING CHECK

Rather than living among family and friends, frontier life left people living among strangers, thus requiring a different set of social skills. The most important of these was probably the ability to judge the trustworthiness of others.

CAPTION **A**NSWERS

Viewing History Clearing land, building a house, cooking, gathering firewood, and tending horses.

VIEWING FINE ART Whether rushed or carefully considered, courtship led to the marriages that were building the new nation. *Country Wedding*, a painting from about 1819, gently pokes fun at young love and informal country life. **Drawing Inferences** *Describe the activities of the participants in the wedding.*

uniform. He soon leaves her penniless and pregnant. The moral of the story is that appearances do not provide enough clues to a person's character.

As American society became less ordered and certain, women became increasingly cautious about marriage. They preferred a long period of getting acquainted with suitors before they committed themselves to marry. This period, called a courtship, was not new but had a new importance in the early 1800s. Women used courtship both to get to know a potential partner and to negotiate the terms of their future life together.

Consider, for example, the proposal of Zadoc Long, a 24-year-old storekeeper in Buckfield, Maine. After a year of courting Julia Davis, he wrote a letter asking her to be his wife. No one knows what their courtship was like. However, his offer—which she accepted—sounds like a response to a long list of demands that Davis may have made:

This wreath was worn by Lucy B. Marsh when she married Hiliah Hawks in 1827.

> 66 *I feel sad when I don't see you. Be married, why won't you? And come to live with me. I will make you as happy as I can. You shall not be obliged to work hard; and when you are tired, you may lie in my lap, and I will sing you to rest. . . . I will play a tune upon the violin as often as you ask and as well as I can; and leave off smoking, if you say so. . . . I would be always very kind to you, I think, because I love you so well. I will not make you bring in wood and water, or feed the pig, or milk the cow, or go to the neighbors to borrow milk. Will you be married?* 99
>
> —Zadoc Long

For most women, getting married was a matter of survival, since few decent employment opportunities existed. Nevertheless, women had other concerns besides marriage. For one thing, American women were becoming increasingly interested in religion. In the early 1800s, a new wave of religious feeling swept the United States. Many Americans, especially women, soon joined this religious movement.

Religious Renewal

During the colonial era, many churches had received financial support from state governments. Government aid continued to flow to Congregational churches in New England well into the 1800s. States had cut support for churches, however, in part because of a drop in church membership. The 1790 census showed that only about one out of ten Americans belonged to a church. Yet in the early 1800s, the pressures of a changing society led many people to renew their religious faith.

The Second Great Awakening The powerful religious movement of the early 1800s is known as the **Second Great Awakening.** The movement began in the backcountry of Kentucky and Tennessee and attracted large numbers of people. Like the Great Awakening a century earlier, it was an **evangelical** movement that affected Protestant Christians. A Christian religious movement is considered evangelical when it emphasizes these three ideas:

1. The Christian Bible, known as the Scripture, is the final authority.
2. Salvation can be achieved only through a personal belief in Jesus.
3. People demonstrate true faith by leading a transformed life and by performing good deeds. This is sometimes called "witnessing for Christ."

In addition to its evangelical nature, the Second Great Awakening was democratic. Anyone, rich or poor, could win salvation if he or she chose to do so. Evangelical religions generally stressed the importance of the **congregation,** or the members of the church, rather than ministers.

One common feature of the Second Great Awakening was the **revival.** In this kind of gathering, people were "revived," or brought back to a religious life, by listening to preachers and accepting belief in Jesus. Revivals were also called camp meetings, because they often took place outdoors in temporary shelters such as tents. One participant described a camp meeting in New Haven, Connecticut, in 1804:

> 66 The power increased during the whole meeting. . . . Triumphing, . . . weeping, people falling, the voice of joy and sorrow mingling, prayer, praise, and shouting, shouting, shouting filled the groves around. 99
> —William Thacher

VIEWING HISTORY Lanterns like this one lit the way to camp meetings similar to the one below. Camp meetings were often dramatic events that could sweep up the whole community. **Drawing Conclusions** *Describe the reactions of the crowd to the speaker at this meeting.*

Women took an active role in the Second Great Awakening. In part this may have reflected the loneliness and unhappiness of many women on the frontier. Religion offered them a chance to connect with others. They might work together to help widows and orphans, to spread the Christian religion, or to improve conditions for mothers. In a world of strangers, they were especially grateful for the company of "beloved sisters" who shared their religious views.

The revival movement brought women increased power, but it was indirect. Few women actually preached or took leadership roles in the Second

Chapter 7 • Section 1   **245**

ACTIVITY

Connecting with Culture

Have students take the perspective of a woman during the Second Great Awakening and write a diary entry describing her life. **(Verbal/Linguistic)**

BACKGROUND

Connections to Culture

Have students work in pairs to develop a graphic organizer to illustrate the characteristics of, and differences in, the Baptist, Methodist, and Unitarian denominations in the early to mid-1800s. Factors that organizers might illustrate include origins, beliefs, clergy, membership, and message. Select pairs to copy their organizers on the chalkboard for the class to evaluate and constructively critique.

VIEWING HISTORY This small Methodist church was built in Pleasant Mills, New Jersey, in 1808. Many communities were visited by circuit riders who traveled from town to town to preach the Gospel. **Recognizing Ideologies** *Which aspects of the Methodist faith are reflected in the simple, undecorated nature of the building?*

Great Awakening. Women did, however, assume greater responsibility for choosing their church ministers. In this way they influenced the beliefs and standards of behavior in their community.

New Denominations During the Second Great Awakening several Protestant **denominations,** or religious subgroups, experienced rapid growth. The United States soon had more different Christian denominations than any other nation. By 1850, Presbyterians and Congregationalists, once the most popular denominations, had fallen to third and fourth place. The fastest-growing denominations included the following:

Baptists Baptists got their name from their beliefs about baptism, a Christian ceremony by which a person is made a member of the church. Unlike other denominations, which tend to baptize people as infants, Baptists believe that only those who are old enough to understand Christian beliefs should be baptized. Also, instead of baptizing people by sprinkling them with water, as other denominations do, Baptists baptize by immersion, or dunking people completely underwater.

Baptist churches had existed in what became the United States since the 1600s. The numbers of Baptists grew rapidly during the Second Great Awakening through their evangelical beliefs and their frequent camp meetings. By 1850, the Baptist church was the nation's second-largest denomination.

Methodists Methodism grew out of the beliefs of a British minister, John Wesley, who lived from 1703 to 1791. His ideas reached the United States in the 1780s and spread rapidly after 1800. By 1850, the Methodists had become the largest Protestant denomination in the United States.

Methodism attracted many followers for four main reasons. First, it focuses on a person's personal relationship with God rather than on religious doctrines that might be hard to understand. Second, unlike ministers in other denominations, Methodist preachers in the early 1800s were common folks instead of highly-educated scholars. They could understand the needs of congregations in the rough-and-tumble frontier world. Third, the Methodists spread their message through a system of traveling ministers called circuit riders. Traveling on horseback in sweeping routes or "circuits" through the wilderness, circuit riders won many new converts. Finally, Methodists held frequent, exciting camp meetings. They held a thousand revivals across the country in one year alone.

Unitarians Although Unitarianism is not an evangelical faith, it gained strength during the Second Great Awakening. Unitarians believe that Jesus was a human messenger of God but not divine himself, and they see God as a loving father, not a stern judge. Unitarianism took root in New England, where many elite churchgoers wanted a modern religion that offered moderation and reason, but not the intensity and emotion found in evangelical congregations.

In 1825, Boston minister William Ellery Channing organized a conference of Congregational ministers that became the American Unitarian Association. He was the perfect spokesperson for the rising denomination. Calm and caring, Channing said that God trained people, as a father would, "by aids and obstructions, by conflicts of reason and passion. . . for union with himself." This Unitarian idea that people are on Earth to improve themselves deeply affected the social reform movement in New England.

CAPTION ANSWERS

Viewing History The simple, unadorned style of the building reflects the fact that Methodists were common people, not wealthy individuals, and many lived in young frontier towns. Also reflected by the architectural style is the Methodist tenet that what is important is an individual's relationship with God rather than a strong institutional church or a complex religious doctrine.

RESOURCE DIRECTORY

Teaching Resources
Learning with Documents booklet (Primary Source Activity) *The American Spirit,* p. 12

Mormons The western and central regions of New York also experienced a lot of activity during the Second Great Awakening. Fiery religious movements swept through this region so often that it became known as the Burned-Over District. Here, in 1830, Joseph Smith published *The Book of Mormon*. According to Smith, the book was a translation of the writing on gold plates that he found buried in the ground, with the help of an angel. The book foretold that God would soon restore a truer, simpler church, free of ministers. This was to take place in North America. Smith went on to start a religion based on the *Book of Mormon*. He called it the Church of Jesus Christ of Latter-day Saints. In time, people began calling members of the church *Mormons*.

Millennialists Many evangelical ministers believed that the United States was leading the world into the millennium, or Earth's final thousand years of glory before the Day of Judgment. They looked for signs of the coming event in everyday life.

One of these ministers, a Baptist preacher named William Miller, studied the Bible closely and determined that Jesus would return to the world between March 1843 and March 1844. This return was called the Advent, or the Second Coming. Miller preached that only the people who knew of the Advent ahead of time and believed in it would be saved and go to heaven. His followers, called Millerites or Adventists, numbered between 50,000 and 100,000, according to his estimate. When Jesus failed to arrive at the predicted time, the Millerites changed the date of the Advent to October 22, 1844.

Many of Miller's followers continued to believe that Jesus would soon return despite the "Great Disappointment" in 1844. In the 1860s, they formed several churches, including the Seventh-Day Adventist Church and the Advent Christian Church.

African American Worship   Like white Americans, great numbers of African Americans turned to evangelical religion. They found a strong sense of community in Methodism and other Protestant denominations. As African Americans joined Christian churches, black and white traditions blended together. One example is the call-and-response method of worship, in which the congregation responds together to a statement made by one member. This is a feature of both older Protestant worship and African music.

Both white and black Christians also sang spirituals, or folk hymns. African American singers, however, often focused on themes that held a double meaning. For example, in the Bible, Moses led the Israelites to freedom from slavery under the Pharaoh, the ruler of Egypt. African Americans used this story as a symbol for winning both spiritual freedom and freedom from physical slavery. One spiritual put it this way:

When Israel was in Egypt's Land
(Let my people go)
Oppressed so hard they could not stand
(Let my people go)
Go down, Moses, way down in Egypt's land,
Tell ol' Pharaoh to let my people go. . . .
O let us all from bondage flee
(Let my people go)
And let us all in Christ be free
(Let my people go). . . .

African American female preachers, such as Juliann Jane Tillman, found a voice within the African Methodist Episcopal Church (AME).

Chapter 7 • Section 1   247

Reading Comprehension

1. (a) Self-reliance, thrift, hard work, and sacrificing individual needs for the good of the community. (b) Americans would need these in the new republic.

2. The most important factor was a great increase in the number of births.

3. Because of the population mobility during this period, a woman was less likely to know much about the status and family background of a suitor. Women now wanted to get to know a potential partner carefully before making a final commitment.

4. Baptist churches grew because they reflected the evangelical zeal of the Second Great Awakening. Methodism was well-suited to frontier life and appealed to common people. Unitarianism offered hope and appealed to reason. The Mormon faith also gained due to the simplicity of its doctrine.

Critical Thinking and Writing

5. The Great Awakening energized people to reject traditional authorities; the Second Great Awakening promised salvation to anyone who was willing to believe in the authority of Christ and the Bible. Both democratized religion.

6. Possible answer: Yes, because Warren made sacrifices and worked hard for the good of a common cause—the Revolution.

7. Essays will vary, but should include the concept that the AME created a place for African Americans to worship and gave them a voice.

Take It to the NET

Graphs will vary, but should give an accurate visual representation of a significant change experienced by the chosen group in America during the 1800s. Students should then write a brief statement explaining what the change in this group meant for American society as a whole.

CAPTION ANSWERS

Viewing History They shared and incorporated elements from each other's traditions.

VIEWING HISTORY One African American church, the Bethel Church of Baltimore, celebrated its good relationship with the minister of a neighboring white congregation in 1845. **Drawing Conclusions** *How did white and African American worshippers influence each other's religious traditions?*

African Americans sometimes felt unwelcome in white-dominated churches. The tensions between whites and blacks increased as African Americans became more assertive about sharing in democratic liberty. In 1787, white worshippers at the St. George Methodist Church in Philadelphia asked the African Americans in the congregation to leave the main floor and sit up in the gallery. They refused. Under the leadership of Richard Allen, the black worshippers left and started a new church of their own. Allen, an African American minister, explained their purpose:

> 66 *Our only design is to secure to ourselves our rights and privileges, to regulate our own affairs, [worldly] and spiritual, the same as if we were white people.* 99
>
> —Richard Allen

African Americans in other cities soon followed Allen's example and started their own churches. Sixteen congregations joined in 1816 to form the African Methodist Episcopal Church (AME). Members elected Allen as their first bishop. By 1831, the African Methodist Episcopal Church included 86 churches with about 8,000 members.

The democratic nature of the Second Great Awakening had attracted many African Americans to the churches of evangelical denominations. Despite setbacks, many remained in predominantly white evangelical churches. Working by themselves, however, the evangelical churches could not establish real equality or overcome racial prejudice against African Americans. Yet they did remind Americans of every background that what mattered in the United States was not wealth or education or color, but what Martin Luther King, Jr., would later call "the content of one's character."

Section   1   Assessment

READING COMPREHENSION

1. (a) What were **republican virtues?** (b) Why were they considered important?

2. What factors drove population growth in the early 1800s?

3. Why did courtship take on new importance in this time period?

4. How did the **Second Great Awakening** lead to the growth of new Christian **denominations?**

CRITICAL THINKING AND WRITING

5. **Making Comparisons** Compare and contrast the Great Awakening of the colonial era and the Second Great Awakening.

6. **Drawing Inferences** Was Mercy Otis Warren a good example of a "republican woman"? Why or why not?

7. **Writing an Expository Essay** Research and write a brief essay explaining the role of the African Methodist Episcopal Church in the evangelical revivals.

Take It to the NET

Activity: Creating a Graph Study census data from the 1800s. Choose one group of people (for example, males aged 16–25) and chart data for this group over 50 years. What does your chart show you about America's population during this period? Use the links provided in the *America: Pathways to the Present* area of the following Web site for help in completing this activity. **www.phschool.com**

RESOURCE DIRECTORY

Teaching Resources
Units 3/4 booklet
• Section 1 Quiz, p. 4
Guide to the Essentials
• Section 1 Summary, p. 37

READING FOCUS

- Why and how did settlers cross the Appalachians?
- How did the United States expand into Florida?
- What factors motivated American migrants bound for the Pacific?

MAIN IDEA

In the early years of the republic, many people traveled west over the Appalachians to settle in the Ohio and Mississippi valleys. Later, settlers would cross the continent to the Great Salt Lake and Pacific Coast.

KEY TERMS

trans-Appalachia
Adams-Onís Treaty
cede
manifest destiny
mountain man
Oregon Trail
pass
Santa Fe Trail
California Gold Rush
ghost town

TAKING NOTES

Fill in the chart below with descriptions of American settlement in each of the following regions.

Region	Description of American Settlement
Trans-Appalachia	• Farmers settled in Ohio Valley •
Oregon Country	
Utah	
California	

SECTION OBJECTIVES

1. Discover how and why settlers crossed the Appalachians.
2. See how the United States expanded into Florida.
3. Find out about factors that motivated American migrants bound for the Pacific.

BELLRINGER

Warm-Up Activity Tell students that in 1810 only one seventh of the American population of 7.2 million lived west of the Alleghenies; by 1840 more than one third of the 17.2 million Americans lived there. Have them consider the impact of such rapid population growth.

Activating Prior Knowledge Ask students to create a list of reasons why people would choose to migrate west of the Alleghenies.

READING STRATEGY

Ask students to skim the section and create an outline using the headings and subheadings. As they read, have them fill in their outlines using supporting evidence from the section.

ACTIVITY
Connecting with Geography

Direct a pair of students to locate, or provide them with, a small-scale topographical map that shows the Cumberland Gap and the surrounding area. Have the students carefully study the map, conduct research about the Gap, and then make a presentation about the Gap to the class. Their presentation should identify the Cumberland Gap, describe it, and explain why it became such a vital avenue to the lands west of the Appalachians. Then students should be prepared to answer questions from the class. **(Visual/Spatial)**

Setting the Scene In the early years of the nation, Americans were bursting with energy and enthusiasm about their new country. Many left their homes in the coastal states and headed inland in search of open land, independence, and prosperity. In 1828, James Hall, a lawyer and writer who lived in the Ohio Valley, captured the mood of a nation on the move in a travel book called *Letters From the West.* In the book, Hall described his voyage down the Ohio River in a keelboat. Hall saw "a great number and a great variety of people" passing through the area on their way west:

> 66 *The innumerable caravans of adventurers, who are daily crowding to the west in search of homes, and the numbers who traverse [cross] these interesting regions from motives of curiosity, produce a constant succession of visitors of every class, and of almost every nation. English, Irish, French and Germans, are constantly emigrating to the new states and territories.* 99

—James Hall

These pioneers had all overcome a geographical barrier to reach the American West. They had crossed the Appalachian Mountains.

Crossing the Appalachians

With a growing and youthful population, the United States needed space to expand. Young couples dreamed of creating a bright and secure future for themselves and their families. Others sought to escape the overcrowding along the Atlantic Coast—to find a place with "elbow room." The area west of the Appalachian Mountains, a region known as **trans-Appalachia,** attracted these

Many pioneers crossed the Appalachians by way of the Cumberland Gap (below).

RESOURCE DIRECTORY

Teaching Resources
Learning Styles Lesson Plans booklet, p. 17
Guided Reading and Review booklet, p. 30

Other Print Resources
Historical Outline Map Book *Western Land Claims,* p. 29

Technology
Section Reading Support Transparencies
Guided Reading Audiotapes (English/Spanish), Ch. 7

Student Edition on Audio CD, Ch. 7
Color Transparencies *Cause-and-Effect Charts,* D3; *Fine Art,* E6; *American Photo,* F2
Prentice Hall Presentation Pro CD-ROM, Ch. 7
Companion Web site, www.phschool.com

Focus Tell students that a young, energetic generation of Americans crossed the Appalachians during this period and moved into the river valleys from the Ohio to the mouth of the Mississippi. Ask what effect this migration had on the original inhabitants of these regions.

Instruct Call students' attention to the quotation by James Hall on the previous page. Point out the author's statements that those traveling west were "adventurers," motivated by "curiosity." Do students agree with this assessment? Discuss with students the fact that Native Americans were forced to move at this time. Discuss the ways in which their experience differed from those who migrated voluntarily.

Assess/Reteach Have students compare and contrast the reasons settlers originally migrated to the United States with the reasons people gave for continuing to travel west in the first half of the nineteenth century.

Focus on TECHNOLOGY

The Log Cabin One reason so many Americans left their homes and migrated westward may have been that they knew it would not be very difficult to build a new shelter. The typical log cabin took only a few days to build and required no expensive nails or spikes. (The builder cut notches in the logs to fit them together.) In fact, a pioneer could build a log cabin with no tools besides an axe, and could even build a small cabin by himself.

Many log cabins had only one room, with blankets or sheets hung from the ceiling to provide a bit of privacy. Glass windows were rare, since glass was both costly and difficult to transport. For floors, some cabins used wooden boards; others simply used packed earth.

Families generally saw their cabins as temporary homes while they cleared the surrounding fields for farming. In time, many built larger, more comfortable homes.

Sounds of an Era

Listen to the words of Morris Birkbeck, a British traveler who observed the westward migration of settlers, and other sounds from the early years of the republic.

Americans. They loaded up their wagons and headed out toward a better life in the wilderness.

In the early 1800s, Americans traveled several main roads over the Appalachians. From New England, they followed the Mohawk Trail into western New York. From Philadelphia, they took Forbes' Road to Pittsburgh, where, like James Hall, they could voyage west on the Ohio River. From Baltimore, they also went to Pittsburgh, on Braddock's Road. From the Middle Atlantic states, settlers used the newly built Cumberland Road, also called the National Road. Southerners followed either the Great Valley Road or the Richmond Road through the mountains to the Cumberland Gap, a low spot in the Appalachians in Southwestern Virginia. From there, they could take the Wilderness Road north, into the Ohio Valley.

Settling the Wilderness As James Hall noted, people from many different backgrounds settled in trans-Appalachia. One settler, Daniel Boone, became a legend in his own lifetime, though in many ways he was no different from thousands of other pioneers. He had hunted in Kentucky as early as 1767 and had survived a clash with a band of Cherokee in 1773. In 1775, the Transylvania Company employed Boone and a group of men to cut the Wilderness Road through the Cumberland Gap. This road became the main route to trans-Appalachia for countless Americans, including Boone's own family. By 1792, nearly 75,000 pioneers had settled in Kentucky, which entered the Union that year as the fifteenth state.

Several other important roads carried the earliest settlers on the long and difficult journey across the Appalachians. Most of these routes ended in the Ohio Valley. In the late 1780s, only a few hundred white Americans lived north of the Ohio River. By 1830, hundreds of thousands of Americans had settled in the region, which by then consisted of Michigan Territory and three new states. These new states were Ohio (with close to 1,000,000 residents), Indiana (with almost 350,000 residents), and Illinois (with more than 150,000 residents).

Settlers usually moved as families, although young men often traveled west alone. Once the newcomers settled on a piece of land, they faced a heavy burden of work. Families toiled to clear trees and underbrush, plant corn or other crops, and build themselves a log cabin—all with hand tools and muscle power.

Although most new settlers were white, many African Americans also crossed the Appalachians. An estimated 98,000 slaves moved west with their owners between 1790 and 1810 to settle in the region south of the Ohio River. The Northwest Ordinance of 1787 had forbidden slavery in territories north of the Ohio.

Forcing Native Americans West Settlers pushing across the Appalachians wanted land, free of competition from the Native Americans living there. The government developed a plan to help settlers by pressuring the eastern tribes to move farther west to the Louisiana Territory. Government leaders saw this as the perfect site for a permanent Indian home. It lay well beyond existing settlements, and most of it, according to reports, was unfit for farming. There the Indians could be isolated from American settlers.

Federal agents carried out the removal plan. Occasionally, they would bribe a dishonest chief into approving a land sale, often against the wishes of his people or of other tribes in his Indian nation. Gradually Native Americans gave

RESOURCE DIRECTORY

Teaching Resources
Biography, Literature, and Comparing Primary Sources booklet (Comparing Primary Sources) *On Peace and Friendship,* pp. 109–110

Other Print Resources
American History Block Scheduling Support *No Neighbors for Miles: The Northwest Territory,* found in the Forging a New Nation folder, includes interdisciplinary lesson suggestions and activities for Geography and History, Primary Sources, Biography, and Literature.

Nystrom *Atlas of Our Country* Early Expansion of the United States, pp. 20–21
Historical Outline Map Book *Land Acquired from Native Americans to 1810,* p. 31

Technology
Color Transparencies *Historical Maps,* A60, A15; *American Diversity,* G3
Sounds of an Era Audio CD *Morris Birkbeck on America Moving Westward* (time: 50 seconds)
RESOURCE PRO Critical Thinking Activity *Making Comparisons: Population Boom,* found on Resource Pro, allows students to apply this skill by analyzing census data from 1790 to 1830.

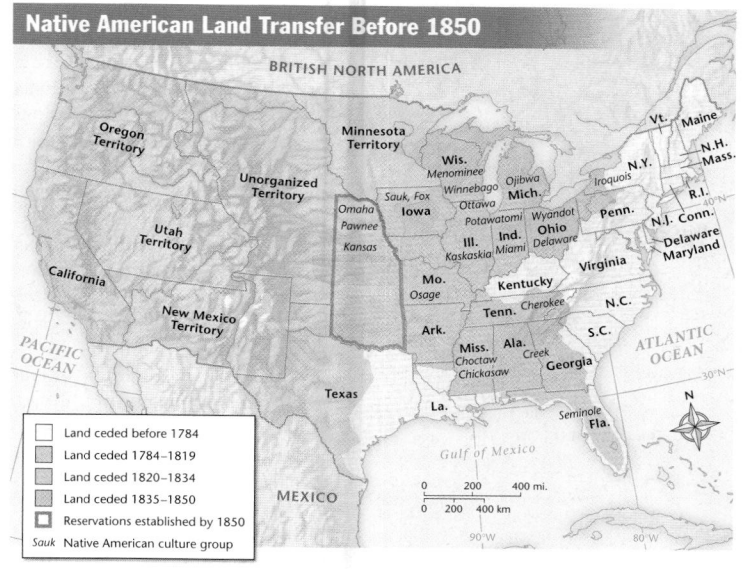

Native American Land Transfer Before 1850

Land ceded before 1784
Land ceded 1784–1819
Land ceded 1820–1834
Land ceded 1835–1850
Reservations established by 1850
Sauk Native American culture group

up their homelands in one treaty after another. Although some Native Americans fought bitterly against removal, most went peacefully.

By 1840, most Native Americans in the eastern states had resettled on reservations west of the Mississippi River, in what had come to be known as Indian country. No matter where Native Americans lived, however, their numbers steadily shrank. The main cause of their decline continued to be diseases brought by white settlers. Devastating epidemics regularly swept through Indian villages on both sides of the Mississippi River.

Expanding Into Florida

Daniel Boone's Kentucky was just one area south of the Ohio River that drew settlers. Americans also swarmed into Tennessee and the Gulf Coast states. The population of Alabama, Mississippi, and Louisiana swelled with pioneers. By 1830, even Florida had 35,000 American settlers, only 11 years after becoming part of the United States.

Spanish Occupation The story of how the United States acquired Florida begins in 1795. In that year the United States and Spain agreed to the Pinckney Treaty, named after Thomas Pinckney, the American diplomat who arranged it. The treaty settled several points, including the following:

1. The southern boundary of the United States was set at 31° N latitude, leaving Florida firmly in Spanish hands.
2. United States citizens would be allowed free use of the Mississippi River through Spanish territory.
3. Spain and the United States agreed to control the Native Americans living within their borders and to prevent them from attacking each other's territory.

By 1810, so many Americans had settled in the western part of Florida that they declared the region's independence. Later, the United States annexed West Florida. Expansionists wanted the rest of the Spanish colony, too, and Americans proceeded to take control of several parts of East Florida. At about

READING CHECK
What were Spain's responsibilites according to the Pinckney Treaty?

Connecting with History and Conflict

Organize students into two groups to debate whether Congress should have condemned Andrew Jackson for his actions in Florida in 1818. Assign one group the affirmative and the other group the negative position. Then call on students for statements that support their assigned point of view. If it is necessary to guide the debate, offer such questions as the following: Did the Seminoles' actions justify Jackson's response? Should Spanish sovereignty in Florida have been recognized? Should Jackson, as a general, have taken it upon himself to set U.S. foreign policy or take military action without approval of the President or Congress? Under what circumstances, if any, do ends justify the means used to achieve them? **(Logical/Mathematical)**

READING CHECK

Americans already occupied Florida; Spain decided to get whatever it could in exchange for the land it would lose anyway.

The Annexation of Florida

MAP SKILLS The United States annexed part of West Florida in 1810 and the rest of West Florida and East Florida nine years later. **Location** Why were the Seminole settlements at Pensacola and St. Marks a threat to the United States?

READING CHECK
Why did Spain agree to give Florida to the United States?

the same time, rebellions arose throughout Spain's South American colonies. Fearing that it would lose its empire, the Spanish government tried desperately to put down the uprisings. In the meantime, it paid little attention to East and West Florida. The Seminoles, a Native American group living in the Floridas, took advantage of Spain's lax rule by stepping up their raids on settlements in southern Georgia. The Seminoles also angered American officials by allowing escaped slaves to live among them.

The general in charge of protecting the settlers was the tough veteran of the War of 1812, Andrew Jackson. When told to put an end to the attacks, Jackson noted that he would have to cross the border into the Spanish Floridas. "Let it be signified to me," Jackson wrote President Monroe, "that the possession of the Floridas would be desirable to the United States, and in sixty days it will be accomplished." Though Monroe did not openly encourage him, Jackson decided to go ahead with his invasion plan.

The Seminole Wars General Jackson proved to be as good as his promise. Setting out in March 1818 with only 2,000 men, he swept across the border, starting what would later be called the First Seminole War. The American troops burned Seminole villages, captured Spanish towns, and within a few weeks claimed possession of the entire western part of the Floridas. Spain expressed outrage, and Congress threatened to condemn Jackson. Most Americans, however, applauded Jackson's bold move.

Monroe and his Secretary of State, John Quincy Adams, decided to make the best of the situation. In late 1818, Adams defined the American position on the issue. Refusing to apologize for Jackson's actions, Adams accused Spain of breaking the Pinckney Treaty by failing to control the Seminoles.

The Spanish were in a poor position to argue. If the United States recognized and supported the independence movements forming in South America, Spain would have no hope of holding on to its colonies there. Besides, by then the Americans had already occupied West Florida and stationed troops in East Florida. The Spanish decided that they might as well try to get something for the land they had already lost.

Spain's representative in Washington, Luiz de Onís, spent weeks working out a treaty with Adams. Finally, in 1819, the two men agreed on what has since been called the **Adams-Onís Treaty.** Spain agreed to **cede,** or give up, Florida to the United States. The treaty also fixed the boundary between the Louisiana Purchase and Spanish territory in the West. To settle the dispute over this boundary, the United States agreed to cede its claims to a huge territory in what is now the southwestern United States, including part of present-day Texas.

252 Chapter 7 • *Life in the New Nation*

CAPTION ANSWERS

Map Skills The settlements harbored escaped slaves and provided a base for Seminole attacks on the United States.

RESOURCE DIRECTORY

Teaching Resources
Biography, Literature, and Comparing Primary Sources booklet (Literature) *The Pioneers,* pp. 47–48

Other Print Resources
Historical Outline Map Book *The War of 1812,* p. 32; *Oregon Country,* p. 38

Technology
Color Transparencies *Fine Art,* E7
RESOURCE PRO® **Primary Source Activity** *Moving West,* found on Resource Pro, uses excerpts from John James Audubon's *Audubon's America* to help students visualize the life of a Kentucky settler.

Bound for the Pacific

Once Americans had crossed the Appalachian barrier, they realized that the entire continent lay open before them. Some began to dream of an American empire stretching from the Atlantic to the Pacific. They believed that the United States had a divine mission to spread liberty across the continent. A New York journalist named John L. O'Sullivan captured this attitude when he coined the phrase **manifest destiny,** meaning "obvious or undeniable fate." Writing in 1845, O'Sullivan claimed that it was the nation's "manifest destiny to overspread and to possess the whole of the continent which Providence has given us for the development of the great experiment of liberty and federated self-government entrusted to us."

The Oregon Country   Americans first began to hear stories of a beautiful land beyond the Rocky Mountains in the 1820s. This vast territory, known as the Oregon Country, stretched from northern California to the southern border of Alaska. The area had magnificent mountains, endless forests, and fertile valleys.

Several Native American groups had lived in the Oregon Country for centuries. Yankee merchants from New England, traveling by ship, first traded for furs with these Indians in the late 1700s. After Lewis and Clark completed their overland expedition in 1806, growing numbers of American fur traders, such as Jedediah Smith and Jim Beckwourth, began to roam the Rocky Mountains in search of beaver pelts. Dubbed **mountain men,** these hardy trappers generally adopted Indian ways, and many of them married Indian women. They also used the Indian trails that led through the Rockies to California and Oregon.

By the early 1800s, four different nations—the United States, Great Britain, Russia, and Spain—claimed rights to the Oregon Country. In 1818, the United States and Britain signed a treaty agreeing to joint occupation of the region. This treaty, called the Convention of 1818, disregarded the wishes of Native Americans who already lived there. A year later, in the Adams-Onís Treaty, Spain gave up its claim to this region, and Russia followed suit in 1825.

As news of the Oregon Country filtered back to the East, a few churches decided to send missionaries to the territory to convert Native Americans to Christianity. The first of these missionaries, a Methodist minister named Jason Lee, arrived in Oregon in 1834. He promptly built a mission school for Indians in the Willamette Valley.

Encouraged by his example, four Presbyterian missionaries joined Lee in Oregon in 1836. Among them was one of the first white women to cross the Rocky Mountains, Narcissa Prentiss Whitman. Whitman and her husband, a doctor, lived and worked among the Cayuse and Nez Percé. Neither Whitman nor the other missionaries who settled in Oregon had much success in converting the region's Indians. In fact, their actions often created more hostility than goodwill.

VIEWING HISTORY Pausing for a photograph in front of their covered wagon, this family was one of many that headed west in the 1840s in search of a better life. **Recognizing Bias** *Why do you think fictional portrayals of the westward journey differ so much from the facts?*

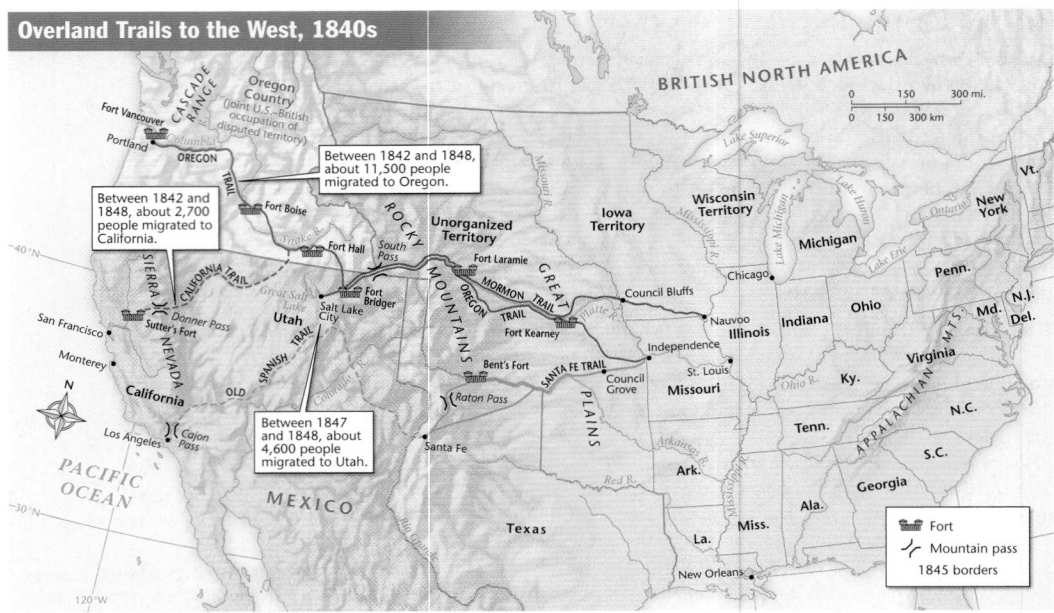

Between 1842 and 1848, about 11,500 people migrated to Oregon.

Between 1842 and 1848, about 2,700 people migrated to California.

Between 1847 and 1848, about 4,600 people migrated to Utah.

Fort
Mountain pass
1845 borders

ACTIVITY
Connecting with Geography

Ask students to assume the roles of pioneers on the Mormon, Oregon, or Santa Fe Trail. Have them create two journal entries with a one-month time span between each. Tell students that each entry should describe life on the trail that day, what their surroundings are like, and the obstacles or hardships their wagon train has recently overcome. Have students use the map on this page to gauge the locations from which to write their entries. Tell them that a wagon train covered about 20 miles a day, or less in rugged terrain. Call on students to read their journal entries and have class members identify the approximate location of each entry from the information it contains. **(Logical/Mathematical; Visual/Spatial; Verbal/Linguistic)**

BACKGROUND
Science and Technology

The "prairie schooners" that carried pioneers across the Great Plains were only about half the size of the Conestoga wagons that moved a previous generation of settlers across the Appalachians. At about 10 feet long and just over 8 feet to the top of the canvas, they carried about a ton of goods. This made them light enough that if two of the six oxen pulling a wagon died, it could still be moved. Despite this design, group travel was necessary. Crossing deep streams and climbing steep slopes required families to combine their teams to move each wagon, one at a time. Also, brakes on loaded wagons were unreliable. Where no trees were available, this required groups going down steep hills to use one wagon as a windlass to ease the others to the bottom.

CAPTION ANSWERS

Map Skills The Columbia River.

MAP SKILLS Thousands of settlers headed west along various overland trails in the 1840s, facing dry country in some parts of the journey and tall, rugged mountains in others. **Movement** Along what important river did the final leg of the Oregon Trail run?

Overland Travelers Starting in 1842, organized wagon trains carried masses of migrants to the West, largely following Indian trails opened up by mountain men. Groups would first meet at a small town in western Missouri called Independence. From there they began the grueling, 2,000-mile trek, or journey, to Oregon. The wagon trains traveled along the **Oregon Trail,** the main route across the vast central plains and the Rocky Mountains.

The journey to the Oregon Country could take from four to six months, and it was expensive. A typical family paid between $500 and $1,000 to make the trip. It was also exhausting. Getting the heavy covered wagons across rivers, through muddy bogs, and up steep hills was backbreaking work.

Why, then, did people head west? The most common reason was to obtain land, which could be settled and farmed or bought and sold at a profit. Another reason was to trade goods, and as the western population grew, the region's attractiveness to merchants grew as well. Beyond these economic factors, many of the pioneers also enjoyed the challenge and independence of life on the frontier.

Movies and television westerns would have us believe that western pioneers and Indians continually fought with each other. In fact, they spent more time trading than fighting. Serious conflict did not develop until the 1850s. Before then, white travelers regularly received food and other items from Indians in return for clothing and tools. Disease was a far more deadly threat to the pioneers than the Native Americans. For example, cholera killed as many as 10,000 pioneers (about 4 percent of the total) between 1840 and 1860.

Normally, pioneers on the Oregon Trail traveled along the Platte River in present-day Nebraska and through the South Pass in present-day Wyoming. A **pass** is a low spot in a mountain range that allows travelers to cross over to the other side. After entering Oregon, they would follow the Snake River to settlements in the Northwest.

RESOURCE DIRECTORY

Teaching Resources
Biography, Literature, and Comparing Primary Sources booklet (Biography) *Brigham Young,* p. 12

Other Print Resources
Historical Outline Map Book *Trails to the West,* p. 40

Technology
Color Transparencies *Historical Maps,* A13, A14

RESOURCE PRO® **Literature Activity** *Song of the Pioneers,* found on Resource Pro, uses the song "Sweet Betsy from Pike" to portray life along the trail to the west.

RESOURCE PRO® **Critical Thinking Activity** *Determining Relevance,* found on Resource Pro, encourages students to consider the relationship between American westward migration from 1841 to 1858 and the expansionist policies of the United States.

Not all westward trails led to Oregon. The **Santa Fe Trail,** which also began in Independence, veered southwest to Santa Fe, New Mexico. Merchants used this route starting in 1821 to carry goods into Mexican territory. From Santa Fe, the Old Spanish Trail carried travelers to southern California. People heading for northern California would follow the Oregon Trail as far as the Snake River. Then they would turn southwest along the California Trail.

By 1845, more than 5,000 Americans had migrated to the Oregon Country, and they demanded complete control of the area. In fact, the Democrats won the 1844 election with the slogan "Fifty-four forty or fight," calling for the northern boundary of American territory to extend past the fifty-fourth parallel (line of latitude). In the Treaty of 1846, however, the United States and Great Britain agreed to divide the Oregon Country along the forty-ninth parallel.

Mormon Migrations You have read about the Mormons, a religious group founded by Joseph Smith in New York State. Harassed by neighbors who condemned their beliefs, the Mormons migrated to Ohio and then to Missouri before finding a home in Nauvoo, Illinois, in 1839. For a while, the Mormons prospered in Illinois. Relations with neighbors broke down, however, in part because Smith revealed that the Mormons allowed men to have more than one wife at the same time. After a hostile mob killed Smith and his brother in 1844, the Mormons moved on once again.

The new leader of the church, Brigham Young, decided that the Mormons' only hope was to live beyond the borders of the United States. He and other leaders chose an area near the Great Salt Lake, in Mexican territory, as the Mormons' new home.

Starting in 1847, hundreds of Mormons left their temporary camps in Iowa for new homes in the valley of the Great Salt Lake. The route they followed came to be called the Mormon Trail. Within three years, more than 11,000 Mormons had settled in the valley. By 1860, about 30,000 Mormons lived in Salt Lake City and more than 90 other towns in what was then Utah Territory. They prospered as farmers and traders by skillfully irrigating their desert region and by selling food and supplies to pioneers heading to California and Oregon.

Gold Rush In January 1848, a carpenter who was building a sawmill for John Sutter, a Swiss immigrant living in California, discovered gold on Sutter's land. The Mexican governor of California had originally granted Sutter the land to build a colony for settlers. By August of that year, some 4,000 gold-crazed prospectors swarmed over the property, destroying the colony and bankrupting Sutter. The **California Gold Rush** had begun. No event was more important in attracting settlers to the West than the gold strike at Sutter's Mill.

The news filled the papers in the eastern United States, and Americans touched by gold fever rushed west by the thousands. California had about 14,000 residents in 1848. A year later the population had exploded to an estimated 100,000, and it reached roughly 200,000 by 1852. Some settlers traveled by ship around the tip of South America or by a combination of ship, rail, and foot via Central America. Most, however, took the direct route, west across the overland trails.

A majority of the new immigrants were unmarried men. In fact, women and children made up only 5 percent of the "forty-niners" who went to

VIEWING HISTORY This gold miner was one of thousands who traveled to California to find his fortune. **Drawing Conclusions** *Describe the typical "forty-niner."*

Reading Comprehension

1. The trans-Appalachia area, primarily the Ohio River valley.

2. As Americans already occupied Florida, Spain saw little hope of keeping Florida and decided to get whatever it could in exchange for the land it would lose anyway.

3. Americans began to believe that it was their right to possess the Oregon Country, which led them to aggressively pursue the acquisition of this territory.

4. It brought hundreds of thousands of people to the state, transformed San Francisco into a major commercial center, and destroyed much of what remained of Native American cultures.

Critical Thinking and Writing

5. Most Native American migrations were forced moves resulting from treaties imposed upon them by the United States. White settlers and immigrants migrated because they chose to.

6. Possible essay topic: Yes, because settling in a new area, especially on the frontier, was very difficult and required a great deal of energy and hard work.

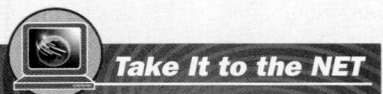

Topics for one-act plays will vary, but should demonstrate knowledge gained from primary sources.

VIEWING HISTORY Within two years of the discovery of gold, Columbia, California, had grown from a small camp in the Sierra Nevadas into the bustling town shown here. After miners extracted most of the area's gold, the town's population declined from a peak of about 6,000 to only 500. **Recognizing Cause and Effect** *Why did the population drop so much when the mining boom ended?*

California in the 1849 gold rush. African Americans, both enslaved and free, also took part in the gold rush. Slaves worked as servants or searched for gold on their owners' work crews, while some free African Americans became independent miners. The gold rush brought settlers not only from the United States but also from Europe and Asia. By 1852, about 10 percent of Californians were Chinese. These Chinese immigrants mainly labored as miners and servants.

The gold rush had a tremendous impact on life in California. For Native Americans, the flood of immigrants was a disaster. Miners forced Indian men to work in the mines and Indian women to work in their households.

Although few miners actually became rich from their efforts, the Gold Rush brought commercial prosperity to cities along the Pacific Coast. The growth of San Francisco was the most impressive. From a small trading village of about 800 people before the gold rush, it had grown to a bustling city of more than 35,000 by 1852.

In the wake of the California Gold Rush came news of more gold strikes. Miners rushed to Cripple Creek in Colorado in the late 1850s, to the Fraser River in western Canada in 1858, and to smaller strikes in Montana and Idaho in the early 1860s.

Whenever reports of a strike circulated, new towns appeared almost overnight. Men and women came to mine, to open stores, or to run saloons. Some stories have exaggerated the number of fights and murders that took place in these boomtowns, but many of the towns were truly wild and violent places.

Mining towns usually had short lives. During the boom, hundreds of new residents arrived and built scores of houses and businesses with amazing speed. Then, when the mines stopped producing, the towns went bust and people moved on. Many mining communities slowly decayed and died, turning into abandoned **ghost towns.** A few of the luckier mining towns were reborn in the late 1900s as tourist and skiing centers.

Section 2 Assessment

READING COMPREHENSION

1. What areas did Americans settle in the early 1800s?

2. Why did Spain **cede** Florida to the United States?

3. How did the idea of **manifest destiny** shape American attitudes regarding the Oregon Country?

4. What were some consequences of the **California Gold Rush?**

CRITICAL THINKING AND WRITING

5. **Making Comparisons** How were the migrations of Native Americans different from those of people of European descent?

6. **Writing to Persuade** In your view, would a young population be more likely to migrate than an older population? Write a brief essay explaining your position.

Activity: Writing a One-Act Play Read first-hand accounts of Americans traveling to the West. Use the primary sources you have read to write a one-act play based on life on the trail or life in the West. Use the links provided in the *America: Pathways to the Present* area of the following Web site for help in completing this activity. www.phschool.com

CAPTION ANSWERS

Viewing History Without a source of gold, miners and the people who sold goods and services to them could no longer earn a living in the town, and many then left.

RESOURCE DIRECTORY

Teaching Resources
Units 3/4 booklet
• Section 2 Quiz, p. 5
Guide to the Essentials
• Section 2 Summary, p. 38

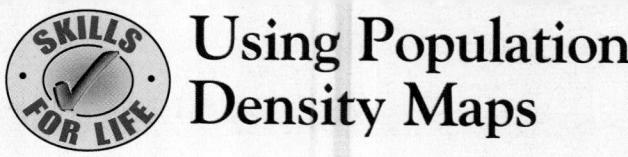

Using Population Density Maps

A population density number represents the average number of persons living in a given area—usually a square mile or a square kilometer. Population density maps can show density for a small area, such as a city, or for a very large area, such as a continent or the entire world. Historians use population density maps to see patterns of human settlement at a particular period of time or changes in population over time.

The maps below represent the population densities in the United States in 1790 and 1830. The figures are based on United States census counts, which, at that time, included whites and African Americans but not Native Americans.

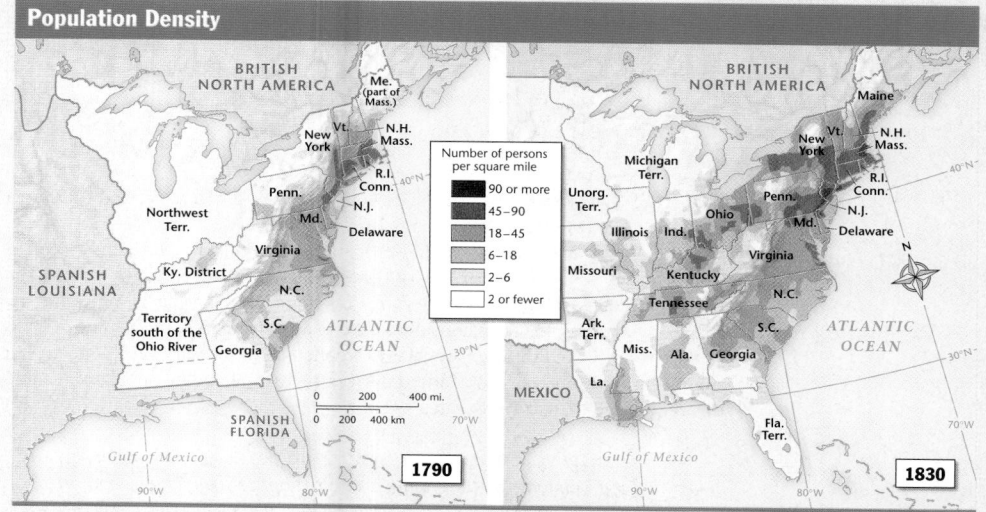

LEARN THE SKILL

Use the following steps to interpret population density maps:

1. **Determine what information each map provides.** Look at the map title and key; then study the map.

2. **Determine the population density of different regions.** Use the map key as your guide.

3. **Analyze population density patterns.** Note where density is the highest and the lowest, and where changes have occurred over time.

4. **Study the maps to draw conclusions.** Relate what you already know about history to what you see on the maps.

PRACTICE THE SKILL

Answer the following questions:

1. **(a)** What kind of information is represented by the colors? **(b)** What do the darkest and lightest colors represent?

2. **(a)** What was the population density of the Northwest Territory in 1790? **(b)** Which states on each map had population densities of 45 or more persons per square mile?

3. **(a)** In general, where was most of the population concentrated in 1790? **(b)** Which was the most densely populated state in 1790? **(c)** Do you think this state also had the largest total population of any state? Explain. **(d)** Which states experienced the greatest and most widespread increase in population density between 1790 and 1830?

4. **(a)** What economic factors do you think accounted for the difference in the population densities of the North and the South, in 1790 and 1830? **(b)** What geographical factors probably contributed to the overall pattern of settlement in 1830? Explain.

APPLY THE SKILL

See the Chapter Review and Assessment for another opportunity to apply this skill.

RESOURCE DIRECTORY

Teaching Resources
Skills for Life booklet, p. 9

Technology
Social Studies Skills Tutor CD-ROM
Interactive Practice in
- Geographic Literacy
- Critical Thinking and Reading
- Visual Analysis
- Communications

USING POPULATION DENSITY MAPS

Focus Analyze and draw conclusions from a population density map.

Instruct Review the concept of population density. Ask: Is your school in a densely populated region? Is your county or township densely populated? What parts of your state are more densely populated than others? Have students read the text on this page.

Extend See the Skills for Life activity in the Resource Directory below.

ANSWERS
PRACTICE THE SKILL

1. **(a)** The number of persons per square mile. **(b)** The darkest colors represent the areas of densest population; the lightest colors represent the areas of least dense population.

2. **(a)** The population density was two or fewer persons per square mile. **(b)** 1790 map: Parts of New York, New Jersey, Pennsylvania, Connecticut, Rhode Island, and Massachusetts. 1830 map: All of Connecticut and Rhode Island, and parts of Ohio, Indiana, Kentucky, Tennessee, Pennsylvania, Maryland, Virginia, New York, Massachusetts, New Hampshire, and Maine.

3. **(a)** In general, the population was concentrated along the New England and Middle Atlantic coast. **(b)** Rhode Island. **(c)** No. It had the smallest area of any state. **(d)** Ohio (was Northwest Territory in 1790), Pennsylvania, and New York.

4. **(a)** The primarily agricultural nature of the South resulted in a much lower population density than that of the North, which had more cities and industries. **(b)** The South was more suited to large farms; the North had harbors that encouraged the growth of cities, trade, and commerce, and its land was often rocky or wooded and supported only small family farms.

Section 3
The Great Plains and the Southwest

SECTION OBJECTIVES

1. Learn how the lives of Plains Indians changed from the 1500s to the 1800s.
2. Discover how Spain integrated California and the Rio Grande valley into Hispanic North America.
3. Find out why Texas fought to win its independence from Mexico.

BELLRINGER

Warm-Up Activity Provide a map of the United States. Ask students to list at least five cities in California, Texas, and New Mexico with names that are Spanish in origin. Ask them if, based on what they know, Mexican and American cultures would be likely to clash.

Activating Prior Knowledge
Ask students to recall from films, books, and other sources the names of Native American groups who lived on the Great Plains. Ask them to consider the cultural images that these sources created.

READING STRATEGY

Ask students to read the section's bold-faced headings. Have them write a question about each heading and look for the answers as they read.

ACTIVITY
Connecting with Culture

Organize the class into small groups. Tell each group to imagine that it is 1880 and that they are visiting a school to tell students about their lives as young men and women in the Southwest of the 1830s. Have each group prepare a short talk to present to the class. Tell groups to present their reminiscences in the roles of Native Americans and Mexicans, as well as white soldiers, settlers, and townspeople. Ask each group to give its talk to the class.
(Bodily/Kinesthetic; Verbal/Linguistic)

The Great Plains and the Southwest

READING FOCUS

• How did the lives of Plains Indians change from the 1500s to the 1800s?
• How did Spain integrate California and the Rio Grande valley into Hispanic North America?
• Why did Texas fight to win its independence from Mexico?

MAIN IDEA

The migration of Spaniards from central Mexico and settlers from the United States into the Great Plains, California, and the Rio Grande valley led to economic and political changes.

KEY TERMS

Great Plains
nomadic
presidio
Texas War for Independence
Battle of the Alamo

TAKING NOTES

As you read, complete the chart below to show how different parts of western North America were affected by settlers and trade in the early 1800s.

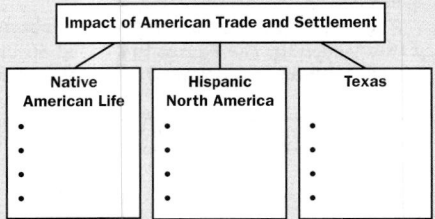

Impact of American Trade and Settlement

Native American Life	Hispanic North America	Texas
•	•	•
•	•	•
•	•	•
•	•	•

Setting the Scene In the 1840s, American settlers followed trails west across the **Great Plains,** the vast grassland that lies between the Mississippi River and the Rocky Mountains. Their destinations included the Oregon Country, California, and New Mexico. Few of these pioneers, however, chose to settle on the Great Plains. They saw this dry, treeless region as a barrier to be overcome as quickly as possible. They considered the plains unsuitable for farming, thanks in part to an expedition led by Major Stephen H. Long in 1820. The report submitted by Long's group painted a bleak picture of the Great Plains, calling this region the "Great American Desert":

> 66 *In regard to this extensive section of country, we do not hesitate in giving the opinion, that it is almost wholly unfit for cultivation, and of course uninhabitable by a people depending upon agriculture for their subsistence. Although tracts of fertile land, considerably extensive, are occasionally to be met with, yet the scarcity of wood and water, almost uniformly prevalent, will prove an insuperable obstacle in the way of settling the country.* 99
> —*Account of an Expedition from Pittsburgh to the Rocky Mountains,* 1823

Many pioneers in the 1840s crossed the prairies of the "Great American Desert" and high mountain ranges in search of fertile land on the Pacific Coast.

RESOURCE DIRECTORY

Teaching Resources
Guided Reading and Review booklet, p. 31

Technology
Section Reading Support Transparencies
Guided Reading Audiotapes (English/Spanish), Ch. 7
Student Edition on Audio CD, Ch. 7
Prentice Hall Presentation Pro CD-ROM, Ch. 7
Companion Web site, www.phschool.com

Plains Indians

Long's description was too harsh. For thousands of years before Long's expedition, Native Americans had thrived in this seemingly inhospitable land. Some of these Plains Indians, especially in the western part of the region, were **nomadic**—continually migrating instead of living permanently in one place. They hunted the bison, or what white settlers called buffalo, on foot, moving their camps to stay close to the huge herds. Plains peoples in the eastern part, where the climate was wetter, hunted buffalo and other game but also established permanent farms and villages. These Native Americans' way of life changed dramatically after Europeans arrived on the Plains.

The Impact of the Horse   One European animal, the horse, had a profound impact on the everyday lives of the Plains Indians. The Spanish had brought horses to their colonies in northern Mexico in the 1500s. Native Americans acquired them through trade and also through raids on Spanish settlements. By the mid-1700s, horses had spread as far north as the Missouri Valley, the Dakotas, and the Oregon Country.

Horses changed much about Native American life, from the nature of warfare to the division of labor between men and women. Many Native Americans, however, took advantage of the horse without allowing it to transform their cultures. The Pawnee, Mandan, and other Native American nations continued to live primarily as farmers, hunters, and gatherers. As in most Native American societies, the women in these villages did most of the farming, while the men took charge of the hunting.

For other Native Americans, the horse completely changed their way of life. Carrying their possessions on the backs of horses, they followed the vast herds of buffalo that crisscrossed the Great Plains. These nomadic Indians of the Plains differed sharply from each other in many respects, but they did share some common practices. They depended heavily on skilled riding, hunting, and fighting—skills that were formally taught to men alone.

By 1800, the Plains Indians had hunted the buffalo on horseback for more than half a century. During that time they discovered countless uses for the buffalo. James R. Walker, a doctor who lived for a time among the Oglala Sioux, described how the buffalo had become an important resource for Native Americans:

> 66 *[They used] the hair for making ropes and pads and for ornamental and ceremonial purposes; the horns and hoofs for making implements and utensils; the bones for making soup and articles to be used in their various occupations and games; the sinews [tendons] for making their sewing thread and their stronger cords such as bowstrings; the skins for making ropes, tipis, clothing . . . ; the flesh and viscera [intestines] for food.* 99
>
> —James R. Walker

READING CHECK
How did the horse change the lives of Native Americans on the Great Plains?

VIEWING FINE ART Alfred Jacob Miller's painting illustrates the nomadic life adopted by many native Americans of the Plains. Both horses and dogs provided hauling power. Using a *travois*, or sled, a dog could pull a 40-pound load 5 or 6 miles a day. **Recognizing Cause and Effect** *How did the nomadic lifestyle affect the roles of men and women?*

This Navajo wall painting shows the Spanish bringing horses and other animals into the Southwest. Horses quickly spread north into the Great Plains.

New Nations and New Settlers Many of the nomads who dominated the Great Plains in the early 1800s were newcomers to that region. The Crow had long lived on the Plains, but the Cheyenne, the Sioux, the Comanche, and the Blackfeet all migrated to the Plains after horses made it easy for them to live on the move.

The seemingly endless herds of buffalo were only one reason that Indian nations migrated to the Plains. Another motivation was the need to avoid the wave of settlers pushing westward toward the Mississippi River and beyond. By the 1830s, white settlers had already penetrated the land set aside as Indian Country. In the North, the steady stream of migrants led to the creation of three new states: Iowa (1846), Wisconsin (1848), and Minnesota (1858). Nomads could stay ahead of this migration, but Indians who had settled in villages had no option but to cope with it.

The Decline of Villages Before the arrival of the horse, the nomadic and village people of the Great Plains had often lived together peacefully. As the 1700s wore on, some nomadic groups developed into warrior cultures. To gain power in their group, Indians joined war parties and rode into battle. Warfare, like the buffalo hunt, became a way of life.

Nomadic Indians engaged in destructive raids on more settled Native American groups. The Comanche drove the Apache and Navajo west into Spanish New Mexico. By the early 1800s, they controlled the southern Plains. The Sioux—in alliance with the Arapaho and Cheyenne—assumed a similar dominance in the northern Plains.

Caught between white Americans advancing from the east and their nomadic neighbors to the west, agricultural Native Americans suffered greatly. Diseases brought by white traders and settlers added to the losses. No group was hit harder by European diseases than the Mandan. From a population of close to 10,000 in the mid-1700s, the number of Mandan already had fallen to a total of around 2,000 in the summer of 1837. Then a smallpox epidemic hit, leaving only a hundred or so Mandan alive.

By 1850, roughly 75,000 nomadic Indians lived on the Great Plains. They still swept across the grasslands, trailing the buffalo and pursuing their enemies. In addition to these nomads, roughly 84,000 Native Americans from the East lived in present-day Oklahoma. The United States government had forced them to relocate from land east of the Mississippi. Together, these two groups made up about 40 percent of the Native American population of North America.

Hispanic North America

In the 1500s, Plains Indians first made contact with Spanish settlers in northern Mexico. This region, in the present-day southwestern United States, lay on the edge of Spain's American empire. Unlike the Aztecs of central Mexico and the Incas of Peru, the Native Americans in northern Mexico did not possess fabulous wealth. Spanish explorers looking for gold and silver established settlements in present-day New Mexico and Texas but found little there to encourage intensive colonization. Missionaries and soldiers tried to control the native people, but most of their efforts failed, thanks in part to Spain's lack of interest in the distant land.

Spanish Colonies After the Pueblo revolt against Spanish settlers in New Mexico in the late 1600s, Spain's commitment to controlling the region had grown even weaker. In the 1700s, surrounded by hostile Indians, the Spanish limited settlement to a string of small towns along the Rio Grande and in Texas.

Once the most powerful nation in Europe, Spain was on the decline. In the late 1700s, it faced growing threats to its North American territory from other European nations. To meet those challenges, the Spanish government tried to establish better relations with the Comanche and Navajo. Their efforts achieved an uneasy peace with these Native American groups.

More dramatic was the Spanish effort to secure the area that is the present-day state of California. The Spanish feared that this land would fall into the hands of either the British or the Russians. In the late 1700s, Spanish soldiers and priests began building a network of missions and **presidios,** or forts, along the rugged California coastline. They created a chain of 21 missions running north from San Diego to San Francisco.

Enthusiastic Franciscan missionaries devoted themselves to converting Native Americans to Christianity. One such missionary, Father Junípero Serra, founded the first of the California missions at San Diego in 1769. By 1782, he had founded eight more missions farther north. While Spain's settlements in present-day New Mexico and Texas remained small, the presidios and missions in California grew and thrived, becoming lively centers of trade.

The missions owed much of their success to the Indians who labored for them. Indians built the missions, tended the cattle and sheep, farmed the land, and wove clothing. In return for their efforts, they usually received only food, clothing, and shelter. Soldiers and priests both treated the Indians harshly. Those who refused to work could be whipped or locked in chains. For these reasons, some Native Americans chose to escape when the opportunity arose. Those who stayed often endured poor living conditions and limited medical care, both of which contributed to tragic epidemics of measles and smallpox. Between 1769 and 1848, the population of Indians in California fell from about 300,000 to about 150,000.

READING CHECK
How did Spain establish control of California?

VIEWING HISTORY Franciscan friars lead a religious procession in this painting of a California mission in the early 1880s.
Drawing Inferences *How were the missions able to develop into centers of trade?*

Settlements in New Mexico began to revive in the late 1700s. Despite continued fighting with Indians, New Mexico benefited from increased attention from Spain. The Mexican population in the region increased from about 3,800 in 1750 to about 19,000 by 1800. Unlike settlers in eastern North America, those in New Mexico did not spread over the countryside in small farms. Instead, the presence of powerful nomadic Indians and the harsh landscape encouraged Mexicans to live close together in large settlements, such as Albuquerque.

Effects of Mexican Independence Mexico won its independence from Spain in 1821, after a 13-year struggle. The independence movement started with demands for self-government and a few local uprisings. In 1810, one of those uprisings, led by a priest named Miguel Hidalgo, triggered a rebellion that spread throughout southern Mexico. Spanish authorities crushed the early rebel groups, but the idea of independence stayed alive. In 1821, when a respected army officer named Agustín de Iturbide joined forces with the remaining rebels, victory came quickly. The Treaty of Córdoba, signed August 24, 1821, officially granted Mexico its independence from Spain.

California, New Mexico, and Texas were far from the fighting. Still, they benefited from being part of an independent Mexico. Political reforms brought greater democracy. As citizens of Mexico, the men in these territories were now free to elect representatives to the new government in Mexico City.

New Mexican policies, on the other hand, did not always benefit the territories. For example, in 1833 the government took control of California's missions, along with their irrigated farmlands, vineyards, and huge herds of cattle and sheep. They granted the rights to these lands to hundreds of wealthy, influential citizens. This action and other new economic policies, designed to bolster the Mexican economy, actually widened the gap between rich and poor in Mexico's northern territories. They did, however, encourage trade with the United States.

In 1821, William Becknell, a nearly bankrupt American, brought a load of goods from Missouri to the New Mexican capital of Santa Fe, where he sold them for mules and silver coins. Other American traders followed. The high quality and low prices of American goods nearly replaced New Mexico's trade with the rest of Mexico. By the early 1830s, caravans of wagons traveled regularly along the Santa Fe Trail.

American fur traders and merchants took advantage of economic openings in other parts of northern Mexico. New Englanders who sailed around South America to reach the West soon dominated the trade with California in fur, cattle hides, and tallow, a waxy substance used to make candles and soap. In return, Californians bought finished goods from the New Englanders. According to one resident of Monterey in the 1840s, "There is not a yard of tape, a pin, or a piece of domestic cotton or even thread that does not come from the United States."

Thus the United States had strong economic ties with New Mexico and California long before it gained political control over these areas. When the Mexican government loosened the rules affecting trade with American merchants, it ensured that Mexico's northern territories would trade more with the nearby United States than with the rest of Mexico. More important, stronger commercial ties encouraged some Americans to settle in northern Mexico.

Texas Fights for Independence

Nowhere was the flow of Americans into Mexican territory more apparent in the 1820s than in Texas. Stephen Austin, 29 years old and a member of the Missouri territorial legislature, led the first organized group of American settlers into Texas in 1822. Austin had received permission from the Mexican government to found a colony of several hundred families in east Texas. By 1825, some 1,800 immigrants lived in Austin's colony. Many of them were farmers from the region south of the Ohio River. On the coastal plains of Texas they found just what they wanted—fertile land for growing cotton.

U.S.-Mexico Trade

The Santa Fe Trail provided an important connection between the United States and New Mexico, but New Mexico was sparsely settled and the volume of trade was low. Traders relied on horse power to carry goods from Independence, Missouri, to Santa Fe along a trail following the Cimarron and Canadian Rivers west.

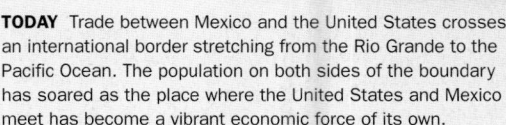

TODAY Trade between Mexico and the United States crosses an international border stretching from the Rio Grande to the Pacific Ocean. The population on both sides of the boundary has soared as the place where the United States and Mexico meet has become a vibrant economic force of its own.

Trade has long been important to the border region, but the North American Free Trade Agreement (NAFTA), which went into effect in 1993, lowered barriers and led to a large expansion of cross-border flows. Exports to Mexico rose from $41 billion in 1992 to $87 billion in 1999, while imports from Mexico tripled from $35 billion to $110 billion in the same period. Much of the increase can be credited to *maquiladoras*, or factories where parts are shipped from the United States and assembled to make goods for re-export to the north. Manufacturers can pay *maquiladora* workers in cities like Tijuana, near San Diego, and Ciudad Juarez, across the Rio Grande from El Paso, less money than workers in American factories are paid. Tijuana and Ciudad Juarez have boomed because of their border location, attracting workers from all parts of Mexico.

Chapter 7 • Section 3 **263**

READING CHECK
How did trade links develop between the United States and northern Mexico?

ACTIVITY
Connecting with History and Conflict

Ask students to analyze the tension caused by the American settlement of Mexico's northern territories. What role might cultural differences have played in the conflict? How do these differences continue to be a source of conflict today in Texas, New Mexico, and California? (**Verbal/Linguistic; Logical/Mathematical**)

BACKGROUND
Art History

Spanish settlers in New Mexico brought Catholicism to Native Americans, who adapted many of their own cultural practices to the new religion. Altarpieces were painted in vivid colors, and saints held local flowers and crops. A popular figure was the Virgin of Guadalupe, who was said to have first appeared to a Spaniard outside Mexico City in 1531. Aztecs and mestizos in New Spain connected her with the dark-skinned Aztec goddess Tonantzin, but they worshipped her as a Catholic saint.

READING CHECK
After achieving independence from Spain, Mexico took control of the missions and the agricultural activity in California. American traders brought coveted goods to New Mexico over the Santa Fe Trail. Goods from New England were transported by sea to California.

☑ **TEST PREPARATION**

Have students read the section "Texas Fights for Independence" starting on this page and then answer the question below.

What was the biggest reason for the conflict between Antonio Lopéz de Santa Anna and the American settlers?

A The settlers and Santa Anna both wanted to control the fate of Mexico.

B Santa Anna was anti-American.

Ⓒ The American settlers did not want to be ruled by a dictator.

D Both wanted control of Mexico's valuable mineral rights.

ACTIVITY

Connecting with History and Conflict

Have students conduct research to locate the full text of William Travis's famous "Victory or Death" letter, in which he pleaded for reinforcements at the Alamo. Have a volunteer provide a dramatic reading of the short but powerful letter to the class. **(Bodily/Kinesthetic)**

BACKGROUND

Connections to Today

The Alamo still stands, and it is "remembered" today by more people than William Travis and James Bowie could ever have imagined. More than 2.5 million people visit the Alamo every year. What most people think of as "The Alamo" is actually an old mission that is just part of a four-acre complex. The complex is owned by the state of Texas and operated by the Daughters of The Republic of Texas. Many visitors are surprised to find the Alamo—in their imagination, a dusty, run-down building in the middle of the Texas wilderness—standing smack in the middle of bustling downtown San Antonio, population: more than one million.

MAP SKILLS General Santa Anna's army far outnumbered the Texan fighters. **Movement** Why do you think Santa Anna expected victory as the Mexican forces moved eastward?

Mexican policy encouraged immigration, promising Americans cheap land, the protection of the Mexican government, and a multi-year tax break if they settled in Texas. By 1830, about 7,000 Americans lived in Texas, more than twice the number of Mexicans in the territory. That year, worried that they were losing Texas through immigration, Mexico passed a law prohibiting further American settlement. Equally important, it outlawed the importation of slaves. Americans continued to cross the border, however, bringing their slaves with them. By 1835, more than 30,000 Americans lived in Texas.

As their numbers swelled, Americans demanded more political control. In particular, they wanted slavery to be guaranteed under Mexican law. Without the labor of slaves, they argued, cotton could not be grown profitably. At the time, some 3,000 African American slaves labored for settlers in Texas. Through his diplomatic efforts, Austin blocked a proposed ban on slavery in the territory. The newcomers continued to push for the same rights from the Mexican government that they had possessed in the United States. Some settlers vowed to fight for independence if Mexico denied their request.

In 1833, General Antonio López de Santa Anna took power in Mexico and soon made himself dictator. Texans condemned Santa Anna's move away from democratic rule. American as well as Mexican settlers sharpened their demand for self-government, but the general refused to give in. Santa Anna's actions united Texans behind the cause of self-rule. In October 1835, these independence-minded settlers clashed with Mexican troops, beginning the **Texas War for Independence.** The settlers named Sam Houston, a recent immigrant from Tennessee, as their commander in chief.

The settlers' defiance of Mexico provoked Santa Anna into action. He led an army of several thousand men north to put down the rebellion. After crossing the Rio Grande, the Mexican general headed for the Alamo, a ruined Spanish mission in San Antonio that had been converted into a fortress. In December 1835, a group of Texas rebels had ousted Mexican troops from the fortress.

The Texans at the Alamo, numbering fewer than 200 men, prepared to resist Santa Anna. Their leaders, William Travis and James Bowie, hoped to be able to slow the general's advance long enough to allow their fellow rebels to assemble an army. The **Battle of the Alamo** lasted 13 days. Under siege by a vastly larger Mexican force, Travis sent this plea for help "to the People of Texas and all Americans in the World":

> 66 Fellow citizens & compatriots, I am besieged by a thousand or more of the Mexicans under Santa Anna. . . . I call on you in the name of Liberty, of patriotism & of everything dear to the American character to come to our aid, with all dispatch [speed]. . . . If this call is neglected, I am determined to sustain myself as long as possible & die like a soldier who never forgets what is due to his own honor or that of his country. 99

—Colonel William B. Travis

CAPTION ANSWERS

Map Skills Sample answer: The Texans had suffered heavy losses, and Santa Anna assumed they were fleeing.

RESOURCE DIRECTORY

Teaching Resources
Units 3/4 booklet
- Section 3 Quiz, p. 6
- Chapter 7 Test, pp. 7, 10
Guide to the Essentials
- Section 3 Summary, p. 39
- Chapter 7 Test, p. 40

Other Print Resources
Historical Outline Map Book *Independence for Texas*, p. 39
Chapter Tests with ExamView® Test Bank CD-ROM, Ch. 7

Technology
ExamView® Test Bank CD-ROM, Ch. 7
Social Studies Skills Tutor CD-ROM
Exploring Primary Sources in U.S. History CD-ROM *Letter from the Alamo, Lt. Col. Comd't. William Barrett Travis*

The Texans inflicted heavy casualties on the roughly 4,000 Mexican troops, but on the morning of March 6, Santa Anna's soldiers forced their way inside the walls. The Mexican general ordered his men to take no prisoners. When the fighting stopped, more than 180 Texans lay dead, including Travis, Bowie, and the legendary frontiersman Davy Crockett.

On March 2, 1836, the rebels formally declared the founding of an independent Republic of Texas. By the end of the month, however, the young republic seemed about to fall to Santa Anna's army. Thousands of Texans were fleeing eastward in what became known as the Runaway Scrape. Sure that victory was near, Santa Anna divided his force to finish off the rebels.

Just when all seemed lost, about 800 Texans regrouped at the San Jacinto River under Sam Houston. There, on April 21, they surprised the overconfident Santa Anna. Rallying to cries of "Remember the Alamo!" they routed the Mexican troops in a matter of minutes.

The Texans captured Santa Anna and, on May 14, forced him to sign the Treaty of Velasco recognizing the Republic of Texas. Mexico later denounced that treaty but did not try to retake Texas. In the fall of 1836, the citizens of Texas elected Sam Houston as their first president. They then drafted a constitution modeled on that of the United States. The constitution included a provision that prohibited the Texas Congress from interfering with slavery. The slavery provision would raise difficult issues in the years to come.

By the end of the 1830s, with almost no help from the United States government, American traders and settlers had established a firm presence in Hispanic North America. They had also succeeded in prying away a large piece of territory from Mexico. The loss of Texas remained a source of considerable tension between the United States and Mexico. Meanwhile, however, Americans kept on pushing west, moving beyond Texas into Mexican territory in present-day New Mexico and California. With these issues unresolved, tensions between Mexico and the United States grew to the point that war became a possibility.

American BIOGRAPHY

Sam Houston
1793–1863

Born in Virginia and raised in the Tennessee wilderness, Sam Houston left home as a teenager to live with Cherokee Indians. He took the name Black Raven and learned the Cherokee language.

During the War of 1812, Houston fought under Andrew Jackson, who later helped him get a job managing the removal of Cherokee Indians from Tennessee. Houston quit in 1818 after the Secretary of War scolded him for wearing his Indian clothes in the Secretary's office.

After studying law and serving in Congress, Houston became governor of Tennessee in 1827, at age 34. After his first term, he moved to Arkansas to trade with the Cherokee and use his knowledge of government to fight for Cherokee rights. In 1832, President Jackson sent Houston to Texas to work out treaties with Indians there. Houston later became a leader of the independence movement.

Section 3 Assessment

READING COMPREHENSION

1. How did horses and traders change the way of life of the Plains Indians?

2. Why was Spain unable to establish firm control over northern Mexico?

3. Why did people in New Mexico trade more with the United States than with the rest of Mexico?

4. What events triggered the **Texas War for Independence?** How did the war end?

CRITICAL THINKING AND WRITING

5. **Drawing Inferences** Why do you think the Mandan chose not to adopt the nomadic way of life?

6. **Recognizing Cause and Effect** Name two effects of increased trade between the United States and northern Mexico.

7. **Writing to Explain** Write a paragraph explaining how Mexican independence from Spain affected California, New Mexico, and Texas.

Take It to the NET

Activity: Virtual Field Trip Visit the Alamo, site of one of the most famous battles in American history. What do the images tell you about the history of the Alamo? Summarize your trip in a brief report. Use the links provided in the *America: Pathways to the Present* area of the following Web site for help in completing this activity.
www.phschool.com

Chapter 7 • Section 3 265

Section 3 Assessment

Reading Comprehension

1. Horses allowed some Native Americans to adopt a nomadic lifestyle, carrying their belongings with them while they followed the buffalo herds. One group of Native Americans, the Mandan, responded to the arrival of French traders by becoming middlemen in the fur trade.

2. Many hostile Native Americans lived in that area, resulting in rebellions against Spanish rule. Also, other European nations were attempting to take control of Spanish possessions in North America.

3. Because of the high quality and low prices of American goods, and the role of the Santa Fe Trail in facilitating trade.

4. Causes: opposition to Mexican laws prohibiting American immigration and the importation of slaves, and the desire by Americans for the same political rights they had enjoyed in the U.S.; Result: Texas gained independence.

Critical Thinking and Writing

5. Sample answer: They enjoyed their status as middlemen in the fur trade; the horse did not have a great impact on their culture.

6. The Santa Fe Trail was established, linking the countries economically and culturally; strong commercial ties gave Americans significant influence in the economy of California even before the Gold Rush.

7. Essays will vary, but should be supported by facts from the text.

Take It to the NET

Invite students to take a Virtual Field Trip at **www.phschool.com**

CUSTOMIZE FOR ...

ESL

List the following terms on the chalkboard and have a volunteer read each one aloud: *mission, Mexico's northern territories, Santa Fe Trail, Stephen Austin, William Travis, the Alamo, General Antonio Lopez de Santa Anna,* and *Sam Houston.* Then ask volunteers to use each term in a sentence that relates to the section content. You may wish to direct students to where the term first appears in the text.

REVIEWING KEY TERMS

Students should refer to the definitions of key terms in the chapter to write sentences that show an understanding of the key aspects of the ways in which culture and settlement patterns were transformed in the years after the Revolution.

REVIEWING MAIN IDEAS

15. People considered education extremely important and began to insist that it be made more widely available to both men and women.

16. The most important factor was the high number of births. Immigration was also a factor, as was (until 1808) the continued importation of slaves.

17. Many people were attracted by the evangelical nature of the movement. They were also attracted to the movement's promise of meaning and community.

18. It was democratic in that it encouraged anyone, rich or poor, to participate in religion and salvation. Hence, people began to expect these ideals from government and politics.

19. African Americans (primarily slaves) were brought in large numbers to the area south of the Ohio River, which they helped their owners to settle.

20. By becoming familiar with the region as they hunted and living peacefully among the Native Americans.

21. To escape persecution for their beliefs by living beyond the border of the United States.

22. Nomadic Native Americans migrated on horseback in search of buffalo, carrying their possessions with them. Their societies were increasingly male-dominated, as males gained wealth and status from the use of horses. As these Native Americans became less dependent on farming and a settled existence, women had less and less influence.

23. They built a network of missions and presidios, strengthened trade, and attempted to convert the Native Americans to Christianity.

24. Many Americans and their slaves moved to Texas, cotton farming developed, and the American population steadily and dramatically increased.

266 • Chapter 7

---

creating a CHAPTER SUMMARY

Copy this chart (right) on a piece of paper and complete it by adding important events and issues that fit each heading.

 iTEXT

For additional review and enrichment activities, see the interactive version of *America: Pathways to the Present*, available on the Web and on CD-ROM.

Important Events	
Cultural, Social, and Religious Life	• Scholars and artists contribute to a new American culture. • Leaders emphasize republican virtues: hard work, self-reliance, self-sacrifice, and harmony. •
Migration to Trans-Appalachia, Utah, and the Pacific Coast	
The Great Plains and the Southwest	

★ Reviewing Key Terms

For each of the terms below, write a sentence explaining how it relates to the growth of the American colonies.

1. republican virtues
2. mobile society
3. evangelical
4. revival
5. denomination
6. trans-Appalachia
7. cede
8. manifest destiny
9. Oregon Trail
10. Santa Fe Trail
11. nomadic
12. presidio
13. Texas War for Independence
14. Battle of the Alamo

★ Reviewing Main Ideas

15. Describe the attitude toward education in the early republic. (Section 1)

16. What was the main cause of the great increase in the population of the United States before 1830? (Section 1)

17. What attracted Americans to the Second Great Awakening? (Section 1)

18. How did the Second Great Awakening contribute to democracy? (Section 1)

19. How did African Americans participate in the development of trans-Appalachia? (Section 2)

20. How did fur traders help open the Oregon Country to settlement? (Section 2)

21. Why did Brigham Young bring his followers to the Great Salt Lake region? (Section 2)

22. Describe the way of life of the nomadic Plains Indians. (Section 3)

23. How did the Spanish try to strengthen their hold on California in the late 1700s? (Section 3)

24. Describe the settlement of Texas before 1836. (Section 3)

★ Critical Thinking

25. **Recognizing Cause and Effect** How did the ideals of the American Revolution continue to influence social developments in the new republic?

26. **Predicting Consequences** You have read that the population of the United States doubled every 20 years during the era of the new republic. What might be the effects on your own town or city if its population doubled in the next 20 years?

27. **Drawing Conclusions** Why were the Spanish missionaries in California more successful than the American missionaries in Oregon?

28. **Making Comparisons** Compare Spain's relations with Native Americans in Florida and the Southwest with relations between American settlers and Native Americans in trans-Appalachia. Why did the two relationships differ so greatly?

CREATING A CHAPTER SUMMARY	
Important Events	
Cultural, Social, and Religious Life	• Scholars and artists contribute to a new American culture. • Leaders emphasize republican virtues: hard work, self-reliance, self-sacrifice, and harmony. • Nationwide renewal of religious faith
Migration to Trans-Appalachia, Utah, and the Pacific Coast	• Settlers moved across the Appalachians. • The United States expanded into Florida. • American settlers crossed the Mississippi, venturing into the Great Plains and the Southwest.
The Great Plains and the Southwest	• The lives of the Plains Indians changed dramatically from the 1500s to the 1800s. • The Spanish integrated California and the Rio Grande valley into Hispanic North America. • Texas won its independence from Mexico.

★ Skills Assessment

Analyzing Political Cartoons ▶

THE WAY THEY GO TO CALIFORNIA.

29. Analyze the images in this cartoon titled "The Way They Go to California," and answer the following questions. (a) Why are the people in this cartoon traveling to California? (b) How does the reader know that this is the reason?

30. (a) List three methods of travel shown in this drawing. (b) According to your reading, which of these methods was actually used by migrants going to California? (c) What point is the cartoonist trying to make by including ridiculous machines?

31. What lesson might be taught by the fact that several people have fallen into the water?

Analyzing Data

Turn to the chart of population growth in the United States on p. 242. Study the chart and use the data presented to answer the questions below.

32. Approximately how much did the African American population increase from 1800 to 1830?

   A 1,300,000
   B 2,300,000
   C 2,300
   D 1,000

33. When did the population of the United States first reach 10 million?

   F Before 1780
   G 1780–1810
   H 1810–1830
   J After 1830

Applying the Chapter Skill:
Reviewing an Economic Activity Map

34. Review the economic activity map on page 257. Based on the crops you see listed, where do you think large-scale slavery existed?

ACTIVITIES

Writing to LEARN

Writing to Compare
Reread the section beginning on page 243 about the effects social mobility had on society. Research and write an essay that answers the following question: Have recent technological changes made the United States more, or less, a nation of strangers? Include evidence to support your conclusions.

Primary Source CD-ROM

Working With Primary Sources Find additional information on life in the early republic on the *Exploring Primary Sources in U.S. History CD-ROM* and use the selection(s) provided to complete the Chapter 7 primary source activity located in the *America: Pathways to the Present* area of the following Web site.
www.phschool.com

Take It to the NET

Chapter Self-Test As a review activity, take the Chapter 7 Self-Test in the *America: Pathways to the Present* area at the Web site listed below. The questions are designed to test your understanding of the chapter content.
www.phschool.com

CRITICAL THINKING

25. The ideal of democracy manifested itself in the evangelical Second Great Awakening; the ideal of beginning a new era was seen in new inventions and faith in human progress.

26. Answers will vary. Students should cite the need for more schools, jobs, housing, and city services; strain on public resources; and expansion of markets.

27. The Spanish used Native American labor to ensure that their missions succeeded; they also fostered a lively network of trade. The missionaries in Oregon focused on converting the Native Americans, which failed.

28. Sample answer: As Spain's hold on New Mexico and Florida grew tenuous (in part due to increased American trade and/or settlement), Native Americans remained in these areas and obtained some autonomy. Native Americans also remained in California but were forced to labor for the Spaniards. American settlers in trans-Appalachia were competing for land and often tried to drive Native Americans off the land. Americans in trans-Appalachia did not need Native Americans for labor, as they often had slaves.

SKILLS ASSESSMENT

29. (a) They are in search of gold. (b) Because they are carrying shovels and picks.

30. (a) Sample answer: Parachute, dirigible, ship. (b) Ship. (c) To show that people desired to get to California by any means possible.

31. In haste, and in desire for wealth, people risk sacrificing that which is truly important.

32. A

33. H

34. Virginia, the Carolinas, and Georgia.

Geography & History

THE CALIFORNIA GOLD RUSH

Focus Ask students to consider how an event, such as the 1848 discovery of gold in relatively unpopulated California, impacted that region's development. Ask them to speculate on effects in the areas of economics, development, immigration, and infra-structure.

Instruct Before the Gold Rush of 1848, California was very thinly settled, and its port cities, such as San Francisco and Los Angeles, small and sleepy. Neither of these cities was considered a major point of entry into the United States. How did the roles of these cities, particularly San Francisco, change with the sudden influx of people who wanted to travel into the Sierra Nevada area? How did the urgency to reach California from many parts of the world affect the development of the region? How did the Gold Rush impact methods of over land travel to California from other parts of the United States? In what ways did the California Gold Rush stimulate the movement towards construction of railroads in the United States?

Extend In what ways can the geographical impact of the California Gold Rush be compared to the geographical impact of other economic booms and surges in this country? Have students do library research to compare and contrast the impact of the Gold Rush with other boom times, such as the movement from cities to suburbs in the late 1940s and 1950s and the surge of population in the Sun Belt in the 1980s.

Panning for Gold
Many early gold miners used pans to collect river sediment that might contain gold flakes.

The California Gold Rush

Before California became part of the United States in 1848, it was a thinly settled Mexican territory inhabited mainly by Native Americans and no more than 8,000 Mexicans, Americans, and Europeans. In 1848, a carpenter was building a sawmill in present-day Sacramento when some sparkling flakes of rock caught his eye. Those flakes were gold. Gold! Headlines around the country and overseas screamed the news. By the next year, tens of thousands of gold seekers streamed to California from all over the world.

Gold Rush California

California's gold fields lay in the foothills of the snow-capped Sierra Nevada. The river ports of Sacramento and Stockton provided key services to the miners, but San Francisco was the state's biggest city, seaport, and commercial center. At the time, Los Angeles was a small cattle town that sent beef cattle north to feed the miners.

Geographic Connection

What aspects of San Francisco's location allowed it to serve as the chief port and commercial center of California during the Gold Rush?

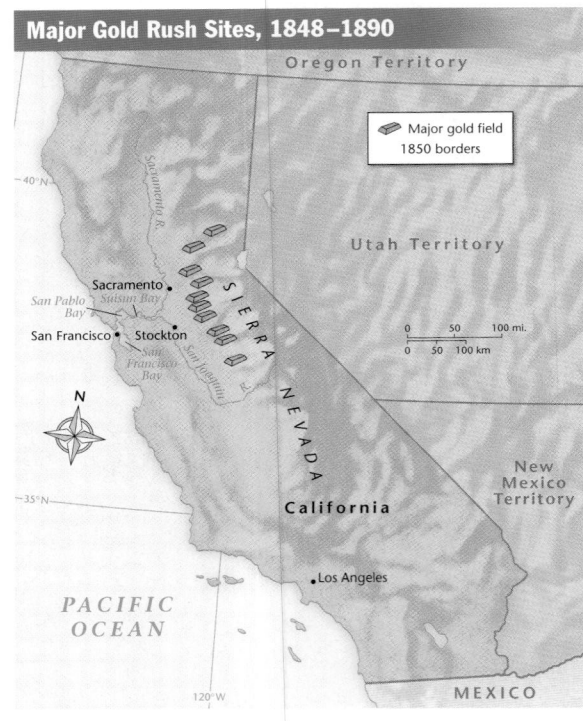

Major Gold Rush Sites, 1848–1890

Major gold field
1850 borders

Oregon Territory
Utah Territory
Sacramento
San Pablo Bay · Suisun Bay
San Francisco · Stockton
San Francisco Bay
SIERRA NEVADA
California
New Mexico Territory
· Los Angeles
PACIFIC OCEAN
MEXICO

0   50   100 mi.
0   50   100 km

268

ANSWERS

1. San Francisco was the seaport closest to the gold fields. It was located along the sheltered coast of San Francisco Bay. A string of bays and rivers provided easy access from San Francisco to river ports near the gold fields, such as Stockton and Sacramento. Other towns in California (such as Los Angeles) lacked San Francisco's unique advantages.

RESOURCE DIRECTORY

Teaching Resources
Geography and History booklet, pp. 6–7

Other Print Resources
Nystrom *Atlas of Our Country* *Early Expansion of the United States,* pp. 20–21

Technology
Prentice Hall United States History Video Collection™ Volume 5, *A New Nation*

A Global Migration

Gold seekers traveled to California over land from Mexico and the Midwest, and by sea from the East Coast, South America, Europe, and China. Sea travelers arrived at the booming port of San Francisco, from which they traveled upriver and over land to the gold fields.

Geographic Connection

What routes might a traveler from the eastern United States take to reach California?

NEW-YORK TRIBUNE.

☞ We are indebted to Hon. JOHN M. BOTTS for a copy of the Report of the Committee on Military Affairs, of which he is Chairman. We are also under obligation to Hon. DAVID FISHER for a copy of his Speech on the Tariff.

The Gold Excitement.

HO! FOR CALIFORIA!

The rage for speculation and adventure, which has been everywhere aroused by the exciting dispatches from California, exceeds anything of the kind ever witnessed in this country. It almost equals in general and pervading interest, the mania for speculation in the South Sea scheme, which was started in Paris more than a century ago.— Fortunately for the subjects of this Gold Fever, their prospects are rather more substantial and tangible than were the promises of the latter speculation, and all those who commence their labors in California with industry and prudence may be sure of reasonable success. The last advices from San Francisco will decide the …

A Diverse Population

By 1852, California had more than 200,000 residents, and roughly 10 percent were Chinese. Many others were migrants from Mexico, South America, or Europe. California still has the ethnic diversity that it had in its first days as a state.

Geographic Connection

Why did California acquire such a diverse population during the Gold Rush?

269

Chapter 8 Planning Guide
Resource Manager

	CORE INSTRUCTION	READING/SKILLS
Chapter-Level Resources	**Teaching Resources** • Pacing Charts booklet • Block Scheduling booklet **Resource Pro® CD-ROM**, Ch. 8 **Prentice Hall Presentation Pro CD-ROM**, Ch. 8 **www.phschool.com** • eTeach	**Guided Reading Audiotapes (English/Spanish)** **Student Edition on Audio CD**, Ch. 8 **Social Studies Skills Tutor CD-ROM** **Color Transparencies**, B4, D4, F3, G4, H5, H6, H7
1 Inventions and Innovations 1. Find out how the Industrial Revolution arrived and spread in the United States, and learn about its impact. 2. Discover how improvements in transportation and communication changed American society. 3. Learn how the U.S. economy expanded during the early 1800s. 4. Read about the role banks had in the growth of the U.S. economy.	**Teaching Resources** **Units 3/4 booklet** • Section 1 Quiz, p. 14 **Learning Styles Lesson Plans booklet,** p. 18	**Guided Reading and Review booklet,** p. 32 **Guide to the Essentials,** p. 41 **Section Reading Support Transparencies**
2 The Northern Section 1. Understand how farming developed in the Old Northwest. 2. See which new industries arose in the Northeast. 3. Find out what caused the growth of cities, and what problems arose as they grew. 4. Learn what kinds of labor disputes arose in factories.	**Teaching Resources** **Units 3/4 booklet** • Section 2 Quiz, p. 15	**Guided Reading and Review booklet,** p. 33 **Guide to the Essentials,** p. 42 **Section Reading Support Transparencies**
3 The Southern Section 1. Learn how the economy of the South remained largely agricultural. 2. Find out how the lives of slaves differed on large and small farms. 3. Discover the results of slave revolts.	**Teaching Resources** **Units 3/4 booklet** • Section 3 Quiz, p. 16	**Guided Reading and Review booklet,** p. 34 **Guide to the Essentials,** p. 43 **Section Reading Support Transparencies**
4 The Growth of Nationalism 1. See some of the signs of a new nationalism after the War of 1812. 2. Find out why the election of 1824 was so controversial. 3. Discover what new political parties emerged in 1828, and find out what views they represent.	**Teaching Resources** **Units 3/4 booklet** • Section 4 Quiz, p. 17	**Guided Reading and Review booklet,** p. 35 **Guide to the Essentials,** p. 44 **Learning with Documents booklet,** pp. 47, 79 **Skills for Life booklet,** p. 10 **Section Reading Support Transparencies**
5 The Age of Jackson 1. Understand how American government and democracy changed with Jackson as President. 2. Learn how Jackson responded to the tariff and Indian crises. 3. See what political strategies prompted the bank war. 4. Find out about the effectiveness of Jackson's presidential successors.	**Teaching Resources** **Units 3/4 booklet** • Section 5 Quiz, p. 18 **Learning Styles Lesson Plans booklet,** p. 19	**Guided Reading and Review booklet,** p. 36 **Guide to the Essentials,** p. 45 **Learning with Documents booklet,** p. 13 **Section Reading Support Transparencies**

ENRICHMENT/PRE-AP

Prentice Hall United States History Video Collection™
www.phschool.com
- Section Activities, Virtual Field Trip, Chapter Activities, Current Events Online

Biography, Literature, and Comparing Primary Sources booklet, p. 13
American History Block Scheduling Support
Exploring Primary Sources in U.S. History CD-ROM

Nystrom *Atlas of Our Country,* pp. 26–27

Biography, Literature, and Comparing Primary Sources booklet, p. 49

Nystrom *Atlas of Our Country,* pp. 24–25
Historical Outline Map Book, pp. 34, 36
Exploring Primary Sources in U.S. History CD-ROM

Biography, Literature, and Comparing Primary Sources booklet, pp. 111–112
American History Block Scheduling Support
Sounds of an Era Audio CD
Exploring Primary Sources in U.S. History CD-ROM
American Pathways Thematic Posters

ASSESSMENT

Core Assessment
  ExamView® Test Bank, Ch. 8
  ExamView® Test Bank CD-ROM, Ch. 8

Standardized Test Preparation
Diagnose and Prescribe
  Diagnostic Tests for High School Social Studies Skills

Review and Reteach
  Review Book for U.S. History

Practice and Assess
  Test-taking Strategies With Transparencies
  Test-taking Strategies Posters
  Test Prep Book for U.S. History
  Alternative Assessment Handbook
  Document-Based Assessment

Teaching Resources
Units 3/4 booklet
- Section Quizzes, pp. 14–18
- Chapter Tests, pp. 19, 22
www.phschool.com Ch. 8 Self-Test

AmericanHeritage RESOURCES

From the Archives of American Heritage®, pp. 275, 282, 292, 299, 302
AmericanHeritage® My Brush with History™ **Videotapes**
www.americanheritage.com

Don't miss the exclusive interactive version of this textbook on the Web and on CD-ROM.

Chapter 8 Planning Guide
In Your Classroom

Gifted and Talented

Teacher's Edition
• Customize for Gifted and Talented, pp. 273, 303

Teaching Resources
• Biography, Literature, and Comparing Primary Sources booklet, pp. 13, 49, 111–112

Technology
• Exploring Primary Sources in U.S. History CD-ROM *A Description of Factory Life in 1846; The Monroe Doctrine; The Sovereignty of the People in America, Alexis de Tocqueville; Our Federal Union: It Must be Preserved, Andrew Jackson; Debate Over Nullification, Daniel Webster and John C. Calhoun*

ESL

Teacher's Edition
• Customize for ESL, p. 287

Teaching Resources
• Guided Reading and Review booklet, pp. 32–36
• Guide to the Essentials (English/Spanish), Chapter 8

Technology
• Student Edition on Audio CD, Chapter 8
• Guided Reading Audiotapes (English/Spanish), Chapter 8
• Section Reading Support Transparencies

Less Proficient Readers

Teacher's Edition
• Customize for Less Proficient Readers, pp. 281, 289, 291

Teaching Resources
• Guided Reading and Review booklet, pp. 32–36
• Guide to the Essentials (English/Spanish), Chapter 8

Technology
• Student Edition on Audio CD, Chapter 8
• Guided Reading Audiotapes (English/Spanish), Chapter 8
• Section Reading Support Transparencies

Less Proficient Writers

Teacher's Edition
• Customize for Less Proficient Writers, p. 275

Teaching Resources
• Guided Reading and Review booklet, pp. 32–36
• Guide to the Essentials (English/Spanish), Chapter 8

Technology
• Student Edition on Audio CD, Chapter 8
• Guided Reading Audiotapes (English/Spanish), Chapter 8
• Section Reading Support Transparencies

CHAPTER 8 – PACING SUGGESTIONS

 For 90-minute Blocks

• Teach sections 1, 4, and 5 using Transparencies B4, D4, F3, G4, H5, H6, and H7, and the Recent Scholarship note on page 287 for class discussions.

 Running Out of Time?

If you are running short on time to cover this chapter, consider the following options:

• Use the Prentice Hall Presentation Pro CD-ROM to create an outline for this chapter.

• Use the Section Summaries for Chapter 8, from **Guide to the Essentials (English/Spanish).**

1 Inventions and Innovations	**Connecting with Science and Technology** Tell students to research a modern American industry. Students might choose to focus on the textile industry, the defense industry, the pharmaceutical industry, or the high-tech industry. Suggest that they consider some of the following questions as they do their research. What products do we make at home? What percentage of our workforce is dedicated to this industry? How have modern inventions changed the way this industry operates? **(Logical/Mathematical)**
2 The Northern Section	**Connecting with Culture** Have students research one major city in the Northeast during the first half of the nineteenth century. Tell students to use library resources to gather information about life in that city. What was the city's population in 1800? How much had it grown by 1850? What were some of the city's significant industries? What kinds of housing did people live in? How safe were the city's streets? What kinds of neighborhoods developed during this period? Have students write about their findings in a short report. **(Verbal/Linguistic)**
3 The Southern Section	**Connecting with Culture** Encourage students to obtain recordings of some of the spirituals that were popular among slaves. Have students bring in the songs and play them for the class. Engage students in a discussion about the feeling that this music creates. How do the lyrics and tunes make them feel? Ask students to consider the role that music plays in bringing people together and providing comfort and inspiration. **(Rhythmic/Musical)**
4 The Growth of Nationalism	**Connecting with History and Conflict** Have students write a letter from President Monroe to his counterpart in Great Britain. Tell students that the letter must express the four main parts of the Monroe Doctrine. Tell students that their letters must be friendly but firm and should give examples to support each part of the document. **(Verbal/Linguistic)**
5 The Age of Jackson	**Connecting with Government** Have students make a poster or newspaper advertisement for Andrew Jackson's reelection campaign. Tell students to include facts or events that prove Jackson's worthiness. Encourage students to convey something about Jackson's background and personality that would appeal to voters. When students finish their posters or ads, have them tape them up around the classroom. **(Visual/Spatial)**

INTRODUCING THE CHAPTER

During the first half of the 1800s, expanding markets and thriving industries and businesses transformed American life. The Market Revolution, as this transformation was called, made the making of money the chief goal of most Americans. The change also created division between the poor and the wealthy, and between those in different regions of the country.

TIME LINE ACTIVITY

To provide students with practice in using the time line, ask questions such as these:

1. In what year did the French Revolution end? *(1799)*

2. When and where was the first centralized textile mill built? *(In 1814 in Waltham, Massachusetts)*

3. When and where was Napoleon defeated? *(In 1815, at Waterloo)*

eTeach

Be sure to check out this month's online discussion with a Master Teacher. Go to **www.phschool.com**.

Chapter 8
The Growth of a National Economy
(1790–1850)

SECTION 1   Inventions and Innovations
SECTION 2   The Northern Section
SECTION 3   The Southern Section
SECTION 4   The Growth of Nationalism
SECTION 5   The Age of Jackson

American Events

1790
Samuel Slater reproduces secret British technology for a textile mill, triggering America's Industrial Revolution.

1794
Eli Whitney patents the cotton gin, causing a cotton production boom in the South.

1807
Using James Watt's steam engine, Robert Fulton demonstrates his steam-powered paddleboat, the *Clermont*.

1808
Congress bans further importing of slaves.

1814
Francis Cabot Lowell builds the world's first centralized textile mill, in Waltham, Massachusetts.

Presidential Terms: George Washington 1789–1797   J. Adams 1797–1801   Thomas Jefferson 1801–1809   James Madison 1809

1780   1790   1800   1810

World Events

Canada is divided into Upper Canada and Lower Canada.
1791

The French Revolution ends.
1799

England wins the Battle of Trafalgar.
1805

Wars of independence begin in South America.
1811

270   Chapter 8 • *The Growth of a National Economy*

RESOURCE DIRECTORY

Teaching Resources
Pacing Charts booklet
Block Scheduling booklet, p. 17
Units 3/4 booklet
 • Chapter Summary, p. 13

Technology
Guided Reading Audiotapes (English/Spanish), Ch. 8
Student Edition on Audio CD, Ch. 8
Prentice Hall United States History Video Collection™ Volume 7, *Democracy and Reform;* Volume 8, *Causes of the Civil War;* Volume 11, *Industrialization and Urbanization*
Prentice Hall Presentation Pro CD-ROM, Ch. 8
Resource Pro® CD-ROM
Social Studies Skills Tutor CD-ROM
Companion Web site, www.phschool.com

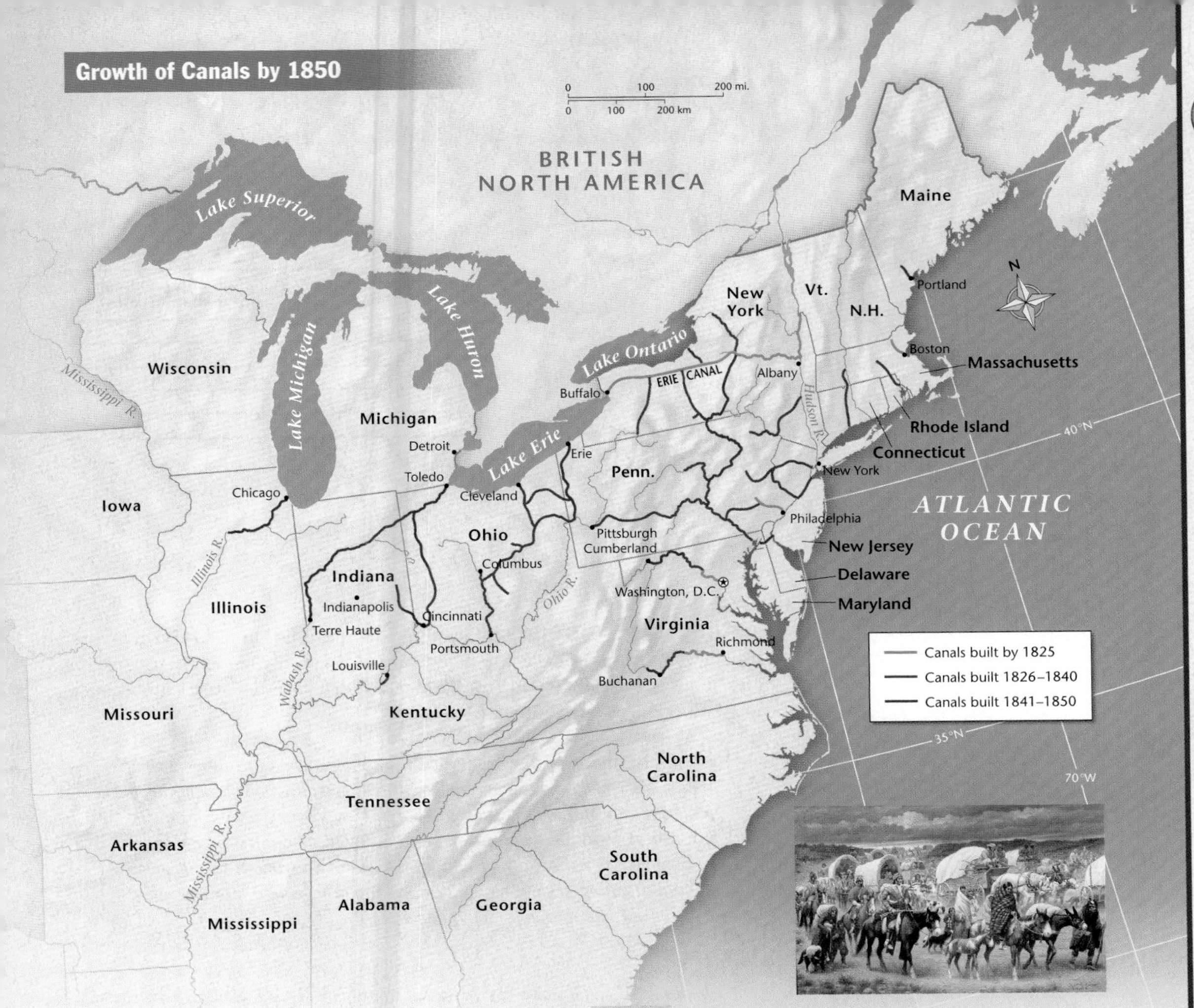

Growth of Canals by 1850

BRITISH NORTH AMERICA

Lake Superior

Wisconsin

Lake Michigan

Lake Huron

Michigan

Detroit

Toledo

Iowa

Chicago

Illinois

Indiana

Indianapolis

Terre Haute

Louisville

Missouri

Kentucky

Tennessee

Arkansas

Alabama

Georgia

Mississippi

Mississippi R.

Illinois R.

Wabash R.

Ohio R.

Cleveland

Lake Erie

Erie

Cincinnati

Portsmouth

Columbus

Ohio

Pittsburgh

Cumberland

Buchanan

Virginia

Richmond

North Carolina

South Carolina

Lake Ontario

Buffalo

ERIE CANAL

Albany

Hudson R.

New York

Vt.

N.H.

Maine

Portland

Boston

Massachusetts

Rhode Island

Connecticut

New York

Philadelphia

New Jersey

Delaware

Maryland

Washington, D.C.

ATLANTIC OCEAN

N

40°N

35°N

70°W

Penn.

	Canals built by 1825
	Canals built 1826–1840
	Canals built 1841–1850

0   100   200 mi.
0   100   200 km

1824
In *Gibbons* v. *Ogden*, the Supreme Court affirms the federal government's authority to regulate interstate commerce.

1828
Two new political parties emerge, the National Republicans and the Jacksonian Democrats.

1838
Cherokees are forcibly relocated westward on a harsh, 116-day walk known as the Trail of Tears.

1850
The U.S. slave population exceeds 3 million. The cotton crop tops a billion pounds.

James Monroe 1817–1825 | John Q. Adams 1825–1829 | Andrew Jackson 1829–1837 | M. Van Buren 1837–1841 | W. Harrison 1841 | John Tyler 1841–45 | J. Polk 1845–49 | Z. Taylor 1849–50

1820 • • **1830** • • **1840** • • **1850**

The French Emperor Napoleon is defeated at Waterloo.
1815

Slavery is abolished in the British Empire.
1833

The Opium Wars between Britain and China begin.
1839

The Irish potato famine begins.
1845

Chapter 8   271

Growth of Canals by 1850

Activating Prior Knowledge When was the Erie Canal built? *(By 1825)*

Previewing Ask students what purposes they think the canals served. *(They facilitated the transportation of both people and goods between places that were previously more difficult to access.)*

BACKGROUND
About the Pictures

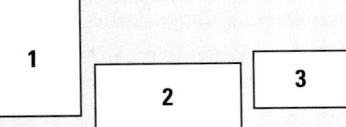

1. Whitney's cotton gin worked by passing the cotton through a set of comb-like wire teeth, which removed the seeds from the cotton.

2. Measuring 133 feet long and 18 feet wide, the Clermont averaged about five miles an hour on her first voyage up the Hudson River.

3. Several of the Cherokees were homeowners and active participants in the American government before they were forced westward, a journey that cost the lives of up to 25 percent of its participants.

TEXT

Don't miss the exclusive interactive version of this textbook on the Web and on CD-ROM.

BIBLIOGRAPHY

For the Teacher

Blassingame, John W. *The Slave Community: Plantation Life in the Antebellum South.* Oxford University Press, 1979. (Presents an analysis of the life of the black slave.)

Remini, Robert V. *Andrew Jackson and His Indian Wars.* Viking, 2001. (The story of Andrew Jackson's relationships with the Indian Nations.)

Sellers, Charles. *The Market Revolution: Jacksonian America 1815–1846.* Oxford University Press, 1994. (A political and social history of the boom years following the war of 1812.)

For the Student

Ehle, John. *Trail of Tears: The Rise and Fall of the Cherokee Nation.* Doubleday, 1989. (Compact account of the forced removal of the Cherokee.)

Feinberg, Barbara Silberdick. *John Marshall: The Great Chief Justice (Justices of the Supreme Court).* Enslow Publishers, 1995. (Emphasizes Marshall's years on the Supreme Court.)

McGrath, Kimberley A. and Bridget E. Travers (eds.). *The World of Invention.* Gale Group, 1998. (This reference work describes the work of both well-known and lesser-known inventors.)

Section 1
Inventions and Innovations

SECTION OBJECTIVES

1. Find out how the Industrial Revolution arrived and spread in the United States, and learn about its impact.
2. Discover how improvements in transportation and communication changed American society.
3. Learn how the U.S. economy expanded during the early 1800s.
4. Read about the role banks had in the growth of the U.S. economy.

BELLRINGER

Warm-Up Activity Have students list ways in which they or other people try to change either their own lives or society in general. Do people always respond favorably to efforts toward change? Why or why not?

Activating Prior Knowledge Ask students to speculate on why changes in industrial capabilities in the early 1800s would lead to a "revolution." What do they think is meant by the phrase "Industrial Revolution"?

READING STRATEGY

As students read, have them look for evidence of the "spirit of improvement" during the late 1700s and early 1800s. Make a list of specific ways in which Americans tried to improve their lives.

ACTIVITY
Connecting with Culture

Have students reread the quotation from Nathaniel Hawthorne on this page. Ask them to write a short essay either agreeing or disagreeing with Hawthorne. Did the introduction of railroads signify a radical assault on traditional ways of life, or were railroads a logical and inevitable manifestation of a growing nation? Discuss both points of view. **(Verbal/Linguistic)**

READING FOCUS

- How did the Industrial Revolution begin and spread in the United States, and what was its impact?
- How did improvements in transportation and communication change American society?
- How did the U.S. economy expand during the early 1800s?
- What role did banks have in the growth of the U.S. economy?

MAIN IDEA

In the early 1800s, the rise of industry, banking, and transportation helped the United States economy expand rapidly.

KEY TERMS

Industrial Revolution
interchangeable parts
cotton gin
patent
Market Revolution
manufacturing
centralized
free enterprise system
specialization
investment capital
bank note

TAKING NOTES

Copy the chart below. As you read, fill in the causes and effects of the Industrial Revolution.

Invention or Innovation	Political, Economic, or Social Effect(s)

Setting the Scene One summer morning in 1844, the writer Nathaniel Hawthorne sat in the woods near Concord, Massachusetts, making notes about the natural world around him. Suddenly, an unnatural sound interrupted him. Hawthorne noted his reaction:

This John Bull locomotive was imported to the United States from Britain in 1831.

> ❝ But, hark! there is the whistle of the locomotive—the long shriek, harsh, above all other harshness, for the space of a mile cannot mollify [calm] it into harmony. It tells a story of busy men, citizens, from the hot street, who have come to spend a day in a country village, men of business; in short of all unquietness; and no wonder that it gives such a startling shriek, since it brings the noisy world into the midst of our slumbrous [sleepy] peace. ❞
>
> —Nathaniel Hawthorne

Unlike Hawthorne, many Americans welcomed the "startling shriek" of the railway locomotive. For them the sound represented a new and exciting time of progress and prosperity. The locomotive, a self-propelled vehicle used for pulling railroad cars, came about during an important period of invention and innovation for the United States.

The Industrial Revolution

As the young republic expanded, Americans developed and profited from a variety of inventions that produced goods and materials faster and more cheaply. Many of the inventions grew out of what is now known as the **Industrial Revolution.** This revolution was an ongoing effort over many decades to increase production by using machines rather than the power of humans or animals.

The Industrial Revolution began in Britain in the 1700s with changes in the textile, or cloth-making, industry. Until that time, craftsworkers spun wool

---

RESOURCE DIRECTORY

Teaching Resources
Learning Styles Lesson Plans booklet, p. 18
Guided Reading and Review booklet, p. 32

Technology
Section Reading Support Transparencies
Guided Reading Audiotapes (English/Spanish), Ch. 8
Student Edition on Audio CD, Ch. 8
Color Transparencies *Cause-and-Effect Charts,* D4
Prentice Hall Presentation Pro CD-ROM, Ch. 8
Companion Web site, www.phschool.com

or fiber and wove cloth at home, using tools powered by hand or by foot. Groups of spinners and weavers gradually began working together in buildings known as mills, usually located on a stream or river, using the power of flowing water to run their tools.

Several British inventions encouraged America's Industrial Revolution. These devices, including the spinning jenny, the water frame, and the power loom, all helped mechanize the processes of spinning and weaving cloth. Increased mechanization, or use of machines, greatly improved the efficiency of textile mills. It also increased the profits earned by the textile industry.

One invention, the steam engine, played a particularly important role in the Industrial Revolution. It worked by harnessing the tremendous energy given off by expanding steam. James Watt developed the first practical steam engine in Britain between 1765 and 1785. His engine eventually provided the energy to pump water out of mines, run textile machines, and do many other tasks. Later improvements by British and American inventors resulted in a high-pressure steam engine powerful enough to drive a locomotive.

Birth of the U.S. Textile Industry The British jealously guarded their knowledge of textile-related inventions, as well as the design and operation of spinning and weaving machines. By law, textile workers could not move out of Britain, and nobody could send drawings of textile machinery to another country.

American textile producers offered generous rewards to anyone who could bring the new technology to the United States. A British textile machinist, Samuel Slater, managed to immigrate to America in 1789. Slater quickly put his knowledge of textile machinery to work. In 1790, in a clothier's shop in Pawtucket, Rhode Island, Slater reproduced the complex British machinery. Slater and his business partners established the nation's first successful water-powered textile mill in 1793, in Pawtucket. He chose the spot because of a waterfall on the nearby Blackstone River, which provided power for the new mill. (The steam engine would not surpass falling water as a power source until well into the 1800s.)

Textile producers soon began copying Slater's methods. By 1814, the United States boasted some 240 textile mills, most of them in Pennsylvania, New York, and New England. Slater and other mill owners grew wealthy by filling the needs of the growing American population for more and more cloth.

Interchangeable Parts Many Americans made important contributions to the Industrial Revolution. One of them, New England inventor Eli Whitney, is credited with developing an idea that changed industry forever. In 1798, he signed a contract with the federal government to make 10,000 guns in a little over two years. It was a bold promise. In those days, a skilled gunsmith made parts for one gun at a time. He would assemble the gun as he went, carefully fitting the new parts together. The process took weeks, because each part fit only one gun. No part could be interchanged, or swapped, with the matching part from another gun.

Whitney realized that if all the corresponding parts were made exactly alike, they could be used on any similar gun. The gunsmith would not have to spend days making parts fit together. He could assemble the parts rapidly, allowing him to produce more goods and make a greater profit.

BIOGRAPHY

**Samuel Slater
1768–1835**

Samuel Slater was born in Derbyshire, England, in 1768. As a boy, he became an apprentice to a mill builder, Jedediah Strutt, who was a pioneer in the use of the new British textile technology. He spent almost seven years working for Strutt.

Once he had settled in the United States, Slater found a company to back him financially. Working from memory alone, he directed the skilled mechanics who built the nation's first successful water-powered textile mill at Pawtucket, Rhode Island, based on the technology used in British mills. Soon he was made a partner in the company.

In 1798, Slater started a new company by himself. He made his own machines and built another mill in Pawtucket. Within a few years, he was expanding his business throughout New England. After he had been in the United States for about 40 years, Slater estimated his wealth at close to $1 million. When he died in 1835, he owned all or part of 13 textile mills.

Whitney worked hard on his new system, but it still had flaws. In fact, he needed ten years to make the 10,000 guns, and in the end he still could not be sure that any given part would fit in every gun. Other inventors later perfected what is now called the system of **interchangeable parts,** in which all parts are made to an exact standard. By 1824, the nation had a reliable method for producing the guns it needed. Other industries, too, gradually adopted the system of interchangeable parts. Today, making factory goods any other way is almost unthinkable.

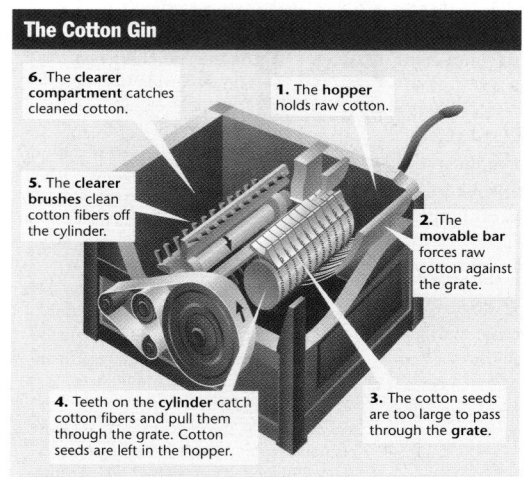

The Cotton Gin

6. The **clearer compartment** catches cleaned cotton.

1. The **hopper** holds raw cotton.

5. The **clearer brushes** clean cotton fibers off the cylinder.

2. The **movable bar** forces raw cotton against the grate.

4. Teeth on the **cylinder** catch cotton fibers and pull them through the grate. Cotton seeds are left in the hopper.

3. The cotton seeds are too large to pass through the **grate.**

INTERPRETING DIAGRAMS By hand, a worker could clean (remove the seeds from) only one pound of cotton per day. With a hand-operated gin like the one shown here, a worker could clean 50 pounds of cotton per day. **Determining Relevance** *How did the invention of the cotton gin lead to the expansion of slavery?*

The Cotton Gin Another of Whitney's inventions also had a lasting effect on the United States. While visiting a Georgia plantation in 1793, Whitney noted the time and effort needed to clean cotton seeds from the cotton fibers. Working by hand, a laborer could clean only one pound of cotton per day. Yet British mills were becoming more efficient, requiring more and more raw cotton. Whitney devised a solution to the problem: the **cotton gin,** a machine that separates the seeds from raw cotton fibers. (The word *gin* means "engine" or "machine.") With a gin powered by water, one worker could now clean 1,000 pounds of cotton per day. (See the diagram of a hand-operated model at left.)

Whitney gained a patent on his invention in 1794. A **patent** is a license from the government giving an inventor the sole right to make, use, and sell an invention for a certain period of time. Whitney's cotton gin had several important effects:

1. The profit per pound of cotton skyrocketed, and with it, the amount of cotton planted for harvest. American exports of cotton boomed as a result, rising 6,000 percent between 1790 and 1815, according to some accounts.

2. Many southern planters began to depend on cotton as their major crop, because it was so profitable.

3. Planters began looking for new land on which they could grow ever larger crops of cotton. They bought up and quickly settled large areas in Alabama, Mississippi, Louisiana, and eventually, Texas.

4. To keep up with the increased demand for raw cotton, planters bought more enslaved Africans to work on the new and expanded cotton plantations. The enslaved population of the South more than doubled between 1790 and 1820, rising from 700,000 to 1.5 million. Many Americans had expected slavery to fade away gradually, but the cotton gin put an end to that dream. Thus the cotton gin helped slavery and agriculture to increase in the South.

Transportation and Communication

Industry was not the only area of American life undergoing a "revolution" in the early 1800s. Innovative building projects and new technologies also produced a transportation revolution.

Roads You have read about the importance of roads to western migration in the early 1800s. Americans also used roads every day to transport goods, deliver the mail, and herd animals to market. As a result, road building boomed in the early republic.

At first, road builders simply carved routes out of forests, cutting down trees as needed. Where the route crossed swampy ground, they laid down logs on the roadway. These were called "corduroy roads" because they looked like the ribbed cloth of the same name. Wagon travel over them was bumpy and uncomfortable. Road builders also used boards to build what were called plank roads. Both types of surfacing soon rotted away, though, and had to be replaced.

In contrast, engineers built the Cumberland Road (also called the National Road) to last. Financed by the federal government, construction began in Cumberland, Maryland, in 1811. By 1833, the road had reached Columbus, Ohio, and in later years it was gradually continued westward. Today it is known as U.S. Route 40.

Despite government interest, private investors built most of the new roads. They expected to make a profit by collecting tolls. At key locations on the road they put up a gate with a bar called a pike that blocked the way. After collecting the toll, the attendant would turn the pike aside. Thus toll roads came to be known as turnpikes.

River Travel   The first roads often functioned mainly to connect one river with another. Rivers provided the country's major transportation routes, and hand-powered keelboats and flatboats served as the main vehicles for travelers and goods. For example, farmers in trans-Appalachia typically floated their products down the Ohio and Mississippi rivers by flatboat to New Orleans. From there, sailing ships carried them east through the Gulf of Mexico, around Florida, and north to ports on the Atlantic Coast. Products following this route took a very long time to get to market. Also, the route did not work in the opposite direction because flatboats could not carry goods upriver, against the current.

American inventor Robert Fulton solved that problem. He developed a boat that ran on steam power, using one of James Watt's steam engines. His paddle-wheeled "North River Steamboat," popularly known as the *Clermont*, steamed up the Hudson River in 1807. The *Clermont* demonstrated the great advantage of the steamboat: It could travel upriver, against the current, much faster even than sailing ships. Fulton's was not the first steamboat to navigate the waters of an American river, but it was the first commercially successful steamboat. Soon his steamboat and others began transporting freight and passengers along eastern rivers and coastal waters.

Within a few years, hundreds of steamboats were operating on the Mississippi and other rivers of the American West. Steam power made it possible for western farmers and southern planters to increase their trade and their profits.

Canals   Farmers and merchants could transport goods most cheaply by water. Unfortunately, waterways did not go everywhere that people wanted them to go. To solve this problem, American innovators built artificial waterways, or canals. By 1840, the nation had some 3,000 miles of canals.

The best-known of these canals, and one that had a huge economic impact, was the Erie Canal, which opened in 1825. Built by the state of New York, this 363-mile waterway linked the Atlantic Coast with the Great Lakes. A typical trip started in New York City. A steamboat would haul a specially built canal

The Industrial Revolution in America		
Date	**Inventor**	**Invention or Innovation**
1787	John Fitch	The first American steamboat
1790	Samuel Slater	Machinery for first U.S. textile mill
1794	Eli Whitney	The cotton gin patented
1795	Robert Fulton	The steam shovel (for digging canals)
1798	Eli Whitney	Mass production of muskets with standard measures and interchangeable parts
1807	Robert Fulton	The *Clermont*, the first commercially successful steamboat
1814	Francis C. Lowell	The first completely mechanized cotton mill
1820	William Underwood	The first U.S. canning factory
1826	Samuel Morey	An internal combustion engine
1828	Joseph Henry	The electromagnet

INTERPRETING CHARTS The Industrial Revolution brought American advances in engineering, medicine, science, agriculture, and technology. In fact, the word *technology* was coined in 1829. **Drawing Inferences** *What aspects of American life did many of these advances affect?*

At the opening of the Erie Canal, New York's governor poured Lake Erie water from this keg into the Atlantic Ocean to symbolize the linking of the two bodies of water via the canal.

ACTIVITY
Connecting with Geography
Assign students the task of writing a brief report entitled "The Erie Canal Today." The report should identify how the canal is currently used, where it runs, who maintains it, and so on. Encourage students to illustrate their reports with photographs or a map and share them with the class. (**Verbal/Linguistic**)

From the Archives of
AmericanHeritage®

Up the River
On April 23, 1823, the riverboat *Virginia* steamed out of St. Louis with a few passengers and a cargo of military supplies bound for Fort St. Anthony, an army post on the site of the present-day St. Paul, Minnesota. Its departure marked the first time a steamboat was going to travel up the Mississippi River all the way to the head of navigation. The low-pressure steam engine employed by Robert Fulton in his famous *Clermont* had been of little use against the powerful currents, treacherous rapids, islands, and shoals that characterized western rivers like the upper Mississippi, so a new type of engine with much higher pressure had to be developed. Although *Virginia*'s voyage was slow, it proved that a steamboat could conquer the upper Mississippi. Before long a fleet of steamers was carrying lead, furs, and grain down the Mississippi and settlers up it. Source: Frederic D. Schwarz, "The Time Machine," *American Heritage*® magazine, April 1998.

CAPTION ANSWERS

Interpreting Charts Answers include: travel, manufacturing, farming.

CUSTOMIZE FOR ...
Less Proficient Writers
Have each student create a poster entitled "New Types of Transportation." Posters should use text and drawings to illustrate how these types of transportation helped America prosper.

ACTIVITY

Connecting with Science and Technology

Have students conduct research necessary for them to create basic but annotated diagrams of steam engines during Watt's time. Consider having one group of students diagram a "pre-Watt" steam engine. Have a second group diagram a "post-Watt" steam engine to highlight the inventor's innovations. Then compare and contrast the two diagrams. **(Visual/Spatial)**

BACKGROUND

Geography in History

Although the early trains solved some problems, they created many of their own. Routes were frequently unfenced or single-tracked, leading trains to collide with livestock or each other. Wood-burning locomotives threw out sparks that set fire to passengers, clothing, and nearby forests. Some trains even included a car stuffed with cotton to protect passengers from locomotive explosions. Train travel became safe and viable only with the introduction of closed cars and new safety devices in the 1850s.

READING CHECK

Transportation: allowed for increased trade and profits; ability to transport goods cheaply; expanded areas where settlement and development were possible; increased rates of settlement. Communication: expanding postal service; national network of information; allowed for connections between different parts of the country.

Along the Erie Canal today, towns stage reenactments of the days when mules towed barges along the waterway.

READING CHECK

What were some of the major effects of the advances in transportation and communication?

boat, loaded with goods and passengers, up the Hudson River to Albany, where the Erie Canal began. Horses or mules towed the canal boat along the canal from the Hudson to Lake Erie.

The opening of the Erie Canal increased the rate of settlement and development of the entire Great Lakes region. Farmers in that area could now ship their products quickly and inexpensively to profitable eastern markets, and merchants could send finished goods in the opposite direction. With its location on the Atlantic Coast at the end of this canal system, New York City grew into a powerful center of business.

Railroads Canals played an important role in transporting goods and people. Railroads, however, proved to be even more efficient. The high-pressure steam locomotive, developed by British and American inventors, could pull more goods and passengers more quickly than canal boats.

In 1828, construction on the first American railroad began in Baltimore, Maryland. It came to be known as the Baltimore and Ohio (B & O) line. By 1840, the nation had several different railway lines and more than 3,300 miles of track, more than any other country in the world. In the coming decades, the nation's system of east-west rail lines would put most canals out of business. The canal network would also forge a strong trading relationship between the West and the Northeast.

Communication The transportation revolution also led to advances in communication. The federal government led the way by expanding its postal service. The number of post offices in the nation leaped from 75 in 1790 to 8,450 in 1830. Regularly scheduled long-distance mail delivery improved communication between individuals and businesses. It also created a national network of information, since the mail included newspapers, magazines, and books.

Before the American Revolution, Americans had access to a relatively small number of newspapers. Most of them came out weekly. By the 1820s, however, advances in education had increased the nation's literacy rate. More than 500 newspapers and magazines of all sorts were being published daily. Improved communication and the free exchange of ideas helped tie together the different parts of the country as it grew in both size and population.

An Expanding Economy

The American genius for invention produced new and better ways to make and transport goods. It also changed the way people did business. A new generation of Americans began buying and selling goods, borrowing and circulating money, and creating wealth. This change in the way Americans made, bought, and sold goods is known as the **Market Revolution.** Thanks to this Market Revolution, the American economy soared in the decades after the War of 1812.

The Rise of Manufacturing In the early 1800s, the United States was mostly a nation of farmers. In the South, farmers continued to profit from the high demand for cotton. In the Old Northwest, farmers put more and more fertile frontier lands into corn and wheat production. In the Northeast, farming continued to be important. However, businesspeople began turning more and more to new enterprises such as **manufacturing,** the use of machinery to make products. They bought cotton, grains, and other raw materials and turned them into products that could be sold for a substantial profit.

American manufacturing began in New England. There, rivers gathered strength as they descended from the mountains, surged through valleys, and plunged over waterfalls. The power generated by these fast-flowing waters ran the new machines in the mills and other factories that sprang up throughout the region.

In 1814, a group of businessmen led by a Boston merchant named Francis Cabot Lowell built a mill in Waltham, Massachusetts, to manufacture textiles. Lowell's mill was the world's first truly **centralized** textile factory—that is, a single facility where all the tasks involved in making a product (in this case, cloth) were carried out. Lowell's Waltham mill and the many later water-powered mills in New England brought together all the tasks of spinning, weaving, and dyeing that turned raw, cleaned cotton into finished cloth. The shift to centralized workplaces dramatically increased production. In 1817, New England's textile mills produced 4 million yards of cotton cloth. By 1840, the amount was 323 million yards.

From the 1820s through the 1840s, manufacturing industries spread from New England across the Northeast and into parts of the old Northwest Territory, such as the Ohio River valley. Manufacturing would soon become the backbone of the North's economy—and a key element in the Market Revolution.

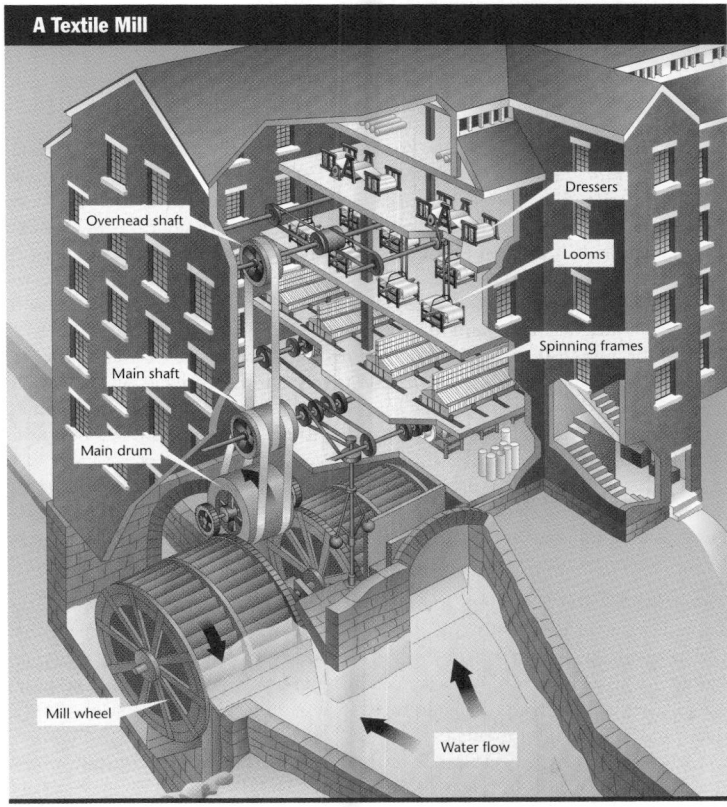

A Textile Mill

Overhead shaft

Dressers

Looms

Main shaft

Spinning frames

Main drum

Mill wheel

Water flow

INTERPRETING DIAGRAMS
New England mill builders adopted a system of belts to harness river power. On the first floor, cotton was combed; on the second floor, it was spun into thread; on the third, thread was woven into cloth; and on the fourth, the cloth was dressed, or finished. **Analyzing Visual Information** *What effect did geography have on the location of a mill?*

Focus on DAILY LIFE

Learning Manners By displaying well-made, store-bought goods in their homes, Americans in the early 1800s showed others that they were respectable as well as prosperous. Another way to make this point was to behave in a refined way—to act like a lady or a gentleman, not a rough pioneer.

Books of etiquette, or proper manners, gave people specific instructions on how to act. They covered such issues as when to use a knife (only for cutting food, not for eating it) and whether it was proper to lean back in one's chair (it wasn't).

The advice these books gave was hardly new. In the past, though, it had been aimed only at the wealthy. In America of the early 1800s, many average people bought these books so they too could learn to behave with dignity and grace.

Manufacturing and other features of the Market Revolution developed within the **free enterprise system,** an economic system in which private companies compete for profits. This system, also called *capitalism,* rewards people who can find better, faster, and more efficient ways of running their businesses. It encourages innovation and the creation of new industries, jobs, and wealth.

Working Outside the Home For most Americans, "going to work" in the 1700s generally meant working in the home or around the farm. Of course, some skilled artisans did produce goods such as books or glass that could not be made easily at home. Others were employed in the shipping industry or the legal or financial professions. Most people, however, worked simply to make the food, clothing, and shelter they needed.

In the 1800s, the rise of manufacturing sharply increased the demand for people who would work outside the home, for a specific number of hours each day and for a certain amount of money. Many young Americans, especially in the Northeast, turned away from farming and went to work in factories for wages.

Factory owners organized the work to maximize production. They increased the use of **specialization,** a system in which each worker performs just one part of an entire production process. For example, unlike earlier clothmakers, who knew all the aspects of spinning and weaving as well as machine repair, the sole job of a textile worker in the 1800s might have been to keep one loom supplied with thread.

The Rise of Shopping Products rolled out of factories at an astounding rate. The growing supply of goods forever changed the patterns of American life. The self-sufficient household, where family members spun their own thread or made their own soap, began to disappear. As products became available and people worked for money, Americans began to shop. In colonial America only the houses of wealthy planters and merchants had been full of goods. The relatively simple homes of the 1700s, however, gave way to the much more decorated and furnished homes of the 1800s.

By the mid-1800s, store-bought items filled the homes of many average Americans. Families bought reproductions of paintings to hang on their walls. They bought manufactured furniture and silverware. Household spinning wheels and looms fell silent as women chose to make their family's clothing out of fabric they had purchased.

The Role of Banks

New types of industries arose during the Market Revolution. Banks quickly rose to the top as the most important of the new enterprises.

The Rise of the Banking Industry The first real banks appeared in the United States in the 1780s and 1790s. By the 1830s, hundreds of new banks had opened up. To start a new bank, a group of private investors generally would obtain a charter from the state. The bank made money by charging interest for the loans it made. It made these loans using the money that customers deposited in the bank for safekeeping.

Many of the loans were made in the form of **investment capital,** money that a business spends in hopes of future gain. The owner of a textile business,

278   Chapter 8 • *The Growth of a National Economy*

for example, might use a bank loan to buy a new power loom. The goal of this investment was to increase production and create more profit for the business.

Banks thus helped the economy grow by providing investment capital. The system generally worked well. Disasters could, and did, occur, however.

Uncontrolled Lending Today, the government insures most deposits. Banks are required to keep a certain amount of cash on hand instead of lending it all out. However, in the 1800s, states did not restrict banks' runaway lending. The new banks often made loans to people who could not pay them back.

Because of these bad loans, a bank might not have enough cash on hand if a large number of depositors wanted their money. A sudden economic crisis, or panic, might cause many customers to try to retrieve their deposits at the same time. The bank, unable to meet its obligations, would go out of business.

In the early 1800s, the economy experienced wild booms followed by panics. These crises led to depressions, bank and business failures, and widespread unemployment. Panics occurred in 1819, 1837, and 1839—the last two so severe that they disrupted the economy well into the 1840s.

Bank Notes In the early republic, the government did not issue paper money. Most people preferred to deal in specie, or coin, mainly of gold or silver. Specie was scarce, however, and difficult to carry around. The most common form of money was the **bank note,** a piece of paper that banks issued to their customers. People used bank notes to pay for goods and services.

Similar to modern-day checks, bank notes were promises to pay specie on demand. In theory, anyone possessing a note could walk into the bank anytime and cash it in for specie. The problem with these notes was that banks simply printed more of them whenever they needed money, so the value of this money was unpredictable. A farmer, for instance, might sell some corn and receive in payment a $100 bank note that could be worth anything from $50 to $200 in specie, depending on the time and place the farmer tried to cash it.

Despite such growing pains, banks played a key role in economic expansion during the 1800s. While different areas of the country grew at different rates, the United States as a whole achieved a new level of prosperity.

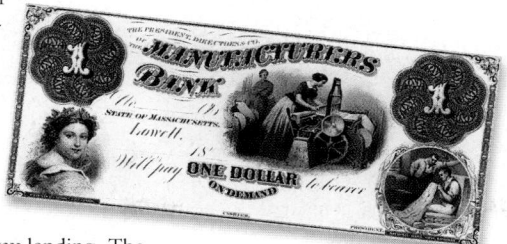

As this bank note shows, people began earning a living outside the home in the early 1800s.

Section 1 Assessment

READING COMPREHENSION

1. What American inventions and new technologies came about during the **Industrial Revolution?**

2. Describe the effects of **manufacturing** and **investment capital** on the U.S. economy.

3. What are the advantages of a **centralized** production process?

4. How did banks help spur economic growth?

CRITICAL THINKING AND WRITING

5. **Synthesizing Information** Create a two-column chart. Label the columns *Transportation* and *Communication*. List at least four innovations in transportation and two in communication.

6. **Writing to Describe** How was the Market Revolution a "revolution"? Write an essay on this topic. Support it with facts from this section.

 Take It to the NET

Activity: Writing a Magazine Article Research the Erie Canal and write the introduction and outline for a magazine article on the canal's history and its impact on America. Use the links provided in the *America: Pathways to the Present* area of the following Web site for help in completing this activity.
www.phschool.com

Reading Comprehension

1. Answers may include: steamboats, cotton gin, steam shovel, interchangeable parts, mechanized cotton mill, canning factory, internal combustion engine, or electromagnet.

2. Manufacturing made more goods available for purchase, so money became more widely used. For the first time, the producers of goods were not the people who used them. Items people used to have to make for themselves were now available for purchase. The availability of investment capital enabled business owners to improve and expand their businesses. This, in turn, enabled the economy as a whole to expand, creating new wealth.

3. Centralization dramatically increased production, which brought great prosperity to the economy of the North.

4. Banks provided the capital entrepreneurs needed to build new factories or expand and improve existing facilities. They did this by loaning out some of the money that depositors had placed in banks. These loans then had to be repaid with interest.

Critical Thinking and Writing

5. Transportation: steam power, new canals, new and better roads, railroads. Communication (two of the following): newspapers, magazines, and more post offices.

6. Essays should show an understanding of the dramatic changes in how and where people worked, in banking, and in transportation and communication.

 **Take It to the NET**

Answers will vary, but should be supported by facts and important dates in the history of the Erie Canal, as well as the Canal's social and economic impact on America.

READING FOCUS

- How did farming develop in the Old Northwest?
- What new industries arose in the Northeast?
- What caused the growth of cities, and what problems arose as they grew?
- What kinds of labor disputes arose in factories?

MAIN IDEA

New technologies helped agriculture prosper in the Old Northwest, while a variety of new industries brought growth—with its benefits and problems—to the Northeast.

KEY TERMS

section
rural
urban
industrialization
tenement
strike
labor union

TAKING NOTES

Copy the chart below. As you read, fill in the blanks with information about the economies of the North.

Economy	Old Northwest	Northeast
Type of economy		Industrial
Urban growth		
Major products		
Economic challenges	Spoiled products	

Setting the Scene In the early 1800s, Americans became more and more aware that their nation could be divided into two distinct regions, or **sections:** the North and the South. Each section had its own unique economy and culture. The French writer Alexis de Tocqueville sought to compare the two sections as he traveled around the country in 1831. When Tocqueville asked a southern lawyer about sectional differences, the man replied with this rather exaggerated comparison:

A woman going to work in one of the busy mills of the North carried her noonday meals in this tin and wood lunch pail.

❝ I should express the difference in this way. What distinguishes the North is its enterprising spirit, what distinguishes the South is l'esprit aristocratique [the spirit of the aristocracy, the wealthy ruling class]. The manners of the inhabitant of the South are frank, open; he is excitable, irritable even, exceedingly touchy of his honour. The New Englander is cold and calculating, patient. While you are with the Southerner you are welcome, he shares with you all the pleasures of his house. The Northerner, after having received you, begins to wonder whether he couldn't do some business with you. ❞
—Alexis de Tocqueville, *Democracy in America*

The North consisted of two main parts. One was the populous Northeast, composed of New England, New York, New Jersey, and Pennsylvania. This area had once been the New England and Middle colonies. The other part was the growing region north and west of the Ohio River—the old Northwest Territory, or simply the Old Northwest. It included land that is now Ohio, Indiana, Illinois, Michigan, Wisconsin, and part of Minnesota.

Farming in the Old Northwest

The highly fertile prairie of the Old Northwest proved to be ideal for growing corn, wheat, and other grains. Still, farmers always looked for ways to make their farms more efficient. New inventions helped. John Deere's steel plow, which he developed in the 1830s, could cut through the heavy soil of the northwestern prairie better than other plows. Cyrus McCormick's mechanical reaper, also developed in the 1830s, made harvesting grains less labor-intensive and thus more profitable.

Once grains were harvested, they tended to spoil. Farmers had to use them, get them to market quickly, or turn them into a product that would not spoil. For example, they used corn as feed for pigs. Pigs provided not only meat but also fat for making soap and bristles for making brushes. Similarly, farmers fed wheat and other crops to cattle. They also sold wheat, oats, barley, and corn to brewers and distillers, who used these crops to make beer and whiskey, products that were easy to store.

Many specialized businesses arose to handle the processing, transport, and selling of farm products. They included slaughterhouses, distilleries, shipping companies, and banks. From Ohio westward into Illinois, agriculture and related industries fueled the growth of cities.

Cincinnati, for example, developed into a hog-processing center. So many hogs were slaughtered in Cincinnati that the city became known as "Porkopolis."

In the early 1800s, farmers sent flour, meal, pork products, whiskey, and other goods by river to New Orleans to be sold in the Caribbean islands, the eastern United States, and Europe. With the transportation revolution, as you have read, farmers from the Old Northwest began shipping their goods east by canal and, later, by rail. Merchants in the Northeast then controlled the further distribution of those goods.

Industries of the Northeast

Farmers in the Old Northwest sold their pork, grains, and beer to a market in which, increasingly, people no longer raised their own food. Most people in the Northeast still lived in **rural** areas, made up of farms and countryside instead of cities. However, an increasing number of people in the region now worked in factories in **urban** areas, or cities. During the early 1800s, the urban population boomed, while the rural population gradually declined.

Industrialization, or the development of industry, increased rapidly in the Northeast. Eli Whitney built a factory near New Haven, Connecticut, to manufacture muskets, using his concept of interchangeable parts. Other

This woodcut shows two men operating machinery in an early textile mill. The machines printed long sheets of a fabric called calico.

Chapter 8 • Section 2 **281**

From the Archives of

AmericanHeritage®

Cooper's Coup

In February 1823 James Fenimore Cooper published *The Pioneers,* which sold over 3,500 copies the first day it went on sale. It became so popular that it would be translated and read around the world. *The Pioneers* introduced America's first great fictional character, Natty Bumppo. Bumppo, also known as Leatherstocking for his deerskin breeches, is an aging frontiersman who has spent decades living off the wilderness until America's burgeoning population begins to encroach on his ways. Bumppo complains about losing his shooting and fishing playground to the settlers' farms. By shunning the settlers' "wasty ways," he sounds an early warning against the American tendency to confuse abundance with inexhaustibility. The popularity of *The Pioneers* led Cooper to write a series of novels called *The Leatherstocking Tales* in which Bumppo was the star. Source: Frederic D. Schwarz, "The Time Machine," *American Heritage®* magazine, February/March 1998.

READING CHECK
In the Northeast.

CAPTION ANSWERS

Interpreting Graphs (a) About 1 million; about 3.5 million. (b) The urban population grew more quickly, but the *total* number of rural dwellers still greatly exceeded the total urban population in 1850.

---

water-powered factories in the state produced furniture, clocks, glass, and tinware. By 1850, more people in Connecticut worked in manufacturing than in farming.

Coal from Pennsylvania's huge coal-mining industry, which started in 1820, fueled the boilers that powered steam engines on boats and locomotives. The state also became a top producer of ships, lumber, iron, leather, textiles, and glass. By 1850, the industrial city of Pittsburgh had 40 glass factories.

In Massachusetts, new industries produced carpet, bricks, and shoes. When Francis Cabot Lowell built the first fully centralized textile mill in Waltham in 1813, he launched another new industry. Similar mills went up along many of New England's rivers. In 1826, nine years after Lowell's death, a mill town in northern Massachusetts was founded and named for him. Lowell, Massachusetts, would become a thriving industrial center.

The mills in Lowell hired young, unmarried women from New England farms to run their spinning and weaving machines. The mill owners promised them a moral environment and a stable income. The young women enjoyed being able to earn and save money before they married.

The young Lowell mill workers made about $3.25 for a 72-hour week in the 1830s. After deducting $1.25 for room and board, the typical woman worker averaged about $2 per week, a fair wage at a time when many basic goods cost only pennies.

Hiring women laborers made economic sense to mill owners. Women were willing to work for about half the pay that men demanded. Women held most factory jobs in the Lowell mills until the 1840s, when they began to be replaced by men, often Irish immigrants who were unable to find better-paying jobs.

Women millworkers usually lived in boardinghouses run by the mill owners. Six days a week, twelve hours a day, from dawn till dusk, they tended the grinding, clattering machines. In the evening they might attend lectures or classes, or gather in sewing or reading circles. Although the work was boring, the women valued the friendships they made. One worker recalled her work in the mill:

READING CHECK
Where did industrialization take hold in the early 1800s?

> 66 *There was a great deal of play mixed with it. We were not occupied more than half the time. The intervals were spent frolicking around among the spinning frames, teasing and talking to the older girls, or entertaining ourselves with games and stories in a corner.* 99
> —Millworker Lucy Larcom

INTERPRETING GRAPHS The changes in the U.S. economy led to changes in its population. **Analyzing Visual Information** (a) *About how many Americans lived in cities in 1830? In 1850? (b) Which grew faster during this period, the urban or rural population?*

Urban and Rural Populations, 1800–1850

SOURCE: *Historical Statistics of the United States, Colonial Times to 1970*

The Growth of Cities

The Northeast brimmed with young people looking for work. Farming opportunities in the region now were limited, because the population had outgrown the available land. Some young workers moved west, but thousands went to the cities of the Northeast. In 1810, only about 6 percent of Americans lived in cities. By 1840, 12 percent lived in cities, an increase shown in the graph on the left.

The largest cities in colonial North America had had no more than 30,000 residents. The rush to the cities in the early 1800s, however, sharply boosted urban populations. For example, the number of people in New York City (Manhattan only) soared from roughly 33,000 in 1790 to 131,000 in 1820, and to

---

RESOURCE DIRECTORY

Other Print Resources
Nystrom *Atlas of Our Country* A Divided Nation, pp. 26–27

Technology

RESOURCE PRO® **Primary Source Activity**
New England Mill Women, found on Resource Pro, helps students examine the pros and cons of factory life.

RESOURCE PRO® **Biography** *Sarah Todd Astor,* found on Resource Pro, profiles Sarah Todd Astor and John Jacob Astor, a couple who exemplified the Market Revolution.

about 516,000 by 1850. The populations of Boston and Philadelphia also rose, as did those of smaller cities such as Baltimore.

Urban life in the 1800s differed greatly from that in colonial times, when human needs such as medical care, education, and care for the elderly had been met within the household. Now, as workers spent more and more time away from the household, they could no longer supply these needs to their families at home. Children, sick relatives, and elderly family members in northern cities often had no support in times of trouble. Gradually, public institutions such as hospitals and schools began to fill this gap.

A growing number of urban poor people lived in areas with cheap, run-down housing. By the 1830s, for example, the Five Points area in lower Manhattan had become known for its **tenements**, crowded apartments with poor standards of sanitation, safety, and comfort. In 1842, the English writer Charles Dickens described the "squalid" (filthy) streets and "hideous tenements" he encountered on a visit to Five Points. He declared that "all that is loathsome, drooping and decayed is here."

Cities simply could not handle the rapid population increase. Police and fire services were primitive at best. Many cities lacked sewage systems and reliable supplies of fresh water. In 1832 and 1833, thousands of people died or fell ill during a major outbreak of cholera, an intestinal disease caused by contaminated water.

Still, cities continued to grow in the Northeast and to dominate the surrounding regions. These urban areas acquired wealth and political influence gained from being centers of industry.

Labor Disputes in Factories

Early industries aimed to make a profit, often at the expense of their workers. Most factory owners of that time paid their employees little and did not try to provide a healthy work environment. Before long, laborers began to demand more from their bosses.

Workers Go on Strike As workers saw factory owners grow rich, they began to want a slice of the wealth that their hard labor produced. Workers complained mainly about long hours and low wages. Since the government set no minimum wage, workers could not go to the legislatures or the courts for help. In fact, they had only one real weapon: They could call for a **strike**, or work stoppage.

Strikes had occurred as early as the 1700s, when sailors and dockworkers walked off the job. Shoemakers also launched strikes in the first decade of the 1800s. From 1834 through 1836, more than 150 strikes took place in the United States, mainly to demand shorter hours and higher pay. In Lowell, 1 out of every 6 women workers went on strike in 1834 when employers, faced with poor sales, cut wages by 15 percent.

The First Labor Unions In 1834, during this period of growing labor activity, workers organized the first national **labor union,** the National Trades Union (NTU). A labor union is an organization of workers formed to protect the

This engraving depicted the poverty-stricken Five Points section of New York City.

ACTIVITY
Connecting with History and Conflict

Divide the class into groups of four. Have one student in each group assume the role of a worker who is trying to persuade his coworkers to strike, while the other students role-play the following: a male worker with a large family and a sick wife at home; an unmarried woman with no children; a woman with a large family and no husband; and a young, unmarried male. Ask students to explain their reasons for wanting or not wanting to strike. (Logical/Mathematical)

BACKGROUND
The Flour Riot

Desperate economic conditions in New York City, where 50,000 people—about one third of the working population—were unemployed, resulted in the Flour Riot of 1837. The New York *Commercial Register* reported, "Barrels of flour, by dozens, fifties and hundreds were tumbled into the street . . . thrown in rapid succession from the windows . . . [And] numbers of women were . . . filling . . . their aprons, with flour, and making off with it."

✓ TEST PREPARATION

Have students read the passage by Lucy Larcom on the previous page and then answer the question below.

How did Lucy characterize her work days?

A They were long and boring.

Ⓑ They had plenty of free time for play and games.

C She had to spend all day at the spinning frames.

D She had no other girls to talk to.

Reading Comprehension

1. The Northeast became industrialized and urban, and workers began to form unions. Industries in the Northeast included shipbuilding, coal mining, and textile manufacturing. With new transportation systems, wheat and corn farming flourished in the Old Northwest, as did the livestock trade.

2. Positive effects: more efficient production and distribution of goods; opportunities for women to work outside the home. Negative effects: overcrowding in cities; poor working conditions; spread of disease; lack of necessary social services.

3. Since the government had not set a minimum wage and did not yet regulate workplace safety issues, workers could not go to the legislatures or courts for help, leaving strikes as their only option.

4. Issues concerning low wages, long hours, hiring practices, and working conditions.

Critical Thinking and Writing

5. Sample answers: People and industries in the North relied on farm products from the South, while the South needed northern markets. Southerners resented the North's wealth and its dependence on banks, while northerners increasingly opposed slavery in the South.

6. Articles should show an understanding of the benefits and drawbacks of factory life.

Take It to the NET

Posters should effectively represent changes in farming methods brought about by mechanization using images, labels, and informative captions.

---

interests of its members, usually by negotiating to resolve issues concerning wages, hiring practices, and working conditions. Close to 300,000 people joined the NTU or other labor unions in the 1830s, a large number for that period.

These early unions soon died out, however. Factory owners obtained court rulings that outlawed labor organizations. The financial panics in 1837 and 1839 also undercut the unions. In the depression that followed the panics, unemployment grew, and workers could not afford to push their demands.

Despite its failures, the early labor movement showed that some workers were willing to take action against their employers. One millworker recalled her response when some women hesitated to strike during a protest against wage cuts:

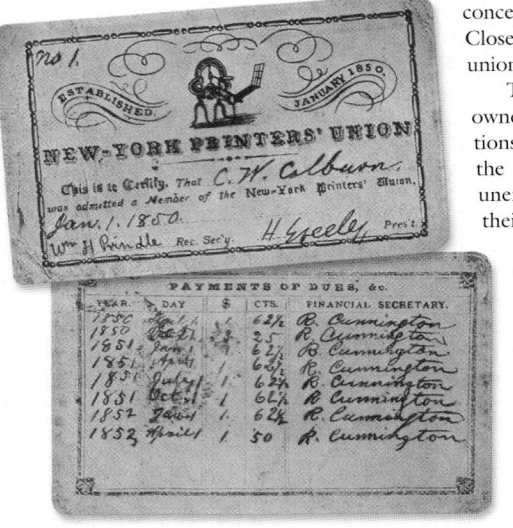

This membership card for the New York Printers' Union was signed by the famous newspaper editor Horace Greeley.

66 Not one of them having the courage to lead off, I . . . became impatient and started on ahead, saying, with childish bravado [boasting], 'I don't care what you do, I am going to turn out [strike], whether any one else does or not'; and I marched out, and was followed by the others. As I looked back at the long line that followed me, I was more proud than I have ever been since at any success I may have achieved. 99

—Lowell millworker Harriet Robinson, 1836

In time, the labor movement would build on the pride of people such as Robinson. By the 1840s, the North had a booming and complex economy with a mixture of industry and agriculture. It was increasingly a region of cities and towns, banks and factories, with all the benefits and problems that come with growth.

Section 2 Assessment

READING COMPREHENSION

1. In what ways did the economy of the North change from 1800 to 1850?

2. What were the good and bad effects of **industrialization** and **urban** growth on the northern **section?**

3. Why were **strikes** the only weapon that workers had with which to fight poor working conditions?

4. What kinds of problems did **labor unions** want companies to address?

CRITICAL THINKING AND WRITING

5. **Expressing Problems Clearly** In what ways did economic change in the North link people together, and in what ways did it push them apart?

6. **Writing a News Story** As a newspaper reporter in the 1840s, write an article describing the life of millworkers and their efforts to improve working conditions.

Take It to the NET

Activity: Making a Poster
Research the inventions of Cyrus McCormick and John Deere. Then create a poster that uses words and visual images to illustrate farming methods before and after machinery came into use. Use the links provided in the *America: Pathways to the Present* area of the following Web site for help in completing this activity.
www.phschool.com

RESOURCE DIRECTORY

Teaching Resources
Units 3/4 booklet
  • Section 2 Quiz, p. 15
Guide to the Essentials
  • Section 2 Summary, p. 42

Setting the Scene

Setting the Scene One famous phrase sums up the economy of the South in the first half of the 1800s: "King Cotton." The phrase came from the book *Cotton Is King* by David Christy, published in 1855. Christy claimed that southern slavery would have ended except for the ever-rising demand for cotton products during the previous 30 years. Even Northerners who criticized slavery, he said, continued to use more and more cotton and other products of slave labor. In addition, the American economy had come to depend on the revenue from the sale of raw cotton:

> 66 *Thus, the very things necessary to the overthrow of American Slavery, were left undone, while those essential to its prosperity, were continued in the most active operation; so that, now, after nearly a 'thirty years' war,' we may say, emphatically, COTTON IS KING, and his enemies are vanquished [defeated].* 99

—David Christy, *Cotton Is King*, 1855

In 1820, the South produced 160 million pounds of raw cotton. By 1830, the harvest had doubled, and the 1850 crop surpassed a billion pounds. In 1860, King Cotton made up two thirds of the total value of American exports. It had created enormous wealth for the South.

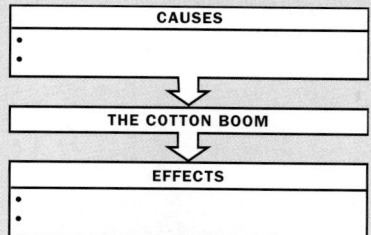

The book *Cotton Is King* is addressed in part "to the Free Colored People of the United States, and to those who hold that Slavery is in itself sinful."

The Economy of the South

In 1820, the South included 6 of the original 13 states: Delaware, Maryland, Virginia (including what would become West Virginia), North Carolina, South Carolina, and Georgia. It also included newer states carved out of former Indian lands south of the Ohio River: Kentucky, Tennessee, Alabama, Mississippi, and Louisiana. By 1850, Arkansas and Texas had joined the Union and become part of the **cotton belt,** a band of states stretching from South Carolina to Texas. The economies of these states relied almost completely on the production of cotton.

Chapter 8 • Section 3   **285**

Focus Explain that most of the South's economy centered on commercial agriculture. Yet it was also a dynamic society based on a free enterprise system. Ask what made its economy flourish.

Instruct Discuss the South's economy. Ask how agriculture differed in the North and South. In what ways were southern planters and farmers as capitalistic as their northern counterparts? How did the Market Revolution affect the South?

Analyze the role that enslaved people played in the southern economy. Would southern commercial agriculture have been possible without slavery?

Assess/Reteach Have students list some ways in which the growth of the southern economy in the early 1800s had its parallel in the growth of the slave trade.

MAP SKILLS The Southern economy relied on cotton more than any other agricultural or industrial product. **Movement** *Describe the route by which cotton farming expanded.*

Products of the South

Cattle	Iron and steel	Rice and sugar cane
Cotton	Lumber	Textiles
Grain	Mining	Tobacco
Spread of cotton, 1820–1860		1860 borders

VIEWING HISTORY Five generations of an African American family—all enslaved—posed for this photograph outside their plantation home in 1862. **Testing Conclusions** *Could this photograph be used as evidence of living conditions during the 1840s? Explain your answer.*

The Geography of Southern Farming   While urban centers developed in the North, the South remained mostly rural. The physical geography of the South made farming highly profitable. Farmers could count on 200 to 290 frost-free days a year in which to grow crops. Fertile soil and plentiful rain encouraged the spread of agriculture.

The development of industry progressed slowly in the early 1800s. Although larger southern cities had banks, farmers often had to rely on British or northern banks for loans. Until later in the century, they depended on textile mills in Britain and the North to process their cotton. Still, few Southerners entered into these industries. Many lawyers, doctors, and preachers hoped to retire eventually and become plantation farmers.

An estimated 15,000 families owned plantations. Plantations used great numbers of enslaved workers to produce a cash crop. By contrast, hundreds of thousands of farm families owned just a few slaves, or none, and raised their own cash crops, food crops, and livestock. In fact, only about one fourth of all slaves lived on plantations with more than 50 slaves. During the early 1800s, farms with six slaves or fewer produced half of the cotton crop. With the invention of the cotton gin in 1793, Southerners scrambled to put more land into cotton production. Small farmers seized this new opportunity, streaming west into uncultivated parts of the trans-Appalachian region. While small farms existed all over the South, in certain areas where the soil was especially fertile and rivers were nearby, plantation owners bought out their poorer neighbors and acquired huge tracts of land for cotton and sugar production.

286   Chapter 8 • *The Growth of a National Economy*

CAPTION ANSWERS

Map Skills Beginning in the 1820s, cotton farming spread westward from South Carolina to Georgia, Florida, Alabama, Mississippi, Arkansas, Louisiana, and Texas.

Viewing History Answers will vary, but might mention that although the photograph was taken during the Civil War, the living conditions of these slaves had probably not improved (and may even have worsened) since the 1840s.

286 • Chapter 8 Section 3

Not all southern states changed over to cotton, however. Virginia and North Carolina continued to be mainly tobacco states. Sugar and rice crops thrived in hot and wet places such as South Carolina. Kentucky developed a varied rural economy that included the breeding of thoroughbred horses.

Slow Urban Growth   Although the South was mainly rural, cities did gradually develop. They included New Orleans, Louisiana; Charleston, South Carolina; and Richmond, Virginia. These cities had smaller populations than those in the North. Yet they shared some of the problems such as run-down housing and poor sanitation that plagued big northern cities such as New York and Boston.

During this period, fewer than 8 percent of white Southerners lived in towns of more than 4,000 people. On the other hand, large numbers of free African Americans made their homes in southern towns and cities. By 1850, of the 3.7 million African Americans nationwide, 12 percent were free. Some lived in the North, but most lived in southern urban areas or rural areas away from the large plantations.

The Slavery System

By 1804, all the northern states had either banned slavery or passed laws to end it gradually. The Constitution had specified that Congress could not end the slave trade before 1808. In that year Congress banned all further importation of slaves to the United States.

In the South, however, population growth among people already enslaved contributed to a sharp increase in the internal slave trade for the next half-century. (Recall that a child born to a slave also became a slave.) In 1820, the slave population numbered about 1.5 million. Just 30 years later, in 1850, the population had more than doubled, to over 3 million. By 1860, African American slaves made up more than half of the population of South Carolina and Mississippi, as well as two fifths of the populations of Florida, Georgia, Alabama, and Louisiana.

Slavery on Small and Large Farms   The lives of enslaved Americans varied. On small farms, slaves often worked side by side with their owners in the fields. They sometimes ate together and slept in the same house. Yet many other enslaved workers on small farms endured all kinds of cruelties without family or friends to turn to for support and protection.

Most slaves, however, did not live on small farms but on large cotton plantations. By 1850, cotton farming employed nearly 60 percent of the enslaved African Americans in the United States. These people lived in sizable communities of slaves, usually numbering 20 or more. On the plantations, life was generally harsher than on small farms. Workers often toiled in large crews under the supervision of foremen.

For women in particular, life could be extremely difficult. In addition to bearing and caring for their own children and taking care of their own households, they cooked for and served food to their owners, cleaned their owners' houses and clothes, and labored

COMPARING PRIMARY SOURCES
Slavery

The issue of slavery opened up a bitter divide between the North and the South. The writers below present viewpoints on whether enslaved people wished to remain in slavery.

Analyzing Viewpoints Compare the main arguments made by the two writers.

In Support of Slavery
"A merrier being does not exist on the face of the globe than the Negro slave of the United States. They are happy and contented, and the master is much less cruel than is generally imagined. Why then . . . should we attempt to disturb his contentment by planting in his mind a vain and indefinite desire for liberty—something which he can't understand?"
—*Prof. Thomas R. Dew, speech to the Virginia legislature, 1832*

In Opposition to Slavery
"I thank God I am not property now, but am regarded as a man like yourself. . . . You may perhaps think hard of us for running away from slavery, but as for myself, I have but one apology to make for it, which is this: I have only to regret that I did not start at any early period."
—*Henry Bibb, who escaped from slavery with his family, in a letter to his former master, 1844*

ACTIVITY
Connecting with Culture

Have students explore different regional lifestyles by dividing into four groups: two groups to represent northern factory owners and factory workers, and two groups to represent southern plantation owners and enslaved people. Have each group write a description of a day in the life of its assigned characters. Then integrate the groups and have students discuss how they want their daily lives to change.
(Verbal/Linguistic)

BACKGROUND
Recent Scholarship

Being born into slavery meant growing up as part of a fractured family. In *Born in Bondage,* Marie Jenkins Schwartz examines the circumstances of slave children, who answered to two distinct sets of authority: their parents and their slave owner. Because children born to slaves automatically became the property of their parents' slave owners, their parents had a limited ability to protect them. Schwartz shows that although slaves had little time to lavish on their children, most did what they could to create a sense of family within the constraints of slavery. She shows that caring for children offered slaves a much-needed break from the grim realities of slave life.

READING CHECK
Physical geography: climate, conducive weather conditions, fertile soil, availability of slaves.

CUSTOMIZE FOR ...
ESL
Ask students to skim the section, noting any unfamiliar words. Help them define these words using context clues or a dictionary.

✓ TEST PREPARATION
Have students read the text under the heading *The Slavery System* and answer the question below.

According to the text, how many years did it take for the number of slaves in 1820 to double?

A Ten years.
Ⓑ Thirty years.
C Twenty years.
D Forty years.

Cotton Production and Slavery, 1800–1860

SOURCE: *Historical Statistics of the United States, Colonial Times to 1970*

INTERPRETING GRAPHS As cotton production rose, so did the number of slaves. **Interpreting Visual Information** (a) How much did cotton production rise from 1820 to 1850? (b) When did the number of slaves rise the most?

in their owners' fields. In addition, some women were subject to physical or sexual abuse by slave owners.

Slaves as Property Most owners saw slaves as mere property that performed labor for their businesses. In a bill of sale from 1811, a slave named Eve and her child, at a price of $156, are listed between a plow for $1.60 and "Eight Fancy Chairs" for $9.25.

As the demand for slaves rose in the early 1800s, so did the prices that slave traders demanded. A "prime" field worker between 18 and 25 years of age cost about $500 in 1832. By 1837, the price had soared to $1,300, a huge amount at that time. Most farmers, therefore, could not afford to acquire enough slaves to start a plantation. Yet after the initial investment, slaves cost only $15 to $60 a year to support.

Because replacing a slave was so costly, slave owners generally kept their slaves healthy enough to work. The system provided little else, however. One enslaved man, Moses Grandy, was standing in the street when he saw his wife go by in a group of African Americans who had been sold to a slaveholder named Rogerson. Grandy later recalled:

❝ Mr. Rogerson was with them on his horse, armed with pistols. I said to him, 'For God's sake, have you bought my wife?' He said he had: when I asked him what she had done, he said she had done nothing, but that her master wanted money. He drew out a pistol and said that if I went near the wagon on which she was, he would shoot me. I asked for leave to shake hands with her, which he refused, but said I might stand at a distance and talk with her. My heart was so full that I could say very little. . . . I have never seen or heard from her [from] that day to this. I loved her as I love my life. ❞
—*Narrative of the Life of Moses Grandy*, 1844

Slave Revolts

Only a small percentage of slaves ever managed to escape their captivity or win their freedom. Rebellion, especially on a large scale, stood little chance of success. While historians have documented scores of slave rebellions, most were small, spontaneous responses to cruel treatment and ended in failure.

Vesey's Plan In 1800, the year of the failed Richmond revolt by Gabriel Prosser, a young slave named Denmark Vesey bought his freedom with $600 he had won in a street lottery. He worked as a carpenter and became a preacher at the local African Methodist Episcopal Church. Self-educated, Vesey started reading antislavery literature. He grew increasingly angry at the sufferings of his fellow African Americans. Vesey preached against slavery, quoting the Declaration of Independence and the Bible. He criticized African Americans who would not stand up to whites.

In 1822, Vesey's anger turned to action. He laid plans for the most ambitious slave revolt in American history. In a conspiracy that reportedly involved hundreds or even thousands of rebels, Vesey plotted to seize the city of Charleston in July 1822. Later accounts said that he had intended to raid the arsenal, kill all the white residents, free the slaves, and burn the city to the ground.

Like Prosser, Vesey was betrayed by some of his followers. In June, South Carolina troops smashed the rebellion before it could get started. Thirty-five African Americans were hanged, including Vesey. Another 32 were expelled from South Carolina. Four white men received fines and prison terms for aiding the rebels.

Turner's Rebellion Nat Turner, a 31-year-old African American preacher, planned and carried out a violent uprising in August 1831 known as **Turner's Rebellion.** Acting under what he believed was divine inspiration, he led up to 70 slaves in raids on white families in southeastern Virginia. In attacks on four plantations, the rebels killed more than 50 white people.

Eventually, local militia captured most of the rebels. The state of Virginia hanged about 20 of the slaves, including Turner. Crowds of frightened and angry whites rioted, killing about a hundred African Americans who had not been involved in the revolt.

White Southerners Alarmed In many communities African Americans outnumbered the white population. For this reason Southerners deeply feared slave revolts. Virginia, which was not primarily a cotton state, briefly considered ending slavery in order to ease this threat. Instead, however, it joined other southern states in tightening restrictions on slaves after the Vesey and Turner rebellions. Virginia and North Carolina passed laws against teaching enslaved people to read. Some states prevented blacks from moving freely or meeting.

VIEWING HISTORY This etching depicts the capture of Nat Turner (left), who claimed that an eclipse of the sun in 1831 was a sign that "I should arise and prepare myself, and slay my enemies with their own weapons." **Recognizing Bias** *Do you think the artist is sympathetic to Turner or not? Explain your reasoning.*

Section 3 Assessment

READING COMPREHENSION

1. Why did the South remain largely rural?

2. Why did farmers in the **cotton belt** resent their relationship to the North?

3. Describe the outcomes of Vesey's attempted revolt and **Turner's Rebellion.**

4. (a) What change did Congress make to the slave trade in 1808? (b) Why did the number of slaves continue to rise after this date?

CRITICAL THINKING AND WRITING

5. **Drawing Conclusions** (a) Why, do you think, did many southerners wish to retire from their professions to become plantation owners? (b) How might this help to explain Southerners' strong defense of slavery?

6. **Journal Writing** From the point of view of a European visitor to the South in 1840, write a journal entry about slave life, both on plantations and on small farms.

Take It to the NET

Activity: Analyzing Perspectives Research one of the slave rebellions listed in this section. Write two newspaper articles on the event, from a Northern perspective and a Southern perspective. Use the links provided in the *America: Pathways to the Present* area of the following Web site for help in completing this activity. **www.phschool.com**

Reading Comprehension

1. The physical geography of the South made farming profitable; fertile soil and much rain encouraged the spread of agriculture.

2. Southern cotton farmers were dependent on textile mills in the North to process their cotton and on northern banks for loans. They also resented the activities of northern abolitionists.

3. Vesey was betrayed by his followers. South Carolina troops quelled the rebellion before it began: 35 African Americans were hanged, 32 were expelled from South Carolina, and 4 white men were fined and imprisoned for aiding rebels. Turner and his followers killed more than 50 whites before the local militia put a stop to the uprising. About 20 slaves were hanged, and riots resulted.

4. (a) Congress banned all further importation of slaves from overseas. (b) Population growth among people already enslaved led to the continuing growth of the slave population.

Critical Thinking and Writing

5. Sample answer: (a) Plantation farmers often enjoyed prestige, wealth, and a comfortable rural lifestyle. (b) Besides being profitable, the plantation tradition became a part of the South's identity that people did not want to give up.

6. Essays should contain factual information from the section.

Take It to the NET

Articles should demonstrate an understanding of either Turner's Rebellion or Vesey's Plan from opposing perspectives. They should also analyze the respective social and political climate that created the chosen rebellion.

CAPTION ANSWERS

Viewing History Allow well-supported answers. Sample answer: The artist is sympathetic to Turner, because Turner is depicted in a proud, fearless stance.

Section 4

The Growth of Nationalism

SECTION OBJECTIVES

1. See some of the signs of a new nationalism after the War of 1812.
2. Find out why the election of 1824 was so controversial.
3. Discover what new political parties emerged in 1828, and find out what views they represent.

BELLRINGER

Warm-Up Activity Ask students with which they feel a stronger identification—the state they live in or the United States. Have them explain their responses.

Activating Prior Knowledge Have a discussion with students about what they think "nationalism" means. List some of their responses on the chalkboard, and review the list with the class after they have read the section.

READING STRATEGY

As students read the section, have them jot down the key events of the presidential elections of 1824 and 1828. Then have them review their list to make sure it is in chronological order.

BACKGROUND
Art History

The Romantic movement of the early nineteenth century encouraged artists to study the natural beauty of the countryside. A group of American painters known as the Hudson River School drew inspiration from New York's Catskill Mountains. These artists' pride in the American wilderness, and their strong wish to split off from European schools of painting, represented the new, nationwide sense of America. Later painters applied the techniques of America's first native artistic movement to the Mississippi River, Grand Canyon, and Yosemite Valley.

READING FOCUS
- What were some signs of a new nationalism after the War of 1812?
- Why was the election of 1824 so controversial?
- What new political parties emerged in 1828, and what views did they represent?

MAIN IDEA
After the War of 1812, a new nationalism among Americans could be seen in Supreme Court rulings and in federal policies at home and abroad. Nationalism also influenced the growth of new political parties.

KEY TERMS
Dartmouth College v. *Woodward*
McCulloch v. *Maryland*
Gibbons v. *Ogden*
Monroe Doctrine
American System

TAKING NOTES
As you read, complete and expand the Venn diagram below. Some categories have been filled in for you already.

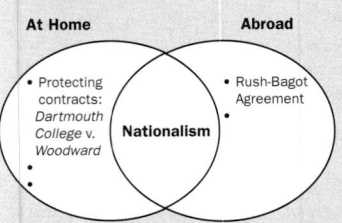

At Home — Abroad
- Protecting contracts: *Dartmouth College* v. *Woodward*
- **Nationalism**
- Rush-Bagot Agreement

This portrait of James Monroe shows him in 1816, at age 58.

Setting the Scene In 1800, residents of Georgia likely considered themselves citizens of their local communities and perhaps of their state, as did Americans in Pennsylvania or Vermont or elsewhere in the young nation. By the 1820s, however, it was becoming clear that national citizenship was growing in importance. Americans increasingly thought of themselves as citizens of the United States as well as members of their state and local communities.

Reflecting this shift, a new generation of American leaders sought to use the powers of the federal government to help unite the country. While traveling around the United States in 1817, President James Monroe encouraged Americans to think in nationalist terms. At a stop in Maine, he said that his tour of the country had given him "many opportunities of seeing and feeling how much we are one people." The President went on to speak about his hopes of putting aside sectional differences to form a "perfect union":

> 66 The United States are certainly the most enlightened people on earth. We are certainly rapidly advancing on the road of national pre-eminence. Nothing but Union is wanting [needed] to make us a great people. The present time affords the happiest presages [indications] that this union is fast consummating [reaching completion]. It cannot be otherwise. I daily see greater proofs of it: the further I advance in my progress, the more I perceive that we are all Americans. 99
>
> —James Monroe, 1817

Nationalism at Home

Many Americans came to think of Monroe's two terms as President (1817–1826) as the Era of Good Feelings. Many people were optimistic about the future. The War of 1812 was fading into the past, and the future looked bright. The Federalist Party was also fading from the scene, leaving just one national

290 Chapter 8 • *The Growth of a National Economy*

RESOURCE DIRECTORY

Teaching Resoures
Guided Reading and Review booklet, p. 35

Technology
Section Reading Support Transparencies
Guided Reading Audiotapes (English/Spanish), Ch. 8
Student Edition on Audio CD, Ch. 8
Color Transparencies *American Photo,* F3
Prentice Hall Presentation Pro CD-ROM, Ch. 8
Companion Web site, www.phschool.com

political party—the Jeffersonian Republicans. Despite the general feeling of hopefulness, however, many problems continued to create tension. As you have read, the economy followed a cycle of boom and bust, and sectional disputes arose concerning the spread of slavery.

To resolve some of its economic and political issues, the nation adopted new, nationalist policies, both at home and abroad. In 1816, for example, Congress passed a protective tariff to encourage the purchase of American-made goods by making foreign goods more expensive. In addition, the Supreme Court under Chief Justice John Marshall made several key decisions that strengthened the federal government's role in the nation's economy.

Protecting Contracts   In an 1819 ruling, the Supreme Court prohibited New Hampshire from changing the charter of Dartmouth College. The college had received its charter during colonial times. In ***Dartmouth College*** v. ***Woodward,*** the Marshall Court reasoned that the charter was a contract and that Dartmouth was a private corporation. The Court ruled that states cannot interfere with such private contracts. This ruling, handed down the same year as the Panic of 1819, proved timely. Its longterm effect was to protect businesses from regulation, which helped stabilize the economy.

Supporting the National Bank   You have read about the Bank of the United States, chartered in 1791. That first national bank lost its charter 20 years later. Then, in 1816, Congress created the second Bank of the United States. This action renewed a longstanding controversy over the existence of a national bank. The Constitution did not specifically grant the federal government the right to charter a national bank. In 1819, the issue made its way to the Supreme Court. The case involved Maryland's attempt to kill the national bank by levying heavy taxes on it. Maryland's action challenged Congress's authority to create such an institution.

In ***McCulloch*** v. ***Maryland,*** Marshall ruled that Congress did have the authority to charter the bank. The powers of the federal government went beyond those spelled out in the Constitution, Marshall said. He based his argument on Article I, Section 8, which states that Congress has the right "to make all laws which shall be necessary and proper" for carrying out the powers granted it under the Constitution. Those who strictly interpreted the Constitution maintained that such a bank was merely a convenience, not a necessity.

READING CHECK
Why did the United States begin to adopt nationalist policies?

Nationalist Supreme Court Decisions, 1819–1824		
Case	**Issues**	**Outcomes**
McCulloch v. *Maryland* (1819)	Does the government have the power to create a national bank? Do states have the right to tax institutions created by the federal government?	Reinforced (1) the doctrine of implied powers and (2) the principle of the power of the national government over state governments.
Dartmouth College v. *Woodward* (1819)	Was Dartmouth's contract protected by the Constitution? Was New Hampshire interfering with the contract?	Prevented state interference in business contracts. Gave stability to the economy by encouraging growth of corporations.
Gibbons v. *Ogden* (1824)	Who has the power to regulate navigation; the states or the federal government?	Established the federal government's right to regulate all aspects of interstate commerce.

INTERPRETING CHARTS
The Supreme Court under Chief Justice John Marshall (above) made several decisions that greatly increased the authority of the federal government. **Drawing Inferences** *How do these decisions reflect the shift toward nationalism?*

Chapter 8 • Section 4   **291**

INTERPRETING POLITICAL CARTOONS This cartoon reflects American nationalism. **Drawing Conclusions** *What do the people in this cartoon represent?*

"Keep Off! The Monroe Doctrine *must* be respected."

Strict constructionists and loose constructionists would continue to disagree over how to interpret the Necessary and Proper Clause.

Furthermore, Marshall stressed that because the national government had created the bank, no state had the power to tax it. "The power to tax is the power to destroy," he pointed out. No state could destroy by taxes what the federal government under the Constitution had created.

Regulating Commerce Events leading to another important Supreme Court case began when a man named Aaron Ogden purchased a state license giving him exclusive rights to operate a New York-to-New Jersey steamboat line. When a competitor, Thomas Gibbons, started a business on the same route, Ogden sued him. Gibbons said he operated under federal license.

In the 1824 case *Gibbons v. Ogden,* the Court declared that states could not interfere with Congress's constitutional right to regulate business on interstate waterways. The ruling advanced the cause of nationalism by reinforcing the federal government's authority over interstate commerce. By taking away the states' right to offer exclusive navigational licenses, the ruling also increased steamboat competition, thus helping open up the American West to settlement.

Nationalism Abroad

As the Supreme Court took steps to strengthen federal authority, Presidents acted to strengthen the nation's foreign policy. The new approach to foreign affairs took shape under the leadership of President Monroe and his Secretary of State, John Quincy Adams, the son of Abigail and John Adams.

One of Monroe's main goals was to ease tensions with Great Britain, which remained high following the War of 1812. In 1817, the United States and Britain signed the Rush-Bagot Agreement, which called on both sides to reduce the number of warships in the Great Lakes region. The following year the two countries agreed to set the northern border of the United States at 49° North latitude from the northern tip of present-day Minnesota west to the Rocky Mountains.

Monroe was also concerned that other European countries, now recovering from several years of warfare, would resume their efforts to colonize the Western Hemisphere. Starting in the early 1800s, Spain's colonies in South America had rebelled and won independence. Monroe had to decide how the United States would relate to these new nations.

President Monroe firmly spelled out American policy on these urgent matters in his yearly address to Congress on December 2, 1823. The speech, influenced by Secretary of State Adams, established a policy that every President since Monroe has followed to some degree. The **Monroe Doctrine,** as it is called, had four main parts:

1. The United States would not become involved in the internal affairs of European countries, nor would it take sides in wars among them.

2. The United States recognized the existing colonies and states in the Western Hemisphere and would not interfere with them.

3. The United States would not permit any further colonization of the Western Hemisphere.

4. Any attempt by a European power to take control of any nation in the Western Hemisphere would be viewed as a hostile action toward the United States.

These points are summed up in this quotation from Monroe's address:

> **KEY DOCUMENTS** " Our policy in regard to Europe . . . is, not to interfere in the internal concerns of any of its powers; to consider the government de facto [in power] as the legitimate government for us; to cultivate friendly relations with it, and to preserve those relations by a frank, firm, and manly policy, meeting in all instances the just claims of every power, submitting to injuries [aggression] from none. . . . It is impossible that the allied [European] powers should extend their political system to any portion of either continent without endangering our peace and happiness. . . . "
>
> —James Monroe, December 2, 1823

The United States did not have the armed forces necessary to back up the warnings in the Monroe Doctrine. Still, this was a bold declaration of policy for a young nation whose Capitol had been burned to the ground by a foreign army less than a decade earlier.

The Controversial Election of 1824

On July 4, 1826, the fiftieth anniversary of the Declaration of Independence, former Presidents Thomas Jefferson and John Adams both died. It was a startling sign that the founding generation of American leaders was passing into history. Another sign had appeared two years earlier. In the presidential election of 1824, for the first time, no candidate could boast of having been a leader during the Revolution.

This election also marked the end of the Era of Good Feelings. Economic problems, the spread of slavery, and other issues had led to conflict among Jeffersonian Republicans. The ambitions of key political leaders also played a role in the end of this era. As Monroe's second term came to an end, several Republicans decided to compete for the presidency. They included Secretary of State John Quincy Adams of Massachusetts, Speaker of the House Henry Clay of Kentucky, and Secretary of War John C. Calhoun of South Carolina. One major figure who prided himself on being an outsider in Washington, General Andrew Jackson of Tennessee, also threw his hat into the ring.

Adams, an Experienced Diplomat No other candidate could match John Quincy Adams's experience in politics and foreign affairs. Adams had first entered national politics in 1803 as a senator from Massachusetts. He arrived in Congress as a Federalist but soon adopted an independent approach to lawmaking. He lost his seat in 1808 after supporting a bill that the Federalists strongly opposed. After several productive years as a diplomat in Europe, Adams returned to the United States to join Monroe's cabinet. As Secretary of State, Adams negotiated the treaty with Britain that extended the American border to the Rockies, played a vital role in acquiring Florida, and helped devise the Monroe Doctrine.

JOHN QUINCY ADAMS.

The Citizens of Cincinnati, friendly to the elevation of this Gentleman to the Presidency of the United States, are requested to meet at the Presbyterian Church, on Walnut street, at 4 o'clock this afternoon, to adopt such measures as shall be deemed most advisable for the attainment of that object.

CINCINNATI, APRIL 24, 1824. THE PEOPLE.

This first-ever photograph of an American President (top) shows John Quincy Adams in the 1840s. The advertisement above invites Adams supporters to a campaign strategy meeting.

ACTIVITY
Connecting with History and Conflict

Engage students in a discussion of the Monroe Doctrine. Ask them how it reflects its time, and whether successive Presidents have upheld or violated the doctrine, and if so, why. Suggest that students consider the relevance of such a document in modern times. **(Verbal/Linguistic)**

BACKGROUND
Connections to Today

As the students read about the contested election of 1824, ask them to think about the chaotic aftermath of the 2000 presidential election. Then have the class discuss the similarities and differences they notice between the 1824 and 2000 presidential elections.

☑ TEST PREPARATION

Have students read the passage by James Monroe on this page and then answer the question below.

According to the Monroe Doctrine, how would the United States meet an attempt by another country to control part of the land on the American continent?

A With an understanding of that country's need for expansion.

B In a spirit of friendship and cooperation.

C By attacking that country and attempting to overthrow its political system.

D With firm, strong opposition.

Connecting with Government

Have students conduct a debate of the presidential candidates in the election of 1824. Ask volunteers to role-play the candidates: John Quincy Adams, Henry Clay, John C. Calhoun, and Andrew Jackson. Encourage students to research their candidate so that they can speak from his viewpoint about the issues of the day. Organize small groups to support each candidate by supplying him with helpful notes. (Verbal/Linguistic)

BACKGROUND

Biography

John Quincy Adams refused to campaign for the presidency. Prior to the election of 1824, Adams wrote, "I never by the most distant hint to anyone ever expressed a wish for any public office, and I should not now begin to ask, for that [the presidency] which of all the others ought to be most freely and spontaneously bestowed." Adams formed his opinions of the ideal American government from his father and the other Founding Fathers, who believed that people should rise to higher office through their achievements, not through their politicking. This attitude toward the presidency proved to be out of step with the times.

BIOGRAPHY

John C. Calhoun 1782–1850

Born to a prominent South Carolina family, John Caldwell Calhoun trained as a lawyer. He married an heiress whose fortune allowed him to become a gentleman farmer and statesman.

Calhoun became a towering figure in Washington. He served in the House of Representatives, as President Monroe's Secretary of War, as Vice President under John Adams and Andrew Jackson, as Secretary of State for Presidents John Tyler and James K. Polk, and in the Senate. John Quincy Adams hailed Calhoun's nationalism, stating that he "is above all sectional and factious [hostile] prejudices. . ."

As South Carolina began to back away from nationalism, so did Calhoun. He saw the industrial North as a threat to the agricultural South and to slavery. Yet even Calhoun's fierce support for slavery reflected his fear that any attempt to address the slavery issue would tear the Union in two.

Calhoun was devoted to his principles. He wrote: "My politics, I think I may say with perfect truth, has . . . been founded on certain fixed principles; and to carry them into effect has been my highest ambition."

Clay, a Passionate Orator Henry Clay was the most colorful politician of his generation. Known as "Harry of the West," Clay loved to drink and gamble. Energetic and charming, he also had a magnificent gift for speechmaking. In Congress he spoke in support of what he called the **American System,** a combination of government-backed economic development and protective tariffs aimed at encouraging business growth. Clay owned slaves but shared Jefferson's discomfort with slavery. He tried and failed to bring slavery in Kentucky to a gradual end, and in his will, Clay freed his own slaves. He had once claimed that he would "rather be right than be President." In 1824, however, he made no secret of his desire to win the presidency.

Calhoun, a Champion of the South John C. Calhoun, an ambitious politician, had served in the House of Representatives and as Monroe's Secretary of War. Early on, Calhoun joined forces with Clay in Congress, speaking out in support of nationalism and sponsoring a variety of economic measures to help unify the nation. He headed committees that created the second Bank of the United States, a national road system, a modernized navy, and protective tariffs. During the 1820s, Calhoun, a slaveholder, turned his attention more toward defending southern sectional interests. Eventually, Calhoun withdrew from the crowded 1824 race. Instead he ran for Vice President, where he stood a better chance of success.

Jackson, Man of the People The 1824 election had a wild card: Andrew Jackson, nicknamed "Old Hickory" for his toughness. Jackson, who had served in Congress in the 1790s, was a slaveholder who now owned a plantation near Nashville, Tennessee. A brilliant general, Jackson had gained widespread popularity for his victories in the War of 1812, his attacks on the Seminole Indians in Florida, and his colorful personality. His opponents, on the other hand, saw him as a poorly educated, ill-tempered roughneck. Yet while other candidates hurled insults and accusations at each other, Jackson avoided such tactics, relying on his popularity as a national hero to attract votes.

The "Corrupt Bargain" In the 1824 election, Jackson won the most votes in the electoral college, but he did not win a majority. Adams came in second. In February 1825, as the Constitution required, the House of Representatives voted to decide the election. Clay used his influence as speaker of the House to swing enough votes to Adams to give him the victory. Just days later, Adams made Clay his Secretary of State. Jackson's supporters charged that Adams and Clay had made a "corrupt bargain" to deny Jackson the win.

Two New Parties Face Off

In his first annual message to Congress, Adams made it clear that he wanted to use federal power to strengthen the nation's economy:

> ❝ The spirit of improvement is abroad upon the earth. . . . While dwelling with pleasing satisfaction upon the superior excellence of our political institutions, let us not be unmindful that liberty is power; and that the tenure [holding] of power by man is . . . to improve the condition of himself and his fellow-men. ❞
>
> —John Quincy Adams, 1825

RESOURCE DIRECTORY

Teaching Resources

Units 3/4 booklet
• Section 4 Quiz, p. 17

Guide to the Essentials
• Section 4 Summary, p. 44

Learning with Documents booklet (Visual Learning Activity) *The Jackson Ticket,* p. 47

Exploring Primary Sources in U.S. History CD-ROM *The Sovereignty of the People in America, Alexis de Toqueville*

Other Print Resources

Nystrom *Atlas of Our Country* *The Second Wave of Immigration,* pp. 24–25

Historical Outline Map Book *Election of 1828,* p. 36

To promote the American System, Adams and Clay pushed for legislation authorizing the federal building of roads, canals, bridges, lighthouses, universities, and many other public improvements. They also backed protective tariffs. Jackson's supporters in Congress, however, blocked these plans at every turn. Meanwhile, Jackson himself prepared for the coming election—and for revenge.

The split among Jeffersonian Republicans became clear during the election of 1828. Supporters of Adams and Clay began calling themselves the Adams Party or National Republicans. (They would later help form the Whig Party.) The National Republicans believed that they were true to the Jeffersonian spirit of improvement. Jackson's followers called themselves Jacksonians or Democratic Republicans. (Historians refer to them as Jacksonian Democrats.) They believed that they were true to Jefferson's ideal of limited government. In other words, unlike most previous elections, the 1828 campaign offered voters a choice between presidential candidates who held sharply differing views.

The 1828 election was notable for another reason: about three times as many men voted that year than in 1824. As you will read in the next section, more and more states were allowing men who did not own property to vote. Many of these new voters threw their support to the man of the people, Andrew Jackson. With this sizable following, Jackson trounced Adams, winning 178 electoral votes to Adams's 83.

During Alexis de Tocqueville's travels around the country in 1831, he noted that "liberty is generally born in stormy weather, growing with difficulty amid civil discords, and only when it is already old does one see the blessings it has brought." The rise of opposition parties in the United States would indeed produce "discords." However, by stirring healthy debates on key issues and strengthening the democratic process, the party system would bring "blessings" as well.

National Republicans vs. Jacksonian Democrats, 1820s

National Republicans	Jacksonian Democrats
Federal government should take a leadership role.	Federal government should remain as inactive as possible.
Federal government should support internal improvements, such as roads and bridges.	The individual states should be responsible for internal improvements.
In favor of a national bank	Against a national bank
Tended to be middle-class or well-established Protestants	Tended to be slaveholders, small farmers, non-Protestants, and working class

INTERPRETING CHARTS
National Republicans and Jacksonian Democrats disagreed on the federal government's role in the economy. **Analyzing Visual Information** How did each party want to make internal improvements?

Section 4 Assessment

READING COMPREHENSION

1. Choose two of these cases and explain how the Supreme Court's ruling in each case supported nationalism: *Dartmouth College v. Woodward; McCulloch v. Maryland; Gibbons v. Ogden.*

2. Why did President Monroe believe it was necessary to create the **Monroe Doctrine?**

3. What two new political parties emerged in the 1820s, and how did their views differ?

CRITICAL THINKING AND WRITING

4. **Synthesizing Information** Describe the rise of nationalism in the early 1800s, and then explain how that sense of national unity was replaced by regional disagreements.

5. **Writing to Persuade** Write a campaign advertisement attempting to persuade voters to support either Adams or Jackson in the 1828 presidential election.

 Take It to the NET

Activity: Participating in Politics Research one of the candidates in the 1824 election. Then create campaign literature, such as a poster or a pamphlet, for your candidate. Use the links provided in the *America: Pathways to the Present* area of the following Web site for help in completing this activity.
www.phschool.com

Reading Comprehension

1. Sample answers: *Dartmouth College v. Woodward*—prevented state interference in business contracts, provided national economic stability by encouraging growth of corporations; *McCulloch v. Maryland*—supported the principle that the national government is free to exercise powers implied by the Constitution with which states cannot interfere; *Gibbons v. Ogden*—established the federal government's right to regulate interstate commerce.

2. To create a policy to ease tensions with Great Britain and formally address the possibility that other European countries might resume their efforts to colonize the Western Hemisphere.

3. National Republicans who supported the Jeffersonian spirit of improvement, and the Jacksonian Democrats, who supported Jefferson's ideal of limited government.

Critical Thinking and Writing

4. Answers will vary, but students should describe nationalistic Supreme Court decisions, the Monroe Doctrine, slavery, and the role of political parties.

5. Advertisements should strongly persuade their audience and be supported with facts from the section.

 **Take It to the NET**

Campaign literature should strongly promote either John Quincy Adams or Andrew Jackson through a factual rendering of their political backgrounds and positions, as well as with persuasive writing and graphics.

CAPTION ANSWERS

Interpreting Charts National Republicans: the federal government should sponsor new roads and bridges; Jacksonian Democrats: such internal improvements are the responsibility of individual states.

 # Determining Relevance

DETERMINING RELEVANCE

Focus Determine the relevance of three tables of political information to specific questions about the Market Revolution.

Instruct Ask students to identify the information presented in each table. For example, ask students to identify the title and headings in Table A. Then have them summarize the information in that table. Repeat this process for Tables B and C. Finally, ask students how these three tables relate to one another and to the Market Revolution.

Extend See the Skills for Life activity in the Resource Directory below.

ANSWERS

PRACTICE THE SKILL

1. **Table A** compares candidates, parties, the popular and electoral votes for the presidential elections of 1824 and 1828. **Table B** compares electoral votes cast in slave states and free states in 1828. **Table C** summarizes the viewpoints of candidates Adams and Jackson about key election issues.

2. **(a)** Tables B and C. **(b)** Table C. **(c)** Table B.

3. **(a)** By using Table C to discover which candidate supported those views (Adams), then using Table B to see which candidate was supported by free states and slave states. **(b)** You could use Table A to show that, in the election of 1828, Jackson had more than twice as many electoral votes as Adams, but the difference in the popular vote was only about 140,000 votes out of approximately one million cast.

Determining relevance means deciding if and how things are related to one another. When you are reading about historical events and trends, you often have to decide whether there is a logical connection between different pieces of information. For example, you have seen that the Market Revolution expanded the American economy and that the debate over federal efforts to promote economic growth helped shape a new political party system in the 1820s. Therefore, you already know that the Market Revolution was relevant to the politics of this decade. The tables on this page present more information about the politics of the 1820s.

LEARN THE SKILL

Use the following steps to determine the relevance of information presented in tables:

1. **Identify the main purpose of each table.** Study each table, including titles and headings.

2. **Determine how the information in the tables might be useful for understanding the time period.** Examine the tables to discover what kinds of issues are addressed by the information in each table. Frame some questions that each table could help you answer.

3. **Use your understanding of the relevance of the information in the tables to support an observation.** Answer the questions that you framed in Step 2. Use your answers to help you understand larger issues that were important in this time period.

PRACTICE THE SKILL
Answer the following questions:

1. What is the purpose of each table?

2. **(a)** If you wanted to know how people who favored slavery voted in 1828, which tables would be relevant? **(b)** If you wanted to know which candidates in 1824 favored tariffs, which table would be most relevant? **(c)** If you wanted to know how each section of the country voted in 1828, which table would be relevant?

3. **(a)** How would you use the tables to support the statement that, generally speaking, tariffs and internal improvements had more favor among northerners than among southerners? **(b)** How would you use the tables to show that, in an election, the popular vote is often closer than the electoral vote?

APPLY THE SKILL
See the Chapter Review and Assessment for another opportunity to apply this skill.

A. Presidential Elections, 1824 and 1828

Year	Candidate	Political Party	Votes Cast Popular	Votes Cast Electoral	House of Representatives
1824	John Quincy Adams	No distinct party designations	108,740	84	13
	Andrew Jackson		153,544	99	7
	Henry Clay		47,136	37	0
	W. H. Crawford		46,618	41	4
1828	Andrew Jackson	Democratic	647,826	178	No vote needed
	John Quincy Adams	National Republican	508,064	83	

SOURCES: *World Almanac & Book of Facts, 1993; Historical Statistics of the United States, Colonial Times to 1970*

B. State Electoral Votes Cast for President, 1828

	Slave States South	Slave States West	Free States North	Free States West	Total
Number of states	9	3	9	3	24
Number of electoral votes	86	28	123	24	261
Number of Democratic electoral votes	77	28	49	24	178
Number of National Republican electoral votes	9	0	74	0	83

SOURCE: *Historical Statistics of the United States, Colonial Times to 1970*

C. Candidate Profiles

Issue	Adams	Jackson
Slavery	Against	For
National bank	For	Against
Protective tariffs	For	Generally against
Federally funded internal improvements	For	Against
Voting rights for propertyless workers	Against	For

SOURCE: *Historical Statistics of the United States, Colonial Times to 1970*

READING FOCUS

- How did American government and democracy change with Jackson as President?
- How did Jackson respond to the tariff and Indian crises?
- What political strategies prompted the bank war?
- How effective were Jackson's presidential successors?

MAIN IDEA

Jackson's presidency strengthened the political power of voters and of the West, brought about a more limited government, and revived the two-party system.

KEY TERMS

patronage
spoils system
Tariff of 1828
nullify
states' rights
secede
Indian Removal Act
Trail of Tears
Black Hawk War
Second Seminole War

TAKING NOTES

Copy the web diagram below. As you read, fill in the blank circles with facts relating to Jackson's presidency. Add circles as necessary.

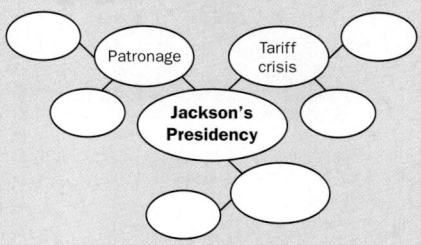

Patronage — *Tariff crisis* — **Jackson's Presidency**

SECTION OBJECTIVES

1. Understand how American government and democracy changed with Jackson as President.
2. Learn how Jackson responded to the tariff and Indian crises.
3. See what political strategies prompted the bank war.
4. Find out about the effectiveness of Jackson's presidential successors.

BELLRINGER

Warm Up Activity Ask students to recall a recent President whose personality played a major role in his popularity. Have them explain what it was that the public found so appealing.

Activating Prior Knowledge Ask students to discuss ways in which reformers have influenced American history. Have them consider times in which reformers were on the outside of the system, and times when the reformers were in power and able to make the changes they sought.

READING STRATEGY

As students read the section, have them make a list of Jackson's policies and the effects that they caused.

BACKGROUND
Connections to Today

Andrew Jackson's Tennessee plantation was named "The Hermitage," and it stands today much as it did when Jackson lived there. Visitors to The Hermitage can enjoy the garden (which is planted in the way it was during Jackson's time) and tour the impressive house. Behind Jackson's huge home, visitors can see the remains of tiny, 20-feet by 20-feet cabins. Each was home to a whole family of people: slaves owned by the seventh President.

Setting the Scene

As Andrew Jackson prepared to take office in March 1829, Americans wondered how his presidency would affect the rapidly changing United States. Politicians and government officials seemed especially anxious. Jackson had campaigned as a reformer, promising to root out corruption in government. Would he sweep great numbers of civil servants from their jobs? Jackson's image as a tough, capable general had gained him many followers. Yet critics saw him as a stubborn, ill-tempered ruffian. Which character would emerge when he came to Washington?

Daniel Webster, a National Republican senator, feared Jackson would worsen the split in the Republican Party. He expressed his concern in a letter he wrote from Washington, D.C., to his brother:

> 66 Gen. J. will be here abt. [about] 15. Feb. Nobody knows what he will do, when he does come. . . . My opinion is that when he comes, he will bring a breeze with him. Which way it will blow, I cannot tell. He will either go with the party, . . . or else, he will . . . be President upon his own strength. . . . My fear is stronger than my hope. 99
> —Daniel Webster, January 17, 1829

Jackson as President

Jackson's inauguration on March 4 did little to ease the fears of Webster and others. The "man of the people" had barely finished receiving the oath of office when the massive crowd of Jackson supporters rushed forward to greet the new President. Jackson, an expert on battle tactics, beat a hasty retreat into the White House. The mob of well-wishers followed him into the building, where they fought over refreshments, smashed china and crystal, and climbed onto fancy furniture to get a look at their hero. Officials finally lured the unruly crowd outside by moving the punch bowls onto the White House lawn.

A navy ship bore this figurehead of Andrew Jackson in 1834.

Chapter 8 • Section 5 297

RESOURCE DIRECTORY

Teaching Resources
Learning Styles Lesson Plans booklet, p. 19
Guided Reading and Review booklet, p. 36

Technology
Section Reading Support Transparencies
Guided Reading Audiotapes (English/Spanish), Ch. 8
Student Edition on Audio CD, Ch. 8
Prentice Hall Presentation Pro CD-ROM, Ch. 8
Companion Web site, www.phschool.com

Focus Explain that Jackson's terms in office were marked by a commitment to minimize the role of the federal government. Ask what events characterized Jackson's presidency.

Instruct Explain that Jackson's actions as President were consistent with the political views he expressed before his election. Ask how these views gave the common man hope and encouraged the spirit of capitalism.

Assess/Reteach Ask students to state some ways in which Jackson's presidency strengthened the power of voters and brought about a more limited government. Did Jackson achieve what he set out to accomplish?

READING CHECK
Use of the patronage system; support for limited government and individual liberty.

This fresco shows Chief Justice John Marshall administering the presidential oath of office to Andrew Jackson on the east front steps of the Capitol, March 4, 1829. The new President would soon defy a landmark ruling by the Marshall Court on Indian rights.

As the inauguration demonstrated, Andrew Jackson came to the presidency on a tidal wave of popular support. His rise to high office thus signaled the start of a new era in American democracy. It also signaled the growing power of the West. Jackson was the first President from west of the Appalachians, where frontier life shaped people's characters. As the country would soon learn, Jackson was a man of strong opinions, accustomed to making tough decisions and fiercely defending them.

Jacksonian Democracy Jackson's support came from thousands of first-time voters. In the previous decade, older states had repealed laws requiring voters to be property holders, and new states such as Indiana and Maine allowed all white adult men to vote. No longer would less-wealthy citizens routinely be denied access to the ballot box. Some states also had begun to let voters, rather than state legislatures, choose presidential electors. As a result of these changes, the votes cast for President tripled from 1824 to 1828, from roughly 356,000 to more than 1.1 million.

The Spoils System For many years, newly elected officials had given government jobs to friends and supporters, a practice known as **patronage.** Unlike earlier Presidents, however, Jackson made patronage an official policy of his administration. He immediately began dismissing presidential appointees and other officeholders and replacing them with Jacksonian Democrats. Although Jackson did not originate the practice of patronage, his support for it infuriated his opponents. Yet, in fact, in his eight-year tenure, he dismissed less than one fifth of all presidential appointees and other federal officeholders.

Critics later labeled Jackson's form of patronage the **spoils system.** Spoils refers to loot taken from a conquered enemy. In politics, the "loot" was jobs for party supporters. Jackson defended his actions on the grounds that any intelligent person could be a competent public official. He also argued that "rotation in office" would prevent a small group of wealthy, well-connected people from controlling the government. His support for the spoils system contributed to Jackson's image as the champion of the common man.

Limited Government Jackson shared the beliefs of Americans who feared the power of the federal government. He attacked politicians whom he considered corrupt and laws that he thought would limit people's liberty. He used his veto power to restrict federal activity as much as possible, rejecting more acts of Congress than the six previous Presidents combined.

For example, Congress voted to provide money to build a road from the town of Maysville, Kentucky, along the Ohio River, southward to the growing city of Lexington, in Kentucky's horse-breeding region. In 1830, when the bill came to Jackson's desk, he vetoed it. Jackson did not object to the road. He just thought that the state of Kentucky, not the national government, should build it.

Yet, no President from Washington to Lincoln did more to increase the power of the presidency than Jackson. His vetoes helped earn him the nickname "King Andrew I."

READING CHECK
What were the main elements of Jacksonian democracy?

The Tariff Crisis

Before Jackson's first term had begun, Congress had passed the **Tariff of 1828,** a heavy tax on imports designed to boost American manufacturing. The tariff greatly benefited the industrial North but forced Southerners to pay higher

RESOURCE DIRECTORY

Teaching Resources
Learning with Documents booklet (Primary Source Activity) *President Jackson's Inauguration*, p. 13

Technology
Color Transparencies *Political Cartoons*, B4

prices for manufactured goods. They called the import tax the "Tariff of Abominations." (An *abomination* is something especially horrible or monstrous.)

The tariff prompted South Carolina to declare that states had the right to judge when the federal government had exceeded its authority. The state maintained that in such cases, states could **nullify,** or reject, federal laws they judged to be unconstitutional.

South Carolina's nullification threat was based on a strict interpretation of states' rights. **States' rights** are the powers that the Constitution neither gives to the federal government nor denies to the states. The concept of states' rights is based on the constitutional principle of divided sovereignty between the federal government and the state government. In other words, each has its own powers that the other cannot take away.

The strict interpretation of states' rights that South Carolina endorsed is what some people call *state sovereignty.* This is the theory that because states created the federal government, they have the right to nullify its acts and even to **secede,** or withdraw, from the Union if they wish to do so.

The tariff issue continued to smolder, finally igniting a famous debate on the floor of the Senate. In January 1830, senators Robert Hayne of South Carolina and Daniel Webster of Massachusetts engaged in a debate that quickly leaped to the broader question of the fate of the Union. The debate peaked on January 26, when Webster, a great orator, delivered a thrilling defense of the Union. "While the Union lasts we have high, exciting, gratifying prospects spread out before us, for us and our children," Webster declared. He attacked Hayne's claim that liberty (meaning, in Hayne's view, states' rights) was more important than the Union.

NOTABLE PRESIDENTS
Andrew Jackson

*7th President
1829–1837*

"Our Federal Union: It must be preserved!"
        **—Andrew Jackson giving a toast at a banquet
        celebrating Thomas Jefferson's birthday, 1830**

Andrew Jackson was born on the frontier, somewhere in the western Carolinas. He had little formal schooling but learned how to get by in the wilderness.

In 1781, Jackson, at age 14, was taken prisoner by British invaders. One of them slashed him across the face with a sword when he refused to shine an officer's boots. Such acts of courage made Jackson a larger-than-life figure: a tough, stubborn man who symbolized the frontier spirit.

After the Revolution, Jackson became a prosecutor in what is now Tennessee. He served briefly in the House and in the Senate before becoming a judge on Tennessee's highest court in 1798. Despite his political success, he never lost his sense of frontier justice. On various occasions Jackson dueled to defend his honor—using a walking stick, a horsewhip, or a pistol.

A major general in the state militia, Jackson assumed a commander's role in the War of 1812. His leadership in the war made him an American hero. In 1818, his invasion of Florida won that territory from Spain.

After losing the 1824 presidential election to what appeared to be a "corrupt bargain," Jackson won easily in 1828, taking his belief in democracy and states' rights with him to the White House.

Despite being ill through much of his presidency, Andrew Jackson proved to be a vigorous leader. He so dominated the national scene that historians often refer to these years as the "Age of Jackson."

Connecting to Today
Do you think that Jackson would have approved of the extent to which democracy is exercised in American politics today? Explain your answer.

Take It to the NET Biography More information about this President is provided at the following Web site: **www.phschool.com**

✓ TEST PREPARATION
Have students reread the section "The Spoils System" and then complete the sentence below.

During Jackson's administration, patronage—

A was abolished.

Ⓑ was openly used.

C became illegal.

D was used to keep Jackson supporters from key positions.

ACTIVITY
Connecting with Citizenship

Share with students the following names given Andrew Jackson, and have them explain how each one reflects Jackson as an individual or Jackson as a public figure, or both: General Andrew Jackson, Hero of the Battle of New Orleans, Hero of the Common Man, King Andrew, Old Hickory, Self-Made Man, and President Andrew Jackson. **(Verbal/Linguistic)**

BACKGROUND
A Diverse Nation

Andrew Jackson differed in several important ways from the Presidents who had preceded him. Unlike the others, Jackson came from a poor background. He was not from New England or Virginia, but from the Tennessee frontier. His experiences on the frontier played a critical role in shaping Jackson's personality, and it was his aggressive nature that characterized his presidency. Jackson's success changed public perception of the presidency, making it possible for any American to dream of becoming President.

From the Archives of
American Heritage®

About the Presidents

Andrew Jackson (1829–1835) embodied the American dream. Born poor, his successes were won by strength, will, effort, and conviction. After his victory in the War of 1812, Jackson became America's greatest hero since George Washington. But Washington had been a gentleman-hero. Jackson was one of the "common people"—a backwoodsman. Source: Saul Braun, "Andrew Jackson," *The American Heritage® Pictorial History of the United States,* vol. 1, 1968.

In 1832, after passage of yet another tariff, South Carolina declared the tariffs null and void. The state threatened to secede from the Union if the federal government did not respect its nullification.

South Carolina's defiance of federal law enraged the President. Jackson believed that the state was disregarding the will of the people. At his urging, in 1833, Congress passed the Force Bill, which required South Carolina to collect the tariff. Jackson threatened to send 50,000 federal troops to enforce the law.

The crisis eased when Senator Henry Clay engineered a compromise. Congress reduced some of the import duties, and South Carolina canceled its nullification act. Refusing to give in completely, however, the state nullified the Force Bill at the same time.

The Indian Crisis

By the 1820s, most Indians east of the Mississippi River had given up their territory and moved west. The remaining Native Americans lived mainly in the Old Northwest and in the South. In the 1820s, cotton farmers in the South and sought to expand into Native American lands. In 1829, when gold was found in western Georgia, whites flooded onto Indian lands.

Indian Relocation The Cherokee, Creek, Choctaw, Chickasaw, and Seminole peoples lived on about 100 million acres of fertile land in western parts of the Carolinas and in Georgia, Florida, Alabama, Mississippi, and Tennessee. These Native Americans were known as the "Five Civilized Tribes."

MAP SKILLS The map at right shows the massive relocation of eastern Native Americans, including the Trail of Tears, depicted in the painting above.
Location (a) Where were most of the Native Americans relocated? (b) Why do you think Americans were willing to give up new lands to the Indians?

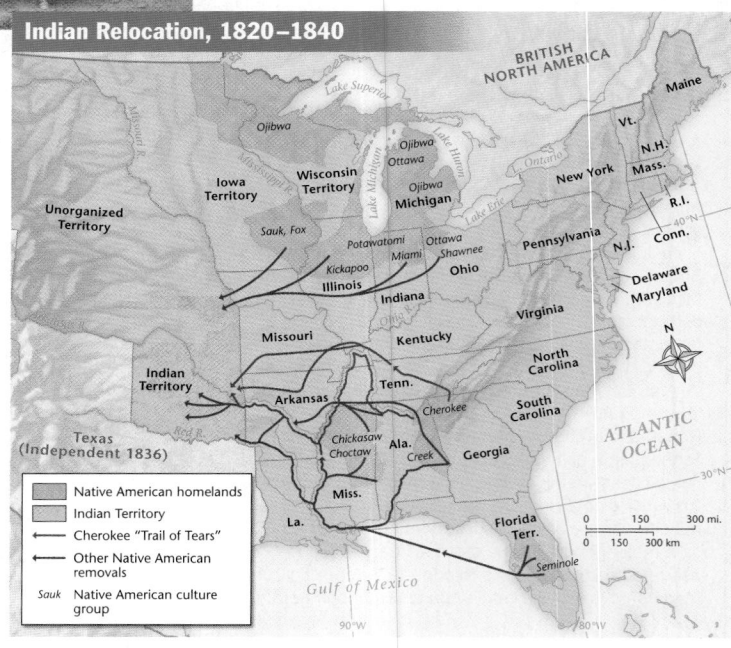

Indian Relocation, 1820–1840

CAPTION ANSWERS

Map Skills (a) Into Indian Territory (or what would become the state of Oklahoma). (b) Sample answer: Many Americans probably thought that the lands west of the Mississippi were barren and of little use.

In 1830, at Jackson's urging, Congress passed the **Indian Removal Act,** which authorized the President to give Native Americans land in parts of the Louisiana Purchase in exchange for land taken from them in the East. The northern groups generally resettled peacefully. But when the Five Tribes refused to move, Jackson forcibly relocated about 100,000 of their members. For their millions of acres of largely cultivated land, the tribes received wild prairie land in Indian Territory (present-day Oklahoma).

Cherokee Resistance   The situation of the Cherokees was unique. More than any other Native American people, they had adopted white culture. Many Cherokees had taken up white farming methods, home styles, clothing styles, and religions. Some had married whites. In 1827, the Cherokees organized a national government modeled upon that of the United States.

Nevertheless, when gold was found on Cherokee land, the state of Georgia seized about 9 million acres of Indian land within its borders. When appeals to Georgia and to the U.S. Senate failed, the Cherokees issued a public statement, trying in vain to rally the support of the American people:

> 66 We wish to remain on the land of our fathers. We have a perfect and original right to remain without interruption. . . . It cannot be that [America], remarkable for its intelligence and religious sensibilities, and preeminent [unmatched] for its devotion to the rights of man, will lay aside this appeal. 99
> —Cherokee public appeal, July 17, 1830

Finally, in 1832, the Cherokees brought their case to the Supreme Court through a missionary from Vermont, Samuel Austin Worcester. In *Worcester* v. *Georgia*, Marshall ruled that Georgia had no authority over Cherokee territory. Georgia defied the Court, with Jackson's backing. "John Marshall has made his decision. Now let him enforce it!" the President is said to have declared. Of course, the Court had no power to enforce its decisions.

Jackson stated his reasons for supporting Indian relocation:

> 66 All preceding experiments for the improvement of the Indians have failed. It seems now to be an established fact that they can not live in contact with a civilized community and prosper. . . . No one can doubt the moral duty of the Government . . . to protect and if possible to preserve and perpetuate the scattered remnants of this race. . . . 99
> —President Jackson, annual address to Congress, December 7, 1835

In 1838, the United States Army rounded up more than 15,000 Cherokees. Then, in a nightmare journey that the Cherokees called the **Trail of Tears,** men, women, and children, most on foot, began a 116-day forced march westward for about 1,000 miles to Oklahoma Territory. Roughly 1 out of every 4 Cherokees died of cold or disease, as troops refused to let them pause to rest.

Indian Uprisings   In Illinois Territory, Fox and Sauk peoples were driven off their lands in 1831. The next spring a warrior named Black Hawk led a group

---

Focus on CULTURE

Sequoyah and Cherokee Writing

Writing is power. Sequoyah, a Cherokee silversmith and painter, recognized that a written language gave white people a great advantage. In 1809, he began to develop a system of writing for the Cherokee people. It was a *syllabary,* in which every symbol represents a syllable. Sequoyah identified some 86 syllables in the Cherokee language and set out to create symbols for them.

As a volunteer in the United States Army in its war against the Creek Indians (1813–1814), Sequoyah envied white soldiers who could write letters home, read orders, or keep a diary. They could easily gather, store, and relay information. Sequoyah returned from battle determined to perfect his syllabary.

In 1821, Sequoyah completed his system, which included adaptations of English, Greek, and Hebrew letters. His system was so simple that nearly the entire Cherokee nation became literate within a short time. During the next few years, Cherokees translated the Bible, hymns, educational materials, religious tracts, and legal documents. In 1828, the *Cherokee Phoenix,* a weekly newspaper, began publication.

ACTIVITY

Connecting with History and Conflict

Have students research some aspect of Cherokee history. Students may choose to learn more about Chief John Ross, who traveled to Washington to lobby on behalf of his people. They might look into the structure of the Cherokee government, which in some ways resembles our own, or research the Cherokee printing press and newspaper. Ask students to present an oral report on their findings. **(Verbal/ Linguistic)**

BACKGROUND

Connections to Today

There are currently three Cherokee tribes that are recognized by the federal government. The Cherokee Nation and the United Keetoowah Band are both headquartered in Oklahoma, and the Eastern Bank of Cherokees is in North Carolina. There are approximately 10,000 full-blooded Cherokee speakers living in Cherokee communities. These people preserve the Cherokee culture by attending Cherokee churches, community meetings, and *gadugi,* gatherings aimed at helping a neighbor in need.

✔ TEST PREPARATION

Have students review the excerpt from the Cherokee public appeal on this page and then complete the sentence below.

According to the quote, the Cherokees are trying to persuade the American people that—

A they should be given land in the West.

B they should be left alone on their ancestral lands.

C they are people of good will who wish peace.

D they will fight for their land with all their might.

Connecting with Economics

Tell students that the Federal Reserve operates with tremendous independence. The members hold their policy meetings in secret and rarely consult with Congress or the President. Engage students in a discussion about the Federal Reserve. Should the nation's central bank be autonomous? What are the advantages of this system? What are its disadvantages? **(Verbal/Linguistic)**

From the Archives of
AmericanHeritage®

About the Presidents

Martin Van Buren (1837–1841) faced the Panic of 1837 just days after his inauguration. "The less government interferes with private pursuits the better for the general prosperity," he said. Van Buren pressed Congress for an independent treasury to deal with the nation's finances. But the permanent independent treasury he hoped for was not established until 1846. Source: Wilson Sullivan, "Martin Van Buren," *The American Heritage® Pictorial History of the Presidents,* vol. 1, 1968.

When William Henry Harrison (1841) ran for President, a Baltimore, Maryland, newspaper insulted his lack of intellectual depth. They said he'd be content with a log cabin and a barrel of hard cider. The Whigs turned the insult to their advantage by giving out log cabin songbooks and cider. Although the Whigs ignored real issues, their "log cabin campaign" won Harrison the presidency. Source: David Jacobs, "William Henry Harrison," *The American Heritage® Pictorial History of the Presidents,* vol. 1, 1968.

CAPTION ANSWERS

Fast Forward to Today Because, as Jefferson recognized, such an institution is not mentioned in the Constitution. Also, many people feel that the economy should be left to regulate itself, according to market forces alone.

 Sounds of an Era

Listen to excerpts on Indian history and on the bank war as well as other sounds from the era of American expansion.

 **Fast** **Forward**
to Today

National Banks

1791 At the urging of Treasury Secretary Alexander Hamilton, Congress creates the Bank of the United States. Hamilton intends that the bank will stabilize the expanding economy and its bank notes will function as currency. Critics, including Thomas Jefferson, oppose a national bank because the Constitution does not explicitly provide for one. In 1811, Congress votes not to renew the bank's 20-year charter.

1816 After the turmoil of the War of 1812, Congress charters a second Bank of the United States. Faced with huge demands for credit in the expanding country, the bank's directors soon relax limits on granting credit. This action helps trigger a major economic crisis in 1819. President Andrew Jackson attacks the bank as a "monster." He vetoes a bill to renew its charter in 1832. The charter expires in 1836.

Today The Federal Reserve System, created in 1913, is one of the nation's most powerful institutions. "The Fed" makes loans to member banks and requires them to keep a percentage of cash in reserve. It sets key interest rates in order to control the money supply and stabilize the economy. The Fed is no less controversial than its predecessors. Critics charge that the system has too much regulatory power. They deplore the role of the Fed chairman, whose economic predictions can send the stock market soaring or plummeting.

? Why has a national bank been controversial since the nation's founding?

of about 1,000 Indians back to their fertile valley in a peaceful effort to reclaim their land. The clashes that followed became known as the **Black Hawk War.** Weakened by hunger and illness, Black Hawk's band retreated into Wisconsin Territory, where most of the Indians were chased down and killed.

In Florida, white settlers wanted the Seminoles to abandon their land, but most refused. In 1835, a group of Seminoles under a chief named Osceola began the **Second Seminole War.** (Recall that in the First Seminole War, General Andrew Jackson had invaded Florida to end Seminole raids.) The bloody war lasted nearly seven years, ending only after Osceola's capture. A few hundred Seminoles managed to remain in Florida, most of them hidden in the thickly forested swamps of the Everglades.

The Bank War

The defining moment of Jackson's presidency came in 1832. Like many Americans, Jackson believed that the Bank of the United States was a "monster" institution controlled by a small group of wealthy Easterners. He held it responsible for the Panic of 1819 and the hard times that had followed.

Under its charter, the Bank of the United States could operate only until 1836 unless Congress issued it a new charter. The president of the bank charter, Nicholas Biddle, supported by Senators Henry Clay and Daniel Webster, decided to recharter the bank four years early, in 1832. If Jackson vetoed the bank charter, the National Republicans planned to use that veto against him in the 1832 election.

Jackson, however, did not bend to the political pressure. He vetoed the bill to recharter the bank, saying, "The bank is trying to kill me, but I will kill it." His successful veto doomed the bank. Jackson justified his action as a protection of the rights of ordinary citizens. He attacked the bank as a tool of greedy, powerful people:

❝ When the laws undertake . . . to make the rich richer and the potent more powerful, the humble members of society—the farmers, mechanics, and laborers— who have neither the time nor the means of securing like favors to themselves, have a right to complain of the injustice of their Government. ❞
—President Jackson, veto message, 1832

The bank's supporters underestimated Jackson. He won reelection in 1832 by a huge margin, defeating Clay, the National Republican candidate. The National Republican Party never recovered from this stunning defeat at the hands of Jackson's Democratic Party. Two years later, the National Republicans would join several other anti-Jackson groups to form the Whig Party. The American Whigs saw themselves as defenders of liberty against a powerful executive.

Jackson's Successors

In poor health, Jackson chose not to run for a third term in 1836. His Vice President, Martin Van Buren, ran and

RESOURCE DIRECTORY

Teaching Resources
Units 3/4 booklet
- Section 5 Quiz, p. 18
- Chapter 8 Test, pp. 19, 22

Guide to the Essentials
- Section 5 Summary, p. 45
- Chapter 8 Test, p. 46

Other Print Resources
Chapter Tests with ExamView® Test Bank CD-ROM, Ch. 8

Technology
Sounds of an Era Audio CD *Andrew Jackson on the Bank of the United States* (time: one minute)
ExamView® Test Bank CD-ROM, Ch. 8
Social Studies Skills Tutor CD-ROM

won. A clever politician committed to modernizing the Democratic Party, Van Buren had served in the Senate and as Jackson's Secretary of State.

As President, Van Buren lacked Jackson's popularity. Jackson shared some of the blame for this. Even before killing the Bank of the United States, Jackson had begun withdrawing federal funds from the bank and depositing them in various "pet banks" around the country. These banks printed and lent paper money recklessly. As a result, in 1836, Jackson was forced to declare that the federal government would accept only gold or silver in payment for public lands. Jackson's order, called the Specie Circular, weakened the "pet banks" and helped cause the Panic of 1837, which occurred during Van Buren's first year in office. In the severe depression that followed, thousands of Americans lost their jobs, and urban poverty mushroomed. Prolonged by a second panic in 1839, the depression dragged on into the 1840 election year.

Taking a lesson from the Democrats' success with Jackson, the Whigs chose military hero William Henry Harrison as their presidential candidate. Unlike Jackson, however, they hoped to win by avoiding the major issues, relying instead on Harrison's popularity and catchy slogans to carry the day. More than 80 percent of eligible voters cast ballots in the election. Many voted in hopes that a change might end the depression.

Harrison soundly defeated President Van Buren, only to be defeated himself by illness. On April 4, 1841, just one month after taking office, Harrison died of pneumonia.

Vice President John Tyler, who took over as President, had won his place on the ticket for reasons of strategy. Tyler was a southern Democrat who strongly supported states' rights, but he had angered his party by taking a public stand against President Jackson. The Whigs had counted on Tyler to draw southern votes away from Van Buren. They never expected him to assume the presidency. As President, Tyler blocked much of the Whig program, including the revival of a national bank. As a result, the Whigs abandoned him. Lacking support from either party, Tyler experienced a tough four years of political deadlock.

HARRISONIAN
BALL ROLLING, **KEEP THE**
RALLY!

A General Meeting

Will be held at the Old COURTROOM, [Riez's building]

On Saturday Evening,

The 18th instant, at early candle light. A punctual attendance is requested.

MESSRS. DAVIS, BOTKIN, KEATING

And others, will address the Meeting.

July 17, 1840. R. P. TODD, *Chairman*
Vigilance Committee.

VIEWING HISTORY This poster announces a campaign rally for William Henry Harrison in July 1840. **Recognizing Bias** *(a) How is Harrison depicted? (b) What leadership qualities does the image try to convey, and what kind of voter might the poster have attracted?*

Reading Comprehension

1. Jackson represented voters rather than established institutions, and he shifted political power toward states and western interests.

2. The tariff greatly benefited the industrial North, supporting the products manufactured there, but it forced southerners to pay higher prices for manufactured goods.

3. South Carolina believed that states could nullify federal laws that they judged to be unconstitutional. South Carolina threatened to secede if the federal government tried to enforce the tariff.

4. The executive and judicial. The Supreme Court ruled in favor of the Cherokees but had no power to enforce its decision. Georgia successfully defied the Court, with Jackson's support.

Critical Thinking and Writing

5. Although Jackson opposed the expansion of federal power under Monroe and Adams, he also opposed states' efforts to defy the federal government's constitutionally delegated powers.

6. Essays should be supported with facts from the section.

Debates might focus on documents such as the text of the Indian Removal Act, Jackson's veto message in regard to the charter of the Bank of the United States, or the text of the Force Bill.

Section 5 Assessment

READING COMPREHENSION

1. In what ways was Jackson's presidency a change from the past?

2. Why did Northerners and Southerners disagree over the **Tariff of 1828?**

3. Why did South Carolina threaten to **secede** over the tariff issue?

4. Which two branches of the federal government came into conflict over the **Indian Removal Act?** Which branch won? Explain.

CRITICAL THINKING AND WRITING

5. **Checking Consistency** Jackson favored states' rights and limited federal government. Was his action to block South Carolina in the tariff crisis consistent with this belief? Explain your answer.

6. **Writing an Opinion** Write a newspaper editorial either for or against Jackson's use of patronage.

 Take It to the NET

Activity: Holding a Debate
Analyze primary sources from Andrew Jackson's presidency. Organize a class debate on whether or not Jackson used his power as chief executive appropriately. Use the links provided in the *America: Pathways to the Present* area of the following Web site for help in completing this activity.
www.phschool.com

CAPTION ANSWERS

Viewing History (a) As a farmer. (b) Strong, hardworking, a friend of farmers; it was intended to attract farmers.

Review and Assessment

REVIEWING KEY TERMS

Students should refer to the definitions of key terms in the chapter to write sentences that show an understanding of the key aspects of U.S. economic growth between 1790 and 1850.

REVIEWING KEY TERMS

Students should refer to the definitions of key terms in the chapter to write sentences that show an understanding of the key aspects of U.S. economic growth between 1790 and 1850.

REVIEWING MAIN IDEAS

11. Possible answers: cotton profits dramatically increased; exports of cotton boomed; led to the purchase and settlement of large areas in the South; purchase of more enslaved Africans.

12. It dramatically increased production.

13. People began to purchase goods that had been made by others. To manufacture these goods, workers would report to a centralized factory, rather than working at home.

14. Banks began to provide the capital needed to build new factories and expand businesses.

15. Cities were unprepared for dramatic population increases. Results included: overcrowding, disease, inadequate housing and social services, poverty.

16. Low pay, long hours, unhealthy conditions.

17. Maintaining secrecy while organizing a large revolt was very difficult.

18. Possible answers—At home: Federal improvement projects, Supreme Court decisions supporting federal control of commerce. Foreign policy: Monroe Doctrine.

19. None of the candidates received a majority of electoral votes, so the House of Representatives had to choose the President. Clay swung Kentucky's votes to Adams, giving him the win. When Adams then chose Clay to be Secretary of State, Jackson supporters accused the two of making a "corrupt bargain."

20. (a) He urged Congress to pass the Force Bill, threatening force if South Carolina refused to pay the Tariff of 1828. (b) He vetoed the rechartering of the Bank of the United States, justifying his action as a protection of the rights of ordinary citizens.

creating a CHAPTER SUMMARY

Copy this cause-and-effect diagram (right) on a piece of paper and complete it by adding information about the Market Revolution. Some entries have been completed for you as examples.

 TEXT

For additional review and enrichment activities, see the interactive version of *America: Pathways to the Present*, available on the Web and on CD-ROM.

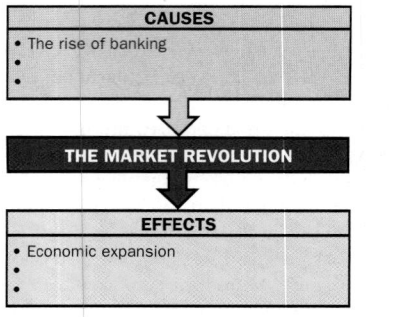

CAUSES
• The rise of banking
•
•

↓

THE MARKET REVOLUTION

↓

EFFECTS
• Economic expansion
•
•

★ Reviewing Key Terms

For each of the terms below, write a sentence explaining how it relates to the growth of the United States in the early 1800s.

1. Market Revolution
2. free enterprise system
3. urban
4. labor union
5. cotton belt
6. *McCulloch* v. *Maryland*
7. Monroe Doctrine
8. spoils system
9. secede
10. Indian Removal Act

★ Reviewing Main Ideas

11. Describe the economic and social effects of the cotton gin on the South. (Section 1)

12. What benefits did centralized manufacturing offer? (Section 1)

13. How did the concept of "going to work" change in the North in the early 1800s? (Section 1)

14. What role did banks have in the nation's economic growth? (Section 1)

15. What were the results of the growth of cities in the North? (Section 2)

16. What conditions led to the formation of labor unions? (Section 2)

17. What caused slave rebellions to end in failure? (Section 3)

18. Give examples of nationalism at home and in foreign policy during the 1820s. (Section 4)

19. Why was the election of 1824 controversial? (Section 4)

20. Explain President Jackson's position in (a) the tariff crisis and (b) the bank war. (Section 5)

21. What were the causes and the outcomes of the Black Hawk War and the Second Seminole War? (Section 5)

★ Critical Thinking

22. **Summarizing Information** What economic changes took place in the frontier lands west of the Appalachian Mountains during the first half of the 1800s?

23. **Recognizing Ideologies** How did the Supreme Court rulings of Chief Justice John Marshall reflect his nationalist beliefs?

24. **Making Comparisons** How did Andrew Jackson's views on the role of government compare with the views of his predecessor, John Quincy Adams?

25. **Identifying Alternatives** (a) Why did Jackson forcibly relocate Native Americans? (b) How else might he have handled the conflict between southern states and Native Americans?

CREATING A CHAPTER SUMMARY

The Market Revolution

Causes	Effects
• The rise of banking	• Economic expansion
• The rise of manufacturing	• Strong economy in northern cities
• New kinds of jobs	• More people working outside the home
• More goods available	• Rise of shopping
• Uncontrolled lending	• Bank failures and depressions

★ Skills Assessment

Analyzing Political Cartoons ▶

26. This cartoon is titled "King Andrew the First."
(a) Who is "King Andrew"? (b) What is he holding in his left hand? (c) What is he standing on?

27. The other documents on the floor are labeled "Internal Improvements" and "U.S. Bank." The book in the foreground is labeled "Judiciary of the United States." To what do these items refer?

28. Why do you think the cartoonist used the image of a king to criticize Jackson?

Analyzing Primary Sources

Reread the excerpt from the Monroe Doctrine in Section 4, and answer the questions that follow.

29. Which statement best represents the meaning of the quotation?

    A The United States considers European governments to have legitimate claims in both North and South America.

    B The United States will not interfere in European matters and will not allow European aggression in the Americas.

    C European powers have injured the peace and prosperity of the United States by engaging in aggressive acts.

    D It is impossible for the United States to have friendly relations with de facto European governments, because they are not legitimate.

30. Monroe's message stated that American foreign policy regarding the internal affairs of European nations would be

    F neutral.
    G de facto but friendly.
    H nationalist.
    J firm but friendly.

Applying the Chapter Skill: _Determining Relevance_

31. How is the topic of shopping in the early 1800s relevant to a discussion of America's system of free enterprise?

ACTIVITIES

Writing to LEARN

Writing an Introduction
Today, the federal government promotes economic prosperity in various ways. Prepare an introduction to an essay comparing today's policies to those of Presidents John Quincy Adams and Andrew Jackson.

Primary Source CD-ROM

Working With Primary Sources Find additional information on the Market Revolution on the _Exploring Primary Sources in U.S. History CD-ROM_ and use the selection(s) provided to complete the Chapter 8 primary source activity located in the _America: Pathways to the Present_ area of the following Web site.
www.phschool.com

Take It to the NET

Chapter Self-Test As a review activity, take the Chapter 8 Self-Test in the _America: Pathways to the Present_ area at the Web site listed below. The questions are designed to test your understanding of the chapter content.
www.phschool.com

---

21. Black Hawk War—Cause: desire of the Fox and Sauk to take back their land; Result: retreat into Wisconsin Territory, where most were killed. Second Seminole War—Cause: Refusal of Seminoles to abandon their land in Florida to white settlers; Result: a nearly seven-year war that ended with most Seminoles being driven off their land.

CRITICAL THINKING

22. As transportation networks reached into the Old Northwest, livestock and grain became big business. In the South, settlement and cotton farming spread westward, displacing Native Americans.

23. They affirmed the delegated and implied powers of the federal government under the U.S. Constitution.

24. Jackson favored limited government and individual liberty. He opposed federally funded infrastructure improvements. Adams favored a larger role for the federal government and felt that his administration had a responsibility to push for federally funded public improvements.

25. (a) Gold was discovered on Native American land, and white settlers demanded that the Five Tribes be moved; the tribes refused.
(b) Possible answers: Negotiate with the tribes; send in the army to protect Indian land.

SKILLS ASSESSMENT

26. (a) Andrew Jackson. (b) A paper saying "veto." (c) The U.S. Constitution.

27. Jackson vetoed both the rechartering of the National Bank and money for internal improvements. The book on the floor is a reminder that Jackson ignored the Court in its ruling that opposed Cherokee relocation.

28. Many Americans believed that Jackson was abusing the power of the presidency.

29. B

30. J

31. Possible answer: People now purchased many of life's necessities. Merchants and entrepreneurs often invested some of their profits in new factories or new retail establishments. The free enterprise system placed no limits on the amount of profit an individual could earn by catering to the need of the public to "go shopping."

American Pathways
GOVERNMENT

The United States Supreme Court

The Supreme Court has played an important role in shaping the political, economic, and social life of the United States. Considered by the Framers to be the "least dangerous" branch of government, the Court has steadily gained power. Today, the decisions put forward by its nine Justices have a profound impact on the lives of Americans.

THE UNITED STATES SUPREME COURT

Focus The Supreme Court plays a pivotal role in determining the political, economic, and social direction of our nation. The nine Justices who make up the country's highest court are entrusted with the power to decide some of the most significant questions of the day. Their decisions impact our rights as individuals, as well as our rights as members of particular groups.

Instruct Tell students to read about the five eras in Supreme Court history. As they read about each period, ask students to think about how the Court's decisions reflect the nation's current mood and shape the country's future. Encourage students to discuss the role of the Chief Justice and consider how his or her perspective affects the Court's overall outlook.

Extend Have students focus on one Supreme Court Chief Justice. Tell students to research that Justice's Court and find out about some of its significant decisions. Encourage students to learn about the ramifications of those decisions. How did the decisions reflect on the Chief Justice? How did they reflect on the Supreme Court members? How did the decisions affect future generations?

1 The Formation and Preservation of the Union

1789–1865 Largely ignored during the early years of its existence, the Supreme Court became more active in 1801 with the appointment of John Marshall as Chief Justice. The Marshall Court encouraged economic growth, nationalism, and fair treatment of Native Americans. Later, under a new Chief Justice, the Court made a historic ruling on slavery.

The Supreme Court building, Washington, D.C. (left)

2 Reconstruction and the Jim Crow South

1866–1896 The Court generally supported the Reconstruction plans of the Radical Republicans, although later, during the Jim Crow era, their decisions tended to limit African American equality. The Supreme Court's decision in *Plessy* v. *Ferguson* in 1896 allowed for "separate but equal" facilities for African Americans.

3 Industrial Expansion and Progressive Reforms

1877–1920 During the first part of this period, the Court allowed the nation's industries to grow freely. In the early 1900s, however, amid mounting public calls for reform, the Court began to accept increased business regulation and more safeguards for labor.

Standard Oil Refinery, Cleveland, Ohio, 1889 (right)

306

RESOURCE DIRECTORY

Teaching Resources
Units 3/4 booklet
• American Pathways Activity, pp. 36–37
American Pathways Thematic Posters

Technology
Companion Web site, www.phschool.com

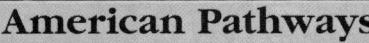

 The New Deal

1933–1939   A majority of the justices on the Supreme Court used their power of judicial review to strike down many of Franklin Roosevelt's economic reforms during the New Deal. Faced with a hostile Court, President Roosevelt tried— and failed—to reshape the Court more to his liking in what is known as the "court-packing" scheme. In the years that followed, though, Roosevelt was able to appoint a number of more liberal justices who supported his programs.

 Expansion and Protection of Americans' Rights

1945–Present   The years after World War II, marked by Earl Warren's appointment as Chief Justice in 1953, saw sweeping changes in the areas of civil rights and criminal procedures. Today's Court grapples with issues of copyright and privacy surrounding the advent of the Internet and other new technologies.

Justices of the U.S. Supreme Court (top); a suspect being read his Miranda rights (middle); and a teenager using the Internet (bottom)

Continuity and Change

1. During which eras has the Supreme Court concerned itself mainly with individual rights?
2. Have the Court's opinions ever shifted within an era? Explain your answer.

 Take It to the NET: Creating a Study Guide
Print and complete the study guide for this topic found in the *America: Pathways to the Present* area of the following Web site. **www.phschool.com**

307

 **Take It to the NET**

Students can print the American Pathways thematic study guide for this topic at the Prentice Hall School Web site, or you can provide students with copies of the study guide, which is found in the Units 3/4 booklet, the American Pathways Activity, pages 36–37. Students should use their texts to fill in a one-sentence description for each event on the study guide. When completed for each of the American Pathways topics, the thematic study guides will aid students in preparing for an end-of-course exam.

ANSWERS

1. Era 2 (Reconstruction and the Jim Crow South) and Era 5 (Expansion and Protection of Americans' Rights).

2. During the late 1800s the Court initially supported Reconstruction but later found the doctrine of "separate but equal" to be constitutional. During the period of Industrial Expansion and Progressive Reforms, the Court at first gave free rein to industry but later supported a more strict regulation of business. During the 1930s the Court was at first hostile toward Franklin Roosevelt's New Deal programs but eventually came to support much of the legislation of the later part of the New Deal.

Chapter 9 Planning Guide
Resource Manager

	CORE INSTRUCTION	READING/SKILLS
Chapter-Level Resources	**Teaching Resources** • Pacing Charts booklet • Block Scheduling booklet **Resource Pro® CD-ROM**, Ch. 9 **Prentice Hall Presentation Pro CD-ROM**, Ch. 9 **www.phschool.com** • eTeach	**Guided Reading Audiotapes (English/Spanish)** **Student Edition on Audio CD**, Ch. 9 **Social Studies Skills Tutor CD-ROM** **Color Transparencies**, G6, G7
1 Reforming Society 1. Learn the message preached by Protestant revivalists. 2. Discover who the transcendentalists were. 3. Find out why reformers launched a temperance movement. 4. See why Horace Mann and others worked to reform public education. 5. Read to find out how Dorothea Dix went about trying to improve conditions in prisons. 6. Understand why many reformers worked to establish utopian communities.	**Teaching Resources** **Units 3/4 booklet** • Section 1 Quiz, p. 26 **Learning Styles Lesson Plans booklet**, p. 20	**Guided Reading and Review booklet**, p. 37 **Guide to the Essentials**, p. 47 **Skills for Life booklet**, p. 11 **Section Reading Support Transparencies**
2 The Antislavery Movement 1. Learn how the antislavery movement arose and grew. 2. Find out about contributions made by Frederick Douglass to the antislavery movement. 3. See what caused divisions to arise among abolitionists. 4. Discover how the Underground Railroad operated. 5. Understand how some Americans demonstrated resistance to abolitionism.	**Teaching Resources** **Units 3/4 booklet** • Section 2 Quiz, p. 27	**Guided Reading and Review booklet**, p. 38 **Guide to the Essentials**, p. 48 **Learning with Documents booklet**, p. 48 **Section Reading Support Transparencies**
3 The Movement for Women's Rights 1. Find out what private roles women were expected to fulfill in the early 1800s. 2. Learn about the public roles gradually adopted by some women. 3. Discover the significance of the Seneca Falls Convention.	**Teaching Resources** **Units 3/4 booklet** • Section 3 Quiz, p. 28	**Guided Reading and Review booklet**, p. 39 **Guide to the Essentials**, p. 49 **Learning with Documents booklet**, p. 80 **Section Reading Support Transparencies**
4 Growing Divisions 1. Read about some causes of the huge rise in immigration to the United States in the 1830s and 1840s. 2. See why reform movements heightened tensions between the North and the South.	**Teaching Resources** **Units 3/4 booklet** • Section 4 Quiz, p. 29 **Learning Styles Lesson Plans booklet**, p. 21	**Guided Reading and Review booklet**, p. 40 **Guide to the Essentials**, p. 50 **Learning with Documents booklet**, p. 14 **Section Reading Support Transparencies**

ENRICHMENT/PRE-AP

Prentice Hall United States History Video Collection™
www.phschool.com
- Section Activities, Virtual Field Trip, Chapter Activities, Current Events Online

Biography, Literature, and Comparing Primary Sources booklet, pp. 113–114
Sounds of an Era Audio CD
Exploring Primary Sources in U.S. History CD-ROM

American History Block Scheduling Support
Nystrom *Atlas of Our Country,* pp. 26–27
Sounds of an Era Audio CD
Exploring Primary Sources in U.S. History CD-ROM

Biography, Literature, and Comparing Primary Sources booklet, p. 14
American History Block Scheduling Support
Sounds of an Era Audio CD
Exploring Primary Sources in U.S. History CD-ROM

Biography, Literature, and Comparing Primary Sources booklet, p. 50
Nystrom *Atlas of Our Country,* pp. 24–25
American Pathways Thematic Posters

ASSESSMENT

Core Assessment
ExamView® Test Bank, Ch. 9
ExamView® Test Bank CD-ROM, Ch. 9

Standardized Test Preparation
Diagnose and Prescribe
Diagnostic Tests for High School Social Studies Skills

Review and Reteach
Review Book for U.S. History

Practice and Assess
Test-taking Strategies With Transparencies
Test-taking Strategies Posters
Test Prep Book for U.S. History
Alternative Assessment Handbook
Document-Based Assessment

Teaching Resources
Units 3/4 booklet
- Section Quizzes, pp. 26–29
- Chapter Tests, pp. 30, 33
www.phschool.com Ch. 9 Self-Test

AmericanHeritage RESOURCES

From the Archives of American Heritage®, pp. 313, 320
AmericanHeritage® My Brush with History™ Videotapes
www.americanheritage.com

Don't miss the exclusive interactive version of this textbook on the Web and on CD-ROM.

Chapter 9 Planning Guide
In Your Classroom

CUSTOMIZE FOR INDIVIDUAL NEEDS

Gifted and Talented

Teacher's Edition
- Customize for Gifted and Talented, pp. 323, 327

Teaching Resources
- Biography, Literature, and Comparing Primary Sources booklet, pp. 14, 50, 113–114

Technology
- Exploring Primary Sources in U.S. History CD-ROM *Civil Disobedience, Henry David Thoreau; Audubon and His Journals: My Style of Drawing Birds, John James Audubon; Meaning of Fourth of July for the Negro, Frederick Douglass; First Issue of the Liberator, William Lloyd Garrison; Seneca Falls Declaration of Sentiments*

ESL

Teacher's Edition
- Customize for ESL, pp. 311, 325

Teaching Resources
- Guided Reading and Review booklet, pp. 37–40
- Guide to the Essentials (English/Spanish), Chapter 9

Technology
- Student Edition on Audio CD, Chapter 9
- Guided Reading Audiotapes (English/Spanish), Chapter 9
- Section Reading Support Transparencies

Less Proficient Readers

Teacher's Edition
- Customize for Less Proficient Readers, pp. 315, 319

Teaching Resources
- Guided Reading and Review booklet, pp. 37–40
- Guide to the Essentials (English/Spanish), Chapter 9

Technology
- Student Edition on Audio CD, Chapter 9
- Guided Reading Audiotapes (English/Spanish), Chapter 9
- Section Reading Support Transparencies

Less Proficient Writers

Teacher's Edition
- Customize for Less Proficient Writers, p. 333

Teaching Resources
- Guided Reading and Review booklet, pp. 37–40
- Guide to the Essentials (English/Spanish), Chapter 9

Technology
- Student Edition on Audio CD, Chapter 9
- Guided Reading Audiotapes (English/Spanish), Chapter 9
- Section Reading Support Transparencies

TEACHER'S EDITION INDEX

CHAPTER 9 – PACING SUGGESTIONS

For 90-minute Blocks

- Teach sections 1 and 4 using Transparencies G6 and G7, and the Recent Scholarship notes on pages 322 and 328 for class discussions.

Running Out of Time?

If you are running short on time to cover this chapter, consider the following options:

- Use the Prentice Hall Presentation Pro CD-ROM to create an outline for this chapter.
- Use the Section Summaries for Chapter 9, from **Guide to the Essentials (English/Spanish).**

ADDITIONAL ACTIVITIES

1 Reforming Society

Connecting with Culture
Tell students to choose one aspect of the reform movement—transcendentalism, temperance, public education, prison reform, and utopian societies. Then have small groups work together to research and present an oral presentation on their topic. Encourage students to consider the following questions: How did this aspect of the reform movement reflect the problems of the day? How successful was the effort? What are its lasting contributions? **(Verbal/Linguistic)**

2 The Antislavery Movement

Connecting with History and Conflict
Tell students that they are going to create their own version of the *North Star*, the antislavery newspaper founded by Frederick Douglass and Martin Delany. Students should divide up the jobs, which include writing articles about abolitionism and the Underground Railroad, making illustrations to accompany the articles, writing editorials, and deciding on the layout of the paper. **(Visual/Spatial; Verbal/Linguistic)**

3 The Movement for Women's Rights

Connecting with Citizenship
Have students present a mock debate on the role of women at the first World Anti-Slavery Convention that took place in London in 1840. Ask for volunteers to play the roles of Lucretia Mott, Elizabeth Cady Stanton, and male abolitionists who objected to women's participation in the convention. Encourage students to prepare a position paper, and present their positions clearly and convincingly. Engage students in a discussion of the issues. **(Bodily/Kinesthetic; Verbal/Linguistic)**

4 Growing Divisions

Connecting with Economics
Tell students to focus on either the North or the South during the period between 1830 and 1850. Have students research the economy of the region to gain a clearer understanding of the division of labor. Suggest that students researching the North look into the kinds of jobs offered to immigrants, as well as the jobs available to non-immigrants. Have students studying the South investigate the role that slavery played in the economy. Tell students to present their economic profiles in a visual display, such as a chart or graph. **(Logical/Mathematical)**

Chapter 9

Religion and Reform

(1815–1855)

INTRODUCING THE CHAPTER

The young republic sped through rapid social change in the early 1800s— change that brought not only new benefits but also new regional and cultural tensions. A growing and dynamic reform movement urged Americans to seek both personal and social improvements, shaping society and the nation for generations to come.

TIME LINE ACTIVITY

To provide students with practice in using the time line, ask questions such as these:

1. When did William Lloyd Garrison found the American Anti-Slavery Society? *(in 1833)*

2. In what year did Sojourner Truth become a leader of the abolitionist movement? *(in 1843)*

3. When did the Irish Potato Famine begin? *(in 1845)*

Chapter 9

Religion and Reform

(1815–1855)

SECTION 1   Reforming Society
SECTION 2   The Antislavery Movement
SECTION 3   The Movement for Women's Rights
SECTION 4   Growing Divisions

Utopian community in New Harmony, Indiana

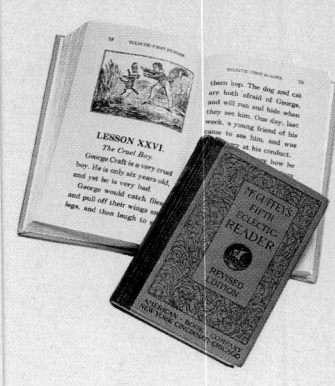
McGuffey's Reader, a popular schoolbook

1837
Reformer Horace Mann becomes the first secretary of the Massachusetts Board of Education.

American Events

1821
The nation's first public high school opens in Massachusetts.

1832
Charles Grandison Finney begins popular religious revival meetings in New York City.

1833
William Lloyd Garrison founds the American Anti-Slavery Society.

Presidential Terms: J. Monroe 1817–1825   John Quincy Adams 1825–1829   Andrew Jackson 1829–1837

1820 • • 1825 • 1830 • • 1835 • •

World Events
The African colony of Liberia is created for free blacks and freed slaves.
1822

Boers (whites of Dutch descent) defeat Zulus in southern Africa.
1838

eTeach

Be sure to check out this month's online discussion with a Master Teacher. Go to **www.phschool.com**.

RESOURCE DIRECTORY

Teaching Resources
Pacing Charts booklet
Block Scheduling booklet, p. 17
Units 3/4 booklet
• Chapter Summary, p. 25

Technology
Guided Reading Audiotapes (English/Spanish), Ch. 9
Student Edition on Audio CD, Ch. 9
Prentice Hall United States History Video Collection™ Volume 7, *Democracy and Reform;* Volume 8, *Causes of the Civil War*
Prentice Hall Presentation Pro CD-ROM, Ch. 9
Resource Pro® CD-ROM
Color Transparencies *American Diversity,* G6
Social Studies Skills Tutor CD-ROM
Companion Web site, www.phschool.com

The Underground Railroad

CANADA
Lake Superior
Lake Michigan
Lake Huron
L. Ontario
L. Erie
Minnesota Territory
Wisconsin
Michigan
Iowa
Unorganized Territory
Missouri
Ill.
Ind.
Ohio
Ky.
Tenn.
Arkansas
Miss.
Alabama
Georgia
La.
Texas
Florida
Va.
N.C.
S.C.
Penn.
New York
Vt.
N.H.
Maine
Mass.
Conn.
R.I.
N.J.
Md.
Del.
MEXICO
Gulf of Mexico
ATLANTIC OCEAN
APPALACHIAN MTS.
Mississippi River
Missouri River
Ohio River
Red River
Montreal
Toronto
Niagara Falls
Boston
New York
Philadelphia
Washington D.C.
Milwaukee
Chicago
Detroit
Cincinnati
Cairo
New Bern
Frederick Douglass established a print shop in Rochester that became a depot.
Portuguese fishermen and the Shinnecock Indians helped transport escaped slaves from Long Island to New England.
John Brown led fugitives on a midwinter journey from Missouri to Canada via Chicago.
Levi Coffin, a Quaker, helped more than 3,000 slaves to escape.
The home of Presbyterian minister John Rankin in Ripley was one of the most active depots.
Harriet Beecher Stowe maintained a depot in Walnut Hills.
Dorchester County was the birthplace of Harriet Tubman. She rescued about 300 slaves on 19 trips to the South.
Seminole Indians in Florida offered safe havens for escaped slaves.
Slavery prohibited
Slavery permitted
Swamp
Underground Railroad
Depot
1849 borders
N
0 150 300 mi.
0 150 300 km
90°W
80°W
70°W
40°N
30°N

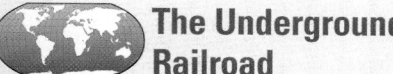

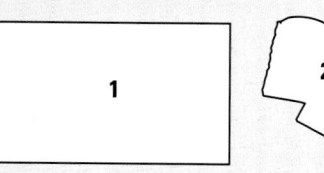

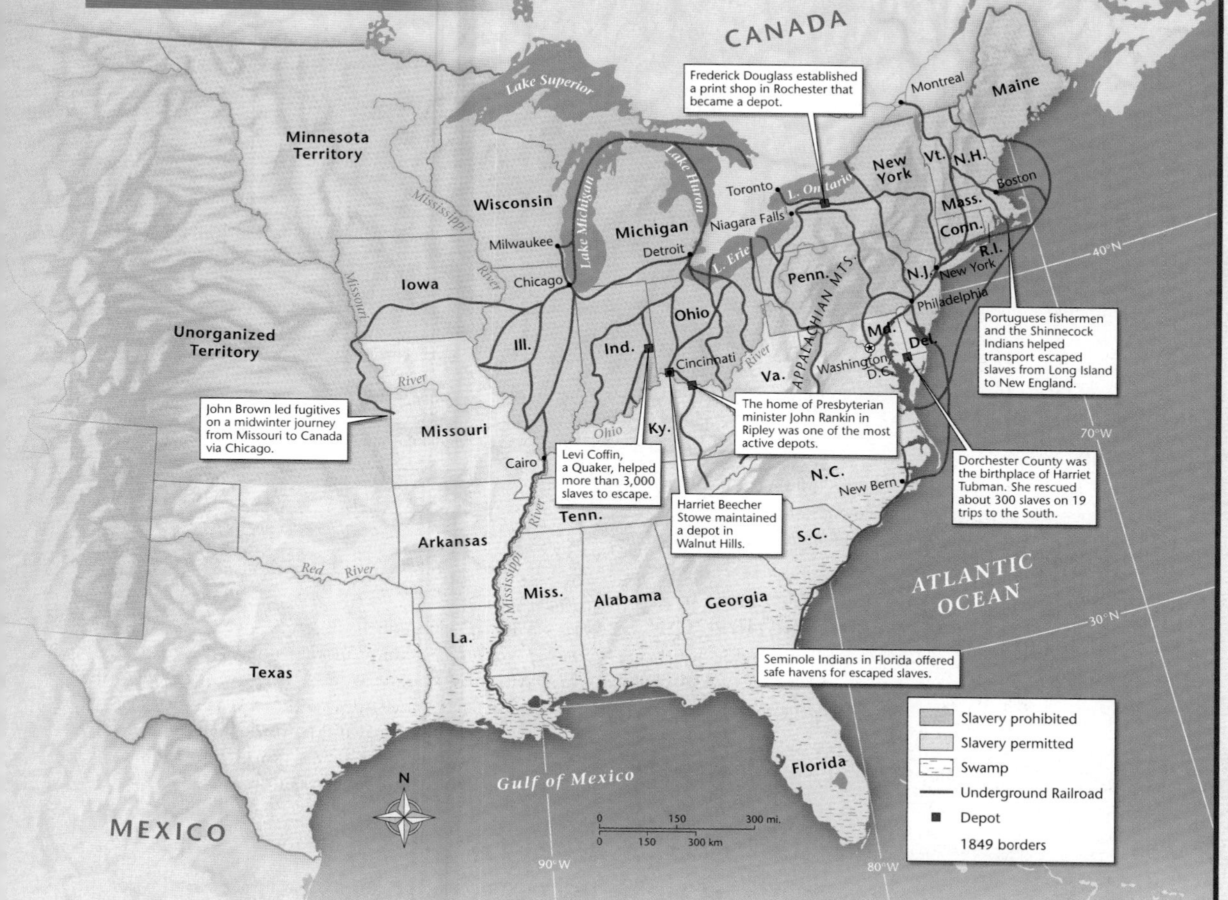

1841 Dorothea Dix visits a Massachusetts jail, triggering her prison reform crusade.

1843 Freed slave Sojourner Truth joins the abolitionist movement.

1847 Escaped slave Frederick Douglass co-founds an abolitionist newspaper, the *North Star.*

1848 The first U.S. women's rights convention is held in Seneca Falls, New York. A wave of German immigration begins.

1850 Escaped slave Harriet Tubman begins to lead others to freedom on the Underground Railroad.

1854 Transcendentalist Henry David Thoreau writes *Walden.*

M. Van Buren 1837–1841 | W. Harrison 1841 | John Tyler 1841–1845 | James K. Polk 1845–1849 | Z. Taylor 1849–50 | M. Fillmore 1850–1853 | F. Pierce 1853–1857

1840 · 1845 · 1850 · 1855

1839 Opium War between Britain and China begins.

1845 Irish potato famine begins.

1854 Russia battles Britain, France, and Turkey in the Crimean War.

The Underground Railroad

Activating Prior Knowledge Where was the common destination of the Underground Railroad? *(Canada; slave hunters were not allowed to pursue the fugitives beyond the U.S. border.)*

Previewing Why was the East Coast route a useful one? *(The swampy areas provided cover for the fugitives.)*

BACKGROUND

About the Pictures

1
2

1. New Harmony was founded by Robert Owen and contained the first free library, kindergarten, trade school, and community-supported public school in the U.S.
2. The readers, written by William Holmes McGuffey, covered a large variety of topics, included excerpts from popular literature, and sold over 125 million copies.

BIBLIOGRAPHY

For the Teacher

Buckmaster, Henrietta and John G. Sproat, eds. ***Let My People Go: The Story of the Underground Railroad and the Growth of the Abolition Movement.*** (Southern Classics Series.) University of South Carolina Press, 1992. (Informative account from an African American point of view.)

Miller, Perry. ***The Transcendentalists: The Classic Anthology.*** Fine Communications, 1997. (Excerpts from and analysis of major transcendentalist texts.)

For the Student

Jacobs, Harriet Ann. ***Incidents in the Life of a Slave Girl, Written by Herself.*** Harvard University Press, 2000. (The author describes her ultimately successful struggle for freedom.)

Parker, John P. and Stuart Seely Sprague, eds. ***His Promised Land: The Autobiography of John P. Parker, Fomer Slave and Conductor on the Underground Railroad.*** W. W. Norton, 1998. (The story of an escaped slave who becomes a conductor on the Underground Railroad.)

iTEXT

Don't miss the exclusive interactive version of this textbook on the Web and on CD-ROM.

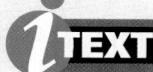

Section 1
Reforming Society

READING FOCUS

- What message did Protestant revivalists preach?
- Who were the transcendentalists?
- Why did reformers launch a temperance movement?
- Why did Horace Mann and others work to reform public education?
- How did Dorothea Dix go about trying to improve conditions in prisons?
- Why did many reformers work to establish utopian communities?

MAIN IDEA

Revivalists and transcendentalists urged Americans to improve themselves and society. Reformers set out to battle social problems such as alcoholism, poor education, and inhumane prisons.

KEY TERMS

transcendentalism
temperance movement
abstinence
segregate
utopian community

TAKING NOTES

Copy the chart below. As you read, fill in the blanks with descriptions of the actions taken by various reform movements.

Reforms During the Mid-1800s	
Reform Effort	**Actions**
Protestant revivalists	• Urged people to reform themselves •
Transcendentalists	• •
Temperance movement	• •
Public education reform	• •
Prison reform	• •

Setting the Scene Poverty, alcoholism, illiteracy, overcrowded housing, poor healthcare, abuse of women, declining moral values—this reads like a list of typical problems in urban areas today. In fact, these were the growing pains that began to plague America's young cities in the early decades of the 1800s. Because these growing pains occurred first in the urban North, it was there that a powerful movement to reform American society first took hold.

Protestant Revivalists

The reform movement was largely rooted in religious faith. Most reformers based their arguments on Protestant principles, whether they preached fiery sermons at camp meetings, risked their lives to help slaves escape, or made speeches to hostile crowds to demand women's right to vote. Their faith gave them purpose and courage.

The democratic principles of the Second Great Awakening stirred the reform movements of the 1830s and 1840s. Reformers generally rejected the Puritan belief that God predetermined people's lives and placed them in rigid social ranks. They believed that God was all-powerful but that God allowed people to make their own destinies.

Charles Grandison Finney This message reached Americans through the preaching of several popular revivalists. The central figure in the revivalist movement was Charles Grandison Finney. A lawyer in Adams, New York, Finney became a Presbyterian minister following a powerful conversion experience in 1821. He addressed his audiences as he had pleaded with juries, with passion and fire.

In *The Bible and Temperance* (circa 1840), illustrator Nathaniel Currier depicts an idle husband sleeping the day away, his job and reputation ruined by alcoholism, while his wife and daughter, in "want and extreme wretchedness," are consoled by a minister reading from the Bible.

Finney sparked revivals in upstate New York before moving to New York City in 1832, where he drew enormous crowds. His common-sense sermons emphasized individuals' power to reform themselves.

Lyman Beecher   Another major revivalist came from New England but later set out to evangelize the West. Lyman Beecher, son of a blacksmith, attended Yale University and became a popular preacher in Boston. In 1832, he moved to Cincinnati to become president of the Lane Theological Seminary, a religion college.

America, Beecher warned, was threatened by "the vast extent of territory, our numerous and increasing population, . . . diversity of local interests, the power of selfishness, and the fury of sectional jealousy and hate." He taught in simple terms that good people would make a good country.

Living up to his own teachings, Beecher himself raised a flock of 13 children, many of whom became major figures in various reform movements. The most famous were the preacher and lecturer Henry Ward Beecher, the writer and antislavery activist Harriet Beecher Stowe, and Catharine Beecher, a key figure in women's education.

The Transcendentalists

The conditions that produced the reform movement also influenced a group of philosophers and writers who rejected traditional religion. The group, centered in Concord, Massachusetts, founded a philosophical movement known as **transcendentalism.** (To *transcend* means to "rise above.") Transcendentalism taught that the process of spiritual discovery and insight would lead a person to truths more profound than he or she could reach through reason.

In writings and lectures from about 1830 to 1855, transcendentalists declared that humans are naturally good. They rejected outward rituals and group worship in favor of private, inward searching. They urged people to be self-reliant and to have the courage to act on their own beliefs. In this way, people could lead moral, meaningful lives. To many, a moral life involved helping to reform society.

Ralph Waldo Emerson   The leader of the transcendental movement was Ralph Waldo Emerson (1803–1882), a Boston-area lecturer and writer who became one of America's greatest thinkers. Following the family tradition passed down from his Puritan ancestors, Emerson entered the ministry, becoming pastor of a Unitarian church in Boston in 1829.

When his young wife died of tuberculosis in 1831, the grieving Emerson began to question his beliefs. He resigned his ministry the following year. He then pursued his growing conviction that people can transcend the material world and become conscious of the spirit that is in all of nature.

In 1834, Emerson settled in Concord, where he started a writing career that would help launch what historians call an "American renaissance" in literature. He gathered his public lectures into two volumes called *Essays,* which gained him worldwide fame. In 1846, Emerson published his first collection of poems. He is now recognized as a major American poet.

Like other transcendentalists, Emerson supported various reform causes and urged others to do so. "What is man born for," Emerson wrote, "but to be a Reformer, a Remaker of what man has made; a renouncer of lies; a restorer of truth and good . . . ?"

Sounds of an Era

Listen to excerpts from Emerson's essay "Self-Reliance" and other sounds from the era of reform.

VIEWING HISTORY After a string of personal tragedies, including a failed engagement in 1840 and the loss of his brother in 1842, Henry David Thoreau sought a quieter life at Walden Pond (below) in Massachusetts. **Drawing Inferences** From what you know about economic and social trends taking place in the Northeast during this time, how might Thoreau's life at Walden Pond have represented a contrast from those trends?

Emerson's work attracted a generation of young thinkers and writers. Among them was a neighbor of Emerson's from Concord, Henry David Thoreau.

Henry David Thoreau Just down the road from the town of Concord is a pine forest surrounding a small pond. This serene setting produced one of the best-known works of American literature—*Walden, or Life in the Woods,* by Henry David Thoreau (1817–1862). A friend and admirer of Emerson's, Thoreau would become an equally renowned figure among New England transcendentalists.

Like Emerson, Thoreau suffered tragedy in his life. An early attempt at teaching failed miserably. A wedding engagement fell through in 1840, and two years later Thoreau's brother died. After trying to break into the literary trade in New York City, Thoreau, unhappy with city life, returned to Concord in 1843.

In 1845, Thoreau began his famous stay at Walden Pond (below), which was located on land owned by Emerson. Thoreau built a small cabin for himself and spent the next two years in a mostly solitary life of thinking, reading, writing, and observing nature. Published in 1854, *Walden* contains 18 essays that describe his experiment in living simply. Among his themes, Thoreau explores the value of leisure and the benefits of living closely with nature:

> ❝ Why should we be in such desperate haste to succeed, and in such desperate enterprises? If a man does not keep pace with his companions, perhaps it is because he hears a different drummer. Let him step to the music which he hears, however measured or far away. ❞
> —Henry David Thoreau, *Walden,* 1854

A strong opponent of the war with Mexico, Thoreau, true to his beliefs, protested in 1846 by refusing to pay his taxes. He was jailed for this act of conscience and later described the episode in his most famous essay, *Civil Disobedience.* In his later years, Thoreau devoted much of his time to the antislavery movement, personally helping escaped slaves to flee northward.

The Temperance Movement

American reformers went to work on numerous social problems in the early 1800s. The first and most widespread of these reform efforts was the **temperance movement,** an organized campaign to eliminate alcohol consumption.

In the early 1800s, Americans consumed more alcoholic beverages per person than at any other time in the country's history. Drinking was so popular

that the Greene and Delaware Moral Society warned in 1815 that the United States was "actually threatened with becoming a nation of drunkards."

Valuing self-control and self-discipline, reformers opposed alcohol consumption because it tended to make people lose control. Women reformers in particular saw drinking as a threat to family life. All too often wives and children suffered abuse at the hands of drunken men.

The Reform Effort Between 1815 and about 1840, thousands of local temperance societies were formed. By 1834, the American Temperance Society boasted about 7,000 local organizations with well over a million members.

Members urged people to take pledges not to drink alcohol. The practice is called **abstinence,** which means to refrain from doing something. Temperance societies also established alcohol-free hotels and passenger boats, encouraged employers to require their workers to sign abstinence pledges, and worked for political candidates who promised to ban the sale of alcohol. Reformers promoted the moral, social, and health benefits of alcohol abstinence as well as its economic benefits (because it reduced employee absenteeism).

Speaking in 1842 in Springfield, Illinois, 33-year-old lawyer Abraham Lincoln equated the temperance revolution with the American Revolution. Lincoln looked forward to the "happy day, when . . . the victory shall be complete—when there shall be neither a slave nor a drunkard on the earth."

Impact of the Temperance Movement In 1851, Maine became the first state to ban the manufacture and sale of all alcoholic beverages. Although other states passed similar laws, the protests of brewers, distillers, and others soon led to the repeal or lax enforcement of most of these laws.

Nevertheless, the temperance movement did have a significant impact on Americans' drinking habits. Between the 1830s and the 1860s, alcohol consumption in the United States dropped dramatically, as the graph above shows.

Public Education

Although reformers stressed the need for self-improvement, they sought to reform America's social institutions as well. Of particular concern was the lack of public education in the nation. Even in New England, where colonial laws had required towns to provide elementary schools, support for public education had declined. Many school buildings were old, textbooks and other materials were scarce, and the quality of teaching was often inadequate.

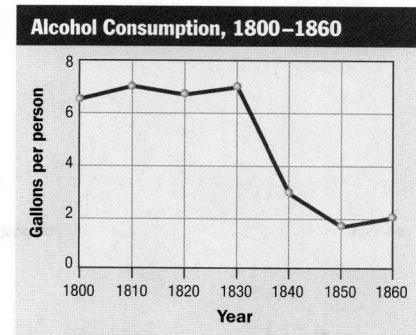

Alcohol Consumption, 1800–1860

INTERPRETING GRAPHS
Temperance societies relied primarily on persuasion to discourage drinking. **Analyzing Visual Information** *Based on the information in this graph, how successful was the temperance movement? Explain.*

Chapter 9 • Section 1   **313**

From the Archives of
AmericanHeritage®

Girls Get a School

The autumn of 1821 saw the opening of two pioneering educational institutions: the Troy Female Seminary, in Troy, New York, and the English Classical School, in Boston. The Troy Female Seminary, founded by the formidable Emma Willard, is generally called the country's first secondary school for girls. It offered course work in everything from zoology to geography, trigonometry to Greek. The English Classical School, in Boston, is usually considered the first truly public high school in the United States. Public education dated back to 1635, when the Boston Latin School was founded, but that institute and its successors were meant only for college-bound boys. The English Classical School (renamed English High School in 1824), was meant to "give a child an education that shall fit him for active life, and shall serve as a foundation for eminence in his profession, whether Mercantile or Mechanical." Source: Frederic D. Schwarz, "The Time Machine," *American Heritage®* magazine, September, 1996.

VIEWING HISTORY This 1857 photograph at top shows a class at a school in Massachusetts, a pioneer in public education. The book above is one of the *McGuffey's Readers*, a series of popular schoolbooks. **Making Comparisons** *How does this classroom scene differ from your classrooms today?*

READING CHECK
What motivated education reform, and why did some people oppose it?

The geography of the mid-Atlantic and southern states further discouraged the building of schools. People in these regions lived on isolated farms separated by poor roads.

Horace Mann Leads Reforms Beginning in the 1820s, many working-class and middle-class citizens began demanding tax-supported public schools. They argued that a democracy could not survive without literate, informed voters and morally upright citizens.

This demand ran into strong opposition. Taxpayers with no children, or those with children who attended private schools, objected to supporting public schools. Many parents did not want to entrust their children's education to the government. Also, many parents relied on their children's labor for their families' survival. They opposed any measures that would keep their children in school until a certain age.

Still, the movement for educational reform gained strength in the 1830s. It owed much of its eventual success to a tireless reformer from Massachusetts named Horace Mann.

Mann grew up in poverty and eventually educated himself at his hometown library. He later earned a law degree and practiced law before winning a seat in the Massachusetts legislature. In 1837, he became that state's first secretary of the Board of Education.

Mann believed in "the absolute right to an education of every human being that comes into the world." He supported the raising of taxes to provide for free public education. Under his leadership, Massachusetts pioneered school reform. Mann began a system in which schools were divided into grade levels. He established consistent curricula and teacher training.

Mann's accomplishments encouraged reformers in other states to establish public schools. By the 1850s, most northern states had free public elementary schools. Massachusetts established the nation's first public high school in 1821. By 1860, the number of public high schools in the United States had risen to 300.

In 1848, Mann took over the seat of John Quincy Adams in the United States House of Representatives and became a fierce opponent of slavery. Later, as president of Antioch College in Ohio, he delivered this advice to his students:

> ❝ I beseech you to treasure up in your hearts these my parting words: Be ashamed to die until you have won some victory for humanity. ❞
> —Horace Mann, speech to graduating class of Antioch College, Yellow Springs, Ohio, June 1859

Two months later Horace Mann died. Presumably he was, indeed, unashamed.

Moral Education Like other middle-class reformers of his time, Horace Mann had a particular kind of education in mind, an education that promoted self-discipline and good citizenship. In Mann's day, public schools taught students how to behave, stand in line and wait their turn, deal with each other politely, and respect authority.

Students learned many of these skills through a series of popular textbooks called the *McGuffey's Readers*. Their creator, William Holmes McGuffey, largely educated himself as a boy and became a teacher in Ohio's frontier schools at age 13. McGuffey became a respected educator and published his first series of *McGuffey's Readers* in 1836. Like other textbooks of the day, McGuffey's books promoted evangelical Protestant values. Besides teaching children to read, the books taught moral values such as thrift, obedience, honesty, and temperance.

The Limits of Reform   Not all parts of the country moved toward free public education at the same pace. Schools were more common in the North than in the South, and they were more common in urban areas than in rural areas.

Where schools did exist, girls often were discouraged from attending or were denied any further education beyond learning to read and write. Schools frequently excluded free black students. In places where African Americans could enroll, such as Boston and New York City, students often were **segregated,** or separated according to race, and African Americans were placed in inferior schools. Opportunities for women and African Americans in higher education were even more limited.

Several private colleges, such as Oberlin, Amherst, and Dartmouth, did open their doors to a small number of African American students. Three black colleges—Avery, Lincoln, and Wilberforce—were founded during this period. In addition, Oberlin, Grinnell, and several other private colleges were coeducational. For the most part, however, white males were the only students welcome at public universities.

Reforming Prisons

In the early 1800s, many states built prisons to house those who had committed crimes. Rather than punish criminals by branding them or putting them on display in public stocks, the states isolated them in institutions for a period of years. The hope was that prisoners would use their time in jail to lead regular, disciplined lives, reflect on their sins, and perhaps become law-abiding citizens.

By the time a Boston schoolteacher named Dorothea Dix visited a Massachusetts jail in 1841, that idealism had given way to a nightmare. Dix discovered men and women, young and old, sane and insane, first-time offenders and hardened criminals, all crowded together in shocking conditions. Many of the inmates were dressed in rags, poorly fed, and chained together in unheated cells.

Dix spent the next two years visiting every prison in Massachusetts. She then submitted a vividly detailed report on her findings to the Massachusetts legislature. Treating the mentally ill as criminals rather than patients "is to condemn them to mental death," she stated. Her powerful testimony convinced the state to improve prison conditions and create separate institutions for the mentally ill. Dix's efforts led 15 other states to build hospitals for the mentally ill.

Utopian Communities

While most reformers worked to improve society at large, some formed **utopian communities,** small societies dedicated to perfection in social and political conditions.

The idea of a utopia had appeared in literature centuries earlier. The term *utopia* described a fictional place where human greed, sin, and egotism did not exist, and where people lived in prosperity as equals. Utopian reformers, disturbed by the ill effects of urban and industrial growth, believed that it was

Prison reformer Dorothea Dix

Chapter 9 • Section 1   315

Reading Comprehension

1. Individuals' power to reform themselves.

2. Transcendentalism grew out of a rejection of traditional religion. The temperance movement was a response to the concern that alcohol was causing people to lose control and was threatening family life. Utopian communities were founded by reformers who wanted to form their own small societies in an attempt to achieve perfect social and political conditions.

3. He believed that every human being has the right to education.

4. Dix's appeals for prison reform led to the improvement of prison conditions and the creation of separate institutions for the mentally ill.

Critical Thinking and Writing

5. Answers should succinctly summarize the motives, aims, and results of the reformer selected.

6. Answers will vary, but students may compare techniques used then and now, including efforts to inform the public of the dangers of alcohol.

Take It to the NET

Essays will vary, but should demonstrate the student's understanding of the factors that led to the growth of the temperance movement, such as the threat to family life, and should recognize the challenges that the movement faced.

---

truly possible to create a place that was free from these troubles.

In the first half of the 1800s, utopian communities arose across the United States. Among the most famous was New Harmony, Indiana, founded in 1825 by Scottish industrialist and social reformer Robert Owen. Owen envisioned a town in which well-educated, hardworking people would share property in common and live in harmony. Like most of the utopias, however, New Harmony fell victim to laziness, selfishness, and quarreling.

Brook Farm, a utopian community near Boston, attracted some of the country's top intellectuals and writers, including transcendentalists from nearby Concord. Its supporters included Bronson Alcott (father of author Louisa May Alcott) and the novelist Nathaniel Hawthorne. Founded in 1841, Brook Farm won considerable fame before dissolving six years later.

Most utopian communities were religiously oriented. Examples include the Ephrata Cloister in Pennsylvania, founded in 1732, and others established in the 1800s: the Oneida community in Putney, Vermont; the Zoar community in Ohio; and the Amana Colony in Iowa.

Far more numerous were the Shakers, an offshoot of the Quakers, who established their first community at New Lebanon, New York, in 1787. The Shakers strived to lead lives of productive labor, moral perfection, and equality among women and men. They are best known today for their simply styled, well-crafted furniture. The Shaker population peaked at about 6,000 in 1840. A few members remain in the twenty-first century.

VIEWING HISTORY Brook Farm, shown in the 1844 painting at top, was once a thriving utopian community that attracted prominent intellectuals. Now, the property has fallen into disuse (right).
Analyzing Visual Information
(a) What feelings does the painting evoke? (b) Why did most utopias fail?

Section 1   Assessment

READING COMPREHENSION

1. What idea did Protestant revivalist Charles Grandison Finney emphasize in his sermons?

2. What social conditions contributed to the growth of **transcendentalism,** the **temperance movement,** and **utopian communities?**

3. Why did Horace Mann favor free public education?

4. What impact did Dorothea Dix have on prison reform during the mid-1800s?

CRITICAL THINKING AND WRITING

5. **Summarizing Information** Choose a reformer mentioned in this section and outline his or her motives, specific goals, and any successes or failures.

6. **Writing to Inform** Write the outline and introduction for an essay in which you compare the temperance movement of the mid-1800s to specific organizations working today to end alcohol abuse and drunken driving.

Take It to the NET

Activity: Writing an Essay
Examine documents and sources from the temperance movement of the early 1800s. Write an essay evaluating the factors that helped the movement grow and the challenges the movement faced. Use the links provided in the *America: Pathways to the Present* area of the following Web site for help in completing this activity.
www.phschool.com

CAPTION ANSWERS

Viewing History (a) Sample answers: rustic tranquility, agricultural bounty, contentedness. (b) Disputes often erupted among the members.

RESOURCE DIRECTORY

Teaching Resources
Units 3/4 booklet
• Section 1 Quiz, p. 26
Guide to the Essentials
• Section 1 Summary, p. 47

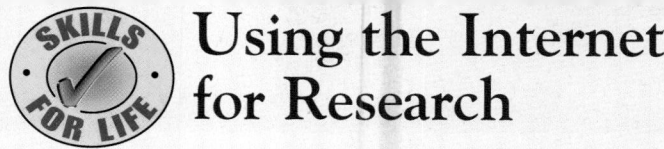

Using the Internet for Research

The Internet is a network of computers that links governments, organizations, and individuals around the world. The World Wide Web is one part of the Internet. Because the Internet has no central organization, finding the information you need can be difficult. To focus your search, you can use search engines—programs that gather and report information located on thousands of Web pages by subject.

You have just read about a number of reform movements of the 1800s. Some of these movements focused on the rights of women, African Americans, immigrant groups, and prisoners—topics still in the headlines today. The United States Department of Justice is just one arm of the government that provides information about these topics through the Internet.

LEARN THE SKILL

Use the following steps when you use the Internet for research:

1. **Plan the scope of your search.** Searching for a very broad subject can yield more results than you could possibly sift through. A vague topic may yield inappropriate listings. Try to state your research topic as a specific question. Then think of search terms that are likely to lead to answers to your question.

2. **Refine your search after you get your first set of results.** Many search engines offer an advanced search option that allows you to narrow your search. For example, you might make your search terms more specific: *"housing discrimination" AND "United States."*

3. **Navigate the sites.** Bookmark promising sites so that you can easily find them again. Once you find a site that meets your needs, explore its home page to determine how to find the specific information you need. Evaluate the site for reliability.

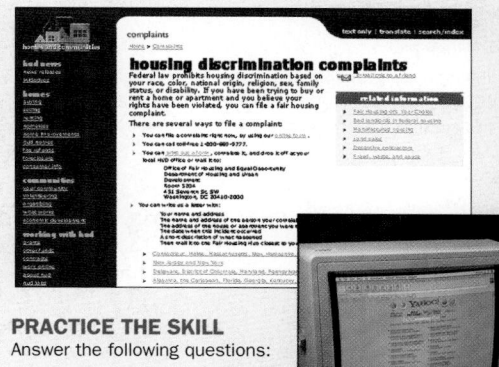

PRACTICE THE SKILL

Answer the following questions:

1. **(a)** Would a search for "discrimination" be likely to yield good results? Explain. **(b)** How might you narrow this topic? **(c)** How might you phrase it as a question?

2. **(a)** If your search engine directed you to the Department of Justice home page, do you think you could use it to find information on housing discrimination? Explain. **(b)** Does the site have its own search tool to help you narrow your search—for example, to *housing discrimination AND immigrants AND* the name of a specific state or city?

3. **(a)** Assuming you return to this site, will it provide links to other Web sites that might help you, such as the Department of Housing and Urban Development? **(b)** To whom does this site belong? **(c)** Do you think it is a reliable source? Explain.

APPLY THE SKILL

See the Chapter Review and Assessment for another opportunity to apply this skill.

USING THE INTERNET FOR RESEARCH

Focus Learn how to use the Internet to research a topic by planning the scope of research, refining a search, and navigating Web sites.

Instruct Explain to students that the Internet can be a tremendous support in researching topics in American history. Like any powerful tool, however, it is necessary for users to master certain skills to maximize its usefulness.

Likewise, it is important for students to recognize the relative strengths and weaknesses of certain Web sites. Some, usually from university or government sources, can be considered reliable resources. Others, posted by uncredentialed amateurs, may be less reliable. Students need to learn how to differentiate between these types of sources as they conduct research.

Just as important is learning the best methods for constructing and refining a search. A search that is too broad-based will yield a frustratingly overwhelming number of possible resources.

Extend See the Skills for Life activity in the Resource Directory below.

ANSWERS

PRACTICE THE SKILL

1. **(a)** This type of search is probably too general to yield good results. **(b)** By adding additional search terms such as "housing" and "United States." **(c)** What is the history of housing discrimination in the United States?

2. **(a)** Yes. It is a topic under "Frequently Asked Questions." You could also search "Discrimination" under "Information for Individuals and Communities." **(b)** Yes; it has a search button in the header.

3. **(a)** Yes, you could use the Search tool or the Site Map Tool. **(b)** This Web site belongs to the United States government. **(c)** Yes. Government Web sites can be considered reliable.

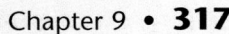

SECTION OBJECTIVES

1. Learn how the antislavery movement arose and grew.
2. Find out about contributions made by Frederick Douglass to the antislavery movement.
3. See what caused divisions to arise among abolitionists.
4. Discover how the Underground Railroad operated.
5. Understand how some Americans demonstrated resistance to abolitionism.

BELLRINGER

Warm-Up Activity Ask students for what act the biblical Moses is most remembered. How do they think the name "Black Moses" might apply to Harriet Tubman? Ask them to explain what they think the nickname means.

Activating Prior Knowledge Do students know the meaning of the word "abolitionist"? Ask them if they can identify the root word in the term.

READING STRATEGY

As students read, write down facts that support the various statements in the Main Idea above.

The Antislavery Movement

READING FOCUS

- How did the antislavery movement arise and grow?
- What contributions did Frederick Douglass make to the antislavery movement?
- What caused divisions to arise among abolitionists?
- How did the Underground Railroad operate?
- How did some Americans demonstrate resistance to abolitionism?

MAIN IDEA

A small but committed antislavery movement arose in the early- to mid-1800s. Leaders, both blacks and whites, used a variety of tactics to combat slavery, facing great dangers in their struggle.

KEY TERMS

abolitionist movement
emancipation
Underground Railroad
gag rule

TAKING NOTES

Copy the chart below. As you read, fill in the blanks with information on the antislavery movement.

Characteristics	Antislavery Movement
Key leaders	• William Garrison • •
Tactics	• • •
Divisions	• • •
Resistance	• • •

Setting the Scene From his modest secondhand clothing store near Boston harbor, a 44-year-old free black man named David Walker fought slavery in a unique way. He bought clothes from sailors returning to port. In the pockets of the pants and jackets, he placed copies of his 1829 antislavery pamphlet, *Appeal to the Colored Citizens of the World*. Then he resold the garments to other sailors departing for southern ports.

Walker's message began to circulate: White people should cooperate so that all Americans could "live in peace and happiness together." But if they would not listen, he warned, then "We must and shall be free . . . in spite of [white people]. . . . [F]or America is as much our country, as it is yours."

An Antislavery Movement Arises

In response to this and other antislavery activities, enraged southern states banned antislavery publications and made it illegal to teach slaves to read. Yet fighters in the **abolitionist movement,** the movement to end slavery, continued their work in the face of southern opposition and even personal danger. In 1830, the year after he published his essay, Walker died in the streets of Boston, possibly poisoned to death.

Walker became one of the heroes of the abolitionist movement. Started by a group of free African Americans and whites, the movement gained momentum in the 1830s. The debate over ending slavery created steadily increasing tensions between the North and the South.

The Roots of Abolitionism The movement against slavery did not spring up overnight. Even during colonial times, a few Americans in both the North and

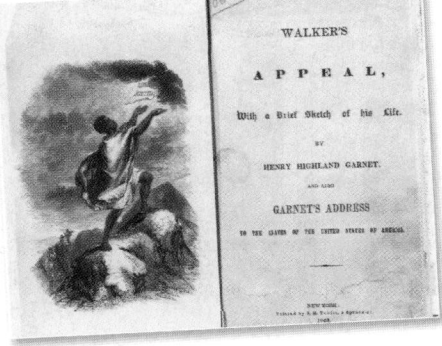

David Walker slipped this pamphlet into the pockets of clothing he sold in Boston to sailors, thus spreading his antislavery message far and wide.

RESOURCE DIRECTORY

Teaching Resources
Guided Reading and Review booklet, p. 38
Learning with Documents booklet (Visual Learning Activity) *Countrymen in Chains,* p. 48

Other Print Resources
Nystrom *Atlas of Our Country* *A Divided Nation,* pp. 26–27.

Technology
Section Reading Support Transparencies
Guided Reading Audiotapes (English/Spanish), Ch. 9
Student Edition on Audio CD, Ch. 9
Prentice Hall Presentation Pro CD-ROM, Ch. 9
Companion Web site, www.phschool.com

the South had spoken out against slavery. In addition, some slaves had petitioned colonial legislatures for their freedom—without success.

The earliest known antislavery protest came from the Mennonites, a Christian sect of German immigrants, who declared in 1688:

> 66 There is a saying, that we should do to all men like as we will be done ourselves; making no difference of what generation, descent, or colour they are. And those who steal or rob men, and those who buy or purchase them, are they not all alike? 99
>
> —Resolutions of Germantown Mennonites, 1688

During the late 1700s, several antislavery societies formed in the North, while abolitionist newspapers appeared in both the North and the South. From 1777 to 1804, every state north of Maryland passed laws that gradually abolished slavery. The legal importing of slaves to the United States also ended in 1808.

At first, most antislavery activists favored a moderate approach. One of the most important of these early abolitionists was a Quaker named Benjamin Lundy. In 1821, Lundy founded an antislavery newspaper in Ohio called *The Genius of Universal Emancipation*. The newspaper called for a gradual program for the **emancipation,** or freeing, of enslaved persons. He favored stopping the spread of slavery to new states and ending the slave trade within the United States as first steps toward full emancipation.

Free blacks had actively opposed slavery long before white reformers became involved in the abolitionist movement. By the end of the 1820s, nearly 50 African American antislavery groups had formed throughout the nation.

The Colonization of Liberia In the early 1800s, some abolitionists favored colonization, a program to send free blacks and emancipated slaves to Africa. Convinced that African Americans would never receive equal treatment in American society, these antislavery advocates founded the American Colonization Society in 1816. To pursue their plan of colonization, the society established the West African country of Liberia (its name taken from *liberty*) in 1822. A white American, Jehudi Ashmun, founded the new refuge. In six years, Ashmun created a trading state with a government and a set of laws. Liberia's first black governor was Joseph Jenkins Roberts, a free black man born in Virginia in 1809.

White supporters of colonization did not all believe in racial equality. Many were eager to rid the United States of both slavery and African Americans. Some southern planters backed colonization as a way to eliminate the threat of free blacks who might encourage slaves to revolt.

The colonization plan offended most African Americans. They considered themselves and their children to be as American as any white people. They wanted to improve their lives in their homeland, not on a faraway continent they had never seen.

Such opposition doomed colonization to failure. By 1831, only about 1,400 free blacks and former slaves had migrated to Liberia. By that time, both

In this illustration, two white children hand an antislavery petition to a gentleman standing beside a pleading slave in chains.

From the Archives of
American Heritage®

Out of Africa!

On December 1, 1822, in what is now Monrovia, Liberia, three dozen former American slaves desperately fought off an armed assault by 1,000 native-born Africans determined to reclaim their land. In 1821, the American Colonization Society had forced a local king at gunpoint to deed them a 130-mile strip of coast-land in return for a few cartloads of hardware and household goods (including place settings for twelve, complete with wineglasses). Ever since, his subjects had been wait-ing for a chance to expel the inter-lopers. When fever had killed or weakened a sufficient number, they struck. Some of the warriors carried spears. Others bore large-caliber muskets, which they loaded with foot-long copper and iron slugs for close-range use. But the settlers had artillery, which made up for their numerical disadvantage. Despite repeated attacks, the colony contin-ued for three more decades until the Civil War made it irrelevant. By that time a mere 15,000 blacks had been resettled. Source: Frederick D. Schwarz, "The Time Machine," *American Heritage®* magazine, December, 1997.

Free and Enslaved Black Population, 1820–1860

Number of persons (in millions)

Year	Free	Enslaved
1820		1.5
1830		2.0
1840		2.4
1850		3.2
1860		4.0

SOURCE: *Historical Statistics of the United States, Colonial Times to 1970*

INTERPRETING GRAPHS
The population of both free and enslaved African Americans rose during the first half of the 1800s. **Analyzing Visual Information** Which population rose more rapidly?

black and white abolitionists were adopting a more aggressive tone in their fight against slavery.

Radical Abolitionism One of the most famous of the radi-cal abolitionists was a white Bostonian named William Lloyd Garrison. In 1831, Garrison began publishing *The Liberator,* an antislavery newspaper supported largely by free African Americans. Garrison denounced moderation in the fight against slavery:

❝ *I do not wish to think, or speak, or write, with modera-tion. . . . I am in earnest—I will not equivocate—I will not excuse—I will not retreat a single inch—AND I WILL BE HEARD.* ❞
—William Lloyd Garrison, in the first issue of *The Liberator,* 1831

In 1833, with the support of both white and African American abolitionists, Garrison founded the American Anti-Slavery Society. As the decade progressed, more middle-class white Northerners began to support the immediate end of slav-ery. By 1835, the American Anti-Slavery Society had some 1,000 local chapters with roughly 150,000 members. With agents traveling throughout the North, the society distributed more than one million antislavery pamphlets a year.

Frederick Douglass

One of the most popular speakers and a key leader of the American Anti-Slavery Society was a former slave, Frederick Douglass. (See American Biography on the following page.) A prominent publisher and brilliant writer, Douglass's accom-plishments are all the more impressive considering how he obtained his education.

The son of a white father whom he did not know and a slave mother from whom he was separated as an infant, Douglass was raised by his grandmother. At age 8 he was sent to Baltimore as a house slave. Although Maryland law pro-hibited the education of slaves, his new owner's wife disregarded the law and

VIEWING HISTORY Abolition-ist Frederick Douglass is shown here speaking at an antislavery meeting. **Formulating Questions** *Write down four or five questions you might have wanted to ask Douglass if you had attended this meeting.*

---

tutored the intelligent young boy. After the owner forbade his wife to teach Douglass, he taught himself, getting help from white children.

Cruel experiences under slavery toughened Douglass's will and would later make him the nation's most influential African American abolitionist. At 17, he was considered unruly, so he was sent to a "slave breaker," a man skilled in punishing slaves to make them passive and cooperative. Subjected to whippings and backbreaking labor for endless hours and days, Douglass did indeed become broken in body and spirit. But after one particularly brutal beating, Douglass reached what he called a "turning point" in his life. He fought back, attacking the slave-breaker with such ferocity that the man never again laid a whip to him. This, Douglass said later, was the story of "how a man became a slave and a slave became a man."

In 1838, the 21-year-old Douglass, working in a ship-yard, disguised himself as a sailor and escaped to New Bedford, Massachusetts. Asked to describe his experiences as a slave to an antislavery convention in 1841, Douglass spoke, unprepared, with passion and eloquence. The event launched Douglass's career with the American Anti-Slavery Society. He wrote and spoke publicly, enduring verbal and physical threats from opponents of abolition.

Douglass also faced skeptics who refused to believe that a slave could be such an articulate spokesperson. This skepticism prompted Douglass to publish his autobiography, *Life and Times of Frederick Douglass*. The book named his former master, so to avoid capture, Douglass went to Europe to continue raising support for the abolitionist movement.

While abroad, Douglass also raised the money to purchase his freedom. He then started an abolitionist newspaper, the *North Star*, which he published from 1847 to 1860. Although Douglass opposed the use of violence, he also believed that slavery should be fought with deeds as well as words:

> 66 They who profess to favor freedom, and yet deprecate [criticize] agitation, are men who want crops without plowing up the ground, they want rain without thunder and lightning. They want the ocean without the awful roar of its many waters. 99
>
> —Frederick Douglass

Divisions Among Abolitionists

While abolitionists shared a common goal, they came from diverse backgrounds and favored a variety of tactics. It is not surprising, therefore, that divisions appeared within the antislavery movement.

Divisions over women's participation One of the first splits occurred over women's participation in the American Anti-Slavery Society. At the time, Americans in general did not approve of women's involvement in political gatherings. When Garrison insisted that female abolitionists be allowed to speak at antislavery meetings, some members resigned in protest.

Two of the most prominent women speakers were Sarah and Angelina Grimké, white sisters from South Carolina who moved north, became Quakers, and devoted their lives to abolitionism. In 1836, Angelina's pamphlet, *An Appeal to the Christian Women of the South,* and Sarah's *Epistle to the Clergy of*

BIOGRAPHY

Frederick Douglass • 1817–1895

The brilliant abolitionist writer and speaker Frederick Douglass was born Frederick Augustus Washington Bailey in Maryland, a slave state, in 1817. First a house slave and then a field hand, Douglass endured abuse that steeled his determination to escape his servitude. In 1838, at age 21, Douglass fled to New Bedford, Massachusetts, where he changed his name from Bailey to Douglass to avoid capture. He soon began lifelong work as an agent of the American Anti-Slavery Society. His autobiography, *Life and Times of Frederick Douglass*, sold thousands of copies.

During the Civil War, Douglass served as an advisor to President Abraham Lincoln. After the war, he fought for the rights of freed slaves, the poor, and women until he died in 1895.

William Lloyd Garrison, an uncompromising abolitionist, grew increasingly stern in his statements. In 1844 he proposed the peaceful secession of the North from the slaveholding states of the South.

the Southern States prompted southern officials to ban and burn the publications.

In the 1840s, a powerful crusader joined the abolitionist cause: Sojourner Truth. Truth was born Isabella Baumfree in Ulster County, New York, in 1797. Freed from slavery in 1827, she found work as a domestic servant in New York City and soon became involved in various religious and reform movements. In 1843, she took the name Sojourner Truth because she believed her life's mission was to sojourn, or "travel up and down the land," preaching the truth about God at revival meetings. That same year she visited a utopian community in Northampton, Massachusetts, where she learned of the abolition movement and took up the cause.

Divisions over race Racial tensions further divided the movement. For African Americans, the movement to end slavery had a personal dimension and an urgency that many white people could never fully understand. In addition, some black reformers felt that white abolitionists regarded them as inferior.

This treatment insulted Martin Delany, an abolitionist who was also one of the first African American students to graduate from Harvard Medical School. In the 1840s, Delany founded a highly respected newspaper, the *Mystery,* and worked closely with Frederick Douglass. A supporter of colonization and a frequent critic of white abolitionists, Delany noted:

> 66 We find ourselves occupying the very same position in relation to our Anti-Slavery friends, as we do in relation to the pro-slavery part of the community—a mere secondary, underling position. 99
> —Dr. Martin Delany, African American abolitionist

Tensions such as these helped lead Frederick Douglass to break with Garrison in 1847 and found, with Delany, his antislavery newspaper, the *North Star.*

Divisions over tactics A third source of tension among abolitionists was political action. Garrison believed that the Constitution supported slavery. Thus, he reasoned, attempting to win emancipation by passing new laws would be pointless, since any such laws would be unconstitutional.

Abolitionists who disagreed, such as Arthur and Lewis Tappan, broke with Garrison to follow a course of political action. Together with former slaveowner and abolitionist James Birney, the Tappans formed the Liberty Party in 1840. The Liberty Party received only a fraction of the presidential vote in 1840 and in 1844. Yet it drew off enough support from the Whig Party in such key states as Ohio and New York to give the 1844 election to James K. Polk, a Democrat.

The Underground Railroad

Some abolitionists insisted on using only legal methods, such as protest and political action. But with tremendous human suffering going on, other people could not wait for long-term legal strategies to work. They attacked slavery in every way they could, legal and illegal.

A Dangerous Operation Risking arrest, and sometimes risking their lives, abolitionists created the **Underground Railroad,** a network of escape routes that provided protection and transportation for slaves fleeing north to freedom. The term *railroad* referred to the paths that Africans Americans traveled, either on foot or in wagons, across the North-South border and finally into Canada, where slave-hunters could not go.

Underground meant that the operation was carried out in secret, usually on dark nights in deep woods. Men and women known as conductors acted as guides. They opened their homes to the fugitives and gave them money, supplies, and medical attention. Historians' estimates on the number of slaves rescued vary widely, from about 40,000 to 100,000.

A Courageous Leader: Harriet Tubman African Americans, some with friends and family still enslaved, made up the majority of the conductors. By far the most famous was a courageous former slave named Harriet Tubman.

Tubman herself escaped from a plantation in Maryland in 1849 and fled north on the Underground Railroad. Remarkably, she returned the next year to rescue family members and lead them to safety. Thereafter, she made frequent trips to the South, rescuing more than 300 slaves and gaining the nickname "the Black Moses." (The name refers to the Bible story of the prophet Moses leading Jewish slaves out of captivity in Egypt.)

The River Route On a map, the routes of the Underground Railroad look like a tangled clump of lines. (See the map on page 309.) One of those pathways came from the West, where the Mississippi River valley offered a natural escape route. Some slaves managed to get a ticket for riverboat passage northward. If they were lucky, they could reach the Underground Railroad routes that started in western Illinois.

The Mississippi River route was dangerous, however. Slave hunters, who often received generous payments for their work, stalked the riverboat towns and boarded the ships looking for slaves on the run.

Through the Eastern Swamps The East Coast, by contrast, had a physical feature that offered protection from human pursuers, but posed serious natural dangers. This feature was the string of low-lying swamps stretching along the Atlantic Coast from southern Georgia to southern Virginia. Fugitives who traveled north through the swamps could link up with one of the eastern Underground Railroad routes to Canada, shown on the map. The travelers faced hazards, however, such as poisonous snakes and disease-bearing mosquitoes.

The Mountain Route The physical feature that most influenced the choice of a route was the Appalachian Mountains. The mountain chain, extending from northern Georgia into Pennsylvania, has narrow, steep-sided valleys separated by forested ridges.

The Appalachians served as an escape route for two reasons. First, the forests and limestone caves sheltered fugitives as they avoided capture on their way north. Second, the Appalachians acted as a barrier for western runaways, leading them northward into a region of intense Underground Railroad activity.

A Refuge for Runaways The center of Underground Railroad activity included Ohio and parts of two states that border it, Indiana and Pennsylvania. This region shared a long boundary with two slave states, Virginia and Kentucky.

Focus on GEOGRAPHY

A Path to Freedom African Americans escaping slavery knew that freedom lay to the north, in the free northern states or in Canada. With no maps to guide them, they followed the North Star. More detailed instructions came in the form of a song passed secretly among some slaves, called "Follow the Drinking Gourd":

"When the sun comes back
    and the first quail calls,
Follow the Drinking Gourd.
For the old man is waiting
    for to carry you to freedom,
If you follow the Drinking Gourd. . . ."

The "Drinking Gourd" is the Big Dipper, which points to the North Star. The first line of the song tells slaves to leave in the winter, when the sun is higher in the sky and quail have migrated to the South. Departing in the winter would give them time to reach the Ohio River by the following winter and cross it on foot over the ice. The "old man" is a man named Peg Leg Joe, who taught slaves the escape route described in the song.

VIEWING HISTORY In this scene depicting the Underground Railroad, weary fugitive slaves disembark from boats and are whisked into waiting carriages for the next leg of their journey to freedom. **Analyzing Visual Information** *What impressions or feelings do you think this picture evokes?*

ACTIVITY
Connecting with Citizenship

Tell students to imagine that they are fugitive slaves. Have them write a poem or song that expresses their experience. Suggest that students think about how they feel toward those who are helping them escape. Have students present their finished work to the rest of the class. **(Musical/Rhythmic)**

READING CHECK

A network of escape routes provided protection and transportation for slaves fleeing north. Men and women known as conductors acted as guides, opening their homes to the fugitives and giving them money, supplies, and medical attention while helping to shepherd them to freedom.

READING CHECK
How did the Underground Railroad operate?

Once the fugitives crossed into Ohio, they found themselves in a region with some measure of safety. Southern Ohio was home to Quakers and others who volunteered their houses as depots, or stations. There, too, lived free blacks as well as whites who had left the South because they opposed slavery. Some white people in the northern and eastern parts of Ohio were antislavery advocates who had resettled from New England. "It is evident," wrote one slave owner, "that there exist some eighteen or nineteen thoroughly organized thoroughfares through the State of Ohio for the transportation of runaway and stolen slaves." Nevertheless, most white Ohioans held deep hostility toward blacks.

Southern Illinois, on the other hand, was an even more dangerous region for fugitives. Settled largely by Southerners, this region remained proslavery. Abolitionists in that area often provided tickets for fugitives on a real railroad, the Illinois Central, for transit to Chicago. From there they continued on toward Canada, often on foot, following the North Star as it marked their route to freedom. (See Focus on Geography, page 323.)

Meanwhile, enraged slave owners offered a $40,000 reward for the capture of Harriet Tubman. Yet she continued. Armed with devout faith—and a handy revolver—she required strict discipline among her escapees, even threatening those who wavered. Tubman later boasted: "I never run my train off the track, and I never lost a passenger."

Resistance to Abolitionism

The activities of the Underground Railroad generated a great deal of publicity and sympathy. Yet the abolition movement as a whole did not receive widespread support. In fact, it provoked intense opposition in both the North and the South.

Opposition in the North In the decades before the Civil War, most white Americans viewed abolitionism as a radical idea, even in the North. Northern merchants, for example, worried that the antislavery movement would further sour relations between the North and South, harming trade between the two regions. White workers and labor leaders feared competition from escaped slaves willing to work for lower wages. Most Northerners, including some who opposed slavery, did not want African Americans living in their communities. They viewed blacks as socially inferior to whites.

324 Chapter 9 • *Religion and Reform*

CAPTION ANSWERS

Viewing History Sample answers: fear, tension, relief, danger, darkness, haste.

RESOURCE DIRECTORY

Teaching Resources
Units 3/4 booklet
• Section 2 Quiz, p. 27
Guide to the Essentials
• Section 2 Summary, p. 48

Opposition to the abolitionists eventually boiled over into violence. At public events on abolition, people hurled stones and rotten eggs at the speakers or tried to drown them out with horns and drums. In 1835, an angry Boston mob assaulted William Lloyd Garrison and paraded him around the city with a rope around his neck. A new hall built by abolitionists in Philadelphia was burned down, as were homes of black residents.

The most brutal act occurred in Alton, Illinois, where Elijah P. Lovejoy edited the *St. Louis Observer,* a weekly Presbyterian newspaper. In his editorials, Lovejoy denounced slavery and called for gradual emancipation. Opponents repeatedly destroyed his printing presses, but each time Lovejoy resumed publication. On the night of November 7, 1837, rioters again attacked the building. Lovejoy, trying to defend it, was shot and killed.

Opposition in the South   Most Southerners were outraged by the criticisms that the antislavery movement leveled at slavery. Attacks by northern abolitionists such as Garrison, together with Nat Turner's 1831 slave rebellion, made many Southerners even more determined to defend slavery. During the 1830s, it became increasingly dangerous and rare for Southerners to speak out in favor of freeing the slaves.

Public officials in the South also joined in the battle against abolitionism. Southern postmasters, for example, refused to deliver abolitionist literature. In 1836, moreover, Southerners in Congress succeeded in passing what Northerners called the **gag rule.** It prohibited antislavery petitions from being read or acted upon in the House for the next eight years. Abolitionists pointed to the gag rule as proof that slavery threatened the rights of all Americans, white as well as black.

VIEWING HISTORY A white mob destroys the printing press of abolitionist Elijah Lovejoy in Alton, Illinois, on November 7, 1837. **Recognizing Bias** *Why did many whites in the North oppose the abolitionist movement?*

Section 2 Assessment

READING COMPREHENSION

1. What tactics did the **abolitionist movement** use to achieve the **emancipation** of slaves?

2. Name four abolitionist leaders and describe their contributions to the movement.

3. Why did divisions emerge within the abolitionist movement?

4. What groups resisted the efforts of abolitionists, and what types of resistance did they carry out?

CRITICAL THINKING AND WRITING

5. **Identifying Central Issues** Explain why the passage of the gag rule was an extraordinary and historically significant act by Congress.

6. **Writing to Inform** Describe how geography (a) affected the course of the Underground Railroad and (b) presented challenges to travelers along the routes.

Take It to the NET

Activity: Recreating History
Find out what escaping slaves took with them on the Underground Railroad. Prepare a list of items you would have taken on that journey. Remember, you could only take what you could carry long distances. Use the links provided in the *America: Pathways to the Present* area of the following Web site for help in completing this activity.
www.phschool.com

Chapter 9 • Section 2   325

CUSTOMIZE FOR ...

ESL

Have students reread the section "Opposition in the South" on this page. Then have students explain the meaning of the word "gag" and why "gag rule" was an appropriate term for the rule passed in the Congress.

Reading Comprehension

1. Protest, political action, publishing, forming groups and societies, developing a colonization program, the Underground Railroad.

2. William Lloyd Garrison: published a newspaper, denounced moderation, founded American Anti-Slavery Society; Frederick Douglass: great speaker and writer, started newspaper, opposed violence; Grimké sisters: involved women by speaking and writing pamphlets; Harriet Tubman: Herself an escaped slave, Tubman led many other slaves to freedom.

3. Leaders disagreed over whether or not to employ illegal tactics, such as helping slaves to escape, and some male members disagreed over whether or not to allow women to play prominent roles in the movement.

4. Northern merchants, white workers and labor leaders who feared competition, most southerners, and public officials in the South; held violent demonstrations, murdered Lovejoy, and passed the gag rule.

Critical Thinking and Writing

5. It was a broad act that prevented any action in Congress on antislavery for a period of eight years.

6. (a) The Underground Railroad led to safety in Canada. The Mississippi River provided a natural escape route North; the swamps of the Atlantic Coast allowed slaves to hide; the Appalachian Mountains provided shelter for fugitives. (b) The Mississippi River was dangerous because slave hunters stalked the riverboat towns; the swamps held dangers such as poisonous snakes; mountains created a challenging barrier.

Take It to the NET

Lists will vary, but may include food, water, clothes or a disguise.

CAPTION ANSWERS

Viewing History Some northern white merchants feared a disruption of North-South trade. Some white workers feared competition from freed slaves. Other white northerners felt that African Americans were inferior to them.

SECTION OBJECTIVES

1. Find out what private roles women were expected to fulfill in the early 1800s.
2. Learn about the public roles gradually adopted by some women.
3. Discover the significance of the Seneca Falls Convention.

BELLRINGER

Warm-Up Activity Have students speculate on how a woman of the early 1800s would react if she were somehow transported to the present day. Which aspects of society might she enjoy? Which would she dislike?

Activating Prior Knowledge Poll students to see if they know when women got the right to vote. Ask if they know what the rights of women were in general in the mid-nineteenth century.

READING STRATEGY

Have students make a list of all the headings in the text of this section. As they read, have them write down one important fact under each heading.

ACTIVITY
Connecting with Citizenship

The public and private spheres were clearly demarcated in the early 1800s. Women in particular were excluded from participating in the public sphere. To help students understand the concept of cultural spheres, ask students of the same gender to sit in circle groupings. Have each "sphere" list five activities in which they participate but the members of the other "sphere" do not. (**Logical/Mathematical; Verbal/Linguistic**)

The Movement for Women's Rights

READING FOCUS
- What private roles were women expected to fulfill in the early 1800s?
- What public roles did some women gradually adopt?
- What is the significance of the Seneca Falls Convention?

MAIN IDEA
Although women were expected to devote their energies to home and family in the early 1800s, some women organized a women's rights movement in the 1840s.

KEY TERMS
Seneca Falls Convention
suffrage

TAKING NOTES
Copy the chart below. As you read, fill in information about restrictions women faced and how they began to challenge those limits.

```
          Women's Roles in the Early 1800s

  Limits on Freedoms              Fight for Freedoms
  • Women expected to             •
    remain in the home            •
  •                               •
  •                               •
                                  •
```

Setting the Scene Catharine Beecher had the spirit of reform in her blood. Daughter of the revivalist Lyman Beecher, Catharine, like her talented siblings, identified a need in society and set about fulfilling it. Like Emerson and Thoreau, Beecher overcame personal tragedy to lead a productive life. In 1822, her fiancé drowned at sea. Beecher never married. Instead she dedicated herself to teaching, writing, and helping.

Private Roles for Women

In the new age of urbanization and industrialization, Beecher was one of many reformers to examine the role of women in American society. Like other reformers, she believed that women were central to the success of a strong, democratic nation. However, while other women of her time were beginning to demand new rights and freedoms, Catharine Beecher took a traditional stand. She advised American women on how to reform society from within their roles in the home.

Cultural and Legal Limits on Women As industrialization and urbanization took hold in the United States, women, especially in the North, felt the impact. Many poorer women took jobs in factories. Women in more comfortable households, however, were freed from chores such as growing their own food and making clothes, as more timesaving products appeared on store shelves.

How, then, should these women spend their energies? Most people believed that women should remain in the home. Middle-class women were expected to raise and educate their children, entertain guests, serve their husbands, do community service, and engage in at-home activities such as needlework and quilting.

In this division of labor, men engaged in public activities such as politics, law, and public speaking. Most people, traditionally minded or not, would have

A mother and son pose for an 1834 portrait. Writer Catharine Beecher spoke for most of society when she declared that women should stay at home and raise their children to be well-educated, moral citizens.

326 Chapter 9 • *Religion and Reform*

RESOURCE DIRECTORY

Teaching Resources
Guided Reading and Review booklet, p. 39

Technology
Section Reading Support Transparencies

been shocked at the idea of American women doing these things. A lady simply did not behave in this way. Even Dorothea Dix, the champion of prison reform, did not personally present her research on prison conditions to state legislatures. She had to rely on men to make these public presentations.

Although some women defied these cultural limits, they still faced strict legal restrictions. For example, federal and state laws did not give women the right to vote. In most states, married women could not own property or make a will. Despite the increasing number of women working outside the home, women generally were not allowed to keep the money they earned. Instead they had to turn it over to a husband or father.

Reform at Home   Catharine Beecher sought reform within the rules of her time and culture. She tried to win respect for women's contributions as wives, mothers, and teachers.

Just a year after her fiancé died, Catharine and her sister Mary Beecher established the Hartford Female Seminary. Teaching was considered a proper occupation for a young woman because it was an extension of the role of mother.

While teaching, Catharine Beecher also started writing about and lobbying for the education of women. She published several books that earned her a national reputation.

Beecher's most popular and important work was *A Treatise on Domestic Economy*. It offered practical advice and household tips and inspired women to help build a strong American society.

"The success of democratic institutions . . . ," she wrote, "depends upon the intellectual and moral character of the mass of the people." In particular, "the formation of the moral and intellectual character of the young is committed mainly to the female hand." Here, then, was the reason why women were so critically important to the nation's welfare:

> ❝ The mother forms the character of the future man; . . . the wife sways the heart, whose energies may turn for good or for evil the destinies of a nation. Let the women of a country be made virtuous and intelligent, and the men will certainly be the same. The proper education of a man decides the welfare of an individual; but educate a woman, and the interests of a whole family are secured. ❞
> —Catharine Beecher, *A Treatise on Domestic Economy*, 1841

Reformist writer Catharine Beecher

Public Roles for Women

Even as Beecher instructed women in their private roles, a restlessness was stirring among a small number of American women. As more women became educated, they grew eager to apply their knowledge and skills beyond the home. Some also became increasingly dissatisfied with the laws and attitudes that prohibited them from doing so.

Fighting for Reform   The religious revivals and reform movements of the early 1800s heightened women's sense of their potential and power. For some, participation in a reform movement was a first, satisfying taste of the world outside the family. Women played a prominent role in nearly every avenue of reform, from temperance to abolition. They marched in parades to support their causes. They participated in economic boycotts. Some even gave lectures at public assemblies.

READING CHECK
Why did Catharine Beecher want women to get an education?

LESSON PLAN

Focus   Women in the early 1800s were expected to dedicate themselves to home and family. Many women, however, were not content with this role. Ask students why people began questioning society's expectations.

Instruct   Explain that radical reform often comes about through a series of changes. Entrenched attitudes such as discrimination are slowly broken down over time as a result of many people's actions. Discuss how some of Catharine Beecher's peers might have considered her views "radical." Compare her views to those of Elizabeth Cady Stanton. In what ways do Stanton's views represent a further development of Beecher's ideas?

Assess/Reteach   Ask students to imagine what it would have been like to be a women's rights advocate in the mid-nineteenth century. What types of attitudes would she have had to break through? Whom might she have had to defy, in order to speak her mind?

READING CHECK
Because in Beecher's view, the development of the morals and intellect of the young, and of the family as a whole, was mainly the responsibility of women, thus women needed to be educated.

CUSTOMIZE FOR ...

Gifted and Talented

Catharine Beecher believed that the role of women in the home was crucial to the nation's welfare. Have students discuss how feminists might have responded to this argument.

This antislavery emblem made many white abolitionist women begin thinking about women's rights.

Through these activities, many northern middle-class women became more conscious of their inferior position in American society. At the same time, they formed strong intellectual and emotional ties with other women in similar positions.

Fighting for Abolition   The battle to end slavery was the primary means by which women entered the public world of politics. By the 1840s, some women were protesting their second-class position within both the antislavery movement and society in general.

Women who participated in the abolition movement saw parallels between the plight of enslaved African Americans and the status of women. Neither group could vote or hold office, for instance, and both were denied the full rights of American citizens.

The fight to end slavery also provided women with a political platform from which they could assert power over public opinion. For example, one famous abolitionist and writer, South Carolina–born Angelina Grimké, demanded that the women of the South fight slavery:

> 66 *If you really suppose you can do nothing to overthrow slavery, you are greatly mistaken. . . . You can read. . . . You can pray. . . . You can speak. . . . You can act.* 99
>
> —Abolitionist Angelina Grimké, 1836

Black women such as Sojourner Truth and white women such as the Grimké sisters began to attend meetings, gather petitions, give public talks, and write pamphlets and books. Abolitionist Lydia Child served on the executive committee of the American Anti-Slavery Society. In 1841, she became editor of the group's publication, the *National Anti-Slavery Standard*.

Female writers had an enormous influence on public opinion about slavery. Harriet Beecher Stowe, Catharine Beecher's sister, opened the eyes of many Northerners with her 1852 abolitionist novel *Uncle Tom's Cabin*. Harriet Ann Jacobs authored the 1861 book *Incidents in the Life of a Slave Girl*. Sojourner Truth could not read or write, but she dictated her experiences to an author to produce *The Narrative of Sojourner Truth*. In 1869, *Scenes in the Life of Harriet Tubman* detailed Tubman's dangerous activities with the Underground Railroad.

VIEWING HISTORY In this watercolor from the early 1800s, students learn geography at a seminary for young women. More such institutions for women began to appear by mid-century. **Synthesizing Information** *What opposition do you think women faced when they wanted to get an education?*

328   Chapter 9 • *Religion and Reform*

Men's Opposition   Many male abolitionists were horrified rather than pleased with women's role in the movement. Some men found it distasteful for women to take part in public meetings. Although many people believed that women were more virtuous than men, they felt that women should use their influence only within their families.

A Women's Rights Movement   In 1840, many American abolitionists attended the first World Anti-Slavery Convention in London, England. The attendees included female delegates from the American Anti-Slavery Society. Despite American women's achievements and devotion to the cause, the convention, after much debate, voted to prohibit women from participating. The action angered and humiliated the women. Two of the American delegates later turned their anger into action.

Born in 1793, Lucretia Mott started teaching at age 15, earning only half the wages of a male teacher. Mott became a Quaker minister in 1821. She and her husband became abolitionists and sheltered fugitive slaves in their home.

Elizabeth Cady Stanton was the daughter of a United States congressman who later became a judge on the New York Supreme Court. She studied law in her father's office and became aware of the legal limitations placed on women. She later married an abolitionist lawyer.

Mott and Stanton both attended the 1840 antislavery convention and resented being prevented from speaking at it. Eight years later, the women organized a convention on women's rights.

The Seneca Falls Convention

The women's rights meeting took place in Stanton's hometown of Seneca Falls, New York, in July 1848. The **Seneca Falls Convention** was the first women's rights convention in United States history.

Women's Rights

The organizers of the Seneca Falls Convention knew they were making history. But they could not have envisioned the legacy they would pass on to future generations of women.

1848 First women's rights convention is held at Seneca Falls, N.Y.
1869 Wyoming Territory grants women full suffrage.
1879 Belva Lockwood becomes the first woman to practice law before the United States Supreme Court.
1920 On August 26, the Nineteenth Amendment becomes law, giving women the right to vote.
1972 Congress passes the Equal Rights Amendment, but the ratification effort fails.
1981 Sandra Day O'Connor is the first woman to become a member of the Supreme Court.
2001 Condoleezza Rice (left) is the first woman to become National Security Advisor. She is a member of the President's inner circle and holds one of the nation's most influential positions.

? What was the legacy of the Seneca Falls Convention?

Chapter 9 • Section 3   **329**

Resolutions

Resolved, That all laws which prevent women from occupying such a station in society as her conscience shall dictate, or which place her in a position inferior to that of man, are contrary to the great precept of nature, and therefore of no force or authority.

Resolved, That woman is man's equal—was intended to be so by the Creator, and the highest good of the race demands that she should be recognized as such...

...solved, That it is the duty of the women of this country to secure to themselves their sacred right to the elective franchise......

...lved, That the speedy success of our cause depends upon the zealous and untiring efforts of both men and women for the overthrow of ...nopoly of the pulpit and for the securing to women an equal participation with men in the various trades, professions and commerce.

...lved, therefore, That, being invested by the Creator with the same capabilities and the same consciousness of responsibility for their exercise, ...monstrate the right and duty of woman, equally with man, to promote every righteous cause by every righteous means; and especially in ...to the great subjects of morals and religion, it is self-evidently her right to participate with her brother in teaching them, both in private and ...lic, by writing and by speaking, by any instrumentalities proper to be used, and in any assemblies proper to be held; and this being a self-evident ...growing out of the divinely implanted principles of human nature, any custom or authority adverse to it, whether modern or wearing the hoary ...tion of antiquity, is to be regarded as a self-evident falsehood, and at war with mankind.

ACTIVITY

Connecting with Science and Technology

As Elizabeth Blackwell and Maria Mitchell pioneered change in the world of medicine and science, they offered new perspectives simply because they were women. Have students research other nineteenth-century women who made significant contributions to science and technology. Suggest that students share their findings in an oral presentation. **(Verbal/Linguistic)**

BACKGROUND

Biography

Elizabeth Blackwell (1821–1910) endured numerous tests of her personal strength and commitment on the road to becoming a doctor. After being rejected by 29 medical schools, Blackwell was finally accepted by Geneva Medical College in New York. Upon arrival, she faced isolation and hostility from her male peers. Despite the lack of support, Blackwell graduated at the head of her class. She was one of the first physicians to campaign for personal hygiene for doctors as a way of reducing the spread of infection. Blackwell was also one of the first physicians to advocate preventive medicine.

VIEWING HISTORY Elizabeth Cady Stanton (above) wrote the Declaration of Sentiments, part of which is shown in the photograph at top right. **Drawing Conclusions** Do you think it was wise of Stanton to insist on a controversial suffrage resolution at such a young stage in the movement? Why or why not?

Focus on GOVERNMENT

Suffrage Suffrage refers to the right to vote.

The Historical Context The Seneca Falls Declaration of Sentiments of 1848 included a resolution calling on women to fight for "their sacred right to the elective franchise," or right to vote. Under the Constitution, each state set its own voting requirements and thus could deny suffrage to any group it chose, such as women or African Americans.

The Concept Today Suffrage in the United States has steadily broadened. Constitutional amendments have guaranteed the vote to African Americans (Fifteenth Amendment, ratified 1870), women (Nineteenth Amendment, ratified 1920), and citizens age 18 or older (Twenty-sixth Amendment, ratified 1971).

At the convention, Stanton herself wrote and presented a historic set of resolutions called a Declaration of Sentiments. The document echoed the language of the Declaration of Independence:

KEY DOCUMENTS ❝ *The history of mankind is a history of repeated injuries and usurpations [seizure of power] on the part of man toward woman, . . . [to establish] absolute tyranny over her. . . . [B]ecause women do feel themselves aggrieved, oppressed, and fraudulently deprived of their most sacred rights, we insist that they have immediate admission to all the rights and privileges which belong to them as citizens of the United States.* ❞

—Elizabeth Cady Stanton, Declaration of Sentiments, 1848

The convention passed 12 resolutions altogether. Signed by 68 women and 32 men, the resolutions protested the lack of legal and political rights for women. They urged women to demand these rights.

The ninth resolution proved to be controversial. It called for women's **suffrage,** or the right to vote. (See Focus on Government, at left.) At Stanton's insistence, the convention passed the resolution. Mott, however, disapproved of the suffrage demand, and so did others at the convention, many of whom withdrew their support for the movement. The resolution also subjected the convention to considerable public criticism.

Slow Progress for Women's Rights The convention did not trigger an avalanche of support for women's rights. Most Americans still shared Catharine Beecher's view that women should influence public affairs indirectly, through their work in the home. Yet the convention marked the beginning of the organized movement for women's rights, including women's suffrage, in the United States.

Whereas no college in the United States admitted women in 1820, thousands of women were graduating from American colleges and universities by 1890. Educated women began appearing in professions from which they once had been excluded.

After becoming the first American woman to earn a medical diploma, Elizabeth Blackwell began practicing medicine in New York City in 1851. Later she founded the first school of nursing in the United States.

CAPTION ANSWERS

Viewing History Possible answers: Yes, because had she not raised the issue, it might have been postponed indefinitely; no, because it attracted extra criticism and might have alienated people who would have otherwise joined the cause.

RESOURCE DIRECTORY

Teaching Resources
Units 3/4 booklet
 • Section 3 Quiz, p. 28
Guide to the Essentials
 • Section 3 Summary, p. 49
Learning with Documents booklet (Key Documents) *Seneca Falls Declaration,* p. 80

Technology
Sounds of an Era Audio CD *"Ain't I a Woman?"* *Sojourner Truth* (time: one minute, 40 seconds)

Maria Mitchell made history by becoming the nation's first female astronomer. Mitchell discovered a new comet in 1847, and in 1848, she became the first woman elected to the American Academy of Arts and Sciences.

In 1845, Margaret Fuller, the editor of an important philosophical journal, also wrote a book, *Woman in the Nineteenth Century,* in which she criticized cultural traditions that restricted women's roles in society. As editor of the popular magazine *Godey's Lady's Book,* Sarah Josepha Hale published articles about women's issues for almost 50 years.

The Role of African American Women No African American women attended the Seneca Falls Convention, and only a handful came to most other women's rights conventions. For most African American women, the abolition of slavery was a more pressing issue.

A frequent participant in such meetings, however, was former slave Sojourner Truth, who joined the abolitionist movement in 1843. She reminded white women that African American women also had a place in the movement for women's rights. Truth became one of a small number of black women in the 1840s and 1850s who were active in the movement for women's rights.

In 1851, the 54-year-old Truth walked into a convention of white women in Akron, Ohio. Over the objections of many delegates, convention president Frances Dana Gage allowed Truth to speak. Truth walked slowly to the front and addressed the group:

VIEWING HISTORY Sojourner Truth's commanding presence and powerful speaking style captured people's attention at many anti-slavery and women's rights meetings. **Recognizing Bias** *Why was women's participation in the abolitionist movement controversial?*

❝ *I am a woman's rights. I have as much muscle as any man, and can do as much work as any man. . . . I can carry as much as any man, and can eat as much too . . . I have heard the Bible and have learned that Eve caused man to sin. Well, if woman upset the world, do give her a chance to set it right side up again.* ❞

—Speech by Sojourner Truth, 1851

Section 3 Assessment

READING COMPREHENSION

1. What private roles did women carry out within the home?

2. What were the results of the **Seneca Falls Convention?**

3. Why did the issue of **suffrage** cause controversy?

4. How did the roles and rights of women change in the mid-1800s, and in what ways did they not change?

CRITICAL THINKING AND WRITING

5. **Recognizing Ideologies** Compare Catharine Beecher's views on women and reform with those of Elizabeth Cady Stanton.

6. **Writing to Explain** How did the various reform movements lead to a greater public role for women?

Take It to the NET

Activity: Writing an Editorial
Read the Declaration of Sentiments from the Seneca Falls Convention. Write a newspaper editorial that might have appeared after the convention, responding to the demands of the signatories. Use the links provided in the *America: Pathways to the Present* area of the following Web site for help in completing this activity.
www.phschool.com

Reading Comprehension

1. Raising and educating their children, instilling moral values in their children and their husbands, entertaining guests, caring for their families, making crafts, and performing other at-home activities.

2. Gains for women were slow in coming. However, the Seneca Falls Convention did pave the way for such events as the granting of female suffrage in the Wyoming territory in 1869.

3. Most Americans still believed that a woman's role was in the home and that her influence should be felt in public affairs only indirectly, through the voices of men.

4. Changed: Women became consumers more than producers, lower-class women took jobs in factories, middle-class women were freed from home chores, and some women became active in reform. Did not change: They still managed home and family, were discouraged from public activities, and could not vote or keep their earnings.

Critical Thinking and Writing

5. Beecher: Women should make the most of their role in the home by influencing men; Stanton: Women should make their voices heard through voting and should have full equal rights.

6. Essays will vary, but should be supported with facts from the section.

Take It to the NET

Students' viewpoints should be expressed in an article addressing the points raised in the Declaration of Sentiments, strongly supporting or opposing suffrage.

CAPTION ANSWERS

Viewing History Many people of that era were opposed to women's involvement in any kind of political or other public activities.

Growing Divisions

SECTION OBJECTIVES

1. Read about some causes of the huge rise in immigration to the United States in the 1830s and 1840s.

2. See why reform movements heightened tensions between the North and the South.

BELLRINGER

Warm-Up Activity Ask students how they might feel if their school administration decided to make changes, such as denying open campus privileges, in order to make the school "safer." Describe the kind of reception such "reformers" might get.

Activating Prior Knowledge Ask students to consider some ways in which the reform movements might lead to heightened tensions between the North and the South.

READING STRATEGY

As students read the section, have them make notes on the beliefs and traditions of groups of Americans mentioned. Then have them note what the groups have in common, and how they differ.

CAPTION ANSWERS

Interpreting Cartoons Sample answer: Ireland is sending its poor and starving citizens to be cared for by America. The boat looks dirty and shabby. It rocks to the side, teeming with poor people.

READING FOCUS

- What were the causes of the huge rise in immigration to the United States in the 1830s and 1840s?
- Why did reform movements heighten tensions between the North and the South?

MAIN IDEA

The United States grew increasingly diverse due to the arrival of new groups of immigrants and the growing cultural differences between the North and South.

KEY TERMS

Irish Potato Famine
naturalize
discrimination

TAKING NOTES

Copy the chart below. As you read, complete the chart with information regarding the causes and effects of immigration during the 1840s and 1850s.

CAUSES
• Demand for cheap labor
•
•

⬇

IMMIGRATION TO THE U.S., 1840s–1850s

⬇

EFFECTS
• Increase in cultural differences
•
•

Setting the Scene People do not always want to hear advice, no matter how sincerely it is offered. Reformers of the early 1800s found this out. From revivalism to temperance to abolition to women's rights, reform movements often did as much to divide American society as to improve it.

One reason was that the nation was becoming more culturally diverse. The North and the South were becoming more distinct. Differences between working people and the middle class were widening. In addition, the young, prosperous nation was attracting immigrants from a variety of European cultures. Some segments of this diverse population did not share the reformers' vision of America.

Rising Immigration

The economic changes of the early 1800s created a growing demand for cheap labor in factories and in the building of canals and railroad lines. These jobs attracted immigrants, most of whom arrived hungry, penniless, and eager to work.

In the entire decade of the 1820s, only about 143,000 immigrants arrived in the United States. During the 1830s, however, the number of new immigrants rose to about 600,000, and in the 1850s, the figure skyrocketed to nearly 2.6 million. Nearly all of these new arrivals settled in the North and the West because the use of slave labor in the South offered few job opportunities in that region.

Almost all of the immigrants to the United States from 1820 to 1860 came from northern Europe. While some immigrated from Scandinavia and England, most were from Ireland and Germany.

The Irish Irish immigration soared in the mid-1840s when Ireland suffered a horrible disaster known as the **Irish Potato Famine.** The famine, which lasted from 1845 to 1849, caused hundreds of thousands of Irish people to flee to the

INTERPRETING CARTOONS
This cartoon depicts a floating poorhouse filled with starving immigrants from the city of Galway, Ireland, fleeing to America.
Recognizing Bias What is the message of the cartoon?

332 Chapter 9 • *Religion and Reform*

RESOURCE DIRECTORY

Teaching Resources
Learning Styles Lesson Plans booklet, p. 21
Guided Reading and Review booklet, p. 40
Biography, Literature, and Comparing Primary Sources booklet (Literature) *A First-Hand Account of the Potato Famine,* p. 50

Technology
Section Reading Support Transparencies
Guided Reading Audiotapes (English/Spanish), Ch. 9
Student Edition on Audio CD, Ch. 9
Color Transparencies *American Diversity,* G7
Prentice Hall Presentation Pro CD-ROM, Ch. 9
Companion Web site, www.phschool.com

United States. Most settled in northeastern cities such as Boston and New York.

Like other immigrant groups, after settling in the United States the Irish became **naturalized.** That is, they applied for and were granted American citizenship. Irish men filled manual labor jobs in factories or on canals or railroads. Once established, the newcomers sent for relatives to join them. Irish communities in northern cities grew steadily.

As their numbers grew, Irish Americans became a political force. Most were Jacksonian Democrats. The Democratic Party had reached out to these potential new voters when they first arrived, and the tactic paid off. In 1855, for example, 34 percent of all New York City voters were first-generation Irish immigrants.

The Germans Many Germans came to America seeking political freedom after a series of failed rebellions across Europe in 1848. The majority of the German immigrants were peasants who bought large tracts of farmland in the Midwest, especially in Wisconsin and Missouri. Many also settled in Texas and, by 1850, made up about 5 percent of the state's population. German artisans and intellectuals tended to settle in northern cities such as New York, Chicago, and Milwaukee.

New Cultures These immigrants brought new cultural traditions to the United States. Most of the Irish and many of the Germans were Roman Catholic. Like Catholics in other countries, they respected the authority of the Pope in Rome as the head of the Church. They looked to Church laws for guidance. Their celebrations followed Church traditions and those of their home country.

Like other laborers, the new immigrants worked long hours in tedious jobs. After work the men gathered in taverns, often the social centers of the neighborhood. Boxing matches, horse races, and new team sports such as baseball were inexpensive diversions from the grind of daily life.

Immigrants Face Hostility Irish and German immigrants often faced **discrimination,** the unequal treatment of a group of people because of their nationality, race, sex, or religion. Discrimination came from Americans who felt threatened by the presence of the newcomers or who disapproved of their culture.

One source of tension was economics. The Irish immigrants, for example, arrived just as new, struggling labor unions were launching strikes to obtain higher wages and better working conditions. Because the Irish would work for lower wages, companies used them as strike breakers. Many of the New England mill girls lost their jobs to Irish men in the 1830s and 1840s.

A second source of tension was religion. Many Protestants disapproved of the Catholic religion. They believed that Catholicism's emphasis on rituals and on the Pope's authority discouraged individual thinking.

Catholics protested when their children in public schools were forced to read the Protestant version of the Bible (the King James version). Textbooks of the time also required students to learn Protestant values. Catholics fought efforts by reformers to enact laws restricting drinking, gambling, and sports, which they did not view as immoral.

Focus on WORLD EVENTS

The Irish Potato Famine The causes of the Irish Potato Famine are the subject of scholarly debate today. In the 1840s, under British rule, three quarters of Irish farmland produced crops to be sold to England. When a fungus from North America destroyed much of Ireland's potato crop—a staple food, especially for the poor—famine spread across the country.

The British government provided some aid to Ireland. Yet British landowners in Ireland refused to put more land into production of other food, such as wheat or oats, for the starving people. Meanwhile, the Irish continued to export food to Britain that they could not afford to buy for themselves. More than one million Irish people died from starvation and related diseases. Up to 1.5 million more Irish people emigrated to places such as the United States or Britain. Many settled in Boston, New York, and other northeastern cities. Ireland's population dropped from 8.4 million in 1844 to 6.6 million by 1851.

READING CHECK
Why did some immigrants face discrimination when they came to America?

Chapter 9 • Section 4   **333**

CUSTOMIZE FOR ...

Less Proficient Writers

Have students photocopy a map of nineteenth-century Europe. Ask them to indicate the main countries from which émigrés came to the United States. Ask them to list reasons why people emigrated from these countries to the United States.

✓ **TEST PREPARATION**

Ask students to review the material on these pages about immigration and then answer the question below.

What is the best definition of the word "naturalized"?

  A Made to feel comfortable in a new place.

  Ⓑ Applied for, and received citizenship.

  C Living in the country in which one was born.

  D Adopting the customs and behavior of one's new country.

LESSON PLAN

Focus As the United States grew increasingly diverse, some segments of society deeply resented middle-class reformers. Ask students why the reformers and their efforts caused such resentment and bitterness.

Instruct Explain that the Market Revolution of the early 1800s created a growing demand for cheap labor, which attracted a huge number of immigrants and caused many Americans to move from farms to the cities. As a result, the working class became larger and society more diverse. Discuss the many differences between middle-class reformers and working-class immigrants. Ask students how life in the North diverged from life in the South.

Assess/Reteach Ask students to draw analogies between divisions that existed between reformers and other segments of society in the nineteenth century and political differences that exist in society today.

***A*CTIVITY**
Connecting with Culture

Refer students to these facts presented under "Rising Immigration" in their textbooks: The number of immigrants arriving in the United States skyrocketed from about 143,000 in the 1820s to some 2.6 million in the 1850s. Have students use these figures to calculate the percentage increase in immigration during this time period and the average number of immigrants that arrived each month during the 1820s and during the 1850s. **(Logical/Mathematical)**

READING CHECK
Discrimination was based on nationality and religion. Some Americans felt threatened by these newcomers and disapproved of their culture or feared they would lose their jobs to immigrants who would work for lower wages.

Connecting with History and Conflict

Tell students to reflect on the morality of slavery. Then have them write an essay expressing their position on this issue. Encourage students to think about what is meant by morality and whether one group of people can force morality on another. Ask them also to think about whether different people have different concepts of morality and if so, whether they can get along, despite their divergent ideas. **(Verbal/Linguistic; Logical/Mathematical)**

BACKGROUND

A Diverse Nation

In the years leading up to the Civil War, southern slave owners condoned slave weddings despite the fact that these marriages lacked legal standing. In order to protect slave owners, who might someday want to sell one half of a "married" couple, ministers deleted the customary "until death do us part" phrase and replaced it with the phrase "until death or distance do you part." Some owners officiated at slave weddings themselves. Usually, they left out the phrase "until death do us part." Some slaveholders used the occasion of a wedding to remind slave couples that their marriage could be dissolved if they didn't comply with the owner's strict code of behavior. This practice gave slave owners a sense of greater control over their slaves.

COMPARING PRIMARY SOURCES
Working Women, North and South

In the excerpts below, writers compare the work done by poor women in the North and the South with work done by slaves.

Analyzing Viewpoints Compare the main arguments made by the two writers.

Southern Women

"Poor white girls never hired [themselves] out to do servants' work, but they would come and help another white woman [with] her sewing or quilting, and take wages for it. . . . That their condition is not as unfortunate by any means as that of negroes, however, is most obvious, since among them, men may sometimes elevate themselves to positions and habits of usefulness and respectability."

—Frederick Law Olmsted,
A Journey in the Seaboard Slave States, 1856

Northern Women

"Thirteen hours per day of monotonous labor are exacted from these young women. So fatigued are the girls that they go to bed soon after their evening meal. It would be a poor bargain from the industrial point of view to own these workers. . . . The greater number of fortunes accumulated by people in the North in comparison with the South shows that hired labor is more profitable than slave labor."

—Report on a visit to the Lowell, Massachusetts, textile mills, published in The Harbinger, 1836

In 1843, anti-immigrant citizens formed the American Republican Party. The party pushed unsuccessfully for a new naturalization law requiring immigrants to live in the United States for 21 years before being eligible for citizenship. When the Philadelphia school board allowed Catholic students to use the Catholic (Douay) version of the Bible and to be excused from religious activities, the American Republicans protested.

In 1844, Irish Catholics attacked American Republicans who were attempting to vote in Philadelphia's Irish districts. The attacks led to riots in the city in May 1844, in which armed mobs burned down Irish homes and churches, and 30 people were killed.

North-South Tensions

Reform movements produced conflict not only in the North. They increased ill will between the North and the South as well. Southerners bitterly resented abolitionists' efforts to prevent the spread of slavery and to shelter escaped slaves. They felt stung by the charge that slaveholders were immoral.

Divided Churches For southern churches, slavery presented a painful dilemma. As southern revivalists began claiming that the Bible supported slavery, their audiences began to grow. On the other hand, Catholic and Episcopal churches in the South were largely silent on the issue.

As the abolition movement intensified, it produced deep rifts in the Methodist and Baptist churches. In 1842, the Methodist Church demanded that one of its southern bishops free his slaves. That action snapped the bonds that had unified northern and southern members for decades. Churches in the slaveholding states left the national organization. They then formed the Methodist Episcopal Church South, which endorsed slavery.

The national membership of the Baptist Church had worked closely together for many years. But it, too, finally splintered, as about 300 churches withdrew in 1845 to form the Southern Baptist Convention.

South Holds on to Traditions Reformers' calls for public schools and equal rights for women further offended many white Southerners. These southern

RESOURCE DIRECTORY

Teaching Resources
Units 3/4 booklet
  • Section 4 Quiz, p. 29
  • Chapter 9 Test, pp. 30, 33
Guide to the Essentials
  • Section 4 Summary, p. 50
  • Chapter 9 Test, p. 51
Learning with Documents booklet (Primary Source Activity) *Plantation Life*, p. 14

Other Print Resources
Chapter Tests with ExamView® Test Bank CD-ROM, Ch. 9
Nystrom *Atlas Of Our Country* *The Second Wave of Immigration*, pp. 24–25

Technology
ExamView® Test Bank CD-ROM, Ch. 9
Social Studies Skills Tutor CD-ROM

men saw these "reforms" as suggestions that they did not properly care for their families. In the South, where personal honor was particularly important, such suggestions provoked offense and outrage.

Most of the South remained untouched by the social turmoil that came with urbanization and industrialization in the North. Thus, Southerners saw no need to reform their society. Families held fast to their traditional family relationships and roles. From small farmers to wealthy planters, for example, southern men had authority over not only their farms and businesses, but their households as well. The master of the plantation was also master of his wife and children.

A few southern white women saw parallels between their role and that of slaves. A South Carolina woman, Mary Boykin Chesnut, confided to her diary that her husband was "master of the house." "To hear is to obey. . . ." she wrote. "All the comfort of my life depends upon his being in good humor." At times Chesnut was sure that "there is no slave . . . like a wife."

Southern women had important roles to play. The wives of small farmers often worked with their husbands in the fields. The wives of plantation owners supervised large households and sometimes helped manage the plantation. Many of these women, rich and poor, oversaw their children's education.

Because farms and plantations were often miles apart, however, opportunities to participate in public organizations and community meetings were rare. The message of reformers such as Elizabeth Cady Stanton and Sojourner Truth did not reach the ears of many southern women, who generally played a less public role than their northern counterparts.

Clearly, the bonds that had united Americans were slipping. As emotions intensified, the North and the South found it increasingly difficult to resolve differences through negotiation and compromise.

VIEWING HISTORY This painting portrays the traditional character of southern plantation life.
Demonstrating Reasoned Judgment *What details in the painting suggest a traditional family structure?*

Section 4 · Assessment

READING COMPREHENSION

1. What impact did growing numbers of **naturalized** immigrants have on the political system in the United States?

2. List some of the factors that contributed to **discrimination** against Irish and German immigrants.

3. Why did reform movements offend many Southerners?

CRITICAL THINKING AND WRITING

4. **Expressing Problems Clearly** Summarize how reform movements deepened hostilities between the North and South.

5. **Writing to Persuade** Write a newspaper column from the 1840s that identifies a problem that divides Americans and proposes constructive solutions.

 Take It to the NET

Activity: Recreating History
Read firsthand accounts and other historic documents about the Irish fleeing the potato famine. Use your research to write an authentic diary entry from the viewpoint of an Irish emigrant. Use the links provided in the *America: Pathways to the Present* area of the following Web site for help in completing this activity.
www.phschool.com

Reading Comprehension

1. The Democratic Party grew by reaching out to immigrant Irish as potential new voters when they first arrived in the country; anti-immigrant groups formed the American Republican Party to press for measures such as restricting citizenship for immigrants, which led to violent conflicts between Catholics and American Republican Party members.

2. Irish and German immigrants were discriminated against by Americans who felt their jobs were being threatened; these immigrants also encountered hostility toward their religious and lifestyle beliefs.

3. They were disturbed by the charge that slaveholders were immoral. Calls for public school and equal rights for women upset southerners who saw these demands as suggestions that they did not properly care for their families. These southerners saw no reason to disrupt their traditional family roles.

Critical Thinking and Writing

4. Southerners resented the charge that slavery was immoral and the efforts of abolitionists to prevent the spread of slavery and provide shelter to escaped slaves. Reformers' calls for public schools and women's rights offended white southerners who took it as an accusation that they did not properly honor their families.

5. Columns will vary, but should be supported by facts from the section.

 **Take It to the NET**

Diary entries should be based on historical facts and should reflect the emigrant's reasons for leaving Ireland, expectations of America, as well as trepidation.

CAPTION ANSWERS

Viewing History The father is at the center of the painting, sitting in a pose that appears dominant; the baby is being cared for by a nurse, who is possibly a slave.

Chapter 9 Review and Assessment

REVIEWING KEY TERMS

Students should refer to the definitions of key terms in the chapter to write sentences that show an understanding of the key aspects of religion and reform in the first half of the nineteenth century.

REVIEWING MAIN IDEAS

12. Emerson: People can transcend the material world and become conscious of the spirit in nature; Thoreau: People should live simply and close to nature.

13. Mann pioneered school reform, establishing the grade level system, making curricula consistent, and instituting teacher training. Dix's appeals for prison reform led to the improvement of prison conditions and separate institutions for the mentally ill.

14. William Lloyd Garrison: published a newspaper, denounced moderation in fighting slavery, founded American Anti-Slavery Society; Frederick Douglass: great speaker and writer, started newspaper, opposed violence; Grimké sisters: involved women in the movement through speaking and writing pamphlets.

15. Answers may include: further split the North and South; ultimately led to emancipation; involved women in public life.

16. Women should become educated so that they can exert a good influence on their husbands and sons.

17. It marked the beginning of the battle for women's rights, especially for female suffrage.

18. A growing need for cheap labor in the United States; poor economic and political conditions in Ireland and Germany.

19. Discrimination was based on nationality and religion and came from Americans who felt threatened by these newcomers, disapproved of their culture, or feared they would lose their jobs to immigrants who would work for lower wages.

20. Reform movements sparked conflict; while the North became industrial, the South remained largely rural; slavery further split the nation.

creating a CHAPTER SUMMARY

Copy this web diagram (right) on a piece of paper and complete it by adding additional ovals and filling in information about reform movements during the mid-1800s.

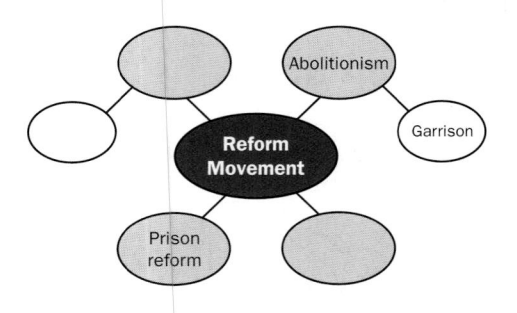

iTEXT

For additional review and enrichment activities, see the interactive version of *America: Pathways to the Present*, available on the Web and on CD-ROM.

★ Reviewing Key Terms

For each of the terms below, write a sentence explaining how it relates to religion and reform in the United States during the mid-1800s.

1. temperance movement
2. segregate
3. utopian community
4. abolitionist movement
5. emancipation
6. Underground Railroad
7. gag rule
8. Seneca Falls Convention
9. suffrage
10. naturalize
11. discrimination

★ Reviewing Main Ideas

12. Name two major transcendentalists and summarize their beliefs. (Section 1)

13. Describe the contributions of Horace Mann and Dorothea Dix. (Section 1)

14. Name three important abolitionists and describe the tactics they used to combat slavery. (Section 2)

15. Describe several effects of the abolitionist movement. (Section 2)

16. What was Catharine Beecher's main message to women? (Section 3)

17. Why was the Seneca Falls Convention important? (Section 3)

18. Why did immigration to the United States increase after the 1820s? (Section 4)

19. Why did German and Irish immigrants sometimes face hostility and discrimination? (Section 4)

20. In what ways were the North and the South growing apart in the mid-1800s? (Section 4)

★ Critical Thinking

21. **Making Comparisons** How did the goals of the abolitionist movement and the women's movement differ?

22. **Recognizing Bias** What issues led to tensions between different ethnic groups during the mid-1800s?

23. **Recognizing Ideologies** Why do you think some abolitionists insisted on using only legal methods to attack slavery while others used both legal and illegal methods?

24. **Drawing Conclusions** If you had lived during the time of the reform movements covered in this chapter, what movement might you have been interesting in joining? Why?

25. **Recognizing Ideologies** (a) What social or personal conditions might have encouraged people to start or to join utopian communities? (b) Do you find the concept appealing? Why or why not?

26. **Distinguishing Fact From Opinion** Reread the quotation from Catharine Beecher in Section 3. Which statements, if any, are opinions, and which, if any, are facts? Explain.

336 Chapter 9 • *Religion and Reform*

CREATING A CHAPTER SUMMARY

Revivalists — Beecher

Abolitionism — Garrison

Reform Movement

Dix — Prison Reform

Public Education — Mann

THE DRUNKARDS PROGRESS.

★ Skills Assessment
Analyzing Political Cartoons ▶

27. Analyze the message of this temperance movement cartoon. (a) What is the title of the cartoon? (b) Characterize the people shown in Steps 1–3. (c) Characterize the people shown on Steps 4–5. (d) Characterize the people shown on Steps 6–9.

28. How does this cartoon help explain why members of the temperance movement were opposed to all alcohol consumption?

29. (a) Who are the figures under the steps? (b) What additional message do they provide?

Interpreting Data

Refer to the chart titled "Free and Enslaved Black Population, 1820–1860" in Section 2 to answer the following questions:

30. About how many more enslaved African Americans were there in 1860 than in 1820?

  A 4 million
  B 1 million
  C 1.5 million
  D 2.5 million

31. In 1860, the number of enslaved African Americans was about how many times larger than that of free African Americans?

  F 2 times
  G 3 times
  H 8 times
  J 11 times

Applying the Chapter Skill: *Using the Internet for Research*

32. Use the steps outlined on the Skills for Life page in this chapter to conduct Internet research on one of the utopian communities mentioned in Section 1. Write a brief report about the community, including information about where the community was located, who founded it, and when and why it was established.

ACTIVITIES

Writing to LEARN

Essay Writing
Choose a reform discussed in this chapter and write an essay on the impact of that reform on American society today. Include answers to these questions: (a) What successes did the reform achieve? (b) How has the reform affected you or someone you know? (c) What work still needs to be done to improve conditions?

Primary Source CD-ROM

Working With Primary Sources Find additional information about life in the United States during the mid-1800s on the *Exploring Primary Sources in U.S. History CD-ROM* and use the selection(s) provided to complete the Chapter 9 primary source activity located in the *America: Pathways to the Present* area at the following Web site.
www.phschool.com

Take It to the NET

Chapter Self-Test As a review activity, take the Chapter 9 Self-Test in the *America: Pathways to the Present* area at the Web site listed below. The questions are designed to test your understanding of the chapter content.
www.phschool.com

Chapter 9 Assessment   **337**

CRITICAL THINKING

21. Abolitionist movement: strove for freedom from slavery, not necessarily full equality; women's movement: worked toward allowing women to vote, hold office, and have the full rights of American citizens.

22. Competition for jobs, different religious beliefs and practices, different political viewpoints.

23. Those who used only legal methods hoped to bring about lasting political change, first by stopping the spread of slavery to new states and then through gradual emancipation. Those who supported using illegal methods hoped to cause change swiftly, because they believed that the suffering and immorality of the slavery system had to be immediately ended in any way possible.

24. Answers will vary, but should be supported with facts from the chapter.

25. (a) Sample answer: Desire for harmony, spiritual growth, and equality between men and women; discontent with the effects of urban and industrial growth. (b) Answers will vary, but should be supported by the text.

26. Students may argue that all the statements are opinions, but allow for well-supported, alternative answers.

SKILLS ASSESSMENT

27. (a) "The Drunkards Progress." (b) Happy and social. (c) Drunk and rowdy. (d) Filthy, ill, violent, suicidal.

28. It shows that the message of the temperance movement was that even social drinking will lead to ruin.

29. (a) A woman and child left widowed and orphaned by a man who was ruined by alcohol. (b) A man's fall to alcohol affects more than himself; it affects his dependents, too.

30. D

31. H

32. Answers should be descriptive and well supported by facts from both the Internet and the chapter.

Writing to LEARN

Essays should include facts from the chapter on the particular reform movement and a comparison of its impact on present-day society.

Primary Source CD-ROM

Direct students to the additional primary sources that can be found on the *Exploring Primary Sources in U.S. History CD-ROM.*

Take It to the NET

Additional support materials and activities for Chapter 9 of *America: Pathways to the Present* can be found in the Social Studies area at the Prentice Hall School Web site. **www.phschool.com**

Chapter 9 • **337**

THE UNDERGROUND RAILROAD

Focus Have students find the meaning of these words in a dictionary before they begin to read: *boarder, verandah.* Ask them to consider, as they read, the risks that Dorr's great-great-grandfather took by helping people in the Underground Railroad.

Instruct Ask volunteers to identify and describe a big change or trauma that they experienced long ago but that still affects their lives. Then have students compare their feelings about their own experience to Dorr's grandmother's feelings about the "secret" of her grandfather's involvement in the Underground Railroad. How are they similar or different? Suggest that students write about their experience either as a journal entry or a memoir.

Analyzing the Document Use this additional question to generate class discussion:

Critical Thinking: Checking Consistency Is the pride that the grandmother feels toward her grandfather for helping runaway slaves consistent with her warning the speaker not to tell anyone? *(Answers will vary. Students should recognize that the grandmother can be simultaneously proud of her grandfather and insecure about her own social standing.)*

The Underground Railroad

Secret rooms, like this one located behind a cabinet, were used to hide escaped slaves.

I n addition to "conductors" like Harriet Tubman, who led escaped slaves out of the South, the Underground Railroad also depended on people who fed and sheltered escaped slaves on their journey north to freedom. In this selection, William M. Dorr explains how he, as a boy, learned of his own family's secret involvement in the Underground Railroad.

THE EARLY 1930s were not good to my grandmother. About all she had left were her memories of her childhood at the old home place. In Grandmother's case the old home place was a

This painting shows escaped slaves arriving at a station on the Underground Railroad.

farm outside of Glasgow, Kentucky. This was the center of her universe and now, in 1937, we were all going on vacation there for a visit.

People today accept a vacation as a God-given right, but in the Depression a vacation was a major event to be planned, discussed, and saved for. Those going were my grandmother, my mother, myself, and our boarder. Mother and Father had divorced, and the boarder had been with us for the past seven or eight years and was considered one of the family. He would do most of the driving and pay for the gasoline.

As I counted off the days, Grandma made the wait even longer by telling me that when we reached Glasgow I would see a big secret. I'd ask, "What secret?" but she would only say that I would have to wait.

338

✓ **TEST PREPARATION**

Have students use the selection on these pages to answer the following question.

Which word best describes the speaker's feelings about his great-great-grandfather's involvement in the Underground Railroad?

A pride

B shame

C horror

D fear

Symbols of the hated institution of slavery, these tags were worn by slaves to identify their owners.

I'd like to say that the trip down to Glasgow from Louisville was all fun and excitement, but that would be far from the truth. Less than twenty miles out of Louisville, the family found out that I had car sickness.

By the time we reached Glasgow I was a hot, sick, and irritable little boy who was making life miserable for all around him. Then the second blow fell: I saw the old home place. I had expected it to look like a Georgia plantation with high columns and wide verandahs. But the house was none of this. Its current owners had not been able to spare a lot of money for upkeep, and to a city boy used to urban newness, it seemed shabby and rundown.

THE SECRET REVEALED But there was a cold pitcher of lemonade and an electric fan in the living room. Grandma asked if I would like to see the bedroom. I didn't really want to see a bedroom, but I was pushed upstairs and into a chamber dominated by a large bed and little else. The headboard of the bed stood solid into the rear wall, and my grandmother told me I was to push against the top left of it. After one missed push, I made part of the headboard slide back into the wall.

The owner of the house came upstairs with a flashlight, and I looked into my first secret panel. I was told I could go in, but all I could see was cobwebs, and I decided I could see all I wanted from the bed. As I shone the light in, Grandma told me that this passage went around the chimney and was three feet wide by three and a half feet tall. The only way in or out was by way of the bed.

Grandma explained that after thinking hard on the subject, her granddaddy had decided that slavery was wrong. Being a man who acted on his beliefs, he had built this room and become part of the Underground Railroad, helping runaway slaves to freedom.

Then Grandma gave a warning. Although the Civil War (or rather the War between the States) had been over for more than seventy years, feelings for the lost cause still ran high. If the purpose of the secret passage were known, we might no longer be socially accepted in Glasgow. I had to promise never to say a word about it.

That night and for a number of nights after, I dreamed of being Great-Great-Granddaddy's helper taking those slaves toward freedom. Mother and Grandma promised that we could come back again to see more of the farm's secrets; but it was not to be.

The 1930s kept us too poor for another vacation, and then came Pearl Harbor. The boarder was drafted and later came home to marry my mother. Grandma did not get back to Glasgow until the late 1940s. By then the owners had sold the property, and the house had been torn down for an industrial plant. Granddaddy's secret passage was gone forever.

I never knew my grandmother's granddaddy, or any of the blacks he helped to spirit North; but occasionally in dreams I still go back to Glasgow to help Great-Great-Granddaddy.

Source: *American Heritage* magazine, September 1993.

Understanding Primary Sources

1. What warning did Dorr's grandmother give to him?
2. What does this warning tell you about racial attitudes in the South in 1937?

American Heritage®
MY BRUSH WITH **HISTORY**™
▶ **Videotapes**

For more information about slavery and the Underground Railroad, view "The Underground Railroad."

339

TEST PREPARATION

Use this sample exam to help your students prepare for standardized tests.

TIPS FOR TEST TAKING

You might want to remind your students of the following:

1. Read the directions carefully.

2. Read each question carefully.

3. For multiple choice questions, try to answer the question before you look at the choices. Read all the choices. Then, eliminate those that are absolutely incorrect.

4. For short answer questions, be sure to answer the question completely if there is more than one part.

5. Answer the easy questions first. Then, go back to the ones that will take more time.

6. Pace yourself. Be sure to set aside enough time for the writing questions.

Write your answers on a separate sheet of paper.

1. Which word pair describes the events of the Second Great Awakening?

   A Christian and Jewish

   B Revival and urban

   C Evangelical and democratic

   D Intolerant and indecent

2. Daniel Boone opened a trail that went from the Atlantic Coastal Plain to the Ohio River valley by going

   A through the Cumberland Gap.

   B along the Erie Canal.

   C across Lake Ontario.

   D up the Hudson River.

3. Which one of the following was added to the United States by the Adams-Onís Treaty?

   A Mississippi

   B Louisiana

   C Kentucky

   D Florida

Use the chart and your knowledge of social studies to answer the following question.

Oregon added to the United States
Texas annexed to the United States
Gold Rush to California
Major migration across trails to the west

4. The events in the chart are part of the movement known as

   A Jacksonian Democracy.

   B Manifest Destiny.

   C Market Revolution.

   D American System.

---

5. Which former slave became a leading abolitionist speaker?

   A Nat Turner

   B Frederick Douglass

   C Noah Webster

   D John Marshall

Use the graph and your knowledge of social studies to answer the following question.

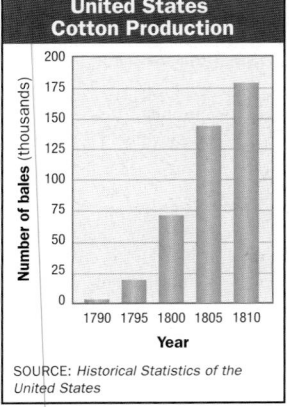

United States Cotton Production

SOURCE: *Historical Statistics of the United States*

6. Which one of the following inventors contributed to the trend shown in the graph?

   A Eli Whitney

   B James Watt

   C Robert Fulton

   D Thomas Edison

340

PRENTICE HALL
ASSESSMENT SYSTEM

Diagnose and Prescribe
• Profile student skills with Diagnostic Tests A&B.
• Address student needs with program materials correlated to test questions.
Review and Reteach
• Provide cumulative content review with the Review Book.
Practice and Assess
• Build test-taking skills with Test-taking Strategies With Transparencies.

7. When Andrew Jackson started giving government jobs to his friends and political supporters, he was practicing what became known as the

A Market Revolution.

B states' rights movement.

C American System.

D spoils system.

8. Horace Mann fought to

A use tax money to provide free public education.

B open up hospitals for mentally ill people.

C provide education for blind and deaf students.

D stop slavery in the states and territories.

9. Who was the most famous conductor on the Underground Railroad?

A Harriet Tubman

B Denmark Vessey

C William Lloyd Garrison

D Phillis Wheatley

10. What was the main result of the Seneca Falls Convention of 1848?

A It led to the movement to abolish slavery.

B It created a national women's rights movement.

C It developed into the Republic Party.

D It started the first national trade union.

11. Which American writer was the leader of the transcendentalist movement?

A Lyman Beecher

B Thomas Jefferson

C Ralph Waldo Emerson

D Thomas Paine

Writing Practice

12. Describe two aspects of the Market Revolution that took place in the United States after the War of 1812.

13. Explain why President Jackson vetoed the renewal charter of the Bank of the United States.

14. Describe two of the divisions that developed in the antislavery movement in the United States.

1. C
2. A
3. D
4. B
5. B
6. A
7. D
8. A
9. A
10. B
11. C
12. Answers will vary, but might explain the rise of manufacturing and centralized factories; the increased demand for people to work outside the home; the increase in shopping; and the rise of the banking industry.
13. Jackson thought the Bank was too big and too powerful. He was also aware that the advocates for the Bank had political motives.
14. Answers might explain the idea of preventing slavery from spreading to the territories versus outright abolition; the debate over popular sovereignty; whether abolitionist tactics should be violent or peaceful; and whether or not abolition should include full civil rights for former slaves.

341

Unit 4

Unit 4

Division and Uneasy Reunion (1846–1877)

INTRODUCING THE UNIT

Division and Uneasy Reunion (1846–1877) Politicians struggled to find compromises that would avoid the division of the United States. But secession and war were inevitable. The Civil War, the bloodiest war in the western world of the nineteenth century, led to the freedom of enslaved African Americans. During the era of Reconstruction, southern society was transformed, and social, political, and economic relationships were redefined throughout the United States.

USING HISTORICAL EVIDENCE

Direct students' attention to the painting on these pages. It depicts the Battle of Kennesaw Mountain, Georgia, on June 27, 1864. The name of the mountain comes from a Cherokee Indian phrase meaning "cemetery" or "burial ground."

Kennesaw Mountain was an extremely important strategic location because it overlooked, and thus protected, the Western & Atlantic Railroad, the supply link to Atlanta. The mountain was well fortified by Confederate Forces, who nonetheless suffered some significant early casualties in skirmishes with Union soldiers in the weeks leading to the ultimate battle.

Ignoring the superiority of the Confederate position, Union General William Tecumseh Sherman led the attack on the mountain that is depicted in the painting. But the action was a bloody failure, resulting in the loss of thousands of lives.

Sherman acknowledged his defeat in this campaign, yet he defended his intentions in his report of the battle: "Failure as it was, and for which I assume the entire responsibility," he wrote, "I yet claim it produced good fruits, as it demonstrated to General Johnston that I would assault, and that boldly."

eTeach

Be sure to check out this month's online discussion with a Master Teacher. Go to **www.phschool.com**.

"With malice toward none; with charity for all; with firmness in the right; as God gives us to see the right, let us strive on to finish the work we are in; to bind up the nation's wounds."

Abraham Lincoln
Second Inaugural Address, March 1865

This lithograph by Kurz and Allison depicts the Battle of Kennesaw Mountain, Georgia, fought on June 27, 1864. ▶

342

RESOURCE DIRECTORY

Teaching Resources
Units 3/4 booklet
- American Pathways Activity, pp. 74–75
- History's Lasting Impact, pp. 76–77
Geography and History booklet, pp. 8–9

Other Print Resources
Prentice Hall Assessment System
- Document-Based Assessment

Chapter 10 The Coming of the Civil War, 1846–1861
Chapter 11 The Civil War, 1861–1865
Chapter 12 Reconstruction, 1865–1877

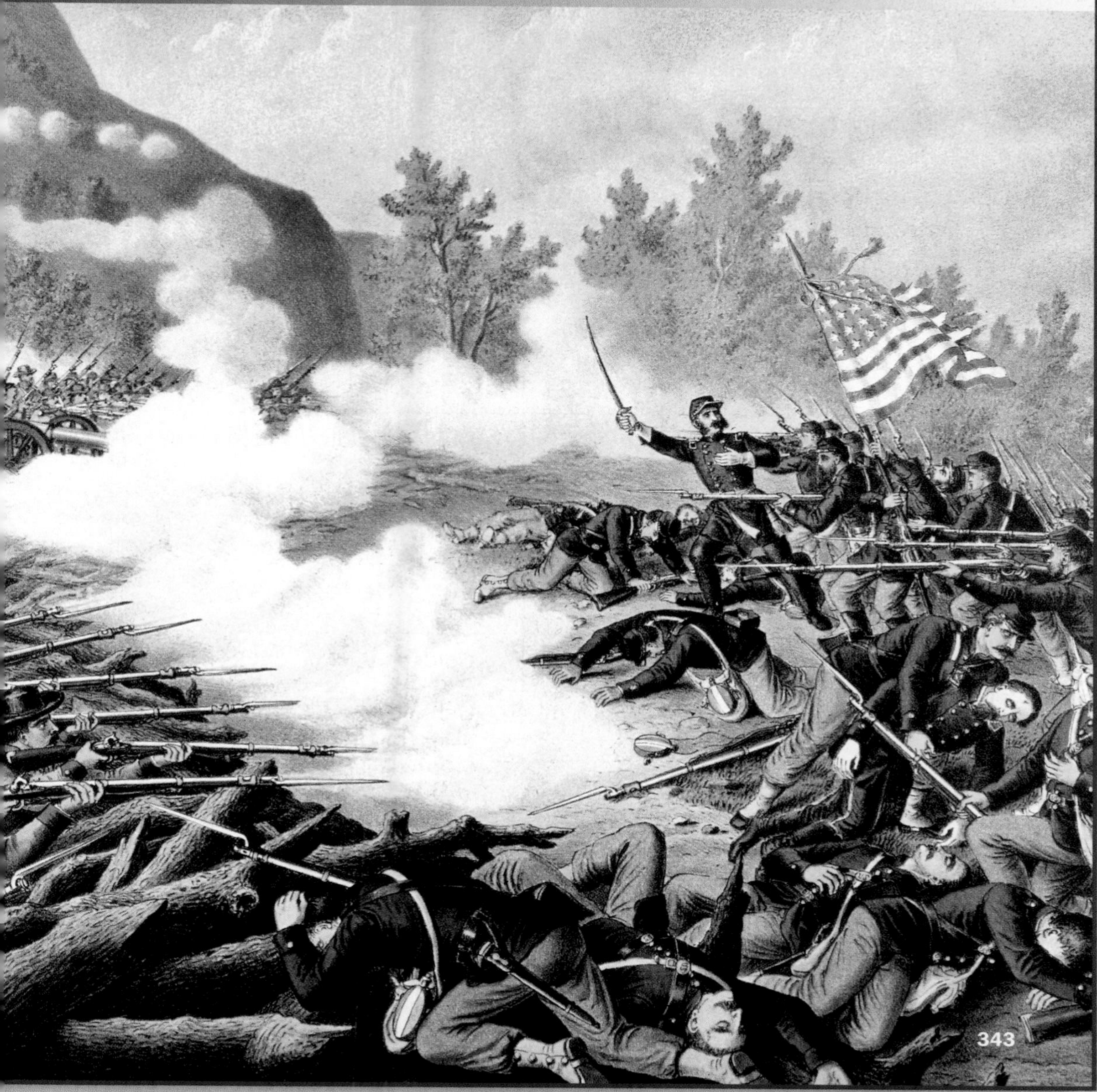

TECHNOLOGY CENTER

Take It to the NET

Prentice Hall School Web site offers student-appropriate Internet activities and links that extend core content. Visit us at the Social Studies area. **www.phschool.com**

AmericanHeritage®

My Brush with History™ Video Program This new video series lets your students learn history from the people who lived it.

RESOURCE PRO®

Teaching Resources on CD-ROM offer lesson-planning flexibility, test-generation capability, and resource manageability.

- **Presentation Pro CD-ROM** Provides you with multimedia lecture notes for each chapter.
- **Social Studies Skills Tutor CD-ROM** Provides interactive practice in Geographic Literacy, Critical Thinking and Reading, Visual Analysis, and Communications.
- **Interactive Constitution CD-ROM** Exploring active citizenship and civic responsibilities, this CD-ROM shows students how the Constitution affects their lives today.
- **Exploring Primary Sources in U.S. History CD-ROM** This interactive exploration of primary sources allows students to analyze and evaluate writing and images from American history.
- **Guided Reading Audiotapes**
- **Student Edition on Audio CD**
- **Sounds of an Era Audio CD** Bring the sounds of American history to life in the classroom with music, speeches, poetry, interviews, and news reports.

iTEXT

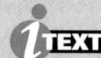

Don't miss the exclusive interactive version of this textbook on the Web and on CD-ROM.

RESOURCE DIRECTORY

Technology

Color Transparencies *Historical Maps,* A18, A19, A20, A22, A23, A24; *Political Cartoons,* B5, B6; *Time Lines,* C4; *Cause-and-Effect Charts,* D5; *Fine Art,* E8, E9; *American Photo,* F4; *American Diversity,* G8; *The Way It Works,* H8
Section Reading Support Transparencies
Prentice Hall United States History Video Collection™ Volume 8, *Causes of the Civil War;* Volume 9, *The Civil War;* Volume 10, *Reconstruction and Segregation (1865–1910)*
Companion Web site, www.phschool.com

Chapter 10 Planning Guide
Resource Manager

	CORE INSTRUCTION	READING/SKILLS
Chapter-Level Resources	**Teaching Resources** • Pacing Charts booklet • Block Scheduling booklet **Resource Pro® CD-ROM**, Ch. 10 **Prentice Hall Presentation Pro CD-ROM**, Ch. 10 **www.phschool.com** • eTeach	**Guided Reading Audiotapes (English/Spanish)** **Student Edition on Audio CD**, Ch. 10 **Social Studies Skills Tutor CD-ROM** **Color Transparencies**, A18, A19, C4, G8
1 Two Nations 1. Find out why some historians think the Civil War was unavoidable. 2. Discover arguments used by abolitionists against slavery. 3. Learn how Southerners viewed slavery. 4. Understand some important differences between the North and the South.	**Teaching Resources** **Units 3/4 booklet** • Section 1 Quiz, p. 41 **Learning Styles Lesson Plans booklet**, p. 22	**Guided Reading and Review booklet**, p. 41 **Guide to the Essentials**, p. 52 **Learning with Documents booklet**, p. 49 **Section Reading Support Transparencies**
2 The Mexican War and Slavery Extension 1. Learn about events that led to the annexation of Texas. 2. Understand why the United States went to war with Mexico. 3. See why the Wilmot Proviso led to conflict.	**Teaching Resources** **Units 3/4 booklet** • Section 2 Quiz, p. 42	**Guided Reading and Review booklet**, p. 42 **Guide to the Essentials**, p. 53 **Section Reading Support Transparencies**
3 New Political Parties 1. Discover some effects of the Missouri Compromise. 2. Learn what was accomplished by the Compromise of 1850. 3. See how political parties changed in the 1850s. 4. Find out why Stephen Douglas proposed the Kansas-Nebraska Act.	**Teaching Resources** **Units 3/4 booklet** • Section 3 Quiz, p. 43	**Guided Reading and Review booklet**, p. 43 **Guide to the Essentials**, p. 54 **Skills for Life booklet**, p. 12 **Section Reading Support Transparencies**
4 The System Fails 1. Learn why violence erupted in Kansas in the mid-1850s. 2. See how slavery affected national politics in this period. 3. Find out about problems caused by the Lecompton constitution. 4. Understand important issues discussed in the Lincoln-Douglas debates. 5. See how John Brown's raid increased tensions between the North and the South.	**Teaching Resources** **Units 3/4 booklet** • Section 4 Quiz, p. 44	**Guided Reading and Review booklet**, p. 44 **Guide to the Essentials**, p. 55 **Learning with Documents booklet**, p. 15 **Section Reading Support Transparencies**
5 A Nation Divided Against Itself 1. Find out how the election of 1860 demonstrated the split between the North and the South. 2. See what concerns led the Lower South to secede from the Union. 3. Discover the event that started the Civil War.	**Teaching Resources** **Units 3/4 booklet** • Section 5 Quiz, p. 45 **Learning Styles Lesson Plans booklet**, p. 23	**Guided Reading and Review booklet**, p. 45 **Guide to the Essentials**, p. 56 **Section Reading Support Transparencies**

ENRICHMENT/PRE-AP

Prentice Hall United States History Video Collection™
www.phschool.com
- Section Activities, Virtual Field Trip, Chapter Activities, Current Events Online

Biography, Literature, and Comparing Primary Sources booklet, pp. 51–52
Sounds of an Era Audio CD
Exploring Primary Sources in U.S. History CD-ROM

Nystrom *Atlas of Our Country*, pp. 20–21
Historical Outline Map Book, p. 41
Sounds of an Era Audio CD

Nystrom *Atlas of Our Country*, pp. 28–29
Historical Outline Map Book, pp. 41, 42, 46, 47
Sounds of an Era Audio CD
Exploring Primary Sources in U.S. History CD-ROM

Exploring Primary Sources in U.S. History CD-ROM

Biography, Literature, and Comparing Primary Sources booklet, pp. 15, 115–116
Historical Outline Map Book, pp. 43, 44, 48, 49
American Pathways Thematic Posters

ASSESSMENT

PRENTICE HALL
ASSESSMENT
SYSTEM

Core Assessment
ExamView® Test Bank, Ch. 10
ExamView® Test Bank CD-ROM, Ch. 10

Standardized Test Preparation
Diagnose and Prescribe
Diagnostic Tests for High School Social Studies Skills

Review and Reteach
Review Book for U.S. History

Practice and Assess
Test-taking Strategies With Transparencies
Test-taking Strategies Posters
Test Prep Book for U.S. History
Alternative Assessment Handbook
Document-Based Assessment

Teaching Resources
Units 1/2 booklet
- Section Quizzes, pp. 41–45
- Chapter Tests, pp. 46, 49
www.phschool.com Ch. 10 Self-Test

AmericanHeritage RESOURCES

From the Archives of American Heritage®, p. 47
AmericanHeritage® My Brush with History™ Videotapes
www.americanheritage.com

iTEXT

Don't miss the exclusive interactive version of this textbook on the Web and on CD-ROM.

Chapter 10 Planning Guide
In Your Classroom

CUSTOMIZE FOR INDIVIDUAL NEEDS

Gifted and Talented

Teacher's Edition
- Customize for Gifted and Talented, p. 365

Teaching Resources
- Biography, Literature, and Comparing Primary Sources booklet, pp. 15, 51–52, 115–116

Technology
- Exploring Primary Sources in U.S. History CD-ROM *Uncle Tom's Cabin, Harriet Beecher Stowe; A Frontier Lady, Sarah Royce; Dred Scott* v. *Sandford*

ESL

Teacher's Edition
- Customize for ESL, p. 353

Teaching Resources
- Guided Reading and Review booklet, pp. 41–45
- Guide to the Essentials (English/Spanish), Chapter 10

Technology
- Student Edition on Audio CD, Chapter 10
- Guided Reading Audiotapes (English/Spanish), Chapter 10
- Section Reading Support Transparencies

Less Proficient Readers

Teacher's Edition
- Customize for Less Proficient Readers, pp. 347, 359

Teaching Resources
- Guided Reading and Review booklet, pp. 41–45
- Guide to the Essentials (English/Spanish), Chapter 10

Technology
- Student Edition on Audio CD, Chapter 10
- Guided Reading Audiotapes (English/Spanish), Chapter 10
- Section Reading Support Transparencies

Less Proficient Writers

Teacher's Edition
- Customize for Less Proficient Writers, p. 371

Teaching Resources
- Guided Reading and Review booklet, pp. 41–45
- Guide to the Essentials (English/Spanish), Chapter 10

Technology
- Student Edition on Audio CD, Chapter 10
- Guided Reading Audiotapes (English/Spanish), Chapter 10
- Section Reading Support Transparencies

TEACHER'S EDITION INDEX

CHAPTER 10 – PACING SUGGESTIONS

 For 90-minute Blocks

- Teach sections 1, 2, 3, and 4 using Transparencies A18, A19, C4, and G8, and the Recent Scholarship note on page 349 for class discussions.

 Running Out of Time?

If you are running short on time to cover this chapter, consider the following options:

- Use the Prentice Hall Presentation Pro CD-ROM to create an outline for this chapter.
- Use the Section Summaries for Chapter 10, from **Guide to the Essentials (English/Spanish).**

ADDITIONAL ACTIVITIES

1 Two Nations

Connecting with Economics
Have students work in pairs to create graphs from the table on page 350 to visually compare the economic differences between the North and South. Assign each pair one of the following three categories: Agriculture, Manufacturing and Finance, or Livestock. Tell students to first decide on the best type of graph for making the comparison. Advise them that in some cases they may decide more than one graph or type of graph is needed. Pairs should then design their graphs and plot the data on them. Call on pairs to present their graphs, explain why they chose their graph types, and describe challenges they had to overcome in constructing their graphs. **(Visual/Spatial; Logical/Mathematical)**

2 The Mexican War and Slavery Extension

Connecting with History and Conflict
Have students assume the role of Northerners or Southerners in 1846 and write letters to the editor either supporting or opposing the United States' war with Mexico. Remind students that the war was controversial. Suggest that, before they write their letters, they consider how any national expansion resulting from the war might influence their opinion about it. Tell students that their letters should identify the role of its writer, state his or her position on the war, and explain his or her reasons for that position. Have students representing "for" and "against" positions from both North and South read their letters to the class. **(Verbal/Linguistic)**

3 New Political Parties

Connecting with Citizenship
Invite students to imagine they are young adults in the mid-1850s. Tell them to think about the issues and events of the late 1840s and early 1850s that would have influenced their political attitudes and values. Have them decide which party—Democratic, Whig, Republican, Free Soil, or American—they would have supported. Tell them to write a one-page statement of their chosen political affiliation, explaining the reasons for their decision. Call on volunteers to read their statements and determine if class members, in their roles, agree with the stated reasons and positions on the issues. **(Verbal/Linguistic)**

4 The System Fails

Connecting with History and Conflict
Organize students into pairs or small groups to create a time line titled "The Road to Civil War." Instruct students to begin their time line with passage of the Kansas-Nebraska Act and end it with John Brown's raid on Harper's Ferry. (You may wish to extend this activity to include related events of the 1840s and early 1850s and subsequent events in 1860 and 1861.) Tell students that events that span a period of time should be so indicated on their time line. Then call on students to explain why specific events on their time lines were "steps" on the road to war. **(Visual/Spatial)**

5 A Nation Divided Against Itself

Connecting with Government
Organize the class into groups of six or eight. Half the students in each group should represent Southerners and the other half Northerners. Tell the groups that their task is to attempt to reach a negotiated settlement of the secession crisis. Remind students on each side that any settlement to which they agree must be politically acceptable to the larger society they represent. Have each group report its negotiated settlement to the class, or explain why no settlement could be reached. Then have the entire class debate and vote, first as Northerners and then as Southerners, whether each settlement the groups have negotiated will be acceptable to their section. **(Verbal/Linguistic)**

INTRODUCING THE CHAPTER

The middle of the nineteenth century was a time of deep distrust and escalating hostility between the North and the South. Many Americans no longer believed that the federal government could settle their differences, and the Union finally shattered.

TIME LINE ACTIVITY

To provide students with practice in using the time line, ask questions such as these:

1. What important event in Mexican and American history took place in 1848, and what was its significance? *(The Treaty of Guadalupe was signed, ending the Mexican War and awarding northern Mexico to the United States.)*

2. In what year was the Kansas-Nebraska Act passed? *(1854)*

3. What important industrial process was discovered in 1856? *(German Henry Bessemer discovered how to mass-produce steel.)*

SECTION 1   Two Nations
SECTION 2   The Mexican War and Slavery Extension
SECTION 3   New Political Parties
SECTION 4   The System Fails
SECTION 5   A Nation Divided Against Itself

Stop the Runaway!

$100 Reward!

Ranaway from the subscriber, living in Clay county, Mo., 3 miles south of Haynesville and 15 miles north of Liberty, a negro boy named SANDY, about 35 years of age, about 5 feet 6 inches high, rather copper color, whiskers on his chin, quick when spoken to, had on when he left brown jeans pants and coat, black plush cap, and coarse boots. If apprehended a reward of $25 will be given if taken in Clay county; $50 if out of the county, and $100 if taken out of the State, and delivered to me or confined in jail so that I can get him.   ROBT. THOMPSON.
April 3, 1860.

American Events

1845
The United States annexes Texas.

1848
The Treaty of Guadalupe Hidalgo ends the Mexican War and awards northern Mexico to the United States.

1850
Congress agrees to the Compromise of 1850, including the Fugitive Slave Act.

1852
Harriet Beecher Stowe publishes *Uncle Tom's Cabin*.

1854
Congress passes the Kansas-Nebraska Act. The Republican Party organizes to oppose the spread of slavery.

Presidential Terms: James Polk 1845–1849   Z. Taylor 1849–50   Millard Fillmore 1850–1853   Franklin Pierce 1853–1857

1845   •   **1850**   •   •   **1855**   •

World Events

The Taiping rebellion begins in China.
1850

Britain and France join the Crimean War against Russia.
1854

Henry Bessemer discovers a way to mass-produce steel.
1856

---

eTeach

Be sure to check out this month's online discussion with a Master Teacher. Go to **www.phschool.com**.

RESOURCE DIRECTORY

Teaching Resources
Pacing Charts booklet
Block Scheduling booklet, p. 18
Units 3/4 booklet
• Chapter Summary, p. 40

Technology
Guided Reading Audiotapes (English/Spanish), Ch. 10
Student Edition on Audio CD, Ch. 10
Prentice Hall United States History Video Collection™ Volume 8, *Causes of the Civil War*
Prentice Hall Presentation Pro CD-ROM, Ch. 10
Resource Pro® CD-ROM
Social Studies Skills Tutor CD-ROM
Companion Web site, www.phschool.com

Slavery by County, 1860

Slaves as percentage of total population

- 70 or more
- 50–70
- 30–50
- 10–30
- 10 or less
- None, or no data

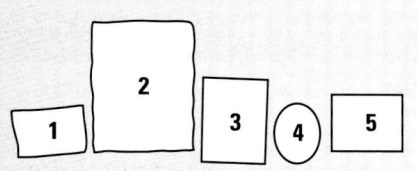

NATIONAL REPUBLICAN CHART
PRESIDENTIAL CAMPAIGN 1860

1857
The Supreme Court rules against Dred Scott.

1860
Abraham Lincoln wins the presidential election with no Southern support.

1860
South Carolina becomes the first of seven Lower South states to secede from the Union.

1861
The attack on Fort Sumter begins the Civil War. Virginia, Tennessee, North Carolina, and Arkansas join the Confederacy.

James Buchanan 1857–1861

Abraham Lincoln 1861–1865

1860

1865

Hindu and Muslim soldiers in India rebel against British rule.

Charles Dickens publishes *A Tale of Two Cities.*

Victor Emmanuel II proclaims a unified Kingdom of Italy.

1857

1859

1861

Chapter 10 **345**

Slavery by County, 1860

Activating Prior Knowledge Why did Missouri have such a low percentage of slaves? *(It was one of the later states to join the Union, and the legality of slavery had been in question there.)*

Previewing What factors may have influenced the percentage of slaves in a population? *(Possible answers may include the types of industries, the cost of labor, and the wealth of the communities.)*

BACKGROUND
About the Pictures

1. Though Texas became a state in the Union once again, it was allowed to keep the title to its public lands.

2. Among other things, the Fugitive Slave Act prohibited fugitives from trials by jury and from testifying in their own cases.

3. *Uncle Tom's Cabin* was initially published as a serial in an antislavery paper called the *National Era.*

4. The *Dred Scott* decision made slavery legal in all of the United States territories.

5. Lincoln's election spurred South Carolina's secession from the Union and, in turn, generated several compromise proposals to guarantee the rights of slave owners.

BIBLIOGRAPHY

For the Teacher

Angle, Paul, ed. **Complete Lincoln-Douglas Debates of 1858**. University of Chicago Press, 1991. (Definitive record of these encounters.)

Ashworth, John. **Slavery, Capitalism, and Politics in the Antebellum Republic: Commerce and Compromise, 1820–1850**. Cambridge University Press, 1996. (A thorough examination of this era.)

Stegmaier, Mark J. **Texas, New Mexico, and the Compromise of 1850: Boundary Dispute & Sectional Crisis**. Kent State University Press, 1996. (Describes this critical region of the country at a crucial point in history.)

For the Student

Bibb, Henry. **The Life and Adventures of Henry Bibb: An American Slave.** University of Wisconsin Press, 2000. (An engrossing self-portrait of a man caught between two worlds.)

Douglass, Frederick. **Narrative of the Life of Frederick Douglass, an American Slave: Written by Himself.** Yale University Press, 2001. (Classic, eloquent account of his life and history.)

Kemble, Fanny, et al. **Journal of a Residence on a Georgian Plantation in 1838–1839.** University of Georgia Press, 1984. (A northern woman discovers that her husband's family holds slaves.)

TEXT

Don't miss the exclusive interactive version of this textbook on the Web and on CD-ROM.

SECTION OBJECTIVES

1. Find out why some historians think the Civil War was unavoidable.

2. Discover arguments used by abolitionists against slavery.

3. Learn how Southerners viewed slavery.

4. Understand some important differences between the North and the South.

BELLRINGER

Warm-Up Activity Ask students to discuss what they know about differences among regions in the United States today. What effect might these differences have on the nation as a whole today?

Activating Prior Knowledge Have students list the types of tensions that arose in the 1840s and 1850s around the issue of slavery.

READING STRATEGY

As students read the section, have them create a chart comparing and contrasting the North's and South's views on slavery, as well as the level of economic development in the two regions.

ACTIVITY
Connecting with Geography

Call students' attention to the argument of some historians that the Civil War resulted from racial, social, and cultural differences in the mid-1800s. Have students speculate on geographical and technological factors that would allow such distinct differences to exist within a nation. Then have each student compile a list of factors in modern America that minimize regional differences and produce a more uniform culture and society. Call on students to share their lists with the class. Discuss the influence of some of the listed items. **(Verbal/Linguistic; Logical/Mathematical)**

Two Nations

READING FOCUS

- Why do some historians think the Civil War was unavoidable?
- What arguments did abolitionists use against slavery?
- How did Southerners view slavery?
- What were some important differences between the North and the South?

MAIN IDEA

In the 1850s, growing numbers of Americans believed that the North and the South were moving in different directions.

KEY TERMS

Union
prejudice
obsolete

TAKING NOTES

Copy the chart below. As you read this section, fill in the chart with the major cultural and economic differences between the North and the South.

Northern States	Southern States
• Diverse, fast-growing population • High concentration of railroads •	

A spool of thread spun in a northern mill and a boll of raw cotton grown in the South symbolize the difference between the industrial power of the North and the agricultural strength of the South in the 1850s.

Setting the Scene Starting in 1861, states of the North clashed with states of the South in a brutal conflict that Americans call the Civil War. The outcome of the war would determine whether the **Union,** as the unified nation was called, would survive or whether the country would split into two independent nations.

The causes of the Civil War were many and complex, and have been debated by historians for decades. This section describes some of the growing cultural and economic differences between the North and the South in the decade before the outbreak of war.

Historians and the Civil War

Some historians have suggested that the United States could have avoided the Civil War. If Americans had elected better leaders and established stronger political institutions at a national level, they believe, extremists on both sides would never have been able to force the nation into war. This view is based on the belief that Americans of the mid-1800s had many cultural and political traditions in common and therefore could have settled their differences. Whether in Alabama, Oregon, Indiana, or Massachusetts, according to this belief, Americans supported democracy, free enterprise, and social equality.

More recently, other historians have rejected this idea that American society was similar everywhere. These historians tend to emphasize the differences between the regions, racial groups, and social classes of the North and the South. Although these historians do not claim that the events of the Civil War had to have happened the way they did, they do believe that some kind of major conflict was bound to occur.

The Case Against Slavery

During the early 1800s, many Americans observed sharp contrasts between the North and the South. They said that the two great sections amounted to distinct nations within the United States. The key difference between the North and the South, and the difference to which all other conflicts were connected, was slavery.

346   Chapter 10 • *The Coming of the Civil War*

RESOURCE DIRECTORY

Teaching Resources
Learning Styles Lesson Plans booklet, p. 22
Guided Reading and Review booklet, p. 41

Technology
Section Reading Support Transparencies
Guided Reading Audiotapes (English/Spanish), Ch. 10
Student Edition on Audio CD, Ch. 10
Sounds of an Era Audio CD *Walt Whitman on America* (time: 45 seconds)
Color Transparencies *American Diversity,* G8

Exploring Primary Sources in U.S. History CD-ROM *Uncle Tom's Cabin, Harriet Beecher Stowe*
Prentice Hall Presentation Pro CD-ROM, Ch. 10
Companion Web site, www.phschool.com

By the 1850s, many white Northerners had come to believe that slavery violated the basic principles of both the United States and the Christian religion. Most white opponents of slavery were members of the democratic Protestant faiths that had been on the rise since the Second Great Awakening. The members of these faiths believed that all humans, free or enslaved, had the right to choose their own destiny and to follow God's laws.

Slavery's white opponents did not necessarily believe that blacks and whites were equal. Many, in fact, were deeply prejudiced against African Americans. (A **prejudice** is an unreasonable, usually unfavorable opinion of another group that is not based on fact.) Nevertheless these people believed that slavery was an evil that could not be tolerated.

Uncle Tom's Cabin   Without question, the most powerful statement made during this period about the impact of slavery was *Uncle Tom's Cabin*, by Harriet Beecher Stowe. Published in 1852, Stowe's novel became an instant bestseller and sold millions of copies in the United States and abroad.

The story is set in the pre–Civil War South. In the novel, a slave named Eliza Harris escapes from her home on Shelby plantation in Kentucky when her child is about to be sold. As Eliza heads north, she avoids the hired slave catchers and finds help along the Underground Railroad. Another slave, Uncle Tom, is "sold down the river" to another owner and is eventually killed by his brutal master, Simon Legree.

Stowe did not depend only on the sharp contrast between the kind slave Uncle Tom and his cruel master to make her case against slavery. She also tried to show that slavery was opposed to beliefs that many Northerners cherished: the importance of women and the ideal of the family. In the novel, the neat, orderly world of Uncle Tom's cabin, formed around his happy family, comes to a tragic end when Uncle Tom's owner has to sell him. Eventually Uncle Tom falls into the hands of the cruel slaveholder, Simon Legree.

By contrast with the saintly Uncle Tom, Simon Legree is everything Stowe's audience in the North feared and despised: an unmarried, anti-Christian, heavy-drinking bully. Not only does he brutalize the enslaved women of his plantation, but in the end he beats Uncle Tom to death with a whip. It was not by accident that Stowe made Legree a Northerner who had moved to the South. She wanted to show that slavery also could corrupt those born outside the system.

To contrast these stark images of the immoral effects of slavery, Stowe wrote powerful scenes in which northern women influence their husbands to do what is right. For example, in one scene set in a house in Ohio, a wife persuades her husband, a senator, to permit some escaped slaves to continue their journey to Canada. When her husband tries to argue with her, she replies:

> 66 *I don't know anything about politics, but I can read my Bible; and there I see that I must feed the hungry, clothe the naked, and comfort the desolate; and that Bible I mean to follow.* 99

Her husband points out that to help escaped slaves would involve breaking the law. The wife replies:

READING CHECK
How did the Second Great Awakening draw people to abolitionism?

VIEWING HISTORY Harriet Beecher Stowe's *Uncle Tom's Cabin* offered antislavery forces new encouragement in resisting the slavery system. **Distinguishing Fact From Opinion** *Identify two ways that the drawing adds drama to Eliza's escape from slavery.*

Chapter 10 • Section 1   **347**

> ❝ *Obeying God never brings on public evils. I know it can't. It's always safest, all round, to do as He bids us.* ❞

Impact of *Uncle Tom's Cabin* Although a work of fiction, *Uncle Tom's Cabin* had as powerful an effect in Stowe's time as Thomas Paine's *Common Sense* had in his. According to a family story, when Stowe met President Lincoln during the Civil War he said, "So this is the little lady who made this big war?"

Stowe's novel presented a vivid picture of slavery in the South that northern readers found believable, even if it was in fact exaggerated. As they read *Uncle Tom's Cabin,* many Northerners became convinced that slavery would be the ruin of the United States. They worried about the impact of slavery not just on African Americans, but on whites and American society in general. Of this they were sure: they would never allow the United States to become a land of Simon Legrees.

Southern Views on Slavery

Southern intellectuals and politicians reacted very differently to *Uncle Tom's Cabin.* To them, Stowe's bestseller was a book of insulting lies. While they admitted that some masters did treat enslaved people badly, they argued that few were as cruel as Simon Legree. Some white Southerners had their own exaggerated view of slavery, in which plantation households were like large and happy families.

Southerners did more than protest northern criticism. Many spoke out to defend slavery and attack the evils they saw in the North. They claimed that most planters took a personal interest in the well-being of the enslaved people who worked for them and provided them with the basic necessities of life. Northern industrialists, they argued, took no personal responsibility for their workers because they had no strong connection to them. Northerners could easily replace their workers and therefore, Southerners believed, northern employers did not care if they paid workers enough to buy decent food, clothing, and shelter. Most Southerners believed that northern business owners mistreated their workers because they were motivated solely by profit.

Perhaps the most direct statement of this point of view appeared in a book by George Fitzhugh published in 1857, titled *Cannibals All!* Attacking northern industrialists, whom he saw as no better than cannibals, Fitzhugh wrote:

> ❝ *You, with the command over labor which your capital gives you, are a slave owner—a master, without the obligations of a master. They, who work for you, who create your income, are slaves, without the rights of slaves. Slaves without a master!* ❞
>
> —George Fitzhugh

Outraged by antislavery Northerners who pretended to be better than Southerners, Fitzhugh exclaimed:

> ❝ *What is falsely called Free Society, is a very recent invention. It proposes to make the weak, ignorant and poor, free, by turning them loose in a world owned exclusively by the few . . . to get a living.* ❞
>
> —George Fitzhugh

THE NEGRO IN HIS OWN COUNTRY.

THE NEGRO IN AMERICA.

Many white Southerners argued that they represented the true spirit of the American Revolution. After all, George Washington, Thomas Jefferson, and many other Revolutionary leaders had owned slaves. These Southerners believed that their households possessed an order, a grace, and a sense of liberty that Northerners could not begin to understand. On one point almost all Southerners agreed: they were not about to let Northerners, whom they saw as arrogant and self-righteous, tell them how to live.

Differences Between the North and the South

The differences between the North and the South were not simply a product of exaggerated fiction and propaganda. Hard facts illustrate how differently the two regions had developed since 1790. Each year the North was becoming ever more urban and industrialized than the South. Its population, already more than twice as large as the South's, was becoming even larger and more diverse as Irish and German immigrants crowded into northern cities. By 1860, nine of the country's ten largest cities were located in the North.

Trains and Trade Like immigration, new technology had a heavier impact on the North than on the South. One critical innovation was the railroad. Railroads dramatically reduced the cost and time needed to ship goods from factory or farm to the marketplace. The most efficient form of transportation the world had yet known, railroads made canals **obsolete,** or outdated, in a matter of years.

By 1840, approximately 3,000 miles of track had been laid in the United States. African American and Irish immigrant workers added another 5,000 miles during the 1840s. It was in the 1850s, however, that the railroads truly came into their own. More than 20,000 miles of track were laid in that decade.

During this railroad boom, remote places suddenly became centers of bustling trade. Railroads took advantage of Chicago's central location to transport goods such as corn and wheat between the east and the west. As a result, Chicago grew from a small trading village to an important regional center in only a few years.

The railroads, however, had a positive effect primarily in the North. In 1860, 70 percent of the railroad track in the United States were in the North. In the 1850s, the South attempted to catch up with the North in terms of transportation. The total length of railroad tracks in the South doubled, and then doubled again in that decade as railroads invested in new links. Railroads contributed to the

VIEWING HISTORY Southern proslavery writers promoted the myth that slavery "raised Africans from savagery" and "civilized" them. These before-and-after pictures are from a pamphlet titled *Bible Defence of Slavery.* **Recognizing Bias** *What other claims did proslavery activists make to justify slavery?*

Reading Comprehension

1. Northerners believed Southerners were morally in the wrong because slavery violated the basic principles of the country and of Christianity. Southerners felt that northern industrialists took no responsibility for workers, paid them meager wages, and were motivated solely by profit.

2. The prejudice that African Americans were inferior.

3. The North was more urban and industrial, had more advanced transportation, and had more immigrants. The South remained agricultural and dependent upon slave labor.

Critical Thinking and Writing

4. Its portrayal of slavery was very dramatic. It showed that slavery was in conflict with the beliefs of many Americans. *Uncle Tom's Cabin* helped convince many Northerners that slavery would be the ruin of the U.S.

5. Sample answer: View 1: Americans were similar in their belief in democracy and could have settled their differences. (Students may infer that a shared goal will unite people despite some differences.) View 2: Americans were not similar. Differences in geography, racial groups, and social class made a major conflict inevitable. (Students may infer that strong differences among people led to conflicts, despite some common goals.)

Take It to the NET

Graphs will vary, but should clearly and effectively represent the chosen data.

CAPTION ANSWERS

Interpreting Charts The North held advantages in finance, industry, population, and railroads; the South had advantages only in certain areas of agriculture and livestock.

Economic Advantages of the North and South

	Northern States	Southern States
Agriculture		
Corn (bushels)	✓ 446 million	280 million
Wheat (bushels)	✓ 132 million	31 million
Oats (bushels)	✓ 150 million	20 million
Cotton (bales)	4 thousand	✓ 5 million
Tobacco (pounds)	✓ 229 million	199 million
Rice (pounds)	50 thousand	✓ 187 million
Finance		
Bank Deposits	✓ $207 million	$47 million
Specie	✓ $56 million	$27 million
Livestock		
Horses	✓ 4.2 million	1.7 million
Donkeys and Mules	300 thousand	✓ 800 thousand
Milk Cows	✓ 5.7 million	2.7 million
Beef Cattle	6.6 million	✓ 7 million
Sheep	✓ 16 million	5 million
Swine	✓ 16.3 million	15.5 million
Manufacturing		
Number of Factories	✓ 110.1 thousand	20.6 thousand
Number of Workers	✓ 1.17 million	111 thousand
Value of Products	✓ $1.62 billion	$155 million
Population	✓ 21.5 million	9 million
Railroad Mileage	✓ 21.7 thousand miles	9 thousand miles

SOURCE: *The American Heritage Picture History of the Civil War*

INTERPRETING CHARTS The economic contrasts between the North and the South were sharp. **Analyzing Information** *Summarize the types of advantages held by the North and the South.*

growth of many southern cities, such as Atlanta, Georgia. Still, in 1860 the southern railroad network was much less developed than railroad networks in New England or the Midwest. Southern planters and farmers were more likely to transport their crops by water than by rail.

The Telegraph Like the railroad, the telegraph magnified the differences between the North and the South. This historic advance in communication, developed by Samuel F. B. Morse in 1844, allowed people to send messages over wires by using a code of short and long pulses of electricity. A combination of "dots" and "dashes" represented each letter of the alphabet. Because telegraph wires were strung along the ever-growing network of railroad tracks, the communications revolution in the North advanced more quickly than in the South.

Together, railroads and improved communications nourished the booming industries of the North. In 1860, the North had 110,000 factories, compared to 20,000 in the South; it produced over $1.6 billion worth of goods, compared to the South's $155 million. In fact, in terms of numbers, the South outranked the North in only two notable ways: it had more enslaved people and it produced more cotton. As the chart illustrates, the South also grew more rice and matched or exceeded the North in many categories of livestock.

Certainly, the North and the South in 1860 had much in common. They both cherished their democratic traditions, for example. Nevertheless, the two regions held competing visions of what American society should become. As economic and political power shifted in favor of the North, people in the South worried that they would lose their voice in the debate.

Section 1 Assessment

READING COMPREHENSION

1. How did slavery affect the views that Northerners and Southerners had of each other?

2. What **prejudice** was common to most whites in all parts of the country?

3. How did the economic trends that occurred in the 1800s affect the North and the South differently?

CRITICAL THINKING AND WRITING

4. **Recognizing Cause and Effect** Why was *Uncle Tom's Cabin* successful in changing many people's attitudes toward slavery?

5. **Writing an Opinion** Write a short paragraph summarizing the two main views held by historians on the issue of whether the Civil War could have been avoided.

Take It to the NET

Activity: Constructing a Graph Use historical census data to construct a graph of agricultural or manufacturing production in different states in 1850 or 1860. What do the data tell you? Use the links provided in the *America: Pathways to the Present* area of the following Web site for help in completing this activity.
www.phschool.com

RESOURCE DIRECTORY

Teaching Resources
Units 3/4 booklet
• Section 1 Quiz, p. 41
Guide to the Essentials
• Section 1 Summary, p. 52
Learning with Documents booklet (Visual Learning Activity) *The Annexation of Texas*, p. 49

The Mexican War and Slavery Extension

READING FOCUS

- What events led to the annexation of Texas?
- Why did the United States go to war with Mexico?
- Why did the Wilmot Proviso lead to conflict?

MAIN IDEA

The annexation of Texas and the Mexican War of 1846–1848 extended the boundaries of the United States from the Atlantic to the Pacific.

KEY TERMS

manifest destiny
annex
Mexican War
Treaty of Guadalupe
 Hidalgo
Gadsden Purchase
Wilmot Proviso

TAKING NOTES

Copy the flowchart below. As you read, fill in the chart with events that led to the acquisition of California and the Southwest.

Texas votes to join the United States.

⬇

⬇

⬇

Treaty gives land in northern Mexico to the United States.

Section 2
The Mexican War and Slavery Extension

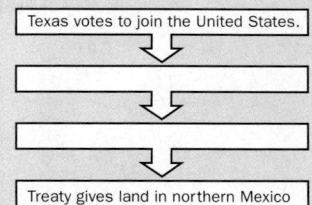

SECTION OBJECTIVES

1. Learn about events that led to the annexation of Texas.
2. Understand why the United States went to war with Mexico.
3. See why the Wilmot Proviso led to conflict.

BELLRINGER

Warm-Up Activity Provide a map of the United States and ask students to list at least five cities in California, Texas, and New Mexico with names that are Spanish in origin. Ask them if, based on what they know, Mexican and American cultures would be likely to clash.

Activating Prior Knowledge Ask students to recall what they have learned about the efforts by Spain to establish settlements east of the Mississippi.

READING STRATEGY

Have students read the section's bold-faced headings. Ask them to write a question about each heading and look for answers as they read.

*A*CTIVITY
Connecting with Culture

Organize students into pairs or small groups to create poems or raps that apply the principle of manifest destiny in the 1840s to the annexation of Texas, to the desire for California, or to going to war with Mexico. Allow time for students to read their poems or perform their raps for the class. (**Musical/Rhythmic; Bodily/Kinesthetic**)

Setting the Scene Migration from the United States into western territories surged in the 1830s and 1840s. That started some Americans dreaming of an empire stretching from the Atlantic to the Pacific. These Americans believed that the United States had a divine mission to spread liberty across the continent. A New York journalist named John L. O'Sullivan captured this sense of mission when he coined the phrase **manifest destiny,** meaning "obvious or undeniable fate."

Writing in 1845, O'Sullivan claimed that it was the nation's "manifest destiny to overspread and to possess the whole of the continent which Providence has given us for the development of the great experiment of liberty and federated self-government entrusted to us." In the 1840s, Americans believed that no other nation should be allowed to keep the United States from fulfilling its destiny.

Annexation of Texas

In 1836, after winning independence from Mexico, Texans voted to be **annexed** by the United States. To annex means to "join" or "attach." Texans encouraged the United States to absorb their new republic, partly to protect themselves from invasion by Mexico.

Americans, however, were far from united on the question of annexation. Most Southerners and Democrats supported it. They looked forward to carving one or more slave states out of the Texas territory. Northerners and Whigs generally opposed it. They feared that the addition of even one slave state would shift the balance of power to the South.

Many people in both the North and the South worried that annexation would lead to war with Mexico. Their fear proved justified in August 1843, when Mexican leader Santa Anna warned that annexation would be "equivalent to a declaration of war against the Mexican Republic." Despite this warning, President John Tyler signed a treaty of annexation with Texas in April 1844. Two months later the Whig-controlled Senate defeated the treaty.

Later that year Democrat James K. Polk won the presidency. The victory of Polk, a strong advocate of expansion, suggested that the majority of Americans

The Texas flag reflects the new republic's informal name: the Lone Star Republic.

RESOURCE DIRECTORY

Teaching Resources
Guided Reading and Review booklet, p. 42

Student Edition on Audio CD, Ch. 10
Prentice Hall Presentation Pro CD-ROM, Ch.10
Companion Web site, www.phschool.com

Other Print Resources
Historical Outline Map Book *War with Mexico, 1846–1848,* p. 41

Technology
Section Reading Support Transparencies
Guided Reading Audiotapes (English/Spanish), Ch. 10

Focus The movement of settlers and traders into Texas, New Mexico, and California caused tension between Mexico and the United States. Ask how Mexico reacted to these new immigrants.

Instruct Discuss the settlement of Hispanic North America. Encourage discussion with questions such as the following: What was Spain trying to do by establishing missions in California? What role did economics play in the American colonization of Mexico's northern territories? How did Mexico unwittingly encourage the American takeover of Texas?

Assess/Reteach Ask students to list ways in which the conflicts between Mexico and the United States resulted in a vastly different North America.

VIEWING HISTORY The election of President James K. Polk in 1844 paved the way for the annexation of Texas. **Recognizing Cause and Effect** How did Mexico react to the annexation?

American settlers in California declared their independence under the Bear Flag in 1846.

wanted to acquire more territory. Legislators' views on the Texas question began to shift. In February 1845, before Polk even took the oath of office, Congress approved annexation. In December 1845, after Texas voters added their approval, Texas became the twenty-eighth state in the Union.

War With Mexico

In March 1845, one month after Congress approved annexation, Mexico broke off diplomatic relations with the United States. The Mexican government had taken the first step toward war. Even if the United States could persuade Mexico to accept the annexation, a dispute about the southern boundary of Texas remained an explosive issue. The United States claimed that the Rio Grande was the official American-Mexican border. Mexico claimed that the Nueces River, located quite a few miles farther north, was the border.

President Polk and other southern Democrats wanted much more from Mexico than just Texas. Polk had dreams of acquiring the entire territory stretching from Texas to the Pacific. In a final attempt to avoid war, he sent Ambassador John Slidell to Mexico City in November 1845 with an offer to buy New Mexico and California for $30 million. But the Mexican government refused even to receive Slidell, let alone consider his offer.

Determined to have his way, Polk sent more than 3,000 American troops under General Zachary Taylor into the disputed area of southern Texas. Taylor crossed the Nueces in March 1846 and set up camp near the Rio Grande. Mexico considered Taylor's advance an invasion of Mexican territory and prepared to take action.

Mexican troops engaged in a skirmish with Taylor's forces in late April 1846. Several Americans were killed. This was the excuse Polk had been waiting for. Expressing outrage at the loss of "American blood on American soil," the President pushed for a declaration of war. Despite some opposition, Congress gave it to him on May 13, 1846, and the **Mexican War** was declared. Meanwhile, an American expedition under the command of Captain John C. Frémont moved into California, probably under orders from President Polk.

Bear Flag Revolt Before news of the war with Mexico even reached California, a group of American settlers took matters into their own hands. Led by William B. Ide, these settlers launched a surprise attack on the town of Sonoma on June 14 and proclaimed the Republic of California. The settlers' flag pictured a grizzly bear and a single star, so the uprising became known as the Bear Flag Revolt. Frémont quickly assumed control of the rebel forces and then drove the Mexican army out of northern California.

In July 1846, United States troops under General Stephen Kearny crossed into New Mexico. Meeting little resistance, American forces occupied Santa Fe by mid-August. Kearny then took part of his army and marched west

352 Chapter 10 • *The Coming of the Civil War*

CAPTION ANSWERS

Viewing History Mexico broke off diplomatic relations with the United States.

RESOURCE DIRECTORY

Other Print Resources
Nystrom *Atlas of Our Country* *Early Expansion of the United States,* pp. 20–21

Technology
Color Transparencies *Historical Maps,* A18
Sounds of an Era Audio CD *"Sovinir de Porto Rico,"* Louis Moreau Gottschalk

to California to join Frémont. Together they defeated the Mexican army. By January 1847 the United States had taken control of the territories of New Mexico and California.

Fighting in Mexico While Frémont and Kearny were securing Mexico's northern territories, General Taylor had taken the war into Mexico. After crossing the Rio Grande, Taylor won a series of victories, leading finally to the Battle of Buena Vista in February 1847.

Here he met Santa Anna, who had brought an army of 20,000 Mexican troops north from Mexico City. Taylor's army won the hard-fought battle, which left hundreds killed and wounded on both sides. When it was over, Santa Anna chose to declare victory and return to Mexico City rather than continue the struggle.

Santa Anna abandoned northeastern Mexico to Taylor in part because of a serious threat to his capital. Pressing for complete victory, Polk had dispatched forces under General Winfield Scott to take Mexico City. In March 1847, Scott captured the port city of Veracruz. Then he marched his army of 10,000 men toward Mexico City along the route once taken by Spanish conquistador Hernán Cortés. After fierce fighting, Scott defeated Santa Anna's forces and captured the Mexican capital on September 14, bringing the war to an end.

The Treaty of Guadalupe Hidalgo With the defeat of its troops and the fall of the country's capital, the Mexican government sought peace. The terms of the **Treaty of Guadalupe Hidalgo,** signed on February 2, 1848, reflected Mexico's weak bargaining position:

1. Mexico gave up its claim to Texas and recognized the Rio Grande as the southern border of Texas.
2. Mexico gave New Mexico and California, which together made up more than two fifths of its territory, to the United States.
3. The United States paid Mexico $15 million.
4. The United States agreed to pay claims made by American citizens against Mexico, which would amount to more than $3 million.

Five years later, in 1853, the Mexican government sold 30,000 square miles of present-day southern New Mexico and Arizona to the United States for $10 million. Known as the **Gadsden Purchase,** this land eventually provided a route for the southern transcontinental railroad.

Although the Mexican War is less well-known than other wars the United States has fought, the American victory over Mexico had important effects. The Treaty of Guadalupe Hidalgo, together with the 1846 division of Oregon and the Gadsden Purchase, established the boundaries of the continental United States as we now know them. Referred to by Mexicans as the North American Invasion, the war also left many Mexicans deeply bitter toward the United States and led to decades of poor relations and misunderstandings. Finally, the acquisition of a vast expanse of territory in the West opened the doors for an even larger wave of western migration.

The Mexican War, 1846–1848

Oregon Country
ROCKY MTS.
Unorganized Territory
Wis. Terr.
UNITED STATES
Iowa
III.
Fort Leavenworth
Mo.
2. Bear Flag Revolt June 14, 1846
San Francisco
3. Monterey occupied July 7, 1846
8. San Gabriel Jan. 8, 1847
4. Santa Fe occupied Aug. 18, 1846
Santa Fe
Ark.
San Diego
6. San Pasqual Dec. 6, 1846
7. El Brazito Dec. 25, 1846
5. Monterrey Sept. 20–25, 1846
1. Palo Alto May 8, 1846
Texas
Nueces R.
La.
MEXICO
Corpus Christi
90°W
10. Sacramento Feb. 28, 1847
Gulf of Mexico
PACIFIC OCEAN
9. Buena Vista Feb. 22–23, 1847
Mazatlán
SANTA ANNA
12. Cerro Gordo Apr. 18, 1847
Tampico
13. Chapultepec Sept. 13, 1847
20°N
14. Mexico City entered Sept. 14, 1847
N
11. Veracruz Mar. 27, 1847
100°W

Disputed territory
American forces
Mexican forces
American victory
Mexican victory
Fort

0   150   300 mi.
0 150 300 km

MAP SKILLS Many Americans, including President Polk, viewed the Mexican War as an opportunity to expand America's borders across the continent. **Movement** *What information on this map can you use to predict who won the war?*

READING CHECK
How did the Mexican War begin?

Reading Comprehension

1. Many Northerners feared that the addition of even one slave state would shift the balance of power to the South. Both Northerners and Southerners worried that annexation could lead to war with Mexico.

2. By adding Texas, New Mexico, and California as a result of it, the war greatly increased the nation's territory.

3. The U.S. purchased 30,000 square miles of present-day southern New Mexico and Arizona. This land eventually provided a route for the southern transcontinental railroad.

4. To prevent slavery from existing in any territory acquired from Mexico.

Critical Thinking and Writing

5. Sample answer: No, because Texas was heavily populated by American settlers.

6. Essays will vary, but students' opinions should be supported with facts from the section.

Take It to the NET

Articles should describe the circumstances leading up to the chosen event, as well as a chronology of the event itself. Students may also choose to discuss the event's potential ramifications.

The Mexican War: Causes and Effects

CAUSES

- United States annexes Texas.
- United States and Mexico disagree about the southern border of Texas.
- Mexico refuses to sell California and New Mexico to the United States.
- Polk sends troops to establish the Rio Grande as the U.S.–Mexico border.
- Polk sends troops to California.

↓

THE MEXICAN WAR

↓

EFFECTS

- Rio Grande is established as the U.S.–Mexico border.
- United States acquires California and New Mexico.
- Debate over the expansion of slavery intensifies.

INTERPRETING CHARTS
The Mexican War was the result of Polk's desire to expand the United States. **Drawing Conclusions** *In what way was the Mexican War a success?*

The Wilmot Proviso

Possibly the most important effect of the Mexican War was helping to bring the question of slavery to the forefront of American politics. Politicians had long avoided dealing with the question of slavery within existing states. But they had to confront the slavery issue directly when they created new territories or states.

A central issue facing Congress in the 1840s and 1850s was whether or not to allow slavery in the territories acquired by the United States from Mexico. Any states carved out of slave territories would, one day, probably become slave states. Likewise, free territories would become free states.

Depending on what Congress did, the balance of political power between North and South (or between free and slave states) could shift. The Senate, where each state had equal representation, would feel the greatest shock as a result of such a power shift. Northerners also feared that adding slave states could cause an economic shift to the South. They did not want to compete with plantation owners, whose use of slavery drove wages down.

In 1846, a bill came before Congress to provide funds for negotiating with Mexico. Pennsylvania Democrat David Wilmot attached a proviso, or amendment, to the bill. The **Wilmot Proviso** stated that "as an express and fundamental condition of the acquisition of any territory from the Republic of Mexico . . . neither slavery nor involuntary servitude shall ever exist in any part of said territory." If the amendment passed, it would have closed California and New Mexico to slavery as a requirement for their annexation. Congress did not pass the amendment.

Northerners continued to attach this proviso to bills related to the new territories. Some Northerners in the House supported the proviso as a weapon against slavery, while others voted for it to show that northern Democrats could challenge southern Democrats for control of the House. The Wilmot Proviso never became law. Each time it came up for discussion, however, the Wilmot Proviso revealed the growing gap between the North and the South over slavery.

Section 2 Assessment

READING COMPREHENSION

1. Why did some Americans oppose the **annexation** of Texas?

2. How did the war against Mexico help the United States achieve its **manifest destiny?**

3. What was the outcome of the **Gadsden Purchase?**

4. What was the purpose of the **Wilmot Proviso?**

CRITICAL THINKING AND WRITING

5. **Identifying Alternatives** Do you think that it would have been possible for Texas to remain separate from the United States? Why?

6. **Writing to Persuade** Write a brief editorial in which you explain why the United States should or should not go to war with Mexico in 1846.

Take It to the NET

Activity: Writing a Newspaper Article Select a key event from the Mexican War or the annexation of Texas. Write a newspaper article describing this event in detail. Use the links provided in the *America: Pathways to the Present* area of the following Web site for help in completing this activity.
www.phschool.com

CAPTION ANSWERS

Interpreting Charts It was a success because it vastly increased the size of the United States.

RESOURCE DIRECTORY

Teaching Resources
Units 3/4 booklet
- Section 2 Quiz, p. 42

Guide to the Essentials
- Section 2 Summary, p. 53

New Political Parties

READING FOCUS

- What were the effects of the Missouri Compromise?
- What did the Compromise of 1850 accomplish?
- How did political parties change in the 1850s?
- Why did Stephen Douglas propose the Kansas-Nebraska Act?

MAIN IDEA

A congressional compromise failed to end disagreement over slavery in the territories. Meanwhile, the political party system broke down as new political parties arose.

KEY TERMS

Compromise of 1850
Fugitive Slave Act
nativism
Kansas-Nebraska Act
popular sovereignty

TAKING NOTES

Copy the web diagram below. As you read this section, fill in the web diagram with important elements of the Compromise of 1850.

Compromise of 1850

SECTION OBJECTIVES

1. Discover some effects of the Missouri Compromise.
2. Learn what was accomplished by the Compromise of 1850.
3. See how political parties changed in the 1850s.
4. Find out why Stephen Douglas proposed the Kansas-Nebraska Act.

BELLRINGER

Warm-Up Activity Ask students to discuss what they know about differences among regions in the United States today. What effect might these differences have on the nation as a whole?

Activating Prior Knowledge Review prior class discussions about the differing economies in the North and the South, which gave rise to a continuation of the use of slaves in the South and the need for new immigrants in the North.

READING STRATEGY

As students read the section, have them write a short essay explaining why the Compromise of 1850 was controversial.

Setting the Scene The differences between the North and the South were bound to cause political conflict, but did they have to lead to a lengthy civil war? The answer to this question requires an understanding of politics in the 1850s. The war occurred when it did and in the way it did because politicians could not solve the question of slavery.

Politicians might have been able to keep slavery from tearing the nation apart if Americans had not annexed and settled new lands to the west of the Mississippi. This newly settled land forced an old question back into politics: whether or not slavery would be allowed in the territories. Each new state that joined the Union could tip the balance in Congress in favor of or against slavery in the future.

In the 1840s, Ralph Waldo Emerson wrote in opposition to the war with Mexico, "The United States will conquer Mexico, but it will be as the man swallows the arsenic; Mexico will poison us." As you have read, the United States won the Mexican War and took a large expanse of territory as a reward. Yet the fight to open or close this and other territories to slavery would ultimately destroy relations between the North and the South.

The end of the Mexican War brought the vast territories of California and New Mexico under American control, raising new questions about the expansion of slavery.

Effects of the Missouri Compromise

Congress had made its first attempt to address the question of whether to extend slavery in the territories with the Missouri Compromise of 1820. In the short run, the compromise maintained the balance in the Senate between slave and free states. It also sought to address the long-term issue of westward expansion by stating that any

MAP
CALIFORNIA
NEW MEXICO TEXAS
NEW YORK
1849

ACTIVITY
Connecting with Government

Ask students to write a paragraph summarizing how the failure of politicians to solve the important issues of the day led to the rise of new political parties in the 1850s. **(Verbal/Linguistic)**

RESOURCE DIRECTORY

Teaching Resources
Guided Reading and Review booklet, p. 43

Other Print Resources
Historical Outline Map Book *The Missouri Compromise, 1820,* p. 45

Technology
Section Reading Support Transparencies
Guided Reading Audiotapes (English/Spanish), Ch. 10

Student Edition on Audio CD, Ch. 10
Prentice Hall Presentation Pro CD-ROM, Ch. 10
Companion Web site, www.phschool.com

Focus Explain that existing political organizations in the 1850s failed to deal with the question of slavery. New political parties emerged in order to try to solve the problem.

Instruct Discuss the inability of politicians to deal with slavery. Ask why the Compromise of 1850 provided only a temporary solution. Why did Senator John C. Calhoun think it was impossible for southern interests to be protected by the existing government? How were both Northerners and Southerners able to justify their stand on slavery in terms of the United States Constitution? Why did the Kansas-Nebraska Act outrage northerners?

Assess/Reteach Can students suggest approaches politicians might have taken to resolve differences between antislavery and pro-slavery states that would have been less inflammatory than the approaches described in this section?

This kerchief celebrated General Zachary Taylor and several important battles of the Mexican War.

MAP SKILLS During the debate that led to the Compromise of 1850, all the great speakers of the Senate had their say. The compromise that resulted is shown in the map below. **Regions** *What issues did the Compromise of 1850 attempt to address?*

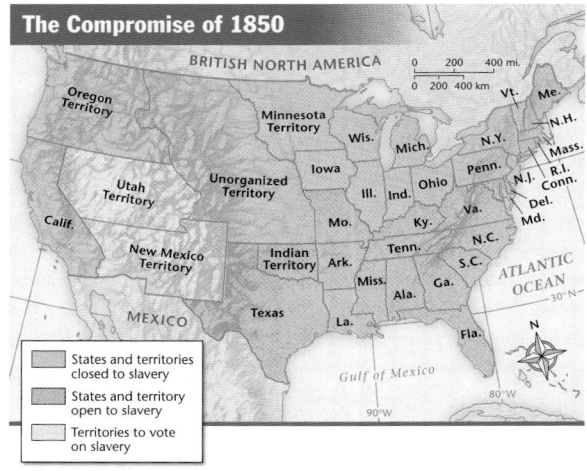

The Compromise of 1850

BRITISH NORTH AMERICA

0   200   400 mi.
0   200 400 km

Oregon Territory

Minnesota Territory

Utah Territory

Unorganized Territory

Calif.

New Mexico Territory

Indian Territory

MEXICO

Texas

Wis. · Mich. · N.Y. · Vt. · Me. · N.H. · Mass.
Iowa · Ill. · Ind. · Ohio · Penn. · N.J. · R.I. · Conn. · Del. · Md.
Mo. · Ky. · Va.
Ark. · Tenn. · N.C. · S.C.
Miss. · Ala. · Ga. · ATLANTIC OCEAN
La. · Fla.

Gulf of Mexico

30°N · 80°W · 90°W

■ States and territories closed to slavery
■ States and territory open to slavery
■ Territories to vote on slavery

states to be created out of lands north of 36° 30' N latitude would be free states. The compromise did not, however, settle the issue of whether slavery would be legal while the lands in the west were still territories.

After the Mexican War, the Treaty of Guadalupe Hidalgo of 1848 gave the United States a large piece of land that had been part of Mexico. Because much of this new territory was south of the line set by the Missouri Compromise, Northerners feared that it would eventually be divided into several slave states. This would give the South a majority vote in the Senate and an advantage in the Electoral College. The best way to prevent the creation of more slave states, reasoned antislavery Northerners, was to keep slavery out of these areas while they were still territories.

Southerners were equally firm in insisting that the national government had no right to prevent free citizens from taking their property to the territories. Property, according to the law, included enslaved people.

In the presidential election of 1848, both major parties hoped to attract voters from all sides of the slavery debate. Thus they nominated candidates who avoided discussing the slavery issue. The Democrats chose Governor Lewis Cass of Michigan, while the Whigs chose a Mexican War general, Zachary Taylor.

Angered by their parties' unwillingness to confront slavery, some members from both parties who opposed slavery in the territories split off and formed the Free Soil Party. The Free Soilers did not win any states in the 1848 election, but they did take enough votes away from Cass to give Taylor a narrow victory.

The Compromise of 1850

The issue of territorial slavery resurfaced in 1849 when California, flooded with migrants during the Gold Rush, asked to join the Union as a free state. Admitting California as a free state would upset the fragile balance between free and slave states in the Senate. The stage was set for one of the most dramatic events in American history.

Clay Proposes a Compromise At the center of this drama were three of the most respected senators of that (or any) era: John C. Calhoun of South Carolina, Henry Clay of Kentucky, and Daniel Webster of Massachusetts. All had begun their long political careers in Congress prior to the War of 1812. When the Senate assembled in 1849, the 73-year-old Clay, who was called "Gallant Harry of the West," tried to solve the nation's dilemma with words rather than blood.

Clay's plan for a compromise over slavery would become known as the **Compromise of 1850.** Seeking a middle ground on the slavery debate, Clay proposed five separate laws, some of which favored the North and some of which favored the South:

1. Congress would admit California as a free state.

RESOURCE DIRECTORY

Other Print Resources
Nystrom *Atlas of Our Country* *Settling the West,* pp. 28–29
Historical Outline Map Book *The Compromise of 1850,* p. 46

Technology
Color Transparencies *Historical Maps,* A19
Sounds of an Era Audio CD *John C. Calhoun for the Compromise of 1850* (time: one minute, 45 seconds)
Exploring Primary Sources in U.S. History CD-ROM *A Frontier Lady,* Sarah Royce

VIEWING HISTORY In February 1850, Henry Clay warned that a failure to compromise would lead to "furious" and "bloody" war. **Cause and Effect** *What led Clay to propose a compromise?*

2. The people of the territories of New Mexico and Utah would decide for themselves whether slavery would be legal.
3. Congress would abolish the sale of slaves, but not slavery, in Washington, D.C.
4. Texas would give up claims to New Mexico for $10 million.
5. A **Fugitive Slave Act** would order all citizens of the United States to assist in the return of enslaved people who had escaped from their owners. It would also deny a jury trial to escaped slaves.

Calhoun Opposes Compromise   Debate over the compromise dragged on for months. On March 4, 1850, the Senate gathered to hear the opinion of John C. Calhoun of South Carolina. Calhoun, a direct and dynamic speaker, would present one of the great summaries of the southern view of the crisis.

Many in the Senate felt great emotion when Calhoun's turn to present his views came. They knew that the 67-year-old senator was ill and that he probably did not have long to live. Calhoun was so weak that he asked James Mason of Virginia to read his speech for him.

As the speech began, Calhoun—through Senator Mason—stated the problem the nation faced:

“ *I have, Senators, believed from the first that . . . the subject of slavery would, if not prevented by some timely and effective measure, end in disunion [of the United States]. . . . It has reached a point when it can no longer be disguised or denied that the Union is in danger. You have thus had forced upon you the greatest and the gravest question that can ever come under your consideration: How can the Union be preserved?* ”

—John C. Calhoun

The "great and primary" cause of the crisis, Calhoun said, was that the North now had "the exclusive power of controlling the Government, which leaves the [South] without any adequate means of protecting itself against . . . encroachment and oppression." Calhoun was referring to the fact that the North's growing population had given it more representatives in the House and more

Sounds of an Era

Listen to Calhoun's speech and other sounds from the 1850s.

VIEWING HISTORY Massachusetts senator Daniel Webster used his powerful oratorical skill to persuade Congress to adopt the Compromise of 1850. **Drawing Inferences** *Why did northern businessmen favor the compromise?*

One controversial part of the Compromise was the Fugitive Slave Act, which made it easier for slaveholders to recapture escaped slaves.

votes in the Electoral College. Calhoun believed that southern states had the right to leave the Union if that were necessary for their own protection.

Calhoun made clear that the South did not *want* to leave the Union. He also stated, however, that the South would not give up its liberty to save the Union: "The South asks for justice, simple justice, and less she ought not to take," he stated. "She has no compromise to offer, but the Constitution; and no concession or surrender to make."

Today, Americans believe that slavery is morally wrong because it robs people of their liberty. Calhoun and other white southern planters believed that stopping slavery was morally wrong, because it interfered with their liberty to own enslaved people as property. Government, they believed, should protect this liberty.

Southern planters held that if the federal government intended to reduce their rights or threaten their property, then it was no longer a government worthy of their respect. From the point of view of Calhoun, it was the northern section, not the southern section, that was twisting the Constitution and the intentions of the Framers. The ringing finale of his speech made this clear: "I have exerted myself . . . with the intention of saving the Union, if it could be done; and if it could not, [with saving] the section . . . which I sincerely believe has justice and the Constitution on its side."

Webster Favors Compromise Three days after Calhoun's speech, Daniel Webster, the nation's leading orator, stood to speak. Webster was a large man with dark, intense eyes. His voice was both magnetic and persuasive. In the past, Webster had opposed any extension of slavery into the territories. Now he surprised his audience by reversing his opinion. Fearing for the existence of the Union, Webster gave his support to each of Clay's proposals:

66 *I wish to speak today, not as a Massachusetts man, nor as a northern man, but as an American. . . . I speak today for the preservation of the Union. 'Hear me for my cause.'* 99

—Daniel Webster

Webster went on to speak for several hours. Believing that slavery would never be practical in New Mexico, he supported Clay's compromise. He also maintained that it was a constitutional duty to return fugitive slaves to their owners. Webster's speech outraged northern abolitionists and many of his longtime supporters. They accused Webster of putting financial matters ahead of issues of freedom and humanity. Northern business owners, however, supported Webster's stance because they feared the loss of valuable southern trade if the Union were dissolved.

Congress Approves the Compromise As the debate continued over the Compromise of 1850, President Taylor set forth his own set of proposals, causing many to fear a presidential veto of the Compromise. Taylor's sudden death in July 1850, however, brought Millard Fillmore to the presidency. Working with Senator Stephen A. Douglas of Illinois, who had taken over for an exhausted Clay, Congress eventually passed the Compromise of 1850.

As Calhoun had foreseen, Southerners were not satisfied with the compromise, although it did bring a brief calm to the nation. In reality, the Compromise of 1850 solved nothing beyond determining that California would be a free state. It did not settle the issue of slavery in the area newly acquired from Mexico. Part of the compromise, the Fugitive Slave Act, actually made the situation worse by infuriating many Northerners—including Harriet Beecher Stowe, who expressed her outrage in her book, *Uncle Tom's Cabin*.

Changes in Political Parties

During the early 1850s, the system of two powerful national parties began to break down. One sign of this breakdown was the decline of the Whig Party. In 1852 the Whigs, rejecting President Fillmore because of his support for the Compromise of 1850, nominated Winfield Scott, a general from the Mexican War. The Democrats chose Franklin Pierce of New Hampshire. Pierce won the election in a landslide.

Decline of the Whigs The Whigs never won another presidential contest, and by the end of the 1850s the Whig Party had largely disappeared. The slavery issue had badly hurt the Whigs. Many of the northern Whigs had been Protestants who became disgusted with the willingness of Whig leaders to compromise on slavery.

Another reason the Whigs faded away was that the old issues that had divided political parties in the 1830s had been resolved. Few people argued about banks as long as the United States was prosperous and expanding. The men at the center of the Jacksonian-Whig struggles—Jackson, Clay, Webster, Calhoun—were either dead or dying. Political parties seemed to exist only to protect their hold on government jobs and contracts.

Many believed the time had come for a new generation of leaders to come forward. Those leaders who rose to power in the 1850s would have to face the new issues dividing the nation.

Rise of the Know-Nothings Slavery and unhappiness with politics were not the only issues that brought down the Whigs. The equally powerful issue of **nativism** also played a part. Nativism was a movement to ensure that native-born Americans received better treatment than immigrants. It arose in response to a surge in immigration between 1846 and 1854, when close to 3 million Europeans arrived in the United States. Many evangelical Protestants were particularly disturbed by the high number of Catholics among the immigrants.

The fear of immigrants led in 1849 to the formation of a secret nativist society called the Order of the Star-Spangled Banner. Within a few years, its membership totaled around one million. Members of the group insisted on complete secrecy, using passwords and special handshakes to identify each other. They always replied to questions about the organization with the answer, "I know nothing."

In 1854, nativists went public by forming a political organization, the American Party. It pledged to work against Irish Catholic candidates and to campaign for laws requiring immigrants to wait longer before they could become citizens. Because it was closely associated with the Order of the Star-Spangled Banner, the American Party was also called the Know-Nothings.

VIEWING HISTORY Democrat Franklin Pierce of New Hampshire defeated the Whig candidate for President in 1852. **Recognizing Cause and Effect** *Why did the Whig Party decline in the 1850s?*

The Know-Nothings called themselves "Native Americans"—by which they meant Americans born in the United States—and whipped up fears against immigrants.

The Kansas and Nebraska Territories

The desire to build a railroad all the way across the continent to unite the East and West was the American dream of the 1850s. No American city could hope for a greater prize than to be chosen as the eastern terminus of the nation's transcontinental railway. New Orleans, Memphis, and St. Louis were among many towns competing with Chicago to be selected and thereby become the bustling headquarters for reaching the wealth and commerce of the West. But Senator Douglas knew that a railroad through the unsettled land of the West could be built only with the aid of government land grants, which could be made only if the region the railroad passed through was already surveyed and organized politically. With this in mind, Douglas introduced a bill to organize the lands west of Iowa and Missouri—the bill that in its final form provided for a Kansas Territory and a Nebraska Territory.

READING CHECK
It angered Northerners because they believed Douglas was selling out to the South; Southerners were pleased because it raised the possibility that Kansas and Nebraska might enter the union as slave states.

Focus on GOVERNMENT

Federalism The term "federalism" describes a system of government in which power is divided between a central government and smaller governments.

The Historical Context A central issue in the debates of the 1850s was the proper division of authority between the federal government and the states. Northerners and Southerners disagreed over whether the federal government could limit slavery in the territories and whether states could secede from the Union.

The Concept Today Through most of the 1900s, the federal government gained power at the expense of the states. In recent years, however, the states have become increasingly active and powerful in areas such as social welfare policy.

READING CHECK
Why did Northerners and Southerners react differently to the Kansas-Nebraska Act?

Know-Nothings claimed that they were committed to "the great work of Americanizing Americans." They declared:

> ❝ [E]very American and naturalized Protestant citizen throughout the Union, [should] use his utmost exertions to aid the cause by organizing and freeing the country from that monster [Catholicism] which . . . is only waiting . . . to approach to plant its flag of tyranny, persecution, and oppression among us. ❞
> —The American Party

The Know-Nothings did very well in local elections in northern states. Their main supporters were voters worried that immigration would lead to crime and vice, and working men fearful of losing jobs to Irish and German immigrants.

The Kansas-Nebraska Act

Amid growing turmoil over immigration and religion, Senator Stephen Douglas of Illinois again raised the issue of slavery in the territories. Douglas had two conflicting ambitions.

First, Douglas wanted Chicago to benefit from the development of the West. The sooner the territories of Kansas and Nebraska became states, the sooner railroads could be built across their land to link Chicago, the largest city in his state, with the West. Chicago would boom as newly-settled farmers in the Midwest sent their crops there via railroads to be sold.

Second, Douglas wanted to run for President. To do that, he needed the support of southern Democrats. Pushing statehood for Kansas and Nebraska would benefit Chicago but it would cost Douglas supporters in the South. Under the terms of the Missouri Compromise of 1820, Kansas and Nebraska would become free states. The North would then become still more powerful as four new free state senators joined Congress, and Southerners would blame Douglas.

To win the support of both Northerners and Southerners, Douglas introduced the **Kansas-Nebraska Act** in the Senate in January 1854. The Kansas-Nebraska Act supported the practice of **popular sovereignty,** or letting the people in a territory decide whether to allow slavery there, instead of restricting the decision-making power to Congress. In effect, Douglas was asking the nation to repeal the Missouri Compromise and its boundary line of 36° 30' N and rely instead on popular sovereignty. As Douglas wrote to a Southerner in April 1854:

> ❝ The great principle of self-government is at stake, and surely the people of this country are never going to decide that the principle upon which our whole republican system rests is vicious and wrong. ❞
> —Stephen A. Douglas

Douglas knew that the Kansas-Nebraska Act would make Southerners happy. After all, it raised the possibility that Kansas and Nebraska might enter the union as slave states, which would have been impossible under the Missouri Compromise. Douglas also thought that Northerners would back the Kansas-Nebraska Act. Northerners, he believed, would decide that slavery would never take hold on the Great Plains, where the weather was relatively harsh and cotton could not grow.

360   Chapter 10 • *The Coming of the Civil War*

RESOURCE DIRECTORY

Teaching Resources
Units 3/4 booklet
 • Section 3 Quiz, p. 43
Guide to the Essentials
 • Section 3 Summary, p. 54

Other Print Resources
Historical Outline Map Book *Kansas-Nebraska Act, 1854,* p. 47

The people of Kansas and Nebraska would no doubt vote peacefully to become free states.

After nine months of debate, Congress passed the Kansas-Nebraska Act. But instead of applauding the bill, as Douglas had expected, Northerners were outraged by it. Senator William Pitt Fessenden of Maine, a Whig, called the Kansas-Nebraska Act "a terrible outrage." He said, "The more I look at it the more enraged I become. It needs but little to make me an out & out abolitionist." Northern members of Douglas's own party, the Democrats, denounced Douglas for what they saw as a sellout to the South. Most northern Democrats in the Senate voted for the Kansas-Nebraska Act out of loyalty to their party, not because they approved of the principles behind it. As you will read, Douglas was also wrong about a peaceful vote in the territories.

The Creation of the Republican Party

During the summer of 1854, people throughout the North held meetings to protest the Kansas-Nebraska bill. During one of these meetings in Michigan, disgusted Northerners launched a new Republican Party, the direct ancestor of today's party by the same name. Its members dedicated themselves to stopping the "Slave Power," as they called the South. They declared that slavery was a great moral evil and vowed to fight against its extension into new territories. They also demanded the repeal of the Kansas-Nebraska Act and the Fugitive Slave Act.

The new Republicans drew their support almost entirely from antislavery Democrats, Whigs, and Free Soilers in the North. Farmers, professionals, small business owners, and craftworkers made up the Republican Party.

New parties appear frequently in American history. Few last very long. In the mid-1850s, however, the disappearance of the Whigs and the emotional issues of nativism and slavery produced two strong parties, the Know-Nothings and the Republicans. It remained to be seen which of the two would become the more powerful.

INTERPRETING POLITICAL CARTOONS Stephen Douglas champions popular sovereignty in this 1858 cartoon. **Recognizing Bias** *What role did Douglas's political ambitions play in his proposal of the Kansas-Nebraska Act?*

Reading Comprehension

1. California was admitted as a free state; the sale of slaves, but not slavery itself, was made illegal in Washington, D.C.; the Fugitive Slave Act was passed; New Mexico and Utah would decide on slavery for themselves; Texas would receive $10 million to settle its border dispute with New Mexico.

2. Calhoun presented the fears and worries of Southerners, explained that they did not wish to leave the Union, and outlined what the South would need in order to remain. Webster supported the Compromise, fearing for the existence of the Union.

3. Fears and mistrust of immigrants contributed to nativism and the formation of the Know-Nothing Party.

4. (a) They felt that northern Democrats had sold out to the South. (b) Many left the Democratic Party for the new Republican Party.

Critical Thinking and Writing

5. The Missouri Compromise did not address the issue of whether slavery would be legal in the territories; the Compromise of 1850 was equally disappointing. It settled only the issue of California as a free state, leaving slavery in the Utah and New Mexico territories unresolved.

6. Possible topics: Southerners were pleased that Kansas and Nebraska could become slave states; Northerners felt Douglas had sold out.

Section 3 Assessment

READING COMPREHENSION

1. List the five parts of the **Compromise of 1850.**

2. What roles did Senator Calhoun and Senator Webster play in passing the Compromise of 1850?

3. Why did some people support the Know-Nothing Party?

4. (a) Why did the **Kansas-Nebraska Act** upset many northern voters? (b) How did northern voters respond to the passage of the Kansas-Nebraska Act?

CRITICAL THINKING AND WRITING

5. **Identifying Point of View** Describe why the Missouri Compromise satisfied neither Northerners nor Southerners. Did the Compromise of 1850 satisfy them? Explain.

6. **Writing to Persuade** Write a persuasive speech from the point of view of either a Southerner or a Northerner supporting or opposing the Kansas-Nebraska Act.

Take It to the NET

Activity: Analyzing Primary Sources Read the text of an important act of Congress from the 1850s and write a thorough analysis. Be sure to discuss how the document was written for a specific audience. Use the links provided in the *America: Pathways to the Present* area of the following Web site for help in completing this activity.
www.phschool.com

Take It to the NET

Students should thoroughly analyze an act of Congress from the 1850s, demonstrating an understanding of the act as well as a recognition of the audience for whom it was written.

CAPTION ANSWERS

Interpreting Political Cartoons
Douglas hoped to be President one day. He saw the implicit repeal of the Missouri Compromise that the Kansas-Nebraska Act entailed as a way to gain the votes of southern Democrats.

✓ TEST PREPARATION

Have students read the excerpt from the American Party on the previous page and then complete the sentence below.

From the passage, you can infer that the only people whom the Know-Nothings welcomed, besides Protestants born in the United States, were—

A Catholic immigrants.

B Protestant immigrants who had become naturalized.

C Catholic immigrants who had become naturalized.

D immigrants who were neither Protestant nor Catholic.

Analyzing Political Speeches

ANALYZING POLITICAL SPEECHES

Focus Students analyze a speech as evidence of the politics, issues, and language style of a historical period.

Instruct Explain that political speeches are a useful tool in a government where politicians' success is based on the ability to win popular support for their views. Henry Clay, a popular politician, was one of the greatest orators of his time and was venerated for his speeches.

Have a volunteer read the excerpt aloud. Then ask students to identify elements that make it extraordinary. How does Clay use language to affect the listener?

Extend See the Skills for Life activity in the Resource Directory below.

ANSWERS
PRACTICE THE SKILL

1. **(a)** Henry Clay is a United States senator from Kentucky. His audience is the U.S. Senate. **(b)** The Compromise of 1850. **(c)** Clay says that "this measure is the reunion of the Union." **(d)** That "our country and our cause" should come before individual concerns.

2. **(a)** "[A]ll resentments, all passions and petty jealousies, all personal desires, all love of place, all hungering after . . . power [and] popular fears." **(b)** He warns that the nation may become the victim of domination by a foreign power if it is disunified. **(c)** He invokes God, country, conscience, and the Union at the beginning, and at the very end he urges patriotism, asking the senators to be willing to sacrifice themselves for their country. **(d)** Very well, as the senators are likely to be swayed by appeals to patriotism and the importance of the Union. **(e)** Possible answer: Clay's appeal to both emotion and reason is very persuasive.

3. **(a)** Clay's speech has an urgent tone, and he reflected concerns shared by the people that sectional conflict was very serious. **(b)** That speakers used very flowery and poetic language and often exaggerated for effect.

The goal of political speeches has always been to persuade listeners to take a particular view. Speeches can also serve as valuable evidence about historical figures and events. Political speakers use a variety of techniques. Sometimes they appeal to the listener's self-interest: "What I propose will make your life better." Sometimes they appeal to social conscience: "What I propose will benefit the community (or the nation, or the world)." Political speeches often appeal to patriotism.

Part of a speech Henry Clay made during the Senate debate over the Compromise of 1850 is shown below.

LEARN THE SKILL
Use the following steps to analyze political speeches:

1. **Identify the main topic of the speech and the speaker's position, or stand, on the issue.** Recall what you already know about the speaker, his or her political ideas, and the circumstances of the speech. Skim through the speech to get a general idea of its topic and purpose.

2. **Analyze the persuasive techniques the speaker uses.** Political speakers appeal to both the hearts and minds of their listeners. Evaluate the speaker's persuasiveness and how he or she achieves it. Be sure to consider the speaker's audience.

3. **Study the speech for clues about the historical period.** Look for hints about events and how people felt about those events, as well as the style of speeches at that time.

PRACTICE THE SKILL
Answer the following questions:

1. **(a)** Who is Henry Clay? Who is the audience for this speech? **(b)** What is the main topic of the speech? **(c)** What evidence in the speech tells you that Clay believes the compromise will work? **(d)** What is Clay's stand on the measure?

2. **(a)** What does Clay tell his listeners to "disregard" and "forget"? **(b)** Where in the speech does he appeal to reason? **(c)** Where in the speech does he appeal to patriotism? **(d)** How well do Clay's techniques suit his audience? **(e)** How would you evaluate the persuasiveness of this speech?

3. **(a)** Based on the speech, do you think that people in 1850 regarded the tensions between the North and the South as somewhat serious or very serious? Explain. **(b)** What does the excerpt tell you about the style of speeches during that period?

APPLY THE SKILL
See the Chapter Review and Assessment for another opportunity to apply this skill.

"I believe from the bottom of my soul that this measure is the reunion of the Union. And now let us disregard all resentments, all passions, all petty jealousies, all personal desires, all love of place, all hungering after the gilded crumbs which fall from the table of power. Let us forget popular fears, from whatever quarter they may spring. Let us . . . think alone of our God, our country, our conscience, and our glorious Union; that Union without which we shall be torn into hostile fragments, and sooner or later become the victims of military despotism, or foreign domination. . . .

What is an individual man? An atom, almost invisible without a magnifying glass—a mere speck upon the surface of the immense universe—not a second in time, compared to immeasurable, never-beginning, and never-ending eternity; a drop of water in the great deep, which evaporates and is borne off by the winds; a grain of sand, which is soon gathered to the dust from which it sprung. Shall a being so small, so petty, so fleeting, so evanescent [quick to disappear], oppose itself to the onward march of a great nation? . . . Let us look at our country and our cause; elevate ourselves to the dignity of pure and disinterested patriots, wise and enlightened statesmen, and save our country from all impending dangers. . . . What are we—what is any man worth who is not ready and willing to sacrifice himself for the benefit of his country when it is necessary?"

—Henry Clay, United States Senator from Kentucky

RESOURCE DIRECTORY
Teaching Resources
Skills for Life booklet, p. 12

Technology
Social Studies Skills Tutor CD-ROM
Interactive Practice in
- Geographic Literacy
- Critical Thinking and Reading
- Visual Analysis
- Communications

The System Fails

READING FOCUS

- Why did violence erupt in Kansas in the mid-1850s?
- How did slavery affect national politics in this period?
- What problems did the Lecompton constitution cause?
- What important issues were discussed in the Lincoln-Douglas Debates?
- How did John Brown's raid increase tensions between the North and the South?

MAIN IDEA

After a series of violent clashes between proslavery and antislavery forces, Americans on both sides of the slavery issue became convinced that the other side was acting against law and morality.

KEY TERMS

free soiler
Dred Scott v. *Sandford*
Lincoln-Douglas Debates
arsenal

TAKING NOTES

Copy the flowchart below. As you read, complete the chart to show some of the violent events leading up to the final split over slavery.

Violence in the 1850s

Setting the Scene After the passage of the Kansas-Nebraska Act in 1854, national attention turned to the Kansas Territory. Under the new law, voters in the territory would decide whether to become a free or slave state. Both proslavery and antislavery groups organized to try to win a majority of voters in the region.

Proslavery forces had won the first battle by successfully passing the Kansas-Nebraska Act. William H. Seward, an antislavery senator from New York, announced to proslavery senators that abolitionists would fight for a free Kansas:

❝ *Since there is no escaping your challenge, I accept it in behalf of the cause of freedom. We will engage in competition for the virgin soil of Kansas, and God give the victory to the side which is stronger in numbers as it is right.* ❞

—William H. Seward

Violence Erupts

Antislavery groups in the Northeast set up so-called Emigrant Aid societies in 1854–1855 to send some 1,200 New Englanders to Kansas to fight against slavery. The new settlers were known as free soilers. Like the Free Soil party founded in 1848, **free soilers** worked to end slavery in the territories. Meanwhile, proslavery settlers in Missouri organized secret societies to oppose the free soilers. Many proslavery settlers crossed into Kansas to vote illegally in territorial elections. By 1855, Kansas had two competing capitals: an antislavery capital at Topeka and a proslavery capital at Lecompton.

VIEWING HISTORY Abolitionists and proslavery forces clash in the "Battle of Hickory Point," about 25 miles outside of Lawrence, Kansas. **Predicting Consequences** *Why did the Kansas-Nebraska Act lead to violent competition for control of the territory?*

SECTION
Section 4

The System Fails

SECTION OBJECTIVES

1. Learn why violence erupted in Kansas in the mid-1850s.
2. See how slavery affected national politics in this period.
3. Find out about problems caused by the Lecompton constitution.
4. Understand important issues discussed in the Lincoln-Douglas debates.
5. See how John Brown's raid increased tensions between the North and the South.

BELLRINGER

Warm-Up Activity Ask students to make a list of controversial issues in the United States that have incited groups to violence in recent years. Ask why people use violence to achieve political ends.

Activating Prior Knowledge Have students consider how politics and economics came together to create a situation in the late 1850s that led inevitably to war.

READING STRATEGY

As students read this section, have them create a time line of events. Then have them write a statement for each event, summarizing its impact on the North and/or the South.

CAPTION ANSWERS

Viewing History Winning control of the government of Kansas would be a major victory for either side of the slavery debate; individuals on both sides were willing to fight for their cause.

RESOURCE DIRECTORY

Teaching Resources
Guided Reading and Review booklet, p. 44

Technology
Section Reading Support Transparencies
Guided Reading Audiotapes (English/Spanish), Ch. 10
Student Edition on Audio CD, Ch. 10
Color Transparencies *Time Lines,* C4
Prentice Hall Presentation Pro CD-ROM, Ch. 10
Companion Web site, www.phschool.com

Focus Ask why the tension between the North and the South increased between 1856 and 1860.

Instruct Discuss the difficulties brought about by the government's inability to solve the slavery issue. Ask students why Kansas became a battleground for pro-slavery and antislavery forces. What was John Brown's role in the escalating violence? How did the *Dred Scott* decision and the Lecompton constitution contribute to the breakdown of trust in the law?

Assess/Reteach Have students list some of the reasons why the pro-slavery and antislavery forces each became convinced that their foes acted against law and morality.

From the Archives of
American Heritage®

About the Presidents

James Buchanan (1857–1861) called for help from Congress at the end of his term. Southern states were pulling away from the Union. Southerners were also capturing forts and arsenals all over the South. Buchanan did not believe he had the power by law to declare war against a state. Instead, he hoped for a legal solution from Congress: an amendment to the Constitution guaranteeing slavery in states that wanted it. Source: Michael Harwood, "James Buchanan," *The American Heritage® Pictorial History of the United States,* vol. 1, 1968.

READING CHECK
The major party candidates had no ties to "Bleeding Kansas"; Democrats supported both the Compromise of 1850 and the Kansas-Nebraska Act; Republicans called for the admission of Kansas as a free state and received strong northern support.

CAPTION ANSWERS

Map Skills Roughly 20 miles; the close proximity of the two capitals probably heightened tensions in the struggle for power in Kansas.

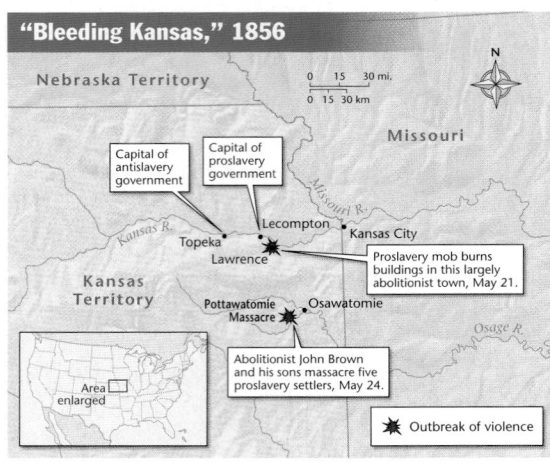

"Bleeding Kansas," 1856

Nebraska Territory

Missouri

Capital of antislavery government

Capital of proslavery government

Lecompton
Topeka • Kansas City
Lawrence

Proslavery mob burns buildings in this largely abolitionist town, May 21.

Kansas Territory

Pottawatomie Massacre • Osawatomie

Osage R.

Area enlarged

Abolitionist John Brown and his sons massacre five proslavery settlers, May 24.

✶ Outbreak of violence

MAP SKILLS Outsiders from both slave and free states tried to influence the political future of Kansas. **Location** *About how far apart were the two Kansas capitals, and what effect might that have had on the political tensions?*

READING CHECK
How did "Bleeding Kansas" affect the presidential election of 1856?

In 1856, tensions in Kansas escalated into open violence. The clashes began on May 21, when a group of Southerners, with the support of a proslavery federal marshal, looted newspaper offices and homes in Lawrence, Kansas, a center of free-soiler activity.

"Bleeding Kansas" The action of the proslavery looters stirred a swift response from Connecticut-born and Ohio-raised John Brown, a stern evangelical who believed that he was God's chosen instrument to end slavery. On the night of May 24, Brown led several New Englanders to a proslavery settlement near Pottawatomie Creek. There, Brown and his men roused five men from their beds, dragged them from their homes, and killed them in front of their families.

The looting in Lawrence and Brown's brutal response at Pottawatomie sparked a summer of murderous raids and counterraids throughout Kansas. The violence won the territory the grim label of "Bleeding Kansas."

"Bleeding Sumner" Violence was not confined to the Kansas frontier. On May 22, it spread to the United States Capitol. Two days earlier, Senator Charles Sumner of Massachusetts had given a fiery speech later titled "The Crime Against Kansas." Sumner, a leading Republican and one of the most powerful antislavery voices in Congress, bitterly attacked Southerners for forcing slavery on the territory. In particular, he made bold insults against Senator Andrew Butler of South Carolina.

Preston Brooks, who was both a member of the House of Representatives and Butler's nephew, was angered by Sumner's remarks and determined to defend the honor of the South. Two days after Sumner's speech, Brooks approached Sumner at his Senate desk and beat him with his cane.

Sumner was badly injured by the attack and never returned to full health. Brooks resigned his House seat, but was immediately reelected. People across the South voiced their support for Brooks. One Southerner sent him a cane inscribed with the words "Hit him again." Northerners were outraged by Brooks's action and the support he received. Sumner's empty Senate seat served as a reminder of that hatred.

Slavery and National Politics

The violence of 1856 passed and peace returned to the country. Still, the issue of slavery continued to dominate national politics, from the presidential election to Supreme Court cases to proposed state constitutions.

The Election of 1856 At their convention in Cincinnati, Democrats nominated James Buchanan for President. Buchanan had been out of the country during the debate over the Kansas-Nebraska Act and the violence in Kansas. The Republicans chose John C. Frémont, a dynamic Mexican War hero with no experience in politics and, like Buchanan, with no ties to "Bleeding Kansas." The American Party, or Know-Nothings, nominated former President Millard Fillmore.

During the campaign, the Democrats supported the Compromise of 1850 and the Kansas-Nebraska Act. In direct opposition, the Republicans declared

RESOURCE DIRECTORY
Technology
Exploring Primary Sources in U.S. History
  CD-ROM Dred Scott *v.* Sandford

that the federal government had the right to restrict slavery in the territories and called for the admission of Kansas as a free state.

While the Republicans received strong northern support, Buchanan won the election with a few key northern states and the solid support of the South. He pledged to his supporters in the South that as President he would stop "the agitation of the slavery issue" in the North.

In fact, Buchanan stated that the slavery issue was now "approaching its end." He expressed his hope that the Supreme Court would use its power to resolve the slavery issue for good. Two days after Buchanan's inauguration, however, the Supreme Court did just the opposite. It announced a decision that would outrage Northerners even more and further divide the country over the issue of slavery.

The *Dred Scott* Decision In March 1857, the Supreme Court handed down one of the most controversial decisions in its history, ***Dred Scott* v. *Sandford*.** The case had started when Dred Scott, an enslaved man living in Missouri, had filed suit against his owner. Scott argued that because he and his wife, Harriet, had once lived in states and territories where slavery was illegal, the couple was in fact free.

The Supreme Court ruled 7 to 2 against Scott. The Justices held that Scott, and therefore all slaves, were not citizens and had no right to sue in court. The Court also ruled that living in a free state or territory, even for many years, did not free Scott from slavery. Finally, the Court found that the Missouri Compromise was unconstitutional. Slaves were the property of their owners, reasoned the Court, and Congress could not deprive people of their property without due process of law according to the Fifth Amendment.

In his written opinion on the case, Chief Justice Roger Taney stated that "the right of property in a slave is distinctly and expressly affirmed in the Constitution." Furthermore, he added:

> 66 No word can be found in the Constitution, which gives Congress a greater power over slave property, or which entitles property of that kind to less protection than property of any other description. The only power conferred [granted] is the power coupled with the duty of guarding and protecting the owner in his rights. 99
>
> —Chief Justice Roger Taney

Antislavery forces were disgusted with the *Dred Scott* decision. It meant that Congress had no power to ban slavery anywhere, including the territories. President Buchanan, however, supported the Court's decision. He hoped that the national government would no longer be required to deal with the slavery issue.

The Lecompton Constitution

Events soon proved that the political fight over slavery was far from over. In the fall of 1857, a small proslavery group in Kansas elected members to a convention to write the constitution required to attain statehood. Called the Lecompton constitution, it was as proslavery as its namesake, the proslavery capital.

Effects of *Scott* v. *Sandford*

- Slaves, because they were not citizens, were denied the right to sue in court.
- Enslaved people could not win freedom simply by living in a free territory or state.
- The Missouri Compromise was ruled unconstitutional and all territories were opened to slavery.

INTERPRETING CHARTS The Supreme Court ruling against Dred Scott (top) was a setback to the antislavery movement. **Predicting Consequences** Why did the *Dred Scott* decision discourage future compromises in Congress?

ACTIVITY
Connecting with Government

Have students assume the roles of associate Justices of the Supreme Court and write concurring or dissenting opinions to Chief Justice Taney's majority opinion in the *Dred Scott* decision. Before students begin writing their opinions, discuss with the class what concurring and dissenting opinions are. Explain the basis on which all Supreme Court decisions are written—various Justices' interpretations of the Constitution. Select students to read their concurring or dissenting opinions to the class. **(Logical/Mathematical; Verbal/Linguistic)**

BACKGROUND
Biography

Dred Scott's original name was Sam Blow. After his master, Peter Blow, died, Sam was sold to John Emerson, a U.S. Army doctor who took Sam with him as he was transferred to Fort Armstrong, Illinois, and then to Fort Snelling in Wisconsin Territory. There, Sam married Harriet, the slave of another army officer. Slaves and master all later returned to St. Louis, where Emerson died in 1843. Sam, who by now had taken the name Dred Scott, sued Emerson's widow for his family's freedom in 1846. As the case made its way to the Supreme Court, some of his legal expenses were paid by the sons of Peter Blow. After the Court's decision, Mrs. Emerson sold the family to the Blows, who immediately freed them. Freedom for Dred Scott was short-lived, however. In 1858 he died of tuberculosis.

CUSTOMIZE FOR ...
Gifted and Talented

Ask students to analyze how the beliefs, principles, and government that had held the United States together for seven decades broke down over the issue of slavery. What led some Americans to abandon the democratic process in favor of violence to settle the slavery issue? Is it possible that a similar situation could happen today in the United States?

✓ TEST PREPARATION

Have students read the quote on this page by Chief Justice Roger Taney and then answer the question below.

What concept in the quote from Chief Justice Roger Taney was probably most painful for abolitionist forces?

- **A** The concept that a slave should be treated as property.
- **B** That slave owners had more rights than slaves.
- **C** That Congress does not have greater control over slaves than over any other property.
- **D** That Congress is obliged to side with slave owners against slaves.

CAPTION ANSWERS

Interpreting Charts The Supreme Court ruled that Congress could not prohibit slavery in the territories, so members of Congress could no longer set aside land as free territory as part of a compromise.

Most Kansans were opposed to slavery and refused to vote in a referendum on the constitution because both options on the ballot would have protected slavery in Kansas. Yet President Buchanan, hoping that the problem of slavery in Kansas would end once the territory became a state, endorsed the Lecompton constitution.

Though Buchanan was a Democrat, his total disregard for popular sovereignty was too much for northern Democrats to swallow. Democratic leader Stephen Douglas spoke sharply against the Lecompton constitution and criticized Buchanan for accepting it. Congress returned the constitution to Kansas for another vote, and the people soundly defeated it in August 1858. For the time being, Kansas remained a territory where slavery was legal according to the *Dred Scott* decision. In reality, however, the free-soiler majority prohibited slavery.

The Lincoln-Douglas Debates

Senator Douglas denounced the Lecompton constitution both out of principle and because he had to be responsive to public opinion. He faced a difficult reelection campaign in Illinois in 1858, where views on slavery were sharply divided.

A short, stout man, Douglas was known as "the Little Giant." Like many white Americans in the 1850s, he believed that white Americans were superior to African Americans. He went even further, however, and tolerated slavery, because he believed in the absolute right of white citizens to choose the kind of society and government they wanted.

Abraham Lincoln told one audience that he was driven "by something higher than an anxiety for office"— desire to defend the principle of equality established by the Declaration of Independence.

Though Douglas was one of the most important senators in the nation's history, he has been overshadowed by the man the Republican Party nominated to run against him, Abraham Lincoln. The campaign drew nationwide attention when Douglas and Lincoln met in the **Lincoln-Douglas Debates,** a series of seven debates on the issue of slavery in the territories.

Abraham Lincoln had been born in a log cabin in Kentucky in 1809. As a young man, he studied law and held various jobs, including jobs as a postmaster and rail splitter. In 1837, he settled in Springfield, Illinois, where he practiced law. He served one term in Congress in the 1840s. Known for his strength of character, Lincoln won further recognition for his skillful performance in the debates against Douglas.

Newspapers throughout the country covered the debates. Many reporters commented on the great difference in appearance between the two candidates. While Douglas was stout, Lincoln was tall, awkward, and thin. While Douglas dressed in an elegant new suit, Lincoln wore plain, everyday clothes.

The debates highlighted two important principles in American government, majority rule and minority rights. Douglas supported popular sovereignty. He believed that the majority of people in a state or territory could rule as they wished, including making slavery legal. Lincoln, on the other hand, did not believe that a majority should have the power to deny a minority their rights to life, liberty, and the pursuit of happiness.

Despite their fundamental differences, Lincoln shared many of Douglas's views on African Americans. During one of the debates Lincoln stated: "I am not nor ever have been in favor of bringing about in any way the social and political equality of the white and black races." He would not propose forbidding slavery in the South because he thought the federal government did not have that power. He hoped that if slavery were confined to the states in which it already existed, it would eventually die out.

Connecting with Government

This activity may take place over several class periods. Divide the class into groups of four to six students. To help students understand that the major issue of contention between Stephen Douglas and Abraham Lincoln was the issue of slavery in the territories, have them select a candidate from this election and develop a political campaign for him. (Verbal/Linguistic; Logical/Mathematical)

The Rivalry Between Lincoln and Douglas

The lives of Abraham Lincoln and Stephen Douglas were intertwined for many years. In addition to their 1858 Senate race, they were linked by common professional, political, and personal backgrounds. Both came from Springfield, Illinois, which, although the state capital, was still a small town in the mid-1800s. Both practiced law there, served together in the Illinois legislature, and represented Springfield in the U.S. House of Representatives in the 1840s. They even competed for the affections of the same woman, 22-year-old Mary Todd, who arrived in Springfield in 1839. Although attracted to Lincoln, she openly flirted with Douglas. In the end, however, Lincoln won this competition, and in 1842 Mary Todd became the future First Lady.

READING CHECK
Because many residents of Kansas opposed slavery.

RESOURCE DIRECTORY

Technology

RESOURCE⊙ **PRO**® **Primary Source Activity**
Lincoln-Douglas Senate Campaign, found on Resource Pro, presents a passage from Gustave Koerner's impressions of the Lincoln-Douglas debates to demonstrate the differences between the two candidates.

Yet Lincoln, like millions of other Northerners, knew that slavery was wrong. Lincoln considered slavery a moral issue. During the debates against Douglas, he quoted both the Bible and the Declaration of Independence to justify his stand:

❝ *The Savior [Jesus] . . . said, 'As your Father in Heaven is perfect, be ye also perfect.' He set that up as a standard, and [whoever] did most towards reaching that standard attained the highest degree of moral perfection. So I say in relation to the principle that all men are created equal, let it be as nearly reached as we can.* ❞

—Abraham Lincoln

In a now-famous speech in Springfield in June 1858, Lincoln foresaw the confrontation that the country would soon face. He stated:

❝ *A house divided against itself cannot stand. I believe this government cannot endure, permanently half slave and half free. I do not expect the Union to be dissolved—I do not expect the house to fall—but I do expect it will cease to be divided. It will become all one thing, or all the other.* ❞

—Abraham Lincoln

Although Lincoln gained a large following in 1858, Douglas won the election. In a letter to a friend after his defeat, Lincoln wrote that he was glad to have taken part in the campaign. "It gave me a hearing on the great and durable question of the age. . . . I believe I have made some marks which will tell for the cause of civil liberty long after I am gone." To another friend he wrote, "The cause of civil liberty must not be surrendered at the end of one, or even, one hundred defeats." Despite his defeat, the tall, gaunt lawyer from Springfield earned a reputation for eloquence and moral commitment that would serve him and the Republicans well just two years later.

Focus on GOVERNMENT

The Purpose of the Debates Very few of the spectators at the Lincoln-Douglas debates had the opportunity to vote for either candidate. Until the ratification of the Seventeenth Amendment in 1913, state legislatures, not voters, elected senators. Public opinion still played an important role because the legislature was elected by the people. By voting for Democratic or Republican candidates for the Illinois state legislature, citizens could vote indirectly for Douglas or Lincoln for senator.

In the 1858 election, Illinois voters cast about the same number of votes for Democratic and Republican legislators, but the Democratic Party won control of the legislature. Although many people believed Lincoln won the debates, Democratic legislators chose their party's spokesman to be the new senator.

Abraham Lincoln speaks at a debate.

Reading Comprehension

1. (a) To make sure Kansas entered the Union as a free state. (b) By settling the territory and defending it against slavery advocates as necessary.

2. Slaves, because they were not citizens, could not sue in court; enslaved people could not win freedom simply by living in a free state or territory; the Missouri Compromise was ruled unconstitutional, and all territories were opened to slavery.

3. Sample answer: Lincoln believed that slavery was wrong. For him it was a moral issue, and he did not believe a majority (in the case of popular sovereignty) could deny minority rights. Douglas was more tolerant of slavery. He believed in the absolute right of white citizens to choose the society and government (i.e., slave or free) that they wanted.

Critical Thinking and Writing

4. The existing political system with its party and sectional divisions was unable to find a compromise over slavery that was acceptable in the long term to the majority of Americans. The illegal action of both pro-slavery and antislavery forces was proof of this failure.

5. Answers will vary, but essays should include the fact that the raid ultimately deepened the division between North and South.

Take It to the NET

Debates should focus on a controversial issue of the 1850s and reflect the style of the Lincoln-Douglas debates.

CAPTION ANSWERS

Viewing History Southerners were outraged by northern support of Brown's actions.

VIEWING HISTORY Behind John Brown's "glittering, gray-blue eyes" lurked a cool willingness to break the law in order to end slavery. **Recognizing Cause and Effect** *How did John Brown's raid deepen the divisions between the North and the South?*

John Brown's Raid

On October 16, 1859, an event took place that raised the worst fears of the South. Three years after his raid at Pottawatomie Creek in Kansas, John Brown attacked the federal **arsenal** at Harpers Ferry, Virginia. (An arsenal is a place where weapons are made or stored.) With him were 21 men, including five African Americans. Brown and his followers hoped to seize the weapons from the arsenal and give them to enslaved people so that they could rebel. They had a dream of an uprising of enslaved Americans that would end slavery, punish slaveholders, and lead the United States to moral renewal.

Alerted to the attack, United States troops under the command of Colonel Robert E. Lee surrounded the arsenal. The troops killed half of Brown's men, including two of his sons, before the rest surrendered. Convicted of treason, John Brown was sentenced to be hanged.

Brown accepted his death sentence. A devout Christian, he believed he was following the example of Jesus by giving up his life for the good of his cause. Just before his execution, Brown wrote a brief note. Although he had failed as a soldier, his final message proved him a prophet:

> 66 *I John Brown am now quite certain that the crimes of this guilty land will never be purged away; but with Blood.* 99
>
> —John Brown

Northerners hailed Brown as a martyr to the cause of justice. In many churches, abolitionist clergy rang bells and led their congregations in solemn prayer on the day that Brown was hanged.

Northern sympathy for John Brown outraged Southerners, who denounced him as a tool of Republican abolitionists. In the eyes of many white Southerners, Brown was a criminal who had tried to launch a rebellion aimed at their very lives. The strong, opposing reactions caused by Brown's raid only deepened the anger between the North and the South.

Section 4 Assessment

READING COMPREHENSION

1. (a) What did **free soilers** hope to accomplish in Kansas? (b) How did they plan to accomplish their goals?

2. What was the legal impact of **Dred Scott v. Sandford** on the issue of slavery in the territories?

3. In your own words, describe the difference between Lincoln's and Douglas's views on slavery.

CRITICAL THINKING AND WRITING

4. **Identifying Central Issues** Explain how the events that occurred in Kansas and in Congress in 1856 support the message of this section's title: "The System Fails."

5. **Writing an Expository Essay** Write a short essay describing what you think was the greatest impact of John Brown's raid.

Take It to the NET

Activity: Organizing a Debate Research the speaking styles and subject matter of the historic Lincoln-Douglas debates. Then, organize a debate on an issue from the 1850s with your classmates. Use the links provided in the *America: Pathways to the Present* area of the following Web site for help in completing this activity.
www.phschool.com

RESOURCE DIRECTORY

Teaching Resources
Units 3/4 booklet
• Section 4 Quiz, p. 44
Guide to the Essentials
• Section 4 Summary, p. 55
Learning with Documents booklet (Primary Source Activity) *An Interview with John Brown*, p. 15

5 | A Nation Divided Against Itself

READING FOCUS

- How did the election of 1860 demonstrate the split between the North and the South?
- What concerns led the Lower South to secede from the Union?
- What event started the Civil War?

MAIN IDEA

After Lincoln's election as President in 1860, seven southern states left the Union. In April 1861, the first shots were fired, and the nation plunged into civil war.

KEY TERMS

Border States
Lower South
secessionist
Confederate States of America
Fort Sumter
Upper South

TAKING NOTES

As you read, prepare an outline of this section. The sample below will help you get started.

> I. The Election of 1860
>   A. Democrats split into northern (Douglas) and southern (Breckenridge) factions.
>   B. Moderates from the South and the Border States form the Constitutional Union Party.
>   C. _____
>   D. _____

Setting the Scene

As 1860 began and a new presidential election approached, it was clear that most Northerners would not accept leadership by a Southerner. Southerners, likewise, would not accept a leader from the ranks of the antislavery Republicans in the North. The next presidential election was looming. Could the Union survive it?

The Election of 1860

When the Democratic Party met in Charleston, South Carolina, in April 1860 to nominate its candidate for President, it was still a national party. For ten days, delegates from both the North and the South debated the issue that had divided the nation for a decade: slavery in the territories. Southern Democrats argued that the government should protect slavery in the territories, while Democrats from the North stood by the doctrine of popular sovereignty.

Unable to gain control of the voting, delegates from eight southern states left the convention and agreed to meet separately to nominate their own candidate. In the months ahead, the split within the Democratic Party became official. Southern Democrats nominated as their candidate John C. Breckinridge, who was committed to an aggressive policy of expanding slavery in the territories. Northern Democrats nominated Stephen Douglas of Illinois, who supported popular sovereignty.

In the meantime, moderate Southerners who had belonged to the Whig and American parties met in Baltimore to form their own new party. These Southerners, along with a few politicians from the **Border States** (Delaware,

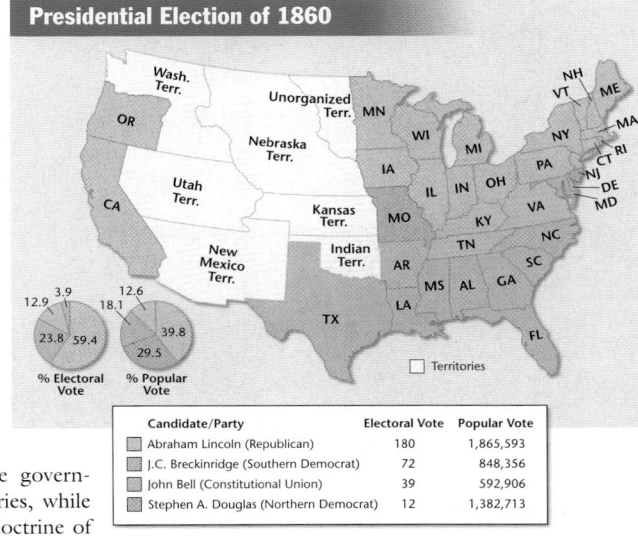

Presidential Election of 1860

Candidate/Party	Electoral Vote	Popular Vote
Abraham Lincoln (Republican)	180	1,865,593
J.C. Breckinridge (Southern Democrat)	72	848,356
John Bell (Constitutional Union)	39	592,906
Stephen A. Douglas (Northern Democrat)	12	1,382,713

MAP SKILLS The results of the 1860 election illustrated the deep political division between the North and the South. **Regions** *Which two candidates achieved dramatically different results in the popular vote and the electoral vote?*

Section 5

A Nation Divided Against Itself

SECTION OBJECTIVES

1. Find out how the election of 1860 demonstrated the split between the North and the South.
2. See what concerns led the Lower South to secede from the Union.
3. Discover the event that started the Civil War.

BELLRINGER

Warm-Up Activity Ask students for names of nations that are currently fighting or have recently fought a civil war, along with the reasons for the conflict. List responses on the chalkboard as a focus for discussion.

Activating Prior Knowledge Can students list reasons why the outcome of the election of 1860 might lead inevitably to the dissolution of the Union?

READING STRATEGY

After students read the section, have them each write a short essay telling what they feel was m___ of no return, Lincoln's ele___ attack on Fort Sumter.

ACTIVITY

Connecting History an___

Ask students to des___ recruiting soldiers___ Confederate or t___ **(Visual/Spatial;**

CAPTION

Map Skil___ who wo___ Brecke___ only 12___ Lincoln___ the e___ only ___ vote.

Focus Point out that the election of a Republican President in 1860 was too much for the South to bear. One by one the southern states seceded from the Union. Ask how the nation finally broke apart.

Instruct Discuss why the southern states seceded from the Union. Ask why Southerners felt it was impossible to trust any Republican President. Why were Southerners so outraged by the election of Lincoln? Why did the secessionists feel that it was their legitimate right to withdraw from the Union?

Assess/Reteach In students' opinion, once the southern states seceded, did Lincoln have any alternative to leading the nation into the Civil War? If they think he had an alternative, have students detail what it was.

READING CHECK
l more moderate views on
standing firmly against
the territories.

READING CHECK
Why was Lincoln chosen as the Republican candidate for President in 1860?

Maryland, Kentucky, and Missouri), formed the Constitutional Union Party. They nominated John Bell of Tennessee, a moderate slaveholder, for President.

When the Republican Party convened in Chicago to nominate their candidate, the man favored to win was William H. Seward of New York. As the days went by, however, many delegates began to worry that Seward was too extreme in his antislavery views to attract the voters they needed.

Another Republican candidate, Abraham Lincoln, offered more moderate views on slavery while at the same time standing firmly against its spread into the territories. Although Lincoln was little known outside his own state, the convention delegates nominated him for President.

The November election proved that the division between North and South was beyond repair. There were no longer any national political parties. In the South, the race was between Bell and Breckinridge. (Lincoln's name did not even appear on many southern ballots.) In the North, voters chose between Lincoln and Douglas. Lincoln won in every free state except New Jersey, where the electoral votes were split between the two candidates. Breckinridge, meanwhile, won North Carolina, Arkansas, Delaware, Maryland, and the states of the **Lower South**—Texas, Louisiana, Mississippi, Alabama, Florida, Georgia, and South Carolina. Bell carried Tennessee, Kentucky, and Virginia. Douglas took Missouri in addition to some of New Jersey's electoral votes.

Lincoln captured the presidency without winning a single electoral vote in the South. While gaining only 39 percent of the popular vote, Lincoln won 180 electoral votes—the majority he needed to win. His was a decisive victory, but a sectional one.

The Lower South Secedes

Southerners were outraged that a President could be elected without any southern electoral votes. The national government, it seemed, had passed completely

COMPARING HISTORIANS' VIEWPOINTS
The Origins of the Civil War

What issue was most important in splitting the North and the South?
Analyzing Viewpoints Compare the main arguments made by the two writers.

The Mexican War Led to Division

"Much of the national harmony had rested upon the existence of a kind of balance between the northern and southern parts of the United States. The decision to fight the war [with Mexico] had disturbed this balance, and the acquisition of a new empire which each section desired to dominate endangered the balance further. Thus, the events which marked the culmination of six decades of exhilarating national growth at the same time marked the beginning of sectional strife which for a quarter of a century would subject American nationalism to its severest testing. Perhaps it may even be said that the developments which gave American nationalism the strength to survive also generated a supreme threat to its survival."

—*David M. Potter,*
The Impending Crisis 1848-1861

Division Grew Over Time

"The Civil War was the second act of America's democratic revolution. The first, in the late eighteenth century, . . . was led by an alliance, a coalition, between predominantly slave-labor and predominantly free-labor communities. Tensions existed between them, but their common interests prevailed. Over the seven decades following the ratification of the Constitution, the growth of both social systems progressively aggravated tensions between the North and South, undermining their political operation. At last, with the sharpening clash of outlooks and interests, the original project of the Founding Fathers—to hold together a society half slave and half free—became untenable. The result was secession, civil war, and ultimately, the irrevocable destruction of chattel slavery."

—*Bruce Levine,* Half Slave and Half Free

RESOURCE DIRECTORY
Other Print Resources
Historical Outline Map Book *The Southern States,* p. 44; *Choosing Sides,* p. 49

out of their hands. Planters and others who backed slavery called for the South to secede, or withdraw, from the Union. An Augusta, Georgia, newspaper editor wrote:

> ❝ [The Republican Party] stands forth today, hideous, revolting, loathsome, a menace not only to the Union of these states, but to Society, to Liberty, and to Law. ❞
>
> —Augusta, Georgia, newspaper editor

The **secessionists,** or those who wanted the South to secede, argued that since the states had voluntarily joined the United States, they also could choose to leave it. Edmund Ruffin of Virginia, a secessionist, claimed that because the Republicans controlled the federal government, they could act constitutionally and legally "to produce the most complete subjection and political bondage, degradation, and ruin of the South."

In response to Lincoln's victory, South Carolina left the Union officially on December 20, 1860. Six other states of the Lower South followed over the next few weeks. In early February 1861, delegates from the seven states met in Montgomery, Alabama. There they created a new nation, the **Confederate States of America,** also called the Confederacy. They elected Jefferson Davis, a former senator from Mississippi, as their president.

The War Starts

The worry on many minds in early 1861 was what the federal government would do about the secession of the southern states. President Buchanan, serving his final months in office, believed that secession was illegal. Still, he declared in a message to Congress that he would not use force to prevent it.

Last-Minute Compromises Fail Some politicians proposed compromises with the South. Senator John J. Crittenden of Kentucky, for example, introduced a plan that would recognize slavery in territories south of 36° 30' N. President-elect Lincoln opposed the plan, however, and convinced the Senate to reject it.

Other Americans, including Horace Greeley, editor of the *New York Tribune,* proposed that the federal government allow the seceding states to go in peace. Many people disagreed with Greeley, especially those who believed strongly in the Union. Many northern businesspeople objected to secession because they feared the loss of business with the South. They insisted that the southern states should be forced to return to the Union. After all, they asked, how could the United States continue to function as a country if its members could come and go as they pleased?

Abraham Lincoln, the one person with the power to decide the government's response, left his home in Springfield, Illinois, for Washington in early 1861. Lincoln believed secession was wrong. He was also strongly committed to stopping the expansion of slavery. Rather than focus on the role of slavery in the South's secession, however, the President-elect emphasized his duty to enforce the laws of the United States.

The Republican ticket of Abraham Lincoln and Hannibal Hamlin nearly attracted 2,000,000 votes, overwhelming in northern states.

ANALYZING CARTOONS This cartoon shows Abraham Lincoln defeating his opponents in the 1860 election. **Drawing Inferences** (a) What might the iron rail represent? (b) What overall point do you think the cartoonist is making?

THE NATIONAL GAME. THREE "OUTS" AND ONE "RUN".
ABRAHAM WINNING THE BALL.

Connecting with History and Conflict

Have students work in pairs to create a recruiting poster to raise troops for either the Union or the Confederacy after the attack on Fort Sumter. Tell pairs that their posters should combine text and graphics to arouse citizens to fight for their nation's cause. Then have the class review selected posters and discuss why they would or would not have likely appealed to the average Northerner or Southerner. (For example, a poster calling on Southerners to fight to save slavery might not have appealed to most southern white males, who were not slaveholders.) **(Visual/Spatial)**

BACKGROUND

The Plot to Kill Lincoln

Lincoln's nearly 2,000-mile train ride from his home in Springfield, Illinois, to his inauguration in Washington, D.C., took nearly two weeks and involved travel on 18 railroads. At every stop were welcoming committees, receptions, and calls for the President-elect to speak. In a time before the Secret Service, Lincoln traveled with little protection except a bodyguard. During a stopover in Philadelphia, the party learned that some secessionists planned to kill him in Baltimore, as he moved from one train station to another to board the final train for Washington. To thwart the plot, the President-elect was disguised as the invalid brother of an undercover female detective of the Pinkerton Detective Agency and put on an earlier train. He secretly passed through Baltimore at 3:15 a.m., hours before the rest of the presidential party.

READING CHECK

It stood as a symbol of the Union that Lincoln had vowed to preserve; it was important to the South because, although South Carolina had seceded, it desired this stronghold that was strategically located in Charleston Harbor.

CAPTION ANSWERS

Fast Forward to Today Because it was a prominent piece of Union military property located in the very heart of the Confederacy.

to Today

Fort Sumter

Although Fort Sumter, South Carolina, held little strategic value to the Union, it was a symbol of the national unity that President Lincoln wished to protect. Instead, the fort became the flash point that ripped apart the Union.

Construction of the fort, on an artificial island at the entrance to the Charleston Harbor, had begun in 1829. One Charleston newspaper described it in 1860 as "a most perfect specimen of civil and military engineering." But the structure was still incomplete and partially unprotected when it came under fire in 1861. Because the fort was built to protect the city from attack by sea, its 60 guns faced outward—not toward the Confederate outposts onshore that shelled the fort—severely damaging it. Further shelling by Union forces—which laid siege to the fort for 22 months until recapturing it in 1865—reduced the massive structure to rubble.

On April 14, 1865, four years to the day that Major General Robert Anderson had surrendered the fort, the aging commander returned to raise the American flag above the fort. (The triumphant ceremony occurred only hours before President Lincoln was assassinated in Washington, D.C., that evening.)

In 1948, Fort Sumter was designated as a national monument. Today, tour boats take visitors on a pleasant harbor cruise out to the island and back to Charleston, a city whose antebellum charm and place in history attracts visitors from around the world.

 Why was Fort Sumter a flash point in tensions between the North and the South?

In his First Inaugural Address on March 4, 1861, Lincoln spoke directly to the Southerners: "In your hands, my dissatisfied fellow-countrymen, and not in mine, is the momentous issue of civil war. . . . You have no oath . . . to destroy the government, while I shall have the most solemn one to preserve, protect, and defend it." Lincoln concluded his address with the following plea:

KEY DOCUMENTS 66 *We must not be enemies. Though passion may have strained, it must not break our bonds of affection. The mystic chords of memory, stretching from every battlefield and patriot grave to every living heart . . . will yet swell the chorus of the Union when again touched, as surely they will be, by the better angels of our nature.* 99
—Abraham Lincoln, First Inaugural Address

Fort Sumter As Lincoln spoke those words, tension was mounting in the waters outside Charleston, South Carolina. Although South Carolina had seceded from the Union, federal troops continued to occupy **Fort Sumter,** a federal fort on an island in Charleston's harbor. A federal ship sent to supply the fort in January had been forced to turn back when Confederate forces fired on it. Federal soldiers under the command of Major Robert Anderson were running out of supplies. If Lincoln did not resupply the fort, it would have to be abandoned to the Confederates.

Lincoln struggled to come to a decision. He had pledged to Southerners in his Inaugural Address that "the government will not assail you. You can have no conflict without being yourselves the aggressors." Yet he had also taken an oath to defend government property. Fort Sumter stood as a vital symbol of the Union he had sworn to preserve. To fight to keep the fort, or even to send new

READING CHECK
Why was Fort Sumter important to both the North and the South?

RESOURCE DIRECTORY

Teaching Resources
Biography, Literature, and Comparing Primary Sources booklet (Biography) *General P.G.T. Beauregard,* p. 15
Biography, Literature, and Comparing Primary Sources booklet (Comparing Primary Sources) *On the Southern Secession,* pp. 115–116

Technology
RESOURCE PRO® **Critical Thinking Activity**
Identifying Assumptions: War Begins, found on

Resource Pro, enhances students' understanding of complex issues through analysis of a contemporary newspaper account of the battle at Fort Sumter.

troops there, might make him responsible for starting a war. Yet to abandon the fort would mean acknowledging the authority of the Confederate government.

Remaining true to both of his pledges, on April 6 Lincoln told the governor of South Carolina that he was sending food, but no soldiers or arms, to Fort Sumter. On April 10, before supplies could arrive, Confederate president Davis ordered General P.G.T. Beauregard to demand that Fort Sumter surrender. If Anderson refused, Beauregard was to take it by force.

Anderson did refuse, and on April 12, 1861, Beauregard opened fire on the fort. After a 34-hour bombardment, Anderson surrendered Fort Sumter to Confederate troops.

The Upper South Secedes By firing on federal property, the Confederate states had committed an act of open rebellion. As the defender of the Constitution, Lincoln had no choice but to respond. When he called for volunteers to fight the seceding states, Southerners saw his action as an act of war against them. The **Upper South** states of Virginia, North Carolina, Tennessee, and Arkansas now seceded and joined the Lower South in the Confederacy. For the time being, the four Border States remained uncommitted to either side in the struggle.

Eighty-four years after it had declared its independence, the United States had come apart. The fighting at Fort Sumter in April 1861 proved that the division between the North and the South could not be settled peacefully. Now a new question was raised: Could the Union be restored by force?

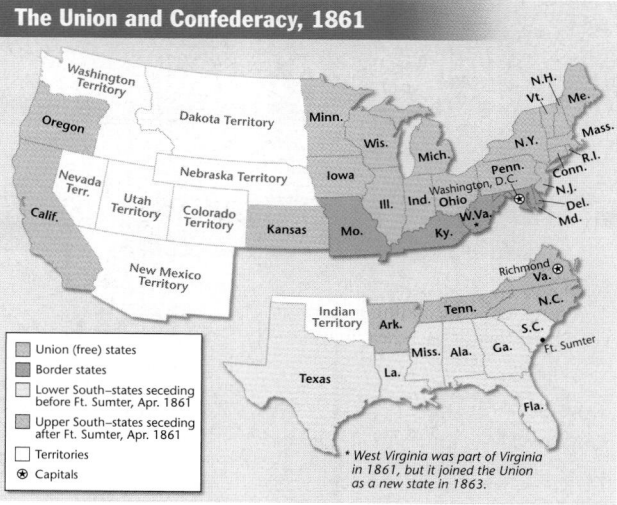

The Union and Confederacy, 1861

* West Virginia was part of Virginia in 1861, but it joined the Union as a new state in 1863.

Union (free) states
Border states
Lower South–states seceding before Ft. Sumter, Apr. 1861
Upper South–states seceding after Ft. Sumter, Apr. 1861
Territories
⊕ Capitals

MAP SKILLS South Carolina was the first state to secede from the Union. It was soon joined by other states, however, making the Confederacy one of the largest republics in the world. **Place** *Name the states that seceded after the surrender of Fort Sumter.*

Section 5 — Assessment

READING COMPREHENSION

1. Why did the Democratic Party split in 1860?

2. How did President Buchanan react to the secession of the southern states?

3. Describe how the **Lower South, Upper South,** and **Border States** responded differently to Lincoln's election and the attack on **Fort Sumter.**

CRITICAL THINKING AND WRITING

4. **Making Comparisons** Many Southerners called the Civil War the Second War for Independence. Many Northerners called it the War of the Rebellion. Explain how each name reflects the point of view of the people who used it.

5. **Writing an Introduction** Write an introduction to an essay on the Civil War, highlighting the importance of what took place at Fort Sumter.

Take It to the NET

Activity: Virtual Field Trip Study political cartoons from the election of 1860. Describe the images and political messages used in these cartoons. Use the links provided in the *America: Pathways to the Present* area of the following Web site for help in completing this activity.
www.phschool.com

Section 5 Assessment

Reading Comprehension

1. Over the issue of slavery.

2. He said it was illegal, but he refused to take action.

3. The Lower South seceded when Lincoln was elected without any southern electoral votes. Senator Crittenden from Kentucky, a Border State, attempted unsuccessfully to mediate. Southerners saw Lincoln's call for volunteers as an act of war against them. This caused the Upper South to secede and join the Lower South in the Confederacy. The Border States remained temporarily uncommitted to either side.

Critical Thinking and Writing

4. The Second War for Independence: Southerners felt they needed to gain independence from the Union and govern themselves. The War of the Rebellion: The Northerners felt that no state had the power to defy the Constitution, and they labeled all who tried as rebels.

5. Answers will vary, but introductions should include the fact that many saw Fort Sumter as a vital symbol of the Union. Northerners were convinced that the Confederate states had committed an undeniable act of open rebellion by firing on federal property.

Take It to the NET

Invite students to take a Virtual Field Trip at **www.phschool.com**

CAPTION ANSWERS

Map Skills Arkansas, North Carolina, Tennessee, and Virginia.

RESOURCE DIRECTORY

Teaching Resources
Units 3/4 booklet
• Section 5 Quiz, p. 45
• Chapter 10 Test, pp. 46, 49
Guide to the Essentials
• Section 5 Summary, p. 56
• Chapter 10 Test, p. 57

Other Print Resources
Chapter Tests with ExamView® Test Bank CD-ROM, Ch. 10

Technology
ExamView® Test Bank CD-ROM, Ch. 10
Social Studies Skills Tutor CD-ROM

REVIEWING KEY TERMS

Students should refer to the definitions of key terms in the chapter to write sentences that show an understanding of the key aspects of the events that led to the Civil War.

REVIEWING MAIN IDEAS

14. They felt it violated the basic principles of both the United States and the Christian religion.

15. Southerners viewed slaves as property. They thought stopping slavery was morally wrong because it interfered with the right to own property, and that the government should protect this right.

16. Congress approved a treaty to annex Texas; war with Mexico broke out one month later.

17. Mexico gave up New Mexico, California, and all claims to Texas, recognizing the Rio Grande as the southern border of Texas. The United States paid Mexico $15 million and agreed to pay claims by American citizens against Mexico amounting to more than $3 million.

18. It dealt definitively only with the issue of California. Stephen Douglas went on to undo the Compromise of 1850 by reopening the issue of slavery in the territories with the Kansas-Nebraska Act.

19. The Republicans attracted former Whigs and many northern Democrats who had opposed the Compromise of 1850 and were appalled by the Kansas-Nebraska Act. The Republicans also capitalized on the abolitionist and antislavery anger over the fact that the *Dred Scott* decision opened all territories to slavery.

20. Because of a series of murderous raids and violent acts in the territory, all of which were related to the slavery question.

21. For Lincoln, slavery was morally wrong. Douglas was more tolerant of slavery and believed strongly in popular sovereignty.

22. Lincoln won by a majority of electoral votes, but he won no electoral votes in the South.

23. Lincoln was an antislavery President elected by Northerners. The South felt that it no longer had a voice in the federal government.

---

creating a CHAPTER SUMMARY

Copy the chart [right] on a piece of paper and complete it by adding important events and issues that fit each heading.

For additional review and enrichment activities, see the interactive version of *America: Pathways to the Present*, available on the Web and on CD-ROM.

Important Events	
Two Nations	• Many historians believe conflict was inevitable. • *Uncle Tom's Cabin* convinced many to oppose slavery. •
Effects of the Mexican War and the Compromise of 1850	
New Political Parties	
Crises in the Late 1850s	
Impact of the Election of 1860	

★ Reviewing Key Terms

For each of the terms below, write a sentence explaining how it relates to the events in the years leading up to the Civil War.

1. prejudice
2. annex
3. Wilmot Proviso
4. Fugitive Slave Act
5. nativism
6. Kansas-Nebraska Act
7. free soiler
8. *Dred Scott* v. *Sandford*
9. arsenal
10. Border States
11. Lower South
12. Confederate States of America
13. Upper South

★ Reviewing Main Ideas

14. Why did many Northerners oppose slavery? (Section 1)

15. How did Southerners respond to Northerners' attacks on slavery? (Section 1)

16. What action by the United States Congress helped lead to the Mexican War? (Section 2)

17. List the basic terms of the Treaty of Guadalupe Hidalgo. (Section 2)

18. Why was the Compromise of 1850 a failure? (Section 3)

19. What issues helped the Republicans in the 1850s? (Section 3)

20. Why was Kansas called "Bleeding Kansas"? (Section 4)

21. How did Lincoln and Douglas differ in their views? (Section 4)

22. Lincoln's victory in the election of 1860 was "a decisive victory, but a sectional one." Explain this statement. (Section 5)

23. Why did Lincoln's election prompt the secession of the southern states? (Section 5)

★ Critical Thinking

24. Determining Relevance The belief that states have the right to secede was not a new concept. How is this belief related to other concepts of government that you have read about?

25. Demonstrating Reasoned Judgment Lincoln's electoral votes in 1860 came entirely from the North. How might voters in the United States respond today if a President were elected by only one region? What challenges might a future President encounter if he or she had only regional support?

26. Identifying Central Issues How did the Supreme Court's *Dred Scott* decision further inflame the slavery issue?

27. Recognizing Ideologies Why did most abolitionists oppose Douglas's idea of popular sovereignty in the territories?

CREATING A CHAPTER SUMMARY

Important Events	
Two Nations	• Many historians believe conflict was inevitable. • *Uncle Tom's Cabin* convinced many to oppose slavery. • The North was heavily industrialized. The South was largely agricultural.
Effects of the Mexican War and the Compromise of 1850	• Greatly aggravated the slavery issue
New Political Parties	• The Republican Party emerged united and powerful.
Crises in the Late 1850s	• The debate over slavery became violent.
Impact of the Election of 1860	• The North wielded its political muscle.

THE EAGLE'S NEST.
"THE UNION—IT MUST AND SHALL BE PRESERVED."

★ Skills Assessment

Analyzing Political Cartoons ▶

28. Examine the images in the cartoon. (a) What is the eagle's nest? (b) What do the eggs represent? (c) Why are some eggs rotten? (d) Why are they hatching?

29. Explain the action of the eagle and what it symbolizes.

30. Read the caption and state the cartoonist's message.

Interpreting Data

Turn to the map on page 373.

31. According to this map, southern states seceded from the Union

   A before the attack on Fort Sumter.
   B after the attack on Fort Sumter.
   C before and after the attack on Fort Sumter.
   D before the election of 1860.

32. Which of the following states was part of the Upper South?

   F Alabama
   G Kentucky
   H Tennessee
   J South Carolina

33. **Writing** Washington, D.C., the capital of the Union, was surrounded on three sides by the Border State of Maryland. Describe why this might have been a difficult situation for the Union.

Applying the Chapter Skill:
Analyzing Political Speeches

34. (a) Summarize the excerpt below. (b) What techniques does Webster use to appeal to his audience?

  ❝ When my eyes shall be turned to behold, for the last time, the sun in heaven, may I not see him shining on the broken and dishonored fragments of a once glorious Union. . . . Nor those . . . words of delusion and folly, Liberty first and Union, now and forever, one and inseparable. ❞

    —Senator Daniel Webster of Massachusetts

ACTIVITIES

Writing to LEARN

Writing to Compare
During his campaign in 1860, Lincoln was portrayed as an ordinary American who was honest, self-made, and hardworking. Compare this portrayal to that of a recent presidential candidate. Are there any similarities? If so, what does this reveal about American values?

Primary Source CD-ROM

Creating a Multimedia Presentation Find additional information on The Coming of the Civil War on the *Exploring Primary Sources in U.S. History CD-ROM* and use the selection(s) provided to complete the Chapter 10 primary source activity located in the *America: Pathways to the Present* area of the following Web site.
www.phschool.com

Take It to the NET

Chapter Self-Test As a review activity, take the Chapter 10 Self-Test in the *America: Pathways to the Present* area at the Web site listed below. The questions are designed to test your understanding of the chapter content.
www.phschool.com

CRITICAL THINKING

24. The social contract, nullification, and states' rights as ideas all have in common the belief that people surrender only limited powers to a central government.
25. Voters would probably feel that they had lost their voice in government. A President with only regional appeal would encounter great difficulties getting bills through Congress.
26. Antislavery forces were opposed to the *Dred Scott* decision because it sent the message that the federal government had no power to keep the territories free from slavery.
27. Because by granting a territory popular sovereignty, the people of the territory could decide to allow slavery.

SKILLS ASSESSMENT

28. (a) The United States. (b) The individual states. (c) They are states that have seceded. (d) To portray rebellion and disloyalty.
29. The eagle is protecting its nest, just as the federal government is protecting the Union.
30. The federal government must preserve the Union.
31. C
32. H
33. Answers should note that if Maryland had joined the Confederacy, the capital of the Union would itself have been in grave peril.
34. (a) Webster is saying that the Union must hold together at all costs. (b) Webster's techniques are eloquence and patriotism.

ANSWERS TO ACTIVITIES

Writing to LEARN

Students' answers will vary. They should discuss the way candidates are portrayed today in the media.

Primary Source CD-ROM

Direct students to the additional primary sources that can be found on the *Exploring Primary Sources in U.S. History CD-ROM*.

Take It to the NET

Additional support materials and activities for Chapter 10 of *America: Pathways to the Present* can be found in the Social Studies area at the Prentice Hall School Web site. **www.phschool.com**

Geography & History

REGIONAL ECONOMIES BEFORE 1860

Focus Help students see that linkages were formed between regional economies in the United States of the eighteenth century based on geographic considerations. Regions would tend to form trade relationships with other regions that were relatively easy to reach.

Instruct Discuss with students the fact that as the United States economy developed in the eighteenth century, trade relationships between regions were often established based on the ease of movement between one area and another. Likewise, strong links and relationships often failed to develop between regions that were separated by geographic barriers, such as mountain ranges. Have students study the map and speculate on the flow of trade between the different areas shown. In the era before train travel, what geographic factors would influence the likelihood of establishing strong trade ties between Cincinnati, Ohio, and Memphis, Tennessee? What factors might hinder strong trade ties between Cincinnati and Richmond, Virginia?

Extend The text notes that the growth of railroads linking the North and West in the 1850s effectively helped preserve the Union during the Civil War. Discuss this fact with students, and ask them to list some supporting evidence for this statement.

Regional Economies Before 1860

During the decades before the Civil War, distinctive economies developed in each major region of the United States: the North (or the Northeast, as we would call it today), the South, and the West (or the Midwest, as it is now known). Each region specialized in a different set of economic activities. Land and sea transportation permitted trade between neighboring regions.

Northern Manufacturing and Commerce
Before 1860, the North was by far the most industrialized region, with machine and textile mills such as the ones shown here. It sold its manufactured goods in the West and the South. The North also housed the biggest banks and shipping firms, which served other regions, particularly the South.

Southern Export Agriculture
The South relied heavily on slave labor to produce cash crops such as cotton and tobacco. It shipped these goods to mills for industrial processing in the North and overseas, particularly Great Britain. Below you see bales of cotton waiting to be loaded onto seagoing ships.

Western Farming and Industry
The West specialized in food production. It produced corn and livestock that it processed and shipped to other regions. In the early 1800s, much of this trade traveled downstream along the Mississippi to the South on riverboats like the one above. The completion of the Erie Canal in 1825 allowed some trade between the West and the North via the Great Lakes. During the mid-1800s, the West's manufacturing sector expanded from food processing to the production of agricultural machinery, such as McCormick's reaper.

Geographic Connection
What were the main items of trade between the regions in the early 1800s?

376

ANSWERS

1. The North exported manufactured products and provided business services to the South and the West. The South exported cotton and tobacco to the North (and overseas). The West exported grains and meat to the South and, to a lesser extent, the North.

RESOURCE DIRECTORY

Teaching Resources
Geography and History booklet, pp. 8–9

Other Print Resources
Nystrom *Atlas of Our Country* *A Divided Nation,* pp. 26–27

Technology
Prentice Hall United States History Video Collection™ Volume 8, *Causes of the Civil War*

	North
	South
	West
——	Canal
——	Navigable river
····	Railroad
	1860 borders

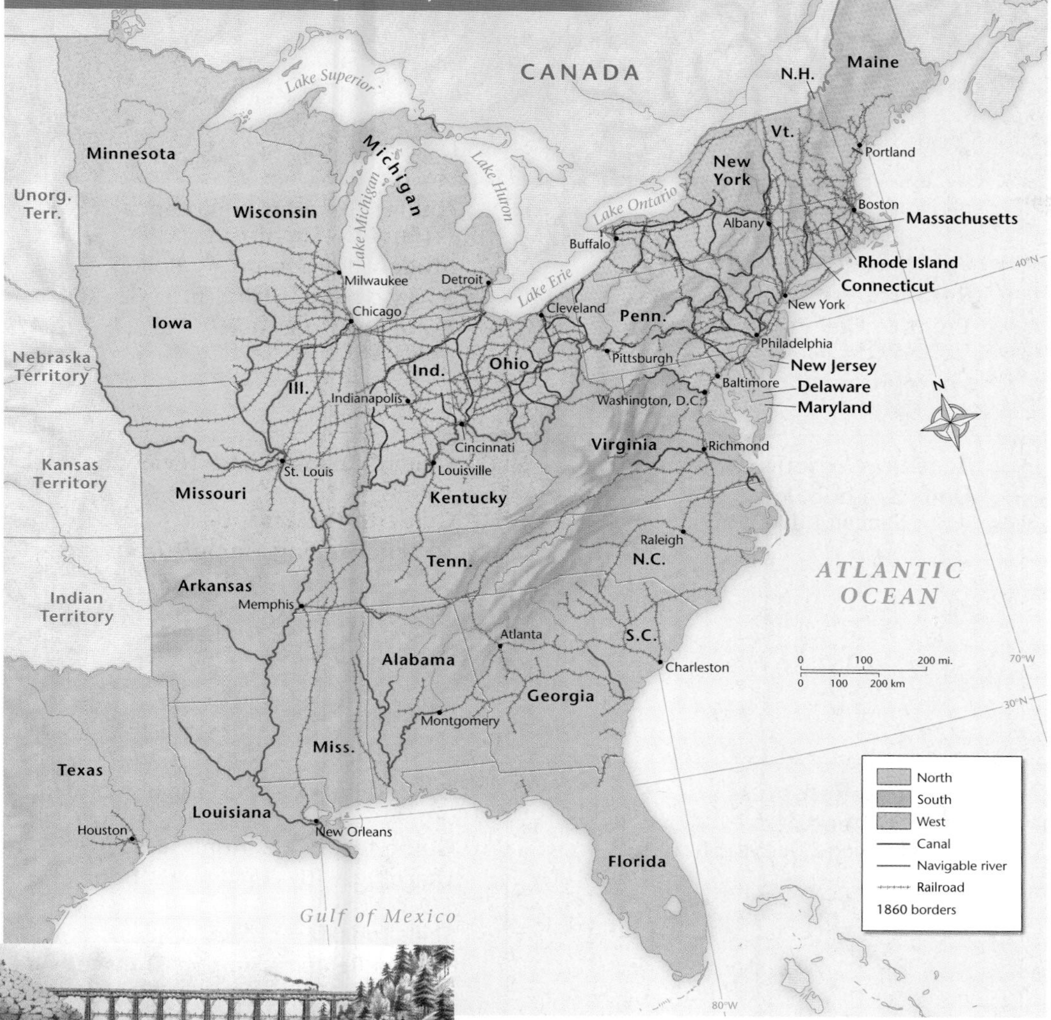

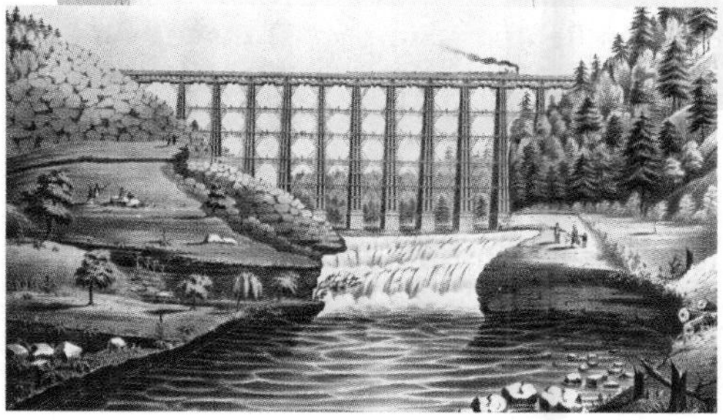

Geographic Connection

How did railroad construction affect each of the three economic regions?

Growing Transportation Links

Railroads gradually expanded after 1828. The densest rail networks developed around the manufacturing cities of the North, but fairly dense networks served the farming country of the West as well. Railroads were the least developed in the South, which continued to rely largely on river transport. By the 1850s, railroads connecting the West with the North allowed the two regions to form closer economic ties. These rail links across the Appalachians would help hold the Union together during the Civil War.

377

Chapter 11 Planning Guide
Resource Manager

	CORE INSTRUCTION	READING/SKILLS
Chapter-Level Resources	**Teaching Resources** • Pacing Charts booklet • Block Scheduling booklet **Resource Pro® CD-ROM**, Ch. 11 **Prentice Hall Presentation Pro CD-ROM**, Ch. 11 **www.phschool.com** • eTeach	**Guided Reading Audiotapes (English/Spanish)** **Student Edition on Audio CD**, Ch. 11 **Social Studies Skills Tutor CD-ROM** **Color Transparencies**, A20, A21, A22, A23, A24, D5, E8, E9, F4, H8
1 From Bull Run to Antietam 1. Understand the significance of the First Battle of Bull Run. 2. Find out how the North and the South prepared for war. 3. Learn why the battles in the West were important. 4. Discover the outcome of each of the battles in the East in 1862.	**Teaching Resources** **Units 3/4 booklet** • Section 1 Quiz, p. 53	**Guided Reading and Review booklet,** p. 46 **Guide to the Essentials,** p. 58 **Section Reading Support Transparencies**
2 Life Behind the Lines 1. Learn how wartime politics affected the Confederate and Union governments. 2. Discover how the Emancipation Proclamation affected both the North and the South. 3. Find out the causes and effects of African Americans' joining the Union army. 4. List the kinds of hardships that befell the North and the South during the war.	**Teaching Resources** **Units 3/4 booklet** • Section 2 Quiz, p. 54	**Guided Reading and Review booklet,** p. 47 **Guide to the Essentials,** p. 59 **Learning with Documents booklet,** p. 81 **Skills for Life booklet,** p. 13 **Section Reading Support Transparencies**
3 The Tide of War Turns 1. Identify the importance of Lee's victories at Fredericksburg and Chancellorsville. 2. Describe how the battles of Gettysburg and Vicksburg turned the tide of the war. 3. Find out why 1863 was a pivotal year in the Civil War. 4. Interpret the message of the Gettysburg Address.	**Teaching Resources** **Units 3/4 booklet** • Section 3 Quiz, p. 55 **Learning Styles Lesson Plans booklet,** p. 24	**Guided Reading and Review booklet,** p. 48 **Guide to the Essentials,** p. 60 **Learning with Documents booklet,** p. 16 **Section Reading Support Transparencies**
4 Devastation and New Freedom 1. Determine General Grant's strategy for defeating the South and how he and General Sherman implemented it. 2. Outline the issues and results of the election of 1864. 3. Explain how the South was finally defeated on the battlefield. 4. State how and why John Wilkes Booth assassinated President Lincoln.	**Teaching Resources** **Units 3/4 booklet** • Section 4 Quiz, p. 56 **Learning Styles Lesson Plans booklet,** p. 25	**Guided Reading and Review booklet,** p. 49 **Guide to the Essentials,** p. 61 **Learning with Documents booklet,** p. 50 **Section Reading Support Transparencies**

ENRICHMENT/PRE-AP

Prentice Hall United States History Video Collection™
www.phschool.com
- Section Activities, Virtual Field Trip, Chapter Activities, Current Events Online

Biography, Literature, and Comparing Primary Sources booklet, pp. 16, 117
Historical Outline Map Book, pp. 49, 50, 51
Sounds of an Era Audio CD
Exploring Primary Sources in U.S. History CD-ROM

American History Block Scheduling Support
Historical Outline Map Book, pp. 43, 44
Exploring Primary Sources in U.S. History CD-ROM

Nystrom *Atlas of Our Country*, pp. 26–27
Historical Outline Map Book, p. 50
Sounds of an Era Audio CD
Exploring Primary Sources in U.S. History CD-ROM

Historical Outline Map Book, p. 52
Exploring Primary Sources in U.S. History CD-ROM
American Pathways Thematic Posters

ASSESSMENT

PRENTICE HALL ASSESSMENT SYSTEM

Core Assessment
> ExamView® Test Bank, Ch. 11
> ExamView® Test Bank CD-ROM, Ch. 11

Standardized Test Preparation
Diagnose and Prescribe
> Diagnostic Tests for High School Social Studies Skills

Review and Reteach
> Review Book for U.S. History

Practice and Assess
> Test-taking Strategies With Transparencies
> Test-taking Strategies Posters
> Test Prep Book for U.S. History
> Alternative Assessment Handbook
> Document-Based Assessment

Teaching Resources
Units 3/4 booklet
- Section Quizzes, pp. 53–56
- Chapter Tests, pp. 57, 60
www.phschool.com Ch. 11 Self-Test

AmericanHeritage RESOURCES

From the Archives of American Heritage®, pp. 392, 402
AmericanHeritage® My Brush with History™ Videotapes
www.americanheritage.com

Don't miss the exclusive interactive version of this textbook on the Web and on CD-ROM.

Chapter 11 Planning Guide
In Your Classroom

CUSTOMIZE FOR INDIVIDUAL NEEDS

Gifted and Talented

Teacher's Edition
- Customize for Gifted and Talented, p. 385, 395, 409, 411

Teaching Resources
- Biography, Literature, and Comparing Primary Sources booklet, pp. 16, 55, 117

Technology
- Exploring Primary Sources in U.S. History CD-ROM *A Diary from Dixie, Mary Chesnut; Civil War Photograph, Mathew Brady; Beat! Beat! Drums!, Walt Whitman; The Education of Henry Adams: Foes or Friends, Henry Adams; Emancipation Proclamation; Gettysburg Address, Abraham Lincoln; In the Wilderness, Thomas J. Halsey; Second Inaugural Address, Abraham Lincoln*

ESL

Teacher's Edition
- Customize for ESL, p. 381, 399

Teaching Resources
- Guided Reading and Review booklet, pp. 46–49
- Guide to the Essentials (English/Spanish), Chapter 11

Technology
- Student Edition on Audio CD, Chapter 11
- Guided Reading Audiotapes (English/Spanish), Chapter 11
- Section Reading Support Transparencies

Less Proficient Readers

Teacher's Edition
- Customize for Less Proficient Readers, p. 387, 391, 403

Teaching Resources
- Guided Reading and Review booklet, pp. 46–49
- Guide to the Essentials (English/Spanish), Chapter 11

Technology
- Student Edition on Audio CD, Chapter 11
- Guided Reading Audiotapes (English/Spanish), Chapter 11
- Section Reading Support Transparencies

Less Proficient Writers

Teacher's Edition
- Customize for Less Proficient Writers, p. 413

Teaching Resources
- Guided Reading and Review booklet, pp. 46–49
- Guide to the Essentials (English/Spanish), Chapter 11

Technology
- Student Edition on Audio CD, Chapter 11
- Guided Reading Audiotapes (English/Spanish), Chapter 11
- Section Reading Support Transparencies

TEACHER'S EDITION INDEX

CHAPTER 11 – PACING SUGGESTIONS

For 90-minute Blocks

- Teach sections 1, 3, and 4 using Transparencies A20, A21, A22, A23, A24, D5, E8, E9, F4, and H8, and the Recent Scholarship notes on pages 382, 388, 398, and 415 for class discussions.

Running Out of Time?

If you are running short on time to cover this chapter, consider the following options:

- Use the Prentice Hall Presentation Pro CD-ROM to create an outline for this chapter.
- Use the Section Summaries for Chapter 11, from **Guide to the Essentials (English/Spanish).**

ADDITIONAL ACTIVITIES

1 From Bull Run to Antietam

Connecting with History and Conflict
The Civil War was the first war to be well covered by newspaper reporters. Their writing was complemented by the work of such photographers as Mathew Brady and Alexander Gardner. Have students research how photography captured the nightmare of the battlefield and its consequences. Ask students to present their information in the form of an essay that examines the effects these images might have had on civilians on the home front. **(Verbal/Linguistic)**

2 Life Behind the Lines

Connecting with History and Conflict
Family loyalties were often divided during the Civil War, with men and women splitting their allegiance between the South and the North. Discuss with students in what kinds of situations such family members might have met, for example, on the battlefield, in a hospital for the wounded, or at a prisoner of war camp. Then have them imagine themselves as one of these men or women and think about how they would treat their kinfolk, given that they were on the enemy's side. Have students role-play the encounter. **(Bodily/Kinesthetic)**

3 The Tide of War Turns

Connecting with History and Conflict
Point out that there is no question that General Sherman's march through Georgia was devastating to Southerners. Ask students to consider, though, how it might have been seen through the eyes of the soldiers of the North who were carrying out Sherman's orders. Suggest that they simulate eyewitness accounts in the form of letters home to family and friends. **(Verbal/Linguistic)**

4 Devastation and New Freedom

Connecting with Economics
Have students research statistics on the casualties for the South during the Civil War, then calculate what percentage of the Southern population was lost. Ask them to use the data to predict how those losses might affect the economy of the postwar South, keeping in mind also the loss of slave labor, as well as livestock and work animals. Suggest they present their calculations and predictions in the form of a graphic organizer, such as a cause-effect chart. **(Logical/Mathematical)**

INTRODUCING THE CHAPTER

"The Civil War," wrote historian Page Smith, "took place because the southern states felt that they could no longer tolerate their status as members of the Union." After the bloodiest war in the western world in the nineteenth century, enslaved African Americans gained their freedom, while the federal government became a strong force in citizens' lives.

TIME LINE ACTIVITY

To provide students with practice in using the time line, ask questions such as these:

1. What event marked the beginning of the Civil War? *(The firing on Fort Sumter by Confederate forces)*
2. Why was the Union victory at Gettysburg hard on both the Union and the Conferacy? *(There were huge losses on both sides, for the winners as well as the losers.)*
3. If the Union forces were winning in 1864, why did Sherman continue his destructive march through the Deep South? *(To help end the war quickly)*

eTeach

Be sure to check out this month's online discussion with a Master Teacher. Go to **www.phschool.com**.

Chapter
11
The Civil War
(1861–1865)

SECTION 1   From Bull Run to Antietam
SECTION 2   Life Behind the Lines
SECTION 3   The Tide of War Turns
SECTION 4   Devastation and New Freedom

The Battle of Missionary Ridge, Tennessee

Civil War cannon

| American Events | **1861** The Confederate attack on Fort Sumter in April signals the start of the Civil War. The South wins the First Battle of Bull Run (Manassas). | **1862** After the Battle of Antietam in September, the Confederate army under the command of General Robert E. Lee retreats into Virginia. In December, the Confederates defeat a Union army at Fredericksburg. | **1863** The Emancipation Proclamation takes effect on January 1. In July, both sides suffer huge losses in the Union victory at Gettysburg. The Union gains control of the Mississippi River. |

Presidential Terms: Abraham Lincoln 1861–1865

	1861	**1862**	**1863**
World Events	Czar Alexander II emancipates Russian serfs. **1861**	Otto von Bismarck becomes prime minister of Prussia. **1862**	French emperor Napoleon III sets up the Austrian Archduke Maximilian as the emperor of Mexico. **1863**

RESOURCE DIRECTORY

Teaching Resources
Pacing Charts booklet
Block Scheduling booklet, p. 18
Units 3/4 booklet
  • Chapter Summary, p. 52

Technology
Guided Reading Audiotapes (English/Spanish), Ch. 11
Student Edition on Audio CD, Ch. 11

Sounds of an Era Audio CD *Senator Robert Toombs on Secession,* 1960s recording (time: 30 seconds); *Former Slave Fountain Hughes,* 1941 recording (time: 20 seconds); *"When Johnny Comes Marching Home Again"* (time: 40 seconds)
Prentice Hall United States History Video Collection™ Volume 9, *The Civil War*
Prentice Hall Presentation Pro CD-ROM, Ch. 11
Resource Pro® CD-ROM
Social Studies Skills Tutor CD-ROM
Companion Web site, www.phschool.com

Major Sites of the Civil War

CANADA

Dakota Territory
Minnesota
Wisconsin
Michigan
New Hampshire
Vermont
Maine
New York
Mass.
Rhode Island
Connecticut
Nebraska Territory
Iowa
Pennsylvania
New Jersey
Delaware
Illinois
Indiana
Ohio
Gettysburg
Antietam
Bull Run
Washington, D.C.
Md.
Chancellorsville
Fredericksburg
Kansas
Missouri
Kentucky
W Va.
Richmond
Va.
Petersburg
Appomattox
Ft. Henry
Ft. Donelson
Tennessee
North Carolina
Bentonville
Indian Territory (Unorganized)
Memphis
Shiloh
Chattanooga
Columbia
South Carolina
Arkansas
Atlanta
Georgia
Ft. Sumter
Alabama
Vicksburg
Mississippi
Texas
Louisiana
New Orleans
Savannah
Florida

Mississippi R.
Ohio R.
Tennessee R.
Alabama R.
Gulf of Mexico
ATLANTIC OCEAN

N

0   150   300 mi.
0   150   300 km

Legend:
- Union state
- Border state
- Upper South—states seceding after Ft. Sumter, Apr. 1861
- Lower South—states seceding before Ft. Sumter, Apr. 1861
- ⊛ Capital city
- ✕ Battle site
- Map shows boundaries of 1863.

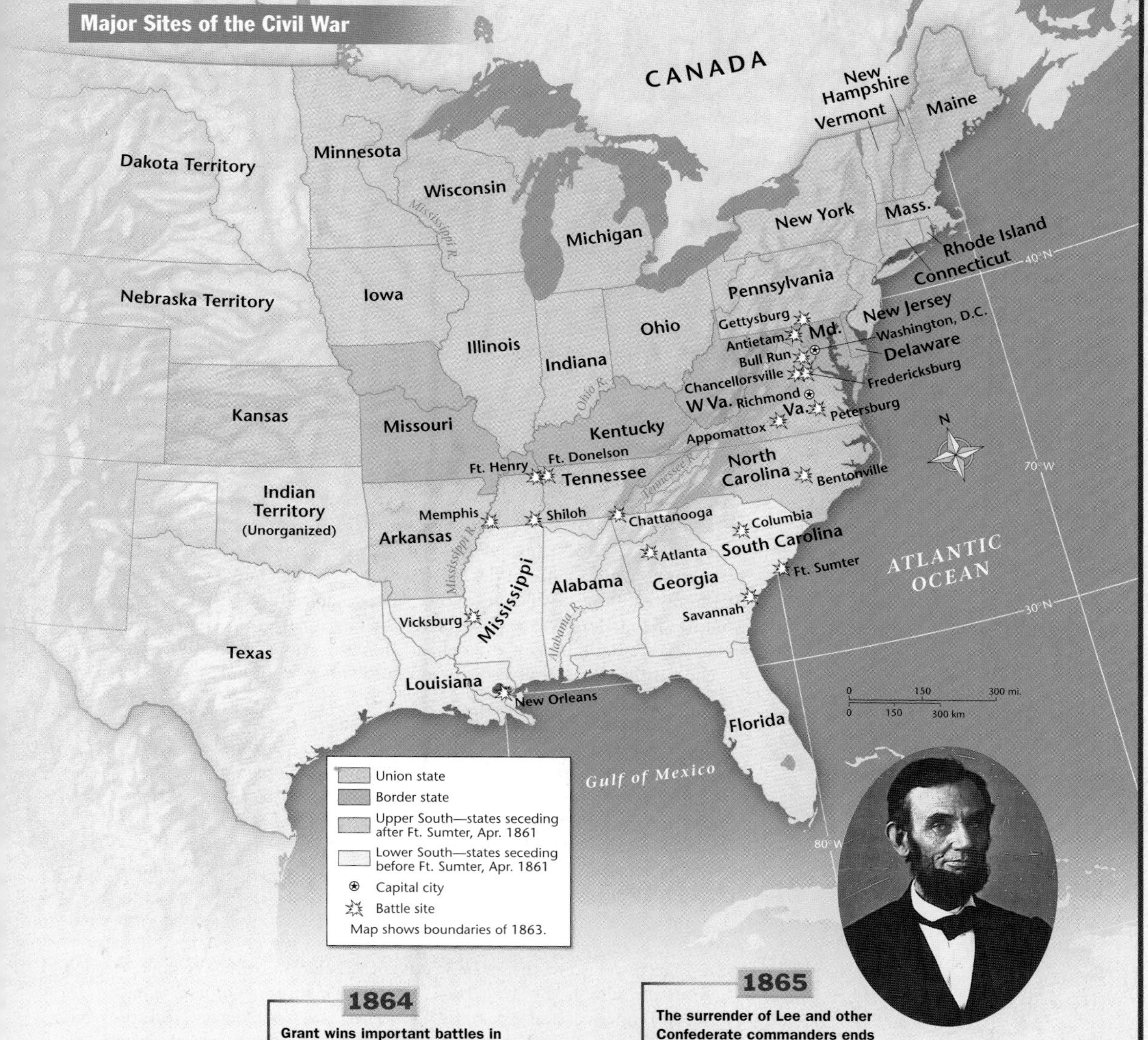

Abraham Lincoln

1864
Grant wins important battles in Virginia; Sherman captures Atlanta and begins his march to the sea. Lincoln wins reelection.

1865
The surrender of Lee and other Confederate commanders ends the Civil War. Ratification of the Thirteenth Amendment abolishes slavery.

Andrew Johnson 1865–1869

1864   1865   1866

1864
After 14 years, the Chinese government finally crushes the Taiping Rebellion.

1865
Work begins on the first undersea transatlantic telegraph cable.

Chapter 11   379

Major Sites of the Civil War

Activating Prior Knowledge
Were most of the battle sites in the Union states or the Confederate states? *(In the Confederate states)*

Previewing How did this affect the Confederate war effort? *(The multiple battles on Confederate sites made it more difficult for the Confederate forces by lowering morale, putting the South in the position of defense rather than offense, and making it possible for Union forces to destroy Southern supplies and supply routes.)*

BACKGROUND
About the Pictures

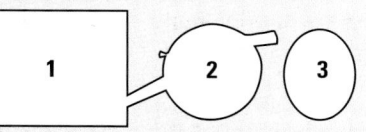

1. This painting by American painter Douglas Volk depicts Union soldiers attacking during the Battle of Missionary Ridge.

2. Cannons such as this one of the Napoleon variety were used to devastating and deadly effect by both sides during the Civil War.

3. Portrait of Abraham Lincoln, United States President from 1861 to 1865. Lincoln, who served as President during the Civil War, was shot by an assassin on April 14, 1865, and died the next day without regaining consciousness.

Don't miss the exclusive interactive version of this textbook on the Web and on CD-ROM.

BIBLIOGRAPHY

For the Teacher

Chesnut, Mary Boykin. ***A Diary from Dixie.*** Random House Value Publishing, 1997. (Observations of the war from the Southern point of view.)

Quarles, Benjamin. ***The Negro in the Civil War.*** De Capo Press, 1989. (The role of African Americans in the Civil War.)

Garry Wills. ***Lincoln at Gettysburg: The Words That Remade America.*** Touchstone, 1993. (Pulitzer Prize–winning examination of the Gettysburg Address.)

For the Student

Crane, Stephen. ***The Red Badge of Courage.*** Washington Square Press, 1996. (Classic novel of a Union soldier in the face of enemy fire; originally published in 1895.)

The Civil War, PBS Video. (Acclaimed, multipart series that combines scholarly analysis and primary sources.)

SECTION OBJECTIVES

1. Understand the significance of the First Battle of Bull Run.
2. Find out how the North and the South prepared for war.
3. Learn why the battles in the West were important.
4. Discover the outcome of each of the battles in the East in 1862.

BELLRINGER

Warm-Up Activity Tell students that at the start of the Civil War, many Northerners expected the war to be over quickly. Some even called it "the six months' war." Write the words *new tactics* and *new technology* on the chalkboard. Ask students to predict how these two factors changed Northerners' expectations.

Activating Prior Knowledge In what ways did the debate over states' rights lead to the Civil War? Does the debate over states' rights versus the governing power of the federal government continue to this day?

READING STRATEGY

Ask students to reread the Main Idea shown on this page. Then, have them rewrite it as a question. As they read, have them take notes about events that help answer the question.

ACTIVITY
Student Portfolio

You may wish to have students add the following to their portfolios: Ask students to write two letters home, one from a Union soldier and one from a Confederate soldier. The Union letter should describe the military strategies of naval blockades. The Confederate letter should describe the military strategy of waging a war of attrition. **(Verbal/Linguistic)**

From Bull Run to Antietam

READING FOCUS

- What was the significance of the First Battle of Bull Run?
- How did the North and the South prepare for war?
- Why were the battles in the West important?
- What was the outcome of each of the battles in the East in 1862?

MAIN IDEA

Bloody fighting during the first two years of the Civil War made it clear to both North and South that the struggle would be long and difficult.

KEY TERMS

Civil War
First Battle of Bull Run
casualty
war of attrition
shell
canister
Battle of Shiloh
Battle of Antietam

TAKING NOTES

Copy the chart below. As you read this section, fill in the advantages of each side at the start of the Civil War. Also include the battles each side won.

Advantages/Battles Won	
North	**South**
More railroad track	First Battle of Bull Run

Setting the Scene The first shots fired on Fort Sumter, South Carolina, in April 1861 signaled the start of the nation's **Civil War**—the war between the Union states of the North and the Confederate states of the South. At the outbreak of hostilities, neither side would have predicted that the war would last four long years. As a matter of fact, in many places in the South, people were both jubilant and defiant. In her memoir, Sallie Hunt, who was a child at the time, recalled the mood in Richmond, Virginia:

Women on both sides contributed to the war effort by sewing uniforms and other supplies. This Southern woman is making caps.

> One spring day in April, 1861, all Richmond was astir. Schools were broken up, and knots of excited men gathered at every street corner. Sumter had been fired upon, and Lincoln had ordered the men of Virginia to rush upon their brethren of the South and put the rebellion down. Now 'the die was cast,' our lot was with theirs, and come weal [well-being] or woe, we would fight for independence. . . . [O]ur hearts swelled with pride to think we could say to our tyrants: 'Thus far shalt thou come, and no further.'
>
> —Sallie Hunt

In response to the call to "put the rebellion down," Virginia seceded from the Union. By May 1861, the Upper South (Virginia, North Carolina, Tennessee, and Arkansas) had joined the Confederacy, and the Confederate capital had been moved from Montgomery, Alabama, to Richmond, Virginia. In July, some 35,000 Northern volunteers were training in Washington, D.C., just 100 miles away. "Forward to Richmond!" urged a headline in the *New York Tribune*. Many Northerners believed that capturing the Confederate capital would bring a quick end to the Civil War.

The First Battle of Bull Run

General Irvin McDowell, commander of the Union troops, was not yet ready to fight. He felt that he needed more time to prepare even though most of his troops had volunteered for just 90 days and their term of service was nearly over. "This is not an army," McDowell told the President. "It will take a long

---

RESOURCE DIRECTORY

Teaching Resources
Guided Reading and Review booklet, p. 46
Biography, Literature, and Comparing Primary Sources booklet (Literature) *The First Battle of Bull Run*, p. 55

Other Print Resources
Historical Outline Map Book *Choosing Sides,* p. 49

Technology
Section Reading Support Transparencies
Guided Reading Audiotapes (English/Spanish), Ch. 11

Student Edition on Audio CD, Ch. 11
Color Transparencies *Cause-and-Effect Charts,* D5; *Fine Art,* E8
Exploring Primary Sources in U.S. History CD-ROM *A Diary from Dixie, Mary Chesnut*
Exploring Primary Sources in U.S. History CD-ROM *Civil War Photograph, Mathew Brady*
Prentice Hall Presentation Pro CD-ROM, Ch. 11
Companion Web site, www.phschool.com

time to make an army." Despite this warning, Lincoln ordered his general into action.

On July 16, McDowell marched his poorly prepared army into Virginia. His objective was the town of Manassas, an important railroad junction southwest of Washington. Opposing him was a smaller Confederate force under General P.G.T. Beauregard, the officer who had captured Fort Sumter. The Confederates were camped along Bull Run, a stream that passed about four miles north of Manassas.

It took the Union army nearly four days to march the 25 miles to Manassas. Lack of training and discipline contributed to the soldiers' slow pace. As McDowell later explained, "They stopped every moment to pick blackberries or get water. . . . They would not keep in the ranks, order as much as you pleased." Meanwhile, Beauregard had no trouble keeping track of McDowell's progress. Accompanying the troops was a huge crowd of reporters, politicians, and other civilians from Washington, planning to picnic and watch the battle. They got a rude surprise.

McDowell's delays had allowed Beauregard to strengthen his army. Some 11,000 additional Confederate troops had been packed into freight cars and sped to the scene. (This was the first time in history that troops were moved by train.) When McDowell finally attacked on July 21, he faced a force nearly the size of his own army. But beyond the Confederate lines lay the road to the Confederate capital at Richmond.

After hours of hard fighting, the Union soldiers appeared to be winning. Their slow advance pushed the Southerners back. However, some Virginia soldiers commanded by General Thomas Jackson refused to give up. Seeing Jackson's men holding firm, another Confederate officer rallied his retreating troops, shouting: "Look! There is Jackson standing like a stone wall! Rally

VIEWING HISTORY This portrait of members of the U.S. Signal Corps is by the famous photographer Mathew Brady. **Making Inferences** *Judging by their expressions, what do these men think of their role in the Civil War?*

COMPARING PRIMARY SOURCES

The Aims of the Civil War

Throughout the years of quarreling between North and South, Southerners protested repeatedly that Northerners were trampling on their rights, including the right to own slaves as property.

Analyzing Viewpoints How did the war aims of each side reflect their quarrel, as described above?

The Aims of the South

"We have vainly endeavored to secure tranquillity and obtain respect for the rights to which we were entitled . . . . If . . . the integrity of our territory and jurisdiction [legal authority] be assailed [attacked], it will but remain for us, with firm resolve, to appeal to arms."

—*President Jefferson Davis,*
Inaugural Address,
February 18, 1861

The Aims of the North

"This war is not waged upon our part in any spirit of oppression, nor for any purpose of conquest or subjugation, nor purpose of overthrowing or interfering with the rights or established institutions of those [seceding] States, but to defend and maintain the supremacy of the Constitution and to preserve the Union."

—*House of Representatives,*
Crittenden Resolution,
July 25, 1861

Chapter 11 • Section 1   **381**

behind the Virginians!" The Union advance was stopped, and "Stonewall" Jackson had earned his famous nickname.

Tired and discouraged, the Union forces began to fall back in late afternoon. Then a trainload of fresh Confederate troops arrived and launched a counterattack. The orderly Union retreat fell apart. Hundreds of soldiers dropped their weapons and ran north. They stampeded into the sightseers who had followed them to the battlefield. As the army disintegrated, soldiers and civilians were caught in a tangle of carriages, wagons, and horses on the narrow road. Terrified that the Confederate troops would catch them, they ran headlong for the safety of Washington, D.C. The Confederates, however, were too disorganized and exhausted to pursue the Union army.

The first major battle of the Civil War was over. It became known as the **First Battle of Bull Run,** because the following year another bloody battle occurred at almost exactly the same site. In the South, this engagement was known as the First Battle of Manassas. The First Battle of Bull Run was not a huge action. About 35,000 troops were involved on each side. The Union suffered about 2,900 **casualties,** the military term for those killed, wounded, captured, or missing in action. Confederate casualties were fewer than 2,000. Later battles would prove much more costly.

Preparing for War

Bull Run caused some Americans on both sides to suspect that winning the war might not be so easy. "The fat is in the fire now," wrote President Lincoln's private secretary. "The preparations for the war will be continued with increased vigor by the Government." Congress quickly authorized the President to raise a million three-year volunteers. In Richmond, a clerk in the Confederate War Department began to worry, "We are resting on our oars, while the enemy is drilling and equipping 500,000 or 600,000 men."

Strengths of the North and the South In several respects, the North was much better prepared for war than was the South. The North had more than twice as much railroad track as the South. This made the movement of troops, food, and supplies quicker and easier in the North. There were also more than twice as many factories in the North, so the Union was better able to produce the guns, ammunition, shoes, and other items needed for its army. The North's economy was well balanced between farming and industry, and the North had far more money in its banks than the South.

What's more, the North already had a functioning government and a small army and navy. Most importantly, two thirds of the nation's population lived in Union states. This made more men available to the Union army, while at the same time allowing for a sufficient labor force to remain behind for farm and factory work.

The Confederates had some advantages, too. Because most of the nation's military colleges were in the South, a majority of the nation's trained officers were Southerners, and they sided with the Confederacy. In addition, the Southern army did not need to initiate any military action to win the war. All they needed to do was maintain a defensive position and keep from being beaten. In contrast, to restore unity to the nation, the North would have to attack and conquer the South. Southerners had an additional advantage: they felt that they were fighting to preserve their way of life and, they believed, their right to self-government.

Patriotism was also important in the North. And there were strongly held beliefs about slavery. The abolitionist Harriet Beecher Stowe responded to the Union call to arms by writing, "This is a cause to die for, and—thanks be to God!—our young men embrace it." There were other reasons that people on both sides were eager to fight. Some enlisted for the adventure, and feared that the war would be over before they got a chance to participate.

Union Military Strategies   After the fall of Fort Sumter, President Lincoln ordered a naval blockade of the seceded states. By shutting down the South's ports along the Atlantic Coast and the Gulf of Mexico, Lincoln hoped to keep the South from shipping its cotton to Europe. He also wanted to prevent Southerners from importing the manufactured goods they needed.

Lincoln's blockade was part of a strategy developed by General Winfield Scott, the hero of the Mexican War and commander of all U.S. troops in 1861. Scott realized that it would take a long time to raise and train an army that was big enough and strong enough to invade the South successfully. Instead, he proposed to choke off the Confederacy with the blockade and to use troops and gunboats to gain control of the Mississippi River, thus cutting the Confederacy in two. Scott believed these measures would pressure the South to seek peace and would restore the nation without a bloody war.

Northern newspapers sneered at Scott's strategy. They scornfully named it the Anaconda Plan, after a type of snake that coils around its victims and crushes them to death. Despite the Union defeat at Bull Run, political pressure for action and a quick victory remained strong in 1861. This public clamor for results led to several more attempts to capture Richmond. Seizing the Confederate capital was another important strategic goal of the Union.

Confederate War Strategies   The South's basic war plan was to prepare and wait. Many Southerners hoped that Lincoln would let them go in peace. "All we ask is to be let alone," announced Confederate president Jefferson Davis, shortly after secession. He planned for a defensive war.

Southern strategy called for a **war of attrition.** In this type of war, one side inflicts continuous losses on the enemy in order to wear down its strength.

Northern Advantages	Southern Advantages
Population 21.5 million N / 9 million S	**Leadership** Seven of the nation's eight military colleges were in the South; most officers sided with the Confederacy.
Railroad Mileage 21,700 miles N / 9,000 miles S	**Military Tactics** Because the South was defending its borders, its army needed only to repel Northern advances rather than initiate military action.
Number of Factories 110,100 N / 20,600 S	**Morale** Many Southerners were eager to fight, considering the war a struggle for their way of life.

READING CHECK
What were the most important strengths of the North and the South?

INTERPRETING DIAGRAMS
This diagram shows the advantages that the North and the South had at the start of the Civil War. **Analyzing Information** *The North and the South had different kinds of advantages. Explain the differences.*

Geography in History

Many Civil War battles have two names, one Northern and one Southern. The names given by the North tend to connect a battle with a physical feature near the battlefield, such as the stream Bull Run. Southerners usually named a battle after the nearest town; they called this one the First Battle of Manassas.

BACKGROUND
Global Connections

One of the most popular forms of ammunition during the Civil War was the Minié ball. A French army officer named Claude-Etienne Minié invented the Minié ball in 1849. This self-cleaning cylindrical bullet had a hollow base and had four times the range of the musket. Soldiers could fire many rounds with a Minié-ball rifle before having to clean the barrel. The use of the Minié ball sped the pace of war. Its use was one of the factors responsible for the high casualties on Civil War battlefields.

READING CHECK
The North had more people, industry, railroad track, governing experience, and money. The South did not need to win, only to survive. Qualified officer candidates were available in large numbers for the Confederate armies.

CAPTION ANSWERS

Interpreting Diagrams The North's advantages were in manpower to fight the war and to keep the economy going at home, and in supplies and transportation. Southern armies had strong leadership and high morale. The South could fight a defensive war.

☑ **TEST PREPARATION**

Have students read the first paragraph under the heading "Preparing for War" on the previous page, and then answer the question below.

After the First Battle of Bull Run, Lincoln's private secretary wrote, "The fat is in the fire now." What did he mean by that?

A There would not be enough food for the Union Army.

B The war would soon consume a tremendous amount of resources.

C The war would soon be over.

D The war might not be over for a long time.

Southerners counted on their forces being able to turn back Union attacks until Northerners lost the will to fight. However, this strategy did not take into account the North's tremendous advantage in resources. In the end, it was the North that waged a successful war of attrition against the South.

Southern strategy in another area also backfired. The South produced some 75 percent of the world's cotton, much of it supplying the textile mills of Great Britain and France. However, Confederate leaders convinced most Southern planters to stop exporting cotton. They believed that the sudden loss of Southern cotton would cause British and French industrial leaders to pressure their governments to help the South gain its independence in exchange for restoring the flow of cotton. Instead, the Europeans turned to India and Egypt for their cotton. By the time Southerners recognized the failure of this strategy, the Union blockade had become so effective that little cotton could get out. With no income from cotton exports, the South could not earn the money it needed to buy guns and maintain its armies.

Tactics and Technology For generations, European commanders had fought battles by concentrating their forces, assaulting a position, and driving the enemy away. The cannons and muskets they used were neither accurate nor capable of repeating fire very rapidly. Generals relied on masses of charging troops to overwhelm the enemy. Most Civil War generals had been trained in these methods, and had seen them work well in the Mexican War.

The newer bullets (at right) were far more accurate than round musket balls like the one shown wedged in a soldier's shoulder plate.

By the time of the Civil War, however, gun makers knew that bullet-shaped ammunition drifted less as it flew through the air than a round ball, the older type of ammunition. They had also learned that rifling, a spiral groove cut on the inside of a gun barrel, would make a fired bullet pick up spin, causing it to travel farther and straighter. Older muskets, which had no rifling, were accurate only to about 100 yards. Bullets fired from rifles, as the new guns were called, hit targets at 500 yards. In addition, they could be reloaded and fired much faster than muskets.

Improvements in artillery were just as deadly. Instead of relying only on iron cannon balls, gunners could now fire **shells,** devices that exploded in the air or when they hit something. Artillery often fired **canister,** a special type of shell filled with bullets. This turned cannons into giant shotguns. Thousands of soldiers went to their deaths by following orders to cross open fields against such weapons. Commanders on both sides, however, were slow to recognize that these traditional strategies exposed their troops to slaughter.

War in the West

After the disaster at Bull Run, President Lincoln named General George McClellan to build and command a new army. While McClellan was involved with this task, Union forces in the West invaded the Confederacy. The states of Arkansas, Louisiana, Mississippi, and Tennessee held the key to control of the Mississippi River, which ran through the heart of the Confederacy. The fighting in these four states is generally referred to as the "war in the West."

The most successful Union forces in the West were led by General Ulysses S. Grant. After the fall of Fort Sumter, Grant's success at organizing and training a group of Illinois volunteers caused Lincoln to promote him from colonel to general. He was assigned to command the Union forces based in Paducah, Kentucky, where the Ohio and Tennessee rivers meet.

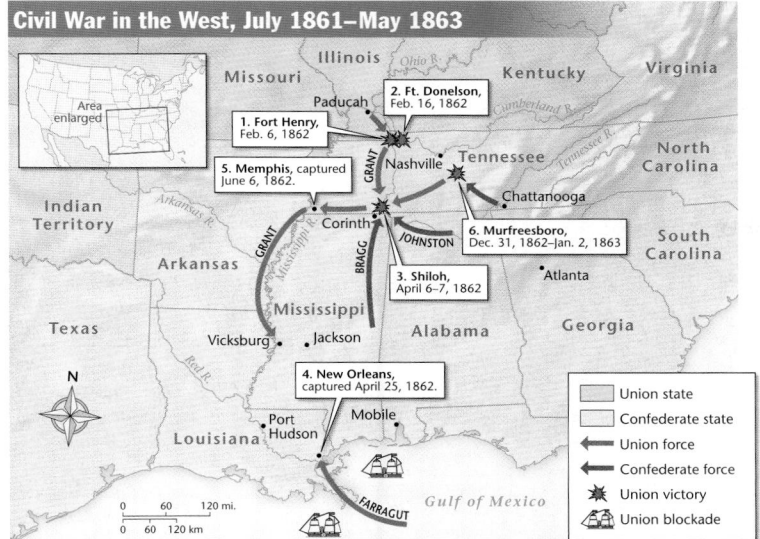

Civil War in the West, July 1861–May 1863

Area enlarged

1. Fort Henry, Feb. 6, 1862
2. Ft. Donelson, Feb. 16, 1862
5. Memphis, captured June 6, 1862.
6. Murfreesboro, Dec. 31, 1862–Jan. 2, 1863
3. Shiloh, April 6–7, 1862
4. New Orleans, captured April 25, 1862.

Illinois • Ohio R. • Kentucky • Virginia
Missouri • Paducah • Nashville • Tennessee • North Carolina
Indian Territory • Arkansas R. • Corinth • Chattanooga • South Carolina
Texas • Mississippi • Atlanta • Georgia • Alabama
Vicksburg • Jackson
Louisiana • Port Hudson • Mobile
Gulf of Mexico

GRANT · JOHNSTON · BRAGG · FARRAGUT

0   60   120 mi.
0   60   120 km

Union state
Confederate state
Union force
Confederate force
Union victory
Union blockade

MAP SKILLS Union generals in the West focused their attention on the Mississippi River. "That Mississippi ruins us, if lost," worried Southern observer Mary Chesnut in 1862. **Place** *What two key cities on the Mississippi had the Union captured by the summer of 1862?*

Forts Henry and Donelson In February 1862, Grant advanced south along the Tennessee River with more than 15,000 troops and several gunboats. Powered by steam and built to navigate shallow bodies of water, these gunboats were basically small floating forts fitted with cannons. Grant's objectives were Fort Henry and Fort Donelson, located just over the border in the Confederate state of Tennessee. The forts protected the Tennessee and Cumberland rivers, important water routes into the western Confederacy.

On February 6 the Union gunboats pounded Fort Henry into surrender before Grant's troops arrived. The general then marched his army east and attacked Fort Donelson on the Cumberland River. Following three days of shelling by the gunboats, Fort Donelson also gave up.

The battles caused a sensation in both the North and the South. Northerners rejoiced that at last the Union had an important victory. Southerners worried that loss of the forts exposed much of the region to attack. Indeed, Nashville soon fell to another Union army. Meanwhile, Grant and some 42,000 soldiers pushed farther south along the Tennessee River to threaten Mississippi and Alabama.

The Battle of Shiloh In late March, Grant's army advanced toward Corinth, Mississippi, an important railroad center near the Tennessee-Mississippi border. Confederate general Albert Sidney Johnston gathered troops from throughout the region to halt the Union advance. By the time Grant's forces approached, Johnston had assembled an army of about 40,000 to oppose them. Grant, however, stopped at Pittsburg Landing, Tennessee, a small river town about 20 miles north of Corinth. Here he waited for more Union troops that General Don Carlos Buell was bringing from Nashville. Johnston decided to launch an attack against Grant's army before the Union force got any larger.

General Grant's demand for the "unconditional and immediate surrender" of Fort Donelson earned him the nickname "Unconditional Surrender Grant."

BACKGROUND
A Diverse Nation

Soldiers on both sides of the war came from a variety of different ethnic groups. Some ethnic groups formed their own fighting units. On the Union side, there were several all-German regiments. About 10,000 Americans of Spanish descent participated in the Civil War, on both the Union and Confederate sides. Many recent Irish immigrants fought in the war, primarily on the Union side, since most Irish immigrants had settled in the North. The 39th New York Infantry Regiment was known as the Garibaldi Guard for the many Italian soldiers in its ranks.

ACTIVITY
Connecting with Geography

Have small groups work together to draw a large map showing the area in which Fort Henry and Fort Donelson were located. Tell students to identify the major geographical features—such as the Tennessee River, the Cumberland River, and the states of Tennessee, Mississippi, and Alabama. Ask students to describe the military actions, taken in sequential order. **(Visual/Spatial)**

CAPTION ANSWERS

Map Skills Memphis and New Orleans.

CUSTOMIZE FOR ...
Gifted and Talented

Ask students to research evidence to support the view that the differences between the North and the South were so great that these two regions were really distinct nations within the United States.

MAP SKILLS McClellan's extreme caution was his own worst enemy. "No one but McClellan would have hesitated to attack," said Confederate general Joseph Johnston during McClellan's slow advance toward Richmond before the Seven Days' Battles.
Movement *What action did Lee take following the Seven Days' Battles?*

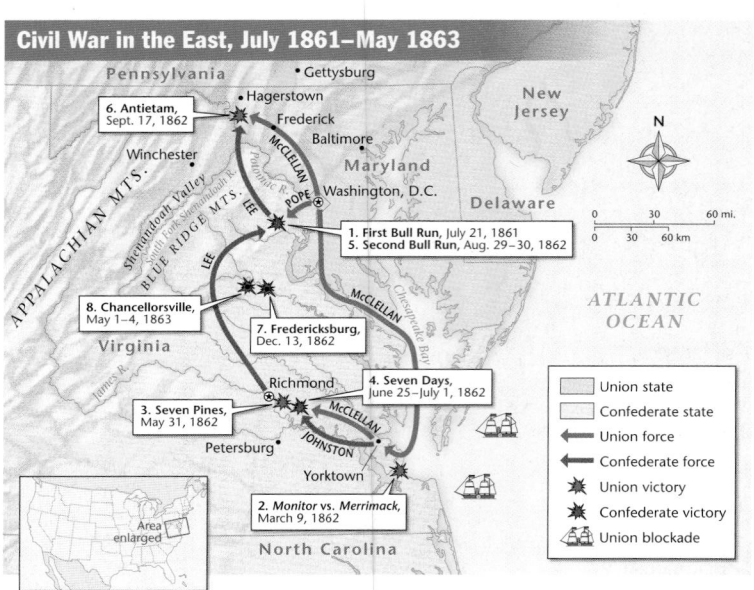

Civil War in the East, July 1861–May 1863

READING CHECK
Briefly describe the Battle of Shiloh.

On April 6, 1862, Johnston's forces surprised some of Grant's troops, who were camped at Shiloh Church outside Pittsburg Landing. Fighting quickly spread along a battle line six miles long. By the end of the first day of the **Battle of Shiloh,** the Southerners had driven the Union forces back, nearly into the Tennessee River. That night, some of Grant's officers advised a retreat before the Confederates could renew their attack the next day. "Retreat?" Grant scoffed. "No. I propose to attack at daylight and whip them."

Fortunately for Grant, Buell's troops arrived during the night. The next day, Union forces counter-attacked and defeated Johnston's army. However, the cost to both sides was very high. The Union suffered more than 13,000 casualties, the Confederates nearly 11,000. General Johnston was among the Confederate dead.

Shiloh was the bloodiest single battle that had taken place on the North American continent to that time. It shattered any remaining illusions either side had about the glory of war, and it destroyed Northern hopes that the Confederacy would soon be defeated.

Action on the Mississippi While Grant advanced into the Confederacy from the north, Union forces were also moving up the Mississippi River from the Gulf of Mexico. In late April 1862, a naval squadron commanded by David Farragut fought its way past two forts in the Louisiana swamps to force the surrender of New Orleans. Pushing upriver, Farragut soon captured Baton Rouge, Louisiana, and Natchez, Mississippi. In her diary, Southerner Mary Chesnut voiced her concerns about the Confederate losses: "Battle after battle—disaster after disaster . . . Are we not cut in two? . . . The reality is hideous."

On June 6, the Union navy seized Memphis, Tennessee. Only two major posts on the Mississippi River now remained in Confederate hands. These were Vicksburg, Mississippi, and Port Hudson, Louisiana. If Northern forces could find some way to capture them, the entire Mississippi River valley would finally be under Union control. The Confederacy would be split into two parts.

War in the East

While the Union army marched through the western Confederacy, Union warships maintained the blockade of Virginia's coast. The Confederates, however, had developed a secret weapon with which to fight the blockade. In early March 1862, a Confederate ship that resembled a floating barn roof steamed out of the James River. When the Union warships guarding the mouth of the river opened fire on the strange-looking vessel, their cannon shots bounced off it like rubber balls. In hours, the Confederate vessel destroyed or heavily damaged three of the most powerful ships in the Union navy.

The *Monitor* and the *Merrimack* Southerners had created the strange-looking vessel by bolting iron plates to an old wooden steamship called the *Merrimack*. (Although the ship was renamed the *Virginia*, it is still called the *Merrimack* in most historical accounts.) The Union's wooden navy was no match for this powerful ironclad warship. Northern leaders feared the new weapon might soon break apart the entire blockade.

Fortunately for the Union, early reports of the Confederates' work on the *Merrimack* had reached the North, and President Lincoln had ordered construction of a similar Union warship. It was made entirely of iron and was rushed to completion in about 100 days. Named the *Monitor*, it looked like a tin can on a raft.

On March 9, the *Monitor* arrived off the Virginia coast to confront the Confederate ironclad. Neither ship was able to do serious damage to the other. After several hours of fighting, the *Merrimack* finally withdrew. The two ships never met again. The Confederates blew up the *Merrimack* at its base in Norfolk, Virginia, in May 1862, rather than let it fall into Union hands. The following December, the *Monitor* sank in a storm. Their one encounter, however, changed the history of warfare. In a single day, the wooden navies of the world became obsolete.

The Peninsular Campaign When Union general George McClellan landed troops near Norfolk in May 1862, he was launching the North's second attempt to capture Richmond. At 36 years old, McClellan was young for a commanding general. However, he was an outstanding organizer, an excellent strategist, and was well liked by his troops. McClellan's great weakness was that he was very cautious and never seemed quite ready to fight. This irritated Lincoln and other Northern leaders, who were impatient to avenge the Union's defeat at Bull Run.

In March 1862, McClellan finally ordered the Army of the Potomac out of Washington. Because he thought that marching to Manassas again would be a mistake, he transported some 100,000 soldiers by boat to a peninsula southeast of Richmond. As the Union troops moved up the peninsula, they encountered some 15,000 Southerners at Yorktown, Virginia, about 60 miles from the Confederate capital.

Although the Confederate force was much smaller than his own, McClellan asked for more troops. Lincoln dispatched a stern message to his general:

VIEWING HISTORY At the center of this painting, the *Merrimack* and the *Monitor* exchange shots at close range. The *Minnesota*, which the *Monitor* was ordered to protect, sits grounded at right. **Drawing Conclusions** *How did this single battle of the ironclads make traditional wooden warships like the Minnesota obsolete?*

ACTIVITY
Connecting with History and Conflict

Ask students to correct each of the following incorrect statements.

- The First Battle of Bull Run was a Union victory that fed the notion that the war could be won quickly.
- The Confederacy planned an offensive war against the Union.
- By 1863 the Union was clearly on its way to winning the war. **(Verbal/Linguistic)**

BACKGROUND
Biography

The Civil War divided the nation in very cruel ways. First Lady Mary Todd Lincoln had four brothers and three brothers-in-law fighting on the Confederate side. Already a controversial figure, accused of extravagance and mental instability, Mrs. Lincoln was also alleged to be a rebel spy. Such rumors led President Lincoln to state: "I, of my own knowledge, know that it is untrue that any of my family hold treasonable communication with the enemy."

CAPTION ANSWERS

Viewing History The battle showed that ironclads could easily destroy wooden battleships and yet not be damaged by them. Only another ironclad could withstand an attack by an ironclad.

BIOGRAPHY

**Robert E. Lee
1807–1870**

A warm and charming Southern gentleman, Robert E. Lee came from an old and distinguished Virginia family. Among his relatives were two signers of the Declaration of Independence. In 1829, Lee graduated second in his class from West Point. Later he was recognized for outstanding service in the Mexican War.

When the Southern states seceded, Lincoln offered Lee the command of Union forces. Although he was opposed to slavery and secession, Lee refused, explaining "I cannot raise my hand against my birthplace, my home, my children." Instead, he resigned from the army and became the top military advisor to Confederate president Jefferson Davis. In May 1862, he took command of the Army of Northern Virginia, a post he held for the rest of the war. As a commander, Lee earned the loyalty and trust of his troops. Stonewall Jackson declared, "I would follow him onto the battlefield blindfolded."

❝ It is indispensable to you that you strike a blow. . . . The country will not fail to note—is now noting—that the present hesitation to move upon an entrenched enemy is but the story of Manassas repeated. . . . I have never written you . . . in greater kindness of feeling than now. . . . But you must act. ❞

—President Lincoln

McClellan, however, did not act. He waited outside Yorktown for about a month. When he finally advanced, the defenders abandoned their positions and retreated toward Richmond. On May 31, as McClellan's army neared the capital, the Southerners suddenly turned and attacked. Although the North claimed victory at the Battle of Seven Pines, both sides suffered heavy casualties. Among the wounded was the Confederate commander, General Joseph Johnston. Command of his army now fell to Robert E. Lee. Like all great generals, Lee believed in good training and planning. However, he also understood that victory sometimes depends on the willingness to take chances.

The South Attacks

With McClellan's forces still threatening Richmond, Lee had his opportunity to take a chance. In early June he divided his 55,000-man army, sending several thousand troops to strengthen Stonewall Jackson's forces in western Virginia. The Seven Pines battle had cut McClellan's army to about 80,000 soldiers. Lee was gambling that the overly cautious McClellan, who was awaiting reinforcements, would not attack Richmond before the Confederates could act.

General Jackson then began a brilliant act of deception: He pretended to prepare for an attack on Washington. Lincoln responded by canceling the order for McClellan's additional troops, keeping them in Washington to protect the Union capital. Jackson then slipped away to join Lee outside Richmond. In late June their combined forces attacked McClellan's larger army in a series of encounters called the Seven Days' Battles. Although the Confederates lost more than 20,000 soldiers, 4,000 more than the Union, McClellan decided to retreat.

The Second Battle of Bull Run After McClellan's failure, Lincoln turned to General John Pope, who was organizing a new army outside Washington. The President ordered McClellan's troops back to Washington and put Pope in overall command. Lee knew that he must draw Pope's army into battle before McClellan's soldiers arrived and made the size of the Union force overwhelming.

Again, Lee divided his army. In late August he sent Jackson's troops north in a sweeping movement around Pope's position. After marching 50 miles in two days, they struck behind Pope's army and destroyed some of his supplies, which were stored at Manassas. Enraged, Pope ordered his 62,000 soldiers into action to smash Jackson. On August 29, while Pope's force was engaged, Lee also attacked it with the main body of the Confederate army.

The battle was fought on virtually the same ground where McDowell had been defeated the year before. And Pope's Union troops met the same fate at this Second Battle of Bull Run. After Pope's defeat, McClellan was returned to command. "We must use what tools we have," Lincoln said in defense of his decision. "If he can't fight himself, he excels in making others ready to fight."

The Battle of Antietam   With Richmond no longer threatened, Lee decided that the time had come to invade the North. He hoped that a victory on Union soil would arouse European support for the South and turn Northern public opinion against the war. So, in early September 1862, Lee's army bypassed the Union troops guarding Washington and slipped into western Maryland. McClellan had no idea where the Confederates were. Then one of his soldiers found a copy of Lee's orders wrapped around some cigars near an abandoned Confederate camp. Now that he knew the enemy's strategy, McClellan crowed, "If I cannot whip Bobbie Lee, I will be willing to go home."

True to his nature, however, McClellan delayed some 16 hours before ordering his troops after Lee. This gave the Confederate general, who had learned that his plans were in enemy hands, time to prepare for the Union attack. The two armies met at Antietam Creek near Sharpsburg, Maryland, on September 17. Lee had about 40,000 troops, McClellan over 75,000, with nearly 25,000 more in reserve.

Union troops attacked throughout the day, suffering heavy losses. In the first three hours of fighting, some 12,000 soldiers from both sides were killed or wounded. By day's end Union casualties had grown to over 12,000. Lee's nearly 14,000 casualties amounted to more than a third of his army. The next day the battered Confederates retreated back into Virginia. Lincoln telegraphed McClellan, "Destroy the rebel army if possible." But the ever-cautious general did not take advantage of his opportunity to destroy Lee's army.

The **Battle of Antietam** became the bloodiest day of the Civil War. "God grant these things may soon end and peace be restored," wrote a Pennsylvania soldier after the battle. "Of this war I am heartily sick and tired."

VIEWING HISTORY This painting depicts two great Confederate generals: Robert E. Lee, left, and Stonewall Jackson. **Drawing Conclusions** *How does the artist show which general is in command?*

Reading Comprehension

1. The Confederacy, because of Jackson's stoic leadership, and the arrival of fresh troops just as the Union army was beginning to fall back.

2. They turned the tactic of attacking a position with massed troops into an act of slaughter.

3. North: implement Anaconda Plan by blockading the South and gaining control of the Mississippi river; seize Richmond. South: fight a war of attrition; apply pressure on Great Britain and France to help by stopping cotton exports.

4. Battle of Shiloh: Johnston's Confederates surprised some of Grant's troops, causing retreat. Buell's troops arrived during the night; Union forces counterattacked and won. Bloodiest battle to date; Johnston killed. Battle of Antietam: Lee decided to invade the North; Union discovered Lee's orders, delayed battle; both sides suffered great losses. Confederates retreated; Union victory. Bloodiest battle of Civil War.

Critical Thinking and Writing

5. Students should choose a battle, such as the Peninsular Campaign, and examine the leadership and strategies used, then analyze the outcome and the variables that could have been changed to alter results.

6. Answers may include a discussion of leadership, skilled troops, manpower, and geography.

Invite students to take a Virtual Field Trip at **www.phschool.com**

CAPTION ANSWERS

Viewing History Lee's gesture indicates he is giving a command. Lee's head is also higher than Jackson's, and he has a white horse and is in sunlight.

Section 1   Assessment

READING COMPREHENSION

1. Which side won the **First Battle of Bull Run?** Why?

2. What were the effects of the invention of new kinds of rifles, bullets, **shells,** and **canister?**

3. Briefly describe the war strategies of the North and the South.

4. Briefly describe the **Battle of Shiloh** and the **Battle of Antietam.**

CRITICAL THINKING AND WRITING

5. **Predicting Consequences** Choose one early Civil War battle that demonstrated the result of a lost opportunity, and describe what might have happened if a different decision had been made.

6. **Writing an Outline** Write an outline for a newspaper editorial of May 1861 in which you will argue why either the North or the South will easily win the Civil War.

 Take It to the NET

Virtual Field Trip Visit the site of the Battle of Antietam, and view photos and paintings from the time of the battle and "tour" the park through current photos. Use the links provided in the *America: Pathways to the Present* area of the following Web site for help in completing this activity.
www.phschool.com

Life Behind the Lines

SECTION OBJECTIVES

1. Learn how wartime politics affected the Confederate and Union governments.

2. Discover how the Emancipation Proclamation affected both the North and the South.

3. Find out the causes and effects of African Americans' joining the Union army.

4. List the kinds of hardships that befell the North and the South during the war.

BELLRINGER

Warm-Up Activity Ask students to think about how the power of the federal government in the United States changed during the nation's first century. Ask them to consider the effects of war on the power of government.

Activating Prior Knowledge How did the Civil War affect the United States' relationships with England and France? Ask students to list reasons why France and England might choose to support either the Union or the Confederacy.

READING STRATEGY

Have students list some possible solutions to the problems that the Confederate and Union governments faced during the war. As they read, have them take specific notes on how both sides actually responded.

READING FOCUS

- How did wartime politics affect the Confederate and Union governments?
- How did the Emancipation Proclamation affect both the North and the South?
- What were the causes and effects of African Americans joining the Union army?
- What kinds of hardships befell the North and the South during the war?

MAIN IDEA

The Union and the Confederacy struggled to raise and support their armies and to provide for the well-being of their citizens. The Emancipation Proclamation had a profound effect on both those efforts.

KEY TERMS

draft
recognition
greenback
Copperhead
martial law
writ of *habeas corpus*
Emancipation
 Proclamation
contraband

TAKING NOTES

As you read, prepare an outline of the first part of this section. Use Roman numerals for the first two major headings, capital letters for subheads, and numbers for supporting details. Include responses to problems as shown in the sample below.

I. Politics in the South
 A. Mobilizing for War
  1. Not enough soldiers to fight/Lee calls for draft.
  2. _____
 B. _____
  1. _____
  2. _____

Setting the Scene By early 1862, the "picnic" atmosphere evident at the beginning of the First Battle of Bull Run was gone. It was clear that the war was going to be neither quick nor easy, and that the resources of both sides would be severely strained. The South, for example, faced a crisis of manpower. As Grant moved toward Mississippi and McClellan's army threatened Richmond, many Confederate soldiers neared the end of their enlistments. Few seemed ready to reenlist. "If I live this twelve months out, I intend to try mighty hard to keep out [of the army]," pledged one Virginia soldier. A young Wisconsin boy who had run away to join the Union Army also had second thoughts:

Soldiers carried their eating implements, or mess kits, with them.

66 *I want to say, as we lay there and the shells were flying all over us, my thoughts went back to my home, and I thought what a foolish boy I was to run away and get into such a mess as I was in. I would have been glad to have seen my father coming after me.* 99

—Elisha Stockwell

Politics in the South

While both sides had to deal with the practical and political problems of a long and costly war, the South had a further difficulty. The branches and powers of the Confederate government were similar to those of the government of the United States. However, the framers of the Confederate constitution had made certain that it recognized states' rights and slavery—two of the main reasons for the South's secession from the Union. These two issues caused problems for the South throughout the war.

Like the government of the North, the Confederate government had to persuade individual citizens to sacrifice their

RESOURCE DIRECTORY

Teaching Resources
Guided Reading and Review booklet, p. 47

Other Print Resources
Historical Outline Map Book *The Southern States,* p. 44

Technology
Section Reading Support Transparencies
Guided Reading Audiotapes (English/Spanish), Ch. 11
Student Edition on Audio CD, Ch. 11
Prentice Hall Presentation Pro CD-ROM, Ch. 11
Companion Web site, www.phschool.com

personal interests for the common good. In addition, Confederate leaders had to find a way to build Southerners' loyalty to their new government. Furthermore, because the South had fewer resources than the North, its war effort depended more on making the best possible use of the resources it had. Since the Southern state governments were strong and sometimes fiercely independent, meeting these objectives would sometimes prove difficult.

Mobilizing for War Fearing the war would be lost if there were not enough soldiers to fight, General Lee called for a **draft,** or required military service. Opponents of strong central government claimed that a draft violated the principles of states' rights that the South was fighting for. A Texas senator disagreed:

> 66 *Cease this child's play. . . . The enemy are in some portions of almost every state in the Confederacy . . . We need a large army. How are you going to get it? . . . No man has any individual rights, which come into conflict with the welfare of the country.* 99
>
> —Senator Louis Wigfall

In April 1862, the Confederate congress passed a draft law requiring three years of military service for white men ages 18 to 35. This automatically extended the service of all volunteers for two more years. After the horrible losses at Antietam, the upper age for the draft became 45. Later it was raised again to 50. The Confederate government also took charge of the South's economy. It determined how much wool, cotton, and leather should be produced, and seized control of Southern railroads from private owners. Farmers were required to contribute one tenth of their produce to the war effort.

To help raise money for the war, the Confederate congress imposed a tax on personal incomes. The Confederate government also authorized the army to seize male slaves for military labor. Though they were paid a monthly fee for borrowed slaves, planters resented this practice because it disrupted work on their plantations.

The Impact of States' Rights Not all of the mobilization efforts described above were successful. A fierce commitment to states' rights worked against the Confederate government and harmed the war effort in many ways. You will recall that the national government under the Articles of Confederation had suffered similar difficulties, and was replaced by the Constitution when Americans of that time felt the need for a stronger central government. Many Americans, especially in the South, had continued to champion states' rights—both under the United States Constitution and under the new Confederacy. The governor of Georgia put it this way:

> 66 *I entered into this revolution . . . to sustain the rights of the states . . . and I am still a rebel . . . no matter who may be in power.* 99
>
> —Governor Joseph Brown

Many Southerners shared the governor's point of view. Local authorities sometimes refused to cooperate with draft officials. Whole counties in some states were ruled by armed bands of draft-dodgers and deserters. It is estimated that perhaps one quarter of Confederate men eligible for the draft failed to cooperate.

Chapter 11 • Section 2   **391**

Focus on WORLD EVENTS

Britain and France While Britain and France had often been rivals and military foes, during the period preceding the American Civil War they had become allies. The two nations had fought on the same side in the Crimean War (1854–1856), and in 1860, Napoleon III of France had negotiated a treaty with Britain to lower tariffs levied on goods traded between them. What's more, by 1864, the German leader Bismarck was changing the balance of power in Europe and posing a threat to France.

LESSON PLAN

Focus The Civil War brought many changes to Northerners and Southerners. The national governments of both sides grew in power. How did the war affect African Americans?

Instruct Discuss the strengths and weaknesses of the Confederate government. List the ways the federal government increased its power during the war. Was Lincoln justified in taking on extraordinary powers to keep the Border States in the Union?

Assess/Reteach Based on what they are learning in the section, ask students to identify the following changes in the federal government as temporary or permanent.

- A draft law supplied troops for the army.
- Congress passed new tax laws, including a federal tax on income.
- Congress created a national currency.
- The President suspended the writ of *habeas corpus*.
- The President shut down newspapers that disagreed with his policies.

ACTIVITY
Connecting with Citizenship

The Confederacy could not rely on its own political unity due to its commitment to individual states' rights. Some believe that this attitude led to the defeat of the South. To help students understand the Unionist and Confederate beliefs about the structure of a nation, divide the class into small groups. Each group member should give an example of one situation in his or her life in which pooling resources was more beneficial than doing something alone, and one in which it was not. (**Verbal/Linguistic**)

CUSTOMIZE FOR ...
Less Proficient Readers

Ask students to turn each of the section's headings and subheadings into a question. Have them then skim the text to answer these questions before reading the section.

VIEWING FINE ART After operating for about 21 months, the Confederate privateer *Alabama* was finally sunk by the U.S.S. *Kearsarge* off the coast of France, as shown in this 1864 painting by Edouard Manet. **Determining Relevance** *Why was the South's ability to capture Union merchant vessels important to the Confederacy?*

"If we are defeated," warned an Atlanta newspaper, "it will be by the people at home."

Seeking Help From Europe Although the Union blockade effectively prevented Southern cotton from reaching Great Britain and France, Southerners continued to hope for British and French intervention in the war. In May 1861, the Confederate government sent representatives to both nations. Even though the Confederacy failed to gain **recognition,** or official acceptance as an independent nation, it did receive some help. Great Britain agreed to allow its ports to be used to build Confederate privateers. One of these vessels, the *Alabama,* captured more than 60 Northern merchant ships. In all, 11 British-built Confederate privateers forced most Union shipping from the high seas for much of the war.

Formal recognition of the Confederacy did seem possible for a time in 1862. Napoleon III, the ruler of France, had sent troops into Mexico, trying to rebuild a French empire in the Americas. He welcomed the idea of an independent Confederate States of America on Mexico's northern border. However, France would not openly support the Confederacy without Great Britain's cooperation.

British opinion about the war was divided. Some leaders clearly sympathized with the Southerners. Many believed an independent South would be a better market for British products. However, there was also strong antislavery feeling in Britain, and there were those who did not want to come to the aid of a slave-owning nation. Others questioned whether the Confederacy would be able to win the war. The British government adopted a wait-and-see attitude. To get foreign help, the South would first have to prove itself on the battlefield.

Politics in the North

After early losses to Confederate forces, President Lincoln and his government had to convince some Northern citizens that maintaining the Union was worth the sacrifices they were being asked to make. As in the South, efforts focused on raising troops and uniting the nation behind the war effort. In addition, the federal government found itself facing international crises as it worked to strengthen civilian support for the war.

Tensions With Great Britain British talks with the South aroused tensions between Great Britain and the United States. Late in 1861, Confederate president Davis again sent two representatives from the Confederacy to England and France. After evading the Union blockade, John Slidell and James Mason boarded the British mail ship *Trent* and steamed for Europe.

Soon a Union warship stopped the *Trent* in international waters, removed the two Confederate officials, and brought them to the United States. An outraged British government sent troops to Canada and threatened war unless Slidell and Mason were freed. President Lincoln ordered their release. "One war at a time," he said.

The Union vigorously protested Great Britain's support of the Confederacy. Lincoln demanded $19 billion compensation from Great Britain for damages done by the privateers built in British ports, and for other British actions on the South's behalf. This demand strained relations between the United States and Great Britain for nearly a decade after the war.

Republicans in Control   With Southern Democrats out of the United States Congress, Republican lawmakers had little opposition. The Civil War Congresses thus became among the most active in American history. Republicans were able to pass a number of laws during the war that would have a lasting impact, even well after the South rejoined the Union.

For example, Southerners had long opposed building a rail line across the Great Plains. It was first proposed by Illinois senator Stephen Douglas in the early 1850s, in part to benefit Chicago by linking that city to the West. In July 1862, however, Congress passed the Pacific Railroad Act with little resistance. The law allowed the federal government to give land and money to companies for construction of a railroad line from Nebraska to the Pacific Coast. The Homestead Act, passed in the same year, offered free government land to people willing to settle on it.

The disappearance of Southern opposition also allowed Congress to raise tariff rates. The tariff became more a device to protect Northern industries than to provide revenue for the government. Union leaders turned to other means to raise money for the war.

Financial Measures   In 1861, the Republican-controlled Congress passed the first federal tax on income in American history. It collected 3 percent of the income of people earning more than $600 a year but less than $10,000, which is the equivalent of about $11,000 to $180,000 today. Those making more than $10,000 per year were taxed at 5 percent. The Internal Revenue Act of 1862 imposed taxes on items such as liquor, tobacco, medicine, and newspaper ads. Nearly all of these taxes ended when the war was over.

During the war, Congress also reformed the nation's banking system. Since 1832, when President Jackson vetoed the recharter of the Second Bank of the United States, Americans had relied on state banks. In 1862, Congress passed an act that created a national currency, called **greenbacks** because of their color. This paper money was not backed by gold, but was declared by Congress to be acceptable for legal payment of all public and private debts.

Opposition to the War   Like the South, the North instituted a draft in order to raise troops for what now looked like a longer, more difficult war. And like the Southern law, this March 1863 measure allowed the wealthy to buy their way out of military service. Riots broke out in the North after the draft law was passed. Mobs of whites in New York City vented their rage at the draft in July 1863. More than 100 people died during four days of destruction. At least 11 of the dead were African Americans, who seemed to be targeted by the rioters.

There was political opposition to the war as well. Although the Democrats remaining in Congress were too few to have much power, one group raised their voices in protest against the war. This group was nicknamed **Copperheads,** after a type of poisonous snake. These Democrats warned that Republican policies would bring a flood of freed slaves to the North. What's more, they predicted that these freed slaves

READING CHECK
What caused tension between the Union and Great Britain?

Focus on
GOVERNMENT

Civil War Conscription   The Civil War marked the first time that conscription, or the draft, was instituted in the United States. Both sides used it to raise troops, and both sides used it unfairly. In the South, owners of 20 or more slaves were excused from serving. A Northerner could pay the government $300 to avoid service. In both the Union and the Confederacy, wealthy men could hire substitutes to fight in their place. No wonder many angry Southerners called the conflict "a rich man's war and a poor man's fight."

ACTIVITY
Connecting with Today

The first income tax was levied during the Civil War. But it did not remain in place for very long. Have students research the history of the income tax in the United States to discover when it was abandoned following the Civil War, when it started up again, and so forth. Can students list the reasons why federal taxes were levied and then rescinded at certain times? How does the 5–10 percent tax rate of the Civil War era compare with tax brackets today? **(Logical/Mathematical)**

BACKGROUND
Interdisciplinary

The term *Copperhead* was first used by James Gordon Bennett, editor of the *New York Herald,* on July 20, 1861. He compared a group opposed to the Civil War to copperhead snakes, which strike savagely without warning. "A rattlesnake rattles, a viper hisses, an adder spits, a black snake whistles, a water snake blows, but a copperhead just sneaks," he wrote.

READING CHECK

The Confederacy found sympathy in Great Britain. The Lincoln administration was enraged that Great Britain built privateers, such as the *Alabama,* for the Confederacy. The *Trent* episode greatly angered the government of Great Britain.

☑ **TEST PREPARATION**

Have students reread the section titled "Seeking Help from Europe" on the previous page and then answer the question below.

Which of the following does not belong?

A Napoleon III supported the Union cause.

B Napoleon III supported the Confederate cause in the Civil War.

C France's effort to gain control of Mexico would be helped by an independent Confederate States of America.

D Great Britain was sympathetic in some ways with the Confederacy.

would take jobs away from whites. Radical Copperheads also tried to persuade Union soldiers to desert the army, and they urged other Northerners to resist the draft.

Emergency Wartime Actions   Like the government of the Confederacy, the United States government exercised great power during the Civil War. To silence the Copperheads and other opponents of the war, Lincoln resorted to extreme measures. He used the army to shut down opposition newspapers and denied others the use of the mails.

The border states provided a special set of problems. Four of them were slave states that remained—at least for the moment—in the Union. Because of their locations, the continued loyalty of Delaware, Maryland, Missouri, and Kentucky was critical to the North. Lincoln considered Delaware, where few citizens held slaves, to be secure. In nearby Maryland, however, support for secession was strong. In September 1861, Lincoln ordered that all "disloyal" members of the Maryland state legislature be arrested. This action prevented a vote on secession and assured that Washington would not be surrounded by the Confederacy.

The Union needed the loyalty of Kentucky and Missouri in order to keep control of the Ohio and Mississippi rivers. In Missouri, Lincoln supported an uprising aimed at overthrowing the pro-Confederate state government. To secure Kentucky, he put the state under **martial law** for part of the war. This is emergency rule by military authorities, during which some Bill of Rights

---

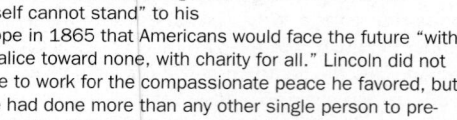

NOTABLE PRESIDENTS
Abraham Lincoln

"A house divided against itself cannot stand."
—**Speech in 1858**

Abraham Lincoln entered the White House with little experience in national politics. Before being elected in 1860, he had been a successful lawyer in Illinois and a one-term member of Congress. Nothing, however, could have prepared him for the extraordinary challenges he would face as President.

Lincoln confronted crises on every side. Southern states began seceding from the Union even before he took office. The border states had to be kept in the Union. Many Northerners who opposed secession did not want to fight the South, and white Northerners disagreed among themselves about slavery.

Lincoln's actions as President all pointed toward one goal: preserve the Union. He changed commanding generals again and again in a desperate search for one who could defeat the Confederate army. He suppressed freedom of speech and assembly. He issued the Emancipation Proclamation to free the slaves living behind Confederate lines, and in 1863 he called upon free blacks to join the Union army.

Along with his commitment to preserve the Union,

Lincoln's greatest strengths were his sense of compassion and his ability to express powerful ideas in simple yet moving language. In fact, his words have come to help define the Civil War, from his warning that "A house divided against itself cannot stand" to his

16th President 1861–1865

hope in 1865 that Americans would face the future "with malice toward none, with charity for all." Lincoln did not live to work for the compassionate peace he favored, but he had done more than any other single person to preserve the Union at its time of greatest danger.

Connecting to Today
How important is it that a President be able to rally people behind a cause?

🖱 **Take It to the NET Biography** To read more about Abraham Lincoln, visit the links provided in the *America: Pathways to the Present* area at the following Web site. **www.phschool.com**

guarantees are suspended. Although Jefferson Davis imposed martial law on parts of the Confederacy, Lincoln is the only United States President ever to exercise this power.

In some places Lincoln suspended the **writ of habeas corpus.** This is a legal protection requiring that a court determine if a person is lawfully imprisoned. Without it, people can be held in jail for indefinite periods even though they are not charged with a crime. The Constitution allows suspension of the writ of *habeas corpus* during a rebellion.

More than 13,000 Americans who objected to the Union government's policies were imprisoned without trial during the Civil War. They included newspaper editors and elected state officials, plus Southern sympathizers and some who actually did aid the Confederacy. Most Northerners approved of Lincoln's actions as necessary to restore the Union.

Emancipation and the War

While the Copperheads attacked Lincoln for making war on the South, abolitionists and others attacked him for not making the military action a war to end slavery. As the Union's battlefield casualties mounted, many Northerners began to question whether it was enough to simply restore the nation. Some, including a group in the Republican Party called the Radical Republicans, thought that the Confederacy should be punished for causing so much suffering. No punishment could be worse, the Radical Republicans argued, than freeing the slaveholders' "property."

Lincoln and Slavery   At first, the President resisted pressure to make the abolition of slavery a goal of the war. He insisted that under the Constitution he was bound only to preserve and protect the Union. Lincoln explained this view in a letter to Horace Greeley, an abolitionist newspaper editor:

> 66 My paramount object in this struggle is to save the Union, and is not to either save or to destroy slavery. If I could save the Union without freeing any slave, I would do it, and if I could save the Union by freeing all the slaves, I would do it; and if I could save it by freeing some and leaving others alone, I would also do that. 99
>
> —President Lincoln

Although Lincoln personally opposed slavery, he did not believe that he had the legal authority to abolish it. He also worried about the effect such an action would have on the loyalty of the border states. However, Lincoln recognized the importance of slavery to the South's war effort. Every slave working in a field or in a factory freed a white Southerner to shoot at Union soldiers. Gradually, Lincoln came to regard ending slavery as one more strategy for winning the war.

The Emancipation Proclamation   In the fall of 1862, as Lee retreated south from Antietam, Lincoln proclaimed that on January 1, 1863, slaves in areas of rebellion against the government would be free. Then, on New Year's Day, 1863, he issued the final **Emancipation Proclamation:**

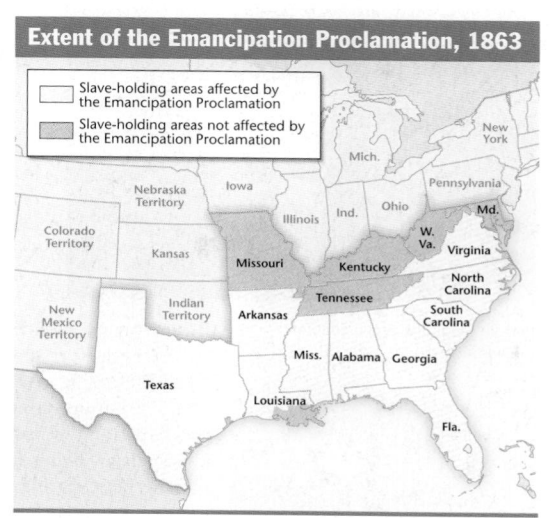

Extent of the Emancipation Proclamation, 1863

Slave-holding areas affected by the Emancipation Proclamation

Slave-holding areas not affected by the Emancipation Proclamation

MAP SKILLS This map shows where the Emancipation Proclamation actually freed the slaves. The state of Tennessee and small areas of Virginia and Louisiana were parts of the Confederacy occupied by Union troops, so they were no longer "in rebellion." **Region** *Where could the emancipation of slaves be enforced? Explain. Why was the Emancipation Proclamation important anyway?*

KEY DOCUMENTS "I, Abraham Lincoln, President of the United States, by virtue of the power in me vested as Commander-in-Chief, of the Army and Navy of the United States in time of actual armed rebellion against the authority and government of the United States, and as a fit and necessary war measure for suppressing said rebellion . . . do order and declare that all persons held as slaves within said designated States, and parts of States, are and henceforward shall be free. . . ."
—President Lincoln, January 1863

Lincoln reads the Emancipation Proclamation to his cabinet.

Reaction to the Proclamation The decree had little direct impact on slavery because it applied only to places that were under Confederate control. Nevertheless, it was condemned in the South and debated in the North. Some abolitionists criticized Lincoln for not having gone far enough. The proclamation did nothing to free people enslaved in the border states, nor did it free slaves living in Confederate areas controlled by Union forces. Other Northerners, fearing that freed people coming north would cause unemployment, criticized even this limited action. After Lincoln's September announcement, the Democratic Party made gains in the congressional elections of November 1862.

The response of black Northerners was much more positive. "We shout for joy that we live to record this righteous decree," abolitionist Frederick Douglass exclaimed. Even if the proclamation brought no immediate end to slavery, it promised, through the word *henceforward*, that an enslaved people would be free when the North won the war.

Perhaps the most significant reaction occurred in Europe. The abolition movement was strong in England. The Emancipation Proclamation, coupled with news of Lee's defeat at Antietam, ended any real chance that France and Great Britain would intervene in the war.

African Americans Join the War

The Emancipation Proclamation had two immediate effects. It inspired Southern slaves who heard about it to free themselves by escaping to the protection of Union troops. It also encouraged African Americans to join the Union army.

The Contraband Issue Union troops had been making gains in the South. Southern slaveholders sometimes fled with their slaves when the Union army approached. Frequently, however, slaves remained behind or escaped to the safety of nearby Union forces. Believing they had no choice, some Union officers gave these slaves back to slaveholders who demanded the return of their "property."

Early in the war, Union general Benjamin Butler devised a legal argument that allowed the Union army to free escaped slaves they captured. It was generally accepted that, during war, one side's possessions could be seized by its enemy. Called **contraband,** these captured items then became the property of the enemy government. Butler maintained that if slaves were property then they could be considered contraband of war. The Union government, as their new owner, could then let the slaves go.

At first, the army employed these freed African Americans to build fortifications, drive wagons, and perform other noncombat jobs. After the Emancipation Proclamation, however, many former slaves enlisted to fight the Confederacy.

396 Chapter 11 • *The Civil War*

African American Soldiers When the Civil War began, black volunteers were not allowed to join the Union army. In July 1862, following McClellan's defeats in Virginia, Congress authorized Lincoln to accept African Americans into the military. Several months later, Lincoln made the announcement in the Emancipation Proclamation.

Given this encouragement, African Americans rushed to join the fight. By 1865, nearly 180,000 African Americans had enlisted in the Union army. More than half were black Southerners who had been freed from slavery by the fighting. For these soldiers, fighting to help free others who were still enslaved held special meaning. Many African Americans viewed the chance to fight against slavery as a milestone in their history. In total, African Americans composed almost 10 percent of the troops who served the North during the war.

On warships, black and white sailors served together. African American soldiers, however, served in all-black regiments under the command of white officers. Until June 1864, African Americans earned less pay than white soldiers.

In July 1863, an African American regiment earned a place in history at Fort Wagner, a stronghold that protected the harbor at Charleston, South Carolina. On July 18, the 54th Massachusetts Infantry, commanded by Colonel Robert Gould Shaw, led the attack on the fort. The regiment's charge across a narrow spit of sand cost it nearly half its men. Sergeant William Carney, the first African American to earn the Congressional Medal of Honor, was among the survivors. So were Frederick Douglass's two sons, one of whom wrote this in a letter to his sweetheart:

> **❝** I have been in two fights . . . The last was desperate. [W]e charged that terrible battery on Morris Island known as Fort Wagner. . . . I escaped unhurt. . . . Should I fall in the next fight killed or wounded I hope I fall with my face to the foe. . . . Remember if I die I die in a good cause. . . .**❞**
>
> —Lewis Douglass

The actions of the 54th Massachusetts demonstrated what Lewis's father, Frederick Douglass, wrote in his newspaper the following month:

> **❝** Once let a black man get upon his person the brass letters, U.S.; let him get an eagle on his button, and a musket on his shoulder and bullets in his pocket, and there is no power on earth which can deny that he has earned the right to citizenship. **❞**
>
> —Frederick Douglass

The Hardships of War

The Emancipation Proclamation and the welcoming of black troops into the Union army drastically changed the culture and the economy in the South. First, these developments prompted thousands of slaves to escape to freedom. Some who remained on plantations resisted the continuation of slavery by not

VIEWING HISTORY Over the course of the Civil War, nearly 180,000 African Americans wore the Union uniform. **Recognizing Cause and Effect** How did the Emancipation Proclamation change the role of African Americans in the military?

doing their work or by destroying farm equipment. These developments hurt the Confederacy in two ways. They depleted or weakened the South's labor force, and they provided the North with even greater numerical advantages in the war effort.

The war produced drastic changes in the lives of both Northerners and Southerners. With the majority of men off fighting, women on both sides took on new responsibilities. Wives and mothers lived with the fear that every day could bring news of the loss of a loved one. In addition, both sides faced labor shortages, inflation, and other economic problems. By 1863, however, it was clear that the North's greater resources were allowing it to meet these challenges, while the South could not.

The Southern Economy Among the problems the Confederacy faced during the war was a food shortage. Invading armies disrupted the South's food-growing regions as well as its production of cotton. In parts of the South not threatened by Union forces, the Confederate draft pulled large numbers of white males out of rural areas. Southern women worked the land, oversaw slaves, and tried to keep farms and plantations operating. However, food production declined in the South as the war progressed.

Many planters made the problem worse by resisting the central government's pleas to shift from raising cotton to growing food crops. While cotton piled up in warehouses due to the Union blockade, food riots erupted in Southern cities. The worst of these occurred in Richmond, where nearly 1,000 women looted bakeries and other shops in April 1863.

INTERPRETING POLITICAL CARTOONS This cartoon was published in a Northern newspaper. At left, Southern women urge their men to go off to war. The panel on the right shows the bread riots resulting from the war. **Recognizing Ideologies** *What is the cartoonist saying about the women's responsibility for their plight?*

Although the Confederacy was never able to provide all the manufactured goods its army needed, Southern industry grew during the war. The Confederate government supervised construction of factories to make railroad track, guns and ammunition, and many other items needed for the war effort. Women filled many of the jobs in these factories.

The labor shortage and lack of goods contributed to inflation. So too did profiteering. Unscrupulous profiteers would buy up large supplies of certain goods, and hold them until the price climbed and they could make a huge profit. Not only did this practice contribute to higher prices, it also helped to *cause* shortages of certain goods. For example, early in the war, profiteers bought up all the nails in Richmond for $4 a keg. Because they had nowhere else to buy nails, the people of Richmond ended up paying the profiteers $10 a keg.

The hardships at home increased desertions in the Confederate army. Some soldiers returned home to work their farms and help provide for their wives and children. "We are poor men and are willing to defend our country but our families [come] first," a Mississippi soldier declared.

The Northern Economy In the North, the war hurt industries that depended heavily on Southern markets or Southern cotton. However, most Northern industries boomed. Unlike the Confederacy, the North had the farms and factories to produce nearly everything its army and civilian population needed. War-related industries fared especially well. Philip Armour made a fortune packaging pork to feed Union soldiers. Samuel Colt ran his factory night and day producing guns for the army.

As in the South, when men went off to war, women filled critical jobs in factories and on farms. Many factory owners preferred women employees because they could be paid less than male workers. This hiring practice kept wages down overall. Prices rose faster than pay during the war.

A few manufacturers made their profits even greater by selling the Union government inferior products: rusty rifles, boats that leaked, hats that dissolved in the rain. Uniforms made from compressed rags quickly fell apart. The soles came off some boots after a few miles of marching. Like the Southern profiteers, these manufacturers took shameful advantage of the needs of their countrymen.

Prison Camps Captured Confederate soldiers were sent to prison camps throughout the North, including Point Lookout in Maryland and Camp Chase in Ohio. The Ohio Penitentiary also housed some Confederate prisoners. The South's prison camps were located wherever there was room. Andersonville, its most notorious camp, was in a field in Georgia. Richmond's Libby Prison was a converted tobacco warehouse.

The North and the South generally treated their prisoners about the same. In most cases officers received better treatment than other prisoners. Andersonville was the exception. Built to hold 10,000 men, it eventually confined nearly 35,000 Northerners in a fenced, 26-acre open area. About 100 prisoners a day died, usually of starvation or exposure. The camp's commander was the only Confederate to be tried for war crimes after the South's defeat. He was convicted and hanged.

Medical Care While soldiers faced miserable conditions in prison camps, life was not much better in the battle camps. Health and medical conditions on both sides were frightful. About one in four Civil War soldiers did not survive the war, but it was disease that killed many of them. Poor nutrition and contaminated food led to dysentery and typhoid fever. Malaria, spread by mosquitoes, was also a killer. Many soldiers died of pneumonia.

A Union soldier was three times more likely to die in camp or in a hospital than he was to be killed on the battlefield. In fact, about one in five Union soldiers wounded in battle later died from their wounds. While most doctors were aware of the relationship between cleanliness and infection, they did not know how to sterilize their equipment. Surgeons sometimes went for days without even washing their instruments.

On both sides, thousands of women volunteered to care for the sick and wounded. Government clerk Clara Barton quit her job in order to provide supplies and first aid to Union troops in camp and during battle. Known to soldiers as the "angel of the battlefield," Barton continued her service after the war by founding the American Red Cross. Mental health reformer Dorothea Dix volunteered to organize and head the Union army's nursing corps. Nursing was a difficult task, as the following letter shows:

Focus on
ECONOMICS

Inflation in the South As the war dragged on and Union armies advanced into the South, shortages and the falling value of Confederate currency caused almost unbelievable inflation. Inflation is a steady increase in prices over time. Even by late 1862, a bag of salt that had cost $2 before the war was selling for $60 in some places. Southerner Rose Frye remembered the price of calico going from 50 cents to $20 per yard, and paying $125 for shoes.

Another way to look at inflation is to compare the value of Confederate currency to $100 worth of gold as shown in this graph.

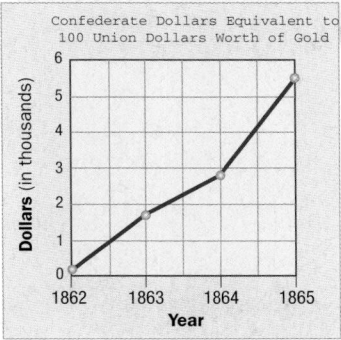

Confederate Dollars Equivalent to 100 Union Dollars Worth of Gold

Section 2 — Assessment

Reading Comprehension

1. Southern draft laws required: three years of military service for white men ages 18 to 35; extended service of all volunteers for two more years; upper age for draft eventually extended to 50; owners of 20 or more slaves were excused. North instituted similar laws, and Northerners could pay the government to avoid service. In both North and South, wealthy men could hire substitutes to fight in their place.

2. Copperheads were Democrats who believed that Republican policies would bring freed slaves to the North, taking jobs away from whites. They tried to persuade Union soldiers to desert the army and urged other Northerners to resist the draft.

3. Lincoln used martial law, suspending some Bill of Rights guarantees, to ensure that Kentucky would remain loyal to the Union. The suspension of the writ of habeas corpus imprisoned, without trial, those who objected to the Union government's policies during the war.

4. Lincoln recognized the importance of slavery to the South's war effort, and came to regard ending slavery as another strategy to end the war.

Critical Thinking and Writing

5. Wigfall's: Allegiance to welfare and preservation of the nation and the ideals on which it was founded.

6. Students' lists should highlight: Southern slaves freed themselves by escaping to the protection of Union troops; encouraged African Americans to join the Union army.

Take It to the NET

Answers will vary. Students should note that the branches and powers of the government were similar in both documents, but the Confederate constitution recognized states' rights and slavery.

Many women served as nurses in the wards of field hospitals. One nurse, Clara Barton (inset), was known as the "angel of the battlefield."

> **❝** *I am very tired tonight; I have been in the field all day. There are no words in the English language to express the sufferings I witnessed today. The men lie on the ground; their clothes have been cut off them to dress their wounds; they . . . have nothing but hardtack to eat. . . . [F]our surgeons, none of whom were idle for fifteen minutes at a time, were busy all day amputating legs and arms. . . . I would get on first rate if they would not ask me to write to their wives; that I cannot do without crying, which is not pleasant to either party.* **❞**
>
> —Cornelia Hancock

Some 4,000 women served as nurses for the Northern army. By the end of the war, nursing was no longer only a man's profession.

Sanitation in most army camps was nonexistent. Rubbish and rotting food littered the ground. Human waste and heaps of animal manure polluted water supplies. Epidemics of contagious diseases, such as mumps and measles, swept through camps. Sick lists were lengthy. At times only half the troops in a regiment were available for fighting.

The United States Sanitary Commission, created in June 1861, attempted to combat these problems. Thousands of volunteers, mostly women, inspected army hospitals and camps. They organized cleanups and provided advice about controlling infection, disease prevention, sewage disposal, and nutrition. Despite these and similar Confederate efforts, about twice as many soldiers on each side died from disease as from enemy gunfire.

Section 2 — Assessment

READING COMPREHENSION

1. Describe the **draft** laws in the North and the South.

2. Who were the **Copperheads?**

3. How were **martial law** and the suspension of the **writ of** *habeas corpus* used to stifle dissent?

4. Why did Lincoln decide to issue the **Emancipation Proclamation?**

CRITICAL THINKING AND WRITING

5. Comparing Points of View Compare the quotes from Senator Louis Wigfall and Governor Joseph Brown. Given the measures President Lincoln used during the war, which position do you think he would have favored?

6. Writing a List Make a list of the effects of the Emancipation Proclamation in both the North and the South. Underline the two most important effects.

Take It to the NET

Activity: Making a Chart Read the constitutions of the United States and the Confederacy. Make a chart showing three important similarities and three important differences between the documents. Use the links provided in the *America: Pathways to the Present* area of the following Web site for help in completing this activity.
www.phschool.com

RESOURCE DIRECTORY
Teaching Resources
Units 3/4 booklet
• Section 2 Quiz, p. 54
Guide to the Essentials
• Section 2 Summary, p. 59

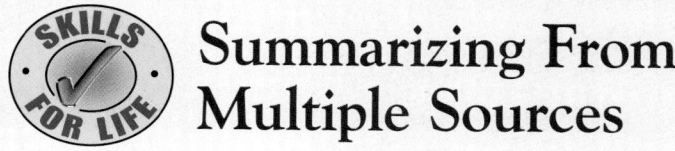

Summarizing From Multiple Sources

When you are doing research, you will often find two or more sources with information about one topic. Combining the main ideas of these sources into a single summary can provide a more complete picture of events than either source could alone. You can also use each source to test the reliability of the others: if the sources do not seem to agree, you should do further research to find out which ones provide the most reliable information.

In February 1865, General Sherman's army began marching through South Carolina, sparing little in its path. Dr. Samuel McGill, a resident of the state, made entries in his diary as the army advanced. Ten years later, in his memoirs, General Sherman would recall his own thinking at the time.

LEARN THE SKILL
Use the following steps to summarize from multiple sources:

1. **Find the main idea of each source.** Sometimes the main idea is stated by the writer, often in the first sentence of a paragraph. In other cases, you may have to use your judgment to identify the main idea from the details in the source.

2. **Identify supporting details in each source.** These include any facts, reasons, explanations, examples, or descriptions that helped you find each main idea.

3. **Write a summary of each source.** State or restate its main idea in your own words.

4. **Create a summary based on the main ideas of all the sources.** Use your own words to tie the sources' main ideas together. If possible, include a supporting detail from each source.

PRACTICE THE SKILL
Answer the following questions:

1. **(a)** Which sentence in Source A states the main idea of the two diary entries? **(b)** Which sentence in Source B provides the main idea of that excerpt?

2. **(a)** What actions are described in Source A? **(b)** How do they support the writer's sense of the mood of the people? **(c)** In Source B, what is the "power" that Sherman planned to use? **(d)** What was Sherman ready to do in order to use it?

3. **(a)** State the main idea of Source A in your own words. **(b)** State the main idea of Source B in your own words.

4. **(a)** What historical event links McGill's diary entries with the excerpt from Sherman's memoirs? **(b)** Do the two sources contradict or complement each other? Explain. **(c)** Drawing information from both sources, describe what happened in the Williamsburg District in 1865 and why it happened.

APPLY THE SKILL
See the Chapter Review and Assessment for another opportunity to apply this skill.

A

February 28, 1865: *"All is gloom and uncertainty, and preparations are being made for the worst. Furniture and provisions are hidden against pending raids. . . . It is feared famine will possess the land; our army is demoralized and the people panic stricken. . . . The power to do [act] has left us. . . . To fight longer seems to be madness; to submit tamely is dishonor."*

March 1, 1865: *"The whole country is in the wildest commotion and many are fleeing to the woods with their wives and daughters, while a few have gone to meet the advance and to give battle."*

—From the diary of Dr. Samuel McGill, Williamsburg District, South Carolina

---

B

"My aim then was, to whip the rebels, to humble their pride, to follow them to their inmost recesses [their inner selves], and make them fear and dread us. . . . It was to me manifest [obvious] that the soldiers and people of the South entertained a . . . fear of our . . . men. . . . [T]his was a power, and I intended to utilize it. . . . and therefore on them should fall the scourge of war in its worst form."

—William Tecumseh Sherman, *Memoirs, Vol. 2*, 1875

Chapter 11 **401**

RESOURCE DIRECTORY

Teaching Resources
Skills for Life booklet, p. 13

Technology
Social Studies Skills Tutor CD-ROM
Interactive Practice in
• Geographic Literacy
• Critical Thinking and Reading
• Visual Analysis
• Communications

SUMMARIZING FROM MULTIPLE SOURCES

Focus Students recognize that an effective way to reconstruct a historical event is to gather sources that recreate the event from various perspectives.

Instruct Ask volunteers to read statements A and B to the class. Divide the class into two groups. Have one group analyze statement A and another group analyze statement B. What are some key words in each that reflect the writer's perspective? *(Statement A: "gloom, uncertainty, famine, demoralized, panic stricken"; Statement B: "whip, humble, fear, dread, the scourge of war.")* How would students characterize the writer's perspective in each statement?

Extend See the Skills for Life activity in the Resource Directory below.

ANSWERS
PRACTICE THE SKILL

1. **(a)** "All is gloom and uncertainty, and preparations are being made for the worst." **(b)** "My aim then was, to whip the rebels, to humble their pride, to follow them to their inmost recesses [their inner selves], and make them fear or dread us. . . ."

2. **(a)** Furniture and provisions being hidden; people fleeing; a few going to the front to fight. **(b)** The actions show fear, confusion, and desperation. **(c)** Fear. **(d)** He was prepared to be as destructive as possible.

3. **(a)** Possible answer: Residents are terrified of the approaching Union army, hiding their belongings, and running away. **(b)** Possible answer: General Sherman plans to show no mercy to the "rebels" and to use fear as a weapon.

4. **(a)** General Sherman's march through the Williamsburg district of South Carolina. **(b)** Complement: the events in excerpt A allow excerpt B to become a reality. **(c)** Sherman's strategy of instilling fear worked. As his army advanced, panicked residents scattered and hid.

SECTION OBJECTIVES

1. Identify the importance of Lee's victories at Fredericksburg and Chancellorsville.

2. Describe how the Battles of Gettysburg and Vicksburg turned the tide of the war.

3. Find out why 1863 was a pivotal year in the Civil War.

4. Interpret the message of the Gettysburg Address.

BELLRINGER

Warm-Up Activity Ask students if they can remember being without electricity for any length of time. If so, ask them to describe how they spent that time. Then ask them how that experience would compare to living in a cave for several months while an enemy army shelled their city.

Activating Prior Knowledge Photography was a new tool used widely for the first time during the Civil War. Can students state some impacts of this new technology? What would it have been like for the general public to be able to see real-life battle scenes, often for the first time? How did photography help generals make their battle plans?

READING STRATEGY

Ask students to write the headings *Gettysburg* and *Vicksburg* on a sheet of paper and take notes about each battle as they read. When they have finished reading the section, ask them to write briefly about why each battle was important in turning the tide of the war.

READING FOCUS

- What was the importance of Lee's victories at Fredericksburg and Chancellorsville?
- How did the Battles of Gettysburg and Vicksburg turn the tide of the war?
- Why was 1863 a pivotal year?
- What is the message of the Gettysburg Address?

MAIN IDEA

Despite Southern victories at Fredericksburg and Chancellorsville, the tide of war turned in the summer of 1863, when the North won at Gettysburg and Vicksburg.

KEY TERMS

Battle of Fredericksburg
Battle of Chancellorsville
Battle of Gettysburg
Pickett's Charge
siege
Gettysburg Address

TAKING NOTES

As you read, complete the following chart. For each battle, fill in the important officers, tell which side won, and write what you consider the most important reason for that side's victory.

Major Battles of 1863			
Battle	Union Officer	Confederate Officer	Victor/Why
Fredericksburg	Burnside	Lee	South/Burnside crossed right in front of Lee's army; kept charging into gunfire.

Setting the Scene   Civil War battles were noisy and smoky. Cannons boomed, rifles fired, men shouted, and the battlefield was wreathed in a haze of gunfire and dust. How did commanders communicate with their troops in this chaos? How did soldiers know when to advance, when to retreat, or even where their units were located? In the early years of the Civil War, it was the sound of the drumbeat that communicated orders. For that reason, drummer boys— usually only 12 to 16 years old—were so important that they were often purposely fired on by the enemy, and hundreds were killed in battle. One drummer boy who was wounded in action at Vicksburg received the Medal of Honor. Another boy described his experience this way:

> 66 A cannon ball came bouncing across the corn field, kicking up dirt and dust each time it struck the earth. Many of the men in our company took shelter behind a stone wall, but I stood where I was and never stopped drumming. An officer came by on horseback and chastised the men, saying 'this boy puts you all to shame. Get up and move forward.' . . . Even when the fighting was at its fiercest and I was frightened, I stood straight and did as I was ordered. . . . I felt I had to be a good example for the others. 99

—A Civil War drummer boy

Victories for General Lee

The Emancipation Proclamation may have renewed enthusiasm for the war among some Northerners, but the war still had to be won in the din and dust of the battlefield. When General George McClellan delayed in following up on his victory over Robert E. Lee at the Battle of Antietam, Lincoln again removed McClellan from command and replaced him with General Ambrose Burnside in November 1862. Sadly for Lincoln, Burnside was better known for his thick whiskers, the origin of the term "sideburns," than for his skills as a military strategist. He soon proved that his poor reputation was justified.

Drummer boys were a vital part of the armies of both the North and the South.

RESOURCE DIRECTORY

Teaching Resources
Guided Reading and Review booklet, p. 48
Learning Styles Lesson Plans booklet, p. 24

Other Print Resources
Nystrom *Atlas of Our Country* *A Divided Nation,* pp. 26–27

Technology
Section Reading Support Transparencies
Guided Reading Audiotapes (English/Spanish), Ch. 11
Student Edition on Audio CD, Ch. 11
Prentice Hall Presentation Pro CD-ROM, Ch. 11
Companion Web site, www.phschool.com

The Battle of Fredericksburg Knowing that McClellan had been fired for being too cautious, Burnside quickly advanced into Virginia. His plan was simple—to march his army of some 122,000 men straight toward Richmond. In response, Lee massed his army of nearly 79,000 at Fredericksburg, Virginia, on the south bank of the Rappahannock River. Lee spread his troops along a ridge called Marye's Heights, behind and overlooking the town.

Incredibly, instead of crossing the river out of range of the Confederate artillery, Burnside decided to cross directly in front of Lee's forces. "The enemy will be more surprised [by this move]," he explained. Lee was surprised—by the poor strategy of Burnside's plan.

Union troops poured across the river on specially constructed bridges and occupied the town. Lee let them cross. He knew that his artillery had the area well covered. Lee believed that if Burnside's army attacked, the Confederate forces could easily deal it a crushing defeat.

On December 13, 1862, the **Battle of Fredericksburg** began. Throughout the day Burnside ordered charge after charge into the Confederate gunfire. Some Union army units lost more than half their men. When the fighting ceased at nightfall, the Union had suffered nearly 13,000 casualties. Confederate losses were just over 5,000. A demoralized Burnside soon asked to be relieved of his command.

The Battle of Chancellorsville After accepting Burnside's resignation, a worried Lincoln turned to yet another general, Joseph "Fighting Joe" Hooker. General Hooker's plan was to move the Union army around Fredericksburg and attack the Confederates' strong defenses from behind. "May God have mercy on General Lee, for I will have none," Fighting Joe promised.

In late April 1863, Hooker put his plan into action. Leaving about a third of his 115,000-man army outside Fredericksburg, he marched the rest of his troops several miles upriver and slipped across the Rappahannock. Lee soon became aware of Hooker's actions. Confederate cavalry commanded by General J.E.B. "Jeb" Stuart discovered Hooker's force camped about ten miles west of Fredericksburg, near a road crossing called Chancellorsville.

Dividing his forces, Lee sent more than 40,000 Confederate soldiers westward to meet Hooker. About 10,000 troops remained in Fredericksburg. Lee ordered them to build many fires at night, so the enemy across the river would not realize that most of the army was gone.

The **Battle of Chancellorsville** began on May 1, 1863. When the Union troops started their march toward Fredericksburg, they suddenly saw Lee's army in front of them. After a brief clash, Fighting Joe ordered them to pull back into the thick woods and build defenses. The next day, when the Confederates did not attack, Hooker assumed they were in retreat. Instead, Lee had daringly divided his forces a second time. He sent General Stonewall Jackson and 26,000 men on a 12-mile march around the Union army for a late-afternoon attack on its right side. The movement of Jackson's troops was concealed by heavy woods that covered the area.

Again, Hooker was taken by surprise. The only warning was a wave of rabbits and deer that poured into the Union camp moments ahead of the Confederate charge. If darkness had not halted his attack, Jackson would have crushed the Union army. That night, Jackson and some other officers left the Confederate camp to scout the Union positions for a renewed attack. As they returned in

Focus on GEOGRAPHY

The Shenandoah Valley One of Stonewall Jackson's deadliest weapons was a detailed map of the Shenandoah Valley, a corridor about 150 miles long and 25 miles wide between the Blue Ridge Mountains and the Alleghenies. Southern armies were able to travel north through the Valley. Although forested, its slopes were not too steep or rocky for troops on foot or horseback, and the main road through the center of the Valley allowed even Robert E. Lee's large army to travel rapidly. What's more, the many gaps in the Blue Ridge Mountains and the pro-Confederate population permitted Southern forces to duck easily in and out of the Valley. However, Union forces that ventured there were harassed by armed raiders. Finally, the Shenandoah's splendid pastures and crops also supplied the Confederate Army with a much-needed source of food.

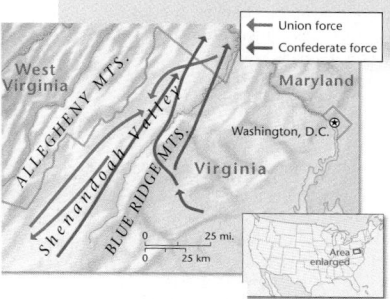

Focus Explain that the turning point of the war came in 1863 with the battles of Vicksburg and Gettysburg. Ask why those battles were so important.

Instruct The capture of Vicksburg was part of the Anaconda Plan, by which the Union intended to divide and squeeze the Confederacy. Tell students that Lincoln said, "Vicksburg is the key. The war cannot be brought to a close until the key is in our pocket." Tell students that General Lee hoped that invading Pennsylvania might encourage foreign countries to recognize and assist the Confederacy and might also dishearten Northern civilians.

Assess/Reteach Have students create a fact file on each of the following battles: Fredericksburg, Chancellorsville, Gettysburg, and Vicksburg. Fact files should include the significance of the battle and a brief summary of what took place.

ACTIVITY
Connecting with Geography

Have students use a map to explain why Vicksburg was so critical to Union strategy. Ask students to trace Lee's route to Gettysburg. (**Visual/Spatial**)

Connecting with History and Conflict

The Battle of Gettysburg was brutal and hard-fought. No soldier who was present and survived would ever have forgotten that day. Ask students to choose a portion of the Battle of Gettysburg to research in depth. Then, have them choose to view that portion of the battle from the perspective of a member of the Union or Confederate army. Have them write an "eyewitness account" of the experience in the form of a letter home to family. (**Verbal/Linguistic**)

BACKGROUND

Geography in History

Roads and railways were poor in the Upper South, so rivers played an important role in the Union planning. Armies covered the most ground in the west, where north-south rivers like the Mississippi and the Tennessee offered an easy route into the Confederacy. In Virginia, however, most rivers flow east from the Appalachians into the Atlantic Ocean. These formed a natural defense for the Confederate troops, since the Union army had to stop to build pontoon bridges across the wider rivers.

---

the darkness, some Confederate soldiers mistook them for enemies and opened fire. Three bullets hit Jackson, one shattering his left arm so badly that it had to be amputated.

On May 3, with Stuart now leading Jackson's command, the Confederate army completed its victory. On May 5, Hooker's badly beaten troops withdrew back across the river. Chancellorsville was Lee's most brilliant victory, but it was also his most costly one. On May 10, Jackson died of complications from his wounds. Stonewall Jackson was probably Lee's most brilliant general. His popularity with the troops was exceeded only by Lee's. His death deprived Lee of a man he called his "strong right arm."

The Battle of Gettysburg

The crushing defeats at Fredericksburg and Chancellorsville were the low point of the war for the Union. The mood in Washington was dark. Rumors swept the capital that Lincoln would resign as President. Some Northern leaders began to talk seriously of making peace with the South. "If there is a worse place than Hell," Lincoln said, "I am in it."

In June 1863, Lee marched his forces northward. The Union blockade and the South's lack of resources were beginning to weaken his army. With all the fighting in Virginia, supplies there had become scarce. Lee hoped to find some in Pennsylvania. More importantly, he hoped that a major Confederate victory on Northern soil would finally push the Union into giving up the war.

As Lincoln prepared to replace Hooker, the Union army moved north, too, staying between the Confederates and Washington. On July 1, some Confederate troops entered the town of Gettysburg, Pennsylvania. Many of them were barefoot, and a supply of shoes was rumored to be stored in the town. There the Confederates encountered a unit of Union cavalry and a fight developed. From this skirmish grew the greatest battle ever fought in North America, the three-day **Battle of Gettysburg.**

MAP SKILLS The Battle of Gettysburg was fought over three days. Notice the changes in troop positions over the course of the battle. **Human-Environment Interaction** How did each side attempt to use the terrain to gain an advantage?

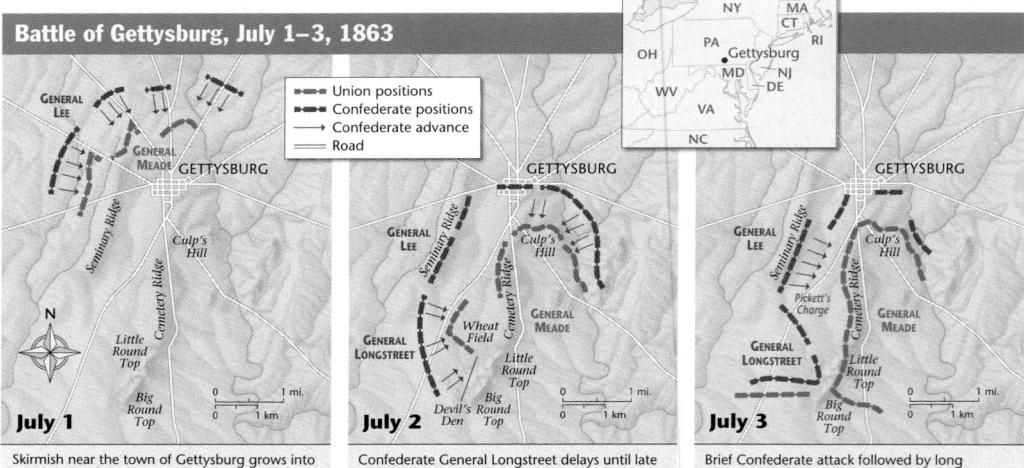

Battle of Gettysburg, July 1–3, 1863

Union positions
Confederate positions
Confederate advance
Road

July 1
Skirmish near the town of Gettysburg grows into a full-scale battle. Confederates push Union troops south; armies gather on both sides. Lee orders an attack on Union position at Cemetery Ridge for the next morning.

July 2
Confederate General Longstreet delays until late afternoon to attack southern end of Union line, giving Union a chance to bring reinforcements. Maine unit defends Union position at Little Round Top; Union lines remain intact.

July 3
Brief Confederate attack followed by long artillery exchange. Thinking his army has destroyed enemy's guns, Lee orders direct infantry attack known as Pickett's Charge. Union is ready with artillery barrage; Confederates prepare to retreat into Virginia.

404   Chapter 11 • *The Civil War*

CAPTION ANSWERS

Map Skills The Confederacy attempted to gain high ground to fire down on the enemy; the Union assumed a defensive position on a ridge, forcing the Confederates to attack.

RESOURCE DIRECTORY

Other Print Resources
Historical Outline Map Book *Major Battles of the Civil War,* p. 50

Technology
Color Transparencies *Historical Maps,* A22

July 1, 1863 Hearing the gunfire coming from Gettysburg, units of both armies rushed to the scene. At first, the Confederates outnumbered the Union forces. Fighting through the day, they pushed the Northerners back onto some hills south of town. Meanwhile, troops on both sides continued to gather. Among the Union soldiers to arrive that night was General George Meade, the new head of the Union army. He had been in command for less than a week.

Each army took up positions on a series of hills. Their lines stretched from the outskirts of town, in a southerly direction, for about four miles. The center of the Union line was a long hill called Cemetery Ridge. Another series of hills, called Seminary Ridge, was the center of the Confederate position. Between these two ridges was a large field several hundred yards wide.

That evening, Lee discussed his battle plan with General James Longstreet, his second-in-command since the death of Stonewall Jackson. Having won the day's fighting, and fresh from his victory at Chancellorsville, Lee's confidence was high. He proposed to continue the battle the next day. Longstreet advised against attacking such a strong Union position, but Lee had made up his mind. "The enemy is there," said Lee, pointing to Cemetery Ridge, "and I am going to attack him there." He ordered Longstreet to lead an attack on the southern end of the Union line the next morning.

July 2, 1863 Although a graduate of West Point, Longstreet preferred more peaceful endeavors. An accountant, he wanted to be in charge of the Confederate army's payroll. Lee made him a field commander instead. "Longstreet is a very good fighter when he . . . gets everything ready," Lee said of him, "but he is so slow."

On this second day of the battle, Longstreet was not ready to attack until about 4:00 P.M. His delays gave Meade the chance to bring up reinforcements. The battle raged into the early evening. Heavy fighting occurred in a peach orchard, a wheat field, and a mass of boulders known locally as the Devil's Den.

At one point, some Alabama soldiers noticed that one of the hills in the Union position, called Little Round Top, was almost undefended. They rushed to capture the hill. From it, Confederate artillery could have bombarded the Union lines. However, Union commanders also had noticed that Little Round Top was vulnerable. About 350 Maine soldiers under Colonel Joshua Chamberlain, a college professor before the war, were ordered to defend the position. They arrived on the hill just before the Alabamans' assault and then held off repeated attacks until they ran out of ammunition. Unwilling to give up, Chamberlain ordered a bayonet charge. The surprised Confederates retreated back down the hill. The Maine soldiers' heroic act likely saved the Union army from defeat. At the end of the day, the Union lines remained intact.

July 3, 1863 The third day of battle began with a brief Confederate attack on the north end of the Union line. Then the battlefield fell quiet. Finally, in the early afternoon, about 150 Confederate cannons began the heaviest artillery barrage of the war. Some Union generals thought the firing might be to protect a Confederate retreat. They were wrong. Lee had decided to risk everything on an infantry charge against the center of the Union position. As he had two days before, Longstreet opposed such a direct attack. Again Lee overruled him.

VIEWING HISTORY This lithograph shows part of the Battle of Gettysburg. **Drawing Inferences** *What can you tell about the military tactics of the battle from the picture?*

READING CHECK
Describe the battle for Little Round Top.

to Today

Photography and War

The Civil War was the first American conflict to be photographed. Mathew Brady and his team of photographers showed its grim realities to great effect.

The Vietnam War was the first to "invade" American homes via television, and the nightly news footage from Vietnam helped turn American public opinion against the war.

During the 1991 Gulf War, CNN's Peter Arnett actually broadcast *live* from Baghdad, Iraq, as American bombs fell on the city.

? Which of these images has the most impact on you, the viewer? Why? What do you learn about war from these images?

After a two-hour artillery duel, the Union guns stopped returning fire. Thinking that the Confederate artillery had destroyed the enemy's guns, Longstreet reluctantly ordered the direct attack. Actually, the Union artillery commander had ceased fire only to save ammunition. Now, however, Northern soldiers on Cemetery Ridge saw nearly 15,000 Confederates, formed in a line a mile long and three rows deep, coming toward them.

Although this event is known in history as **Pickett's Charge,** General George Pickett was only one of three Southern commanders on the field that day. Each led an infantry division of about 5,000 men. As the Confederates marched across about a mile of open ground between the two ridges, the Union artillery resumed firing. Hundreds of canister shells rained down on the approaching soldiers, tearing huge gaps in their ranks. When the Southern troops closed to within about 200 yards of the Union lines, Northern soldiers poured rifle fire into those who remained standing.

Only a few hundred Confederates reached the Union lines—at a bend in a stone wall that became known as the Angle. A survivor described the fighting:

> 66 Men fire into each other's faces, not five feet apart. There are bayonet-thrusts, sabre-strokes, pistol-shots; . . . men going down on their hands and knees, spinning round like tops, throwing out their arms, falling; legless, armless, headless. There are ghastly heaps of dead men. 99
>
> —Soldier at Gettysburg

In about 30 minutes it was over. Scarcely half the Confederate force returned to Seminary Ridge. Lee ordered Pickett to reform his division in case Meade counterattacked. "General Lee, I have no division," Pickett replied.

Pickett's Charge ended the bloodiest battle of the Civil War. Losses on both sides were staggering. The Union army of about 85,000 suffered over 23,000 casualties. Of some 75,000 Southerners, about 28,000 were casualties. For the second time, Lee had lost more than a third of his army. The next day, July 4, the Confederates began their retreat back to Virginia.

Vicksburg

While armies clashed in the East, a Union force in the West struggled to capture the city of Vicksburg, Mississippi. Only this stronghold and a fortress at Port Hudson, Louisiana, stood in the way of the Union's complete control of the Mississippi River. Vicksburg seemed safe from attack. It sat on a bluff, high above a sharp bend in the river. From this bluff, Confederate artillery could lob shells at any Union ships that approached the city. In addition, much of Vicksburg was surrounded by swamps. The only approach to the city over dry land was from the east, and Confederate forces held that territory.

Grant Attacks The Union general who faced these difficult challenges was Ulysses S. Grant. Between December 1862 and April 1863, he made several attempts either to capture or to bypass the city. First, he sent General William Tecumseh Sherman and several thousand troops in an unsuccessful attack on Vicksburg from the north. Next he had his army dig a canal across the bend in the river, so Union boats could bypass the city's guns. However, the canal turned out to be too shallow. Then he tried to attack from the north by sending gunboats down another river. This too failed.

An attempt to approach the city through a swampy backwater called Steele's Bayou nearly ended in disaster. The Confederates cut down trees to slow the Union boats and fired on them from shore. Finally, Sherman's troops had to come and rescue the fleet.

By mid-April 1863, the ground had dried out enough for Grant to try a daring plan. He marched his army down the Louisiana side of the river and crossed into Mississippi south of Vicksburg. Then he moved east and attacked Jackson, the state capital. This maneuver

MAP SKILLS Lincoln called capturing Vicksburg "the key" to winning the war. Jefferson Davis considered the city to be "the nailhead that holds the South's two halves together." **Movement** *(a) Trace Grant's route on the map and explain the strategy behind it. (b) According to the painting, what made the attempt to attack the city by gunboat so difficult?*

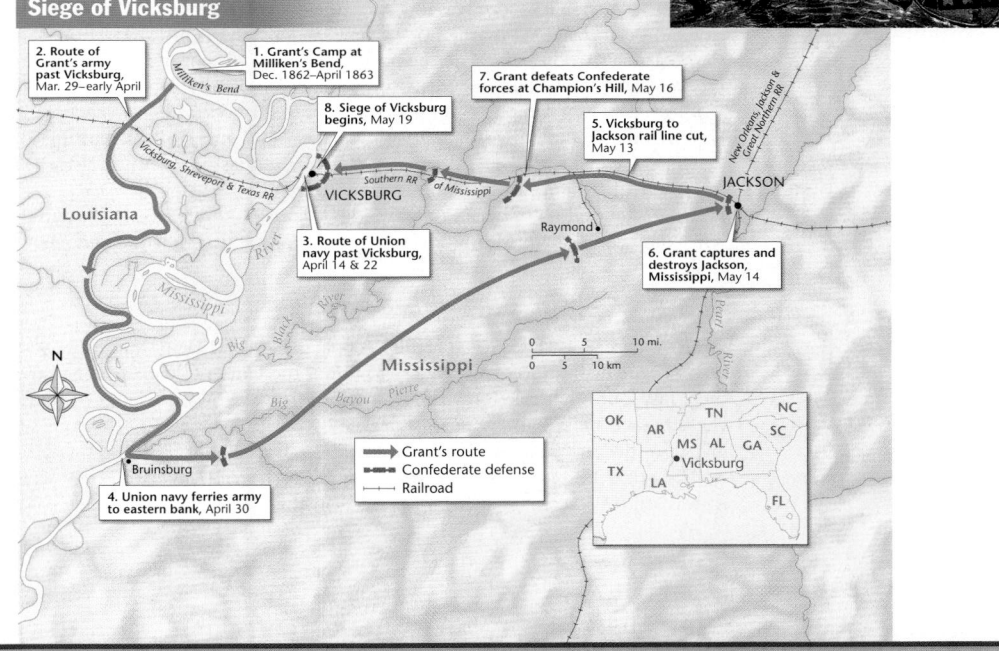

Siege of Vicksburg

2. Route of Grant's army past Vicksburg, Mar. 29–early April

1. Grant's Camp at Milliken's Bend, Dec. 1862–April 1863

7. Grant defeats Confederate forces at Champion's Hill, May 16

8. Siege of Vicksburg begins, May 19

5. Vicksburg to Jackson rail line cut, May 13

Milliken's Bend

New Orleans, Jackson & Great Northern RR

Vicksburg, Shreveport & Texas RR

Southern RR of Mississippi

VICKSBURG

JACKSON

Louisiana

3. Route of Union navy past Vicksburg, April 14 & 22

Raymond

6. Grant captures and destroys Jackson, Mississippi, May 14

Mississippi River

Big Black River

Mississippi

0 5 10 mi.
0 5 10 km

N

Bruinsburg

4. Union navy ferries army to eastern bank, April 30

→ Grant's route
Confederate defense
Railroad

OK   AR   TN   NC
         MS AL GA   SC
TX   LA   FL
         Vicksburg

407

Focus on DAILY LIFE

Life Underground A young mother described living in a cave during the siege of Vicksburg: "Our new habitation was an excavation made in the earth, a cave in the shape of a T. In one of the wings my bed fitted; the other I used as a kind of a dressing room. In this the earth had been cut down a foot or two below the floor of the main cave. I could stand erect here and when tired of sitting in other portions of my residence, I bowed myself into it and stood impassively resting at full height. Our quarters were close indeed, yet I was more comfortable than I expected I could have been under the earth.

"We were safe at least from fragments of shell—and they were flying in all directions—though no one seemed to think our cave any protection should a mortar shell happen to fall directly on top of the ground above us."

—Mary Ann Loughborough

Sounds of an Era

Listen to the Gettysburg Address and other sounds from the Civil War era.

---

drew out the Confederate forces from Vicksburg, commanded by General John Pemberton, to help defend the capital. Before they could arrive, Grant captured the city of Jackson. Then he turned his troops west to fight Pemberton.

On May 16, the two armies clashed at Champion's Hill, halfway between Jackson and Vicksburg. Although Grant won the battle, he could not trap Pemberton's army. The Confederates were able to retreat back to Vicksburg's fortifications. In late May, after two more unsuccessful attacks, Grant began a **siege,** a tactic in which an enemy is surrounded and starved in order to make it surrender.

The Siege of Vicksburg When Union cannons opened fire on Vicksburg from land and water, a bombardment began that would average 2,800 shells a day. For more than a month, the citizens of Vicksburg endured a nearly constant pounding from some 300 guns. The constant schedule of shelling took over everyday life.

To avoid being killed by the shells falling on their homes, residents dug caves in hillsides, some complete with furniture and attended by slaves. "It was living like plant roots," one cave dweller said. As the siege dragged on, residents and soldiers alike were reduced to eating horses, mules, and dogs. Rats appeared for sale in the city's butcher shops.

By late June, Confederate soldiers' daily rations were down to one biscuit and one piece of bacon per day. On July 4, some 30,000 Confederate troops marched out of Vicksburg and laid down their arms. Pemberton thought he could negotiate the best terms for the surrender on the day that celebrated the Union's independence.

The Importance of 1863

For the North, 1863 had begun disastrously. However, the Fourth of July, 1863, was for some the most joyous Independence Day since the first one 87 years earlier. For the first time, thousands of former slaves could truly celebrate American independence. The holiday marked the turning point of the Civil War.

In the West, Vicksburg was in Union hands. For a time, the people of that city had been sustained by the hope that President Jefferson Davis would send some of Lee's troops to rescue them. But Lee had no reinforcements to spare. His weakened army had begun its retreat into Virginia; it would never again seriously threaten Union soil. Four days later, Port Hudson surrendered to Union forces. The Mississippi River was now in Union hands, cutting the Confederacy in two. "The Father of Waters again goes unvexed [undisturbed] to the sea," announced Lincoln in Washington, D.C.

In Richmond there began to be serious talk of making peace. Although the war would continue for nearly two years more, for the first time the end seemed in sight.

The Gettysburg Address

On November 19, 1863, some 15,000 people gathered at Gettysburg. The occasion was the dedication of a cemetery to honor the Union soldiers who had died there just four months before. The featured guest was Edward Everett of Massachusetts, the most famous public speaker of the time. President Lincoln was invited to deliver "a few appropriate remarks" to help fill out the program.

Everett delivered a grand crowd-pleasing speech that lasted two hours. Then it was the President's turn to speak. In his raspy, high-pitched voice,

Lincoln delivered his remarks, which became known as the **Gettysburg Address.** In a short, two-minute speech he eloquently reminded listeners of the North's reason for fighting the Civil War: to preserve a young country unmatched by any other country in history in its commitment to the principles of freedom, equality, and self-government:

 KEY DOCUMENTS 66 *Fourscore and seven years ago our fathers brought forth on this continent, a new nation, conceived in Liberty, and dedicated to the proposition that all men are created equal.*

Now we are engaged in a great civil war, testing whether that nation, or any nation so conceived and so dedicated, can long endure. . . .

It is for us the living, rather, to be dedicated here to the unfinished work which they who fought here have thus far so nobly advanced. It is rather for us to be here dedicated to the great task remaining before us—that from these honored dead we take increased devotion to that cause for which they gave the last full measure of devotion—that we here highly resolve that these dead shall not have died in vain—that this nation, under God, shall have a new birth of freedom—and that government of the people, by the people, for the people, shall not perish from the earth. 99

—Lincoln's Gettysburg Address,
November 19, 1863

VIEWING HISTORY "In times like the present," Lincoln said, "men should utter nothing for which they would not willingly be responsible through time. . . ." **Identifying Central Issues** *How do Lincoln's words at Gettysburg represent the noblest goals of the Union cause?*

In 1863, most Americans did not pay much attention to Lincoln's speech. Some thought it was too short and too simple. Lincoln's fellow speaker, Edward Everett, was an exception. He wrote to Lincoln the next day, "I wish I could flatter myself that I had come as near to the central idea of the occasion in two hours as you did in two minutes." Future generations have agreed with Everett. The Gettysburg Address has become one of the best-loved and most-quoted speeches in English. It expresses simply and eloquently both grief at the terrible cost of the war and the reasons for renewed efforts to preserve the Union and the noble principles for which it stands.

Section 3 Assessment

READING COMPREHENSION

1. Briefly describe the **Battle of Fredericksburg** and the **Battle of Chancellorsville.**

2. Why was the **Battle of Gettysburg** a turning point in the war?

3. What were three effects of Grant's **siege** of Vicksburg?

4. Summarize the main points of the **Gettysburg Address.**

CRITICAL THINKING AND WRITING

5. **Determining Relevance** How did the superior manpower of the North and its greater ability to produce both crops and manufactured goods begin to affect the war in 1863?

6. **Writing to Persuade** Which do you think was a more significant turning point: Vicksburg or Gettysburg? Write the opening paragraph of a persuasive essay supporting your choice.

 Take It to the NET

Activity: Writing an Ad Read more about the equipment and clothing that Civil War soldiers typically carried, and create an advertisement aimed at selling these items to the soldiers. Use the links provided in the *America: Pathways to the Present* area of the following Web site for help in completing this activity. **www.phschool.com**

Reading Comprehension

1. Battle of Fredericksburg: In an attempt to surprise the Confederacy, Burnside approached Lee's troops directly. Union losses extremely heavy. Confederate victory, Burnside demoralized. Battle of Chancellorsville: General Hooker led the Union, Lee became aware of Hooker's plan and strategically divided and subdivided troops, resulting in a Confederate victory.

2. It defined how each side would be able to operate thereafter. The North had now seized the initiative in the east. After Gettysburg, Lee was restricted to operating defensively within the South.

3. The siege caused Confederate residents to move into underground dwellings, reduced supplies and soldiers' rations, and ultimately forced a surrender.

4. It summarized the North's reasons for fighting the Civil War: to preserve the country's commitment to the principles of freedom, equality, and self-government.

Critical Thinking and Writing

5. Union blockade and South's lack of resources began to weaken the Confederate army. Union had a large pool of new recruits, and could sustain farming, manufacturing, and fighting. Confederate troops were depleted.

6. Essays should use facts from the section to persuade readers of their point.

 **Take It to the NET**

Sample answer: Soldiers could buy a better mess kit, containing more than the standard knife, fork, cup, and plate.

CAPTION ANSWERS

Viewing History They stress the importance of the nation. Lincoln's primary goal in the war was to preserve the nation by any means necessary.

Section 4 · Devastation and New Freedom

Section 4 · Devastation and New Freedom

SECTION OBJECTIVES

1. Determine General Grant's strategy for defeating the South and how he and General Sherman implemented it.
2. Outline the issues and results of the election of 1864.
3. Explain how the South was finally defeated on the battlefield.
4. State how and why John Wilkes Booth assassinated President Lincoln.

BELLRINGER

Warm-Up Activity Ask students to think about what it means to surrender. Have them describe the feeling of giving up a fight. How does it feel to win a long-fought struggle?

Activating Prior Knowledge The submarine was used for the first time in the Civil War, when the Confederate-operated submarine *Hunley* sneaked up on and sank the Union ship *Housatonic*. Ask students to imagine and describe the impact of such an unexpected surprise attack from a completely new type of weapon.

READING STRATEGY

Lincoln ended his Second Inaugural Address with these words: "With malice towards none; with charity for all; with firmness in the right, as God gives us to see the right, let us strive on to finish with work we are in; to bind up the nation's wounds; to care for him who shall have borne the battle, and for his widow, and his orphan—to do all which may achieve and cherish a just and lasting peace, among ourselves, and with all nations." As students read about the end of the Civil War, ask them to consider ways in which Lincoln's words were an attempt to help the nation begin the process of reconciliation.

READING FOCUS

- What was General Grant's strategy for defeating the South, and how did he and General Sherman implement it?
- What were the issues and results of the election of 1864?
- How was the South finally defeated on the battlefield?
- How and why did John Wilkes Booth assassinate President Lincoln?

MAIN IDEA

After years of fighting, countless casualties, and considerable devastation, the South finally surrendered in April 1865.

KEY TERMS

Battle of the Wilderness
Battle of Spotsylvania
Battle of Cold Harbor
Thirteenth Amendment
guerrilla

TAKING NOTES

Copy this flowchart. As you read, fill in the boxes with some of the important events that led to the surrender of the South.

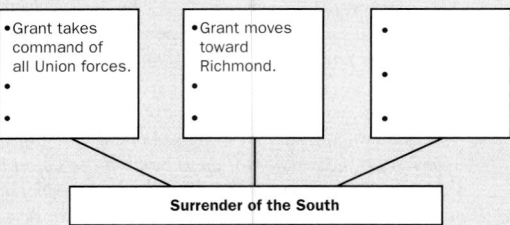

- Grant takes command of all Union forces.
- •
- •

- Grant moves toward Richmond.
- •
- •

- •
- •
- •

Surrender of the South

Setting the Scene In April 1865 the city of Richmond, which had welcomed the war with such enthusiasm four years earlier, was a very different place. The war was nearly over, and both the Confederate government and its army abandoned the city. While many Southern cities, towns, and farms were set ablaze by conquering Union armies, the fires in the Confederate capital were set by retreating Southern troops in an effort to keep stored provisions from falling into the hands of the enemy. One Union soldier described the scene as he approached the city:

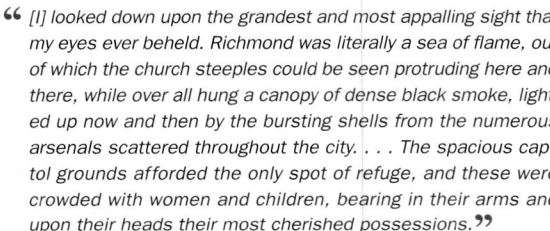

Retreating Confederate troops and citizens flee their burning capital.

> 66 [I] looked down upon the grandest and most appalling sight that my eyes ever beheld. Richmond was literally a sea of flame, out of which the church steeples could be seen protruding here and there, while over all hung a canopy of dense black smoke, lighted up now and then by the bursting shells from the numerous arsenals scattered throughout the city. . . . The spacious capitol grounds afforded the only spot of refuge, and these were crowded with women and children, bearing in their arms and upon their heads their most cherished possessions. 99
>
> —R. B. Prescott

While there was certainly much destruction and misery, there were also pockets of rejoicing. African Americans joyously welcomed Union troops. Prescott went on to say that the freed slaves "hailed our appearance with the most extravagant expressions of joy. . . . 'God bless you' and 'Thank God, the Yankees have come' resounded on every side."

Grant Takes Command

At the beginning of 1864, the Confederates still hoped to keep the Union forces out of Richmond. Their war strategy was a simple one—to hold on. They knew that the North would have a presidential election in November. If the war dragged on and casualties mounted, some Southerners felt that Northern voters

RESOURCE DIRECTORY

Teaching Resources
Guided Reading and Review booklet, p. 49
Learning Styles Lesson Plans booklet, p. 25

Technology
Section Reading Support Transparencies
Guided Reading Audiotapes (English/Spanish), Ch. 11
Student Edition on Audio CD, Ch. 11
Color Transparencies *Historical Maps,* A20, A21, A24
Exploring Primary Sources in U.S. History CD-ROM *In the Wilderness, Thomas J. Halsey*
Prentice Hall Presentation Pro CD-ROM, Ch. 11
Companion Web site, www.phschool.com

might replace Lincoln with a President willing to grant the South its independence. "If we can only subsist," wrote a Confederate official, "we may have peace."

At the same time, President Lincoln understood that his chances for reelection in 1864 depended on the Union's success on the battlefield. In March he summoned Ulysses S. Grant to Washington and gave him command of all Union forces. Grant's plan was to confront and crush the Confederate army and end the war before the November election.

Placing General William Tecumseh Sherman in charge in the West, Grant remained in the East to battle General Lee. He realized that Lee was running short of men and supplies. Grant now proposed to use the North's superiority in population and industry to wear down the Confederates. He ordered Sherman to do the same in the West.

Battle of the Wilderness   In early May 1864, Grant moved south across the Rapidan River in Virginia with a force of some 115,000 men. Lee had about 64,000 troops. The Union army headed directly toward Richmond. Grant knew that to stop the Union advance, Lee would have to fight. In May and June the Union and Confederate armies clashed in three major battles. This was exactly what Grant wanted.

The fighting began on May 5 with the two-day **Battle of the Wilderness.** This battle occurred on virtually the same ground as the Battle of Chancellorsville the year before. The two armies met in a dense forest. The fighting was so heavy that the woods caught fire, causing many of the wounded to be burned to death. Unable to see in the smoke-filled forest, units got lost and fired on friendly soldiers, mistaking them for the enemy. One of these casualties was General Longstreet, Lee's second-in-command. He was accidentally shot and wounded by his own soldiers only three miles from where Stonewall Jackson had been shot the year before.

Grant took massive losses at the Battle of the Wilderness. However, instead of retreating as previous Union commanders had done after suffering heavy casualties, he moved his army around the Confederates and again headed south. Despite the high number of casualties, Union soldiers were proud that under Grant's leadership they would not retreat so easily.

Spotsylvania and Cold Harbor   Two days later, on May 8, the Confederates caught up to the Union army near the little town of Spotsylvania Court House. The series of clashes that followed over nearly two weeks is called the **Battle of Spotsylvania.** The heaviest fighting took place on May 12. In some parts of the battlefield, the Union dead were piled four deep. When Northerners began to protest the huge loss of life, a determined Grant notified Lincoln, "I propose to fight it out on this line [course of action] if it takes all summer." Then he moved the Union army farther south.

In early June the armies clashed yet again at the **Battle of Cold Harbor,** just eight miles from Richmond. In a dawn attack on June 3, Grant launched two direct charges on the Confederates, who were behind strong fortifications. Some 7,000 Union soldiers fell—many in the first hour.

The Siege of Petersburg   Unable to reach Richmond or defeat Lee's army, Grant moved his army around the capital and attacked Petersburg, a railroad center south of the city. He knew that if he could cut off shipments of food to Richmond, the city would have to surrender. However, the attack failed. In less than two months, Grant's army had suffered some 65,000 casualties. This toll

---

Focus on TECHNOLOGY

Civil War Submarine   In 1864, the South had a secret weapon. Nothing like it had ever been seen before. It was the world's first successful military submarine, and the first such vessel to sink a ship in battle—something that would not happen again until World War I. Made from an old steam engine boiler, and cranked by hand, the Confederate *Hunley* was just 40 feet long. Once the craft submerged, the only light came from a candle. The flame would go out after about 25 minutes from lack of oxygen—a sign that the crew had better surface soon.

In February 1864, near Charleston, South Carolina, the *Hunley* rammed its torpedo into the *Housatonic,* and sank the Union ship. Then, mysteriously, the *Hunley* also sank. Now, in one of the largest recovery projects of its kind, the sub is being recovered and restored, and its crew of nine given heroes' burials.

READING CHECK

What happened at Spotsylvania and Cold Harbor?

Chapter 11 • Section 4   **411**

Focus   Explain that Lee finally surrendered at Appomattox Court House, Virginia, in April 1865. Ask students to consider the costs of the Civil War. What were its major results?

Instruct   Have students trace Sherman's route through Georgia. Ask how Sherman's march and Grant's dogged pursuit of Lee show the commitment of both generals to the idea of total war. Discuss how Lincoln's reelection led to the passage of the Thirteenth Amendment.

Assess/Reteach   Ask students to identify the significance of the following in relation to the end of the Civil War and the redefinition of the nation: Gettysburg Address, Thirteenth Amendment, Appomattox Court.

ACTIVITY
Connecting with Culture

Ask students to prepare an oral reading of one of the following: the Gettysburg Address, selections from Stephen Vincent Benet's "John Brown's Body," or Walt Whitman's poem mourning the death of Lincoln, "O Captain! My Captain!" **(Verbal/Linguistic)**

READING CHECK

Union casualties were extremely heavy at Spotsylvania and Cold Harbor in May and June of 1864. At Cold Harbor, Grant ordered Union troops to make frontal assaults against extremely strong Confederate defenses.

CUSTOMIZE FOR ...
Gifted and Talented

Railroads played a central role in widening the economic gap between the North and the South. Later, they also played a leading part in the war that erupted between the two regions. Ask students to research the development of railroads in the United States and to draw a map showing the routes of the major railroads in both the North and the South in the 1850s.

Connecting with History and Conflict

Remind students that war is really about individual people, and that relationships between individuals often affect the lives of thousands. Sherman and Grant had a relationship built on loyalty. Despite what other Union commanders thought, Grant stood by Sherman. Divide students into groups. Have them research the lives of both men. Then have each group prepare and present a short skit demonstrating the personalities and philosophies of both men as Sherman convinces Grant to permit a daring move to "make Georgia howl." **(Verbal/Linguistic)**

BACKGROUND

Cryptology in the Civil War

Nearly as old as writing itself, secret codes have been used in times of war for thousands of years. During the Civil War, both the Union and Confederate armies relied on codes for their military communication. The code used by the Confederacy was easily broken by Union cryptanalysts. But the Union's code defied the Confederate's code-breakers. The coded Union messages were sometimes published in Confederate newspapers, with pleas to readers for deciphering help.

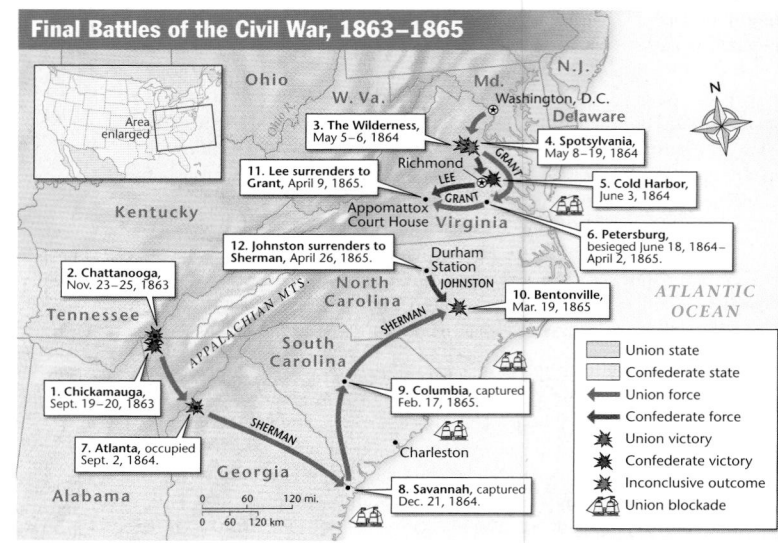

MAP SKILLS Grant's stubbornness and Sherman's campaign of total war brought the Civil War to a bloody close. **Movement** Compare the size and movement of the Union and Confederate forces in the final months of the war. Why do you think Sherman met with little resistance?

Final Battles of the Civil War, 1863–1865

had a chilling effect on the surviving Union troops. At Cold Harbor, many soldiers pinned their names and addresses on their uniforms so their bodies could be identified.

Grant then turned to the tactic he had successfully used at Vicksburg. On June 18, 1864, he began the siege of Petersburg. Lee responded by building defenses. While he had lost many fewer men than Grant, it was becoming difficult for Lee to replace all of his casualties. He was willing to stay put and wait for the Northern election in November.

In the Shenandoah Grant recognized the importance of the Shenandoah Valley, both strategically and as a source of Southern supplies. In the summer of 1864, he decided to shut down that supply source once and for all. He told General Phil Sheridan, "Do all the damage to railroads and crops you can. . . . If the war is to last another year, we want the Shenandoah Valley to remain a barren waste." Sheridan carried out these orders to the letter. In the fall of 1864 he wrote Grant: "The people here are getting sick of the war." Grant answered: "Keep on, and your good work will cause the fall of Richmond."

In July 1864, one house that became a victim of Grant's policy belonged to Henrietta E. Lee. Her husband—the grandson of Revolutionary patriot and "rebel" Richard Henry Lee and a relative of Confederate General Robert E. Lee—was not at home. Henrietta Lee could not defend her home with weapons; all she had were words. She wrote the Union General a letter that began this way:

> **❝**General Hunter:
>   Yesterday your underling, Captain Martindale, of the First New York Cavalry, executed your infamous order and burned my house. . . . the dwelling and every outbuilding, seven in number, with their contents, being burned. I, therefore, a helpless woman whom you have cruelly wronged, address you, a Major-General of the United States Army, and demand why this was done? What was my offence? My

CAPTION ANSWERS

Map Skills Union manpower has become a vital factor. With his hands full facing Grant in Virginia, Lee could not reinforce Johnston and Hood against Sherman in Georgia.

RESOURCE DIRECTORY

Other Print Resources
Historical Outline Map Book *Union Advances,* p. 52

Technology
Color Transparencies *Fine Art,* E9
(RESOURCE•**PRO**ᴮ) **Primary Source Activity**
A Teenager's Account of War, found on Resource Pro, uses excerpts from Emma LeDonte's diary to show how young Southerners viewed and experienced the war.

husband was absent—an exile. He has never been a politician or in any way engaged in the struggle now going on . . . The house was built by my father, a Revolutionary soldier, who served the whole seven years for your independence. There I was born; there the sacred dead repose. . . ."

—Henrietta Lee, July 20, 1864

Little did Henrietta Lee know that this was just the beginning of the devastation of the South.

Sherman in Georgia

As Grant's army advanced against Lee, Sherman began to move south from Chattanooga, Tennessee, to threaten the city of Atlanta. Sherman's strategy was identical to Grant's in Virginia. He would force the main Confederate army in the West to attempt to stop his advance. If the Southern general took the bait, Sherman would destroy the enemy with his huge 98,000-man force. If the Confederates refused to fight, he would seize Atlanta, an important rail and industrial center.

The Capture of Atlanta Sherman's opponent in Georgia was General Joseph Johnston, the Confederate commander who had been wounded at the Battle of Seven Pines in Virginia in 1862. Johnston's tactics were similar to Lee's. He would engage the Union force to block its progress. At the same time, he would not allow Sherman to deal him a crushing defeat. In this way, he hoped to delay Sherman from reaching Atlanta before the presidential elections could take place in the North.

Despite Johnston's best efforts, by mid-July 1864 the Union army was just a few miles from Atlanta. Wanting more aggressive action, Confederate president Jefferson Davis replaced Johnston with General James Hood.

The new commander gave Davis—and Sherman—exactly what they wanted. In late July, Hood engaged the Union force in a series of battles. With each clash the Southern army lost thousands of soldiers. Finally, with the Confederate forces reduced from some 62,000 to less than 45,000, General Hood retreated to Atlanta's strong defenses. Like Grant at Petersburg, Sherman laid siege to the city. Throughout the month of August, Sherman's forces bombarded Atlanta. In early September the Confederate army pulled out and left the city to the Union general's mercy.

Sherman Marches to the Sea "War is cruelty," Sherman once wrote. "There is no use trying to reform it. The crueler it is, the sooner it will be over." It was from this viewpoint that the tough Ohio soldier conducted his military campaigns. Although a number of Union commanders considered Sherman to be mentally unstable, Grant stood by him. As a result, Sherman was fiercely loyal to his commander.

Now, Sherman convinced Grant to permit a daring move. Vowing to "make Georgia howl," in November 1864, Sherman led some 62,000 Union troops on a march to the sea to capture Savannah, Georgia. Before abandoning Atlanta, however, he ordered the city evacuated and then burned. After leaving Atlanta in ruins, Sherman's soldiers cut a

VIEWING HISTORY *General Sherman's March to the Sea* shows the destruction caused by the Union advance. **Drawing Inferences** *What kinds of destruction are the Union troops causing here? What are the strategic purposes of this destruction?*

Chapter 11 • Section 4   **413**

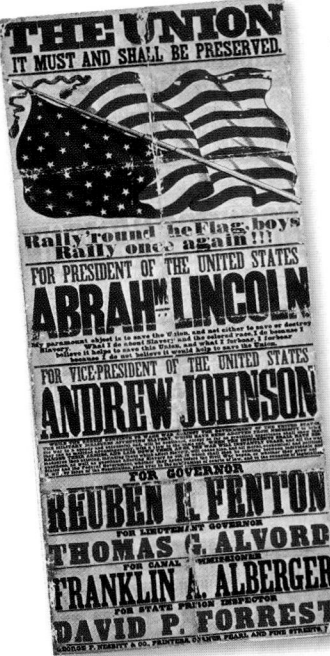

VIEWING HISTORY This campaign poster shows Lincoln running on the Union Party ticket. **Drawing Conclusions** *Do you think calling themselves the Union Party was a good strategy for the Republicans in 1864? Explain your answer.*

nearly 300-mile-long path of destruction across Georgia. The Union troops destroyed bridges, factories, and railroad lines. They seized and slaughtered livestock. Grain that had recently been harvested for the Confederate troops went to Union soldiers instead.

As the Northerners approached Savannah, the small Confederate force there fled. On December 21, the Union army entered the city without a fight. "I beg to present you, as a Christmas gift, the city of Savannah," read General Sherman's message to Lincoln. For the President, it was the second piece of good news since the November election.

The Election of 1864

"I am going to be beaten," Lincoln said of his reelection chances in 1864, "and unless some great change takes place, badly beaten." Lincoln not only had to face a Democratic candidate, he also faced a brief challenge for the nomination of his own party. This challenge came from the Radical Republicans, those who were committed to emancipation and to "punishing" the South for the war. They were so angered when Lincoln pocket-vetoed the Wade-Davis Bill (which required stringent requirements for Southern states re-entering the Union), that they supported John C. Frémont for the nomination. Frémont eventually withdrew.

In an attempt to broaden Lincoln's appeal, the Republicans temporarily changed their name to the Union Party. They also dropped Vice President Hannibal Hamlin from the ticket and nominated Andrew Johnson of Tennessee to run with the President. Johnson was a Democrat and a pro-Union Southerner.

The Democrats nominated General George McClellan as their candidate. McClellan was only too happy to oppose Lincoln, who had twice fired him. The general was still loved by his soldiers, and Lincoln feared that McClellan would find wide support among the troops. McClellan promised that if elected, he would negotiate an end to the war.

Sherman's capture of Atlanta, however, changed the political climate in the North. Sensing that victory was near, Northerners became less willing to support a negotiated settlement. In November, with the help of ballots cast by Union soldiers, Lincoln won an easy victory, garnering 212 out of a possible 233 electoral votes.

A New Birth of Freedom

By reelecting Lincoln, voters showed not only their approval of his war policy, but also their increasing acceptance of his stand against slavery. Three months later, in February 1865, Congress joined Lincoln in that stand and passed the **Thirteenth Amendment** to the Constitution. It was ratified by the states and became law on December 18, 1865. In a few words, the amendment ended slavery in the United States forever:

> ❝ *Neither slavery nor involuntary servitude, except as a punishment for crime whereof the party shall have been duly convicted, shall exist within the United States, or any place subject to their jurisdiction.* ❞
> —Thirteenth Amendment to the Constitution

In his Second Inaugural Address, in March 1865, Lincoln noted how slavery had divided the nation, but he also laid the groundwork for the effort to "bind up the nation's wounds."

> " . . . It may seem strange that any men should dare ask a just God's assistance in wringing their bread from the sweat of other men's faces; but let us judge not that we be not judged."
>
> —Lincoln's Second Inaugural, March 1865

As President Lincoln prepared to begin his second term, it was clear to most Northerners that the war was nearly over. Lincoln said, "Fondly do we hope, fervently do we pray, that this mighty scourge of war may speedily pass away."

The End of the War

As Grant strangled Richmond and Sherman prepared to move north from Savannah to join him, gloom deepened in the South. President Davis claimed that he had never really counted on McClellan's election, or on a negotiated peace. "The deep waters are closing over us," Mary Chesnut observed in her diary.

Sherman Moves North   In February 1865, General Sherman's troops left Savannah and headed for South Carolina. Since it had been the first state to secede from the Union, many Northerners regarded South Carolina as the heart of the rebellion. "Here is where the treason began and, by God, here is where it shall end," wrote one Union soldier as the army marched northward.

Unlike Virginia and many other Confederate states, the Carolinas had seen relatively little fighting. Sherman had two goals as he moved toward Grant's position at Petersburg: to destroy the South's remaining resources and to crush Southerners' remaining will to fight. In South Carolina he did both. The Confederate army could do little but retreat in front of Sherman's advancing force. South Carolina was treated even more harshly than Georgia. In Georgia, for example, Union troops had burned very few of the houses that were in their path. In South Carolina, few houses were spared.

On February 17, the Union forces entered the state capital, Columbia. That night a fire burned nearly half of the city to the ground. Although no one could prove who started the fire, South Carolinians blamed Sherman's troops for the destruction. When the Union army moved into North Carolina, all demolition of civilian property ceased.

Surrender at Appomattox   By April 1865, daily desertions had shrunk the Confederate army defending Richmond to fewer than 35,000 starving men. Realizing that he could no longer protect the city, on April 2 Lee tried to slip around Grant's army. He planned to unite his troops with those of General Johnston, who was retreating before Sherman's force in North Carolina. Lee hoped that together they would be able to continue the war.

Units of General Grant's army tracked the Confederates as they moved west. Each time Lee tried to turn his soldiers south, Grant's troops cut them off. On April 9, Lee's army arrived at the small Virginia town of Appomattox

Fast Forward to Today

Arlington National Cemetery

Arlington National Cemetery is located in Arlington, Virginia, across the Potomac River from Washington, D.C. This parcel of land once belonged to George Custis, who was the adopted

son of George Washington. After Custis's daughter Mary inherited the property, she married a young army officer named Robert E. Lee, and they lived in the mansion Custis had built. During the Civil War, the Union army seized the property and used the mansion as a headquarters. The land became a military cemetery in 1864. In an 1882 Supreme Court case, Lee's

descendants finally succeeded in having the U.S. government declared a trespasser on their property. The next year, Congress appropriated $150,000 to buy the property from the Lee family. Today, Arlington is the final resting place for many of the nation's military dead, and the mansion serves as a memorial to Robert E. Lee.

?   Given the circumstances of the Civil War, do you think the Union was justified in seizing this property? Explain.

Connecting with History and Conflict

How did the generosity of Grant's terms of surrender parallel his stated desire to support restoration of peaceful relations between North and South? Have students list the ways Grant, by word and deed, took a leadership role in restoring the unity of the nation. Ask students to write a brief essay describing situations in their own lives when they have been part of a dispute's settlement. Can they compare ways in which they achieved reconciliation with the approach used by Grant? **(Verbal/Linguistic)**

INTERPRETING GRAPHS
After four years and more than 10,500 battles, the Civil War claimed a staggering number of casualties. **Drawing Conclusions** *How does the total number of Civil War dead compare to those killed in other U.S. wars? Why do you think this is so? How does the information in the pie chart help to explain the outcome of the war?*

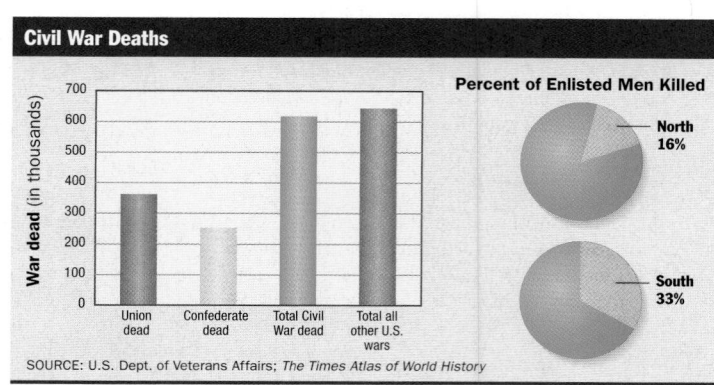

Civil War Deaths

SOURCE: U.S. Dept. of Veterans Affairs; *The Times Atlas of World History*

Court House. There, the Confederates were surrounded by a much larger Union force. Some of Lee's officers suggested that the army could scatter and continue to fight as **guerrillas**—soldiers who use surprise raids and hit-and-run tactics. Lee rejected this idea, fearing that it would bring more devastation to Virginia. Reluctantly he admitted, "There is nothing left for me to do but go and see General Grant, and I would rather die a thousand deaths." He knew the war was over.

That afternoon Lee and Grant met in a private home in the town. The house belonged to Wilmer McLean. He had not lived there long. In 1861, McLean had been living in Manassas, and the opening shots of the First Battle of Bull Run had landed in his front yard. To ensure the safety of his family, he had moved them away from the war—or so he thought—to the town of Appomattox Court House. Now the war was ending in his parlor.

When they met in McLean's house, General Lee was in his dress uniform, a sword at his side, and Grant was wearing his usual private's uniform, which was splattered with mud. They briefly chatted about the weather and their service in the Mexican War. Then Lee asked Grant about the terms of the surrender. These were generous. Southern soldiers could take their horses and mules and go home. They would not be punished as traitors so long as they obeyed the laws where they lived. Grant also offered to feed the starving Confederate army. After the two men signed the surrender papers, they talked for a few more minutes. Then Lee mounted his horse and rode away.

As news of the surrender spread through the Union army, soldiers began firing artillery salutes. Grant ordered the celebration stopped. He did not want rejoicing at the Southerners' misfortune because, as he pointed out, "the rebels are our countrymen again."

In the South, the news also met with mixed feelings. Nancy De Saussure recalled how she felt: "Joy and sorrow strove with each other. Joy in the hope of having my husband . . . return to me, but oh, such sorrow over our defeat!"

Lincoln Is Assassinated

A few weeks after Lee's surrender, General Johnston surrendered to Sherman in North Carolina. Throughout May, other Confederate forces large and small also gave up.

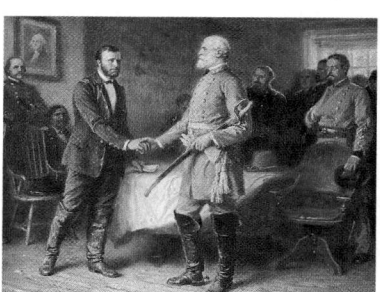

VIEWING HISTORY Lee surrenders to Grant at Appomattox Court House. **Making Inferences** *What do the expressions, dress, and other details of the two generals indicate about the surrender? Do you think the artist's sympathies were with the North or the South? Explain.*

CAPTION ANSWERS

Interpreting Graphs It almost equals those in all other U.S. wars because both sides were American and the obsolete tactics combined with new technology caused huge casualties. The pie charts show that the South lost a much larger percentage of its forces, and thus was short of manpower by the end of the war.

Viewing History General Lee looks dignified, elegant, and sadly heroic; his sword gives him the look of authority. Grant looks smaller and slightly deferential; he is positioned farther back in the painting. Both men look cordial and respectful of the other. Answers will vary about the artist's sympathies.

RESOURCE DIRECTORY

Teaching Resources
Units 3/4 booklet
 • Section 4 Quiz, p. 56
 • Chapter 11 Test, pp. 57, 60
Guide to the Essentials
 • Section 4 Summary, p. 61
 • Chapter 11 Test, p. 62

Other Print Resources
Chapter Tests with ExamView® Test Bank CD-ROM, Ch. 11

Technology
ExamView® Test Bank CD-ROM, Ch. 11
Social Studies Skills Tutor CD-ROM

Tragically, Abraham Lincoln did not live to see the official end of the war. Throughout the winter of 1864–1865, a group of Southern conspirators in Washington, D.C., had worked on a plan to aid the Confederacy. Led by John Wilkes Booth, a Maryland actor with strong Southern sympathies, the group plotted to kidnap Lincoln and exchange him for Confederate prisoners of war. After several unsuccessful attempts, Booth revised his plan. He assigned members of his group to kill top Union officials, including General Grant and Vice President Johnson. Booth himself would murder the President.

On April 14, 1865, Booth slipped into the back of the President's unguarded box at Ford's Theater in Washington, D.C. Inside, the President and Mrs. Lincoln were watching a play. Booth pulled out a pistol and shot Lincoln in the head. Leaping over the railing, he fell to the stage, breaking his leg in the process. Booth then limped off the stage and escaped out a back alley. The army tracked Booth to his hiding place in a tobacco barn in Virginia. When he refused to surrender, they set the barn on fire. In the confusion that followed, Booth was shot to death, either by a soldier or by himself.

Mortally wounded, the unconscious President was carried to a boardinghouse across the street from the theater. While doctors and family stood by helplessly, Lincoln lingered through the night. He died early the next morning without regaining consciousness.

In the North, citizens mourned for the loss of the President who had led them through the war. Lincoln's funeral train took 14 days to travel from the nation's capital to his hometown of Springfield, Illinois. As the procession passed through towns and cities, millions of people lined the tracks to show their respect.

Both the North and the South had suffered great losses during the war, but both also gained by it. They gained an undivided nation, a democracy that would continue to seek the equality Lincoln had promised for it. They also gained new fellow citizens—the African Americans who had broken the bonds of slavery and claimed their right to be free and equal, every one.

VIEWING HISTORY Lincoln's body was displayed in several major cities, including New York as shown here, on its way from Washington, D.C., to its resting place in Springfield, Illinois. **Drawing Conclusions** *Why do you think Lincoln was given such an elaborate funeral?*

Section 4 · Assessment

READING COMPREHENSION

1. What did the **Battle of the Wilderness** reveal about Grant's strategy?
2. What happened at the **Battle of Spotsylvania** and the **Battle of Cold Harbor?**
3. What had the South hoped for in the election of 1864? Why did the election turn out differently?
4. What did the **Thirteenth Amendment** accomplish?
5. Who was John Wilkes Booth?

CRITICAL THINKING AND WRITING

6. **Analyzing Information** General Sherman said this about war: "The crueler it is, the sooner it will be over." Do you agree or disagree? Use examples from 1864 and 1865 to support your opinion.
7. **Writing an Editorial** Review the terms of surrender. Were they fair or too generous? Write the opening paragraph of an editorial stating your opinion.

 **Take It to the NET**

Activity: Preparing an Oral Report Read about the events leading up to Lee's surrender to Grant. Report to your class on what you think is most interesting and important about the occasion. Use the links provided in the *America: Pathways to the Present* area of the following Web site for help in completing this activity.
www.phschool.com

Reading Comprehension

1. Under Grant's leadership, troops would not retreat quickly.
2. At Spotsylvania, despite huge losses, Grant persevered; at Cold Harbor, 7,000 Union troops fell in less than one hour.
3. For Lincoln's defeat, and McClellan's victory, as the latter had promised to negotiate to end the war. Sherman's capture of Atlanta changed the political climate in the North, leaving Northerners less willing to support negotiation.
4. The Thirteenth Amendment ended slavery in the United States forever.
5. He was a Southern conspirator who assassinated President Lincoln.

Critical Thinking and Writing

6. Students should assess military tactics and determine to what extent Union tactics such as Sheridan's Shenandoah campaign and Sherman's march to the sea contributed to ending the war.
7. Those who feel the terms were fair might claim it was necessary to offer easy terms because the former enemies were once again parts of one nation. Students who feel the terms were too generous might suggest that secession could be seen as treason and should be punished.

 **Take It to the NET**

Students should demonstrate an understanding of the events that led to the end of the Civil War, including the Battle of Appomattox.

CAPTION ANSWERS

Viewing History Sample answers: He was respected for leading the Union to victory; an elaborate funeral was a display of Union solidarity and sorrow over Lincoln's death.

REVIEWING KEY TERMS

Students should refer to the definitions of key terms in the chapter to write sentences that show an understanding of the Civil War era.

REVIEWING MAIN IDEAS

11. North: more railroad track; more factories for production of goods needed; a well-balanced economy; more money; functioning government; small army and navy; two-thirds of the nation's population lived there. South: home of most of the nation's military colleges; army did not need to initiate military action to win the war; fighting to preserve their way of life and self-government.

12. Union forces took control of the Cumberland and Tennessee rivers and seized parts of Mississippi, Tennessee, and Louisiana.

13. Union troops under Irvin McDowell were repulsed at Manassas in 1861; under McClellan were repulsed by Lee in 1862; under Burnside were beaten at Fredericksburg in 1862; under Hooker were beaten at Chancellorsville in 1863.

14. In May 1861 the Confederate government sent representatives to France and Great Britain. Though the South did not gain recognition, Great Britain did allow its ports to be used to build Confederate privateers.

15. He used the army to shut down opposition newspapers and denied others the use of the mails; used martial law to keep Kentucky in the Union camp. Kentucky citizens lost some of their constitutional rights.

16. While it did not bring an immediate end to slavery, it promised freedom when the North won the war. It caused many African American men to enlist in the military. It influenced both Great Britain and France in deciding not to intervene in the war.

17. There was some industrial growth. Women joined the Southern workforce in large numbers. The disruption of Southern farming, combined with the labor shortage and profiteering, caused shortages of food and other goods, as well as great inflation.

---

creating a **CHAPTER SUMMARY**

Copy the time line (right) on a piece of paper and complete it by adding the important military and political events of the Civil War. Include a brief explanation of why each event was important. You may need to continue on several sheets of paper.

For additional review and enrichment activities, see the interactive version of *America: Pathways to the Present*, available on the Web and on CD-ROM.

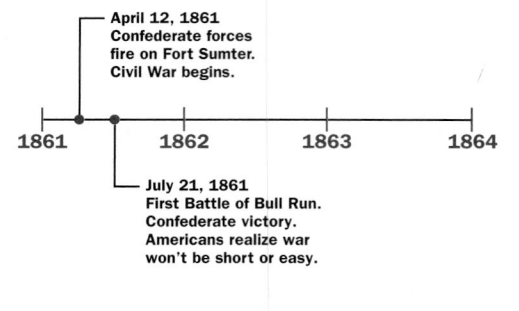

April 12, 1861
Confederate forces fire on Fort Sumter. Civil War begins.

1861   1862   1863   1864

July 21, 1861
First Battle of Bull Run. Confederate victory. Americans realize war won't be short or easy.

★ **Reviewing Key Terms**

For each of the terms below, write a sentence explaining how it relates to the Civil War.

1. First Battle of Bull Run
2. war of attrition
3. Battle of Antietam
4. Copperhead
5. martial law
6. writ of *habeas corpus*
7. contraband
8. Pickett's Charge
9. siege
10. Thirteenth Amendment

★ **Reviewing Main Ideas**

11. List three strengths of the North and three strengths of the South. (Section 1)

12. What gains did Union forces make in the western part of the Confederacy in the first two years of the war? (Section 1)

13. Summarize Union efforts to capture Richmond in 1861–1863. (Section 1)

14. How and why did the South seek help from Europe? (Section 2)

15. Briefly describe three emergency measures Lincoln took during the war. (Section 2)

16. How did the Emancipation Proclamation affect the war? (Section 2)

17. How was the South's economy affected by the war? (Section 2)

18. What was the significance of the Battle of Gettysburg? (Section 3)

19. Why did Vicksburg surrender, and what was the importance of this Union victory? (Section 3)

20. What were the immediate and the long-term effects of Sherman's march to the sea? (Section 4)

21. What events led to Lee's surrender? (Section 4)

★ **Critical Thinking**

22. Making Comparisons Compare the Union and Confederate military strategies.

23. Predicting Consequences How might the war have been different if Lincoln had appointed Grant to lead the Union forces in July 1861? Explain your answer.

24. Testing Conclusions Lincoln came to believe that the Union could not survive if slavery were preserved. Give evidence to support this conclusion.

25. Synthesizing Information Why did the Civil War cost so many more American lives than wars before or since?

CREATING A CHAPTER SUMMARY	
Year	**Events**
1861	• April 12 Confederate forces fire on Fort Sumter. Civil War begins. • July 21 First Battle of Bull Run, Confederate victory
1862	• March 9 Battle between the *Merrimack* and the *Monitor* • April 6–7 Battle of Shiloh • September 17 Battle of Antietam • December 13 Battle of Fredericksburg
1863	• January Emancipation Proclamation takes effect. • May 1–4 Battle of Chancellorsville • July 1–3 Battle of Gettysburg • July 4 Vicksburg surrenders. • November 19 Lincoln presents Gettysburg Address.
1864	• May 5–6 Battle of the Wilderness • June 3 Battle of Cold Harbor • September 2 Sherman occupies Atlanta. • December 21 Sherman captures Savannah. • April 9 Lee surrenders to Grant at Appomattox. • April 14 President Lincoln assassinated.

★ Skills Assessment

Analyzing Political Cartoons ▶

26. In this cartoon, England and France look on as a pair of combatants fight. Identify the two fighters.

27. In addition to the figure on the left, what other threat does the figure on the right face? Explain how you know.

28. What is being trampled? What does it stand for?

29. What do you think the political leanings of the cartoonist are? Explain your answer.

Interpreting Data

Turn to the "Civil War Deaths" graphs on page 416.

30. Which statement best describes the number of Civil War dead?

   A More Confederate soldiers died than Union soldiers.

   B More soldiers died in the Civil War than in all other U.S. wars combined.

   C More Union soldiers died than Confederate soldiers.

   D Twice as many Union soldiers died than Confederate soldiers.

31. Which statement best describes the percent, or fraction, of the total number of enlisted men killed?

   F Half of the soldiers who fought in the Civil War were killed.

   G A higher percentage of Confederate soldiers were killed than Union soldiers.

   H One third of all Union soldiers were killed.

   J More than a quarter of all Union soldiers were killed.

Applying the Chapter Skill: *Summarizing from Multiple Sources*

32. Reread two descriptions of battle by young boys who served in the Civil War: the quotation from Elisha Stockwell at the beginning of Section 2 and the one from the drummer boy at the beginning of Section 3. Create a summary of the two sources that expresses how it felt to be in a Civil War battle.

ACTIVITIES

Writing to LEARN

Writing to Persuade
In your view, would Lincoln have won the election of 1864 if the South had continued to triumph on the battlefield? Write an essay explaining your opinion. Include at least two reasons for your opinion, and support your reasons with specific details.

Primary Source CD-ROM

Working With Primary Sources Find additional information on the Civil War on the *Exploring Primary Sources in U.S. History CD-ROM* and use the selection(s) provided to complete the Chapter 11 primary source activity located in the *America: Pathways to the Present* area of the following Web site.
www.phschool.com

Take It to the NET

Chapter Self-Test As a review activity, take the Chapter 11 Self-Test in the *America: Pathways to the Present* area at the Web site listed below. The questions are designed to test your understanding of the chapter content.
www.phschool.com

---

18. After numerous defeats, Lee was forced to retreat, though both sides suffered huge losses. Lee never returned to Northern soil.

19. The siege depleted Confederate troops' rations, forcing them to surrender. The victory gave the Union control of the Mississippi River.

20. It brought widespread destruction to the South and created a long-lasting resentment of Southerners for Northerners.

21. Sheridan and Grant cut off Lee's supplies, forcing him to abandon Petersburg and Richmond. Then, hemmed in by Union forces, Lee surrendered at Appomattox Court House.

CRITICAL THINKING

22. The Union implemented the Anaconda Plan. Sherman and Grant were also able to win victories deep in southern territory. The Confederacy fought a primarily defensive war, hoping to wear down the Union's appetite for battle. But General Lee did march his troops into northern territory on two occasions.

23. Students may include a discussion of Grant's strong commanding skills, which may suggest that under his leadership the war might have been shorter, and more brutal.

24. Northerners were no longer content to let the slave system stand. Lincoln knew that slavery in the South would be an enduring source of friction even if the South could be brought back into the Union.

25. Advances in technology—both military and medical; the fact that both armies comprised Americans.

SKILLS ASSESSMENT

26. The seceding states, or the Confederacy, and the Union.

27. Copperheads, or anti-war Democrats, symbolized by the snake wrapped around the figure's leg.

28. The American flag: the United States and its ideals.

29. The cartoonist expresses the sentiments of a Union Democrat who supports the war. The Union figure is treated sympathetically, wearing white clothing and fighting two adversaries simultaneously—the Confederacy and the Copperheads.

30. C

31. F

32. Elisha Stockwell wants to go home, while the drummer boy wants to do his duty, regardless of the danger.

A CIVIL WAR SOLDIER'S STORY

Focus Have students find the meaning of each of these words in a dictionary before they begin to read: *bantering, conscripted, pallor, execration, forage, escritoire, depredator, debris.* Ask them to think, as they read, about the factors that make civil wars different from other wars.

Instruct Point out that Union and Confederate soldiers shared a life-changing experience in the Civil War. For many soldiers, their military service was the first time they had ever been away from home. Have students identify an instance when a promise made to men on the enemy side superseded loyalty to the soldiers' own army. *(Some Confederates deserted into enemy lines after their major fired at a Union soldier during a truce.)*

Explain the allusion to Puritan leader Oliver Cromwell. *(The most important leader of the English Civil War, Cromwell was a commander of the army of Parliament that defeated the forces of King Charles I in 1645 and later used vicious massacres to subdue Scotland and Ireland. Conyngham asserts that Sherman's soldiers thought, like Cromwell, that by mercilessly destroying the enemy they were following the will of God.)*

Analyzing the Document Use this additional question to generate class discussion:

Critical Thinking: Determining Relevance The description in the excerpt of the destruction wrought by Union troops passing through Georgia illustrates the savagery of the war. Remind students of Conyngham's point that soldiers from opposing sides enjoyed socializing together. Ask students how, in their respective opinions, such a contradiction could be possible. *(Answers will vary. Students might point out that although the Civil War was extremely brutal, it was fought between people of the same country. The fraternization between Union and Confederate soldiers may have been an indication of how much people on opposing sides of the conflict actually had in common.)*

A Civil War Soldier's Story

One day soldiers from the North and the South are shooting at each other in a life-and-death struggle; the next day they're trading coffee and conversation. Although it sounds too strange to be true, the following eyewitness account, selected by the editors of *American Heritage* magazine, describes just such a scene. The account is written by David Conyngham, an officer in the army of William T. Sherman and a journalist. As you read the following excerpt, think about why such "private truces" might have taken place.

IT WAS NO UNUSUAL THING to see our pickets and skirmishers enjoying themselves very comfortably with the rebels, drinking bad whiskey, smoking and chewing worse tobacco, and trading coffee and other little articles. The rebels had no coffee, and our men plenty, while the rebels had plenty of whiskey; so they very soon came to an understanding. It was strange to see these men, who had been just pitted in deadly conflict, trading, and bantering, and chatting, as if they were the best friends in the world. They discussed a battle with the same gusto they would a cock-fight, or horse-race, and made inquiries about their friends, as to who was killed, and who not. . . .

In those improvised truces, the best possible faith was observed by the men. These truces were brought about chiefly in the following manner. A rebel, who was heartily tired of his crippled position in his pit, would call out, "I say, Yank!"

"Well, Johnny Reb," would echo from another hole or tree.

"I'm going to put out my head; don't shoot."

"Well, I won't."

The reb would pop up his head; the Yank would do the same.

"Hain't you got any coffee, Johnny?"

"Na'r a bit, but plenty of rot-gut."

"All right; we'll have a trade."

They would meet, while several others would follow the example, until there would be a regular bartering mart established. In some cases the men would come to know each other so well, that

---

RESOURCE DIRECTORY

Technology
AmericanHeritage® My Brush with History™ Videotapes *A Civil War Soldier's Story*

✓ TEST PREPARATION

Have students use the excerpt on these pages to answer the following question.

What two main topics does Conyngham treat?

A The accuracy of Civil War rifles and Sherman's campaign.

(B) Friendly interactions between northern and southern soldiers and the northern campaign through central Georgia and South Carolina.

C Soldiers' abuse of alcohol and tobacco and the campaign through central Georgia.

D The Civil War and its effects on soldiers' morale.

Blasted by Union artillery fire, the Potter house in Atlanta was one of countless buildings damaged or destroyed by Sherman's forces.

they would often call out, "Look out, reb; we're going to shoot," or "Look out, Yank, we're going to shoot," as the case may be.

On one occasion the men were holding a friendly reunion of this sort, when a rebel major came down in a great fury, and ordered the men back. As they were going back, he ordered them to fire on the Federals. They refused, as they had made a truce. The major swore and stormed, and in his rage he snatched the gun from one of the men, and fired at a Federal soldier, wounding him. A cry of execration at such a breach of faith rose from all the men, and they called out, "Yanks, we couldn't help it." At night these men deserted into our lines, assigning as a reason, that they could not with honor serve any longer in an army that thus violated private truces. . . .

THE PICNIC THROUGH GEORGIA Our campaign all through Central Georgia was one delightful picnic. We had little or no fighting, and good living. The farm-yards, cellars, and cribs of the planters kept ourselves and animals well stored with provisions and forage. . . .

In passing through the camp one night, I saw a lot of jolly soldiers squatted outside the huts . . . , and between them a table richly stocked with meats and fowls of different kinds, flanked by several bottles of brandy. . . . They thought campaigning in Georgia about the pleasantest sort of life out, and they wondered what would become of the poor dog-gone folks they had left with their fingers in their mouths, and little else to put in them.

Many of our foragers, scouts, and hangers-on of all classes, thought, like Cromwell, that they were doing the work of the Lord, in wantonly destroying as much property as possible. Though this was done extensively in Georgia, it was only in South Carolina that it was brought to perfection. . . .

A planter's house was overrun in a jiffy; boxes, drawers, and escritoires were ransacked with a laudable zeal, and emptied of their contents. If the spoils were ample, the depredators were satisfied, and went off in peace; if not, everything was

torn and destroyed, and most likely the owner was tickled with sharp bayonets into a confession where he had his treasures hid. . . . Sorghum barrels were knocked open, bee hives rifled, while their angry swarms rushed frantically about. Indeed, I have seen a soldier knock a planter down because a bee stung him. Hogs are bayonetted, and then hung in quarters on the bayonets to bleed; chickens, geese, and turkeys are knocked over and hung in garlands from the saddles . . . ; cows and calves, so wretchedly thin that they drop down and perish on the first day's march, are driven along, or, if too weak to travel, are shot, lest they should give aid to the enemy.

Should the house be deserted, the furniture is smashed in pieces, music is pounded out of four-hundred-dollar pianos with the ends of muskets. . . . After all was cleared out, most likely some set of stragglers wanted to enjoy a good fire, and set the house, debris of furniture, and all the surroundings, in a blaze. This is the way Sherman's army lived on the country. They were not ordered to do so, but I am afraid they were not brought to task for it much either.

Source: *Sherman's March Through the South* by David Conyngham, Sheldon & Co., 1865.

Understanding Primary Sources

1. (a) How were the private truces arranged? **(b)** How did the soldiers react when a truce was violated?

2. Why did the Union soldiers destroy so much property as they made their way through Georgia and South Carolina?

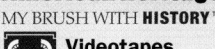
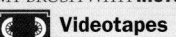

American Heritage®
MY BRUSH WITH **HISTORY**™

For more information about the Civil War, view "A Civil War Soldier's Story."

📼 **Videotapes**

421

Chapter 12 Planning Guide
Resource Manager

Chapter-Level Resources	**CORE INSTRUCTION**	**READING/SKILLS**
	Teaching Resources • Pacing Charts booklet • Block Scheduling booklet **Resource Pro® CD-ROM**, Ch. 12 **Prentice Hall Presentation Pro CD-ROM**, Ch. 12 **www.phschool.com** • eTeach	**Guided Reading Audiotapes (English/Spanish)** **Student Edition on Audio CD**, Ch. 12 **Social Studies Skills Tutor CD-ROM** **Color Transparencies**, B5, B6
1 Presidential Reconstruction 1. Learn about conditions in the South following the Civil War. 2. Analyze Lincoln's and Johnson's Reconstruction plans for similarities. 3. Find out how newly freed slaves began to rebuild their lives.	**Teaching Resources** **Units 3/4 booklet** • Section 1 Quiz, p. 64 **Learning Styles Lesson Plans booklet,** p. 26	**Guided Reading and Review booklet,** p. 50 **Guide to the Essentials**, p. 63 **Learning with Documents booklet,** p. 51 **Section Reading Support Transparencies**
2 Congressional Reconstruction 1. Discover how black codes and the Fourteenth Amendment were related. 2. Analyze the differences between Congress's Reconstruction plan and Andrew Johnson's. 3. Learn the significance of the Fifteenth Amendment. 4. Find out who supported the Republican governments of the South.	**Teaching Resources** **Units 3/4 booklet** • Section 2 Quiz, p. 65	**Guided Reading and Review booklet,** p. 51 **Guide to the Essentials**, p. 64 **Learning with Documents booklet,** p. 82 **Section Reading Support Transparencies**
3 Birth of the "New South" 1. Find out how farming in the South changed after the Civil War. 2. Explore how the growth of cities and industry began to change the South's economy after the war. 3. Learn how money designated for Reconstruction projects was used.	**Teaching Resources** **Units 3/4 booklet** • Section 3 Quiz, p. 66 **Learning Styles Lesson Plans booklet,** p. 27	**Guided Reading and Review booklet,** p. 52 **Guide to the Essentials**, p. 65 **Learning with Documents booklet,** p. 17 **Skills for Life booklet**, p. 14 **Section Reading Support Transparencies**
4 The End of Reconstruction 1. Learn about tactics used by the Ku Klux Klan to spread terror throughout the South. 2. Find out why Reconstruction ended. 3. Review the major successes and failures of Reconstruction.	**Teaching Resources** **Units 3/4 booklet** • Section 4 Quiz, p. 67	**Guided Reading and Review booklet,** p. 53 **Guide to the Essentials**, p. 66 **Section Reading Support Transparencies**

ENRICHMENT/PRE-AP

Prentice Hall United States History Video Collection™

www.phschool.com
- Section Activities, Virtual Field Trip, Chapter Activities, Current Events Online

Biography, Literature, and Comparing Primary Sources booklet, pp. 17, 54–56
Great Debates booklet, p. 6
Historical Outline Map Book, p. 53
Sounds of an Era Audio CD

Biography, Literature, and Comparing Primary Sources booklet, pp. 119–120
American History Block Scheduling Support
Sounds of an Era Audio CD

Nystrom *Atlas of Our Country,* pp. 28–29

American History Block Scheduling Support
Historical Outline Map Book, p. 54
American Pathways Thematic Posters

ASSESSMENT

PRENTICE HALL ASSESSMENT SYSTEM

Core Assessment
ExamView® Test Bank, Ch. 12
ExamView® Test Bank CD-ROM, Ch. 12

Standardized Test Preparation
Diagnose and Prescribe
Diagnostic Tests for High School Social Studies Skills

Review and Reteach
Review Book for U.S. History

Practice and Assess
Test-taking Strategies With Transparencies
Test-taking Strategies Posters
Test Prep Book for U.S. History
Alternative Assessment Handbook
Document-Based Assessment

Teaching Resources
Units 3/4 booklet
- Section Quizzes, pp. 64–67
- Chapter Tests, pp. 68, 71

www.phschool.com Ch. 12 Self-Test

AmericanHeritage RESOURCES

From the Archives of American Heritage®, pp. 432, 443, 444
AmericanHeritage® My Brush with History™ Videotapes
www.americanheritage.com

TEXT

Don't miss the exclusive interactive version of this textbook on the Web and on CD-ROM.

Chapter 12 Planning Guide
In Your Classroom

CUSTOMIZE FOR INDIVIDUAL NEEDS

Gifted and Talented

Teacher's Edition
- Customize for Gifted and Talented, p. 429

Teaching Resources
- Biography, Literature, and Comparing Primary Sources booklet, pp. 17, 54–56, 119–120

ESL

Teacher's Edition
- Customize for ESL, p. 431

Teaching Resources
- Guided Reading and Review booklet, pp. 50–53
- Guide to the Essentials (English/Spanish), Chapter 12

Technology
- Student Edition on Audio CD, Chapter 12
- Guided Reading Audiotapes (English/Spanish), Chapter 12
- Section Reading Support Transparencies

Less Proficient Readers

Teacher's Edition
- Customize for Less Proficient Readers, pp. 427, 445

Teaching Resources
- Guided Reading and Review booklet, pp. 50–53
- Guide to the Essentials (English/Spanish), Chapter 12

Technology
- Student Edition on Audio CD, Chapter 12
- Guided Reading Audiotapes (English/Spanish), Chapter 12
- Section Reading Support Transparencies

Less Proficient Writers

Teacher's Edition
- Customize for Less Proficient Writers, pp. 425, 437

Teaching Resources
- Guided Reading and Review booklet, pp. 50–53
- Guide to the Essentials (English/Spanish), Chapter 12

Technology
- Student Edition on Audio CD, Chapter 12
- Guided Reading Audiotapes (English/Spanish), Chapter 12
- Section Reading Support Transparencies

TEACHER'S EDITION INDEX

CHAPTER 12 – PACING SUGGESTIONS

 For 90-minute Blocks
- Teach sections 2 and 4 using Transparencies B5 and B6, and the Recent Scholarship note on page 463 for class discussions.

 Running Out of Time?

If you are running short on time to cover this chapter, consider the following options:

- Use the Prentice Hall Presentation Pro CD-ROM to create an outline for this chapter.
- Use the Section Summaries for Chapter 12, from **Guide to the Essentials (English/Spanish)**.

ADDITIONAL ACTIVITIES

1 Presidential Reconstruction	**Connecting with Culture** The Freedmen's Bureau helped to establish Howard University in Washington, D.C., as a predominantly African American university. Have students research the history of the institution, including, if possible, information about some of its notable graduates. Have students present the information in the form of a proposal to produce a documentary film about the school. **(Verbal/Linguistic)**
2 Congressional Reconstruction	**Connecting with Economics** Students can assume the roles of various carpetbaggers, honest as well as those with less honorable intentions. Suggest that they have each person present his or her story in the form of testimony at a legislative hearing on the economic motives behind their journey south. **(Bodily/Kinesthetic)**
3 Birth of the "New South"	**Connecting with Government** Tell students that the Congressional Black Caucus is an organization of African American members of the U.S. Congress. Have students gather information on the history, membership, and goals of this group and present it either in writing or in the form of a mock interview with one of its members. **(Verbal/Linguistic)**
4 The End of Reconstruction	**Connecting with Government** Explain to students that before the South's final surrender, there were some on both sides who called for a negotiated settlement, based on a compromise. Have students conduct a debate that might have been held at the time on the practicality of a compromise, given the country's previous experience with the Missouri Compromise. Divide students into two groups, one arguing for compromise and the other against. Allow time for the debaters to rehearse their arguments. **(Bodily/Kinesthetic)**

INTRODUCING THE CHAPTER

Though the outcome of the Civil War cemented the Union, the years that followed plunged the nation into dramatic social and economic changes. While African Americans obtained their liberty and southern society was transformed, Reconstruction involved a redefinition of social, economic, and political relationships between the North and the South as well as between the races.

TIME LINE ACTIVITY

To provide students with practice in using the time line, ask questions such as these:

1. What important events occurred in 1865? *(The Civil War ended, plans to pardon the South and restore the Union were made, and the Thirteenth Amendment ended slavery.)*

2. What did the Fourteenth Amendment do? *(It granted citizenship to all African Americans.)*

3. Where were slave markets abolished in 1873? *(Zanzibar)*

eTeach

Be sure to check out this month's online discussion with a Master Teacher. Go to **www.phschool.com**.

Chapter 12 Reconstruction (1865–1877)

SECTION 1	Presidential Reconstruction
SECTION 2	Congressional Reconstruction
SECTION 3	Birth of the "New South"
SECTION 4	The End of Reconstruction

Andrew Johnson

Following the Civil War, the South faced the challenge of rebuilding.

American Events

1865 The Civil War ends, and Presidents Lincoln and Johnson put forth plans to pardon the South and restore the Union. The Thirteenth Amendment ends slavery.

1866 The Ku Klux Klan forms, using terror to maintain white supremacy in the South.

1867 Angered by the southern states' attempts to limit rights of African Americans, Congress takes over Reconstruction and places the South under military rule.

1868 The Fourteenth Amendment grants blacks citizenship.

1870 The Fifteenth Amendment gives blacks the right to vote, and Republicans, including hundreds of freedmen, are elected to public office in the South.

Presidential Terms: Abraham Lincoln 1861–1865   Andrew Johnson 1865–1869   Ulysses S. Grant 1869–1877

1863   •   •   **1866**   •   •   **1869**   •

World Events

Archduke Maximilian of Austria is made emperor of Mexico.

Russia sells Alaska to the United States.

The French-built Suez Canal opens in Egypt.

1864   **1867**   **1869**

422   Chapter 12 • *Reconstruction*

RESOURCE DIRECTORY

Teaching Resources
Pacing Charts booklet
Block Scheduling booklet, p. 15
Units 3/4 booklet
  • Chapter Summary, p. 63

Technology
Guided Reading Audiotapes (English/Spanish), Ch. 12
Student Edition on Audio CD, Ch. 12
Sounds of an Era Audio CD *Senator Robert Toombs on Secession,* 1960s recording (time: 30 seconds); *Former Slave Fountain Hughes,* 1941 recording (time: 20 seconds)

Prentice Hall United States History Video Collection™ Volume 10, *Reconstruction and Segregation (1865–1910)*
Prentice Hall Presentation Pro CD-ROM, Ch. 12
Resource Pro® CD-ROM
Social Studies Skills Tutor CD-ROM
Companion Web site, www.phschool.com

CANADA

Dakota Territory

Minnesota

Wisconsin

Michigan

New York

Maine

Vt.

N.H.

Mass.

Rhode Island

Connecticut

Nebraska Territory

Iowa

Pennsylvania

40°N

Colorado Territory

Illinois

Indiana

Ohio

New Jersey

Md.

Delaware

70°W

Kansas

Missouri

Kentucky

West Virginia

Virginia (1870)

N

Indian Territory (Unorganized)

Arkansas (1868)

Tennessee (1866)

North Carolina (1868)

South Carolina (1868)

ATLANTIC OCEAN

Miss. (1870)

Alabama (1868)

Georgia (1870)

Texas (1870)

Louisiana (1868)

Florida (1868)

Gulf of Mexico

30°N

80°W

	Confederate states
	Other states and territories
(1868)	Date of readmission to the Union

Map shows 1863 borders.

0   150   300 mi.
0   150   300 km

1872

By 1872, all southern states have established public schools based in part on the success of the Freedmen's Bureau schools.

1877

Reconstruction ends when President Hayes withdraws federal troops from the South and Democrats regain control of southern politics.

Rutherford B. Hayes 1877–1881

• **1872** • **1875** • **1878**

Britain legalizes labor unions.

1871

Slave markets are abolished in Zanzibar.

1873

Chapter 12   423

Reuniting a War-Torn Nation

Activating Prior Knowledge What was the first state to be readmitted to the Union? *(Tennessee was readmitted in 1866.)*

Previewing According to Johnson's Presidential Reconstruction plan, states were required to void secession, abolish slavery, and repudiate the confederate debt to be readmitted to the Union. Looking at the map, which states were last to meet these requirements? *(Texas, Mississippi, Georgia, and Virginia)*

BACKGROUND
About the Pictures

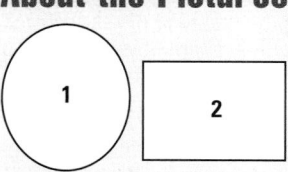

1
2

1. Contemporary engraving of Andrew Johnson, the seventeenth President of the United States.
2. The South was the main battleground of the Civil War, with hardly a farm or a family remaining unscarred by the time it was over.

iTEXT

Don't miss the exclusive interactive version of this textbook on the Web and on CD-ROM.

BIBLIOGRAPHY

For the Teacher

Du Bois, W.E.B. ***Black Reconstruction.*** University of Notre Dame Press, 2001. (Classic account by the famous African American scholar.)

Foner, Eric. ***A Short History of Reconstruction.*** HarperCollins, 1990. (Abridgment of a definitive historical study of the era.)

Franklin, John Hope. ***Reconstruction After the Civil War.*** University of Chicago Press, 1995. (Sympathetic treatment of congressional efforts to reconstruct the old Confederacy.)

For the Student

Lester, Julius. ***This Strange New Feeling.*** Scholastic, 1997. (Three short stories about slavery and freedom, based on true accounts.)

Smith, John David. ***Black Voices from Reconstruction, 1865–1877.*** University Press of Florida, 1997. (Uses primary source material to detail the hopes, dreams, and disappointments of black people during the period after slavery.)

Presidential Reconstruction

READING FOCUS

- What condition was the South in following the Civil War?
- How were Lincoln's and Johnson's Reconstruction plans similar?
- How did the newly freed slaves begin to rebuild their lives?

MAIN IDEA

Lincoln's and Johnson's Reconstruction plans focused on pardoning the Confederate states and restoring the Union quickly.

KEY TERMS

Reconstruction
pardon
Radical Republicans
pocket veto
Freedmen's Bureau

TAKING NOTES

Copy the diagram below. As you read, fill in the two circles with information about the two Presidents' Reconstruction plans. Place items that are similar in both plans in the area where the two circles overlap.

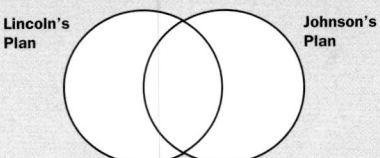

Lincoln's Plan — Johnson's Plan

Setting the Scene The Civil War was over, and throughout the summer and fall of 1865, the soldiers who had made up the great armies of the Union and the Confederacy headed home. One was former Confederate soldier Val C. Giles, of Texas:

> 66 *I reached home in Govalle, outside of Austin . . . after an absence of four years and five months. Father and mother were not expecting me and were not at home, but my dog, Brave, was on guard. . . . It was not a 'deep-mouth welcome' that greeted me as I drew near, but a gruff emphatic warning to keep out. 'Brave, old boy,' I said, 'don't you know me?' He cocked up one ear and looked at me sideways. It finally dawned on him who I was, and he . . . circled wildly all around me, expressing in his dumb way his delight at my return. . . .* 99
> —Val C. Giles

VIEWING HISTORY Many families eagerly awaited the return of loved ones at the end of the war. **Making Inferences** What evidence is there in this photograph that this soldier's return home is an important event?

Often the Confederate soldiers' homecomings contained as much sorrow as delight. Their cause had been defeated and their homes, in many cases, completely destroyed. Charleston, for example, was described by a journalist as a "city of ruins, of desolation, of vacant houses, of widowed women, of rotting wharves, of deserted warehouses, of weed-wild gardens, of miles of grass-grown streets, of acres of pitiful . . . barrenness."

Between 1865 and 1877, the federal government carried out a program to repair the damage to the South and restore the southern states to the Union. This program, known as **Reconstruction,** was hugely controversial at the time, and historians continue to debate its successes and failures to this day.

The War's Aftermath

At the start of Reconstruction, it was clear that the nation—especially the South—had been changed forever by the war. The changes reached into families and farms.

The Physical Toll War had destroyed two thirds of the South's shipping industry and about 9,000 miles of railroads. It had devoured farmland, farm buildings, and farm machinery; work animals and one third of all livestock; bridges, canals, and levees; and thousands of miles of roads. Factories, ports, and cities lay smoldering. The value of southern farm property had plunged by about 70 percent.

The Human Toll The Civil War destroyed a generation of young, healthy men—fathers, brothers, and husbands. The North lost 364,000 soldiers, including more than 38,000 African Americans. The South lost 260,000 soldiers, one fifth of its adult white men. One out of three southern men were killed or wounded. Many of the survivors were permanently scarred in mind or body. Fighting also resulted in countless civilian deaths. Children were made orphans; brides became widows.

VIEWING HISTORY This photograph of grave diggers by Alexander Gardner reminds viewers in grisly detail of the horrible human cost of the Civil War.

Southerners' Hardships The postwar South was made up of three major groups of people. Each group faced its own hardships and fears.

Black southerners Some 4 million freed people were starting their new lives in a poor region with slow economic activity. As slaves, they had received food and shelter, however inadequate. Now, after a lifetime of forced labor, many found themselves homeless, jobless, and hungry. Some freed slaves did choose to continue working on the plantations of their former masters. Others sought new jobs in the cities and in the West.

Plantation owners Planters lost slave labor worth about $3 billion. In addition, the Captured and Abandoned Property Act of 1863 allowed the federal government to seize $100 million in southern plantations and cotton. With worthless Confederate money, some farmers couldn't afford to hire workers. Others had to sell their property to cover debts.

Poor white southerners Many white laborers could not find work because of the new job competition from freedmen. Poor white families began migrating to frontier lands such as Mississippi and Texas to find new opportunities.

Punishment or Pardon? The fall of the Confederacy and the end of slavery raised difficult questions. How and when should southern states be allowed to resume their role in the Union? Should the South be punished for its actions, or be forgiven and allowed to recover quickly? Now that black southerners were free, would the races have equal rights? If so, how might those rights be protected? Did the Civil War itself point out a need for a stronger federal government? In Washington the debate over these questions launched new battles so fierce that some historians call Reconstruction an extension of the Civil War.

At stake were basic issues concerning the nation's political system. Yet it was not even clear which branch of government had the authority to decide these matters. On these key questions, the Constitution was silent. The Framers had made no provisions for solving the problems raised by the Civil War.

 **Sounds of an Era**

Listen to "When Johnny Comes Marching Home Again" and other sounds from the Reconstruction period.

Chapter 12 • Section 1   425

VIEWING HISTORY Grant's Union army entered the Confederate capital of Richmond, Virginia on April 3, 1865. Retreating troops set fire to warehouses filled with cotton, tobacco, and ammunition, leaving only the shells of buildings behind (below). **Analyzing Visual Information** *Can you find evidence of rebuilding efforts already underway in this April 1865 photograph of The Circular Church in Charleston, South Carolina (above)?*

Lincoln's Reconstruction Plan

With no road map for the future, Lincoln had begun postwar planning as early as December 1863, when he proposed a Ten Percent Plan for Reconstruction. The plan was forgiving to the South:

1. It offered a **pardon,** an official forgiveness of a crime, to any Confederate who would take an oath of allegiance to the Union and accept federal policy on slavery.
2. It denied pardons to all Confederate military and government officials and to southerners who had killed African American war prisoners.
3. It permitted each state to hold a convention to create a new state constitution only after 10 percent of voters in the state had sworn allegiance to the Union.
4. States could then hold elections and resume full participation in the Union.

Lincoln's plan did not require the new constitutions to give voting rights to black Americans. Nor did it "readmit" southern states to the Union, since in Lincoln's view, their secession had not been constitutional. Lincoln set a tone of forgiveness for the postwar era in his Second Inaugural Address:

KEY DOCUMENTS ❝With malice toward none; with charity for all; with firmness in the right, as God gives us to see the right, let us strive on to finish the work we are in; to bind up the nation's wounds . . . to do all which may achieve and cherish a just, and a lasting peace, among ourselves, and with all nations.❞

—Lincoln's Second Inaugural Address, March 1865

Congress, however, saw Lincoln's Reconstruction plan as a threat to congressional authority. The Republican leadership warned that Lincoln "should confine himself to his executive duties—to obey and execute, not make the laws . . . and leave political reorganization to Congress."

426

Much of the opposition to Lincoln's plan for Reconstruction came from a group of congressmen from his own party. The group, known as the **Radical Republicans,** believed that the Civil War had been fought over the moral issue of slavery. The Radicals insisted that the main goal of Reconstruction should be a total restructuring of society to guarantee black people true equality.

The Radical Republicans viewed Lincoln's plan as too lenient. In July 1864 Congress passed its own, stricter Reconstruction plan, the Wade-Davis Act. Among its provisions, it required ex-Confederate men to take an oath of past and future loyalty and to swear that they had never willingly borne arms against the United States. Lincoln let the bill die in a **pocket veto.**

Lincoln's hopes came to a violent end less than a month after his second inauguration. As discussed in the previous chapter, Lincoln was murdered on April 14, 1865, by John Wilkes Booth. The assassination plunged the nation into grief and its politics into chaos.

Johnson's Reconstruction Plan

With Lincoln's death, Reconstruction was now in the hands of a one-time slave owner from the South: the former Vice President, Andrew Johnson. Born poor in North Carolina, Johnson grew up to become a tailor. He learned to read and write with the help of his wife and later entered politics in Tennessee as a Democrat.

Johnson had a profound hatred of rich planters and found strong voter support among poor white southerners. He served Tennessee first as governor, then in Congress. Johnson was the only southern senator to remain in Congress after secession. Hoping to attract Democratic voters, the Republican Party chose Johnson as Lincoln's running mate in 1864.

When Johnson took office in April 1865, Congress was in recess until December. During those eight months, Johnson pursued his own plan for the South. His plan, known as Presidential Reconstruction, included the following provisions:

1. It pardoned southerners who swore allegiance to the Union.
2. It permitted each state to hold a constitutional convention (without Lincoln's 10 percent allegiance requirement).
3. States were required to void secession, abolish slavery, and repudiate the Confederate debt.
4. States could then hold elections and rejoin the Union.

Presidential Reconstruction reflected the spirit of Lincoln's Ten Percent Plan but was more generous to the South. Although officially it denied pardons to all Confederate leaders, in reality Johnson often issued pardons to those who asked him personally. In 1865 alone, he pardoned 13,000 southerners.

The Taste of Freedom

As politicians debated, African Americans celebrated their new freedom. No longer were they mere property, subject to the whims of white slave owners. The feeling was overwhelming. "Everybody went wild," said Charles Ames, a Georgia freedman. "We all felt like horses. . . . We was free. Just like that, we was free."

Booker T. Washington, a future leader in black education, was 9 years old when the news came: "[W]e were told that we were all free and could go when and where we pleased. My mother, who was standing by my side, leaned over and kissed her children, while tears of joy ran down her cheeks."

Focus on GOVERNMENT

Pocket Veto If Congress adjourns its session within ten days of submitting a bill to the President, and the President does not act, the bill dies. This is known as a pocket veto.

The Historical Context In an effort to balance the powers of the President and the Congress, the Constitution grants the President the power to veto, or "refuse to sign," congressional legislation. Although it is rare, the House or Senate may pass a bill over the President's veto by a two-thirds vote of the members present in each house.

The Concept Today Most Presidents use the pocket veto frequently because Congress regularly passes a large number of measures in the closing days of its annual session.

READING CHECK
How did the Radical Republicans' Reconstruction plan differ from Lincoln and Johnson's plans?

Chapter 12 • Section 1 **427**

ACTIVITY
Student Portfolio

You may wish to have students add the following to their portfolios: Frederick Douglass was the most famous African American leader in the years following the Civil War. Ask each student to evaluate the impact of this great reform leader and to write and perform a one-person skit about his accomplishments.

BACKGROUND
A Diverse Nation

Freedom for emancipated African American slaves was not always immediate. In one first-hand account, *Memories of Childhood's Slavery Days,* published in 1909, Annie L. Burton recalled when news of the Emancipation Proclamation reached the plantation where she lived.

"My mother came for us at the end of the year 1865, and demanded that her children be given up to her," wrote Annie. "This, mistress refused to do, and threatened to set the dogs on my mother if she did not at once leave the place." Annie's mother returned and helped the children escape. When caught, she refused to give up her children. "Upon her offering to go with them to the Yankees headquarters to find out if it were really true that all the Negroes had been made free, the young men left, and troubled us no more."

READING CHECK
Radical Republicans: Wanted to punish white southerners, secure equal rights for African Americans, and issue a harsh loyalty test for former Confederate soldiers. Lincoln and Johnson: Wanted quick pardons for most former Confederate soldiers and early constitutional conventions for southern states, and felt that ending slavery was more important than securing full equal rights for African Americans.

CUSTOMIZE FOR ...

Less Proficient Readers

Have students construct a chart showing the major points of the two Reconstruction plans. Headings should include *Lincoln's Plan* at the top of one column and *Johnson's Plan* at the top of the other.

✓ TEST PREPARATION

Have students read these pages and then answer the question below.

How did Congress view President Lincoln's Reconstruction plan?

A Congress supported the plan.

B Congress did not offer an opinion of Lincoln's plan.

C Congress was divided over Lincoln's plan.

Ⓓ Congress did not support Lincoln's plan.

VIEWING HISTORY Freedom brought new educational opportunities for African Americans both young and old. The young boy pictured below is holding a book furnished by the Freedmen's Bureau. **Drawing Inferences** *(a) Which person in the photograph to the right is the teacher? (b) What is the approximate age span of the students?*

Edmund Commander after your boys came

Freedom of Movement

During the war, enslaved people had simply walked away from the plantations upon hearing that a northern army was approaching. "Right off colored folks started on the move," said James, a freed cowhand from Texas. "They seemed to want to get closer to freedom, so they'd know what it was like—like it was a place or a city." Many freed people took to the roads looking for family members who had been torn from them by slavery. Not all were successful in finding loved ones, but many joyful reunions did occur.

Freedom to Own Land

Black leaders knew that emancipation—physical freedom—was only a start. True freedom would come only with economic independence, the ability to get ahead through hard work.

Freed people urged the federal government to redistribute southern land. They argued that they were entitled to the land that slaves had cleared and farmed for generations. A Virginia freedman put it this way: "We have a right to the land where we are located. For why? I tell you. Our wives, our children, our husbands, have been sold over and over again to purchase the lands we now locate upon; for that reason we have a divine right to the land."

Proposals to give white-owned land to freedmen got little political support. In 1865, Union general William Tecumseh Sherman had set up a land-distribution experiment in South Carolina. He divided confiscated coastal lands into 40-acre plots and gave them to black families. Soon the South buzzed with rumors that the government was going to give all freedmen "forty acres and a mule." Sherman's project was short-lived, however. President Johnson eventually returned much of the land to its original owners, forcing the freedmen out. In place of programs like Sherman's, small-scale, unofficial land redistribution took place. For example, in 1871 Amos Morel, a freedman who stayed on to work on the plantation where he had been enslaved in Georgia, used his wages to buy more than 400 acres of land. He sold pieces to other freedmen and later bought land for his daughter.

Focus on CULTURE

Marriage and Family Upon gaining their freedom, African Americans could live together without fear of separation from their family members. Many legalized their marriages and adopted the children of deceased friends and relatives rather than send them to Freedmen's Bureau orphanages. Although a far higher percentage of black than white women and children continued to work outside their homes, African American families now had control of their own labor.

Freedom to Worship In their struggle to survive, African Americans looked to each other for help. New black organizations arose throughout the South. The most visible were churches. African Americans throughout the South formed their own churches. They also started thousands of voluntary groups, including mutual aid societies, debating clubs, drama societies, and trade associations.

Freedom to Learn Historians estimate that in 1860, nearly 90 percent of black adults were illiterate, partly because many southern states had banned educating slaves. One supporter of black education was Charlotte Forten, a wealthy black woman from Philadelphia. In 1862, after Union troops occupied Port Royal, South Carolina, Forten went there to teach. She observed:

> ❝ I never before saw children so eager to learn. Coming to school is a constant delight and recreation to them. . . . Many of the grown people [also] are desirous of learning to read. It is wonderful how a people who have been so long crushed to the earth . . . can have so great a desire for knowledge, and such a capability for attaining it. ❞
>
> —Charlotte Forten

Help came from several directions. White teachers, often young women, went south to start schools. Some freed people taught themselves and one another. Between 1865 and 1870, black educators founded 30 African American colleges.

The Freedmen's Bureau To help black southerners adjust to freedom, Congress created the **Freedmen's Bureau** in March 1865, just prior to Lincoln's death. It was the first major federal relief agency in United States history.

The Freedmen's Bureau lacked strong support in Congress, and the agency was largely dismantled in 1869. Yet in its short existence the bureau gave out clothing, medical supplies, and millions of meals to both black and white war refugees. More than 250,000 African American students received their first formal education in bureau schools.

Ho for Kansas!

Brethren, Friends, & Fellow Citizens:
I feel thankful to inform you that the
REAL ESTATE
AND
Homestead Association,
Will Leave Here the
15th of April, 1878,
In pursuit of Homes in the Southwestern Lands of America, at Transportation Rates, cheaper than ever was known before.
For full information inquire of
Benj. Singleton, better known as old Pap,
NO. 5 NORTH FRONT STREET.
Beware of Speculators and Adventurers, as it is a dangerous thing to fall in their hands.
Nashville, Tenn., March 18, 1878.

VIEWING HISTORY This ad from a Nashville, Tennessee, newspaper invites African Americans to emigrate to Kansas to find new homes. **Drawing Inferences** (a) What can you infer were some of the chief obstacles to emigration for African Americans? (b) Who was Benjamin Singleton?

Section 1 Assessment

Reading Comprehension

1. To repair damage to the South and restore southern states to the Union.

2. Southerners who swore allegiance to the Union.

3. A group of congressmen from Lincoln's party who believed that the Civil War had been fought over the moral issue of slavery. They insisted that the main goal of Reconstruction be a total restructuring of society to guarantee black people true equality.

4. Created by Congress, it was the first major federal relief agency in United States history, designed to help black southerners adjust to freedom.

Critical Thinking and Writing

5. Economic challenges included: finding homes, food, and jobs; selling property to cover debts; migrating to find new opportunities. Also, planters must now pay their workers either in wages or in kind.

6. Answers will vary. Students may want to focus on whether or not former slaves were entitled to compensation in the form of free land for having suffered the indignity and the hardship of living as slaves, and for the contributions to the southern economy they had made while working as slaves.

Posters should advertise the benefits of Freedmen's Bureau projects such as securing land for African Americans, building schools, providing education, and enforcing anti-slavery laws.

Section 1 Assessment

READING COMPREHENSION

1. Why was a period of **Reconstruction** necessary following the end of the Civil War?

2. Who was **pardoned** under Johnson's Reconstruction plan?

3. Who were the **Radical Republicans**?

4. What was the **Freedmen's Bureau**?

CRITICAL THINKING AND WRITING

5. **Analyzing Information** Create a list of economic challenges that southerners faced after the Civil War.

6. **Writing an Outline** Create an outline for a persuasive essay in which you argue in favor of or against the redistribution of land from whites to blacks during Reconstruction.

Take It to the NET

Activity: Creating a Poster
Research a Freedmen's Bureau project and create a poster to inform freedmen about the project. Use the links provided in the *America: Pathways to the Present* area of the following Web site for help in completing this activity.
www.phschool.com

CUSTOMIZE FOR ...

Gifted and Talented

Have students decide where they would go if they were recently freed from bondage and how they would provide for their food, shelter, and clothing. Students should list three changes that would occur in their lives.

CAPTION ANSWERS

Viewing History (a) Finding and securing land and financing the price of a home. (b) Benjamin Singleton was an African American who helped organize an effort to obtain land in Kansas for a settlement for freed slaves leaving the South.

Section 2

SECTION OBJECTIVES

1. Discover how black codes and the Fourteenth Amendment were related.
2. Analyze the differences between Congress's Reconstruction plan and Andrew Johnson's.
3. Learn the significance of the Fifteenth Amendment.
4. Find out who supported the Republican governments of the South.

BELLRINGER

Warm-Up Activity Ask students to think about times in their lives when they experienced change. How did they and others react to the change? Did they want to go back to the way it had been before the change?

Activating Prior Knowledge Freed African American slaves and defeated Confederates alike experienced a great deal of upheaval during the Reconstruction years. Ask students to list some feelings, both positive and negative, that members of each group might have felt at that time.

READING STRATEGY

In the late 1800s, southern states were putting ex-Confederates back in power and trying to keep freedmen in slave-like conditions. Ask students to analyze the social issue of treatment of minorities by listing some possible solutions to this problem. As they read, have them take specific notes on how Congress actually responded.

CAPTION ANSWERS

Viewing History The African American men are being forced to allow their labor to be auctioned off by the white men on the porch, similar to the manner in which slaves had been auctioned off.

Section 2 · Congressional Reconstruction

READING FOCUS

- How were black codes and the Fourteenth Amendment related?
- How did Congress's Reconstruction plan differ from Johnson's plan?
- What was the significance of the Fifteenth Amendment?
- Who supported the Republican governments of the South?

MAIN IDEA

As southern states moved to limit freedmen's rights, Congress took over Reconstruction and passed new laws to protect African Americans' freedom.

KEY TERMS

black codes
Fourteenth Amendment
civil rights
impeach
Fifteenth Amendment
carpetbagger
scalawag

TAKING NOTES

Create a cause-and-effect diagram like the one below. As you read, fill in the chart with the causes and effects discussed in the section.

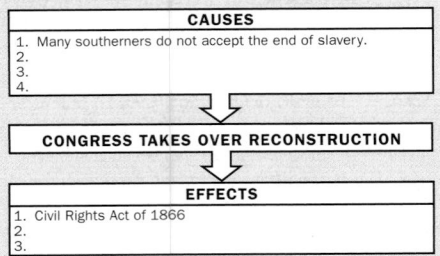

CAUSES
1. Many southerners do not accept the end of slavery.
2.
3.
4.

CONGRESS TAKES OVER RECONSTRUCTION

EFFECTS
1. Civil Rights Act of 1866
2.
3.

Setting the Scene For many African Americans, the initial surge of joy at gaining freedom quickly faded as they realized how many obstacles stood between them and true equality. Defeat in war had not changed the fact that white people still dominated southern society. As one white Georgian noted:

❝ [The freedman] has no land; he can make no crops. . . . He can scarcely get work anywhere but in the rice-fields and cotton plantations. . . . What sort of freedom is that?❞

Under Johnson's plan for Reconstruction, former Confederates were pardoned, state governments were restored, and the white leaders of those governments acted quickly to pass laws that severely restricted African Americans' newfound freedoms. These laws were known collectively as black codes.

Black Codes

One by one, southern states met Johnson's Reconstruction demands and were restored to the Union. The first order of business in these new, white-run governments was to enact **black codes,** laws that restricted freedmen's rights. The black codes established virtual slavery with provisions such as these:

Curfews Generally, black people could not gather after sunset.

Vagrancy laws Freedmen convicted of vagrancy—that is, not working—could be fined, whipped, or sold for a year's labor.

Labor contracts Freedmen had to sign agreements in January for a year of work. Those who quit in the middle of a contract often lost all the wages they had earned.

Land restrictions Freed people could rent land or homes only in rural areas. This restriction forced them to live on plantations.

VIEWING HISTORY According to Florida's black codes, a freedman without visible means of support could be fined. If the fine was not paid, the freedman's services could be auctioned off, as shown here. **Drawing Conclusions** *How does this photograph support the claim that black codes established virtual slavery?*

RESOURCE DIRECTORY

Teaching Resources
Guided Reading and Review booklet, p. 51

Technology
Section Reading Support Transparencies
Guided Reading Audiotapes (English/Spanish), Ch. 12
Student Edition on Audio CD, Ch. 12
Prentice Hall Presentation Pro CD-ROM, Ch. 12
Companion Web site, www.phschool.com

The Fourteenth Amendment

Southern defiance of Reconstruction enraged northern Republicans in Congress who blamed President Johnson for southern Democrats' return to power. Determined to bypass Johnson and put an end to his Reconstruction plan, Congress used one of its greatest tools: the power to amend the Constitution.

In early 1866, Congress passed a Civil Rights Act that outlawed the black codes. Johnson vetoed the measure. As President, Johnson was head of the Republican Party. Yet instead of leading congressional Republicans, he often found himself at odds with them. As an unelected former Democrat, Johnson had no real mandate to govern. (A mandate is voter approval of a politician's policies that is implied when he or she wins an election.) Lack of a mandate greatly limited Johnson's ability to influence Congress.

Congress overrode the President's veto. Then it took further action. Concerned that courts might strike down the Civil Rights Act, Congress decided to build equal rights into the Constitution. In June 1866, Congress passed the **Fourteenth Amendment,** which was ratified by the states in 1868. The amendment was a turning point, and its effects have echoed throughout American history. The amendment states:

> **KEY DOCUMENTS** " All persons born or naturalized in the United States . . . are citizens of the United States and of the State wherein they reside. No State shall make or enforce any law which shall abridge the privileges or immunities of citizens of the United States; nor shall any State deprive any person of life, liberty, or property, without due process of law; nor deny to any person within its jurisdiction the equal protection of the laws. . . . "
>
> —Fourteenth Amendment, Section 1

Radical Reconstruction

The congressional Republicans who drafted the Fourteenth Amendment consisted of two major groups. One group was the Radical Republicans. Radicals were small in number but increasingly influential. Most Republicans, however, saw themselves as moderates. In politics, a moderate is someone who supports the mainstream views of the party, not the more extreme positions.

Moderates and Radicals both opposed Johnson's Reconstruction policies, opposed the spread of black codes, and favored the expansion of the Republican Party in the South. But moderates were less enthusiastic over the Radicals' goal of granting African Americans their **civil rights,** citizens' personal liberties guaranteed by law, such as voting rights and equal treatment. (See Focus on Government.) Racial inequality was still common in the North, and moderates did not want to impose stricter laws on the South than those in the North.

The North Grows Impatient This reluctance to grant civil rights began to dissolve in early 1866, as word spread of new violence against African Americans. In April, the famous Civil War nurse Clara Barton gave graphic testimony in Congress about injured black victims she had treated. During the next three months, white rioters went on rampages against African Americans in Memphis, Tennessee; New Orleans, Louisiana; and New York City. White police sometimes joined in the stabbings, shootings, and hangings that killed hundreds.

Focus on GOVERNMENT

Civil Rights The rights to which every citizen is entitled.

The Historical Context The first Civil Rights Act, in 1866, guaranteed citizenship to African Americans. The second, in 1875, guaranteed them equal rights in public places. More fundamentally, in 1868, the Fourteenth Amendment made protection of civil rights part of the Constitution.

The Concept Today Violations of African Americans' civil rights continued and even increased following Reconstruction. Nearly a century later, the civil rights movement of the 1950s and 1960s fought to erase laws that discriminated against African Americans. Today it is illegal to discriminate on the basis of race.

READING CHECK
How did moderate Republicans in Congress differ from the Radical Republicans?

LESSON PLAN

Focus Explain that once southern state governments were reestablished under Johnson's plan, they began to undermine the plan. Ask students what southern states did to undermine Reconstruction. How did Congress respond?

Instruct Discuss how Republicans were able to bring radical political and social changes to the South. Ask students why Congress wanted to take over Reconstruction. How did the dissatisfaction of Congress with Johnson eventually lead to his impeachment? What was Congress hoping to accomplish by passing the Fourteenth and Fifteenth Amendments? What impact did the Fifteenth Amendment have on Reconstruction legislatures?

Assess/Reteach What was the intention of Congress in passing the Fourteenth Amendment? How did most members of Congress in the years just after the Civil War probably feel about black codes?

ACTIVITY
Connecting with Government

The phrases "due process" and "equal protection of the laws" in the Fourteenth Amendment are the foundations upon which many civil rights cases are argued today. Have students trace the historical development of the civil rights movement in the nineteenth century by supposing they are going to defend someone who has been discriminated against in employment, housing, education, or health care. Have them draw up the case to present to a court based on the Fourteenth Amendment. They should outline the case, explain the evidence, and lay out arguments based on due process and equal protection clauses. Students may then write up their cases or present them orally to the class. (**Logical/ Mathematical; Verbal/Linguistic**)

READING CHECK

Moderate Republicans did not want full civil rights for African Americans, and felt threatened by the desire of Radical Republicans for a level of racial equality exceeding that found in northern states.

CUSTOMIZE FOR ...
ESL

Ask a volunteer to read aloud the excerpt from the Fourteenth Amendment on this page. Then have students take turns summarizing each sentence in the passage in their own words.

✓ TEST PREPARATION

Have students read the excerpt from the Fourteenth Amendment on this page and then complete the sentence below.

The word abridge in the passage means—

 A enforce.
 Ⓑ take away.
 C connect.
 D grant.

MAP SKILLS President Lincoln had hoped to restore southern state governments to "successful operation, with order prevailing and the Union reestablished," by December 1865. Under Radical Republican rule, however, this did not happen for more than a decade. Because of its adherence to Congressional demands, Tennessee was the only southern state not placed under northern military rule. **Place** *(a) Which state was the first to rejoin the Union? (b) How do you think southerners reacted to military rule by northern generals?*

Radical Rule of the South

Military District and Commander	
	General Phillip Sheridan
	General Edward Ord
	General John Pope
	General Daniel Sickles
	General John Schofield
(1868)	Date of readmission to Union

Senator Charles Sumner of Massachusetts (top) and Thaddeus Stevens, a Congressman from Pennsylvania, were both leading spokesmen for the Radical Republicans in their fight to win civil rights for African Americans.

Despite public outrage against the brutality, Johnson continued to oppose equal rights for African Americans. In the 1866 congressional elections, he gave speeches urging states not to ratify the Fourteenth Amendment. Angry northern voters responded by sweeping Radical Republicans into Congress. Now, Radicals could put their own Reconstruction plans into action.

Strict Laws Imposed Calling for "reform, not revenge," Radicals in Congress passed the Reconstruction Act of 1867. Historians note that this was indeed a "radical" act in American history. These are its key provisions:

1. It put the South under military rule, dividing it into five districts, each governed by a northern general. (See the map on this page.)
2. It ordered southern states to hold new elections for delegates to create new state constitutions.
3. It required states to allow all qualified male voters, including African Americans, to vote in the elections.
4. It temporarily barred those who had supported the Confederacy from voting.
5. It required southern states to guarantee equal rights to all citizens.
6. It required the states to ratify the Fourteenth Amendment.

Congress and the President The stage was now set for a showdown that pitted President Johnson against two powerful Radical Republicans in Congress. Massachusetts Senator Charles Sumner, a founder of the Republican Party, was a passionate abolitionist who sought voting rights for black Americans. In the House, Johnson faced Thaddeus Stevens, a Pennsylvania congressman with a stern face and a personality to match. Stevens led the charge that threatened to bring down Johnson's presidency.

At face value, the contest was a test of wills between the President and his congressional adversaries. Yet it was also a power struggle between the legislative and executive branches of government, a test of the system of checks and balances established by the Constitution.

A Power Struggle The crisis began in early 1868, when Johnson tried to fire Secretary of War Edwin Stanton, a Lincoln appointee. Johnson wanted Stanton removed because, under the new Reconstruction Act, Stanton, a friend of the Radicals, would preside over military rule of the South.

The firing of Stanton directly challenged the Tenure of Office Act just passed by Congress in 1867. The act placed limits on the President's power to hire and fire government officials. Under the Constitution, the President must seek Senate approval for candidates to fill certain jobs, such as Cabinet posts.

The Tenure of Office Act demanded that the Senate approve the firing of those officials as well, thereby limiting the President's power to create an administration to his own liking. The act also took away the President's constitutional powers as commander in chief of the armed forces.

Johnson Is Impeached Led by the fiery Stevens, the House found that Johnson's firing of Stanton was unconstitutional. On February 24, 1868, House members voted 126 to 47 to **impeach** him—to charge him with wrongdoing in office. The House drafted 11 articles of impeachment, including violation of the Tenure of Office Act and bringing "into disgrace, ridicule, hatred, contempt, and reproach the Congress of the United States." Johnson became the first President in United States history to be impeached.

As called for by the Constitution, the Senate tried President Andrew Johnson for "high crimes and misdemeanors." Chief Justice Salmon P. Chase presided over the proceedings. If two thirds of the senators were to vote for conviction, Johnson would become the only President ever removed from office. The historic vote took place on May 16, 1868. When all the "ayes" and "nays" were counted, Johnson had escaped by the closest of margins: one vote. The crisis set the precedent that only the most serious crimes, and not merely a partisan dispute with Congress, could remove a President from office.

Grant Is Elected President Johnson, as the saying goes, "won the battle but lost the war." He served the remaining months of his term, but with no mandate and no real power. Rejected by the party that had never really embraced him, Johnson went back to Tennessee and regained his Senate seat—as a Democrat.

In the 1868 election, Republicans chose a trusted candidate who was one of their own: the victorious Civil War general, Ulysses S. Grant. In a close race, Grant beat Democrat Horatio Seymour, former governor of New York. Now, Congress and the President were allies, not enemies.

The Fifteenth Amendment

Across the South, meanwhile, freedmen were beginning to demand the rights of citizenship: to vote, to hold public office, to serve on juries, and to testify in court. In a letter to the Tennessee constitutional convention, Nashville freedmen eloquently presented the case for black voting rights:

> 66 If [freedmen] are good law-abiding citizens, praying for its [the nation's] prosperity, rejoicing in its progress, paying its taxes, fighting its battles, making its farms, mines, work-shops and commerce more productive, why deny them the right to have a voice in the election of its rulers? 99
> —The "black citizens of Nashville," January 9, 1865

The letter received no known response. Yet African Americans, and their supporters in Congress, pressed on.

President Johnson was the first President to be impeached by the House of Representatives. The Senate found Johnson innocent, and he was not removed from office.

COMPARING PRIMARY SOURCES
Voting Rights for African Americans

The question of whether to extend voting rights to African Americans was hotly debated in the 1860s.
Analyzing Viewpoints Compare the main arguments made by the two writers.

In Favor of Voting Rights
"If impartial suffrage is excluded in rebel States, then every one of them is sure to send a solid rebel representative delegation to Congress, and cast a solid rebel electoral vote. They . . . would always elect the President and control Congress. . . . I am for negro suffrage in every rebel state. If it be just, it should not be denied; if it be necessary, it should be adopted; if it is a punishment to traitors, they deserve it."
—Speech by Thaddeus Stevens, Radical Republican, January 3, 1867

Opposed to Voting Rights
"Most of the whites are disenfranchised [not legally able to vote] and ineligible for office, whilst the Negroes are [granted] the right of voting. The political power is therefore thrown into the hands of a mass of human beings who, having just emerged from a state of servitude [slavery], are ignorant of the forms of government and totally unfit to exercise this, the highest privilege of a free people."
—Henry William Ravenel, South Carolina planter, journal entry for February 24, 1867

Chapter 12 Section 2 • **433**

BIOGRAPHY

**Blanche K. Bruce
1841–1898**

A boy born into slavery in 1841 could expect little more than a life of servitude. Blanche K. Bruce was more fortunate than some. Growing up in Virginia and Missouri, he shared a tutor with his master's son. Later he attended Oberlin College in Ohio, until his money ran out. Bruce then moved to Mississippi and began recruiting Republicans from among freedmen on the plantations. In 1871 he ran for sheriff of Bolivar County, Mississippi. Bruce won the sheriff's post, and later held other government jobs as well. As a public servant, he worked to ease racial and political tensions, earning respect from Radical and moderate Republicans—even white planters. In 1874 Bruce won election to the United States Senate.

READING CHECK
How did the Fifteenth Amendment influence the composition of southern state legislatures?

In February 1869, at the peak of Radical power, Congress passed the **Fifteenth Amendment** to the Constitution. It stated that no citizen may be denied the right to vote "by the United States or by any State on account of race, color, or previous condition of servitude." Ratified in March 1870, the Fifteenth Amendment was one of the enduring legacies of Reconstruction.

The Supreme Court added its weight to the federal Reconstruction effort in 1869. In *Texas* v. *White,* the Court ruled that it was illegal for any state to secede from the Union. The case also upheld Congress's right to restructure southern governments. The ruling added new support for federal power over states' rights.

The First Votes   Even before the Fifteenth Amendment was ratified, the military had begun to register freedmen under the Reconstruction Act of 1867. Nearly 735,000 African Americans joined the voting rolls and their electoral power transformed politics in the South.

In 1867 and 1868, voters in southern states chose delegates to draft new state constitutions. Nearly 80 percent of the newly registered African American voters went to the polls, while most registered white voters did not participate. As a result, one quarter of the more than 1,000 delegates elected to the ten state conventions were black. In two states where African Americans outnumbered whites, Louisiana and South Carolina, voters chose majority-black delegations.

These integrated conventions wrote radical new constitutions for their states. Provisions in the new constitutions guaranteed the civil rights of all residents, opened political office to individuals without regard to wealth, and set up a system of public schools and orphanages. Ten Reconstruction state governments quickly adopted the new constitutions.

Electing Black Leaders   In 1870, with federal troops stationed across the South and with the Fifteenth Amendment in place, southern black men proudly voted in legislative elections for the first time. Most voted Republican, while many angry white voters again stayed home.

The results were dramatic. Before the election, African American voters made up a majority in five states—Alabama, Florida, Louisiana, Mississippi, and South Carolina—and a substantial minority in the other states undergoing Reconstruction. The unique circumstances of the election swept Republicans, including hundreds of freedmen, into public office in the South.

More than 600 African Americans were elected to state legislatures. However, African Americans remained the minority in nearly every state house in the South. The sole exception was South Carolina, where black legislators controlled the lower house and even, for a short time, the state senate. Individual black leaders could rise to positions of power in state government through alliances with white Republicans.

Louisiana gained a black governor, P.B.S. Pinchback, who had settled in that state after fighting for the Union during the Civil War. During Reconstruction, Pinchback had served as a state senator and eventually became lieutenant governor and then governor in 1872.

Integrating the Capitol   The extension of the vote to freedmen led to the election of the first African Americans to the House of Representatives. Despite resistance from other representatives, their number gradually rose to eight by 1875.

In 1870, Hiram Revels of Mississippi became the first African American elected to the Senate. Four years later, Mississippi's state legislature sent to the Senate a former slave, Blanche K. Bruce. (See American Biography.) Louisiana chose P.B.S. Pinchback to represent it in the Senate, but other senators voted not to seat him in 1876. By that time, the climate in Washington, D.C., and the southern states had begun to shift against African American legislators.

A northerner's carpetbag

The Republican South

During Radical Reconstruction, the Republican Party was a mixture of people who had little in common but a desire to prosper in the postwar South. This bloc of voters included freedmen and two other groups.

Carpetbaggers Northern Republicans who moved to the postwar South became known as **carpetbaggers.** Southerners gave them this insulting nickname, which referred to a type of cheap suitcase made from carpet scraps. The name implied that these northerners had stuffed some clothes into a carpetbag and rushed in to profit from southern misery.

Carpetbaggers were often depicted as greedy men seeking to grab power or make a fast buck. Certainly the trainloads of northerners who disembarked in southern cities included some profiteers and swindlers. Yet historians point out that most carpetbaggers were honest, educated men. They included former union soldiers, black northerners, Freedmen's Bureau officials, businessmen, clergy, and political leaders.

Scalawags In the postwar South, to be white and a southerner and a Republican was to be seen as a traitor. Southerners had an unflattering name for white southern Republicans as well: **scalawag,** originally a Scottish word meaning "scrawny cattle." Some scalawags were former Whigs who had opposed secession. Some were small farmers who resented the planter class. Still others were former planters. Many scalawags, but not all, were poor.

Many southern whites, resenting the power of freedmen, carpetbaggers, and scalawags, criticized the Reconstruction governments as corrupt and incompetent. In reality, Reconstruction legislatures included honest men and dishonest men, qualified politicians and incompetent ones, literate men and a few illiterate ones. Today, most historians agree that these officials were no worse and no better than officials in other regions of the country at that time.

Section 2 Assessment

READING COMPREHENSION

1. Why were northern Republicans in Congress enraged by the **black codes** and the reports of violence against African Americans?

2. How did the moderate and Radical Republicans in Congress disagree over African American **civil rights?**

3. Who were the **carpetbaggers** and the **scalawags?**

CRITICAL THINKING AND WRITING

4. **Drawing Conclusions** How was the impeachment of Andrew Johnson a test of the Constitution's system of checks and balances?

5. **Comparing Points of View** Describe the gains made by African Americans under Radical Reconstruction governments in the South. How did white Democrats perceive Radical rule?

 **Take It to the NET**

Activity: Drawing a Political Cartoon Learn more about southerners' perceptions of carpetbaggers, and then draw your own cartoon of a carpetbagger. Use the links provided in the *America: Pathways to the Present* area of the following Web site for help in completing this activity.
www.phschool.com

Chapter 12 • Section 2 435

Reading Comprehension

1. Black codes created virtual slavery, rather than freedom and equality. The hypocrisy of these codes exemplified southern defiance of Reconstruction, as did incidents of violence in which African Americans were killed or wounded.

2. Moderates were less eager to support the Radicals' goal of granting civil rights to African Americans. Racial inequality in the North was still common, and moderates did not want to impose stricter laws on the South than those in the North.

3. Carpetbaggers were northern Republicans who moved to the postwar South. The nickname implied that these northerners had rushed in to profit from southern misery. Scalawags were white southern Republicans who, at the time, were viewed as traitors.

Critical Thinking and Writing

4. Congress used its constitutionally granted power to impeach a President who had been accused of acting unconstitutionally.

5. Answers may include the following: end of black codes; granting of civil rights, such as voting and equal treatment; ratification of the Fourteenth Amendment; election to public office. Southern white Democrats despised the Reconstruction governments. They felt that carpetbaggers and scalawags were the corrupt representatives of those governments, and that freedmen had been given too much power and protection.

 **Take It to the NET**

Illustrations should show the carpetbaggers' exploitation of the defeated South.

Birth of the "New South"

SECTION OBJECTIVES

1. Find out how farming in the South changed after the Civil War.
2. Explore how the growth of cities and industry began to change the South's economy after the war.
3. Learn how money designated for Reconstruction projects was used.

BELLRINGER

Warm-Up Activity Ask students to think about the term *economic reorganization*. What do they suppose it means? Ask students if they know of any countries that have undergone economic reorganization in the last decade.

Activating Prior Knowledge Ask students to consider the types of people who might be drawn to help rebuild the South. Would it be likely that their interests would be mainly for the good of society, for their own personal gain, or both?

READING STRATEGY

Have students read the Main Idea on this page. Ask them to rewrite it as a question. As they read, have them take notes that help answer that question and that help them support a point of view on one of the social studies issues or events described in the section.

CAPTION ANSWERS

Viewing Fine Art Similarities: the great size of the cotton fields is clear. The facial expressions are also very similar between the two illustrations. Differences: in the photo, the whole family is present in the field; the painting only shows two women. The dirt and dust that can be seen on each family member's clothing in the photo conveys the difficulty of the work.

READING FOCUS

- How did farming in the South change after the Civil War?
- How did the growth of cities and industry begin to change the South's economy after the war?
- How was the money designated for Reconstruction projects used?

MAIN IDEA

The end of slavery brought about new patterns of agriculture in the South, while expansion of cities and industry led to limited economic growth.

KEY TERMS

sharecropping
tenant farming
infrastructure

TAKING NOTES

Copy the chart below. As you read, fill in details about economic changes that occurred in the South during Reconstruction.

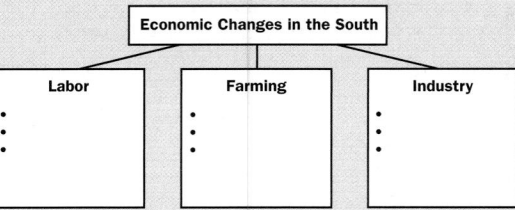

Economic Changes in the South

Labor	Farming	Industry
•	•	•
•	•	•
•	•	•

Setting the Scene Writing to a South Carolina newspaper late in 1865, a black soldier in the United States Army stated:

> ❝ We have been faithful in the field . . . and think that we ought to be considered as men, and allowed a fair chance in the race of life. It has been said that a black man can not make his own living, but give us opportunities and we will show the whites that we will not come to them for any thing. ❞
>
> —Black Union soldier

VIEWING FINE ART Despite emancipation, the cotton still needed to be picked. This painting by Winslow Homer (1876) shows young women in the fields, probably working just as their mothers had before the war, except for some small wages. **Making Comparisons** *Compare the details in this painting to the photograph on the next page.*

This demand for a "fair chance in the race of life" was echoed by freedmen across the South. For most of them, the key to that fair chance was land. "Give us our own land and we can take care of ourselves," said one freedman, "but without land, our old masters can hire us or starve us as they please."

As you read in Section 1, proposals to distribute formerly white-owned land to freedmen received little political support. Few freedmen had the money to buy their own land, and even those who did often found that whites refused to sell or rent land to them. As a result, most freedmen had little choice but to work the land of others. They soon discovered, in one freedman's words, that "No man can work another man's land [without getting] poorer and poorer every year."

One black family in Alabama learned this lesson the hard way. The Holtzclaw family worked on the cotton farm of a white planter. Every year at harvest time they received part of the cotton crop as payment for their work. Most years, however, the Holtzclaws' share of the harvest didn't earn them enough money to feed themselves. Some years the planter gave them nothing at all. To earn more money, Mrs. Holtzclaw worked as a cook, while Mr. Holtzclaw hauled logs at a sawmill for 60 cents a day. Their children waded knee-deep in swamps gathering anything edible. This was not the freedom they had hoped for.

Changes in Farming

The Holtzclaws were part of an economic reorganization in the "New South" of the 1870s. It was triggered by the ratification of the Thirteenth Amendment in 1865, which ended slavery and shook the economic foundations of the South.

The loss of slave labor raised grave questions for southern agriculture. Would cotton still be king? If so, who would work the plantations? Would freed people flee the South or stay? How would black emancipation affect the poor white laborers of the South? No one really knew.

Wanted: Workers Although the Civil War left southern plantations in tatters, the destruction was not permanent. Many planters had managed to hang on to their land, and others regained theirs after paying off their debt. Planters complained, however, that they couldn't find people willing to work for them. Nobody liked picking cotton in the blazing sun. It seemed too much like slavery. Workers often disappeared to look for better, higher-paying jobs. For instance, railroad workers in Virginia in the late 1860s earned $1.75 to $2 a day. Plantation wages came to 50 cents a day at best. Women in the fields earned as little as 6 cents a day. In simple terms, planters had land but no laborers, while freedmen had their own labor but no land. Out of these needs came new patterns of farming in the South.

Sharecropping The most common new farming arrangement was known as **sharecropping.** A sharecropping family, such as the Holtzclaws, farmed some portion of a planter's land. As payment, the family was promised a share of the crop at harvest time, generally one third or one half of the yield. The planter usually provided housing for the family.

Sharecroppers worked under close supervision and under the threat of harsh punishment. They could be fined for missing a single workday. After the harvest, some dishonest planters simply evicted the sharecroppers without pay. Others charged the families for housing and other expenses, so that the sharecroppers often wound up in debt at the end of the year. Since they could not leave before paying the debt, these sharecroppers were trapped on the plantation.

INTERPRETING DIAGRAMS
Whether white or black, most southern farmers remained poor in the years following the Civil War—as did this Florida family (below right), thought to be sharecroppers or tenant farmers. The chart (below left) shows the cycle of debt that poor families faced. **Drawing Conclusions** *How did farmers get caught in a cycle of debt?*

Sharecropping and the Cycle of Debt

1. Poor whites and freedmen have no jobs, no homes, and no money to buy land.

2. Poor whites and freedmen sign contracts to work a landlord's acreage in exchange for a part of the crop.

3. Landlord keeps track of the money that sharecroppers owe him for housing and food.

4. At harvest time, the sharecropper owes more to the landlord than his share of the crop is worth.

5. Sharecropper cannot leave the farm as long as he is in debt to the landlord.

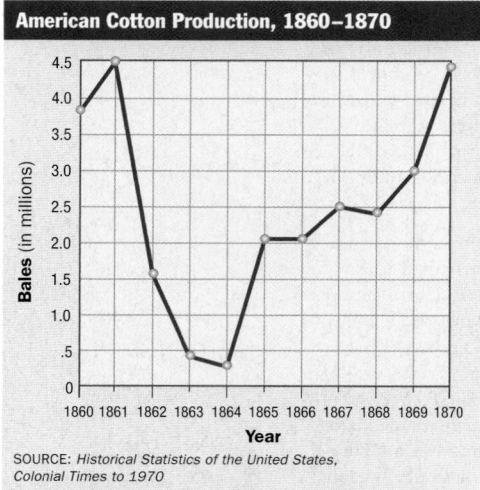

American Cotton Production, 1860–1870

SOURCE: *Historical Statistics of the United States, Colonial Times to 1970*

INTERPRETING GRAPHS
Cotton production was the South's main economic activity until 1930. **Making Inferences** *What accounts for the drop in production in the middle of this graph?*

READING CHECK
In what ways did the end of slavery change agriculture in the South?

ACTIVITY

Connecting with Economics

Select students to take the roles of the following: sharecropper, tenant farmer, merchant. Have them tell one another about their situations and compare their lives. How are they similar? How are they different? Each group might also discuss how they would like to improve their situations. You might also suggest that groups present their situations, and then have them take questions from the class. **(Verbal/Linguistic)**

BACKGROUND

Recent Scholarship

The story of Reconstruction for African Americans is a story of 4 million people who experienced freedom only to find that freedom had its limitations. Nonetheless, they persevered. Generally, their stories are similar. Those who left rural life and farming traveled to southern urban centers, such as Atlanta, Georgia. In *To 'Joy My Freedom: Southern Black Women's Lives and Labors After the Civil War,* Tera W. Hunter details the individual stories of newly free African American women who moved to Atlanta. Atlanta was a key city in the South after the Civil War because it became the symbol in the New South of urbanization and industrial growth. And black women are key to understanding the African American community because their lives, work, and sacrifices informed the activities of the men, children, and other women in their communities.

READING CHECK
Sharecropping and tenant farming by emancipated African Americans and poor whites allowed destitute planters to get their land worked. Cash crops became the focus. Some former slaves found higher-paying non-agricultural jobs.

CAPTION ANSWERS

Interpreting Graphs The Civil War.

Tenant Farming If a sharecropper saved enough money, he might try **tenant farming.** Like sharecroppers, tenant farmers did not own the land they farmed. Unlike sharecroppers, however, tenant farmers paid to rent the land, just as you might rent an apartment today. Tenants chose which crops to plant and when and how much to work. As a result, the tenant farmers had a higher social status than sharecroppers.

The Holtzclaws managed to move from sharecropping to tenant farming. They rented 40 acres of land. They bought a mule, a horse, and a team of oxen. William Holtzclaw was a child at the time. "We were so happy at the prospects of owning a wagon and a pair of mules, and having only our father for boss, that we shouted and leaped for joy," he later recalled.

Effects on the South Changes in farming during Reconstruction affected the long-term health of the South's economy in several important ways:

Changes in the labor force Before the Civil War, 90 percent of the South's cotton was harvested by slaves. By 1875, white laborers, mostly tenant farmers, picked 40 percent of the crop.

Emphasis on cash crops Sharecropping and tenant farming encouraged planters to grow cash crops, such as cotton, tobacco, and sugar cane, rather than food crops. The South's postwar cotton production soon surpassed prewar levels. As a result of the focus on cash crops, the South had to import much of its food.

Cycle of debt By the end of Reconstruction, rural poverty was deeply rooted in the South, among blacks and whites alike. Both groups remained in a cycle of debt, in which this year's profits went to pay last year's bills. The Southern Homestead Act of 1866 attempted to break that cycle by offering low-cost land to southerners, black or white, who would farm it. By 1874, black farmers in Georgia owned 350,000 acres. Still, most landless farmers could not afford to participate in the land-buying program. In the cotton states, only about one black family in 20 owned land after a decade of Reconstruction.

Rise of merchants Tenant farming created a new class of wealthy southerners: the merchants. Throughout the South, stores sprang up around plantations to sell supplies on credit. "We have stores at almost every crossroad," a journalist observed. By 1880, the South had more than 8,000 rural stores. Some merchants were honest; others were not. Landlords frequently ran their own stores and forced their tenants to buy there at high prices.

After four years of tenant farming, the Holtzclaws watched as creditors carted away everything they owned. "They came and took our corn and, finally, the vegetables from our little garden, as well as the chickens and the pig," Holtzclaw said. The family had no choice but to return to sharecropping.

Cities and Industry

Southerners who visited the North after the Civil War were astounded at how industrialized the North had become. The need for large-scale production of war supplies had turned small factories into big industries that dominated the North's economy. Industrialization had produced a new class of wage earners.

RESOURCE DIRECTORY

Teaching Resources
Learning with Documents booklet (Primary Source Activity) *A Bleak Future for Freedmen,* p. 17

Other Print Resources
Nystrom *Atlas of Our Country* *Settling the West,* pp. 28–29

It had ignited city growth and generated wealth. Could all this happen in the South?

Some southern leaders saw a unique opportunity for their region. They urged the South to build a new, industrialized economy. One of the pro-business voices was that of Henry Grady, editor of the *Atlanta Constitution*. He called for a "New South" of growing cities and thriving industries.

The Growth of Cities   Atlanta, the city so punished by Sherman's army, took Grady's advice. Only months after the war, the city was on its way to becoming a major metropolis of the South, as one observer noted:

> 66 *A new city is springing up with marvelous rapidity. The narrow and irregular and numerous streets are alive from morning till night . . . with a never-ending throng of . . . eager and excited and enterprising men, all bent on building and trading and swift fortune-making.* 99
> —Visitor to Atlanta, 1865

A major focus of Reconstruction, and one of its greatest successes, was the rebuilding and extension of southern railroads. By 1872, southern railroads were totally rebuilt and about 3,300 miles of new track laid, a 40 percent increase. Railroads turned southern villages into towns, and towns into cities where businesses and trade could flourish. Commerce and population rose not only in Atlanta, but also in Richmond, Nashville, Memphis, Louisville, Little Rock, Montgomery, and Charlotte. On the western frontier, the Texas towns of Dallas, Houston, and Fort Worth were on the rise.

Limits of Industrial Growth   Despite these changes, Reconstruction did not transform the South into an industrialized, urban region like the North. Most southern factories did not make finished goods such as furniture. They handled only the early, less profitable stages of manufacturing, such as producing lumber or pig iron. These items were shipped north to be made into finished products and then sold.

Most of the South's postwar industrial growth came from cotton mills. New factories began to spin and weave cotton into undyed fabric. The value of cotton mill production in South Carolina rose from about $713,000 in 1860 to nearly $3 million by 1880. However, the big profits went to northern companies that dyed the fabric and sold the finished product.

Funding Reconstruction

The Republicans who led Congress agreed with southern legislatures on the importance of promoting business. The strong conviction that the growth of business would bring better times for everyone was called the "gospel of prosperity." It guided the Reconstruction efforts of Congress and the Reconstruction legislatures throughout the 1870s.

Raising Money   In a sense, the postwar South was one giant business opportunity. The region's **infrastructure,** the public property and services that a society uses, had to be almost completely rebuilt. That included roads, bridges, canals, railroads, and telegraph lines. In addition to the rebuilding effort, some states used Reconstruction funds

San Antonio, Texas, prospered following the Civil War as a mercantile and cattle center. This 1872 photo shows a view of the east side of Main Plaza.

Focus on
CITIZENSHIP

Achievements of Black Legislators
Thomas E. Miller defended the work of the South Carolina legislature in which he served: "We had built school

houses, established charitable institutions . . . rebuilt bridges and reestablished ferries. In short, we had reconstructed the State and placed it upon the road to prosperity." The lithograph above shows seven African Americans who were elected to the United States Congress.

Chapter 12 • Section 3   **439**

Chapter 12 Section 3 • **439**

Reading Comprehension

1. The work too closely resembled slavery; workers often left to look for better jobs and more money.

2. Tenant farmers rented land from a planter, chose which crops to plant, and decided how much to work, whereas sharecroppers farmed a portion of a planter's land in exchange for a share of the crop at harvest, and, oftentimes, housing.

3. As railroads were rebuilt in the South, and new track vastly extended, towns and villages were transformed into cities, trade and businesses flourished, allowing an increase in commerce and population.

4. Southern factories often did not make finished goods, but rather focused on the early stages of manufacturing. Profits from the cotton industry shifted to northern companies. Cotton from southern mills went north to facilities that dyed the fabric and sold the finished product.

5. Congress, private investors, and the levying of heavy taxes on individuals.

Critical Thinking and Writing

6. To increase and ensure profits; the subsequent need to import food into southern states would create further expense for those living in poverty.

7. Answers will vary. Students may want to mention that southern cities like Atlanta were devastated by the war.

Take It to the NET

Invite students to take a Virtual Field Trip at **www.phschool.com**

INTERPRETING POLITICAL CARTOONS This cartoon, which appeared in *Harper's Weekly* in 1876, poked fun at President Grant's promise to "get to the bottom" of the corruption in government. **Making Inferences** *What does the cartoon imply about Grant's ability to investigate and put an end to corruption?*

to expand services to their citizens. For instance, following the North's example, all southern states created public school systems by 1872.

Reconstruction legislatures poured money into infrastructure. Some of the money came from Congress and from private investors. The rest, however, was raised by levying heavy taxes on individuals, many of whom were still deeply in debt from the war. White southerners, both wealthy and poor, resented this added financial burden. Spending by Reconstruction legislatures added another $130 million to southern debt. What further angered southerners was evidence that much of this big spending for infrastructure was being lost to corruption.

Corruption Today, corruption in government and business is vigorously uncovered and prosecuted. That was not the case a century ago. During Reconstruction, enormous sums of money changed hands rapidly in the form of fraudulent loans and grants. Participants in such schemes included blacks and whites, Republicans and Democrats, southerners and northern carpetbaggers. "You are mistaken if you suppose that all the evils . . . result from the carpetbaggers and negroes," a Louisiana man wrote to a northern fellow Democrat. Democrats and Republicans cooperated "whenever anything is proposed which promises to pay," he observed. The South Carolina legislature even gave $1,000 to the Speaker of the House to cover his loss on a horse race!

Scandal and corruption also reached to the White House. Early in Grant's second term, a scandal emerged involving the Credit Mobilier Company. Credit Mobilier had been set up by the owners of the Union Pacific Railroad to build their portion of the transcontinental railroad westward from Omaha. The Union Pacific gave the Credit Mobilier enormous sums of federal money. While some of this money paid for work, much of it went into the pockets of the Union Pacific officers and politicians who were bribed into ignoring the fraud.

Section **3** Assessment

READING COMPREHENSION

1. Why did planters have trouble finding people to work for them?

2. How did **sharecropping** and **tenant farming** differ?

3. How did railroads contribute to the growth of cities?

4. Why was southern industrial growth limited?

5. What were the sources of funding for Reconstruction programs?

CRITICAL THINKING AND WRITING

6. **Predicting Consequences** Why did sharecropping and tenant farming encourage planters to grow cash crops rather than food crops? What impact might this have had on people living in poverty?

7. **Creating an Outline** Create an outline for an essay in which you explain why the physical reconstruction of the South was necessary.

Take It to the NET

Activity: Virtual Field Trip Visit the Levi Jordan Plantation in Brazoria County, Texas, and learn how freed African Americans working on this plantation adapted to life as tenant farmers and sharecroppers after the Civil War. Use the links provided in the *America: Pathways to the Present* area of the following Web site for help in completing this activity.
www.phschool.com

CAPTION ANSWERS

Interpreting Political Cartoons
President Grant is "in over his head," meaning he is unaware of the scope and magnitude of the corruption problem he has promised to address. From the number of papers and notes coming from the barrel, the cartoonist is suggesting that the corruption comes from all parts of the government.

RESOURCE DIRECTORY

Teaching Resources
Units 3/4 booklet
• Section 3 Quiz, p. 66
Guide to the Essentials
• Section 3 Summary, p. 65

Using Maps to Show Change Over Time

Historians compare maps to help them identify changes over time. One far-reaching change that took place after the Civil War was the breakup of Southern plantations. The maps below show 2,000 acres of land before and after the Civil War.

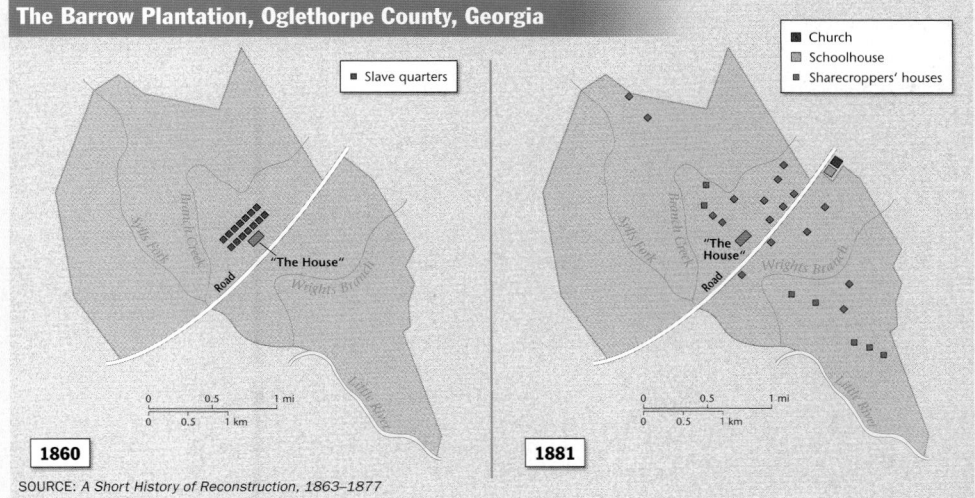

The Barrow Plantation, Oglethorpe County, Georgia

■ Slave quarters

■ Church
□ Schoolhouse
■ Sharecroppers' houses

1860

1881

SOURCE: *A Short History of Reconstruction, 1863–1877*

LEARN THE SKILL

Use the following steps to analyze maps for evidence of change over time:

1. **Identify the location and time periods of the maps.** Most maps are labeled with the location and subject. If a date is not included, historians can often determine the date based on the style and content of the map.

2. **Identify the subject of the maps.** Maps can include information about geographic features as well as man-made features, such as buildings and roads.

3. **Analyze the map key and scale.** The key identifies what different symbols and colors represent on the map. The scale helps you determine the actual distance between features shown on the map.

4. **Analyze the data on the maps.** Compare the data to draw conclusions about change over the time period the maps indicate. Also use what you already know about events in the time period.

PRACTICE THE SKILL

Answer the following questions:

1. **(a)** What specific area of land do both maps show? **(b)** What dates are given on the maps? How long a time period is represented? **(c)** Is there anything unusual about the style of the maps? Explain.

2. **(a)** What geographic features are shown on both maps? **(b)** What man-made features are shown on each map? Are they the same on both maps?

3. **(a)** According to the key, what do the red squares on the 1860 map represent? **(b)** According to the key, what do the blue squares on the 1881 map represent? **(c)** How did the mapmaker show the difference between a church and a schoolhouse on the 1881 map? **(d)** What do you think the label "The House" means on each map? **(e)** On the 1881 map, approximately how far is "The House" from any other dwelling?

4. **(a)** How has the location of dwellings on the plantation changed during this time period? **(b)** What type of dwelling has disappeared? **(c)** What type of dwelling has been added? **(d)** What other new buildings have been added? **(e)** Summarize the changes to this plantation over time. What historical events helped produce these changes?

APPLY THE SKILL

See the Chapter Review and Assessment for another opportunity to apply this skill.

Chapter 12   **441**

RESOURCE DIRECTORY

Teaching Resources
Skills for Life booklet, p. 14

Technology
Social Studies Skills Tutor CD-ROM
Interactive Practice in
• Geographic Literacy
• Critical Thinking and Reading
• Visual Analysis
• Communications

USING MAPS TO SHOW CHANGE OVER TIME

Focus Students compare two historical maps to identify changes in the cultural landscape over time.

Instruct Explain that historical maps provide information about the cultural, or human-made, traits of a place. Ask students to use visual evidence from the maps, along with information they already have about the time periods, to suggest at least one cultural change that may have taken place. Then ask students what a map of this same area might be likely to show today.

Extend See the Skills for Life activity in the Resource Directory below.

ANSWERS

PRACTICE THE SKILL

1. **(a)** The Barrow Plantation in Oglethorpe County, Georgia. **(b)** 1860 and 1881. 21 years. **(c)** The maps label "The House" on the map but use a key for other buildings. "The House" is not identified.

2. **(a)** Rivers and creeks. **(b)** 1860 map: Road, "The House," slave quarters; 1881 map: Road, "The House," church, schoolhouse, sharecroppers' houses. No.

3. **(a)** Slave quarters. **(b)** Sharecroppers' houses. **(c)** By color. **(d)** "The House" is the Barrow Plantation's main house, where the plantation owners lived. **(e)** Less than 1/8 mile (1/4 kilometer).

4. **(a)** In 1860 they were concentrated in a single area; by 1881 they had spread out across the entire plantation. **(b)** Slave quarters. **(c)** Sharecroppers' houses. **(d)** A church and a school. **(e)** The Civil War emancipated slaves, eliminating the need for slave quarters. By 1881 many former slaves had become sharecroppers and worked scattered plots of land.

Section 4 · The End of Reconstruction

READING FOCUS
- What tactics did the Ku Klux Klan use to spread terror throughout the South?
- Why did Reconstruction end?
- What were the major successes and failures of Reconstruction?

MAIN IDEA
In the 1870s, white Democrats regained power in the South, and public interest in Reconstruction declined.

KEY TERMS
Enforcement Act of 1870
solid South
Compromise of 1877

TAKING NOTES
Copy the web diagram below. As you read, fill in supporting details for each heading.

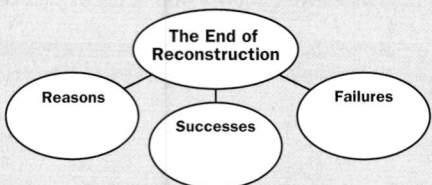

The End of Reconstruction — Reasons — Successes — Failures

Members of the Ku Klux Klan (pictured below) left miniature coffins like this, containing written death threats, at the doors of many freedmen and their white supporters.

Setting the Scene In 1866, six former Confederate soldiers living in Pulaski, Tennessee, decided to form a secret society. Someone suggested they name their group "Kuklos" (the Greek word for "circle"), and they voted to modify that to "Ku Klux Klan" (KKK). Members wore robes and masks and pretended to be the ghosts of Confederate soldiers, returned from the dead in search of revenge against the enemies of the South.

The Klan spread rapidly through the South, fueled by a blend of rage and fear over the Confederacy's defeat and toward the newly won freedom of black southerners. Klansmen pledged to "defend the social and political superiority" of whites against what they called the "aggressions of an inferior race." The membership consisted largely of ex-Confederate officials and plantation owners who had been excluded from politics. The group also attracted merchants, lawyers, and other professionals. While the Klan was supposed to be a secret society, most members' identities were well known in their communities.

In 1867, at a convention in Nashville, Tennessee, the Klan chose its first overall leader, or "grand wizard," Nathan Bedford Forrest. Before the war, Forrest had grown wealthy as a cotton planter and slave trader. During the war, he had become known as one of the Confederacy's most brilliant generals. He also had ordered the massacre of more than 300 black men, women, and children when his troops captured Fort Pillow, Tennessee, in 1864.

As Reconstruction proceeded, Klan violence intensified. Arkansas Klansmen killed more than 300 Republicans, including a United States congressman, in 1868 alone. That year Klansmen murdered 1,000 people in Louisiana. Fully half of the adult white male population of New Orleans belonged to the KKK.

Spreading Terror

During Radical Reconstruction, the Klan sought to eliminate the Republican Party in the South by intimidating Republican voters, both white and black. The Klan's long-term goal was to keep African Americans in the role of submissive laborers.

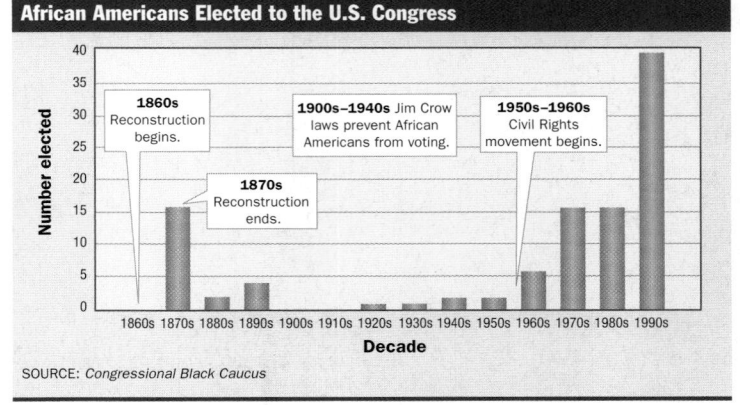

African Americans Elected to the U.S. Congress

1860s Reconstruction begins.

1870s Reconstruction ends.

1900s–1940s Jim Crow laws prevent African Americans from voting.

1950s–1960s Civil Rights movement begins.

SOURCE: *Congressional Black Caucus*

The Klan's terror tactics varied from place to place. Often, horsemen in long robes and hoods appeared suddenly at night, carrying guns and whips. They encircled the homes of their victims, and planted huge burning crosses in their yards. People were dragged from their homes and harassed, tortured, kidnapped, or murdered.

Anyone who didn't share the Klan's goals and hatreds could be a victim: carpetbaggers, scalawags, freedmen who had become prosperous—even those who had merely learned to read. With chilling frequency, black women went to claim the dead bodies of their husbands and sons.

The Federal Response The violence kindled northern outrage. At President Grant's request, Congress passed a series of anti-Klan laws in 1870 and 1871. The **Enforcement Act of 1870** banned the use of terror, force, or bribery to prevent people from voting because of their race. Other laws banned the KKK entirely and strengthened military protection of voters and voting places.

Using troops, cavalry, and the power of the courts, the government arrested and tried thousands of Klansmen. Within a year the KKK was virtually wiped out. Still, the thinly spread federal army could not be everywhere at once. As federal troops gradually withdrew from the South, black suffrage all but ended.

Reconstruction Ends

President Grant, who won reelection in 1872, continued to pursue the goals of Reconstruction, sometimes with energy. However, the widespread corruption in his administration reminded voters of all that was wrong with Reconstruction.

A Dying Issue By the mid-1870s, voters had grown weary of Republicans and their decade-long concern with Reconstruction. There were four main factors contributing to the end of Reconstruction:

Corruption Reconstruction legislatures, as well as Grant's administration, came to symbolize corruption, greed, and poor government.

The economy Reconstruction legislatures taxed and spent heavily, putting southern states deeper into debt. In addition, a nationwide economic

---

Focus on WORLD EVENTS

Alaska, the Midway Islands, and Mexico For the most part, Americans focused on rebuilding the nation during Reconstruction. Secretary of State William H. Seward, however, took a number of actions to expand the country's resources and trade. In 1866, Seward convinced the Senate to ratify his purchase of Alaska from Russia for $7.2 million. His opponents referred to Seward's purchase of Alaska's "walrus-covered icebergs" as "Seward's Folly." In an effort to expand trade with China, in 1867 Seward also annexed the Midway Islands, where coal-powered naval steamships could stop for refueling and repair on their voyages across the Pacific. Closer to home, Seward sent 50,000 American troops, who were already in Texas at the end of the Civil War, to Mexico to force the French to withdraw their troops from the country.

From the Archives of
AmericanHeritage®

Ku Klux Klan

In May 1867 the ex-Confederate general and guerrilla leader Nathan Bedford Forrest took his place as the first Grand Wizard in the recently formed Ku Klux Klan in Pulaski, Tennessee. As the 1868 elections approached, violence against former slaves hoping to vote became general throughout Tennessee. By the next spring, Grand Wizard Forrest oversaw an empire with toeholds in fourteen southern states. The Klan led riots against black suffragists in Mississippi, burned schools and whipped or lynched northern schoolteachers, and intimidated former slaves. Testifying before Congress in 1871, Forrest explained, "this organization was got up to protect the weak, with no political intention at all. . . ." Source: Nathan Ward, "The Time Machine," *American Heritage®* magazine, May/June 1992.

READING CHECK

The heavy taxes and corrupt public officials involved in Reconstruction were unpopular. The violence of the Ku Klux Klan was unsettling. President Rutherford B. Hayes ended the military occupation of southern states in the compromise settlement of the disputed presidential election of 1876.

MAP SKILLS In the tarnished election of 1876, the electoral votes in three states under federal control were disputed, but went to Hayes when he promised to end Reconstruction. **Location** *In which states were election results disputed?*

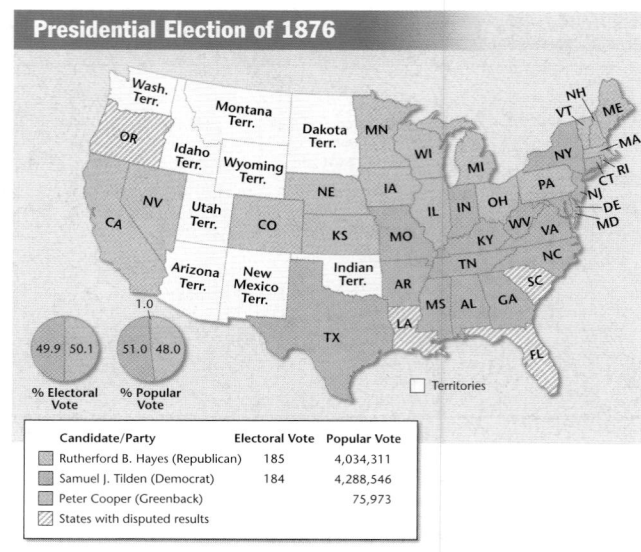

Presidential Election of 1876

Candidate/Party	Electoral Vote	Popular Vote
Rutherford B. Hayes (Republican)	185	4,034,311
Samuel J. Tilden (Democrat)	184	4,288,546
Peter Cooper (Greenback)		75,973
States with disputed results		

% Electoral Vote: 49.9 / 50.1
% Popular Vote: 51.0 / 48.0

downturn in 1873 diverted public attention from the movement for equal rights. In fact, northern voters had never fully supported the Radical Republicans' goal of racial equality.

Violence As federal troops withdrew from the South, some white Democrats were freer to use violence and intimidation to prevent freedmen from voting. This allowed white southerners to regain control of state governments.

The Democrats return to power The era of Republican control of the South was coming to a close. In 1872, the last ex-Confederates had been pardoned. They combined with other white southerners to form a new bloc of Democratic voters known as the **solid South.** Democrats of the solid South blocked many federal Reconstruction policies and reversed many reforms of the Reconstruction legislatures.

Supreme Court Limits Scope of Amendments The Supreme Court also played a role in bringing about the end of Reconstruction. In a series of cases, including the *Slaughterhouse Cases* in 1873, *United States* v. *Reese* in 1876, and *United States* v. *Cruikshank* in 1876, the Supreme Court narrowly interpreted the Fourteenth and Fifteenth amendments and placed the control of Americans' basic civil rights in the hands of the states. In short, the Court's decisions in these cases limited the federal government's ability to protect the civil and voting rights of African Americans.

READING CHECK
What factors contributed to the end of Reconstruction?

The Compromise of 1877 Reconstruction politics took a final, sour turn in the presidential election of 1876. In that election, Republican Rutherford B. Hayes lost the popular vote to Democrat Samuel Tilden, who had the support of the solid South. The electoral vote, however, was disputed. The map above shows the results.

Hayes claimed victory based partly on wins in Florida, Louisiana, and South Carolina. Those states were still under Republican and federal control. Democrats submitted another set of tallies showing Tilden as the winner in those

Successes and Failures of Reconstruction

Successes	Failures
Union is restored.	Many white southerners remain bitter toward the federal government and the Republican Party.
The South's economy grows and new wealth is created in the North.	The South is slow to industrialize.
Fourteenth and Fifteenth amendments guarantee African Americans the rights of citizenship, equal protection under the law, and suffrage.	After federal troops are withdrawn, southern state governments and terrorist organizations effectively deny African Americans the right to vote.
Freedmen's Bureau and other organizations help many black families obtain housing, jobs, and schooling.	Many black and white southerners remain caught in a cycle of poverty.
Southern states adopt a system of mandatory education.	Racist attitudes toward African Americans continue, in both the South and the North.

INTERPRETING TABLES
Until recently, many historians believed that Reconstruction was a dismal failure. Today most historians argue that the truth is more complex. The cartoon below shows President Hayes "plowing under" Reconstruction programs. **Drawing Conclusions** *Do you think Reconstruction was more of a success or a failure? Why?*

states, and thus in the presidential race. (The eligibility of one Republican elector from Oregon was also called into question.) Congress set up a special commission to resolve the election crisis. Not surprisingly, the commission, which included more Republicans than Democrats, named Hayes the victor. However, Democrats had enough strength in Congress to reject the commission's decision.

Finally the two parties made a deal. In what became known as the **Compromise of 1877,** the Democrats agreed to give Hayes the victory in the presidential election he had not clearly won. In return, the new President agreed to remove the remaining federal troops from southern states. He also agreed to support appropriations for rebuilding levees along the Mississippi River, and to give huge subsidies to southern railroads. The compromise opened the way for Democrats to regain control of southern politics and marked the end of Reconstruction.

Section 4 — Assessment

READING COMPREHENSION

1. Why did Congress pass the **Enforcement Act of 1870?**
2. What four factors contributed to the end of Reconstruction?
3. What was the **solid South?**
4. What was the **Compromise of 1877?** Why do you think the two parties made this compromise?

CRITICAL THINKING AND WRITING

5. **Drawing Conclusions** Do you agree with historian Samuel Eliot Morison, who said that "the North may have won the war, but the white South won the peace"?
6. **Writing an Opinion** What was the most significant success of Reconstruction? What was the most significant failure? Write an outline for an essay in which you state your opinions.

 Take It to the NET

Activity: Writing a News Article
Prepare a newspaper article about the election of 1876. Use the links provided in the *America: Pathways to the Present* area of the following Web site for help in completing this activity.
www.phschool.com

Reading Comprehension

1. It banned the use of terror, force, or bribery as methods of preventing people from voting on the basis of race.
2. Corruption, the economy, violence, and the Democratic return to power in the South.
3. A new bloc of Democratic voters who blocked many federal Reconstruction policies and reversed many reforms of the Reconstruction legislatures.
4. The disputed results of the election of 1876 led to the Compromise of 1877 in which Democrats agreed to give Hayes the victory in the presidential election. In return, Hayes agreed to remove the remaining federal troops from southern states, and to give huge subsidies to southern railroads. Tilden and the Democrats made this compromise to open the way for Democrats to regain control of southern politics and end Reconstruction.

Critical Thinking and Writing

5. Students who agree might point to the long interval between the end of the war and the attainment of true civil rights by African Americans in the South.
6. Successes: rebuilt Union, stimulated economy; amendments passed; education in South; jobs and housing for freedmen; failures: corruption, poverty, and debt remained; freedmen prevented from voting; concerns of farmers and women not met.

 **Take It to the NET**

Students should demonstrate knowledge of the controversial circumstances surrounding the 1876 election.

CAPTION ANSWERS

Interpreting Tables Answers will vary. Successes: the election of many African Americans to public office; African Americans were given rights they had never held under slavery. Failures: many white people ignored the rights newly granted to African Americans; many southern localities established "black codes," which returned African Americans to a position of near-slavery.

CUSTOMIZE FOR ...

Less Proficient Readers
Ulysses S. Grant was a very popular leader in wartime, but an unpopular President. Have students make two lists about Grant. In one, have them list actions by Grant that made him popular. In the other, have them list actions taken by Grant that made him unpopular.

✓ TEST PREPARATION

Have students read the section on the previous page called "The Democrats return to power," and then answer the question below.

What is the meaning of the phrase "solid South"?

A It refers to a group of southern states that supported Reconstruction.

Ⓑ It refers to a bloc of voters that opposed Reconstruction.

C It refers to a group of southern states that resisted rejoining the Union.

D This phrase refers to the heavy, claylike soil of many southern states.

REVIEWING KEY TERMS

Students should refer to the definitions of key terms in the chapter to write sentences that show an understanding of the Reconstruction era.

REVIEWING MAIN IDEAS

11. Reconstituting southern state governments, cycle of debt, and loss of labor on plantations.

12. Lincoln's plan was tougher on the South. He supported a 10 percent allegiance requirement.

13. They attempted to create a new social order in the South and gain equal rights as citizens.

14. Congress blamed Johnson for southern Democrats' return to power and the southern defiance of Reconstruction. Johnson violated the Tenure of Office Act.

15. Through Reconstruction efforts, a Supreme Court decision that upheld the right of Congress to restructure southern governments, and through the Republican votes of freedmen who were benefiting from the Fifteenth Amendment.

16. They guaranteed the civil rights of all residents, opened political office to individuals without regard to wealth, and set up a system of public schools and orphanages.

17. The South became more industrialized and had to adjust to a new labor system. Still, it remained largely a farming economy.

18. It ended with the Compromise of 1877, which created an understanding between Democrats and Republicans. Hayes removed federal troops from southern states and opened the way for Democrats to regain control of southern politics.

CRITICAL THINKING

19. (a) Reconstruction efforts helped to provide aid but sharecropping resulted in greater debt for farmers; (b) Former Confederates may have reluctantly accepted Reconstruction or turned to activities such as Klan membership; (c) Carpetbaggers benefited from southern poverty; (d) Much was accomplished despite the corruption and the blockage of policies by southern states.

446 • Chapter 12

---

creating a CHAPTER SUMMARY

Copy the chart (right) on a piece of paper, and then complete it by adding information about key legislation passed during Reconstruction. Some entries have been completed for you as examples.

For additional review and enrichment activities, see the interactive version of *America: Pathways to the Present*, available on the Web and on CD-ROM.

Major Reconstruction Legislation		
Date	**Legislation**	**Description**
1865	13th Amendment	Abolished slavery
1865, 1866	Freedmen's Bureau	Provided services for war refugees and newly freed people
1867	Reconstruction Acts	
1868	14th Amendment	
1870	15th Amendment	
1875	Civil Rights Act	

★ **Reviewing Key Terms**

For each of the terms below, write a sentence explaining how it relates to the post-Civil War period.

1. Reconstruction
2. pardon
3. black codes
4. impeach
5. carpetbagger
6. scalawag
7. sharecropping
8. tenant farming
9. infrastructure
10. solid South

★ **Reviewing Main Ideas**

11. Name the three major problems the South faced at the end of the Civil War. (Section 1)

12. How did Lincoln's plan for Reconstruction compare to Johnson's plan? (Section 1)

13. How did African Americans try to improve their lives after emancipation? (Section 1)

14. Why did Johnson and Congress clash over Reconstruction? (Section 2)

15. How did Republicans gain control of southern governments? (Section 2)

16. In what ways were the new state constitutions radical? (Section 2)

17. In what ways did the economy of the South change after the Civil War, and in what ways did it remain unchanged? (Section 3)

18. Why did Reconstruction end? (Section 4)

★ **Critical Thinking**

19. Comparing Points of View Evaluate Reconstruction from the point of view of (a) a black sharecropper, (b) an ex-Confederate, (c) a carpetbagger, (d) a Radical Republican.

20. Identifying Assumptions Congress accused President Johnson of abusing his presidential powers, and Johnson thought that Congress overstepped its authority in carrying out Radical Reconstruction. What differing assumptions led to these conclusions?

21. Recognizing Ideologies Why were the strong policies of Radical Reconstruction largely ineffective in changing the attitudes of white southerners toward African Americans?

22. Identifying Central Issues Refer to the political cartoon depicting corruption during Grant's presidency in Section 3. Conduct research to learn more about one of the scandals pictured in the cartoon, such as the Whiskey Fraud, Secretary of War W. W. Belknap's impeachment, or the Back Pay Grab. Write a summary of the scandal and explain its impact on Reconstruction.

CREATING A CHAPTER SUMMARY

Major Reconstruction Legislation

Date	Legislation	Description
1865	13th Amendment	Abolished slavery
1865, 1866	Freedman's Bureau	Provided services for war refugees and newly freed people
1867	Reconstruction Acts	Put the South under military rule, ordered these states to hold new elections, required states to allow all qualified males to vote, temporarily barred Confederacy supporters from voting, required southern states to guarantee equal rights to all citizens, required states to ratify the 14th Amendment
1868	14th Amendment	Established right of citizenship for all people born in the United States
1870	15th Amendment	Stated that no citizen would be denied the right to vote because of race, color, or previous condition of servitude
1875	Civil Rights Act	Stated that African Americans shall have unrestricted access to public places

★ Skills Assessment

Analyzing Political Cartoons ▶

23. This cartoon depicts President Grant riding in a carpetbag. (a) What does Grant represent? (b) What do the soldiers represent? (c) What does the woman represent?

24. State the central message of this cartoon.

Analyzing Primary Sources

Read this excerpt, and then answer the questions that follow.

> ❝ If [freedmen] are good law-abiding citizens, praying for its [the nation's] prosperity, rejoicing in its progress, paying its taxes, fighting its battles, making its farms, mines, work-shops and commerce more productive, why deny them the right to have a voice in the election of its rulers? ❞
> —the "black citizens of Nashville," January 9, 1865

25. Which statement best represents the meaning of the quotation?

   A Freedmen are responsible citizens.
   B Freedmen deserve the right to vote because they earn money for the country.
   C Freedmen deserve the right to vote because they are fulfilling the responsibilities of citizenship.
   D Freedmen deserve to rule themselves.

26. What is the most likely reason the writers never received a response?

   F White Tennesseans did not want freedmen to vote.
   G White Tennesseans did not want freedman to become citizens.
   H White Tennesseans thought freedmen should have economic rights, not political rights.
   J White Tennesseans had already guaranteed freedmen the right to vote.

Applying the Chapter Skill: *Comparing Maps Over Time*

27. Refer to the maps on page 441. If the years of the maps were not labeled, would you be able to tell which map showed the plantation in 1860, and which showed the land in 1881? Explain your answer.

ACTIVITIES

Writing to LEARN

Writing an Opinion
Should Congress have accepted Johnson's Reconstruction plan, which allowed white Democrats and ex-Confederates to rejoin the political system (through voting and office holding)? Should Congress have worked with white southerners to uphold civil rights for African Americans? What were the consequences of not allowing the defeated Democrats to participate in the political process?

Primary Source CD-ROM

Working With Primary Sources Find additional information related to Reconstruction on the *Exploring Primary Sources in the U.S. History CD-ROM* and use the selection(s) provided to complete the Chapter 12 primary source activity located in the *America: Pathways to the Present* area of the following Web site.
www.phschool.com

Take It to the NET

Chapter Self-Test As a review activity, take the Chapter 12 Self-Test in the *America: Pathways to the Present* area at the Web site listed below. The questions are designed to test your understanding of the chapter content.
www.phschool.com

Chapter 12 Assessment   447

---

20. Both sides assumed that the other was overstepping boundaries and should have its power limited.
21. White southerners believed African Americans were inferior and that the government was treating them better than whites, themselves, were being treated. Plantation owners resented the changes because they lost their workforce.
22. Answers will vary, but should include a detailed summary, supported by facts, of one of the following scandals: Whiskey Fraud had whiskey distillers avoiding high taxes by bribing government officials; W. W. Belknap was Grant's Secretary of War who resigned to avoid impeachment for supposedly receiving bribes; Salary Grab, when the entire Republican Party was implicated for retroactively raising pay for congressmen and the President.

SKILLS ASSESSMENT

23. (a) Republican government. (b) Bayonet rule. (c) Southern Democrats.
24. Grant is oppressing the South, aided by martial rule.
25. C
26. G
27. On the earlier map, the slave quarters are all central to the main house. The later map shows the sharecroppers' houses spread out, demonstrating more independence and autonomy. The later map also has a church and a schoolhouse, buildings that would not have been available for slaves.

ANSWERS TO ACTIVITIES

Writing to LEARN

Sample answer: Congress opposed Johnson's Reconstruction policies, and with them the imposition of black codes. Had there been some room for compromise, some of the chaotic developments that characterized the era of Reconstruction might have been avoided, along with the growth and spread of the Ku Klux Klan.

Primary Source CD-ROM

Direct students to the additional primary sources that can be found on the *Exploring Primary Sources in U.S. History CD-ROM.*

Take It to the NET

Additional support materials and activities for Chapter 12 of *America: Pathways to the Present* can be found in the Social Studies area at the Prentice Hall School Web site. **www.phschool.com**

American Pathways
GOVERNMENT

Federalism and States' Rights

The Framers of the Constitution based the American system of government on federalism, which is the sharing of power between the national, or federal, government and state governments. This system set up a struggle for power between the two levels of government. The Supreme Court has served as the referee in this ongoing contest, which reached its climax in the Civil War.

 The Growth of Nationalism

1787–1828 The Constitution created a federal system of government that strengthened what had been a weak national government. In the early 1800s, a sense of nationalism, along with westward expansion, prompted Congress and the Supreme Court to become more involved in issues affecting the states.

 Sectionalism and Civil War

1828–1865 Nationalism turned into sectionalism as the federal government's policies in support of business and trade benefited the industrial North more than the agricultural South. Southern states, demanding their states' rights, denounced tariffs imposed by the federal government as well as calls for the abolition of slavery. The inability to resolve sectional conflicts, especially the slavery issue, ignited the Civil War.

Industry in Whitneyville, Connecticut (above left), and growing cotton along the Mississippi River (below left)

 Reconstruction

1865–1877 The federal government's power over the states peaked during Reconstruction, when Congress put the Southern states under military rule and set the conditions for their reentry into the Union.

Federal troops in Atlanta, Georgia (right)

448

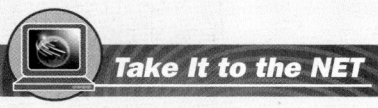

 Progressive Reforms

1890–1920 Cities and states often led the way in promoting Progressive reforms, which the federal government in some cases then applied to the entire nation. During this period, Congress took numerous actions to ensure the health and welfare of citizens and to prevent big businesses from limiting competition.

Two women protesting child labor (right)

 From New Deal to Great Society

1932–1970 During the Great Depression, President Franklin Roosevelt's New Deal introduced many programs to assist the needy and regulate the economy. The federal government's involvement in areas formerly controlled by the states expanded.

 The Civil Rights Movement

1954–1971 The Supreme Court, and later Congress, supported African Americans' efforts to secure their civil rights, despite firm resistance from state governments in the South.

Thurgood Marshall (left, center) outside the Supreme Court in Washington, D.C.

 The Reagan Revolution

1980–Present President Ronald Reagan sought to limit the size—and the power—of the federal government while giving more responsibility to the states. He focused especially on cutting taxes, reducing government regulations, and reforming social welfare programs. Reagan's view of government has influenced politics to the present day.

Continuity and Change

1. Why did Southern states dislike the tariffs that Congress imposed?
2. Has power been evenly balanced between the federal government and the state governments? Explain your answer.

   Take It to the NET: Creating a Study Guide
   Print and complete the study guide for this topic found in the *America: Pathways to the Present* area of the following Web site. www.phschool.com

449

Take It to the NET

Students can print the American Pathways thematic study guide for this topic at the Prentice Hall School Web site, or you can provide students with copies of the study guide, which is found in the Units 3/4 booklet, the American Pathways Activity, pages 74–75. Students should use their texts to fill in a one-sentence description for each event on the study guide. When completed for each of the American Pathways topics, the thematic study guides will aid students in preparing for an end-of-course exam.

ANSWERS

1. The tariffs were a heavy tax on imports designed to discourage foreign imports and encourage American manufacturing. The tariff greatly benefited the industrial North, but it forced southerners to pay higher prices for manufactured goods. Also, southerners believed in states' rights and wanted to limit the power of the federal government.

2. Possible answer: The balance has shifted over time, reflecting the different views on the issue held by elected federal leaders. During Reconstruction, the federal government assumed its greatest control over the states. During the New Deal, the role of the federal government was greatly expanded into areas formerly controlled by the states. Since Ronald Reagan's presidency in the 1980s, most federal leaders have favored expanded powers for state governments and a reduction in the size of the federal government.

Use this sample exam to help your students prepare for standardized tests.

TIPS FOR TEST TAKING
You might want to remind your students of the following:

1. Read the directions carefully.

2. Read each question carefully.

3. For multiple choice questions, try to answer the question before you look at the choices. Read all the choices. Then, eliminate those that are absolutely incorrect.

4. For short answer questions, be sure to answer the question completely if there is more than one part.

5. Answer the easy questions first. Then, go back to the ones that will take more time.

6. Pace yourself. Be sure to set aside enough time for the writing questions.

Write your answers on a separate sheet of paper.

1. To many people in the North, Harriet Beecher Stowe's book *Uncle Tom's Cabin* was

   A an accurate picture of life in the South.

   B a defense of the slave-owning planters.

   C an explanation for the *Dred Scott* case.

   D a reason to vote against Abraham Lincoln.

2. Keeping a balance in the United States Senate of slave and free states was one of the purposes of the

   A Lecompton constitution.

   B Missouri Compromise.

   C *Dred Scott* decision.

   D Lincoln-Douglass Debates.

3. Which one of the following was a cause of the nativism that appeared in the United States in the 1850s?

   A The Lecompton constitution

   B The Fugitive Slave Act

   C Railroad construction

   D Immigration

4. The shots fired on which piece of federal property marked the start of the Civil War?

   A The Pentagon in Washington, D.C.

   B Fort Sumter in North Carolina

   C Independence Hall in Philadelphia

   D Fort Henry in Tennessee

5. What was the effect of the Union Army capture of Vicksburg, Mississippi?

   A It brought Missouri back into the Union.

   B It ended most southern cotton exports.

   C It required General Lee to turn back from Gettysburg.

   D It divided the Confederacy into two parts.

6. The Emancipation Proclamation of 1863

   A officially freed the slaves in the Confederate states.

   B ended all slavery in the United States.

   C caused England and France to assist the South.

   D prevented African Americans from joining the army.

7. What problem plagued the Confederacy throughout the Civil War?

   A Declining industrial and manufacturing output

   B Failure of the cotton crop

   C Food shortages

   D Women not working outside the home

450

Diagnose and Prescribe
- Profile student skills with Diagnostic Tests A&B.
- Address student needs with program materials correlated to test questions.

Review and Reteach
- Provide cumulative content review with the Review Book.

Practice and Assess
- Build test-taking skills with Test-taking Strategies With Transparencies.

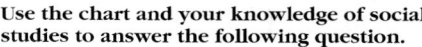
Use the chart and your knowledge of social studies to answer the following question.

Reconstruction Plan
Southerners who take an oath of allegiance to the United States are pardoned.
Each state in the South can have a constitutional convention.
Each state in the South must abolish slavery.
Each southern state can hold elections and then rejoin the Union.

8. Which reconstruction plan is outlined in the chart?

   A The Wade-Davis plan

   B The plan of Abraham Lincoln

   C The plan of Andrew Johnson

   D The Radical Republican plan

9. Which statement about sharecropping is correct?

   A A sharecropper did not own land.

   B A sharecropper paid rent to use the land.

   C Cotton was never grown by a sharecropper.

   D Debt was not a problem facing a sharecropper.

10. Which of the following areas of the southern economy grew the most during Reconstruction?

   A Furniture manufacturing

   B Railroads

   C Tourism

   D Clothing manufacturing

> "A house divided against itself cannot stand."
>
> —*Abraham Lincoln*

11. To what was Lincoln referring when he made this statement?

   A The poor construction of many southern buildings

   B The division of the United States into factions during the Civil War

   C Conflicts among members of the Supreme Court during Reconstruction

   D His new White House visitation policy

Writing Practice

12. Describe two of the five laws in the Compromise of 1850.

13. What was the purpose of the Black Codes? How did they work?

14. What effect did sharecropping have on the South after Reconstruction?

---

1. A
2. B
3. D
4. B
5. D
6. A
7. C
8. C
9. A
10. B
11. B
12. Any two of the following: Congress would admit California as a free state; New Mexico and Utah would decide on the issue of slavery for themselves; Congress would abolish the sale of slaves in Washington, D.C.; slavery would remain legal in Washington, D.C.; and the Fugitive Slave Act would require the federal government to return escaped slaves to their owners.
13. Their purpose was to restrict the rights of newly freed blacks in the South immediately after the Civil War. They used curfews, vagrancy laws, labor contracts, and restrictions on land use and ownership.
14. Sharecropping caused planters to grow cash crops, rather than food crops. As a result, the South had to import much of its food. Sharecropping also created a cycle of continual debt for farmers.

451

Unit 5

Expansion: Rewards and Costs (1850–1915)

INTRODUCING THE UNIT

Expansion: Rewards and Costs (1850–1915) The Industrial Revolution was a tremendous agent for change in the United States, particularly in urban areas of the North. But progress for industry brought bad conditions for workers, who arose in protest. Elsewhere, Americans migrated west of the Mississippi, staking claims to Native American land, a process that often resulted in violence and bloodshed. Opportunities seemed limitless in the United States at this time, drawing many people to cross both the Atlantic and Pacific oceans to seek their fortunes in the "Land of Opportunity." As America grew and prospered, it became ever more a country of many voices and factions. The rapid pace of change brought resistance in some quarters, but the burgeoning nation's growth and progress was unstoppable.

USING HISTORICAL EVIDENCE

Direct students' attention to the painting on these pages. It depicts Americans migrating west along the Oregon Trail. This great migratory route to the United States Northwest runs from Independence, Missouri, about 2,000 miles west to the Columbia River in Oregon.

The Oregon Trail was first broken by fur traders and missionaries. By the mid-1800s, it was a popular route, with more than half a million travelers from 1843 to 1869. In the late 1840s many "gold bugs" traveled the trail on their way to California. At about that same time, Mormons traveled portions of the trail on their way to Utah.

The use of the trail was continuous until the completion of the transcontinental railroad in 1869. Even then, the trail was still used by cowboys and sheepherders who were moving their stock from one settlement to another.

eTeach

Be sure to check out this month's online discussion with a Master Teacher. Go to **www.phschool.com**.

> *"Up to our own day American history has been in a large degree the history of the colonization of the Great West. The existence of an area of free land, its continuous recession, and the advance of American settlement westward, explain American development."*
>
> Frederick Jackson Turner, 1893

The prospect of prosperity in the West lured many Americans along the Oregon Trail, as in this painting by Albert Bierstadt. ▶

452

RESOURCE DIRECTORY

Teaching Resources
Units 5/6 booklet
- American Pathways Activity, pp. 47–48
- History's Lasting Impact, pp. 49–50

Geography and History booklet, pp. 10–11

Other Print Resources
Prentice Hall Assessment System
- Document-Based Assessment

453

TECHNOLOGY CENTER

Take It to the NET

Prentice Hall School Web site offers student-appropriate Internet activities and links that extend core content. Visit us at the Social Studies area. www.phschool.com

AmericanHeritage®

My Brush with History™ Video Program This new video series lets your students learn history from the people who lived it.

RESOURCE PRO®

Teaching Resources on CD-ROM offer lesson-planning flexibility, test-generation capability, and resource manageability.

PRESENTATION PRO CD-ROM Provides you with multimedia lecture notes for each chapter.

SOCIAL STUDIES SKILLS TUTOR CD-ROM Provides interactive practice in Geographic Literacy, Critical Thinking and Reading, Visual Analysis, and Communications.

INTERACTIVE CONSTITUTION CD-ROM Exploring active citizenship and civic responsibilities, this CD-ROM shows students how the Constitution affects their lives today.

EXPLORING PRIMARY SOURCES IN U.S. HISTORY CD-ROM This interactive exploration of primary sources allows students to analyze and evaluate writing and images from American history.

GUIDED READING AUDIOTAPES

STUDENT EDITION ON AUDIO CD

SOUNDS OF AN ERA AUDIO CD Bring the sounds of American history to life in the classroom with music, speeches, poetry, interviews, and news reports.

 **TEXT**

Don't miss the exclusive interactive version of this textbook on the Web and on CD-ROM.

RESOURCE DIRECTORY

Technology
Color Transparencies *Historical Maps,* A25, A26, A58, A60; *Political Cartoons,* B7, B8; *Cause-and-Effect Charts,* D6; *Fine Art,* E10, E11, E12, E13, E14, E15; *American Photo,* F5; *American Diversity,* G9, G10; *The Way It Works,* H9, H10, H11, H12, H13, H14
Section Reading Support Transparencies
Prentice Hall United States History Video Collection™ Volume 10, *Reconstruction and Segregation (1865–1910);* Volume 11, *Industrialization and Urbanization;* Volume 12, *Immigration and Cultural Change*
Companion Web site, www.phschool.com

Chapter 13 Planning Guide
Resource Manager

	CORE INSTRUCTION	READING/SKILLS
Chapter-Level Resources	**Teaching Resources** • Pacing Charts booklet • Block Scheduling booklet **Resource Pro® CD-ROM**, Ch. 13 **Prentice Hall Presentation Pro CD-ROM**, Ch. 13 **www.phschool.com** • eTeach	**Guided Reading Audiotapes (English/Spanish)** **Student Edition on Audio CD**, Ch. 13 **Social Studies Skills Tutor CD-ROM** **Color Transparencies**, B7, D6, F5, H9, H10, H11
1 A Technological Revolution 1. Learn how daily lives changed in the decades following the Civil War. 2. Find out how advances in electric power and communication affected people and businesses in this era. 3. Discover the effects the development of railroads had on industrial growth. 4. Think about the impact of the Bessemer process on American culture.	**Teaching Resources** **Units 5/6 booklet** • Section 1 Quiz, p. 6 **Learning Styles Lesson Plans booklet**, p. 28	**Guided Reading and Review booklet**, p. 54 **Guide to the Essentials**, p. 68 **Skills for Life booklet**, p. 15 **Section Reading Support Transparencies**
2 The Growth of Big Business 1. Read to find out why American industrialists of the late 1800s were called both "robber barons" and "captains of industry." 2. Discover how social Darwinism affected Americans' views on big business. 3. Analyze the ways in which big businesses differed from smaller businesses. 4. Learn how industrialists gained a competitive edge over their rivals.	**Teaching Resources** **Units 5/6 booklet** • Section 2 Quiz, p. 7	**Guided Reading and Review booklet**, p. 55 **Guide to the Essentials**, p. 69 **Learning with Documents booklet**, p. 18 **Section Reading Support Transparencies**
3 Industrialization and Workers 1. Find out about factors that led to a growing American work force betweeen 1860 and 1900. 2. Learn what factory work at the turn of the century was like. 3. Discover why it was sometimes necessary for entire families to work.	**Teaching Resources** **Units 5/6 booklet** • Section 3 Quiz, p. 8 **Learning Styles Lesson Plans booklet**, p. 29	**Guided Reading and Review booklet**, p. 56 **Guide to the Essentials**, p. 70 **Learning with Documents booklet**, p. 52 **Section Reading Support Transparencies**
4 The Great Strikes 1. Discover the impact of industrialism on the gulf between rich and poor. 2. Find out the goals of the early labor unions in the United States. 3. Learn why Eugene V. Debs formed the American Railway Union. 4. Study the causes and outcomes of the major strikes in the late 1800s.	**Teaching Resources** **Units 5/6 booklet** • Section 4 Quiz, p. 9	**Guided Reading and Review booklet**, p. 57 **Guide to the Essentials**, p. 71 **Section Reading Support Transparencies**

ENRICHMENT/PRE-AP

Prentice Hall United States History Video Collection™
www.phschool.com
- Section Activities, Virtual Field Trip, Chapter Activities, Current Events Online

Great Debates booklet, p. 30
American History Block Scheduling Support
Nystrom *Atlas of Our Country,* pp. 28–29
Historical Outline Map Book, p. 82
Sounds of an Era Audio CD
Exploring Primary Sources in U.S. History CD-ROM

Great Debates booklet, p. 8
Sounds of an Era Audio CD
Exploring Primary Sources in U.S. History CD-ROM

Biography, Literature, and Comparing Primary Sources booklet, p. 57
American History Block Scheduling Support
Nystrom *Atlas of Our Country,* pp. 24–25, 30–31
Exploring Primary Sources in U.S. History CD-ROM

Biography, Literature, and Comparing Primary Sources booklet, pp. 18, 121
Sounds of an Era Audio CD
American Pathways Thematic Posters

ASSESSMENT

PRENTICE HALL ASSESSMENT SYSTEM

Core Assessment
ExamView® Test Bank, Ch. 13
ExamView® Test Bank CD-ROM, Ch. 13

Standardized Test Preparation
Diagnose and Prescribe
Diagnostic Tests for High School Social Studies Skills

Review and Reteach
Review Book for U.S. History

Practice and Assess
Test-taking Strategies With Transparencies
Test-taking Strategies Posters
Test Prep Book for U.S. History
Alternative Assessment Handbook
Document-Based Assessment

Teaching Resources
Units 5/6 booklet
- Section Quizzes, pp. 6–9
- Chapter Tests, pp. 10, 13
www.phschool.com Ch. 13 Self-Test

AmericanHeritage RESOURCES

From the Archives of American Heritage®, pp. 474, 480
AmericanHeritage® My Brush with History™ Videotapes
www.americanheritage.com

Don't miss the exclusive interactive version of this textbook on the Web and on CD-ROM.

Chapter 13 Planning Guide
In Your Classroom

CUSTOMIZE FOR INDIVIDUAL NEEDS

Gifted and Talented

Teacher's Edition
- Customize for Gifted and Talented, pp. 471, 481

Teaching Resources
- Biography, Literature, and Comparing Primary Sources booklet, pp. 18, 57, 121

Technology
- Exploring Primary Sources in U.S. History CD-ROM *The Tall Office Building Artistically Considered, Louis H. Sullivan; Wealth, Andrew Carnegie; Spindle Top Gusher*

ESL

Teacher's Edition
- Customize for ESL, pp. 457, 469

Teaching Resources
- Guided Reading and Review booklet, pp. 54–57
- Guide to the Essentials (English/Spanish), Chapter 13

Technology
- Student Edition on Audio CD, Chapter 13
- Guided Reading Audiotapes (English/Spanish), Chapter 13
- Section Reading Support Transparencies

Less Proficient Readers

Teacher's Edition
- Customize for Less Proficient Readers, pp. 461, 479

Teaching Resources
- Guided Reading and Review booklet, pp. 54–57
- Guide to the Essentials (English/Spanish), Chapter 13

Technology
- Student Edition on Audio CD, Chapter 13
- Guided Reading Audiotapes (English/Spanish), Chapter 13
- Section Reading Support Transparencies

Less Proficient Writers

Teacher's Edition
- Customize for Less Proficient Writers, p. 475

Teaching Resources
- Guided Reading and Review booklet, pp. 54–57
- Guide to the Essentials (English/Spanish), Chapter 13

Technology
- Student Edition on Audio CD, Chapter 13
- Guided Reading Audiotapes (English/Spanish), Chapter 13
- Section Reading Support Transparencies

TEACHER'S EDITION INDEX

CHAPTER 13 – PACING SUGGESTIONS

For 90-minute Blocks

- Teach sections 1 and 2 using Transparencies B7, D6, F5, H10, and H11, and the Recent Scholarship note on page 469 for class discussions.

Running Out of Time?

If you are running short on time to cover this chapter, consider the following options:

- Use Prentice Hall Presentation Pro CD-ROM to create an outline for this chapter.
- Use the Section Summaries for Chapter 13, from **Guide to the Essentials (English/Spanish)**.

ADDITIONAL ACTIVITIES

1 A Technological Revolution

Connecting with Science and Technology
Have students research an invention that had its beginning in this era of technological advance, then decide what its modern counterpart is. Tell them to imagine what a day in our lives—at home, in school, or at work—might have been like if this device had not been invented. Students can present their ideas visually in the form of an illustrated poster, chart, or cartoon strip. **(Visual/Spatial)**

2 The Growth of Big Business

Connecting with Culture
Initiate a discussion about the hardships laborers from other countries might have endured while working on the transcontinental railroad in the United States. Have students consider what the workers encountered that might have been very different from what they were used to, such as new climate, food, culture, and language. Then have students individually or in pairs create a presentation in which they speak directly to the audience as they describe what their life was like. Presentations should also include factors that affected all the workers, such as physical dangers, strenuous labor, discrimination, and separation from their families. **(Bodily/Kinesthetic)**

3 Industrialization and Workers

Connecting with Culture
Students may know that during the early Industrial Revolution, young women who left home to work in the textile mills of Lowell, Massachusetts, published their own magazine, the *Lowell Offering,* in which they used a variety of genres to present their thoughts about life and work. Ask students to imagine a similar magazine as it might have been written during the period of intense labor strife. Ask for volunteers to form an editorial staff to coordinate such a publication. Invite all students to research the era, then submit poems, first-person essays, and fiction about workers' lives. Students with drawing skills can illustrate the selections. **(Verbal/Linguistic)**

4 The Great Strikes

Connecting with Economics
Have students research and identify the resources that are available today to settle, or at least to end, labor-management strife. These might include arbitration, boycotts, injunctions, lockouts, and mediation. In presenting the material—either in a written report or chart format—students should define and give examples of how each method works. You may wish to have students present their work orally, then discuss how each works to the benefit of either the workers or the employers. **(Verbal/Linguistic)**

Chapter 13

The Expansion of American Industry

(1850–1900)

INTRODUCING THE CHAPTER

Beginning before the Civil War, rapid industrial progress transformed the United States, but relations between those who managed the industries and those who labored in them were filled with tensions. Conditions for workers grew worse.

TIME LINE ACTIVITY

To provide students with practice in using the time line, ask questions such as these:

1. What railroad was the first to connect the east and west coasts of the United States? *(The transcontinental railroad)*

2. What issues were the cause of the Great Railroad Strike? *(Dangerous working conditions and pay cuts)*

3. What railroad was completed that links eastern and western Canada? *(The Canadian Pacific Railway)*

eTeach

Be sure to check out this month's online discussion with a Master Teacher. Go to **www.phschool.com**.

Chapter 13
The Expansion of American Industry
(1850–1900)

SECTION 1	A Technological Revolution
SECTION 2	The Growth of Big Business
SECTION 3	Industrialization and Workers
SECTION 4	The Great Strikes

The steel-framed Syndicate Building in New York City.

American Events

1856
The Bessemer process is patented, paving the way for the mass production of steel and a new industrial age in America.

1859
Edwin L. Drake strikes oil in Titusville, Pennsylvania, marking the first successful oil well and the beginning of the commercial use of oil.

1869
Workers finish construction on the transcontinental railroad, the first railroad to connect the east and west coasts.

Presidential Terms: Franklin Pierce 1853–1857 | James Buchanan 1857–1861 | Abraham Lincoln 1861–1865 | Andrew Johnson 1865–1869 | Ulysses S. Grant 1869–1877

1850 • •1860• •1870

World Events

Charles Darwin publishes *On the Origin of Species.*
1859

Louis Pasteur introduces pasteurization.
1861

The Suez Canal is completed.
1869

454   Chapter 13 • *The Expansion of American Industry*

RESOURCE DIRECTORY

Teaching Resources
Pacing Charts booklet
Block Scheduling booklet, p. 19
Units 5/6 booklet
 • Chapter Summary, p. 3

Technology
Guided Reading Audiotapes (English/Spanish), Ch. 13
Student Edition on Audio CD, Ch. 13

Sounds of an Era Audio CD *"Dallas Railway,"* 1930s recording (time: 30 seconds)
Prentice Hall United States History Video Collection™ Volume 11, *Industrialization and Urbanization*
Prentice Hall Presentation Pro CD-ROM, Ch. 13
Resource Pro® CD-ROM
Social Studies Skills Tutor CD-ROM
Companion Web site, www.phschool.com

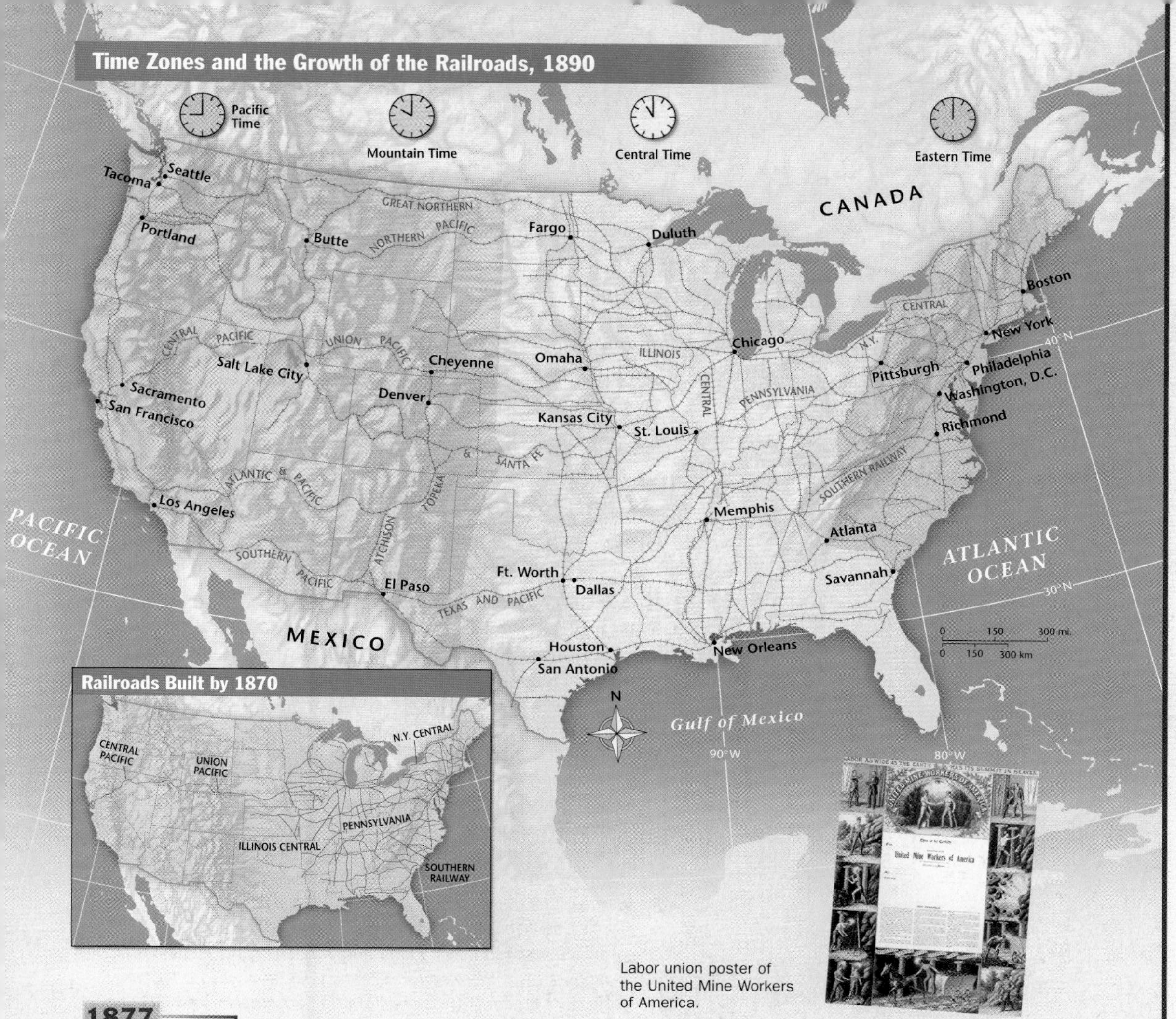

Time Zones and the Growth of the Railroads, 1890

Pacific Time · Mountain Time · Central Time · Eastern Time

Seattle · Tacoma · Portland · Butte · Fargo · Duluth · CANADA · Boston

GREAT NORTHERN · NORTHERN PACIFIC

CENTRAL PACIFIC · UNION PACIFIC · Salt Lake City · Cheyenne · Omaha · ILLINOIS · Chicago · N.Y. · New York · Pittsburgh · Philadelphia · Washington, D.C.

Sacramento · San Francisco · Denver · PENNSYLVANIA · Richmond

Los Angeles · ATLANTIC & PACIFIC · Kansas City · St. Louis · SOUTHERN RAILWAY

& SANTA FE · ATCHISON · TOPEKA

SOUTHERN PACIFIC · El Paso · Memphis · Atlanta

MEXICO · TEXAS AND PACIFIC · Ft. Worth · Dallas · Savannah · ATLANTIC OCEAN

Houston · San Antonio · New Orleans

PACIFIC OCEAN

0 150 300 mi. · 0 150 300 km

Gulf of Mexico

N

Railroads Built by 1870

CENTRAL PACIFIC · UNION PACIFIC · N.Y. CENTRAL · PENNSYLVANIA · ILLINOIS CENTRAL · SOUTHERN RAILWAY

Labor union poster of the United Mine Workers of America.

Activating Prior Knowledge
Which time zones had the greatest number of railroad lines in 1890? *(The Central and Eastern time zones)*

Previewing In which time zones did the number of railroad lines grow the most from 1870 to 1890? *(The Pacific and Mountain time zones)*

BACKGROUND
About the Pictures

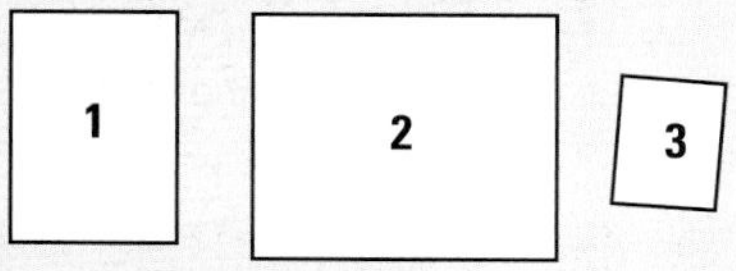

1 · 2 · 3

1. The Syndicate Building, also known as the Park Row Building, was constructed in lower Manhattan from 1896 to 1899 and stands 30 stories tall.

2. Constructing the transcontinental railroad required thousands of laborers such as these to perform dangerous, backbreaking work.

3. The United Mine Workers of America was founded in Columbus, Ohio, in 1890 when the Knights of Labor Trade Assembly No. 135 and the National Progressive Union of Miners and Mine Laborers joined together.

1877
Dangerous working conditions and wage cuts spark violent protests by railway workers in the Great Railroad Strike.

1882
Samuel Dodd and John Rockefeller form the Standard Oil Trust, which would soon dominate the nation's oil industry.

1890
Congress passes the Sherman Antitrust Act.

1894
The Pullman Strike leads President Cleveland to use federal force against striking workers.

| Rutherford B. Hayes 1877–1881 | James Garfield 1881 C. Arthur 1881–1885 | Grover Cleveland 1885–1889 | Benjamin Harrison 1889–1893 | Grover Cleveland 1893–1897 | William McKinley 1897–1901 |

1880 · 1890 · 1900

1876
Korea becomes an independent nation.

1885
The Canadian Pacific Railway opens, linking eastern and western Canada.

1889
The Eiffel Tower is completed.

Chapter 13 455

BIBLIOGRAPHY

For the Teacher

Boorstin, Daniel J. ***The Americans: The Democratic Experience.*** Random House, 1985. (A description of post–Civil War America, this book won the Pulitzer Prize when first published in 1973.)

Josephson, Matthew. ***The Robber Barons.*** Harvest Books, 1962. (This book was written in the 1930s at the height of the Depression, but it is still considered an important look at the rise of the titans of nineteenth-century American industry.)

For the Student

Riis, Jacob. ***How the Other Half Lives.*** Bedford/St. Martin's, 1996. (The wretchedness of urban slums in 1890 as described by a young New York reporter.)

Weisberger, Bernard. ***Captains of Industry.*** American Heritage Publishing, 1996. (A fast-moving, well-illustrated description of industrial leaders.)

TEXT

Don't miss the exclusive interactive version of this textbook on the Web and on CD-ROM.

SECTION OBJECTIVES

1. Learn how daily lives changed in the decades following the Civil War.
2. Find out how advances in electric power and communication affected people and businesses in this era.
3. Discover the effects the development of railroads had on industrial growth.
4. Think about the impact of the Bessemer process on American culture.

BELLRINGER

Warm-Up Activity Write the following list of inventions on the chalkboard: typewriter, phonograph, telegraph, telephone. Ask students to decide which they consider the most important.

Activating Prior Knowledge Ask students to imagine how many times during the day they use a telephone. Have them list the number and types of calls they make on a given day. If they lived before the telephone was invented, how do they imagine they would have communicated the same types of information? How would their lives be different without telephones?

READING STRATEGY

Tell students that they will be reading about daily life in the United States between 1865 and 1900. As they read, have them list the ways in which the United States changed during those 35 years to help them analyze economic issues such as the growth of railroads.

ACTIVITY
Connecting with Science and Technology

Share this quotation from the philosopher Alfred North Whitehead with students: "The greatest invention of the nineteenth century was the invention of the method of invention." Ask students to write paragraphs explaining what Whitehead meant, speculating on what "the method of invention" might be. **(Verbal/Linguistic)**

A Technological Revolution

READING FOCUS

• Why did people's daily lives change in the decades following the Civil War?

• How did advances in electric power and communication affect life for people and businesses?

• What effects did the development of railroads have on industrial growth?

• What was the impact of the Bessemer process on American culture?

MAIN IDEA

In the years after the Civil War, new technology revolutionized American life.

KEY TERMS

patent
productivity
transcontinental railroad
Bessemer process
mass production

TAKING NOTES

As you read, complete this table listing some of the major technological innovations of the decades following the Civil War and their impact on American life.

A Technological Revolution		
Technology	**Examples**	**Impact on Daily Life and Business**
Electric power	Refrigerator	Reduced food spoilage

Below, Samuel Morse sends the first successful telegraph message, using Morse code, from the Supreme Court in Washington, D.C. Morse Code (inset) is still used today in amateur radio.

Setting the Scene Samuel Morse had worked for years on improving the telegraph and finally began to run out of money. Nearly broke, he anxiously awaited a bill to pass through Congress, which would provide him with funds to complete his work. The bill narrowly passed, to the surprise of many. Morse was greatly relieved. The next year he reached the climax of his success.

> 66 And now at last the supreme moment had arrived. The line from Washington to Baltimore was completed, and on the 24th day of May, 1844, the company invited by the inventor . . . assembled to witness his triumph. True to his promise to Miss Annie Ellsworth, he had asked her to indite the first public message which should be flashed over the completed line, and she . . . chose the now historic words . . . 'What hath God wrought!' . . . Calmly he seated himself at the instrument and ticked off the inspired words in the dots and dashes of the Morse alphabet . . . the electromagnetic telegraph was no longer the wild dream of a visionary, but an accomplished fact. 99
> —Samuel F.B. Morse

Little did Americans know as they entered the second half of the nineteenth century what other "wild dreams" would become reality. Samuel Morse's first successful telegraph message sent in 1844 marked the beginning of a second industrial revolution. The United States was on the verge of a major transformation. In the years after the Civil War, the United States developed into an industrial powerhouse. Inventors and scientists, backed by business leaders, created an explosion of inventions and improvements. Their efforts brought about a technological revolution that energized American industry and forever changed people's daily lives.

RESOURCE DIRECTORY

Teaching Resources
Learning Styles Lesson Plans booklet, p. 28
Guided Reading and Review booklet, p. 54

Technology
Section Reading Support Transparencies
Guided Reading Audiotapes (English/Spanish), Ch. 13
Student Edition on Audio CD, Ch. 13
Prentice Hall United States History Video Collection™ Volume 11, *Industrialization and Urbanization*
Prentice Hall Presentation Pro CD-ROM, Ch. 13
Companion Web site, www.phschool.com

Changes in Daily Life

Most Americans today can flip a switch for light, turn a faucet for water, and talk to a friend a thousand miles away just by pressing a few buttons. It is hard for us to imagine life without these conveniences. In 1865, however, daily life was vastly different.

Daily Life in 1865 Indoor electric lighting did not exist in 1865. Instead, the rising and setting of the sun dictated the rhythm of a day's work. After dark, people lit candles or oil lamps if they could afford them. If they could not, they simply went to sleep, to rise at the first light of dawn.

Think about summers without the benefits of refrigeration! Ice was available in 1865, but only at great cost. People sawed blocks of ice out of frozen ponds during the winter, packed them in sawdust, and stored them in icehouses for later use.

By modern standards, long-distance communication was agonizingly slow. In 1860, most mail from the East Coast took ten days to reach the Midwest and three weeks to get to the West. An immigrant living on the frontier would have to wait several months for news from relatives in Europe.

Investing in Technology By 1900, this picture of daily life had changed dramatically for millions of Americans. The post–Civil War years saw tremendous growth in new ideas and inventions. Between 1790 and 1860, the Patent and Trademark Office of the federal government issued just 36,000 **patents**—licenses that give an inventor the exclusive right to make, use, or sell an invention for a set period of time. In contrast, 500,000 patents were issued between 1860 and 1890 for inventions such as the typewriter, telephone, and phonograph.

European and American business leaders began to invest heavily in these new inventions. The combination of financial backing and American ingenuity helped create new industries and expand old ones. By 1900, Americans' standard of living was among the highest in the world. This achievement was a result of the nation's growing industrial **productivity**—the amount of goods and services created in a given period of time.

New Forms of Energy

The blossoming of American inventive genius in the late 1800s had a profound effect on millions of people's lives. For example, scientists began developing new uses for petroleum, including fuels that would help power new machines. Electricity proved to be another productive energy source. It led to many important advances in the nation's industrial development and changed people's eating, working, and even sleeping habits.

Drake Strikes Oil In 1858, the Pennsylvania Rock Oil Company sent Edwin L. Drake to Titusville, Pennsylvania to drill for oil. The idea to drill for oil was new and many were skeptical of the project. Previously, oil had been obtained by either melting the fat from a whale or by digging large pits and waiting for oil to seep above ground—both of which were time-consuming and expensive. If the new method worked, it would be cheaper and more efficient.

READING CHECK

What were the benefits of Drake's new method of oil extraction?

Chapter 13 • Section 1 **457**

ACTIVITY

Connecting with Science and Technology

Have small groups of students make presentations to the class that explain the differences between alternating current (AC) and direct current (DC). Their presentation should then describe the great "AC versus DC debate" of the 1880s and 1890s, in which Westinghouse eventually prevailed. **(Verbal/Linguistic)**

BACKGROUND

Art History

The earliest existing photographs date from the 1820s. Technological advances in the mid-1800s allowed photographers to produce pictures on paper rather than glass. In the 1880s, George Eastman developed a hand-held camera that could be used by professionals and amateurs alike.

After spending nearly a year raising money and building the equipment needed for the project, Drake finally set up an oil well and began drilling using a steam-powered engine. In 1859, just as nervous investors had decided to call off the project, Drake struck oil. Oil quickly became a major industry.

As new uses for oil began to appear, the oil business grew rapidly. Titusville soon became one of several boom towns in northwestern Pennsylvania. Oil refineries, which transformed crude oil into kerosene, sprang up around the country. A byproduct of this process, gasoline, would eventually make oil even more valuable. Until the invention of the automobile in the late 1880s, however, gasoline was seen as a waste product and simply thrown away.

Edison's favorite invention, the phonograph, shown above, recorded sounds on metal foil wrapped around a rotating cylinder. The first words Edison recorded and then replayed on his phonograph were "Mary had a little lamb." This wondrous machine, introduced in 1877, gained Edison the nickname the "Wizard of Menlo Park."

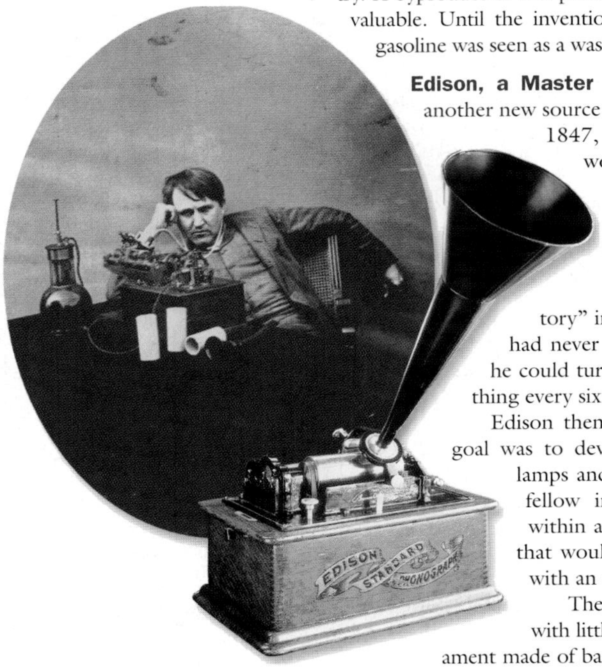

Edison, a Master of Invention Thomas A. Edison helped make another new source of energy, electric power, widely available. Born in 1847, Edison grew up tinkering with electricity. While working for a New York company, he improved the stock tickers that sent stock and gold prices to other offices. When his boss awarded him a $40,000 bonus, the 23-year-old Edison left his job and set himself up as an inventor.

In 1876, Edison moved into his "invention factory" in Menlo Park, New Jersey. The young genius, who had never received any formal science training, claimed that he could turn out "a minor invention every ten days and a big thing every six months or so."

Edison then began experimenting with electric lighting. His goal was to develop affordable, in-home lighting to replace oil lamps and gaslights. Starting around 1879, Edison and his fellow inventors tried different ways to produce light within a sealed glass bulb. They needed to find a material that would glow without quickly burning up when heated with an electric current.

The team experimented with various threadlike filaments with little success. In 1880, they finally found a workable filament made of bamboo fiber. This filament glowed, Edison said, with "the most beautiful light ever seen."

Until the early 1880s, people who wanted electricity had to produce it with their own generator. Hoping to provide affordable lighting to many customers, Edison developed the idea of a central power station. In 1882, to attract investors, Edison built a power plant that lit dozens of buildings in New York City. Investors were impressed, and Edison's idea spread. By 1890, power stations across the country provided electricity for lamps, fans, printing presses, and many other newly invented appliances.

Electricity Is Improved Other inventors later improved upon Edison's work. Lewis Latimer, the son of an escaped slave, patented an improved method for producing the filament in light bulbs. He worked in Edison's laboratories, where he helped develop new advances in electricity. Latimer later wrote a landmark book about electric lighting.

Another major advance for electric lighting came from inventor George Westinghouse. In 1885, Westinghouse began to experiment with a form of electricity called alternating current. Edison had used direct current, which was expensive to produce and could only travel a mile or two. Alternating current could be generated more cheaply and travel longer distances.

RESOURCE DIRECTORY

Technology

Color Transparencies *The Way It Works,* H11

Sounds of an Era Audio CD *Thomas Edison on the Electric Age,* 1908 recording (time: one minute)

Westinghouse also used a device called a transformer to boost power levels at a station so that electricity could be sent over long distances. Another transformer at a distant substation could reduce power levels as needed. These aspects of Westinghouse's system made home use of electricity practical.

By the early 1890s, investors had used Edison's and Westinghouse's ideas and inventions to create two companies, General Electric and Westinghouse Electric. These companies' products encouraged the spread of the use of electricity. By 1898, nearly 3,000 power stations were lighting some 2 million light bulbs across the land.

Electricity's Impact on Business and Daily Life   Electricity helped to improve the productivity of the business world and transform the nature of the workplace. Electric power was cheaper and more efficient than some previously existing power sources. For example, the electric sewing machine, first made in 1889, led to the rapid growth of the ready-made clothing industry. Before the electric sewing machine, workers had to physically push on a foot pedal to generate power. With electricity, a worker could produce more clothing in less time. As a result, the costs of producing each item of clothing decreased.

Rapidly growing industries, such as the ready-made clothing industry, opened up thousands of jobs for Americans looking for employment. Many of the country's new immigrants, especially women and children, found work making clothing in factories powered by electricity.

Household use of electric current revolutionized many aspects of daily life. To take but one example, electricity made the refrigerator possible. This invention reduced food spoilage and relieved the need to preserve foods by time-consuming means, such as smoking or salting.

Yet all Americans did not receive the benefits of electricity equally. Rural areas, especially, went without electricity for many decades. Even where electric power was available, many people could not afford the home appliances or other conveniences that ran on electricity.

Advances in Communications

In the late 1800s, thousands of people left their homes in Europe and the eastern United States to seek a new life in the West. One of the greatest hardships for these immigrants was leaving their loved ones behind. Would they ever hear from family and friends again? By 1900, thanks to many advances in communications, such fears of isolation had diminished.

The Telegraph   The idea of sending messages over wires had occurred to inventors in the early 1700s. Several inventors actually set up working telegraph systems well before an American, Samuel F. B. Morse, took out a patent on telegraphy.

Morse may not have invented the telegraph, but he perfected it. He devised a code of short and long electrical impulses to represent the letters of the alphabet. Using this system, later called Morse code, he sent his first message in 1844. His success signaled the start of a communications revolution.

VIEWING HISTORY Here, visitors marvel at the electricity building, on display at the 1893 World's Columbian Exposition in Chicago. The building boasted more than 18,000 electric light bulbs and hosted other exhibits that showed the practical and entertainment value of electricity. **Drawing Conclusions** *Why do you think expositions such as this one were important? Who attended them?*

Chapter 13 • Section 1   **459**

Student Portfolio

You may wish to have students add the following to their portfolios: Many popular American folk songs concern the building of the railroads. Ask students to research the history of railroad songs and to prepare a written report or an oral presentation using an audiotape of the songs they researched. Suggest that students begin their research with books of American folk songs, such as Carl Sandburg's *The American Songbag.* (**Musical/Rhythmic**)

BACKGROUND

A Diverse Nation

Not everyone greeted the improvements in railroad transportation and travel with enthusiasm. *The Boston Courier* printed the following assertion as part of an editorial in 1827: "The project of a railroad from Boston to Albany is impracticable, as every one knows who knows the simplest rule of arithmetic, and the expense would be little less than the market value of the whole of Massachusetts; and which, if practicable, every person of common sense knows would be as useless as a railroad from Boston to the moon."

After the Civil War, several telegraph companies joined together to form the Western Union Telegraph Company. In 1870, Western Union had more than 100,000 miles of wire, over which some 9 million telegraph messages were transmitted. By 1900, the company owned more than 900,000 miles of wire and was sending roughly 63 million telegraph messages a year.

The Telephone   In 1871, Alexander Graham Bell of Scotland immigrated to Boston, Massachusetts, to teach people with hearing difficulties. After experimenting for several years with an electric current to transmit sounds, Bell patented the "talking telegraph" on March 7, 1876. He had just turned 29. In 1885, Bell and a group of partners set up the American Telephone and Telegraph Company to build long-distance telephone lines.

The earliest local phone lines could connect only two places, such as a home and a business. Soon central switchboards with operators could link an entire city. The first commercial telephone exchange began serving 21 customers on January 28, 1878, in New Haven, Connecticut. The next year President Rutherford B. Hayes had a telephone installed at the White House. By 1900, 1.5 million telephones were in use.

Railroads Create a National Network

In 1850, steam-powered ships still provided much of the nation's transportation. Over the following decades, however, improvements in train and track design, plus the construction of new rail lines, gave railroads a big boost.

Before the Civil War, most of the nation's railroad tracks were in short lines that connected neighboring cities, mainly in the East. Since there was no standard track width, or gauge, each train could only travel on certain tracks. As a result, goods and passengers often had to be moved to different trains, which caused costly delays. To make matters worse, train travel was dangerous. No system of standard signals existed, and train brakes were unreliable.

The Transcontinental Railroad   The rail business expanded greatly after the Civil War. The key event was the completion of the **transcontinental railroad,** a railway extending from coast to coast. When the project began in 1862, rail lines already reached from the East Coast to the Mississippi River. Now new rails were laid between Omaha, Nebraska, and Sacramento, California.

Because private investors did not see any likelihood of profit in building railroads beyond the line of settlement, the federal government stepped in to fund the completion of the transcontinental railroad. Members of Congress believed that the completion of a coast-to-coast railway would strengthen the country's economic infrastructure. Thus the federal government awarded huge loans and land grants to two private companies. The Central Pacific Railroad began laying track eastward out of Sacramento. The Union Pacific Railroad began work toward the west in Omaha.

Historians disagree as to whether it was a good idea for the government to provide funds for this project. Many believe that the government gave a much needed boost to

Fast Forward to Today

The World Wide Web

The growth and influence of the Internet in the second half of the 1990s was a turning point in the nation's economy, similar in scope to the vast economic changes brought about by the telegraph and railroads in the late 1800s. Estimates show that from 1996 to 2001, the number of people using the Internet worldwide skyrocketed from 45 million to over 400 million. Also during that time, the amount of revenue generated by the Internet jumped from $2.9 billion to over $700 billion.

Just as in the late 1800s, the world of business and daily life at the end of the twentieth century changed drastically with the advent of new technologies resulting from the Internet. The Internet became the next step in a process that began with the telegraph and the railroads to connect people and ideas in faster, more efficient ways. Moving beyond telegraph wires and railroad tracks, the United States, and indeed the world, is now connected through an infinite and invisible World Wide Web.

? **What other recent technological innovations have changed the world of communications? What do you think will be the next step in this process? Explain.**

CAPTION **A**NSWERS

Fast Forward to Today Possible answer: Faxes, cell phones, pagers, camcorders, digital cameras, high-speed passenger trains. Such innovations will continue to speed up the pace of everyday life. People are likely to become less reliant on traditional hard-wired telephones as they turn more and more to e-mail and cell phones.

RESOURCE DIRECTORY

Teaching Resources
Great Debates booklet (Decision-Making Activities) *Using Chinese Laborers to Build the Transcontinental Railroad,* p. 30

Other Print Resources
American History Block Scheduling Support *Linking the Nation: The Railroads,* found in the Expansion, Reconstruction, and Immigration folder, includes interdisciplinary lesson suggestions and activities for Geography and History, Primary Sources, Biography, and Literature.

Nystrom *Atlas of Our Country Settling the West,* pp. 28–29
Historical Outline Map Book *Political United States,* p. 82

Technology
Color Transparencies *The Way it Works,* H9
RESOURCE PRO® **Primary Source Activity** *Working on the Railroad,* found on Resource Pro, introduces students to a folk song by Thomas Casey about the hard life of an 1880s worker.

VIEWING HISTORY Workers from the Union and Central Pacific Railroads met at Promontory Summit, Utah, in 1869. The driving of the golden spike (inset) marked the completion of the transcontinental railroad. **Synthesizing Information** *Some have called this the greatest historical event in transportation in this country. Why was it such a joyous and momentous occasion?*

the railroad industry when the private sector was hesitant to invest. However, others argue that the government should not have gotten involved. One reason is that railroads built with federal aid did not operate as efficiently and profitably as those built by the private sector. For example, James J. Hill's Great Northern Railroad in the 1880s and 1890s had both lower rates and higher profits than the railroads built with federal aid.

Most of the workers on the transcontinental railroad were immigrants. Irish workers on the Union Pacific line used pickaxes to dig and level rail beds across the Great Plains at the rate of up to 6 miles a day. Chinese workers brought to the United States by the Central Pacific chiseled, plowed, and dynamited their way through the Sierra Nevada. Workers took pride in their labor. One work crew set a record for putting down track—an amazing ten miles in one day.

Finally, after seven years of grueling physical labor, the two crews approached each other in what is now Utah. On May 10, 1869, at a place called Promontory Summit, Central Pacific president Leland Stanford raised his hammer to drive the final golden spike into position. A telegraph operator beside the track tapped out a message to crowds throughout the country: "Almost ready now. Hats off. Prayer is being offered. . . . Done!" The nation had its first transcontinental railroad.

Railroad Developments By 1870, railroads could carry goods and passengers from coast to coast, but they still had problems. Trains were often noisy, dirty, and uncomfortable for travelers. The huge engines, spewing smoke and cinders as they thundered through the countryside, sometimes aroused fear and distrust.

In spite of the problems, train travel continued to expand and improve. The various new technologies emerging at this time all aided in the development of the national railroad system. Steel rails replaced iron rails, and track gauges and signals became standardized. Railroad companies also took steps to improve safety. In 1869, George Westinghouse developed more effective air

READING CHECK
What types of problems did railroads have in the late 1800s?

ACTIVITY
Connecting with Geography

Have students work in groups to create an illustrated and annotated map of the first transcontinental railroad. Their map should be illustrated with the major geographical barriers the builders faced, and annotated with notes that explain how each obstacle was overcome. (**Visual/Spatial**)

BACKGROUND
Biography

African American engineer Elijah McCoy (1843–1929) was born in Canada to escaped slaves. He studied in Edinburgh, Scotland, before settling in the United States. In 1872, while working for the Michigan Central Railroad, McCoy invented the lubricating cup—a device that continuously oiled the moving parts of factory machinery. Over the years he invented and sold nearly 60 kinds of devices and machine parts. It is sometimes said that the expression "the real McCoy," meaning the genuine article, came about because people insisted that the machinery they bought be equipped with McCoy's invention.

READING CHECK
The trains sometimes aroused fear because of their enormity, and passengers found the trains to be loud, unclean, and uncomfortable.

CUSTOMIZE FOR ...
Less Proficient Readers
Ask students to construct a cause-and-effect chart showing the effects of the growth of railroads, improved communications, and the availability of electric power.

CAPTION ANSWERS

Viewing History Joyous for workers because they spent seven years working on it; joyous for railroad owners because their profits and businesses would expand; momentous in history because it revolutionized transportation, businesses, and daily life.

VIEWING HISTORY Citadel rock looms over the construction of the Union Pacific Railroad through Wyoming Territory in 1868. **Identifying Central Issues** *In what ways did the nation's growing transportation system help promote industrial growth?*

brakes. In 1887, Granville Woods patented a telegraph system for communicating with moving trains, thus reducing the risk of collision.

The growth of railroads also led to the development of many towns throughout the western part of the United States. Railroad owners, looking to expand their businesses and increase profits, began building towns near their railroads on land granted to them by the government.

Railroads and Time Zones Scheduling proved to be another problem for railroads. Throughout much of the 1800s, most towns set their clocks independently, according to solar time. But when trains started regular passenger service, time differences from town to town created confusion. So, in 1883, the railroads adopted a national system of time zones to improve scheduling. As a result, clocks in broad regions of the country showed the same time, a system we still use today.

Rail improvements such as this made life easier not only for passengers but also for businesses that shipped goods. By the end of the century, some 190,000 miles of rails linked businesses and their customers. Shipping costs dropped enormously. In 1865, shipping a barrel of flour from Chicago to New York cost $3.45. In 1895, it cost just 68 cents.

Railroads and Industry Although the development of canals, turnpikes, and steam-powered ships in the first half of the century had improved transportation, the transport of goods over long distances was still costly and inefficient. Railroads played a key role in revolutionizing business and industry in the United States in several ways.

A faster and more practical means of transporting goods Railroads were not as severely limited by geographic and natural factors, such as poor weather conditions. They could travel at higher speeds, and transport larger items in much greater quantities.

Lower costs of production Railroads were a cheaper way to transport goods. As shipping costs dropped, more goods could be sent at lower prices. As a result, businesses were able to receive the raw materials and resources needed to produce their products at much lower costs and in much less time.

Creation of national markets Higher speeds and lower costs now allowed a business to market and sell its finished products to locations nationwide, rather than just in a local region. Also, the resources needed to produce these goods could be obtained from anywhere in the country. These advances in commerce helped to link distant regions of the United States, furthering the national network of business, transportation, and communication.

A model for big business Because of the complexity and size of the railroad companies, with railroads came new administrative techniques for handling large numbers of workers and large quantities of materials and money. New methods of management also arose. The professional manager and the specialized department grew out of the railroad business.

Stimulation of other industries The growth of the railroad industry encouraged innovation in other industries. The replacement of iron rails with steel rails, for example, promoted the growth of the steel industry.

The Bessemer Process

Through the mid-1800s, the nation depended on iron for railroad rails and the frames of large buildings. But in the 1850s, Henry Bessemer in England and William Kelly in Kentucky independently developed a new process for making steel. In 1856, Bessemer received the first patent for the **Bessemer process.** Steel had long been produced by melting iron, adding carbon, and removing impurities. The Bessemer process made it much easier and cheaper to remove the impurities.

Locomotives, such as this Erie Locomotive from 1903, were an impressive sight to many Americans at the turn of the century.

463

ACTIVITY
Connecting with Science and Technology

Have students conduct research to identify the major steps in both the Bessemer process of producing steel and in the traditional method of producing steel. Have students create illustrated flowcharts that depict each process, and compare and contrast them. **(Visual/Spatial)**

BACKGROUND
Biography

John Roebling, the engineer who began to build the Brooklyn Bridge, died six months after construction began, in 1869, of injuries resulting from a construction accident. His son Colonel Washington Roebling took over, but he contracted the "bends," or caisson disease, in 1872 and was confined to his bed. His wife, Emily, acted as his messenger through the final phases of construction, which ended in 1883.

✔ **TEST PREPARATION**

Have students read the section "Railroads and Industry" on these pages and then answer the question below.

Which of the following was NOT true of railroads in the 1800s?

A They could transport larger quantities than ships.

B They helped create nationwide markets.

Ⓒ They made shipping by water obsolete.

D They promoted the growth of other industries.

Steel is lighter, stronger, and more flexible than iron. The Bessemer process made possible the **mass production,** or production in great amounts, of steel. As a result, a new age of building began. A majestic symbol of this new age that endures is the Brooklyn Bridge.

The Brooklyn Bridge After the Civil War, New York City grew in size as well as population. Many people who worked on the island of Manhattan lived in nearby Brooklyn. The only way to travel between Brooklyn and Manhattan was by ferry across the East River. In winter, ice or winds often shut down the ferry service. Could a bridge high enough to clear river traffic be built across such a large distance? Engineer John A. Roebling, a German immigrant, thought it could.

Roebling designed a suspension bridge with thick steel cables suspended from high towers to hold up the main span. That span, arching 1,595 feet above the

ACTIVITY
Connecting with Economics

Present the following facts to students: the Brooklyn Bridge cost $18 million to build. On the day it opened, 150,300 pedestrians crossed the bridge. Each paid a penny ($.01) for the privilege. Also on the first day, 1,800 vehicles crossed the bridge. Vehicles had to pay a nickel ($.05) to cross. Have students calculate the revenue earned on the Brooklyn Bridge's first day of operation. Then have them determine the percentage of the construction cost this amount represents. **(Logical/ Mathematical)**

BACKGROUND
Geography in History

The distance people could travel to work, as well as natural boundaries such as rivers and seashores, determined early city boundaries. In the late 1800s, bridges and streetcar lines eliminated these barriers and opened up an era of urban expansion in the east. Between 1855 and 1873, Boston absorbed several towns to the west and south and expanded north across its harbor. Fifteen years after the Brooklyn Bridge opened, New York City annexed the independent cities of Brooklyn and Queens.

READING CHECK

It allowed impurities to be removed cheaply and easily, enabling steel to be produced in mass quantities.

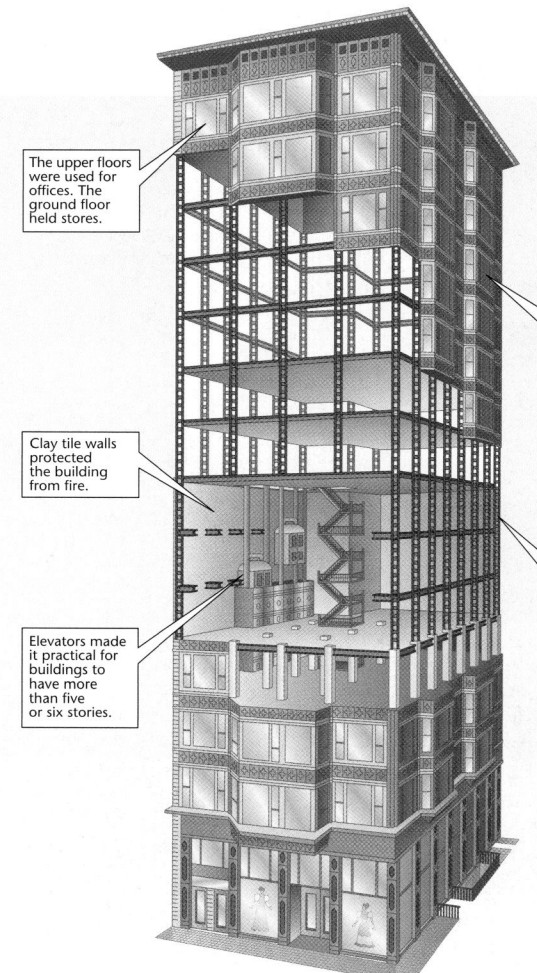

The upper floors were used for offices. The ground floor held stores.

Clay tile walls protected the building from fire.

Elevators made it practical for buildings to have more than five or six stories.

The Chicago Reliance Building

Bay windows let in light and air. This was important at a time when few buildings had electric lights and no one had even dreamed of air conditioning.

The steel frame carried the weight of the building.

VIEWING HISTORY The Bessemer process paved the way for the use of steel in building construction. Before steel, frameworks consisted of heavy iron. Steel acted as a much lighter framework and allowed the construction of taller buildings. The Reliance Building in Chicago, shown here, was built 16 stories high in the 1890s. At the time, 16 stories was enough to make a building a "skyscraper." **Analyzing Information** *How did various technologies combine to make skyscrapers possible?*

CAPTION ANSWERS

Viewing History The Bessemer process made possible the mass production of steel, which made steel cheap and easy to use for the construction of new buildings and bridges. Electricity aided the development of elevators.

RESOURCE DIRECTORY

Teaching Resources
Units 5/6 booklet
 • Section 1 Quiz, p. 4
Guide to the Essentials
 • Section 1 Summary, p. 68

Technology
Color Transparencies *The Way It Works,* H10; *American Photo,* F5
Exploring Primary Sources in U.S. History
 CD-ROM *The Tall Office Building Artistically Considered, Louis H. Sullivan*

river, would be the longest in the world. Roebling died shortly after construction of the Brooklyn Bridge began in 1869, so his son Washington took over the project. Washington was disabled in 1872 by a severe attack of decompression sickness ("the bends") while inspecting a foundation deep under the river. Other disasters followed, from explosions and fires, to dishonest dealings by a steel-cable contractor.

A Symbol of American Success Despite these problems, the Brooklyn Bridge was completed and opened with a ceremony on May 24, 1883. In the keynote address, congressman and future New York City mayor Abram Hewitt remarked on this great triumph:

> 66 *It is not the work of any one man or any one age. It is the result of study, of the experience, and of the knowledge of many men in many ages. It is not merely a creation; it is a growth. It stands before us today as the sum and epitome of human knowledge; as the very heir of the ages; as the latest glory of centuries of patient observation, profound study and accumulated skill. . . .* 99
>
> —Abram Stevens Hewitt

At nightfall, crowds gasped as electric light bulbs, which had been strung along the bridge, lit up the darkness and shimmered on the river below. The city celebrated with a magnificent fireworks display. Indeed, the entire United States celebrated, its inventive genius and hard work plainly visible for all the world to see.

VIEWING HISTORY This 1883 lithograph by Currier and Ives reveals the atmosphere of triumph and celebration that accompanied the opening of the Brooklyn Bridge. **Demonstrating Reasoned Judgment** *How do you think images such as this influenced people's perceptions of the changes taking place in society?*

Reading Comprehension

1. Due to new technology, the great increase in inventions, and the investments to fund them.

2. Using Drake's type of well made it much less expensive and easier to obtain large amounts of oil. The new process allowed an increase in demand to be satisfied.

3. They extended the usable hours of the day, allowed for efficient long-distance communication, and made possible the creation of entirely new industries.

4. Answers may include: reduce cost and increase efficiency of transportation; facilitate commerce; create national markets; stimulate other industries, like the steel industry.

5. Mass production of steel; large suspension bridges; steel frame construction in buildings.

Critical Thinking and Writing

6. By giving inventors and investors ownership of their ideas and creations, and the resulting profits.

7. Sample answers: personal computers or contact lenses.

8. Sample answers: A nationwide rail system made for a reduction in shipping prices. The Internet allows one to obtain news updates at any time throughout the day.

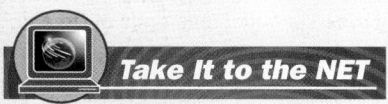

Invite students to take a Virtual Field Trip at **www.phschool.com**

Section 1 Assessment

READING COMPREHENSION

1. Why did the nation's industrial **productivity** rise in the late 1800s?

2. Why did the oil business change after Drake found oil in Pennsylvania?

3. How did inventions such as the light bulb and the telegraph change daily life in the late 1800s?

4. What were the advantages of building the **transcontinental railroad?**

5. What innovations did the **Bessemer process** encourage?

CRITICAL THINKING AND WRITING

6. **Determining Relevance** How did the system of patents encourage innovation and investment?

7. **Making Comparisons** Think of a modern convenience that you rely on. What benefits does this item bring to your life? Are there any drawbacks associated with this item?

8. **Writing a List** Create a list that compares the changes in business and daily life resulting from the telegraph and the railroad in the late 1800s with the changes resulting from the Internet in the late 1900s.

 Take It to the NET

Virtual Field Trip Visit the Central Pacific Railroad Photographic History Museum to learn more about the completion of the transcontinental railroad and life surrounding the railroads in the middle of the nineteenth century. Use the links provided in the *America: Pathways to the Present* area of the following Web site for help in completing this activity.
www.phschool.com

CAPTION ANSWERS

Viewing History They glorified and celebrated the new technologies and achievements of the time. The celebratory atmosphere depicted the public's view of American technological/business success and suggested that the United States was on the brink of something greater.

USING CROSS-SECTIONAL MAPS

Focus Students compare the data provided in a cross-sectional map with that in a physical-political map.

Instruct To be sure students understand the information presented in the cross-sectional map, ask them to identify the locations on the map at elevations of 1,000 feet and 7,000 feet. Have them indicate the elevation at Bitter Creek. Ask students to think about some other useful subjects for cross-sectional maps. *(The ocean floor, rivers, and other waterways)*

Extend See the Skills for Life activity in the Resource Directory below.

ANSWERS

PRACTICE THE SKILL

1. **(a)** The Rocky Mountains, Salt Lake Valley, Humboldt Valley, and the Sierra Nevada are on both maps. The Wyoming Basin and Independence Range appear only on the physical-political map. **(b)** No. The cross-sectional maps do not show the land area that lies north or south of the railroads. **(c)** No. The physical-political map shows some land to the east of Omaha, while the cross-sectional map ends at Omaha.

2. **(a)** Union Pacific: the highest elevation was about 7,500 feet above sea level, the lowest about 1,000 feet. Central Pacific: the highest elevation was just over 7,000 feet above sea level, the lowest about 300 feet. **(b)** The sharpest changes occurred heading east from Sacramento. **(c)** The most gradual changes occurred heading west from Omaha. **(d)** The Central Pacific Railroad: 700 miles; the Union Pacific Railroad: 1,100 miles.

3. **(a)** The Central Pacific Railroad was shorter but had more extreme changes in elevation. **(b)** Those working east from Sacramento, because of the Sierra Nevada mountains. **(c)** Union Pacific Railroad workers, because their route was longer and included more terrain at high elevation.

Using Cross-Sectional Maps

It is sometimes helpful to use more than one type of map to understand a particular piece of land. Physical-political maps show the land as if viewed from above, revealing distances across the surface. Cross-sectional maps show how the land would look if viewed from the side; they indicate the heights of mountains and valleys. The cross-sectional map below shows the changes in elevation along the route of the first transcontinental railroad. These changes posed a great challenge to workers building the railroad between 1862 and 1869.

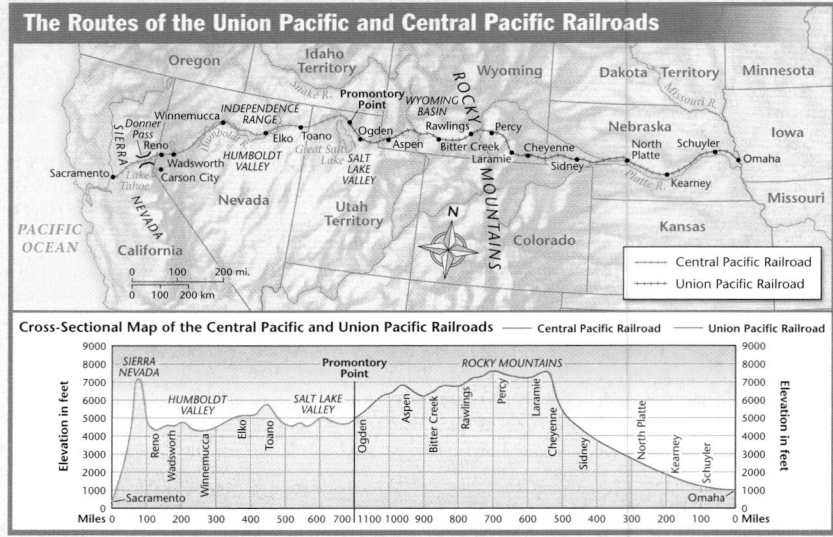

LEARN THE SKILL

Use the following steps to analyze a cross-sectional map:

1. **Study the region shown on both maps.** Compare the area covered and the elements shown on each map. Find several points that appear on both maps, and notice how they are depicted on each map.

2. **Analyze the information shown on the cross-sectional map.** Notice how changes in elevation are shown on the map (in this case, as the rising and falling of the green and red lines). Study the scale on the map, and notice both the distance covered across land and the elevation.

3. **Draw conclusions about the places or events depicted on the maps.** Use what you learn from both maps to better understand the landforms and the human activity in that area.

PRACTICE THE SKILL

Answer the following questions:

1. **(a)** Which landforms on the physical-political map correspond to those on the cross-sectional map?

Which landforms appear on only one map? **(b)** Does the cross-sectional map show the same land area as the physical-political map? Explain. **(c)** Does the cross-sectional map cover the same east-west distance as the physical-political map? Explain.

2. **(a)** What were the highest and lowest elevations of each railroad route? **(b)** Which 100-mile section on each route had the sharpest changes? **(c)** Which 100-mile section on each route had the most gradual changes? **(d)** How long was each route?

3. **(a)** How do the length and elevation changes of the two routes compare? **(b)** Which railroad workers faced the greatest challenge at the start of the project: those working east from Sacramento, or those working west from Omaha? Explain. **(c)** Which workers faced the greatest overall challenge? Explain.

APPLY THE SKILL

See the Chapter Review and Assessment for another opportunity to apply this skill.

466 Chapter 13 • *The Expansion of American Industry*

RESOURCE DIRECTORY

Teaching Resources
Skills for Life booklet, p. 15

Technology
Social Studies Skills Tutor CD-ROM
Interactive Practice in
• Geographic Literacy
• Critical Thinking and Reading
• Visual Analysis
• Communications

READING FOCUS

• Why were American industrialists of the late 1800s called both "robber barons" and "captains of industry"?

• How did social Darwinism affect Americans' views on big business?

• In what ways did big businesses differ from smaller businesses?

• How did industrialists gain a competitive edge over their rivals?

MAIN IDEA

Big business created wealth for its owners and for the nation, but it also prompted controversy and concern over its methods.

KEY TERMS

social Darwinism
oligopoly
monopoly
cartel
vertical consolidation
economies of scale
horizontal consolidation
trust
Sherman Antitrust Act

TAKING NOTES

Copy the web diagram below. As you read, fill in examples relating to the growth of big business in the late 1800s.

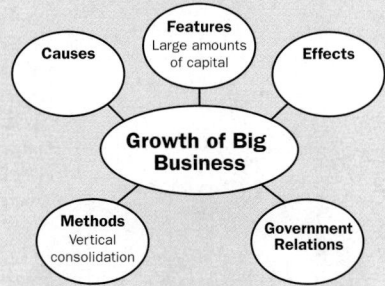

Causes

Features
Large amounts of capital

Effects

Growth of Big Business

Methods
Vertical consolidation

Government Relations

SECTION OBJECTIVES

1. Read to find out why American industrialists of the late 1800s were called both "robber barons" and "captains of industry."

2. Discover how social Darwinism affected Americans' views on big business.

3. Analyze the ways in which big businesses differed from smaller businesses.

4. Learn how industrialists gained a competitive edge over their rivals.

BELLRINGER

Warm-Up Activity Have students describe a "mom and pop" business. Then have them write a definition of "big business" and explain how the two differ.

Activating Prior Knowledge Ask students to list reasons why this period in history saw the birth and rapid growth of many different types of big businesses.

READING STRATEGY

Have students read the paragraphs under the heading "Robber Barons or Captains of Industry?" on the next page. Have them look for evidence to support each of these views of industrialists to help them understand and analyze the issue of industrialization and the rise of big business and the impact of the Sherman Antitrust Act on business.

Setting the Scene

> 66 *A very important incident in my life occurred when one day in a train, a nice, farmer-looking gentleman approached me. . . . He pulled from a small green bag the model of the first sleeping car. This man was Mr. Woodruff, the inventor. Its value struck me like a flash. . . . [He] offered me an interest in the venture, which I promptly accepted. . . . I had not the money, and I did not see any way of getting it. But I finally decided to visit the local banker and ask him for a loan. . . . I really made my first considerable sum from this investment in the Woodruff Sleeping Car Company.* 99

—Andrew Carnegie

One of the most successful of all business leaders and industrialists in the late 1800s was Andrew Carnegie. He came from humble beginnings, but quickly understood and embraced the concept that "money could make money." He just needed a way to find it. Carnegie had an eye for recognizing a good investment. Making wise and sometimes risky investments would soon make him one of the richest and most successful businessmen in the world.

The period of invention after the Civil War set the stage for great industrial growth. Still, more than technology would be needed to transform the United States. It would take shrewd businesspeople and many investors willing to gamble on new products. Without huge amounts of capital, businesses could not build factories or market their inventions. To succeed, business leaders often combined funds and resources to create large companies. Thus was born the age of big business.

Wall Street in New York City was a prominent financial center in the late 1800s.

467

RESOURCE DIRECTORY

Teaching Resources
Guided Reading and Review booklet, p. 55

Technology
Section Reading Support Transparencies
Guided Reading Audiotapes (English/Spanish), Ch. 13
Student Edition on Audio CD, Ch. 13
Prentice Hall Presentation Pro CD-ROM, Ch. 13
Companion Web site, www.phschool.com

Focus Explain that organizational changes in late nineteenth century businesses brought both great wealth and great hardship to the country. Ask students what those changes were and how they affected Americans.

Instruct Explain that in order to control the large amounts of money needed to produce new inventions and build railroads, bridges, and factories, American businesses grew into giant enterprises. Ask students how industrialists expanded their businesses. Discuss how the powerful industrialists of the late 1800s were both captains of industry and robber barons. Ask students who they think would be most likely to advocate the theory of social Darwinism—industrialists or workers.

Assess/Reteach Ask students to discuss which aspects of the growth of big business in the late nineteenth century were beneficial to society at large and which aspects were more hurtful than helpful. In what ways do the problems and the benefits of big business still affect us today?

BACKGROUND
Interdisciplinary

The term *robber baron* dates back to Medieval England. Then, the term referred to a nobleman, a baron, who was known for accosting and robbing anyone unlucky enough to cross his lands. The term fell into obscurity until it was revived in the late 1870s. To those who used it, the term seemed appropriate: the original robber barons became wealthy by exploiting defenseless travelers. The modern robber barons became wealthy by exploiting defenseless workers.

Robber Barons or Captains of Industry?

Historians have used the terms "robber barons" and "captains of industry" to describe the powerful industrialists who established large businesses in the late 1800s. The two terms suggest strikingly different images.

"Robber barons" implies that the business leaders built their fortunes by stealing from the public. According to this view, they drained the country of its natural resources and persuaded public officials to interpret laws in their favor. At the same time, these industrialists ruthlessly drove their competitors to ruin. They paid their workers meager wages and forced them to toil under dangerous and unhealthful conditions.

The term "captains of industry," on the other hand, suggests that the business leaders served their nation in a positive way. This view credits them with increasing the supply of goods by building factories, raising productivity, and expanding markets. In addition, the giant industrialists created the jobs that enabled many Americans to buy new goods and raise their standard of living. They also established outstanding museums, libraries, and universities, many of which still serve the public today.

Most historians believe that both views of America's early big business leaders contain elements of truth. The big business railroad giants of the late 1800s, such as Cornelius Vanderbilt, Edward Harriman, and James J. Hill, all exhibited qualities of both "robber barons" and "captains of industry." Consider how the examples of John D. Rockefeller and Andrew Carnegie, two of the country's first great industrialists, reflect this dual nature.

John D. Rockefeller John D. Rockefeller was on his way to accumulating a great fortune when he formed the Standard Oil Company in 1870. Some of the methods Rockefeller used to gain control of a large share of the oil industry were called into question, as you will read later in this section.

By the end of his life, however, Rockefeller had given over $500 million to establish or improve charities and institutions that he believed would benefit humanity. His philanthropy helped found the University of Chicago and the Rockefeller Foundation, which gave aid to institutions working in the fields of public health, the arts, social research, and many others.

Carnegie's "Gospel of Wealth" Andrew Carnegie's story is similar to Rockefeller's. (See the American Biography on the next page.) While expanding his steel business, Carnegie became a major public figure. In his books and speeches, he preached a "gospel of wealth." The essence of his message was simple: People should be free to make as much money as they can. After they make it, however, they should give it away.

More than 80 percent of Carnegie's fortune went toward some form of education. By the turn of the century, Carnegie had donated the money for nearly 3,000 free public libraries worldwide, supported artistic and research institutes, and set up a fund to study how to abolish war. By the time he died in 1919, Carnegie had given away some $350 million.

Still, not everyone approved of Carnegie's methods. As you will read later in this chapter, workers at his steel plants protested against his company's labor practices. Many others questioned the motives behind his good works. In reply, Carnegie argued that the success of men like him helped the nation as a whole:

Industrial growth required the contributions of both workers and business owners, as this illustration suggests.

RESOURCE DIRECTORY

Teaching Resources
Learning with Documents booklet (Primary Source Activity) *Tenement Factories,* p. 18
Great Debates booklet (Great Debates) *How Should Business Leaders Affect the Economy?* p. 8

Technology
Sounds of an Era Audio CD *"Gospel of Wealth,"* 1901 recording (time: 35 seconds)
RESOURCE PRO® **Primary Source Activity** *Carnegie's Gospel of Wealth,* found on Resource Pro, uses an excerpt from the

writing of Andrew Carnegie to explain his philosophy regarding money and philanthropy.
RESOURCE PRO® **Critical Thinking Activity** *Making Comparisons: Business Consolidations,* found on Resource Pro, uses a diagram on consolidating business to help students apply this skill.
Exploring Primary Sources in U.S. History CD-ROM *Wealth, Andrew Carnegie*

> *It will be a great mistake for the community to shoot the millionaires, for they are the bees that make the most honey, and contribute most to the hive even after they have gorged themselves full.*
>
> —Andrew Carnegie

Social Darwinism

In statements such as these, Carnegie also suggested that the wealthy were somehow the most valuable group in society. This idea, popular in the late 1800s, was inferred from Charles Darwin's theory of evolution, first published in 1859. According to Darwin, all animal life had evolved by a process of "natural selection," a process in which only the fittest survived to reproduce.

A theory soon emerged that applied Darwin's theory to society as a whole. Called **social Darwinism,** it held that society should do as little as possible to interfere with people's pursuit of success. In thinking about the relations between workers and employers, social Darwinists believed that if the government would stay out of the affairs of business, those who were most "fit" would succeed and become rich. Society as a whole would benefit from the success of the fit and the weeding out of the unfit.

Most Americans agreed that the government should not interfere with private businesses. As a result, the government neither taxed businesses' profits nor regulated their relations with their workers.

Business on a Larger Scale

Many factors combined to create a new kind of business in the United States in the late 1800s. Businesses grew to include much greater sums of money, more workers, and more products than had previously existed in American business. Several characteristics help to explain how big business differed from earlier forms of business in the United States.

Larger pools of capital The most basic feature of the new giant industries was the huge amount of money, or capital, needed to run them. In order to pay for new, expensive technology, and to run large plants across the country, entrepreneurs had to invest massive amounts of capital themselves or borrow huge sums from investors. The high start-up costs also limited the ability of smaller businesses to enter an industry.

Wider geographic span The advent of railroads and the telegraph aided the geographic expansion of businesses. Big businesses often had factories and sales offices in several different regions throughout the country.

Broader range of operations Prior to big business, most businesses in the United States were highly specialized. Big businesses often combined multiple operations. They were responsible for all or almost all the stages of production.

Revised role of ownership The increased scope of operations, workers, products, and money changed the nature of ownership and management. Owners had less of a connection to all aspects of their businesses because their businesses were simply too large. In most cases, owners would hire a "professional manager" to run their business. The manager had no ownership in the business, but was responsible for overseeing its operations.

New methods of management Innovations, such as more complex systems of accounting, were also necessary for controlling these large amounts of

BIOGRAPHY

Andrew Carnegie 1835–1919

Born in Scotland in 1835, Andrew Carnegie knew something about the harsh side of industrialization. His father was a skilled weaver, but the invention of the power loom caused the market for skilled craftsworkers to collapse. Carnegie's family faced hard times. As a result, they immigrated to the United States in 1848, settling near Pittsburgh, Pennsylvania.

At 12 years old, Carnegie found work in a cotton mill at $1.20 a week. At age 18, he attained the post of secretary to the superintendent in the Pennsylvania Railroad Company. His boss there encouraged him to invest $500 in the Adams Express Company. Although this amount exceeded the available assets of his whole family, Carnegie's parents agreed to mortgage their house in order to come up with the money. He was amazed that he made money from this stock "without any attention." Carnegie had begun his career as a businessman.

READING CHECK

Why did owners hire managers to manage certain aspects of their business?

resources. As a result, big businesses developed new systems of formal, written rules and created specialized departments.

Gaining a Competitive Edge

In their efforts to compete and earn higher profits, industrialists used many methods, fair or unfair, to gain a competitive edge over their rivals. They attempted to pay as little as they could for raw materials, labor, and shipping, hoping to maintain the most efficient businesses in their industry.

New Market Structures The lure of gaining enormous profits from new booming industries attracted many investors and entrepreneurs. However, the start-up costs of creating certain types of businesses were high and, as a result, only a few companies could compete in those industries. A market structure such as this, which is dominated by only a few large, profitable firms, is called an **oligopoly.** Many industries today are oligopolies, such as those that produce breakfast cereals, cars, and household appliances.

Some companies set out to gain a **monopoly,** or complete control of a product or service. To do this, a business bought out its competitors or drove them out of business. Once consumers had no other place to turn for a given product or service, the sole remaining company would be free to raise its prices.

Toward the end of the 1800s, federal and state governments passed laws to prevent certain monopolistic practices. Those laws did not prevent or destroy all monopolies, however. One reason was that political leaders refused to attack the powerful business leaders.

Forming monopolies was not the only way to control an industry. Sometimes industrialists prospered by taking steps to limit competition with other firms. One way was to form a **cartel**—a loose association of businesses that make the same product. Members of the cartels agreed to limit the supply of their product and thus keep prices high.

Neither the monopolies nor the cartels were foolproof. Monopolies faced the threat of government action, and cartels tended to fall apart during hard economic times. To achieve a more reliable arrangement, industrialists came up with new strategies that would help them dominate their markets.

Carnegie Steel By the time he was 30, in 1865, Andrew Carnegie was making $50,000 a year, and he wanted to invest his wealth. The development of the Bessemer process persuaded Carnegie that steel would soon replace iron in many industries. During the early 1870s, near Pittsburgh, he founded the first steel plants to use the Bessemer process. These holdings would eventually grow into the Carnegie Steel Company, which he established in 1889.

Carnegie's business prospered. The company's wealth enabled him to make it even stronger. He soon had enough money to buy the companies that performed all the phases of steel production, from the mines that produced iron ore to the furnaces and mills that made pig iron and steel. He even bought the

THE PROTECTORS OF OUR INDUSTRIES

INTERPRETING POLITICAL CARTOONS Some Americans were offended by the argument that business leaders protected jobs. **Drawing Conclusions** What does this cartoon suggest about the relationship of workers to business leaders?

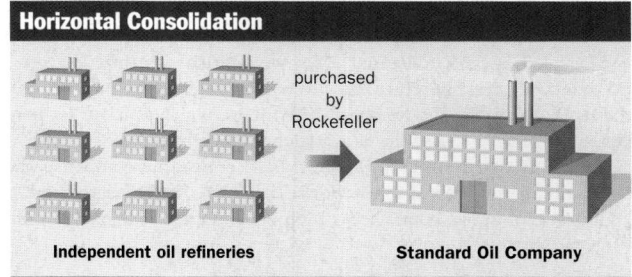

Horizontal Consolidation

Independent oil refineries → purchased by Rockefeller → Standard Oil Company

Vertical Consolidation

Coke fields → purchased by Carnegie

Iron ore deposits → purchased by Carnegie

Steel mills → purchased by Carnegie

Ships → purchased by Carnegie

Railroads → purchased by Carnegie

Carnegie Steel Company — Owns all phases of production

shipping and rail lines necessary to transport his products to market. Gaining control of the many different businesses that make up all phases of a product's development is known as **vertical consolidation.** (See diagram at right.)

This method of industrial control allowed Carnegie Steel to maintain very low production costs. This enabled Carnegie to cut his prices. He could charge less because of a phenomenon known as **economies of scale.** That is, as production increases, the cost of each item produced is lower. As Carnegie Steel expanded, its cost per item went down. Smaller companies were then at a disadvantage. Since they did not have the wealth to purchase all the phases of production, they were unable to cut their prices.

The Standard Oil Trust Oil was another industry that was about to become huge. In 1859, when Edwin L. Drake discovered oil in Titusville, Pennsylvania, many new opportunities for oil arose. The new ease of attaining oil and oil's growing usefulness excited many wealthy businessmen, including John D. Rockefeller. He had become rich from a grain and meat partnership during the Civil War, and he saw the oil business as a way to become even richer. In 1863, Rockefeller built an oil refinery near Cleveland, Ohio. The refinery expanded rapidly. In 1870, Rockefeller and several associates formed the Standard Oil Company of Ohio.

The large size of Standard Oil helped Rockefeller cut some of his production costs. For example, Standard Oil did not need to use all of the railroad services that other companies used, such as insurance and storage. Therefore, Rockefeller was able to negotiate with railroad companies to obtain refunds on part of the cost of transporting his oil. As a result of these refunds, he could set Standard Oil's prices lower than those of his competitors. As Rockefeller's company sold more oil, he was able to undersell his competitors by charging even less.

Rockefeller knew that he could expand his business further. He figured that if he could own his competitors' oil refineries, he would be able to create a giant oil company that had even lower production costs. This is another method of industrial control, called **horizontal consolidation,** which involves the bringing together of many firms in the same business. (See diagram above.)

Rockefeller soon had enough money to buy out his competitors, but the law stood in his way. State laws prohibited one company from owning the stock of another. If Rockefeller were to "buy out" his competitors, he would in effect be owning their stock. State governments feared that this practice would reduce competition and restrain, or hold back, free trade.

INTERPRETING DIAGRAMS
Some companies grew more powerful through horizontal consolidation, in which companies simply bought competitors in their field (above left). Other companies grew more powerful through vertical consolidation, in which they controlled all the phases of production (above right). **Analyzing Information** *What problems might a business face when trying to compete with a company that has a vertical monopoly? With a company that has a horizontal monopoly?*

Section 2 Assessment

Reading Comprehension

1. Social Darwinism encouraged laissez faire policies because of the belief that society should not interfere with people's successes.

2. Answers may include: large amounts of capital, diversification to encompass the total production of a product, revised role of ownership, and new management methods.

3. Mainly by getting rid of competitors, thus forcing consumers to pay artificially high prices.

4. Public concerns over large trusts led Congress to attempt to stop trusts from limiting industrial competition and from restraining interstate commerce.

Critical Thinking and Writing

5. Both had enough wealth to invest in industries on the brink of expansion. Both gained industry-wide control by lowering production costs and realizing economies of scale. Rockefeller formed a trust; Carnegie did not.

6. Answers may include: industrialists increased the availability of goods, provided jobs, and endowed cultural institutions. However, many were ruthless and corrupt, stopping at nothing to gain control over the competition.

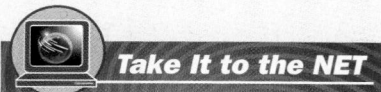

Take It to the NET

Encourage students to learn more about the personal histories and professional accomplishments of both Carnegie and Rockefeller.

Focus on ECONOMICS

The Panic of 1893 In 1893, a period of business expansion suddenly ended, sending a severe shock to the economy. During the "Panic of 1893," hundreds of banks closed, and more than 15,000 businesses failed, sinking the economy into a four-year depression. The resulting unemployment caused widespread misery, especially among workers and their families.

How does such a panic happen? At some point, businesses may begin churning out more goods than consumers want or can afford. Then they have to lower prices in order to sell their products. To cover their losses, they often cut wages and lay off workers. In turn, investors begin to fear that key businesses, heavily in debt, might not be able to repay their loans. Investors rush to sell stock, stock prices fall, and companies go bankrupt.

Samuel Dodd, Rockefeller's lawyer, had an idea to get around this ban. In 1882, the owners of Standard Oil and the companies allied with it agreed to combine their operations. They would turn over their assets to a board of nine trustees. In return, they were promised a share of the profits of the new organization. The board of trustees, which Rockefeller controlled, managed the companies as a single unit called a **trust.**

In time, 40 companies joined the trust. Because the companies did not officially merge, they did not violate any laws. Rockefeller's trust, a new kind of monopoly, controlled a high percentage of the nation's oil-refining capacity.

The Government Response Many Americans were skeptical and wary of trusts and other large business organizations. Americans who feared that trusts were limiting industrial competition began to demand government action to break up these industrial giants.

Despite questions about their practices, the large industrialists found sympathy and support from many government officials and leaders. The government was hesitant to interfere with the actions of big business. After all, these firms contributed mightily to the country's rising level of wealth. By the turn of the century, such mammoth companies as American Telephone and Telegraph, Swift and Armour, General Electric, Westinghouse, and Dupont were some of America's greatest success stories.

Congress did pass a law, however, in 1890, in an attempt to limit the amount of control a business could have over an industry. The **Sherman Antitrust Act** outlawed any combination of companies that restrained interstate trade or commerce.

The act, however, proved ineffective against trusts for nearly 15 years. Its vague wording essentially meant that the courts had to determine what the law said. As a result, the courts, which were largely pro-business in their views, enforced the law infrequently. The law actually *aided* giant corporations when it was applied successfully against labor unions. Federal officials argued that labor unions restrained trade because workers were combining to gain an advantage.

Section 2 Assessment

READING COMPREHENSION

1. How did the theory of **social Darwinism** affect the government's relationship to big business?

2. What were some features of the new big businesses?

3. How did methods such as **vertical** and **horizontal consolidation,** and factors such as **economies of scale** help companies dominate their markets?

4. Why did the **Sherman Antitrust Act** seek to stop big business from forming **trusts?**

CRITICAL THINKING AND WRITING

5. **Making Comparisons** Andrew Carnegie and John D. Rockefeller were both giant industrialists. Compare and contrast the ways they entered into, controlled, and dominated their respective industries.

6. **Writing to Persuade** Create an outline for a persuasive essay in which you explain why you view the nation's early industrialists as either "robber barons" or "captains of industry."

Take It to the NET

Biography To learn more about Andrew Carnegie or John D. Rockefeller, visit the links provided in the *America: Pathways to the Present* area of the following Web site.
www.phschool.com

RESOURCE DIRECTORY

Teaching Resources
Units 5/6 booklet
- Section 2 Quiz, p. 5
Guide to the Essentials
- Section 2 Summary, p. 69

Technology
Color Transparency *Political Cartoons,* B7

Industrialization and Workers

READING FOCUS
- What factors led to a growing American work force between 1860 and 1900?
- What was factory work like at the turn of the century?
- Why was it necessary for entire families to work?

MAIN IDEA
Industry relied on its laborers, who worked in low-paying, unskilled jobs and often in unsafe factories.

KEY TERMS
piecework
sweatshop
division of labor

TAKING NOTES
As you read, complete the following chart to show some of the positive and negative effects of industrialization on workers.

Effects of Industrialization		
Event/Aspect	**Positive Effects**	**Negative Effects**
Growing work force	Opens up many new jobs for immigrants and ex-farmers	Supply of workers drives wages down; whole families forced to work

Setting the Scene The abundant natural resources, inventive minds, and risk-taking entrepreneurs of the United States all contributed to the nation's industrial expansion. This expansion would not have been possible, however, without the millions of laborers who allowed the companies to succeed.

Sadie Frowne immigrated to the United States from Poland in 1899 when she was 13 years old. Her family, like so many others, hoped that America would provide greater opportunities for making money and living comfortably. Sadie began working in New York City, where she made skirts by machine.

> 66 I was new at the work and the foreman scolded me a great deal. . . . I did not know at first that you must not look around and talk, and I made many mistakes with my sewing, so that I was often called a 'stupid animal.' . . . The machines go like mad all day, because the faster you work, the more money you get. Sometimes in my haste I get my finger caught and the needle goes right through it. It goes so quick, tho[ugh], that it does not hurt much. . . . We all have accidents like that. . . . 99
> —Garment worker Sadie Frowne

The Growing Work Force

Around 14 million people immigrated to the United States between 1860 and 1900. Most came in the hope of finding work in the country's booming industrial centers. During the Civil War, when labor was scarce, the federal government encouraged immigration by passing the Contract Labor Act in 1864. This law allowed employers to enter into contracts with immigrants. Employers would pay the cost of their passage in return for immigrants' agreeing to work for a certain amount of time, up to a year. Employers soon began actively recruiting foreign laborers.

In another dramatic population shift, some 8 or 9 million Americans moved to cities during the late 1800s. Most of them fled poor economic conditions on the nation's farms. A long drought beginning in 1887, combined with

VIEWING HISTORY Industrialization led to a growing work force and new work environment. **Identifying Central Issues** How did industrial workers respond to their working conditions?

Chapter 13 • Section 3 **473**

RESOURCE DIRECTORY

Teaching Resources
Learning Styles Lesson Plans booklet, p. 29
Guided Reading and Review booklet, p. 56

Other Print Resources
Nystrom *Atlas of Our Country* *The Second Wave of Immigration,* pp. 24–25; *The Third Wave of Immigration,* pp. 30–31

Technology
Section Reading Support Transparencies
Guided Reading Audiotapes (English/Spanish), Ch. 13
Student Edition on Audio CD, Ch. 13
Prentice Hall United States History Video Collection™ Volume 12, *Immigration and Cultural Change*
Prentice Hall Presentation Pro CD-ROM, Ch. 13
Companion Web site, www.phschool.com

SECTION OBJECTIVES

1. Find out about factors that led to a growing American work force between 1860 and 1900.
2. Learn what factory work at the turn of the century was like.
3. Discover why it was sometimes necessary for entire families to work.

BELLRINGER

Warm-Up Activity Have students write down the words and phrases that they associate with the idea of work. Ask them to circle all the positive words and phrases on their list.

Activating Prior Knowledge Ask students what they know about child labor in the United States in the late 1800s. Are children permitted to work in this country today? Do other countries in the world permit child labor?

READING STRATEGY

Before students read this section, ask them to look at the section's pictures and main headings. Have them write a prediction of what life was like for factory workers in late nineteenth-century America. As they read, have students compare their predictions with the information presented in the text to help analyze the social issue of immigrants and child labor.

CAPTION ANSWERS

Viewing History Workers often became frustrated by dangerous conditions, strict work environments, and the repetitive nature of their work. Such sentiments eventually led large numbers of workers to join unions. Nevertheless, many others, including children, accepted harsh working conditions as a part of life and struggled on as best they could.

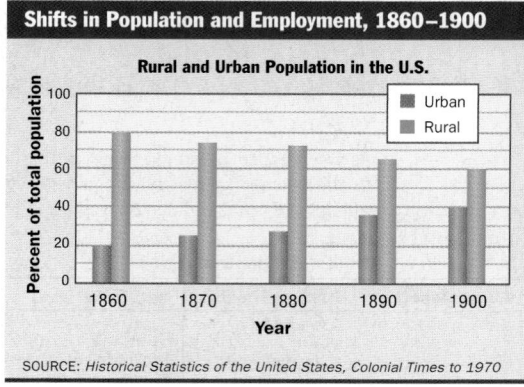

Rural and Urban Population in the U.S.

SOURCE: *Historical Statistics of the United States, Colonial Times to 1970*

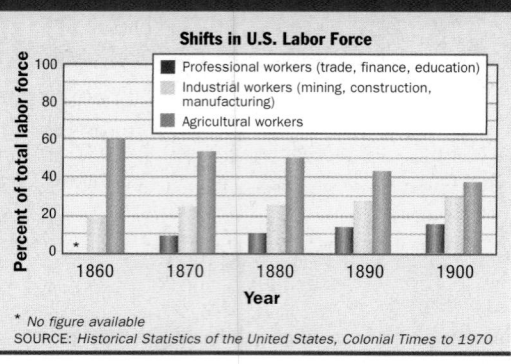

Shifts in U.S. Labor Force

* *No figure available*
SOURCE: *Historical Statistics of the United States, Colonial Times to 1970*

INTERPRETING GRAPHS
Industrial growth in the mid- to late 1800s led to shifts in population and the work force. **Drawing Conclusions** *What do you think accounted for the rise in the percentage of professional workers?*

low prices and more competition from foreign wheat producers, left many farm families penniless. Plentiful work in the factories lured the former farmers, as did many of the new attractions of city life.

Factory Work

By 1860, most states had established a ten-hour workday, yet they rarely enforced it. Thus, most laborers worked twelve hours, six days a week—and even more when they had to meet production goals. An 1868 federal law granted government employees an eight-hour day, but this did not affect private industry.

In many industries, employers paid workers not by the time worked but by what they produced. Workers received a fixed amount for each finished piece they produced—for example, a few cents for a garment or a number of cigars. This system of **piecework** meant that those who worked the fastest and produced the most pieces earned the most money. Most piecework was performed in what came to be known as a **sweatshop**—a shop where employees worked long hours at low wages and under poor working conditions.

Increasing Efficiency In 1881, Frederick Winslow Taylor set out to improve worker efficiency in the steel plant where he was chief engineer. He began to study the workers, trying to see how much time they took to do various jobs. Then he broke down each task into a number of steps and determined how long each step should take. In the same way he also studied each motion needed in a task. The goal of Taylor's time and motion studies was to increase worker productivity and thereby increase profits.

Taylor used his studies as the foundation of an entire system for the scientific management of workers. In 1911, he described this system in his book, *The Principles of Scientific Management*:

> 66 The work of every workman is fully planned out by the management at least one day in advance, and each man receives in most cases complete written instructions, describing in detail the task which he is to accomplish, as well as the means to be used in doing the work . . . and the exact time allowed for doing it. 99

—Frederick Winslow Taylor

Focus on TECHNOLOGY

Technology and the Arts The emergence of clanging, greasy machines at the end of the nineteenth century entirely changed the American landscape. Many Americans, including writers and artists, were delighted with the new machines and the human progress they represented. Nathaniel Hawthorne described trip hammers as "very pleasant objects to look at, working so massively as they do, and yet so accurately, chewing up, as it were, the hot iron, and fashioning it into shape, with a sort of mighty and gigantic gentleness in their mode of action."

Some employers had their own, unscientific methods of improving efficiency. They simply increased the speed of factory machines or gave each employee more work. Increases in productivity, however, did not always translate into higher pay for workers. On the contrary, greater factory efficiency often led to layoffs because businesses no longer needed as many workers. In addition, many workers felt that these methods gave owners too much control over their work. As a result, most workers came to resent them.

The Division of Labor Although its goal was to increase worker productivity, the methods used in scientific management brought about a change in the relationship between the worker and the product he or she created. Artisans traditionally made a product from start to finish. Doing so required them to perform a variety of tasks. In contrast, factory workers usually performed only one small task, over and over, and rarely even saw the finished product. This **division of labor** into separate tasks proved to be efficient, but it took much of the joy out of the work.

The relationship between workers and owners also changed. In smaller businesses, owners and workers had day-to-day interactions with each other. Because of the large size of new big businesses, owners seldom even visited the factory floor where workers toiled. In the worst cases, the workers, called "hands" or "operatives," were viewed as interchangeable parts in a vast and impersonal machine. One factory manager in 1883 declared, "I regard my people as I regard my machinery. So long as they can do my work for what I choose to pay them, I keep them, getting out of them all I can."

The Work Environment Unlike farmers, who had more flexibility in the pace they worked, factory workers were ruled by the clock, which told them when to start, take any breaks, and stop work. In addition, discipline within the factory was strict. To make a profit, factory managers needed to run an efficient operation. Thus they might fine or fire workers for a range of offenses, such as being late, talking, or refusing to do a task.

Workplaces were not always safe. The noise of the machines was deafening. Lighting and ventilation were poor. Fatigue, faulty equipment, and careless training resulted in frequent fires and accidents. Despite the harsh conditions, employers suffered no shortage of labor. Factory work offered higher pay and more opportunities than most people could hope to find elsewhere.

Laboring in factories or mines and performing dangerous work was unhealthy for all workers. But it especially threatened growing children. Many children became stunted in both body and mind. In 1892, social reformer Jacob Riis explained the impact of factory work on children in a book titled *Children of the Poor*. Riis wrote that people who spent their whole childhood on the factory floor grew "to manhood and womanhood . . . with the years that should have prepared them for life's work gone in hopeless and profitless drudgery." Thanks to Riis and others, the practice of child labor came under broad attack in the 1890s and early 1900s, prompting states to begin curbing this practice through legislation.

VIEWING FINE ART John Ferguson Weir's painting *Gun Foundry* presents a vivid image of the nation's industrial might. **Drawing Inferences** *What does the painting suggest about the conditions faced by workers?*

READING CHECK
What was the goal of Taylor's studies?

ACTIVITY
Connecting with History and Conflict

Direct students' attention to the quotation from the factory manager at the end of "The Division of Labor." Have students generate a rebuttal to this statement, following its construction, from the point of view of a factory worker. Students' statements should begin "I regard my managers as. . . ." **(Verbal/Linguistic)**

BACKGROUND
Biography

Frederick Taylor is often thought of as an apologist for management, but he went to great pains to argue that "scientific management" would actually benefit workers and, moreover, even lead to the end of labor conflicts. He wrote that "The majority of [employees and employers] believe that the fundamental interests of employees and employers are necessarily antagonistic. Scientific management, on the contrary, has for its very foundation the firm conviction that the true interests of the two are one and the same; that prosperity for the employer cannot exist through a long term of years unless it is accompanied by prosperity for the employee and vice versa; and that it is possible to give the workman what he most wants—high wages—and the employer what he wants—a low labor cost—for his manufactures."

READING CHECK
To increase the output of each worker, thus making the business more profitable.

CUSTOMIZE FOR ...
Less Proficient Writers
Have students create a "handbill" that states the rules of employment in a factory of this era. They can base the employment rules on the information included in the paragraph on this page headed "The Work Environment."

☑ **TEST PREPARATION**
Have students reread the quotation from Frederick Winslow Taylor on the previous page and then answer the question below.

What was one of the results of using Taylor's theories of management?

 A Factory workers took more pride in their work.

 B Factory owners lost money.

 C Owners visited factories more often.

 D More factory workers were laid off.

CAPTION ANSWERS

Viewing Fine Art Conditions were dangerous and emphasized production over worker safety.

Section 3 Assessment

Reading Comprehension

1. Two population shifts occurred; farm to city and immigrants arriving in the U.S. Both groups sought work in the factories.

2. Piecework rewarded workers for products completed, not time worked. This led to inequity as not all workers could complete the same amount of product.

3. While increasing efficiency, the division of labor and Taylor's studies had a dehumanizing effect. Workers were treated like pieces of machinery whose performance could be precisely calculated.

4. Their income was often vital for family survival; no laws existed to prohibit child labor at this time. Families had no insurance for illness or unemployment.

Critical Thinking and Writing

5. Workers on farms may have had more of a connection to the work they were doing. Farm work was dictated more by nature than by technology—farmers could not work at night or in severe weather.

6. Outlines will vary. Possible answers include: lengthy work day, unpleasant working conditions, low pay.

Take It to the NET

Invite students to take a Virtual Field Trip at www.phschool.com

VIEWING HISTORY Many children worked in hazardous conditions. The boys above worked in coal mines. The grime that covers their faces also clogged their lungs, leading to disease. The girl in the photo on the right operated heavy machinery in a textile mill. **Drawing Conclusions** *How do you think Americans at the time reacted to photos such as these?*

Working Families

In the 1880s, children made up more than 5 percent of the industrial labor force. By the end of the 1800s, nearly one in five children between the ages of 10 and 16 was employed. For many households, children's wages meant the difference between going hungry or having food on the table.

As a result, children often left school at the age of 12 or 13 to work. Girls sometimes took factory jobs so that their brothers could stay in school. If a mother could not make money working at home, she might take a factory job, leaving her children with relatives or neighbors. If an adult became ill, died, or could not find or keep a job, children as young as 6 or 7 had to bring in cash.

In the 1800s, families in need relied on private charities. These charities could not afford to help everyone, however. They had limited resources, so only the neediest received the food, clothing, and shelter that charities had to offer. Except in rare cases, government did not provide public assistance. Unemployment insurance, for example, did not exist, so workers received no payments as a result of layoffs or factory closings. The popular theory of social Darwinism held that poverty resulted from personal weakness. Many thought that offering relief to the unemployed would encourage idleness.

Section 3 Assessment

READING COMPREHENSION

1. Why did the American work force grow in the late 1800s?

2. How did **piecework** change the nature of factory work?

3. What were the effects of Taylor's scientific management studies and the **division of labor** on workers?

4. Why did children work?

CRITICAL THINKING AND WRITING

5. **Identifying Alternatives** Although it differed from factory work, work on family farms was also difficult and dangerous. Explain what you think were the key differences between the two types of work.

6. **Writing to Describe** Prepare an outline for an essay describing the daily life of a typical factory worker.

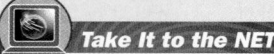

Take It to the NET

Virtual Field Trip Visit the Smithsonian Institute to learn more about sweatshops and labor conditions in the late 1800s and find out what they are like today. Use the links provided in the *America: Pathways to the Present* area of the following Web site for help in completing this activity. www.phschool.com

CAPTION ANSWERS

Viewing History Most probably began to sympathize with the children and advocate an end to child labor.

RESOURCE DIRECTORY

Teaching Resources
Units 5/6 booklet
• Section 3 Quiz, p. 6
Guide to the Essentials
• Section 3 Summary, p. 70

READING FOCUS

- What impact did industrialization have on the gulf between rich and poor?
- What were the goals of the early labor unions in the United States?
- Why did Eugene V. Debs organize the American Railway Union?
- What were the causes and outcomes of the major strikes in the late 1800s?

MAIN IDEA

In the late 1800s, workers organized labor unions to improve their wages and working conditions.

KEY TERMS

socialism
craft union
collective bargaining
industrial union
scab
anarchist
Haymarket Riot
Homestead Strike
Pullman Strike

TAKING NOTES

As you read, complete the chart below, filling in the successes and failures of the labor unions.

Labor Unions	
Successes	Failures
The Knights of Labor protect railroad wages from being cut in 1885 through the use of the strike.	The Great Railroad Strike of 1877 turns violent, giving the public and the government a bad taste for unions.

Setting the Scene

66 *What shall the workers do? Sit idly by and see the vast resources of nature and the human mind be utilized and monopolized for the benefit of the comparative few? No. The laborers must learn to think and act, and soon, too, that only by the power of organization, and common concert of action, can . . . their rights to life . . . be recognized, and liberty and rights secured.* 99

—Samuel Gompers

Industrialization had lowered the prices of consumer goods, but in the late 1800s most factory workers did not earn enough to buy them. The successful entrepreneurs of the era had worked hard. Many, like Carnegie, had used their wealth to provide money for good works. Still, in hard times only the poor went hungry. Increasingly, working men and women took their complaints directly and forcefully to their employers.

Gulf Between Rich and Poor

In 1890, the richest 9 percent of Americans held nearly 75 percent of the national wealth. In the best of times, the average worker could earn only a few hundred dollars a year. Many workers resented the extravagant lifestyles of many factory owners. Poor families had little hope of relief when hard times hit. Some suffered in silence, trusting that tomorrow would be better. Others became politically active in an effort to improve their lives. A few of these individuals were drawn to the idea of **socialism,** which was then gaining popularity in Europe.

Socialism is an economic and political philosophy that favors public instead of private control

VIEWING HISTORY Many wealthy industrialists enjoyed great personal wealth and luxurious comforts (left). In stark contrast, many workers lived in crowded boarding houses (right). **Identifying Central Issues** How did many workers respond to the contrast between the rich and poor?

Focus Explain to students that industrialization caused great inequalities in wealth in the late nineteenth century. Big business owners grew wealthy while workers toiled for low wages. Ask students how workers tried to improve their wages and working conditions.

Instruct Discuss why workers resented the wealth of business owners. Ask how socialism, anarchism, and labor unions were different approaches to solving the problems of workers. Ask how socialism and anarchism promised to improve workers' lives but ran counter to some American ideals. What did labor unions do to address workers' problems? Ask students to describe public reaction to the strikes. What pattern of events did the Pullman Strike set in motion?

Assess/Reteach Have students list the types of grievances experienced by workers that led to the development of labor unions.

BACKGROUND
Interdisciplinary

Though the cost of manufactured consumer goods dropped because of industrialization, working-class women had difficulty affording them. Women's wages and job opportunities were far below those of men. African American women were even worse off, being excluded from most factory positions until World War I. Consider the average earnings of a working woman and the price of consumer goods: factories paid the average woman worker $5 a week, department stores paid $2 a week plus 5 percent commission, and families paid domestic servants $3 a week plus board. A ready-made blouse cost $1, a skirt $2, and a pair of shoes $1.50. Carfare for sales clerks was a nickel each way, and a dormitory bed cost $2.50 a week.

of property and income. Socialists believe that society at large, not just private individuals, should take charge of a nation's wealth. That wealth, they say, should be distributed equally to everyone.

Socialism began in the 1830s as an idealistic movement. Early Socialists believed that people should cooperate, not compete, in producing goods. Socialism then grew more radical, reflecting the ideas of a German philosopher named Karl Marx. In 1848, Marx, along with Friedrich Engels, wrote a famous pamphlet called the *Communist Manifesto*. In it they denounced the capitalist economic system and predicted that workers would one day overturn it.

Most Americans opposed socialism. The wealthy saw it as a threat to their fortunes. Politicians saw it as a threat to public order. Americans in general, including most workers, saw it as a threat to the deeply rooted American ideals of private property, free enterprise, and individual liberty.

The Rise of Labor Unions

A small percentage of American workers did become Socialists and called for an end to free enterprise. Far more workers, however, chose to work within the system by uniting to form labor unions.

Meeting posters and labor union badges such as these appeared around the country as labor unions grew more popular.

Early Labor Unions The early years of industrialization had spawned a few labor unions, organized among workers in certain trades, such as construction and textile manufacturing. The first national labor organization was the National Trades Union, which was open to workers from all crafts. It survived only a few years before being destroyed by the panic and depression of 1837.

Strong local unions resurfaced after the Civil War. They began by providing help for their members in bad times, but soon became the means for expressing workers' demands to employers. These demands included shorter workdays, higher wages, and better working conditions.

National unions also began to reappear at this time. In Baltimore in 1866, labor activists formed the National Labor Union, representing some 60,000 members. In 1872, this union nominated a candidate for President. It failed, however, to survive a depression that began the following year. Indeed, unions in general suffered a steep decline in membership as a result of the poor economy.

The Knights of Labor Another national union, the Noble and Holy Order of the Knights of Labor, formed in Philadelphia in 1869. The Knights hoped to organize all working men and women, skilled and unskilled, into a single union. Membership included farmers and factory workers as well as shopkeepers and office workers. The union recruited African Americans, 60,000 of whom joined. After 1881, the union also recruited women members.

Under the leadership of former machinist Terence Powderly, the Knights pursued broad social reforms. These included equal pay for equal work, the eight-hour workday, and an end to child labor. They did not emphasize higher wages as their primary goal.

The leaders of the Knights preferred not to use the strike as a tool. Most members, however, differed with their leadership on this issue. In fact, it was a strike that helped the Knights achieve their greatest strength. In 1885, when unions linked to the Knights forced railroad owner Jay Gould to give up a wage cut, membership quickly soared to 700,000. Yet a series of failed strikes followed, some of them violent. Membership dropped off, and public support for the Knights waned. By the 1890s, the Knights had largely disappeared as a national force.

The American Federation of Labor A third national union, the American Federation of Labor (AFL) formed in 1886 under the leadership of Samuel Gompers, a London-born cigar maker. Unlike the Knights of Labor, the AFL was a **craft union.** Rather than organizing all workers, the AFL sought to organize only skilled workers in a network of smaller unions, each devoted to a specific craft.

Between 1886 and 1892, the AFL gained some 250,000 members. Yet they still represented only a tiny portion of the nation's total labor force. Few African Americans joined. In theory the AFL was open to African Americans, but local unions often found ways to exclude them from membership. Women, too, were not welcome in the AFL. Gompers opposed the membership of women because he believed that their presence in the work force would drive wages down.

Gompers and the AFL focused mainly on issues of workers' wages, hours, and working conditions. This so-called bread-and-butter unionism set the AFL apart from the Knights of Labor. The Knights had sought to help their members through political activity and education. The AFL relied on economic pressure, such as strikes and boycotts, against employers. By using these tactics, the AFL tried to force employers to participate in **collective bargaining,** a process in which workers negotiate as a group with employers. Workers acting as a group had more power than a single worker acting alone. To strengthen its collective bargaining power, the AFL pressed for a "closed shop," a workplace in which only union members would be hired.

The Wobblies The AFL's policies did not suit all workers. In 1905, in Chicago, 43 groups opposed to the AFL founded the Industrial Workers of the World (IWW), or Wobblies. The IWW, which focused on unskilled workers, was a radical union that included many Socialists among its leadership. A number of IWW strikes were violent on both sides. During World War I, many IWW leaders were convicted of promoting strikes in war-related industries.

Reaction of Employers By and large, employers disliked and feared unions. They preferred to deal with employees as individuals. In addition, they feared that if they had to pay higher wages and meet the other demands of unions, their costs would go up and they would be less competitive in the marketplace. As a result, employers took measures to stop unions, such as
1. forbidding union meetings;
2. firing union organizers;
3. forcing new employees to sign "yellow dog" contracts, in which workers promised never to join a union or participate in a strike;
4. refusing to bargain collectively when strikes did occur;
5. refusing to recognize unions as their workers' legitimate representatives.

In 1902, George F. Baer, the president of a mining company, reflected the opinions of many business leaders when he wrote: "The rights and interests of the laboring man will be protected and cared for—not by the labor agitators, but by the Christian men to whom God . . . has given control of the property interests of the country. . . . "

Focus on CULTURE

Labor Day The Knights of Labor sponsored the first Labor Day on September 5, 1882, as a tribute to the American worker. As the labor force grew, so did support for making this day an official national holiday. In 1887, five states passed laws giving Labor Day legal status. Finally, in 1894, days after President Cleveland sent troops to suppress the Pullman Strike, Congress passed the bill making Labor Day a national holiday. The "workingman's holiday," celebrated the first Monday of every September, has now also come to be associated with the end of summer vacations, a return to school, and one last long weekend for family barbecues and outdoor picnics before the autumn months arrive.

 Sounds of an Era

Listen to the IWW song "The Commonwealth of Toil" and other sounds from the period of industrial expansion.

Chapter 13 • Section 4   **479**

Railroad Workers Organize

The first major incident of nationwide labor unrest in the United States occurred in the railroad industry. The violent strike of 1877 touched off a wave of strikes and bitter confrontations between labor, management, and the government in the decades to follow. It also led to reform and reorganization within the labor movement itself.

The Great Railroad Strike of 1877   The strike began in July 1877, when the Baltimore and Ohio Railroad announced a wage cut of 10 percent in the midst of a depression. This was the second wage cut in eight months. Railroads elsewhere imposed similar cuts, along with orders to run "double headers," trains with two engines and twice as many cars as usual. The unusually long trains increased the risk of accidents and the chance of worker layoffs.

Railway workers reacted with violence. Workers in Martinsburg, West Virginia, were the first to declare a strike. Strikers and sympathizers there were strong enough to turn back the local militia. Rioting spread rapidly to Pittsburgh, Chicago, St. Louis, and other cities. The governors in some of these states requested assistance from the federal government. President Rutherford B. Hayes responded by sending in federal troops to put down the strikes.

A week later in Pittsburgh, soldiers fired on rioters, killing and wounding many. A crowd of 20,000 angry men and women reacted to the shootings by setting fire to railroad company property, causing more than $5 million in damage. President Hayes again sent in federal troops. From the 1877 strike on, employers relied on federal and state troops to repress labor unrest. A new and violent era in labor relations had begun.

Debs and the American Railway Union   At the time of the 1877 strike, railroad workers mainly organized into various "brotherhoods," which were basically craft unions. Eugene V. Debs had taken a leadership role in the Brotherhood of Locomotive Firemen. He spoke out against the 1877 strike. The mission of the brotherhood, according to Debs, was "not to antagonize capital." Although he was initially opposed to strikes because of their confrontational nature, Debs gained sympathy for the strike as he became more involved in the labor movement.

COMPARING PRIMARY SOURCES
Labor Unions

In 1883, the Senate Committee on Education and Labor held a series of hearings concerning the relationship between workers and management. The committee heard these opposing views about the need for labor unions.

Analyzing Viewpoints   Compare the main arguments made by the two speakers.

Testimony of a Labor Leader

"The laws written [by Congress] and now in operation to protect the property of the capitalist and the moneyed class generally are almost innumerable, yet nothing has been done to protect the property of the workingmen, the only property that they possess, their working power, their savings bank, their school, and trades union."

—*Samuel Gompers,
labor leader*

Testimony of a Factory Manager

"I think that . . . in a free country like this . . . it is perfectly safe for at least the lifetime of this generation to leave the question of how a man shall work, and how long he shall work, and what wages he shall get to himself."

—*Thomas L. Livermore,
manager of a manufacturing company*

Debs, however, never thought violence had a place in strikes. He believed that the violence of the 1877 strike had resulted in part from the disorganization and corruption that existed within the brotherhoods. As a solution to this problem, and in an attempt to avoid future violent strikes, Debs proposed a new **industrial union** for all railway workers. Industrial unions organized workers from all crafts in a given industry. The American Railway Union (A.R.U.), formed in 1893, would replace the existing craft brotherhoods and unite all railroad workers, skilled and unskilled. Its primary purpose would be to protect the wages and rights of all the employees.

> 66 If fair wages [were] the return for efficient service, [then] harmonious relations may be established and maintained . . . and the necessity for strike and lockout, boycott and blacklist, alike disastrous to employer and employee, and a perpetual menace to the welfare of the public, will forever disappear. 99
>
> —Eugene V. Debs

Strikes Rock the Nation

From 1881 to 1900, the United States faced one industrial crisis after another. Some 24,000 strikes erupted in the nation's factories, mines, mills, and rail yards during those two decades alone. Three events were particularly violent: the Haymarket Riot and the Homestead and Pullman strikes.

Haymarket, 1886   On May 1, 1886, groups of workers mounted a national demonstration for an eight-hour workday. "Eight hours for work, eight hours for rest, eight hours for what we will," ran the cry. Strikes then erupted in a number of cities.

On May 3, at Chicago's McCormick reaper factory, police broke up a fight between strikers and **scabs.** (A scab is a negative term for a worker called in by an employer to replace striking laborers. Using scabs allows a company to continue operating and to avoid having to bargain with the union.) The police action caused several casualties among the workers.

Union leaders called for a protest rally on the evening of May 4 in Chicago's Haymarket Square. A group of **anarchists,** radicals who oppose all government, joined the strikers. Anarchists addressed workers with fiery speeches, such as this one by newspaper editor August Spies:

> 66 You have endured the pangs of want and hunger; your children you have sacrificed to the factory-lords. In short, you have been miserable and obedient slaves all these years. Why? To satisfy the insatiable greed, to fill the coffers of your lazy thieving master! 99
>
> —August Spies

At the May 4 event, someone threw a bomb into a police formation, killing one officer. In the riot that followed, gunfire between police and protesters killed dozens on both sides. Investigators never found the bomb thrower, yet eight anarchists were tried for conspiracy to commit murder. Four were

VIEWING HISTORY Eugene V. Debs was arrested following the Pullman Strike in 1894. While in jail, Debs gained an interest in socialism. He would later combine his energetic style and his belief in socialism to conduct several unsuccessful presidential campaigns as leader of the Socialist Party. **Drawing Inferences** What factors, including his core beliefs, ultimately led Debs to become a Socialist?

READING CHECK
What led to the riot in Haymarket?

482 • Chapter 13 Section 4

VIEWING HISTORY The violence of the Haymarket Riot, depicted here, troubled many Americans. **Recognizing Cause and Effect** *What were the effects of the incident at Haymarket on the union cause?*

READING CHECK
What were the benefits and drawbacks of Pullman's town?

hanged. Another committed suicide in jail. Governor John P. Altgeld of Illinois decided later that the convictions resulted from public outrage rather than evidence. He pardoned the remaining three anarchists.

To many unionists, the anarchists who took part in the **Haymarket Riot** would be heroes forever. To employers, however, they remained vicious criminals determined to undermine law and order. Much of the American public came to associate unions in general with violence and radical ideas.

Homestead, 1892 In the summer of 1892, while Andrew Carnegie was in Europe, his partner Henry Frick tried to cut workers' wages at Carnegie Steel. The union at the Carnegie plant in Homestead, Pennsylvania, called a strike.

Frick had a plan for defeating the union. On July 1, he called in the Pinkertons, a private police force known for their ability to break strikes. Under cover of darkness on July 5, some 300 Pinkertons moved up the Monongahela River on barges. In a shootout with strikers on shore, several people died and many were wounded.

At first Americans generally sympathized with the striking workers. Then, on July 23, anarchist Alexander Berkman tried and failed to assassinate Frick. Although Berkman was not connected with the strike, the public associated his act with the rising tide of labor violence.

The union admitted defeat and called off the **Homestead Strike** on November 20. Homestead reopened under militia protection. "I will never recognize the union, never, never!" Frick declared. Carnegie believed in unions and accepted their right to strike, as long as no violence took place. However, Carnegie Steel (and its successor, U.S. Steel) remained nonunionized until the late 1930s.

Pullman, 1894 Like the strike of 1877, the last of the great strikes involved the railroad industry. Inventor George Pullman had developed a luxury sleeping car that was slightly larger than existing railroad cars. Known as Pullman cars, they were so successful that Pullman needed a steady source of labor to meet growing demands. He believed he could attract a solid, dedicated labor force by constructing a town made just for workers.

Built in 1880, twelve miles south of Chicago's business district, the town of Pullman provided its workers with everything they could possibly need: parks, a miniature lake, schools, a theater, a church, and paved sidewalks lined with shade trees. Pullman also maintained remarkable health and sanitation conditions, athletic programs, and a military band.

However, Pullman held his town to high standards, which workers sometimes viewed as unfriendly. Many workers felt that Pullman exercised too much control over their lives. Pullman's ban on alcohol in the town, for example, angered many residents. While these factors did not directly cause a strike, they provided a tense backdrop for the events about to occur. Conditions in the town took a turn for the worse after the Panic of 1893. Pullman laid off workers and cut wages by 25 percent. Meanwhile, he kept rent and food prices in his town at the same levels.

In May 1894, a delegation of workers went to him to protest. In response, Pullman fired three of the workers, which led the local union to go on strike.

Pullman refused to bargain and instead shut down the plant. Badly needing help, the workers turned to the newly formed American Railway Union and Eugene V. Debs for support.

One month earlier, the A.R.U. had achieved success when they supported striking workers on James J. Hill's Great Northern Railroad. Following that victory, membership in the union rose to over 150,000 members, 3,000 percent more than the previous year. The A.R.U.'s triumph led many railway workers to feel optimistic about their cause.

Although Debs was hesitant to join this strike, the delegates of the A.R.U. voted to support the strike and called for a boycott of Pullman cars throughout the country. Widespread local strikes followed. By June 1894, some 260,000 railway workers had joined in the **Pullman Strike.** Debs instructed strikers not to interfere with the nation's mail, but the strike got out of hand. It completely disrupted western railroad traffic, including delivery of the mail.

Railroad owners, organized as the General Managers Association, turned to the federal government for help. By arguing that the mail had to get through and citing the Sherman Antitrust Act, Attorney General Richard Olney won a court order forbidding all union activity that halted railroad traffic. The American Railway Union, he argued, had formed an illegal trust and was restraining free trade. Two days later, on July 4, President Grover Cleveland sent in 2,500 federal troops to ensure that strikers obeyed the court order. A week later the strike was over.

The Pullman strike and its outcome set an important pattern. In the years ahead, factory owners appealed frequently for court orders against unions. The federal government regularly approved these appeals, denying unions recognition as legally protected organizations. This official government opposition helped limit union gains for more than 30 years.

VIEWING HISTORY Angry railroad strikers look on as federal troops ride in to restore order. **Synthesizing Information** *Why did the government intervene in the Pullman Strike? Why did the government side against labor unions?*

Section 4 — Assessment

READING COMPREHENSION

1. Why did **socialism** appeal to some Americans in the late 1800s?

2. How did early labor unions in the United States differ in their organization and in the methods they used to achieve their goals?

3. Why did the railroad strike in 1877 prompt Eugene V. Debs to create an **industrial union?**

4. How successful were labor unions at the end of the century?

CRITICAL THINKING AND WRITING

5. **Making Comparisons** Compare socialism and the labor movement as two different responses to the growing gulf between the rich and the poor. How did their goals differ?

6. **Writing a Letter** Write a letter to President Hayes regarding the strike in Martinsburg, West Virginia, in 1877. Try to persuade the President either to send troops in to stop the strike or to refuse to intervene.

Take It to the NET

Activity: Creating a Fact Sheet
Prepare a fact sheet outlining a specific aspect of labor unions, for example, the role of labor unions in our society, or the experience of a labor union member in the late 1800s. Use the links provided in the *America: Pathways to the Present* area of the following Web site for help in completing this activity.
www.phschool.com

Section 4 — Assessment

Reading Comprehension

1. The gap between rich and poor was vast. Socialism seemed to offer a political and economic philosophy which favored the public at large, rather than a few wealthy individuals.

2. Organization: inclusion of skilled or unskilled workers; by trade, or including all trades. Methods: collective bargaining, strikes, boycotts.

3. He disliked the violence of the strike. He felt that separate railway unions were too fractured, and that one union for the entire railroad industry would be efficient and effective.

4. Labor unions had only limited success at that time. They brought many of labor's pressing issues to light, but often met with violence and government opposition during strikes.

Critical Thinking and Writing

5. Socialists hoped to see all Americans share equally in the nation's wealth. The labor movement worked mostly within the free enterprise system, attempting to attain fair treatment for workers and owners.

6. Letters requesting federal troops might stress that the strikers had defied the state militia. Letters opposing intervention might say that the use of federal troops would only increase the violence.

Take It to the NET

Answers will vary. Students might note the solidarity of the unions, the level of support they received, and the success or failure rate they had in achieving their goals.

CAPTION ANSWERS

Viewing History The government was sympathetic to big business at the time. The government also felt that rail transport was a vital industry that must not be interrupted, particularly since railroads carried the nation's mail.

Chapter 13

Chapter 13 Review and Assessment

REVIEWING KEY TERMS

Students should refer to the definitions of key terms in the chapter to write sentences that show an understanding of the era of American industrial expansion.

REVIEWING MAIN IDEAS

15. Railroad expansion created great demand for steel rails; manufacturers could use railroads to sell their products nationwide; towns benefited from being located along rail lines.
16. Free enterprise was invaluable to the stimulation of big business because the lure of profits and success encouraged investment and innovation.
17. Horizontal consolidation, vertical consolidation, formation of trusts, underselling competitors.
18. It made the United States wealthy, opened up thousands of jobs, and created many new products at low costs. However, the safety and well-being of labor was not a priority.
19. They often resented these attempts for increased efficiency, as it gave employers too much control over their work and made the work less interesting.
20. Many young children left school and worked at hard labor in unhealthy conditions in order to help support their families.
21. They disallowed union meetings; fired union organizers; forced new employees to sign yellow dog contracts; refused to bargain collectively or recognize unions as workers' legitimate representatives.
22. Causes: the confining structure of Pullman's town, layoffs, and wage cuts. Effects: the federal government sent troops to restore order and end the strike. Union gains were minimal for years to come.

CRITICAL THINKING

23. Answers will vary. Students might mention the impact of computers or other new electronic inventions.

---

creating a CHAPTER SUMMARY

Copy this chart (right) on a piece of paper and complete it by adding information about how each of these important figures contributed to the period of industrial expansion in the United States.

 iTEXT

For additional review and enrichment activities, see the interactive version of *America: Pathways to the Present*, available on the Web and on CD-ROM.

Person	Impact
Thomas Edison	Helped bring electric power to businesses and homes. This new form of energy stimulated the growth of big business.
Henry Bessemer	
Andrew Carnegie	
John D. Rockefeller	
Frederick Winslow Taylor	
Samuel Gompers	
Eugene V. Debs	
George Pullman	

★ Reviewing Key Terms

For each of the terms below, write a sentence explaining how it relates to the period of industrial expansion in the United States.

1. transcontinental railroad
2. Bessemer process
3. mass production
4. social Darwinism
5. monopoly
6. vertical consolidation
7. economies of scale
8. trust
9. Sherman Antitrust Act
10. piecework
11. division of labor
12. socialism
13. collective bargaining
14. scab

★ Reviewing Main Ideas

15. How did new railroads and improvements in railway technology help spur economic growth? (Section 1)
16. Evaluate the impact of the free enterprise system in stimulating the age of big business. (Sections 1 and 2)
17. Name four methods that industrialists may have used to dominate their industry. (Section 2)
18. What were some positive and negative effects of rapid industrial growth? (Section 2)
19. How did workers react to attempts by employers to increase factory efficiency? (Section 3)

20. What problems did children face in industrialized America? (Section 3)
21. What steps did employers take to fight labor unions? (Section 4)
22. Analyze the causes and effects of the Pullman Strike. (Section 4)

★ Critical Thinking

23. **Making Comparisons** How have recent inventions such as the personal computer and the cell phone changed your daily life?
24. **Demonstrating Reasoned Judgment** Choose two visuals from the chapter and explain how they reflect the impact of industrialism on American society.
25. **Drawing Conclusions** Why do you think the federal government was friendly to the industrialists even when much of the public did not support them?
26. **Recognizing Ideologies** How did the emergence of beliefs in social Darwinism and/or socialism reflect the new challenges facing American society in the late 1800s?
27. **Expressing Problems Clearly** What challenges did labor unions have to overcome in order to achieve their main goals?

CREATING A CHAPTER SUMMARY

Person	Impact
Thomas Edison	Helped bring electric power to businesses and homes, stimulating the growth of big business
Henry Bessemer	Developed less expensive process for manufacturing steel
Andrew Carnegie	One of the most successful business leaders and industrialists of the late 1800s; first fortune in railroads, second in steel
John D. Rockefeller	Founded Standard Oil Company; great American philanthropist
Frederick Winslow Taylor	An "efficiency expert," invented the process of time and motion studies
Samuel Gompers	Founded American Federation of Labor
Eugene V. Debs	Established the American Railway Union to clean up corruption in unions and to eradicate violence in strikes
George Pullman	Pullman gave his workers good places to live, but he tried to control their lives. This led to the Pullman Strike of 1894, involving 120,000 railway workers.

★ Skills Assessment

Analyzing Political Cartoons ▶

28. In the background of this cartoon, a concerned citizen tries to alert Uncle Sam to the dangerous scene in the foreground. (a) What is the snake a symbol of? (b) How do you know? (c) Who is the woman? (d) How do you know?

29. What is the snake doing?

30. What is the cartoon's overall message?

Interpreting Data

Turn to the population and labor graphs in Section 3.

31. Which statement best summarizes the information shown in both graphs?

   A The rural population decreased between 1860 and 1900.

   B The number of industrial workers and city dwellers rose between 1860 and 1900.

   C The percentage of professional workers decreased as people began moving away from farms.

   D As people moved to the cities, a higher percentage of the population became industrial or professional workers.

32. What was the main reason for shifts in population and employment in the late 1800s?

   F increasing immigration and decreasing farm prices

   G the lure of new attractions in the nation's growing cities

   H the growth of railroads and expansion of American industry

   J high wages and incentives offered by factory owners

Applying the Chapter Skill: *Using Cross-Sectional Maps*

33. Use map resources to plot a route across the Appalachian Mountains from Raleigh, North Carolina, to Columbus, Ohio. Then draw a cross-sectional map of your route.

ACTIVITIES

Writing to LEARN

Writing to Describe
The Bessemer process helped create what has been termed the "age of steel" in the United States. Is the United States still in the age of steel? If not, how might you describe the present era? Write an essay expressing your view. Include specific examples.

Primary Source CD-ROM

Working With Primary Sources Find additional information on the period of industrial expansion on the *Exploring Primary Sources in U.S. History CD-ROM* and use the selection(s) provided to complete the Chapter 13 primary source activity located in the *America: Pathways to the Present* area of the following Web site. **www.phschool.com**

Take It to the NET

Chapter Self-Test As a review activity, take the Chapter 13 Self-Test in the *America: Pathways to the Present* area at the Web site listed below. The questions are designed to test your understanding of the chapter content. **www.phschool.com**

---

24. Answers might focus on the disparity in wealth represented in the illustration at the beginning of Section 4, or the heroism of railroad track gangs depicted in the photograph in Section 1.

25. Because of their contributions to the rising wealth of the country and the political power wielded by many of the industrialists.

26. Social Darwinism reflected free enterprise and laissez faire. Socialism emphasized the problems of wealth and the desire for its equal distribution to all, preserving the greater good rather than individual success.

27. They had to overcome their differences in order to remain united; deal with hostile employers who attempted to stop all union activity; and face disapproval by the federal government.

SKILLS ASSESSMENT

28. (a) Monopolies. (b) It is labeled, "Monopoly." (c) Liberty. (d) Lady Liberty is a common political symbol.

29. The snake has control of the Capitol and is attacking liberty.

30. That monopolies control the government and threaten freedom.

31. D

32. F

33. Answers will vary, but students should try to map out a direct route.

Chapter 14 Planning Guide
Resource Manager

	CORE INSTRUCTION	**READING/SKILLS**
Chapter-Level Resources	Teaching Resources • Pacing Charts booklet • Block Scheduling booklet **Resource Pro® CD-ROM**, Ch. 14 **Prentice Hall Presentation Pro CD-ROM**, Ch. 14 **www.phschool.com** • eTeach	**Guided Reading Audiotapes (English/Spanish)** **Student Edition on Audio CD**, Ch. 14 **Social Studies Skills Tutor CD-ROM** **Color Transparencies**, A25, A26, A60, B8, E10, E11, E12, E13, H12, H13, H14
1 Moving West 1. Learn about the kinds of conditions that lured people to migrate to the West. 2. Find out where western settlers came from. 3. Describe how the American frontier shifted westward.	Teaching Resources **Units 5/6 booklet** • Section 1 Quiz, p. 15	**Guided Reading and Review booklet**, p. 58 **Guide to the Essentials**, p. 73 **Learning with Documents booklet**, p. 19 **Section Reading Support Transparencies**
2 Conflict with Native Americans 1. Study the factors that caused changes in the life of the Plains Indians. 2. Find out how government policies and battlefield challenges affected the Indian Wars. 3. Learn about changes that occurred in federal Indian policies by 1900.	Teaching Resources **Units 5/6 booklet** • Section 2 Quiz, p. 16 **Learning Styles Lesson Plans booklet**, p. 30	**Guided Reading and Review booklet**, p. 59 **Guide to the Essentials**, p. 74 **Learning with Documents booklet**, p. 53 **Section Reading Support Transparencies**
3 Mining, Ranching and Farming 1. Learn how mining spread in the West. 2. Find out what caused the western cattle boom. 3. See what life was like for a cowboy on the Chisholm Trail. 4. Discover how settlers overcame barriers in farming the plains.	Teaching Resources **Units 5/6 booklet** • Section 3 Quiz, p. 17	**Guided Reading and Review booklet**, p. 60 **Guide to the Essentials**, p. 75 **Section Reading Support Transparencies**
4 Populism 1. See why farmers complained about federal post–Civil War economic policies. 2. Find out how the government responded to organized protests by farmers. 3. Discover the Populists' key goals. 4. Understand the main point of William Jennings Bryan's Cross of Gold speech. 5. Learn about the legacy of Populism.	Teaching Resources **Units 5/6 booklet** • Section 4 Quiz, p. 18 **Learning Styles Lesson Plans booklet**, p. 31	**Guided Reading and Review booklet**, p. 61 **Guide to the Essentials**, p. 76 **Learning with Documents booklet**, p. 83 **Skills for Life booklet**, p. 16 **Section Reading Support Transparencies**

ENRICHMENT/PRE-AP

Prentice Hall United States History Video Collection™
www.phschool.com
- Section Activities, Virtual Field Trip, Chapter Activities, Current Events Online

Nystrom *Atlas of Our Country,* pp. 28–29
Sounds of an Era Audio CD

Biography, Literature, and Comparing Primary Sources booklet, p. 125
Nystrom *Atlas of Our Country,* pp. 32–33
Historical Outline Map Book, p. 55
Sounds of an Era Audio CD
Exploring Primary Sources in U.S. History CD-ROM

Biography, Literature, and Comparing Primary Sources booklet, p. 19, 58
American History Block Scheduling Support
Historical Outline Map Book, p. 56
Sounds of an Era Audio CD
Exploring Primary Sources in U.S. History CD-ROM

Great Debates booklet, p. 10
American History Block Scheduling Support
Sounds of an Era Audio CD
American Pathways Thematic Posters

ASSESSMENT

PRENTICE HALL
ASSESSMENT SYSTEM

Core Assessment
ExamView® Test Bank, Ch. 14
ExamView® Test Bank CD-ROM, Ch. 14

Standardized Test Preparation
Diagnose and Prescribe
Diagnostic Tests for High School Social Studies Skills

Review and Reteach
Review Book for U.S. History

Practice and Assess
Test-taking Strategies With Transparencies
Test-taking Strategies Posters
Test Prep Book for U.S. History
Alternative Assessment Handbook
Document-Based Assessment

Teaching Resources
Units 5/6 booklet
- Section Quizzes, pp. 15–18
- Chapter Tests, pp. 19, 22

www.phschool.com Ch. 14 Self-Test

AmericanHeritage RESOURCES

From the Archives of American Heritage®, pp. 501, 503, 505, 511
AmericanHeritage® My Brush with History™ Videotapes
www.americanheritage.com

Don't miss the exclusive interactive version of this textbook on the Web and on CD-ROM.

Chapter 14 Planning Guide
In Your Classroom

CUSTOMIZE FOR INDIVIDUAL NEEDS

Gifted and Talented

Teacher's Edition
• Customize for Gifted and Talented, p. 489

Teaching Resources
• Biography, Literature, and Comparing Primary Sources booklet, pp. 19, 58, 125

Technology
• Exploring Primary Sources in U.S. History CD-ROM *Geronimo: His Own Story, S. M. Barrett, ed.; The Old Chisholm Trail, Cowboy Song; Peary Reaches the North Pole, Robert E. Peary*

ESL

Teacher's Edition
• Customize for ESL, p. 499

Teaching Resources
• Guided Reading and Review booklet, pp. 58–61
• Guide to the Essentials (English/Spanish), Chapter 14

Technology
• Student Edition on Audio CD, Chapter 14
• Guided Reading Audiotapes (English/Spanish), Chapter 14
• Section Reading Support Transparencies

Less Proficient Readers

Teacher's Edition
• Customize for Less Proficient Readers, pp. 495, 511

Teaching Resources
• Guided Reading and Review booklet, pp. 58–61
• Guide to the Essentials (English/Spanish), Chapter 14

Technology
• Student Edition on Audio CD, Chapter 14
• Guided Reading Audiotapes (English/Spanish), Chapter 14
• Section Reading Support Transparencies

Less Proficient Writers

Teacher's Edition
• Customize for Less Proficient Writers, p. 505

Teaching Resources
• Guided Reading and Review booklet, pp. 58–61
• Guide to the Essentials (English/Spanish), Chapter 14

Technology
• Student Edition on Audio CD, Chapter 14
• Guided Reading Audiotapes (English/Spanish), Chapter 14
• Section Reading Support Transparencies

TEACHER'S EDITION INDEX

CHAPTER 14 – PACING SUGGESTIONS

For 90-minute Blocks

• Teach sections 1–4 using Transparencies A25, A26, A60, B8, E10, E11, E12, E13, H12, H13, and H14, and the Recent Scholarship note on page 503 for class discussions.

Running Out of Time?

If you are running short on time to cover this chapter, consider the following options:

• Use the Prentice Hall Presentation Pro CD-ROM to create an outline for this chapter.

• Use the Section Summaries for Chapter 14, from **Guide to the Essentials (English/Spanish).**

1 Moving West

Connecting with Geography
Point out that settlers moving west probably encountered many things that were new to them in terms of landforms, climate, wildlife, and vegetation. Have students work in small groups to create an annotated map showing these new aspects of the settlers' lives. You may wish to limit students to certain geographical areas. For example, students might assume the identity of a family from Vermont that has decided to settle in Kansas. Their map, therefore, would be limited to what they might have encountered en route and when they arrived. **(Visual/Spatial)**

2 Conflict with Native Americans

Connecting with Culture
Divide the class into groups that will report on various aspects of the culture of the Plains Indians. These might include tribal organization, daily life, spiritual beliefs and practices, housing, transportation, clothing, art, and legends. You may wish to approach the study either from the perspective of one particular Native American group or apply the topic to Native Americans in general. Have students present their information in written form, then share what they learned with the class. Encourage students to illustrate their reports. **(Verbal/Linguistic)**

3 Mining, Ranching and Farming

Connecting with Economics
Explain to students that many of the mining towns that sprang up in areas where minerals were found eventually became large cities: Helena, Montana; Virginia City, Nevada; and Denver, Colorado, are examples. However, some of the towns faded as conditions changed. Have students research ghost towns and diagram the process by which a boom town that developed in a mining area eventually became a ghost town. **(Visual/Spatial)**

4 Populism

Connecting with Economics
Point out to students that many of the financial terms introduced in this section will reappear as they continue reading in the textbook. Therefore, they will find it useful to create a dictionary of the financial terms discussed in this section, such as *money supply, inflation,* and *deflation.* Students might begin by creating an index card for each entry and its definition, or they can use a computer database. Encourage students to add to their dictionaries as they read and to add terms from present-day financial pages, on-line sites, and television business news. **(Verbal/Linguistic)**

Chapter 14
Looking to the West
(1860–1900)

INTRODUCING THE CHAPTER

After the Civil War, Americans moved west of the Mississippi River, taking over the land for farms, ranches, and mines, forcing out the original users, the Native Americans. The taming of the West became one of the great American myths.

TIME LINE ACTIVITY

To provide students with practice in using the time line, ask questions such as these:

1. What began the push of Indians off their traditional lands in the 1860s and 1870s? (*Federal land grants starting in 1862 spurred settlement of the West.*)

2. Which country began to move Indians onto reservations in 1871? (*Canada*)

3. What were two key battles between U.S. forces and Native Americans? (*The Battle of Little Bighorn in 1876 and the Wounded Knee Massacre in 1890*)

Chapter 14

Looking to the West
(1860–1900)

SECTION 1   Moving West
SECTION 2   Conflict With Native Americans
SECTION 3   Mining, Ranching, and Farming
SECTION 4   Populism

Grand Canyon of the Yellowstone, by Thomas Moran, 1872

Longhorn steer

A Ute settlement in the Great Basin region

American Events

1862 Federal land grants ignite western settlement.

1867 Founding of Abilene, Kansas, spurs era of Texas cattle drives.

1872 Yellowstone National Park is created.

1876 Custer and his men are killed at Battle of Little Bighorn.

Presidential Terms: A. Lincoln 1861–1865   A. Johnson 1865–1869   U. S. Grant 1869–1877   R. Hayes 1877–1881

1860 · · · 1870 · · ·

World Events

Swedish scientist Alfred Nobel invents dynamite. **1867**

Canada begins forcing Indians onto reservations. **1871**

eTeach

Be sure to check out this month's online discussion with a Master Teacher. Go to **www.phschool.com**.

RESOURCE DIRECTORY

Teaching Resources
Pacing Charts booklet
Block Scheduling booklet, p. 20
Units 5/6 booklet
• Chapter Summary, p. 14

Technology
Guided Reading Audiotapes (English/Spanish), Ch. 14
Student Edition on Audio CD, Ch. 14
Sounds of an Era Audio CD *"The Cowboy's Life Is a Very Dreary Life,"* 1942 recording (time: 30 seconds)

Prentice Hall United States History Video Collection™ Volume 11, *Industrialization and Urbanization*
Prentice Hall Presentation Pro CD-ROM, Ch. 14
Resource Pro® CD-ROM
Social Studies Skills Tutor CD-ROM
Companion Web site, www.phschool.com

Statehood in the West

Map

CANADA

Washington
1889

Montana
MONTANA
1889

North Dakota
1889
Minnesota

Oregon
STATE OF OREGON 1859
1859

Idaho
1890

South Dakota
1889

Wyoming
1890

Nebraska
1867
Iowa

Nevada
1864

Utah
1896

Colorado
1876

Kansas
KANSAS
1861

Missouri

California
CALIFORNIA REPUBLIC
1850

Arizona
1912

New Mexico
1912

Oklahoma
OKLAHOMA
1907

Arkansas

Texas
1845

Louisiana

PACIFIC OCEAN

40°N

30°N

120°W

MEXICO

0   100   200 mi.
0   100   200 km

90°W

N

1890 Date of statehood

State flag today

Chapter 14   **487**

Time line

1887
The Dawes Act allots land to individual Indians.

1889
"Boomers" race to stake claims as tracts of Indian Territory open in Oklahoma.

1890
Wounded Knee Massacre marks the end of the Indian wars. The Sherman Silver Purchase Act aims to boost silver currency.

1896
Democratic presidential candidate William Jennings Bryan gives pro-silver "Cross of Gold" speech.

J. Garfield 1881
C. Arthur 1881–1885   G. Cleveland 1885–1889   B. Harrison 1889–1893   G. Cleveland 1893–1897   W. McKinley 1897–1901

1880   •   •   • **1890**   •   •   **1900**

Britain takes sole control of Egypt.
1882

Canada's transcontinental railroad completed despite uprising by Plains Indians.
1885

Russia's last czar, Nicholas II, begins his reign.
1895

Australian nationhood is approved by Britain.
1900

Statehood in the West

Activating Prior Knowledge Why do you think the dates of statehood are so close for many of the states shown? *(The western areas were settled rapidly in a wave of pioneers.)*

Previewing Many of the states shown have very regular shapes, unlike the shapes of states on the East Coast. What might be one reason? *(Possible answers: State boundaries were sometimes determined by natural borders, such as mountains. There were fewer of these natural borders in some of the country's midwestern plains areas, so the borders that were created had a very regular look.)*

BACKGROUND
About the Pictures

1. The teepee was an ideal shelter for the Utes because it was easy to disassemble and transport as they moved from place to place in pursuit of game animals and better land.

2. Longhorn cattle, originally bred in Texas, were a tough and hardy breed ideally suited for grazing on the sparse western plains. Soldiers returning from the Civil War found millions of Longhorns wandering wild in Texas.

3. American artist Thomas Moran painted the *Grand Canyon of Yellowstone* while on an expedition to document the natural wonders of the area. This painting was one of the major influences in convincing the government to set aside the area as the first national park.

TEXT

Don't miss the exclusive interactive version of this textbook on the Web and on CD-ROM.

BIBLIOGRAPHY

For the Teacher

Moynihan, Ruth B., Susan Armitage, and Christine Fischer Dichamp, eds. ***So Much to Be Done: Women Settlers on the Mining and Ranching Frontier.*** University of Nebraska Press, 1990. (Nineteen narratives by women from diverse environments and backgrounds in the nineteenth-century West.)

Unruh, John D., Jr., ***The Overland Emigrants and the Trans-Mississippi West, 1840–60.*** University of Illinois Press, 1993. (Reissue of a prizewinning account of the opening of the Oregon Trail.)

For the Student

Time-Life Books editors. ***Time-Life Books: The Old West.*** Prentice Hall, 1990. (A richly illustrated companion volume to a ten-hour miniseries, ***Faces and Voices of the Wild West.***)

"The Donner Party," KCTS Video, 90 minutes. (Part of the PBS series, ***The American Experience;*** an ill-fated journey west.)

Dakota Wars and Reservation Life. University of Nebraska. Film. (Depicts the lives of Native Americans of the Plains and their wars, including Custer's last stand.)

Chapter 14 • **487**

READING FOCUS

- What conditions lured people to migrate to the West?
- Where did the western settlers come from?
- How did the American frontier shift westward?

MAIN IDEA

With the help of the federal government, Americans and immigrants settled the region west of the Mississippi in a major migration during the second half of the 1800s.

KEY TERMS

push-pull factors
Pacific Railway Acts
Morrill Land-Grant Act
land speculator
Homestead Act
Exoduster

TAKING NOTES

Copy the diagram below. As you read, fill in factors relating to settlement of the West.

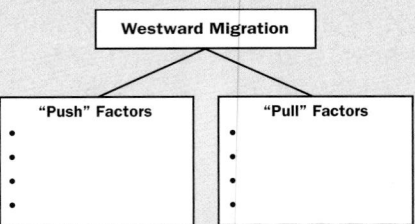

VIEWING HISTORY Buffalo dot the landscape today in South Dakota's Badlands National Park. Majestic prairie scenes like this greeted early settlers. **Expressing Problems Clearly** To many newcomers, the first sight of the Great Plains was both dazzling and daunting. Explain this statement.

Setting the Scene   At minus 50 degrees, a Montana winter night could turn a fatted steer into a furry icicle. In the Southwest, heat topping 110 degrees left the bleached bones of prospectors strewn across the desert. Describing the harsh winters of the open plains, one newspaper editor called western Kansas "a prairie where the cows give blue milk and the wind whips the long-tailed pigs to death."

After the Civil War, pioneers settled from the Mississippi River to the partly populated California coast. Newcomers from Vermont, or Kentucky, or Germany wrote home with fantastic tales of these strange lands:

> 66 The wind was too fierce. . . . It actually blows the feathers off the chickens' backs. . . . I can't put up many pictures and things for everytime the door opens they all blow off the wall. . . . [W]e noticed how terrible loud everyone talks out here and now we find ourselves just shouting away at the top of our voices. . . . [U]nless you yell you can't be heard at all. 99
> —South Dakota settler Mary Clark

Truly, you have to wonder: What moved people like Mary Clark to journey to this land of known and unknown dangers?

The Lure of the West

The settlers of the American West had many reasons for giving up their old, sometimes comfortable, lives for a new start in the wilderness. The West seized the American imagination. It kindled people's sense of adventure, their entrepreneurial spirit, and their appetite for profit and conquest.

When scholars study the reasons for major migrations, they look at what they call **push-pull factors**—events and conditions that either force (push) people to move elsewhere or strongly attract (pull) them to do so.

Push Factors   Various conditions urged settlers westward. The Civil War had displaced thousands of farmers, former slaves, and other workers. Eastern

488   Chapter 14 • *Looking to the West*

farmland was increasingly costly, certainly for many African Americans or for impoverished immigrants. Failed entrepreneurs sought a second chance in a new location. Ethnic and religious repression caused both Americans (such as the Mormons) and Europeans to seek freedom in the West. The open spaces also sheltered outlaws on the run.

Yet the West was more than just a refuge for discouraged people and shady characters. The region offered temptations and adventures that lured—pulled—settlers westward.

Pull Factor: Government Incentives   Before the Civil War, the North and South had fought bitterly over whether the new territories of the West would allow or prohibit slavery. After the war, with those issues behind it, the federal government opened the way to western migration by giving away public lands—or selling them at rock-bottom prices.

Under the **Pacific Railway Acts** of 1862 and 1864, the government gave large land grants to the Union Pacific and Central Pacific railroads. The original act granted 10 square miles of public land on each side of the track for every mile of track laid. From 1850 to 1871, the railroads received more than 175 million acres of public land—an area more than one tenth the size of the whole United States and larger than the state of Texas.

Railroad expansion provided new avenues of migration into the American interior. The railroads sold portions of their land to arriving settlers at a handsome profit. Lands closest to the tracks drew the highest prices, because farmers and ranchers wanted to locate near railway stations.

To further encourage western settlement, Congress passed the **Morrill Land-Grant Act** of 1862. It gave state governments millions of acres of western lands, which the states could then sell to raise money for the creation of "land grant" colleges specializing in agriculture and mechanical arts. The states sold their land grants to bankers and **land speculators,** people who bought up large areas of land in the hope of selling it later for a profit.

The government program that really set the wagons rolling west was the **Homestead Act,** signed by President Lincoln in 1862. Under the act, for a small fee settlers could have 160 acres of land—a quarter-mile square—if they met certain conditions: They were at least 21 years old or the heads of families. They were American citizens or immigrants filing for citizenship. They built a house of a certain minimum size (usually 12 feet by 14 feet) on their claims and lived in it at least six months a year. Finally, they had to farm the land for five years in a row before claiming ownership.

The act created more than 372,000 farms. By 1900, settlers had filed 600,000 claims for more than 80 million acres under the Homestead Act.

Pull Factor: Private Property   A key incentive to western settlement was the availability of legally enforceable, transferable property rights. The Homestead Act and state and local laws helped to limit settlers' risks and avoid a total free-for-all. Miners, cattle ranchers, and farmers all received certain rights to land and possessions. Land parcels were measured, registered, and deeded. Cattle branding established ownership. Enforcement of water rights provided stable water sources for crops and for human and animal consumption.

In time, established American economic concepts of private property, private enterprise, and a free market extended across the continent. One editor, hoping to raise the standards of a rather lawless town, reminded his readers that

---

LESSON PLAN

Focus Tell students that after the Civil War, large numbers of Americans and Europeans continued moving into "the West," the area between the settled West Coast and the Mississippi River. Ask students what these people hoped to find.

Instruct Discuss the conditions that inspired people to head west. Explain that many Civil War veterans from New England sought larger, more fertile fields. Many African Americans wanted to leave the restrictive South and obtain land of their own. Ask students why the government gave land to homesteaders. How did railroads profit from the land the federal government granted to them? Who were the most successful homesteaders? What special challenges did frontier life present for African Americans? For women?

Assess/Reteach The second half of the nineteenth century was marked by a major migration of settlers from the eastern portion of the United States to the western portion. Can students list some areas to which these new settlers journeyed?

BACKGROUND
Geography in History

African Americans who left the South for a better life in the West were met with both acceptance and rejection in their new homes. When a group of Exodusters arrived in Kansas in 1879, the governor vowed to help them. A Freedman's Relief Association provided food and medical supplies, and many white people offered jobs and homes. Within a few years, African Americans had bought more than twenty thousand acres of land and created the towns of Dunlap, Singleton, and Nicodemus. While life in the West was generally better than it had been in the South, African Americans still faced discrimination. In Denver the locals would not rent to or hire African Americans, and in communities such as Lincoln, Nebraska, African American migrants were expelled.

CUSTOMIZE FOR ...

Gifted and Talented

Explain that pressure for a homestead law began long before 1862. Ask students to discuss why Northerners opposed such a law until the Civil War. What factors might have made life easier for African Americans in the West?

✓ **TEST PREPARATION**

Have students reread the section on this page titled "Pull Factor: Government Incentives" and then answer the question below.

Which of these activities would a land speculator be likely to undertake?

A Creating a large agricultural college.

B Overseeing the donation of public lands for the creation of railroads.

C Inducing settlers to establish homestead farms.

D Buying up large areas of land very cheaply in the hope of selling it later for a profit.

Section 1 Assessment

Reading Comprehension

1. The Homestead Act offered land for a nominal fee, encouraging people to move to the West to begin farming. Settlers were attracted by the prospect of legal ownership of property.

2. The Pacific Railway Acts granted an enormous amount of territory to railroads. People followed the railroads west, either to lay track or to purchase some railroad land.

3. (a) Answers may include: white Easterners, African Americans, Germans, Irish, Italians, European Jews, Chinese, Mexicans.
(b) Different religions, languages, and traditions. For example, Germans and Scandinavians brought the Lutheran religion, which stressed hard work and education.

Critical Thinking and Writing

4. Answers will vary, but may include: The West had a spirit of equality; there were fewer class divisions; the hard work of any group of people was highly valued.

5. Answers may include references to the richness of the soil, the beauty of the prairie, and the joy of farming one's own land.

Take It to the NET

Flyers should highlight the advantages of moving to one of these new settlements. They should advertise plenty of land, inexpensive prices, favorable climate, and other selling points.

VIEWING HISTORY Settlers registered their claims at this land office in Round Pond, Oklahoma Territory. **Determining Relevance** *How did the surveying and registration of land claims encourage settlement and free enterprise in the West?*

"people who have money to invest go where they are protected by law."

Settlers From Far and Wide

New groups of settlers soon joined the mainly white easterners who first cut trails into the western wilderness. Cheap land and new jobs attracted people of other countries and ethnic groups. In growing towns and cities throughout the region, settlers spoke a rich mixture of languages and practiced a variety of customs.

German immigrants arrived in the last half of the 1800s, mainly seeking land to farm. They built orderly, tight-knit settlements from Texas to the upper Missouri River. They brought the Lutheran religion, with its strict ethics, and their traditional emphasis on hard work and education. Lutherans from Scandinavia settled the northern plains from Iowa to Minnesota to the Dakotas, many pursuing dairy farming.

Irish, Italians, European Jews, and Chinese tended to settle in concentrated communities, initially in West Coast cities. Eventually they gravitated to growing cities in the American interior, taking jobs in mining, railroad construction, and other trades. Ranching, mining, farm labor, and jobs in boom towns drew Americans and foreigners alike. Mexicans and Mexican Americans contributed to the growth of ranching.

After the Civil War, thousands of African Americans rode or even walked westward, often fleeing the violence and exploitation that followed Reconstruction. In 1879, Benjamin "Pap" Singleton led groups of southern blacks on a mass "Exodus," a trek inspired by the biblical account of the Israelites' flight from Egypt to a prophesied homeland. Hence, the settlers called themselves **Exodusters.** Some 50,000 or more Exodusters migrated west.

The Shifting Frontier

The "frontier" was not a line that moved westward in a unified motion. Various regions were settled at different times. Yet by 1890, settlements dotted the prairie every 10 miles or so. Towns gave rise to cities at a stunning pace. But one reality remained: The West was already occupied—by Native Americans.

Section 1 Assessment

READING COMPREHENSION

1. Why was the **Homestead Act** such a significant factor in the westward migration?

2. How did the **Pacific Railway Acts** influence Western settlement?

3. (a) What main groups of Americans and immigrants settled the West? (b) Describe the contrasting cultural influences they brought to the region.

CRITICAL THINKING AND WRITING

4. **Drawing Inferences** Why do you think some African Americans faced less discrimination in the West than they had experienced in the East?

5. **Writing to Inform** You were an unemployed eastern factory worker with a family who moved to Kansas. Write a letter to a friend back East, describing this new place and explaining why you made this risky move.

Take It to the NET

Activity: Creating a Flyer
Research Exoduster towns such as Nicodemus, Kansas. Create a flyer to attract migrants to such a town. Use the links provided in the *America: Pathways to the Present* area of the following Web site for help in completing this activity.
www.phschool.com

Conflict With Native Americans

READING FOCUS
- What caused changes in the life of the Plains Indians?
- How did government policies and battlefield challenges affect the Indian wars?
- What changes occurred in federal Indian policies by 1900?

MAIN IDEA
American expansion into the West led to the virtual elimination of Native Americans.

KEY TERMS
Great Plains
nomad
reservation
Battle of Little Bighorn
Ghost Dance
Massacre at Wounded Knee
assimilation
Dawes Act
boomers
sooners

TAKING NOTES
As you read, complete this chart, listing federal Indian policies in the West and their outcomes.

Federal Indian Policies	Results
Treaties	Often violated by U.S.

SECTION OBJECTIVES

1. Study the factors that caused changes in the life of the Plains Indians.
2. Find out how government policies and battlefield challenges affected the Indian wars.
3. Learn about changes that occurred in federal Indian policies by 1900.

BELLRINGER

Warm-Up Activity Discuss with students the tremendous gulf of understanding implied between the Easterners' perception of the "Indian problem," versus the Native Americans' perception that what was at stake was their own existence as a civilization.

Activating Prior Knowledge Ask students to describe what they know already about the impact of western settlement on Native American people. Direct the class to list the areas of conflict that were most likely to arise between natives and new settlers.

READING STRATEGY

Have students use the headings and subheadings to create an outline of the section. Then, as they read, have them fill in supporting details and analyze how the contributions of Native Americans have helped to shape the national identity.

Setting the Scene Easterners called it "the Indian problem." What could and should be done with western Indians so that their lands could be used productively, as they saw it, for mining, ranching, and farming?

To Native Americans, the "problem" was a life-or-death battle. In the second half of the 1800s, they resisted an all-out assault on their warriors, their women and children, their homelands, their sources of food and shelter, and their ways of life. It was a race against time. They faced their fate in varying ways—with blood-thirsty anger, solemn faith, and cautious compromise. At last, when their time ran out, they faced resignation, fatigue, and heartbreak.

The Life of the Plains Indians

Long before eastern settlers arrived, changes had affected the lives of Native Americans on the **Great Plains,** the vast grassland between the Mississippi River and the Rocky Mountains. The changes blended with and altered traditions that had existed for generations.

Well into the 1800s, millions of buffalo ranged the Great Plains. These huge beasts provided life-sustaining supplies to the Plains Indians: meat, hides for making shelters and clothing, and a wealth of other uses. The opening of relations with French and American fur traders in the 1700s allowed the Plains Indians to exchange hides for guns, making buffalo hunting easier.

By the mid-1700s, horses' hooves thundered across the plains. The Spanish had brought horses to Mexico in the 1500s, and Native Americans obtained them through trading and raids. The impact of the horse on Native American culture was profound.

While many Indian nations continued to live mainly as farmers, hunters, and gatherers, others became **nomads.** These are people who travel from place to place, usually following available food sources, instead of living in one location. With horses, nomadic peoples were better able to carry their possessions as they followed the vast buffalo herds across the plains.

VIEWING FINE ART Artist George Catlin lived with the Plains Indians for years, producing more than 500 sketches and paintings of Native American life, including this work, *Buffalo Chase—Single Death.* **Analyzing Visual Information** *How does Catlin depict the equipment, skills, and character needed to hunt the buffalo?*

CAPTION ANSWERS

Viewing Fine Art The hunter is depicted on a speeding horse with only a bow and arrow. He and the horse must move in closely to the thundering buffalo in order to hit it, a maneuver that appears to require courage, horsemanship, good timing, and good aim.

RESOURCE DIRECTORY

Teaching Resources
Learning Styles Lesson Plans booklet, p. 30
Guided Reading and Review booklet, p. 59
Learning with Documents booklet (Visual Learning Activity) *Western Expansion into Native American Land,* p. 53
Biography, Literature, and Comparing Primary Sources booklet (Comparing Primary Sources) *On Cultural Ties,* p. 125

Other Print Resources
Historical Outline Map Book *Indian Lands After 1850,* p. 55

Technology
Section Reading Support Transparencies
Guided Reading Audiotapes (English/Spanish), Ch. 14
Student Edition on Audio CD, Ch. 14
Prentice Hall Presentation Pro CD-ROM, Ch. 14
Companion Web site, www.phschool.com

Focus Explain that as settlers from the U.S. and Europe poured into the West, they took up land that had been home to Native Americans for many generations. Ask students how Native Americans of the West were affected.

Instruct Discuss how cultural beliefs can lead to misunderstandings and even war. In what ways did Native American groups and settlers hold conflicting beliefs about land use and government? What role did their differences play in the Indian Wars of the late 1800s? How did attempts to "civilize" Native Americans contribute to their ruin?

Ask students to consider the results of dividing up Native American land. What was the effect of the homesteading rush in 1889?

Assess/Reteach Can students list alternative approaches to settlement of the West that might have avoided the terrible consequences to Native American peoples?

BACKGROUND
A Diverse Nation

Some native peoples were outraged by the encroachment of the transcontinental railroad. On August 7, 1867, about 40 Cheyenne, led by Chief Pawnee Killer, derailed a train near Plum Creek in central Nebraska. At a Peace Commission conference in September 1867, General William Sherman told several chiefs, "We will build iron roads, and you cannot stop the locomotive any more than you can stop the sun or the moon, and you must submit, and do the best you can."

READING CHECK
Plains Indians began to obtain firearms and horses in the 1700s. Horses were used in Indian wars against rival Indian nations. These battles were quite fierce. Some Indians took to their horses and became nomads.

READING CHECK
What changes occurred in the culture of Plains Indians before the arrival of settlers?

The arrival of the horse also brought upheaval. Warfare among Indian nations, to gain possessions or for conquest, rose to a new intensity when waged on horseback. Success in war brought wealth and prestige. The rise of warrior societies led to a decline in village life, as nomadic Native Americans raided more settled groups.

Indian Wars and Government Policy

Before the Civil War, Native Americans west of the Mississippi continued to inhabit their traditional homelands. An uneasy peace prevailed, punctured by occasional hostilities as workers laid railroad track deeper into Indian lands and as the California gold rush of 1848 drew wagon trains across the plains. By the 1860s, however, Americans had discovered that the interior concealed a treasure chest of resources. The battle for the West was on.

Causes of Clashes   Settlers' views of land and resource use contrasted sharply with Native American traditions. Many settlers felt justified in taking Indian land because, in their view, they would make it more productive. To Native Americans, the settlers were simply invaders. Increasing intrusions, especially into sacred lands, angered even chiefs who had welcomed the newcomers.

Making Treaties   Initially, the government tried to restrict the movements of nomadic Native Americans by negotiating treaties. Some treaties arranged for the federal purchase of Indian land, often for little in return. Other treaties restricted Native Americans to **reservations,** federal lands set aside for them.

The treaties produced misunderstandings and outright fraud. The government continued its longtime practice of designating as "tribes" groups that often had no single leadership or even related clans or traditions. Federal agents selected "chiefs" to sign treaties, but the signers often did not represent the majority of their people. Honest government agents negotiated some pacts in good faith; others had no intention of honoring the treaties. Some sought bribes or dealt violently with tribes until they signed. Indian signers often did not know that they were restricted to the reservations, and that they might be in danger if they left.

The federal Bureau of Indian Affairs (BIA), a part of the Interior Department, was supposed to manage the delivery of critical supplies to the reservations. But widespread corruption within the BIA and among its agents resulted in supplies being mishandled or stolen.

The government made some attempts to protect the reservations, but their poorly manned outposts were no match for waves of land-hungry settlers. Unscrupulous settlers stole land, killed buffalo, diverted water supplies, and attacked Indian camps. After a treaty violation in 1873, Kicking Bird, a Kiowa, declared: "I have taken the white man by the hand, thinking him to be a friend, but he is not a friend; government has deceived us. . . ."

Native Americans reacted in frustration and anger. Groups who disagreed with the treaties refused to obey. Acts of violence on both sides set off cycles of revenge that occurred with increasing brutality.

Battlefield Challenges

Federal lawmakers came to view the treaties as useless. In 1871, the government declared that it would make no more treaties and recognize no chiefs.

Focus on
GOVERNMENT

Acquiring Indian Lands From the 1860s to 1900, presidential administrations gained Native American lands however they could: through treaties, land purchases, forced relocation of Indians to reservations, wars—or simply looking the other way and letting settlers solve the problem. In 1875, after failed attempts to purchase the mineral-rich but sacred Black Hills of the Sioux, President Ulysses S. Grant gave General William T. Sherman the go-ahead for mining the treaty-protected territory. Sherman wrote that if the miners were to pour in, "I understand that the president and the Interior Department will wink at it." Word got out, and soon the hills were crawling with prospectors.

RESOURCE DIRECTORY

Other Print Resources
Nystrom ***Atlas of Our Country*** *Later Expansion of the United States,* pp. 32–33

Technology
Color Transparencies *Fine Art,* E10

Inconclusive Battles In 1865, one general urged the government to "finish this Indian war this season, so that it will stay finished." Yet the tragic conflicts would drag on for nearly three more decades.

Both sides lacked a coherent strategy along with the resources to achieve one. They reacted to each others' attacks in a long, exhausting dance of death. The Indians were outgunned, and suffered far more casualties. Yet in the end, they succumbed less to war than to disease and to lack of food and shelter.

The United States Army, spread across the South to monitor Reconstruction, had slim resources to send to the West. With infantry, cavalry, and artillery units spread thinly across the vast region, the Army could not build coordinated battle fronts. Battle lines constantly shifted as settlers moved into new areas. Most confrontations were small hit-and-run raids with few decisive outcomes. Still, experienced army generals managed to lead successful campaigns in some regions.

Indian warriors fought mostly on their own turf, employing tactics they had used against their traditional enemies for generations. Profit-seeking whites sold guns to the warriors. Native American groups made some alliances in attempts to defeat the intruders, but their efforts usually failed. Moreover, the army often pitted Indian groups against one another.

The Soldier's Life on the Frontier Who would volunteer for this army? Living conditions: $13 a month; a leftover Civil War uniform; rotten food. Duties: build forts; drive settlers from reservations; escort the mail; stop gunfights; prevent liquor smuggling and stagecoach robberies; protect miners, railroad crews, and visiting politicians; and—occasionally—fight Indians. Hazards: smallpox, cholera, and flu; accidents; endless marching; and death in battle. In fact, thousands of recruits—former Civil War soldiers, freed slaves, jobless men—did join the frontier army. Unlike the typical Indian warrior, the average soldier on the plains rarely saw battle. Up to a third of the men deserted.

Key Battles

Native Americans and the army met in battles throughout the interior West. In major engagements, the army usually prevailed.

The Sand Creek Massacre, 1864 The southern Cheyenne occupied the central plains, including parts of Colorado Territory. After some gruesome Cheyenne raids on wagon trains and settlements east of Denver, Colorado's governor took advantage of a peace campaign led by Cheyenne chief Black Kettle. Promised protection, Black Kettle and other chiefs followed orders to camp at Sand Creek.

Colonel John Chivington, who had so far failed to score a big military victory against the Cheyenne, now saw his chance. On November 29, 1864, his force of 700 men descended upon the encamped Cheyenne and Arapaho. While Black Kettle frantically tried to mount an American flag and a white flag of surrender, Chivington's men slaughtered between 150 and 500 people—largely women and children. The next year, many southern Cheyenne agreed to move to reservations.

> 66 *Nothing lives long.*
> *Only the earth and the mountains.* 99
> —death song sung by a Cheyenne killed at Sand Creek, 1864

BIOGRAPHY

Chief Joseph 1840–1904

Born in 1840, *Hin-mah-too-yah-lat-kekt,* or "Thunder Rolling Down the Mountain," was better known by the name he got from his father, Joseph, a converted Christian. As his father lay dying in 1871, he made Joseph promise never to sell their scenic, fruitful homeland in the Northwest. The promise proved impossible to keep.

Forced to flee in 1877, the Nez Percé fought skillfully, but their chief found no joy in it. In his surrender speech, Joseph reportedly declared, "Hear me, my chiefs! I am tired. My heart is sick and sad. From where the sun now stands I will fight no more forever."

Chief Joseph's band was exiled to Indian Territory (Oklahoma), where all six of Joseph's children died. In 1885, the chief was returned to the modern-day state of Washington, but not to his father's land. He died in 1904 "of a broken heart," his doctor said.

This 1864 poster promises cavalry recruits "all horses and other plunder taken from the Indians."

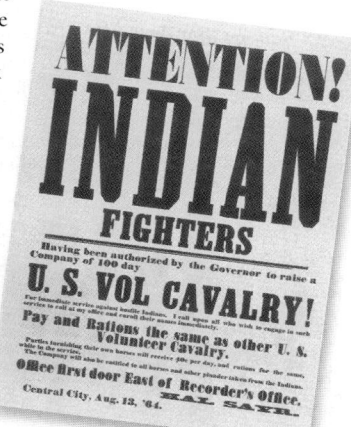

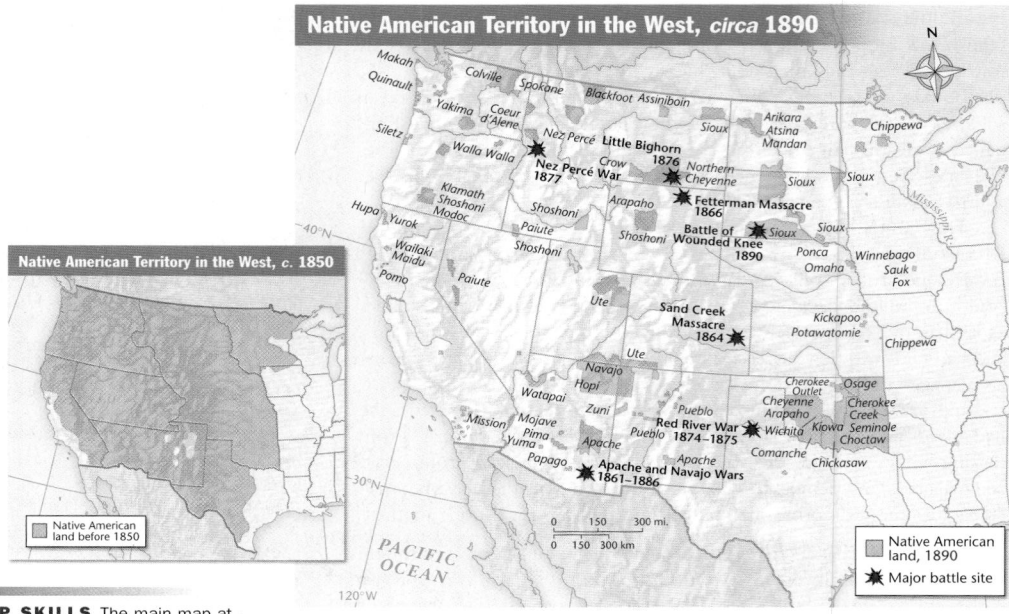

MAP SKILLS The main map at right shows Indian lands in 1890, compared with the land they roamed in 1850, shown in the inset map above. **Regions** In what directions were Native Americans pushed as they lost territory?

 Sounds of an Era

Listen to *Black Elk Speaks*, an eyewitness account of the Battle of Little Bighorn, and other sounds from the era of the western settlement.

The Battle of Little Bighorn, 1876 The Sioux of the northern plains—Dakota, Wyoming, and Montana territories—powerfully resisted white expansion. In 1865, the government enraged the Sioux by deciding to build a road, the Bozeman Trail, through prime Sioux hunting grounds in the Bighorn Mountains.

Sioux chief Red Cloud launched a two-year war to block the project. In 1866, Sioux warriors slaughtered more than 80 soldiers under Captain W. J. Fetterman near Fort Phil Kearny. The war ended in the Fort Laramie Treaty of 1868, under which the United States abandoned the Bozeman Trail and created a large Sioux reservation in what is half of South Dakota today.

Sioux land protected by the treaty included the Black Hills—tall, dramatic, pine-covered mountains in South Dakota and Wyoming territories, held sacred by many Sioux. But in 1874, the government sent Lieutenant Colonel George A. Custer to investigate rumors of gold in the Black Hills. He reported that the hills cradled gold "from the grass roots down." This news was the starting gun in a mining race that overran the region.

The government offered to buy the Black Hills, and Red Cloud entered negotiations. But two Sioux chiefs, Sitting Bull and Crazy Horse, who had never signed the Fort Laramie Treaty, left the reservation. Hostilities resumed.

494 Chapter 14 • *Looking to the West*

In June 1876, Custer was sent to round up the Indians. He moved his cavalry toward the Little Bighorn River in what is now Montana. There he met the full fury of the Sioux: nearly 2,000 warriors, the largest Indian force ever gathered on the plains. Custer, expecting a smaller enemy, had split his forces. The Sioux fell on their prey, wiping out Custer and his more than 200 soldiers within an hour.

The **Battle of Little Bighorn,** or "Custer's Last Stand," stunned Americans. The army flooded the area with troops and swiftly forced most of the Sioux back to their reservations. Crazy Horse was killed after surrendering in 1877. Sitting Bull and some remaining Sioux escaped to Canada, but starvation forced them to surrender and return to a reservation four years later.

The Battle of Wounded Knee, 1890 Under stress for a half-century, Native Americans saw the rise of religious prophets predicting danger or prosperity. A prophet of the plains, Wovoka, promised a return to traditional life if people performed purification ceremonies. These included the **Ghost Dance,** a ritual in which people joined hands and whirled in a circle.

The Ghost Dance caught on among the Teton Sioux, who, still struggling to adjust to reservation life, practiced it with great urgency, encouraged by Sitting Bull. In 1890, word spread that the Indians were becoming restless. The government agent at the Pine Ridge Reservation in South Dakota wired the army: "Indians are dancing in the snow and are wild and crazy. . . . We need protection and we need it now." The army dispatched the Seventh Cavalry, Custer's old unit, to the scene.

Hoping to calm the crisis, Indian police officers tried to arrest Sitting Bull. When he hesitated, the officers shot and killed him. His grieving followers, some 120 men and 230 women and children, surrendered and were rounded up at a creek called Wounded Knee. As they were being disarmed, someone fired a shot. Soldiers opened fire, killing more than 200 Sioux. The **Massacre at Wounded Knee** was the last major episode of violence in the Indian wars.

New Policies Toward Native Americans

"I am the last Indian," Sitting Bull is reported to have said. Indeed, he was among the last to have lived the life of a free Native American, roaming with the buffalo herds across unobstructed plains, practicing traditional customs.

Critics of Federal Indian Policies While many white Americans called for the destruction of Native Americans, others, horrified by the government's policies, formed a growing peace movement. It found inspiration in Helen Hunt Jackson's 1881 publication *A Century of Dishonor*. Protesting what she

BIOGRAPHY

George Armstrong Custer
1839–1876

He had the stuff of a legendary hero: charming, fearless, and memorable in his long, golden curls and flamboyant uniform. He was also vain, heedless of authority, and foolhardy—qualities that would prove fatal.

Custer seemed to be born for war. Daring in battle, he achieved great distinction in the Civil War. At the war's end, he was sent to fight Indians, a job he relished. To the Sioux, he was the "chief of thieves" for entering their sacred Black Hills and spreading word of their gold wealth.

Court-martialed twice for various offenses, Custer at last found fame and adoration in his final impulsive act: rushing to his death in 1876 at the Battle of Little Bighorn. At "Custer's Last Stand," he became the heroic victim of legend and song.

Apache chief Geronimo leads a band of renegades. Apache resistance ended with his surrender in 1886, the year of this photograph.

The town of Wounded Knee has become a continuing symbol of Native American suffering. In March 1973 more than 200 members of the American Indian Movement (AIM) seized the trading post at Wounded Knee in an attempt to draw national attention to their platform. AIM leaders wanted reforms in the tribal government and demanded Senate hearings on United States treaties with Native American nations. In response federal law officers surrounded the area. "You have here," said one government official, "an arguable case of treason." The AIM occupation ended in surrender to the federal authorities, but it mobilized other Native American groups and focused attention on recovering the titles to their tribal territories.

ACTIVITY
Connecting with Culture

Tell students to research the Sioux. Have them investigate how the Sioux lived in the nineteenth century and how their culture has survived in the twenty-first century. How has their way of life changed over the years? Where do the Sioux live? What is their approximate population? After students complete their research, have them deliver an oral presentation on their findings. **(Verbal/Linguistic)**

BACKGROUND
Art History

In addition to relying on the buffalo for basic needs, the Native Americans of the Plains created beautiful things from the skins of buffalo and deer. Women's dresses, children's clothes, men's ceremonial shirts, shields, and robes were all made from the hides of the animals that roamed the plains. Each tribe had its own unique patterns and ways of applying decorations such as porcupine quills, beads, and feathers of the eagle, hawk, and crow. In *Buckskin & Buffalo*, author Colin F. Taylor examines the details and symbols that turned everyday objects into works of art.

CUSTOMIZE FOR ...
Less Proficient Readers
Ask students to rewrite the following incorrect statements:
• In the massacres at Sand Creek and Wounded Knee, Native Americans killed large numbers of United States cavalry.
• Most Native Americans were eager to become farmers like the white settlers.

Connecting with Economics

As students review the chart of Key Events in the Indian Wars, have them discuss the role that economics played in these battles. Encourage students to consider why the United States government felt compelled to acquire territories where native groups had lived. What were the forces that drove white people to conquer the land? Why was the drive to "strike it rich" such a powerful force in this chapter of history? Have students analyze the relationship between private property rights and the settlement of the Great Plains. How did the clash of values play out in the conflicts between Native Americans and whites? **(Verbal/Linguistic)**

BACKGROUND

Connections to Today

Despite pressure from white Americans to assimilate, Native American tribes have managed to maintain their cultural identity. There are now more than 300 federally recognized tribes. Many of these tribes have prospered since the federal courts ruled that tribes could operate casinos on reservations if that type of gambling is legal in the states in which the reservations are located. As a result of the Indian Gaming Regulatory Act of 1988, many tribes have a chance to become self-sufficient. With economic success comes political clout as local officials seek out tribal leaders for their support.

CAPTION ANSWERS

Interpreting Charts (a) These battles often resulted from attempts by U.S. forces to confine Native Americans to reservations. The fighting often occurred on the Great Plains. (b) Sometimes the army triggered the violence, and sometimes Native Americans did.

Key Events in the Indian Wars, 1861–1890

Wars / Battles	Native American Nations / Homelands	Key Players	Description / Outcome
Apache and Navajo Wars 1861–1886	Apache in Arizona, New Mexico, and Colorado territories; Navajo in New Mexico, Colorado territories	• Geronimo • Col. Christopher "Kit" Carson	Carson kills or relocates many Apache to reservations in 1862. Clashes drag on until Geronimo's surrender in 1886. Navajo told to surrender in 1863, but before they can, Carson attacks, killing hundreds, destroying homelands. Navajos moved to New Mexico reservation in 1865.
Sand Creek Massacre 1864	Southern Cheyenne, Arapaho, in central plains	• Black Kettle • Col. John Chivington	Cheyenne massacres prompt Chivington to kill up to 500 surrendered Cheyenne and Arapaho led by Black Kettle.
Red River War 1874–1875	Comanche and southern branches of Cheyenne, Kiowa, and Arapaho, in southern plains	• Comanche war parties • Gen. William T. Sherman • Lt. Gen. Philip H. Sheridan	Southern plains Indians relocated to Oklahoma Indian Territory under 1867 Treaty of Medicine Lodge. After buffalo hunters destroy the Indians' food supply, Comanche warriors race to buffalo grazing areas in Texas panhandle to kill hunters. Sherman and Sheridan defeat warriors and open panhandle to cattle ranching.
Battle of Little Bighorn 1876	Northern plains Sioux in Dakota, Wyoming, and Montana territories	• Sitting Bull • Crazy Horse • Red Cloud • Lt. Col. George A. Custer	U.S. tries to buy gold-rich Black Hills from Sioux. Talks fail. Custer's 7th Cavalry is sent to round up Sioux, but meets huge enemy force. Custer and some 200 men perish in "Custer's Last Stand."
Nez Percé War 1877	Largest branch of Nez Percé, in Wallowa Valley of Idaho and Washington territories and Oregon	• Chief Joseph • Gen. Oliver O. Howard • Col. Nelson Miles	Howard orders Nez Percé to Idaho reservation; violence erupts. Joseph leads some 700 men, women, and children on 1,400-mile flight. His 200 warriors hold off Miles's 2,000 soldiers until halted 40 miles short of Canada. Sent to Indian Territory, many die of disease. In 1885, survivors moved to reservation in Washington Territory.
Battle of Wounded Knee 1890	Sioux at Pine Ridge Reservation, South Dakota	• Sitting Bull • U.S. 7th Cavalry	Ghost Dance raises fears of Sioux uprising; Sitting Bull killed in attempted arrest. His followers surrender and camp at Wounded Knee. Shots are fired; some 200 Sioux die.

INTERPRETING CHARTS
This chart provides a brief summary of some of the key battles that were fought in various areas of the western interior. **Making Comparisons** (a) What factors did many of these clashes have in common? (b) In what ways did they differ?

saw as the government's broken promises and treaties, Jackson wrote, "It makes little difference . . . where one opens the record of the history of the Indians; every page and every year has its dark stain."

Attempts to Change Native American Culture As sincere as the reformers may have been, most believed that Native Americans still needed to be "civilized." That is, they should be made to give up their traditions, become Christians, learn English, adopt white dress and customs, and support themselves by farming and trades. Tribal elders were ordered to give up their religious beliefs and rituals. Christian missionaries ran schools on the reservations.

In 1879, Army Captain Richard H. Pratt opened the United States Indian Training and Industrial School in Carlisle, Pennsylvania. Children as young as 5 years old were taken from the reservations by coaxing, trickery, or force, and sent to Carlisle and other such schools to be educated "as Americans." The children were to be integrated into white society. This policy is called **assimilation,** the process by which one society becomes a part of another, more dominant society by adopting its culture.

In 1887, a federal law dismantled the Native American concept of shared land in favor of the principle of private property highly valued by Americans. The **Dawes Act** divided reservation land into individual plots. Each Native American family headed by a man received a plot, usually 160 acres. These landholders were granted U.S. citizenship and were subject to local, state, and federal laws. Many Indian sympathizers believed that the land allocations would make families self-supporting and create pride of ownership.

But the idea of taking up farming offended the beliefs of many Native Americans. Smohalla, a religious teacher from the Northwest, retorted: "You

RESOURCE DIRECTORY

Technology
Color Transparencies *Historical Maps,* A60
Sounds of an Era Audio CD *John G. Neihardt* (time: 35 seconds)
Exploring Primary Resources in U.S. History CD-ROM *Geronimo: His Own Story, S. M. Barrett,* ed.

ask me to cut grass and make hay and sell it, and be rich like white men! But how dare I cut off my mother's hair?"

In reality, much reservation land was not suitable for farming. Many Native Americans had no interest or experience in agriculture. Some sold their land to speculators or were swindled out of it. Between 1887 and 1932, some two thirds of the 138 million acres of Indian land wound up in the hands of whites.

The Opening of Indian Territory   For the some 55 Indian nations that had been forced into Indian Territory, worse trouble loomed. The territory contained the largest unsettled farmland in the United States—about 2 million unassigned acres. During the 1880s, as squatters overran the land, Congress agreed to buy out Indian claims to the region.

On the morning of April 22, 1889, tens of thousands of homesteaders lined up at the territory's borders. At the stroke of noon, bugles blew, pistols fired, and the eager hordes surged forward, racing to stake a claim.

> 66 [W]ith a shout and a yell the swift riders shot out, then followed the light buggies or wagons and last the lumbering prairie schooner and freighters' wagons, with here and there even a man on a bicycle and many too on foot—above all a great cloud of dust hovering like smoke over a battlefield. 99
>
> —newspaper reporter, 1889

By sundown, these settlers, called **boomers,** had staked claims on almost 2 million acres. Many boomers discovered that some of the best lands had been grabbed by **sooners,** people who had sneaked past the government officials earlier to mark their claims. Under continued pressure from settlers, Congress created Oklahoma Territory in 1890. In the following years, the remainder of Indian Territory was opened to settlement.

It took a half-century, more than a thousand battles, and the deaths of about 950 United States soldiers to conquer the Native Americans. The clashes also took the lives of countless Indians used by the army as scouts and fighters; of settlers killed in Indian attacks; and of millions of Native American men, women, and children who died in battles or on squalid reservations.

VIEWING HISTORY Officials at the Carlisle, Pennsylvania, Indian school took before-and-after photographs of their students. **Analyzing Visual Information** List details that show the changes undergone by these boys.

Section 2 · Assessment

READING COMPREHENSION

1. Describe early changes in the lifestyle of the Plains Indians.

2. Why were Indian treaties often unsuccessful?

3. How did the **Ghost Dance** lead to a tragic conflict?

4. Describe two major federal **assimilation** policies.

CRITICAL THINKING AND WRITING

5. **Identifying Assumptions** What assumptions about Native Americans did sympathetic easterners make when proposing improvements on the reservations?

6. **Writing a News Story** As an eastern reporter traveling with an army unit, report on one of the battles discussed in this section.

 Take It to the NET

Activity: Creating a Presentation Prepare a presentation on attempts to assimilate Indian students. Use the links provided in the *America: Pathways to the Present* area of the following Web site for help in completing this activity. **www.phschool.com**

RESOURCE DIRECTORY

Teaching Resources
Units 5/6 booklet
 • Section 2 Quiz, p. 16
Guide to the Essentials
 • Section 2 Summary, p. 74

Section 2   Assessment

Reading Comprehension

1. Some early changes were caused by guns and horses, which facilitated buffalo hunting; the horses also supported the nomadic lifestyle and helped to confer status and wealth upon warriors.

2. Treaties were often fraught with misunderstandings and fraud. The government frequently designated "tribes" and "chiefs" to suit its own needs. Treaty violations resulted in violence on both sides.

3. A ritual dance was misinterpreted as an act of aggression and led to the Massacre at Wounded Knee. Chief Sitting Bull was killed. Further violence erupted as his followers were being disarmed. More than 200 Sioux were killed.

4. Reeducation forced elders to give up their traditions and beliefs; schools for Native American children instilled only "white" cultural ideas. The Dawes Act divided shared reservation land into separate plots.

Critical Thinking and Writing

5. Answers will vary, but may include that eastern "reformers" assumed that Native American ways of life, religion, education, and work were inferior to the ways of whites.

6. Answers may include that the Native Americans were usually heavily outgunned but not always outnumbered, or that the Native Americans were good fighters and worthy adversaries.

Student presentations should reflect the aspects of assimilation described in the chapter, focusing on the attempts by whites to do away with Native American culture.

CAPTION ANSWERS

Viewing History Answers include: Their traditional garments were replaced with military-style uniforms; their long hair was cut; the traditional head scarf worn by the boy on the left was replaced with a cap.

Section 3
Mining, Ranching and Farming

SECTION OBJECTIVES

1. Learn how mining spread in the West.
2. Find out what caused the western cattle boom.
3. See what life was like for a cowboy on the Chisholm Trail.
4. Discover how settlers overcame barriers in farming the plains.

BELLRINGER

Warm-Up Activity Write the words *modernization* and *mechanization* on the chalkboard. Ask students to think about the positive and negative effects of these processes.

Activating Prior Knowledge How long do students think it took for word to spread throughout the country of gold's discovery in California in 1849? What are some ways students think this information might have traveled? How long would it take the information to travel around the country today?

READING STRATEGY

As students read, have them notice the ways in which the farming, mining and ranching industries changed in the second half of the nineteenth century. Have students explain how scientific discoveries and technological innovations in agriculture resulted from specific needs.

CAPTION ANSWERS

Viewing History The site is full of activity. Factories and homes for the workers are spread across the city. The mound in the center appears to be refuse produced by mining. Tracks indicate the presence of railroads for hauling the ore. The overall appearance is dirty and unappealing.

Section 3

Mining, Ranching and Farming

READING FOCUS

- How did mining spread in the West?
- What caused the western cattle boom?
- What was life like for a cowboy on the Chisholm Trail?
- How did settlers overcome barriers in farming the plains?

MAIN IDEA

Mining, ranching, and farming developed from individual and family enterprises into major industries, transforming the West.

KEY TERMS

placer mining
long drive
homesteader
soddie
dry farming
bonanza farm
Turner thesis
stereotype

TAKING NOTES

As you read, complete this diagram to show the effects of settlement by various groups.

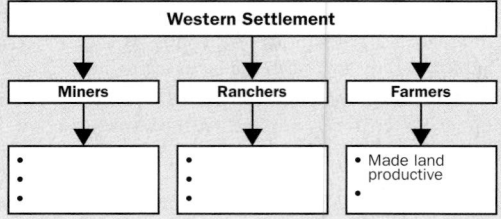

Western Settlement		
Miners	Ranchers	Farmers
• • •	• •	• Made land productive •

Setting the Scene Along with the armies of Custer and Sherman came virtual armies of miners, ranchers, and farmers that descended on the American West from the end of the Civil War to the end of the nineteenth century. Once unleashed, this force would remake the West. One railroad worker saw the transformation coming:

> *The time is coming, and fast, too, when, in the sense it is now understood, THERE WILL BE NO WEST.*
>
> —from the diary of a Union Pacific engineer

VIEWING HISTORY With the arrival of large mining operations, mining sites became sprawling industrial towns, like Virginia City, Nevada, shown here. **Analyzing Visual Information** *Describe the character and appearance of this mining site, using details from the photograph.*

He was right. By the late 1800s, the West of the Native Americans, of unplowed prairie, of thundering buffalo, had vanished. A new breed of Westerners had come here, they believed, on a mission: to unlock the potential of this land and make it fruitful.

The Spread of Western Mining

After the stunning discovery of gold at Sutter's Mill, California, in 1848, a surge of fortune-hunters, from single men to whole families, set their sights on the West Coast. Little did they know that on the way to California, their wagon wheels rolled over mountains even more rich in precious minerals.

Mining Moves Inland In 1859, rumors of gold "everywhere you stick your shovel" at Pikes Peak, Colorado, brought on a stampede of wagons painted with the slogan "Pikes Peak or Bust!" The rumors turned out to be exaggerated. But later that year, one of the biggest strikes ever, Nevada's Comstock Lode, sent prospectors converging on the ore-laden western mountain ranges. Over the next 30 years, the Comstock Lode would yield $400 million in gold and silver.

Almost simultaneously, a gold strike west of the little town of Denver, in what was then Kansas Territory, threw open the gates to the American interior.

RESOURCE DIRECTORY

Teaching Resources
Guided Reading and Review booklet, p. 60
Literature, Biography, and Comparing Primary Sources booklet (Literature) *The Californian's Tale*, p. 58

Other Print Resources
Historical Outline Map Book *Opening the West*, p. 56

Technology
Section Reading Support Transparencies
Guided Reading Audiotapes (English/Spanish), Ch. 14
Student Edition on Audio CD, Ch. 14
Prentice Hall Presentation Pro CD-ROM, Ch. 14
Companion Web site, www.phschool.com

By 1861, the swarm of settlers caused the federal government to carve out Colorado Territory from western Kansas. The Homestake mine, opened in 1877 in the Black Hills of Dakota, was possibly the richest single mine ever uncovered in the world, producing a billion dollars' worth of ore.

One miner, William Parsons, perceived the national significance of the gold rush: "The Atlantic and Pacific coasts, instead of being, as they are now, divided countries, will become parts of a compact whole, joined and cemented together by bonds of mutual interest."

Early Mining, and Mining Towns At first, miners searched for metal in surface soil or in streambeds. The simplest tool was a shallow pan in which the miner scooped dirt and water, and then swished it around. Lighter particles washed over the edge while the gold stayed in the bottom of the pan. A technique called **placer mining** used this method on a larger scale. Miners shoveled loose dirt into boxes and then ran water over the dirt to separate it from gold or silver particles. (The word *placer,* of Spanish origin, rhymes with *passer.*)

These methods could be used by individuals, small groups of men, or even families. They came at the first whisper of a new strike, and tent communities popped up almost overnight. Larger strikes led to settled towns, even cities. Merchants, farmers, and other entrepreneurs came to supply miners' needs.

The easily gathered precious metal was skimmed off quickly. By the late 1850s and early 1860s, most of the precious metals that remained in the West lay locked in quartz and deeply buried. At that point, many prospectors straggled home, leaving mining settlements deserted ghost towns.

The large, deep veins of ore attracted the money and sophisticated technologies of large corporations. Using large work crews, they diverted streams and dug into the exposed beds. Workers tunneled into mountains and plunged into rickety mine shafts that sometimes became their graves. Huge drills replaced pickaxes. Hydraulic pumps pounded mountainsides with water. With the arrival of dynamite in the 1870s, miners blasted ore out of hillsides. Like other industries, mining had become the realm of big business.

The Cattle Boom

Mexicans taught Americans cattle ranching in the early 1800s. The Americans adopted Mexican ranching equipment and dress. They also learned from Mexican cattlemen the advantages of raising the hardy Texas longhorn cattle that thrived on the dry, grassy plains.

Demand Spurs Growth Several changes launched the West's legendary cattle industry. During the Civil War, many Texans left their ranches to serve in the Confederate army. They returned home to find up to 5 million cattle roaming wild in the grasslands, making available ample supplies of beef.

Prior to the war, pork had been Americans' meat of choice. But when cookbooks began snubbing pork as "difficult to digest" and "unwholesome," the nation went on a beef binge. Cattle that had sold for only $3 to $6 a head in Texas at the war's end now brought $40 a head in Illinois and $80 in New York. Soon, however, consumers began to complain about the tough beef from the Texas

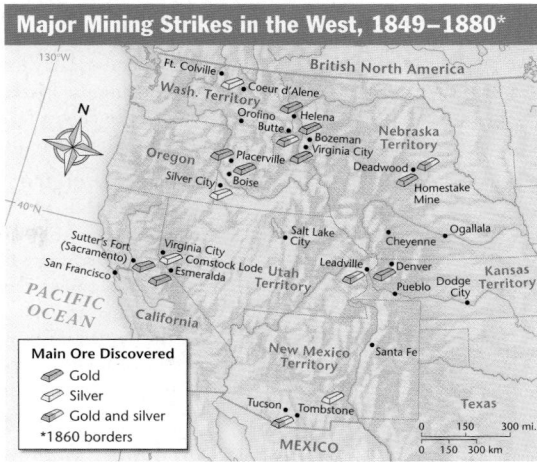

Major Mining Strikes in the West, 1849–1880*

Main Ore Discovered
- Gold
- Silver
- Gold and silver
*1860 borders

MAP SKILLS Mining spread throughout the interior West in the 1860s after a gold strike outside of Denver. **Place** *From the map, what can you tell about the characteristics of places where key mining strikes occurred?*

Connecting with Geography

Tell students that according to the 2000 census, there are about 300,000 buffalo now roaming the Plains states and more Native Americans there than at any time since the late 1870s. Have students conduct research to find out how and why these changes have taken place. Then have students write a brief report explaining what they have learned. They may create a thematic map, graph, chart, model or database representing their findings. **(Verbal/Linguistic; Visual/Spatial)**

Geography in History

At the beginning of the cattle drives, the frontier settlement of Abilene, Kansas, was lawless. It was not yet an organized town and therefore was not entitled to public services, including a police force. People formed "vigilance committees," which operated like volunteer fire departments. When there was trouble, committee members were summoned to mediate the problem. Sometimes, members of the vigilance committees called for swift punishment before they had gathered all the facts. In 1869 the citizens of Abilene formed a town that was run by an elected council. Laws were passed, a courthouse and a jail were built, and a town marshal was appointed to enforce the laws.

READING CHECK

Wild herds of longhorn cattle grew quite large during the Civil War. After the war, Americans came to prefer beef to pork. Selective breeding and refrigeration allowed high-quality beef to be shipped anywhere in the country.

longhorn, known as "the butcher's nightmare: eight pounds of hamburger on 800 pounds of bone and horn." Breeders then began importing eastern purebreds to make a better-quality longhorn.

Shipping the live cows to the East by rail was expensive. But with the invention of refrigerated railroad cars in the 1870s, animals were slaughtered before shipping. This development cut transportation costs in half.

Destruction of the Buffalo Widespread cattle ranching became possible with the removal of Native Americans and the near-extinction of the buffalo. Of some 25 million buffalo on the Great Plains in 1840, as few as 1,100 remained in the entire country by 1889. Several factors caused the destruction. Buffalo-fur robes became popular in the East, and buffalo-hide leather made sturdy belts to drive machines in factories. Buffalo hunting became a popular sport, and the huge beasts with poor eyesight made easy targets for individuals or organized hunting groups. "The biggest killing I ever made was 106 buffalo before breakfast," boasted one hunter. The government also sought to wipe out the buffalo, to force Indians to grow their food and to make room for settlers.

Cow Towns At first, Texas herds were driven north across the open range all the way to their markets. Then, in 1867, J. G. McCoy established the town of Abilene, Kansas, on the Hannibal & St. Joseph Railroad—the first town built specifically for receiving cattle. Other "cow towns" sprang up along the rail lines: Cheyenne in Wyoming; and in Kansas, Dodge City, Wichita, and Ellsworth.

Cow towns were a truly *wild* part of the West—at least until farmers came along and settled in as year-round residents, determined to make the towns respectable and law-abiding. Cattle trades, banking, and other commerce took place in larger towns.

Abilene thrived for only a few years but saw some 700,000 head of cattle pass through its stockyard gates in 1871 alone. By 1872, the cattle business had shifted to Wichita; but within about three years, that town, like Abilene, had become fenced in by farmers. Dodge City, on the Santa Fe Trail, proclaimed

Cowboys with their herd in the 1880s

500   Chapter 14 • *Looking to the West*

RESOURCE DIRECTORY
Technology
Color Transparencies *Historical Maps,* A26

itself the "cowboy capital of the world." All told, in the cattle industry's two decades of great prosperity (roughly 1867 to 1887), as many as 8 million Texas cattle were rounded up and shipped east.

A Cowboy's Life: Cattle Drive on the Chisholm Trail

In the year of Abilene's founding, cowboys drove some 35,000 cattle up the Chisholm Trail. Within two decades, 2 million animals had made the trek. The story of the Chisholm Trail typifies the cowboy's experience on the **long drive,** the herding of thousands of cattle to railway centers scattered across the plains.

Geography of the Trail The Chisholm Trail was one of several trails that linked the good grazing lands of Texas's San Antonio region with cow towns to the north. The trail was a network of routes, many of which converged at Fort Worth, the largest town on the trail. From there, the trail led north to the Red River, one of several rivers that required a hazardous crossing of men, horses, and cows.

The Red River marked the border between Texas and Indian Territory, which had to be crossed to reach Kansas. Cowboys had to be on the lookout for Indian raids. Some enterprising Native Americans set up what were virtually toll booths on the trail, demanding payment in steers for passage through their land. Once into Kansas, the Chisholm Trail branched out to various end-of-the-line towns.

The Cowboy The men of the Chisholm Trail were a tough lot. They included Americans, Native Americans, and immigrants. About a fifth of all cowboys were African American or Mexican. Cowhands had trail names, like "Busted Snoot Johnny" and "Teddy Blue." They survived on their physical endurance, little need for sleep, sense of humor, and perhaps a touch of eccentricity. Neither Union nor Confederate, the cowboy became a unifying national hero. His past didn't matter; only how he did his job. And what a job!

66 *After you have . . . learned not to dread getting in mud up to your ears, jumping your horse into a swollen stream when the water is freezing, nor . . . trying to stop a stampeded herd, on a dark night, when your course has to be guided by the sound of the frightened steer's hoofs—you command good wages [$25 to $60 a month].* 99
—cowboy Charles A. Siringo

A cowboy earned more the farther north he worked, partly because he had to buy warmer clothes. A no-frills cowboy outfit cost $77: pony, $25; leggings, $5; saddle, $25; saddle blankets, $5; spurs, bridle, and rope, $5; revolver, $12.

The Long Drive For all the stories of the supposed joys and freedoms of cowboy life, the job was mostly bone-tiring drudgery; boring and at the same time tense. The men were up at 3:30 A.M. and in the saddle by 4:00. On the trail, the cowhands spread out across tens of miles. As the cattle moved along the trail, two experienced cowboys rode in front of the herd, guiding the animals along the route. Other men rode beside the herd to keep the cattle all together, and still others rode in the dust at the rear, pushing the stragglers along. A cowhand

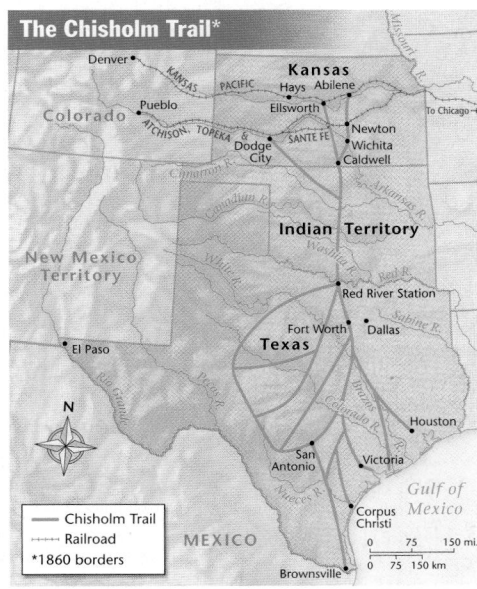

The Chisholm Trail*

MAP SKILLS The Chisholm Trail was probably named after Jesse Chisholm, a trader in the region. The trail originated south of San Antonio, Texas, and ended in Kansas cow towns along the railroad lines. **Movement** *Why do you think ranchers risked driving their herds through Indian Territory?*

Connecting with Culture

Tell students to find photographs and paintings depicting cowboy life. Encourage students to spend time in the local library looking for books containing artistic and photographic reproductions. Suggest that students look for examples by Frederic Remington, Charles M. Russell, and N. C. Wyeth. Have students bring in their examples, and discuss what these works of art express about this time in history. **(Visual/Spatial)**

From the Archives of
American Heritage®

"East to the Slaughter"

On September 5, 1867, the first of many thousands of Texas longhorns were packed into twenty waiting cattle cars of the Kansas Pacific Railway and left Abilene, Kansas, for eastern slaughterhouses. The event marked the birth of the era of great cattle drives along the Chisholm Trail and the culmination of Joseph McCoy's work. He had bought the 480-acre town for $2,400, then made a deal with the railway company and persuaded ranchers to drive their herds to his northern shipping point. The route followed by most of the drivers came to be known for an Indian trader, Jesse Chisholm, whose wagon ruts had worn it over the years. By 1871, 700,000 cattle had followed the Chisholm Trail to be packed off at Abilene and slaughtered in Kansas City and Chicago. Source: Nathan Ward, "The Time Machine," *American Heritage®* magazine, September 1992.

CAPTION ANSWERS

Map Skills Going through Indian Territory was by far the most direct route from the Texas panhandle to the markets and railroad in Kansas.

Texas Cattle Driven North, 1867–1881	
Year	Number of Cattle
1867	35,000
1868	75,000
1869	350,000
1870	300,000
1871	600,000
1872	350,000
1873	405,000
1874	166,000
1875	151,618
1876	321,998
1877	201,159
1878	265,646
1879	257,927
1880	394,784
1881	250,000

SOURCE: *The Cowboys,* William H. Forbis

VIEWING HISTORY Frederic Remington's famous 1902 painting *The Cowboy* (top) captures the skill and spirit of the cowboy legend. The cowboy's heyday was relatively brief, as the table above shows. **Interpreting Tables** *When did the Texas cattle drives peak?*

could spend up to 18 hours a day in the saddle and still had to be on constant alert.

A cowboy's greatest nightmare was the stampede. A mere breath of wind could spook a nervous herd, sending thousands of cattle into crushing, headlong flight. The men learned that singing calmed the cattle at night, and they invented endless lullabies and ballads, accompanied by a harmonica or a fiddle. One of the best known songs was "The Old Chisholm Trail":

> ❝ I'm up in the mornin' afore daylight
> And afore I sleep the moon shines bright. . . .
> I went to the boss to draw my roll [pay],
> He had it figured out I was nine dollars in the hole. ❞
>
> —"The Old Chisholm Trail"

During the era of the cattle drives, the leading cause of cowboy deaths was being dragged by a horse. Diseases such as pneumonia, tuberculosis, fevers, and infections also took many a young life, as did lightning and, of course, stampedes and gunfights. Not the least of the hardships on the trail was loneliness, with only fellow cowhands as company for months on end. In cattle country, men outnumbered women 10 to 1. In the West as a whole, men outnumbered women about 2.5 to 1 in 1870 (not counting Native Americans).

The Cattle Barons As the cattle business grew, a new breed of wealthy ranchers created huge cattle operations. Some of these new lords of the Texas plains owned more than 100,000 cattle that grazed over millions of acres. On such a grand scale, the annual roundup, said one cowhand, was like "a farmer in Massachusetts turning a cow out to graze and finding her months later in Delaware." By 1885, about three dozen cattle barons reigned over more than 20 million acres of rangeland.

Often, these entrepreneurs were cowboys who had struck out on their own. One of the most famous, Charles Goodnight, arrived in Texas as a child. He made a study of ranching. He determined that a cow needed 10 acres of grass in the Texas panhandle to graze for a year, if the soil was good, and it could drink up to 30 gallons of water a day. Thus, success depended on ownership of water sources and plenty of land. He acquired these by clearing out the Native Americans and their buffalo herds in the Palo Duro Canyon and beyond.

After fighting in the Civil War, Goodnight joined the Texas-wide roundup to recover his free-roaming cattle. He built a mighty business with the help of his wife, Mary Ann (who ran the operation after his death). With business partner Oliver Loving, he blazed the Goodnight-Loving Trail through the Southwest all the way up to Cheyenne, Wyoming.

The cattle bonanza ended in the mid-1880s, when a combination of over-expansion, price declines, cold winters, dry summers, and cattle fever drove thousands into bankruptcy. Cattle ranching survived, but on a much smaller scale.

Farming the Plains

Prairie life is romanticized in novels and films. But for most **homesteaders**—those who farmed claims under the Homestead Act—life was relentlessly rugged.

Hardships for Homesteaders The first order of business for a homesteader was building a home. In the early days, wood-frame homes were rare on the virtually treeless plains. Most people built either a dugout or a soddie. A dugout was actually carved out of the side of an embankment. The earthen structure cost about $3 to build. It was insulated from winter chill and summer heat. A **soddie,** or sod home, was a structure with the walls and roof made from blocks of sod—strips of grass with the thick roots and earth attached. Construction cost: less than $10.

Once the soddie was up, farmers faced the grim task of sodbusting—plowing the fields for planting. Oscar Micheaux, a black homesteader in South Dakota, tried to plow his whole claim in one season, to prove his ability. But, he noted, "as it had taken a 1,400-mile walk to follow the plow in breaking the 120 acres, I was about 'all in' physically when it was done." Backbreaking labor became heartbreaking when floods, prairie fires, dust storms, or drought left the year's work in ruins.

Then there were the bugs. Grasshoppers, locusts, and boll weevils ravaged fields of wheat, rye, sorghum, and corn. Various sources describe a mammoth column of grasshoppers stretching 150 miles by 100 miles that gnawed its way through Kansas. Mosquitoes and flies showed no mercy to people or animals, and could carry disease. Insects crawled out of the walls of dugouts and soddies.

Like the rattlesnakes that hung from the roof of a soddie, money worries hung on farmers' minds. Creating a livable homestead could cost $1,000, beyond the reach of many newcomers. Some settlers who lacked farming skills could not hold on for five years in order to receive their claim.

Falling crop prices created rising farm debt. Once farmers invested in machines, they had to focus on raising the crop for which the machines were designed. If prices for that crop dipped, farmers could not pay off their debts, which carried crippling interest rates of up to 25 percent or more.

Conditions proved so difficult that in the mid-1880s, following a series of droughts, hordes of prairie schooners took off and headed back east. About 18,000 wagons with returning homesteaders crossed over the Missouri River from Nebraska to Iowa in 1891 alone.

Families Pull Together Among the families who stayed, most husbands and wives had fairly well-defined roles. Yet in a pinch, it didn't much matter what was "men's work" or "women's work."

In general, men did the sodbusting, often walking miles to borrow a neighbor's ox or plow. They "dragged" the field to break up clots; they planted, hoed, and harvested. They did the threshing and binding. In the off-season, or to raise money in a bad year, husbands lent themselves out for labor in construction or other jobs.

In most families, women raised and schooled children, cooked, cleaned, made and washed clothes, and preserved food. They also raised food crops, made soap and butter, raised chickens, milked the cows, spun wool for sale, and managed the money.

Although most homesteaders went west as families, women could file claims on their own. Married or not, farm women often faced long periods of solitude and hardship. "My Husband went a way to find work and came home last night and told me that we would have to Starve he has

VIEWING HISTORY A family of Nebraska homesteaders pose in front of their soddie. **Analyzing Visual Information** *From looking at this photograph, describe what might have been the challenges of building a soddie.*

Focus on CITIZENSHIP

Women's Suffrage in the West
The West pioneered efforts to grant women suffrage. Western women launched campaigns to gain the vote at city and state levels. In 1887, two Kansas towns, Syracuse and Argonia, passed women's suffrage. Syracuse then elected an all-female town council, and Argonia the nation's first female mayor. Wyoming, which entered the union in 1890, became the first state whose constitution included women as voters.

Chapter 14 • Section 3 **503**

bin in ten countys and did not Get no work," a desperate Susan Orcutt wrote the governor of Kansas in 1894. "It is Pretty hard for a woman to do with out any thing to Eat. . . ."

Under these conditions, children's labor was crucial to the family's survival. Boys and girls as young as 4 years old collected wood for fuel or carried water. Some parents were forced to hire out their older children for work. In this unforgiving land, settlers relied heavily on each other, raising houses and barns together, sewing quilts, husking corn, and providing other forms of support.

New Technology Eases Farm Labor The dry climate in parts of the West greatly reduced the land's productivity. In response, farmers practiced water conservation techniques called **dry farming.** These techniques included planting crops that do not require a great deal of water, such as sorghum, keeping the fields free of weeds, and digging deep furrows so water could reach the plant roots.

Farmers welcomed any machines that would save time and effort. During the 1870s, improvements in farm implements multiplied. Soon farmers were riding behind a plow that made several furrows at once. Other inventions included harrows, implements with spring teeth to dislodge debris and break up the ground before planting, and automatic drills to spread grain. Steam-powered threshers arrived by 1875, and cornhuskers and cornbinders by the 1890s.

Knowledge of farming techniques improved during this period as well. In the 1880s and 1890s, the United States Department of Agriculture (USDA), which was created under the 1862 Morrill Land-Grant Act, collected statistics on markets, crops, and plant diseases. The USDA provided information on crop rotation, hybridization (cross-breeding plants), and soil and water conservation.

Farming Becomes Big Business New farm machines and techniques increased farm output enormously. Owners of large farms hoped to reap a "bonanza" by supplying food to growing eastern populations. They applied to farming the organizational ideas taking hold in industry. As one observer noted:

> ❝ It is no longer left to the small farmer, taking up 160 acres of land. . . . Organized capital is being employed in the work, with all the advantages which organization implies. Companies and partnerships are formed for the cultivation precisely as they are for building railroads, manufactures, etc. ❞
> —*Commercial and Financial Chronicle,* 1879

The result was **bonanza farms,** operations controlled by large businesses, managed by professionals, and raising massive quantities of single cash crops. The farms' huge output caused problems, however. When the supply of a crop rose faster than the demand, prices fell. To make up for falling prices, farmers produced ever larger quantities of the product, adding to the oversupply.

Farmers Prevail on the Plains Despite the growth of large-scale farms in the Red River Valley along the Texas border and around Salt Lake City in Utah, the Great Plains remained a region of small family farms well into the 1900s. Despite continual setbacks, the farmer's way of life prevailed in

Farming Innovations on the Prairie, 1860–1900	
Mechanized Reaper	Reduces labor force needed for harvest. Allows farmers to maintain larger farms.
Barbed Wire	Keeps cattle from trampling crops and uses a minimal amount of lumber, which was scarce on the plains.
Dry Farming	Allows cultivation of arid land by using drought-resistant crops and various techniques to minimize evaporation.
Steel Plow	Allows farmers to cut through dense, root-choked sod.
Harrow	Smoothes and levels ground for planting.
Steel Windmill	Powers irrigation systems and pumps up ground water.
Hybridization	Cross-breeding of crop plants, which allows greater yields and uniformity.
Improved Communication	Creation of the U.S. Department of Agriculture in 1862 provides farmers with information about improved farming practices.
Grain Drill	Array of multiple drills used to carve small trenches in the ground and feed seed into the soil.

INTERPRETING CHARTS An agricultural revolution took place in the late 1800s with the introduction of farm machinery and new growing techniques. While it took a farmer an average of about 61 hours to harvest an acre of land by hand, a farmer with a machine could do it in about 3 hours. **Drawing Conclusions** *Choose one of the items in the chart and describe the effect it might have had on a farm family on the plains.*

the West, as mines closed down and the song of the cowboy slowly faded. Farmers triumphed in a showdown with ranchers that shaped the economy of the West. (See Geography and History: The End of the Open Range, on pages 516–517.)

Frontier Myths

The "Wild West": Was it the rootin'-tootin', hard-livin', free-for-all of sharp-shootin' marshals, quick-witted outlaws, rough-talkin' women, and handsome Indian fighters? To be sure, the West was all this and more: boxing matches and animal fights; traveling minstrels, jugglers, magicians, and zoos; rodeos and carnivals. Yet in truth, many wild towns of the West calmed down fairly quickly or disappeared.

Taming the Frontier In Colorado after about 1880, residents had a choice of at least seven church denominations. They might join a social group such as the Masons, the Odd Fellows, or a Civil War veterans' group. Most social clubs had a women's auxiliary devoted to charitable work. There were clubs for railroad engineers, ranchers, teachers; for hunters and equestrians; for lovers of literature, science, and Shakespearean drama. Major theatrical productions toured growing western cities. The East had come West.

The End of the Frontier In 1870, most of the Great Plains and the Rocky Mountains had a population of less than two people per square mile. (The census did not count Native Americans.) As populations swelled, unorganized lands became U.S. territories, then states. In 1872, the government moved to preserve western lands, establishing Yellowstone National Park in northwest Wyoming, southern Montana, and eastern Idaho. It was the nation's first national park.

Finally, in 1890, the head of the Census Bureau announced the official end of the frontier. The country's "unsettled area has been so broken into by isolated bodies of settlement," he declared, "that there can hardly be said to be a frontier line." The days of free western land were over.

Turner's Frontier Thesis In 1893, historian Frederick Jackson Turner claimed that the frontier had played a key role in forming the American character. "American intellect owes its striking characteristics [to the frontier]," Turner declared. Frontier life, he said, had created Americans who were socially mobile, ready for adventure, bent on individual self-improvement, and committed to democracy.

Historians have since modified the **Turner thesis,** as his view came to be called. His theory of frontier life did not include the contributions of women and of various ethnic groups. It emphasized the effects of individual effort but played down the effects of federal subsidies and business investments on development and on Native Americans.

Myths in Literature, Shows, and Song Despite today's deeper understanding of the history of the American West, frontier myths continue to influence how Americans think about themselves. The romantic image of the American cowboy, for example, began as early as the 1870s, in dime novels often based on the lives of real people. Writers created characters such as Wild Bill Hickok, Calamity Jane, and Deadwood Dick. The stories promoted **stereotypes,** exaggerated or oversimplified descriptions of reality. The stereotypical hero might be an

VIEWING HISTORY Buffalo Bill's Wild West shows (above) toured America and Europe. African American cowboy Nat Love (below) became the larger-than-life hero of a novel. **Distinguishing False From Accurate Images** What details in the images above and below might have given Americans a romanticized image of the West?

Chapter 14 • Section 3 **505**

Reading Comprehension

1. Large drills, hydraulic pumps, and dynamite replaced placer mining.

2. Texans returned to their ranches after the Civil War to find a cattle population boom. Increased demand for beef, refrigerated railroad cars, and the extension of rail lines into the West caused cattle ranching to become successful.

3. Cow towns were specifically developed along railroad lines to receive cattle on their way to market. These towns would often thrive until they became surrounded by farms.

4. Answers may include: building homes without wood, floods, prairie fires, dust storms, drought, insects that ravaged the crops, disease-carrying mosquitoes, financial worries.

5. The West was romanticized as a place full of outlaws, Indian fighters, cowboys, and happily prosperous farmers. Another stereotype is that issues of right and wrong were clearly defined in the West.

Critical Thinking and Writing

6. Drills, hydraulic pumps, and dynamite favored large mining corporations. Refrigerated railroad cars and open land with water resulted in vast cattle-ranching operations. Machines like automatic grain drills and techniques like dry farming and crop rotation created bonanza farms.

7. Answers might try to debunk some of the myths by explaining the difficulties and hardships involved in homesteading.

Invite students to take a Virtual Field Trip at **www.phschool.com**

The 1943 Rodgers and Hammerstein musical "Oklahoma" is a love story that takes place during the settlement of Oklahoma Territory, where "the corn is as high as an elephant's eye." One song declares that "the farmer and the cowman should be friends," a reference to the frequent land feuds between the two groups.

outlaw, a miner, a gang leader, or a cowboy—anyone who dealt out righteous justice against evil.

Edward Wheeler's novel *Deadwood Dick, The Prince of the Road: or, the Black Rider of the Black Hills* was based on a real person. But the real Deadwood Dick was no outlaw. He was an African American named Nat Love. Entering a rodeo contest in a Dakota Territory mining town named Deadwood, Love won several roping and shooting contests. In his autobiography, Love wrote, "Right there the assembled crowd named me 'Deadwood Dick' and proclaimed me champion roper of the Western cattle country."

In 1883, William F. ("Buffalo Bill") Cody created his fantastically popular Wild West shows, contributing further to frontier myths. These events drew thousands of spectators to steer-roping contests, rodeos, and battle enactments between "good" cavalry regiments and "bad" Native Americans. One season featured the real-life Sitting Bull.

Most stories from the West supported stereotypes about men. The West was the place where a young man could find freedom and opportunity. He could lead a virtuous life and resist the forces of civilization that had made easterners soft. Many writers praised the West for having toughened the bodies and souls of young men. In his histories of the West, future President Theodore Roosevelt urged American men to experience the "strenuous life" of the West before they became too weak from the comforts of modern civilization.

Some male themes also appealed to women. In 1912, Juliette Low founded the American Girl Scouts in part because she feared that civilization had made girls too soft. Praising women homesteaders for their strength and intelligence, she made the scouting techniques of tracking, woodcraft, and wilderness survival the core of her program.

The Wild West remains fixed in popular culture, from the Dallas lawyer in a cowboy hat to western movies. Cowboy songs—"Home on the Range" and "Don't Fence Me In"—celebrate images of wide-open spaces and freedom from civilization. While myths of the Old West are more dramatic than the reality, the era produced many of the nation's most cherished images of itself.

Section 3 Assessment

READING COMPREHENSION

1. What technologies gradually replaced **placer mining?**

2. Why did cattle ranching become so successful after the Civil War?

3. Describe the rise of cow towns.

4. What hardships did **homesteaders** face?

5. What kinds of **stereotypes** were created about the Old West?

CRITICAL THINKING AND WRITING

6. **Analyzing Information** Describe the impact of new technologies and other factors on small entrepreneurs in mining, ranching, and farming.

7. **Writing to Narrate** Create a historical fiction narrative describing the experience of a homesteading family on the Great Plains.

Take It to the NET

Virtual Field Trip Travel the Chisholm Trail. Read about the challenges of getting Texas cattle herds to market. See how the trail's history is being preserved. Use the links provided in the *America: Pathways to the Present* area of the following Web site for help in completing this activity.
www.phschool.com

506 Chapter 14 • *Looking to the West*

RESOURCE DIRECTORY

Teaching Resources
Units 5/6 booklet
• Section 3 Quiz, p. 17
Guide to the Essentials
• Section 3 Summary, p. 75

Populism

READING FOCUS

- Why did farmers complain about federal post–Civil War economic policies?
- How did the government respond to organized protests by farmers?
- What were the Populists' key goals?
- What was the main point of William Jennings Bryan's Cross of Gold speech?
- What was the legacy of Populism?

MAIN IDEA

Economic crises led to organized protests by farmers seeking government relief. Economic reform became an election issue and led to the rise of Populism.

KEY TERMS

money supply
deflation
monetary policy
bimetallic standard
free silver
Bland-Allison Act
Sherman Silver Purchase Act
the Grange
Interstate Commerce Act
Populist
Cross of Gold speech

TAKING NOTES

Copy the web diagram below. As you read, fill in the blank circles to show the effects of economic instability from 1870 to 1900. Add more circles if needed.

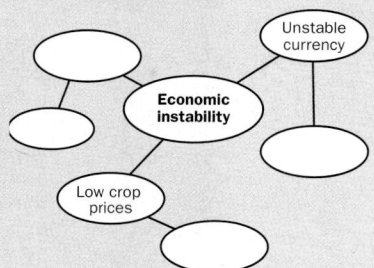

SECTION OBJECTIVES

1. See why farmers complained about federal post–Civil War economic policies.
2. Find out how the government responded to organized protests by farmers.
3. Discover the Populists' key goals.
4. Understand the main point of William Jennings Bryan's Cross of Gold speech.
5. Learn about the legacy of Populism.

BELLRINGER

Warm-Up Activity Ask students why merchants and service industries accept paper money or coins in return for goods and services. What gives these items value?

Activating Prior Knowledge In the years following the Civil War the government took steps to ensure the strength of the country's economy. What types of steps does the government take today?

READING STRATEGY

Imagine you are a farmer in the late 1800s. List some of the problems you face and identify some of the organizations that promise to help you.

ACTIVITY

Connecting with Economics

Ask students to research the ways in which the federal government controls the money supply. Have them locate magazine and newspaper articles that focus on the Federal Reserve Bank's influence in recent times. Tell students to write a short report describing the influence of the Federal Reserve Bank on the economy. (**Logical/Mathematical**)

Setting the Scene American farmers have always struggled against two forces: nature and the economy. In the late 1800s, economic perils were as devastating to farmers as locusts or boll weevils. Ever since the end of the Civil War, farm production had risen. So too had debt, as farmers borrowed heavily to purchase the expensive new equipment that made possible such increased productivity.

Indebted farmers found themselves in an increasingly dangerous, even hopeless, position, as competition from abroad increased and crop prices went into a prolonged decline. Tenant farming increased as homesteaders lost their farms when they couldn't make their loan payments. The crisis struck farmers throughout the West and the South, both whites and blacks.

In 1890, a Congregational minister described the plight of the farmer:

> 66 The farmers . . . are the bone and sinew of the nation; they produce the largest share of its wealth; but they are getting, they say, the smallest share for themselves. The American farmer is steadily losing ground. His burdens are heavier every year and his gains are more meager. 99

—Washington Gladden

The Farmers' Complaint

The American economy rested on shaky ground in the post–Civil War era. Twice, in 1873 and 1893, the collapse of a financially ailing railroad led to a cascading national panic. Banks failed. Businesses—which, like farmers, had also

Wheat Prices 1866–1890

SOURCE: Historical Statistics of the United States, Colonial Times to 1970

INTERPRETING CHARTS

Farmers often suffered from unpredictable crop prices. **Drawing Conclusions** (a) What might have caused the sharpest price drop? (b) What happened to prices during the Panic of 1873?

Chapter 14 • Section 4 **507**

RESOURCE DIRECTORY

Teaching Resources
Learning Styles Lesson Plans booklet, p. 31
Guided Reading and Review booklet, p. 61

Technology
Section Reading Support Transparencies
Guided Reading Audiotapes (English/Spanish), Ch. 14
Student Edition on Audio CD, Ch. 14
Prentice Hall Presentation Pro CD-ROM, Ch. 14
Companion Web site, www.phschool.com

CAPTION ANSWERS

Interpreting Charts Sample answer: (a) A sharp drop in demand after the war. (b) Wheat prices dropped sharply.

Focus Explain that as farmers' incomes declined, they began to join together, many by supporting the Populist Party. Ask students what the farmers' complaints were. What reforms did the Populist Party promise to help them institute?

Instruct Discuss why Americans in the late 1800s were divided over the issue of tariffs. Ask how industrialists profited from tariffs and why farmers ultimately protested against them.

Assess/Reteach As the country expanded, many different groups raised their voices to seek the government's support. One such group was the Populists. Have students list the aims of the Populists. Are there groups today whose interests and main opinions resemble those of the Populists?

BACKGROUND
Global Connections

As the world has become more complex, and countries more economically dependent on one another, international efforts to balance trade have grown in importance. In 1947, 23 countries signed on to GATT, the General Agreement on Tariffs and Trade. This set of trade agreements, designed to eliminate quotas and reduce tariff duties, played a key role in increasing world trade in the second half of the twentieth century. By 1995, when GATT was replaced by the World Trade Organization (WTO), 125 countries had become signatories to its agreements. GATT's most significant policy was to promote trade without discrimination, which required every member nation to open its markets equally to every other. Under GATT when a nation and its largest trading partners agreed to a tariff reduction, the cut applied to all other GATT members.

READING CHECK
The economic strength of the nation fluctuated wildly after the Civil War. Farm earnings plummeted during hard times while farm loans were being called.

READING CHECK
Why did farmers begin to ask for government help in solving their problems?

Focus on
ECONOMICS

Monetary Policy The federal government's plan for the size of the nation's money supply.

The Historical Context Farmers in the late 1800s called for an increase in the money supply, which would cause higher prices and thus raise their incomes. Their opponents called for a continued "tight money" policy, in which the money supply is kept low.

The Concept Today The Federal Reserve System, established in 1913, controls the nation's money supply today. Led by its chairman, the "Fed" seeks to promote steady economic growth without causing high inflation.

RESOURCE DIRECTORY
Teaching Resources
Great Debates booklet (Great Debates) *How Should People Treat the Land?* p. 10

---

over-borrowed—went under. Unemployment soared. During both panics, farmers suffered the double disasters of falling crop prices and loans called in by banks desperate for cash.

Historically, the federal government rarely had intervened to stabilize the nation's economy, nor would most people have expected it to. But in their distress, farmers increasingly began to view government help as a right. In small but rapidly growing numbers, they voiced their demands.

Farmers and Tariffs   One federal policy of concern to farmers was tariffs. Tariffs on imported goods discourage people from buying imports by making them more expensive. Thus, tariffs encourage the sale of goods produced at home.

Americans in the late 1800s were divided on the benefit of tariffs. Businesses claimed that tariffs protected American factory jobs—and their own profits. But because tariffs reduced foreign competition, they also encouraged American firms to raise their prices, which harmed workers and consumers in general.

Tariffs helped farmers by protecting them against competition from farm imports. But tariffs hurt farmers in two ways. First, they raised the prices of manufactured goods, such as farm machinery. Second, they kept foreigners from earning the U.S. currency they needed to buy American crops. Thus, tariffs indirectly reduced the world market for American farm products.

Whenever the government raised tariffs to benefit industry, farmers protested. They viewed tariff increases as proof that the government favored eastern manufacturers over western farmers.

The Money Issue   Tariffs were not farmers' only concern in the late 1800s. For many, the key issue was the silver supply. The value of money is linked to the **money supply,** the amount of money in the national economy. If the government increases the money supply, the value of every dollar drops. This drop in value shows up as inflation, a widespread rise in prices on goods of all kinds.

People who borrow money benefit from inflation because the money they eventually pay back is worth less than the money they borrowed. Inflation also helps sellers, such as farmers, because it raises the prices of the goods they sell.

In contrast, if the government reduces the money supply, the value of each dollar becomes greater. This causes **deflation,** or a drop in the prices on goods. People who lend money are helped by deflation because the money they receive in payment of a loan is worth more than the money they lent out.

In the years following the Civil War, the nation's money supply shrank as the federal government took out of circulation the paper money issued during the war. As a result, the nation experienced a prolonged period of deflation.

Monetary policy, the federal government's plan for the makeup and quantity of the nation's money supply, thus emerged as a major political issue. Supporters of inflation pushed for an increase in the money supply. Supporters of deflation wanted a "tight money" policy of less currency in circulation.

Gold Bugs   In 1873—the year of the worst economic panic in U.S. history to that point—supporters of tight money won a victory. Until that time, United States currency had been on a **bimetallic standard.** That is, currency consisted of gold or silver coins or United States treasury notes that could be traded in for gold or silver. In 1873, in order to prevent inflation and stabilize the economy, Congress put the nation's currency on a gold standard. This move reduced the amount of money in circulation because the money supply was limited by the amount of gold held by the government. Conservative "gold bugs" were pleased. Many of them were big lenders, and they liked the idea of being repaid in currency backed by the gold standard.

Silverites The move to a gold standard enraged "silverites," mostly silver-mining interests and western farmers. They claimed that ending silver as a monetary standard would depress farm prices. Silverites called for **free silver,** the unlimited coining of silver dollars to increase the money supply.

The **Bland-Allison Act** of 1878, was, for the silverites, a step in the right direction. This act required the federal government to purchase and coin more silver, increasing the money supply and causing inflation. Passed by Congress, the Bland-Allison Act was vetoed by President Rutherford B. Hayes because he opposed the inflation it would create. Congress overrode Hayes's veto. Yet the act had only a limited effect, because the Treasury Department refused to buy more than the minimum amount of silver required under the act. The Treasury also refused to circulate the silver dollars that the law required it to mint.

In 1890, Congress passed the **Sherman Silver Purchase Act.** While not authorizing the free and unlimited coinage of silver that the silverites wanted, it increased the amount of silver the government was required to purchase every month. The law required the Treasury to buy the silver with notes that could be redeemed for either silver or gold. That plan backfired, as people turned in their silver Treasury notes for gold dollars, thus depleting the government's gold reserves. To protect the gold supply, President Grover Cleveland oversaw the repeal of the Silver Purchase Act in 1893.

Gold vs. silver: an 1891 silver dime and an 1873 $20 gold coin

COMPARING PRIMARY SOURCES

Gold Bugs *vs.* Silverites

In this famous exchange, one "silverite" proposes the return to a bimetallic standard along with the unlimited coining of silver, while his opponent, a "gold bug," criticizes the proposal.

Analyzing Viewpoints Compare the main arguments made by the two scholars.

In Favor of Free Silver

"Our forefathers showed much wisdom in selecting silver, of the two metals, out of which to make the unit [of currency]. . . . [T]hey were led to adopt silver because it was the most reliable. It was the most favored as money by the people. It was scattered among all the people. . . . Gold was considered the money of the rich. . . . [With the coining of silver,] you increase the value of all property by adding to the number of monetary units in the land. You make it possible for the debtor to pay his debts; business to start anew, and revivify all the industries of the country. . . . The money lenders in the United States, who own substantially all our money, have a selfish interest in maintaining the gold standard."

—pamphlet by Professor W. H. "Coin" Harvey,
of Coin's Financial School, 1894

Opposed to Free Silver

"Do you suppose that the farmers of this country really believe that with each ton of silver taken out of the mines by the silver law-makers in the Senate that there are created bushels of wheat[?] . . . Free coinage of silver then is absolutely certain to drive all our gold out of circulation. . . . [Hence] there will be no increase in the quantity of money. . . . The only way it would act would be by increasing the price of everything. . . . A dozen eggs, now selling at 15 cents, would sell for about 30 cents. . . . As [it] would inevitably result in a rise of prices it would immediately result in the fall of wages. . . . Are we willing to sacrifice the interests of the laboring classes to the demands of certain owners of silver mines . . . ?"

—University of Chicago economist James Laurence
Laughlin, in a public debate with "Coin" Harvey, 1895

Organizing Farmer Protests

Because farmers lived far from one another and usually relied on their own efforts, they tended not to organize protests against policies they opposed. In the late 1800s, however, farmers took advantage of improvements in communication and transportation to form several powerful protest groups.

The Grange   In 1866, the Department of Agriculture sent Oliver H. Kelley on an inspection tour of southern farms. Disturbed by the farmers' isolation, the following year he founded the Patrons of Husbandry, or **the Grange.**

The Grange soon began helping farmers form cooperatives, through which they bought goods in large quantities at lower prices. The Grange also pressured state legislators to regulate businesses on which farmers depended, such as the operators of grain elevators that stored farmers' crops and the railroads that shipped goods to market.

Farmers' Alliances   Although the Grange was popular (and still exists today), eventually farmers formed other political groups. In the 1880s, many farmers joined a network of Farmers' Alliances that were formed around the nation. The alliances launched harsh attacks on monopolies, such as those that controlled the railroads.

The Farmers' Alliance in the South, formed in Texas in the mid-1870s, grew especially powerful. It called for actions that many of the nation's farmers could support: federal regulation of the railroads, more money in circulation, creation of state departments of agriculture, antitrust laws, and farm credit.

Farmers' Alliances held special importance for women, who served as officers and won support for women's political rights. One of the most popular speakers was Kansas lawyer Mary Elizabeth Lease, who reportedly urged farmers to raise "less corn and more Hell!" African Americans worked through a separate but parallel "Colored Farmers' Alliance." Formed in 1886 in Lovelady, Texas, the group had a quarter of a million members by 1891.

A series of natural disasters gave special urgency to Farmers' Alliance programs. The Mississippi River flooded in 1882. In 1886 and 1887, Texas suffered a 21-month drought. Terrible blizzards, which killed thousands of cattle, struck the West in 1887. Increasingly, farmers wanted to know why the federal government was unwilling to respond to these disasters.

Government Responses   Political power and influence were splintered during this period. Farmers often differed on how much federal help was needed, if any. On the other hand, business interests were not always strong enough to prevent legislation they disliked from becoming law. As one historian put it, "Big business was powerful; it was by no means all-powerful."

Meanwhile, fragmented political parties had difficulty rallying support for controversial proposals among their members in various regions of the country as well as among different economic and ethnic groups. In every election from 1880 to

VIEWING HISTORY A teacher who farmed, studied law, and raised a family, Mary Elizabeth Lease (above) became a leading speaker and educator for Farmers' Alliance groups. The illustration below is from a book of Farmer's Alliance songs. **Drawing Inferences** *Why do you think education and a spirit of unity were key goals of these groups?*

1892, no candidate won a majority of the popular vote. Only rarely did the President's party command a majority in Congress. Presidents thus lacked the power to take bold action. In addition, some Presidents were influenced by promises of support from powerful business interests.

In 1887, Congress passed the Texas seed bill, which provided seed grain to drought victims. But President Cleveland, a Democrat, vetoed the bill, expressing the commonly held view that "though the people support the government, the government should not support the people."

On the issue of railroad regulation, some consensus emerged. Even some railroad owners backed moderate regulations, fearing more drastic measures. In 1887, Cleveland signed the **Interstate Commerce Act.** It regulated the prices that railroads charged to move freight between states, requiring the rates to be set in proportion to the distance traveled. The law also made it illegal to give special rates to some customers. While the act did not control the monopolistic railroad practices that angered farmers, it established the principle that Congress could regulate the railroads, a significant expansion of federal authority. The act also set up the Interstate Commerce Commission (ICC) to enforce the laws.

In 1890, President Benjamin Harrison approved the Sherman Antitrust Act. This act was meant to curb the power of trusts and monopolies. But during its first decade, enforcement was lax.

The Populists

In 1890, the various small political parties associated with the Farmers' Alliances began to enjoy success at the ballot box, especially in the South. In 1891, the Alliances founded the People's Party, a new national party that demanded radical changes in federal economic and social policies. The **Populists,** as followers of the new party were known, built their platform around the following issues:

1. An increased circulation of money.
2. The unlimited minting of silver.
3. A progressive income tax, in which the percentage of taxes owed increases with a rise in income. This tax would place a greater financial burden on wealthy industrialists and a lesser one on farmers.
4. Government ownership of communications and transportation systems.

Seeking the support of urban industrial workers, the Populists endorsed an eight-hour work day. For the same reason, they opposed the use of Pinkertons, the private police force that had been involved in the bloody Homestead Strike of 1892, as strikebreakers. Breaking through deeply rooted racial prejudice, Populists sought a united front of African American and white farmers. The poor of both races had a common cause, they argued. "You are kept apart that you may be separately fleeced of your earnings," said one party leader. The party drew some black sharecroppers and tenant farmers away from the Republican Party.

During the 1892 campaign, populism generated great excitement among its followers. But the party's presidential candidate, Iowan James B. Weaver, won barely a million votes. Cleveland returned to the presidency.

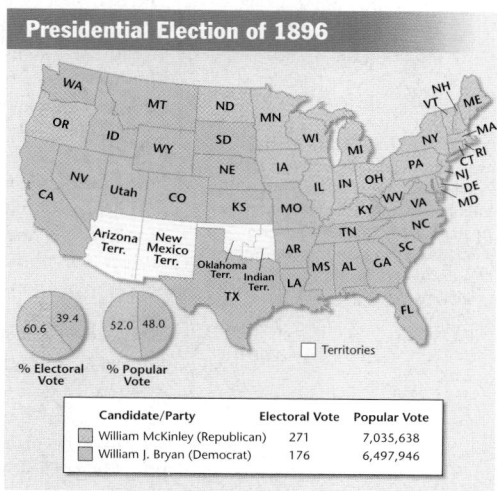

Presidential Election of 1896

Candidate/Party	Electoral Vote	Popular Vote
William McKinley (Republican)	271	7,035,638
William J. Bryan (Democrat)	176	6,497,946

MAP SKILLS William Jennings Bryan was the candidate of the Democrats and the Populists in 1896. As the map shows, he won most of the western and southern states and nearly half the popular vote, yet he lost the election. **Analyzing Visual Information** *Explain the reasons for Bryan's defeat.*

ACTIVITY
Connecting with Government

Tell students to research recent presidencies to find out whether the administration in power corresponded with a party majority in Congress. Have students look into the benefits a President has when his party has a majority in Congress. Tell students also to find out how a President's efforts can be stymied when the opposition party is in the majority. As students discuss recent presidencies, have them cite specific examples of both situations. **(Verbal/Linguistic)**

From the Archives of
AmericanHeritage®

About the Presidents

William McKinley (1897–1901) enjoyed a big advantage over William Jennings Bryan in his first election, which was a well-financed campaign. Businessman Marcus A. Hanna raised millions of dollars on McKinley's behalf. McKinley's campaign chest paid for pamphlets, posters, and buttons, as well as train fare for those wishing to visit McKinley in his home town of Canton, Ohio. On one day alone McKinley spoke to some 30,000 visitors. By contrast, Bryan's campaign had little money. Although Bryan crossed the country with his "silverite" message, warning that wealthy eastern financial interests should not be allowed to "crucify" ordinary working Americans "upon a cross of gold," McKinley beat Bryan with a comfortable electoral margin. Source: Donald Young, "William McKinley," *The American Heritage® Pictorial History of the Presidents of the United States,* vol. 2, 1968.

CUSTOMIZE FOR ...
Less Proficient Readers

Ask students to make a chart with two headings: *The Farmers* and *The Populists.* On one side students should list the complaints of farmers in 1896 about the money supply, the transportation system, and the disparity between the incomes of the rich and the poor. On the other side, they should list the promises of the Populist Party that addressed those complaints.

☑ TEST PREPARATION

Have students reread the quote from President Cleveland on this page. Then have them answer the question below.

Which sentence below most closely paraphrases the quote from President Cleveland?

A The government is responsible for providing goods and services to citizens.

B The government and the people do not have a connection.

C The government should not be responsible for providing its people a living or food.

D The government exists for the people's good.

CAPTION ANSWERS

Map Skills Bryan failed to capture many of the most populous urbanized states in the East and Midwest, which had more electoral votes. Elections are determined by the electoral count, not by the popular vote.

Reading Comprehension

1. Increase in money supply, free silver, higher tariffs, regulation of rates charged by railroads and grain elevators.

2. Gold standard: limited the money supply to match the gold held by the government. Bimetallic standard: gold or silver coins or treasury notes that could be traded for gold or silver. Free silver: unlimited coining of silver dollars to increase the money supply.

3. The Bland-Allison Act put more silver into circulation and was inflationary. The Sherman Silver Purchase Act increased the government's silver supply but caused a depletion of its gold reserves. The Interstate Commerce Act made interstate rail shipping prices equitable.

4. It appealed to many Democrats, especially in the West and South, as well as many Populists, farmers, and other silverites. They applauded its support of free silver and the preservation of farming.

Critical Thinking and Writing

5. Political parties were fractured, leaving an opening for a new party. Populism appealed to diverse groups, including rural voters. Populism also drew on existing organizations like the Grange and the Farmers' Alliance.

6. Answers will vary, but might focus on inflation and deflation, or on the transformation of the United States from an agricultural into an industrial nation.

Take It to the NET

Fact sheets should compare the Grange's early activities, such as helping farmers form unions, with its modern-day activities of providing support to families involved in agriculture, as well as its involvement in broader environmental and conservation issues.

CAPTION ANSWERS

Viewing History The cartoon portrays him in a negative light, suggesting that he is using the symbols of Christianity —the cross, the crown of thorns, and the Bible—to further his political career.

VIEWING HISTORY This cartoon shows William Jennings Bryan holding a crown of thorns and a cross of gold, biblical images that he used in his famous speech. **Analyzing Visual Information** *Does this cartoon present Bryan in a positive or a negative light?*

Bryan's "Cross of Gold"

Populists renewed their vigor in the 1896 presidential campaign. In an election that focused mainly on currency issues, the Republicans ran moderate Ohio governor William McKinley on a gold-standard platform. William Jennings Bryan, a former silverite congressman from Nebraska and a powerful speaker, captured the Democratic nomination with an emotional plea for free silver.

Bryan addressed the 1896 Democratic Convention in Chicago on July 8, at the close of the debate over the party platform. Using images from the Bible, he stood with head bowed and arms outstretched and cried out at the climax of his speech, "You shall not press down upon the brow of labor this crown of thorns. You shall not crucify mankind upon a cross of gold!" So stunning was Bryan's speech that both the Democrats and the Populists nominated him for President. The **Cross of Gold speech** is one of the most famous in American history.

The 1896 campaign was one of marked contrasts. Bryan created a whirlwind of activity, traveling all over the country and making speeches at every stop. McKinley ran a more traditional campaign. He remained in his hometown of Canton, Ohio, greeting visitors and making a few speeches from his front porch.

Despite his best efforts, Bryan lost the election. He carried the Democratic West and South but none of the urban and industrial midwestern and northern states. In these states, factory workers feared that free silver might cause inflation, which would eat away the buying power of their wages. Thus, despite populism's broad appeal, it could not bridge the gap between America's cities and farms. Nor could populism slow America's transition from an agricultural nation to an industrial nation.

Populism's Legacy

By 1897, McKinley's administration had raised the tariff to new heights. In 1900, after gold discoveries in South Africa, the Canadian Yukon, and Alaska had increased the world's gold supply by more than $100 million, Congress returned the nation to a gold standard. To the surprise of many farmers, crop prices began a slow rise. The silver movement died, as did populism.

The goals of populism, however, lived on. In the decades ahead, other reformers, known as Progressives, applied populist ideas to urban and industrial problems. In so doing, they launched a new, historic era of reforms.

Section 4 Assessment

READING COMPREHENSION

1. What changes in economic policy did many farmers seek?

2. Explain the difference between a gold standard, a **bimetallic standard**, and **free silver**.

3. What did the government do to address farmers' complaints?

4. To whom did Bryan's **Cross of Gold speech** appeal, and why?

CRITICAL THINKING AND WRITING

5. **Drawing Conclusions** Few strong third parties such as the Populists have arisen in the nation's history. What caused the Populist Party to enjoy relative success in its time?

6. **Writing an Outline** Set up an outline for an analysis of the gold-versus-silver debate. Include facts on the currency plans put forward and who favored and opposed them.

 Take It to the NET

Activity: Creating a Fact Sheet Write a fact sheet comparing the Grange's early activities with its modern-day ones. Browse the Web site of the National Grange by using the link provided at the *America: Pathways to the Present* area of the following Web site for help in completing this activity.
www.phschool.com

RESOURCE DIRECTORY

Teaching Resources
Units 5/6 booklet
- Section 4 Quiz, p. 18
- Chapter 14 Test, pp. 19, 22

Guide to the Essentials
- Section 4 Summary, p. 76
- Chapter 14 Test, p. 77

Learning with Documents booklet (Key Documents) *William Jennings Bryan, Cross of Gold Speech*, p. 83

Other Print Resources
Chapter Tests with ExamView® Test Bank CD-ROM, Ch. 14

Technology
Color Transparencies *Political Cartoons*, B8
Sounds of an Era Audio CD *"Cross of Gold"* (time: 40 seconds)
ExamView® Test Bank CD-ROM, Ch. 14
Social Studies Skills Tutor CD-ROM

Expressing Problems Clearly

Expressing a problem clearly is the first step toward understanding and solving it. Problems often arise out of situations that have many elements; this makes them complex or puzzling. Other problems are difficult because there are clearly several possible solutions; this makes these problems open to debate. The ability to express a problem clearly means being able to describe a complex situation or body of information so that possible solutions can be evaluated, and the problem can be solved.

In 1877, the United States was in the midst of a depression. On July 14, the Baltimore and Ohio Railroad announced a 10 percent wage cut. The passage below is from an editorial, "The Railroad Strike," which appeared in a business journal.

LEARN THE SKILL
Use the following steps to express problems clearly:

1. **Analyze the information.** Identify the difficulties faced by the persons or groups involved. Consider what led to the problem, including the historical context. Be aware of the point of view of those who are describing the problem.

2. **Identify the basic concepts involved.** Problems usually arise out of a specific set of circumstances. However, they often revolve around a general principle, such as fairness. To identify this concept, try to express the problem in terms of what each side wants for itself.

3. **Identify the function of the supporting details.** Note details that are not basic to the problem. Eliminating them from consideration can help you see the problem more clearly.

4. **Express the problem as simply and completely as possible.** Once you have identified the main area of dispute and have stripped away irrelevant details, you are ready to express the problem clearly.

PRACTICE THE SKILL
Answer the following questions:

1. **(a)** What difficulty were the railroad companies facing? What actions did they take? **(b)** What difficulty were the workers facing? What action did they take? **(c)** Who else may have been affected by the problem? Why? **(d)** How does the historical context affect this situation? **(e)** What is the point of view of the writer of this editorial?

2. **(a)** Explain what each party wants for itself. **(b)** Do you think the writer is interested in fairness, or unfairly favors one side? Explain.

3. **(a)** Is the detail that the Baltimore & Ohio Company is paying 10 percent to its stockholders important to understanding the problem? Explain. **(b)** Are there any details in this excerpt that are irrelevant to the problem? Explain.

4. **(a)** Describe the problem caused by the railroad strike. **(b)** Evaluate the editorial's proposed solution. **(c)** What other solutions might be possible?

"The present strike among the employees of most of our principal railroad lines, is an illustration of errors in judgment . . . committed by the employers as well as by the employees of the railroad companies. None can deny, as a fundamental principle, the absolute necessity of . . . 'making both ends meet.' This principle is as applicable to every line of business, whether small or large, as to every family, whether poor or rich. Now, the railroad companies, in order to make ends meet, had the choice of three different means: 1st, to pay less dividends to the stockholders, in case dividends are paid; 2d, to raise the rates of freight; 3d, to reduce expenses. . . .

Of these three ways to make ends meet, the railroad companies, or rather those who are supposed to have sound judgment enough to be entrusted with their management . . . chose the latter means; and this was unjust to the employees and unfortunate for the stockholders, and especially unfortunate for the community at large, which is highly interested in reliable railroad transportation. . . .

It should not be lost sight of that the railroad on which the strike began (the Baltimore & Ohio) has been paying, and has thus far continued to pay, 10 per cent dividends to its stockholders. We ask if it would not be more just all around to pay only 8 or 9, or even 6 or 7 per cent dividend, and thus, instead of reducing the already too scanty wages of their employees, enable the railroad company to increase their pay. They forget that the interest on the capital invested must be earned by the men they employ, without whom they could not earn anything. . . ."

—*The Manufacturer and Builder*, August 1877

APPLY THE SKILL
See the Chapter Review and Assessment for another opportunity to apply this skill.

EXPRESSING PROBLEMS CLEARLY

Focus Students clearly express the dispute between railroad companies and their workers.

Instruct Have students write the following headings on a piece of paper: *Employees* and *Employers.* As they read the passage, have them list aspects of it that apply to each side in the dispute. Have them use this chart to organize information for the "Learn the Skill" activities. For more practice, have students bring in and analyze editorials from current newspapers.

Extend See the Skills for Life activity in the Resource Directory below.

ANSWERS
PRACTICE THE SKILL

1. **(a)** They were having trouble making ends meet. Railroad management reduced expenses. **(b)** Their pay was reduced. They went out on strike. **(c)** People who use the railroad, because they rely on it to be dependable. **(d)** The nationwide depression contributed to the railroad's financial problems. **(e)** That it would be better to reduce the dividends than to cut workers' salaries.

2. **(a)** The railroad wants to remain profitable; the workers want to continue to earn the same amount of money. **(b)** More sympathetic to the workers, though he suggests a compromise, asking the railroads to consider lower dividends. He suggests this will benefit workers, patrons, and, ultimately, the railroad.

3. **(a)** Yes. This is a figure that the editorial writer thinks could be lowered to solve the problem. **(b)** Every family must make ends meet. The problem does not deal with family finances.

4. **(a)** Service to patrons is disrupted, workers earn no wages, and the railroad loses money. **(b)** The solution seems fair, but it might be difficult to get the stockholders to accept it. **(c)** Some possibilities include raising rates of freight, improving operating efficiency, combining routes, or closing underused stations.

REVIEWING KEY TERMS

Students should refer to the definitions of key terms in the chapter to write sentences that show an understanding of the era of westward expansion.

REVIEWING MAIN IDEAS

11. Pacific Railway Acts opened the West. Morrill Land Grant Act allowed states to sell western lands. Homestead Act sold land cheaply, luring settlers. Congress in the 1880s began to open Native American lands to white settlers.

12. Treaties lacked clarity and often were administered fraudulently. White settlers complicated the situation. Western army units were undermanned.

13. Capital, sophisticated equipment, and large firms were necessary to extract deep gold and silver deposits. Ranching grew after 1865 due to large herds of cattle, disappearance of buffalo, and expulsion of Native Americans from open lands. New devices and techniques made large farms possible.

14. They brought diversity of religion, education, and work ethics.

15. Gold standard: conservatives, lenders. Free silver: silver miners, western farmers.

16. Populism had wide appeal, other parties fractured. Goals: increase circulation; free silver; government ownership of some vital industries; eight-hour workday; progressive income tax.

17. Issue: currency. Players: Republican William McKinley on a gold-standard platform; Democrat William Jennings Bryan, a silverite. Outcome: McKinley wins election; Bryan strong in West and South.

18. Answers may refer to: stereotypes, characters in dime novels, Wild West shows.

CRITICAL THINKING

19. Settlers wanted to farm the land. Native Americans co-existed with the land. Settlers tried to force their priorities on Native Americans, often leading to conflict.

---

creating a CHAPTER SUMMARY

Copy this chart (right) on a piece of paper and complete it by adding information about major influences on western development. Some entries have been completed for you as examples.

For additional review and enrichment activities, see the interactive version of *America: Pathways to the Present*, available on the Web and on CD-ROM.

Forces That Shaped the West		
Cause(s)	Event	Effect(s)
Gold and silver strikes in California and the western interior	Mining rushes	
	Ranching	
	Homesteading	Immigrants populate the West.
	Indian wars	
	Populism	

★ Reviewing Key Terms

For each of the terms below, write a sentence explaining how it relates to the period of frontier development in the West.

1. Pacific Railway Acts
2. Exoduster
3. reservation
4. Battle of Little Bighorn
5. long drive
6. soddie
7. bonanza farm
8. free silver
9. the Grange
10. Interstate Commerce Act

★ Reviewing Main Ideas

11. Describe four ways that the federal government encouraged the settlement of the West. (Section 1)

12. Why did it take decades for the government to bring the Indian wars to an end? (Section 2)

13. How did large mining, ranching, and farming industries evolve in the West? (Section 3)

14. How did the arrival of American and immigrant settlers change the culture of the West? (Section 3)

15. Which groups supported the gold standard, and which favored free silver? (Section 4)

16. Why did Populism take hold in the late 1800s, and what were its main goals? (Section 4)

17. Identify the key issues, the key players, and the outcome of the 1896 presidential election. (Section 4)

18. Describe the origins of some of the frontier myths around the turn of the century. (Section 4)

★ Critical Thinking

19. **Recognizing Ideologies** Analyze the beliefs of settlers and Native Americans that brought them into conflict.

20. **Drawing Conclusions** Evaluate the impact of the federal government's policy of assimilation of Native Americans in the late 1800s.

21. **Synthesizing Information** Explain the roles played by the following people in the development of the West: (a) Lieutenant Colonel George Armstrong Custer; (b) Chief Joseph of the Nez Percé; (c) Native American sympathist writer Helen Hunt Jackson; (d) cattle baron Charles Goodnight.

22. **Testing Conclusions** Give evidence to support these statements: (a) Private property rights encouraged the settlement of the West. (b) Homesteaders caused the spread of traditional values such as democracy and a strong work ethic.

23. **Recognizing Cause and Effect** Analyze the effects of the federal government's monetary policies, such as tariffs and the gold standard, on the following groups: (a) farmers; (b) businesses and banks.

CREATING A CHAPTER SUMMARY		
Forces That Shaped the West		
Cause(s)	**Event**	**Effect(s)**
Gold and silver strikes in California and the western interior	Mining rushes	Fortune hunters on their way to California find rich mineral strikes in other areas, too.
Increased supply *and* demand for beef after Civil War	Ranching	A cattle boom
Government incentives	Homesteading	Immigrants populate the West.
Usurpation of Native American land and resources by settlers	Indian wars	Annihilation of majority of Indian population
Farmers heavily in debt, facing stiff foreign competition and collapsing prices	Populism	Though eventually defeated, the movement gave voice to many for the first time and later gave rise to other movements.

Analyzing Political Cartoons ▶

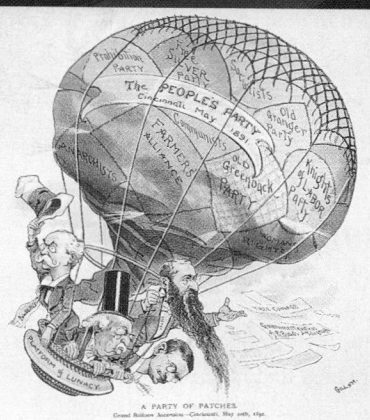

A PARTY OF PATCHES
Grand Balloon Ascension—Cincinnati, May 20th, 1891.

24. This hot-air balloon holds aloft several Populist figures. (a) How do you know these men are Populists? (b) What is the balloon made of, and what do its components suggest?

25. What is the message of the words on the basket, "Platform of Lunacy"?

26. Analyze the elements of this cartoon and state the cartoonist's main message.

Analyzing Primary Sources

Reread the two quotations in Comparing Primary Sources in Section 4, and then answer the questions that follow.

27. What is Professor Harvey's main reason for supporting free silver?

    A Gold was considered the money of the rich.

    B The Founding Fathers selected silver as the preferred coinage, and the people preferred it.

    C Silver is a more reliable type of currency than gold.

    D Coining silver would put more money in circulation, enabling debtors to clear their debts.

28. According to Laughlin, who would be harmed by the coinage of free silver?

    F miners, farmers, and consumers

    G consumers and silver lawmakers

    H laborers, farmers, and consumers

    J mine owners and pro-silver Senators

Applying the Chapter Skill: *Expressing Problems Clearly*

Review the skill on page 513. Then refer to Section 2 to write a paragraph that addresses these questions:

29. What was the central conflict between Native American groups and the United States, and how did their goals differ?

30. (a) What attempts were made to resolve the conflict, and what circumstances usually caused the efforts to fail? (b) What other solutions to the conflict could have been pursued?

ACTIVITIES

Writing to LEARN

Writing to Narrate

From what you have read in this chapter about the settlement of the West, create your own mythical frontier story. Choose for your hero a man or a woman who is one of these characters: a homesteader, a Native American, a cattle rancher, an army officer, or a miner. Use realistic details to demonstrate your understanding of life during that time. Also draw on what you have read about popular western stereotypes to make your hero larger than life.

Primary Source CD-ROM

Working With Primary Sources Find additional information on settlers in the West on the *Exploring Primary Sources in U.S. History CD-ROM* and use the selection(s) provided to complete the Chapter 14 primary source activity located in the *America: Pathways to the Present* area of the following Web site. **www.phschool.com**

Take It to the NET

Chapter Self-Test As a review activity, take the Chapter 14 Self-Test in the *America: Pathways to the Present* area at the Web site listed below. The questions are designed to test your understanding of the chapter content. **www.phschool.com**

Chapter 14 Assessment   **515**

20. Possible answers: the heavy-handed and arrogant nature of government assimilation efforts limited their effectiveness; cultural differences made assimilation impossible.

21. (a) Army moves vigorously against Sioux after Custer and troops were killed; (b) Chief Joseph and his people symbolize pain and upheaval experienced by Native Americans who were moved to reservations; (c) Jackson's writings publicize plight of Native Americans; (d) Charles Goodnight helped create booming cattle business in Texas.

22. (a) Private property rights allowed people to safely buy and settle western property; (b) Traditional values did move west with immigrant homesteaders, particularly German and Scandinavian Lutherans.

23. (a) Farmers: high tariffs bad, expenses rise, foreign markets close; gold standard bad, reduces farm income, tightens credit. (b) Business and banks: high tariffs good, industrial prices rise; gold standard good, makes lending profitable.

SKILLS ASSESSMENT

24. (a) "The People's Party" was the Populist Party. (b) A frail patchwork of Populist groups and causes, suggesting instability and division.

25. That Populists support crazy ideas.

26. Populists are full of hot air, expounding a patchwork of unrelated, unrealistic ideas.

27. C

28. H

29. The U.S. government wanted to mine, ranch, and farm Native American land.

30. (a) The government negotiated treaties but offered little in return for the purchase of the land or restricted the Native Americans. The government often did not honor the treaties or protect the reservations, and Native American groups who disagreed with the treaties refused to obey them. (b) Answers will vary.

ANSWERS TO ACTIVITIES

Writing to LEARN

Stories will vary but should include specific details from the chapter.

Primary Source CD-ROM

Direct students to the additional primary sources that can be found on the *Exploring Primary Sources in U.S. History CD-ROM.*

Take It to the NET

Additional support materials and activities for Chapter 14 of *America: Pathways to the Present* can be found in the Social Studies area at the Prentice Hall School Web site. **www.phschool.com**

Geography & History

SETTLING THE GREAT PLAINS

Focus Explain that the two main groups that arrived on the Great Plains and drove off the Native Americans were ranchers and farmers. Ranchers and farmers had different needs and fought for control of the grasslands until the farmers finally won out.

Instruct Divide the class into two groups: farmers and ranchers. Ask the farmers to suppose that they are new settlers on an unplowed homestead on the Great Plains. Ask them to list their minimum needs (tools, seeds, etc.) for creating a successful farm on the plains. Ask the ranchers to suppose that they are starting a ranch in northern Texas after the Civil War. What are their minimum needs for creating a successful ranch? After students have completed their lists, determine which needs bring the two groups into conflict.

Discuss with students how the coming of railroads affected this process. What was the impact of railroads on farmers? How did the railroads impact ranchers?

Extend Ask students to find out about the other group that entered into the conflict over the use of the Great Plains: the sheepherders. Why did ranchers oppose the sheepherders?

Settling the Great Plains

Native Americans once hunted buffalo on the Great Plains and farmed its river valleys. By the 1860s, especially in Texas, cattle ranchers had taken over the open ranges of the Plains. That all changed with the expansion of railroads and the invention of barbed wire.

Transformation of the Plains

In 1870, no railroads crossed the Texas plains. Ranchers drove their cattle over long trails to railroad towns in Kansas and Colorado. This was the heyday of the open range. As railroads expanded, though, farmers settled in areas of higher rainfall and put up barbed-wire fences to keep cattle off their land. Ranchers sometimes responded violently, but the government stood by the farmers. By 1890, railroads crisscrossed the Plains, and ranchers were forced to retreat to their own fenced ranges.

Geographic Connection
Why might farmers prefer areas with more rain?

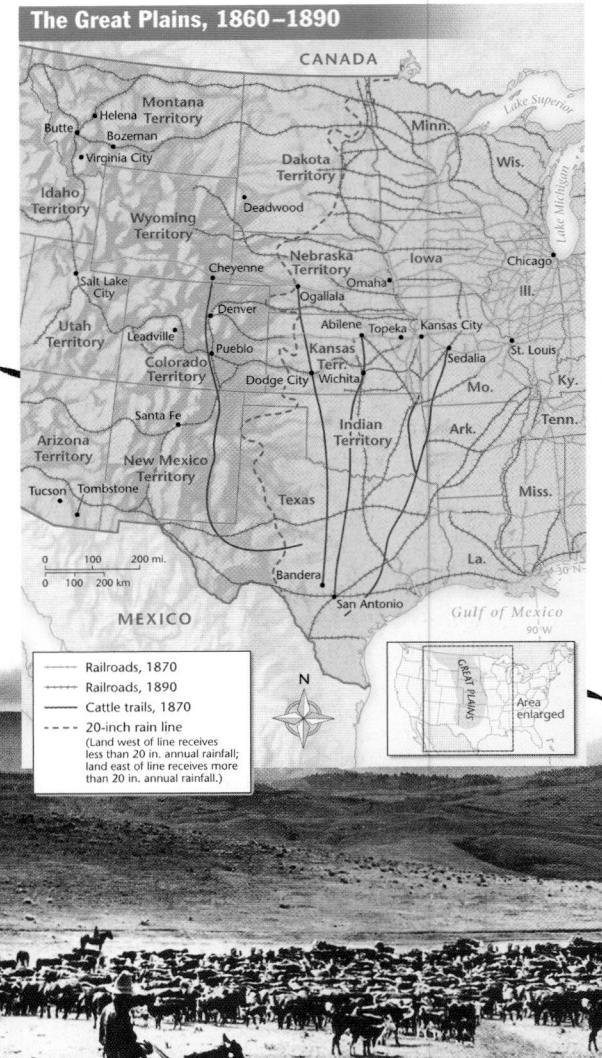

The Great Plains, 1860–1890

Railroads, 1870
Railroads, 1890
Cattle trails, 1870
20-inch rain line
(Land west of line receives less than 20 in. annual rainfall; land east of line receives more than 20 in. annual rainfall.)

516

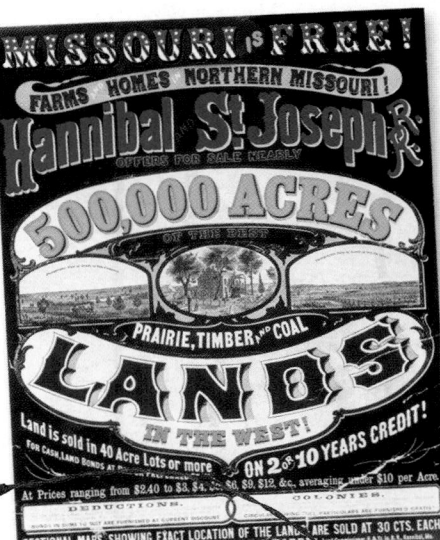

Attracting Farmers

The government gave railroads generous land grants for building lines across unsettled country on the Great Plains and in other parts of the country. Railroads such as the Hannibal and St. Joseph could cover expenses—and win future customers—by recruiting farmers to purchase and settle their land, as advertised in glowing posters like the one shown here.

A Rough Start

The first settlers on the Plains lacked wood for building houses and had to build "soddies," or houses made of sod, which consists of dirt and grass. They also had to contend with hostile, gun-slinging cattlemen, whose herds trampled their crops until the farmers could build barbed-wire fences.

The Nation's Breadbasket

Early explorers had called the treeless Great Plains the "Great American Desert," fit only for buffalo and cattle herds. However, farmers proved them wrong and made the region one of the world's most productive grain belts. This poster contrasts the reputation of Kansas as "drouthy" (or drought-prone) with images of abundant rainfall and crops.

Geographic Connection
How did the physical and human geography of the Great Plains allow farmers to displace ranchers?

517

Chapter 15 Planning Guide
Resource Manager

	CORE INSTRUCTION	READING/SKILLS
Chapter-Level Resources	Teaching Resources • Pacing Charts booklet • Block Scheduling booklet **Resource Pro® CD-ROM,** Ch. 15 **Prentice Hall Presentation Pro CD-ROM,** Ch. 15 **www.phschool.com** • eTeach	**Guided Reading Audiotapes (English/Spanish)** **Student Edition on Audio CD,** Ch. 15 **Social Studies Skills Tutor CD-ROM** **Color Transparencies,** A58, E14, G9, G10
1 Politics in the Gilded Age 1. Find out how business influenced politics during the Gilded Age. 2. Learn the ways in which government reformed the spoils system and regulated railroads. 3. Discover the effect the transition from depression to prosperity had on politics in the 1890s.	Teaching Resources **Units 5/6 booklet** • Section 1 Quiz, p. 26 **Learning Styles Lesson Plans booklet,** p. 32	**Guided Reading and Review booklet,** p. 62 **Guide to the Essentials,** p. 78 **Section Reading Support Transparencies**
2 People on the Move 1. Share the experiences of immigrants in the late 1800s and early 1900s. 2. Analyze the different challenges faced by immigrants from Europe, Asia, and Mexico.	Teaching Resources **Units 5/6 booklet** • Section 2 Quiz, p. 27 **Learning Styles Lesson Plans booklet,** p. 33	**Guided Reading and Review booklet,** p. 63 **Guide to the Essentials,** p. 79 **Learning with Documents booklet,** p. 54 **Section Reading Support Transparencies**
3 The Challenge of the Cities 1. Find out why cities expanded in the late 1800s and early 1900s. 2. Review new developments that helped cities grow. 3. Learn how living conditions in cities changed. 4. State the results of city growth.	Teaching Resources **Units 5/6 booklet** • Section 3 Quiz, p. 28	**Guided Reading and Review booklet,** p. 64 **Guide to the Essentials,** p. 80 **Learning with Documents booklet,** p. 20 **Skills for Life booklet,** p. 17 **Section Reading Support Transparencies**
4 Ideas for Reform 1. Study the ways in which different movements helped the needy. 2. Learn how and where sociology developed. 3. Examine efforts to control immigration and personal behavior in the late 1800s.	Teaching Resources **Units 5/6 booklet** • Section 4 Quiz, p. 29	**Guided Reading and Review booklet,** p. 65 **Guide to the Essentials,** p. 81 **Section Reading Support Transparencies**

Politics, Immigration, and Urban Life ★ 1870–1915 (pp. 518–547)

ENRICHMENT/PRE-AP

Prentice Hall United States History Video Collection™
www.phschool.com
- Section Activities, Virtual Field Trip, Chapter Activities, Current Events Online

American History Block Scheduling Support
Sounds of an Era Audio CD

Biography, Literature, and Comparing Primary Sources booklet, pp. 61, 125
American History Block Scheduling Support
Nystrom *Atlas of Our Country,* pp. 30–31
Sounds of an Era Audio CD
Exploring Primary Sources in U.S. History CD-ROM

Biography, Literature, and Comparing Primary Sources booklet, p. 20
American History Block Scheduling Support
Sounds of an Era Audio CD

American History Block Scheduling Support
Nystrom *Atlas of Our Country,* pp. 30–31
Exploring Primary Sources in U.S. History CD-ROM
American Pathways Thematic Posters

ASSESSMENT

PRENTICE HALL ASSESSMENT SYSTEM

Core Assessment
ExamView® Test Bank, Ch. 15
ExamView® Test Bank CD-ROM, Ch. 15

Standardized Test Preparation
Diagnose and Prescribe
Diagnostic Tests for High School Social Studies Skills

Review and Reteach
Review Book for U.S. History

Practice and Assess
Test-taking Strategies With Transparencies
Test-taking Strategies Posters
Test Prep Book for U.S. History
Alternative Assessment Handbook
Document-Based Assessment

Teaching Resources
Units 5/6 booklet
- Section Quizzes, pp. 26–29
- Chapter Tests, pp. 30, 33
www.phschool.com Ch. 15 Self-Test

AmericanHeritage RESOURCES

From the Archives of American Heritage®, pp. 523, 524, 535
AmericanHeritage® My Brush with History™ Videotapes
www.americanheritage.com

i TEXT

Don't miss the exclusive interactive version of this textbook on the Web and on CD-ROM.

Chapter 15 Planning Guide
In Your Classroom

CUSTOMIZE FOR INDIVIDUAL NEEDS

Gifted and Talented

Teacher's Edition
- Customize for Gifted and Talented, pp. 523, 545

Teaching Resources
- Biography, Literature, and Comparing Primary Sources booklet, pp. 20, 61, 125

Technology
- Exploring Primary Sources in U.S. History CD-ROM *The New Colossus, Emma Lazarus; Poems by Chinese Immigrants at Angel Island; Twenty Years at Hull House, Jane Addams*

ESL

Teacher's Edition
- Customize for ESL, p. 529

Teaching Resources
- Guided Reading and Review booklet, pp. 62–65
- Guide to the Essentials (English/Spanish), Chapter 15

Technology
- Student Edition on Audio CD, Chapter 15
- Guided Reading Audiotapes (English/Spanish), Chapter 15
- Section Reading Support Transparencies

Less Proficient Readers

Teacher's Edition
- Customize for Less Proficient Readers, pp. 525, 533

Teaching Resources
- Guided Reading and Review booklet, pp. 62–65
- Guide to the Essentials (English/Spanish), Chapter 15

Technology
- Student Edition on Audio CD, Chapter 15
- Guided Reading Audiotapes (English/Spanish), Chapter 15
- Section Reading Support Transparencies

Less Proficient Writers

Teacher's Edition
- Customize for Less Proficient Writers, p. 537

Teaching Resources
- Guided Reading and Review booklet, pp. 62–65
- Guide to the Essentials (English/Spanish), Chapter 15

Technology
- Student Edition on Audio CD, Chapter 15
- Guided Reading Audiotapes (English/Spanish), Chapter 15
- Section Reading Support Transparencies

TEACHER'S EDITION INDEX

CHAPTER 15 – PACING SUGGESTIONS

 For 90-minute Blocks

- Teach sections 2 and 3 using Transparencies A58, E14, G9, and G10, and the Recent Scholarship notes on pages 521, 525, 530, and 544 for class discussions.

 Running Out of Time?

If you are running short on time to cover this chapter, consider the following options:

- Use Prentice Hall Presentation Pro CD-ROM to create an outline for this chapter.

- Use the Section Summaries for Chapter 15, from **Guide to the Essentials (English/Spanish).**

1 **Politics in the Gilded Age**	**Connecting with Government** Have students review the party platforms and issues of the presidential campaigns of this time period, then create political posters that "sell" one candidate's position. Issues might include corruption, the Civil War, and economic conditions. You may wish to pair students, so that at least one student works on a campaign poster for each of the opposing candidates. Have students display the posters and discuss what their appeal would have been at the time. **(Visual/Spatial)**	
2 **People on the Move**	**Connecting with Citizenship** Have students role-play immigrants to the United States as they might have presented themselves to an interviewer. Players should identify themselves by country of birth, year of immigration, destination, family status (single, married, dependent, and so forth), then discuss their expectations for the future, based on their plans, skills, and ambitions. You may wish to have the same students role-play similar interviews that would have taken place a year or two later, with players describing what has happened to them since they arrived. **(Bodily/Kinesthetic)**	
3 **The Challenge of the Cities**	**Connecting with Geography** Explain to students that using population density is one way of comparing large urban areas. Have students choose four large cities in the United States—such as New York City, Chicago, Miami, Atlanta, Boston, Houston, Cleveland, Denver, Indianapolis, Philadelphia, Los Angeles, and Washington, D.C.—and calculate their population density per square mile. Have students research other statistics for each city, such as percentage of unemployment and per capita income, then discuss whether they can assume any correlation between population density and quality of life in those cities. **(Logical/Mathematical)**	
4 **Ideas for Reform**	**Connecting with Culture** Tell students about the Ashcan School, a group of American artists of the early 1900s whose works showed realistic city scenes, presenting such realities as factories, slums, and crowded streets. Explain that critics gave this group of artists this name because of their realistic subject matter. Students should find reproductions of one or more of the group's work, then make an oral presentation that connects the paintings' subject matter to the activities of social reformers of the period. **(Visual/Spatial)**	

Chapter 15
Politics, Immigration, and Urban Life
(1870–1915)

Chapter 15

Politics, Immigration, and Urban Life

(1870–1915)

SECTION 1 Politics in the Gilded Age
SECTION 2 People on the Move
SECTION 3 The Challenge of the Cities
SECTION 4 Ideas for Reform

INTRODUCING THE CHAPTER

The years from 1870 to 1915 saw a continuation of the social, economic, and political divisions that had characterized the nation even before the Civil War. This was not a "nation united" as much as it was a collection of political factions and machines, ghettos, neighborhoods, ethnic enclaves, and extremes of rich and poor all competing to realize their version of the "American Dream."

TIME LINE ACTIVITY

To provide students with practice in using the time line, ask questions such as these:

1. What did the events of 1873 and 1883 say about public attitudes about corruption? *(The arrest and imprisonment of Boss Tweed and changes in federal hiring practices showed a growing intolerance of corruption.)*

2. Where did new immigration centers open in 1892 and 1910 and why were the centers in these areas? *(In 1892 New York was a popular destination for European immigrants, while in 1910 San Francisco attracted heavier Asian immigration.)*

3. What was one of the defining events in Woodrow Wilson's presidency? *(The beginning of World War I in 1914)*

Boss Tweed
cartoon

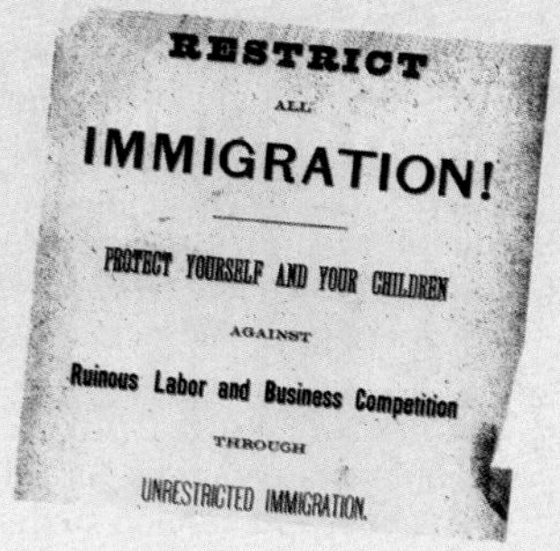

RESTRICT ALL IMMIGRATION!
PROTECT YOURSELF AND YOUR CHILDREN AGAINST
Ruinous Labor and Business Competition
THROUGH
UNRESTRICTED IMMIGRATION.

American Events

1873 New York City's Boss Tweed is sent to prison for corruption in city government.

1882 The Chinese Exclusion Act closes the door to new immigration from China.

1883 In response to scandals, the Pendleton Civil Service Act changes how the federal government hires and promotes workers.

1886 The United States officially accepts the Statue of Liberty as a gift from France.

Presidential Terms: U.S. Grant 1869–1877   R. Hayes 1877–1881   J. Garfield 1881 / C. Arthur 1881–1885   G. Cleveland 1885–1889   B. Harrison 1889–1893

1870   1880   1890

World Events

European powers meet at Berlin to divide up Africa.
1884

Sherlock Holmes debuts in *A Study in Scarlet.*
1887

eTeach

Be sure to check out this month's online discussion with a Master Teacher. Go to **www.phschool.com**.

RESOURCE DIRECTORY

Teaching Resources
Pacing Charts booklet
Block Scheduling booklet, p. 20
Units 5/6 booklet
• Chapter Summary, p. 25

Technology
Guided Reading Audiotapes (English/Spanish), Ch. 15
Student Edition on Audio CD, Ch. 15

Sounds of an Era Audio CD *"The Sidewalks of New York,"* 1895 recording (time: 30 seconds)
Prentice Hall United States History Video Collection™ Volume 12, *Immigration and Cultural Change*
Prentice Hall Presentation Pro CD-ROM, Ch. 15
Resource Pro® CD-ROM
Social Studies Skills Tutor CD-ROM
Companion Web site, www.phschool.com

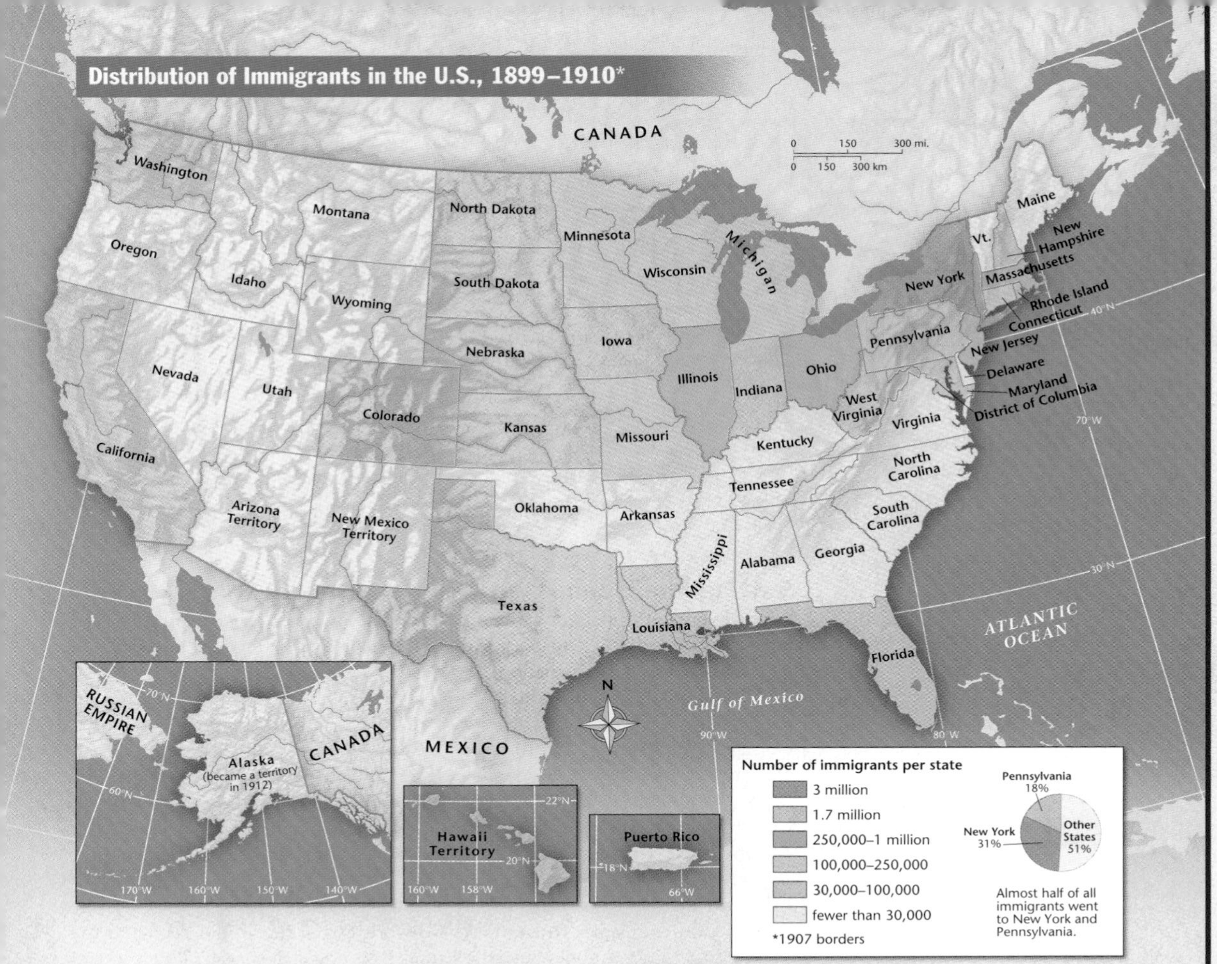

Distribution of Immigrants in the U.S., 1899–1910*

CANADA

Washington
Montana
North Dakota
Minnesota
Oregon
Idaho
Wyoming
South Dakota
Wisconsin
Michigan
Maine
Vt.
New Hampshire
New York
Massachusetts
Rhode Island
Connecticut
Nevada
Utah
Colorado
Nebraska
Iowa
Illinois
Indiana
Ohio
Pennsylvania
New Jersey
Delaware
Maryland
District of Columbia
California
Kansas
Missouri
West Virginia
Virginia
Kentucky
North Carolina
Arizona Territory
New Mexico Territory
Oklahoma
Arkansas
Tennessee
South Carolina
Mississippi
Alabama
Georgia
Texas
Louisiana
Florida

ATLANTIC OCEAN
Gulf of Mexico
MEXICO

0   150   300 mi.
0   150   300 km

RUSSIAN EMPIRE
Alaska (became a territory in 1912)
CANADA

Hawaii Territory

Puerto Rico

Number of immigrants per state

- 3 million
- 1.7 million
- 250,000–1 million
- 100,000–250,000
- 30,000–100,000
- fewer than 30,000

*1907 borders

Pennsylvania 18%
New York 31%
Other States 51%

Almost half of all immigrants went to New York and Pennsylvania.

1892
A new reception center for immigrants opens at Ellis Island.

1907
Immigration to the United States reaches an all-time high.

1910
The federal government begins processing immigrants at Angel Island in San Francisco Bay.

G. Cleveland 1893–1897   W. McKinley 1897–1901   T. Roosevelt 1901–1909   W.H. Taft 1909–1913   W. Wilson 1913–1921

1900   **1910**

1900
Boxer Rebellion occurs in China.

1905
Albert Einstein publishes the *Special Theory of Relativity*.

1912
The Titanic sinks.

1914
World War I begins in Europe.

Chapter 15   519

BIBLIOGRAPHY

For the Teacher

Miller, Kerby A. *Emigrants and Exile: Ireland and the Irish Exodus to North America.* Oxford University Press, 1988. (The first "transatlantic" history of the Irish, the book offers a full account of the diverse waves of Irish emigration to North America.)

Schlereth, Thomas J. *Victorian America: Transformations in Everyday Life, 1876–1915 (The Everyday Life in America Series, Vol. 4).* Harperperennial Library, 1992. (A portrait of the daily life of Americans during the Victorian era.)

Takaki, Ronald. *Strangers from a Different Shore: A History of Asian Americans.* Little, Brown, 1989. (A comprehensive account of the Asian American immigrant experience.)

For the Student

Addams, Jane. *Twenty Years at Hull House.* Signet, 1999. (The autobiography of a pioneer of the settlement house movement, first published in 1910.)

Immigration: Growth of a Nation. Random House Media, 1985. Sound filmstrip. (A two-part feature in color.)

Distribution of Immigrants in the U.S., 1899–1910

Activating Prior Knowledge Have students study the map on this page and then answer the following question, based on their prior knowledge: The east-west population distribution of immigrants to the United States at the end of the 1800s mirrors what earlier population movement? *(The western migration of settlers in the early 1800s)*

Previewing Ask students to study the map on this page and ask the following question: Based on the population distribution of immigrants shown on the map, which of the following three regions do you think contributed the most immigrants to the United States in the years 1899–1910: China, Mexico, or Europe? Why? *(Europe; because the state that gained the largest immigrant population is New York, gateway for European immigration to the U.S.)*

BACKGROUND
About the Pictures

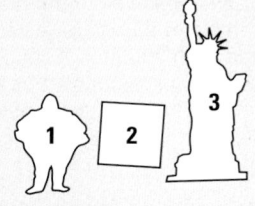

1. Published in 1871 by Thomas Nast, this political cartoon suggests William Marcy "Boss" Tweed is concerned only with money. Tweed, head of New York City's Democratic party during the 1870s, amassed millions of dollars in illegal funds. He was arrested and jailed in 1873.

2. During the 1880s cities like New York City saw a huge influx of immigrants. This created serious overcrowding, leading many Americans to oppose unrestricted immigration.

3. The Statue of Liberty, a gift from France, was erected in New York harbor in 1886. The statue has come to symbolize the values of the United States.

Don't miss the exclusive interactive version of this textbook on the Web and on CD-ROM.

Section 1
Politics in the Gilded Age

1. Find out how business influenced politics during the Gilded Age.
2. Learn the ways in which government reformed the spoils system and regulated railroads.
3. Discover the effect the transition from depression to prosperity had on politics in the 1890s.

BELLRINGER

Warm-Up Activity Ask students to list ideas they associate with the word *reformer.* In what areas of life are reformers trying to make changes today? What factors work against them?

Activating Prior Knowledge Certain private individuals made vast fortunes in the railroad industry in this era. Ask students to list some of the impacts of the expansion of the railroads on the life of the average person in the United States to help them analyze how technological innovations such as those in transportation have changed the standard of living in the United States.

READING STRATEGY

Have students write the following headings from the section on a sheet of paper, leaving room under each: *The Business of Politics; Reforming the Spoils System; Regulating Railroads; Depression to Prosperity.* As they read, have them list important details under each of these headings.

CAPTION ANSWERS

Interpreting Political Cartoons The cartoonist takes a very negative view of Gould. The cartoon demonstrates the viewpoint that Gould has far too much power, and that he abuses this power.

Section 1
Politics in the Gilded Age

READING FOCUS

- How did business influence politics during the Gilded Age?
- In what ways did government reform the spoils system and regulate railroads?
- What effect did the transition from depression to prosperity have on politics in the 1890s?

MAIN IDEA

From 1877 to 1900, national politics was dominated by issues of corruption and reform.

KEY TERMS

Gilded Age
laissez-faire
subsidy
blue law
civil service
Pendleton Civil
  Service Act
rebate
Munn v. Illinois

TAKING NOTES

Copy the diagram below. As you read, fill in the two circles with events and issues of the Gilded Age that you can categorize as related to business or politics. Place events and issues that involved both politics and business in the area where the two circles overlap.

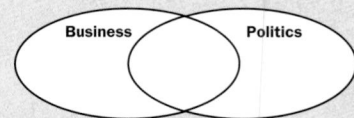

INTERPRETING POLITICAL CARTOONS Jay Gould's wealth and social connections gave him tremendous power in the financial world, as this cartoon shows. **Making Inferences** *How did the cartoonist feel about Gould's power? Explain your answer.*

JAY GOULD'S NEW YORK BOWLING ALLEY

Setting the Scene Jay Gould never formally learned how to run a railroad, but he understood the stock market. By 1871, he had become the most powerful railroad man in New York. A decade later he controlled the largest rail network in the nation.

Gould began buying and selling shares of small railways in 1859 and rose to the position of Director of New York's Erie Railroad Company. In 1867, Cornelius Vanderbilt moved to buy stock in the Erie to combine it with his own New York Central Railroad. Gould, seeking to keep control out of Vanderbilt's hands, swiftly issued 50,000 new shares. Knowing the stock issue was illegal, Gould bribed members of the New York State Legislature to legalize his stock sale and to forbid the combination of the New York Central and Erie railroads. Vanderbilt had been stopped.

Now securely in control, Gould directed the Erie to pay his own private construction companies to lay track. No work was done. Gould pocketed the money, and the Erie's share price fell sharply. When several British shareholders tried to stop him, Gould refused to recognize their voting rights. A judge ruled against the shareholders when they sued.

Gould lived in a time when corruption was common among judges, politicians, and presidential advisors. Some corrupt individuals were caught and punished. Jay Gould, on the other hand, died a very wealthy man. His story illustrates the remarkable flavor of politics and business in the **Gilded Age**—a term coined by Mark Twain to describe the post-Reconstruction era. Gilded means "covered with a thin layer of gold," and "Gilded Age" suggests that a thin but glittering layer of prosperity covered the poverty and corruption of much of society. This was a golden period for America's industrialists. Their wealth helped hide the problems faced by immigrants, laborers, and farmers. It also helped cover up the widespread abuse of power in business and government.

520   Chapter 15 • *Politics, Immigration, and Urban Life*

RESOURCE DIRECTORY

Teaching Resources
Learning Styles Lesson Plans booklet, p. 32
Guided Reading and Review booklet, p. 62

Technology
Section Reading Support Transparencies
Guided Reading Audiotapes (English/Spanish), Ch. 15
Student Edition on Audio CD, Ch. 15
Prentice Hall Presentation Pro CD-ROM, Ch. 15
Companion Web site, www.phschool.com

The Business of Politics

The United States faced great challenges in Gould's day as it emerged from Reconstruction. Industrial expansion raised the output of the nation's factories and farms. Some Americans, such as speculators in land and stocks, quickly rose "from rags to riches." At the same time, depressions, low wages, and rising farm debt contributed to discontent among working people.

Laissez-faire Policies   In the late 1800s, businesses operated largely without government regulation. This hands-off approach to economic matters, known by the French phrase **laissez-faire,** holds that government should play a very limited role in business. Supporters of this strategy maintain that if government does not interfere, the strongest businesses will succeed and bring wealth to the nation as a whole.

The term *laissez-faire* translates roughly as "allow to be" in French. Although the term probably originated with French economists in the mid-1700s, the theory of *laissez-faire* economics was primarily developed by Adam Smith in his 1776 book, *The Wealth of Nations.* A university professor in Scotland, Smith argued that government should promote free trade and allow a free marketplace for labor and goods.

In the late 1800s, most Americans accepted *laissez-faire* economics in theory. In practice, however, many supported government involvement when it benefited them. For example, American businesses favored high tariffs on imported goods to encourage people to buy American goods instead. American businesses also accepted government land grants and subsidies. A **subsidy** is a payment made by the government to encourage the development of certain key industries, such as railroads.

To ensure government aid, business giants during the Gilded Age supported friendly politicians with gifts of money. Some of these contributions were legal and some were illegal. Between 1875 and 1885, the Central Pacific Railroad reportedly budgeted $500,000 each year for bribes. Central Pacific co-founder Collis P. Huntington explained, "If you have to pay money to have the right thing done, it is only just and fair to do it."

Credit Mobilier Scandal   Washington's generous financial support for railroad-building after the Civil War invited corruption. A notorious scandal developed when Congress awarded the Union Pacific Railroad Company loans and western land to complete the first transcontinental railroad. Like Jay Gould and the Erie Railroad, the owners of the Union Pacific hired an outside company—Credit Mobilier—to build the actual tracks that Union Pacific trains would ride upon. Credit Mobilier charged Union Pacific far beyond the value of the work done, and money flowed from the federal government through the Union Pacific railroad to the shareholders of Credit Mobilier.

Credit Mobilier's managers needed Congress to continue funding the Union Pacific. They gave cheap shares of valuable Credit Mobilier stock to those who agreed to support more funding. Congress did not investigate Credit Mobilier until 1872—three years after the Union Pacific had completed the transcontinental railroad. It was discovered that Credit Mobilier gave stock to representatives of both parties, including a future President, a future Vice President, several cousins of President Grant, and as many as thirty other officials. Unfortunately, Credit Mobilier was only one of many scandals that marked Grant's eight years as President.

In this political cartoon, monopolies and trusts are depicted as controlling the government.

READING CHECK

How did the government help private businesses in the Gilded Age?

LESSON PLAN

Focus National politics during the Gilded Age was uninspired at best. Ask how business affected politics during the Gilded Age. Why were reformers unable to end corruption in politics and business?

Instruct Review with students the reasons some Americans demanded reform. Discuss the positions of the two major political parties. Which party was favored by wealthy Americans? Which party opposed blue laws? How did the cycle of depression of the early 1890s hurt Democrats and help Republicans? Ask students to list the efforts of Presidents Hayes and Arthur to end the spoils system and analyze civil service reform.

Assess/Reteach There was a great deal of corruption and scandal during this period of time. Ask students to discuss why they think neither state nor federal governments seemed able to control this widespread problem.

BACKGROUND
Recent Scholarship

In *Nothing Like It in the World* author Stephen E. Ambrose provides an account of the construction of the transcontinental railroad. Ambrose documents the amazing brainpower and manpower that made the project a success. He compares the two railroad companies—the Union Pacific and the Central Pacific—to Civil War armies. At the peak of the project, both companies employed as many as 15,000 workers. Men toiled in all kinds of weather to lay tracks stretching from Omaha, Nebraska, to Sacramento, California. Ambrose shows that the Central Pacific workers—mostly Chinese—and the Union Pacific workers—mostly Irish—came together to create one of the last big projects done mostly by hand.

READING CHECK
Business regulation was lacking due to laissez faire policies. Also, government officials accepted bribes from business in return for subsidies, land grants, and other favorable action.

Connecting with Government

Tell students to find out the philosophical and political differences between the Democrats and the Republicans today. One way would be to obtain copies of the party platforms from the last presidential election. Another way would be to read recent newspaper articles detailing the way Democrats and Republicans have voted on important issues. Have students share their findings with the class. **(Verbal/Linguistic)**

BACKGROUND

The Rotation System

Corrupt party officials used the so-called rotation system to reward lower-level party members. This is how the system worked: workers would stay at a position for a brief period—a month, a few weeks, or even a few days—and then be dropped from that position and go into the rotation to wait for another job. This form of corruption allowed powerful politicians to offer at least partial employment to a great many Loyalists—far more than were actually needed for the requirements of each position. This practice was common around the country at many federal offices—but not in Washington, where observers would have scrutinized it more closely. At the Port of New York, for example, the customs collector removed about one employee every three days.

The Spoils System Bribery was one consequence of the reliance of American politics on the spoils system. Under this system, elected officials appointed friends and supporters to government jobs, regardless of their qualifications. By the Gilded Age, government swarmed with unqualified, dishonest employees.

The spoils system appealed to many politicians because it ensured them a loyal group of supporters in future elections. Both Democrats and Republicans handed out jobs to pay off the people who had helped them get elected. But the system led to corruption when dishonest appointees used their jobs for personal profit.

Opposing Political Parties During the Gilded Age, the Democratic and Republican parties had roughly the same number of supporters. They differed greatly, however, in who those supporters were and in the positions that the parties took on major issues.

Republicans appealed to industrialists, bankers, and eastern farmers. The party was strongest in the North and the upper Midwest and was weak to nonexistent in the South. In general, Republicans favored a tight money supply backed by gold, high tariffs to protect American business, generous pensions for Union soldiers, government aid to the railroads, strict limits on immigration, and enforcement of **blue laws,** regulations that prohibited certain private activities that some people considered immoral.

As a rule, the Democratic Party attracted those in American society who were less privileged, or at least felt that way. These groups included northern urban immigrants, laborers, southern planters, and western farmers. Claiming to represent the interests of ordinary people, Democrats favored an increased money supply backed by silver, lower tariffs on imported goods, higher farm prices, less government aid to big business, and fewer blue laws.

Reforming the Spoils System

Since the two parties had roughly equal strength, presidential candidates needed the votes of almost all members of their party in order to win an election. To avoid offending party members, candidates generally avoided taking well-defined stands on controversial issues. Most states had very strong ties to one party or the other, so candidates often came from the few states that could swing either Democratic or Republican. Seven of the eight presidents who followed Andrew Johnson came from Ohio or New York.

Republicans whipped up support by "waving the bloody shirt." This meant recalling the bloodshed of the Civil War, a conflict they blamed on the Democrats. This tactic helped Republicans hold on to the presidency for much of the post-Reconstruction era.

Presidents of this period did make some efforts to exercise leadership. Indeed, the Gilded Age witnessed some important reforms in such areas as the spoils system and the railroads.

Hayes Fights the Spoils System After his election in 1877, Rutherford B. Hayes surprised many supporters by refusing to use the patronage system. Instead he appointed qualified political independents to Cabinet posts and fired employees who were not needed. By these actions Hayes began to reform the **civil service,** or the government's nonelected workers.

The Spoils System

White House

Favors
Subsidies
Political Support
Government Jobs
Government Contracts

INTERPRETING DIAGRAMS
Under the spoils system, individuals offered candidates their votes and support. If the candidate won office, he rewarded his supporters with jobs in his administration. More broadly, the spoils system also gave supporters access to money and political favors.
Determining Relevance *Why did the spoils system weaken the effectiveness of government?*

CAPTION ANSWERS

Interpreting Diagrams Politicians gave government jobs to their friends and supporters, who may have been unqualified, dishonest, or both.

RESOURCE DIRECTORY

Technology

RESOURCE◦**PRO**® **Critical Thinking Activity**
Distinguishing False from Accurate Images: Honest Graft, found on Resource Pro, helps students apply this skill by examining a politician's attempted justification of "honest graft."

Hayes undertook these reforms without congressional backing, even from members of his own Republican Party. He further angered his party on July 11, 1878, when he removed fellow Republican Chester A. Arthur from an important patronage position in New York. Then, with the help of congressional Democrats, he replaced Arthur with one of his own appointments. These moves especially upset Senator Roscoe Conkling, a supporter of patronage in New York State.

Hayes had announced at the beginning of his presidency that he would not seek a second term. After his bold attack on the spoils system, he probably could not have won his party's nomination in any case. That attack strengthened the government but also helped weaken the Republicans.

Garfield's Term Cut Short   As the 1880 presidential election approached, the Republican Party was split into three factions. The Stalwarts, followers of Senator Conkling, defended the spoils system. The Half-Breeds, who followed Senator James G. Blaine of Maine, hoped to reform the spoils system while remaining loyal to the party. Independents opposed the spoils system altogether.

James A. Garfield, an Ohio congressman and ally of the Half-Breeds, won the party's presidential nomination. To balance the ticket, the Republicans chose as their vice-presidential candidate Chester A. Arthur, a New York Stalwart.

Garfield won a narrow victory over the Democratic candidate, General Winfield S. Hancock. However, his term was cut short. On July 2, 1881, a mentally unstable lawyer named Charles Guiteau shot Garfield as the President walked through a Washington, D.C., railroad station. When he fired his fatal shot, Guiteau cried out, "I am a Stalwart and Arthur is President now!" Garfield died three months later.

The public later learned that Guiteau, a loyal Republican, had expected a job from Garfield. When Garfield passed him over, Guiteau became so enraged that he decided to murder the President. The murder caused a public outcry against the spoils system.

Arthur Reforms the Civil Service   Upon Garfield's death, Vice President Chester Arthur became President. Arthur had fought for (and benefited from) patronage in New York. Once in office, however, he urged Congress to support reform of the spoils system. With Garfield's assassination fresh in the nation's mind, President Arthur was able to obtain congressional support for this reform. As a result, the **Pendleton Civil Service Act** became law in 1883.

The act created a Civil Service Commission, which classified government jobs and tested applicants' fitness for them. It also stated that federal employees could not be required to contribute to campaign funds and could not be fired for political reasons.

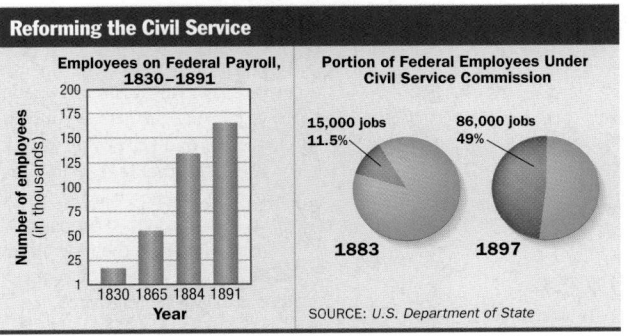

A GREAT NATION IN GRIEF

PRESIDENT GARFIELD SHOT BY AN ASSASSIN

THOUGH SERIOUSLY WOUNDED HE STILL SURVIVES

THE WOULD-BE MURDERER LODGED IN PRISON.

President Garfield's assassination made the nation aware of the need for reform of the spoils system.

INTERPRETING GRAPHS
Arthur's reforms protected thousands of jobs from political concerns. **Synthesizing Information** *Why did the rapid growth of the government work force encourage the spoils system?*

Reforming the Civil Service

Employees on Federal Payroll, 1830–1891

Number of employees (in thousands): 1, 25, 50, 75, 100, 125, 150, 175, 200

Year: 1830, 1865, 1884, 1891

Portion of Federal Employees Under Civil Service Commission

1883: 15,000 jobs 11.5%

1897: 86,000 jobs 49%

SOURCE: U.S. Department of State

From the Archives of
AmericanHeritage®

About the Presidents

James Abram Garfield (1881) had just appointed a new Postmaster General when *The New York Times* brought the "Star Route Frauds" to light. The *Times'* investigation revealed that thousands of dollars were being spent for deliveries to places that received mail no more than three times a year. With Garfield's approval, the Postmaster General began a thorough public investigation. In the scandal that unfolded, several high-ranking Republicans were implicated. Nevertheless, Garfield called on the Postmaster General to continue releasing his report. As it turned out, the scandal outlived Garfield. In time, it helped lead to civil service reform. Source: David Jacobs, "James Abram Garfield," *The American Heritage® Pictorial History of the Presidents of the United States,* vol. 2, 1968.

CAPTION ANSWERS

Interpreting Graphs An expanding government created more job openings for political appointees and was also difficult to police for corruption.

Connections to Today

In the twentieth century, the growing popularity of air travel resulted in a major decline in railroad use. In 1950 there were about 9,000 passenger trains in service, but by 1970 there were only about 450 trains still in operation. That year Congress created Amtrak, a federally supported corporation that operates almost all intercity passenger trains in the country. In recent years, decreased federal funding of Amtrak has caused controversy. Public concern over traffic and air congestion has caused many people to call for increased governmental support of rail travel.

From the Archives of

AmericanHeritage®

About the Presidents

When Chester Alan Arthur (1881–1885) took over as President, many Americans were worried. For good reason: he was seen as a tool of New York political boss Roscoe Conkling. He'd also been a firm supporter of the spoils system. But Arthur filled his new role with honesty and ability. He supported and signed into law the Pendleton Bill, which created the Civil Service Commission. He became a popular Chief Executive, but could not pacify feuding factions in his party. He never got a chance to run for a presidential term in his own right. Source: Michael Harwood, "Chester Alan Arthur," *The American Heritage® Pictorial History of the Presidents of the United States,* vol. 2, 1968.

CAPTION ANSWERS

Fast Forward to Today At that time many of the veterans of the Union army were still alive. They would certainly have looked with great disfavor upon any proposal to return Confederate flags that they and their comrades had captured during hard-fought battles.

Democrats Take Power In 1884, the Republicans nominated James G. Blaine, a former Secretary of State and senator from Maine, for President. The Democrats chose Grover Cleveland, former mayor of Buffalo and governor of New York.

Serious issues confronted the nation that year, such as high tariffs, unfair business practices, and unregulated railroads. Yet the campaign focused mostly on scandals. Had James G. Blaine received railroad stock options in return for favorable votes while he was in Congress? No one could prove that he had. Had Cleveland fathered a child out of wedlock while a bachelor in Buffalo? Cleveland admitted the rumor was true. Republicans jeered, "Ma, Ma, where's my Pa?" Democrats responded, "Going to the White House, ha, ha, ha!"

Cleveland became the first Democrat to capture the presidency since 1856. He owed at least some of his success to Republican independents who decided that Blaine was too corrupt to support. An unsympathetic newspaper editor called these Cleveland voters "Little Mugwumps." (*Mugwump* was an Algonquin word meaning "important chief.") The editor was suggesting that the independents were little men who wanted to be big chiefs.

Cleveland favored tight money policies, so most business interests backed him. Yet not all his policies were pro-business. He opposed high tariffs and took back from the railroads and other interests some 80 million acres of federal land that had been granted to them. In addition, Cleveland supported more government regulation of the powerful railroad companies.

Regulating Railroads

Railroad regulation had begun in 1869, when Massachusetts investigated claims that railroad companies were overcharging customers. By 1880, about 14 states had railroad commissions that looked into complaints about railroad practices. One of those practices was charging more for a short haul than for a long haul over the same track. Another practice was to offer **rebates,** or partial refunds, to favored customers. Others included keeping rates secret and charging different rates to different people for the same service.

Some of these practices can be justified by the economics of operating a railroad. For example, a short haul is more costly per mile than a long haul because the cost of loading and unloading the cargo is equal in both cases. Rebates were one legal way that railroads competed for customers. In any event, farmers and businesses opposed them because they favored some customers and kept others from predicting their costs.

In 1877 the Supreme Court, in **Munn v. Illinois,** allowed states to regulate certain businesses within their borders, including railroads. But railroad traffic often crossed state boundaries. Lawyers for the railroads argued that under the Constitution only the federal government could regulate interstate commerce. In 1886, in the *Wabash* case, the Supreme Court agreed. Interstate railroad traffic thus remained unregulated.

Fast Forward to Today

Confederate Battle Flags

Memories of the Civil War still divided Americans after Reconstruction. In 1887, President Cleveland proposed returning captured Confederate battle flags held by the federal government to southern states. Cleveland was the first Democrat and non-veteran President elected since the Civil War, and his request unleashed a firestorm of anger from the 400,000 veterans of the Grand Army of the Republic. Governor Foraker of Ohio said, "The patriotic people of this state are shocked and indignant beyond anything I can express." Shaken by the reaction, Cleveland retreated from his proposal.

Today President Theodore Roosevelt returned the battle flags held by the federal government in 1905, but individual states and societies still hold other battle flags today. In 2000, the Virginia Senate urged the Minnesota Historical Society to return the battered flag of the 28th Virginia Infantry. The Minnesota 1st Volunteer had captured the flag at the Battle of Gettysburg after suffering terrible losses. "Absolutely not," replied Minnesota Gov. Jesse Ventura. "We took it. That makes it our heritage."

? Why were many northerners upset by Cleveland's proposal to return the flags?

RESOURCE DIRECTORY

Other Print Resources

American History Block Scheduling Support *Linking the Nation: The Railroads,* found in the Expansion, Reconstruction, Immigration folder, includes interdisciplinary lesson suggestions and activities for Geography and History, Primary Sources, Biography, and Literature.

Pressure mounted on Congress to curb these abuses. As you read in the last chapter, in 1887 Congress responded by passing the Interstate Commerce Act. The act required that rates be set in proportion to the distance traveled and that rates be made public. It also outlawed the practice of giving special rates to powerful customers. Finally, it set up the nation's first federal regulatory board, the Interstate Commerce Commission (ICC), to enforce the act.

The Interstate Commerce Act did not give the ICC the power to set railroad rates. Also, to enforce its rulings, the ICC had to take the railroads to court, where it usually lost. Of the 16 cases involving the ICC that came before the Supreme Court between 1887 and 1905, the Court ruled against the ICC 15 times.

Depression to Prosperity

Boosted by vigorous industrial growth, American business generally grew during the late 1880s and into the 1890s. But in 1893 a depression struck, and prosperity did not return until around 1900. These ups and downs made the economy the hottest political issue of this period.

Focus on Tariffs Cleveland lost the 1888 presidential election to Republican Benjamin Harrison. The campaign had focused on tariffs. Cleveland favored a minor reduction in tariffs, while Harrison wanted an increase. Harrison's position won him plenty of business support and, ultimately, the presidency.

Among President Harrison's achievements was the signing of the Sherman Antitrust Act in 1890, described earlier. Like the Interstate Commerce Act, however, this seemingly bold action failed to curb the power of the largest corporations until well after the turn of the century.

Meanwhile, Harrison made good his campaign promise to business by approving a huge tariff increase in 1890. He also supported legislation on behalf of special business interests. Although he was thought to be conservative with public funds, Harrison dipped deep into the Treasury to award huge new pensions to dependents of Civil War soldiers.

These actions would later damage the economy, and they did not help Harrison in the election of 1892. Many new immigrants had swelled the ranks of the Democratic Party. Campaigning again for lower tariffs, Grover Cleveland was returned to the presidency.

Cleveland's Second Term Cleveland's second term started badly. Thanks in part to the drained treasury, a panic hit the country in 1893. This began a long depression, during which millions of workers lost their jobs or had their wages slashed. Despite the suffering, the government offered no help.

In 1894, Jacob S. Coxey, a wealthy Ohio quarry owner, demanded that government create jobs for the unemployed. Coxey called on unemployed workers to march on the nation's capital. "We will send a petition to Washington with boots on," he declared.

Many small "armies" started out on the protest march, but only Coxey's army reached Washington. Police arrested him and a few others for illegally carrying banners on the Capitol grounds and for trampling the grass. A song sung by

These campaign ribbons illustrate how presidential candidates attracted support from different groups of people.

Chapter 15 • Section 1   **525**

Reading Comprehension

1. Negative. It suggests that the positive and prosperous aspects of society were a thin, golden layer masking numerous problems, such as poverty and corruption.

2. To promote the expansion of industries deemed essential by the government.

3. It created a Civil Service Commission that classified government jobs, tested applicants, and stipulated that federal employees could not be required to contribute to campaign funds. In addition, federal workers could no longer be fired for political reasons.

4. It forced railroads to set rates according to distance and to make rates public and universal for all customers.

Critical Thinking and Writing

5. Sample answer: They voted for increased tariff regulation because it would help the businesspeople who had made contributions.

6. Outlines will vary but should be supported with facts from the text, and may include tariffs, government spending, and the gold standard.

Resumes will vary but should be supported with research and should reference appropriate skills for the desired position.

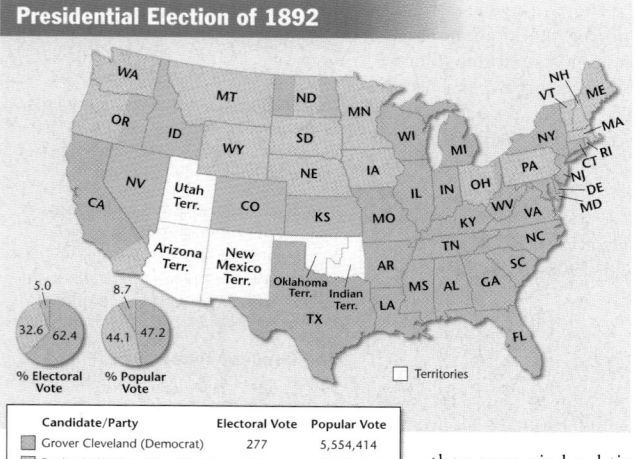

Presidential Election of 1892

Candidate/Party	Electoral Vote	Popular Vote
Grover Cleveland (Democrat)	277	5,554,414
Benjamin Harrison (Republican)	145	5,190,802
James Weaver (People's)	22	1,027,329

5.0 8.7
32.6 62.4   44.1 47.2
% Electoral Vote   % Popular Vote

☐ Territories

MAP SKILLS Grover Cleveland returned to the White House after the 1892 election with the support of Southern Democrats and immigrants. **Place** *Compare this map to the map on page 519. How did the states that later attracted many immigrants vote in 1892?*

Coxey's supporters mocked the government for worrying more about its lawns than its citizens.

In his second term Cleveland managed to anger not only the unemployed but almost everyone else. In 1893, he upset farmers by repealing the Sherman Silver Purchase Act, which had become law just three years before. He enraged unions when he sent federal troops to Chicago during the Pullman strike of 1894.

By the time of his party's convention in 1896, Cleveland had turned many fellow Democrats against him. Hence, the President failed to win his party's nomination.

McKinley Wins in 1896 The Populists had emerged as a political power during the economic hard times of the early 1890s and had made gains in the 1894 elections. But in 1896, William Jennings Bryan, the presidential candidate of the Populists and Democrats, lost to the Republican candidate, William McKinley. McKinley was supported by urban workers and the middle class.

President McKinley oversaw a new tariff bill and a stronger gold standard. These actions brought Republicans an even more decisive victory against Bryan in 1900. McKinley won 292 electoral votes while Bryan only won 155. As the economy began to climb out of the 1890s depression, Republicans claimed credit with their slogan "A Full Dinner Pail."

McKinley did not live long enough to enjoy the effects of the returning prosperity. On September 6, 1901, McKinley went on a tour of the Pan-American Exposition in Buffalo, New York. Leon Czolgosz, a mentally ill man who called himself an anarchist, shot the President as he greeted the public there. McKinley died days later.

Section 1 Assessment

READING COMPREHENSION

1. Is the term **Gilded Age** a positive or negative description of this period? Explain.

2. What is the purpose of a **subsidy?**

3. How did the **Pendleton Civil Service Act** address the problems of the spoils system?

4. How did the Interstate Commerce Act affect railroads?

CRITICAL THINKING AND WRITING

5. **Recognizing Cause and Effect** Businesses sought political influence by making large contributions to politicians. How do you think these politicians voted on tariff legislation? Why?

6. **Creating an Outline** Create an outline for an essay in which you explain how economic issues affected the outcome of presidential elections during the Gilded Age.

Activity: Finding a Job Research a job from the variety of employment options offered by the federal government and civil service. Create a résumé that you could submit for the job you researched. Use the links provided in the *America: Pathways to the Present* area at the following Web site for help in completing this activity. **www.phschool.com**

526 **Chapter 15 • *Politics, Immigration, and Urban Life***

CAPTION ANSWERS

Map Skills Many of the states destined for an influx of immigrants voted for Harrison in 1892. However, Cleveland benefited by winning large future immigrant haven states such as New York and Texas.

RESOURCE DIRECTORY

Teaching Resources
Units 5/6 booklet
• Section 1 Quiz, p. 26
Guide to the Essentials
• Section 1 Summary, p. 78

Technology
Sounds of an Era Audio CD *William McKinley*
(time: one minute)

Section 2
People on the Move

READING FOCUS

- What were the experiences of immigrants in the late 1800s and early 1900s?
- What different challenges did immigrants from Europe, Asia, and Mexico face?

MAIN IDEA

Millions of immigrants, representing many different cultures, arrived in the United States during the late 1800s and early 1900s.

KEY TERMS

pogrom
steerage
quarantine
ghetto
restrictive covenant
Chinese Exclusion Act
Gentlemen's Agreement
alien

TAKING NOTES

As you read, complete this chart listing the reasons why immigrants came to America and their experiences in their new land.

Place of Origin	Reasons for Immigration	Experiences in the United States
Europe	To escape religious persecution	Settled in cities in the East and the Midwest
Asia		
Mexico		

Setting the Scene

Peter Mossini was born in 1898 into a poor family in Sicily. He shared a small two-bedroom house with his parents and seven brothers and sisters. Peter's parents could not afford to send him to school, so at age ten he went to work in a factory. He earned about ten cents a day for eleven or twelve hours of work.

When Peter was still an infant, his father left home to find work in the coal mines of Pennsylvania. Peter's family survived on the money his father sent back in addition to the children's wages from the factory. Peter's father returned to Sicily in 1913, and the family once again struggled to get by. Following World War I, Peter saw no future for himself in his hometown of Santa Teresa di Riva:

66 During the First World War, I was in the army, and I held to my idea about coming to America. Then, in 1919, my sister Josephine came [to America]. I was very close to her . . . She came by herself and she got married. She was doing very well over here. And I wanted to build a new life, better myself. Eventually, all my brothers and sisters came to the United States. 99

—Peter Mossini

At age 22, Peter boarded a ship, the *Pesaro*, bound for America. Three months later he joined his sister in Portage, Pennsylvania.

It was sometimes said that America's streets were paved with gold. This myth held a grain of truth for the millions of immigrants who left a life of poverty behind. Like Peter, they came to America because it offered, if not instant wealth, then at least the chance to improve their lives. Some immigrants did get rich through hard work and determination. Many more managed to carve out a decent life for themselves and their families. For these immigrants, the chance to come to the United States was indeed a golden opportunity.

A family of immigrants arrives at Ellis Island in 1905.

RESOURCE DIRECTORY

Teaching Resources
Learning Styles Lesson Plans booklet, p. 33
Guided Reading and Review booklet, p. 63
Learning with Documents booklet (Visual Learning Activity) *Passage to America,* p. 54

Other Print Resources
Nystrom *Atlas of Our Country* *The Third Wave of Immigration,* pp. 30–31

Technology
Section Reading Support Transparencies
Guided Reading Audiotapes (English/Spanish), Ch. 15
Student Edition on Audio CD, Ch. 15
Prentice Hall Presentation Pro CD-ROM, Ch. 15
Companion Web site, www.phschool.com

SECTION OBJECTIVES

1. Share the experiences of immigrants in the late 1800s and early 1900s.
2. Analyze the different challenges faced by immigrants from Europe, Asia, and Mexico.

BELLRINGER

Warm-Up Activity Ask students what immigrants entering the United States in 1900 might have thought as they saw the Statue of Liberty. Ask them to explain why the Statue of Liberty remains a potent symbol today, despite the fact that few immigrants now arrive by sailing into New York harbor.

Activating Prior Knowledge How do students think the experiences of new Americans around 1900 would compare to experiences of immigrants arriving in this country today?

READING STRATEGY

Have students write down several questions they might ask about the experiences of immigrants around 1900. As they read the chapter, have them note the answers to their questions to help them analyze social issues such as the problems of immigrants.

ACTIVITY
Connecting with Geography

Have students trace the journey of an immigrant from a city in southern Italy, Russia, Japan, or China at the end of the nineteenth century. Using a world map, students should calculate the distance from the immigrant's former home to Boston, New York, or San Francisco. Students should map out two possible routes and state which route was probably more popular, and why. **(Visual/Spatial; Logical/Mathematical)**

Focus Explain that the Gilded Age was marked by the arrival of new immigrants to the United States. Ask students what immigrants' lives were like.

Instruct Ask what drew immigrants to the United States. Have them compare the experiences of Europeans, Asians, and Mexicans. What special problems did Asian immigrants encounter? Ask students to analyze the role of fear and racism in discrimination against Asians. How did Americans respond to Asian customs, their willingness to work for low wages, and their success in California agriculture?

Assess/Reteach Ask students to write a first-person essay describing the experience, as they imagine it, of immigrating to a new country. Have them imagine that as new immigrants, they do not speak the language in the new country, and they find the customs and regulations completely unfamiliar. In the essay, have them reflect on the circumstances that may have caused them to immigrate to a new country.

BACKGROUND
Global Connections

The emergence of the steamship resulted from fierce competition among several countries. The United Kingdom, Germany, the Netherlands, and the United States engaged in a development race that lasted from the late 1850s until the 1860s. Although the public was initially wary of traveling aboard steamships, eventually people accepted the greater speed of the steamship as a big advantage over its predecessor, the more sluggish sailing ship. In 1856 more than 95 percent of all immigrants journeyed to America on sailing ships. By 1873 only 3.2 percent came on sailing ships; the rest arrived on steamships.

CAPTION ANSWERS

Viewing History Steerage passengers paid much less than other passengers. Also, there was no shortage of immigrants wishing to cross to America. For these reasons, ship owners had no incentive to improve conditions.

VIEWING HISTORY While crossing the Atlantic, some passengers escaped crowded conditions in steerage by sleeping on deck in the open air. **Making Inferences** Why did shipowners provide such poor conditions for immigrants in steerage?

In the late 1800s, millions of immigrants brought their belongings and their dreams to the United States in a single steamer trunk.

The Immigrant Experience

In the late 1800s, people in many parts of the world were on the move from farms to cities and from one country to another. Immigrants from around the globe were fleeing crop failures, shortages of land and jobs, rising taxes, and famine. Some were also escaping religious or political persecution.

Immigrants' Hopes and Dreams The United States received a huge portion of this global migration. In 1860, the resident population of the United States was 31.5 million people. Between 1865 and 1920, close to 30 million additional people entered the country.

Some of these newcomers dreamed of getting rich, or at least of securing free government land through the Homestead Act. Others yearned for personal freedoms. In America, they had heard, everyone could go to school, young men were not forced to serve long years in the army, and citizens could freely take part in a democratic government. Conditions in two countries, Italy and Russia, illustrate how economic problems and political persecution encouraged millions to immigrate to the United States.

"There [were] two classes of people in Sicily," Peter Mossini said, "the rich and the very poor." A few people owned most of the land and the poor lived as sharecroppers. In the late 1800s, the economy of southern Italy slipped into decline. The land was very poor, but the government of Italy demanded more and more money in taxes. Thousands of farmers lost their livelihood when a parasite killed many of the region's grapevines. Many tenant farmers found they simply could not afford to stay in their homes and still take care of their families. Skilled workers, too, could not find jobs. The United States offered a solution.

In Russia, Jews faced hostility from their Christian neighbors and the government. In the 1880s, a wave of **pogroms,** or violent massacres of Jews, swept across the country. The czar responded to the pogroms by sharply limiting where Jews could live and how they could earn a living. America offered freedom of religion and the opportunity to build a new life.

Crossing the Ocean In the late 1800s, steam-powered ships could cross the Atlantic Ocean in two to three weeks. By 1900, on more powerful steamships, the crossing took just one week. Even this brief journey, however, could be difficult, especially for those who could not afford cabins. Most immigrants traveled in **steerage,** a large open area beneath the ship's deck. Steerage offered limited toilet facilities, no privacy, and poor food, but tickets were relatively cheap.

Crossing the vast Pacific Ocean took much longer, but the arrangements were similar. Passengers traveled in steerage, with few comforts. A person's country of origin, however, could make a difference in the conditions aboard a ship. Immigrants from Japan, whose power in the world was growing, often received better treatment than those from China, which at that time was a weak country.

528 Chapter 15 • *Politics, Immigration, and Urban Life*

Arriving in America Information about the number and origins of the nation's immigrants is not precise. Officials often misidentified the origins of immigrants. About one third of them were "birds of passage." These were usually young, single men who worked for a number of months or years and then returned home.

Historians estimate that about 10 million immigrants arrived between 1865 and 1890. Most came from northwestern and central European countries: about 2.8 million from Germany, another 1.8 million from Great Britain, and nearly 1.4 million from Ireland.

In the 1890s, the pattern of immigration shifted dramatically. Most new immigrants came from the countries of central, southern, and eastern Europe and the Middle East. Between 1890 and 1920 about 10 million Italians, Greeks, Slavs, Jews, and Armenians arrived. Around 3.8 million immigrants came from Italy alone. Another 3 million, primarily Jews, came from Russia.

Until the 1880s, decisions about whom to allow into the country were left to the states. In 1882, the federal government began excluding certain categories of immigrants. In 1891, the Office of the Superintendent of Immigration was formed to determine who was fit to settle in America and who was not.

Immigrants entered the United States through several port cities. European newcomers might come through Boston, Philadelphia, or Baltimore. Asians might enter through San Francisco or Seattle. Yet more than 70 percent of all immigrants came through New York City, which was called the "Golden Door."

Immigrants From Europe

Throughout most of the 1800s, immigrants arriving in New York entered at the Castle Garden depot, near the southern tip of Manhattan. In 1892, the federal government opened a huge reception center for steerage passengers on Ellis Island in New York harbor, near where the Statue of Liberty had been erected in 1886. The statue, a gift from France, celebrated "Liberty Enlightening the World." It became a symbol of the United States as a place of refuge and hope.

Physical Exams In 1892, the federal government required all new immigrants to undergo a physical examination. Those who were found to have a contagious disease such as tuberculosis faced **quarantine**, a time of isolation to prevent the spread of a disease. They could even be deported. People with trachoma, an eye disease common among immigrants, were automatically sent back to their country.

Fiorello La Guardia, who later became mayor of New York City, worked as an interpreter at Ellis Island. "It was harrowing to see families separated," he remembered in the book *The Making of an Insurgent:*

INTERPRETING GRAPHS
Beginning in the 1890s, large numbers of immigrants arrived from eastern and southern Europe.
Analyzing Information *Which region provided the greatest number of immigrants in 1910?*

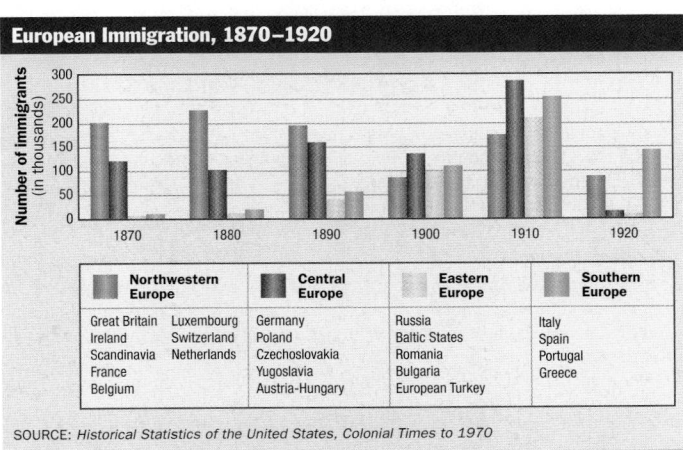

European Immigration, 1870–1920

Number of immigrants (in thousands)

	Northwestern Europe	Central Europe	Eastern Europe	Southern Europe
	Great Britain	Germany	Russia	Italy
	Ireland	Poland	Baltic States	Spain
	Scandinavia	Czechoslovakia	Romania	Portugal
	France	Yugoslavia	Bulgaria	Greece
	Belgium	Austria-Hungary	European Turkey	
	Luxembourg			
	Switzerland			
	Netherlands			

SOURCE: *Historical Statistics of the United States, Colonial Times to 1970*

Connecting with Economics

Have students research the standard of living in certain cities in the United States at the turn of the century, when millions of immigrants settled here. Tell students to find out how much money workers earned from various jobs and how much they paid in rent. Suggest that students also find out the cost of everyday items, such as food, soap, toothpaste, and clothing. **(Logical/Mathematical)**

BACKGROUND

Recent Scholarship

One topic often ignored by historians is *return migration*—the phenomenon of immigrants deciding to go back to their home country. In *Round-Trip to America* (Cornell University Press, 1996), historian Mark Wyman examines why nearly 4 million Europeans who crossed the Atlantic from 1880 to 1930 ultimately returned home. Many immigrants stayed in the United States for several years and brought home new ideas and skills. Some returning immigrants had learned how to organize labor unions; others had participated in political campaigns. Three returning immigrants ended up as prime ministers of their homelands, in Norway, Finland, and Latvia.

Focus on WORLD EVENTS

Argentina Open prairies, busy ports, ranches and mines desperate for workers—Argentina was a Latin American land of opportunity for Italian and Spanish immigrants. With only 1.8 million people in 1869, Argentina welcomed nearly six million immigrants over the next 45 years. Slightly more than half stayed. By 1914, foreigners made up two thirds of the population in the largest cities. Italian is still spoken by some in the capital, Buenos Aires.

ARGENTINA

> " Sometimes, if it was a young child who suffered from trachoma, one of the parents had to return to the native country with the rejected member of the family. When they learned their fate, they were stunned. They . . . had no homes to return to. "
>
> —Fiorello La Guardia

After their physicals, immigrants showed their documents to officials and then collected their baggage. If they had the address of friends or relatives, they headed off to find them. Those who were on their own had a harder time. Criminals hung around ports with fake offers of lodgings and jobs, stealing money and baggage from the unwary.

Where Immigrants Settled Immigrants often sought to live in communities established by previous settlers from their homelands. These communities formed not only in ports of entry, such as New York and Boston, but also in inland cities. In this way, large settlements of Poles and Italians grew in Buffalo, Cleveland, Detroit, and Milwaukee. A diverse group of immigrants found a home in Chicago, a growing port, railroad hub, and industrial center. Some immigrants continued on to mining towns of the West. Only 2 percent went to the South, an area that offered newcomers few jobs.

Once settled, immigrants looked for work. When jobs were scarce, employers (many of whom were immigrants themselves) took advantage of the newcomers. They paid them less than other workers and paid the women even less than the men. Female seamstresses, for example, did the same job as male tailors, working up to 14 hours a day, 6 days a week, but earning only half as much as the men.

Ghettos Some urban neighborhoods became **ghettos**, areas in which one ethnic or racial group dominated. Many newly arrived immigrants chose to live near others of their ethnic group because of the comfort of familiar language and traditions. These ethnic communities strongly reflected the culture of the homeland. In 1904, Emily Dinwiddie, a tenement-house inspector, wrote a joyful description of Philadelphia's "Little Italy":

COMPARING PRIMARY SOURCES
Cultural Ties

Many people held opinions on how immigrants could best adjust to their new lives in the United States. Some thought they should give up their own language and customs as quickly as possible. Others thought they should hold on to their heritage.

Analyzing Viewpoints Compare the statements of the two speakers.

Breaking Cultural Ties

"We wanted to be Americans so quickly that we were embarrassed if our parents couldn't speak English. My father was reading a Polish paper. And somebody was supposed to come to the house. I remember sticking it under something. We were that ashamed of being foreign."

—Louise Nagy,
a Polish immigrant, 1913

Preserving Cultural Ties

"We ate the same dishes, spoke the same language, told the same stories, [as in Syria]. . . . To me the colony [neighborhood] was a habitat so much like the one I had left behind in Syria that its home atmosphere enabled me to maintain a firm hold on life in the face of the many difficulties which confronted me in those days."

—Abraham Ribahny, on his
neighborhood in New York, 1893

530 Chapter 15 • *Politics, Immigration, and Urban Life*

RESOURCE DIRECTORY

Teaching Resources
Biography, Literature, and Comparing Primary Sources booklet (Comparing Primary Sources) *On Cultural Ties,* p. 125

Technology
Sounds of an Era Audio CD *Ellis Island Immigrants* (time: 50 seconds)
RESOURCE PRO® **Visual Learning Activity**
The Chinese Question, found on Resource Pro, encourages students to analyze one common sentiment about immigration and understand the effect of political cartoons.

> *The black-eyed children rolling and tumbling together, the gaily colored dresses of the women and the crowds of street vendors all give the neighborhood a wholly foreign appearance.*
>
> —Emily Dinwiddie

Dinwiddie's delight with the neighborhood did not lessen her distress at the slum conditions and poverty that she saw.

Other ghettos formed when ethnic groups isolated themselves, in part because of threats from whites. San Francisco's Chinatown had well-known street boundaries: "From Kearny to Powell, and from California to Broadway," recalled one resident. "If you ever passed them and went out there, the white kids would throw stones at you."

Still other urban ghettos resulted from **restrictive covenants.** Restrictive convenants were agreements among homeowners not to sell real estate to certain groups of people. These covenants often prevented African Americans, Mexicans, Asian Americans, and Jews from buying land or houses in the better neighborhoods.

Immigrants From Asia

Most of the immigrants who entered the United States through West Coast ports came from Asia. Chinese and Japanese formed the largest groups by far. Culturally, Asian immigrants differed greatly from both Americans and European immigrants, and those differences made them targets of suspicion and even hostility. As a result, Asian immigrants often found that the path to acceptance was especially difficult.

Chinese Excluded In the mid-1800s, American railroad companies recruited about a quarter of a million Chinese workers. Thousands helped build the transcontinental railroad, completed in 1869.

Chinese immigrants had to work for their companies until they had paid the cost of their passage and upkeep. Many Chinese immigrants paid their debts, settled down, and began to work in other fields, often side by side with white Americans and European immigrants. Those occupations included mining, farming, fishing, factory work, food preparation, and laundering.

Like many European immigrants, the Chinese tended to live in their own ethnic communities. This was not only more comfortable for Chinese Americans, but it also helped them avoid conflicts with non-Asian neighbors.

American labor unions fought hard to exclude Chinese immigrants. Because the Chinese accepted low wages, they affected the rates of pay of all workers. The unions maintained that if Chinese laborers kept coming to California, wage rates there would continue to drop.

Other groups claimed the Chinese simply were not worthy of being Americans. Using scientific-sounding but faulty reasoning, anti-Asian movements

Chinese Immigration

The vast majority of Chinese immigrants who came to the United States in the 1850s were men from the rural villages of Guangdong Province to the north of Hong Kong. In California, they took jobs as farmers, fishermen, laborers, and cooks. Most intended to return to China.

Today A recent immigrant from China is as likely to be a graduate student in Georgia, a chemical engineer in Ohio, or a textile worker in Los Angeles. Congress lifted the Chinese Exclusion Act in 1943, and about 40,000 people immigrate to the United States each year from China. Many Chinese immigrants also come from Taiwan, Hong Kong, the Philippines, and Southeast Asia. California is still a popular destination, but it is only one of many. More than 80,000 residents of China, Taiwan, and Hong Kong have come to study at American colleges and universities. Other Chinese immigrants earn college degrees in their home countries and move to the United States to work.

? Why do Chinese immigrants have a wider range of job opportunities today?

Sounds of an Era

Listen to interviews with immigrants and other sounds from the late 1800s and early 1900s.

ACTIVITY
Connecting with Geography

Ask students to interview an immigrant to the United States. Before the interview, students should prepare questions about the immigrant's country of origin, the date he or she arrived, reasons for immigrating, impressions of the political system of the United States, and opinions concerning problems currently facing the United States, such as crime and poverty. Students should also ask if the immigrant keeps in touch with friends and relatives in his or her country of origin. Remind students to be sensitive about asking for personal information regarding finances and visa status. If your school does not have students who have immigrated from another country, students might contact religious, ethnic, or fraternal organizations for help in locating a subject to interview. **(Verbal/Linguistic)**

BACKGROUND
Art History

As ships docked in New York, photographer Alfred Stieglitz (1864–1946) captured images of the poor immigrants in steerage. Stieglitz is considered by many to be the father of modern photography. He tested the limits of the camera in the 1890s, taking the first successful photos at night, in rain, and in snow. Stieglitz also convinced people to accept photography as an art form, not just a scientific curiosity.

READING CHECK

Labor unions were hostile to Chinese laborers who would work for less money than white Americans. Contemporary racist theories questioned the fitness of Asians for American citizenship.

CAPTION ANSWERS

Viewing History Japanese immigrants faced hostility from white Americans. At times they were excluded from schools, prevented from purchasing farms, or discouraged from entering the United States at all.

READING CHECK
Why did many Chinese immigrants face hostility in the United States?

claimed that Asians were physically and mentally inferior to white Americans. These claims helped spread racist attitudes toward Asian immigrants.

Congress responded to the demands of unions and others by passing the **Chinese Exclusion Act** in 1882. The act prohibited Chinese laborers from entering the country. It did not, however, prevent entry by those who had previously established residence in the United States. The act was renewed in 1892 and 1902 and then made permanent. It was not repealed until 1943. The number of residents of Chinese ancestry fell considerably from 1890 to 1940.

In 1910, the federal government built an immigration center on Angel Island in San Francisco Bay, similar to the center on Ellis Island in New York harbor. There immigrants underwent a lengthy examination. Besides having to pass medical checks, the Chinese newcomers also had to prove that they should not be excluded.

Japanese Restricted   Many of the earliest Japanese to immigrate to the United States came from Hawaii. They had migrated to Hawaii to work on sugar plantations, and when the United States annexed Hawaii in 1898, a number of Japanese saw an opportunity for a better life in America.

By 1920 some 200,000 Japanese immigrants had arrived in the United States through West Coast ports. Most Japanese settled in the Los Angeles area, and soon they were producing a large percentage of southern California's fruits and vegetables. Mainly involved in private business, the Japanese did not compete with union laborers as the Chinese had. Still, labor unions and the political leaders who supported them fought to stop Japanese immigration.

More than economic motives were at work, for some acts reflected prejudice against Asians generally. In 1906, for example, the school board in San Francisco ruled that all Chinese, Japanese, and Korean children should attend a separate school. The Japanese government condemned this policy, claiming it violated an 1894 treaty that gave Japanese citizens the right to enter the United States freely. The issue threatened to become an international crisis.

VIEWING HISTORY These immigrants from Japan, shown in traditional dress, were known as "picture brides." Their parents arranged their marriages to Japanese men in America by exchanging photos across the Pacific. **Drawing Conclusions** *What challenges did these immigrants face in the United States?*

In response, President Theodore Roosevelt reached a compromise with Japanese officials in 1907. Named the **Gentlemen's Agreement** because it was not an official government document, the compromise called on San Francisco to end its school policy and Japan to stop issuing passports to laborers.

Anti-Japanese feeling, however, did not decline. In 1913, California passed the Webb Alien Land Law, which banned **alien** (noncitizen) Asians from owning farmland.

Immigration From Mexico

In 1902, Congress passed the Newlands National Reclamation Act to promote the irrigation of southwestern lands. Over the next decade, irrigation turned millions of acres of desert into fertile farmland across Texas, Arizona, New Mexico, and California.

The new farmland meant new jobs in the sparsely populated Southwest. Employers hired Mexican laborers to work on farms and ranches as well as in

---

RESOURCE DIRECTORY

Teaching Resources
Units 5/6 booklet
 • Section 2 Quiz, p. 27
Guide to the Essentials
 • Section 2 Summary, p. 79

Technology
Color Transparencies *American Diversity,* G9
Exploring Primary Sources in U.S. History
 CD-ROM *Poems by Chinese Immigrants at Angel Island*

---

mines. Like Chinese immigrants before them, Mexican workers helped construct railroads, including the Southern Pacific and Santa Fe. Employers valued Mexican immigrants for their skills and their willingness to take difficult jobs at low wages. Roughly 50,000 Mexicans headed north between 1900 and 1910. When the United States entered World War I in 1917, demand increased sharply for laborers to grow and harvest food and mine the copper, coal, and other vital minerals needed for the war effort.

New opportunities were a "pull" factor that drew Mexican workers to America. Turmoil at home was a "push" factor that encouraged them to leave Mexico. The 1910 Mexican Revolution, and the civil war that followed, increased the flow northward over the next decade. One person who lived in a small Mexican village at the time noted:

> *"Martial law was declared. At the end of 1913, and into 1914, you couldn't even step out of the village because if the government came and found you walking, they killed you. The first village to be burned was Santa Maria, in 1913. . . . It was entirely destroyed. The [soldiers] had burned everything."*
>
> —Pedro Martínez

Peasants lost their crops, possessions, and homes to looting and destruction. Soldiers killed many men and drafted others to fight. Perhaps a million Mexicans, ten percent of Mexico's population, lost their lives between 1910 and 1920. Hundreds of thousands chose to come to the United States to escape the violence during this decade.

When the Immigration Restriction Act of 1921 limited immigration from Europe and Asia, labor shortages again drew Mexicans across the border. By 1925, Los Angeles had the largest Spanish-speaking population of any North American city outside of Mexico.

VIEWING HISTORY This Mexican family crossed the Rio Grande into Texas with their possessions. **Making Inferences** *How was the experience of entering the United States different for immigrants from Mexico and Europe?*

Section 2 Assessment

READING COMPREHENSION

1. How did **pogroms** affect life for Jews in Russia?
2. Describe conditions in the **steerage** section of a ship.
3. What were the shared goals of the **Chinese Exclusion Act** and the **Gentlemen's Agreement?**
4. Why did immigrants leave Mexico for the United States between 1910 and 1920?

CRITICAL THINKING AND WRITING

5. **Drawing Conclusions** Why do you think only steerage passengers were required to pass through Ellis Island, instead of all passengers?
6. **Writing to Inform** It is 1890 and you are a young immigrant who has recently arrived in America. Write a letter home to your parents describing your journey and your impressions of life in America.

Take It to the NET

Activity: Virtual Field Trip Take a virtual tour of Ellis Island to view exhibits of immigrant life. Use the links provided in the *America: Pathways to the Present* area of the following Web site for help in completing this activity.
www.phschool.com

Section 2 Assessment

Reading Comprehension

1. Pogroms made life very dangerous for Russian Jews. Thereafter, Jews were restricted to living in certain designated areas and were denied access to many professions and trades.
2. A large, open, overcrowded area below deck with limited toilet facilities, no privacy, and poor food.
3. To limit further Asian immigration into the United States; to keep Asians out of the American labor force.
4. Turmoil in their home country encouraged them to leave; new opportunities (largely due to the irrigation of southwestern lands) encouraged them to emigrate to America.

Critical Thinking and Writing

5. Sample answer: To try to prevent the entry of "less desirable" foreigners into the United States.
6. Letters will vary but should be supported with facts from the section, such as the unpleasantness of steerage accommodations while at sea.

Take It to the NET

Invite students to take a Virtual Field Trip at **www.phschool.com**

CUSTOMIZE FOR ...
Less Proficient Readers

Ask students to write a one-sentence answer for each of the following questions:
- Why did immigrants come to the United States during the Gilded Age?
- From what part of Europe did most European immigrants come before 1890?
- From what part of Europe did most European immigrants come after 1890?
- How did the United States restrict Asian immigration?

CAPTION ANSWERS

Viewing History Immigrants from Mexico entered the United States by crossing the Rio Grande or by traveling north over land. European immigrants had to travel across the Atlantic and be admitted by immigration officials in port cities.

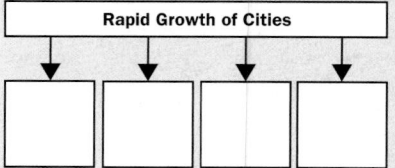
Section 3

The Challenge of the Cities

SECTION OBJECTIVES

1. Find out why cities expanded in the late 1800s and early 1900s.
2. Review new developments that helped cities grow.
3. Learn how living conditions in cities changed.
4. State the results of city growth.

BELLRINGER

Warm-Up Activity Ask students to think about the expression "bright lights, big city." Then have them list the advantages and disadvantages of city life.

Activating Prior Knowledge Ask students if they know much about the history of immigration and settlement in their area. Can they identify some of the predominant ethnic groups in the community? Do they know at what point in time these ethnic groups settled in the area?

READING STRATEGY

As students read, ask them to find evidence to support the following statement: "The arrival of large numbers of newcomers, from both within and outside the nation, radically changed the face of the nation's cities."

ACTIVITY

Connecting with Culture

Tell students to imagine that they are living around the year 1900. Their family has decided to abandon the family farm and move to a fast-growing city. Have students write a diary entry that describes how it feels to move from the country to a city. Encourage students to tell how everyday life in the city differs from life on a farm. **(Verbal/Linguistic)**

READING FOCUS

- Why did cities expand in the late 1800s and early 1900s?
- What new developments helped cities grow?
- How did living conditions in cities change?
- What were the results of city growth?

MAIN IDEA

Millions of people moved into the cities, creating new growth and new challenges.

KEY TERMS

suburb
tenement
dumbbell tenement
political machine
graft

TAKING NOTES

Copy the flowchart below. As you read, complete the following chart to show some of the effects of rapid population growth in the cities.

Rapid Growth of Cities			

Setting the Scene New York's first European settlers lived at the southern tip of Manhattan Island. To the north, along the East River, colonial families like the Rutgers and Delanceys established estates in the countryside. As the city grew, wealthy sea captains and merchants built large houses there to be near the docks. Later, the city government planned a grid of roads in the fields. Developers divided the land for rows of narrow single-family homes to house the large middle-class families of the early 1800s.

These residents moved uptown as Irish and German immigrants began to arrive in the 1840s. Builders tore down single-family row houses to make room for five- and six-story apartment buildings that fit several families on each floor. An influx of Italian and Jewish immigrants in the 1890s again changed the character of the Lower East Side, as the area came to be known. The streets teemed during the day with merchants, shoppers, and children.

A Council of Hygiene and Public Health studied how these immigrants lived. To their shock, they found the old Delancey and Rutgers farms housed an amazing 240,000 people per square mile. The Council wrote:

Most immigrants in New York City lived in cramped, overcrowded apartments. This family posed in a space that served as both a kitchen and a bedroom.

66 It is only because this rate of packing is somewhat diminished by intervening warehouses, factories, private dwellings, and other classes of buildings that the entire [apartment] population is not devastated by the domestic pestilences and infectious epidemics that arise from overcrowding and uncleanness. . . . Such concentration and packing of a population has probably never been equaled in any city as may be found in particular localities in New York. 99

—Council of Hygiene and Public Health

RESOURCE DIRECTORY

Teaching Resources
Guided Reading and Review booklet, p. 64
Learning with Documents booklet (Primary Source Activity) *New York Gangs,* p. 20

Technology
Section Reading Support Transparencies
Guided Reading Audiotapes (English/Spanish), Ch. 15
Student Edition on Audio CD, Ch. 15
Color Transparencies *Historical Maps,* A58
Sounds of an Era Audio CD *"The Bowery,"* 1893 recording (time: 45 seconds)
Prentice Hall Presentation Pro CD-ROM, Ch. 15
Companion Web site, www.phschool.com

Expanding Cities

But New York was not alone. Philadelphia, Chicago, St. Louis, New Orleans, and many other cities were bursting at the seams with newcomers. While millions of immigrants from around the world were settling in the cities of the United States, growing numbers of native-born Americans were moving there, too. Between 1880 and 1920, 11 million Americans left behind the economic hardship of their farms and headed for the opportunities of the cities. This migration within the country, combined with the new immigration, brought explosive growth to the nation's urban centers.

Women and men alike took part in the migration from rural to urban America. As factories produced more of the goods that farm women had once made, the need for women's labor on farms declined. In addition, as new machines replaced manual labor on many farms, the need for male farmhands shrank. The result was a striking shift in the nation's population. Between 1880 and 1910, the percentage of the nation's population living on farms fell from 72 to 54 percent.

Many African Americans took part in this internal migration. In 1870, fewer than a half million of the nation's 5 million African Americans lived outside the South. But after Reconstruction ended in 1877, segregation and acts of racial violence against African Americans increased. By 1890, partly as a result of these pressures, another 150,000 black southerners had left the South, and many rural African Americans had moved into nearby cities. Then, in the 1910s, the boll weevil destroyed cotton crops and floods ruined Alabama and Mississippi farmlands. These disasters drove several hundred thousand more African Americans out of the South, mostly to northern cities.

How Cities Grew

The arrival of large numbers of newcomers, from both within and outside the nation, radically changed the face of the nation's cities. Between 1865 and 1900 many features of modern city life, both good and bad, first appeared—from subways and skyscrapers to smog and slums.

Before the Civil War, cities were small in area, rarely extending more than three or four miles across. Most people lived near their workplace and walked wherever they had to go. The introduction of public, horse-drawn carriages that traveled on rails began to change this pattern. Appearing in many cities in the 1850s, they allowed people who could afford the fares to move outside the cities. Those people made their homes in the **suburbs,** or residential communities surrounding the cities.

Later in the 1800s, motorized methods of transportation made commuting much easier and advanced suburban growth. The first elevated trains, opened in 1868 in New York,

VIEWING FINE ART These two drawings give a bird's-eye view of Chicago in 1871 and many years later in 1916. **Making Comparisons** *What happened to the farmland at the city's edge between 1871 and 1916? What changes do you observe in the buildings in the city center?*

CHICAGO 1871

CHICAGO 1916

LESSON PLAN

Focus Tell students that people flocked to the nation's cities during the Gilded Age. Ask how this changed the cities.

Instruct To help students analyze the factors contributing to migration within the U.S., ask students about the Industrial Revolution's role in migration from rural areas to cities.

Assess/Reteach Have students research the population of New York City in 1860 and in 1900.

From the Archives of
American Heritage®

Two Fires

On the evening of October 7, 1871, Chicago firemen encountered the latest and biggest in a series of fires the city had seen during an unusually dry summer and fall. The next evening, around a quarter of nine, a fresh load of hay caught on fire in Catherine and Patrick O'Leary's barn at the corner of DeKoven and Jefferson streets. A tale sprang up almost instantly that one of their milk cows had kicked over a lantern, but there is no evidence for this; other possible explanations include arson, spontaneous combustion, and a discarded cigar or cigarette. Whatever the cause, high winds swiftly spread the flames, and the fire department, weary from the previous night's marathon effort, was slow to respond. The first company to reach the site attacked the wrong end of the fire, while the second one found its steam pumper broken and without fuel. By the time the whole department could be mobilized, the blaze was out of control. A couple of hours later a gasworks exploded, intensifying the conflagration, and then at 7:00 A.M. hydrants ran dry when the city waterworks caught fire. From then on, all anyone could do was pray for rain. Source: Frederic D. Schwarz, "The Time Machine," *American Heritage*® magazine, October 1996.

CAPTION ANSWERS

Viewing Fine Art The open land near Chicago filled with streets and buildings as the city grew. Newer, taller buildings were built in the city center.

Focus on GEOGRAPHY

Streetcar Suburbs The spread of streetcar lines created a new type of town: the streetcar suburb. Streetcars doubled or tripled the distance people could live from the central city while still traveling there to work each day. In many places, the same company that operated the streetcar line built middle-class homes and apartments in leafy suburbs to create demand for their services. Streetcar suburbs included West Philadelphia; East Cleveland; Piedmont Park near Charlotte, North Carolina; Roxbury and Dorchester near Boston; and Harlem, north of downtown New York. Many of these first suburbs later merged with their parent cities.

Growing cities drew people from rural areas. This woman found work as a porter in a subway.

allowed commuters to bypass the congested streets. Cable cars, introduced in San Francisco in 1873, allowed quick access to the city's steep hills. Electric trolleys, first used in Richmond, Virginia, in 1888, replaced horse-drawn cars and reached even farther into the suburbs. Subway trains first appeared in Boston in 1897. Finally, the automobile, invented in the 1890s and mass-produced beginning in the 1910s, guaranteed that expansion into the suburbs would continue.

Cities grew upward as well as outward. Before the Civil War, buildings stood no more than five stories high. Yet as urban space became scarce, buildings were made taller and taller. To build these mammoth structures, engineers needed the strength of Bessemer steel girders.

To reach the upper floors, people relied on the speed and efficiency of elevators. In 1852 Elisha Graves Otis, an American, invented a safety device that made passenger elevators possible. The first one went into operation five years later. The first skyscraper, Chicago's Home Insurance Company Building, appeared in 1885. Ten stories tall, it was built with a framework of iron and steel and had four passenger elevators. Architect Louis Sullivan completed the ten-story Wainwright building in St. Louis in 1891. The Wainwright building consisted of a steel skeleton sheathed in red sandstone, granite, brick, and a form of baked red clay called terra cotta.

As cities expanded, specialized areas emerged within them. Banks, financial offices, law firms, and government offices were located in one central area. Retail shops and department stores were located in another central neighborhood. Industrial, wholesale, and warehouse districts formed a ring around the center of the city.

Urban Living Conditions

Some urban workers moved into housing built especially for them by mill and factory owners. The rest found apartments wherever they could. Many middle-class residents who moved to the suburbs left empty buildings behind. Owners converted these buildings into multifamily units for workers and their families.

Speculators also built many **tenements**, low-cost apartment buildings designed to house as many families as the owner could pack in. A group of dirty, run-down tenements could transform an area into a slum.

Conditions in the Slums Before long, because of poverty, overcrowding, and neglect, the old residential neighborhoods of cities gradually declined. Trees and grass disappeared. Hundreds of people were crammed into spaces meant for a few families. Soot from coal-fired steam engines and boilers made the air seem dark and foul even in daylight. Open sewers attracted rats and other disease-spreading vermin.

In 1905, journalist Eleanor McMain quoted a university student who described a block of tenements in the Italian district of New Orleans as "death traps, closely built, jammed together, with no side openings. Twenty-five per cent of the yard space is damp and gloomy. . . . Where the houses are three or more rooms in depth, the middle ones are dark, without outside ventilator. . . . There is no fire protection whatever."

Fire was a constant danger in cities. With tenement buildings so closely packed together, even a small fire could quickly consume a neighborhood. Once a fire started, it leaped easily from roof to roof. As a result, most large cities had major fires during this period. Chicago experienced one of the most devastating: the Great Chicago Fire of 1871. Nobody knows for sure what started it, but before it was over, 18,000 buildings had burned, leaving some 250 people dead and 100,000 homeless. Property damage estimates reached $200 million, the equivalent of $2 billion today. A similar fire in Boston caused the equivalent of nearly $1 billion in damage.

Contagious diseases, including cholera, malaria, tuberculosis, diphtheria, and typhoid, thrived in crowded tenement conditions. Epidemics, such as the yellow fever that swept through Memphis, Tennessee, in the late 1870s and through New Orleans in the early 1900s, took thousands of lives. Children were especially vulnerable to disease. In one district of tenements in New York City, six out of ten babies died before their first birthday.

Diseases spread rapidly, especially during the summer months when apartments heated up like ovens. A heat wave lasting from August 5 to 13, 1896, took the lives of over 400 New Yorkers. The Chicago Health Department found that at least 80 percent of summer deaths among children under two were caused by preventable diseases. Chicago and New York City established fresh-air havens on their waterfronts for sick children to escape the deadly conditions of the slums.

Light, Air, and Water Scientists believed that lack of good ventilation helped disease spread. They pushed for reforms to improve air flow and natural light in tenements. One wrote:

> *"Simple ordinary outdoor air is a most valuable health resource . . . a balcony on a city street is a thousand times better than a room in a house closed for fear of drafts, curtained for fear of fading the furniture, and lighted by a lamp."*
>
> —Ellen Swallow Richards

In 1879, a change in New York laws required an outside window in every room. To accommodate windows in rows of buildings, an architect designed the **dumbbell tenement,** named for its dumbbell shape. Each building narrowed in the middle, and gaps on either side formed air shafts to bring light and air to inside rooms.

While an improvement, the gloomy air shaft was certainly not an open balcony. The tenement-dweller looked across the closed space to a brick wall and a neighbor's window only a few feet away. Rotting garbage collected at the bottom of the shaft. Little sunlight or fresh air reached apartments this way.

Scientists also linked diseases like cholera and typhoid to contaminated drinking water, which tenement residents drew from a common pipe or pump in the yard. Authorities feared that polluted city water drawn from local springs and rivers could cause epidemics. Boston, Cincinnati, and New York built reservoirs or waterworks to collect clean water far from the city and filter out impurities. City water companies later introduced chlorination and filtration. A 1901 New York City law required that hallway bathrooms replace

INTERPRETING DIAGRAMS
Architects designed the dumbbell tenement to fit as many people as possible into a city block while providing all rooms with light and air. **Drawing Conclusions** *How successful was the dumbbell tenement at meeting these two goals?*

The Dumbbell Tenement

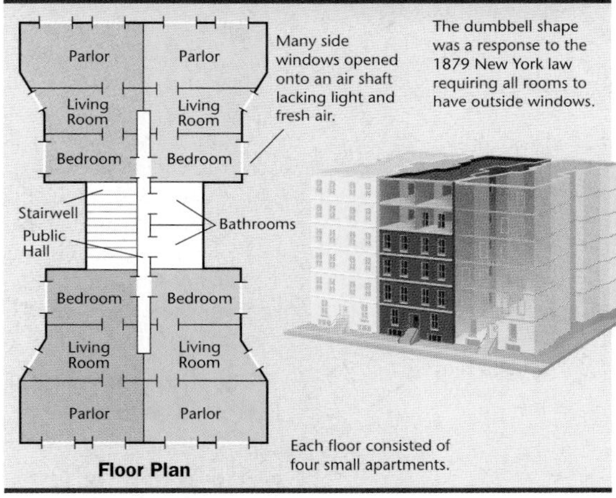

Parlor
Parlor
Living Room
Living Room
Bedroom
Bedroom
Stairwell
Public Hall
Bathrooms
Bedroom
Bedroom
Living Room
Living Room
Parlor
Parlor
Floor Plan
Many side windows opened onto an air shaft lacking light and fresh air.
The dumbbell shape was a response to the 1879 New York law requiring all rooms to have outside windows.
Each floor consisted of four small apartments.

ACTIVITY
Connecting with Science and Technology

Tell students to research some of the medical discoveries that have made many of the common nineteenth-century diseases obsolete or rare. Of the contagious diseases—yellow fever, cholera, malaria, tuberculosis, diphtheria, and typhoid—that claimed many lives, which ones are still a threat? Which of these diseases do we no longer see? How have we eradicated them? **(Verbal/Linguistic)**

BACKGROUND
Geography in History

Thanks to the foresight of Andrew Jackson Downing, America's first major landscape architect, residents of crowded New York City enjoy the trees and wide-open spaces of Central Park. In 1848, after living through numerous riots and epidemics, Downing suggested creating a vast "lung" for the city. In 1858 a competition was held for the design of the park. The winners of the contest were Calvert Vaux and Frederick Law Olmsted. The result—Central Park—has been used as a model for public parks all over the world.

CUSTOMIZE FOR ...
Less Proficient Writers

This section refers to the first development of urban parklands as "lungs of the cities." Ask students to think about nearby parklands, and to write a brief essay or poem about what that open space means to them.

CAPTION ANSWERS

Interpreting Diagrams Dumbbell tenements did allow a great many people to be crammed into each city block. However, they were largely unsuccessful in providing adequate ventilation and sunlight.

Student Portfolio

You may wish to have students add the following to their portfolios: Frederick Law Olmsted is considered by many to be America's greatest landscape architect. He designed New York City's Central Park, Boston's city park system, and about 38 other major parks. Have students find out more about Olmsted's life and present a report about one of his major projects. **(Visual/Spatial)**

BACKGROUND

Biography

David Sarnoff (1891–1971) arrived in New York City from Russia in 1900 and exceeded the immigrant promise of America beyond his wildest dreams. Self-educated in Morse code, he got a job as a radio operator. By 1930 he was president of the Radio Corporation of America (RCA). By 1932 Sarnoff had added the National Broadcasting Corporation (NBC) to the ranks of RCA-owned companies. During World War II Sarnoff served as General Eisenhower's communications consultant. After the war he aggressively promoted the new color television industry for NBC.

READING CHECK

Urban growth caused city governments to become larger and more powerful. Revenue from increased taxes financed better fire fighting, drinking water, public transportation, and other city services.

BIOGRAPHY

**Jacob Riis
1849–1914**

Some reformers worked to improve the lives of the urban poor. One was Jacob Riis. A native of Denmark, Riis had boarded a steamship bound for America in 1870 at the age of 21 and settled in New York City. There he personally experienced the dreadful conditions in which many new Americans lived.

Riis held various jobs before he landed a position as a police reporter in 1873. Riis honed his writing skills while covering New York's Lower East Side, a tenement slum bursting with immigrant families. He worked for the *New York Tribune* from 1877 to 1888 and the *New York Evening Sun* from 1888 to 1899. While working at the *Sun*, Riis wrote *How the Other Half Lives*.

READING CHECK
Why did urban growth change the role of city government?

backyard outhouses. Landlords installed small bathtubs and sinks with running water in most apartments.

How the Other Half Lives   The American public learned about the horrors of tenement life in 1890 when a reporter named Jacob Riis published *How the Other Half Lives.* Hoping to generate public support for reform of the tenement "system," Riis painted a bleak picture of New York's future:

❝ Today three-fourths of [New York's] people live in the tenements. . . . We know now that there is no way out; that the 'system' that was the evil offspring of public neglect and private greed has come to stay, a storm-centre forever of our civilization. Nothing is left but to make the best of a bad bargain. ❞

—Jacob Riis, *How the Other Half Lives,* 1890

In order to document his reporting, Riis mastered the new technology of flash photography. Drawings based on these photographs appeared in his book, and he showed the actual photographs of overcrowded rooms and run-down buildings in his lectures on the plight of immigrants. As a result of Riis's work, New York State passed the nation's first meaningful laws to improve tenements.

The Results of City Growth

Some city residents could avoid urban problems simply by leaving the cities. The middle and upper classes began moving to the suburbs in the late 1800s. As a result, the gap between the well-to-do and the poor widened.

A few cities preserved neighborhoods of mansions and luxury townhouses near the city center for the wealthiest residents. These areas included Beacon Hill in Boston, the Gold Coast in Chicago, and Nob Hill in San Francisco. Often, people living in these neighborhoods also owned country estates and were quite isolated from the nearby poverty.

Political Divisions   Rapidly growing cities proved difficult to govern. Urban growth put pressure on city officials to improve police and fire protection, transportation systems, sewage disposal, electrical and water service, and health care. To deliver these services, cities raised taxes and set up offices to deal with people's needs.

Increased revenue and responsibilities gave city governments more power. Competition among groups for control of city government grew more intense. Some groups represented those members of the middle and upper classes who still lived in the cities. Other groups represented new immigrants, migrants from the countryside, and workers—people that now made up the majority of the population in most cities.

The Rise of Political Bosses   The **political machine** was born out of these clashing interests. A political machine was an unofficial city organization designed to keep a particular party or group in power and usually headed by a single powerful "boss." Sometimes the boss held public office. More often, he handpicked others to run for office and then helped them win.

Political machines worked through the exchange of favors. Machines used an army of ward leaders, each of whom managed a city district, to hand out city jobs and contracts to residents of their ward and do other favors for them. In return, those residents were expected to give their votes to the machine's

RESOURCE DIRECTORY

Teaching Resources
Units 5/6 booklet
 • Section 3 Quiz, p. 28
Guide to the Essentials
 • Section 3 Summary, p. 80
Biography, Literature, and Comparing Primary Sources booklet (Biography) *Thomas Nast,* p. 20

candidates on election day. Similarly, individuals or companies wanting a favor from the city could get it by first paying some money to the machine. **Graft,** or the use of one's job to gain profit, was a major source of income for the machines.

Many people blamed the success of political machines on the large number of urban immigrants. They charged that corrupt politicians easily took advantage of immigrants who were poorly educated and unfamiliar with democracy. Immigrants tended to support political machines because they helped poor people at a time when neither government nor private industry would.

Cincinnati's George B. Cox, a former saloon owner, was an unusual example of a fairly honest political boss. A Republican, in 1879 he won election to the city council. In true machine fashion he used this post to guarantee election victories and business contracts for the party faithful. But he also worked with local reformers to improve the quality of the police force and city services.

Perhaps the most notorious boss was William Marcy Tweed. "Boss" Tweed controlled Tammany Hall, the political club that ran New York City's Democratic Party. Once Tweed and his pals gained access to the city treasury in 1870, they used various illegal methods to plunder it. Tweed and his friends padded bills for construction projects and supply contracts with fake expenses and kept the extra money for themselves. Through countless such instances of fraud and graft, the Tweed ring amassed many millions of dollars.

The brilliant political cartoons of German immigrant Thomas Nast helped bring Tweed down by exposing his methods to the public. Nast's cartoons depicted Tweed as a thief and a dictator who manipulated New York City politics for his own benefit. Convicted of crimes in 1873, Tweed eventually died in jail. Under new leaders, however, Tammany Hall dominated New York politics for another half century.

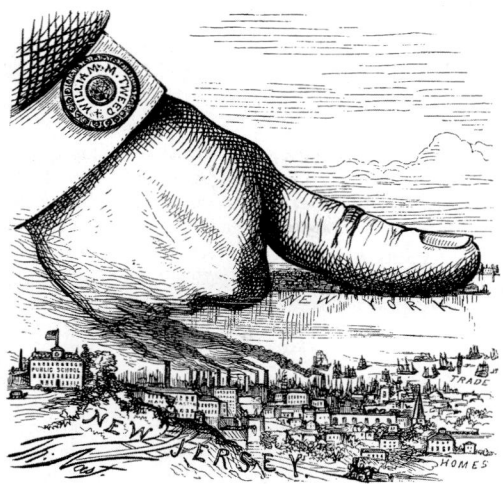
UNDER THE THUMB.

INTERPRETING POLITICAL CARTOONS This cartoon by Thomas Nast illustrates Boss Tweed's total control over New York City. **Recognizing Point of View** *Why did some people believe Boss Tweed's leadership helped New York City?*

Section 3 Assessment

Reading Comprehension

1. Overcrowded, unsanitary, disease-ridden, and run-down; but low-cost.

2. Answers should describe advancements in transportation and construction methods, and may include the invention of the elevator, the subway, and the cable car.

3. As city governments grew in size, wealth, and power, they became prizes to control. The machine enabled a local faction of one party to maintain control.

4. Graft is distasteful because it involves using one's position of power to exploit others.

Critical Thinking and Writing

5. Himself and his cohorts in Tammany Hall, revealing political machines as largely self-serving and detrimental to the population at large.

6. Answers will vary but may include: overcrowding, disease, danger of fires, contaminated water, lack of indoor plumbing.

Section 3 Assessment

READING COMPREHENSION

1. Describe the living conditions in a **tenement** apartment.

2. What were three technological developments that enabled cities to house more people?

3. What contributed to the rise of **political machines?**

4. Why did some people criticize **graft?**

CRITICAL THINKING AND WRITING

5. **Drawing Inferences** Who benefited most from Boss Tweed's control of New York City? What does this tell you about the effects of political machines?

6. **Writing an Outline** Create an outline of the challenges city dwellers faced in the 1880s and 1890s.

 **Take It to the NET**

Activity: Virtual Field Trip Visit the Lower East Side Tenement Museum in New York and learn how immigrants from Germany, Italy, and Russia lived from the 1850s to the 1930s. Use the links provided in the *America: Pathways to the Present* area of the following Web site for help in completing this activity. **www.phschool.com**

 **Take It to the NET**

Invite students to take a Virtual Field Trip at **www.phschool.com**

✓ **TEST PREPARATION**

Have students read the passage by Jacob Riis on the previous page and then complete the sentence below.

Based on the passage, you can tell that—

A Riis felt optimistic about the future of the tenements.

B Riis blamed only tenement owners for the plight of the poor.

C half of New York's population lived in tenements.

(D) Riis thought the tenement system was entrenched in city life and would be difficult to overcome.

Analyzing Tables and Statistics

Statistical tables present large amounts of numerical data concisely and clearly. The patterns suggested by statistics must be carefully analyzed, however, and their sources evaluated for reliability. Once you have analyzed the data, you can draw conclusions about historical periods or trends.

ANALYZING TABLES AND STATISTICS

Focus Students learn to analyze statistics to see what they show, what they distort, and what they hide.

Instruct Begin the activity by asking students to review the data in the table. To give them warm-up practice in working with the statistics provided, ask them to identify peak years of immigration for these various population groups: Eastern Europeans, Southern Europeans, Central Europeans. Before they begin the Learn the Skill activity, ask the class to brainstorm various types of analyses they can do, using the statistics.

Extend See the Skills for Life activity in the Resource Directory below.

ANSWERS

PRACTICE THE SKILL

1. **(a)** Estimated Number of Immigrants to the United States, by Region, 1871–1920. **(b)** Northwestern Europe, Central Europe, Eastern Europe, Southern Europe, Asia, the Americas, Africa, and Oceania. **(c)** *Historical Statistics of the United States, Colonial Times to 1970.* **(d)** Government data is considered reliable.

2. **(a)** 65,727. **(b)** Central Europe provided the largest number of immigrants. Africa provided the smallest number of immigrants.

3. **(a)** Central Europe. **(b)** 1891–1900.

4. When the U.S. unemployment rate was high, the immigration rate was relatively low. When unemployment was low, the immigration rate increased dramatically. A low unemployment rate may have signaled the availability of jobs in the United States and attracted immigrants.

5. **(a)** Answers will vary. **(b)** Answers will vary.

Estimated Number of Immigrants to the United States, by Region, 1871–1920

Years	Northwestern Europe	Central Europe	Eastern Europe	Southern Europe	Asia[1]	The Americas[2]	Africa	Oceania
1871–1875	858,325	549,610	15,580	37,070	65,727	193,345	205	6,312
1876–1880	493,866	254,511	24,052	39,248	58,096	210,690	153	4,602
1881–1885	1,121,477	1,128,528	63,443	120,297	60,432	403,977	331	4,406
1886–1890	1,131,844	729,967	157,749	211,399	7,948	22,990	526	8,168
1891–1895	745,433	762,216	251,405	314,625	19,255	14,734	163	2,215
1896–1900	392,907	432,363	270,421	389,608	51,981	24,238	187	1,750
1901–1905	761,517	1,121,234	711,546	1,061,406	115,941	63,774	1,829	6,134
1906–1910	807,020	1,365,530	1,058,024	1,260,424	127,626	298,114	5,539	6,890
1911–1915	652,189	1,027,138	978,931	1,137,539	123,719	528,098	5,847	6,126
1916–1920	201,304	23,276	33,547	322,640	68,840	615,573	2,596	7,301

[1]No record of immigration from Korea prior to 1948. [2]No record of immigration from Mexico for 1886 to 1893.
SOURCE: *Historical Statistics of the United States, Colonial Times to 1970*

LEARN THE SKILL

Use the following steps to analyze tables and statistics:

1. **Determine what type of information is presented and decide whether the source is reliable.** The title of the table and the labels for the rows and columns tell you what information is presented. The source is most often found below the table. Government publications are usually reliable sources.

2. **Read the information in the table.** Note how the statistics are organized. This table provides the total number of immigrants who came from each region for a given five-year period.

3. **Find relationships among the statistics.** In this case, you can compare the number of immigrants who came to the United States from different regions or trace changes in the pattern of immigration from one region over time.

4. **Use the data to draw conclusions.** You can also use what you know from other sources. Compare patterns in the two sets of data.

5. **Share your data and conclusions.** Present and support your conclusions in a report, or create graphs or charts that help explain your data.

APPLY THE SKILL

See the Chapter Review and Assessment for another opportunity to apply this skill.

PRACTICE THE SKILL

Answer the following questions:

1. **(a)** What is the title of the table? **(b)** What geographical areas are covered? **(c)** What is the source of the statistics? **(d)** Are the data reliable?

2. **(a)** Between 1871 and 1875, how many immigrants came to the United States from Asia? **(b)** Between 1881 and 1885, which region provided the largest number of immigrants? The smallest number of immigrants?

3. **(a)** Between 1871 and 1920, which region provided the largest total number of immigrants? **(b)** During which decade did the Americas show the sharpest drop in the number of immigrants?

4. Between 1891 and 1900, the unemployment rate in the United States averaged 10.5 percent. Between 1901 and 1910, it averaged 4.5 percent. What conclusions can you draw about the relationship between the unemployment rate and the immigration rate for these time periods?

5. **(a)** Write a paragraph summarizing the conclusions you reached in Question 4. Support your conclusions with data from the table. **(b)** Create a line graph showing the pattern of immigration from one region from 1871–1920.

RESOURCE DIRECTORY

Teaching Resources
Skills for Life booklet, p. 17

Technology
Social Studies Skills Tutor CD-ROM
Interactive Practice in
• Geographic Literacy
• Critical Thinking and Reading
• Visual Analysis
• Communications

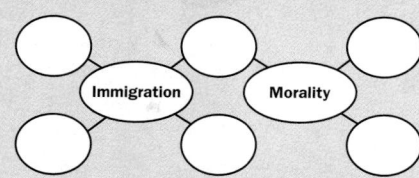
READING FOCUS

- How did different movements help the needy?
- How and where did sociology develop?
- What efforts were made to control immigration and personal behavior in the late 1800s?

MAIN IDEA

A variety of groups worked to improve social, economic, and political conditions in the cities.

KEY TERMS

social gospel movement
settlement house
sociology
nativism
temperance movement
prohibition
vice

TAKING NOTES

Copy the web diagram below. As you read, fill in each blank circle with important movements that focused on immigration, morality, or both.

```
  (   )        (   )        (   )
       \      /    \       /
     [Immigration]  [Morality]
       /      \    /       \
  (   )        (   )        (   )
```

SECTION OBJECTIVES

1. Study the ways in which different movements helped the needy.
2. Learn how and where sociology developed.
3. Examine efforts to control immigration and personal behavior in the late 1800s.

BELLRINGER

Warm-Up Activity Ask students to list what they consider the most effective ways to help needy people. Ask them to consider the pros and cons of each.

Activating Prior Knowledge Ask students to list some efforts in the local community to help people in need. Can students also name global organizations designed to help people? Have students list in order the types of help they consider most important to needy people.

READING STRATEGY

Have students write down these headings: *Controlling Immigrants* and *Helping the Needy.* As they read, have students list under the correct heading strategies used to reform cities.

ACTIVITY
Connecting with Citizenship

Have students investigate ways in which religious and civic groups promote social welfare in today's culture. What kinds of charitable efforts are made by churches, synagogues, and other organized religious or civic groups? How successful are these campaigns? Can students list such activities that take place in their community? Have students participated in any efforts to help those less fortunate than themselves? If so, what have they done? **(Verbal/Linguistic)**

Setting the Scene During the Gilded Age, saloons, places where men could meet to drink and gamble, could be found in nearly every city and town. Frances Willard paid her first visit to one at the age of 35. Unlike the customers, she arrived with a prayer group. Willard later wrote:

> 66 The tall, stately lady who led us placed her Bible on the bar and read a psalm . . . and then one of the older women whispered to me softly that the leader wished to know if I would pray. It was strange, perhaps, but I felt not the least reluctance, and kneeling on the sawdust floor, with a group of earnest hearts around me, and behind them . . . a crowd of unwashed, unkempt, hard-looking drinking men, I was conscious that perhaps never in my life, save beside my sister Mary's dying bed, had I prayed as truly as I did then. 99
>
> —Frances Willard

Frances Willard described the experience as her "baptism" in the "Crusade." One week later she became president of the Chicago chapter of the Woman's Christian Temperance Union, an anti-alcohol group. Frances Willard was a reformer. Like many Americans of her time, she observed a problem in society and chose to confront it, motivated by her faith and her concern for the well-being of others. However, not everyone agreed with her wish to ban alcohol. Like many other crusaders, Frances Willard found that her personal goals could lead to conflict.

Helping the Needy

Many middle-class people were genuinely shocked by poor living and working conditions in the slums. One group of reformers, moved by social conscience or religious idealism, worked to improve society by helping the needy. They argued that prosperous Americans should fight poverty and improve unwholesome social conditions in cities.

Temperance advocates pray outside a saloon.

RESOURCE DIRECTORY

Teaching Resources
Guided Reading and Review booklet, p. 65

Other Print Resources
Nystrom *Atlas of Our Country* The Third Wave of Immigration, pp. 30–31

Technology
Section Reading Support Transparencies
Guided Reading Audiotapes (English/Spanish), Ch. 15
Student Edition on Audio CD, Ch. 15
Prentice Hall Presentation Pro CD-ROM, Ch. 15
Companion Web site, www.phschool.com

Focus Point out that the rapid growth of the nation's cities led to many urban problems. Reformers worked to improve social, economic, and political conditions in the cities. How successful were they?

Instruct Discuss the events and trends that made some Americans wary of immigration. Examples include the assassination of President McKinley, corruption in city governments, and poor conditions in slums. How did members of groups like the nativists and the temperance movement try to control immigration and personal behavior?

Have students compare reformers who tried to outlaw certain behaviors with those who developed a "helping" approach. Which group more successfully achieved its goals?

Assess/Reteach Throughout the history of the United States, immigrants have had a hard time being accepted in their new country. Have students research other periods when immigration was a contentious political issue.

BACKGROUND
Biography

Jane Addams wrote a memoir, *Twenty Years at Hull House,* in which she details her efforts to create the now-famous community center. In the introduction to a recent reprinting of Addams's memoir, author Ruth Sidel notes that Addams was influenced by the thinking of two men: Abraham Lincoln and her own father. Her father, a Quaker and state legislator, helped Addams develop her social conscience, reminding her every day of those less fortunate than she. Addams graduated from Rockford College and went on to study medicine. She was forced to halt her studies because of a medical condition. While visiting London in 1883, Addams saw the Toynbee Hall settlement house, which became her inspiration for Hull House.

CAPTION ANSWERS

Viewing History She is learning how to cook an American breakfast like an American woman.

The Charity Organization Movement In 1882, Josephine Shaw Lowell founded the New York Charity Organization Society (COS). The COS tried to make charity a scientific enterprise. Members kept detailed files on those who received help. In this way, COS leaders could more easily determine how to serve their clients. Yet keeping detailed files also allowed COS leaders to distinguish between the poor whom they considered worthy of help and those whom they deemed unworthy. This attitude sometimes led to unkind treatment of the needy.

Many COS members wanted immigrants to adopt American, middle-class standards of child-raising, cooking, and cleaning. They did not care how strange these customs seemed to people with different cultural backgrounds. This disturbed some immigrants, but others were grateful for the assistance.

The Social Gospel Movement In the 1880s and 1890s, urban churches began to provide social services for the poor who now surrounded them. They also tried to aim some reform campaigns in new directions. Instead of blaming immigrants for drinking, gambling, and other behaviors, the churches sought to treat the problems that drove people into such activities.

Soon a social reform movement developed within religious institutions. It was called the **social gospel movement** and it sought to apply the gospel (teachings) of Jesus directly to society. The movement focused on the gospel ideals of charity and justice, especially by seeking labor reforms. In 1908, followers of such views formed the Federal Council of the Churches of Christ. This organization supported providing improved living conditions and a larger share in the national wealth for all workers. Other religious organizations, including some Jewish synagogues, adapted the social gospel ideal for themselves.

The Settlement Movement Thousands of young, educated women and men put the social gospel into practice in an innovative reform program called the settlement movement. These young reformers settled into a house in the midst of a poor neighborhood. From this **settlement house,** a kind of community center, they eventually offered social services.

The settlement movement had begun in Britain. Its founders believed that simply giving money to the poor never really helped them. In order to find out what would be most helpful, the young settlers had to live in poor neighborhoods. There they could witness the effects of poverty firsthand.

In 1889, inspired by the British settlement movement, Jane Addams and Ellen Gates Starr bought the run-down Charles Hull mansion in Chicago. They repaired it and opened its doors to their immigrant neighbors. At first, Starr and Addams simply wanted to get to know their neighbors, offering help when needed. Soon they began anticipating and responding to the needs of the community as a whole.

Over the decades that followed, Addams and Starr turned Hull House into a center of community activity. At Hull House, neighbors could attend cultural events, take classes, or display exhibits of crafts from their home countries. The

VIEWING HISTORY Some reformers focused their efforts on helping immigrants adjust to life in the United States. This immigrant is learning English. **Analyzing Information** *What else is she learning?*

RESOURCE DIRECTORY

Other Print Resources

American History Block Scheduling Support *Ellis Island: Gateway to America,* found in the Expansion, Reconstruction, Immigration folder, includes interdisciplinary lesson suggestions and activities for Geography and History, Primary Sources, Biography, and Literature.

Technology

RESOURCE PRO® **Biography** *Lillian Wald,* found on Resource Pro, profiles the public-health nurse, activist, fund-raiser, and champion of child welfare and women's rights.

RESOURCE PRO® **Primary Source Activity** *Hull House,* found on Resource Pro, uses excerpts from the writings of founder Jane Addams to encourage students' investigations of social service organizations.

Exploring Primary Sources in U.S. History CD-ROM *Twenty Years at Hull House,* Jane Addams

VIEWING HISTORY Reformers offered help to newcomers by watching over their children while they worked. **Synthesizing Information** *What other services did settlement houses offer?*

settlement set up child-care centers, playgrounds, clubs, and summer camps for boys and girls; offices to help people find jobs and deal with legal problems; and health-care clinics. It also launched investigations of city economic, political, and social conditions. These actions laid the foundation for many later reforms.

Settlement houses like Hull House sprang up across the country. The Henry Street Settlement, founded by Lillian Wald on New York's Lower East Side, was originally a nurses' settlement to offer home health care to the poor. Its programs soon expanded to resemble many of those at Hull House. Missionaries, too, founded settlement houses, in part to gain converts but also to apply the social gospel in practical ways.

By 1910 there were more than 400 settlement houses. Most were supported by donations and staffed by volunteers or people willing to work for low wages and free room and board. Hundreds of college graduates, especially women excluded from other professions, became settlement workers. Except for leaders, such as Addams and Wald, most workers spent only a few years in these jobs. Many moved on to professional careers in social work, education, or government.

Few ever forgot their settlement experience. "I don't know that my attitude changed," wrote one former settlement worker, "but my point of view certainly did, or perhaps it would be more true to say that now I have several points of view." By helping its workers see social issues in new ways, the settlement houses energized the reform movement while improving the lives of the urban poor.

The Development of Sociology

While settlement workers observed first-hand the problems of the slums, scholars in America and Europe were developing a scientific way of looking at how people lived. Philosopher Auguste Comte coined the term **sociology** to describe the study of how people interact with one another in a society. Sociology is a social science. Like a biologist studying animals, a sociologist collects data on societies, and measures the data against theories of human behavior.

READING CHECK
What were the effects of the settlement movement?

544 • Chapter 15 Section 4

Connecting with Culture

Instruct students to research ways in which the sentiments of the nativists may have influenced immigration policies in the United States and how those policies have evolved. Students should include the Comprehensive Immigration Law (1924) and the Immigration Bill (1965) in their research. Have students write a short essay on their findings. (**Verbal/Linguistic**)

BACKGROUND

Recent Scholarship

Were settlement movement founders altruists who respected the cultural pluralism of immigrant communities? Or were they "social controllers" trying to check the chaos of a rapidly urbanizing society and bent on Americanization? Focusing solely on the nationally important settlement houses can be misleading, suggests Ruth Crocker in *Social Work and Social Order: The Settlement Movement in Two Industrial Cities, 1889–1930.* Crocker looks at "second-tier" settlements, notably those founded by religious groups in Indiana. By highlighting the evangelical side of the movement and the support it received from the business community, she reveals a tendency toward social control that historians often do not discuss.

READING CHECK

Nativists felt threatened by urban immigrants who had attained political and financial power. They blamed immigrants for the problems, such as crime and poverty found in cities in the late 1800s.

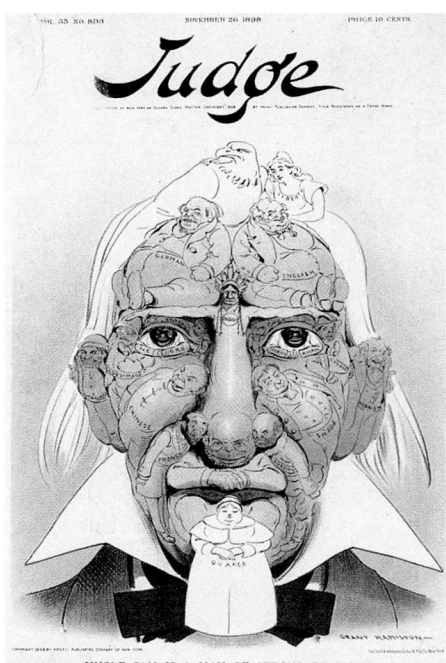

VOL. 35 NO. 890   NOVEMBER 26 1898   PRICE 10 CENTS

Judge

UNCLE SAM IS A MAN OF STRONG FEATURES.

INTERPRETING POLITICAL CARTOONS The caption on this magazine cover reads, "Uncle Sam is a man of strong features." **Recognizing Point of View** *What does this cartoon suggest about the artist's view of immigration?*

READING CHECK

Why did nativists oppose immigration?

Sociology provided a scientific counterpart to the settlement houses' practical experience.

Sociologists studied cultures around the world to learn what institutions and practices define a society. The institutions in an American community might include houses of worship, local governments, schools, libraries, and museums. Practices might include the way that children relate to their parents or a community teaches students. In the late nineteenth century, many sociologists studied the effects of industrialization and urbanization on established communities. America's rapidly changing population provided them with many examples.

Controlling Immigration and Behavior

Many Americans linked the problems of the cities to the new immigrants. By controlling immigrants, they hoped to restore what they believed had been a past of purity and virtue. Groups were formed to pursue this goal. Some sought to keep immigrants out of the United States, while others wanted to change their behavior.

Nativism   In the 1850s, the Know-Nothing Party had gained many followers by vowing to restrict immigration. Thirty years later this policy of **nativism,** or favoring native-born Americans over immigrants, reappeared. The rise of immigrants to positions of power in the cities helped provoke this new wave of antiforeign bias. Passage of the Chinese Exclusion Act in 1882 showed how politically effective the new nativists were.

Nativists did not oppose only Asian immigration. The American Protective Association, a nativist group founded in 1887, targeted immigrants in general as well as the Catholic Church. It called for the teaching of only American culture and the English language in schools and demanded tighter rules on citizenship and employment of aliens. Members of this secret society took an oath to hire and vote for Protestants alone.

Nativists won a victory in 1885, when Congress repealed the Contract Labor Act. Passed in 1864, the law had allowed employers to recruit foreign laborers. Even after the law's repeal, however, employers often illegally brought in foreign workers to replace striking employees. Such actions only heightened nativist feelings among workers.

There were nativists among the wealthy as well. The Immigration Restriction League was organized in 1894 by some Harvard College graduates. The League hoped to exclude immigrants considered unfit by requiring them to pass literacy tests. Its main targets were immigrants from southern and eastern Europe, whose cultures differed greatly from those of League members.

Prohibition   Like nativism, another movement begun before the Civil War saw a revival later in the 1800s: the **temperance movement,** an organized campaign to eliminate alcohol consumption. Three groups dominated the new temperance movement: the Prohibition party, founded in 1869, the Woman's Christian Temperance Union, founded in 1874, and the Anti-Saloon League, founded in 1893. These groups opposed drinking on the grounds that it led to personal tragedies. They supported **prohibition,** a ban on the manufacture and sale of alcoholic beverages. One activist, Carry Nation, won fame by smashing illegal saloons with a hatchet in her home state of Kansas.

CAPTION ANSWERS

Interpreting Political Cartoons The cartoonist believed that immigration built the United States and continued to make it stronger.

RESOURCE DIRECTORY

Teaching Resources
Units 5/6 booklet
 • Section 4 Quiz, p. 29
 • Chapter 15 Test, pp. 30, 33
Guide to the Essentials
 • Section 4 Summary, p. 81
 • Chapter 15 Test, p. 82

Other Print Resources
Chapter Tests with ExamView® Test Bank CD-ROM, Ch. 15

Technology
ExamView® Test Bank CD-ROM, Ch. 15
Social Studies Skills Tutor CD-ROM

Prohibition groups also opposed drinking because of what they saw as the links among saloons, immigrants, and political bosses. Immigrant men often used saloons as social clubs, where they could relax and also find information about jobs. Prohibitionists believed that saloons undermined public morals. Some prohibitionists even claimed that saloons formed the center of a movement to take over the United States. "Foreign control or conquest is rapidly making us un-Christian, with immorality throned in power," one prohibitionist wrote in 1908.

At first, progress was slow. Early prohibitionists measured their success by towns and counties that agreed to ban alcohol. By 1890, only three states had gone completely "dry" and embraced prohibition: Maine, Kansas, and North Dakota.

Purity Crusaders As cities grew, drugs, gambling, prostitution, and other forms of vice became big business. **Vice** (immoral or corrupt behavior) was not unique to the cities. But large urban populations made vice highly visible and very profitable. Then as now, many residents fought to rid their communities of unwholesome and illegal activities.

"Purity crusaders" led the way. In 1873, Anthony Comstock founded the New York Society for the Suppression of Vice. The following year he won passage of a law that prohibited sending obscene materials through the United States mail. Material deemed obscene included descriptions of methods to prevent unwanted pregnancy. For decades the Comstock Law, as it came to be known, slowed the distribution of information about birth control.

Other purity crusaders attacked urban political machines, saying that machine-controlled police forces profited from vice. Police were known to demand payment from gamblers in return for ignoring illegal activities. On occasion, purity crusaders joined forces with other reformers to run for public office. By campaigning on an anti-vice platform, some succeeded in throwing machine candidates out of office. Usually the political machines regained power in later elections by mocking the self-righteous tone of many purists and by arguing that morality was a personal issue.

Reading Comprehension

1. To take a scientific approach to providing charity. Also, to encourage immigrants to behave like middle-class Americans.

2. To examine, scientifically, how people live and interact with one another in a society.

3. To favor native-born Americans over immigrants.

4. Temperance groups and purity crusaders focused on banning alcohol and vice. The other groups focused on improving society by providing help to the needy.

Critical Thinking and Writing

5. Sample: Less wealthy nativists might have argued to restrict immigration so they would not have to compete for jobs. Wealthy nativists opposed immigrant cultures.

6. Answers will vary, but may include: morality is a personal issue; vice was big business; protection of First Amendment rights.

7. Answers will vary, but may include being shocked at the depth of poverty, or finding the work to be fulfilling.

Take It to the NET

Posters will vary but should demonstrate knowledge of the services offered to immigrants and the poor at Hull House.

Section 4 Assessment

READING COMPREHENSION

1. What was the purpose of the New York Charity Organization Society?

2. What is the purpose of **sociology?**

3. What was the goal of **nativist** movements?

4. How did **temperance** groups and purity crusaders differ from charity, **social gospel,** and **settlement** movements?

CRITICAL THINKING AND WRITING

5. **Identifying Assumptions** How might the anti-immigrant arguments of wealthy nativists have differed from those of less-affluent nativists?

6. **Drawing Inferences** What were two possible reasons for people to oppose purity crusaders?

7. **Journal Writing** Write three brief fictional journal entries from the point of view of a settlement house worker.

 Take It to the NET

Activity: Creating a Poster
Research Hull House and create a poster designed to inform neighbors about the services offered at that settlement house. Use the links provided in the *America: Pathways to the Present* area of the following Web site for help in completing this activity.
www.phschool.com

REVIEWING KEY TERMS

Students should refer to the definitions of key terms in the chapter to write sentences that show an understanding of politics, immigration, and urban life in the Gilded Age.

REVIEWING MAIN IDEAS

15. Business interests tried to influence politicians to vote in their favor by giving gifts and money.

16. The hiring of unqualified and often dishonest government employees. Corruption in government became an accepted practice.

17. Immigrants fled poor farming, working, and living conditions in their home countries.

18. More new immigrants during this period come from southern and eastern Europe.

19. Middle-class residents moved to the suburbs. Urban landowners built cheap tenements that became neglected, overcrowded, unsanitary, and unsafe.

20. Advantages: They helped poor immigrants when no help was given by government or private industry. Disadvantages: They illegally skimmed money from the city's income and hurt businesses.

21. By offering social services in community centers, such as classes, childcare, and health care. They also launched investigations of city economic, political, and social conditions, laying the foundation for later reforms.

22. They influenced the passage of the Chinese Exclusion Act and the repeal of the Contract Labor Act. They also founded the Immigration Restriction League.

---

creating a CHAPTER SUMMARY

Copy this chart (right) on a piece of paper and complete it by adding important events and issues that fit each heading. Some entries have been completed for you as examples.

For additional review and enrichment activities, see the interactive version of *America: Pathways to the Present*, available on the Web and on CD-ROM.

Politics, Immigration, and Urban Life in the Gilded Age	
Immigration and Nativism	• More immigrants arrive from eastern and southern Europe. • Mexican immigrants settle in the Southwest. • Asian immigrants face challenges in the West. •
Presidential Politics	
Urban Growth	
Political Machines	
Social Reform	

★ Reviewing Key Terms

For each of the terms below, write a sentence explaining how it relates to the Gilded Age.

1. Gilded Age
2. *laissez-faire*
3. blue law
4. civil service
5. steerage
6. ghetto
7. Chinese Exclusion Act
8. suburb
9. tenement
10. political machine
11. graft
12. settlement house
13. nativism
14. prohibition

★ Reviewing Main Ideas

15. How did business influence politicians during the Gilded Age? (Section 1)

16. What problems did the spoils system create? (Section 1)

17. Why did so many people want to come to the United States between 1870 and 1915? (Section 2)

18. Starting in the 1890s, where did large numbers of immigrants come from? (Section 2)

19. How did slums develop in cities? (Section 3)

20. What were the advantages and disadvantages of political machines for urban residents? (Section 3)

21. How did the settlement movement seek to help the needy? (Section 4)

22. What actions did nativists take to restrict immigration? (Section 4)

★ Critical Thinking

23. Drawing Inferences What character trait did President Rutherford B. Hayes exhibit by his actions regarding the spoils system? Explain.

24. Drawing Conclusions What conclusion(s) can you draw from the fact that Tammany Hall dominated New York City for more than 50 years?

25. Predicting Consequences What might have been the effect if the United States had adopted all the ideas of the nativists?

26. Making Comparisons How and why did the experiences of Chinese immigrants differ from the experiences of immigrants from Italy and Russia?

27. Recognizing Bias Read the following quote about a charity reformer's visit to an immigrant home: "[they] upset the usual routine of their lives, opening windows, undressing children, giving orders not to eat this and that, not to wrap babies in swaddling clothes." (a) What does this quote reveal about the author's opinions? (b) How might a charity reformer describe the visit?

CREATING A CHAPTER SUMMARY

Politics, Immigration, and Urban Life in the Gilded Age	
Immigration and Nativism	• More immigrants arrive from eastern and southern Europe. • Mexican immigrants settle in the Southwest. • Asian immigrants face challenges in the West.
Presidential Politics	• Corruption common at high levels in government • Laissez faire attitude by government toward business • Credit Mobilier scandal in Grant's administration • Hayes reformed spoils system • Garfield shot and later died • Arthur ended spoils system.
Urban Growth	• Populations of cities swelled in years 1871–1900. • Slums and ghettos developed. • Suburbs developed. • Transportation caused cities to grow.
Political Machines	• Bosses arose to control problems in cities. • Graft a source of income for political machines
Social Reform	• Social service organizations sprang up to try to help immigrants and so improve city life. • Many people wrote about the problems of the cities and tried to suggest solutions.

★ Skills Assessment

Analyzing Political Cartoons ▶

28. This scene shows a strength contest once popular at fairs. The goal was to test one's strength in an attempt to ring the bell at the top of the column. Examine the scene. Who are the contestants?

29. Examine the game. (a) What are the contestants hitting? (b) What is the bell? (c) What is the mallet?

30. Read the caption. Describe the cartoonist's message in a brief paragraph.

Interpreting Data

Turn to the graph titled "European Immigration, 1870–1920" in Section 2.

31. In which of the following years did immigrants from central Europe outnumber immigrants from every other region?

    A 1870
    B 1880 and 1890
    C 1900 and 1910
    D 1920

32. Which sentence best describes immigration from eastern Europe from 1870 to 1920?

    F Immigration increased steadily and then fell to near zero.
    G The number of immigrants declined steadily.
    H The number of immigrants increased steadily every decade.
    J The number of immigrants stayed constant.

Applying the Chapter Skill: *Analyzing Tables and Skills*

33. Look back at the table on the Skills for Life page. World War I was fought from 1914 to 1918. How does the table reflect the influence of the war on immigration to the United States?

TRY YOUR STRENGTH, GENTS!

ACTIVITIES

Writing to LEARN

Writing to Compare and Contrast
Today, the Democratic and Republican parties both try to appeal to the large American middle class. Write an essay comparing and contrasting the major parties of today with those in the Gilded Age. Be sure to address this question: Did all levels of society have a political voice in both eras?

Primary Source CD-ROM

Working With Primary Sources Find additional information on immigration and urban life on the *Exploring Primary Sources in the U.S. History CD-ROM* and use the selection(s) provided to complete the Chapter 15 primary source activity located in the *America: Pathways to the Present* area of the following Web site.
www.phschool.com

Take It to the NET

Chapter Self-Test As a review activity, take the Chapter 15 Self-Test in the *America: Pathways to the Present* area of the Web site listed below. The questions are designed to test your understanding of the chapter content.
www.phschool.com

Chapter 15 Assessment   **547**

American Pathways
GEOGRAPHY

Immigrants in Search of the American Dream

The United States is a nation of immigrants. For hundreds of years, people have come, pushed by events and circumstances in their home countries and pulled by the freedom and opportunity available to them in the United States. Immigrants arrive with optimism, in search of their own American dream. Through hard work, most achieve success as American citizens.

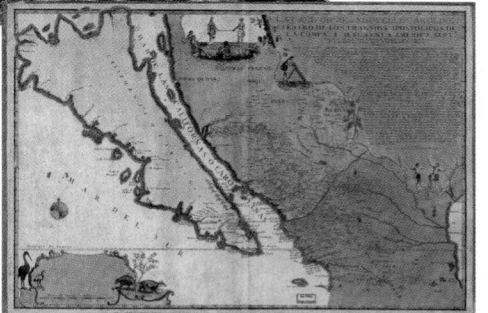

1 Earliest European Settlements

1565–1634 The earliest settlers in the present-day United States came with a variety of goals, from finding gold, to opening new trading markets, to avoiding religious persecution.

French explorers on the Mississippi River (left) and a 1720 map showing California as an island (below)

2 Northern Europeans

1820–1890 Northern European immigrants, most of whom were of Irish or German descent, settled mainly in the cities of the Northeast and the farmlands of the Midwest. Members of the Know-Nothing Party and other nativists feared that these immigrants would increase crime and vice.

 Asians

1849–1924 During these years, many Asians immigrated to the United States to find jobs and seek their fortunes in the land of opportunity. Many faced hostility and new laws aimed at limiting their numbers.

Chinese gold prospectors in California (right)

548

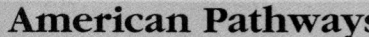

5 Mexicans

1902–1930 Large numbers of Mexicans came to the United States during these years to work on farms, in mines, and in factories. Some were escaping political turmoil in their own country. Others were looking for higher-paying work than they had had at home.

6 More Latin Americans and Asians

1945–Present The Immigration Act of 1965 removed a long-standing ban on immigration from Asia and relaxed other quotas. Immigration increased steadily during the 1960s and 1970s. During the 1980s, more than 1,000,000 more Mexicans and nearly 1,200,000 more Asians arrived in the United States than had come in the 1970s. Immigration from Central America more than tripled during this same time period. By the early 1990s, an overwhelming majority of immigrants were coming from Asia and Central America.

A portrait of American diversity (right)

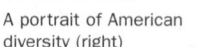

4 Southern and Eastern Europeans and Middle Easterners

1890–1924 Huge numbers of people from southern and eastern Europe and the Middle East arrived in the United States during this period. When immigration rose sharply after World War I, Congress responded by passing laws restricting the number of foreigners who could enter the United States.

Italian immigrants at Ellis Island (above)

Continuity and Change

1. Did the government encourage immigration after World War II or discourage it? Explain.
2. How has the United States benefited from its ethnic and cultural diversity?

 Take It to the NET: Creating a Study Guide
Print and complete the study guide for this topic found in the *America: Pathways to the Present* area of the following Web site. **www.phschool.com**

549

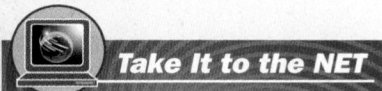 **Take It to the NET**

Students can print the American Pathways thematic study guide for this topic at the Prentice Hall School Web site, or you can provide students with copies of the study guide, which is found in the Units 5/6 booklet, the American Pathways Activity, pages 47–48. Students should use their texts to fill in a one-sentence description for each event on the study guide. When completed for each of the American Pathways topics, the thematic study guides will aid students in preparing for an end-of-course exam.

★ ANSWERS

1. The government began encouraging immigration with the Immigration Act of 1965, although calls for limits continue, as reflected in the passage of California's Proposition 187.

2. The ethnic and cultural diversity in the United States has led to an openness to new ideas, as well as a tolerance of and respect for differences. Ethnic and cultural differences also make the United States a very interesting place to live and work.

Chapter 16 Planning Guide
Resource Manager

	CORE INSTRUCTION	READING/SKILLS
Chapter-Level Resources	**Teaching Resources** • Pacing Charts booklet • Block Scheduling booklet **Resource Pro® CD-ROM**, Ch. 16 **Prentice Hall Presentation Pro CD-ROM**, Ch. 16 **www.phschool.com** • eTeach	**Guided Reading Audiotapes (English/Spanish)** **Student Edition on Audio CD**, Ch. 16 **Social Studies Skills Tutor CD-ROM** **Color Transparency**, E15
1 The Expansion of Education 1. Learn how and why public schools expanded during the late 1800s. 2. Find out how opportunities for higher education increased after the Civil War. 3. Discover the views of Booker T. Washington and W.E.B. Du Bois regarding African American education.	**Teaching Resources** **Units 5/6 booklet** • Section 1 Quiz, p. 37 **Learning Styles Lesson Plans booklet**, p. 21	**Guided Reading and Review booklet**, p. 66 **Guide to the Essentials**, p. 83 **Learning with Documents booklet**, pp. 84, 85 **Skills for Life booklet**, p. 18 **Section Reading Support Transparencies**
2 New Forms of Entertainment 1. Discover the new kinds of performances and recreation that Americans enjoyed at the turn of the century. 2. Find out what people were reading for education and entertainment. 3. Learn how American music was changing.	**Teaching Resources** **Units 5/6 booklet** • Section 2 Quiz, p. 38 **Learning Styles Lesson Plans booklet**, p. 34	**Guided Reading and Review booklet**, p. 67 **Guide to the Essentials**, p. 84 **Section Reading Support Transparencies**
3 The World of Jim Crow 1. Probe the kinds of discrimination encountered by African Americans after Reconstruction. 2. Find out how African Americans resisted this discrimination.	**Teaching Resources** **Units 5/6 booklet** • Section 3 Quiz, p. 39	**Guided Reading and Review booklet**, p. 68 **Guide to the Essentials**, p. 85 **Section Reading Support Transparencies**
4 The Changing Role of Women 1. Examine the issues in the debate over women's equality. 2. Discover how women's work in the home changed at the turn of the century. 3. Learn how stores and catalogs served women's new role as consumers. 4. Find out about the kinds of work that women did outside the home.	**Teaching Resources** **Units 5/6 booklet** • Section 4 Quiz, p. 40 **Learning Styles Lesson Plans booklet**, p. 35	**Guided Reading and Review booklet**, p. 69 **Guide to the Essentials**, p. 86 **Learning with Documents booklet**, p. 55 **Section Reading Support Transparencies**

ENRICHMENT/PRE-AP

Prentice Hall United States History Video Collection™
www.phschool.com
- Section Activities, Virtual Field Trip, Chapter Activities, Current Events Online

Sounds of an Era Audio CD

Biography, Literature, and Comparing Primary Sources booklet, p. 62
Sounds of an Era Audio CD

Great Debates booklet, pp. 32–35
American History Block Scheduling Support
Nystrom *Atlas of Our Country,* pp. 30–31

Biography, Literature, and Comparing Primary Sources booklet, p. 127
Great Debates booklet, p. 34
American Pathways Thematic Posters

ASSESSMENT

PRENTICE HALL
ASSESSMENT SYSTEM

Core Assessment
 ExamView® Test Bank, Ch. 16
 ExamView® Test Bank CD-ROM, Ch. 16

Standardized Test Preparation
Diagnose and Prescribe
 Diagnostic Tests for High School Social Studies Skills

Review and Reteach
 Review Book for U.S. History

Practice and Assess
 Test-taking Strategies With Transparencies
 Test-taking Strategies Posters
 Test Prep Book for U.S. History
 Alternative Assessment Handbook
 Document-Based Assessment

Teaching Resources
Units 5/6 booklet
- Section Quizzes, pp. 37–40
- Chapter Test, p. 41, 44

www.phschool.com Ch. 16 Self-Test

AmericanHeritage RESOURCES

From the Archives of American Heritage®, p. 570
AmericanHeritage® **My Brush with History™ Videotapes**
www.americanheritage.com

i TEXT

Don't miss the exclusive interactive version of this textbook on the Web and on CD-ROM.

Chapter 16 Planning Guide
In Your Classroom

CUSTOMIZE FOR INDIVIDUAL NEEDS

Gifted and Talented

Teacher's Edition
- Customize for Gifted and Talented, p. 563

Teaching Resources
- Biography, Literature, and Comparing Primary Sources booklet, pp. 21, 62, 127

ESL

Teacher's Edition
- Customize for ESL, p. 553

Teaching Resources
- Guided Reading and Review booklet, pp. 66–69
- Guide to the Essentials (English/Spanish), Chapter 16

Technology
- Student Edition on Audio CD, Chapter 16
- Guided Reading Audiotapes (English/Spanish), Chapter 16
- Section Reading Support Transparencies

Less Proficient Readers

Teacher's Edition
- Customize for Less Proficient Readers, p. 557

Teaching Resources
- Guided Reading and Review booklet, pp. 66–69
- Guide to the Essentials (English/Spanish), Chapter 16

Technology
- Student Edition on Audio CD, Chapter 16
- Guided Reading Audiotapes (English/Spanish), Chapter 16
- Section Reading Support Transparencies

Less Proficient Writers

Teacher's Edition
- Customize for Less Proficient Writers, p. 561

Teaching Resources
- Guided Reading and Review booklet, pp. 66–69
- Guide to the Essentials (English/Spanish), Chapter 16

Technology
- Student Edition on Audio CD, Chapter 16
- Guided Reading Audiotapes (English/Spanish), Chapter 16
- Section Reading Support Transparencies

TEACHER'S EDITION INDEX

CHAPTER 16 – PACING SUGGESTIONS

 For 90-minute Blocks
- Teach section 4 using Transparency E15, and the Recent Scholarship notes on pages 556 and 571 for class discussions.

 Running Out of Time?
If you are running short on time to cover this chapter, consider the following options:

- Use the Prentice Hall Presentation Pro CD-ROM to create an outline for this chapter.

- Use the Section Summaries for Chapter 16, from **Guide to the Essentials (English/Spanish)**.

1 **The Expansion of Education**	**Connecting with Citizenship** Remind students that the message of the Niagara Movement was somewhat different from that of Tuskegee Institute. Ask students, working in pairs, to prepare a pamphlet that presents each organization's message. The pamphlets should highlight what the founders feel is the organization's strongest appeal to African Americans of that time. Encourage students to give each pamphlet strong visual appeal. **(Verbal/Linguistic; Visual/Spatial)**
2 **New Forms of Entertainment**	**Connecting with Culture** Remind students of Mark Twain's statement about baseball being "the very symbol, the outward and visible expression of the drive and push and rush and struggle of the raging, tearing, booming nineteenth century." Initiate a discussion based on the following question: Does Twain's statement hold true for the twenty-first century? Have students give reasons for their answers. If they disagree, invite them to suggest another sport that they feel is more representative of the present time. You may prefer to have students present their arguments in writing. **(Verbal/Linguistic)**
3 **The World of Jim Crow**	**Connecting with Culture** Point out to students that poet Paul Laurence Dunbar often wrote about the problems faced by fellow African Americans. Have students locate Dunbar's poem "The Haunted Oak" in *The Complete Poems of Paul Laurence Dunbar*. A group of students might take turns reading stanzas of the poem, then compare its presentation of lynching with that in the text. You might then ask such questions as these: Which best captures the passion and pain of the events? Why did the poet choose to give the oak a voice? What audience was Dunbar trying to reach? How might audiences of the time have reacted to such a story told in poetic form? **(Verbal/Linguistic)**
4 **The Changing Role of Women**	**Connecting with Economics** Point out to students some contemporary icons, such as those found on most computer screens. Tell them that icons are intended to be symbolic representations of important concepts. Therefore, they must be immediately identifiable as standing for a particular function. Have students in small groups brainstorm icons that might be representative of women's lives in the period covered by this chapter (1870–1915). Each icon should symbolize some aspect of women's lives, such as clothing, communication, work inside the home, and work outside of the home. Suggest that students research photographs and illustrations of the period before creating their icons. You may wish to limit each group's work to a specific 10–15 year period. **(Visual/Spatial)**

Chapter 16

Life at the Turn of the Twentieth Century

(1870–1915)

INTRODUCING THE CHAPTER

The growth of industry and urban areas in the late 1800s brought many cultural and social transformations to the United States. At the time, many Americans feared change and clung to old ideas about social roles, particularly those that affected women and African Americans.

TIME LINE ACTIVITY

To provide students with practice in using the time line, ask questions such as these:

1. What country granted voting rights to women in 1893? *(New Zealand)*

2. How did the outcome of *Plessy* v. *Ferguson* affect the cause of civil rights in the United States? *(The Supreme Court ruled in favor of separate but equal facilities for African Americans and whites, effectively making segregation legal.)*

3. What organization was formed in 1909 to advance the cause of African Americans? *(The NAACP)*

eTeach

Be sure to check out this month's online discussion with a Master Teacher. Go to **www.phschool.com**.

Chapter 16

Life at the Turn of the Twentieth Century

(1870–1915)

SECTION 1   The Expansion of Education
SECTION 2   New Forms of Entertainment
SECTION 3   The World of Jim Crow
SECTION 4   The Changing Roles of Women

The justices of the Supreme Court

1890
Local women's clubs join together to form influential national organizations, such as the General Federation of Women's Clubs.

1895
In his speech at the Atlanta Exposition, Booker T. Washington urges blacks to postpone demands for equality while educating themselves for productive work.

1896
In *Plessy* v. *Ferguson*, the Supreme Court upholds segregation and the concept of "separate but equal."

American Events

Presidential Terms: B. Harrison 1889–1893   G. Cleveland 1893–1897   W. McKinley 1897–1901

1890   •   **1895**   •   **1900**   •

World Events

New Zealand grants women the right to vote.
1893

The first motion picture, made by the Lumière brothers, opens in Paris.
1895

The first "foolproof" vacuum cleaner is invented in England.
1901

RESOURCE DIRECTORY

Teaching Resources
Pacing Charts booklet
Block Scheduling booklet, p. 21
Units 5/6 booklet
• Chapter Summary, p. 36

Technology
Guided Reading Audiotapes (English/Spanish), Ch. 16
Student Edition on Audio CD, Ch. 16
Sounds of an Era Audio CD *"Blue Back Speller,"* vowel exercise (time: 30 seconds)
Prentice Hall United States History Video Collection™ Volume 11, *Immigration and Cultural Change*
Prentice Hall Presentation Pro CD-ROM, Ch. 16
Resource Pro® CD-ROM
Social Studies Skills Tutor CD-ROM
Companion Web site, www.phschool.com

Daily Expenditure per Pupil in Public Schools, 1909–1910

CANADA

Washington
Montana
North Dakota
Minnesota
Maine
Oregon
Idaho
Wyoming
South Dakota
Wisconsin
Michigan
New York
Vt.
New Hampshire
Massachusetts
Rhode Island
Connecticut
Nevada
Utah
Colorado
Nebraska
Iowa
Illinois
Indiana
Ohio
Pennsylvania
New Jersey
Delaware
Maryland
California
Kansas
Missouri
Kentucky
West Virginia
Virginia
North Carolina
Arizona Territory
New Mexico Territory
Oklahoma
Arkansas
Tennessee
South Carolina
ATLANTIC OCEAN
Texas
Mississippi
Alabama
Georgia
Louisiana
Gulf of Mexico
Florida

0 150 300 mi.
0 150 300 km

In dollars:
24 and above
19–23
14–18
0–13

N

THE GREAT TRAIN ROBBERY
SENSATIONAL AND STARTLING HOLD UP OF THE GOLD EXPRESS, BY FAMOUS WESTERN OUTLAWS

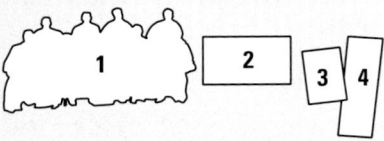

WOMAN'S HOME COMPANION

A DAILY PAPER FOR ONE CENT A DAY.
THE CHICAGO DAILY NEWS
CHICAGO WEEKLY NEWS

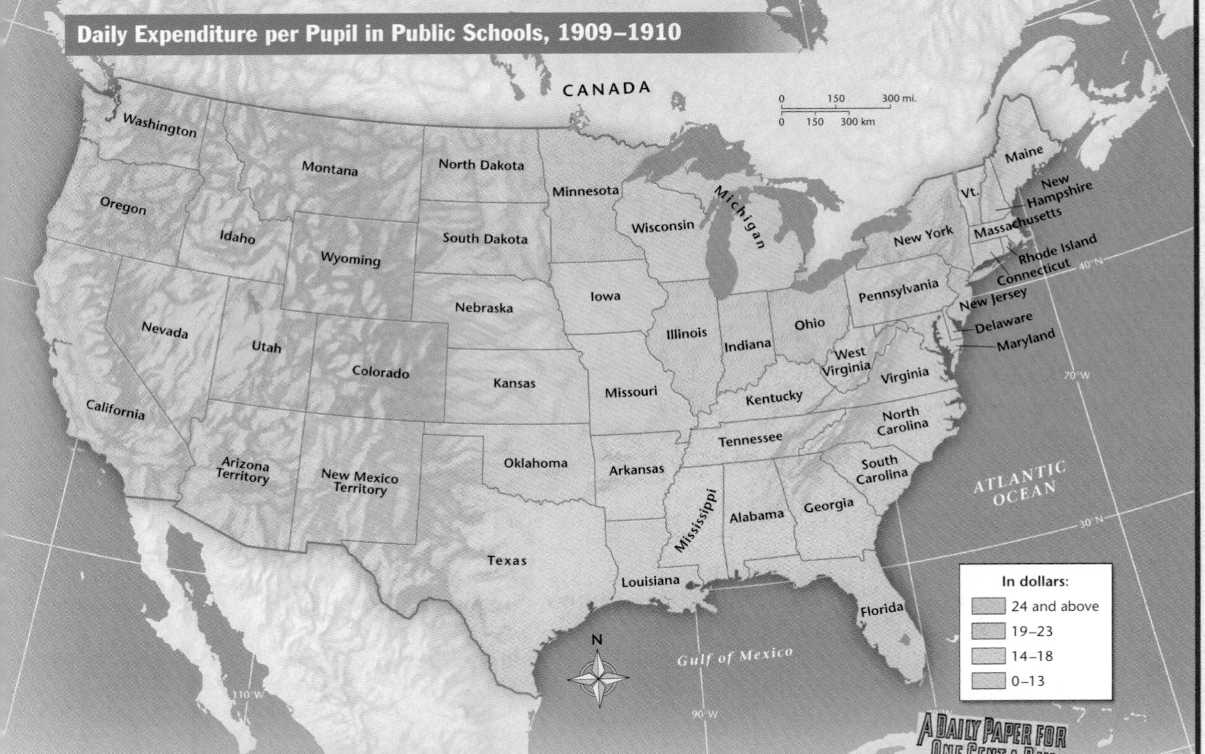

Newspapers and magazines offer information and entertainment.

1903
The huge success of the movie *The Great Train Robbery* signals the beginning of the silent movie era.

1905
W.E.B. Du Bois helps found the Niagara Movement, which promotes full civil liberties for African Americans.

1909
The National Association for the Advancement of Colored People is founded to fight for civil rights.

T. Roosevelt 1901–1909

W. Taft 1909–1913

W. Wilson 1913–1921

1905 • **1910** • **1915**

Italian tenor Enrico Caruso makes his first recording.

Marcus Garvey founds the Universal Negro Improvement Association in Jamaica.

1902

1914

Chapter 16   551

Daily Expenditure per Pupil in Public Schools, 1909–1910

Activating Prior Knowledge
Which states had a daily expenditure of between 19 and 23 dollars per pupil? *(Oregon, Utah, Minnesota, Illinois, Indiana, Ohio, New York, and New Jersey)*

Previewing By looking at the map, why do you think the western states were able to spend so much more money per student than states like New York and Maryland? *(There were probably fewer students in western schools, so there was more money to spend per student.)*

BACKGROUND
About the Pictures

1   2   3   4

1. The judges of the Supreme Court who ruled on the *Plessy* v. *Ferguson* case in 1896.
2. Poster from *The Great Train Robbery,* one of the first movies to attract a vast, nationwide audience.
3. & 4. Newspapers such as the *Chicago Daily News* offered readers both information and entertainment. Magazines also expanded in this era, assisted by lowered postal rates.

BIBLIOGRAPHY

For the Teacher

Abrahams, Roger D. *Singing the Master: The Emergence of African Culture in the Plantation South.* Penguin USA, 1993. (Uses primary sources to trace the impact of plantation traditions and songs on African American performance styles in the nineteenth and twentieth centuries.)

Lewis, David Levering. *W.E.B. Du Bois: Biography of a Race, 1868–1919.* Henry Holt, 1994. (The first 51 years of the life of the brilliant African American leader.)

For the Student

Blacks and the Constitution. PBS Video, 1987.

Ward, Geoffrey C. *Baseball: An Illustrated History.* Alfred A. Knopf, 1996. (Based on the acclaimed PBS series, this book recounts the history of baseball from its earliest days.)

Washington, Booker T. *Up from Slavery.* Oxford University Press, 2000. (Classic autobiography of the famous civil rights leader.)

iTEXT

Don't miss the exclusive interactive version of this textbook on the Web and on CD-ROM.

The Expansion of Education

SECTION OBJECTIVES

1. Learn how and why public schools expanded during the late 1800s.
2. Find out how opportunities for higher education increased after the Civil War.
3. Discover the views of Booker T. Washington and W.E.B. Du Bois regarding African American education.

BELLRINGER

Warm-Up Activity Ask students if they think changes need to be made in American education in order to better prepare students for their future roles. Ask them to explain what they think these changes should be.

Activating Prior Knowledge What are some ways in which your students' educational experience would be different if they had attended a nineteenth-century-style one-room schoolhouse rather than a modern high school? Have them list some of the differences.

READING STRATEGY

As students read this section, have them make a list of examples of how educational opportunities expanded between 1870 and 1910. How did industrialization, the growth of railroads, the growth of labor unions, farm issues, and the rise of big business affect education?

READING FOCUS

- How and why did public schools expand during the late 1800s?
- How did opportunities for higher education increase after the Civil War?
- What were the views of Booker T. Washington and W.E.B. Du Bois regarding African American education?

MAIN IDEA

Education was a lofty goal that was out of reach of most nineteenth-century Americans. However, as the new century began, more and more Americans took advantage of educational opportunities.

KEY TERMS

literacy
assimilation
philanthropist
Niagara
  Movement

TAKING NOTES

Copy the diagram below. As you read, fill in the causes and effects of the expanding opportunities for education in America. You may add circles as needed.

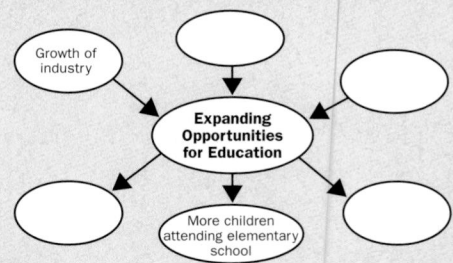

Growth of industry → Expanding Opportunities for Education → More children attending elementary school

Setting the Scene From sparsely populated prairie towns to crowded city neighborhoods, schools were becoming more common and more important to Americans at the end of the nineteenth century. In frontier areas, families banded together to hire teachers for their one-room schoolhouses. City schools were larger and more crowded, and often served many immigrants. Mary Antin, whose father sent for his family from Russia after he had established himself in Boston, describes the importance of free schools to her family:

A teacher (far left) and her students stand in front of their sod school in Thomas County, Kansas, around 1880. The adult man is probably an immigrant who wants to learn English.

66 *Education was free. That subject my father had written about repeatedly, as comprising his chief hope for us children, the essence of American opportunity, the treasure that no thief could touch, not even misfortune or poverty. . . . A little girl from across the alley came and offered to conduct us to school. . . . No application made, no question asked, no examinations, no fees. The doors stood open for every one of us. The smallest child could show us the way.* 99

—Mary Antin

The Growth of Public Schools

Americans had long understood that a democratic society functioned best when its citizens could read and write. By the late 1800s, however, an education had become more than just a worthy goal. For a growing number of Americans, it was a necessary first step toward economic and social success. In recognition of this fact and in response to public demand, educational opportunities expanded.

By the time of the Civil War, more than half of the nation's white children were attending the nation's free public schools. Because most children had to help their families earn a living, however, many left school at an early age. A high school diploma was still the exception. In 1870, only 2 percent

RESOURCE DIRECTORY

Teaching Resources
Guided Reading and Review booklet, p. 66

Technology
Section Reading Support Transparencies
Guided Reading Audiotapes (English/Spanish), Ch. 16
Student Edition on Audio CD, Ch. 16

RESOURCE PRO **Literature Activity** *The Promised Land,* found on Resource Pro, uses an excerpt from the autobiography of Mary

Antin, a Jewish immigrant from Russia living in Boston, to show the importance of education to immigrant families.
Prentice Hall Presentation Pro CD-ROM, Ch. 16
Companion Web site, www.phschool.com

of all 17-year-olds graduated from high school. An even lower percentage of students went on to college.

The vast majority of American children attended school for only a few years and learned only to "read, and write, and 'cipher [do basic arithmetic]." What's more, in farm communities, older children often attended school only from November to April so that they could help in the fields. As industries grew after the Civil War, parents came to realize that their children needed more than basic skills to advance in life. They began pressuring local governments to increase school funding and to lengthen the school year. At the same time, reformers pressured state governments to limit child labor.

By 1900, 31 states had laws requiring children between the ages of 8 and 14 to attend school. Although unevenly enforced, these laws had a powerful effect. By 1910, nearly 72 percent of American children attended school, with more than a million students in high school.

School Days   Early in the 1900s, about half of the nation's children attended one-room schools. There, children aged 6 to 14 were taught by a single teacher; often the older students helped the younger ones with their lessons. In the classic *Little House* novels based on her own life, Laura Ingalls Wilder describes these schools. *These Happy Golden Years* tells how Laura becomes a teacher when she is only 15 years old. She boards with a rural family, teaches in a drafty shanty, and has only five students—three of whom are older than she is!

Students in both rural and city schools learned many of their lessons by rote. They read aloud from texts such as the *McGuffey Readers*, and recited passages and facts from memory. As they got older, they studied geography, history, and grammar in addition to the "three Rs." Teachers often kept discipline with the threat of physical punishment. Erwin House was a student in 1876: "To a nervous child the discipline was indeed terrible. The long birch switches hanging on hooks against the wall haunted me day and night, from the time I entered school."

Other students loved school. Tony Longo, son of an Italian immigrant, went to a city school:

> ❝ I liked school. . . . The teacher told us stories about General Grant and Abraham Lincoln and other great Americans. She also taught us how to read and write in English. . . . For the Centennial celebration we had a pageant at school. I wore a white wig and played the role of George Washington. My father was very proud. ❞
>
> —Tony Longo

Immigrants and Education   Like the parents of Tony Longo and Mary Antin, many immigrants placed a high value on American public education. It was a way for their children to become successful Americans.

One of the most important functions of the public schools was to teach literacy skills. **Literacy** is the ability to read and write. For many immigrants, learning to read and write English was an important step in their quest to succeed in the United States. And it was not only children who went to school. Adults attended school at night to learn English and civics, which they needed to qualify for citizenship.

Public schools also played a role in assimilating immigrants. **Assimilation** is the process by which people of one culture become part of another culture.

The *McGuffey Readers*   At the end of the nineteenth century, all across America, schoolchildren could be heard reciting from their *McGuffey Eclectic Readers*. This series of textbooks was by far the most popular in the nation. The first *Reader* was published in 1830, and by 1922, about 122 million texts had been sold. Graded from first to sixth, *McGuffey Readers* included excerpts from great books. For rural families who lived far from libraries, the *Readers* might be their only exposure to good literature, such as works by Wordsworth and Shakespeare. *McGuffey Readers* also contained tales designed to teach moral lessons and good citizenship. Children often memorized verses like these:

> "'Tis a lesson you should heed,
> Try, try again;
> If at first you don't succeed,
> Try, try again. . . ."

READING CHECK
What were schools like in the early 1900s?

LESSON PLAN

Focus Explain that as the United States became more industrialized and urbanized after the Civil War, education became more important.

Instruct Discuss the expansion of education after the Civil War. What was the result of compulsory school laws? How did education encourage immigrants to assimilate? Who benefited from increased opportunities for higher education?

   Ask students to analyze the impact of educational expansion on African Americans, on women, and on American society as a whole. How did Booker T. Washington's and W.E.B. Du Bois's approaches toward education for African Americans differ?

Assess/Reteach Have students discuss the types of changes that would result in a society in which education gradually, but steadily, became available to a wider variety of people.

READING CHECK
Many schools had only one room and one teacher with older students helping the younger ones. There were a growing number of city schools that were larger, however. Discipline was often imposed with physical force, and attendance was mandatory in most states for school-age children.

CUSTOMIZE FOR ...

ESL

Write the words *public education, literacy,* and *assimilation* on the chalkboard. Have volunteers define the words. Make sure that all students understand what they mean. Then lead a discussion about the importance of public education for literacy and the importance of literacy for assimilation. Encourage students to speak from their own experience.

Public school teachers taught their students about American standards of the times, such as thrift, patriotism, and hard work. Students also learned how to cook traditional American foods and play American games such as baseball. As a result of their schooling, many immigrant children became Americanized.

Some immigrants resisted Americanization. Fearing that their children would forget their heritage, many parents sent them to religious schools where they could learn their own cultural traditions in their native languages. For example, Polish parents in Chicago in the early 1900s sent their children to Roman Catholic schools. There, Polish history and religion were taught in Polish, while American history, bookkeeping, and algebra were taught in English.

Of course, the process of Americanization was not a one-way street. The contact between those born in America and newer immigrants, both in public schools and in the wider society, encouraged a constant sharing of cultural traditions that helped to enrich and redefine American culture itself.

Uneven Support for Schools Although state and local government support for education was expanding, not everyone benefited equally. Whites and African Americans usually attended separate schools, and the schools for African Americans received far less money. Writing of her upbringing in Durham, North Carolina, in the 1910s, civil rights activist Pauli Murray remembered the contrast between "what we had and what the white children had." She noted:

> 66 We got the greasy, torn, dog-eared books; they got the new ones. They had field day in the city park; we had it on a furrowed, stubby hillside. They got wide mention in the newspaper; we got a paragraph at the bottom. . . . We came to know that whatever we had was always inferior. 99
> —Pauli Murray

Mexican Americans in parts of the Southwest and many Asians in California were also sent to separate schools that received less funding than schools for white children. In 1900, only a small percentage of Native American children were receiving any formal schooling at all. The Native American boarding schools that did exist required students to live far from their families and forced them to give up their language, dress, customs, and culture.

Higher Education Expands

Between 1880 and 1900, more than 150 new American colleges and universities opened to train young people in the skills needed by a growing industrial economy. Wealthy Americans often endowed, or gave money or property to, institutions of higher learning. Leland Stanford, the entrepreneur who had helped build the transcontinental railroad, is one example. In 1885, he and his wife, Jane Lathrop Stanford, founded Stanford University in memory of their son. John D. Rockefeller and his philanthropic organizations made donations to the University of Chicago that eventually totaled more than $75 million.

With the opening of these new schools, college enrollment more than doubled between 1890 and 1910. Still, only a small percentage of Americans went to college. In the 1890s, annual family incomes averaged under a thousand

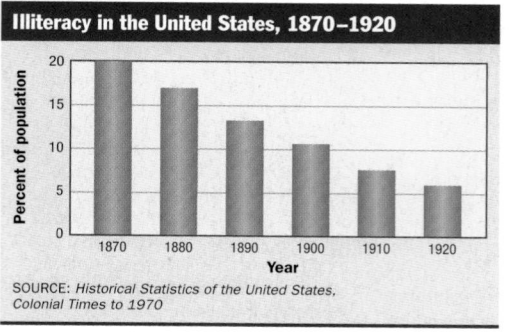

Illiteracy in the United States, 1870–1920

SOURCE: *Historical Statistics of the United States, Colonial Times to 1970*

INTERPRETING GRAPHS
This graph shows the percentage of Americans who were illiterate during a 50-year period. **Analyzing Information** *Describe the change in the illiteracy rate during this period? What effects do you think this change had on American society? Explain your answer.*

RULES FOR TEACHERS

1. Teachers each day will fill lamps, clean chimneys.
2. Each teacher will bring a bucket of water and a scuttle of coal for the day's session.
3. Make your pens carefully. You may whittle nibs to the individual taste of the pupils.
4. Men teachers may take one evening each week for courting purposes, or two evenings a week if they go to church regularly.
5. After ten hours in school, the teachers may spend the remaining time reading the Bible or other good books.
6. Women teachers who marry or engage in unseemly conduct will be dismissed.
7. Every teacher should lay aside from each day's pay a goodly sum of his earnings for his benefit during his declining years so that he will not become a burden on society.
8. The teacher who performs his labor faithfully and without fault for five years will be given an increase of twenty-five cents per week in his pay, providing the Board of Education approves.

VIEWING HISTORY These rules for teachers date from 1872. **Recognizing Ideologies** *(a) What do they reveal about society's view of teaching as a profession? (b) What do they suggest about society's view of men and of women?*

dollars, and parents were hard-pressed to meet college costs. A few gifted students did win scholarships or manage to work their way through college. By 1915, some middle-income families were beginning to send their children to college. The availability of advanced education for a large number of its citizens would come to distinguish the United States from other industrialized countries.

Women and Higher Education   After the Civil War, there was a call for greater educational opportunities for women. In response, educators and **philanthropists,** people who give donations to worthy causes, established private women's colleges with high academic standards. The first was New York's Vassar College, which opened in 1865.

In the 1880s and 1890s, there was increased pressure on men's colleges to admit women. Rather than do so, some schools founded separate institutions for women that were related to the men's schools. Harvard University in Massachusetts established Radcliffe College in 1879. Tulane University in Louisiana became the only major southern university to take this step when it opened Sophie Newcomb College in 1886. Shortly thereafter, Columbia University in New York founded Barnard, and Brown University in Rhode Island established Pembroke in 1891.

Opportunities for men and women to study together—coeducation—also increased. A number of religiously based colleges, including Oberlin, Knox, Antioch, Swarthmore, and Bates, had been coeducational since long before the Civil War. In the postwar years, they were joined by other institutions including Cornell University. In 1873, Boston University announced that it welcomed women not only as students but also as professors.

Because most scholarships went to men, women had a harder time obtaining a college education. Even those who could afford the cost faced society's prejudice against educating women. Many parents feared that college would make their daughters too independent or "unmarriageable," or that it would bring them in contact with unacceptable friends. When Martha "Minnie" Carey Thomas finally persuaded her Quaker father to allow her to take the Cornell University entrance exams, he said to her, "Well, Minnie, I am proud of thee, but this university is an awful place to swallow thee up." However, college life agreed with Thomas; she eventually became president of Bryn Mawr College in Pennsylvania.

Women also had to struggle to gain access to most state-funded institutions, and once they got there they often faced prejudice within the colleges. For example, in 1863 the University of Wisconsin was coeducational, but it did not treat women equally. For one thing, it required female students in a class to remain standing until all male students had found seats. After 1867, Wisconsin directed women into a "Female College." In 1873, however, when women refused to attend separate classes, the university was forced to reestablish coeducation.

African Americans and Higher Education
In spite of strong prejudice against their doing so, many African Americans also wanted to enroll in institutions of higher learning. Only a few of the nation's colleges,

Focus on
CULTURE

Public Libraries   In addition to endowing colleges, philanthropists also funded public libraries. Increased education and literacy meant that there was a wider audience for books. And the educated elite of the time believed that exposing working people to the best that had been thought and written in the world would help to make them better citizens. In some states, legislation established libraries. But many public libraries were started by private individuals, such as Andrew Carnegie, who spent roughly $40 million to help fund libraries in about 1,400 communities across the country. Free to all, the American public library provided another means of self-help for those who wanted to share in the American success story.

VIEWING HISTORY The women in this 1880 Smith College chemistry class were among the first to benefit from new opportunities for higher education. **Drawing Conclusions** *Do you think these women would have had as much of an opportunity to study science in a coeducational college? Explain your answer.*

ACTIVITY
Connecting with Economics

Have students research the cost of a college education around the turn of the twentieth century. Suggest that students obtain information about tuition at private colleges, such as Harvard University or the University of Chicago, as well as at public institutions, such as a state university. Then have students investigate the current cost of a college education and make a graph showing the relationship between average income and college tuition at the turn of the century and now. (**Logical/Mathematical**)

BACKGROUND
Biography

Martha Carey Thomas (1857–1935) was relentless in her pursuit of education. After graduating from Cornell University, Thomas did graduate work at Johns Hopkins University in Baltimore, her hometown. She studied at the University of Leipzig for three years but was refused a degree because she was a woman. Thomas went on to the University of Zurich, from where she received her Ph.D. summa cum laude in 1882. She spent a year studying at the Sorbonne in Paris, then returned to the United States. In 1884 Thomas became an English professor and dean at Bryn Mawr College for women. In addition to her dedication to women's education, Thomas was a devoted suffragist and an early supporter of the equal rights amendment to the U.S. Constitution.

CAPTION ANSWERS

Viewing History Sample answer: No. They would probably have been discouraged from such rigorous studies, and men would have been given precedence in science courses.

✔ TEST PREPARATION

Have students read the passage on the previous page by Pauli Murray and then complete the sentence below.

The main point of the passage is that—

A she disliked torn, greasy books.

B she resented not being in the newspaper more often.

C she felt that black children were made to feel inferior by how they were treated.

D she was sent to school during segregation.

including Oberlin, Bates, and Bowdoin, accepted blacks. In 1890, only 160 African Americans were attending white colleges.

Many more were studying at the nation's African American institutions. During Reconstruction, a number of black colleges, including Atlanta University, Fisk University, Hampton Institute, and Howard University, had been founded through the efforts of the American Missionary Association and the Freedmen's Bureau. The nation's oldest private African American school, Wilberforce University, had been incorporated even before the Civil War, in 1856. These schools provided an opportunity for blacks to become doctors and lawyers and educators. By 1900, more than 2,000 students had graduated from 34 African American colleges.

Schools founded for African Americans after the Civil War generally accepted women as well as men. The number of women attending remained small, however, because most of the scholarships went to male students. Anna Julia Cooper, an Oberlin graduate who later became an educator, estimated that there were only 30 black women studying in American colleges in 1891.

Two Perspectives on African American Education Among the African American college graduates of this era were Booker T. Washington and W.E.B. Du Bois. They both became educators, but they had different opinions on the kind of education that would best serve African Americans.

Booker T. Washington dedicated his life to a school for African Americans, Tuskegee Institute, which he founded in Alabama in 1881. Washington taught his students the skills and attitudes that he thought would help them succeed in American society. He told them to put aside their desire for political equality for now and instead to focus on building economic security by gaining vocational skills. Washington urged his students to prepare for productive, profitable work and to bring their intellect "to bear upon the everyday practical things of life, upon something that is needed to be done, and something which they will be permitted to do in the community in which they reside." African Americans could win white acceptance eventually, he predicted, by succeeding economically.

Washington spelled out his ideas in a speech he delivered in 1895 at the Atlanta Exposition:

> 66 To those of my race who depend on bettering their condition . . . I would say: 'Cast down your bucket where you are'—cast it down . . . in agriculture, mechanics, in commerce, in domestic service, and in the professions. . . . No race can prosper till it learns that there is as much dignity in tilling a field as in writing a poem. 99
>
> —Booker T. Washington

In addition to appealing to many African Americans, Washington's ideas reassured those whites who worried that educated African Americans would seek more equality within society. Whites began to consult Washington on many issues concerning race relations, and President Theodore Roosevelt invited him to the White House in 1901. Booker T. Washington's autobiography, *Up From Slavery* (1901), became a classic, and he became an influential force in the African American community.

BIOGRAPHY

Although famous as an educator, Booker T. Washington had no formal schooling during his childhood. Even after their emancipation from slavery, his family was too poor to send him to school. Instead, at the age of 9, Washington went to work in a salt furnace, and then in a coal mine, but he never gave up his desire for an education. In 1872, Washington began working as a janitor to pay his way through the Hampton Normal and Agricultural Institute. After graduating, he became a teacher. Then Washington was given a huge opportunity—and a huge challenge. In 1881, he became the head of a new African American normal school. When it opened, the Tuskegee Institute had only two ramshackle buildings and almost no funds. It became Washington's life's work. When he died, Tuskegee was a respected institution with a large campus, more than 1,500 students, and an endowment of over $2 million.

Booker T. Washington 1856–1915

Sounds of an Era

Listen to Booker T. Washington's speech and other sounds from the turn of the twentieth century.

W.E.B. Du Bois led the next generation of African Americans in a different direction. Born in Massachusetts, Du Bois graduated from Fisk University and in 1895 became the first African American to earn a Ph.D. from Harvard.

Du Bois rejected Washington's message, which he mockingly called the Atlanta Compromise. Instead, Du Bois argued that the brightest African Americans had to step forward to lead their people in their quest for political and social equality and civil rights. He urged those future leaders to seek an advanced liberal arts education rather than the vocational education that Washington was promoting. Only when they had developed "intelligence, broad sympathy, knowledge of the world that was and is, and of the relation of men to it," he wrote, would they be equipped to lead "the Negro race."

In an essay published in the 1903 book *The Negro Problem*, Du Bois wrote:

> 66 *I insist that the true object of all true education is not to make men carpenters, it is to make carpenters men. . . . The Talented Tenth of the Negro race must be made leaders of thought and missionaries of culture among their people. No others can do this work and Negro colleges must train men for it.* 99
>
> — W.E.B. Du Bois

VIEWING HISTORY The scholar and activist W.E.B. Du Bois is shown here in his NAACP office. **Synthesizing Information** *Briefly explain how Du Bois's views differed from those of Booker T. Washington.*

In writings such as *The Souls of Black Folk*, Du Bois urged blacks not to define themselves as whites saw them. Instead, he insisted that they take pride in both their African and their American heritages.

In 1905, Du Bois helped found the **Niagara Movement**, a group of African Americans that called for full civil liberties, an end to racial discrimination, and recognition of human brotherhood. Five years later, he left his teaching post at Atlanta University to work as publications director at the National Association for the Advancement of Colored People (Section 3). Du Bois would remain associated with the NAACP for many years, becoming one of the best-known black leaders of the first half of the twentieth century.

Section 1 Assessment

READING COMPREHENSION

1. What is **literacy**?

2. How did public schools help with the **assimilation** of new immigrants?

3. Describe how one **philanthropist** contributed to higher education.

4. How did educational opportunities for women change at this time?

5. What was the **Niagara Movement**?

CRITICAL THINKING AND WRITING

6. **Making Comparisons** Compare and contrast the educational goals and opportunities for immigrants and African Americans at the turn of the century.

7. **Writing a Speech** It is 1900, and your town wants to raise taxes to improve town schools. Take a position either for or against the plan, and write the introduction to a speech to give at the town meeting.

 Take It to the NET

Activity: Creating a Debate Dialogue Read more about both W.E.B. Du Bois and Booker T. Washington. Write a debate they might have had about the best way for African Americans to achieve equality. Use the links provided in the *America: Pathways to the Present* area of the following Web site for help in completing this activity.
www.phschool.com

Section 1 Assessment

Reading Comprehension

1. The ability to read and write.

2. Students were taught English, American values, traditional American cooking, and American games.

3. Possible answers: Leland Stanford and the founding of Stanford University; John D. Rockefeller and his donations to the University of Chicago.

4. Coeducational opportunities increased; private women's colleges were founded; men's colleges were pressured to admit women; institutions for women were established within some male colleges and universities.

5. It was a group of African Americans calling for full civil liberties and denouncing all forms of discrimination.

Critical Thinking and Writing

6. Answers might include: that both groups wanted to attain literacy. However, inequality resulted from African Americans attending separate schools while European immigrants attended white public schools.

7. Speeches will vary, but should persuade the reader with facts from the section and focus on whether or not public education is a worthwhile investment for the community.

 **Take It to the NET**

Students should demonstrate knowledge of both men's points of view on African American education: Washington advocated concentrating on vocational skills to further their position through success and wealth; Du Bois encouraged studying politics and the liberal arts to become social leaders.

CAPTION ANSWERS

Viewing History Booker T. Washington felt African Americans should put off their demands for equality and seek a vocational education to prepare them for a trade. Du Bois demanded equality now and advocated the creation of a highly educated African American elite who could be the leaders of African American society.

ANALYZING POLITICAL CARTOONS FOR POINT OF VIEW

Focus Students learn to analyze a political cartoon as historical evidence of ideas and attitudes about a past event.

Instruct Explain to students that one way of gaining insight into the views of a society of a bygone era is by studying political cartoons created in that era. Political cartoons, though prone to bias, often offer an inside perspective on past events not available from reading secondary sources. Post examples of present-day political cartoons, and ask students to analyze them using the techniques described in the activity.

Extend See the Skills for Life activity in the Resource Directory below.

ANSWERS

PRACTICE THE SKILL

1. **(a)** She is a teacher. **(b)** He represents most men, who are happy to see a woman teaching school. **(c)** She is petitioning for suffrage, or the right to vote. **(d)** The man is opposed to her petition.

2. **(a)** Yes. **(b)** No. **(c)** Possible answer: In the first panel, the woman is teaching a classroom of children, which the man approves of. In the second panel, the woman is petitioning for the right to vote, but the man rejects her ideas.

3. **(a)** Women's right to vote. **(b)** The cartoonist implies that the man is hypocritical to be praising the woman for holding a job and guiding the development of the next generation (including boys), but to be angry with her for demanding the right to vote. **(c)** The man in the cartoon has the more typical viewpoint. **(d)** The cartoonist appears to support the woman's demand for suffrage. It is likely that the cartoon was not that effective at the time, as most people in society shared the man's point of view.

Analyzing Political Cartoons for Point of View

Political cartoons can tell you a great deal about the past. Political cartoonists try to influence public opinion about issues by exaggerating or highlighting certain details about the facts. A cartoon can often make a point more strongly than words alone. When you look at a political cartoon from the past, however, it is important to remember that there were different points of view when the event took place. To analyze the cartoon, be sure to consider the cartoonist's frame of reference—the place, time, and circumstances when the cartoon was created.

"The woman question" provided a wealth of material for cartoonists at the turn of the last century. The cartoon below was published early in the 1900s.

LEARN THE SKILL
Use the following steps to analyze a political cartoon for point of view:

1. **Identify the symbols used in the cartoon.** Cartoons often use visual images that stand for some other idea or event. For example, a heart is a commonly used symbol for love. A dove is a symbol for peace.

2. **Analyze the meaning of the symbols and words.** Use what you already know about the historical period and the cartoon itself to decide what the symbols refer to and how they are used as shorthand to represent actions or ideas. Summarize what is happening in the cartoon in your own words.

3. **Interpret the cartoon.** Determine what the cartoonist is saying about the political issue. Consider the cartoonist's frame of reference, and compare the cartoonist's representation with other opinions of the time and with the facts. Finally, draw conclusions about the cartoonist's point of view.

APPLY THE SKILL
See the Chapter Review and Assessment for another opportunity to apply this skill.

PRACTICE THE SKILL
Answer the following questions:

1. **(a)** In the left panel, what job is the woman doing? **(b)** What does the man represent, and what is his reaction to what the woman is doing? **(c)** In the right panel, what is the woman doing? **(d)** What is the man's reaction?

2. **(a)** In the early 1900s, would women have been likely to do the job shown in the left panel? **(b)** Would women have been likely to do what is shown in the right panel? **(c)** Summarize the action in the two panels; be sure to include the man's reaction.

3. **(a)** What political issue is the cartoon about? **(b)** What point is the cartoonist making by showing the man's two reactions side by side? **(c)** Which point of view—the man's or the cartoonist's—is more typical of the early 1900s? Explain. **(d)** What action is the cartoonist advocating? Do you think the cartoon was effective at the time? Explain.

RESOURCE DIRECTORY

Teaching Resources
Skills for Life booklet, p. 18

Technology
Social Studies Skills Tutor CD-ROM
Interactive Practice in
• Geographic Literacy
• Critical Thinking and Reading
• Visual Analysis
• Communications

READING FOCUS

- What new kinds of performances and recreation did Americans enjoy at the turn of the century?
- What were people reading for information and entertainment?
- How was American music changing?

MAIN IDEA

Americans flocked to new forms of entertainment, sports, and music during the period from the late 1880s to 1915.

KEY TERMS

vaudeville
yellow journalism
ragtime

TAKING NOTES

Copy the chart below. As you read, add types of entertainment to the first column, and details to the other two columns.

Type of Entertainment	How It Developed	Why People Enjoyed It
• Vaudeville	• Grew out of minstrel shows	• Inexpensive
•	•	• Lots of variety
•	•	•

SECTION OBJECTIVES

1. Discover the new kinds of performances and recreation that Americans enjoyed at the turn of the century.
2. Find out what people were reading for education and entertainment.
3. Learn how American music was changing.

BELLRINGER

Warm-Up Activity Ask students how they like to entertain themselves during their free time. Ask them if they spend money on entertainment.

Activating Prior Knowledge Ask students what they know about the history of such popular American pastimes as baseball, basketball, visiting amusement parks, and going to movies. Do they know how long such amusements have been popular?

READING STRATEGY

As students read the section, have them take notes to help analyze the relationship between culture and economy in the late nineteenth century. What impact did leisure activities have on the U.S. economy?

Setting the Scene You can probably hum the following song, even though it was written in 1908. It has been baseball's "anthem" since that time, and is still sung at the seventh-inning stretch in ballparks today. But "Take Me Out to the Ballgame" also captures the spirit of the turn of the twentieth century in America.

> 66 *Take me out to the ball game*
> *Take me out with the crowd*
> *Buy me some peanuts and Cracker Jack*
> *I don't care if I never get back . . .* 99
> —Jack Norworth

Many of the changes occurring in America at that time are reflected in this verse: more leisure time for working people, more money to spend on entertainment, the craze for sports, the introduction of snack foods, and a spirit of fun. The United States was becoming a more urban nation, and city dwellers began looking for entertainment in their own neighborhoods, as well as for recreation away from the dirty, crowded streets where they lived and worked. These factors would fuel a whole new commercial recreation industry designed to supply inexpensive entertainment for all Americans.

Performances and Recreation

Many kinds of performances attracted audiences at this time. They ranged from live theater to a new medium: the moving picture show, or the "movies."

Vaudeville and Minstrel Shows The most popular kind of live theatrical performance was **vaudeville,** a type of inexpensive variety show that first appeared in the 1870s. Vaudeville performances consisted of comic sketches based on ethnic or racial humor; song-and-dance routines; magic acts; and performances by ventriloquists, jugglers, and animals. In 1899, the actor Edwin Milton Royle wrote, "The vaudeville theatre is an American invention. There is nothing like it anywhere else in the world." Although early vaudeville was

By 1898, baseball had become the American pastime. From 1891 to 1899, there was one professional league, with teams from Boston to St. Louis. The ball and glove shown above commemorate an 1899 college game.

RESOURCE DIRECTORY

Teaching Resources
Learning Styles Lesson Plans booklet, p. 34
Guided Reading and Review booklet, p. 67
Biography, Literature, and Comparing Primary Sources booklet (Biography) *George M. Cohan,* p. 21

Technology
Section Reading Support Transparencies
Guided Reading Audiotapes (English/Spanish), Ch. 16
Student Edition on Audio CD, Ch. 16

Sounds of an Era Audio CD *"Mr. Moonman, Turn Out Your Light"* (time: 45 seconds)

RESOURCE PRO® **Critical Thinking Activity** *Recognizing Cause and Effect: America's Game,* found on Resource Pro, focuses on the development of American baseball to help students apply the skill.
Prentice Hall Presentation Pro CD-ROM, Ch. 16
Companion Web site, www.phschool.com

Focus Explain that urbanization and industrialization brought in their wake a new commercial entertainment industry. Ask students what the new forms of amusement were in the late 1800s. Did men and women prefer different forms of entertainment?

Instruct Discuss the kinds of popular amusements that emerged in the late 1800s. Ask what part sports played in mass entertainment. What was the influence of African American art on popular entertainment?

Assess/Reteach Have students list the forms of entertainment that were popular in the United States in the years between 1880 and 1915. Which of those amusements are still popular today?

ACTIVITY

Connecting with Culture

Many well-known American entertainers got their start in vaudeville. Have students research the early careers of W. C. Fields, Charlie Chaplin, Will Rogers, Lillian Russell, or another star who began in vaudeville for a description of the performer's act. Have students identify the impact of these popular performers on Americans and on the rest of the world. Then have students write and perform a skit based on their chosen performer's act. **(Verbal/Linguistic; Kinesthetic; Musical/Rhythmic)**

Focus on TECHNOLOGY

Snapshots Although professional photographers had been taking portraits for decades, it was not until the 1880s that ordinary people could become their own family photographers—and the snapshot was born. In 1888, George Eastman marketed a handheld camera that he had developed. The Kodak was so easy to use that its motto was, "You press the button—We do the rest." "The rest" included developing the film when the camera was sent to the company, and then returning the camera reloaded and ready to take more pictures. However, at $25 the Kodak was expensive. In 1900, Eastman came out with a new and even simpler camera called the Brownie (below right). It was marketed to children and cost only one dollar. Families all over America began snapping pictures of each other, and the family snapshot album became a staple of American culture.

geared to male spectators, the shows soon sought a wider audience and presented themselves as family entertainment.

One of the sources of vaudeville was the minstrel show. A popular form of entertainment from the 1840s, minstrel shows began to die out as vaudeville gained popularity. Minstrel shows featured white actors in "blackface" (exaggerated make-up caricaturing African Americans). The shows perpetuated racial stereotypes with exaggerated imitations of African American music, dance, and humor. Nevertheless, black performers—also wearing blackface—sometimes performed in minstrel shows, as these were often the only stage jobs they could get. Once they were able to, many African American performers switched to vaudeville.

Movies As the twentieth century began, vaudeville started getting competition from the movies. *The Great Train Robbery*, released in 1903, was a huge success and clearly demonstrated that profits could be made from movies. By 1908, the nation had 8,000 nickelodeons—theaters set up in converted stores or warehouses that charged a nickel admission. They showed short slapstick comedies and other films to as many as 200,000 people a day.

Improving technology and the increasing popularity of films led to longer, better movies and to bigger, more elaborate movie houses. Full-length dramas featured new stars such as Mary Pickford and Douglas Fairbanks. Charlie Chaplin began appearing in comedies. Early movies were silent and often accompanied by a live piano player. Soon audiences flocked to new movie palaces with names like The Empress and The Riviera, which often had full orchestras to accompany their films.

The Circus While circuses have a long history, it was the introduction of the circus train in 1872 that made the annual visit of the circus an anticipated event all over America. First, "advance men" arrived in a town to promote the performances. They often recruited young boys to hand out printed advertisements. Several days later, the circus train pulled in, and the big top went up. This was a show in itself, and hundreds of people often gathered to watch. Then the circus parade kicked off, and all the circus acts and performers marched through town to great fanfare. After the parade and advertising created great anticipation, the paid performances were held. At the turn of the century, there was hardly a town or a city in America where a youngster did not dream of running away to join the circus.

Amusement Parks The technology of the trolley—and the trolley lines themselves—led to the development of amusement parks. A similar technology helped to create their main attractions: mechanical rides like the steeplechase, the Ferris wheel, and the roller coaster.

As trolley lines were extended from the central cities out to less populated areas, "trolley parks" began to spring up at the end of the lines. Although many people still worked ten hours a day, a half-holiday on Saturday was becoming more common. Transportation companies encouraged ridership on weekends, and the inexpensive excursion from the city to an amusement park was just what the public wanted. These parks often featured music, games of skill, vaudeville productions, bathing beaches, and exciting rides. The business of the amusement park, according to the manager of Coney Island's Luna Park, was "the business of amusing the million."

Sports   Another way "the million" were amused was by watching or participating in sports. While many enjoyed the spectator sports of boxing and horse racing, baseball was by far the most popular.

By 1860, groups such as firefighters, police officers, and teachers had formed baseball clubs in many American cities. When it became clear that there were large audiences for these games, entrepreneurs enclosed fields and charged admission. Teams formed leagues and began to play championship games. In 1869, the first true professional team, the Cincinnati Red Stockings, was formed. By the 1870s, the sport's best players were being paid. What Americans loved most about baseball was the speed, daring, and split-second timing of the game. Mark Twain called baseball "the very symbol, the outward and visible expression of the drive and push and rush and struggle of the raging, tearing, booming nineteenth century."

Two other games captured the interest of Americans during the late 1800s. Football emerged as a popular American sport when Walter Camp began adapting the European game of rugby during the 1880s. Basketball, the only major sport of exclusively American origin, was invented in 1891 by a physical education teacher, Dr. James Naismith of Springfield, Massachusetts, to keep athletes fit during winter.

Women also participated enthusiastically in many sports. When a bicycling fad swept the nation in the late 1800s, women joined in. Whether women were riding "bicycles built for two" or the new safety bicycles deemed suitable for female riders, the sport required practical clothing. Women athletes abandoned corsets, which wrapped tightly around their torsos and restricted their breathing. Women's involvement in sports also led to the popularity and acceptance of shirtwaists (ready-made blouses) that were tucked into shorter or split skirts.

Female college students also began playing basketball. However, recreation specialists thought that stiff competition and hard physical exertion were unhealthy for women, so they devised less demanding "women's rules." Ice-skating had long been a favorite recreation for women. Now they also played tennis, learned gymnastics, and swam, although society's strict dress codes required women to wear black cotton stockings under short dresses or bloomers.

What People Were Reading

The increase in education that you read about in the last section meant that reading for entertainment became a popular pastime for many Americans. Writers and publishers were quick to take advantage of this new, larger audience.

Newspapers   For generations, newspapers had been a vital source of information for city dwellers. In the late 1800s, they became a popular form of entertainment as well. Taking advantage of new typesetting machinery that allowed printers to set whole lines of type quickly, publishers created larger and more interesting publications. They introduced new features, such as comics, sports sections, Sunday editions, women's pages, stories "hot off the wires," and graphic pictures.

Between 1870 and 1900, newspaper circulation soared from 2.6 to 15.1 million copies a day. Because of heated competition, publishers urged their reporters to discover lurid details of murders, vice, and scandal—anything to sell more papers. Such sensational news coverage came to be called **yellow journalism,** a reference to the yellow ink used in a popular comic strip of the era.

Hungarian-born Joseph Pulitzer, who owned the *St. Louis Post-Dispatch* and the *New York World*, said his purpose was to "expose all fraud and sham,

VIEWING HISTORY Coney Island, the most spectacular of the turn-of-the-century amusement parks, was really three parks along the beach in Brooklyn, New York. By 1900, it had tens of thousands of visitors every day. **Drawing Conclusions** *How does this 1904 guidebook help explain Coney Island's appeal?*

Connecting with Culture

Tell students to research the origin of a professional sports team in your area. Have students find out when the team was formed, where the team plays, how much money players earn, and how much community support the team receives. Then have students present an oral report on their findings. If possible, students should supply visuals, such as photographs and newspaper accounts. (**Verbal/Linguistic**)

BACKGROUND

Biography

The game of basketball was invented in 1891 by Canadian American James A. Naismith (1861–1939). As head of the physical education department at Springfield College in Massachusetts, Naismith was asked to devise a safe, indoor game for play during the cold winter months. Blending aspects of soccer, field hockey, football, and other sports, and removing (in theory) physical contact, Naismith invented a basketball game for nine players on each side. He coached the game at the University of Kansas, Lawrence, until 1908.

READING CHECK

They introduced spirituals to white audiences and earned enough money to save Fisk University.

Focus on
ECONOMICS

The Newsboys' Strike "Extra! Extra!" and "Hot off the presses!" These were the cries of "newsies," the children who sold newspapers at the turn of the century. Aged 8 to 15, newsies were independent business persons. They bought their papers from the publishers and sold them at a small profit, but they could not get refunds on unsold papers. Marketing their papers aggressively, newsies vied with each other for the best street corners.

In 1899, New York newspaper sales were slowing. Hearst and Pulitzer feared that raising prices would cause them to lose customers—so they raised the cost to the newsies instead, cutting into their profits. Newsboys insisted that the *Journal* and the *World* roll back the increase. When the publishers refused, the newsboys boycotted their papers. Circulation went way down. After two weeks, the newsboys won a partial victory: the increase remained but unsold papers would now be refunded.

READING CHECK
What were the accomplishments of the Fisk Jubilee Singers?

---

fight all public evils and abuses." Californian William Randolph Hearst used his father's gold-mining millions to put out the even more sensational *New York Journal*. While popular with many readers, yellow journalism troubled some observers. Critics charged that the "yellow press" intruded into private lives, invented facts, and sensationalized ordinary events by exaggerating them.

Magazines   In 1879, Congress passed a law lowering the postal rates for periodicals. One result was the increased circulation and popularity of magazines, such as *McClure's*, *Cosmopolitan*, and *Munsey's*. Magazines appeared weekly or monthly and contained helpful articles, advertising, and fiction.

Many of the popular magazines of this era featured stories appealing to the average American's desire and determination to succeed. In many of Horatio Alger's stories, for example, the main character embodies the American dream of rising from "rags to riches" through cheerfulness, honesty, and hard work. Stories of this kind reminded the working poor of the seemingly boundless opportunities available to them in the nation's industrial cities.

Popular Fiction   Rags-to-riches stories as well as adventure yarns also appeared as "dime novels," inexpensive books with a wide readership. More educated readers turned instead to serious novels by such writers as Henry James and Edith Wharton and to the social protest novels of Upton Sinclair and other reformers. Even the humorist Mark Twain satirized the attitudes and practices of the time in his popular novels, such as the classic *The Adventures of Huckleberry Finn* (1884).

Huck Finn was also an example of local color, a type of writing that describes the people and places of particular regions of the United States in accurate detail. In an author's note at the beginning of *Huck Finn*, Twain explains that seven different dialects used in the book have been written "pain-stakingly, and with the trustworthy guidance and support of personal familiarity with these several forms of speech." Local color writers satisfied their audience's hunger for information about distant parts of the country. For example, Sarah Orne Jewett depicted the people of Maine and many of New England's disappearing traditions, Bret Harte captured the excitement of the California Gold Rush, and Willa Cather described life on the Great Plains.

Musical Diversions

Music was an important part of life in the late 1800s. People went to concerts, operettas, and dances, or gathered around the piano at home. But this era also saw important changes that would influence American music forever.

The Negro Spiritual   One series of concerts in 1871 helped make American music more inclusive by introducing African American religious folk songs called spirituals to white audiences. These concerts also helped save a struggling black university from financial ruin. When Fisk University found itself deeply in debt in 1871, the school's music teacher organized a highly successful fundraising concert tour featuring nine gifted students. The Fisk Jubilee Singers, all of whom had been slaves or were the children of former slaves, toured the United States, England, and Europe—and eventually raised $150,000 to secure their school's future.

In the process of making the Negro spiritual acceptable to white audiences, the Jubilee Singers and similar groups transformed the musical form. It acquired

---

RESOURCE DIRECTORY

Teaching Resources
Units 5/6 booklet
• Section 2 Quiz, p. 38
Guide to the Essentials
• Section 2 Summary, p. 84
Biography, Literature, and Comparing Primary Sources booklet (Literature) *Around the World in 72 Days*, p. 62

Technology
Sounds of an Era Audio CD *"Maple Leaf Rag,"* 1916 recording (time: one minute); *"Florida Rag,"* 1907 recording (time: one minute)

characteristics of the European musical tradition with which whites were familiar. This new spiritual became identified as an American art form, as opposed to a purely African American one.

Ragtime and Jazz **Ragtime** originated among black musicians in the South and Midwest in the 1880s. This infectious music featured melodies with shifting accents over a steady, marching-band beat. In 1899, composer and piano player Scott Joplin wrote "Maple Leaf Rag," which was recorded in 1903. It became a huge hit, and ragtime became a rage all across the country.

Jazz grew out of the vibrant musical culture of New Orleans, a city with a heritage that included African, Spanish, French, and Latin American influences. The city also had a popular marching-band tradition. After the Civil War, African American bands experimented with new styles, such as "raggy" rhythms and a style based on the call-and-response patterns of some church services. These bands also played jazzed-up versions of familiar melodies, such as hymns or the mournful "blues" songs of Southern slaves and sharecroppers. New Orleans jazz styles slowly worked their way northward through towns along the Mississippi River. By 1915, thanks in part to the success of the phonograph, jazz and the dances associated with it were becoming a national passion.

Music at Home While African American influences were beginning to enrich American music, two new ways of enjoying music at home appeared on the scene. Both allowed people access to music without having to produce it themselves. In the player piano, a paper roll was "played" by wooden "fingers" to reproduce the music recorded on the roll. Foot pedals activated the machine, requiring no skill on the part of the human player. The phonograph was invented in 1877 by Thomas Edison, and was selling at a rate of more than 500,000 per year by 1914.

These two technological advances allowed new musical styles to spread quickly, thus creating nationwide hits and stars. And the popularity of the phonograph signaled the birth of the music business that is so important to America's culture and economy today.

VIEWING HISTORY This painting of the Jubilee Singers by a British artist is on view at Fisk University. **Making Inferences** *Why do you think the group chose to be painted in formal clothing and posed against a classical backdrop?*

Section 2 Assessment

READING COMPREHENSION

1. What was **vaudeville,** and why did it become popular?
2. How did movies change during this period?
3. What was the most popular spectator sport at this time?
4. What was **yellow journalism?**
5. Describe **ragtime** music.

CRITICAL THINKING AND WRITING

6. **Drawing Inferences** What role do you think compulsory education played in creating a larger market for newspapers and magazines?
7. **Writing to Explain** Briefly explain how the growth of cities led to the growth of entertainment and recreation.

Take It to the NET

Activity: Drawing a Cartoon
Read more about baseball or basketball in the late 1800s, and draw a cartoon about the sport. Use the links provided in the *America: Pathways to the Present* area of the following Web site for help in completing this activity.
www.phschool.com

Chapter 16 • Section 2 **563**

Section 2 Assessment

Reading Comprehension

1. Vaudeville was a type of live variety show with comedy, magicians, song-and-dance routines, ventriloquists, jugglers, and animals. It appealed to an increasingly urban nation, where city dwellers sought affordable, local, mass entertainment.
2. Improving technology allowed longer, better movies to be made. Movies were often accompanied by small orchestras rather than by a single piano.
3. Baseball.
4. Sensational news coverage focusing on lurid details of murders, vice, and scandal.
5. Ragtime mixed shifting melodies with marching-band beats.

Critical Thinking and Writing

6. Sample answer: Increased literacy expanded the demand for magazines and newspapers.
7. Answers might point out that urban workers were gaining more leisure time and that the entertainment industry grew to cater to city customers who had more money to spend.

Take It to the NET

Cartoons will vary, but might show the uniforms and equipment used at the time.

CAPTION ANSWERS

Viewing History Answers will vary, but students may note that it was probably important to the group to be taken seriously and to have their music taken as seriously as was classical music from the European tradition.

READING FOCUS

- How were African Americans discriminated against after Reconstruction?
- How did African Americans resist this discrimination?

MAIN IDEA

African Americans found their hopes of equality dashed after Reconstruction by white attitudes, customs, and the law. Yet many blacks not only resisted discrimination but achieved success in spite of it.

KEY TERMS

poll tax
grandfather clause
segregation
Jim Crow
Plessy v. *Ferguson*
lynching
National Association for the Advancement of Colored People (NAACP)

TAKING NOTES

Copy the web diagram below. As you read, fill in the circles with examples of discrimination against African Americans and with examples of how blacks resisted discrimination.

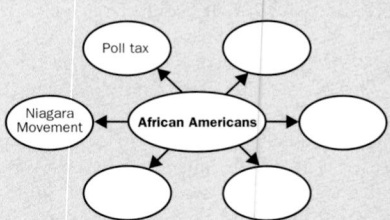

Setting the Scene Within a few years after the end of Reconstruction in the 1870s, African Americans began to see many of their newly won freedoms disappear. In the South, black Americans were prevented from voting and were subjected to repressive laws and intimidating violence. It did not take young African Americans long to recognize their inferior status in Southern society. Albon Holsey, who was a teenager in the first decade of the twentieth century, later recalled:

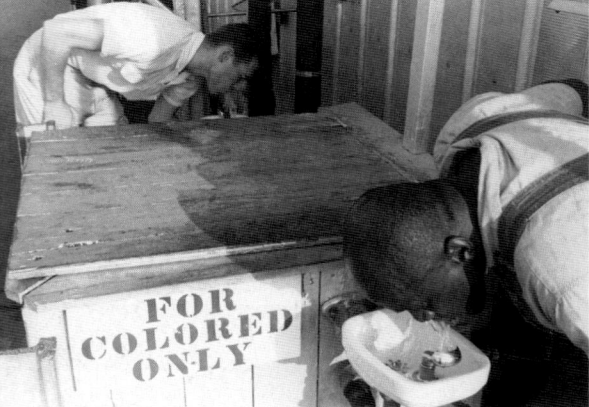

66 *At fifteen, I was fully conscious of the racial difference. . . . I knew then that I could never aspire to be President of the United States, nor Governor of my State, nor mayor of my city; I knew that the front door of white homes in my town were not for me to enter except as a servant; I knew that I could only sit in the peanut gallery at our theatre, and could only ride on the back seat of the electric car and in the Jim Crow car on the train. I had bumped into the color line. . . .* 99

—Albon Holsey

VIEWING HISTORY By the turn of the century, segregation was integral to life in the South. African American (then called *colored*) and white citizens had separate facilities, ranging from drinking fountains to public schools. **Making Inferences** *What effect do you think this separation had on both blacks and whites?*

Discrimination was also widespread in the North, but it was in the South that the color line was clearly drawn in all aspects of daily life. Nevertheless, in spite of the many obstacles placed in their path, African Americans at this time began to work together to fight discrimination and to become successful in spite of it.

Post-Reconstruction Discrimination

Booker T. Washington's belief that white Americans would be willing to accept hard-working African Americans as equal citizens was proving too optimistic.

Voting Restrictions	States										
	AL	AR	FL	GA	LA	MS	NC	SC	TN	TX	VA
Grandfather Clause	▣			▣	▣		▣				
Property Test	▣			▣	▣		▣				▣
Literacy Test	▣			▣	▣	▣	▣	▣			▣
Poll Tax	▣	▣	▣		▣	▣	▣	▣	▣	▣	▣

Voting Restrictions for African Americans in the South, 1889–1908

SOURCE: *The American Record: Images of the Nation's Past*

INTERPRETING CHARTS This chart shows how southern states tried to prevent African Americans from voting. **Analyzing Information** Which kind of restriction was used by the most states? Which states had the widest variety of voting restrictions?

Some southern whites, who in the past had used slavery to repress African Americans, now turned to other methods of oppression.

Voting Restrictions In many southern communities, whites were concerned that if African Americans were allowed to exercise their right to vote, they would gain too much political power. As a result, during the 1890s southern states began using several tactics to deny the vote to blacks. Some states required voters to own property or to pay a **poll tax,** a special fee that must be paid before a person was permitted to vote. Both of these requirements were beyond the financial reach of most African Americans. Voters also had to pass literacy tests. These tests were supposed to demonstrate that a voter could read, write, and meet minimum standards of knowledge. But, like the property requirement and the poll tax, literacy tests were really designed to keep African Americans from voting. In fact, blacks were often given much more difficult tests than whites.

To ensure that the literacy tests did not keep too many poor whites from voting, some states passed special laws with **grandfather clauses.** These laws exempted men from certain voting restrictions if they had already voted, or if they had ancestors (grandfathers) who had voted prior to blacks being granted suffrage. African Americans, of course, did not meet these qualifications and thus were required to take the literacy tests. All of these laws kept African Americans from voting while not singling out the group by name, which would have been unconstitutional.

Segregation During this period many states also instituted a system of legal **segregation.** This system ensured that African Americans were treated as second-class citizens. Segregation means separation of people by race. When this separation is the result of custom, it is called *de facto* segregation (meaning the condition exists in fact, but not in law). In the South, segregation was required by statutes called **Jim Crow** laws. The name came from a minstrel show routine called "Jump Jim Crow," in which a white entertainer in blackface and baggy clothes grinned broadly as he performed unflattering caricatures of African American song and dance.

Although segregation laws are usually associated with the South, they first appeared in the 1830s, when Massachusetts allowed railroad companies to separate black and white passengers. It was in the South,

INTERPRETING POLITICAL CARTOONS Literacy tests were designed to keep African Americans from voting. **Drawing Inferences** According to this cartoon, what unexpected results did these tests sometimes have?

"BY TH' WAY, WHAT'S THAT BIG WORD?"

VOTERS TAKE LITERACY TESTS HERE

Chapter 16 • Section 3   **565**

LESSON PLAN

Focus Tell students that although African Americans were free, white society found many ways to suppress them. Despite this, many reached high levels of achievement after Reconstruction. Ask in what ways white society denied African Americans their freedom.

Instruct Review discrimination after Reconstruction. Which tactics did whites use to legally prohibit African Americans from doing certain things, inhibiting them from exercising their full rights? Have students analyze the African American response to discrimination. How did "community" help them overcome discrimination?

Assess/Reteach Have students research ways in which late-nineteenth-century African Americans helped their people make progress in spite of society's obstacles.

ACTIVITY
Connecting with Government

Tell students to learn about the voting patterns of African Americans in the most recent presidential election. Have students look into whether certain issues drew voters to a particular candidate or party, and if so, what those issues were. **(Logical/Mathematical)**

CAPTION ANSWERS

Interpreting Charts All but one of these states used the poll tax. Alabama, Louisiana, and North Carolina had the widest variety of restrictions.

Interpreting Political Cartoons They exposed the fact that there were many illiterate whites who would themselves have failed literacy tests if they had had to take the same difficult tests that African Americans were forced to take.

Connecting with Economics

Many African Americans had done skilled work as slaves, but between 1865 and 1890, the number of southern blacks working in skilled areas dropped sharply. Tell students to research the kind of work that southern African Americans could find at the end of the nineteenth century. Have students look into the reasons that African Americans were allowed to do certain jobs, but not others. Then have students write a short report describing what they learned. (**Verbal/Linguistic**)

A Diverse Nation

African American demography has changed rapidly over the past century. In the mid-1870s more than 90 percent of all African Americans lived in the rural South. Today the major geographic centers of African American population are the rural South (about 15 percent), the urban South (more than 30 percent), and the urban Northeast, Midwest, and West (roughly 55 percent).

---

however, that Jim Crow became firmly established. These laws began appearing there a few years after the end of Reconstruction. By the early 1900s, Jim Crow laws dominated almost every aspect of southern daily life. They required the separation of blacks and whites in schools, parks, public buildings, hospitals, and on transportation systems. African Americans and whites were not allowed to use the same water fountains or public toilets. They could not sit in the same sections of theaters. Facilities designated for blacks were almost always inferior.

Plessy v. Ferguson At the end of the nineteenth century, the Supreme Court upheld many Jim Crow laws. In the *Civil Rights Cases* of 1883, the Court overturned the Civil Rights Act of 1875, which had guaranteed African American rights in public places. According to the Supreme Court, the Fourteenth Amendment did not give the federal government the power to prevent private organizations from discriminating against individuals.

Perhaps the greatest setback to African American equality came with the Supreme Court's establishment of the "separate-but-equal" doctrine in the case **Plessy v. Ferguson.** In this 1896 case, African American Homer Plessy argued that his right to "equal protection of the laws" was violated by a Louisiana law that required separate seating for white and black citizens on public railroads. In its decision, the Court held that segregation was legal as long as the separate facilities provided for blacks were equal to those provided to whites. The Fourteenth Amendment, the Court stated, was "not intended to give Negroes social equality but only political and civil equality." The "equal" part of the "separate-but-equal" ruling in *Plessy* proved hard to enforce, however, and African American schools and other facilities in the South were rarely if ever made equal.

Violence Forcing blacks to use separate but clearly unequal facilities and to attend inferior schools was a way to ensure that African Americans were aware of their inferior status in southern society. There were also other ways of keeping blacks "in their place." One was the system of customs or etiquette that required that blacks always show deference to whites. White men called adult African American men "boy" or by their first names but insisted that blacks address them as "mister" or "sir." Blacks had to remove their hats or step off the curb to let whites pass. Even small breaches of this racial etiquette could lead to serious trouble for African Americans, who could lose their jobs or even be subjected to violence.

The worst kind of violence against blacks was **lynching,** or the murder of an accused person by a mob without a lawful trial. An estimated 1,200 African Americans were lynched between 1882 and 1892. Sometimes the victims were suspected criminals. Often they had merely overstepped their status as second-class citizens or had shown too little respect to whites. Occasionally they were in financial competition with whites. After the African American owners of a Memphis, Tennessee, grocery store were lynched, Frederick Douglass said, "The men lynched at Memphis were murdered because they were prosperous."

The fact that lynchings sometimes included a mock trial shows that their purpose was partly to set an example that would intimidate other African Americans. To add to the fear, lynching victims were sometimes mutilated before being hanged and riddled with bullets. Those who carried out these horrors were rarely pursued or caught, much less punished. Although most lynchings

INTERPRETING CHARTS
Violence against African Americans was alarmingly frequent around the turn of the century. White mobs had killed more than 3,000 African Americans by the 1920s. **Drawing Conclusions** *In what timespan did the most lynchings occur? Why do you think lynchings peaked at that time and then tapered off?*

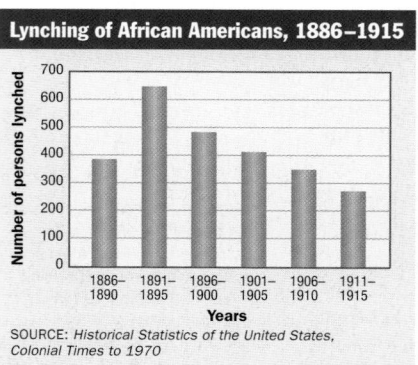

Lynching of African Americans, 1886–1915

SOURCE: *Historical Statistics of the United States, Colonial Times to 1970*

CAPTION ANSWERS

Interpreting Charts The greatest number of lynchings occurred between 1891 and 1895. Some African Americans were beginning to become financially successful. Whites began to fear financial competition and demands for social equality from blacks. Lynchings began to diminish after 1895. This decline was undoubtedly due, at least in part, to the vigorous anti-lynching crusade begun in 1892 by Ida B. Wells and others.

took place in the South, African Americans in the North were sometimes lynched as well.

Race Relations in the North   Although they realized that life in the North was not perfect, many African Americans moved there to escape violence and legal segregation. What they found instead was de facto discrimination—discrimination "in fact" instead of by law—in northern schools, housing, and employment.

As many African Americans moved to northern industrial cities, they began to compete with American-born whites and with recent immigrants for work. Whites' fears of racial equality—and of losing their jobs to blacks—erupted in the form of race riots in New York City in 1900 and in Springfield, Illinois, in 1908. The Springfield riot was touched off when authorities refused to release a black prisoner charged with rape to a crowd of whites. After learning that the prisoner had been secretly transferred to another city, a mob of several thousand whites attacked, looted, and burned black businesses and homes and killed two elderly African Americans. It took the Illinois state militia two days to restore order.

Resisting Discrimination

As conditions for African Americans deteriorated, black leaders began to seek new approaches to race problems. For example, Bishop Henry M. Turner of the African Methodist Episcopal church advocated black pride and emigration to Africa. Others still felt that blacks could succeed in the United States. Some criticized Booker T. Washington for his silence on such issues as lynching, but in fact Washington quietly supported legal cases against segregation and gave financial support for civil rights and black businesses.

As you read in Section 1, a number of outspoken African Americans came together under the leadership of W.E.B. Du Bois in 1905 to denounce all discrimination. Meeting in Niagara Falls, Ontario, Canada, they vowed never to accept "inferiority," bow to "oppression," or apologize "before insult." "We do not hesitate to complain, and to complain loudly and insistently," they warned. The Niagara Movement, as this group came to be called, gained only about 400 members and won few victories. After the 1908 Springfield race riot, however, its members joined with concerned white citizens to discuss solutions to the conflict between the races.

The NAACP and Civil Rights   Mary White Ovington, a white social worker who had worked in black neighborhoods, was among those concerned about race relations at this time. She helped organize a national conference on the "Negro Question" to be held on Lincoln's birthday in 1909. Leaders of the Niagara Movement attended. This event marked the founding of the interracial **National Association for the Advancement of Colored People (NAACP).** Its purpose was to abolish segregation and discrimination, to oppose racism, and to gain civil rights for African Americans.

By 1914, the NAACP had 50 branches and 6,000 members. Its magazine, *Crisis*, edited by Du Bois, reached more than 30,000 readers. The organization worked primarily through the courts. It won its first major victory when the Supreme Court declared grandfather clauses in voting laws unconstitutional in 1915. In the decades ahead, the NAACP would remain a vital force in the fight for civil rights.

Focus on CITIZENSHIP

Ida B. Wells's Anti-Lynching Crusade   The daughter of slaves, Ida B. Wells attended Fisk University and then became a teacher and a journalist. In 1884, she refused to leave a segregated first-class railroad car, and won a lawsuit against the railroad company for forcibly removing her from her seat. The Tennessee Supreme Court overturned that decision in 1887.

When three Memphis friends were lynched in 1892, Wells began an editorial campaign and speaking tour against lynching. Her newspaper office was destroyed. Fearing for her own safety, she moved to Chicago, where she married Ferdinand Barnett, a lawyer and the publisher of the *Chicago Conservator*. Wells-Barnett continued to write about lynching in the *Conservator* and in other publications. She also became active in civil rights groups, organizations for African American women, and the woman's suffrage movement. In 1989, Wells was featured on the postage stamp shown below.

READING CHECK
Describe the origin and accomplishments of the NAACP.

Reading Comprehension

1. African Americans often could not afford to pay the poll tax and were given more complex literacy tests than were whites. Grandfather clauses allowed illiterate white men to vote while excluding all African Americans.

2. Statutes that required segregation.

3. The murdering of an African American by white mob action without a lawful trial was used to intimidate other African Americans. Victims were sometimes mutilated or shot before being hanged.

4. The NAACP was formed in 1909 to abolish segregation and discrimination, to oppose racism, and to gain civil rights for African Americans.

Critical Thinking and Writing

5. The separate facilities set aside for African Americans that *Plessy* v. *Ferguson* declared legal were never, in fact, as comfortable or convenient as facilities for whites. African Americans were thus left with unequal treatment.

6. Answers might claim that preventing African Americans from voting was a violation of the Fifteenth Amendment.

Take It to the NET

Answers will vary, but should include key events, including the founding of the NAACP, important legal victories, protests, and recent social and political actions.

In this photograph, taken at Tuskegee Institute around 1900, Booker T. Washington (front, center) poses with some distinguished guests, including Charles W. Eliot, President of Harvard University (front, far left) and Andrew Carnegie (to the right of Washington).

Overcoming Obstacles In the early 1900s, African American mutual aid and benefit societies multiplied, and social workers and church groups founded settlement houses in black neighborhoods. The Young Men's and Young Women's Christian Associations developed separate recreational and guidance programs for African American youth. The National Urban League, founded in 1911, improved job opportunities and housing for blacks.

Also during this period, African American intellectuals began to publish literature, history, and groundbreaking sociological studies. George Washington Carver became known for his scientific and agricultural research at Tuskegee Institute. In 1897, Alexander Crummell founded the American Negro Academy, which promoted scholarly publications about African American culture and history. Academy members included Du Bois, the poet Paul Dunbar, and educator Anna Julia Cooper.

Black-owned businesses began appearing everywhere. To help these businesses, Booker T. Washington founded the National Negro Business League in 1900. By 1907, it had 320 branches.

In 1912, Madam C. J. Walker spoke at the annual meeting of the Negro Business League. By any standards, she was a successful business person. Walker came from a family of ex-slaves and sharecroppers and had worked as a servant and as a laundress. "I got myself a start by giving myself a start," Walker would later say. She did so by developing her own preparations for styling the hair of African American women. Walker moved to Denver, Colorado, in 1905, and set up a prosperous mail-order business for her hair products. She also established a chain of beauty parlors and training schools. By 1916 her company had 20,000 employees.

With her business a success, Walker moved to New York City. Her home became a gathering place for African American leaders. Walker supported black welfare, education, and civil rights with large contributions. She also made many speeches for the anti-lynching drives of the NAACP and for African American women's organizations. "The girls and women of our race must not be afraid to take hold of business endeavor," she said in her 1913 speech to the Negro Business League. "I want to say to every Negro woman present, don't sit down and wait for the opportunities to come. . . . Get up and make them!"

Section 3 Assessment

READING COMPREHENSION

1. How did the **poll tax**, literacy tests, and **grandfather clauses** limit African American suffrage?

2. What were **Jim Crow** laws?

3. How was **lynching** used to intimidate African Americans?

4. When and why was the **National Association for the Advancement of Colored People** formed?

CRITICAL THINKING AND WRITING

5. **Expressing Problems Clearly** How did *Plessy* v. *Ferguson* contribute to the denial of equal rights for African Americans?

6. **Writing an Editorial** Write an editorial criticizing the denial of suffrage to African Americans that might have appeared at the turn of the century.

Take It to the NET

Activity: Creating a Time Line
Read more about the NAACP from its founding until today, and create a time line of the major events in the NAACP's history. Use the links provided in the *America: Pathways to the Present* area of the following Web site for help in completing this activity.
www.phschool.com

RESOURCE DIRECTORY

Teaching Resources
Units 5/6 booklet
• Section 3 Quiz, p. 39
Guide to the Essentials
• Section 3 Summary, p. 85

The Changing Roles of Women

READING FOCUS

- What were the issues in the debate over women's equality?
- How did women's work in the home change at the turn of the century?
- How did stores and catalogs serve women's new role as consumers?
- What kind of work did women do outside the home?

MAIN IDEA

Changes in women's lives, including new jobs, new educational opportunities, and new roles in the home and in the market-place, fueled a debate over the proper role of women in society.

KEY TERMS

department store
rural free delivery
 (RFD)
mail-order catalog

TAKING NOTES

As you read, use a chart like the one below to keep track of the changes in women's activities during this period.

In the Home	Outside the Home
Cleaning/traditional	
Buying processed foods/new	

SECTION OBJECTIVES

1. Examine the issues in the debate over women's equality.
2. Discover how women's work in the home changed at the turn of the century.
3. Learn how stores and catalogs served women's new role as consumers.
4. Find out about the kinds of work that women did outside the home.

BELLRINGER

Warm-Up Activity Ask students if they think women have full equality with men in American society today. Encourage them to explain their answers.

Activating Prior Knowledge Ask students to state their impression of the rights women had at the turn of the century. What were the short and long-term goals of those who struggled to increase opportunities for women? How did those rights compare to rights still sought today?

READING STRATEGY

As students read this section, have them look for evidence to support the following statement: "Although much had changed in women's lives by the turn of the century, much had stayed the same." Have students reflect on this statement as they identify the political, social, and economic contributions of women to American society at this time.

Setting the Scene "Women hain't no business a votin'," pronounced Josiah Allen, a fictional creation of the popular turn-of-the-century humorist Marietta Holley. "They had better let the laws alone, and tend to their house-work. The law loves wimmin and protects 'em." His wife, Samantha, replied, "If the law loves wimmin so well, why don't he give her as much wages as men get for doin' the same work?" Most Americans around 1900 would have known exactly what Samantha and Josiah were arguing about. They would have called it *the woman question*, a wide-ranging debate about the roles of women in society. This debate grew out of several major developments of the era.

The Debate Over Women's Equality

For women like Samantha Allen, the woman question boiled down to a few key demands: Women should be able to vote. They should be able to control their own property and income, and they should have access to higher education and professional jobs. Women's rights advocates were countered by those who insisted that giving women economic and political power would upset the social order. Some argued that allowing women more public roles would destroy their femininity.

Sometimes the debate about the role of women occurred within one individual. Frederic Howe was a writer and reformer who believed in women's equality. When Howe married a woman who was a Unitarian minister, however, he found that he didn't want her to work anymore.

These ladies are enjoying the annual horse show at the Islip Polo Club in 1915. They are also enjoying looser-fitting, more comfortable clothing than had been the style in the 1800s.

> 66 *I wanted my old-fashioned picture of a wife rather than [an] equal partner. Men and women fell in love, they married, had children; the wife cooked the meals, kept the house clean, entertained friends . . . cared for the family when sick, got the children ready for school and church, arranged the men's clothes . . . made cakes and pies for the church sociables. . . . She was careful of her conduct, and only had an opinion of her own in a whisper.* 99

—Frederic Howe

Chapter 16 • Section 4   **569**

ACTIVITY
Connecting with Culture

For many women in the late 1800s, club membership provided the means for involvement in public life for the first time. Have groups choose a focus for a club and develop an agenda of activities around that focus. Have a recorder from each group report to the class, and discuss common activities. **(Verbal/Linguistic)**

RESOURCE DIRECTORY

Teaching Resources
Learning Styles Lesson Plans booklet, p. 35
Guided Reading and Review booklet, p. 69
Learning with Documents booklet (Visual Learning Activity) *The New Woman and the New Man*, p. 55

Technology
Section Reading Support Transparencies
Guided Reading Audiotapes (English/Spanish), Ch. 16
Student Edition on Audio CD, Ch. 16
Prentice Hall Presentation Pro CD-ROM, Ch. 16
Companion Web site, www.phschool.com

Focus Explain that women's lives were undergoing rapid changes in the late 1800s. Ask what women's rights advocates wanted. Why were they opposed by some people?

Instruct Discuss the ways in which women's lives were different in the late 1890s from what they were in the 1840s. Why did women want more economic and political rights?

Ask students why the demand for equal economic and political rights for women stirred up so much controversy. Why did many men feel threatened by the demands of women's rights advocates? How might some women feel threatened? Why does the gender question continue to inspire emotional debate today?

Assess/Reteach Have students list some of the changes that took place for women at the turn of the century. Then have them list some aspects of women's lives that stayed the same.

From the Archives of
American Heritage®

Margaret Sanger

After visiting several contraception-advice centers in the Netherlands during a tour of Europe, Margaret Sanger, a nurse and midwife, returned home in October 1916, to open the nation's first birth-control clinic, in Brooklyn. Sanger, along with her sister, counseled 488 women in just 10 days before the police shut it down on the legal grounds that contraception information passed on by anyone but a doctor was obscenity. The judge upheld the 1873 Comstock Act, the Federal law under which they'd been prosecuted, and ruled against the sisters. Sanger, who introduced the phrase "birth control," made the issue her life's work. In 1923, she opened the country's first birth-control clinic staffed entirely by doctors. In 1936, Sanger and her group helped overturn the Comstock Act. By 1938, 300 clinics had spread across the country. Source: Nathan Ward, "The Time Machine," *American Heritage*® magazine, October 1991.

The new technology of the washing machine cut down on the full day formerly needed to do the family laundry. That had included carrying and boiling huge tubs of water, scrubbing against washboards, and wringing clothes by hand.

What was the reality of women's lives at the turn of the century? Women worked in most sectors of the economy and in many areas of public life, but their work at home continued to be essential. At the same time, a small number of women were earning advanced degrees and entering professions. Others were building volunteer organizations that took leading roles in reforming education, labor relations, public health, and other areas of society.

Women's Work in the Home

As they had for centuries, women continued to perform most of the jobs in the home. Thanks to the era's technological revolution, some aspects of this work became less physically demanding and less time-consuming. However, women still had much to do. For example, just cleaning a house could amount to a full-time job. The 1908 book *The Cost of Cleanliness* estimated that merely removing dust and tracked-in dirt from an eight-room house took 18 hours a week. If the house had a furnace in addition to fireplaces, and oil lighting fixtures that produced soot, 27 hours per week should be spent on keeping the house clean. In the 1880s, technology had begun to reduce this burden with the popular and affordable carpet sweeper. Electric vacuum cleaners became available in 1908. However, even as late as 1917, only one quarter of American homes had electricity; therefore, the development of electric appliances had a limited effect on the average American home.

By 1900, fewer urban women were making their own bread or butchering and preserving their own meat. The number of foods available in tin cans increased fourfold between 1870 and 1880. By 1910, quick cereals and factory-made biscuits were easily available. Ready-made clothing was becoming as common as ready-made foodstuffs. At the turn of the century, few women produced their family's clothing from start to finish anymore. Instead, they shopped for these items at stores and through the mail.

COMPARING PRIMARY SOURCES
Equality for Women

Americans debated the social, political, and economic roles of women in the late 1800s and early 1900s.

Analyzing Viewpoints Restate the arguments presented in the excerpts below in your own words.

For Women's Rights

"These things the women want to do and be and have are not in any sense masculine. They do not belong to men. They never did. They are departments of our social life, hitherto monopolized [until now controlled] by men."

—*Charlotte Perkins Gilman, "Are Women Human Beings?" Harper's Weekly, May 25, 1912*

Against Women's Rights

"So I say deliberately that the so-called woman movement is an attempt to escape the function of woman, a revolt against the fact that woman is not a man. . . . It is a rising against nature. It is a revolt against God."

—*Dr. Cyrus Townsend Brady, from a sermon given October 17, 1915*

From Producer to Consumer

As more and more ready-made goods became available commercially, women began to spend more of their time purchasing food, clothing, and furnishings than they did producing these items. Since women were the prime consumers, stores, catalogs, and advertising were geared to attracting their business.

Growing urban populations, an abundance of manufactured goods, the expansion of public transportation, and electric lighting led to the development of **department stores.** These large retail establishments carried such a wide variety of goods they were divided into departments. Unlike small general stores, which carried only a few choices, each department offered a variety of items in one category, such as men's shoes or furniture. Marshall Field in Chicago and Macy's in New York City were among the earliest department stores.

The end of the nineteenth century also saw the rise of chain stores, or retail outlets located in different sites but owned by the same company. Chain stores such as F. W. Woolworth's, which opened its first two stores in 1879, could offer their customers

RESOURCE DIRECTORY
Teaching Resources
Biography, Literature, and Comparing Primary Sources booklet (Comparing Primary Sources) *On the Woman Question,* p. 127
Great Debates booklet (Decision-Making Activities) *Promoting Women's Rights,* p. 34

Technology
RESOURCE PRO® Biography *Lucy Stone,* found on Resource Pro, profiles the fervent abolitionist and pioneer in the struggle for women's rights.

Fast Forward to Today

Shopping at Home

Mail-order catalogs enabled rural Americans to purchase a wide variety of goods without leaving home. By 1910, approximately 10 million Americans were shopping by mail. Others took advantage of another innovation: telephone ordering from department stores.

After the automobile made "going shopping" easier, technology changed shopping habits again in 1977, when the television Home Shopping Network went on the air.

The next revolution was the Internet. Shopping online was available as early as 1994, and in the 2000 holiday season, Americans spent some $8.7 billion online.

 Which change in shopping do you think had the greatest effect on people's lives? Which one had the greatest effect on the American economy?

---

lower prices because they were able to buy larger quantities from manufacturers. Both department and chain stores helped popularize another retailing innovation: the use of brand names.

Of course, farm families in rural areas of the Midwest also wanted access to manufactured items at low prices. Despite the protests of local shopkeepers, the United States Post Office began offering **rural free delivery (RFD)** in 1896 to any group of farmers who petitioned their congressman. By 1905, the Post Office was delivering mail on over 32,000 RFD routes. This free service gave farm families access to big-city goods through **mail-order catalogs,** or printed materials advertising a wide range of goods that could be purchased by mail. Two of the largest mail-order companies were Montgomery Ward and Sears, Roebuck and Company. Both of these companies worked hard to gain their customers' trust by offering money-back guarantees.

Working Outside the Home

In 1870, nearly two million women and girls, or one in every eight females over the age of 10, worked outside the home. Women worked in each of the 338 occupations listed in the United States census. Most Americans believed that for women, careers and married life did not mix, and so many of these working women were single. In the decades that followed, however, a rising proportion of married women would also go to work.

Domestic work was an important source of income for many women. In 1900, about one in fifteen American homes employed live-in servants, mostly immigrants or African Americans. Working from dawn to dusk, six-and-a-half days a week, these women cooked, cleaned, washed, ironed, and cared for children. Many supported their own families, who lived elsewhere.

Chapter 16 • Section 4   571

VIEWING HISTORY These telephone operators are on the cutting edge of a new technology and a new industry. **Drawing Conclusions** *Why do you think this job was deemed acceptable for women at the turn of the century?*

Most single female workers were between the ages of 16 and 24. Employers assumed that they would leave when they got married and rarely gave them supervisory jobs or advanced training. They also paid women an average of $3 to $5—about 30 to 60 percent—a week less than men. Self-supporting women were discouraged from entering fields that put them in competition with men. Many educated young women who wanted or needed to work became nurses or teachers. Then new technology opened up two other areas for female workers where they would not be competing with men. The typewriter appeared on the scene in the 1870s, and by 1900 more than one third of American clerical workers were women—usually typists supervised by men. The spread of telephone networks also provided jobs for women, who took telephone orders for department stores and worked as operators.

Much of American society believed that women did not have the mental capacity for professional training. In 1873, retired Harvard Medical School professor Edward H. Clarke warned that young women could not engage in studying and learning while retaining "uninjured health and a future secure from [sickness], hysteria, and other derangements of the nervous system." Three years before Clarke made this warning, the United States had 525 physicians, 67 ministers, and 5 lawyers who were women. Still, women professionals found most of their opportunities in women's colleges and in hospitals.

Volunteering for a Larger Role in Society   Women in both the North and the South had performed important voluntary service during the Civil War. Afterward, their interest in voluntary work exploded. They formed hundreds of clubs and associations to facilitate their activities. At first, women joined these organizations primarily for intellectual and social reasons. They studied subjects of common interest, gave talks, or heard lectures by distinguished guests. Some groups, such as the New England Woman's Club, promoted specific causes such as temperance and girls' education. Others worked to establish new libraries and playgrounds. African American club women in Atlanta participated in a national adult education program. The Chicago Woman's Club read Karl Marx's writings and other theoretical works.

Whatever their focus, these clubs gave their members invaluable experience in speaking, writing, and finance. They helped women increase

READING CHECK
What kinds of activities were popular in women's clubs?

572   Chapter 16 • *Life at the Turn of the Twentieth Century*

their self-confidence and take their first steps toward public life. To increase their influence, women's groups combined into national associations. The Association for the Advancement of Women was formed in 1873, followed by the General Federation of Women's Clubs in 1890. These groups took on increasingly ambitious projects, including suffrage and the reform of political abuses. In doing so, they joined with other groups founded to pursue specific reforms, such as the Woman's Christian Temperance Union, established in 1874, and the National American Woman Suffrage Association, formed in 1890. This last group would carry the cause of women's suffrage to victory some 30 years later.

New Women, New Ideas By the early 1900s, the woman question had grown to include a number of issues besides economic and political rights. One was the question of lifestyle: How should women dress and behave? As more women entered the work force or went to college, they took this matter into their own hands. Because they valued convenience, they began to wear shorter hairstyles, raise their hemlines, and wear skirts and blouses that were more suited to their new activities.

Courting and marriage customs also changed. For example, instead of being limited to entertaining a man at home under the watchful eyes of their parents, many young women now went out on dates without supervision. "New women," as they were sometimes called, still hoped to marry. Yet they seemed to have higher expectations of fulfillment in marriage than earlier generations of women did. As a result, the divorce rate rose from one in twelve in 1900 to one in nine by 1916. Many "new women" who married began to push for the legalized spread of information about birth control, a campaign led by New York nurse Margaret Sanger. Such developments were shocking to more traditional Americans.

What was the consensus among women on the woman question? Although the majority wanted "their rights," most women still saw domestic fulfillment as their chief goal. The right to vote was another matter. The issue of the vote prompted huge numbers of women to support the suffrage movement in some way. Soon the vote would be the one issue on which women from many walks of life would unite.

Focus on **CULTURE**

The Gibson Girl Who was the most popular young woman in 1890s America? Definitely the Gibson Girl. In reality, she was the pen-and-ink creation of illustrator Charles Gibson, whose sketches in *Life* and other magazines helped set the fashion of the time. The Gibson Girl was modern but respectable, and changes in her appearance and activities mirrored the changing roles of women. She often wore the proper business attire of a shirtwaist and skirt; she participated in sports; and eventually she even appeared as a college graduate in cap and gown.

Section 4 Assessment

READING COMPREHENSION

1. Name three traditional household tasks that women no longer had to do at home after 1900.

2. How did the new system of **rural free delivery** lead to the popularity of **mail-order catalogs?**

3. (a) What kinds of jobs were acceptable for women in 1900? (b) What made these jobs acceptable?

4. How did volunteer work prepare women to be influential in public life?

CRITICAL THINKING AND WRITING

5. **Recognizing Cause and Effect** Use a flowchart to show which changes in society at large led to changes in the roles of women in this era.

6. **Writing a Letter** Parents of young women often objected to their daughters going to work outside the home. Write a letter from a young woman of 1900 in which she tries to convince her parents that she should get a clerical job.

 Take It to the NET

Activity: Creating an Advertisement Read about the history of Sears, Roebuck and Company. Draw a poster that might have been used in 1900 to advertise the young company to potential shoppers. Use the links provided in the *America: Pathways to the Present* area of the following Web site for help in completing this activity.
www.phschool.com

Chapter 16 • Section 4 **573**

Section 4 Assessment

Reading Comprehension

1. Baking bread, sewing clothing, butchering.

2. Rural free delivery made department store goods accessible to farming families in rural areas of the Midwest through mail-order catalogs.

3. (a) Teaching, nursing, clerical work, telephone operators, domestic work. (b) These jobs were low-paying, did not lead to promotion, and did not put women in competition with men.

4. Volunteer work gave women experience in speaking, writing, and finance, giving them the skills and confidence to pursue political and social change.

Critical Thinking and Writing

5. Flowcharts will vary, but changes might include: increase in educational opportunities, new technology in the workplace, less time needed for housework.

6. Possible answer: Perhaps the woman has a college education. She might then argue that she has an obligation to put her education to use.

 **Take It to the NET**

Posters will vary, but should advertise practical, high-quality, reliable products aimed at the average person.

REVIEWING KEY TERMS

Students should refer to the definitions of key terms in the chapter to write sentences that show an understanding of daily life between 1870 and 1915.

REVIEWING MAIN IDEAS

11. Legislation in many states began to limit child labor and require children to attend school; newly arrived immigrants were eager to send their children to public schools.
12. Washington urged African Americans to strengthen their vocational job skills. Du Bois called for full civil liberties for African Americans, urging them to use education to become leaders in professional fields.
13. Amusement parks and vaudeville appealed to city dwellers who now had the time and the money to seek entertainment near their homes. The technology of the trolley aided both the development and the accessibility of amusement parks.
14. Bicycling, basketball, ice skating, tennis, gymnastics, swimming. Women's participation in sports led to new clothing styles and the development of "women's rules" in competitive sports.
15. Ragtime evolved in the South and Midwest by combining shifting melodies with marching-band beats. Jazz originated in New Orleans and synthesized a variety of musical styles, including traditional hymns and the newer ragtime rhythms.
16. Requirements to own property and pay poll taxes in order to vote; court decisions overturning the Civil Rights Act and *Plessy* v. *Ferguson;* Jim Crow laws, which required discrimination.
17. The NAACP worked through the courts system to gain civil rights for African Americans.
18. People were able to shop more conveniently at chain stores with low prices, at department stores, and through mail-order catalogs.
19. Work at home became less demanding, increased opportunities for education existed, volunteer experience gave women skills and confidence.

creating a CHAPTER SUMMARY

Copy this chart (right) and complete it by adding important information about changes in education, entertainment, the situation for African Americans, and the roles of women in the period from 1870 to 1915.

For additional review and enrichment activities, see the interactive version of *America: Pathways to the Present*, available on the Web and on CD-ROM.

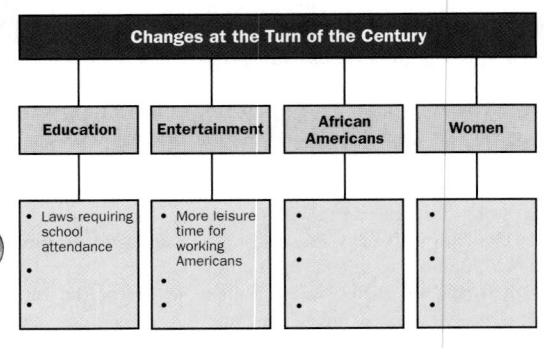

Changes at the Turn of the Century

Education	Entertainment	African Americans	Women
• Laws requiring school attendance	• More leisure time for working Americans	•	•
•	•	•	•

★ Reviewing Key Terms

For each of the terms below, write a sentence explaining how it relates to daily life at the turn of the century.

1. literacy
2. assimilation
3. Niagara Movement
4. yellow journalism
5. ragtime
6. poll tax
7. grandfather clause
8. Jim Crow
9. *Plessy* v. *Ferguson*
10. rural free delivery

★ Reviewing Main Ideas

11. Why did public schools gain more students in the late 1800s? (Section 1)
12. Compare the ideas of Booker T. Washington and W.E.B. Du Bois. (Section 1)
13. Why were vaudeville and amusement parks popular during this time? (Section 2)
14. Which sports did women participate in, and what effects did their participation have? (Section 2)
15. Where and how did ragtime and jazz originate? (Section 2)
16. Describe three ways African Americans were discriminated against after Reconstruction. (Section 3)
17. How did the NAACP help African Americans during the early 1900s? (Section 3)

18. How did new sources of manufactured goods change how people shopped? (Section 4)
19. Why were more women entering the work force in the early 1900s? (Section 4)

★ Critical Thinking

20. **Analyzing Information** Use the following data to make a bar graph showing the increase in students earning bachelor's degrees from 1890 to 1920.

    1890: males—12,857; females—2,682
    1900: males—22,173; females—5,237
    1910: males—28,762; females—8,437
    1920: males—31,980; females—16,642

    During which decade did women make the most significant gains compared to men? Why?

21. **Testing Conclusions** Cite evidence to support this statement: The turn of the century saw the birth of the American mass entertainment industry.
22. **Identifying Central Issues** Why do you think southern whites were so determined to use custom and law to keep blacks separate from whites?
23. **Recognizing Bias** (a) What views of men and women are reflected in the quotation by Frederic Howe on page 337? (b) How did women challenge these views?

CREATING A CHAPTER SUMMARY

Changes at the Turn of the Century

Education	Entertainment	African Americans	Women
• Laws requiring school attendance	• More leisure time for working Americans	• Increased discrimination after end of Reconstruction	• Invention of the washing machine frees homemakers
• Expansion of higher education	• People began attending movies	• Segregation is legal	• Availability of ready-made food
• Increased opportunities for coeducation	• Popularity of attending sporting events	• Growth of civil rights organizations	• More women in the work-force

A GOVERNMENT OF THE PEOPLE BY THE PEOPLE FOR THE PEOPLE

ARE NOT THE WOMEN HALF THE NATION?

★ **Skills Assessment**

Analyzing Political Cartoons ▶

24. Read the words at the top of the cartoon. To what government do they refer? Describe how that kind of government should treat its citizens.

25. Identify the figures. (a) What does each figure represent? (b) How do you know?

26. Analyze the woman on the right. (a) Why is she shackled? (b) Why is she appealing to the man on the left? (c) Why does the cartoonist show the woman in the middle supporting the woman on the right?

27. Read the words at the bottom of the cartoon. What is the message of the cartoon?

Interpreting Data

Turn to the graph on illiteracy in the United States in Section 1.

28. In which year were illiteracy rates the highest?

    A 1870
    B 1880
    C 1890
    D 1920

29. Which of the following statements best summarizes the information in the graph?

    F Few people were able to read and write in the late 1800s.
    G About 10 percent of the United States population was illiterate in 1900.
    H During the period from 1870 to 1920, illiteracy rates dropped in the United States.
    J Literacy was an important requirement for citizenship in the United States.

Applying the Chapter Skill: *Analyzing Political Cartoons for Point of View*

30. Look back at the cartoon on page 565. Use the steps presented on the Skills for Life page in this chapter to analyze the cartoon. (a) What was the cartoonist's frame of reference? Explain. (b) Do you think his point of view is the same as that of the two men in the cartoon? Explain. (c) What is the point of view of the cartoonist? What action might he advocate?

ACTIVITIES

Writing to LEARN

Writing an Outline
Many kinds of social and cultural changes occurred in America at the turn of the century. Make five of these changes the main headings of an outline. Under each heading, write who welcomed each change and why, and also who resisted the change (if anyone) and why. Finally, write a short paragraph summarizing how these changes affected American society at the beginning of the twentieth century.

Primary Source CD-ROM

Working With Primary Sources Find additional information on life at the turn of the twentieth century on the *Exploring Primary Sources in U.S. History CD-ROM* and use the selection(s) provided to complete the Chapter 16 primary source activity located in the *America: Pathways to the Present* area of the following Web site.
www.phschool.com

Take It to the NET

Chapter Self-Test As a review activity, take the Chapter 16 Self-Test in the *America: Pathways to the Present* area at the Web site listed below. The questions are designed to test your understanding of the chapter content.
www.phschool.com

LIVING UNDER JIM CROW

Focus Have students find the meaning of each of these words in a dictionary before they begin to read: *vehement, rookery, hovel, locality, consternation, glimpse.* Ask them to think, as they read, about how segregation shaped the attitudes of blacks and whites toward one another. Explain the allusion to Spanish-American heroes. *(In 1898 the United States declared war on Spain. African American troops served with distinction in the Spanish-American War, which the United States won resoundingly in just three months.)*

Instruct Ask students to think about a typical day in their family's life. Discuss with students how the presence of Jim Crow would affect such a day. Elicit specific examples.

To ensure that students grasp the writer's subtle points, call on volunteers to explain sentences such as the following:

- "There is no wonder that we die; the wonder is that we persist in living."
- "We had ruined his neighborhood of poor people; poor as we, poorer in manners at least."

Analyzing the Document Use this additional question to generate class discussion:

Critical Thinking: Demonstrating Reasoned Judgment Give evidence to support the speaker's statement: "I have seen very small white children hang their black dolls. It is not the child's fault, he is simply an apt pupil." *(Adult whites hanged African Americans under Jim Crow.)*

Living Under Jim Crow

The editors of *American Heritage* magazine have selected this account, published in 1902 and written by an unnamed African American woman living in the South. In it she described the world of Jim Crow—the daily frustrations and humiliations that African Americans had to endure as they struggled to build successful lives.

I AM A COLORED WOMAN, wife and mother. I have lived all my life in the South, and have often thought what a peculiar fact it is that the more ignorant the Southern whites are of us the more vehement they are in their denunciation of us. They boast that they have little intercourse with us, never see us in our homes, churches or places of amusement, but still they know us thoroughly.

They also admit that they know us in no capacity except as servants, yet they say we are at our best in that single capacity. What philosophers they are! The Southerners say we Negroes are a happy, laughing set of people, with no thought of tomorrow. How mistaken they are! The educated, thinking Negro is just the opposite. There is a feeling of unrest, insecurity, almost panic among the best class of Negroes in the South. In

Even well-educated African Americans were often restricted to low-paying jobs.

our homes, in our churches, wherever two or three are gathered together, there is a discussion of what is best to do. Must we remain in the South or go elsewhere? Where can we go to feel that security which other people feel? Is it best to go in great numbers or only in several families? These and many other things are discussed over and over. . . .

I know of houses occupied by poor Negroes in which a respectable farmer would not keep his cattle. It is impossible for them to rent elsewhere. All Southern real estate agents have "white property" and "colored property." In one of the largest Southern cities there is a colored minister, a graduate of Harvard, whose wife is an educated, Christian woman, who lived for weeks in a tumble-down rookery because he could neither rent nor buy in a respectable locality.

Many colored women who wash, iron, scrub, cook or sew all the week to help pay the rent for these miserable hovels and help fill the many small mouths, would deny themselves some of the necessaries of life if they could take their little children and teething babies on the cars to the parks of a Sunday afternoon and sit under trees, enjoy the cool breezes and breathe God's pure air for only two or three hours; but this is denied them. Some of the parks have

576

---

signs, "No Negroes allowed on these grounds except as servants." Pitiful, pitiful customs and laws that make war on women and babes! There is no wonder that we die; the wonder is that we persist in living.

A NEIGHBORHOOD OF POOR PEOPLE

Fourteen years ago I had just married. My husband had saved sufficient money to buy a small home. On account of our limited means we went to the suburbs, on unpaved streets, to look for a home, only asking for a high, healthy locality. Some real estate agents were "sorry, but had nothing to suit," some had "just the thing," but we discovered on investigation that they had "just the thing" for an unhealthy pigsty. Others had no "colored property." One agent said that he had what we wanted, but we should have to go to see the lot after dark, or walk by and give the place a casual look; for, he said, "all the white people in the neighborhood would be down on me." Finally, we bought this lot. When the house was being built we went to see it. Consternation reigned. We had ruined his neighborhood of poor people; poor as we, poorer in manners at least. The people who lived next door received the sympathy of their friends. When we walked on the street (there were no sidewalks) we were embarrassed by the stare of many unfriendly eyes.

Two years passed before a single woman spoke to me, and only then because I helped one of them when a little sudden trouble came to her. Such was the reception, I a happy young woman, just married, received from people among whom I wanted to make a home. Fourteen years have now passed, four children have been born to us, and one has died in this same home, among these same neighbors. Although the neighbors speak to us . . . , not one woman has ever been inside of my house, not even at the times when a woman would doubly appreciate the slightest attention of a neighbor. . . .

White agents and other chance visitors who come into our homes ask questions that we must not dare ask their wives. They express surprise that our children have clean faces and that their hair is combed. . . .

We were delighted to know that some of our Spanish-American heroes were coming where

Jim Crow laws continued into the second half of the twentieth century, as this woman discovered in a Dallas, Texas, bus station in 1961.

we could get a glimpse of them. Had not black men helped in a small way to give them their honors? In the cities of the South, where these heroes went, the white school children were assembled, flags waved, flowers strewn, speeches made, and "My Country, 'tis of Thee, Sweet Land of Liberty," was sung. Our children who need to be taught so much, were not assembled, their hands waved no flags, they threw no flowers, heard no thrilling speech, sang no song of their country. And this is the South's idea of justice. Is it surprising that feeling grows more bitter, when the white mother teaches her boy to hate my boy, not because he is mean, but because his skin is dark? I have seen very small white children hang their black dolls. It is not the child's fault, he is simply an apt pupil. . . .

Source: Anonymous, *Independent* magazine, 1902.

Understanding Primary Sources

1. At what time of day did this woman and her husband have to go to look at a new house they were thinking of buying?

2. When she refers to her neighbors as "poor people," what does she mean?

American Heritage®
MY BRUSH WITH HISTORY™
 Videotapes

For more information about segregation and Jim Crow laws, view "Living Under Jim Crow."

577

CUSTOMIZE FOR ...

Gifted and Talented

Discuss the speaker's tone in the first two paragraphs. *(Sarcastic)* Have students read aloud examples that illustrate this tone.

Ask students to think of a time that they used sarcasm, humor, or "put-downs" to deal with a painful situation. Have them write a description of the situation and the strategy that they used to protect themselves.

CUSTOMIZE FOR ...

ESL

Students may need help with the following words and phrases:
denunciation harsh criticism
capacity role
on account of because of
assembled gathered together

CUSTOMIZE FOR ...

Less Proficient Readers

Discuss the differences between the lives of white and black children under Jim Crow. (Refer students particularly to the last paragraph in the selection.) Then discuss the challenges that confronted African American parents raising children under Jim Crow. The discussion might include areas such as schools and teachers, safety precautions, and places to play.

CUSTOMIZE FOR ...

Less Proficient Writers

In this passage, the writer lists many injustices experienced by her and her family. Ask students to select one of these injustices and state their own opinion about it in two or three sentences.

ANSWERS

1. After dark.

2. "Poorer in manners," she calls them. They greet her with unfriendly eyes and do not speak to her.

Use this sample exam to help your students prepare for standardized tests.

TIPS FOR TEST TAKING

You might want to remind your students of the following:

1. Read the directions carefully.

2. Read each question carefully.

3. For multiple choice questions, try to answer the question before you look at the choices. Read all the choices. Then, eliminate those that are absolutely incorrect.

4. For short answer questions, be sure to answer the question completely if there is more than one part.

5. Answer the easy questions first. Then, go back to the ones that will take more time.

6. Pace yourself. Be sure to set aside enough time for the writing questions.

Write your answers on a separate sheet of paper.

1. What is the process by which a company gains control over the businesses that make up all phases of a product's development?

   A Monopolization

   B Vertical consolidation

   C Horizontal consolidation

   D Exportation with the intent to deliver

2. What issue did the Sherman Antitrust Act address?

   A The treatment of Confederate soldiers after the Civil War

   B The right to bear arms

   C A banking crisis

   D A new kind of business monopoly

3. What was discovered at Sutter's Mill in California, in 1848?

   A Gold

   B Oil

   C Uranium

   D Silver

4. Which of the following laws divided Native American reservation land into individual plots?

   A The Lecompton constitution

   B The Interstate Commerce Act

   C The Dawes Act

   D The Compromise of 1859

5. Which one of the following nineteenth-century business leaders is correctly paired with his area of industry?

   A John D. Rockefeller and oil

   B Andrew Carnegie and railroads

   C Edwin Drake and steel

   D Thomas A. Edison and the telephone

6. The Sherman Antitrust Act initially was unsuccessful because

   A it was not passed into law by the Congress.

   B it was enforced infrequently by the courts.

   C President Harrison refused to support it.

   D John D. Rockefeller turned his employees against it.

Use the chart and your knowledge of social studies to answer the following question.

Which Early Labor Union?
• Represented skilled workers
• Consisted of a network of smaller "craft" unions
• Focused on wages, hours, and working conditions
• Excluded women and African Americans
• Used strikes, boycotts, and collective bargaining
• Wanted "closed shops"

7. The chart describes which one of the following early labor unions?

   A The National Labor Union

   B The Knights of Labor

   C The American Federation of Labor

   D The Industrial Workers of the World

PRENTICE HALL
ASSESSMENT
SYSTEM

Diagnose and Prescribe
• Profile student skills with Diagnostic Tests A&B.
• Address student needs with program materials correlated to test questions.
Review and Reteach
• Provide cumulative content review with the Review Book.
Practice and Assess
• Build test-taking skills with Test-taking Strategies With Transparencies.

8. What was the long-term result of the Pullman Strike of 1894?

   A The federal government sided with business against labor unions.

   B The Knights of Labor membership grew after they won the strike.

   C Nonviolent methods helped the unions win the strike.

   D Unskilled workers formed their own labor unions.

9. The Pendelton Civil Service Act

   A limited government assistance to businesses.

   B provided special jobs for Civil War veterans.

   C opened up government jobs to African Americans.

   D helped to end the spoils system.

Use the chart and your knowledge of social studies to answer the following question.

Immigration to U.S. From Italy	
Year	**Number of Immigrants**
1900	100,135
1901	135,996
1902	178,375
1903	230,622
1904	193,296
1905	221,479
SOURCE: *Historical Statistics of the United States, Colonial Times to 1970*	

10. Which of the following factors contributed to the rise in U.S. immigration from Italy around the turn of the century?

   A Pogroms

   B Steerage and quarantines

   C High taxes and crop failures

   D Revolution and civil war

11. Jane Addams operated Hull House as a center to

   A assist the urban poor.

   B fight immigration to the U.S. from Asia.

   C aid men who fought in the Civil War.

   D support Populist Party candidates.

Writing Practice

12. Describe some of the farming innovations that occurred in the United States during the late 1800s.

13. Explain the methods businesses used to limit the power of unions.

14. What actions did the federal government take to encourage people to move to the West following the Civil War?

1. B
2. D
3. A
4. C
5. A
6. B
7. C
8. A
9. D
10. C
11. A
12. Answers will vary but might mention the mechanized reaper, barbed wire, dry farming, the steel plow, the harrow, the steel windmill, hybridization of plants, the USDA, and the grain drill.
13. Answers should include forbidding union meetings; firing union organizers; forcing new employees to sign contracts promising not to join unions; refusing to bargain with unions; refusing to recognize unions as representatives of workers; and benefiting from the actions of government officials in the breaking of strikes.
14. Answers should mention the Pacific Railway Acts, which greatly expanded railway construction; the Morrill Land-Grant Act, which provided land for the founding of agricultural colleges; and the Homestead Act, which gave settlers small parcels of western land if they agreed to settle and farm them.

579

INTRODUCING THE UNIT

The United States on the Brink of Change (1890–1920) This unit presents the United States as it first begins to look outward and form its role as an important leader among nations of the world. Global situations and conflicts began to engage the United States as the nineteenth century came to a close. Meanwhile, at home, there were conflicts between different factions of society: between the rich and the poor, the working class and business owners, new immigrants and older settlers, former slaves and American society at large. As Americans dealt with their problems at home, tension between the great powers continued in Europe, resulting finally in the Great War (World War I), which compelled the United States to join in a worldwide conflict for the first time.

USING HISTORICAL EVIDENCE

Direct students' attention to the painting on these pages. It depicts the U.S. fleet's return to New York harbor after a victory in the Spanish-American War. This war took place as imperialism spread worldwide. Under imperialism, stronger, richer nations took control of smaller, poorer nations. America's role as an imperialist nation is a sign of how much the new country had grown in power and strength.

Discuss this change with students. What were some positive aspects of this type of strength and power? What were some pitfalls? How did this imperialist posture affect America as the era of global conflict got under way?

eTeach

Be sure to check out this month's online discussion with a Master Teacher. Go to **www.phschool.com**.

"Whether they will or no, Americans must begin to look outward."

Alfred T. Mahan
The Interest of America in Sea Power, 1897

This 1898 painting by Fred Pansing shows part of the U.S. fleet entering New York harbor following the Spanish-American War. ▶

580

RESOURCE DIRECTORY

Teaching Resources
Units 5/6 booklet
- American Pathways Activity, pp. 85–86
- History's Lasting Impact, pp. 87–88

Geography and History booklet, pp. 12–13

Other Print Resources
Prentice Hall Assessment System
- Document-Based Assessment

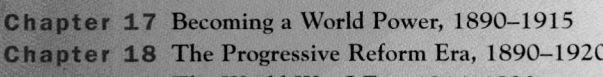

581

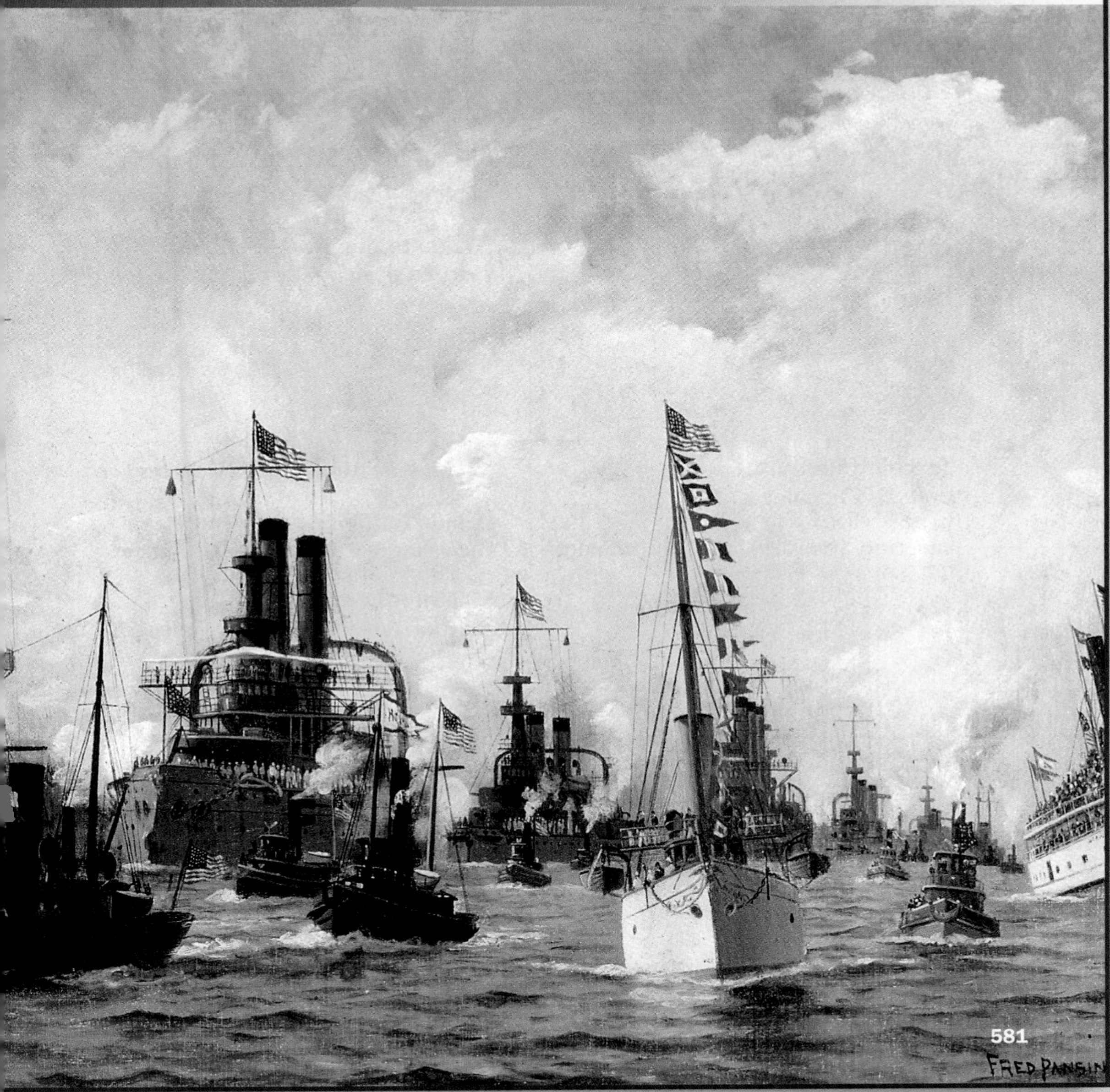

FRED PANSING

RESOURCE DIRECTORY

Technology
Color Transparencies *Historical Maps,* A27,
A28, A29, A30, A31, A33, A34; *Political
Cartoons,* B9, B10, B11; *Time Lines,* C5, C6;
Cause-and-Effect Charts, D7, D8; *Fine Art,*
E16; *American Photo,* F6; *American Diversity,*
G11; *The Way It Works,* H15, H16
Section Reading Support Transparencies
Prentice Hall United States History Video
Collection™ Volume 14, *The Progressive
Movement;* Volume 15, *The United States and
the World;* Volume 16, *The Great War*
Companion Web site, www.phschool.com

TECHNOLOGY CENTER

 Take It to the NET

Prentice Hall School Web site
offers student-appropriate Internet
activities and links that extend
core content. Visit us at the Social
Studies area. www.phschool.com

American Heritage®

**My Brush with History™ Video
Program** This new video series
lets your students learn history
from the people who lived it.

RESOURCE PRO®

Teaching Resources on CD-ROM
offer lesson-planning flexibility,
test-generation capability, and
resource manageability.

PRESENTATION PRO CD-ROM
Provides you with multimedia
lecture notes for each chapter.

**SOCIAL STUDIES SKILLS TUTOR
CD-ROM** Provides interactive
practice in Geographic Literacy,
Critical Thinking and Reading,
Visual Analysis, and
Communications.

**INTERACTIVE CONSTITUTION
CD-ROM** Exploring active
citizenship and civic responsibilities, this CD-ROM shows
students how the Constitution
affects their lives today.

**EXPLORING PRIMARY SOURCES IN
U.S. HISTORY CD-ROM** This
interactive exploration of primary sources allows students
to analyze and evaluate
writing and images from
American history.

GUIDED READING AUDIOTAPES

STUDENT EDITION ON AUDIO CD

SOUNDS OF AN ERA AUDIO CD
Bring the sounds of American
history to life in the classroom
with music, speeches, poetry,
interviews, and news reports.

 **TEXT**

Don't miss the exclusive interactive version of this textbook on
the Web and on CD-ROM.

Chapter 17 Planning Guide
Resource Manager

Chapter-Level Resources	CORE INSTRUCTION	READING/SKILLS
	Teaching Resources • Pacing Charts booklet • Block Scheduling booklet **Resource Pro® CD-ROM**, Ch. 17 **Prentice Hall Presentation Pro CD-ROM**, Ch. 17 **www.phschool.com** • eTeach	**Guided Reading Audiotapes (English/Spanish)** **Student Edition on Audio CD**, Ch. 17 **Social Studies Skills Tutor CD-ROM** **Color Transparencies**, A27, A28, A29, A30, B9, B10, C5, D7, E16, G11
1 The Pressure to Expand 1. Find out about the factors that led to the growth of imperialism around the world. 2. Learn about the ways in which the United States began to expand its interests abroad in the 1800s. 3. See the arguments made in favor of United States expansion in the 1890s.	**Teaching Resources** **Units 5/6 booklet** • Section 1 Quiz, p. 52	**Guided Reading and Review booklet**, p. 70 **Guide to the Essentials**, p. 88 **Section Reading Support Transparencies**
2 The Spanish-American War 1. Read about United States activities in Latin America that set the stage for war with Spain. 2. Find out about events leading up to and following the Spanish-American War. 3. Discover challenges faced by the United States after the war. 4. Learn why the United States sought to gain influence in the Pacific.	**Teaching Resources** **Units 5/6 booklet** • Section 2 Quiz, p. 53 **Learning Styles Lesson Plans booklet**, p. 36	**Guided Reading and Review booklet**, p. 71 **Guide to the Essentials**, p. 89 **Learning with Documents booklet**, p. 56 **Skills for Life booklet**, p. 19 **Section Reading Support Transparencies**
3 A New Foreign Policy 1. Find out why the United States wanted to build the Panama Canal. 2. Learn about the goals of Roosevelt's "big stick" diplomacy. 3. Discover some ways in which the foreign policies of Presidents Taft and Wilson differed from those of President Roosevelt.	**Teaching Resources** **Units 5/6 booklet** • Section 3 Quiz, p. 54	**Guided Reading and Review booklet**, p. 72 **Guide to the Essentials**, p. 90 **Learning with Documents booklet**, pp. 22, 85 **Section Reading Support Transparencies**
4 Debating America's New Role 1. Examine the main arguments raised by the anti-imperialists. 2. See why imperialism appealed to many Americans. 3. Find out how American imperialism was viewed from abroad.	**Teaching Resources** **Units 5/6 booklet** • Section 4 Quiz, p. 55 **Learning Styles Lesson Plans booklet**, p. 37	**Guided Reading and Review booklet**, p. 73 **Guide to the Essentials**, p. 91 **Section Reading Support Transparencies**

ENRICHMENT/PRE-AP

Prentice Hall United States History Video Collection™
www.phschool.com
• Section Activities, Virtual Field Trip, Chapter Activities, Current Events Online

Nystrom *Atlas Of Our Country,* pp. 32–33
Historical Outline Map Book, pp. 58, 81
Exploring Primary Sources in U.S. History CD-ROM

Biography, Literature, and Comparing Primary Sources booklet, p. 22
Great Debates booklet, p. 14
American History Block Scheduling Support
Historical Outline Map Book, p. 57
Sounds of an Era Audio CD
Exploring Primary Sources in U.S. History CD-ROM

Biography, Literature, and Comparing Primary Sources booklet, p. 63
American History Block Scheduling Support
Nystrom *Atlas of Our Country,* pp. 32–33
Historical Outline Map Book, p. 59
Sounds of an Era Audio CD
Exploring Primary Sources in U.S. History CD-ROM

Biography, Literature, and Comparing Primary Sources booklet, p. 129
American Pathways Thematic Posters

ASSESSMENT

PRENTICE HALL ASSESSMENT SYSTEM

Core Assessment
ExamView® Test Bank, Ch. 17
ExamView® Test Bank CD-ROM, Ch. 17

Standardized Test Preparation
Diagnose and Prescribe
Diagnostic Tests for High School Social Studies Skills

Review and Reteach
Review Book for U.S. History

Practice and Assess
Test-taking Strategies With Transparencies
Test-taking Strategies Posters
Test Prep Book for U.S. History
Alternative Assessment Handbook
Document-Based Assessment

Teaching Resources
Units 5/6 booklet
• Section Quizzes, pp. 52–55
• Chapter Tests, pp. 56, 59
www.phschool.com Ch. 17 Self-Test

AmericanHeritage RESOURCES

From the Archives of American Heritage®, pp. 591, 602
AmericanHeritage® My Brush with History™ Videotapes
www.americanheritage.com

TEXT

Don't miss the exclusive interactive version of this textbook on the Web and on CD-ROM.

Chapter 17 Planning Guide
In Your Classroom

CUSTOMIZE FOR INDIVIDUAL NEEDS

Gifted and Talented

Teacher's Edition
- Customize for Gifted and Talented, p. 603

Teaching Resources
- Biography, Literature, and Comparing Primary Sources booklet, pp. 22, 63, 129

Technology
- Exploring Primary Sources in U.S. History CD-ROM *Roosevelt Corollary*

ESL

Teacher's Edition
- Customize for ESL, p. 585

Teaching Resources
- Guided Reading and Review booklet, pp. 70–73
- Guide to the Essentials (English/Spanish), Chapter 17

Technology
- Student Edition on Audio CD, Chapter 17
- Guided Reading Audiotapes (English/Spanish), Chapter 17
- Section Reading Support Transparencies

Less Proficient Readers

Teacher's Edition
- Customize for Less Proficient Readers, p. 591

Teaching Resources
- Guided Reading and Review booklet, pp. 70–73
- Guide to the Essentials (English/Spanish), Chapter 17

Technology
- Student Edition on Audio CD, Chapter 17
- Guided Reading Audiotapes (English/Spanish), Chapter 17
- Section Reading Support Transparencies

Less Proficient Writers

Teacher's Edition
- Customize for Less Proficient Writers, p. 607

Teaching Resources
- Guided Reading and Review booklet, pp. 70–73
- Guide to the Essentials (English/Spanish), Chapter 17

Technology
- Student Edition on Audio CD, Chapter 17
- Guided Reading Audiotapes (English/Spanish), Chapter 17
- Section Reading Support Transparencies

TEACHER'S EDITION INDEX

CHAPTER 17 – PACING SUGGESTIONS

 For 90-minute Blocks

- Teach sections 1–4 using Transparencies A27, A28, A29, A30, B9, B10, C5, D7, and G11, and the Recent Scholarship note on page 601 for class discussions.

 Running Out of Time?

If you are running short on time to cover this chapter, consider the following options:

- Use Prentice Hall Presentation Pro CD-ROM to create an outline for this chapter.
- Use the Section Summaries for Chapter 17, from **Guide to the Essentials (English/Spanish).**

1	**The Pressure to Expand**	**Connecting with History and Conflict** Have students create cause-effect diagrams to summarize in graphic form the different forces whose influence and power led to the build-up of the U.S. Navy. Diagrams could use illustrations as well as text to identify the various factors involved. You may wish to have students make an oral presentation of their diagrams. **(Visual/Spatial)**
2	**The Spanish-American War**	**Connecting with Citizenship** Point out that while sensational journalism sold well, there were still newspapers that gave thoughtful analyses of events with the aim of informing citizens of their significance. Suggest that students imagine they are columnists assigned to analyze—in a calm and lucid manner—the motives behind the country's expansionist policies. Have them develop an outline for their story that will examine the following driving forces: economic profit, military strategy, patriotism, religion, and a sense of cultural and racial superiority. **(Verbal/Linguistic)**
3	**A New Foreign Policy**	**Connecting with Science and Technology** Even those who might have protested the building of the Panama Canal could not deny the fact that it was an engineering marvel. Have students work in pairs to create parallel journal entries for two people who might have been present on August 15, 1914, the day the S.S. *Ancon* became the first ship to complete a trip through the canal. One entry is that of an American engineer, in which he celebrates the technical and scientific achievements of the work. The other is that of a Jamaican-born workman, in which he expresses his feelings on that day as he recalls the costs in labor and lives during the time it took to build the canal. **(Verbal/Linguistic)**
4	**Debating America's New Role**	**Connecting with Government** Ask students to consider the voices that spoke up against American imperialism. Propose a hypothetical situation in which those individuals tried to create either a law or a constitutional amendment that prohibited imperialism. Have students work in small groups to compose such a law. Point out that the wording would, first, have to define imperialism; second, have to avoid closing off the government's ability to defend itself and its allies. Have students present their draft in character and invite comment and discussion from the class. **(Verbal/Linguistic; Bodily/Kinesthetic)**

Chapter 17

Becoming a World Power

(1890–1915)

INTRODUCING THE CHAPTER

By the 1890s, business and political leaders with dreams of empire were expanding into new markets and seizing control of territory abroad. Imperialism on the part of a country founded on freedom from colonialism troubled many United States citizens. The responsibilities of world power brought the government's conflicting domestic and international agendas to the forefront.

TIME LINE ACTIVITY

To provide students with practice in using the time line, ask questions such as these:

1. Who was President at the time the United States overthrew Hawaii's Queen Liliuokalani? *(Grover Cleveland)*

2. What act led the United States to declare war on Spain? *(The explosion of the U.S.S.* Maine *in 1898)*

3. What later action resulted from Austria's annexation of Bosnia and Herzegovina? *(The outbreak of World War I)*

Becoming a World Power
(1890–1915)

SECTION 1   The Pressure to Expand

SECTION 2   The Spanish-American War

SECTION 3   A New Foreign Policy

SECTION 4   Debating America's New Role

1890

Alfred T. Mahan's *The Influence of Sea Power Upon History, 1660–1783* urges the United States to build a powerful navy to protect markets abroad.

American Events

1893

American business groups, with the help of United States Marines, overthrow Hawaii's Queen Liliuokalani and set up a provisional government.

1898

The U.S.S. *Maine* explodes off the coast of Havana, Cuba, killing more than 250 American sailors. An outraged American public convinces Congress to declare war on Spain.

Presidential Terms: Grover Cleveland 1893–1897   William McKinley 1897–1901

| 1890 | • | 1894 | • | 1898 | • |

World Events

Cuba rebels against Spanish rule.

The Boxer Rebellion erupts in China.

1895

1900

582   Chapter 17 • *Becoming a World Power*

eTeach

Be sure to check out this month's online discussion with a Master Teacher. Go to **www.phschool.com**.

RESOURCE DIRECTORY

Teaching Resources
Pacing Charts booklet
Block Scheduling booklet, p. 21
Units 5/6 booklet
  • Chapter Summary, p. 51

Technology
Guided Reading Audiotapes (English/Spanish), Ch. 17
Student Edition on Audio CD, Ch. 17
Sounds of an Era Audio CD *"The Washington Post March,"* 1897 recording
Prentice Hall United States History Video Collection™ Volume 15, *The United States and the World*
Prentice Hall Presentation Pro CD-ROM, Ch. 17
Resource Pro® CD-ROM
Social Studies Skills Tutor CD-ROM
Companion Web site, www.phschool.com

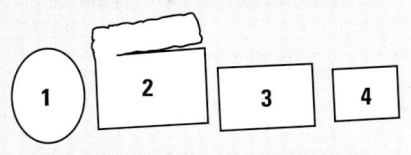

Map Legend

① UNITED STATES — American possessions
② BELGIUM — Belgian possessions
③ UNITED KINGDOM — British possessions
④ CHINA — Chinese possessions
⑤ DENMARK — Danish possessions
⑥ NETHERLANDS — Dutch possessions
⑦ FRANCE — French possessions
⑧ GERMANY — German possessions
⑨ ITALY — Italian possessions
⑩ JAPAN — Japanese possessions
⑪ OTTOMAN EMPIRE — Ottoman possessions
⑫ PORTUGAL — Portuguese possessions
⑬ RUSSIAN EMPIRE — Russian possessions
⑭ SPAIN — Spanish possessions
Independent country

Timeline

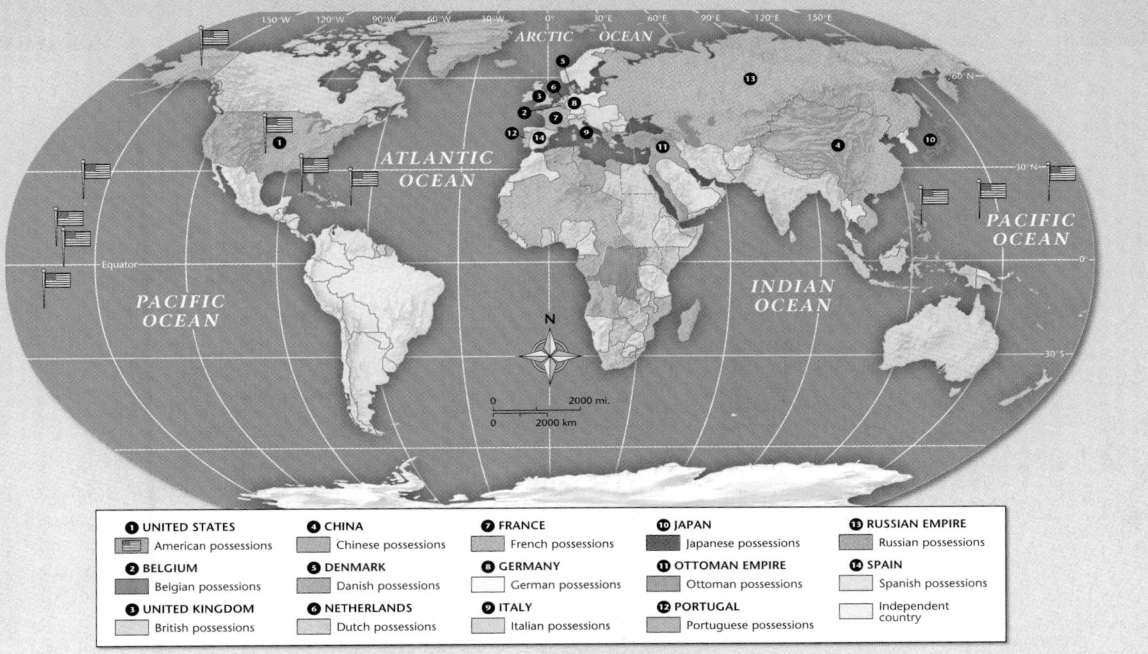

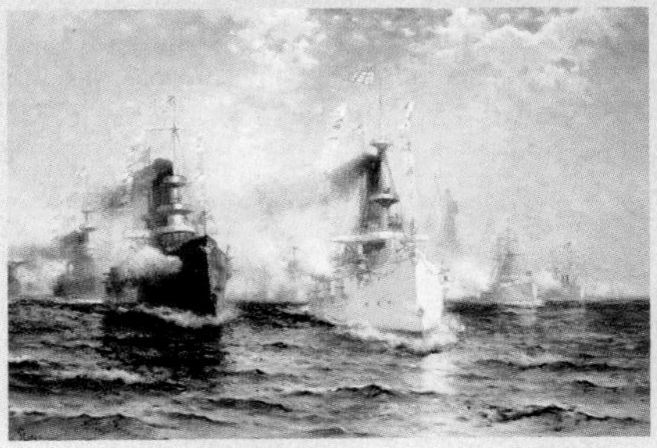

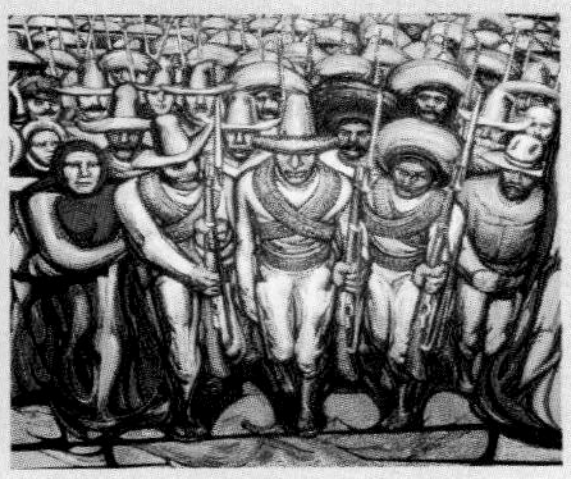

1903 Panama gives the United States control over the Panama Canal Zone for $10 million.

1904 President Roosevelt issues the Roosevelt Corollary to the Monroe Doctrine.

1907 The Great White Fleet tours the world as a display of the impressive naval power of the United States.

1914 President Wilson sends troops to Mexico to assist Mexican revolutionaries.

Theodore Roosevelt 1901–1909

William Howard Taft 1909–1913

Woodrow Wilson 1913–1921

1902 • • • **1906** • • • **1910** • • • **1914**

1905 Japan defeats Russia in the Russo-Japanese War.

1908 Austria annexes Bosnia and Herzegovina.

1912 The First Balkan War begins.

1914 World War I begins.

BIBLIOGRAPHY

For the Teacher

McCullough, David. **The Path Between the Seas: The Creation of the Panama Canal, 1870–1914.** Simon & Schuster, 1977. (Lively and full account contains excerpts from original sources and reads as an epic adventure.)

Traxel, David. **1898: The Birth of the American Century.** Vintage, 1999. (A historian pinpoints 1898 as the year America entered the world stage.)

For the Student

O'Toole, G.J.A. **The Spanish War: An American Epic—1898.** Norton, 1986. (An anecdotal discussion of the explosion of the *Maine* with recent evidence and an analysis of the McKinley administration's role in the expansion of the conflict.)

Friar, William. **Portrait of the Panama Canal: From Construction to the 21st Century.** Graphic Arts Center Publishing Company, 1999. (A lively collection of historic and contemporary photos.)

World Imperialism, circa 1900

Activating Prior Knowledge
Looking at the map, explain the saying current at this time that "the sun never sets on the British Empire." *(Great Britain had acquired so much territory that it was always daytime in some place under Britain's control.)*

Previewing Why do you think the United States bought Alaska and annexed islands in the Pacific? *(The United States was trying to intimidate the British in Canada by placing American territory on two sides of Canada. The annexed islands were to be used as refueling and repair stations for the rebuilt U.S. Navy.)*

BACKGROUND
About the Pictures

1   2   3   4

1. Until the 1893 overthrow of Queen Liliuokalani, Hawaii had been the only state in the United States to have a monarchical government.

2. The exact cause of the February 1898 explosion of the U.S.S. *Maine* was never discovered, but the speculation was sabotage by the Spanish.

3. British artist Edward Moran painted *Return of the Conquerors* in 1899. Moran moved to America in 1844, and by the time of his death in 1901 he was widely regarded as one of the foremost American painters of maritime subjects.

4. From 1911 until 1917, the United States was involved in the Mexican civil war. In 1916 General Pershing was dispatched to Mexico to apprehend the Mexican revolutionary leader Pancho Villa, who had been raiding American towns across the border. Pershing failed, however, and Pancho Villa escaped.

Don't miss the exclusive interactive version of this textbook on the Web and on CD-ROM.

Section 1
The Pressure to Expand

SECTION OBJECTIVES

1. Find out about the factors that led to the growth of imperialism around the world.
2. Learn about the ways in which the United States began to expand its interests abroad in the 1800s.
3. See the arguments made in favor of United States expansion in the 1890s.

BELLRINGER

Warm-Up Activity Write the following on the chalkboard: "The sun never sets on the British Empire." Ask students what they think the saying means. Explain that in the late 1800s, when this saying was popular, the United States was beginning to build its own empire. Ask what an empire is.

Activating Prior Knowledge Ask students, "Which of the current United States became part of this country's territory in the 1890s?" *(Hawaii)*

READING STRATEGY

Before they read, ask students to write a question about each heading in the section. As they read, have them note answers to their questions.

CAPTION ANSWERS

Viewing History The United States, now industrialized, faces its past (the frontier) and must look to the future (a new frontier). Industrialized man appears confident about future expansion, yet somewhat nostalgic for the past.

The Pressure to Expand

READING FOCUS

- What factors led to the growth of imperialism around the world?
- In what ways did the United States begin to expand its interests abroad in the late 1800s?
- What arguments were made in favor of United States expansion in the 1890s?

MAIN IDEA

In the late 1800s, as European nations took over vast areas in Africa and Asia, American leaders looked to extend American influence abroad.

KEY TERMS

imperialism
nationalism
annex
banana republic

TAKING NOTES

As you read, complete the diagram below to show some of the causes that led the United States to adopt a policy of political and economic expansion overseas.

CAUSES
• Growth of imperialism in Europe and Asia
•
•

→ **United States Expansion**

Setting the Scene By the dawn of the twentieth century, industrialization had forever changed the national landscape and the daily lives of all Americans. The rise of cities, the beginnings of mass culture, westward expansion, and new coast-to-coast networks of travel and communications all strengthened the country's national identity. Americans wondered what these changes meant for the future of the country.

The development of the United States into an industrial powerhouse not only revolutionized the lives of all Americans, it also forced them to strengthen their ties to other nations more than ever before. Many Americans began to believe that the country had to protect its economic, political, and social interests internationally. A surge in European conquests for new lands and resources reinforced this new way of thinking about America's role in the world. Some Americans, such as Senator Henry Cabot Lodge, believed that the time was right for the United States to expand its interests abroad.

VIEWING HISTORY This 1902 photograph shows a man in a car overlooking the Grand Canyon. **Determining Relevance** *What does this photograph suggest about the new pressures facing the United States?*

66 *Small States are of the past and have no future. The modern movement is all toward the concentration of people and territory into great nations and large dominions. The great nations are rapidly absorbing for their future expansion and their present defence all the waste places of the earth. . . . As one of the great nations of the world, the United States must not fall out of the line of march.* 99
—Senator Henry Cabot Lodge, speech to Congress, 1895

Growth of Imperialism

As the map on the previous page shows, Europe had reached new heights in its quest for territories to rule. The late 1800s marked the peak of European **imperialism**, with much of Africa and Asia under foreign domination. Under imperialism, stronger nations attempt to create

584 Chapter 17 • *Becoming a World Power*

RESOURCE DIRECTORY

Teaching Resources
Guided Reading and Review booklet, p. 70

Other Print Resources
Nystrom *Atlas of Our Country* *Later Expansion of the United States*, pp. 32–33

Technology
Section Reading Support Transparencies
Guided Reading Audiotapes (English/Spanish), Ch. 17
Student Edition on Audio CD, Ch. 17
Color Transparencies *Time Lines*, C5
Prentice Hall Presentation Pro CD-ROM, Ch. 17
Companion Web site, www.phschool.com

empires by dominating weaker nations—economically, politically, culturally, or militarily.

Why Imperialism Grew Several factors accounted for the burst of imperialistic activity in the late 1800s.

Economic factors The growth of industry in Europe created an increased need for natural resources, such as rubber and petroleum, which came from undeveloped areas of the world. Manufacturing nations also required new markets in which to sell their manufactured goods.

Nationalistic factors Competition among European nations for large empires was the result of a rise in **nationalism,** or devotion to one's nation. Nationalism usually suggests that a nation's people believe themselves, their ideals, and their goals to be superior to those of other nations. In the late 1800s, nationalist feelings grew stronger in many countries, causing several European nations to take strong actions to protect their interests. For example, when France acquired colonies in West Africa in the late 1800s, rival nations Great Britain and Germany seized lands nearby to stop French expansion.

Military factors Advances in military technology produced European armies and navies that were far superior to those in Africa and Asia. Also, Europe's growing navies required bases around the world for taking on fuel and supplies.

Humanitarian factors Humanitarian and religious goals spurred on imperialists. Colonial officials, doctors, and missionaries believed they had a duty to spread the blessings of Western civilization, including its law, medicine, and Christian religion.

Europe Leads the Way Improved transportation and communication made it easier for Great Britain, France, and Russia, all with long imperialist traditions, to extend their grip over far-flung lands. Great Britain, in particular, acquired so much new territory around the globe that people began to say "the sun never sets on the British Empire." Competition for new territory grew even more intense when Germany, unified in 1871, seized colonies in Africa and Asia.

By 1890, the United States was eager to join the competition for new territories. Supporters of expansion denied that the United States sought to **annex** foreign lands. (To annex is to join a new territory to an existing country.) Yet annexation did take place.

Expanding U.S. Interests

In his Farewell Address in 1796, President George Washington had advised Americans to "steer clear of permanent alliances" with other countries. For the next century, Americans generally followed Washington's advice. The nation's rapid economic growth along with the settlement of the West left the United States with little interest in foreign affairs.

As early as the 1820s, the Monroe Doctrine had been the main principle of foreign policy in the United States. Taking Washington's advice, under this doctrine, the United States had declared itself neutral in European wars and

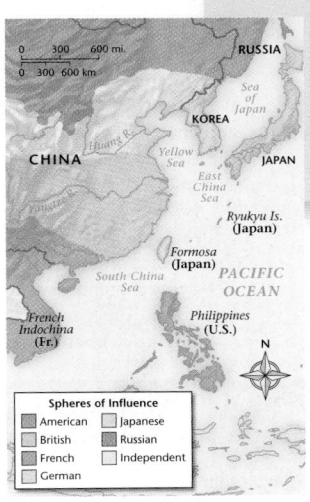

Spheres of Influence
- American
- British
- French
- German
- Japanese
- Russian
- Independent

Connecting with Culture

Discuss how nationalism affects a country's identity. Suggest that students think about how nationalism discourages friendly relations with other countries and fosters an insular feeling within a country. Encourage students to consider how cultivating a sense of superiority affects national pride. Have students identify and explain reasons for changes in political boundaries, such as those resulting from statehood and international conflicts. How do such events affect the nationalistic attitude of a country? You might challenge students to name countries that have suffered as a result of adopting a nationalist attitude. **(Verbal/Linguistic)**

BACKGROUND
Art History

Europeans who visited Japan in the 1850s and 1860s often returned with Japanese art. Wall scrolls were marked by clear, well-defined lines, a spare layout, and flat, bold colors. Impressionist painters, including Monet, Degas, and Toulouse-Lautrec, collected Japanese art and applied these techniques to their own work. An 1868 show of Japanese decorative arts made Japanese interior design popular in France.

READING CHECK

An expanded form of the Monroe Doctrine was used to justify American acquisition of territories from Mexico, the annexation of Texas and Midway, the purchase of Alaska, and highly favorable trade terms with Hawaii.

READING CHECK
What was the role of the Monroe Doctrine in shaping U.S. foreign policy?

---

warned other nations not to interfere in the Western Hemisphere. There were instances, however, when Americans "looked outward." Over time the Monroe Doctrine would be broadened to support American imperialism.

From the 1830s to 1850s, belief in the idea of Manifest Destiny helped the United States to justify its policies toward Mexico. The annexation of Texas and the acquisition of California and other southwestern lands were early steps toward claiming an American empire.

After the Civil War, American secretaries of state continued to apply the principles of the Monroe Doctrine. In 1866, for example, Secretary of State William H. Seward sent 50,000 troops to the Mexican border after France placed an emperor on the Mexican throne. In the face of this army, the French abandoned their colonial venture in Mexico. Then, in 1867, Seward bought Alaska from Russia. In addition to gaining more territory, Seward hoped that the presence of the United States on two sides of Canada would force the British out of that region. Most Americans ridiculed the undertaking. Seward, they said, was buying "walrus-covered icebergs" in a "barren, worthless, God-forsaken region." Seward, however, waged a successful campaign to educate the nation about Alaska's rich resources. In the end, the Senate ratified the purchase, and the United States took possession of what was then called "Seward's Folly."

Americans also showed their interest in the Pacific. In 1853, an American fleet led by Commodore Matthew C. Perry sailed into Tokyo Bay and convinced Japan to open trade relations with the United States. By the 1860s, the United States and several European countries had signed a series of treaties that allowed for expanded trade with China.

Now the U.S. government wanted control of some Pacific islands to use as refueling and repair stations for its naval vessels. To this end, Seward championed the annexation of the uninhabited Midway Islands in 1867. Eight years later the U.S. government signed a treaty with Hawaii. This agreement allowed Hawaiians to sell sugar in the United States duty-free, as long as they did not sell or lease territory to any foreign power.

COMPARING HISTORIANS' VIEWPOINTS
The Motivation Behind American Imperialism

Historians offer many different explanations for why the United States sought to expand its influence abroad.
Analyzing Viewpoints What factors do these historians describe as contributing to American expansionism?

Expansion to Solve Domestic Problems	**Expansion to Restore a Sense of Security**
"Spurred by a fantastic industrial revolution, which produced ever larger quantities of surplus goods, depressions, and violence, and warned by a growing radical literature that the system was not functioning properly, the United States prepared to solve its dilemmas with foreign expansion. Displaying a notable lack of absentmindedness, Americans set out to solve their problems by creating an empire whose dynamic and characteristics marked a new departure in their history." —*Walter LaFeber*, The New Empire: An Interpretation of American Expansion 1860–1898	"In a period of drastic social change, old maxims lost their sway over people who had good reason to take them for granted no longer; calm and thoughtful Americans, as well as frightened and anxious ones, felt compelled by events to reexamine the precepts of U.S. foreign policy. . . . Perhaps the United States could reaffirm its soundness by thrashing some country in a war or, more subtly, by demonstrating its ability to govern 'inferior' peoples in a colonial empire. Once indifferent to events outside their boundaries, Americans now searched abroad for means to internal salvation." —*Robert L. Beisner*, From the Old Diplomacy to the New, 1865–1900

586   Chapter 17 • *Becoming a World Power*

RESOURCE DIRECTORY

Other Print Resources
Historical Outline Map Book *The United States in the Caribbean, 1898–1917,* p. 58; *Central America and the Caribbean,* p. 81

Technology
Color Transparencies *Political Cartoons,* B9
RESOURCE PRO® **Visual Learning Activity**
Expansionism, found on Resource Pro, uses a political cartoon from the British magazine *Puck* to present a critical view of United States territorial expansion.

Also of great concern to the United States were the Caribbean islands and Latin America. In 1870, President Ulysses S. Grant announced that in the future the Monroe Doctrine would protect all territories in these two regions from "transfer to a European power." Not long after, the United States was playing an active role in several diplomatic and military conflicts in Latin America.

Arguments for U.S. Expansion

By the 1890s, Americans were debating what foreign policy would best serve the United States. Some argued that the country should continue to avoid foreign entanglements. Others offered a variety of reasons for increased American involvement in international affairs.

Promoting Economic Growth   A chief argument in favor of expansion was economic. By the late 1800s, the industrialists, inventors, and workers of the United States had built a powerful industrial economy. Americans alone, however, could not consume everything their nation produced. The overproduction of food and goods led to financial panics and frequent economic depressions. Protesting their plight, workers and farmers helped to convince business and political leaders that the United States must secure new markets abroad.

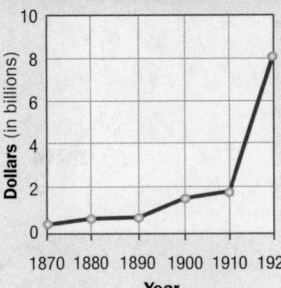

Many business leaders agreed that the economic problems of the nation could be solved only by expanding its markets. For this reason, they threw their support behind expansionist policies. Some American businesses already dominated international markets. Firms such as Rockefeller's Standard Oil and American Telephone and Telegraph had all become international businesses.

Other American business leaders had gone a step further and invested directly in the economies of other countries. In some cases their investments gave them political influence in those countries. In Central America, for example, an American named Minor C. Keith provided financial services to the Costa Rican government. In return, he won long-term leases for lands and railroad lines. By 1913, Keith's United Fruit Company not only exported 50 million bunches of bananas a year to the United States, it also dominated the governments and economies of Costa Rica, Guatemala, and Honduras. As a result, some people began calling the Central American nations **banana republics.**

Protecting American Security   Lobbyists who favored a strong United States Navy formed a second force pushing for expansion. By the 1880s, U.S. warships left over from the Civil War were rusting and rotting. Naval officers joined with business interests to convince Congress to build modern steam-powered, steel-hulled ships to protect overseas trade.

The most influential of these officers was Captain (later Admiral) Alfred T. Mahan. In his 1890 book, *The Influence of Sea Power Upon History, 1660–1783,* Mahan argued that the nation's economic future hinged on gaining new markets abroad. In his view, the United States needed a powerful navy to protect these markets from foreign rivals.

Influenced by supporters of an expanded navy, Congress established a Naval Advisory Board in 1881. The board pushed to increase the navy's budget. Two years later, Congress authorized the building of three cruisers and two battleships, including the U.S.S. *Maine.* Finally, the Naval Act of 1890 called for the construction of more battleships, gunboats, torpedo boats, and

Value of United States Exports, 1870–1920

SOURCE: *Historical Statistics of the United States, Colonial Times to 1970*

INTERPRETING GRAPHS
Businesses eagerly sought new markets abroad in the late 1800s and early 1900s. **Analyzing Information** *By how much did U.S. exports increase between 1870 and 1920?*

Reading Comprehension

1. Industrial growth; nationalism; advances in military technology; humanitarian and religious goals.

2. To keep the Western Hemisphere free from intervention by European powers; to justify Manifest Destiny as well as the acquisition of overseas territories, such as Midway.

3. Foreign markets were seen as necessary to sell the nation's surplus products. American industrial and agricultural goods could not be consumed fast enough domestically to prevent recurring cycles of panic and depression.

4. They worried that the closing of the frontier would deplete the nation's energy; a quest for an empire might restore America's pioneer spirit. There was a belief that Americans could civilize and Christianize other peoples.

Critical Thinking and Writing

5. It created a sense of urgency for Americans. Many believed that the United States would need to acquire overseas territories in order to continue on the path toward becoming a great nation.

6. Answers should include territory acquired during westward expansion, as well as Alaska and Midway.

Take It to the NET

Answers will vary. For: the need for more land and new trading markets, Alaska's natural resources, and the potential to force the British out of Canada. Against: the cost involved, and the isolationist views of many Americans who did not want to be involved in European affairs.

CAPTION ANSWERS

Interpreting Political Cartoons The United States is represented by the largest rooster and is in charge of the chicken coop (the Western Hemisphere). The U.S. protects its own interests and weaker nations by blocking strong European powers.

INTERPRETING POLITICAL CARTOONS As this 1901 political cartoon suggests, the United States relied on the principles of the Monroe Doctrine to block European involvement in Latin America. **Drawing Inferences** *What is the cartoonist suggesting about the role of the United States in world affairs?*

cruisers. By 1900, the United States had one of the most powerful navies in the world. The expanded fleet suggested that the United States was willing and able to confront an enemy on the open sea.

Preserving American Spirit A third force for expansion consisted of people who feared that the United States was losing its vitality. Among them were Massachusetts Senator Henry Cabot Lodge, historian Frederick Jackson Turner, and a young politician from New York named Theodore Roosevelt. Worried that the closing of the frontier would sap the nation's energy, they argued that a quest for an empire might restore the country's pioneer spirit.

These and other leaders of the day drew on the doctrine of social Darwinism to justify the takeover of new territories, just as they had done earlier to defend the conquest of Native Americans. In the opinion of respected leaders such as Congregationalist minister Josiah Strong and Indiana senator Albert J. Beveridge, the civilizations produced by Anglo-Saxon and Teutonic (Germanic) peoples were superior to the societies they conquered. Social Darwinists believed that expansionism was not only this nation's destiny but also a noble pursuit, for it introduced Christianity and modern civilization to other "heathen" peoples around the world. This was an age when many intellectuals believed that certain racial and national groups were superior to others.

Americans Lean Toward Expansion Gradually public opinion warmed to the idea of expansionism. Although most Americans had accepted the conquest of Native Americans as right and inevitable, they did not see themselves as potential rulers of oppressed foreign peoples. Moreover, they did want new markets abroad and favorable trade relations. What they soon discovered was that political and military entanglements tended to follow. The United States would find itself in difficult, bloody, and painful foreign conflicts.

Section 1 Assessment

READING COMPREHENSION

1. Why did **imperialism** grow in Europe at the end of the 1800s?

2. How did the United States apply the Monroe Doctrine to its foreign policy throughout the 1800s?

3. Why did U.S. policymakers feel the need to secure new markets abroad?

4. Why did some believe that U.S. expansion was needed to preserve the "American spirit"?

CRITICAL THINKING AND WRITING

5. **Recognizing Cause and Effect** What effect did the growth of European imperialism have on United States attitudes toward foreign policy and expansion?

6. **Writing a List** Beginning with the Louisiana Purchase, write a chronological list tracing specific examples of American expansionism before 1880.

Take It to the NET

Activity: Writing a Letter If you were alive in 1867, would you have supported or opposed Seward's purchase of Alaska? Write a letter to the editor explaining your position. Use the links provided in the *America: Pathways to the Present* area of the following Web site for help in completing this activity.
www.phschool.com

RESOURCE DIRECTORY

Teaching Resources
Units 5/6 booklet
• Section 1 Quiz, p. 52
Guide to the Essentials
• Section 1 Summary, p. 88

Technology
Color Transparencies *American Diversity,* G11

READING FOCUS

- How did the activities of the United States in Latin America set the stage for war with Spain?

- What were the events leading up to and following the Spanish-American War?

- What challenges did the United States face after the war?

- Why did the United States seek to gain influence in the Pacific?

MAIN IDEA

A swift victory in the Spanish-American War confirmed the status of the United States as a world power, but it left some people arguing over how to govern newly acquired territories.

KEY TERMS

arbitration
jingoism
Platt Amendment
sphere of influence
Open Door Policy

TAKING NOTES

As you read, complete this chart listing the effects of United States foreign policies on other nations after the Spanish-American War.

Effects of United States Foreign Policy

Nation	Policy and Effects
Philippines	Annexed by U.S. after Spanish-American War. U.S. soldiers remain there. Fighting between U.S. and Philippines occurs. U.S. occupation continues until 1946.
Cuba	
Puerto Rico	
Hawaii	
China	

SECTION OBJECTIVES

1. Read about United States activities in Latin America that set the stage for war with Spain.

2. Find out about events leading up to and following the Spanish-American War.

3. Discover challenges faced by the United States after the war.

4. Learn why the United States sought to gain influence in the Pacific.

BELLRINGER

Warm-Up Activity Write the word *sensationalism* on the chalkboard and ask students to define it and explain how it can trigger public reactions. Discuss news that might be called sensational.

Activating Prior Knowledge Can students name the country that had sovereignty over Cuba in the nineteenth century? *(Spain)*

READING STRATEGY

As students read, have them jot down the key events that led to the Spanish-American War in 1898. Then have them review their list to make sure it is in chronological order. Ask students to briefly summarize the economic effects of the Spanish-American War on the United States. Have them state the importance of the year 1898 in American history.

Setting the Scene The United States was poised on the edge of becoming a world power. All that was needed was something to push the country in that direction. The cautious McKinley administration resisted the growing demands of those in Congress and throughout the country who hungered for expansion. The time was not yet right. As they waited for action, Americans woke up to this newspaper headline in October 1897:

> ❝ EVANGELINA CISNEROS RESCUED BY THE JOURNAL: AN AMERICAN NEWSPAPER ACCOMPLISHES AT A SINGLE STROKE WHAT THE RED TAPE OF DIPLOMACY FAILED UTTERLY TO BRING ABOUT IN MANY MONTHS. ❞
>
> —Headline in the *New York Journal*, October 10, 1897

Many would have been shocked to read in big, bold letters that a newspaper had acted outside the law to protect liberty and justice abroad. In this instance, the *Journal* staged the rescue of someone they described as a beautiful, young Cuban girl being held prisoner by the Spanish. Vivid headlines such as this attracted readers craving controversy and excitement. The sensational stories that followed increased newspaper circulations and resulted in huge profits for newspaper publishers.

Another year would pass before the United States fought a war that would forever change its role in world affairs. The newspapers did not cause the war, but they did help to reinforce and magnify a new set of assumptions among the American people regarding their place in the world. Americans began to feel that their nation was growing bigger and stronger. They were ready and willing to take action outside U.S. borders. In the process of expanding and becoming a world power, however, the United States increasingly found itself in conflict with other nations.

VIEWING HISTORY This illustration by Thure de Thulstrup depicts Cuban rebels charging into battle with the Spanish. **Analyzing Visual Information** *What do the details in the illustration tell you about the artist's view of the Cuban rebellion?*

CAPTION ANSWERS

Viewing History The viewer is riding with the Cuban rebels and feels a sense of purpose and triumph. The machetes held high indicate charging forward and success. The artist most likely supports the rebellion.

RESOURCE DIRECTORY

Teaching Resources
Learning Styles Lesson Plans booklet, p. 36
Guided Reading and Review booklet, p. 71

Technology
Section Reading Support Transparencies
Guided Reading Audiotapes (English/Spanish), Ch. 17
Student Edition on Audio CD, Ch. 17
Color Transparencies *Historical Maps,* A27
Prentice Hall Presentation Pro CD-ROM, Ch. 17
Companion Web site, www.phschool.com

Focus An aggressive foreign policy brought the United States into conflict with other nations.

Ask what problems the United States faced as a new world power.

Instruct Discuss how United States intervention in Latin America and the Pacific resulted in conflict. Ask how conflict in the Caribbean developed into war with Spain. What were the major causes of the Spanish-American War? What lands did the United States gain?

Discuss how national pride and an aggressive foreign policy could be seen at work in events in Chile, Cuba, the Philippines, and Hawaii in the late 1800s. In what areas in the Pacific did the United States pursue an expansionist policy?

Assess/Reteach Ask students how the United States' position among nations changed as a result of the Spanish-American War.

READING CHECK

The United States forced Great Britain to accept the Cleveland administration's plan for resolving a dispute over South American territory. Thus, the United States proved itself to be the dominant power in the Western Hemisphere.

READING CHECK
How did the 1895 dispute between the United States and Great Britain reaffirm the validity of the Monroe Doctrine?

Setting the Stage for War

American expansionists paid close attention to the political and economic actions of countries in the Western Hemisphere. In the 1890s, several incidents took place that allowed the United States to strengthen its role in Latin American affairs.

Displays of United States Power In 1891, an angry Chilean mob attacked a group of American sailors on shore leave in Valparaíso. They killed two Americans and injured seventeen others. The U.S. government reacted strongly, forcing Chile to pay $75,000 to the families of the sailors who were killed or injured. Two years later, when a rebellion threatened the friendly republican government of Brazil, President Cleveland ordered naval units to Rio de Janeiro to protect United States shipping interests. This show of force broke the back of the rebellion.

In the third and most important incident of the era, the United States confronted the nation then considered the most powerful in the world, Great Britain. Since the 1840s, Britain and Venezuela had disputed ownership of a piece of territory located at the border between Venezuela and British Guiana. In the 1880s, the dispute intensified when rumors surfaced of mineral wealth in this border area. President Cleveland's Secretary of State, Richard Olney, demanded in July 1895 that Britain acknowledge the Monroe Doctrine and submit the boundary dispute to **arbitration.** (Arbitration is the settlement of a dispute by a person or panel chosen to listen to both sides and come to a decision.) The British government replied that the doctrine had no standing in international law.

Eventually Britain backed down and agreed to arbitration. Concerned about the rising power of Germany in Africa, the British government realized that it needed to stay on friendly terms with the increasingly powerful United States.

The Cuban Rebellion By the mid-1890s, the United States had not only reaffirmed the Monroe Doctrine, it had also forced the world's most powerful nation to bow to its will. Events in Cuba soon paved the way for a far more spectacular display of American power.

An island nation off the coast of Florida, Cuba first rebelled against Spain in 1868. After ten years of fighting the rebels, Spain finally put in place a few meager reforms to appease the Cuban people. In 1895, after the island's economy had collapsed, Cubans rebelled again. This time Spain sent 150,000 troops and its best general, Valeriano Weyler, to put down the rebellion. In a desperate attempt to prevent civilians from aiding the rebels, Weyler instituted a policy of "reconcentration." He forced hundreds of thousands of Cubans into guarded camps. The prisoners, including women, children, and the elderly, lived in miserable conditions with little food or sanitation. Over two years, disease and starvation killed an estimated 200,000 Cubans.

Cuban exiles living in the United States, led by the journalist José Martí, urged the United States to intervene. Both Presidents Cleveland and McKinley refused. They were unwilling to spend the money that intervention would require and feared the United States would be saddled with colonial responsibilities it could not handle. Frustrated, Cuban guerrillas turned to the one tactic they knew would attract the U.S. government's attention: the destruction of American sugar plantations and mills in Cuba. As a result, business owners increased their pressure on the government to act.

Focus on WORLD EVENTS

José Martí Fights for Cuban Independence José Martí (1853–1895) dedicated his life to achieving Cuban independence. A patriot and a revolutionary, Martí had dreamed of *Cuba Libre* (a free Cuba) since the age of 15. A gifted writer, he wrote poems as a teenager and soon founded his own newspaper, *La patria libre (The Free Fatherland).*

Because of his revolutionary activity, Martí was forced to leave Cuba in 1871. He was deported to Spain, where he received a master's degree and a law degree. Martí finally settled in New York City in 1881, where he led the Cuban Revolutionary Party. In 1895, Martí left New York to stage attacks in Cuba with other revolutionaries. Later that year, he was killed in battle, just a few years before *Cuba Libre* became a reality.

RESOURCE DIRECTORY

Other Print Resources

American History Block Scheduling Support *The Spanish-American War: Door to Imperialism,* found in the Prosperity, Depression, and War folder, includes interdisciplinary lesson suggestions and activities for Geography and History, Primary Sources, Biography, and Literature.

Historical Outline Map Book *The Spanish-American War,* p. 57

Technology

Color Transparencies *Historical Maps,* A30

RESOURCE PRO® **Literature Activity** *The Open Boat,* found on Resource Pro, describes the harrowing experience of Stephen Crane, who survived the sinking of a munitions supply steamer returning from Cuba in 1897.

RESOURCE PRO® **Critical Thinking Activity** *Drawing Conclusions: The Explosion of the Maine,* found on Resource Pro, presents contemporary reports about the mysterious explosion of the *Maine* to help students apply this skill.

Yellow Journalism Demands for United States intervention in Cuba also came in large part from American newspapers. In the 1890s, a fierce competition for readers broke out between two New York City newspapers, the *New York World* and the *New York Morning Journal*. Both newspapers reported exaggerated and sometimes false stories about the events in Cuba in order to increase circulation. The battle pitted the *World's* established publisher, Joseph Pulitzer, against a newcomer to the city, the *Journal's* William Randolph Hearst.

Hearst bought the *Journal* when it was struggling in 1895. By luring experienced journalists from other papers, including the *World*, he managed to turn it into a success. Hearst used a variety of other techniques to increase the *Journal's* circulation, including printing sensational crime stories, using illustrations and vivid headlines to draw in the reader, and lowering the price to one penny.

Both Hearst and Pulitzer took advantage of the horrifying stories coming from Cuba about the "Butcher" Weyler and his barbed-wire concentration camps. Their sensational headlines and stories, known as yellow journalism, whipped up American public opinion in favor of the rebels. The intense burst of national pride and the desire for an aggressive foreign policy that followed came to be known as **jingoism.** The name came from a line in a British song of the 1870s: "We don't want to fight, yet by Jingo! if we do, We've got the ships, we've got the men, and got the money too."

The Spanish-American War

The stories printed in newspapers such as the *Journal* strengthened American sympathy for the Cuban rebels. Slowly the demand for U.S. intervention began to build.

Steps to War Early in 1898, riots erupted in Havana, the capital of Cuba. In response, President McKinley moved the battleship U.S.S. *Maine* into the city's harbor to protect American citizens and property. Several events followed that pushed the United States to war.

The de Lôme letter A few weeks later, in early February 1898, United States newspapers published a letter stolen from the Spanish ambassador to Washington, Dupuy de Lôme. The de Lôme letter, which described McKinley as "weak and a bidder for the admiration of the crowd," caused an outcry in the United States. The letter raised a commotion not just because it ridiculed McKinley, but mostly because of the sensationalism surrounding it. Because de Lôme was a Spaniard, the press now had a golden opportunity to intensify anti-Spanish sentiments.

The explosion of the U.S.S. Maine Then, on February 15, an explosion sank the *Maine*, killing more than 250 American sailors. The blast probably had been caused by a fire that set off ammunition, but the American public put the blame on Spain. (The exact cause of the explosion has never been determined.) The papers jumped on the chance to arouse more bitter feelings toward Spain. The *New York Morning Journal* asked, "How long shall the United States sit idle and indifferent within sound and hearing of rapine and murder? How long?" The Spanish were willing to enter into arbitration talks to determine more decisively if they were responsible, but that did not matter. An enraged American public called for war. Still, McKinley hesitated.

American BIOGRAPHY

William Randolph Hearst 1863–1951

William Randolph Hearst's first venture into newspaper publishing came in 1887, when he took control of the *San Francisco Examiner,* a faltering paper owned by his father. Hearst used a combination of investigative reporting and sensationalistic stories to increase circulation.

After achieving success with the *New York Morning Journal* several years later, Hearst went on to serve briefly in the United States House of Representatives. He continued to expand his publishing empire, acquiring newspapers in cities throughout the country. By 1935, he owned 28 major newspapers, 18 magazines, and several radio stations and news services. Although the era of rabid yellow journalism declined following the turn of the century, the innovations of Hearst and his competitors continue to influence journalism today.

INTERPRETING TABLES
Sales of Hearst's *New York Morning Journal* soared in 1898.
Synthesizing Information *What factors led to the increased demand for papers such as the* Journal?

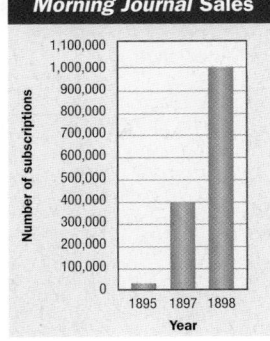

Morning Journal Sales

Number of subscriptions vs. Year (1895, 1897, 1898)

From the Archives of
American Heritage®

Sousa's Greatest

On May 14, 1897, John Philip Sousa premiered his most inspired and glorious march, "The Stars and Stripes Forever." The march, which he had composed in his head as he strolled the deck of the steamship *Teutonic* while crossing from Liverpool to New York the previous November, brought down the house. A joyous audience made the Sousa Band repeat it twice more. Critics in the next day's papers were just as ecstatic. One called the piece "stirring enough to rouse the American eagle from his crag and set him to shriek exultantly while he hurls his arrows at the aurora borealis." The march's "jingoistic" character, as many critics called it, reflected the times—war with Spain was brewing. Although Sousa was already known as the March King, it took "The Stars and Stripes Forever" to make him immortal. Until his death in 1932, no audience would let him leave the podium without conducting it at least once. Source: Frederic D. Schwarz, "The Time Machine," *American Heritage®* magazine, May 1997.

Preparing in the Philippines On the other side of the world, the people of another of Spain's last remaining possessions, the Philippine Islands, also were rebelling. In the view of Theodore Roosevelt, then Assistant Secretary of the Navy, the Philippines could become a key base from which the United States might protect its Asian trade. On February 25, while his boss, the Secretary of the Navy, was out of the office, Roosevelt cabled naval commanders in the Pacific to prepare for military action against Spain. When President McKinley discovered what Roosevelt had done, he ordered most of the cables withdrawn, but he made an exception in the case of the cable directed to Admiral George Dewey. Dewey was told to attack the Spanish fleet in the Philippines if war broke out with Spain.

McKinley's war message Late in March, in a final attempt at a peaceful solution, McKinley sent a list of demands to Spain. These included compensation for the *Maine*, an end to the reconcentration camps, a truce in Cuba, and Cuban independence. Eager to find a peaceful settlement to the crisis, Spain accepted all but the last. McKinley decided he could not resist the growing cries for war. On April 11, he sent a war message to Congress. A few days later, rallying to the cry of "Remember the *Maine*!" Congress recognized Cuban independence and authorized force against Spain.

"A Splendid Little War" The war's first action took place not in Cuba but in the Philippines, as shown on the map on this page. On May 1, 1898, Admiral Dewey launched a surprise attack on Spanish ships anchored in Manila Bay, destroying Spain's entire Pacific fleet in just seven hours. In Cuba, meanwhile, United States warships quickly bottled up Spain's Atlantic fleet in the harbor at Santiago.

American army troops gathered in Tampa, Florida, to prepare for an invasion of Cuba. The group that received the most publicity was the First Volunteer Cavalry, known as the Rough Riders. Its leader, Theodore Roosevelt, had resigned his position as Assistant Secretary of the Navy and recruited a diverse group of volunteers that included cowboys, miners, policemen, and college athletes. On July 1, 1898, Roosevelt led the Rough Riders in a charge up San Juan Hill. This charge became the most famous incident of the war.

The Spanish fleet made a desperate attempt to escape Santiago harbor on July 3. In the ensuing battle, the United States Navy sank every Spanish ship,

MAP SKILLS Although the Spanish-American War was fought in two locations on opposite sides of the world, the United States defeated Spain in just nine weeks. **Location** *At what specific sites were the major battles of the war fought?*

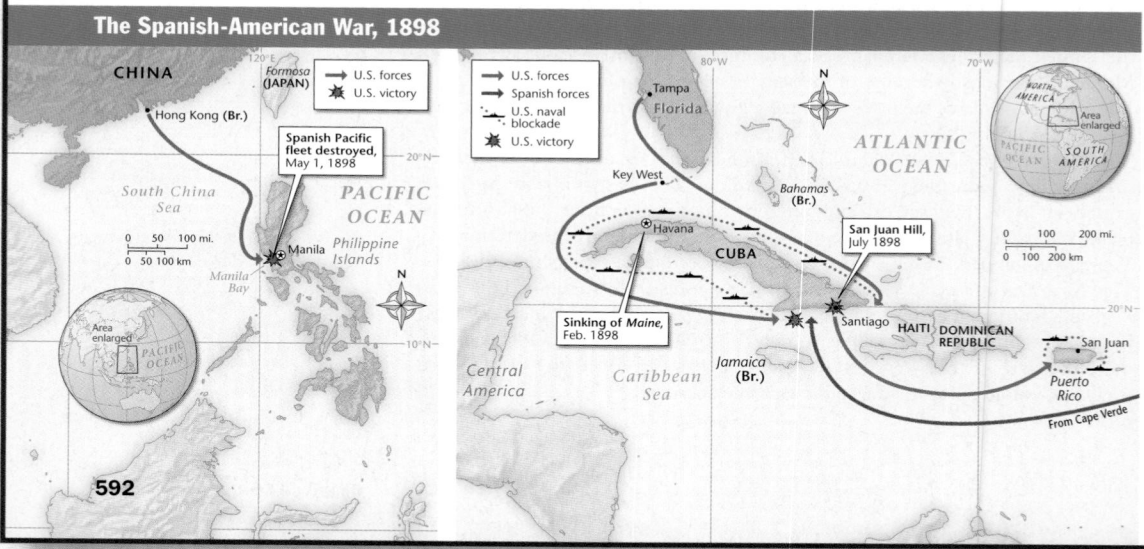

The Spanish-American War, 1898

setting off wild Independence Day celebrations back in the United States.

It had all seemed quite simple. Although 2,500 Americans had died in the short war, fewer than 400 died in battle. The remainder died from food poisoning, yellow fever, malaria, and inadequate medical care. Future Secretary of State John Hay captured the public mood when he wrote his friend Teddy Roosevelt that it had been "a splendid little war."

The Treaty of Paris The United States signed the Treaty of Paris with Spain in December 1898. In the treaty, the Spanish government recognized Cuba's independence. In return for a payment of $20 million, Spain also gave up the Philippines, Puerto Rico, and the Pacific island of Guam to the United States. These became "unincorporated" territories of the United States, which meant that these lands were not intended for eventual statehood.

The Senate ratified the treaty in February 1899, but not without great debate. A majority of senators supported the annexation of these territories, but many senators still remained passionately against such policies. Although the outnumbered anti-imperialists held their ground, the treaty narrowly passed by only one vote more than the two-thirds majority needed.

New Challenges After the War

With many in the United States divided over the issue of imperialism, developing a policy for dealing with the new territories proved to be difficult. How could the United States become a colonial power without violating the nation's most basic principle—that all people have the right to liberty?

Dilemma in the Philippines President McKinley was forced to justify this seeming departure from American ideals with his policy toward the Philippines.

> 66 We could not leave them to themselves—they were unfit for self-government, and they would soon have anarchy and misrule worse than Spain's was. . . . There was nothing left for us to do but to take them all, and to educate the Filipinos, and uplift and civilize and Christianize them. . . . 99
>
> —President McKinley

Despite the fact that most Filipinos were already Christian, McKinley pressed on with his arguments for annexation. He made what was perhaps a more convincing argument when he warned that if the United States did not act first, European powers might try to seize the islands and new conflicts could result.

Filipino rebels had fought alongside American troops in the war against Spain with the expectation that victory would bring independence. But when rebel leader Emilio Aguinaldo issued a proclamation in January 1899 declaring the Philippines a republic, the United States ignored him. Mounting tensions between the rebel forces and American soldiers finally erupted into war in February. In the bitter three-year war that followed, more than 4,000 Americans were killed and nearly 3,000 more wounded. Fighting without restraint—and sometimes with great brutality—American forces killed some 16,000 Filipino

INTERPRETING POLITICAL CARTOONS European powers and Uncle Sam look on as the United States Navy defeats the Spanish. **Drawing Inferences** Why do you think most of the European powers look upset by this turn of events?

READING CHECK
Why did President McKinley want to annex the Philippines?

Connecting with History and Conflict

Have students write a short essay on U.S. intervention in foreign affairs. Suggest that students reflect on events at the end of the nineteenth century as they formulate their opinions on U.S. foreign intervention. Have students consider some of the following questions as they prepare their essay: Why and when should our government become involved in the affairs of another country? What specific situations warrant U.S. intervention? When should the U.S. stay out of another country's affairs? **(Verbal/Linguistic)**

BACKGROUND

Biography

Walter Reed (1851–1902) was a U.S. Army doctor who proved that yellow fever was transmitted by mosquitoes. Yellow fever is an infectious tropical and subtropical disease that affects humans, monkeys, and some other small mammals. Yellow fever was first recorded in the sixteenth century in South America. For the next 300 years, it was one of the greatest plagues in history. During the nineteenth century, many people believed that yellow fever was spread by *fomites*—bedding and clothing that had been used by a yellow-fever victim. Reed went to Cuba in 1899 after an outbreak of yellow fever in the U.S. garrison in Havana. After Reed's discovery, yellow fever was practically eliminated from Havana. The last outbreak of yellow fever in the U.S. took place in 1905 in New Orleans and other southern ports.

READING CHECK

Anti-imperialists in Congress had formulated the Teller Amendment to ensure that Cuba became independent after the war. The Teller Amendment forbade the United States from annexing Cuba.

CAPTION ANSWERS

Fast Forward to Today Balkans as peacekeeper; South Korea as peacekeeper; Iraq—enforcing the no-fly zones.

READING CHECK
What was the purpose of the Teller Amendment?

---

rebels and as many as 200,000 Filipino civilians. Occasional fighting continued for years. The Philippines did not gain complete independence until 1946.

The Fate of Cuba Supporters of Cuban independence had attached an amendment, called the Teller Amendment, to Congress's 1898 war resolution against Spain. The document promised that the United States would not annex Cuba. Yet American involvement in Cuba did not end with the victory over Spain in 1898. In order to protect American business interests in the chaotic environment that followed the war, President McKinley installed a military government in Cuba led by General Leonard Wood. The military government would remain in place for three years. This government organized a school system and restored economic stability. It also established a commission led by Major Walter Reed of the Army Medical Corps that discovered a cure for the deadly disease yellow fever.

Many Cubans felt that the United States had betrayed its goal of securing independence for Cuba. To some, it seemed that the United States had simply replaced Spain as Cuba's sovereign nation. In 1900, the U.S. military government authorized the Cubans to begin to draft a constitution. The new constitution was modeled on the United States Constitution and did not allow for continued American involvement in Cuba. The U.S. government, however, only agreed to remove its troops if the Cubans included provisions outlined in a document called the **Platt Amendment.** The Platt Amendment stipulated that the Cuban government could not enter any foreign agreements, must allow the United States to establish naval bases as needed on the island, and must give the United States the right to intervene whenever necessary. Cuba, which wanted an end to U.S. occupation, reluctantly agreed to the amendment. The

Fast Forward to Today

U.S. Foreign Intervention

Victory in the Spanish-American War touched off a new era in the United States. Its role in world affairs forever changed, the United States became involved in many foreign conflicts over the next century.

1898 The United States enters the Spanish-American War.

1917 After a time of neutrality, the United States enters World War I on the side of the Allies.

1941 After Japan bombs Pearl Harbor, the United States enters World War II.

1950 Following North Korea's invasion of South Korea, President Truman calls on American troops to defend South Korea.

1964 Congress passes the Gulf of Tonkin Resolution, authorizing the use of American military force in the war in Vietnam.

1991 The United States and its allies free Kuwait from Iraqi occupation in the Gulf War.

1999 After NATO launches airstrikes against Serbia, the United States commits troops to a NATO peacekeeping force in Kosovo.

? Since the Spanish-American War, the United States has become involved in many foreign conflicts. What foreign conflicts does the United States play a part in today? What is its role in these conflicts?

594 Chapter 17 • *Becoming a World Power*

RESOURCE DIRECTORY

Teaching Resources
Biography, Literature, and Comparing Primary Sources booklet (Biography) *Walter Reed,* p. 22
Great Debates booklet (Great Debates) *Should the United States Have Colonies?* p. 14

Technology
Color Transparencies *Historical Maps,* A28; *Cause-and-Effect Charts,* D7

United States intervened militarily in Cuban affairs only twice while the Platt Amendment remained in force until 1934.

The United States and Puerto Rico
Unlike Cuba, Puerto Rico did not become independent. The United States maintained a military government in the territory until 1900. The military aided in the development of infrastructure and education, and also acted as a police force. With the passage of the Foraker Act in 1900, the United States removed its military control and established a civil government, still under U.S. control. Gradually, the United States ceded more freedom and control to the Puerto Rican people.

In an attempt to stem a growing independence movement, the United States government granted Puerto Ricans American citizenship with the passage of the Jones Act in 1917. However, because the Constitution did not apply to United States territories, this citizenship was based only on the act of Congress. In addition, although Puerto Ricans could now elect their local legislatures, the United States retained the power to appoint key officials, such as the governor.

Other Gains in the Pacific

The United States government intervened in other parts of the Pacific at the same time that events played out in the Spanish-American War. This intervention eventually brought about changes in the relationships of the United States with Hawaii, Samoa, and China.

Annexation of Hawaii Hawaii had become increasingly important to U.S. business interests in the late 1800s. In 1887, Hawaii and the United States renewed a trade treaty that allowed Hawaiian sugar to be sold duty-free in the United States. Hawaii also leased Pearl Harbor to the United States as a fueling and repair station for naval vessels. That same year, white Hawaiian-born planters forced the Hawaiian king, Kalakaua, to accept a new constitution that, in effect, gave them control of the government.

When the king died in 1891, his sister Liliuokalani came to the throne. A strong nationalist, Queen Liliuokalani opposed U.S. control of the islands and sought to reduce the power of foreign merchants. In 1893, with the help of the United States Marines, pineapple planter Sanford B. Dole removed Queen Liliuokalani from power. He proclaimed Hawaii a republic and requested that it be annexed by the United States.

When William McKinley was elected President, he supported the annexation. "We need Hawaii just as much and a good deal more than we did California. It is Manifest Destiny," McKinley said in early 1898. After briefly considering whether the Hawaiian people wished to be annexed, Congress was swayed by arguments that the United States needed naval stations in Hawaii in order to protect its world trade. In 1898, Congress approved the annexation of Hawaii.

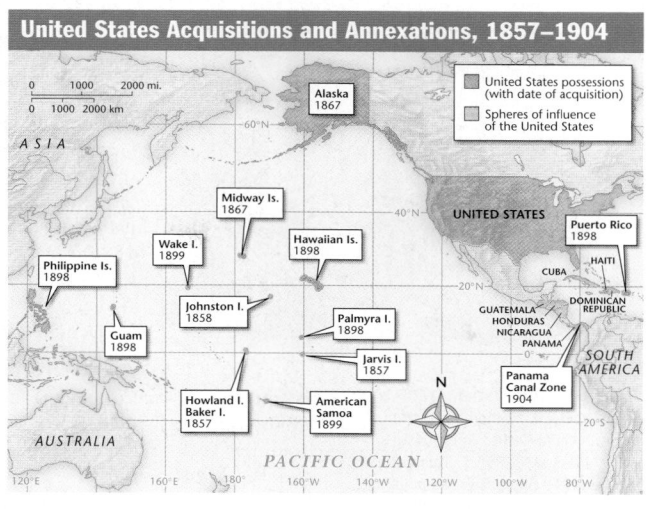

United States Acquisitions and Annexations, 1857–1904

- ■ United States possessions (with date of acquisition)
- ■ Spheres of influence of the United States

Alaska 1867
Midway Is. 1867
Wake I. 1899
Hawaiian Is. 1898
Philippine Is. 1898
Johnston I. 1858
Guam 1898
Palmyra I. 1898
Jarvis I. 1857
Howland I. Baker I. 1857
American Samoa 1899
Panama Canal Zone 1904
Puerto Rico 1898

UNITED STATES
CUBA
HAITI
DOMINICAN REPUBLIC
GUATEMALA
HONDURAS
NICARAGUA
PANAMA
SOUTH AMERICA
ASIA
AUSTRALIA
PACIFIC OCEAN

MAP SKILLS Between 1857 and 1904, the United States acquired many new territorial possessions around the globe. **Regions** *Why were so many of these new possessions located in the Pacific Ocean?*

Chapter 17 • Section 2   **595**

Reading Comprehension

1. Strengthened American sympathy for the Cuban rebels; nationalism and a demand for U.S. intervention began to build.

2. The war was short and victorious. American deaths in battle were relatively few.

3. The Platt Amendment made Cuba into an American satellite. The Treaty of Paris made the Philippines, Guam, and Puerto Rico American possessions outright. American forces fought a brutal campaign against Filipino rebels.

4. The United States proclaimed an Open Door trade policy in regard to China. The United States acquired partial control over Samoa by treaty and by declaring protectorate status. Hawaii was annexed to the United States in 1898.

Critical Thinking and Writing

5. In both wars the U.S. swiftly defeated weak and disorganized enemies and acquired important new territories from the defeated nations in the ensuing peace treaties.

6. Essays will vary, but should reflect the style presented in the section.

Answers will vary. Students may note that Hawaii was not annexed peacefully, but by subterfuge and force; the U.S. economic interests in Hawaii; the tone of the apology.

Samoa The Polynesian islands of Samoa represented another possible stepping stone to the growing trade with Asia. Back in 1878, the United States had negotiated a treaty with Samoa offering protection in return for a lease on Samoa's fine harbor at Pago Pago. When Britain and Germany began competing for control of these islands in the 1880s, tension between these European powers and the United States almost led to war. Eventually the three nations arranged a three-way protectorate of Samoa in 1889. The withdrawal of Great Britain from Samoa in 1899 left Germany and the United States to divide up the islands. A year after the annexation of Hawaii, the United States had acquired the harbor at Pago Pago as well.

An Open Door to China China's huge population and its vast markets became increasingly important to American trade by the late 1800s. But the United States was not the only nation interested in China. Countries such as Russia, Germany, Britain, France, and Japan were seeking **spheres of influence,** or areas of economic and political control, in China. In 1899, John Hay, President McKinley's Secretary of State, wrote notes to the major European powers trying to persuade them to keep an "open door" to China. He wanted to ensure through his **Open Door Policy** that the United States would have equal access to China's millions of consumers. Hay's suggestions met with a cool response from the other countries.

Meanwhile, many Chinese resented foreign influence of any kind. A secret society called the Righteous and Harmonious Fists (the Western press called them "Boxers") started a rebellion in the spring of 1900 that led to the massacre of 300 foreigners and Christian Chinese. Although the European powers eventually defeated the Boxers, Secretary Hay feared that these imperialist nations would use the rebellion as an excuse to seize more Chinese territory. Thus, he issued a second series of Open Door notes. These notes reaffirmed the principle of open trade in China and made an even stronger statement about the intention of the United States to preserve it.

INTERPRETING POLITICAL CARTOONS Competition for trade in China led to Secretary Hay's Open Door Policy. This cartoon depicts Uncle Sam as holding the "key" to China's "open door." **Drawing Inferences** *Is the cartoonist being sympathetic toward, or critical of, Hay's Open Door Policy?*

Section 2 Assessment

READING COMPREHENSION

1. How did yellow journalism and **jingoism** influence Americans' views of the Cuban rebellion?

2. What did John Hay mean when he called America's war with Spain a "splendid little war"?

3. How did U.S. policies, such as the **Platt Amendment,** secure control over its newly acquired territories?

4. What methods did the United States use to gain land and influence in the Pacific region?

CRITICAL THINKING AND WRITING

5. **Making Comparisons** In what ways was the Spanish-American War similar to the war between the United States and Mexico in 1846?

6. **Writing a News Story** Using information from this section, write a brief newspaper story with a sensational headline in the same style that was used in William Randolph Hearst's newspapers around the turn of the century.

Activity: Writing a Letter
Research the history of the American annexation of Hawaii in 1898 and the apology offered by our government in 1993. Consider whether you think the apology was sufficient. Write a letter to your representative in Congress expressing your views on the subject. Use the links provided in the *America: Pathways to the Present* area of the following Web site for help in completing this activity. **www.phschool.com**

CAPTION ANSWERS

Interpreting Political Cartoons Both. On the one hand, the cartoonist believes that "American diplomacy" is the key to China's open door. On the other hand, the cartoonist seems concerned about the U.S. having too large a role in the process.

RESOURCE DIRECTORY

Teaching Resources
Units 5/6 booklet
• Section 2 Quiz, p. 53
Guide to the Essentials
• Section 2 Summary, p. 89

Using a Time Zone Map

A system of worldwide standard time was devised in 1884. It divides the world into 24 time zones based on meridians of longitude. The time is the same throughout each zone. The Prime Meridian of 0°, which passes through Greenwich, England, is the starting point for calculating the time in each zone. The meridian of 180° longitude, halfway around the world, is the International Date Line. The calendar date to the east of this line is one day later than the date to the west.

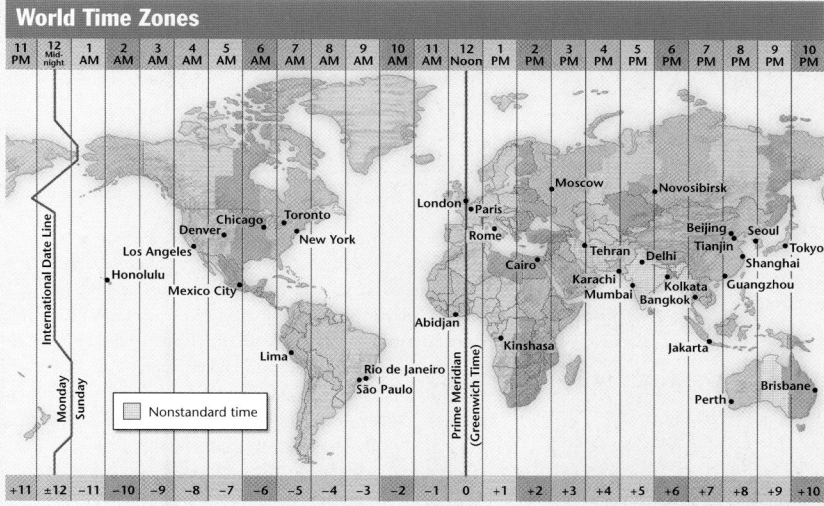

World Time Zones

Nonstandard time

LEARN THE SKILL

Use the following steps to read a time zone map:

1. **Study the information on the map.** Locate the Prime Meridian and the International Date Line. Study any keys, labels, and color-coding. On this map, the 24 time zones are shown by colored bands. The numbers at the bottom of the map indicate the number of hours each time zone differs from time at the Prime Meridian (Greenwich time). For example, +3 means that local time is three hours later than Greenwich time. The numbers at the top of the map provide examples of how this system works if it is 12:00 noon in Greenwich.

2. **Determine where the time zones and date change.** Notice how closely the time zones correspond to the meridians of longitude and where they vary from these lines. Compare time zones in different areas.

3. **Compare the time in your zone with other zones around the world.** Find your time zone on the map. Determine how it differs from Greenwich time.

APPLY THE SKILL

See the Chapter Review and Assessment for another opportunity to apply this skill.

PRACTICE THE SKILL

Answer the following questions:

1. **(a)** How does the map indicate which line is the Prime Meridian? **(b)** What time is it at the International Date Line when it is noon in Greenwich? **(c)** How many different time zones does South America have?

2. **(a)** If it is 12:00 noon, Greenwich time, what time is it in Moscow, Russia? In Denver, United States of America? **(b)** If it is 2 P.M. in Abidjan, Cote d'Ivoire, what time is it in the zone labeled +7? In the zone labeled –4? **(c)** Why do you think some of the time zones follow geographical features and political boundaries rather than the meridians of longitude?

3. **(a)** If it is 12:00 noon in Greenwich, what time is it in your time zone? **(b)** If it is 1 A.M. in your time zone, what time is it in Karachi, Pakistan? In Guangzhou, China? **(c)** If it is 12:00 noon in São Paulo, Brazil, what time is it where you live? **(d)** If it is 9 P.M. on Wednesday where you live, what are the day and time in Brisbane, Australia?

Chapter 17   597

RESOURCE DIRECTORY

Teaching Resources
Skills for Life booklet, p. 19

Technology
Social Studies Skills Tutor CD-ROM
Interactive Practice in
• Geographic Literacy
• Critical Thinking and Reading
• Visual Analysis
• Communications

USING A TIME ZONE MAP

Focus Students will use a time zone map to calculate times in various locations in the world.

Instruct Ask students if they have seen pictures of Earth from space. Do they show a clear dividing line between day and night? Explain that as areas of Earth pass out of darkness and into sunlight, people experience sunrise. We say that sunrise occurs at a specific time in a certain area, but sunrise occurs continuously as Earth turns. Ask why people on Earth need agreed-upon times and time zones.

Extend See the Skills for Life Activity in the Resource Directory below.

ANSWERS

PRACTICE THE SKILL

1. **(a)** It is a clearly labeled, bright red line. **(b)** Midnight. **(c)** Three.

2. **(a)** Moscow: 2:00 P.M.; Denver: 5:00 A.M. **(b)** 9:00 P.M.; 10:00 A.M. **(c)** For convenience so that people doing business with one another are in the same time zone.

3. **(a)** Answers will vary. **(b)** Answers will vary. **(c)** Answers will vary. **(d)** Answers will vary.

Section

3

A New Foreign Policy

SECTION OBJECTIVES

1. Find out why the United States wanted to build the Panama Canal.
2. Learn about the goals of Roosevelt's "big stick" diplomacy.
3. Discover some ways in which the foreign policies of Presidents Taft and Wilson differed from those of President Roosevelt.

BELLRINGER

Warm-Up Activity Display a world map. Ask students how much time they think it took a ship to travel from New York to San Francisco before and after the building of the Panama Canal. Ask for an estimate of the distance between the two cities.

Activating Prior Knowledge
Do students know the status of the Panama Canal today? *(By treaty, control of the Canal Zone territory was given over to the government of Panama on December 31, 1999.)*

READING STRATEGY

As students read the section, have them note the effects of physical and human geographic factors on such events as the building of the Panama Canal and the establishment of the National Park Service. What are some ways in which the existence of the canal has changed the world? How has the establishment of the National Park Service impacted American life?

ACTIVITY
Connecting with Geography

Tell students to use either a globe or a map of the world to chart routes from the Atlantic Ocean to the Pacific, without going through the Panama Canal. How many routes are possible between London and Los Angeles? How many routes are possible between Tokyo and New York? How does the Panama Canal shorten each route? **(Visual/Spatial; Logical/Mathematical)**

READING FOCUS

- Why did the United States want to build the Panama Canal?
- What were the goals of Theodore Roosevelt's "big stick" diplomacy?
- In what ways did the foreign policies of Presidents Taft and Wilson differ from those of President Roosevelt?

MAIN IDEA

President Theodore Roosevelt conducted a vigorous foreign policy that suited the new status of the United States as a world power. Presidents Taft and Wilson took a different approach to influencing other nations.

KEY TERMS

concession
Roosevelt Corollary
dollar diplomacy

TAKING NOTES

Copy the flowchart below. As you read, fill in the boxes with some of the major effects of the new United States foreign policy.

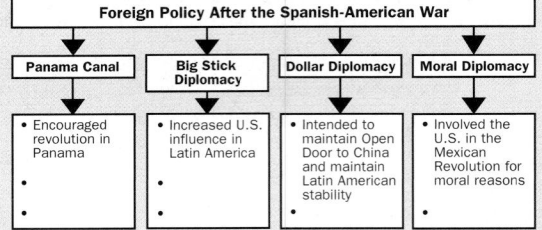

Foreign Policy After the Spanish-American War			
Panama Canal	**Big Stick Diplomacy**	**Dollar Diplomacy**	**Moral Diplomacy**
• Encouraged revolution in Panama • •	• Increased U.S. influence in Latin America • •	• Intended to maintain Open Door to China and maintain Latin American stability	• Involved the U.S. in the Mexican Revolution for moral reasons

Setting the Scene By 1900, the United States had emerged as a genuine world power. It controlled several overseas territories and had a large and vigorous economy. These circumstances contributed to William McKinley's decisive victory in the presidential election of 1900. One year later McKinley was dead, cut down by an assassin's bullet. Theodore Roosevelt, McKinley's Vice President, was now President. The new President developed a foreign policy to support the nation's new role in the world. Under his leadership, the United States continued to intervene in the affairs of countries that were of economic and strategic interest to the nation.

The Panama Canal

The Spanish-American War brought home to Americans the need for a shorter route between the Pacific and Atlantic oceans. A canal built across Central America would link the two oceans, making global shipping much faster and cheaper. It would also allow the United States Navy to move quickly from one ocean to the other in time of war.

Building the Canal The Isthmus of Panama was an ideal location for such a route. At that time, Panama was a province of the South American nation of Colombia. In 1879, a French company headed by Ferdinand de Lesseps had bought a 25-year **concession** from Colombia to build a canal across Panama. (A concession is a grant for a piece of land in exchange for a promise to use the land for a specific purpose.) Defeated by yellow fever and severe mismanagement, the company abandoned the project ten years later. It offered its remaining rights to the United States for $100 million. When the price fell to $40 million, Congress

Because of the uneven elevation in the canal zone, engineers had to design a series of locks to raise and lower the ships so that they could pass through the canal.

RESOURCE DIRECTORY

Teaching Resources
Guided Reading and Review booklet, p. 72

Other Print Resources
Nystrom *Atlas of Our Country* *Later Expansion of the United States,* pp. 32–33
Historical Outline Map Book *The Panama Canal,* p. 59

Technology
Section Reading Support Transparencies
Guided Reading Audiotapes (English/Spanish), Ch. 17
Student Edition on Audio CD, Ch. 17
Color Transparencies *Historical Maps,* A29
Prentice Hall Presentation Pro CD-ROM, Ch. 17
Companion Web site, www.phschool.com

passed the Spooner Act in 1902 that authorized the purchase of the French assets. The act required that the United States work out a treaty with Colombia for a lease on the land.

Treaty negotiations went nowhere. Colombia was waiting for the French concession to expire in 1904 so that it could offer the isthmus at a higher price. Roosevelt was enraged by this attempt of Colombian "bandits" to "rob" the United States. Secretary of State John Hay sent a message to the American minister in Colombia in June 1903 essentially threatening Colombia if it did not reconsider.

> 66 If Colombia should now reject the treaty or unduly delay its ratification, the friendly understanding between the two countries would be so seriously compromised that action might be taken by the Congress next winter which every friend of Colombia would regret. 99
>
> —Secretary of State John Hay

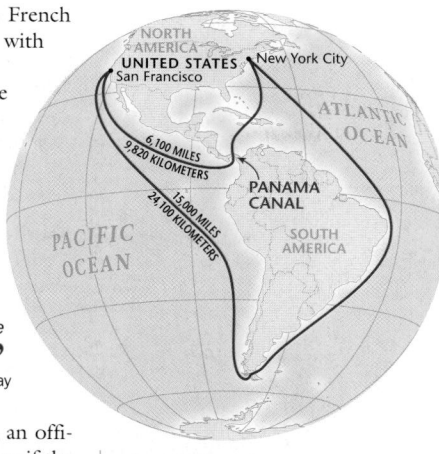

Meanwhile, Roosevelt secretly made it clear to Philippe Bunau-Varilla, an official with the French company, that the United States would not interfere if the company organized a Panamanian revolution against Colombia.

The revolt took place in November 1903 with U.S. warships waiting offshore to provide support for the rebels. The United States immediately recognized an independent Panama and became its protector. In return, Panama signed the Hay-Bunau-Varilla Treaty in November 1903. The treaty gave the United States a permanent grant of a 10-mile-wide strip of land for a Canal Zone over which the United States would have complete sovereignty. In return, the Panamanians received a payment of $10 million.

Construction of the canal began in 1904. To complete this mammoth task, workers were brought in from several countries. Many of them had no construction experience whatsoever. After receiving proper training, the workers surpassed all expectations. They finished the canal in 1914, six months ahead of schedule and $23 million under budget.

MAP SKILLS Compare the sea route from New York City to San Francisco (above) with and without the canal. **Movement** By how many miles did the Panama Canal reduce the journey?

Reaction to the Canal Roosevelt's opponents did not appreciate the methods he had used to secure the Canal Zone. A newspaper published by William Hearst commented, "Besides being a rough-riding assault upon another republic over the shattered wreckage of international law . . . , it is a quite unexampled instance of foul play in American politics."

Most Americans, however, convinced that the canal was vital to national security and prosperity, approved of President Roosevelt's actions in Panama. Two years after leaving office, Roosevelt gave a speech at the University of California at Berkeley in which he justified his methods:

> 66 If I had followed traditional, conservative methods I would have submitted a dignified State paper of probably 200 pages to Congress and the debates on it would have been going on yet; but I took the Canal Zone and let Congress debate; and while the debate goes on the canal does also. 99
>
> —Theodore Roosevelt, 1911

Workers on the Panama Canal wore identification badges like the ones shown here.

Despite the success of the Panama Canal as a link between the Atlantic and Pacific, its acquisition left a legacy of ill will among Latin Americans toward the United States. In recognition of the illegal means used to acquire the Canal

Chapter 17 • Section 3   **599**

LESSON PLAN

Focus The foreign policies of Presidents Roosevelt and Taft were crafted to suit America's new role as a world power. Ask how their approaches differed.

Instruct Point out that the United States did not settle in the territories it acquired in the late 1800s and early 1900s as the British did in parts of the British Empire. Ask: Why did Roosevelt and Taft pursue policies that involved American control of other countries? Why did the United States want to build the Panama Canal? How did Roosevelt get Colombia to agree? How did the tactics he used in Latin American countries differ from those he used in Asia?

Assess/Reteach President Roosevelt relied on the power of his personality to further his goals for American foreign policy. Though many Americans were opposed to his approach, he made a great deal of progress in a short amount of time. Can students state their own opinions of his methods? Do Presidents use the "personality" approach today?

CAPTION ANSWERS

Map Skills By about 8,900 miles.

Zone, Congress voted to pay $25 million to Colombia in 1921, two years after Roosevelt had died.

Roosevelt's Big Stick Diplomacy

In 1901, Roosevelt reminded an audience at the Minnesota State Fair of an old African proverb: "Speak softly and carry a big stick; you will go far." In his view, the "big stick" was the United States Navy. Indeed, the threat of military force allowed Roosevelt to conduct an aggressive foreign policy.

The Roosevelt Corollary In December 1904, Roosevelt issued a message to Congress that became known as the **Roosevelt Corollary** to the Monroe Doctrine. Roosevelt began this corollary, or extension of a previously accepted idea, by denying that the United States wanted any more territory.

KEY DOCUMENTS

❝ *It must be understood that under no circumstances will the United States use the Monroe Doctrine as a cloak for territorial aggression. We desire peace with all the world, but perhaps most of all with the other peoples of the American continent. . . . It is always possible that wrong actions toward this nation . . . may result in our having to take action to protect our rights; but such action will not be taken with a view to territorial aggression.* ❞

—Roosevelt Corollary to the Monroe Doctrine, Theodore Roosevelt, 1904

INTERPRETING POLITICAL CARTOONS Published after the announcement of the Roosevelt Corollary, this cartoon depicts Roosevelt as the world's police officer, using his "big stick" to maintain order and stability in Latin America. **Making Comparisons** *Compare this cartoon to the others in this chapter. What similarities can you find? What conclusions can you draw?*

The United States wanted only "to see neighboring countries stable, orderly, and prosperous," he said. But if the countries engaged in activities harmful to the interests of the United States or if their governments collapsed, inviting intervention from stronger nations, then the United States would be forced to exercise "an international police power." In other words, the U.S. government would intervene to prevent intervention from other powers. This was the central point of the Roosevelt Corollary.

The first test of the Roosevelt Corollary concerned the small Caribbean island republic of Santo Domingo (now the Dominican Republic). When the island went bankrupt, European nations threatened to intervene to collect their money. Roosevelt moved quickly to establish American supervision of customs collections. Bankers in the United States took over the country's finances and paid its European debt. Congress initially blocked Roosevelt's actions. However, the President was able to get around congressional opposition by creating an executive agreement with Santo Domingo's president.

Under Roosevelt, U.S. intervention in Latin America became common. This development angered many Latin Americans. Congress also was displeased with Roosevelt's single-handed foreign policies that seemed to strengthen the President's powers while weakening their own.

Roosevelt as Peacemaker In Asia, the President's chief concern was to preserve an open door to trade with China. However, growing conflicts between Japan and Russia posed a threat to Asian security. These conflicts came to a head in the Russo-Japanese War, which began in 1904. As the war progressed it was clear that Japan's military power outmatched Russia's. Finally, after a key naval victory for Japan, Russia requested peace talks.

READING CHECK
What were the main points of the Roosevelt Corollary?

Meanwhile, President Roosevelt had grown increasingly concerned over Japan's expanding military power. Japan had crushed China a decade earlier in the Sino-Japanese War and had been growing stronger ever since. He also saw potential problems resulting from certain policies then being proposed in California that would discriminate against and exclude Japanese immigrants. In a letter to his friend Senator Henry Cabot Lodge, Roosevelt wrote:

66 I hope that we can persuade our people on the one hand to act in a spirit of generous justice and genuine courtesy toward Japan, and on the other hand to keep the navy respectable in numbers and more than respectable in the efficiency of its units. If we act thus we need not fear the Japanese. But if, as Brooks Adams says, we show ourselves 'opulent, aggressive, and unarmed,' the Japanese may sometime work us an injury. 99

—President Theodore Roosevelt, June 1905

Two months later, in August 1905, Roosevelt mediated a peace agreement to the Russo-Japanese War. He invited delegates from the two nations to Portsmouth, New Hampshire, where he persuaded Japan to be satisfied with small grants of land and control over Korea instead of a huge payment of money. He also secured a promise from Russia to vacate Manchuria, which remained part of China. Roosevelt succeeded in keeping trade in China open to all nations. His role as mediator won him the Nobel peace prize.

NOTABLE PRESIDENTS
Theodore Roosevelt

*26th President
1901–1909*

"Speak softly and carry a big stick; you will go far."
—1901 speech at the Minnesota State Fair

Born into a wealthy New York family, Theodore ("Teddy") Roosevelt had asthma as a child, but at his father's insistence he overcame it with rigorous physical exercise. "TR" developed a stocky body, a fighter's toughness, and a love for strenuous living.

As a Republican politician in New York in the 1880s, TR called for a larger government role in the economy, a stand that made him a leader of the Progressives. TR believed in honest as well as active government. During a six-year term on the U.S. Civil Service Commission, he enforced the merit system. TR later attacked corruption as head of the New York City Police Board.

In 1897, TR was appointed Assistant Secretary of the Navy. There he built up a two-ocean fleet and urged a more aggressive American foreign policy. When the Spanish-American War was declared in 1898, TR, though nearly 40 and with poor eyesight, demanded to see combat. He organized the "Rough Riders" and led them on a famous charge up Cuba's San Juan Hill.

The war made TR a national hero. Returning to New York, he won the governorship in 1898. Two years later, President McKinley chose TR as his running mate. In 1901, McKinley was assassinated. Roosevelt became,

at age 42, the nation's youngest President up to that time.

TR saw the presidency as a "bully pulpit," or a wonderful stage from which to win public support for his brand of strong leadership. His economic policies included regulating big business and supporting labor unions. His foreign policies reflected the "big stick" approach described in the quotation above. Roosevelt was also a vocal conservationist, acting to preserve the nation's natural resources and wildlife. Most importantly, TR's boldness and constant activity helped create the modern image of the President.

Connecting to Today
Do you think that American foreign policy today should be guided by the principle "speak softly and carry a big stick"? Explain your answer.

Take It to the NET **Biography** More information about this President is provided at the following Web site: **www.phschool.com**

Chapter 17 • Section 3   **601**

Foreign Policy After Roosevelt

Under the presidency of Theodore Roosevelt, the United States assumed a forceful new role in foreign affairs. Roosevelt's successors were thrown into a complex mix of political alliances and world events that would require careful and creative policymaking. William Howard Taft and Woodrow Wilson continued the Roosevelt legacy, but each brought with them their own unique methods of diplomacy.

MAP SKILLS This map shows how frequently the United States intervened in the affairs of Latin American countries in the early 1900s. **Place** *What form did most of these interventions take?*

Taft and Dollar Diplomacy   William Howard Taft, elected to the presidency in 1908, was not as aggressive as Roosevelt in pursuing foreign policy aims. A distinguished lawyer from Ohio, Taft had served as Roosevelt's Secretary of War and had headed the commission that governed the Philippines.

Taft's main foreign policy goals were to maintain the open door to Asia and preserve stability in Latin America. As for the rest, he preferred "substituting dollars for bullets." By this he meant maintaining orderly societies abroad through increased American investment in foreign economies. Although some of Taft's contemporaries mocked his approach, calling it **dollar diplomacy,** Taft himself later used this term with pride.

Dollar diplomacy did not succeed as well as Taft had hoped. Although it increased the level of United States financial involvement abroad, the results were not always profitable. For example, when Taft's Secretary of State, Philander Knox, persuaded bankers from the United States to invest in railroad projects in China and Manchuria, Russia and Japan united in an effort to block the influence of the Americans. In addition, many U.S. investments in China were lost when the country's government collapsed in revolution in 1911.

Dollar diplomacy also created enemies in Latin America, especially in the Caribbean and Central America, where local revolutionary movements opposed American influence. Although the United States reached new heights as an international power under Roosevelt and Taft, anti-colonialism abroad and anti-imperialism at home provided a growing check to further expansion.

Wilson and the Mexican Revolution   American intervention in Mexico under President Woodrow Wilson led to even more anti-American feeling in Latin America. In 1911, a revolution forced Mexico's longtime dictator, Porfirio Diaz, to resign. The new president, Francisco Madero, promised democratic reforms but could not unite his deeply divided and impoverished country. In 1913, General Victoriano Huerta overthrew him and had him killed.

The United States was unsure how to respond to Huerta's illegal action. Americans had invested over $1 billion in Mexican oil, mines, land, and railways. When Huerta promised to protect foreign investments, most European countries recognized him. American investors urged President Wilson to do the same, but he refused. To him, Huerta was a "butcher" ruling without the consent of the

Map: United States Interventions, 1898–1934

- U.S. expeditionary force, 1916–1917
- UNITED STATES
- ATLANTIC OCEAN
- Parral
- U.S. occupation, 1915–1934
- U.S. occupation, 1898–1902, 1906–1909, 1912, 1917–1922
- Bahamas (Br.)
- MEXICO
- U.S. seizure, 1914
- Havana
- U.S. possession, 1898
- Tampico
- CUBA
- DOMINICAN REPUBLIC
- Mexico City
- Guantanamo
- Purchased from Denmark, 1917
- Veracruz
- Puerto Rico
- Virgin Is.
- Antigua (Br.)
- Br. Honduras (Br.)
- Jamaica (Br.)
- HAITI
- Guadeloupe (Fr.)
- Dominica (Br.)
- GUATEMALA
- HONDURAS
- U.S. leased naval base, 1903
- Martinique (Fr.)
- Barbados (Br.)
- United Fruit Co. organized for banana trade, 1899
- EL SALVADOR
- NICARAGUA
- St. Lucia (Br.)
- Grenada (Br.)
- U.S. occupation, 1916–1924
- Trinidad (Br.)
- U.S. occupation, 1924–1925
- COSTA RICA
- PANAMA
- VENEZUELA
- U.S. occupation, 1909–1910, 1912–1925, 1926–1933. Canal proposed, 1916
- U.S. leased Corn Is., 1914
- COLOMBIA
- U.S. acquired Canal Zone, 1904. Canal completed, 1914
- PACIFIC OCEAN
- 0   250   500 mi.
- 0   250   500 km

Sounds of an Era

Listen to a campaign speech by William Howard Taft in 1908 and other sounds from the age of imperialism.

people. With this refusal, Wilson was announcing the end of Taft's "dollar diplomacy." From now on, the United States would apply moral and legalistic standards to foreign policy decisions.

Wilson's policy led him into a complex and bloody confrontation with Mexico. First, he interfered in Mexican politics. Another Mexican leader, Venustiano Carranza, began making military progress against Huerta. Wilson demanded that a truce be declared and that Mexico hold democratic elections in which Huerta could not run. When Huerta refused, Wilson decided to support Carranza and blocked all munitions from reaching Huerta's forces.

In April 1914, the brief arrest of American sailors in Tampico gave Wilson an excuse to act militarily. He sent the American navy to occupy Veracruz, Mexico's port on the Gulf of Mexico. Over a hundred Mexicans died resisting the occupation, and Mexico's political factions united against the United States. Deprived by the occupation of customs revenue and munitions, on July 15 Huerta resigned in favor of Carranza.

Wilson withdrew the navy, but was soon drawn into Mexican affairs again by the actions of peasant rebel leader Francisco "Pancho" Villa. Villa had once supported Carranza but now opposed him and gathered his armed forces in his strongholds in northern Mexico. The threat of civil war in Mexico again worried President Wilson, who encouraged Carranza and Villa to meet and negotiate. When neither of the two leaders would agree to such a meeting, Wilson felt he had to choose between them. He chose Carranza as the more stable of the two.

Wilson's decision to support Carranza infuriated Pancho Villa, who then began to pursue a more radical path in Mexico. Villa began terrorizing Americans in Mexico and raiding border towns in the United States. On March 9, 1916, his men crossed the U.S. border into Columbus, New Mexico, and burned the town, killing more than 15 people.

Wilson's "moral diplomacy" had not worked well. Carranza's government eventually adopted a constitution that curbed foreign ownership of Mexico's resources. Many American and Mexican lives had been lost, and American financial interests had lost ground. Wilson's interference in Mexican affairs soured relations between the two countries for years to come.

Focus on WORLD EVENTS

In Pursuit of Pancho Villa Besides wanting to take revenge on Wilson, Villa's other likely motive for terrorizing Americans along the border was to weaken Mexican support for the Carranza government. Villa knew that Wilson would respond to the terrorism with force. Any attempt by Wilson to interfere with Mexican affairs would make Carranza look weak.

Villa was right. Wilson sent General John J. "Black Jack" Pershing at the head of more than 5,000 American troops into Mexico to pursue Villa. Carranza authorized Wilson to do this, only to regret his decision later on. His strongest supporters were nationalists who saw American intervention as a violation of Mexican sovereignty. Threatened with a loss of power, Carranza demanded that the American troops leave, but was refused. Bloody clashes took place between Mexican and American troops. Pershing's pursuit of Villa failed. In 1917, with the United States on the brink of war in Europe, Wilson withdrew his troops.

Section 3 Assessment

READING COMPREHENSION

1. How did the United States secure the rights to build the Panama Canal?

2. (a) Why did Roosevelt issue the **Roosevelt Corollary?** (b) How did people in Latin America and the United States react to Roosevelt's declaration?

3. Why did Taft's **dollar diplomacy** and Wilson's actions in Mexico anger many Latin Americans?

CRITICAL THINKING AND WRITING

4. **Making Comparisons** How were Teddy Roosevelt and Andrew Jackson similar in the way in which they used the power of the presidency to achieve policy goals?

5. **Writing an Opinion** In two or three paragraphs, explain why you think that the United States adopted a new foreign policy in the 1900s and whether or not you think this policy was justified.

 Take It to the NET

Activity: Creating a Time Line Read more about President Taft (1909–1913), and create a time line of his career. What do you consider his most important achievement? What did Taft consider his most important achievement? Use the links provided in the *America: Pathways to the Present* area of the following Web site for help in completing this activity. **www.phschool.com**

Section 3 Assessment

Reading Comprehension

1. It secretly encouraged a revolution in Panama and sent military forces to protect it. It received a 10-mile-wide strip of land across the isthmus in return.

2. (a) It would allow U.S. intervention if Latin American countries took actions harmful to the U.S. or if their governments collapsed, inviting intervention from stronger nations. (b) Latin Americans were angered. The U.S. Congress was displeased, as these measures strengthened Roosevelt's powers while weakening those of Congress.

3. In Latin America, increased American investment in the economy angered local revolutionaries that opposed American influence. Wilson's moral stance during his direct intervention in Mexican affairs dictated how the civil war would go, angering many Mexicans.

Critical Thinking and Writing

4. Both were active Presidents who used high-handed tactics in pursuit of their policy goals. For example, Jackson refused to enforce the Supreme Court's decision stating that the removal of the Cherokee people was illegal. Roosevelt stage-managed the Panamanian revolution.

5. Essays will vary but should be supported with facts from the section.

 **Take It to the NET**

Answers will vary. Students should include Taft's accomplishments both as a judge and as President. Taft considered his Supreme Court work to be his most important.

CUSTOMIZE FOR ...

Gifted and Talented

Next to Washington, Jefferson, and Lincoln, the fourth stone face on the slopes of Mount Rushmore is that of Theodore Roosevelt. Have students write one or two paragraphs explaining why some people might have wanted Roosevelt to be on this monument, while others felt that he did not belong.

SECTION OBJECTIVES

1. Examine the main arguments raised by the anti-imperialists.
2. See why imperialism appealed to many Americans.
3. Find out how American imperialism was viewed from abroad.

BELLRINGER

Warm-Up Activity Write the following sentence on the chalkboard: "Americans are always searching for a new frontier." Ask students what this might mean for other nations.

Activating Prior Knowledge Ask students to describe some situations that demonstrate the ways in which the debate concerning United States involvement in international affairs continues to this day.

READING STRATEGY

Have students skim the section and use the headings and subheadings to create an outline. Then, as they read the section, have them fill in supporting details.

CAPTION ANSWERS

Interpreting Political Cartoons The other powers appear ready to fight over their "share" of China as the United States looks on. The cartoonist seems to believe that imperialism perpetuates greed and violence.

Section 4 — Debating America's New Role

READING FOCUS

- What were the main arguments raised by the anti-imperialists?
- Why did imperialism appeal to many Americans?
- How was American imperialism viewed from abroad?

MAIN IDEA

After the Spanish-American War, the debate intensified over whether the United States should build an empire.

KEY TERMS

racism
compulsory
Great White Fleet

TAKING NOTES

As you read, complete this chart listing all of the arguments for and against imperialism.

Pro-Imperialism	Anti-Imperialism
• Offers new "frontier" for the American imagination and spirit	• Rejects the foundation of American ideals and democracy
•	•
•	•

Setting the Scene Before the Spanish-American War, U.S. citizens were already debating the consequences of an expanded role in world affairs. Walter Gresham, President Cleveland's Secretary of State in 1894, cautioned against "the evils of interference in affairs that do not specially concern us." Until the annexation of the Philippines in 1898, however, most citizens supported overseas involvement. The U.S. occupation of the Philippines quickly raised the voices of those wary of imperialism.

66 *Much as we abhor the 'criminal aggression' in the Philippines, greatly as we regret that the blood of the Filipinos is on American hands, we more deeply resent the betrayal of American institutions at home. The real firing line is not in the suburbs of Manila. The foe is of our own household. The attempt of 1861 was to divide the country. That of 1899 is to destroy its fundamental principles and noblest ideals.* 99

—From the platform of the Anti-Imperialist League

INTERPRETING POLITICAL CARTOONS This cartoon depicts the imperialist powers about to carve up a slain China. **Analyzing Visual Information** *What is the cartoonist's attitude toward imperialism?*

The Anti-Imperialists

In November 1898, opponents of U.S. policy in the Philippines established the Anti-Imperialist League. Most of its organizers were well-to-do professionals. They included editor E. L. Godkin, Democratic politician William Jennings Bryan, settlement house leader Jane Addams, and novelist Mark Twain.

Moral and Political Arguments To support their position, the anti-imperialists used a variety of arguments. The strongest of these were moral and political in nature. Expansionist behavior, the anti-imperialists asserted, was a rejection of the nation's foundation of "liberty for all." As one prominent Republican and former senator from Missouri explained in 1899:

604 Chapter 17 • *Becoming a World Power*

RESOURCE DIRECTORY

Teaching Resources
Learning Styles Lesson Plans booklet, p. 37
Guided Reading and Review booklet, p. 73

Technology
Section Reading Support Transparencies
Guided Reading Audiotapes (English/Spanish), Ch. 17
Student Edition on Audio CD, Ch. 17
Prentice Hall Presentation Pro CD-ROM, Ch. 17
Companion Web site, www.phschool.com

> " We regret that it has become necessary in the land of Washington and Lincoln to reaffirm that all men, of whatever race or color, are entitled to life, liberty, and the pursuit of happiness. "
>
> —Carl Schurz

Other anti-imperialists promoted the idea that "the Constitution must follow the flag," by which they meant that the American flag and laws went together. They argued that people in territories controlled by the United States should be entitled to the same guarantees in the Constitution as U.S. citizens. For example, labor leader Samuel Gompers objected to taking over countries in which U.S. labor laws did not apply. He pointed out that in Hawaii, half of the population consisted of "contract laborers, practically slaves," who did not benefit from the laws that protected American workers.

In response to such an argument, expansionists claimed that the people of the Caribbean and the Pacific were not ready for democracy and that the United States was preparing them for liberty. Major General Douglas MacArthur, military governor of the Philippines in 1900, said, "We are planting in those islands . . . the best traditions, the best characteristics of Americanism." Anti-imperialists, however, did not believe that any group of people should be forced to wait to enjoy liberty.

Finally, anti-imperialists noted that imperialism threatened the nation's democratic foundations. The large standing armies that were employed to bring other nations under American control could be used just as easily to crush dissent at home.

Racial Arguments   Other anti-imperialists saw racism at work in imperialism. **Racism** is a belief that differences in character or intelligence are due to one's race. Many Americans of this period believed that people of Anglo-Saxon heritage were superior to other races. Many of the public officials who developed the country's policies shared these sentiments.

African Americans were at first torn about imperialistic issues. As U.S. citizens, they wanted to support their country. But they recognized the racism that underlay imperialism. A leader of the A.M.E. Zion Church had this to say in 1899:

> " Had the Filipinos been white and fought as bravely as they have, the war would have been ended and their independence granted a long time ago. "
>
> —Bishop Alexander Walters

Although most southern Democrats also opposed imperialism, they did so for different reasons. Many southern politicians feared the effects of having to absorb more people of different races into the United States. Consequently, southern Democrats led the movement in the Senate against ratifying the treaty with Spain after the Spanish-American War. A number of anti-imperialists outside the South also feared that imperialist policies would encourage people

COMPARING PRIMARY SOURCES
Imperialism

The Spanish-American War heightened the debate between imperialist and anti-imperialist factions at home.
Analyzing Viewpoints Which of the viewpoints do you think most Americans supported?

Anti-Imperialist
"We assume that what we like and practice, and what we think better, must come as a welcome blessing to Spanish-Americans and Filipinos. This is grossly and obviously untrue. They hate our ways. They are hostile to our ideas. Our religion, language, institutions, and manners offend them."
—William G. Sumner, Yale University professor, in an 1898 speech

Pro-Imperialist
"Think of the tens of thousands of Americans who will invade mine and field and forest in the Philippines when a liberal government, protected and controlled by this republic, if not the government of the republic itself, shall establish order and equity there!"
—Albert J. Beveridge, leading imperialist and later United States senator, in an 1898 speech

READING CHECK
Why did some anti-imperialists believe that "the Constitution must follow the flag"?

VIEWING FINE ART Edward Moran captured the triumph of the United States Navy in his 1899 painting *Return of the Conquerors.* **Identifying Central Issues** How does this painting both reinforce and reflect imperialism's appeal to many Americans?

READING CHECK

How did the "closing" frontier make imperialism more appealing to some Americans?

of different racial backgrounds to move to the United States.

Economic Arguments Finally, anti-imperialists raised economic objections to expansionist policies. In their view, the time was not right for the United States to expand. First, expansion involved too many costs. Maintaining the necessary armed forces required more taxation, debt, and possibly even **compulsory,** or required, military service.

Samuel Gompers raised another concern. He argued that laborers coming to the United States from annexed territories would compete with American workers for jobs. Since these immigrants would work for lower wages, their presence would drive all wages down. The nation's industrialists raised yet another concern. They pointed out that goods produced cheaply in annexed countries could be imported to the United States without customs duties. This competition would hurt many American industries.

Imperialism's Appeal

Despite the strength of these arguments, imperialism maintained a powerful hold on the American imagination. Some people looked to a new frontier abroad to keep Americans from losing their competitive edge. The America of explorers and pioneers, who bravely chartered unknown territories and overcame great obstacles, was fast disappearing into the shadows of memory. In 1890, the director of the census had declared the frontier "closed." Imperialism offered a new kind of frontier for American expansion. Some proponents of expansionism believed that imperialism was a celebration of American tradition and creative spirit. In this editorial, Walter Hines Page dismissed the anti-imperialist notion that imperialism was a betrayal of American ideals:

> 66 It is temperament that tells, and not schemes of national policy, whether laid down in Farewell Addresses or in Utopian books. No national character was ever shaped by formula or by philosophy; for greater forces than these lie behind it,—the forces of inheritance and of events. Are we, by virtue of our surroundings and institutions, become a different people from our ancestors, or are we yet the same race of Anglo-Saxons, whose restless energy in colonization, in conquest, in trade, in 'the spread of civilization,' has carried their speech into every part of the world, and planted their habits everywhere? 99
> —Walter Hines Page, editor of the *Atlantic Monthly,* 1898

The growth and popularity of youth scouting programs during this period shows that many Americans shared a "frontier mentality." Sir Robert Baden-Powell, an army officer of the British Empire, had used scouting techniques (tracking, woodcraft, and wilderness survival) to great success in a battle in South Africa. A few years after he returned to Britain as a war hero, Baden-Powell founded the Boy Scout movement. Scouting appeared in the United States in 1910 and soon became immensely popular. Two years later, Juliette

Low, a close friend and admirer of Baden-Powell, founded the American Girl Scouts. Low hoped to use the program both to build moral character in girls and to teach them skills that would make them "hardy" and "handy."

Many people were swayed by the practical advantages of imperialism. They agreed with the economic arguments that emphasized the need to gain access to foreign markets. Others embraced the strategic military reasons for expansion.

In December 1907, Roosevelt sent part of the United States Navy on a cruise around the world. The trip was designed to demonstrate the nation's impressive naval power to other nations. The **Great White Fleet,** as the gleaming white ships were called, made a big impression everywhere it sailed. For American citizens, the fleet clearly showed the benefits of having a powerful navy.

Imperialism Viewed From Abroad

Having begun a pattern of international involvement, the United States discovered that these actions frequently took on a life of their own. In the Caribbean and Central America, for example, the United States often had to defend governments that were unpopular with local inhabitants. In Latin America, the cry "Yankee, Go Home!" began to be heard. Even before the Panama Canal was completed in 1914, Panamanians began to complain that they suffered from discrimination.

On the other hand, because the United States was quickly becoming so powerful, other countries—even those fearful about maintaining their independence—began to turn to the United States for help. Both welcomed and rejected, the United States would spend the rest of the century trying to decide the best way to reconcile its growing power and national interests with its relationships with other nations.

Focus on CULTURE

The Media and Imperialism In addition to the pro-imperialist yellow journalism of the time, much of the popular media glorified the accomplishments of imperialist frontier heroes. Theodore Roosevelt's book on his heroic charge, *The Rough Riders,* drew much praise. However, satirist Finley Peter Dunne's character, "Mr. Dooley," suggested the book should be called *Alone in Cuba* to emphasize Roosevelt's boastfulness.

Another book of this era, *Conquest of the Tropics* (1914), describes the history of the United Fruit Company, portraying railroad entrepreneur Minor Keith as one of "the hardy American type which listens and responds eagerly to the call of the wild."

Section 4 Assessment

READING COMPREHENSION

1. Why did some people believe that **racism** was at work in imperialism?

2. What were three economic arguments raised by the anti-imperialists?

3. How did imperialism's appeal go beyond what many saw as its practical advantages?

4. What was significant about the tour of the **Great White Fleet?**

CRITICAL THINKING AND WRITING

5. **Identifying Assumptions** How did expansionists and anti-imperialists view imperialism in relation to original principles of American democracy? What different assumptions did people on the two sides make about the roots and goals of the United States?

6. **Writing an Opinion** Based on the arguments they made against imperialism, what role do you think the anti-imperialists believed the United States should play in world affairs?

Take It to the NET

Activity: Creating a Poster Research the itinerary, composition, and purpose of the Great White Fleet. Create a tour poster advertising "appearances" along the route. Keep in mind the political purpose of the tour. Use the links provided in the *America: Pathways to the Present* area of the following Web site for help in completing this activity.
www.phschool.com

Reading Comprehension

1. Through the desire to bring American values to other countries, imperialism perpetuated the belief that Anglo-Saxons were superior, and other races were inferior and in need of "Americanization."

2. Expansion was too costly; laborers coming to the U.S. from annexed territories would compete with American workers for jobs; cheap, duty-free goods imported from overseas possessions would hurt American industries.

3. Imperialism was seen by some Americans as a way to reinvigorate the American frontier spirit. It would also give American missionaries the opportunity to spread Christianity.

4. It reinforced imperialism's appeal to Americans as it demonstrated the nation's impressive naval power to the world.

Critical Thinking and Writing

5. Anti-imperialists: expansion rejected the "liberty for all" aspect of American life. People in overseas U.S. territories should have full constitutional rights. Expansionists: Imperialism was a rebirth of the American frontier spirit and would spread civilization to other lands.

6. Defender of democratic ideals and institutions around the world to which all peoples deserved access.

Take It to the NET

Student posters should advertise where the fleet was going, how many vessels there were, and why it was on tour.

CUSTOMIZE FOR ...

Less Proficient Writers

Ask students to imagine that they are a resident of one of the countries that the United States sought to rule. Can they write a list of words to describe how they would feel about this action?

Chapter 17 Review and Assessment

creating a CHAPTER SUMMARY

Copy this cause-and-effect diagram (right) on a separate sheet of paper to show some of the causes and effects of American expansion during the late 1800s and early 1900s. Provide at least four causes and four effects.

TEXT

For additional review and enrichment activities, see the interactive version of *America: Pathways to the Present*, available on the Web and on CD-ROM.

CAUSES
- Pressure to find new markets abroad
-
-
-

↓

AMERICAN EXPANSIONISM

↓

EFFECTS
- Purchase of Alaska from Russia
-
-
-

★ Reviewing Key Terms

For each of the terms below, write a sentence explaining how it relates to the era of imperialism in the United States.

1. imperialism
2. nationalism
3. annex
4. banana republic
5. arbitration
6. jingoism
7. Platt Amendment
8. sphere of influence
9. concession
10. dollar diplomacy
11. racism
12. compulsory
13. Great White Fleet

★ Reviewing Main Ideas

14. Why were the major European powers scrambling to seize new territory in the late 1800s? (Section 1)

15. Briefly explain the arguments of Alfred T. Mahan, Henry Cabot Lodge, and Albert J. Beveridge regarding expansionism. (Section 1)

16. Why did the American public favor war with Spain in 1898? (Section 2)

17. What was the Open Door Policy, and why was it important to the United States? (Section 2)

18. How did the Roosevelt Corollary affect United States policy in Latin America? (Section 3)

19. Describe the foreign policy goals of Taft and Wilson. (Section 3)

20. Explain why anti-imperialists believed that imperialism betrayed basic American principles. (Section 4)

★ Critical Thinking

21. Synthesizing Information In what sense were the expansionist policies of the United States in the late 1800s a continuation of the concept of Manifest Destiny?

22. Identifying Central Issues How did the popular theory of social Darwinism make it easier for some Americans to embrace imperialist policies in the late 1800s?

23. Drawing Conclusions During the late 1800s, the press fanned the flames of the Spanish-American War by publishing sensational stories about Spanish cruelties in Cuba. On what current issues has the press played a major role in influencing public opinion?

24. Distinguishing Fact From Opinion President McKinley's Secretary of State, John Hay, referred to the Spanish-American War as "a splendid little war." Can you think of any Americans, in addition to anti-imperialists, who might disagree with Hay's opinion?

CREATING A CHAPTER SUMMARY

American Expansionism

Causes	Effects
Pressure to find new markets abroad	Purchase of Alaska from Russia
Desire to protect American security	Spanish-American War
Desire to preserve American spirit of vitality	Annexation of Hawaii and Puerto Rico
Need for outposts for shipping traffic and steamship refueling	Construction of the Panama Canal

★ Skills Assessment
Analyzing Political Cartoons ▶

25. The caption to this 1904 political cartoon was "HIS 128th BIRTHDAY. 'Gee but this is an awful stretch!'" (a) Whose birthday is it? (b) How do you know? (c) What does the "awful stretch" refer to? (d) How do you know?

26. What is the cartoonist's view of United States imperialism?

Analyzing Primary Sources

Read this excerpt, and then answer the questions that follow.

> ❝ I hope that we can persuade our people on the one hand to act in a spirit of generous justice and genuine courtesy toward Japan, and on the other hand to keep the navy respectable in numbers and more than respectable in the efficiency of its units. If we act thus we need not fear the Japanese. But if . . . we show ourselves 'opulent, aggressive, and unarmed,' the Japanese may sometime work us an injury. ❞
> —President Theodore Roosevelt

27. This statement best reflects Roosevelt's support for

A the Monroe Doctrine.

B "Speak softly and carry a big stick."

C the Open Door Policy.

D the Roosevelt Corollary.

28. What is the most likely reason for Roosevelt's concern over Japan?

F He knew their military could easily defeat the military of the United States.

G The Japanese threatened to intervene if Western nations pursued trade with China.

H Laws were being proposed in the United States that discriminated against Japanese immigrants.

J The United States was interested in acquiring Japanese land.

Applying the Chapter Skill: *Using a Time Zone Map*

29. Review the time zone map on page 597. Name two cities on the map that are in the same time zone as New York City.

ACTIVITIES

Writing to LEARN

Writing a Persuasive Essay
The United States still intervenes in foreign countries when its interests are threatened. Write a letter to the editor of a newspaper in which you argue either for or against an interventionist foreign policy. Research recent examples of United States intervention in foreign countries and use them to support your arguments.

Primary Source CD-ROM

Working With Primary Sources Find additional information on American imperialism on the *Exploring Primary Sources in the U.S. History CD-ROM* and use the selection(s) provided to complete the Chapter 17 primary source activity located in the *America: Pathways to the Present* area of the following Web site:
www.phschool.com

Take It to the NET

Chapter Self-Test As a review activity, take the Chapter 17 Self-Test in the *America: Pathways to the Present* area at the Web site listed below. The questions are designed to test your understanding of the chapter content.
www.phschool.com

21. Expansionism built on the belief that the U.S. was destined to expand across North America. The closing of the frontier led to the belief that the U.S. should acquire overseas territory.

22. Social Darwinism promoted the racist idea that Europeans and Americans were superior to other cultures and peoples. Social Darwinists applauded imperialism as a way to bring civilization to "inferior" countries.

23. Answers will vary. Students might cite press coverage of any issue currently in the news. Students may point out that the degree of sensationalism usually depends on the source that is covering the story.

24. The families of people who were injured or killed in the war would probably disagree with Hay, as would anyone who suffered as a result of the war.

SKILLS ASSESSMENT

25. (a) The birthday of the United States. (b) The eagle with the banner is a common symbol of the nation. (c) U.S. imperialism. (d) The eagle's wings stretch from Puerto Rico and Panama to the Philippines—places of strong U.S. involvement.

26. Sample response: The cartoonist may be suggesting that the United States is not justified in its involvements far from home.

27. B

28. H

29. Toronto and Lima.

ANSWERS TO ACTIVITIES

Writing to LEARN

Students' letters should take into account the imperialist and anti-imperialist arguments advanced in the chapter.

Primary Source CD-ROM

Direct students to the additional primary sources that can be found on the *Exploring Primary Sources in U.S. History CD-ROM.*

Take It to the NET

Additional support materials and activities for Chapter 17 of *America: Pathways to the Present* can be found in the Social Studies area at the Prentice Hall School Web site. **www.phschool.com**

BUILDING THE PANAMA CANAL

Focus Point out that the building of the Panama Canal is all the more remarkable when one realizes that it was undertaken with the earliest types of earth-moving equipment and without surveillance, computerized geological models, or even thorough knowledge of Panama's rugged jungle environment.

Instruct Explain that the Panama Canal was the largest engineering accomplishment of its day. The main challenges of the project fell into the categories of location, human-environmental interaction, and the movement of people and goods—three key factors in the study of geography.

Before they read, have students make a chart using these three factors as headings. Ask them to speculate about what specific challenges engineers might have faced in building the canal and to write down their ideas under the appropriate heading.

Extend After they read, have students add to their chart by filling in factual information under each of the three headings and comparing it with their original, speculative answers.

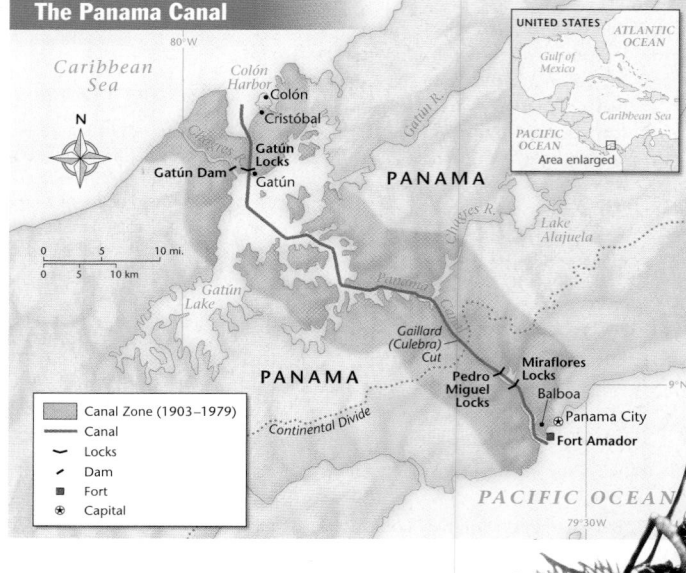

Building the Panama Canal

Constructing the Panama Canal was one of the greatest engineering feats of all time. Panama's physical and human geography presented several obstacles to the canal's planners and builders, but they overcame each challenge. When the canal was completed in 1914, it linked the Atlantic and Pacific Oceans, as well as the East and West Coasts of the United States.

The Panama Canal

Flooding a River Valley

The greatest challenge was how to move ships across the Continental Divide, with an elevation of 312 feet above sea level. Digging a canal at sea level across the entire isthmus would have been much too expensive and time-consuming. However, the proposed route of the canal partly followed the course of the wild Chagres River, which had a record of violent floods. Engineers solved these problems by damming the Chagres River to create Gatún Lake, 85 feet above sea level. A series of locks would raise ships from the Atlantic Ocean to the lake. Ships could then travel across most of the isthmus at the level of the lake.

Canal Zone (1903–1979)
Canal
Locks
Dam
Fort
Capital

Cutting Across the Continental Divide

Workers would cut a deep gorge, later known as the Gaillard Cut (or Culebra Cut), to allow ships to cross the continental divide at the level of Gatún Lake before descending through another set of locks to the Pacific.

Geographical Connection The inset map shows that the Atlantic Ocean lies east of the Pacific Ocean. According to the main map, in what direction do ships passing from the Pacific to the Atlantic actually travel through the Panama Canal?

610

ANSWERS

1. They actually travel northwest. This is because of the peculiar orientation of the Isthmus of Panama.

RESOURCE DIRECTORY

Teaching Resources
Geography and History booklet, pp. 12–13

Other Print Resources
Nystrom *Atlas of Our Country* *Later Expansion of the United States,* pp. 32–33

Technology
Prentice Hall United States History Video Collection™ Volume 15, *U.S. and the World*

Solving Problems of Movement

One of the greatest challenges for planners was assembling a labor force to build the canal, because Panama did not have enough workers for the project. As a solution, workers were brought in from overseas, mainly from the United States and the West Indies. Another challenge was removing rock and soil from the canal bed and bringing in machinery and supplies for the workers. The engineers' solution was an extensive rail system.

How Locks Work

The canal's massive locks are an engineering marvel. The locks' lower gates serve as temporary dams to hold water so that ships can float in at the level of the canal above the locks. Then, the upper gates close, the lower gates open, and water flows out of the lock chamber. This lets ships float down to the next-lowest level. When the lower gates close and the gates at the upper end open, water floods in and raises ships. This drawing shows a lock chamber and gates under construction.

Eradicating Disease

Two deadly mosquito-borne diseases—malaria and yellow fever—threatened the canal's work force, but army physician William Gorgas devised an effective mosquito eradication program that saved thousands of lives.

Geographic Connection

What kinds of obstacles did the human and physical geography of Panama pose for the builders of the Panama Canal? How did they overcome those obstacles?

611

2. Obstacles posed by the physical geography: The elevation of the Continental Divide, which required that ships be raised or that a deep gap be cut in the earth across the divide. Solution: A combination of both options—construction of locks to raise ships and the Gaillard Cut across the divide; the need to remove large amounts of earth and rock. Solution: Construction of a rail system; flooding along the Chagres River. Solution: Construction of a dam and the creation of Gátun Lake; the presence of disease-bearing mosquitoes. Solution: A mosquito eradication program.

Obstacle posed by the human geography: The lack of an adequate labor force in Panama. Solution: Recruitment and transport of workers from other countries.

Chapter 18 Planning Guide
Resource Manager

	CORE INSTRUCTION	**READING/SKILLS**
Chapter-Level Resources	Teaching Resources • Pacing Charts booklet • Block Scheduling booklet **Resource Pro® CD-ROM**, Ch. 18 **Prentice Hall Presentation Pro CD-ROM** **www.phschool.com** • eTeach	Guided Reading Audiotapes (English/Spanish) Student Edition on Audio CD, Ch. 18 Social Studies Skills Tutor CD-ROM Color Transparencies, B11, F6
1 The Origins of Progressivism 1. Learn the key goals of Progressives. 2. Find out how the ideas of progressive writers helped inspire new reform movements. 3. Discover which reform organizations and which women reformers took up progressive causes. 4. Understand why progressive reforms met with resistance.	Teaching Resources **Units 5/6 booklet** • Section 1 Quiz, p. 63 **Learning Styles Lesson Plans booklet**, p. 38	Guided Reading and Review booklet, p. 74 Guide to the Essentials, p. 93 Skills for Life booklet, p. 20 Section Reading Support Transparencies
2 Progressive Legislation 1. Read about how Progressives wished to expand the role of government. 2. Discover the municipal and state reforms achieved by Progressives. 3. Learn what federal reforms Theodore Roosevelt championed as President.	Teaching Resources **Units 5/6 booklet** • Section 2 Quiz, p. 64	Guided Reading and Review booklet, p. 75 Guide to the Essentials, p. 94 Learning with Documents booklet, p. 57 Section Reading Support Transparencies
3 Progressivism Under Taft and Wilson 1. Study the political conflicts that marked the presidency of William Howard Taft. 2. Find out who contended in the Election of 1912 and learn the outcome of that election. 3. Learn about the major policies that President Woodrow Wilson put into place. 4. Discover the limitations placed on the achievements of progressivism.	Teaching Resources **Units 5/6 booklet** • Section 3 Quiz, p. 65	Guided Reading and Review booklet, p. 76 Guide to the Essentials, p. 95 Section Reading Support Transparencies
4 Suffrage at Last 1. Learn the ways in which Susan B. Anthony and Elizabeth Cady Stanton formed a "bridge" to the twentieth-century suffrage effort. 2. Discover two main strategies pursued by suffrage leaders. 3. Read about the status of the suffrage movement by the turn of the century. 4. Find out why a new generation of leaders was needed in the suffrage effort. 5. Study the factors that led to a final victory for suffrage.	Teaching Resources **Units 5/6 booklet** • Section 4 Quiz, p. 66 **Learning Styles Lesson Plans booklet**, pp. 38–39	Guided Reading and Review booklet, p. 77 Guide to the Essentials, p. 96 Section Reading Support Transparencies

ENRICHMENT/PRE-AP

Prentice Hall United States History Video Collection™
www.phschool.com
- Section Activities, Virtual Field Trip, Chapter Activities, Current Events Online

Biography, Literature, and Comparing Primary Sources booklet, pp. 23, 64
American History Block Scheduling Support
Sounds of an Era Audio CD
Exploring Primary Sources in U.S. History CD-ROM

Great Debates booklet, p. 57
Nystrom *Atlas of Our Country,* pp. 30–31

Sounds of an Era Audio CD

Biography, Literature, and Comparing Primary Sources booklet, p. 131
Sounds of an Era Audio CD
Exploring Primary Sources in U.S. History CD-ROM

ASSESSMENT

PRENTICE HALL **ASSESSMENT SYSTEM**

Core Assessment
ExamView® Test Bank, Ch. 18
ExamView® Test Bank CD-ROM, Ch. 18

Standardized Test Preparation
Diagnose and Prescribe
Diagnostic Tests for High School Social Studies Skills

Review and Reteach
Review Book for U.S. History

Practice and Assess
Test-taking Strategies With Transparencies
Test-taking Strategies Poster
Test Prep for U.S. History
Alternative Assessment Handbook
Document-Based Assessment

Teaching Resources
Units 5/6 booklet
- Section Quizzes, pp. 63–66
- Chapter Tests, pp. 67, 70
www.phschool.com Ch. 18 Self-Test

AmericanHeritage RESOURCES

From the Archives of American Heritage®, pp. 626, 631
AmericanHeritage® My Brush with History™ Videotapes
www.americanheritage.com

TEXT

Don't miss the exclusive interactive version of this textbook on the Web and on CD-ROM.

Chapter 18 Planning Guide
In Your Classroom

CHAPTER 18 – PACING SUGGESTIONS

 For 90-minute Blocks
- Teach sections 3 and 4 using Transparencies B11 and F6, and the Recent Scholarship note on pages 623 and 637 for class discussions.

 Running Out of Time?

If you are running short on time to cover this chapter, consider the following options:

- Use the Prentice Hall Presentation Pro CD-ROM to create an outline for this chapter.
- Use the Section Summaries for Chapter 18, from **Guide to the Essentials (English/Spanish).**

ADDITIONAL ACTIVITIES

1 The Origins of Progressivism	**Connecting with Citizenship** Have students choose one of the individuals who made a name for her- or himself as a proponent of progressive legislation. Students should research that person's life and political opinions, then write a character profile that could have appeared in a progressive magazine at the time. Students can use their research to role-play a speech that person might have made at the time. **(Verbal/Linguistic; Bodily/Kinesthetic)**
2 Progressive Legislation	**Connecting with Government** Have students select one piece of progressive legislation—especially one that resulted in the establishment of a government agency or department—that passed during this period, then track it through present times. Have them present their findings in a chart or diagram form, labeled to indicate what changes have been made over the years. **(Visual/Spatial)**
3 Progressivism Under Taft and Wilson	**Connecting with Citizenship** Have students work in pairs or small groups to develop what they consider to be a thorough definition of progressivism. Before they begin to work, remind students that they have read about individuals and movements that would have agreed on some aspects of progressivism but not others. Students' definitions should account for such differences. Encourage students to use their own thinking and words, though at some point you may wish to have them compare their definitions with those they find in dictionaries, textbooks, and other reference sources. **(Verbal/Linguistic)**
4 Suffrage at Last	**Connecting with History and Conflict** Remind students that the Nineteenth Amendment received added impetus from World War I because of women's new responsibilities on the home front. Have students create a time line from 1791 up to the present of constitutional amendments and other laws that extended suffrage. Then have them add to the time line the major conflicts in which this country has fought, such as the Revolutionary War, the Civil War, World War I, World War II, and the Vietnam War. When students present their time lines, have them suggest what, if any, connections they see between the amendments or legislation and the involvement in the conflicts by those groups whose voting rights were extended. **(Logical/Mathematical; Visual/Spatial)**

INTRODUCING THE CHAPTER

At the turn of the century, many Americans hoped to change American society for the better. These reform-minded citizens, who were called Progressives, worked for many different causes at the national, state, and local levels. Many of their reforms had lasting effects on American society.

TIME LINE ACTIVITY

To provide students with practice in using the time line, ask questions such as these:

1. What was the aim of the Boxer Rebellion? *(To drive foreigners out of China)*

2. Which happened first: Theodore Roosevelt's third Presidential campaign, or the passage of the Clayton Antitrust Act? *(Roosevelt's third presidential campaign in 1912)*

3. What was Upton Sinclair's intention in publishing *The Jungle*? *(To expose the horrors of the meatpacking industry)*

eTeach

Be sure to check out this month's online discussion with a Master Teacher. Go to **www.phschool.com**.

Chapter 18

The Progressive Reform Era
(1890–1920)

SECTION 1 The Origins of Progressivism
SECTION 2 Progressive Legislation
SECTION 3 Progressivism Under Taft and Wilson
SECTION 4 Suffrage at Last

Elephants carry a suffrage "plank" in a New York rally.

American Events

1890	1899	1900
The National American Woman Suffrage Association is founded.	National Consumers' League is founded.	Hurricane devastates Galveston, Texas; recovery produces new model for city government.

Presidential Terms: B. Harrison 1889–1893 | Grover Cleveland 1893–1897 | William McKinley 1897–1901 | Theodore Roosevelt 1901–1909

1890	1900

World Events

The Boxer Rebellion fails to drive foreigners out of China. **1900**

Albert Einstein puts forth his special theory of relativity. **1905**

RESOURCE DIRECTORY

Teaching Resources
Pacing Charts booklet
Block Scheduling booklet, p. 22
Units 5/6 booklet
• Chapter Summary, p. 62

Technology
Guided Reading Audiotapes (English/Spanish), Ch. 18
Student Edition on Audio CD, Ch. 18
Prentice Hall United States History Video Collection™ Volume 14, *The Progressive Movement*
Prentice Hall Presentation Pro CD-ROM, Ch. 18
Resource Pro® CD-ROM
Social Studies Skills Tutor CD-ROM
Companion Web site, www.phschool.com

Theodore Roosevelt's Conservation Legacy

CANADA

0   150   300 mi.
0   150   300 km

RUSSIA

Alaska (U.S.)   CANADA

Gulf of Alaska

MEXICO

ATLANTIC OCEAN

Gulf of Mexico

- ■ Present-day national parks that originated prior to Roosevelt's administration
- ▲ Present-day national monuments that originated prior to Roosevelt's administration
- ■ Present-day national parks that originated during Roosevelt's administration
- ▲ Present-day national monuments that originated during Roosevelt's administration
- ▢ Present-day national forests that originated during Roosevelt's administration

This first-edition copy of *The Jungle* was given by Sinclair to author Mark Twain.

THE JUNGLE

UPTON SINCLAIR

1906
Upton Sinclair's *The Jungle* exposes unsanitary conditions in the meatpacking industry.

1912
Roosevelt runs for President under the new Progressive ("Bull Moose") Party and splits the GOP vote, giving the election to Wilson.

1914
The Clayton Antitrust Act gives the federal government broad anti-monopoly power.

1920
The Nineteenth Amendment is ratified.

William H. Taft 1909–1913

Woodrow Wilson 1913–1921

1910

1920

American Robert Peary reaches the North Pole.
1909

The Mexican Revolution begins.
1910

World War I begins in Europe.
1914

The Russian Revolution begins.
1917

The Treaty of Versailles is signed.
1919

Chapter 18   **613**

BIBLIOGRAPHY

For the Teacher

Cott, Nancy F., editor. ***Root of Bitterness: Documents of the Social History of American Women.*** New York: Oxford, 1996. (Examines the range and depth of women's experience through historical sources such as diaries, letters, and petitions.)

Norris, Frank. ***The Octopus.*** Penguin, 1994. (Originally published in 1901, this is a classic turn-of-the-century epic of California wheat farmers struggling against the forces of greedy railroad interests.)

For the Student

Life History of the United States. Vols. 8–10. *The Progressive Era.* (Richly illustrated series by editors of *Life* magazine.)

The Progressives. McGraw Hill Films. (A brief history of the period.)

Theodore Roosevelt's Conservation Legacy

Activating Prior Knowledge What was the majority of the land set aside by Theodore Roosevelt intended for? *(National forests)*

Previewing Theodore Roosevelt viewed the presidency as a "bully pulpit" that he could use to rally Americans to support his causes. How does his conservation legacy illustrate this notion? *(He saw the enjoyment and appreciation of nature as an important part of American life. By setting aside so much land, he encouraged all Americans to utilize the land.)*

BACKGROUND
About the Pictures

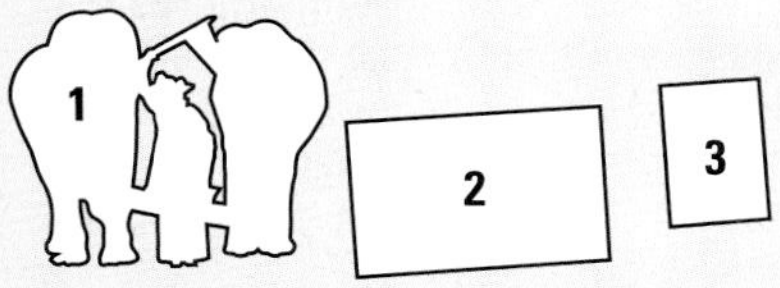

1. Elephants, the symbol of the Republican Party since the 1840s, are shown using their force and strength to represent the determination of women to gain the right to vote on a national basis.

2. The unnamed hurricane that hit Galveston, Texas, in 1900 stands as the deadliest natural disaster in United States history.

3. Upton Sinclair and other writers, dubbed "muckrakers" by President Theodore Roosevelt, used their journalistic skills to stimulate reforms.

TEXT

Don't miss the exclusive interactive version of this textbook on the Web and on CD-ROM.

Section 1
The Origins of Progressivism

The Origins of Progressivism

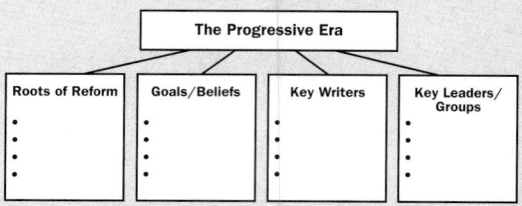

READING FOCUS

- What were the key goals of Progressives?
- How did the ideas of progressive writers help to inspire new reform movements?
- What reform organizations and what women reformers took up Progressive causes?
- Why did Progressive reforms meet with resistance?

MAIN IDEA

At the end of the 1800s, problems resulting from rapid industrialization, immigration, and urban growth spurred the creation of many reform movements during what is known as the Progressive Era.

KEY TERMS

Progressive Era
muckraker
injunction

TAKING NOTES

Copy the chart below. As you read, fill in factors relating to the Progressive Era.

The Progressive Era

Roots of Reform	Goals/Beliefs	Key Writers	Key Leaders/ Groups
• • •	• • •	• • •	• • •

Setting the Scene In 1906, Upton Sinclair turned the nation's stomachs. That year, the writer and journalist published *The Jungle*, a novel based on his investigations of the turn-of-the-century meatpacking industry. Besides depicting the violent accidents, horrible illnesses, and painful deaths that came to packinghouse workers themselves, Sinclair sickened the public with descriptions of how meat—and what was *called* meat—was processed on the way to their dinner tables.

Workers at a Chicago stockyard package boiled hams on dingy tables. Sinclair and others pressed for tough sanitary standards in meatpacking plants.

The main character in *The Jungle* is a naive, hard-working new immigrant from Lithuania who gratefully takes a job at a meatpacking house. Gradually, Sinclair's readers learn, as the worker does, the ugly secrets of what goes on inside the plant.

> 66 *It seemed they must have agencies all over the country, to hunt out old and crippled and diseased cattle to be canned. There were cattle which had been fed on 'whisky-malt,' the refuse [garbage] of the breweries, and had become what the men called 'steerly'—which means covered with boils. . . . It was stuff such as this that made the 'embalmed beef' that had killed several times as many United States soldiers as all the bullets of the Spaniards [in the Spanish-American War].* 99
> —Upton Sinclair, *The Jungle*, 1906

The Progressive Era

Revelations like these sent shock waves across a country that prided itself in being a modern land of progress and prosperity. Sinclair and others like him became leading figures in an era of reform movements that spread throughout American society at the turn of the twentieth century.

The Roots of Twentieth-Century Reform Many of these new reform movements were an outgrowth of earlier reform groups, such as the Populists. But while populism thrived mainly among western and southern farmers, many of the new reform movements arose in the cities of the Northeast, Midwest, and West Coast. They had their roots in movements such as nativism, prohibition, purity crusades, electoral reform, charity reform, social gospel philosophy, and the settlement houses.

The new reformers were reacting to the effects of rapid industrialization, immigration, and urbanization in the United States during the last decades of the 1800s. These changes contributed to the growth of the nation's cities and population.

Industrialization had brought a national prosperity that had come at a cost to some members of society. Industrial workers, like the farmers of the post–Civil War decades, suffered from low incomes and cycles of unemployment. Working conditions for men, women, and children in the factories were deplorable. Political corruption plagued governments at all levels.

Many Progressives maintained that private efforts to address the needs of workers, such as initiatives made by charities, were inadequate. What action, then, was needed? An active political debate produced a variety of attempts to bring about progress in society. Hence, historians refer to the period from about 1890 to 1920 as the **Progressive Era.**

The Progressives: Their Goals and Beliefs Progressivism was not a single unified movement. People who called themselves Progressives did not all share the same views. For the most part, their goals fell into four categories: social, moral, economic, and political. Some of these goals overlapped; some in fact conflicted.

Progressives included Republicans, Democrats, and members of other political parties. Yet in general, most reformers were people of average wealth who held in common at least four basic beliefs:

1. Government should be more accountable to its citizens.
2. Government should curb the power and influence of wealthy interests.
3. Government should be given expanded powers so that it could become more active in improving the lives of its citizens.
4. Governments should become more efficient and less corrupt so that they could competently handle an expanded role.

Reform in Modern Times

Urban changes and industrialization led to a period of social reforms in the 1960s and 1970s, as they had at the start of the century. Following World War II, many Americans moved from cities to new

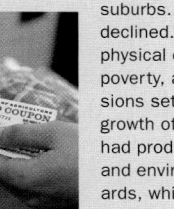

suburbs. City tax revenues declined. Economic and physical decay, inner-city poverty, and racial tensions set in. Wartime growth of heavy industry had produced workplace and environmental hazards, which were exposed by citizen activists.

Responding to these needs, in 1964 President Lyndon B. Johnson launched his Great Society program. It established a permanent Food Stamp program; Medicare and Medicaid; and federal programs for education, immigration, literacy, jobs, and urban renewal.

Johnson's successor, Richard M. Nixon, sought to trim social programs, yet he promoted other reforms. In 1970, Nixon created the Environmental Protection Agency (EPA) to oversee the cleanup of pollution in the air, water, and soil. That same year the Occupational Safety and Health Administration (OSHA) was created to monitor workplace safety.

? **What beliefs did Johnson and Nixon share with the Progressives regarding the functions of government? Explain.**

Focus In the 1880s and 1890s, many concerned citizens worked to reform American society. Their efforts became known as progressivism. How did progressivism affect American life?

Instruct Discuss the theme of reform. In what ways does progressivism resemble populism? What reform ideas were new? Ask students to compare the ideas of Henry George and Edward Bellamy. What actions did each think the government should take to transform society?

Discuss the various progressive movements. How did journalists work to bring about reform? What kinds of reforms did women and labor unions hope to effect?

Assess/Reteach Ask students to suggest the types of Americans who would be drawn to support the various progressive movements. Which of the movements established at the turn of the twentieth century would be likely to find supporters today?

BACKGROUND
Global Connections

In 1905, as progressivism caught fire in the United States, Einstein's theory of relativity—the idea that space and time are connected and that nothing is absolute, that even the passage of time is not uniform but varies in relation to an object's velocity—set the stage for a major rethinking of scientific truth. Publication of the more sweeping theory of general relativity in 1916 brought with it a questioning of the status quo and justified, some felt, revolutionary calls for change.

CUSTOMIZE FOR ...
ESL

Write the words *progress* and *progressive* on the chalkboard. Explain to students that progress is the root word of progressive. Have a volunteer look up *progress* in a dictionary and read the definition aloud. Have another student look up the word *progressive* and read its definition. Tell students that historians refer to the period between 1890 and 1920 as the Progressive Era. Ask them why.

CAPTION ANSWERS

Fast Forward to Today Sample answer: They shared the belief that the federal government had a responsibility to provide certain services that affected Americans' health and well-being.

Connections to Today

Since *The Jungle* spurred reform in 1906, the federal government has worked to ensure the safety of the nation's food supply. Yet despite new technologies to protect food and oversight of the food industry by the Food and Drug Administration, about 5,000 deaths and about 76 million illnesses are caused by food poisoning each year. Experts say people are eating more raw and precooked foods, thus increasing the chances of infection from bacteria or viruses. Also, the variety of foods available from all over the globe has increased much faster than the FDA's ability to inspect them. Still, the American food supply remains the safest in the world.

ACTIVITY

Connecting with Citizenship

Tell students that in 1799 Thomas Jefferson wrote: "Our citizens may be deceived for awhile, and have been deceived; but as long as the presses can be protected, we may trust to them for light." Discuss the quotation's meaning as a class. Then ask: Would Thomas Jefferson have approved of the muckrakers? Have students write brief essays in response. **(Verbal/Linguistic)**

READING CHECK

Progressives pressed for efficient, honest, accountable government. They wanted government to be strong enough to protect the public from abuse at the hands of capitalists and bankers.

READING CHECK
In your own words, summarize the main beliefs of Progressives.

INTERPRETING POLITICAL CARTOONS Theodore Roosevelt himself was willing to wield the muckrake to attack social problems. Here, he tries to clean up the meatpacking industry. **Determining Relevance** (a) What does the rake represent, and how would the President use it to solve the problem? (b) What is the significance of the U.S. Capitol in the background?

A DISGUSTING JOB BUT IT MUST BE DONE.

Igniting Reform: Writers and Their New Ideas

From the 1880s into the new century, lively debates emerged about how to reform society. The ideas of journalists and other writers had enormous influence on public opinion.

Two Early Reformers   In 1879, reformer Henry George wrote *Progress and Poverty,* an effort to explain why poverty continued to plague such an advanced civilization. George, a journalist and self-taught economist, concluded that poverty arose because some people bought and held on to land until its price went up. This practice, known as speculation, prevented others from using the land productively.

To solve this problem, George proposed that the government charge landowners a single tax on the value of the land itself. In the past, landowners had been taxed on improvements to the land, such as houses and cultivation. A single tax would make speculation in land less attractive by increasing the cost of holding land without using it. George's ideas had a powerful effect. "Single tax" clubs sprang up everywhere.

In 1888, newspaper editor Edward Bellamy published *Looking Backward.* In this novel, a Boston man undergoes hypnosis in 1887 and wakes up in the year 2000. Upon waking, the man finds the United States transformed. In place of harsh working conditions, poverty, and political corruption, he finds a utopian country where the government has taken over the largest companies. The government has also reorganized the companies with the goal of meeting human needs rather than making profits. Bellamy wrote:

> ❝ In a word, the people of the United States concluded to assume the conduct of their own business, just as . . . years before they had assumed the conduct of their own government. ❞
> —Edward Bellamy, *Looking Backward,* 1888

Bellamy's novel was a phenomenal bestseller. In response, more than 150 "Nationalist" clubs formed to promote his ideas. Bellamy's views also influenced the Populist Party platform in 1892.

The Muckrakers   Many reformers at the turn of the century worked to bring about change in a systematic manner. Relying heavily on scientific data and expert testimony, they first investigated issues of concern, such as conditions in slums and sweatshops. They then publicized the results of their investigations, so that the public would pressure legislators to pass and enforce new laws. Women's clubs and charitable groups provided leadership in pressuring officials to implement reforms.

Journalists such as Upton Sinclair played a key role in alerting the public to wrongdoing in politics and business. Theodore Roosevelt called such writers **muckrakers.** A *muckrake* is a rake or pitchfork used to clean manure and hay out of stables. Roosevelt took the term *muckraker* from John Bunyan's 1678 book *Pilgrim's Progress,* in which one of the characters was too busy raking filth on Earth to lift his eyes to heaven.

While Roosevelt approved of the legitimate exposure of wrongdoing, he condemned those who "earn their

---

CAPTION ANSWERS

Interpreting Political Cartoons (a) The rake represents federal regulations and standards intended to clean up the meatpacking industry and make meat products safe for consumers. (b) The Capitol refers to the pressure Roosevelt put on Congress to pass laws regulating the industry.

RESOURCE DIRECTORY

Teaching Resources
Biography, Literature, and Comparing Primary Sources booklet (Biography) *Ida Tarbell,* p. 23

livelihood by telling . . . scandalous falsehoods about honest men." Yet when Roosevelt read Upton Sinclair's *The Jungle,* he wrote the young novelist that "the specific evils you point out shall, if their existence be proved, and if I have power, be eradicated."

Despite the exaggerations of some authors, the muckrakers included many respected writers who identified and exposed serious abuses. Journalist Lincoln Steffens uncovered political corruption in St. Louis and other cities. In the 1904 book *The History of the Standard Oil Company,* Ida Tarbell, an investigative journalist, editor, teacher, and lecturer, revealed the abuses committed by the Standard Oil Trust.

Progressive Reform Organizations

Americans read the muckrakers' novels and newspaper accounts with enthusiasm. Whether angered or sickened by what they read, many Americans were inspired to take action by joining reform groups.

The Labor Movement The union movement grew in the 1890s, but only slowly. Employers discouraged union membership, preferring to deal with individual workers. If unions succeeded in forming, business leaders could often count on courts to issue **injunctions,** court orders that prohibit a certain activity. Courts often issued injunctions preventing workers from going on strike. Unions, however, continued to fight for better working conditions through collective rather than individual bargaining.

Socialists The Progressive Era saw a rise in the popularity of socialism, an economic and political philosophy favoring public or government control of property and income. Many American Socialists of this era wanted to end the capitalist system, distribute wealth more equally, and have government ownership of American industries. Writers Edward Bellamy and Upton Sinclair, among others, promoted Socialist ideas. Bellamy's *Looking Backward,* in particular, appealed to a wide spectrum of Americans, from military men to progressive women. Socialism also attracted some union members who hoped for fundamental change in the way the economy was organized.

Most Socialists hoped to accomplish their goals through the ballot box, not through revolution. In 1901 they formed the Socialist Party of America. By

---

ACTIVITY

Connecting with History and Conflict

While they did not have voting power, women often created ways to push progressive reform when legislators were slow to cooperate. Businesses that supported progressive social reform, for example, were put on a list of places where women should do their shopping. In order to be named to this "White List," businesses needed to meet certain criteria in harmony with reform. Divide students into groups to create at least five criteria suitable for a White List of today. Then have the groups compare their lists and justify their choices. (**Logical/Mathematical**)

BACKGROUND

Art History

The spirit of iconoclasm that marked the Progressive Era produced an important new movement in art known as the Ashcan school. Emerging in the early 1900s, it was led by a diverse group of painters known as "the Eight." These artists, among them Robert Henri, John Sloan, and Arthur B. Davies, rejected the conventional portraits and landscapes that had been the staple of nineteenth-century art. Instead, they depicted urban scenes, showing city life in all its shabby vitality. While the style of the art was conservative, the gritty realism of its content was entirely new.

READING CHECK

Women's groups, labor unions, and Socialists.

VIEWING HISTORY The International Ladies Garment Workers Union was formed in 1900. Activists such as those shown above fought hard to organize the garment industry. **Recognizing Cause and Effect** *Why do you think women activists targeted the garment industry, in particular, for reforms?*

READING CHECK

What types of groups became involved in Progressive reforms?

1912 the party had won more than 1,000 city government offices.

Unlike the Socialists and some more radical reformers, most Progressives did not support sweeping economic and political changes. They did not want to lose the high standard of living and personal liberties that democracy and a free enterprise system had given them. Instead, Progressives wanted to free the existing government of corruption and refocus its energies toward guarding the welfare of workers and the poor.

Women's Groups Rising to new levels of civic activism, women played a pivotal role in the reform movements of the Progressive Era. Influential women's organizations formed around nearly every major reform issue.

One leading women's group was the National Consumers' League (NCL), organized in 1899 to unite local consumers' leagues. Through these groups, women investigated the conditions under which goods were made and sold. They also encouraged consumers to purchase goods only at shops that did not employ children or require overtime. Leagues insisted that factories obey state factory inspection laws and pay a minimum wage.

Although they shared many goals, Progressive women did not all agree on methods for reforming society. For example, from her perspective in an impoverished urban neighborhood, social worker Jane Addams made an argument that not all reformers shared. She maintained that women in cities needed government help in order to care for their families:

> 66 Women who live in the country sweep their own dooryards and may either feed the refuse [scraps] of the table to a flock of chickens or allow it innocently to decay in the open air and sunshine. In a crowded city quarter, however, if the street is not cleaned by the city authorities no amount of private sweeping will keep the tenement free from grime; if the garbage is not properly collected and destroyed a tenement house mother may see her children sicken and die of diseases. 99
> —Jane Addams, *Ladies' Home Journal* article, 1910

Whatever their interests, many women agreed that they needed the right to vote. The cause of women's suffrage was important to many Progressives.

Two Women Reformers

Because so many urban women and children worked in factories, women's organizations took a special interest in workplace reforms. Among the numerous women who rose to national prominence in labor movements were Florence Kelley and Mary Harris "Mother" Jones.

Florence Kelley A leader in the work for labor reform, Florence Kelley joined Jane Addams's Hull House in Chicago in 1891. When federal officials asked Addams to investigate local labor conditions, she recommended Kelley for the job. Largely through Kelley's efforts, in 1893 Illinois passed a law prohibiting child labor, limiting working hours for women, and regulating

618 Chapter 18 • *The Progressive Reform Era*

CAPTION ANSWERS

Viewing History Workplace conditions in the garment industry were some of the worst. That industry also employed large numbers of women and children.

RESOURCE DIRECTORY

Teaching Resources
Units 5/6 booklet
• Section 1 Quiz, p. 63
Guide to the Essentials
• Section 1 Summary, p. 93

sweatshop conditions. The governor put Kelley in charge of enforcing the law. She became so frustrated by the district attorney's refusal to prosecute cases that she earned a law degree in order to take legal action herself.

Kelley later served as general secretary of the National Consumers' League. Under her leadership, the NCL spearheaded national movements to outlaw child labor and protect workers, especially women. When criticized, Kelley would ask why "seals, bears, reindeer, fish, wild game in the national parks, buffalo" and numerous other creatures were worthy of government protection, "but not the children of our race and their mothers."

Mother Jones Irish immigrant Mary Harris Jones came to the reform movement late in her life, inspired by personal convictions and tragedies. Her husband, an iron worker, and her four children died in a yellow fever epidemic in Tennessee in 1867. She rebuilt her life, establishing a successful dressmaking business. Then, in 1871, she lost everything in the Great Chicago Fire.

From her laborer husband, Jones had learned of the difficult working conditions in factories. Now she also discovered what it meant to be poor and alone. She appealed to the Knights of Labor for assistance, and became interested in its efforts to improve workplace conditions. In the labor movement, "Mother Jones," as she came to be called, found her life's work. Across the country, she organized unions for workers, both men and women. A tireless worker, Jones became best known for organizing unions in the mines of West Virginia and Colorado. These mines had some of the worst working conditions. Company resistance to unions often turned violent. Well into her eighties, Jones gave fiery speeches at rallies, uttering her famous call, "Join the union, boys!"

Jones became a national speaker on behalf of both unions and child labor laws. In 1905, she helped found the International Workers of the World (IWW).

Progressive Reforms Meet With Resistance

Progressives sought increased government involvement in people's lives—in housing, health care, and even in the content of the movies. This aspect of progressivism provoked resistance, often among the very people Progressives hoped to help. For example, Progressives saw child labor laws as critical to social progress. Yet, poor families who could not survive without the wages of their working children opposed the laws. Such disputes added to the perception that Progressives were insensitive to the poor.

Florence Kelley (top) and Mary Harris "Mother" Jones (below) were two of the nation's most active women reformers.

Section 1 Assessment

Reading Comprehension

1. Answers may include: nativism; prohibition; purity crusades; charity reform; social gospel philosophy; settlement houses.

2. Henry George: Combat poverty by charging a single tax to landowners based on the value of the land itself, discouraging speculation and decreasing poverty. Edward Bellamy: Government should take over the largest companies and reorganize them to focus more on human needs than on profits. Led to the development of "Nationalist" clubs; influenced the Populist Party platform.

3. They made it more difficult to go on strike. However, unions continued to fight through collective bargaining.

4. Answers may include: International Ladies Garment Workers Union to organize the garment industry; National Women's Trade Union League fought for labor laws; National Consumers' League fought to outlaw child labor and protect workers.

Critical Thinking and Writing

5. In general, Progressives wanted to rid the government of corruption and expand its role to regulate economic activity and enhance human welfare.

6. Answers will vary, but might state that while muckraking articles tend to be somewhat one-sided, they also point out some of the worst abuses in an industrializing society.

Section 1 Assessment

READING COMPREHENSION

1. What were some of the historical roots of the **Progressive Era?**

2. How did Henry George and Edward Bellamy influence the rise of progressivism?

3. How did **injunctions** affect the growth of labor unions?

4. Identify some Progressive women's groups and their causes.

CRITICAL THINKING AND WRITING

5. **Recognizing Ideologies** What beliefs did most Progressives share?

6. **Writing to Persuade** Write a letter to the editor of a 1905 newspaper arguing why the paper should publish articles by muckrakers.

Take It to the NET

Activity: Writing a Summary
Choose a reform issue or organization from the Progressive Era and write a summary on how it survives today. Use the links provided in the *America: Pathways to the Present* area of the following Web site for help in completing this activity.
www.phschool.com

Take It to the NET

Sample answer: The Food and Drug Administration was founded during the Progressive Era and initially had limited powers. Through public support and legal initiatives, the FDA became the official regulating group for all food and drugs. It continues to oversee food and drug testing and regulations today.

DRAWING AND TESTING CONCLUSIONS

Focus Students learn to analyze data to support a conclusion, and also how to test statements or opinions against facts to check a conclusion's validity.

Instruct Discuss with students the steps necessary to draw a conclusion and test its validity. Ask students to brainstorm ways to gather the necessary information to reach a conclusion. How can they check the validity of information they've gathered? How will they know when they have enough data? What steps should they take to sort through the information that is gathered so they may focus just on those pieces that are necessary to use in forming a conclusion? To validate the approach suggested in the book, ask students to describe other situations in which they would follow the same steps to draw and test conclusions.

Extend See the Skills for Life activity in the Resource Directory below.

ANSWERS
PRACTICE THE SKILL

1. **(a)** The "Work Force and Labor Union Membership" chart. **(b)** Conclusion 2: Data is from "Average Union and Nonunion Hours and Earnings in Manufacturing Industries" chart. Conclusion 3: Data is from "Work Force and Labor Union Membership" chart. Conclusion 4: There is not sufficient data in the charts to test this conclusion. **(c)** The data support conclusions 1 and 2. They contradict conclusion 3, and are insufficient to evaluate conclusion 4.

2. **(a)** Conclusion 1 deals with a trend. **(b)** No.

3. **(a)** Percentage of total workforce in unions increased by 8.9% in the years between 1900 and 1920. **(b)** The data contradict conclusion 3. **(c)** No data is given that indicates the earnings that were last due to work stoppages. Therefore, Conclusion 4 is not valid.

Drawing and Testing Conclusions

Drawing conclusions involves using available and reliable information to find an answer or to form an opinion. Testing conclusions means checking statements or opinions against data known to be valid. If the data support the conclusion, then you have reason to believe the conclusion is sound.

Read the conclusions below. Note that the first one has been left for you to complete. Then examine the data in the tables.

Conclusions:

1. The 20-year period between 1900 and 1920 saw a steady and significant _____ in union membership.
2. By 1920, union workers earned more money than nonunion workers while working fewer hours.
3. In terms of a percent of the work force, more workers were union members in 1910 than in 1920.
4. The reason the vast majority of workers did not join labor unions in the early 1900s was that work stoppages led to pay stoppages and decreased earnings.

LEARN THE SKILL
Use the following steps to draw conclusions and to test their validity:

1. **Identify the type of data that is necessary to draw conclusions about your topic or to verify existing conclusions.** Consider the issue about which you want to draw a conclusion, or study existing conclusions you wish to verify. If supporting data are provided, decide if they are useful for the conclusions.

2. **Decide on the criteria by which the conclusions could be made or tested.** Conclusions based on trends require data that cover a period of time. Other more specific conclusions may need exact data.

3. **Draw conclusions by analyzing the data, or test the conclusions by comparing them with the data.** Decide whether there are sufficient data to draw a sound conclusion, and be sure you interpret the data correctly. To test conclusions, decide whether the data support or contradict the conclusions and whether additional information is needed to determine the validity of some conclusions.

PRACTICE THE SKILL
Answer the following questions:

1. **(a)** Consider the data needed to complete Conclusion 1. Which chart supplies these data?

Work Force and Labor Union Membership

Year	Total Workers	Total Union Membership	Percentage of Work Force in Unions
1900	29,073,000	868,000	3.0
1910	37,371,000	2,140,000	5.7
1920	42,434,000	5,048,000	11.9

Union Membership by Industry

Year	Building	Textiles	Public Service
1900	153,000	8,000	15,000
1910	459,000	21,000	58,000
1920	888,000	149,000	161,000

Average Union and Nonunion Hours and Earnings in Manufacturing Industries

Year	Union		Nonunion	
	Weekly Hours	Hourly Earnings	Weekly Hours	Hourly Earnings
1900	53.0	$0.341	62.1	$0.152
1910	50.1	$0.403	59.8	$0.188
1920	45.7	$0.884	53.5	$0.561

SOURCE: *Historical Statistics of the United States, Colonial Times to 1970*

(b) Upon what data is each of the other conclusions based? **(c)** Are these data useful for either supporting or contradicting these conclusions?

2. **(a)** Does Conclusion 1 deal with a trend or with a specific point in time? **(b)** Would data covering a period of time be needed to support Conclusion 2?

3. **(a)** Use the data to complete Conclusion 1. **(b)** Do the data support or contradict Conclusion 3? **(c)** Do the data give you reason to agree with Conclusion 4? Explain.

APPLY THE SKILL
See the Chapter Review and Assessment for another opportunity to apply this skill.

620 Chapter 18 • *The Progressive Reform Era*

RESOURCE DIRECTORY

Teaching Resources
Skills for Life booklet, p. 20

Technology
Social Studies Skills Tutor CD-ROM
Interactive Practice in
- Geographic Literacy
- Critical Thinking and Reading
- Visual Analysis
- Communications

620 • Chapter 18

Progressive Legislation

READING FOCUS

- How did Progressives wish to expand the role of government?
- What municipal and state reforms did Progressives achieve?
- What federal reforms did Theodore Roosevelt champion as President?

MAIN IDEA

Because of public demand, local, state, and federal officials enacted major Progressive reforms in the early 1900s.

KEY TERMS

social welfare program
municipal
home rule
direct primary
initiative
referendum
recall
holding company

TAKING NOTES

In the left-hand column of the chart below, list Progressive reforms. As you read, place checkmarks to indicate what level(s) of government initiated each type of reform.

Progressive Reform	Municipal	State	Federal
Fight government corruption	√	√	√
Home rule	√		

Setting the Scene On March 25, 1911, about 500 workers, mostly Italian and Jewish girls, were on the job at the Triangle Shirtwaist Company. The company, which occupied the upper floors of a 10-story building in New York City, made tailored women's blouses. In the supposedly fireproof building, a small fire broke out. Feeding on fabric and rubbish, it swelled into an inferno.

Some workers fled to safety through the one open stairway to the roof. Surging to the other exits, employees found doors locked from the outside. Others piled onto the single, rusted fire escape; it collapsed, plunging them to their deaths. Ladders on the fire trucks were not long enough to reach the upper floors, so desperate women, their dresses aflame, leaped into the firemen's nets below. The nets tore open, killing many who fell to the pavement. Those trapped above perished in smoke and flames, some still hunched over their sewing machines. A total of 146 workers died.

In the aftermath, 29-year-old labor leader Rose Schneiderman addressed a public meeting held to discuss the causes of the fire. A Jewish immigrant from Poland, Schneiderman would become one of the nation's best-known women labor leaders. She attacked government resistance to reform:

> 66 Every week I must learn of the untimely death of one of my sister workers. . . . But every time the workers come out in the only way they know to protest against conditions which are unbearable, the strong hand of the law is allowed to press down heavily upon us. 99
> —Rose Schneiderman, public address, 1911

Schneiderman helped stir powerful public support for reforms. Public and private groups called on the city to appoint fire inspectors, to make fire drills compulsory, to unlock and fireproof exits, and to require automatic sprinklers in buildings more than seven stories high. New York's Tammany government bowed to the pressure and adopted new workplace protections.

Firefighters wage a losing battle against the deadly blaze in the upper floors of the 10-story, 135-foot Asch Building housing the Triangle Shirtwaist Company.

Chapter 18 • Section 2   **621**

SECTION OBJECTIVES

1. Read about how Progressives wished to expand the role of government.
2. Discover the municipal and state reforms achieved by Progressives.
3. Learn what federal reforms Theodore Roosevelt championed as President.

BELLRINGER

Warm-Up Activity Ask students to consider this statement by former Speaker of the House Thomas P. "Tip" O'Neill, Jr.: "All politics is local [politics]." Do students agree or disagree?

Activating Prior Knowledge After a period of rapid change, it is often necessary to slow down for a bit and regroup to assess the larger impacts of the changes that have taken place. In some ways, the era of progressive legislation marked such a point in United States history. Can students pinpoint a time in their own lives during which they experienced rapid change, followed by a period of reassessment?

READING STRATEGY

As students read the chapter, have them create a cause-and-effect chart. Under the heading "cause," have them list events that served as stimuli to reforms. Under the heading "effect," have them list legislation that resulted.

Focus Progressives succeeded in passing many reform bills in local, state, and federal legislatures. What were these laws, and what did they accomplish?

Instruct Discuss the alliance between machine politicians and reformers. What were they able to accomplish together? Why were they able to make more improvements by working together?

Ask what state and federal reforms were passed to protect workers. What was done to improve social conditions in the cities? Ask why it was important for city dwellers that utilities be regulated.

Discuss how state legislatures empowered voters. In what ways did voters gain more influence in government during the Progressive Era?

Assess/Reteach Ask students to list some ways in which demands from the public stirred the movement toward reform. Were there some types of reform that people in general wanted to see, but that government failed to provide?

ACTIVITY
Connecting with Economics

Discussing social welfare programs raises the question of how such programs should be financed. Progressives opposed the tariff as being unfair to poor people. They supported a progressive income tax to distribute the burden of taxation more fairly. Stage a classroom debate over the relative merits and fairness of the tariff versus the progressive income tax. To further the discussion, have students study the relative merits of three different types of tax codes—proportional, progressive, and regressive—and have them write brief descriptions of the positive and negative aspects of each. **(Logical/Mathematical)**

READING CHECK
Curbing the power of state governments and political bosses through home rule and civil service reform, respectively; ensuring the equitable delivery of services, such as public utilities and welfare programs.

Focus on GOVERNMENT

Good Government Clubs Determined to clean up corruption and make governments operate with business efficiency, a Good Government movement arose in the 1880s. Good Government clubs throughout the country promoted Progressive reforms and attracted new recruits, creating fertile ground for the future Progressive Party. In 1894, the clubs held a national conference in Philadelphia, with future President and Progressive Party candidate Theodore Roosevelt as the key speaker. The conference led to the founding of the National Municipal League. Municipal leagues thrive in many cities today.

READING CHECK
Describe some of the goals of municipal reformers.

An Expanded Role for Government

Rose Schneiderman was one of many Progressive leaders who sought more government regulation to protect workers' rights and business competition. But most Progressives opposed government control of businesses, except for companies that supplied essential services such as water and electricity.

Progressives also believed that government ought to increase its responsibility for the welfare, or well-being, of people. They sought more **social welfare programs,** which help ensure a minimum standard of living. Progressives pressed for social welfare programs such as unemployment benefits, accident and health insurance, and a social security system for the disabled and the elderly. Progressives envisioned a government that relied on experts and scientists to plan efficient programs managed by professionals, not politicians.

Municipal Reforms

Many of the earliest Progressive reforms were made at the city, or **municipal,** level. Those seeking reform of municipal governments came from within and outside of those governments. Cities were home to most of the settlement workers, club members, and professionals who pressed for changes. Some municipal reformers worked for **home rule,** a system that gives cities a limited degree of self-rule. Home rule allowed cities to escape domination by state governments controlled by political machines or by business or rural interests.

Municipal reformers sometimes seemed naive in their belief that they could abolish corruption. Some reformers also held negative views of immigrants, who they felt were responsible for many city problems. Still, the ideas of municipal activists formed an important part of the era's spirit of reform.

Attacking the Bosses Municipal reformers opposed the influence of political bosses. They argued that only a civil service system based on merit instead of favors would keep political appointees out of important jobs, such as those enforcing labor and public safety laws.

For the most part, political machines and bosses survived such attacks. In 1896, for example, Columbia University president Seth Low ran for mayor of New York City, supported by municipal reformers. To help in his campaign

622 Chapter 18 • The Progressive Reform Era

against Tammany Hall's ward bosses, settlement houses sent children out to post handbills in their neighborhoods. Low lost that election but won in 1901. Still, the Tammany Hall machine returned to power in the next election.

In some cities, however, voter support for reforms prompted machine politicians to work with reformers. Together they improved city services, established public health programs and workplace reforms, and enforced tenement codes.

New Forms of Municipal Government   Like the Triangle Shirtwaist fire, other catastrophes served to bring about reforms. On September 8, 1900, a powerful hurricane in the Gulf of Mexico slammed into the city of Galveston, Texas. The storm left more than 6,000 people dead when its 120-mile-per-hour winds and surging waves pounded the unprotected city for 18 hours. To manage the huge relief and rebuilding effort needed, the city created an emergency commission of five administrators to replace the mayor and aldermen. The commission handled the rebuilding with such efficiency that Galveston permanently instituted the commission form of government. Other cities rapidly adopted the Galveston model, adapting it to their needs.

In March 1913, Ohio's Great Miami River Basin flooded the city of Dayton, killing 360 people and causing damage of more than $100 million. In the aftermath, Dayton became the first large city to adopt a council-manager government. Typically, this system includes an elected city council, which sets laws and appoints a professional city manager to run city services.

Cities Take Over Utilities   Reformers made efforts to regulate or dislodge the monopolies that provided city utilities such as water, gas, and electricity. Reform mayors Hazen S. Pingree of Detroit (1889–1897), Samuel M. Jones of Toledo (1897–1904), and Tom Johnson of Cleveland (1901–1909) worked within existing government structures to pioneer city control or ownership of utilities. By 1915, nearly two out of three cities had some city-owned utilities.

Providing Welfare Services   Some reform mayors led movements for city-supported welfare services. Pingree provided public baths, parks, and a work-relief program for Detroit. Jones opened playgrounds, free kindergartens, and lodging houses for the homeless in Toledo. In his view, all people would become good citizens if social conditions were good.

VIEWING HISTORY The coastal city of Galveston, Texas, lacked a retaining wall to protect it from the powerful hurricanes that blow ashore from the Gulf of Mexico. In 1900, after a huge storm left wind and flood devastation, the city needed a new type of government to manage the relief and rebuilding effort. **Drawing Inferences** *What features or qualities would a municipal government need to handle a reconstruction job of the magnitude seen here?*

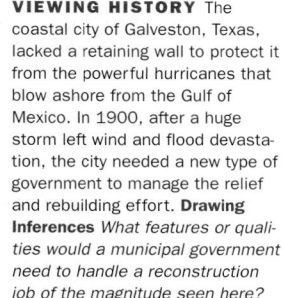

Texas

Galveston

Chapter 18 • Section 2   **623**

ACTIVITY

Connecting with Government

After discussing how progressive reforms at the state level gave more power to citizens, ask students: What law would you like to see passed if you had the power? Then have them work individually or in groups to write their own ballot initiatives or referenda. Have students explain how participation in the democratic process reflects our national identity. Afterward, discuss and vote on students' initiatives as a class.

ACTIVITY

Connecting with Science and Technology

In 1913 the new technology of moving pictures was used to improve the efficiency of factory workers. In a time-and-motion study at a factory in Providence, Rhode Island, a motion picture camera operator filmed a worker assembling a braiding machine. Based on the film, "waste motions" were eliminated. Afterward the worker assembled the machine in less than a quarter of the time previously needed.

Have students with access to video cameras use them to conduct their own time-and-motion studies. They should study a daily activity, such as making lunch, to see how quickly and efficiently it can be done. As they work, have them analyze the impact of technological innovations, such as the motion picture, on the nature of work. Have groups share their results with the class. **(Visual/Spatial; Bodily/Kinesthetic)**

CAPTION ANSWERS

Interpreting Diagrams The measures address voting reform, without which, the Progressives believed, citizens could not participate fully in the process of cleaning up government and making it more efficient and responsive.

State Reforms

Some governors and state legislators also promoted progressive reforms. Like the reform mayors, Progressives at the state level first worked to oust party bosses and give more power to citizens. Then they passed laws to increase the role of government in business regulation and social welfare.

More Power to Voters During the Progressive Era, voters gained more direct influence in lawmaking and in choosing candidates. (See diagram below.) Throughout the country, party leaders traditionally had handpicked candidates for public office. In Wisconsin, reform governor Robert M. La Follette instituted a **direct primary**, an election in which citizens vote to select nominees for upcoming elections. By 1916, all but three states had direct primaries. Many states also instituted the **initiative,** a process in which citizens can put a proposed new law directly on the ballot in the next election by collecting voters' signatures on a petition. Another lawmaking reform was the **referendum,** a process that allows citizens to approve or reject a law passed by the legislature. The **recall** procedure permits voters to remove public officials from office before the next election.

In 1904, Oregon began allowing voters, rather than the state legislature, to choose their United States senators. In 1913, the Seventeenth Amendment, allowing the direct election of senators, was ratified by the states.

Progressive Political Reforms

Before	Reforms	After
Party leaders choose candidates for state and local offices.	**Direct Primaries** Voters select their party's candidates.	Power moves to voters.
State legislatures choose U.S. senators.	**17th Amendment** U.S. senators are elected by popular vote.	
Only members of the state legislature can introduce bills.	**Initiative** Voters can put bills before the legislature.	
Only legislators pass laws.	**Referendum** Voters can vote on bills directly.	
Only courts or the legislature can remove corrupt officials.	**Recall** Voters can remove elected officials from office.	

INTERPRETING DIAGRAMS This diagram shows the effects of some of the major reforms achieved by Progressives at all levels of government. **Synthesizing Information** *What type of reform do all these measures address, and why were such changes so important to Progressives?*

Reforms in the Workplace Motivated in part by the Triangle Shirtwaist fire, state reformers worked to curb workplace hazards. Some states established labor departments to provide information and dispute-resolution services to employers and employees. Other states developed workers' accident insurance and compensation systems. However, government efforts to control working conditions met legal opposition. Business owners contended that the government could not interfere with their constitutional right to make contracts with their employees. They also maintained that government workplace regulations violated their private property rights by attempting to dictate how they used their property.

The courts generally upheld these views. Reformers argued that the Constitution reserves police powers to the states, and the states could use these powers to intervene in the workplace to protect workers.

In principle, the courts acknowledged the reformers' reasoning. But in the case of *Lochner* v. *New York* (1905), the Supreme Court struck down a law setting maximum hours for bakers. The Court said that since the law had not been shown to protect public health, the law constituted an improper use of the state's police power and "an illegal interference with the rights of individuals . . . to make contracts."

The justices left open the possibility that if such a law *could* be shown to protect workers' health, it would be permissible. Reformers used this strategy in

Muller v. *Oregon*. In this 1908 case, the Court upheld an Oregon law that limited hours for female laundry workers to 10 hours a day. Reform lawyer Louis D. Brandeis represented the interests of the laundry workers. Using scientific evidence gathered by activists in the National Consumers' League, he argued that women's long work hours in laundries harmed their health.

Labor reformers succeeded on other fronts as well. By 1907, nearly two thirds of the states had abolished child labor, often defined as employment of children under the age of 14. Minimum wage laws for women and children also made headway, with Florence Kelley leading a national campaign. After Massachusetts adopted a minimum wage in 1912, eight other states followed.

Wisconsin's Reform Governor One of the most determined Progressives in U.S. politics was Robert M. La Follette of Wisconsin. "Fighting Bob" earned his nickname through efforts to clean up government and produce social welfare reforms. In three terms as a Progressive Republican governor (1901–1906), La Follette ousted party bosses and brought about structural changes such as a direct primary and civil service reform.

La Follette introduced a new way of running state government. He called on academic experts to help draft reform legislation. To get it passed, he had the voting roll call read publicly in the districts of legislators who opposed reform. He drew on academics and citizen committees to run regulatory agencies. The "Wisconsin Idea" of a public–academic alliance to improve government became known nationwide.

> 66 *If it can be shown that Wisconsin is a happier and better state to live in, that its institutions are more democratic, that the opportunities of all its people are more equal, that social justice more nearly prevails, that human life is safer and sweeter—then I shall rest content in the feeling that the Progressive movement has been successful. . . . [T]here is no reason now why the movement should not expand until it covers the entire nation.* 99
>
> —Robert M. La Follette, from his autobiography,
> *A Personal Narrative of Political Experiences*, 1913

La Follette took his ideas to the U.S. Senate, where he served from 1906 until his death in 1925. Famous for his independence from business interests, he successfully promoted Progressive legislation on the federal level. As the Progressive Party's candidate for President in 1924, La Follette lost, but received one sixth of the vote.

Federal Reforms

A number of important Progressive reforms were made at the federal level. Beginning with President Theodore Roosevelt in 1901, the White House became a powerful voice for change. In a major expansion of federal authority, Roosevelt used his presidential powers vigorously in domestic matters, just as he did overseas. He viewed the presidency as a "bully pulpit"—an ideal platform from which to guide or rally the American public to support moral, worthy causes. In the process he created the modern presidency, in which the chief executive is a strong political force.

TR's "Square Deal" TR got a chance to flex his political muscle in May 1902, when the United Mine Workers called a strike to protest

Progressive reform politician Robert M. La Follette earned the nickname "Fighting Bob."

La Follette on the Firing Line

SNAPSHOT WHILE ADDRESSING AN AUDIENCE OF 12,000 PEOPLE AT LOG AN CO EN IN 1912

ROBERT MARION LA FOLLETTE

Candidate for Republican Nomination as U. S. Senator at Primary, September 9th.

ACTIVITY
Connecting with Government

Have students review the quote on this page by Robert La Follette. His goals as a Progressive reformer are clearly stated. Did the movement succeed in achieving the aims he described? Have groups of students research and then list the pros and cons of several of La Follette's reforms, such as the direct primary, civil service reforms, and incorporation of academics and citizen committees to run regulatory agencies. **(Verbal/Linguistic)**

BACKGROUND
Biography

One of the most effective reform governors in the nation was the plain-spoken governor of California, Hiram Johnson (1866–1945). The son of a Republican politician, Johnson ran for governor vowing to "kick the Southern Pacific out of politics." The Southern Pacific Railroad was not only the state's most powerful corporation, it was his own father's close political ally. But Johnson was, in his own words, a "natural rebel." He fought against "rotten big business and crooked politics," enacting so many progressive reforms that one journalist called his tenure a "political revolution."

CUSTOMIZE FOR ...

Gifted and Talented

Tell students that most Progressives were financially comfortable. Ask how much self-interest was involved in the Progressives' desire to maintain order and stability and the nation's high standard of living. Does self-interest on the part of reformers affect the value of their reforms?

READING CHECK

By getting involved in labor disputes, breaking up harmful trusts, and successfully pushing Congress to regulate railroads and the food-processing industry.

CAPTION ANSWERS

Interpreting Charts Legislation such as the Hepburn Act and the Meat Inspection Act exemplify progressive reforms that allowed the federal government to intervene forcefully in the sphere of private business in order to protect the well-being of consumers.

Progressive Era Legislation

Legislation	Purpose
Sherman Antitrust Act, 1890	Outlawed monopolies and practices that restrained trade, such as price fixing.
National Reclamation Act, 1902	Created to plan and develop irrigation projects.
United States Forest Service, 1905	Created to manage the nation's water and timber resources.
Hepburn Act, 1906	Authorized the Interstate Commerce Commission to regulate railroad rates.
Pure Food and Drug Act, 1906	Banned interstate shipping of impure food and deliberate mislabeling of food and drugs.
Meat Inspection Act, 1906	Required federal inspection of meat processing to ensure sanitary conditions.
Department of Labor, 1913	Cabinet department created to promote the welfare and employment of working people.
16th Amendment, 1913	Gave Congress the power to levy an income tax.
17th Amendment, 1913	Provided for the direct election of senators.
Federal Reserve Act, 1913	Created Federal Reserve System of government banks to supervise private banks and provide a flexible money supply.
National Park Service, 1916	Created to administer the nation's parks.
18th Amendment, 1919	Prohibited the manufacture and sale of liquor. (Repealed in 1933.)
19th Amendment, 1920	Granted women full suffrage.
Women's Bureau, 1920	Created within the Department of Labor to improve the status of working women.

INTERPRETING CHARTS
Progressive reform touched many aspects of American life, including business, natural resources, labor, voting, and consumer protection. **Analyzing Information** *How did Progressive reforms result in a major expansion of federal power?*

READING CHECK
How did Roosevelt expand presidential authority?

---

their low wages. As winter approached and mine owners continued to refuse to talk to the union, TR decided to intervene. Lacking coal, the nation would be without a major source of heating fuel.

Roosevelt insisted that both sides submit to arbitration, a settlement in which an impartial third party decides on a legally binding solution. To pressure mine owners, TR threatened to use the army to seize and operate the mines. In 1903, arbitrators granted the miners a 10 percent raise and reduced their workday from 10 hours to 9. The arbitrators did not officially recognize the union, however. When Roosevelt called this a "square deal" for both sides in the coal strike, the phrase became a slogan of his presidency.

Antitrust Activism Although the Sherman Antitrust Act in 1890 was in place as a check on big business, it had never been vigorously enforced. Reversing this trend, Roosevelt's Attorney General used the act to sue the Northern Securities Company. Northern Securities was a **holding company,** a firm that buys up stocks and bonds of smaller companies. In doing so, it can create a monopoly. Northern Securities had brought about a modest decline in railroad rates by forming such a monopoly. But in 1904 the government convinced the Supreme Court that the company was in violation of the Sherman Act. The Court dissolved the company.

The Roosevelt administration filed 42 antitrust actions. The beef trust, Standard Oil, and the American Tobacco Company were either broken up or forced to reorganize. Like most Progressives, TR was not antibusiness. He did not wish to destroy trusts that did not harm the public. But he believed that government should regulate them.

Railroad Regulation An unelected President facing congressional opposition, Roosevelt proceeded with caution in his first term. He used his executive powers to achieve change, creating a political platform and a record on which to run in 1904. His comfortable victory over his Democratic opponent, Alton B. Parker, gave Roosevelt a mandate for his pursuit of reforms. He soon used his position to achieve a long-sought Progressive goal: regulation of the railroads.

After a battle with Congress, Roosevelt won passage of the 1906 Hepburn Act. The act moved the Interstate Commerce Commission (ICC) out of its largely weak advisory role and gave it strong enforcement powers that were essentially both legislative and judicial. The act authorized the ICC to set and limit railroad rates. Thus, the ICC became the first true federal regulatory agency.

Protecting Public Health Although Roosevelt denounced the muckrakers at first, public horror over numerous exposés of the food and drug industries persuaded him to respond. The result was the Pure Food and Drug Act and the Meat Inspection Act. The 1906 laws required accurate labeling of ingredients, strict sanitary conditions, and a rating system for meats.

A New Labor Department In response to pressure from labor and women's groups, in 1912 the government established a Children's Bureau. A Cabinet-level Department of Labor was added in 1913, and a Women's Bureau in 1920. The two new bureaus, both part of the Department of Labor, supported laws to benefit women and children. Julia Lathrop and Mary Anderson, the heads of these bureaus, became the first women in such federal posts.

Protecting the Environment TR also urged Congress to take further steps to protect the nation's natural resources. At the urging of explorers and nature writers such as John Wesley Powell and John Muir, Congress had established Yellowstone in Wyoming as the nation's first national park in 1872. Yosemite National Park in California had been created in 1890. Presidents Harrison and Cleveland had preserved some 35 million acres of forest land.

In 1905, Roosevelt named Gifford Pinchot, a forester, to head a new United States Forest Service. Pinchot sought to develop a policy for land and water use based on scientific data. At his recommendation, TR set aside more than 200 million acres for national forests, mineral reserves, and water projects. The National Reclamation Act, passed in 1902, used money from the sale of public lands to build irrigation systems in arid states.

New Constitutional Amendments During the Progressive Era, constitutional restraints on federal power gradually diminished. The Sixteenth Amendment, ratified in 1913, authorized Congress to collect federal income taxes. Previously, the government had relied on income from tariffs. Progressives had argued that tariffs pushed up the prices of goods for the working poor. The Sixteenth Amendment enabled the government to get more revenues from people with higher incomes. The Seventeenth Amendment (allowing direct election of senators) also was ratified in 1913. The Eighteenth Amendment, ratified in 1919, banned the production, sale, or import of alcoholic beverages. Not all Progressives favored Prohibition, but many thought it would protect society from the poverty and violence associated with drinking.

Roosevelt and conservationist John Muir pose against the magnificent landscape of California's Yosemite National Park in this 1906 photograph.

Section 2 Assessment

READING COMPREHENSION

1. Summarize the Progressives' views on regulating business.

2. Give examples of government reforms and **social welfare programs** at the municipal and state levels during the Progressive Era.

3. Describe the effect of each of these reforms: (a) **home rule;** (b) **direct primary;** (c) **initiative.**

4. What reforms did TR achieve under his square deal?

CRITICAL THINKING AND WRITING

5. **Synthesizing Information** Choose two constitutional amendments passed during the Progressive Era and explain how they expanded the role of government in citizens' lives.

6. **Writing a Conclusion** From what you know about TR's personality, beliefs, and leadership style, draw conclusions about how these characteristics affected his pursuit of Progressive reforms.

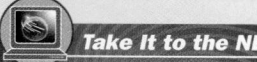

Activity: Virtual Field Trip To learn more about the Triangle Shirtwaist Factory fire, visit the links provided in the *America: Pathways to the Present* area of the following Web site.
www.phschool.com

Section 2 Assessment

Reading Comprehension

1. Progressives sought government regulation to protect workers' rights and business competition. They opposed government control, except in the cases of companies that supplied services like water and electricity.

2. Possible answers: Municipal: public baths in Detroit, free kindergartens in Toledo. State: workers' accident insurance, child labor legislation.

3. (a) Home rule: frees cities from domination by state governments; (b) direct primary: voters, not party leaders, choose candidates; (c) initiative: voters introduce a bill, then vote on it at the next election.

4. Antitrust activism; railroad regulation; transforming ICC into first regulatory agency; Pure Food and Drug Act, Meat Inspection Act; protecting the environment.

Critical Thinking and Writing

5. Answers may include: Sixteenth Amendment: introduced a graduated income tax. Eighteenth Amendment: prohibited alcohol manufacture, sale, and consumption.

6. Answers will vary, but might mention that TR's dynamic personality and energetic leadership style was well suited to the Progressive Era. He was not afraid to take on the railroads and large trusts.

Invite students to take a Virtual Field Trip at **www.phschool.com**

Section 3

Progressivism Under Taft and Wilson

Progressivism Under Taft and Wilson

SECTION OBJECTIVES

1. Study the political conflicts that marked the presidency of William Howard Taft.
2. Find out who contended in the election of 1912 and learn the outcome of that election.
3. Learn about the major policies that President Woodrow Wilson put into place.
4. Discover the limitations placed on the achievements of progressivism.

BELLRINGER

Warm-Up Activity Have students consider an election for class president with four students running for office. If half the class agreed to vote for one nominee and half the class voted for several, who would win? Explain how the election of 1912 was determined in a similar fashion.

Activating Prior Knowledge The elections of 1992 and 2000, like the election of 1912, each involved challenges by a third-party candidate. In students' opinions, what might the outcome of these elections have been without these third-party challenges?

READING STRATEGY

As students read this section, have them each create a time line of reforms made during the Taft and Wilson presidencies.

CAPTION ANSWERS

Viewing History Taft had neither Roosevelt's sheer energy nor his ability to line up congressional support for his reforms. He also did not place Progressives in his Cabinet, and he disappointed Progressives on a few key issues, such as tariff reduction.

READING FOCUS

- What political conflicts marked the presidency of William Howard Taft?
- Who were the contenders in the Election of 1912, and what was the outcome?
- What major policies did President Woodrow Wilson help put in place?
- In what ways were the achievements of progressivism limited?

MAIN IDEA

Despite his solid record of reforms, President Taft alienated many Progressives. They broke away and formed their own party with Roosevelt as their candidate. Democrat Woodrow Wilson beat both men in 1912 and continued progressive reforms.

KEY TERMS

conservationist
New Nationalism
Bull Moose Party
Clayton Antitrust Act
Federal Trade
Commission (FTC)
Federal Reserve System

TAKING NOTES

Copy the Venn diagram below. As you read, fill in the two circles with facts about the policies of Presidents Taft and Wilson. Where the circles overlap, fill in policies endorsed by both Presidents.

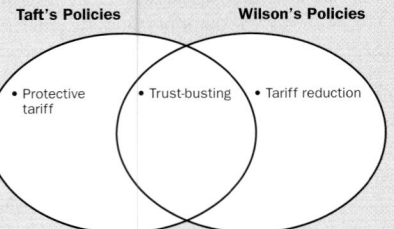

Taft's Policies — Wilson's Policies

- Protective tariff
- Trust-busting
- Tariff reduction

Setting the Scene The day after his election in 1904, Theodore Roosevelt announced he would not seek another term as President. One evening, as the 1908 campaign approached, Roosevelt was entertaining the Secretary of War, William Howard Taft, and his wife, Helen, at the White House. Suddenly the mischievous TR pretended to fall into a fortune teller's trance. "I see a man standing before me weighing about 350 pounds." (Taft was a portly man, more than 6 feet tall.)

"There is something hanging over his head. I cannot make out what it is; it is hanging by a slender thread. At one time it looks like the Presidency—then again it looks like the Chief Justiceship."

"Make it the Presidency!" exclaimed Mrs. Taft.

"Make it the Chief Justiceship!" cried Mr. Taft.

Helen Taft, a key political advisor to her husband, had her way. TR persuaded the reluctant Taft to run for the job, and made him his hand-picked nominee on the Republican ticket in 1908.

Perhaps Taft should have listened instead to his mother: "I do not want my son to be President. His is a judicial mind and he loves the law." Taft would, in time, become the nation's highest judge, a job he dearly loved. But not until he served a fairly miserable four years as President.

Taft's Presidency

With TR's backing, Taft easily won the 1908 election over Democrat William Jennings Bryan, who tried for a third and last time to win the office. Taft pledged to carry on TR's progressive program. But from the beginning, Taft found his predecessor's shoes difficult to fill. He had neither Roosevelt's energy nor strength of personality to battle the powerful Republican congressmen who opposed progressive reforms. He created disappointment from the start by not appointing any Progressives to his Cabinet. Although in many ways he would fulfill his pledge to continue Roosevelt's reforms, in the

VIEWING HISTORY President Taft accomplished as much as or more than TR in some areas of progressive reform, yet he took several steps for which Progressives never forgave him. **Identifying Central Issues** What factors made Taft's job so difficult?

RESOURCE DIRECTORY

Teaching Resources
Guided Reading and Review booklet, p. 76

Technology
Section Reading Support Transparencies
Guided Reading Audiotapes (English/Spanish), Ch. 18
Student Edition on Audio CD, Ch. 18
Prentice Hall Presentation Pro CD-ROM, Ch. 18
Companion Web site, www.phschool.com

end he alienated Progressives and caused a crisis in the Republican Party.

Conflict Over Tariffs In 1908, Taft had run on a Republican platform of lower tariffs, a Progressive goal that Roosevelt had not addressed. Taft promptly called a special session of Congress in 1909 to pass tariff reductions. The effort backfired on him. The House passed some reductions, while more traditional Republicans in the Senate added some highly protective tariff increases. The compromise measure, which Taft signed enthusiastically, was the Payne-Aldrich Tariff. Although not as protective as the McKinley Tariff Act of 1890, Payne-Aldrich was a protective measure. Progressives were furious with Taft.

The Ballinger-Pinchot Affair Progressives felt betrayed by Taft on another issue: the management of public lands. Taft's choice for Secretary of the Interior, Richard A. Ballinger, angered **conservationists,** people who favor the protection of natural resources. Ballinger opposed conservation policies on federal lands in the West, siding with business interests that sought unrestricted development.

Ballinger's views put him in conflict with Gifford Pinchot, head of the U.S. Forest Service. Pinchot favored scientific management of wilderness lands to allow both preservation and development. He had crafted many of TR's conservation policies. Pinchot's relationship with Taft, however, was strained.

In 1909, it became known that Ballinger had allowed a private group of businesspeople to obtain several million acres of Alaskan public lands containing rich coal deposits. Pinchot charged that Ballinger had improperly shown special preference to the purchasing group. When Pinchot protested to a congressional committee and aired suggestions of corruption on Ballinger's part, Taft fired Pinchot. Ballinger, although never found guilty of wrongdoing, eventually resigned. Pinchot remained a public hero, while Taft's popularity continued to slump.

Turmoil in the Republican Party

Angry Republican Progressives in the House now teamed up with Democrats to attack opponents of reform in the Republican Party. This so-called "old guard" of traditional Republicans controlled the House Rules Committee, which decides whether and how bills will be referred for action by the House. Through the Rules Committee, the old guard had been able to block much reform legislation.

To break this stranglehold, the progressive faction sought to curtail the powers of the old guard member and House Speaker, Joseph G. Cannon. In 1910, the House passed a resolution allowing the full membership, instead of the Speaker, to appoint the Rules Committee. The Speaker was barred from serving on the committee. The Republican Party was now bitterly split.

The Midterm Elections of 1910 Following Taft's election in 1908, Roosevelt had set off on a long safari to East Africa. He returned to the United States to a wildly cheering crowd in New York and a storm of protest against Taft. At first, Roosevelt refrained from criticizing his old

"GOODNESS GRACIOUS! I MUST HAVE BEEN DOZING!"

INTERPRETING POLITICAL CARTOONS Taft's presidency quickly became entangled in controversy and conflict. **Drawing Inferences** What details illustrate Taft's troubles? What does the cartoon suggest about TR's reaction to Taft's predicament?

Focus on
GEOGRAPHY

Environmental Management The nation's forests should be managed for "the greatest good of the greatest number in the long run." This summarizes the philosophy of conservationist Gifford Pinchot, head of the U.S. Forest Service from 1898 to 1909. After studying forestry in France, the young Pinchot returned home to find that "the nation was obsessed by a flurry of development." At that point he devoted his life to making forestry and conservation recognized professions and to promoting the scientific study and management of American forests.

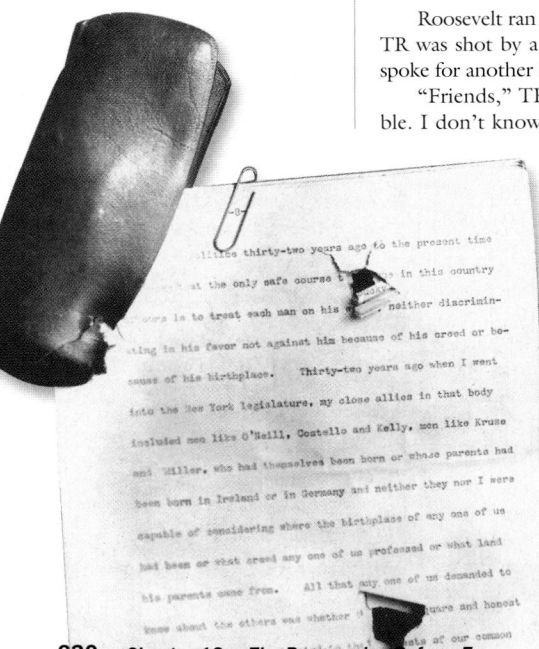

The Republicans had their elephant mascot, the Democrats had their donkey, and the Progressives added a Bull Moose (above) to the zoo of political symbols. The "Bull Moose" himself, TR, escaped assassination, possibly thanks to the speech and eyeglass case (below) tucked inside his coat.

friend, but before long he plunged into the battle between Taft and the Progressives. Roosevelt campaigned for Progressive candidates for the 1910 midterm elections. He called for business regulation, welfare laws, workplace protection for women and children, income and inheritance taxes, and voting reform. TR called his plan the **New Nationalism.**

The congressional elections brought down the old guard. Democrats gained control the House and Senate, with Progressive Democrats and Republicans firmly in place in both houses.

The Election of 1912

In early 1912, Roosevelt challenged Taft for the Republican presidential nomination. In the GOP primaries, voters preferred Roosevelt. But Taft, who controlled the Republican convention in Chicago, won the nomination handily.

Charging Taft's group with fraud, the Progressive Republicans marched out. Now Progressives vowed to form their own party. In August the Progressive Party held its convention. Spontaneous and intense, it had the feel of a religious revival. Gone were the party bosses. More women and young people attended. State delegations prayed together for their candidates: Roosevelt and his running mate, California Governor Hiram Johnson, a Progressive crusader.

When TR was asked about his physical readiness for a campaign, he said, "I feel fit as a bull moose!" The **Bull Moose Party** became the nickname of the Progressive Party—and the moose a symbol to challenge the Republican elephant and the Democratic donkey.

The Bull Moose Party The Bull Moose platform included tariff reduction, women's suffrage, more regulation of business, a child labor ban, an eight-hour workday, a federal workers' compensation system, and the direct election of senators. Many women joined the Progressive Party and campaigned for candidates. In states where women could vote, women ran for state and local offices.

Roosevelt ran a vigorous campaign. On October 14, at a speech in Milwaukee, TR was shot by a would-be assassin. With a bullet lodged in his lung, Roosevelt spoke for another hour and a half before seeking medical aid.

"Friends," TR addressed the crowd, "I shall ask you to be as quiet as possible. I don't know whether you fully understand that I have just been shot; but it takes more than that to kill a Bull Moose." He showed the crowd his bloodstained shirt, then continued his speech. It was classic TR.

Taft's Record Taft's frequent complaints about his job ("politics makes me sick") are so often quoted that they threaten to overshadow his presidential legacy. Yet Taft did achieve a notable record on progressive causes. He reserved more public lands and brought more antitrust suits in four years than TR had in seven. He supported the Children's Bureau, the Sixteenth and Seventeenth amendments, and the Mann-Elkins Act of 1910. This act gave the Interstate Commerce Commission the power to regulate telephone and telegraph rates. Yet Taft remained at odds with Republican Progressives.

Wilson's New Freedom To head the Democratic ticket, the party chose New Jersey Governor Woodrow Wilson. Like Roosevelt, Wilson ran on a reform platform.

630 Chapter 18 • *The Progressive Reform Era*

Unlike Roosevelt, he criticized both big business and big government. As part of his "New Freedom" policy, he promised to enforce antitrust laws without threatening economic competition. His position was pure progressivism:

> ❝ A trust is an arrangement to get rid of competition. . . . I am for big business, and I am against the trusts. Any man who can survive by his brains, any man who can put the others out of the business by making the thing cheaper to the consumer at the same time that he is increasing its intrinsic value and quality, I take off my hat to, and I say: 'You are the man who can build up the United States. . . .' ❞
>
> —Woodrow Wilson, campaign speech, 1912

A Four-Way Election Four main candidates sought the presidency in 1912. Taft, despite his distaste for the job, fought to keep it for the Republicans. Roosevelt, eager to get his job back, represented his Bull Moose Progressives. Wilson headed the Democratic ticket. Labor leader Eugene V. Debs made the third of his eventual five presidential runs for the Socialists.

With the Republican vote split between Taft and Roosevelt, Wilson emerged the victor. He gained only about 42 percent of the popular vote, but he won the electoral vote by a landslide: 435 votes to TR's 88 and Taft's mere 8. (See election map, above.) The Democrats also took control of both houses of Congress.

Taft left office with few regrets. "I'm glad to be going," he told his successor. "This is the lonesomest place in the world."

Wilson's Policies as President

As president of Princeton University (1902–1910) and then as the governor of New Jersey (1911–1913), Wilson had acquired a reputation as a dedicated reformer. A former professor of political science, Wilson believed that one of his main duties as President was to offer major legislation to Congress, promote it publicly, and help guide it to passage. In that role he worked the Congress vigorously, keeping it in session for a full year and a half for the first time ever.

Tariffs and Taxes Wilson's first major victory was tariff reduction, a long-unfulfilled goal of Progressives. The Underwood Tariff Act of 1913 reduced average tariff rates from 40 percent to 25 percent. To make up for that loss of government revenue, in October 1913 Wilson signed into law a federal income tax, made legal with ratification of the Sixteenth Amendment earlier in the year.

Attacking the Trusts Despite the Sherman Act and the trustbusting under Roosevelt and Taft, a congressional committee concluded that a relatively small group of powerful men still controlled much of the nation's wealth, businesses, and credit. Wilson believed strongly that monopolies and trusts led

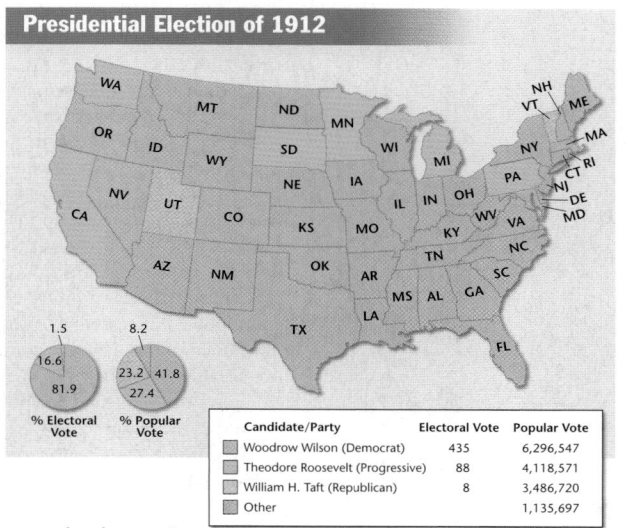

Presidential Election of 1912

Candidate/Party	Electoral Vote	Popular Vote
Woodrow Wilson (Democrat)	435	6,296,547
Theodore Roosevelt (Progressive)	88	4,118,571
William H. Taft (Republican)	8	3,486,720
Other		1,135,697

% Electoral Vote: 1.5 / 16.6 / 81.9
% Popular Vote: 8.2 / 23.2 / 41.8 / 27.4

MAP SKILLS In the 1912 presidential election, progressive ideas influenced the party platforms of the three major contenders. **Predicting Consequences** What would have happened if Roosevelt had not run and Taft had received Roosevelt's votes?

 Sounds of an Era

Listen to speeches from 1912 by Roosevelt and Wilson, and other sounds from the Progressive Era.

BACKGROUND
Art History

The year after his defeat in the presidential election, Theodore Roosevelt was back in the public eye as art critic. In 1913 he attended the International Exhibition of Modern Art in New York City. Organized by the avant-garde artists known as "the Eight," the show introduced French cubist and post-impressionist painting to America. Roosevelt's review of the show was mixed. Referring to cubists and futurists as the "lunatic fringe," he compared a painting entitled "A Naked Man Going Downstairs" to the Navajo rug in his bathroom. "From the standpoint of decorative value, of sincerity, and of artistic merit," he wrote, "the Navajo rug is infinitely ahead of the picture."

From the Archives of
American Heritage®

About the Presidents

Woodrow Wilson (1913–1921) met with Louis D. Brandeis in August 1912. It may have been the most important event of his campaign. Brandeis helped to convert Wilson to a progressive agenda. During his campaign, Wilson articulated the New Freedom, as preached to him by Brandeis. After Wilson's inauguration, progressivism took the form of far-reaching reforms. Lowering the tariff was one top priority. To emphasize its importance, the new President called a special session of Congress. The result was a tariff reform bill. As it turned out, however, a law attached to that bill had a more far-reaching effect: establishing the U.S. income tax. Source: Joseph L. Gardner, "Woodrow Wilson," *The American Heritage® Pictorial History of the Presidents of the United States*, vol. 2, 1968.

CUSTOMIZE FOR ...

Less Proficient Readers

Ask students to list the names of the presidential candidates in 1912—Debs, Taft, Roosevelt, and Wilson—at the top of a piece of paper. Then have them make notes under each name as they read, identifying each candidate, his political party in 1912, and his claim to be called a Progressive, even if he was not a member of the progressive party.

CAPTION ANSWERS

Map Skills Taft would have won the popular vote with 7,605,291 votes to Wilson's 6,296,547. But Taft still would have lost the election with a total of only 96 electoral votes to Wilson's 435.

to economic instability and the restriction of free enterprise. He did not want to create more government to monitor the trusts. He sought to get rid of trusts altogether.

With Wilson's guidance, in 1914 Congress passed the **Clayton Antitrust Act** to strengthen the Sherman Antitrust Act of 1890. Instead of simply making trusts illegal, as the Sherman Act had done, the Clayton Act spelled out specific activities that big businesses could not do. Companies could not prevent their buyers from purchasing goods from competitors. Some types of holding companies used to create monopolies were banned. Price cutting in local markets to squeeze out competitors was forbidden, as were some rebates.

Prior to the Clayton Act, courts often treated labor unions as monopolies. Clayton stated that unions could not be regarded as "illegal combinations [monopolies] in restraint of trade under the antitrust laws" because "the labor of a human being is not a commodity or article of commerce." The act therefore legalized unions as well as their key weapons: strikes, peaceful picketing, and boycotts. Courts were prevented from issuing injunctions against unions unless their activities led to "irreparable injury to property."

To enforce the Clayton Act and set up fair-trade laws, in 1914 Wilson and the Congress created the **Federal Trade Commission (FTC).** The FTC was given the power to order firms to "cease and desist" the practice of business tactics found to be unfair. Still, later court rulings weakened the Clayton Act.

The Federal Reserve System Congress did not give the FTC authority over banks. Wilson sought a total overhaul of the American banking system to promote competition in the industry and to ease the frequent panics that destabilized the U.S. economy. Bankers, however, had their own ideas about how to reform the system, and many viewed Wilson's plans as radical.

After a long, heated debate, Congress passed the Federal Reserve Act of 1913. The act created the **Federal Reserve System.** It divided the country into 12 districts, each with a Federal Reserve bank owned by its member

MAP SKILLS Initially, the 12 regional banks in the Federal Reserve System acted independently, sometimes in conflict. Changes to the system over the years have improved coordination among the regional banks while still allowing them to represent the interests of their member banks. **Analyzing Visual Information** *Which regions' banks might represent a large proportion of (a) farm interests; (b) urban interests; (c) manufacturing interests?*

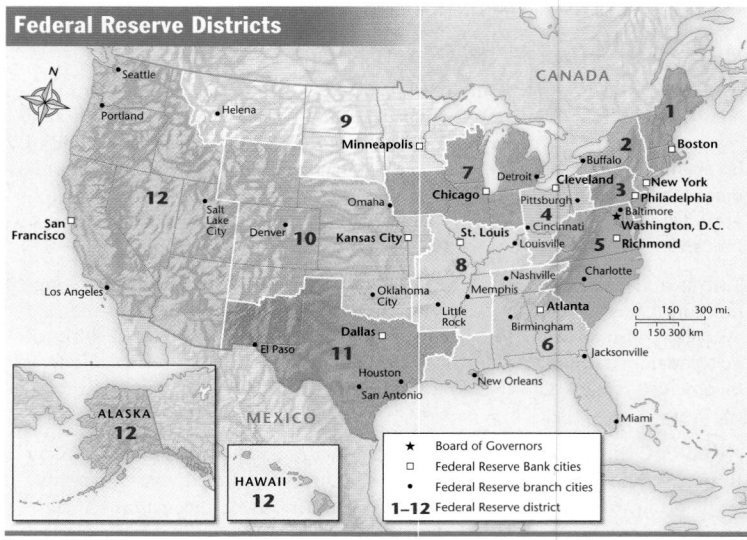

Federal Reserve Districts

banks. The system was supervised by a Federal Reserve Board appointed by the President.

The Federal Reserve banks were the central banks for their regions—the "bankers' banks." Every national bank was required to become a member of the Federal Reserve bank in its district and to deposit some of its capital and cash reserves in that bank. Member banks could borrow from the Federal Reserve to meet short-term demands. This helped to prevent bank failures that occurred when large numbers of depositors withdrew funds during an economic panic.

The system also created a new national currency known as Federal Reserve notes. The Federal Reserve could now expand or contract the amount of currency in circulation according to economic needs.

Another Wilson financial reform was the establishment of the Federal Farm Loan Board in 1916. This board and a system of Farm Loan Banks made loans available to farmers. Farmers could borrow money for five to forty years at rates lower than those offered by commercial banks.

Brandeis to the Supreme Court   In 1916, with the presidential election approaching, Wilson took a number of steps aimed partly at attracting progressive voters. Early that year, Wilson nominated progressive lawyer Louis D. Brandeis to the Supreme Court. Brandeis was known for his brilliance and for fighting many public causes. He was known as "the people's lawyer."

Wilson's nomination of Brandeis to the Supreme Court drew a storm of protest. Opponents, including former President Taft, accused Brandeis of being too radical. Anti-Semitism also played a part in the opposition; Brandeis was the first Jewish Supreme Court nominee. Nevertheless, he was confirmed by the Senate and served on the Court with distinction until 1939. The appointment of Brandeis marked the peak of federal progressive reforms.

Also in the months preceding the 1916 election, Wilson oversaw federal legislation limiting the use of child labor in industry. Most states already had such laws. Yet the federal provision was struck down by the Supreme Court two years later. A federal ban on child labor would take another two decades.

Wilson Wins a Second Term   By 1916, the historic progressive drive was winding down. TR did not want to run again. Instead, Roosevelt and the Bull Moose Party endorsed Wilson's Republican opponent, Charles Evans Hughes, a former governor of New York and Supreme Court justice. Wilson ran on the slogan that he had kept the country out of World War I, which had erupted in Europe two years before. He barely defeated Hughes, with 277 electoral votes to 254.

The Limits of Progressivism

By the mid-1910s, Progressives had made broad changes in society, government, and business. They had redefined and enlarged the role of government. Yet their influence was limited to certain sectors of society. Focused mainly on municipal problems, Progressives did little to aid tenant and migrant farmers

VIEWING HISTORY In 1916, Wilson had the election momentum of an incumbent, suggested in the campaign button above. The campaign truck at top publicized Wilson's record during his first term as President. **Analyzing Information** *Which of the slogans shown on this truck probably contributed most to Wilson's reelection?*

READING CHECK
List some progressive reforms achieved by Wilson.

Reading Comprehension

1. (a) Reserved public lands; antitrust suits; supported the Children's Bureau; supported the Sixteenth and Seventeenth Amendments and the Mann-Elkins Act. (b) By appointing Richard A. Ballinger, then firing Pinchot; Ballinger resigns; continued decline in Taft's popularity.

2. Split Republican vote, allowing Democratic candidate, Wilson, to win.

3. Reducing tariffs; eliminating trusts; overhaul of the American banking system; attempted to impose federal limits on child labor.

4. (a) Legalized unions and strikes, limited the issuing of injunctions against unions. (b) Worked to eliminate unfair business tactics. (c) Established national banking system; created new form of currency; stabilized banking as a whole.

Critical Thinking and Writing

5. Payne-Aldrich: the Senate insisted on protective measures. Underwood: congressional acquiescence secured for significant cuts. Payne-Aldrich: Progressives furious with Taft. Underwood: major victory for Wilson.

6. Answers will vary, but should include references to: curbing the power of trusts; regulating business; creating Federal Reserve System, Federal Trade Commission, and Federal Farm Loan Board.

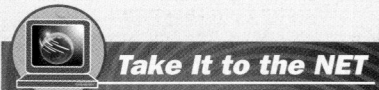
Take It to the NET

Answers will vary. Students should note the background, political position, and influence of the Progressive. They should also note to what extent the reformer's goals were achieved, and whether they were satisfied with their work.

At right, the journal of the NAACP. At top, the offices of the NAACP, with W.E.B. Du Bois standing to the right at the back of the photograph.

and nonunionized workers. Some Progressives supported immigration limits and literacy tests.

Social Justice and Progressivism The progressive Presidents took little action to pursue social justice reforms. Wilson allowed his Cabinet officers to extend the Jim Crow practice, begun under Taft, of separating the races in federal offices. Wilson also initially opposed a constitutional amendment on women's suffrage because his party platform had not endorsed it.

Many African Americans felt ignored by Progressives. Only a tiny group of Progressives, those who helped found the National Association for the Advancement of Colored People (NAACP) in 1909, concerned themselves with the worsening race relations and continued lynchings of the era. Although Roosevelt invited Booker T. Washington to the White House in 1901, he did little else to support African American rights. At the 1912 Progressive Party convention, Roosevelt declined to seat black delegates from the South for fear of alienating white southern supporters. In addition, some white southern Progressives who favored the women's vote did so because they realized that women's suffrage could double the white vote, putting African Americans further behind.

The End of Progressivism As more and more nations became involved in World War I, Americans worried about how long they could remain uninvolved. Soon, calls to prepare for war drowned out calls for reform in America. By the end of 1916, the reform spirit had nearly sputtered out. But one reform movement grew bolder: the drive for women's suffrage.

Section 3 Assessment

READING COMPREHENSION

1. (a) What progressive reforms did Taft achieve? (b) How did he offend **conservationists,** and what was the result?

2. What effect did the Bull Moose Party have on the election of 1912?

3. What reforms did Wilson seek?

4. What reforms resulted from the establishment of (a) the **Clayton Antitrust Act;** (b) **the Federal Trade Commission;** (c) the **Federal Reserve System?**

CRITICAL THINKING AND WRITING

5. **Making Comparisons** Compare and contrast the Payne-Aldrich Tariff and the Underwood Tariff Act. Describe the political battles and the outcomes of each.

6. **Writing an Introduction** Write a one-paragraph introduction to an essay on how reforms under President Wilson changed the size, scope, and role of the federal government.

Take It to the NET

Activity: Writing a Biography Write a brief biography of a Progressive mentioned in this section. Discuss your subject's success or failure in achieving Progressive goals. Use the links provided in the *America: Pathways to the Present* area of the following Web site for help in completing this activity. **www.phschool.com**

RESOURCE DIRECTORY

Teaching Resources
Units 5/6 booklet
• Section 3 Quiz, p. 65
Guide to the Essentials
• Section 3 Summary, p. 95

READING FOCUS

- In what ways were Susan B. Anthony and Elizabeth Cady Stanton a "bridge" to the twentieth-century suffrage effort?
- What two main strategies did suffrage leaders pursue?
- What was the status of the suffrage movement by the turn of the century?
- Why was a new generation of national leaders needed in the suffrage effort?
- What factors led to a final victory for suffrage?

MAIN IDEA

Demonstrating their skills as organizers and activists, women won the right to vote with the ratification of the Nineteenth Amendment in 1920.

KEY TERMS

civil disobedience
National American Woman Suffrage Association (NAWSA)
Congressional Union (CU)

TAKING NOTES

As you read, complete this chart, adding causes that led to the passage of women's suffrage.

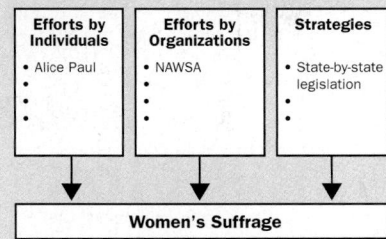

Efforts by Individuals	Efforts by Organizations	Strategies
• Alice Paul	• NAWSA	• State-by-state legislation
•	•	•
•	•	•

Women's Suffrage

Setting the Scene

For roughly 70 years, women's organizations actively campaigned for the right to vote. As the movement grew, so did resistance to it. Opponents included men and women from all age groups and income levels. Many viewed the idea of women's suffrage as unnecessary, at best. At worst, they saw it as a threat to the stability of American society and government.

In speeches and articles, anti-suffragists voiced the genuine fears of many Americans: Would women become "too masculine," as critics suggested? Would they be easily manipulated by politicians? Would politics distract them from their duties in the home?

One of the most persuasive arguments against suffrage was that women simply did not want to vote—a fact that was confirmed by some opinion polls in some areas. Yet note the language this popular magazine used to make generalizations about all women:

> 66 *This is the negative reason why woman does not wish the ballot: she does not wish to engage in that conflict of wills which is the essence of politics; she does not wish to assume the responsibility for protecting person and property which is the essence of government. The affirmative reason is that she has other, and in some sense, more important work to do.* 99
> —Lyman Abbott, "Why Women Do Not Wish the Suffrage," *The Atlantic Monthly*, September 1903

Anthony and Stanton: Preparing the Way

From the beginning, suffragists heard such arguments, and more. In their long struggle, they faced confrontations, ridicule, threats, and even violence.

INTERPRETING CARTOONS
As the women's suffrage movement gained strength, criticisms grew louder. **Drawing Inferences** *Give at least one possible explanation for the word* delusion *in the title of this cartoon.*

HUGGING A DELUSION

COPYRIGHTED BY LIFE PUBLISHING CO.

Chapter 18 • Section 4   **635**

SECTION OBJECTIVES

1. Learn the ways in which Susan B. Anthony and Elizabeth Cady Stanton formed a "bridge" to the twentieth-century suffrage effort.
2. Discover two main strategies pursued by suffrage leaders.
3. Read about the status of the suffrage movement by the turn of the century.
4. Find out why a new generation of leaders was needed in the suffrage effort.
5. Study the factors that led to a final victory for suffrage.

BELLRINGER

Warm-Up Activity Ask students if they intend to vote when they turn 18. How would they feel if a constitutional amendment raised the voting age to 25?

Activating Prior Knowledge Can students determine why some people would deny others the right to vote? Are they aware that voting rights are not universal in all nations?

READING STRATEGY

As students read, have them construct a time line of events that led to the enactment of the Nineteenth Amendment. Time lines should start in 1848 and end in 1920.

CAPTION ANSWERS

Interpreting Cartoons Possible answers: the delusion that women would get the right to vote; that women wanted the right to vote; that women were capable of making good voting choices.

Focus Women won the right to vote in 1920 after a long, bitter fight. Ask students how the suffrage campaign achieved success.

Instruct Read students the following comment from a 1974 interview with the suffragist Alice Paul, then 89 years old: "I always feel . . . the movement is a sort of mosaic. Each of us puts in one little stone, and then you get a great mosaic at the end." (Quoted in Garraty, John A., ed. *Historical Viewpoints,* Vol. II. Harper & Row, 1983, p. 195.) Ask students what role civil disobedience played in Susan B. Anthony's efforts to gain suffrage. Have students compare the tactics of Catt and the NAWSA with those of Paul and the CU. How did the actions of both help the suffragists gain victory?

Assess/Reteach Gaining the right to vote was a long, arduous process for the women of the United States. Without dedication and persistence, this right might never have been won. As a class, discuss the ways in which the eventual passage of the Nineteenth Amendment opened the way toward ensuring equal rights for all Americans.

ACTIVITY
Connecting with Citizenship

Susan B. Anthony was one of many American activists who have used civil disobedience to protest an unfair law. Have students research other examples of civil disobedience in U.S. history, then use their findings to create original skits or role-plays.
(Bodily/Kinesthetic)

READING CHECK
By personally lobbying Congress; cofounding the American Equal Rights Association; engaging in civil disobedience; and leading the National American Woman Suffrage Association.

BIOGRAPHY

Susan B. Anthony
1820–1906

Like her father, a Quaker abolitionist, Susan B. Anthony was a crusader. She founded her own temperance group. She campaigned hard to get schools to open their doors to women and former slaves. As an abolitionist, Anthony faced armed mobs and threats. She fought for equal pay and an eight-hour workday for women.

Anthony ran a tireless campaign for women's voting rights as head of the National Woman Suffrage Association. For nearly 40 years, Anthony appeared before every Congress to demand a suffrage amendment. Anthony cofounded the National American Woman Suffrage Association, which she led for eight years, retiring in 1900. Devoting her life to her many causes, Anthony never married.

"Failure is impossible," Anthony declared before her death in 1906. Fourteen years later, her words came true with the ratification of the Nineteenth Amendment.

READING CHECK
How did Susan B. Anthony contribute to the suffrage movement?

American women activists first formally demanded the right to vote in 1848 at the Seneca Falls Convention in New York. The meeting made famous the names of Lucretia Mott and Elizabeth Cady Stanton. A few years later, a young woman joined their cause: Susan B. Anthony. She, along with Stanton, would become the nation's most celebrated champions of women's suffrage.

Together, Anthony, a tireless strategist and organizer, and Stanton, a skilled speaker and writer, would take the women's suffrage movement into the twentieth century. In 1866, they founded the American Equal Rights Association and soon began publication of a newspaper, *The Revolution.* On its banner was emblazoned ". . . men, their rights and nothing more; women, their rights and nothing less."

The movement later split into two groups. Stanton and Anthony continued, as the National Woman Suffrage Association, to fight for a constitutional amendment for suffrage. Meanwhile, the newly formed American Woman Suffrage Association worked on the state level to win voting rights. When Wyoming entered the union in 1890, it became the first state to grant women full suffrage.

In 1872, Anthony led a group of women to the polls in Rochester, New York, where she insisted on voting. Anthony was arrested for this act of **civil disobedience.** Civil disobedience is a nonviolent refusal to obey a law in an effort to change it. While she awaited her trial, Anthony set out on a highly publicized lecture tour. During one of these lectures she asserted:

> ❝ The preamble of the Federal Constitution says: 'We, the people of the United States. . . . ' It was we, the people; not we, the white male citizens; nor yet we, the male citizens; but we, the whole people, who formed the Union. And we formed it, not to give the blessings of liberty, but to secure them; not to the half of ourselves and the half of our posterity, but to the whole people—women as well as men. ❞
> —Susan B. Anthony

Anthony was convicted at her trial and fined $100. She refused to pay the fine but was set free anyway. Legal maneuvering by the judge and her court-appointed lawyer prevented her from appealing the conviction and further pursuing her case.

Suffragist Strategies

Suffragists continued to follow two paths toward their goal. One path was to press for a constitutional amendment giving women the vote. The most commonly used method of amending the Constitution required two thirds of each house of Congress to pass a measure. The measure then had to be ratified by three fourths of the state legislatures.

The other path pursued by suffragists was to get individual states to let women vote. At first this approach was more successful, especially in the western states. There, survival on the frontier required the combined efforts of men and women and encouraged a greater sense of equality between them.

Pushing for a federal amendment proved to be the more difficult approach. The first amendment introduced in Congress in 1868 stalled. In 1878, suffragists introduced a new amendment that adopted the wording of

---

RESOURCE DIRECTORY

Teaching Resources
Biography, Literature, and Comparing Primary Sources booklet (Comparing Primary Sources) *On the Nineteenth Amendment,* p. 131

Technology
Exploring Primary Sources in U.S. History CD-ROM *Are Not the Women Half the Nation?*

RESOURCE PRO® **Literature Activity** *The "New" Woman,* found on Resource Pro, provides insight into the oppression of women at the turn of the century, with excerpts from Kate Chopin's novel, *The Awakening.*

RESOURCE PRO® **Visual Learning Activity** *When Women Have Rights,* found on Resource Pro, uses a 1913 cartoon to illustrate a popular antisuffrage argument.

Susan B. Anthony: "The right of citizens of the United States to vote shall not be denied or abridged by the United States or by any state on account of sex."

With this language, the proposed amendment received its first committee hearing. Elizabeth Cady Stanton described the chair of the committee, Senator Bainbridge Wadleigh of New Hampshire, as a picture of "inattention and contempt." "He stretched, yawned, gazed at the ceiling, cut his nails, sharpened his pencil, changing his occupation and position every two minutes."

Stalled again, the bill was not debated until 1887. It was then defeated in the Senate by a vote of 16 for, 34 against, and 26 absent. Supporters reintroduced the "Anthony Amendment," as the bill came to be called, every year until 1896. Then it disappeared, and did not resurface again until 1913.

Suffrage at the Turn of the Century

In 1890, veteran leaders of the suffrage movement, including Anthony, Stanton, and Lucy Stone, were joined by younger leaders in forming the **National American Woman Suffrage Association (NAWSA).** Anthony served as president of NAWSA from 1892 until 1900.

By the time of NAWSA's founding, women had won many rights. For example, married women could now buy, sell, and will property. By 1900, growing numbers of women were demanding the vote. Some were participating in voluntary organizations that investigated social conditions. These women were publicizing their findings, suggesting reforms, lobbying officials, and monitoring enforcement of new laws. Working women were becoming more active in unions, picketing, and getting arrested. To many of these women, being denied the right to vote seemed ridiculous.

Yet from the late 1890s to 1910, the suffrage movement was in "the doldrums," as one historian put it. Years of legal efforts to win suffrage had failed. The rise of progressivism brought new political support, but it was not enough to turn the tide. The beloved leaders of the suffrage movement, Stanton and

Focus on CITIZENSHIP

Women in Law Practice Suffrage workers confronted strongly held attitudes about women and their proper social roles. When lawyer Myra Bradwell of Chicago was denied a state license to practice law in 1869, she took her case to the Supreme Court. In *Bradwell* v. *Illinois* (1873), the Court upheld the denial, reaffirming the "wide difference in the respective spheres and destinies of man and woman." Although Illinois had given Bradwell her license by 1890, most Americans believed that woman's proper sphere remained the home, not the workplace.

COMPARING PRIMARY SOURCES

Voting Rights for Women

In the early 1900s, the longtime debate over women's suffrage entered a heated, final stage prior to the passage of the Nineteenth Amendment.

Analyzing Viewpoints Summarize the arguments made in the two quotations below.

In Favor of Women's Suffrage

"The great doctrine of the American Republic that 'all governments derive their just powers from the consent of the governed' justifies the plea of one-half of the people, the women, to exercise the suffrage. The doctrine of the American Revolutionary War that taxation without representation is unendurable justifies women in exercising the suffrage."

—*Robert L. Owen,*
senator from Oklahoma, 1910

Opposed to Women's Suffrage

"In political warfare, it is perfectly fitting that actual strife and battle should be apportioned [given out] to man, and that the influence of woman, radiating from the homes of our land, should inspire to lofty aims and purposes those who struggle for the right. I am thoroughly convinced that woman can in no better way than this usefully serve the cause of political betterment."

—*Grover Cleveland,*
Ladies' Home Journal, October 1905

Student Portfolio

You may wish to have students add the following to their portfolios: Ask students to use an almanac to find the percentage of eligible women voting in each of the presidential elections since 1920 and to compare it with the percentage of eligible males voting. Students can show the statistics in a series of simple bar graphs or a table. **(Logical/Mathematical)**

BACKGROUND

Recent Scholarship

African American women and men supported the movement for women's suffrage from the beginning. However, the movement, which was led by white women, included instances of racism and divisiveness, as Rosalyn Terborg-Penn's *African American Women in the Struggle for the Vote, 1850–1920* makes clear. In fact, some southern women suffrage leaders sought to both enfranchise the "best white women in the South" and disenfranchise American black women, thus preserving the inequalities of race and class.

BACKGROUND

Biography

Born into slavery, Ida Bell Wells-Barnett (1862–1931) founded what was probably the first African American women's suffrage group, Chicago's Alpha Suffrage Club. As a journalist she was a strident crusader against the lynching of African Americans in the South, and in 1909 she helped organize the National Association for the Advancement of Colored People (NAACP). Her memoirs, *Crusade for Justice,* were published posthumously in 1970.

CUSTOMIZE FOR ...

Less Proficient Writers

Have students review the quote on this page from Susan B. Anthony. Then have them paraphrase the quote using their own words.

✓ TEST PREPARATION

Have students read the quotation by Elizabeth Cady Stanton on this page and then complete the sentence below.

Based on Stanton's description of New Hampshire senator Bainbridge Wadleigh's behavior as he listened to a hearing about the Nineteenth Amendment, you can infer that Senator Wadleigh—

A avidly supported the proposed amendment.

B wanted to know more about Elizabeth Cady Stanton.

C did not like being a senator.

(D) did not support the proposed amendment.

VIEWING HISTORY At the 1913 suffrage rally hundreds of participants were taunted and injured by opponents, yet the event was considered a success. **Drawing Conclusions** *What reasons might suffragists have had for viewing the rally as a victory?*

This suffrage poster urges parents to consider the future of their daughters.

Anthony, died in 1902 and 1906, respectively—without seeing the realization of their life's work. It was time for a new generation to create momentum and take the cause of suffrage to victory.

A New Generation

One new leader who emerged to re-energize the movement was Carrie Chapman Catt, a former high school principal and superintendent of schools in Mason City, Iowa. A talented speaker and organizer, she headed NAWSA from 1900 to 1904, and then again after 1915. As head of NAWSA, Catt insisted on precinct-by-precinct political work with close coordination among districts.

Alice Paul also rose as a leader in the women's suffrage movement. She had learned tactics from the aggressive English suffrage movement while she was a student in England. In January 1913, she and a friend, Lucy Burns, took over the NAWSA committee that was working on congressional passage of the federal suffrage amendment.

Two months later, the two women had organized a parade of 5,000 women in Washington, D.C. The parade took place on the day before Woodrow Wilson's inauguration. It drew so much attention that few supporters greeted Wilson when he arrived at the train station. After the success of the rally, Paul transformed her committee into a new organization, the **Congressional Union (CU).**

A Split in the Movement Following Paul's action, a split occurred within the suffrage movement. Paul's CU called for an aggressive, militant campaign for the constitutional amendment. She planned to bypass existing state suffrage organizations and set up new ones in each state.

The leadership of NAWSA opposed Paul's plan, believing it would alienate moderate supporters. In February 1914, they expelled the Congressional Union from the organization. The CU went on to stage militant protests. They demonstrated in front of the White House. They set aflame a life-size dummy of Wilson, who was still refusing to back the suffrage amendment. They burned copies of his speeches. Exasperated authorities arrested CU members and sent them to prison, where they went on hunger strikes to protest horrible prison conditions.

Meanwhile, NAWSA continued to back the state suffrage campaigns. The group focused its efforts on winning the vote in four eastern states: New York, Pennsylvania, Massachusetts, and New Jersey. In 1915, the suffrage campaigns failed in all four states. At that point, Carrie Chapman Catt was reinstated as NAWSA president and given free rein to bring about victory. Out of this challenge came her "Winning Plan."

This plan consisted of developing a large group of full-time leaders to work in "red-hot" campaigns for six years. In addition, NAWSA decided to focus on getting Congress to re-introduce the federal suffrage amendment.

By 1917, NAWSA had grown into the largest volunteer organization in the country, with 2 million members. In the fall of that year, it won an important victory when New York State voted for women's suffrage. New York, with its large number of electoral votes in presidential elections, would now be courted by candidates seeking the support of the state's women voters.

Impact of World War I The United States entered World War I in April 1917. Women across the country hastened to do their patriotic duty by volunteering for ambulance corps and for medical work and by taking on jobs left by men. Arguments of separate spheres for women and men were forgotten during wartime.

In addition, Congress adopted the Eighteenth Amendment, prohibiting the sale of liquor. As a result of this action, liquor interests no longer had reason to fight suffrage.

Victory for Suffrage

In 1918, Congress formally proposed the suffrage amendment. Its members finally succumbed to the political forces of states that had passed suffrage and to the unrelenting work of NAWSA. They also had been keenly embarrassed and disturbed by the treatment that the women of Alice Paul's Congressional Union had received in filthy jails, where some hunger strikers were force-fed. After the amendment was proposed in Congress, the ratification battle began. It would end in August, 1920, when Tennessee became the 36th state necessary to ratify the suffrage amendment.

As suffragist Carrie Chapman Catt commented when the exhausting battle of many decades was finally over, "It is doubtful that any man . . . ever realized what the suffrage struggle came to mean to women. . . . It leaves its mark on one, such a struggle." The Nineteenth Amendment marked the last major reform of the Progressive Era.

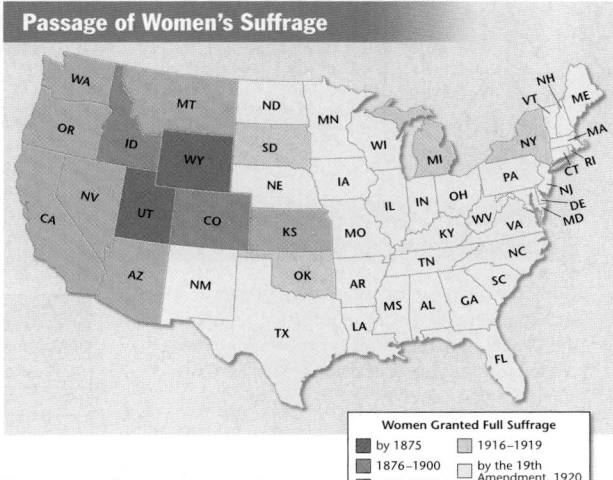

Passage of Women's Suffrage

Women Granted Full Suffrage
- ■ by 1875
- ■ 1876–1900
- ■ 1901–1915
- ▢ 1916–1919
- ▢ by the 19th Amendment, 1920

Map shows present-day borders.

MAP SKILLS Women's suffrage was already in place in many states by the time the Nineteenth Amendment was ratified. **Analyzing Visual Information** *What pattern do you see in the locations of states that did and did not pass suffrage at the state level?*

Reading Comprehension

1. Founded the American Equal Rights Association; published *The Revolution;* worked for a voting rights constitutional amendment; formed National American Woman Suffrage Association.

2. Suffrage efforts were failing; deaths of Stanton and Anthony.

3. CU: aggressive, militant tactics, wanted new state suffrage organizations. NAWSA opposed CU, fearing CU would alienate moderate supporters; NAWSA worked with old state organizations toward a federal suffrage amendment.

4. (a) Women in voluntary organizations and unions began to demand the right to vote. They pressed for a constitutional amendment and for individual states to allow women to vote. Ratification came in 1920. (b) Widely held attitudes about role of women; loss of momentum in suffrage movement; amendment bill stalled in Congress.

Critical Thinking and Writing

5. Successes in individual states contributed support for federal amendment allowing female suffrage.

6. Answers will vary but should be supported with facts from the section.

Take It to the NET

Answers will vary. Students might compare the opposition to, the tactics of, and the level of violence of the suffrage movement to other struggles for liberty, as well as the successfulness of each movement.

Section 4 Assessment

READING COMPREHENSION

1. Describe how Anthony and Stanton worked together to lead the suffrage movement.

2. Why was the suffrage movement in need of new leadership after the turn of the century?

3. How did the **National American Woman Suffrage Association** and the **Congressional Union** differ in their tactics?

4. (a) How did passage of the Nineteenth Amendment come about? (b) Why did the battle take so long?

CRITICAL THINKING AND WRITING

5. **Drawing Inferences** How do you think the state-by-state efforts of suffragists affected the effort to win a constitutional amendment on suffrage?

6. **Writing an Opinion** Identify the goals, strategies, and tactics of two of the suffrage leaders described in this section. Which leader or group do you think was most effective? Why? Write a brief paragraph expressing your opinion.

 Take It to the NET

Activity: Writing an Essay Study the suffrage movement online. Write an essay comparing the suffrage movement to other struggles for liberty. Use the links provided in the *America: Pathways to the Present* area of the following Web site for help in completing this activity.
www.phschool.com

Chapter 18 • Section 4 **639**

Map Skills The states that adopted suffrage soonest were mostly in the West. The Northeast, Midwest, and South were slower to accept women as voters.

CUSTOMIZE FOR ...

Gifted and Talented

Ask students to list arguments used against women's suffrage. Then ask them to refute each of the arguments.

REVIEWING KEY TERMS

Students should refer to the definitions of key terms in the chapter to write sentences that show an understanding of the Progressive Reform Era.

REVIEWING MAIN IDEAS

11. People: George, Bellamy, Kelley, Jones. Muckrakers such as Sinclair, Tarbell, Steffens. Ideas: honest government, government involvement in social welfare, giving more power to voters.

12. Progressives studied social problems using scientific methods. They publicized their results to pressure lawmakers. Muckrakers used investigative journalism to publicize progressive causes.

13. State reformers wanted to give more power to voters, for example, through direct primaries. They also championed labor and factory legislation. Urban reformers attacked political machines, took over utilities, and expanded welfare services.

14. Theodore Roosevelt sponsored antitrust initiatives; conserved natural resources; regulated railroads; and spearheaded reform of the meatpacking industry. Constitutional amendments expanded the power of the federal government.

15. He had not been elected, and he faced congressional opposition.

16. Taft achieved many progressive goals, such as increased prosecution of antitrust cases. He lost progressive support, however, because of events such as the Ballinger-Pinchot affair and his failure to lower the tariff.

17. His progressive beliefs and a split Republican vote.

18. Preparations for war began to occupy the nation.

19. To win suffrage in individual states and to pass a constitutional amendment allowing female suffrage.

20. Answers will vary but should be supported with facts from the section.

CRITICAL THINKING

21. Possible answers: Henry George and the "single tax"; Upton Sinclair's expose of problems in the

---

creating a CHAPTER SUMMARY

Copy the chart (right) on a piece of paper and complete it by adding information about the Progressive Era. Some entries have been completed for you as examples. Add as many entries as you can.

For additional review and enrichment activities, see the interactive version of *America: Pathways to the Present*, available on the Web and on CD-ROM.

Progressive Era Reforms

Municipal Level	State Level	Federal Level
Regulating utilities		Pure Food and Drug Act

★ Reviewing Key Terms

For each of the terms below, write a sentence explaining how it relates to the Progressive reforms.

1. Progressive Era
2. muckraker
3. injunction
4. municipal
5. holding company
6. conservationist
7. New Nationalism
8. Bull Moose Party
9. Federal Reserve System
10. civil disobedience

★ Reviewing Main Ideas

11. What people and ideas contributed to the rise of progressivism? (Section 1)
12. What were the typical methods of Progressive reformers? (Section 1)
13. Summarize progressive reforms at the municipal and state levels. (Section 2)
14. Describe progressive reforms at the national level. (Section 2)
15. Why did TR have to proceed with caution on pushing for reforms in his first term? (Section 2)
16. What were the main successes and failures of Taft's presidency? (Section 3)
17. What factors contributed to the election of Wilson in 1912? (Section 3)
18. Why did progressivism decline? (Section 3)

19. What two main approaches did women's organizations take to win suffrage? (Section 4)
20. Choose two leaders of the suffrage movement and describe their contributions to the cause. (Section 4)

★ Critical Thinking

21. **Drawing Conclusions** In what ways did reform movements benefit from the contributions of both men and women? Give examples.
22. **Drawing Inferences** Why do you think reformers at the municipal and state levels began by passing voting reforms and tackling corruption?
23. **Synthesizing Information** How did Roosevelt use the "bully pulpit," and how did his style shape the modern presidency?
24. **Making Comparisons** How did TR, Taft, and Wilson compare in their approaches to reform?
25. **Identifying Central Issues** What was the Clayton Antitrust Act, and why was it important to progressive reformers and labor leaders?
26. **Recognizing Cause and Effect** What kinds of reforms contributed to an increase in the size and role of government?
27. **Analyzing Information** What shift in public attitudes was necessary for social welfare programs to gain support and passage?

CREATING A CHAPTER SUMMARY

Progressive Era Reforms

Municipal Level	State Level	Federal Level
Regulating utilities	Voting reforms, i.e., direct primary, initiative, referendum, recall	Pure Food and Drug Act
Workplace protections	Workplace protections	Sherman Antitrust Act
Home rule	Abolition of child labor	Constitutional amendments 16, 17, 18 and 19
Providing welfare services	Minimum wage laws	Establishment of Department of Labor, U.S. Forest Service, National Park Service, Women's and Children's Boards

★ Skills Assessment

Analyzing Political Cartoons ▶

28. Examine this 1904 cartoon at right. (a) What does the octopus represent? (b) What does the octopus hold in its tentacles? (c) What is it reaching for?

29. Why is the octopus pictured on a globe?

30. (a) What overall point is the cartoonist trying to make? (b) Why was an octopus such a good choice for making this point?

Analyzing Primary Sources

Read the quotation from Jane Addams on page 618, and answer the questions that follow.

31. In comparing the lives of rural and urban women, Addams' main purpose was to point out

   A the problems that united women throughout the country.

   B their differing lifestyles and roles in American society.

   C the ways in which urban living presented new problems for women.

   D the reasons that rural children were healthier.

32. In this quotation, Addams made the argument for

   F better health services for children.

   G more and better government services in cities, to help families survive.

   H the need for garbage collection in rural areas, to prevent the spread of disease.

   J programs to get women and children out of tenement houses.

Applying the Chapter Skill: *Testing Conclusions*

33. Based on the results of the election of 1912, is it reasonable to conclude that most Americans favored some amount of progressive reform? Explain.

ACTIVITIES

Writing to LEARN

Writing a News Story
Write a brief newspaper or broadcast story on the 1900 Galveston hurricane. Identify the basic facts of the event, as well as immediate and long-term effects of the tragedy. Include fictional quotations from city government officials, reformers, and survivors of the devastation.

Primary Source CD-ROM

Working With Primary Sources Find additional information on the Progressive era on the *Exploring Primary Sources in U.S. History CD-ROM* and use the selection(s) provided to complete the Chapter 18 primary source activity located in the *America: Pathways to the Present* area of the following Web site.
www.phschool.com

Take It to the NET

Chapter Self-Test As a review activity, take the Chapter 18 Self-Test in the *America: Pathways to the Present* area at the Web site listed below. The questions are designed to test your understanding of the chapter content.
www.phschool.com

---

meatpacking industry; Florence Kelley and Mother Jones working for labor reform.

22. Reformers needed to attack political machines in order to make governments honest and more accountable to voters before progressive reform legislation could be passed.

23. Roosevelt used his authority as President to push for reform. He believed in and exerted the power of the presidency.

24. TR: used personal skills to push aggressively for certain reforms. Taft: lacked TR's ability to push for reform legislation, compromised more, yet still made significant achievements. Wilson: believed it was the President's duty to submit bills to Congress. Thus, he pushed for progressive reform.

25. The Clayton Antitrust Act strengthened the Sherman Antitrust Act by specifying actions businesses could not do and by supporting unions. It showed that government was committed to regulating business and protecting workers.

26. New federal regulatory agencies such as the Federal Trade Commission and the Federal Reserve System increased the federal budget and the federal work force. Measures such as prohibition and federal income tax increased the role of government in citizens' lives.

27. Americans became accustomed to an increasing government role in their lives.

SKILLS ASSESSMENT

28. (a) Standard Oil Company.
    (b) Government and industry.
    (c) The White House.

29. To imply that Standard Oil was trying to control the entire world.

30. (a) That Standard Oil had a stranglehold on government and industry.
    (b) It demonstrates the powerful, far-reaching control of the Standard Oil Company.

31. C

32. G

33. Yes. Roosevelt and Wilson, who both supported progressivism, between them gained almost 70 percent of the popular vote.

ANSWERS TO ACTIVITIES

Writing to LEARN

Answers will vary but should focus on the area hit, the amount of destruction, deaths, and how the rebuilding efforts led to a commission form of government.

Primary Source CD-ROM

Direct students to the additional primary sources that can be found on the *Exploring Primary Sources in U.S. History CD-ROM.*

 ### Take It to the NET

Additional support materials and activities for Chapter 18 of *America: Pathways to the Present* can be found in the Social Studies area at the Prentice Hall School Web site. **www.phschool.com**

American Pathways
HISTORY

Fighting for Freedom and Democracy

Throughout the nation's history, Americans have stepped forward to risk their lives to protect freedom and democracy. More than 40 million Americans have fought in the nation's wars both at home and abroad, and more than one million have given their lives to preserve their country's cherished ideals.

From Colonies to Nation

1565–1783 As Europeans established a presence in North America, conflicts occurred among the competing nations as well as with Native Americans. Ultimately, the colonists' struggle to gain independence from Britain resulted in the creation of a new country built on the foundations of freedom, equality, and self-government.

Emanuel Gottlieb Leutze's *George Washington Crossing the Delaware* (left)

The New Nation Asserts Its Authority

1812–1848 In the first half of the nineteenth century, the United States asserted its sovereignty during the War of 1812 and the Mexican-American War, as well as with the proclamation of the Monroe Doctrine.

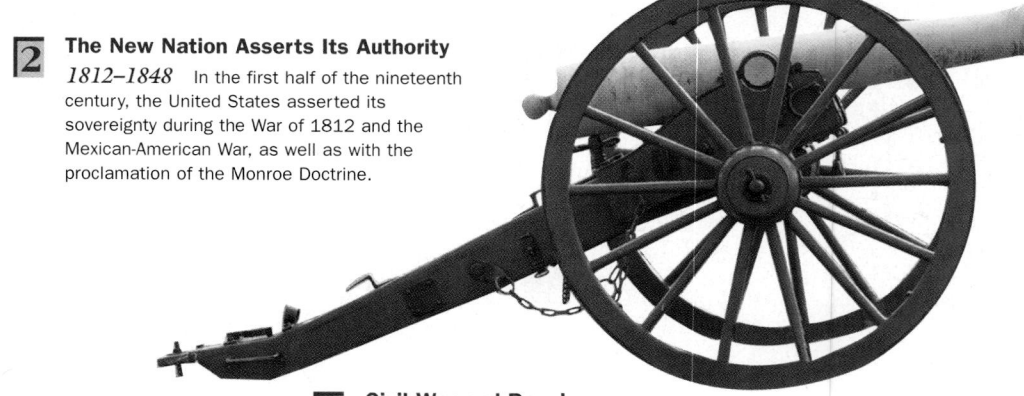

Civil War and Reunion

1861–1890 From 1861 to 1865, the Civil War split the nation in two as armies from the North and the South battled over the issues of states' rights and slavery. Although the Union was restored, conflicts developed over the status of freed African Americans during the Reconstruction period. In the West, Native Americans continued to resist the expansion of the United States.

A cannon used in the Battle of Gettysburg (above)

642

 Becoming a World Power and World War I

1890–1918   As a result of the industrial boom at the turn of the century, the United States expanded its foreign trade. When German submarines attacked neutral American merchant ships, the United States entered World War I and helped the French and English defeat the Germans. In the words of President Wilson, Americans fought "to make the world safe for democracy."

Allied troops fighting in the trenches during World War I (left)

 Isolationism

1920–1940   The horrors of World War I convinced many Americans that the country should end foreign entanglements and curtail military expenditures.

 World War II and the Cold War

1941–1991   Tensions between the United States and the Soviet Union developed at the end of World War II and lasted for 50 years until the collapse of the Soviet Union in 1991. Throughout that time, the goal of U.S. foreign policy was to prevent the spread of communism.

American troops landing in Normandy, France, on D-Day, June 6, 1944 (above)

Regional Conflicts and Terrorism

1991–Present   In the post–Cold War period, the United States played a role in resolving many regional ethnic conflicts. The nation also struggled to preserve its freedoms in the face of terrorism.

Firemen raise an American flag amid the rubble of the World Trade Center following the terrorist attacks on New York and Washington, D.C., on September 11, 2001 (above).

Continuity and Change

1. What factors contributed to the country's relative isolationism between the two World Wars?
2. Explain how the Cold War began and ended.

Take It to the NET: Creating a Study Guide
Print and complete the study guide for this topic found in the *America: Pathways to the Present* area of the following Web site. **www.phschool.com**

643

 Take It to the NET

Students can print the American Pathways thematic study guide for this topic at the Prentice Hall School Web site, or you can provide students with copies of the study guide, which is found in the Units 5/6 booklet, the American Pathways Activity, pages 85–86. Students should use their texts to fill in a one-sentence description for each event on the study guide. When completed for each of the American Pathways topics, the thematic study guides will aid students in preparing for an end-of-course exam.

ANSWERS

1. The savagery of World War I made Americans wary of involvement in foreign affairs. The stock market crash of 1929 and subsequent Depression limited American resources and kept American military budgets low.

2. The Cold War arose out of tensions between the United States and the Soviet Union at the end of World War II and from the deeply held philosophical differences between Soviet-backed communism and U.S.–supported capitalism. The Cold War ended following Soviet leader Mikhail Gorbachev's glasnost ("political openness") policies in the late 1980s, the subsequent collapse of Eastern European Communist governments, the destruction of the Berlin Wall, Strategic Arms Reduction agreements, and the dissolution of the Soviet Union at the beginning of 1992.

Chapter-Level Resources

Teaching Resources
- Pacing Charts booklet
- Block Scheduling booklet

Resource Pro® CD-ROM, Ch. 19
Prentice Hall Presentation Pro CD-ROM, Ch. 19
www.phschool.com
- eTeach

Guided Reading Audiotapes (English/Spanish)
Student Edition on Audio CD, Ch. 19
Social Studies Skills Tutor CD-ROM
Color Transparencies, A32, A33, A34, D8, H15, H16

---

1 The Road to War

1. Identify the main causes of World War I.
2. Understand how the conflict expanded to draw in much of Europe.
3. Analyze how the United States responded to the war in Europe.

Teaching Resources
Units 5/6 booklet
- Section 1 Quiz, p. 74

Learning Styles Lesson Plans booklet, p. 40

Guided Reading and Review booklet, p. 78
Guide to the Essentials, p. 98
Learning with Documents booklet, p. 24
Skills for Life booklet, p. 21
Section Reading Support Transparencies

---

2 The United States Declares War

1. Discover how Germany's use of submarines affected the war.
2. Find out the steps the United States took toward war in early 1917.

Teaching Resources
Units 5/6 booklet
- Section 2 Quiz, p. 75

Guided Reading and Review booklet, p. 79
Guide to the Essentials, p. 99
Section Reading Support Transparencies

---

3 Americans on the European Front

1. Analyze the preparations of the United States for World War I.
2. Study the ways in which the American troops helped turn the tide of the war.
3. Learn about conditions in Europe and the United States at the end of the war.

Teaching Resources
Units 5/6 booklet
- Section 3 Quiz, p. 76

Guided Reading and Review booklet, p. 80
Guide to the Essentials, p. 100
Section Reading Support Transparencies

---

4 Americans on the Home Front

1. Learn about the steps the government took to finance the war and manage the economy.
2. Describe how the government enforced loyalty to the war effort.
3. Find out how the war changed the lives of Americans on the home front.

Teaching Resources
Units 5/6 booklet
- Section 4 Quiz, p. 77

Guided Reading and Review booklet, p. 81
Guide to the Essentials, p. 101
Learning with Documents booklet, p. 58
Section Reading Support Transparencies

---

5 Global Peacemaker

1. Discover the expectations that Wilson and the Allies brought to the Paris peace conference.
2. Learn about the important provisions of the peace treaty.
3. Find out how the federal government and ordinary Americans reacted to the end of the war.

Teaching Resources
Units 5/6 booklet
- Section 5 Quiz, p. 78

Learning Styles Lesson Plans booklet, p. 41

Guided Reading and Review booklet, p. 82
Guide to the Essentials, p. 102
Learning with Documents booklet, p. 86
Section Reading Support Transparencies

ENRICHMENT/PRE-AP

Prentice Hall United States History Video Collection™
www.phschool.com
- Section Activities, Virtual Field Trip, Chapter Activities, Current Events Online

Biography, Literature, and Comparing Primary Sources booklet, p. 66
American History Block Scheduling Support
Historical Outline Map Book, p. 60
Sounds of an Era Audio CD

Biography, Literature, and Comparing Primary Sources booklet, p. 24
Sounds of an Era Audio CD
Exploring Primary Sources in U.S. History CD-ROM

Historical Outline Map Book, p. 61
Sounds of an Era Audio CD
Exploring Primary Sources in U.S. History CD-ROM

American History Block Scheduling Support
Nystrom *Atlas of Our Country,* pp. 30–31
Sounds of an Era Audio CD

Biography, Literature, and Comparing Primary Sources booklet, p. 133
Historical Outline Map Book, p. 62
Exploring Primary Sources in U.S. History CD-ROM
American Pathways Thematic Posters

ASSESSMENT

Core Assessment
ExamView® Test Bank, Ch. 19
ExamView® Test Bank CD-ROM, Ch. 19

Standardized Test Preparation
Diagnose and Prescribe
Diagnostic Tests for High School Social Studies Skills

Review and Reteach
Review Book for U.S. History

Practice and Assess
Test-taking Strategies With Transparencies
Test-taking Strategies Posters
Test Prep Book for U.S. History
Alternative Assessment Handbook
Document-Based Assessment

Teaching Resources
Units 5/6 booklet
- Section Quizzes, pp. 74–78
- Chapter Tests, pp. 79, 82
www.phschool.com Ch. 19 Self-Test

AmericanHeritage RESOURCES

From the Archives of American Heritage®, pp. 666, 671
AmericanHeritage® My Brush with History™ Videotapes
www.americanheritage.com

Don't miss the exclusive interactive version of this textbook on the Web and on CD-ROM.

Chapter 19 Planning Guide
In Your Classroom

CUSTOMIZE FOR INDIVIDUAL NEEDS

Gifted and Talented

Teacher's Edition
- Customize for Gifted and Talented, pp. 661, 665

Teaching Resources
- Biography, Literature, and Comparing Primary Sources booklet, pp. 24, 66, 133

Technology
- Exploring Primary Sources in U.S. History CD-ROM *Zimmermann Telegram; Diary of a World War I Ambulance Driver, William Stevenson; The Fourteen Points*

ESL

Teacher's Edition
- Customize for ESL, p. 647

Teaching Resources
- Guided Reading and Review booklet, pp. 78–82
- Guide to the Essentials (English/Spanish), Chapter 19

Technology
- Student Edition on Audio CD, Chapter 19
- Guided Reading Audiotapes (English/Spanish), Chapter 19
- Section Reading Support Transparencies

Less Proficient Readers

Teacher's Edition
- Customize for Less Proficient Readers, p. 655

Teaching Resources
- Guided Reading and Review booklet, pp. 78–82
- Guide to the Essentials (English/Spanish), Chapter 19

Technology
- Student Edition on Audio CD, Chapter 19
- Guided Reading Audiotapes (English/Spanish), Chapter 19
- Section Reading Support Transparencies

Less Proficient Writers

Teacher's Edition
- Customize for Less Proficient Writers, p. 673

Teaching Resources
- Guided Reading and Review booklet, pp. 78–82
- Guide to the Essentials (English/Spanish), Chapter 19

Technology
- Student Edition on Audio CD, Chapter 19
- Guided Reading Audiotapes (English/Spanish), Chapter 19
- Section Reading Support Transparencies

TEACHER'S EDITION INDEX

CHAPTER 19 – PACING SUGGESTIONS

 For 90-minute Blocks

- Teach sections 1 and 3 using Transparencies A31, A32, A33, A34, C6, D8, H15, and H16, and the Recent Scholarship note on page 667 for class discussions.

 Running Out of Time?

If you are running short on time to cover this chapter, consider the following options:

- Use the Prentice Hall Presentation Pro CD-ROM to create an outline for this chapter.

- Use the Section Summaries for Chapter 19, from **Guide to the Essentials (English/Spanish)**.

1 The Road to War

Connecting with History and Conflict
Explain to students that, though it may sound strange, nations of the world have established certain rules of war. The first Geneva Convention, or Treaty, was signed in 1864 and updated in 1906, 1929, 1949, and 1977. Similarly, there are rules of neutrality. In 1907 the second Hague Peace Conference set the rules of neutrality on land and sea, which spell out how neutral and belligerent nations are supposed to act. Have students research either the Geneva Conventions or the rules of neutrality, then pair up to role-play a radio host interviewing an expert guest on the subject. **(Verbal/Linguistic)**

2 The United States Declares War

Connecting with Culture
Share the following information with students: Advances in the speed and quality of color presses during the nineteenth century allowed for the mass production of posters. Posters served both decorative and advertising purposes. They were also used for propaganda, that is, any effort to bring the public to believe certain ideas. Have students design a propaganda poster that attempts to do one of the following: convert or strengthen public opinion in support of the United States joining the war; recruit soldiers, nurses, ambulance drivers, or women workers to replace men serving in the armed forces; or collect relief funds. **(Visual/Spatial)**

3 Americans on the European Front

Connecting with Culture
Have students look for examples of war poetry in the work of such English poets as Siegfried Sassoon, Rupert Brooke, Wilfred Owen, and Isaac Rosenberg, and American Malcolm Cowley. (You may wish to explain that Brooke, Owen, and Rosenberg died in the war. Cowley, who served as an ambulance driver, and Sassoon survived.) Have students take turns reading the poems aloud. Then pose and discuss this question: Can any poet possibly communicate the experience of war through poetry? **(Verbal/Linguistic)**

4 Americans on the Home Front

Connecting with Government
Have students discuss or debate this question: Should true patriots be willing to give up the right to free speech in order to support a war effort? As preparation, have students compare the Espionage Act of 1917 and the Sedition Act of 1918 with the Alien and Sedition acts of 1798 so that they understand the effect of such laws on the expression of dissent. You might also remind students of similar restrictions during the American Civil War. **(Verbal/Linguistic)**

5 Global Peacemaker

Connecting with Citizenship
Explain to students that the first reliable public opinion polls were conducted in the 1930s. Have students research how such polls are created and conducted, then create one that might have been used to assess how the public felt about United States membership in the League of Nations. Point out that pollsters, in order to get accurate results, have to frame their questions on the poll very carefully. Students might then poll their classmates on whether the United States should have joined the League and use graphs to summarize the results. **(Logical/Mathematical; Verbal/Linguistic)**

INTRODUCING THE CHAPTER

In the second decade of the twentieth century, a terrible war began in Europe, with the death toll eventually totaling an estimated 8 million combatants—and many more civilians. At first the United States vowed to maintain its neutrality. However, the nation finally declared war in order to support its allies and defend its commercial interests.

TIME LINE ACTIVITY

To provide students with practice in using the time line, ask questions such as these:

1. What impact did the assassination of Archduke Francis Ferdinand have on the United States? *(His 1914 assassination caused many people to call for the United States to enter the war, but President Wilson declared that the country would stay neutral.)*

2. Explain the significance of the following dates: 1914–1918. *(World War I was fought between 1914 and 1918.)*

3. Did the sinking of the *Lusitania* cause the United States to enter World War I? *(Not directly, but it did cause more Americans to be in favor of the entry of the United States into the war.)*

eTeach

Be sure to check out this month's online discussion with a Master Teacher. Go to **www.phschool.com**.

Chapter 19

The World War I Era
(1914–1920)

SECTION 1   The Road to War
SECTION 2   The United States Declares War
SECTION 3   Americans on the European Front
SECTION 4   Americans on the Home Front
SECTION 5   Global Peacemaker

Assassination of Archduke
Francis Ferdinand

The New York Times. EXTRA

LUSITANIA SUNK BY A SUBMARINE, PROBABLY 1,260 DEAD;
TWICE TORPEDOED OFF IRISH COAST; SINKS IN 15 MINUTES;
CAPT. TURNER SAVED, FROHMAN AND VANDERBILT MISSING;
WASHINGTON BELIEVES THAT A GRAVE CRISIS IS AT HAND

American Events

1914
President Wilson announces American neutrality in the war.

1915
The sinking of the *Lusitania* angers Americans.

1916
With the Sussex pledge, Germany promises the United States that U-boats will warn ships before attacking.

Presidential Terms: Woodrow Wilson 1913–1921

1912   **1914**   **1916**

World Events

1914
Assassination of Archduke Francis Ferdinand triggers World War I.

1915
Poison gas is first used against the Allies.

1916
Millions of British, French, and German soldiers die in failed offensives at Verdun and the Somme River.

644   Chapter 19 • *The World War I Era*

RESOURCE DIRECTORY

Teaching Resources
Pacing Charts booklet
Block Scheduling booklet, p. 22
Units 5/6 booklet
  • Chapter Summary, p. 73

Technology
Guided Reading Audiotapes (English/Spanish), Ch. 19
Student Edition on Audio CD, Ch. 19
Color Transparencies *Historical Maps,* A31;
  Time Lines, C6

Sounds of an Era Audio CD *"It's a Long Way to Tipperary,"* 1917 recording
Prentice Hall United States History Video Collection™ Volume 16, *The Great War*
Prentice Hall Presentation Pro CD-ROM, Ch. 19
Resource Pro® CD-ROM
Social Studies Skills Tutor CD-ROM
Companion Web site, www.phschool.com

The World at War, 1914–1918

Legend:
- Allies, 1914
- Allies at end of war
- Colonial possessions of Allies
- Central Powers
- Colonial possessions of Central Powers

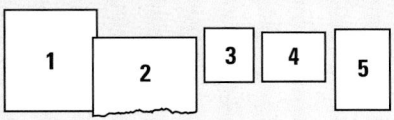

Allied soldiers on the Western Front

After the Welcome Home — a JOB!
U.S. EMPLOYMENT SERVICE, Dept of Labor

Department of Labor poster

1917
Germany ends Sussex pledge and resumes undeclared submarine warfare. Wilson declares war and sends the first units of the AEF to France under General Pershing.

1918
American troops fight at Belleau Wood, Château-Thierry, and the Argonne Forest.

1919
United States Senate rejects the Treaty of Versailles and membership in the League of Nations as American soldiers return from Europe.

Warren G. Harding 1921–1923

1918 • 1920 1922

1917
Revolutions in Russia overthrow the czar and bring the Bolsheviks to power.

1918
Central Powers agree to a truce with the Allies.

1919
Germany signs the Treaty of Versailles.

Chapter 19   645

The World at War, 1914–1918

Activating Prior Knowledge What country in South America had joined forces with the European Allies by the end of World War I? *(Brazil)*

Previewing Ask students to study the map and explain how the Great War eventually became known as World War I. *(Because most of the countries in the world had allegiance to one side or the other in the war)*

BACKGROUND
About the Pictures

1 2 3 4 5

1. Archduke Francis Ferdinand and his wife, Sophia, were assassinated on June 28, 1914. Carried out by a Serbian named Gavrilo Princip, the assassination was one of the events that led to World War I.

2. The front page of *The New York Times* on May 7, 1915, the day following the sinking of the cruise ship *Lusitania,* which went down with many Americans on board.

3. General John J. Pershing (center) inspects British troops in Brest, France, during World War I.

4. Allied soldiers begin the dangerous task of going "over the top"—leaving the protection of the trenches and crossing "No Man's Land," an action often performed under heavy artillery and machine gun fire.

5. Poster used by the Department of Labor encouraging veterans of World War I to return to the workforce after their welcome home.

TEXT

Don't miss the exclusive interactive version of this textbook on the Web and on CD-ROM.

BIBLIOGRAPHY

For the Teacher

Horne, Alistaire. *The Price of Glory.* Penguin, 1994. (In-depth account of the grueling ten-month Battle of Verdun.)

Tuchman, Barbara W. *The Guns of August.* Macmillan, 1962. (Chronicle of the events that resulted in World War I.)

Winter, Denis. *Soldiers of the Great War.* Penguin, 1985. (Distillation of soldiers' personal experiences during World War I.)

For the Student

Remarque, Erich Maria. *All Quiet on the Western Front.* Ballantine, 1996. (Classic novel of the war from the German viewpoint; first published in 1929.)

Lawrence, T. E. *The Seven Pillars of Wisdom.* Anchor, 1991. (The author is the real Lawrence of Arabia, who helped unify various Arab factions against a common Turkish invader during World War I.)

Time-Life Books editors. *Time-Life Books: This Fabulous Century, Vol. 2. 1910–1920.* Time-Life, 1969. (Richly illustrated, comprehensive study of the era.)

SECTION OBJECTIVES

1. Identify the main causes of World War I.
2. Understand how the conflict expanded to draw in much of Europe.
3. Analyze how the United States responded to the war in Europe.

BELLRINGER

Warm-Up Activity Ask students to define the word *neutral*. Ask them to think of situations in which they remained neutral and others in which they took a stand. What conditions affected their choices?

Activating Prior Knowledge What impact might the presence of many first-generation European immigrants have had on the position of the United States toward entering the war?

READING STRATEGY

As World War I began and then expanded throughout much of Europe, the United States remained neutral. Ask students to rewrite the statement above as a question. As they read the section, have them write down the answers to their question.

ACTIVITY
Student Portfolio

You may wish to have students add the following to their portfolios. Britain's Queen Victoria, who reigned from 1837 to 1901, has been called "Europe's grandmother" because so many monarchs were descended from her five children. Ask students to make a family tree tracing Victoria's descendents up to 1920. Have them highlight the names of the cousins who reigned during World War I. **(Logical/Mathematical)**

CAPTION ANSWERS

Viewing History Nationalism.

READING FOCUS

- What were the main causes of World War I?
- How did the conflict expand to draw in much of Europe?
- In what ways did the United States respond to the war in Europe?

MAIN IDEA

As World War I began and then spread to much of Europe, the United States tried to remain neutral as long as possible.

KEY TERMS

militarism
mobilization
Central Powers
Allies
stalemate
autocrat
propaganda

TAKING NOTES

As you read, complete the following cause-and-effect diagram that shows why World War I began.

CAUSES
• Assassination of Archduke Francis Ferdinand in Sarajevo
• Competition for colonies in Africa, Asia, and the Pacific
•
•

↓

WORLD WAR I

Setting the Scene On June 28, 1914, Archduke Francis Ferdinand and his wife made a state visit to Sarajevo, the capital of Bosnia. Bosnia was a new province within the Austro-Hungarian Empire, and Francis Ferdinand was heir to the empire's throne. Although many Bosnians were upset with Austro-Hungarian rule, Francis Ferdinand decided to disregard growing tensions and visit his government's soldiers in Sarajevo.

The morning of his visit, a bomb thrown by a terrorist bounced off the archduke's car and exploded, injuring two officers in another car. Unfazed, Francis Ferdinand attended a state ceremony and then rode to the hospital to see the wounded officers. Gavrilo Princip, a second terrorist, just 19 years old, happened to spot the car as it slowly moved down a narrow street. One of Princip's friends saw what happened next:

VIEWING HISTORY The assassination of Archduke Francis Ferdinand and his wife Sofia in Sarajevo triggered a series of events that led to war. **Recognizing Cause and Effect** Which of the four causes of World War I contributed most directly to the murder in Sarajevo?

Sarajevo ★

❝ As the car came abreast he stepped forward from the curb, drew his automatic pistol from his coat and fired two shots. The first struck the wife of the Archduke, the Archduchess Sofia, in the abdomen. . . . She died instantly. The second bullet struck the Archduke close to the heart. He uttered only one word; 'Sofia'—a call to his stricken wife. Then his head fell back and he collapsed. He died almost instantly. ❞
—Borijove Jevtic

Princip, a Bosnian nationalist, believed that Austria-Hungary had no right to rule Bosnia. Little did he know that his act of terrorism in Sarajevo would have grave consequences.

646 Chapter 19 • *The World War I Era*

RESOURCE DIRECTORY

Teaching Resources
Learning Styles Lesson Plans booklet, p. 40
Guided Reading and Review booklet, p. 78

Technology
Section Reading Support Transparencies
Guided Reading Audiotapes (English/Spanish), Ch. 19
Student Edition on Audio CD, Ch. 19
Color Transparencies *Historical Maps,* A32
Sounds of an Era Audio CD *"Castle Walk,"* 1914 recording by Europe's Society Orchestra (time: 45 seconds)
Prentice Hall Presentation Pro CD-ROM, Ch. 19
Companion Web site, www.phschool.com

Causes of World War I

The assassination of Archduke Francis Ferdinand ignited what was then called the Great War, later known as World War I. However, the main causes of the war existed well before 1914. Those causes included imperialism, militarism, nationalism, and a tangled system of alliances.

Imperialism A great scramble for colonies took place in the late 1800s. European powers rushed to claim the remaining uncolonized areas of the world, particularly in Africa, Asia, and the Pacific. Japan joined the roster of colonial powers when it won the Sino-Japanese War in 1895 and moved to acquire Korea, Taiwan, and territory on China's mainland.

By 1910, the most desirable colonies had been taken. Competition for the lands that remained led to conflict among the powers of Europe. Germany's leaders envied Britain and France—two countries that had begun colonizing early and controlled large, resource-rich empires. Leaders in Germany and other countries recognized that they could only expand in Africa by taking land away from other colonizers.

Militarism By the early 1900s in Europe, diplomacy had taken a back seat to **militarism.** This policy involved aggressively building up a nation's armed forces in preparation for war and giving the military more authority over the government and foreign policy. The great powers of Europe—Austria-Hungary, France, Germany, Great Britain, and Russia—all spent large sums of money on new weapons and warships for expanding their armed forces. Their endless planning for war made war much more likely.

Nationalism Two kinds of nationalism contributed to World War I. The first was the tendency for countries such as the great powers to act in their own

READING CHECK
How did competition for colonies help lead to war?

The War in Europe, 1914–1918

MAP SKILLS Before the war, Europe was a land of empires and alliances. When Austria-Hungary declared war on Serbia, much of the continent was drawn into the conflict. **Location** *Based on this map, which side, if any, had a geographical advantage in the war? Explain.*

Focus Explain that when war first broke out in Europe, most Americans wished to remain neutral. However, as the war continued, the United States moved to more active involvement. Ask what prompted this change.

Instruct Remind students that World War I did not erupt overnight. Ask about long-standing causes and discuss the reasons why each European nation became involved. Why did the system of secret European alliances fail to maintain peace? Discuss being both neutral and prepared. Did arms and troops buildup ensure United States entry into the war? Why or why not?

Assess/Reteach Ask students to consider the underlying causes of World War I: imperialism, militarism, and nationalism. In what ways did these trends lead to war? How did conflicts in central Europe (especially in Bosnia) cause the scope of the war to grow? Ask them to consider how new weapons changed the way soldiers fought.

READING CHECK
Competition for colonies led to frequent disputes between the Great Powers in the 1895–1914 period.

ESL

Have students read the material under the heading "Causes of World War I." Then have them use the map on this page titled "The War in Europe, 1914–1918" to explain the causes of the war in their own words.

✓ **TEST PREPARATION**

Have students reread the section "Causes of World War I" on this page and then answer the question below.

Which of the below is an example of nationalism?

A The desire of a powerful nation to expand by seizing control of a smaller nation.

B The growth of a nation's military power in the interest of waging war.

Ⓒ The longing of an ethnic minority for independence.

D The decision by a government to remain neutral in wartime.

CAPTION ANSWERS

Map Skills The Allies, because the Central Powers were nearly surrounded by enemy nations.

Connecting with Government

Have students divide into groups of four to six. Each group will become the expert on one European nation. Each group is to prepare a "briefing book" for President Wilson—a document describing one of the major nations of Europe in June 1914. The document should include sections on the head of state and form of government; geographical features; economy, including major products and trade partners; military leaders; and ethnic and religious composition of the population. Each student should assume responsibility for one section of the document for the group's nation. **(Verbal/Linguistic)**

BACKGROUND

Getting to Stalemate

Before reaching stalemate, both sides suffered tremendous losses. In just the first five months of the war, approximately one million French soldiers were seriously injured or killed. The Germans also experienced huge losses in what was considered the world's worst bloodbath. Although the Germans had built up a formidable military, they had failed to anticipate the combined strength of their enemies. The result was a stalemate and a new form of battle known as *trench warfare.*

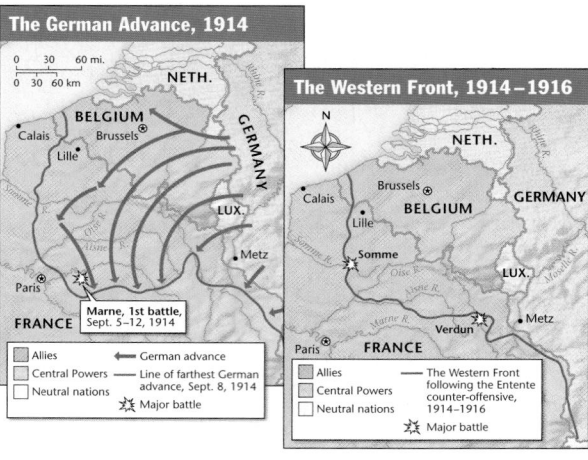

MAP SKILLS German troops advanced deep into French territory before British and French armies stopped them at the Battle of the Marne. **Movement** *Why did the battle lines change little after 1914?*

As the need for soldiers increased, the British government used powerful national symbols to draw young people into Britain's all-volunteer army.

national interest. When such action went against the national interest of another nation, warfare could result.

One source of trouble was the German region of Alsace-Lorraine, a strip of land along Germany's border with France. The French people considered the return of Alsace-Lorraine, which had been conquered by Germany in 1871, a matter of national pride. German leaders valued the region's strong defenses and historic ties to Germany. These conflicting goals soured relations between France and Germany.

The second kind of nationalism occurred in countries with diverse ethnic populations, particularly those in central and eastern Europe. In Austria-Hungary, Hungarians and German-speaking Austrians governed millions of Czechs, Slovaks, Poles, and others who sought self-government. The empire also included Italians, Romanians, and Serbs who wished to join their compatriots in neighboring lands. Poles in Russia, Germany, and Austria-Hungary wanted to reunite and build an independent Poland. The longing of an ethnic minority for independence often led to violence.

As the most powerful Slavic country, Russia protected Slavs in Serbia and those under Austro-Hungarian rule. Russia's strong ties to the Serbs would play an important role in expanding the conflict beyond Serbia in 1914.

Alliances A complicated system of alliances developed among the nations of Europe during the late nineteenth century. Designed to bolster each nation's security, the alliances bound the great powers to come to each other's aid in the event of attack. Germany and Austria-Hungary were linked by treaty, as were Russia and France. Great Britain and France shared a looser alliance called the Entente Cordiale, or simply Entente. In 1914, this fragile balance of power, which had kept the peace for decades, led its creators into war.

The Conflict Expands

At the time of the assassination of Francis Ferdinand, Bosnia was the focal point of a nationalist dispute between Austria-Hungary, which had recently annexed Bosnia, and its neighbor Serbia, which shared a language and common history with Bosnia. Convinced that Serbia was behind the assassination, Austria-Hungary used the event as an excuse to crush its small enemy. On July 28, 1914, Austria-Hungary declared war on Serbia.

This declaration of war set off a chain reaction that rapidly worked its way through Europe's complex web of alliances. On July 29, Russia, as Serbia's protector, began **mobilization**—the readying of troops for war. Germany, Austria-Hungary's chief ally, demanded that Russia stop mobilizing. Russia refused. At that point, Russia's ally, France, began to ready its troops, as did Germany.

On August 1, Germany declared war on Russia. Germany's military leaders had long prepared for this day. Their country lay between France to the west and Russia to the east. To avoid fighting both the French and Russian armies at the same time, Germany had developed a first-strike strategy. Known as the Schlieffen Plan, it called for a quick sweep through France to knock the French out of the war. Then, the German army would turn east and defeat Russia.

CAPTION ANSWERS

Map Skills Due to trenches.

RESOURCE DIRECTORY

Teaching Resources
Learning with Documents booklet (Primary Source Activity) *Thoughts on the War,* p. 24
Biography, Literature, and Comparing Primary Sources booklet (Literature) *A War Song,* p. 66

Other Print Resources
■ **American History Block Scheduling Support** *Liberty Bread and War Bonds: Supporting Our Soldiers in World War I,* found in the Prosperity, Depression, and War folder, includes interdisciplinary lesson suggestions and activities for Geography and History, Primary Sources, Biography, and Literature.

Historical Outline Map Book *Europe in World War I,* p. 60

Technology
Color Transparencies *Historical Maps,* A33, A34

Germany put the plan into action. To reach France as quickly as possible, the German army had to pass through Belgium, a country whose neutrality was protected by an international treaty. Germany had hoped that Britain would stay out of the war, but the invasion of Belgium brought Britain into the conflict on August 4.

One week after the war started, all the great powers of Europe had been drawn into it. The conflict divided them into two sides. Germany and Austria-Hungary made up the **Central Powers.** Russia, France, Serbia, and Great Britain were called the **Allies.**

Stalemate   Each side felt confident of swift victory. A few months, experts said, and the war would be over. The experts were wrong.

Using the Schlieffen Plan, the German army quickly swept through Belgium and northern France. By September, they had advanced to within 30 miles of Paris. There, at the river Marne, a combined French and British force stopped their progress. Both sides then dug in and fortified their lines. Relatively equal in size and strength, the two sides reached a bloody **stalemate,** a situation in which neither side is able to gain the advantage.

Holed up in lines of muddy, rat-infested trenches, the two sides faced each other across an empty "no man's land." For months, each side tried to reach the other's lines to push back the enemy. But neither side was able to gain more than a few miles, and then only at an appalling human cost.

In the east, the poorly-armed Russian army invaded Germany and Austria-Hungary. Under the Schlieffen Plan, Germany expected to give some ground in the east to the Russian army while the bulk of the German army dealt a knock-out blow to France. After capturing Paris, German troops would travel east to defeat the Russian army. However, Russia's early victories frightened Germany into sending soldiers to the Eastern Front ahead of schedule. There, German forces pushed the invading Russian armies back. However, the early transfer of troops away from France may have prevented a German victory in the west.

At the end of 1914, the Ottoman Empire, centered in what is now Turkey, entered the war on the side of the Central Powers. In the spring of 1915, Italy joined the Allies. Bulgaria joined the Central Powers that October, and Romania joined the Allies the following year. Each side hoped that a new ally would attack the enemy in a weak spot and break the stalemate. Instead, fronts in northern Italy and at Gallipoli, southwest of the Ottoman capital of Constantinople, brought the familiar pattern of trench warfare and costly, unsuccessful attacks.

Modern Warfare   In 1914, the youth of Europe had marched off to fight, eager for a chance to be heroic. In earlier wars, a strong, swift offense led by troops on horseback often had been enough to secure victory in battle. The soldiers of World War I, however, came up against new killing machines of amazing efficiency. Defensive forces could use modern firepower, such as machine guns and rapid-fire

Focus on TECHNOLOGY

Gas Masks The German army first released chlorine gas into the Allied trenches in April 1915. The gas attacked the lungs and the eyes, causing panic, pain, and even death in enemy trenches. At first, soldiers covered their mouths with wet gauze for protection. Later, they received gas masks that allowed the wearer to breathe in and draw air through a canister that filtered out poisons. Putting on the clumsy, heavy gas mask became an essential part of a soldier's drill. Unfortunately, these masks could not protect against the more dangerous mustard gas used later in the war.

VIEWING HISTORY Trenches ranged from crudely dug foxholes (below) to a series of elaborate trenches stretching for miles. The German soldier at left wears a gas mask and holds a grenade. **Drawing Conclusions** *Why do you think the armies resorted to poison gas to attack fortifications like this?*

Focus on CULTURE

The War Poets The horrors of modern warfare had a major impact on British culture. Wilfred Owen was one of several soldiers in their late teens and twenties whose poems expressed anger at older leaders who sent them to fight and die under ghastly circumstances. Owen's poem, "Dulce et Decorum Est," contrasts school lessons that "it is fitting and sweet to die for one's country" with harsh images of death in a gas attack. Another poem, "The Parable of the Old Man and the Young," compares the war to a biblical story in which Abraham is asked to sacrifice his son, Isaac, but is told not to kill him at the last minute. Owen's poem has a different ending:

> "But the old man would not so, but slew his son,
>
> And half the seed of Europe, one by one."

artillery, to stop advancing soldiers. Ripped apart by machine guns, hand grenades, or artillery shells, and choked by poison gases, soldiers found that heroism came at a terrible price.

If soldiers charging across no man's land toward the enemy survived the artillery shells that rained down upon them, the enemy's machine guns, firing 450 rounds a minute, mowed them down. The generals, unaccustomed to the new weaponry, assumed that superiority in troop numbers would bring them victory. They repeatedly ordered soldiers to go "over the top" of the trenches to attack the enemy. That strategy, however, produced only a mounting pile of dead infantry. In the Battle of the Somme in 1916, for example, the British suffered some 20,000 deaths in a single day of combat.

Morale sank. Desperate, the armies began using any tactic available. Erasing the distinction between soldier and civilian, they burned fields, killed livestock, and poisoned wells. They tunneled under the no man's land to plant bombs below enemy trenches. German submarines torpedoed any ship they believed to be carrying arms to the Allies. A British naval blockade slowly starved the German people. None of these tactics brought a quick end to the conflict.

The American Response

Newspapers in the United States had recorded the march toward war in bold headlines. "Austria Declares War, Rushes Vast Army into Serbia; Russia Masses 80,000 Men on Border." Americans read the news with mounting alarm. How could all of these great countries of beauty and culture be at war with one another?

Some Americans felt personally involved. More than a third of the nation's 92 million people were immigrants or the children of immigrants. About a quarter of these were German American, and another eighth were Irish American. Both of these groups felt hostility toward Great Britain because of past conflicts and the current war. For that reason, they favored the Central Powers over the Allies.

Most Americans, however, opposed the Central Powers. Millions of Americans traced their roots to Britain, and others identified with British history, literature, and culture. Recent immigrants from Italy and parts of Austria-Hungary hoped that a defeat of the Central Powers would lead to independence for or expansion of their homelands.

Another source of mistrust was Kaiser Wilhelm II of Germany. The Kaiser, or emperor, was an **autocrat**—a ruler with unlimited power. His rule offended supporters of democracy. Americans also saw the Germans as a people of frightening militarism and cold-blooded efficiency. Reporters who had rushed to Europe to witness the German advance fueled this view. Richard Harding Davis described the August 1914 invasion as "not men marching, but a force of nature like a tidal wave, an avalanche, or a river flooding its banks." Americans read that the Germans killed civilians and destroyed libraries, cathedrals, and even entire towns in Belgium and France.

While civilians suffered severely under German occupation, some of the worst stories of German crimes were not true. British newspapers published false **propaganda,** or information intended to sway public opinion, that spread throughout the United States. These stories turned American public opinion against Germany.

American Neutrality Trade strongly influenced the American position on the war. Between 1897 and 1914, American commercial investments overseas had increased five-fold, from $700 million to $3.5 billion. German submarines and a British naval blockade of the North Sea placed those investments at risk. To protect the investments, on August 4, 1914, President Wilson officially proclaimed the United States a neutral country. The American government protested the actions of both sides and tried to act as peacemaker.

The Preparedness Movement American business leaders welcomed the proclamation of neutrality. Still, those who had strong commercial ties to Great Britain urged that the United States get ready for war. Their watchword was "preparedness." They wanted their country to be in a position to aid Great Britain if necessary. In December 1914, preparedness supporters organized a National Security League to "promote patriotic education and national sentiment and service among people of the United States."

By the late summer of 1915, the movement's leaders had persuaded the government to set up camps to train American men for combat. By the summer of 1916, Wilson had worked out an agreement with Congress for large increases in the armed forces.

The Peace Movement When World War I broke out, a peace movement also swung into gear. Its members consisted primarily of former Populists, Midwest progressives, and social reformers. Women were particularly active. On August 29, 1914, suffragists, dressed in black and carrying a banner of a dove, marched down New York City's Fifth Avenue. In November 1915, a group of social reformers founded the American Union Against Militarism.

Congress also included some peace advocates. They insisted on paying for preparedness through a tax on the makers of arms and through higher income taxes. Claude Kitchin, a member of Congress from North Carolina, predicted that when people discovered "that the income tax will have to pay for the increase in the army and navy, . . . preparedness will not be so popular." Congress increased taxes, but the preparedness movement remained strong.

VIEWING HISTORY This "peace ship" traveled to Europe in 1915 with hopes of ending the war. Jane Addams, second from the left in the front row, joined the delegation. **Recognizing Ideologies** *How did the peace movement differ from the preparedness movement?*

Section 1 — Assessment

READING COMPREHENSION

1. How did nationalism contribute to the start of World War I?

2. Which countries were known as the **Allies?** Which countries were known as the **Central Powers?**

3. What were two causes of the **stalemate** in the West?

4. What was the main reason that the United States stayed neutral at the start of World War I?

CRITICAL THINKING AND WRITING

5. **Checking Consistency** The alliance system in Europe was designed to maintain peace. Yet it seemed to make the conflict worse once the fighting began. Explain the apparent inconsistency.

6. **Writing to Persuade** Write an essay in which you express your support for the preparedness movement. Persuade your readers that the United States had no choice but to be ready to go to war.

Take It to the NET

Activity: Interpreting a Poem
Read a poem about World War I and write a short essay about the meaning of the poem. Discuss how the writer felt about the war. What symbols does the writer use? Use the links provided in the *America: Pathways to the Present* area of the following Web site for help in completing this activity.
www.phschool.com

Chapter 19 • Section 1   651

Section 1 — Assessment

Reading Comprehension

1. The tendency for countries such as the Great Powers to act in their own national interest, which sometimes went against the national interest of another nation; in countries with diverse ethnic populations, the longing of an ethnic minority for independence often led to violence.

2. Allies: Russia, France, Serbia, Great Britain. Central Powers: Germany, Austria-Hungary, Turkey.

3. Answers should include two of the following: similar size and strength of opposing armies; neither side had an ally to break the stalemate and attack; early transfer of troops away from France.

4. President Wilson wanted to protect American commercial investments overseas.

Critical Thinking and Writing

5. Sample answer: Alliances tend to widen the conflict by involving nations that have no concern with the issues that caused the war.

6. Essays should use facts from the section to persuade readers of their point. Answers may describe American support for neutrality, the National Security League, and the need to protect commercial ties to Great Britain.

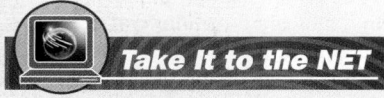
Take It to the NET

Essays will vary, but might address the horrors of war or the soldier's desire to return home to loved ones.

CAPTION ANSWERS

Viewing History The peace movement was an effort to keep the United States out of war, while the preparedness movement advocated that the U.S. become prepared to defend Great Britain.

Identifying and Analyzing Alternatives

Identifying alternatives means finding one or more possible ways to achieve a goal or to solve a problem. You have read about the conflict in the United States over how to respond to the war escalating in Europe. President Woodrow Wilson favored one response. Former President Theodore Roosevelt favored another.

IDENTIFYING AND ANALYZING ALTERNATIVES

Focus Students will identify and analyze alternative solutions to a problem.

Instruct As a class, work through the question in steps 1–3. You might want to divide students into small groups for consideration of step 4. Ask each group to submit a sentence stating the goal of the United States regarding the war in Europe and at least three steps likely to achieve that goal. Have each group tell which of these steps the nation actually took.

Extend See the Skills for Life activity in the Resource Directory below.

ANSWERS

PRACTICE THE SKILL

1. **(a)** World War I and the United States response to it. **(b)** Answers will vary but should reflect an understanding of chapter material.

2. **(a)** Neutrality. **(b)** Intervening to protect small, democratic nations against German aggression.

3. Possible answers: **(a)** It is difficult to expect people not to judge or feel strong sympathy when small, democratic nations suffer aggression. **(b)** It may lead to wider war or unnecessary bloodshed. American interests may be injured. **(c)** No. **(d)** No. It is presumed that this standard is clearly understood by all. **(e)** No, because the standard for action is not clear.

4. **(a)** Answers will vary. **(b)** Make sure students explain their answers and demonstrate an understanding of the problem. **(c)** Answers will vary.

LEARN THE SKILL

Use the following steps to identify and analyze alternatives:

1. **Identify the nature of the problem under discussion.** Before you can identify alternative solutions to a problem, you must understand what the problem is.

2. **Note the solutions proposed.** Write down the main points of each proposed solution.

3. **Evaluate the potential effectiveness of each solution.** Consider the strengths and weaknesses of each proposal.

4. **Consider other alternatives.** Recall the nature of the problem under discussion. Then, using the insights you gained by following the preceding steps, think of other possible solutions.

PRACTICE THE SKILL

Answer the following questions:

1. **(a)** What is the issue that both passages address? **(b)** What do you already know about this issue from your reading?

2. **(a)** What does Passage A suggest is the proper response of the United States to the war in Europe? **(b)** What does Passage B suggest is the proper response?

3. **(a)** What difficulties do you see in Wilson's suggestion that the United States not judge the actions of other nations? **(b)** What might happen if the United States acts in a "disinterested" way, as Wilson suggests? **(c)** Is Roosevelt clear about what he means when he refers to a nation that "does ill"? **(d)** Does Roosevelt explain how nations should be judged "highly civilized" or "well-behaved"? **(e)** Is his solution practical?

4. **(a)** What do you think should have been the goal of the United States in responding to the war in Europe? **(b)** What steps were most likely to achieve that goal? **(c)** Write a brief paragraph outlining your alternative solution.

APPLY THE SKILL

See the Chapter Review and Assessment for another opportunity to apply this skill.

A

"My thought is of America. . . .[T]his great country of ours . . . should show herself in this time of peculiar trial a nation fit beyond others to exhibit the fine poise of undisturbed judgment, the dignity of self-control, the efficiency of dispassionate [unemotional] action; a nation that neither sits in judgment upon others nor is disturbed in her own counsels and which keeps herself fit and free to do what is honest and disinterested and truly serviceable for the peace of the world."

—Woodrow Wilson, *Appeal for Neutrality*
August 18, 1914

B

"Our true course should be to judge each nation on its conduct, unhesitatingly to antagonize every nation that does ill [at the point] it does ill, and equally without hesitation to act. . . .

One of the greatest of international duties ought to be the protection of small, highly civilized, well-behaved and self-respecting states from oppression and conquest by their powerful military neighbors. . . .

I feel in the strongest way that we should have interfered, at least to the extent of the most emphatic diplomatic protest and at the very outset—and then by whatever further action was necessary—[when Germany invaded Belgium]."

—Theodore Roosevelt
America and the World War, 1915

RESOURCE DIRECTORY

Teaching Resources
Skills for Life booklet, p. 21

Technology
Social Studies Skills Tutor CD-ROM
Interactive Practice in
- Geographic Literacy
- Critical Thinking and Reading
- Visual Analysis
- Communications

The United States Declares War

READING FOCUS
- How did Germany's use of submarines affect the war?
- What moves did the United States take toward war in early 1917?

MAIN IDEA
German submarine warfare helped push the United States into World War I.

KEY TERMS
U-boat
Sussex pledge
Zimmermann note
Russian Revolution

TAKING NOTES
Copy this flowchart. As you read, fill in the boxes with some of the major events that caused the United States to declare war on Germany. The first box has been completed to help you get started.

German U-boats begin sinking Allied ships, killing 1,200 aboard the *Lusitania* in 1915.
↓
↓
Wilson asks Congress to declare war on Germany.

SECTION OBJECTIVES

1. Discover how Germany's use of submarines affected the war.
2. Find out the steps the United States took toward war in early 1917.

BELLRINGER

Warm-Up Activity Ask students what makes a country one of the great nations of the world. What domestic conditions and foreign alliances characterize a great nation? What countries are great nations today? Why?

Activating Prior Knowledge Did everyone in the United States agree that going to war was the best approach? In what ways did President Wilson take a political risk by keeping the United States out of the war in its early years?

READING STRATEGY

Ask students to imagine that they are members of Congress in 1917, and they helped decide that the United States would go to war against Germany and the other Central Powers. As they read the section, have them identify the reasons for U.S. involvement in World War I, including unrestricted submarine warfare.

ACTIVITY
Connecting with History and Conflict

Have students discuss the impact of Germany's aggressive use of U-boats. In small groups, have them examine the issue and suggest that they consider why the submarine attacks proved to be the turning point in American sentiment toward the war. **(Logical/Mathematical)**

Setting the Scene The fighting in Europe continued with no end in sight. In October 1916, *The New York Times* explained why American voters wanted a leader who would keep the United States out of war:

> 66 The voters . . . have seen lives lost, property ruined, privations suffered, on a greater scale than the world had ever known, and they have seen existence become harder, not only for the men who are fighting, but for all the inhabitants of the stricken countries. They have seen nation after nation drawn in, until the roll of the original combatants has been doubled. 99

Many Americans hoped that the United States would not be the next country to be drawn in. Nevertheless, friction between the United States and Germany increased from 1914 to 1917. The preparedness movement continued to gain support in the United States, and the pressure to join in the war intensified. Ultimately, actions by the Central Powers pushed Congress and the President into entering the war on the side of the Allies.

German Submarine Warfare

One action that provoked angry calls for war in the United States was the German use of submarine warfare. This tactic was effective militarily, but it cost the Germans dearly in terms of American public opinion.

The German **U-boat,** short for *Unterseeboot,* or submarine, was a terrifying new weapon that changed the rules of naval warfare. Germany deployed them to prevent munitions and food from reaching Britain's ports. At first, U-boats rose to the surface to allow the crew of merchant ships to abandon ship before their ship was attacked. After Britain armed merchant ships to fire on exposed U-boats, Germany abandoned the old rules and permitted U-boats to remain hidden and fire on merchant ships without warning.

The U-boat enabled Germany to break a stalemate at sea. In the years leading up to the war, Britain and Germany competed to build the largest, strongest

This German poster urged U-boats on their mission. The translation is "U-boats: Go out!"

Chapter 19 • Section 2   653

RESOURCE DIRECTORY

Teaching Resources
Guided Reading and Review booklet, p. 79

Technology
Section Reading Support Transparencies
Guided Reading Audiotapes (English/Spanish), Ch. 19
Student Edition on Audio CD, Ch. 19
Sounds of an Era Audio CD *"I Didn't Raise My Boy to be a Soldier,"* 1916 recording (time: one minute)
Prentice Hall Presentation Pro CD-ROM, Ch. 19
Companion Web site, www.phschool.com

Focus Explain that from 1915 to 1917, relations between the United States and Germany deteriorated. Ask why the United States finally declared war on the Central Powers.

Instruct Discuss why Germany's use of submarines caused outrage among Americans. Ask students to respond to the German argument that they should not be denied their weapon of surprise.

Discuss the events that moved the United States toward war with Germany. How did Germany violate the Sussex pledge? Ask students how they think the Zimmermann note affected American public opinion. What roles did the Russian Revolution, British propaganda, big business, and idealism play in the American decision to enter the war?

Assess/Reteach Ask students to describe the changing role of Russia in World War I. Have them create a simple time line that shows events that led to a change in Russia's position from 1915 to 1917. What impact do they think Russia's changing situation had on the overall conduct of the war?

The New York Times. EXTRA 5:30 A.M.

LUSITANIA SUNK BY A SUBMARINE, PROBABLY 1,260 DEAD; TWICE TORPEDOED OFF IRISH COAST; SINKS IN 15 MINUTES; CAPT. TURNER SAVED, FROHMAN AND VANDERBILT MISSING; WASHINGTON BELIEVES THAT A GRAVE CRISIS IS AT HAND

NOTICE!
TRAVELLERS intending to embark on the Atlantic voyage are reminded that a state of war exists between Germany and her allies and Great Britain and her allies; that the zone of war includes the waters adjacent to the British Isles; that, in accordance with formal notice given by the Imperial German Government, vessels flying the flag of Great Britain, or of any of her allies, are liable to destruction in those waters and that travellers sailing in the war zone on ships of Great Britain or her allies do so at their own risk.

IMPERIAL GERMAN EMBASSY,
WASHINGTON, D. C., APRIL 22, 1915.

CUNARD
EUROPE VIA LIVERPOOL
LUSITANIA
Fastest and Largest Steamer now in Atlantic Service Sails
SATURDAY, MAY 1, 10 A. M.

VIEWING HISTORY Germany warned travelers—including passengers on the *Lusitania*—to stay out of the war zone (top, left). Nevertheless, the sinking of the *Lusitania* and the deaths of 1,200 passengers shocked Americans. Germany did not show much remorse and even designed this medal (above) to commemorate the attack. **Drawing Inferences** *How strongly did Wilson respond to the sinking of the* Lusitania?

navy in Europe. When war came, Germany chose not to risk the loss of its ships and kept all but the U-boats in port.

The German High Seas Fleet did make one attempt to enter the North Sea and confront the British fleet in 1916. The British encountered the Germans north of Denmark, where at the ensuing Battle of Jutland both fleets suffered heavy losses. Neither Britain nor Germany could claim victory, and the German fleet returned to port after the battle. This stalemate meant that the U-boat was the only tool the Germans had to fight the British blockade and to target Allied shipping and transport.

Passenger and merchant ships had no defense against the submarine, which could go undetected nearly anywhere in the ocean. Only gradually did the British develop devices called hydrophones that could detect the sound of a submarine underwater. Although Americans generally accepted Britain's blockade of Germany, the German efforts to blockade Britain with submarine attacks struck many as uncivilized.

The British encouraged such anti-German feelings. Shortly after the war began, the British cut the transatlantic cable connecting Germany and the United States. All news of the European front henceforth flowed through London. The pro-Allied bias of news reports helped shape the opinion of the people in the United States in favor of punishing Germany for its use of submarines against Britain.

American public opinion of the Germans declined further on May 7, 1915, when a U-boat sighted the *Lusitania*, a British passenger liner, in the Irish Sea. Suspecting correctly that the ship carried weapons for the Allies, the U-boat fired on the liner. Eighteen minutes later, the *Lusitania* disappeared beneath the waves along with almost 1,200 passengers. Included among the dead were 128 Americans, who had boarded the *Lusitania* in spite of German warnings to stay off British ships. Nevertheless, the American press wildly denounced what they called Germany's act of "barbarism."

Viewing History At first urging patience, Wilson insisted that Germany change its policy and demanded reparations, but did not go to war.

RESOURCE DIRECTORY
Technology
RESOURCE **PRO**® **Critical Thinking Activity**
Identifying Central Issues: Provocations of War, found on Resource Pro, encourages students to apply this skill by examining a 1917 political cartoon.
RESOURCE **PRO**® **Visual Learning Activity**
Uncle Sam's Pledge, found on Resource Pro, uses a Library of Congress drawing to show how symbols were used to promote public support for World War I.
Exploring Primary Sources in U.S. History
CD-ROM *Zimmermann Telegram*

Wilson urged patience. He demanded that Germany stop its submarine warfare and make payments to the victims' families. Germany's reply that the *Lusitania* carried small arms and ammunition did not quiet American anger. Wilson sent a second, stronger note of protest. In response, Germany promised to stop sinking passenger ships without warning, as long as the ship's crew offered no resistance to German search or seizure.

Still, U-boats continued to torpedo Allied ships. On March 24, 1916, a German submarine torpedoed the *Sussex,* a French passenger steamship. The attack killed or injured 80 passengers, including two Americans. The United States threatened to cut diplomatic ties to Germany. In what came to be called the **Sussex pledge,** the German government again promised that U-boats would warn ships before attacking.

The series of demands and broken promises that led up to the Sussex pledge frustrated Wilson. He could not threaten force without entering the war. During this time, however, Wilson did embrace the concept of preparedness. He also authorized bankers to make a huge loan to the Allies. American neutrality was beginning to weaken.

Moving Toward War

In the presidential election of 1916, Wilson ran for reelection on the slogan "He kept us out of war." The Republicans, who nominated Supreme Court Justice Charles Evans Hughes, criticized Wilson for not taking a stronger stand against Germany. American voters gave Wilson a narrow victory.

Germany soon tested Wilson's patience. On January 31, 1917, Germany informed the United States that it would end the Sussex pledge and resume unrestricted submarine warfare the following day. German strategists knew that it might bring the United States into the war. But they gambled that they could defeat Britain and win the war in France before American entry could make a difference.

Germany's action dashed Wilson's hope of maintaining freedom of the seas—and American neutrality. On February 3, the United States broke off diplomatic relations with Germany. A few weeks later, Wilson asked Congress for permission to arm American merchant ships.

The Zimmermann Note   Despite the announcement, the German Navy avoided attacking American ships in February. As a result, the American public continued to hope for peace. In the Senate, a group of antiwar senators tried to prevent a vote on Wilson's initiative to arm ships. While these senators stalled the initiative, the British revealed the contents of an intercepted German telegram. In the note, Arthur Zimmermann, Germany's foreign secretary, made a secret offer to Mexico. If Mexico declared war on the United States, he wrote, Germany would reward it with American land in the Southwest.

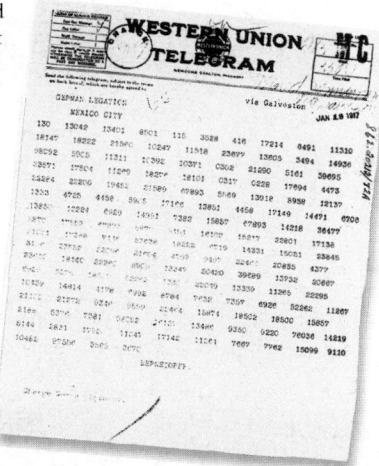

> ❝ *We shall endeavor to keep the United States neutral. In the event of this not succeeding, we make Mexico a proposal of alliance. . . : Make war together, make peace together, . . . and . . . Mexico is to reconquer the lost territory in Texas, New Mexico, and Arizona.* ❞
> —Arthur Zimmermann

VIEWING HISTORY The Zimmermann note, shown here in its original code, infuriated many Americans with its promise to give American land to Mexico.
Recognizing Cause and Effect *Why did the Zimmermann note threaten Americans more directly than German submarine attacks?*

Section 2 Assessment

Reading Comprehension

1. Answers should include: ships had no warning or defense against U-boats; submarines attacked American and other neutral ships; the German government broke its promises about restricting its submarines.

2. (a) It created a temporary peace. (b) By resuming unrestricted submarine warfare, Germany hoped to defeat Britain and win the war in France before American entry into the war could make a difference.

3. Though Wilson did not take it seriously, the Zimmermann note enraged Americans because it was an attempt to secretly draw Mexico into the war and ultimately reward it with U.S. territory.

Critical Thinking and Writing

4. Sample answer: The United States would have had to keep its commercial vessels out of waters patrolled by U-boats. This would have been politically unpopular and economically damaging.

5. Answers may vary, but should chronicle Germany's use of the submarine, the sinking of unarmed ships, and the dissolving of the Sussex pledge.

Take It to the NET

Posters will vary, but should convey the importance of the specific job, the idea that women in the workforce were vital to the country's success, and a sense of patriotism.

Focus on CITIZENSHIP

The Price of Pacifism One of the fifty votes against the House war resolution came from Montana's Representative Jeannette Rankin, the first woman elected to Congress. Elected only a few months earlier, she said, "I want to stand by my country, but I cannot vote for war." Rankin faced a strong backlash over her vote. The Republican Party refused to nominate her for the Senate in 1918. She ran as an independent candidate but lost.

Rankin returned to Congress in 1941. When Japan bombed Pearl Harbor that December and the President asked Congress for a declaration of war, Rankin voted no once again.

Neither Wilson nor Mexico took the **Zimmermann note** seriously. Already divided by civil war, Mexico could not have launched a successful invasion of the United States. The telegram's release, however, scored another public relations victory for Great Britain. The United States edged closer to war.

Revolution in Russia By early 1917, Russia already had suffered enormous casualties in the war: more than 1.5 million killed, roughly 2.5 million taken prisoner, and millions more wounded. Austro-Hungarian and German forces had advanced deep into Russian territory. Poorly fed and miserably equipped, the Russians fell back farther and farther into their country's interior.

Then, in March 1917, Czar Nicholas II, Russia's autocratic leader, was forced to give up the throne. The Russian monarchy was replaced with a republican government. This **Russian Revolution** cheered the prowar faction in the United States. Concern over being allied with the autocratic government of the czar had slowed the nation's move toward entry into the war. The fall of the czar removed a last stumbling block to joining the Allies.

The War Resolution Between March 16 and March 18, Germany sank the United States ships *City of Memphis, Illinois,* and *Vigilancia.* Wilson's patience had run out. On March 20, the President's Cabinet voted unanimously for war. Casting the issue in idealistic terms, Wilson told Congress on April 2 that "the world must be made safe for democracy." He stated:

> ❝ It is a fearful thing to lead this great peaceful people into war, the most terrible and disastrous of all wars, civilization itself seeming to be in the balance. But the right is more precious than peace. ❞
> —Woodrow Wilson

Members of Congress, ambassadors, and Supreme Court justices stood up and cheered the President's call to war. A war resolution passed 82 to 6 in the Senate and 373 to 50 in the House. On April 6, 1917, the President signed it.

Section 2 Assessment

READING COMPREHENSION

1. Why did Germany's use of **U-boats** lead to conflict with the United States?

2. (a) How did the **Sussex pledge** affect relations between the United States and Germany? (b) Why did Germany end the pledge?

3. Why did the **Zimmermann note** enrage Americans?

CRITICAL THINKING AND WRITING

4. **Identifying Alternatives** Consider the causes that brought the United States into World War I. (a) What would the United States have had to do to avoid the conflict altogether? (b) Why did the United States not take such steps?

5. **Writing to Inform** Write a paragraph explaining why President Wilson asked Congress to arm American merchant ships.

Take It to the NET

Activity: Creating a Poster
Research some of the women's organizations that contributed to the war effort in Europe. Create a recruitment poster encouraging women to join one of these organizations. Use the links provided in the *America: Pathways to the Present* area of the following Web site for help in completing this activity.
www.phschool.com

RESOURCE DIRECTORY

Americans on the European Front

READING FOCUS

- How did the United States prepare to fight in World War I?
- In what ways did American troops help turn the tide of war?
- What were conditions like in Europe and in the United States at the end of the war?

MAIN IDEA

American troops helped the Allies defeat the Central Powers in World War I.

KEY TERMS

Selective Service Act
American Expeditionary Force (AEF)
convoy
zeppelin
armistice
genocide

TAKING NOTES

Copy this flowchart. As you read, fill in the boxes with significant events, beginning with the declaration of war by the United States and ending with the Allied victory. The first box has been completed to help you get started.

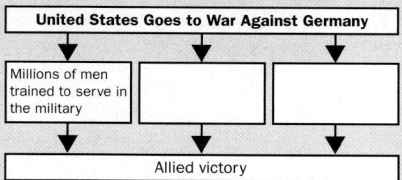

United States Goes to War Against Germany

Millions of men trained to serve in the military

Allied victory

SECTION OBJECTIVES

1. Analyze the preparations of the United States for World War I.
2. Study the ways in which the American troops helped turn the tide of the war.
3. Learn about conditions in Europe and the United States at the end of the war.

BELLRINGER

Warm-Up Activity Are allies automatically equals? Can allies exist without a common enemy? Ask students what kinds of relationships allies share.

Activating Prior Knowledge Have students list five ways in which the entry of the United States into the war would change the Allies' situation. Then have them list five ways in which the entry of the United States into the war would change the Central Powers' situation.

READING STRATEGY

Ask students to create a list of this section's boldfaced headings and sub-headings. Under each one, have them write a one-sentence prediction of what the content will be. Then have them check their predictions against the actual text.

Setting the Scene Woodrow Wilson brought the United States into war with the support of Congress and most of the country. But in April 1917, despite the success of the preparedness movement, the United States was far from ready to send an army to the European front. With a little more than 100,000 men in uniform, the United States army was outranked in size by the armies of 16 other countries. The country's 15,500 marines were far from Europe, patrolling several Central American countries and American possessions in the Pacific. The National Guard, 132,000 strong, needed training. The United States was simply not ready for war.

The Allies desperately needed replacement troops. In June, President Wilson agreed to send a small force to Europe under the command of General John J. Pershing. A veteran of the Spanish-American War, the general had also taught for a time at West Point. Pershing would need all his experience and skills to lead the American forces against a determined German army.

Preparing for War

Instead of a full-sized army, a cautious Congress sent the Allies naval support, supplies, arms, and $3 billion in loans. The token force of 14,500 men led by General Pershing served mainly to boost Allied morale. After landing in France, Pershing realized that he needed more troops. He recommended that the army number 1 million men by 1918 and 3 million the following year.

Draftees and Volunteers Congress passed a **Selective Service Act** in May 1917, authorizing a draft of young men for military service. During the Civil War, the draft had sparked riots. Now, however, the general feeling that this was the "war to end all wars" led to wide acceptance of the draft. By November 1918, more than 24 million men had registered for the draft. From those, a lottery picked 3 million draftees to serve in the war. Volunteers and National Guardsmen made up the remainder of what was called the **American Expeditionary Force (AEF).**

VIEWING HISTORY James Montgomery Flagg's poster called on Americans to join the military. **Drawing Inferences** *Why do you think this poster was effective?*

CAPTION ANSWERS

Viewing History It inspired patriotism while at the same time bringing the war to a personal level, making a direct appeal to the viewer.

RESOURCE DIRECTORY

Teaching Resources
Guided Reading and Review booklet, p. 80

Technology
Section Reading Support Transparencies
Guided Reading Audiotapes (English/Spanish), Ch. 19
Student Edition on Audio CD, Ch. 19
Color Transparencies *Cause-and-Effect Charts,* D8

RESOURCE PRO® **Primary Source Activity**
Women on the War Front, found on Resource Pro, uses an excerpt from *Two Colored*

Women with the American Expeditionary Forces to show how African American women contributed to the war effort.
Prentice Hall Presentation Pro CD-ROM, Ch. 19
Companion Web site, www.phschool.com

Focus Point out that the United States quickly became fully involved in the war. Ask what roles Americans played abroad. How did American efforts affect the war?

Instruct Discuss why President Wilson preferred to send money and supplies to the Allies rather than troops. Ask students what the difficulties are in organizing an army in a short amount of time. Have them list the steps required to create an army large enough to fight a war on the scale of World War I.

Ask students to locate on a map the major battles of the war involving Americans and to describe their outcomes.

Ask what events turned the tide of the war. What role did American troops play in ending the war? Ask students why they think the Allies insisted on total surrender.

Assess/Reteach Have students list the European countries involved in World War I. Ask students to create lists of descriptive phrases to describe each country's likely response to the entry of the United States into the war.

ACTIVITY

Connecting with Citizenship

Tell students to form two groups—one made up of American soldiers just arriving in France and the other made up of British and French soldiers who have been stationed at the Western Front. Have students conduct a role-playing exercise in which the Allied soldiers orient the Americans. Tell members of the American Expeditionary Force to ask questions about what has been going on and what they can expect to do and see. **(Bodily/Kinesthetic)**

CAPTION ANSWERS

Viewing History Most soldiers were new to the armed forces and needed to learn how to dig trenches and fight with bayonets and modern weapons.

VIEWING HISTORY New soldiers learn how to attack with bayonets at a training camp in the United States. **Recognizing Cause and Effect** *Why was training important to the war effort?*

Among the Americans who served their country were thousands of women. Some 11,000 women volunteered to serve in uniform as nurses, drivers, and clerks. Another 14,000 women served abroad, as civilians working for the government or for private agencies.

Training for War The military's next challenge was to transform draftees into soldiers who were armed and ready to fight. In September, draftees began to arrive at new and expanded training camps around the country. At these camps, they learned how to use a bayonet and a rifle, dig a trench, put on a gas mask, and throw a grenade. American and British lecturers told them about German crimes in Belgium and the strategies of trench warfare.

The military planned to give new soldiers several months of training in the United States and France before shipping them off to battle. In reality, soldiers did not always receive that much training. The task of building an army of millions and transporting it to France in time to be of help meant that training would sometimes be cut short.

The Convoy System In addition to building a fighting force, the War Department had to worry about transporting its troops overseas safely. In April 1917 alone, German U-boats had sunk more than 400 Allied and neutral ships.

Starting in May 1917, all merchant and troop ships traveled in a **convoy.** A convoy consisted of a group of unarmed ships surrounded by a ring of destroyers, torpedo boats, and other armed naval vessels equipped with hydrophones to track and destroy submarines. Between April and December 1917, merchant marine losses dropped by half.

The convoy system was remarkably successful in carrying American troops to Europe. Despite several scares, U-boats did not sink a single United States troopship traveling to Europe. A relatively small number of Americans lost their lives on the return trip.

Focus on CITIZENSHIP

Conscientious Objectors Some men refused to fight when they were drafted. Most of these men belonged to religious groups that opposed war, such as the Quakers. They were known as "conscientious objectors" because they objected to fighting as a matter of conscience. Most conscientious objectors were allowed to serve in a noncombatant (nonfighting) position. Sometimes they were resented by other soldiers. General Leonard Wood called conscientious objectors "enemies of the Republic, fakers and active agents of the enemy."

American Soldiers in Europe From the time the AEF arrived in France in June 1917, Pershing kept American troops independent of the Allied armies. In Pershing's view, the Allies had become too accustomed to defensive action. He wanted to save his men's strength for offensive moves.

American troops surprised the British and French soldiers on the front lines with their strength, good health, and energy. They resembled the European soldiers who had gone to war in 1914, not the exhausted forces that survived after several years of fighting. By 1918, European armies could only recruit new soldiers among much older men, boys turning 18, and wounded soldiers returning from the hospital.

Members of the American Expeditionary Force were called doughboys, although no one is sure why. The nickname had been in use for years, but it stuck with World War I soldiers. The name could have come from the white adobe dust that stuck to the boots of soldiers during the Mexican War. On the other hand, Civil War soldiers might have picked up the nickname from their uniform buttons, which looked like flour dumplings, or from the white flour they used to keep their belts white.

RESOURCE DIRECTORY

Technology
Sounds of an Era Audio CD *General Pershing,* 1917 recording (time: 30 seconds)
RESOURCE PRO® **Biography** *Henry Johnson,* found on Resource Pro, profiles the most famous African American soldier of World War I.

The more than 300,000 African Americans who volunteered or were drafted served in segregated units. Most black soldiers never saw combat, though many fought with distinction and nearly 4,000 died or were wounded. The marines refused to accept African Americans altogether, and the navy used them for menial tasks only. The army, too, used African Americans mostly for manual labor.

These assignments distressed many African Americans. The 369th Infantry Regiment, which came to be known as the Harlem Hell Fighters, was especially eager to fight. Its members persuaded their white officers to loan the regiment to the French, who integrated the regiment into the French army. Because of their distinguished service, the entire regiment received France's highest combat medal, the Croix de Guerre.

Turning the Tide of War

As American involvement in the war expanded, events in Russia shook the alliance. In November 1917, followers of Vladimir Lenin, called Bolsheviks, violently overthrew Russia's republican government. Until that spring, Lenin had been living in Switzerland. He had promised to make peace with Germany if he successfully won control of his native land, and for that reason Germany helped arrange his return to Russia.

Lenin signed a truce with Germany in December and a final peace treaty on March 3, 1918. Germany won vast territories in western Russia that included much of the country's industry and richest farmland. More important, Russia's exit from the war freed the Germans from the two-front war they had been forced to fight. Germany sent hundreds of thousands of troops west for one final offensive before American troops could reinforce the British and French armies in large numbers.

German forces attacked British lines on March 21, 1918. For the first time since 1914, they successfully broke through the trenches and advanced deep into Allied territory. Their aim was to split British troops in northern France from French armies to the east, and eventually to capture Paris. From March through May 1918, German forces turned all their energies toward pounding the French and British lines. By the end of May, they were only about 50 miles from Paris.

Americans Save Paris American forces came to the rescue. General Pershing dispatched troops to the front to turn back the German offensive. American troops attacked and recaptured the village of Cantigny on May 28. One week later, soldiers from the Marine Corps and the army stopped German attacks at Belleau Wood and Château-Thierry, east of Paris. Marching out from Paris, the men received this word from their leader, Brigadier General James G. Harbord: "We dig no trenches to fall back on. The Marines will hold where they stand." At the battle of Château-Thierry, they did just that.

The Western Front, 1917–1918

Allies
Central Powers
Neutral nations
Limit of final German advance, 1918
American Expeditionary Force attacks
Armistice Line, Nov. 11, 1918
Major battle

Ypres, 3rd battle, July 31–Nov. 10, 1917
Cantigny, May 28, 1918
Belleau Wood, June 6–July 1, 1918
Meuse-Argonne offensive, Sept. 26–Nov. 11, 1918
Château-Thierry, June 4, 1918
St. Mihiel, Sept. 12–16, 1918
Marne, 2nd battle, July 18–Aug. 6, 1918

MAP SKILLS After the final German offensive faltered, American troops helped the British and French push the Germans back across land Germany had held since the start of the war. General Pershing (above, center) directed American forces in Europe. **Place** *In what region of France did American troops have the greatest impact?*

Chapter 19 Section 3 • **659**

TEST PREPARATION

Have students read the first two paragraphs under the heading "Turning the Tide of War" and then answer the question below.

How did Lenin's victory in the Russian Revolution affect the course of World War I?

A There was no effect.

Ⓑ Germany and Russia signed a truce.

C France and Russia signed a truce.

D Lenin's victory caused the United States to enter the war.

ACTIVITY
Connecting with History and Conflict

Ask students to research the impact of John J. Pershing during World War I. Have students analyze his actions and their importance to the war effort, including his determination not to mix American troops with those of other countries. **(Verbal/Linguistic)**

BACKGROUND
A Diverse Nation

African Americans entered the war only after passage of the Selective Service Act, which allowed *all* able-bodied American men between the ages of 21 and 31 to enlist. The Harlem Hell Fighters got their name from the French and Germans, who were impressed with the persistence of the 369th Infantry. On September 29, 1918, this unit engaged in heavy combat, capturing the town of Sechault, along with prisoners, cannons, and machine guns. Then the 369th Infantry led a dawn assault on the enemy, overpowering the Germans.

CAPTION ANSWERS

Map Skills American troops had the greatest impact on France east of Paris.

Trench Warfare on the Western Front

Artillery bombardments turned the "no man's land" into rough terrain that slowed advancing infantry.

Underground "dugout" shelters allowed soldiers to take cover during enemy bombardment.

Periscopes allowed soldiers to observe the enemy without making themselves vulnerable to gunfire.

Sandbags protected soldiers from enemy bullets.

A "fire step" boosted troops above sandbags to shoot at the enemy.

ACTIVITY
Connecting with Geography

To analyze significant events such as the battle of Argonne Forest, have students make a detailed map of France showing the locations mentioned in the text—the Marne river, Paris, Amiens, St. Mihiel, the Argonne Forest, and the region of the Meuse river. Tell students to identify where and when the battles took place. **(Visual/Spatial)**

BACKGROUND
Geography in History

The Meuse-Argonne Offensive was a very difficult campaign. There were numerous obstacles. The land to the north of Verdun was in disarray as a result of previous battles. It was difficult for tanks to get through the Argonne Forest, which was located in a mass of rivers and ridges. In addition to the physical obstacles, the American soldiers were inexperienced. Fortunately, the British had secured a huge supply of high-explosive shells, as well as a copy of the Germans' battle plans.

READING CHECK

American soldiers drove the Germans out of their heavily defended position at St. Mihiel in September 1918. Later that month, more than one million men of the American Expeditionary Force participated in a major Allied offensive in the Meuse-Argonne region of northern France. This attack routed the Germans and forced the German army into headlong retreat.

INTERPRETING DIAGRAMS
Protected by rows of barbed wire, sandbags, and armed soldiers, trenches were very difficult to capture. Neither side could advance on the Western Front without losing thousands of men in the attack. **Drawing Inferences** *How did tanks overcome the obstacles of barbed wire, sandbags, and enemy guns?*

READING CHECK
How did American soldiers contribute to the Allied counterattack?

At a loss of over half of their troops, they helped the French save Paris, blunted the edge of the German advance, and began to turn the tide of the war.

In mid-July, the Germans launched a massive attack on French positions on the river Marne. The French were joined by 28,000 American troops in a counter-attack that forced the Germans back across the river and into retreat. The Second Battle of the Marne ended any German hopes for victory.

Allied Counterattack   After turning back the Germans outside Paris, the Allies took heart. About 250,000 new American soldiers were arriving in France each month, and thousands more were ready to leave training camps in France for the front line.

Using a new weapon, the tank, which could cross trenches and roll through barbed wire, the Allies began to break the German lines. On August 8, at the battle of Amiens, the Allied armies stopped the German advance in the north and recaptured Germany's gains from earlier in the year. General von Ludendorff, sensing the end was near, called it the "black day of the German army." He advised Kaiser Wilhelm to seek a peace settlement. The Allies, however, insisted on total surrender before peace talks.

In September, some 500,000 American troops, assisted by 100,000 French soldiers, began to hit the final German strongholds. In the battle of St. Mihiel, the first major military effort entirely in American hands, General Pershing and his troops ousted the Germans from a long-held position. The final Allied assault, the Meuse-Argonne Offensive, began on September 26, 1918. Over a million AEF troops began the drive to expel the Germans from France and to cut their supply lines. Soon after, the German army was in full retreat from the Argonne Forest and the region of the Meuse river.

War in the Air   The Americans entered the war with only 55 planes, all too primitive to use in war. The United States quickly manufactured hundreds of planes to match the technology used by the Allies. Very different from modern aircraft, World War I planes were built from wooden frames covered with cloth. The pilot, and sometimes a copilot, sat in an open-air cockpit.

CAPTION ANSWERS

Interpreting Diagrams Tanks were able to roll right over these obstacles with their heavy, durable treads.

RESOURCE DIRECTORY

Other Print Resources
Historical Outline Map Book *The Western Front, 1914–1918,* p. 61

Technology
Color Transparencies *The Way It Works,* H15, H16

RESOURCE PRO® **Literature Activity**
A Poet Describes War, found on Resource Pro, uses e. e. cummings's short poem, "look at this," to express the tragedy of war.

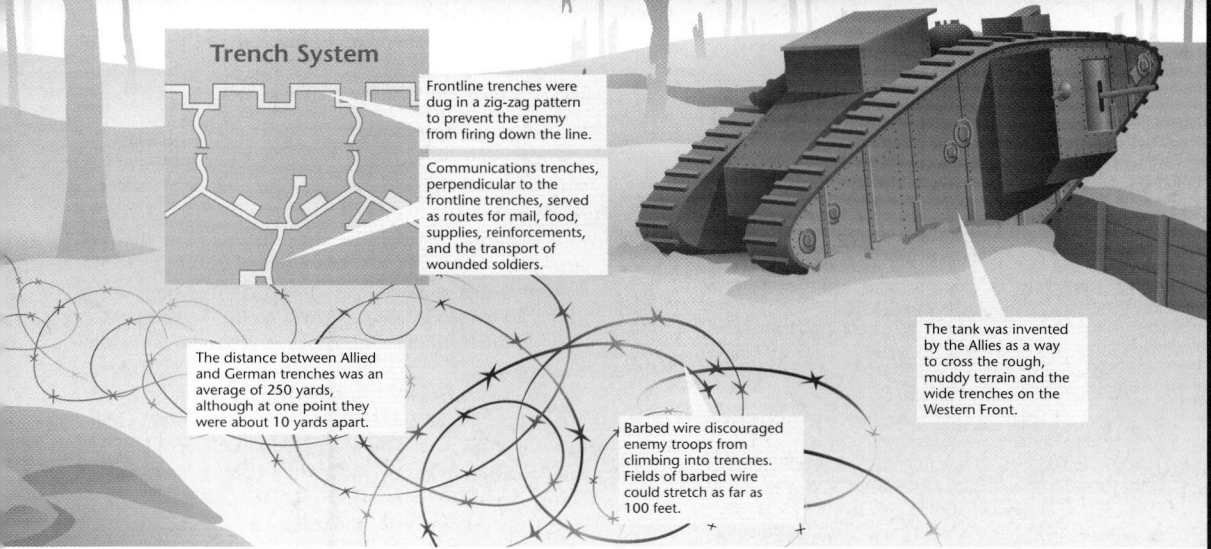

Trench System

Frontline trenches were dug in a zig-zag pattern to prevent the enemy from firing down the line.

Communications trenches, perpendicular to the frontline trenches, served as routes for mail, food, supplies, reinforcements, and the transport of wounded soldiers.

The distance between Allied and German trenches was an average of 250 yards, although at one point they were about 10 yards apart.

Barbed wire discouraged enemy troops from climbing into trenches. Fields of barbed wire could stretch as far as 100 feet.

The tank was invented by the Allies as a way to cross the rough, muddy terrain and the wide trenches on the Western Front.

Aircraft were first used to scout enemy positions, but soon flyers engaged each other in dogfights with pistols and later with machine guns. Each side had its "aces," such as the American Captain Eddie Rickenbacker, who downed 26 enemy fighters. Pilots also shot down hot-air balloons that were used for observation, and fired on individual soldiers on the ground. German **zeppelins**, or floating airships, and German bombers launched more than 100 raids on London, killing almost 1,500 civilians.

The airplane took on a new role in the 1918 offensive. American Colonel Billy Mitchell organized a fleet of more than 1,400 planes to drop bombs on enemy positions and on the railroads that carried supplies to the front. Bombing was not very effective at destroying targets, but frequent bombing raids frightened and confused enemy soldiers. Bombing raids would become a devastating weapon in the future.

Ending the War

The Allies pressed on against their enemy. The Central Powers collapsed, one by one, in the face of Allied attacks and domestic revolutions. Two of Germany's allies, Bulgaria and the Ottoman Empire, made a separate peace with the Allies in autumn. Austria-Hungary splintered in October as Poles, Hungarians, Czechs, and Slovaks declared their independence from the emperor.

The German commanders begged for peace, still hoping to dictate some terms before the fighting crossed onto German soil. The Allies refused. In the last week of October, the German naval command ordered the fleet to leave port and confront the British Navy for one final battle. Sailors in the German port of Kiel recognized that defeat was only a matter of time and further fighting would cause needless loss of life, so they mutinied on October 29. The revolt quickly spread to other ships and ports as well as to factories and industrial cities, pressuring the generals to bring the war to an end. By November 10, the Kaiser had fled to Holland. A civilian representative of the new German

James Cochran was an American soldier from Philadelphia who died in the war at the age of 19. His family honored his memory with a locket containing a photograph and a lock of his hair.

to Today

Bomber Planes

Airplanes equipped with bombs came late to the war and played a minor role in the fighting. Early planes were limited by how far and how fast they could fly and how well they could attack other planes. World War I-era planes averaged a speed of 100 miles per hour and carried about 1,750 pounds of bombs. Their guns were only effective on targets up to about 200 yards away.

Today Once a helpful tool for armies, fighter and bomber planes have replaced ground troops altogether in some campaigns. In the 1990s, the United States attacked Yugoslavia with air power alone. Bombers can launch airstrikes against factories, roads, railroads, and enemy positions with a much smaller risk of casualties.

The most advanced bombers are no longer limited by distance from a home base. In March 1999, two B-2 bombers took off from an air force base in Missouri and flew across the Atlantic to bomb targets in Yugoslavia. They returned to Missouri after the mission was completed—a total of 30 hours in the air without landing.

Modern planes fly faster and higher than their predecessors. B-2 bombers can fly at speeds approaching 600 miles per hour. The B-1B bomber can break the speed of sound, reaching 900 miles an hour, and carry 80,000 pounds of bombs.

? Why does the military rely so heavily on air power today?

Republic signed an **armistice,** or cease-fire, in a French railroad car at 5:00 AM on November 11, 1918. Six hours later, as agreed, the guns finally fell silent.

The Influenza Epidemic The last months of the war were darkened by an epidemic that killed more people worldwide than all of the wartime battles. American troops arriving in France in the spring of 1918 carried with them a new strain of an influenza virus that had been first detected in a military training camp in Kansas in March. The virus swept across the Western Front in June, disabling 500,000 German troops at the peak of their summer offensive, and then it vanished. But worse was to come.

The first cases were followed by a second, deadlier wave in the fall and a third wave in the winter. Unlike other flu viruses, the new variant struck people of all ages equally hard and could kill within a few days. A doctor described the effects of the disease at Fort Devens in Massachusetts, where an average of 100 people died each day:

> 66 *These men start with what appears to be an attack of LaGrippe or Influenza, and when brought to the [hospital] they very rapidly develop the most viscous type of Pneumonia that has ever been seen. Two hours after admission they have the Mahogany spots over the cheek bones. . . . It is only a matter of a few hours then until death comes, and it is simply a struggle for air until they suffocate. It is horrible.* 99
>
> —Anonymous

The virus spread easily in crowded, unsanitary conditions. Military bases and cities were particularly susceptible to outbreaks of influenza. San Francisco required citizens to wear surgical masks in public. After a parade led to an outbreak in Philadelphia, officials closed all schools, churches, and theaters. At the peak of the second wave in October, so many people died in a short period of time that gravediggers could not dig graves quickly enough.

Conditions were no better among American soldiers in Europe. The AEF suffered 16,000 cases of influenza in the first week of October alone, and the death rate in some units reached 32 percent. In a little under a year, more American soldiers died from influenza than from battle. Over half a million Americans and perhaps 30 million people worldwide died before the epidemic came to an end.

Results of the War The physical and mental scars of the war ran deep. About 50,000 American soldiers died in battle, and many more died of disease, mainly influenza. The toll would have been even greater but for the efforts of volunteer nurses serving their country through the Red Cross and other agencies.

Corporal Elmer Sherwood of Indiana, just 21 years old, wrote after one bloody battle in August 1918:

> 66 *Hundreds of bodies of our brave boys lie on Hill 212, captured with such a great loss of blood. We will never be able to explain war to our loved ones back home even if we . . . live and return.* 99
>
> —Corporal Elmer Sherwood

American losses were tiny compared with those suffered by the Europeans. The total death toll of 8 million soldiers and sailors is only an estimate. Still, this figure averages out to more than 5,000 soldiers killed on each day of the war. Germany, Austria-Hungary, Russia, and France all suffered more than a million dead. About 900,000 troops from Britain and its empire died. While most of the fighting and dying took place in Europe, there were battles in the Middle East and Africa as well. Survivors sensed that the war had destroyed a whole generation of young men. Their deaths were mourned not only by those who knew them, but by their countries, which would suffer the loss of their talents and abilities as well as the loss of future generations.

In every major country, the sick and wounded outnumbered the dead. Thousands of soldiers had lost limbs to bullets and artillery shells. Doctors amputated feet infected with "trench foot," a disease developed from spending too much time in wet, muddy trenches. Poison gas attacks blinded many soldiers permanently and caused long-lasting lung damage.

The suffering extended beyond the battlefields. Millions of civilians died during and immediately after the fighting, from starvation, disease, or war-related injuries. These deaths included hundreds of thousands of Armenian civilians. In a campaign of **genocide,** or the organized killing of an entire people, Ottoman forces deported and murdered Armenians, whom they suspected of disloyalty to the government. The killings of Armenians would continue into the early 1920s.

BIOGRAPHY

Corporal York 1887–1964

Many acts of heroism shone during the final months of the war. But the bravery of Corporal Alvin York during the Meuse-Argonne offensive stood out above the rest. On October 8, York's patrol tried to destroy a German machine-gun nest, losing half its men in the attempt. Facing heavy machine-gun fire, the remaining soldiers took cover. York continued the attack on his own, killing 25 machine-gunners with his rifle and pistol and capturing 132 German soldiers.

When a general asked about his exploits, York replied, "General, I would hate to think I missed any of them shots; they were all at pretty close range—50 or 60 yards." For his heroism above and beyond the call of duty, York received the Congressional Medal of Honor as well as the French Croix de Guerre.

Reading Comprehension

1. They enabled new recruits to be protected and safely transported to Europe.

2. (a) The U.S. army was outranked in size, marines were patrolling Central American countries and Pacific possessions, and the National Guard needed training. (b) President Wilson sent the Allies a token force of 14,500 men, led by General Pershing; naval support; supplies; arms; and $3 billion in loans.

3. The collapse of the Central Powers, due to Allied attacks and domestic revolutions, led troops to recognize that defeat was imminent. A mutiny at the port of Kiel led to other German troop revolts on ships, as well as at ports, factories, and industrial cities.

4. The tank, which could cross trenches and roll through barbed wire, enabled Allies to break the German lines. Aircraft were used to scout enemy positions, in direct combat, and to drop bombs.

Critical Thinking and Writing

5. (a) American losses: about 50,000 soldiers to battle, many more to disease. German and French losses: more than a million each. British losses: just under 900,000. (b) Answers will vary, but should include reference to the wounded, loss to future generations, and the extensive, ongoing physical and psychological suffering.

6. Students' time lines may vary, but should include entries chronicling the events from April 1917 to November 1918.

Section 3 Assessment

READING COMPREHENSION

1. Why were **convoys** important to American war efforts?

2. (a) In what ways was the United States unprepared to help the Allies in 1917? (b) In what ways did the United States offer immediate help?

3. Why did Germany agree to an **armistice** in November 1918?

4. How did new weapons change the way that soldiers fought during the war?

CRITICAL THINKING AND WRITING

5. **Analyzing Information** (a) How did America's losses in the war compare to those of Germany, France, and Britain? (b) How might these losses have affected how the people in these countries remember World War I?

6. **Creating a Time Line** Create a time line of all the major wartime events that involved the United States.

 Take It to the NET

Enrichment Explore how the influenza epidemic of 1918 affected soldiers and civilians in Europe and in the United States. Then write a brief summary of a section that interested you. Use the links provided in the *America: Pathways to the Present* area of the following Web site for help in completing this activity.
www.phschool.com

 **Take It to the NET**

Answers will vary, but could focus on the epidemic in the United States on the battlefield or international effects of the flu. Students should note the high infection and mortality rates and any measures taken to contain the epidemic.

Americans on the Home Front

SECTION OBJECTIVES

1. Learn about the steps the government took to finance the war and manage the economy.
2. Describe how the government enforced loyalty to the war effort.
3. Find out how the war changed the lives of Americans on the home front.

BELLRINGER

Warm-Up Activity Ask students what the term *home front* implies about the nature of American life during the war. Why could life not continue normally while the nation was involved in a war overseas?

Activating Prior Knowledge World War I brought many women into the paid labor force for the first time. How might this change have affected American families? Ask students to name some other periods of time during the twentieth century when women entered the paid labor force in large numbers.

READING STRATEGY

Tell students that as they read, they should look for evidence to support the following statement, which appears on this page: "Waging war required many sacrifices at home." On a sheet of paper, have students describe the economic effects of World War I on the United States.

CAPTION ANSWERS

Viewing History They are not depicted as human, but rather as savage and bloodthirsty.

READING FOCUS

- What steps did the government take to finance the war and manage the economy?
- How did the government enforce loyalty to the war effort?
- How did the war change the lives of Americans on the home front?

MAIN IDEA

Americans and their government took extraordinary steps at home to support the war effort.

KEY TERMS

Liberty Bond
price controls
rationing
daylight saving time
sedition
vigilante

TAKING NOTES

As you read, prepare an outline of this section. Use Roman numerals to indicate the major headings of this section, capital letters for the subheadings, and numbers for the supporting details. The sample below will help you get started.

> **I. Financing the War**
> **II. Managing the Economy**
>   **A. New agencies are founded to organize the economy.**
>   **1. War Industries Board oversees production.**
>   **2.** _____
>   **3.** _____
>   **B.** _____

Setting the Scene

> " *I hate war, because war is murder, desolation and destruction. If one-tenth of what has been spent on preparedness for war had been spent on the prevention of war the world would always have been at peace.* "
>
> —Henry Ford

Henry Ford's words appeared in the *Detroit Free Press* on August 12, 1915, when the United States still practiced neutrality. Ford vowed that he would burn down his factories before allowing them to make goods for the war in Europe.

Two years later, the United States was at war, and Ford had orders to build 16,000 tanks and 20,000 tractors for the United States government. A new Ford factory that would build anti-submarine ships was rising in Dearborn, Michigan, with the help of $10 million in federal aid. Henry Ford and his workers, along with the rest of the nation, had joined the war effort.

Waging war required many sacrifices at home. Despite the efforts of the preparedness movement, the American economy was not ready to meet the demands of modern warfare. War required huge amounts of money and personnel. As President Wilson explained, now "there are no armies . . . ; there are entire nations armed."

Financing the War

The government launched a vigorous campaign to raise money from the American people. It borrowed money by selling **Liberty Bonds,** special war bonds to support the Allied cause. Like all bonds, they could later be redeemed for the original value of the bonds plus interest. By selling war bonds to enthusiastic Americans, Secretary of the Treasury William Gibbs McAdoo raised more than $20 billion. These funds allowed the United States to pay about one quarter of its war costs and still loan more than $10 billion to the Allies during and just after the war.

VIEWING HISTORY The United States government used posters to whip up sentiment against the "Huns"—the Germans—and to sell bonds to fund the war effort. **Recognizing Bias** *How does this poster depict German soldiers?*

RESOURCE DIRECTORY

Teaching Resources
Guided Reading and Review booklet, p. 81

Technology
Section Reading Support Transparencies
Guided Reading Audiotapes (English/Spanish), Ch. 19
Student Edition on Audio CD, Ch. 19
Sounds of an Era Audio CD *"Over There,"* 1917 recording (time: 40 seconds)

RESOURCE PRO® **Literature Activity**
Selling the War, found on Resource Pro, uses an excerpt from the propaganda folder *Why America Fights Germany* to show how the government galvanized popular sentiment against Germany.
Prentice Hall Presentation Pro CD-ROM, Ch. 19
Companion Web site, www.phschool.com

Responding to the slogan "Every Scout to Save a Soldier," Boy Scouts and Girl Scouts set up booths on street corners and sold bonds. The government hired popular commercial artists to draw colorful posters and recruited famous screen actors to lead public rallies to buy bonds. An army of 75,000 "four-minute men" gave brief (four-minute) speeches before movies, plays, and school or union meetings to persuade audiences to buy bonds.

Buying war bonds was one of several ways that civilians could support Americans at the front and demonstrate their patriotism. Patriotism is the love of one's country and the willingness to fight to defend its ideals and institutions.

Managing the Economy

The government also called on industry to switch from producing commercial goods to war goods. In 1918, Wilson won authority to set up a huge bureaucracy to manage this process. Business leaders flocked to Washington to take up posts in thousands of new agencies. Because they gave their service for a token salary, they were called "dollar-a-year" men and women.

New Agencies A War Industries Board, headed by financier Bernard Baruch, oversaw the nation's war-related production. The board had far-reaching powers. It doled out raw materials, told manufacturers what and how much to produce, and even fixed prices.

A War Trade Board licensed foreign trade and punished firms suspected of dealing with the enemy. A National War Labor Board, set up in April 1918 under former President Taft, worked to settle any labor disputes that might disrupt the war effort. Labor leader Samuel Gompers promised to limit labor problems in war-production industries. A separate War Labor Policies Board, headed by Harvard law professor Felix Frankfurter, set standards for wages, hours, and working conditions in the war industries. Labor unions won limited rights to organize and bargain collectively.

Regulating Food and Fuel Consumption In August 1917, Congress passed the Lever Food and Fuel Control Act. This act gave the President the power to manage the production and distribution of foods and fuels vital to the war effort.

Using the slogan "Food will win the war," the government began to manage how much food people bought. Under the leadership of engineer and future President Herbert Hoover, the Food Administration worked to increase farm output and reduce waste. Hoover had the power to impose **price controls,**

Sounds of an Era

Listen to "Over There" and other sounds from the World War I era.

VIEWING HISTORY At this shipyard, women workers replaced men who left to join the military. **Synthesizing Information** *Based on this photograph, describe some of the changes that wartime brought to the workplace.*

665

שפּײַז װעט געװינען די קריעג!

איהר קומט אהער צו געפינען פֿרײַהײם.
יעצט מוזט איהר העלפֿען די צו בעשיצען
סיר מוזען די עללײַס פֿערזארגען מיט הײַ.
לאָזט קײן זאַך ניט גײן אין פֿערלוסט.

יונגשער סטײַטס פֿוד אַדמיניסטראציאן.

FOOD WILL WIN THE WAR
You came here seeking Freedom
You must now help to preserve it
WHEAT is needed for the allies
Waste nothing

VIEWING HISTORY The poster on the left, written in Yiddish, encouraged Jewish people who had immigrated to the United States from Eastern Europe to conserve food for the war effort. It was also printed in English and other languages to appeal to as many immigrants as possible. **Determining Relevance** *How does this poster link the decision to come to America with aiding the war effort?*

---

a system of pricing determined by the government, on the sale of food. He also had the power to begin a system of **rationing**, or distributing goods to consumers in a fixed amount. But Hoover thought both these approaches went too far. He hoped instead that voluntary restraint and increased efficiency would accomplish the Food Administration's goals.

Women played a key role in Hoover's program. Writing to women in August 1917, he preached a "Gospel of the Clean Plate." He appealed:

> ❝ Stop, before throwing any food away, and ask 'Can it be used?' . . . Stop catering to different appetites. No second helpings. Stop all eating between meals. . . . One meatless day a week. One wheatless meal a day. . . . No butter in cooking: use substitutes. ❞
> —Herbert Hoover

"The American woman and the American home," Hoover concluded, "can bring to a successful end the greatest national task that has ever been accepted by the American people." Eager to take part in the war effort, women across the country responded to this patriotic challenge.

The Lever Food and Fuel Control Act also created an agency called the Fuel Administration. It sponsored gasless days to save fuel. This agency also began the practice of **daylight saving time**—turning clocks ahead one hour for the summer. By shifting an hour of sunlight from the early morning, when most people were asleep, to the evening, it increased the number of daylight hours available for work. Daylight saving time also reduced the need for artificial light and lowered fuel consumption.

Enforcing Loyalty

News and information also came under federal control during World War I. The government imposed censorship on the press and banned some publications from the mails. A film was banned and the producer jailed because it depicted British troops, America's allies, killing women and children during the American Revolution. The government challenged any media influences that threatened the war effort.

In 1917, George Creel, a Denver journalist and former muckraker, was appointed the head of the Committee on Public Information. His job was to rally popular support for the war. Creel's office coordinated the production of short films, pamphlets explaining war aims, and posters advertising recruitment and Liberty Bonds. Some of the slogans used were "Buy Bonds Till It Hurts" and "The Soldier Gives—You Must Lend."

Fear of Foreigners As in all wars, the fear of espionage, or spying, was widespread. A few months after the sinking of the *Lusitania*, a staff member of the German embassy left his briefcase on an American train. Inside the briefcase were plans for turning Americans against the Allies and disrupting the American economy.

The government feared that secret agents might try to undermine the war effort by destroying transportation or communication networks. The possibility of such acts of sabotage put the government on alert. It also generated calls for restrictions on immigration.

The National Security League, having won its battle for preparedness, began to preach "100 Percent Americanism." Early in 1917, the League got Congress to pass, over Wilson's veto, a literacy test for immigrants. This test

---

excluded those who could not read English or any other language. As it turned out, relatively few immigrants failed the test. Still, the test had set the stage for a vigorous revival of nativism.

"Hate the Hun!" Once the United States declared war, alertness for spies approached hysteria. The war also spurred a general hostility toward Germans. People began calling them Huns, in reference to a people who had brutally invaded Europe in the fourth and fifth centuries. High schools stopped teaching German. Books by German authors disappeared from library shelves, and German composers and musicians were banned from symphony concerts. German measles became "liberty measles," and a hamburger (which was named after Hamburg, a German city) became a Salisbury steak. Nervous dog-owners even renamed their German shepherds, calling them "police dogs" instead.

Anti-German sentiment had a more serious dimension. In April 1918, a mob lynched a German-born citizen named Robert Prager near St. Louis. Despite his German heritage, Prager had in fact tried to enlist in the navy. His lynching was but one of many wartime attacks on people of German descent.

Repression of Civil Liberties In his 1917 call for war on Germany, Wilson had claimed that the United States would be fighting for liberty and democracy. In that same war message, Wilson warned that disloyalty would be "dealt with with a firm hand of stern repression." His efforts to unite Americans against the enemy often prevailed over his promise to fight for liberty.

In 1917, Congress passed the Espionage Act, which made it illegal to interfere with the draft. The Espionage Act was amended in 1918 by the Sedition Act. (**Sedition** is any speech or action that encourages rebellion.) The Sedition Act made it illegal to obstruct the sale of Liberty Bonds or to discuss anything "disloyal, profane, scurrilous, or abusive" about the American form of government, the Constitution, or the army and the navy. The Sedition Act violated the First Amendment's guarantee of freedom of speech, but many felt that the needs of war required harsh measures.

The government pursued more than 1,500 prosecutions and won more than 1,000 convictions. Socialist and former presidential candidate Eugene V. Debs drew a ten-year jail sentence for criticizing the American government and business leaders and for urging people to "resist militarism."

Controlling Political Radicals Socialists such as Debs argued that the war was merely a fight among imperialist capitalists and that workers had no stake in the outcome. This view became a rallying point for antiwar sentiment. In the elections of 1917 in New York, Ohio, and Pennsylvania, Socialists made impressive gains.

The radical labor organization Industrial Workers of the World (IWW) also won new supporters from among western miners, migrant farm workers, and other unskilled laborers. They supported the IWW's goal of overthrowing capitalism and tried to interfere with copper mining during the war.

The views of Socialists and the IWW upset moderate labor leaders like Samuel Gompers, who had promised that unions would work with the war effort. The police hounded the IWW. Raids in September 1917 led to the conviction of nearly 200 members in trials held in Illinois, California, and Oklahoma. Groups of **vigilantes,** citizens who take the law into their own hands, lynched and horsewhipped others.

The IWW gained strength during World War I. It also became the target of the government's effort to control political radicals.

Chapter 19 • Section 4   **667**

ACTIVITY
Connecting with Citizenship

In 1917 Charles Schenck, General Secretary of the Socialist Party of the United States, printed and distributed a leaflet urging American men to resist the World War I army draft. He was arrested and tried under the Espionage Act. His case went all the way to the Supreme Court, where Chief Justice Oliver Wendell Holmes, writing for the majority, ruled that the government had a right to limit speech when there was a "clear and present danger" to other people. He compared Schenck's act to that of falsely yelling "Fire!" in a crowded theater.

Stage a debate in your classroom based on Justice Holmes's comparison. Have those who support and those who reject Justice Holmes's argument present examples to reinforce their opinions. (**Verbal/Linguistic**)

BACKGROUND
Recent Scholarship

Shortly after the United States declared war, Frances Witherspoon, suffragist, socialist, and daughter of a Mississippi congressman, was walking along New York's Fifth Avenue when she saw a foreigner being arrested after he asked an army recruiter questions. Appalled, she not only helped get the man released but later established the New York Bureau of Legal Advice to help others whose civil rights had been violated. After the war the Bureau coordinated amnesty campaigns for conscientious objectors and helped form the American Civil Liberties Union (ACLU). See Frances Early's *A World Without War: How U.S. Feminists and Pacifists Resisted World War I.*

Reading Comprehension

1. Price controls and rationing gave the President the ability to control the production and distribution of foods and fuels vital to the war effort.

2. Answers may include: Liberty Bonds, rationing, price controls, daylight savings time.

3. The government censored the press and banned certain films, thereby challenging any media influences that threatened the war effort.

Critical Thinking and Writing

4. (a) To raise money for the war costs. (b) By purchasing Liberty Bonds, civilians had a way of demonstrating their patriotism and supporting America's war efforts.

5. Answers will vary, but should include a discussion of being identified with the enemy, loyalty, and fear of espionage.

Take It to the NET

Graphs should be clearly constructed and should accurately present the historical data provided.

With the help of workers in the Woman's Land Army, farmers were able to harvest crops despite a labor shortage.

Changing People's Lives

American patriotism and war fever made military styles and activities more acceptable at home. Children joined scouting programs with military-style uniforms, marching, and patriotic exercises. Military drill became part of many school programs. By the summer of 1918, all able-bodied males in colleges and universities had become army privates, subject to military discipline.

Social Mobility for Minorities and Women After the war, Americans would turn away from military trends and other war-related activities. But other social changes that occurred during the war would have more lasting effects. The war virtually stopped the flow of immigrants from Europe, and the armed forces had taken many young men out of the labor pool. Businesses, especially war-related industries, suddenly needed workers. These wartime conditions drew some people into higher paying jobs. Factory owners and managers that had discriminated against African Americans and Mexican Americans now actively recruited them.

The African Americans who had left the South to work in northern factories added to a steady stream of migrants that had already started in the late 1800s. The stream turned into a flood during the war, when some 500,000 African Americans joined what came to be called the Great Migration.

The diminished work force also created new opportunities for women. Some women found jobs on farms, thanks to organizations such as the Woman's Land Army. Others moved into jobs as telegraph messengers, elevator operators, letter carriers, and similar jobs that were previously open only to men. A few earned management positions.

As a result of the war, about 400,000 women joined the industrial work force for the first time. In 1917, a speaker for the Women's Trade Union League proclaimed, "At last, after centuries of disabilities and discrimination, women are coming into the labor and festival of life on equal terms with men." Such pronouncements, while premature, celebrated what seemed to be a major social change.

Section 4 Assessment

READING COMPREHENSION

1. What was the role of **price controls** and **rationing** on the home front in World War I?

2. What were three ways that the government intervened in the economy to help the war effort?

3. How did the government deal with newspapers, magazines, and movies during the war?

CRITICAL THINKING AND WRITING

4. **Drawing Inferences** (a) What was the primary purpose of selling Liberty Bonds? (b) What else did the government's efforts to sell bonds accomplish?

5. **Writing an Opinion** Write a short speech discussing anti-German sentiment. Why do you think people reacted the way they did to the use of German words in the United States?

Take It to the NET

Activity: Creating a Graph
Interpret historical data to create a bar graph of the financial costs of World War I. Use the links provided in the *America: Pathways to the Present* area of the following Web site for help in completing this activity.
www.phschool.com

668 Chapter 19 • *The World War I Era*

RESOURCE DIRECTORY

Teaching Resources
Units 5/6 booklet
• Section 4 Quiz, p. 77
Guide to the Essentials
• Section 4 Summary, p. 101
Learning with Documents booklet (Visual Learning Activity) *Women's Roles in World War I*, p. 58

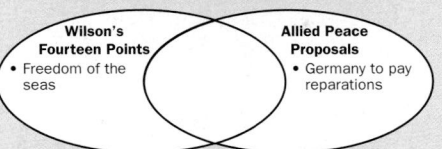
READING FOCUS

- What expectations did Wilson and the Allies bring to the Paris Peace Conference?
- What were the important provisions of the peace treaty?
- How did the federal government and ordinary Americans react to the end of war?

MAIN IDEA

When the fighting ended in Europe, President Wilson pressed for a treaty that would bring peace to the postwar world.

KEY TERMS

Fourteen Points
self-determination
spoils
League of Nations
reparations
Versailles Treaty

TAKING NOTES

Copy this incomplete Venn diagram. As you read, write the key peace proposals offered by President Wilson and the Allied leaders in the appropriate sections. If both sides supported a proposal, include it in the space where the circles overlap.

Wilson's Fourteen Points
- Freedom of the seas

Allied Peace Proposals
- Germany to pay reparations

SECTION OBJECTIVES

1. Discover the expectations that Wilson and the Allies brought to the Paris peace conference.
2. Learn about the important provisions of the peace treaty.
3. Find out how the federal government and ordinary Americans reacted to the end of the war.

BELLRINGER

Warm-Up Activity Ask students to explain the expression "At what cost peace?" How could this expression be applied to other wars the United States has fought?

Activating Prior Knowledge How did actions taken by President Wilson before and during the war affect his ability to negotiate a peace settlement? Would he be likely to have the support of the United States Congress?

READING STRATEGY

As students read, have them analyze major issues raised by U.S. involvement in World War I, such as the changing role of the U.S. in world affairs and changes the war brought to the American home front.

ACTIVITY
Connecting with Government

When Wilson presented the Versailles Treaty to Congress with the provision to establish the League of Nations, he asked: "Dare we reject it and break the heart of the world?" Discuss Wilson's statement with students. Have them write essays in which they analyze major issues raised by the Treaty of Versailles. **(Verbal/Linguistic)**

CAPTION ANSWERS

Viewing History Many people wanted the United States to withdraw from European affairs and focus on issues at home.

Setting the Scene On January 8, 1918, President Wilson stood before the Congress of the United States. The war had not ended, yet Wilson talked about peace. He hoped that the world could "be made safe for every peace-loving nation which, like our own, wishes to live its own life, determine its own institutions, be assured of justice and fair dealing by the other peoples of the world as against force and selfish aggression."

Wilson's program for reaching these goals came to be called the **Fourteen Points,** for the number of provisions it contained. Wilson's first point called for an end to entangling alliances, a key cause of the war. He wrote:

❝ Open covenants of peace, openly arrived at, after which there shall be no private international understandings of any kind but diplomacy shall proceed always frankly and in the public view. ❞

—Woodrow Wilson

The remaining provisions of the Fourteen Points dealt with a variety of issues related to keeping the peace after the war. They included the removal of trade barriers among nations and the reduction of military forces. Wilson also called for the right of Austria-Hungary's ethnic groups to **self-determination,** or the power to make decisions about one's own future.

Wilson hoped that these points would form the basis of peace negotiations. Germany assumed that they would. At first, the Allies appeared to cooperate. But it soon became clear that Wilson's colleagues did not share his idealism. The Allies discarded Wilson's proposals one by one as they met to map out a future for Europe.

The Paris Peace Conference

In January 1919, an international peace conference convened in Paris. Wilson decided to head the United States delegation. Although the Republican-controlled Senate would have the final word on the treaty,

VIEWING HISTORY Crowds greet returning soldiers at a victory parade in New York City. **Drawing Inferences** How did American attitudes toward Europe change in 1919 and 1920?

Chapter 19 • Section 5   669

RESOURCE DIRECTORY

Teaching Resources
Guided Reading and Review booklet, p. 82
Learning Styles Lesson Plans booklet, p. 41
Learning with Documents booklet (Key Documents) *Woodrow Wilson, The Fourteen Points,* p. 86

Technology
Section Reading Support Transparencies
Guided Reading Audiotapes (English/Spanish), Ch. 19
Student Edition on Audio CD, Ch. 19
Exploring Primary Sources in U.S. History CD-ROM *The Fourteen Points*
Prentice Hall Presentation Pro CD-ROM, Ch. 19
Companion Web site, www.phschool.com

Focus Explain that President Wilson's vision of postwar peace, summarized in his Fourteen Points, was not shared by the Allies or the United States Congress. Ask what Wilson's Fourteen Points were. What were the provisions of the Versailles Treaty?

Instruct Explain that Wilson made several political mistakes that cost him support for his peace plan. Ask how the loss of Republican support hurt Wilson's efforts to negotiate and fulfill his promise to "make the world safe for democracy."

Discuss why such harsh conditions were imposed on Germany. Ask students if they agree that the seeds of World War II were sown in the Versailles Treaty.

Ask why many Americans had trouble adjusting to life after the war. Why were Americans disillusioned?

Assess/Reteach The Versailles peace treaty involved many different countries. Each country came to the peace table hoping for certain outcomes. What were some outcomes the Allies looked for? What did Germany hope to achieve? How was the U.S. position different from that of the Allies?

BACKGROUND

Global Connections

When he sought to establish the League of Nations, Woodrow Wilson demonstrated his belief in the concept of *collective security*. In a collective security arrangement, a country that wants to wage war against one country must consider itself waging wars against all of the countries that are part of the arrangement. The concept is intended to prevent or stop wars. First practiced by the League of Nations, it is the system that is used today by the United Nations.

It is an imperfect system, but the League of Nations and the United Nations have provided the world with a neutral forum in which to discuss solutions and alternatives to war.

CAPTION ANSWERS

Interpreting Tables It encouraged them to seek reparations and to punish Germany.

British Prime Minister David Lloyd George (left), French Prime Minister Georges Clemenceau (center), and Wilson negotiated at the Paris Peace Conference.

INTERPRETING TABLES
Many American soldiers died either from disease or in battle, but European countries on both sides of the conflict suffered even greater losses. **Understanding Point of View** How did high casualties in Britain and France influence how Lloyd George and Clemenceau acted at the Paris Peace Conference?

Casualties of World War I *		
Allies	**Killed**	**Wounded**
Russia	1,700,000	4,950,000
France	1,358,000	4,266,000
British Empire	908,000	2,090,000
Italy	462,000	954,000
United States	51,000	206,000
Others	410,000	343,000
Total	**4,889,000**	**12,809,000**
Central Powers	**Killed**	**Wounded**
Germany	1,809,000	4,247,000
Austria-Hungary	923,000	3,620,000
Turkey	325,000	400,000
Bulgaria	76,000	152,000
Total	**3,133,000**	**8,419,000**

SOURCE: *Encyclopedia of Military History*
*Numbers rounded to thousands

Wilson chose not to name any senior Republicans to the group, with the exception of one elderly diplomat.

When Wilson arrived in Paris, the Parisians greeted the American President as a conquering hero and threw flowers in his path. Wilson claimed that he was not interested in the **spoils,** or rewards, of war. That is, he did not expect the United States to take money or land from the war's losers. His only goal was to establish a permanent agency where countries could work together to resolve disputes peacefully and guarantee international stability. As Wilson had declared two years earlier, "There must be not a balance of power, but a community of power; not organized rivalries, but an organized common peace."

Wilson Forced to Compromise All would not go Wilson's way. Wilson shared power at the conference with other members of the Big Four: David Lloyd George of Britain, Georges Clemenceau of France, and Vittorio Orlando of Italy. Wilson's three allies were interested in making the Central Powers pay for their part in the war with land, goods, livestock, and money. In particular, they wanted to divide up Germany's colonies.

Russia, although absent from the conference, was still on everyone's mind. Civil war had erupted between Lenin's Bolsheviks and the armies loyal to the old government. British, French, and American forces had become involved in the civil war on the side of Lenin's opponents. Would Lenin's government survive? Would it present a set of war claims? Lenin called for workers everywhere to overthrow their governments, and the Allies feared a Bolshevik Russia as much as they feared Germany. As it turned out, Lenin's government held on to power, but refused to claim any spoils of war. Lenin's government would, in fact, sign a Treaty of Friendship and Cooperation with Germany in 1922.

From the start of the Paris Peace Conference, Wilson was forced to compromise on the principles outlined in the Fourteen Points. He had to give up, for example, the idea of respecting the rights of native peoples in Germany's colonies in Africa, China, and the Pacific. He finally agreed that the Allied powers could simply take over the colonies.

The League of Nations Wilson did, however, convince the other powers to postpone further discussion of Germany's fate and talk about his ideas for global security. After ten days of hard work, he produced a plan for the **League of Nations,** an organization in which the nations of the world would join together to ensure security and peace for all its members. Wilson then left France for home, hoping to persuade Congress and the nation to accept his plan.

For Wilson, the heart of his proposal for the League of Nations was Article 10 of the plan. This provision pledged that members of the League would regard an attack on one country as an attack on all. Since the League would not have any military power, the force of the article depended on the will of members to back it up with their armies. Nevertheless, 39 Republican senators or senators-elect signed a statement rejecting it. They feared that Article 10 could be used to drag the United States into unpopular foreign wars.

RESOURCE DIRECTORY

Teaching Resources
Biography, Literature, and Comparing Primary Sources booklet (Comparing Primary Sources) *On the League of Nations,* p. 133

The Peace Treaty

In March 1919, Wilson returned to the peace conference. The Big Four dominated the proceedings. Although the Allies accepted Wilson's plan for the League of Nations, opposition to the League from Congress and many Americans had weakened Wilson's position at the conference.

French premier Georges Clemenceau took advantage of that weakness to demand harsh penalties against Germany. Wilson feared that these demands would lead to future wars, but he could not get Clemenceau to budge.

Redrawing the Map of Europe Wilson also had to compromise elsewhere. Self-determination for the peoples of Central Europe proved hard to apply. As the map on the following page shows, the conference created nine new nations out of the territory of Austria-Hungary, Russia, and Germany. Several of these nations were created to form a north-south buffer zone dividing Bolshevik Russia from the rest of Europe. Most borders were drawn with the ethnic populations of the region in mind, but clean divisions were impossible. The boundaries created new ethnic minorities in several countries, including millions of Germans and Hungarians whose homes became part of Poland, Czechoslovakia, or Romania. These arrangements failed to resolve all ethnic tensions.

In the Middle East, the Allies reduced the Ottoman Empire to a small remnant that became the nation of Turkey. Britain took control of Palestine, Transjordan, and Iraq. France was awarded Syria and Lebanon.

Wilson had more luck opposing the demands of Vittorio Orlando, Italy's prime minister. To convince Italy to join the Allies in 1915, Britain had secretly promised Italy several pieces of territory controlled by Austria-Hungary. At the conference, however, Wilson and the other Allied leaders refused to support Italy's claims. As a result, Italy gained less territory than it had expected. Orlando had to resign as prime minister because of his failure at the conference.

War Guilt and Reparations Wilson met his greatest defeat when he gave in to French insistence on German war guilt and financial responsibility. The French, with the support of Britain, wanted to cripple Germany. They insisted that Germany supply **reparations,** or payment for economic injury suffered during a war. In 1921, a Reparations Commission ruled that Germany owed the Allies $33 billion, an amount far beyond its ability to pay. As Wilson had feared, Germany never forgot or forgave this humiliation.

Signing the Treaty The Allies presented the treaty to the Germans on May 7, 1919. Insisting that the treaty violated the Fourteen Points, the Germans at first refused to sign it. They gave in, however, when threatened with a French invasion. On June 28, the great powers signed the treaty at Versailles, the former home of French kings, outside of Paris. Thus, the treaty is known as the **Versailles Treaty.** Even the location offered an opportunity to

---

COMPARING PRIMARY SOURCES
League of Nations

The debate over joining the League of Nations often hinged on the effect that joining would have on American sovereignty or independence.

Analyzing Viewpoints On what basis does each speaker support or oppose American entry into the League?

In Favor of Joining the League of Nations

"The United States will, indeed, undertake . . . to 'respect and preserve as against external aggression the territorial integrity and existing political independence of all members of the League,' and that engagement constitutes a very grave and solemn moral obligation. But it is a moral, not a legal, obligation, and leaves our Congress absolutely free to put its own interpretation upon it."
—*Woodrow Wilson, testifying before the Foreign Relations Committee, August 19, 1919*

Opposed to Joining the League of Nations

"Shall we go there, Mr. President, to sit in judgment, and in case that judgment works for peace join with our allies, but in case it works for war withdraw our cooperation? How long would we stand as we now stand, a great Republic commanding the respect and holding the leadership of the world, if we should adopt any such course?"
—*Senator William Borah (Idaho), testifying in the Senate, November 19, 1919*

READING CHECK
How did Wilson's allies react to the Fourteen Points?

From the Archives of
AmericanHeritage®

Ending the War to End All Wars

In 1921, three years after the end of the Great War, Americans dealt with some unfinished business from that conflict. On November 8, President Warren Harding signed a joint resolution to end the war. Then, three days later on November 11, the remains of an unknown American soldier, exhumed from a French grave, were buried in Washington, D.C. Military men from all nations paid tribute with medals, ribbons, and decorations, including a Native American who laid a coup stick and war bonnet on the bier. In a moving address, Harding asked the American people to give of their influence and strength "…to put mankind on a little higher plane, exulting and exalting, with war's distressing and depressing tragedies barred from the state of righteous civilization." Source: Frederic D. Schwarz, "The Time Machine," *American Heritage*® magazine, November 1996.

READING CHECK

The Allies were vehemently opposed to some aspects of Wilson's program, and lacked enthusiasm for the Fourteen Points as a whole. Clemenceau, Lloyd George, and Orlando were determined to extract reparations and territory from the defeated nations. The Allies also defied Wilson by insisting that Germany accept guilt for starting the war.

CAPTION ANSWERS

Comparing Primary Sources Wilson supports joining the League to attain collective security; Borah views League membership as an excuse for drawing the United States into foreign quarrels and wars.

Europe After World War I

MAP SKILLS Britain, France, and the United States redrew the map of Europe at the Paris Peace Conference. **Regions** Which three participants in the war lost the most territory in central and eastern Europe?

Focus on GEOGRAPHY

Multinational States Two countries created at the Paris Peace Conference were designed as multinational states. These were Czechoslovakia, a country dominated by Czechs and Slovaks, and Yugoslavia, or the Kingdom of the South Slavs, which included Serbs, Croats, Slovenes, and others. Czechoslovakia flourished as a democracy between the two world wars, but Yugoslavia stayed intact only under the strong hand of kings and dictators. Czechoslovakia split peacefully in 1993. Yugoslavia broke up violently into several countries in the 1990s, and many borders are still unsettled.

humiliate Germany. In 1871, the new German Empire had been founded in the same hall at Versailles.

Reactions at Home

On July 8, treaty in hand, Wilson returned home to great acclaim. But many legislators had doubts about the results of the peace conference. Some senators opposed the treaty because it committed the United States to the League of Nations. These senators were called the "irreconcilables," because they could not be reconciled to, or made to accept, the treaty. Irreconcilables argued that joining the League would threaten American independence.

Senator Henry Cabot Lodge, chair of the Foreign Relations Committee, led another group called the "reservationists." This group accepted the League of Nations but wanted to impose reservations, or restrictions, on American participation. In particular, they wanted a guarantee that the Monroe Doctrine would remain in force. Wilson's point that compliance with the League's decisions was "binding in conscience only, not in law," failed to persuade them.

Wilson Tours the Country Determined to win grass-roots support for the League, Wilson took to the road in September. In 23 days, he delivered three dozen speeches across the country. After this tremendous effort, he suffered a stroke that paralyzed one side of his body. He would remain an invalid, isolated from his Cabinet and visitors, for the rest of his term.

During his illness, Wilson grew increasingly inflexible. Congress would have to accept the treaty and the League as he envisioned it, or not at all. In November 1919, the Senate voted on the treaty with Lodge's reservations included. The Senate rejected the treaty by a vote of 39 for, 55 against. When the treaty came up without the reservations, it failed again, 38 to 53. In the face of popular dismay at this outcome, the Senate reconsidered the treaty in March 1920, but once again the treaty was rejected.

A Formal End to Hostilities On May 20, 1920, Congress voted to disregard the Treaty of Versailles and declare the war officially over. Steadfast to his principles, Wilson vetoed the resolution. Finally, on July 2, 1921, another joint resolution to end the war passed. By that time, a Republican President, Warren G. Harding, was in office, and he signed it. Congress ratified separate peace treaties with Germany, Austria, and Hungary that October.

Difficult Postwar Adjustments The war spurred the United States economy, giving a big boost to American businesses. The United States was now the world's largest creditor nation. In 1922, a Senate debt commission calculated that European countries owed $11.5 billion to the United States.

The decline of the European powers thrust the United States into a position of unexpected strength. Britain, once the banker to the world and center of the greatest colonial empire, had spent much of its great wealth on the war. Britain's economy never adjusted to peacetime, and the nation's power declined in comparison to that of the United States. The German invasion had devastated France, and Germany was weakened by the Treaty of Versailles. Yet even though the United States enjoyed unparalleled power, it chose to turn away from international affairs and focus on its concerns at home.

The return to peace had caused problems for the country at large. By April 1919, about 4,000 servicemen a day were being mustered out of the armed forces. But nobody had devised a plan to help returning troops merge back into society. The federal agencies that controlled the economy during the war had abruptly canceled war contracts. As a result, jobs proved scarce. The women who had taken men's places in factories and offices also faced readjustment. To free up jobs for returning soldiers, many women left their jobs voluntarily or were fired.

Like white troops, black soldiers came home to a hero's welcome. When they went to find jobs, however, their reception was different. Their contributions to the war had not earned black soldiers more respect from others. African Americans still faced discrimination in housing and employment, and lynchings and race riots continued.

Postwar Gloom Many artists and intellectuals in the United States entered the postwar years with a sense of gloom or disillusionment. They expressed their feelings in books and other artistic works. Social reformers had been encouraged by the government-business collaboration during the war. For most of them, the end of the war also ended an era of optimism. Alice Lord O'Brian, a military post exchange director from Buffalo who was twice decorated by the French, expressed the views of many who took part in the war. In a letter home she stated:

> 66 We all started out with high ideals. . . . [A]fter being right up here almost at the front line . . . I cannot understand what it is all about or what has been accomplished by all this waste of youth. 99
> —Alice Lord O'Brian

Focus on GOVERNMENT

Checks and Balances This is the system, established by the Constitution, that enables each of the three branches of the federal government to check the other branches.

The Historical Context After President Wilson signed the Versailles Treaty, the treaty went to the Senate. There, a two-thirds vote in favor of the treaty was needed for the treaty to become official in the United States. The Senate, however, failed to approve the treaty.

The Concept Today Many people complain today that the branches of government should work together more and check each other less. Yet the system of checks and balances helps keep government responsible to the voters.

Section 5 · Assessment

READING COMPREHENSION

1. Describe three of Woodrow Wilson's **Fourteen Points.**

2. How did the Allies both encourage and discourage **self-determination** in Europe?

3. Why did France and Britain demand **reparations** from Germany?

4. How did the United States eventually make peace with Germany?

CRITICAL THINKING AND WRITING

5. **Synthesizing Information** Why do you think many Americans opposed the Versailles Treaty?

6. **Drawing Inferences** Why did the Fourteen Points fail as a basis of peace negotiations?

7. **Writing a List** Compile a list of ten descriptive phrases that characterize the United States and Europe after the war.

Take It to the NET

Activity: Historical Recreations Choose one of the Big Four leaders. Research your representative and recreate a meeting of the conference in your class. Use the links provided in the *America: Pathways to the Present* area of the following Web site for help in completing this activity.
www.phschool.com

Chapter 19 • Section 5   673

Section 5   Assessment

Reading Comprehension

1. Answers should include three of the following: an end to entangling alliances; removal of trade barriers among nations; reduction of military forces; the right of Austria-Hungary's ethnic groups to self-determination.

2. Encouraged by giving independence to some countries; discouraged by disregarding the wishes of other countries. Allies were inconsistent in their application of self-determination.

3. To punish Germany for its role in the war.

4. The U.S. Senate approved a separate peace treaty with Germany in October 1921. Prior to that, President Warren G. Harding had signed a Congressional resolution declaring an end to the conflict without regard to the Treaty of Versailles in the summer of 1921.

Critical Thinking and Writing

5. It committed the United States to the League of Nations, which caused concern about American independence and whether or not the Monroe Doctrine would remain in effect.

6. Sample answer: The Fourteen Points did not serve the ends of the other Allies; especially France and Britain; they wanted to cripple Germany by taking its territory and demanding reparations.

7. Answers will vary but should be supported by facts from the section. Sample answer: postwar gloom.

Take It to the NET

Answers will vary, but should focus on the disagreement between the Allies over postwar conduct.

CUSTOMIZE FOR ...

Less Proficient Writers

Ask students to list a set of three or four reasons either for or against the United States' participation in the League of Nations. Additionally, they could illustrate one of their reasons as a political cartoon.

✓ TEST PREPARATION

Have students read the section on the previous page under "Reactions at Home" and then answer the question below.

What United States political figure, active in 1921, supported the position of the "irreconcilables"?

A Woodrow Wilson

B Henry Cabot Lodge

Ⓒ Warren G. Harding

D none of the above

REVIEWING KEY TERMS

Students should refer to the definitions of key terms in the chapter to write sentences that show an understanding of the World War I era.

REVIEWING MAIN IDEAS

15. Imperialism, militarism, nationalism, and alliances were the deeper causes. The triggering cause was the assassination of Archduke Francis Ferdinand.

16. Answers should include the objectives of the Schlieffen Plan and the fact that it failed, the failure of the Russian invasion of Germany, the beginning of trench warfare, and the fact that modern weapons gave the overwhelming advantage to defending forces.

17. Most Americans favored the Allies. President Wilson decided on a position of neutrality. Both the preparedness movement, which urged the United States to get ready for war, and the peace movement began promoting their views.

18. The triggering cause was the continued sinking of neutral ships, which harmed American commercial interests. Other causes included the Zimmermann note, the Russian Revolution, and an anti-German bias among Americans.

19. Machine guns, hand grenades, long-range artillery, poison gases, tanks, the convoy system, and the use of airplanes as fighters and bombers.

20. They stopped the German advance on Paris and then led a counter-attack that helped end the war.

21. To be sure that the United States would produce enough for the war effort, the government established new federal agencies to oversee industry and labor, as well as food consumption.

22. The government censored printed material and films to promote the Allied cause to the American people and to ensure that spies did not gain access to damaging material. The Espionage and Sedition Acts blunted criticism of the government.

23. There was widespread popular support for the treaty, but many senators opposed membership in the League.

creating a CHAPTER SUMMARY

Copy this chart (right) on a piece of paper and complete it by adding important events that occurred in each year. Some entries have been completed for you as examples.

TEXT

For additional review and enrichment activities, see the interactive version of *America: Pathways to the Present*, available on the Web and on CD-ROM.

Year	Events
1914	• Gavrilo Princip assassinates Archduke Francis Ferdinand. • War breaks out between the Central Powers and the Allies. •
1915	
1916	
1917	
1918	
1919	
1920	

★ Reviewing Key Terms

For each of the terms below, write a sentence explaining how it relates to World War I.

1. militarism
2. Central Powers
3. Allies
4. stalemate
5. U-boat
6. Zimmermann note
7. American Expeditionary Force (AEF)
8. convoy
9. armistice
10. Liberty Bond
11. sedition
12. Fourteen Points
13. League of Nations
14. Versailles Treaty

★ Reviewing Main Ideas

15. What were the main causes of World War I? (Section 1)

16. Describe the first three months of the war in Europe in your own words. (Section 1)

17. What were the reactions in the United States to the outbreak of the war in Europe? (Section 2)

18. Why did the United States declare war on Germany? (Section 2)

19. Name some of the military innovations introduced during World War I. (Section 3)

20. How did American troops help turn the tide of the war on the battlefield? (Section 3)

21. Why and how did the government try to control the economy at home? (Section 4)

22. Why and how did the government influence what people said about the war? (Section 4)

23. What was the American reaction to the Versailles Treaty and to the League of Nations? (Section 5)

★ Critical Thinking

24. Predicting Consequences What might have happened on the European front if General Pershing had decided to combine the American troops with other Allied armies instead of keeping them independent?

25. Drawing Inferences Do you think that women played a key role in World War I? Why or why not?

26. Testing Conclusions Many young people in Europe and the United States felt that they bore the heaviest costs of the war. Cite evidence showing whether they were correct.

27. Supporting a Position Do you think the Sedition Act was a good way to deal with critics during wartime? Explain.

28. Identifying Central Issues It is often said that Woodrow Wilson won World War I, but then "lost the peace." Explain your understanding of this statement.

CREATING A CHAPTER SUMMARY

Year	Events
1914	• Gavrilo Princip assassinates Archduke Francis Ferdinand. • War breaks out between the Central Powers and the Allies. • United States declares its neutrality.
1915	• British ship *Lusitania* is sunk by Germans. • Poison gas used on Western Front in an attempt to break stalemate.
1916	• Germany signs the Sussex pledge. • Huge offensives at Verdun and the Somme River; many German, French, and British casualties.
1917	• Russian revolution. • Germany ends Sussex pledge. • United States enters war.
1918	• American troops finally end stalemate, pushing back the Western Front. • Influenza epidemic spreads throughout the world. • Central Powers agree to a cease-fire.
1919	• United States Senate rejects Versailles Treaty and refuses to join League of Nations. • Germany signs the Treaty of Versailles.
1920	• Congress votes to disregard the Treaty of Versailles and declares the war officially over.

★ **Skills Assessment**

Analyzing Political Cartoons ▶

29. Analyze the images in this 1919 cartoon. (a) Who is the man? (b) What does the little boy represent? (c) How can you tell?

30. Who does the man in the cartoon want the "child" to play with?

31. Why does the "child" want to play alone?

32. Explain the meaning of the cartoon.

Interpreting Data

Turn to the table of casualties in Section 5.

33. Which two countries suffered the greatest number of soldiers killed?

   A Russia and France
   B Germany and Austria-Hungary
   C Russia and Austria-Hungary
   D Germany and Russia

34. What can you conclude about casualties in "Other" Allied countries from this table?

   F These countries suffered as many casualties as the British Empire and France.
   G Their casualties were comparable to the total casualties in Bulgaria.
   H Unlike soldiers from France or Russia, soldiers in Romania, Serbia, and other small Allied countries were more likely to be killed in battle than wounded.
   J "Other" Allies suffered fewer casualties because they entered the war in 1916 or later.

Applying the Chapter Skill: *Identifying Alternatives*

35. The United States chose to go to war with Germany in 1917 largely because of continued German submarine attacks on neutral shipping. Identify alternative solutions to this problem of U-boat attacks. Discuss your alternative in a written proposal to President Wilson.

THE CHILD WHO WANTED TO PLAY BY HIMSELF.
President Wilson: "Now come along and enjoy yourself with the other nice children. I promised that you'd be the life and soul of the party."

ACTIVITIES

Writing to LEARN

Writing to Compare
Compare the peacemaking ability of the United States today with its peacemaking ability after the war. What characteristics does it take for a country to serve as a peacemaker? Does the United States have these characteristics today? Did it have them in Wilson's time?

Primary Source CD-ROM

Working With Primary Sources Find additional information on World War I on the *Exploring Primary Sources in U.S. History CD-ROM* and use the selection(s) provided to complete the Chapter 19 primary source activity located in the *America: Pathways to the Present* area of the following Web site.
www.phschool.com

Take It to the NET

Chapter Self-Test As a review activity, take the Chapter 19 Self-Test in the *America: Pathways to the Present* area at the Web site listed below. The questions are designed to test your understanding of the chapter content.
www.phschool.com

Chapter 19 Assessment **675**

---

adopted the Europeans' defensive posture and not have taken the offensive against the Germans outside Paris; Paris might have fallen; the war might have been lost.

25. Yes; they moved into important jobs, helped Food Administration programs succeed, served in the American Expeditionary Force at home and at the front.

26. Historians agree that the young men of all the major European combatant nations were, as a generational group, largely wiped out by the war (American casualties were lower). Young soldiers could sense that their leaders had failed to adapt their battle plans to the realities of the enormous firepower of twentieth century weapons.

27. Possible answer: the Sedition Act was a bad idea because, in disregarding the First Amendment, it undermined the goals President Wilson claimed the United States was fighting for.

28. Sample answer: Wilson had directed the victorious U.S. war effort, yet was unable to influence the Allies in the peace settlement.

SKILLS ASSESSMENT

29. (a) President Wilson. (b) The U.S. (c) "U.S.A." is printed on his hat.

30. He wants him to play with the other children in the "Temple of Peace." In other words, Wilson wants the U.S. to join the League of Nations.

31. Congress was reluctant to involve the nation in alliances that could pull it into international disputes.

32. Wilson looks foolish to the world because he can't get the U.S. to agree to an organization he proposed.

33. D

34. H

35. Answers might include suggesting to Wilson that he prohibit American ships from entering the war zone, or that he prohibit Americans from traveling to or from Great Britain.

ANSWERS TO ACTIVITIES

Writing to LEARN

Essays might focus on characteristics such as power and influence, and on the role of military might and democratic values.

Primary Source CD-ROM

Direct students to the additional primary sources that can be found on the *Exploring Primary Sources in U.S. History CD-ROM.*

 ### Take It to the NET

Additional support materials and activities for Chapter 19 of *America: Pathways to the Present* can be found in the Social Studies area at the Prentice Hall School Web site. **www.phschool.com**

A FLYER ON THE EDGE

Focus Have students find the meaning of each of these words in a dictionary before they begin to read: *flinching, burlesque, strafing, airdrome, grotesque, contemptible, cur.* Ask them to consider, as they read, the long-term emotional effects of the war on those who fought it.

Instruct Ask students to review the passage from the viewpoint of a World War I historian. What information about World War I can you gain from the pilot's diary? What information can you discern from it about the emotions and morale of fighting men? What other types of sources would you need to consult to become an expert on World War I?

Analyzing the Document Use this additional question to generate class discussion:

Critical Thinking: Testing Conclusions Do you think that the pilot is correct when he writes that, after a war has ended, defeated enemies become objects of charity, while politicians look for another war? Give examples to support your answer. *(Answers will vary. Some students may argue that the pilot is correct; for example, the United States gave aid to Germany after World War II and then went to war against North Korea. Other students may answer that compassion dictates that a vanquished population receive aid and that subsequent wars are unavoidable.)*

AmericanHeritage®
MY BRUSH WITH HISTORY™

by ANONYMOUS

A Flyer on the Edge

The dangers of war took a heavy toll on the men who served in uniform, not only the soldiers in the trenches but also those who fought in the skies overhead. The passage below, selected by the editors of *American Heritage* magazine, is from the diary of an unknown pilot in World War I. As you read the following excerpt, think about how the psychological stresses of modern warfare affected those who fought to defend freedom.

———⇒●⇐———

WE'VE LOST A LOT OF GOOD MEN. It's only a question of time until we all get it. I'm all shot to pieces. I only hope I can stick it. I don't want to quit. My nerves are all gone and I can't stop. I've lived beyond my time already.

It's not the fear of death that's done it. I'm still not afraid to die. It's this eternal flinching from it that's doing it and has made a coward out of me. Few men live to know what real fear is. It's something that grows on you, day by day, that eats into your constitution and undermines your sanity. I have never been serious about anything in my life and now I know that I'll never be otherwise again. But my seriousness will be a burlesque for no one will recognize it.

Here I am, twenty-four years old, I look forty and I feel ninety. I've lost all interest in life beyond the next patrol. No one Hun will ever get me and I'll never fall into a trap, but sooner or later I'll be forced to fight against odds that are too long or perhaps a stray shot from the ground will be lucky and I will have gone in vain. Or my motor will cut out when we are trench strafing or a wing will pull off in a dive. Oh, for a parachute! The Huns are using them now. I haven't a chance, I know, and it's this eternal waiting around that's killing me. I've even lost my taste for liquor. It doesn't seem to do me any good now. I guess I'm stale. Last week I actually got frightened in the air and lost my head. Then I found ten Huns and took them all on and I got one of them down out of control. I got my nerve back by that time and came back home and slept like a baby for the first time in two months. What a blessing sleep is! I know now why men go out and take such long chances

Airplanes, originally used for reconnaissance, fought in aerial "dogfights" toward the end of the war.

676

✓ TEST PREPARATION

Have students use the excerpt on these pages to answer the following question.

Based on the passage, you can tell that—

A the pilot's mental and emotional health is very frail.

B the pilot is mourning the loss of things that he may never experience, such as getting married and having children.

C the pilot is angry with himself for not using his family connections to stay out of the war.

D the pilot has post-traumatic stress syndrome.

and pull off such wild stunts. No discipline in the world could make them do what they do of their own accord. I know now what a brave man is. I know now how men laugh at death and welcome it. I know now why Ball went over and sat above a Hun airdrome and dared them to come up and fight with him. It takes a brave man to even experience real fear. A coward couldn't last long enough at the job to get to that stage. What price salvation now?

More than 8 million soldiers died in World War I, making it the costliest war in history to that time.

THOUGHTS ABOUT WAR

War is a horrible thing, a grotesque comedy. And it is so useless. This war won't prove anything. All we'll do when we win is to substitute one sort of Dictator for another. In the meantime we have destroyed our best resources. Human life, the most precious thing in the world, has become the cheapest. After we've won this war by drowning the Hun in our own blood, in five years' time the sentimental fools at home will be taking up a collection for these same Huns that are killing us now and our fool politicians will be cooking up another good war. Why shouldn't they? They have to keep the public stirred up to keep their jobs and they don't have to fight and they can get soft berths for their sons and their friends' sons. To me the most contemptible cur in the world is the man who lets political influence be used to keep him away from the front. For he lets another man die in his place.

The worst thing about this war is that it takes the best. If it lasts long enough the world will be populated by cowards and weaklings and their children. And the whole thing is so useless, so unnecessary, so terrible! . . .

The devastation of the country is too horrible to describe. It looks from the air as if the gods had made a gigantic steam roller, forty miles wide and run it from the coast to Switzerland, leaving its spike holes behind as it went. . . .

I've lost over a hundred friends, so they tell me—I've seen only seven or eight killed—but to me they aren't dead yet. They are just around the corner, I think, and I'm still expecting to run into them any time. I dream about them at night when I do sleep a little and sometimes I dream that some one is killed who really isn't. Then I don't know who is and who isn't. I saw a man in Boulogne the other day that I had dreamed I saw killed and I thought I was seeing a ghost. I can't realize that any of them are gone. Surely human life is not a candle to be snuffed out. . . .

Source: Anonymous, *War Birds: Diary of an Unknown Aviator,* Doran, 1926.

Understanding Primary Sources

1. (a) What is the writer's attitude toward war? **(b)** How does he feel about politicians and their role in war? **(c)** Why does the writer feel this way?

2. (a) In the author's opinion, what are his chances of surviving the war? **(b)** From what you've learned about World War I, is this a reasonable position?

American Heritage®
MY BRUSH WITH **HISTORY**™

📼 **Videotapes**

For more information about the experience of World War I, view "A Flyer on the Edge."

677

Use this sample exam to help your students prepare for standardized tests.

TIPS FOR TEST TAKING

You might want to remind your students of the following:

1. Read the directions carefully.

2. Read each question carefully.

3. For multiple choice questions, try to answer the question before you look at the choices. Read all the choices. Then, eliminate those that are absolutely incorrect.

4. For short answer questions, be sure to answer the question completely if there is more than one part.

5. Answer the easy questions first. Then, go back to the ones that will take more time.

6. Pace yourself. Be sure to set aside enough time for the writing questions.

Write your answers on a separate sheet of paper.

Use the information in the map to answer the following question.

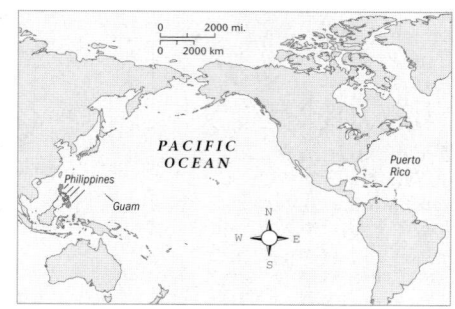

United States Overseas Possessions, 1900

1. How did the United States gain the territories labeled on the map?

   A Through the Monroe Doctrine

   B By treaty after World War II

   C Through a ruling of the United Nations

   D By winning the Spanish-American War

2. Who argued that naval power was crucial to the success of United States involvement overseas?

   A Samuel Gompers

   B William Randolph Hearst

   C Alfred T. Mahan

   D William Howard Taft

---

3. Which one of these was the main argument for those who supported United States imperialism?

   A Colonies would give the United States a place to sell products.

   B Colonies would provide students for United States colleges and universities.

   C The Constitution must go wherever the flag goes.

   D The United States needed naval bases in China and Japan.

Use the chart and your knowledge of social studies to answer the following question.

?????
• Settled the United Mine Workers' strike
• Passed the Hepburn Act, giving the ICC the power to limit railroad rates
• Created the Department of Labor
• Was a leader in the conservation of natural resources
• Changed the Monroe Doctrine
• Won the Nobel peace prize for ending the Russo-Japanese War

4. Which one of these is a correct title for the information in the chart?

   A Progressive reforms of Woodrow Wilson

   B Accomplishments of Theodore Roosevelt

   C Accomplishments of Admiral Alfred T. Mahan

   D Actions of Roosevelt canceled by Taft

5. What did the Muckrakers do in the Progressive Era?

   A They helped sell war bonds during World War I.

   B They were the leaders in the Red Scare.

   C They exposed problems present in American society.

   D They did not want the United States to have colonies.

678

Diagnose and Prescribe
- Profile student skills with Diagnostic Tests A&B.
- Address student needs with program materials correlated to test questions.

Review and Reteach
- Provide cumulative content review with the Review Book.

Practice and Assess
- Build test-taking skills with Test-taking Strategies With Transparencies.

6. How did the Clayton Antitrust Act differ from the Sherman Antitrust Act?

  A The Sherman Antitrust Act divided the nation into 12 banking districts.

  B The Clayton Antitrust Act applied equally to businesses and unions.

  C The Sherman Antitrust Act applied only to railroads and transportation.

  D The Clayton Antitrust Act listed specific actions businesses could not do.

Use the information in the chart to answer the following question.

1912 Election Results			
Candidate	Party	Popular Vote	Percentage
Woodrow Wilson	Democrat	6,293,152	41.8%
Theodore Roosevelt	Progressive	4,119,207	27.4
William Howard Taft*	Republican	3,486,333	23.2
Eugene V. Debs	Socialist	900,369	6.0

*Incumbent

SOURCE: *New York Times Almanac 2001*

7. Which one of the following conclusions is correct?

  A Most of the Republican votes came from the Western states.

  B The American people voted for change in 1912.

  C The Democrats spent more money than the Republicans.

  D Taft would have won if Debs had not been in the race.

8. Susan B. Anthony and Carrie Chapman Catt were two of the leaders in the fight for the

  A rejection of prohibition.

  B approval of the Treaty of Versailles.

  C right of women to vote.

  D passage of the Clayton Antitrust Act.

9. Which one of the following contributed to the decision of the United States to enter World War I?

  A Germany's unrestricted submarine warfare

  B Mobilization of their armies by the Central Powers

  C The failure of the convoy system

  D The success of the czar in ending the Russian Revolution

10. Who was the commander of the American Expeditionary Force (AEF) in World War I?

  A Louis D. Brandeis

  B Arthur Zimmermann

  C John J. Pershing

  D David Lloyd George

11. Which of the following best describes Woodrow Wilson's Fourteen Points?

  A A statement of the goals for peace put forth by the United States following World War I

  B The American fighting plan for World War I

  C A list of Progressive Era reforms

  D The constitutional amendments planned by Progressives

Writing Practice

12. What actions did the Progressives take to change the United States government?

13. Describe the major reasons for the entry of the United States into World War I.

14. What steps did the government take to manage the economy during World War I?

1. D
2. C
3. A
4. B
5. C
6. D
7. B
8. C
9. A
10. C
11. A
12. Answers might mention reform-oriented writers and muckrakers; labor unions and women's groups; social welfare programs; implementation of workplace safety, minimum wage, and child labor reforms; new antitrust legislation; establishment of the Federal Trade Commission and the Federal Reserve System; and others.
13. Answers might mention the German use of the submarine, especially against neutral ships and passenger liners; and British control of U.S.–German communications and encouragement of anti-German sentiment among the American public.
14. Answers might mention the establishment of government agencies to oversee war-related production and labor, rationing, and the regulation of food and fuel consumption, and the enforcement of daylight saving time.

679

Unit 7

Boom Times to Hard Times
(1920–1938)

Boom Times to Hard Times (1920–1938) The decades between World War I and World War II saw dramatic changes in society and the economy. The 1920s were an era of social experimentation, flourishing of the arts, and rapid economic growth. They were also a decade of political corruption and financial collapse, resulting in a world-wide economic Depression. Though challenged by this economic crisis, Americans pulled together and were able to help one another through the hard times, spurred on by massive governmental programs designed to restore the country's infrastructure while keeping its citizens busily engaged.

USING HISTORICAL EVIDENCE

In the 1920s, New York City's Times Square first came into prominence as a crossroads of culture. As the painting on these pages shows, it was a lively scene, even in the dark of night. Crowds thronged there to enjoy the theater, the cinema, and simply the activity.

As students study the painting, discuss ways in which it depicts the liveliness of the Roaring Twenties. It was painted in 1925—at the height of an era of prosperity and optimism. How do students think the painting might be different if it had been painted six years later—during the heart of the Depression? Would the lively crowds be there? How many of the theater marquees would be brightly lit? How would people be dressed?

"We are moving forward to a greater freedom, to greater security for the average man than he has ever known before in the history of America."

Franklin D. Roosevelt
Fireside chat, September 1934

Howard Thain's painting, *The Great White Way, Times Square, 1925*, captures the upbeat mood of the 1920s. ▶

680

eTeach

Be sure to check out this month's online discussion with a Master Teacher. Go to **www.phschool.com**.

RESOURCE DIRECTORY

Teaching Resources
Units 7/8 booklet
- American Pathways Activity, pp. 44–45
- History's Lasting Impact, pp. 46–47
Geography and History booklet, pp. 14–15

Other Print Resources
Prentice Hall Assessment System
- Document-Based Assessment

Chapter 20 Postwar Social Change, 1920–1929
Chapter 21 Politics and Prosperity, 1920–1929
Chapter 22 Crash and Depression, 1929–1933
Chapter 23 The New Deal, 1933–1941

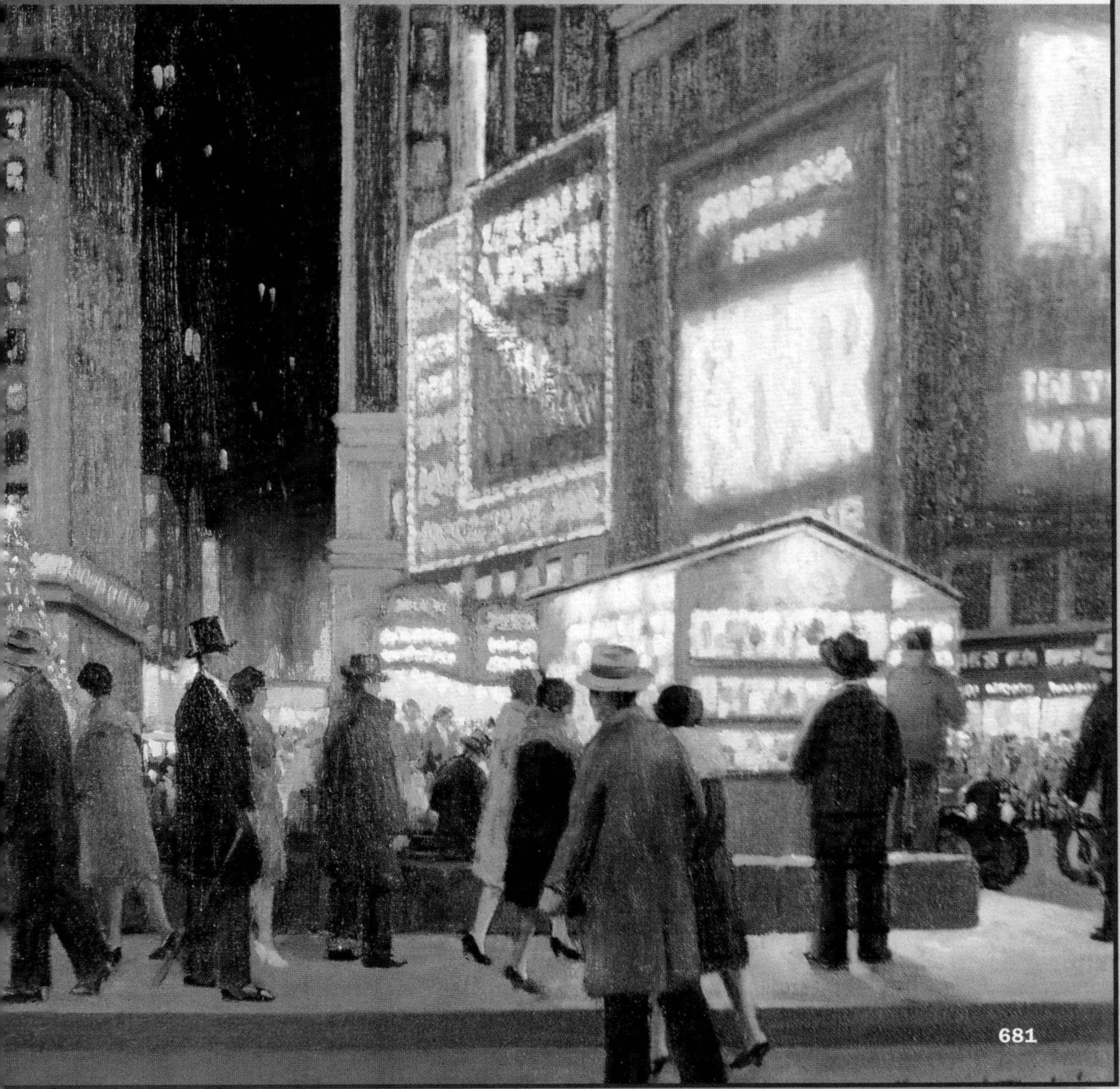

TECHNOLOGY CENTER

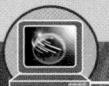

Take It to the NET

Prentice Hall School Web site offers student-appropriate Internet activities and links that extend core content. Visit us at the Social Studies area. **www.phschool.com**

AmericanHeritage®

My Brush with History™ Video Program This new video series lets your students learn history from the people who lived it.

RESOURCE PRO®

Teaching Resources on CD-ROM offer lesson-planning flexibility, test-generation capability, and resource manageability.

- **PRESENTATION PRO CD-ROM** Provides you with multimedia lecture notes for each chapter.
- **SOCIAL STUDIES SKILLS TUTOR CD-ROM** Provides interactive practice in Geographic Literacy, Critical Thinking and Reading, Visual Analysis, and Communications.
- **INTERACTIVE CONSTITUTION CD-ROM** Exploring active citizenship and civic responsibilities, this CD-ROM shows students how the Constitution affects their lives today.
- **EXPLORING PRIMARY SOURCES IN U.S. HISTORY CD-ROM** This interactive exploration of primary sources allows students to analyze and evaluate writing and images from American history.
- **GUIDED READING AUDIOTAPES**
- **STUDENT EDITION ON AUDIO CD**
- **SOUNDS OF AN ERA AUDIO CD** Bring the sounds of American history to life in the classroom with music, speeches, poetry, interviews, and news reports.

iTEXT

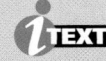

Don't miss the exclusive interactive version of this textbook on the Web and on CD-ROM.

RESOURCE DIRECTORY

Technology

Color Transparencies *Historical Maps,* A35; *Political Cartoons,* B12, B13; *Cause-and-Effect Charts,* D9; *Fine Art,* E17; *American Photo,* F7; *American Diversity,* G9, G12; *The Way It Works,* H17

Section Reading Support Transparencies

Prentice Hall United States History Video Collection™ Volume 17, *The Roaring Twenties;* Volume 18, *The Great Depression and the New Deal*

Companion Web site, www.phschool.com

Chapter 20 Planning Guide
Resource Manager

	CORE INSTRUCTION	READING/SKILLS
Chapter-Level Resources	**Teaching Resources** • Pacing Charts booklet • Block Scheduling booklet **Resource Pro® CD-ROM**, Ch. 20 **Prentice Hall Presentation Pro CD-ROM**, Ch. 20 **www.phschool.com** • eTeach	**Guided Reading Audiotapes (English/Spanish)** **Student Edition on Audio CD**, Ch. 20 **Social Studies Skills Tutor CD-ROM** **Color Transparencies**, E17, G19
1 Society in the 1920s 1. Learn how women's roles changed in the 1920s. 2. Find out how the nation's cities and suburbs were affected by Americans on the move from rural areas. 3. Read about America's heroes of the 1920s, and come to see the reasons for their popularity.	**Teaching Resources** **Units 7/8 booklet** • Section 1 Quiz, p. 4	**Guided Reading and Review booklet**, p. 83 **Guide to the Essentials**, p. 104 **Learning with Documents booklet**, p. 25 **Section Reading Support Transparencies**
2 Mass Media and the Jazz Age 1. See how the mass media helped create common cultural experiences. 2. Realize why the decade of the 1920s was called the Jazz Age, and learn how the jazz spirit affected the arts. 3. Discover how the writers of the Lost Generation responded to popular culture. 4. Find out about some of the subjects explored by the writers of the Harlem Renaissance.	**Teaching Resources** **Units 7/8 booklet** • Section 2 Quiz, p. 5 **Learning Styles Lesson Plans booklet**, p. 42	**Guided Reading and Review booklet**, p. 84 **Guide to the Essentials**, p. 105 **Learning with Documents booklet**, p. 59 **Skills for Life booklet**, p. 22 **Section Reading Support Transparencies**
3 Cultural Conflicts 1. Learn about the effects of Prohibition on society. 2. Discover the issues of religion that were at the core of the Scopes trial. 3. Find out how racial tensions changed after World War I.	**Teaching Resources** **Units 7/8 booklet** • Section 3 Quiz, p. 6 **Learning Styles Lesson Plans booklet**, p. 43	**Guided Reading and Review booklet**, p. 85 **Guide to the Essentials**, p. 106 **Learning with Documents booklet**, p. 59 **Section Reading Support Transparencies**

ENRICHMENT/PRE-AP

Prentice Hall United States History Video Collection™
www.phschool.com
- Section Activities, Virtual Field Trip, Chapter Activities, Current Events Online

Biography, Literature, and Comparing Primary Sources booklet, p. 25
Great Debates booklet, p. 38
Sounds of an Era Audio CD
Exploring Primary Sources in U.S. History CD-ROM

Biography, Literature, and Comparing Primary Sources booklet, p. 67
American History Block Scheduling Support
Sounds of an Era Audio CD
Exploring Primary Sources in U.S. History CD-ROM

Biography, Literature, and Comparing Primary Sources booklet, p. 135
Sounds of an Era Audio CD
American Pathways Thematic Posters

ASSESSMENT

PRENTICE HALL ASSESSMENT SYSTEM

Core Assessment
ExamView® Test Bank, Ch. 20
ExamView® Test Bank CD-ROM, Ch. 20

Standardized Test Preparation
Diagnose and Prescribe
Diagnostic Tests for High School Social Studies Skills

Review and Reteach
Review Book for U.S. History

Practice and Assess
Test-taking Strategies With Transparencies
Test-taking Strategies Posters
Test Prep Book for U.S. History
Alternative Assessment Handbook
Document-Based Assessment

Teaching Resources
Units 7/8 booklet
- Section Quizzes, pp. 4–6
- Chapter Tests, pp. 7, 10

www.phschool.com Ch. 20 Self-Test

AmericanHeritage RESOURCES

From the Archives of American Heritage®, pp. 692, 701
AmericanHeritage® My Brush with History™ Videotapes
www.americanheritage.com

iTEXT

Don't miss the exclusive interactive version of this textbook on the Web and on CD-ROM.

Chapter 20 Planning Guide
In Your Classroom

CUSTOMIZE FOR INDIVIDUAL NEEDS

Gifted and Talented

Teacher's Edition
- Customize for Gifted and Talented, pp. 693, 705

Teaching Resources
- Biography, Literature, and Comparing Primary Sources booklet, pp. 25, 67, 135

Technology
- Exploring Primary Sources in U.S. History CD-ROM *A Flapper's Appeal to Parents, Ellen Welles Page; Charles Lindbergh's Transatlantic Flight, The Japan Times; The Report of the Committee on Recent Economic Changes; As I Grew Older, Langston Hughes*

ESL

Teacher's Edition
- Customize for ESL, pp. 695, 701

Teaching Resources
- Guided Reading and Review booklet, pp. 83–85
- Guide to the Essentials (English/Spanish), Chapter 20

Technology
- Student Edition on Audio CD, Chapter 20
- Guided Reading Audiotapes (English/Spanish), Chapter 20
- Section Reading Support Transparencies

Less Proficient Readers

Teacher's Edition
- Customize for Less Proficient Readers, p. 703

Teaching Resources
- Guided Reading and Review booklet, pp. 83–85
- Guide to the Essentials (English/Spanish), Chapter 20

Technology
- Student Edition on Audio CD, Chapter 20
- Guided Reading Audiotapes (English/Spanish), Chapter 20
- Section Reading Support Transparencies

Less Proficient Writers

Teacher's Edition
- Customize for Less Proficient Writers, p. 687

Teaching Resources
- Guided Reading and Review booklet, pp. 83–85
- Guide to the Essentials (English/Spanish), Chapter 20

Technology
- Student Edition on Audio CD, Chapter 20
- Guided Reading Audiotapes (English/Spanish), Chapter 20
- Section Reading Support Transparencies

TEACHER'S EDITION INDEX

CHAPTER 20 – PACING SUGGESTIONS

 For 90-minute Blocks
- Teach section 1 using Transparencies E17 and G19, and the Recent Scholarship note on page 693 for class discussions.

 Running Out of Time?

If you are running short on time to cover this chapter, consider the following options:

- Use the Prentice Hall Presentation Pro CD-ROM to create an outline for this chapter.
- Use the Section Summaries for Chapter 20, from **Guide to the Essentials (English/Spanish).**

ADDITIONAL ACTIVITIES

1	**Society in the 1920s**	**Connecting with Culture** Have students locate and share photographs of events and people taken during the 1920s that they think capture the themes of this section, such as the changing roles of women, the youth culture, the changing demographics, and aviation and sports heroes. You may wish to have students make an oral presentation to the class during which they explain what they see in the examples they chose. **(Visual/Spatial)**
2	**Mass Media and the Jazz Age**	**Connecting with Culture** Have students re-create a 15-minute radio broadcast of the period that might have featured a jazz artist like Louis Armstrong or Duke Ellington. They can tape their introductions and selections so that other students can listen to them. **(Musical/Rhythmic)**
3	**Cultural Conflicts**	**Connecting to Today** Students can examine how modern-day restrictions on the sale of cigarettes compare to Prohibition. They can then use that evaluation to take a position on a total ban on the sale of cigarettes in the form of a persuasive essay for or against. **(Verbal/Linguistic)**

Chapter 20

Postwar Social Change

(1920–1929)

INTRODUCING THE CHAPTER

American society changed in many ways following World War I, as the Jazz Age introduced a variety of new styles, tastes, and manners. Conflict arose between Americans ready to adopt these new manners and new ways and Americans who tried to resist the forces of change.

TIME LINE ACTIVITY

To provide students with practice in using the time line, ask questions such as these:

1. What spurred the nationwide popularity of jazz? *(Broadcasting live jazz performances by radio)*

2. What famous discovery of this era changed the way we look at the ancient past? *(The discovery of King Tutankhamen's tomb in Egypt)*

3. What achievement combined bravery and technology to enthrall the world? *(Charles Lindbergh's successful transatlantic solo flight in 1927)*

Chapter 20

Postwar Social Change

(1920–1929)

SECTION 1   Society in the 1920s

SECTION 2   Mass Media and the Jazz Age

SECTION 3   Cultural Conflicts

Newspaper headline shows unrest in Chicago.

Campaign for Prohibition succeeds.

The Shadow of Danger

Heavyweight champion Jack Dempsey, sports hero of the 1920s.

American Events

1919
Race riots erupt in Chicago and other cities. Marcus Garvey launches the first of his Black Star Line ships for the Universal Negro Improvement Association.

1920
The Eighteenth Amendment institutes Prohibition. The Nineteenth Amendment gives women the right to vote.

1923
Louis Armstrong makes his first jazz recording. Duke Ellington begins playing in Harlem's jazz clubs. Jazz is made more popular by a growing radio audience.

1924
Women governors are elected in Wyoming and Texas.

Presidential Terms: Woodrow Wilson 1913–1921   Warren G. Harding 1921–1923   Calvin Coolidge 1923–1929

1918   •   1920   1922   •   1924

World Events

Dutch painter Piet Mondrian publishes his ideas on "neoplastic" style.
1920

King Tutankhamen's tomb is discovered in Egypt.
1922

First Winter Olympic games are held in Chamonix, France.
1924

eTeach

Be sure to check out this month's online discussion with a Master Teacher. Go to **www.phschool.com**.

RESOURCE DIRECTORY

Teaching Resources
Pacing Charts booklet
Block Scheduling booklet, p. 23
Units 7/8 booklet
  • Chapter Summary, p. 3

Technology
Guided Reading Audiotapes (English/Spanish), Ch. 20
Student Edition on Audio CD, Ch. 20
Sounds of an Era Audio CD *"Livery Stable Blues"* (time: 45 seconds)

Prentice Hall United States History Video Collection™ Volume 17, *The Roaring Twenties*
Prentice Hall Presentation Pro CD-ROM, Ch. 20
Resource Pro® CD-ROM
Social Studies Skills Tutor CD-ROM
Companion Web site, www.phschool.com

The Growth of Urban Areas, 1900–1920

CANADA

ATLANTIC OCEAN

MEXICO

Gulf of Mexico

Population by 1900
- Cities over 10,000
- Cities over 100,000

Population by 1920
- Cities over 10,000
- Cities over 100,000

People Per Square Mile 1920
- 45–90
- 18–45
- 2–18
- under 2

0   150   300 mi.
0   150   300 km

Sixth Avenue Elevated at Third Street, 1928, by John Sloan.

Actress Lillian Gish, star of silent films and "talkies."

1925
The Scopes trial stirs a national debate on evolution.

1926
Gertrude Ederle becomes the first woman to swim across the English Channel.

1927
Aviator Charles Lindbergh completes the first nonstop transatlantic solo flight.

Herbert Hoover 1929–1933

1926   1928   1930

Japan enacts universal male suffrage.

1925

The Threepenny Opera by Bertolt Brecht and Kurt Weill debuts in Berlin.

1928

The term *apartheid* is introduced in South Africa.

1929

Chapter 20   683

BIBLIOGRAPHY

For the Teacher

Delany, Sarah Louise and Elizabeth. *Having Our Say: The Delany Sisters' First 100 Years.* Dell, 1996. (Two noted African American centenarians share their memories, in memorable fashion.)

Lemann, Nicholas. *The Promised Land, The Great Black Migration and How It Changed America.* Vintage, 1992. (Scholarly examination of the tremendous impact of this mass movement on both cities and rural areas.)

For the Student

Editors of Time-Life Books. *The Jazz Age: The 20s (Our American Century).* Time-Life, 1998. (Colorful, lively account of an interesting era.)

Willis-Thomas, Deborah, et al. *Van Der Zee.* Harry N. Abrams, 1998. (Harlem in its heyday as seen by its most famous photographer.)

The Growth of Urban Areas, 1900–1920

Activating Prior Knowledge Where were more people per square mile concentrated—in the eastern or western part of the United States? *(Eastern)*

Previewing Between 1900 and 1920, there were changes regarding the places many people chose to live. Looking at the map, find one such change that took place. *(More people chose to live in large cities in 1920 than in 1900.)*

BACKGROUND
About the Pictures

1   2   3   4   5

1. The Chicago Race Riots of 1919 shocked the nation and after five days of rioting left 38 people dead and hundreds more injured.

2. During the 1920s, anti-alcohol groups attempted to sway the public toward supporting Prohibition because the enforcement of Prohibition laws was proving to be nearly impossible without public support.

3. The heavyweight boxing match between American Jack Dempsey and Frenchman Georges Carpentier was the first boxing match broadcast over the radio. Grossing over one million dollars in ticket sales, the fight lasted only 11 minutes as Dempsey completely overpowered Carpentier.

4. New York's trolley system was extensive, providing transportation to most parts of the city. New York was also one of the first cities to run its trolleys through underground tunnels, or subways.

5. One of the most prolific and popular actresses of the twentieth century, Lillian Gish had a career that spanned 75 years, beginning with her first film in 1912 and ending with her last in 1987.

i TEXT

Don't miss the exclusive interactive version of this textbook on the Web and on CD-ROM.

Section 1
Society in the 1920s

SECTION OBJECTIVES

1. Learn how women's roles changed in the 1920s.
2. Find out how the nation's cities and suburbs were affected by Americans on the move from rural areas.
3. Read about America's heroes of the 1920s, and come to see the reasons for their popularity.

BELLRINGER

Warm-Up Activity Ask students if they have ever moved and, if so, for what reasons. Which state or region of the country do they think currently provides the best opportunity for good jobs and advancement?

Activating Prior Knowledge Have students research the populations of several major American cities based on data from the 1920 census and the 1930 census. Which cities experienced the greatest growth in population?

READING STRATEGY

Have students copy the headings in this section. As they read, they should write down at least two key points under each heading.

CAPTION ANSWERS

Viewing History The flapper wears a carefree smile and kicks up her leg, as though dancing the Charleston. Her knee-length skirt, short hair, and cloche hat are some of the new fashions appearing in the 1920s.

READING FOCUS

• How were women's roles changing during the 1920s?
• How were the nation's cities and suburbs affected by Americans on the move from rural areas?
• Who were some American heroes of the 1920s? What made them popular with the American public?

MAIN IDEA

The 1920s were a time of rapid social change, in which many young people, particularly young women, adopted new lifestyles and attitudes. As its rural population decreased, the United States became an urban nation, and traditional values were increasingly challenged.

KEY TERMS

flapper
demographics
barrio

TAKING NOTES

Copy the chart below. As you read, fill in details relating to various social changes of the 1920s.

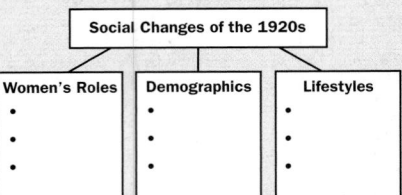

Social Changes of the 1920s
- Women's Roles
- Demographics
- Lifestyles

VIEWING HISTORY Flappers defined a new style of dress. **Drawing Inferences** *How does this young woman's attitude reflect the mood of the 1920s?*

Setting the Scene The decade of the 1920s stands out as a time of rapid change in American society. Much of the change had its roots in the previous century. In the late 1800s, industrialization and immigration began transforming the United States into an urban nation. Farm families streamed into the cities. Along with masses of immigrants, the new arrivals helped form a more complex urban culture.

The Great War accelerated those changes. Millions of young people had marched off to war full of enthusiasm. Many returned bearing the scars of that war: shell shock, permanent injury, and the effects of poison gas. Many also came back disillusioned, a condition they shared with others who had stayed home during the war. Together, they questioned the ideas and attitudes that had led to the war. Their challenge of traditional values helped ignite a revolution in manners and morals.

The **flapper** symbolized this revolution. The term described a new type of young woman: rebellious, energetic, fun-loving, and bold. One author depicted the flapper this way:

> 66 *Breezy, slangy, and informal in manner; slim and boyish in form; covered in silk and fur that clung to her as close as onion skin; with carmined [vivid red] cheeks and lips, plucked eyebrows and close-fitting helmet of hair; gay, plucky and confident.* 99
> —Preston Slosson, *The Great Crusade and After*, 1930

Many older Americans held more traditional views of how young women were supposed to behave in public. They disapproved not only of the flappers' display of free manners but also of the behavior of the young men who flocked around them.

Of course, not all young women became flappers, and not everyone questioned traditional values. Still, those who did had a lasting effect on society. They helped create what we think of today as modern America.

RESOURCE DIRECTORY

Teaching Resources
Guided Reading and Review booklet, p. 83
Learning with Documents booklet (Primary Source Activity) *The Younger Generation,* p. 25

Technology
Section Reading Support Transparencies
Guided Reading Audiotapes (English/Spanish), Ch. 20
Student Edition on Audio CD, Ch. 20

Sounds of an Era Audio CD *"Have You Seen Rosie's Sister?"* 1925 recording (time: one minute)
Exploring Primary Sources in U.S. History CD-ROM *A Flapper's Appeal to Parents, Ellen Welles Page*
Prentice Hall Presentation Pro CD-ROM, Ch. 20
Companion Web site, www.phschool.com

Women's Changing Roles

Women stood at the center of much of the social change in the 1920s. Both single and married women had been in the work force for a long time. During the war, their numbers rose and they moved into better, higher-paying jobs. After the Nineteenth Amendment was adopted in 1920, all American women could vote. These experiences made them eager for still greater equality with men. Without intending to, the rebellious flapper brought all women closer to that goal.

The Flapper Image The flapper represented only a small number of American women, yet her image had a wide impact on fashion and on behavior. Stylish young women began wearing dresses shorter than their mothers did, to the dismay of some guardians of decency. The fashion page of the *New York Times* declared in July 1920 that "the American woman . . . has lifted her skirts far beyond any modest limitation." At that time, hemlines had risen to just nine inches above the ground. By 1927, they would rise to knee-length or even higher. Between 1913 and 1928, the average amount of fabric used to make a woman's outfit shrank from 19.5 yards to just 7 yards.

Women also broke with the past in other ways. While most of their mothers had grown their hair long and then pinned it up, young women bobbed, or cut short, their hair. Instead of wide-brimmed hats, they wore the close-fitting "cloche," whose bell shape accentuated the new hairstyles. They also began wearing heavy makeup, a practice formerly associated only with actresses or prostitutes.

Women's manners changed as well. Before the 1920s, "proper" women rarely drank anything much stronger than wine, much less smoked, in public. By the end of the decade, many women were doing both, in part to defy Prohibition, but also to express their new freedom. Between 1918 and 1928, the number of cigarettes produced in the United States more than doubled. Though men were smoking more (many switching from cigars and pipes to cigarettes), the new woman smoker accounted for a large part of the increase. All these changes shocked American society and enraged many parents.

Women Working and Voting Although many women bobbed their hair and wore shorter skirts, most did not embrace a flapper lifestyle. Some women adopted the new fashions simply because they were more convenient.

Convenience was an issue for young working women, as they had less time to spend maintaining elaborate wardrobes or hairstyles. During the 1920s, about 15 percent of wage-earning women became professionals and about 20 percent held clerical positions. Generally, these were single white women, although the percentage of married women working increased from 23 percent of the total female work force in 1920 to 29 percent in 1930.

Businesses remained prejudiced against women seeking professional posts. Many hospitals refused to hire female doctors, and many legal firms rejected female lawyers or offered them secretarial jobs. Employers seldom trained women for jobs beyond the entry level or paid them on as high a scale as men. Few women advanced to leadership positions. Employers expected women to quit if they married and became pregnant.

Fast Forward to Today

Women in the Workplace

Over time, the nature of women's work has changed to accommodate the needs of the labor market and changes in attitudes about women working outside the home. In a rural setting, women looking for outside work have typically found their choices more limited than in a city. As more and more people moved from rural areas in the 1920s, growing urban economies made room for women to enter the paid work force. The 1920s saw many women securing clerical jobs, work once reserved for men. From the 1920s to today, work available to women in the United States has expanded from jobs women have traditionally held, such as teaching and nursing, to include a range of options never before available.

As shown by the chart below, the percentage of women in the labor force has risen from the 1920s to the 1990s.

? What types of jobs are limited to rural areas or to cities today?

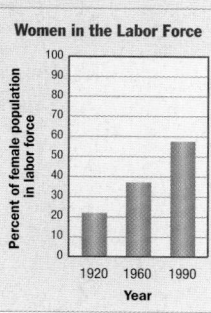

Women in the Labor Force

(bar graph: vertical axis "Percent of female population in labor force" 0–100; horizontal axis "Year" 1920, 1960, 1990)

READING CHECK

In a very limited manner. Many women failed to vote. Women who did vote had little effect on national politics, but did impact local campaigns. By the end of the decade, many women had been elected to state legislatures, and two female state governors had been elected.

CAPTION ANSWERS

Viewing History Disinterest; difficulty finding child care; family members may have discouraged it.

VIEWING HISTORY In 1920, women in New York City vote after the adoption of the Nineteenth Amendment. **Drawing Conclusions** *Why do you think more women did not turn out to vote in the early 1920s?*

READING CHECK
How did women influence politics in the 1920s?

Like the situation of women at work, women's status in politics changed little. As of 1920, women could vote in all elections. At first, some politicians feared that women might vote as a bloc, or special-interest group. That did not happen. Most women voted along the same lines as men. Moreover, relatively few women voted at all, especially in the early years after gaining national suffrage. Only about 35 percent of women voters went to the polls in 1920. In 1923, a survey asked women in Chicago why they did not vote in the mayoral election. Most notably, about a third said that they lacked interest. Another eleven percent said that they did not think women should vote at all.

Early on, women did not exercise their right to vote for a number of reasons. Women who lived in rural areas or had children to look after had to make special arrangements to get to the polls. Sometimes women's families discouraged them from voting. Other women were not comfortable with the idea of voting. In short, women had yet to make voting a habit, and it would take time for the habit to develop.

As the decade wore on, more women voted, but their choices did not change politics greatly. In national elections, women voted in patterns similar to men's. In local elections, however, women's votes often differed from men's, perhaps because women were more familiar with the candidates and issues.

After the Nineteenth Amendment was adopted, the alliance that worked for suffrage split, weakening its ability to push bills through Congress. Progressive reformers did lobby successfully for the Sheppard-Towner Act of 1921, the first major federal welfare measure concerned with women's and children's health. A constitutional amendment calling for an end to child labor failed, however. So did the Equal Rights Amendment (ERA), introduced in Congress for the first time in 1923. The original wording of the ERA stated that "Men and women shall have equal rights throughout the United States and every place subject to its jurisdiction." Some reformers opposed the ERA because it would make the laws requiring special working conditions for women unconstitutional.

Despite their disagreements, women worked together to win political office. Jeannette Rankin of Montana won election to the U.S. House of Representatives in 1916, becoming the first woman to serve in either house of Congress. Miriam A. Ferguson from Texas and Nellie Tayloe Ross of Wyoming, both wives of former governors, were elected governors themselves in 1924. By 1928, there were 145 women in 38 state legislatures. Thus, although women did not increase their political power as quickly as suffragists had hoped, they did lay a foundation for future participation in government on a larger scale.

Americans on the Move

In addition to social changes, many changes in **demographics** occurred in the 1920s. Demographics are the statistics that describe a population, such as data on race or income. The major demographic change of the 1920s was a movement away from the countryside. The 1920 census showed that for the first time in the nation's history, more Americans lived in urban areas than in rural areas.

Rural-Urban Split The 1920s magnified the gap between rural and urban society. One aspect of that gap was economic. Farmers had done well for the first two decades of the century. After the war, however, market prices dropped while the costs of operation rose. By the early 1920s, many farmers were economically stressed.

Meanwhile, the industrial and commercial economy began to boom. This prosperity bypassed much of rural America. Many farmers reluctantly left the land and headed to cities. During the decade, some 6 million people moved from rural to urban areas.

This migration, combined with urban prosperity, had important effects on society. Attendance at public high schools rose from 2.2 million in 1920 to 4.4 million by 1930. Some of this rise came from an increase in urban population and greater prosperity, but an important part of it resulted from a change in the labor pool. On farms, most older children played vital roles as laborers, so they often had to drop out of school to help their parents. In cities, children needed more education to compete in urban-based industry.

Rural and urban America also split over cultural issues. You read earlier about the change in manners and morals. This general shift away from traditional values took place mainly in the cities. Most rural populations wanted to preserve traditional values, not defy them. They frowned on the flappers and other aspects of society that they deemed immoral or dangerous.

African Americans in the North As you have read, the passage of Jim Crow laws, as well as new job opportunities in the North, produced the Great Migration of blacks from the South to northern cities. This migration continued from the late 1800s through World War I. The boom in northern industries further encouraged this demographic shift.

Throughout the early 1900s, jobs for African Americans in the South had been scarce and low-paying. Many factories refused to hire blacks for anything other than menial jobs. As industries expanded during the 1920s, many jobs opened up for African Americans in the North. In 1860, 93 percent of all African Americans lived in the South. By 1910, this figure had dropped to 89 percent. By 1930, it had fallen far more, to 80 percent.

Yet the North was no promised land. African American factory workers often faced anger and hatred from whites, who believed that migrants would work for lower wages and take their jobs. African American women generally worked for very low wages as household help for whites.

Other Migration After World War I, masses of refugees applied for entry into the United States. During the 1920s, Congress acted to limit immigration, especially from southern and eastern Europe and also from China and Japan. Since the limits did not apply to nations in the Americas, employers turned to immigrants from Mexico and Canada to fill low-paying jobs.

In the West, Mexicans supplied most of this labor, migrating to work on the farms of California and the ranches of Texas. In the Northeast, Canadians from the French-speaking province of Quebec traveled south to work in the paper mills, potato fields, and forests of New England and New York.

Migrants also took jobs in the cities. Los Angeles, for example, became a magnet for Mexicans and developed a distinct **barrio,** or Spanish-speaking neighborhood. New York also attracted a Spanish-speaking population— Puerto Ricans migrating in the hope of a better life in the United States.

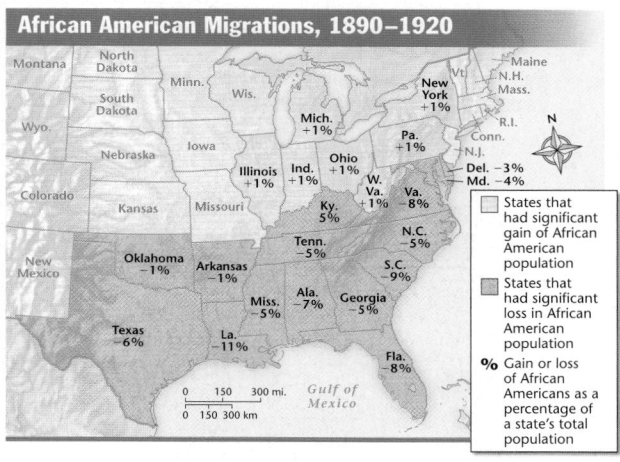

African American Migrations, 1890–1920

States that had significant gain of African American population

States that had significant loss in African American population

% Gain or loss of African Americans as a percentage of a state's total population

MAP SKILLS The migration of African Americans from the South to the North helped alter the populations of both regions. **Movement** *Which states lost the largest percentages of their black populations?*

ACTIVITY
Connecting with Geography

Have half of your students conduct research to find out the percentage of Americans who were living in rural areas and the percentage of Americans who were living in urban areas in 1920. Have the second half find the same data for the year 1930. Then have students cooperate to create a line graph that shows the changes during the 1920s. Ask them how the graph emphasizes the demographic changes of 1920s America. **(Visual/Spatial)**

BACKGROUND
Connections to Today

Most African Americans who migrated to the North during the late nineteenth and early twentieth centuries settled in urban areas. Urban areas were the seats of the economic opportunities the migrants sought. Upon arrival, a combination of poverty on the part of the new migrants and racism on the part of property owners ensured that African Americans were forced to settle in less desirable parts of towns. This settlement pattern is still in evidence today: many northern cities still have segregated neighborhoods, and many primarily African American areas are the same ones that were created during the early twentieth-century migrations from the South.

CUSTOMIZE FOR ...
Less Proficient Writers
Have students create two lists with the headings: *Jobs in the Country* and *Jobs in the City.* Have them list some of the jobs they could imagine someone a little older than themselves holding in the country and in the city in the 1920s. Have them put a star next to each job that would require a high school education or more.

✓ TEST PREPARATION
Have students review the material on the previous page about migration of Mexicans to United States cities and then complete the sentence below.

According to the text, the word *barrio* **means—**

A region.

Ⓑ neighborhood.

C country.

D state.

CAPTION ANSWERS

Map Skills Louisiana lost 11 percent of its African American population. South Carolina lost 9 percent.

MAP SKILLS Charles Lindbergh's transatlantic flight helped foster the development of commercial aviation. Lindbergh is shown below with his *Spirit of St. Louis.* **Location** *What body of water did Lindbergh cross from New York to Paris?*

Lindbergh's Famous Route

Lindbergh begins record-setting test flight May 10, 1927, stopping in St. Louis and landing in New York the next day.

Lindbergh lands at Le Bourget Field, 33 hours and 30 minutes after leaving New York.

Lindbergh's transatlantic journey begins at Roosevelt Field on Long Island, May 20, 1927.

→ Charles Lindbergh's route

688

Growth of the Suburbs As a result of the migrations of the 1920s, American suburbs grew. Suburban growth had begun to accelerate in the late nineteenth century. Cities built transportation systems that used electric trolleys—cars that ran on rails laid in the streets, and were powered by overhead wires. Trolleys allowed people to get from their suburban homes to jobs and stores in the city cheaply.

During the 1920s, buses replaced trolleys in many areas. Buses did not need rails and overhead wires, and thus were less expensive and easier to route. By the mid-1920s, about 70,000 buses were operating throughout the United States. At the same time, the automobile became more affordable to middle-class families and offered even greater flexibility in travel.

New York City provides a good example of the demographic changes that occurred during the 1920s. The number of residents decreased in Manhattan, the heart of the city, while the suburb of Queens saw its population double.

American Heroes

The changing morals of the 1920s made many Americans hungry for the values of an earlier time. Many in the nation became fascinated with heroes. Some were admired for their bravery and modesty, others for the way they showed Americans how to meet new challenges, with spirit and vitality. Among the decade's heroes, none became more famous than Charles Lindbergh.

"Lucky Lindy" The sky was drizzling rain at Roosevelt Field on Long Island, New York, on the morning of May 20, 1927. A 25-year-old Minnesotan, Charles Lindbergh, climbed into the cockpit of his plane, the *Spirit of St. Louis,* and revved the engine. He had not slept much, but he did not dare wait any longer. Two other teams were waiting on the airfield, hoping to be the first to fly nonstop from

The Last Flight of Amelia Earhart

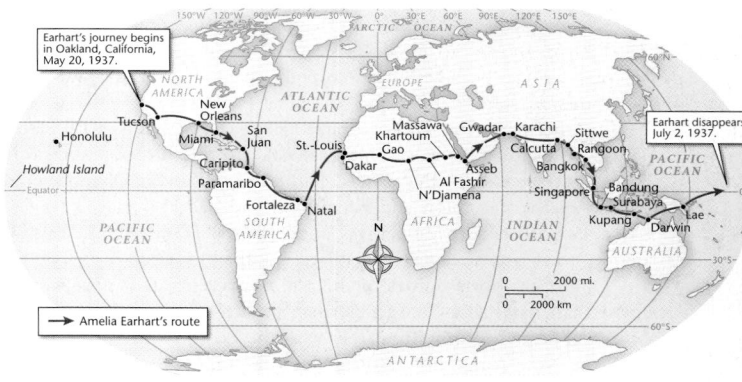

Earhart's journey begins in Oakland, California, May 20, 1937.

Earhart disappears July 2, 1937.

→ Amelia Earhart's route

MAP SKILLS The map shows the route aviator Amelia Earhart and navigator Fred Noonan took in their attempt to fly around the world. **Regions** *What continents did Earhart and Noonan fly over on their journey?*

Amelia Earhart helped open the field of aviation to more women.

New York to Paris. The prize was $25,000, and Lindbergh was determined to capture it.

In those days, flying was an infant science. Orville and Wilbur Wright had achieved the first powered, sustained, and controlled airplane flight only two decades earlier, in 1903. Radio and navigation equipment were primitive at best, and Lindbergh had no autopilot to switch on if he grew tired. Flying solo, he would have to stay awake and alert for the entire flight.

The minute Lindbergh's plane was aloft, the news flashed by telegraph and telephone to news desks around the nation. Americans everywhere took notice and began to wait eagerly for the latest word. The newspapers fed this hunger, printing some 27,000 columns of information about Lindbergh in the first few days after his departure.

After a brutal flight over the Atlantic Ocean, battling icy weather and fighting off sleep, "Lucky Lindy" landed safely in an airfield outside Paris, 33½ hours after he had left New York. America went wild with jubilation. Lindbergh was brought home on a navy cruiser, given the Congressional Medal of Honor, and celebrated with parades throughout the nation.

Yet despite this frenzy of hero-worship, Lindbergh remained modest and calm. He refused offers of millions of dollars in publicity fees. To millions of Americans, Lindbergh was proof that the solid moral values of the old days lived on in the heartland of America. The public's fascination with Lindbergh may have played a role in a great tragedy for him, however, when one night his firstborn son was kidnapped from his crib. The child was later found murdered. Ironically, the murder case brought Lindbergh and his family more media attention than ever before.

Amelia Earhart   Lindbergh's feat inspired later flyers, including Amelia Earhart. In 1928, Earhart became the first woman to fly across the Atlantic, although she was only a passenger. In 1932, she made the trip on her own, becoming the first woman to fly solo across the Atlantic. Later Earhart set another record, as the first person to fly solo from Hawaii to California, a challenge that had resulted in the deaths of many aviators before her. In 1937, Earhart and her navigator, Fred Noonan, tried to fly around the world. After completing two thirds of the trip, they disappeared mysteriously while crossing the Pacific Ocean.

Reading Comprehension

1. The bold and rebellious spirit of the flapper inspired women of the 1920s to pursue equality and to challenge their roles in society.

2. Low market prices and higher operational costs caused many farmers to move to cities, which were experiencing an economic boom. Job opportunities in expanding industries drew African Americans north. Mexicans and Canadians arrived to fill low-paying positions as immigration from Europe and Asia became restricted. Expanded transportation systems spurred the growth of suburbs.

3. Many Mexicans seeking work moved to Los Angeles, where they lived in a common neighborhood in which Spanish was the primary language.

Critical Thinking and Writing

4. Sample answer: Young people today question traditional values; challenge traditional roles; and favor fashions, manners, and morals that might shock the older generation.

5. Answers will vary, but might point out that voter turnout among women in the early 1920s was surprisingly low.

Students should note the achievements of and important facts about both aviators: Lindbergh's solo, non-stop, transatlantic flight, the kidnapping of his baby, and his involvement in politics; Earhart becoming the first woman to fly solo across the Atlantic Ocean, creating opportunities for American women in aviation, and her mysterious disappearance.

CAPTION ANSWERS

Viewing History The spectators are wearing coats. Thus, the air and the water are probably cold. The grease is probably to keep Ederle warm and to help her swim faster. It is a highly publicized swim since there are spectators and someone helping her to prepare.

Sports Heroes Though spectator sports had long been popular with the American public, they became big business in the 1920s. The new, heavy commercialization of sports led to larger audiences and more revenues. A highly publicized fight between boxers Jack Dempsey and Georges Carpentier in 1921 broke the record for ticket sales, taking in $1 million. Dempsey won the fight to become the heavyweight champion of the world and a new American hero.

Another hero, Jim Thorpe, starred as a professional football player in the 1920s. By then he was in the late stages of his career, and his role was to attract fans to the games. Earlier, he had won Olympic gold medals in the decathlon and pentathlon and had also played professional baseball. Thorpe, a Native American, was elected the first president of what later became the National Football League.

Of all the sports heroes of the era, none generated more excitement than baseball's George Herman "Babe" Ruth, known as "the Sultan of Swat." During his career with the Boston Red Sox and then with the New York Yankees, Ruth hit 714 home runs, a record that was unbroken for nearly 40 years. In 1927, the champion enthralled Americans by setting the legendary record of 60 home runs in a 154-game season.

VIEWING HISTORY At Cape Gris Nez, France, Gertrude Ederle is greased up in preparation for her swim across the English Channel. **Analyzing Visual Information** What does the photograph show about the difficulties of a Channel swim and what the feat might mean to the public?

Women who excelled in sports included Hazel Wightman and Helen Wills, Olympic and Wimbledon tennis stars, and Gertrude Ederle, who smashed record after record in women's freestyle swimming. Ederle won one gold and two bronze medals in the 1924 Olympic Games. Newspapers hailed her as the "bob-haired, nineteen-year-old daughter of the Jazz Age." Her coach explained that her feat was a product of modern times. Thirty years previously, he said, "corsets and other ridiculously unnecessary clothing" would have hampered her physical conditioning. In 1926, Ederle became the first woman to swim the English Channel, having made an unsuccessful attempt the year before. She covered some 35 miles, taking into account crosscurrents and rough water. Her time beat the men's record by nearly two hours.

Besides being eager spectators, more Americans participated in amateur sports during the 1920s. With wide-ranging transportation, such as buses and automobiles, plus more leisure time, people took up golf, tennis, swimming, and many other types of recreation.

Section 1 Assessment

READING COMPREHENSION

1. How did the **flapper** symbolize change for women in the 1920s?

2. What conditions brought about the **demographic** shifts of the 1920s?

3. How did a **barrio** develop in Los Angeles during the 1920s?

CRITICAL THINKING AND WRITING

4. **Making Comparisons** How is today's youth culture similar to the youth culture of the 1920s?

5. **Writing a News Brief** Write a short news article and headline reporting on women voting in 1920 after the adoption of the Nineteenth Amendment.

Take It to the NET

Activity: Writing a Biography Research the lives of Charles Lindbergh and Amelia Earhart. Use the links provided in the *America: Pathways to the Present* area of the following Web site for help in completing this activity. **www.phschool.com**

RESOURCE DIRECTORY

Teaching Resources
Units 7/8 booklet
• Section 1 Quiz, p. 4
Guide to the Essentials
• Section 1 Summary, p. 104

Technology
Exploring Primary Sources in U.S. History
CD-ROM *The Report of the Committee on Recent Economic Changes*

READING FOCUS

- How did the mass media help create common cultural experiences?
- Why are the 1920s called the Jazz Age, and how did the jazz spirit affect the arts?
- How did the writers of the Lost Generation respond to the popular culture?
- What subjects did the Harlem Renaissance writers explore?

MAIN IDEA

In the 1920s, the mass media provided information and entertainment as never before. The decade was an especially creative period for music, art, and literature.

KEY TERMS

mass media
Jazz Age
Lost Generation
Harlem Renaissance

TAKING NOTES

Copy the web diagram below. As you read, fill in the blank circles with details on how the mass media affected American life.

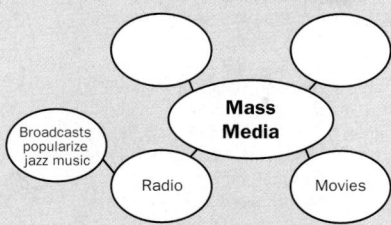

Setting the Scene

Before 1900, few people outside Los Angeles had even heard of a dusty little subdivision northwest of the city. Its founder, a religious man, hoped that it would remain a quiet town, where citizens valued proper behavior. In the early 1900s, however, filmmakers began moving there. They were attracted by the large work force in nearby Los Angeles; by the variety of landscapes, from desert to snowy mountains; and by the warm climate and the sun they needed to light their films.

These pioneer filmmakers faced many difficulties. Director Cecil B. DeMille set up his first studio in a rented barn, which he shared with horses and a carriage. DeMille later wrote, "I expected to be working like a horse: what did it matter being housed like one?"

In the early 1920s, DeMille became known for his stylish comedies that dealt with the changing romance customs of the time, and for his epics, which were designed to appeal to mass audiences. The barn he rented grew into a huge movie complex and the small suburb it was located in—Hollywood—soon became the center of the entertainment film industry. The town's main avenue displayed a strip of expensive shops and bars. Stars drove the streets in luxurious cars, trailed by reporters. In turn, what grew out of Hollywood in the 1920s—its culture of movies, movie stars, and entertainment reporters—helped create the beginnings of a common national culture.

The Mass Media

Hollywood's new fame reflected a major trend of the 1920s. Before that time, the United States had been largely a collection of regional cultures. Interests, tastes, and attitudes varied widely from one region to another. Most Americans simply did not know much about the rest of the country, talk with people in other regions, or even read the same news as other Americans.

VIEWING HISTORY Hollywood's Mulholland Drive is shown in this 1924 photo. The now-famous sign in the hills was erected to promote a real-estate development. **Analyzing Visual Information** *What details in the photograph show Hollywood's past and future?*

Chapter 20 • Section 2   691

Section 2

Mass Media and the Jazz Age

SECTION OBJECTIVES

1. See how the mass media helped create common cultural experiences.
2. Realize why the decade of the 1920s was called the Jazz Age, and learn how the jazz spirit affected the arts.
3. Discover how the writers of the Lost Generation responded to popular culture.
4. Find out about some of the subjects explored by the writers of the Harlem Renaissance.

BELLRINGER

Warm-Up Activity Ask students what new source of information became popular in the 1990s. *(The Internet)* How has it affected communication? In what other ways has it affected life in the United States?

Activating Prior Knowledge Many artists, writers, and performers of this era are still known today. Ask students if they can identify individuals such as Duke Ellington, Louis Armstrong, Ernest Hemingway, Greta Garbo, and Charlie Chaplin.

READING STRATEGY

As students read, have them write down facts that will help them define what the Jazz Age was. Then have them use their notes to write a one-sentence definition.

CAPTION ANSWERS

Viewing History The road looks new and barren. Thus, Hollywood in the 1920s had not yet been built up very much. The future is indicated by the sign which, in shortened form, would signify that the word "Hollywood" had become synonymous with "movies."

Focus In the 1920s developments in communication, entertainment, and the arts contributed to the growth of a distinctly American culture. Ask students what these developments were. How did they affect life in the United States?

Instruct Discuss the role of the mass media. How did newspapers and radio help to create a national culture?

Ask students how radio helped make jazz a part of American culture. Who were some of the most well-known jazz musicians during the 1920s?

Discuss the role of other art forms and artists in the 1920s. How did writers of the Lost Generation express their discontent with American culture? What was the contribution of the Harlem Renaissance to American literature?

Assess/Reteach Ask students to discuss some of the reasons why the decade of the 1920s saw such an outpouring of creativity in all areas of the arts.

BACKGROUND
Interdisciplinary

The stunning growth of the popularity of films during the 1920s was accompanied by the growth of their influence on American culture. For the first time, movies set trends. In 1929 a study revealed that chorus girls and flappers, as portrayed on the big screen, had become the standards by which women judged their appearance and behavior. "These modern pictures," a sixteen-year-girl of the time said, "give me a feeling to imitate their ways."

Focus on
TECHNOLOGY

Adding Sound to Movies The system used to record and play sound in *The Jazz Singer* (below) was known as Vitaphone, which used a 16-inch rotating wax disk to record the movie's singing and speech. The sound was then synchronized with the film and amplified by loudspeakers in the theater. The Vitaphone system offered the best sound quality of its time.

Another method of making sound movies involved recording sound directly onto film. Although the early use of this method produced poor sound quality and distortion, by the 1930s it became the preferred technology for making "talkies."

The 1920s changed all that. Films, nationwide news gathering, and the new industry of radio broadcasting produced the beginnings of a national culture. As you have read, early in the decade few American women dressed in the flapper style or smoked and drank in public. Such customs became common cultural experiences because of the growth of the mass media. The **mass media** are print and broadcast methods of communicating information to large numbers of people.

Movies From their beginnings in the 1890s, motion pictures had been a wildly popular mass medium, and through the 1920s, audiences grew. Between 1910 and 1930, the number of theaters rose from about 5,000 to about 22,500. By 1929, when the total population was less than 125 million, the nation's theaters sold roughly 80 million tickets each week. Moviemaking had become the fourth largest business in the country.

This growth occurred throughout the silent film era. In 1927, the success of the first sound film, *The Jazz Singer,* changed the course of the movie industry. Starring vaudeville performer Al Jolson, the movie included speech, singing, music, and sound effects. Audiences loved it. As more theaters played "talkies," the industry's boom continued.

Some actors never made the shift from silent films to sound films. Foreign actors, for example, often faced the choice of learning English or giving up their movie careers. Other actors moved more smoothly to talkies. Greta Garbo, a glamorous star of the silent screen, retained her popularity in speaking roles despite a heavy Swedish accent. Silent screen actress Lillian Gish won renown for playing the part of the delicate heroine. She readily transferred her expressive gestures and heart-rending glances to speaking roles. Charlie Chaplin extended the silent era. Dressed in his famous tattered suit, derby hat, and cane, Chaplin had delighted American audiences since 1914 with his silent comedy. In the era of sound, Chaplin added music to his films and successfully continued his soundless portrayal of the "little tramp."

Newspapers and Magazines Americans followed the off-screen lives of their favorite stars in two other mass media—newspapers and magazines. During the 1920s, newspapers increased both in size and in circulation, or readership. In 1900, a hefty edition of the *New York Times* totaled only 14 pages. By the mid-1920s, however, newspapers even in mid-sized American cities often totaled more than 50 pages a day, and Sunday editions were enormous. In fact, the use of newsprint roughly doubled in the United States between 1914 and 1927.

Even as newspapers grew and gained more readers, the number of independently owned newspapers fell. Many disappeared as a result of mergers. A newspaper chain, owned by a single individual or company, often bought up two of a city's established papers and merged them. Thus they created one newspaper with potentially twice the circulation. The larger the circulation, the more money that advertisers would pay to market their products in the paper and the greater the profits for the publisher. Between 1923 and 1927, the number of chains doubled, and the total number of newspapers they owned rose by 50 percent.

Profits, not quality, drove most of these newspaper chains. To attract readers, especially in the cities, many chains published tabloids. A tabloid is a compact newspaper that relies on large headlines, few words, and many pictures to tell a story. Tabloids of the 1920s replaced serious news with entertainment that focused on fashion, sports, and sensational stories about crimes and scandals. This content sold papers, as publisher William Randolph Hearst knew well. Hearst once said that he wanted his New York tabloid the *Daily Mirror* to be "90 percent entertainment, 10 percent information—and the information without boring you."

During the 1920s, sales of magazines rose, too. By 1929, Americans were buying more than 200 million copies of such popular magazines as the *Saturday Evening Post, Reader's Digest, Ladies' Home Journal,* and *Time*. These magazines provided a variety of information in a form that most people could easily digest. Advertisers, eager to reach so many potential customers, often ran full-page ads promoting their products.

With the rise of newspapers and magazines as mass media, Americans began to share the same information, read about the same events, and encounter the same ideas and fashions. Thus newspapers and magazines helped create a common popular culture.

Radio As a mass medium, radio barely existed until the 1920s. Before that time, relatively few Americans had radio sets, and those they had were all homemade. They used their radios to communicate with each other one-on-one. In 1920, Frank Conrad, an engineer with the Westinghouse Electric Company, set up a radio transmitter in his garage in Pittsburgh. As an experiment, he began sending recorded music and baseball scores over the radio. The response was so great that Westinghouse began broadcasting programs on a regular basis. Soon the nation had its first commercial radio station, Pittsburgh's KDKA.

At first, the only advertising on KDKA was the occasional mention of its sponsor, Westinghouse. Yet even that was enough to increase the sales of Westinghouse products, mainly home appliances. In the coming years, radio would become a profitable medium for advertisers.

Radio enjoyed tremendous growth. By 1922, more than 500 stations were on the air, and Americans eagerly bought radios to listen to them. To reach more people, networks such as the National Broadcasting Company (NBC) linked many individual stations together. Each station in the network played the same programming. Soon much of the country was listening to the same jokes, commercials, music, sports events, religious services, and news. Other companies imitated NBC, building networks of their own.

The Jazz Age

Both the growing radio audience and the great African American migration to the cities helped make a music called jazz widely popular in the 1920s. This music features improvisation, a process by which musicians make up music as they are playing it rather than relying completely on printed scores. It also has a type of off-beat rhythm called syncopation.

Jazz Arrives Jazz grew out of the African American music of the South, especially ragtime and blues. By the early 1900s, bands in New Orleans were

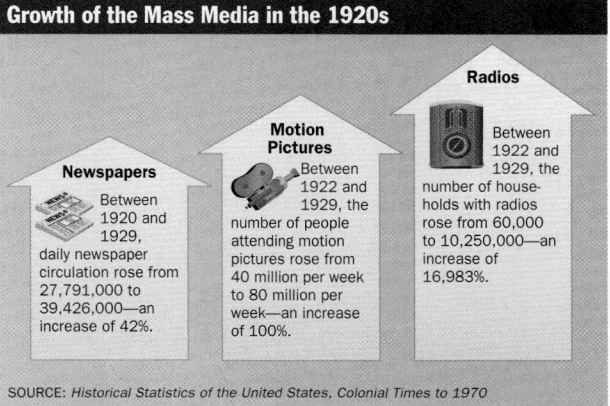

Growth of the Mass Media in the 1920s

Newspapers Between 1920 and 1929, daily newspaper circulation rose from 27,791,000 to 39,426,000—an increase of 42%.

Motion Pictures Between 1922 and 1929, the number of people attending motion pictures rose from 40 million per week to 80 million per week—an increase of 100%.

Radios Between 1922 and 1929, the number of households with radios rose from 60,000 to 10,250,000—an increase of 16,983%.

SOURCE: *Historical Statistics of the United States, Colonial Times to 1970*

INTERPRETING DIAGRAMS
The decade of the 1920s saw an explosion in forms of mass communication. **Making Comparisons** *Which form of mass communication grew the most during this decade?*

READING CHECK
What social changes were brought about by the mass media?

Chapter 20 • Section 2   693

Connecting with Culture

Provide Paul Whiteman's recording of "Rhapsody in Blue" to the class. Direct them to listen to the recording with the aim of interpreting the music in light of George Gershwin's description of it. Then have students discuss what makes it, in Gershwin's words, "a sort of musical kaleidoscope of America." **(Musical/Rhythmic)**

BACKGROUND

Biography

James van der Zee (1886–1983) turned his pride in his Harlem neighbors and his skill as a photographer into a priceless archive of images. The son of Ulysses S. Grant's maid and butler, van der Zee first thought of a career as a musician. But it was with his camera, in the elaborately decorated studio area of his "Guarantee Photo" shop, that he made his reputation. Acknowledged to be the first great African American photographer, van der Zee made more than 75,000 photo portraits during his career, photographing people both ordinary and famous.

The heyday of van der Zee's career corresponded with the years of the Harlem Renaissance. By the 1940s more individuals owned cameras themselves, and people did not often go to a studio to have portraits made. Van der Zee continued to work during these years, largely in obscurity. Then in 1968 his work was rediscovered and became a major portion of an exhibit, "Harlem On My Mind," at New York's Metropolitan Museum of Art.

BIOGRAPHIES

Duke Ellington (1899–1974)

Edward Kennedy Ellington was born in Washington, D.C. At 17, "Duke," as Ellington was called, played in Washington's clubs at night and painted signs during the day. In 1923, Ellington and several other musicians moved to New York City and formed a band. This band, under various names and in one form or another, continued to play with Ellington until his death at age 75.

Although Ellington was an excellent pianist, his greatest talents were as a band leader, an arranger, and a composer. He wrote at least a thousand pieces in his long career, including music for concerts, Broadway shows, films, and operas. Among his most memorable tunes are "Mood Indigo," "Solitude," "In a Sentimental Mood," "Blue Harlem," and "Bojangles."

Louis Armstrong, nicknamed "Satchmo," was born and grew up in New Orleans, where he learned to sing and play the trumpet. In 1922, Armstrong was invited to play the trumpet in Chicago, and in 1923, he made his first recordings with King Oliver's Creole Jazz Band. Armstrong's showmanship and virtuosity soon became evident, especially when he performed his improvised extended solos. Because of Armstrong, long solos became key elements of jazz ensemble performances.

Louis Armstrong (1901–1971)

Armstrong also improvised with his voice, replacing words with nonsense syllables in a style known as "scat" singing. His first scat recording, "Heebie Jeebies," encouraged many jazz vocalists to sing scat. His Hot Five and Hot Seven ensemble recordings are among his most notable early recordings.

Sounds of an Era

Listen to a 1927 recording of "East St. Louis Toodle-oo" by Duke Ellington.

---

playing the new mix of styles. Although jazz recordings were available in the 1910s, many radio listeners began hearing the new sound for the first time in the 1920s. Soon jazz became a nationwide craze. Younger people in particular loved to dance to the new music. By 1929, a survey of stations showed that two thirds of all radio air time was devoted to jazz.

Some Americans were horrified by jazz. Its syncopated rhythms and improvisations were too suggestive of the free manners and morals of the age. Eventually, however, Americans from many walks of life embraced the music. The great symphony conductor Leopold Stokowski declared that jazz was "an expression of the times, of the breathless, energetic, superactive times in which we are living." The 1920s came to be called the **Jazz Age.**

Jazz Clubs and Dance Halls One of the most popular places to listen to jazz was Harlem, a district on the northern end of the island of Manhattan. By one count, Harlem had some 500 jazz clubs. A dozen of them, including the Cotton Club, Connie's Inn, and the Saratoga Club, catered to the rich and famous. At clubs such as these, musicians, most of whom were black, performed for audiences that were primarily white.

Nearly all the great jazz musicians played in the Harlem clubs at one time or another. Jelly Roll Morton, a jazz pianist from New Orleans, arranged his band's music in a way that encouraged group improvisation. This gave his band a smooth, modern sound. Benny Goodman, known as the "King of Swing," began playing jazz professionally as a teenager in the early 1920s. His "big band" helped make jazz popular with white audiences. Goodman's 1936 quartet, which included African American musicians Lionel Hampton and Teddy Wilson, was the first popular racially mixed jazz group. Two musicians, in particular, made important contributions to jazz beginning in the 1920s: Louis Armstrong, who wowed audiences with his brilliantly improvised trumpet solos, and Duke Ellington, an arranger, composer, and bandleader, whose works are played widely to this day.

When flappers danced to jazz on the radio or to a live jazz band, most likely they did the Charleston. This dance took over the dance halls and ballrooms in the 1920s and became a national fad. The Charleston embodied the Jazz Age. It was wild and reckless, full of kicks and twists and pivots. Unlike traditional ballroom dancing, the Charleston could be danced with a partner, in a group, or all alone.

The Jazz Spirit The jazz spirit ran through all the arts of the 1920s. People spoke of "jazz poetry" and "jazz painting." However, jazz most strongly influenced other forms of music. Composers in the Jazz Age, such as George Gershwin, mixed jazz elements into more familiar-sounding music. Gershwin, the son of

694 Chapter 20 • Postwar Social Change

RESOURCE DIRECTORY

Teaching Resources
Biography, Literature, and Comparing Primary Sources booklet (Literature) *The Weary Blues,* p. 67

Other Print Resources
American History Block Scheduling Support *The Harlem Renaissance During the Jazz Age,* found in the Prosperity, Depression, and War folder, includes interdisciplinary lesson suggestions and activities for Geography and History, Primary Sources, Biography, and Literature.

Technology
Sounds of an Era Audio CD *"Rhapsody in Blue"* (time: one minute, 30 seconds); *"West End Blues"* (time: 45 seconds); *"East St. Louis Toodle-oo,"* 1927 recording (time: one minute, 15 seconds)

RESOURCE PRO® **Literature Activity** *Tales of the Jazz Age,* found on Resource Pro, highlights the shallow, carefree rebellion of the flapper culture.

Russian immigrants, won overnight success in 1924 with his *Rhapsody in Blue*. First played by bandleader Paul Whiteman's orchestra, this piece throbbed with jazz rhythms. Not quite jazz and not quite symphony, it was, instead, a magical blend of the two. The basic form of this rhapsody came to Gershwin in a sudden rush of insight while riding a train. He said that he heard the music in the rhythmic noise of the train:

    66 *I heard it as a sort of musical kaleidoscope of America—of our vast melting pot, of our unduplicated national pep, of our blues, our metropolitan madness.* 99

        —George Gershwin, 1924

Painting Like jazz musicians, American painters of the 1920s did not shy away from taking the pulse of American life. Painters such as Edward Hopper and Rockwell Kent showed the nation's rougher side, from cities to coal mines, from the streets to the barrooms.

By contrast, a young artist named Georgia O'Keeffe painted natural objects such as flowers, animal bones, and landscapes. However simple her images, they always suggest something greater than themselves. A range of hills, for example, seems almost to shudder with life. O'Keeffe continued to paint until her death in 1986 at the age of nearly 100.

Literature Several modern writers began fruitful careers during the 1920s. Novelist Sinclair Lewis attacked American society with savage irony. His targets included the prosperous conformist (*Babbit*, 1922), the medical business (*Arrowsmith*, 1925), and dishonest ministers (*Elmer Gantry*, 1927). In *Main Street* Lewis, showing no mercy, depicts small-town Americans as a

    66 *savorless people, gulping tasteless food, and sitting afterward, coatless and thoughtless, in rocking-chairs prickly with inane decorations, listening to mechanical music, saying mechanical things about the excellence of Ford automobiles, and viewing themselves as the greatest race in the world.* 99

        —Sinclair Lewis, *Main Street* (1920)

Lewis refused a Pulitzer Prize in 1926, but in 1930 he became the first American to receive the Nobel prize for literature.

Another writer destined for the Nobel prize was playwright Eugene O'Neill. In a career stretching from the 1920s into the 1950s, he wove dark, poetic tragedies out of the material of everyday American life. Until his time, most American theaters had shown only European plays or light comedies. The power of O'Neill's work proved to the public that the American stage could achieve a greatness rivaling that of Europe.

The Lost Generation American society in the 1920s troubled one group of important writers. This group rejected the quest for material possessions that

VIEWING HISTORY Edward Hopper painted this scene, titled *Automat*, in 1927. The Automat was a popular restaurant chain in which one could purchase a snack or meal from a vending machine and then eat at a table. **Drawing Inferences** *What does the painting suggest about Hopper's view of the culture of the times?*

ACTIVITY
Student Portfolio
You may wish to have students add the following to their portfolios: Ask students to research the life and writings of F. Scott Fitzgerald in order to determine whether he invented the concept of the "flapper." Have them write a brief essay defending their point of view. **(Verbal/Linguistic)**

BACKGROUND
Art History
Edward Hopper's (1882–1967) paintings reflected the character of the people and the land realistically and objectively. Hopper saw America as a lonely place, often silhouetted in harsh shades of light, as depicted in his paintings "Early Sunday Morning" (1930) or "Room in Brooklyn" (1932). In the midst of the Depression, Hopper's works achieved national recognition when New York's Museum of Modern Art mounted a one-man retrospective show in 1933.

CAPTION ANSWERS

Viewing History Sample answer: It shows a view of a lonely, isolated, impersonal world.

Artists of the Jazz Age (left to right): Writer F. Scott Fitzgerald and his wife, Zelda Sayre Fitzgerald, a writer and painter; poet Edna St. Vincent Millay; and writer and anthropologist Zora Neale Hurston.

ACTIVITY
Connecting with Culture

Have students choose one of the expatriate writers of the Lost Generation listed on this page and read one or more of his or her shorter works (poem, short story, or essay). Students should search for evidence of the writer's dissatisfaction with American culture at the time. Have the students present brief readings of the work to the class, along with an interpretation of its cultural critique. **(Verbal/Linguistic)**

BACKGROUND
A Diverse Nation

The Harlem Renaissance inspired many artists to create masterpieces of language and tone. Claude McKay's "The Tropics in New York," Jean Toomer's "Cane," and Georgia Douglas Johnson's "Common Dust" are among the many works that express the feelings of both urban and rural African Americans. Langston Hughes's poem "I, Too" epitomizes the sense of possibility and the deep frustrations that African Americans felt at the time. Carl Van Doren, the editor of *Century* magazine and a Pulitzer Prize winner for biography, observed: "What American literature decidedly needs at this moment is color, music, gusto, the free expression of gay or desperate moods. If the Negroes are not in a position to contribute to these items, I don't know what Americans are."

seemed to occupy so many Americans. Its members also scorned American popular culture as artless and uninspired. Postwar society so repelled them that they left the United States for Europe. These expatriates, or people who live outside their homeland, found Europe more intellectually stimulating.

The most prominent of these writers settled in Paris. They included Sherwood Anderson, Archibald MacLeish, Hart Crane, E. E. Cummings, John Dos Passos, Ernest Hemingway, and F. Scott Fitzgerald. Another notable American writer, Gertrude Stein, had been living in Paris for some time and had come into contact with many of the expatriates. Stein remarked to Hemingway that he and the other expatriate writers were all a **Lost Generation,** a group of people disconnected from their country and its values. Hemingway introduced Stein's term to the reading public when he used it in his 1926 novel *The Sun Also Rises.*

F. Scott Fitzgerald was both part of the Lost Generation and part of the Jazz Age. Some people believe Fitzgerald helped create the flapper culture with his novel *This Side of Paradise,* published in 1920. His 1925 masterpiece *The Great Gatsby* focused on the wealthy, sophisticated Americans of the Jazz Age whom he found to be self-centered and shallow.

After Hemingway made the term *Lost Generation* famous, it was taken up by the flappers. They liked to imagine themselves as rebels against the culture of their time, living a fast and dangerous life. The words of a popular poet of the day, Edna St. Vincent Millay, captured the flapper's attitude toward life:

> 66 *My candle burns at both ends;*
> *It will not last the night;*
> *But ah, my foes, and oh, my friends—*
> *It gives a lovely light!* 99
>
> —Edna St. Vincent Millay, "First Fig," 1920

The Harlem Renaissance

For African Americans, New York City's Harlem was becoming the cultural center of the United States. The number of African Americans living in Harlem grew from 50,000 in 1914 to about 200,000 in 1930. Not just a national center for jazz, Harlem also became the home of an African American literary awakening of the 1920s known as the **Harlem Renaissance.**

James Weldon Johnson emerged as a leading writer of the Harlem group. Johnson lived in two worlds, the political and the literary. As executive secretary of the National Association for the Advancement of

Focus on CULTURE

Twenties Slang Every generation coins its own terms and phrases. The youth culture of the 1920s was no different. In addition to "flappers" and "speakeasies," the decade spoke its share of slang, some of which is still in use today.

baloney *Nonsense; untrue*
bee's knees *The best; cutest*
copacetic *Excellent, used as an exclamation*
gold digger *A woman in search of a wealthy man*
goofy *Silly, clumsy, stupid*
hard-boiled *Unfeeling or tough*
jazz baby *Another word for flapper*
peppy *Energetic*
ritzy *High class*
swell *Terrific*

696 Chapter 20 • *Postwar Social Change*

RESOURCE DIRECTORY

Teaching Resources
Units 7/8 booklet
 • Section 2 Quiz, p. 5
Guide to the Essentials
 • Section 2 Summary, p. 105

Technology
Sounds of an Era Audio CD *"I, Too, Am America"* (time: 35 seconds)
Exploring Primary Sources in U.S. History CD-ROM *As I Grew Older, Langston Hughes*

Colored People (NAACP), he led the group during an active period in its history. At the same time, he pursued a writing career that inspired younger members of the Harlem group. His most famous work, *God's Trombones* (1927), is a collection of sermons in rhythmic verse modeled after the style of traditional black preaching.

Other writers followed Johnson's lead. Alain Locke's 1925 book *The New Negro* celebrated the blossoming of African American culture. Locke noted that both African and American heritages could be enriching, not conflicting. Zora Neale Hurston came to New York in 1925, became an anthropologist, and gained fame as a writer with her poignant novel *Their Eyes Were Watching God* (1937). Dorothy West, another accomplished writer, tackled the dual themes of being black and being a woman.

The leading poets of the Harlem Renaissance were Claude McKay and Countee Cullen. McKay produced a large body of work, including *Harlem Shadows* (1922), and was a voice of protest against the sufferings of African Americans in white society. The gifted Cullen is best known for his 1925 collection of poems called *Color*. He also brought to light the talents of fellow writers in *Caroling Dusk: An Anthology of Verse by Negro Poets* (1927).

The Harlem writer perhaps most studied today is Langston Hughes, a poet, short story writer, journalist, and playwright whose career stretched into the 1960s. Hughes spoke with a clear, strong voice about the joys and difficulties of being human, being American, and being black:

Harlem Renaissance poet and writer Langston Hughes

 I, too, sing America.
I am the darker
brother.
They send me to eat
in the kitchen
When company comes,
But I laugh,
And eat well,
And grow strong. . . .

Tomorrow,
I'll be at the table
When company
comes.
Nobody'll dare
Say to me,
'Eat in the
kitchen,'
Then.

Besides,
They'll see how
beautiful I am
And be
ashamed—

I, too, am
America. **99**

—Langston Hughes,
"I, Too," 1926

Section 2 Assessment

READING COMPREHENSION

1. What social changes were brought about by the **mass media?**

2. Who were some of the major figures of the **Jazz Age?**

3. Why is the term **Lost Generation** used to describe some writers of the 1920s?

4. How might the jazz spirit have influenced the poetry that came out of the **Harlem Renaissance?**

CRITICAL THINKING AND WRITING

5. **Making Comparisons** What do the novels of Sinclair Lewis and F. Scott Fitzgerald say about Americans in the 1920s?

6. **Writing an Opinion** What do you think about the balance of entertainment and information in today's news media?

 **Take It to the NET**

Activity: Drawing a Cartoon
Learn more about popular entertainment in the 1920s, and then draw a cartoon about the music, movies, sports, or arts of the Jazz Age. Use the links provided in the *America: Pathways to the Present* area of the following Web site for help in completing this activity.
www.phschool.com

Reading Comprehension

1. Encouraged a national popular culture to develop: affected fashion, consumerism, and what music became popular (jazz).

2. Sample answer: Louis Armstrong, Duke Ellington, Langston Hughes, George Gershwin, Edna St. Vincent Millay.

3. Gertrude Stein first used the term to describe American writers who felt disconnected from their country and its values. The country lost these writers; they, in turn, lost their country.

4. Possible answer: the jazz spirit contributed rhythm and subject matter to poetry.

Critical Thinking and Writing

5. Beneath a transparent sophistication, Americans were represented as shallow, uncouth, and self-centered.

6. Answers will vary but might compare the present news media with the mass media represented within the section.

Take It to the NET

Cartoons will vary. Students should demonstrate an understanding of the trends in 1920s music, movies, sports, and arts, including the increasing influence of African Americans on popular entertainment.

Supporting a Position

When you take a position on an issue, you have a better chance of winning others to your side if you can back up your argument with solid reasons and evidence.

The movie industry introduced the first "talkie"—a movie with sound—in 1927. At that time, many people predicted that these films would replace traditional stage productions. (In recent years, some people have made a similar prediction with regard to computers replacing books, newspapers, and magazines.) In 1929, Irving Norton Fisher discussed this issue in a letter to his father. Fisher would later become a drama critic and author. In his letter, he takes a position on talkies.

LEARN THE SKILL
Use the following steps to support a position:

1. **State your position clearly in a sentence.** To take a position on any issue, you must be clear as to what that position is. Writing it out in a sentence forces you to organize your thoughts.

2. **Identify at least three reasons for your position.** To be convincing, you must do more than say what you believe; you must say why you believe it. Think of reasons for your side—or against the opposing position. Pointing out the weakness of an opposing idea can be very effective. Also consider your audience. Think of what reasons will be most effective with those you are trying to persuade.

3. **Support each reason with evidence.** To build a solid case for your position, use facts to support each reason.

4. **Add a conclusion.** This is your chance to sum up and drive your point home.

PRACTICE THE SKILL
Answer the following questions:

1. **(a)** What position does Irving Norton Fisher take on the issue of talkies replacing live theater? **(b)** What part of his letter states this position? **(c)** Restate Fisher's position in your own words, as if you were using it to begin an essay or a speech.

2. **(a)** What reasons does Fisher give for his position? **(b)** How does Fisher treat the opposing position? **(c)** Does this strengthen or weaken his argument? Explain your reasoning.

3. **(a)** What evidence does Fisher give for each of his reasons? **(b)** Is the evidence factual, or just opinion masquerading as fact?

4. **(a)** Fisher's argument is part of an informal letter and does not have a conclusion. Write a conclusion for his argument. **(b)** Write a short paragraph that takes one of these positions: the position of Fisher's father (that talkies would become popular

Nov. 14, 1929.

Dear Father:—

Yours of the 10th just here. For which many thanks, as I know how pressed for time you must be. It's incredible that the stock market can go any lower, and yet each new day seems to be worse than the day before. . . .

I'm free to confess I don't entirely agree with all you say about "talkies" replacing the theatre. Any more than I believe that artificial flowers can ever replace those produced by nature. There is no mechanical way of thrilling the human mind as the actual presence of an actor or singer thrills it. And from what Sidney Howard said after directing three "talkies" in Hollywood himself, the whole thing is still in the balance. No talkie has yet paid for itself.—They are so much more expensive than other films, and the whole foreign market (formerly so lucrative) is automatically cut out, except for English-speaking countries. Formerly, movies didn't _begin_ to make money until the returns began accumulating from the small towns in U.S. (which are still unequipped for "talkies") and from foreign countries. Of course Hollywood is optimistic, who wouldn't be if his livelihood [sic] depended on it, but it is by no means an assured thing! . . .

—Your very loving son,
Irving N. Fisher

and replace live theater); or the position that, in the future, computers will (or will not) replace books, newspapers, and magazines.

APPLY THE SKILL
See the Chapter Review and Assessment for another opportunity to apply this skill.

READING FOCUS

- What were the effects of Prohibition on society?
- What issues of religion were at the core of the Scopes trial?
- How did racial tensions change after World War I?

READING FOCUS

- What were the effects of Prohibition on society?
- What issues of religion were at the core of the Scopes trial?
- How did racial tensions change after World War I?

MAIN IDEA

Rapid social change after World War I caused conflicts among people with differing beliefs and values.

KEY TERMS

bootleggers
speakeasies
fundamentalism
Scopes trial

TAKING NOTES

Create a chart like the one below. As you read, fill the chart with some of the effects of Prohibition.

PROHIBITION

⬇

EFFECTS
• Alcoholic beverages are no longer sold legally. • •

Setting the Scene

Setting the Scene Prohibition of all alcoholic beverages became the law of the land when the Eighteenth Amendment to the Constitution took effect on January 16, 1920. Yet for many people, life went on as before. Even President Harding did not heed the law, as the daughter of former President Theodore Roosevelt witnessed:

> 66 *Though violation of the Eighteenth Amendment was a matter of course in Washington, it was rather shocking to see the way Harding disregarded the Constitution he was sworn to uphold. . . . there were always, at least before the unofficial dinners, cocktails in the upstairs hall outside the President's room. . . . One evening . . . a friend of the Hardings asked me if I would like to go up to the study. . . . No rumor could have exceeded the reality; . . . trays with bottles containing every imaginable brand of whiskey stood about. . . .* 99
>
> —Alice Roosevelt Longworth, *Crowded Hours*, 1933

Prohibition

The main goals of Prohibition seemed worthy: (1) Eliminate drunkenness and the resulting abuse of family members and others. (2) Get rid of saloons, where prostitution, gambling, and other forms of vice thrived. (3) Prevent absenteeism and on-the-job accidents stemming from drunkenness. Congress passed the Volstead Act in 1919 to provide a system for enforcing the Eighteenth Amendment, but it was widely ignored—especially in the large cities along the coasts and in the upper Midwest. A 1924 report showed Kansans obeying the law at a rate of about 95 percent and New Yorkers at a rate of only about 5 percent. Thus Prohibition sharpened the contrast between urban and rural moral values during the 1920s.

Bootlegging Liquor, beer, and wine could no longer be manufactured, sold, or transported in the United States. Americans who chose to defy the Volstead Act needed to find a private source of alcoholic beverages. For this they turned to a new type of criminal: the bootlegger.

Prohibition forced many beer companies to find new beverages to brew, as these labels show.

Focus Explain that rapid changes in American life after World War I led to differences in values among Americans. Ask students what major conflicts arose.

Instruct Discuss the institution of Prohibition and its failure. How did Prohibition contribute to the expansion of organized crime? Ask students to explain why some Americans argued that even though alcohol was bad, it should be legal.

Ask students how the Scopes trial pointed out divisions in American society. Why was the trial of lasting importance?

Discuss racial tensions in the 1920s. Why did violence by whites against blacks increase in the North? Why did membership in the Klan grow? How did African Americans react to the violence?

Assess/Reteach Many complex and divisive issues faced the United States after World War I. Have students list some of society's major conflicts at this time. Then, have them state which of those conflicts have been resolved by now, and which still cause problems.

VIEWING HISTORY The government struggled to stop the illegal flow of liquor during Prohibition. Federal agents are shown destroying cases of beer during a raid in Philadelphia. **Analyzing Information** *What were the biggest problems in enforcing Prohibition?*

In the old days, **bootleggers** merely had been drinkers who hid flasks of liquor in the leg of their boots. Now the term was used to describe suppliers of illegal alcohol. Some bootleggers operated stills—devices used to produce alcohol from corn, grain, potatoes, or other fruit and vegetable sources. Others smuggled liquor overland from Canada or by ship from the Caribbean. A smuggler's ship might anchor far off the coast, where its illegal cargo would be loaded onto speedboats fast enough to outrace Coast Guard cutters. The boats would then head to secluded harbors where trucks were waiting to carry the liquor to warehouses. From there, it would be transported to retail outlets. Those outlets included restaurants, nightclubs, and speakeasies.

Speakeasies were bars that operated illegally. These bars flourished in the cities. One observer estimated that there were 700 speakeasies and 4,000 bootleggers in Washington, D.C., a city with only 300 licensed saloons before Prohibition. The whole state of Massachusetts had 1,000 saloons before Prohibition, while during it Boston alone had 4,000 speakeasies and 15,000 bootleggers. A customer could not just stroll into a speakeasy. A heavy gate usually blocked the entrance, and the customer had to show a membership card or be recognized by a guard. A

COMPARING PRIMARY SOURCES
The Eighteenth Amendment

Violations of Prohibition led Congress to hear testimony on whether the Eighteenth Amendment should be repealed.

Analyzing Viewpoints Compare the main arguments made by the two speakers.

In Favor of Repeal	*Against Repeal*
"I will concede that the saloon was odious [offensive], but now we have delicatessen stores, pool rooms, drug stores, millinery shops, private parlors, and 57 other varieties of speakeasies selling liquor and flourishing." —*Representative Fiorello La Guardia of New York, 1926*	"Instead of lowering our standards, we urge that the law be strengthened. . . .The closing of the open saloon . . . has resulted in better national health; children are born under better conditions, homes are better, and the mother is delivered from the fear of a drunken husband." —*Ella A. Boole, president of the National Woman's Christian Temperance Union, 1926*

Viewing History Bootleggers and owners of speakeasies were clever in eluding the police. Many people disregarded Prohibition laws. There was not enough money to enforce Prohibition properly. Organized crime was hard to fight.

RESOURCE DIRECTORY

Teaching Resources
Biography, Literature, and Comparing Primary Sources booklet (Comparing Primary Sources) *On the Eighteenth Amendment,* p. 135

number of speakeasies rejected the standard gate for a more creative entrance, as a French diplomat observed in New York City:

> " Some speakeasies are disguised behind florists' shops, or behind undertakers' coffins. I know one, right in Broadway, which is entered through an imitation telephone-box; it has excellent beer. . . . "
>
> —Paul Morand, 1929

Organized Crime Supplying illegal liquor was a complex operation, involving manufacture, transportation, storage, and sales. This complexity, and bootlegging's huge potential for profit, helped lead to the development of organized crime.

At first, local gangsters operated independently, competing to supply liquor. Then some of them found that by joining forces they could create an organization large and efficient enough to handle the entire bootlegging operation. When these organizations tried to expand their territory, they clashed with other gangs. As rival groups fought for control with machine guns and sawed-off shotguns, gang wars and murder became commonplace. The streets of American cities became a battleground.

Successful bootlegging organizations often moved into other illegal activities, including gambling, prostitution, and a highly profitable business called racketeering. In one kind of "racket," gangsters bribed police or other government officials to ignore their illegal operations. In another, gangsters forced local businesses to pay a fee for "protection." Those who refused to pay might be gunned down or have their businesses blown to bits. In one period of a little more than a year, racketeers set off 157 bombs in Chicago. Terrified citizens went along with the gangsters' demands. The supporters of Prohibition had never dreamed that their ideals would bear such evil fruit.

Al Capone The most notorious of the gangster organizations operated in Chicago. There, bootlegging had added immense wealth to an already successful gambling, prostitution, and racketeering business that reached into nearly every neighborhood, police station, and government office.

In 1925, a young gangster murdered his way to the top of Chicago's organized crime network. He was Al Capone, nicknamed "Scarface." Capone was a ruthless criminal with a talent for avoiding jail. With so much money at his disposal ($60 million a year from bootlegging alone), Capone easily bought the cooperation of police and city officials. Politicians, even judges, took orders from him.

The government fought back with improved law enforcement. The Federal Bureau of Investigation (FBI), headed by J. Edgar Hoover, became a dedicated, independent force against organized crime during the 1920s. Still, Capone managed for years to slip out of any charges brought against him. Finally, in 1931, a federal court convicted him of income-tax evasion and sent him to prison. Bootlegging remained a problem, however, until Prohibition ended in 1933.

Issues of Religion

Prohibition highlighted the differences between urban and rural areas of the country. Another issue that tended to split Americans along urban and rural lines was the teaching of evolution. Many Americans felt that the theory of evolution conflicted with their

VIEWING HISTORY Chicago gangster Al Capone (left) confers with his lawyer in this 1929 photo. **Synthesizing Information** *Why was it so difficult for the government to bring Capone to justice?*

701

702

ACTIVITY

Connecting with Culture

Have students cooperate in conducting research and creating a Venn diagram that compares and contrasts the lives and careers of Billy Sunday and Aimee Semple McPherson. The students' diagram should include such things as biographical backgrounds, numbers of followers, promotional techniques, use of media, and so on. Have the students share the diagram with the class, highlighting remarkable similarities and differences between the two evangelists. **(Visual/Spatial)**

BACKGROUND

Biography

John T. Scopes, whose name lives in history as the moniker of the famous trial, led a life otherwise free from conflict and the media spotlight. After the trial, he refused his old teaching position (which was offered to him) and instead accepted a scholarship funded by scientists and journalists to attend the prestigious University of Chicago. He studied geology for two years, and then went to work for Gulf Oil Corporation, which sent him to Venezuela in 1925. He returned to the United States in 1929. Scopes later worked as a geologist for the United Gas Corporation. From 1940 to 1963, when he retired, he worked at the company's headquarters in Louisiana. Scopes died in 1970.

CAPTION ANSWERS

Viewing History Freedom of speech.

Fundamentalist preacher Billy Sunday drew large crowds at religious revivals.

VIEWING HISTORY William Jennings Bryan (right) and Clarence Darrow (left) faced off on the issue of evolution in Dayton, Tennessee, in 1925. **Drawing Inferences** *What constitutional issue was at the heart of the matter?*

---

religious beliefs. The teaching of this theory in some public schools during the 1920s touched off a debate that continues today.

Fundamentalism   Before the teaching of evolution became an issue, many Americans already felt uneasy with certain changes in society. During the early part of the century, challenges to traditional beliefs came from several directions:

1. Science and technology were taking a larger role in everyday life.
2. War and the widespread problems of modern society were causing more people to question whether God took an active role in human affairs or if God even existed.
3. Some scholars were saying that the Bible was a document written by humans and that it contained contradictions and historical inaccuracies.

In response to these challenges, between 1910 and 1915, religious traditionalists published a series of 12 pamphlets called *The Fundamentals*. They stated a set of beliefs that have since come to be called **fundamentalism.** In addition to supporting traditional Christian ideas about Jesus, fundamentalists argued that God inspired the Bible, so it cannot contain contradictions or errors. They declared that the Bible is literally true and that every story in it actually took place as described.

Fundamentalism gained tremendous attention in the 1920s. The most famous fundamentalist preacher of the time was Billy Sunday, a former professional baseball player. Sunday's sermons on the evils of alcohol made him an influential figure in the Prohibition movement. His series of more than 300 religious revival meetings attracted an estimated total attendance of 100 million. Another popular preacher, Aimee Semple McPherson, was a master of theatrical presentation. Her followers gave $1.5 million to build her the massive Angelus Temple in Los Angeles, where she preached to huge crowds. "Sister Aimee," as she was called, owned her own radio station, which allowed her to broadcast her revival meetings. By doing so, she used radio in an innovative way: to broaden the reach of her ministry.

Evolution and the Scopes Trial   The theory of evolution deeply disturbed fundamentalists. This theory states that human beings and all other living species developed over time from simpler life forms.

Fundamentalists denounced the evolution theory, saying that it contradicts the history of creation as stated in the Bible. They worked for the passage of laws to prevent public schools from teaching evolution. When Tennessee passed such a ban in 1925, a science teacher named John T. Scopes agreed to challenge it as unconstitutional, thus denying him personal and religious freedom. He defied the law and was arrested for teaching evolution. Thus began the case popularly known as the **Scopes trial.**

The case became a battle between two of the country's greatest lawyers. William Jennings Bryan, an outspoken fundamentalist, volunteered to help prosecute Scopes. Clarence Darrow, a passionate supporter of free speech, volunteered to help defend him. Both men were known for their debating skills. Bryan had run for President three times. Darrow had won fame for defending political and labor activists such as Eugene V. Debs.

The trial took place in the small town of Dayton, Tennessee, in the withering heat of July 1925. In this new era of mass media, journalists swarmed around the courthouse, telegraphing some 2 million words of

702   Chapter 20 • *Postwar Social Change*

RESOURCE DIRECTORY

Technology
Sounds of an Era Audio CD   *Billy Sunday,* 1923 recording (time: one minute)

RESOURCE PRO®   **Visual Learning Activity**
The Ku Klux Klan, found on Resource Pro, uses a 1923 drawing from *Life* magazine to enhance students' understanding of how artists use symbols to convey political viewpoints.

reporting to their papers over the ten days of the trial. This was the first trial ever broadcast over American radio.

On the surface, the case was a simple one. The judge ruled that the jury should determine only whether Scopes had taught evolution, which he readily admitted he had. The jury took just a few minutes to find Scopes guilty, and the judge fined him $100. However, more complex issues were at stake, including the clash between the country's modern beliefs and its traditional values.

The dramatic climax of the case came when Darrow put Bryan himself on the stand to testify as an expert on the Bible. Darrow set about testing the logic of Bryan's faith by citing passages from the Bible and forcing him to try to explain them. In the process, Darrow ridiculed fundamentalist beliefs. Under Darrow's intense, often brutal, questioning, Bryan admitted that even he did not interpret all of the Bible literally. He kept fighting back, however, at one point saying, "I am simply trying to protect the word of God."

This grueling battle exhausted Bryan, who died just a few days after the trial ended. Fundamentalists saw Bryan as a martyr for their cause. Modernists saw Darrow as a defender of science and reason. Although fundamentalists considered the trial a setback, their movement remained active. In later decades, it would grow in membership and strength.

Racial Tensions

Americans clashed over race in the 1920s. African Americans took part in the Great Migration to the North in the early 1900s for two main reasons. They wanted to take advantage of greater job opportunities in the North, and they wanted to escape the increasing violence against African Americans in the South. Many of them, however, found both racial prejudice and violence in the North.

Violence Against African Americans   During the summer of 1919, mob violence between white and black Americans erupted in about 25 cities. That summer became known as the "Red Summer" for all the blood that was spilled. Omaha, Tulsa, and Washington, D.C., all suffered periods of racial turmoil. The worst of these race riots, however, occurred in Chicago.

The African American population of Chicago had doubled since 1910. This increase led to overcrowded neighborhoods and heightened tensions between blacks and whites. An incident at a beach on Lake Michigan touched off the violence. On one especially hot July day, stone-throwing had erupted between whites and blacks on a beach typically used only by whites. Meanwhile, a 17-year-old black boy, swimming just offshore with his friends, accidentally floated into the "whites only" area. A white man, who had been throwing rocks at the swimmers for some time, struck the boy, and he drowned. Furious blacks accused the whites of killing him, and more fights broke out. The riot spread through the city. For several days, chaos reigned in parts of Chicago. By the end, some 23 African Americans and 15 whites were dead, another 537 people were wounded, and the destruction caused by rioting had left hundreds homeless.

Race riots broke out in several cities in the summer of 1919.

Some whites also directed racial violence against specific individuals. During the 1920s, the lynchings of the Jim Crow era continued. Many of these new crimes were the work of an old enemy of racial harmony, the Ku Klux Klan.

Revival of the Klan During Reconstruction, President Grant's campaign against the Ku Klux Klan had largely eliminated it. However, in 1915 a former Methodist circuit preacher from Atlanta, Colonel William J. Simmons, revived the organization. The Klan used modern fundraising and publicity methods to increase its influence and size. By 1922, Klan membership had grown to about 100,000. Two years later, it had ballooned to 4 million. The new Klan was no longer just a southern organization. In fact, the state with the greatest number of Klansmen was Indiana. The Klan's focus shifted, too. The organization vowed to defend their own white-Protestant culture against any group, not just blacks, that seemed to them un-American:

This 1920s poster illustrates the Ku Klux Klan's views on immigration.

> 66 *Klansmen are to be examples of pure patriotism. They are to organize the patriotic sentiment of native-born white, Protestant Americans for the defense of distinctively American institutions. Klansmen are dedicated to the principle that America shall be made American through the promulgation [circulation] of American doctrines, the dissemination [spread] of American ideals, the creation of wholesome American sentiment, the preservation of American institutions.* 99
> —Klansman's Manual, 1925

During the early 1920s, Klan members carried out many crimes against African Americans, Catholics, Jews, immigrants, and others. They rode by night, beating, whipping, even killing their victims, terrorizing blacks and whites alike. Then, in 1925, the head of the Klan in Indiana was sentenced to life imprisonment for assaulting a girl who later poisoned herself. The nation was finally shocked into action, and police began to step up enforcement. By 1927, Klan activity had diminished once again.

Fighting Discrimination Increasing violence against African Americans rallied the efforts of the NAACP. During the 1920s, the NAACP worked in vain to pass federal anti-lynching laws. A proposed law passed the House of Representatives in 1922 but died in the Senate. Law enforcement improved at the state level, and the number of lynchings gradually decreased. Ten lynchings were reported in 1929.

During the 1920s, the NAACP also worked to protect the voting rights of African Americans, but again it had only limited success. For example, the Supreme Court struck down as unconstitutional a Texas law prohibiting blacks from voting in the Democratic primary. Yet the Texas legislature got around the law by giving political parties the right to decide who could vote in primary elections. African Americans in the South still could not exercise their full political rights.

READING CHECK
Where and how did racial issues surface in the 1920s?

The Garvey Movement Some African Americans, frustrated by continued violence and discrimination, dreamed of a new homeland where they could live in peace. An African American named Marcus Garvey worked to make that dream a reality. Garvey had come to New York City from his native Jamaica in 1916 to establish a new headquarters for his Universal Negro Improvement Association (UNIA).

Through the UNIA, Garvey sought to build up African Americans' self-respect and economic power. African Americans were encouraged to buy shares in Garvey's Negro Factories Corporation, a set of small black-owned businesses. He also urged African Americans to return to "Motherland Africa" to create a self-governing nation. Garvey's message of racial pride and independence attracted a large number of followers to his black nationalist movement. Garvey held regular UNIA meetings in Harlem, and his followers could be seen in military-style uniforms reflecting their status, whether as members of the marching band, the Black Cross Nurses, or the African Legion. Several respected African American leaders, such as W.E.B. Du Bois, criticized the movement, however. They objected to Garvey's call for separation of the races, as well as his careless business practices.

Garvey gathered $10 million for a steamship company, the Black Star Line, that would carry his followers back to the motherland. Corruption and mismanagement plagued the shipping line, however, and in 1925, Garvey was jailed on mail fraud charges relating to the sale of stock in the steamship company. From prison the same year, he wrote in an essay: "Why should we be discouraged because somebody laughs at us today? Who [is] to tell what tomorrow will bring forth? . . . We see and have changes every day, so pray, work, be steadfast and be not dismayed."

Garvey's sentence was later commuted, and he was deported to Jamaica in 1927. Without his leadership, the UNIA in America collapsed. Still, Garvey's ideas remained an inspiration to later "black pride" movements.

VIEWING HISTORY This ship belonged to Marcus Garvey's Black Star Line steamship company, founded in 1919. It was one of many enterprises Garvey (left) hoped would strengthen the African American community. **Drawing Conclusions** *Was Marcus Garvey a successful leader?*

Section 3 Assessment

READING COMPREHENSION

1. What were the goals of Prohibition?

2. How did organized crime profit from **bootleggers** and **speakeasies** during Prohibition?

3. How were religious issues and **fundamentalism** at odds with the teaching of evolution?

4. Which positions did William Jennings Bryan and Clarence Darrow each represent in the **Scopes trial?**

5. Why were many African Americans drawn to Marcus Garvey's message and movement?

CRITICAL THINKING AND WRITING

6. **Predicting Consequences** How might life in the 1920s have been different without Prohibition?

7. **Synthesizing Information** Consider the racial tensions that existed in the 1920s and those that exist today. Why are racial issues difficult to resolve?

8. **Writing a Conclusion** Write a short essay that supports the following conclusion: Differences between traditional and modern beliefs were responsible for the cultural conflicts of the 1920s.

 Take It to the NET

Activity: Creating a Poster Research arguments for and against Prohibition, and then create a poster that either promotes Prohibition or calls for its repeal. Use the links provided in the *America: Pathways to the Present* area of the following Web site for help in completing this activity.
www.phschool.com

Reading Comprehension

1. Eliminate drunkenness and the abuses it caused; eliminate saloons, where vice thrived; prevent job absenteeism and accidents stemming from drunkenness.

2. Organized crime had the resources necessary to handle all aspects of the illegal liquor trade. In return, each gang made money from each speakeasy and bootlegger operating within its territory.

3. Fundamentalists believe the Bible is true in a literal sense. The theory of evolution contradicts the history of creation as stated in the Bible.

4. Bryan: fundamentalist; prosecution. Darrow: supporter of free speech; defense.

5. His movement seemed to offer an escape from continued violence and discrimination. Garvey urged his followers to take pride in being African American and to strive for economic advancement.

Critical Thinking and Writing

6. Sample answer: Organized crime may not have developed at all, or at least not to the extent that it did.

7. Answers will vary, but might include references to the long history of racial tension in the United States.

8. Essays will vary, but might focus on the Scopes trial, or the fact that Prohibition was more effective in rural areas than it was in large cities.

 **Take It to the NET**

Answers will vary. For: the elimination of family or workplace problems caused by drunkenness; the elimination of crime associated with alcohol. Against: the interference with individuals' rights; the economic loss involved.

CAPTION ANSWERS

Viewing History Sample answer: Garvey was successful as a symbol of both African American pride and the hope of economic advancement. He performed poorly, however, in the day-to-day management of his various business enterprises. Consequently, his empire collapsed.

CUSTOMIZE FOR ...

Gifted and Talented

Have students research Marcus Garvey and the Universal Negro Improvement Association (UNIA), then have them write a paragraph from the point of view of one of Garvey's followers that explains why they joined the UNIA.

REVIEWING KEY TERMS

Students should refer to the definitions of key terms in the chapter to write sentences that show an understanding of the social changes of the 1920s.

REVIEWING MAIN IDEAS

11. Women started smoking, wearing makeup, and drinking. Women began moving into office jobs, but were still denied equal pay and leadership positions. Some began to seek political offices.
12. A great number of people moved to cities; African Americans moved north; immigrants from Mexico and Canada entered the country; American suburbs greatly expanded.
13. Sample answer: Charles Lindbergh for his bravery and ability to meet a new challenge; Gertrude Ederle, as a sports hero, for her swim across the English Channel.
14. Development of national popular culture, expansion of movie industry, expansion of size and circulation of newspapers and magazines, development of radio.
15. Growing radio audiences helped to popularize jazz.
16. A group of expatriate American writers in the 1920s. They were troubled by what they saw as a greedy, materialistic world that lacked moral values.
17. Their work explored traditional black culture, being female, being Americans, the experiences of African Americans in society, and being human.
18. Differences between urban and rural moral values: speakeasies flourished in cities. Large numbers of formerly law-abiding citizens were willing to break the law by drinking.
19. The division between fundamentalist, traditional values and modern scientific belief.
20. Mob violence between African Americans and whites, lynchings, and the revival of the Ku Klux Klan.

---

creating a CHAPTER SUMMARY

Copy this chart (right) on a piece of paper and complete it by adding information about the effects of important social changes and conflicts that occurred in the 1920s. Some entries have been completed for you as examples.

For additional review and enrichment activities, see the interactive version of *America: Pathways to the Present*, available on the Web and on CD-ROM.

Conflict and Change in the 1920s	
Change/Conflict	**Impact on Society**
Women win the right to vote.	Their vote influences local politics.
Prohibition takes effect.	
Farm prices drop.	

★ Reviewing Key Terms

For each of the terms below, write a sentence explaining how it relates to the 1920s.

1. flapper
2. demographics
3. barrio
4. mass media
5. Jazz Age
6. Lost Generation
7. bootleggers
8. speakeasies
9. fundamentalism
10. Scopes trial

★ Reviewing Main Ideas

11. How did women's roles change during the 1920s? (Section 1)
12. What types of demographic change occurred during the 1920s? (Section 1)
13. Name two American heroes from the 1920s and tell why they were popular at that time. (Section 1)
14. What types of changes occurred with the rise of mass media in the 1920s? (Section 2)
15. Explain the significance of radio broadcasting in the Jazz Age. (Section 2)
16. What was the Lost Generation? What trends in society did they find troubling? (Section 2)
17. How were the experiences of African Americans reflected by the writers of the Harlem Renaissance? (Section 2)

18. What cultural conflicts did Prohibition highlight? (Section 3)
19. What divisions in American society did the Scopes trial reflect? (Section 3)
20. Describe the racial conflicts experienced in the 1920s. (Section 3)

★ Critical Thinking

21. **Drawing Conclusions** Why did women fail to have an immediate impact on national elections after the passage of the Nineteenth Amendment?
22. **Drawing Inferences** Evaluate the possible impact of racial tensions of the 1920s on the growth of the Universal Negro Improvement Association (UNIA).
23. **Comparing Points of View** Evaluate Prohibition from the point of view of (a) a law officer, (b) the owner of a legal bar, (c) a bootlegger, (d) a member of the National Woman's Christian Temperance Union.
24. **Demonstrating Reasoned Judgment** Explain the meaning of this statement: "For many African Americans, migration to the North was a mixed success."

CREATING A CHAPTER SUMMARY

Conflict and Change in the 1920s	
Change/Conflict	**Impact on Society**
Women win the right to vote.	Their vote influences local politics.
Prohibition takes effect.	Organized crime grows.
Farm prices drop; urban economy grows.	Migration from rural to urban areas
Mass media develops, including radio.	Heightened awareness of national issues and figures; instant transmission of news
Scopes teaches theory of evolution.	"Showdown" between supporters of theory of evolution versus fundamentalists
Racial tensions increase after WWI.	Urban riots

"YES, IT'S A NOBLE EXPERIMENT."

★ Skills Assessment

Analyzing Political Cartoons ▶

25. Herbert Hoover famously referred to Prohibition as a "noble experiment." Who does the nurse to the right of Hoover represent? Why would the cartoonist choose this particular nurse to assist in the "experiment"?

26. Why are the doctor and his syringe made to seem frightening?

27. What is the cartoonist's message?

Analyzing Primary Sources

Reread the poem below, "First Fig" by Edna St. Vincent Millay, from Section 2:

(1) **❝** My candle burns at both ends;

(2)   It will not last the night;

(3)   But ah, my foes, and oh, my friends—

(4)   It gives a lovely light! **❞**

28. Which of the following best expresses the speaker's meaning in lines one and two?

   A She feels bright.

   B She lives in a dark world.

   C She stays up all night.

   D The pace of her life is dangerously fast.

29. Which of the following best expresses the meaning of lines three and four?

   F Her lifestyle is exciting while it lasts.

   G She feels bright and lovely.

   H Her friends and foes approve of her lifestyle.

   J Her life is quiet.

Applying the Chapter Skill: *Supporting a Position*

30. Review the steps involved in supporting a position outlined on page 698. Then reread the Comparing Primary Sources quotes on page 700. What reasons does each speaker give as evidence to support his or her position on the Eighteenth Amendment?

ACTIVITIES

 Writing to LEARN

Writing to Describe
Consider that radio broadcasts were a new experience for Americans in the 1920s. Imagine turning on a radio and hearing jazz for the first time. Describe what the experience might have been like for a teenager, for the teenager's parents, and for the grandparents.

Primary Source CD-ROM

Working With Primary Sources Find additional information on the 1920s on the *Exploring Primary Sources in U.S. History CD-ROM* and use the selection(s) provided to complete the Chapter 20 primary source activity located in the *America: Pathways to the Present* area of the following Web site.
www.phschool.com

 Take It to the NET

Chapter Self-Test As a review activity, take the Chapter 20 Self-Test in the *America: Pathways to the Present* area at the Web site listed below. The questions are designed to test your understanding of the chapter content.
www.phschool.com

CRITICAL THINKING

21. Relatively few women voted, and those who did voted largely along the same lines as men.

22. A postwar recession increased competition between blacks and whites for the same jobs.

23. (a) Difficult to enforce, and not enough resources to properly enforce it. (b) Bars could not legally sell alcohol and faced a loss of livelihood. (c) Lucrative. (d) In favor of Prohibition as a social reform.

24. Although they came in search of a better life, African Americans still met with racism in the North. For instance, African American women often had to work as household help for whites at low wages that kept them trapped in poverty.

SKILLS ASSESSMENT

25. Virtue. She looks tough, as if Prohibition was an effort to force Americans to live virtuous lives.

26. Possible answer: To suggest that the "cure" (Prohibition) was worse than the "disease" (drinking alcoholic beverages).

27. It is a bad idea to forcibly inflict the preferences of a minority (temperance advocates) onto the nation as a whole.

28. D

29. F

30. For repealing: Prohibition has led to alcohol being sold successfully, and in great quantities, from many new sources other than saloons. Against repealing: Prohibition has increased the general health of the nation, leading to better conditions for children and families, and has lessened instances of domestic abuse.

ANSWERS TO ACTIVITIES

Writing to LEARN

Sample answer: Teenagers would have enjoyed the exciting new sound of jazz—a sound that they had probably never heard before. They would have loved to dance to it. Parents may have resisted jazz at first but could have grown to like it as it influenced other forms of familiar music. Grandparents probably did not approve of the suggestive music that reflected the morals of the time.

Primary Source CD-ROM

Direct students to the additional primary sources that can be found on the *Exploring Primary Sources in U.S. History CD-ROM.*

 Take It to the NET

Additional support materials and activities for Chapter 20 of *America: Pathways to the Present* can be found in the Social Studies area at the Prentice Hall School Web site. **www.phschool.com**

American Pathways
CULTURE

The Arts in America

Throughout the nation's history, the arts have reflected the era in which they were created. Newspapers and magazines have brought the latest information into American homes. Books, movies, and music often have focused on issues of national concern.

 Early American Arts and Crafts

1732–1776 The colonial period abounded with artisans such as Paul Revere, news printers such as Benjamin Franklin, and writers such as Franklin, Thomas Paine, and Thomas Jefferson.

A bowl made by Paul Revere (right)

 A New Nation

1783–1860 A spirit of improvement swept the new nation, leading to increased interest in education and the arts. Transcendental writers Ralph Waldo Emerson and Henry David Thoreau celebrated both the individual and the natural world, and female intellectuals like Margaret Fuller sought to raise awareness of women's new roles in society.

Henry David Thoreau (far left) and Ralph Waldo Emerson (left)

 Civil War to World War I

1861–1918 Following the Civil War, Americans embraced new forms of popular entertainment, including vaudeville, minstrel shows, ragtime music, jazz, and motion pictures.

A poster for the 1903 film *The Great Train Robbery* (right)

708

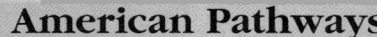
4 The Jazz Age

1920–1929 The popularity of jazz soared during the Roaring Twenties, and its spirit ran through many of the other arts of the time.

Louis Armstrong's Hot Five jazz band (below) and record labels from the 1920s (right)

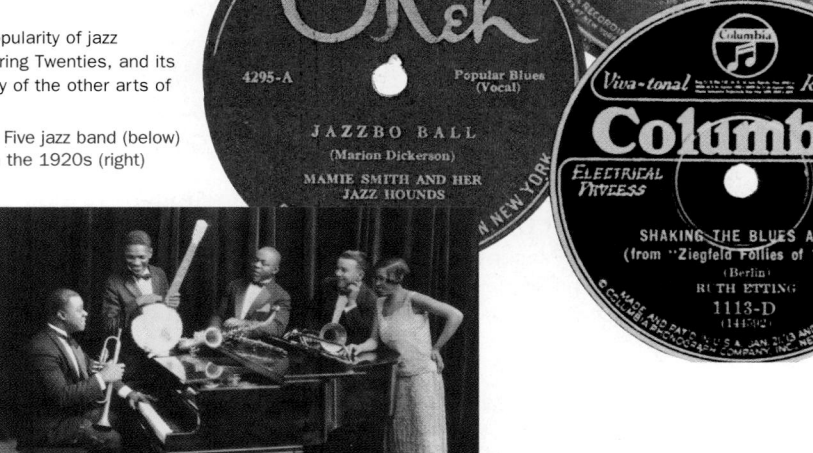

6 Postwar Turmoil and Change

1945–Present After World War II, Americans experienced a time of rapid cultural and social change. Writers and other artists explored subjects such as youthful rebellion, civil rights, environmental issues, and the Vietnam War.

American artist Georgia O'Keeffe (above)

5 The Great Depression and World War II

1929–1945 During this period, serious works of art dealt with the despair of the Depression and the war, while entertainment largely sought to offer a means of escape from these harsh realities.

American author John Steinbeck (above)

Continuity and Change

1. What work of art created in colonial times helped bring about the American Revolution? Explain.
2. How did Ernest Hemingway and F. Scott Fitzgerald view the era in which they lived?

 Take It to the NET: Creating a Study Guide
Print and complete the study guide for this topic found in the *America: Pathways to the Present* area of the following Web site. **www.phschool.com**

709

Take It to the NET

Students can print the American Pathways thematic study guide for this topic at the Prentice Hall School Web site, or you can provide students with copies of the study guide, which is found in the Units 7/8 booklet, the American Pathways Activity, pages 44–45. Students should use their texts to fill in a one-sentence description for each event on the study guide. When completed for each of the American Pathways topics, the thematic study guides will aid students in preparing for an end-of-course exam.

ANSWERS

1. Possible answers: *Common Sense* and the Declaration of Independence both called on Americans to throw off British tyranny.
2. Possible answer: As part of the "lost generation," they rejected American popular culture and the postwar society's quest for material possessions.

Chapter 21 Planning Guide
Resource Manager

	CORE INSTRUCTION	READING/SKILLS
Chapter-Level Resources	**Teaching Resources** • Pacing Charts booklet • Block Scheduling booklet **Resource Pro® CD-ROM**, Ch. 21 **Prentice Hall Presentation Pro CD-ROM**, Ch. 21 **www.phschool.com** • eTeach	**Guided Reading Audiotapes (English/Spanish)** **Student Edition on Audio CD**, Ch. 21 **Social Studies Skills Tutor CD-ROM** **Color Transparencies**, G12, H17
1 A Republican Decade 1. Learn about events that fueled the Red Scare of the early 1920s. 2. Find out about conflicts that led to the major labor strikes of 1919. 3. See how Republican leadership during the Harding and Coolidge presidencies shaped the 1920s. 4. Discover the issues that shaped the presidential election of 1928.	**Teaching Resources** **Units 7/8 booklet** • Section 1 Quiz, p. 14 **Learning Styles Lesson Plans booklet**, p. 44	**Guided Reading and Review booklet**, p. 86 **Guide to the Essentials**, p. 108 **Skills for Life booklet**, p. 23 **Section Reading Support Transparencies**
2 A Business Boom 1. Understand the role businesses and consumers play in a consumer economy. 2. Find out how Henry Ford and the automobile were important to the 1920s. 3. Discover the ways in which industrial growth affected the economy of the 1920s. 4. See how the economic boom bypassed some people and benefited others.	**Teaching Resources** **Units 7/8 booklet** • Section 2 Quiz, p. 15 **Learning Styles Lesson Plans booklet**, p. 45	**Guided Reading and Review booklet**, p. 87 **Guide to the Essentials**, p. 109 **Section Reading Support Transparencies**
3 The Economy in the Late 1920s 1. See why the economy in the late 1920s appeared healthy to most Americans. 2. Observe the danger signs that were present in the economy of the late 1920s.	**Teaching Resources** **Units 7/8 booklet** • Section 3 Quiz, p. 16	**Guided Reading and Review booklet**, p. 88 **Guide to the Essentials**, p. 110 **Section Reading Support Transparencies**

ENRICHMENT/PRE-AP

Prentice Hall United States History Video Collection™
www.phschool.com
• Section Activities, Virtual Field Trip, Chapter Activities, Current Events Online

Biography, Literature, and Comparing Primary Sources booklet, p. 26
American History Block Scheduling Support
Sounds of an Era Audio CD

Biography, Literature, and Comparing Primary Sources booklet, pp. 68–69, 137–138
Nystrom *Atlas of Our Country*, pp. 30–32
Sounds of an Era Audio CD

American Pathways Thematic Posters

ASSESSMENT

PRENTICE HALL
ASSESSMENT
SYSTEM

Core Assessment
ExamView® Test Bank, Ch. 21
ExamView® Test Bank CD-ROM, Ch. 21

Standardized Test Preparation
Diagnose and Prescribe
Diagnostic Tests for High School Social Studies Skills

Review and Reteach
Review Book for U.S. History

Practice and Assess
Test-taking Strategies With Transparencies
Test-taking Strategies Posters
Test Prep Book for U.S. History
Alternative Assessment Handbook
Document-Based Assessment

Teaching Resources
Units 7/8 booklet
• Section Quizzes, pp. 14–16
• Chapter Test, pp. 17, 20
www.phschool.com Ch. 21 Self-Test

AmericanHeritage RESOURCES

From the Archives of American Heritage®, pp. 718, 720
AmericanHeritage® My Brush with History™ Videotapes
www.americanheritage.com

TEXT

Don't miss the exclusive interactive version of this textbook on the Web and on CD-ROM.

Chapter 21 Planning Guide
In Your Classroom

CUSTOMIZE FOR INDIVIDUAL NEEDS

Gifted and Talented

Teacher's Edition
- Customize for Gifted and Talented, pp. 713, 725

Teaching Resources
- Biography, Literature, and Comparing Primary Sources booklet, pp. 26, 68–69, 137–138

ESL

Teacher's Edition
- Customize for ESL, p. 727

Teaching Resources
- Guided Reading and Review booklet, pp. 86–88
- Guide to the Essentials (English/Spanish), Chapter 21

Technology
- Student Edition on Audio CD, Chapter 21
- Guided Reading Audiotapes (English/Spanish), Chapter 21
- Section Reading Support Transparencies

Less Proficient Readers

Teacher's Edition
- Customize for Less Proficient Readers, p. 715

Teaching Resources
- Guided Reading and Review booklet, pp. 86–88
- Guide to the Essentials (English/Spanish), Chapter 21

Technology
- Student Edition on Audio CD, Chapter 21
- Guided Reading Audiotapes (English/Spanish), Chapter 21
- Section Reading Support Transparencies

Less Proficient Writers

Teacher's Edition
- Customize for Less Proficient Writers, pp. 719, 733

Teaching Resources
- Guided Reading and Review booklet, pp. 86–88
- Guide to the Essentials (English/Spanish), Chapter 21

Technology
- Student Edition on Audio CD, Chapter 21
- Guided Reading Audiotapes (English/Spanish), Chapter 21
- Section Reading Support Transparencies

TEACHER'S EDITION INDEX

CHAPTER 21 – PACING SUGGESTIONS

For 90-minute Blocks
- Teach sections 1 and 2 using Transparencies G12 and H17, and the Recent Scholarship note on page 719 for class discussions.

Running Out of Time?
If you are running short on time to cover this chapter, consider the following options:

- Use the Prentice Hall Presentation Pro CD-ROM to create an outline for this chapter.
- Use the Section Summaries for Chapter 21, from **Guide to the Essentials (English/Spanish).**

1 A Republican Decade	**Connecting with Government** Have students use a graphic organizer to summarize President Harding's major legislative and diplomatic moves as described in the text and other sources. Students should categorize each move as "positive" or "negative," based on what they believe the effects of the actions were on the country. Have students use their organizer as the basis for an evaluation of Harding's administration. **(Verbal/Linguistic)**	
2 A Business Boom	**Connecting with Economics** Suggest that students reread this section so that they can assemble a list of those practices that appear to be the basis for certain businesses becoming more successful than others. Students can follow up their assessment by discussing, in small groups, whether such practices would be effective in modern businesses. You may wish to have each group summarize their discussion in writing. **(Verbal/Linguistic)**	
3 The Economy in the Late 1920s	**Connecting with Economics** Point out the graphs in this section, which show personal debt and income distribution in the 1920s. Ask students to find comparable data for a recent year and present it in graphic form. Invite a discussion on how the two compare. What has changed over the years? What has not? **(Logical/Mathematical)**	

INTRODUCING THE CHAPTER

Coming out of World War I, Americans were focused on returning to normal and improving the nation's economy. Through three one-term presidencies, the country saw an economic boom, labor troubles, and the seeds of an economic disaster that loomed as the decade ended.

TIME LINE ACTIVITY

To provide students with practice in using the time line, ask questions such as these:

1. What impact did the Russian Revolution have on the public's perception of Communists in the United States? *(Communists were viewed as "subversives" whose movements and actions were held under suspicion.)*

2. What incident revealed the Harding administration's corruption? *(The Teapot Dome scandal of 1923)*

3. What medical breakthrough occurred during this decade? *(The 1928 discovery of penicillin by Scottish scientist Alexander Fleming)*

eTeach

Be sure to check out this month's online discussion with a Master Teacher. Go to **www.phschool.com**.

Chapter 21

Politics and Prosperity (1920–1929)

SECTION 1   A Republican Decade

SECTION 2   A Business Boom

SECTION 3   The Economy in the Late 1920s

Coolidge backers sang this song to show their support.

THE OFFICIAL
CAMPAIGN SONG of the HOME TOWN COOLIDGE CLUB
of
PLYMOUTH, VERMONT

KEEP COOL AND KEEP COOLIDGE

MUSIC BY BRUCE HARPER   WORDS BY IDA CHEEVER GOODWIN

American Events

1919
During a Red Scare, the Palmer raids target suspected Communists and other "subversives." Labor strikes are widespread.

1920
Sacco and Vanzetti are arrested and later tried and convicted for murder. They are executed in 1927.

1923
Senate hearings on Teapot Dome reveal corruption in the Harding administration.

Presidential Terms: Woodrow Wilson 1913–1921   Warren G. Harding 1921–1923   Calvin Coolidge 1923–1929

1918	1920	1922	1924

World Events

The Russian Civil War ends.
1920

The Chinese Communist Party is founded.
1921

In Germany, Hitler's Beer Hall Putsch fails.
1923

Soviet leader Vladimir Ilyich Lenin dies.
1924

710   Chapter 21 • *Politics and Prosperity*

RESOURCE DIRECTORY

Teaching Resources
Pacing Charts booklet
Block Scheduling booklet, p. 23
Units 7/8 booklet
• Chapter Summary, p. 13

Technology
Guided Reading Audiotapes (English/Spanish), Ch. 21
Student Edition on Audio CD, Ch. 21
Prentice Hall United States History Video Collection™ Volume 17, *The Roaring Twenties*
Prentice Hall Presentation Pro CD-ROM, Ch. 21
Resource Pro® CD-ROM
Social Studies Skills Tutor CD-ROM
Companion Web site, www.phschool.com

Air Routes, 1927–1930

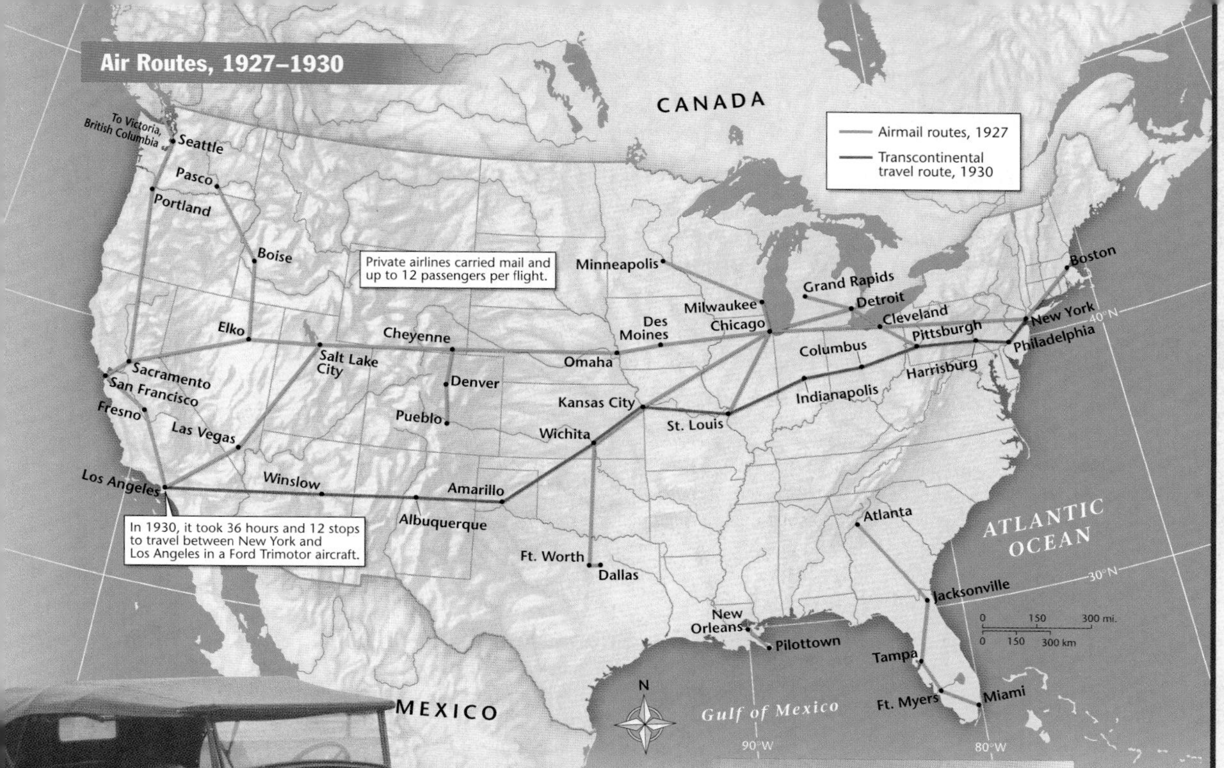

Air Routes, 1927–1930 (map)

Legend:
— Airmail routes, 1927
— Transcontinental travel route, 1930

CANADA

Private airlines carried mail and up to 12 passengers per flight.

In 1930, it took 36 hours and 12 stops to travel between New York and Los Angeles in a Ford Trimotor aircraft.

Cities labeled: To Victoria, British Columbia; Seattle; Pasco; Portland; Boise; Elko; Cheyenne; Salt Lake City; Sacramento; San Francisco; Fresno; Las Vegas; Los Angeles; Winslow; Amarillo; Albuquerque; Ft. Worth; Dallas; Denver; Pueblo; Wichita; Kansas City; Omaha; Des Moines; St. Louis; Minneapolis; Milwaukee; Chicago; Grand Rapids; Detroit; Cleveland; Columbus; Indianapolis; Harrisburg; Pittsburgh; New York; Philadelphia; Boston; Atlanta; Jacksonville; New Orleans; Pilottown; Tampa; Ft. Myers; Miami

MEXICO

ATLANTIC OCEAN

Gulf of Mexico

A 1929 Model A Ford Phaeton

Hard times forced many farmers to auction their land, equipment, animals, and homes.

1927
Ford's Model A automobile replaces the Model T.

1928
Nations signing the Kellogg-Briand Pact vow to resolve disputes peacefully.

1929
Home building falls by 25 percent. Two hundred companies own nearly half of all industry. Stock values reach $87 billion in October.

Herbert Hoover 1929–1933

1926 • 1928 • 1930

1928
Penicillin is discovered by Scottish scientist Alexander Fleming.

1929
The National Revolutionary Party is established in Mexico.

Air Routes, 1927–1930

Activating Prior Knowledge Did airlines of this time serve people in all parts of the country? *(No. Mail and passenger routes were limited.)*

Previewing How do you think the achievements of Charles Lindbergh and Amelia Earhart affected the airlines? *(Their exploits helped popularize the industry.)*

BACKGROUND
About the Pictures

1 2 3 4

1. The trial and execution of Nicola Sacco and Bartolomeo Vanzetti caused great controversy not only in the United States but also internationally. In France a mob of people protesting the case besieged the American embassy, requiring French police and soldiers to defend the building.

2. During the 1920s most presidential campaign paraphernalia consisted of printed material, such as this song book endorsing Calvin Coolidge.

3. Originally introduced in 1927, the Ford Model A was a drastic improvement over the earlier Model T. The Model A had hydraulic brakes, a three-speed transmission complete with clutch, and safety glass for the front windshield.

4. Farmers unable to pay their bills would be forced to auction off their farm equipment and possessions at extremely low prices, reducing many of them to poverty.

TEXT

Don't miss the exclusive interactive version of this textbook on the Web and on CD-ROM.

BIBLIOGRAPHY

For the Teacher

Coolidge, Calvin (author), and Peter Hannaford (editor). *The Quotable Calvin Coolidge: Sensible Words for a New Century.* New York: Images from the Past, 2001. (Fascinating collection of Coolidge quotations, with an insightful introduction.)

Sacco, Nicola, and Bartolomeo Vanzetti (authors), and Marian Denman Frankfurter (editor), *The Letters of Sacco and Vanzetti.* New York: Penguin, 1997. (This collection of letters from the condemned prisoners, originally published in 1928, was reissued to coincide with the seventieth anniversary of their execution.)

For the Student

Gourley, Catherine. *Wheels of Time: A Biography of Henry Ford.* Brookfield, Connecticut: Millbrook Press, 1997. (Written in association with the Henry Ford Museum, this book contains many archival photographs.)

Monroe, Judy. *The Sacco and Vanzetti Controversial Murder Trial: A Headline Court Case.* New York: Enslow Publishers, 2000. (Did Sacco and Vanzetti get a fair trial? This book will stimulate classroom debate.)

SECTION OBJECTIVES

1. Learn about events that fueled the red scare of the early 1920s.
2. Find out about conflicts that led to the major labor strikes of 1919.
3. See how Republican leadership during the Harding and Coolidge presidencies shaped the 1920s.
4. Discover the issues that shaped the presidential election of 1928.

BELLRINGER

Warm-Up Activity Write on the chalkboard: "The business of the American people is business." Ask students what they think the quote means and why it might have appealed to Americans after World War I.

Activating Prior Knowledge Can students state their impressions of the American economy as World War I ended? What type of direction do students think most people wanted from the government at this time?

READING STRATEGY

Have students copy the headings in this section. As they read, have them write down at least two key points under each heading. Have them focus particularly on the causes and effects of significant issues such as the red scare.

CAPTION ANSWERS

Viewing History Americans wanted strong, reassuring leaders who promised stability and prosperity.

READING FOCUS

- What events fueled the Red Scare of the early 1920s?
- What conflicts led to the major labor strikes of 1919?
- How did Republican leadership during the Harding and Coolidge presidencies shape the 1920s?
- What issues influenced the presidential election of 1928?

MAIN IDEA

Republican administrations of the 1920s pursued pro-business economic policies and an isolationist foreign policy.

KEY TERMS

communism
Red Scare
isolationism
disarmament
quota
Teapot Dome scandal
Kellogg-Briand Pact

TAKING NOTES

Copy the cause-and-effect diagram below. As you read, fill in the causes leading to the red scare and the effects the scare had on domestic issues.

CAUSES
• Communism is hostile to American values. •

⬇

THE RED SCARE

⬇

EFFECTS
• • •

Setting the Scene In 1920, the memory of World War I remained fresh. The Senate still refused to accept the Versailles Treaty, and debates on America's participation in the League of Nations continued. At the same time, a harsh economic downturn had begun, bringing an end to a brief postwar boom. Emerging from the shadow of the war and putting the economy back on track became significant issues in the 1920 presidential race.

The eventual winner, Republican Warren G. Harding, had the style of a leader. With his deep voice and dignified manner of speaking, he impressed people as honest and kind. But Harding doubted his own ability to serve as President, as did many of his critics. One Democrat called Harding's speeches "an army of pompous phrases moving across the landscape in search of an idea."

Nonetheless, one of his campaign speeches struck a chord with Americans. In it, Harding spelled out what the nation required in order to shake off the gloom of war:

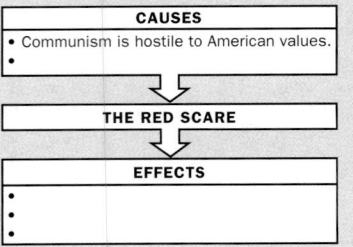

VIEWING HISTORY President Warren G. Harding had promised a return to "normalcy." **Drawing Inferences** *What sort of leadership were Americans seeking in the early 1920s?*

❝ *America's present need is not heroics, but healing; not nostrums [fake cures] but normalcy; not revolution, but restoration; not agitation, but adjustment; not surgery, but serenity; not the dramatic, but the dispassionate; not experiment, but equipoise [stability]; not submergence in internationality, but sustainment in triumphant nationality.* ❞
—Warren G. Harding, Boston, May 14, 1920

Harding's call for a return to "normalcy" became a hallmark of his campaign speeches. Voters got the message. In a nation weary of war abroad and sacrifice at home, the mere promise of "normalcy" gave Harding a landslide victory over Democrat James Cox and his running mate, Franklin D. Roosevelt.

712   Chapter 21 • *Politics and Prosperity*

RESOURCE DIRECTORY

Teaching Resources
Learning Styles Lesson Plans booklet, p. 44
Guided Reading and Review booklet, p. 86
Learning with Documents booklet (Primary Source Activity) *Industrializing the USSR,* p. 26
Biography, Literature, and Comparing Primary Sources booklet (Biography) *Walter Lippmann,* p. 26

Technology
Section Reading Support Transparencies
Guided Reading Audiotapes (English/Spanish), Ch. 21
Student Edition on Audio CD, Ch. 21
Prentice Hall Presentation Pro CD-ROM, Ch. 21
Companion Web site, www.phschool.com

The Red Scare

"Normalcy" appealed to Americans in 1920 because events within the country and abroad seemed anything but normal. Upheaval in faraway Russia and a series of strikes and bombings at home convinced many people that political violence posed a real threat to the United States.

The Russian Revolution As you read in an earlier chapter, Russia's absolute ruler, Czar Nicholas II, lost his hold on power in March 1917. The czar's popularity had been declining as a result of several tragically poor decisions, including leading his country into World War I. The war brought devastating casualties and severe food shortages. With riots in the streets and the army too weak to protect him, Nicholas was forced to abdicate. A new government formed, led by Alexander Kerensky. Kerensky pledged to remain in the European war, a decision that hurt him politically. Weary of war and political turmoil, Russia's workers and peasants fell under the sway of more radical ideas.

Promising "peace, land, and bread," revolutionary leader Vladimir I. Lenin undermined Kerensky's power. Although in the minority, Lenin and his followers took the name Bolsheviks, Russian for "majority," and adopted the red flag as their party's emblem. With such slogans as "End the war! All land to the peasants!" the Bolsheviks overthrew Kerensky's government on November 6, 1917. They then made peace with Germany and put all privately owned farms, industries, land, and transportation under government ownership.

Civil war broke out almost immediately. Lenin's Red Army, often simply called the Reds, met resistance from several armies, known collectively as the Whites. The Whites included former landowners, government officials, Russian army leaders and others. Britain, France, Japan, and the United States, whose investments in Russia had been seized by Bolsheviks, backed the Whites.

After more than two and a half years, the Reds triumphed in 1920. Two years later, their new nation became known as the Union of Soviet Socialist Republics (USSR), or the Soviet Union.

Lenin made communism the official ideology of Russia and, later, the Soviet Union. This ideology was openly hostile to American beliefs and values, such as capitalism, private ownership of land and business, and First Amendment freedoms. For Lenin and his followers, **communism** meant the following:
1. The government owned all land and property.
2. A single political party controlled the government.
3. The needs of the country always took priority over the rights of individuals.
If isolated, a Communist country could be open to attack. For communism to survive, Lenin believed that it would have to be spread throughout the world.

To a working class long oppressed by czarist rule, communism's appeal lay in the promise of a classless society, its wealth shared according to need. In practice communism evolved into something far different, especially when shaped by Joseph Stalin, who led the Soviet Union after Lenin's death in 1924. Instead of "peace, land, and bread," Stalin used terror to force the peasantry onto collectivized farms. The result was great famine.

American Fears Russia's intention to spread communism to other countries alarmed many Americans. They distrusted Europeans already, blaming them for starting World War I. Some Americans grew concerned that among the masses of

Focus on GOVERNMENT

The Origins of Communism The communal sharing of wealth is an old concept, one often embraced by religious groups. The Shakers, who settled in New York in the mid-eighteenth century, worked together and shared wealth and property, as did the later Amana colonies of Iowa. Eventually, the huge disparities of wealth created by industrialization transformed communism into a general social ideal.

Followers of this ideal soon split into factions. Both Socialists and Communists believed that wealth should be shared according to need but differed on how to achieve this goal. Some socialists put their hopes in democratic processes and labor unions, others in terrorism. Communists adopted Lenin's idea of the "dictatorship of proletariat," which referred to a period when workers would rule through a single authoritarian party. The party would regulate all activities until it had achieved a classless society and a world union of socialist republics. At left, Lenin addresses a crowd.

714 • Chapter 21 Section 1

INTERPRETING POLITICAL CARTOONS Anarchists on American soil were a matter of concern at the time of this 1919 illustration. **Analyzing Visual Information** *How does the artist use symbolism to convey a message?*

ACTIVITY

Connecting with Economics

To help students understand the red scare, propose that communism will replace the capitalist system. Divide students into groups and assign to each one of the following roles: factory worker, factory owner, investor, government official, consumer. From the perspective determined by each of their roles, have students decide if the new system would improve or worsen their lives. How might the wish for "normalcy" have intensified these views? **(Verbal/Linguistic)**

BACKGROUND

Connections to Today

During the Red Scare, when then–U.S. Attorney General A. Mitchell Palmer relentlessly pursued "subversives," thousands of people—mainly immigrants—were arrested and held without trial. In the immediate aftermath of the September 11, 2001, terrorist attacks in New York City, Washington, D.C., and Pennsylvania, the United States government showed that it had learned from history's lessons. Congress quickly passed House Concurrent Resolution 227, declaring "that in the quest to identify, bring to justice and punish the perpetrators and sponsors of the terrorist attacks. . . the civil rights and civil liberties of all Americans, including Arab Americans, American Muslims, and Americans from South Asia, should be protected. . . ."

READING CHECK

Abroad: The Bolshevik seizure of power in Russia; Communist agitation in Germany; a Communist regime in Hungary. In U.S.: red scare; strikes; bomb explosions; mistrust of recent immigrants.

READING CHECK

What events abroad and in the United States caused concern among war-weary Americans?

European immigrants entering the United States were Communists and other radicals. American worries about foreigners from Europe reached new heights.

In early 1919, Russian-backed Communists tried to overthrow the new German government, and Communists came to power in Hungary. Similar chaos threatened to seep into the United States, or so many people thought. In February, shipyard workers went on strike in Seattle, and the mayor proclaimed them "revolutionists." In April, a number of bombs were sent through the mail, addressed mainly to government officials—including Seattle's mayor. One of the bombs reached its destination and exploded, severely injuring a Georgia senator's housekeeper. Newspapers whipped up the public's anxiety with sensational stories about these events. Soon the United States was in the grip of a **Red Scare,** an intense fear of communism and other politically radical ideas. Americans called for known Communists to be jailed or driven out of the country.

Schenck v. U.S. To some people, a 1919 Supreme Court decision seemed to justify jailing Communists. During World War I, a war opponent named Charles Schenck had mailed letters to men who were drafted, urging them not to report for duty. He was convicted of breaking the Espionage Act, a wartime law aimed at spies and people who opposed the war. Schenck appealed the case, claiming that he was only exercising his right to speak freely.

In the Court's written opinion, Justice Oliver Wendell Holmes, Jr., said that the government is justified in silencing free speech when there is a "clear and present danger" to the nation. He compared what Schenck had done to shouting "Fire!" in a crowded theater. Such an action could cause a dangerous panic. Some have argued that in equating what was reasonable with what was constitutional, Holmes expanded the powers of the Supreme Court beyond the original intent of the Constitution.

Gitlow v. New York The Supreme Court's decision in another radical speech case in this period had later significance. The state of New York had convicted Bernard Gitlow, a Socialist, of "criminal anarchy" for publishing calls in 1919 to overthrow the government by force. Gitlow appealed on the basis that New York had violated his constitutional guarantees of freedom of speech and of the press.

In the past, the Supreme Court had argued that the Bill of Rights protected individuals only against actions of the federal, not the state, governments. In this case, the Court upheld Gitlow's conviction, saying that he had indeed urged people to violent revolution. At the same time, it affirmed that the Fourteenth Amendment protected civil rights against restriction by state governments. Since *Gitlow,* the Court has used the Fourteenth Amendment to make other provisions of the Bill of Rights apply to state actions.

The Palmer Raids In June 1919, bombs exploded in several cities. One explosion severely damaged the home of A. Mitchell Palmer, the Attorney General of the United States. Although Palmer escaped injury, the bombings convinced him that radicals were conspiring to overthrow the government. He began a campaign to identify and root out groups whose activities posed a "clear and present danger" to the country.

Later that year the Justice Department, headed by Palmer, set up a special force to conduct raids and arrest suspected "subversives" (people trying to subvert, or overthrow, the government). Targets included Communists, Socialists,

CAPTION ANSWERS

Interpreting Political Cartoons The American flag, a symbol of freedom and democracy, is used to show how the United States can be destroyed by the "flames" of anarchy.

and anarchists, or people who oppose all government. Palmer approached the task zealously. On the night of December 31, 1919, he stated: "Any movement, however cloaked or dissembled, designed to undermine the government, will be met with unflinching, persistent, aggressive warfare."

On January 2, 1920, federal agents in 33 cities arrested thousands of suspected radicals, and without evidence, charged them with anarchy. Most of the suspects had been born overseas. Many were completely innocent. Still, more than 500 of them were later deported, or sent back to their homeland.

At first, Palmer received strong support for his actions. The army's chief of staff urged that those deported be sent away on "ships of stone with sails of lead." Popular preacher Billy Sunday suggested that a firing squad would save money on ships.

The Red Scare created such a frenzy that in April 1920, the New York State Assembly voted to expel five recently elected Socialist members. Many people protested that the assembly was violating the public's right to choose its own representatives, but the Socialists never took office.

Americans expected the worst on May 1, 1920, an annual Socialist holiday honoring workers and labor organizations. On that day, according to Palmer, the nation would experience a general labor strike and widespread bombings. Newspapers predicted a major crisis. When May 1 came and went quietly, the press turned on Palmer, and Americans lost faith in him.

Sacco and Vanzetti The Red Scare played a part in one of the most controversial events in United States history. The story began on April 15, 1920, when gunmen robbed and killed the guard and paymaster of a shoe factory in South Braintree, Massachusetts. A few weeks later, police arrested two Italian immigrants in connection with the crime.

One, Nicola Sacco, was a shoemaker, and the other, Bartolomeo Vanzetti, was a fish peddler. Both of them were also anarchists. Police found guns on both men when they were arrested; Sacco's gun was the same model used in the crime. Yet many Americans suspected that the two men were arrested mainly because they were immigrants with radical beliefs. The case drew international attention and controversy.

After a trial that many observers called unfair, a jury found Sacco and Vanzetti guilty. Their lawyers appealed the case to higher courts again and again for years, but the convictions were upheld. The two men were sentenced to death in April 1927, and despite mass protests, they died in the electric chair four months later.

Labor Strikes

A wave of strikes helped fuel the Red Scare in 1919. Strikers included telephone operators in New England, machinists in Ohio, and construction workers in Texas. The number of strikes per month climbed from around 175 in March of that year to around 370 in August. Many Americans believed that Communist "agitators" were behind this labor unrest. Most of the strikes, however, had a simpler cause. In

COMPARING HISTORIANS' VIEWPOINTS
The Sacco and Vanzetti Verdict

Over the years, historians have examined and reexamined evidence and transcripts from the Sacco and Vanzetti trial. Opinions regarding their guilt or innocence, and the fairness of the trial, have changed over time.

Analyzing Viewpoints Compare the main arguments made by the writers.

Vanzetti Was Innocent

"Even if one accepts the possibility that someone other than Sacco fired the [murder weapon], Sacco knew who that someone was.

Vanzetti's innocence is, at least for me, confirmed by . . . contradictions to the court testimony. . . . Yet it would have been like Vanzetti to go to the chair rather than betray a friend."

—*Francis Russell*, Tragedy in Dedham: The Story of the Sacco-Vanzetti Case

Opposed to the Verdict

"Any attempt to establish the guilt or innocence of Sacco and Vanzetti must be based upon an analysis of the evidence. . . . The revelations of the state police files, the grand jury proceeding, and the prosecution notebooks show that virtually every piece of evidence against the two men ultimately rested upon falsehoods and fabrications."

—*William Young and David E. Kaiser*, Postmortem: New Evidence in the Case of Sacco and Vanzetti

Chapter 21 • Section 1   **715**

early 1919, prices of food, clothing, housing, and other necessities soared. By 1920, inflation brought the cost of living to twice that of prewar levels. Most workers went on strike because the standard of living they had achieved during World War I had declined.

The Boston Police Strike Boston police officers had not received a pay increase since the start of the war. In September 1919, they took steps to organize a union, even though department rules banned labor unions. After the Boston police commissioner fired 19 officers for union activity, the whole force voted to strike.

Rioting broke out in Boston within hours after the police walked off the job, and it lasted through the night. In the morning, the mayor sent out a volunteer police force to restore order. Later in the day, Massachusetts governor Calvin Coolidge called out the state guard, but by then, calm had largely returned to Boston. "There is no right to strike against the public safety by anybody, anywhere, anytime," Coolidge stated. The future President gained national attention for his firm response to the strike.

Steel and Coal Strikes Later in September, steelworkers launched a strike against the United States Steel Corporation. At the time, steelworkers put in 12-hour shifts, and their work week averaged more than 65 hours. Backed by the American Federation of Labor (AFL), the workers asked for an 8-hour day and a 48-hour week. Some 350,000 workers walked off the job.

The strike nearly shut down a huge steel mill in Gary, Indiana, and it affected plants in several other cities as well. Claiming that the strike was the work of Communists, U.S. Steel set out to stop it. The company hired a private police force, which killed 18 strikers and beat hundreds more.

The company also brought in thousands of African American workers from the South to break the strike. The state and federal governments supported management by supplying troops to control the strikers and protect the strikebreakers. After ten weeks, the AFL called off the strike when workers, realizing that they could not win, started heading back to work.

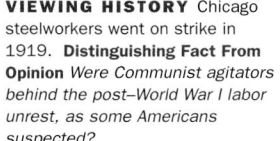

VIEWING HISTORY Chicago steelworkers went on strike in 1919. **Distinguishing Fact From Opinion** *Were Communist agitators behind the post–World War I labor unrest, as some Americans suspected?*

Soft-coal miners also went on strike in that troubled fall of 1919, demanding higher wages. Their union, the United Mine Workers of America (UMW), had made a no-strike agreement during the war that they claimed had ended with the armistice. The Wilson administration argued that the agreement was still in effect. When the miners struck in November, Attorney General Palmer persuaded a court to order the strikers back to work. Regardless, the miners continued their walkout until early December, when a coal shortage developed. To end the strike, a government-established coal commission granted the miners a 14 percent pay raise.

Strikes Decline Most Americans opposed strikes. They saw them as anti-American and likely to result in violence. They also distrusted labor unions and the immigrant workers they represented, assuming they were influenced by radical ideas. Actually, the largest labor union by far in the United States, the AFL, did not fit this description at all. At its convention in 1919, the AFL went out of its way to declare its opposition to labor radicalism and to communism. Nevertheless, the union stuck by its main goals—to fight for higher wages, shorter hours, and the right to organize workers.

Membership in labor unions peaked at 5 million workers during the Red Scare of 1919–1920. Then it dropped sharply to a level that stayed fairly steady throughout the 1920s. When union growth leveled, the number of strikes declined. These changes to organized labor had a range of causes. Public opposition hurt unions, as did the lack of support from the government. President Wilson called the Boston police strike a "crime against civilization" and warned that striking for higher wages only drove up prices. Other causes were economic. The economic downturn that began in 1920 severely reduced the number of employed workers. The following economic boom brought higher wages, which undercut both the workers' desire to seek union representation and their need to strike.

Republican Leadership

The Red Scare had important political consequences. Americans felt that the Republican Party was more likely to restore stability than the Democratic Party. Starting with the 1920 election, Republicans solidified their power and dominated all three branches of government for the rest of the decade. Republican Presidents Warren G. Harding, Calvin Coolidge, and Herbert Hoover served from 1921 to 1933. Republicans held the majority in Congress during this period. In addition, Supreme Court decisions of the era reflected the influence of its new chief justice, former President William Howard Taft, appointed by Harding in 1921.

Republican leaders agreed on basic policies and goals. Generally, they favored business and sought social stability. Many of these leaders were, in fact, businessmen who believed that social stability promoted economic growth.

The Harding Presidency

President Harding took office as the Red Scare and the labor strikes were beginning to subside. In that respect, the country did seem to be getting back to "normalcy."

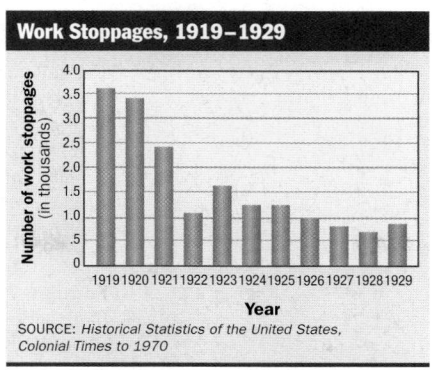

Work Stoppages, 1919–1929

SOURCE: *Historical Statistics of the United States, Colonial Times to 1970*

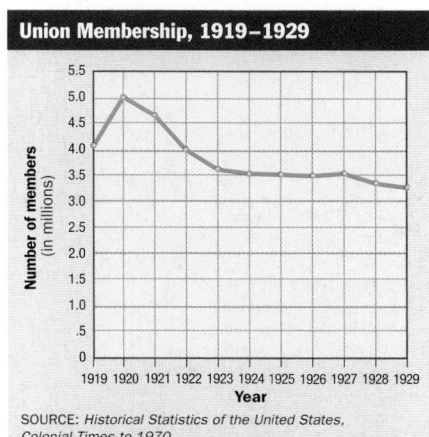

Union Membership, 1919–1929

SOURCE: *Historical Statistics of the United States, Colonial Times to 1970*

INTERPRETING GRAPHS
The post–World War I years were stormy ones for labor and business, until a booming economy caused wages to rise. **Making Comparisons** *How do union membership and the number of work stoppages reflect changes in labor?*

 Sounds of an Era

Listen to President Harding's speech "Return to Normalcy" and other sounds from the 1920s.

Chapter 21 • Section 1   **717**

ACTIVITY
Connecting with Citizenship

Harding's election was the first ever broadcast by radio, on station KDKA in Pittsburgh. Have students research this election, and then have a group of interested students create a radio play in which they simulate a portion of the broadcast election results.
(Verbal/Linguistic)

BACKGROUND
A Diverse Nation

Many advances in aviation technology occurred during the 1920s, allowing the business of carrying passengers by air to expand. New navigational instruments were available by the end of the decade which allowed aircraft to be flown safely in conditions of poor visibility, such as bad weather or darkness. There were also powerful and reliable new aircraft engines of an improved air-cooled radial design (such as the engine which powered Charles Lindbergh's *Spirit of St. Louis* on his transatlantic flight). These and other advances allowed commercial air travel to begin to be seen as a realistic alternative for the traveling public.

TEST PREPARATION

Have students read the paragraphs under "The Boston Police Strike" on the previous page and then complete the sentence below.

Based on the passage, you can infer that—

(A) Coolidge believed this strike should be stopped, as it presented a danger to the general public.

B Coolidge did not support strikes under any circumstances.

C Coolidge favored expanding the role of government to stop all strikes.

D Coolidge sympathized with the police officers.

CAPTION ANSWERS

Interpreting Graphs As union membership leveled off throughout the 1920s, work stoppages fell to a much lower level than had been the case in 1919–1920.

Chapter 21   Section 1 • **717**

Harding made some wise Cabinet appointments. An able administrator, Herbert Hoover reorganized the office of Secretary of Commerce. Charles Evans Hughes, a former Supreme Court justice, worked for world peace as Secretary of State. One of the nation's most powerful businessmen, Andrew Mellon, became Treasury Secretary. Serving under Harding and his two Republican successors, Mellon shaped the economic policies of the 1920s.

Harding showed poor judgment in many of his other appointments, however. He gave important jobs to friends and acquaintances, many of whom were inexperienced, incompetent, or dishonest. These choices eventually overwhelmed his presidency and his life.

Foreign Policy After the war, many Americans wished to avoid political or economic alliances with foreign countries, a policy called **isolationism.** Harding's opposition to American membership in the League of Nations reflected those wishes, and he made no attempt to join. Yet the President wanted to establish international peace and stability. To reach this goal, he worked with other nations, while carefully avoiding "entangling alliances" that might threaten the independence of the United States.

One road to peace and stability involved finding ways to prevent war. Harding called for **disarmament,** a program in which the nations of the world would voluntarily give up their weapons. He convened the Washington Conference in 1921 to discuss this plan. At the conference, several major military powers signed a treaty limiting the size of their navies.

The United States, now a major economic power, continued to engage in trade throughout the world. Harding promoted the expansion of trade, saying that American business must "go on to the peaceful commercial conquest of the world." He also acted to protect business at home. In 1922, Congress, with Harding's support, passed the Fordney-McCumber Tariff, which raised import taxes to historically high levels. The tariff especially discouraged imports that competed with goods made by new American industries, such as china, toys, and chemicals.

The new tariff angered the European nations who faced demands from the United States to pay their American war debts. To raise the money necessary to pay off those debts, Europeans needed to sell goods to the United States. Yet the tariff acted as a barrier to their exports. Great Britain and France argued forcefully for the cancellation of their debts. To resolve the issue, Congress agreed in 1922 to scale back those debts to a level that better suited each country's ability to pay.

The United States hoped to apply the same approach to another sensitive international issue, German war reparations. In the early 1920s, inflation left Germany's economy in ruins. The German government simply could not afford the huge bill for war costs that the Allies demanded in the Versailles Treaty. Along with the British, the United States pushed for a plan to help the German economy recover enough to pay its debts. A special commission developed the Dawes Plan, which the Allies and Germany signed in 1924. The plan set a payment

VIEWING HISTORY President Harding (seated center) with (seated from left) Henry Ford, Thomas Edison, tire manufacturer Harvey Firestone, and William Anderson, Methodist Bishop of Cincinnati. **Drawing Inferences** *What goals and ideals might Harding and his companions in this photo have had in common?*

schedule, reorganized the German national bank, and approved a loan to Germany.

Domestic Issues As Americans became more isolationist, they also became more nativist. Nativism is a movement favoring native-born Americans over immigrants. It had first appeared in the 1800s, but after World War I it flared up again, for several reasons:

Patriotism Many Americans believed that foreigners could never be fully loyal to the United States.

Religion Nativists, who were mostly Protestants, had long mistrusted immigrants who were Catholics, Orthodox Christians, or Jews.

Urban conditions Americans often blamed the problems in cities, such as slums and corruption, on the immigrants who lived in them.

Jobs Workers feared that immigrants would take their jobs away from them.

Red Scare Some immigrants came from the most unstable parts of Europe, where World War I had started. Nativists believed that these immigrants might hold or adopt radical political ideas, and spread them to the United States.

Nativists reacted to the sharp postwar rise in immigration with calls for government action. In 1921, at Harding's request, Congress passed a law restricting immigration. Although only a temporary measure, the law included an important feature whose impact would long be felt: a **quota,** or numerical limit, imposed on immigrants representing certain ethnic groups or nations. According to the law, a group's numerical limit equaled 3 percent of that group's total United States population as of the 1910 census.

A permanent measure, the National Origins Act, passed in 1924. This law reduced the quota to 2 percent and based it on the census of 1890. In 1890, the population of immigrants from Italy, Poland, Russia, and other southern and eastern European countries was low. As a result, the law severely limited continued immigration from those countries. The law went further, prohibiting the entry of "aliens ineligible to citizenship," a category that referred specifically to the Japanese. (The Chinese Exclusion Act had already shut down immigration from China.)

Recall that social stability became a basic goal of Republicans in the 1920s. President Harding believed that restrictions on immigration helped the cause of social stability. He also believed that restrictions on the civil rights of American citizens hurt that cause. In 1921, in front of a segregated audience in Birmingham, Alabama, Harding made a surprisingly bold speech on equality:

> ❝ I want to see the time come when black men will regard themselves as full participants in the benefits and duties of American citizenship; . . . We cannot go on . . . with one great section of our population . . . set off from real contribution to solving national issues, because of division on race lines. ❞
>
> —Warren G. Harding, October 26, 1921

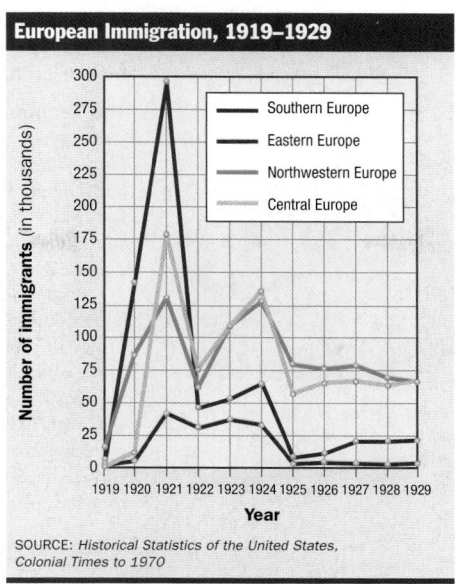

European Immigration, 1919–1929

Number of immigrants (in thousands)

Legend: Southern Europe, Eastern Europe, Northwestern Europe, Central Europe

Year: 1919 1920 1921 1922 1923 1924 1925 1926 1927 1928 1929

SOURCE: *Historical Statistics of the United States, Colonial Times to 1970*

INTERPRETING GRAPHS
The graph shows European immigration to the United States before and after immigration legislation was passed. **Analyzing Information** *Describe the effect of Harding's immigration policies on the number of immigrants from eastern and southern Europe as shown by the graph.*

Connecting with Citizenship

As he left office in 1969, Charles de Gaulle, then president of France, commented: "Patriotism is when love of your own people comes first; nationalism, when hate for people other than your own comes first." Hold a classroom discussion about this statement, and then ask students to write brief essays in response to it. Have students include their own definitions of patriotism and nationalism in the essays and give examples of each, either contemporary or historical. (**Verbal/Linguistic**)

BACKGROUND

Recent Scholarship

One outgrowth of virulent nativist sentiment was legislation such as the Chinese Exclusion Act of 1882. This act, which remained in force in the U.S. until 1943, arose from anti-Chinese demonstrations in San Francisco in the 1870s and 1880s. It was intended to protect American jobs and wages from what was seen as an uncontrollable influx of immigrants from China.

Claiming America: Constructing Chinese American Identities During the Exclusion Era is a collection of essays about the formation of an ethnic identity during the time that immigration from China was barred and the rights of Chinese living in America were severely restricted. The book presents accounts of Chinese immigrants as well as essays that describe the struggle of members of the next generation to define their identity as Chinese Americans and to achieve the kinds of opportunities afforded other immigrant populations.

CUSTOMIZE FOR ...

Less Proficient Writers
Have students reread the section "The Coolidge Presidency." Then have students list specific actions or decisions by Coolidge that supported his opinion that "the chief business of the American People is business."

CAPTION ANSWERS

Interpreting Graphs Immigration legislation was passed in 1921 and in 1924. These acts caused a sharp drop in the number of immigrants from both southern and eastern Europe, but especially from southern Europe.

African American onlookers cheered the President's words, but the white members of the audience responded with shocked silence. Later, Harding introduced federal anti-lynching legislation, but his proposal died in the Senate.

The Teapot Dome Scandal At the start of 1923, the economy was growing steadily. A period of prosperity had begun, and Harding enjoyed strong popularity. Then, major corruption scandals in Harding's administration came to light. There was no evidence that the President was involved in the scandals. In fact, Harding became terribly disturbed when he heard of the scandals, and the strain may have contributed to his death, possibly from heart problems, on August 2, 1923.

By 1924, the extent of the corruption in Harding's administration was widely known. One official had stolen government funds. Others had taken bribes in return for help in getting contracts approved or laws passed. Several other officials were also accused of wrong-doing, and two committed suicide.

The worst Harding scandal came to be known as the **Teapot Dome scandal.** In 1921 and 1922, Harding's Secretary of the Interior, Albert B. Fall, secretly gave oil-drilling rights on government oil fields in Elk Hills, California, and Teapot Dome, Wyoming, to two private oil companies. In return, Fall received more than $300,000 in illegal payments and gifts disguised as loans.

The Democrats in 1924 tried to use public anger over the Teapot Dome affair to defeat the Republicans, as this campaign artifact shows.

The Coolidge Presidency

Vice President Calvin Coolidge was visiting his parents in Vermont on August 3, 1923, when word arrived of Harding's death. At 2:30 A.M., by the light of a kerosene lamp, Coolidge's father, a justice of the peace, administered to him the oath of office of President of the United States.

Coolidge was still widely respected for his actions as governor of Massachusetts. He had played no part in the Harding scandals. In fact, one Democrat said that Coolidge's "great task was to restore the dignity and prestige of the presidency when it had reached the lowest ebb in our history." After finishing Harding's term, Coolidge ran in the 1924 election, defeating Democrat John W. Davis and Progressive Robert M. La Follette with the slogan "Keep cool with Coolidge." Coolidge had a reputation as a skilled public speaker, but in private he was a man of few words. Someone said of him that "he could be silent in five languages."

Laissez Faire In one sentence, Coolidge summed up a major theme of the Republican decade: "The chief business of the American people is business." The best that the government could do, he believed, was to leave business alone and allow it to grow. This laissez-faire business policy helped fuel the tremendous economic boom of the 1920s.

For the most part, Congress supported a laissez-faire approach to business. It lowered income and inheritance tax rates and approved higher tariffs that benefited domestic manufacturing. Coolidge was so insistent on a minimal role for government that when Herbert Hoover, his Secretary of Commerce, urged him to regulate the buying of stocks on easy credit, he refused. When Mississippi River flood victims appealed to him for help, he said that government had no duty to protect citizens "against the hazards of the elements."

Coolidge's effort to have government do less drew criticism from those who saw it as a failure to take action. In 1926, the noted newspaper columnist Walter Lippmann said: "Mr. Coolidge's genius for inactivity is developed to a very high point. It is a grim, determined, alert inactivity, which keeps Mr. Coolidge occupied constantly."

Kellogg-Briand Pact Coolidge continued Harding's approach to international issues. He wanted peace and stability without getting the United States too deeply involved with other nations. Coolidge, however, left most foreign-policy decisions up to his Secretary of State, Frank B. Kellogg.

In 1927, Kellogg received an unusual suggestion from French Foreign Minister Aristide Briand. Briand thought that their two countries should formally agree not to declare war on each other. An isolationist at heart, Kellogg feared that such a treaty might entangle the United States with France. When other nations agreed to participate, however, Kellogg helped Briand iron out the details. Under the **Kellogg-Briand Pact,** 15 nations pledged not to use the threat of war in their dealings with one another. More than 60 nations eventually joined the pact. Outlawing war seemed to be a good idea, but the pact was unrealistic and unworkable because it had no provisions for enforcement. By 1941, many of the nations that had signed the pact would be at war.

The Election of 1928

As Coolidge neared the end of his first full term, he was asked about his political plans. "I do not choose to run for President in 1928" was his brief and famous reply. In his place, Republicans nominated Herbert Hoover. During and after World War I, Hoover had won respect for programs he ran in Europe to ease hunger. He had held Cabinet posts under Harding and Coolidge.

Hoover's main opponent was Alfred E. Smith of New York, a popular Democratic governor. Prohibition emerged as a major issue of the presidential campaign, as did religion. Smith was the first Roman Catholic to be nominated for President, and he opposed Prohibition. Hoover, a Protestant, vigorously supported Prohibition, which he called a "noble experiment." The contest reflected the basic urban-rural split in the country, as Smith drew most of his votes from the large cities, while Hoover did best in small towns. Drawn especially by the Prohibition debate, women voted in fairly large numbers for the first time and made a strong impact on both parties. Hoover captured about 21 million popular votes to 15 million for Smith, and he won in the electoral college by a huge margin. Americans expected that what they called the "Coolidge prosperity" would continue under Hoover.

INTERPRETING POLITICAL CARTOONS Calvin Coolidge, shown here with a saxophone, was known for his support of big business. **Analyzing Information** *What does this cartoon say about Coolidge and big business? Write a caption for the cartoon.*

Section 1 Assessment

READING COMPREHENSION

1. Why did **communism** seem to pose a threat to capitalist nations?

2. How did the **Red Scare** contribute to America's policy of **isolationism** in the 1920s?

3. What was the **Teapot Dome scandal?**

4. What was the **Kellogg-Briand Pact** and how did it reflect Republican foreign policy in the 1920s?

CRITICAL THINKING AND WRITING

5. **Identifying Central Issues** What led Americans to suspect that Communists were the source of labor unrest in the 1920s?

6. **Write a Letter to the Editor** Suppose you observed the trial of Sacco and Vanzetti. Write a letter telling whether or not you think the defendants received a fair trial.

Take It to the NET

Activity: Writing a Biography
Write a brief biography of one of the three Republican Presidents of the 1920s. Include stands on important issues and highlights from the presidency. Use the links provided in the *America: Pathways to the Present* area of the following Web site for help in completing this activity.
www.phschool.com

Section 1 Assessment

Reading Comprehension

1. Communist system: government owns all land and property; one-party government, needs of the nation supersede individual rights. Communism antithetical to capitalist philosophies of free enterprise and private sector ownership of industrial facilities.

2. Many of the suspected radicals swept up in the Palmer raids were immigrants. This contributed to the desire of Americans to adopt an isolationist stance.

3. Corruption in the Harding administration.

4. The Kellogg-Briand Pact was an agreement declaring warfare to be illegal. The United States, France, and some 60 other nations were signatories. This pact reflected the Republican desire to avoid foreign wars.

Critical Thinking and Writing

5. With the red scare as a backdrop, the number of strikes per month more than doubled in mid-1919. Blaming Communists was related to the prevalent belief that labor unions contained large numbers of immigrant radicals.

6. Letters will vary, but should be supported with facts from the section.

Take It to the NET

Answers will vary. Students should demonstrate knowledge of the major policies and accomplishments of Presidents Warren Harding, Calvin Coolidge, or Herbert Hoover.

CAPTION ANSWERS

Interpreting Political Cartoons Big business likes what Coolidge has to say. Possible caption: "Dancing to Coolidge's tune."

Evaluating Advertisements

Advertisements offer more than evidence of the consumer goods and services produced in a historical period. They often hold clues to widely held ideas, attitudes, and values. However, when using advertisements as historical evidence, keep in mind that their stated or unstated messages may reflect what the advertisers want readers to believe, value, or desire—rather than the reality for most people of the time.

By the 1920s, "situational" ads depicted not only products and what they did, but also the ways these products might enhance the lives of typical consumers. One such ad from the 1920s is shown below.

LEARN THE SKILL
Use the following steps to evaluate historical advertisements:

1. **Identify the subject of the advertisement.** What product or service does the advertisement promote?

2. **Analyze the advertisement's reliability as historical evidence.** Consider both the product itself and the way it is advertised.

3. **Study the advertisement to learn more about the historical period.** Consider the product and its purpose, the situation depicted in the advertisement, the text, and the visuals.

PRACTICE THE SKILL
Answer the following questions:

1. **(a)** What product or service does this advertisement promote? **(b)** What facts about the product does it provide? **(c)** What is the situation of the ad—in other words, what "problem" will this product solve for the people depicted in the ad? **(d)** What strategy does this advertisement use to appeal particularly to men? How does the ad try to appeal to women?

2. **(a)** Do you think the people depicted in the advertisement represent typical consumers of the 1920s? Explain. **(b)** In this ad, what is the unstated message that the advertiser is using to persuade people to buy the product?

3. **(a)** What social or cultural values are promoted in the advertisement? **(b)** What clues to the time period are given in the photograph? **(c)** In general, do you think advertisements reflect consumers' desires for products or create the desire for such products? Explain your reasoning.

APPLY THE SKILL
See the Chapter Review and Assessment for another opportunity to apply this skill.

Focus Students learn to analyze an advertisement as a historical document to gain insight into ideas, attitudes, and values of an era.

Instruct As you and your students analyze the historical ad shown in the book, focus particularly on the ad's message and its possible historical interpretations. Ask students to discuss their impressions of the effectiveness of the ad. Particularly, do they think it is likely that the lady would reject the man for "slovenliness" for the reason stated in the ad? Ask students to think of, or bring in, examples of modern-day advertisements that use the type of persuasion shown in this ad.

Extend See the Skills for Life Activity in the Resource Directory below.

ANSWERS
PRACTICE THE SKILL

1. **(a)** Garters to hold up men's socks. **(b)** The ad shows two available garter styles; gives price range; states that no metal can touch the wearer. **(c)** The "problem" the ad promises to solve is the rejection of the man's proposal because he appears slovenly to the woman due to his sagging socks and exposed calves. **(d)** Men: the need to present a neat appearance and to be successful; the concern about being rejected by women. Women: the concern about having husbands who will not be embarrassments in social situations.

2. **(a)** Answers will vary but should be based on facts about the 1920s. **(b)** That men will be more desirable to women if they use Paris Garters.

3. **(a)** Being neat, well-dressed, successful, and attractive to the opposite sex; caring about others' opinions. **(b)** The dress of the people in the ad, the furnishings of the room, the art-deco style border around the ad. **(c)** Answers will vary but should be well supported. Sample answer: Ads create a desire for products and manipulate people into buying them.

RESOURCE DIRECTORY

Teaching Resources
Skills for Life booklet, p. 23

Technology
Social Studies Skills Tutor CD-ROM
Interactive Practice in
- Geographic Literacy
- Critical Thinking and Reading
- Visual Analysis
- Communications

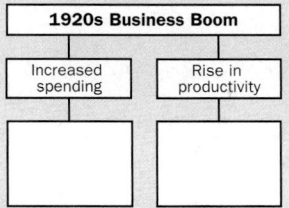

READING FOCUS

- What role do businesses and consumers play in a consumer economy?
- How were Henry Ford and the automobile important to the 1920s?
- In what ways did industrial growth affect the economy of the 1920s?
- Why did the economic boom bypass some people and benefit others?

MAIN IDEA

During the 1920s, new products and Americans' power to purchase them grew rapidly, producing a decade of enormous business growth.

KEY TERMS

consumer economy
installment plan
Gross National Product (GNP)
assembly line

TAKING NOTES

Copy this flowchart. As you read, fill in the boxes with some of the factors that caused a business boom in the 1920s.

```
                1920s Business Boom
         ┌──────────────┬──────────────┐
         │  Increased   │   Rise in    │
         │  spending    │ productivity │
         └──────┬───────┴──────┬───────┘
         ┌──────┴──────┐┌──────┴──────┐
         │             ││             │
         │             ││             │
         └─────────────┘└─────────────┘
```

SECTION OBJECTIVES

1. Understand the role businesses and consumers play in a consumer economy.
2. Find out how Henry Ford and the automobile were important to the 1920s.
3. Discover the ways in which industrial growth affected the economy of the 1920s.
4. See how the economic boom bypassed some people and benefited others.

BELLRINGER

Warm-Up Activity Ask students what items are commonly bought on credit. Ask how American life would be different if credit disappeared.

Activating Prior Knowledge What, in students' opinions, constitutes a consumer society? Have the class list some aspects of a consumer society. Then have them list some positive and negative aspects of such a society.

READING STRATEGY

Have students reread the Main Idea on this page. Then have them rewrite it as a question. As they read, have them take notes about events that help answer the question.

Setting the Scene

Until the 1920s, shopping centers did not exist. Food was not "fast." Billboards did not line the nation's highways, because there were no highways, few cars, and relatively few advertisements.

The decade of the 1920s gave birth to much of the popular culture we know in modern America. The nation's first shopping center opened in Kansas City, giving consumers a more convenient way to shop. The first fast-food chain, A&W Root Beer, began selling burgers and soft drinks.

A popular roadside advertising campaign for shaving cream found its start in the mid-1920s. Signs that were evenly spaced apart compelled motorists to read each successive message: "Your shaving brush . . . has had its day . . . so why not . . . shave the modern way." Advertising became big business in the 1920s, with companies spending $3.2 billion on ads in 1927.

A Consumer Economy

After a period of uncertainty following World War I, the United States economy made a rapid adjustment. By 1920, incomes had resumed the upward trend begun during the war. Between 1914 and 1926, average wages rose more than 28 percent. The number of millionaires in the United States more than doubled in the same period.

Much of this growth resulted from a new focus on the consumer. In fact, the 1920s saw the development of a **consumer economy,** one that depends on a large amount of spending by consumers—individuals who use, or consume, products. Increased spending leads to larger profits for businesses, which in turn pushes up wages and encourages even more spending.

Traditionally, Americans valued thrift. They bought mainly what they needed, and much less of what they merely wanted, or what was nonessential. Several factors helped spark more buying in this decade, including higher wages, clever advertising, new products, lower costs, and the widespread availability of credit.

VIEWING HISTORY The nation's first modern shopping center, the Country Club Plaza, opened in Kansas City, Missouri, in 1922. **Making Comparisons** *How does it compare to the shopping malls of today?*

Chapter 21 • Section 2   723

CAPTION ANSWERS

Viewing History The first shopping mall was large, but not nearly as large as many malls are today.

RESOURCE DIRECTORY

Teaching Resources
Learning Styles Lesson Plans booklet, p. 45
Guided Reading and Review booklet, p. 87

Other Print Resources
Nystrom *Atlas of Our Country* *The Third Wave of Immigration,* pp. 30–32

Technology
Section Reading Support Transparencies
Guided Reading Audiotapes (English/Spanish), Ch. 21
Student Edition on Audio CD, Ch. 21
Prentice Hall Presentation Pro CD-ROM, Ch. 21
Companion Web site, www.phschool.com

Catalogs brimming with exciting new goods tempted consumers to buy on credit.

Spending on Goods and Services, 1928	
Item	**Percent of Budget Spent**
Food	27%
Clothing	13%
Shelter	12%
Fuel and light	4%
Furniture and furnishings	2%
Health and education	3%
Automobile	5%
Sundries:	
Tobacco, candy, soft drinks, gum	5%
Recreation (theater, ball games)	3%
Miscellaneous (trolley, stationery)	4%
Savings and insurance	12%
Taxes	10%
Total	**100%**

SOURCE: *Setting a Course: American Women in the 1920s*

INTERPRETING TABLES A study of family spending habits during the late 1920s reveals lifestyle choices as well as economic realities. **Drawing Conclusions** *What does the sundries category say about life in the 1920s?*

Buying on Credit Until the 1920s, middle-class Americans generally paid cash for everything. Borrowing money for any purchase but a house or land was considered unthrifty, even immoral. During the 1920s, new kinds of consumer goods, such as automobiles and refrigerators, became widely available. Americans wanted these modern conveniences, but they cost a great deal. Unless manufacturers sold more of these goods, they would go out of business. To increase their profits, manufacturers developed and financed buying on the **installment plan.** On an installment plan, the customer makes partial payments (installments) at set intervals over a period of time until the total debt is paid. Installment plans fueled the growth of consumer spending.

Clever advertising made this form of buying acceptable to the American people. People who otherwise would not spend beyond their means were encouraged to buy all kinds of items, even though interest charges ranged from 11 to 40 percent. By 1929, Americans were using the installment plan to buy 60 percent of all cars sold; 70 percent of all furniture; 80 percent of all vacuum cleaners, radios, and refrigerators; and 90 percent of all washing machines.

Electric Power Refrigerators, washing machines, and other power-hungry appliances created a surge in the demand for electricity. Between 1913 and 1927, the number of electric power customers more than quadrupled. The number of people who had electric lights jumped from 16 percent to 63 percent in about the same time. Part of this increase came from the expanding housing industry. New homes, wired for electricity, could now be filled with electric appliances.

Although cities gained electric power rapidly, the countryside did not. By 1925, for example, power plants supplied only 4 percent of American farms with electricity. Running power lines to scattered farming communities simply cost too much. Instead, some farmers created their own source of electricity by building wind-powered generators.

The growth of General Electric Company illustrates how the increasing use of electricity went hand in hand with the jump in consumer sales. General Electric was formed in 1892 to take over Thomas Edison's electric light business. During the 1920s, the company grew dramatically by selling a variety of household electric appliances. It also sold electric motors and other products for industry. Between 1919 and 1929, the value of electrical products of this kind more than doubled, from nearly $1 billion to $2.3 billion. General Electric rode this wave of consumer buying to become one of the world's largest companies.

Advertising General Electric's product line included electric toasters, ovens, sewing machines, coffee pots, irons, and vacuum cleaners. Other companies offered similar appliances, as well as a vast array of other goods, from telephones to cosmetics. To rise above the competition, manufacturers needed an edge: mass-media advertising.

By the 1920s, marketers had developed a new approach to advertising. In the past, advertisements had provided fairly basic information about a product. A magazine ad for clothing, for example, might have noted its quality of fabric, smart design, and affordable price. Advertising in the 1920s, especially in mass magazines, spoke less about the product and more about how the product could enhance the consumer's image. "A woman is only as old as her complexion," stated one cosmetics ad from 1923. For postal service, consumers were advised, "Air mail is socially correct." Ads like these appealed to such emotions as insecurity and fear. Other ads used celebrities to associate an image with their products. This kind of ad might show a movie star using a product and claiming to adore it. The ad implied that anyone who used the product could be as stylish as a movie star.

The new advertising had its critics. Some saw it as a waste of time and money. Others condemned its use of psychology to persuade people to buy products. Advertising also had its defenders. One professional "ad man" claimed that advertising for modern products served a vital educational purpose:

> 66 The vacuum cleaner was introduced by educational advertising. The advertising was done partly by manufacturers anxious to sell vacuum cleaners, and partly by electric-light companies anxious to sell current. . . . But the result has been a public benefit, an increasing willingness to spend money to lighten the human burden, to cut down the waste of human energy spent in the operation of living. 99
> —Earnest Elmo Calkins, *Business the Civilizer*, 1928

Rise in Productivity Electric power, persuasive advertising, and the installment plan all helped consumers go on a buying spree in the 1920s. Without an increased volume of goods to buy, however, the consumer economy could not have developed as rapidly as it did. In order to meet consumer demand, productivity needed to increase. Productivity is a worker's level of output, whether in goods or in services, over a given period. One measure of productivity is the **Gross National Product (GNP),** which is the total value of goods and services a country produces annually. From 1921 to 1929, the GNP grew at an average rate of 6 percent per year. The preceding decade had seen a growth rate of less than 1 percent.

Productivity rose in part because the nation developed new resources, new management methods, and new technologies. Major oil fields had been discovered in Texas, Oklahoma, and California around the turn of the century. These discoveries provided the resources to power industrial growth. You have read about Frederick Winslow Taylor's time-and-motion studies in the late 1800s, designed to increase worker efficiency. By the 1920s, industrial managers as well as labor leaders had come to accept Taylor's management principles. Application of those principles helped workers produce more goods. The increasing use of new machines and other kinds of technology also significantly increased workers' output. In addition, technology proved useful in solving production problems, such as how to make more automobiles in less time.

Ford and the Automobile

The first automobile appeared in Germany in the 1880s. In 1892, Charles and Frank Duryea of Springfield, Massachusetts, developed a marketable car, and several other American inventors soon followed their lead. Over the next 28 years, about 8 million cars rolled out of factories and onto America's roads. Yet in the ten years after that period, during the 1920s, the number of registered cars rose by more than 15 million. Much of this rapid growth in production resulted from the efforts of the inventive businessman Henry Ford.

Twice the cleaning...
twice the leisure!

Premier Duplex

Electrical appliances such as the vacuum cleaner changed the nature of housework.

READING CHECK
What factors allowed for a rise in productivity in the 1920s?

BACKGROUND
The Model T

There is some debate about whether Henry Ford was oblivious to consumer tastes regarding color. Ford biographer Robert Lacey says in *Ford: The Men and the Machine* that the only reason Ford's Model T was offered to customers in "any color so long as it's black" was because an engineer in the Ford plant discovered that black dried faster than any other color. Tin Lizzies originally came in green with a red stripe.

Ford and the "Model T"   In the late 1880s, Ford worked as an engineer with a lighting company. In his spare time he began inventing a "horseless carriage." In 1896, Ford perfected his first version of a lightweight, gas-powered car he called the "quadricycle." By 1903, he had started his own automobile company. Five years later, Ford sold 30,000 of an improved vehicle that he called the Model T.

Ford's Assembly Line   Ford wanted to "democratize the automobile," producing even more cars and selling them at prices ordinary people could afford. This goal set him apart from all other car makers and made him one of the most influential people of the century.

To achieve his goal, he adapted the **assembly line** for his factories. An assembly line is a manufacturing process in which each worker does one specialized task in the construction of the final product. In the past, an individual worker might build an entire product from start to finish. Since that type of manufacturing process required each worker to master hundreds of tasks, it was too inefficient for the mass production of something as complex as an automobile. On an assembly line, one worker might install windshields on all the cars. Another might mount the tires or weld a certain part in place or apply the paint.

Ford did not invent the assembly line, but he made it more efficient. His specially designed assembly line moved while each worker stayed in place, instead of moving from vehicle to vehicle. Critics of Ford's system claimed that the assembly line, with its endless repetition of tasks, strained workers both physically and mentally. Ford admitted that he would be bored working on an assembly line but insisted that his employees enjoyed it. At Ford's Highland Park, Michigan, factory, the assembly line turned out a Model T every 24 seconds. Between 1908 and 1927, Ford built half of the automobiles produced in the entire world, more than 15 million cars.

By making large numbers of identical automobiles in an identical way, Ford could take advantage of economies of scale, a concept you have read about in an earlier chapter. The more automobiles he made, the less each one cost. In 1914,

---

INTERPRETING DIAGRAMS
The layout of the main buildings at Ford's River Rouge facility was designed to maximize efficiency. Locate the power house in the late 1920s photo by its eight smoke stacks. **Analyzing Information** *Trace the work process from delivery of raw materials to finished automobile. What steps must be taken along the way?*

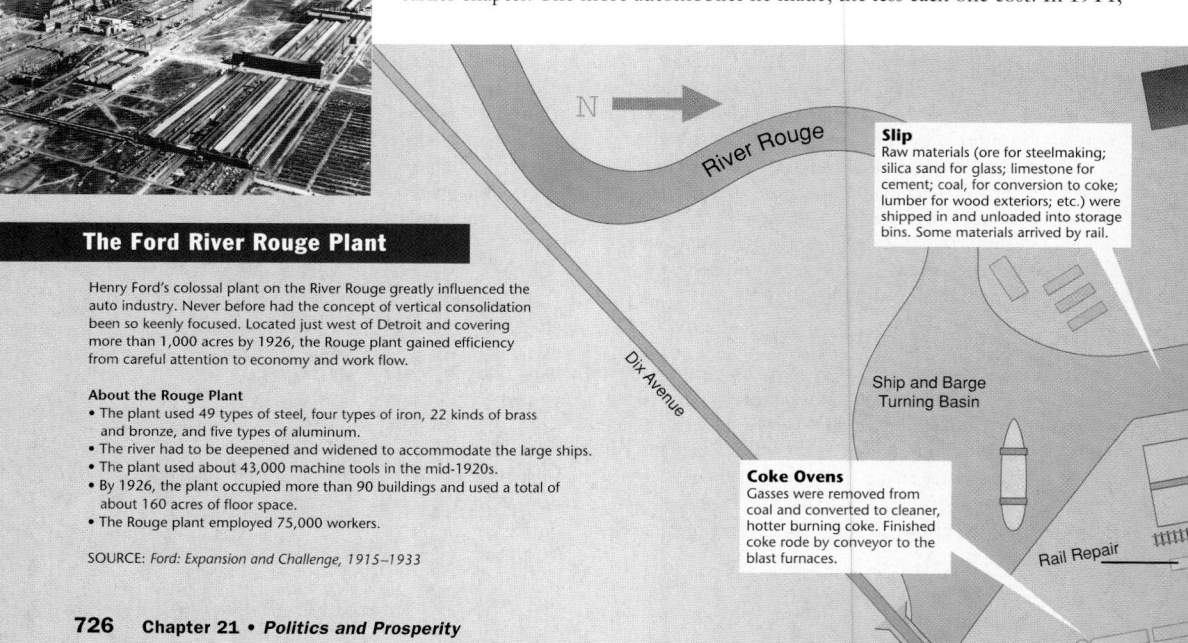

The Ford River Rouge Plant

Henry Ford's colossal plant on the River Rouge greatly influenced the auto industry. Never before had the concept of vertical consolidation been so keenly focused. Located just west of Detroit and covering more than 1,000 acres by 1926, the Rouge plant gained efficiency from careful attention to economy and work flow.

About the Rouge Plant
• The plant used 49 types of steel, four types of iron, 22 kinds of brass and bronze, and five types of aluminum.
• The river had to be deepened and widened to accommodate the large ships.
• The plant used about 43,000 machine tools in the mid-1920s.
• By 1926, the plant occupied more than 90 buildings and used a total of about 160 acres of floor space.
• The Rouge plant employed 75,000 workers.

SOURCE: *Ford: Expansion and Challenge, 1915–1933*

N

River Rouge

Dix Avenue

Slip
Raw materials (ore for steelmaking; silica sand for glass; limestone for cement; coal, for conversion to coke; lumber for wood exteriors; etc.) were shipped in and unloaded into storage bins. Some materials arrived by rail.

Ship and Barge Turning Basin

Coke Ovens
Gasses were removed from coal and converted to cleaner, hotter burning coke. Finished coke rode by conveyor to the blast furnaces.

Rail Repair

CAPTION ANSWERS

Interpreting Diagrams Work flow: Raw materials are delivered over water into the slip (or by rail) and are deposited into bins. The "High Line" transports materials from bins for processing: ore goes to blast furnaces, then (as metals) to foundry. Open hearth rolling mill makes steel. Engines, steel, windshields, etc. proceed to "B Building" for assembly. Coke ovens provide fuel for the plant. The power house produces electricity.

RESOURCE DIRECTORY
Technology
Color Transparencies   *The Way It Works,* H17

the first year Ford's assembly line was in full swing, his company sold Model T's at $490 each. This price was almost half of what a car had cost in 1910. The following year he dropped the price to $390.

The Model T was a utilitarian, or practical, vehicle. It was available in a limited range of styles, but built with essentially the same engine and other basic parts. While early Model T's came in a variety of colors, Ford eventually switched to cheaper and more durable black paint. Ford's competitors, however, realized that the American public wanted different colors and styles of cars. When General Motors introduced its low-priced Chevrolet in several colors, Ford lost many customers. Not until 1925 did he introduce a choice of colors for his "improved" Model T. The last Model T was produced in 1927, making way for the Model A.

Ford's success came partly from vertical consolidation, which, as you have read, means controlling the businesses that make up phases of a product's development. From Ford's huge new plant built on the River Rouge, he was able to take a load of raw ore on any morning and roll it off the line as a car the next day. Much of the ore came from Ford's own iron mines and was forged in his own blast furnaces and steel mills, which were fired by coal from his 16 coal mines. Wood used in the car came from his 700,000 acres of forests, and glass for windshields from his own glassworks. He hauled materials over his own railroad and on his own fleet of ships. Company workshops made nearly all the tools used in his factories. Furthermore, he built this entire empire with profits from the Model T.

A Complex Businessman   Like the empire he ran, Henry Ford was complex. He had both admirable qualities and personal failings. For example, he won praise in 1914 for introducing a $5-a-day pay rate for many of his workers. At the time, other factories paid only about half that amount. Yet he was not always so generous. He ran his company harshly and used violence to fight unions. During World War I, Ford devised an Americanization program for his

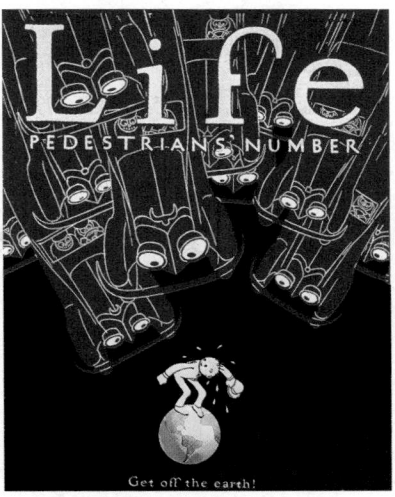

ANALYZING VISUAL INFORMATION Automobiles are the subject of this 1925 *Life* magazine cover. **Making Comparisons** *What do the illustration and its caption, "Get off our earth," say about the impact of the automobile on society in the 1920s?*

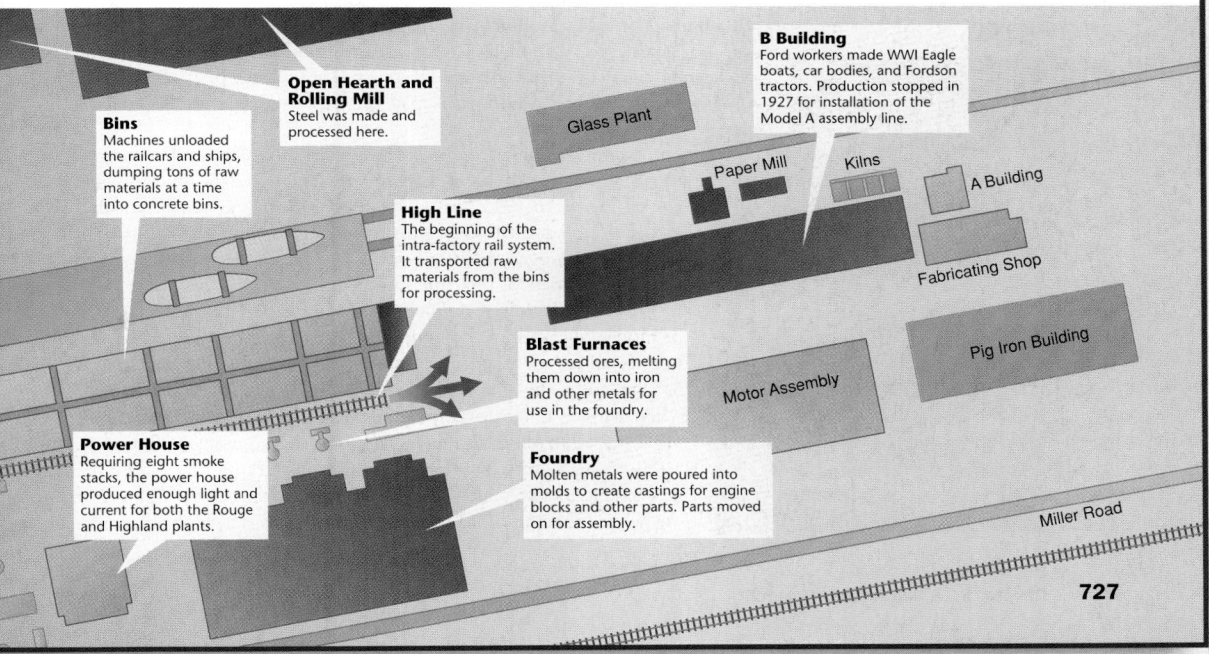

Bins
Machines unloaded the railcars and ships, dumping tons of raw materials at a time into concrete bins.

Open Hearth and Rolling Mill
Steel was made and processed here.

B Building
Ford workers made WWI Eagle boats, car bodies, and Fordson tractors. Production stopped in 1927 for installation of the Model A assembly line.

Glass Plant

Paper Mill   Kilns

A Building

High Line
The beginning of the intra-factory rail system. It transported raw materials from the bins for processing.

Fabricating Shop

Blast Furnaces
Processed ores, melting them down into iron and other metals for use in the foundry.

Motor Assembly

Pig Iron Building

Power House
Requiring eight smoke stacks, the power house produced enough light and current for both the Rouge and Highland plants.

Foundry
Molten metals were poured into molds to create castings for engine blocks and other parts. Parts moved on for assembly.

Miller Road

727

☑ **TEST PREPARATION**

Have students read the paragraph that begins "Ford's success came partly from vertical consolidation . . .", then answer the question below.

How did Ford acquire the raw materials (such as coal) needed to operate the River Rouge plant?

A   The Standard Oil Trust provided all of Ford's raw materials at a special discount.

B   Ford worked with independent contractors.

C   Rival automobile manufacturers sold raw materials to Ford.

Ⓓ   Ford owned coal mines, forests, iron mines, and rail and shipping resources.

CAPTION ANSWERS

Analyzing Visual Information The man standing on the globe is threatened by the cars surrounding him. It seems to say that there are so many cars that they are taking over the planet.

Connecting with Economics

Have students research the growth in auto ownership during the 1920s. If they can, have them find out what percentage of these cars were manufactured by the Ford Motor Company. Have them use transfer information from one medium to another to present the first set of findings as a graph, and the second set of findings as a pie chart. **(Logical/Mathematical)**

BACKGROUND

Interdisciplinary

Though some people heralded the rise in productivity brought about by mass production, others found the development profoundly dehumanizing. One artist who applied his satirical genius to this situation was the actor and filmmaker Charlie Chaplin. The 1936 film *Modern Times* portrayed Chaplin's popular Little Tramp character as a victim of modern factory efficiency.

The most hilarious scenes in the film depict the Tramp as a hapless assembly-line worker who suffers the indignity of being fed by a remorseless "lunch-machine" and is whirled away on the cogs of a monstrous piece of equipment.

BIOGRAPHY

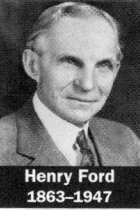

Henry Ford 1863–1947

Henry Ford was born on a Michigan farm during the Civil War, the son of Irish immigrants. Although Ford is best known as an industrialist, not all his energies were devoted to the Ford Motor Company. His pursuits were diverse, at the very least.

In 1915, he sailed a rented ocean liner across the Atlantic in a hopeless effort to talk Europe out of fighting World War I. He purchased the *Dearborn Independent* in 1918, but then used his newspaper to run a series of articles that blamed Jews for the world's problems. In 1927, however, after being sued for slander, he apologized for these attacks and sold the paper.

As a nod to his early years on the farm, he recreated a rural American town, Greenfield Village, as well as a museum of American artifacts that can still be visited today.

Electric power fueled homes, businesses, and a consumer economy. Workers stand on an electric power generator in 1924.

foreign-born workers. In return for higher pay, workers had to enroll in English and civics classes and let investigators inspect their homes. The company held elaborate graduation ceremonies in which workers shed their previous ethnic identities and became "Americans." When postwar inflation made the pay incentive less attractive, the program declined. Although he showed genius in giving millions of Americans a car they could afford, he stubbornly refused to keep up with their changing tastes. By 1936, the Ford Motor Company had slipped to third place in the automobile industry.

Industrial Growth

Through Ford's genius, automobile making became the nation's biggest single manufacturing industry in the 1920s. By the late twenties, automakers used 15 percent of America's steel, 80 percent of its rubber, half of its glass, 65 percent of its leather upholstery, and 7 billion gallons of its gasoline every year. Naturally, the industries that provided those materials, such as steelmaking and oil refining, also grew.

Thousands of new businesses arose to serve automobile travel, including garages, car dealerships, motels ("motor hotels"), campgrounds, gas stations, and restaurants. Thanks to the automobile, suburbs expanded, in turn boosting the housing industry. Truck lines began hauling the nation's freight, and motorized buses traveled new routes through both city and countryside. By 1929, about 3.7 million people owed their jobs directly or indirectly to the automobile industry. In that year, the nation spent nearly $2 billion to build and maintain its roads and bridges.

Businesses unrelated to the automobile industry also boomed. As you have read, movie making, radio broadcasting, and publishing all flourished. One industry that greatly expanded during the late 1920s was aviation. This industry had begun to develop during the war, with the production of military aircraft. The first domestic airlines, however, had limited success. They flew small planes, mainly over local routes, and many of them stayed in business only a short time. The public's fascination with Charles Lindbergh and Amelia Earhart helped boost the industry's fortunes. Aircraft companies began designing larger, faster planes. By late in the decade, air transport of mail and other goods, as well as passengers, had improved.

Under Republican laissez-faire policies, which limited government regulation of business, the value of the nation's businesses soared. Between 1919 and 1929, the 200 top American companies nearly doubled their total worth, which rose from $43 billion to $81 billion. Government and industry seemed eager to prove that the chief business of the American people truly was business.

Even with limited regulation and a business boom, the power of monopolies declined. Rapid business expansion opened up new opportunities for smaller companies. These competitors rushed in to challenge the giant steel and oil monopolies. For example, when banker J. P. Morgan created the U.S. Steel Corporation in 1901, it controlled about 60 percent of the steel business. By 1930, it had grown enormously. Yet its competitors also had grown, and in that year, U.S. Steel controlled only about 39 percent of the steel business. Likewise, the companies that had once made

728 Chapter 21 • *Politics and Prosperity*

RESOURCE DIRECTORY

Teaching Resources
Units 7/8 booklet
  • Section 2 Quiz, p. 15
Guide to the Essentials
  • Section 2 Summary, p. 109
Biography, Literature, and Comparing Primary Sources booklet (Comparing Primary Sources)
On the McNary-Haugen Bill (1927), pp. 137–138

up the Standard Oil Trust grew with the demand for oil products during the 1920s. Even so, by 1930 they controlled only about half of the nation's oil business.

Bypassed by the Boom

While most Americans enjoyed a better standard of living, others struggled to survive. Unskilled laborers, including many African American migrants, remained poor. Their wages and working conditions did not improve, nor did those for workers in several major industries, including agriculture.

For some sectors of the farm economy, the 1920s brought not prosperity but devastation. Farm prices had stayed high during the war and just afterward, as American farmers supplied food to the United States and to war-torn Europe. After the war, however, the recovering European farm industry and cheaper food imports helped to push American products out of the European market. The huge wartime demand shrank, and American farm prices, especially for wheat and hogs, plummeted.

During more prosperous times, many farmers had borrowed money to buy new tractors and other machinery. Their new equipment allowed them to expand their operations, so they bought more land as well. In the late 1920s, when most Americans spent freely on consumer goods, these farmers could not even pay back their loans. Many of them abandoned agriculture. Others hung on to the only way of life they had ever known, going even further into debt every day.

The same dwindling demand for goods hurt producers of cotton textiles and bituminous (soft) coal. These industries had expanded to meet wartime needs, but after the war they failed to uncover new markets for their products. The resulting low profits kept wage rates down. Railroads suffered, too, not just from shrinking demand but also from mismanagement, competition from trucking firms, and labor unions that fought against wage cuts and layoffs.

Purchasing expensive tractors and other equipment helped put many farmers into debt in the 1920s.

Reading Comprehension

1. Increased wages and incomes; technologically advanced new consumer products; lower costs; clever advertising; widespread availability of credit.

2. A payment plan in which the customer makes partial payments at set intervals over a period of time until the total debt is paid.

3. It grew markedly, at an average rate of 6 percent per year.

4. His assembly line moved, while the workers stayed in place.

Critical Thinking and Writing

5. Automobile workers benefited from new businesses that fostered auto travel. However, the postwar recovery of European agriculture and cheaper food imports helped to reduce European demand for American farm products. Prices plummeted as the wartime demand shrank.

6. Higher wages; higher incomes; clever advertising; new products; lower costs; availability of credit.

Take It to the NET

Answers will vary. Examples may include inventions or scientific developments such as the television, the discovery of penicillin, and the liquid-fueled rocket.

Section 2 Assessment

READING COMPREHENSION

1. What conditions made a **consumer economy** possible in the 1920s?

2. What is an **installment plan?**

3. How did the **Gross National Product** change during the 1920s?

4. How did Henry Ford change his **assembly line** to increase efficiency?

CRITICAL THINKING AND WRITING

5. **Making Comparisons** How did postwar economic conditions favor automobile workers and yet undermine the farming industry?

6. **Writing a List** List all the factors that led to increased consumer spending in the 1920s.

 Take It to the NET

Activity: Writing a Summary
Research several inventions from the 1920s and write a summary of how they affected consumer goods or business in general. Use the links provided in the *America: Pathways to the Present* area of the following Web site for help in completing this activity.
www.phschool.com

Chapter 21 • Section 2   729

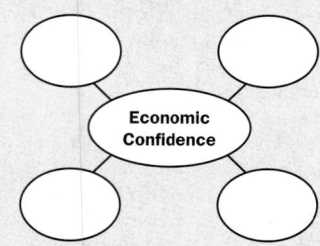

Section 3

The Economy in
the Late 1920s

SECTION OBJECTIVES

1. See why the economy in the late 1920s appeared healthy to most Americans.

2. Observe the danger signs that were present in the economy of the late 1920s.

BELLRINGER

Warm-Up Activity Discuss with students the many elements that combine to influence the economy for a country as diverse and globally interconnected as the United States. Talk about ways in which an economic situation in this country could have worldwide implications.

Activating Prior Knowledge Ask students to talk about what they know about the current state of the United States economy. Can they state some descriptive terms that they may have heard or read about in the news? How does today's economy compare with the economy of the late 1920s?

READING STRATEGY

Have students write down three questions they might ask to help them better understand the economy of the 1920s. As they do so, have them analyze the causes of economic growth and prosperity in the 1920s.

READING FOCUS

- Why did the economy of the late 1920s appear healthy to most Americans?
- What danger signs were present in the economy of late 1920s?

MAIN IDEA

During the 1920s, rising wealth and a booming stock market gave Americans a false sense of faith in the economy. In fact, there were signs that the economy was in trouble.

KEY TERMS

welfare capitalism
speculation
buying on margin

TAKING NOTES

Copy the web diagram below. As you read, add reasons showing that Americans in the 1920s had confidence in the nation's economy.

Economic Confidence

Many Americans expected Herbert Hoover to oversee continued prosperity.

Setting the Scene   The mood of most Americans in the late 1920s was optimistic, and with good reason. Medical advances had greatly reduced deaths from whooping cough, diphtheria, and other serious diseases. Since 1900 the number of infant deaths had declined, and life expectancy had increased by more than 10 years, to an average of 59 years for men and 63 years for women.

The brightest hopes seemed to come from the economy. During a campaign speech in 1928, Herbert Hoover reflected on Republican economic policies. Hoover sought to keep the government out of business in order to preserve "the American system of rugged individualism," and to continue prosperity:

❝ [T]he greatness of America has grown out of a political and social system and a method of control of economic forces distinctly its own—our American system—which has carried this great experiment in human welfare further than ever before in all history. We are nearer today to the ideal of the abolition of poverty and fear from the lives of men and women than ever before in any land. ❞

—Herbert Hoover, New York City, October 1928

Economy Appears Healthy

As you have read, Hoover easily won the 1928 election, benefiting from years of prosperity under previous Republican presidents. Americans widely admired this self-made millionaire for the way he had organized food relief in Europe during and after World War I. He had also worked effectively as Secretary of Commerce under Presidents Harding and Coolidge. People expected that the good times would get even better under Hoover.

"Wonderful Prosperity"   As Hoover took office, the American economy seemed to be in fine shape. In 1925, the market value of all stocks was $27 billion. Over the next few years, stocks soared. In 1928 alone, stock values rose by more than $11 billion. Because the stock market was widely regarded as the nation's economic weathervane, the *New York Times* could describe the

730   Chapter 21 • *Politics and Prosperity*

RESOURCE DIRECTORY

Teaching Resources
Guided Reading and Review booklet, p. 88

Technology
Section Reading Support Transparencies
Guided Reading Audiotapes (English/Spanish), Ch. 21
Student Edition on Audio CD, Ch. 21
Prentice Hall Presentation Pro CD-ROM, Ch. 21
Companion Web site, www.phschool.com

year as one "of unprecedented advance, of wonderful prosperity." By early October 1929, stock values hit $87 billion.

Many working people had prospered in the post-World War I period. Since 1914, the value of workers' wages had risen more than 40 percent. Although certain industries were troubled and some workers lost jobs in the shift to new technologies, unemployment averaged below 4 percent. Even such critics of capitalism as journalist Lincoln Steffens made optimistic predictions: "Big business in America," Steffens said in 1928, "is producing what the Socialists held up as their goal: food, shelter and clothing for all. You will see it during the Hoover administration."

"Everybody Ought to Be Rich"   People had unusually high confidence in the business world during the 1920s. For some, business success became almost a religion. One of the decade's best-selling books was *The Man Nobody Knows* (1925). Written by Bruce Barton, an advertising executive, it told the biblical story of Jesus' life in business terms. Barton portrayed Jesus as a managerial genius who "picked up twelve men [a reference to Jesus' 12 apostles, or followers] from the bottom ranks of business and forged them into an organization that conquered the world."

Similarly, Americans trusted the advice of corporate leaders such as John J. Raskob. In a 1929 article titled "Everybody Ought to Be Rich," Raskob stated that savings of only $15 a week over 20 years could bring a $400-a-month income from investments. "I am firm in my belief," Raskob said, "that anyone not only can be rich, but ought to be rich." Statements such as this encouraged Americans to make investments that in an earlier era would have seemed far too risky.

Welfare Capitalism   Following the violent labor strikes of 1919, the postwar economy stabilized. Many larger companies launched strategies to meet some of their workers' demands. By doing so, they believed they could avoid union intervention, prevent strikes, and keep productivity high. This new approach to labor relations became known as **welfare capitalism.** Employers raised wages and provided such benefits as paid vacations, health plans, recreation programs, and English classes for recent immigrants, all in the interest of strengthening company loyalty and morale. Employers also set up "company unions," which they controlled, as channels for workers to express their concerns. As a result of welfare capitalism, organized labor lost members during the 1920s.

Economic Danger Signs

A climbing stock market, consumer confidence, and labor stability all pointed the way to a bright future. Yet despite the apparent prosperity, all was not well. Only later did many people recognize the warning signs of an unsound economy.

Uneven Prosperity   Despite the stock market success stories, it was mainly the rich who got richer. Huge corporations rather than small businesses

Market Speculation

Stock market speculation was almost a sport in the 1920s: The cartoon at left shows stockbrokers fishing for new clients from the top of the New York Stock Exchange. Though market investment is now more regulated than it was in the 1920s, Americans continue to speculate on stocks, both by buying on margin and by practicing other forms of high-risk trading.

One trading method involves what are known as call options. An investor may buy the right to purchase a certain stock before an expiration date, but at a price set near its current value (the "strike price"). Profit is made this way: If the stock goes up in price, the investor then "calls" in that option. In other words, he or she exercises the right to buy the stock at the lower rate set earlier. The investor then turns around and sells the same stock at its currently higher market price, or the option itself may be sold.

Some brokers have used the Internet to lure option speculators into making unwise investments. While the stock market has more government oversight than it did in the 1920s, buyers must still make their decisions carefully.

 How could investors lose money by buying call options? Explain.

Connecting with Economics

An "installment" purchase is one in which a consumer buys an expensive item, such as a car or furniture, by making many small payments over a long time. In the years between 1920 and 1929, the number of installment purchases quintupled, reaching $6 billion per year. Have students research the growth of installment purchases during this decade and create a graph or table that demonstrates this growth. **(Logical/Mathematical)**

BACKGROUND

Geography in History

Hoover Dam, on the Nevada-Arizona border, controls the flow of the Colorado River. It has had more than one name. The project was begun while Herbert Hoover was Secretary of Commerce in the Harding administration, and he is generally credited with helping solve a series of problems that made the dam possible. When the dam was dedicated in 1936, it was named after him.

However, after Hoover left office, the dam became known as the Boulder Canyon Dam or the Boulder Dam. This change may have occurred because the new administration of Franklin D. Roosevelt did not want to promote such an impressive reminder of its immediate predecessor. Nonetheless, in 1947, the name Hoover Dam was officially restored to the project, and it retains that name to this day.

READING CHECK

Wealth was very unevenly distributed. Many families were on the brink of poverty. Large corporations dominated the industrial scene. Individual wealth was concentrated amongst a very small segment of the population.

CAPTION ANSWERS

Interpreting Diagrams Sixty-five percent of families earned below $2,000 a year.

READING CHECK

Describe the distribution of wealth in the United States in the 1920s. How were families affected?

dominated industry. In 1929, some 200 large companies controlled 49 percent of American industry.

Similarly, a small proportion of families held most of the nation's personal wealth. In 1929, the richest Americans—24,000 families, or just 0.1 percent of the population—had incomes of more than $100,000. They also held 34 percent of the country's total savings.

By contrast, 71 percent of individuals and families earned less than $2,500 a year, an amount some budget experts at the time considered the minimum standard of living. Nearly 80 percent of all families had no savings. Many people earned so little that almost every family member, children included, had to work just to get by.

Government tax policy contributed to this imbalance. Andrew Mellon, Secretary of the Treasury and one of the richest people in the nation, successfully pushed Congress to reduce taxes. Mellon's tax plan, however, gave the largest tax cuts to the wealthiest Americans. He believed that continued high taxation of the wealthy, imposed during the war, would hinder business expansion.

Personal Debt   Many Americans became accustomed to credit spending during the 1920s. However, the resulting increase in personal debt signaled trouble. As you have read, assembly-line production made consumer items more affordable and available. People bought radios, vacuum cleaners, refrigerators, and other exciting new products, whether or not they had the money to pay for them. They believed that they could count on future income to cover their debts. Traditionally, Americans had feared debt and postponed buying goods until they had the cash to pay for them. Now, however, talk of unending prosperity eased worries about going into debt. Installment plans, boasting of "easy terms," made even luxury items seem affordable.

Playing the Stock Market   Fed by the optimism of the age, a "get-rich-quick" attitude prevailed during the 1920s. The dizzying climb of stock prices encouraged widespread **speculation,** the practice of making high-risk investments in hopes of getting a huge return.

Before World War I, only the wealthy played the stock market. Now the press reported stories of how ordinary people were making fortunes. Many small investors entered the market, often spending their life savings. To attract these less wealthy investors, stockbrokers encouraged a practice called **buying on margin.** This option allowed investors to purchase a stock for only a fraction of its price (10 to 50 percent) and borrow the rest. The brokers charged high interest rates and could demand payment of the loan at any time. If the stock price went up, however, borrowers could sell the stock at a price high enough to pay off both the loan and the interest charges and still make money.

Too Many Goods, Too Little Demand   Rising productivity had brought prosperity, but eventually it created a problem. By the late 1920s, the country's warehouses were overstocked; they held more goods than consumers would

Personal Debt and Income Distribution in the 1920s

Personal Debt
Net private noncorporate debt (in billions of dollars)

Income Distribution, 1929

- ■ $10,000 and over
- ■ $5,000–$9,999
- $2,000–$4,999
- $1,999 and under

SOURCE: *Historical Statistics of the United States, Colonial Times to 1970*

INTERPRETING DIAGRAMS
The circle graph (right) shows how unevenly the country's wealth was distributed in the 1920s. The line graph (left) shows the rise in personal debt. **Analyzing Information** *What percentage of American families earned less than $2,000 a year in 1929?*

RESOURCE DIRECTORY

Teaching Resources
Units 7/8 booklet
- Section 3 Quiz, p. 16
- Chapter 21 Test, pp. 17, 20

Guide to the Essentials
- Section 3 Summary, p. 110
- Chapter 21 Test, p. 111

Other Print Resources
Chapter Tests with ExamView® Test Bank CD-ROM, Ch. 21

Technology
ExamView® Test Bank CD-ROM, Ch. 21
Social Studies Skills Tutor CD-ROM

buy. Wages had risen, but people still could not afford to buy goods as fast as the assembly lines turned them out.

Although the stock market kept rising, overproduction caused some industries to slow in the late 1920s. The automobile industry, which had helped create American prosperity, slumped after 1925. Industries that depended on it, including steel, rubber, and glass, also declined. Housing construction, which also caused a "ripple effect" on the economy, fell by 25 percent between 1928 and 1929.

Trouble for Farmers and Workers   As you have read, falling farm prices left many farmers unable to repay their debts for land and machinery. These farmers often lost their farms. Some rural banks gave farmers extra time to meet their obligations, but those banks struggled when loans were not repaid. About 6,000 rural banks failed during the 1920s.

Congress responded to the farm problem with the McNary-Haugen farm relief bill. This measure was designed to increase the prices farmers received for their crops. Congress passed the bill twice, in 1927 and 1928, but each time President Coolidge vetoed it, believing that it was not the government's job to provide such assistance. Farmers continued to suffer.

Life remained exceedingly hard for many factory workers as well. While companies grew wealthy, most laborers still worked long hours for low wages. Conditions were especially bad in distressed industries, such as coal mining and textiles. In the rayon mills of Elizabethton, Tennessee, for instance, women worked 56-hour weeks, earning 16 to 18 cents an hour—about $10 a week.

To some observers, these factors—uneven wealth, rising debt, stock speculation, overproduction, and the hardships of farmers and workers—clearly signaled trouble in the economy. In 1928, Belle Moskowitz, who had managed Al Smith's losing presidential campaign that year, predicted that "growing unemployment, business depression, or some false step" would soon trigger a reaction against Republican policies.

VIEWING HISTORY Auctioneers grew increasingly busy through the late 1920s, as distressed farmers defaulted on loans for expensive equipment and other items. **Identifying Alternatives** *What economic choices did farmers face after they repaid their loans?*

Section 3 Assessment

READING COMPREHENSION

1. What reasons did corporations have for practicing **welfare capitalism** in the 1920s?

2. Why was **speculation** in the stock market so popular in the 1920s?

3. How does a stockbroker profit from an investor **buying on margin?**

CRITICAL THINKING AND WRITING

4. **Recognizing Cause and Effect** How does a widespread increase in personal debt affect a nation's economy?

5. **Writing to Persuade** Write an essay from the perspective of someone living in the 1920s and feeling optimistic about his or her finances. Persuade your readers that the economy is sound, despite all the existing danger signs.

 Take It to the NET

Activity: Creating a Diagram
Research more on how the economy of the 1920s functioned. Create a chart or diagram showing what factors affected the economy and how the economy affected people's lives. Use the links provided in the *America: Pathways to the Present* area of the following Web site for help in completing this activity.
www.phschool.com

Section 3   Assessment

Reading Comprehension

1. They hoped to meet workers' demands while avoiding union intervention, preventing strikes, and keeping productivity high.

2. The optimism of the age, the prevalence of a "get-rich-quick" mentality, and the rise in stock values.

3. The brokers charge high interest rates and could demand payment of the loan at any time.

Critical Thinking and Writing

4. If future earning potential is curtailed by an economic downturn, people become unable to pay back their loans. This, in turn, devastates the finances of lenders.

5. Essays will vary, but should persuade the reader and be supported with facts from the section.

 **Take It to the NET**

Sample answer: Mass production made goods easier to manufacture in large quantities; more production often led to higher wages and lower unemployment; higher wages led to more consumer spending; and the presence of mass-marketed goods made consumer spending easy to accomplish.

CAPTION ANSWERS

Viewing History They could continue to farm, and probably incur more debt doing so. They could try to work in another industry, but that might involve moving to a city. Such a change would be difficult for those who had never done any other work besides farming.

REVIEWING KEY TERMS

Students should refer to the definitions of key terms in the chapter to write sentences that show an understanding of the era of politics and prosperity.

REVIEWING MAIN IDEAS

11. Labor strikes and terrorist acts. The government responded with the Palmer raids.

12. Though Schenck contended that he was only exercising free speech, the Supreme Court declared that Schenck's actions created a "clear and present danger" to the nation.

13. It raised import taxes, with special protection for new American industrial products, furthering a break from foreign countries. It also impeded European repayment of American war debt.

14. Harding appointed dishonest and incompetent friends and acquaintances to high office. This resulted in widespread corruption, such as the Teapot Dome Scandal. Coolidge was respected for his actions as governor of Massachusetts; he had no part in the Harding scandals; he was a skilled public speaker.

15. Advertising no longer sold only products; it also sought to make new consumer goods seem glamorous. Fewer hard facts about the products were presented. Instead, advertising focused on such things as how the product would make one more stylish.

16. An increase in productivity due to the development of new resources, new management methods, and new technologies.

17. Ford produced cars that working people could afford. Auto-making became the nation's biggest single manufacturing industry. Scores of related new businesses arose.

18. Republican laissez-faire policies caused rapid business expansion, opening up new opportunities for competitors to the giant monopolies. The automobile, steel, oil and electrical industries boomed as did the publishing, motion picture, and machine-making industries.

19. It furthered the imbalance, giving the largest tax cuts to the wealthiest Americans.

creating a CHAPTER SUMMARY

Copy this chart (right) on a piece of paper and complete it by showing how Republican leadership affected American life and the economy in the 1920s.

For additional review and enrichment activities, see the interactive version of *America: Pathways to the Present*, available on the Web and on CD-ROM.

Administrations	Policies, Legislation, and Major Events
Wilson	Labor strikes, Palmer raids
Harding	"Normalcy"
Coolidge	
Hoover	

★ Reviewing Key Terms

For each of the terms below, write a sentence explaining how it relates to the post–World War I period.

1. communism
2. disarmament
3. quota
4. Teapot Dome scandal
5. Kellogg-Briand Pact
6. installment plan
7. assembly line
8. welfare capitalism
9. speculation
10. buying on margin

★ Reviewing Main Ideas

11. What events of 1919 caused the Red Scare? How did the government respond? (Section 1)

12. Explain why the Supreme Court decision in *Schenck* v. *U.S.* seemed to justify jailing Communists. (Section 1)

13. Describe how the Fordney-McCumber Tariff of 1922 reflects a policy of isolationism. (Section 1)

14. What events brought disgrace upon the Harding presidency? How did Coolidge restore respect to the office? (Section 1)

15. How did the advertising industry help to develop a consumer economy? (Section 2)

16. What helped the growth of the Gross National Product (GNP) during the 1920s? (Section 2)

17. Describe Henry Ford's impact on American business and society. (Section 2)

18. How did a decade of Republican government affect the economy? (Section 3)

19. Evaluate the impact of the government's tax policy on income distribution in 1929. (Section 3)

20. What issues faced farm and factory workers in the late 1920s? (Section 3)

★ Critical Thinking

21. **Comparing Points of View** Evaluate welfare capitalism from the point of view of (a) a factory worker, (b) a labor union leader, and (c) a factory owner.

22. **Expressing Problems Clearly** Explain the American public's opposition to the wave of labor strikes that occurred from 1919 to 1920.

23. **Recognizing Bias** How did the bombing of A. Mitchell Palmer's home in 1919 affect Palmer's actions as Attorney General of the United States?

24. **Determining Relevance** How might changing social customs and attitudes have affected the spending habits of Americans during the 1920s?

25. **Recognizing Ideologies** Identify the domestic issues that led to passage of immigration legislation in the 1920s. Why were immigration quotas favored? What was the impact of the legislation?

CREATING A CHAPTER SUMMARY

Administrations	Policies, Legislation, and Major Events
Wilson	Labor strikes, Palmer raids
Harding	"Normalcy"
Coolidge	Laissez-faire business policy, Kellogg-Briand Pact
Hoover	Rising productivity, rising personal debt, stock market boom, stock market crash

★ Skills Assessment

Analyzing Political Cartoons ▶

26. This cartoon appeared in 1924. (a) Who was President in 1924? (b) What were the major news items regarding the presidential administration in 1924?

27. Describe the scene in the cartoon. What is it satirizing?

28. Why are Cabinet members advertised as being for sale?

Analyzing Primary Sources

Reread President Harding's quote from the first page of Section 1, and then answer the questions that follow.

29. Which statement best represents the meaning of the quotation?

   A Americans need to commit to radical reforms.

   B The nation's problems can be solved with international assistance.

   C The nation should look calmly inward and proceed with caution.

   D The nation's heroes will lead the country to triumph.

30. Harding's message was effective because

   F the heroic actions taken in World War I were no longer admired.

   G Americans were seeking the stability and normalcy Harding promised.

   H voters were looking for Harding to deliver dramatic solutions to their problems.

   J sustaining international ties was important to the American public.

31. **Applying the Chapter Skill: Analyzing Advertising** Turn to the vacuum cleaner ad in Section 2. What does the ad say about life in the 1920s? What does the ad promise that the vacuum cleaner will do for the consumer?

ACTIVITIES

Writing to LEARN

Writing an Opinion
Consider the beliefs and fears that helped fuel the Red Scare in the 1920s. What events led up to the Red Scare? How did fears of Communism develop, and were those fears justified? Explain your reasoning.

Primary Source CD-ROM

Working With Primary Sources Find additional information about the 1920s on the *Exploring Primary Sources in U.S. History CD-ROM* and use the selection(s) provided to complete the Chapter 21 primary source activity located in the *America: Pathways to the Present* area of the following Web site.
www.phschool.com

Take It to the NET

Chapter Self-Test As a review activity, take the Chapter 21 Self-Test in the *America: Pathways to the Present* area at the Web site listed below. The questions are designed to test your understanding of the chapter content.
www.phschool.com

---

20. Falling farm prices left farmers unable to repay their debts, facing the loss of their farms. Factory workers faced long hours for low wages and in poor conditions.

CRITICAL THINKING

21. (a) Support, due to increased wages and benefits. (b) Oppose, as it would mean a decrease in union membership. (c) Mixed, had to offer employees more money and benefits, but avoided strikes and could thereby maintain increased productivity.

22. They believed Communists and other radicals were behind the labor unrest. This activity was thought to be un-American.

23. It caused him to believe that radicals were conspiring to overthrow the government, leading him to create a campaign to identify and eliminate groups like Communists, Socialists, and anarchists.

24. New advertising techniques made it seem acceptable to purchase on credit. Advertising also sold "image" as well as products. Such changes in the 1920s encouraged people to purchase what they wanted, not just items they needed.

25. Americans associated immigrants with Communism and radical politics. Laborers feared immigrant competition for jobs. Nativism was on the rise in the U.S. Quotas were favored because they sharply restricted immigration from eastern and southern Europe as well as Japan.

SKILLS ASSESSMENT

26. (a) Calvin Coolidge. (b) Financial scandals, such as the Teapot Dome scandal, that had characterized the previous Harding administration.

27. The scene shows the Capitol, White House, Washington Monument, the armed forces, and members of Harding's administration for sale. It is satirizing the scandals in Harding's administration.

28. In the Teapot Dome affair, a Cabinet secretary (Albert Fall) gave away oil rights on government land in exchange for money.

29. C

30. G

31. The advertisement exemplifies the excitement over new consumer goods. It promises that cleaning can be done more thoroughly in much less time with the vacuum cleaner, thus increasing one's leisure time.

ANSWERS TO ACTIVITIES

Writing to LEARN

Sample response: The belief that communism would spread to America and the fear of violence. It was understandable to a certain extent since Lenin vowed to stir up revolutions in other countries, but the widespread paranoia that took place in America resulted in raids and arrests of innocent people.

Primary Source CD-ROM

Direct students to the additional primary sources that can be found on the *Exploring Primary Sources in U.S. History CD-ROM.*

 Take It to the NET

Additional support materials and activities for Chapter 21 of *America: Pathways to the Present* can be found in the Social Studies area at the Prentice Hall School Web site. **www.phschool.com**

Geography & History

TAKING TO THE HIGHWAY

Focus Explain that when automobiles were first invented, they were purchased more by sports enthusiasts or hobbyists than as a practical means of transportation. Early automobiles had no roofs and traveled slowly on dirt roadways built for horses and buggies. The first cars were owned by very few individuals and were relatively expensive.

Instruct Ask students to list the types of changes that would be necessary in order for American society to increase its reliance on cars for transportation. Have them consider the design of early cars, including the fact that they did not have roofs, as well as the fact that they were relatively expensive to purchase. How did design modifications and the introduction of mass production influence the popularity of automobiles?

Discuss with students the 1921 establishment of the federal highway system. Have them consider how this uniform system of connected roads would have influenced the increased use of cars. Ask students to list the ways in which the increased use of cars across the United States affected the development of the country.

Extend Ask students to compare and contrast the development of the national railway system with the development of the interstate highway system. In what ways are the two systems similar? How are they different? How did the rise of auto travel ultimately affect the railroads?

Taking to the Highway

Car ownership expanded rapidly during the 1910s and the 1920s. By 1927, some 54 percent of American families owned a car. The growing popularity of car travel and the usefulness of trucks during World War I led to calls for federally funded highways. In 1926, the first nationwide system of numbered highways was introduced, as shown on this map.

Principal U.S. Highways, 1926

— Principal U.S. highways
(80) Route numbers

Aid for Highways

The first paved highways were built with state and local funding. The Federal Highway Act of 1921 provided federal funding for the first time for a national system of paved highways.

Geographic Connection
How would a federal highway system with uniform route numbers make long-distance travel easier than separate systems of numbered highways in each state?

The Difficulties of Early Car Travel
When cars were first introduced in the 1890s and early 1900s, they had to travel on poorly maintained dirt roads that often turned to mud when it rained.

736

RESOURCE DIRECTORY

Teaching Resources
Geography and History booklet, pp. 14–15

Other Print Resources
Nystrom *Atlas of Our Country* United States
Political Map, pp. 38–39

Technology
Prentice Hall United States History Video Collection™ Volume 17, *The Roaring Twenties*

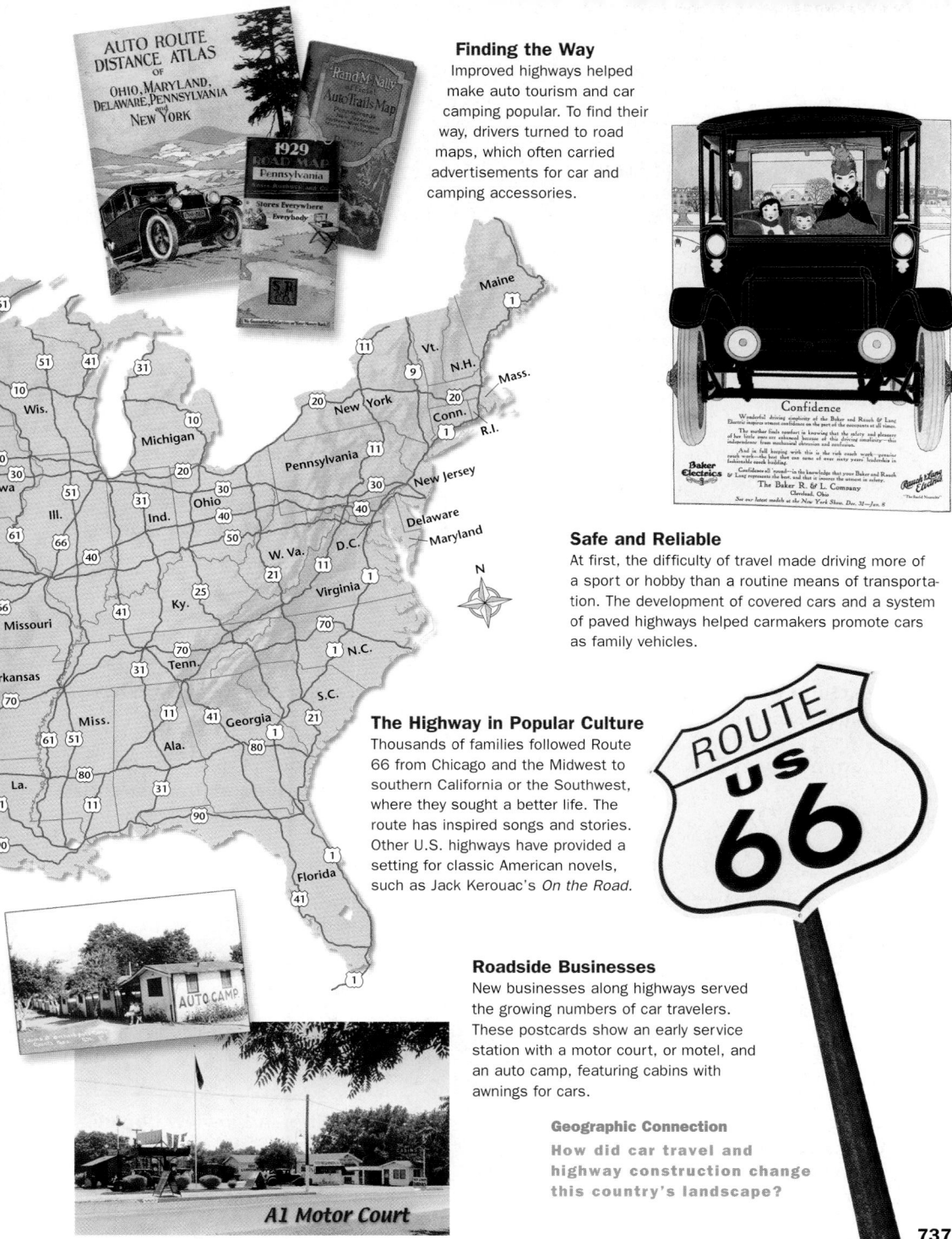

Finding the Way

Improved highways helped make auto tourism and car camping popular. To find their way, drivers turned to road maps, which often carried advertisements for car and camping accessories.

Safe and Reliable

At first, the difficulty of travel made driving more of a sport or hobby than a routine means of transportation. The development of covered cars and a system of paved highways helped carmakers promote cars as family vehicles.

The Highway in Popular Culture

Thousands of families followed Route 66 from Chicago and the Midwest to southern California or the Southwest, where they sought a better life. The route has inspired songs and stories. Other U.S. highways have provided a setting for classic American novels, such as Jack Kerouac's *On the Road*.

Roadside Businesses

New businesses along highways served the growing numbers of car travelers. These postcards show an early service station with a motor court, or motel, and an auto camp, featuring cabins with awnings for cars.

Geographic Connection

How did car travel and highway construction change this country's landscape?

A1 Motor Court

737

Chapter 22 Planning Guide
Resource Manager

	CORE INSTRUCTION	READING/SKILLS
Chapter-Level Resources	Teaching Resources • Pacing Charts booklet • Block Scheduling booklet **Resource Pro® CD-ROM**, Ch. 22 **Prentice Hall Presentation Pro CD-ROM**, Ch. 22 **www.phschool.com** • eTeach	**Guided Reading Audiotapes (English/Spanish)** **Student Edition on Audio CD**, Ch. 22 **Social Studies Skills Tutor CD-ROM** **Color Transparencies**, A35, B12, F7
1 The Stock Market Crash 1. Learn about events that led to the stock market's Great Crash in 1929. 2. See how the Great Crash produced a ripple effect throughout the nation's economy. 3. Become familiar with the main causes of the Great Depression.	Teaching Resources **Units 7/8 booklet** • Section 1 Quiz, p. 24	**Guided Reading and Review booklet**, p. 89 **Guide to the Essentials**, p. 112 **Section Reading Support Transparencies**
2 Social Effects of the Depression 1. Understand how poverty spread during the Great Depression. 2. Find out about social problems that were caused by poverty in the 1930s. 3. Discover how some people struggled to survive hard times.	Teaching Resources **Units 7/8 booklet** • Section 2 Quiz, p. 25 **Learning Styles Lesson Plans booklet**, p. 46	**Guided Reading and Review booklet**, p. 90 **Guide to the Essentials**, p. 113 **Skills for Life booklet**, p. 24 **Section Reading Support Transparencies**
3 Surviving the Great Depression 1. Read about ways Americans pulled together to survive the Great Depression. 2. See the signs of change Americans began to notice in the early 1930s.	Teaching Resources **Units 7/8 booklet** • Section 3 Quiz, p. 26	**Guided Reading and Review booklet**, p. 91 **Guide to the Essentials**, p. 114 **Section Reading Support Transparencies**
4 The Election of 1932 1. Find out how President Hoover responded to the Great Depression. 2. Learn what Roosevelt meant when he offered Americans a "new deal." 3. Realize why the election of 1932 was a significant turning point in American politics.	Teaching Resources **Units 7/8 booklet** • Section 4 Quiz, p. 27 **Learning Styles Lesson Plans booklet**, p. 47	**Guided Reading and Review booklet**, p. 92 **Guide to the Essentials**, p. 115 **Learning with Documents booklet**, p. 87 **Section Reading Support Transparencies**

ENRICHMENT/PRE-AP

Prentice Hall United States History Video Collection™

www.phschool.com
- Section Activities, Virtual Field Trip, Chapter Activities, Current Events Online

Biography, Literature, and Comparing Primary Sources booklet, p. 70

American History Block Scheduling Support

American History Block Scheduling Support

Sounds of an Era Audio CD

Exploring Primary Sources in U.S. History CD-ROM

Biography, Literature, and Comparing Primary Sources booklet, p. 27

Exploring Primary Sources in U.S. History CD-ROM

Biography, Literature, and Comparing Primary Sources booklet, p. 139

Sounds of an Era Audio CD

American Pathways Thematic Posters

ASSESSMENT

Core Assessment
ExamView® Test Bank, Ch. 22
ExamView® Test Bank CD-ROM, Ch. 22

Standardized Test Preparation
Diagnose and Prescribe
Diagnostic Tests for High School Social Studies Skills

Review and Reteach
Review Book for U.S. History

Practice and Assess
Test-taking Strategies With Transparencies
Test-taking Strategies Posters
Test Prep Book for U.S. History
Alternative Assessment Handbook
Document-Based Assessment

Teaching Resources
Units 7/8 booklet
- Section Quizzes, pp. 24–27
- Chapter Tests, pp. 28, 31

www.phschool.com Ch. 22 Self-Test

AmericanHeritage® RESOURCES

From the Archives of American Heritage®, p. 758
AmericanHeritage® My Brush with History™ Videotapes
www.americanheritage.com

Don't miss the exclusive interactive version of this textbook on the Web and on CD-ROM.

Chapter 22 Planning Guide
In Your Classroom

CUSTOMIZE FOR INDIVIDUAL NEEDS

Gifted and Talented

Teacher's Edition
- Customize for Gifted and Talented, p. 759

Teaching Resources
- Biography, Literature, and Comparing Primary Sources booklet, pp. 27, 70, 139

Technology
- Exploring Primary Sources in U.S. History CD-ROM *The Grapes of Wrath, John Steinbeck; Depression Photograph, Dorothea Lange; This Land Is Your Land, Woody Guthrie*

ESL

Teacher's Edition
- Customize for ESL, p. 749

Teaching Resources
- Guided Reading and Review booklet, pp. 89–92
- Guide to the Essentials (English/Spanish), Chapter 22

Technology
- Student Edition on Audio CD, Chapter 22
- Guided Reading Audiotapes (English/Spanish), Chapter 22
- Section Reading Support Transparencies

Less Proficient Readers

Teacher's Edition
- Customize for Less Proficient Readers, p. 741

Teaching Resources
- Guided Reading and Review booklet, pp. 89–92
- Guide to the Essentials (English/Spanish), Chapter 22

Technology
- Student Edition on Audio CD, Chapter 22
- Guided Reading Audiotapes (English/Spanish), Chapter 22
- Section Reading Support Transparencies

Less Proficient Writers

Teacher's Edition
- Customize for Less Proficient Writers, p. 755

Teaching Resources
- Guided Reading and Review booklet, pp. 89–92
- Guide to the Essentials (English/Spanish), Chapter 22

Technology
- Student Edition on Audio CD, Chapter 22
- Guided Reading Audiotapes (English/Spanish), Chapter 22
- Section Reading Support Transparencies

TEACHER'S EDITION INDEX

CHAPTER 22 – PACING SUGGESTIONS

 For 90-minute Blocks
- Teach sections 1, 2, and 4 using Transparencies A35, B12, and F7, and the Recent Scholarship note on page 747 for class discussions.

 Running Out of Time?

If you are running short on time to cover this chapter, consider the following options:

- Use Prentice Hall Presentation Pro CD-ROM to create an outline for this chapter.
- Use the Section Summaries for Chapter 22, from **Guide to the Essentials (English/Spanish).**

1 The Stock Market Crash	**Connecting with Economics** Remind students of the diagram in this section that shows the ups and downs of the business cycle. Have students choose another decade in history (such as the 1950s or 1980s) and locate data on the business cycle over that ten-year period. Have them make or reproduce one graph that shows the business cycles and one that shows the behavior of the stock market during the same period to see whether the surges and falls of the two correspond. **(Logical/Mathematical)**
2 Social Effects of the Depression	**Connecting with the Arts** Ask students to research the work of Dorothea Lange so that they can select those photographs of hers that they find most moving and report on how and why she took them. After students make an oral presentation to the class, encourage a discussion on what effect the photographs might have had at the time and how they affect today's audience. **(Visual/Spatial)**
3 Surviving the Great Depression	**Connecting with Culture** Students can find an anthology of first-person recollections of the Great Depression, such as Studs Terkel's *Hard Times: An Oral History of the Great Depression*. Have students organize and present a play that uses the recollections to tell the story of the Depression through the eyes and words of those who were there. **(Bodily/Kinesthetic)**
4 The Election of 1932	**Connecting with Citizenship** Students will recall that the song "Happy Days Are Here Again" was closely associated in 1932 with the Democratic candidate, Franklin Delano Roosevelt. Have students research other popular songs that became campaign songs and share what they learn with the class. **(Musical/Rhythmic)**

Chapter 22

Crash and Depression

(1929–1933)

Crash and Depression (1929–1933)

SECTION 1	The Stock Market Crash
SECTION 2	Social Effects of the Depression
SECTION 3	Surviving the Great Depression
SECTION 4	The Election of 1932

INTRODUCING THE CHAPTER

When the economy of the high-flying 1920s crashed in 1929, the bleak years of the Great Depression began. Behind the headlines and photos of stock-buying-and-selling frenzy and destitution grew a debate that cut to the very political, social, and economic fiber of the country and changed forever how Americans look at government.

TIME LINE ACTIVITY

To provide students with practice in using the time line, ask questions such as these:

1. What event led to the Great Depression? *(The Great Crash of October 29, 1929)*

2. What famous building was completed at the height of the Depression? *(The Empire State Building)*

3. What were conditions like in the Soviet Union in 1932? *(There was widespread famine.)*

Tickertape machines delivered investors news about their stocks.

The Long and the Short of it

American Events

1929

Oct. 29: Stock prices tumble in what is known as the Great Crash. Investors lose millions of dollars, and the economy sinks into a devastating depression.

1930

Congress passes the Hawley-Smoot tariff, the highest import tax in American history, in an effort to protect domestic industries. World trade suffers as a result.

1931

The Empire State Building, the world's tallest, opens in New York City.

Presidential Terms: Herbert Hoover 1929–1933

1929 **1930** **1931**

World Events

The term *apartheid* is introduced in South Africa.

1929

Five nations meet at the London Naval Conference.

1930

Japanese troops occupy Manchuria.

1931

738 Chapter 22 • *Crash and Depression*

eTeach

Be sure to check out this month's online discussion with a Master Teacher. Go to **www.phschool.com**.

RESOURCE DIRECTORY

Teaching Resources
Pacing Charts booklet
Block Scheduling booklet, p. 24
Units 7/8 booklet
- Chapter Summary, p. 23

Technology
Guided Reading Audiotapes (English/Spanish), Ch. 22
Student Edition on Audio CD, Ch. 22
Sounds of an Era Audio CD *"Brother Can You Spare a Dime?"* 1932 recording
Prentice Hall United States History Video Collection™ Volume 18, *The Great Depression and the New Deal*
Prentice Hall Presentation Pro CD-ROM, Ch. 22
Resource Pro® CD-ROM
Social Studies Skills Tutor CD-ROM
Companion Web site, www.phschool.com

The Dust Bowl, 1933–1940

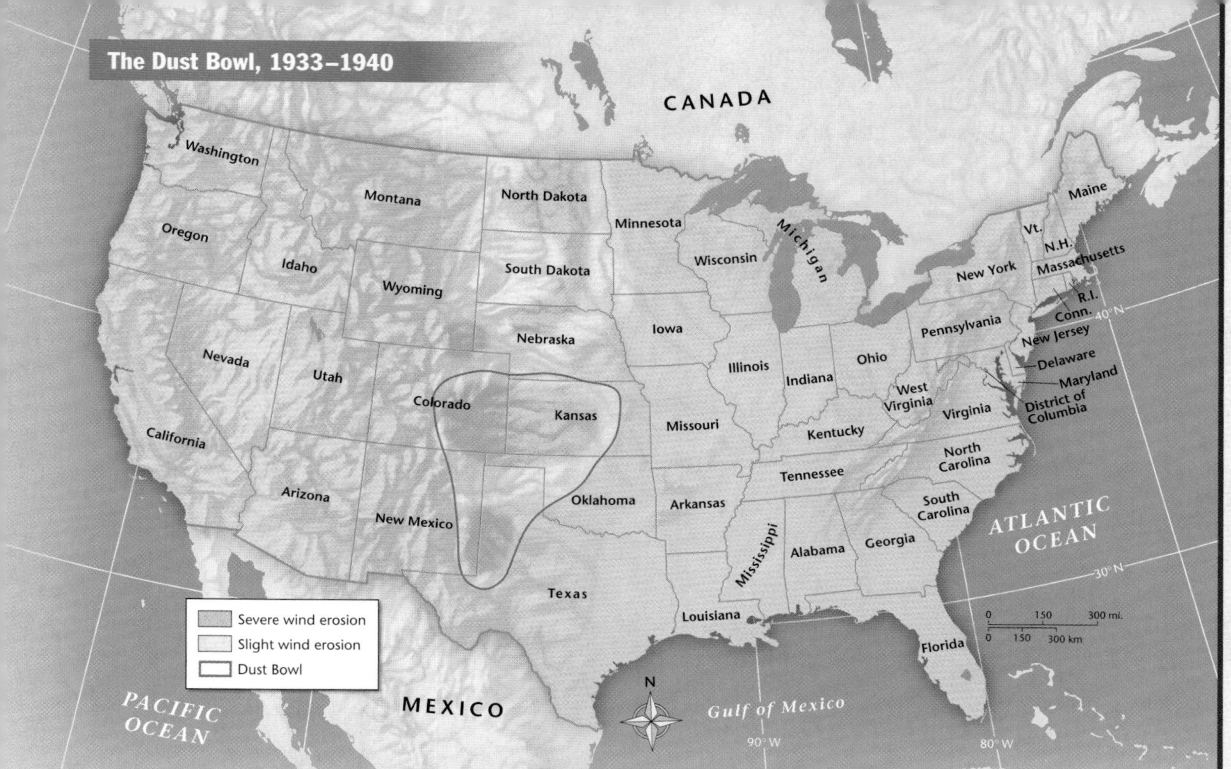

CANADA

Washington
Montana
North Dakota
Minnesota
Maine
Oregon
Idaho
Wyoming
South Dakota
Wisconsin
Michigan
Vt.
N.H.
New York
Massachusetts
Nevada
Utah
Nebraska
Iowa
Illinois
Indiana
Ohio
Pennsylvania
R.I.
Conn.
New Jersey
Delaware
Maryland
District of Columbia
California
Colorado
Kansas
Missouri
Kentucky
West Virginia
Virginia
North Carolina
Arizona
New Mexico
Oklahoma
Arkansas
Tennessee
South Carolina
Georgia
Alabama
ATLANTIC OCEAN
Texas
Mississippi
Louisiana
Florida

PACIFIC OCEAN
MEXICO
Gulf of Mexico

- Severe wind erosion
- Slight wind erosion
- Dust Bowl

0   150   300 mi.
0   150   300 km

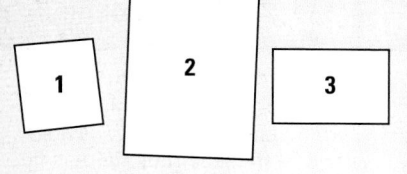

Franklin D. Roosevelt at his inauguration in 1933.

1932
President Hoover authorizes troops to remove Bonus Army protesters after Congress refuses to give them an advance on a pension bonus.

1932
The American people, hopeful about Franklin Delano Roosevelt's "New Deal," overwhelmingly elect him to be the nation's 32nd President.

1933
Congress passes the Twenty-first Amendment, which repeals Prohibition.

Franklin D. Roosevelt 1933–1945

1932

1933

1932
Famine strikes the Soviet Union.

1933
Hitler and the Nazis take over Germany.

1932

1933

Chapter 22   739

BIBLIOGRAPHY

For the Teacher

Brendon, Piers. **The Dark Valley: A Panorama of the 1930s.** Knopf, 2000. (A vivid portrait of conditions around the world during the 1930s.)

Watkins, T. H. **The Great Depression: America in the 1930s.** Little, Brown, 1995. (Companion volume to the PBS video.)

For the Student

The Great Depression. 420 minutes. PBS Video, 1993. (Seven one-hour segments produced by the Public Broadcasting Service.)

The Grapes of Wrath. 129 minutes. Zenger. Black-and-white film. (Dramatization of John Steinbeck's novel about the Depression.)

The Dust Bowl, 1933–1940

Activating Prior Knowledge What region of the United States was most heavily affected by the drought that caused the Dust Bowl? *(The Midwest)*

Previewing What role did climatic conditions play in creating the Dust Bowl? *(Overcultivated areas with severe wind erosion and a lack of rainfall experienced the worst effects.)*

BACKGROUND
About the Pictures

1   2   3

1. The stock ticker machine was a small telegraph receiver connected to the New York Stock Exchange. It would print out the stock trade information on long, thin rolls of paper known as ticker tape. The phrase "ticker-tape parade" originated when brokerage offices on Wall Street threw their used ticker-tape rolls out of the windows during parades.

2. At the time it was completed, the Empire State Building in New York City was the tallest in the world. All 100 stories were completed in just over 400 days, an average of 4½ stories built each week. Over 7 million hours of work were required to complete the building.

3. Franklin Delano Roosevelt's inauguration was on March 4, 1933.

iTEXT

Don't miss the exclusive interactive version of this textbook on the Web and on CD-ROM.

Section 1
The Stock Market Crash

SECTION OBJECTIVES

1. Learn about events that led to the stock market's Great Crash in 1929.
2. See how the Great Crash produced a ripple effect throughout the nation's economy.
3. Become familiar with the main causes of the Great Depression.

BELLRINGER

Warm-Up Activity Ask students to take the perspective of a bank customer who wants to withdraw savings and is told by the teller that there is no money. What might be the cause of such a situation? What options would the customer have?

Activating Prior Knowledge Ask students if they have ever heard a description of conditions during the Great Depression. What are their impressions of that time?

READING STRATEGY

Have students copy the time line on the previous pages. Then, as they read, have them add more information to the time line. Have them apply absolute and relative chronology through the sequencing of significant individuals, events, and time periods as they analyze how one event led to the next. Have them analyze the causes of the Great Depression, including the decline in worldwide trade, the stock market crash, and bank failures.

CAPTION ANSWERS

Viewing History As stock prices dropped sharply, investors began to lose millions of dollars. Many tried to sell their stocks as soon as they could to avoid losing their entire investments. They believed they faced financial ruin.

READING FOCUS

- What events led to the stock market's Great Crash in 1929?
- Why did the Great Crash produce a ripple effect throughout the nation's economy?
- What were the main causes of the Great Depression?

MAIN IDEA

In October 1929, panic selling caused the United States stock market to crash. The crash led to a worldwide economic crisis called the Great Depression.

KEY TERMS

Dow Jones Industrial Average
Black Tuesday
Great Crash
business cycle
Great Depression

TAKING NOTES

As you read, complete the following diagram to show some of the causes and effects of the Stock Market's Great Crash in 1929.

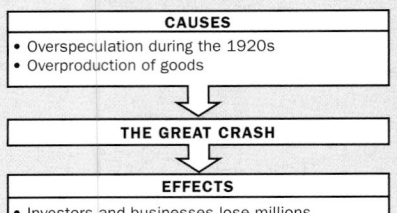

CAUSES
• Overspeculation during the 1920s
• Overproduction of goods

⬇

THE GREAT CRASH

⬇

EFFECTS
• Investors and businesses lose millions
• Thousands of banks fail, savings are wiped out

Setting the Scene On October 29, 1929, fear gripped the floors of the New York Stock Exchange as investors watched millions of dollars slip away. The "wonderful prosperity" of the 1920s had come to an abrupt end. Writers Gordon Thomas and Max Morgan-Witts captured the scene:

VIEWING HISTORY As stock market prices fell, the ticker tape could not report market activity fast enough. Nervous investors crowded into Wall Street hoping to hear the latest news. **Identifying Central Issues** *Why did investors panic in October 1929?*

> 66 *A messenger struggling through the crowd suddenly found himself yanked by his hair off his feet. The man who held him kept screaming he had been ruined. He would not let the boy go. The terrified youth at last broke free, leaving the man holding tufts of his hair. Crying in pain, the messenger fled the Exchange. His hair never regrew.*
>
> *Behind, he left a scene of increasing pandemonium. As huge blocks of shares continued to be dumped, . . . 1,000 brokers and a support army of 2,000 page boys, clerks, telephonists . . . and official recorders could sense this was going to be the 'day of the millionaire's slaughter.'*
>
> *William Crawford, swept along helplessly by the great tide of people, would always remember how 'they roared like a lot of lions and tigers. They hollered and screamed, they clawed at one another's collars. It was like a bunch of crazy men.'* 99
>
> —Gordon Thomas and Max Morgan-Witts from *The Day the Bubble Burst*

The Market Crashes

Before the panic on that fateful October day, most people saw no reason to worry. In early 1928, the **Dow Jones Industrial Average,** an average of stock prices of major industries, had climbed to 191. By Hoover's Inauguration

---

RESOURCE DIRECTORY

Teaching Resources
Guided Reading and Review booklet, p. 89
Biography, Literature, and Comparing Primary Sources booklet (Literature) *The Stock Market Crash,* p. 70

Other Print Resources
American History Block Scheduling Support *The Great Depression: A Struggle to Survive,* found in the Prosperity, Depression, and War folder, includes interdisciplinary lesson suggestions and activities for Geography and History, Primary Sources, Biography, and Literature.

Technology
Section Reading Support Transparencies
Guided Reading Audiotapes (English/Spanish), Ch. 22
Student Edition on Audio CD, Ch. 22
RESOURCE PRO® Biography *Woody Guthrie,* found on Resource Pro, profiles the folk songwriter and singer who chronicled the woes of ordinary Americans during the Depression.
Prentice Hall Presentation Pro CD-ROM, Ch. 22
Companion Web site, www.phschool.com

Day, March 4, 1929, it had risen another 122 points. By September 3, the Dow Jones average reached an all-time high of 381.

The rising stock market dominated the news. Keeping track of prices became almost as popular as counting Babe Ruth's home runs. Eager, nervous investors filled brokerage houses to catch the latest news coming in on the ticker tape. Prices for many stocks soared far above their real value in terms of the company's earnings and assets.

Black Thursday   After the peak in September, stock prices fell slowly. Some brokers began to call in loans, but others continued to lend even more. One bank official assured the nervous public: "Although in some cases speculation has gone too far, . . . the markets generally are now in a healthy condition."

When the stock market closed on Wednesday, October 23, the Dow Jones average had dropped 21 points in an hour. The next day, Thursday, October 24, worried investors began to sell, and stock prices fell. Investors who had bought General Electric stock at $400 a share sold it for $283 a share.

Again, business and political leaders told the country not to worry. Another banking executive said that only a nation as rich as the United States could "withstand the shock of a $3 billion paper loss on the Stock Exchange in a single day without serious effects to the average citizen." President Hoover maintained that the nation's business "is on a sound and prosperous basis."

Black Tuesday   To stop the panic, a group of bankers pooled their money to buy stock. This action stabilized prices, but only for a few days. By Monday, prices were falling again. Investors all over the country raced to get their money out of the stock market. On October 29, **Black Tuesday,** a record 16.4 million shares were sold, compared with the average 4 million to 8 million shares a day earlier in the year.

This collapse of the stock market is known as the **Great Crash.** Despite efforts to halt it, the Crash continued beyond Black Tuesday. By November 13, the Dow Jones average had fallen from its September high of 381 to 198.7. Overall losses totaled $30 billion. The Great Crash was part of the nation's **business cycle,** a span in which the economy grows, then contracts.

The Ripple Effect of the Crash

Initially the effects of the Crash were felt only by those who were heavily invested in the stock market. By 1929, that number was about 4 million people out of a population of 120 million. Some investors lost everything. One wealthy Bostonian who lost heavily in the market wrote in his diary, "The profit in my little book melted yesterday to seven thousand. It is probably nil [nothing] today. . . . My dreams of a million—where are they?"

Within a short time, however, the effects of the Great Crash began to ripple throughout the nation's economy. Soon millions of people who had never owned a share of stock were affected. The following list explains how the effects of the Crash spread to all Americans.

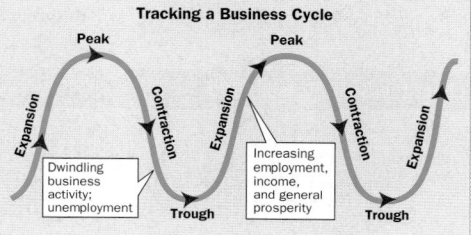

Tracking a Business Cycle

Peak — Expansion — Contraction — Trough

Dwindling business activity; unemployment

Increasing employment, income, and general prosperity

READING CHECK
Who felt the effects of the Great Crash?

Connecting with Economics

Invite students to imagine that they are living in the early 1930s. To help them analyze the effects of the Great Depression on the U.S. economy and government, organize them into small groups to discuss how their lives would be affected if the banks in their region closed. After discussions have proceeded for a few minutes, point out that there were no credit cards in the 1930s. Advise them to consider this fact as they continue their discussions. (Groups will have to confront such issues as how to negotiate paychecks to raise funds for everyday expenses and how to pay for needs in such an environment.) Have a spokesperson from each group report its conclusions to the class. **(Verbal/Linguistic)**

BACKGROUND
Economics

Most bank runs lasted just a day or two, and sometimes only hours. So bankers tried to combat them by slowing down the rate of withdrawals while reassuring customers that the bank would not fail. One Arkansas bank resisted a run by paying only in silver coins and making customers provide their own bags. Forced to carry away heavy bags of savings, some customers changed their minds and left their money in the bank. In 1932, banks in Urbana, Illinois, prevented a run in nearby Champaign from spreading to Urbana by closing for five days. Meanwhile, teams of volunteers pressured depositors into signing no-withdrawal pledges. When the strategy worked, the concept of a "bank holiday" spread. The following year, a national bank holiday was the first action ordered by new President Franklin D. Roosevelt.

CAPTION ANSWERS

Interpreting Diagrams Sample answer: Businesses and consumer spending suffer when investors lose money. Layoffs occur. Loans go unpaid. Banks fail. Tariffs prevent Europeans from purchasing U.S. goods. Reparations payments and declining U.S. overseas investments severely harm European economies.

Risky loans hurt banks Banks earn their profits on the interest they earn from lending out their deposits. Throughout the 1920s, banks loaned huge sums of money to many high-risk businesses. When stock prices fell, these businesses were unable to repay their loans.

Consumer borrowing Banks also make money on loans they lend to consumers. Consumers had borrowed heavily from banks throughout the 1920s to purchase consumer goods. When banks called in their loans, customers did not have cash to pay them.

Bank runs The Great Crash resulted in widespread bank runs. Fearful that banks would run out of money, people rushed to make withdrawals from their accounts. To pay back these deposits, banks had to recall loans from borrowers. However, many businesses and consumers hurt by falling stock prices could not repay their loans. Even if loans were repaid, banks could not get the money fast enough to pay all the depositors demanding their money.

Bank failures The combination of unpaid loans and bank runs meant that many banks across the country failed. Thousands of banks closed their doors when they could not return their depositors' money. In just a few years, more than 5,500 banks failed.

Savings wiped out Bank failures wiped out what little savings people had. By 1933, the money from 9 million savings accounts had vanished.

Cuts in production Businesses now could not borrow money to use to produce more goods. In addition, businesses lacked any incentive to spend money producing goods. Few people had money to buy them.

Rise in unemployment As businesses cut back on production, they laid off workers. Unemployment grew.

INTERPRETING DIAGRAMS
After the Great Crash, each sector of the economy experienced a damaging cycle of events. Each cycle also directly influenced the others. **Expressing Problems Clearly** *How did the events following the Great Crash interact and affect one another?*

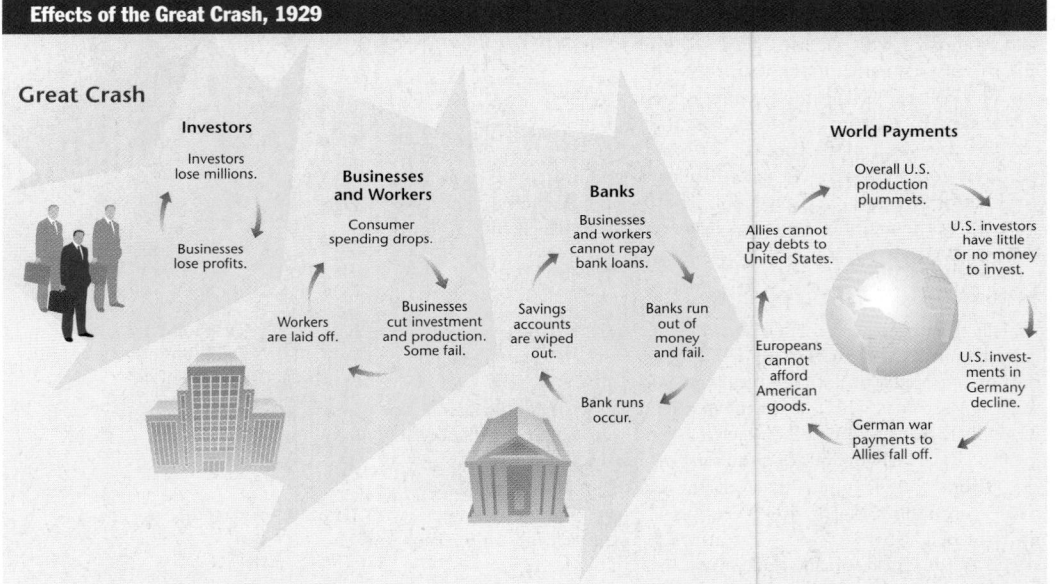

Effects of the Great Crash, 1929

RESOURCE DIRECTORY

Technology
Color Transparencies *American Photo*, F7
(RESOURCE•PRO®) **Critical Thinking Activity**
Identifying Central Issues: Signs of Trouble, found on Resource Pro, helps students apply the skill by analyzing a graph of income distribution in the United States in 1929.

Further cuts in production As unemployment grew and incomes shrank, consumers spent less and less money and businesses produced still fewer goods. The overall output of goods in the economy dropped.

Economic Contraction The results of the Great Crash described above are all symptoms of an economy beginning to contract. A contraction is an economic decline marked by a falling output of goods and services. A particularly long and severe contraction is known as a depression. The contraction that began with the Great Crash triggered the most severe economic downturn in the nation's history—the **Great Depression.** The Great Depression lasted from 1929 until the United States entered World War II in 1941.

Impact on Workers and Farmers With no money and little incentive to produce more goods, factories throughout the country began to close. Thousands of workers lost their jobs or endured pay cuts. In August 1931, Henry Ford shut down his Detroit automobile factories, putting at least 75,000 people out of work.

Soon after local factories closed, small local businesses began to suffer as well. Restaurants and other small businesses closed because customers could no longer afford to go to them. Formerly wealthy families dismissed household workers. Farm prices, already low, fell even more, bringing disaster to many families. In 1929, a bushel of wheat had sold for $1.18; in 1932 it brought a mere 49 cents. Cotton dropped from 19 to 6.5 cents a pound.

By 1932, more than 12 million people were unemployed, which accounted for about a quarter of the labor force. (See the graph to the right.) Others worked only part-time or had their wages cut. The Gross National Product (GNP)—the total value of goods and services a country produces annually—dove from $103 billion in 1929 to just $56 billion in 1933.

Impact on the World By the 1930s, international banking, manufacturing, and trade had made nations around the world interdependent. For example, Latin America depended on U.S. markets for its goods. Europeans depended on the United States for investments and loans. When the world's leading economy fell, the global economic system began to crumble or contract in much the same way the U.S. economy had.

After World War I, the United States had insisted that France and Britain, its wartime allies, repay their war debts. At the same time, Congress kept import taxes high, making it hard for European nations to sell goods in the United States. With economies weakened by the war and little chance of selling goods in the United States, the Allies had to rely on Germany's reparations payments for income.

As long as American companies invested in Germany, reparations payments continued. But with the Depression, investments fell off. German banks failed, Germany suspended reparations, and the Allies, in turn, stopped paying their debts. Industrial production fell by 40 percent in Germany, 14 percent in Britain, and 29 percent in France. Europeans could no longer afford to buy American-made goods. Thus the American stock market crash started a downward cycle in the global economy.

Economic Impact of the Great Depression

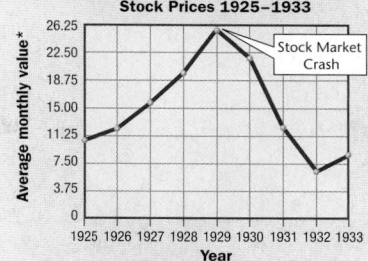

Stock Prices 1925–1933
*Based on Standard and Poor's index of common stocks

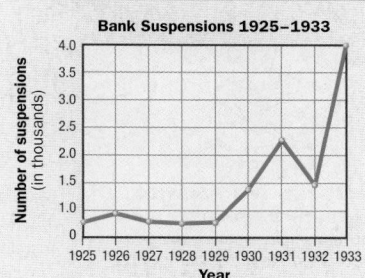

Bank Suspensions 1925–1933

Unemployment 1925–1933

SOURCE: *Historical Statistics of the United States, Colonial Times to 1970*

INTERPRETING GRAPHS
The stock market crash caused a series of economic disasters.
Analyzing Information *Roughly how many people became unemployed between 1929 and 1933?*

Reading Comprehension

1. The average of stock prices of major industries.

2. A record 16.4 million shares of stock were sold off on Wall Street, causing the stock market to crash.

3. A trough.

4. Widespread unemployment resulting from a lack of demand for products and the inability of businesses to obtain loans with which to finance their manufacturing operations.

5. The unbalanced economy had no stable base to fall back upon. Production far outstripped demand; wealth was unevenly distributed; the boom in stock market prices was based mainly on borrowed money, not real value.

Critical Thinking and Writing

6. Interdependence of the world's economies; high U.S. tariffs; the breakdown of reparations payments; declining European demand for American goods.

7. Answers will vary, but should display an understanding of how the credit situation and the distribution of wealth in the 1920s differed from today.

8. Answers should reflect the shock and sense of panic that swept the nation at that time.

Take It to the NET

Students should research the weaknesses of the stock market. They may also note a sense of optimism before the Great Depression set in, noting that during the Great Crash it appeared as if only the very wealthy would be hit hardest.

CAPTION ANSWERS

Interpreting Political Cartoons The cartoonist predicts prolonged hard times ahead. The investor clings to the bear's tail in a desperate attempt to slow down a bear market gaining speed. The twisted buildings suggest a Wall Street losing its sense of order and stability.

INTERPRETING POLITICAL CARTOONS This cartoon was published three weeks before the Great Crash, at the beginning of a "bear market." A bear market exists when the stock market falls for a period of time. **Analyzing Visual Information** *What effect did the cartoonist predict the bear market would have on Wall Street?*

Underlying Causes of the Depression

The stock market crash of 1929 did not cause the Great Depression. Rather, both the Great Crash and the Depression were the result of deep underlying problems with the country's economy.

An Unstable Economy Overall, the seemingly prosperous economy of the 1920s lacked a firm base. National wealth was unevenly distributed, with most money in the hands of a few families who tended to save or invest rather than buy goods. Industry produced more goods than most consumers wanted or could afford. Farmers and many workers had not shared in the economic boom. The uneven prosperity of the 1920s made rapid recovery from an economic downturn impossible.

Overspeculation During the 1920s, speculators bought stocks with borrowed money and then pledged those stocks as *collateral* to buy more stocks. Collateral is an item of value that a borrower agrees to forfeit to the lender if the borrower cannot repay the loan. Brokers' loans went from under $5 billion in mid-1928 to $850 billion in September 1929. The stock market boom was based on borrowed money and optimism instead of real value.

Government Policies Mistakes in monetary policy were also to blame. During the 1920s, the Federal Reserve system, which regulates the amount of money in circulation, cut interest rates to spur economic growth. Then in 1929, worried about overspeculation, the Federal Reserve limited the money supply to discourage lending. As a result, there was too little money in circulation to help the economy recover after the Great Crash.

Section 1 Assessment

READING COMPREHENSION

1. What is the **Dow Jones Industrial Average?**

2. What happened on **Black Tuesday?**

3. Which part of the **business cycle** did the **Great Depression** represent?

4. What could cause a country's Gross National Product to decrease?

5. How did the unstable economy in the 1920s contribute to the Great Depression?

CRITICAL THINKING AND WRITING

6. **Recognizing Cause and Effect** How did the Great Depression have such a huge impact on the economies of other countries?

7. **Making Comparisons** Many people today use credit cards and charge accounts to buy on credit. Is this practice as dangerous now as it was in 1929? Why or why not?

8. **Writing to Inform** It is the day after Black Tuesday. Write a brief newspaper report describing the scene at local banks.

Take It to the NET

Activity: Writing a Diary Entry
Research the events of October 1929 leading up to the Great Crash. Then write a diary entry from the perspective of a stockbroker in New York noting your experiences. How are you affected by the crash? What is your reaction? Use the links provided in the *America: Pathways to the Present* area of the following Web site for help in completing this activity.
www.phschool.com

RESOURCE DIRECTORY

Teaching Resources
Units 7/8 booklet
• Section 1 Quiz, p. 24
Guide to the Essentials
• Section 1 Summary, p. 112

Social Effects of the Depression

READING FOCUS

- How did poverty spread during the Great Depression?

- What social problems were caused by poverty in the 1930s?

- How did some people struggle to survive hard times?

MAIN IDEA

By the early 1930s, wage cuts and growing unemployment had brought widespread suffering across the United States.

KEY TERMS

Hooverville
Dust Bowl

TAKING NOTES

As you read, complete this chart by listing examples of how the Great Depression affected different parts of American society.

Effects of the Great Depression	
Social Groups	**Effects**
City laborers	Many lost their jobs, became homeless, lived in poverty, some resorted to living in "Hoovervilles"
Farmers	
Women	
Children	
Men	
Racial minorities	

Setting the Scene Many Americans thought the Depression would not last. They were soon proved wrong. Hard times continued and eventually spread to all levels of society. Those who never imagined they would one day have to ask friends, neighbors, or even the government for money found themselves with no other option. In this account from 1934, a "middle-class" college graduate details the awkwardness and pain associated with what she described as "becoming one of them," or joining the ranks of the poor:

66 *Two years ago I was living in comfort and apparent security. My husband had a good position in a well-known orchestra and I was teaching a large and promising class of piano pupils. When the orchestra was disbanded we started on a rapid down-hill path. My husband was unable to secure another position. My class gradually dwindled away. We were forced to live on our savings.*

In the early summer of 1933 I was eight months pregnant and we had just spent our last twelve dollars on one month's rent for an apartment. . . . [which] lacked the most elementary comforts such as steam heat, bathtubs, sunlight, and running hot water. They usually are infested with mice and bedbugs. Ours was. . . .

What then, did we do for food when our last money was spent on rent? So strong was the influence of our training that my husband kept looking feverishly for work when there was no work, and blaming himself because he was unable to find it. . . . An application to the Emergency Home Relief Bureau was the last act of our desperation. 99

—From Ann Rivington [pseudonym],
"We Live on Relief," *Scribner's Magazine*, April 1934

Poverty Spreads

Imagine that the bank where you have a savings account suddenly closes. Your money is gone. Or your parents lose their jobs and cannot pay the rent or mortgage. One day you come home to find your furniture and all of your belongings on the sidewalk—you have been evicted.

VIEWING HISTORY The number of people without jobs rose dramatically after the Crash. **Drawing Inferences** *What can you tell from this man's sign about the social view of charity in the 1930s?*

Chapter 22 • Section 2   **745**

SECTION OBJECTIVES

1. Understand how poverty spread during the Great Depression.

2. Find out about social problems that were caused by poverty in the 1930s.

3. Discover how some people struggled to survive hard times.

BELLRINGER

Warm-Up Activity Ask students to discuss how they would cut back on their expenses if their cash funds were limited. Have students describe how they might feel if this happened.

Activating Prior Knowledge Do students know anyone who was directly affected by the Depression? Ask students to interview that person about his or her memories. Can the interview subject state how living through the Depression affected him or her in later life?

READING STRATEGY

Before students read, have them list the section headings and one sentence telling what they think each section might be about. Then, as they read, have them review the sentences they wrote and modify them if necessary.

CAPTION ANSWERS

Viewing History Many people did not look favorably upon charity. Most unemployed people wanted to work for food or money and not receive handouts or direct aid. To accept charity without working may have been shameful or damaging to one's pride.

VIEWING HISTORY Makeshift huts served as homes for the homeless and unemployed in this New York City Hooverville. **Making Comparisons** Do "Hoovervilles" exist today? Under what conditions do the homeless now live?

People at all levels of society faced these situations during the Great Depression. Professionals and white-collar workers, who had felt more secure in their jobs than laborers, suddenly were laid off with no prospects of finding another position. Those whose savings disappeared could not understand why banks no longer had the money they had deposited for safekeeping.

"Hoovervilles" The hardest hit were those at the bottom of the economic ladder. Some unemployed laborers, unable to pay their rent, moved in with relatives. Others drifted around the country. In 1931, census takers estimated the homeless population in New York City alone at 15,000.

Homeless people sometimes built shanty towns, with shacks of tar paper, cardboard, or scrap material. These shelters of the homeless came to be called **Hoovervilles,** mocking the President, whom people blamed for not resolving the crisis.

A woman living in Oklahoma visited one Hooverville: "Here were all these people living in old, rusted-out car bodies," she noted. "There were people living in shacks made of orange crates. One family with a whole lot of kids were living in a piano box."

Many homeless and jobless people, rather than staying in one place, became drifters, hitchhiking from one "hobo jungle" to another. Thousands rode the rails—or jumped on trains illegally to travel across the country. They slept in boxcars or open freight cars. By 1933, an estimated one million people were on the move, risking jail, injury, or death.

Farm Distress Farm families suffered as low crop prices cut their income. When they could not pay their mortgages, they lost their farms to the banks, which sold them at auction. In the South, landowners expelled tenant farmers and sharecroppers. In protest against low prices, farmers dumped thousands of gallons of milk and destroyed crops. These desperate actions shocked a hungry nation.

The Dust Bowl For thousands of farm families in the Midwest, the harsh conditions of the Depression were made even more extreme by another major crisis of the decade. The origin of this one was not economic, but environmental. Between 1931 and 1940, so much soil blew out of the central and southern Great Plains that the region became known as the **Dust Bowl.**

Focus on GEOGRAPHY

Weather in the Dust Bowl The Great Plains is called "America's breadbasket." Deep, fertile soils, a long growing season, and flat land make it ideal for farming. But the region has always experienced severe weather. Hot and humid tropical air masses come from the Gulf of Mexico. Cold polar air masses rush southward from above the Arctic Circle. When these air masses collide, powerful storms with fierce updrafts are created. The complex root systems of the grasslands had protected the soil from weather. As you have read, however, when farmers plowed the land, this natural protection was lost.

The Dust Bowl was created, in part, by dust storms that began in the early 1930s. Farmers said the storms were the result of a severe drought. While drought was a major factor in creating the Dust Bowl, it was not the only factor. Farming practices also contributed.

As long as there was a thick layer of prairie grasses to protect topsoil, severe weather could not harm the land. When farmers plowed the land, however, they stripped the soil of its natural protection. Winds picked up the dark, nutrient-rich topsoil and carried it eastward, sometimes for hundreds of miles, leaving behind barren, shifting dunes of grit and sand. The map below shows the extent of soil erosion across the plains.

The most severe storms of the dry years were called "black blizzards." Time after time, dirt was swept up and dropped by the ton over states and cities far to the east. The dirt darkened the sky in New York City and Washington, D.C. It stained the snows of New England red and dropped on ships hundreds of miles off the Atlantic Coast. The drought and winds persisted for more than seven years, bringing ruin to the farmers.

The combination of terrible weather and low prices for farm products caused about 60 percent of Dust Bowl families to lose their farms. More than 440,000 people left Oklahoma during the 1930s. Nearly 300,000 people left Kansas. Thousands of families in Oklahoma, Texas, Kansas, and other southwestern Plains states migrated to California. Many found work on California's farms as laborers. About 100,000 of the Dust Bowl migrants headed to cities such as Los Angeles, San Francisco, and San Diego. Relief did not come to the Dust Bowl region until the early 1940s, when the rains finally arrived and World War II drove farm prices up.

Poverty Strains Society

As the Depression wore on, it took a serious physical and psychological toll on the entire nation. Unemployment and fear of losing a job caused great anxiety. People became depressed; many considered suicide, and some did take their own lives.

Impact on Health "No one has starved," President Hoover declared, but some did, and thousands more went hungry. Impoverished people who could not afford food or shelter got sick more easily. Children suffered most from the long-term effects of poor diet and inadequate medical care.

"All last winter we never had a fire except about once a day when Mother used to cook some mush or something," one homeless boy recalled. "When the kids were cold they went to bed. I quit high school, of course."

In the country, people grew food. In cities, they sold apples and pencils, begged for money to buy food, and fought over the contents of restaurant garbage cans. Families who had land planted "relief gardens" to feed themselves or so they could barter food for other items. One historian recalled:

Sounds of an Era

Listen to a reading from John Steinbeck's *The Grapes of Wrath* and other sounds from the Great Depression.

MAP SKILLS Drought combined with over-farming to reduce the Great Plains to dust. **Regions** How did farmers destroy the region's natural protection against severe weather?

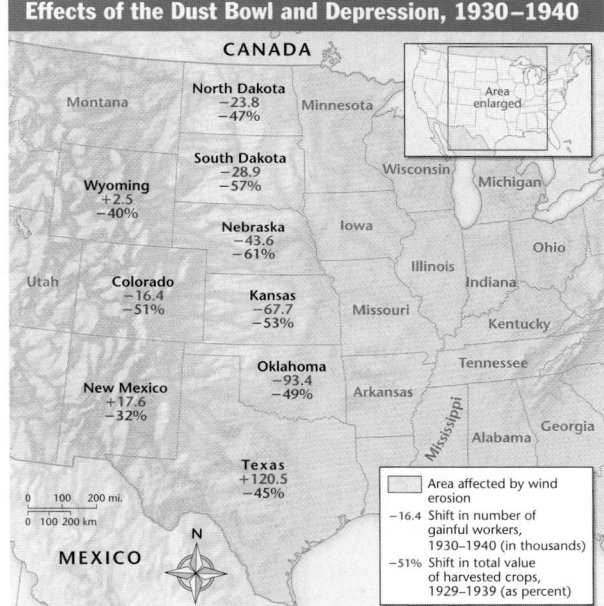

Effects of the Dust Bowl and Depression, 1930–1940

CANADA

Montana

North Dakota
−23.8
−47%

Minnesota

South Dakota
−28.9
−57%

Wisconsin

Michigan

Wyoming
+2.5
−40%

Nebraska
−43.6
−61%

Iowa

Ohio

Illinois

Indiana

Utah

Colorado
−16.4
−51%

Kansas
−67.7
−53%

Missouri

Kentucky

New Mexico
+17.6
−32%

Oklahoma
−93.4
−49%

Arkansas

Tennessee

Mississippi

Alabama

Georgia

Texas
+120.5
−45%

Area enlarged

MEXICO

0   100   200 mi.
0 100 200 km

N

Area affected by wind erosion
−16.4 Shift in number of gainful workers, 1930–1940 (in thousands)
−51% Shift in total value of harvested crops, 1929–1939 (as percent)

Connecting with Geography

Point out that the Dust Bowl was the result of decades of natural and human conditions and developments. Then organize the class into five groups. Have each locate and use primary and secondary sources such as computer software, databases, media and news services, biographies, interviews, and artifacts to investigate one of the following areas of Great Plains history: (1) its physical geography and natural environment; (2) native inhabitants and their lifestyles; (3) the role of technology in frontier agriculture; (4) climate, conditions, and population trends in the late 1800s; and (5) soil conservation methods in use today. Have each group select a spokesperson to present its findings to the class. **(Verbal/Linguistic)**

BACKGROUND
Recent Scholarship

In *Bad Land: An American Romance,* Jonathan Raban observes that most people date the "downfall" of the midwestern homesteaders to the "Dirty Thirties." Raban's reading of 800 family memoirs collected in Montana, however, leads him to conclude that the exodus from midwestern farmlands began much earlier. In fact, Raban found that more people left their farms between 1917 and 1928 than between 1929 and 1940. The dry spell actually began with a rainless spring in 1917 and culminated in the terrible winter of 1919. The roots of the already-overgrazed grasses died. Ruined farmers went on to other jobs in nearby towns. Those who had held on through the first dry spell went west when the second one occurred.

TEST PREPARATION

Have students read the quotation by the homeless boy under "Impact on Health" on this page and then complete the sentence below.

Based on the passage, you can infer that the reason the writer quit high school was—

A he was too cold to go to school.

(B) his first priority was getting enough to eat and staying warm.

C he was not interested in studying.

D he had to help his mother make dinner.

CAPTION ANSWERS

Map Skills Farmers destroyed the sod by cultivating the land too extensively. This exhausted the soil and broke up the prairie grass that had held topsoil in place, thus allowing the topsoil to erode.

ACTIVITY

Connecting with Culture

Organize students into groups to create collages that compare and contrast life during the Depression with life today. Have each group search current newspapers and magazines, as well as books about modern times and the Depression, for photos that show similarities or differences in the experiences of farmers, workers, homeless people, women, and others now and then. Remind students to photocopy the images they select so as not to damage the source materials. Groups should then arrange, label, and mount their images on a piece of posterboard to complete their collage. **(Visual/Spatial)**

BACKGROUND

Preserving the Past

Jobless men in worn-out clothes, hungry babies, and desperate mothers—Dorothea Lange's photos stirred public attention in the 1930s and created a powerful historical record of the decade's suffering. "She told me . . . that she was thirty-two," Lange recalled of the migrant mother. "She said that they had been living on frozen vegetables and the birds that the children killed. She had just sold the tires from her car to buy food. There she sat in that lean-to tent with her children huddled around her, and seemed to know that my pictures might help her." Indeed, images such as this helped lead to the creation of government camps for migrant workers. Lange's photographs also inspired John Steinbeck's important Depression-era novel *The Grapes of Wrath*.

READING CHECK

Widespread malnutrition led to reduced resistance to diseases such as tuberculosis. The increase of such diseases, poor diet, and lack of medical care seriously weakened millions of Americans, especially children.

CAPTION ANSWERS

Viewing Fine Art They aroused public attention and helped to create political support for aid to unemployed and homeless people.

READING CHECK
How did the Great Depression impact people's health?

> *"In Detroit nearly one out of every seven persons was on relief [government aid]. Children scavenged through the streets like animals for scraps of food, and stayed away from school. . . . Among high school students in the inner city the incidence of tuberculosis tripled. Each day four thousand children stood in bread lines. With their sunken, lifeless eyes, sallow cheeks, and distended bellies, some resembled the starving children in Europe during the war."*
>
> —Robert Conot

Stresses on Families Living conditions declined as families moved in together, crowding into small houses or apartments. The divorce rate dropped because people could not afford separate households. People gave up even small pleasures like an ice cream cone or a movie ticket.

Men who had lost jobs or investments often felt like failures because they could no longer provide for their families. If their wives or children were working, men thought their own status had fallen. Many were embarrassed to be seen at home during normal work hours. They were ashamed to ask friends for help.

Women faced other problems. Those who had depended on a husband's paycheck worried about feeding their hungry children. Working women were accused of taking jobs away from men. Even in the better times of the 1920s, Henry Ford had fired married women. "We do not employ married women whose husbands have jobs," he explained. During the Depression, this practice became common. In 1931, the American Federation of Labor endorsed it. Most school districts would not hire married women as teachers, and many fired those who got married.

Many women continued to find work, however, because poor-paying jobs such as domestic service, typing, and nursing were considered "women's work." The greatest job losses

VIEWING FINE ART Dorothea Lange's most famous photographs, the "Migrant Mother" series (1936, right), have become a symbol of the Depression. The face of the undernourished mother displays a numbness to her destitute surroundings, yet a certain determination to pull through it all. Above is another of Lange's most famous photographs, "White Angel Breadline." **Determining Relevance** *What effect did Lange's photographs have on the general public?*

RESOURCE DIRECTORY

Technology

Exploring Primary Sources in U.S. History
CD-ROM *Depression Photograph, Dorothea Lange*

of the Depression were in industry and other areas that seldom hired women.

Discrimination Increases Hard economic times put groups of Americans in competition with one another for a shrinking number of jobs. This produced a general rise in suspicions and hostilities against minorities. African Americans, Hispanics, and in the West, Asian Americans all suffered as white laborers began to demand the low-paying jobs typically filled by these minorities. Hispanics and Asian Americans lost not only their jobs but also their country. Thousands were deported—even those born in the United States.

Black unemployment soared—about 56 percent of black Americans were out of work in 1932. Some white citizens declared openly that blacks had no right to jobs if whites were out of work. Gordon Parks, a photographer who rode the rails to Harlem, later wrote:

> 66 *To most blacks who had flocked in from all over the land, the struggle to survive was savage. Poverty coiled around them and me with merciless fingers.* 99

—Photographer Gordon Parks

Because government relief programs often discriminated against African Americans, black churches and organizations like the National Urban League gave private help. The followers of a Harlem evangelist known as Father Divine opened soup kitchens that fed thousands every day. Discrimination was even worse in the South, where African Americans were denied civil rights such as access to education, voting, and health care. Lynchings increased.

The justice system often ignored the rights of minority Americans. In March 1931, near Scottsboro, Alabama, nine black youths who had been riding the rails were arrested and accused of raping two white women on a train. Without being given the chance to hire a defense lawyer, eight of the nine were quickly convicted by an all-white jury and sentenced to die.

The case of the "Scottsboro boys" was taken up, and sometimes exploited, by northern groups, most notably the Communist Party. The party helped supply legal defense and organized demonstrations, which, after many years, helped overturn the convictions, but four of the "boys" spent many years in jail.

Stories of Survival

A generation of Americans would live to tell their grandchildren how they survived the Depression. Wilson Ledford first felt the effects of the Depression in March 1930 when he was 15, living in Chattanooga, Tennessee, with his mother and younger sister. Wilson had worked part time and after school in a grocery store since he was 11. By 1930, his family could no longer afford Chattanooga. They moved back to Cleveland, Tennessee, a nearby small town. They survived on the rent Wilson's mother received on a house and 15 acres of land, which she still owned. The property brought in $6 a month in rent—except when the tenants were out of work. After taxes and insurance, the family had about a dollar a week to live on. Wilson "swapped work with neighbors." He looked after the family horse and cow, chopped wood for the fireplace, tended the garden that provided family food, and raised corn to feed the animals:

BIOGRAPHY

Dorothea Lange 1895–1965

"The camera is an instrument that teaches people how to see without a camera," said photographer Dorothea Lange. Born in New Jersey in 1895, Lange decided at a young age to be a photographer. In 1919, Lange opened a portrait studio in San Francisco where she photographed wealthy clients. Beyond the windows of her studio, she could see the spreading effects of the Depression. She thought about the vast difference "between what I was working on in the printing frames [in the studio] and what was going on in the street."

Lange's first exhibition, in 1934, landed her an assignment to photograph the hundreds of migrant workers streaming into California from the Dust Bowl. Lange's photographs showed the world the desperation and bravery of families displaced by the Depression.

Lange continued to document the suffering and mistreatment of other Americans until her death in 1965. But she will be forever linked in people's minds to the 1930s and the human courage that she made a part of the nation's permanent record.

Section 2 Assessment

Reading Comprehension

1. Unemployed laborers and their families.

2. Exposure of topsoil due to overintensive agriculture, drought, and wind erosion.

3. Causes: Competition for scarce, low-paying jobs, and a legal system that continued to disregard civil rights for nonwhites. Effects: Deportations, lynchings, high African American unemployment.

4. His experiences demonstrate the hardships of finding work, which was often only temporary or was located far from home. Yet, he and his family made the best of the situation in order to survive.

Critical Thinking and Writing

5. Answers will vary, but students might note the feelings of hopelessness and the loss of pride many Americans felt. Well-educated people could not find jobs. Many people had to rely on friends, family, or the government for help. The goals and expectations of most people were only to survive, not to prosper.

6. Questions will vary but should be supported with facts from the section.

Take It to the NET

Articles should describe weather and environmental conditions faced by farmers in the Dust Bowl. Students should note both the great size of the storms and the damage they caused.

❝ We had to raise most of what we ate since money was so scarce. . . . Sometimes I plowed for other people when I could get the work. . . . I got 15 cents an hour for plowing, and I furnished the horse and plow. ❞
—Wilson Ledford

Nothing was wasted. Wilson's mother kept chickens and traded eggs at the store for things they could not grow or raise. Overalls cost 98 cents; shoes were $2. She bought a pig for $3 and raised it for meat, and she made jelly from wild blackberries. Despite the family's own poverty, she gave extra milk and butter to "some poor people, a woman with three small children who lived in a one-room shack with a dirt floor."

VIEWING HISTORY Many Americans reluctantly waited in "souplines" such as this when they did not have enough money to buy food. **Drawing Inferences** What do you think was the hardest part of such an experience? What made it easier?

Wilson never got to high school, "as survival was more important." The Ledfords had no radio, but Wilson made his own entertainment. Wilson and some other boys cleaned the rocks off a field, graded it, and made a baseball diamond. Baseballs were precious. "You could buy a pretty good baseball for a quarter and a real good one for 50 cents. . . . If we lost a ball during the game, everyone had to go hunt for it."

In the summer of 1932, when he was 17, Wilson got a job in Chattanooga delivering ice. He worked there again the next summer: "I worked twelve hours a day, six days a week, and made $3.00 a week." When the icehouse closed in the fall, Wilson hitchhiked throughout the Southeast looking for work, but never had any success. "I pumped up so many tires for people I rode with, I had blisters all in my hands. Finally I got back home."

Later Wilson bought a truck to haul coal, cotton, and oranges, then worked nights in a woolen mill while carrying ice during the day. Finally, "I got a call from Chickamauga Dam and I went to work there. That was a good job working on the dam. I made 60 cents an hour. Times were better by then, but did not start booming until World War II started."

Section 2 Assessment

READING COMPREHENSION

1. Who lived in **Hoovervilles?**

2. What factors led to the creation of the **Dust Bowl** in the 1930s?

3. What were some causes and effects of increased discrimination during the Great Depression?

4. What can you learn about the Depression from Wilson Ledford's experiences?

CRITICAL THINKING AND WRITING

5. **Identifying Central Issues** Explain the effect the Depression had on the psychology of many Americans. Why do you think the Depression changed people's goals and expectations?

6. **Writing an Interview** In an effort to learn firsthand what it was like to live during the Great Depression, write ten questions that you might ask someone who lived through it.

Take It to the NET

Activity: Writing a Newspaper Article Write a newspaper article describing the conditions faced by those living in the Dust Bowl during the Great Depression. Be sure to include a lot of details for the readers back home. Use the links provided in the *America: Pathways to the Present* area of the following Web site for help in completing this activity. **www.phschool.com**

Drawing Inferences

Drawing inferences is a way of interpreting what you read. When you draw inferences about a person's character, you add what you know to what an author tells you, including facts about the person's words and actions, and ideas that are implied but not directly stated in the text.

Gordon Parks eventually became a successful photographer and writer. But when the Great Depression hit, he was only a teenager, on his own and desperately in need of a job and a place to live. When he tried to get a room in a cheap hotel, he was refused because he was black (Passage A). Later, Parks determined to become a photographer (Passage B).

LEARN THE SKILL

Use the following steps to draw inferences:

1. **Identify stated facts.** Identify what the person actually said and did. Determine what information is directly stated.

2. **Identify unstated ideas.** Distinguish between what is implied by the facts and what is suggested by the perspective of the author.

3. **Add what you know.** Use information you know about the historical period and about human nature to help you understand the person's actions.

4. **Draw inferences about the person's character.** Keep the point of view of the author in mind, and be wary of authors who may have a bias.

PRACTICE THE SKILL

Answer the following questions:

1. Summarize the facts in each passage.

2. (a) What does Passage A suggest about Parks's reaction to racism? Explain. (b) Where does Parks suggest what he wants you to think? (c) What do you think the author of Passage B wants you to feel about Parks? Explain.

3. (a) How does your knowledge of the Depression help you understand what Parks does in Passage A? (b) How does your understanding of human nature help you evaluate Parks's decision to tell the truth in Passage B? Explain.

4. (a) From the passages, what inferences can you draw about Parks as a teenager? As an adult? (b) How do the two passages help you understand Gordon Parks?

APPLY THE SKILL

See the Chapter Review and Assessment for another opportunity to apply this skill.

A

"Mike tells me you're looking for a room and work. That so?" [the manager] asked, squinting down . . . at me.

"That's right."

"You look like a clean-cut colored boy."

"I'm a boy. I don't know what my color's got to do with it."

"Don't go gittin' your dander up. I think I got a proposition for you." I waited. "How'd you like to have a room and a job both?"

"Where?"

"Right here. I'm needin' a boy to clean this place. You'll git a room in the back and a half a buck a day. . . ."

"I'd like to know why I can't just pay and sleep here?"

"Look, I ain't no expert on race problems," the . . . man said impatiently. "I'm just givin' you a proposition. Whyn't you try it and see how things work out?"

"Give me twenty-five cents more a day and some food."

"Hell, fellow, you'll be makin' a buck a day with all that. That's big dough round these parts."

"Sorry," I said, turning as if I were going.

"Just a second." I had bluffed him into a decision. "Okay. . . ."

—Gordon Parks, *Voices in the Mirror: An Autobiography*

B

"Early in 1938, Parks walked through the door of an upscale women's clothing store in St. Paul and asked if they might need any fashions photographed. The manager wasn't interested, but the fellow's wife convinced him to give Parks a chance. Parks borrowed a Speed Graphic camera on credit, and spent a day photographing models. But when he developed the film, he was devastated to find that he had double-exposed all but one shot. [His wife] suggested he take a chance and blow up the one good picture. When the store manager saw it, he was thrilled. Where were the rest? Parks told the truth. He was allowed to reshoot. Soon his pictures filled the windows of Frank Murphy's store. That was the beginning. . . ."

—Dick Russell, *Black Genius and the American Experience*

Chapter 22   751

RESOURCE DIRECTORY

Teaching Resources
Skills for Life booklet, p. 24

Technology
Social Studies Skills Tutor CD-ROM
Interactive Practice in
- Geographic Literacy
- Critical Thinking and Reading
- Visual Analysis
- Communications

DRAWING INFERENCES

Focus Students will learn how to use historical material to draw inferences about a person's character.

Instruct Discuss with students what life was like for a young African American artist such as Gordon Parks in the first part of the last century. What opportunities might come his way? What obstacles would he have to overcome? Have students read passage A. Ask them to describe how Parks must have felt as he had to assert himself to get what he needed. What do his actions indicate about his character? Have students read passage B. Ask students to describe ways in which his behavior in this passage is consistent with his behavior in passage A.

Extend See the Skills for Life activity in the Resource Directory below.

ANSWERS
PRACTICE THE SKILL

1. Sample answers: A: Parks is looking for a job and a place to live; he resents being referred to as "colored"; he rejects the first offer by the hotel manager. B: Parks was first rejected for a photographer's job at a clothing store; the manager's wife intervened; only one photograph came out; when asked, Parks told the truth; he was allowed to shoot more photos and was hired; it was the start of his career.

2. (a) It angered him, but he dealt with the situation calmly. (b) At the end of the passage. (c) To respect his determination, honesty, and talent.

3. (a) He was desperate for a job, food, and a place to live. He took a big chance, as jobs were scarce. (b) That telling the truth is the right thing to do even when it isn't easy.

4. (a) As a teenager, he was proud and determined with a bit of a temper, and good at manipulating people. As an adult, he was still determined but showed integrity and no temper. (b) They show his development from a headstrong, rather desperate boy to a mature, honest man.

Section 3
Surviving the Great Depression

SECTION OBJECTIVES

1. Read about ways Americans pulled together to survive the Great Depression.
2. See the signs of change Americans began to notice in the early 1930s.

BELLRINGER

Warm-Up Activity Ask students to recall a time in their lives when friends, neighbors, or strangers worked together to solve a problem or helped one another through an unpleasant situation.

Activating Prior Knowledge Have students find out about the history of the Depression in your local area. What government programs were put in place to help out-of-work citizens? Are there examples of Depression-era government-funded buildings, bridges, or highways that students can find?

READING STRATEGY

As students read the section, have them make a list of the strategies that helped Americans survive the Depression years.

CAPTION ANSWERS

Viewing History These symbols pointed fellow hobos toward welcoming places and away from dangerous ones. The system was mutually beneficial. It was in each person's best interest to keep the system alive. By sticking together, these people could survive the Depression.

READING FOCUS

- In what ways did Americans pull together to survive the Great Depression?
- What signs of change did Americans begin to notice in the early 1930s?

MAIN IDEA

Americans survived the Great Depression with determination and even humor. They helped one another, looked for solutions, and waited for the hard times to pass.

KEY TERMS

penny auction
Twenty-first Amendment

TAKING NOTES

As you read, prepare an outline of this section. Use Roman numerals to indicate the major headings of this section, capital letters for the subheadings, and numbers for the supporting details.

I. Americans Pull Together
  A. Farmers Stick Together
    1. Worked together to minimize impact of Great Depression
    2. _____
    3. _____
  B. Young People Ride the Rails
    1. Young people left home to seek a better life.
    2. _____
    3. _____

Setting the Scene No one who lived through the Great Depression ever forgot it. Long after the economy rebounded, many from the "Depression generation," even those who recovered enough to live a very comfortable life, would continue to pinch pennies as if financial ruin were just around the corner. Many Americans avoided buying on credit, instead saving for years to pay cash for needed items. Others even stuffed money under their mattresses rather than trust their life savings to banks.

Americans Pull Together

Not all the memories of the Depression were bad or despairing, as one reporter noted:

> 66 The great majority of Americans may be depressed. They may not be well pleased with the way business and government have been carried on, and they may not be at all sure that they know exactly how to remedy the trouble. They may be feeling dispirited. But there is one thing they are not, and that is—beaten. 99
>
> —Journalist Gerald W. Johnson, 1932

Throughout the country people pulled together to help one another. Tenant groups formed to protest rent increases and evictions. Neighbors, in difficult circumstances themselves, helped those they saw as worse off than themselves. One woman remembered:

> 66 There were many beggars, who would come to your back door, and they would say they were hungry. I wouldn't give them money because I didn't have it. But I did take them in and put them in my kitchen and give them something to eat. 99
>
> —Depression survivor Kitty McCulloch

VIEWING HISTORY Traveling hobos gave each other helpful information about certain areas with symbols such as these. They were usually written on sidewalks, fences, or buildings using chalk or coal. **Drawing Inferences** *How did such a symbol system help hobos and the homeless? Why do you think they wanted to help each other?*

Hobo Symbols

(cat)	Kind-hearted woman lives here
+⌐	Food for work
⊗	Good place for a handout
⌣	Can sleep in barn
◠◠◠	Bad-tempered owner
###	Unsafe place
o×o	Good water
+☹	Doctor won't charge

RESOURCE DIRECTORY

Teaching Resources
Guided Reading and Review booklet, p. 91
Biography, Literature, and Comparing Primary Sources booklet (Biography) *Babe Didrickson Zaharias,* p. 27

Technology
Section Reading Support Transparencies
Guided Reading Audiotapes (English/Spanish), Ch. 22
Student Edition on Audio CD, Ch. 22

RESOURCE PRO® Primary Source Activity
The Forgotten Man, found on Resource Pro, uses two letters written to President Hoover during the Depression to show the way many American workers viewed their President and the economic breakdown of the country.
Exploring Primary Sources in U.S. History CD-ROM *This Land Is Your Land,* Woody Guthrie
Prentice Hall Presentation Pro CD-ROM, Ch. 22
Companion Web Site, www.phschool.com

McCulloch also gave one beggar a pinstripe suit belonging to her husband, who, she explained, already had three others.

Farmers Stick Together Farmers also worked together to minimize the impact of the Depression. When a farmer was unable to pay the mortgage on his farm, the bank would foreclose on the property and then sell it at an auction. In some farm communities, local farmers met secretly and agreed to keep bids low during the auction. In what were known as **penny auctions,** farmers would bid mere pennies on land and machines auctioned by the banks in order to help their struggling neighbors. Buyers then returned the farms and machinery to their original owners. As one farmer recalled about his farming community:

> “ The aim of our organization was pure survival. All the farmer asked was more time to see him through the depression years. If they won, they had saved (temporarily at least) their home and means of livelihood, and the means of paying their just debts. If they lost, they would be no worse off. They knew they had nothing to lose, so they decided to fight. . . .”
>
> —Harry Haugland

In the first two months of 1933, more than 70 foreclosure sales on farms were blocked by penny auctions. The success of penny auctions as well as the threat of violence at some farm auctions led some states to pass laws suspending foreclosures on farms. For example, in February 1933, the Iowa state legislature passed a "foreclosure moratorium law," which gave farmers more time to pay back their mortgages.

Young People Ride the Rails At the height of the Great Depression, many young people left their homes, either out of necessity or the desire to seek a better life. In the mid-1930s roughly 250,000 teenagers were living on the road, illegally riding the rails of freight trains. Some rode the rails to find work; others hungered for adventure. Clarence Lee, who left home when he was 16, recalled:

> “ I wanted to stay home and fight poverty with my family. But my father told me I had to leave. . . . But I didn't have it in my mind to leave until he told me, 'Go fend for yourself. I cannot afford to have you around any longer.'”
>
> —Clarence Lee

Jim Mitchell also left home at 16. He was not forced to leave, but he could not deal with the pressures of home life after his father lost his job and was unable to support the family. "The quickest and easiest way to get out," he recalled, "was go jump a train and go somewhere."

Young people riding the rails faced danger every day. They were vulnerable to train-related injuries, the possibility of being arrested by police, or even the threat of being shot at by angry farmers. These hobos, as they are sometimes called, witnessed the Depression in all parts of the country firsthand. Many who rode the rails described their experiences as some of the loneliest times of their

Focus on CULTURE

Monopoly With everyday life so difficult during the Depression, people needed a way to get their minds off their troubles. In response to this need, Charles B. Darrow, an unemployed man living in Germantown, Pennsylvania, created a compelling board game. Called Monopoly®, the game allowed people to live the fantasy of acquiring land, houses, and hotels that they could rent or sell to fellow players. Darrow brought Monopoly to executives at Parker Brothers, a leading board game company, to see if they would produce it. The company rejected Darrow's game, saying that it had 52 design errors. Determined to make the game a success, Darrow worked on correcting the flaws and produced Monopoly on his own. Darrow sold so many sets so quickly that Parker Brothers reconsidered its decision and agreed to produce it. The game was introduced in 1935 and was a bestseller in its first year. Since then, an estimated 500 million people have played Monopoly.

READING CHECK

Why did so many young people ride the rails in the 1930s?

Focus Explain that Americans who lived through the Great Depression never forgot the pain of that time, and their feelings about banks, business, government, and money changed forever. Ask what characteristics helped Americans to survive those troubled times.

Instruct Discuss how living through the Great Depression brought out courage, kindness, charity, and humor in many Americans. Ask students why crises bring out these characteristics. You might want to have students share their recollections from the Warm-Up Activity. Discuss the signs of changing times that gave Americans hope. Ask students to explain the impact of the repeal of Prohibition.

Assess/Reteach Ask students to discuss some favorite pastimes of the Depression, such as going to movies and playing board games, like Monopoly. How do they think such diversions helped people cope with their situations?

B*ACKGROUND*
Homelessness

Evictions were commonplace during the 1930s. Those already marginalized before the Depression, including many African Americans, suffered especially heavily. Writer Langston Hughes observed, "[T]he Depression had brought everyone down a peg or two. And the Negroes had but a few pegs to fall."

☑ TEST PREPARATION

Have students review the quote by Clarence Lee on this page and then complete the sentence below.

Clarence Lee's attitude toward leaving his family during the Depression could best be described as—

A indifferent.

Ⓑ reluctant.

C hostile.

D eager.

INTERPRETING POLITICAL CARTOONS Showing the darker side of Depression humor, an end-of-the-year cartoon in *Life* magazine summed up the hopes and disasters of 1929. **Drawing Conclusions** *Why did Americans use humor to fight their despair?*

lives. Yet, most managed to survive and pull themselves together when the Depression came to an end.

Seeking Political Solutions As bad as conditions were, few Americans called for radical political change. In Europe, economic problems brought riots and political upheaval, but in the United States most citizens trusted the democratic process to handle their problems. As one writer wryly observed:

> 66 *Ten million unemployed continue law-abiding. No riots, no trouble, no multi-millionaires cooked and served with cranberry sauce, alas.* 99
> —William Saroyan, 1936

For some Americans, however, radical and reform movements offered new solutions to the country's problems, by promising a fairer distribution of wealth. The Communist Party had about 14,000 members, mainly intellectuals and labor organizers. In the 1932 election, the Communist candidate polled just over 100,000 votes. Socialists, who called for gradual social and economic changes rather than revolution, did better. Their presidential candidate, Norman Thomas, won 881,951 votes in 1932, about 2.2 percent of the total vote.

Voting figures and party membership do not reflect the notable interest in radical and reform movements in the 1930s. Those who were part of those movements remember the decade as a high point of cooperation among different groups of Americans—students, workers, writers, artists, and professionals of all races. They worked together for social justice in cases such as that of the Scottsboro boys.

Depression Humor For the most part, Americans gritted their teeth and waited out the hard times. Jokes and cartoons helped people through their troubles. The term "Hooverville" was at first a joke. People who slept on park benches huddled under "Hoover blankets"—old newspapers. Empty pockets turned inside out were "Hoover flags." When Babe Ruth was criticized for requesting a salary of $80,000, higher than Hoover's, he joked, "I had a better year than he did."

People fought despair by laughing at it. In 1929, humorist Will Rogers quipped, "When Wall Street took that tail spin, you had to stand in line to get a window to jump out of." A cartoon that showed two men jumping out of a window arm-in-arm was captioned "The speculators who had a joint account."

Signs of Change

Looking back, we know that the Great Depression began to ease when the United States entered into World War II in 1941. Americans suffering through the Depression, of course, had no idea when the hard times would end. They looked for signs of change, and even in the early 1930s there were some.

Prohibition Is Repealed In February 1933, just 15 years after it passed the Eighteenth Amendment banning the sale of alcoholic beverages, Congress passed the **Twenty-first Amendment,** repealing Prohibition. The amendment was ratified by the end of the year.

Some people, including President Hoover, regretted the repeal, but most welcomed it as an end to a failed social experiment and as a curb on gangsters who profited from bootlegging. Control of alcohol returned to the states, eight of which chose to continue the ban on liquor sales.

754 Chapter 22 • *Crash and Depression*

The Empire State Building For many, a dramatic symbol of hope was the new Empire State Building, begun in 1930. John J. Raskob, the developer of the gleaming new skyscraper, won the race to build the world's tallest building. Some 2,500 to 4,000 people worked on its construction on any given day. The cost of the construction was about $41 million (including land). Because of the Depression, projected building costs were cut in half.

The 102-story Empire State Building soared 1,250 feet into the sky and was topped with a mooring mast for blimps. The building's 67 elevators, traveling 1,000 feet per minute, brought visitors to its observation deck. The building officially opened on May 1, 1931, when President Hoover pressed a button in Washington, D.C. that turned on the building lights, illuminating the New York City skyline. On the first Sunday after it opened, more than 4,000 people paid a dollar each to make the trip to the top.

The End of an Era By the mid-1930s, it was clear that an era was ending. One by one, symbols of the 1920s faded away. In 1931, organized crime gangster Al Capone was at last brought down, convicted of tax evasion and sent to prison. The frugal former President Calvin Coolidge, who presided over the freewheeling prosperity of the 1920s, died in January 1933. Baseball legend Babe Ruth retired in 1935. The Depression-era labor policies of automaker Henry Ford, once admired for his efficiency, made him labor's prime enemy.

In 1932, the nation was horrified when the infant son of aviation hero Charles Lindbergh and Anne Morrow Lindbergh was kidnapped and murdered. Somehow this tragedy seemed to echo the nation's distressed condition and its fall from the heights of its energy and heroism in the 1920s.

VIEWING HISTORY Workers like the man shown above looked out over New York City as they labored to complete the Empire State Building. **Determining Relevance** How was the Empire State Building a symbol of hope?

Section 3 — Assessment

READING COMPREHENSION

1. What were **penny auctions** and how did they help farmers overcome some of the hardships of the Great Depression?

2. Why was there an interest among some Americans in radical and reform movements? How did American involvement in these movements differ from the political movements occurring in some parts of Europe at the same time?

3. Why was the **Twenty-first Amendment** passed? Why do you think it was passed during the Great Depression?

CRITICAL THINKING AND WRITING

4. **Making Comparisons** Cite three events in American history that reflect the same qualities of cooperation and endurance exhibited by Americans during the Depression.

5. **Writing an Opinion** In a time of crisis, the building of an expensive skyscraper such as the Empire State Building might have been seen as wasteful. Instead, many Americans found it inspiring. What might account for this view of the project?

 Take It to the NET

Activity: Virtual Field Trip Take a tour showing the construction of the Empire State Building. What kinds of conditions did the workers encounter? Write a poem or an essay based on the images you see. Use the links provided in the *America: Pathways to the Present* area of the following Web site for help in completing this activity.
www.phschool.com

Reading Comprehension

1. A penny auction occurred when a bank foreclosed on a farm and put it up for auction. Neighbors of the fore-closed farmer would buy his property for only pennies, then return it to him in order to help him out.

2. Many Americans became interested in radical social movements because they felt the current government had failed them. Unlike the situation in many European countries, American involvement in these movements was nonviolent and did not seriously challenge the government.

3. It passed because many people wanted to lift the ban on the sale and consumption of alcohol. It was passed during the Depression to help people socialize during tough times and to lessen the activity of gangsters and bootleggers.

Critical Thinking and Writing

4. Answers will vary but might include the American Revolution, the war efforts for both World War I and II, the civil rights movement, and the women's movement.

5. Sample answer: The skyscraper was a symbol of American pride in spite of the Depression, and the project provided jobs for many people.

 **Take It to the NET**

Invite students to take a Virtual Field Trip at **www.phschool.com**

CAPTION ANSWERS

Viewing History The tallest building in the world symbolized progress and success in a time when people were losing hope.

Section 4 The Election of 1932

READING FOCUS

- How did President Hoover respond to the Great Depression?
- What did Roosevelt mean when he offered Americans a "new deal"?
- Why was the election of 1932 a significant turning point for American politics?

MAIN IDEA

As the Depression worsened, people blamed Hoover and the Republicans for their misery. The 1932 presidential election brought a sweeping victory for Democrat Franklin D. Roosevelt and profound changes in the role of government.

KEY TERMS

Hawley-Smoot tariff
Reconstruction Finance Corporation (RFC)
Bonus Army

TAKING NOTES

As you read, complete this chart listing some ideas of the presidential candidates in 1932.

Candidate	Ideas on Government
Herbert Hoover	• Believed in minimal government action • Strict view of government (less government is better) •
Franklin Delano Roosevelt	• Willing to experiment with government roles • Supported broadening the role of government •

Setting the Scene In 1932, President Hoover asked the popular singer Rudy Vallee to come up with a theme song for his campaign. Hoover wanted a song that would help people forget about their troubles during the Depression. The song that Vallee produced, "Brother, Can You Spare a Dime?" was taken from the Broadway musical "New Americana," and soon became a fitting symbol for the Depression years. Although embraced by Americans, it was not quite the rousing song of optimism Hoover would have preferred as a campaign song.

> 66 Once I built a railroad
> I made it run
> Made it race against time.
> Once I built a railroad
> Now it's done
> Brother, can you spare a dime? 99

In contrast, the Democratic candidate for President in 1932, Franklin Delano Roosevelt, built his campaign around a much different tune:

> 66 Happy days are here again,
> The skies above are clear again
> Let us sing a song of cheer again—
> Happy days are here again. 99

VIEWING HISTORY This *New Yorker* cover drawing of FDR's inauguration in 1933 shows Roosevelt, the new President, in contrast with Hoover. **Recognizing Bias** *Do you think this drawing is being critical of Hoover or of the American public's perception of the two candidates?*

As the election approached, Hoover, known as the "great engineer" for his exceptional engineering career, tried desperately to "engineer" the United States out of the Depression. His strict adherence to his political beliefs, however, would put severe limits on what he was able to accomplish.

Hoover's Limited Strategy

For a few months after the stock market crash, President Hoover, along with business leaders, insisted that the key to recovery was confidence. Hoover

756 Chapter 22 • *Crash and Depression*

blamed the Great Depression on "world-wide economic conditions beyond our control"—not on problems in the United States economy. Taking Hoover's advice, business and government leaders tried to maintain public confidence in the economy. Even as factories closed, Hoover administration officials insisted that conditions would improve soon.

Voluntary Action Fails   Hoover believed that voluntary controls by businesses in the United States were the best way to end the economic crisis. He quickly organized a White House conference of business leaders and got their promise to maintain wage rates. At first, many firms did keep wages up. By the end of 1931, however, companies were quietly cutting workers' pay.

Hoover held rigidly to his principle of voluntary action. A shy man, he was successful in business but inexperienced in politics. As a result, he showed less flexibility when it came to political compromise. Often unwilling to budge from his views, Hoover was ultimately unable to make his plan attractive to the American people. After a year of misery, the public began to blame him and the Republicans for the crisis.

The Government Acts   Despite his staunch beliefs and continual reassurances to the public, Hoover knew that he had to do something to alleviate the suffering of so many Americans. Even before the Depression began, Congress, with the support of Hoover, passed the Agricultural Marketing Act in June 1929. The act provided a form of relief for farmers by creating a Federal Farm Board, which was designed to stabilize the prices of farm crops. The program proved to be a failure, however, losing over $150 million and sending farm prices on another downward spiral.

As a result of the worsening Depression, the Republicans took a beating in the 1930 midterm elections. After the election, Republicans no longer controlled the House, and their majority in the Senate was reduced to just one seat. As the hardships continued and criticisms increased, Hoover took an even more active approach. To create jobs, the government spent more on new public buildings, roads, parks, and dams. Construction on Boulder Dam (later renamed Hoover Dam) began in 1930. A President's Emergency Committee on Employment advised the President to create local relief programs.

In an attempt to protect domestic industries from foreign imports, in 1930 Congress passed the **Hawley-Smoot tariff,** the highest import tax in history. The tariff backfired. European countries raised their own tariffs, bringing a sudden slowdown in international trade. Hoover suspended the Allies' payments of their war debts, but Europe's economies grew weaker.

In early 1932, Hoover set up the **Reconstruction Finance Corporation (RFC),** which gave government credit to a number of institutions, such as large industries, railroads, and insurance companies. The act also lent money to banks so that they could extend loans. Also that year, Congress passed the

VIEWING HISTORY Boulder Dam, seen here under construction, was built with massive steel bar columns, and used as much steel as the Empire State Building. **Synthesizing Information** *What did Hoover hope to accomplish by spending money to build Boulder Dam?*

Home Loan Bank Act, which, by discounting mortgage rates, helped homeowners save their homes and farmers keep their farms. The RFC reflected the theory that prosperity at the top would help the economy as a whole. To many people, however, it seemed that the government was helping bankers and big business leaders while ordinary people went hungry. Despite the RFC, banks continued to fail.

Hoover's Unpopularity Grows Despite his support of these programs, Hoover insisted that state and local governments should handle relief. Hoover argued that direct federal relief would destroy people's self-respect and create a large bureaucracy. His refusal to provide direct aid brought bitter public reaction and negative publicity. Although his World War I relief work had earned him the title "Great Humanitarian," Hoover's attitude toward Depression relief made him seem cold and hard-hearted.

Many people blamed Hoover, not always fairly, for their problems. While people went hungry, newspapers showed a photograph of him feeding his dog on the White House lawn. People booed when he said such things as "Our people have been protected from hunger and cold."

Private charities and local officials could not meet the demands for relief as Hoover wanted. Finally, in 1932, Hoover broke with tradition and let the RFC lend the states money for unemployment relief. But it was too little and too late.

As the Depression deepened, some economists backed the ideas of British economist John Maynard Keynes. Keynes argued that massive government spending could help a collapsing economy and encourage more private spending and production of goods and services. This economic theory was not yet widely accepted, however.

Veterans March on Washington A low point for Hoover came in the summer of 1932, when 20,000 jobless World War I veterans and their families encamped in Washington, D.C. The **Bonus Army,** as they called themselves,

Fast Forward to Today

Philosophy of Government

FDR's New Deal represented the birth of a new philosophy of the government's role in American life. Since the days of FDR, Americans have had differing opinions on what the size and role of the government should be.

1933 Roosevelt's New Deal greatly expands the role of government for social and welfare programs.

1964 In the tradition of FDR, President Johnson promises a "Great Society," which would provide legislation to combat poverty and offer health care.

1981 Conservatives, who believe in a minimal role for the government, score a victory when President Reagan begins to cut social welfare spending.

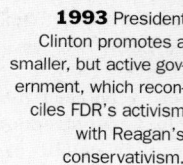

1993 President Clinton promotes a smaller, but active government, which reconciles FDR's activism with Reagan's conservativism.

? What are possible consequences of both a large government role in social welfare and a limited government role?

758   Chapter 22 • *Crash and Depression*

wanted immediate payment of a pension bonus that had been promised for 1945. The House of Representatives agreed, but the Senate said no. Most of the Bonus Army then went home, but a few thousand stayed, living in shacks.

Although the bonus marchers were generally peaceful, a few violent incidents prompted Hoover to call in the army. General Douglas MacArthur decided to use force to drive the marchers out of Washington. Armed with bricks and stones, the Bonus Army veterans faced their own country's guns, tanks, and tear gas. Many people were injured. Hoover was horrified, but he took responsibility for MacArthur's actions. In the next election, the lingering image of this ugly scene would help defeat him.

A "New Deal" for America

"I pledge myself to a new deal for the American people," announced presidential candidate Franklin Delano Roosevelt as he accepted the Democratic Party's nomination at its Chicago convention in July 1932. Delegates cheered, and an organ thundered out the song "Happy Days Are Here Again." The Republicans, in June, had again named Hoover as their candidate. As the presidential campaign took shape, the differences between the two candidates became very clear.

In Franklin and Eleanor Roosevelt, the Democrats had a remarkable political couple ready to bring them to victory. Franklin, nicknamed "FDR" by the press, was born in 1882. He graduated from Harvard University and took a job in a law firm, although his main interest was politics. He was elected twice to the New York State Senate before becoming Assistant Secretary of the Navy under President Wilson.

In 1920, FDR ran for Vice President but lost. The following summer, he came down with polio and never walked without help again. He spent much of the 1920s recovering at Warm Springs, Georgia, but with his wife's help kept up his political interests.

Eleanor Roosevelt, a niece of Theodore Roosevelt, was born in 1884 into a wealthy family. She married her distant cousin Franklin in 1905. During the 1920s, in New York State, Eleanor worked for several causes, including public housing legislation, state government reform, birth control, and better conditions for working women. By 1928,

> ## Focus on GOVERNMENT
>
> **The Twentieth Amendment** On March 2, 1932, Congress proposed the Twentieth Amendment to the Constitution. Called the "Lame Duck Amendment," its purpose was to shorten the period between election day in November and the time when congressional representatives and the President take office. Prior to this amendment, elected officials took office on March 4. During this post-election period of over four months, those who had lost the election were "lame ducks," and would spend this time without having much influence or effectiveness. The amendment changed the inauguration date to January 20, cutting the lame duck period in half. By October 15, 1933, every state had ratified the amendment. The first presidential term to be affected would be FDR's second term, which began on January 20, 1937.

Connecting with Citizenship

Analyze with students the problems of image in a presidential campaign. Ask in what ways image is unavoidable. In what ways can image mask the truth? Did Hoover's image mask his real strengths? What was FDR's image? What about his image appealed to many Americans? (**Verbal/Linguistic**)

BACKGROUND

Connections to Today

In one respect, the 1932 election was the first modern presidential campaign. The Democratic National Committee had hired Charles Michelson as the first publicity specialist in American politics in 1928. Armed with a large budget, he developed a well-planned and coordinated media campaign. Michelson wrote the speeches for prominent Democrats and got anti-Hoover stories placed in newspapers and on radio. These tactics reflected Michelson's decision to make Hoover himself, and not the Depression, the issue in the campaign. The nation's widespread suffering facilitated this strategy. In such circumstances, the shy Hoover was no match for a public relations genius like Michelson.

READING CHECK

Democrats, Republicans, immigrants, laborers, and urban workers.

---

when FDR was persuaded to run for governor of New York, Eleanor was an experienced political worker and social reformer.

After FDR's success as governor of New York (1929–1932), his supporters believed him ready to try for the presidency. With his broad smile and genial manner, he represented a spirit of optimism that the country badly needed.

Unlike Hoover, FDR was ready to experiment with governmental roles. Though from a wealthy background, he had genuine compassion for ordinary people, in part because of his disability. He was also moved by the great gap between the nation's wealthy and the poor.

As governor of New York, Roosevelt had worked vigorously for Depression relief. In 1931, he set up an unemployment commission and a relief administration, the first state agencies to aid the poor in the Depression era. When, as a presidential candidate, FDR promised the country a "new deal," he had similar programs in mind.

The Election of 1932

Hoover, the incumbent candidate for President, summed up the choice that voters had in 1932:

> ❝ This campaign is more than a contest between two men. . . . It is a contest between two philosophies of government. ❞
> —President Herbert Hoover, October 1932

This statement also accurately describes the long-term impact of the 1932 presidential election. It was a historic battle between those who believed that the federal government could not and should not try to fix people's problems, and those who felt that large-scale problems such as the Depression required the government's help. The election would have an enormous effect on public policy for decades to come.

Still arguing for voluntary aid to relieve the Depression, Hoover attacked the Democratic platform. If its ideas were adopted, he said, "this will not be the America which we have known in the past." He sternly resisted the idea of giving the national government more power.

Roosevelt, by contrast, called for "a reappraisal of values" and controls on business:

> ❝ I feel that we are coming to a view through the drift of our legislation and our public thinking in the past quarter century that private economic power is . . . a public trust as well. ❞
> —Franklin Delano Roosevelt, 1932

While statements like this showed FDR's new approach, many Americans did not support Roosevelt because of his ideas as much as they opposed Hoover because he had been too passive. Even longtime Republicans deserted him. A reserved man by nature, Hoover became grim and isolated. He gave few campaign speeches. Crowds jeered his motorcade.

FDR won the presidency by a huge margin of 7 million popular votes. Much of his support came from groups that had begun to turn to the

---

COMPARING PRIMARY SOURCES

Fighting the Depression

Sharp philosophical differences characterized the presidential campaign of 1932.

Analyzing Viewpoints Compare the statements made by the two candidates.

Against Drastic Measures

"We are told by the opposition that we must have a change, that we must have a new deal. It is not the change . . . to which I object but the proposal to alter the whole foundations of our national life which have been built through generations of testing and struggle."
—Herbert Hoover, speech at Madison Square Garden, October 31, 1932

For Drastic Measures

"I have recounted to you in other speeches, and it is a matter of general information, that for at least two years after the Crash, the only efforts made by the [Hoover administration] to cope with the distress of unemployment were to deny its existence."
—Franklin D. Roosevelt, campaign address, October 13, 1932

READING CHECK

From what groups did FDR receive support in the 1932 election?

RESOURCE DIRECTORY

Teaching Resources

Units 7/8 booklet
- Section 4 Quiz, p. 27
- Chapter 22 Test, pp. 28, 31

Guide to the Essentials
- Section 4 Summary, p. 115
- Chapter 22 Test, p. 116

Learning with Documents booklets (Key Documents) *Franklin D. Roosevelt, First Inaugural Address,* p. 87

Other Print Resources

Chapter Tests with ExamView® Test Bank CD-ROM, Ch. 22

Technology

ExamView® Test Bank CD-ROM, Ch. 22
Social Studies Skills Tutor CD-ROM

Democrats in 1928: urban workers, coal miners, and immigrants of Catholic and Jewish descent.

On a rainy day in 1933, FDR stood before a Depression-weary crowd and took the oath of office of President of the United States. As reporter Thomas Stokes observed, a stirring of hope moved through the crowd when Roosevelt said, "This nation asks for action and action now."

Phrases like this foreshadowed a sweeping change in the style of presidential leadership and government response to its citizens' needs. Ultimately, such changes altered the way many Americans viewed their government and its responsibilities.

In the depths of the Great Depression, many Americans had to give up cherished traditional beliefs in "making it on their own." They turned to the government as their only hope. Thus, as you will read in the next chapter, the Roosevelt years saw the beginning of many programs that changed the role of government in American society.

The words of FDR's Inaugural Address gave much of the country renewed hope for the future:

> 66 *So first of all let me assert my firm belief that the only thing we have to fear is fear itself.* 99
>
> —President Franklin Delano Roosevelt,
> First Inaugural Address, 1933

Having overcome fear in his own life many times, Roosevelt spoke with conviction and confidence, reassuring a frightened nation.

Presidential Election of 1932

11.1 / 88.9
% Electoral Vote

2.9 / 39.7 / 57.4
% Popular Vote

Candidate/Party	Electoral Vote	Popular Vote
Franklin D. Roosevelt (Democrat)	472	22,821,857
Herbert Hoover (Republican)	59	15,761,841
Other		1,160,615

MAP SKILLS Franklin D. Roosevelt and the Democratic Party won the popular vote in 1932 as well as a huge margin of electoral votes. **Location** Which states' electoral votes did Hoover win?

Section 4 Assessment

READING COMPREHENSION

1. How did President Hoover hope to end the Depression and its hardships?

2. What was the intent of the **Hawley-Smoot tariff** and the **Reconstruction Finance Corporation?**

3. How did the **Bonus Army** conflict contribute to Hoover's downfall?

4. Describe Franklin Delano Roosevelt's appeal to the American voter in 1932.

CRITICAL THINKING AND WRITING

5. **Distinguishing Fact From Opinion** Do you think the criticisms of Hoover were justified, or might the Depression have brought failure for any President? Explain.

6. **Writing a News Story** Take the position of a reporter covering FDR's inaugural speech. Write a brief newspaper report describing what the President said and how Americans responded to the speech.

 Take It to the NET

Activity: Analyzing Primary Sources Read several of FDR's campaign speeches. What issues did he focus on? Referring to the map of the election of 1932 above or online, did FDR win the states in which he made campaign stops? Use the links provided in the *America: Pathways to the Present* area of the following Web site for help in completing this activity. **www.phschool.com**

Chapter 22 • Section 4 761

Section 4 Assessment

Reading Comprehension

1. Hoover believed that the economy would correct itself if Americans remained confident. He relied on voluntary actions from businessmen to maintain this confidence. He finally, and reluctantly, agreed to allow some direct federal assistance to be used for relief efforts.

2. Hawley-Smoot tariff: to protect American products from cheaper foreign imports, keeping money in the United States economy. RFC: to stabilize large banks and corporations with government aid.

3. It made Hoover appear unconcerned with the problems of the average American, who made up the largest part of the voting public.

4. He intended to bring in a new philosophy of government, one that would expand the government to provide more for the common people.

Critical Thinking and Writing

5. Possible answer: no single person's policies and personality could have compensated for the deep flaws in the economy. On the other hand, Hoover appeared cold and hard-hearted, unwilling to provide enough government money either for relief or to stimulate economic recovery.

6. Answers will vary, but might mention that FDR seemed to symbolize hope and action.

 **Take It to the NET**

Students should note FDR's concern for the economic situation in the United States, which was suffering from the Great Depression.

CAPTION ANSWERS

Map Skills Maine, New Hampshire, Vermont, Connecticut, Pennsylvania, and Delaware.

REVIEWING KEY TERMS

Have students refer to the definitions of key terms in the chapter to write sentences that show an understanding of the causes and effects of both the stock market crash and the Great Depression.

REVIEWING MAIN IDEAS

13. Speculation resulted in enormous blocks of stocks being purchased with borrowed money. Thus, the rise in stock prices during the 1920s had no solid foundation.

14. The Great Depression affected other countries by slowing or halting World War I reparation payments and international trade. The world's economies had also become heavily interdependent in many ways during the 1920s.

15. Those at the bottom of the economic scale were hit hardest by the Depression. Many people were left homeless and jobless.

16. Farmers could not meet their payments on loans for land and machinery; natural disasters such as the Dust Bowl ruined farms; prices for farm products fell sharply.

17. Sample answers: soup kitchens were set up; people agreed to keep bids low on foreclosed farm property; some poor people gave food to those who were even worse off.

18. The repeal of Prohibition symbolized a nationwide desire to ease the psychological rigors of the Depression. Repeal also greatly weakened the organized crime networks that had plagued the 1920s.

19. Americans thought that under Hoover's leadership, the government was not doing enough to relieve their problems. What assistance he did offer was too little and too late.

20. Hoover planned to end the Depression through voluntary actions from businessmen and restoring consumer confidence; FDR planned to end the Depression through government intervention, increasing the role government played in helping citizens.

creating a CHAPTER SUMMARY

Copy this cause-and-effect diagram (right) on a piece of paper and complete it by filling in the major causes and effects of the Great Depression.

i TEXT

For additional review and enrichment activities, see the interactive version of *America: Pathways to the Present*, available on the Web and on CD-ROM.

CAUSES
• Inflated stock prices and uneven economy of the 1920s
• Stock market crash of 1929
•

THE GREAT DEPRESSION

EFFECTS
• Thousands lose their jobs, homes, farms, and other property.
• Discrimination against minorities increases.
•

★ Reviewing Key Terms

For each of the terms below, write a sentence explaining how it relates to the Great Depression.

1. Dow Jones Industrial Average
2. Black Tuesday
3. Great Crash
4. business cycle
5. Great Depression
6. Hooverville
7. Dust Bowl
8. penny auction
9. Twenty-first Amendment
10. Hawley-Smoot tariff
11. Reconstruction Finance Corporation (RFC)
12. Bonus Army

★ Reviewing Main Ideas

13. How did overspeculation in the stock market endanger the economy? (Section 1)

14. Why did the Great Depression in the United States affect countries worldwide? (Section 1)

15. How did the Depression affect those at the bottom of the economic scale? (Section 2)

16. Why were farm families hit particularly hard by the Depression? (Section 2)

17. Give specific examples of Americans helping one another to survive the Depression. (Section 3)

18. In what ways did the end of Prohibition mark the end of an era? (Section 3)

19. Why was President Hoover criticized for his handling of the Great Depression? (Section 4)

20. Compare and contrast Hoover's strategy for ending the Great Depression with Roosevelt's. (Section 4)

★ Critical Thinking

21. Determining Relevance During the Depression, some economists turned to the ideas of British economist John Maynard Keynes, who argued that massive government spending could help a collapsing economy. Do you agree with Keynes's approach? To what extent are Keynes's views still at work in the American economy today?

22. Drawing Conclusions The Great Depression led to hardships for almost everyone, from the very wealthy to the very poor. Do you think this had an impact on traditional American assumptions regarding the work ethic and the theory of social Darwinism?

23. Demonstrating Reasoned Judgment Think about some of the examples of Depression humor in this chapter, such as the cartoon in Section 3, and the use of President Hoover's name to describe certain symbols of the Depression. (a) What is the tone of this "humor"? (b) Would you describe it as funny? (c) Think about examples of humor in today's culture. What differences and similarities can you find between now and then?

24. Recognizing Ideologies How did the political ideologies of Hoover and Roosevelt affect their decision making?

CREATING A CHAPTER SUMMARY
Causes
• Inflated stock prices and uneven economy of the 1920s
• Stock market crash of 1929
• Congress passes the Hawley-Smoot tariff.
Effects
• Thousands lose their jobs, homes, farms, and other property.
• Discrimination against minorities increases.
• Loan failures, bank runs, bank failures, cuts in production, rise in unemployment
• "Hoovervilles"
• Farm distress
• Election of FDR with his promise of a "new deal"

★ **Skills Assessment**

Analyzing Political Cartoons ▶

25. This political cartoon appeared in 1931. Who is the figure at the center of the cartoon?

26. What is the crowd doing?

27. Do you think the cartoonist is criticizing Hoover or those who are blaming him? Explain.

Interpreting Data

Turn to the series of three graphs in Section 1.

28. About how many banks suspended their business in 1933?

    A about 2,000
    B about 2,300
    C about 1,500
    D about 4,000

29. Which of the following statements best summarizes the data on the unemployment graph?

    F The numbers of unemployed people peaked in 1929.
    G Unemployment was low in 1925.
    H Unemployment increased dramatically between 1929 and 1933.
    J Unemployment decreased after 1933.

30. Which of the following can you NOT tell from these graphs?

    A the percentage of Americans unemployed in 1930
    B the average monthly value of stock prices in 1932
    C the change in stock prices from 1927 to 1932
    D the total number of bank suspensions from 1925 to 1933

Applying the Chapter Skill: *Drawing Inferences*

31. Review the steps needed to draw inferences in the Skills for Life feature on page 751. Then, reread the American Biography on Dorothea Lange on page 749 and study her photographs. Taking into account what you know about the Depression, what inferences can you draw about Lange's attitude toward the Depression? Why do you think she depicts it the way she does?

ACTIVITIES

Writing to LEARN

Writing a Letter

It is 1932. You want to preserve this period in history in a letter that your grandchildren can read in the 2000s. List the main events leading up to the Depression. Include details of daily life in difficult economic times, as well as the upcoming presidential election. Note how your life has been permanently changed by the Depression. Then write a draft of your letter in which you explain your experiences and those of the people around you. Make sure you use enough detail to bring your experiences to life.

Primary Source CD-ROM

Working With Primary Sources Find additional information on the Great Depression on the *Exploring Primary Sources in U.S. History CD-ROM* and use the selection(s) provided to complete the Chapter 22 primary source activity located in the *America: Pathways to the Present* area of the following Web site.
www.phschool.com

Take It to the NET

Chapter Self-Test As a review activity, take the Chapter 22 Self-Test in the *America: Pathways to the Present* area at the Web site listed below. The questions are designed to test your understanding of the chapter content.
www.phschool.com

CRITICAL THINKING

21. Answers will vary, but students should demonstrate a knowledge of Keynesian theory and the ability to give examples from today's economy.

22. Sample answer: Yes, because even those individuals who worked hard were not able to make ends meet. The government had to intervene in people's lives in order to help them to survive.

23. (a) It is dark and sarcastic. (b) In a way. This type of humor gave people a way to laugh in spite of their misery and despair. (c) Answers will vary but should be supported by examples from today.

24. Hoover believed that government should be as unobtrusive as possible. He was hesitant to use the government to provide direct relief, even during the Depression. Roosevelt believed in social welfare programs and was willing to expand the role of government in order to help people.

SKILLS ASSESSMENT

25. President Hoover.
26. Blaming their problems on Hoover.
27. The cartoonist is criticizing both sides. The cartoon seems to be mocking the fact that Hoover is blamed for everyone's troubles, but it also shows Hoover as ineffective.
28. D
29. H
30. A
31. Students should infer that Lange felt that the Great Depression was a tragedy for America, but one that America would survive. Her depictions of Depression-era Americans are meant to show both the crisis they were facing and their perseverance.

AFTERNOON IN THE BALLPARK

Focus Have students find the meaning of each of these words in a dictionary before they begin to read: *revered, buoyant, bunting, luster, jaunty.* Ask them to think about the selection's two themes as they read: the historic opening game of the 1932 World Series and the emergence of FDR as the front runner on the presidential "playing field."

Instruct Ask students to describe what they already know about the social, political, and economic climate of the country in 1932. Write key ideas on the chalkboard. Then ask them to explain the significance to the writer of the "bright autumn afternoon" of October 1, 1932. Ask a volunteer to read aloud the last two paragraphs of the selection. Discuss the significance to the writer of seeing then-Governor Roosevelt.

Ask students to consider today's baseball heroes and their feats (for example, Mark McGwire and Sammy Sosa's 1998 shattering of Roger Maris's single-season home run record). How might they respond to seeing a famous baseball player or other sports star today?

Analyzing the Document Use this additional question to generate class discussion:

Critical Thinking: Predicting Consequences Based on the passage, which candidate do you think the people of Chicago supported in the election of 1932? *(Franklin D. Roosevelt. Fleming remarks that Hoover was booed in Chicago. Americans blamed Hoover and the Republicans for the Depression.)*

Afternoon in the Ballpark

Both the boom times of the 1920s and the hard times of the 1930s produced numerous heroes and celebrities. Thanks to advances such as radio, these national heroes were familiar to Americans all across the country. Seeing one in person was a memorable experience. In the passage below, Tom Fleming recalls the day he saw three: the President, the man who would become the next President, and the greatest baseball player of his era.

LIKE EVERY AMERICAN BOY in the twenties and thirties, I revered Babe Ruth as the greatest name in baseball. What made him come alive for me was a genuine American League baseball that my father brought home after one of his trips to New York. Ruth had fouled it off, and Dad had jumped up and caught it one-handed. "Just for you," he said. That was at Yankee Stadium, the "House that Ruth built."

Of course, I wanted to see Babe Ruth play too, but this wasn't easy. Dad and I were Cub fans. Ruth was an American Leaguer with the Yankees, so when they came to Chicago, they played the White Sox in Comiskey Park on the South Side.

In the fall of 1932 it became clear that Babe would be coming to Wrigley Field (the Cubs and Yankees had reached the World Series). It was beyond expectation that I would actually get to see those games; I hoped that perhaps I could sneak into the coach's office in the high school locker room and catch a few plays on his radio before the bell rang for afternoon classes.

One evening in September Dad came home in an unusually buoyant mood. I was doing a jigsaw puzzle at the family game table in the den. I watched him take off his suit coat and drape it deliberately over the back of his desk chair. As he unbuttoned his vest, he leaned forward and took a small envelope from his inside coat pocket.

Inside the envelope was a pair of tickets to the October 1 home opener of the World Series—the Cubs and the Yankees at Wrigley Field.

"Now you can see Babe Ruth," he said.

Our beloved Wrigley Field had been transformed for the Series, with red, white, and blue bunting draped everywhere. Temporary stands had been set up in the outfield to accommodate the huge crowd. Our seats were only six rows back from the playing field on the left-field side, between the end of the Cubs' dugout and third base.

"There's your man," Dad said, pointing to left field as we settled in. Sure enough, there he

Babe Ruth in action, 1929

764

RESOURCE DIRECTORY

Technology
AmericanHeritage® **My Brush with History**™
Videotapes *Afternoon in the Ballpark*

☑ **TEST PREPARATION**

Have students use the excerpt on these pages to answer the following question.

What is the main idea of the excerpt?

A Roosevelt was a popular governor.

B Fleming's father applauded Hoover while other spectators booed.

C Many people lost their jobs during the Depression.

D Seeing Roosevelt made Fleming realize that he was part of the larger world of politics.

was warming up with his teammates—the Bambino, the Sultan of Swat, the Colossus of Clout—Babe Ruth, all six feet two inches and 215 pounds of him.

When the players left the field, the announcer introduced President Hoover, who was in the stands for the big game. The applause was scattered, and I was shocked to hear boos. (As a Boy Scout I thought you didn't do such a thing to a President.) When Governor Franklin D. Roosevelt was introduced, there was much more applause and fewer boos. Both men were on the campaign trail for the presidential election coming up that November. If I had been politically conscious, I would have known right then that Mr. Hoover was in trouble, for it seemed most fans felt Hoover wasn't having nearly as good a year as Ruth.

Charlie Root took the mound for the Cubs. He was in trouble from the first pitch. With the first two Yankees on base on a walk and a throwing error by the shortstop Billy Jurges, Ruth lumbered up to the plate. He promptly did what he was famous for—lofted one of his patented homers out to the center field seats.

The Cubs lifted our hearts with some good hitting, especially from Kiki Cuyler, but they never seemed to get real control of the game. The score was 4 to 4 when Ruth stepped into the box at the top of the fifth inning.

RUTH CALLS HIS SHOT How lucky we were to be on the third-base side. As a left-handed batter, Ruth faced us, and we could see his every move and gesture. Root was very careful. After each strike the Babe raised his right arm, showing one finger for a strike, then two, to keep the stands posted on the duel between him and the pitcher. The crowd reacted wildly. When the count stood at 2 and 2, Ruth stepped back a bit and then pointed grandly to the outfield, making a big arc with his right hand.

Dad poked me in the ribs.

"Look at him point, son! Look at him point! He's calling a home run!"

The very air seemed to vibrate. I held my breath, digging my fingernails into my palms.

Ruth stepped back into the batter's box, ready for Root's next pitch. It came in knee-high, and the Babe connected solidly with his great swing. The crowd let out a volcanic, spontaneous gasp

of awe. Everybody knew it was gone, gone, gone as it soared high and out over the center-field score board for one of the longest homers ever hit out of Wrigley Field.

The Babe started his trip around the bases. When he rounded second and came toward us, we saw a triumphant smile on his face. Past third, he leaned over and pointed into the Cub dugout. I can only guess what he said to the Cub bench jockeys, although I probably wouldn't have known all the words then.

Root and Hartnett, the Cub battery, later denied that Ruth had called his shot or pointed. I guess that as great competitors they didn't want to give Ruth any more luster than he already had. Dad and I knew that Babe Ruth had pointed though. The Yankees went on to win, 7 to 5, and four of their runs were provided by Babe Ruth. That was the Sultan of Swat at his greatest.

As we were leaving the ballpark, a loud siren wailed just below us, and we rushed over to the ramp railing to see what was going on. Below was the big white touring car of the city greeter, and beside him on the back seat was Governor Roosevelt—gray felt hat and cigarette holder at the jaunty angle cartoonists loved to draw. For a brief moment my eyes locked with his as he looked up at the people lining the railing.

At that moment I realized I was seeing a new star about to enter a more serious arena. That day was a capsule of life. I passed from my boyhood interests to those of the greater game of politics on that bright autumn afternoon of October 1, 1932.

Source: *American Heritage* magazine, November 1990.

Understanding Primary Sources

1. What was the public's reaction when President Herbert Hoover was introduced?
2. Why was this reaction particularly significant in 1932?

American Heritage®
MY BRUSH WITH **HISTORY**™
⬛ Videotapes

For more information about life during the Great Depression and the 1932 election, view "Afternoon in the Ballpark."

765

Chapter 23 Planning Guide
Resource Manager

	CORE INSTRUCTION	READING/SKILLS
Chapter-Level Resources	**Teaching Resources** • Pacing Charts booklet • Block Scheduling booklet **Resource Pro® CD-ROM**, Ch. 23 **Prentice Hall Presentation Pro CD-ROM**, Ch. 23 **www.phschool.com** • eTeach	**Guided Reading Audiotapes (English/Spanish)** **Student Edition on Audio CD**, Ch. 23 **Social Studies Skills Tutor CD-ROM** **Color Transparencies**, B13, D9
1 Forging a New Deal 1. Explore Franklin and Eleanor Roosevelt's roles in restoring the nation's hope. 2. Learn about the major New Deal programs that were created in the first hundred days, and find out about some of FDR's key players in these programs. 3. Discover what caused the New Deal to falter. 4. Review the key goals and accomplishments of the Second New Deal. 5. Interpret the significance of the outcome of the 1936 election.	**Teaching Resources** **Units 7/8 booklet** • Section 1 Quiz, p. 35 **Learning Styles Lesson Plans booklet**, p. 48	**Guided Reading and Review booklet**, p. 93 **Guide to the Essentials**, p. 117 **Learning with Documents booklet**, pp. 28, 62 **Section Reading Support Transparencies**
2 The New Deal's Critics 1. Learn about some of the New Deal's shortcomings and limitations. 2. Discover the chief complaints of FDR's critics inside and outside of politics. 3. See how the court-packing fiasco harmed FDR's reputation.	**Teaching Resources** **Units 7/8 booklet** • Section 2 Quiz, p. 36 **Learning Styles Lesson Plans booklet**, p. 49	**Guided Reading and Review booklet**, p. 94 **Guide to the Essentials**, p. 118 **Skills for Life booklet**, p. 25 **Section Reading Support Transparencies**
3 Last Days of the New Deal 1. Learn about factors that led to the recession of 1937 and about the Roosevelt administration's response to this situation. 2. Find out about triumphs and setbacks experienced by unions during the New Deal era. 3. Discover some effects of the New Deal on American culture. 4. See what lasting effects can be attributed to the New Deal.	**Teaching Resources** **Units 7/8 booklet** • Section 3 Quiz, p. 37	**Guided Reading and Review booklet**, p. 95 **Guide to the Essentials**, p. 119 **Section Reading Support Transparencies**

ENRICHMENT/PRE-AP

Prentice Hall United States History Video Collection™
www.phschool.com
- Section Activities, Virtual Field Trip, Chapter Activities, Current Events Online

Great Debates booklet, pp. 16, 18
American History Block Scheduling Support
Nystrom *Atlas of Our Country,* pp. 34–35
Sounds of an Era Audio CD
Exploring Primary Sources in U.S. History CD-ROM

Biography, Literature, and Comparing Primary Sources booklet, pp. 71, 141–142
Sounds of an Era Audio CD

Biography, Literature, and Comparing Primary Sources booklet, p. 28
Sounds of an Era Audio CD
American Pathways Thematic Posters

ASSESSMENT

PRENTICE HALL ASSESSMENT SYSTEM

Core Assessment
ExamView® Test Bank, Ch. 23
ExamView® Test Bank CD-ROM, Ch. 23

Standardized Test Preparation
Diagnose and Prescribe
Diagnostic Tests for High School Social Studies Skills

Review and Reteach
Review Book for U.S. History

Practice and Assess
Test-taking Strategies With Transparencies
Test-taking Strategies Posters
Test Prep Book for U.S. History
Alternative Assessment Handbook
Document-Based Assessment

Teaching Resources
Units 7/8 booklet
- Section Quizzes, pp. 35–37
- Chapter Tests, pp. 38, 41

www.phschool.com Ch. 23 Self-Test

AmericanHeritage RESOURCES

From the Archives of American Heritage®, p. 770
AmericanHeritage® My Brush with History™ Videotapes
www.americanheritage.com

iTEXT

Don't miss the exclusive interactive version of this textbook on the Web and on CD-ROM.

Chapter 23 Planning Guide
In Your Classroom

CUSTOMIZE FOR INDIVIDUAL NEEDS

Gifted and Talented

Teacher's Edition
• Customize for Gifted and Talented, pp. 771, 787

Teaching Resources
• Biography, Literature, and Comparing Primary Sources booklet, pp. 28, 71, 141–142

Technology
• Exploring Primary Sources in U.S. History CD-ROM *First Inaugural Address, Franklin D. Roosevelt*

ESL

Teacher's Edition
• Customize for ESL, pp. 773, 781

Teaching Resources
• Guided Reading and Review booklet, pp. 93–95
• Guide to the Essentials (English/Spanish), Chapter 23

Technology
• Student Edition on Audio CD, Chapter 23
• Guided Reading Audiotapes (English/Spanish), Chapter 23
• Section Reading Support Transparencies

Less Proficient Readers

Teacher's Edition
• Customize for Less Proficient Readers, p. 779

Teaching Resources
• Guided Reading and Review booklet, pp. 93–95
• Guide to the Essentials (English/Spanish), Chapter 23

Technology
• Student Edition on Audio CD, Chapter 23
• Guided Reading Audiotapes (English/Spanish), Chapter 23
• Section Reading Support Transparencies

Less Proficient Writers

Teacher's Edition
• Customize for Less Proficient Writers, p. 769

Teaching Resources
• Guided Reading and Review booklet, pp. 93–95
• Guide to the Essentials (English/Spanish), Chapter 23

Technology
• Student Edition on Audio CD, Chapter 23
• Guided Reading Audiotapes (English/Spanish), Chapter 23
• Section Reading Support Transparencies

TEACHER'S EDITION INDEX

CHAPTER 23 – PACING SUGGESTIONS

For 90-minute Blocks

• Teach sections 1 and 2 using Transparencies B13 and D9, and the Recent Scholarship notes on pages 771, 779, and 782 for class discussions.

Running Out of Time?

If you are running short on time to cover this chapter, consider the following options:

• Use the Prentice Hall Presentation Pro CD-ROM to create an outline for this chapter.

• Use the Section Summaries for Chapter 23, from **Guide to the Essentials (English/Spanish)**.

1 Forging a New Deal

Connecting with Economics
Read students the following statements: "In time, the REA brought power to 98 percent of U.S. farms. Demand for electric appliances grew, benefiting manufacturing companies and local merchants." Have students locate a supply and demand diagram and use it as the basis for an illustrated diagram that shows how rural electrification benefited both businesses and consumers. You may wish to discuss with students how these events might be used as an argument to convince doubters that government action can be beneficial to business. **(Visual/Spatial; Logical/Mathematical)**

2 The New Deal's Critics

Connecting with Economics
Remind students that in the 1940s, an African American domestic worker might work 14-hour days and earn only $6.50 per week. Domestic workers were not covered by the minimum wage. Have students research which workers currently are covered by the minimum wage law and which are not. Similarly, students might look into who is eligible to receive unemployment benefits when out of work and Social Security payments upon retirement. Have students present a written report on what they learn. **(Verbal/Linguistic)**

3 Last Days of the New Deal

Connecting with Culture
Point out that among the artworks completed under the WPA program were a number of murals, which were often painted in such public buildings as post offices and schools. The works frequently represented subjects of social concern. Many of the New Deal muralists were inspired by the work of Mexican muralists José Orozco and Diego Rivera. Have students design a mural for their school that deals with subjects of concern to society today. Students can find photographs of original New Deal murals in various reference sources, as well as on the Internet. **(Visual/Spatial)**

Chapter 23

The New Deal

(1933–1941)

INTRODUCING THE CHAPTER

President Roosevelt's New Deal—the name given to the vast collection of programs and policies formulated to combat the Depression—proved to be only partially successful at ending the nation's misery. But though critics were quick to point to the New Deal's many failures, it was hard to argue against its resounding success in bringing hope to a weary nation. Moreover, the New Deal influenced the social, political, and cultural life and attitudes of Americans in ways that are still apparent today.

TIME LINE ACTIVITY

To provide students with practice in using the time line, ask questions such as these:

1. Who was a popular opponent of FDR and the New Deal? *(Father Coughlin, whose radio show attracted up to 10 million listeners)*

2. What important project was completed in 1937? *(The Golden Gate Bridge in San Francisco)*

3. Name an event that took place in 1938 and foreshadowed World War II. *(Germany invaded and annexed Austria.)*

Chapter

23

The New Deal

(1933–1941)

SECTION 1   Forging a New Deal
SECTION 2   The New Deal's Critics
SECTION 3   Last Days of the New Deal

Campaigning in 1932, Roosevelt greets a miner in Elm Grove, West Virginia.

Union poster from an oil painting by Ben Shahn, late 1930s

1933
FDR's New Deal is launched, creating new legislation and several major federal agencies.

1934
The American Liberty League is founded. Father Coughlin attracts millions of listeners to his radio show.

1935
As the Depression continues, FDR launches the Second New Deal. The Social Security system is created.

1936
Workers stage a sit-down strike at automobile plants in Michigan.

American Events

Presidential Terms: Franklin D. Roosevelt 1933–1945

1932   •   **1934**   •   **1936**

World Events

Germany opens the first concentration camps.
1933

Communists begin the 6,000-mile "Long March" across China.
1934

The Spanish Civil War begins.
1936

eTeach

Be sure to check out this month's online discussion with a Master Teacher. Go to **www.phschool.com**.

RESOURCE DIRECTORY

Teaching Resources
Pacing Charts booklet
Block Scheduling booklet, p. 24
Units 7/8 booklet
- Chapter Summary, p. 34

Technology
Guided Reading Audiotapes (English/Spanish), Ch. 23
Student Edition on Audio CD, Ch. 23
Sounds of an Era Audio CD *Will Rogers April 30, 1933 recording* (time: one minute, 30 seconds)
Prentice Hall United States Video Collection™ Volume 18, *The Great Depression and the New Deal*
Prentice Hall Presentation Pro CD-ROM, Ch. 23
Resource Pro® CD-ROM
Social Studies Skills Tutor CD-ROM
Companion Web site, www.phschool.com

P.W.A. IN ACTION

Transportation
Trans-Mountain highway to Glacier Park

Bonneville Dam
Washington-Oregon border

Indian School
For Sioux in South Dakota

Low-rent Housing
Indianapolis, Indiana

Conservation Project
Tree planting in New York State

Rebuilt Schools
After earthquake in Los Angeles

Art Museum
Wichita, Kansas

Aircraft Carriers
Built in Newport News, Virginia

Navigational Beacons
For air traffic from Washington, D.C., to Nashville, Tennessee

Flood Control
Along Rio Grande in Texas

State Hospital
Saline County, Arkansas

Sea Walls
Storm protection along Florida coast

Pacific Ocean

Atlantic Ocean

Gulf of Mexico

OFF RELIEF ROLLS ON TO PAY ROLLS
A map showing how the Public Works program is building a greater nation, making jobs for men and factories. How it conserves resources and harnesses rivers. How finer transportation is being created and land saved for better use.

Adapted from New Deal-era P.W.A. map

1937

San Francisco's Golden Gate Bridge is completed. FDR attempts to "pack" the Supreme Court. The U.S. economy collapses into recession again.

1941

James Agee's *Let Us Now Praise Famous Men* is published.

The Wizard of Oz (1939) delighted Depression-era audiences.

1938

The Sino-Japanese War breaks out.
1937

1940

Germany invades and annexes Austria.
1938

1942

The United States enters World War II.
1941

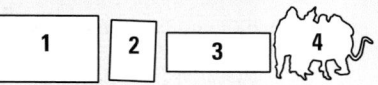

P.W.A. in Action

Activating Prior Knowledge What is an example of a public works program that improved ground transportation? *(The Trans-Mountain highway to Glacier Park.)*

Previewing How did the public works programs help boost Americans' morale? *(The programs provided jobs and improved the country by providing housing, improving transportation, harnessing energy, and building schools and museums.)*

BACKGROUND
About the Pictures

1 2 3 4

1. When accepting the Democratic Party's nomination in 1932, Roosevelt said, "I pledge you, I pledge myself, to a new deal for the American people."

2. Shahn was a painter and graphic artist who used his artwork to champion important social and political causes.

3. Constructed under the supervision of Joseph B. Strauss, this enormous suspension bridge is 4,200 feet wide at its main span and has "earthquake-proof" foundations.

4. Written by L. Frank Baum, the book *Wonderful Wizard of Oz* was first made into a musical stage performance in 1901 and later became the cinematic adventure beloved by children of all generations.

i TEXT

Don't miss the exclusive interactive version of this textbook on the Web and on CD-ROM.

BIBLIOGRAPHY

For the Teacher

Allan, Frederick Lewis. *Since Yesterday: The 1930s in America, September 3, 1929–September 3, 1939.* HarperCollins, 1986. (A close-up view of the era by a respected magazine editor.)

Steinbeck, John. *The Harvest Gypsies: On the Road to* The Grapes of Wrath. Heyday Books, 1996. (A collection of newspaper articles written by Steinbeck in 1936, based on interviews with workers in federal migrant labor camps.)

For the Student

Leuchtenberg, William E. *Franklin D. Roosevelt and the New Deal, 1932–1940.* HarperCollins, 1963. (An introduction to the New Deal.)

Warren, Robert Penn. *All the King's Men.* Harvest Books, 1996. (A fictionalized account of the life of Huey Long.)

Section 1

Forging a New Deal

SECTION OBJECTIVES

1. Explore Franklin and Eleanor Roosevelt's roles in restoring the nation's hope.

2. Learn about the major New Deal programs that were created in the first hundred days, and find out about some of FDR's key players in these programs.

3. Discover what caused the New Deal to falter.

4. Review the key goals and accomplishments of the second New Deal.

5. Interpret the significance of the outcome of the 1936 election.

BELLRINGER

Warm-Up Activity Have students imagine a situation in which all members of their household were out of work, had no hope of finding a job, and had no government benefits. Ask them how they would want their government leaders to respond.

Activating Prior Knowledge Ask students to list some current government programs that are designed to help families that are out of work.

READING STRATEGY

Have students write two column headings on a sheet of paper: *New Deal* and *Second New Deal*. As they read, have them list details from the section in the appropriate column, note the significance of each detail, and evaluate the effectiveness of New Deal measures in ending the Depression.

CAPTION ANSWERS

Viewing History (a) Republican public officeholders put out of work when Roosevelt, a Democrat, took office. They are looking for work. (b) The cartoonist is pointing out the irony that the failure of Hoover, a Republican, to ease severe unemployment at the start of the Great Depression caused him and those in his administration to lose their own jobs.

Section 1

Forging a New Deal

READING FOCUS

- How did Franklin and Eleanor Roosevelt work to restore the nation's hope?
- What major New Deal programs were created in the first hundred days, and who were some of FDR's key players in these programs?
- What caused the New Deal to falter?
- What were the key goals and accomplishments of the Second New Deal?
- What did the outcome of the 1936 election indicate?

MAIN IDEA

President Roosevelt sought to end the Great Depression through the federal programs of the New Deal.

KEY TERMS

New Deal
hundred days
public works program
Civilian Conservation Corps (CCC)
Agricultural Adjustment Administration (AAA)
Tennessee Valley Authority (TVA)
Second New Deal
Wagner Act
closed shop
Social Security system

TAKING NOTES

As you read, fill in the chart below with key goals of the first and second phases of the New Deal.

```
        Key Goals of the New Deal
    ┌───────────────┴───────────────┐
The First                      The Second
Hundred Days                   Hundred Days
    │                               │
• Restore the                  • Pass new
  nation's hope                  labor laws
•                              •
•                              •
```

Setting the Scene A desperate nation anticipating Franklin Delano Roosevelt's "new deal" for America had to wait an agonizingly long time for it to begin. Presidential elections took place in November, but the inauguration of the victor did not occur until the following March 4—a full four-month wait. The lengthy time interval had made sense in earlier days, when vote counting took longer and the President-elect often needed more time to travel to the capital.

By 1933, however, improvements in communication and transportation had eliminated the need for such a long wait, and the disadvantages of the delay were abundantly clear. Hoover remained in office as a "lame duck"—a leader whose authority is weakened because he or she is about to leave office. Meanwhile, the Depression deepened.

The situation prompted Congress to pass the Twentieth Amendment—nicknamed the "lame-duck amendment"—which changed the date of the inaugural to January 20. Ratified in early 1933, the amendment did not take effect until the next election. Roosevelt, therefore, became the last President to be inaugurated in March. While the nation waited, FDR prepared for what would be the biggest change in the federal government since its inception.

Restoring the Nation's Hope

As he prepared plans for rescuing the economy, FDR, along with the new First Lady, Eleanor, went about restoring Americans' sense of hope. Building public confidence in the future was essential to calming panic and creating support for the President's plans.

A test of the new administration's approach to crises came shortly after he took office. World War I veterans staged a second Bonus March on Washington. This time, the White House provided campsites for the veterans. Even more astounding, Eleanor Roosevelt paid them a visit.

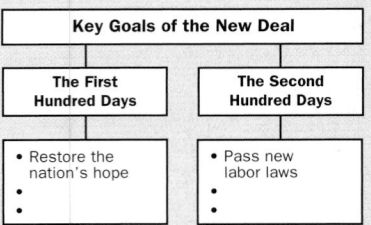

VIEWING HISTORY Whenever a presidential administration changes hands from one political party to another, many members of the old administration lose their government jobs. **Drawing Inferences** *(a) Who are the elephants in this cartoon, and what are they doing? (b) What point is the cartoonist trying to make?*

768   Chapter 23 • *The New Deal*

RESOURCE DIRECTORY

Teaching Resources
Learning Styles Lesson Plans booklet, p. 48
Guided Reading and Review booklet, p. 93

Other Print Resources
Nystrom *Atlas of Our Country* *People on the Move,* pp. 34–35

Technology
Section Reading Support Transparencies
Guided Reading Audiotapes (English/Spanish), Ch. 23

Student Edition on Audio CD, Ch. 23
Sounds of an Era Audio CD *President Roosevelt's First Inauguration Speech, 1933 recording* (time: 50 seconds); *President Roosevelt's First "Fireside Chat," March 12, 1933* (time: 45 seconds)
Exploring Primary Sources in U.S. History CD-ROM *First Inaugural Address, Franklin D. Roosevelt*
Prentice Hall Presentation Pro CD-ROM, Ch. 23
Companion Web site, www.phschool.com

When she walked up to a group of marchers, "They looked at me curiously and one of them asked my name and what I wanted," she recalled later. By the time she left, the veterans were waving and calling out, "Good-bye and good luck to you!" The First Lady told reporters afterward how polite the marchers had been. By this act, she demonstrated compassion and soothed popular fears about renewed radical agitation.

FDR, in his First Inaugural Address, March 4, 1933, told Americans, "The only thing we have to fear is fear itself." The first Sunday after taking office, Roosevelt spoke to the nation over the radio in the first of what became regular "fireside chats." His easy manner and confidence helped renew people's hopes for the future.

In campaigning for the White House, FDR had promised "bold, persistent experimentation." No one knew exactly what that meant—only that someone was going to do something. As reporter Arthur Krock noted, Washington "welcomes the 'New Deal,' even though it is not sure what the New Deal is going to be."

Even Roosevelt himself had no sure plan for government under his leadership. Nevertheless, the new President's optimism and willingness to experiment won him the support of the American people. He had promised "a new deal for the American people," and he kept his word. The term **New Deal** came to refer to the relief, recovery, and reform programs of FDR's administration that were aimed at combating the Great Depression.

The First Hundred Days

From his inauguration in March through June 1933, a period known as the **hundred days,** Roosevelt pushed program after program through Congress to provide relief, create jobs, and stimulate economic recovery. He based some of these programs on the work of federal agencies that had controlled the economy during World War I and on agencies set up by states to ease the Depression. Former Progressives figured prominently, inspiring New Deal legislation or administering programs.

Stabilizing Financial Institutions FDR's first step was to restore public confidence in the nation's banks. On March 5, 1933, he ordered all banks to close for the next four days. He then pushed Congress to pass the Emergency Banking Act, which was approved on March 9. The act authorized the government to inspect the financial health of all banks.

Many Americans had been terrified by the prospect of losing all their savings in a bank failure. By his actions, FDR hoped to assure the American people that their banks would not fail. Indeed, government inspectors found that most banks were healthy, and two thirds had reopened by March 15.

After the brief "bank holiday," Americans regained confidence in the banking system. They began to put more money back into their accounts than they took out. These deposits allowed banks to make loans that would help stimulate the economy. Congress increased public confidence further by passing the Glass-Steagall Banking Act of 1933. It established a Federal Deposit Insurance Corporation (FDIC) to insure bank deposits.

Sounds of an Era

Listen to excerpts from FDR's First Inaugural Address, one of his fireside chats, and other sounds from the New Deal era.

VIEWING HISTORY A Detroit, Michigan, bank opens under a new charter following the "bank holiday" ordered by FDR. **Drawing Inferences** (a) Why do you think the bank is so crowded? (b) How would you react to the bank closings if you were a bank customer in March 1933?

LESSON PLAN

Focus Explain that FDR fulfilled his promise to take action to combat the Depression. Though the New Deal suffered setbacks, FDR's attitude and programs uplifted the nation.

Instruct Explain that the Depression had deeply demoralized the nation by the time FDR became President. Ask students to name the programs FDR created. What were the problems with this New Deal? How did the Second New Deal address the shortcomings of the first one?

Discuss FDR's choice of advisers and policymakers. How did FDR's political appointments reflect his commitment to change? Ask how Eleanor Roosevelt redefined the role of First Lady.

Assess/Reteach Ask students to discuss the underlying assumption of the New Deal: that government can and should help restore economic stability through creation of jobs and funding of economic initiatives. Do students agree or disagree with that basic premise?

ACTIVITY
Connecting with Government

Ask students to discuss ways in which the government can build and maintain public confidence. Encourage students to consider why it is important for the government to win the public's trust and what happens when the government loses the public's trust. Have students list some current government programs that create positive feelings among the public. Make sure students understand the changes in the role of government over time. **(Verbal/Linguistic)**

CAPTION ANSWERS

Viewing History (a) Many of the people in the photograph probably showed up simply to reassure themselves that the bank was indeed open again and functioning properly. Some customers undoubtedly came in order to withdraw their savings. However, there were probably some in the photograph who actually deposited money that day. (b) Answers might mention that such an occurrence would be very frightening to experience. A bank closing might make one reluctant to ever put any more money into a bank.

CUSTOMIZE FOR ...

Less Proficient Writers

To construct an outline of the section, have students first list each boldfaced title in the section and then write a sentence or phrase about each title.

During the first 100 days of FDR's administration, many federal programs passed through Congress to provide relief, create jobs, and stimulate the economy. Stage a classroom discussion in which students evaluate the effectiveness of New Deal measures in ending the Great Depression. To help students understand these New Deal programs, have them create public works programs within their school. Divide students into small groups to develop a public works project. Each group should identify the goal of the project, the people who would qualify to work on it, and the way in which it would affect the school community. **(Logical/Mathematical)**

From the Archives of
AmericanHeritage®

About the Presidents

Franklin Delano Roosevelt (1933–1945) used two forms of public communication that contributed to his administration's success. First, he met with the press about twice a week. These free-and-easy, back-and-forth sessions put his achievements and plans in the headlines. Even more important were his radio "fireside chats." On these occasions, Roosevelt talked about his programs and purposes to the nation. His soothing voice inspired confidence. Source: Wilson Sullivan, "Franklin Delano Roosevelt," *The American Heritage® Pictorial History of the Presidents of the United States,* vol. 2, 1968.

Congress also moved to correct problems that had led to the stock market crash. The Federal Securities Act, passed in May 1933, required companies to provide information about their finances if they offered stock for sale. The next year Congress set up the Securities and Exchange Commission (SEC) to regulate the stock market. Congress also gave the Federal Reserve Board power to regulate the purchase of stock on margin.

In July 1933, Roosevelt took a further step to stimulate the economy. He decreased the value of U.S. currency by taking it off the gold standard. He hoped that this action would raise the prices of farm products and other goods. He also hoped that a devalued American currency would stimulate export trade. FDR's move pleased many in Congress, who thought it would make paying off New Deal debts easier. Others, including his budget director, Lewis Douglas, thought it was "the end of Western civilization."

Providing Relief and Creating Jobs   FDR's next step was to help overburdened local relief agencies. He persuaded Congress in May to establish a Federal Emergency Relief Administration (FERA), which sent funds to these agencies. Harry Hopkins, a former settlement worker and a longtime Roosevelt friend and advisor, directed this agency. Hopkins professed a strong belief in helping people find work:

> 66 Give a man a dole [handout], and you save his body and destroy his spirit. Give him a job and pay him an assured wage and you save both the body and the spirit. 99
>
> —FERA administrator Harry Hopkins

To help people who were out of work, the FERA also put federal money into **public works programs,** government-funded projects to build public facilities. One of these programs, set up in November 1933, was the Civil Works Administration (CWA). The CWA put the unemployed to work building or improving roads, parks, airports, and other facilities. The agency was a tremendous morale booster to its 4 million employees. As a former insurance salesman

VIEWING HISTORY This worker for the Civilian Conservation Corps (right) is planting seedlings in Montana. The poster below proclaims the benefits of CCC labor. **Drawing Conclusions** If you had been a young person during the Depression, what effect might these images have had on you? Why?

CAPTION ANSWERS

Viewing History These images would undoubtedly have inspired hope for Depression-era youths who would be given the opportunity to earn wages for performing interesting, useful, and healthy outdoor work. These workers would also receive free lodging and meals—in and of themselves powerful inducements for a generation of young people who often found it difficult to get enough to eat.

RESOURCE DIRECTORY

Teaching Resources
Learning with Documents booklet (Primary Source Activity) *A Fireside Chat: The NIRA,* p. 28
Great Debates booklet (Great Debates) *Who Is Responsible for the Elderly and Unemployed?* p. 18

NOTABLE PRESIDENTS
Franklin Delano Roosevelt

"The only thing we have to fear is fear itself."
—First Inaugural Address, 1933

Courage in times of crisis was perhaps Franklin Delano Roosevelt's greatest strength. His first crisis was personal rather than political. In 1921, Roosevelt was stricken with polio, which paralyzed his legs and threatened to destroy what had been a promising political career. (Roosevelt had been the Democratic vice-presidential candidate the year before.)

Roosevelt returned to politics in 1928, running for governor of New York. Despite having to be helped or carried onto podiums to speak, Roosevelt campaigned energetically and won the election. Four years later he ran for President. In a campaign dominated by the gloom of the Great Depression, FDR's confidence helped bring him victory.

As President, Roosevelt fought the Depression through what he called "bold, persistent experimentation." "It is common sense to take a method and try it," he explained. "If it fails, admit it frankly and try another. But above all, try something." This commitment to action gave Americans much-needed hope.

Roosevelt showed a similar commitment as commander in chief during World War II. After the attack on Pearl Harbor in 1941, Roosevelt rallied a shocked nation and oversaw the creation of the greatest

32nd President 1933–1945

military force ever seen up to that time. Elected President for a record fourth time in 1944, Roosevelt died in April 1945, just months before the victorious end of the war.

Connecting to Today
Should government programs to help the elderly and the poor be temporary responses to crises such as the Great Depression, or should such programs be permanent? Defend your position.

Take It to the NET Biography To read more about Franklin Delano Roosevelt, visit the links provided in the *America: Pathways to the Present* area at the following Web site. **www.phschool.com**

---

from Alabama remarked, "When I got that [CWA identification] card, it was the biggest day in my whole life. At last I could say, 'I've got a job.'"

The **Civilian Conservation Corps (CCC)** became FDR's favorite program. Established in March 1933, the CCC put more than 2.5 million young, unmarried men to work maintaining forests, beaches, and parks. CCC workers earned only $30 a month, but they lived in camps free of charge and received food, medical care, and job training. Eleanor Roosevelt persuaded the CCC to fund similar programs for young women.

Public works programs also helped Native Americans. John Collier, FDR's commissioner of Indian Affairs, used New Deal funds and Native American workers to build schools, hospitals, and irrigation systems. The Indian Reorganization Act of 1934 ended the sale of tribal lands begun under the Dawes Act (1887) and restored some lands to Indian owners.

Regulating the Economy The sharp decline of industrial prices in the early 1930s had caused many business failures and much unemployment. The National Industrial Recovery Act (NIRA) of June 1933 sought to bolster those prices. The NIRA established the National Recovery Administration (NRA), which set out to balance the unstable economy through extensive planning.

This planning took the form of industry-wide codes to spell out fair business practices. The federal codes regulated wages, restraining wage competition. They controlled working conditions, production, and prices, and set a minimum wage. They gave organized labor collective bargaining rights, which allowed workers to negotiate as a group with employers. NRA officials wrote some of the codes, and they negotiated the details of some codes with the affected businesses. Many codes, however, were drawn up by the largest companies in an

VIEWING HISTORY The National Recovery Administration (NRA) attempted to stabilize the economy by regulating business practices.

Connecting with Economics

Have students find out about local or regional projects, such as bridges or buildings, that were carried out by the Public Works Administration (PWA) or the Works Progress Administration (WPA). Suggest that students contact your local or state public works department for information. If possible, encourage students to bring in photos and other pertinent information about these projects. Have students share their findings, including how many people worked on the project, how long it took them to complete it, and how much they were paid. **(Verbal/Linguistic)**

BACKGROUND

A Diverse Nation

In the late 1920s, farming was still a way of life for many Americans. In 1929 two-fifths of the country's citizens lived in rural places. (The U.S. Census defined *rural* as any place with fewer than 2,500 inhabitants.) One-quarter of the country's jobs were related to agriculture. When a worldwide agricultural depression began in 1926, many Americans were affected, especially those in the cotton belt—the area going west from South Carolina to Texas—and those in the wheat belt—the area running south from Minnesota and North Dakota to Kansas and Oklahoma. When the financial crisis struck at the end of the decade, farmers were ill prepared to cope.

Focus on GEOGRAPHY

Florida's Overseas Highway: A New Deal Project Like a string of pearls, the Florida Keys dangle from the tip of Florida out into the Gulf of Mexico. In the early 1900s, the Florida East Coast Railroad connected the mainland to the popular island of Key West. But in 1935, the strongest hurricane ever recorded in the Western Hemisphere smacked into the Keys with winds of up to 250 miles an hour, destroying the railroad. The Public Works Administration stepped in with a $3.6 million loan that largely financed the construction of a highway over the old railroad bed. Officially opened on July 4, 1938, the 110-mile-long Overseas Highway is the longest overwater road in the world. Part of U.S. Highway 1, it links the Keys with 42 bridges. FDR celebrated this engineering feat by driving the route from Miami to Key West in 1939.

industry. This practice pleased businesses but drew criticism from people concerned that industry influence would bias the codes against workers.

For a brief time, the codes stopped the tailspin of industrial prices. But by the fall of 1933, when higher wages went into effect, prices rose, too. Consumers stopped buying. The cycle of rising production and falling consumption returned, and many more businesses failed, causing more unemployment. Businesses complained that the codes were too complicated and the NRA's control was too rigid.

To this day, one of the most visible parts of the NIRA's efforts is the work carried out by its Public Works Administration (PWA). Directed by Secretary of the Interior Harold Ickes, the PWA launched projects ranging from the Grand Coulee Dam on the Columbia River in Washington State, to New York City's Triborough Bridge, to the causeway that connects Key West to the Florida mainland.

Assisting Homeowners and Farmers The Depression caused many middle-income homeowners to fall behind in paying their mortgages. The Home Owners' Loan Corporation (HOLC) refinanced mortgages— that is, changed the terms of the mortgages—to make the payments more manageable. Between June 1933 and June 1936, the HOLC made about 1 million low-interest loans. Even with these low-interest-rate loans, however, many owners lost their homes because they could not pay their mortgages.

The National Housing Act of 1934 established the Federal Housing Administration (FHA), a government-owned corporation. The FHA, which exists today, was created to improve housing standards and conditions, to insure mortgages, and to stabilize the mortgage market.

Many farmers were losing their homes and their land because of the low prices they received for their products. The **Agricultural Adjustment Administration (AAA),** set up in May 1933, tried to raise farm prices through subsidies, or government financial assistance. The AAA used proceeds from a new tax to pay farmers *not* to raise certain crops and livestock. Lower production, it was hoped, would cause prices to rise.

Under this program, some farmers plowed under crops that were already growing. Many Americans could not understand how the federal government could encourage the destruction of food while so many people were hungry.

The TVA One public works project proved especially popular. The **Tennessee Valley Authority (TVA),** created in May 1933, helped farmers and created jobs in one of the country's least developed regions. By reactivating a hydroelectric power facility started during World War I, the TVA provided cheap electric power (in cooperation with the Rural Electrification Administration), flood control, and recreational opportunities to the entire Tennessee River valley, as shown on the map on the next page.

Key Players in the New Deal

Roosevelt surrounded himself with eager and hard-working advisors. Some became members of the Cabinet or, like Harry Hopkins, headed one of the new agencies. Columbia University Professors Raymond Moley, Adolf A. Berle, and Rexford G. Tugwell became the three key members of FDR's so-called "brain trust," an informal group of intellectuals who helped draft policies.

772   Chapter 23 • *The New Deal*

RESOURCE DIRECTORY

Teaching Resources
Great Debates booklet (Great Debates) *Should the Federal Government Interfere in Local Matters?,* p. 16

Other Print Resources
American History Block Scheduling Support *Alphabet Soup: New Deal Legislation,* found in the Prosperity, Depression, and War folder, includes interdisciplinary lesson suggestions and activities for Geography and History, Primary Sources, Biography, and Literature.

Historical Outline Map Book *Tennessee Valley Authority,* p. 63

Technology
Color Transparencies *Cause-and-Effect Charts,* D9

RESOURCE PRO **Primary Source Activity**
Providing Emergency Relief, found on Resource Pro, uses excerpts from Frances Perkins's *The Roosevelt I Knew* to demonstrate her impressions of the New Deal President.

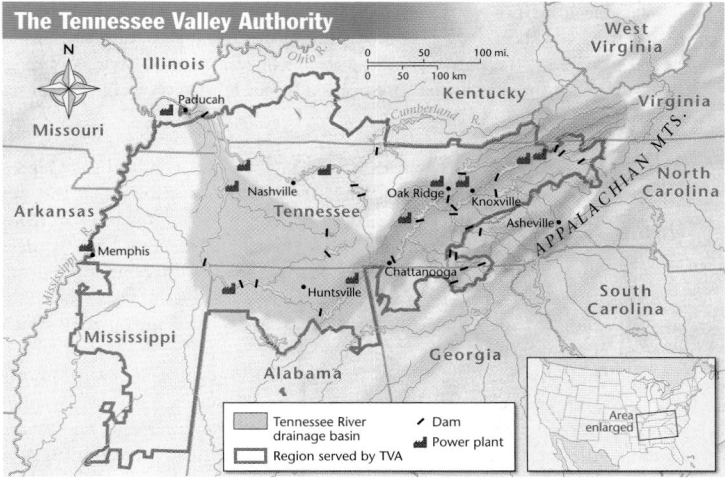

The Tennessee Valley Authority

Legend:
- Tennessee River drainage basin
- Region served by TVA
- Dam
- Power plant

MAP SKILLS The massive TVA project combined the activities of many government agencies to control flooding of the Tennessee River, provide hydroelectric power and irrigation for farms, improve navigation, and provide recreation. The photograph below shows the interior of a dam in Norris, Tennessee. **Regions** *(a) Which states benefited from the TVA? (b) What formed the boundary of TVA activity in the East?*

READING CHECK
What historic appointments did FDR make to his administration?

Groundbreaking Appointments

Roosevelt was the first President ever to appoint a woman to a Cabinet post. Frances Perkins, a former Progressive who had headed the New York State Industrial Commission, became Secretary of Labor. She held this job until 1945. Perkins successfully pressed for laws that would help both wage earners and the unemployed. Perkins was one of more than two dozen women who held key New Deal positions.

FDR's administration also broke new ground by hiring African Americans in more than a hundred policymaking posts. One of Roosevelt's key appointees, Mary McLeod Bethune, held the highest position of any African American woman in the New Deal. Bethune was a former elementary school teacher, a college president, and the founder of the National Council of Negro Women. She entered government service with a reputation as one of the country's most influential spokespersons for African American concerns.

Appointed director of the Division of Negro Affairs of the National Youth Administration (NYA) in 1936, Bethune advised FDR on programs that aided African Americans. In the process, she increased her level of influence. She forged a united stand among black officeholders by organizing a Federal Council on Negro Affairs. This unofficial group, known as the "black Cabinet," met weekly to hammer out priorities and increase African American support for the New Deal.

Eleanor Roosevelt

Among FDR's most important colleagues was his wife, Eleanor. She threw herself into supporting the New Deal and traveled widely for her husband, whose disability made traveling difficult. She reported to him on conditions in the country and on the effects of his programs. At times, the First Lady took stands that embarrassed her husband. For example, in 1938, she attended a Birmingham, Alabama, meeting of the Southern Conference for Human Welfare, an interracial group. She knew she was expected to obey local Jim Crow laws that required blacks and whites to sit on opposite sides of the auditorium. In protest, she sat in the center of the aisle, between the divided races. Her act received wide publicity, and no one missed its symbolism.

Connecting with Citizenship

Tell students to explore the interests and accomplishments of a recent First Lady. As students do their research, have them consider the following questions: What kinds of issues did she address and how? How did the public receive her efforts? How assertive can a First Lady be in pursuing her own national agenda? Invite students to share their findings in an oral report. **(Verbal/Linguistic)**

BACKGROUND

The First Lady

Eleanor Roosevelt was personally responsible for persuading Harry Hopkins to create a women's division within the Federal Emergency Relief Administration (FERA). And in late 1933, Mrs. Roosevelt sponsored a White House Conference on the Emergency Needs of Women. By spring 1934, more than 300,000 women—more than 50 percent of those who qualified for relief—were employed on various public works projects. At the same time, these women were usually paid less than men.

BIOGRAPHY

Anna Eleanor Roosevelt, a niece of Theodore Roosevelt, was born in New York City on October 11, 1884. A member of a wealthy family, Eleanor attended private schools. In 1905, she married her distant cousin Franklin, and they had six children.

Eleanor Roosevelt 1884–1962

During World War I, Eleanor Roosevelt joined the war effort as a volunteer for the Red Cross. After the war, she became involved in social and political reforms. In 1922, she joined the Women's Trade Union League and became a leader in the New York State Democratic Party.

Eleanor Roosevelt reshaped the role of First Lady. Besides traveling widely to observe the effects of the New Deal on Americans, she held her own press conferences at the White House, which were for women correspondents only. She lectured widely, and in 1935, she started a newspaper column called "My Day." She used the column to drum up support for the New Deal.

Within a year after Franklin's death in 1945, Eleanor gained further admiration as a delegate to the United Nations. In that role, she led the campaign to approve a Declaration of Human Rights. She worked vigorously for human rights causes until her death in 1962.

Eleanor Roosevelt's activities troubled some Americans. In their view, a First Lady should act only as a gracious hostess at state dinners. Gradually, however, the public got used to her unconventional style, and many came to admire her for her political skills, her humanity, and her idealism.

The New Deal Falters

The zeal and energy with which New Dealers attacked the Depression pleased many observers, at least at first. But when the new programs failed to bring about significant economic improvement, criticism began to mount. Many worried that New Deal agencies were giving increasing power to the federal government. Former President Hoover warned against "a state-controlled or state-directed social or economic system. . . . That is not liberalism; it is tyranny," he said.

The Supreme Court also attacked FDR's programs. In 1935, the Court declared the NIRA unconstitutional because it gave the President lawmaking powers and regulated local, rather than interstate, commerce. The following year, the Court also struck down the tax that funded AAA subsidies to farmers. Two of the most important elements of the New Deal had crumbled. It was time to reassess.

A Second New Deal

Most of the public remained behind Roosevelt. The midterm elections of 1934 showed overwhelming nationwide support for FDR's administration. In 1935, the President launched a new, even bolder burst of activity. Many historians call this period and the legislation it produced the **Second New Deal,** or the Second Hundred Days. In part, it was FDR's response to critics who said he was not doing enough for ordinary Americans. The Second New Deal included more social welfare benefits, stricter controls over business, stronger support for unions, and higher taxes on the rich.

New and Expanded Agencies New agencies attacked joblessness even more aggressively than before. The Works Progress Administration (WPA), an agency set up in 1935 and lasting eight years, provided work for more than 8 million citizens. The WPA built or improved tens of thousands of playgrounds, schools, hospitals, and airfields, and it supported the creative work of many artists and writers. The National Youth Administration, established in June 1935 within the WPA, provided education, jobs, recreation, and counseling for young men and women ages 16 through 25.

The Second New Deal responded to the worsening plight of agricultural workers. The original AAA had ignored many of the farm workers who did not own land. In the Southwest, for example, Mexican American farm workers struggled to survive. Many of these migrant workers were forced to return to Mexico. Others tried to form unions, causing fierce resistance from farming associations. In the South, when landlords accepted the AAA subsidies and took land out of production, many tenants and sharecroppers were left without land to farm.

In May 1935, Rexford Tugwell, an economist in FDR's Department of Agriculture, set up the Resettlement Administration. The agency loaned money to owners of small farms and helped resettle tenants and sharecroppers on productive land. In 1937, the Farm Security Administration (FSA) replaced

774 Chapter 23 • *The New Deal*

Tugwell's agency. It loaned more than $1 billion to farmers and set up camps for migrant workers.

Rural Electrification   The New Deal also brought electricity to the American countryside. By the 1930s, nearly 90 percent of Americans in urban areas had electricity, compared to only about 10 percent in rural areas. The free market did not encourage private companies to provide power because of the high cost of running power lines to remote areas.

Roosevelt believed that the government had an obligation to provide this essential service where private enterprise would not. In 1935, Congress created the Rural Electrification Administration (REA), which offered loans to electric companies and farm cooperatives for building power plants and extending power lines, as well as to farmers and other rural residents to wire their homes and barns.

Within four years, about 25 percent of rural households had electricity. In time, the REA brought power to 98 percent of U.S. farms. Demand for electric appliances grew, benefiting manufacturing companies and local merchants.

New Labor Legislation   Labor unions had liked the NIRA provision known as 7a, which granted them the right to organize and bargain collectively. When the NIRA was declared unconstitutional, workers began to demand new legislation to protect their rights.

In July 1935, Congress responded. It passed the National Labor Relations Act, called the **Wagner Act** after its leading advocate, New York Senator Robert Wagner. The Wagner Act legalized such union practices as collective bargaining and **closed shops,** which are workplaces open only to union members. It also outlawed spying on union activities and blacklisting, a practice in which employers agreed not to hire union leaders. The act set up the National Labor Relations Board (NLRB) to enforce its provisions. The

READING CHECK
Why did Roosevelt see a need to launch a second New Deal?

INTERPRETING CHARTS
The New Deal created an alphabet soup of new federal agencies, greatly expanding the bureaucracy and authority of the government. **Synthesizing Information** *Write a statement explaining the major goals of these agencies.*

Major New Deal Agencies

Agency	Purpose
Federal Emergency Relief Act (FERA), 1933	Provided funds to state relief agencies.
Civil Works Administration (CWA), 1933	Provided federal jobs in building and improving roads and public facilities.
Tennessee Valley Authority (TVA), 1933	Provided hydroelectric power, flood control, and recreational opportunities to the Tennessee River Valley and surrounding areas.
Home Owners Loan Corporation (HOLC), 1933	Provided low-cost mortgage refinancing to homeowners facing foreclosure.
Civilian Conservation Corps (CCC), 1933	Provided jobs to young, unmarried men (and, later, women) to work on conservation and resource development projects.
Public Works Administration (PWA), 1933	Sponsored massive public works projects such as dams and hydroelectric plants.
National Recovery Administration (NRA), 1933	Worked with industries to establish codes outlining fair business and labor practices.
Federal Deposit Insurance Corporation (FDIC), 1933	Insured bank deposits up to $5,000.
Agricultural Adjustment Administration (AAA), 1933	Attempted to raise farm prices by paying farmers to lower farm output.
Federal Housing Administration (FHA), 1934	Improved housing standards and conditions and provided home financing.
Securities and Exchange Commission (SEC), 1934	Regulated the stock market and protected investors from dishonest trading practices.
Works Progress Administration (WPA), 1935	Gave the unemployed work in building construction and arts programs.
National Labor Relations Board (NLRB), 1935	Enforced provisions of the Wagner Act, which included the right to collective bargaining and other union rights.
National Youth Administration (NYA), 1935	Provided education, jobs, recreation, and counseling for youth ages 16 to 25.
Rural Electrification Administration (REA), 1935	Provided loans for building power plants, extending power lines to rural areas, and wiring homes.
Social Security Administration (SSA), 1935	Provided old-age pensions, disability payments, and unemployment benefits.

Connecting with Economics

Tell students to learn about migrant farm workers in the West and Southwest. Encourage students to find answers to some of the following questions. Which countries do migrant workers come from? How do they get here? Do they belong to unions? Do the unions provide ample protection? Who was César Chávez and what did he accomplish? Who are some of the contemporary leaders of the farm workers' movement? Have students explain actions taken by migrant farm workers to expand their economic opportunities and political rights in American society. (**Verbal/ Linguistic**)

BACKGROUND

FDR

By passing legislation that redistributed corporate wealth and empowered unions, FDR made enemies among the country's business leaders. In his acceptance speech for the Democratic nomination in June 1936, FDR addressed a crowd in Philadelphia. He compared the patriots' efforts in 1776 to free themselves from "royalists who held special privileges from the crown" to his own fight against the new "economic royalists . . . who sought to regiment the people, their labor, and their property." Although FDR's policies were unpopular with business leaders, they made him a hero among the working class.

READING CHECK

It was an effort to assist agricultural workers and to silence critics who claimed that FDR was giving more aid to businesses and wealthy people than to the average citizen.

CAPTION ANSWERS

Interpreting Charts Sample answer: The major New Deal agencies aimed to promote economic recovery, stabilize the nation's financial system, improve the nation's infrastructure, and improve the quality of life for all Americans.

✓ TEST PREPARATION

Ask students to study the chart "Major New Deal Agencies" on this page and then answer the question below.

Which of the following agencies provided benefits when a worker was unemployed?

A Home Owners Loan Corporation.

B Public Works Administration.

Ⓒ Social Security Administration.

D Rural Electrification Administration.

Reading Comprehension

1. His easy, confident manner; his direct communication to the American people in "Fireside Chats" helped create hope; he renewed confidence in economic institutions through such actions as the Bank Holiday of 1933; the Glass-Steagall Banking Act of 1933; the creation of the SEC.

2. They employed a great number of people to build and maintain public facilities such as roads and public beaches. This activity rejuvenated people through employment. The nation itself benefited through the work that was being accomplished.

3. It helped farmers and created jobs in one of the country's least developed regions. The TVA provided cheap electric power, flood control, and recreational opportunities.

4. It legalized important union practices such as collective bargaining and closed shops, while outlawing both spying on union activities and blacklisting. The National Labor Relations Board was established to enforce the provisions of the Wagner Act.

Critical Thinking and Writing

5. The first New Deal was energetic, but it failed to create economic recovery by itself. Two of its lynchpin programs, the NILB and the AAA, were declared unconstitutional by the Supreme Court. The Second New Deal instituted bolder programs than the first, reaching out to more Americans and increasing FDR's popularity.

6. Answers will vary but should be supported with facts from the section.

Take It to the NET

Answers will vary, but should demonstrate a knowledge of the origins of the TVA and an understanding of how it has changed to remain a part of present-day society.

The Social Security system marked a major expansion of the federal government's role as a caretaker of its citizens.

Supreme Court upheld the constitutionality of the Wagner Act in *NLRB* v. *Jones and Laughlin* (1939). The landmark case established the federal government's ability to regulate interstate commerce. In 1938, the Fair Labor Standards Act banned child labor and established a minimum wage for all workers covered under the act.

Social Security In 1935, Congress also passed the Social Security Act. The act established a **Social Security system** to provide financial security, in the form of regular payments, to people who could not support themselves. This system offered three types of insurance:

Old-age pensions and survivors' benefits Workers and their employers paid equally into a national insurance fund. Retired workers or their surviving spouses were eligible to start receiving Social Security payments at age 65. The act did not cover farm and domestic workers until it was amended in 1954.

Unemployment insurance Employers with more than eight employees funded this provision by paying a tax. The government distributed the money to workers who lost their jobs. States administered their own programs, with federal guidance and financial support.

Aid for dependent children, the blind, and the disabled The federal government gave grants to states to help support needy individuals in these categories.

The 1936 Election

No one expected the Republican presidential candidate of 1936, Kansas governor Alfred M. Landon, to beat the popular incumbent President. But few could have predicted the extent of FDR's landslide. Roosevelt carried every state except Maine and Vermont, winning 523–8 in the electoral college.

FDR's landslide victory showed that most Americans supported the New Deal. Yet the New Deal still had many critics with their own sizable followings.

READING COMPREHENSION

1. What steps did FDR take to restore the nation's hope and boost public confidence in economic institutions?

2. What role did **public works programs** play in Roosevelt's plans for economic recovery?

3. What benefits did the **Tennessee Valley Authority** bring about?

4. How was the **Wagner Act** a triumph for organized labor?

CRITICAL THINKING AND WRITING

5. **Making Comparisons** Compare the success of the early New Deal programs with those of the Second New Deal. Explain why the early programs faltered, and how the Second New Deal gave FDR a boost in the 1936 election.

6. **Writing a Conclusion** Write a statement that analyzes the types of programs created under the New Deal and then draws conclusions about FDR's view of the role of government. Give evidence to support your conclusions.

Take It to the NET

Activity: Yesterday and Today A New Deal program that survives today is the Tennessee Valley Authority (TVA). Research the TVA's beginnings and find out how it has changed to meet present-day needs. Summarize your findings in a brief report. Use the links provided in the *America: Pathways to the Present* area of the following Web site for help in completing this activity.
www.phschool.com

The New Deal's Critics

Section 2
The New
Deal's Critics

READING FOCUS

- What were some of the shortcomings and limits of the New Deal?
- What were the chief complaints of FDR's critics inside and outside of politics?
- How did the court-packing fiasco harm FDR's reputation?

MAIN IDEA

A variety of critics pointed out the shortcomings of the New Deal as well as its potential for restricting individual freedom.

KEY TERMS

American Liberty League
demagogue
nationalization
deficit spending

TAKING NOTES

Copy the chart below. As you read, fill in criticisms of the New Deal.

Criticisms of the New Deal

Goes Too Far	Not Far Enough
• Overtaxes the rich • •	• Should create a new economic system

SECTION OBJECTIVES

1. Learn about some of the New Deal's shortcomings and limitations.
2. Discover the chief complaints of FDR's critics inside and outside of politics.
3. See how the court-packing fiasco harmed FDR's reputation.

BELLRINGER

Warm-Up Activity Write the following statement on the chalkboard: "I feel that our President is doing an outstanding job, and I agree with his policies." Do students agree? Ask them to consider the reasons people criticize their leaders.

Activating Prior Knowledge Have students speculate on some possible objections to the New Deal. List these on the chalkboard. What groups might feel that the New Deal did not represent their best interests?

READING STRATEGY

Have students scan the section and note the main headings. Have them turn each main heading into a question. As they read, have them answer the questions they have created.

Setting the Scene To the poor and the jobless who benefited from New Deal programs, Franklin Delano Roosevelt was a true hero. One mill worker expressed the thoughts of many citizens:

> 66 *Roosevelt is the only President we ever had that thought the Constitution belonged to the pore [poor] man too. . . . Yessir, it took Roosevelt to read in the Constitution and find out them folks way back yonder that made it was talkin' about the pore man right along with the rich one.* 99
>
> —Testimony by mill worker George Dobbin in 1939, collected in *These Are Our Lives*, Federal Writers Project of the Works Progress Administration (1939)

Letters thanking the President poured into the White House. One letter read, "There ain't no other nation in the world that would have sense enough to think of WPA and all the other *A*'s."

Yet the New Deal inspired its share of critics, and the criticism would swell as the Depression dragged on. One critic wrote, "If you could get around the country as I have and seen the distress forced upon the American people, you would throw your darn NRA and AAA, and every other . . . *A* into the sea."

The Limitations of the New Deal

For all its successes, the New Deal fell short of many people's expectations. The Fair Labor Standards Act, for example, covered fewer than one quarter of all gainfully employed workers. It set the minimum wage at 25 cents an hour, which was well below what most covered workers already made. New Deal agencies also were generally less helpful to women and minority groups than they were to white men.

Women Many aspects of New Deal legislation put women at a disadvantage. The NRA codes, for example, permitted lower wages for women's work in almost a quarter of all cases. In relief and job programs, men and boys received strong preference. In accordance with the social customs of the time, jobs went to male "heads of families," unless the men were unable to work.

"COME ALONG. WE'RE GOING TO THE TRANS-LUX TO HISS ROOSEVELT."

INTERPRETING POLITICAL CARTOONS In this cartoon, rich people are going to a fancy hotel to "hiss"—that is, protest—FDR. **Analyzing Visual Information** How does the cartoonist depict wealth? Why did some rich people oppose Roosevelt's policies?

CAPTION ANSWERS

Interpreting Political Cartoons Wealthy people are portrayed in the cartoon as being selfish and elitist. The New Deal antagonized some wealthy people who opposed the "Wealth Tax Act," the requirement to pay Social Security taxes, and the general principle of government intervention in the economy.

RESOURCE DIRECTORY

Teaching Resources
Learning Styles Lesson Plans booklet, p. 49
Guided Reading and Review booklet, p. 94
Biography, Literature, and Comparing Primary Sources booklet (Literature) *In Search of Work: African Americans*, p. 71

Technology
Section Reading Support Transparencies
Guided Reading Audiotapes (English/Spanish), Ch. 23
Student Edition on Audio CD, Ch. 23
Prentice Hall Presentation Pro CD-ROM, Ch. 23
Companion Web site, www.phschool.com

LESSON PLAN

Focus Explain that the many far-reaching programs of the New Deal did not provide benefits to all people. Ask students why President Roosevelt and the New Deal sparked criticism.

Instruct Ask how the New Deal failed to address the problems of many women and African Americans. Ask students to describe the opposition from the right and the left, respectively. Discuss the role of anti–New Dealers such as Huey Long and Father Coughlin, and ask students to consider why such demagogues often find eager audiences.
Explore the court-packing scheme. Ask students how that episode provoked widespread public disapproval of Roosevelt and damaged his standing in Congress.

Assess/Reteach Have students discuss the ways that the New Deal and its supporters and detractors demonstrated the effectiveness of America's system of checks and balances in government.

No New Deal provision protected domestic service, the largest female occupation. In 1942, an African American domestic worker in St. Louis pleaded with the President to ask employers, the "rich people," to "give us some hours to rest in and some Sundays off and pay us more wages." Working 14-hour days, she earned only $6.50 per week. A brutally honest official wrote back to her:

> 66 *State and Federal labor laws, which offer protection to workers in so many occupations, have so far not set up standards for working conditions in domestic situations. There is nothing that can be done . . . to help you and others in this kind of employment.* 99
>
> —Roosevelt administration official

African Americans Federal relief programs in the South, including public works projects, reinforced racial segregation. As a rule, African Americans were not offered jobs at a professional level. They were kept out of skilled jobs on dam and electric power projects, and they received lower pay than whites for the same work. Because the Social Security Act excluded both farmers and domestic workers, it failed to cover nearly two thirds of working African Americans. One black American expressed deep disappointment with FDR's policies:

> 66 *All the prosperity he had brought to the country has been legislated and is not real. Nothing he has ever started has been finished. My common way of expressing it is that we are in the middle of the ocean like a ship without an anchor. No good times can come to the country as long as there is so much discrimination practiced. . . . I don't see much chance for our people to get anywhere when the color line instead of ability determines the opportunities to get ahead economically.* 99
>
> —Testimony by Sam T. Mayhew in 1939, collected in *Such As Us* (1978)

VIEWING HISTORY This photograph, taken at a relief center in Louisville, Kentucky, highlights the struggle of African Americans to overcome the effects of both the Depression and prejudice. **Analyzing Visual Information** *What contrast was the photographer trying to point out in this picture?*

Yet the New Deal did nothing to end discriminatory practices in the North. In many black neighborhoods, for example, white-owned businesses continued to employ only whites. In the absence of help from the federal government, African Americans took matters into their own hands. Protesters picketed and boycotted such businesses with the slogan "Don't shop where you can't work."

The early Depression had seen an alarming rise in the number of lynchings. The federal government again offered no relief. A bill to make lynching a federal crime was abandoned by Congress in 1938. NAACP leader Walter White recalled in 1948 that FDR had given this explanation for his refusal to support these measures:

> 66 *Southerners, by reason of seniority rule in Congress, are chairmen or occupy strategic places on most of the Senate and House committees. If I come out for the anti-lynching bill now, they will block every bill I ask Congress to pass to keep America from collapsing. I just can't take that risk.* 99
>
> —President Franklin Roosevelt

CAPTION ANSWERS

Viewing History All of the people on the billboard, which touts the nation's high standard of living, are white. All the people in the relief line are African Americans. The photographer might have been commenting on discrimination in New Deal relief programs.

RESOURCE DIRECTORY
Technology
Sounds of an Era Audio CD *Marian Anderson*

Although African Americans in the North had not supported FDR in 1932, by 1936 many had joined his camp. Often the last hired and first fired, they had experienced the highest unemployment rates of any group during the Depression. For this reason, those who did gain employment appreciated many of the New Deal programs.

Other aspects of Roosevelt's record also had some appeal to many African Americans. He appointed more African Americans to policymaking posts than any President before him. The Roosevelts also seemed genuinely concerned about the fate of African Americans. These factors help to explain FDR's wide support among black voters.

Political Critics

Under the desperate conditions of the Great Depression, reactions to the New Deal ran strong. People with widely differing political views criticized the New Deal, both for what it did and for what it did not do.

New Deal Does Too Much   A number of Republicans, in Congress and elsewhere, opposed Roosevelt. They knew something had to be done about the Depression, but they believed that the New Deal went too far.

These critics included many wealthy people who regarded FDR as their enemy. Early in the New Deal, they had disapproved of certain programs, such as the TVA and rural electrification, that they considered to be socialistic. The Second New Deal gave them even more to hate, as FDR pushed through a series of higher taxes aimed at the rich. One of these was the Revenue Act of 1935, also known as the Wealth Tax Act. This act raised the tax rate on individual incomes over $50,000 as well as on the income and profits of corporations.

The Social Security Act also aroused political opposition. Some of FDR's enemies claimed that it penalized successful, hardworking people by forcing them to pay into the system. Others saw the assignment of Social Security numbers as the first step toward a militaristic, regimented society. They predicted that soon people would have to wear metal dog tags engraved with their Social Security numbers.

A group called the **American Liberty League,** founded in 1934, spearheaded much of the opposition to the New Deal. It was led by former Democratic presidential candidate Alfred E. Smith, the National Association of Manufacturers, and leading business figures.

The league charged the New Deal with limiting individual freedom in an unconstitutional, "un-American" manner. To them, programs such as compulsory unemployment insurance smacked of "Bolshevism," a reference to the political philosophy of the founders of the Soviet Union.

New Deal Does Not Do Enough   Many Progressives and Socialists also attacked the New Deal. But these critics charged that FDR's programs did not provide enough help.

Muckraking novelist Upton Sinclair believed that the nation's entire economic system needed to be reformed in order to cure what he believed to be a "permanent crisis." A Socialist, he sought solutions that went far beyond New Deal–style reforms. In 1934, Sinclair ran for governor of California on the Democratic ticket. His platform, "End Poverty in California" (EPIC), called for a new economic system in which the state would take over factories and farms.

Focus on CULTURE

Marian Anderson and the DAR One of the greatest concert singers of her time, Marian Anderson first achieved widespread fame in Europe. At the time, opportunities for African Americans in the United States were limited. In 1935, however, Anderson successfully debuted in New York City. The following year, at the Roosevelts' invitation, she became the first African American to perform at the White House. In 1939, Anderson attempted to rent Constitution Hall in Washington, D.C., to stage a concert. The owners of the hall, the prestigious Daughters of the American Revolution (DAR), denied Anderson's request. In protest, Eleanor Roosevelt and other important members resigned from the group and then arranged for Anderson to perform on the steps of the Lincoln Memorial. An audience of some 75,000, including both blacks and whites, attended the concert on Easter, April 9, 1939. Anderson's moving performance included a patriotic rendering of "America."

READING CHECK
What were the main criticisms of the New Deal?

EPIC clubs formed throughout the state, and Sinclair won the primary. Terrified opponents then used shady tactics to discredit him. They produced fake newsreels showing people who spoke with a Russian accent endorsing Sinclair. Associated unfairly with communism, Sinclair lost the election.

The New Deal had only limited success in eliminating poverty. This fact contributed to a revival of progressivism in Minnesota and Wisconsin. Running for the United States Senate, Wisconsin Progressive Robert La Follette, Jr., argued that "devices which seek to preserve the unequal distribution of wealth . . . will retard or prevent recovery." His brother Philip also took a radical stand, calling for a redistribution of income. Philip's ideas persuaded the state Socialist Party to join the Progressives after he won the Wisconsin governorship in 1934.

Other Critics

Some New Deal critics were **demagogues,** leaders who manipulate people with half-truths, deceptive promises, and scare tactics. Two such demagogues attracted strong followings during the Depression.

Father Coughlin One such demagogue was Father Charles E. Coughlin (CAWG-lin), a dynamic speaker who used the radio to broadcast his message. Throughout the 1930s, the so-called Radio Priest held listeners spellbound from his studio in Detroit. In 1934, Father Coughlin's weekly broadcasts reached an audience estimated at more than 10 million people.

Coughlin achieved popularity even though he sometimes contradicted himself. One time he advocated the **nationalization,** or government takeover and ownership, of banks and the redistribution of their wealth. Another time he defended the sanctity of private property, including banks. At first he supported FDR and the New Deal. Later he denounced them, through his radio show and through the organization he formed in 1934 called the National Union for

780 Chapter 23 • *The New Deal*

Social Justice. Coughlin's attacks on FDR grew increasingly reckless. In 1936, he called him "Franklin 'Double-crossing' Roosevelt" and described him as a "great betrayer and liar."

By the end of the 1930s, Coughlin was issuing openly anti-Jewish statements. He also began showering praise on Adolf Hitler and Benito Mussolini, two menacing leaders who were rising to power in Europe. Coughlin's actions alarmed many Americans, and he lost some of his support. In 1942, Roman Catholic officials ordered him to stop broadcasting his show.

Huey Long A powerful figure in Louisiana politics, Huey Long was a different type of demagogue. Long was a country lawyer who had grown up in poverty. He won the governorship of Louisiana in 1928 and became a United States senator in 1932. Unlike many other southern Democrats, Long never used racial attacks to build a base of power. Instead, he worked to help the underprivileged by improving education, medical care, and public services. He also built an extraordinarily powerful and ruthless political machine in his home state.

Originally a supporter of FDR, Long broke with him early in the New Deal. "Unless we provide for redistribution of wealth in this country, the country is doomed," he said. While in the Senate, Long developed a program called Share-Our-Wealth. It would limit individual income to $1 million and inheritance to $5 million. The government would take the rest in steep progressive income taxes. Thus the plan would confiscate large fortunes. It would then redistribute that wealth by giving every family a minimum $5,000 "household estate" and a minimum annual income of $2,500. Long also sought other improvements for Americans: shorter working hours, more veterans' benefits, payments for education, and pensions for the elderly.

At top, Father Coughlin addresses some 6,000 members of his National Union for Social Justice in Detroit, 1936. Above, Louisiana's Huey Long gestures in the flamboyant style for which he was famous.

COMPARING HISTORIANS' VIEWPOINTS
Roosevelt and the New Deal

Historians disagree on the effectiveness of the New Deal in combating the Depression and improving the lives of Americans.

Analyzing Viewpoints Compare the viewpoints of these two historians.

Criticism of the New Deal

"[New Deal measures] have not been administered with any special care to preserve the best features of private industry and encourage it to bring about recovery. The relief measures have been inefficient and expensive. They have resulted in a tremendous burden of taxation. . . . There has been no effort to preserve conditions under which a man, striving for a private job and doing his job well, shall be encouraged and preferred to the man on WPA. . . . More men have gone out of business in the last five years than have gone into business because of the complete uncertainty whether they can survive a constant Government interference."

—*Robert A. Taft, "A Conservative Critique: The New Deal and the Republican Program"*

Praises for the New Deal

"What then did the New Deal do? . . . [It] expanded the authority of the presidency, recruited university-trained administrators, won control of the money supply, established central banking, imposed regulations on Wall Street, . . . rescued debt-ridden farmers and homeowners, . . . fostered unionization of the factories, drastically reduced child labor, . . . established minimal working standards, enabled thousands of tenants to buy their own farms, built camps for migrants, introduced the Welfare State with old-age pensions, unemployment insurance, . . . subsidized painters and novelists, composers and ballet dancers, . . . [and] gave women greater recognition. . . ."

—*William E. Leuchtenburg, The FDR Years: On Roosevelt and His Legacy*

Focus on
ECONOMICS

Deficit and Debt The terms *federal deficit* and *federal debt* (or *national debt*) are often confused. A federal <u>deficit</u> occurs when the government spends more money in its annual budget than it receives in revenues during that year. To cover a deficit, the government borrows money by issuing bonds, which are essentially IOUs to those who buy the bonds. The federal <u>debt</u> is the money the government owes to its bondholders. The government could have a great deal of federal debt, but not be practicing deficit spending. That is, it could be spending no more than it earns each year, yet it still could be paying off old debt, much like individuals who owe money on their credit cards. The chart below, for example, shows the deficit rising and falling during the Depression, as federal revenues and spending varied. The debt chart at the bottom, however, shows steady increases in government borrowing for New Deal programs.

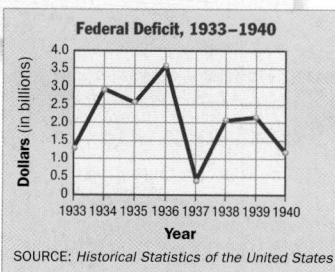

Federal Deficit, 1933–1940

SOURCE: *Historical Statistics of the United States*

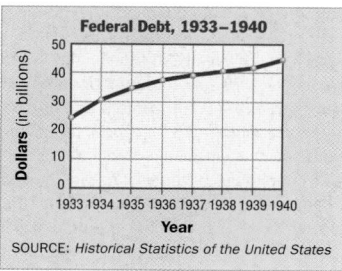

Federal Debt, 1933–1940

SOURCE: *Historical Statistics of the United States*

Long's program for helping all Americans achieve wealth attracted many followers. His success helped push FDR to propose new taxes on wealthy Americans in the Second New Deal. Meanwhile, Long himself began to eye the presidency. But in September 1935, the son-in-law of one of Long's political enemies shot and killed him.

Long and Coughlin never seriously threatened FDR or the New Deal. But their influence warned Roosevelt that if he failed to solve the nation's problems, he risked losing mass support.

Modern-Day Critics

Although many of the people who directly benefited from the New Deal are now gone, their children and grandchildren still pass down individual stories of hope and help that came to their families through programs like the WPA. To many Americans, FDR's bold actions place him among the nation's greatest Presidents. Yet some modern-day critics question whether the New Deal achieved the greatest good for the greatest number of Americans.

Some historians and economists have examined this question in recent years and found the New Deal lacking. They say that New Deal programs actually hindered economic progress and threatened America's core beliefs in free enterprise. Further, they charge that the programs created a bloated and dangerously powerful federal bureaucracy and encouraged inefficient use of resources.

For example, critics maintain that New Deal employment programs created "make work" jobs instead of allowing the free market to determine what jobs, and how many, were needed. These job programs were financed by heavy tax increases, which took money out of the economy and gave people less money to spend on products that would boost production and create jobs.

Modern critics also attack the policy of paying farmers not to plant. They contend that market demand should have been allowed to determine the supply and price of farm products. In a time of hunger, the program wasted precious resources, they note—from dumped milk to burned wheat. The program encouraged some farmers to plant crops on poor land just so that they could later take the land out of production and get paid for doing so. This caused marginal soil to erode further and become depleted. Farm production quotas penalized efficient and less-efficient farmers equally, while the free market would have weeded out inefficiency and rewarded productivity.

Finally, the New Deal receives criticism from people who oppose **deficit spending**—paying out more money from the annual federal budget than the government receives in revenues. Deficit spending to fund New Deal programs required the government to borrow money. Government borrowing produced what economists call the "crowding-out effect"—making less money available for private borrowing by businesses and consumers.

At the heart of the question is a difference in ideologies. Some people believe that the New Deal violated the free-market system that Americans have traditionally cherished. Others believe that providing direct relief to many of the nation's suffering citizens was worth the compromise. These debates continue today.

The Court-Packing Fiasco

Roosevelt received criticism not only for his programs, but also for his actions. No act aroused more opposition than his attempt to "pack" the Supreme Court.

Throughout the early New Deal, the Supreme Court had caused FDR his greatest frustration. The Court had invalidated the NIRA, the AAA, and many state laws from the Progressive Era. In February 1937, FDR proposed a major court-reform bill.

The Constitution had not specified the number of Supreme Court justices. Congress had last changed the number in 1869. By Roosevelt's time, the number nine had become well established. Arguing that he merely wanted to lighten the burden of the aging justices, FDR asked Congress to allow him to appoint as many as six additional justices, one for each justice over 70 years old. Roosevelt's real intention was to "pack" the Court with judges supportive of the New Deal.

Negative reaction came swiftly from all sides. Critics blasted the President for trying to inject politics into the judiciary. They warned Congress not to let him undermine the constitutional principle of separation of powers. With several dictators ruling in Europe, the world seemed already to be tilting toward tyranny. If Congress let FDR reshape the Supreme Court, critics worried, the United States might head down the same slope.

Strong opposition forced FDR to withdraw his reform bill. He also suffered political damage. Many Republicans and Southern Democrats united against further New Deal legislation. This alliance remained a force for years to come.

In the end, FDR still wound up with a Court that tended to side with him. Some older justices retired, allowing the President to appoint justices who favored the New Deal. Even earlier, however, the Court, acting on lawsuits filed by New Deal adversaries, had begun to uphold measures from the Second New Deal, including the Wagner Act. The Court may have been reacting to public opinion, or it may have decided that those measures were better thought out and more skillfully drafted than earlier ones.

INTERPRETING POLITICAL CARTOONS FDR's request to Congress to allow him to appoint more Supreme Court justices (friendly to his New Deal programs) caused an uproar that damaged the President politically. **Analyzing Visual Information** *In this cartoon, what do you think the donkey represents, and what is the cartoonist trying to portray?*

Section 2 · Assessment

READING COMPREHENSION

1. What effects did the New Deal have on women and minorities?

2. Why did the **American Liberty League** view the New Deal as unconstitutional and un-American?

3. Why did Upton Sinclair and Robert La Follette believe that the New Deal did not go far enough?

4. Describe FDR's "court-packing" maneuver and its outcome.

CRITICAL THINKING AND WRITING

5. **Making Comparisons** Compare and contrast the criticisms of two New Deal–era demagogues, Father Coughlin and Huey Long.

6. **Writing an Opinion** Review the arguments made by modern-day supporters and critics of the New Deal, and reread Comparing Historians' Viewpoints. Write a statement explaining which arguments you agree with, and why.

 **Take It to the NET**

Activity: Analyzing Primary Sources Read or listen to the "fireside chat" in which FDR explains his controversial court-packing plan to the nation. What is his argument? Do you agree or disagree with it? Explain. Use the links provided in the *America: Pathways to the Present* area of the following Web site for help in completing this activity.
www.phschool.com

Reading Comprehension

1. It allowed lower wages for their work and favored white males in job programs. Federal relief programs in the South enforced racial segregation. The Social Security Act excluded farmers and domestic workers, the primary areas in which African Americans and women worked.

2. It felt the New Deal limited individual freedom too radically and that its compulsory programs resembled Bolshevik philosophies.

3. Sinclair believed that the nation's entire economic system needed to be reformed along Socialist lines. La Follette believed that wealth needed to be evenly distributed.

4. After the court struck down some early New Deal programs, FDR pressed for legislation to increase the number of Supreme Court justices, hoping to appoint justices friendly to the New Deal. The resulting negative reaction caused political damage to FDR and increased opposition to New Deal legislation.

Critical Thinking and Writing

5. Coughlin and Long shared strident and combative methods to present their views, but only Coughlin used racial attacks. Also, Coughlin retracted his early support for wealth redistribution, while Long never lost faith in his Share-the-Wealth philosophy.

6. Answers will vary, but should be persuasive and supported by facts from the section.

 **Take It to the NET**

Answers will vary but should include an examination of FDR's desire to gain support for the New Deal by adding justices to the Supreme Court bench who would approve of his programs.

CAPTION ANSWERS

Viewing History The donkey represents Democrats, most likely in the Democrat-controlled Congress. They, like many other critics, balked at FDR's request to add Justices to the Supreme Court.

Distinguishing Fact From Opinion

DISTINGUISHING FACT FROM OPINION

Focus Analyze a speaker's use of facts and opinions in a political speech.

Instruct Divide students into small groups to examine the speech and identify the various facts and opinions used by the speaker. Ask each group to report its findings. If groups draw different conclusions about which statements are facts and which are opinions, have the whole class discuss the examples. Then ask students whether or not they think the speaker in this case has made an effective argument. What facts might he have used to strengthen his points?

Extend See the Skills for Life activity in the Resource Directory below.

ANSWERS
PRACTICE THE SKILL

1. **(a)** The decisions of the Supreme Court are matters of public record and can thus be easily verified. **(b)** Possible answers: the statements about the growth of the national debt, billions spent by government, higher taxes, the percent of income paid in taxes, and the growth in the number of public officials. They could be verified in government publications.

2. **(a)** It is an appeal to emotion and does not define "foundations of freedom." **(b)** Possible answers: "must" has invaded independence of Congress; Congress has abandoned its responsibility; torrent of waste; freedom has changed to slavery to the government; and New Deal developments have polluted the foundation of liberty. They are opinions because they cannot be proven or verified, and they contain sweeping generalizations and emotion-packed words.

3. **(a)** He states that they were overthrown by the Supreme Court, the guardian of constitutional rights. **(b)** No, he gives no specific examples—he just makes a sweeping accusation. **(c)** Answers will vary, but should note the unsupported statements listed in question 2.

A fact is something that can be proved to be true by checking an encyclopedia or other trusted source. An opinion is a judgment that reflects beliefs or feelings. Historical materials such as speeches, letters, and diaries often contain both facts and opinions. The ability to distinguish between facts and opinions will help you determine the soundness of a writer's ideas and reach your own conclusions about historical events.

In the excerpt below from a speech given at the 1936 Republican National Convention, Herbert Hoover criticizes the New Deal.

LEARN THE SKILL
Use the following steps to distinguish between fact and opinion in historical materials:

1. **Determine which statements are facts.** Remember that facts can be verified in other sources.

2. **Determine which statements are opinions.** Sometimes authors signal opinions with phrases such as "I believe" or "I think," but often they do not. Other clues that indicate opinions are emotion-packed words and sweeping generalizations. (A sweeping generalization is a broad statement about a group of people, things, or events, such as, "Politicians are corrupt.")

3. **Evaluate opinions as you read.** Generally, an opinion is more reliable when the author gives facts to support it.

PRACTICE THE SKILL
Answer the following questions:

1. **(a)** For what reason is Hoover's first statement, about the Supreme Court, easily recognizable as a fact? **(b)** Find two other statements of fact in the excerpt. How might you prove each one is a statement of fact?

2. **(a)** What indicates that the final sentence of the first paragraph is an opinion rather than a fact? **(b)** Find two other statements of opinion in the excerpt. What indicates that they are opinions?

3. **(a)** How does Hoover support his opinion that many New Deal acts "were a violation of the rights of men and of self-government"? **(b)** Does he present any facts to support his statement that the Congress has "abandoned its responsibility"? **(c)** In your opinion, how good a job has Hoover done in supporting his opinions? Explain your answer.

APPLY THE SKILL
See the Chapter Review and Assessment for another opportunity to apply this skill.

"The Supreme Court has reversed some ten or twelve of the New Deal major enactments. Many of these acts were a violation of the rights of men and of self-government. Despite the sworn duty of the Executive and Congress to defend these rights, they have sought to take them into their own hands. That is an attack on the foundations of freedom.

More than this, the independence of the Congress, the Supreme Court, and the Executive are pillars at the door of liberty. For three years the word 'must' has invaded the independence of Congress. And the Congress has abandoned its responsibility to check even the expenditures [spending] of money. . . .

We have seen these gigantic expenditures and this torrent of waste pile up a national debt which two generations cannot repay. . . .

Billions have been spent to prime the economic pump. . . . We have seen the frantic attempts to find new taxes on the rich. Yet three-quarters of the bill will be sent to the average man and the poor. He and his wife and his grandchildren will be giving a quarter of all their working days to pay taxes. Freedom to work for himself is changed into a slavery of work for the follies of government. . . .

We have seen the building up of a horde of political officials. We have seen the pressures upon the helpless and destitute to trade political support for relief. Both are a pollution of the very foundations of liberty."

—Herbert Hoover, *American Ideals Versus the New Deal*

RESOURCE DIRECTORY

Teaching Resources
Skills for Life booklet, p. 25

Technology
Social Studies Skills Tutor CD-ROM
Interactive Practice in
• Geographic Literacy
• Critical Thinking and Reading
• Visual Analysis
• Communications

Last Days of the New Deal

READING FOCUS

- What factors led to the recession of 1937, and how did the Roosevelt administration respond?
- What triumphs and setbacks did unions experience during the New Deal era?
- What effects did the New Deal have on American culture?
- What lasting effects can be attributed to the New Deal?

KEY TERMS

recession
national debt
revenue
coalition
sit-down strike

TAKING NOTES

Copy the chart below on a piece of paper. As you read, fill in the blanks by listing various effects of the New Deal.

Effects of the New Deal			
Economic	Political	Social	Cultural

MAIN IDEA

Ultimately, the New Deal did not end the Depression. Yet it had lasting effects on many aspects of American life.

Setting the Scene In 1936, writer James Agee and photographer Walker Evans made a six-week journey among the nation's poorest citizens, the tenant farmers of Alabama. Evans's photographs and Agee's descriptions were later published as *Let Us Now Praise Famous Men*, a book that left powerful images of the Great Depression in the nation's consciousness. The book bore witness to the survival of human dignity in the midst of deepest poverty. Here Agee, who shared meager lodgings with families, describes one farmer's revolving door of debt and despair:

> 66 *Years ago the Ricketts were, relatively speaking, almost prosperous. Besides their cotton farming they had ten cows and sold the milk, and they lived near a good stream and had all the fish they wanted. Ricketts went $400 into debt on a fine young pair of mules. One of the mules died before it had made the first crop; the other died the year after; against his fear . . . Ricketts went into debt for other, inferior mules; his cows went one by one . . . ; he got congestive chills; his wife got pellagra [a disease caused by dietary deficiencies]; a number of his children died; . . . for ten consecutive years now . . . they have not cleared or had any hope of clearing a cent at the end of the year. . . .*
>
> *WPA work is available to very few tenants: they are, technically, employed, and thus have no right to it: and if by chance they manage to get it, landlords are more likely than not to intervene. They feel it spoils a tenant to be paid wages, even for a little while.* 99
> —James Agee, *Let Us Now Praise Famous Men*, 1941

VIEWING HISTORY Walker Evans's photographs captured both the plight and the dignity of the impoverished farm families he visited. **Analyzing Visual Images** What impressions come to mind when you study this picture? Explain.

RESOURCE DIRECTORY

Teaching Resources
Guided Reading and Review booklet, p. 95

Technology
Section Reading Support Transparencies
Guided Reading Audiotapes (English/Spanish), Ch. 23
Student Edition on Audio CD, Ch. 23
Prentice Hall Presentation Pro CD-ROM, Ch. 23
Companion Web site, www.phschool.com

SECTION OBJECTIVES

1. Learn about factors that led to the recession of 1937 and about the Roosevelt administration's response to this situation.
2. Find out about triumphs and setbacks experienced by unions during the New Deal era.
3. Discover some effects of the New Deal on American culture.
4. See what lasting effects can be attributed to the New Deal.

BELLRINGER

Warm-Up Activity Write the term *federal government* on the chalkboard. Ask students to brainstorm a list of words they associate with the term. Explain that many modern attitudes and beliefs concerning the government stem from the New Deal era.

Activating Prior Knowledge Ask students to discuss whether government alone has the power to reverse an economic crisis. What other factors must come into play for a steady recovery to occur?

READING STRATEGY

Before students read the section, have them make a table. Across the top, have them list these categories: *economics, culture, citizenship,* and *society.* Then, as they read the section, have students list the works of art, literature, or music in a column at the side of the table, and then indicate which aspects of New Deal society they reflect. Have students describe how characteristics and issues of the New Deal era are reflected in these works.

CAPTION ANSWERS

Viewing History Sample answers: The family's shack and their tattered, dirty clothing suggest extreme poverty. The individuals and their facial expressions suggest resignation, malnutrition, weariness, dignity amid misfortune, and family togetherness.

Focus Point out that the New Deal did not succeed in ending the Depression but that it did have a great impact on the nation's political, social, and cultural life. Ask students to list ways that this impact is felt today.

Instruct Ask students what the recession of 1937 revealed about the New Deal and the economy. Discuss the changes that the New Deal introduced to the nation. Ask students to describe changes affecting labor unions. Ask them to consider the role of government in helping to make union gains possible.

Discuss government support for the arts as an important part of the New Deal. Ask students to discuss the benefits and drawbacks of government funding of the arts.

Assess/Reteach Ask students to discuss the ways in which government-funded art programs of the New Deal era helped creative people make a record of the time in which they lived. If students were recipients of similar types of grants today, which aspects of society would they choose to depict, and how?

BACKGROUND
Art History

Mexican-born muralist Diego Rivera (1886–1957) was commissioned to work on several building lobbies during the Depression, including that of the Detroit Institute of the Arts. Rivera's bright, expansive murals integrated elements of Mexican folk art and modern industrial themes.

CAPTION ANSWERS

Interpreting Graphs (a) New Deal jobs programs provided initial relief, but only for certain segments of society. Critics charged that government spending on jobs programs and public works projects wasted resources, interfered with free market economics, and needlessly expanded the government bureaucracy. Also, the WPA and certain other jobs programs had their funding reduced in 1937. (b) By approximately four million workers.

Unemployment, 1933–1940

SOURCE: *Historical Statistics of the United States, Colonial Times to 1970*

INTERPRETING GRAPHS
Combating unemployment was one of Roosevelt's greatest challenges during the Depression. **Analyzing Visual Information** *(a) From your reading of Section 2, explain why unemployment rose during 1937. (b) By about how much did unemployment decline over the course of the New Deal?*

CIO chief John L. Lewis addresses 10,000 textile workers in Massachusetts in 1937.

786

The Recession of 1937

The New Deal was no miracle cure for the Great Depression. While massive government spending led to some temporary economic improvement, in August 1937, the economy collapsed again. Industrial production fell, as did employment levels. The nation entered a **recession,** a period of slow business activity.

The new Social Security tax was partly to blame for this recession. The tax came directly out of workers' paychecks, through payroll deductions. With less money in their pockets, Americans bought fewer goods.

Americans also had less money because FDR had cut way back on expensive programs such as the WPA. The President had become distressed at the rising **national debt,** or the total amount of money the federal government borrows and has to pay back. (See Focus on Economics, page 550.) The government borrows when its **revenue,** or income, does not keep up with its expenses. To fund the New Deal, the government had to borrow massive amounts of money. As a result, the national debt rose from $21 billion in 1933 to $43 billion by 1940.

After 1937, Harry Hopkins and other advisors persuaded FDR to expand the WPA and other programs that had been cut back. The increased spending provided some economic relief. Still, hard times lasted until well into the 1940s.

Unions Triumph

The New Deal changed the way many Americans thought about labor unions. New federal protections for unions under the 1935 Wagner Act made union membership more attractive to workers. Membership rose from about 3 million in 1933 to 10.5 million by 1941, a figure representing 11.3 percent of the nonagricultural work force. By 1945, some 36 percent were unionized, the all-time high for unions in the United States.

A New Labor Organization Activism by powerful union leaders helped increase membership. The cautious and craft-based American Federation of Labor (AFL) had done little to attract unskilled industrial workers during the half-century of its existence. In 1935, United Mine Workers President John L. Lewis joined with representatives of seven other AFL unions to try to change this situation. They created a Committee for Industrial Organization (CIO) within the AFL.

Although the AFL did not support its efforts, the CIO sought to organize the nation's unskilled workers in mass-production industries. It sent organizers into steel mills, auto plants, and southern textile mills and encouraged all workers to join. In response, the AFL suspended CIO unions in 1936.

Two years later, the CIO had 4 million members. In November 1938, this **coalition,** or alliance of groups with similar goals, changed its name to the Congress of Industrial Organizations. John L. Lewis became its first president. The aim of this coalition of industrial unions was to challenge conditions in industry. Their main tool was the strike.

RESOURCE DIRECTORY

Teaching Resources
Biography, Literature, and Comparing Primary Sources booklet (Biography) *Emma Tenayuca,* p. 28

Technology
RESOURCE PRO® **Literature Activity**
In Search of Work: Migrant Farmers, found on Resource Pro, uses an excerpt from John Steinbeck's *The Grapes of Wrath* to illustrate the plight of tenant farmers during the Depression.

VIEWING HISTORY
Automobile workers stage a successful sit-down strike during the winter of 1936–1937 at the Fisher Body Plant No. 1, in Flint, Michigan. Here, workers guard a window during the strike. **Drawing Inferences** *Make a list of the possible challenges these men faced during this long sit-down strike.*

An Era of Strikes The Wagner Act legalized collective bargaining and required companies to bargain in good faith with certified union representatives. But the act did not force companies to accept unions' demands. Although the Wagner Act was designed to bring about industrial peace, in the short term it led to a wave of dramatic strikes.

Many of these work stoppages took the form of sit-down strikes. A weapon often used by the Congress of Industrial Organizations, the **sit-down strike** is a strike in which laborers stop working but refuse to leave the building. Supporters outside the workplace set up picket lines. Together, the strikers and the picket lines prevent the company from bringing in scabs, or non-union substitute workers. In areas where local authorities were New Deal Democrats, the workers' actions sometimes went unchallenged, making the sit-down strike an effective tool.

The first sit-down strikes took place in early 1936 at three huge rubber-tire plants in Akron, Ohio. The success of the sit-downs led to similar strikes later in the year at several General Motors (GM) auto plants. The most famous began on December 31, 1936. In this strike, laborers associated with the United Auto Workers (UAW) occupied GM's main plants in Flint, Michigan, and refused to leave.

GM executives turned off the heat and blocked entry to the plants so that the workers could not receive food. They also called in the police against the picketers outside. Violence erupted. The wife of a striker grabbed a bullhorn and urged other wives to join the picketers.

Women—both workers' wives and female employees—later organized food deliveries to supply the strikers. They set up a speakers' bureau to present the union's position to the public, and formed a Women's Emergency Brigade to take up picket duty. Governor Frank Murphy of Michigan and President Roosevelt refused to use the militia against the strike. By early February General Motors had given in.

Not all labor strikes were as successful. Henry Ford continued to resist unionism. In 1937, at a Ford Motor Company plant near Detroit, his men beat UAW officials when the unionists tried to distribute leaflets. Walter Reuther, a future UAW president, later testified about the incident:

READING CHECK
What made sit-down strikes effective to some extent?

788

ACTIVITY

Connecting with Culture

Tell students to bring in books, such as *The Good Earth, The Grapes of Wrath, Their Eyes Were Watching God*, and *Let Us Now Praise Famous Men*, that were written during the 1930s and early 1940s. Encourage students to read one of these books and write a summary telling what the book is about and how it describes the characteristics and issues of the era of the Great Depression. **(Verbal/Linguistic)**

BACKGROUND

Interdisciplinary

Technological developments changed the culture of the New Deal period. Specifically, the integration of sound with moving pictures revitalized the motion picture industry. Adding sound was first accomplished by using a sound-on-film synchronization system, Phonofilm, patented by Lee DeForest in 1919. By 1933, when techniques had been developed to eliminate camera noise from recordings, improve microphones (so that actors could move while they spoke), and edit a sound-track, all of the major studios had converted to sound, increasing their profits by 600 percent.

> " They picked me up about eight different times and threw me down on my back on the concrete. While I was on the ground they kicked me in the face, head, and other parts of my body. . . . I never raised a hand. "
> —Walter Reuther

Companies and the police were not the only instigators of violence. Mobs of striking unionists sometimes attacked strikebreakers trying to enter or leave a plant, or they destroyed company property. Unions generally opposed such actions, instead encouraging passive resistance. Still, strikers often fought back with bottles, bricks, stones, and bats.

Like Ford, the Republic Steel Company refused to sign with steelworkers' unions until war loomed in 1941. At one strike against Republic Steel on May 30, 1937, Chicago police killed several picketers and injured dozens. This Memorial Day tragedy was a sign that labor, despite its triumphs, still faced many challenges. Another sign came in the form of a Supreme Court ruling. In 1939, the Court outlawed the sit-down strike as being too potent a weapon and an obstacle to negotiation.

The New Deal's Effects on Culture

Artists created enduring cultural legacies for the nation during the Great Depression. They were aided by federal funds allocated by Congress to support the popular and fine arts and to provide jobs.

Literature Several works of literature destined to become classics emerged during this period. One example is Pearl Buck's novel *The Good Earth* (1931), a saga of peasant struggle in China. In 1937, folklorist Zora Neale Hurston published *Their Eyes Were Watching God*, a novel about a strong-willed African American woman and the Florida town in which she lives. John Steinbeck wrote *The Grapes of Wrath* (1939), a powerful tale about Dust Bowl victims who travel to California in search of a better life. Funding from *Fortune* magazine allowed James Agee and Walker Evans to live for weeks with Alabama sharecroppers. The result of their experiences was the nonfiction masterpiece *Let Us Now Praise Famous Men* (1941).

Radio and Movies The new medium of radio became a major source of entertainment for American families. Comedy shows of the 1930s produced stars such as Jack Benny, Fred Allen, George Burns, and Gracie Allen. The first daytime dramas, called soap operas because soap companies often sponsored them, emerged in this period. These 15-minute stories, designed to provoke strong emotional responses, were meant to appeal to women who remained at home during the day. Symphonic music and opera also flourished on the radio.

By 1933, the movies had recovered from the initial setback caused by the early Depression. Americans needed an escape from hard times, and the movies provided that escape. For a quarter, customers could see a double feature (introduced in 1931) or take the whole family to a drive-in theater (introduced in 1933). Federal agencies used motion pictures to publicize their work. The Farm Security Administration, for example, produced documentaries of American agricultural life.

Some Hollywood studios concentrated on optimistic films about common people who triumphed over evil, such as Warner Brothers' *Mr. Smith Goes to Washington* (1939). Comedies were

Focus on CULTURE

The Grapes of Wrath The 1939 novel by John Steinbeck epitomizes the despair of downtrodden farmers during the Depression. The story pits powerful banks and corporate farming interests against powerless farmers. This bitter critique is told through the experiences of the Joad family, "Okies" forced to travel to California in an endless search for migrant labor. The family finds human kindness in the midst of misfortune, cruelty, hunger, and hopelessness. Steinbeck's intimate, searing portrayals shocked the nation and aroused sympathy for migrant workers.

RESOURCE DIRECTORY

Technology

Sounds of an Era Audio CD *"King Porter Stomp,"* Benny Goodman (time: one minute); *"The People, Yes,"* Carl Sandburg (time: 50 seconds)

RESOURCE PRO® Biography *Jacob Lawrence,* found on Resource Pro, profiles one of the finest artists of the WPA Federal Arts Project, long considered the foremost African American painter of his time.

Fast Forward to Today

Social Security

1935 "Young people have come to wonder what would be their lot when they came to old age," says FDR, signing into law the Social Security Act. It provides retirement pensions financed by a tax on employers and employees. Initally, retirees received a one-time payment, averaging $58.08.

1939 Act is amended to include benefits for spouses, minor children, and survivors, paid in monthly checks.

1950 Act is amended to increase the number of workers covered in the program from about 50 percent to nearly all workers; cost-of-living increases are enacted.

1956 Act is amended to cover disabled Americans.

1965 Creation of Medicare gives Social Security recipients health insurance.

2000 Social Security Trustees report that payment of full benefits can be guaranteed only through 2037. With the huge "baby boom" generation nearing retirement, concern about funding for the system prompts intense debate on proposals to reform Social Security.

? Why do you think the federal government kept enlarging the Social Security system and extending its benefits?

very popular, too. In this era, the zany Marx Brothers produced such comic classics as *Monkey Business* (1931) and *Duck Soup* (1933), both of which had first premiered as stage shows.

The greatest box-office hits were movies that distracted Americans from the gloom of the Depression. *The Wizard of Oz,* released in 1939, allowed viewers to escape to a whole different world. Moviegoers flocked to musicals that featured large orchestras and lavishly choreographed dance numbers. No one understood the needs of Depression-era audiences better than Walt Disney, whose Mickey Mouse cartoons delighted moviegoers everywhere. Disney also released the classic cartoon *Snow White and the Seven Dwarfs* (1938) during this period.

The WPA and the Arts FDR believed that the arts were not luxuries that people should have to give up in hard times. For this reason, he earmarked WPA funds to support unemployed artists, musicians, historians, theater people, and writers. The Federal Writers' Project, established in 1935, assisted more than 6,000 writers, including Richard Wright, Saul Bellow, Margaret Walker, and Ralph Ellison. Historians with the project surveyed the nation's local government records, wrote state guidebooks, and collected life stories from about 2,000 former slaves.

Other government projects supported music and the visual arts. The Federal Music Project started community symphonies and organized free music lessons. It also sent music specialists to lumber camps and small towns to collect and preserve a fast-disappearing folk music heritage.

The Federal Art Project, begun in 1935, put thousands of artists to work. They painted some 2,000 murals, mainly in public buildings. They also produced about 100,000 other paintings, 17,000 sculptures, and many other works of art.

VIEWING FINE ART New Deal support for the arts led to many lasting works, including this mural painted by Thomas Hart Benton in 1930 for the New School of Social Research in New York City.
Analyzing Visual Information *How does this mural celebrate the values and spirit of the era? Support your answer with specifics from the painting.*

READING CHECK
Why did the federal government fund new arts programs during the Depression?

The Federal Theatre Project, directed by Vassar College Professor Hallie Flanagan, was the most controversial project. Flanagan used drama to create awareness of social problems. Her project launched the careers of many actors, playwrights, and directors who later became famous, including Burt Lancaster, Arthur Miller, John Houseman, and Orson Welles.

Accusing the Federal Theatre Project of being a propaganda machine for international communism, the House Un-American Activities Committee (HUAC) investigated the project in 1938 and 1939. In July 1939, Congress eliminated the project's funding.

Lasting New Deal Achievements

The New Deal attacked the Great Depression with a barrage of programs that affected nearly every American. The New Deal did not end the nation's suffering, but it led to some profound changes in American life. Voters began to expect a President to formulate programs and solve problems. People accepted more government intervention in their lives, and they grew accustomed to a much larger government. Laborers demanded more changes in the workplace.

The New Deal did not vanish completely when the Depression ended. Its accomplishments continued in many forms. This legacy ranges from physical monuments that dot the American landscape to towering political and social achievements that still influence American life.

Public Works and Federal Agencies Many New Deal bridges, dams, tunnels, public buildings, and hospitals exist to this day. These durable public works are visual reminders of this extraordinary period of government intervention in the economy.

Some of the federal agencies from the New Deal era have also endured. The Tennessee Valley Authority remains a model of government planning. The Federal Deposit Insurance Corporation still guarantees bank deposits. The Securities and Exchange Commission continues to monitor the workings of the stock exchanges.

And in rural America, farmers still plant according to federal crop allotment policies adopted after the Supreme Court struck down AAA crop-reduction plans.

Social Security Despite its enduring support throughout American society, the Social Security system has had many critics. At first, Social Security came under attack because its payments were very low.

For a long time the system discriminated against women. It assumed, for example, that the male-headed household was typical. A mother could lose benefits for her children if a man, whether providing support for her or not, lived in her house. Women who went to work when their children started school rarely stayed in the work force long enough or earned high enough wages to receive the maximum benefits from the system. In addition, when a male recipient died, his benefits ended, leaving his family without an income.

In 1939, Congress and the Social Security Administration developed a series of amendments to the system attempted to address some of the weaknesses in the system. The amendments raised benefit amounts and provided monthly benefit checks instead of one-time payments. They also provided benefits for recipients' dependents and survivors. Later amendments included farm workers and others previously excluded from coverage, and added disability coverage.

A Legacy of Hope Of all of its achievements, perhaps the New Deal's greatest was to restore a sense of hope. People poured out their troubles to the President and First Lady. Eleanor and Franklin Roosevelt received thousands of letters daily during the late Depression era. Every letter contained a story of continued personal suffering. In their distress, people looked to their government for support. Indeed, government programs did mean the difference between survival and starvation for millions of Americans.

Nevertheless, economic recovery in the United States would not come until well into the 1940s, and it did not come through more New Deal programs. The return of a robust economy was set in motion on the battlefields of Europe in the late 1930s, where another test of American character was brewing: a second world war.

Sample Social Security card, with zeroes representing an individual's Social Security number

Reading Comprehension

1. Social Security taxes meant that workers had less money to spend and bought fewer goods; consumers also had less money because programs such as the WPA had been reduced in size.

2. New Deal programs had required borrowing massive amounts of money, causing the national debt to rise dramatically.

3. (a) Wagner Act protections and activism by union leaders allowed unions to grow dramatically. Strikes were used as a tool, sometimes successfully, but sometimes leading to violent opposition. Eventually the sit-down type of strike was outlawed by the Supreme Court. (b) The CIO helped to unite and organize the nation's unskilled workers in mass-production industries, using the strike as the main tool in the quest for better wages and working conditions.

4. The payments were low, and women were discriminated against.

Critical Thinking and Writing

5. They advised restoring the programs that had been reduced in scope; they were proven right, as economic conditions slowly improved.

6. Essays will vary, but should address both the overall impact of the New Deal and the question of whether or not federal funding for the arts was justified.

Section **3** Assessment

READING COMPREHENSION

1. Why did the United States slide back into a **recession** in 1937?

2. Why did FDR become concerned about the **national debt?**

3. (a) What gains and setbacks did unions experience during the New Deal era? (b) What impact did the Congress of Industrial Organizations (CIO) have on union strategies?

4. What did critics dislike about the Social Security system?

CRITICAL THINKING AND WRITING

5. **Testing Conclusions** FDR's advisors concluded that certain actions were needed to combat the recession of 1937. What actions did they recommend, and what were the consequences?

6. **Writing an Opinion** Write an essay that examines the legacy of the New Deal. In your opinion, what positive or negative effects did it have on the country? Should the federal government have become involved in creating jobs in theater and the other arts?

 **Take It to the NET**

Activity: Interdisciplinary Connections Examine examples of federally funded arts projects during the New Deal. State your opinion on whether federal sponsorship of the arts was valuable and appropriate. Explain your reasoning. Use the links provided in the *America: Pathways to the Present* area of the following Web site for help in completing this activity.
www.phschool.com

Chapter 23 • Section 3 **791**

 **Take It to the NET**

Opinions will vary and may include a discussion of how the New Deal arts projects provided work for a great number of jobless artists who could convey themes of the time through their work. Art could provide enjoyment for the public during a time of tremendous trial and change. At the same time, such programs were opposed by some politicians who claimed that government funds were being used to create Communist propaganda.

Chapter
23

Review and Assessment

creating a CHAPTER SUMMARY

Copy this web diagram (right) on a piece of paper and complete it by adding information about New Deal programs and laws. Add as many circles as you need. Some entries have been completed for you as examples.

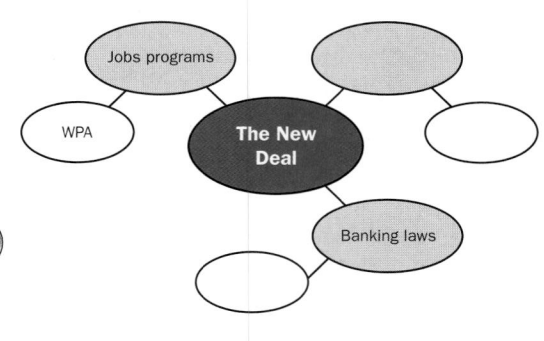

For additional review and enrichment activities, see the interactive version of *America: Pathways to the Present*, available on the Web and on CD-ROM.

★ Reviewing Key Terms

For each of the terms below, write a sentence explaining how it relates to the New Deal era.

1. New Deal
2. hundred days
3. Tennessee Valley Authority (TVA)
4. Second New Deal
5. Wagner Act
6. Social Security system
7. demagogue
8. nationalization
9. national debt
10. sit-down strike

★ Reviewing Main Ideas

11. Why did FDR begin the New Deal by closing the nation's banks? (Section 1)
12. How did the National Industrial Recovery Act aim to help businesses? (Section 1)
13. What did the 1936 election reveal about voters' attitudes toward the New Deal? (Section 1)
14. What were some of the limitations of the New Deal? (Section 2)
15. What was the main criticism of the New Deal by the American Liberty League? (Section 2)
16. Why did President Roosevelt attempt to "pack" the Supreme Court? (Section 2)
17. What factors led to the recession of 1937? (Section 3)

18. What permanent changes took place for labor unions as a result of the New Deal? (Section 3)
19. How did the New Deal support the popular and fine arts in America? (Section 3)

★ Critical Thinking

20. **Identifying Central Issues** Do you think that the New Deal was a success or a failure? Explain, citing information from the chapter.
21. **Comparing Points of View** (a) How did Eleanor Roosevelt view her role as First Lady? (b) How did her critics view that role? (c) How and why did these view point differ?
22. **Demonstrating Reasoned Judgment** (a) Why did the Supreme Court strike down the National Industrial Recovery Act? (b) Do you agree with the court's decision? Why or why not?
23. **Identifying Alternatives** Choose a present-day social or economic problem and state whether a New Deal type of approach would help to solve it. Explain your reasoning.
24. **Recognizing Ideologies** Compare the viewpoints of supporters and critics of the New Deal. Describe the beliefs and values that influenced the opinions of each side.

CREATING A CHAPTER SUMMARY

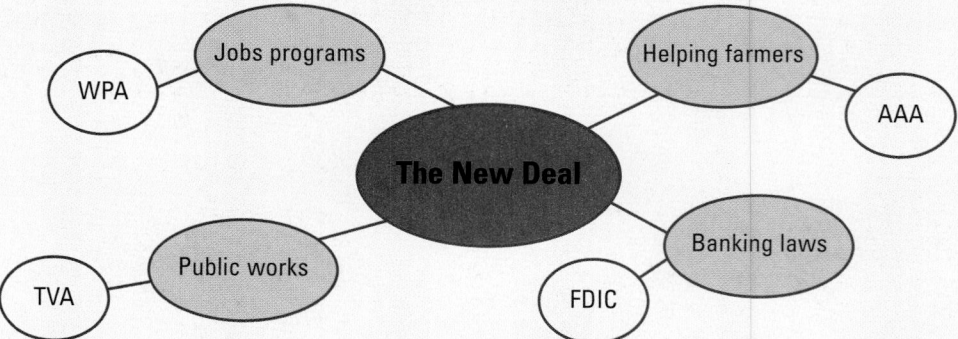

THIS IS ONE RABBIT THAT NEVER FAILED ME!

SPENDING

OLD RELIABLE!

★ Skills Assessment

Analyzing Political Cartoons ▶

25. In this New Deal–era cartoon, (a) Who is the magician? (b) What does the rabbit represent?

26. (a) What does the caption "Old Reliable" mean? (b) Summarize the cartoon's message.

Analyzing Primary Sources

Turn to the quotation from Sam T. Mayhew in Section 2. Then answer the questions that follow.

27. What statement *best* summarizes Mayhew's opinion of the New Deal?

   A Roosevelt's policies were harmful to all Americans because they were never put into action.

   B Roosevelt should have provided more leadership during the Depression instead of letting the country drift.

   C The New Deal failed to bring prosperity to all of America because its benefits were given out by race, not ability.

   D Discrimination on the basis of color caused the Great Depression to worsen in the United States.

28. What does Mayhew mean when he says, "All the prosperity he had brought to the country has been legislated and is not real"?

   F Laws to relieve the Depression were passed but not carried out.

   G Congress passed laws to create new opportunities for Americans, but those opportunities did not become a reality for African Americans.

   H Politicians misled Americans into believing that the New Deal had brought prosperity.

   J Roosevelt himself did not bring any real prosperity to the country; Congress did, through the legislation it passed.

Applying the Chapter Skill: *Distinguishing Fact From Opinion*

29. Suppose you could use these three sources for a report on the 1936 election: (a) a speech by Alfred M. Landon, (b) a political encyclopedia, (c) Franklin Roosevelt's diary for 1936. Which source would you turn to for verifiable facts about the election? Why? Which sources would you turn to for opinions? Why?

ACTIVITIES

Writing to LEARN

Writing an Interview
By the late 1930s, the TVA was well established. Write an interview that might have taken place between a reporter and a farmer, a homeowner, a banker, or some other person living in the region affected by the TVA. Begin the interview by reviewing the purpose of the TVA project.

Primary Source CD-ROM

Creating a Multimedia Presentation Find additional information on the New Deal on the *Exploring Primary Sources in U.S. History CD-ROM* and use the selection(s) provided to complete the Chapter 23 primary source activity located in the *America: Pathways to the Present* area of the following Web site.
www.phschool.com

Take It to the NET

Chapter Self-Test As a review activity, take the Chapter 23 Self-Test in the *America: Pathways to the Present* area at the Web site listed below. The questions are designed to test your understanding of the chapter content.
www.phschool.com

Chapter 23 Assessment   793

CRITICAL THINKING

20. Answers will vary but should be supported with specific facts from the chapter.

21. Answers will vary but should show an understanding that Eleanor Roosevelt performed many active roles in promoting government programs and in alleviating suffering.

22. (a) It gave the President legislative powers and regulated local, not interstate, commerce. (b) Opinions will vary, but should reflect an understanding of the separation of powers and Congress's power to regulate interstate commerce.

23. Essays will vary, but should be supported with specific examples and address themes and topics introduced in the chapter.

24. Supporters: the government has a responsibility to provide aid to its citizens in times of crisis, justifying huge New Deal spending. Though the New deal did not end the Depression, it provided relief and hope for many people. Opponents: were angered by government interference in a free enterprise economy. They felt that free market policies would have been more effective than the New Deal at ameliorating the Depression. Opponents also felt that the New Deal imposed an inordinately large tax burden upon the wealthy. Some critics opposed the crop subsidies paid to farmers, the creation of a huge bureaucracy, and massive spending.

SKILLS ASSESSMENT

25. (a) FDR. (b) New Deal spending.

26. (a) That FDR can be relied on to think he has solved Depression-era problems. (b) FDR's answer to the ills of the Depression is always more government spending.

27. C

28. G

29. For reliable facts about the election, you would choose the encyclopedia as a source because it presents facts that have been checked and confirmed. For opinions, you would choose the Landon and Roosevelt sources because they are first-person accounts and reflect the participants' personal beliefs and feelings, unconfirmed by other sources.

TEST PREPARATION

Use this sample exam to help your students prepare for standardized tests.

TIPS FOR TEST TAKING

You might want to remind your students of the following:

1. Read the directions carefully.
2. Read each question carefully.
3. For multiple choice questions, try to answer the question before you look at the choices. Read all the choices. Then, eliminate those that are absolutely incorrect.
4. For short answer questions, be sure to answer the question completely if there is more than one part.
5. Answer the easy questions first. Then, go back to the ones that will take more time.
6. Pace yourself. Be sure to set aside enough time for the writing questions.

Write your answers on a separate sheet of paper.

1. Charles Lindbergh was admired by many Americans in the 1920s after he

   A made many popular silent films.

   B set records in Major League baseball.

   C flew alone across the Atlantic Ocean.

   D became a commercial radio announcer.

2. Which one of the following best describes the Harlem Renaissance?

   A A system of registering African Americans to vote

   B A very popular nightclub in New York City

   C A program to end Jim Crow laws in the southern states

   D An African American literary and artistic movement

3. Support for African American businesses and a back-to-Africa movement were part of whose program?

   A Marcus Garvey

   B W.E.B. Du Bois

   C James Weldon Johnson

   D Jim Thorpe

4. Which one of the following best describes the Red Scare of the 1920s?

   A A part of the Ku Klux Klan program

   B A type of popular music, especially among teenagers

   C A period of fear of communism and radical ideas

   D A plan to limit immigration from eastern Europe

Use the information in the graph to answer the following question.

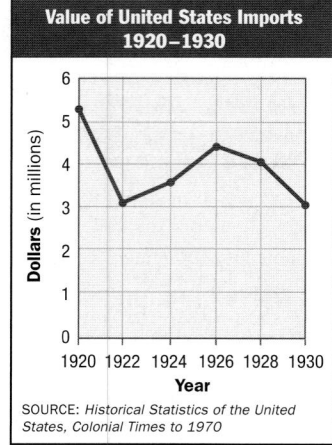

Value of United States Imports 1920–1930

SOURCE: *Historical Statistics of the United States, Colonial Times to 1970*

5. Which one of the following statements best explains the information in the graph?

   A United States tariffs reduced imports into the country during the 1920s.

   B No one had money in the 1920s to buy imports.

   C World War I effectively ended all international trade.

   D New immigrants bought many things from their former countries.

6. The assembly line was first used in manufacturing by

   A J. P. Morgan.

   B Walter Chrysler.

   C A. Mitchell Palmer.

   D Henry Ford.

794

PRENTICE HALL ASSESSMENT SYSTEM

Diagnose and Prescribe
- Profile student skills with Diagnostic Tests A&B.
- Address student needs with program materials correlated to test questions.

Review and Reteach
- Provide cumulative content review with the Review Book.

Practice and Assess
- Build test-taking skills with Test-taking Strategies With Transparencies.

Use the information in the chart to answer the following question.

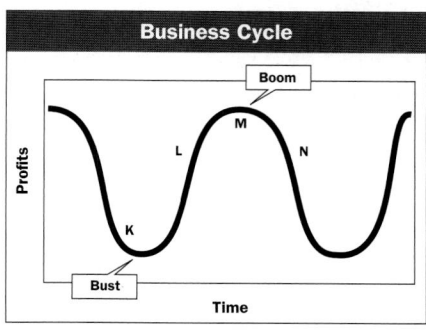

Business Cycle

7. At what point in the business cycle was the U.S. economy just before the Great Crash occurred?

   A K

   B L

   C M

   D N

8. Which one of the following was an action taken by President Hoover to fight the Depression?

   A Giving assistance directly to individuals

   B Closing down all the nation's banks

   C Establishing the Social Security Act

   D Providing jobs through public works programs

9. Which one of the following was one of the first actions taken by Franklin D. Roosevelt when he became President?

   A Ending prohibition in the country

   B Creating the Reconstruction Finance Corporation

   C Closing down all the nation's banks

   D Establishing the 12 Federal Reserve Banks

10. The New Deal–era law that gives money to people who are retired or without work is the

    A Wagner Act.

    B National Youth Administration.

    C Social Security Act.

    D National Industrial Recovery Act.

11. Putting young men to work restoring and maintaining forests, beaches, and parks was the purpose of Roosevelt's

    A Civilian Conservation Corps.

    B American Federation of Labor.

    C Tennessee Valley Authority.

    D Federal Emergency Relief Administration.

12. Which one of the following effectively ended the Depression and restored the U.S. economy?

    A The Public Works Administration

    B The Security and Exchange Commission

    C World War II

    D The Bonus Army march on Washington

Writing Practice

13. Describe the changing role of women in the 1920s.

14. What were the three major causes of the Depression?

15. Describe the actions taken during the New Deal to change the financial system of the United States.

1. C
2. D
3. A
4. C
5. A
6. D
7. C
8. D
9. C
10. C
11. A
12. C
13. Answers might mention that women worked outside the home more often, adopted more casual social manners, and in a few instances were elected to public office.
14. Answers should explain the unstable economy, overspeculation, and mistakes in government economic policies.
15. Answers might include the Glass-Steagall Banking Act, the establishment of the Securities and Exchange Commission, the Social Security Act, and the refinancing of home mortgages.

795

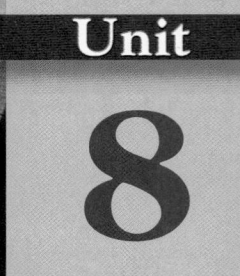

Unit 8

Hot and Cold War
(1931–1960)

Hot and Cold War (1931–1960)
World War II was a devastating world-wide experience. Americans fought to defend democracy against German and Japanese forces. Americans at home endured shortages and hardships in a spirit of cooperation and patriotism. After the war ended there were new problems to confront. The shaky alliance between the United States and the Soviet Union, established for the sake of convenience during the war, fell into a state of undeclared belliger-ence called the Cold War. As that hos-tility intensified, and as the United States sought to contain the expansion of communism around the world, some Americans were accused of disloyalty and even treason.

USING HISTORICAL EVIDENCE

Direct students' attention to the photo-graph on these pages. Reflect with them on the fact that the soldiers landing on the shores of Normandy are heading into a terrifying battle situation. Note that the soldiers in the photograph look eager. Note particularly the body position of the man in the foreground on this page. He seems to be leaning forward, almost as though he were eager to meet the enemy. Note also the expressions of others as they leap off the end of the landing craft.

Discuss with students the soldiers' attitude and spirit. What do students think lay behind that? What do stu-dents think it would have been like to be one of these soldiers?

"It is not enough to fight. It is the spirit which we bring to the fight that decides the issue. It is morale that wins the victory."

George C. Marshall
Military Review, October 1948

U.S. soldiers disembark from Coast Guard landing craft on the shores of Normandy after the main D-Day invasion. ▶

796

eTeach

Be sure to check out this month's online discussion with a Master Teacher. Go to **www.phschool.com**.

RESOURCE DIRECTORY

Teaching Resources
Units 7/8 booklet
• American Pathways Activity, pp. 92–93
• History's Lasting Impact, pp. 94–95
Geography and History booklet, pp. 16–17

Other Print Resources
Prentice Hall Assessment System
• Document-Based Assessment

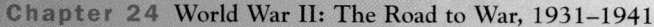

Chapter 24 World War II: The Road to War, 1931–1941
Chapter 25 World War II: Americans at War, 1941–1945
Chapter 26 The Cold War, 1945–1960
Chapter 27 The Postwar Years at Home, 1945–1960

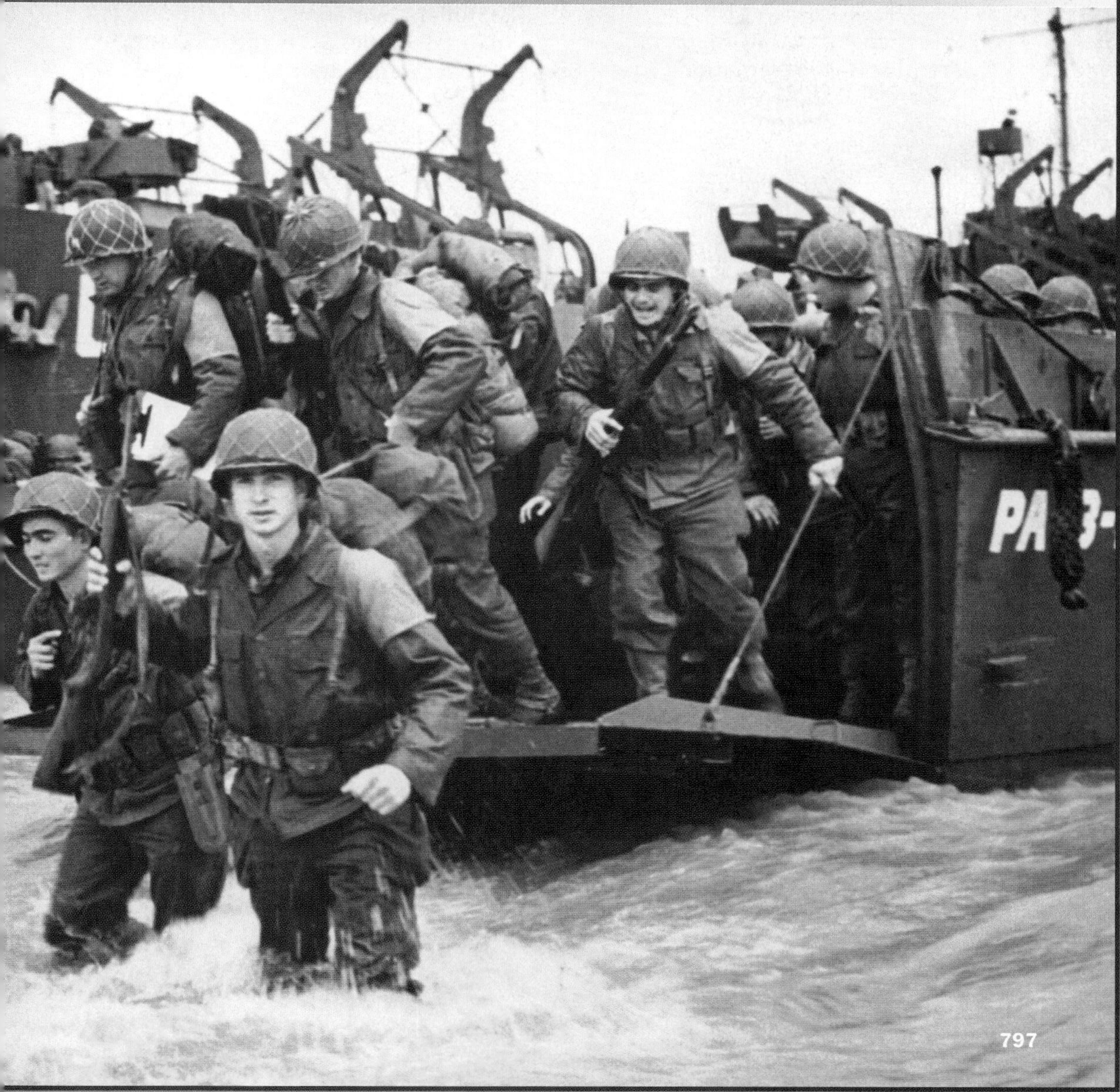

TECHNOLOGY CENTER

Take It to the NET

Prentice Hall School Web site offers student-appropriate Internet activities and links that extend core content. Visit us at the Social Studies area. **www.phschool.com**

AmericanHeritage®

My Brush with History™ Video Program This new video series lets your students learn history from the people who lived it.

RESOURCE PRO®

Teaching Resources on CD-ROM offer lesson-planning flexibility, test-generation capability, and resource manageability.

- **Presentation Pro CD-ROM** Provides you with multimedia lecture notes for each chapter.
- **Social Studies Skills Tutor CD-ROM** Provides interactive practice in Geographic Literacy, Critical Thinking and Reading, Visual Analysis, and Communications.
- **Interactive Constitution CD-ROM** Exploring active citizenship and civic responsibilities, this CD-ROM shows students how the Constitution affects their lives today.
- **Exploring Primary Sources in U.S. History CD-ROM** This interactive exploration of primary sources allows students to analyze and evaluate writing and images from American history.
- **Guided Reading Audiotapes**
- **Student Edition on Audio CD**
- **Sounds of an Era Audio CD** Bring the sounds of American history to life in the classroom with music, speeches, poetry, interviews, and news reports.

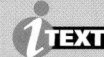

iTEXT

Don't miss the exclusive interactive version of this textbook on the Web and on CD-ROM.

RESOURCE DIRECTORY

Technology

Color Transparencies *Historical Maps,* A36, A37, A38, A39, A40, A41, A42, A43, A44, A45, A46, A47; *Political Cartoons,* B14, B15; *Time Lines,* C7; *Cause-and-Effect Charts,* D10; *Fine Art,* E18; *American Photo,* F8; *The Way it Works,* H18
Section Reading Support Transparencies
Prentice Hall United States History Video Collection™ Volume 19, *World War II;* Volume 20, *Post-War USA*
Companion Web site, www.phschool.com

Chapter 24 Planning Guide
Resource Manager

	CORE INSTRUCTION	READING/SKILLS
Chapter-Level Resources	**Teaching Resources** • Pacing Charts booklet • Block Scheduling booklet **Resource Pro® CD-ROM**, Ch. 24 **Prentice Hall Presentation Pro CD-ROM**, Ch. 24 **www.phschool.com** • eTeach	**Guided Reading Audiotapes (English/Spanish)** **Student Edition on Audio CD**, Ch. 24 **Social Studies Skills Tutor CD-ROM** **Color Transparencies**, A36, A37, A38, A39, A40
1 The Rise of Dictators 1. Find out how the government and the economy of the Soviet Union changed under Stalin. 2. Discover the origins and goals of Italy's fascist government. 3. See how Hitler rose to power in Germany and Europe in the 1930s. 4. Learn about the causes and results of the Spanish Civil War.	**Teaching Resources** **Units 7/8 booklet** • Section 1 Quiz, p. 49 **Learning Styles Lesson Plans booklet**, p. 50	**Guided Reading and Review booklet**, p. 96 **Guide to the Essentials**, p. 121 **Section Reading Support Transparencies**
2 Europe Goes to War 1. Understand how the German invasion of Poland led to war with Britain and France. 2. See what wartime victories and setbacks Germany experienced in Western Europe. 3. Find out why the Battle of Britain was an important victory for Britain.	**Teaching Resources** **Units 7/8 booklet** • Section 2 Quiz, p. 50 **Learning Styles Lesson Plans booklet**, p. 51	**Guided Reading and Review booklet**, p. 97 **Guide to the Essentials**, p. 122 **Learning with Documents booklet**, p. 63 **Skills for Life booklet**, p. 26 **Section Reading Support Transparencies**
3 Japan Builds an Empire 1. Discover the causes and effects of Japan's growing military power. 2. See why the Manchurian Incident was a turning point for Japan's civil government. 3. Find out about the initial outcome of Japan's war against China. 4. Learn why Japan looked beyond China for future expansion.	**Teaching Resources** **Units 7/8 booklet** • Section 3 Quiz, p. 51	**Guided Reading and Review booklet**, p. 98 **Guide to the Essentials**, p. 123 **Section Reading Support Transparencies**
4 From Isolationism to War 1. Find out why the United States chose neutrality in the 1930s. 2. See how American involvement in the European conflict grew from 1939 to 1941. 3. Discover why Japan's attack on Pearl Harbor led the United States to declare war.	**Teaching Resources** **Units 7/8 booklet** • Section 4 Quiz, p. 52	**Guided Reading and Review booklet**, p. 99 **Guide to the Essentials**, p. 124 **Learning with Documents booklet**, p. 88 **Section Reading Support Transparencies**

ENRICHMENT/PRE-AP

Prentice Hall United States History Video Collection™
www.phschool.com
- Section Activities, Virtual Field Trip, Chapter Activities, Current Events Online

Biography, Literature, and Comparing Primary Sources booklet, p. 29
Historical Outline Map Book, p. 64
Exploring Primary Sources in U.S. History CD-ROM

Biography, Literature, and Comparing Primary Sources booklet, pp. 72, 143
Historical Outline Map Book, p. 65
Sounds of an Era Audio CD

Historical Outline Map Book, p. 66

Great Debates booklet, p. 20
Sounds of an Era Audio CD
Exploring Primary Sources in U.S. History CD-ROM
American Pathways Thematic Posters

ASSESSMENT

PRENTICE HALL
ASSESSMENT
SYSTEM

Core Assessment
ExamView® Test Bank, Ch. 24
ExamView® Test Bank CD-ROM, Ch. 24

Standardized Test Preparation
Diagnose and Prescribe
Diagnostic Tests for High School Social Studies Skills

Review and Reteach
Review Book for U.S. History

Practice and Assess
Test-taking Strategies With Transparencies
Test-taking Strategies Posters
Test Prep Book for U.S. History
Alternative Assessment Handbook
Document-Based Assessment

Teaching Resources
Units 7/8 booklet
- Section Quizzes, pp. 49–52
- Chapter Tests, pp. 53, 56

www.phschool.com Ch. 24 Self-Test

AmericanHeritage RESOURCES

From the Archives of American Heritage®
AmericanHeritage® My Brush with History™ Videotapes
www.americanheritage.com

TEXT

Don't miss the exclusive interactive version of this textbook on the Web and on CD-ROM.

Chapter 24 Planning Guide
In Your Classroom

CUSTOMIZE FOR INDIVIDUAL NEEDS

Gifted and Talented

Teacher's Edition
- Customize for Gifted and Talented, p. 801

Teaching Resources
- Biography, Literature, and Comparing Primary Sources booklet, pp. 29, 72, 143

Technology
- Exploring Primary Sources in U.S. History CD-ROM *Berlin Diary, William Shirer; Lend Lease; Pearl Harbor, Daniel K. Inouye*

ESL

Teacher's Edition
- Customize for ESL, p. 809

Teaching Resources
- Guided Reading and Review booklet, pp. 96–99
- Guide to the Essentials (English/Spanish), Chapter 24

Technology
- Student Edition on Audio CD, Chapter 24
- Guided Reading Audiotapes (English/Spanish), Chapter 24
- Section Reading Support Transparencies

Less Proficient Readers

Teacher's Edition
- Customize for Less Proficient Readers, p. 815

Teaching Resources
- Guided Reading and Review booklet, pp. 96–99
- Guide to the Essentials (English/Spanish), Chapter 24

Technology
- Student Edition on Audio CD, Chapter 24
- Guided Reading Audiotapes (English/Spanish), Chapter 24
- Section Reading Support Transparencies

Less Proficient Writers

Teacher's Edition
- Customize for Less Proficient Writers, p. 819

Teaching Resources
- Guided Reading and Review booklet, pp. 96–99
- Guide to the Essentials (English/Spanish), Chapter 24

Technology
- Student Edition on Audio CD, Chapter 24
- Guided Reading Audiotapes (English/Spanish), Chapter 24
- Section Reading Support Transparencies

TEACHER'S EDITION INDEX

CHAPTER 24 – PACING SUGGESTIONS

For 90-minute Blocks

- Teach sections 1, 2, 3, and 4 using Transparencies A36, A37, A38, A39, and A40, and the Recent Scholarship note on page 809 for class discussions.

Running Out of Time?

If you are running short on time to cover this chapter, consider the following options:

- Use the Prentice Hall Presentation Pro CD-ROM to create an outline for this chapter.

- Use the Section Summaries for Chapter 24, from **Guide to the Essentials (English/Spanish)**.

1 The Rise of Dictators

Connecting with Culture

From the first, Picasso's *Guernica* has been internationally recognized as condemning fascism and war. Explain to students that while the painting is not strictly representative of events in the city of Guernica, it can qualify as a historical painting. Point out that artists before Picasso used their skills to represent battle scenes. Like Picasso's work, these works could be used for propaganda purposes. An example might be the familiar painting by Emanuel Leutze, *Washington Crossing the Delaware,* which emphasized the general's heroic leadership, though the event probably happened in a less dramatic fashion. Ask students to research other historical paintings and analyze how they might have contributed to the public's feelings about a particular war or war in general. Such artists include Benjamin West, John Trumbull, Eugène Delacroix, and Francisco de Goya. **(Visual/Spatial)**

2 Europe Goes to War

Connecting with History and Conflict

Have students do research on the events and participants in the evacuation of Dunkirk. They might, for example, view a video of the 1942 film *Mrs. Miniver,* which won six Academy Awards and is regarded, because of its subject matter, as having contributed to the Allied effort. Then have students imagine themselves as participants in the evacuation and write journal entries describing what part they played and their feelings about their roles. **(Verbal/Linguistic)**

3 Japan Builds an Empire

Connecting with Culture

Point out to students that, as in World War I, popular music composers often wrote works in response to the war. Some songs, such as Jerome Kern and Oscar Hammerstein II's 1940 hit "The Last Time I Saw Paris," are sad and melancholy, while others, such as the 1942 song "Don't Sit Under the Apple Tree" by Lew Brown, Charles Tobias, and Sam H. Stept, are lively and optimistic. Have students find and share some of the songs of World War II, either by performing them or playing recorded versions. **(Rhythmic/Musical)**

4 From Isolationism to War

Connecting with Government

Remind students that many Americans felt comfortable with writing letters to President or Mrs. Roosevelt. Ask students to imagine themselves in the days before America entered the war. Have them write letters to one of the White House residents expressing their feelings about what is going on in the world and their opinions about whether the country should retain its isolationist position or help Great Britain. Ask each student to adopt a persona and identify it, for example: farmer, industrial worker, pacifist. **(Verbal/Linguistic)**

Chapter 24

World War II:
The Road
to War

(1931–1941)

INTRODUCING THE CHAPTER

Economic conditions in Europe and Russia following the end of World War I and the Russian Revolution were devastating. Conditions were ripe for the rise to power of new leaders, totalitarian in approach, who promised to relieve countries of poverty and chaos. Joseph Stalin in Russia, Adolf Hitler in Germany, and (to a lesser extent) Benito Mussolini in Italy each took actions, ostensibly to revitalize their countries, which would result in further devastation and vast destruction.

The prevailing mood in the United States during the 1930s was isolationist as Americans coped with the economic crisis of the depression. But when Japanese forces struck Pearl Harbor on December 7, 1941, the United States could remain neutral no longer.

TIME LINE ACTIVITY

To provide students with practice in using the time line, ask questions such as these:

1. What action taken by Japan in 1931 would have far-reaching global consequences? *(The Japanese army invaded Manchuria.)*

2. What 1938 meeting between two leaders failed to forestall World War II? *(The meeting between Neville Chamberlain and Adolf Hitler)*

3. What 1939 action began World War II? *(The invasion of Poland by Germany)*

eTeach

Be sure to check out this month's online discussion with a Master Teacher. Go to **www.phschool.com**.

Chapter
24

World War II:
The Road to War

(1931–1941)

SECTION 1 The Rise of Dictators
SECTION 2 Europe Goes to War
SECTION 3 Japan Builds an Empire
SECTION 4 From Isolationism to War

This German election poster translates to "Our Last Hope: Hitler."

Adolf Hitler

		1934		1935
American Events		The United States cuts tariffs on foreign goods to benefit trade and international relations.		Congress passes the first Neutrality Act banning the sale of arms to countries at war.

Presidential Terms: Herbert Hoover 1929–1933   Franklin D. Roosevelt 1933–1945

1931	**1933**	•	**1935**

World Events	Japanese army overruns Manchuria.	Adolf Hitler is named Chancellor of Germany.	Joseph Stalin begins the Great Purge of Soviet citizens.
	1931	1933	1934

798   Chapter 24 • *World War II: The Road to War*

RESOURCE DIRECTORY

Teaching Resources
Pacing Charts booklet
Block Scheduling booklet, p. 25
Units 7/8 booklet
 • Chapter Summary, p. 48

Technology
Guided Reading Audiotapes (English/Spanish), Ch. 24
Student Edition on Audio CD, Ch. 24
Prentice Hall United States History Video Collection™ Volume 19, *World War II*
Prentice Hall Presentation Pro CD-ROM, Ch. 24
Resource Pro® CD-ROM
Social Studies Skills Tutor CD-ROM
Companion Web site, www.phschool.com

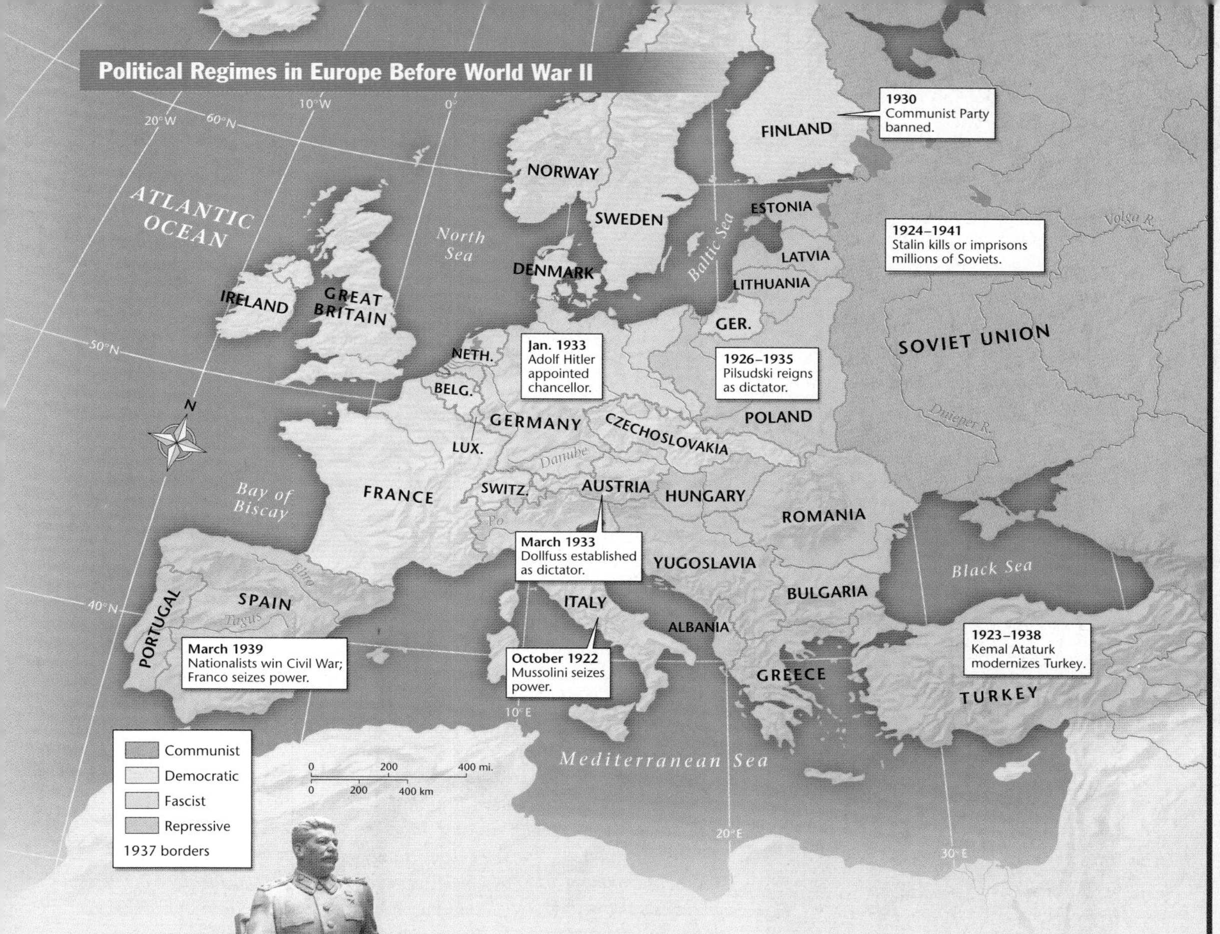

Political Regimes in Europe Before World War II

1930 Communist Party banned.

1924–1941 Stalin kills or imprisons millions of Soviets.

Jan. 1933 Adolf Hitler appointed chancellor.

1926–1935 Pilsudski reigns as dictator.

March 1933 Dollfuss established as dictator.

March 1939 Nationalists win Civil War; Franco seizes power.

October 1922 Mussolini seizes power.

1923–1938 Kemal Ataturk modernizes Turkey.

Communist
Democratic
Fascist
Repressive
1937 borders

Joseph Stalin

1939
Congress repeals the arms embargo.

1940
Roosevelt sends 50 destroyers to Britain in exchange for military bases in the Western Hemisphere.

1941
Roosevelt proposes lend-lease program to aid the Allies. Japan bombs Pearl Harbor and brings the United States into the war.

1937 ● **1939** ● **1941**

Italy conquers Ethiopia.
1936

Marco Polo Bridge incident leads Japan to invade China.
1937

Chamberlain and Hitler meet at the Munich Conference.
1938

Invasion of Poland begins World War II.
1939

Germany defeats France and attacks Britain by air.
1940

Chapter 24   799

Political Regimes in Europe Before World War II

Activating Prior Knowledge What was the political system of the Allied countries? *(Democratic)*

Previewing Czechoslovakia was one of the first countries to become dominated by Germany. Looking at the map, give two reasons for this. *(Czechoslovakia was the lone democratic country surrounded by more repressive political regimes, and a section of Czechoslovakia was bordered by Germany on three sides.)*

BACKGROUND
About the Pictures

1. One of Hitler's campaign strategies was using propaganda like this poster to manipulate the voters he was trying to reach.

2. On August 2, 1934, Hitler assumed both the role of Führer (German for *the leader*) and Chancellor of Germany.

3. Through statues like this, Stalin became widely recognizable and inspired a cult-like fanaticism among his people.

TEXT

Don't miss the exclusive interactive version of this textbook on the Web and on CD-ROM.

BIBLIOGRAPHY

For the Teacher

Kershaw, Ian. *Hitler, 1936–1945: Nemesis.* W. W. Norton, 2000. (A chilling, definitive biography.)

Prange, Gordon William. *At Dawn We Slept: The Untold Story of Pearl Harbor.* Penguin, 2001. (Exhaustively researched, detailed account of the attack on Pearl Harbor.)

Radzinsky, Edvard. *Stalin: The First In-Depth Biography Based on Explosive New Documents from Russia's Secret Archives.* Anchor, 1997. (From behind the iron curtain comes one of the first biographies written with access to previously secret information.)

For the Student

Raymer, Edward C. *Descent Into Darkness: Pearl Harbor, 1941: A Navy Diver's Memoir.* Presidio Press, 1996. (Find out what it was like to dive at Pearl Harbor following the attack, trying to salvage ships and search for remains.)

Rooney, Andy. *My War.* Public Affairs, 2000. (A first-hand account of the war experiences of a 19-year-old.)

Section 1

The Rise of Dictators

READING FOCUS

- How did Stalin change the government and the economy of the Soviet Union?
- What were the origins and goals of Italy's fascist government?
- How did Hitler rise to power in Germany and Europe in the 1930s?
- What were the causes and results of the Spanish Civil War?

MAIN IDEA

Dictators in the Soviet Union, Italy, Germany, and Spain formed brutal, repressive governments in the 1920s and 1930s. They were motivated by their political beliefs and a desire for power.

KEY TERMS

totalitarian
fascism
purge
Nazism
Axis Powers
appeasement

TAKING NOTES

As you read, complete this chart listing the actions of dictators in the Soviet Union, Italy, and Germany in the 1930s.

Country	Actions Taken
Soviet Union	• Combined farms into collectives • Sent millions to labor camps in Siberia •
Germany	
Italy	

SECTION OBJECTIVES

1. Find out how the government and the economy of the Soviet Union changed under Stalin.
2. Discover the origins and goals of Italy's fascist government.
3. See how Hitler rose to power in Germany and Europe in the 1930s.
4. Learn about the causes and results of the Spanish Civil War.

BELLRINGER

Warm-Up Activity The world of the 1930s was a tremendously unstable place, due to economic crisis and a slow recovery from the devastation of World War I. Several leaders catapulted to power on this shaky foundation, including Joseph Stalin, Adolf Hitler, and Benito Mussolini. Ask students to reflect on the global conditions that created opportunities for those leaders.

Activating Prior Knowledge What do students know about conditions in Europe and Russia in the 1930s? Ask students to recall what they learned about the terms of the Versailles Treaty, in relation to Germany. In what ways might France's fury with Germany, and its desire for punishment and revenge, now give rise to a bitter harvest?

READING STRATEGY

As students read the section, have them make notes on conditions that led to a growth of dictatorships in the 1930s.

Adolf Hitler presided over massive party rallies, including this one at Nuremberg.

Setting the Scene In September 1936, German dictator Adolf Hitler called hundreds of thousands of his followers to a week-long rally in the German city of Nuremberg. Included with political meetings and parades was a nighttime ceremony: the Oath under the Cathedral of Light. A Nazi Party booklet described the beginning of the ceremony.

❝ *180,000 people look to the heavens. 150 blue spotlights surge upward hundreds of meters, forming overhead the most powerful cathedral that mortals have ever seen.*

There, at the entrance, we see [Hitler]. He too stands for several moments looking upward, then turns and walks, followed by his aides, past the long, long columns, 20 deep, of the fighters for his idea. An ocean of Heil-shouts and jubilation surrounds him. ❞
—*The Party Rally of Honor*

Amid waving red banners and circling searchlights, Hitler led the audience of 180,000 in a "holy oath" to Germany.

Grand spectacles like the Nuremberg Party Rally were essential to Hitler's **totalitarian** rule. A totalitarian government exerts total control over a nation. It dominates every aspect of life, using terror to suppress individual rights and silence all forms of opposition. The pride and unity of the Nuremberg rally hid the fact that people who disagreed with Hitler were silenced, beaten, or killed. Hitler's power rested on the destruction of the individual.

Hitler and Italy's Benito Mussolini governed by a philosophy called **fascism.** Fascism emphasizes the importance of the nation or an ethnic group and the supreme authority of the leader. In the Soviet Union, Joseph Stalin based his totalitarian government on a vicious form of communism. Like fascism, communism relies upon a strong, dictatorial government that does not respect individual rights and freedoms. Historically, however, Communists and Fascists have been natural enemies.

RESOURCE DIRECTORY

Teaching Resources
Learning Styles Lesson Plans booklet, p. 50
Guided Reading and Review booklet, p. 96

Technology
Section Reading Support Transparencies
Guided Reading Audiotapes (English/Spanish), Ch. 24
Student Edition on Audio CD, Ch. 24
Prentice Hall Presentation Pro CD-ROM, Ch. 24
Companion Web site, www.phschool.com

Stalin's Soviet Union

While Lenin led the Soviet Union, the worldwide Communist revolution he sought never materialized. Even in his own country, economic failure threatened Communist control of the government. Lenin eased up on the drive to convert all property to public ownership. His New Economic Policy (NEP) allowed some private business to continue. Stalin took over after Lenin's death in 1924. Stalin decided to abandon the NEP and take "one great leap forward" to communism. He launched the first of a series of five-year plans to modernize agriculture and build new industries from the ground up.

Stalin's Economic Plans To modernize agriculture, Stalin encouraged Soviet farmers to combine their small family farms into huge collective farms owned and run by the state. Facing widespread resistance, Stalin began forcing peasants off their land in the late 1920s.

The state takeover of farming was completed within a few years, but with terrible consequences. In the Ukraine and other agricultural regions, Stalin punished resistant farmers by confiscating much or all of the food they produced. Millions of people died from starvation, and millions more fled to the cities. Stalin also sent approximately 5 million peasants to labor camps in Siberia and northern Russia. In addition to the human cost, the collectivization campaign caused agricultural production to fall dramatically. Food shortages forced Stalin to introduce rationing throughout the country.

Stalin pursued rapid industrialization with more success. He assigned millions of laborers from rural areas to build and run new industrial centers where iron, steel, oil, and coal were produced. Because Stalin poured money and labor into these basic industries rather than housing, clothing, and consumer goods, the Soviet people endured severe shortages of essential products, and their standard of living fell sharply. Still, by 1940 Stalin had achieved his goal of turning the Soviet Union into a modern industrial power.

Stalin's Reign of Terror During the economic upheaval, Stalin completed his political domination of the Soviet Union through a series of **purges.** In political terms, a purge is the process of removing enemies and undesirable

Labor Camps in the Western Soviet Union, *circa* 1936

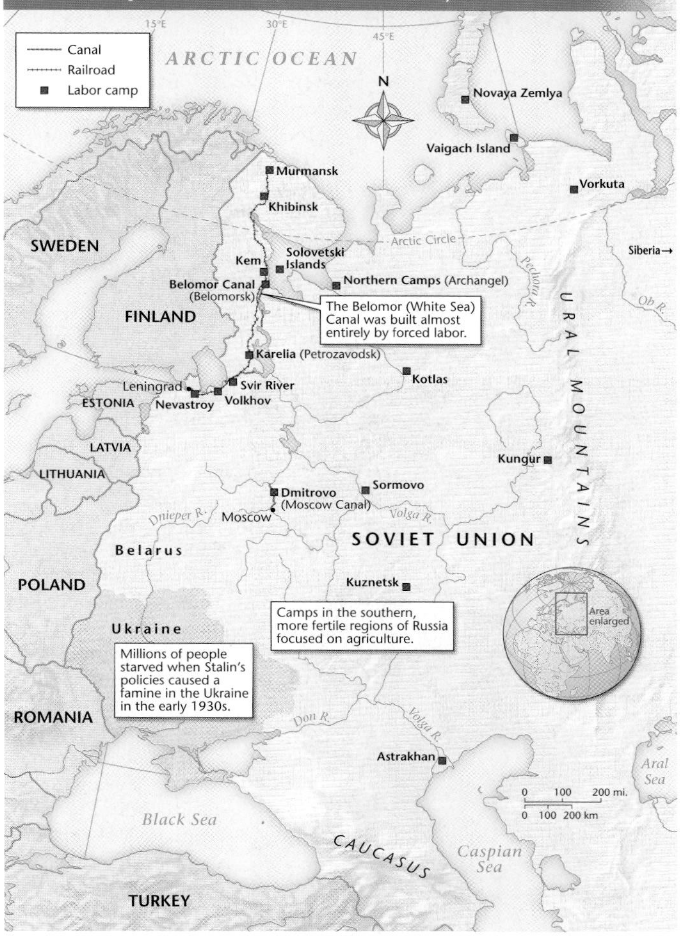

Legend:
— Canal
···· Railroad
■ Labor camp

The Belomor (White Sea) Canal was built almost entirely by forced labor.

Camps in the southern, more fertile regions of Russia focused on agriculture.

Millions of people starved when Stalin's policies caused a famine in the Ukraine in the early 1930s.

Area enlarged

0 100 200 mi.
0 100 200 km

MAP SKILLS Stalin presided over a vast expansion of the Soviet Union's system of labor camps. **Place** *What hardships did prisoners experience in the northernmost camps?*

Connecting with Citizenship

Ask students to write letters to the editor, in the role of Italians of the 1920s or 1930s, explaining why they support (or do not support) Mussolini as the leader of Italy. Ask several students from each side of the issue to read their letters to the class. **(Verbal/Linguistic)**

BACKGROUND

Daily Life

As he made war in Africa, Mussolini preserved the appearance of Italy's economic "miracle" by keeping the nation on a peacetime footing. As a result, when restrictions finally came, they were very harsh. In 1939 sugar and soap were rationed throughout Italy, followed by fats in 1940 and other foodstuffs in 1941. Most civilians were limited to less than 1,000 calories a day, although a well-organized black market in food flourished. Italians were permitted one new pair of shoes or a few articles of clothing per year, but not both. Newspapers were limited to four pages, later reduced to two. By the end of 1941, all civilian gasoline-powered vehicles had been forbidden on the nation's streets and highways. Only a few cars and buses continued to run, powered by methane from Italy's Po Valley.

READING CHECK

Stalin removed his enemies from government through purges. He had his enemies arrested, often on false charges. Stalin used show trials to find these individuals guilty, after which they were executed, deported, or imprisoned.

CAPTION ANSWERS

Viewing History Mussolini's head is pictured prominently over a map of Italy's conquest, giving him credit for the victory. His image is surrounded by a light glow.

READING CHECK

How did Stalin establish total control of the Soviet Union?

individuals from power. Stalin "purified" the Communist Party by getting rid of his opponents and anyone else he believed to be a threat to his power or to his ideas. The Great Purge began in 1934 with a series of "show trials," in which the only possible verdict was "guilty." Stalin's reign of terror did not stop there, however. He and his followers purged local party offices, collective farms, the secret police, and the army of anyone whom he considered a threat.

By 1939, his agents had arrested more than 7 million people from all levels of society. A million were executed, and millions more ended up in forced labor camps. Nearly all of the people were innocent victims of Stalin's paranoia. But the purges successfully eliminated all threats to Stalin's power, real or imagined.

Fascism in Italy

As in the Soviet Union, Italy's totalitarian government arose from the failures of World War I. Benito Mussolini had fought and been wounded in the war. He believed strongly that the Versailles Treaty should have granted Italy more territory. A talented speaker, Mussolini began to attract followers, including other dissatisfied war veterans, opponents of the monarchy, Socialists, and anarchists. In 1919, Mussolini and his supporters formed the revolutionary Fascist Party.

Calling himself *Il Duce* ("the leader"), Mussolini organized Fascist groups throughout Italy. He relied on gangs of Fascist thugs, called Blackshirts because of the way they dressed, to terrorize and bring under control those who opposed him. By 1922, Mussolini had become such a powerful figure that when he threatened to march on Rome, the king panicked and appointed him prime minister.

Strikes and riots had plagued Italy since World War I. Mussolini and the Fascists vowed to end Italy's economic problems. In the name of efficiency and order, they suspended elections, outlawed all other political parties, and established a dictatorship.

Italy's ailing economy improved under *Il Duce*'s firm command. Other European nations noted his success with the Italian economy and applauded him as a miracle worker. They would soon choke on their words of praise, however, for Mussolini had dreams of forging a new Roman Empire. A Fascist slogan summed up Mussolini's expansionist goals: "The Country Is Nothing Without Conquest."

In October 1935, Mussolini put those words into practice by invading the independent African kingdom of Ethiopia. The Ethiopians resisted fiercely, but the large Italian army, using warplanes and poison gas, overpowered the Ethiopian forces. By May 1936, Ethiopia's emperor had fled to England and the capital, Addis Ababa, was in Italian hands.

Hitler's Rise to Power

While Mussolini was gaining control in Italy, a discontented Austrian painter was rising to prominence in Germany. Like Mussolini, Adolf Hitler had been wounded while serving in World War I. He, too, felt enraged by the terms of the peace settlement, which stripped Germany of land and colonies and imposed a huge burden of debt to pay for the damage done to France, Belgium, and Britain. He especially hated the war-guilt clause—the section of the Versailles Treaty that forced Germany to accept the blame for starting the war.

VIEWING HISTORY This poster announced, "Italy finally has its empire," after the conquest of Ethiopia. The letters *A.O.* are the Italian abbreviation for East Africa—the site of Mussolini's empire. **Drawing Inferences** *How does this poster glorify Mussolini?*

The Nazi Party In 1919, Hitler joined a small political group that became the National Socialist German Workers' Party, or Nazi Party. The philosophy and policies of this party came to be called **Nazism.** Nazism was a form of fascism shaped by Hitler's fanatical ideas about German nationalism and racial superiority.

Hitler's powerful public-speaking abilities quickly made him a leader of his party. The Nazis held mass meetings at which Hitler spoke passionately against Germany's national humiliation. One such meeting in 1921 drew more than 8,000 people. Nazi posters helped to boost attendance:

> 66 *White collar and manual workers of our people, you alone have to suffer the consequences of this unheard-of treaty. Come and protest against Germany being burdened with the war guilt. Protest against the peace treaty of Versailles which has been forced upon us. . . .* 99
>
> —Nazi poster, Munich, Germany, March 1921

In November 1923, with some 3,000 followers, Hitler tried to overthrow the German government. Authorities easily crushed the uprising. Although a German court sentenced Hitler to five years in prison, he spent only nine months in confinement.

Adolf Hitler spoke with a charismatic passion that helped him expand the reach of the Nazi Party. The party's symbol, the swastika, is shown here.

While in prison, Hitler began writing an autobiography, *Mein Kampf* ("My Struggle"). In it Hitler outlined the Nazi philosophy, his views of Germany's problems, and his plans for the nation. According to *Mein Kampf,* Germany had been weakened by certain groups that lived within its borders. In particular, Hitler bitterly criticized the nation's Jewish population, which he blamed for Germany's defeat in World War I.

In *Mein Kampf,* Hitler proposed, in defiance of the Versailles Treaty, strengthening Germany's military and expanding its borders to include Germans living in other countries. He also called for purifying the so-called "Aryan race" (blond, blue-eyed Germans) by removing from Germany those groups he considered undesirable. In time, removal came to mean the mass murder of millions of Jews and other peoples.

After Germany's economy recovered from an inflationary crisis in the mid-1920s, the Great Depression hit in the early 1930s. The German people, facing more poverty, looked to their political leaders for help. In response, Hitler and the Nazis promised to stabilize the country, rebuild the economy, and restore the empire that had been lost.

Hitler Becomes Chancellor Hitler's promises gradually won him a large following. In the 1930 elections, the Nazi Party became the largest group in the *Reichstag* (the lower house of the German parliament). In 1932, Hitler placed second to Paul von Hindenburg, a general in World War I, in the presidential election. In January 1933, the elderly President Hindenburg made Hitler chancellor, or head of the German government.

Hitler soon moved to suspend freedom of speech and freedom of the press. Thousands of Nazi thugs, called storm troopers or Brownshirts, waged a violent campaign that silenced those opposed to Hitler's policies. In the March elections, the Nazis gained enough seats to

Focus on CULTURE

The Berlin Olympics Hitler used the 1936 Olympic Games, hosted by Berlin, to spotlight his theory of the racial superiority of "Aryan" Germans. To link the Nazi regime with the heritage of ancient Greece, Hitler introduced the custom of carrying a torch from the birthplace of the Olympics to the modern games. Hitler hoped that German athletes would sweep the competition and awe the world. Instead, an African American runner, Jesse Owens, won four gold medals, as well as the support of the crowd.

Connecting with Government

Have half the class create flow charts showing the process by which Mussolini came to power in Italy. Have the other half chart Hitler's rise in Germany. Then pair students from each half to compare their flow charts and find similarities and differences in how these two leaders gained control of their nations. Call on pairs to report their findings to the class. **(Visual/Spatial)**

*B*ACKGROUND
Global Connections

The swastika, a hooked cross with arms facing in a clockwise-rotating direction, is an ancient symbol with cultural significance in many parts of the world. Its name derives from the Sanskrit word *svastika,* which means "conducive to well-being." The swastika denoted good fortune and appeared on ancient Mesopotamian coins, as well as in early Christian and Byzantine art. It was also present in Mayan and other pre-Columbian cultures in the Americas. In India, Hindus continue to use the swastika today to mark doorways and the opening pages of account books. To Buddhists it symbolizes the footprints of the Buddha, and Tibetan Buddhists use it as a clothing decoration. In 1910 German poet Guido von List, mistakenly believing the swastika to be Teutonic in origin, suggested it as an anti-Semitic symbol. The Nazi party adopted it in 1919.

804 • Chapter 24 Section 1

ACTIVITY
Connecting with History and Conflict

Organize students into small groups. Ask them to speculate how history would have been affected if Britain and France had resisted Germany's militarization of the Rhineland in 1936. Have a spokesperson from each group summarize its discussion for the class. Then springboard from the groups' conclusions to a general class discussion of the value of appeasement as an instrument of foreign policy. **(Logical/Mathematical)**

BACKGROUND
Biography

Jesse Owens (1913–1980), the tenth child of African American sharecroppers in the South, gave an outstanding performance at the 1936 Olympic Games in Berlin, Germany. The Nazi dictator Adolf Hitler expected the Games to showcase German athletes' superiority since he believed that the Nazis were destined to rule "non-Aryan," or inferior, peoples. Before the eyes of the world, Owens proved Hitler wrong by winning four gold medals in track and field events. After the Games, Owens said, "[I] learned that the false leaders and sick movements of this earth must be stopped in the beginning, for they turn humanity against itself."

VIEWING HISTORY Germany's democratically elected assembly, the *Reichstag*, gave Hitler dictatorial powers in March 1933.
Drawing Conclusions *What does this photograph indicate about the* Reichstag*'s independence from Hitler?*

MAP SKILLS Germany annexed Austria and dismembered Czechoslovakia without triggering a war. **Place** *What advantage did Germany gain by stationing troops in the Rhineland?*

dominate the *Reichstag*. Less than three weeks later, the *Reichstag* building burned down in a suspicious fire. Hitler blamed the Communists and used the disaster to convince the parliament to pass an Enabling Bill which gave him dictatorial powers. When Hindenburg died in August 1934, Hitler became both chancellor and president. He gave himself the title *Der Führer* ("the leader").

Germany Rearms Determined to put Germans to work while restoring Germany's military might, the Nazis secretly began spending money on rearming and expanding the armed forces in violation of the Versailles Treaty. They also hired unemployed workers to build massive public buildings and a network of highways known as the *autobahn*. Unemployment fell to near zero, industry prospered, and, by 1936, the Depression had ended in Germany. In addition, the Nazis were now in a position to put Hitler's expansion plans into action.

Like Mussolini, Hitler saw expansion as a way to bolster national pride. He also longed to see Germany return to a dominant position in the world. To do this, he believed, Germans needed more territory, or what he called *lebensraum* ("living space"), to the east. Hitler's main goal, therefore, became the conquest of eastern Europe and the Soviet Union. First, he needed to assert German military power within Germany's own borders.

On March 7, 1936, German troops entered the Rhineland, a region in western Germany. The Versailles Treaty had expressly banned German military forces from this region, which Germany had used as a base for the 1914 attack on France and Belgium. Since the Allies had taken no action in 1935 when Hitler revealed Germany's illegal rearmament, he had reason to believe that the Allies would not enforce the treaty.

German Aggression, 1936–1939

LITHUANIA · DENMARK · Baltic Sea · North Sea · NETH. · GERMANY · East Prussia · POLAND · BELG. · LUX. · FRANCE · CZECHOSLOVAKIA · AUSTRIA · SWITZ. · ITALY · HUNGARY

Area enlarged

0 50 100 mi.
0 50 100 km

- ◻ Rhineland re-occupied, March 1936
- ◻ Germany and Austria united (*Anschluss*), March 1938
- ◻ Sudetenland annexed, Oct. 1938
- ◼ Czech. territory to Poland, 1938
- ◻ Annexed by Hungary, 1938–1939
- ◻ Memel annexed, March 1939
- ◻ Western Czech. occupied, March 1939
- ◻ Slovakia made satellite state, March 1939

CAPTION ANSWERS

Viewing History The swastikas on the banners and the eagle sculpture illustrate the Nazi Party's total control of the Reichstag.

Map Skills With troops in the Rhineland, Hitler could threaten Belgium and France with invasion more easily. This event also convinced Hitler that Britain and France would acquiesce to additional German territorial demands.

RESOURCE DIRECTORY

Other Print Resources
Historical Outline Map Book *Aggression in Europe,* p. 64

Technology
Exploring Primary Sources in U.S. History CD-ROM *Berlin Diary, William Shirer*

Still, Hitler took an enormous gamble in remilitarizing the Rhineland. The German army was not ready for war. However, neither Britain nor France chose to react to this blatant violation of the Versailles Treaty. The British and French had not forgotten the awful costs of World War I, and their leaders were reluctant to challenge Hitler.

Also in 1936, Hitler signed an alliance with the Italian dictator, Mussolini. Their agreement created what Mussolini called an "axis" between Rome and Berlin, the capitals of the two nations. Germany and Italy, joined later by Japan, became known as the **Axis Powers.**

Germany Expands Two years later, the German Army was much stronger. Hitler began to press his homeland of Austria for *Anschluss,* or political union with Germany. In March 1938, after Austria's chancellor refused to surrender his country to Germany, Hitler ordered German troops into the country. Most Austrians warmly welcomed the Nazis, who were often presented with flowers by cheering crowds. When Britain and France protested the German actions, Hitler replied that the affair concerned only the German people.

Several months later, Hitler demanded the Sudetenland, an industrial region of western Czechoslovakia with a heavily German population and many fortifications crucial to Czechoslovakia's defense. Neville Chamberlain, the British prime minister, met with Hitler twice to try to resolve the issue. Chamberlain pursued a policy of **appeasement,** or giving in to a competitor's demands in order to keep the peace. Hitler kept increasing his demands, so Chamberlain and the French president, Édouard Daladier, met with Hitler and Mussolini in Munich, Germany, in September 1938.

Because Britain and France were unprepared for a conflict, they agreed to sacrifice the Sudetenland, in the hopes that Hitler's appetite for territory would be satisfied. Although France was bound by treaty to defend Czechoslovakia, Daladier and Chamberlain agreed to let Hitler annex the Sudetenland on his own terms. No one consulted Czechoslovakia's leaders. British crowds cheered Chamberlain upon his return home for achieving what he called "peace for our time."

The Spanish Civil War

While Britain and France struggled to maintain peace with Germany, civil war was raging in Spain. Spain's democratic government held what would be the country's last free elections under the old republic in February 1936.

Numerous political parties vied for power, including small Fascist and Communist organizations. In this atmosphere, labor strikes, assassinations, and street battles became commonplace.

A group backed by liberal parties won, and five months later the military began a rebellion against the newly elected government, whose supporters were called the Republicans. General Francisco Franco led the rebels, who became known as the Nationalists. By October, the Nationalists had formed their own government, a military dictatorship under the rule of Franco.

The uprising turned into a fierce civil war between the Nationalists and the Republicans. Both sides turned to foreign powers for help. Germany and Italy provided planes, tanks, and soldiers to the Nationalists. Their aid attracted international attention in 1937 when Hitler's Condor Legion

VIEWING HISTORY Upon his return to London from Munich in September 1938, Neville Chamberlain showed crowds the agreement that promised "peace in our time." **Drawing Conclusions** *Why did Chamberlain sign the Munich Agreement?*

German bombers left the Spanish city of Guernica in ruins.

Chapter 24   Section 1 • **805**

Section 1 **Assessment**

Reading Comprehension

1. (a) In an attempt to modernize agriculture and other industries, he created a system of collective farming and poured money into other basic industries, turning the Soviet Union into a modern industrial power. (b) Stalin confiscated land of resistant farmers and sent peasants to distant labor camps, causing food shortages and the need for rationing.

2. At the onset of the Great Depression, Hitler and the Nazis promised to stabilize the country, rebuild the economy, and restore the empire that had been lost. Through these promises, he gained the support of many Germans.

3. Still feeling the aftermath of World War I, neither country was prepared for war; they desired peace.

4. Both Spanish Nationalists and Republicans sought help from foreign powers. Germany and Italy provided support to the Nationalists; the Soviet Union supported the Republicans; Britain, France, and the United States did not intervene, but people came from many countries, including the U.S., to aid the Republicans.

Critical Thinking and Writing

5. (a) Totalitarian leaders felt free to act against other nations, or against domestic opponents. (b) Democratic nations were reluctant to use force.

6. Sample answer: 1933–Hitler became chancellor; 1935–Hitler admitted that Germany was rearming; 1936–German troops entered the Rhineland, Hitler signed an alliance with Mussolini, 1938–Britain and France sacrifice the Sudentenland, Hitler takes over Austria.

Take It to the NET

Editorials should mention concern about German aggression and note that most Americans felt that European conflicts did not concern the United States.

CAPTION ANSWERS

Viewing Fine Art Answers will vary, but may mention that the painting includes more elements of human suffering than does the photograph.

VIEWING FINE ART Spanish artist Pablo Picasso painted *Guernica* to convey the horrors of the Spanish Civil War to a world audience. **Making Comparisons** *Which do you think illustrates the raid more effectively,* Guernica *or the photograph on the previous page? Explain.*

bombed the northern Spanish town of Guernica into ruins. Attacking on a market day, German pilots incinerated the town center and fired on civilians from the air. One person, watching the attack from nearby hills, described it as "a preview of the end of the world." In fact, the attack was a preview of the destruction that would strike hundreds of cities in Britain, Germany, Poland, and other countries a few years later.

The Soviet Union sent arms and supplies to the Republicans. Although Britain, France, and the United States did not intervene, some 40,000 foreigners volunteered to fight for the Republicans as part of the International Brigades. Mostly young and many of them Communist, the soldiers of the International Brigades came from about 50 countries, including the United States.

In March 1939, the Nationalist army finally took the Spanish capital of Madrid and ended the civil war. Franco kept firm control of the government after the war and ruled Spain until his death in 1975.

Section 1 Assessment

READING COMPREHENSION

1. (a) How did Stalin change the Soviet economy? (b) How did he change the lives of the Soviet people?

2. Why did many Germans support Hitler and **Nazism** in the early 1930s?

3. Why did Britain and France pursue a policy of **appeasement** with Hitler?

4. How did the Spanish Civil War highlight divisions in Europe?

CRITICAL THINKING AND WRITING

5. Making Comparisons (a) How did leaders of totalitarian states feel about using force against people and nations they considered their enemies? (b) How did that compare with how leaders of democratic countries such as Britain and France felt about using force against other nations?

6. Creating a Time Line Create a time line of important events in Germany in the 1930s.

Take It to the NET

Activity: Writing an Editorial Take notes on the reaction to German aggression in Europe, particularly following the Munich Conference. Write an editorial for an American newspaper reacting to the events you've studied. Use the links provided in the *America: Pathways to the Present* area of the following Web site for help in completing this activity.
www.phschool.com

RESOURCE DIRECTORY

Teaching Resources
Units 7/8 booklet
• Section 1 Quiz, p. 49
Guide to the Essentials
• Section 1 Summary, p. 121
Biography, Literature, and Comparing Primary Sources booklet (Biography) *Winston Churchill,* p. 29

Technology
Color Transparencies *Historical Maps,* A36, A37

Europe Goes to War

READING FOCUS

- How did the German invasion of Poland lead to war with Britain and France?
- What wartime victories and setbacks did Germany experience in western Europe?
- Why was the Battle of Britain an important victory for Britain?

MAIN IDEA

After war began in September 1939, Germany easily conquered Poland, France, and several smaller countries, but Britain successfully defended itself against German air attacks.

KEY TERMS

blitzkrieg
collaboration
Resistance
Allies

TAKING NOTES

As you read, prepare an outline of this section. Use Roman numerals to indicate the major headings of the section, capital letters for the subheadings, and numbers for the supporting details.

> I. Invasion of Poland
>   A. Hitler invades Czechoslovakia.
>   B. Stalin and Hitler agree to divide Eastern Europe between them.
>   C. German *blitzkrieg* attack overwhelms Poland in three weeks.
> II. War in the West

SECTION OBJECTIVES

1. Understand how the German invasion of Poland led to war with Britain and France.
2. See what wartime victories and setbacks Germany experienced in western Europe.
3. Find out why the Battle of Britain was an important victory for Britain.

BELLRINGER

Warm-Up Activity Germany's initial forays in World War II were vastly successful, largely thanks to the form of attack they pioneered, called *blitzkrieg* ("lightning war"), which combined air and land attacks plus the element of surprise. This approach resulted in rapid victories in Poland, the Netherlands, Luxembourg, Belgium, and France. What types of tactical advantages did these early victories give Germany?

Activating Prior Knowledge In war, opposing sides often benefit from new techniques and approaches. *Blitzkreig* was the new technique applied by the Germans in World War II. What are some techniques students recall from their reading that were pioneered in the Civil War and World War I?

READING STRATEGY

Ask students to rewrite the Main Idea of this section as a question. As they read the section, have them write down answers to their question.

Setting the Scene Neville Chamberlain's triumphant return from the Munich Conference in 1938 did not cheer everyone. Winston Churchill, a member of the British Parliament, believed that sacrificing part of Czechoslovakia to preserve peace was a fatal mistake. He made a dire prediction about this choice: "Britain and France had to choose between war and dishonor," Churchill said. "They chose dishonor. They will have war."

Churchill thought that Hitler had no intention of stopping his military machine and that Chamberlain's peace agreement would give Britain only a few more months of peace. He and other members of Parliament urged Chamberlain to reconsider Britain's policy toward Germany. Alfred Duff Cooper, the head of the British navy, chose to resign rather than accept that policy. In his resignation speech to Parliament, he insisted that Hitler had to be confronted with British might, not appeased:

> 66 *That is the deep difference between the Prime Minister and myself throughout these days. The Prime Minister has believed in addressing Herr Hitler through the language of sweet reasonableness. I have believed that he was more open to the language of the mailed [armored] fist.* 99
> —Alfred Duff Cooper, First Lord of the Admiralty, 1938

Hitler had promised that the Sudetenland was all he wanted. But in March 1939, only six months after annexing the Sudetenland, Hitler occupied the western half of Czechoslovakia and divided the rest of the country among his allies. Most Czechs were hostile to Hitler and bitterly opposed to the German occupation. The following month, Italian forces invaded and occupied Albania, a nation on the Balkan Peninsula north of Greece. Although no shots had been fired, peace in Central Europe was rapidly breaking down.

Winston Churchill succeeded Neville Chamberlain as prime minister in May 1940.

Chapter 24 • Section 2 807

RESOURCE DIRECTORY

Teaching Resources
Learning Styles Lesson Plans booklet, p. 51
Guided Reading and Review booklet, p. 97
Biography, Literature, and Comparing Primary Sources booklet (Comparing Primary Sources) *On Arming Europe,* p. 143

Technology
Section Reading Support Transparencies
Guided Reading Audiotapes (English/Spanish), Ch. 24
Student Edition on Audio CD, Ch. 24

Sounds of an Era Audio CD *Winston Churchill,* 1940 recording (time: 15 seconds)
Prentice Hall Presentation Pro CD-ROM, Ch. 24
Companion Web site, www.phschool.com

Focus Germany's momentum afforded the country an early advantage. Yet forces in Britain were determined to beat back the enemy. What advantages did Britain have over Germany as the Battle of Britain was waged?

Instruct Discuss with students how Hitler combined military and strategic advances to gain momentum at the beginning of the war. In what ways did he catch others in Europe by surprise? Was his early onslaught inevitable, or could it have been prevented? In retrospect, how did Chamberlain's policy of appeasement wind up affording Hitler an advantage?

Assess/Reteach Have students create a time line of major events in the first years of World War II. Have them suggest an answer to this question: By the end of 1941, which country held the advantage?

ACTIVITY

Connecting with Citizenship

Have students create political cartoons about appeasement and the results of the Munich Conference. Tell them that their cartoons can either support or oppose Chamberlain's action at Munich, but should express a point of view from 1938—in other words, without taking into account what students know about subsequent events. Select cartoons for interpretation by the class. **(Visual/Spatial)**

READING CHECK

Britain and France had promised to help Poland in the case of a German attack. However, the invasion of Poland was so rapid that Poland was devoured by Germany and Russia before Britain and France could offer the Poles any substantive assistance.

CAPTION ANSWERS

Interpreting Political Cartoons It implies that the terms of the pact will not last long.

Invasion of Poland

The March invasion of Czechoslovakia ended Chamberlain's hope of working peacefully with Hitler. Britain and France abandoned their policy of appeasement and prepared for war. After Hitler took Czechoslovakia, British and French leaders warned him that any further German expansion would risk war. On March 31, 1939, they formally pledged their support to Poland, agreeing to come to its aid if Germany invaded. By now, however, Hitler did not believe their warning.

Hitler did have one major concern. As in 1914, Germany could ill afford to fight a war on two fronts at the same time. Hitler wanted to deal with Britain and France, his foes to the west, without having to fear an attack from the east.

Hitler's Pact With Stalin Nazi Germany and the Soviet Union had been sworn enemies, but Hitler and Stalin recognized that they had much to gain by working together. Stalin refused to believe that Hitler's long-term plans included conquering the Soviet Union. In August, he and Hitler signed a ten-year Nonaggression Pact, which eliminated the danger of a Soviet invasion from the east.

A secret document attached to the pact divided up the independent states of eastern Europe between Germany and the Soviet Union. One week later, on September 1, 1939, Hitler invaded Poland. On September 3, Britain and France declared war on Germany.

Lightning War Britain, France, and Poland together made an impressive alliance, at least on paper. They had more soldiers and more infantry divisions than Germany. Each German division, however, had superior firepower—more machine guns, artillery, and other weapons. Germany also boasted six panzer, or armored, divisions organized around more than 2,000 tanks.

In addition, the Germans practiced a new form of attack that they unveiled in the invasion of Poland. Called *blitzkrieg* ("lightning war"), this new military tactic included a fast, concentrated air and land attack that took the enemy's army by surprise. The German *stuka*, a divebombing warplane, began the *blitzkrieg* by shattering defenses and terrorizing civilians. Then the tanks and mobile artillery of the panzer divisions punched through enemy lines, encircling and capturing opposing troops. Finally, the infantry moved in to defeat the enemy and occupy the country.

Using the *blitzkrieg* tactic, German troops overran Poland in less than a month. Britain and France watched helplessly from hundreds of miles away, unable to aid Poland in time. Meanwhile, in mid-September, Soviet forces joined the German attack. Under the secret terms of his Nonaggression Pact with Hitler, Stalin seized eastern Poland for the Soviet Union.

War in the West

After Poland fell, the war entered a quiet period. The British and French held back their troops, fearing tremendous losses. The American press dubbed this lack of combat the "phony war." The Germans labeled the lull in fighting the *sitzkrieg* ("sit-down war"). For the next several months, German troops sat and waited while French forces held their defenses.

The key to these defenses was the Maginot Line, a massive string of fortifications along France's border with Germany. A triumph of modern technology, the Maginot Line provided housing for troops, recreational areas, and even air

INTERPRETING POLITICAL CARTOONS The unlikely alliance between Nazi Germany and the Communist Soviet Union stunned western observers. **Drawing Inferences** What does the caption imply about the Nonaggression Pact?

READING CHECK
How did Britain and France react to the fall of Poland?

RESOURCE DIRECTORY
Other Print Resources
Historical Outline Map Book *World War II in Europe and North Africa,* p. 65

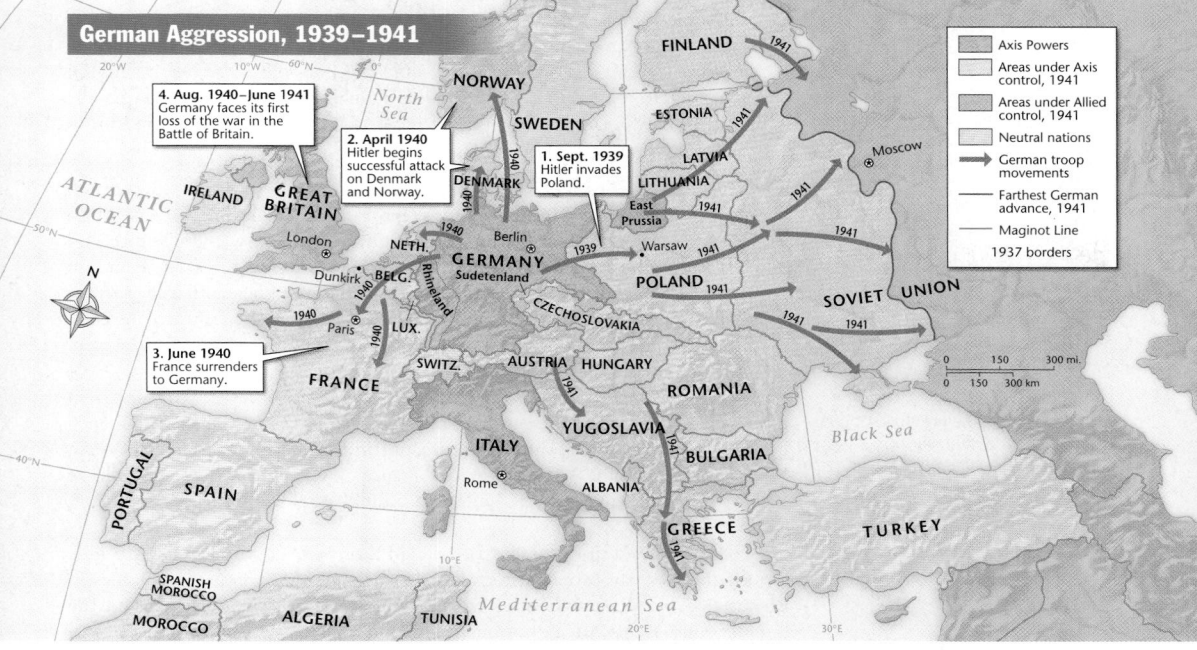

German Aggression, 1939–1941

4. Aug. 1940–June 1941 Germany faces its first loss of the war in the Battle of Britain.

2. April 1940 Hitler begins successful attack on Denmark and Norway.

1. Sept. 1939 Hitler invades Poland.

3. June 1940 France surrenders to Germany.

	Axis Powers
	Areas under Axis control, 1941
	Areas under Allied control, 1941
	Neutral nations
→	German troop movements
—	Farthest German advance, 1941
—	Maginot Line
	1937 borders

conditioning. Underground rail lines connected its main sections. Thick concrete walls and extra-heavy artillery stood ready to fend off any invading army. The Maginot Line had two major problems, however. It protected only the part of the French border that faced Germany, leaving France open to an attack through Belgium. In addition, all of its heavy guns pointed east, toward Germany. If the Germans got around the line, those guns would be useless.

Germany Attacks On April 9, 1940, the phony war came to an end as Hitler began a successful attack on Denmark and Norway. Then, on May 10, German troops launched a *blitzkrieg* on the Netherlands, Belgium, and Luxembourg. Although British and French troops rushed to Belgium to defend their neighbor, they were too late. The German army overran Luxembourg in a day, the Netherlands in five days, and Belgium in less than three weeks. Meanwhile, in mid-May, German motorized divisions in Belgium invaded northern France, skirting the end of the Maginot Line. They raced from there all the way to the English Channel, splitting the main French armies to the south from the British and French troops in northern France and Belgium.

Dunkirk The German drive west divided British and French troops into two pockets, one in the north and one in the south. In the face of Germany's advance, French and British forces in the north retreated to the coastal city of Dunkirk. There, over a nine-day period in late May and early June, one of the greatest rescues in the history of warfare took place. While some troops fought to slow the advancing Germans, others hastily

MAP SKILLS Germany overran northern and western Europe in 1940, conquered Yugoslavia and Greece in the spring of 1941, and invaded the Soviet Union in June 1941. **Location** How does this map illustrate the dire situation of the Allies in 1941?

This 1940 British painting depicts the difficult circumstances surrounding the retreat from Dunkirk.

ACTIVITY
Connecting with Geography

Pair students to take the role of generals in the German military writing memos to Hitler. Each pair's memo should explain why German control of Austria, Czechoslovakia, Poland, Belgium, Denmark, or France is important to Hitler's goal of conquering all of Europe. Call on at least one pair for each country to read its memo to the class. **(Verbal/Linguistic)**

BACKGROUND
Recent Scholarship

World War II was the greatest military conflict ever known. In *A World at Arms: A Global History of World War II,* Gerhard L. Weinberg argues that this struggle was qualitatively different from World War I. While the first major war of the twentieth century brought unprecedented casualties and unveiled horrific new weapons, World War II was a struggle for the total reordering of the globe. It resulted in an Allied victory at last, but only after mobilizing huge numbers of soldiers and civilians and concluding in a series of titanic battles around the world.

CUSTOMIZE FOR ...
ESL

Photocopy a map of Europe, and ask students to use a pencil to shade in the countries conquered by Hitler by 1941.

✓ TEST PREPARATION

Have students read the material on these pages under the heading "War in the West." Then ask them to complete the sentence below.

One main weakness of the Maginot Line was that—

A it did not have enough heavy artillery.

B it faced Belgium, rather than Germany.

C it was too far away from Germany.

D it only protected the part of the French border that faced Germany.

CAPTION ANSWERS

Map Skills By 1941 the Axis controlled most of continental Europe, and the invasion of the Soviet Union had nearly reached the capital, Moscow.

Adolf Hitler posed before the Eiffel Tower during a victory tour of German-occupied Paris.

VIEWING HISTORY London's St. Paul's Cathedral survived the Battle of Britain while surrounding buildings were reduced to rubble. The cathedral became a powerful symbol of Britain's spirit of defiance. **Drawing Conclusions** *How did this spirit help defeat the* Luftwaffe?

assembled a makeshift fleet consisting mainly of tugboats, yachts, and other small private craft. Braving merciless attacks by the *Luftwaffe* (the German air force), about 900 vessels carried some 340,000 soldiers across the English Channel to Great Britain. Although Dunkirk marked a retreat for the British, the remarkable boatlift saved British and some French forces from almost certain capture by the Germans.

The Fall of France Hitler's armies turned and swept south through France. On June 10, the French government abandoned Paris. With France's defeat only a matter of time, Italy declared war on France and Britain on the same day. On June 14, German troops entered Paris, and on June 22 France and its more than 1.5 million soldiers officially surrendered. Adolf Hitler himself traveled to France to join the armistice negotiations and to make a brief victory tour of Paris. The British and French were stunned by the speed of Germany's conquest of France.

According to the surrender terms, Germany occupied the northern three fifths of France and the entire Atlantic Coast southward to Spain. The French government supervised the unoccupied south from the vacation resort of Vichy, and this zone became known as Vichy France. Under General Henri-Philippe Pétain, Vichy France adopted a policy of **collaboration,** or close cooperation, with Germany.

Free France, a government-in-exile in London, continued the struggle against the German invaders from bases in Britain and in France's colonies in Africa. Led by General Charles de Gaulle, the Free French also backed the underground **Resistance** movement in France. The Resistance consisted of groups of French citizens whose activities ranged from distributing anti-German leaflets to sabotaging German operations in France.

Until the summer of 1940, Hitler had experienced nothing but success. German armies had conquered most of Western Europe. He seemed to be on the verge of destroying the **Allies,** the group of countries who opposed the Axis Powers. Eventually, the United States and the Soviet Union would join the Allies, but at that time Great Britain stood alone.

The Battle of Britain

As France fell, Hitler amassed troops on the French coast. His next invasion target, Great Britain, lay just 20 miles away, across the English Channel. Winston Churchill, now Britain's prime minister, pledged that the British would defend their island at all costs:

> 66 We shall fight on the beaches, we shall fight on the landing grounds, we shall fight in the fields and in the streets, we shall fight in the hills; we shall never surrender. 99
>
> —Winston Churchill

Relentless Attack Britain's large and well-equipped navy stood between Hitler and England. To neutralize the British navy, Germany would have to control the air. Hitler turned to the *Luftwaffe* to destroy Britain's air defenses. In August 1940, he launched the greatest air assault the world had yet seen. This intense attack, called the Battle of Britain, would continue well into September. Day after day, as many as 1,000 planes rained bombs on Britain.

The 1923 Hague Draft Rules of Air Warfare prohibited attacks on civilians. At first, the Germans only targeted British ports, airfields, and radar installations. Later they attacked aircraft factories and oil storage tanks. In late August, a

---

group of German bombers strayed off course and dropped their bombs on London. Two nights later, perhaps in retaliation, British planes bombed Berlin. A new, more deadly type of air war was about to begin.

In early September, Hitler ordered massive bombing raids on London and other cities to try to break the British people's will to resist. These attacks included firebombs, which carried a mix of chemicals that burned at a temperature high enough to set buildings on fire. The bombing of London, called the Blitz, would continue off and on until May 1941. The bombing of population centers, by both sides, would continue throughout the war.

Courageous Defense Britain's Royal Air Force (RAF), although greatly outnumbered, stoutly defended its homeland. In a typical raid, slow-moving German bombers, accompanied by speedy fighter planes, would cross the English Channel at a height of about 15,000 feet. RAF pilots in British Spitfires and Hurricanes dodged the German fighter planes while trying to shoot down the bombers. They inflicted heavy damage on the attackers, sometimes flying six or seven missions a day. Hundreds of RAF pilots died defending Britain, but German losses were higher. "Never in the field of human conflict was so much owed by so many to so few," said Churchill, praising the courageous resistance of the RAF.

The British people showed equal bravery. In December 1940, German bombing of London started some 1,500 fires, setting the center of the historic city ablaze. Despite massive losses, the British people kept their will to fight. By the end of 1941, when the German air raids ended, some 20,000 Londoners had been killed and more than 70,000 injured.

Besides courageous pilots and citizens, Britain had another advantage. By February 1940, scientists in Britain had cracked the code that Germany used for top-secret communications. By deciphering coded messages, the British military could get a general idea of Hitler's battle plans. They knew, for example, that Hitler would not invade Britain until the *Luftwaffe* established air superiority—which it never did.

Focus on DAILY LIFE

London in the Blitz Some Londoners sought nighttime shelter from the Blitz in the stations of London's Underground subway system. The authorities tried to discourage the practice for safety reasons, but they were overwhelmed by the number of people who hurried underground in advance of air raids. Eventually, London Transport allowed civilians to spend the night on the tracks and platforms and even provided special trains to supply them with coffee and snacks.

Section 2 Assessment

READING COMPREHENSION

1. How did relations between Britain and Germany change between the Munich Conference and the invasion of Poland?

2. What were three reasons why Germany was able to defeat Poland in less than a month?

3. What was the French policy of **collaboration** with Germany?

4. Why were aircraft crucial to Germany's planned invasion of Britain?

CRITICAL THINKING AND WRITING

5. **Identifying Alternatives** (a) Why did Britain and France choose not to attack Germany in 1939 and 1940? (b) What were the possible disadvantages of attacking Germany?

6. **Demonstrating Reasoned Judgment** Do you think bombing cities is a fair act of war? Explain your answer.

7. **Creating a Time Line** Construct a time line of important events in Europe in 1939 and 1940.

 Take It to the NET

Virtual Field Trip The Maginot Line was designed to shield France from German aggression following World War I. Take a virtual tour of these historic fortifications and write a summary of what you learn on the journey. Use the links provided in the *America: Pathways to the Present* area of the following Web site for help in completing this activity.
www.phschool.com

Section 2 Assessment

Reading Comprehension

1. The invasion of Czechoslovakia ended Chamberlain's hope of working peaceably with Hitler. Britain abandoned its policy of appeasement and prepared for war.

2. Answers may include: use of *blitzkrieg* for the first time; more advanced military than Poland; France and Britain were unable to aid Poland in time; Soviet Union came to Germany's aid, and under the secret terms of the Nonaggression Pact, seized eastern Poland.

3. Answers will vary. Students may note that the policy of collaboration allowed southern France to remain temporarily free of German occupying troops.

4. To neutralize Britain's navy so that German troops could invade with some hope of success.

Critical Thinking and Writing

5. (a) They felt safe behind the Maginot Line. Also, Britain and France lacked enthusiasm for the war. (b) The risks consisted of defeat and high casualties.

6. Answers will vary, but should pertain to issues and events described in the section.

7. Time lines will vary and may include: Hitler's takeover of Czechoslovakia; invasion of Poland; Hitler's attacks against Denmark and Norway; the fall of France; Battle of Britain.

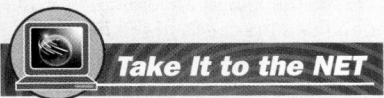 **Take It to the NET**

Invite students to take a Virtual Field Trip at **www.phschool.com**

RESOURCE DIRECTORY

Teaching Resources
Units 7/8 booklet
  • Section 2 Quiz, p. 50
Guide to the Essentials
  • Section 2 Summary, p. 122

Technology
Sounds of an Era Audio CD *Edward R. Murrow on the London Blitz,* 1940 recording (time: one minute)

EXAMINING PHOTOGRAPHS

Focus Analyze a photograph as historical evidence, taking into account the point of view of the photographer.

Instruct If possible, display collections of World War II photographs. Ask students to note the subjects, background, quality of light, and mood. Encourage them to try to determine the photographer's style or point of view. Discuss the importance of being able to analyze a photographer's point of view.

Extend See the Skills for Life activity in the Resource Directory below.

ANSWERS

PRACTICE THE SKILL

1. **(a)** A group of soldiers watching other soldiers wading to their ship. **(b)** It tells when and where the photo was taken and explains why the soldiers are wading to the ship. **(c)** The soldiers are in very deep water and are struggling to reach the ship.

2. **(a)** Yes, the situation was desperate, and soldiers were willing to wade to the ships. **(b)** Answers will vary. Sample answer: a feeling of aloneness, of grim determination. **(c)** Answers will vary. Sample answers: there is open water on both sides of the wading men, making them look lost. The tilted angle makes the image unsettling, and you don't see the faces of the men on the ship. **(d)** Sample answers: the photographer may have chosen the angle of the photograph and to stand behind the men on the ship. **(e)** Answers will vary. Sample answer: the photographer might have taken a picture of one of the men being pulled into the ship, happy at being rescued, or a man on the ship shouting encouragement. A change in the camera angle would have made the image less unsettling.

3. **(a)** Answers will vary. **(b)** Answers will vary. Sample answer: photographs can convey the feeling and immediacy of an event in ways that aren't always possible in writing.

Examining Photographs

Photographs are a form of visual evidence that can provide valuable information about an event or a historical period. Photographers, however, like other observers of events, have their own points of view. By their choice of subject, lighting, and camera angle, photographers can influence what is seen and how it is perceived. They may also distort the appearance of objects in their photographs to create an illusion or to convey a particular mood. For these reasons, you should always analyze photographs carefully.

LEARN THE SKILL
Use the following steps to examine photographs:

1. **Study the photograph to identify the subject.** Look at the photograph as a whole; then study the details. If a title and a caption are provided, refer to them for more information.

2. **Analyze the reliability of the photograph as a source of information.** Note how the photograph conveys information and how it creates a mood or an emotion. Think about other ways the event or scene might have been photographed.

3. **Study the photograph to learn more about the historical period.** Think about how the photograph fits with what you already know. Consider what the photograph adds to your understanding of the historical period.

PRACTICE THE SKILL
Answer the following questions:

1. **(a)** What do you see in the picture? **(b)** How does the caption help you understand the photograph? **(c)** What visual details of the men in the water help you understand what happened at Dunkirk?

2. **(a)** Do you think the photograph depicts the situation accurately? Explain. **(b)** What mood or emotion do you think the photographer wanted viewers to feel? **(c)** What aspects of the photograph help to create this feeling? **(d)** What choices might the photographer have made before taking this picture? **(e)** What other choices (of subject or camera angle, for example) might the photographer have made to give a different impression of Dunkirk? Explain.

3. **(a)** Briefly summarize what you already know about the evacuation at Dunkirk. Does this photograph in any way contradict what you already know, or does it add to your understanding? Explain. **(b)** What can photographs like this contribute to your knowledge of an event that written sources cannot?

APPLY THE SKILL
See the Chapter Review and Assessment for another opportunity to apply this skill.

▲ Soldiers of the British Expeditionary Force wade to the safety of one of 900 vessels that evacuated Allied troops trapped on the beaches of Dunkirk, France, May 1940.

RESOURCE DIRECTORY

Teaching Resources
Skills for Life booklet, p. 26

Technology
Social Studies Skills Tutor CD-ROM
Interactive Practice in
- Geographic Literacy
- Critical Thinking and Reading
- Visual Analysis
- Communications

Japan Builds an Empire

READING FOCUS

- What were the causes and effects of Japan's growing military power?
- Why was the Manchurian Incident a turning point for Japan's civilian government?
- What was the initial outcome of Japan's war against China?
- Why did Japan look beyond China for future expansion?

MAIN IDEA

The Japanese military expanded Japan's power into China and southeast Asia and came to dominate Japan's government.

KEY TERMS

Manchurian Incident
puppet state
Burma Road
Greater East Asia
  Co-Prosperity Sphere

TAKING NOTES

Copy this flowchart. As you read this section, fill in the boxes with some of the major events that led to Japan's invasion of China in 1937.

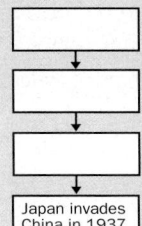

| Japan invades China in 1937. |

Setting the Scene   Japan emerged from isolation in the mid-1800s. The United States forced Japan to open its markets to foreigners when Matthew Perry sailed into Tokyo Bay in 1853. That event pushed Japan to strengthen its military and modernize its economy in order to defend itself. Japan also developed a constitutional government, although the emperor remained a respected figure and the divine leader of the nation.

By engaging in wars against China (1894–1895) and Russia (1904–1905), Japan expanded its sphere of influence in East Asia. It took control of Korea and gained considerable influence over the northern Chinese province of Manchuria, where it stationed soldiers. By the eve of World War I, Japan had developed into the strongest nation in East Asia and one of the most powerful nations in the world.

Growing Military Power

During World War I, Japan joined the Allies. Although Japan played just a minor military role, it conquered several German possessions in the Pacific and won access to markets abandoned by the Europeans. As a result, Japan's economy prospered.

After the war, Japan enacted political reforms that resulted in a two-party parliamentary system and a sharp increase in the number of people allowed to vote. Japan also slowed its territorial expansion. It helped found the League of Nations and signed international agreements designed to keep the peace. By signing the 1928 Kellogg-Briand Pact, Japan condemned war and pledged to solve all disagreements peacefully. Japan would soon show how little influence such international peace agreements really had.

Democracy in Crisis   In the early 1920s, a series of recessions rocked Japan's economy. As in Germany, conditions grew worse after 1930 because of the Great Depression. Japan's industries depended on selling their goods to foreign countries, but many of the nation's trading partners put high tariffs on Japanese goods to protect their own businesses. The resulting industrial decline led to

VIEWING HISTORY The rising sun was the symbol of Imperial Japan. **Synthesizing Information** *Why was this an appropriate symbol for Japan in the early 1900s?*

Chapter 24 • Section 3   813

RESOURCE DIRECTORY

Teaching Resources
Guided Reading and Review booklet, p. 98

Technology
Section Reading Support Transparencies
Guided Reading Audiotapes (English/Spanish), Ch. 24
Student Edition on Audio CD, Ch. 24
Prentice Hall Presentation Pro CD-ROM, Ch. 24
Companion Web site, www.phschool.com

SECTION OBJECTIVES

1. Discover the causes and effects of Japan's growing military power.
2. See why the Manchurian Incident was a turning point for Japan's civil government.
3. Find out about the initial outcome of Japan's war against China.
4. Learn why Japan looked beyond China for future expansion.

BELLRINGER

Warm-Up Activity Though Japan sided with the Allies in World War I, during the 1920s and 1930s a series of economic and political crises changed the balance of power in Japan. Eventually, a more militaristic regime took control and launched an invasion of China. This action was a turning point in Japan's relationships with the rest of the world.

Activating Prior Knowledge Ask students to state what they know about Japan's role in world affairs prior to World War I. Were the Japanese primarily nationalist or internationalist in outlook at that time?

READING STRATEGY

Have students write down the main headings of this section. As they read, have them take notes about the contents under each heading. Then, have students write a brief sentence to summarize material under each of the headings.

CAPTION ANSWERS

Viewing History Japan was extending its military and economic reach across Asia and the Pacific.

Focus Japan was a very isolated nation in the 1930s, by choice. As militaristic Japanese leaders sought to increase Japanese territory, there was a very strong, negative global response. What was the response of the Japanese military leaders to this attempt to thwart Japanese nationalistic intentions?

Instruct Though Japan was never actually ruled by the military, this aspect of the government came to hold more and more control over decisions that were made. Ask students to discuss the impact of the increased efforts by Japan to dominate China. The response of the United States was to attempt to "quarantine" Japan. But there could be no further response from the United States because of a series of "neutrality acts." Ask students to speculate about what might have happened if these neutrality acts had not been in place.

Assess/Reteach What risk did the United States and other nations run by condemning Japanese actions in China? Could this risk have been avoided?

ACTIVITY

Connecting with History and Conflict

Invite students to create time lines comparing events related to Japan's rise in Asia with those associated with Germany's rise in Europe. Suggest to students that they plot German events on one side of their time line and Japanese events on the other. Then have students use information from their time lines to write a paragraph summarizing how the paths Germany and Japan followed were similar and how they differed. **(Visual/Spatial)**

Japanese troops in Manchuria

BIOGRAPHY

General Joseph Stilwell 1883–1946

One high-ranking American soldier witnessed Japan's aggression in China from a local perspective. A West Point graduate, Joe Stilwell served in the Philippines and France before returning to the United States where he learned Chinese. From 1926 to 1929 and 1932 to 1946, Stilwell lived in China, where he represented the United States Army and developed close ties to Jiang Jieshi. Stilwell rose from Jiang's chief of staff to commander of U.S. forces in China, Burma, and India. During World War II, he played an important role in defending South Asia from Japan and in keeping China's links to the West open.

massive layoffs, strikes, and widespread political discontent. Many Japanese blamed the new multiparty system of government. Politicians, they believed, had taken too long to deal with the mounting economic problems. While economic conditions were worsening, some politicians had enriched themselves by taking bribes from the huge family-owned companies that dominated the economy.

The Japanese military, too, expressed dissatisfaction with democracy. At the Washington Conference in 1922, the Japanese government had accepted limits on the size of its navy. Later it had cut the strength of the army and prevented the military from challenging the Chinese troops in Manchuria.

Rise of Nationalism Several radical nationalist groups formed in response to the government's perceived weaknesses. They demanded a return to traditional ways and an end to multiparty rule, powerful businesses, and other Western-style institutions. Radicals assassinated several business and political leaders. By committing terrorism, they hoped to force the military to take over the government. Some members of the military, especially younger officers, supported the radicals.

The Manchurian Incident

Japan, located on a chain of volcanic islands, experienced a population explosion in the 1900s. By 1930, the population neared 65 million, and it was growing by about one million people per year. Japan lacked the land needed to feed its rising population and the raw materials and markets needed to power the Japanese economy. Many Japanese saw the acquisition of Manchuria as a solution to these problems, both for its coal and iron ore and for its immense areas of undeveloped land.

In September 1931, a Japanese army stationed in Manchuria took matters into its own hands. Claiming that Chinese soldiers had tried to blow up a railway line, they captured several cities in southern Manchuria. Chinese troops withdrew from the area. Japan's civilian government tried but failed to prevent the army from taking further action. By February 1932, the army had seized all of Manchuria. World leaders and most Japanese expressed shock at what came to be called the **Manchurian Incident.**

In response, Japan announced that Manchuria was now the independent state of Manchukuo, under Japanese protection. Japan installed a new head of state—P'u-I, China's last emperor from a Manchurian dynasty—with Japanese advisors to run the government. In fact, Manchukuo was a **puppet state,** or a supposedly independent country under the control of a powerful neighbor. Japan sent more than a million farmers, entrepreneurs, and soldiers with the goal of securing Manchuria as a Japanese colony.

The United States and Britain protested that Japan had broken the Kellogg-Briand Pact, but they did not act to halt Japan's aggression. The League of Nations ordered Japan to end its occupation of Manchuria. Japan refused and withdrew from the League instead.

The Manchurian Incident greatly increased the army's power over the government, but some radicals in the military wanted complete control. In 1932, naval officers helped assassinate the prime minister. Other military leaders did not support the assassins, but they used this opportunity to end the multiparty government, putting the parliamentary system itself in danger. In 1936, an uprising by junior military officers resulted in the murder of several high government officials. The uprising failed, but it gave the military even greater power. Civilian politicians began to

Other Print Resources
Historical Outline Map Book *World War II in the Pacific,* p. 66

Technology
Color Transparencies *Historical Maps,* A39

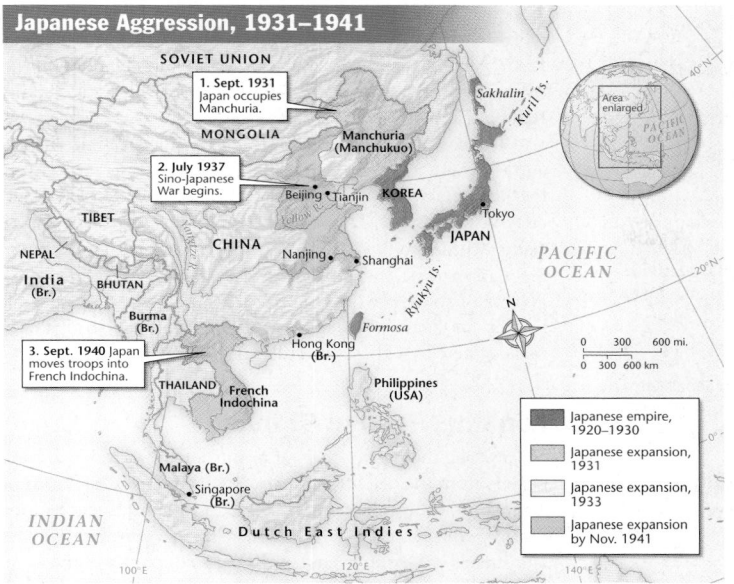

Japanese Aggression, 1931–1941

1. Sept. 1931 Japan occupies Manchuria.

2. July 1937 Sino-Japanese War begins.

3. Sept. 1940 Japan moves troops into French Indochina.

Japanese empire, 1920–1930

Japanese expansion, 1931

Japanese expansion, 1933

Japanese expansion by Nov. 1941

0 300 600 mi.
0 300 600 km

MAP SKILLS Japan's gradual expansion in Asia led to an outright war with China in 1937. **Location** List three countries or colonial possessions that appeared to be likely targets of Japanese aggression in November 1941. Explain your reasoning.

fear for their lives so much that they dared not criticize the military. The new prime minister said:

> 66 The military are like an untamed horse left to run wild. If you try head-on to stop it, you'll get kicked to death. The only hope is to jump on from the side and try to get it under control while still allowing it to have its head to a certain extent. 99
>
> —Hirota Koki

Japan's military leaders never actually seized control of the government. However, they took a much stronger hand in governing the nation, especially in the area of foreign policy. They began to develop Manchuria as a base for even further Japanese expansion in Asia.

War Against China

In July 1937, Japan resumed its invasion of China. The Japanese army turned a minor clash at the Marco Polo Bridge outside Beijing into a full-scale war. By the end of the month, Japanese forces occupied the major cities of Beijing and Tianjin and threatened the rest of northern China. The Chinese Nationalist army, led by General Jiang Jieshi (jyawng jeh SHEE), fiercely resisted the invasion. In battle after battle, however, Japan's superior weapons overcame China's huge manpower advantage. Japanese warplanes ruthlessly bombed Chinese cities. During the "Rape of Nanjing," Japanese soldiers brutalized or killed at least 100,000 civilians, including women and children, in the former capital of China.

The United States and other nations condemned Japan's actions. President Roosevelt spoke out against international aggression, saying that "the epidemic of world lawlessness is spreading" and calling for a "quarantine" to protect peaceful nations. Meanwhile, Congress passed a series of Neutrality Acts that prevented the United States from becoming involved in foreign conflicts. The

READING CHECK
How successful was Japan's 1937 invasion of China?

Chapter 24 • Section 3 **815**

Reading Comprehension

1. (a) A Japanese army stationed in Manchuria. (b) The Manchurian incident was launched by the Japanese Army on its own, not by the civilian government; whereas Germany's attack on Poland was launched by Hitler.

2. Though Japanese troops controlled the cities, Mao Zedong's Chinese guerrillas dominated the countryside, causing a stalemate.

3. (a) To liberate Asia from European colonizers. (b) Japan needed the region's natural resources to carry on its war against China.

Critical Thinking and Writing

4. Answers will vary somewhat, but should show an understanding of how the effects of a population boom in Japan led the Japanese to look overseas for resources and for land upon which to expand.

5. Paragraphs will vary, but should reflect an understanding of the growing power that the military began to wield in Japan's government during the 1930s, and the waning influence of Japanese civilian government officials at that time.

Take It to the NET

Entries should note that after the initial shock of the attack, most sailors tried to man battle stations and carry out their duties. The severity of the attacks should be conveyed through the amount of damage done and the number of casualties.

CAPTION ANSWERS

Fast Forward to Today America protested Japan's aggression against China in the 1930s. The United States government feared for the security of the Philippines, which was an American possession at that time. FDR cut off American oil exports to Japan in 1941 in response to the Japanese occupation of French Indochina. Amidst worsening U.S.–Japanese relations, Japan attacked the U.S. Pacific Fleet at Pearl Harbor, killing more than 2,000 Americans.

Fast Forward to Today

An American Partner in the Pacific

Since the 1930s and 1940s, when they competed for control of the Pacific, Japan and the United States have become important allies and trading partners. The two countries share concerns about aggressive moves by North Korea and China.

Japan had renounced war and had limited the use of its much-reduced military to defense purposes after World War II. In 1998, the Japanese government announced that Japan would offer noncombat support to American troops in "areas surrounding Japan." This bill upset many Japanese who were unwilling to send any troops overseas, even in noncombat roles, to avoid association with Japan's wartime past.

? Why did the United States and Japan come into conflict in the 1930s and 1940s?

Soviet Union also voiced its concern and backed up its words with arms, military advisors, and warplanes for China. Later, Britain sent a steady stream of supplies to the Chinese over the **Burma Road**, a 700-mile-long highway linking Burma (present-day Myanmar) to China.

The war brought two longtime enemies together. Jiang and Chinese Communist leader Mao Zedong, who were locked in a bitter struggle for power, put aside their differences to fight the Japanese. When direct resistance failed, Jiang withdrew his armies to the mountains of remote Sichuan province in the south. Mao split his army into small groups of soldiers who organized bands of Chinese guerrilla fighters to harass the Japanese. While Japanese troops controlled the cities, these guerrillas dominated the countryside. By 1939, the war in China had reached a stalemate.

Looking Beyond China

Meanwhile, the start of the war in Europe distracted European powers from the defense of their colonies in East Asia. Japanese leaders took this opportunity to expand their influence in the region to its south. In 1940, Japan's prime minister announced a **Greater East Asia Co-Prosperity Sphere** to be led by the Japanese, extending from Manchuria in the north to the Dutch East Indies in the south. Japan declared it would liberate Asia from European colonizers. In reality, Japan needed the region's natural resources, especially oil and rubber, to carry on its war against China. In this way, Japan's co-prosperity sphere resembled Hitler's invasion of other countries for *lebensraum* ("living space").

In September 1940, Japan allied itself with Germany and Italy through the Tripartite Pact. That same month, Japan moved troops into the northern part of French Indochina, with the reluctant permission of the Vichy government of France. With the Netherlands in German hands, Japan also set its sights on the oil-rich Dutch East Indies. Then, in April 1941, the Japanese signed a neutrality pact with the Soviet Union. The stage was now set for Japan to challenge the Europeans and Americans for supremacy in Asia.

Section 3 Assessment

READING COMPREHENSION

1. (a) Who among the Japanese was responsible for the conquest of Manchuria? (b) How was this invasion different from Germany's invasion of Poland?

2. Why was Japan unable to win the war in China?

3. (a) According to Japan, what was the purpose of the **Greater East Asia Co-Prosperity Sphere?** (b) What was Japan's real goal?

CRITICAL THINKING AND WRITING

4. **Drawing Conclusions** What do Japan's actions indicate about the way economic problems affect foreign policy? Cite evidence from your reading.

5. **Writing an Opinion** Read the quote from Hirota Koki. Write a paragraph defending or criticizing Hirota's response to the military's actions.

Take It to the NET

Activity: Writing a Newspaper Article The massacre at Nanjing was a terrible episode of World War II. Using eyewitness accounts and other primary sources, write a newspaper article on this topic. Use the links provided in the *America: Pathways to the Present* area of the following Web site for help in completing this activity.
www.phschool.com

RESOURCE DIRECTORY

Teaching Resources
Units 7/8 booklet
• Section 3 Quiz, p. 51
Guide to the Essentials
• Section 3 Summary, p. 123

READING FOCUS

- Why did the United States choose neutrality in the 1930s?
- How did American involvement in the European conflict grow from 1939 to 1941?
- Why did Japan's attack on Pearl Harbor lead the United States to declare war?

MAIN IDEA

United States foreign policy changed slowly from neutrality to strong support for the Allies. Japan's surprise attack on Pearl Harbor immediately brought the United States into the war with the full support of the people.

KEY TERMS

Neutrality Acts
cash and carry
America First Committee
Lend-Lease Act

TAKING NOTES

As you read, complete this chart by listing reasons why people supported or opposed the involvement of the United States in the war.

Supported Involvement in the War	Opposed Involvement in the War
• Britain was defending American ideals of freedom and democracy. • The Axis Powers would eventually declare war on the United States. •	

Setting the Scene

During the 1930s, the United States largely turned away from international affairs. Instead, the government focused its energies on solving the domestic problems brought about by the Great Depression. Even as Italy, Germany, and Japan threatened to shatter world peace, the United States clung to its policy of isolationism. The horrors of World War I still haunted many Americans who refused to be dragged into another foreign conflict. President Franklin Roosevelt assured Americans that he felt the same way:

> ❝ I have seen war. I have seen war on land and sea. I have seen blood running from the wounded. I have seen men coughing out their gassed lungs. I have seen the dead in the mud. I have seen cities destroyed. I have seen two hundred limping, exhausted men come out of line—the survivors of a regiment of one thousand that went forward forty-eight hours before. I have seen children starving. I have seen the agony of mothers and wives. I hate war. ❞
>
> —Franklin D. Roosevelt, address at Chautauqua, New York, August 1936

Few people in the United States agreed with the actions or the ideas of the Fascists, the Nazis, or the Japanese radicals. Most Americans sympathized with the victims of aggression. Still, nothing short of a direct attack on the United States would propel Americans into another war.

The United States Chooses Neutrality

American isolationism increased in the early 1930s, although President Roosevelt, elected in 1932, favored more international involvement. The demands of carrying out the New Deal kept Roosevelt focused on domestic issues, however. He was more concerned with lifting the United States out of the Depression than with addressing foreign concerns.

VIEWING HISTORY Franklin Roosevelt used "fireside chats" to speak directly to Americans during the Depression and later as the United States drew closer to war.

Chapter 24 • Section 4 817

SECTION OBJECTIVES

1. Find out why the United States chose neutrality in the 1930s.
2. See how American involvement in the European conflict grew from 1939 to 1941.
3. Discover why Japan's attack on Pearl Harbor led the United States to declare war.

BELLRINGER

Warm-Up Activity Ask students to choose a place in the world where there is currently armed conflict and to describe the involvement of the United States in that area, if any. Ask them to consider under what conditions the United States should intervene in a conflict between other nations.

Activating Prior Knowledge Ask students if they recall the word "isolationism" from the class study of World War I. Can they define it? What situations in the United States might cause the country to adopt an isolationist attitude in the years leading up to World War II?

READING STRATEGY

Have students create a concept map by drawing five large circles on a piece of paper and labeling each circle with a heading from the section. Have them add supporting information in smaller circles and draw lines connecting them to the large circles.

RESOURCE DIRECTORY

Teaching Resources
Guided Reading and Review booklet, p. 99

Technology
Section Reading Support Transparencies
Guided Reading Audiotapes (English/Spanish), Ch. 24
Student Edition on Audio CD, Ch. 24
Prentice Hall Presentation Pro CD-ROM, Ch. 24
Companion Web site, www.phschool.com

BACKGROUND
American Isolationism

American isolationism in the late 1930s had significant support. The America First Committee was not only vocal but also influential in gathering support from a cross-section of Americans against intervening in the war in Europe. Among the public figures who supported the America First Committee were former President Herbert Hoover; labor leader John L. Lewis; historian Charles Beard; architect Frank Lloyd Wright; chairman of Sears, Roebuck Robert Wood; and possibly the most famous American of his generation, Charles Lindbergh.

THESE SPRING DAYS IT'S HARD TO KEEP YOUR MIND ON YOUR WORK!

INTERPRETING POLITICAL CARTOONS Domestic issues kept Congress and the President from focusing on the increasingly tense situation in Europe. **Predicting Consequences** *What did this cartoonist believe would happen if the United States did not act against Hitler and Mussolini?*

In 1930, Congress had passed the Hawley-Smoot tariff to protect American industries from foreign competitors. In response, other nations raised their tariff walls against American goods. Although they were reduced in 1934, these trade barriers prolonged the Depression and isolated the United States.

Congress again prevented international involvement by passing a series of **Neutrality Acts.** The first of these, in 1935, banned the United States from providing weapons to nations at war. The second, in 1936, banned loans to such nations. The third, in 1937, permitted trade with fighting nations in nonmilitary goods as long as those nations paid cash and transported the cargo themselves. This policy became known as **cash and carry.**

The Neutrality Acts prevented the United States from selling arms even to nations that were trying to defend themselves from aggression. By doing this, as FDR pointed out later, the Neutrality Acts encouraged aggression. By the end of 1938, Italy had conquered Ethiopia, Japan had invaded China, and Germany had taken Austria and the Sudetenland. The United States watched warily from a distance, protected by the Atlantic and Pacific oceans.

American Involvement Grows

As the decade wore on, the American economy recovered somewhat. Unemployment and business failures no longer required the nation's full attention. At the same time, Germany and Japan stepped up their aggression against neighboring countries. This combination of events softened Americans' isolationist views.

American opinion shifted even further against the Axis Powers in September 1939, when Germany invaded Poland. At that time, almost no one believed that America should enter the war against Germany. But many people felt that the United States shared Britain's interests, and given the constraints of neutrality, President Roosevelt began to look for ways to send more aid to the Allies.

COMPARING PRIMARY SOURCES
Assistance for Britain

After France fell and Britain stood alone against Germany, Americans debated whether to assist Britain and what form that assistance should take.

Analyzing Viewpoints Compare the statements of the two speakers.

Opposed to Aid

"When England asks us to enter this war, she is considering her own future, and that of her Empire. In making our reply, I believe we should consider the future of the United States and that of the Western Hemisphere. . . . I ask you to look at the map of Europe today and see if you can suggest any way in which we could win this war if we entered it. . . . If we concentrate on our own and build the strength that this nation should maintain, no foreign army will ever attempt to land on American shores."

—*Charles Lindbergh, Address to the America First Committee, April 23, 1941*

In Favor of Aid

"The Nazi masters of Germany have made it clear that they intend . . . to enslave the whole of Europe, and then to use the resources of Europe to dominate the rest of the world. . . . the Axis not merely admits but proclaims that there can be no ultimate peace between their philosophy of government and our philosophy of government. . . . [Britain is] putting up a fight which will live forever in the story of human gallantry."

—*Franklin D. Roosevelt, Arsenal of Democracy speech, December 29, 1940*

818 Chapter 24 • *World War II: The Road to War*

Debating the American Role   Three weeks after the invasion of Poland, Roosevelt asked Congress to revise the Neutrality Acts to make them more flexible. Congress did so by repealing the arms embargo and providing Britain and France with the weapons they needed. A later amendment allowed American merchant ships to transport these purchases to Britain. The neutrality legislation was effectively dead.

In June 1940, France fell to the Germans, and Hitler prepared to invade Britain. France's rapid collapse shocked Americans, who had expected the Allies to defend themselves effectively against Germany. Now Britain stood alone against Hitler, and many Americans supported "all aid short of war" for Britain. Roosevelt successfully pressed Congress for more aid. On September 2, the United States agreed to send 50 old destroyers to Britain in return for permission to build bases on British territory in the Western Hemisphere. Some Americans saw this exchange as a dangerous step toward direct American military involvement. Two days after the trade, a group of isolationists formed the **America First Committee** to block further aid to Britain. At its height, this group attracted more than 800,000 members, including Charles Lindbergh.

During the presidential campaign of 1940, both Roosevelt and his Republican opponent, Wendell Willkie, supported giving aid to the Allies. They disagreed, however, on how much aid should be given and on what the aid should be. As election day approached, Willkie sharpened his attack, saying that if FDR won, he would plunge the nation into war. To counter this charge, FDR assured all parents: "Your boys are not going to be sent into any foreign wars." In reality, both men knew that war would be hard to avoid.

Lend-Lease   In November 1940, Roosevelt won reelection to a third term as President. His easy victory encouraged him to push for greater American involvement in the Allied cause. To continue battling Germany, Britain needed American equipment. Britain, however, faced a financial crisis. Prime Minister Churchill, in a letter to FDR, confessed that his country was nearly bankrupt. "The moment approaches," he wrote in December, "when we shall no longer be able to pay cash for shipping and other supplies."

In December 1940, Roosevelt introduced a bold new plan to keep supplies flowing to Britain. He proposed providing war supplies to Britain without any payment in return. Roosevelt explained his policy to the American people by

VIEWING HISTORY Members of the "Mothers' Crusade" knelt and prayed outside the Capitol to stop Congress from passing the Lend-Lease Act, Bill 1776. **Drawing Inferences** *How did these protesters hope to sway votes?*

Chapter 24 • Section 4   **819**

ACTIVITY
Connecting with Government

Have students substantiate or refute these two explanations offered by historians as the reasons for American involvement in World War II: (a) Roosevelt saw the war as a way to end the economic depression in the United States. (b) Roosevelt knew that involvement in the war would guarantee the United States a key role in the postwar peace process. **(Logical/Mathematical; Verbal/Linguistic)**

BACKGROUND
Geography in History

The Axis occupation of Europe and North Africa made getting Lend-Lease supplies to the Soviets difficult and dangerous. Goods had to be transported north on the Arctic Ocean to the Barents Sea port of Murmansk, or south around Africa to present-day Iran and then by rail to the USSR. The long southern route maximized exposure to German submarines. (The southern route became much shorter and somewhat safer after the Mediterranean was reopened to Allied shipping in late 1943 in the wake of the defeat of Italy.) The northern route was hazardous because of the extreme weather. Arctic ice sometimes forced ships close to the coast of German-held Norway, where they came within range of air attack. Some Lend-Lease planes headed for Russia were flown across the Bering Strait from Alaska. Others flew in stages from the United States to Brazil, across the Atlantic to West Africa, across Africa to British-held Egypt, and finally north to the Soviet Union.

READING CHECK
With France and Poland already under Nazi control, Britain was the last remaining European power opposing the Nazis (until Hitler invaded the Soviet Union). In that situation, President Roosevelt's lobbying of Congress on behalf of aiding Britain was in keeping with the sentiments of many Americans.

CAPTION ANSWERS

Viewing History The protestors used their roles as mothers to attack the aid bill as a threat to their sons' lives. By praying, they hoped to appeal to the lawmakers' religious beliefs by equating religion with pacifism.

CUSTOMIZE FOR ...
Less Proficient Writers

Have students read the quote on this page in which FDR justifies the Lend-Lease Act. Then ask them to rewrite his quote in their own words, to offer a similarly logical justification of the program.

☑ TEST PREPARATION

Have students read the section "Lend-Lease" on this page and then answer the question below.

What did Roosevelt mean when he said that when your neighbor's house is on fire you lend, not sell, him a hose?

A America should charge Britain lower rates for supplies.

Ⓑ America should send Britain what it needs in an emergency without payment.

C America should stay out of foreign problems.

D It was time for America to join the fight on Britain's side.

BACKGROUND
Connections to Today

Few events in U.S. history have forever changed the very course of the country itself. Pearl Harbor was one of those events. The same can be said of September 11, 2001. Addressing Congress nine days after the terrorist attacks on the World Trade Center and the Pentagon, President George W. Bush said, "Americans have known wars—but for the past 136 years, they have been wars on foreign soil, except for one Sunday in 1941 . . . . Americans have known surprise attacks—but never before on thousands of civilians. All of this was brought upon us in a single day—and night fell on a different world, a world where freedom itself is under attack."

BACKGROUND
Global Connections

The idea of a surprise attack on Pearl Harbor came from Admiral Osoroku Yamamoto, the commander-in-chief of the Japanese navy. It appears to have been inspired by a fictional book he read and by an actual historic air attack. In the 1925 book *The Great Pacific War,* British author Hector Bywater presented a fictional account of a war between the United States and Japan that began with the destruction of the U.S. fleet. The actual air attack was a British strike in November 1940 on the Italian fleet at its base at Taranto, in southern Italy. Launched from an aircraft carrier 180 miles out to sea, the raid took the Italians completely by surprise. Three battleships and a cruiser were hit; three of the battleships were heavily damaged. That same month Yamamoto began planning a similar attack on Pearl Harbor.

the use of a simple comparison: If your neighbor's house is on fire, you don't sell him a hose. You lend it to him and take it back after the fire is out.

The America First Committee campaigned strongly against this new type of aid. Nevertheless, Congress passed the **Lend-Lease Act** in March 1941, authorizing the President to aid any nation whose defense he believed was vital to American security. FDR immediately began sending aid to Britain. After Germany attacked the Soviet Union, the United States extended lend-lease aid to the Soviets as well. By the end of the war, the United States had loaned or given away more than $49 billion worth of aid to some 40 nations.

Japan Attacks Pearl Harbor

Although Roosevelt focused his attention on Europe, he was aware of Japan's aggressive moves in the Pacific. In July 1940, Roosevelt began limiting what Japan could buy from the United States. In September, he ended sales of scrap iron and steel. He hoped to use the threat of further trade restrictions to stop Japan's expansion. A year later, however, Japanese forces took complete control of French Indochina. In response, Roosevelt froze Japanese financial assets in the United States. Then he cut off all oil shipments. As you have read, Japan desperately needed raw materials, and this embargo encouraged Japan to look to the lightly defended Dutch East Indies for new supplies of oil. For the next few months, leaders in the United States and Japan sought ways to avoid war with each other.

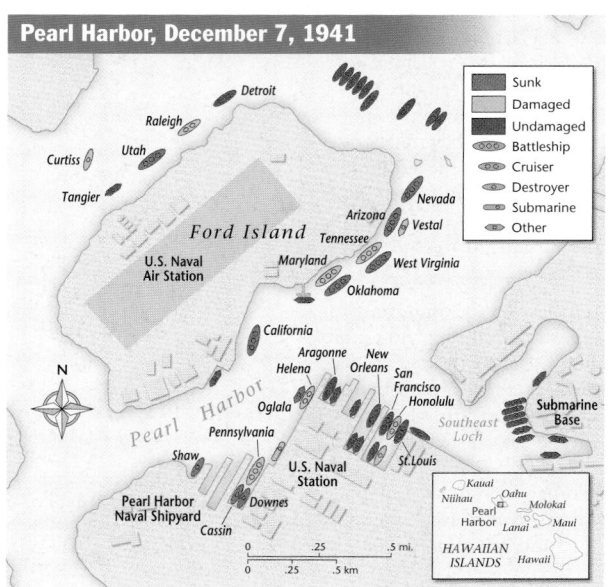

Pearl Harbor, December 7, 1941

Legend: Sunk / Damaged / Undamaged / Battleship / Cruiser / Destroyer / Submarine / Other

MAP SKILLS The Japanese attack on Pearl Harbor was surprising and swift. **Location** *Where did the Japanese inflict the most damage?*

Final Weeks of Peace While Japanese and American diplomats negotiated, a militant army officer took power in Japan. General Tojo Hideki, who supported war against the United States, became prime minister in October 1941. Yet Roosevelt still hoped for peace, and he continued negotiations.

More than a year earlier, American technicians had cracked a top-secret Japanese code. Knowing this code allowed them to read intercepted diplomatic messages. By November 27, based on decoded messages, American military leaders knew that Japanese aircraft carriers were on the move in the Pacific. They expected an attack, but they did not know where.

Indeed, a Japanese fleet of 6 aircraft carriers and more than 20 other ships was already on the move. Its target was Pearl Harbor, the naval base on the Hawaiian island of Oahu that served as the home of the U.S. Pacific Fleet. Japan's leaders had gambled that they could cripple the American fleet and then achieve their goals in Asia before the United States could rebuild its navy and challenge Japan.

The Attack Shortly after 7:00 on the morning of December 7, an American army radar operator on Oahu noticed a large blip on his radar screen. He called his headquarters to report that planes were headed toward the island. The only officer on duty that Sunday morning believed that the planes were American. "Don't worry about it," the officer told the radar operator, and he hung up the

RESOURCE DIRECTORY

Teaching Resources
Learning with Documents booklet (Key Documents) *Franklin D. Roosevelt, Message Asking for War Against Japan,* p. 88

Technology
Color Transparencies *Historical Maps,* A40
Exploring Primary Sources in U.S. History CD-ROM *Pearl Harbor, Daniel K. Inouye*

phone. Less than an hour later, more than 180 Japanese warplanes streaked overhead. Half of the Pacific Fleet lay at anchor in Pearl Harbor, crowded into an area less than three miles square.

Japanese planes bombed and strafed (attacked with machine-gun fire) the fleet and the airfields nearby. By 9:45, the attack was over. In less than two hours, some 2,400 Americans had been killed and nearly 1,200 wounded. Nearly 200 American warplanes had been damaged or destroyed; 18 warships had been sunk or heavily damaged, including 8 of the fleet's 9 battleships. Japan had lost just 29 planes.

United States Declares War

The attack on Pearl Harbor stunned the American people. Calling December 7, 1941, "a date which will live in infamy," Roosevelt the next day asked Congress to declare war on Japan:

> 66 Hostilities exist. There is no blinking at the fact that our people, our territory, and our interests are in grave danger. With confidence in our armed forces—with the unbound determination of our people—we will gain the inevitable triumph—so help us God. 99
>
> —Franklin D. Roosevelt, December 8, 1941

Within hours after Roosevelt finished speaking, Congress passed a war resolution. Only one of its members, pacifist Jeannette Rankin of Montana, voted against declaring war. Even the America First Committee called on its members to back the war effort.

On December 11, Germany and Italy declared war on the United States. For the second time in the century, Americans had been drawn into a world war. Once more, their contributions would make the difference between victory and defeat for the Allies.

Wearing a black armband to mourn those killed at Pearl Harbor, Roosevelt signed a declaration of war against Japan on December 8, 1941.

 Sounds of an Era

Listen to Roosevelt's speech and other sounds from World War II.

Reading Comprehension

1. (a) The Neutrality Acts required: banning the United States from providing weapons and loans to nations at war; nations at war to pay cash for all nonmilitary goods and be responsible for transporting the goods from the United States—cash and carry. (b) Yes, for a limited time, until the revisions which created a more flexible Neutrality Act of 1939. Events such as the German invasion of Poland convinced the American public of the need for America to provide weapons to nations fighting the Axis powers.

2. Because the nations which needed American military equipment were running out of money with which to pay for it. Lend-Lease allowed nations such as Great Britain to pursue their war efforts with the idea that they would pay back their debts to the United States at a later date.

3. Answers will vary. Students might state that relations were cool; the United States was unhappy with Japan's expansionist policies.

Critical Thinking and Writing

4. (a) He wanted to right the American economy before becoming involved in foreign affairs, and he moved slowly in regard to the war in Europe because he felt he needed the support of the American people before taking action. (b) Because no American President can succeed in anything without popular support. Also, FDR hoped to win the 1940 Presidential election and to get legislation he favored (such as scrapping the neutrality laws) passed.

5. Articles will vary but should be supported with facts from the section.

Section 4   Assessment

READING COMPREHENSION

1. (a) What was required by the **Neutrality Acts?** (b) Did they succeed in keeping the United States neutral? Why or why not?

2. Why did Roosevelt ask Congress to pass the **Lend-Lease Act?**

3. In your own words, describe relations between Japan and the United States before the attack on Pearl Harbor.

CRITICAL THINKING AND WRITING

4. **Recognizing Cause and Effect** (a) How much did President Roosevelt consider American public opinion when deciding how to respond to the conflict in Europe? (b) Why did he need to consider public opinion at all?

5. **Writing a News Story** Write a short newspaper article on the fall of France from an American point of view. Explain the consequences for the United States.

 Take It to the NET

Activity: Writing a Diary Entry
Read eyewitness accounts of the Pearl Harbor bombing online. Next, write a personal diary entry as if you were present for this historic event. Use the links provided in the *America: Pathways to the Present* area of the following Web site for help in completing this activity.
www.phschool.com

Chapter 24 • Section 4   **821**

RESOURCE DIRECTORY

Teaching Resources
Units 7/8 booklet
- Section 4 Quiz, p. 52
- Chapter 24 Test, pp. 53, 56

Guide to the Essentials
- Section 4 Summary, p. 124
- Chapter 24 Test, p. 125

Other Print Resources
Chapter Tests with ExamView® Test Bank CD-ROM, Ch. 24

Technology
Sounds of an Era Audio CD *Broadcast from KGU, Honolulu,* December 7, 1941, recording (time: 15 seconds); *Broadcast from Washington,* December 7, 1941, recording (time: 15 seconds); *Roosevelt's Declaration of War,* 1941 recording (time: one minute); *"We Hold These Truths,"* December 15, 1941, recording (time: one minute, 30 seconds)
ExamView® Test Bank CD-ROM, Ch. 24
Social Studies Skills Tutor CD-ROM

 **Take It to the NET**

Student articles should note the brutality of the Nanjing Massacre. Students should note that all of the casualties were either surrendered soldiers or civilians.

REVIEWING KEY TERMS

Students should refer to the definitions of key terms in the chapter to write sentences that show an understanding of the decade of tension and conflict leading up to World War II.

REVIEWING MAIN IDEAS

15. (a) Germany was suffering economically at the time, and Hitler attracted Germans with promises of stabilizing the economy and restoring Germany to a strong international position. The growing strength of the Nazi party forced President Hindenburg to appoint Hitler Chancellor in January 1933. (b) Mussolini believed strongly that the Versailles Treaty should have granted Italy more territory, and he would later seek it himself. His talent as a public speaker attracted followers and led to the founding of the Italian Fascist party. Through terror and threats, his power grew.

16. Sample answer: peasants were forced off their lands in favor of large, collective farms; food shortages and rationing occurred; purges exiled and executed large numbers of people.

17. Aircraft, which play a central role in *blitzkrieg*, allowed fast, concentrated, surprise attacks, contributing significantly to a quick victory in Poland.

18. (a) The Blitz was destructive, and many sought shelter in subway stations at night. (b) No, they kept their will to fight. In 1940 they cracked Germany's code for top-secret communications. The superb performance of the Royal Air Force in the Battle of Britain inspired the nation.

19. The military gradually took power away from the civilian government.

20. In China, the war had reached a stalemate. At home, the lack of raw materials was hurting the Japanese economy, particularly after July 1940, when the United States began to curtail exports to Japan.

21. The Neutrality Act of 1939 allowed Britain to buy goods on a cash-and-carry basis; a later amendment allowed American merchant ships to transport these purchases to Britain; the United States sent 50 destroyers to Britain in return for permission to build bases on British territory in the Western Hemisphere; the Lend-Lease

creating a CHAPTER SUMMARY

Copy this diagram (right) on a piece of paper and complete it by adding important events and issues that fit each heading.

For additional review and enrichment activities, see the interactive version of *America: Pathways to the Present*, available on the Web and on CD-ROM.

Time Period	Important Events
The Rise of Dictators	• Stalin takes control of the Soviet Union and nationalizes most of the economy. • Millions die during Stalin's collectivization campaign and Communist purges. • Mussolini overthrows the Italian government shortly after World War I.
Europe Goes to War	
Japan Builds an Empire	
From Isolationism to War	

★ Reviewing Key Terms

For each of the terms below, write a sentence explaining how it relates to the years leading up to the entry of the United States into war.

1. totalitarian
2. fascism
3. Nazism
4. Axis Powers
5. appeasement
6. *blitzkrieg*
7. collaboration
8. Allies
9. Manchurian Incident
10. puppet state
11. Neutrality Acts
12. cash and carry
13. America First Committee
14. Lend-Lease Act

★ Reviewing Main Ideas

15. (a) How did Hitler come to power in Germany? (b) How did Mussolini come to power in Italy? (Section 1)

16. List three ways that individuals in the Soviet Union suffered under Stalin. (Section 1)

17. What role did aircraft play in the German attacks on Poland? (Section 2)

18. (a) How did the Blitz affect life in Britain? (b) Did it succeed in discouraging Britain from resisting? Why or why not? (Section 2)

19. Describe the relationship between the military and the civilian government in Japan in the 1930s. (Section 3)

20. What problems did Japan face in China in 1939 and 1940? (Section 3)

21. What steps did Roosevelt take to help Britain up until the attack on Pearl Harbor? (Section 4)

22. Describe the events leading up to and following the attack on Pearl Harbor. (Section 4)

★ Critical Thinking

23. **Predicting Consequences** If Britain and France had not adopted a policy of appeasement, would Adolf Hitler have been as successful as he was in overrunning Europe?

24. **Making Comparisons** (a) What characteristics did fascism under Mussolini and Hitler have in common with communism under Stalin? (b) What are two important differences between fascism and communism?

25. **Synthesizing Information** In what ways did the Spanish Civil War foreshadow the events that occurred in 1939 and later, throughout Europe?

26. **Recognizing Ideologies** How was the idea of the Greater East Asia Co-Prosperity Sphere designed to appeal to Asians? (b) Why do you think Japan failed to win lasting support from most non-Japanese within this region?

27. **Identifying Central Issues** Why didn't Roosevelt declare war on Germany in 1939?

CREATING A CHAPTER SUMMARY

Time Period	Important Events
The Rise of Dictators	• Stalin takes control of the Soviet Union and nationalizes most of the economy. • Millions die during Stalin's collectivization campaign and Communist purges. • Mussolini overthrows the Italian government shortly after World War I.
Europe Goes to War	• Hitler makes a pact with Stalin. • Germany invades Poland. • Germany conquers Denmark, Norway, Luxembourg, and the Netherlands. • Germany invades and conquers France. • Germany loses the Battle of Britain.
Japan Builds an Empire	• Rise of militaristic nationalism in Japan • Japan invades Manchuria. • Japan continues its invasion of China.
From Isolationism to War	• United States remains neutral in early years of the war. • Interest grows in America to become involved on European front. • America First Committee opposes war. • FDR establishes Lend-Lease program to aid allies. • Japan attacks Pearl Harbor. • U.S. enters the war.

"Sometimes I wonder -- would we speed things up if we used turtles instead of snails?"

"ALL OUT" AID TO BRITAIN

★ Skills Assessment

Analyzing Political Cartoons ▶

28. Analyze the images in this May 4, 1941, cartoon. (a) What does the tank represent? (b) Whom do the men represent?

29. Why is it significant that the tank is riding on the backs of snails?

30. What point is the cartoonist making by having the men ask this question?

Analyzing Primary Sources

Read the excerpt from Roosevelt's speech asking Congress to declare war on Japan. Then answer the questions below.

31. How would you describe the tone of Roosevelt's speech?

A serious but optimistic
B joyful
C pessimistic
D angry

32. What is the most likely reason that Roosevelt began this speech with the words, "hostilities exist"?

F to inform members of Congress that Japan has bombed Pearl Harbor.
G to inform the Japanese that the United States is hostile to the Axis Powers.
H to give Japan an opportunity to make peace with the United States.
J to convince members of Congress that their only option is to declare war.

Applying the Chapter Skill: *Examining Photographs*

33. Study the photograph of St. Paul's Cathedral in London on p. 810. (a) What do you think was the purpose of this photo? (b) How did the photographer add drama to a picture of St. Paul's among damaged buildings? (c) Do you think this photo reflects the experiences of ordinary Londoners during the Blitz? Explain your answer.

ACTIVITIES

Writing to LEARN

Writing an Opinion
If a foreign power threatens a neighbor of the United States, and American intervention can stop the aggression, should the United States intervene? Does the United States have a responsibility to act? How should the President and Congress determine when to act and when to avoid a conflict? Write an essay to explain your answer.

Primary Source CD-ROM

Working With Primary Sources Find additional information on World War II on the *Exploring Primary Sources in U.S. History CD-ROM* and use the selection(s) provided to complete the Chapter 24 primary source activity located in the *America: Pathways to the Present* area of the following Web site.
www.phschool.com

Take It to the NET

Chapter Self-Test As a review activity, take the Chapter 24 Self-Test in the *America: Pathways to the Present* area at the Web site listed below. The questions are designed to test your understanding of the chapter content.
www.phschool.com

Chapter 24 Assessment **823**

act allowed for the flow of supplies to Britain without pay.

22. Japan's actions in China and Indochina led the U.S. to freeze Japanese assets in the United States and stop exporting raw materials to Japan. Japanese and American diplomats negotiated to avoid war, while General Tojo Hideki came to power in Japan. Tojo's regime planned and carried out the Japanese attack on Pearl Harbor. After the attack the United States declared war on Japan. Subsequently, Germany and Italy declared war on the United States.

CRITICAL THINKING

23. Sample answer: Probably not; Hitler might not have been able to fight Czechoslovakia in the east and Britain and France in the west at the same time.
24. (a) Single-party control of the government; lack of individual rights. (b) Communist governments have complete ownership of land and property, and call for worldwide revolution. Fascist regimes allow private business ownership and do not favor worldwide revolution.
25. Other countries were drawn into a civil war within Spain. Similarly, the German attack on Poland eventually plunged virtually all of Europe into war.
26. (a) As a way to liberate Asia from European colonizers. (b) Their method of colonization was similar to that of European powers, and thus met with objection.
27. American Presidents cannot declare war. Only Congress can declare war. Americans were unwilling to fight then, and had no commitments in Europe at the time.

SKILLS ASSESSMENT

28. (a) Aid to Britain. (b) Americans policy makers and weapons manufacturers supplying aid to Britain.
29. The flow of aid was slow in starting.
30. America was not doing enough to send aid, though it claimed to be.
31. A
32. J
33. (a) To show the cathedral, which survived the bombing, as an example of Britain's refusal to surrender. (b) By capturing one of the buildings in the foreground as the upper stories fell to the ground. (c) Yes, because many areas of London were damaged during the blitz, but like the cathedral, British people refused to give in despite the bombing.

ANSWERS TO ACTIVITIES

Writing to LEARN

Pro-intervention: Students may cite the dangers to American interests abroad and the suffering of innocent people living under tyranny. Anti-intervention: Students may note the possibility of American casualties and the idea that America should not intervene in the business of other nations.

Primary Source CD-ROM

Direct students to the additional primary sources that can be found on the *Exploring Primary Sources in U.S. History CD-ROM.*

Take It to the NET

Additional support materials and activities for Chapter 24 of *America: Pathways to the Present* can be found in the Social Studies area at the Prentice Hall School Web site. **www.phschool.com**

Chapter 25 Planning Guide
Resource Manager

	CORE INSTRUCTION	READING/SKILLS
Chapter-Level Resources	**Teaching Resources** • Pacing Charts booklet • Block Scheduling booklet **Resource Pro® CD-ROM**, Ch. 25 **Prentice Hall Presentation Pro CD-ROM**, Ch. 25 **www.phschool.com** • eTeach	**Guided Reading Audiotapes (English/Spanish)** **Student Edition on Audio CD**, Ch. 25 **Social Studies Skills Tutor CD-ROM** **Color Transparencies**, A41, A42, A43, A44, E18, F8, H18
1 Mobilization 1. Find out how Roosevelt mobilized the armed forces. 2. Learn about ways in which the government prepared the economy for war. 3. See how the war affected daily life on the home front.	**Teaching Resources** **Units 7/8 booklet** • Section 1 Quiz, p. 60 **Learning Styles Lesson Plans booklet**, p. 52	**Guided Reading and Review booklet,** p. 100 **Guide to the Essentials**, p. 126 **Section Reading Support Transparencies**
2 Retaking Europe See Teacher's Edition p. 600 for Section Objectives 1–5.	**Teaching Resources** **Units 7/8 booklet** • Section 2 Quiz, p. 61	**Guided Reading and Review booklet,** p. 101 **Guide to the Essentials**, p. 127 **Section Reading Support Transparencies**
3 The Holocaust 1. Find out about some ways in which Germany persecuted Jews in the 1930s. 2. See how Germany's policies toward Jews developed from murder into genocide.	**Teaching Resources** **Units 7/8 booklet** • Section 3 Quiz, p. 62	**Guided Reading and Review booklet,** p. 102 **Guide to the Essentials**, p. 128 **Section Reading Support Transparencies**
4 The War in the Pacific 1. Learn about advances Japan made in Asia and the Pacific in late 1941 and 1942. 2. See which Allied victories turned the tide of war in the Pacific. 3. Read about the strategy of the United States in the struggle to reconquer the Pacific Islands. 4. Discover why the battles of Iwo Jima and Okinawa were important. 5. Understand how the Manhattan Project brought the war to an end.	**Teaching Resources** **Units 7/8 booklet** • Section 4 Quiz, p. 63	**Guided Reading and Review booklet,** p. 103 **Guide to the Essentials**, p. 129 **Learning with Documents booklet,** p. 30 **Skills for Life booklet**, p. 27 **Section Reading Support Transparencies**
5 The War's Social Impact 1. Learn how African Americans, Mexican Americans, and Native Americans experienced the war at home. 2. Find out about difficulties Japanese Americans faced. 3. See how the war changed conditions for working women.	**Teaching Resources** **Units 7/8 booklet** • Section 5 Quiz, p. 64 **Learning Styles Lesson Plans booklet**, p. 53	**Guided Reading and Review booklet,** p. 104 **Guide to the Essentials**, p. 130 **Learning with Documents booklet,** p. 64 **Section Reading Support Transparencies**

ENRICHMENT/PRE-AP

Prentice Hall United States History Video Collection™
www.phschool.com
- Section Activities, Virtual Field Trip, Chapter Activities, Current Events Online

Historical Outline Map Book, pp. 65, 67
Sounds of an Era Audio CD
Exploring Primary Sources in U.S. History CD-ROM

Sounds of an Era Audio CD
Exploring Primary Sources in U.S. History CD-ROM

Biography, Literature, and Comparing Primary Sources booklet, p. 74
Historical Outline Map Book, p. 66
Sounds of an Era Audio CD
Exploring Primary Sources in U.S. History CD-ROM

Biography, Literature, and Comparing Primary Sources booklet, pp. 30, 145
American History Block Scheduling Support
Nystrom *Atlas of Our Country*, pp. 32–33, 34–35
Sounds of an Era Audio CD
Exploring Primary Sources in U.S. History CD-ROM
American Pathways Thematic Posters

ASSESSMENT

PRENTICE HALL ASSESSMENT SYSTEM

Core Assessment
> ExamView® Test Bank, Ch. 25
> ExamView® Test Bank CD-ROM, Ch. 25

Standardized Test Preparation
Diagnose and Prescribe
> Diagnostic Tests for High School Social Studies Skills

Review and Reteach
> Review Book for U.S. History

Practice and Assess
> Test-taking Strategies With Transparencies
> Test-taking Strategies Posters
> Test Prep Book for U.S. History
> Alternative Assessment Handbook
> Document-Based Assessment

Teaching Resources
Units 7/8 booklet
- Section Quizzes, pp. 60–63
- Chapter Tests, pp. 64, 67
www.phschool.com Ch. 25 Self-Test

AmericanHeritage RESOURCES

From the Archives of American Heritage®, pp. 828, 848
AmericanHeritage® My Brush with History™ Videotapes
www.americanheritage.com

iTEXT

Don't miss the exclusive interactive version of this textbook on the Web and on CD-ROM.

Chapter 25 Planning Guide
In Your Classroom

CUSTOMIZE FOR INDIVIDUAL NEEDS

Gifted and Talented

Teacher's Edition
• Customize for Gifted and Talented, pp. 827, 833, 849, 853, 859

Teaching Resources
• Biography, Literature, and Comparing Primary Sources booklet, pp. 30, 74, 145

Technology
• Exploring Primary Sources in U.S. History CD-ROM *What Should You Bring Overseas? Bill Steele; "Gee, Mom, I Want to Go Home," Army Song; Night, Elie Wiesel; Japanese Internment Photograph; Rosie the Riveter Poster*

ESL

Teacher's Edition
• Customize for ESL, p. 843

Teaching Resources
• Guided Reading and Review booklet, pp. 100–104
• Guide to the Essentials (English/Spanish), Chapter 25

Technology
• Student Edition on Audio CD, Chapter 25
• Guided Reading Audiotapes (English/Spanish), Chapter 25
• Section Reading Support Transparencies

Less Proficient Readers

Teacher's Edition
• Customize for Less Proficient Readers, pp. 835, 837, 845

Teaching Resources
• Guided Reading and Review booklet, pp. 100–104
• Guide to the Essentials (English/Spanish), Chapter 25

Technology
• Student Edition on Audio CD, Chapter 25
• Guided Reading Audiotapes (English/Spanish), Chapter 25
• Section Reading Support Transparencies

Less Proficient Writers

Teacher's Edition
• Customize for Less Proficient Writers, p. 857

Teaching Resources
• Guided Reading and Review booklet, pp. 100–104
• Guide to the Essentials (English/Spanish), Chapter 25

Technology
• Student Edition on Audio CD, Chapter 25
• Guided Reading Audiotapes (English/Spanish), Chapter 25
• Section Reading Support Transparencies

TEACHER'S EDITION INDEX

CHAPTER 25 – PACING SUGGESTIONS

For 90-minute Blocks

• Teach sections 1, 2, 3, 4, and 5 using Transparencies A41, A42, A43, A44, E18, F8, and H18, and the Recent Scholarship notes on pages 844, 849, and 859 for class discussions.

Running Out of Time?

If you are running short on time to cover this chapter, consider the following options:

• Use the Prentice Hall Presentation Pro CD-ROM to create an outline for this chapter.

• Use the Section Summaries for Chapter 25, from **Guide to the Essentials (English/Spanish).**

1 Mobilization	**Connecting with Government** Have students prepare written reports that compare the role of the federal government during World War I with its role in World War II. Students might examine such factors as efforts to mobilize industry, direct public opinion, or control the movement of foreign-born citizens. **(Verbal/Linguistic)**
2 Retaking Europe	**Connecting with History and Conflict** Ask students to create a biographical profile of a well-known personality of the period in the form of a multimedia presentation. Have them select an individual whose voice was well known to the radio-listening public during the war, such as Edward R. Murrow, Franklin Delano Roosevelt, or Bob Hope. Suggest that they find recordings, film clips, photographs, and published materials dealing with or featuring their subject. You may wish to have students make their presentations to the class, or you could set aside a section of the classroom as a viewing-listening area. **(Verbal/Linguistic; Bodily/Kinesthetic)**
3 The Holocaust	**Connecting with History and Conflict** Explain that the charges against the defendants in the Nuremberg Trials were of four types: crimes against peace; war crimes; crimes against humanity; and conspiracy to commit war crimes, crimes against humanity, and crimes against peace. Have students examine what was meant by each charge, then do further research on the nature of the crimes against humanity. If possible, have them find the court transcript and take the role of the prosecutor in making an oral presentation of that charge. **(Verbal/Linguistic; Bodily/Kinesthetic)**
4 The War in the Pacific	**Connecting with Geography** Have students use a series of outline maps to trace the year-by-year advances and retreats of the Japanese military beginning in 1931. The maps should distinguish where the military had ground forces (such as China) and where the Japanese struck with air power (such as Pearl Harbor, Hawaii). **(Visual/Spatial)**
5 The War's Social Impact	**Connecting with Economics** Have students calculate what percentage of the American female population was working out of the home during World War II. Have them also use pie charts to show the number of women who served in the Women's Army Corps (WAC). You may wish to have students discuss how this data might have influenced women's career expectations in the years after the war. **(Logical/Mathematical)**

INTRODUCING THE CHAPTER

"The peace, freedom, and security of 90 percent of the world is being jeopardized by the remaining 10 percent . . ." said President Roosevelt about the war raging in Europe. Many Americans, opposed to intervention, were convinced only after the attack on Pearl Harbor that the United States should be involved in the war. With the American entry into World War II, there was no longer any question about the role of the United States in world affairs.

TIME LINE ACTIVITY

To provide students with practice in using the time line, ask questions such as these:

1. In what year did the United States declare war on Japan, Germany, and Italy? *(1941)*

2. Which two countries were engaged in the Battle of Midway, and which country was victorious? *(The United States and Japan; the United States)*

3. In what year did the Japanese begin *kamikaze* attacks? *(1944)*

Chapter 25

World War II: Americans at War

(1941–1945)

SECTION 1   Mobilization
SECTION 2   Retaking Europe
SECTION 3   The Holocaust
SECTION 4   The War in the Pacific
SECTION 5   The Social Impact of the War

Ration cards and points

American troops in the South Pacific

	1941		**1942**
American Events	A. Philip Randolph threatens to march on Washington to end discrimination in war industries. The United States declares war on Japan, Germany, and Italy.		Japan conquers the Philippines. The United States defeats the Japanese navy at the Battle of Midway. Japanese Americans are interned in camps.
Presidential Terms:		Franklin D. Roosevelt 1933–1945	
	1940	**1941**	**1942**
World Events	Hitler invades the Soviet Union. Hong Kong falls to Japan.		Allied troops land in North Africa. The Battle of Stalingrad begins.
		1941	**1942**

---

eTeach

Be sure to check out this month's online discussion with a Master Teacher. Go to **www.phschool.com**.

RESOURCE DIRECTORY

Teaching Resources
Pacing Charts booklet
Block Scheduling booklet, p. 25
Units 7/8 booklet
• Chapter Summary, p. 59

Technology
Guided Reading Audiotapes (English/Spanish), Ch. 25
Student Edition on Audio CD, Ch. 25
Prentice Hall United States History Video Collection™ Volume 19, *World War II*
Prentice Hall Presentation Pro CD-ROM, Ch. 25
Resource Pro® CD-ROM
Social Studies Skills Tutor CD-ROM
Companion Web site, www.phschool.com

Map Legend

- Axis powers
- Occupied by Axis
- Axis satellites
- Allied territory
- Occupied by Allies
- Neutral nations

Map Labels

ATLANTIC OCEAN
North Sea
IRELAND
GREAT BRITAIN
NORWAY
SWEDEN
FINLAND
DENMARK
Baltic Sea
Reichskommissariat Ostland
SOVIET UNION
NETH.
BELG.
GREATER GERMANY
Occupied Poland
Reichskommissariat Ukraine
Occupied Soviet Union
OCCUPIED FRANCE
SWITZ.
Rhine R.
Danube R.
Oder R.
SLOVAKIA
HUNGARY
Dnieper R.
Bay of Biscay
VICHY FRANCE
Po R.
ITALY
CROATIA
SERBIA
MONT.
ROMANIA
BULGARIA
Black Sea
PORTUGAL
Tagus R.
SPAIN
Ebro R.
ALBANIA
GREECE
TURKEY
SPANISH MOROCCO
MOROCCO (Fr.)
ALGERIA (Fr.)
TUNISIA (Fr.)
Mediterranean Sea
LEBANON (Fr.)
PALESTINE (Br.)

Scale: 0 — 200 — 400 mi. / 0 — 200 — 400 km

A Soviet soldier raises his country's flag over the ruined *Reichstag* in Berlin.

A letter written by Albert Einstein led to the development of the atomic bomb.

Timeline

1943
Americans help defeat Axis armies in North Africa and invade Italy. Troops in the Pacific take Guadalcanal and begin island-hopping campaign.

1944
American and British troops lead the D-Day invasion of France.

1945
Harry S Truman becomes President after Roosevelt's death. American troops liberate Western Germany. The United States drops atomic bombs on Hiroshima and Nagasaki.

Harry S Truman 1945–1953

1943 | **1944** | **1945**

1943
Jews in Warsaw ghetto rebel. Germany invades Italy after Mussolini is overthrown.

1944
Japan begins *kamikaze* attacks. De Gaulle leads Allies into Paris.

1945
Hitler commits suicide. Germany and Japan surrender.

Chapter 25   825

Hitler's Europe, 1942

Activating Prior Knowledge
According to this map, how many countries were Allied territory? *(Two: Great Britain and the Soviet Union)*

Previewing Considering the location of the Allied territories, what advantage did the Allies have? *(They were positioned on either side of the Axis powers, satellites, and territories, so they could attack on both fronts.)*

BACKGROUND
About the Pictures

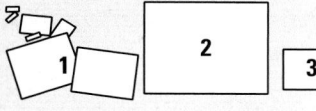

1. Ration cards were distributed to help limit quantities and to conserve resources during wartime.

2. The everyday hardships and difficult conditions the soldiers faced together during war helped them create strong bonds of friendship among themselves.

3. After breaking their pact with the Soviet Union and launching a large-scale attack, Germany was finally defeated.

4. Despite the fact that Einstein's name became closely associated with atomic weaponry, he was a pacifist, wishing to prevent any further use of atomic bombs.

Don't miss the exclusive interactive version of this textbook on the Web and on CD-ROM.

BIBLIOGRAPHY

For the Teacher

Brokaw, Tom. *The Greatest Generation.* Random House, 2001. (The veteran television announcer has assembled a moving collection of first-hand reminiscences based on hundreds of letters and interviews with people who lived through World War II.)

Prange, Gordon William. *At Dawn We Slept: The Untold Story of Pearl Harbor.* Penguin, 2001. (This minutely researched book provides a definitive account of the attack on Pearl Harbor, from both the Japanese and United States perspectives.)

Roeder, George. *The Censored War: American Visual Experience During World War II.* Yale University Press, 1993. (A collection of wartime photographs, many used for propaganda, and many from the National Archives.)

For the Student

Hersey, John. *Hiroshima.* Vintage, 1989. (Harrowing account of the bombing.)

Selden, Kyoko, and Mark Selden, eds. *The Atomic Bomb: Voices from Hiroshima and Nagasaki.* Sharpe, 1989. (Accounts of the bombing by survivors.)

SECTION OBJECTIVES

1. Find out how Roosevelt mobilized the armed forces.
2. Learn about ways in which the government prepared the economy for war.
3. See how the war affected daily life on the home front.

BELLRINGER

Warm-Up Activity Ask students to suppose they were President Roosevelt on December 8, 1941. What are the three most important things that must be done to prepare the country for war?

Activating Prior Knowledge Ask students to list some facts they know about the United States' involvement in World War II. In particular, do they know in what year the U.S. entered the war? In what year did the war end?

READING STRATEGY

Have students write the heading "Economic Effects of World War II" on a piece of paper. As they read the chapter, have them list effects that are described. These should include rationing, female employment, and the end of the Great Depression.

BACKGROUND
Geography in History

The United States' "Good Neighbor Policy" paid dividends during the war. The Latin American nations provided vital war materials—rubber, quinine, tin—along with naval and air bases. Brazil sent troops to Europe, and Mexico had an air squadron in the Pacific. The Mexican and Cuban navies patrolled the Caribbean for German submarines. In return, the U. S. provided military equipment and loans to these nations.

Section 1
Mobilization

READING FOCUS

- How did Roosevelt mobilize the armed forces?
- In what ways did the government prepare the economy for war?
- How did the war affect daily life on the home front?

MAIN IDEA

The United States quickly mobilized millions of Americans to fight the Axis powers. The government organized the economy to supply the military.

KEY TERMS

Selective Training and Service Act
GI
Office of War Mobilization
Liberty ship
victory garden

TAKING NOTES

As you read, complete the following flow-chart to show some of the effects that America's entry into war had on the economy of the United States.

United States Enters the War			
Industries adapt to produce war goods.			

Setting the Scene   Well before the Japanese attack on Pearl Harbor, officials in the United States had begun to prepare for war. President Roosevelt made his concerns and worries clear to the American people in a radio address in December 1940. He stated that the Axis nations, especially Germany, posed a direct threat to the security of the United States. He appealed to American business owners and workers to support Britain's defensive efforts or face the ultimate task of defending their own land against the "brute force" of the Axis.

> 66 *We must be the great arsenal of democracy. For us this is an emergency as serious as war itself. We must apply ourselves to our task with the same resolution, the same sense of urgency, the same spirit of patriotism and sacrifice as we would show were we at war.* 99
> —Franklin D. Roosevelt, fireside chat, December 29, 1940

Millions of Americans traded their civilian clothes for military fatigues (above) as the United States prepared to fight the Axis.

FDR understood that the outcome of the war in Europe ultimately depended on his country's ability to produce planes, tanks, guns, uniforms, and other war materials for the Allies.

Mobilizing the Armed Forces

FDR realized that a crucial step that he had to take was to strengthen the armed forces if the United States were to enter the war on the side of the Allies. In September 1940, Congress authorized the first peacetime draft in the nation's history. The **Selective Training and Service Act** required all males aged 21 to 36 to register for military service. A limited number of men was selected from this pool to serve a year in the army. The United States also boosted its defense spending from $2 billion at the start of the year to more than $10 billion in September.

As the United States prepared for the possibility of war, thousands of American men received official notices to enter the army. In what came to be known as the "Four Freedoms speech," FDR shared his vision of what these troops would be fighting for:

RESOURCE DIRECTORY

Teaching Resources
Learning Styles Lesson Plans booklet, p. 52
Guided Reading and Review booklet, p. 100

Technology
Section Reading Support Transparencies
Guided Reading Audiotapes (English/Spanish), Ch. 25
Student Edition on Audio CD, Ch. 25
Color Transparencies *Time Lines,* C7

RESOURCE ◉ P R O® **Primary Source Activity**
Experiences of an African American Soldier, found on Resource Pro, uses narrative by World War II veteran Timuel Black to show some of the hardships and injustices African American soldiers faced.
Exploring Primary Sources in U.S. History CD-ROM *What Should You Bring Overseas? Bill Steele*
Prentice Hall Presentation Pro CD-ROM, Ch. 25
Companion Web site, www.phschool.com

> 66 *We look forward to a world founded upon four essential freedoms. The first is freedom of speech and expression. . . . The second is freedom of every person to worship God in his own way. . . . The third is freedom from want [need]. . . . The fourth is freedom from fear.* 99
> —Franklin D. Roosevelt, State of the Union Message, January 6, 1941

Artist Norman Rockwell illustrated these four freedoms in a series of paintings that the government distributed in poster form during the war. After the attack on Pearl Harbor, feelings of patriotism swept over the United States. Tens of thousands of men volunteered to serve in the military.

The GI War   World War II greatly changed the lives of the men and women who were uprooted from home and sent far away to fight for their country. More than 16 million Americans served as soldiers, sailors, and aviators in the war. They called themselves **GIs**, an abbreviation of "Government Issue."

During the war, American GIs slogged through swamps, crossed hot deserts and turbulent seas, and flew through skies pounded by enemy guns. Soldiers on the front lines often found their experience in the war was a daily struggle just to stay alive. Between battles, the typical GI dreamed of home and a cherished way of life. When asked what he was fighting for, a young marine replied, "What I'd give for a piece of blueberry pie." American soldiers knew that they were fighting to preserve the freedoms that they held dear.

Diversity in the Armed Forces   Americans from all ethnic and racial backgrounds fought during World War II. More than 300,000 Mexican Americans served their country, primarily in the army.

Some 25,000 Native Americans also served in the military. A group of Navajos developed a secret code, based on their language, that the enemy could not break. The marines recruited more than 400 Navajos to serve as radio operators. These "code talkers," as they became known, provided an important secure communications link in several key battles of the war.

Nearly a million African Americans joined the military. At first, officials limited most black troops to supporting roles. By late 1942, however, faced with mounting casualties, military authorities reluctantly gave African Americans the opportunity to fight. African Americans fought in separate units. One such group, called the Tuskegee Airmen, became the first African American flying unit in the United States military. In late 1944, heavy casualties forced the army to accept African Americans into some white combat units.

Women in the Military   Not all who served in the military were men. By the war's end, roughly 350,000 American women had volunteered for military service. Faced with a personnel shortage, officials agreed to use women in almost all areas except combat. Many worked as clerks, typists, airfield control tower operators, mechanics, photographers, and drivers. Others ferried planes around the country and towed practice targets for antiaircraft gunners.

Preparing the Economy for War

The United States entered the war at a time when the production levels of the other Allies had dropped sharply. Bombing campaigns and German advances had affected production in Britain and the Soviet Union, and Japan's conquests in the Pacific threatened to cut off

OURS...to fight for

FREEDOM FROM WANT

Norman Rockwell's *Freedom From Want* was widely reproduced during the war.

INTERPRETING POLITICAL CARTOONS Bill Mauldin created the characters of GIs Willie and Joe for the Army newspaper, *Stars and Stripes.* **Distinguishing False From Accurate Images** *What does this cartoon say about the GIs who fought in World War II?*

"Me future is settled, Willie. I'm gonna be a perfessor on types o' European soil."

supplies of such vital raw materials as rubber, oil, and tin. President Roosevelt pushed industries to move quickly into the production of war equipment.

War Production FDR knew that the federal government would have to coordinate the production of American businesses to meet Allied demand. The government had already assumed tremendous power over the economy during the New Deal. Now the Supreme Court, filled with Roosevelt appointees, tended to support FDR's attempts to boost the government's power even further.

In January 1942, the government set up the War Production Board (WPB) to direct the conversion of peacetime industries to industries that produced war goods. It quickly halted the production of hundreds of civilian consumer goods, from cars to lawn mowers to bird cages, and encouraged companies to make goods for the war. The armed forces decided which companies would receive contracts to manufacture military hardware, but the WPB set priorities and allocated raw materials.

As the war went on, the government established dozens of additional agencies to deal with war production, labor questions, and scarce resources. In May 1943, the President appointed James F. Byrnes, a longtime member of Congress and a close presidential advisor, to head the **Office of War Mobilization.** The office would serve as a super-agency in the centralization of resources. Working from a makeshift office in the White House, Byrnes had such broad authority that he was often called the "assistant president." Some people said that Byrnes ran the country while FDR ran the war.

As production of consumer goods stopped, factories converted to war production. The Ford Motor Company built a huge new factory to make B-24 Liberator bombers using the same assembly-line techniques used to manufacture cars. Henry J. Kaiser introduced mass production techniques into shipbuilding and cut the time needed to build one type of ship from 200 days to 40 days. The vessels that made Kaiser famous were called **Liberty ships.** They were large, sturdy merchant ships that carried supplies or troops.

To motivate businesses and guarantee profits, the government established the "cost-plus" system for military contracts. The military paid development and production costs and added a percentage of costs as profit for the manufacturer. Pride and patriotism also motivated business executives. As in World War I, thousands went to Washington, D.C., to work in the new federal agencies that coordinated war production. They received a token "dollar-a-year" salary from the government while still remaining on their own companies' payrolls.

Each year of the war, the United States raised its production goals for military materials, and each year it met these goals. In 1944, American production levels doubled those of all the Axis nations put together. By the middle of 1945, the nation had produced approximately 300,000 airplanes; 80,000 landing craft; 100,000 tanks and armored cars; 5,600 merchant ships (including about 2,600 Liberty ships); 6 million rifles, carbines, and machine guns; and 41 billion rounds of ammunition.

The Wartime Work Force War production benefited workers, too, ending the massive unemployment of the 1930s. As the graphs on the next page show, unemployment virtually vanished during the war. Not only did people find

VIEWING HISTORY Henry J. Kaiser's Liberty ship *Robert E. Peary* (above) was built in a matter of days. A button (right) shows the spirit of workers building airplanes for the war effort. **Drawing Conclusions** *Why was military production so important to winning the war?*

jobs, they also earned more money for their work. Average weekly wages in manufacturing, adjusted for inflation, rose by more than 50 percent between 1940 and 1945. Under pressure to produce high-quality goods in a hurry, the American labor force delivered. A journalist wrote of a war production factory: "Not a day passes but you'll hear somebody say to a worker who seems to be slowing down, 'There's a war on, you know!'"

With more people working, union membership rose. From 1940 to 1941, the number of workers belonging to unions increased by 1.5 million. Union membership continued to rise sharply once the United States entered the war, increasing from 10.5 million in 1941 to 14.8 million in 1945.

Two weeks after the attack on Pearl Harbor, labor and business representatives agreed to refrain from strikes and "lockouts." A lockout is a tactic in which an employer keeps employees out of the workplace to avoid meeting their demands. As the cost of living rose during the war, however, unions found the no-strike agreement hard to honor. The number of strikes rose sharply in 1943 and continued to rise in the last two years of the war.

The most serious strikes occurred in the coal industry. John L. Lewis, head of the United Mine Workers union, called strikes on four occasions in 1943. Lewis and the miners had watched industry profits and the cost of living soar while their wages stayed the same. Secretary of the Interior Harold L. Ickes finally negotiated an agreement with Lewis. Meanwhile, Congress passed the Smith-Connally Act in June 1943, limiting future strike activity.

Financing the War The United States government vowed to spend whatever was necessary to sustain the war effort. Federal spending increased from $8.9 billion a year in 1939 to $95.2 billion in 1945. The Gross National Product (GNP) more than doubled. Overall, between 1941 and 1945, the federal government spent about $321 billion—ten times as much as it had spent in World War I.

Higher taxes paid for about 41 percent of the cost of the war. The government borrowed the rest of the money from banks, private investors, and the public. The Treasury Department launched bond drives to encourage Americans to buy war bonds to help finance the war. Total war bond sales brought in about $186 billion.

During the Depression, British economist John Maynard Keynes had argued in favor of deficit spending to get the economy moving. While spending did increase during the 1930s, the government failed to generate large deficits until World War II. The country could not afford to pay all the costs of war, so deficits provided a way to postpone some payments until after the war. High levels of deficit spending helped the United States field a well-equipped army and navy, bring prosperity to workers, and pull the United States out of the Depression. It also boosted the national debt from $43 billion in 1940 to $259 billion in 1945.

Unemployment and Armed Service Enlistment, 1940–1945

INTERPRETING CHARTS Ten years of high unemployment came to an end as workers joined the military or found jobs in defense industries. **Analyzing Information** *In what year did the number of people in the armed forces increase by 5 million?*

READING CHECK
How did the government pay for the war effort?

Chapter 25 • Section 1   **829**

Focus on DAILY LIFE

Black Markets Despite rationing and shortages, people could buy rare goods if they were willing to pay a high price. Nylon stockings could be found for $5 a pair in most cities, if not in the stores. Gas stations, shoe stores, and groceries sold rationed goods to trusted customers "off-ration," or without ration coupons, at a higher price. These deals were known as the black market. They hurt the war effort by taking resources away from war production and upsetting Americans who played by the rules and stuck to their rations. Because it depended on thousands of personal relationships and small trades, the black market was impossible to defeat.

Daily Life on the Home Front

The war affected the daily lives of most Americans. Nearly everyone had a relative or a friend in the military, and people closely followed war news on the radio. During the war, nearly 30 million people moved, including soldiers, families of soldiers, and civilians relocating to take jobs in military production. The end of the Depression helped lift Americans' spirits. One measure of people's optimism was an increase in the birthrate. The population grew by 7.5 million between 1940 and 1945, nearly double the rate of growth for the 1930s.

Shortages and Controls Wartime jobs gave many people their first extra cash since the Depression. Still, shortages and rationing limited the goods that people could buy. Familiar consumer items were simply unavailable "for the duration." Metal to make zippers or typewriters went instead into guns, and rubber went to make tires for army trucks instead of for bicycles. Nylon stockings, introduced in 1939, vanished from shops because the nylon was needed for parachutes.

The supply of food also fell short of demand. The government needed great amounts of food for the military. In addition, the closing of shipping lanes and enemy occupation of foreign countries cut off some of America's supplies of sugar, tropical fruits, and coffee.

Worried that shortages would cause price increases, the government used tough measures to head off inflation. In April 1941, the Office of Price Administration (OPA) was established by an executive order. The OPA's job was to control inflation by limiting prices and rents. Such controls sometimes backfired, however. For example, companies would cut back on the production of goods whose prices did not allow for a substantial profit. Such cutbacks could cause the very shortages they were supposed to prevent. Also, people found ways of getting around the limits. Still, the OPA accomplished its main task, keeping inflation under control. The cost of living rose, but not nearly as much as it had in World War I.

The OPA also oversaw rationing during the war. The goal of rationing was a fair distribution of scarce items. Beginning in 1943, the OPA assigned point values to items such as sugar, coffee, meat, butter, canned fruit, and shoes. It issued ration books of coupons worth a certain number of points for categories of food or clothing. Once consumers had used up their points, they could not buy any more of those items until they received new ration books or traded coupons with neighbors. Gasoline for cars was strictly rationed, too, on the basis of need. Signs asked, "Is this trip necessary?" Customers found some shortages and ration rules confusing, but any complaint could be answered with the question, "Don't you know there's a war on?"

VIEWING HISTORY Shoppers needed ration points (right) as well as cash to buy rationed goods. **Drawing Inferences** *Why did Americans support rationing?*

Popular Culture With so many goods unavailable, Americans looked for other ways to spend their money. Civilians bought and read more books and magazines. They purchased recordings of popular songs, such as "White Christmas" by Irving Berlin, a sentimental favorite of both soldiers and civilians. They flocked to baseball games, even though most of their favorite players had gone off to war. Millions of Americans—about 60 percent of the population—also went to the movies every week.

Enlisting Public Support The government understood the need to maintain morale. It encouraged citizens to participate in the war effort while persuading them to accept rationing and conserve precious resources. Roosevelt established the Office of War Information in June 1942 to work with magazine publishers, advertising agencies, and radio stations. It hired writers and artists to create posters and ads that stirred Americans' patriotic feelings.

One popular idea was the **victory garden,** a home vegetable garden planted to add to the home food supply and replace farm produce sent to feed the soldiers. Soon people in cities and suburbs were planting tomatoes, peas, and radishes in backyards, empty parking lots, and playgrounds. By 1943, victory gardens produced about one third of the country's fresh vegetables.

The war became a part of everyday life in many ways. People drew their shades for nighttime "blackouts," which tested their readiness for possible bombing raids. Men too old for the army joined the Civilian Defense effort, wearing their CD armbands as they tested air raid sirens. Women knit scarves and socks or rolled bandages for the Red Cross.

The government encouraged efforts to recycle scrap metal, paper, and other materials for war production. In one drive, people collected tin cans, pots and pans, razor blades, old shovels, and even old lipstick tubes. The collection drives kept adults and children actively involved in the war effort. "Play your part." "Conserve and collect." "Use it up, wear it out, make it do or do without." These slogans echoed throughout the United States and reminded people on the home front of their important contributions to the war effort.

Victory gardens gave people a chance to help the war effort and to add fresh vegetables to their food rations.

Section 1 Assessment

READING COMPREHENSION

1. Describe three ways that individual Americans contributed to the war effort.
2. How did the government pay for the war effort?
3. What was the purpose of the **Office of War Mobilization?**
4. What effect did shortages have on the economy?

CRITICAL THINKING AND WRITING

5. **Making Comparisons** (a) How were African Americans in the military treated differently from white soldiers? (b) How were women in the military treated differently from men? (c) Why do you think the military insisted on these differences at the start of the war?
6. **Writing to Describe** Write a paragraph detailing daily life from the point of view of an American in the early 1940s. Include the effects of the mobilization for war.

Activity: Analyzing Primary Sources Select a primary source from the American home front during World War II (for example, a letter, a poster, or an oral history). Describe the source you selected in a brief report. What did the source reveal about the home front? Use the links provided in the *America: Pathways to the Present* area at the following Web site for help in completing this activity.
www.phschool.com

Reading Comprehension

1. Sample answers: Volunteering for military service; planting victory gardens; joining the Civilian Defense effort.
2. Through higher taxes, borrowing money, sale of war bonds, and deficit spending.
3. It served as an agency specializing in the centralization of resources.
4. They limited the goods people could buy; rationing occurred; supply of consumer goods fell short of demand.

Critical Thinking and Writing

5. (a) At first, African American troops were limited to supporting roles, and even when given the opportunity to fight, they were generally assigned to separate units. (b) Women were used in many different roles, but were excluded from combat. (c) These differences reflected existing roles in society at that time.
6. Paragraphs will vary, but should be descriptive and use supporting facts from the section.

Take It to the NET

Reports will vary, but should demonstrate insight into the wartime mood and conditions on the home front.

READING FOCUS

- Where did Americans join the struggle against the Axis?
- How did the war in the Soviet Union change from 1941 to 1943?
- What role did air power play in the war in Europe?
- Why did the invasion of Western Europe succeed?
- What events marked the end of the war in Europe?

MAIN IDEA

To secure victory in Europe, the Allies waged war in the Atlantic Ocean, North Africa, the Soviet Union, and Western Europe between 1941 and 1945.

KEY TERMS

Atlantic Charter
carpet bombing
D-Day
Battle of the Bulge

TAKING NOTES

As you read, complete the following chart by listing wartime events in different regions of Europe and North Africa.

Region	Events
Western Europe	• Allied navies battle Germany for control of the Atlantic Ocean. •
Eastern Europe	
North Africa and Italy	

Setting the Scene In August 1941, unknown to the rest of the world, two warships quietly lay at anchor off the coast of Newfoundland. Aboard were Prime Minister Winston Churchill and President Franklin D. Roosevelt. Both men believed that the United States would soon join Great Britain militarily as an ally in war. The two leaders met in secret to discuss the war's aims and to agree on a set of principles to guide them in the years ahead. After several days of talks, they issued a joint declaration of those principles, which included the following:

Churchill and Roosevelt met secretly to negotiate the Atlantic Charter while the United States was still neutral.

❝ First, their countries seek no aggrandizement [enlargement], territorial or other.

Second, they desire to see no territorial changes that do not accord with the freely expressed wishes of the peoples concerned.

Third, they respect the right of all peoples to choose the form of government under which they will live; . . .

Sixth, after the final destruction of the Nazi tyranny, they hope to see established a peace which will afford to all nations the means of dwelling in safety within their own boundaries, . . .

Eighth, they believe that all of the nations of the world . . . must come to the abandonment of the use of force. . . .❞

—Franklin D. Roosevelt and Winston S. Churchill, August 14, 1941

The declaration of principles became known as the **Atlantic Charter.** After the war, this charter would form the basis for the United Nations.

Americans Join the Struggle

The United States entered the war in December 1941, at a critical time for the Allies. London and other major British cities had suffered heavy damage during the Battle of Britain. The Germans' *blitzkrieg* had extended Nazi control across most of Europe. In North Africa, a mixed German and Italian army was bearing down on British forces. Many people feared that Germany could not be stopped.

The Battle of the Atlantic At sea, Britain and the United States desperately struggled to control the Atlantic trade routes vital to British survival. Britain relied on shipments of food and supplies from the United States and from its territories overseas. As allied merchant ships crossed the Atlantic, German U-boats, or submarines, sailed out from ports in France to attack them. To protect themselves better, Allied ships formed convoys led by American and British warships. The Germans countered with groups of as many as 20 U-boats, called wolf packs, that carried out coordinated nighttime attacks on the convoys.

After the United States entered the war, U-boats began attacking merchant ships within sight of the American coast. Although Allied warships used underwater sound equipment called sonar to locate and attack U-boats, the wolf packs experienced great success. In the Atlantic, they sank nearly 175 ships in June 1942 alone. Allied convoys later developed better defensive strategies, including the use of long-range sub-hunting aircraft, and the U-boat success rate plummeted.

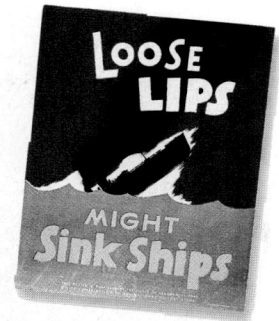

Posters warned people not to discuss what they knew about military movements for fear of espionage.

MAP SKILLS After stopping the German offensive, the Allies were able to reconquer Europe from the south, east, and west. **Place** *Which regions saw fighting in 1943?*

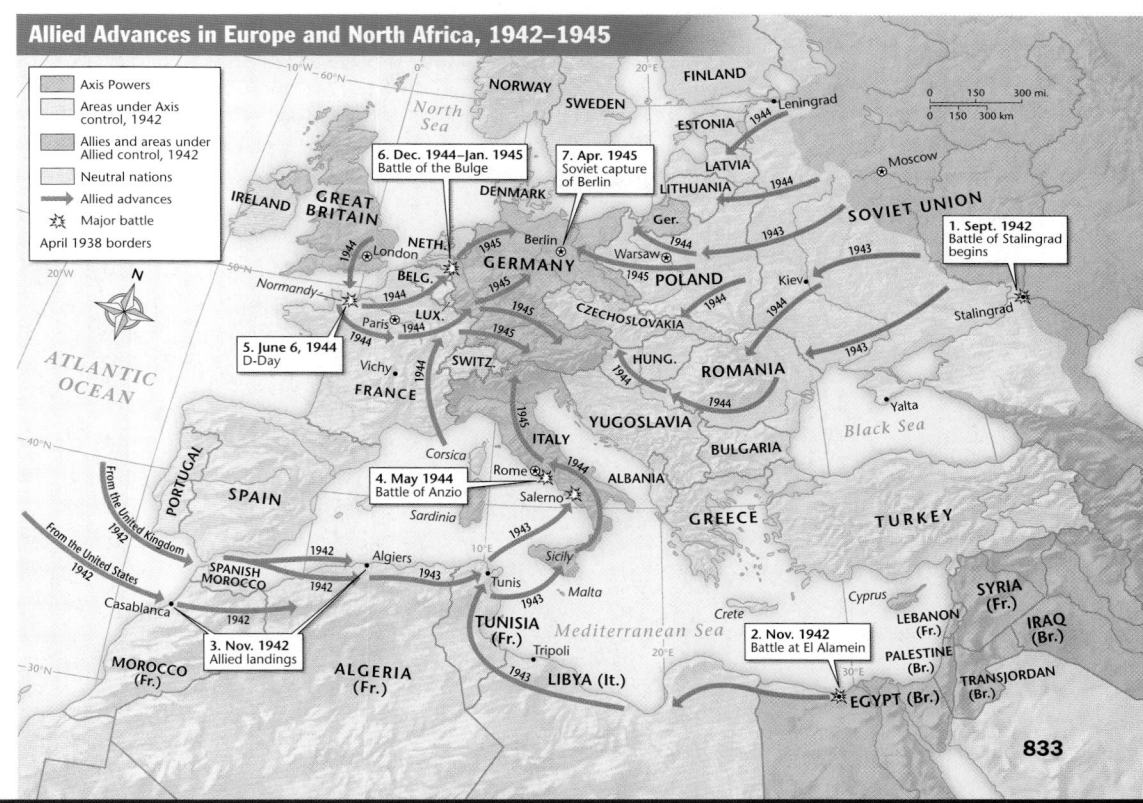

Allied Advances in Europe and North Africa, 1942–1945

Legend:
- Axis Powers
- Areas under Axis control, 1942
- Allies and areas under Allied control, 1942
- Neutral nations
- Allied advances
- Major battle

April 1938 borders

5. June 6, 1944 D-Day

6. Dec. 1944–Jan. 1945 Battle of the Bulge

7. Apr. 1945 Soviet capture of Berlin

1. Sept. 1942 Battle of Stalingrad begins

4. May 1944 Battle of Anzio

3. Nov. 1942 Allied landings

2. Nov. 1942 Battle at El Alamein

833

General Dwight D. Eisenhower (left) was named commander of U.S. troops in Europe in June 1942.

The North Africa Campaign   Starting in August 1940, a British army had successfully battled Italian troops in the Egyptian and Libyan deserts of North Africa. Then, in February 1941, Hitler sent General Erwin Rommel and a German division to reinforce the Italians. Rommel, who earned the nickname "Desert Fox" for his shrewd tactics, won several battles. The Germans pushed deep into British-controlled Egypt and threatened the Middle East. Rommel's offensive failed, however, in November 1942, when the British under General Bernard Montgomery won a decisive victory at El Alamein. The German army retreated west.

A few days later, Allied troops landed in the French territories of Morocco and Algeria on the northwest coast of North Africa. This largely American force, under the command of American General Dwight D. Eisenhower, quickly pushed eastward. Meanwhile, British troops chased Rommel westward from Egypt. In response, Hitler sent some 20,000 combat troops across the Mediterranean Sea from Italy to reinforce Rommel's army in Tunisia. There, in February 1943, the inexperienced Americans suffered a major defeat of the war while trying to defend the Kasserine Pass. They learned from their defeat, however, and by early May 1943, the Allied armies had the Axis forces in North Africa trapped. Despite Hitler's instructions to fight to the death, about 240,000 Germans and Italians surrendered.

Churchill and Roosevelt met again in January 1943 at Casablanca, Morocco. At this Casablanca Conference, they mapped out their strategy for the rest of the war. They decided to maintain the approach of dealing with Europe first. They would continue to concentrate Allied resources on Europe before trying to win the war in the Pacific. Churchill and Roosevelt also agreed to accept nothing less than the unconditional surrender of Italy, Germany, and Japan.

The Invasion of Italy   Control of North Africa freed the Allies to make the next move toward retaking Europe. They decided to target Italy, which lay to the north, across the Mediterranean. In July 1943, the U.S. Seventh Army, under General George S. Patton, invaded the large island of Sicily with British forces.

VIEWING HISTORY The ancient monastery at Monte Cassino was destroyed in the battle to break through German defenses in Italy. **Expressing Problems Clearly** *Describe the obstacles Allied troops faced in Italy.*

With the Italian mainland in jeopardy, Italians lost faith in Mussolini's leadership. An official Fascist council voted to remove him from office, and King Victor Emmanuel III had him arrested. The Fascist Party was promptly disbanded, but the Germans freed Mussolini and evacuated him to northern Italy.

In September 1943, as Allied troops threatened to overrun the south and take Rome, Italy's new government surrendered. On October 13, the government declared war on Germany. The German army in Italy, however, continued to resist, blocking roads and destroying bridges as it retreated northward through the mountainous Italian peninsula. The Germans set up Mussolini as the puppet ruler of a fascist Italian state in northern Italy.

By November, the Allied advance had stalled in the face of a stiffened German defense. The town of Cassino, the key to the German defensive line, stood between the Allies and Rome. In January 1944, the Allies made a surprise move. They landed an American army unit behind German lines on the beach at Anzio, just 35 miles south of Rome. However, the American commander took too long to organize his forces. A German force blocked off the beach in time to trap the Allied troops. For the next four months, the Germans fiercely attacked the trapped soldiers. Before the Americans finally broke through German defenses in May 1944, tens of thousands of American soldiers had been killed or wounded.

Meanwhile, the Allies attacked Cassino and succeeded in breaking through the German line. Joining with the forces from Anzio, the Allied army quickly captured Rome. They faced more months of heavy fighting, however, before the Germans in northern Italy finally surrendered in April 1945. That same month, Mussolini was shot and killed by Italians as he tried to flee across the northern Italian border.

War in the Soviet Union

As the Allies battled their way across North Africa and into Italy, an epic struggle unfolded in eastern Europe. In *Mein Kampf*, Hitler had called for the conquest of the Soviet Union, to give the German people "living space." Hitler believed that Germany had to be self-sufficient, which meant that it needed its own sources of oil and food. By 1941, Hitler had taken control of huge oilfields in Romania. Now he planned to seize the farmlands of the Ukraine. After losing the Battle of Britain, Hitler decided to turn his war machine to the east. He broke his pact with Stalin and launched an attack against the Soviet Union.

The Germans Advance, 1941–1942 The attack began in the early morning hours of June 22, 1941. Nearly 3.6 million German and other Axis troops poured across the length of the Soviet border, from Finland in the north to Romania in the south. Nearly 3 million Red Army soldiers, poorly trained and badly equipped, mobilized to oppose the *blitzkrieg*.

The intensity and the brutality of the German attack took the Soviet defenders by surprise. The *Luftwaffe* quickly gained control of the air, and German ground troops drove deep into Soviet territory. Germany captured hundreds of thousands of Soviet soldiers who were trapped by the German army's quick advances. Soviet citizens who suffered badly under Stalin, including Ukrainians and Lithuanians, welcomed the Germans as liberators. Their enthusiasm ended quickly as German troops introduced forced labor and began executing civilians.

Chapter 25 • Section 2 835

Focus on WORLD EVENTS

The Siege of Leningrad At the northern reaches of the Eastern Front, Hitler's armies began a nearly three-year siege of Leningrad in September 1941. Despite German artillery attacks, the Soviets sustained a heroic effort to transport food and supplies to the city's three million inhabitants across the frozen surface of Lake Ladoga, Leningrad's only link to the Soviet Union. About 660,000 residents died of starvation and disease before the Germans retreated in January 1944. Leningrad was awarded the Order of Lenin and the title "Hero City of the Soviet Union" in gratitude for its stand against Hitler.

READING CHECK
How successful was the invasion of the Soviet Union in its first few months?

ACTIVITY
Connecting with Geography

Ask students to work in groups to make a detailed map of the theater of war in either Europe or North Africa, including battle lines and the dates of important events. **(Visual/Spatial)**

BACKGROUND
Military Technology

One of the obstacles facing the landing at Anzio was a shortage of LSTs. LST stood for "Landing Ship Tank." Many different types of landing craft were used by the Allies to land troops on beaches. Of these, the LST was the largest and arguably the most important. They were so crucial to the war effort that Winston Churchill once remarked, "Sometimes I think the whole war depends on some damned thing called an LST." In some ways, he was right: it was a critical piece of equipment. (Naval personnel, who knew the LSTs were prime targets for enemy attack, sometimes said that LST stood for "Large Slow Target.")

READING CHECK
It was widely successful in the first few months. The German air forces gained near total control of the air, and German ground troops took hundreds of thousands of Russian prisoners and penetrated deep into Russian territory.

Student Portfolio

You may wish to have students add the following to their portfolios: Ask students to prepare a detailed report about one battle of World War II or about one military leader, such as Omar Bradley, Dwight Eisenhower, or Douglas MacArthur. Suggest that students locate old issues of *Yank* magazine in the library and read eyewitness accounts written by soldiers who actually participated in the battles as background for their reports. **(Verbal/Linguistic)**

BACKGROUND

Interdisciplinary

It is instructive to compare Soviet and American casualties from World War II. About 27 million Soviets died as a result of the war. The comparable figure for Americans is about 40,000 lives lost. As one historian put it, "More Russian soldiers died in the one great battle for Stalingrad than Americans did in *all* the battles in the *entire* war." The Battle of Stalingrad stands as the deadliest battle in human history. Before the battle, about 500,000 people lived in Stalingrad. At the end of the battle, only about 1,500 of them were still alive. All told, this single battle claimed more than one million lives—a mind-boggling death toll. Soviet resentment of a perceived lack of American appreciation of such facts as these helped fuel the Cold War.

to Today

The *Reichstag*

In the final days of World War II, a Soviet soldier celebrated the final conquest of Berlin by raising a Soviet flag over the ruined *Reichstag* building. His act was only one of many turning points in German history that occurred at the *Reichstag* (left).

On February 27, 1933, four weeks after Hitler became chancellor, the main chamber of the *Reichstag* burned in a suspicious fire attributed to the Communists. Hitler used the fire as a pretext to win dictatorial powers and end the legislature's independence. The *Reichstag* building housed Nazi exhibitions in the late 1930s and suffered from Allied bombing during World War II.

After 1945, the heavily damaged *Reichstag* was located within West Berlin, but the new east-west boundary divided it from nearby buildings. The West German government, uncomfortable with Berlin's isolated location and its Nazi associations, chose the university town of Bonn as its capital instead. Partially restored as a museum, the *Reichstag* occasionally served as a backdrop for speeches and concerts protesting Communist acts in the east.

Today When Germany reunited in 1990, Chancellor Helmut Kohl opted to move the national capital back to unified Berlin. Germany chose to replace part of the old building so as to create a new *Reichstag* unburdened by its past history. To replace the destroyed roof, British architect Norman Foster designed a futuristic glass dome that reflected light into the building and opened the parliamentary chamber up to the outside. Visitors may climb to the very top of the dome for views of Berlin. In 1999, 60 years after World War II began, the German Parliament returned to the *Reichstag* building.

 How did the history of the *Reichstag* building parallel the history of democracy in Germany?

Ten days after the invasion began, Stalin broadcast a message to his people: "In case of a forced retreat of the Red Army," he said, "all rolling stock [trains] must be evacuated; to the enemy must not be left a single engine, a single railway car, not a single pound of grain or gallon of fuel." Now, as the army began to retreat, it carried out this policy, destroying everything that might be useful to the enemy. In the meantime, Stalin asked Roosevelt for help through the Lend-Lease program. American aid began to flow and lasted until the end of the war.

By that autumn, German armies had advanced several hundred miles into the Soviet Union. German troops threatened the capital, Moscow, and nearly surrounded the historic city of Leningrad, now known as St. Petersburg. Stalin desperately urged his allies to launch an attack on Western Europe. This action would take pressure off the Soviet Union's Red Army by forcing Hitler to fight on two fronts at once. Churchill did not feel ready to commit to a risky invasion. Later, at Casablanca, he would persuade Roosevelt instead to invade Italy, which he called the "soft underbelly" of Europe. The Soviet people would have to confront the bulk of the German army on their own.

The Battle of Stalingrad The cold Russian winter stopped Germany's advance in October, and the Soviets regained some of their lost territory. The next summer brought a new German offensive aimed at oil fields to the southeast. The Red Army decided to make its stand at Stalingrad, a major rail and industrial center on the Volga River. In mid-September 1942, the Germans began a campaign of firebombing and shelling that lasted more than two months. Soviet fighters took up positions in the charred rubble that remained of Stalingrad. There they engaged the advancing German troops in bitter house-to-house combat, but lost most of the city.

In mid-November, taking advantage of harsh winter weather, Soviet forces launched a fierce counterattack. As Hitler had ruled out a retreat, the German army was soon surrounded in the ruined city with few supplies and no hope of escape. In late January, the Red Army launched a final assault on the freezing enemy. A German soldier later described the experience:

> ❝ Completely cut off, the men in field grey just slouched on, invariably filthy and invariably louse-ridden, their weary shoulders sagging, from one defence position to another. The icy winds of those great white wastes which stretched for ever beyond us to the east lashed a million crystals of razor-like snow into their unshaven faces, skin now loose-stretched over bone, so utter was the exhaustion, so utter the starvation. ❞
> —A German infantryman at Stalingrad, December 1942

Fast Forward to Today The 1933 Reichstag fire and its aftermath served as a reminder that democracy in Germany had come to a grinding halt. The 1999 reopening of the renovated Reichstag building symbolized that democracy had returned to all of Germany.

RESOURCE DIRECTORY

Technology

RESOURCE PRO® Literature Activity
Dispatches from the Battle Front, found on Resource Pro, features war correspondent Ernie Pyle's descriptions of the front lines of the European theater and the lives of the U.S. servicemen who fought there.

On January 31, 1943, more than 90,000 surviving Germans surrendered. In all, Germany lost some 330,000 troops at Stalingrad. Soviet losses are unknown, but estimates range as high as 1,100,000.

The Battle of Stalingrad proved to be the turning point of the war in the east. Germany's seemingly unstoppable offensive was over. After their victory, Soviet forces began a long struggle to regain the territory lost to the Germans. As the Red Army slowly forced the German invaders back, Stalin continued to push for the long-promised Soviet invasion of Western Europe.

The Allied Air War

To be successful, a major invasion of Western Europe by land forces needed the support of air power. By 1943, Allied pilots had gained plenty of battle experience. Aside from fighting off German attacks, Britain's Royal Air Force (RAF) had carried out long-range bombing of Germany, as well as Germany's oil facilities in Romania.

As you read earlier, German warplanes started to target cities during the Battle of Britain and British warplanes followed suit. After abandoning attempts to pinpoint targets, the RAF developed a technique called **carpet bombing,** in which planes scattered large numbers of bombs over a wide area. German cities suffered heavy damage as a result.

Allied bombing of Germany intensified after the United States entered the war. In a typical American raid, hundreds of B-17 Flying Fortresses took off from Britain, escorted by fighters. They rained bombs on German aircraft factories, railway lines, ball-bearing plants, bridges, and cities. With these massive raids, the Allies aimed to destroy Germany's ability to fight the war.

In the spring of 1943, the Allies stepped up their bombing campaign yet again in preparation for an eventual Allied invasion. Like British civilians during the Blitz, Germans came to spend nights in underground air raid shelters while enemy planes flew above. On the night of July 28, 1943, firebombing turned Hamburg into one huge blaze. A survivor recalled that "a storm started, a shrill howling in the street. It grew into a hurricane so that we had to abandon all hope of fighting the fire." The Hamburg fire department coined the term "firestorm" to describe this combination of flames driven by fierce heat-generated winds. More than 40,000 civilians died in four attacks on Hamburg.

By 1944, British and American commanders were conducting coordinated air raids—American planes bombing by day and RAF planes bombing by night. At its height, some 3,000 planes took part in this campaign.

The Invasion of Western Europe

Stalin was not the only leader calling for an invasion of Western Europe. George Marshall, the top American general and FDR's Chief of Staff, voiced the same opinion. At every Allied strategy conference after the United States entered the war, he pushed for an attack on the German forces occupying France. In late 1943, the British finally agreed to go along with Marshall's proposal. The invasion, code-named Operation Overlord, would be launched from Great Britain. Marshall chose General Eisenhower to be the supreme commander of the invasion forces.

The Allies began a massive military buildup in southern England. Polish, Dutch, Belgian, and French troops joined the American, British, and Canadian forces already in place. In response, the Germans strengthened their defenses

BIOGRAPHY

**George Marshall
1880–1959**

A graduate of Virginia Military Institute, George Marshall had served in France during World War I, where he aided in planning major Allied victories. He became Army Chief of Staff in 1939 and used his position to urge President Roosevelt to strengthen the army in preparation for war. As the highest-ranking general in the United States during the war, he was among the first leaders to recommend an early invasion of Western Europe. After the war, he left his post as Army Chief of Staff to become Secretary of State under President Truman. His work to rebuild Europe with American aid gained him the Nobel peace prize in 1953.

ACTIVITY
Connecting with History and Conflict

Have student groups research the use of carpet bombing versus targeted bombing in different conflicts, such as the Vietnam War and the Gulf War. Have students list the strengths and weaknesses and parameters for the use of each method. **(Verbal/Linguistic)**

BACKGROUND
Connections to History and Conflict

In contrast to the Royal Air Force's "carpet bombing," the American bomber command focused on its opposite: "precision bombing." In precision bombing, bombers attacked specific targets, such as factories or road junctions. The Americans felt they could achieve such precision because of a device called the Norden bombsight. Named for its inventor, Carl Norden, the bombsight was basically an early analog computer consisting of gyroscopes, mirrors, and a telescope. By sighting through it, bombardiers could calculate the exact moment to release their bomb loads. Theoretically, the bombsight was so accurate that a bombardier could hit a 100-foot circle from an altitude of four miles. In practice, it was less accurate, but still fairly effective. Airmen often claimed it could "put a bomb in a pickle barrel." The bombsight was a closely guarded military secret, and bombardiers had to swear to guard its secret with their lives.

CUSTOMIZE FOR ...
Less Proficient Readers

Have students read the section on the Battle of Stalingrad. Ask them to write a paragraph briefly explaining what they feel to be the most important reason for the massive German defeat at Stalingrad.

838 • Chapter 25 Section 2

Connecting with Today

Divide the class into small groups. Assign each group the task of creating an illustrated travel brochure for a trip to the Normandy beaches today. The students' brochure should identify the ruins, monuments, and other attractions that modern visitors to the site of the historic invasion can view. **(Visual/Spatial)**

BACKGROUND

Etymology

Today, the term *D-Day* is used almost exclusively to refer to June 6, 1944, when the great Allied invasion of Europe began. Originally, however, D-Day referred to the day on which any military operation or offensive was set to commence. The time of the day that operations began was called "H-Hour." These terms were used most often in the case of amphibious operations—i.e., landings from the sea, such as the island campaigns in the Pacific. The etymology of the two terms follows the same pattern: the "D" in D-Day is simply an abbreviation for "day"; the "H" in H-Hour is an abbreviation for "hour."

CAPTION ANSWERS

Map Skills The Allies divided the attacking forces into five groups with assigned landing points and defined goals to meet in the first day. Allied forces entered the English Channel from different ports and met at a gathering point in the Channel before attacking.

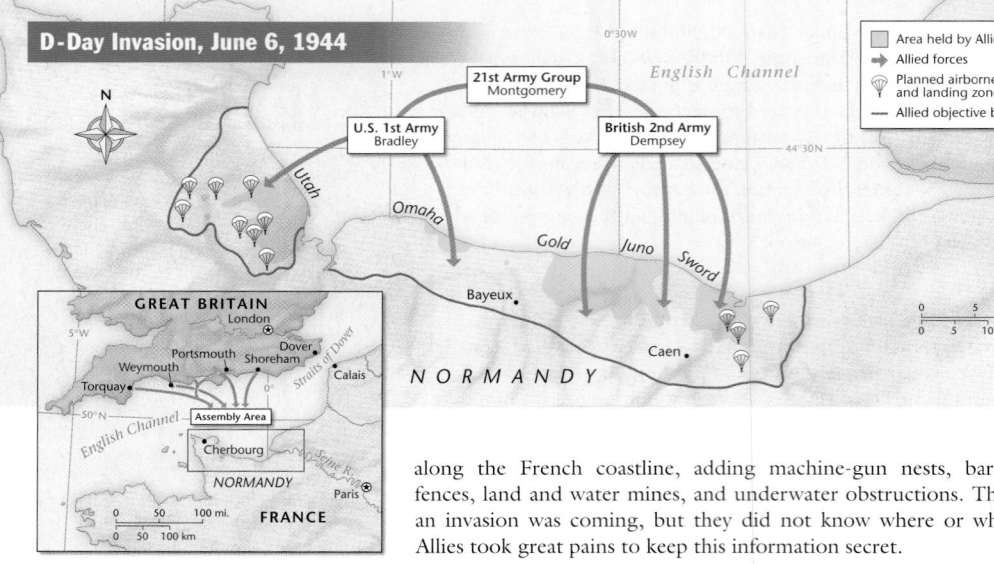

D-Day Invasion, June 6, 1944

MAP SKILLS Allied troops began the liberation of Western Europe on the beaches of Normandy on June 6, 1944. **Movement** *Cite evidence to show that the Allies carefully planned most aspects of the invasion.*

Sounds of an Era

Listen to a live description of the D-Day invasion and other sounds from World War II.

along the French coastline, adding machine-gun nests, barbed-wire fences, land and water mines, and underwater obstructions. They knew an invasion was coming, but they did not know where or when. The Allies took great pains to keep this information secret.

D-Day Shortly after midnight on June 6, 1944, some 4,600 invasion craft and warships slipped out of their harbors in southern England. As the ships crossed the English Channel, about 1,000 RAF bombers pounded German defenses at Normandy. Meanwhile, some 23,000 airborne British and American soldiers, in a daring nighttime maneuver, parachuted behind enemy lines.

At dawn on **D-Day**, the day the invasion of Western Europe began, Allied warships in the channel began a massive shelling of the coast. Some 1,000 American planes continued the RAF's air bombardment. Then, around 150,000 Allied troops and their equipment began to come ashore along 60 miles of the Normandy coast in the largest landing by sea in history.

Despite the advice of his generals to launch a quick counterattack, Hitler hesitated. Thanks to a complex Allied deception, he feared a second, larger invasion at the narrowest part of the English Channel near Calais. Nevertheless, the limited German force at Normandy resisted fiercely. At Omaha Beach, the code name for one landing site, the Allies suffered some 2,000 casualties. One Allied soldier later explained his experience of landing at Omaha Beach:

❝ *It seemed like the whole world exploded. There was gunfire from battleships, destroyers, and cruisers. The bombers were still hitting the beaches. . . . As we went in, we could see small craft from the 116th Infantry that had gone in ahead, sunk. There were bodies bobbing in the water, even out three or four miles.* ❞

—Lieutenant Robert Edlin

In spite of the heavy casualties of D-Day, within a week a half million men had come ashore. By late July, the Allied force in France numbered some 2 million troops.

Liberating France Air power helped the Allies establish a beachhead at Normandy and also held off German reinforcements by blowing up bridges throughout the region. Allied troops engaged in intense fighting on the ground. In early August, General Patton used a *blitzkrieg* to open a hole in the German

RESOURCE DIRECTORY

Other Print Resources
Historical Outline Map Book *Germany Divided,* p. 67

Technology
Color Transparencies *Historical Maps,* A42
Sounds of an Era Audio CD *D-Day Invasion,* 1944 recording (time: 40 seconds)

lines and burst out of Normandy. Armored units of his U.S. Third Army drove deep into enemy territory and then encircled and destroyed the opposing forces. After breaking German defenses, Patton led his army on a successful sweep across northern France.

In Paris, an uprising started by the French Resistance freed the city from German control. On August 25, 1944, a French division of the U.S. First Army officially liberated Paris. That same day, General Charles de Gaulle arrived in the city, prepared to take charge of the French government.

British and Canadian forces freed Brussels and Antwerp in Belgium a few days later. In mid-September, a combined Allied force attacked the Germans occupying the Netherlands. At about the same time, American soldiers crossed the western border of Germany.

The Battle of the Bulge The Nazis fought desperately to defend their conquests. To the north, the Allied attack on the Netherlands faltered at the Rhine River. Meanwhile, Hitler reinforced the army with thousands of additional draftees, some as young as 15. Then, in mid-December 1944, Germany launched a counterattack in Belgium and Luxembourg. The German attack smashed into the U.S. First Army and pushed it back, forming a bulge in the Allied line. The resulting clash came to be known as the **Battle of the Bulge.**

Many small units, cut off from the rest of the American army, fought gallantly against overwhelming odds. From his headquarters near Paris, Eisenhower ordered more troops to the scene. General Patton rapidly moved his U.S. Third Army north to help stop the German advance. In just a few weeks, the First and Third armies, under the overall direction of General Omar N. Bradley, knocked the Germans back and restarted the Allied drive into Germany.

The Battle of the Bulge was the largest battle in Western Europe during World War II, and the largest battle ever fought by the United States Army. It involved some 600,000 GIs, of whom about 80,000 were killed, wounded, or captured. German losses totaled about 100,000. After this battle, most Nazi leaders recognized that the war was lost.

The War in Europe Ends

In March 1945, as Allied bombers continued to strike German cities, American ground forces under General Bradley crossed the Rhine River and moved toward Berlin from the west. Meanwhile, Soviet troops pushed into Germany from the east.

Soviet Forces Advance The struggle between German and Soviet forces from 1941 to 1945 dwarfed the fighting in France. At any given time, more than 9 million soldiers were fighting on the eastern front. The costs of this struggle were horrific. Some 11 million Soviet and 3 million German soldiers died, accounting for more than two thirds of the soldiers killed in all of World War II. Current estimates place the total of Soviet civilian and military deaths at about 18 million.

After the hardships their nation had endured, Soviet leaders considered the capture of Berlin, Germany's capital, a matter of honor. In late April 1945, Soviet troops fought their way into Berlin. As they had in Stalingrad, they fought German soldiers for each ruined house and street in the destroyed city.

Allied soldiers parachute into France during the D-Day invasion.

839

Reading Comprehension

1. It contained terms agreed to by Great Britain and the U.S. to govern war behavior and define their aims.

2. (a) The intensity of the attack took the Soviets by surprise. (b) During the retreat, the Soviets destroyed any items that could be of use to the Germans; the cold, harsh weather; the vast size of the Soviet Union.

3. (a) To drop many bombs over a wide area, causing heavy damage. (b) Carpet bombing, along with more precise American bombing, enabled the Allies to strike all over Germany with lower risk for Allied casualties.

4. It represented the opening of the Allied invasion of Western Europe.

Critical Thinking and Writing

5. The Soviet Union bore the heaviest cost of fighting Germany.

6. Battle of Stalingrad: Turning point of war in the east; German surrender and loss showed that Germany's seemingly unstoppable offensive was over. Battle of the Bulge: Battle resulted in great German losses, after which most Nazi leaders recognized that the war was lost.

7. Entries may include: February 1941: Hitler sends General Rommel to reinforce Italian troops in North Africa; November 1942: British victory at El Alamein, and U.S. and British forces land in northwest Africa; July 1943: U.S. and British forces invade Sicily; Winter 1942–1943: Battle of Stalingrad; June 1944: D-Day; August 1944: Paris liberated; December 1944: Battle of the Bulge; May 1945: Germany surrenders.

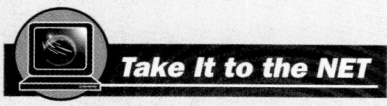

Take It to the NET

Invite students to take a Virtual Field Trip at **www.phschool.com**

CAPTION ANSWERS

Viewing History Soviet troops invaded Germany from the east and conquered Berlin with heavy losses in the final weeks of the war in Europe.

VIEWING HISTORY A United States soldier (left) and a Soviet soldier (right) share a moment of camaraderie after meeting at the Elbe River in April 1945. **Recognizing Cause and Effect** *How did Soviet assaults in 1945 help end the war?*

While some Soviet troops attacked Berlin, other elements of the Red Army continued to drive west. On April 25, at the Elbe River, they connected with American troops pushing east.

Germany Surrenders As the Soviet army surrounded Berlin, Hitler refused to take his generals' advice to flee the city. Instead, he chose to commit suicide in his underground bunker in Berlin on April 30, 1945. A few days later, on May 8, 1945, Germany's remaining troops surrendered.

When the fighting in Europe came to an end, American soldiers rejoiced, and civilians on the home front celebrated V-E Day (Victory in Europe Day). They knew, however, that the war would not be over until the Allies had defeated Japan.

The Yalta Conference In February 1945, months before the fall of Berlin, Roosevelt, Churchill, and Stalin met at Yalta, a city in the Soviet Union near the Black Sea. Building on discussions at Teheran, in Iran, at the end of 1943, they gathered to plan the final defeat of Germany and to decide the shape of the postwar world. The leaders agreed to split Germany into four zones, each under the control of one of the major Allies, including France. They planned a similar division of the city of Berlin, which would lie deep inside the Soviet zone. Stalin promised to allow elections in the nations of Eastern Europe that his army had liberated from the Germans. He also promised to enter the war against Japan within three months of Germany's surrender.

Stalin did not fulfill his promises at Yalta. He refused, for example, to honor his pledge of free elections in Eastern Europe. Critics of Yalta accused Roosevelt and Churchill of not doing enough to prevent Soviet domination of half of Europe. The issue of Eastern Europe would be at the heart of the conflict that later arose between the Soviet Union and the Western Allies.

Section 2 Assessment

READING COMPREHENSION

1. Why was the **Atlantic Charter** significant?

2. (a) Why did the German invasion of the Soviet Union succeed at first? (b) What factors helped the Soviet army defeat the Germans?

3. (a) What was the goal of **carpet bombing**? (b) What advantage did carpet bombing have over a conventional attack on Germany?

4. Explain the significance of the D-Day invasion.

CRITICAL THINKING AND WRITING

5. **Identifying Alternatives** How did the Allied decision to delay an invasion of Western Europe and fight instead in North Africa and Italy affect the Soviet Union?

6. **Making Comparisons** Explain why Stalingrad and the Battle of the Bulge marked two different turning points for Germany during the war.

7. **Writing a Time Line** Create a time line that lists important events in the war in Europe and in North Africa between 1941 and 1945.

Take It to the NET

Activity: Virtual Field Trip D-Day is one of the most memorable events of World War II. Take a virtual field trip examining different aspects of the Normandy invasion. Then, write a summary of your field trip. Use the links provided in the *America: Pathways to the Present* area of the following Web site for help in completing this activity. **www.phschool.com**

RESOURCE DIRECTORY

Teaching Resources
Units 7/8 booklet
• Section 2 Quiz, p. 61
Guide to the Essentials
• Section 2 Summary, p. 127

READING FOCUS

- In what ways did Germany persecute Jews in the 1930s?
- How did Germany's policies toward Jews develop from murder into genocide?

MAIN IDEA

During World War II, the Nazis carried out a brutal plan that resulted in the deaths of 6 million Jews and millions of other victims.

KEY TERMS

anti-Semitism
Holocaust
concentration camp
Kristallnacht
Warsaw ghetto
Wannsee Conference
death camp
War Refugee Board
  (WRB)
Nuremberg Trials

TAKING NOTES

Copy the web diagram below and fill in the circles with examples of German persecution of Jews.

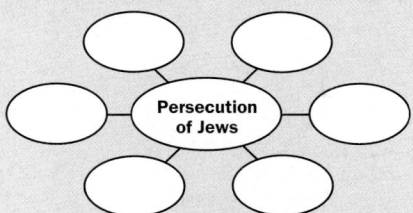

Persecution of Jews

SECTION OBJECTIVES

1. Find out about some ways in which Germany persecuted Jews in the 1930s.
2. See how Germany's policies toward Jews developed from murder into genocide.

BELLRINGER

Warm-Up Activity Ask students to define the word *genocide*. Ask students if they are aware of any racial, ethnic, or cultural groups in the past or in the present against which genocide has been committed.

Activating Prior Knowledge Ask students to search for the dictionary definition of *holocaust*. Can they state a list of synonyms for that word? Have a discussion about the power of certain words in our language, such as *holocaust*, to call up a host of emotions. What are some emotions that are stirred amongst students by the word *holocaust*?

READING STRATEGY

As students read the section, have them create a time line of the events related to the Holocaust. For each event, have students write a sentence that analyzes the event's historic importance.

ACTIVITY

Connecting with History and Conflict

Assign segments of *Mein Kampf* as outside reading to students. Have students summarize and analyze their excerpts in written or oral reports. (**Verbal/Linguistic**)

Setting the Scene

Jews in Europe faced persecution for their religious beliefs for centuries. In the mid-1800s, a new form of anti-Jewish prejudice arose based on racial theories. Some thinkers claimed that Germanic peoples whom they called "Aryans" were superior to Middle Eastern peoples called Semites. Semitic peoples included Arabs and Jews, but the term often applied only to Jews.

Although most scholars rejected those theories, others used them to justify the continued persecution of "non-Aryans." By the 1880s, Europeans used the term **anti-Semitism** to describe discrimination or hostility, often violent, directed at Jews. Despite the rise of anti-Semitism, most European countries repealed old anti-Jewish laws between the mid-1800s and World War I.

The suffering caused by World War I and the hardships of the Great Depression led many to look to these old theories to restore national pride and a sense of purpose. In *Mein Kampf*, Adolf Hitler revived the idea of Aryan superiority and expressed an especially hateful view of Jews. In particular, he despised the mixing of the two "races":

> ❝ Let the desolation which Jewish hybridization daily visits on our nation be clearly seen, this blood-poisoning that can be removed from our body national only after centuries or nevermore; let it be pondered, further, how racial decay drags down, indeed often annuls, the final Aryan values of our German nation. . . .❞
>
> —Adolf Hitler, from *Mein Kampf*, 1925

Persecution in Germany

When Hitler became Germany's leader in 1933, he made anti-Semitism the official policy of the nation. No other persecution of Jews in modern history equals the extent and brutality of the **Holocaust,** Nazi Germany's systematic murder of European Jews. In all, some six million Jews, about two thirds of Europe's

Building upon historic anti-Semitism, the Nazis planned to exclude Jews from all areas of German life. A sign turns away shoppers from a Jewish-owned store during the April 1, 1933, boycott.

Chapter 25 • Section 3 **841**

RESOURCE DIRECTORY

Teaching Resources
Guided Reading and Review booklet, p. 102

Technology
Section Reading Support Transparencies
Guided Reading Audiotapes (English/Spanish), Ch. 25
Student Edition on Audio CD, Ch. 25
Prentice Hall Presentation Pro CD-ROM, Ch. 25
Companion Web site, www.phschool.com

Focus During World War II, the Nazis undertook the annihilation of Jews, Romany, people with physical and mental disabilities, and others whom they considered to be inferior. Ask students how the Nazis tried to accomplish this task.

Instruct Ask students why Germany might have wanted a scapegoat during the 1930s. How did anti-Semitism become official government policy? In what ways did the Nazis use this policy to persecute Jews during the 1930s?

Assess/Reteach Ask students to contemplate the enormity of the Nazis' plan, "The Final Solution," to systematically annihilate many millions of people. Hold a classroom discussion that analyzes both the stark cruelty of the "Solution" and the horrific brutality experienced as it was carried out.

READING CHECK
It was meant to exclude German Jews from all aspects of political, economic, and social life.

READING CHECK
What was the goal of Nazi persecution of Jews in the mid-1930s?

VIEWING HISTORY At bottom, a Jewish shopkeeper sweeps up shop windows left shattered by *Kristallnacht.* Below, the "J" stamp on this girl's identification paper identifies her as Jewish.
Synthesizing Information *In what other ways did the Nazis organize the persecution of the Jews?*

Jewish population, would lose their lives. Some 5 to 6 million other people would also die in Nazi captivity.

Nazi Policies Early Nazi persecution aimed to exclude Germany's Jews from all aspects of the country's political, social, and economic life. On April 1, 1933, the Nazis ordered a one-day boycott of businesses owned by Jews. In 1935, the Nuremberg laws stripped Jews of their German citizenship, and outlawed marriage between Jews and non-Jews. Nazi-controlled newspapers and radio constantly attacked and caricatured Jews as enemies of Germany.

In 1938, the Nazis enacted new policies to make life even more difficult for the Jewish people. Most Jews had already lost their jobs. The Nazis now forced Jews to surrender their own businesses to Aryans for a fraction of their value. Jewish doctors and lawyers were forbidden to serve non-Jews, and Jewish students were expelled from public schools.

A Jew was defined as any person who had three or four Jewish grandparents, regardless of his or her current religion, as well as any person who had two Jewish grandparents and practiced the Jewish religion. At the request of Switzerland, the destination of many refugees, the Nazis marked Jews' identity cards with a red letter "J." The Nazis also gave Jews new middle names—"Sarah" for women and "Israel" for men—which appeared on all documents. Eventually, Jews in Germany and German-occupied countries were forced to sew yellow stars marked "Jew" on their clothing. These practices exposed Jews to public attacks and police harassment.

Hitler's Police When Hitler first came to power, the Gestapo, Germany's new secret state police, was formed to identify and pursue enemies of the Nazi regime. Hitler also formed the SS, or *Schutzstaffel,* an elite guard that developed into the private army of the Nazi party. By 1939, the Gestapo had become part of the SS.

The duties of the SS included guarding the **concentration camps,** or places where political prisoners are confined, usually under harsh conditions. In addition to Communists, the Nazi camps soon held many other classes of people whom they considered "undesirable"—mainly Jews, but also homosexuals, Jehovah's Witnesses, Gypsies, and the homeless.

Kristallnacht Despite the ever-increasing restrictions on their lives, many Jews believed they could endure persecution until Hitler lost power. Older people believed staying in Germany was safer than starting a new life with no money in a foreign country. Their illusions were destroyed on the night of November 9, 1938, when Nazi thugs throughout Germany and Austria looted and destroyed Jewish stores, houses, and synagogues.

This incident became known as ***Kristallnacht,*** or "Night of the Broken Glass," a reference to the broken windows of the Jewish shops. Nearly every synagogue was destroyed. The Nazis arrested thousands of Jews that night and shipped them off to concentration camps. These actions were followed by an enormous fine to make Jews pay for the damage of *Kristallnacht.* After that night, Germany's remaining Jews sought any means possible to leave the country.

Refugees Seek an Escape From 1933 through 1937, about 130,000 Jews, or one in four, fled Germany with Nazi encouragement. At first, most refugees moved to neighboring European nations. As the numbers grew, however, Jews began to seek protection in the United States, Latin America,

---

CAPTION ANSWERS

Viewing History They set up concentration camps and death camps, and organized mobile killing units.

RESOURCE DIRECTORY
Technology
Color Transparencies *Historical Maps,* A43
Exploring Primary Sources in U.S. History CD-ROM *Night,* Elie Wiesel

---

and British-ruled Palestine. Few countries, however, welcomed Jewish refugees as long as the Depression prevented their own citizens from finding work.

Responding to criticism, President Roosevelt called for an international conference to discuss the growing numbers of Jewish refugees. The Evian Conference, held in France in July 1938, failed to deal with the situation. With the exception of the Dominican Republic, each of the 32 nations represented, including the United States, refused to open its doors to more immigrants.

From Murder to Genocide

As German armies overran most of Europe, more and more Jews, including many who had fled Germany, came under their control. In 1939, for example, the invasion of Poland brought some 2 million additional Jews under German control. Nazi plans for dealing with these Jews included the establishment of ghettos, areas in which members of a minority group are concentrated. In Warsaw, the Nazis rounded up more than 400,000 Jews, about 30 percent of the Polish capital's population, and confined them in an area that was less than 3 percent of the entire city. They sealed off the **Warsaw ghetto** with a wall topped with barbed wire and guarded by Germans. Jews received little food, and hunger, overcrowding, and a lack of sanitation brought on disease. Each month, thousands of Jews died in the ghetto. The Nazis, however, sought more efficient ways of killing Jews.

The *Einsatzgruppen* During the invasion of the Soviet Union, Hitler ordered *Einsatzgruppen*, or mobile killing squads, to shoot Communist political leaders as well as all Jews in German-occupied territory. Typically, they rounded up their victims, drove them to gullies or freshly dug pits, and shot them. In a ravine called Babi Yar outside Kiev, the Nazis killed more than 33,000 Jews in two days.

Although Hitler considered mass murder by firing squad acceptable in a war zone, he found the method unsuitable for the conquered nations of western and central Europe. In January 1942, Nazi officials met at the **Wannsee Conference** outside Berlin to agree on a new approach. They developed a plan to achieve what one Nazi leader called the "final solution to the Jewish question." Ultimately, the plan would lead to the construction of special camps in Poland where **genocide,** or the deliberate destruction of an entire ethnic or cultural group, was to be carried out against Europe's Jewish population.

The Death Camps The Nazis chose poison gas as the most effective way to kill people. A pesticide called Zyklon B proved to be the most efficient killer. In January 1942, the Nazis opened a specially designed gas chamber disguised as a shower room at the Auschwitz camp in western Poland. The Nazis outfitted six such camps in Poland. Unlike concentration camps, which functioned as prisons and centers of forced labor, these **death camps** existed primarily for mass murder.

Jews in Poland, the Netherlands, Germany, and other lands were crowded into train cars built for cattle and transported to these extermination centers. Most of them were told they were going to "the East" to work. At four of the six death camps, nearly all were murdered soon after they arrived. On arrival at the two largest camps, Auschwitz and Majdanek, prisoners were organized into a line and quickly inspected. The elderly, women with children, and those who looked too weak to work were herded into gas chambers and killed. Jewish

VIEWING HISTORY The Nazis forced Jews to wear armbands or bright yellow stars marked "Jew" in Germany (top), in occupied lands, including France (center), and in the Netherlands (bottom). Jews caught without a star were deported or killed. **Predicting Consequences** *Why did the stars make life more difficult for Jews?*

Focus on WORLD EVENTS

Rescue in Denmark One country managed to save almost its entire Jewish community from destruction during the war. In October 1943, Danish fishermen secretly ferried nearly all of Denmark's 8,000 Jews across the water to neutral Sweden. A German official had alerted the Danish resistance that the Jews were about to be deported. Denmark's success was as rare as it was remarkable. Rescue was much more difficult in countries where the Jewish population was much greater than in Denmark, where the non-Jewish population was unwilling to help, or where there was no safe haven nearby.

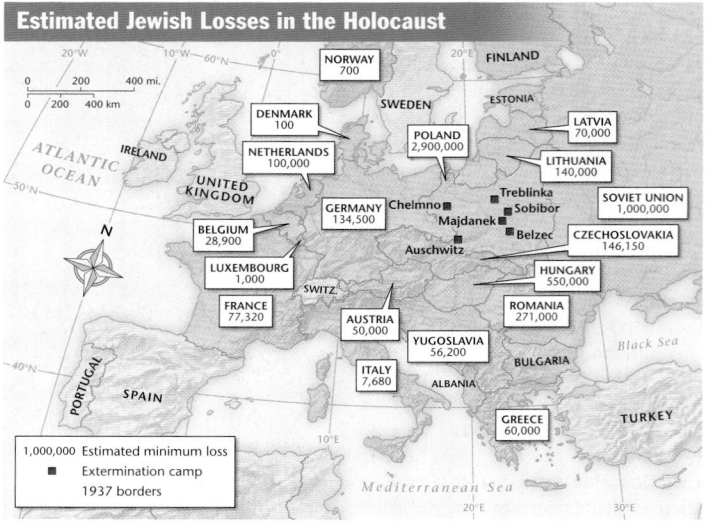

Estimated Jewish Losses in the Holocaust

NORWAY 700
DENMARK 100
NETHERLANDS 100,000
POLAND 2,900,000
LATVIA 70,000
LITHUANIA 140,000
GERMANY 134,500
SOVIET UNION 1,000,000
BELGIUM 28,900
CZECHOSLOVAKIA 146,150
LUXEMBOURG 1,000
HUNGARY 550,000
FRANCE 77,320
AUSTRIA 50,000
ROMANIA 271,000
YUGOSLAVIA 56,200
ITALY 7,680
GREECE 60,000

Chelmno • Treblinka • Sobibor • Majdanek • Belzec • Auschwitz

1,000,000 Estimated minimum loss
■ Extermination camp
1937 borders

MAP SKILLS The horror of the Holocaust touched many nations in Europe. **Place** *Which country do you think was most altered by the Holocaust?*

Jews in the Lodz ghetto in Poland board a train for deportation to the Chelmno death camp. The Germans seized the Jews' belongings and did not tell the deportees where they were going.

prisoners carried the dead to the crematoria, or huge ovens where the bodies were burned.

Those who were selected for work endured almost unbearable conditions. The life expectancy of a Jewish prisoner at Auschwitz was a few months. Men and women alike had their heads shaved and a registration number tattooed on their arms. They were given one set of clothes and slept in crowded, unheated barracks on hard wooden pallets. Their daily food was usually a cup of imitation coffee, a small piece of bread, and thin, foul-tasting soup made with rotten vegetables. Diseases swept through the camps and claimed many who were weakened by harsh labor and starvation. Others died from torture or from cruel medical experiments. At periodic "selections," German overseers sent weak prisoners to the gas chambers.

The number of people killed in the labor and death camps is staggering. At Auschwitz, the main Nazi killing center, 12,000 victims could be gassed and cremated in a single day. There the Nazis killed as many as 1.5 million people, some 90 percent of them Jews.

Fighting Back Some Jews resisted the Nazis. In Poland, France, and elsewhere, Jews joined underground resistance groups. Jews in several ghettos and camps took part in violent uprisings. In August 1943, rioting Jews damaged the Treblinka death camp so badly that it had to be closed. However, uprisings often came too late to save many people, and they were quickly crushed by the Germans.

Escape was the most common form of resistance. Most attempts failed, and most of those who escaped were later caught, but a few people managed to bring word of the death camps to the outside world. After several prisoners escaped from Treblinka, word got back to the Warsaw ghetto about the fate of nearly 300,000 Jews from Warsaw who had been sent there in 1942. As a result, in April 1943, the approximately 50,000 Jews still in the Warsaw ghetto rose up against a final deportation to Treblinka. For some 27 days, Jews armed with little more than pistols and homemade bombs held out against more than 2,000 Germans with tanks and artillery. Although the Germans defeated the rebellion, Warsaw's Jews had brought the deportation drive to a standstill, if only for a time.

Rescue and Liberation The United States government knew about the mass murder of Jews by the Nazis as early as November 1942. The press showed little interest in reporting the story. Congress did not raise immigration quotas, and even the existing quotas for Jews went unfilled.

Finally, in January 1944, over the objection of the State Department, Roosevelt created the **War Refugee Board (WRB)** to try to help people threatened by the Nazis. Despite

844 Chapter 25 • *World War II: Americans at War*

its late start, the WRB's programs helped save some 200,000 lives. With WRB funding, for example, Swedish diplomat Raoul Wallenberg rescued thousands of Hungarian Jews by issuing them special Swedish passports. A WRB effort to bring Jews to the United States met with less success. Some 1,000 refugees were rescued and brought to an army camp in Oswego, New York, but Roosevelt would not expand the program.

As Allied armies advanced in late 1944, the Nazis abandoned the camps outside Germany and moved their prisoners to camps on German soil. On the eve of liberation, thousands of Jews died on death marches from camp to camp as their German guards moved them ahead of advancing armies. In 1945, American troops were able to witness the horrors of the Holocaust for the first time. A young soldier described the conditions he discovered as he entered the barracks at Buchenwald:

66 The odor was so bad I backed up, but I looked at a bottom bunk and there I saw one man. He was too weak to get up; he could just barely turn his head. . . . He looked like a skeleton; and his eyes were deep set. He didn't utter a sound; he just looked at me with those eyes, and they still haunt me today. 99

—Leon Bass, American soldier

VIEWING HISTORY The faces of these newly liberated prisoners reflect the starvation and horrors they experienced in a concentration camp in Ebensee, Austria. **Recognizing Cause and Effect** *How did the liberation of the camps lead to the Nuremberg trials?*

Horrified by the death camps and by Germany's conduct during the war, the Allies placed a number of former Nazi leaders on trial. They charged them with crimes against peace, crimes against humanity, and war crimes. An International Military Tribunal composed of members selected by the United States, Great Britain, the Soviet Union, and France conducted the **Nuremberg Trials** in November 1945. Of the 24 Nazi defendants, 12 received the death sentence. More significant than the number of convictions, the trials established the important principle that individuals must be responsible for their own actions. The tribunal firmly rejected the Nazis' argument that they were only "following orders."

Section 3 Assessment

READING COMPREHENSION

1. Why was *Kristallnacht* a critical event for Jews living under Nazi control?

2. (a) What was the purpose of a **concentration camp?** (b) What was the purpose of a **death camp?**

3. How did the United States respond to news of the **Holocaust** during the war?

CRITICAL THINKING AND WRITING

4. **Identifying Central Issues** How did the Nazis implement their plans for genocide?

5. **Writing to Inform** Write a short paragraph from the point of view of a Jewish teenager living in the Warsaw Ghetto in 1942.

Take It to the NET

Activity: Virtual Field Trip Visit the United States Holocaust Memorial Museum online. Select one of the several online exhibits available and write an essay describing the exhibit's effectiveness. Use the links provided in the *America Pathways to the Present* area of the following Web site for help in completing this activity.
www.phschool.com

Section 3 Assessment

Reading Comprehension

1. Many Jews living under Nazi rule thought they could endure persecution until Hitler lost power. The devastation of *Kristallnacht* forced them to realize that outlasting Hitler would not be possible and that they should try to leave Germany by any means possible.

2. (a) To confine Jews, political prisoners, and others, and act as a forced labor camp. (b) The mass murder of (primarily) Jews.

3. At first the United States was unresponsive, showing little interest in reporting the stories, not raising immigration quotas, and not filling the existing quota for Jews. Later, Roosevelt, over the objection of the State Department, created the War Refuge Board to try to help people threatened by the Nazis.

Critical Thinking and Writing

4. During the invasion of Russia, German *Einsatzgruppen* (mobile killing units) carried out mass shootings of Russian Jews. At the Wannsee Conference in January 1942, the Nazis decided to set up death camps to systematically murder Jews using poison gas.

5. Paragraphs will vary, but should reflect an understanding of ghettoization as it is described in the chapter.

Invite students to take a Virtual Field Trip at **www.phschool.com**

CAPTION ANSWERS

Viewing History The Allies called for Nazi leaders to be put on trial due in large part to the horrors revealed when the camps were liberated.

CUSTOMIZE FOR ...

Less Proficient Readers

Have students read the section "From Murder to Genocide," and examine the map on the previous page. Ask them to make a list of the names of the six death camps. Have the students indicate which two death camps were also work camps by underlining the names of those camps.

Section 4
The War in the Pacific

Section 4
The War in the Pacific

SECTION OBJECTIVES

1. Learn about advances Japan made in Asia and the Pacific in late 1941 and 1942.
2. See which Allied victories turned the tide of war in the Pacific.
3. Read about the strategy of the United States in the struggle to reconquer the Pacific Islands.
4. Discover why the battles of Iwo Jima and Okinawa were important.
5. Understand how the Manhattan Project brought the war to an end.

BELLRINGER

Warm-Up Activity Ask students to write one sentence describing what they think is the most important way the use of nuclear weapons has changed the world.

Activating Prior Knowledge Can students recall and list some significant events that led up to the war between Japan and the United States? What was the single most significant event?

READING STRATEGY

Have students sketch a map that shows the areas where fighting took place in the Pacific Ocean. As they read the section, have them mark the major battle sites on their map. Also have them note who won each battle.

CAPTION ANSWERS

Viewing History American troops were surprised by the Japanese, and the Philippines were too distant from the United States to reinforce with new American troops in time to make a difference.

READING FOCUS

- What advances did Japan make in Asia and the Pacific in late 1941 and 1942?
- Which Allied victories turned the tide of war in the Pacific?
- What was the strategy of the United States in the struggle to reconquer the Pacific islands?
- Why were the battles of Iwo Jima and Okinawa important?
- How did the Manhattan Project bring the war to an end?

MAIN IDEA

Fierce fighting and heavy casualties characterized the war in the Pacific Ocean as the Allied forces struggled to turn back Japanese advances.

KEY TERMS

Bataan Death March
Geneva Convention
Battle of the Coral Sea
Battle of Midway
Battle of Guadalcanal
island-hopping
Battle of Leyte Gulf
kamikaze
Battle of Iwo Jima
Battle of Okinawa
Manhattan Project

TAKING NOTES

As you read, prepare an outline of this section. The sample below will help you get started.

> I. Japan attacks American and British bases across the Western Pacific.
>   A. American troops at Bataan and Corregidor surrender.
>   B. POWs are forced on Bataan Death March.
>   C. Allies defend India and extend aid to China.
>   D. Battle of the Coral Sea ends threat to Australia.
> II. _____

VIEWING HISTORY A Japanese soldier patrols the ruins of Bataan in the Philippines. **Drawing Inferences** Why was the United States unable to defend the Philippines successfully?

Setting the Scene The bombing of Pearl Harbor was only the first of several sudden attacks across the Pacific. Japanese forces attacked American bases on Wake Island on December 8 and on Guam on December 10. Just hours after striking Pearl Harbor, Japanese warplanes bombed Clark Field, the main American air base in the Philippines. Although news of Pearl Harbor had reached Douglas MacArthur, the commanding general, the Americans at Clark Field failed to prepare for an attack. The Japanese destroyed about half of MacArthur's airplanes, which were lined up in rows on the ground.

Within days, a large Japanese force landed on the main Philippine island of Luzon. MacArthur withdrew most of his troops southward to the Bataan Peninsula. There he set up defenses, hoping the navy would be able to evacuate his army to safety.

American and Filipino troops held out on the Bataan Peninsula under Japanese fire for several months as hopes of rescue dimmed. Realizing that the situation was hopeless, President Roosevelt ordered MacArthur to escape to Australia. In March 1942, the general reluctantly boarded a torpedo boat and set off through Japanese-controlled waters to the safety of the southern Philippines. There, he boarded an airplane for Australia. Upon his arrival, MacArthur made a promise to the people of the Philippines and to his army: "I shall return."

The Japanese Advance, 1941–1942

The Japanese struck Pearl Harbor and Clark Field to try to gain military control of the Western Pacific. By shattering American forces everywhere in the region, they hoped that the United States would withdraw, leaving them easy access to the natural resources of Southeast Asia. Oil from the Dutch East Indies and rubber from British Malaya would give Japan the economic independence it

RESOURCE DIRECTORY

Teaching Resources
Guided Reading and Review booklet, p. 103

Other Print Resources
Historical Outline Map Book *World War II in the Pacific*, p. 66

Technology
Section Reading Support Transparencies
Guided Reading Audiotapes (English/Spanish), Ch. 25
Student Edition on Audio CD, Ch. 25
Color Transparencies *Historical Maps*, A44
Exploring Primary Sources in U.S. History CD-ROM *Japanese Internment Photograph*
Prentice Hall Presentation Pro CD-ROM, Ch. 25
Companion Web site, www.phschool.com

needed. With this goal in mind, the Japanese attacked a number of other Allied colonies in December 1941. By early March 1942, they had overrun the British strongholds of Hong Kong and Singapore, seized the Dutch East Indies and Malaya, and invaded Burma. Japan's southern offensive swept aside British, American, and Dutch naval power in Southeast Asia and brought a wide band of colonies into the Japanese empire. Japan then turned its attention to securing the Philippines.

The Philippines Fall Facing starvation and renewed Japanese attacks, most of Bataan's defenders surrendered in early April 1942. About 2,000 soldiers and nurses escaped to the fortified island of Corregidor, just off the tip of the peninsula, to join the fort's defenders. American troops on Corregidor survived another month of continual Japanese bombardment by living in the rock tunnels of the fortress. Finally, running low on ammunition and food, more than 11,000 Americans and Filipinos surrendered to invading Japanese forces on May 6.

With the fall of the Bataan Peninsula in early April and Corregidor in May, the Japanese captured about 76,000 Filipinos and Americans as prisoners of war. Already weakened by disease and lack of food, these prisoners faced a grueling test in the tropical heat. Their Japanese captors split them into groups of 500 to 1,000 and force-marched them some 60 miles to a railroad junction. There, the prisoners were boarded on a train that took them to within eight miles of an army camp and then walked the rest of the way.

During the march, many prisoners were treated brutally. They were denied water and rest and many were beaten and tortured. At least 10,000 prisoners died during the 6- to 12-day journey. Many were executed by the guards when they grew too weak to keep up. Their ordeal became known as the **Bataan Death March.** Those who survived were sent to primitive prison camps, where an additional 15,000 or more died.

The brutality of Japanese soldiers in Bataan defied accepted international standards of conduct toward prisoners of war. Those standards had been spelled out in 1929 in the third **Geneva Convention.** "Prisoners of war," the convention stated, "shall at all times be humanely treated and protected, particularly against acts of violence. . . ."

Defending China and Burma China joined the Allies on December 9, 1941, by officially declaring war on Germany, Italy, and its longtime foe, Japan. The United States had already sent military advisors and Lend-Lease arms and equipment to China. They hoped to strengthen China and thus divert Japan from the drive to conquer Southeast Asia.

Shortly after the war began, China's Nationalist leader Jiang Jieshi asked an American general, Joseph Stilwell, to serve as his chief of staff. Stilwell led the Chinese armies defending Burma, an important link between the Allies and Jiang's base in southwestern China. Despite the support of volunteer American aviators called the "Flying Tigers," China's ragtag forces fared poorly against the well-trained Japanese. They lost control of China's lifeline, the Burma Road, and retreated back into China. British and Indian troops in Burma fled west into India, which now also faced the threat of Japanese invasion.

American and Filipino prisoners captured by the Japanese in the Philippines

Focus on GOVERNMENT

War Crimes in the Pacific Word of the Bataan Death March did not reach the American public until a few years later when three soldiers escaped from their prison camp. As at Nuremberg, Japanese leaders accused of crimes against humanity faced a trial after the war. A United States military commission tried and convicted the general blamed for organizing the march. He was one of seven Japanese executed for war crimes.

Focus As Allied forces struggled to defeat the Axis Powers in Europe, they were also fighting fiercely against the Japanese in the Pacific.

Instruct Explain that initially the Japanese had the upper hand in the Pacific. Ask students why they think this was so. What military successes did Japan have between 1941 and 1942?

Discuss the strategies used by the Allies in the Pacific from 1943 to 1945. Why was it important that the Allies get control of the islands? Why did so many casualties result? Ask students to explain the significance of the Battle of Okinawa.

Discuss the history of the atomic bomb and have students explain the Manhattan Project. Ask them if they think Truman would have dropped the atomic bomb if he had known the bomb's delayed effects. Ask students to compare the use of the atomic bomb with the Allied conventional bombing raids against German cities discussed in Section 2.

Assess/Reteach Ask students to consider Truman's position as he contemplated the use of the atomic bomb. American casualties in the Pacific were heavy and mounting. The bombing of Germany with conventional bombs had been an accepted practice in the war in Europe. He saw in the use of the atomic bomb a quick and certain way to bring the war to a close. In students' opinions, did this justify the use of the atomic bomb?

ACTIVITY
Connecting with Government

Douglas MacArthur's statement, "I shall return," is among the most famous utterances to come out of World War II. Have students include it in a booklet they make that records the most famous quotations of the war era. Quotations should be selected for their historical importance and their fame. Students should write an annotation for each quotation that identifies its author and explains its context. **(Verbal/Linguistic)**

☑ TEST PREPARATION

Have the students read the section dealing with the American defeat in the Philippines, and then answer the following question.

On what date did the last American troops in the Philippines surrender to the Japanese?

A December 7, 1941

Ⓑ May 6, 1942

C December 10, 1941

D August 5, 1943

From the Archives of AmericanHeritage®

Thirty Seconds over Tokyo

Four months after Pearl Harbor it turned out that Japan could be surprised, too. On April 18, 1942, the world-renowned aviator Lt. Col. James H. Doolittle commanded a daring raid by sixteen B-25 bombers on Japan. Doolittle's bombers took off from the carrier *Hornet* while it was deep in Japanese-controlled waters but still 800 miles from Japan itself. There was no thought of returning to the carrier. The planes would drop their bombs, then fly on another 1,000 miles to land in China. True to plan, the pilots bombed military and industrial targets in Tokyo, Yokohama, and other cities. One bomber went down inside the Soviet border, where its surveying crew was detained; three of eight Americans captured in Japanese territory were executed. The raid had caused little damage, but it offered a gleam of triumph in a theater where the Allies had thus far known little but disaster. Its leader was made a brigadier general the very next day. Source: Nathan Ward, "The Time Machine," *American Heritage*® magazine, April 1992.

MAP SKILLS United States forces advanced from island to island across the Pacific toward Japan. **Location** *Why was the Battle of the Coral Sea important to the Allied cause?*

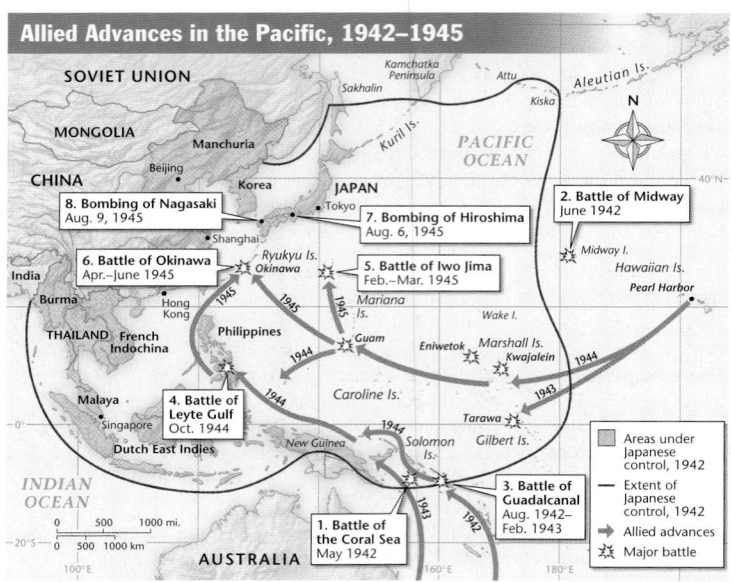

Allied Advances in the Pacific, 1942–1945

The War at Sea   At Pearl Harbor, Japan had not achieved one of its main goals: to destroy the three aircraft carriers that formed the heart of the Pacific Fleet. Two of the carriers, the *Lexington* and the *Enterprise*, had been away at sea during the attack, accompanied by the fleet's heavy cruisers. The third, the *Saratoga*, was undergoing repairs in California. These carriers would prove to be important American weapons in the war at sea.

Since World War I, the design of carriers and the aircraft that relied on them had improved tremendously. Carriers had become floating airfields, greatly extending the area in which warplanes could fly. These planes now included dive bombers and torpedo bombers capable of destroying enemy ships. Japan had used aircraft carriers as a base for the attack on Pearl Harbor.

In April 1942, a group of American B-25 medium bombers took off from the aircraft carrier *Hornet* on their own secret mission. Led by Lieutenant Colonel James Doolittle, the planes flew 650 miles to Japan to carry out a daring American counterattack. Doolittle's squadron dropped bombs on Tokyo and other cities before crash landing in China. Most of the pilots survived. The Doolittle raid caused little physical damage, but it shocked Japan's leadership and boosted Allied morale at a crucial time.

Japanese forces continued to advance across the Pacific, and the battered American navy fought desperately to stop them. The fall of the Dutch East Indies opened the way to Australia. In May 1942, a largely American naval group engaged a superior Japanese fleet in the Coral Sea, northeast of Australia. In the **Battle of the Coral Sea,** aircraft launched from aircraft carriers bombed and strafed enemy ships more than 70 miles away. The five-day battle cost both sides more than half their planes. The Japanese destroyed the *Lexington* and badly damaged the *Yorktown*, another carrier. One Japanese carrier sank, another lost most of its planes, and a third was put out of action. The battle was a draw, but it prevented the Japanese from invading Australia.

The Battle of the Coral Sea also opened a new chapter in naval warfare. It was the first naval combat carried out entirely by aircraft. The enemy ships never came within sight of one another. From now on, aircraft and aircraft carriers would play the central role in naval battles.

Allied Victories Turn the Tide

In the summer of 1942, while the Soviet Union resisted German attacks and the Allies prepared to invade North Africa, two critical battles took place in the Pacific. The fight for Midway Island, near Hawaii, and for Guadalcanal, near the Coral Sea, changed the course of the war in the Pacific.

The Battle of Midway   Japanese Admiral Yamamoto Isoroku, architect of the Pearl Harbor attack, hoped to destroy what remained of the United States Pacific Fleet by luring it into battle near Midway Island, some 1,100 miles northwest of Hawaii. Yamamoto committed a large part of Japan's navy to his planned invasion of Midway. He believed, correctly, that American Admiral Chester Nimitz would use all his resources to protect the island so vital to the defense of Hawaii.

The **Battle of Midway** opened on June 4, 1942, with a wave of Japanese bomber attacks on the island and a simultaneous, unsuccessful American strike on the Japanese fleet. As in the Battle of the Coral Sea, the Battle of Midway was fought entirely from the air. At first, American planes based on Midway's airfields tried to fend off the Japanese carrier-based bombers. Then the American carriers intervened. Their warplanes surprised Japan's carriers at a vulnerable time as the Japanese were refueling planes and loading them with bombs. Aboard the targeted Japanese ships, fuel hoses caught fire and bombs stacked on the decks exploded. The Americans swiftly sank three of the four heavy Japanese carriers and finished off the fourth, the *Hiryu,* the next day. Before the *Hiryu's* destruction, planes from that carrier had managed to disable the *Yorktown,* which was later sunk by a Japanese submarine. The other two American carriers, the *Enterprise* and the *Hornet,* emerged undamaged.

Japanese planes attack an American aircraft carrier during the Battle of Midway. The black clouds of smoke come from antiaircraft fire.

The sinking of four Japanese carriers, combined with the loss of some 250 planes and most of Japan's skilled naval pilots, was a devastating blow to the Japanese navy. The American victory owed much to Commander Joseph Rochefort, who broke the Japanese code JN-25 in time to learn crucial information before the attack began. After the Battle of Midway, Japan was unable to launch any more offensive operations in the Pacific.

The Battle of Guadalcanal   The victory at Midway allowed the Allies to take the offensive in the Pacific. Their first goal was to capture Guadalcanal in the Solomon Islands, where the Japanese were building an airfield to threaten nearby Allied bases and lines of communication with Australia.

When more than 11,000 marines landed on the island in August 1942, the 2,200 Japanese who were defending the island fled into the jungle. The **Battle of Guadalcanal** provided the marines with their first taste of jungle warfare. They slogged through swamps, crossed rivers, and hacked through tangles of vines in search of the enemy. The marines made easy targets for Japanese snipers hidden in the thick underbrush or in the tops of palm trees.

Estimated World War II Deaths

Country	Military Deaths	Civilian Deaths	Total Deaths
Axis			
Germany	3,250,000	2,350,000	5,600,000
Italy	226,900	60,000	286,900
Japan	1,740,000	393,400	2,133,400
Allies			
France	122,000	470,000	592,000
Great Britain	305,800	60,600	366,400
United States	405,400	—	405,400
Soviet Union	11,000,000	6,700,000	17,700,000
China	1,400,000	8,000,000	9,400,000

SOURCE: *World War II: A Statistical Survey*

INTERPRETING TABLES
Accurate death tolls are hard to determine, but scholars do not dispute the horrific human cost of the war. **Analyzing Information** *Which nation suffered the greatest human loss?*

READING CHECK
Why were *kamikaze* attacks effective?

Both sides landed thousands of reinforcements in five months of fighting. After several fierce naval battles, the American navy took control of the waters around the island in November, limiting Japanese troop landings. Japan's outnumbered forces finally slipped off the island in February 1943. The Allies had conquered their first piece of Japanese-held territory. Now they made plans for rolling back Japan's other conquests.

Struggle for the Islands

From Guadalcanal, American forces began **island-hopping,** a military strategy of selectively attacking specific enemy-held islands and bypassing others. By capturing only a few crucial islands, the United States effectively cut off the bypassed islands from supplies and reinforcements and rendered those islands useless to the Japanese. This strategy also allowed the Americans to move more quickly toward their ultimate goal—Japan itself.

Island-Hopping in the Pacific In 1943 and 1944, the Allies pushed north from Australia and west across the Central Pacific. Forces under General MacArthur and Admiral William Halsey leapfrogged through the Solomon Islands while Admiral Nimitz led a similar island-hopping campaign in the Gilbert Islands. After seizing the island of Tarawa, Nimitz used it to launch bombing raids on Japanese bases in the Marshall Islands. By February 1944, these attacks had crippled Japanese air power, allowing Nimitz's forces to seize Kwajalein and Eniwetok at the northwest end of the island group.

From the Marshalls, Nimitz captured parts of the Mariana Islands in June. For the first time, Japan was within reach of long-range American bombers. By the end of 1944, B-29 Superfortresses were dropping tons of explosives on Japanese cities.

The Philippines Campaign As American forces pushed toward Japan in the summer of 1944, military planners decided to bypass the Philippine Islands. MacArthur vigorously opposed this strategy, claiming that the United States had an obligation to free the Filipino people. The general's arguments persuaded Roosevelt, who reversed the decision.

In mid-October, some 160,000 American troops invaded the Philippine island of Leyte. After the beach was secure, General MacArthur dramatically waded ashore from a landing craft. News cameras recorded the historic event as MacArthur proclaimed, "People of the Philippines, I have returned."

While American troops fought their way inland, the greatest naval battle in world history developed off the coast. More than 280 warships took part in the three-day **Battle of Leyte Gulf.** The Japanese high command directed nearly every warship still afloat to attack the United States Navy. This was the first battle in which Japanese **kamikazes,** or suicide planes, were used. *Kamikaze* pilots loaded their aircraft with bombs and then deliberately crashed them into enemy ships to inflict maximum damage. Despite this tactic, the American force virtually destroyed the Japanese navy and emerged victorious.

Japanese land forces in the Philippines continued to resist, however. American troops needed two months to liberate Leyte. Some 80,000 Japanese defenders were killed and fewer than 1,000 Japanese surrendered. The battle for the Philippines' capital city of Manila, on the island of Luzon, was equally hard fought. Fighting left most of Manila in ruins and some 100,000 Filipino civilians dead. Not until June 1945 did the Allies control the Philippines.

Iwo Jima and Okinawa

The fighting grew deadlier as American troops moved closer to Japan. One of the bloodiest battles of the war took place on the tiny volcanic island of Iwo Jima, less than 700 miles from Japan. The island's steep, rocky slopes were honeycombed with caves and tunnels. The natural terrain protected more than 600 Japanese guns, many encased in concrete bunkers. In November 1944, American bombers, based in the recently conquered Marianas, began to pound Iwo Jima from the air. For 74 days, American planes and warships poured nearly 7,000 tons of bombs and more than 20,000 shells onto Iwo Jima's defenders.

In mid-February 1945, marines stormed the beaches. They encountered furious resistance from the Japanese. After three days of combat, the marines had advanced only about 700 yards inland. Eventually nearly 110,000 American troops took part in the campaign. Although opposed by fewer than 25,000 Japanese, the marines needed almost a month to secure the island. The enemy fought almost to the last defender. Only 216 Japanese were taken prisoner.

In the **Battle of Iwo Jima**, American forces suffered an estimated 25,000 casualties. The United States awarded 27 Medals of Honor for actions on Iwo Jima, more than in any other single operation of the war. Admiral Nimitz described the island as a place in which "uncommon valor was a common virtue." A photo of servicemen raising the United States flag on Mt. Surabachi came to symbolize the struggles and sacrifices of American troops during World War II.

The **Battle of Okinawa**, fought from April to June 1945, was equally bloody. The small island of Okinawa, little more than 350 miles from Japan itself, was historically Japanese soil. It was the last obstacle to an Allied invasion of the Japanese home islands. With this in mind, many of the island's nearly 100,000 defenders had pledged to fight to the death.

The Allies gathered some 1,300 warships and more than 180,000 combat troops to drive the enemy from Okinawa in an effort second only to the Normandy invasion in size. Japanese pilots flew nearly 2,000 *kamikaze* attacks against this fleet. As American soldiers stormed ashore, defenders made equally desperate *banzai* charges—attacks in which the soldiers tried to kill as many of the enemy as possible until they themselves were killed.

On February 19, 1945—the first day of the invasion—Marines fought to win a foothold on Iwo Jima under intense Japanese fire.

Kamikaze attacks took a toll on the United States Navy in the final year of the war.

One soldier described the long, hard-fought campaign to take Okinawa:

> ❝ Our attack pattern was: barrage a hill with bombs and shells, move up the foot soldiers, hold it against counterattacks, fight down the reverse slope, then start on the next one. We would attack during the day, dig in for the night—not for sleep, but for safety. A hole was never deep enough when the Japanese started their barrage. And then, at night, they would come, a screaming banzai or a single shadow. ❞
> —An American GI at Okinawa

In June, when the Japanese resistance finally ended after almost three months, only 7,200 defenders remained to surrender. For American forces, the nearly 50,000 casualties made the Battle of Okinawa the costliest engagement of the Pacific war. At long last, however, the Allies had a clear path to Japan.

The Manhattan Project

The next challenge for American soldiers was to prepare themselves for the invasion of Japan. After the grueling battles at Iwo Jima and Okinawa, they knew how costly such an invasion would be. Unknown to them, however, work was nearly complete on a bomb that would make the invasion unnecessary.

In August 1939, Roosevelt had received a letter from Albert Einstein, a brilliant Jewish physicist who had fled from Europe. In his letter, Einstein suggested that an incredibly powerful new type of bomb could be built by the Germans. Determined to build the bomb before Germany did, Roosevelt organized the top secret **Manhattan Project** to develop an atomic bomb.

Scientists had already succeeded in splitting the nucleus of the uranium atom. To make an atomic bomb, however, they had to discover how to create a chain reaction. In such a reaction, particles released from the splitting of one atom would cause another atom to break apart, and so on. In theory, the energy released by the splitting of so many atoms would produce a massive explosion. In 1942, Enrico Fermi produced the first controlled chain reaction in a laboratory at the University of Chicago. Scientists worked to design a bomb that could store the raw materials and trigger a much more powerful chain reaction on demand.

On July 16, 1945, Manhattan Project scientists field-tested the world's first atomic bomb in the desert of New Mexico. With a blinding flash of light, the explosion blew a huge crater in the earth and shattered windows some 125 miles away. As he watched, J. Robert Oppenheimer, who had supervised the building of the bomb, remembered the words of the *Bhagavad Gita*, the Hindu holy book: "Now I am become Death, the destroyer of worlds."

VIEWING HISTORY A single atomic bomb leveled the city of Hiroshima. **Making Comparisons** *How was the atomic bomb different from other war technology?*

The Decision to Drop the Bomb Once the bomb was ready, the question became whether or not to use it against Japan. There were a number of alternative possibilities for ending the war:

1. a massive invasion of Japan, expected to cost millions of Allied casualties
2. a naval blockade to starve Japan, along with continued conventional bombing
3. a demonstration of the new weapon on a deserted island to pressure Japan to surrender

852   Chapter 25 • *World War II: Americans at War*

4. a softening of Allied demands for an unconditional surrender

An advisory group of scientists, military leaders, and government officials, called the Interim Committee, met in the spring of 1945 to debate these ideas. It could not recommend any of the alternatives. Heavy American casualties at Iwo Jima and Okinawa were a factor in the committee's support for using the bomb.

The final decision, however, rested with President Harry S Truman, who had taken office barely three months earlier, after Roosevelt's sudden death in April 1945. Truman had no difficulty making up his mind. He considered the bomb to be a military weapon and had no doubt that it should be used. Truman never regretted his decision. "You should do your weeping at Pearl Harbor," he said to his critics in 1963.

Japan Surrenders On August 6, 1945, an American plane, the *Enola Gay*, dropped a single atomic bomb on Hiroshima, a city in southern Japan and the site of a large army base. A blast of intense heat annihilated the city's center and its residents in an instant. Many buildings that survived the initial blast were destroyed by fires spread by powerful winds. Perhaps 80,000 died and at least as many were injured by fire, radiation sickness, and the force of the explosion. At least 90 percent of the city's buildings were damaged or totally destroyed. A Hiroshima resident described the scene after the bombing:

Japanese officials signed documents of surrender aboard the USS *Missouri*.

> 66 Wherever you went, you didn't bother to take the roads. Everything was flat, nothing was standing, no gates, pillars, walls, or fences. You walked in a straight line to where you wanted to go. Practically everywhere you came across small bones that had been left behind. 99
>
> —Hiroshima survivor

Three days later, a second bomb was dropped on Nagasaki. On August 14, the government of Japan accepted the American terms for surrender. The next day, Americans celebrated V-J Day (Victory in Japan Day). The formal surrender agreement was signed on September 2, 1945, aboard the USS *Missouri* in Tokyo Bay. The long and destructive war had finally come to an end.

Section 4 Assessment

READING COMPREHENSION

1. What was Japan's military strategy immediately after the attack on Pearl Harbor?

2. How did the **Battle of Midway** and the **Battle of Guadalcanal** change the course of the war in the Pacific?

3. How did the **Battle of Okinawa** influence the decision to use the atomic bomb against Japan?

CRITICAL THINKING AND WRITING

4. **Making Comparisons** (a) In what ways did naval power play a different role in the Pacific war than it did in the war in Europe? (b) Why were aircraft carriers crucial to the Japanese and American war efforts?

5. **Writing to Explain** Write a brief essay that explains why the Japanese were able to advance so easily in 1941 and early 1942.

 Take It to the NET

Activity: Writing a Magazine Article Select a battle, issue, or military unit from the War in the Pacific. Research your subject online, and then write a magazine article on that theme. Be sure to incorporate primary sources. Use the links provided in the *America: Pathways to the Present* area of the following Web site for help in completing this activity.
www.phschool.com

Chapter 25 • Section 4 **853**

Section 4 Assessment

Reading Comprehension

1. To continue attacking in several different areas of the Pacific, before the United States would have time to respond. In this way, the Japanese hoped to gain unrestricted access to territory in Southeast Asia.

2. The losses sustained by Japan during the Battle of Midway prevented the Japanese from launching any further offensive operations in the Pacific. In the Battle of Guadalcanal, the Americans conquered their first piece of Japanese-held territory.

3. The vast number of casualties at Okinawa led to the decision to use the atomic bomb, rather than sustain the heavy losses that would undoubtedly be incurred if Japan itself were invaded.

Critical Thinking and Writing

4. (a) Europe: Allied naval power used primarily to defeat the German U-boats; Pacific: Naval battles there were the most significant of the war. Establishing naval supremacy in the Pacific was essential to the success of the American island-hopping strategy. (b) Carrier-based aircraft could attack the opposing fleet from a great distance without the need for a land base. Aircraft carriers themselves were (and are) highly mobile. Thus, air strikes could be carried out anywhere in the Pacific.

5. Answers will vary, but should reflect an understanding of the following elements: surprise attacks; time America needed to respond; Britain, Netherlands preoccupied with war in Europe.

 **Take It to the NET**

Articles will vary but should thoroughly represent the chosen topic, and be supported with various primary sources.

MAKING DECISIONS

Focus Students will gain insight into the process of decision-making by reading about the process of deciding to drop the atomic bomb on Japan.

Instruct Review with students the historical context of this document. America was at the end of a war that had been very costly in terms of lives and resources. President Truman had at his disposal a new kind of weapon that would bring the war to a rapid end. Should he use it? It was a heart-wrenching decision, because dropping the bomb would cause many innocent people to be injured or killed. Have students review his options. How many of them would have made the same decision?

Extend See the Skills for Life activity in the Resource Directory below.

ANSWERS

PRACTICE THE SKILL

1. (a) Whether to use the atomic bomb or not. To end the war in Japan. **(b)** Yes. Truman had to find a way to end the war.

2. (a) Truman knew that Japan still had 5,000 attack planes, 17 garrisons on Kyushu, and more than 2 million soldiers. **(b)** The United States would probably lose between a quarter of a million and a half million men.

3. (1) Attacking the island of Kyushu, then Honshu; (2) blockading Japan and using conventional weaponry; (3) dropping the bomb in an area with a very small population; (4) dropping the atomic bomb on military-manufacturing areas.

4. (a) 1 and 2 would lead to great loss of American life but no definite end of the war, and 3 would not be shocking enough to force surrender. **(b)** Pros: 1 and 2 didn't have the bomb's horrific results; 3 had fewer Japanese civilian casualties. Cons: In 1 and 2 the war would go on longer, with many casualties on both sides. In 3 the Japanese would not surrender.

5. (a) To drop the bomb on military-manufacturing areas. **(b)** He felt this would bring the war to a faster end with fewest American casualties.

Making Decisions

Some decisions are more difficult to make than others. A good way to learn decision-making skills is to look at the choices others have made and how they made them.

One of the most famous—and most analyzed—decisions in history was President Harry S Truman's decision to drop the atomic bomb on Japan during World War II. The decision was made after Germany had surrendered. Truman feared that defeating Japan might be more difficult because "the Japanese were self-proclaimed fanatic warriors who made it all too clear that they preferred death to defeat in battle." He describes his decision at right.

LEARN THE SKILL

Use the following steps to make decisions:

1. **Identify the problem and express it clearly.** First determine *whether* a decision is needed; then clarify *what* needs to be decided. What is the issue you want to resolve or the goal you want to achieve?

2. **Gather information.** Find out facts about the issue. Be sure that your sources are reliable.

3. **Identify options.** Be sure to consider all the ways an issue might be handled. Stating the options clearly will help you decide.

4. **Predict consequences.** Identify the pros and cons of each choice.

5. **Make a decision.** Evaluate your options; choose the one with the most acceptable consequences.

PRACTICE THE SKILL

Answer the following questions:

1. **(a)** What issue did President Truman need to resolve? What was his goal? **(b)** Was a decision necessary? Explain your answer.

2. **(a)** What information was Truman given about Japan's military strength? **(b)** What information was he given on the projected casualties should the United States invade Japan?

3. What options did Truman identify?

4. **(a)** What did Truman think would be the consequences of each of these options? **(b)** What pros and cons did he consider?

5. **(a)** What did President Truman decide? **(b)** What was his reasoning?

APPLY THE SKILL

See the Chapter Review and Assessment for another opportunity to apply this skill.

"[O]n June 18, I met with the Joint Chiefs of Staff to discuss what I hoped would be our final push against the Japanese. We still hadn't decided whether or not to use the atomic bomb, and the chiefs of staff suggested that we plan an attack on Kyushu, the Japanese island on their extreme west, around the beginning of November, and follow up with an attack on the more important island of Honshu. But the statistics that the generals gave me were as frightening as the news of the big bomb. The chiefs of staff estimated that the Japanese still had five thousand attack planes, seventeen garrisons on the island of Kyushu alone, and a total of more than two million men on all of the islands of Japan. General Marshall then estimated that, since the Japanese would unquestionably fight even more fiercely than ever on their own homeland, we would probably lose a quarter of a million men and possibly as many as a half million in taking the two islands. I could not bear this thought, and it led to the decision to use the atomic bomb.

We talked first about blockading Japan and trying to blast them into surrender with conventional weaponry; but Marshall and others made it clear that this would never work, pointing out that we'd hit Germany in this way and they hadn't surrendered until we got troops into Germany itself. Another general also pointed out that Germany's munitions industries were more or less centralized and that our constant bombings of these facilities never made them quit, and Japan's industries were much more spread apart and harder to hit. Then, when we finally talked about the atomic bomb, on July 21, coming to the awful conclusion that it would probably be the only way the Japanese might be made to surrender quickly, we talked first about hitting some isolated area, some low-population area where there would not be too many casualties but where the Japanese could see the power of the new weapon. Reluctantly, we decided against that as well, feeling that that just wouldn't be enough to convince the fanatic Japanese. And we finally selected four possible target areas, all heavy military-manufacturing areas: Hiroshima, Kokura, Nagasaki, and Niigata."

—*Where the Buck Stops: The Personal and Private Writings of Harry S Truman*, Margaret Truman (ed.)

RESOURCE DIRECTORY

Teaching Resources
Skills for Life booklet, p. 27

Technology
Social Studies Skills Tutor CD-ROM
Interactive Practice in
- Geographic Literacy
- Critical Thinking and Reading
- Visual Analysis
- Communications

READING FOCUS

- How did African Americans, Mexican Americans, and Native Americans experience the war at home?

- What difficulties did Japanese Americans face?

- In what ways did the war change conditions for working women?

MAIN IDEA

While the war brought new opportunities for women and some racial and ethnic minorities, Japanese Americans were the victims of widespread intolerance.

KEY TERMS

Congress of Racial Equality (CORE)
bracero
barrio
interned
Nisei

TAKING NOTES

As you read, complete this chart listing the experiences of women and minorities during the war.

Women	• Women fill jobs at factories and shipyards.
	•
African Americans	
Mexican Americans	
Japanese Americans	

SECTION OBJECTIVES

1. Learn how African Americans, Mexican Americans, and Native Americans experienced the war at home.

2. Find out about difficulties Japanese Americans faced.

3. See how the war changed conditions for working women.

BELLRINGER

Warm-Up Activity Write the words *injustice* and *inequality* on the chalkboard. Have students describe an incident that they associate with these words.

Activating Prior Knowledge Ask students what they know about the involvement of minorities, particularly African Americans, Native Americans, Hispanics, and Japanese Americans, in World War II.

READING STRATEGY

As students read the section, have them list and then analyze how the contributions of people of various racial, ethnic, and religious groups helped shape the national identity during World War II.

Setting the Scene To win the war, the United States needed to draw upon all its resources, including its people. For several groups in American society, this need opened up opportunities that had not existed before the war. Taking advantage of those opportunities proved difficult, however, especially for racial and ethnic minorities. Prejudice still blocked many people from advancing freely.

Early in the war, most defense industries refused to accept African Americans. A. Philip Randolph, a powerful union leader, thought that mass protest might force the government to end this discrimination. He called for a march on Washington, D.C., under the slogan "We loyal Negro American citizens demand the right to work and fight for our country." Critics, including President Roosevelt, feared that a protest march by African Americans might hurt national unity and lead to violence. Randolph replied:

66 *We seek the right to play our part in advancing the cause of national defense and national unity. But certainly there can be no national unity where one tenth of the population are denied their basic rights as American citizens. . . . One thing is certain and that is if Negroes are going to get anything out of this national defense, which will cost the nation 30 or 40 billions of dollars that we Negroes must help pay in taxes as property owners and workers and consumers, we must fight for it and fight for it with gloves off.* 99

—A. Philip Randolph, press release, January 15, 1941

African Americans

African Americans had struggled for decades to end discrimination. Yet the Jim Crow system still endured in the South, and African Americans in the North faced unofficial discrimination in employment, education, and housing.

Economic Discrimination In 1941, industries searched for millions of new workers to meet the demands of the Lend-Lease program. Still, one out of five potential African American workers remained jobless. Government

Segregation in the military mirrored conditions at home. Members of an African American field artillery unit (above) fire shells in Germany.

RESOURCE DIRECTORY

Teaching Resources
Learning Styles Lesson Plans booklet, p. 53
Guided Reading and Review booklet, p. 104

Technology
Section Reading Support Transparencies
Guided Reading Audiotapes (English/Spanish), Ch. 25
Student Edition on Audio CD, Ch. 25
Prentice Hall Presentation Pro CD-ROM, Ch. 25
Companion Web site, www.phschool.com

Focus Point out that women and Americans of different ethnic groups were recruited to support the war effort. Ask what impact the war had on these Americans.

Instruct Although the war provided opportunities for African Americans, it did not end discrimination. Have students list examples of continued discrimination and describe efforts to promote racial equality.

Ask students what new job opportunities opened for Mexican Americans and Native Americans. How did both groups face cultural challenges as their interaction with the dominant society increased? Discuss why Japanese Americans were treated so harshly during the war. What civil rights were violated by their internment?

Assess/Reteach While World War II hastened the demand for and the rate of social change on the home front, it also caused many Americans to experience new kinds of discrimination. Have students list each ethnic group that experienced discrimination in the United States during World War II.

BACKGROUND
Biography

Adam Clayton Powell, Jr. (1908–1972), charismatic minister from Harlem, used the pulpit and his oratorical skills to mobilize frustrated African Americans into positive political action. He echoed the sentiments of many fellow African Americans of his time when he said: "If the Negro is good enough to drive tanks on the battlefronts of Europe and Asia, he's good enough to work on the assembly lines of America." In 1944 Powell became one of only two African Americans in Congress and gained admiration for his "Powell Amendments"—attachments to bills that called for the cut-off of federal funds to any organization that practiced racial discrimination.

American BIOGRAPHY

**A. Philip Randolph
1889–1979**

While working his way through college in New York and later as a ship's waiter, A. Philip Randolph began work as a union organizer. Starting in 1925, Randolph gradually won recognition for the Brotherhood of Sleeping Car Porters, a railway union composed largely of African Americans. The union won higher wages and cuts in working hours and travel requirements in 1937.

After World War II, Randolph continued as a labor leader, and became a vice president of the combined AFL and CIO labor union in 1955. When the civil rights movement got under way, the march that Randolph had wanted to hold years before finally took place. In August 1963, he directed the March on Washington, D.C., and stood beside Martin Luther King, Jr., as King gave his famous "I Have a Dream" speech.

agencies set up to help the unemployed during the Depression honored employers' requests for "whites only." Randolph hoped that his March on Washington would persuade the President to end this discrimination. He told Roosevelt to expect thousands of marchers in the capital on July 4. Roosevelt tried to talk Randolph out of the march, but Randolph refused.

Finally, on June 25, 1941, the President signed Executive Order 8802, opening jobs and job training programs in defense plants to all Americans "without discrimination because of race, creed, color, or national origin." The order also created the Fair Employment Practices Committee (FEPC) to hear complaints about job discrimination in defense industries and government. The committee had no real power, and many defense employers ignored its recommendations. Still, it was a beginning. For the first time in American history, the government acted against discrimination in employment. Randolph called off his march.

As a result, African Americans shared in some of the wartime prosperity. During the 1940s, more than 2 million African Americans migrated from the South to cities in the North. They found new job opportunities but also encountered new problems. Segregation forced most African Americans to live in poor housing in overcrowded urban ghettos. A 1941 survey showed that 50 percent of all African American homes were substandard, compared to only 14 percent of white homes.

To make matters worse, white workers and homeowners often feared and resented the newcomers. Resentments escalated into violence in some cities. In June 1943, a race riot in Detroit killed 34 people and caused millions of dollars worth of damage. Later that summer, a riot also broke out in New York City.

Soldiers and Segregation African American and white soldiers risked their lives equally in the war. Yet the American military strictly segregated white and African American troops. When they came home on leave, African Americans in army uniform still faced prejudice. Alexander J. Allen, who worked for the Baltimore Urban League during the war, remarked, "It made a mockery of wartime goals to fight overseas against fascism only to come back to the same kind of discrimination and racism here in this country." In Kansas, for instance, the owner of a lunch counter refused to serve a group of African American GIs. One GI recalled:

> ❝ 'You know we don't serve coloreds here,' the man repeated. . . .We ignored him, and just stood there inside the door, staring at what we had come to see—the German prisoners of war who were having lunch at the counter. . . . We continued to stare. This was really happening. It was no jive talk. The people of Salina would serve these enemy soldiers and turn away black American GIs. ❞
>
> —Lloyd Brown

Divided Opinions In a 1942 poll, six out of ten whites believed that black Americans were satisfied with existing conditions and needed no new opportunities. Government attitudes mirrored this lack of concern. Roosevelt declined to disrupt the war effort to promote social equality. "I don't think, quite frankly," he said in late 1943, "that we can bring about the millennium [a period of human perfection] at this time."

856 Chapter 25 • *World War II: Americans at War*

RESOURCE DIRECTORY

Other Print Resources
Nystrom *Atlas of Our Country* *Later Expansion of the United States,* pp. 32–33; *People on the Move,* pp. 34–35

These attitudes forced African Americans to work for change on their own. The *Pittsburgh Courier,* an African American newspaper, launched a "Double V" campaign. The first *V* stood for victory against the Axis powers, the second for victory in winning equality at home.

Another step was the founding of the **Congress of Racial Equality (CORE)** in Chicago in 1942. CORE believed in using nonviolent techniques to end racism. In May 1943, it organized its first sit-in at a restaurant called the Jack Spratt Coffee House. Groups of CORE members, including at least one African American, filled the restaurant's counter and booths. They refused to leave until everyone was served. The sit-in technique ended Jack Spratt's discriminatory policies and quickly spread to CORE groups in other cities. These efforts paved the way for the civil rights movement that would begin in the next decade.

Mexican Americans

Like African Americans, both Mexican American citizens and Mexicans working in the United States faced discrimination during the war. Mexican Americans joined the armed forces, and the wartime economy brought new job opportunities in defense industries. By 1944, about 17,000 Mexican American citizens and Mexicans working in the United States held jobs in the Los Angeles shipyards, where none had worked three years before. Mexican Americans also found jobs in shipyards and aircraft factories in California and in Washington, Texas, and New Mexico. Some headed for other war production centers such as Detroit, Chicago, Kansas City, and New York.

The *Bracero* Program   In agriculture, a shortage of farm laborers led the United States to seek help from Mexico. In 1942, an agreement between the two nations provided for transportation, food, shelter, and medical care for thousands of **braceros,** Mexican farm laborers brought to work in the United States. Between 1942 and 1947, more than 200,000 *braceros* worked on American farms and, occasionally, in other industries. The program brought a rise in the Latino population of Los Angeles and other cities in southern California. Many lived in Spanish-speaking neighborhoods called **barrios.** Crowded conditions and discrimination often created tensions, however.

The "Double V" campaign urged victory over enemies overseas and over racial discrimination at home. This man (above) protested outside a Chicago milk company in 1941.

COMPARING PRIMARY SOURCES
Integration of the Armed Forces

Discussion about desegregating the armed forces during World War II aroused strong feelings on both sides.
Analyzing Viewpoints   What arguments does each side use to support its viewpoint?

In Favor of Integration	*Opposed to Integration*
"Though I have found no Negroes who want to see the United Nations lose this war, I have found many who, before the war ends, want to see the stuffing knocked out of white supremacy. . . . If freedom and equality are not vouchsafed [granted] the peoples of color, the war for democracy will not be won. . . We demand the abolition of segregation and discrimination in. . . [all] branches of national defense." —*A. Philip Randolph, African American labor and civil rights leader, November 1942*	"In this hour of national crisis, it is much more important that we have the full-hearted co-operation of the thirty million white southern Americans than that we satisfy the National Association for the Advancement of Colored People. . . .If they be forced to serve with Negroes, they will cease to volunteer; and when drafted, they will not serve with that enthusiasm and high morale that has always characterized the soldiers and sailors of the United States." —*W. R. Poage, Texas state representative, 1941*

Chapter 25 • Section 5   **857**

Zoot Suit Riots In the 1940s, some young Mexican Americans in Los Angeles began to wear an outfit known as the "zoot suit," featuring a long draped jacket and baggy pants with tight cuffs. "Zoot-suiters" often wore a slicked-back "ducktail" haircut. This look offended many people, especially sailors who came to Los Angeles on leave from nearby military bases. Groups of sailors roamed the streets in search of zoot-suiters, whom they beat up and humiliated for looking "un-American." One Spanish newspaper, *La Opinión*, urged Mexican American youths not to respond with more violence, but some took revenge on the sailors when they could.

Early in June 1943, the street fighting grew into full-scale riots. Local newspapers usually blamed Mexican Americans for the violence. Police often arrested the victims rather than the sailors who had begun the attacks. Army and navy officials finally intervened by restricting GIs' off-duty access to Los Angeles.

Native Americans

The war also changed the lives of Native Americans. In addition to the 25,000 Native Americans who joined in the armed forces, many others migrated to urban centers to work in defense plants. Roughly 23,000 Native Americans worked in war industries around the country.

Life in the military or in the cities was a new experience for many Native Americans who had lived only on reservations. They had to adapt quickly to white culture. At the end of the war, those who had moved away often did not return to reservation life. For some, the cultural transition brought a sense of having lost their roots.

VIEWING HISTORY To defeat the Japanese in the Pacific, United States Marines had to keep their strategies from the enemy. Navajo code talkers, using a Native American language, allowed the Allies to stay one step ahead of the Japanese. **Synthesizing Information** *How else did the armed forces benefit from diversity?*

Japanese Americans

Japanese Americans suffered official discrimination during the war. In late 1941, they were a tiny minority in the United States, numbering only 127,000 (about 0.1 percent of the entire population). Most lived on the West Coast, where racial prejudice against them had always been strong. About two thirds of Japanese Americans had been born in the United States. Although they were native-born citizens, they still often met hostility from their white neighbors.

Hostility grew into hatred and hysteria after Japan attacked Pearl Harbor. Rumors flew about sabotage on the West Coast. The press increased people's fears with inaccurate reports carrying headlines such as "Jap Boat Flashes Message Ashore" and "Japanese Here Sent Vital Data to Tokyo." Such reports left Americans feeling that Japanese spies were everywhere.

Japanese Internment As a result of these prejudices and fears, the government decided to remove all "aliens" from the West Coast. On February 19, 1942, President Roosevelt signed Executive Order 9066. It authorized the Secretary of War to establish military zones on the West Coast and remove "any or all persons" from such zones. Officials told foreign-born Italians and Germans to move away from the coast, but within a few months they canceled those orders. The government set up the War Relocation Authority to move out everyone of Japanese ancestry—about 110,000 people, both citizens and noncitizens. They would be **interned,** or confined, in camps in remote areas far from the coast.

Relocation took place so fast that Japanese Americans had little time to secure their property before they left. Many lost their businesses, farms, homes, and other valuable assets. Henry Murakami, a resident of California, remembers losing the $55,000 worth of fishing nets that had been his livelihood:

> 66 When we were sent to Fort Lincoln [in Bismarck, North Dakota] I asked the FBI men about my nets. They said, 'Don't worry. Everything is going to be taken care of.' But I never saw the nets again, nor my brand-new 1941 Plymouth, nor our furniture. It all just disappeared. I lost everything. 99
>
> —Henry Murakami

Japanese Americans had no idea where they were going when they boarded buses and trains for the camps. Monica Sone, who lived in Seattle, imagined her camp would be "out somewhere deep in a snow-bound forest, an American Siberia. I saw myself plunging chest deep in the snow, hunting for small game to keep us alive." She and her family packed their winter clothes, only to end up in Camp Minidoka, on the sun-baked prairie of central Idaho, where the normal July temperature is about 90 degrees Fahrenheit.

All the camps were located in desolate areas. Families lived in wooden barracks covered with tar paper, in rooms equipped only with cots, blankets, and a light bulb. People had to share toilet, bathing, and dining facilities. Barbed wire surrounded the camps, and armed guards patrolled the grounds. Although the government referred to these as relocation camps, one journalist pointed out that they seemed "uncomfortably close to concentration camps."

Legal Challenges A few Japanese Americans challenged the internment policy in the courts. Four cases eventually reached the Supreme Court, which ruled that the wartime relocation was constitutional. In one case, California resident Fred Toyosaburo Korematsu, a defense-plant worker, was arrested for refusing to report to a relocation center. Korematsu appealed, saying that his civil rights had been violated.

The Supreme Court, in *Korematsu* v. *United States* (1944), ruled that the relocation policy was not based on race. The majority opinion said that "the military urgency of the situation demanded that all citizens of Japanese ancestry be segregated from the West Coast temporarily." The dissenting opinion, however, labeled the policy "an obvious racial discrimination."

Early in 1945, the government allowed Japanese Americans to leave the camps. Some returned home and resumed their lives, but others found that they had lost nearly everything. As time passed, many Americans came to believe that the internment had been a great injustice. In 1988, Congress passed a law awarding each surviving Japanese American internee a tax-free payment of $20,000. More than 40 years after the event, the United States government also officially apologized.

Japanese Americans in the Military During the war, the military refused to accept Japanese Americans into the armed forces until early 1943. Despite the government's harsh treatment of Japanese civilians, thousands volunteered and eventually more than 17,000 fought in the United States armed services. Most were **Nisei**, or citizens born in the United States to Japanese immigrant parents, and some volunteered while in internment camps. Many all-Nisei units won recognition for their courage in Europe. In fact, the soldiers of the

VIEWING HISTORY Five months after the attack on Pearl Harbor, the Mochida family waits for a bus to take them from Hayward, California, to a camp. **Recognizing Bias** *Why did the United States intern Japanese Americans like the Mochidas?*

READING CHECK
What was the record of Japanese American soldiers in World War II?

ACTIVITY

Connecting with Culture

Have students provide dramatic readings from sections of the book *The Good War* by Studs Terkel, an oral history of World War II that includes many descriptions of life in the United States at the time. Focus students' attention on the role of women. (**Verbal/Linguistic**)

BACKGROUND

Connections to Today

In June 2000 President Bill Clinton presented the Medal of Honor, the nation's highest military award, to 22 Nisei veterans of World War II (15 of these were awarded posthumously). All but two of the recipients were members of the 442nd Regimental Combat Team. Many of the recipients volunteered for service right out of internment camps. At the ceremony, President Clinton said that these soldiers "did not give up on their country when too many of their countrymen gave up on them." He added, "They risked their lives above and beyond the call of duty, and in doing so, they did more than defend America. In the face of painful prejudice, they helped to define America at its best."

Working Women

Women of all ages and ethnic and economic backgrounds went to work in the wartime economy. Many of them joined the work force out of a sense of patriotism. They wanted to support their husbands, boyfriends, sons, and brothers who had marched off to war. Others realized that the war gave them an opportunity to work at jobs that would otherwise be closed to them.

New Kinds of Jobs Before the war, most women who worked for wages were single and young. They worked mainly as secretaries, sales clerks, household servants, and in other low-paying jobs traditionally held by women. Except for teaching and nursing, few women entered professional careers. Women with factory jobs usually worked in industries that produced clothing, textiles, and shoes, while men dominated the higher-paying machinery, steel, and automobile industries. Almost everywhere, women earned less than men.

The motto of the women's Auxiliary Reserve Pool (top) during World War II was "Prepared and Faithful." The worker (bottom) is assembling an aircraft.

Like World War I, World War II brought women into different parts of the work force. As men were drafted into the armed forces, many factory jobs fell vacant. These higher-paying positions lured many women away from traditional women's jobs. They moved eagerly into manufacturing, particularly in the defense industries. Many women who had never worked outside the home also took jobs in the aircraft factories, shipyards, and other industrial sites that directly supported the war effort. The number of working women rose by almost one third, from 14.6 million in 1941 to about 19.4 million in 1944. Women at one point made up about 35 percent of the total civilian labor force.

A popular song in 1942 told the story of a fictional young woman called Rosie the Riveter. Rosie was a home front hero. She worked in a defense plant, driving rivets into the metal plates of aircraft, while her boyfriend Charlie served in the marines. The government used images of Rosie in posters and recruitment films of the 1940s to attract new women workers. In time, Rosie the Riveter became the popular name for all women who worked in war-production jobs, including riveters, steelworkers, and welders.

Benefits and Problems of Employment On the whole, women enjoyed working in war-related industries. Employment outside the home made a big difference in their lives, giving them self-confidence as well as economic independence. For example, Josephine McKee, a Seattle mother of nine who worked at the Boeing Aircraft Company, used her earnings to pay off debts from the Depression. Other women found the work more interesting and challenging than what they had done before. Evelyn Knight left a job as a cook to work in a navy yard. She explained, "After all, I've got to keep body and soul together, and I'd rather earn a living this way than to cook over a hot stove." Many women took jobs for patriotic reasons. One rubber plant worker declared, "Every time I test a batch of rubber, I know it's going to help bring my three sons home quicker."

African American women had long worked in greater proportion than white women. Generally, though, only cooking, cleaning, child care, and other domestic jobs were open to them. When they applied for defense jobs, African American women often faced prejudice based on both their gender and race. Some women fought back. Through lawsuits and other forms of protest,

Sounds of an Era

Listen to "Rosie the Riveter" and other sounds from World War II.

RESOURCE DIRECTORY

Teaching Resources
Units 7/8 booklet
 • Section 5 Quiz, p. 64
 • Chapter 25 Test, pp. 65, 68
Guide to the Essentials
 • Section 5 Summary, p. 30
 • Chapter 25 Test, p. 131
Learning with Documents booklet (Visual Learning Activity) *Campaigns on the Home Front,* p. 64

Other Print Resources
Chapter Tests with ExamView® Test Bank CD-ROM, Ch. 25

Technology
Sounds of an Era Audio CD *Mary Anderson, Director of the Women's Bureau,* 1942 recording (time: 30 seconds); *"Rosie the Riveter"* (time: one minute, 30 seconds)
Exploring Primary Sources in U.S. History CD-ROM *Rosie the Riveter Poster*
ExamView® Test Bank CD-ROM, Ch. 25
Social Studies Skills Tutor CD-ROM

African American women improved their chances in the work force. From 1940 to 1944, the percentage of African American women in industrial jobs increased from 6.8 percent to 18 percent. The number working in domestic service dropped from 59.9 percent to 44.6 percent.

In spite of the benefits of working, women faced a number of problems both inside and outside the workplace. They often encountered hostile reactions from other workers, particularly in jobs previously filled only by men. They also earned much less pay than men doing the same jobs. The National War Labor Board declared in the fall of 1942 that women who performed "work of the same quality and quantity" as men should receive equal pay. Employers widely ignored this policy.

Working women had to figure out what to do with their children while they were on the job. More than half a million women with children under the age of 10 worked during the war, and day-care centers were scarce. They were forced to rely on family members and friends to care for their children. Furthermore, a typical woman's workday did not end after eight hours at the plant. Most working women also shouldered the burden of cooking, cleaning, and otherwise maintaining the household.

After the War The government drive to bring women to defense plants assumed that when the war was over, women would leave their jobs and return home. War work was just "for the duration." While many women wanted to continue working at the war's end, the pressures to return home were intense. Returning servicemen expected to get their jobs back.

As the economy returned to peacetime, twice as many women as men lost factory jobs. Some women were content to leave once the wartime sense of urgency ended. Others, however, had discovered new satisfactions in the workplace that made them want to keep on working. Some women also continued to work part time to bring in additional income.

What's Become of Rosie the Riveter?

VIEWING HISTORY Government campaigns aimed at women changed their message once the war was over. Posters such as this one tried to persuade women to give up their factory jobs and return to full-time homemaking. **Drawing Inferences** *Why were women being urged out of the work force?*

Reading Comprehension

1. (a) For African Americans to gain the right to work and fight for their country. (b) Through its nonviolent search for equality, CORE paved the way for the civil rights movement.

2. They joined the armed forces, worked in defense industries, and *braceros* worked primarily on farms, but also in other industries.

3. (a) They often encountered hostile reactions from male workers; they earned much less than men doing the same jobs; they had to arrange child care while at work; and they had to maintain their household responsibilities in addition to their work outside the home. (b) Promoted self-confidence and economic independence; it was interesting and challenging and gave them opportunities to work in fields that were not previously open to women.

Critical Thinking and Writing

4. That women's place was still in the home, and that their work for the war effort was only temporary. Men returning from the war needed their jobs back, and women were expected to relinquish those jobs and resume their roles at home.

5. Paragraphs will vary, but should discuss the feelings of many Americans after the attack on Pearl Harbor—the growing prejudices and fears that Japanese Americans would sabotage facilities on the West Coast. That the war brought long-simmering animosity toward Japanese Americans into the open should also be mentioned. Bias against Japanese in the United States was stronger than bias against European immigrants at that time.

Entries will vary, but should reflect an understanding of the key activities of American women in the war.

CAPTION ANSWERS

Viewing History To accommodate the employment needs of men returning from the war.

Section **5** Assessment

READING COMPREHENSION

1. (a) What was the goal of A. Philip Randolph's march? (b) What was the significance of **CORE**?

2. How did Mexican Americans contribute to the war effort through the *bracero* program and in other ways?

3. (a) What challenges did women confront when taking jobs outside the home? (b) What were some benefits of wartime jobs for women?

CRITICAL THINKING AND WRITING

4. **Recognizing Bias** Although women workers were recruited during the war, they were pressured to leave their jobs and return to domestic work once it ended. What underlying beliefs does this series of events suggest?

5. **Writing an Opinion** Write a short paragraph explaining why you think the government acted more harshly against Japanese Americans than against people of Italian and German ancestry.

 Take It to the NET

Activity: Writing an Encyclopedia Entry Investigate key roles women played during World War II. Take detailed notes. Then using your findings, write an encyclopedia entry for "Women's Roles During World War II." Use the links provided in the *America: Pathways to the Present* area of the following Web site for help in completing this activity. **www.phschool.com**

Chapter 25 • Section 5 861

REVIEWING KEY TERMS

Students should refer to the definitions of key terms in the chapter to write sentences that show an understanding of the World War II era.

REVIEWING MAIN IDEAS

16. The economy was boosted by the massive production of goods to supply the Allied forces.
17. They stopped producing consumer goods, converting to weapons and other wartime production. American businesses also built new factories and developed new mass production techniques.
18. In the Atlantic, North Africa, Sicily, and Italy; and by bombing German cities from the air.
19. The invasion of Western Europe begun by Allied forces at Normandy on June 6, 1944. D-Day was the largest landing by sea in history.
20. They believed that they could endure persecution, which would be easier than starting a new life in a foreign country, until Hitler lost power.
21. To annihilate all Jews and others considered "undesirable" by the Nazis. The killing was done by mobile killing squads in Russia and in six death camps in Poland.
22. (a) By selectively attacking specific enemy-held islands and bypassing others, the United States effectively cut off the bypassed islands from supplies and reinforcements, rendering them useless to Japan, and allowing Americans to move more quickly toward their ultimate goal—Japan. (b) Possible answer: Guadalcanal, Tarawa, Kwajalein, Iwo Jima, Okinawa.
23. To prevent the further loss of American troops and to end the war.
24. They launched the "Double V" campaign to win equality at home, founded CORE, and used activism to try to end discrimination.
25. Before the war women worked mainly as secretaries, sales clerks, household servants, and with the exception of teaching and nursing, seldom entered professional careers. In wartime, women worked in higher-paying positions in manufacturing and the defense industry.

creating a CHAPTER SUMMARY

Copy this chart (right) on a piece of paper and complete it by adding important events and issues that fit each heading. Some entries have been completed for you as examples.

 TEXT

For additional review and enrichment activities, see the interactive version of *America: Pathways to the Present*, available on the Web and on CD-ROM.

Time Period	Important Events
The Home Front	• The armed forces draft millions of men to fight. • The economy converts to meet the needs of war. • Food and consumer goods are rationed. •
War in Europe (1941–1945)	
War in Asia and the Pacific (1941–1945)	
The Holocaust	

★ Reviewing Key Terms

For each of the terms below, write a sentence explaining how it relates to the role of the United States in World War II.

1. Selective Training and Service Act
2. Office of War Mobilization
3. victory garden
4. Atlantic Charter
5. carpet bombing
6. D-Day
7. Holocaust
8. concentration camp
9. death camp
10. Bataan Death March
11. Battle of Midway
12. *kamikaze*
13. Manhattan Project
14. *bracero*
15. Nisei

★ Reviewing Main Ideas

16. How did World War II end the Depression? (Section 1)
17. What changes did American businesses make at the start of the war? (Section 1)
18. Where did the United States battle Germany and Italy in 1942 and 1943? (Section 2)
19. What was the D-Day operation? (Section 2)
20. Why did many Jews remain in Germany after 1933? (Section 3)
21. What was Hitler's "final solution"? (Section 3)

22. (a) What were the benefits of "island-hopping"? (b) List three islands or island groups in the order that they were captured by the United States. (Section 4)
23. Why did Truman decide to use the atomic bomb against Japan? (Section 4)
24. What strategies did African Americans use to gain equal rights during World War II? (Section 5)
25. What changes took place in the kinds of jobs women held before and during World War II? (Section 5)

★ Critical Thinking

26. **Recognizing Cause and Effect** Why were there shortages of sugar, coffee, and gasoline during World War II?
27. **Testing Conclusions** Some historians claim that Germany made a fatal mistake by declaring war on the United States in December 1941. Cite evidence to defend or disprove this claim.
28. **Identifying Assumptions** Why did military planners believe that an attack on Japan would be much more costly and dangerous than the D-Day invasion and eventual defeat of Germany?
29. **Predicting Consequences** How might the changes that the war brought for African Americans have affected the later civil rights movement?

862 Chapter 25 • *World War II: Americans at War*

CREATING A CHAPTER SUMMARY

Time Period	Important Events
The Home Front	• The armed forces draft millions of men to fight. • The economy converts to meet the needs of war. • Food and consumer goods are rationed. • The national debt rises to finance the wartime economy.
War in Europe (1941–1945)	• The Germans invade the Soviet Union. • Americans join the war in 1941. • The North African campaign is conducted. • The Allied air war intensifies. • Western Europe is invaded on D-Day. • The Allies invade Germany.
War in Asia and the Pacific (1941–1945)	• Japanese attack Pearl Harbor in 1941. • Japan attacks the Philippines and British and Dutch possessions in the Far East. • U.S. aircraft bomb Tokyo and Yokohama. • The Americans defeat the Japanese at Midway and Guadalcanal. • American victories in the Solomon, Gilbert, and Marshall islands, the Philippines, and at Iwo Jima and Okinawa • The U.S. drops atomic bombs on Hiroshima and Nagasaki. • World War II ends.
The Holocaust	• Germany builds concentrations camps. • *Kristallnacht* takes place in Germany. • Jews seek to escape Germany. • Jews, Romany, and other ethnic minorities are captured and transferred to concentration camps. • German mobile killing squads and death camps begin the mass murder of Jews. • The death camps and the concentration camps are liberated in 1945 after six million Jews had been murdered by the Nazis.

★ Skills Assessment

Analyzing Political Cartoons ▶

30. What does the woman in the cartoon symbolize?

31. What is the significance of her having her own "man-size" pay?

32. What point does the man's speech make?

33. Examine both figures. What message is conveyed by the woman's huge size and by the man's clothing?

Analyzing Primary Sources

Turn to the quotation in Section 4 about fighting in Okinawa.

34. Which phrase best describes the American campaign on Okinawa?

   A long and hard-fought

   B easy

   C completely safe

   D over in one day

35. According to the description of the fighting, you can infer that the terrain on Okinawa was

   F flat and sandy.

   G heavily wooded.

   H rocky.

   J hilly.

36. Writing Write a brief paragraph describing how you think the GIs felt during the long nights on Okinawa.

Applying the Chapter Skill: *Making Decisions*

37. Turn to Section 4 and to page 854, and read again about the decision to drop the atomic bomb. (a) What were the potential consequences of a naval blockade to starve Japan? (b) Why do you think Truman and the Interim Committee rejected this option?

ACTIVITIES

Writing to LEARN

Writing a Persuasive Essay
The horrible slaughter of six million Jews during the Holocaust is an example of genocide. Research and write an essay on a more recent case where one group tried to carry out a campaign of genocide against another ethnic group. In your essay, include the global community's reaction to the killings.

Primary Source CD-ROM

Working With Primary Sources Find additional information on World War II on the *Exploring Primary Sources in U.S. History CD-ROM* and use the selection(s) provided to complete the Chapter 25 primary source activity located in the *America: Pathways to the Present* area of the following Web site. **www.phschool.com**

Take It to the NET

Chapter Self-Test As a review activity, take the Chapter 25 Self-Test in the *America: Pathways to the Present* area at the Web site listed below. The questions are designed to test your understanding of the chapter content. **www.phschool.com**

Chapter 25 Assessment 863

CRITICAL THINKING

26. The closing of shipping lanes and enemy occupation of foreign countries limited the supply of sugar and coffee to the United States during World War II. Gasoline was rationed because it was needed for the war effort.

27. Answers will vary but should be supported with facts from the chapter.

28. The Japanese were reluctant to surrender and fought to the last defender. The D-Day landings took place in an occupied country, rather than in Germany proper. Also, British and American D-Day planners knew that the vast majority of German troops were pinned down on the Eastern Front fighting the Russians.

29. For the first time in American history, the government acted (with Executive Order 8802) against discrimination in employment. Also, the founding of CORE and the creation of the sit-in technique paved the way for the civil rights movement that would later follow.

SKILLS ASSESSMENT

30. Women who entered the labor force in support of the war effort.

31. It means that women enjoyed working in traditionally male jobs and making good wages while doing so.

32. Women were expected to give up their new jobs once men returned home from the war.

33. Women empowered by gainful employment are threatening to men. Such women might become the dominant partner in a marriage, and might force their husbands to wear aprons.

34. A

35. J

36. Paragraphs will vary, but should be descriptive and should mention that nights on Okinawa were very frightening and dangerous.

37. (a) No definite end to the war, humanitarian disaster in Japan. (b) Primarily because it would delay the ending of the war and could only be successful if the blockade were accompanied by an Allied ground invasion of Japan's home islands.

LOCKING HORNS WITH THE BULL

Focus Have students find the meaning of each of these words in a dictionary before they begin to read: *transmission, meteorologist, keen, court-martial, insubordination.* Ask them to think, as they read, about the responsibilities that Roddewig had despite his young age.

Instruct Explain that the work of radio operators was critical during World War II. After World War I, the U.S. Navy led the world in radio innovation. (Unlike the telegraph and telephone, radio was developed mainly for military use.) The interception of radio transmissions became routine during World War II. When decoded, such transmissions significantly influenced the movements of all naval forces. Discuss Roddewig's responsibilities as a radio operator during the war.

Analyzing the Document Use this additional question to generate class discussion:

Critical Thinking: Identifying Assumptions Why did Roddewig think that his naval career was sure to end in disgrace? *(Because he, a lowly third-class radioman, had told a four-star admiral to "shut up.")*

AmericanHeritage®

MY BRUSH WITH **HISTORY**™

by ROBERT RODDEWIG

Locking Horns With the Bull

In the passage below, Robert Roddewig, a sailor on the battleship USS *Missouri* in the final months of World War II, describes a nerve-wracking experience in the waters near Japan. As you read, think about the responsibilities that Roddewig had despite his young age.

United States Navy radiomen at work during World War II

Admiral William F. "Bull" Halsey

THE YEAR WAS 1945. As an eighteen-year-old eligible for the draft, I had enlisted in the Navy before graduation from high school in Davenport, Iowa. After boot camp and radio school, at Farragut, Idaho, I was assigned to the staff of Adm. William F. "Bull" Halsey aboard the *Missouri,* an *Iowa*-class battleship.

I felt honored to pull duty as a staff member with a four-star admiral. Halsey usually selected the *New Jersey,* another *Iowa*-class ship, but the *Jersey* had steamed stateside for some badly needed maintenance and repair. The *Missouri* got the call.

There were seven radio transmitting-and-receiving stations aboard the *Missouri,* and I usually spent my four hours handling routine communications among ships of the fleet. I had been onboard several weeks and had not even seen the admiral. Then I was transferred to the radio station just behind the ship's bridge. I would be copying coded messages from several military shore stations. When decoded, these transmissions would help our meteorologists map weather conditions over possible Japanese bombing targets. I quickly came to realize the importance of my work. The safety of our carrier pilots might well depend upon the accuracy and thoroughness of the radiomen on duty behind the bridge.

To obtain weather information I usually copied station NPG Honolulu or an Army station from Andrews Air Force Base on Guam. These were clear stations with little interference of any kind. But station KCT from Vladivostok, U.S.S.R., was different.

If our planes were to raid the Japanese islands of Hokkaido or Honshu, we needed the weather report from KCT. The Japanese, knowing this, constantly jammed the KCT frequency with music, loud laughter, foreign languages—anything and everything to drown out the signal. It required keen concentration to find our signal and stay on it while totally ignoring all the "trash."

864

✓ **TEST PREPARATION**

Have students use the excerpt above to answer the following question.

From what you read, which statement best describes Admiral Halsey?

A He understood the importance of the contributions of all his staff members.

B He hated war.

C His nickname came from the way he bullied his staff.

D He had little interest in the task that Roddewig was carrying out.

INTERFERENCE FROM A LOUD VOICE

One evening I was copying KCT with the usual Japanese garbage jamming my frequency. I had my eyes closed, and I was concentrating totally on that faint but distinctive signal: Dit dah dit. I automatically hit the R key on the typewriter (or mill, as the Navy called it). Dah dit dit dit, B. Dit dit dit, S.

Then a loud voice behind me asked, "Are they jamming our station?"

"Yes, sir," I replied, my concentration broken. I hit the space bar of the mill several times to indicate missed letters. I found the signal once again.

"Are you able to copy it?" The voice again. I hit the space bar several more times before finding my signal once more. "Will you be able to get enough for us?" And the space-bar routine again. But this time I blurted out, "Shut up!"

When the transmission was complete, I pulled the message from my machine. Wondering if the blank spaces would ruin our mapmaking effort, I turned in my seat—and looked up at four stars on each lapel of a brown shirt. I had just met Admiral Halsey.

Oh my . . . , I thought. I was an insignificant radioman, third class, and I had told an admiral to shut up.

At nineteen years my life would end. I would be fortunate to get a court-martial for insubordination along with a dishonorable discharge from the Navy.

"Sir, are you the one I told to 'shut up'?"

This tough-looking admiral was standing there with arms folded and legs apart in a mild inverted Y, brown naval field cap pulled to his brow, jaw jutting menacingly with lips pressed firmly together. I could see now why they called him Bull Halsey.

"Yes, lad," he blared.

"I apologize, sir. I did not know it was you. I have no excuse, sir."

The admiral broke his stance and began to pace the floor. "Lad," he bellowed, "when I come into this radio shack and speak to you while you are on that radio, you do not tell me to shut up! Do you understand?"

His voice boomed like the nine 16-inch guns attached to the ship's three main turrets.

Launched in 1944, the battleship USS Missouri *was nearly 900 feet long and had a crew of 1,900.*

"Yes, sir, I understand." I was frozen at attention and, I am certain, tears were welling in my eyes.

Then, stopping in front of me and looking me straight in the eye, he went on in a very calm and friendly voice. "If I or anyone else ever bothers you while you are on that radio, you do not tell them to shut up. What you tell them is to get the . . . out of here and that's an order. Do you understand, lad?"

I could only look at him and stammer, "Yes, sir."

We saluted. Admiral Halsey went on his way. I never met him again.

Source: *American Heritage* magazine, September 1997.

Understanding Primary Sources

1. How did Admiral Halsey respond when an underling told him to "shut up" under these circumstances?

2. What does this response imply about Halsey's character and leadership ability?

American Heritage®
MY BRUSH WITH **HISTORY**™
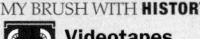 **Videotapes**

For more information about World War II in the Pacific, view "Locking Horns With the Bull."

865

Chapter 26 Planning Guide
Resource Manager

	CORE INSTRUCTION	READING/SKILLS
Chapter-Level Resources	**Teaching Resources** • Pacing Charts booklet • Block Scheduling booklet **Resource Pro® CD-ROM,** Ch. 26 **Prentice Hall Presentation Pro CD-ROM,** Ch. 26 **www.phschool.com** • eTeach	**Guided Reading Audiotapes (English/Spanish)** **Student Edition on Audio CD,** Ch. 26 **Social Studies Skills Tutor CD-ROM** **Color Transparencies,** A45, A46, A47, B14, D10
1 Origins of the Cold War 1. Learn why 1945 was a critical year in United States foreign relations. 2. Discover some of the postwar goals of the United States and the Soviet Union. 3. Find out how the iron curtain tightenend the Soviet hold over Eastern Europe. 4. See how the Truman Doctrine complemented the policy of containment.	**Teaching Resources** **Units 7/8 booklet** • Section 1 Quiz, p. 72	**Guided Reading and Review booklet,** p. 105 **Guide to the Essentials,** p. 132 **Learning with Documents booklet,** pp. 31, 68 **Skills for Life booklet,** p. 28 **Section Reading Support Transparencies**
2 The Cold War Heats Up 1. Find out how the Marshall Plan, the Berlin airlift, and NATO helped to achieve American goals in postwar Europe. 2. Realize how Communist advances affected American foreign policy. 3. See how the Cold War affected American life at home.	**Teaching Resources** **Units 7/8 booklet** • Section 2 Quiz, p. 73 **Learning Styles Lesson Plans booklet,** p. 54	**Guided Reading and Review booklet,** p. 106 **Guide to the Essentials,** p. 133 **Section Reading Support Transparencies**
3 The Korean War 1. Observe the ways Communist expansion in Asia set the stage for the Korean War. 2. Learn who fought in the Korean War and about the war's three stages. 3. Discover the different effects of the Korean War.	**Teaching Resources** **Units 7/8 booklet** • Section 3 Quiz, p. 74	**Guided Reading and Review booklet,** p. 107 **Guide to the Essentials,** p. 134 **Learning with Documents booklet,** p. 89 **Section Reading Support Transparencies**
4 The Continuing Cold War 1. Discover some characteristics of the McCarthy era. 2. See how the Cold War was waged in Southeast Asia, the Middle East, and Latin America during the 1950s. 3. Understand how the arms race developed.	**Teaching Resources** **Units 7/8 booklet** • Section 4 Quiz, p. 75 **Learning Styles Lesson Plans booklet,** p. 55	**Guided Reading and Review booklet,** p. 108 **Guide to the Essentials,** p. 135 **Section Reading Support Transparencies**

ENRICHMENT/PRE-AP

Prentice Hall United States History Video Collection™
www.phschool.com
- Section Activities, Virtual Field Trip, Chapter Activities, Current Events Online

Biography, Literature, and Comparing Primary Sources booklet, p. 31
Historical Outline Map Book, pp. 68, 77
Sounds of an Era Audio CD

Biography, Literature, and Comparing Primary Sources booklet, pp. 147–148
American History Block Scheduling Support
Sounds of an Era Audio CD

American History Block Scheduling Support
Historical Outline Map Book, p. 69
Sounds of an Era Audio CD

Biography, Literature, and Comparing Primary Sources booklet, p. 75
Historical Outline Map Book, p. 78
Sounds of an Era Audio CD
American Pathways Thematic Posters

ASSESSMENT

PRENTICE HALL
ASSESSMENT SYSTEM

Core Assessment
ExamView® Test Bank, Ch. 26
ExamView® Test Bank CD-ROM, Ch. 26

Standardized Test Preparation
Diagnose and Prescribe
Diagnostic Tests for High School Social Studies Skills

Review and Reteach
Review Book for U.S. History

Practice and Assess
Test-taking Strategies With Transparencies
Test-taking Strategies Posters
Test Prep Book for U.S. History
Alternative Assessment Handbook
Document-Based Assessment

Teaching Resources
Units 7/8 booklet
- Section Quizzes, pp. 72–75
- Chapter Tests, pp. 76, 79
www.phschool.com Ch. 26 Self-Test

AmericanHeritage RESOURCES

From the Archives of American Heritage®, p. 871
AmericanHeritage® My Brush with History™ Videotapes
www.americanheritage.com

TEXT

Don't miss the exclusive interactive version of this textbook on the Web and on CD-ROM.

Chapter 26 Planning Guide
In Your Classroom

CUSTOMIZE FOR INDIVIDUAL NEEDS

Gifted and Talented

Teacher's Edition
• Customize for Gifted and Talented, pp. 870, 885

Teaching Resources
• Biography, Literature, and Comparing Primary Sources booklet, pp. 31, 75, 147–148

ESL

Teacher's Edition
• Customize for ESL, p. 893

Teaching Resources
• Guided Reading and Review booklet, pp. 105–108
• Guide to the Essentials (English/Spanish), Chapter 26

Technology
• Student Edition on Audio CD, Chapter 26
• Guided Reading Audiotapes (English/Spanish), Chapter 26
• Section Reading Support Transparencies

Less Proficient Readers

Teacher's Edition
• Customize for Less Proficient Readers, pp. 873, 877

Teaching Resources
• Guided Reading and Review booklet, pp. 105–108
• Guide to the Essentials (English/Spanish), Chapter 26

Technology
• Student Edition on Audio CD, Chapter 26
• Guided Reading Audiotapes (English/Spanish), Chapter 26
• Section Reading Support Transparencies

Less Proficient Writers

Teacher's Edition
• Customize for Less Proficient Writers, p. 879

Teaching Resources
• Guided Reading and Review booklet, pp. 105–108
• Guide to the Essentials (English/Spanish), Chapter 26

Technology
• Student Edition on Audio CD, Chapter 26
• Guided Reading Audiotapes (English/Spanish), Chapter 26
• Section Reading Support Transparencies

TEACHER'S EDITION INDEX

CHAPTER 26 – PACING SUGGESTIONS

For 90-minute Blocks

• Teach sections 2, 3, and 4 using A45, A46, A47, B14, and D10, and the Recent Scholarship notes on pages 879 and 881 for class discussions.

Running Out of Time?

If you are running short on time to cover this chapter, consider the following options:

• Use the Prentice Hall Presentation Pro CD-ROM to create an outline for this chapter.

• Use the Section Summaries for Chapter 26, from **Guide to the Essentials (English/Spanish).**

1 Origins of the Cold War	**Connecting with Culture** Point out to students that the American presence in war-torn countries was often the local populations' first encounter with American values. Have students research Japan under occupation and record what changes the American presence engendered in the cultural values of its people. They might demonstrate what they learned in the form of a diagram showing past and present attitudes in Japan about specific issues—such as voting rights, women's issues, and forms of government. **(Visual/Spatial)**
2 The Cold War Heats Up	**Connecting with Today** Have students each make an oral presentation to compare what NATO was like at its inception and how it functions today. Students' presentations should take into account any changes in the following: membership, statement of purpose, and the perceived enemy. You may wish to have students discuss or debate what a modern NATO should be. **(Verbal/Linguistic)**
3 The Korean War	**Connecting with History and Conflict** Students should research the history of the split between North Korea and South Korea, then use art, graphics, or dance movements to illustrate the significance and effects of having one's country arbitrarily divided. You might begin by referring students to stories about reunions (first allowed in the year 2000) of family members who had been separated by this division since the Korean War. **(Visual/Spatial)**
4 The Continuing Cold War	**Connecting with Culture** Have students research the work of Walt Kelly, who, even before Joseph McCarthy was officially discredited, used his comic strip *Pogo* to satirize the senator with the character Simple J. Malarkey. Have students choose one or more of the strips that feature Malarkey to write a comparison of the flesh-and-blood senator and his cartoon caricature. **(Visual/Spatial)**

Chapter 26

The Cold War
(1945–1960)

INTRODUCING THE CHAPTER

American foreign policy after World War II remained consistent with the nation's wartime activities: force would be used to oppose authoritarian regimes that the United States considered a threat to the free world. At home the federal government would use strong, and sometimes questionable, measures to counter what it perceived to be threats to the nation's internal security.

TIME LINE ACTIVITY

To provide students with practice in using the time line, ask questions such as these:

1. Why did Churchill, Truman, and Stalin meet in Potsdam? *(To plan the postwar world)*

2. What was the stated purpose of the Eisenhower Doctrine? *(To defend Middle East countries against Communist aggression)*

3. What two events in 1949 would have been very threatening to those who opposed the worldwide expansion of communism? *(The Communist victory in China and the successful Soviet test of an atomic bomb)*

eTeach

Be sure to check out this month's online discussion with a Master Teacher. Go to **www.phschool.com**.

Chapter 26 The Cold War
(1945–1960)

SECTION 1   Origins of the Cold War
SECTION 2   The Cold War Heats Up
SECTION 3   The Korean War
SECTION 4   The Continuing Cold War

Churchill, Truman, and Stalin (left to right) at the Potsdam Conference

1945
The United States, Britain, and the Soviet Union meet at Yalta, and later at Potsdam, to plan the postwar world. The United Nations is founded.

1947
The Truman Doctrine promises support to nations resisting Communist aggression.

1948
The Marshall Plan provides U.S. aid to Europe. The Berlin airlift brings supplies to West Berlin.

1949
NATO is formed to defend Europe against the Communists.

1950
The Korean War begins. Senator Joseph McCarthy launches his anti-Communist campaign.

American Events

Presidential Terms:
F.D. Roosevelt 1933–1945   Harry S Truman 1945–1953

1944   •   **1946**   •   **1948**   •   **1950**

World Events

Soviet leader Joseph Stalin predicts the worldwide triumph of communism.
1946

Communists win control of China. The Soviets test an atomic bomb.
1949

RESOURCE DIRECTORY

Teaching Resources
Pacing Charts booklet
Block Scheduling booklet, p. 26
Units 7/8 booklet
 • Chapter Summary, p. 71

Technology
Guided Reading Audiotapes (English/Spanish), Ch. 26
Student Edition on Audio CD, Ch. 26
Prentice Hall United States History Video Collection™ Volume 20, *Post-War USA*
Prentice Hall Presentation Pro CD-ROM, Ch. 26
Resource Pro® CD-ROM
Social Studies Skills Tutor CD-ROM
Companion Web site, www.phschool.com

NATO and the Warsaw Pact, 1955

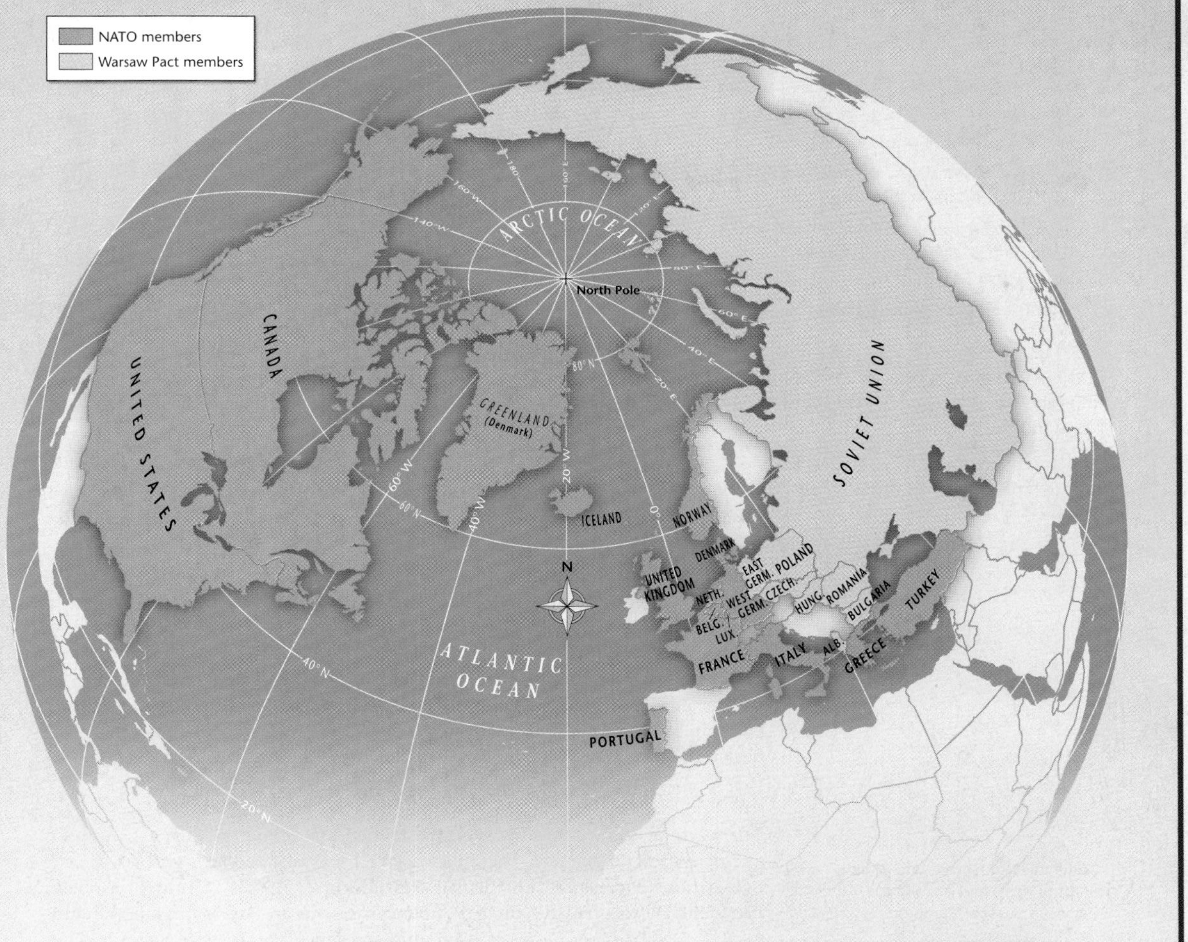

NATO members
Warsaw Pact members

Map labels: ARCTIC OCEAN, North Pole, UNITED STATES, CANADA, GREENLAND (Denmark), ICELAND, SOVIET UNION, NORWAY, DENMARK, UNITED KINGDOM, NETH., BELG., LUX., EAST GERM., WEST GERM., POLAND, CZECH., HUNG., ROMANIA, BULGARIA, TURKEY, FRANCE, ITALY, ALB., GREECE, PORTUGAL, ATLANTIC OCEAN

Activating Prior Knowledge Ask students to explain where the term "iron curtain" comes from. *(It is the imaginary line drawn between NATO and the Warsaw Pact members.)*

Previewing Why was the formation of NATO necessary? *(To create an alliance that would counterbalance the threat of communism)*

BACKGROUND
About the Pictures

| 1 | 2 |

1. Though the three men met as allies, the ties that bound them were very weak. Each was heavily focused on his own motives and interests.

2. Through the Marshall Plan, over $13 billion worth of aid was distributed to European nations over the course of four years.

1953

The Rosenbergs are executed for spying for the Soviets.

1954

Senator Joseph McCarthy is formally censured by the Senate.

1957

The President proclaims the Eisenhower Doctrine, promising to use force to defend Middle Eastern countries against Communist aggression.

Dwight D. Eisenhower 1953–1961

| 1952 | • | 1954 | • | 1956 | • | 1958 |

The Soviets test a hydrogen bomb.
1953

The Warsaw Pact is formed.
1955

The Soviet Union launches the *Sputnik* satellite.
1957

Chapter 26 **867**

BIBLIOGRAPHY

For the Teacher

Kennan, George F. *Memoirs: 1925–1950.* Knopf, 1983. (A personal view of the era by the definitive statesman of the policy of "containment.")

McCullough, David. *Truman.* Touchstone, 1993. (A comprehensive biography of the Cold War President.)

For the Student

Orwell, George. *Nineteen Eighty-Four.* New American Library Classics, 1990. (A haunting, futuristic indictment of the totalitarian state.)

Solzhenitsyn, Aleksandr I. *One Day in the Life of Ivan Denisovich.* Signet Classic, 1998. (A famous Russian dissident's moving account of life in a Soviet prison camp.)

TEXT

Don't miss the exclusive interactive version of this textbook on the Web and on CD-ROM.

SECTION OBJECTIVES

1. Learn why 1945 was a critical year in United States foreign relations.
2. Discover some of the postwar goals of the United States and the Soviet Union.
3. Find out how the iron curtain tightened the Soviet hold over Eastern Europe.
4. See how the Truman Doctrine complemented the policy of containment.

BELLRINGER

Warm-Up Activity Write the following questions on the chalkboard and ask students to write an answer: What do you think a "cold war" is? Why was this war considered "cold" and not "hot"? What made it a war?

Activating Prior Knowledge Ask students to describe the relationship between the United States and the Soviet Union at the end of World War II. What were their areas of agreement? What were some areas of conflict?

READING STRATEGY

As students read, have them make a list of events that led to the development of the Cold War. Have students list the date of each event. Then, have students arrange the dates in chronological order.

ACTIVITY
Student Portfolio

You may wish to have students add the following to their portfolios: Have student write an essay in response to this question: Had the United States and the Soviet Union been able to avoid the deep split that made them enemies and to instead remain allies, what benefits might have resulted? In the essay, have students describe U.S. responses to Soviet aggression after World War II, including the Truman Doctrine, the Marshall Plan, the North Atlantic Treaty Organization, and the Berlin airlift.

Origins of the Cold War

READING FOCUS

- Why was 1945 a critical year in United States foreign relations?
- What were the postwar goals of the United States and the Soviet Union?
- How did the iron curtain tighten the Soviet Union's hold over Eastern Europe?
- How did the Truman Doctrine complement the policy of containment?

MAIN IDEA

At the end of World War II, conflicting goals for the future of Europe led to growing hostility between the United States and the Soviet Union.

KEY TERMS

satellite nation
iron curtain
Cold War
containment
Truman Doctrine

TAKING NOTES

As you read, complete this chart to show how the Soviets tightened their hold on Eastern Europe and how the United States responded to the increasing Soviet threat. Add as many rows as you need.

Soviet Actions	U.S. Actions
Stalin refuses to allow free elections in Poland.	Truman criticizes Soviets for not allowing Polish elections.

Setting the Scene "I know you will not mind my being brutally frank when I tell you that I can personally handle Stalin," President Roosevelt told Winston Churchill during World War II. "He thinks he likes me better, and I hope he will continue to." By 1944, Roosevelt was so sure of Stalin's cooperation that he began calling the Soviet dictator "Uncle Joe."

A Roosevelt advisor later wrote that the President did not have "any real comprehension of the great gulf that separated [their] thinking." Nor did he understand just what a wily and difficult adversary Stalin would turn out to be. Churchill, however, clearly understood the situation. "Germany is finished," he declared. "The real problem is Russia. I can't get the Americans to see it."

1945—A Critical Year

The wartime cooperation between the United States and the Soviet Union was a temporary arrangement. There had been a history of bad feelings between the two nations ever since the Russian Revolution of 1917. During that revolt, President Wilson had dispatched American troops to Russia to support anti-Communist resistance. The United States had not even recognized the legal existence of the Soviet government until 1933. These actions caused considerable resentment in the Soviet Union.

As wartime allies, the Soviets disagreed bitterly with their American and British partners over battle tactics and postwar plans. The United States was angered by the nonaggression pact that Stalin had signed with Hitler (which Hitler had broken), and Stalin was angry that the Allies had not invaded Europe sooner, to take the pressure off the Russian front. As the end of the war approached, relations between the Communist Soviet Union and the two Western democracies grew increasingly tense.

Churchill, Roosevelt, and Stalin (left to right) met at Yalta to discuss postwar Europe.

868 Chapter 26 • *The Cold War*

RESOURCE DIRECTORY

Teaching Resources
Guided Reading and Review booklet, p. 105
Learning with Documents booklet (Primary Source Activity) *Uncle Joe,* p. 31

Other Print Resources
Historical Outline Map Book *Europe After World War II,* p. 68

Technology
Section Reading Support Transparencies
Guided Reading Audiotapes (English/Spanish), Ch. 26
Student Edition on Audio CD, Ch. 26
Prentice Hall Presentation Pro CD-ROM, Ch. 26
Companion Web site, www.phschool.com

Differences at Yalta In February 1945, Roosevelt met with Stalin and Churchill at Yalta to work out the future of Germany and Poland. They agreed on the division of Germany into American, British, French, and Soviet occupation zones. (Later, the American, British, and French zones were combined to create West Germany. The Soviet zone became East Germany.) Roosevelt and Churchill rejected Stalin's demand that Germany pay the Soviet Union $20 billion in war damages.

At the meeting, Roosevelt pressed Stalin to declare war on Japan. The atomic bomb had not yet been tested, and the President wanted Soviet help if an invasion of Japan became necessary. Stalin promised to enter the war against Japan soon after Germany surrendered, in exchange for Soviet control over two Japanese islands.

Poland proved the most difficult issue at Yalta. The Red Army had occupied that country and supported the Communist-dominated government. Stalin opposed the return of Poland's prewar government, then in exile in London. Historically, Poland provided an invasion route into Russia, as Hitler had just demonstrated. The Polish government, Stalin insisted, must be sympathetic to Soviet security needs. The Yalta meeting stalled until Stalin agreed on elections to let Poles choose their government, using the Communist-dominated regime as a framework. However, disputes about Poland were not over; they would continue to strain American-Soviet relations for years to come.

The United Nations One item on which the leaders at Yalta all agreed was the creation of the United Nations (UN), a new international peacekeeping organization. The League of Nations, founded after World War I, had failed largely because the United States refused to join. This time, policymakers got congressional support for the UN.

In April 1945, delegates from 50 nations met in San Francisco to adopt a charter, or statement of principles, for the UN. The charter stated that members would try to settle their differences peacefully and would promote justice and cooperation in solving international problems. In addition, they would try to stop wars from starting and "take effective collective measures" to end those that did break out.

All member nations belonged to the UN's General Assembly. Representatives of 11 countries sat on a Security Council. The United States, the Soviet Union, Great Britain, France, and China had permanent seats on the Security Council and a veto over proposed policies.

VIEWING HISTORY President Truman called the United Nations "a victory against war itself." In this photograph, Truman and representatives from other member nations look on as Secretary of State Edward Stettinius signs the UN charter in June 1945. **Drawing Conclusions** *Why do you think Congress agreed to United States membership in the UN even though it had not supported the League of Nations?*

Truman Takes Command Roosevelt never lived to see his dream of the United Nations fulfilled. On April 12, 1945, just two weeks before the UN's first meeting, the President died while vacationing at Warm Springs, Georgia. Although he was in poor health and noticeably tired, his unexpected death shocked the nation. No one was more surprised than Vice President Harry S Truman, who suddenly found himself President.

Few Vice Presidents have been less prepared to become President. Although he had spent ten years in Congress, Truman had been Vice President for only a few months. Roosevelt had never involved him in major foreign policy

Focus Having defeated a common enemy in World War II, the United States and the Soviet Union then became enemies themselves. Ask students what both sides sought to gain after World War II.

Instruct Discuss how the United States and the Soviet Union became bitter rivals after World War II. Was the Cold War the result of a mistake, or were there powerful forces at work that made the conflict inevitable? Point out the differing views of Joseph Stalin held by Roosevelt and Churchill, and discuss what effect the personalities of Western leaders might have had on Soviet policy.

Assess/Reteach Can students think of any way that the hostility between the United States and the Soviet Union could have been avoided? Are there any safeguards in place today that would prevent a cold war from erupting again?

CUSTOMIZE FOR ...

Gifted and Talented

Have students enact a meeting of the United Nations General Assembly. Ask them to choose a current or historical world event to discuss and conduct research to prepare them for the meeting. Students can assume the roles of the secretary-general and delegates from member nations. Students should debate the situation and vote on a proposed solution.

CAPTION ANSWERS

Viewing History Sample Answer: The lack of American participation in the League of Nations led to that organization's downfall, and thus to global war. American participation in the UN was thought of as a way to prevent another global war.

Connecting with History and Conflict

Your students may take several periods to complete the following activity: Their task is to reenact a meeting between President Truman and Soviet Foreign Minister Molotov. Divide the class into several groups of four to six students each. Each group should assign two students to role-play the officials and two students to act as coaches. Each team should develop a list of overall goals and specific demands for the meeting. Students should consider the desires, fears, and political systems of their respective countries.

The goal of the activity is to help students understand the political perspective of each official and his respective nation. **(Verbal/Linguistic)**

READING CHECK

Postwar plans for Poland and Germany continued to create divisions between the views of Attlee and Truman on the one hand, and Stalin on the other. Truman informed Stalin, in general terms only, of U.S. possession of an atomic bomb.

---

discussions. Truman at first seemed willing to compromise with the Soviets. But before long his attitude hardened.

The Potsdam Conference Truman's first meeting with Stalin occurred in July 1945 in the Berlin suburb of Potsdam. During the conference, Churchill was replaced by Clement Attlee, who had just won the British election. Thus, new representatives from Britain and the United States now faced off against Stalin. They continued to debate the issues that had divided them at Yalta, including the future of Germany and of Poland. Stalin renewed his demand for war payments from Germany, and Truman insisted on the promised Polish elections.

At Potsdam, Truman got word that the atom bomb had been tested in New Mexico. Hoping to intimidate Stalin, Truman told him that the United States had a new weapon of extraordinary force. Stalin, who already knew of the bomb from Soviet spies, simply nodded and said that he hoped it would be put to good use. Stalin's casual manner hid his concern over America's new strategic advantage.

READING CHECK
Summarize what happened at the Potsdam Conference.

Conflicting Postwar Goals

Shortly after Truman took office, he scolded the Soviet Foreign Minister, Vyacheslav Molotov, for the Soviet Union's failure to allow Polish elections. Molotov was offended by Truman's bluntness. "I have never been talked to like that in my life," Molotov protested. "Carry out your agreements and you won't get talked to like that," Truman snapped.

The American View Tensions over Poland illustrated the differing views of the world held by American and Soviet leaders. Americans had fought to bring democracy and economic opportunity to the conquered nations of Europe and

---

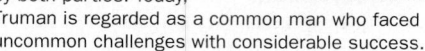

NOTABLE PRESIDENTS
Harry S Truman

"We must build a new world, a far better world— one in which the eternal dignity of man is respected."

—Radio address to the UN conference, 1945

Harry S Truman has been called the ultimate common man—but he was a common man who became President. Truman tried careers as a bank clerk, a farmer, and a haberdasher, but he was more successful as a military officer during World War I. He entered politics in Missouri in 1922. In spite of his connection to corrupt Democratic Party boss Thomas Prendergast, Truman earned a reputation for personal integrity and skillful management, both as a judge and as a United States senator.

When Vice President Truman was catapulted into the presidency by FDR's death in 1945, he expressed shock and asked reporters to pray for him. He also put a sign on his desk that said, "The buck stops here," and took responsibility for dropping the atomic bombs on Japan that ended World War II, the Truman Doctrine, the Berlin airlift, sending troops to Korea, integrating

the military, and initiating other civil rights reforms. His election to a second term surprised the pundits of his day, and the reforms of his Fair Deal were eventually supported by both parties. Today, Truman is regarded as a common man who faced uncommon challenges with considerable success.

33rd President 1945–1953

Connecting to Today
Truman's reputation for personal integrity no doubt contributed to his reelection in 1948. How did the issue of personal integrity influence the election of 2000, between George W. Bush and Al Gore?

Take It to the NET Biography To read more about Harry S Truman, visit the links provided in the *America: Pathways to the Present* area of the following Web site. **www.phschool.com**

RESOURCE DIRECTORY

Teaching Resources
Learning with Documents booklet (Visual Learning Activity) *What They Fear Most,* p. 68

Other Print Resources
Historical Outline Map Book *Europe,* p. 77

Asia. The United States hoped to see these goals achieved in the postwar world. An economically strong and politically open world would also serve American interests by providing markets for its products.

The Soviet View After losing more than 20 million people during the war and suffering widespread destruction, the Soviet Union was determined to rebuild in ways that would protect its own interests. One way was to establish **satellite nations,** countries subject to Soviet domination, on the western borders of the Soviet Union. These governments would be sympathetic to Communist goals.

The Soviet Union also looked forward to the spread of communism throughout the world. According to Communist doctrine, revolution to overthrow the capitalist system was inevitable, and the role of Communist governments was to support and speed up these revolutionary processes in other countries. Stalin thus refused to cooperate with new agencies such as the World Bank and the International Monetary Fund, intended to help build strong capitalist economies. Instead, Stalin installed or supported totalitarian Communist governments in Eastern Europe.

Soviets Tighten Their Hold

The Soviet Union quickly gained political control over nations that the Red Army had freed from the Nazis. The promised elections in Poland did not take place for nearly two years. By that time, Poland's Soviet-installed government had virtually eliminated all political opposition. The Soviets sponsored similar takeovers in other nations of Eastern Europe.

Albania and Bulgaria In Albania, Communist guerrilla forces had driven out the Germans by 1944. When elections were held the following year, all anti-Communist leaders had been silenced. Soviet troops rolled into Bulgaria in 1944, and the Communists secured their hold on the country by 1948.

Czechoslovakia The Czechs desperately tried to hold on to their democratic multiparty political system. The Communist candidate won 40 percent of the vote in free elections in 1946, but Communist repression in neighboring nations hurt the popularity of the Czech Communists. They plotted to take power, therefore, by replacing all non-Communist police officers with party members. Sure of support from the Soviet Union, they also staged rallies, strikes, and a violent uprising. By 1948, Czechoslovakia was a Soviet satellite nation.

Hungary and Romania After Communist candidates lost elections in Hungary in late 1945, Soviet troops remained there and demanded Communist control of the police. The arrest of anti-Communist leaders allowed the Communists to

---

COMPARING HISTORIANS' VIEWPOINTS
The Origins of the Cold War

Early in the Cold War, the United States and the Soviet Union blamed each other for increased tensions. Historians continue to analyze the outbreak of the Cold War.

Analyzing Viewpoints Would Gaddis agree that "Soviet policies were reasonably cautious and conservative"?

American Policy Led to the Cold War

"By overextending policy and power and refusing to accept Soviet interests, American policy-makers contributed to the Cold War. . . . There is evidence that Soviet policies were reasonably cautious and conservative, and that there was at least a basis for accommodation. But . . . [a]s American demands for democratic governments in Eastern Europe became more vigorous, as the new administration delayed in providing economic assistance to Russia and in seeking international control of atomic energy, policy-makers met with increasing Soviet suspicion and antagonism. Concluding that Soviet-American cooperation was impossible, they came to believe that the Soviet state could be halted only by force or the threat of force."

—Barton Bernstein, "American Foreign Policy and the Origins of the Cold War," 1989

Stalin's Actions Led to the Cold War

"Would there have been a Cold War without Stalin? Perhaps. Nobody in history is indispensable. But Stalin had certain characteristics that set him off from others in authority. . . . He alone pursued personal security by depriving everyone else of it: no Western leader relied on terror to the extent that he did. He alone transformed his country into an extension of himself: no Western leader could have succeeded at such a feat, and none attempted it. He alone saw war and revolution as acceptable means with which to pursue ultimate ends: no Western leader associated violence with progress to the extent that he did. Did Stalin therefore seek a Cold War? The question is a little like asking: 'Does a fish seek water?'"

—John Lewis Gaddis, We Now Know: Rethinking Cold War History, 1997

ACTIVITY
Connecting with Government

Fearing the threat of communism, the United States government established a containment policy to provide financial and military support to countries potentially subject to Communist influence. To help students understand this policy, have them describe an example of a current threat their parents fear might influence them (the students). Ask them to list three ways their parents could try to "contain" this threatening influence. Then, as a group, make a list of parental containment policies and compare them with the postwar containment policies of the United States government.
(Verbal/Linguistic)

From the Archives of
American Heritage®

Naming the New War

On April 16, 1947, Bernard Baruch gave a name to something that had been developing for several years but was still inchoate in the public mind: the Cold War. In a speech before the legislature of his native South Carolina, on the occasion of the unveiling of his portrait, the venerable financier, humanitarian, and presidential adviser said: "Let us not be deceived—we are today in the midst of a Cold War. Our enemies are to be found abroad and at home. Let us never forget this: Our unrest is the heart of their success." The phrase was not original with Baruch. In his autobiography he attributed it to his longtime friend the journalist Herbert Bayard Swope. As early as October 1945 George Orwell had used the same words to refer to a hostile peace, and the following March the London Observer employed them to describe Soviet policy toward Britain. Neither one drew much attention, so commentators made do with references to "current world events" or "Russia's actions in Europe" until Baruch crystallized the situation in a compact, convenient form. Source: Frederic D. Schwarz, "The Time Machine," American Heritage® magazine, April 1997.

872 • Chapter 26 Section 1

ACTIVITY

Connecting with Culture

Have students locate and use primary source materials from the Cold War era. They could do library research to find newspaper and magazine articles from 1946. Students might focus on how journalists reported on the speeches made by Stalin and Churchill. Or they might search for editorials and cartoons that reflect the political and emotional climate at the time. Have students present an oral report on their findings. **(Verbal/Linguistic)**

BACKGROUND

Geography in History

Despite its geographical proximity to the Soviet Union, Finland remained neutral during the Cold War. Finland is one of the world's most geographically remote countries. Approximately one-third of the country lies north of the Arctic Circle. Because of its location, Finland experiences harsh weather conditions. The mean annual temperature in Helsinki, the capital, is 5.3 degrees Celsius, or 42 degrees Fahrenheit. More than 5 million people live in Finland. Three-quarters of the country's surface area is covered with forests. The country is also known for its many lakes and islands. During the 1940s, Finland surrendered about one-tenth of its land to the Soviet Union.

VIEWING HISTORY Not only did Stalin dominate the Soviet Union and its satellites, he was also a commanding figure on the world stage. **Synthesizing Information** *Why do you think the Allies found Stalin such a difficult adversary?*

Winston Churchill coined the phrase "iron curtain."

win new elections held in 1947. The Red Army also stayed in Romania, and in 1945 the Soviets forced the Romanian king to name a Communist as prime minister. Less than two years later, the prime minister forced the king to step down.

East Germany   While the Western Allies wanted a strong, rebuilt Germany at the center of Europe, Stalin was determined that the Germans would never threaten his nation again. He established national control of all East German resources and installed a brutal totalitarian government there. In 1949, under the Communist government, the country became known as the German Democratic Republic.

Finland and Yugoslavia   In spite of the Soviet successes occurring all around them, two countries did manage to maintain a degree of independence from the Soviet Union. Finland signed a treaty of cooperation with the Soviets in 1948. The treaty required Finland to remain neutral in foreign affairs but allowed it to manage its own domestic affairs. In Yugoslavia, Communists gained control in 1945 under the leadership of Josip Broz, better known as Tito. A fiercely independent dictator, Tito refused to take orders from Stalin, who unsuccessfully tried to topple him in 1948. For the next three decades, Tito would pursue his own brand of communism relatively free from Soviet interference.

The Iron Curtain

In a February 1946 speech, Stalin predicted the ultimate triumph of communism over capitalism. Yet he knew that it would be years before the Soviets were strong enough militarily to directly confront the United States. In the meantime, Stalin called on Communists to spread their system by other means. He established Cominform, an agency intended to coordinate the activities of Communist parties around the world.

A month after Stalin's speech, Winston Churchill responded. Although recently defeated for reelection as prime minister, Churchill remained a powerful voice of opposition to the Soviet Union. Speaking in Fulton, Missouri, he condemned the division of Europe that Stalin had already accomplished:

> **KEY DOCUMENTS** ❝ *From Stettin in the Baltic to Trieste in the Adriatic, an iron curtain has descended across the Continent. Behind that line lie all the capitals of . . . Central and Eastern Europe. . . . The Communist parties, which were very small in all these Eastern States of Europe, have been raised to pre-eminence and power far beyond their numbers and are seeking everywhere to obtain totalitarian control. . . . This is certainly not the Liberated Europe we fought to build up. Nor is it one which contains the essentials of permanent peace.* ❞
> —"Iron Curtain" speech, Winston Churchill, March 5, 1946

Churchill also called on Americans to help keep Stalin from enclosing any more nations behind the **iron curtain** of Communist domination and oppression.

These two speeches of 1946—by Stalin and by Churchill—set the tone for the **Cold War,** the competition that developed between the United States and the Soviet Union for power and influence in the world. For nearly 50 years, until the collapse of the Soviet Union in 1991, the Cold War was characterized by political and economic conflict and military tensions. The rivalry stopped just short of a

CAPTION ANSWERS

Viewing History Answers will vary, but students may note that Stalin was ruthless and secretive and not above lying to allies and adversaries alike.

RESOURCE DIRECTORY

Teaching Resources
Biography, Literature, and Comparing Primary Sources booklet (Biography) *George F. Kennan,* p. 31

Technology
Sounds of an Era Audio CD *"Iron Curtain Speech," Winston Churchill* (time: 50 seconds)

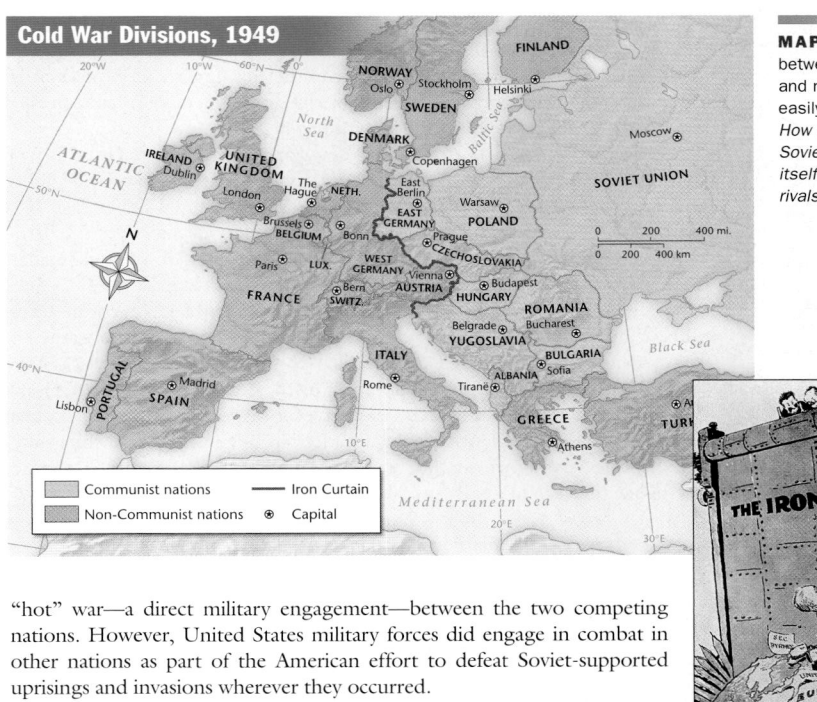

Cold War Divisions, 1949

MAP SKILLS The division between Soviet-controlled nations and non-Communist countries is easily seen on this map. **Location** *How does the map illustrate the Soviet Union's policy of protecting itself from its non-Communist rivals in Europe?*

THE IRON CURTAIN

INTERPRETING POLITICAL CARTOONS In this cartoon, United States Secretary of State James Byrnes is portrayed as a determined suitor. **Drawing Inferences** *(a) Whom is Byrnes courting? (b) How does the cartoonist rate his chances of success? (c) Explain how the cartoon conveys this opinion.*

"hot" war—a direct military engagement—between the two competing nations. However, United States military forces did engage in combat in other nations as part of the American effort to defeat Soviet-supported uprisings and invasions wherever they occurred.

Containment

In a long telegram to the State Department in early 1946, George Kennan, a top American diplomat stationed in Moscow, analyzed Soviet behavior and policy. Later, in an anonymous journal article, Kennan warned that the Soviets had "no real faith in the possibility of a permanently happy coexistence of the Socialist and capitalist worlds" and that they also believed in the inevitable triumph of communism. Therefore, Kennan concluded that the Soviet Union "cannot be easily defeated or discouraged by a single victory on the part of its opponents . . . but only by intelligent long-range policies." According to Kennan, the "United States policy toward the Soviet Union must be that of a long-term, patient but firm and vigilant containment of Russian expansive tendencies."

The American policy of **containment** emerged from Kennan's analysis. This policy recognized the possibility that Eastern Europe was already lost to communism. It called for the United States to resist Soviet attempts to form Communist governments elsewhere in the world.

Critics saw containment as too moderate an approach to Soviet-American relations. They called for action to push the Communists out of Eastern Europe, Russia, and anywhere else they had taken power. Kennan, however, argued that the Soviet system "bears within it the seeds of its own decay" and would eventually crumble. Thus, although containment remained controversial, it became the cornerstone of America's Cold War foreign policy.

The Truman Doctrine

President Truman soon had an opportunity to apply the policy of containment. Since 1945, the Soviet Union had been making threats against Turkey.

Reading Comprehension

1. Satellites were countries subject to Soviet domination. Stalin wanted satellites in order to speed up communism's spread and to protect the Soviet western border in case of another war.

2. It seemed that there was an impermeable barrier between the capitalist West and the Communist East.

3. A cold war has no direct military fighting between the main antagonists. It is instead a stealthy contest to gain influence in world affairs. A "hot" war is a direct military engagement.

4. The policy of containment set out the United States aim to stop the spread of communism, and the Truman Doctrine gave justification for American efforts to intervene against communism on behalf of oppressed nations.

Critical Thinking and Writing

5. Sample answer: The two speeches outlined the opposing positions in the Cold War.

6. Letters will vary but should be supported with facts from the section.

Take It to the NET

Students may summarize the Yalta or Potsdam conferences, which focused mainly on the future of Germany and Poland.

TIME
THE WEEKLY NEWSMAGAZINE

MAN OF THE YEAR
A popular victory and a new kind of hope.

VIEWING HISTORY President Truman was named Man of the Year by *Time* in 1949. Behind him on the *Time* cover is the Doomsday Clock, showing how close the world was to nuclear destruction. **Drawing Inferences** *What reason for honoring Truman does the* Time *cover suggest?*

Stalin wanted control of the Dardanelles, a narrow strait in Turkey that would give Soviet ports on the Black Sea access to the Mediterranean. In addition, a civil war had broken out in nearby Greece in the closing days of World War II. There, Communists fought to overthrow the government that had returned to power after the Axis invaders had withdrawn.

Still suffering from the economic devastation of the war, Great Britain announced in February 1947 that it could no longer afford to provide aid to Greece and Turkey. The British suggested that the United States take over responsibility for defending the region. Undersecretary of State Dean Acheson reported that at that moment Great Britain "handed the job of world leadership, with all its burdens and all its glory, to the United States."

State Department officials developed a plan to provide American aid to Greece and Turkey. To head off congressional opposition, Acheson warned of grave dangers if the United States failed to act. "Only two great powers remain in the world," he observed, "the United States and the Soviet Union."

In March 1947, in a speech before a joint session of Congress, Truman called on the United States to take a leadership role in the world. In a statement of principles known as the **Truman Doctrine,** he established another major policy that would guide American actions in the Cold War.

KEY DOCUMENTS

> " Nearly every nation must choose between alternative ways of life. The choice is too often not a free one. One way of life is based upon the will of the majority. . . . The second way of life is based upon the will of a minority forcibly imposed upon the majority. . . . I believe that it must be the policy of the United States to support free peoples who are resisting attempted subjugation [conquest] by armed minorities or by outside pressures. I believe that we must assist free peoples to work out their own destinies in their own way. "
>
> —Truman Doctrine, March 12, 1947

Responding to Truman's appeal, Congress approved $400 million in aid for Greece and Turkey. In addition, the United States soon established military bases in both countries. During the next four decades, the Truman Doctrine and the policy of containment would lead the United States into controversial involvements in both "hot" and "cold" conflicts around the world.

Section 1 — Assessment

READING COMPREHENSION

1. What is a **satellite nation?** Why did Stalin want these satellites?

2. Why was the term **iron curtain** a good description of the Soviet presence in Eastern Europe?

3. What is the difference between the **Cold War** and a "hot" war?

4. How do the policy of **containment** and the **Truman Doctrine** complement one another?

CRITICAL THINKING AND WRITING

5. Drawing Conclusions What effect do you think the Stalin and Churchill speeches of 1946 had on American public opinion? Explain your answer.

6. Writing a Letter to the Editor In 1947, some Americans thought that containment was a wise policy and others felt that it was too moderate. Support one of these positions in a 1947 letter to the editor.

Take It to the NET

Activity: Writing a News Article Select an important international conference of the Cold War period, and write an article summarizing what was accomplished at the conference. Use the links provided in the *America: Pathways to the Present* area of the following Web site for help in completing this activity. **www.phschool.com**

874 Chapter 26 • *The Cold War*

Recognizing Cause and Effect

History is more than a list of events; it is a study of relationships among events. Recognizing cause and effect means examining how one event or action brings about another—which, in turn, may bring about still more events. Each one becomes a link in a growing chain of events. The statements below deal with the events and attitudes leading to the Cold War.

LEARN THE SKILL

Use the following steps to recognize cause and effect:

1. **Identify the two parts of a cause-effect relationship.** A cause is an event, action, or idea that brings about an effect. As you read, look for key words that signal a cause-effect relationship. Words and phrases such as *because, due to,* and *on account of* signal causes. Words and phrases such as *so, thus, therefore,* and *as a result* signal effects.

2. **Remember that events can have more than one cause and more than one effect.** Several causes can combine to lead to one event. So, too, can a single cause have more than one effect.

3. **Understand that an event can be both a cause and an effect.** A cause can lead to an effect, which in turn can be the cause of another event—forming a chain of related events. You can illustrate the chain by making a cause-effect diagram like this one:

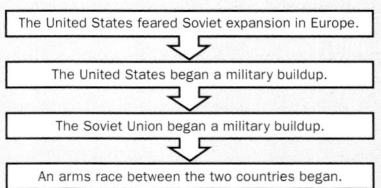

PRACTICE THE SKILL

Answer the following questions:

1. **(a)** Read statements A through C. Which statements contain both a cause and an effect? **(b)** Which is the cause and which is the effect in each statement? **(c)** Which words, if any, signal the cause-effect relationship?

2. **(a)** In Statement D, find an example of a cause that has more than one effect. **(b)** Give an example of an effect that has more than one cause in Statement D.

3. **(a)** What is the chain of related events in Statement D? Explain it in one or two sentences. **(b)** Draw a diagram showing the chain of related events.

APPLY THE SKILL

See the Chapter Review and Assessment for another opportunity to apply this skill.

A

Because President Roosevelt believed that post-war cooperation with the Soviet Union was necessary, he viewed Stalin as a partner—if not an ally—in formulating a peace.

B

Unlike Roosevelt, President Truman was persuaded by advisors that the Soviet Union would become a "world bully" after the war. As a result, he adopted a "get tough" policy whose aim was to block any possibility of Soviet expansion.

C

The Soviets, for their part, believed that the United States was intent on global domination and meant to encircle the Soviet Union with anti-Communist states.

D

Due to mounting distrust between the United States and the Soviet Union, each power came to view the postwar peace negotiations as an opportunity to test the other's global objectives. Thus, negotiating the status of Poland became the first such test. Other tests included the plans for former German satellite states and the policies for the occupation of Germany. Each power regarded its own positions in these negotiations as essentially defensive, but each viewed the other's stances as aggressive and expansionist. Together these tests and stances produced the Cold War, an armed and dangerous truce that lasted for 45 years.

Chapter 26   875

RESOURCE DIRECTORY

Teaching Resources
Skills for Life booklet, p. 28

Technology
Social Studies Skills Tutor CD-ROM
Interactive Practice in
• Geographic Literacy
• Critical Thinking and Reading
• Visual Analysis
• Communications

RECOGNIZING CAUSE AND EFFECT

Focus Students distinguish between causes and effects and recognize multiple causes and effects.

Instruct Present this quotation from Harry Truman: "There is nothing new in the world except the history you do not know." Why, then, is it important to study the causes and effects of historical events?

Ask students to cite causes of the Cold War. Discuss events in the world today that are similar to those that caused the Cold War.

Extend See the Skills for Life activity in the Resource Directory below.

ANSWERS

PRACTICE THE SKILL

1. **(a)** A and B. **(b)** A: Cause—Roosevelt believed that postwar cooperation with the Soviet Union was necessary; Effect—He viewed Stalin as a partner in formulating peace. B: Cause—Truman was persuaded that the Soviet Union would become a "world bully"; Effect—he adopted a tough policy to block Soviet expansion. **(c)** *Because* signals cause. *As a result* signals effect.

2. **(a)** Cause: mounting distrust between the U.S. and the Soviet Union. Effects: negotiations on Poland, the former German satellite states, and the occupation of Germany used as ways to test the other nation's global objectives. **(b)** Effect: the Cold War. Causes: mounting distrust; negotiations viewed as tests; defensive positions seen as aggressive stances.

3. **(a)** Mistrust of one another, led the United States and the Soviet Union to test each other's objectives in postwar peace negotiations over the future of Poland, the former German satellite states, and the occupation of Germany. These tests and the distrust they caused led to the Cold War. **(b)** Diagrams should include events described in **3 (a)**.

The Cold War Heats Up

READING FOCUS

- How did the Marshall Plan, the Berlin airlift, and NATO help to achieve American goals in postwar Europe?
- How did Communist advances affect American foreign policy?
- How did the Cold War affect American life at home?

MAIN IDEA

As the Cold War intensified, American foreign policy focused on rebuilding and unifying Western Europe. At home, Americans began to suspect Communist infiltration of their own society and government.

KEY TERMS

Marshall Plan
Berlin airlift
North Atlantic Treaty Organization (NATO)
collective security
Warsaw Pact
House Un-American Activities Committee (HUAC)
Hollywood Ten
blacklist
McCarran-Walter Act

TAKING NOTES

Copy the chart below. As you read, fill in details illustrating the effects of the Cold War on American foreign policy and on life at home.

The U.S. Responds to the Cold War		
In Europe	**Regarding Nuclear Weapons**	**At Home**

Setting the Scene The end of World War II caused a profound change in the way world leaders and ordinary citizens thought about war. The devastation caused by the atomic bombs dropped on Japan and the efforts of the Soviet Union to acquire similar weapons instilled fear in both East and West. In his last State of the Union address, President Truman declared:

> 66 [W]e have entered the atomic age and war has undergone a technological change which makes it a very different thing from what it used to be. War today between the Soviet empire and the free nations might dig the grave not only of our Stalinist opponents, but of our own society, our world as well as theirs. . . . Such a war is not a possible policy for rational men. 99
>
> —President Harry S Truman

A 1946 American atomic bomb test creates the signature mushroom cloud over the Pacific Ocean.

Anxiety about a "hot" and catastrophic nuclear war became a backdrop to the Cold War policies of both the United States and the Soviet Union.

The Marshall Plan

In addition to worrying about the new threat of nuclear war, American policymakers were determined not to repeat the mistakes of the post–World War I era. This time the United States would help restore the war-torn nations so that they might create stable democracies and achieve economic recovery. World War II had devastated Europe to a degree never seen before. About 21 million people had been made homeless. In Poland, some 20 percent of the population had died. Nearly 1 of every 5 houses in France and Belgium had been damaged or destroyed. Across

Europe, industries and transportation were in ruins. Agriculture suffered from the loss of livestock and equipment. In France alone, damage equaled three times the nation's annual income.

These conditions led to two fundamental shifts in American foreign policy that were designed to strengthen European democracies and their economies. The first was the Truman Doctrine. The other was the **Marshall Plan,** which called for the nations of Europe to draw up a program for economic recovery from the war. The United States would then support the program with financial aid.

The plan was unveiled by Secretary of State George C. Marshall in 1947. The Marshall Plan was a response to American concerns that Communist parties were growing stronger across Europe, and that the Soviet Union might intervene to support more of these Communist movements. The plan also reflected the belief that United States aid for European economic recovery would create strong democracies and open new markets for American goods.

Marshall described his plan in a speech at Harvard University in June 1947:

> **KEY DOCUMENTS** 66 It is logical that the United States should do whatever it is able to assist in the return of normal economic health in the world, without which there can be no political stability and no assured peace. Our policy is directed not against any country or doctrine but against hunger, poverty, desperation, and chaos. Its purpose should be the revival of a working economy in the world so as to permit the emergence of political and social conditions in which free institutions can exist. 99
> —Marshall Plan speech, George C. Marshall, June 5, 1947

The Soviet Union was invited to participate in the Marshall Plan, but it refused the help and pressured its satellite nations to do so too. Soviet Foreign Minister Vyacheslav Molotov called the Marshall Plan a vicious American scheme for using dollars to "buy its way" into European affairs. In fact, Soviet leaders did not want outside scrutiny of their country's economy.

In 1948, Congress approved the Marshall Plan, which was formally known as the European Recovery Program. Seventeen Western European nations joined the plan: Austria, Belgium, Denmark, France, Greece, Iceland, Ireland, Italy, Luxembourg, the Netherlands, Norway, Portugal, Sweden, Switzerland, Turkey, the United Kingdom, and West Germany. Over the next four years, the United States allocated some $13 billion in grants and loans to Western Europe. The region's economies were quickly restored, and the United States gained strong trading partners in the region.

The Berlin Airlift

One of the nations that benefited from the Marshall Plan was West Germany. By 1948, American, British, and French leaders had become convinced that Stalin was not going to allow the reunification of Germany. Therefore the

Shipments Financed by the Marshall Plan, 1948–1951	
Shipment	Total Value (in millions of dollars)
Food, feed, fertilizer	3,209.5
Fuel	1,552.4
Cotton	1,397.8
Other raw materials	2,327.6
Machinery and vehicles	1,428.1
Other	88.9
Total	**10,004.3**

SOURCE: *Statistical Abstract of the United States*

ANALYZING TABLES The photo shows a parade in Athens, Greece, following the unloading of sacks of flour delivered by the Marshall Plan. The table identifies the kinds of goods the Marshall Plan provided. **Drawing Conclusions** *What made up the largest percentage of goods delivered? Why do you think this was so?*

Divided Germany and Berlin, 1949

North Sea

NETH.

POLAND

Berlin

EAST GERMANY

LUX.

WEST GERMANY

CZECH.

FRANCE

SWITZ.

AUSTRIA

Berlin

East Berlin

West Berlin

EAST GERMANY

MAP SKILLS The map shows the location of West Berlin within East Germany. In the photo below, German children wave to an American airplane during the Berlin airlift. **Location** How did Berlin's location make it difficult to supply?

Western Allies prepared to merge their three occupation zones to create a new nation, the Federal Republic of Germany, or West Germany. The western part of Berlin, which lay in the Soviet zone, would become part of West Germany. The Soviets responded in 1949 by forming a Communist state, the German Democratic Republic, or East Germany.

Capitalist West Berlin and Communist East Berlin became visible symbols of the developing Cold War struggle between the Soviet Union and the Western powers. Hundreds of thousands of Eastern Europeans left their homes in Communist-dominated nations, fled to East Berlin, and then crossed into West Berlin. From there they booked passage to freedom in the United States, Canada, or Western Europe.

Stalin decided to close this escape route by forcing the Western powers to abandon West Berlin. He found his excuse in June 1948, when a new German currency was introduced in West Germany, including West Berlin. Stalin considered the new currency and the new nation it represented to be a threat. The city of West Berlin—located within East Germany—was a symbol of that threat. The Soviets used the dispute over the new currency as an excuse to block Allied access to West Berlin. All shipments to the city through East Germany were banned. The blockade threatened to create severe shortages of food and other supplies needed by the 2.5 million people in West Berlin.

Truman did not want to risk starting a war by using military force to open the transportation routes. Nor did he want to give up West Berlin to the Soviets. Instead, Truman decided on an airlift, moving supplies into West Berlin by plane. During the next 15 months, British and American military aircraft made

878

CAPTION ANSWERS

Map Skills It was isolated within Communist East Germany (and lies inland, not on the coast). Therefore, supplies being moved overland to West Berlin from western Europe had to pass through Soviet-controlled territory.

more than 200,000 flights to deliver food, fuel, and other supplies. At the height of the **Berlin airlift,** nearly 13,000 tons of goods arrived in West Berlin daily.

The Soviets finally gave up the blockade in May 1949, and the airlift ended the following September. By that time, the Marshall Plan had helped achieve economic stability in the capitalist nations of Western Europe, including West Germany. Berlin, however, remained a focal point of East-West conflict.

NATO

In the early postwar period, the international community looked to the United Nations to protect nations from invasion or destabilization by foreign governments, and to maintain world peace. However, the Soviet Union's frequent use of its veto power in the Security Council prevented the UN from effectively dealing with a number of postwar problems. Thus it became clear that Western Europe would have to look beyond the UN for protection from Soviet aggression. In 1946, the Canadian foreign minister, Louis St. Laurent, proposed creating an "association of democratic peace-loving states" to defend Western Europe against attack by the Soviet Union.

American officials expressed great interest in St. Laurent's idea. Truman was determined to prevent the United States from returning to pre–World War II isolationism. The Truman Doctrine and the Marshall Plan soon demonstrated his commitment to making America a leader in postwar world affairs. Yet Truman did not want the United States to be the only nation in the Western Hemisphere pledged to defend Western Europe from the Communists. For this reason, a Canadian role in any proposed organization became vital to American support.

Not all Americans agreed that such an organization was a good idea. Ohio Senator Robert Taft thought that the pact was "not a peace program; it is a war program." He continued, "We are undertaking to arm half the world against the other half. We are inevitably starting an armament race." On the other hand, Senator Tom Connally favored joining such an association:

> 66 From now on, no one will misread our motives or underestimate our determination to stand in defense of our freedom. . . . The greatest obstacle that stands in the way of complete recovery [from World War II] is the pervading and paralyzing sense of insecurity. The treaty is a powerful antidote to this poison. . . . With this protection afforded by the Atlantic Pact, Western Europe can breathe easier again. 99
> —Texas Senator Tom Connally, 1949

In April 1949, Canada and the United States joined Belgium, Britain, Denmark, France, Iceland, Italy, Luxembourg, the Netherlands, Norway, and Portugal to form the **North Atlantic Treaty Organization (NATO).** Member nations agreed that "an armed attack against one or more of them . . . shall be considered an attack against them all." This principle of mutual military assistance is called **collective security.** Having dropped its opposition to military treaties with Europe for the first time since the Monroe Doctrine, the United States now became actively involved in European affairs. In 1955,

Early Cold War Crises, 1944–1949

Year	Crisis	Significance
1944–1949	Poland, Albania, Bulgaria, Czechoslovakia, Hungary, Romania, and East Germany become Soviet satellite nations.	Communist power grows with the Soviet Union's domination of Eastern Europe.
1948–1949	The Soviet Union blockades West Berlin. Truman initiates Berlin airlift to supply the city with food, fuel, and other necessities.	Tensions increase between the United States and the Soviet Union, with Berlin a focal point of East-West conflict.
1949	The Soviet Union develops nuclear weapons technology. China falls to Communist dictator Mao Zedong.	The United States no longer has the upper hand in weapons technology. Communism spreads to the most populous nation in Asia.

INTERPRETING CHARTS
A series of crises stepped up demands on the American government to deal effectively with the spread of communism. **Making Comparisons** *(a)* How are the two entries in the last row different from those that came before? *(b)* How did they affect American public opinion?

READING CHECK
Describe how China fell to the Communists.

the Soviet Union responded to the formation of NATO by creating the **Warsaw Pact,** a military alliance with its satellite nations in Eastern Europe.

Communist Advances

In 1949, two events heightened American concerns about the Cold War. The first was President Truman's terrifying announcement that the Soviet Union had successfully tested an atomic bomb. Then, just a few weeks later, Communist forces took control of China.

The Soviet Atomic Threat "We have evidence that within recent weeks an atomic explosion occurred in the USSR," Truman told reporters in September 1949. The news jolted Americans. New York, Los Angeles, and other American cities were now in danger of suffering the horrible fate of Hiroshima and Nagasaki.

Truman's response to the Soviet atomic threat was to forge ahead with a new weapon to maintain America's nuclear superiority. In early 1950, he gave approval for the development of a hydrogen, or thermonuclear, bomb that would be many times more destructive than the atomic bomb. The first successful thermonuclear test occurred in 1952, reestablishing the United States as the world's leading nuclear power.

At about the same time, Truman organized the Federal Civil Defense Administration. The new agency flooded the nation with posters and other information about how to survive a nuclear attack. These materials included plans for building bomb shelters and instructions for holding air raid drills in schools. Privately, however, experts ridiculed these programs as almost totally ineffective. Not until the late 1950s did civil defense become a more important federal government priority.

China Falls to the Communists The Communist takeover of China also came as a shock to many Americans. However, in actuality the struggle between China's Nationalists and Communists had been going on since the 1920s. (See Section 3.) During World War II, the Communist leader Mao Zedong and the Nationalist leader Jiang Jieshi (also known as Chiang Kai-shek) grudgingly cooperated to resist the invading Japanese. But the war also enabled Mao to strengthen his forces and to launch popular political, social, and economic reforms in the regions of China that he controlled.

As World War II drew to a close, the fighting between the Communists and government forces resumed. The Truman administration at first provided economic and military assistance to Jiang. Despite this aid, by 1947 Mao's forces had occupied much of China's countryside and had begun to take control of the northern cities. When Jiang asked for more American help, Truman and his advisors concluded that Mao's takeover of China probably could not be prevented. While continuing to give some aid to Jiang, the United States decided to focus instead on saving Western Europe from Soviet domination.

In early 1949, China's capital of Peking (now Beijing) fell to the Communists. A few months later, Mao proclaimed the creation of a Communist state, the People's Republic of China. The defeated Jiang and his followers withdrew to the island of Taiwan, off the Chinese mainland. There they continued as the Republic of China, claiming to be the legitimate government of the entire

Chinese nation. With American support, the Republic of China also held on to China's seats in the UN's General Assembly and Security Council.

Many Americans viewed the "loss of China" as a stain on the record of the Truman administration. Members of Congress and others who held this view called for greater efforts to protect the rest of Asia from communism. Some Americans also began to suspect the loyalties of those involved in making military and foreign policy.

The Cold War at Home

Throughout the Great Depression, tens of thousands of Americans had joined the Communist Party, which was a legal organization. Many were desperate people who had developed serious doubts about the American capitalist system, partly because of the economic collapse of the 1930s. Others were intellectuals who were attracted to Communist ideals. After World War II, however, improved economic times, as well as the increasing distrust of Stalin, caused many people to become disillusioned with communism. Most American Communists quit the party, although some remained members, whether active or not. Now, as a new red scare began to grip America, their pasts came back to haunt them.

During the presidencies of Truman and his successor, Dwight D. Eisenhower, concern about the growth of world communism raised fears of a conspiracy to overthrow the government, particularly when a number of Communist spies were caught and put on trial. These fears launched an anti-Communist crusade that violated the civil liberties of many Americans. Anyone who had ever had Communist party ties and many who had never even been Communists were swept up in the wave of persecutions.

The Loyalty Program As the Truman administration pursued its containment policy abroad, government officials launched programs to root out any element of communism that might have infiltrated the United States. Exposure of a number of wartime spy rings in 1946 increased the anxiety of many Americans. (In recent years, new evidence of Soviet infiltration has come to light. It is known, for instance, that Soviet spies gathered information on the United States nuclear program that helped the Soviet Union advance its own atomic development.)

When Republicans made big gains in the 1946 congressional elections, Truman worried that his rivals would take political advantage of the loyalty issue. To head off this possibility, he began his own investigation, establishing a federal employee loyalty program in 1947. Under this program, all new employees hired by the federal government were to be investigated. In addition, the FBI checked its files for evidence of current government employees who might be engaged in suspicious activities. Those accused of disloyalty were brought before a Loyalty Review Board.

While civil rights were supposed to be safeguarded, in fact those accused of disloyalty to their country often had little chance to defend themselves. Rather than being considered innocent until proven guilty, they found that the accusation alone made it difficult to clear their names. The Truman program examined several million government employees, yet only a few hundred were actually removed from their jobs. Nonetheless, the loyalty program added to a climate of suspicion taking hold in the nation.

Focus on CULTURE

The Rise of the Spy Novel The Cold War produced real spies, as well as the fear of spies where none existed. But perhaps the most famous Cold War spies were the fictional espionage agents in spy novels. James Bond, for example, is a postwar British Secret Service agent whose exploits continue in countless movies. The author of the Bond novels, Ian Fleming, had served in British naval intelligence during the war. John Le Carré, who was in the British Foreign Service in West Germany, created another famous British intelligence agent, George Smiley, who battles the Soviet master spy Karla in a series of novels. In Le Carré's classic *The Spy Who Came in From the Cold*, agents and double agents struggle to cross (and get doublecrossed!) at the Berlin Wall. Len Deighton's *Funeral in Berlin* also features a dangerous passage between East and West in the divided city of Berlin, where heroes and villains, secrets and spies, often slipped through the iron curtain on their shadowy missions.

ACTIVITY
Connecting with Culture

To help students understand the "red scare," have them research communism to gain a better grasp of its ideals. Tell students to find out why thousands of Americans had been drawn to the Communist Party during the 1920s and the Depression. What did it offer that our capitalist system didn't? Engage students in a discussion about communism and its appeal at the time. **(Verbal/Linguistic)**

BACKGROUND
Recent Scholarship

In 1943 the U.S. Army built a secret laboratory at Los Alamos, New Mexico. Sitting high atop a mesa, the laboratory was far removed from the people whom it was designed to protect. Two years later the lab had created two atomic bombs, both of which were used to end World War II. In 1993, 50 years after the lab had opened, the workers at Los Alamos faced another daunting task: providing advice on how to disassemble portions of the deadly nuclear arsenal. In *The Good Servant: Making Peace with the Bomb at Los Alamos*, Janet Bailey examines how the scientists at Los Alamos coped with the dramatic change brought about by the end of the Cold War.

✓ TEST PREPARATION

Have students review the section entitled "The Cold War at Home," and then have them answer the question below.

In 1947, how did Truman demonstrate his concern about Communist infiltration?

A He put suspected Communists on trial.

(B) He required government employees to have background checks before they started their jobs.

C He campaigned in favor of officials who were committed to rooting out Communists.

D He took no action.

Connecting with Culture

In the late 1940s and early 1950s, the film and television industries were often a target of investigation by the House Un-American Activities Committee (HUAC). Have students work in small groups to list three activities by the film and television industry today that might be considered un-American, and three activities that would be considered "good" for Americans. **(Logical/Mathematical)**

BACKGROUND

Biography

Dalton Trumbo (1905–1976) was arguably the most talented member of the Hollywood Ten. As a result of his refusal to testify before the House Un-American Activities Committee, he spent 11 months in prison in 1950 and was blacklisted. After his blacklisting, he continued to write, but under pseudonyms. Trumbo won an Oscar in 1956 for the script for *The Brave One*, written under the name Robert Rich. By 1960 Trumbo was writing under his own name again, creating the scripts for the epics *Exodus* and *Spartacus*. He was also the author of the searing antiwar novel *Johnny Got His Gun*.

HUAC As the Loyalty Review Board carried out its work, Congress pursued its own loyalty programs. The **House Un-American Activities Committee,** known as **HUAC,** had been established in 1938 to investigate disloyalty on the eve of World War II. Now it began a postwar probe of Communist infiltration of government agencies and, more spectacularly, a probe of the Hollywood movie industry.

Claiming that movies had tremendous power to influence the public, in 1947 HUAC charged that numerous Hollywood figures had Communist leanings that affected their filmmaking. In fact, some Hollywood personalities were or had been members of the Communist Party. Others in the industry had openly supported various causes and movements with philosophical similarities to communism (which, of course, did not make them Communists or disloyal in any way). With government encouragement, Hollywood had also produced some movies favorable to the Soviet Union and its people. These films had been made during the war, when the United States and the Soviet Union had been allies.

Many movie stars protested HUAC's attitude and procedures. Actor Frederic March asked Americans to consider where it all could lead: "Who's next? . . . Is it you, who will have to look around nervously before you can say what's on your mind? . . . This reaches into every American city and town."

The Hollywood Ten In September and October of 1947, HUAC called a number of Hollywood writers, directors, actors, and producers to testify. They were a distinguished group, responsible for some of Hollywood's best films of the previous decade. Facing the committee, celebrities who were accused of having radical political associations had little chance to defend themselves. The committee chairman, Republican Representative J. Parnell Thomas of New Jersey, first called witnesses who were allowed to make accusations based on rumors and other flimsy evidence. Then the accused were called.

Over and over the committee asked, "Are you now or have you ever been a member of the Communist Party?" When some of those called before HUAC attempted to make statements, they were denied permission. Invoking their Constitutional rights, ten of the accused declined to answer the committee's questions. The **Hollywood Ten** were cited for contempt of Congress and served jail terms ranging from six months to a year.

The HUAC investigations had a powerful impact on filmmaking. Nervous motion picture executives denounced the Hollywood Ten for having done a disservice to their industry. The studios compiled a **blacklist,** a list circulated among employers, containing the names of persons who should not be hired. Many other entertainment figures were added to the Hollywood blacklist simply because they seemed subversive or because they opposed *the idea* of a blacklist. The list included actors, screenwriters, directors, and broadcasters.

In the past, Hollywood had been willing to make movies on controversial subjects such as racism and anti-Semitism. Now studios resisted all films dealing with social problems and concentrated on pure entertainment.

The McCarran-Walter Act While HUAC carried out its work in the House, Democrat Pat McCarran led a Senate hunt for Communists in the movie industry, labor unions, the State Department, and the UN. Senator McCarran became convinced that most disloyal Americans were immigrants from Communist-dominated parts of the world.

VIEWING HISTORY Actor Humphrey Bogart protested HUAC's actions against other actors, and then ended up having to clear his own name. *Red Channels* was an index of blacklisted actors published in 1950. **Drawing Inferences** *How do these two items demonstrate the climate of suspicion at that time?*

CAPTION ANSWERS

Viewing History The poster shows that people, especially prominent people in the arts, felt they had to prove their loyalty to the United States by denouncing communism. The blacklist shows that there were many people whose loyalty was suspect and that retaliation against them caused them to lose their livelihoods.

RESOURCE DIRECTORY

Teaching Resources

Units 7/8 booklet
- Section 2 Quiz, p. 73

Guide to the Essentials
- Section 2 Summary, p. 133

Technology

Sounds of an Era Audio CD *House Un-American Activities Committee Testimony,* 1948 recording (time: 40 seconds)

RESOURCE PRO® Primary Source Activity *The Rise of Joseph McCarthy,* found on Resource Pro, provides students with an insider's description of how the stage was set for the McCarthy hearings with a chapter from Senator Charles E. Potter's book *Days of Shame.*

At his urging, Congress passed the **McCarran-Walter Act** in 1952. This law reaffirmed the quota system for each country that had been established in 1924. It discriminated against potential immigrants from Asia and from Southern and Central Europe. President Truman vetoed McCarran's bill, calling it "one of the most un-American acts I have ever witnessed in my public career." Congress, however, passed the bill over the President's veto.

Spy Cases Inflame the Nation   Two famous spy cases helped fuel the suspicion that a conspiracy within the United States was helping foreign Communists gain military and political successes overseas. In 1948, HUAC investigated Alger Hiss, who had been a high-ranking State Department official before he left government service. Whittaker Chambers, a former Communist who had become a successful *Time* magazine editor, accused Hiss of having been a Communist in the 1930s. Hiss denied the charge and sued Chambers for slander. Chambers then declared that Hiss had been a Soviet spy.

Too much time had passed for the spying charge to be pressed. After two trials, Hiss was convicted of perjury for lying in the slander case. In 1950, he went to prison for four years. Not all Americans were convinced that he was guilty, and the case was debated for years. For most people, however, the case seemed to prove that there was a real Communist threat in the United States.

Several months after Hiss's conviction, Julius and Ethel Rosenberg, a married couple who were members of the Communist Party, were accused of passing atomic secrets to the Soviets during World War II. After a highly controversial trial, the Rosenbergs were convicted of espionage and executed in 1953. The case was another event that inflamed anti-Communist passions and focused attention on a possible internal threat to the nation's security.

Like the Hiss case, the Rosenbergs' convictions were debated for years afterward. Careful work by historians in once-classified American records and in secret Soviet records opened at the end of the Cold War indicate that both Alger Hiss and Julius Rosenberg were guilty. While Ethel Rosenberg may have had some knowledge of her husband's activities, it now appears that she was not guilty of espionage.

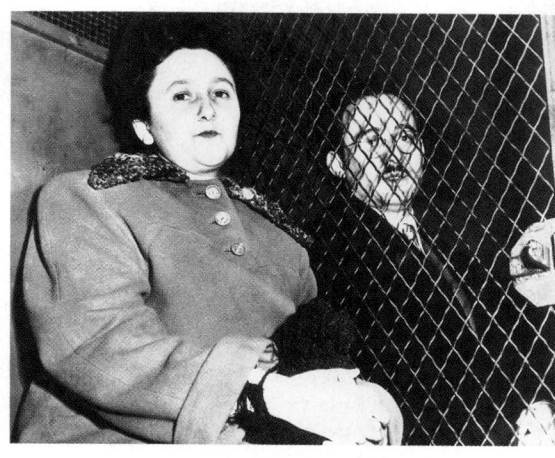

VIEWING HISTORY Ethel and Julius Rosenberg were the first U.S. civilians to be executed for espionage. **Drawing Conclusions** *How did spy cases affect Americans' perception of a Communist threat to society?*

Section 2 Assessment

READING COMPREHENSION

1. What was the **Marshall Plan,** and why was it instituted?

2. What was the importance of the **Berlin airlift?**

3. How did **NATO** demonstrate the principle of **collective security?**

4. What did the **HUAC** hearings and the **McCarran-Walter Act** show about American attitudes?

CRITICAL THINKING AND WRITING

5. Identifying Central Issues What dangers to a free society are posed by the kind of tactics used by HUAC and by the creation of blacklists?

6. Writing a Conclusion How well did the United States respond to Cold War threats? Support your conclusion with three examples.

 **Take It to the NET**

Activity: Writing an Editorial
Read more about the Marshall Plan. Then write a newspaper editorial supporting or criticizing the plan. Use the links provided in the *America: Pathways to the Present* area of the following Web site for help in completing this activity.
www.phschool.com

Reading Comprehension

1. A program for the economic recovery of postwar Europe. American policymakers hoped it would keep Communist governments from gaining more power, and strengthen European economies as well as foreign trade.

2. The Berlin Airlift allowed West Berlin to remain free from Communist domination and allowed President Truman to avoid using military force to end an early Cold War standoff.

3. Every nation that joined NATO had to agree that a military attack on any member nation would be viewed as an attack upon the alliance as a whole, and that all NATO member nations would defend the nation that had been attacked.

4. They demonstrated the paranoia and distrust on the part of Americans toward communism.

Critical Thinking and Writing

5. HUAC used mainly rumors and false accusations to gather information, leading to innocent people being accused and imprisoned; the movie industry suffered greatly, as no one wanted to make films that might appear controversial; Americans in general were fearful of speaking their minds, thinking anyone could be a government informer.

6. Answers will vary but should be supported with facts from the section.

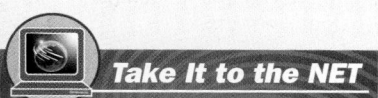 **Take It to the NET**

Sample answer: It was important to fight communism and to boost U.S. exports.

CAPTION ANSWERS

Viewing History The spy cases made Americans more convinced of the existence of a Communist conspiracy within the nation.

Section 3 — The Korean War

READING FOCUS

- How did Communist expansion in Asia set the stage for the Korean War?
- Who fought in the Korean War, and what were the three stages of the war?
- What were the effects of the Korean War?

MAIN IDEA

To repel a North Korean invasion of South Korea, American and other UN troops fought against Communist forces for three years. The result was a return to prewar Korean borders.

KEY TERMS

38th parallel
Korean War
military-industrial complex

TAKING NOTES

Copy the diagram below. As you read, fill in the causes and effects of the Korean War.

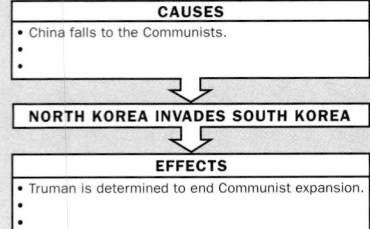

```
              CAUSES
• China falls to the Communists.
•
•
                 ⬇
   NORTH KOREA INVADES SOUTH KOREA
                 ⬇
              EFFECTS
• Truman is determined to end Communist expansion.
•
•
```

Setting the Scene The Korean War is sometimes called America's forgotten war, but the soldiers who fought in Korea never forgot it. In June of 1950, American troops struggled to push back the Communists, who had made huge advances. One American marine recalled the fierce fighting:

> 66 To push the North Koreans back across the river we had to kick them off a series of ridges. . . . It was straight uphill. No cover. There were machine guns, mortars, grenades going off. The volume of fire was terrific. They were pouring everything they had into us. Guys were cursing and yelling and dropping all around me. . . . 99
>
> —Arnold Winter

Later in 1950, both sides dug in to hold their positions. Infantryman Tom Clawson said later, "I didn't realize it at the time, but when I got to Korea the war of movement had just ended. What they called the sitting war had taken its place." He described what "the sitting war" was like:

American soldiers dig in during the Korean War.

> 66 You spent hours every day improving your position, working on the foxholes and trenches and bunkers. But I never liked to get too fancy, because sooner or later we'd be shifted to a different position. . . . Most times [after going on patrol] you'd return to the place you started from, but the day would always come when you wouldn't. You'd come back and move directly to a new position. But all the positions were always somewhere on the same ridgeline. 99
>
> —Tom Clawson

Although it lacked the glory of World War II and the turmoil of the Vietnam War, the Korean conflict had important effects on the United States.

884 Chapter 26 • *The Cold War*

Communist Expansion in Asia

While the attention of most Americans was focused on the Communist threat in Europe, events were unfolding in Asia that would cause the Cold War to flare up into a "hot" military confrontation. The roots of this armed conflict were found in the Chinese Civil War and in Japanese aggression in both China and Korea before and during World War II.

The Chinese Civil War As you recall, before World War I, foreign powers exerted considerable influence in China and even held some Chinese territory. One of these powers was Japan. Another was Germany. After Germany was defeated in World War I, the Allies gave Japan control over former German possessions, thus increasing Japanese power in China. In 1919, Chinese protesters began calling for a stronger, more independent China. Some demanded democracy and nationalism. Others, impressed by the results of the Russian Revolution of 1917, thought that communism was the way to build a strong nation.

In the mid-1920s, the Nationalist Party led by Jiang Jieshi gained strength in northern China and captured Beijing. Meanwhile, the Communists had made gains around Shanghai. In 1927, Jiang sent troops to attack the Communists and their supporters. The result was a massacre that would lead to civil war.

The Communists were led by Mao Zedong. He gained support for the Communist cause in southeastern China by redistributing land to the peasants and offering them schooling and health care. Determined to consolidate his power, Jiang continued to pursue the Communists. In 1934, Mao and his followers began retreating before Jiang's forces. After the Long March, Mao began rebuilding his forces in the north of China.

As you read in Section 2, the Nationalists and the Communists had cooperated to resist invading Japanese forces, but after World War II the Chinese Civil War became more intense. The Nationalists lost support because of their harsh treatment of the population, high taxes, and corruption. Mao's land reforms and his promise of equality, as well as his military victories, led the Communists to power in 1949. The Nationalists fled to Taiwan, where they still claimed to be the legitimate government of China.

Dividing Korea In addition to seeking territory and influence in China before World War I, Japan had also annexed the Korean peninsula. Japanese rule of Korea was harsh, and Koreans hoped that their nation would be restored after the Japanese were finally defeated in World War II. However, the war ended before careful plans for Korean independence could be worked out. In 1945, the Allies agreed on a temporary solution. Soviet soldiers accepted the surrender of Japanese troops north of the **38th parallel**, the latitude line running across Korea at approximately the midpoint of the peninsula; American forces did the same south of the parallel. While the dividing line was never intended to be permanent, Korea was divided—temporarily—into a Soviet-occupied northern zone and an American-occupied southern zone. Soon a pro-American government formed in South Korea and a Communist regime was established in North Korea. Occupying forces withdrew from both zones in 1948 and 1949.

The Long March In the fall of 1934, some 85,000 Communist troops found themselves surrounded by Nationalist forces in southeastern China. They broke through the Nationalist lines and began a 6,000-mile, year-long trek to Northwest China, near the Soviet border. Constantly under both air and ground attack by the Nationalists, they crossed 24 rivers and 18 mountain ranges. In the first three months, the Communists lost more than half their army, and only about 8,000 survivors finally reached their destination. During the Long March, Mao Zedong's leadership made him the undisputed head of the Chinese Communist Party. In spite of their often desperate circumstances, the Communist troops treated the peasants with respect, paid for goods they needed, and did not damage crops. This behavior—and the heroic ordeal of the Long March itself—inspired many young Chinese to join the Communist cause.

READING CHECK

How did Korea become a divided nation?

Chapter 26 • Section 3 **885**

LESSON PLAN

Focus The momentum of the Cold War carried the United States into troubled political waters. The Korean War was a costly, difficult conflict, fought primarily to help suppress the spread of communism in Asia.

Instruct Explain that in its efforts to fight Communist aggression, the United States engaged in its own aggressive policies, both at home and abroad. Discuss whether those actions were justified in order to oppose communism. Encourage students to support their opinions with facts and reasoning.

Assess/Reteach Looking back from today, what do students think about efforts such as the Korean War? Does the end—the suppression of communism—justify the means—a costly, bloody war?

BACKGROUND
Geography in History

A few months before North Korea launched the Korean War, Secretary of State Dean Acheson gave a speech on American postwar military commitments at Washington, D.C.'s National Press Club. In the case of Soviet attack, Acheson said, the United States would only defend countries within its Pacific defense perimeter. Because China had recently fallen to the Communists, Acheson drew this line off the coast of Asia. The islands of Japan, the Philippines, and Okinawa fell under American protection, but South Korea did not. Although American historians have found no proof, many suspect that Acheson's speech encouraged Communist leaders to invade South Korea.

READING CHECK

Japan had occupied Korea prior to World War I. After Japan's defeat in World War II, Korea was temporarily occupied by Russian troops in the north and American troops in the south. The departure of all occupation troops in the late 1940s left a Communist government north of the 38th parallel and a Western-oriented non-Communist government in the south.

CUSTOMIZE FOR ...

Gifted and Talented

Have students research the route of the Long March. Then have them make a map detailing the route, noting dates and events along an accompanying time line.

The Korean Conflict

Koreans on both sides of the dividing line wanted to unify their nation. In June 1950, the **Korean War** broke out when North Korean troops streamed across the 38th parallel, determined to reunite Korea by force. The invasion took the United States by surprise. It also alarmed Americans, who were sure—wrongly, it turned out—that the action had been orchestrated by the Soviet Union. The fall of China to the Communists had been a shock to the United States; now it seemed as though communism was on the advance again. Faced with what he viewed as a clear case of aggression, President Truman was determined to respond. He recalled earlier instances "when the strong had attacked the weak." Each time that the democracies failed to act, Truman remembered, it had encouraged the aggressors. "If this [invasion of South Korea] was allowed to go unchallenged, it would mean a third world war, just as similar incidents brought on the second world war," Truman said.

The UN Police Action After the defeat of the Chinese Nationalists in 1949, the United States had blocked Communist China's admission to the United Nations. The Soviet delegation had walked out in protest, and thus could not exercise its veto when President Truman brought the issue of North Korean aggression to the UN. The United States gained unanimous approval for resolutions that branded North Korea an aggressor and that called on member states to help defend South Korea and restore peace.

President Truman wasted no time. He commanded the American Seventh Fleet to protect Taiwan, and he ordered American air and naval support for the South Koreans. Later he sent ground troops as well. Although Truman did not go to Congress for a declaration of war as required by the Constitution, both Democrats and Republicans praised him for his strong action. Members of the House stood and cheered when they heard of it.

The UN set up the United Nations Command and asked the United States to choose the commander of the UN forces. Eventually, 16 member nations contributed troops or arms, but Americans made up roughly 80 percent of the troops that served in the UN police action in Korea.

MAP SKILLS These maps show the back-and-forth nature of the fighting in the Korean War.
Movement *Examine the maps and the movements of UN troops. Why do you think China entered the war when it did?*

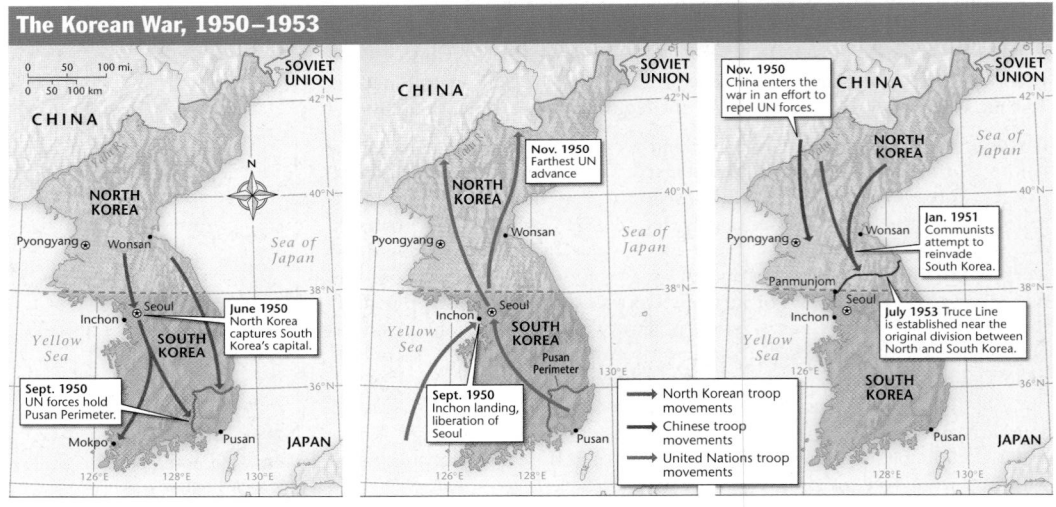

The Korean War, 1950–1953

0 50 100 mi.
0 50 100 km

SOVIET UNION
CHINA
NORTH KOREA
Pyongyang · Wonsan
Sea of Japan
Inchon · Seoul
SOUTH KOREA
Yellow Sea
Mokpo · Pusan
JAPAN

June 1950 North Korea captures South Korea's capital.
Sept. 1950 UN forces hold Pusan Perimeter.

SOVIET UNION
CHINA
NORTH KOREA
Pyongyang · Wonsan
Sea of Japan
Inchon · Seoul
SOUTH KOREA
Pusan Perimeter
Yellow Sea
Pusan
JAPAN

Nov. 1950 Farthest UN advance
Sept. 1950 Inchon landing, liberation of Seoul

Nov. 1950 China enters the war in an effort to repel UN forces.

SOVIET UNION
CHINA
NORTH KOREA
Pyongyang · Wonsan
Sea of Japan
Panmunjom
Inchon · Seoul
SOUTH KOREA
Yellow Sea
Pusan
JAPAN

Jan. 1951 Communists attempt to reinvade South Korea.
July 1953 Truce Line is established near the original division between North and South Korea.

→ North Korean troop movements
→ Chinese troop movements
→ United Nations troop movements

Waging the War A hero of two world wars and a strong anti-Communist, General Douglas MacArthur was Truman's choice to lead the UN forces in Korea. MacArthur was based in Japan, where he headed the postwar occupation. He was responsible for establishing Western democracy there and for creating Japan's new democratic constitution. He had been less successful in implementing democracy in South Korea, where he also commanded American occupation forces. There, MacArthur had supported Korean president Syngman Rhee, despite Rhee's brutal elimination of his opponents.

Despite a difficult personality, MacArthur was an excellent military strategist, and he developed a bold plan to drive the invaders from South Korea. With Soviet tanks and air power, the North Koreans had swept through South Korea in just weeks. Only a small part of the country, near the port city of Pusan, remained unconquered.

MacArthur suspected that the North Koreans' rapid advance had left their supply lines stretched thin. He decided to strike at this weakness. After first sending forces to defend Pusan, in September 1950 he landed troops at Inchon in northwestern South Korea, and attacked enemy supply lines from behind.

MacArthur's strategy worked. Caught between UN forces in the north and in the south, and with their supplies cut off, the invaders fled back across the 38th parallel. UN troops pursued them northward. American and South Korean leaders began to boast of reuniting Korea under South Korean control. Such talk alarmed the Chinese Communists, who had been in power less than a year and who did not want a pro-Western nation next door.

As UN troops approached North Korea's border with China, the Chinese warned them not to advance any farther. MacArthur ignored the warning. On November 24, 1950, the general announced his "Home by Christmas" offensive, designed to drive the enemy across the North Korean border at the Yalu River into China and end the war. However, Chinese troops poured across the Yalu to take the offensive. The Chinese and the North Koreans pushed the UN forces back into South Korea. A stalemate developed.

MacArthur favored breaking the stalemate by opening a second front. He wanted the Chinese opposition forces of Jiang Jieshi on the island of Taiwan to return to the mainland to attack the Chinese Communists. Truman opposed this strategy, fearing it could lead to a widespread war in Asia. Unable to sway Truman, MacArthur sent a letter to House Minority Leader Joseph Martin in March 1951, attacking the President's policies. Martin made the letter public. On April 11, Truman fired MacArthur for insubordination.

MacArthur returned home to a hero's welcome. In an address to a joint session of Congress on April 19, he made an emotional farewell:

> 66 Since I took the oath at West Point, the hopes and dreams [of youth] have all vanished. But I still remember the refrain of one of the most popular barracks ballads of that day, which proclaimed most proudly that old soldiers never die, they just fade away. And like the old soldier of that ballad, I now close my military career and just fade away, an old soldier who tried to do his duty as God gave him the light to see that duty. Good-bye. 99
>
> —General Douglas MacArthur, 1951

BIOGRAPHY

Douglas MacArthur 1880–1964

The son of an army officer, Douglas MacArthur graduated from West Point at the top of his class. Cited for bravery in World War I, he became a general by the time he was 38, and Army Chief of Staff in 1930.

During World War II, MacArthur commanded American forces in Asia. He organized the defense of the Philippines and the island-hopping campaign against the Japanese in the Pacific. After commanding American Occupation forces in both Japan and South Korea, MacArthur led the UN forces in the Korean War. His dispute with President Truman led the President to fire him for insubordination.

Although a hero to those he commanded and to much of the American public, MacArthur was disliked by many political leaders, who viewed him as overly ambitious. MacArthur, in turn, had little respect for either Roosevelt or Truman; he thought both were soft on communism. His attitude made MacArthur an anti-Communist hero. Yet his characteristic contempt for anyone with authority over him led him to take actions that undermined his otherwise brilliant career.

Sounds of an Era

Listen to MacArthur's speech to Congress and other sounds from the Cold War period.

ACTIVITY
Connecting with History and Conflict

Have students work in small groups to analyze the conflict between President Truman and General MacArthur. Have them list two or three beliefs held by each. What goals did they have in common? Why did they come into conflict? Whose views do students favor more? (Verbal/Linguistic)

BACKGROUND
MacArthur's Dismissal

Although President Truman had no qualms about his decision to dismiss General MacArthur, his decision prompted a huge outcry from the public, as well as from members of the Republican Party. In the first two days after the firing, the White House received 250,000 telegrams protesting the decision. During a private meeting of Republican members of Congress, one senator proposed that Congress impeach Truman. After MacArthur delivered his famous farewell speech, members of Congress rushed to touch the fired general. Meanwhile, back at the White House, President Truman and his aides watched in disbelief. Despite the outpouring of support for MacArthur, Truman knew he had made the right decision.

✓ TEST PREPARATION

Have students review the text in the section "Waging the War," and then ask them to complete the sentence below.

The main reason Truman fired MacArthur was that—

A they did not agree on the best way to fight the Korean War.

B Truman did not like MacArthur.

Ⓒ MacArthur was insubordinate to his commander in chief.

D MacArthur did not like Truman.

Reading Comprehension

1. It is the latitude line that divides Korea in half. After World War II, Communists controlled the northern half, while the south was supported by the United States.

2. (a) It began when North Korean troops crossed the 38th parallel in an attempt to reunite North and South Korea by force. (b) The North Koreans were aided by the Chinese; the South Koreans had the aid of the United States, along with some other UN member countries.

3. For insubordination after MacArthur wrote a letter to a U.S. Congressman blasting Truman's policies.

4. Answers can include: the frustration caused in the United States, ambiguities of the war, a huge increase in defense spending, and the beginning of the military-industrial complex.

Critical Thinking and Writing

5. Success: the Communist forces were successfully evicted from South Korea. Failure: North Korea remained under Communist control, and many American lives were sacrificed for little apparent gain.

6. Time lines will vary but should be supported with facts from the section.

Collages should accurately reflect the nature of the Korean War.

U.S. Defense Spending, 1941–1961

Dollars (in billions) plotted against *Year* (1941 to 1961), with values ranging from 0 to 90.

SOURCE: *Historical Statistics of the United States, Colonial Times to 1970*

INTERPRETING GRAPHS
The competition for world leadership led to an arms race between the United States and the Soviet Union. **Recognizing Cause and Effect** What was the cause of the sharpest rise in American defense spending in the post–World War II era? Why do you think spending did not drop off abruptly again, the way it did after World War II?

Once tempers cooled, MacArthur did, in fact, fade from view, and Truman was able to keep the war limited. However, the struggle dragged on for over two more years, into the presidency of Dwight D. Eisenhower. When peace talks stalled, Eisenhower's threat to use atomic weapons got the talks going again. Finally, a truce was signed in 1953, leaving Korea divided at almost exactly the same place as before the war, near the 38th parallel.

The Effects of the Korean War

The Korean War caused enormous frustration in the United States. Americans wondered why roughly 34,000 of their soldiers had been killed and 103,000 wounded for such limited results. They questioned whether their government was serious about stopping communism. On the other hand, Communist forces had been pushed back beyond the 38th parallel. What's more, this containment had occurred without nuclear war. It seemed that Americans would have to get used to more limited wars and more limited victories.

Americans would have to get used to other changes as well. One change was in the military itself. Although President Truman had ordered the integration of the armed forces in 1948, the Korean War was the first war in which white Americans and African Americans served in the same units.

The Korean War also led to a huge increase in military spending. The military had taken less than a third of the federal budget in 1950; a decade later, military spending made up about half of federal expenditures. At the same time, the United States came to accept the demands of permanent mobilization. Over a million American soldiers were stationed around the world. At home, the military establishment became more powerful as it developed links to the corporate and scientific communities. These ties created a powerful **military-industrial complex** that employed 3.5 million Americans by 1960.

The Korean War also helped to shape future U.S. policy in Asia. Hoping that Japan could help to maintain the balance of power in the Pacific, the United States signed a peace treaty with that nation in September 1951. In addition, the Korean War further poisoned relations with Communist China, leading to a diplomatic standoff that would last more than 20 years.

Section 3 Assessment

READING COMPREHENSION

1. What was the importance of the **38th parallel**?

2. (a) How did the **Korean War** begin? (b) Who fought on each side?

3. Why did President Truman fire General MacArthur?

4. Name two effects of the war.

CRITICAL THINKING AND WRITING

5. **Drawing Conclusions** Considering containment and the Truman Doctrine, do you think the Korean War was a success or a failure? Why?

6. **Creating a Time Line** Make a time line of the important events of the Korean War.

 **Take It to the NET**

Activity: Creating a Collage
Make a collage about one aspect of the Korean War. Download or copy maps, photos, newspaper headlines, and quotes from soldiers. Use the links provided in the *America: Pathways to the Present* area of the following Web site for help in completing this activity.
www.phschool.com

888 Chapter 26 • The Cold War

CAPTION ANSWERS

Interpreting Graphs The Korean War. Americans felt that the enemy had not been totally defeated in the sense that the Nazis and the Japanese had been defeated in World War II. Americans felt that the Communist threat continued, and that the U.S. must remain ready for another war.

RESOURCE DIRECTORY

Teaching Resources
Units 7/8 booklet
• Section 3 Quiz, p. 74
Guide to the Essentials
• Section 3 Summary, p. 134
Learning with Documents booklet (Key Documents) *General Douglas MacArthur, Address to Congress,* p. 89

Technology
RESOURCE PRO **Visual Learning Activity**
Civilian Control of the Military, found on Resource Pro, uses a cartoon to present one view of Truman's controversial firing of General MacArthur during the Korean War.

READING FOCUS

- What were the characteristics of the McCarthy era?
- How was the Cold War waged in Southeast Asia, the Middle East, and Latin America during the 1950s?
- How did the arms race develop?

MAIN IDEA

During the 1950s, the Cold War spread around the world. At home, McCarthyism caused fear and distrust.

KEY TERMS

McCarthyism
arms race
deterrence
brinkmanship
ICBM
Sputnik
U-2 incident

TAKING NOTES

As you read, prepare an outline of the first section. Follow the model below.

The McCarthy Era

I. McCarthy's Rise to Power
   A. McCarthy needed a popular issue for the 1952 election.
      1. _____
      2. _____
   B. _____

Setting the Scene Communist aggression in Korea was already heightening Americans' fear of communism when Wisconsin Senator Joseph McCarthy held up a piece of paper and declared, "I have here in my hand a list of 205 [people] who were known to the secretary of state as being members of the Communist Party and who, nevertheless, are still working and shaping policy at the State Department." In the Cold War atmosphere of 1950, McCarthy's charges quickly gained so much support that only the most courageous spoke out against him. One such person was Edward R. Murrow, who concluded his TV show on McCarthy by saying that "[t]his is no time for men who oppose Senator McCarthy to keep silent." He explained:

❝ [T]he line between investigating and persecuting is a very fine one and the junior Senator from Wisconsin has stepped over it repeatedly. . . . We must not confuse dissent with disloyalty. We must remember always that accusation is not proof. . . . We can deny our heritage and our history, but we cannot escape responsibility for the result. . . . ❞

—Edward R. Murrow

The McCarthy Era

In 1950, it seemed to many Americans that the events in Asia supported McCarthy's sensational charges. However, the famous list of 205 known State Department Communists turned out to be the names of people who were still employed by the government, even though they had been accused of disloyalty under Truman's loyalty program. When pressed for details, the senator reduced the number from 205 to 57. Nevertheless, McCarthy's accusations sparked an anti-Communist hysteria and national search for subversives that caused suspicion and fear across the nation.

McCarthy's Rise to Power Joseph McCarthy's first term in the Senate had been undistinguished and he needed an issue to arouse public support. He found that issue in the menace of communism. Piling baseless accusations on top of unprovable charges, McCarthy took his crusade to the floor of the Senate and engaged in the smear tactics that came to be called **McCarthyism.** Not only was McCarthy reelected, but he became

ANALYZING POLITICAL CARTOONS The caption of this cartoon cites Senator McCarthy's famous claim to have proof of subversion "in his hand." **Drawing Conclusions** (a) According to the cartoon, what does McCarthy really have, instead of proof? (b) What is the message of the cartoon?

"I Have Here In My Hand—"

Chapter 26 • Section 4   **889**

SECTION OBJECTIVES

1. Discover some characteristics of the McCarthy era.
2. See how the Cold War was waged in Southeast Asia, the Middle East, and Latin America during the 1950s.
3. Understand how the arms race developed.

BELLRINGER

Warm-Up Activity Discuss with students the concepts of loyalty and patriotism. Do they think that it is possible to be a "true American" while supporting an ideology or belief such as communism?

Activating Prior Knowledge Ask students if they are familiar with the concept of "blacklisting" as practiced during the McCarthy era.

READING STRATEGY

As students read, have them list some of the ways in which the United States government sought to suppress and contain the spread of communism in the 1950s.

CAPTION ANSWERS

Analyzing Political Cartoons (a) Bogus evidence that "stinks." (b) McCarthy is a liar and not to be believed.

Focus The Cold War era created many tense and difficult political situations for the United States. The new availability of the atomic bomb complicated the situation enormously. Discuss whether there was any precedent in United States history for the ideological warfare of the 1950s.

Instruct Discuss the ways in which America's military strategy changed from the end of World War II to the 1950s, as the enemy shifted from Hitler's German army to forces in Stalin's Russia. Discuss with students the ways in which the beginnings of the nuclear weapons race complicated matters still further.

Assess/Reteach Ask students to state ways in which the tension between the United States and the Soviet Union spilled over into U.S. domestic affairs, such as the Senate hearings conducted by Joseph McCarthy.

ACTIVITY

Connecting with Culture

Have students research the media's coverage of the McCarthy era. Have them look for news stories and editorials from the early 1950s. Tell students to photocopy several articles and bring them to class. Engage students in a discussion of the way in which the news media handled the story. What did the news coverage reveal about a newspaper or magazine and its particular slant? Why was this story difficult to cover? What were the complexities of the story? **(Verbal/Linguistic)**

VIEWING HISTORY Army counsel Joseph Welch listens as Senator Joseph McCarthy discusses Communist infiltration into the army. **Analyzing Visual Information** (a) What emotion do you think Welch is experiencing? Why do you think he feels that way? (b) What was the result of the Army-McCarthy hearings?

Focus on
CITIZENSHIP

Declaration of Conscience
Margaret Chase Smith's declaration to the Senate made it clear that Senator McCarthy, far from protecting American values as he claimed, was really putting American principles in danger:

"Those of us who shout the loudest about Americanism in making character assassinations are all too frequently those who, by our own words and acts, ignore some of the basic principles of Americanism—

The right to criticize;
The right to hold unpopular beliefs;
The right to protest;
The right of independent thought.

The exercise of these rights should not cost one single American citizen his right to a livelihood nor should he be in danger of losing his reputation nor should he be in danger . . . merely because he happens to know someone who holds unpopular beliefs."

---

chairman of an investigations subcommittee. Merely being accused by McCarthy caused people to lose their jobs and reputations.

McCarthy soon took on larger targets. He attacked former Secretary of State George Marshall, a national hero and a man of unquestioned integrity. McCarthy claimed that Marshall was involved in "a conspiracy so immense and an infamy so black as to dwarf any previous venture in the history of man," because of his inability to stop the Communist triumph in China.

Even other senators came to fear McCarthy. They worried that opposition to his tactics would brand them as Communist sympathizers. But there were a few exceptions. As early as June 1950, Republican Senator Margaret Chase Smith of Maine presented a Declaration of Conscience to the Senate. She denounced McCarthy for having "debased" the Senate "to the level of a forum of hate and character assassination sheltered by the shield of congressional immunity. . . ."

McCarthy's Fall In early 1954, when one of his assistants was drafted, McCarthy charged that even the army was full of Communists. Army officials, in turn, charged McCarthy with seeking special treatment for his aide. As charges and countercharges flew back and forth, the senator's subcommittee voted to investigate the claims.

The Army-McCarthy hearings began in late April 1954. Democrats asked that the hearings be televised, hoping that the public would see McCarthy for what he was. Ever eager for publicity, the senator agreed. For weeks, Americans were riveted to their television sets. Most were horrified by McCarthy's bullying tactics and baseless allegations.

By the time the hearings ended in mid-June, the senator had lost even his strongest supporters. The Senate formally condemned him for his reckless actions. Unrepentant, McCarthy charged his accusers with being tools of the Communists, but he no longer had credibility. Although McCarthy remained in the Senate, his power was gone.

Eventually this second red scare, much like the one that followed World War I, subsided. But the nation was damaged by the era's suppression of free speech and open, honest debate.

The Cold War in the 1950s

American Cold War policy entered a new phase when Republican Dwight D. Eisenhower became President in 1953. Eisenhower's Secretary

---

Viewing History (a) Answers may vary from despair to disgust. Welch knows that McCarthy is both a liar and a dangerous person. (b) They brought about McCarthy's downfall because they showed him as a bully whose accusations were baseless and unfair.

RESOURCE DIRECTORY

Other Print Resources
Historical Outline Map Book *The Middle East,* p. 78

Technology
Color Transparencies *Political Cartoons,* B14
Sounds of an Era Audio CD *Army-McCarthy Hearings,* 1954 recording (time: 40 seconds)
RESOURCE PRO® Literature Activity *The Hunt for Witches and Communists,* found on Resource Pro, focuses on *The Crucible,* Arthur Miller's play about the Salem witch trials of 1692, which he wrote in response to the McCarthy hearings.

of State, John Foster Dulles, was a harsh anti-Communist who considered winning the Cold War to be a moral crusade. Dulles believed that Truman's containment policy was too cautious. Instead, he called for a policy to roll back communism where it had already taken hold.

As a military leader, Eisenhower recognized the risks of confronting the Soviets. He acted as a brake on Dulles's more extreme views. In Eisenhower's judgment, the United States could not intervene in the affairs of the Soviet Union's Eastern European satellites. So when East Germans revolted in 1953, and Poles and Hungarians in 1956, the United States kept its distance as Soviet troops crushed the uprisings. Eisenhower felt that any other response risked war with the Soviet Union. He wanted to avoid that at all costs. Thus containment remained an important part of American foreign policy in the 1950s.

Southeast Asia   In July 1953, Eisenhower fulfilled a campaign promise to bring the Korean War to an end. The sudden death of Stalin in March and the rapid rise of more moderate Soviet leaders contributed to the resolution of this conflict. Meanwhile, the United States began providing substantial military aid to support France, which was trying to retain control of its colony, Vietnam. When an international conference divided Vietnam, like Korea, into a Communist north and an anti-Communist south, the United States provided aid to South Vietnam, but—for the time being—resisted greater involvement. (See Chapter 31.)

The Middle East   The Cold War was also played out in the historic tensions of the Middle East. In the 1930s and 1940s, the Holocaust had forced many Jews to seek safety in Palestine, the Biblical home of the Jewish people, now controlled by the British. Calls for a Jewish state intensified. In 1947, the British turned the question over to the UN, which created two states in the area, one Jewish and one Arab. In May 1948, the Jews in Palestine proclaimed the new nation of Israel. Israel's Arab neighbors, who also viewed Palestine as their ancient homeland, attacked the Jewish state in 1948. Israel repelled the Arab assault, and the UN mediated new borders. As Arab hostility to the idea of a Jewish state continued, the United States supported Israel, while the Soviet Union generally backed Arab interests.

Meanwhile, the United States also worked to prevent oil-rich Arab nations from falling under the influence of the Soviet Union. In 1952, a nationalist leader gained control in Iran. Fearful that he would be neutral—or worse, sympathetic to Communism—the United States backed groups that overthrew the nationalist government and restored the pro-American Shah of Iran to power.

Next came the Suez crisis of 1956. When Egypt's ruler, Gamal Abdel Nasser, sought Soviet support, the United States and Great Britain cut off their aid to Egypt. Nasser responded by seizing the British-owned Suez Canal. This canal was a vital waterway that passed through Egypt and allowed Middle East oil to reach Europe via the Mediterranean. In late 1956, British and French forces attacked Egypt to regain control of the canal, despite prior assurances they would not rely on force. Reacting to Soviet threats of "dangerous consequences," a furious Eisenhower persuaded his NATO allies to withdraw from Egypt, which retained control of the canal.

To combat further Soviet influence in the Middle East, the President announced the Eisenhower Doctrine in

MAP SKILLS Following the 1948 war, Israel controlled most of what had been Palestine, but Egypt barred Israel and all nations trading with Israel from using the Suez Canal. **Location** *(a) Why do you think the Suez Canal was important to Israel and to its trading partners? (b) What do you think Egypt's purpose was in denying access to Israel?*

Israel After the 1948 War

- Palestine prior to the creation of Israel
- Israeli-held territory, 1948
- Arab-held territory, 1948
- Suez Canal

LEBANON
SYRIA
Sea of Galilee
West Bank
Jordan R.
N
-32°N
Mediterranean Sea
Gaza Strip
Jerusalem
Dead Sea
ISRAEL
JORDAN
Suez Canal
EGYPT
0   25   50 mi.
0   25   50 km
SINAI PENINSULA
Gulf of Aqaba
Gulf of Suez

Fast Forward to Today

From *Sputnik* to Space Station

When the Soviets launched *Sputnik* in 1957, they also launched the space race. NASA was established in 1958 to oversee an American space program that could compete with the Soviets. However, in 1961, the Soviets scored another win: the first man in space. Competition continued through the 1960s, but the Americans raised the stakes by landing on the moon in 1969.

The two nations also continued to launch orbiting satellites. In 1973, the American *Skylab* became the first successful space station, but the Soviet *Mir*, launched in 1986, was the most successful, remaining in orbit until 2001. *Mir*, which means "peace" in Russian, also changed the nature of space exploration: it became a cooperative venture. Crews from many nations visited *Mir*, including the United States beginning in 1995. And in 1998, when the United States and Russia began assembling the International Space Station, to which many nations will eventually contribute, a new era of cooperation had truly begun.

? Which kind of "space race" do you think would lead to more progress: competition or cooperation? Explain your reasoning.

January 1957. This policy stated that the United States would use force "to safeguard the independence of any country or group of countries in the Middle East requesting aid against [Communist-inspired] aggression." Eisenhower used his doctrine in 1958 to justify landing troops in Lebanon to put down a revolt against its pro-American government.

Latin America The United States also acted to support pro-American governments and to suppress Communist influences in Latin America, especially where American companies had large investments. Since the mid-1920s, the United States had exercised control over the economies of some ten Latin American nations. In Central America, United States troops had invaded Nicaragua and Honduras to prop up leaders who supported American interests. In 1947, the United States signed the Rio Pact, a regional defense alliance with 18 other nations in the Western Hemisphere. The next year, the United States led the way in forming the Organization of American States (OAS) to increase cooperation among the nations of the hemisphere.

In 1954, the CIA helped overthrow the government of Guatemala on the grounds that its leaders were sympathetic to radical causes. The CIA takeover restored the property of an American corporation, the United Fruit Company, which had been seized by the Guatemalan government. Such actions fueled a Soviet perception that America was escalating the Cold War.

The Arms Race

Throughout the 1950s, the United States and the Soviet Union waged an increasingly intense struggle for world leadership. Nowhere was this competition more dangerous than in the **arms race,** the struggle to gain weapons superiority.

The Growth of Nuclear Arsenals In August 1953, less than a year after the United States exploded its first thermonuclear device, the Soviet Union successfully tested its own hydrogen bomb. As part of the policy of deterrence begun by President Truman, Eisenhower stepped up American weapons development. **Deterrence** is the policy of making the military power of the United States and its allies so strong that no enemy would dare attack for fear of retaliation. Between 1954 and 1958, the United States conducted 19 hydrogen bomb tests in the Pacific. One of these explosions, in March 1954, was over 750 times more powerful than the atomic bomb that had been dropped on Nagasaki in World War II. Japanese fishermen some 90 miles from the blast suffered severe radiation burns. The test was a chilling warning that nuclear war could threaten the entire world with radioactive contamination.

Brinkmanship American policymakers used the fear of nuclear war to achieve their Cold War objectives. In 1956, Secretary of State John Dulles made it clear that the United States was prepared to risk war to protect its national interests. Dulles explained the policy of **brinkmanship** this way: "The ability to get to the verge without getting into the war is the necessary art. If you cannot master it, you inevitably get into war. If you try to run away from it, if you are scared to go to the brink, you are lost." Many Americans agreed with the reaction of Illinois senator Adlai Stevenson: "I am shocked that the Secretary of State is willing to play Russian roulette with the life of our nation." Still, the Eisenhower administration relied on the policy of brinkmanship.

Cold War in the Skies To carry hydrogen bombs to their targets, American military planners relied mainly on airplanes. Unable to match this strength, the Soviets focused on long-range rockets known as intercontinental ballistic missiles, or **ICBMs.** Americans also worked to develop ICBMs. However, in part because of its dependence on conventional air power, the United States lagged behind the Soviet Union in missile development.

The size of this technology gap became apparent in 1957, when the Soviets used one of their rockets to launch ***Sputnik,*** the first artificial satellite to orbit Earth. The realization that the rocket used to launch *Sputnik* could carry a hydrogen bomb to American shores added to American shock and fear.

In May 1960, the Soviet military again demonstrated its arms capabilities by using a guided missile to shoot down an American U-2 spy plane over Soviet territory. Because these spy planes flew more than 15 miles high, American officials had assumed that they were invulnerable to attack. The **U-2 incident** shattered this confidence, and made Americans willing to expend considerable resources to catch up to—and surpass—the Soviet Union.

One legacy of the Cold War was the creation of what Eisenhower called a "permanent armaments industry of vast proportions." As he left office, he warned that the existence of this military-industrial complex, employing millions of Americans and having a financial stake in war-making, could become a threat to peace:

KEY DOCUMENTS
   ❝ *Our arms must be mighty, ready for instant action. . . . We recognize the imperative need for this development. Yet we must not fail to comprehend its grave implications. . . . [In] government, we must guard against the acquisition of unwarranted [unnecessary] influence, whether sought or unsought, by the military-industrial complex. The potential for the disastrous rise of misplaced power exists and will persist.* ❞
—Dwight D. Eisenhower, Farewell Address, 1961

This 1959 *Newsweek* illustration shows Soviet leader Khruschev (left) and President Eisenhower (right) using missiles to maintain a balance of power.

Reading Comprehension

1. Using baseless rumors and unfounded accusations to destroy someone's reputation and career, a tactic perfected by Senator Joseph McCarthy.

2. The struggle between the United States and the Soviet Union to achieve weapons superiority, particularly in the area of nuclear weapons.

3. It allowed Secretary of State John Foster Dulles to use brinkmanship as a strategy. Dulles's actions put the United States in diplomatic positions where threatening to apply military force presented the danger of starting a war.

4. Americans were shocked and frightened that the Soviet Union was technologically ahead of the United States in the arms race and in space travel. This caused U.S. public opinion and policy to favor a large military buildup to surpass the Soviet Union.

Critical Thinking and Writing

5. Sample answer: President Eisenhower could have intervened when Soviet troops crushed an East German uprising in 1953. This would have caused the United States and the Soviet Union to get into a "hot" war with one another.

6. Answers will vary but should be supported with facts from the section.

Take It to the NET

Sample response: Americans were afraid of the dangers posed by Soviet missile development.

Section 4 Assessment

READING COMPREHENSION

1. What was **McCarthyism?**

2. What was the **arms race?**

3. How did the policy of **deterrence** influence U.S. actions during the Cold War?

4. How did *Sputnik* and the **U-2 incident** affect American public opinion and policy?

CRITICAL THINKING AND WRITING

5. **Identifying Alternatives** When could President Eisenhower have chosen an alternative to containment and the arms race? How might history have been different if he had done so?

6. **Writing a Letter** Write a letter urging a senator of 1952 to oppose Senator McCarthy.

Take It to the NET

Activity: Writing a Diary Entry
Learn more about *Sputnik* and how Americans reacted to it. Write a diary entry as if you were an American of 1957 who has just heard about the launch of the Soviet satellite. Use the links provided in the *America: Pathways to the Present* area of the following Web site for help in completing this activity.
www.phschool.com

Chapter 26 • Section 4   893

CUSTOMIZE FOR ...

ESL

Ask students to write the column headings "Problem" and "Solution" on a piece of paper. In the first column have them list the problems the United States faced in Asia, the Middle East, and Latin America, and in the second column have them write the solutions the United States attempted to carry out.

REVIEWING KEY TERMS

Students should refer to the definitions of key terms in the chapter to write sentences that show an understanding of the Cold War.

REVIEWING MAIN IDEAS

11. Yalta: Germany be divided into zones, Poland hold elections, and the United Nations be formed. Potsdam: Truman and Stalin tried to resolve outstanding issues from Yalta, and Truman alluded to the atomic bomb to intimidate Stalin.

12. U.S.: to bring economic prosperity back to Europe and install democratic governments in recovering nations. Soviet Union: to dominate the satellite nations on its western border and spread communism.

13. Through containment, the U.S. hoped to prevent additional domination by the Soviet Union or internal Communist governments. The Truman Doctrine made it U.S. policy to intervene on behalf of nations in danger of having elected governments overthrown by Communist forces.

14. It helped European nations rebuild economies and gave the U.S. new allies and trading partners.

15. (a) A U.S.–Soviet war could result in the destruction of both nations. (b) By authorizing work on the hydrogen bomb.

16. To provide collective security against Soviet aggression.

17. The Soviet test of an atomic bomb and the establishment of a Communist government in mainland China.

18. (a) The administration began to investigate the background of prospective federal government employees. Congress investigated communism in Hollywood and passed the McCarran-Walter Act, restricting immigration from Communist-leaning regions. (b) They created paranoia and mistrust.

19. China's Nationalist government lost popular support due to corruption and harsh policies, while the Communists won the people's loyalty with reforms.

20. One: Communist invasion of South Korea. Two: United Nations' forces drive North Koreans across the 38th parallel. Three: Stalemate as the

creating a CHAPTER SUMMARY

Copy the diagram (right) onto a piece of paper. Complete it by filling in the the most important causes and effects of the Cold War.

 TEXT

For additional review and enrichment activities, see the interactive version of *America: Pathways to the Present*, available on the Web and on CD-ROM.

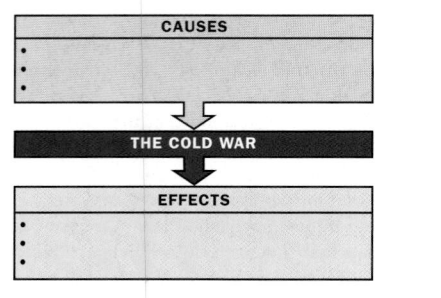

CAUSES
• • •

THE COLD WAR

EFFECTS
• • •

★ Reviewing Key Terms

For each of the terms below, write a sentence explaining how it relates to the Cold War.

1. satellite nation
2. iron curtain
3. containment
4. Marshall Plan
5. Warsaw Pact
6. HUAC
7. blacklist
8. 38th parallel
9. brinkmanship
10. U-2 incident

★ Reviewing Main Ideas

11. What decisions were reached at Yalta and Potsdam? (Section 1)

12. Summarize the postwar goals of the United States and the Soviet Union. (Section 1)

13. How did the United States hope to use the policy of containment and the Truman Doctrine to respond to the Soviet creation of an iron curtain? (Section 1)

14. What did the Marshall Plan accomplish in Europe? (Section 2)

15. (a) What was the Soviet atomic threat? (b) How did President Truman respond to it? (Section 2)

16. What was the purpose of NATO? (Section 2)

17. What Communist advances worried Americans in 1949? (Section 2)

18. (a) Describe the efforts by the Truman administration and Congress to stop Communist influence

in the United States. (b) How did this anti-Communist effort affect the nation? (Section 2)

19. How did the Communists gain control of China? (Section 3)

20. Describe the three phases of the Korean War. (Section 3)

21. Describe the rise and fall of Senator Joseph McCarthy. (Section 4)

22. How did the Cold War play out in Southeast Asia, the Middle East, and Latin America? (Section 4)

23. Describe the arms race of the 1950s. (Section 4)

★ Critical Thinking

24. Recognizing Ideologies Explain how the differing ideologies of the Soviets and the United States were reflected in their Cold War policies.

25. Predicting Consequences (a) What principles of American foreign policy did the Berlin airlift put into action? (b) What do you think might have happened if the United States and Britain had not tried the airlift or if the airlift had failed?

26. Identifying Central Issues Why do you think that Americans were so willing to believe that Communists had infiltrated the movie industry and the American government?

27. Expressing Problems Clearly General MacArthur wanted to pursue the Korean War more aggressively, but President Truman was more cautious. Explain the pros and cons of each position.

894 Chapter 26 • *The Cold War*

CREATING A CHAPTER SUMMARY

The Cold War

Causes	Effects
• U.S. and Soviet Union have had a bad relationship since the Russian Revolution of 1917. • U.S. is angered by Stalin's nonaggression pact with Hitler. • Stalin is angry that U.S. did not invade Europe sooner. • U.S. rejects Soviet Union's demand for war reparations. • Soviets expand sphere of influence. • Stalin predicts triumph of communism over capitalism and urges expansion of communism. • Soviets gain nuclear capability. • China becomes Communist.	• Winston Churchill describes the "iron curtain." • Truman adopts policy of containment (the Truman Doctrine). • NATO is established. • Truman establishes a Loyalty Program for government employees. • McCarthy uses the issue of communism to become a powerful senator. • Korean War is fought. • Eisenhower tries to defeat communism in Southeast Asia, the Middle East, and Latin America. • Beginning of U.S. involvement in Vietnam; beginning of U.S.–Soviet arms buildup • Beginning of U.S.–Soviet space race

June 17, 1949

★ Skills Assessment

Analyzing Political Cartoons ▶

28. Examine the images in this 1949 cartoon. (a) What is the flame that the man is about to douse? (b) What does the flame represent?

29. (a) What does the man represent? (b) How can you tell?

30. What is the cartoonist's message?

Analyzing Primary Sources

Turn to the excerpt from the Truman Doctrine at the end of Section 1.

31. What was the main purpose of Truman's speech?

   A to frighten the Soviet government
   B to make clear how the United States would respond to Communist aggression
   C to win congressional approval of his containment policy
   D to expand the Cold War

32. What group or groups did Truman promise to help?

   F subjugated minorities
   G armed resistance movements
   H majorities whose freedom was threatened
   J all of the above

33. According to Truman, what two groups might try to subjugate free peoples?

   A free peoples and armed minorities
   B subjugated minorities and outside forces
   C the majority and outsiders
   D outside forces and armed minorities

Applying the Chapter Skill: _Recognizing Cause and Effect_

34. Look back at the Skills for Life page, and review the steps for recognizing cause and effect. Then create a cause-and-effect chain to explain what led to the Marshall Plan and what impact it had.

ACTIVITIES

Writing to LEARN

Writing to Persuade
Review the policy of brinkmanship as stated by John Foster Dulles in Section 4 as well as Adlai Stevenson's objection to that policy. Take a position for or against brinkmanship, and write an editorial that might have appeared in 1956. Create a well-reasoned argument, and support it with specific details.

Primary Source CD-ROM

Working With Primary Sources Find additional information on the Cold War on the _Exploring Primary Sources in U.S. History CD-ROM_ and use the selection(s) provided to complete the Chapter 26 primary source activity located in the _America: Pathways to the Present_ area of the following Web site.
www.phschool.com

Take It to the NET

Chapter Self-Test As a review activity, take the Chapter 26 Self-Test in the _America: Pathways to the Present_ area at the Web site listed below. The questions are designed to test your understanding of the chapter content.
www.phschool.com

Chapter 26 Assessment   895

Chinese Communists enter the fighting, resulting in stalemate.

21. McCarthy gained popularity by crusading against communism, and he lost power when he accused the army of housing Communists.

22. Southeast Asia: The U.S. attempted to prevent a Vietnamese Communist government from coming to power in the 1950s. Middle East: The Soviets supported Arab nations; the U.S. supported Israel. Latin America: The U.S. helped bring down a Communist-leaning government in Guatemala.

23. A competition for weapons superiority between the U.S. and the Soviet Union. Both nations tried to build enough nuclear weapons to frighten other nations (but mainly each other).

CRITICAL THINKING

24. The Soviet Union worked to rebuild itself and protect its borders. The U.S. helped rebuild European countries that opposed communism.

25. (a) The Truman Doctrine and the policy of containment. (b) West Berlin could have fallen under Soviet domination.

26. Students may note that both the government and the movie industry had significant influence over Americans' everyday lives. Perhaps this made both seem susceptible to infiltration.

27. MacArthur's position might have ended all Communist domination in China and Korea, but it also could have led to larger war. Truman's position was safer for the U.S., but would not end Communist influence in Asia.

SKILLS ASSESSMENT

28. (a) The torch held by the Statue of Liberty. (b) Liberty.

29. (a) Cold War hysteria; exaggerated fear of communism. (b) The cartoon's date, and the "hysteria" label.

30. Cold War hysteria is threatening American civil liberties.

31. C

32. H

33. D

34. European countries suffer huge losses in World War II; Soviet Union attempts to dominate nearby nations; U.S. uses Marshall Plan to intervene on behalf of non-Communist European countries; the economies of these countries begin to recover; U.S. gains influence and trading partners.

ANSWERS TO ACTIVITIES

Writing to LEARN

Sample responses may include: In certain situations, the threat of massive retaliation is worth the price of peace; it is a dangerous policy that could easily lead to all-out war and destruction.

Primary Source CD-ROM

Direct students to the additional primary sources that can be found on the _Exploring Primary Sources in U.S. History CD-ROM._

 Take It to the NET

Additional support materials and activities for Chapter 26 of _America: Pathways to the Present_ can be found in the Social Studies area at the Prentice Hall School Web site. **www.phschool.com**

American Pathways
SCIENCE & TECHNOLOGY

American Innovations in Technology

Technological innovation has always spurred the nation's economic growth. From the Industrial Revolution to the Information Age, American inventiveness has resulted in new and improved products for consumers and increased profits for businesses.

1 **A Young and Growing Economy**
1790–1850 As the nation expanded westward, a number of innovations such as the cotton gin, the mechanical reaper, and centralized textile factories improved agriculture and encouraged trade.

A textile mill label from Lowell, Massachusetts (left)

2 **Industrial Expansion**
1850–1890 New inventions such as the telephone and the light bulb, as well as other technological advances such as the first electric power stations, played an important role in the massive industrial expansion that occurred after the Civil War.

Corliss steam engine at the 1876 Centennial Exhibition (left) and the receiving device for Alexander Graham Bell's first telephone call (above)

896

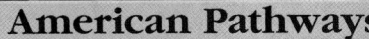

3 Becoming a Superpower

1900–1945 The Allies won two world wars in part because of American technological skills, including the ability to apply assembly-line and other mass-production techniques to the manufacture of war materials.

Boeing B-17 bomber production during the 1940s (above)

4 A Modern Economy

1945–Present The modern American economy has benefited from a steady stream of innovations, especially in the fields of biotechnology, electronics, plastics, aerospace, and computer science.

High-tech devices (above) and an implantable replacement heart (left)

Continuity and Change

1. How did the Erie Canal encourage the growth of agriculture in the West?
2. How did the assembly line improve productivity in the automobile industry?

Take It to the NET: Creating a Study Guide
Print and complete the study guide for this topic found in the *America: Pathways to the Present* area of the following Web site. **www.phschool.com**

897

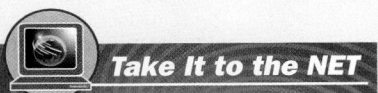

Take It to the NET

Students can print the American Pathways thematic study guide for this topic at the Prentice Hall School Web site, or you can provide students with copies of the study guide, which is found in the Units 7/8 booklet, the American Pathways Activity, pages 92–93. Students should use their texts to fill in a one-sentence description for each event on the study guide. When completed for each of the American Pathways topics, the thematic study guides will aid students in preparing for an end-of-course exam.

ANSWERS

1. By improving east-west transportation, the Erie Canal helped populate the West and provided farmers there with a faster route to east coast markets.

2. Workers stayed in one place while the assembly line moved the vehicles to them. Also, workers specialized in just one part of the assembly. These factors enabled the assembly line to greatly speed the production of vehicles.

Chapter 27 Planning Guide
Resource Manager

	CORE INSTRUCTION	READING/SKILLS
Chapter-Level Resources	Teaching Resources • Pacing Charts booklet • Block Scheduling booklet **Resource Pro® CD-ROM**, Ch. 27 **Prentice Hall Presentation Pro CD-ROM**, Ch. 27 **www.phschool.com** • eTeach	**Guided Reading Audiotapes (English/Spanish)** **Student Edition on Audio CD**, Ch. 27 **Social Studies Skills Tutor CD-ROM** **Color Transparency**, B15
1 The Postwar Economy 1. Find out how businesses reorganized after World War II. 2. Learn how technology transformed life after World War II. 3. Discover ways in which the nation's workforce changed after World War II. 4. See how subways and highway systems grew after World War II. 5. Understand how postwar conditions affected consumer credit.	Teaching Resources **Units 7/8 booklet** • Section 1 Quiz, p. 83 **Learning Styles Lesson Plans booklet,** p. 56	**Guided Reading and Review booklet,** p. 109 **Guide to the Essentials,** p. 137 **Learning with Documents booklet,** p. 66 **Section Reading Support Transparencies**
2 The Mood of the 1950s 1. Find out why comfort and security were so important to Americans in the 1950s. 2. Learn about the accepted roles of men and women during the 1950s. 3. See how some people challenged conformity in the 1950s.	Teaching Resources **Units 7/8 booklet** • Section 2 Quiz, p. 84 **Learning Styles Lesson Plans booklet,** p. 57	**Guided Reading and Review booklet,** p. 110 **Guide to the Essentials,** p. 138 **Section Reading Support Transparencies**
3 Domestic Politics and Policy 1. Discover Truman's Domestic policies as outlined in the Fair Deal. 2. Learn how Truman won the election of 1948. 3. Understand the Republican approach to government during the Eisenhower presidency.	Teaching Resources **Units 7/8 booklet** • Section 3 Quiz, p. 85	**Guided Reading and Review booklet,** p. 111 **Guide to the Essentials,** p. 139 **Learning with Documents booklet,** p. 32 **Skills for Life booklet,** p. 29 **Section Reading Support Transparencies**

ENRICHMENT/PRE-AP

Prentice Hall United States History Video Collection™
www.phschool.com
- Section Activities, Virtual Field Trip, Chapter Activities, Current Events Online

Biography, Literature, and Comparing Primary Sources booklet, p. 20
American History Block Scheduling Support
Sounds of an Era Audio CD
Exploring Primary Sources in U.S. History CD-ROM

Biography, Literature, and Comparing Primary Sources booklet, pp. 149–150
Sounds of an Era Audio CD

Biography, Literature, and Comparing Primary Sources booklet, pp. 76–77
Sounds of an Era Audio CD
American Pathways Thematic Posters

ASSESSMENT

PRENTICE HALL ASSESSMENT SYSTEM

Core Assessment
ExamView® Test Bank, Ch. 27
ExamView® Test Bank CD-ROM, Ch. 27
Standardized Test Preparation

Diagnose and Prescribe
Diagnostic Tests for High School Social Studies Skills

Review and Reteach
Review Book for U.S. History

Practice and Assess
Test-taking Strategies With Transparencies
Test-taking Strategies Posters
Test Prep Book for U.S. History
Alternative Assessment Handbook
Document-Based Assessment

Teaching Resources
Units 7/8 booklet
- Section Quizzes, pp. 83–85
- Chapter Tests, pp. 86, 89
www.phschool.com Ch. 27 Self-Test

AmericanHeritage RESOURCES

From the Archives of American Heritage®, pp. 914, 915, 916
AmericanHeritage® My Brush with History™ Videotapes
www.americanheritage.com

iTEXT

Don't miss the exclusive interactive version of this textbook on the Web and on CD-ROM.

Chapter 27 Planning Guide
In Your Classroom

CUSTOMIZE FOR INDIVIDUAL NEEDS

Gifted and Talented

Teacher's Edition
- Customize for Gifted and Talented, p. 909

Teaching Resources
- Biography, Literature, and Comparing Primary Sources booklet, pp. 20, 76–77, 149–150

Technology
- Exploring Primary Sources in U.S. History CD-ROM *Dr. Salk and His Vaccine*

ESL

Teacher's Edition
- Customize for ESL, p. 901

Teaching Resources
- Guided Reading and Review booklet, pp. 109–111
- Guide to the Essentials (English/Spanish), Chapter 27

Technology
- Student Edition on Audio CD, Chapter 27
- Guided Reading Audiotapes (English/Spanish), Chapter 27
- Section Reading Support Transparencies

Less Proficient Readers

Teacher's Edition
- Customize for Less Proficient Readers, p. 905

Teaching Resources
- Guided Reading and Review booklet, pp. 109–111
- Guide to the Essentials (English/Spanish), Chapter 27

Technology
- Student Edition on Audio CD, Chapter 27
- Guided Reading Audiotapes (English/Spanish), Chapter 27
- Section Reading Support Transparencies

Less Proficient Writers

Teacher's Edition
- Customize for Less Proficient Writers, p. 915

Teaching Resources
- Guided Reading and Review booklet, pp. 109–111
- Guide to the Essentials (English/Spanish), Chapter 27

Technology
- Student Edition on Audio CD, Chapter 27
- Guided Reading Audiotapes (English/Spanish), Chapter 27
- Section Reading Support Transparencies

TEACHER'S EDITION INDEX

CHAPTER 27 – PACING SUGGESTIONS

 For 90-minute Blocks
- Teach sections 1 and 3 using Transparency B15, and the Recent Scholarship note on page 917 for class discussions.

 Running Out of Time?

If you are running short on time to cover this chapter, consider the following options:

- Use the Prentice Hall Presentation Pro CD-ROM to create an outline for this chapter.
- Use the Section Summaries for Chapter 27, from **Guide to the Essentials (English/Spanish).**

1 The Postwar Economy	**Connecting with Citizenship** Have students research the G.I. Bill of Rights and use an illustrated format to explain its history and intentions, then examine its effects on both the individuals involved and American society in general. Students can supplement their presentations by providing statistics in graph form or with summaries of interviews with community members who directly benefited from the legislation. **(Visual/Spatial; Logical/Mathematical)**	
2 The Mood of the 1950s	**Connecting with Culture** Have students research public reaction to rock-and-roll and compare the 1950s to other periods when the younger generation embraced a new form of music, such as jazz. Have them write a brief essay that cites the similarities and differences, then conclude with the students' own interpretation of the reasons behind such generational differences and/or similarities. Students might read their essays aloud, accompanied by audio examples of the music they describe. **(Verbal/Linguistic; Rhythmic/Musical)**	
3 Domestic Politics and Policies	**Connecting with Citizenship** Have students prepare a flow chart that clearly shows the steps taken when an opinion poll is conducted and how the data are interpreted. Students should use graphic representations of the data and, in an oral presentation, explain the data's significance. **(Visual/Spatial; Logical/Mathematical)**	

Chapter 27

The Postwar Years at Home
(1945–1960)

SECTION 1   The Postwar Economy
SECTION 2   The Mood of the 1950s
SECTION 3   Domestic Politics and Policy

INTRODUCING THE CHAPTER

As the United States emerged from World War II, the American Dream of having a secure job and owning a house came within reach for many Americans. Fueled by the postwar baby boom, the economy rocketed forward in the late 1940s and 1950s.

TIME LINE ACTIVITY

To provide students with practice in using the time line, ask questions such as these:

1. What event took place in 1947 that would have a huge impact on later technological development? *(The transistor was invented.)*

2. What 1951 event would eventually lead to a cultural revolution? *(Alan Freed played the first rock-and-roll music on a Cleveland radio station.)*

3. What 1957 event would lead to a space race between the United States and the Soviet Union? *(The Soviet Union launched* Sputnik.*)*

A Levittown suburb

Plastic flamingos were popular lawn ornaments in the 1950s.

The BUCK STOPS *here*

This sign sat on President Truman's desk.

American Events

1944
Congress passes the GI Bill of Rights.

1946
Dr. Spock publishes *The Common Sense Book of Baby and Child Care.*

1947
Congress passes the Taft-Hartley Act. The first transistor is invented, spurring growth in computers and electronics.

Presidential Terms: Franklin D. Roosevelt 1933–1945   Harry S Truman 1945–1953

1940	•	1945	•	•	•	1950

World Events

Thor Heyerdahl and his crew sail the raft *Kon-Tiki* from Peru to Polynesia.
1947

English novelist George Orwell's *Nineteen Eighty-Four* is published.
1949

eTeach

Be sure to check out this month's online discussion with a Master Teacher. Go to **www.phschool.com**.

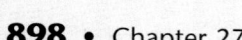

Regional Migration, 1940–1960

CANADA

Washington
Montana
North Dakota
Minnesota
Maine
Oregon
Idaho
Wyoming
South Dakota
Wisconsin
Michigan
Vt.
N.H.
Mass.
New York
Nevada
Nebraska
Iowa
Pa.
R.I.
Conn.
New Jersey
Utah
Colorado
Kansas
Illinois
Indiana
Ohio
Delaware
Maryland
California
Missouri
W. Va.
Virginia
D.C.
Ky.
Arizona
New Mexico
Oklahoma
Arkansas
Tenn.
North Carolina
Mississippi
Alabama
Georgia
South Carolina
Texas
Louisiana
ATLANTIC OCEAN
Florida

PACIFIC OCEAN

MEXICO

Gulf of Mexico

Singer, songwriter, and guitarist Chuck Berry greatly influenced rock-and-roll.

Net regional migration by race, 1940–1960

— Limit of population zone

Black migration   White migration

2,000   2,000
1,000   1,000
0   0

Approximate number of migrants (in thousands)

The Growth of Suburban St. Louis, Missouri 1950–1960

N

City of St. Louis

Increases in percentages:
■ 100
■ 70
■ 50
□ 20
□ Decrease
□ No basis for comparison

0   5   10 mi.
0   5   10 km

1951
Disc jockey and music promoter Alan Freed begins hosting a radio show, featuring music that comes to be known as "rock-and-roll."

1954
Successful tests are conducted on a polio vaccine.

1956
The Federal-Aid Highway Act funds an interstate highway system.

1958
Congress passes the National Defense Education Act and establishes the National Aeronautics and Space Administration.

Dwight D. Eisenhower 1953–1961

1955   •   •   •   •   •   1960

1953
The double-helix model for DNA is formulated in London.

1957
The Soviet Union launches *Sputnik*.

1959
The Soviet Union launches three lunar probes.

Chapter 27   **899**

BIBLIOGRAPHY

For the Teacher

Halberstam, David. *The Fifties.* Fawcett, 1994. (A comprehensive look at the social, political, economic, and cultural history of the 1950s.)

Marling, Karal Ann. *As Seen on TV: The Visual Culture of Everyday Life in the 1950s.* Harvard University Press, 1996. (Combines social commentary with a vivid recapturing of the dawn of the television era.)

For the Student

Drake, Albert. *Fifties Flashback: A Nostalgic Trip!* California Bill's Automotive, 2000. (A car buff offers nostalgic memories of the way things were in the 1950s.)

Stolley, Richard B. *The American Dream: The 50s.* Time-Life Books, 2000. (Richly illustrated and comprehensive study of the 1950s.)

Regional Migration, 1940–1960

Activating Prior Knowledge Most of the migrating African Americans moved in what general direction? *(Northward)*

Previewing What does the map of suburban St. Louis show about regional migration? *(People were leaving the city for the suburbs.)*

BACKGROUND
About the Pictures

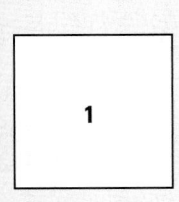

1

2
3
4

1. Designed and built by Levitt and Sons, Inc. in the 1950s, Levittown was a planned suburban development in Pennsylvania that was then reproduced in communities across the United States.

2. Flamingos, along with dogs, ducks, and frogs, began appearing on lawns in two-dimensional forms in 1946. In 1957 a man named Don Featherstone sculpted the first three-dimensional plastic flamingo, soon to be found on suburban lawns everywhere.

3. This phrase is a reply to the act of "passing the buck," or transferring responsibility from one person to the next and avoiding blame. Truman wanted to make clear that he would take all responsibility for the actions of his administration.

4. Berry's music drew from a broad range of influences, including rhythm and blues, country-western, gospel, and music from the Caribbean to create his brand of rock-and-roll.

iTEXT

Don't miss the exclusive interactive version of this textbook on the Web and on CD-ROM.

SECTION OBJECTIVES

1. Find out how businesses reorganized after World War II.

2. Learn how technology transformed life after World War II.

3. Discover ways in which the nation's workforce changed after World War II.

4. See how suburbs and highway systems grew after World War II.

5. Understand how postwar conditions affected consumer credit.

BELLRINGER

Warm-Up Activity Have students think of an invention that would be totally new to a person from the 1950s who was suddenly transported to the present.

Activating Prior Knowledge Television was a new phenomenon in the 1950s. Can students list some ways they think the introduction of television into homes changed families' lives?

READING STRATEGY

Have students make a chart with two headings, one reading *Causes of Prosperity,* the other reading *Effects of Prosperity.* As they read the section, have them identify the causes and effects of prosperity in the 1950s.

CAPTION ANSWERS

Viewing History After the war, servicemen and their families wanted to be able to buy items that they couldn't afford during the Depression, or that were rationed during the war.

The Postwar Economy

READING FOCUS

- How did businesses reorganize after World War II?

- How did technology transform life after World War II?

- In what ways did the nation's work force change following World War II?

- Why did suburbs and highway systems grow after World War II?

- How did postwar conditions affect consumer credit?

MAIN IDEA

The "American Dream," characterized by a home in the suburbs and a car in the garage, became reality for many people in the postwar years.

KEY TERMS

per capita income
conglomerate
franchise
transistor
baby boom
GI Bill of Rights

TAKING NOTES

Copy the outline below. As you read, fill in information about the postwar economy. Use Roman numerals to indicate the major headings, capital letters for the subheadings, and numbers for the supporting details.

> **1950s Economic Expansion**
> **I. Businesses Reorganize**
>   **A. Corporate expansion accompanies growth.**
>   1. _____
>   2. _____
>   **B.** _____

VIEWING HISTORY A wounded World War II soldier returns to his family in New York. **Drawing Conclusions** *What were some expectations of former servicemen and their families after the war?*

Setting the Scene When American soldiers returned from the battlefields, they wanted to put the horrors of the war behind them and enjoy the comforts of home. During the war, many items were rationed or not produced at all. Many people had simply put their money into savings. Now most Americans were eager to acquire everything the war—and before that, the Depression—had denied them.

The marriage rate increased dramatically after the war, and the population boomed. Fueled by a growing economy, suburbs sprang up with look-alike houses in answer to a postwar housing shortage. One writer observed:

> 66 *Socially, these communities have neither history, tradition, nor established structure. . . . Everybody lives in a 'good neighborhood'; there is, to use that classic American euphemism, no 'wrong side of the tracks.'* 99
> —Harry Henderson, "The Mass-Produced Suburbs,"
> *Harper's,* 1953

Suburban families enjoyed incomes that were considerably higher than those in rural communities. They spent large sums of money on recreation. By the end of the 1950s, about 75 percent of families owned a car, and even more owned a TV set. America's consumer economy was thriving.

Businesses Reorganize

During the postwar years, the United States embarked on one of its greatest periods of economic expansion. The gross national product (GNP) more than doubled, jumping from $212 billion in 1945 to $504 billion in 1960. **Per capita income,** the average annual income per person, increased from $1,223 to $2,219 during the same period.

Major corporate expansion accompanied economic growth. Industrialists fully intended to provide consumers the goods they desired, as they reconverted their businesses to civilian production at the end of the war. At the same time, American industry had benefited from technological advances made during the war. Research and development—funded by the government—helped create a variety of new products, such as radar and the computer, that could be used in the civilian economy.

In the 1950s, a few large firms dominated many industries. General Motors, Ford, and Chrysler overshadowed all competitors in the automobile industry; General Electric and Westinghouse enjoyed similar positions in the electrical industry. The Great Depression, however, had made many giant corporations wary of investing all their resources in a single business. A **conglomerate,** a corporation made up of three or more unrelated businesses, was better able to defend against economic downturns. For this reason, some corporations chose to become conglomerates. In the event one industry or area of the economy failed, the conglomerate could rely on its earnings in another industry. International Telephone and Telegraph, for example, purchased Avis Rent-a-Car, Sheraton Hotels, Hartford Fire Insurance, and Continental Baking.

At the same time, another kind of expansion took place. In 1954, salesman Ray Kroc was amazed when two brothers who owned a restaurant in San Bernardino, California, gave him an order for their eighth Multimixer, a brand of milkshake machine. With eight machines, the restaurant could make 40 milkshakes at once. Because of the restaurant's fast, efficient service and its prime location along a busy highway, it was experiencing great success. Intrigued by the possibilities, Kroc purchased the two brothers' idea of assembly-line food production. He also acquired the restaurant's name: McDonald's. Kroc built a nationwide chain of fast-food restaurants by selling eager entrepreneurs the right to open a **franchise**—a business that contracts to offer certain goods and services from a larger parent company. Franchise agreements vary from one company to the next, but generally the contracts allow each owner to use the company's name, suppliers, products, and production methods. Each franchise, then, is operated as a small business whose owners profit from the parent company's guidance. Franchise owners assume less risk than small business owners, in that they sell a product that is well known—and presumably liked by the consumer. Many other restaurant franchises followed.

The franchise system flourished in the 1950s. Other kinds of businesses, such as clothing stores and automobile muffler shops, also adopted the franchise method. Some small businesses suffered from the growth of the franchise system. As nationwide chains grew popular with consumers, independent businesses declined, unable to compete successfully.

Technology Transforms Life

Meanwhile, developments in technology spurred industrial growth. Rushing to keep up with demand, businesses produced hundreds of new products, such as dishwashers and gas-powered lawnmowers, aimed at saving the consumer time and money. Eager Americans filled their homes with the latest inventions.

Television Americans fell in love with television in the 1950s. The technology for television had been developed throughout the late 1920s and 1930s, but then stalled during the war. After World War II, television became enormously

This sign at the original fast-food restaurant in San Bernardino, California, advertised the McDonald brothers' hamburgers.

Westerns featuring Hopalong Cassidy aired on TV during the 1950s.

Chapter 27 • Section 1   901

popular. Although taped programs later became the norm, live broadcasts in the early days of television made the shows especially exciting to watch.

In 1955, the average American family watched television four to five hours a day. Children grew up on such programs as *Howdy Doody* and *The Mickey Mouse Club*. Teenagers danced to rock-and-roll music played on *American Bandstand*, a forerunner to today's MTV. Other viewers followed comedies, including *I Love Lucy* and *Father Knows Best*. A 1949 *McCall's* article described the importance of television at the time: "Many couples credit television, which simultaneously eased baby-sitting, entertainment, and financial problems, with having brought them closer. . . . Though often contemptuous of many programs, they speak of TV gratefully as 'something we can share.' . . ."

Three large networks controlled television programming. As had been the case with radio, they raised the money to broadcast their shows by selling advertising time. Television became a powerful new medium for advertisers, allowing them to reach millions of viewers. As a result, Americans watched their favorite shows interrupted by commercials, a practice that continues today.

The Computer Industry Another innovation appeared in the 1950s that would transform American life in the years to come. Wartime research led to the development of ever more powerful calculators and computers. During the 1950s, American businesses reached out to embrace the computer industry. Grace Hopper, a research fellow at Harvard University's computation laboratory, pioneered the creation of software that ran computers. She also introduced the term *debugging*—which was born when she removed a moth that had become caught in a relay switch and had caused a large computer to shut down. Today the term means "ridding a computer program of errors."

In 1947, scientists at Bell Telephone Laboratories invented the first **transistor**, a tiny circuit device that amplifies, controls, and generates electrical signals. The transistor could do the work of a much larger vacuum tube, but took up less

Fast Forward to Today

Television Viewing

After inventor Philo Taylor Farnsworth transmitted the first electronic television image in 1927, he hoped that television would become an important educational tool. Instead, he was dismayed at the programs he saw on television in the 1950s and 1960s, as well as the amount of time people spent watching TV. He refused to allow his children to watch television when they were growing up, telling them, "I don't want it in your intellectual diet."

Today many adults share Farnsworth's concerns about television content and viewing habits. Researchers have suggested links between TV viewing and lower reading scores for children, obesity, and violent behavior. The introduction of program rating systems and the v-chip, which allows parents to block out programs that have certain ratings, came about in response to such concerns.

The graph (left) and chart (above) indicate television's popularity with the American public over time.

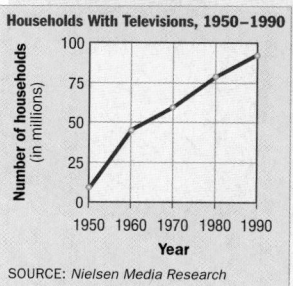

Households With Televisions, 1950–1990

Number of households (in millions)

SOURCE: *Nielsen Media Research*

Average Household TV Viewing Hours, 1950–1990	
Year	Average Daily Viewing per Household
1950	4 hours, 35 minutes
1960	5 hours, 6 minutes
1970	5 hours, 56 minutes
1980	6 hours, 36 minutes
1990	6 hours, 55 minutes

SOURCE: *Nielsen Media Research*

? Study the graph (left), "Households With Televisions, 1950–1990." Why would more people have acquired TV sets in the 1950s than in any of the other decades shown? Explain.

space and generated less heat. The transistor could be used in radios, computers, and other electronic devices, and greatly changed the electronics industry. Because of the transistor, giant machines that once filled whole rooms could now fit on a desk. Calculations that had taken hours could now be performed in fractions of a second. The Census Bureau purchased one of the first new computer systems to tally the 1950 census.

Nuclear Power An entirely new industry, the generation of electrical power through the use of atomic energy, resulted from the research that had produced the atomic bomb. Nuclear fission, which involves splitting uranium or plutonium atoms, could produce a huge explosion if the reaction occurred quickly. But fission, carefully controlled, could also produce heat to generate steam and drive electrical turbines. In 1954, the Navy produced the first nuclear-powered submarine, which had a small reactor in the hull. The submarine's technology provided a model for the first nuclear power plant on land, which opened in Shippingport, Pennsylvania, in 1957. The 1956 children's book *The Walt Disney Story of Our Friend the Atom*, by scientist Heinz Haber, explored the potential uses of atomic energy during peacetime. The accompanying Disney film, *Our Friend the Atom*, gave many children their first glimpse into what has since been referred to as the atomic age.

Advances in Medicine Americans also found hope in developments made in medicine. In 1954, Dr. Jonas Salk and Dr. Thomas Francis conducted a successful field test of a vaccine to prevent one of the most feared diseases—poliomyelitis. Before the vaccine, the disease, known commonly as polio, had killed or disabled more than 20,000 children in the United States every year. As you have read, Franklin D. Roosevelt suffered the effects of polio throughout much of his life. Just before the polio vaccine's success was to be reported, Salk wrote to FDR's widow Eleanor: "The scientific report, that may mark the beginning of the end of the scourge of polio, is to be made on the Tenth Anniversary of Mr. Roosevelt's untimely death. Wherever you may be, or whatever your thoughts, I would like you to know that a part of his great spirit will be within me, living as it was during his great life, while we all share the knowledge that may bring the fulfillment of the dream he had many years ago." Salk's injected vaccine, together with an oral version developed later by Dr. Albert Sabin, effectively eliminated the threat of polio.

Research in the development of drugs used to fight bacterial infections had been underway long before the start of World War II. By 1944, advances in the production of antibiotics such as penicillin were saving countless lives. During the 1950s, doctors discovered other antibiotics that were effective against penicillin-resistant bacteria.

Doctors who had served during the war saving the lives of wounded soldiers helped usher in a new era of surgical advances. Surgical techniques developed during the war allowed doctors to correct heart defects, and the specialty of heart surgery grew rapidly.

Changes in the Work Force

In earlier years, most Americans made a living as blue-collar workers, producing goods or performing services that depended on manual labor. After the war, however, new machines performed many of the jobs previously done by people. Some blue-collar workers found their way into white-collar jobs. Young people, particularly former servicemen with new college degrees,

VIEWING HISTORY The vacuum tube (top left) was used in radios prior to the invention and development of the transistor (bottom left). The transistor radio (top) was among many new electronic products the invention made possible. **Making Comparisons** *Compare the size of the vacuum tube to that of the transistor. How did the size of the tube limit its uses?*

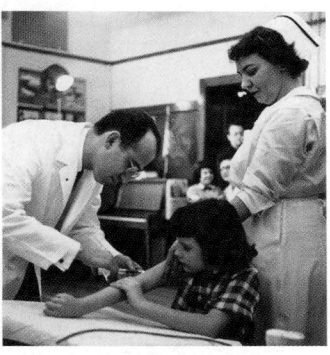

VIEWING HISTORY Jonas Salk is shown administering his new polio vaccine. **Drawing Inferences** *How did the availability of the vaccine change the lives of Americans?*

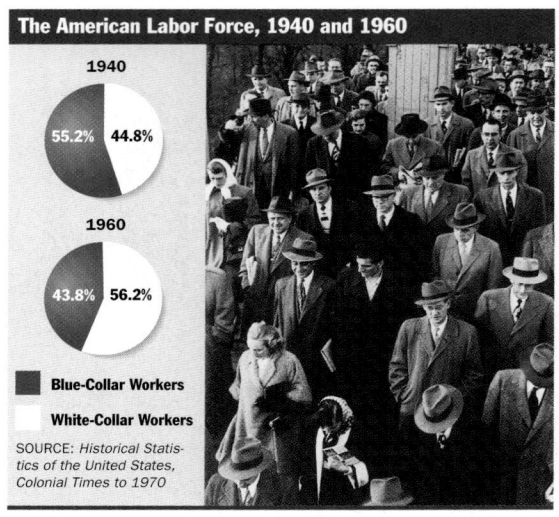

The American Labor Force, 1940 and 1960

1940
55.2% 44.8%

1960
43.8% 56.2%

■ Blue-Collar Workers
□ White-Collar Workers

SOURCE: *Historical Statistics of the United States, Colonial Times to 1970*

INTERPRETING GRAPHS
These Chicago-area commuters (above right) display some of the conformity that characterized the labor force in the 1950s. The graph above shows the American labor force in 1940 and 1960. **Making Comparisons** *How did the labor force change from 1940 to 1960? Be specific.*

INTERPRETING GRAPHS
The graph shows the trend in the birthrate from 1930 to 1960. **Synthesizing Information** *Overall, which decade shows the lowest number of births, and which shows the highest number of births?*

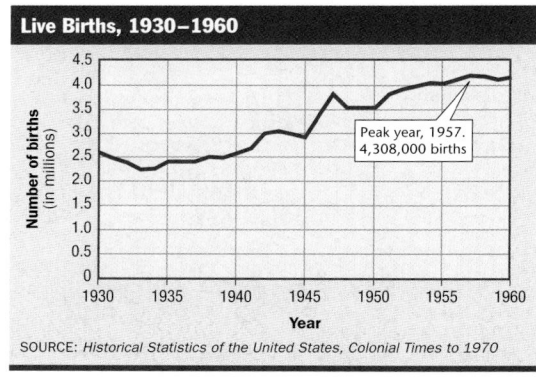

Live Births, 1930–1960

Peak year, 1957. 4,308,000 births

Number of births (in millions) — 4.5, 4.0, 3.5, 3.0, 2.5, 2.0, 1.5, 1.0, 0.5, 0

Year — 1930, 1935, 1940, 1945, 1950, 1955, 1960

SOURCE: *Historical Statistics of the United States, Colonial Times to 1970*

also gravitated toward white-collar jobs as they entered the work force for the first time. Corporate expansion meant that more people were needed to keep growing organizations running. By 1956, a majority of American workers held white-collar jobs, managing offices, working in sales, and performing professional and clerical duties in which manual labor was not an essential element.

The growth of the service industry had a great effect on the lives of Americans. The new white-collar workers felt encouraged by the working conditions they found: the buildings were clean, the offices bright. Physically, the work was less exhausting than blue-collar labor, it was not as dangerous, and some workers had the opportunity to rise into executive positions. But office jobs had their drawbacks. Employment in large corporations was often impersonal. White-collar workers in large companies had less connection with the products and services that their companies provided. Employees sometimes felt pressure to dress, think, and act alike. Sociologist C. Wright Mills commented: "When white-collar people get jobs, they sell not only their time and energy but their personalities as well."

In the blue-collar sector, working conditions and wages improved during the 1940s and 1950s. During this period, workers in some unions won important gains, such as guaranteed cost-of-living increases, designed to adjust wages to keep up with the rate of inflation. By 1955, nearly 33 percent of the total labor force in the United States was unionized. In that year, the two largest unions, the American Federation of Labor (AFL) and the Congress of Industrial Organizations (CIO), merged. The new and more powerful organization, called the AFL-CIO, remains a major force today.

Suburbs and Highways

With so many people working and making a better living than ever before, the **baby boom** that had begun in the mid-1940s continued. The birthrate, which had fallen to 19 births per 1,000 people during the Depression, soared to more than 25 births per 1,000 in its peak year of 1957.

Moving to the Suburbs Seeking more room, growing families retreated from the noise and pollution of aging cities and bought new houses in suburbs that ringed the urban areas. World War II veterans expanded their economic opportunities with the help of the Servicemen's Readjustment Act of 1944, commonly known as the **GI Bill of Rights,** which gave them low-interest mortgages to purchase new homes and provided them with educational stipends to go to college or graduate school.

Developers like William J. Levitt began to cater to the demand for housing. Levitt built new communities in the suburbs, pioneering mass-production techniques in home building. He bought precut and preassembled materials, and built houses in just weeks instead of months. Proud of his creations, Levitt gave his name to the new towns. By the late 1940s, there was a Levittown on Long Island that included more than 17,000 homes. Another in Bucks County, Pennsylvania, had about 16,000 homes, and a third Levittown in Willingsboro, New Jersey, appeared in the late 1950s. Other developers adopted Levitt's techniques, and new communities sprang up all over the United States.

For the first time, many average Americans could afford to buy their own home. While most fully enjoyed life in their new houses, others complained that the developments all looked too much alike. Folk singer Malvina Reynolds expressed her distaste for the new communities with these words from "Little Boxes," a popular song of the era:

> 66 *Little boxes on the hillside*
> *Little boxes made of ticky-tacky*
> *Little boxes on the hillside*
> *Little boxes all the same.*
>
> *There's a green one and a pink one*
> *And a blue one and a yellow one*
> *And they're all made out of ticky-tacky*
> *And they all look just the same.* 99

—Malvina Reynolds, "Little Boxes"

Cars and Highways Suburban growth brought with it other changes. Following their customers, some stores began to move from cities to shopping centers located in the suburbs. Many Americans, living in suburbs built beyond the reach of public transportation, depended more and more on automobiles. Suburban resident Agnes Geraghty recalled, "When we came here [to the suburbs] our first goal was to buy a new car. I mean with all the traveling that we needed to do, our old car just didn't cut it. We soon realized that task was a little more complicated than we anticipated. A car was a real status symbol and hey, who didn't want to impress the neighbors?"

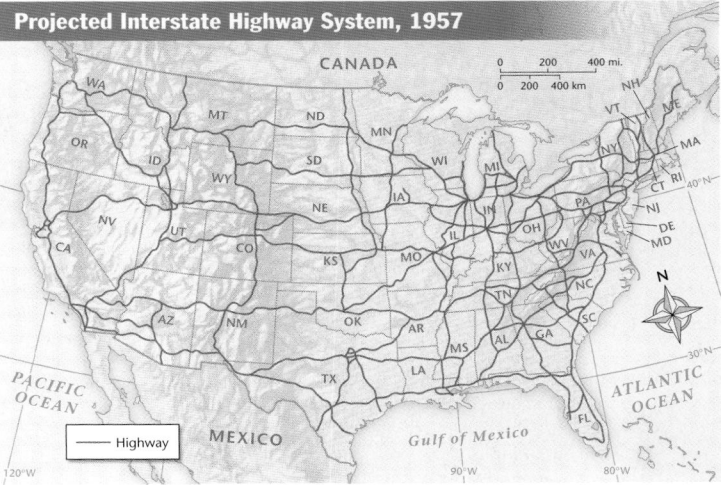

Levitt and other developers built not just houses, but entire communities.

MAP SKILLS Increasingly dependent on the automobile, Americans needed new and better roads. **Place** *How did roads built under the Interstate Highway Act contribute to changes in American culture?*

Projected Interstate Highway System, 1957

CANADA

0   200   400 mi.
0   200   400 km

PACIFIC OCEAN

MEXICO

Gulf of Mexico

ATLANTIC OCEAN

— Highway

Connecting with Geography

Assign students the task of obtaining a copy of a map of a Levittown, or provide one for them. Direct the students to compare and contrast that community's layout with the layout of an earlier American city and a contemporary American suburb. Have students point out similarities and differences in the communities' structures. Have them pose and answer questions about geographic distributions and patterns shown on their maps. Use the presentation as a springboard into a discussion about changes in the geography of population centers in the United States. (Visual/Spatial)

Connections to Today

While the houses of Levittown, New York, were commonly criticized as "little boxes" and as symbols of a cheapened mass culture, many commentators think they look better as time goes on. Historian Alexander O. Boulton, for instance, has pointed out that far from being "made of ticky-tacky," the Levittown houses were unusually well-designed and built. In addition, Levittown residents have modified their homes in so many ways through the years that those homes still in original condition are sought after as rarities. In Boulton's words, Levittown "now seems not the model of mass conformity, but a monument to American individualism."

✔ **TEST PREPARATION**

Have students read the excerpt from the song "Little Boxes" on this page and then complete the sentence below.

The main reason the songwriter dislikes the new housing development is that—

A the houses resemble boxes.

Ⓑ all the houses look the same.

C the houses are in poor taste.

D she dislikes pastel colors.

CUSTOMIZE FOR ...

Less Proficient Readers

Ask students to write one or two sentences showing how each of the following developments changed American life during the postwar period: corporate expansion, technological advances, changes in the workforce, changes in farm work and life, the move to the suburbs, and consumer credit.

CAPTION ANSWERS

Map Skills Roads are shorter and have more intersections on the East Coast. Roads in the West are spaced farther apart and intersect less often.

Section 1 Assessment

Reading Comprehension

1. Average annual income per person.

2. Conglomerates allowed more security for a company, through investing in multiple businesses rather than just one. Franchises allowed a larger parent company to expand to many locations, operated locally as small businesses, while still under the parent company's guidance.

3. To amplify, control, and generate electrical signals. Transistors greatly impacted the electronics industry because they took up much less physical space and made possible rapid improvements in early computers.

4. Couples with children increasingly left cities to raise their children in the suburbs. The GI Bill of Rights gave World War II veterans economic and educational opportunities that helped them gain better-paying jobs, enabling them to purchase homes in the suburbs.

Critical Thinking and Writing

5. Students should note that the author's bias is to assume that television viewers will consist almost entirely of married couples who have children.

6. Answers will vary, but should be descriptive, and supported with facts from the section.

Take It to the NET

Research should chronicle the phases of development and testing of the vaccine, including dates, milestones, and advancements in technology, from 1908 to 1961.

Focus on DAILY LIFE

1950s Car Culture In the 1950s, cars increasingly became part of many social and cultural events. Families took long vacations traveling by car with campers hitched to the rear and went on Sunday drives in their station wagons. Teenagers would cruise about town with no particular destination. Drivers sat in their parked cars at outdoor movie theaters and watched double features, with the sound coming through a speaker hooked onto the car door. At drive-in restaurants, waitresses delivered food right to the car, placing orders on trays that attached to the door.

You'll get BIG-CAR quality at lowest cost

The car culture was fed by consumer demand for the latest "dream car" to come from the Detroit automakers. Such cars were large and stylish, with powerful engines, chrome accents, and long tail fins projecting off the rear fenders.

The ad above prompts consumers to "See the USA" by automobile.

To meet the demand, automakers started introducing new car designs every year. People eagerly awaited the unveiling of the latest models. During the 1950s, American automakers produced up to 8 million new cars each year. From 1948 to 1958, passenger car sales increased by more than 50 percent.

Growth in the car industry created a need for more and better roads. The 1956 Federal-Aid Highway Act—sometimes called the Interstate Highway Act—provided $25 billion to build an interstate highway system more than 40,000 miles long. The project provided a national web of new roads and theoretically allowed for the evacuation of major cities in the event of nuclear attack.

The car culture inspired the development of many new businesses including gas stations, repair shops, and parts stores. Americans, especially teenagers, flocked to drive-in movies and restaurants. Families, encouraged by car advertisements that urged them to "See the USA," headed off for vacations at national parks, seaside resorts, and amusement parks.

The Growth of Consumer Credit

Eager to cash in on the increasing number of cars on the road, gasoline companies began offering credit cards to loyal customers. These cards allowed people to charge gas purchases when they were traveling. Americans found the cards convenient and easy to use.

Lending agencies picked up the credit card idea and made borrowing easy. Just as installment plans of the 1920s encouraged consumers to purchase beyond their means, credit cards introduced in the 1950s encouraged similar spending. The Diner's Club credit card appeared in 1950, followed at the end of the decade by the American Express card, and then by the BankAmericard (later called Visa). Total consumer credit debt rose from more than $8 billion in 1946 to more than $56 billion in 1960.

Americans used their credit to purchase washing machines, vacuum cleaners, and television sets. The United States had become, in the words of economist John Kenneth Galbraith, "the affluent society."

Section 1 Assessment

READING COMPREHENSION

1. What is **per capita income?**

2. How did **conglomerates** and **franchises** evolve in the postwar economy?

3. What is the purpose of a **transistor** and how did it contribute to other developments?

4. How did the **baby boom** and the **GI Bill of Rights** affect suburban growth?

CRITICAL THINKING AND WRITING

5. **Recognizing Bias** Reread the excerpt from the article on television viewing that begins, "Many couples credit television. . . ." What is the author's bias in the article?

6. **Writing to Describe** Write a paragraph that shows in detail what it would be like to move from an apartment in the city to a house in a Levittown after World War II.

Take It to the NET

Activity: Creating a Fact Sheet Research the history of polio up to the creation and testing of a vaccine in the 1950s. Use the links provided in the *America: Pathways to the Present* area of the following Web site for help in completing this activity.
www.phschool.com

RESOURCE DIRECTORY

Teaching Resources
Units 7/8 booklet
• Section 1 Quiz, p. 83
Guide to the Essentials
• Section 1 Summary, p. 137

READING FOCUS

- Why were comfort and security so important to Americans in the 1950s?
- What were the accepted roles of men and women during the 1950s?
- How did some people challenge conformity during the 1950s?

KEY TERMS

rock-and-roll
beatnik

TAKING NOTES

Copy the chart below. As you read, fill in details that describe the mood of the 1950s.

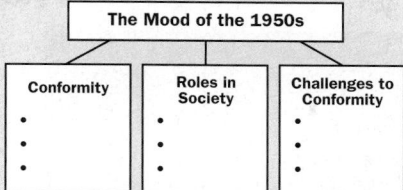

The Mood of the 1950s

Conformity	Roles in Society	Challenges to Conformity
•	•	•
•	•	•
•	•	•

MAIN IDEA

After World War II, many Americans enjoyed economic prosperity. While some welcomed the conformity of the 1950s, others felt it was restrictive and rebelled against it.

SECTION OBJECTIVES

1. Find out why comfort and security were so important to Americans in the 1950s.
2. Learn about the accepted roles of men and women during the 1950s.
3. See how some people challenged conformity in the 1950s.

BELLRINGER

Warm-Up Activity Ask students to decide what they consider to be the "proper" roles for men and women in their society today. Do their views of gender-based roles differ from those of their parents or grandparents? If so, how?

Activating Prior Knowledge Have the class list some aspects of 1950s culture with which they are familiar, under such headings as *Art, Music, Television, Theater, Fashion,* etc.

READING STRATEGY

Have students write two headings on a piece of paper: *Conformity* and *Nonconformity.* As they read the section, have them note relevant information in the appropriate column. Then have them write a sentence explaining whether conformity or nonconformity was more prevalent in the 1950s than it is in American life today.

Setting the Scene Most Americans were comfortable during the 1950s. They valued security over adventure, reflecting the mood of a nation still recovering from years of economic depression and war. One historian who grew up in the 1950s wrote:

> 66 The spreading of huge organizations, the rapidity of technological change, the rise of suburbia, the standardization of life posed new challenges, but for the most part people coped with them. That may not be very dramatic. But it is the truth about daily life as most people knew it and lived it. . . . Life in the 1950s . . . was a better life than they, or almost anyone else, had ever known. 99
>
> —Geoffrey Perrett, *A Dream of Greatness: The American People, 1945–1963*

Americans applauded the apparent harmony between individuals and groups in the United States that conformity seemed to encourage. Compromise, rather than conflict, was the way disagreements could be settled. People wanted to enjoy their newly won prosperity and provide even better opportunities for their children.

Comfort and Security

In the past, sociologist David Riesman observed, Americans had valued individuality. Now most preferred conformity. Riesman cited *Tootle the Engine*, a children's story in the popular Little Golden Book series. Tootle, a young train engine, found it was more fun to play in the fields than it was to stay on the tracks. His fellow citizens in "Engineville" worked hard to break him of the habit. Tootle finally absorbed the lesson of his peers: "Always stay on the track no matter what." The story, Riesman believed, was a powerful parable for the young people of the 1950s.

One of many 1950s fads: By wearing special glasses, audiences could see "3-D movies," films that produced an effect of three dimensions.

ACTIVITY
Connecting with Culture

This activity may take place over several class periods: Have groups of four to six students brainstorm topics concerning life in the 1950s, write questions for potential interviews, and select possible subjects to interview. Students may focus their interview questions on a specific population, for example, women. The goal of the project is to identify significant aspects of life in the 1950s and learn about them through first-person accounts.
(Verbal/Linguistic)

Chapter 27 • Section 2   907

RESOURCE DIRECTORY

Teaching Resources
Learning Styles Lesson Plans booklet, p. 57
Guided Reading and Review booklet, p. 110

Technology
Section Reading Support Transparencies
Guided Reading Audiotapes (English/Spanish), Ch. 27
Student Edition on Audio CD, Ch. 27
Prentice Hall Presentation Pro CD-ROM, Ch. 27
Companion Web site, www.phschool.com

Focus In the 1950s, many Americans enjoyed unprecedented prosperity and security. Ask students if this comfort was worth the price of conformity.

Instruct Ask students how people behave when they want to fit into a group. How did the Great Depression and World War II affect Americans' need for security? Discuss other factors, such as the fear of communism, that led to increased conformity. Remind students that not everyone wanted to conform. Ask how rock and roll challenged middle-class mores in the 1950s. What distinguished the beatniks?

Discuss men's and women's roles in the postwar era. Ask students to define those roles and to compare them with the roles of men and women today.

Assess/Reteach Ask students to discuss conformity in American life today. How does the proliferation of franchise clothing stores and restaurants contribute to that sense of conformity? What approaches would students who do not wish to conform take toward clothing and entertainment?

READING CHECK

Fearing communism and threats of nuclear war, many Americans sought comfort in their religion. Attendance in churches and at synagogues increased. Evangelists catered to the trend toward religion by delivering sermons over the radio or on television.

BIOGRAPHY

Billy Graham b. 1918

Evangelist Billy Graham gained a wide following during the 1950s. Born in Charlotte, North Carolina, William Franklin Graham, Jr., was the son of a prosperous dairy farmer. In 1939, he was ordained as a Southern Baptist minister, and he went on to graduate from college in 1943.

Graham then joined an organization founded to minister to young soldiers during World War II. Following the war, he appeared at tent revivals and religious rallies in the United States and Europe.

Thousands of Americans flocked to hear Graham preach throughout the United States. His direct style of speaking made religion accessible, and he became known as fundamentalism's chief spokesperson. In addition to his televised crusades, Graham founded *Decision* magazine and wrote several books. Graham's prominence continued to grow, and in 1996, he was awarded the Congressional Gold Medal.

READING CHECK
Why did some Americans return to religion in the 1950s?

Youth Culture Some called the youth of the 1950s the "silent generation." The silent generation seemed to have little interest in the problems and crises of the larger world.

The strong economy of the 1950s allowed more young people to stay in school rather than having to leave early to find a job. Before World War I, most youths left school in their mid-teens to help support their families. In the 1920s, however, more and more children were able to complete secondary school. Because jobs were scarce during the Depression, many teenagers stayed in school. By the 1950s, most middle-class teenagers were expected to stay in school, holding only part-time jobs, if they worked at all. With more leisure time, some young people appeared to devote all their energies to organizing parties and pranks, joining fraternities and sororities, and generally pursuing entertainment and fun.

Some teenagers, most of them girls, baby-sat in their spare time. Young parents who moved to the suburbs were less able to turn to members of their extended family for help with child-care. By the 1950s, baby-sitting had for the first time become a job done not by relatives, but by the young daughters of friends and neighbors. By the end of the decade, half of all teenage girls were employed as part-time baby sitters.

Businesses seized the opportunity to sell products to the youth market. Advertisements and movies helped to build an image of what it meant to be a teenager in the 1950s. The girls were shown in bobby socks and poodle skirts, and the boys wore letter sweaters. These images created a greater sense of conformity in style. The media's ideal of the clean-cut teen could also be seen on such television shows as *Leave It to Beaver* and *Father Knows Best.* Magazines targeting youth, including *Seventeen, Datebook, Teen,* and *Cool,* offered plenty of advice to teenagers—not only on how to dress, but on how best to behave, especially when it came to dating.

Teenage girls collected items such as silver and linens in anticipation of marriage, which was often just after high school. The number of teenage brides rose in the 1950s, so that by 1954, close to half of all brides were in their teens, typically marrying grooms just slightly older.

A Resurgence in Religion In the 1950s, Americans, who had drifted away from religion in earlier years, flocked back to their churches and synagogues. The renewed interest in religion was a response in part to the Cold War struggle against "godless communism." Some looked to religion to find hope in the face of the threat of nuclear war.

Evidence of the newfound commitment to religion was abundant. In 1954, Congress added the words "under God" to the Pledge of Allegiance, and the next year it required the phrase "In God We Trust" to appear on all American currency. Like other aspects of American life, religion became more commercial. Those in need could call Dial-a-Prayer, and new slogans that sounded a lot like advertising—"the family that prays together stays together," for example—became commonplace. Evangelists used radio and television to carry their messages to more people than ever before. By the end of the 1950s, about 95 percent of all Americans said they felt connected to some formal religious group.

Men's and Women's Roles

Americans in the post–World War II years were keenly aware of the roles that they were expected to play as men and women. These roles were defined by

RESOURCE DIRECTORY

Teaching Resources
Biography, Literature, and Comparing Primary Sources booklet (Comparing Primary Sources) *On Rock and Roll,* pp. 149–150

Technology
Sounds of an Era Audio CD The Feminine Mystique, *Betty Friedan*
RESOURCE PRO® Critical Thinking Activity
Determining Relevance: Wages, Hours, and Unions, found on Resource Pro, uses graphs of American work statistics between 1900 and 1960 to help students apply this skill.

RESOURCE PRO® Literature Activity
Nonconformity in the 1950s, found on Resource Pro, features a passage from the novel *On the Road* by Jack Kerouac, the author whose work and life are often considered synonymous with the "Beat Generation."

social and religious traditions that had broad appeal to Americans. Men were expected to go to school and then find jobs to support wives and children. Theirs was the public sphere, the world away from home, where they earned money and made important political, economic, and social decisions.

Women were expected to play a supporting role in their husbands' lives. They kept house, cooked meals, and raised children. Many parents turned to pediatrician Dr. Benjamin Spock for child-care advice. His book *The Common Sense Book of Baby and Child Care* (1946) had a major impact on child-rearing practices. Most middle-class women settled into the domestic role and took on the demands of raising children and maintaining their suburban homes. In 1956, *Life* magazine published "Busy Wife's Achievements." The article profiled a housewife who had married at the age of 16, had four children, and kept busy with the PTA, Campfire Girls, and charity causes. She served as "home manager, mother, hostess, and useful civic worker." Her family duties and community service were typical of many middle-class suburban women.

Challenges to Conformity

Social conformity made it easy to mask the differences among individuals and groups. Not all Americans fit the model of American middle-class life described above, however.

Women at Work Many women had enjoyed working outside the home during World War II and were reluctant to give up their good jobs. Some women, single and married, worked simply to make ends meet. Although the norm was for women to leave their jobs once they were married, not all women did. In 1950, about 24 percent of all married American women had jobs. By 1960, the figure had risen to 31 percent. Married women with jobs had first begun to outnumber unmarried women with jobs near the end of World War II; in the postwar years, the gap grew even larger.

Most of the women who worked outside the home held jobs as secretaries, teachers, nurses, and sales clerks. Besides the satisfaction of earning their own money, women wanted to be able to buy the items that were part of "the good life," such as cars and electric appliances.

In 1963, Betty Friedan published a critique of the 1950s ideal of womanhood. In *The Feminine Mystique*, Friedan lashed out at the culture that made it difficult for women to choose alternative roles. Millions of women, Friedan charged, were frustrated with their roles in the 1950s:

> 66 It was unquestioned gospel [in the 1950s] that women could identify with nothing beyond the home—not politics, not art, not science, not events large or small, war or peace, in the United States or the world, unless it could be approached through female experience as a wife or mother or translated into domestic detail! 99
>
> —Betty Friedan, *The Feminine Mystique*

Youthful Rebellions Young people also challenged the norms of 1950s society. Some young people rejected the values of their parents and felt

Focus on DAILY LIFE

Tupperware Parties Tupperware, a line of flexible plastic containers designed by Earl Silas Tupper, became popular after World War II. Many women sold Tupperware from their homes in the 1950s, making the "Tupperware party" a fixture of the suburban social scene. Sales "hostesses" invited friends and acquaintances over for product demonstrations in an atmosphere designed to make the buyer feel relaxed and at home. At the party's end, the hostess took product orders, earning a commission from her sales. As buyers and sellers, some women found home-based sales to be less intimidating than the door-to-door sales that were also popular in the 1950s. In 1954, Tupperware vice president Brownie Wise, the pioneer of home parties, was the first woman to appear on the cover of *BusinessWeek*. Above is a 1946 ad for Tupperware.

INTERPRETING GRAPHS
The graph shows the numbers of single and married women in the labor force from 1900 to 1960.
Making Comparisons *Which years show more single women than married women in the work force?*

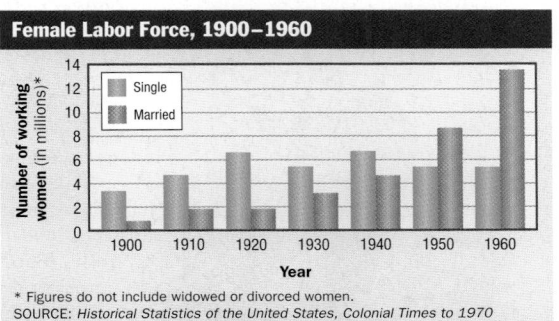

Female Labor Force, 1900–1960

Number of working women (in millions)*

Legend: Single, Married

Years: 1900, 1910, 1920, 1930, 1940, 1950, 1960

* Figures do not include widowed or divorced women.
SOURCE: *Historical Statistics of the United States, Colonial Times to 1970*

COMPARING PRIMARY SOURCES
Rock-and-Roll Music

When the defiant beat of rock-and-roll burst onto the American scene in the mid-1950s, few people remained impartial about its sound or its impact.

Analyzing Viewpoints What does each viewpoint below say about the relationship between rock-and-roll music and juvenile delinquency?

In Favor of Rock-and-Roll

"If my kids are home at night listening to my radio program, and get interested enough to go out and buy records and have a collection to listen to and dance to, I think I'm fighting delinquency."
—*Radio disc jockey Alan Freed,*
the New York Times,
January 12, 1958

Opposed to Rock-and-Roll

"Rock 'n' roll . . . is sung, played and written for the most part by [mentally deficient] goons and by means of its almost imbecilic repetition and sly, lewd, in plain fact, dirty lyrics . . . it manages to be the [warlike] music of every sideburned delinquent on the face of the earth."
—*Singer Frank Sinatra,*
the New York Times,
January 12, 1958

Teenagers listened to the new rock-and-roll music on record players.

Elvis Presley was a star performer in the early days of rock-and-roll.

misunderstood and alone. A few films, such as *Rebel Without a Cause*, released in 1955, captured these feelings of alienation. The movie's young star, James Dean, became a teen idol and a film legend.

Holden Caulfield, the main character in J. D. Salinger's 1951 novel *The Catcher in the Rye*, is troubled by the "phonies" he sees at boarding school and in the world around him. Throughout the book, Holden struggles to preserve his own integrity despite the fierce pressure to conform. Many readers could relate to this experience.

Young people sought a style they could call their own. In 1951, disc jockey Alan Freed began hosting a radio show in Cleveland, Ohio, playing what was called black rhythm-and-blues music for a largely black audience. Though other white—and black—disc jockeys were playing rhythm-and-blues at the time, the music did not have a wide audience. Freed's charismatic on-air style quickly drew a broad audience of teenage listeners, both black and white. Freed's program, "Moondog Rock 'n' Roll Party" gave important exposure to the music, which grew out of rhythm-and-blues and came to be called **rock-and-roll.** Teenagers across the nation quickly became fans of the driving beat and simple melodies that characterized rock-and-roll. They rushed to buy records of their favorite performers: African American stars such as Chuck Berry, Little Richard, and Fats Domino; and white musicians including Bill Haley and the Comets, Jerry Lee Lewis, and Buddy Holly.

One of the best-known rock-and-roll singers was Elvis Presley. Presley's performances showcased his flamboyant style and good looks. He attracted hordes of screaming teenage girls everywhere he went. Presley released many records that became huge hits, including "Don't Be Cruel," "Hound Dog," and "Heartbreak Hotel." From the United States, rock music spread to Europe and Asia, becoming popular with listeners and influencing musicians. Early songs by The Beatles, a British group that first performed in 1957, were inspired by American rock-and-roll.

Many adults disliked the new music, fearing it would cause a rise in immorality. For some people, opposition to rock-and-roll had to

910 Chapter 27 • *The Postwar Years at Home*

do with race. Rock-and-roll, in its appeal to both black and white teenagers, and in its black rhythm-and-blues origins, threatened many who were comfortable with racial segregation in the 1950s and who were uncomfortable with the idea of black and white teenagers attending the same concerts and dancing to the same music. Despite some efforts to ban rock concerts and keep records out of stores, rock-and-roll's popularity continued to soar.

Members of the "Beat Generation," called **beatniks,** launched a different kind of challenge. Beatniks, some of them writers, some artists, some simply participants in the movement, promoted spontaneity, or acting at a moment's notice without planning. They stressed spirituality and the need for release from the world of money and property. Beatniks challenged traditional patterns of respectability and shocked other Americans with their more open sexuality and their use of illegal drugs.

Author Jack Kerouac, whom many considered the leader of the beat generation, gathered with others in coffee houses in San Francisco, California, to share ideas and experiences. The unconventional Kerouac published his best-selling novel *On the Road* in 1957. He typed the first complete draft in less than a month, and on one continuous roll of paper. This was a reflection of his free-flowing, spontaneous writing method. The novel's "wild form," as Kerouac described it, was meant to reflect an open approach to life. One of Kerouac's friends, Allen Ginsberg, used the unstructured and chaotic style of the Beat Movement to write his influential epic poem "Howl," which begins, "I saw the best minds of my generation destroyed by madness . . ."

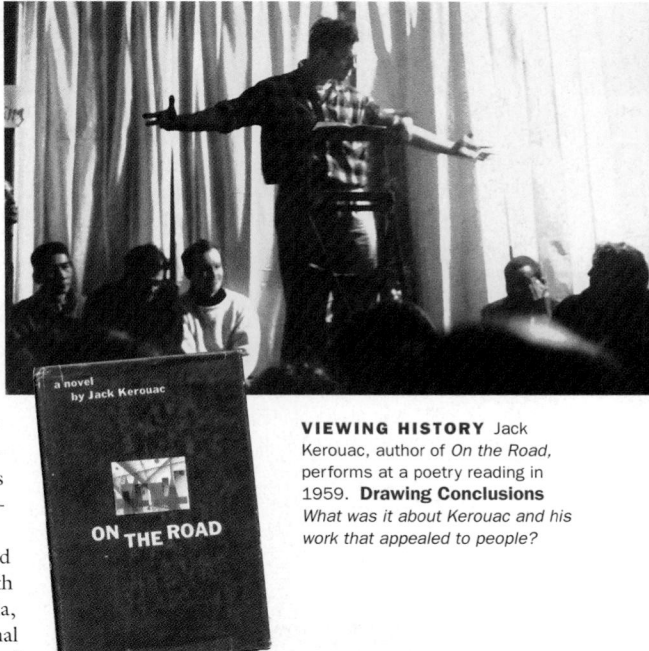

VIEWING HISTORY Jack Kerouac, author of *On the Road*, performs at a poetry reading in 1959. **Drawing Conclusions** *What was it about Kerouac and his work that appealed to people?*

Section 2 · Assessment

READING COMPREHENSION

1. Why did some people call 1950s youth the "silent generation"?

2. Why did Americans renew their interest in religion during the 1950s?

3. How did **rock-and-roll** influence life in the 1950s?

4. How did **beatniks** challenge conformity?

CRITICAL THINKING AND WRITING

5. **Making Comparisons** Describe the roles of men and women in 1950s society.

6. **Writing an Interview** Ask a relative, a neighbor, or a friend who grew up in the 1950s about what life was like for young people at that time. Write your interview in question-and-answer format.

Activity: Writing a Report
Research the history of rock-and-roll and write a brief report on its social impact. Use the links provided in the *America: Pathways to the Present* area of the following Web site for help in completing this activity.
www.phschool.com

Chapter 27 • Section 2   **911**

Reading Comprehension

1. They seemed to have little interest in the problems of the larger world; the stronger economy allowed the youth generation to stay in school, delaying their entry into the workforce and "real world" responsibilities.

2. In part as a response to the Cold War's "godless communism," Americans turned to religion to find hope in the face of the threat of nuclear war. As a result, religion grew more commercial, thereby attracting even more interest.

3. It gave young people a style of their own, causing adults to fear a rise in immorality and some to oppose this type of music on a racial basis, preferring segregation to watching young blacks and whites enjoy attending concerts together.

4. Stressing spirituality and the need for release from the material world, beatniks challenged traditional patterns of respectability.

Critical Thinking and Writing

5. Men assumed the public sphere. They worked outside the home and brought in money to support the family. Women primarily played a supporting role, working within the home, raising children, and managing the family, though some women did work outside the home.

6. Answers will vary, but questions included in the interview should reflect themes from the section.

Take It to the NET

Reports should focus on the social impact of rock-and-roll, including its effects on racial issues, youth culture, and the relationship between the generations. Students should demonstrate an understanding of the connection between social identity, age, class, and musical style that continues today.

CAPTION ANSWERS

Viewing History Kerouac's fans found his spontaneity and his writing style to be refreshing.

Chapter 27 Section 2 • **911**

Domestic Politics and Policy

READING FOCUS

- What were Truman's domestic policies as outlined in his Fair Deal?
- How did Truman win the election of 1948?
- What was the Republican approach to government during the Eisenhower presidency?

MAIN IDEA

Presidents Harry Truman and Dwight Eisenhower used two very different styles of leadership to meet the challenges they faced during the postwar period.

KEY TERMS

reconversion
Taft-Hartley Act
Modern Republicanism
National Aeronautics and
   Space Administration
   (NASA)
National Defense
   Education Act

TAKING NOTES

Copy the web diagram below. As you read, fill in each blank circle with details about Eisenhower's policies.

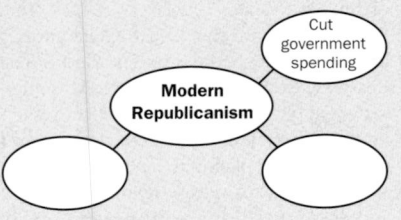

Setting the Scene The 1950s were conservative years— politically as well as culturally. The government felt public pressure to maintain the nation's newly won prosperity. Democrat Harry Truman first struggled with the problems of moving to a peacetime economy, and then fought for a reform program blocked repeatedly by Congress.

Republican Dwight Eisenhower took a more low-key approach to the presidency. One economic advisor, Gabriel Hauge, recalled that Eisenhower was "very decent, wholesome in his instincts, terribly free of the little meannesses that often plague great men's lives." His genial, reassuring manner made him one of the most popular Presidents in the years following World War II.

Truman's Domestic Policies

Harry Truman wanted to follow in Franklin Roosevelt's footsteps, but he often appeared ill-prepared for the presidency. He seemed to have a scattershot approach to governing, offering a new batch of proposals in every speech. People wondered where his focus lay.

The Peacetime Economy Truman's first priority was **reconversion**—the social and economic transition from wartime to peacetime. Soldiers wanted to return home, and politicians were flooded with messages that warned, "No boats, no votes." Truman responded quickly and got most soldiers home by 1946.

Lifting the economic controls that had kept wartime inflation in check proved a more difficult challenge. Most Americans had limited access to consumer goods during World War II. Now they wanted those goods, and they wanted them right away. In an effort to make the economy more responsive to consumer preferences, the government eased the controls in July 1946, and prices soared almost 25 percent. Since wages failed to keep up with prices, many people still could not enjoy the fruits of their years of sacrifice.

VIEWING HISTORY These former servicemen are picketing the entrance to a Pennsylvania coal mine in 1946 to demand jobs. **Analyzing Information** One of the signs held in the photo reads "Fought for U.S.A., Now Discarded." What is the complaint this man is making?

In some ways, the economic issues facing the United States at the end of World War II were similar to those at the end of World War I. Workers demanded wage increases that they had forgone for the sake of the war effort. In 1946, nearly 4.6 million workers went on strike, more than ever before in the United States. Strikes hit the automobile, steel, electrical, coal, and railroad industries, and affected nearly everyone in the country.

Although Truman agreed that workers deserved higher wages, he thought that their demands were inflationary. That is, he feared that such increases would push the prices of goods still higher. In his view, workers failed to understand that big wage increases might destroy the health of the economy.

In the spring of 1946, a railroad strike caused a major disruption in the economy. In response, Truman asked Congress for the power to draft the striking workers into the army. He would then be able to order them as soldiers to stay on the job. Determining that Truman's request was an overreaction to the strike, the Senate refused to go along.

Truman's White House took other steps to limit the power of labor unions as well. When John L. Lewis and his United Mine Workers defied a court order against a strike, the Truman administration asked a judge to serve Lewis with a contempt of court citation. The court fined Lewis $10,000 and his union $3.5 million.

Congress went even further than Truman: In 1947, it passed the **Taft-Hartley Act.** This act allowed the President to declare an 80-day cooling-off period during which strikers had to return to work, in strikes in industries that affected the national interest. Reflecting the widespread anti-Communist feelings gripping the United States at the time, the measure also required union officials to sign oaths that they were not Communists. Furious union leaders complained bitterly about the measure, and Truman vetoed it. Congress, however, passed the act over Truman's veto.

Truman's Fair Deal Truman had supported Roosevelt's New Deal, and now, playing on the well-known name, he devised a program he called the Fair Deal. The Fair Deal extended the New Deal's goals.

Truman agreed with FDR that government needed to play an active role in securing economic justice for all American citizens. As the war ended, he introduced a 21-point program that included legislation designed to promote full employment, a higher minimum wage, greater unemployment compensation for workers without jobs, housing assistance, and a variety of other items. Over the next ten weeks, Truman added more proposals to the Fair Deal. By early 1946, he had asked for a national health insurance program and legislation to control atomic energy.

Truman ran into tremendous political opposition in Congress from a coalition of conservative Democrats and Republicans. Opponents rejected the majority of the Fair Deal initiatives. One measure that passed was the Employment Act of 1946, which created a Council of Economic Advisors to advise the President.

As the 1946 midterm elections approached, it seemed to many people that Truman was little more than a bungling bureaucrat. Among the remarks often heard about Truman were, "You just sort of forget about Harry until he makes another mistake," and "To err is Truman," adapted

VIEWING HISTORY Truman sits at his desk in the White House. **Analyzing Information** Why would Truman place a sign reading "The buck stops here" on his desk?

The leader of the United Mine Workers, John Lewis (left), opposed the Taft-Hartley Act cosponsored by Senator Robert Taft (right).

Focus Presidents Truman and Eisenhower presented Americans with different approaches to government and to the challenges facing the post-war nation. How did they disagree about the proper role of government and the way to solve the nation's social problems?

Instruct Discuss the tasks that needed to be accomplished to return the nation to stability after World War II. Ask students to assess how well Truman carried out each of these tasks and show how he was a New Dealer in his view of the appropriate role of government in American life. Ask how the Fair Deal extended Roosevelt's New Deal.

Assess/Reteach Ask students to summarize the differences in Truman and Eisenhower's governing styles. In what ways was each leader most effective?

ACTIVITY
Connecting with Economics

Have students conduct research to determine the total numbers of American servicemen and women who were overseas at the end of World War II. Have them also determine the total population of the United States at the time. Direct students to calculate the percentage of the country's population that was repatriated at the end of the war to analyze the effects of changing demographic patterns resulting from migration within the United States. Have students speculate on the effects such a percentage of returning people might have had on the American economy. **(Logical/Mathematical)**

TEST PREPARATION

Have students reread the section "Truman's Fair Deal" on this page and then have them answer the question below.

Which of the following statements is NOT correct?

A The Fair Deal extended FDR's New Deal.

(B) Truman was able to gain wide support for the Fair Deal from both parties.

C The aim of the Fair Deal was economic justice.

D The Fair Deal proposed an increase in the minimum wage.

CAPTION ANSWERS

Viewing History Truman means that as President, he is the man responsible for what happens in his administration, and that he is not afraid of making decisions.

from a well-known saying. Truman's support in one poll dropped from 87 percent just after he assumed the presidency to 32 percent in November 1946. The results of the 1946 elections reflected many people's feelings that Truman was not an effective leader. Republicans won majorities of both houses of Congress.

The 80th Congress battered the President for the next two years. Under the leadership of the conservative Republican senator Robert A. Taft of Ohio, commonly known as "Mr. Republican," the Republican Party worked hard to reduce the size and the power of the federal government, to decrease taxes, and to block Truman's liberal goals. On civil rights initiatives, in particular, Truman found opposition throughout his presidency.

Truman on Civil Rights   While holding in private many of the racial prejudices he had learned growing up, Truman recognized that as President he had to take action on civil rights. In a letter to a friend, he wrote, "I am not asking for social equality, because no such things exist, but I am asking for equality of opportunity for all human beings, and, as long as I stay here, I am going to continue that fight."

Truman had publicly supported civil rights for many years. In September 1946, he met with a group of African American leaders to discuss the steps that needed to be taken to achieve their goals. They asked Truman to support a federal anti-lynching law, abolish the poll tax as a voting requirement, and establish a permanent board to prevent discriminatory practices in hiring. Congress refused to address any of these concerns, so in December 1946, Truman appointed a biracial Committee on Civil Rights to look into race relations. This group produced a report demanding action on the concerns listed above. It also recommended that a permanent civil rights commission be established.

A majority of the members of Congress disagreed with the report, and as a result, Congress took no action. In July 1948, Truman banned discrimination in the hiring of federal employees. He also ordered an end to segregation and discrimination in the armed forces. Real change came slowly, however. Only with the onset of the Korean War in 1950 did the armed forces make significant progress in ending segregation.

VIEWING HISTORY Harry Truman became the first President ever to campaign in Harlem, the heart of New York City's African American community. The campaign button (top) supports his civil rights stance. **Synthesizing Information** *How did Truman's support of civil rights cause a split in the Democratic Party?*

The Election of 1948

Truman decided to seek another term as President in 1948. He had no reason to expect victory, however, because even in his own party, his support was disintegrating. The southern wing of the Democratic Party, protesting a moderate civil rights plank in the party platform, split off from the main party. These segregationists formed the States' Rights, or Dixiecrat Party and nominated Governor J. Strom Thurmond of South Carolina for President.

Meanwhile, the liberal wing of the Democratic Party deserted Truman to follow Henry Wallace, who headed the Progressive Party ticket. Wallace had been Franklin Roosevelt's second Vice President, and many Democrats believed that he was the right person to carry out the measures begun by Roosevelt. Most recently Wallace had served as Truman's Secretary of Commerce. Wallace had resigned, however, because he did not support Truman's Cold War policies.

CAPTION ANSWERS

Viewing History Segregationist southern Democrats formed a separate party, the States' Rights Party.

Running against Republican Thomas E. Dewey, governor of New York, Truman crisscrossed the country by train. He campaigned not so much against Dewey as against the Republican Congress, which the President repeatedly mocked as the "do-nothing" 80th Congress. Truman's campaign style was blunt and effective. In off-the-cuff speeches, he challenged all Americans: "If you send another Republican Congress to Washington, you're a bigger bunch of suckers than I think you are." "Give 'em hell, Harry," the people yelled as Truman got going. And he did.

Among other things, Truman vehemently attacked Congress's farm policy. In the past, a federal price-support program had permitted farmers to borrow money to store surplus crops until someone bought the produce. Recently, however, Congress had kept the Commodity Credit Corporation, responsible for buying the surplus, from buying or leasing storage bins. Unforeseen by legislators of either party, the 1948 harvest was especially good. With commercial storage space filled, farmers were forced to sell their surpluses on the open market at very low prices. Truman attacked Congress, saying it had "stuck a pitchfork in the farmers' backs."

On election day, although virtually all experts and polls had picked Dewey to win, Truman scored an astounding upset. Furthermore, Democrats won control of Congress. With this victory, Truman stepped out of FDR's shadow to claim the presidency in his own right.

Truman looked forward to a chance to push further for his legislative goals. Over the next four years, however, the Fair Deal scored only occasional successes. Instances of corruption among federal officials hurt Truman's image.

Longtime Democratic control over the White House frustrated many Republicans, who were opposed to any legacy of the New Deal. Debate over presidential term limits had flared up after Roosevelt won his unprecedented third and fourth terms. Up until that time, the two-term presidency had been upheld by custom—as set by George Washington—rather than by law. Republicans, together with southern Democrats, moved for the passage of a constitutional amendment limiting a President to two terms. The amendment won more than enough votes in both houses. Truman was silent on the matter, and Americans showed little concern for the issue. It was in the absence of public opposition, rather than with any overwhelming public support, that the Twenty-second Amendment was adopted in 1951. It states, in part:

> **KEY DOCUMENTS** 66 *No person shall be elected to the office of the President more than twice, and no person who has held the office of President, or acted as President, for more than two years of a term to which some other person was elected President shall be elected to the office of the President more than once.* 99
>
> —The Twenty-second Amendment

The amendment's passage did little to keep politicians from debating the issue. Since then analysts have wondered if term limitations render a second-term President less effective than one empowered to seek reelection.

The *Chicago Daily Tribune* was so certain of Truman's defeat that it printed this edition before all the votes were tallied.

The "I like Ike" message was seen in many places in 1952, even on cosmetics containers.

The amendment contained specific language that allowed Truman to be reelected. Nonetheless, he decided not to run again in 1952. Instead, the Democrats chose Adlai Stevenson, governor of Illinois, as their presidential candidate.

Eisenhower and the Republican Approach

Running against Stevenson for the Republicans was Dwight Eisenhower, former commander in chief of the Allied forces. As a public figure, Eisenhower's approach to politics differed from that of Harry Truman. Whereas Truman was a scrappy fighter, Ike—as the people affectionately called Dwight Eisenhower—had always been a talented diplomat. During World War II, Eisenhower forged agreements among Allied military commanders. His easygoing charm gave Americans a sense of security.

By 1952, Americans across the land were chanting, "I like Ike." The Republicans devised a "K_1C_2" formula for victory, which focused on three problems: Korea, communism, and corruption. Eisenhower promised to end the Korean War, and the Republican Party guaranteed a tough approach to the Communist challenge. Eisenhower's vice-presidential running mate, Californian Richard M. Nixon, hammered on the topic of corruption in government.

The Checkers Speech In spite of his overwhelming popularity, Eisenhower's candidacy hit a snag in September 1952. Newspapers accused Richard Nixon of having a special fund, set up by rich Republican supporters. "Secret Nixon Fund!" and "Secret Rich Man's Trust Fund Keeps Nixon in Style Beyond His Salary," screamed typical headlines. In fact, Nixon had done nothing wrong, but the accusation that he had received illegal gifts from political friends was hard to shake.

Nixon's broadcast of his "Checkers" speech on national television was well received by viewers.

Soon, cries arose for Eisenhower to dump Nixon from the ticket. Eisenhower decided to allow Nixon to save himself, if he could. In response to the allegation, Nixon delivered a televised speech, emotionally denying wrongful use of campaign funds. He also gave a detailed account of his personal finances. In response to the charge that he was living above his means, he described his wife, Pat, as wearing a "respectable Republican cloth coat."

The emotional climax of the speech came when Nixon admitted that he had, in fact, received one gift from a political supporter:

> ❝ It was a little cocker spaniel dog. . . . Black and white spotted. And our little girl—Tricia, the 6-year-old—named it Checkers. And you know the kids love that dog and I just want to say this right now, that regardless of what they say about it, we're going to keep it. ❞
> —Richard Nixon, September 23, 1952

Sounds of an Era

Listen to part of Richard Nixon's "Checkers" speech and other sounds from the postwar years.

At the end of his speech, Nixon requested that the American people contact the Eisenhower campaign to register their opinions as to whether or not he should stay on the Republican ticket. People from all across the nation called, wired, and wrote to Eisenhower, demanding that Nixon continue as his running mate. Nixon had turned a political disaster into a public relations bonanza.

Support for Eisenhower continued to grow through the fall. Ike got 55 percent of the popular vote and swept into office with a Republican Congress.

Eisenhower as President Ike's natural inclination was to work behind the scenes. "I am not one of those desk-pounding types that likes to stick out his jaw and look like he is bossing the show," Eisenhower said. Critics misinterpreted his apparent lack of leadership, joking about an Eisenhower doll—you wound it up and it did nothing. Eisenhower defended his approach, declaring:

> ❝ I'll tell you what leadership is. It's persuasion—and conciliation—and education—and patience. It's long, slow tough work. That's the only kind of leadership I know or believe in—or will practice. ❞
>
> —Dwight Eisenhower

The American people approved of Ike's style. In 1956, Eisenhower once again faced Stevenson and easily won reelection. This time he garnered an even greater margin of victory, with almost 58 percent of the vote. The Democrats, however, having regained control of Congress in midterm elections, continued to lead both houses after the 1956 election.

Modern Republicanism   In domestic matters, Eisenhower was determined to slow the growth of the federal government. He also wanted to limit the President's power and increase the authority of Congress and the courts. Eisenhower was not, however, interested in completely reversing the New Deal.

Ike's priorities included cutting spending, reducing taxes, and balancing the budget. He called this approach to government "dynamic conservatism" or **Modern Republicanism.** He intended to be "conservative when it comes to money, liberal when it comes to human beings."

In the tradition of past Republican Presidents such as Coolidge and Hoover, Eisenhower favored big business. His Cabinet was composed mostly of successful businessmen, plus one union leader. Critics charged that the Eisenhower Cabinet consisted of "eight millionaires and a plumber."

Modern Republicanism sought to encourage and support corporate America. Eisenhower's administration transferred control of about $40 billion worth of

READING CHECK
What were Eisenhower's domestic priorities?

NOTABLE PRESIDENTS
Dwight D. Eisenhower

34th President
1953–1961

"I am no politician as you well know."
—Eisenhower, as he prepared to assume the presidency

Born in Texas in 1890, Dwight Eisenhower grew up in Abilene, Kansas. After high school he attended the United States Military Academy at West Point. As supreme commander of the Allied Expeditionary Force during World War II, Eisenhower oversaw the D-Day landings in France and the final defeat of Germany. After the war, he served as Army Chief of Staff, president of Columbia University, and then head of NATO, the North Atlantic Treaty Organization. In 1952, he ran for President as a Republican and won a landslide victory in the general election.

Eisenhower was a strong defender of American interests abroad, yet he also feared that high military spending would harm the economy. Therefore, Eisenhower endorsed a military strategy of relying on nuclear weapons, rather than more costly conventional armies, in conflicts around the world.

At home, Eisenhower generally favored restraint in government actions and spending.

Eisenhower's critics sometimes complained about his low-key approach to the presidency and accused him of providing weak leadership. Yet he offered the nation stability and reassurance during a dangerous period of the Cold War.

Connecting to Today
How might experience as a military leader help a President? Can you think of any ways in which such experience might not be helpful? Explain.

Take It to the NET Biography To read more about Dwight Eisenhower, visit the links provided in the *America: Pathways to the Present* area at the following Web site. **www.phschool.com**

Section 3 Assessment

Reading Comprehension

1. Answers may include: lifting economic controls while attempting to check inflation; workers demanding wage increases; 1946 railroad strike.

2. It allowed the President to declare an 80-day cooling-off period when strikes occurred in industries affecting national interests. During this time, strikers had to return to work while the government conducted an investigation. It also stipulated that union leaders had to declare under oath that they did not belong to the Communist party.

3. Policies of cutting spending, reducing taxes, and balancing the budget. He was determined to slow the growth of the government and support big business.

4. As a response to the concern that the U.S. was losing its technological edge to Russia and the fear that a nuclear attack was forthcoming.

5. A law designed to improve science and mathematics instruction in the schools so that the U.S. could meet the scientific and technical challenge from the Soviet Union.

Critical Thinking and Writing

6. Truman believed in an active, positive role for the federal government in social and economic matters; Eisenhower wanted to curb the role of the federal government in these areas.

7. Letters will vary, but should be supported with facts from the section.

Take It to the NET

Students' answers will vary, but may include an exploration of the reasons for the founding of NASA in 1958 and descriptions of the growth and development of early operations.

CAPTION ANSWERS

Viewing History As a world power, the United States wanted to compete with the Soviet Union on many levels. Soviet advances in space exploration, such as *Sputnik,* made NASA a priority.

VIEWING HISTORY Scientists (left to right) William Pickering, James Van Allen, and Wernher von Braun raise a model of the first U.S. satellite, *Explorer-I.* The scientists participated in the satellite program. **Drawing Conclusions** *Why did the government find it important to establish a space program in the 1950s?*

offshore oil lands from the federal government to the states so that the states could lease oil rights to corporations. It worked to end government competition with big business.

Ike's attempt to balance the budget backfired. His cuts in government spending caused the economy to slump. When that happened, tax revenues dropped, and the deficit grew larger instead of smaller. Economic growth, which had averaged 4.3 percent between 1947 and 1952, fell to 2.5 percent between 1953 and 1960. The country suffered three economic recessions during Eisenhower's presidency, from 1953 to 1954, from 1957 to 1958, and again from 1960 to 1961.

Despite America's economic troubles, Eisenhower helped the country maintain a mood of stability. He also underscored the basic commitment the government had made during the New Deal: to ensure the economic security of all Americans. For example, in 1954 and 1956, Social Security was extended to make eligible 10 million additional workers. In 1955, the minimum wage was raised from 75 cents to $1 an hour.

Meeting the Technology Challenge When the Soviet Union launched *Sputnik* in 1957, as described in the previous chapter, many Americans grew concerned that the United States was losing its competitive edge. Others feared a nuclear attack would soon follow. In 1958, the United States government responded by creating the **National Aeronautics and Space Administration (NASA),** as an independent agency for space exploration.

The same year, Congress passed and President Eisenhower signed into law the **National Defense Education Act.** The measure was designed to improve science and mathematics instruction in the schools so that the United States could meet the scientific and technical challenge from the Soviet Union. The act provided millions of dollars in low-cost loans to college students and significant reductions in repayments if they ultimately became teachers. The federal government also granted millions to state schools for building science and foreign language facilities.

Section 3 Assessment

READING COMPREHENSION

1. What issues did Truman face during the period of **reconversion?**

2. What was the **Taft-Hartley Act?**

3. What was **Modern Republicanism?** Why did Eisenhower embrace it?

4. Why was the **National Aeronautics and Space Administration (NASA)** created?

5. What was the **National Defense Education Act?**

CRITICAL THINKING AND WRITING

6. **Making Comparisons** Compare what President Truman and President Eisenhower each saw as the federal government's role in domestic matters.

7. **Writing a Letter** Review the issues that led to the passage of the Twenty-second Amendment. Write a letter to your state senator registering your opinion as to whether the amendment should be repealed.

Take It to the NET

Activity: Writing a News Article Investigate the early years of America's space program. Write an article on some aspect of NASA's first operations. Use the links provided in the *America: Pathways to the Present* area of the following Web site for help in completing this activity.
www.phschool.com

RESOURCE DIRECTORY

Teaching Resources
Units 7/8 booklet
 • Section 3 Quiz, p. 85
 • Chapter 27 Test, pp. 86, 89
Guide to the Essentials
 • Section 3 Summary, p. 139
 • Chapter 27 Test, p. 140

Other Print Resources
Chapter Tests with ExamView® Test Bank CD-ROM, Ch. 27

Technology
ExamView® Test Bank CD-ROM, Ch. 27
Social Studies Skills Tutor CD-ROM

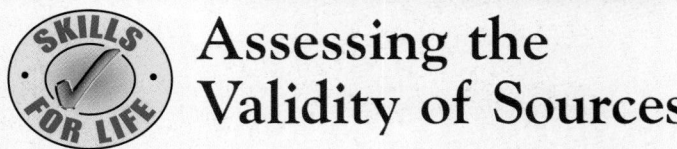

Assessing the Validity of Sources

Sometimes it seems that information is everywhere: in newspapers, magazines, and books; on television, radio, and the Internet. How can you tell which information is reliable? Your teacher or librarian can point you toward good sources, such as well-respected encyclopedias, publishers, and Web sites, but you can also make judgments about the validity of sources yourself. The sources at right discuss President Truman's veto of the 1947 Taft-Hartley Act.

LEARN THE SKILL

Use the following steps to assess the validity of sources:

1. **Determine what kind of information you need.** For current statistics, you need an up-to-date source. To learn about a historical event, you may want a primary source from the time. Remember, however, that causes and effects may have been unclear to the people writing when the event occurred.

2. **Ask yourself if the information is generally accurate.** Does it agree with sources you already know are reliable, such as a current encyclopedia?

3. **Check the qualifications of the author or publisher.** Is the author an expert on the subject? Is the magazine generally well respected? Is the Web site hosted by a reliable organization?

4. **Consider whether the author seems objective or biased.** An author who is trying to persuade might mention only certain facts, use "loaded" language, or state opinions as if they are proven facts.

PRACTICE THE SKILL

Answer the following questions:

1. **(a)** Do you need recent information to research this event? Explain. **(b)** What are the benefits of using a primary source such as A? **(c)** What might be one benefit of using a secondary source such as B?

2. **(a)** How might you check the information found in Source A for accuracy? **(b)** Source B includes extensive footnotes citing bibliographic sources. How does this information help you judge its reliability?

3. **(a)** What are the qualifications of the author of Source A for writing about this subject? **(b)** Do you have confidence in the author and publisher of Source B? Explain.

4. **(a)** Why is the author of Source A writing about this subject? Is he likely to be objective? Explain. **(b)** Does Source B seem to be objective or biased? Explain.

APPLY THE SKILL

See the Chapter Review and Assessment for another opportunity to apply this skill.

A

"My fellow countrymen:

At noon today I sent the Congress a message vetoing the Taft-Hartley labor bill. I vetoed this bill because I am convinced it is a bad bill. It is bad for labor, bad for management, bad for the country. . . .

This bill is deliberately designed to weaken labor unions. When the sponsors of the bill claim that by weakening unions, they are giving rights back to individual working men, they ignore the basic reason why unions are important in our democracy. Unions exist so that laboring men can bargain with their employers on a basis of equality. . . .

We have been told, by the supporters of the Taft-Hartley bill, that it would reduce industrial strife.

On the contrary, I am convinced that it would increase industrial strife. . . . because a number of its provisions deprive workers of legal protection of fundamental rights. They would then have no means of protecting those rights except by striking. . . ."

—Harry S Truman, radio address,
June 20, 1947

B

"Several quite important political factors indicated that signing the measure would be [Truman's] wisest course. The . . . desire of the nation for remedial labor legislation, plus the large majorities given the bill by Congress, made it fairly obvious that a veto would be overridden. Thus Truman would be placed in the embarrassing position of having tried to withhold legislation that the people demanded. . . .

But . . . [s]igning the proposal would be inconsistent with . . . the requests made in [Truman's] State of the Union message. . . . Then there was the apparently honest conviction that the bill would actually increase industrial strife. Reports of various competent advisers . . . indicated that the legislation was fundamentally unworkable. . . . "

—R. Alton Lee, Truman and Taft-Hartley: a
question of mandate,
University of Kentucky Press, 1966

ASSESSING THE VALIDITY OF SOURCES

Focus Students learn to compare and contrast the validity of primary and secondary material in seeking to understand a historical situation.

Instruct After students have read passage A, ask them to discuss the ways in which President Truman attempted to justify his actions. Do his arguments make sense? Next, have students read passage B, in which they gain more background on the situation. Truman's decision was very costly politically. How do students view his decision now, with more information on the background of the situation? Have students explain the usefulness of analyzing both primary and secondary sources in attempting to reconstruct a historical event.

Extend See the Skills for Life activity in the Resource Directory below.

ANSWERS
PRACTICE THE SKILL

1. **(a)** No. Most facts about the event are already known. **(b)** It is possible to find out Truman's views on the situation and how he thought he could convince the nation. **(c)** It is possible to gain more perspective and to hear an unbiased view.

2. **(a)** Though it might be helpful to read the bill itself for more background, the statements made by Truman are statements of opinion, not fact. **(b)** Footnotes and extensive bibliographic citation help support the validity of the author's assertions.

3. **(a)** The author of source A is the man who made the actual decision— President Truman. **(b)** A university press is generally considered a reliable source because the material it publishes is usually reviewed by experts for accuracy.

4. **(a)** Because he is trying to defend an unpopular stance he has taken by vetoing a bill. He is unlikely to be objective, because he is involved in the decision. **(b)** Source B appears to be objective because he presents both sides of the argument.

REVIEWING KEY TERMS

Students should refer to the definitions of key terms in the chapter to write sentences showing an understanding of domestic issues during the postwar era.

REVIEWING MAIN IDEAS

11. The conglomerate system led to the formation of giant corporations that owned businesses in many different areas of the economy. The franchise system meant that local businesses were sometimes pushed out of business by large chains.

12. New electronic components, such as transistors, aided in the development of new and improved products. Peaceful uses of atomic energy were also explored.

13. Suburbs developed because of urban decay, an increase in population, cheap and plentiful housing, improved roads, and availability of automobiles and fuel.

14. They seemed to have little interest in national and international issues; the stronger economy allowed the youth generation to stay in school; teenagers seemed to be mainly interested in enjoying themselves.

15. Men working as breadwinners, active in society and politics. Women at home in suburbia, tending to the house and children. Young people in school, pursuing fun in their free time. The media encouraged conformity in appearance and behavior, promoting, for example, the image of bobby socks and letter sweaters for teens.

16. They gave young people identities of their own as they rebelled against rigid societal roles and expectations.

17. The Fair Deal promoted full employment, a higher minimum wage, greater unemployment compensation, housing assistance, national health insurance, and atomic energy legislation. A coalition of conservative Democrats and Republicans in Congress opposed most of the Fair Deal initiatives.

18. He supported civil rights, appointing a biracial Committee on Civil Rights and banning discrimination in the hiring of federal employees and

creating a CHAPTER SUMMARY

Copy this flowchart (right) on a piece of paper and complete it by adding information about life in the United States after World War II.

 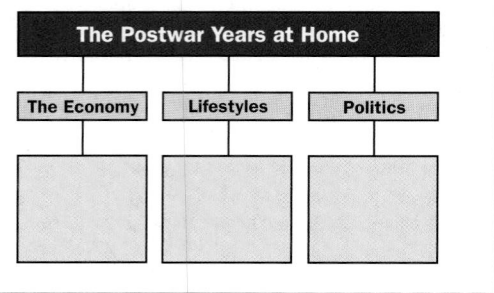

For additional review and enrichment activities, see the interactive version of *America: Pathways to the Present*, available on the Web and on CD-ROM.

The Postwar Years at Home

The Economy   Lifestyles   Politics

★ **Reviewing Key Terms**

For each of the terms below, write a sentence explaining how it relates to the postwar years.

1. per capita income
2. conglomerate
3. franchise
4. transistor
5. GI Bill of Rights
6. reconversion
7. Taft-Hartley Act
8. modern republicanism
9. National Aeronautics and Space Administration (NASA)
10. National Defense Education Act

★ **Reviewing Main Ideas**

11. How did the conglomerate and the franchise system change the American economy after World War II? (Section 1)

12. What technological advances took place during the postwar years? (Section 1)

13. What factors contributed to the development of the suburbs from 1945 to 1960? (Section 1)

14. Explain why children of the baby boom were sometimes called the "silent generation." (Section 2)

15. What was the model middle-class lifestyle of the 1950s? Give examples showing how the media fostered expectations of "the good life." (Section 2)

16. Why did young people identify with rock-and-roll and the beat movement in the 1950s? (Section 2)

17. Describe Truman's Fair Deal program and the congressional response to it. (Section 3)

18. What was Truman's stand on civil rights issues? (Section 3)

19. What effect did Eisenhower's leadership style have on his presidency? (Section 3)

★ **Critical Thinking**

20. **Recognizing Cause and Effect** How did Americans' experiences throughout the Depression and World War II affect consumer spending during the 1950s?

21. **Demonstrating Reasoned Judgment** Which technological advance of the 1950s—atomic energy, computers, or television—do you think has had the most far-reaching impact on the way Americans live? Explain why you think so.

22. **Identifying Central Issues** What economic changes occurred in the United States from 1945 to 1960? Explain why the changes occurred.

23. **Making Comparisons** Analyze the conflicts between labor unions and the Truman administration just after World War II. How did the situation compare to labor disputes that followed World War I?

24. **Identifying Assumptions** Why was the outcome of the 1948 election a surprise to some people? What issues did Truman raise in his campaign that helped secure his victory?

920 Chapter 27 • *The Postwar Years at Home*

CREATING A CHAPTER SUMMARY

The Postwar Years at Home

The Economy	Lifestyles	Politics
Businesses reorganize.	Alan Freed begins playing rock-and-roll in Cleveland.	Congress passes the GI Bill.
Efforts to reconvert the economy from wartime to peacetime	Americans begin to buy televisions.	Congress passes the Taft-Hartley Act.
The Fair Deal	Baby boom begins.	Very close election of 1948
	Housing boom in suburbs	White House is Republican for the first time in 20 years in 1953.
	Surge of auto use, highway construction	

Analyzing Political Cartoons ▶

25. A cartoonist drew this view of suburban life in 1952. (a) What is most striking about this community? (b) What do you know about such communities?

26. Read the caption. What is the cause of the woman's dilemma?

27. What is the cartoonist saying about life in a 1950s suburb?

Interpreting Data

Turn to the chart "Average Household TV Viewing Hours, 1950–1990" in Section 1.

28. During what year was TV viewing at its lowest point?
   A 1950
   B 1960
   C 1970
   D 1980

29. By how much time did average daily television viewing per household increase from 1950 to 1960?
   F 1 hour, 29 minutes
   G 31 minutes
   H 29 minutes
   J 45 minutes

Applying the Chapter Skill: *Assessing the Validity of Sources*

30. Using the library or the Internet, find five other sources of information on the Taft-Hartley Act. How does the validity of those five sources compare to that of the two sources used on the skill page at the end of this chapter?

"I'm Mrs. Edward M. Barnes. Where do I live?"

ACTIVITIES

Writing to LEARN

Journal Writing
What it would be like to return to life at home after serving in World War II? Finding a job, reconnecting with friends and family, and adjusting to postwar social and economic conditions were some of the issues that returning soldiers faced. Write a journal entry from a returning soldier's point of view that addresses some of these topics.

Primary Source CD-ROM

Working With Primary Sources Find additional information on the post–World War II years on the *Exploring Primary Sources in U.S. History CD-ROM* and use the selection(s) provided to complete the Chapter 27 primary source activity located in the *America: Pathways to the Present* area of the following Web site. **www.phschool.com**

Take It to the NET

Chapter Self-Test As a review activity, take the Chapter 27 Self-Test in the *America: Pathways to the Present* area at the Web site listed below. The questions are designed to test your understanding of the chapter content. **www.phschool.com**

Chapter 27 Assessment **921**

19. Eisenhower's behind-the-scenes leadership increased his popularity with the American people. The stability and reassurance he offered led to his reelection.

CRITICAL THINKING

20. People were eager to buy everything that the war and the Depression had denied them.

21. Answers will vary. Students may point out that television has been blamed for such problems as violence and consumerism; computers have become elements of daily life, changing both work and recreation; and atomic energy has raised concerns about waste disposal, accidents, and terrorism.

22. Answers may vary, but should include: under President Truman, inflation set in as wartime economic controls were lifted and wages remained low. There was overall prosperity during Eishenhower's term, with three recessions caused by his efforts to reduce federal government size and balance the budget.

23. In both cases, workers demanded increases that they had forgone for the war effort; the number of strikes soared and affected many industries; in both time periods unemployment was a problem, and strong anti-Communist feelings dominated.

24. Truman's support, even from his own party, had fallen. Truman stressed that the Republican Congress did little to effect progress. He attacked its farm policy, giving him the farmers' support.

SKILLS ASSESSMENT

25. (a) Its uniformity. (b) Prefabricated communities were built of affordable, mass-produced houses in the postwar years by Levitt and other developers.

26. She cannot distinguish her home from the others.

27. It lacks individuality and originality.

28. A

29. G

30. Answers will vary, but students should check the qualifications of the author or publisher for the five sources. For example, they should note if a Web site is a personal home page or if it is hosted by a reliable organization, such as the government or a university.

ANSWERS TO ACTIVITIES

Writing to LEARN
Answers will vary, but should explore social, economic, and political themes discussed in the chapter.

Primary Source CD-ROM
Direct students to the additional primary sources that can be found on the *Exploring Primary Sources in U.S. History CD-ROM*.

Take It to the NET
Additional support materials and activities for Chapter 27 of *America: Pathways to the Present* can be found in the Social Studies area at the Prentice Hall School Web site. **www.phschool.com**

THE RISE OF THE SUBURBS

Focus Explain that before the postwar building boom, only the wealthy could afford to live in the suburbs. After the war, prosperity and government programs to finance mortgages started a suburban building boom that changed the way many Americans lived.

Instruct Show students a detailed map of the nearest large city and its surrounding suburbs. Ask students to point out the core city, beltways, and "edge cities."

Ask students to list ways in which the development of suburban housing changed American life. Ask them to consider:

- The family: How did suburban housing encourage nuclear, as opposed to extended, families?

- The environment: What impact did the growth of suburbs have on wildlife, quality of air and water, and amount of farmland?

- Integration: Did the growth of suburbs encourage or discourage integration of housing and schools?

Extend Many observers thought that the shopping mall would become the "community center" of the suburbs, filling the roles of Main Street, the town common, the city square, and the neighborhood playground. Ask students how successful they think shopping malls have been in creating a sense of community. What activities other than shopping, such as eating meals, taking an exercise class, or going to a movie, are available in shopping malls?

The Rise of the Suburbs

In the decades after World War II, millions of Americans moved from older cities to new suburban developments. By the 1960s, a new landscape of single-family homes and shopping malls had spread across the land. This phenomenon was not new: Commuter suburbs on rail and streetcar lines had attracted affluent and middle-class home buyers since the 1800s. What was new was the massive scale of the movement, made possible by government subsidies and widespread car ownership.

The Government's Role

The Federal Housing Administration offered low-cost loans to homebuyers, and the GI Bill made these loans even cheaper for veterans. These loans promoted suburban development by favoring new single-family houses over existing multifamily housing in cities. Meanwhile, the Interstate Highway Act of 1956 provided government funding for superhighways that gave cars easy access to the suburbs.

Urban Decay

City residents moved to the suburbs to fulfill dreams of home ownership and to flee crime and congestion. Increasingly, city neighborhoods, such as this one in Washington, D.C., fell victim to decay and abandonment.

Geographic Connection

Why did people move from the inner cities to the suburbs?

922

ANSWERS

1. City dwellers sought to pursue dreams of home ownership and to flee crime and congestion. Government programs (subsidized loans, highway construction) promoted suburban single-family development over multifamily urban housing.

RESOURCE DIRECTORY

Teaching Resources
Geography and History booklet, pp. 16–17

Other Print Resources
Nystrom *Atlas of Our Country* Land Use, Population, and Ethnicity, pp. 46–47

Technology
Prentice Hall United States History Video Collection™ Volume 20, *Post-War USA*

The Suburbanization of Houston

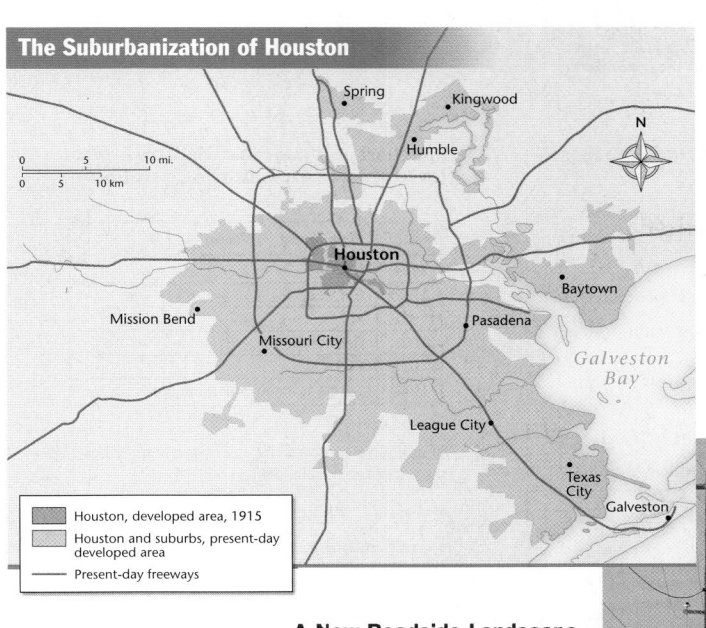

Spring

Kingwood

Humble

Houston

Mission Bend

Baytown

Missouri City

Pasadena

Galveston Bay

League City

Texas City

Galveston

0   5   10 mi.
0   5   10 km

N

Houston, developed area, 1915
Houston and suburbs, present-day developed area
Present-day freeways

One City's Example

In 1915, before most people owned cars, Houston, Texas, was a compact city, and most people walked or took a streetcar to work. With the growth in car ownership and the construction of freeways and suburban developments, Houston has expanded to cover a much larger area, organized around car travel and major highways.

A New Roadside Landscape

Billboards and retail businesses sprang up along suburban highways to serve a growing population of drivers.

Geographic Connection

How did the geography of cities and suburbs change as a result of growth along suburban highways?

New Commercial Centers

At first, suburbs were mainly residential, and people traveled into the city to shop and work. Then open-air malls were built to serve suburban shoppers. By the 1960s, covered malls and office parks had begun to replace traditional downtown city districts as places to shop and work.

Geographic Connection

How do you think the growth of suburban malls and roadside businesses affected traditional downtown businesses?

923

TEST PREPARATION

TIPS FOR TEST TAKING

You might want to remind your students of the following:

1. Read the directions carefully.
2. Read each question carefully.
3. For multiple choice questions, try to answer the question before you look at the choices. Read all the choices. Then, eliminate those that are absolutely incorrect.
4. For short answer questions, be sure to answer the question completely if there is more than one part.
5. Answer the easy questions first. Then, go back to the ones that will take more time.
6. Pace yourself. Be sure to set aside enough time for the writing questions.

Write your answers on a separate sheet of paper.

1. Which one of the following is a correct statement about Stalin's "show trials" in the Soviet Union in the 1930s?

   A The rights of the accused were fully protected.

   B The juries always found Communists not guilty.

   C Guilt was determined before the trial began.

   D Few people were actually punished by the trials.

2. Why did British and French leaders follow a policy of appeasement when dealing with Germany?

   A They were not ready to fight a war with Hitler.

   B The two countries were following isolationist policies.

   C As Axis Powers, they could ignore the growing German strength.

   D Their main interests were in East Asia and not Western Europe.

> "Never . . . was so much owed by so many to so few."
>
> —Winston Churchill

3. British Prime Minister Winston Churchill was speaking about

   A American military forces who invaded France during D-Day.

   B British pilots who defeated the Germans in the Battle of Britain.

   C British troops who ended German expansion in North Africa.

   D Soviet soldiers who stopped the Germans in central Russia.

Use the chart and your knowledge of social studies to answer the following question.

The Road to World War II	
Year	**Event**
1936	Germany occupies the Rhineland
1938	Austria taken over by Germany
1938	Germany divides up Czechoslovakia
1939	???
1940	Germany invades and conquers France

4. Which one of the following items replaces the question marks on the chart?

   A England begins bombing raids on Germany.

   B Italy and Germany invade Spain.

   C Germany declares war on the Soviet Union.

   D Germany invades and conquers Poland.

5. During World War II, why did the government ration sugar, butter, and other foods?

   A To stop the Germans from buying up foods and exporting them to Germany

   B To prevent deflation of the nation's money

   C To make sure items in short supply were available for all people

   D To keep the military from getting more food than it needed

6. Which battle in World War II ended Japan's ability to carry out offensive operations in the Pacific?

   A Midway

   B Coral Sea

   C Leyte Gulf

   D Okinawa

924

Use the information in the map to answer the following question.

Western Europe

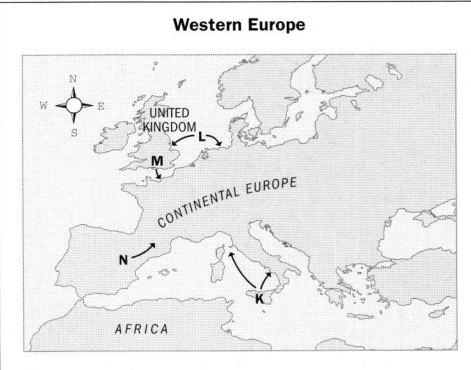

7. Which one of the arrows represents Operation Overlord on D-Day, June 6, 1944, when Western Europe was invaded by Allied forces?

A K

B L

C M

D N

"The President shall be Commander in Chief of the Army and Navy of the United States. . . ."

—Article II, Section 2,
United States Constitution

---

8. This part of the United States Constitution provided the basis for President Harry S Truman to

A open up trade with China.

B make General Dwight Eisenhower the next President.

C help rebuild the Soviet Union after World War II.

D fire General Douglas MacArthur.

Use the information in the graph and your knowledge of social studies to answer the following question.

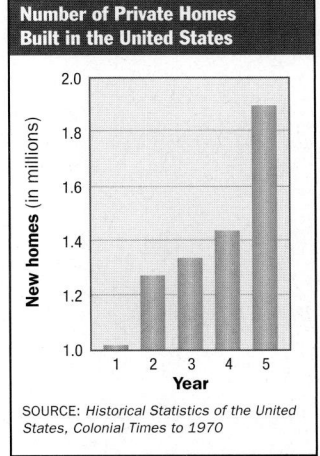

SOURCE: *Historical Statistics of the United States, Colonial Times to 1970*

9. The information on housing best describes which five-year period?

A 1930–1935

B 1936–1940

C 1941–1945

D 1946–1950

Writing Practice

10. What was the intended purpose of the U. S. Neutrality Acts passed during the 1930s? What was their actual effect? Explain why this happened.

11. What promises were made at the Yalta Conference and which of these were kept?

12. Describe three components of the Fair Deal as proposed by President Harry S Truman.

---

1. C
2. A
3. B
4. D
5. C
6. A
7. C
8. D
9. D
10. The purpose was to keep the U.S. out of future wars. In effect, the acts encouraged German aggression, because they made it difficult for the United States to help countries trying to defend themselves against German attacks.
11. Stalin promised to enter the war against Japan and to allow Poland to have free elections. He kept the first promise (just barely) and allowed Polish elections only after a long delay in which he eliminated political opposition to communism there.
12. Answers could discuss any three of the following: legislation to promote full employment; a higher minimum wage; increased unemployment compensation; housing assistance; a national health insurance program; or congressional action in regard to controlling atomic energy.

Unit 9

A Period of Turmoil and Change
(1950–1975)

A Period of Turmoil and Change (1950–1975) The third quarter of the twentieth century found many Americans restless for change. For African Americans, it was a time to demand equal opportunities in education, housing, and citizenship. Many American students supported these demands, and the movement for civil rights evolved into a protest movement that opposed the United States policies in Vietnam as well as in domestic activities. President Kennedy offered a steadying hand in the early days of civil rights protests; after Kennedy was assassinated in 1963, President Johnson had to deal with the unrest. He also inherited the deteriorating situation in Vietnam. Johnson's decision to escalate United States involvement in that war and the growing United States protest movement combined to cripple his presidency.

USING HISTORICAL EVIDENCE

Direct students' attention to the photograph on these pages. Have students list the various factions they see represented in the photograph. Also note that there are protestors from many different parts of the country. Point out that many protestors are African American, but there are also members of other ethnic groups.

Talk with students about why Washington, D.C., became the focus of so many civil rights and antiwar protests. Who were the protestors trying to reach? Do students agree with the strategy of gathering large groups of protestors in the nation's capital?

eTeach

Be sure to check out this month's online discussion with a Master Teacher. Go to **www.phschool.com**.

"In a democratic society like ours, relief must come through an aroused popular conscience that sears the conscience of the people's representatives."

Felix Frankfurter, Supreme Court Justice
Baker v. Carr, 1962

Thousands showed their support for the civil rights movement at the March on Washington in 1963. ▶

926

RESOURCE DIRECTORY

Teaching Resources
Units 9/10 booklet
• American Pathways Activity, pp. 47–48
• History's Lasting Impact, pp. 49–50
Geography and History booklet, pp. 18–19

Other Print Resources
Prentice Hall Assessment System
• Document-Based Assessment

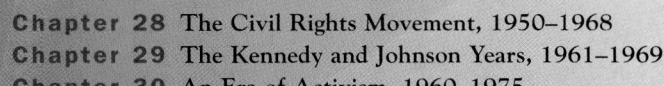

TECHNOLOGY CENTER

Take It to the NET

Prentice Hall School Web site offers student-appropriate Internet activities and links that extend core content. Visit us at the Social Studies area. www.phschool.com

AmericanHeritage®

My Brush with History™ Video Program This new video series lets your students learn history from the people who lived it.

RESOURCE PRO®

Teaching Resources on CD-ROM offer lesson-planning flexibility, test-generation capability, and resource manageability.

- **PRESENTATION PRO CD-ROM** Provides you with multimedia lecture notes for each chapter.

- **SOCIAL STUDIES SKILLS TUTOR CD-ROM** Provides interactive practice in Geographic Literacy, Critical Thinking and Reading, Visual Analysis, and Communications.

- **INTERACTIVE CONSTITUTION CD-ROM** Exploring active citizenship and civic responsibilities, this CD-ROM shows students how the Constitution affects their lives today.

- **EXPLORING PRIMARY SOURCES IN U.S. HISTORY CD-ROM** This interactive exploration of primary sources allows students to analyze and evaluate writing and images from American history.

- **GUIDED READING AUDIOTAPES**

- **STUDENT EDITION ON AUDIO CD**

- **SOUNDS OF AN ERA AUDIO CD** Bring the sounds of American history to life in the classroom with music, speeches, poetry, interviews, and news reports.

iTEXT

Don't miss the exclusive interactive version of this textbook on the Web and on CD-ROM.

927

RESOURCE DIRECTORY

Technology
Color Transparencies *Historical Maps,* A48, A49, A50, A51; *Political Cartoons,* B16, B17; *Time Lines,* C8; *American Photo,* F9; *The Way It Works,* H19
Section Reading Support Transparencies
Prentice Hall United States History Video Collection™ Volume 20, *Post-War USA*
Companion Web site, www.phschool.com

Chapter 28 Planning Guide
Resource Manager

	CORE INSTRUCTION	READING/SKILLS
Chapter-Level Resources	**Teaching Resources** • Pacing Charts booklet • Block Scheduling booklet **Resource Pro® CD-ROM**, Ch. 28 **Prentice Hall Presentation Pro CD-ROM**, Ch. 28 **www.phschool.com** • eTeach	**Guided Reading Audiotapes (English/Spanish)** **Student Edition on Audio CD**, Ch. 28 **Social Studies Skills Tutor CD-ROM** **Color Transparencies**, B16, F9
1 Demands for Civil Rights 1. Learn about events that led to a rise in African American influence in the twentieth century. 2. Find out how Americans responded to the *Brown* v. *Board of Education* decision. 3. Discover how the Montgomery bus boycott affected the civil rights movement. 4. See how other minorities began to demand civil rights in the 1960s.	**Teaching Resources** **Units 9/10 booklet** • Section 1 Quiz, p. 4 **Learning Styles Lesson Plans booklet,** p. 58	**Guided Reading and Review booklet,** p. 112 **Guide to the Essentials,** p. 141 **Learning with Documents booklet,** pp. 33, 92 **Section Reading Support Transparencies**
2 Leaders and Strategies 1. Find out how early groups laid the foundation for the civil rights movement. 2. Understand the philosophy of nonviolence. 3. Realize how SNCC gave students a voice in the civil rights movement.	**Teaching Resources** **Units 9/10 booklet** • Section 2 Quiz, p. 5	**Guided Reading and Review booklet,** p. 113 **Guide to the Essentials,** p. 142 **Learning with Documents booklet,** p. 67 **Section Reading Support Transparencies**
3 The Struggle Intensifies 1. Identify the goals of sit-ins and Freedom Rides. 2. Find out the reaction to James Meredith's integration at the University of Mississippi. 3. Understand how the Birmingham events affected attitudes toward the civil rights movement.	**Teaching Resources** **Units 9/10 booklet** • Section 3 Quiz, p. 6 **Learning Styles Lesson Plans booklet,** p. 59	**Guided Reading and Review booklet,** p. 114 **Guide to the Essentials,** p. 143 **Learning with Documents booklet,** p. 33 **Skills for Life booklet,** p. 30 **Section Reading Support Transparencies**
4 The Political Response 1. Learn about Kennedy's approach to civil rights. 2. Find out why civil rights leaders proposed a march on Washington. 3. Learn the goals of the Civil Rights Act of 1964.	**Teaching Resources** **Units 9/10 booklet** • Section 4 Quiz, p. 7	**Guided Reading and Review booklet,** p. 115 **Guide to the Essentials,** p. 144 **Learning with Documents booklet,** p. 91 **Section Reading Support Transparencies**
5 The Movement Takes a New Turn 1. Learn about Malcolm X's approach to gaining civil rights. 2. Become familiar with the major goals of the black power movement. 3. See why violent riots erupted in many urban streets. 4. Find out how the tragic events of 1968 affected the nation.	**Teaching Resources** **Units 9/10 booklet** • Section 5 Quiz, p. 8	**Guided Reading and Review booklet,** p. 116 **Guide to the Essentials,** p. 145 **Section Reading Support Transparencies**

ENRICHMENT/PRE-AP

Prentice Hall United States History Video Collection™
www.phschool.com
• Section Activities, Virtual Field Trip, Chapter Activities, Current Events Online

Biography, Literature, and Comparing Primary Sources booklet, p. 33
Great Debates booklet, p. 40
Sounds of an Era Audio CD
Exploring Primary Sources in U.S. History CD-ROM

Biography, Literature, and Comparing Primary Sources booklet, pp. 78–79, 151–152
American History Block Scheduling Support

Sounds of an Era Audio CD
Exploring Primary Sources in U.S. History CD-ROM

American History Block Scheduling Support
Sounds of an Era Audio CD
Exploring Primary Sources in U.S. History CD-ROM

Sounds of an Era Audio CD
American Pathways Thematic Posters

ASSESSMENT

PRENTICE HALL ASSESSMENT SYSTEM

Core Assessment
ExamView® Test Bank, Ch. 28
ExamView® Test Bank CD-ROM, Ch. 28

Standardized Test Preparation
Diagnose and Prescribe
Diagnostic Tests for High School Social Studies Skills

Review and Reteach
Review Book for U.S. History

Practice and Assess
Test-taking Strategies With Transparencies
Test-taking Strategies Posters
Test Prep Book for U.S. History
Alternative Assessment Handbook
Document-Based Assessment

Teaching Resources
Units 9/10 booklet
• Section Quizzes, pp. 4–8
• Chapter Tests, pp. 9, 12
www.phschool.com Ch. 28 Self-Test

AmericanHeritage® RESOURCES

From the Archives of American Heritage®, pp. 933, 951, 958
AmericanHeritage® My Brush with History™ Videotapes
www.americanheritage.com

TEXT

Don't miss the exclusive interactive version of this textbook on the Web and on CD-ROM.

Chapter 28 Planning Guide
In Your Classroom

CUSTOMIZE FOR INDIVIDUAL NEEDS

Gifted and Talented

Teacher's Edition
• Customize for Gifted and Talented, pp. 943, 945

Teaching Resources
• Biography, Literature, and Comparing Primary Sources booklet, pp. 33, 78–79, 151–152

Technology
• Exploring Primary Sources in U.S. History CD-ROM *Brown v. Board of Education; Letter from a Birmingham Jail, Martin Luther King, Jr.; I Have a Dream, Martin Luther King, Jr.; Reynolds v. Sims*

ESL

Teacher's Edition
• Customize for ESL, p. 951

Teaching Resources
• Guided Reading and Review booklet, pp. 112–116
• Guide to the Essentials (English/Spanish), Chapter 28

Technology
• Student Edition on Audio CD, Chapter 28
• Guided Reading Audiotapes (English/Spanish), Chapter 28
• Section Reading Support Transparencies

Less Proficient Readers

Teacher's Edition
• Customize for Less Proficient Readers, pp. 935, 937, 953

Teaching Resources
• Guided Reading and Review booklet, pp. 112–116
• Guide to the Essentials (English/Spanish), Chapter 28

Technology
• Student Edition on Audio CD, Chapter 28
• Guided Reading Audiotapes (English/Spanish), Chapter 28
• Section Reading Support Transparencies

Less Proficient Writers

Teacher's Edition
• Customize for Less Proficient Writers, p. 957

Teaching Resources
• Guided Reading and Review booklet, pp. 112–116
• Guide to the Essentials (English/Spanish), Chapter 28

Technology
• Student Edition on Audio CD, Chapter 28
• Guided Reading Audiotapes (English/Spanish), Chapter 28
• Section Reading Support Transparencies

TEACHER'S EDITION INDEX

Activities Connecting with Citizenship, 931, 943; Connecting with Culture, 937, 945, 955, 957; Connecting with Economics, 933; Connecting with Geography, 942, 952; Connecting with Government, 932, 938; Connecting with History and Conflict, 934, 939, 950, 956; Connecting with Science and Technology, 950; Student Portfolio, 944, 958; Time Line, 928
American Heritage 933, 951, 958
Assessment 935, 940, 946, 953, 959, 960–961
Background Notes About the Pictures, 929; Biography, 932, 934, 939; Connections to Today, 945, 950, 957; A Diverse Nation, 938; Geography in History, 952; Interdisciplinary, 944, 956; Recent Scholarship, 943
Bellringer 930, 936, 941, 948, 954
Civil Rights Act of 1964, 951
CORE, 940
Customize For . . . ESL, 951; Gifted and Talented Students, 943, 945; Less Proficient Readers, 935, 937, 953; Less Proficient Writers, 957
Fayer, Steve, 943
Hampton, Henry, 943
Jackson, Jesse, 939
Johnson, Lyndon Baines, 951
King, Coretta Scott, 938
March on Washington, 950
Marshall, Thurgood, 932
My Life with Martin Luther King, Jr., 938
National Urban League, 940
"Next Stop: the North," 952
New Frontier, 944
PUSH (People United to Save Humanity), 939
Race riots, 957, 958
Racism (football game, 1946), 933
Reading Strategies 930, 936, 941, 948, 954
Sixteenth Street Baptist Church, 945
Skills for Life 947
Songs (of the civil rights movement), 937
"Soul," 956
Test Preparation 933, 939, 945, 950, 955
Voices of Freedom: An Oral History of the Civil Rights Movement from the 1950s through the 1980s, 943
Warren, Earl, 934
Weltner, Representative Charles, 951

CHAPTER 28 – PACING SUGGESTIONS

 For 90-minute Blocks

• Teach section 3 using Transparencies B16 and F9, and the Recent Scholarship note on page 943 for class discussions.

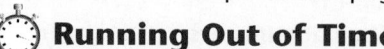 Running Out of Time?

If you are running short on time to cover this chapter, consider the following options:

• Use the Prentice Hall Presentation Pro CD-ROM to create an outline for this chapter.

• Use the Section Summaries for Chapter 28, from **Guide to the Essentials (English/Spanish).**

ADDITIONAL ACTIVITIES

1 Demands for Civil Rights

Connecting with Citizenship
Have students present an audio documentary on the National Guard, describing its history, duties, and how it is used in both peacetime and wartime. The documentaries should include reports on the Guard's participation in significant moments of U.S. history, such as during periods of civil unrest and natural disasters. **(Verbal/Linguistic)**

2 Leaders and Strategies

Connecting with Citizenship
Have students read and report on the experiences of a woman who was a major participant in the civil rights movement. For example, they might learn about major events in the life of either Rosa Parks or Diane Nash in such books as Douglas Brinkley's *Rosa Parks,* David Halberstam's *The Children,* and Lynne Olson's *Freedom's Daughters.* Have them present the highlights of each woman's experiences in the form of a time line. **(Visual/Spatial)**

3 The Struggle Intensifies

Connecting with Culture
Have students read Henry David Thoreau's essay "Civil Disobedience" and write an evaluation on how closely Martin Luther King, Jr., and others followed its ideas. You may also want to extend the comparison to Mahatma Gandhi's campaign for India's independence. **(Verbal/Linguistic)**

4 The Political Response

Connecting with Government
Ask students to find the answer to these questions: What parts of John F. Kennedy's legislative agenda did Lyndon B. Johnson inherit? Which ones did Johnson put before the Congress? Which did he succeed in having Congress enact? Have students present their research in chart form. **(Visual/Spatial)**

5 The Movement Takes a New Turn

Connecting with Citizenship
Have students give their own responses, in the form of personal essays, poems, or rap songs, to the question posed by Barbara Jordan: "Do the black people who were born on this soil, who are American citizens, do they really feel that this is the land of opportunity, the land of the free?" **(Verbal/Linguistic)**

INTRODUCING THE CHAPTER

The 1950s and 1960s were a time of great progress and great frustration for African Americans. Through nonviolent protests and an extremely focused civil rights struggle, African Americans ended institutional segregation and secured voting rights in the South. Lack of progress on economic issues, especially in urban areas, however, drove some to vent their anger through bitter violence.

TIME LINE ACTIVITY

To provide students with practice in using the time line, ask questions such as these:

1. What event took place in 1954 that would forever change the United States? *(The Supreme Court's historic* Brown *v.* Board of Education *of Topeka, Kansas, ending school segregation)*

2. What did President Eisenhower do in 1957 that supported the Supreme Court's 1954 decision? *(He sent troops to Little Rock, Arkansas, to assist the integration of a high school.)*

3. What important international leader was jailed in 1962? *(Nelson Mandela)*

Chapter 28
The Civil Rights Movement
(1950–1968)

SECTION 1   Demands for Civil Rights
SECTION 2   Leaders and Strategies
SECTION 3   The Struggle Intensifies
SECTION 4   The Political Response
SECTION 5   The Movement Takes a New Turn

This protester picketed a restaurant in Georgia.

1954
In a unanimous decision, the Supreme Court rules that segregation in public schools is unconstitutional in *Brown* v. *Board of Education of Topeka, Kansas.*

1955
Thousands of African Americans participate in the Montgomery, Alabama, bus boycott to protest discrimination in public transportation.

1957
Eisenhower sends troops to Little Rock, Arkansas, to facilitate integration at Central High School.

American Events

Presidential Terms: Harry S Truman 1945–1953   Dwight D. Eisenhower 1953–1961

1950   1954   •   •   •   1958

World Events

Vietnamese Communists defeat the French at Dien Bien Phu.
1954

Sudan becomes an independent nation.
1956

928   Chapter 28 • *The Civil Rights Movement*

---

eTeach

Be sure to check out this month's online discussion with a Master Teacher. Go to **www.phschool.com**.

RESOURCE DIRECTORY

Teaching Resources
Pacing Charts booklet
Block Scheduling booklet, p. 27
Units 9/10 booklet
 • Chapter Summary, p. 3

Technology
Guided Reading Audiotapes (English/Spanish), Ch. 28
Student Edition on Audio CD, Ch. 28
Prentice Hall United States History Video Collection™ Volume 20, *Post-War USA*
Prentice Hall Presentation Pro CD-ROM, Ch. 28
Resource Pro® CD-ROM
Social Studies Skills Tutor CD-ROM
Companion Web site, www.phschool.com

Civil Rights Events, 1945–1968

Civil Rights Events, 1945–1968

Activating Prior Knowledge In which state was there the greatest number of peaceful demonstrations? *(Alabama)*

Previewing Were there more incidents of racial violence and fewer peaceful demonstrations during the period from 1945 to 1965 or during the period from 1966 to 1968? *(There were more incidents of racial violence and fewer peaceful demonstrations from 1966 to 1968.)*

▲ Seven days of race-related riots occurred in the Watts area of Los Angeles, California, in 1965.

More than 200,000 black and white Americans peacefully marched on Washington, D.C., to further civil rights in 1963.

▲	Racial violence, 1945–1965
▲	Racial violence, 1966–1968
■	Peaceful demonstration, 1945–1965
■	Peaceful demonstration, 1966–1968

The Watts riot in the summer of 1965.

BACKGROUND
About the Pictures

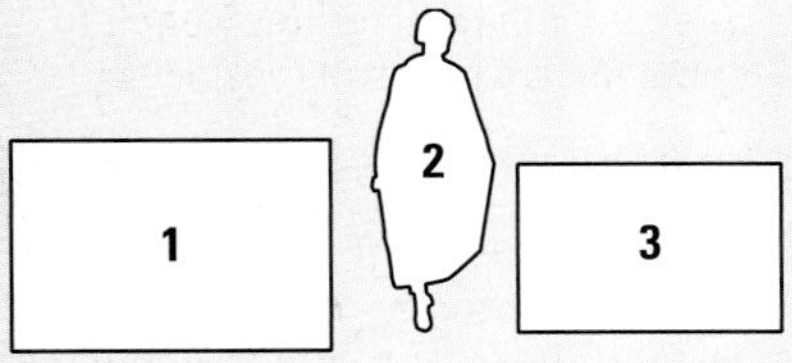

1. This protest began in response to the arrest of Rosa Parks, who had refused to remove herself from the "whites only" section of a bus.

2. After the success of the bus boycotting, which led to the desegregation of seating on buses, picketing and protests broke out all over for various American rights to be upheld.

3. Frustrated by social injustice, many African Americans burned stores and wrought havoc in this riot, which eventually ended in 34 deaths and over 1,000 injuries.

1961
Freedom Riders challenge segregation on interstate buses.

1964
Congress passes the Civil Rights Act of 1964.

1968
The assassinations of Martin Luther King, Jr., and Robert F. Kennedy mark a tragic point in the civil rights movement.

John F. Kennedy 1961–1963

Lyndon B. Johnson 1963–1969

1962

1966

1959
Fidel Castro rises to power in Cuba.

1962
Nelson Mandela is jailed in South Africa.

1966
The Chinese Cultural Revolution begins.

Chapter 28   929

BIBLIOGRAPHY

For the Teacher

Branch, Taylor. *Parting the Waters: America in the King Years, 1954–1963*. Touchstone, 1989. (Chronicles the times from Eisenhower to Kennedy.)

Raines, Howell. *My Soul Is Rested: Movement Days in the Deep South Remembered*. Viking, 1983. (First-person accounts of participants in major civil rights events.)

For the Student

Ellison, Ralph. *Invisible Man.* Random House, Vintage, 1995. (Awarded the 1952 National Book Award for fiction, uses the experiences of an idealistic young African American to depict the alienation of American society.)

Eyes on the Prize. PBS Video. (Comprehensive six-part series on the history of the civil rights movement from 1954.)

TEXT

Don't miss the exclusive interactive version of this textbook on the Web and on CD-ROM.

SECTION OBJECTIVES

1. Learn about events and cultural trends that led to a rise in African American influence in the twentieth century.
2. Find out how Americans responded to the Supreme Court's decision in *Brown* v. *Board of Education.*
3. Discover how the Montgomery bus boycott affected the civil rights movement.
4. See how other minorities began to demand civil rights in the 1960s.

BELLRINGER

Warm-Up Activity Ask students to consider the role of sports in American life. Ask if sports stars should be considered heroes. What qualities does a "hero" possess? Ask students who their heroes are. Why?

Activating Prior Knowledge Ask students if they are familiar with the term *boycott.* If they are, have them describe some situations where boycotts might be used to influence political decisions. What impressions do students have of the use of boycotts as a political tool?

READING STRATEGY

This section describes some significant events in the historical development of the civil rights movement in the twentieth century. As students read the section, have them make a list of the important events described and write a one-sentence description of the importance of each of these events.

CAPTION ANSWERS

Viewing History Robinson publicly broke a professional race barrier and was an inspirational role model.

Section 1
Demands for Civil Rights

READING FOCUS

• What events and cultural trends led to a rise in African American influence in the twentieth century?

• How did Americans respond to the Supreme Court's decision in *Brown* v. *Board of Education?*

• How did the Montgomery bus boycott affect the civil rights movement?

• How did other minorities begin to demand civil rights in the 1950s?

MAIN IDEA

Following World War II, African Americans began to push harder in the civil rights movement and brought about significant results.

KEY TERMS

Brown v. *Board of Education of Topeka, Kansas*
Montgomery bus boycott
integration

TAKING NOTES

As you read, complete the following chart to show how each person affected the civil rights movement in its early years.

Person	Impact on Civil Rights
Branch Rickey	Hired Jackie Robinson, ending segregation in the Major Leagues
Thurgood Marshall	
Earl Warren	
Jo Ann Robinson	
Dwight Eisenhower	
Rosa Parks	
Orval Faubus	

Setting the Scene In August 1945, Branch Rickey, the general manager of the Brooklyn Dodgers, called a young man named Jackie Robinson into his office. Rickey told Robinson of his plan to challenge the rule in Major League Baseball that required African Americans to play in a separate Negro League. Rickey wanted Robinson, a promising athlete in college and a World War II veteran, to be the first player to break the color barrier.

To test how Robinson would respond to the pressure he was likely to face, Rickey acted the part of those who might try to discourage him. He roared insults at Robinson and threatened him with violence. "Mr. Rickey," Robinson finally said, "do you want a ballplayer who's afraid to fight back?" Rickey answered, "I want a player with guts enough not to fight back."

In 1947, Robinson joined the Brooklyn Dodgers, becoming the first African American to play in the Major Leagues. Despite many instances of prejudice, Robinson behaved with dignity and had a sparkling first season. He was named Rookie of the Year in 1947. In 1949, he was voted the league's most valuable player. Just as important, Robinson fostered pride in African Americans around the country and paved the way for other African Americans to follow him into professional sports.

The Rise of African American Influence

Before and during World War II, African Americans were not treated as equals by a large portion of American society. After the war, however, the campaign for civil rights began to accelerate. Millions of people believed that the time had come to demand that the nation live up to its creed that all are equal before the law. Several factors contributed to this growing demand.

African American Migration After the Civil War, many African Americans migrated to large northern cities. Between 1910 and 1940, the black population of New York City leaped from 60,000 to 450,000. Other cities experienced a similar growth in black population. Out of these expanding black communities

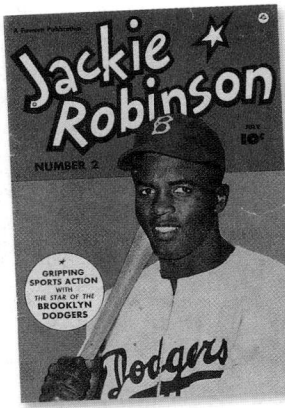

VIEWING HISTORY After his brilliant first season with the Brooklyn Dodgers, Jackie Robinson was featured on baseball cards like the one above, issued in 1951. **Determining Relevance** *How did Robinson's career serve the cause of civil rights?*

RESOURCE DIRECTORY

Teaching Resources
Learning Styles Lesson Plans booklet, p. 58
Guided Reading and Review booklet, p. 112

Technology
Section Reading Support Transparencies
Guided Reading Audiotapes (English/Spanish), Ch. 28
Student Edition on Audio CD, Ch. 28
Sounds of an Era Audio CD, *Reaction to* Brown v. Board of Education, 1954 (time: about one minute)
Prentice Hall Presentation Pro CD-ROM, Ch. 28
Companion Web site, www.phschool.com

emerged a number of prominent African American citizens, including doctors and lawyers, who gained political influence. They were able to form alliances with political machines. In effect, they could offer their votes in return for social gains.

The New Deal During the Depression, Roosevelt and the Democrats began to court black votes and gain African Americans' support for New Deal policies. Under Roosevelt, the number of African Americans working for the federal government increased significantly.

World War II Perhaps the greatest stimulus to the changing racial climate in the United States was World War II. During the war, increased demands for labor in northern cities led to a rise in the black population in the North. This increase in numbers gave African Americans considerable voting power in some northern cities.

Another impact of World War II was ideological. The war, fought largely over the racism and discrimination taking place in Europe, opened many people's eyes to the racism and discrimination taking place in the United States. This realization did not spread to everyone, nor did it have a sudden impact. Rather, these new ideas crept into the ideological climate of the country.

Rise of the NAACP Amidst these cultural changes, the NAACP—the National Association for the Advancement of Colored People—worked hard in the courts to challenge segregation laws throughout the country. For years the NAACP had tried to get the 1896 *Plessy v. Ferguson* decision overturned. That decision held that segregation of the races in public institutions and accommodations was constitutional as long as facilities were "separate but equal." In practice, equal facilities were rarely—if ever—the case.

One of the NAACP's greatest assets was its legal team. Leading the NAACP's Legal Defense Fund was Thurgood Marshall, who had joined the association in the 1930s. Known as "Mr. Civil Rights," Marshall fought many battles over segregation in the courts and achieved great gains. His success was bolstered by the support of an exceptional team of lawyers.

One lawyer in particular, Oliver Hill, from Virginia, won many civil rights suits that focused on issues of discrimination in education and wages. According to the *Washington Post*, Hill's team of lawyers had succeeded in winning more than $50 million in higher pay and better educational facilities for black students and teachers. Little by little, Marshall and Hill managed to chip away at the "separate but equal" clause of *Plessy v. Ferguson*. Finally, in 1951, they took on the greatest and most important fight of all.

Brown v. Board of Education

In 1951, Oliver Brown sued the Topeka, Kansas, Board of Education to allow his 8-year-old daughter Linda to attend a school that only white children were allowed to attend. She passed the school on her way to the bus that took her to a distant school for African Americans. After appeals, the case reached the Supreme Court. There, Thurgood Marshall argued on behalf of Brown and against segregation in America's schools.

On May 17, 1954, in ***Brown v. Board of Education of Topeka, Kansas,*** the Supreme Court issued its historic ruling.

VIEWING HISTORY Thurgood Marshall talks to reporters in New York City in 1955, after the Supreme Court ordered the desegregation of public schools. Marshall later became the first African American Supreme Court Justice.
Analyzing Information *How did Marshall's efforts lead to gains in civil rights and prepare him for the Brown v. Board of Education case?*

LESSON PLAN

Focus Point out to students that many alterations in social, economic, and demographic conditions coalesced in the 1950s to create a sense that gains in civil rights were possible.

Instruct Ask the students to voice their opinions as to what issues, in addition to the gains made by African Americans during World War II, made the 1950s seem like the right time to mount a serious challenge to the legality of *Plessy* v. *Ferguson.*

Assess/Reteach Discuss with students the role of the NAACP. Ask students to explain why the NAACP was well positioned in the 1950s to move ahead on civil rights issues.

ACTIVITY
Connecting with Citizenship

The civil rights movement included different groups with many priorities, all working toward the larger goal of social equality. To help students understand this concept, divide the class into three groups. Have groups form organizations with the common goal of social equality for all young adults. Have each group state its own aims, create an acronym for itself, and describe one way it will attempt to achieve its aims. Discuss how groups might support each other in their aims. **(Logical/Mathematical)**

READING CHECK

Due to the demands for labor in northern cities, the black population in the North grew, giving African Americans considerable voting power in some northern cities. The war heightened awareness of racial discrimination in the United States.

CAPTION ANSWERS

Viewing History Marshall was a successful lawyer who possessed a superb understanding of desegregation cases. He had won many civil rights battles in court in the 1930s and 1940s. These successes paved the way for victory in *Brown* v. *Board of Education.*

❝ Does segregation of children in public schools solely on the basis of race . . . deprive the children of the minority group of equal educational opportunities? We believe that it does. . . . To separate them from others of similar age and qualifications solely because of their race generates a feeling of inferiority as to their status in the community that may affect their hearts and minds in a way unlikely to ever be undone. . . . We conclude that in the field of public education the doctrine of 'separate but equal' has no place. Separate educational facilities are inherently unequal. ❞

—Chief Justice Earl Warren

In a unanimous decision, the Court declared that the "separate but equal" doctrine was unconstitutional and could not be applied to public education. A year later, the Court ruled that local school boards should move to desegregate "with all deliberate speed."

Reaction to *Brown* v. *Board of Education*

The public's reaction to the Supreme Court's ruling was mixed. African Americans rejoiced. Many white Americans, even if they did not agree, accepted the decision and hoped that desegregation could take place peacefully. President Eisenhower, who privately disagreed with the *Brown* ruling, said only that "the Supreme Court has spoken and I am sworn to uphold the constitutional processes in this country, and I am trying. I will obey." Not everyone, however, was willing to obey.

The ruling in *Brown* v. *Board of Education* caused many southern whites, especially in the Deep South, to react with fear and angry resistance. In Georgia, Governor Herman Talmadge made it clear that his state would "not tolerate the mixing of the races in the public schools or any other tax-supported institutions." The Ku Klux Klan also became more active, threatening those who advocated acceptance of the *Brown* decision. The congressional representatives of states in the Deep South joined together in March 1956 to protest the Supreme Court's order to desegregate public schools.

More than 90 members of Congress expressed their opposition to the Court's ruling in what was known as the "Southern Manifesto." The congressmen asserted

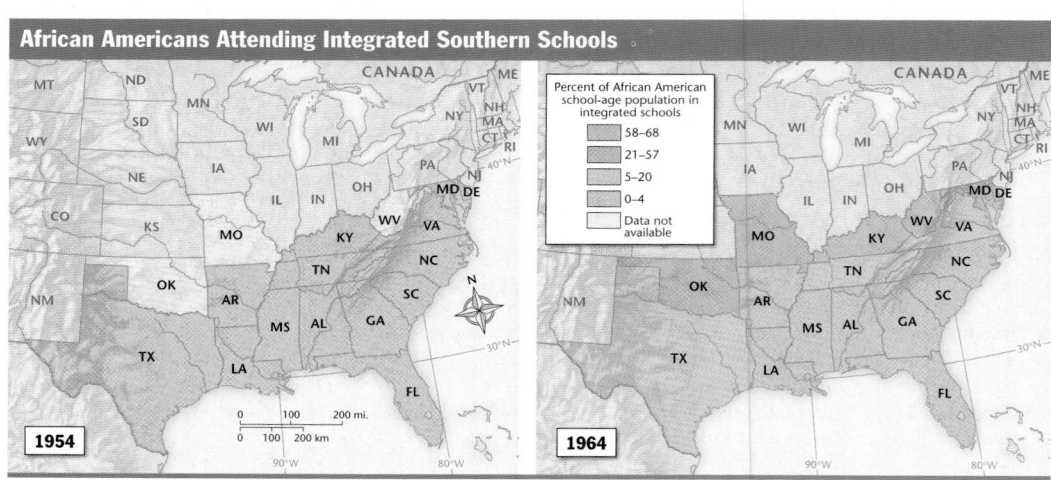

African Americans Attending Integrated Southern Schools

Percent of African American school-age population in integrated schools
- 58–68
- 21–57
- 5–20
- 0–4
- Data not available

1954

1964

that the Supreme Court had overstepped its bounds and had "no legal basis for such action." The decision, they claimed, violated states' rights and was an example of "judicial usurpation." Many believed that desegregation would lead to violence and chaos in several southern states. As a result, they refused to comply with the court's ruling:

> 66 We pledge ourselves to use all lawful means to bring about a reversal of this decision, which is contrary to the Constitution, and to prevent the use of force in its implementation. 99
>
> —From the Congressional Record, 84th Congress, 2nd session

The Montgomery Bus Boycott

In 1955, the nation's attention shifted from the courts to the streets of Montgomery, Alabama. In December, Rosa Parks, a seamstress who had been the secretary of the Montgomery NAACP for 12 years, took a seat in the middle section of a bus, where both African Americans and whites usually were allowed to sit. African Americans, however, were expected to give up their seats for white passengers if no available seats remained. When a white man got on at the next stop and had no seat, the bus driver ordered Parks to give up hers. She refused. Even when threatened with arrest, she held her ground. At the next stop, police seized her and ordered her to stand trial for violating the segregation laws.

Civil rights leaders in Montgomery quickly met and, after Jo Ann Robinson of the Women's Political Council (WPC) suggested the idea, decided to organize the **Montgomery bus boycott.** The plan called for African Americans to refuse to use the entire bus system until the bus company agreed to change its segregation policy. Robinson and other members of the WPC wrote and distributed leaflets announcing the boycott. Martin Luther King, Jr., the 26-year-old minister of the Baptist church where the original boycott meeting took place, soon became the spokesperson for the protest movement. He proclaimed:

> 66 There comes a time when people get tired . . . tired of being segregated and humiliated, tired of being kicked about by the brutal feet of oppression. We have no alternative but to protest. 99
>
> —Martin Luther King, Jr.

The morning of the first day of the boycott, King roamed the streets of Montgomery. He was anxious to see how many African Americans would participate, and recorded his observations:

> 66 During the rush hours the sidewalks were crowded with laborers and domestic workers, many of them well past middle age, trudging patiently to their jobs and home again, sometimes as much as twelve miles. They knew why they walked, and the knowledge was evident in the way they carried themselves. And as I watched them I knew that there is nothing more majestic than the determined courage of individuals willing to suffer and sacrifice for their freedom and dignity. 99
>
> —Martin Luther King, Jr.

Over the next year, 50,000 African Americans in Montgomery walked, rode bicycles, or joined car pools to avoid the city buses. Despite losing money,

Rosa Parks's arrest in 1955 touched off the successful Montgomery bus boycott. Here, one year later, she smiles after the Supreme Court ruled bus segregation to be unconstitutional.

Fast Forward to Today

The Boycott

The boycott has often been an effective form of protest throughout United States history. When Britain passed the Stamp Act in 1765, the colonists responded by organizing a boycott of certain British goods. The boycott proved to be effective when the British merchants who had lost profits on their goods pressured Parliament into repealing the act.

The actual term "boycott" did not come into use until the 1880s in Ireland. A land agent there, Charles Boycott, had refused to comply with a new land reform law designed to lower rents. As a result, his tenants and employees turned against him. He soon found himself isolated and poor.

In modern times, boycotts are often initiated to protest the actions of corporations. Recently, a successful boycott was waged on the tuna industry. The nets used to catch tuna had killed many dolphins and raised environmental concerns. Now, almost all commercial tuna fishing is "dolphin-friendly." Other boycotts have centered around religious, political, and civil or human rights issues.

? Why do you think boycotts are effective? What types of boycotts are the hardest for boycotters to endure? Explain.

---

the bus company refused to change its policies. Finally, in 1956, the Supreme Court ruled that bus segregation, like school segregation, was unconstitutional.

The Montgomery bus boycott encouraged a new generation of leaders in the African American community, most notably Martin Luther King, Jr. In addition, it gave minority groups hope that steps toward equality could be made through peaceful protest.

Resistance in Little Rock

In the fall of 1957, Arkansas Governor Orval Faubus declared that he could not keep order if he had to enforce **integration,** or the bringing together of different races. In blatant defiance of the Supreme Court's *Brown* decision, Governor Faubus posted Arkansas National Guard troops at Central High School in Little Rock, Arkansas, and instructed them to turn away the nine African American students who were supposed to attend the school that year. Outside the school, mobs of angry protesters gathered to prevent the entry of the black students. One of those students, 15-year-old Elizabeth Eckford, remembered that day:

VIEWING HISTORY African American students like Elizabeth Eckford (below, right) had to endure the insults of white students who disagreed with the the Court's *Brown* v. *Board* decision. **Recognizing Cause and Effect** *What finally caused President Eisenhower to support desegregation?*

66 *[The Arkansas national guardsmen] glared at me with a mean look and I was very frightened and didn't know what to do. I turned around and the crowd came toward me. They moved closer and closer. Somebody started yelling 'Lynch her! Lynch her!' I tried to see a friendly face somewhere in the mob—someone who maybe would help. I looked into the face of an old woman and it seemed a kind face, but when I looked at her again, she spat on me.* 99

—Elizabeth Eckford

President Eisenhower could no longer avoid the issue of segregation. Faubus's actions were a direct challenge to the Constitution and to Eisenhower's authority as President. Eisenhower acted by placing the National Guard under federal command. He then sent soldiers to Arkansas to protect

934 Chapter 28 • *The Civil Rights Movement*

the nine students. In a speech to the nation on September 24, 1957, Eisenhower justified his actions:

> 66 Our personal opinions about the decision have no bearing on the matter of enforcement; the responsibility and authority of the Supreme Court to interpret the Constitution are very clear. . . . Mob rule cannot be allowed to override the decisions of our courts. . . . In the present case the troops are there, pursuant to law, solely for the purpose of preventing interference with the orders of the Court. 99
>
> —President Eisenhower

Other Voices of Protest

African Americans were not the only minority group to demand equal rights after World War II. Mexican Americans, for example, also struggled to achieve equality. In one case, a funeral home in Texas refused to bury Felix Longoria, a World War II veteran who had died in the Philippines. Protests in the Mexican American community over the refusal finally led to the soldier's burial in Arlington National Cemetery in Washington, D.C. Groups like the Community Service Organization and the Asociación Nacional México-Americana found that peaceful protest could slowly bring about some of the results Mexican Americans desired.

Native Americans faced a unique situation. The federal government managed the reservations where most Native Americans lived in terrible poverty. In 1953, however, the government adopted a new approach, known as "termination," which sought to eliminate reservations altogether. The government's goal was to assimilate Native Americans into the mainstream of American life.

The policy of termination met with resistance, and in time the federal government discarded it. Yet the problems of the Native Americans remained: poverty, discrimination, and little real political representation. For Native Americans, the civil rights advances of the 1950s were mere tokens of the real gains that were needed.

Focus on CITIZENSHIP

Dr. Hector Garcia

When Latino veterans returned to the United States from battle in World War II, they faced discrimination and prejudice at every turn. Latino veterans were often denied employment, housing, and military benefits afforded to white Americans. Many were still denied the right to vote and hold office.

Dr. Hector P. Garcia, who served as a combat surgeon during the war, decided that he had to act. In 1948, he organized a group that would protect the interests and rights of Latino veterans: the American G.I. Forum. Through the years, the G.I. Forum worked tirelessly to battle discrimination and improve conditions for Latinos in the United States. The Forum's activities included providing funds for higher education, raising money to help poor Latinos pay poll taxes so they could vote, and winning a Supreme Court case allowing Latinos to serve on juries. Today, the G.I. Forum continues to thrive as it works to promote and protect Latino rights.

Section 1 Assessment

Section 1 Assessment

READING COMPREHENSION

1. What was the principle behind the Supreme Court's ruling in **Brown v. Board of Education?**

2. What were the goals of the Southern Manifesto?

3. How did President Eisenhower react to the incident over **integration** in Little Rock, Arkansas?

4. How did Mexican Americans and Native Americans assert their rights in the 1950s?

CRITICAL THINKING AND WRITING

5. **Making Comparisons** The Montgomery bus boycott proved to be an effective form of nonviolent protest against segregation. Can you find other examples of effective boycotts in American history?

6. **Writing a News Story** Take the position of a reporter stationed at Central High School in Little Rock, Arkansas, on the day when nine African American students are to be integrated into the school. Write a brief news story describing the scene.

 Take It to the NET

Activity: Analyzing Primary Source Access the full *Brown* v. *Board of Education of Topeka, Kansas,* unanimous Supreme Court decision. Read the entire majority opinion. What arguments were used? How was the Constitution cited? Use the links provided in the *America: Pathways to the Present* area of the following Web site for help in completing this activity. **www.phschool.com**

Reading Comprehension

1. That what the "separate but equal" doctrine really meant is that African Americans were forced to use public facilities that were vastly inferior to the facilities routinely made available to whites.

2. To oppose desegregation of schools, asserting that the Supreme Court had no legal basis for its decision, and that the decision violated states' rights.

3. He placed the Arkansas National Guard under federal command and sent additional soldiers from the regular army to Arkansas to protect the students. He was determined to uphold the rule of law and to prevent one state from flouting the Supreme Court and the Constitution.

4. Mexican Americans—through peaceful protest; Native Americans—through resistance to the termination policy.

Critical Thinking and Writing

5. Answers will vary but may include: the colonists' boycott of certain British goods after the passage of the Stamp Act in 1765; the more recent boycott of the tuna industry, which has helped raise environmental awareness and protect dolphins.

6. Answers will vary, but should be supported with facts from the section.

 **Take It to the NET**

Answers will vary, but should explore arguments and constitutional references made in the *Brown* v. *Board of Education* case, such as: that segregated schools will always be of unequal quality, and that a segregated educational system violates the equal protection section of the Fourteenth Amendment.

SECTION OBJECTIVES

1. Find out how early groups laid the foundation for the civil rights movement.
2. Understand the philosophy of nonviolence.
3. Realize how SNCC gave students a voice in the civil rights movement.

BELLRINGER

Warm-Up Activity Ask students to think of ways that people can protest without resorting to violence. What advantages do these tactics have?

Activating Prior Knowledge Are students familiar with nonviolent protest strategies? Ask if they can list some, such as sit-ins, boycotts, and peaceful demonstrations.

READING STRATEGY

Have students analyze nonviolent protest as a means of achieving equality of political rights. As they read the section, they should list various strategies described, and then offer a one-sentence response stating which of the various approaches, in their opinion, is most effective.

CAPTION ANSWERS

Viewing History (a) The images show positive interaction between African Americans and white Americans, either enjoying life together or working together to create "one" society.
(b) The NAACP is portrayed as an organization working for an integrated society in which different racial groups can coexist happily for the benefit of all.

Section

2 **Leaders and Strategies**

READING FOCUS

- How did early groups lay the groundwork for the civil rights movement?
- What was the philosophy of nonviolence?
- How did SNCC give students a voice in the civil rights movement?

MAIN IDEA

The civil rights movement of the 1960s consisted of many separate groups and leaders. While the methods used by these groups differed, they shared the same goal of securing equal rights for all Americans.

KEY TERMS

interracial
Congress of Racial Equality (CORE)
Southern Christian Leadership Conference (SCLC)
nonviolent protest
Student Nonviolent Coordinating Committee (SNCC)

TAKING NOTES

As you read, complete the chart below listing the prominent civil rights organizations in the early 1960s and their goals and characteristics.

Civil Rights Group	Features
NAACP	Focused on gaining legal equality. Appealed mainly to middle- and upper-class African Americans.
National Urban League	
CORE	
SCLC	
SNCC	

Setting the Scene

VIEWING HISTORY The NAACP was one of many civil rights groups committed to improving the status of African Americans. **Analyzing Visual Information** *(a) How are the images in this poster intended to rally support for the NAACP? (b) What does the poster tell you about the goals of this organization?*

NAACP-ONE SOCIETY

National Association for the Advancement of Colored People, 1790 Broadway, New York, N.Y. 10019
(212) 245-2100

66 *It really hit me when I was fifteen years old, when I heard about Martin Luther King, Jr., and the Montgomery bus boycott. Black people were walking the streets for more than a year rather than riding segregated buses. To me it was like a great sense of hope, a light. . . . That more than any other event was the turning point for me, I think. It gave me a way out.*

When I graduated from high school, I enrolled at the American Baptist Theological Seminary in Nashville. . . . While I was there I began attending these workshops, studying the philosophy and discipline of nonviolence: the life and times of Gandhi, the works of Henry Thoreau, and the philosophy of civil disobedience. And we began to think about how we could apply these lessons to the problem of segregation. 99

—John Lewis

In the 1960s, many young people, like John Lewis, became active in the struggle for civil rights. They knew that battling segregation and gaining civil rights would require organization and strong commitment.

Laying the Groundwork

The civil rights movement of the 1950s and 1960s was a grass-roots effort of ordinary citizens determined to end racial injustice in the United States. Although no central organization directed the movement, several major groups formed to share information and coordinate civil rights activities. Each of these groups had its own priorities, strategies, and ways of operating, but they all helped to focus the energies of thousands of Americans committed to securing civil rights for all citizens.

NAACP Behind the case of *Brown* v. *Board of Education* was the National Association for the Advancement of Colored People (NAACP),

RESOURCE DIRECTORY

Teaching Resources
Guided Reading and Review booklet, p. 113

Technology
Section Reading Support Transparencies
Guided Reading Audiotapes (English/Spanish), Ch. 28
Student Edition on Audio CD, Ch. 28
Prentice Hall Presentation Pro CD-ROM, Ch. 28
Companion Web site, www.phschool.com

one of the oldest civil rights organizations in the United States. The group formed in 1909 as an **interracial** organization—one with both African Americans and white Americans as members.

W.E.B. Du Bois, a prominent African American scholar, was a founding member. Du Bois had been the first African American to receive a doctoral degree from Harvard University. He served as the NAACP's director of publicity and research and also edited the NAACP magazine, *Crisis*. Du Bois summarized the NAACP's goals this way:

> 66 The main object of this association is to secure for colored people, and particularly for Americans of Negro descent, free and equal participation in the democracy of modern culture. This means the clearing away of obstructions to such participation . . . and it means also the making of a world democracy in which all men may participate. 99

—W.E.B. Du Bois

From the start, the NAACP focused on challenging the laws that prevented African Americans from exercising their full rights as citizens. The NAACP worked to secure full legal equality for all Americans and to remove barriers that kept them from voting.

In the 1920s and 1930s, lynching was still a threat to African Americans, particularly in the South. Working to end such violence, the NAACP succeeded in getting two anti-lynching bills passed by the House of Representatives in the 1930s. Southern leaders in the Senate prevented the bills from becoming law, but the NAACP continued to keep the issue of lynching in the public eye.

The NAACP was more successful in its lawsuits that challenged segregation laws. In the 1920s and 1930s, it won a number of legal battles in the areas of housing and education.

The NAACP appealed mainly to educated, middle- and upper-class African Americans and some liberal white Americans. Critics charged that it was out of touch with the basic issues of economic survival faced by many poorer African Americans.

National Urban League   One organization that took on economic issues was the National Urban League, founded in 1911. The League sought to assist people moving to major American cities. It helped African Americans moving out of the South find homes and jobs and ensured that they received fair treatment at work. League workers also looked for migrant families on ship docks and at train stations and found safe, clean apartments for them. They also insisted that factory owners and union leaders allow African American workers the opportunity to learn the skills that could lead to better jobs.

CORE   Founded by pacifists in 1942, the **Congress of Racial Equality (CORE)** was dedicated to bringing about change through peaceful confrontation. It too was interracial, with both African American and white members. During World War II, CORE organized demonstrations against segregation in cities including Baltimore, Chicago, Denver, and Detroit.

In the years after World War II, CORE director James Farmer worked without pay in order to keep the organization alive. The growing interest in civil rights in the 1950s gave him a new base of support and allowed him to

Focus Explain that the civil rights movement was not a monolithic organization under the sway of a single leader. The groups were as diverse as the people in the movement. Ask students to note in what ways the movement was diverse and in what ways it was united.

Instruct Ask students to read the first quotation by Martin Luther King, Jr., under the subheading "A New Voice For Students." Then discuss these questions: Do you agree with King's view that the failure to fight oppression made African Americans guilty of cooperating with evil? What values and beliefs did King hold that caused him to view the struggle this way?

Assess/Reteach Ask students to analyze the significance of the inclusion of students into the civil rights movement.

ACTIVITY
Connecting with Culture

"We Shall Overcome" is one of many songs sung by 1960s civil rights marchers and their supporters. Have students locate the music and lyrics to other notable songs of the movement, such as "Oh Freedom," "Which Side Are You On?" "We Shall Not Be Moved," "Keep Your Eyes on the Prize," "Woke Up This Morning with My Mind Stayed on Freedom," "Ain't Gonna Let Nobody Turn Me Around," and "This Little Light of Mine." Students can perform the songs for the class, or have the class listen to recordings. Have them describe how characteristics and issues of the civil rights era are reflected in these songs. **(Musical/Rhythmic)**

Focus on CULTURE

"We Shall Overcome" The anthem of the civil rights movement, which brought together activists from all backgrounds, similarly arose through a combination of diverse efforts. "We Shall Overcome" has its roots in an African American spiritual from the days of slavery and from a gospel song called "I'll Overcome Someday," by Minister Charles Albert Tindley.

In 1945, tobacco strikers in South Carolina adopted the song, which had been passed by oral tradition down through the generations. The song later reached white folk singers Pete Seeger and Guy Carawan, who changed the lyrics and altered the melody. They renamed the song "We Shall Overcome," and began teaching it to young activists. The song spread quickly across the nation, unifying all those fighting for civil rights. The successful folk group Peter, Paul, and Mary made the song popular to audiences across the country.

"We Shall Overcome" soon became not only a symbol of the movement, but also a source of pride and determination. An SCLC leader remarked: "You really have to experience it to understand the kind of power it has for us. When you get through singing it, you could walk over a bed of hot coals, and you wouldn't even feel it!"

STUDENT NONVIOLENT
WE SHALL OVERCOME
COORDINATING COMMITTEE

Less Proficient Readers

As they read the section, have students list the key organizations and people mentioned and describe the contributions of each to the civil rights movement.

ACTIVITY

Connecting with Government

At this time, Martin Luther King, Jr.'s, birthday—January 15—is celebrated as a national holiday. But the process of officially designating it as such was a long and difficult one. Have students research the governmental process by which King's birthday was made a holiday, as well as the controversy surrounding it. Ask students to share their findings with the class. **(Verbal/Linguistic)**

BACKGROUND

A Diverse Nation

After the death of Martin Luther King, Jr., in 1968, his widow, Coretta Scott King (b. 1927), remained active in various civil rights issues. In the 1993 edition of her book, *My Life with Martin Luther King, Jr.,* she wrote: "One reason so many young people became involved in the Movement was television. The Movement began in Montgomery just when the electronic era was beginning. Students were educated about social issues through the nightly news."

American BIOGRAPHY

Martin Luther King, Jr. 1929–1968

Born in Atlanta, Georgia, in 1929, King grew up amid all the symbols of southern segregation—separate schools, stores, churches, and public places. Although he had white playmates as a child, those social ties ended when he reached school age. King's father, Martin Luther King, Sr., and his grandfather were both prominent and respected Baptist preachers. He was raised with a sense of personal pride and dignity that went beyond the limitations of segregation.

Even in high school, young Martin was an inspiring and eloquent public speaker. Graduating early from high school, he went to Morehouse College in Atlanta. He earned a divinity degree at Crozer Theological Seminary in Pennsylvania, and then a doctorate in theology at Boston University in 1955. There he met and married Coretta Scott.

King's opponents would attack him physically and verbally, and he would often go to jail for his beliefs. Death threats were frequent. As King had sometimes predicted, he did not live to see the success of the movement. He was assassinated in Memphis, Tennessee, in April 1968, at the age of 39. King's accused killer, a white southerner named James Earl Ray, was convicted in 1969 and sentenced to 99 years in prison.

turn CORE into a national organization, one that would play a major role in the confrontations that lay ahead.

The Philosophy of Nonviolence

Growing opposition to the gains made by African Americans through the *Brown* decision and the Montgomery bus boycott resulted in increasing violence and hostility toward African Americans. Even so, rising new leaders such as Martin Luther King, Jr., preached a philosophy of nonviolence. They asked anyone involved in the fight for civil rights not to retaliate with violence out of fear or hate.

The SCLC In 1957, Martin Luther King, Jr., and other African American clergymen began a new and significant civil rights organization, the **Southern Christian Leadership Conference (SCLC).** SCLC advocated the practice of **nonviolent protest,** a peaceful way of protesting against restrictive racial policies. Nonviolent protesters do not resist even when attacked by opponents. In its first official statement, SCLC set out this principle:

> 66 To understand that nonviolence is not a symbol of weakness or cowardice, but as Jesus demonstrated, nonviolent resistance transforms weakness into strength and breeds courage in the face of danger. 99
> —SCLC statement

SCLC shifted the focus of the civil rights movement to the South. Earlier organizations had been dominated by northerners. Now southern African American church leaders moved into the forefront of the struggle for equal rights. Among them, Martin Luther King, Jr., became a national figure. (See the American Biography on this page.)

Dr. King Leads the Way When the Montgomery bus boycott began, Martin Luther King, Jr., was a young Baptist preacher. Within a few years he would become one of the most loved and admired—and also one of the most hated—people in the United States. King became not only a leader in the African American civil rights movement but also a symbol of nonviolent protest for the entire world.

As he became more and more involved in the civil rights movement, King was influenced by the beliefs of Mohandas K. Gandhi. Gandhi had been a leader in India's long struggle to gain independence from Great Britain, an effort that finally succeeded in 1947. Gandhi preached a philosophy of nonviolence as the only way to achieve victory against much stronger foes. Those who fight for justice must peacefully refuse to obey unjust laws, Gandhi taught. They must remain nonviolent, regardless of the violent reactions such peaceful resistance might provoke—a tactic that requires tremendous discipline and courage.

The philosophy of protest advocated by King had other sources as well. American author Henry David Thoreau had been an advocate of civil disobedience in the mid-1800s. Thoreau, who opposed the 1846 war with Mexico, refused to pay his taxes, and as a result, was jailed. He then wrote about this experience and the principles behind his actions in his famous essay "*Civil Disobedience.*"

As the Montgomery boycott ended and boycotters prepared to ride the newly-integrated buses, King began training volunteers for what they might expect in the months ahead. Films, songs, and skits showed Gandhi's activities

RESOURCE DIRECTORY

Teaching Resources

Biography, Literature, and Comparing Primary Sources booklet (Comparing Primary Sources) *On School Integration,* pp. 151–152

Biography, Literature, and Comparing Primary Sources booklet (Literature) *SNCC Workers,* pp. 78–79

Learning with Documents booklet (Visual Learning Activity) *Nonviolent Resistance,* p. 67

Other Print Resources

American History Block Scheduling Support *Martin Luther King, Jr.'s, Nonviolent Way to Civil Rights,* found in the Nation After World War II folder, includes interdisciplinary lesson suggestions and activities for Geography and History, Primary Sources, Biography, and Literature.

and demonstrated the success of passive resistance in India. Bus riders were advised to follow 17 rules for maintaining a nonviolent approach in case they encountered confrontations on the buses as they traveled through the South. These rules included the following:

> 66 Pray for guidance and commit yourself to complete nonviolence in word and action as you enter the bus. . . . Be loving enough to absorb evil and understanding enough to turn an enemy into a friend. . . . If cursed, do not curse back. If pushed, do not push back. If struck, do not strike back, but evidence love and good will at all times. . . . If another person is being molested, do not arise to go to his defense, but pray for the oppressor and use moral and spiritual force to carry on the struggle for justice. . . . 99
> —Leaflet distributed throughout the city

As a result of his role in the Montgomery boycott, King gained national prominence. He went on to play a key role in almost every major civil rights event. His work earned him the Nobel peace prize in 1964.

A New Voice for Students

Nonviolent protest was a practical strategy in the civil rights struggle. It also represented a moral philosophy. "To accept passively an unjust system is to cooperate with that system; thereby the oppressed become as evil as the oppressor," King said. "Noncooperation with evil is as much a moral obligation as is cooperation with good."

The Formation of SNCC   A new, student organization conceived by the SCLC took a somewhat different approach. The **Student Nonviolent Coordinating Committee,** usually known as **SNCC** (pronounced "snick"), began in 1960 at a meeting in Raleigh, North Carolina, for students active in the struggle. SCLC executive director Ella Baker thought that the NAACP and SCLC were not keeping up with the demands of young African Americans. She wanted to give them a way to play an even greater role in the civil rights movement.

Nearly 200 students showed up for the first SNCC meeting. Most came from southern communities, but some northerners attended as well. Baker delivered the opening address. "The younger generation is challenging you and me," she told the adults present. "They are asking us to forget our laziness and doubt and fear, and follow our dedication to the truth to the bitter end."

Martin Luther King, Jr., spoke next to the young audience, calling the civil rights movement "a revolt against the apathy and complacency of adults in the Negro community. . . ." At the end of the meeting, the participants organized a temporary coordinating committee.

A month later, student leaders met with Baker and other SCLC and CORE leaders and voted to maintain their independence from other civil rights groups. By the end of the year, the Student Nonviolent Coordinating Committee was a permanent and separate organization. It was interracial at first, though that changed in later years.

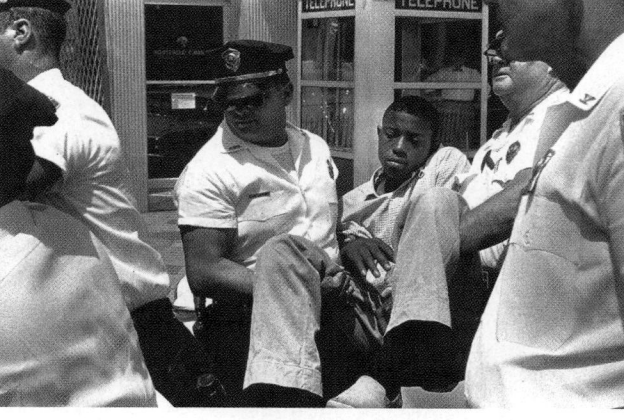

VIEWING HISTORY Police arrested SNCC member Eddie Brown at a 1962 protest rally in Albany, Georgia. **Analyzing Visual Information** *How do Brown's actions reflect the philosophy of nonviolent protest?*

READING CHECK
What led to the formation of SNCC?

Reading Comprehension

1. The National Urban League assisted poor African Americans economically by helping them move to cities, obtain employment there, and find a place to live. CORE leaders concentrated on bringing about change through peaceful confrontation. CORE organized demonstrations against segregation during World War II.

2. Nonviolence, civil disobedience.

3. It gave the movement a younger focus and energy. Its members were idealistic activists who pushed for social change and forced others to confront their demands.

4. He was soft-spoken, and seemed humble and accessible. He was a sincere speaker and a strong leader.

Critical Thinking and Writing

5. Strengths: Nonviolent protest preserves the moral integrity of the protesters because they refuse to use violence against their oppressors. In this way, they may also win the respect and support of other people. Weaknesses: Nonviolent protesters often encounter violent resistance but have no way to protect themselves.

6. Agendas will vary, but should be supported with facts from the section.

Take It to the NET

Students should create a chart comparing past goals and accomplishments of the organization they select with that group's present endeavors. Encourage students to highlight both similarities and differences.

CAPTION ANSWERS

Viewing History The sincere, low-key style of Bob Moses was well suited to the SNCC because he was able to earn the trust of his audiences.

SNCC filled its own niche in the American civil rights movement. The focus of the civil rights movement shifted away from church leaders alone and gave young activists a chance to make decisions about priorities and tactics. SNCC also sought more immediate change, as opposed to the gradual change advocated by most of the older organizations.

Robert Moses One of SNCC's most influential leaders was Robert Moses, a Harvard graduate student and a mathematics teacher in Harlem. As the civil rights movement developed, he wanted to be involved. He first went to work for SNCC in Atlanta, and later headed for Mississippi to recruit black and white volunteers to help rural blacks register to vote.

While Martin Luther King, Jr., spoke with eloquence and passion, Moses was more soft-spoken. He took time to gather his thoughts, and then he spoke slowly. Todd Gitlin, a white student-activist leader, later noted that Moses was loved and trusted "precisely because he seemed humble, ordinary, accessible." Gitlin went on to describe Moses's style of oratory:

VIEWING HISTORY Robert Moses helped train SNCC volunteers in Ohio in 1964. **Drawing Conclusions** Why was Bob Moses well suited to be a leader of SNCC?

> 66 He liked to make his points with his hand, starting with palm down-turned, then opening his hand outward toward his audience, as if delivering the point for inspection, nothing up his sleeve. The words seemed to be extruded [thrust forth], with difficulty, out of his depths. What he said seemed earned. . . . To teach his unimportance, he was wont [accustomed] to crouch in the corner or speak from the back of the room, hoping to hear the popular voice reveal itself. 99
>
> —Todd Gitlin

With fresh new ideas and strong leaders like Bob Moses, SNCC became a strong and vital organization for students wanting to take part in the civil rights movement. As the struggle intensified, SNCC became a powerful force, and many students found that they would risk almost anything for their beliefs.

Section 2 Assessment

READING COMPREHENSION

1. What functions did the National Urban League and **CORE** serve for African Americans?

2. What was Dr. King's approach to civil rights?

3. What role did **SNCC** play in the movement?

4. Why was Bob Moses an effective leader?

CRITICAL THINKING AND WRITING

5. **Determining Relevance** What do you think are some of the strengths and weaknesses of nonviolent protest as a means to bring about social change?

6. **Writing a List** As a student in the 1960s, you have been asked to help organize a local chapter of SNCC. Write an agenda for organizing such a group, listing strategies you would use to recruit members and to work for change.

Take It to the NET

Activity: Yesterday and Today Select one of the civil rights organizations discussed in this section and research its goals and strategies in the present day. Create a chart comparing this group's historic actions to its actions today. Use the links provided in the *America: Pathways to the Present* area of the following Web site for help in completing this activity.
www.phschool.com

RESOURCE DIRECTORY

Teaching Resources
Units 9/10 booklet
• Section 2 Quiz, p. 5
Guide to the Essentials
• Section 2 Summary, p. 142

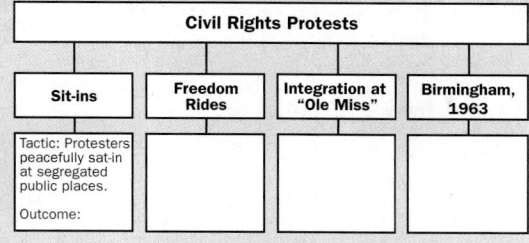

Setting the Scene As a child in the rural Mississippi town of Centreville, Anne Moody grew up wondering what "the white folks' secret" was. "Their homes were large and beautiful with indoor toilets and every other convenience that I knew of at the time," she observed. "Every house I had ever lived in was a one- or two-room shack with an outdoor toilet." Moody was horrified when 14-year-old Emmett Till, visiting from Chicago, was killed in Mississippi supposedly because he had whistled at a white woman.

While in college, Moody became involved in the civil rights movement. She joined the NAACP and also worked with CORE and SNCC. She took part in the first sit-ins in Jackson, Mississippi, in 1963. Like so many other students in the 1960s, Moody was jailed for taking part in civil rights demonstrations.

Worse was the reaction from her family at home. Her mother, afraid for the lives of her relatives, begged Moody to end her involvement with the civil rights movement. The local sheriff had warned that Moody should never return to her hometown. Moody's brother had been beaten up and almost lynched by a group of white boys. Her sister angrily told her that her activism was threatening the life of every African American in Centreville.

Against all that resistance, Moody persevered. She participated in demonstrations, helped force the desegregation of local facilities, and remained determined to do everything she could to make the South a better place for African Americans. But it was never easy, and the gains came at tremendous personal cost. Like many other Americans committed to changing society through nonviolent means, Moody learned that challenging white supremacy often provoked an ugly and violent reaction.

Sit-ins Challenge Segregation

As you read in an earlier chapter, the Congress of Racial Equality (CORE) created the **sit-in** in 1943 to desegregate the Jack Spratt Coffee House in Chicago. In this technique, a group of CORE members simply sat down at a segregated lunch counter or other public place. If they were refused service at first, they simply stayed where they were.

Anne Moody joined a SNCC voter registration drive during her first year at Tougaloo College. She said of her fellow SNCC workers, "I had never known people so willing and determined to help others."

Focus Explain that as civil rights activists put the philosophy of nonviolence into action, protests began to sweep the South. Ask students to describe what happened as a result of these protests.

Instruct Discuss what issues made the civil rights movement so unstoppable. Ask students to consider the following factors in their examination of the movement: the people involved, the tactics, the moral philosophy of the movement, the reactions of whites, and television and newspaper images of the violence.

Assess/Reteach At the time of nonviolent protests, many people who sympathized with the aims of the civil rights movement nonetheless did not agree with the methods used. In students' opinions, did the end justify the means?

ACTIVITY
Connecting with Geography

Have students use a historical atlas of the United States to broaden their understanding of Anne Moody's background growing up in Centreville, Mississippi. Have them use the appropriate mathematical skills to interpret social studies information as they use an atlas to do the following: locate Centreville on a map, find out its population, calculate the town's distance from a major city, identify transportation routes by which a person could travel to Centreville, and describe the economy of the area in which the town is located. Then discuss the picture that emerges from this information. (Visual/Spatial; Logical/Mathematical)

READING CHECK

They were subjected to physical abuse and often served time in jail.

CAPTION ANSWERS

Viewing History It forced business owners to decide between serving the protesters or risking a disruption of business.

VIEWING HISTORY Signs like the one below were clear indications of how institutionalized segregation was in the South. At right, John Salter, Jr., Joan Trumpauer, and Anne Moody (left to right) held a sit-in in at a Jackson, Mississippi, lunch counter in May 1963. A hostile crowd registered their response by mocking and pouring food on the three activists. **Synthesizing Information** *Why was the sit-in often a successful tactic?*

CITY CAFE
COLORED ENTRANCE

This tactic was a popular form of protest in the early 1960s. It often worked because it forced business owners to decide between serving the protesters or risking a disruption and loss of business. In some places, sit-ins brought strong reactions. John Lewis, a SNCC activist, participated in sit-ins in Nashville, Tennessee, in the 1960s. He remembered the experience:

> 66 *It was a Woolworth in the heart of the downtown area, and we occupied every seat at the lunch counter, every seat in the restaurant. . . . A group of young white men came in and they started pulling and beating primarily the young women. They put lighted cigarettes down their backs, in their hair, and they were really beating people. In a short time police officials came in and placed all of us under arrest, and not a single member of the white group, the people that were opposing our sit-in, was arrested.* 99
>
> —John Lewis

READING CHECK
What often happened to those who participated in sit-ins?

Soon, thousands of students were involved in the sit-in campaign, which gained the support of SCLC. Martin Luther King, Jr., told students that arrest was a "badge of honor." By the end of 1960, some 70,000 students had participated in sit-ins, and 3,600 had served time in jail. The protests began a process of change that could not be stopped.

The Freedom Rides

In *Boynton* v. *Virginia* (1960), the Supreme Court expanded its earlier ban on segregation on interstate buses. As a result, bus station waiting rooms and restaurants that served interstate travelers could not be segregated either.

In 1961, CORE, with aid from SNCC, organized and carried out the **Freedom Rides.** They were designed to test whether southern states would obey the Supreme Court ruling and allow African Americans to exercise the rights newly granted to them.

Violence Greets the Riders The first Freedom Ride departed Washington, D.C., on May 4, 1961. Thirteen freedom riders, both African Americans and

RESOURCE DIRECTORY

Teaching Resources
Learning with Documents booklet (Primary Source Activity) *Protecting the Freedom Riders,* p. 33

Technology
Color Transparencies *American Photo,* F9
Sounds of an Era Audio CD *A Sit-in in Nashville, Tennessee* (time: one minute, 30 seconds)
RESOURCE **PRO**® **Biography** *Sidney Poitier,* found on Resource Pro, profiles the actor whose movies in the 1950s and 1960s dramatically portrayed the evils of racism in United States society.

white Americans, boarded two interstate buses heading south. (See the map of the route below.) At first the group encountered only minor conflicts. In Atlanta the two buses split up and headed for the Deep South. There the trip turned dangerous.

In Anniston, Alabama, a heavily armed white mob met the first bus at the terminal. The bus attempted to leave. CORE director James Farmer described what happened next:

> 66 *Before the bus pulled out, however, members of the mob took their sharp instruments and slashed tires. The bus got to the outskirts of Anniston and the tires blew out and the bus ground to a halt. Members of the mob had boarded cars and followed the bus, and now with the disabled bus standing there, the members of the mob surrounded it, held the door closed, and a member of the mob threw a firebomb into the bus, breaking a window to do so. Incidentally, there were some local policemen mingling with the mob, fraternizing with them while this was going on.* 99
>
> —James Farmer

The riders escaped before the bus burst into flames, but many were beaten by the mob as they stumbled out of the vehicle, choking on the smoke. They had anticipated trouble, since they meant to provoke a confrontation. The level of violence, however, took them by surprise.

As a result of the savage response, Farmer considered calling off the project. SNCC leaders, though, begged to go on. Farmer warned, "You know that may be suicide." Student activist Diane Nash replied, "If we let them stop us

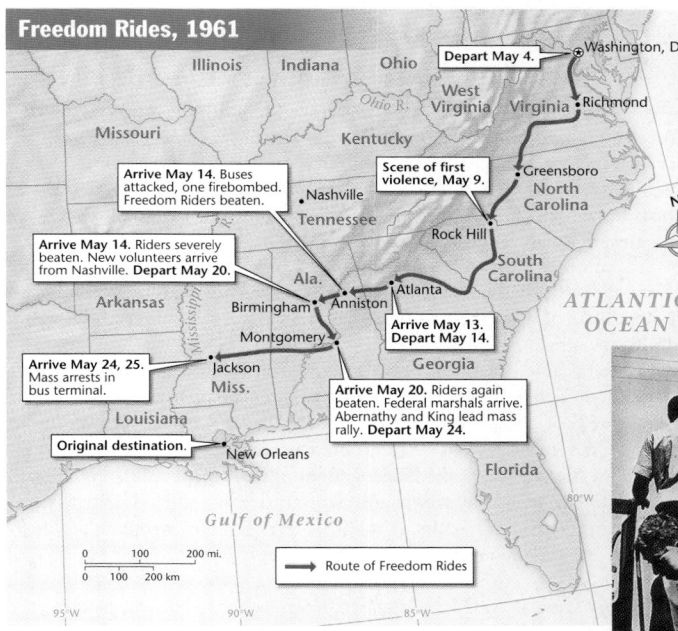

Freedom Rides, 1961

Depart May 4. — Washington, D.C.
Richmond
Scene of first violence, May 9. — Greensboro
Arrive May 14. Buses attacked, one firebombed. Freedom Riders beaten. — Nashville — North Carolina
Arrive May 14. Riders severely beaten. New volunteers arrive from Nashville. **Depart May 20.** — Rock Hill — South Carolina
Birmingham — Anniston — Atlanta — Arrive May 13. Depart May 14.
Montgomery — Georgia
Arrive May 24, 25. Mass arrests in bus terminal. — Jackson — Arrive May 20. Riders again beaten. Federal marshals arrive. Abernathy and King lead mass rally. **Depart May 24.**
Original destination. — New Orleans — Florida

ATLANTIC OCEAN

Gulf of Mexico

0 100 200 mi.
0 100 200 km

→ Route of Freedom Rides

MAP SKILLS The Freedom Riders left Washington, D.C., for New Orleans, Louisiana, to test southern compliance with desegregation laws. The bus below was firebombed by white men in Anniston, Alabama, who then beat the fleeing activists. Local hospitals refused to treat the wounded riders. **Movement** *(a) Through how many states did they pass? (b) What kinds of opposition did they face?*

Major Civil Rights Protests, 1954–1965

Year	Event and Outcome
1954	**Brown v. Board of Education** Supreme Court ruled against the "separate but equal" doctrine and ordered the desegregation of all public schools. Violent protests in southern states followed.
1955–1956	**Montgomery Bus Boycott** Bus company desegregated its buses. Martin Luther King, Jr., emerged as an important civil rights leader.
1960s	**Sit-ins** Peaceful actions sparked violent reactions and many protesters were jailed. The tactic gained momentum for the civil rights movement.
1961	**Freedom Rides** Attempts to desegregate interstate travel led to mob violence. The Interstate Commerce Commission banned segregation in interstate transportation.
1962	**James Meredith Enrolls at the University of Mississippi** The Supreme Court upheld Meredith's right to enter the all-white institution. Violence erupts on the campus.
1963	**Protest Marches and Boycotts in Birmingham, Alabama** Violence against peaceful demonstrators shocked the nation. Under pressure, Birmingham desegregated public facilities.
1963	**March on Washington** More than 200,000 people demonstrated in an impressive display of support for civil rights.
1965	**Selma March** State troopers attacked marchers. President Johnson used federal force to protect the route from Selma to Montgomery, and thousands joined the march, which was designed to call attention to the issue of voting rights.

INTERPRETING CHARTS The visibility of early civil rights protests led to advances in civil rights on both the local and national level. **Making Comparisons** *What do most of these protests have in common? How do they differ?*

with violence, the movement is dead! . . . Your troops have been badly battered. Let us pick up the baton and run with it."

National Reactions Photographs of the smoldering bus in Anniston horrified the country. Burke Marshall, the Assistant Attorney General who headed the Justice Department's Civil Rights Division, was astonished "that people—presumably otherwise sane, sensible, rational—would have this kind of reaction simply to where people were sitting on a bus."

The violence intensified in Birmingham and Montgomery. Upon their arrival in Jackson, Mississippi, the riders met no mobs but were arrested immediately. New volunteers arrived to replace them and were also arrested. This first Freedom Ride died out in Jackson, but about 300 Freedom Riders continued the protest throughout that summer. Attorney General Robert Kennedy had at first been reluctant to lend federal support to the protest, but now he sent federal marshals to protect the Freedom Riders.

Kennedy then took further measures. He pressured the Interstate Commerce Commission to issue a ruling that prohibited segregation in all interstate transportation—trains, planes, and buses. The Justice Department sued local communities that did not comply.

Integration at "Ole Miss"

In 1961, James Meredith, an African American Air Force veteran, fought a personal battle for equal rights. Meredith was a student at Jackson State College, but he wanted to transfer to the all-white University of Mississippi, known as "Ole Miss." After being rejected, Meredith got legal help from the NAACP. It filed a lawsuit claiming that Meredith's application was turned down on racial grounds.

In the summer of 1962, the Supreme Court upheld Meredith's claim. Mississippi Governor Ross Barnett, however, declared that Meredith could not enroll, regardless of what the Court said. Barnett personally blocked the way to the admissions office.

The issue became a standoff between the governor and the Justice Department. President Kennedy sent federal marshals to accompany Meredith to the campus. Crowds of angry white protesters, who had gathered around campus, destroyed their vehicles. As violence erupted on campus, tear gas covered the grounds. Two bystanders were killed and hundreds of people hurt. Finally, President Kennedy sent army troops to restore order, but federal marshals continued to escort Meredith to class. A month later, Meredith wrote an article for the *Saturday Evening Post* describing his experiences:

❝ *It hasn't been all bad. Many students have spoken to me very pleasantly. They have stopped banging doors and throwing bottles into my dormitory now. One fellow from my home town sat down at my table in the cafeteria. 'If you're here to get an education, I'm for you,' he said. 'If you're here to cause trouble, I'm against you.' That seemed fair enough to me.* **"**

—James Meredith, 1962

Clash in Birmingham

Elsewhere, civil rights leaders looked for chances to protest segregation nonviolently. The Reverend Fred Shuttlesworth, head of the Alabama Christian Movement for Human Rights, in Birmingham, invited Martin Luther King, Jr., and the SCLC to visit the city in April 1963. Birmingham's population was 40 percent African American, but King called it "the most segregated city in America." Victory there could be a model for resistance.

King and Shuttlesworth planned boycotts of downtown stores and attempts to integrate local churches. Business leaders, fearing disruptions and lost sales, tried to negotiate with Shuttlesworth to call off the plan, without success.

When reporters wanted to know how long King planned to stay, he drew on a biblical story and told them he would remain until "Pharaoh lets God's people go." Birmingham police commissioner Eugene "Bull" Connor, a determined segregationist, replied, "I got plenty of room in the jail."

From Birmingham Jail The campaign began nonviolently with protest marches and sit-ins. City officials declared that the marches violated a regulation prohibiting parades without a permit. They obtained a court injunction, which directed the protesters to cease demonstrations. King decided to disobey the court orders and set an example of civil disobedience. Connor then arrested King and other demonstrators. When a group of white clergy criticized the campaign as an ill-timed threat to law and order by an "outsider," King responded from his cell. In his "Letter from Birmingham Jail," he defended his tactics and his timing:

" *Frankly, I have yet to engage in a direct-action campaign that was 'well timed' in the view of those who have not suffered unduly from the disease of segregation. For years now I have heard the word 'Wait!' It*

VIEWING HISTORY President Kennedy supported the Supreme Court's decision to allow James Meredith to enroll at the University of Mississippi. **Synthesizing Information** *How did the various branches and levels of government interact over this issue?*

COMPARING PRIMARY SOURCES
Integrating Schools

In parts of the Deep South, the battle for equal rights continued to be fought at the nation's schoolhouse doors each September, long after the Supreme Court ordered schools to desegregate in 1954.

Analyzing Viewpoints How do these two speeches, made about a month apart, reflect the divisions in the country?

For School Integration

"Nearly nine years have elapsed since the Supreme Court ruled that state laws requiring or permitting segregated schools violate the Constitution. . . . Since that time it has become increasingly clear that neither violence nor legalistic measures will be tolerated as a means of thwarting court-ordered desegregation."
—President Kennedy, message to Congress February 28, 1963

Against School Integration

"I draw the line in the dust and toss the gauntlet before the feet of tyranny and I say segregation now, segregation tomorrow, segregation forever."
—Alabama Governor George Wallace, Inaugural Address, January 14, 1963

ACTIVITY
Connecting with Culture

This activity may take place over several class periods: Divide the class into groups of three. Have each student in the group make or find three images relating to the civil rights movement to include in a collage. The group should decide on a title for the artwork, perhaps borrowing a film or television series title (such as *Mississippi Burning* or *Eyes on the Prize*), using a line from a speech (such as "I have a dream"), or making up a title. One student from each group should present the finished collage to the class. (**Visual/Kinesthetic**)

BACKGROUND
Connections to Today

On September 15, 1963, a bomb exploded outside the Sixteenth Street Baptist Church in Birmingham, Alabama, killing four black girls. Although an FBI investigation concluded that four Ku Klux Klansmen were responsible, FBI director J. Edgar Hoover closed the case without filing any charges. In the 1970s Alabama's attorney general reopened the case and succeeded in convicting one suspect of murder. An FBI review of the case in the early 1990s led to the conviction of a second suspect in May 2001. Other cases from the civil rights era have also recently been reopened. In 1994 a jury convicted the assassin of civil rights leader Medgar Evers, who was killed in 1963.

CUSTOMIZE FOR ...
Gifted and Talented

After students have read the statement on the previous page by Assistant Attorney General Burke Marshall, ask them to analyze why whites reacted as they did to the Freedom Rides. What was at stake from the point of view of white segregationists? Why did African Americans riding a bus alongside whites seem so threatening to them?

 TEST PREPARATION

Have students read the quotation by Martin Luther King, Jr., on these pages and then complete the statement below.

The reason King gives to defend the timing of his campaign note is that—

A only segregationists can plan well timed campaigns.

B African Americans only know how to wait.

C there is no such thing as perfect timing in a fight to overcome segregation.

D direct-action campaigns cannot be well timed.

CAPTION ANSWERS

Viewing History The U.S. Supreme Court ruled that Meredith could enroll at the University of Mississippi. President Kennedy sent troops and federal marshals to uphold the Supreme Court's decision in the face of Mississippi Governor Barnett's defiance of the Court.

Section 3 Assessment

Reading Comprehension

1. Angry white mobs harassed, and sometimes physically attacked, the sit-in participants. Sit-ins generated tremendous publicity around the country, which aided the civil rights movement as a whole.

2. The nation was shocked by the violence; the federal government began to support the protesters.

3. In both cases the President supported the Supreme Court's decision to allow the students to be integrated. The government supported the students, intervening and sending escorts to accompany them to school in the face of resistance.

4. Martin Luther King, Jr., wanted to bring about the integration of public facilities and to end discrimination in hiring practices. He also wanted to use Birmingham as a model for the desegregation of other southern cities.

Critical Thinking and Writing

5. Answers will vary but may include: working through established political channels, voting for candidates who supported their cause, or initiating letter-writing campaigns.

6. Answers will vary. Encourage students to support their responses by considering their own views toward the strategy of nonviolence.

Take It to the NET

Invite students to take a Virtual Field Trip at **www.phschool.com**

VIEWING HISTORY Police in Birmingham, Alabama, used high-powered hoses to break up civil rights marches in 1963. Television coverage of this brutal treatment of peaceful demonstrators prompted widespread sympathy for the movement. **Identifying Central Issues** *What was the outcome of the Birmingham crisis?*

rings in the ear of every Negro with piercing familiarity. This 'Wait!' has almost always meant 'Never.' **"**

—"Letter from Birmingham Jail," Martin Luther King, Jr., 1963

After more than a week, King was released on bail. Soon after, he made a difficult decision: to let young people join the campaign. Though dangerous, it would test the conscience of the Birmingham authorities and the nation.

As they marched with the adults, "Bull" Connor arrested more than 900 of the young people. Police used high-pressure fire hoses, which could tear the bark from trees, on the demonstrators. They also brought out trained police dogs that attacked marchers' arms and legs. When protesters fell to the ground, policemen beat them with clubs and took them off to jail.

The Nation Watches Television cameras brought the scenes of violence to people across the country. Even those unsympathetic to the civil rights movement were appalled. As reporter Eric Sevareid observed, "A newspaper or television picture of a snarling police dog set upon a human being is recorded in the permanent photo-electric file of every human brain."

In the end, the protesters won. A compromise arranged by Assistant Attorney General Burke Marshall led to desegregation of city facilities and fairer hiring practices. An interracial committee was set up to aid communication.

The success of the Birmingham marches was just one example that proved how effective nonviolent protest could be. Sometimes the technique did not work, or worked only slowly. Nevertheless, nonviolent protest as a means to social change had earned itself a place of honor in the history of civil rights in the United States.

Section 3 Assessment

READING COMPREHENSION

1. What reaction did **sit-ins** provoke?

2. How did the violent response to the **Freedom Rides** and the Birmingham marches aid the civil rights movement?

3. Compare the government's response to the controversy at "Ole Miss" with its response to the Little Rock controversy in 1957.

4. What was the aim of the Birmingham campaign?

CRITICAL THINKING AND WRITING

5. **Identifying Alternatives** If student protesters had not chosen nonviolent protest, what other peaceful options might they have used?

6. **Writing to Persuade** In May 1961, an article in the *New York Times* urged the Freedom Riders to call off their plans, saying, "Non-violence that deliberately provokes violence is a logical contradiction." Write two paragraphs explaining why you agree or disagree with this opinion.

Take It to the NET

Activity: Virtual Field Trip Visit the National Civil Rights Museum online and tour the exhibits it has provided. Select the exhibit in the museum that interests you the most and summarize what you see in that exhibit in a brief essay. Use the links provided in the *America: Pathways to the Present* area of the following Web site for help in completing this activity. **www.phschool.com**

946 Chapter 28 • *The Civil Rights Movement*

CAPTION ANSWERS

Viewing History City facilities were desegregated, more equitable hiring practices were instituted, and an interracial committee was established to aid in communication.

RESOURCE DIRECTORY

Teaching Resources
Units 9/10 booklet
• Section 3 Quiz, p. 6
Guide to the Essentials
• Section 3 Summary, p. 143

Technology
Exploring Primary Sources in U.S. History
CD-ROM *Letter from Birmingham Jail, Martin Luther King, Jr.*

Understanding Public Opinion Polls

Elected officials are always interested in public opinion—first, so they can support the policies their constituents favor; and second, so they can be reelected. Public opinion polls that use scientific polling techniques are a good way of finding out what the public thinks at a particular time and how these opinions change over time. Professional polling organizations follow a complex process to provide reliable public opinion data. In the 1960s, civil rights was a divisive issue. Samples of polling about civil rights conducted by the Gallup Organization appear at right.

LEARN THE SKILL

Use the following steps to understand opinion polls:

1. **Define the universe being polled.** In polling, a *universe* is the whole population that the poll aims to measure—for example, all adults in the country or all the members of a political party or region. After defining the universe, pollsters interview a randomly selected sample of people representing that universe. Unless noted, the universe is assumed to be all the adults in the nation or region being polled.

2. **Examine the questions.** Polling questions should be simply worded and objective, and should not lead toward a particular answer.

3. **Analyze the results.** If they include answers from subgroups of the universe, ask yourself why the pollster chose these groups. What are the differences between the groups? Use your knowledge of the historical period to determine what events might have affected results. Consider how the polling results might be used by a politician or other decision-maker.

PRACTICE THE SKILL

Answer the following questions:

1. **(a)** What is the universe of Poll C? **(b)** Of Poll D? **(c)** What subgroup is singled out in Poll A?

2. **(a)** How is the first question in Poll C different from the questions in the other polls? **(b)** Why do you think the pollster gives "No opinion" or "Don't know" as options? **(c)** Do you think the polls contain any leading questions? Explain.

3. **(a)** Why do you think Poll A breaks out only one region of the country? **(b)** Why do you think the pollster asks the same question in Polls B and D? **(c)** What kind of information can you learn from Poll C that you cannot learn from the others? **(d)** How might decision-makers or candidates use each of these polls?

A. Integration, June 23, 1961

The United States Supreme Court has ruled that racial segregation in the public schools is illegal. This means that all children, no matter what their race, must be allowed to go to the same schools. Do you approve or disapprove of this decision?

		South Only	
Approve	62%	Approve	24%
Disapprove	33%	Disapprove	69%
No opinion	5%	No opinion	7%

B. Integration, Nov. 14, 1962

Do you think the Kennedy Administration is pushing racial integration too fast, or not fast enough?

Too fast	42%	About right	31%
Not fast enough	12%	No opinion	15%

C. Most Important Problem, Oct. 2, 1963

What do you think is the most important problem facing this country today?

Racial problems	52%
International problems (Russia—threat of war)	25
Unemployment	5
Cost of living	3
Other problems	13
Don't know	5
	108%

Which political party do you think can do a better job of handling the problem you just mentioned—the Republican Party or the Democratic Party?

Democratic	30%
Republican	20
No opinion	50

(Note: table [at left] adds to more than 100% since some persons named more than one problem.)

D. Integration, Oct. 13, 1963

Do you think the Kennedy Administration is pushing integration too fast, or not fast enough?

Too fast	50%	About right	27%
Not fast enough	11%	No opinion	12%

APPLY THE SKILL

See the Chapter Review and Assessment for another opportunity to apply this skill.

Chapter 28   947

UNDERSTANDING PUBLIC OPINION POLLS

Focus Students learn how to study historical polling data to gain insight into the opinions of the American people about a pressing or divisive issue.

Instruct Discuss with students why it is important in a democracy to monitor public opinion. Ask students to describe how shifts in public opinion could impact the results of elections. Do students think officials should modify their stances in response to opinions?

Extend See the Skills for Life activity in the Resource Directory below.

ANSWERS

PRACTICE THE SKILL

1. **(a)** All adults in the nation. **(b)** All adults in the nation. **(c)** Adults in the South.

2. **(a)** It is the only question that allows individuals to suggest and rank national problems rather than having them react to a stated issue. **(b)** Some people may not have enough information to offer an opinion in answer to a given question. **(c)** The question in Polls B and D might be considered a leading question because of the word "pushing." While each question leaves out the possibility that people feel the Kennedy Administration is moving at the right speed, that is one of the answer options.

3. **(a)** That is the region of the country that is most concerned with the issues of integration and segregation. **(b)** The pollster wants to see how opinions have changed over time. **(c)** What other issues are on the minds of Americans and how important the issue of racial integration is to the population, compared with other issues. **(d)** These polls might be used to influence government policies and election platforms.

SECTION OBJECTIVES

1. Learn about President Kennedy's approach to civil rights.
2. Find out why civil rights leaders proposed a march on Washington.
3. Learn the goals of the Civil Rights Act of 1964.
4. Discover how African Americans fought to gain voting rights.

BELLRINGER

Warm-Up Activity Ask students if they plan to vote when they reach voting age. Why or why not? How many students would vote if it meant facing possible harassment or violence? Explain that protection of voters' rights was an important aspect of the civil rights movement.

Activating Prior Knowledge Ask students to recall stories of elections where votes were in dispute. Focus particularly on the 2000 presidential election, when some voters in Florida claimed that their votes went uncounted, or were counted improperly. Ask students to talk about how they would feel if they were one of those voters.

READING STRATEGY

As students read, have them analyze how effective the civil rights movement was by making a list of all the major cause-and-effect relationships they can find.

READING FOCUS

- What was President Kennedy's approach to civil rights?
- Why did civil rights leaders propose a march on Washington?
- What were the goals of the Civil Rights Act of 1964?
- How did African Americans fight to gain voting rights?

MAIN IDEA

Continuous civil rights protests in the 1960s gradually made politicians respond to public opinion and move forward with strong civil rights legislation.

KEY TERMS

March on Washington
filibuster
cloture
Civil Rights Act of 1964
Voting Rights Act of 1965
Twenty-fourth Amendment

TAKING NOTES

As you read, complete this chart showing some of the provisions of major civil rights legislation passed in the 1960s.

Legislation	Provisions
Civil Rights Act of 1964	• Increased Justice Department authority to enforce school desegregation and ensure fair voting practices •
Voting Rights Act of 1965	
Twenty-fourth Amendment	

Setting the Scene In October 1960, just weeks before the presidential election, John F. Kennedy had an opportunity to make a powerful gesture of goodwill toward African Americans. Martin Luther King, Jr., had been arrested in Georgia and sentenced to four months of hard labor. His family feared for his life in the prison camp. Kennedy called Coretta Scott King, Dr. King's wife, and offered his help. Then, Robert Kennedy, John's younger brother, persuaded the Georgia sentencing judge to release King on bail. Word of the Kennedys' actions spread quickly throughout the African American community, and many switched their votes from Nixon to Kennedy. These votes were crucial in Kennedy's slim margin of victory in the election.

Kennedy on Civil Rights

As a senator from Massachusetts, John F. Kennedy had voted for civil rights measures but had never actively pushed the issue. During his presidential campaign, however, Kennedy had sought and won many African American votes with bold rhetoric. In 1960, he proclaimed, "If the President does not himself wage the struggle for equal rights—if he stands above the battle—then the battle will inevitably be lost."

Once in office, however, Kennedy moved slowly on issues such as fair housing. He did not want to anger southern Democratic senators whose votes he needed on other issues. Yet Kennedy did appoint a number of African Americans to prominent positions. For example, Thurgood Marshall joined the United States Circuit Court and later became the first African American Supreme Court Justice. At the same time, however, Kennedy also named a number of segregationists to federal courts.

As the civil rights movement gained momentum and violence began to spread, Kennedy could no longer avoid the issue. He was deeply disturbed by the scenes of violence in

President Kennedy confers with his brother, Attorney General Robert Kennedy, outside the White House in 1962. Both Kennedy brothers played key roles in the civil rights movement.

RESOURCE DIRECTORY

Teaching Resources
Guided Reading and Review booklet, p. 115

Technology
Section Reading Support Transparencies
Guided Reading Audiotapes (English/Spanish), Ch. 28
Student Edition on Audio CD, Ch. 28
Prentice Hall Presentation Pro CD-ROM, Ch. 28
Companion Web site, www.phschool.com

the South that flooded the media. The race riots surrounding the Freedom Rides in 1961 embarrassed the President when he met with Soviet leader Nikita Khrushchev. Observers around the world watched the brutality in Birmingham early in 1963. Aware that he had to respond, Kennedy spoke to the American people on television:

66 We preach freedom around the world, and we mean it, and we cherish our freedom, here at home, but are we to say to the world, and much more importantly, to each other that this is the land of the free except for the Negroes? . . . The time has come for this nation to fulfill its promise. 99

—President John F. Kennedy, television address, June 1963

Hours after Kennedy's broadcast, civil rights leader Medgar Evers was gunned down outside his home. Evers had been an NAACP field secretary in Mississippi. He worked on recruiting NAACP members and organized various voter-registration drives throughout the state. Police charged a white supremacist, Byron de la Beckwith, with the murder. After two hung juries failed to convict him, Beckwith was set free in 1964. (Beckwith was convicted of murder in 1994 after the case was reopened.) The timing of the Evers murder made it clear that the government needed to take action.

Earlier in his term, Kennedy had proposed a modest civil rights bill. After the crisis in Birmingham, he introduced a far stronger one. The bill would prohibit segregation in public places, ban discrimination wherever federal funding was involved, and advance school desegregation. Powerful southern segregationists in Congress, however, kept the bill from coming up for a vote.

The March on Washington

To focus national attention on Kennedy's bill, civil rights leaders proposed a march on Washington, D.C. Kennedy feared the march would alienate Congress and cause racial violence. Yet when he could not persuade organizers to call off the march, he gave it his support.

The **March on Washington** took place in August 1963. More than 200,000 people came from all over the country to call for "jobs and freedom," the official slogan of the march. Labor leader A. Philip Randolph directed the march. Participants included religious leaders and celebrities such as writer James Baldwin, entertainer Sammy Davis, Jr., and baseball player Jackie Robinson. Leading folk singers of the early 1960s, such as Joan Baez and Bob Dylan, were also there. Dylan's powerful protest song "Blowin' in the Wind" was performed at the march by the popular group Peter, Paul, and Mary:

66 How many years can a mountain exist
Before it's washed to the sea?
Yes, 'n' how many years can some people exist
Before they're allowed to be free.
Yes, 'n' how many times can a man turn his head,
Pretending he just doesn't see?
The answer, my friend, is blowin' in the wind,
The answer is blowin' in the wind. 99

—Bob Dylan, ©1962

READING CHECK
Why did civil rights violence embarrass Kennedy when he met with world leaders?

VIEWING HISTORY Bob Dylan raised social consciousness about civil rights issues with his songs. Here, he plays on the back porch of the SNCC office in Greenwood, Mississippi, in 1963. **Determining Relevance** Why do you think music played an important role in the civil rights movement?

Chapter 28 • Section 4   949

Martin Luther King, Jr. (above), delivers his famous "I Have a Dream" speech at the March on Washington (below) in 1963.

Sounds of an Era

Listen to Martin Luther King, Jr.'s "I Have a Dream" speech and other sounds from the civil rights movement.

The march was peaceful and orderly. After many songs and speeches, Martin Luther King, Jr., delivered what was to become his best-known address. With power and eloquence, he spoke to all Americans:

> **KEY DOCUMENTS** ❝ I have a dream that one day this nation will rise up and live out the true meaning of its creed, 'We hold these truths to be self-evident, that all men are created equal.' I have a dream that one day on the red hills of Georgia, the sons of former slaves and the sons of former slave owners will be able to sit down together at the table of brotherhood. . . . I have a dream that my four little children will one day live in a nation where they will not be judged by the color of their skin, but by the content of their character. . . . When we allow freedom to ring, when we let it ring from every village and every hamlet, from every state and every city, we will be able to speed up that day when all of God's children, black men and white men, Jews and Gentiles, Protestants and Catholics, will be able to join hands and sing in the words of the old Negro spiritual: 'Free at last. Free at last. Thank God Almighty, we are free at last.' ❞
> —"I Have a Dream" speech, Martin Luther King, Jr., August 28, 1963

King's words echoed around the country. President Kennedy, watching the speech on television, was impressed with King's skill. But still the civil rights bill remained stalled in Congress.

The Civil Rights Act of 1964

Three months after the March on Washington, President Kennedy was assassinated, and his civil rights bill was not much closer to passage. The new President, Lyndon Johnson, was finally able to move the legislation along.

Johnson's Role Lyndon Johnson, a former member of Congress from Texas, had voted against civil rights measures during the Truman administration. As Senate majority leader, however, he had worked successfully to get a civil rights bill passed in 1957. Upon becoming President, he was eager to use his

950

political skills to build support for Kennedy's bill. In his first public address, he told Congress and the country that nothing "could more eloquently honor President Kennedy's memory than the earliest possible passage of the civil rights bill." Johnson promised African American leaders that he would push for the measure "with every energy [he] possessed," and he made good on that commitment.

Johnson let Congress know that he would accept no compromise on civil rights. After the House of Representatives passed the bill, civil rights opponents in the Senate started a lengthy **filibuster,** exercising their right of unlimited day-and-night debate. (A filibuster is a tactic in which senators prevent a vote on a measure by taking the floor and refusing to stop talking.) Johnson finally enlisted his former colleague, Republican minority leader Everett Dirksen, to support the rarely used procedure called **cloture**—a three-fifths vote to limit debate and call for a vote. In June 1964, the Senate voted for cloture, which successfully ended the filibuster. Soon after, the bill passed with support from both Democrats and Republicans.

The Provisions of the Act The **Civil Rights Act of 1964** had an impact on many areas, including voting, schools, and jobs. It gave the Justice Department the authority to act vigorously in school desegregation and voting rights cases. The law's major sections (called titles) included these provisions:

1. Title I banned the use of different voter registration standards for blacks and whites.
2. Title II prohibited discrimination in public accommodations, such as motels, restaurants, gas stations, theaters, and sports arenas.
3. Title VI allowed the withholding of federal funds from public or private programs that practice discrimination.
4. Title VII banned discrimination on the basis of race, sex, religion, or national origin by employers and unions, and also created the Equal Employment Opportunity Commission (EEOC) to investigate charges of job discrimination.

Focus on CITIZENSHIP

A Profile in Courage When Congress voted on the Civil Rights Act of 1964, southern Congressmen opposed to racial discrimination faced a difficult choice: They could vote for their beliefs, or risk losing reelection. Only one representative from a state in the Deep South, Charles Weltner of Georgia, voted for the bill.

In 1966, Weltner faced another moral dilemma. At that time, the Democratic Party required all its members to take an oath of support for all Democratic candidates. The oath meant that Weltner would have to support a vehement segregationist, Lester Maddox, for governor of Georgia. Weltner shocked the country when he decided to give up his seat in Congress rather than support Maddox. Weltner's action meant the end of his congressional career. Years later, in 1991, he received the prestigious "Profile in Courage" Award for his heroism.

951

Civil Rights Measures

Measure	Purpose
Truman's Executive Orders, 1948	• Required equality in the armed forces • Established the Committee on Equality of Treatment and Opportunity in the Armed Services • Banned discrimination in the hiring of federal employees
Civil Rights Act of 1957	• Established a federal Civil Rights Commission • Created a Civil Rights Division in the Department of Justice • Increased efforts to protect voting rights
Civil Rights Act of 1960	• Strengthened the 1957 act by giving courts more power to enforce fair voting practices • Prescribed criminal penalties for bombing and bomb threats
Kennedy's Executive Orders, 1962	• Increased enforcement of previous acts and the *Brown* v. *Board of Education* ruling • Prohibited racial and religious discrimination in housing built or purchased with federal aid
Twenty-fourth Amendment, 1964	• Eliminated the poll tax as a voting requirement
Civil Rights Act of 1964	• Banned discrimination in public accommodations • Authorized the attorney general to institute suits to desegregate schools • Outlawed discrimination in employment on the basis of race, sex, or religion • Furthered efforts at protecting voting rights
Voting Rights Act of 1965	• Eliminated literacy tests as a voting requirement • Gave federal officials the power to supervise voter registration
Open Housing Law, 1968	• Prohibited discrimination in the sale or rental of most housing

INTERPRETING CHARTS The federal government passed a significant number of civil rights measures following World War II. **Analyzing Information** *(a) Which civil rights issues did each of these measures address? (b) Which do you think were the most effective?*

Fighting for the Vote

Even with a strong new law, change came slowly. Civil rights leaders pushed harder for expanded rights, most notably voting rights.

Freedom Summer In 1964, leaders of the major civil rights groups organized a voter registration drive in Mississippi. About a thousand African American and white volunteers, mostly college students, joined in what came to be called Freedom Summer. Many white Mississippians were already angry about the new Civil Rights Act before the volunteers arrived. The Ku Klux Klan held rallies to intimidate the volunteers.

Soon, three young civil rights workers, James Chaney, Andrew Goodman, and Michael Schwerner, were reported missing. Later in the summer, FBI agents found their bodies buried in a new earthen dam a few miles from where their burned-out station wagon had been found. These three murders were only part of the turbulence reported that summer. Civil rights leaders also reported about 80 mob attacks. Volunteers were beaten up and a few wounded by gunfire. About a thousand were arrested. African American churches and homes were burned or firebombed.

The Democratic Convention Newly registered Mississippi voters, along with members of SNCC, organized the Mississippi Freedom Democratic Party (MFDP). The MFDP sent delegates to the Democratic national convention in the summer of 1964. The delegates argued that they, not politicians from the segregated party organization, were the rightful representatives.

One delegate was Fannie Lou Hamer, who had lost her job on a cotton plantation when she tried to register to vote. She told the convention about her experiences in one voter drive:

> 66 *I began to scream, and one white man got up and began to beat me on my head and tell me to 'hush.'. . . All of this is on account we want to register, to become first class citizens, and if the Freedom Democratic Party is not seated now, I question America.* 99
>
> —Fannie Lou Hamer

President Johnson offered a compromise to the Freedom Party: he would choose two MFDP delegates to sit among Mississippi's 68 seats. Johnson also promised that the rules of the convention would be changed in 1968 to eliminate discrimination. Leaders of the MFDP rejected Johnson's offer, believing that it fell short of the gains they were seeking.

The Selma March Many black southerners still had trouble obtaining their voting rights. In Selma, Alabama, police and sheriff's deputies arrested people just for standing in line to register to vote. To call attention to the voting rights issue, King and other leaders decided to organize a protest march. They would walk from Selma to the state capital, Montgomery, about 50 miles away.

As the marchers set out on a Sunday morning in March 1965, armed state troopers on horseback charged into the crowd with whips, clubs, and tear gas. TV pictures of the attack again shocked many viewers. In response, President Johnson put the Alabama National Guard under federal control. He sent members of the National Guard, along with federal marshals and army helicopters, to protect the march route. When the Selma marchers started out again, supporters from all over the country flocked to join them. By the time the march reached Montgomery, its ranks had swelled to about 25,000 people.

The Voting Rights Act Reacting to Selma, Johnson went on national television, promising a strong new law to protect voting rights. Raising his arms, Johnson repeated, "And . . . we . . . shall . . . overcome!" That summer, despite another filibuster, Congress passed the **Voting Rights Act of 1965.**

Under the act, federal officials could register voters in places where local officials were blocking registration by African Americans. The act also effectively eliminated literacy tests and other barriers. In the year after the law passed, more than 400,000 African Americans registered to vote in the Deep South.

Legal Landmarks Together, the Civil Rights Act of 1964 and the Voting Rights Act of 1965 created an entirely new voting population in the South. This new block of voters meant that more black Americans would be elected to political office. Another legal landmark was the **Twenty-fourth Amendment** to the Constitution, ratified in 1964. This amendment outlawed the poll tax, which was still being used in several southern states to keep poor African Americans from voting.

For some African Americans, new laws were not nearly enough. Impatient with the slow pace of progress, they were ready to listen to more militant leaders.

VIEWING HISTORY The Selma March, led here by Martin Luther King, Jr., and his wife, Coretta Scott King, impelled President Johnson to push for the Voting Rights Act of 1965. Between 1960 and 1970, about 2 million new African American voters registered to vote. **Recognizing Cause and Effect** *How did the Selma March focus attention on the issue of voting rights?*

Section 4 Assessment

Reading Comprehension

1. Having won the presidency by a very narrow margin, JFK was afraid of alienating white southerners in Congress, whose votes he needed to support other measures. He soon decided to back stronger civil rights legislation.

2. President Johnson urged the Senate to take a cloture vote to limit debate and call for a vote. This was done, and the bill passed with bipartisan support.

3. The violence that occurred during the 1965 Selma-to-Montgomery march.

Critical Thinking and Writing

4. Johnson used his skills as a political consensus builder and played on the nation's sorrow over Kennedy's death to ensure passage of the Civil Rights Act of 1964 and the Voting Rights Act of 1965.

5. Answers will vary, but should be descriptive and supported with facts from the section.

Take It to the NET

Responses will vary, but should note that the speech was addressed to all Americans. They should cite specific examples of King's persuasiveness, a result of the eloquence of his language.

Section 4 Assessment

READING COMPREHENSION

1. Why did President Kennedy hesitate at first to support civil rights wholeheartedly? How did his position change?

2. How did the **Civil Rights Act of 1964** overcome the **filibuster** some senators used to try to block it?

3. What events led to the passage of the **Voting Rights Act of 1965**?

CRITICAL THINKING AND WRITING

4. **Recognizing Cause and Effect** How did President Johnson's previous experience in Congress help achieve the passage of civil rights legislation?

5. **Writing a News Story** Write a short news story describing the scene at the March on Washington.

Take It to the NET

Activity: Analyzing Primary Sources Access the full text of Martin Luther King, Jr.'s "I Have a Dream" speech. Then write an analysis of the speech. To whom was the speech addressed? What terms did King use for persuasion? Use the links provided in the *America: Pathways to the Present* area of the following Web site for help in completing this activity.
www.phschool.com

Chapter 28 • Section 4   953

CAPTION ANSWERS

Viewing History The idea to march from Selma to Montgomery was daring and was certain to attract attention. Police brutality shown on television led many to sympathize with the marchers. It also caused President Johnson to act to protect the marchers, and later, to sign the 1965 Voting Rights Act.

The Movement Takes a New Turn

SECTION OBJECTIVES

1. Learn about Malcolm X's approach to gaining civil rights.
2. Become familiar with the major goals of the black power movement.
3. See why violent riots erupted in many urban streets.
4. Find out how the tragic events of 1968 affected the nation.

BELLRINGER

Warm-Up Activity Ask students what kinds of activities go on in schools that are against the rules. Then explain the difference between the terms *de jure* and *de facto*.

Activating Prior Knowledge Why do students think that some parts of the civil rights movement became nonviolent? Why do students think that some parts of the civil rights movement became violent? Do they think the movement needs to exist today?

READING STRATEGY

As students read this section, have them identify the significant leaders at this stage of the civil rights movement. Have students list ways in which these leaders' strategies differed from those who were most influential before.

READING FOCUS

- What was Malcom X's approach to gaining civil rights?
- What were the major goals of the black power movement?
- Why did violent riots erupt in many urban streets?
- How did the tragic events of 1968 affect the nation?

MAIN IDEA

Gains in civil rights came so slowly that some African Americans rejected nonviolence and called for more radical action. Increases in social unrest culminated in 1968 with the assassinations of Martin Luther King, Jr., and Robert F. Kennedy.

KEY TERMS

Nation of Islam
black nationalism
black power
de jure segregation
de facto segregation

TAKING NOTES

As you read, prepare an outline of this section. Use Roman numerals to indicate the major headings of this section, capital letters for subheadings, and numbers for the supporting details.

I. Malcolm X and Black Nationalism
  A. Black Nationalism
  B. Opposition to Integration
    1. Malcolm X rejects ideas of integration and nonviolent protest.
    2. _____
II. The Black Power Movement
  A. _____

VIEWING HISTORY Author James Baldwin wrote movingly of the black experience. **Identifying Central Issues** *What did Baldwin foresee happening to African Americans in the 1960s?*

Setting the Scene James Baldwin's essays and novels included powerful descriptions of the African American experience that touched both black and white Americans deeply. As a strong voice for the civil rights movement, Baldwin wrote about the damaging effects of segregation in the United States. He recounted "the Negro's past, of . . . death and humiliation; fear by day and night; fear as deep as the marrow of the bone; doubt that he was worthy of life, since everyone around him denied it. . . ."

In 1963, in the bestseller *The Fire Next Time*, Baldwin told how generations of oppression and suffering had set African Americans apart but had also made them stronger. Now, he said, African Americans were tired of promises. Their anger was ready to erupt. As Baldwin put it, "The Negro himself no longer believes in the good faith of white Americans—if, indeed, he ever could have."

Over time, the passage of two civil rights acts would help African Americans to win court battles that would tear down segregation. But in the meantime, African Americans still faced economic and social discrimination. Many were angry at the slow pace of change. Growing anger led to a deep divide within the civil rights movement.

Malcolm X and Black Nationalism

Outside the mainstream civil rights movement, more radical and militant political leaders emerged. The most well known of these was Malcolm X, born Malcolm Little in Omaha, Nebraska, in 1925. His father, a Baptist minister who spread the "back-to-Africa" message of Marcus Garvey, died when Little was a child. Growing up in ghettos in Detroit, Boston, and New York, Little turned to crime. At age 20, he was arrested for burglary and served seven years in prison. While in jail he joined the **Nation of Islam**, a group often called the Black Muslims. Viewing white society as oppressive, it preached black separation and self-help.

CAPTION ANSWERS

Viewing History He believed their anger was ready to erupt.

RESOURCE DIRECTORY

Teaching Resources
Guided Reading and Review booklet, p. 116

Technology
Section Reading Support Transparencies
Guided Reading Audiotapes (English/Spanish), Ch. 28
Student Edition on Audio CD, Ch. 28
RESOURCE PRO Literature Activity *Sins of the Father,* found on Resource Pro, uses an essay from Eldridge Cleaver's *Soul on Ice* to show Cleaver's view that there could be mutual respect between the races if "white youth" could repudiate the evils of the past.
Prentice Hall Presentation Pro CD-ROM, Ch. 28
Companion Web site, www.phschool.com

Black Nationalism   Elijah Muhammad, the leader of the Nation of Islam, taught that Allah (the Muslim name for God) would bring about a "Black Nation," a union among all nonwhite peoples. According to Elijah Muhammad, one of the keys to self-knowledge was knowing one's enemy. For him, the enemy of the Nation of Islam was white society.

Members of the Nation of Islam did not seek change through political means but waited for Allah to create the Black Nation. In the meantime, they tried to lead righteous lives and worked hard to become economically self-sufficient.

Released from prison in 1952, Malcolm Little changed his name to Malcolm X. (The name Little, he said, had come from slaveowners.) He spent the next 12 years as a minister of the Nation of Islam, winning followers with his fiery speeches. He spread the ideas of **black nationalism,** a belief in the separate identity and racial unity of the African American community.

Opposition to Integration   Malcolm X disagreed with both the tactics and the goals of the early civil rights movement. He called the March on Washington the "Farce on Washington," and voiced his irritation at "all of this non-violent, begging-the-white-man kind of dying . . . all of this sitting-in, sliding-in, wading-in, eating-in, diving-in, and all the rest." Instead of preaching brotherly love, he rejected ideas of integration. Asking why anyone would want to join white society, he noted:

> 66 No sane black man really wants integration! No sane white man really wants integration! No sane black man really believes that the white man ever will give the black man anything more than token integration. No! The Honorable Elijah Muhammad teaches that for the black man in America the only solution is complete separation from the white man. . . . The American black man should be focusing his effort toward building his own businesses, and decent homes for himself. As other ethnic groups have done, let the black people, wherever possible, however possible, patronize their own kind, hire their own kind, and start in those ways to build up the black race's ability to do for itself. That's the only way the American black man is ever going to get respect. 99
>
> —Malcolm X

Malcolm X and Elijah Muhammad came to disagree about many things, including political action. In 1964, Malcolm X left the Nation of Islam and formed his own religious organization, called Muslim Mosque, Inc. He then made a pilgrimage, or religious journey, to Mecca, the holy city of Islam, in Saudi Arabia.

Seeing millions of Muslims of all races worshipping together peacefully had a profound effect on Malcolm X. It changed his views about separatism and hatred of white people. When he returned, he was ready to work with other civil rights leaders and even with white Americans on some issues. It seemed as if Malcolm X might become one of the leaders in a unified civil rights movement. His change of heart, however, had earned him some enemies.

Malcolm X had only nine months to spread his new beliefs. In February 1965, he was shot to death at a rally in New York. Three members of the Nation of Islam were charged with the murder. Malcolm X's message of black nationalism lived on, however. He particularly influenced younger members of SNCC, the Student Nonviolent Coordinating Committee.

VIEWING HISTORY Malcolm X was a leading minister of the Nation of Islam until 1964. **Making Comparisons** How did black nationalism differ from other kinds of civil rights activism?

READING CHECK

How did Malcolm X's views change after his pilgrimage in 1964?

Focus Explain that nonviolent protests resulted in early gains, but that progress subsequently seemed to stall. Ask students how African Americans reacted to continuing discrimination.

Instruct Discuss the alternatives to nonviolent confrontation that evolved in the civil rights movement. How did the views of Malcolm X differ from those of Martin Luther King, Jr.?

Point out President Johnson's comment on the last page of the section. Then discuss the answers to his and the following questions: Why, after so much progress for civil rights, did anger and violence erupt? Why did African Americans become cynical about the goal of nonviolent integration pursued by Martin Luther King, Jr.?

Assess/Reteach Have students evaluate the progress made in civil rights since the 1960s. In what areas have gains in equality been made? In what areas does inequality still prevail?

*A*CTIVITY
Connecting with Culture

Have students research black nationalism in America, beginning with abolitionist David Walker, whose *Appeal to the Coloured Citizens of the World* (1829) articulated the fundamental beliefs of black nationalism for the first time. Allow individuals or small groups to focus on an aspect of the topic in depth: e.g., chronology of black nationalism, explanation of black nationalist thought, profiles of individual leaders, or readings from black nationalist texts. Have groups present their findings orally, in writing, or in a chart or diagram. **(Verbal/Linguistic; Visual/Spatial)**

READING CHECK

He changed his views about separatism and white people.

CAPTION ANSWERS

Viewing History Leaders like Malcolm X hoped to see African Americans succeed economically and politically without joining white society. They were thus opposed to Dr. King's desire for an integrated society (although Malcolm X himself eventually softened on this issue).

The Black Power Movement

One SNCC leader who heard Malcolm's message was Stokely Carmichael. Born in Trinidad, in the West Indies, in 1941, Carmichael came to the United States at the age of 11 and was soon involved in protests. At Howard University in Washington, D.C., he and other students became actively involved in the Washington chapter of SNCC.

SNCC Shifts Gears As Carmichael rose to SNCC leadership, the group became more radical. After being beaten and jailed for his participation in demonstrations, he was tired of nonviolent protest. He called on SNCC workers to carry guns for self-defense. He wanted to make the group exclusively black, rejecting white activists.

The split in the civil rights movement became obvious in June 1966. At a protest march in Greenwood, Mississippi, while King's followers were singing "We Shall Overcome," Carmichael's supporters drowned them out with "We Shall Overrun." Then Carmichael, just out of jail, jumped into the back of an open truck to challenge the moderate leaders:

> 66 *This is the twenty-seventh time I have been arrested, and I ain't going to jail no more! . . . The only way we gonna stop them white men from whippin' us is to take over. We been saying freedom for six years—and we ain't got nothin'. What we gonna start saying now is 'black power!'* 99
> —Stokely Carmichael, public address, June 1966

VIEWING HISTORY Members of the Black Panthers marched in New York City in 1968 to protest the trial of Huey P. Newton. Newton had been convicted of voluntary manslaughter in the death of a police officer. His conviction was later overturned. **Identifying Central Issues** *What efforts did the Black Panthers make to improve the quality of life in black communities?*

As he repeated "We . . . want . . . black . . . power!" the audience excitedly echoed the new slogan. Carmichael's idea of **black power** resonated with many African Americans. It was a call "to unite, to recognize their heritage, to build a sense of community . . . to begin to define their own goals, to lead their own organizations and support those organizations."

The Black Panthers In the fall of 1966, a new militant political party, the Black Panthers, was formed by activists Bobby Seale and Huey Newton. The Panthers wanted African Americans to lead their own communities. They demanded that the federal government rebuild the nation's ghettos to make up for years of neglect. The Panthers also wanted to combat what they saw as police brutality in the ghettos. Often, as a result of their monitoring the police, they became engaged in direct confrontation with white authorities. Newton repeated the words of Chinese Communist leader Mao Zedong: "Power flows from the barrel of a gun." Although they did organize some beneficial community programs, the Panthers more often found themselves in violent encounters with police.

Black power gave rise to the slogan "Black is beautiful," which fostered racial pride. It also led to a serious split in the civil rights movement. More radical groups like SNCC and the Black Panthers moved away from the NAACP and other more moderate organizations.

Riots in the Streets

The early civil rights movement focused on battling *de jure* **segregation,** racial separation created by law. Changes in the law, however, did not address the more difficult issue of *de facto* **segregation,** the separation caused by social conditions such as poverty. *De facto* segregation was a fact of life in most American cities, not just in the South.

There were no "whites only" signs above water fountains in northern cities, yet discrimination continued in education, housing, and employment. African Americans were kept out of well-paying jobs, job-training programs, and suburban housing. Inner-city schools were run-down and poorly equipped.

Residents of ghetto neighborhoods viewed police officers as dangerous oppressors, not upholders of justice. James Baldwin remarked that a white police officer in one of these neighborhoods was "like an occupying soldier in a bitterly hostile country." Eventually, frustration and anger boiled over into riots and looting. In 1964, riots ravaged Rochester, New York; New York City; and several cities in New Jersey.

One of the most violent riots occurred in the Los Angeles neighborhood of Watts. On August 11, 1965, police in Watts pulled over a 21-year-old black man for drunk driving. At first the interaction was friendly among the police, the suspect, and a crowd of Watts residents that had gathered. When the suspect resisted arrest, however, one police officer panicked and began swinging his riot baton. The crowd was outraged, and the scene touched off six days of rioting.

Thousands of people filled the streets, burning cars and stores, stealing merchandise, and sniping at firefighters. When the national guard and local police finally gained control, 34 people were dead and more than a thousand had been injured. Violence spread to other cities in 1966 and 1967. Cries of "Burn, baby, burn" replaced the gentler slogans of the earlier civil rights movement.

A concerned federal government set up a special National Advisory Commission on Civil Disorders, headed by former Illinois Governor Otto Kerner, to investigate. In 1968, the Kerner Commission report declared flatly that the riots were an explosion of the anger that had been smoldering in the inner-city ghettos. It declared that "our nation is moving toward two societies, one black, one white—separate and unequal."

Tragedy Strikes in 1968

In the troubled decade of the 1960s, the most shattering year was 1968. A series of tragic events hit with such force that, month by month, the nation seemed to be coming apart. Against a backdrop of domestic violence, chaos, and confrontation, many Americans began to believe that the chance of achieving peaceful social change through political activism was hopeless.

For many Americans, the memory of President Kennedy's assassination in 1963 was still vivid and haunting five years later. They looked to other leaders to carry on the spirit and idealism of the Kennedy years. But in 1968, people's hopes were again shattered by the burst of bullets from assassins' guns.

Martin Luther King, Jr., Is Assassinated In 1968, Dr. King turned his attention to economic issues. Convinced that poverty bred violence, he broadened his approach to attack economic injustice. Calling his new crusade the

---

Focus on ECONOMICS

***De facto* Challenges** The fight against *de facto* segregation faced different challenges than the fight against *de jure* segregation. One problem was that the civil rights movement lost much of its political support as the Nixon administration assumed power in 1969. Another had to do with changes taking place within the African American community. Not all civil rights organizations joined in this fight. Some activists believed that the real struggle was against legal barriers and not against residential patterns. Because there was less solidarity among civil rights groups, protests lost much of their strength.

African American solidarity was also weakened as a result of the increasing number of black Americans who had "made it" by the early 1970s. Many began moving to suburbs, attending college, and obtaining better jobs. As a result, some African Americans became disconnected from the intense struggle with poverty in the city ghettos.

Overall, the statistics looked promising. The number of black Americans living in poverty decreased from more than 40 percent in 1959 to about 20 percent in 1968. Between 1960 and 1977, the number of African Americans enrolled in college increased by 500 percent. Yet, for those African Americans living in inner cities, conditions had not improved. For example, in 1970, 60 percent of African Americans living in cities had low-level service jobs, compared to 33 percent of white Americans also living in cities.

---

*A*CTIVITY
Connecting with Culture

Ask students to locate protest poems, prose, songs, and art from the 1960s and to include several in a notebook. Suggest that they begin by examining the writings of James Baldwin and Malcolm X. **(Verbal/Linguistic)**

*B*ACKGROUND
Connections to Today

In 1992 race riots again paralyzed the city of Los Angeles. The cause was eerily similar to that of 1965: outrage over the mistreatment of a black citizen by white police officers. In April 1992 four white LAPD officers, who had been caught on videotape beating a black motorist, were found innocent of brutality by a jury. As news of the acquittal spread, riots and mayhem erupted around the city. Five days later, 58 people were dead and thousands more were injured. Since then, the LAPD has come under scrutiny for brutality, corruption, and fabricating testimony. As a result of the most recent investigation, dozens of convictions were overturned.

CUSTOMIZE FOR ...

Less Proficient Writers

Have students make a chart illustrating the key occurrences in the chain of events that led from nonviolent protests to the ghetto riots.

VIEWING HISTORY Assassinations in 1968 shocked the nation. Above, Martin Luther King, Jr., lies mortally wounded, while companions point frantically to the direction from which shots were fired. At right, busboy Jay Romero is the first to reach Robert Kennedy after he was shot in a hotel kitchen just after winning the California primary. **Identifying Central Issues** *What effect did these murders have?*

Poor People's Campaign, King began planning a Poor People's March on Washington. Traveling around the United States to mobilize support, he went to Memphis, Tennessee, in early April. There he offered his assistance to striking garbage workers who were seeking better working conditions.

King spoke eloquently, referring to threats made against his life:

> 66 *We've got some difficult days ahead. But it doesn't matter with me now, because I've been to the mountain top. And I don't mind. Like anybody, I would like to live a long life. . . . But I'm not concerned about that now. I just want to do God's will. And He's allowed me to go up to the mountain. And I've looked over. And I've seen the promised land.* 99
> —Martin Luther King, Jr., April 3, 1968

The next day, as King stood on the balcony of his motel, a bullet fired from a high-powered rifle tore into him. An hour later, King was dead.

King's assassination sparked violent reactions across the nation. In an outburst of rage and frustration, some African Americans rioted, setting fires and looting stores in more than 120 cities. The riots, and the police response to them, left close to 50 people dead. President Johnson ordered flags on federal buildings to be flown at half mast to honor King, but it took more than 50,000 troops to quell the violence. For many Americans of all races, King's death eroded faith in the idea of nonviolent change.

Robert F. Kennedy Is Assassinated Senator Robert F. Kennedy, who had served his brother John as Attorney General, was another major crusader for civil rights. In 1968, he decided to enter the race for the Democratic presidential nomination. President Johnson had lost support from many Democrats because of America's involvement in the Vietnam War. After Senator Eugene McCarthy lost to Johnson in the New Hampshire primary by only six percentage points, Kennedy realized that Johnson was vulnerable. On March 16, Kennedy entered the campaign. His candidacy received a critical boost on March 31, when Johnson stunned the nation by announcing that he would not run for a second term as President.

In the years since his brother's death, Robert Kennedy had reached out to many Americans, including Chicanos in the California farm fields, Native Americans in the Southwest, African Americans in the Mississippi delta, and poor white families in New York tenements. Opposed to the Vietnam War, he condemned the killing of both Americans and Vietnamese. He criticized the Johnson administration for financing a war instead of funding the programs needed to help the poor and disadvantaged at home.

Kennedy spent the spring of 1968 battling McCarthy in the Democratic primary elections. On June 4, he won a key victory in California's primary. But just after midnight, after giving his victory speech in a Los Angeles hotel, Robert Kennedy was shot by an assassin. He died the next day.

When the shooting was reported, several campaign workers who had watched the speech on TV were waiting for Kennedy in his hotel room. One of them, civil rights leader John Lewis, later said, "We all just fell to the floor and started crying. To me that was like the darkest, saddest moment." Kennedy's death ended many people's hopes for an inspirational leader who could heal the nation's wounds.

Legacy of the Movement

At times, both black and white Americans wondered whether real progress in civil rights was possible. Many young activists felt frustrated and discouraged when the movement failed to bring changes quickly. Lyndon Johnson was devastated by the violence that exploded near the end of his presidency. "How is it possible," he asked, "after all we've accomplished?" Still, the measures passed by his administration had brought tremendous change. Segregation was now illegal. Because of voter registration drives, thousands of African Americans could now vote. The power they wielded changed the nature of American political life.

Between 1970 and 1975, the number of African American elected officials rose by 88 percent. Black mayors were elected in Atlanta, Detroit, Los Angeles, and Newark, New Jersey. Others served in Congress and state legislatures. In 1966, Barbara Jordan became the first African American elected to the Texas state senate since Reconstruction. Six years later she was elected to the United States Congress. Jordan noted what made the movement necessary:

> ❝ The civil rights movement called America to look at itself in a giant mirror. . . . Do the black people who were born on this soil, who are American citizens, do they really feel that this is the land of opportunity, the land of the free? . . . America had to say no. ❞
>
> —Texas Representative Barbara Jordan

Section 5 Assessment

Reading Comprehension

1. It rejected the idea of racial integration and suggested that blacks needed to develop a separate identity and racial unity.

2. By stressing that African Americans should build their own communities, just as Carmichael had wanted to make SNCC an all-black organization. Both Carmichael and the Black Panthers disdained nonviolence and became more radical.

3. That the riots were a result of pent-up anger, and that the nation was moving toward two separate and unequal societies of African Americans and whites.

4. They marked an end to the civil rights movement; Americans lost faith in nonviolent protest, in their leaders, and in affecting change through political action.

Critical Thinking and Writing

5. Possible answer: The statement is an opinion; it expresses Malcolm X's conclusion about the complex problem of race relations in the United States.

6. Answers will vary, but should build a case for the student's viewpoint and be supported with facts from the section.

Take It to the NET

Student time lines should indicate events in the civil rights movement from 1965 to 1970.

Section 5 Assessment

READING COMPREHENSION

1. How did **black nationalism** reflect a change from the early days of the civil rights movement?

2. How did the Black Panthers reflect Stokely Carmichael's idea of **black power?**

3. What did the Kerner Commission conclude about the race riots occurring in American cities?

4. What impact did the 1968 assassinations have on the legacy of the civil rights movement?

CRITICAL THINKING AND WRITING

5. **Distinguishing Fact From Opinion** Malcom X once said that for African Americans "the only solution is complete separation from the white man." Do you believe this statement to be a fact or an opinon? Explain your answer.

6. **Writing to Persuade** Black nationalists believed that African Americans should establish separate communities. Write a brief paper defending or opposing this position.

Take It to the NET

Activity: Creating a Time Line
Do further research on the civil rights movement from 1965–1970. Create a poster-sized time line for these years, incorporating images and quotations you find in your research. Be sure to include events covered in this section. Use the links provided in the *America: Pathways to the Present* area of the following Web site for help in completing this activity.
www.phschool.com

Chapter 28 — Review and Assessment

REVIEWING KEY TERMS

Students should refer to the definitions of key terms in the chapter to write sentences that show an understanding of the civil rights movement.

REVIEWING MAIN IDEAS

13. By declaring "separate but equal" unconstitutional, and finding support as well as violent opposition to this ruling, the nation faced dilemmas of integration and racial uprisings.

14. Sample answers: By law, blacks were permitted to attend the same school as whites; the Ku Klux Klan became more active; the Southern Manifesto was created.

15. Sample answer: The NAACP had many legal successes, including *Brown* v. *Board of Education*. CORE organized demonstrations against segregation and became a national organization by the 1950s.

16. King's approach of nonviolent protest was influenced by Mohandas Gandhi's ideas, espoused during India's struggle for independence from Britain.

17. Activists placed groups of African Americans and whites on Freedom Rides to the South. After the groups were attacked at bus terminals, the federal government forced local authorities to uphold desegregation policies for interstate bus travelers.

18. After Kennedy's assassination, Johnson lobbied Congress to pass the Civil Rights Act of 1964 and the Voting Rights Act of 1965.

19. Civil Rights Act: created consistent standards for voter registration; prohibited discrimination in public places; allowed withholding of federal funds from programs that practiced discrimination; outlawed discrimination in the workplace; created the EEOC. Voting Rights Act: allowed federal officials to register voters in places where local officials were blocking African American registration; eliminated literacy tests and other barriers to voting; allowed for federal supervision of voter registration.

---

creating a CHAPTER SUMMARY

Copy this web diagram (right). Add more circles to each of the four categories of civil rights participants. Fill in the circles with details about each person you add.

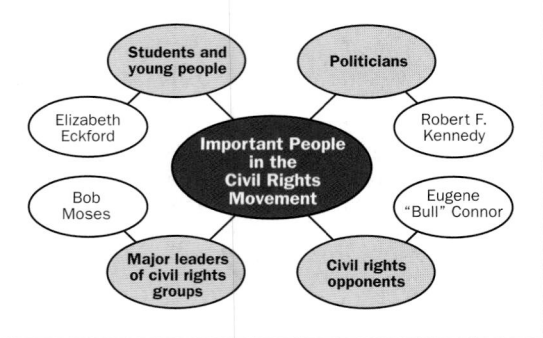

For additional review and enrichment activities, see the interactive version of *America: Pathways to the Present*, available on the Web and on CD-ROM.

★ Reviewing Key Terms

For each of the terms below, write a sentence explaining how it relates to the civil rights movement.

1. Montgomery bus boycott
2. integration
3. interracial
4. nonviolent protest
5. sit-in
6. Freedom Ride
7. filibuster
8. cloture
9. Twenty-fourth Amendment
10. black nationalism
11. black power
12. *de facto* segregation

★ Reviewing Main Ideas

13. How did the Supreme Court's decision in *Brown v. Board of Education* set the stage for a civil rights movement? (Section 1)
14. What were three effects of the *Brown* decision? (Section 1)
15. Name two groups that worked for African American rights *before* the 1960s. What did they accomplish? (Section 2)
16. What new approach did Martin Luther King, Jr., bring to the civil rights movement? What was the inspiration for his philosophy? (Section 2)
17. How did activists work to desegregate the interstate bus system? (Section 3)

18. What was President Johnson's role in passing civil rights legislation? (Section 4)
19. What did the Civil Rights Act of 1964 and the Voting Rights Act of 1965 accomplish? (Section 4)
20. What is the Nation of Islam? (Section 5)
21. What major changes occurred in the civil rights movement in the mid- to late 1960s? (Section 5)

★ Critical Thinking

22. **Identifying Assumptions** What assumptions did the federal government make when it created the termination policy to promote Native American assimilation into mainstream American culture?
23. **Formulating Questions** Make a list of five questions that you might ask a student activist from the 1960s to find out his or her reasons for taking part in the civil rights movement.
24. **Synthesizing Information** SNCC began as an alternative to existing civil rights groups. How did SNCC maintain itself as an alternative organization, and how did it change over time?
25. **Demonstrating Reasoned Judgment** Many people who lived through the 1960s would agree that the country lost its sense of hope after the deaths of Martin Luther King, Jr., and Robert F. Kennedy. Do you think that people in the United States today have regained a sense of hope?

One of the first African American students to attend a white Arkansas high school

Students and young people

Politicians

Civil rights crusader

U.S. Attorney General

Elizabeth Eckford

Robert F. Kennedy

Important People in the Civil Rights Movement

SNCC leader

Teacher

Bob Moses

Eugene "Bull" Connor

Birmingham police commissioner

Directed violent police actions against civil rights protestors

Major leaders of civil rights groups

Civil rights opponents

★ Skills Assessment

Analyzing Political Cartoons ▶

26. Examine both panels of the cartoon. What does the man represent?

27. (a) What does the first pit represent? (b) What does the second pit represent?

28. What is the man's overall goal, and what obstacles does he face?

29. What point is the cartoonist trying to make?

Analyzing Primary Sources

Read the excerpt from Martin Luther King, Jr.'s "I Have a Dream" speech in Section 4. Then answer the following questions.

30. Which of the following best *summarizes* King's dream?

   A that Americans of all religions will be free at last
   B that all Americans will achieve true equality and freedom
   C that African Americans will form a brotherhood
   D that children will not be judged by their color

31. King hopes that his dream will be fulfilled

   F sometime in the future.
   G in his children's lifetime.
   H in the twentieth century.
   J today.

Applying the Chapter Skill: *Using Autobiography and Biography*

32. Reread the excerpt on the Skills for Life page.
   (a) Why was Ralph Abernathy a reliable source for information about the civil rights movement?
   (b) How might Abernathy's association with Martin Luther King, Jr., have affected his point of view toward those events?

ACTIVITIES

Writing to LEARN

Writing to Inform
Reread the list of provisions of the 1964 Civil Rights Act in Section 4. Look through current newspapers and news magazines. Then write an essay describing how these laws and regulations still affect American life and politics today.

Primary Source CD-ROM

Working With Primary Sources Find additional information on the civil rights movement on the *Exploring Primary Sources in U.S. History CD-ROM* and use the selection(s) provided to complete the Chapter 28 primary source activity located in the *America: Pathways to the Present* area of the following Web site.
www.phschool.com

Take It to the NET

Chapter Self-Test As a review activity, take the Chapter 28 Self-Test in the *America: Pathways to the Present* area at the Web site listed below. The questions are designed to test your understanding of the chapter content.
www.phschool.com

---

20. An organization dedicated to black separation and self-help.
21. It changed from a mainstream, non-violent movement to a collection of splinter groups advocating various degrees of militancy. It also became younger and less church-inflenced.

CRITICAL THINKING

22. The government assumed that Native Americans wanted to assimilate into mainstream American culture, and that the best way to improve their existing living conditions was for them to abandon their traditional ways of life and become "Americanized."
23. Sample questions: Why did you join the civil rights movement? Did your opinions of race relations change as a result of your participation? Do you agree that the use of nonviolent confrontation is the most effective way of achieving equality?
24. SNCC gave a voice to the youth generation. It maintained its individuality by deliberately choosing to remain autonomous, seeking immediate change, and through such activities as helping to organize the Mississippi Freedom Democratic Party. SNCC became less interracial and more radical over time.
25. Students' outlooks are likely to vary depending on individual situations, but they should reflect thoughtful consideration of today's major issues in relation to the issues that were current at the time of the 1968 assassinations.

SKILLS ASSESSMENT

26. African Americans.
27. (a) Racial inequality. (b) Economic inequality.
28. He is seeking equality in American society, but racism and lack of economic opportunity prevent him from achieving it.
29. Economic inequality is as effective as racism in preventing equality between blacks and whites.
30. B
31. G
32. (a) He was a firsthand observer, his tone is matter-of-fact, and he doesn't seem to exaggerate.
(b) He was a strong partisan of King's views and worked closely with him, meaning that his views would be favorable.

ANSWERS TO ACTIVITIES

Writing to LEARN

Students' answers will vary, but should demonstrate the relevance of the Civil Rights Act in American life and politics today. For example, more recent cases of discrimination in the workplace sometimes appear in current newspaper accounts.

Primary Source CD-ROM

Direct students to the additional primary sources that can be found on the *Exploring Primary Sources in U.S. History CD-ROM.*

Take It to the NET

Additional support materials and activities for Chapter 28 of *America: Pathways to the Present* can be found in the Social Studies area at the Prentice Hall School Web site. **www.phschool.com**

ENCOUNTERS WITH SEGREGATION

Focus Have students find the meaning of each of these words in a dictionary before they begin to read: *defunct, premise, freestanding, sparse, Jim Crow.* Ask them to consider, as they read, how a greater understanding of segregation might have changed white Americans' attitudes toward civil rights.

Instruct Have students role-play Bruce Killebrew and Joan W. Musbach talking to each other, as adults, about their childhood experiences of race. Have students work in pairs to outline conversations and choose roles. Tell them to construct conversations so that they give information in a manner that is consistent with both characters. Then have them perform their conversations for the class.

Analyzing the Document Use this additional question to generate class discussion:

Critical Thinking: Making Comparisons How were Bruce Killebrew's and Joan W. Musbach's experiences alike? How were they different? *(They were alike in that both students became aware of current issues dealing with race through personal experience. They were different in that Killebrew was inspired by integration, whereas Musbach was shocked and saddened by segregation.)*

AmericanHeritage®
MY BRUSH WITH **HISTORY**™

by BRUCE KILLEBREW and JOAN W. MUSBACH

Encounters With Segregation

COLORED ← WAITING ROOM

The two passages below describe how two white Americans became aware of the system of racial segregation that existed in many parts of the country. In the first account, Bruce Killebrew recalls the integration of his third-grade class. In the second account, Joan W. Musbach remembers the day that she, as a high school student, came face to face with her own ignorance about segregation.

A VIRGINIA CLASSROOM In 1954 my father was stationed at the Pentagon in Washington, D.C., and we lived on the now-defunct South Post of Fort Myer. My friends and I had a grand time romping through the nearby Civil War battlefields, taking turns being Yankee and Rebel. I couldn't decide whether to favor the Blue or the Gray. At the age of eight I'd really never thought about the issues that fueled the fighting.

Then, one day in the first week of September 1954, at the beginning of the year for our small military elementary school at Fort Myer, there were new faces in my class—and reporters from United Press and *Army Times* taking pictures. They were photographing the class while I led the Pledge of Allegiance for the first integrated class in the formerly Confederate state of Virginia. The two new students were black, and to me and the rest of my third-grade classmates they did not seem any different from the rest of us kids. But I was very proud to have been chosen to lead the Pledge of Allegiance on that day.

The event would help shape this nation's future, and my own. It brought

Bruce Killebrew (far left) leads the Pledge of Allegiance for one of the first integrated classes in Virginia.

RESOURCE DIRECTORY

Technology
AmericanHeritage® **My Brush with History**™
Videotapes *Encounters With Segregation*

✔ **TEST PREPARATION**

Have students use the excerpt on these pages to answer the following question.

Why did newspaper reporters appear in Bruce Killebrew's class in the first week of school?

A Newspaper reporters in every town cover the beginning of the school year.

B Killebrew's school was particularly noteworthy because it was located on a military base.

C The reporters expected violence in the newly integrated school.

D Killebrew's was the first integrated class in Virginia.

home to me the idea that all men are created equal and have the right to equal opportunity. Much of my life as an individual and a social worker has been based on the premise I learned in that classroom in 1954.

A MIDWESTERN CAFÉ On a crisp, cool, sunny Saturday in January, a Midwestern café—a free-standing building with one counter, stools in front, grill behind—became the site of the most memorable experience of my high school years.

It was 1960. I was a senior member of the debate team from John J. Ingels High School, in Atchison, Kansas. I was growing up within sixty miles of the origin of the 1954 Supreme Court case, *Brown* v. *Board of Education*, but, as of 1960, had never heard of Linda Brown or the case that bears her name. I was soon to discover that there was a great deal about which I was unaware.

We finished the Saturday-morning rounds and then went out for lunch before returning to the college to hear the semifinalists announced. We chose an appealing-looking cafeteria near the college. I was the only girl on the trip, and I was still just entering when Mr. Phipps and the boys turned around and came back out. I was busy talking and didn't ask why we had left. I assumed the cafeteria was too crowded. We got into Mr. Phipps's old car and drove a few blocks to a café. Business was sparse, and we spread out down the red-plastic-covered stools along the counter. John, my partner, was seated beside me. The waitress came down the counter distributing menus. John did not get one. We called this to her attention, and she quickly informed us that blacks were not served in there. I was shocked. I had never heard of such a thing. We all got up and went to the car, and Mr. Phipps went to a nearby hamburger stand and bought hamburgers and sodas for us all to eat in the car.

John wouldn't eat. He sat in the corner of the back seat, speechless. We didn't know what to say either. We just ate our hamburgers and went back to the college.

As I thought about the incident, I realized that John was the victim of our ignorance as well as of the prejudice of the management of the cafeteria and the café. He had probably never been exposed to such humiliation before,

The countless small conflicts of a segregated society flared up nationwide in diners and lunchrooms such as this one.

protected by parents or other adults who would have avoided such an incident. Strange as it may seem, a carful of high school students and their teacher were unaware of the segregation of public services just across the river from where they lived.

The look on John's face as we ate our hamburgers ensured that I would never forget that crisp January Saturday or the Kansas City café where I met Jim Crow.

Source: *American Heritage* magazine, April 1991 and April 1994.

Understanding Primary Sources

1. What do Mr. Phipps and the boys do after they go into the first cafeteria near the college?

2. Why might they have done this?

American Heritage®
MY BRUSH WITH **HISTORY**™
📼 **Videotapes**

For more information about the fight against segregation, view "Encounters With Segregation."

963

American Pathways
CITIZENSHIP

Expanding Civil Rights

When the Constitution was written, only white male property owners had the right to vote. Over the past two centuries, though, the term "government by the people" has become more of a reality. Civil rights have been expanded for many groups, including Native Americans, African Americans, women, and young adults.

1 **The Bill of Rights**

1791 The first ten amendments to the United States Constitution were added in 1791. Known as the Bill of Rights, these amendments guaranteed freedom of belief and expression, freedom and security of the person, and fair and equal treatment before the law. Throughout American history, many people have worked to make these constitutional guarantees a reality for all Americans.

President Washington's cabinet (right)

2 **Rights for African Americans**

1868 and 1870 Two amendments ratified during the Reconstruction period sought to improve the civil rights of African Americans. The Fourteenth Amendment, ratified in 1868, granted citizenship to African Americans and declared that states could not "deprive any person of life, liberty, or property, without due process of law" or "deny to any person . . . the equal protection of the laws." The Fifteenth Amendment, ratified in 1870, was intended to protect any citizen from being denied the right to vote because of race or color. Still, for nearly another century, African Americans were systematically prevented from voting.

African American voters casting ballots in the 1876 election (left)

3 **Suffrage for Women**

1900–1920 Women made important civil rights gains with the ratification of the Nineteenth Amendment in 1920, which gave all American women the right to vote.

An American suffragette (left)

964

RESOURCE DIRECTORY

Teaching Resources
Units 9/10 booklet
• American Pathways Activity, pp. 47–48
American Pathways Thematic Posters

Technology
Companion Web site, www.phschool.com

EXPANDING CIVIL RIGHTS

Focus Remind students that the acquisition of civil rights has been a long and gradual process. At the time of the writing of the Constitution, only white males could vote. Over the course of the last 200 years, groups such as African Americans, Native Americans, and women have gained the right to vote. Laws have been passed banning discrimination against such groups.

Instruct Tell students to read the text carefully and look over the photographs. Ask students to think about why it has been necessary to pass laws to enforce civil rights. Ask students whether legislation is all that's needed to change people's attitudes. What else needs to happen to ensure "liberty and justice for all"?

Extend Encourage students to focus on one aspect of the struggle for civil rights. For example, students might choose to explore the suffrage movement or the civil rights era of the 1950s and 1960s. Tell students to research this era. Who were some of the prominent leaders? What were some of the biggest obstacles to obtaining civil rights?

Rights for Native Americans

1924 As European settlers migrated westward, they pushed many Indian groups off their lands. The result for many Native Americans was the loss of their sovereignty, culture, and territory. To help prevent further losses, Congress ratified the General Citizenship Act in 1924. It granted Native Americans the rights of citizenship, including the right to vote in federal elections.

 ### The Civil Rights Era

1954–1968 In the period following World War II, thousands of ordinary Americans worked to end racial and ethnic injustice in the United States. The civil rights movement, especially, won significant victories in the battle to secure equal rights for all Americans, including African Americans, Latinos, Native Americans, and women.

Martin Luther King, Jr., and his wife, Coretta Scott King, lead a protest march from Selma to Montgomery, Alabama, in 1965 (above).

 ### Suffrage for Young Adults

1971 Ratified in 1971, the Twenty-sixth Amendment set the minimum voting age at 18. Many of those who backed the amendment began to work for its passage during World War II. Its ratification was spurred by the Vietnam War.

An 18-year-old voter (left)

 ### Rights for the Disabled

1990 The Americans with Disabilities Act guarantees disabled Americans equal opportunity in employment and public accommodations. The act has succeeded in breaking down many of the barriers that prevented the disabled from achieving equality.

Continuity and Change

1. How long did the system of Jim Crow, or legal segregation, last? What finally ended it?
2. What did minority groups do to try to gain their civil rights?

 Take It to the NET: Creating a Study Guide
Print and complete the study guide for this topic found in the *America: Pathways to the Present* area of the following Web site. **www.phschool.com**

965

 ## Take It to the NET

Students can print the American Pathways thematic study guide for this topic at the Prentice Hall School Web site, or you can provide students with copies of the study guide, which is found in the Units 9/10 booklet, the American Pathways Activity, pages 47–48. Students should use their texts to fill in a one-sentence description for each event on the study guide. When completed for each of the American Pathways topics, the thematic study guides will aid students in preparing for an end-of-course exam.

ANSWERS

1. Jim Crow lasted from about 1877 to 1954. It ended with the Supreme Court's decision in *Brown* v. *Board of Education of Topeka*.
2. Minority groups formed organizations, such as the NAACP and the American Indian Movement, to push the government to end discrimination.

Chapter 29 Planning Guide
Resource Manager

	CORE INSTRUCTION	READING/SKILLS
Chapter-Level Resources	Teaching Resources • Pacing Charts booklet • Block Scheduling booklet **Resource Pro® CD-ROM**, Ch. 29 **Prentice Hall Presentation Pro CD-ROM**, Ch. 29 **www.phschool.com** • eTeach	**Guided Reading Audiotapes (English/Spanish)** **Student Edition on Audio CD**, Ch. 29 **Social Studies Skills Tutor CD-ROM** **Color Transparencies**, A48, A49, B17, H19
1 The New Frontier 1. Learn about factors that affected the election of 1960. 2. Find out about domestic programs pursued by President Kennedy. 3. Read about circumstances that surrounded Kennedy's assassination.	Teaching Resources **Units 9/10 booklet** • Section 1 Quiz, p. 16 **Learning Styles Lesson Plans booklet**, p. 60	**Guided Reading and Review booklet**, p. 117 **Guide to the Essentials**, p. 147 **Learning with Documents booklet**, p. 68 **Skills for Life booklet**, p. 31 **Section Reading Support Transparencies**
2 The Great Society 1. Discover Lyndon Johnson's path to the presidency. 2. Find out about some of the goals and programs of the Great Society. 3. Learn about some of the cases that made the Warren Court both important and controversial.	Teaching Resources **Units 9/10 booklet** • Section 2 Quiz, p. 17	**Guided Reading and Review booklet**, p. 118 **Guide to the Essentials**, p. 148 **Learning with Documents booklet**, pp. 34, 94 **Section Reading Support Transparencies**
3 Foreign Policy in the Early 1960s 1. Understand the goals and the outcome of the Bay of Pigs invasion. 2. Read to find out about events that led to the Berlin Crisis and the Cuban Missile Crisis. 3. Discover the goals of the Alliance for Progress and the Peace Corps. 4. Find out about Cold War conflicts in which Johnson became involved.	Teaching Resources **Units 9/10 booklet** • Section 3 Quiz, p. 18 **Learning Styles Lesson Plans booklet**, p. 61	**Guided Reading and Review booklet**, p. 119 **Guide to the Essentials**, p. 149 **Learning with Documents booklet**, p. 93 **Section Reading Support Transparencies**

ENRICHMENT/PRE-AP

Prentice Hall United States History Video Collection™
www.phschool.com
- Section Activities, Virtual Field Trip, Chapter Activities, Current Events Online

Biography, Literature, and Comparing Primary Sources booklet, p. 80
Sounds of an Era Audio CD
Exploring Primary Sources in U.S. History CD-ROM

American History Block Scheduling Support
Sounds of an Era Audio CD

Biography, Literature, and Comparing Primary Sources booklet, pp. 34, 153
American History Block Scheduling Support
Sounds of an Era Audio CD
American Pathways Thematic Posters

ASSESSMENT

Core Assessment
ExamView® Test Bank, Ch. 29
ExamView® Test Bank CD-ROM, Ch. 29

Standardized Test Preparation
Diagnose and Prescribe
Diagnostic Tests for High School Social Studies Skills

Review and Reteach
Review Book for U.S. History

Practice and Assess
Test-taking Strategies With Transparencies
Test-taking Strategies Posters
Test Prep Book for U.S. History
Alternative Assessment Handbook
Document-Based Assessment

Teaching Resources
Units 9/10 booklet
- Section Quizzes, pp. 16–18
- Chapter Tests, pp. 19, 22

www.phschool.com Ch. 29 Self-Test

AmericanHeritage RESOURCES

From the Archives of American Heritage®, pp. 972, 988
AmericanHeritage® My Brush with History™ Videotapes
www.americanheritage.com

Don't miss the exclusive interactive version of this textbook on the Web and on CD-ROM.

Chapter 29 Planning Guide

In Your Classroom

CUSTOMIZE FOR INDIVIDUAL NEEDS

Gifted and Talented

Teacher's Edition
- Customize for Gifted and Talented, pp. 985, 989

Teaching Resources
- Biography, Literature, and Comparing Primary Sources booklet, pp. 34, 80, 153

Technology
- Exploring Primary Sources in U.S. History CD-ROM *Colonel Glenn Rides into Space; On the Cuban Missile Crisis, John F. Kennedy and Nikita Khrushchev*

ESL

Teacher's Edition
- Customize for ESL, p. 969

Teaching Resources
- Guided Reading and Review booklet, pp. 117–119
- Guide to the Essentials (English/Spanish), Chapter 29

Technology
- Student Edition on Audio CD, Chapter 29
- Guided Reading Audiotapes (English/Spanish), Chapter 29
- Section Reading Support Transparencies

Less Proficient Readers

Teacher's Edition
- Customize for Less Proficient Readers, p. 987

Teaching Resources
- Guided Reading and Review booklet, pp. 117–119
- Guide to the Essentials (English/Spanish), Chapter 29

Technology
- Student Edition on Audio CD, Chapter 29
- Guided Reading Audiotapes (English/Spanish), Chapter 29
- Section Reading Support Transparencies

Less Proficient Writers

Teacher's Edition
- Customize for Less Proficient Writers, p. 981

Teaching Resources
- Guided Reading and Review booklet, pp. 117–119
- Guide to the Essentials (English/Spanish), Chapter 29

Technology
- Student Edition on Audio CD, Chapter 29
- Guided Reading Audiotapes (English/Spanish), Chapter 29
- Section Reading Support Transparencies

TEACHER'S EDITION INDEX

CHAPTER 29 – PACING SUGGESTIONS

For 90-minute Blocks

- Teach sections 2 and 3 using Transparencies A48, A49, B17, and H19, and the Recent Scholarship notes on pages 980, 986, and 989 for class discussions.

Running Out of Time?

If you are running short on time to cover this chapter, consider the following options:

- Use the Prentice Hall Presentation Pro CD-ROM to create an outline for this chapter.

- Use the Section Summaries for Chapter 29, from **Guide to the Essentials (English/Spanish).**

ADDITIONAL ACTIVITIES

1 The New Frontier	**Connecting with Science and Technology** Have students research the scientific goals of the first mission to the moon and ascertain in what ways this exploit advanced scientific knowledge. Students can create a mock-up of the mission and use what they learned to create informative labels. Invite participants to present their displays to the class and answer questions. Encourage students to also be prepared to respond to questions about the political implications of the mission. **(Visual/Spatial)**
2 The Great Society	**Connecting with Culture** Have students measure the scope of the Head Start program by using graphs to show how many students the program has reached each year. They should also graph year-to-year expenditures of the program. Have students present their findings in chart form, accompanied by a summary of the stated goals of the program. Encourage a discussion of whether the statistics support those goals. **(Logical/Mathematical)**
3 Foreign Policy in the Early 1960s	**Connecting with History and Conflict** Suggest that students imagine themselves living during the Cuban Missile Crisis, with daily news reports building a high level of concern among the public. Have the class discuss how they would have behaved during the crisis and in particular how they would have helped younger family members or other children in their care cope with the situation. Encourage students to draw on their own experiences in similar situations. **(Verbal/Linguistic)**

Chapter 29
The Kennedy and Johnson Years
(1961–1969)

INTRODUCING THE CHAPTER

The contrast between the presidencies of John F. Kennedy and Lyndon Johnson is striking. While Kennedy articulated plans for domestic reform, few of his programs actually advanced through Congress, perhaps because of his pre-occupation with foreign affairs. When Johnson took office after Kennedy's death, he used his legislative skills to push through Congress some of the most significant social programs in the nation's history.

TIME LINE ACTIVITY

To provide students with practice in using the time line, ask questions such as these:

1. In what year did the first U.S. astronaut go into space? *(1961)*

2. In what year did a country in Africa gain independence from France, and what was that country? *(1962; Algeria)*

3. What 1966 Supreme Court ruling gave rights to people accused of crimes? *(The Miranda ruling)*

eTeach

Be sure to check out this month's online discussion with a Master Teacher. Go to **www.phschool.com**.

Chapter

29

The Kennedy and Johnson Years

(1961–1969)

SECTION 1   The New Frontier
SECTION 2   The Great Society
SECTION 3   Foreign Policy in the Early 1960s

The Kennedys host renowned cellist Pablo Casals at a White House gala in 1961.

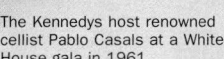

Lyndon Johnson rides his horse, Lady B, at his Texas ranch in 1963.

American Events

1960
Kennedy and Johnson win election by a razor-thin margin.

1961
Kennedy launches his New Frontier program. The first U.S. astronaut goes into space. The failed Bay of Pigs invasion is a U.S. foreign policy disaster.

1962
The Cuban Missile Crisis brings the superpowers to the brink of nuclear war.

1963
On November 22, Kennedy is assassinated in Dallas; Johnson becomes President.

1964
Johnson wins election. He launches a "war on poverty" with a series of programs known as the Great Society.

Presidential Terms: John F. Kennedy 1961–1963   Lyndon B. Johnson 1963–1969

1960   •   **1962**   •   **1964**

World Events

1961
In a showdown with Kennedy, Soviets build the Berlin Wall.

1962
Algeria wins independence from France, a colonial power in Africa.

1964
UN peacekeepers are sent to Cyprus amid Greek-Turk hostilities.

966   Chapter 29 • *The Kennedy and Johnson Years*

RESOURCE DIRECTORY

Teaching Resources
Pacing Charts booklet
Block Scheduling booklet, p. 27
Units 9/10 booklet
 • Chapter Summary, p. 15

Technology
Guided Reading Audiotapes (English/Spanish), Ch. 29
Student Edition on Audio CD, Ch. 29

Sounds of an Era Audio CD *"The President Twist"* (time: 45 seconds)
Prentice Hall United States History Video Collection™ Volume 20, *Post-War USA*
Prentice Hall Presentation Pro CD-ROM, Ch. 29
Resource Pro® CD-ROM
Social Studies Skills Tutor CD-ROM
Companion Web site, www.phschool.com

Nuclear Threat From Cuba

Teacher and students in the federal Head Start program begun under Johnson.

Map labels:
- Seattle
- CANADA
- 0 150 300 mi.
- 0 150 300 km
- Chicago
- New York
- Washington, D.C.
- Denver
- ATLANTIC OCEAN
- 40°N
- Los Angeles
- 2,843 miles
- 2,000 miles, 17 minutes
- 1,500 miles, 15 minutes
- 1,819 miles
- 2,299 miles
- 1,333 miles
- Atlanta
- 1,139 miles
- 1,317 miles
- 30°N
- 1,000 miles, 12 minutes
- Houston
- 924 miles
- 761 miles
- Miami
- Gulf of Mexico
- About 5,000 miles
- UNITED STATES
- SOVIET UNION
- Nuclear Threat From the U.S.S.R.
- MEXICO
- 243 miles
- Havana
- CUBA
- 90°W
- 80°W
- 1,103 miles
- Mexico City

Timeline

1965 — Johnson sends the Marines to support a U.S.-backed government in the Dominican Republic. U.S. involvement in Vietnam deepens. Medicare and Medicaid programs are created.

1966 — The Warren Court's landmark *Miranda* ruling gives rights to persons accused of crimes.

1968 — Amid race riots and Vietnam War protests, Johnson's popularity plummets. He announces he will not run for reelection.

1966

1968

1965 — Rhodesia declares independence from Britain.

1966 — China's Cultural Revolution begins.

Nuclear Threat From Cuba

Activating Prior Knowledge Which is greater, the distance between Cuba to Washington, D.C., or the distance from Russia to the continental United States? By about how much? *(The distance from Russia to the United States is greater. The difference is about 4,000 miles.)*

Previewing Why would the United States object to Soviet missiles in Cuba? *(The proximity of Cuba to the United States meant that missiles from Cuba could arrive in the United States very quickly, giving the United States very little time to respond.)*

BACKGROUND
About the Pictures

1  2  3 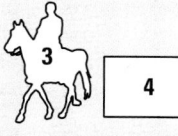 4

1. Kennedy's narrow win (only 118,550 out of 70 million votes) over the Republican candidate, Richard Nixon, spurred allegations of vote fraud in the state of Illinois.

2. The Kennedys become well known for their associations with people of glamour, style, and intellect.

3. Wishing to honor President Kennedy's memory, one of Johnson's highest priorities became signing the Civil Rights Act into law.

4. The Head Start program, created under the Economic Opportunity Act, provided needed social services, including preschool, for children in low-income families.

BIBLIOGRAPHY

For the Teacher

Bechschloss, Michael, editor. *Taking Charge: The Johnson White House Tapes.* Simon & Schuster, 1997. (Warts-and-all, behind-the-scenes glimpse of Johnson as President.)

Freedman, Lawrence. *Kennedy's Wars: Berlin, Cuba, Laos, Vietnam.* Oxford University Press, 2000. (Uses newly released material to insightfully analyze Kennedy's performance.)

Reeves, Richard. *President Kennedy: Profile of Power.* Touchstone, 1994. (Comprehensive account of Kennedy's 1960 presidential campaign.)

For the Student

Brown, Claude. *Manchild in the Promised Land.* Simon & Schuster, 1999. (Autobiography of an African American youth from poverty in Harlem to a law degree from Howard University.)

Kennedy, John F. *Profiles in Courage.* Harperperennial, 2000. (A first-rate book about political integrity.)

Kennedy, Robert F. *Thirteen Days.* Norton, 1999. (Gripping account of the Cuban missile crisis by the President's brother and closest adviser, who served as attorney general of the United States.)

 **TEXT**

Don't miss the exclusive interactive version of this textbook on the Web and on CD-ROM.

SECTION OBJECTIVES

1. Learn about factors that affected the election of 1960.

2. Find out about domestic programs pursued by President Kennedy.

3. Read about circumstances that surrounded Kennedy's assassination.

BELLRINGER

Warm-Up Activity Ask students to picture a political campaign for President waged without television appearances, interviews, or campaign commercials. How would voters learn about the candidates? What do voters learn about candidates from television?

Activating Prior Knowledge What do students know about the Kennedy presidency? Ask if students are familiar with the famous phrase from Kennedy's inauguration: "Ask not what your country can do for you; ask what you can do for your country." Ask students to explain why this statement had a tremendous impact on the American people.

READING STRATEGY

As students read this section, have them make a list, in chronological order, of the programs that Kennedy proposed.

READING FOCUS

- What factors affected the election of 1960?
- What domestic programs did President Kennedy pursue?
- What circumstances surrounded Kennedy's assassination?

MAIN IDEA

Following a narrow election victory, President John F. Kennedy proposed a number of changes in domestic policy, many of which were defeated in Congress.

KEY TERMS

mandate
New Frontier
Warren Commission

TAKING NOTES

Copy the chart below. As you read, fill in details relating to Kennedy's New Frontier program.

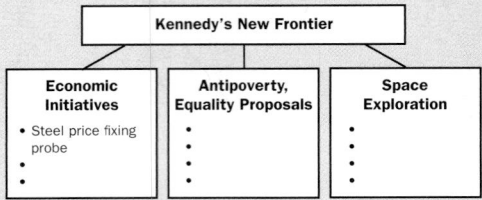

Kennedy's New Frontier		
Economic Initiatives • Steel price fixing probe • • •	**Antipoverty, Equality Proposals** • • • •	**Space Exploration** • • • •

Setting the Scene On September 26, 1960, American politics changed forever. From a CBS television studio in Chicago, two presidential candidates—Republican Richard Nixon and Democrat John F. Kennedy—faced off in the first of four live, televised debates broadcast by all the networks. This debate focused on domestic issues.

Nixon was a tough, veteran campaigner who had gained plenty of political experience as a member of Congress and as Eisenhower's Vice President. Yet he was not in peak form. He had kept a grueling campaign schedule and had been sidelined in the hospital for two weeks with a serious knee injury. Nixon arrived at the studio 10 pounds underweight, having ignored advice to get a new shirt with a collar that fit. He refused makeup, except for a pasty beard stick called "Lazy Shave" to cover his perpetual "five o'clock shadow." According to biographer Stephen A. Ambrose, Nixon stood under the hot studio lights "half slouched, his 'Lazy Shave' powder faintly streaked with sweat, his eyes exaggerated hollows of blackness, his jaw, jowls, and face dropping with strain." Nixon had prepared his mind for the battle, but not his appearance.

Senator Kennedy, on the other hand, arrived in Chicago after a campaign swing through California that included plenty of rest and sunshine. Tanned, relaxed, and smiling, he breezed into the studio. The camera favored his young, handsome face, and Kennedy spoke directly to the camera, paying little attention to his opponent and addressing the viewing voters instead.

Who won the debate? Surveys showed that most of the 70 million TV viewers thought Kennedy won. Yet many radio listeners gave the victory to Nixon. Analysts still disagree over whether the debate was the turning point in the election.

The undisputed winner that night was television itself. The presidential debates of 1960 put TV in the national spotlight and made it the communications vehicle of choice for politicians.

In a CBS studio in Chicago, a relaxed John Kennedy (seated) browses his notes as he prepares to meet Richard Nixon (at the podium) in the first of their four televised debates in the fall of 1960.

968   Chapter 29 • *The Kennedy and Johnson Years*

The Election of 1960

Kennedy, a Massachusetts Democrat, had served in the United States House of Representatives and Senate for 14 years, following distinguished service in the United States Navy in World War II. Yet the senator faced serious obstacles in his quest for the presidency.

A New Type of Candidate   John Kennedy was only 43 years old, and many questioned whether he had the experience needed for the nation's highest office. (While he was the youngest person ever to be *elected* President, Kennedy was not the youngest ever to serve. Theodore Roosevelt became President at age 42 when William McKinley was assassinated.) In addition, Kennedy was a Roman Catholic, and no Catholic had ever been elected President. Kennedy helped put an end to the religion issue when he won the primary of the largely Protestant state of West Virginia.

With that hurdle behind him, he campaigned hard, promising to spur the sluggish economy. During the last years of the Eisenhower administration, the Gross National Product (GNP) had grown very slowly, and the economy had suffered several recessions. During the campaign, Kennedy proclaimed that it was time to "get America moving again."

A Narrow Kennedy Victory   Kennedy and his running mate, Lyndon Baines Johnson, won the election by an extraordinarily close margin. Although the electoral vote was 303 to 219 in Kennedy's favor, he won by fewer than 119,000 popular votes out of nearly 69 million cast. In Illinois and Texas, Nixon could have inched by Kennedy with just a few thousand more votes, and accusations were made that the Democrats had won these states through fraud.

As a result of this razor-thin victory, Kennedy entered office without a strong **mandate,** or public endorsement of his proposals. Without a mandate, Kennedy would have difficulty pushing his more controversial measures through Congress.

Senator John F. Kennedy, the 1960 Democratic presidential candidate, greets supporters during a campaign stop.

Sounds of an Era

Listen to John F. Kennedy's Inaugural Address and other sounds from the Kennedy-Johnson era.

Presidential Election of 1960

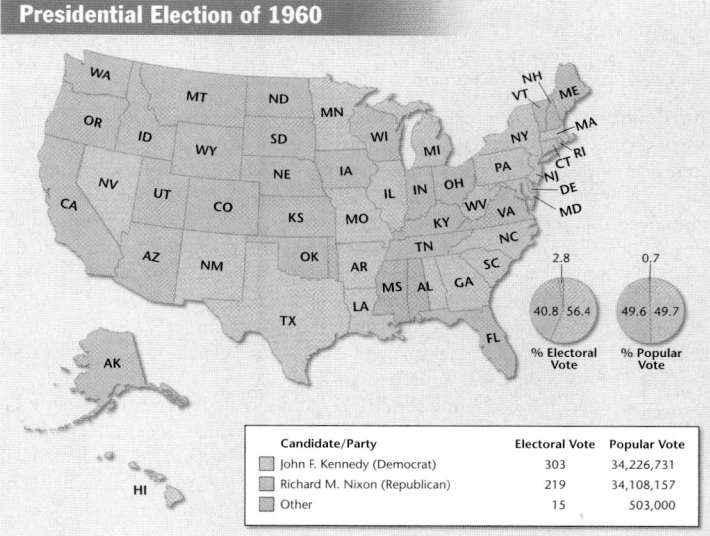

Candidate/Party	Electoral Vote	Popular Vote
John F. Kennedy (Democrat)	303	34,226,731
Richard M. Nixon (Republican)	219	34,108,157
Other	15	503,000

MAP SKILLS Kennedy and Nixon fought a head-to-head contest in the 1960 presidential election. **Regions** *(a) From what areas did each candidate draw the most votes? (b) Compare the popular vote and the electoral college vote, and explain the election outcome.*

You may wish to have students add the following to their portfolios: Ask students to research and prepare either a written or oral report on the folk revival in popular music in the early 1960s (focusing on artists such as Bob Dylan and Joan Baez) and its relation to increasing demands for social reform in the nation. How does this music reflect the life and times in which it was created? **(Verbal/Linguistic)**

BACKGROUND
Connections to Earlier Events

Kennedy's phrase "Ask not what your country can do for you; ask what you can do for your country" is arguably his most famous utterance. Yet it is not entirely original. In 1884 Oliver Wendell Holmes wrote, "It is now the moment . . . to recall what our country has done for each of us, and to ask ourselves what we can do for our country in return." In 1904 LeBaron Russell Briggs wrote, "As has often been said, the youth who loves his Alma Mater will always ask, not 'What can she do for me?' but 'What can I do for her?'" And, in 1916, Warren Harding said, ". . . we must have a citizenship less concerned about what the government can do for it and more anxious about what it can do for the nation."

READING CHECK
Improving the economy, assisting the poor and disadvantaged, environmental issues, advancing the space program.

The President's children, Caroline Kennedy and John F. Kennedy, Jr., created an atmosphere of fun and family life in the Oval Office.

Kennedy nevertheless took office with vigor and confidence. In his Inaugural Address, he inspired a generation of young people by urging them to put patriotism before personal interests:

> 66 My fellow Americans, ask not what your country can do for you; ask what you can do for your country. 99
> —John F. Kennedy, Inaugural Address, 1961

Kennedy's Domestic Programs

In a speech early in his presidency, Kennedy said that the nation was poised at the edge of a **"New Frontier."** The name stuck. It referred to Kennedy's proposals to improve the economy, assist the poor, and speed up the space program.

The Economy Concerned about the continuing recession, Kennedy hoped to work with business leaders to promote economic growth. Often, however, he faced resistance from executives who were suspicious of his plans. Their worst fears were realized in the spring of 1962. When the U.S. Steel Company announced that it was raising the price of steel by $6 a ton, other firms did the same. Worried about inflation, Kennedy called the price increase unjustifiable and charged that it showed "utter contempt for the public interest." He ordered a federal investigation into the possibility of price fixing.

Under that pressure, U.S. Steel and the other companies backed down. Business leaders remained angry, and the stock market fell in its steepest drop since the Great Crash of 1929.

To help end the economic slump, in 1963 Kennedy proposed a large tax cut over three years. At first, the measure would reduce government income and create a budget deficit. Kennedy believed, however, that the extra cash in taxpayers' wallets would stimulate the economy and eventually bring in added tax revenues. However, as often happened, the President's proposal became stuck in Congress.

READING CHECK
What domestic issues did President Kennedy attempt to address?

Combating Poverty and Inequality Kennedy also was eager to take action against poverty and inequality. In his first two years in office, he hoped that he could help the poor simply by stimulating the economy. In 1962, though, author Michael Harrington described the lives of the poor in his powerful book, *The Other America*. Harrington's book revealed that while many Americans were enjoying the prosperity of the 1950s, a shocking one fifth of the population was living below the poverty line. Kennedy became convinced that the poor needed direct federal aid.

Kennedy's ambitious plans for federal education aid and medical care for the elderly both failed in Congress. Some measures did make it through Congress, however. Congress passed both an increase in the minimum wage and the Housing Act of 1961, which provided $4.9 billion for urban renewal. Congress also approved the Twenty-fourth Amendment, which outlawed the poll tax. In June 1963, Congress passed the Equal Pay Act. Added into the Fair Labor Standards Act of 1938, a New Deal program, the Equal Pay Act stated that all employees doing substantially the same work in the same workplace must be given equal pay.

Other Kennedy Initiatives In the face of congressional roadblocks, Kennedy, like many Presidents, sought to achieve his goals through executive orders. Among them were orders on providing equal opportunity in housing and establishing an expanded program of food distribution to needy families. Other orders established the President's Committee on Equal Employment, the President's Commission on the Status of Women, and the President's Council on Aging.

Other acts in Kennedy's shortened presidency—some carried out in collaboration with Congress—included the following:
1. an executive order providing improved surplus food to unemployed Americans;
2. the largest, fastest defense buildup in peacetime history, as Kennedy boosted missile programs;
3. an Area Redevelopment law to help communities plagued with long-term unemployment;
4. changes in Social Security extending benefits to 5 million people and allowing Americans to retire and collect benefits at age 62;
5. a law doubling federal resources to combat water pollution;
6. the creation of National Seashore Parks, a part of the National Park System;
7. the expansion and increase of the minimum wage;
8. the creation of the first federal program to address juvenile delinquency;
9. changes in the welfare system aimed at helping ailing families instead of encouraging dependency on government benefits;
10. the construction of the world's largest nuclear power plant, in Hanford, Washington;
11. tightening of food and drug laws to protect against untested drugs;
12. signing of a Trade Expansion Act to reduce American protectionism and encourage free trade;
13. signing of the Nuclear Test Ban Treaty, the first nuclear weapons agreement.

INTERPRETING GRAPHS
At bottom, Defense Department workers inspect the *Friendship 7* capsule after John Glenn's historic flight and splashdown. The chart below shows changes in NASA funding over two decades. **Analyzing Visual Information** *What accounts for the sudden surge in funding during the late 1950s?*

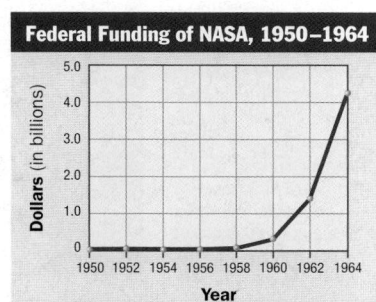

Federal Funding of NASA, 1950–1964

Dollars (in billions) — vertical axis: 0, 1.0, 2.0, 3.0, 4.0, 5.0
Year — horizontal axis: 1950 1952 1954 1956 1958 1960 1962 1964

SOURCE: *Historical Statistics of the United States, Colonial Times to 1970*

ACTIVITY
Connecting with History and Conflict

Have pairs or small groups of students cooperate to compare Kennedy's domestic programs with those of the New Deal. Ask them to create a chart that presents the results of their comparison.

BACKGROUND
The Nuclear Test Ban Treaty

Signed during Kennedy's administration, the Nuclear Test Ban Treaty had its origins in concern about the dangers of radioactive fallout from nuclear weapons testing. Discussions had been underway since the mid-1950s, but the Cuban Missile Crisis of 1962 threw the problem into sharp focus. The world's three nuclear powers of the time, the Soviet Union, the United States, and Great Britain, agreed on the basic terms of a treaty with only ten days of discussion in the summer of 1963.

The treaty banned nuclear weapons testing in the atmosphere, in outer space, and underwater. Underground testing was still permitted, as was the maintenance of nuclear stockpiles and nuclear weapons buildup. Still, the treaty was regarded as an important first step. Within a few months, more than 100 other countries had signed the treaty.

✓ TEST PREPARATION

Ask students to read the material in the section "The Space Program" on the next page and then answer the question below.

What 1961 event caused NASA to accelerate its space program and send a person into outer space?

A The Cuban Missile Crisis.

B The Cold War.

C A decision to send humans to the moon.

(D) The Soviet's successful launch of a peopled spacecraft.

CAPTION **A**NSWERS

Interpreting Graphs The launch of the Soviet satellite *Sputnik* in 1957 frightened and energized the United States into building a first-rate space program.

From the Archives of AmericanHeritage®

Rush to Judgment

By 1967 theories about the assassination of President Kennedy were many. One magazine offered a review of 25 alternative theories grown up since the Warren Commission's report. They included the suggestion that original autopsy pictures had been destroyed to arguments over how many shots had been fired to the assertion that the killer's killer had been injected with cancer while in prison. But the most spectacular theory belonged to New Orleans district attorney Jim Garrison, who arrested respected New Orleans businessman Clay Shaw. According to Garrison, Shaw was part of a conspiracy funded by a rightist Cuban anti-Castro group that was angry with Kennedy for the failed Bay of Pigs invasion. After a trial filled with ever-widening charges and shadowy figures, Shaw was acquitted in 1969. Source: Nathan Ward, "The Time Machine," *American Heritage®* magazine, May/June 1992.

Focus on CULTURE

Camelot The name *Camelot* came to represent the energetic, idealistic image of the Kennedy White House. The Broadway musical *Camelot,* which opened in 1960, portrayed the legendary kingdom of the British King Arthur. Arthur dreamed of transforming medieval Britain from a country in which "might makes right," or the strong always get their way, into one in which power would be used to achieve what is right.

The Kennedys themselves embodied the royal, romantic spirit of Camelot. The President and First Lady made the White House a stage for high culture, inviting the best artists, musicians, and thinkers. Jacqueline Kennedy, an intelligent and beautiful woman, brought an atmosphere of style and grace to the White House. She personally supervised its renovation and redecoration, acquiring tasteful furnishings that reflected the Kennedys' interest in American cultural history.

The couple's young children, Caroline and John, Jr., added to the lively atmosphere. They played with their father in the Oval Office and in a swimming pool and treehouse on the White House lawn. The fact that the Kennedys had young children made it all the more tragic when Camelot came to a sudden end.

The Space Program Kennedy was also successful in his effort to breathe life into the space program. Following the Soviet Union's launch of the *Sputnik* satellite in 1957, government agencies and private industries had been working furiously with the National Aeronautics and Space Administration (NASA) to place a manned spacecraft in orbit around Earth. As part of the Mercury program, seven test pilots were chosen to train as astronauts in 1959. Government spending and the future of NASA became uncertain, however, when a task force appointed by Kennedy recommended that NASA concentrate on exploratory space missions without human crews.

All of that changed in April 1961. The Soviet Union announced that Yuri Gagarin had circled Earth on board the Soviet spacecraft *Vostok,* becoming the first human to travel in space. Gagarin's flight rekindled Americans' fears that their technology was falling behind that of the Soviet Union.

On May 5, 1961, the United States made its own first attempt to send a person into space. Astronaut Alan Shepard made a 15-minute flight that reached an altitude of 115 miles. Unlike Gagarin's flight, Shepard's flight did not orbit Earth. Nevertheless, its success convinced Kennedy to move forward. On May 25, Kennedy issued a bold challenge to the nation. He said the United States "should commit itself to achieving the goal, before this decade is out, of landing a man on the moon."

The nation accepted the challenge, and funding for NASA was increased. Less than a year later, on February 20, 1962, John Glenn successfully completed three orbits around Earth and landed in the Atlantic Ocean near the Bahamas. Later that year Kennedy outlined the reasons for American space exploration:

> 66 We set sail on this new sea because there is new knowledge to be gained, and new rights to be won, and they must be won and used for the progress of all people. . . . [O]nly if the United States occupies a position of preeminence can we help decide whether this new ocean will be a sea of peace or a new, terrifying theater of war. 99
> —John F. Kennedy, speech at Rice University, Houston, Texas, 1962

Over the course of the decade, NASA flights brought the country closer and closer to its goal. Finally, on July 20, 1969, astronaut Neil Armstrong became the first person to walk on the moon. Unfortunately, Kennedy would not live to see the fulfillment of the goal he set in motion.

Kennedy Is Assassinated

On November 22, 1963, as Kennedy looked ahead to the reelection campaign the following year, he traveled to Texas to mobilize support. Texas Governor John Connally and his wife, Nelly, met the President and the First Lady, Jacqueline Kennedy, at the airport in Dallas. Together they rode through the streets of downtown Dallas in an open limousine, surrounded by Secret Service agents. Newspapers had published the parade route ahead of time, and it was jammed with thousands of supporters hoping for a glimpse of the President.

The motorcade slowed as it turned a corner in front of the Texas School Book Depository. Its employees had been sent to lunch so they could watch the event outside. Yet one man stayed behind. From a sixth-floor window, he aimed his rifle.

Suddenly shots rang out. Bullets struck both Connally and Kennedy. Connally would recover from his injuries. The President, slumped over in Jacqueline's lap, was mortally wounded.

The motorcade sped to nearby Parkland Memorial Hospital, where doctors made what they knew was a hopeless attempt to save the President. Kennedy was pronounced dead at 1:00 P.M. An aide delivered the news to a dazed Lyndon Johnson, addressing him as "Mr. President."

As the news spread by radio and TV bulletins, the country came to a halt in stunned disbelief. By the time Air Force One arrived in Washington, thousands of people had gathered in the streets. They stood in near silence, except for the sounds of weeping. America was shattered. Millions remained glued to their televisions for days as the impact of the tragedy sank in.

The prime suspect in Kennedy's murder was Lee Harvey Oswald, a former marine and supporter of Cuban leader Fidel Castro. He was apprehended within an hour of the President's death, but revealed little information to the police.

Two days after Kennedy's assassination, the TV cameras rolled as Oswald was being transferred from one jail to another. As the nation watched, a Dallas nightclub owner, Jack Ruby, stepped through the crowd of reporters and fatally shot Oswald.

On November 29, President Johnson appointed The President's Commission on the Assassination of President John F. Kennedy. It was better known as the **Warren Commission,** after its chairman, Supreme Court Chief Justice Earl Warren. After months of investigation, the Warren Commission determined that Oswald had acted alone in shooting the President. Neither Oswald, Jack Ruby, nor any other American or foreigner was involved in a conspiracy to commit the crime, the commission concluded.

Since then, the case has been explored in millions of pages of books, magazine and newspaper accounts, and formal and informal reports. It continues to be the topic of reenactments and television documentaries. Some investigations support the theory that Oswald was involved in a larger conspiracy, and that he was killed in order to protect others who had helped plan Kennedy's murder. The whole story probably will never be known.

On his third birthday, November 25, 1963, John F. Kennedy, Jr., salutes as his father's casket passes by in the funeral procession for President Kennedy. Other family members, from left, are JFK's brother Edward M. Kennedy; the late President's daughter, Caroline, almost age 6; his wife, Jacqueline Kennedy; and his brother Robert F. Kennedy.

Section 1 Assessment

READING COMPREHENSION

1. Explain the role of television in the 1960 presidential election, and describe the election outcome.

2. How did lack of a **mandate** affect Kennedy's administration?

3. Describe some of the successes and failures of Kennedy's **New Frontier.**

4. What were the conclusions of the **Warren Commission?**

CRITICAL THINKING AND WRITING

5. **Making Comparisons** Compare the advantages and disadvantages that Richard Nixon had going into the 1960 debates with John F. Kennedy.

6. **Writing a Conclusion** Why do you think the goal of a moon landing was so important to Kennedy? What effects do you think the successful NASA mission had on the country?

Take It to the NET

Activity: Virtual Field Trip Visit the John F. Kennedy Memorial and Library to learn more about JFK's life and work. Use the links provided in the *America: Pathways to the Present* area of the following Web site for help in completing this activity.
www.phschool.com

Section 1 Assessment

Reading Comprehension

1. It marked the beginning of television as a major influence on political campaigns. TV viewers thought Kennedy won the first debate; radio listeners felt the victory belonged to Nixon. Ultimately, Kennedy did win the election, but by a narrow margin.

2. Without a mandate, Kennedy had difficulty pushing his more controversial measures through Congress.

3. Successes: the space program, passage of the Twenty-fourth Amendment, Housing Act of 1961. Failures: the stock market decline, inability to push through education, medical care, or tax-cutting plans.

4. It determined that Oswald had acted alone in shooting the President and ruled out any conspiracy theories.

Critical Thinking and Writing

5. Disadvantages: Nixon felt and looked exhausted due to vigorous campaigning and his recent hospitalization for a knee injury. Nixon was not telegenic, which proved to be a disadvantage in televised debates. John F. Kennedy was well-rested and telegenic. Advantages: Nixon was mentally prepared. In addition, he had a great deal of campaign experience. As a Vice President and former Senator and Congressman, Nixon had considerable experience in high public office.

6. To remain technologically competitive with the Soviet Union, and to determine how space would be used in the times ahead. It renewed Americans' pioneer spirit and gave them a sense of security in this accomplishment.

Take It to the NET

Invite students to take a Virtual Field Trip at **www.phschool.com**

Exploring Oral History

EXPLORING ORAL HISTORY

Focus Students will analyze the content of oral history excerpts.

Instruct Ask student groups to consider the following: Twenty Americans have been selected to answer questions about the presidency of John Kennedy. Ask each group to write questions about the 20 citizens that might provide useful information when historians try to evaluate their testimony. (Questions might include age, level of political activity, level of education).

Extend See the Skills for Life activity in the Resource Directory below.

ANSWERS

PRACTICE THE SKILL

1. **(a)** John Lewis, Atlanta city council member and civil rights leader. **(b)** In 1983, 20 years after the event. **(c)** He loved and admired President Kennedy because of his concern for civil rights. **(d)** No. Lewis's admiration has not lessened over time.

2. **(a)** Lewis heard the news of the assassination on the radio. But his organization had worked closely with Kennedy on racial issues, and Lewis felt he knew the President. **(b)** As a civil rights leader who saw Kennedy as supportive, Lewis probably viewed the event as especially tragic. **(c)** The civil rights legislation passed after Kennedy's death probably made Lewis view Kennedy as a man who played a pivotal role in progress. **(d)** That he favored government intervention on domestic issues such as civil rights, and that he believed government should be accessible to the people.

3. **(a)** That it gave people a feeling of hope about issues such as civil rights. **(b)** That although Kennedy's administration may not have made big changes in the laws, they did begin to change attitudes and made minorities feel hopeful and that they had a friend in the White House.

Oral history is made up of people's verbal accounts and recollections of former times and events. Historians collect oral history through interviews, which may take place at the time of an event or at some later date, perhaps even decades later. These interviews are primary sources that record not only facts about the past, but also people's opinions, feelings, and impressions—all important for putting together a picture of the past.

The excerpt below is from an interview with John Lewis on the twentieth anniversary of President Kennedy's death. In 1963, Lewis was chairperson of the Student Nonviolent Coordinating Committee and one of the leaders of the civil rights March on Washington.

LEARN THE SKILL
Use the following steps to analyze an oral history:

1. **Identify the nature of the oral account.** Determine who was interviewed, that person's relationship to the event, and any factors that might have influenced the person's recollection of the event.

2. **Determine the reliability of the evidence.** Consider whether the person was in a position to observe events first-hand, or to judge events impartially. Also consider the length of time between the event and the interview.

3. **Study the evidence to learn more about the historical event.** Note any new facts you learn from the interview, as well as new insights into people's attitudes at the time of the event.

PRACTICE THE SKILL
Answer the following questions:

1. **(a)** Who was interviewed? **(b)** When did the interview take place? **(c)** What was Lewis's attitude toward Kennedy at the time of his death? Why? **(d)** Did that attitude change in any way over time?

2. **(a)** What was Lewis's relationship to the event he is describing? **(b)** How might Lewis's role in the civil rights movement have affected his interpretation of the event? **(c)** How might events after Kennedy's death have affected the account? **(d)** What do Lewis's views reveal about his political perspective?

3. **(a)** What impact does Lewis think Kennedy's presidency had on government policy and the nation? **(b)** What can you learn about Kennedy's presidency from Lewis's account?

APPLY THE SKILL
See the Chapter Review and Assessment for another opportunity to apply this skill.

An Interview with John Lewis: Remembering President Kennedy's Assassination

"I was living in Atlanta then, but I had gone back to Nashville for a trial. I was getting into a car to go to the Nashville airport when I heard it on the radio. And to me, it was the saddest moment in my life. I had grown up to love and to admire President Kennedy. I remember crying on the plane.

I saw him as a sort of guy that listened. Sincere. Caring. People argue and say that he didn't really do anything. But he did listen, and during that period from 1961 to 1963, I'll tell you, I think probably for the first time in modern American history, we felt, 'Well, we have a friend in the White House.' On some things we disagreed. We'd call them up and argue and debate with them on some issue, and we said a lot of different things, and sometimes it was harsh. But we saw the Kennedy administration during that period as a sympathetic referee in the whole struggle for civil rights.

His campaign had created a sense of hope, a sense of optimism for many of us. When someone asked him about the civil rights sit-ins that year, he said, 'By sitting down, these young people are standing up for the very best in American tradition.'"

—*Newsweek*, November 28, 1983

RESOURCE DIRECTORY

Teaching Resources
Skills for Life booklet, p. 31

Technology
Social Studies Skills Tutor CD-ROM
Interactive Practice in
• Geographic Literacy
• Critical Thinking and Reading
• Visual Analysis
• Communications

READING FOCUS

- What was Lyndon Johnson's path to the presidency?
- What were some of the goals and programs of the Great Society?
- What were some of the cases that made the Warren Court both important and controversial?

MAIN IDEA

President Johnson's Great Society programs aimed to improve America's economy and provide substantial government aid to its citizens, especially the poor.

KEY TERMS

Great Society
Head Start
Volunteers in Service to America (VISTA)
Medicare
Medicaid
Immigration Act of 1965
Miranda rule
apportionment

TAKING NOTES

Copy the web diagram below. As you read, fill in details relating to President Johnson's Great Society programs.

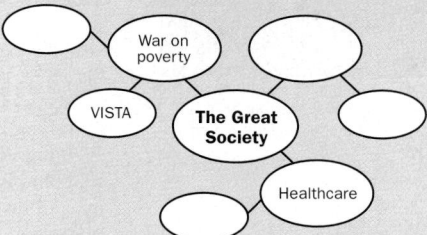

War on poverty

VISTA

The Great Society

Healthcare

SECTION OBJECTIVES

1. Discover Lyndon Johnson's path to the presidency.
2. Find out about some of the goals and programs of the Great Society.
3. Learn about some of the cases that made the Warren Court both important and controversial.

BELLRINGER

Warm-Up Activity Ask students what they think is great about American society. Was it as great in Johnson's time? What differences are evident?

Activating Prior Knowledge Ask students if they can name some Great Society initiatives that are still part of the federal government today. *(Head Start, Medicare and Medicaid, the Department of Housing and Urban Development)*

READING STRATEGY

As students read, ask them to create a chart describing the key elements of Johnson's Great Society program. Have them identify ways in which actions made by the government in introducing the Great Society program expanded economic opportunities for all citizens.

*A*CTIVITY
Connecting with Today

Have students ask appropriate older adults to share their recollections of the day Kennedy was assassinated and Lyndon Johnson became the thirty-sixth President of the United States. Have students share what they learn with the class. **(Verbal/Linguistic)**

Setting the Scene At 2:35 P.M. on November 22, 1963, about 90 minutes after John F. Kennedy was pronounced dead, Lyndon Baines Johnson stood inside Air Force One on an airstrip at Dallas's Love Field. He was flanked by his wife, Lady Bird, and by Jacqueline Kennedy, who was bearing up with "amazing strength and calm," according to an account by the *Houston Chronicle*. According to the Constitution, LBJ had *immediately* become the thirty-sixth President from the moment of Kennedy's death. Johnson, however, insisted on taking the oath of office before leaving Dallas.

Federal District Judge Sarah T. Hughes was rushed to the airport to administer the oath. "The President and Mrs. Johnson were very serious and very calm," Judge Hughes told the *Chronicle* afterward. "He thanked us and told us he would rely on God's help."

Two minutes later, Air Force One took off for the capital, bearing Kennedy's body. Lady Bird Johnson, the new First Lady, began her White House diary that day.

"Friday, November 22, 1963 DALLAS

"It all began so beautifully. . . ."

LBJ's Path to the White House

The grief of a nation, and the responsibility for healing it, hung heavily upon the new President. Johnson began the recovery process in a speech to Congress:

“ *All I have I would have given gladly not to be standing here today. . . . No words are sad enough to express our sense of loss. No words are strong enough to express our determination to continue the forward thrust of America that [Kennedy] began. . . . [T]he ideas and the ideals which he so nobly represented must and will be translated into effective action.* ”

—Lyndon Johnson, address to a joint session of Congress, November 27, 1963

A sad and solemn Lyndon Johnson is sworn in as President aboard Air Force One shortly after President Kennedy's assassination. On Johnson's right is his wife, Lady Bird, and on his left is Kennedy's grief-stricken widow, Jacqueline.

Chapter 29 • Section 2 975

RESOURCE DIRECTORY

Teaching Resources
Guided Reading and Review booklet, p. 118

Technology
Section Reading Support Transparencies
Guided Reading Audiotapes (English/Spanish), Ch. 29
Student Edition on Audio CD, Ch. 29
Sounds of an Era Audio CD *"The Times They Are A-Changing,"* Bob Dylan (time: almost two minutes)
Prentice Hall Presentation Pro CD-ROM, Ch. 29
Companion Web site, www.phschool.com

Focus After taking office following Kennedy's assassination, Lyndon Johnson moved many reform bills through Congress as part of his goal of achieving a "Great Society." Ask what Johnson's most important reform bills were. Why did some Americans criticize Johnson's program?

Instruct Discuss why LBJ was able to succeed where Kennedy had failed. Remind students that Congress, as well as LBJ, wanted to pass legislation proposed by the slain President as a memorial and as a way of reassuring the country. Ask to what extent LBJ's political experience helped him move legislation through Congress.

Ask students to describe the impact of Chief Justice Earl Warren on the Supreme Court. What were some landmark cases handed down by the Court under Warren?

Assess/Reteach When Johnson assumed the Presidency, the nation was in mourning. He demonstrated his leadership capabilities by moving ahead with an aggressive domestic program. Ask students to discuss the impact of Johnson's programs on American life, both in his time and today.

Johnson's nose-to-nose form of persuasion could be intimidating.

Although he came to the Oval Office through tragedy, Johnson found himself in a job he had long sought. LBJ's road to the presidency was laid carefully and cunningly, through years of skillful political maneuvering and strong leadership.

Lyndon Johnson arrived in the United States House of Representatives in 1937 as a New Deal Democrat from Texas. In 1948, he won a seat in the Senate, but only by a tiny margin of 87 votes. He was jokingly dubbed "Landslide Lyndon"—a nickname that stuck for the rest of his career.

In the Senate, Johnson demonstrated both political talent and an unstoppable ambition. In 1953, he became the youngest Senator ever to be elected Minority Leader. When the Democrats won control of the Senate the following year, LBJ became Majority Leader. In this powerful post he became famous for his ability to use the political system to accomplish his goals. He controlled the legislative agenda and the votes to get bills passed by rewarding his friends and punishing his enemies. Johnson inspired fear and awe among his colleagues.

He was "not a likeable man," former Secretary of State Dean Acheson once told him. But Johnson was more concerned with accomplishment than popularity, and his single-minded intensity enabled him to get his way. Other senators marveled at the "Johnson treatment," in which he carefully researched a bill, and then approached in a hallway or office the legislator whose vote he needed. If he thought it was the best way to persuade the legislator, he would attack, "his face a scant millimeter from his target, his eyes widening and narrowing, his eyebrows rising and falling," according to columnists Rowland Evans, Jr.,

NOTABLE PRESIDENTS
Lyndon Baines Johnson

36th President 1963–1969

"In a land of great wealth, families must not live in hopeless poverty."

—**Inaugural Address, January 20, 1965**

Lyndon Johnson rose to the presidency under the worst of circumstances—the assassination of President John F. Kennedy—and governed during one of the nation's most divisive periods. President Johnson waged war on poverty in America. But another war, half a world away, drained funds from his ambitious domestic agenda.

Born to a financially struggling political family in Texas, Johnson became a school teacher during the 1920s, witnessing the harsh poverty of his students, mostly Mexican Americans. His concerns led him into politics. Johnson served for nearly 12 years in the House as a New Deal Democrat. In 1948, he won election to the Senate. Shrewd and determined, LBJ fought his way up to become, at age 46, the youngest-ever Senate Majority Leader.

In the 1960 Democratic primaries, Johnson had to settle for the No. 2 spot on Kennedy's ticket. As Vice President, Johnson was restless and powerless. But power came all too soon, when Kennedy's death launched him into the Oval Office.

LBJ moved quickly to pursue his Great Society programs, designed to lift Americans out of poverty and promote equal rights. But Johnson had inherited a problem: the escalating war against communism in Vietnam. The conflict was political and military quicksand.

In the 1968 primaries, facing low public support and a growing challenge from Robert F. Kennedy, a war-weary LBJ withdrew his candidacy. At the end of his term, he retired to his beloved Texas ranch with his wife, Claudia "Lady Bird" Johnson.

Connecting to Today
Have crises overseas had a strong effect on any recent presidencies? Why or why not?

Take It to the NET **Biography** To read more about Lyndon Johnson, visit the links provided in the *America: Pathways to the Present* area of the following Web site. **www.phschool.com**

RESOURCE DIRECTORY

Teaching Resources
Learning with Documents booklet (Primary Source Activity) *President Johnson's Thanksgiving Address*, p. 34

Technology
Color Transparencies *Political Cartoon*, B17
Sounds of an Era Audio CD *"Great Society Speech,"* 1964 recording (time: 40 seconds)

and Robert Novak. Johnson might grab his victim by the lapels or by the shoulders, flattering, cajoling, and shouting in turn. Nearly without fail, he got the vote he wanted.

When Johnson's bid for the Democratic nomination failed in 1960, he accepted Kennedy's invitation to run for the vice presidency. Once elected, however, Johnson was frustrated with the job, which lacked any real power. He was also unhappy being away from Congress, where he had been so effective.

Yet Johnson was not powerless for long. While it had been a long journey to the vice presidency, it was a tragically short trip to the Oval Office in 1963.

The Great Society

Johnson was aware that the American people needed some action that would help heal the wound caused by the loss of their President. To that end, he used all the talents he had developed as Senate Majority Leader to push through Congress an extraordinary program of reforms on domestic issues.

Johnson's agenda included Kennedy's civil rights and tax-cut bills. It also embraced laws to aid public education, provide medical care for the elderly, and eliminate poverty. By the spring of 1964, he had begun to use the phrase *Great Society* to describe his goals. In a speech that year he told students:

> ❝ Your imagination, your initiative, and your indignation will determine whether we build a society where progress is the servant of our needs, or a society where old values and new visions are buried under unbridled [unrestrained] growth. For in your time we have the opportunity to move not only toward the rich society and the powerful society, but upward toward the Great Society. ❞
>
> —Lyndon Johnson, speech at the University of Michigan, May 1964

Johnson's **Great Society** was a series of major legislative initiatives that continued into his second term. The Great Society programs included major poverty relief, education aid, healthcare, voting rights, conservation and beautification projects, urban renewal, and economic development in depressed areas.

The Election of 1964 Johnson's early successes paved the way for his landslide victory over Republican Barry Goldwater in the election of 1964. Goldwater, a senator from Arizona, held conservative views that seemed excessive to many Americans, as well as to many members of his own party.

For example, he opposed civil rights legislation, and he believed that military commanders should be allowed to use nuclear weapons as they saw fit on the battlefield. The Johnson campaign took advantage of voters' fears of nuclear war. It aired a controversial television commercial in which a little girl's innocent counting game turned into the countdown for a nuclear explosion.

Johnson received 61 percent of the popular vote and an overwhelming 486 to 52 tally in the electoral college. The Democrats won majorities in both houses of Congress: 295 Democrats to 140 Republicans in the House of Representatives and 68 to 32 in the Senate. "Landslide Lyndon" now had the mandate to move ahead even more aggressively.

Sounds of an Era
Listen to Lyndon Johnson's Great Society speech and other sounds from the Kennedy-Johnson era.

Focus on GOVERNMENT

The "Daisy" Campaign Commercial
It aired only once, on September 7, 1964. Yet the Johnson campaign's chilling, black-and-white "daisy" commercial became one of the most famous in history. The camera zeroes in on a little girl holding a daisy. She counts the petals as she pulls them off: "One, two, three, four . . ." At "nine," a man's voice begins counting down to zero: ". . . three, two, one . . ." The image of the girl fades to the mushroom cloud of a nuclear blast.

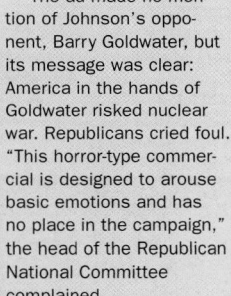

The ad made no mention of Johnson's opponent, Barry Goldwater, but its message was clear: America in the hands of Goldwater risked nuclear war. Republicans cried foul. "This horror-type commercial is designed to arouse basic emotions and has no place in the campaign," the head of the Republican National Committee complained.

The protest backfired. Although the ad was pulled, the controversy caused TV news shows to play it over and over. The little girl with the daisy appeared on the cover of *Time* magazine.

ACTIVITY
Connecting with Citizenship

Share with students Johnson's description of the Great Society in the Background note below. Lead a class discussion in which students, using Johnson's description as a springboard, identify the qualities that any "great society" would have. Record and organize responses on the board. **(Verbal/ Linguistic)**

BACKGROUND
Interdisciplinary

In the speech described on this page, Johnson went on to describe the "Great Society." He said the "Great Society rests on abundance and liberty for all. It demands an end to poverty and racial injustice. . . . The Great Society is a place where every child can find knowledge to enrich his mind and to enlarge his talents. It is a place where leisure is a welcome chance to build and reflect. . . . It is a place where man can renew contact with nature. . . . But most of all, the Great Society is not a safe harbor, a resting place, a final objective, a finished work. It is a challenge constantly renewed, beckoning us toward a destiny where the meaning of our lives matches the marvelous products of our labor. . . ."

 TEST PREPARATION

Have students read Johnson's quotation on this page and then answer the question below.

What does Johnson mean when he speaks of the "rich" society, the "powerful" society, and the "Great" society?

A He envisions a society where no one will be either rich or poor.

(B) He sees a society that treats all its citizens with decency and respect.

C He does not think it matters if individual citizens are wealthy.

D He does not think it matters if the United States is powerful.

INTERPRETING GRAPHS
The cartoon above depicts Johnson playing Congress like a piano, with Great Society programs flowing forth like music. One of those programs, the Elementary and Secondary Education Act, was passed by Congress in 1965. **Analyzing Visual Information** *How does the graph illustrate the overall effect of this legislation?*

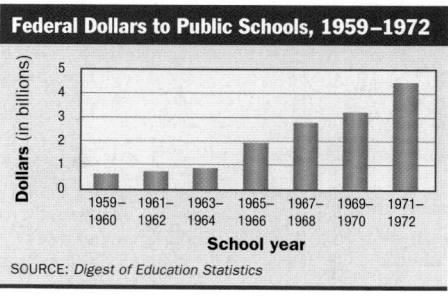

Federal Dollars to Public Schools, 1959–1972

SOURCE: *Digest of Education Statistics*

The Tax Cut Like Kennedy, Johnson believed that a budget deficit could be used to improve the economy. Not everyone agreed. To gain conservatives' support for Kennedy's tax-cut bill, which was likely to bring about a deficit, Johnson also agreed to cut government spending. With that agreement, the measure passed and worked just as planned. When the tax cut went into effect, the Gross National Product (GNP) rose by 7.1 percent in 1964, by 8.1 percent in 1965, and by 9.5 percent in 1966. The deficit, which many people feared would grow, actually shrank because the renewed prosperity generated new tax revenues. Unemployment fell, and inflation remained in check.

The War on Poverty Growing up in an impoverished area of rural Texas, Johnson had experienced the pain of poverty first-hand. He now pressed for the antipoverty program that Kennedy had begun to consider.

In his 1964 State of the Union message, Johnson vowed, "This administration today, here and now, declares unconditional war on poverty in America." The Economic Opportunity Act, passed in the summer of 1964, was created to combat several causes of poverty, including illiteracy, unemployment, and inadequate public services. The act provided nearly $950 million for 10 separate projects, including work training programs. The act also gave poor people a voice in defining housing, health, and education policies in their own neighborhoods.

Two of the best-known programs created under the act were Head Start and VISTA. **Head Start** is a preschool program for children from low-income families that also provides healthcare, nutrition services, and social services. **Volunteers in Service to America (VISTA)** sent volunteers to help people in poor communities. Under Presidents Bush and Clinton, VISTA was merged with other national service programs.

Aid to Education Johnson's education initiatives moved through Congress as well. The Elementary and Secondary Education Act of 1965 provided $1.3 billion in aid to states, based on the number of children in each state from low-income homes. The funds went to public and private schools, including parochial schools. Johnson signed the Education Act into law in the small Texas school he had attended as a child. The graph at left shows federal aid to schools from 1959 to 1972.

Medicare and Medicaid President Johnson also focused attention on the increasing cost of medical care. Harry Truman had proposed a medical assistance plan as part of his Fair Deal program, but it had never been passed into law. In 1965, Johnson used his leadership skills to push through Congress two new programs, Medicare and Medicaid.

Medicare provides hospital and low-cost medical insurance to most Americans age 65 and older. "No longer will older Americans be denied the healing miracle of modern medicine," Johnson declared. "No longer will illness crush and destroy the savings that they have so carefully put away." **Medicaid** provides low-cost health insurance coverage to poor Americans of any age who cannot afford their own private health insurance.

978 Chapter 29 • *The Kennedy and Johnson Years*

Great Society Legislation, 1964–1966

Legislation	Purpose
Economic Opportunity Act, 1964	Created to combat causes of poverty such as illiteracy. Set up community action programs to give the poor a voice in defining local housing, health, and education policies.
Volunteers in Service to America (VISTA), 1964	Sent volunteers to help people in poor communities.
Medicare, 1965	Provided hospital and low-cost medical insurance for most Americans age 65 and older.
Medicaid, 1965	Provided low-cost health insurance for poor Americans of any age who could not afford their own private health insurance.
Elementary and Secondary Education Act of 1965	Provided education aid to states based on the number of children from low-income homes.
Immigration Act of 1965	Eliminated strict quotas for individual countries and replaced them with more flexible limits.
The Department of Housing and Urban Development (HUD), 1965	Established to oversee the nation's housing needs and to develop and rehabilitate urban communities. HUD also provided money for rent supplements and low-income housing.
The National Foundations of the Arts and Humanities, 1965	Offered grants to artists and scholars.
Water Quality Act, 1965; Clean Water Restoration Act, 1966	Brought about water and air quality standards and provided funding for environmental research.
The National Traffic and Motor Vehicle Safety Act, 1966	Established safety standards for all vehicles to protect consumers.

INTERPRETING CHARTS As this chart shows, Great Society legislation addressed a wide range of topics. **Synthesizing Information** *Which pieces of legislation attempted to combat poverty?*

These broad-based healthcare programs were the most important pieces of social welfare legislation since the passage of the Social Security Act in 1935. They demonstrated the government's commitment to provide help to needy Americans.

Immigration Reform The Great Society also revised the immigration policies that had been in place since the 1920s. Laws passed in 1921 and 1924 had set quotas, or numerical limits, for newcomers from each foreign nation. Low quotas—based on the 1890 census, before the arrival of new waves of immigrants—had been established for countries from southern and eastern Europe.

The **Immigration Act of 1965** replaced the varying quotas with a limit of 20,000 immigrants per year from any one country outside the Western Hemisphere. In addition, the act set overall limits of 170,000 immigrants from the Eastern Hemisphere and 120,000 from the Western Hemisphere. Family members of United States citizens were exempted from the quotas, as were political refugees. In the 1960s, some 350,000 immigrants entered the United States each year; in the 1970s, the number rose to more than 400,000 a year.

The Warren Court

The Kennedy-Johnson years featured many of the landmark decisions of the famous, and controversial, Warren Court. As it had in earlier civil rights cases,

READING CHECK
Under President Johnson, how did the role of the federal government change?

Connecting with Culture

Ask students to draw a political cartoon illustrating either a criticism of Johnson's Great Society legislation or a response to LBJ's critics. In the latter case, have students reflect on LBJ's contributions as President of the United States. **(Visual/Spatial)**

BACKGROUND
Biography

In 1965 lawyer Marian Wright Edelman (b. 1939) became the first African American woman admitted to the Mississippi bar. Edelman is the founder and president of the Children's Defense Fund, an advocacy group that promotes the health and welfare of children. Edelman summarizes the Fund's philosophy as follows: "Children cannot eat rhetoric and they cannot be sheltered by commissions. I don't want to see another commission that studies the needs of kids. We need to help them."

READING CHECK
It became more activist. The primary focus of Johnson's Great Society program was to vastly increase to government's role in tackling social problems.

CAPTION ANSWERS

Interpreting Charts The Economic Opportunity Act, VISTA, Medicare, Medicaid, Elementary and Secondary Education Act, and HUD.

The members of the Warren Court, shown here on Nov. 22, 1965 are: (standing, left to right) Byron White, William Brennan, Potter Stewart, Abe Fortas; (seated, left to right) Tom Clark, Hugo Black, Earl Warren, William Douglas, and John Marshall Harlan.

VIEWING HISTORY The Warren Court issued rulings that angered many Americans, as this popular sign below shows. **Recognizing Ideologies** *What beliefs might have caused critics to oppose some of these rulings?*

the Supreme Court under Chief Justice Earl Warren overturned many old laws and rulings and established new legal precedents.

Social Issues The Warren Court made the first attempt to define obscenity in the 1957 case *Roth* v. *United States,* ruling that obscene materials were "utterly without redeeming social importance." In an explosive 1962 case, the Court ruled that religious prayer in public schools was unconstitutional according to the First Amendment principle of separation of church and state *(Engel* v. *Vitale).* In 1965, the Court struck down a Connecticut law that prohibited the use of birth control *(Griswold* v. *Connecticut).*

Criminal Procedure The Warren Court was concerned with safeguarding the constitutional rights of the individual against the power of the government. In particular, the Court handed down several decisions protecting the rights of persons accused of crimes.

Mapp v. *Ohio* (1961) established the exclusionary rule, which states that evidence seized illegally cannot be used in a trial. The Court's decision in *Gideon* v. *Wainwright* (1963) stated that suspects in criminal cases who could not afford a lawyer had the right to free legal aid. In *Escobedo* v. *Illinois* (1964), the justices ruled that accused individuals had to be given access to an attorney while being questioned.

The Court's decision in *Miranda* v. *Arizona* (1966) stated that a suspect must be warned of his or her rights before being questioned. As a result of this **Miranda rule,** police must inform accused persons that they have the right to remain silent; that anything they say can be used against them in court; that they have a right to an attorney; and that if they cannot afford an attorney, one will be appointed for them.

"One Person, One Vote" The Warren Court also handed down a series of decisions on **apportionment,**

or the distribution of the seats in a legislature among electoral districts. Over the years, many Americans had moved from rural to urban areas, but most state governments had not reapportioned their electoral districts to reflect that fact. As a result, in many states, rural areas had more power in state legislatures—and urban areas had less power—than their populations should have given them.

The Warren Court's decision in the case of *Baker v. Carr* (1962) declared that state legislative districts had to be divided on the basis of "one person, one vote." In other words, each person's vote should carry the same weight, regardless of where in the state the person lived. This decision prevented the party in power from drawing district lines in unfair ways to give itself more potential votes. In *Reynolds v. Sims* (1964), the Supreme Court held that state legislative districts not based on the "one person, one vote" formula violated the equal protection clause of the Fourteenth Amendment.

Many of these decisions were, and remain, controversial. Some people argued that the justices had gone too far in their "loose construction" of the Constitution. A number of Warren Court rulings are under vigorous attack from conservatives today.

Effects of the Great Society

At first, the Great Society seemed enormously successful. Opinion polls taken in 1964 showed Johnson to be more popular than Kennedy had been at a comparable point in his presidency.

In time, however, criticisms began to surface. New programs raised expectations that often could not be met. From 1965 through 1968, bloody race riots erupted in poor areas of major cities, giving urgency to Johnson's plans for Great Society programs. But military spending on Vietnam took ever-bigger bites out of the federal budget.

BIOGRAPHY

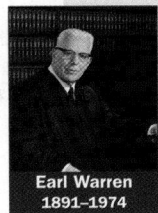
**Earl Warren
1891–1974**

One of the most important chief justices in history, Earl Warren led a Supreme Court that brought sweeping changes to American law and society. His decisions delighted liberals but surprised and angered many in his own Republican Party.

Earl Warren earned his law degree at the University of California at Berkeley. From 1925 to 1953, he won various posts in California: Alameda County district attorney, state attorney general, and finally governor. Warren's only election defeat was as Thomas E. Dewey's vice presidential running mate in 1948. In 1953, President Eisenhower appointed him the fourteenth Chief Justice of the United States—a choice Ike would later regret. Warren served as Chief Justice until he retired in 1969.

COMPARING HISTORIANS' VIEWPOINTS
The Great Society

Historians disagree about the effectiveness of President Johnson's Great Society programs.
Analyzing Viewpoints Compare the main arguments made by the two writers.

In Support of the Great Society

"In 1965 and early 1966 . . . the President and his economic advisors gratefully accepted the fiscal dividends provided by the booming economy as a means of bringing the Great Society closer to reality. Prosperity helped in two vital ways: by creating new jobs and by generating additional federal income that could be used to fund new social programs. Congress, which frequently approves new federal activities but then starves them to death by providing little or no money for their operation, funded the programs it authorized during 1965 and 1966 quite generously."

—Jim F. Heath,
The Decade of Disillusionment:
The Kennedy-Johnson Years

In Opposition to the Great Society

"In fact the war on poverty was destined to be one of the great failures of twentieth-century liberalism. Most of its programs could be grouped under two strategies. One of these emphasized opening new opportunities for poor people. . . . The other strategy, recognizing that mere opportunity would not be enough for many of the poor, provided subsidies to increase their consumption of food, shelter, and medical care. . . . Taken together, the programs spawned by these two strategies did little to diminish inequality and therefore, by definition, failed measurably to reduce poverty."

—Allen J. Matusow,
The Unraveling of America:
A History of Liberalism in the 1960s

ACTIVITY
Connecting with History and Conflict

Assign student pairs or small groups the task of creating a table that identifies and describes the landmark decisions of the Warren Court. The students should write a brief introduction to or caption for their table, which should at least include the names, parties to, dates, and impact of each of the decisions. **(Verbal/Linguistic)**

BACKGROUND
Connections to Today

An enduring legacy of LBJ's aid to education is Head Start—a program begun in 1965 to prepare economically disadvantaged preschoolers for school. Now administered by the Department of Health and Human Services, Head Start works through local communities to provide nutritious lunches, medical and family services, and educational preparation. Head Start receives bipartisan support in Congress and serves more than 11 million children, mostly under the age of five.

CUSTOMIZE FOR ...
Less Proficient Writers

Have students reread the section "Criminal Procedure." Then, have students list the four cases mentioned in the section and write a brief description of each case in their own words.

VIEWING HISTORY A teacher instructs young students in the Head Start program. **Predicting Consequences** What long-term effects do you think the Johnson administration hoped to achieve through the Head Start program?

Meanwhile, some Americans complained that too many of their tax dollars were being spent on poor people. For decades following the Great Society, a major political debate continued over the criticism that antipoverty programs encouraged poor people to become dependent on government aid and created successive generations of families on welfare instead of in jobs. Other critics argued that Great Society programs put too much authority into the hands of the federal government. They opposed the expansion of the federal bureaucracy that accompanied the new programs.

Nevertheless, the number of Americans living in poverty in the United States was cut in half during the 1960s and early 1970s. Michael Harrington, author of *The Other America*, argued that the federal government should have allocated even more public funds to fight poverty. He noted, "What was supposed to be a social war turned out to be a skirmish and, in any case, poverty won."

In the midst of praise and criticism, Johnson himself was proud of his Great Society programs. In his view, they were "major accomplishments without equal or close parallel in the present era."

Before his death, John Kennedy had focused more on foreign affairs than domestic. When Johnson took office, he threw his energies into problems at home. The next section describes Kennedy's actions on the world stage and, after JFK's death, the beginnings of the conflict in Southeast Asia that would eventually consume the resources that Johnson had hoped to spend on domestic programs. LBJ's inability to contain that conflict undermined and finally ended the Great Society.

Section 2 Assessment

READING COMPREHENSION

1. Briefly outline LBJ's rise to the presidency.

2. List the key goals of the **Great Society** and some of the programs created to meet those goals.

3. Describe the changes made by the **Immigration Act of 1965.**

4. How did the **Miranda rule** change law enforcement in the United States?

CRITICAL THINKING AND WRITING

5. Demonstrating Reasoned Judgment Do you think Johnson's Great Society programs were a success? What questions would you ask yourself in order to make this judgment?

6. Writing an Opinion What positive or negative effects do you think the Warren Court has had on society today? Use examples to support your opinion.

Take It to the NET

Activity: Creating a Fact Sheet Read about the lives and activities of either Jacqueline Kennedy or Lady Bird Johnson. Create a fact sheet that describes the contributions of these First Ladies to their husbands' presidencies and to the nation. Use the links provided in the *America: Pathways to the Present* area of the following Web site for help in completing this activity.
www.phschool.com

Foreign Policy in the Early 1960s

READING FOCUS

- What were the goals of the Bay of Pigs invasion, and what was the outcome?
- What events led to the Berlin crisis and to the Cuban Missile Crisis?
- What were the goals of the Alliance for Progress and the Peace Corps?
- Which Cold War conflicts did Johnson become involved in?

MAIN IDEA

The Cold War intensified as President Kennedy and President Johnson became involved in anti-Communist conflicts in Latin America, Europe, and Southeast Asia.

KEY TERMS

Bay of Pigs invasion
Berlin Wall
Cuban Missile Crisis
Limited Test Ban Treaty
Alliance for Progress
Peace Corps

TAKING NOTES

Copy the chart below. As you read, fill in facts about the outcomes of Cold War crises under Kennedy and Johnson.

Cold War Crises Under Kennedy and Johnson	Outcomes
Bay of Pigs	Failed invasion; United States humiliated

SECTION OBJECTIVES

1. Understand the goals and the outcome of the Bay of Pigs invasion.
2. Read to find out about events that led to the Berlin Crisis and the Cuban Missile Crisis.
3. Discover the goals of the Alliance for Progress and the Peace Corps.
4. Find out about Cold War conflicts in which Johnson became involved.

BELLRINGER

Warm-Up Activity Ask students to think about the way the United States pursues relationships with other countries. Ask them to list what they think should be the goals of our foreign policy.

Activating Prior Knowledge Ask students to discuss ways in which United States foreign policy changed after World War II. In particular, how did the worsening relationship between the Soviet Union and the United States impact decisions that were made in Washington?

READING STRATEGY

Before students read this section, have them write one question for each of the main headings. As they read, have them look for answers to those questions. Have them reflect on the impact of significant international decisions that took place during this era.

Setting the Scene Although they would have liked to dedicate more of America's resources to improving conditions at home, both Kennedy and Johnson found themselves in the front lines of the Cold War. It was a dangerous and expensive battle, but, as Kennedy argued, it was one worth fighting:

> ❝ Let every nation know, whether it wishes us well or ill, that we shall pay any price, bear any burden, meet any hardship, support any friend, oppose any foe to assure the survival and the success of liberty. ❞
> —John F. Kennedy, Inaugural Address, 1961

As President at the height of the Cold War between the Soviet Union and the United States, Kennedy spoke boldly. In the crises he faced as President, though, Kennedy found that he had to act more cautiously to prevent a local conflict from sparking a global war.

The Bay of Pigs Invasion

Kennedy's first foreign crisis arose in Cuba, an island about 90 miles off the Florida coast. The United States had been concerned about Cuba ever since 1959, when Fidel Castro overthrew the U.S.-backed dictator Fulgencio Batista. Some Cubans had supported Castro because he promised to improve the lives of poor people. Castro claimed that the poor were being exploited by wealthy Cubans and by United States companies operating in Cuba.

Once in power, the Castro government seized large, privately owned plantations and property owned by foreign corporations, including some U.S. businesses. The United States broke diplomatic relations with Cuba and refused to accept Castro as the country's legitimate leader. When Castro developed ties to the Soviet Union, American officials began to fear that Cuba could become a model for revolutionary upheaval throughout Latin America.

A Plan to Overthrow Castro After Kennedy became President, he was informed about a plan that President Eisenhower had approved in 1960. Under

Cuba's Fidel Castro (left) poses with his ally and supporter, Soviet leader Nikita Khrushchev, at a United Nations meeting.

RESOURCE DIRECTORY

Teaching Resources
Learning Styles Lesson Plans booklet, p. 61
Guided Reading and Review booklet, p. 119
Learning with Documents booklet (Key Documents) *John F. Kennedy, Inaugural Address,* p. 93

Technology
Section Reading Support Transparencies
Guided Reading Audiotapes (English/Spanish), Ch. 29
Student Edition on Audio CD, Ch. 29
Prentice Hall Presentation Pro CD-ROM, Ch. 29
Companion Web site, www.phschool.com

A CTIVITY
Connecting with History and Conflict

Have student groups research and prepare a brief (one page or less) biography of Fidel Castro's early life (before the revolution in Cuba). Have student groups compare their biographies and together compile a list of facts about Castro. **(Verbal/Linguistic)**

Focus The foreign policies of Presidents Kennedy and Johnson were grounded in the Cold War. Ask how Kennedy reacted to Communist challenges. How did Johnson continue many of Kennedy's foreign policies?

Instruct Discuss the Bay of Pigs fiasco. Why was the United States concerned about Castro? Why did Kennedy agree to support the invasion? Have students make a time line of the Cuban Missile Crisis events on the chalkboard. Ask them to identify the most critical time period of the crisis.

Ask students to explain the underlying political goal of the Alliance for Progress and the Peace Corps. How successful were these programs?

Assess/Reteach In what ways has the end of the Cold War modified the relationship between the United States and the former Soviet Union? Ask students to discuss the changes in attitudes that have resulted from this altered situation.

READING CHECK

Fidel Castro had seized U.S. property and was on good terms with the Soviet Union. The United States did not recognize Castro's government. Kennedy was motivated to act because he believed that the Cuban example might trigger revolutionary upheavals in other Latin American nations.

READING CHECK
Why did President Kennedy want to overthrow Fidel Castro?

MAP SKILLS This map traces the ill-fated Bay of Pigs invasion authorized by President Kennedy in 1961. The photo below shows a Cuban beachfront resort littered with artillery shells following the invasion. **Regions** (a) How many countries played a role in the incident in some form? (b) How do you think this complexity affected the outcome of the operation?

this plan, the Central Intelligence Agency (CIA) was training a group of Cubans to invade Cuba and overthrow Castro. The training took place in Guatemala, a nearby Central American country. Kennedy and his advisors expected the Cuban people to help the invaders defeat Castro.

Resistance to the plan soon surfaced, however. When Democratic Senator J. William Fulbright, head of the Foreign Relations Committee, learned of the scheme, he called it an "endless can of worms." He warned the President:

❝ To give this activity even covert [secret] support is of a piece with the hypocrisy and cynicism for which the United States is constantly denouncing [condemning] the Soviet Union in the United Nations and elsewhere. This point will not be lost on the rest of the world—nor on our own consciences. . . . The Castro regime is a thorn in the flesh; but it is not a dagger in the heart.❞
—Senator J. William Fulbright, memorandum to Kennedy, March 29, 1961

Despite such reservations and those of some military leaders, Kennedy accepted the advice of the CIA and agreed to push ahead with the invasion plan.

A Military Catastrophe The **Bay of Pigs invasion,** shown on the map below, took place on April 17, 1961. It was a total disaster. An airstrike failed to destroy Cuba's air force, and Cuban troops were more than a match for the 1,500 U.S.-backed invaders. When Kennedy's advisors urged him to use American planes to provide air cover for the attackers, he refused. Rather than continue a hopeless effort, he chose simply to accept defeat.

The United States lost a great deal of prestige in the disastrous attack. To begin with, the invasion was clumsy and incompetent. Furthermore, America's support of an effort to overthrow another nation's government was exposed to the world. The United States faced anger from other countries in Latin America for violating agreements not to interfere in the Western Hemisphere. European

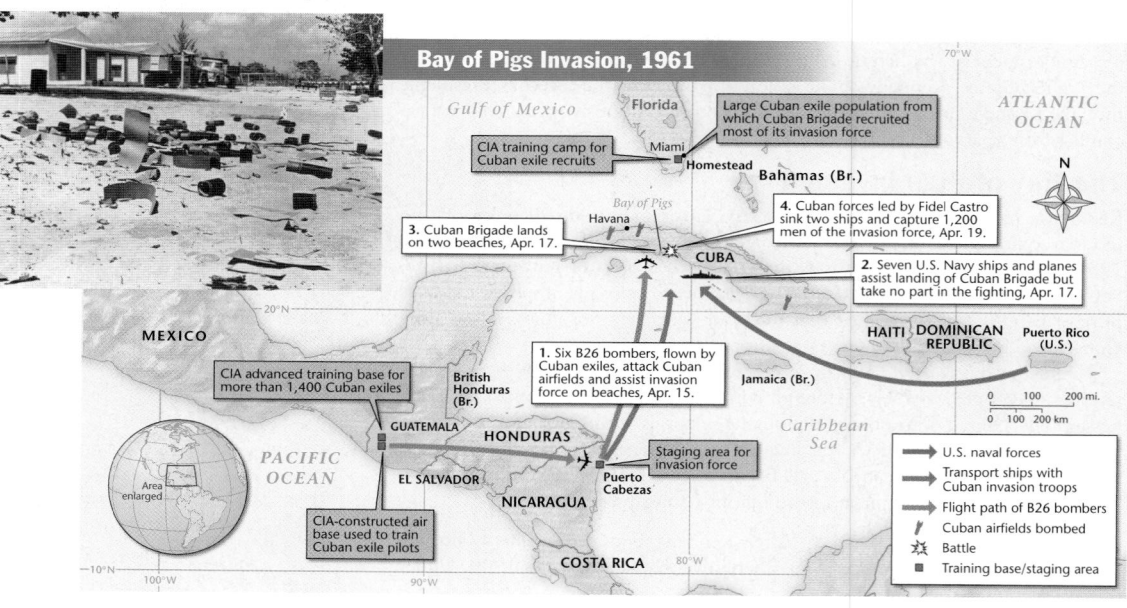

Bay of Pigs Invasion, 1961

Gulf of Mexico — Florida — ATLANTIC OCEAN
Large Cuban exile population from which Cuban Brigade recruited most of its invasion force
CIA training camp for Cuban exile recruits — Miami — Homestead
Bahamas (Br.)
Bay of Pigs — Havana
3. Cuban Brigade lands on two beaches, Apr. 17.
4. Cuban forces led by Fidel Castro sink two ships and capture 1,200 men of the invasion force, Apr. 19.
CUBA
2. Seven U.S. Navy ships and planes assist landing of Cuban Brigade but take no part in the fighting, Apr. 17.
MEXICO
HAITI — DOMINICAN REPUBLIC — Puerto Rico (U.S.)
CIA advanced training base for more than 1,400 Cuban exiles
British Honduras (Br.)
1. Six B26 bombers, flown by Cuban exiles, attack Cuban airfields and assist invasion force on beaches, Apr. 15.
Jamaica (Br.)
GUATEMALA — HONDURAS
PACIFIC OCEAN
Area enlarged
EL SALVADOR
NICARAGUA
Puerto Cabezas
Staging area for invasion force
Caribbean Sea
CIA-constructed air base used to train Cuban exile pilots
COSTA RICA

0   100   200 mi.
0   100   200 km

→ U.S. naval forces
→ Transport ships with Cuban invasion troops
→ Flight path of B26 bombers
✈ Cuban airfields bombed
⚔ Battle
■ Training base/staging area

★ **CAPTION ANSWERS**

Map Skills (a) Four (the United States, Cuba, Nicaragua, and Guatemala; the U.S. territory of Puerto Rico was involved as well). (b) Sample answer: It probably hampered the coordination of the operation, contributing to its failure.

RESOURCE DIRECTORY

Other Print Resources

American History Block Scheduling Support *The Berlin Wall: Past and Present,* found in The Nation After World War II folder, includes interdisciplinary lesson suggestions and activities for Geography and History, Primary Sources, Biography, and Literature.

Technology
Color Transparencies *Historical Maps,* A48

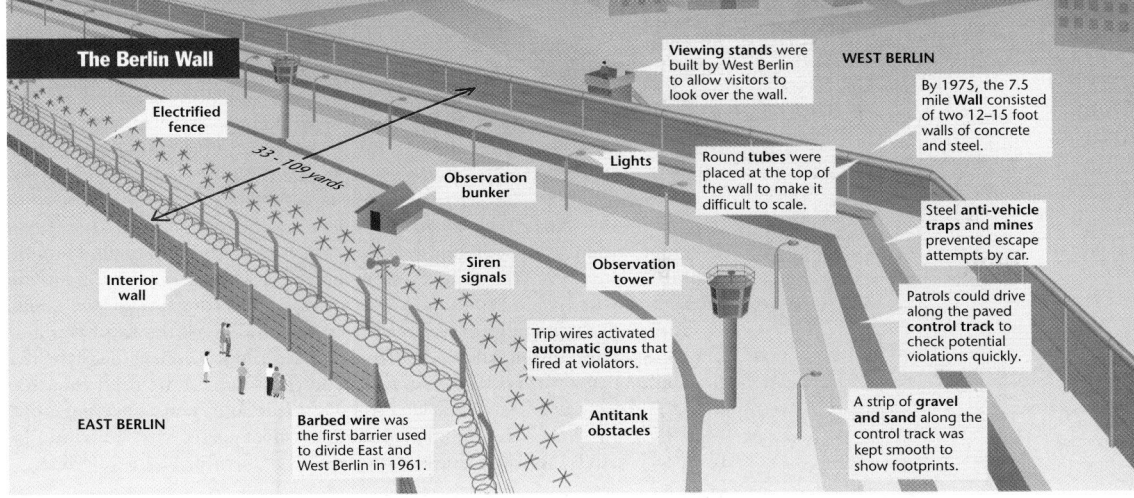

The Berlin Wall

Electrified fence

Viewing stands were built by West Berlin to allow visitors to look over the wall.

WEST BERLIN

By 1975, the 7.5 mile Wall consisted of two 12–15 foot walls of concrete and steel.

Round tubes were placed at the top of the wall to make it difficult to scale.

33–109 yards

Observation bunker

Lights

Steel anti-vehicle traps and mines prevented escape attempts by car.

Interior wall

Siren signals

Observation tower

Patrols could drive along the paved control track to check potential violations quickly.

Trip wires activated automatic guns that fired at violators.

EAST BERLIN

Barbed wire was the first barrier used to divide East and West Berlin in 1961.

Antitank obstacles

A strip of gravel and sand along the control track was kept smooth to show footprints.

leaders, who had high hopes for the new President, were concerned about the kind of leadership he would provide.

The Berlin Crisis

Upset by the failure at the Bay of Pigs, Kennedy was now even more determined to prove his toughness against communism. Later in 1961, he had another opportunity when a new crisis arose over a familiar issue: Berlin.

Rekindled Tensions Over Germany After World War II, the Allies had divided Germany into zones. The United States, Great Britain, the Soviet Union, and France each controlled one sector of the country. While the zones were meant to be temporary, the lines between them had hardened as Cold War tensions increased among the former Allies. In time, the western regions had been combined to form the nation of West Germany. The sector controlled by the Soviet Union became East Germany. The city of Berlin, although located completely inside East Germany, had also been divided among the World War II victors.

The Soviet attempt to cut off access to Berlin in 1948 had failed as a result of President Truman's successful Berlin airlift. Now the Soviets made another effort to resolve problems in Berlin on their own terms. They demanded a peace treaty that would make the division of the city permanent. Their goal was to cut off the large flow of East Germans escaping into West Germany, particularly through Berlin.

Kennedy feared that the Soviet effort in Germany was part of a larger plan to take over the rest of Europe. Adding to his fears, his first meeting with Soviet leader Nikita Khrushchev, in Vienna, Austria, in June 1961, went poorly. When Khrushchev made a public ultimatum regarding Germany, Kennedy felt bullied by the Soviet leader.

Kennedy Takes Action Upon returning home, Kennedy decided to show the Soviets that the United States would not be intimidated. He asked Congress for a huge increase of more than $3 billion for defense. He doubled the number of young men being drafted into the armed services and called up reserve forces for active duty. At the same time, he sought more than $200 million for a

INTERPRETING DIAGRAMS
Below, West Berliners peer through the newly built Berlin Wall into East Berlin near Checkpoint Charlie. Initially, tubes on the top of the wall were supposed to prevent escapees from getting a grip to pull themselves over. Later, as shown in the diagram of a typical checkpoint in the 1980s (top), a whole range of deadly deterrents were installed. **Analyzing Visual Information** As depicted in the diagram, what other hazards were added to prevent escape?

ACTIVITY

Connecting with Geography

Have students use a historical atlas or help small groups conduct Internet research to locate a map of Berlin, circa 1961. Have the students research and organize information on the city at that time, using the map as a visual aid. **(Verbal/Linguistic)**

BACKGROUND

Connections to Today

When the Berlin Wall that divided East and West Germany for 28 years was torn down on November 9, 1989, a witness said that spectators "seemed to be drawn by the sense that . . . the barrier of concrete and steel that had figured so prominently in the history of this city and the world might soon be relegated to history." The reunification of Germany one year later proved to be just part of the collapse of the iron curtain.

CAPTION ANSWERS

Interpreting Diagrams Reinforced walls, barbed wire, sirens, electrified fencing, trip wires that activated automatic weapons, patrol vehicles, anti-vehicle traps and mines, bright lights, and a smooth sand-and-gravel strip that showed footprints.

CUSTOMIZE FOR ...

Gifted and Talented

Have students analyze the impact of the construction of a physical barrier, such as the Berlin Wall, in your city or town. Ask them to consider the implications of such a construction from political, economic, social, and purely practical perspectives. Have them write a "newspaper editorial" that expresses an opinion about this action.

TEST PREPARATION

Have students read the quotation by Senator Fulbright on the previous page and then answer the question below.

What is the main reason that the senator opposed the plan to overthrow Castro?

A He had no objection to the Castro regime.

Ⓑ He thought it was wrong for the United States to take the kind of actions it denounced other nations for taking.

C He wanted the plan to be carried out openly, not secretly.

D He thought the Soviet Union would retaliate.

program to build fallout shelters across the country. He argued that the United States had to be prepared if the crisis led to nuclear war.

Kennedy appeared on television to tell the American people that West Berlin was "the great testing place of Western courage and will, a focal point where our solemn commitments . . . and Soviet ambitions now meet in basic confrontation." The United States, he said, would not be pushed around: "We do not want to fight—but we have fought before."

In August 1961, the Soviets responded by building a wall to separate Communist and non-Communist Berlin. The **Berlin Wall** became a somber symbol of the Cold War. Still, by stopping the flow of East Germans to the West, the Soviet Union had found a way to avoid a showdown over East Berlin.

Although the immediate crisis was over, the tensions of the Cold War continued. Speaking in Frankfurt, Germany, in June 1963, Kennedy declared that the United States "will risk its cities to defend yours because we need your freedom to protect ours." Two days later, the President addressed a cheering crowd near the Berlin Wall. To symbolize his commitment to the city, he concluded his speech with the rousing words, *"Ich bin ein Berliner,"* or "I am a Berliner."

The Cuban Missile Crisis

Kennedy also had a chance to restore American prestige in another crisis with Cuba. The Soviet Union, disturbed by the attempted Bay of Pigs invasion, had pledged to support Castro's government. On October 16, 1962, photographs taken from an American spy plane revealed that the Soviets were building missile bases on Cuban soil—only about 90 miles from the Florida coast. What followed was the **Cuban Missile Crisis**, a terrifying standoff between the United States and the Soviet Union that brought the superpowers to the brink of nuclear war.

MAP SKILLS U.S. spy plane photographs such as the one at right showed missile bases under construction in Cuba. The map shows the naval blockade of Cuba, put in place during tense diplomatic negotiations to avert a nuclear disaster. Khrushchev offered to withdraw the missiles from Cuba if Kennedy promised not to invade the island. **Location** What details in the map help to explain (a) why the Soviet Union wanted a military presence in Cuba, and (b) why Kennedy was determined to prevent that from happening?

Kennedy's Options The Soviet missiles in Cuba did not radically change the military balance between the United States and

Cuban Missile Crisis, 1962

Florida
Miami
BAHAMAS
ATLANTIC OCEAN

1. **Oct. 16** CIA provides President Kennedy with evidence of Soviet missile bases under construction in Cuba.

2. **Oct. 22** President Kennedy announces a naval "quarantine" of Cuba.

3. **Oct. 24** Soviet ships reverse course upon learning of the blockade.

4. **Oct. 28** Premier Khrushchev offers to withdraw missiles from Cuba in exchange for removal of the quarantine and a U.S. pledge not to invade Cuba.

5. **Oct. 28** President Kennedy accepts the offer. Soviet missile bases are dismantled by mid-November.

Havana
CUBA
Guantanamo
HAITI
DOMINICAN REPUBLIC
JAMAICA
Caribbean Sea

- ⬤ Soviet missile base
- ▬ U.S. naval quarantine
- ■ U.S. naval base

N

0   100   200 mi.
0   100   200 km
80°W   70°W   20°N

the Soviet Union. The Soviets could already inflict serious damage on the United States from bases within their own country. Yet installing missiles so close to the United States seemed to be an effort by the Soviets to intimidate the Americans. Kennedy was convinced that the missiles presented a direct challenge to which he must respond.

But how? The President quickly assembled his top advisors in a series of secret meetings. They outlined four possible responses:

1. Engage in further negotiations with Khrushchev. This option, although peaceful, would give the Soviets more time to finish building the missile bases. It also risked making Kennedy look hesitant and weak in the face of the bold Soviet move.

2. Invade Cuba. This would eliminate the missile threat and achieve the additional goal of ousting Fidel Castro. A Cuban invasion had failed before, though, and this plan risked all-out nuclear war with the Soviets.

3. Blockade Cuba. This action would prevent Soviet ships from making further missile deliveries. It would force Khrushchev either to back off or to take aggressive action against U.S. warships. However, no one knew how the Soviet leader might react to this step.

4. Bomb the missile sites. A series of airstrikes could quickly knock out the missiles. Yet would the Soviets launch a counterstrike, and where?

Attorney General Robert Kennedy argued against the airstrike option. It seemed, he said, too much like the Japanese attack on Pearl Harbor that had launched the United States into World War II. At one point former Secretary of State Dean Acheson joined the discussions and declared that the United States had to knock out the Soviet missiles. He was asked what would happen next. His response points out the very real danger of a local conflict escalating, or expanding, into a widespread war:

Acheson: I know the Soviet Union well. I know what they are required to do in the light of their history and their posture around the world. I think they will knock out our missiles in Turkey.

An advisor: Well, then what do we do?

Acheson: I believe under our NATO treaty . . . we would be required to respond by knocking out a missile base inside the Soviet Union.

Another advisor: Then what do they do?

Acheson: That's when we hope that cooler heads will prevail, and they'll stop and talk.

Kennedy Decides   President Kennedy ordered United States forces on full alert. U.S. bombers were armed with nuclear missiles. The navy was ready to move, and army and marine units prepared to invade Cuba.

Kennedy listened to the different views of his advisors, grilling them with questions. Then, in solitude, he weighed the options, facing one of the most dangerous and agonizing decisions any President has had to make.

On Monday, October 22, Kennedy went on television and radio to confirm the press reports that had begun to circulate about Cuba. "[U]nmistakable evidence has established the fact that a series of offensive missile sites is now in

VIEWING HISTORY This famous photograph shows Kennedy in the Oval Office. The photo is often used to evoke the loneliness of the presidency. **Drawing Inferences** *From what you know about Kennedy's previous foreign policy experiences, what factors might have weighed heavily on him as he made his decision on the Cuban missiles?*

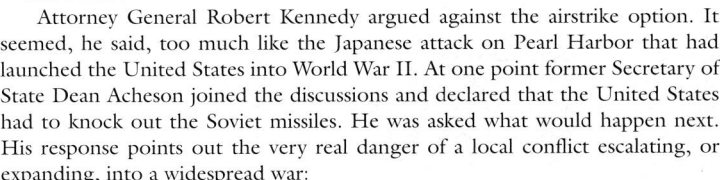

ACTIVITY
Connecting with History and Conflict

The threat of a nuclear holocaust was very real in the 1960s. Ask students to use the *Reader's Guide to Periodical Literature* or the Internet to locate and report on contemporary magazine articles about building, stocking, and living in fallout shelters. **(Verbal/Linguistic)**

BACKGROUND
Cuba and the United States

Since the Communist revolution in 1959, Cuban leader Fidel Castro has insisted that the small United States naval base in Guantanamo Bay on the eastern coast of Cuba is "a dagger plunged into Cuban soil." It has been there since 1903—five years after the end of the Spanish-American War—and some 70,000 United States military personnel and their families live and work at the base.

CUSTOMIZE FOR ...
Less Proficient Readers

Have students write two column headings on a piece of paper: *Kennedy's Trouble Spots* and *Johnson's Trouble Spots.* After they read the section, ask them to list each of the foreign affairs crises discussed in the section in the appropriate column and briefly describe the crisis and its resolution.

CAPTION **A**NSWERS

Viewing History Sample answer: He did not want to repeat the embarrassment of the failed Bay of Pigs invasion. He needed to take a firm stand against the Soviet Union for several reasons: to curb aggressive designs on the part of the Russians; to uphold the Monroe Doctrine; and to restore America's position of strength in foreign affairs.

Connecting with Today

Have students ask appropriate older adults to share their recollections of the Cuban Missile Crisis and the Cold War in general. Have students share what they learn with the class. **(Verbal/Linguistic)**

From the Archives of

AmericanHeritage®

About the Presidents

John Fitzgerald Kennedy (1961–1963) won rave reviews for the first three months of his presidency. He announced the formation of the Peace Corps to send volunteer workers to developing countries. His administration continued Eisenhower's Food for Peace Program, helping to solve the problem of agricultural surplus while winning friends abroad. He also launched the Alliance for Progress for Latin-American economic cooperation and social development. Kennedy's live press conferences only added to his glamour. Some commentators suggested that Kennedy's first 100 days might surpass FDR's. Then came the Bay of Pigs. The disaster cost him prestige abroad and the support of liberals at home. Source: Joseph L. Gardner, "John Fitzgerald Kennedy," *The American Heritage® Pictorial History of the Presidents of the United States,* vol. 2, 1968.

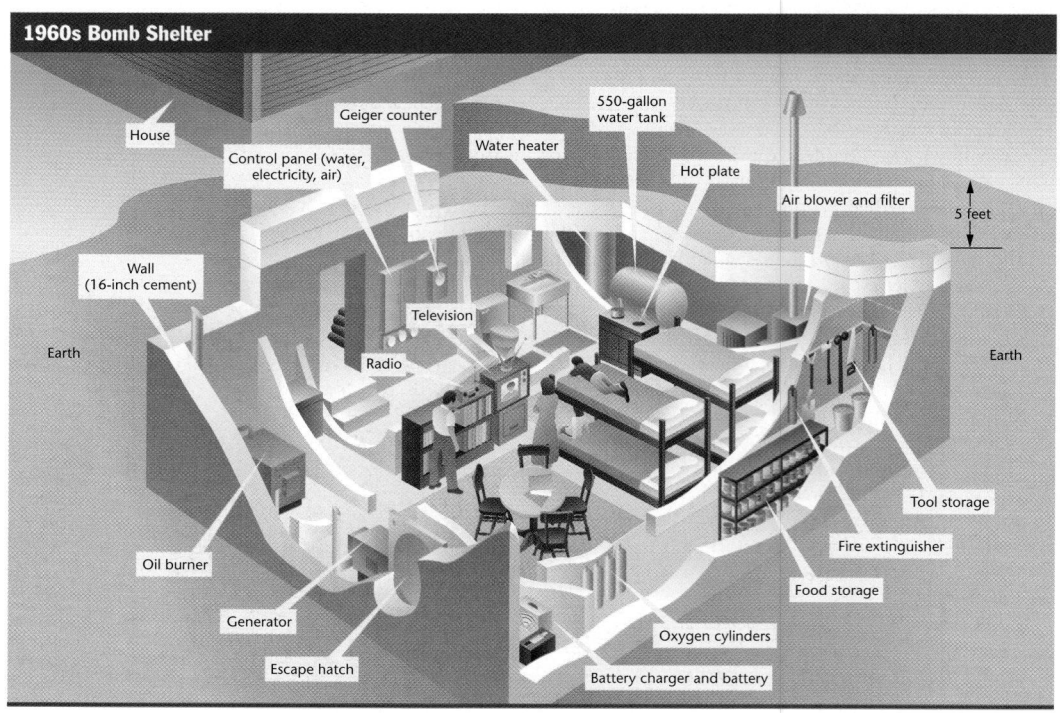

1960s Bomb Shelter

House — Geiger counter — 550-gallon water tank — Water heater — Hot plate — Air blower and filter — 5 feet — Control panel (water, electricity, air) — Wall (16-inch cement) — Television — Radio — Earth — Earth — Oil burner — Tool storage — Fire extinguisher — Food storage — Generator — Oxygen cylinders — Escape hatch — Battery charger and battery

INTERPRETING DIAGRAMS
Many Americans hoped they could survive a nuclear war in a basement shelter that would protect them from radioactive fallout, the deadly particles that rain down after an atomic blast. **Analyzing Visual Information** *Which features of this fallout shelter are intended to provide safety for the family, and which provide comfort and necessities for living?*

preparation on that imprisoned island," he said. The President then announced his decision: He had authorized a naval "quarantine" around Cuba. He was careful not to call the action a "blockade" because a blockade is an act of war. He demanded that Khrushchev "halt and eliminate this clandestine, reckless and provocative threat. . . ."

America did not desire confrontation, Kennedy said, but neither would it shrink from aggression. He told Americans:

> 66 *The path we have chosen for the present is full of hazards. . . . The cost of freedom is always high—and Americans have always paid it. And one path we shall never choose, and that is the path of surrender or submission.* 99
>
> —President Kennedy, television and radio address to the nation, October 22, 1962

The World Waits The two most powerful nations in the world stood teetering on the brink of disaster. "The immediate public reaction was a mixture of anger and fear—but no panic—as they rallied in support of the president," one reporter later recalled. Some people huddled in their bomb shelters, expecting the worst.

The naval quarantine went into effect on Wednesday, October 24. On October 25, a Soviet ship reached the quarantine line and was stopped by the navy. Because it was carrying only oil, it was allowed to proceed. Meanwhile, a dozen more Soviet cargo ships were steaming toward the blockade. Then, to

---

CAPTION ANSWERS

Analyzing Diagrams Accept reasonable answers. Safety: thick cement walls, Geiger counter, air filter, escape hatch, oxygen cylinders, fire extinguisher. Comfort and necessities: television, radio, oil burner, generator, battery charger, food storage, tool storage, hot plate, water tank and heater.

RESOURCE DIRECTORY

Teaching Resources
Biography, Literature, and Comparing Primary Sources booklet (Comparing Primary Sources) *On the Cold War,* p. 153

Technology
Color Transparencies *The Way It Works,* H19

everyone's great relief, the Soviet ships suddenly reversed direction. Khrushchev had called them back.

Disaster Avoided   The crisis was not yet over, however. In Cuba, construction on the existing missile sites continued. On October 26, Khrushchev sent Kennedy a long letter in which he pledged to remove the missiles if Kennedy promised that the United States would end the quarantine and stay out of Cuba. A second letter delivered the next day demanded that the United States remove its missiles from Turkey in exchange for the withdrawal of Soviet missiles in Cuba. Kennedy publicly accepted the terms of the first note. He responded to the second note through secret negotiations and eventually met the demand.

With that, the crisis ended. As Secretary of State Dean Rusk observed to President Kennedy, "We have won a considerable victory. You and I are still alive."

The Cuban Missile Crisis brought the world closer than ever before to nuclear war. Such a war would have caused unimaginable death and destruction—far more, for example, than the atomic bombings of Japan in 1945, in part because more-powerful hydrogen bombs had replaced those early atomic weapons.

Kennedy emerged from the confrontation as a hero. He had stood up to the Soviets and shown that the United States would not be pushed around. His reputation, and that of the Democratic Party, improved just in time for the midterm congressional elections that were only weeks away.

The Aftereffects   The Cuban Missile Crisis led to a number of efforts to reduce the risk of nuclear war. Once the confrontation was over, Kennedy and Khrushchev established a "hot line" between their two nations to allow the Soviet and American leaders to communicate quickly in the event of a future crisis. In addition, in the summer of 1963 the two countries (along with Great Britain) signed the first nuclear treaty since the development of the atomic bomb.

This agreement, the **Limited Test Ban Treaty,** banned nuclear testing above the ground. By doing so, it sought to eliminate the radioactive fallout that threatened to contaminate human, animal, and plant life.

The treaty still permitted underground nuclear testing, and the United States and the Soviet Union continued to build bigger and bigger bombs. Nonetheless, as Kennedy noted, the treaty marked "an important first step toward peace, a step toward reason, a step away from war."

The Alliance for Progress

The Soviet Union and the United States competed not only by building up their military forces, but also by seeking allies in the developing countries of Latin America, Asia, and Africa. Many of these countries were terribly poor. Communist revolutionary movements in some of these countries were gaining support by promising people a better future.

To counter these revolutionary movements, Kennedy tried to promote "peaceful revolution"—that is, to help build stable governments that met the needs of their citizens and also were allied with the democratic countries of the West. Two months after taking office, Kennedy called on all the people of the Western Hemisphere to join in a new **Alliance for Progress,** or *Alianza para Progreso.* The Alliance would be

As a U.S. Navy patrol plane flies overhead, the American destroyer U.S.S. *Barry* pulls alongside the Soviet freighter *Anesov* during the American naval blockade of Cuba.

Focus on WORLD EVENTS

Memoirs of the Crisis   Many policymakers on both sides of the Cuban Missile Crisis composed memoirs of the event. In *Thirteen Days: A Memoir of the Cuban Missile Crisis,* Robert F. Kennedy recalled with awe what the American team had experienced:

> "We saw as never before the meaning and responsibility in the power of the United States, . . . the responsibility we had to people around the globe who had never heard of us, who had never heard of our country or of the men sitting in that room determining their fate. . . ."

Likewise, Russian leader Nikita Khrushchev set down his recollections in *Khrushchev Remembers:*

> "I found myself in the difficult position of having to decide on a course of action which would answer the American threat but which would also avoid war. Any fool can start a war, and once he's done so, even the wisest of men are helpless to stop it— especially if it's a nuclear war."

Chapter 29 • Section 3   989

Connecting with Economics

During President Kennedy's administration, Social Security benefits were extended, and the age of eligibility for Social Security was lowered from 65 to 62. Have students research the current eligibility requirements for Social Security today, the current benefit rates, and the long-term prospects for this program. Have them present their findings in a chart, graph, or table. **(Logical/Mathematical)**

BACKGROUND

Connections to Geography

In speaking of the Alliance for Progress, Kennedy was always careful to include Spanish words and phrases to forge a closer bond with Latin American officials. Thus he spoke of *Alianza para Progreso* as "a vast cooperative effort, unparalleled in magnitude and nobility of purpose, to satisfy the basic needs of the American people for homes, work and land, health and schools—*techo, trabajo y tierra, salud y escuela.*" "Our motto," Kennedy said, "is what it has always been—progress yes, tyranny no—*progreso si, tirania no!*"

a vast cooperative effort to satisfy the basic needs of people in North, Central, and South America for homes, work, land, health, and schools.

The task was a huge undertaking. The administration pledged $20 billion over ten years to promote economic development and social reform and to prevent revolution. All citizens in the Western Hemisphere, Kennedy declared, had "a right to social justice," and that included "land for the landless, and education for those who are denied education."

Soon, however, Latin Americans began to question the benefits of the Alliance. Some viewed it simply as a tool of the United States to stop the spread of communism. Because of such doubts, the Alliance for Progress never lived up to Kennedy's expectations.

The Peace Corps

Kennedy's hope for a world in which nations worked together peacefully to solve problems was also reflected in his establishment of the **Peace Corps** in 1961. This program sent volunteers abroad as educators, health workers, and technicians to help developing nations around the world.

Paul Cowan was typical of many Peace Corps volunteers. After graduating from college in 1963, he worked in the civil rights movement, tutoring African American children in Maryland. In 1965, Cowan and his wife, Rachel, joined the Peace Corps and prepared to work in South America. After a training program at the University of New Mexico, they went to the city of Guayaquil in Ecuador to do community development work. Their job was to raise the standard of living in

The Peace Corps

The idea for an overseas voluntary service organization began late at night on October 14, 1960. Kennedy, in an unscheduled speech to students at the University of Michigan, challenged them to devote two years of their lives helping people in developing countries. The idea took off. With the official creation of the Peace Corps a year later, the first volunteers accepted assignments in a handful of countries.

The mission of the Peace Corps, as set by Congress in 1961, was to meet the need for trained workers in participating countries and to promote mutual understanding between Americans and other peoples. "Life in the Peace Corps will not be easy," President Kennedy said in authorizing the organization. The more than 163,000 Peace Corps volunteers who served during the last four decades discovered the truth of Kennedy's statement. They have served in 135 countries, working side by side with local citizens—for low wages and only basic provisions—to improve impoverished areas of the world.

The mission and reach of the Peace Corps has expanded in recent years. In 1990, President George Bush celebrated the

"talented Americans who are . . . to become the first Peace Corps volunteers to serve in Eastern Europe"—in Hungary and Poland. A special "Crisis Corps," created in 1995, provided workers who were trained to respond to humanitarian and natural disasters such as hurricanes. And in 2000, the Peace Corps announced that volunteers in Africa and in the Crisis Corps would be trained to provide education on HIV/AIDS. A "domestic Peace Corps," Americorps, founded in 1994, trains workers in local community service projects in the United States. Volunteers receive various benefits, including money for college, in return for their service.

 What is the meaning of the Peace Corps slogan, "The toughest job you'll ever love"?

CAPTION **A**NSWERS

Fast Forward to Today It means that service in the Peace Corps is demanding and difficult, but that it also offers a highly rewarding sense of accomplishment.

RESOURCE DIRECTORY

Teaching Resources
Units 9/10 booklet
• Section 3 Quiz, p. 18
• Chapter 29 Test, pp. 19, 22
Guide to the Essentials
• Section 3 Summary, p. 149
• Chapter 29 Test, p. 150

Other Print Resources
Chapter Tests with ExamView® Test Bank CD-ROM, Ch. 29

Technology
ExamView® Test Bank CD-ROM, Ch. 29
Social Studies Skills Tutor CD-ROM

poor areas and to work with local governments to provide services such as garbage removal and clean water.

Johnson's Foreign Policy

In 1963, Lyndon Johnson assumed the presidency upon Kennedy's death. His foreign policy, like Kennedy's, focused on containing communism around the world.

The Dominican Republic In 1965, Johnson received word that the military-backed government in the Dominican Republic, a Caribbean nation close to Cuba, had been attacked by rebels. Johnson feared that the disruption might endanger American citizens living there. Arguing (wrongly, it turned out) that Communist elements were causing the disruption, Johnson sent 22,000 marines to the Dominican Republic. Their presence tipped the balance away from the rebels. Within a few months a provisional government backed by the United States was put in place. Elections were held the following year.

Vietnam Johnson also became deeply involved in the ongoing conflict in Southeast Asia between Communist North Vietnam and non-Communist South Vietnam. Like Kennedy, Johnson was determined to prevent the spread of communism there. By 1963, about 16,000 American military advisors were in South Vietnam. The United States was also contributing economic aid to the South Vietnamese government.

In his 1964 campaign for President, Johnson opposed more direct United States involvement in the war. Yet, before long he faced the prospect of a Communist takeover of South Vietnam, which he could not tolerate. During 1965, American involvement in the conflict deepened as more and more troops and money were sent to prop up the South Vietnamese government.

COMPARING PRIMARY SOURCES
The Cold War

The United States and its allies continued to battle Communist expansion in the 1960s.
Analyzing Viewpoints What strategy did each of the speakers below want to pursue during the Cold War?

For Moderation in the Cold War

"The issues called the cold war . . . must be met with determination, confidence, and sophistication. . . . [C]hannels of communication should be kept open. . . . Our discussion, public or private, should be marked by civility; our manners should conform to our own dignity and power and to our good repute throughout the world."

—Secretary of State Dean Rusk, speech at the University of California, Berkeley, March 20, 1961

For Aggressiveness in the Cold War

"[I]t is really astounding that our government has never stated its purpose to be that of complete victory over the tyrannical forces of international communism. . . . And we need an official act, such as the resumption of nuclear testing, to show our own peoples and the other freedom-loving peoples of the world that we mean business."

—Arizona Senator Barry Goldwater, address to the United States Senate, July 14, 1961

Section 3 Assessment

READING COMPREHENSION

1. Describe the causes and effects of the **Bay of Pigs invasion.**

2. (a) Why did tensions reignite over the division of Germany? (b) Why was the **Berlin Wall** built?

3. What goals did the **Alliance for Progress** and the **Peace Corps** attempt to fulfill?

4. In what ways did Johnson continue Kennedy's approach to the Cold War?

CRITICAL THINKING AND WRITING

5. **Drawing Inferences** What can you infer about the Soviet Union's foreign policy goals from its actions in the Cold War crises of the 1960s?

6. **Journal Writing** Write a fictional entry from a personal journal of President Kennedy during the Cuban Missile Crisis. Include details that demonstrate your understanding of the difficulties Kennedy faced.

 Take It to the NET

Activity: Creating a Brochure
Create a brochure about the Peace Corps. Include facts about why people volunteer, where they serve, and what kinds of work they do. Use the links provided in the *America: Pathways to the Present* area of the following Web site for help in completing this activity.
www.phschool.com

Section 3 Assessment

Reading Comprehension

1. Causes: Castro's seizure of American property and his friendship with Soviet leaders; to prevent other revolutionary upheavals throughout Latin America. Effects: The United States lost prestige; European leaders began to have doubts about Kennedy, other Latin American nations expressed anger.

2. (a) The Soviets demanded a peace treaty that would make the division of the city permanent. (b) To separate Communist and non-Communist Berlin and stop the flow of East Germans escaping into West Germany, particularly through Berlin.

3. Alliance for Progress: to create a vast cooperative effort to improve the lives of people in North, Central and South America, and to stop the threat of communism. Peace Corps: to send American volunteers to work in developing countries on programs, such as public health and sanitation, which would help the local inhabitants make better lives for themselves. Both initiatives were part of Kennedy's vision for cooperation among nations to solve problems.

4. Johnson's dispatch of United States marines to the Dominican Republic showed that he shared Kennedy's concern over the threat of communism in Latin America; Johnson also continued, and greatly expanded, Kennedy's policy of supporting South Vietnam.

Critical Thinking and Writing

5. Students might infer that the Soviet Union was determined to increase its political influence and spread communism to many different parts of the world; the Russians also worked to weaken United States influence globally.

6. Entries will vary but should reflect the issues, both humanitarian and political, that President Kennedy faced.

 **Take It to the NET**

Brochures should highlight the purposes and practices of volunteerism in the Peace Corps.

REVIEWING KEY TERMS

Students should refer to the definitions of key terms in the chapter to write sentences that show an understanding of the respective administrations of John F. Kennedy and Lyndon Johnson.

REVIEWING MAIN IDEAS

11. According to television viewers, Kennedy was the victor, as he appeared far more composed than Nixon. Radio listeners, however, favored Nixon, as he was well-prepared to discuss the issues.
12. Kennedy wanted to cut taxes, offer health care and other benefits to the elderly, aid education, help poor Americans, protect the environment, and help troubled young people. Many of Kennedy's proposals died in Congressional committees. This was due in part to Kennedy's lack of a broad electoral mandate.
13. That Lee Harvey Oswald bore sole responsibility for killing President Kennedy.
14. The Civil Rights Act and the Voting Rights Act, tax relief, medical benefits for the elderly and the poor, educational assistance, programs to fight poverty, easing immigration restrictions, funding for cultural and consumer measures, environmental protection.
15. *Griswold* v. *Connecticut* (1965): the Court ruled that states could not prohibit birth control; *Baker* v. *Carr* (1962): held that state reapportionment had to be on the basis of "one person, one vote"; *Miranda* v. *Arizona* (1966): the Court ruled that police must make suspects aware of their rights before questioning begins.
16. Sample answer: It created new social programs and used government to attack social problems head-on, especially through the launching of the war on poverty. Gains were limited by the increase in military spending for the Vietnam War.
17. Kennedy appeared inexperienced in the eyes of European leaders; the Bay of Pigs was a blow to American prestige; Latin American leaders were angry at the U.S. attempt to overthrow a government in the Western Hemisphere.

992 • Chapter 29

---

creating *a* CHAPTER SUMMARY

Copy this chart (right) on a piece of paper and complete it by adding information about key events and policies of the Kennedy and Johnson administrations. Some entries have been completed for you as examples.

For additional review and enrichment activities, see the interactive version of *America: Pathways to the Present*, available on the Web and on CD-ROM.

Major Events/ Actions	Kennedy	Johnson
Domestic Policy	• 1960 debates • •	• Tax cut • •
Foreign Policy	• Bay of Pigs • •	• Dominican Republic uprising • •

★ Reviewing Key Terms

For each of the terms below, write a sentence explaining how it relates to the Kennedy-Johnson years.

1. mandate
2. New Frontier
3. Great Society
4. Medicare
5. Medicaid
6. Immigration Act of 1965
7. Miranda rule
8. apportionment
9. Limited Test Ban Treaty
10. Peace Corps

★ Reviewing Main Ideas

11. Describe the outcome of the first Nixon-Kennedy debate and the reasons for that outcome. (Section 1)
12. What domestic programs did Kennedy propose, and why were they largely unsuccessful? (Section 1)
13. What actions were taken to investigate Kennedy's assassination? (Section 1)
14. What domestic programs did Johnson propose? (Section 2)
15. Describe three landmark decisions handed down by the Supreme Court under Chief Justice Earl Warren. (Section 2)

16. Identify the major effects of the Great Society. (Section 2)
17. What consequences to President Kennedy and the United States resulted from the failed Bay of Pigs invasion? (Section 3)
18. Describe the Berlin crisis of 1961. (Section 3)
19. Why did Kennedy establish the Peace Corps? (Section 3)
20. What was Johnson's approach to foreign policy? (Section 3)

★ Critical Thinking

21. **Making Comparisons** What policies and programs would you recommend as part of an effort to eliminate poverty? How would they be similar to, or different from, the programs of Johnson's Great Society?
22. **Predicting Consequences** How did the beliefs of Presidents Kennedy and Johnson about the spread of communism influence their foreign policy decisions?
23. **Drawing Inferences** In what ways did the Warren Court help to uphold the principle that a person is "innocent until proven guilty"?
24. **Drawing Conclusions** Would you characterize Johnson as a weak or a powerful politician? Explain your reasoning.

CREATING A CHAPTER SUMMARY

Major Events/Actions	Kennedy	Johnson
Domestic Policy	• 1960 debates • The New Frontier • Space program	• Tax cut • The Great Society • War on poverty • Aid to education • Medicare and Medicaid
Foreign Policy	• Bay of Pigs • Berlin Crisis • Cuban Missile Crisis • Peace Corps • Alliance for Progress	• Dominican Republic uprising

★ Skills Assessment

Analyzing Political Cartoons ▶

25. This cartoon was printed in November 1962. (a) Who are the two men? (b) What are they trying to do?

26. What does the monster represent?

27. (a) What is the message of the cartoon? (b) What event do you think inspired the cartoon?

Analyzing Primary Sources

Reread the two quotations in Comparing Primary Sources in Section 3 and then answer the questions that follow.

28. Which statement best describes Secretary of State Dean Rusk's view of the Cold War?

  A The Cold War is not a serious threat to the United States and does not require a strong American response.

  B The United States should be cautious in its discussions with the Soviet Union.

  C The United States should be firm but honorable in its Cold War diplomacy.

  D The United States must live up to its reputation as a superpower by being tough on communism.

29. Which statement best describes Senator Barry Goldwater's view of the Cold War?

  F A strong statement of America's goal of eliminating communism should be backed up by military action.

  G The United States should use nuclear weapons to protect people's freedom.

  H The United States government has waged a tyrannical fight against communism.

  J American businesses should help fight communism and protect freedom-loving peoples.

Applying the Chapter Skill: *Exploring Oral History*

30. Interview one or two adults who remember Kennedy's assassination. Ask them if they can recall what they were doing when they heard the news. Have them describe their reaction to the tragedy as well as its impact on the nation.

LET'S GET A LOCK FOR THIS THING.

ACTIVITIES

Writing to LEARN

Writing to Inform
What advantages and disadvantages did Kennedy and Johnson have as Presidents? Write a summary that includes factors such as their backgrounds, their leadership styles, their personality traits, public opinion of them, and the circumstances surrounding their presidencies. In what ways were the two men alike, and in what ways did they differ?

Primary Source CD-ROM

Working With Primary Sources Find additional information on the Kennedy and Johnson administrations on the *Exploring Primary Sources in U.S. History CD-ROM.* Use the selection(s) provided to complete the Chapter 29 primary source activity located in the *America: Pathways to the Present* area of the following Web site. **www.phschool.com**

Take It to the NET

Chapter Self-Test As a review activity, take the Chapter 29 Self-Test in the *America: Pathways to the Present* area at the Web site listed below. The questions are designed to test your understanding of the chapter content. **www.phschool.com**

Chapter 29 Assessment   **993**

18. Tensions mounted when the Russians pressed for a permanent division of Berlin to prevent East Germans from fleeing to the West. Kennedy's June 1961 meeting with Kruschev failed to resolve the issue; Kennedy took steps to strengthen U.S. military forces; the immediate crisis passed when the Russians built the Berlin Wall in August 1961 to prevent escapes, but Berlin continued to be a source of tension.

19. Because he felt that nations should work together to solve problems peacefully.

20. Like Kennedy, Johnson was determined to contain communism. This led Johnson to dramatically expand the American role in the war in Vietnam.

CRITICAL THINKING

21. Answers will vary, but should either support or refute Johnson's approach to the war on poverty.

22. Sample answer: It led them to attempt to counter communism everywhere. One result was foreign policy disasters such as the Bay of Pigs. Other aspects, such as Kennedy's strong stand in the Cuban Missile Crisis, were more successful. Actions by Kennedy and Johnson made it much more difficult for the U.S. government to consider withdrawing from South Vietnam.

23. In general, the Warren Court tended to uphold the rights of individuals against what the Court regarded as the arbitrary power of national, state, and local government. The *Miranda* case, in its protection of the rights of criminal suspects, is a perfect example of this philosophy.

24. Answers will vary, but should be supported with facts from the section, and reflect students' consideration of the issues.

SKILLS ASSESSMENT

25. John F. Kennedy and Nikita Kruschev.
26. The threat of nuclear war.
27. (a) That the superpowers need to do more to prevent the outbreak of nuclear war. (b) The Cuban Missile Crisis.
28. C
29. F
30. Answers will vary. Students' questions should pursue themes introduced in the chapter.

ANSWERS TO ACTIVITIES

Writing to LEARN

Answers will vary but should be supported with facts from the section.

Primary Source CD-ROM

Direct students to the additional primary sources that can be found on the *Exploring Primary Sources in U.S. History CD-ROM.*

Take It to the NET

Additional support materials and activities for Chapter 29 of *America: Pathways to the Present* can be found in the Social Studies area at the Prentice Hall School Web site. **www.phschool.com**

Chapter 30 Planning Guide
Resource Manager

	CORE INSTRUCTION	READING/SKILLS
Chapter-Level Resources	Teaching Resources • Pacing Charts booklet • Block Scheduling booklet **Resource Pro® CD-ROM**, Ch. 30 **Prentice Hall Presentation Pro CD-ROM**, Ch. 30 **www.phschool.com** • eTeach	**Guided Reading Audiotapes (English/Spanish)** **Student Edition on Audio CD**, Ch. 30 **Social Studies Skills Tutor CD-ROM** **Color Transparencies**, E20, G12, H20
1 The Women's Movement 1. Discover the background of the women's movement. 2. Find out how women organized to gain support and to effect change. 3. Observe the impact of feminism. 4. Learn which groups opposed the women's movement and why.	Teaching Resources **Units 9/10 booklet** • Section 1 Quiz, p. 26	**Guided Reading and Review booklet**, p. 120 **Guide to the Essentials**, p. 151 **Learning with Documents booklet**, p. 35 **Skills for Life booklet**, p. 32 **Section Reading Support Transparencies**
2 Ethnic Minorities Seek Equality 1. Learn how Latinos sought equality during the 1960s and the early 1970s. 2. Find out how Asian Americans fought discrimination during this period. 3. See the ways in which Native Americans confronted their unique problems.	Teaching Resources **Units 9/10 booklet** • Section 2 Quiz, p. 27	**Guided Reading and Review booklet**, p. 121 **Guide to the Essentials**, p. 152 **Section Reading Support Transparencies**
3 The Counterculture 1. Find out about social changes promoted by the counterculture. 2. Learn how the music world of the 1960s and 1970s contributed to the cultural changes of this era.	Teaching Resources **Units 9/10 booklet** • Section 3 Quiz, p. 28 **Learning Styles Lesson Plans booklet**, p. 62	**Guided Reading and Review booklet**, p. 122 **Guide to the Essentials**, p. 153 **Section Reading Support Transparencies**
4 The Environmental and Consumer Movements 1. Read about efforts begun in the 1960s to protect the environment. 2. Understand how the government tried to balance jobs and environmental protection. 3. Find out how the consumer movement began, and what it tried to accomplish.	Teaching Resources **Units 9/10 booklet** • Section 4 Quiz, p. 29 **Learning Styles Lesson Plans booklet**, p. 63	**Guided Reading and Review booklet**, p. 123 **Guide to the Essentials**, p. 154 **Learning with Documents booklet**, p. 69 **Section Reading Support Transparencies**

ENRICHMENT/PRE-AP

Prentice Hall United States History Video Collection™
www.phschool.com
  • Section Activities, Virtual Field Trip, Chapter Activities, Current Events Online

Biography, Literature, and Comparing Primary Sources booklet, pp. 155–156
Great Debates booklet, p. 22
American History Block Scheduling Support
Sounds of an Era Audio CD
Exploring Primary Sources in U.S. History CD-ROM

Biography, Literature, and Comparing Primary Sources booklet, pp. 35, 82
Great Debates booklet, p. 42
Nystrom *Atlas of Our Country,* pp. 32–33, 36–37
Sounds of an Era Audio CD

American History Block Scheduling Support
Sounds of an Era Audio CD
American Pathways Thematic Posters

ASSESSMENT

PRENTICE HALL ASSESSMENT SYSTEM

Core Assessment
  ExamView® Test Bank, Ch. 30
  ExamView® Test Bank CD-ROM, Ch. 30

Standardized Test Preparation
Diagnose and Prescribe
  Diagnostic Tests for High School Social Studies Skills

Review and Reteach
  Review Book for U.S. History

Practice and Assess
  Test-taking Strategies With Transparencies
  Test-taking Strategies Posters
  Test Prep Book for U.S. History
  Alternative Assessment Handbook
  Document-Based Assessment

Teaching Resources
Units 9/10 booklet
  • Section Quizzes, pp. 26–29
  • Chapter Tests, pp. 30, 33
www.phschool.com Ch. 30 Self-Test

AmericanHeritage RESOURCES

From the Archives of American Heritage®, p. 998
AmericanHeritage® My Brush with History™ Videotapes
www.americanheritage.com

iTEXT

Don't miss the exclusive interactive version of this textbook on the Web and on CD-ROM.

Chapter 30 Planning Guide
In Your Classroom

CUSTOMIZE FOR INDIVIDUAL NEEDS

Gifted and Talented

Teacher's Edition
• Customize for Gifted and Talented, p. 1005

Teaching Resources
• Biography, Literature, and Comparing Primary Sources booklet, pp. 35, 82, 155–156

Technology
• Exploring Primary Sources in U.S. History CD-ROM *Debate on the Equal Rights Amendment, Representatives Emmanuel Celler and Edith Green*

ESL

Teacher's Edition
• Customize for ESL, p. 1011

Teaching Resources
• Guided Reading and Review booklet, pp. 120–123
• Guide to the Essentials (English/Spanish), Chapter 30

Technology
• Student Edition on Audio CD, Chapter 30
• Guided Reading Audiotapes (English/Spanish), Chapter 30
• Section Reading Support Transparencies

Less Proficient Readers

Teacher's Edition
• Customize for Less Proficient Readers, pp. 997, 1007

Teaching Resources
• Guided Reading and Review booklet, pp. 120–123
• Guide to the Essentials (English/Spanish), Chapter 30

Technology
• Student Edition on Audio CD, Chapter 30
• Guided Reading Audiotapes (English/Spanish), Chapter 30
• Section Reading Support Transparencies

Less Proficient Writers

Teacher's Edition
• Customize for Less Proficient Writers, p. 1015

Teaching Resources
• Guided Reading and Review booklet, pp. 120–123
• Guide to the Essentials (English/Spanish), Chapter 30

Technology
• Student Edition on Audio CD, Chapter 30
• Guided Reading Audiotapes (English/Spanish), Chapter 30
• Section Reading Support Transparencies

TEACHER'S EDITION INDEX

CHAPTER 30 – PACING SUGGESTIONS

For 90-minute Blocks

• Teach section 2 using Transparencies E20, G12, and H20, and the Recent Scholarship note on page 1005 for class discussions.

Running Out of Time?

If you are running short on time to cover this chapter, consider the following options:

• Use Prentice Hall Presentation Pro CD-ROM to create an outline for this chapter.

• Use the Section Summaries for Chapter 30, from **Guide to the Essentials (English/Spanish)**.

1 The Women's Movement

Connecting with Citizenship
Have students review the history of the women's movement in the nineteenth century to inform themselves of its stated goals and actual achievements, then do the same for the twentieth century. Have students present their findings by role-playing a major figure in each time period, such as Susan B. Anthony or Betty Friedan. You might extend the idea by having the two historical figures converse across time about their respective campaigns. **(Bodily/Kinesthetic)**

2 Ethnic Minorities Seek Equality

Connecting with History and Conflict
Have students write one or two paragraphs explaining, in their own words, why they think the years 1960–1975 saw so much activism and protest. Bring students together in small groups to examine and evaluate the various theories. Suggest that students imagine how they might have behaved at the time and explain why. **(Verbal/Linguistic)**

3 The Counterculture

Connecting with Culture
Have students listen, on their own, to some of the popular music hits of the 1960s and 1970s. When they find a selection they feel is particularly representative of the time, have them make a presentation to the class and explain what they hear in the music and the lyrics and what, if any, connection the music helps them make to that time period. **(Musical/Rhythmic)**

4 The Environmental and Consumer Movements

Connecting with Science and Technology
Rachel Carson's efforts to protect the environment were recognized in 1981 by a stamp in her honor. Have students research the process by which a noted person is nominated and finally honored by a stamp. Then have them choose another person they feel should be recognized for his or her efforts to protect Earth's natural resources and write a nomination. Student letters should provide strong arguments on behalf of their nominees. Students should also make certain that their nominees have not already been honored by a postage stamp. **(Verbal/Linguistic)**

Inspired by the civil rights movement, women, Latinos, and Native Americans struggled to achieve equality in the 1960s and 1970s through protests. The movement for social change affected almost every aspect of American society from the environment to consumer awareness.

TIME LINE ACTIVITY

To provide students with practice in using the time line, ask questions such as these:

1. What was an important outcome of the publication of Rachel Carson's *Silent Spring*? *(Many people credit that book with launching the environmental movement.)*

2. Who was India's first woman prime minister? *(Indira Gandhi)*

3. What important environmental events took place in 1970? *(The first Earth Day was celebrated, the Environmental Protection Agency was established, and Congress passed the Clean Air Act.)*

eTeach

Be sure to check out this month's online discussion with a Master Teacher. Go to **www.phschool.com**.

Chapter 30

An Era of Activism
(1960–1975)

SECTION 1 The Women's Movement
SECTION 2 Ethnic Minorities Seek Equality
SECTION 3 The Counterculture
SECTION 4 The Environmental and Consumer Movements

American Events

1962
Rachel Carson's book *Silent Spring* launches the environmental movement.

1963
The Feminine Mystique by Betty Friedan inspires the women's movement.

1965
Ralph Nader's *Unsafe at Any Speed* is published, initiating the consumer protection movement.

1966
The National Organization for Women is formed.

1967
César Chávez's United Farm Workers organize a nationwide boycott of grapes picked on nonunion farms.

Presidential Terms: D. Eisenhower 1953–1961   John F. Kennedy 1961–1963   Lyndon B. Johnson 1963–1969

1960 • • **1965** • •

World Events

In Ceylon (now Sri Lanka), Sirimavo Bandaranaike is elected the world's first female prime minister. **1960**

Soviet cosmonaut Valentina Tereshkova becomes the first woman in space. **1963**

Indira Gandhi becomes prime minister of India. **1966**

RESOURCE DIRECTORY

Teaching Resources
Pacing Charts booklet
Block Scheduling booklet, p. 28
Units 9/10 booklet
• Chapter Summary, p. 25

Technology
Guided Reading Audiotapes (English/Spanish), Ch. 30
Student Edition on Audio CD, Ch. 30
Prentice Hall United States History Video Collection™ Volume 20, *Post-War USA*
Prentice Hall Presentation Pro CD-ROM, Ch. 30
Resource Pro® CD-ROM
Social Studies Skills Tutor CD-ROM
Companion Web site, www.phschool.com

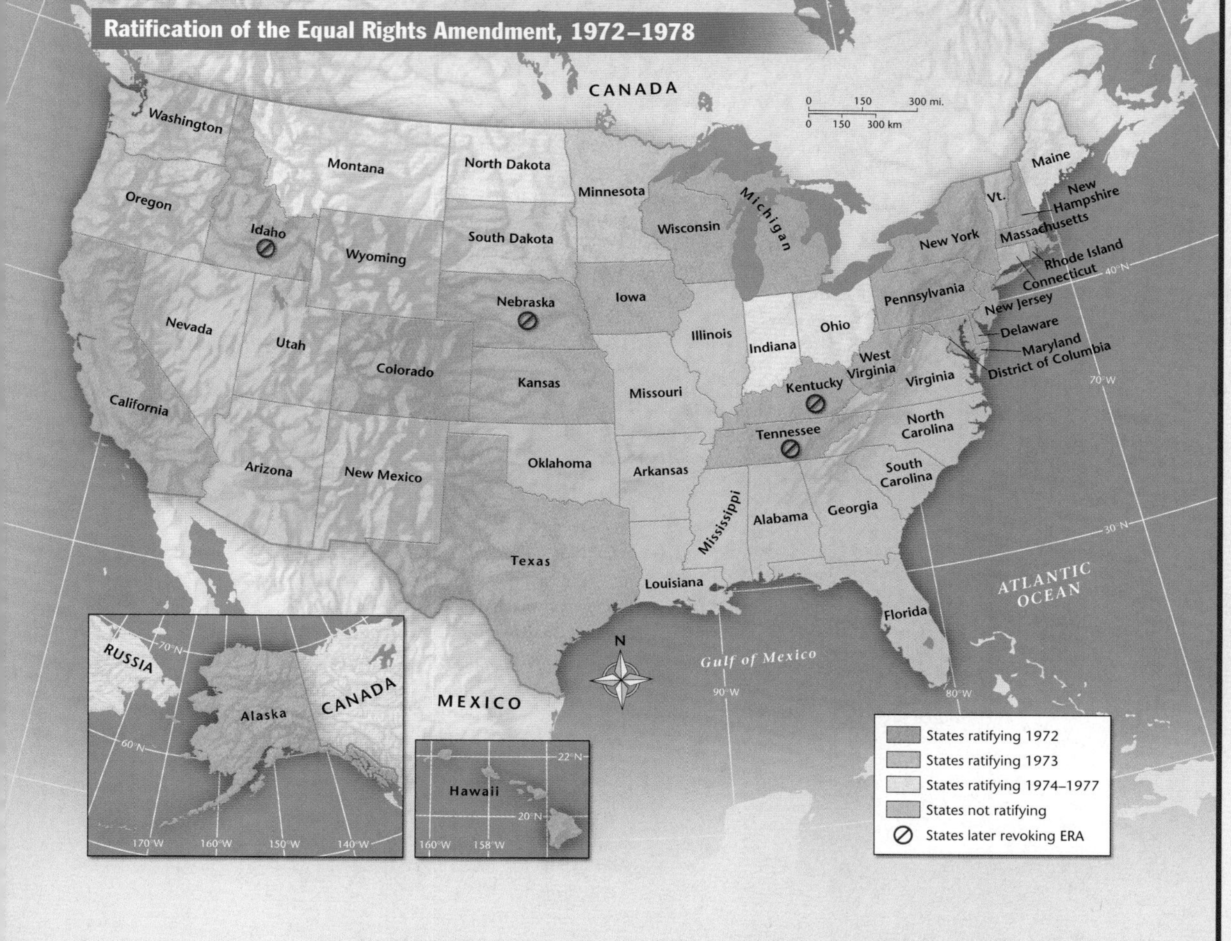

Ratification of the Equal Rights Amendment, 1972–1978

CANADA

Washington
Montana
North Dakota
Minnesota
Maine
Oregon
Idaho
Wyoming
South Dakota
Wisconsin
Michigan
Vt.
New Hampshire
New York
Massachusetts
Nevada
Utah
Nebraska
Iowa
Illinois
Indiana
Ohio
Pennsylvania
Rhode Island
Connecticut
New Jersey
Delaware
Maryland
District of Columbia
California
Colorado
Kansas
Missouri
Kentucky
West Virginia
Virginia
Arizona
New Mexico
Oklahoma
Arkansas
Tennessee
North Carolina
South Carolina
Mississippi
Alabama
Georgia
Texas
Louisiana
Florida

ATLANTIC OCEAN

Gulf of Mexico

RUSSIA
CANADA
Alaska
MEXICO

Hawaii

0 150 300 mi.
0 150 300 km

N

	States ratifying 1972
	States ratifying 1973
	States ratifying 1974–1977
	States not ratifying
⊘	States later revoking ERA

Timeline

1969
The Woodstock festival celebrates rock music and the counterculture.

1970
The first Earth Day is celebrated, the Environmental Protection Agency is established, and Congress passes the Clean Air Act.

1973
The Supreme Court legalizes abortion in *Roe v. Wade.* Protesters from the American Indian Movement take over the reservation at Wounded Knee.

Richard M. Nixon 1969–1974   Gerald R. Ford 1974–1977

• **1970** • • **1975**

1971
Greenpeace is founded in Vancouver, Canada.

1973
The Vietnam War ends with the signing of a formal peace agreement in Paris.

Chapter 30   **995**

BIBLIOGRAPHY

For the Teacher

Carson, Rachel. *Silent Spring.* Houghton Mifflin, 1994. (Classic, groundbreaking book on environmental awareness.)

Friedan, Betty. *The Feminine Mystique.* W. W. Norton, 2001. (A critique of postwar inequities and discrimination against women.)

For the Student

Momaday, N. Scott. *House Made of Dawn.* HarperCollins, 1999. (The Pulitzer Prize–winning novel of a young Native American caught between the white world and the ways of his people; written by an Oklahoma Kyowa.)

Unger, Irwin, and Unger, Debi (editors). *The Times Were a Changin': The Sixties Reader.* Three Rivers Press, 1998. (A collection of documents that brings central 1960s issues to life.)

Ratification of the Equal Rights Amendment,
1972–1978

Activating Prior Knowledge
Which states ratified the Equal Rights Amendment (ERA) between 1974 and 1977? *(Indiana, Ohio, Montana, Maine, and North Dakota)*

Previewing To become law, the ERA had to be ratified by 38 states within 10 years of its introduction in 1972. By looking at the map, calculate whether the ERA was passed into law by 1978. *(By 1978 there were not 38 states that had ratified the ERA, so it did not pass into law.)*

*B*ACKGROUND
About the Pictures

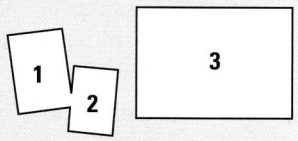

1. *Silent Spring* illustrated the harmful environmental effects of heavy chemical pesticide use and discouraged dependence on them in favor of a more varied approach to pest control.

2. Friedan's book shed light on women's feelings of frustration and inadequacy stemming from their reliance on their husbands for economic, emotional, and intellectual stability.

3. The boycott and strike lasted five years and, after many conflicts and court battles, ended in favor of the United Farm Workers.

 **TEXT**

Don't miss the exclusive interactive version of this textbook on the Web and on CD-ROM.

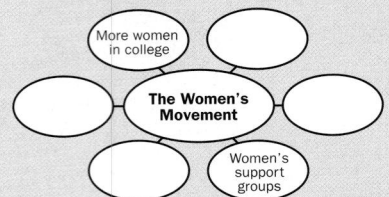

Setting the Scene Songwriter Bob Dylan's 1964 hit "The Times They Are A-Changin'" reflected the atmosphere of the sixties. The fifties had been primarily a time of unprecedented prosperity and security, but not all groups had participated equally. The sixties ushered in an era of activism, as these groups and their supporters seized the opportunity to make their voices heard. One demand for change came from women who did not want to be limited to the traditional roles of wife and mother. These women demanded the same opportunities as men. Pop singer Helen Reddy's 1971 song exemplified this new point of view:

> 66 *I am woman, hear me roar*
> *In numbers too big to ignore,*
> *And I know too much to go back*
> *and pretend. . . .*
> *Yes, I've paid the price*
> *But look how much I gained.*
> *If I have to, I can do anything.*
> *I am strong, I am invincible,*
> *I am woman.* 99

—Ray Burton and Helen Reddy

On August 26, 1970, the anniversary of the passage of the constitutional amendment granting women suffrage, thousands of women took the day off from jobs and household chores to observe Women's Equality Day.

These lyrics reflect the sense of self-confidence and strength that helped to create the new women's movement in the 1960s and continued to drive it forward into the 1970s.

Background of the Women's Movement

The crusade for women's rights was not new in 1960. In the late 1800s, particularly, women had worked for the right to vote and for equality in education and in jobs. The term **feminism,** which came to be associated with the 1960s, had first come into recorded use in 1895 to describe the theory of political, economic, and social equality of men and women. Feminists were those who believed in this equality or took action to bring it about.

While much progress had been made since the 1890s, the full equality sought by feminists had not been achieved. The women's movement of the 1960s sought to change aspects of American life that had been accepted for decades. The 1950s stereotype of women still placed them in the home, married and raising children. For many women, this stereotype did not reflect either reality or necessity. As had been the case in earlier decades, many women needed to work in order to support themselves or to help support their families. Furthermore, World War II had opened many new employment opportunities for women. During and after the war, more and more women entered the labor force. By the beginning of the 1960s, about 38 percent of all women held jobs. In addition, many women were educated, and looked forward to putting their education to use in professional careers.

Education and Employment An increasing number of women began going to college after World War II. In 1950, only 25 percent of all Bachelor of Arts degrees were earned by women. Twenty years later, in 1970, the number was 43 percent. Better-educated women had high hopes for the future, but they were often discouraged by the discrimination they faced when they looked for jobs or tried to advance in their professions.

In many cases, employers were reluctant to invest in training women because they expected female employees to leave their jobs after a few years to start families. Other employers simply refused to hire qualified women because they believed that home and family should be a woman's only responsibility.

Women who did enter the work force often found themselves underemployed, performing jobs and earning salaries below their abilities. Working women earned less than working men doing similar or even identical jobs. In 1963, women, on average, were paid only 59 cents for each dollar that men earned. By 1973, this figure had dropped to 57 cents. This financial inequality created a growing sense of frustration among women and led to renewed demands for equal pay for equal work.

The Impact of the Civil Rights Movement While social, educational, and economic conditions set the scene for the women's movement, the civil rights movement provided a "how-to" model for action. It also provided inspiration. Black and white women had joined in the struggle for civil rights and gained valuable skills from their work in the movement. At the same time, they had endured frustration over their second-class status in civil rights organizations. As they worked to end racial discrimination, women were expected to make coffee and do clerical work while men made most of the policy decisions. Frustrated over their assigned roles, women began to apply the techniques that had been successful in the civil rights movement to a new movement that would address their own concerns.

The civil rights movement also provided women with legal tools to fight discrimination. One such tool was the 1964 Civil Rights Act. Originally, the section of the act called Title VII prohibited discrimination based on race, religion, or national origin. When Congress debated the bill, however, some opponents of civil rights added an amendment to outlaw discrimination on the basis of gender. This action was a strategy to make the entire bill look ridiculous, so that it would fail in the final vote. To the dismay of its opponents, both the amendment and the bill passed. The

The new women's movement chose symbols of power to represent its cause.

INTERPRETING GRAPHS
Women's incomes continued to lag behind men's earnings, partly because many low-paying jobs were traditionally considered "women's work." **Making Comparisons** *How did the gap change between 1950 and 1975?*

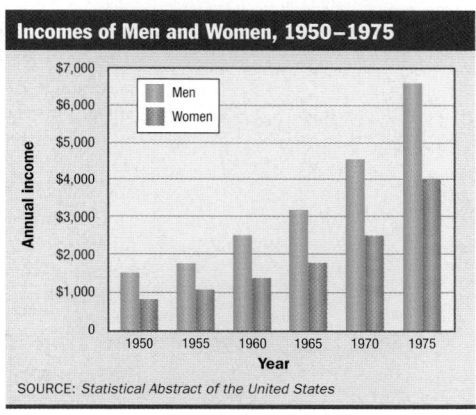

Incomes of Men and Women, 1950–1975

Legend: Men, Women

Y-axis: Annual income — $7,000, $6,000, $5,000, $4,000, $3,000, $2,000, $1,000, 0
X-axis: Year — 1950, 1955, 1960, 1965, 1970, 1975

SOURCE: *Statistical Abstract of the United States*

LESSON PLAN

Focus Women were among the first groups to note the successes of the civil rights movement and to apply them to the inequalities of their own lives. Ask students how the women's movement affected American society.

Instruct Discuss the conditions in American society that feminists wanted to change. Ask students to list the ways in which employers discriminated—and in some cases continue to discriminate—against women.

Ask students to list the kinds of action taken by feminists to improve conditions for women. Which were most successful?

Assess/Reteach Ask students to consider the ways in which the Women's Liberation Movement improved women's lives. Are there also ways in which this movement created more challenges for women? Have students list some of those challenges.

BACKGROUND
Workplace Opportunities

In the late 1960s and early 1970s, women created a vast network of health clinics, legal centers, newspapers, counseling centers, and professional caucuses for their needs. But since "men and institutions resisted radical challenges," according to one historian, women found it difficult to break through the "glass ceiling" in business. Women with college degrees were earning half as much as men with similar education, and one-third of all working women held clerical jobs. Even by the late 1970s, very few women were executives or upper-level managers.

CAPTION ANSWERS

Interpreting Graphs In dollar amounts, the gap grew larger. In percentages, it grew smaller.

Connecting with Citizenship

During the civil rights movement, women learned protest tactics that they then used to fight their own battle against discrimination. To help students understand how protest tactics allowed the civil rights movement to bring about changes in the United States, divide them into small groups to design a campaign for youth rights. Each group should create an identifying acronym, give one example of a discriminatory practice against youth, and describe a peaceful tactic that could be used to change this practice. **(Verbal/Linguistic)**

From the Archives of

AmericanHeritage®

ERA

On March 22, 1972, by a vote of 84 to 8, the Senate passed the Equal Rights Amendment, a goal of feminists for half a century. Since the House had given equally lopsided approval the previous fall, the amendment went to the states for ratification. Thirty-two minutes after the Senate vote, Hawaii became the first to ratify; New Hampshire and Nebraska followed the next day. Support for the idea of equality quickly swept the country, with both major parties endorsing the amendment. Within a year of the Senate vote, 30 of the required 38 states had passed the ERA. Boosters confidently predicted a quick completion of the process. Over the remainder of 1973, though, no more states added their names to the list. In 1974, even as polls showed three-quarters of Americans in favor, just three states gave their consent. One state ratified in 1975 and one in 1977, raising the total to 35, but that was all. The ERA's time limit expired in 1982, and since then, there has been no serious attempt to get it through Congress again. Source: Frederic D. Schwarz, "The Time Machine," *American Heritage*® magazine, February 1997.

Focus on
CULTURE

The Feminine Mystique Betty Friedan's book *The Feminine Mystique* caused a sensation in the suburbs of America. It addressed the women who had everything that society said they should want: husbands who were good providers, healthy children, a house in the suburbs—often even the time and money to furnish and refurnish the comfortable homes they ran for their families. But many of these women were not happy, and when they said so, they were often called "neurotic" or not normal. Friedan called it "the problem that had no name"—the dissatisfaction of not being able to realize one's own full potential. Many women were dissatisfied with being regarded only as support services for their families, with constantly subordinating their own need for personal growth and fulfillment to the needs of their families, and with second-class citizenship in law and in the marketplace. Friedan gave these women the courage to ask, "Is this all?"—and her book helped women realize that it doesn't have to be.

---

new Civil Rights Act now had a provision that gave women a legal framework to challenge discrimination.

Even with the added boost of the new legislation, progress took time. Women soon discovered that the Equal Employment Opportunity Commission (EEOC) set up by the bill did not take women's discrimination claims seriously. Nevertheless, Title VII would be tremendously important as the women's movement gained strength.

Women's Groups Organize

As the 1960s unfolded, women began to meet in groups to compare experiences. Women active in the civil rights movement met to look for ways in which they could play a larger role in that struggle. Soon they went beyond politics, exploring other aspects of their lives. The growing movement drew women who were active in other forms of protest and reform. They included student radicals, opponents of the Vietnam War and the draft, and workers for welfare rights and other social issues. Another important influence was Betty Friedan's 1963 book *The Feminine Mystique*. The dissatisfied housewives that Friedan described in her book began meeting, too, to discuss their lives and their roles in society.

Support Groups Meeting in kitchens and living rooms, women began gathering in consciousness-raising groups, which were dedicated to increasing their members' awareness of women's situation in society. One participant, Nancy Hawley, who was a community activist in Boston, Massachusetts, was troubled by patterns she saw at work. "Though many of us were working harder than the men," she noted, "we realized we were not listened to and often ignored." Growing numbers of women recognized the negative attitudes, or sexism, directed toward them. Many told of being ridiculed for attending women's groups. Such lack of support outside the group made their bond stronger within the group.

Organizing NOW In 1966, a group of 28 professional women, including Betty Friedan, established the **National Organization for Women (NOW).** These women were frustrated that existing women's groups were unwilling to pressure the Equal Employment Opportunity Commission to take women's grievances more seriously. The goal of NOW was "to take action to bring American women into full participation in the mainstream of American society now."

NOW sought fair pay and equal job opportunities. It attacked the "false image of women" in the media, such as advertising that used sexist slogans or photographs. NOW also called for more balance in marriages, with men and women sharing parenting and household responsibilities. A year after NOW was founded, it had 1,000 members. Only four years later, some 15,000 women had joined.

For some women, NOW seemed too extreme; for others, it was not extreme enough. Some saw NOW—and the women's movement in general—as mainly benefiting white, middle-class women. Nonetheless, NOW served as a rallying point to end sex discrimination and to promote equality for all women.

The Impact of Feminism

The women's movement came of age in the early 1970s. In August 1970, a New York City march celebrating the fiftieth anniversary of women's suffrage drew

---

RESOURCE DIRECTORY

Teaching Resources
Biography, Literature, and Comparing Primary Sources booklet (Comparing Primary Sources) *On Working Mothers*, pp. 155–156

Technology
Color Transparencies *Fine Art*, E20

tens of thousands of demonstrators supporting women's equality. More women began identifying themselves as feminists. Even those who did not join feminist groups could now find new kinds of information and opinions on women's issues. One new source was a book called *Our Bodies, Ourselves*. This handbook, published in 1970 by a women's health collective in Boston, encouraged women to understand their own health issues. It sold 200,000 copies in the first several years after its publication and three million by 1990.

In 1972, journalist Gloria Steinem and several other women founded *Ms.* magazine. Devoted to feminist issues, *Ms.* provided women with viewpoints that were decidedly different from those in *Good Housekeeping, Ladies' Home Journal,* and other women's magazines of the day. All 300,000 copies of the preview issue sold out in eight days. Only one year later, *Ms.* had nearly 200,000 subscribers. While not all readers considered themselves feminists, the magazine familiarized its audience with the arguments and issues of the women's movement.

READING CHECK
What were some of the effects of the women's movement?

A Shift in Attitudes   Slowly the women's movement brought a shift in attitudes and in the law. For example, in 1972, Congress passed a prohibition against gender discrimination as part of the Higher Education Act. A survey of first-year college students revealed a significant change in career goals—and opportunities. In 1970, men interested in fields such as business, law, engineering, and medicine outnumbered women by eight to one. Five years later, the margin had dropped to three to one. More women entered law school and medical school. Women were finally admitted to military academies to be trained as officers.

In 1971, the National Women's Political Caucus was formed to expand women's participation in politics. By working from within the system, women were able to gain broader support for the goals of the women's movement. Women also became more influential in politics. New Yorker Shirley Chisholm, who was a founder of the National Women's Political Caucus, served in the House of Representatives from 1969 to 1983. In 1972, she ran for President, winning 152 delegates to the Democratic National Convention before she withdrew from the race. Chisholm's candidacy demonstrated that an African American woman

---

COMPARING PRIMARY SOURCES
Working Mothers

In the early years of the women's movement, experts disagreed over the issue of working mothers.

Analyzing Viewpoints   What assumptions and biases about women and about children are revealed by each author? What reasonable argument does each author use?

In Favor of Working Mothers	*Opposed to Working Mothers*
"At the present time, one can say anything—good or bad—about children of employed mothers and support the statement by some research finding. But there is no definitive evidence that children are less happy, healthy, adjusted, because their mothers work. The studies that show working women to be happier, better, more mature mothers do not get much publicity." —Betty Friedan, The Feminine Mystique, *1963*	"To work or not to work? Some mothers have to work to make a living. Usually their children turn out all right, because some reasonably good arrangement is made for their care. But others grow up neglected and maladjusted. . . . It doesn't make sense to let mothers go to work making dresses in a factory or tapping typewriters in an office, and have them pay other people to do a poorer job of bringing up their children." —Benjamin Spock, M.D., Baby and Childcare, *1957 first published in 1946*

ACTIVITY
Connecting with Culture

Challenge students to write short stories about a woman in the early 1960s who finds herself wanting or needing to enter the workplace and the obstacles she must confront in doing so. As they write their stories, have students consider and identify the political, social, and economic contributions of women to society. **(Verbal/Linguistic)**

BACKGROUND
Biography

In 1970 Betty Friedan (b. 1921) helped create the National Women's Political Caucus, and led a national Women's Strike for Equality. Friedan continually encouraged women "to march, to picket, and to speak up for equal rights." A frequent target of her attacks was the advertising industry, which she claimed promoted an image of women as the "weaker sex." In her 1981 book *The Second Stage*, Friedan assumed a more moderate stance, and criticized earlier feminists for trying to emulate the male realm rather than "affirm the differences between men and women."

READING CHECK
The formation of NOW and women's support groups; increasing numbers of women enrolled in law schools and medical schools in the 1970s. Gender discrimination in higher education is outlawed by Congress.

✓ TEST PREPARATION

Have students read the section "The Impact of Feminism" on these pages and then answer the question below.

In what way did the 1972 Higher Education Act reflect the influence of the women's movement?

A The act included a prohibition against gender discrimination.

B The act did not reflect the influence of the women's movement.

C The act supported the continuation of gender discrimination.

D The act explicitly supported equal rights for men and women.

VIEWING HISTORY Gloria Steinem, above, was one of the founders of *Ms.* magazine. The first issue is shown at right. **Analyzing Visual Information** *How does the* Ms. *cover show the many roles women were expected to fill?*

could gain support for national office. And she paved the way for Geraldine Ferraro's selection as the Democratic Party's vice presidential candidate in 1984.

Many women did not actively participate in or support the women's movement. Still, most agreed with NOW's goal to provide women with better job opportunities. Many were also pleased that the women's movement brought a greater recognition of issues important to women. These issues included the need for child-care facilities, shelters for homeless women, more attention to women's health concerns, and increased awareness of sexual harassment.

Despite many shared concerns, the women's movement continued to be divided regarding some of its goals and strategies. Radical feminists emphasized the need to end male domination, sometimes even rejecting men, marriage, and childbearing. Other women rejected the strong opinions of the radicals, fearing they would cause a split in the women's movement. These women emphasized that they sought only equality with men, not rejection of them.

Roe v. Wade One issue that had the potential to divide the movement was abortion. NOW and other groups worked to reform the laws governing a woman's decision to choose an abortion instead of continuing an unwanted pregnancy. Many states outlawed or severely restricted access to abortion. Women who could afford to travel to another state or out of the country could usually find legal medical services, but poorer women often turned to abortion methods that were not only illegal but unsafe.

A landmark social and legal change came in 1973, when the Supreme Court legalized abortion in the controversial **Roe v. Wade** decision. The justices based their decision on the constitutional right to personal privacy, and struck down state regulation of abortion in the first three months of pregnancy. However, the ruling still allowed states to restrict abortions during the later stages of pregnancy. The case was, and remains, highly controversial, with radical thinkers on both sides of the argument.

Many women demonstrated in favor of ratification of the ERA.

The Equal Rights Amendment Many women also took part in the campaign for a change to the Constitution that would make discrimination based on a person's sex illegal. In 1972, Congress approved passage of the **Equal Rights Amendment (ERA)** to the Constitution:

KEY DOCUMENTS

❝*Equality of rights under the law shall not be denied or abridged by the United States or by any State on account of sex.*❞
—Equal Rights Amendment, 1972

To become law, the amendment had to be ratified by 38 states. Thirty states did so quickly. When a few others also ratified it, approval seemed certain. By 1977, 35 states had ratified the amendment, but opposition forces were gaining strength. The effort to add the ERA to the Constitution limped along until the 1982 deadline for ratification and then died.

1000 Chapter 30 • *An Era of Activism*

Opposition to the Women's Movement

It was a woman, conservative political activist Phyllis Schlafly, who led a national campaign to block ratification of the ERA. She said this about the amendment:

> **66** It won't do anything to help women, and it will take away from women the rights they already have, such as the right of a wife to be supported by her husband, the right of a woman to be exempted from military combat, and the right . . . to go to a single-sex college. **99**
>
> —Phyllis Schlafly

Women already had legal backing for their rights, Schlafly argued. ERA supporters contested Schlafly's charges about the supposed effects of the ERA, such as the establishment of coed bathrooms and the end of alimony. Nevertheless, arguments such as Schlafly's were instrumental in preventing the ERA from being ratified before the deadline.

Schlafly was not alone in her opposition to the ERA and to the women's movement in general. Many men were also hostile to the feminist movement, which was sometimes scornfully called "women's liberation" or "women's lib."

Nor were all women sympathetic to the goals of the women's movement. Some women responded by stressing their desire to remain at home and raise children. They were happy with women's traditional roles and resented being told that they should feel dissatisfied. These women felt that their roles as wives, and particularly as mothers, were being undervalued by the women's movement. The result, as these women saw it, was less rather than more respect for women and for the important task of raising the next generation.

Opposition came from other quarters as well. Some African American women felt that combating racial discrimination was more important than battling sex discrimination. In 1974, NOW's African American president, Aileen Hernandez, acknowledged that "Some black sisters are not sure that the feminist movement will meet their current needs." Many working-class women felt removed from the movement, too. They believed they were being encouraged to give up homemaking in order to take up undesirable paid labor.

Nevertheless, the women's movement continued to make gains, to change minds, and to expand opportunities for women. In so doing, it became one of several important strands of reform in the era of activism.

VIEWING HISTORY Phyllis Schlafly spoke out against the ERA. **Determining Relevance** *Do you think the fact that Schlafly was a woman made her a more effective or less effective advocate for her point of view? Explain your answer.*

Section 1 Assessment

READING COMPREHENSION

1. What is **feminism?**

2. (a) When was **NOW** formed? (b) What was its purpose?

3. Who was Shirley Chisholm?

4. Explain the **Roe v. Wade** decision.

5. (a) What was the **ERA?** (b) How many states eventually ratified it?

CRITICAL THINKING AND WRITING

6. **Identifying Assumptions** (a) What beliefs led many women to support the women's movement? (b) What beliefs led others to oppose it?

7. **Writing an Opinion** Would there have been a successful women's movement without the example of the civil rights movement? Support your opinion in a paragraph.

Take It to the NET

Activity: Making a Poster Learn more about the battle over ratification of the ERA. Make a poster either for or against ratification. Use the links provided in the *America: Pathways to the Present* area of the following Web site for help in completing this activity.
www.phschool.com

Chapter 30 • Section 1 **1001**

RECOGNIZING BIAS

Focus Students will practice recognizing bias in two written selections.

Instruct After students have read the selections, have them analyze the following quotation using the feature skills.

"As radical feminists we recognize that we are engaged in a power struggle with men, and that the agent of our oppression is man insofar as he identifies with and carries out the supremacy privileges of the male role. For while we realize that the liberation of women will ultimately mean the liberation of men from their destructive role of oppressor, we have no illusion that men will welcome this liberation without a struggle."

Extend See the Skills for Life activity in the Resource Directory below.

ANSWERS
PRACTICE THE SKILL

1. **(a)** A: ERA passage will give too much power to the federal government. B: ERA passage will end legal discrimination against women. **(b)** No, each one is one-sided.

2. **(a)** Stated: the opening statement notes the passage will be an "objection to ERA." **(b)** Unstated: the author does not state her position clearly.

3. **(a)** A: none. B: The 14th and 15th amendments information; the date and events when Susan B. Anthony voted; the number of "legal discriminations" against women on state books; the ERA language. **(b)** Yes. Possible answers: A: The ERA is a power grab by Washington. States rights pertaining to women will go to the national government. B: The ERA will give women 100 percent protection of the Constitution.

4. **(a)** A: Supreme Court actions over the last 25 years have been bad. The federal government has too much power and wants more. B: Discrimination against women is built into the government. Women deserve equality and can only get it through "their own" Amendment. **(b)** A, by saying that everyone who doesn't agree is a fool. **(c)** B has more material that can be verified.

1002 • Chapter 30

Recognizing Bias

Recognizing bias means being aware of information and ideas that are one-sided or that present only a partial view of a subject. Bias may be stated or unstated. A writer may admit partisanship, or bias, and then support one side of an issue. Unstated bias—when a source presents only one side of an issue while suggesting that it presents the whole picture—is more difficult to detect. The ability to spot bias will help you analyze information and make sound judgments about the reliability of sources.

Bias is often attached to issues that have emotional impact—issues that also inspire strong expressions of different points of view. One such issue was the Equal Rights Amendment (ERA).

LEARN THE SKILL
Use the following steps to recognize bias:

1. **Decide whether or not the source presents only one side of an issue.** Writing from a single viewpoint signals imbalance—and bias.

2. **Look for unstated as well as stated bias.** Look for clear statements of a position that signal stated bias. Also look for indications that a source is presenting only one side of the issue while suggesting it covers all sides; that is unstated bias.

3. **Determine whether the presentation of the issue is supported by opinions or verifiable facts.** Sometimes what appear to be facts are actually opinions disguised as facts. Remember, you can check the accuracy of facts in other sources.

4. **Examine the source for hidden assumptions or generalizations that are not supported by facts.** Look for sweeping generalizations and for claims that opposing opinions are worthless.

PRACTICE THE SKILL
Answer the following questions:

1. **(a)** What is the overall message of each passage? **(b)** Does either passage present both sides of the issue? Explain.

2. **(a)** Is the bias in Passage A stated or unstated? Explain. **(b)** Is the bias in Passage B stated or unstated? Explain.

3. **(a)** Which details in the passages can be checked for accuracy? **(b)** Are any opinions presented as though they were facts? Give an example.

4. **(a)** What hidden assumptions or generalizations do you find in the passages? **(b)** Which passage ridicules the opposing point of view? How does it do so? **(c)** How much would you rely on each passage for information about the ERA? Explain your reasoning.

APPLY THE SKILL
See the Chapter Review and Assessment for another opportunity to apply this skill.

A.

"My primary objection to ERA is that it's a broad, general amendment which is open to interpretation. I think only an absolute fool would give an open amendment to the Supreme Court in light of what the Court has done in the last twenty-five years.

The ERA is a power grab by Washington. States' rights pertaining to women will go to the national government. We've already given up power to the feds in other Constitutional amendments. Why give up more power?"

—Opponent of ERA, in *The Politics of the Equal Rights Amendment*, 1979

B.

"The 14th and 15th amendments, written in 1868 and 1870, said: 'All persons born or naturalized in the U.S. are citizens and have the right to vote.'

Susan B. Anthony, considering herself to be a person, registered and voted in 1872. She was arrested, brought to trial, convicted of the crime of voting—because she was a woman, and the word persons *mentioned in our Constitution did not mean women.* . . . If she were alive today, Susan B. Anthony might vote, but she would still see 1000 legal discriminations against women upon various state statute books. . . .

The solution of the problem of giving women 100 per cent protection of the Constitution . . . is the adoption of the Equal Rights for Women Amendment which reads: Equality of rights under law shall not be denied or abridged by the United States or by any state on account of sex."

——Proponent of ERA, in *Delta Kappa Gamma Magazine*, Fall 1969

RESOURCE DIRECTORY

Teaching Resources
Skills for Life booklet, p. 32

Technology
Social Studies Skills Tutor CD-ROM
Interactive Practice in
• Geographic Literacy
• Critical Thinking and Reading
• Visual Analysis
• Communications

Ethnic Minorities Seek Equality

READING FOCUS

- How did Latinos seek equality during the 1960s and early 1970s?
- How did Asian Americans fight discrimination during this period?
- In what ways did Native Americans confront their unique problems?

MAIN IDEA

Inspired by the civil rights movement, Latinos, Asian Americans, and Native Americans organized to seek equality and to improve their lives.

KEY TERMS

Latino
migrant farm worker
United Farm Workers (UFW)
Japanese American Citizens League (JACL)
American Indian Movement (AIM)
autonomy

TAKING NOTES

As you read, complete the chart below to describe each group's struggle for equality.

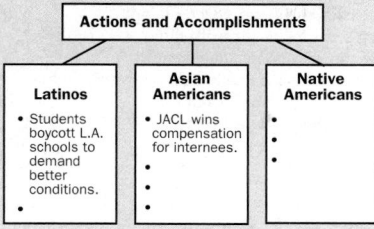

Actions and Accomplishments

Latinos	Asian Americans	Native Americans
• Students boycott L.A. schools to demand better conditions.	• JACL wins compensation for internees.	•
•	•	•
•	•	•

Setting the Scene

Inspired by the civil rights and women's movements, other ethnic and racial groups began to fight for equality during the 1960s and 1970s. In May 1970, journalist Rubén Salazar predicted the future of one of these new movements, the Chicano movement in Los Angeles, California. "We are going to overthrow some of our institutions," he said. "But in the way Americans have always done it: through the ballot, through public consensus. That's a revolution." Three months later, Salazar was killed in the rioting that broke out after police tried to stop a Chicano anti–Vietnam War demonstration.

After his death, Salazar became a martyr to the Chicano movement. His ideals and his death also point to the connection between the Chicano movement and other activist causes of the era, such as the antiwar and civil rights movements. In addition, Salazar's words show how these movements of the 1960s and 1970s fit into the long tradition of American reform—a tradition that is marked by change "through the ballot, through public consensus"—and occasionally marred by violence.

Latinos Fight for Change

People whose family origins are in Spanish-speaking Latin America, or **Latinos,** come from many different places, but they share the same language and some elements of culture. Whether their origins are in Puerto Rico, Cuba, Mexico, or other parts of the Americas, Latinos have often been regarded as outsiders by other Americans. They have frequently been denied equal opportunities in many important areas, including employment, education, and housing.

The Latino Population Spanish-speaking people lived in many parts of the present-day United States before English-speaking settlers arrived, and their numbers have grown steadily. In the late 1960s and early 1970s, for example, immigration from Central and South America increased, and between 1970 and 1980, census figures for people "of Spanish origin" rose from 9 million to 14.6 million. Specific groups

VIEWING HISTORY César Chávez leads a United Farm Workers Union march in 1965. **Checking Consistency** *Does this peaceful protest by Latino migrant workers correspond to the description of the "revolution" described by Rubén Salazar? Explain your answer.*

Chapter 30 • Section 2   1003

RESOURCE DIRECTORY

Teaching Resources
Guided Reading and Review booklet, p. 121

Technology
Section Reading Support Transparencies
Guided Reading Audiotapes (English/Spanish), Ch. 30
Student Edition on Audio CD, Ch. 30
Prentice Hall Presentation Pro CD-ROM, Ch. 30
Companion Web site, www.phschool.com

SECTION OBJECTIVES

1. Learn how Latinos sought equality during the 1960s and early 1970s.
2. Find out how Asian Americans fought discrimination during this period.
3. See the ways in which Native Americans confronted their unique problems.

BELLRINGER

Warm-Up Activity Ask students to consider the dilemma faced by all ethnic Americans from the early days of mass immigration: whether to assimilate or to try to retain their native culture. Ask students to note what is gained and lost by assimilation.

Activating Prior Knowledge Ask students to consider the ways in which the civil rights movement, originally launched to improve the circumstances of African Americans, became a model for other minority groups. What techniques were adapted to support various struggles?

READING STRATEGY

Have students skim the section and use the headings and subheadings to create an outline. Then, as they read, have them fill in appropriate details in the section outline.

CAPTION ANSWERS

Viewing History Yes, in that it is a peaceful protest designed to change minds and laws.

Focus Inspired by the civil rights movement, other ethnic minorities such as Latinos, Asian Americans, and Native Americans began to struggle for greater equality. Ask how their struggles differed.

Instruct Discuss how cultural differences among different groups of Latinos have led to many Latino movements rather than a single unified effort for equality in American society. Read this comment by Daniel Villanueva, a TV executive: "We need a Spanish Bobby Kennedy or Martin Luther King. Right now he's just not there." Discuss what a "Spanish Martin Luther King" might have been able to do that Cesar Chavez did not do.

Assess/Reteach Ask students to consider Latino, Asian American, and Native American groups' efforts to fight discrimination and secure equal rights. What were the primary concerns of each group? In what areas have the various groups succeeded in accomplishing their goals? In what areas does more work remain to be done?

ACTIVITY
Connecting with Citizenship

Have students work in groups to research and create time lines that compare major events in the civil rights movement for Asian Americans, Latinos, or Native Americans with major events in the African American civil rights movement. Be sure students focus on actions taken by people from these various ethnic groups to expand economic opportunities and political rights in American society. Display time lines for each movement and have students hypothesize how one movement might have influenced another. (Visual/Spatial)

CAPTION ANSWERS

Viewing History Elements such as family values (the father and son); music (the blue note); the ancient and sophisticated cultures of Mexico (the Aztec eagle); the power of the UFW (its flag); Chicano political and labor power (the fist and the words).

VIEWING HISTORY Mexico's northern neighbors, California and Texas, traditionally received the majority of Mexican immigrants. This mural is located in Los Angeles. **Analyzing Visual Information** *What elements does the mural use to show Chicano cultural pride?*

Focus on WORLD EVENTS

The Cuban Revolution In the 1950s, a young Cuban lawyer began organizing opposition to the corrupt regime of the Cuban dictator Fulgencio Batista. By 1959, Fidel Castro and his small band of guerrilla fighters had driven Batista from the country. When he took power, Castro promised an honest administration, full civil and political liberties, and moderate reforms. Instead, he imposed a one-party dictatorship, nationalized farms and industries, and suppressed all political dissent. Many Cubans—skilled workers, educated professionals, wealthy owners of businesses and farms, intellectuals and journalists—felt betrayed by Castro and chose to emigrate. Hundreds of thousands left Cuba, and many settled in the United States.

tended to settle in certain areas. In the 1960s, Cubans, fleeing Fidel Castro's Communist rule, went first to Florida. Many of these refugees were educated professionals, and they became successful citizens of Miami and other American cities. The Puerto Ricans who moved to the Northeast, and the Mexicans who settled in the West and Southwest, usually had less education and found it harder to succeed in American society.

Mexican Americans, also known as Chicanos, have always made up the largest group of Latinos in the United States. In the 1960s, they began to organize against discrimination in education, employment, and the legal system, leading to *el Movimiento Chicano*—the Chicano movement.

Cultural Identity Chicano activists began encouraging Mexican Americans to take pride in their culture and its dual heritage from Spain and the ancient cultures of Mexico. Some of these activists also claimed that Anglos—white, English-speaking non-Latinos—had undermined Mexican Americans' control over their lives through economic pressure and through institutions such as the Roman Catholic Church, the media, and the schools.

This claim was supported by conditions in the Los Angeles barrios, or Latino neighborhoods. There, schools were crowded and run-down, with high dropout rates. In March 1968, 10,000 Mexican American students walked out of five such Los Angeles high schools to protest their unequal treatment. Latino students in other parts of California, and in the states of Colorado and Texas, followed their example. They demanded culturally sensitive courses, better facilities, and Latino teachers and counselors.

Organizing to Fight Discrimination The students were not the only protesters in the Latino community. Throughout the 1960s, organizers struggled to unite Latino farm workers. César Chávez became a hero to millions of Americans, both Latino and Anglo, in his effort to improve conditions for migrant workers. Moving from farm to farm, and often from state to state to provide the labor needed to plant, cultivate, and harvest crops, **migrant farm workers** were some of the most exploited workers in the country. They spent long hours doing backbreaking work for low pay, and their children had little opportunity for education.

Growing up among these farm workers, Chávez came to believe that unions offered them the best opportunity to gain bargaining power and

RESOURCE DIRECTORY

Teaching Resources
Biography, Literature, and Comparing Primary Sources booklet (Biography) *Delores Huerta*, p. 35

Technology
Color Transparencies *American Diversity*, G12
Sounds of an Era Audio CD *César Chávez*, 1973 recording (time: 30 seconds)
RESOURCE PRO® **Literature Activity**
Perspectives of Women of Color, found on Resource Pro, expresses the hopes of women of color with a poem by Puerto Rican–born poet Judith Ortiz Cofer.

to resist the economic power of their employers. In the 1960s, he and fellow-activist Dolores Huerta began to organize Mexican field hands into what became the **United Farm Workers (UFW).** They went from door to door and field to field. By 1965, the union had 1,700 members.

The UFW's first target was the grape growers of California. Chávez, like Martin Luther King, Jr., believed in nonviolent action. In 1967, when growers refused to grant more pay, better working conditions, and union recognition, Chávez organized a successful nationwide consumer boycott of grapes picked on nonunion farms. Later boycotts of lettuce and other crops also won consumer support across the country.

Chávez's efforts generated angry opposition and even brought him death threats. He responded this way:

> 66 It's not me who counts, it's the Movement. And I think that in terms of stopping the Movement—this one or other movements by poor people around the country—the possibility is very remote. . . . The tide for change now has gone too far. 99
>
> —César Chávez

In 1975, California passed a law requiring collective bargaining between growers and union representatives. Workers finally had a legal basis to ask for better working conditions. By encouraging them to demand equality, the UFW had brought Latino migrant farm workers into the movement for civil rights.

While Chávez was organizing farm workers, other Chicanos took a different approach: they sought political power. In 1961, voters in San Antonio, Texas, elected Henry B. González to Congress. Another Texan, Elizo "Kika" de la Garza, went to the House of Representatives in 1964. Joseph Montoya of New Mexico was elected to the Senate in 1962. At the same time, new political groups formed to support Latino interests. In Texas, José Angel Gutiérrez spearheaded the formation of the political party *La Raza Unida* in 1970. This new party worked for better housing and jobs, and also backed Latino political candidates.

Yet a different approach was taken by Reies López Tijerina, who argued that the Anglo culture had stolen the Chicanos' land and heritage. To call attention to broken treaties, his *Alianza Federal de Mercedes* ("Federal Alliance of Land Grants") marched on the New Mexico state capital, Santa Fe, in 1966. At about the same time, the Mexican American Legal Defense and Educational Fund (MALDEF) began providing legal aid to help Mexican Americans defend their rights. It also encouraged Mexican American students to become lawyers.

Asian Americans Fight Discrimination

Ever since they first arrived in the United States, Americans of Chinese and Japanese ancestry have faced racial discrimination. Prejudice against Japanese Americans reached a peak during World War II, and the Communist takeover of China in 1949 caused negative feelings toward Chinese Americans. Still, the years after the war brought positive changes for Asian Americans.

Japanese Americans After the War   As you have read, Japanese American citizens living along the West Coast were interned in camps during World War II. The government had feared that they were a risk to American security following Japan's attack on Pearl Harbor. Not only had they been unjustly detained and deprived of their rights as citizens, but they had also lost hundreds of millions of

BIOGRAPHY

César Chávez
1927–1993

Before the Depression, César Chávez's father was a successful farmer and a local postmaster in Yuma, Arizona. In 1937, when César was 10, the family lost their farm because they could not afford the taxes. They became migrant workers in California. Because the family was always on the move, young César attended more than 30 different schools while working part time in the fields. Even so, the Chávez family fostered a powerful sense of independence. Chávez recalled, "I don't want to suggest we were that radical, but I know we were probably one of the strikingest families in California." After serving in the Navy, Chávez returned to California and worked as an organizer for the Community Services Organization before launching his own farm workers union.

   Sounds of an Era

Listen to a speech by César Chávez and other sounds from the activist movements of the 1960s and 1970s.

Connecting with Government

Divide the class into four groups. Have each student in Group One write a newspaper editorial supporting the compensation of Native Americans for the loss of their tribal lands. Tell students in Group Two to write editorials on why Native Americans should *not* be compensated. Have those in Groups Three and Four write similar editorials for each side on the compensation of Japanese Americans for their internment during World War II. You may then wish to have Groups One and Three and Groups Two and Four exchange editorials. Each student should write a letter to the editor opposing the position taken in the editorial he or she receives. **(Verbal/Linguistic)**

BACKGROUND

A Diverse Nation

Attempts to correct injustices against Native Americans often created other problems. When the Chippewa in Minnesota sued the government in 1975 to regain 100,000 acres that they claimed had been taken, in the words of one sympathetic historian, "through theft, trickery, ignorance, or for failing to pay taxes that were, in fact, illegal," the suit hurt white farmers who had bought the land in good faith. Because of the pending claims, banks wouldn't lend these farmers money to buy machinery, and no one would buy the land.

Asian Immigration, 1951–1978

SOURCE: *Statistical Abstract of the United States*

INTERPRETING GRAPHS
The photo above shows the JACL participating in the 1963 Civil Rights March in Washington, D.C. Patterns of immigration from Asia changed dramatically from the 1950s to the 1970s. **Analyzing Information** (a) Which two countries did the greatest number of Asian immigrants come from in the 1950s? In the 1970s? (b) What do you think might have accounted for this change?

dollars in homes, farms, and businesses. After the war, many of those who had been interned sought compensation for these losses through the **Japanese American Citizens League (JACL).** In 1948, the JACL won passage of the Japanese American Claims Act. Under this act, Congress eventually paid relatively small amounts for property losses, with some claims not being settled until 1965. (It was not until 1988, however, that the United States apologized to Japanese American internees and paid them further monetary compensation.)

Economic and Political Advances   Although Asian Americans as a group were well educated, in 1960 they earned less than white Americans. In California, for example, for each $51 a white man was paid, a Chinese man would earn $38 and a Japanese man, $43. College graduates faced prejudice when they tried to move into management positions. In the 1960s and 1970s, Asian Americans made economic gains faster than other minorities. Nonetheless, they still faced discrimination and relied on the example of the civil rights movement to push for change.

When Hawaii became a state in 1959, Asian Americans gained a voice in Congress. The new state sent Hiram Leong Fong, a Chinese American, to the Senate, and Daniel K. Inouye, a Japanese American, to the House of Representatives.

Native Americans Face Unique Problems

As the original inhabitants of North America, Native Americans have always occupied a unique social and legal position in the United States. Although the cultures and languages of Indian peoples varied, white society tended to view all Native Americans as one group. By 1871, the United States government no longer recognized Indian nations as independent powers. At the same time, it did not extend full citizenship to Native Americans, either. Instead, state and federal agencies limited self-government for Native Americans and often worked to destroy their traditional lifestyles. In 1924, the Snyder Act granted citizenship to all Native Americans born in the United States, but they continued to be recognized as citizens of their own nations or tribal groups as well. Even then, many states denied suffrage to Native Americans. It was not until 1948 that Arizona and New Mexico granted Indians the right to vote.

As a whole, Native Americans have routinely been denied equal opportunities. They have had higher rates of unemployment, alcoholism, and suicide, as well as a shorter life expectancy, than white Americans. Many communities have suffered from poverty and poor living conditions. Like other nonwhite groups, Native Americans have been the victims of centuries-old stereotypes reinforced by the images in movies and other media.

Native Americans also have had some grievances unique to their situation. The land now occupied by the United States was once theirs, and treaties made between Indian nations and the United States have repeatedly been broken by the American government.

Land Claims   Traditional lands have a special role in most Native American cultures. "Everything is tied to our homeland," declared D'Arcy McNickle, a

CAPTION **A**NSWERS

Interpreting Graphs (a) 1950s: Japan and China. 1970s: the Philippines and Korea. (b) Answers will vary. They may include the fact that Japan's economy greatly improved over this period, so fewer Japanese may have felt the need to emigrate for economic reasons. At the same time, the Communists were tightening their hold over China and refusing to let Chinese people emigrate.

RESOURCE DIRECTORY

Teaching Resources
Great Debates booklet (Decision-Making Activities) *Native American Fishing Rights on Trial,* p. 42

Other Print Resources
Nystrom *Atlas of Our Country*   *Later Expansion of the United States,* pp. 32–33; *The Fourth Wave of Immigration,* pp. 36–37

Technology
RESOURCE PRO® **Visual Learning Activity** *Changing Attitudes Toward Native Americans,* found on Resource Pro, portrays attempts made in the 1960s and 1970s to challenge stereotypes about Native Americans.

RESOURCE PRO® **Biography** *Vine Deloria Jr.,* found on Resource Pro, profiles the man who, through his books, emerged as the leading spokesman for Native American nationalism.

Native American anthropologist, in 1961. Yet, many years after pioneers first moved onto Native American territory, state and federal governments continued to take over traditional tribal lands. Protecting what was left became a major goal of Native American activists.

A government project in New York State triggered one early protest. According to a 1794 treaty, the Seneca Nation owned the land on its Allegany reservation. In 1956, when the federal government wanted to build a dam there, Congress held hearings that did not include the Seneca. Legal actions by the tribe and a 1961 appeal to President John Kennedy failed to halt the project. After the Kinzua Dam was completed, however, Congress agreed to pay $15 million in damages to the Seneca, but this award did not restore their hunting and fishing lands, homes, and sacred sites. In response, other Native American tribes, such as the Seminole, brought successful lawsuits for violations of treaty rights and failure to make promised payments.

The American Indian Movement In 1968, two Chippewa activists, Dennis Banks and George Mitchell, set out the goals of a new activist organization, the **American Indian Movement (AIM).** Banks called it "a new coalition that will fight for Indian treaty rights and better conditions and opportunities for our people." Following the example of militant black groups, AIM focused first on the special problems of Native Americans living in cities by setting up patrols and encouraging racial and cultural pride in young people. Eventually, AIM also fought for Native American legal rights, including **autonomy,** or self-government. It also sought control of natural resources on Native American lands, and the restoration of lands illegally taken from Indian nations. Many people, both white and Native American, criticized AIM's militant approach. Nevertheless, AIM continued to confront the government over Indian-rights issues.

Confronting the Government Native American activists used standoffs with the federal government to call attention to issues that mainstream America had long ignored. In 1972, demonstrators protesting the violation of treaties between the United States and various Indian groups formed the Broken Treaties Caravan. They traveled to Washington, D.C., and occupied the Bureau of Indian Affairs' offices for six days. Other protests were even more dramatic.

In 1969, more than 75 Native American protesters landed on Alcatraz Island in San Francisco Bay. They claimed the 13-acre rock under the terms of the Fort Laramie Treaty of 1868, which allowed male Native Americans to file homestead claims on federal lands. Others joined the group, planning to turn the deserted island into an educational and cultural center. The occupation failed. Federal marshals eventually removed the last protesters after a year and a half. But the episode drew national attention to Native American grievances.

An even more dramatic confrontation came in 1973 at the Oglala Sioux village of Wounded Knee, South Dakota. In 1890, the army's Seventh Cavalry had massacred more than 200 Sioux men, women, and children there. The Pine Ridge reservation around the village was one of the country's poorest, with half of its families living on welfare. In February 1973, AIM took over the village and

VIEWING HISTORY AIM leader Dennis Banks leads a protest march in South Dakota. **Drawing Inferences** *Why do you think Banks chose to pose in front of Mount Rushmore?*

READING CHECK
Describe two Native American protests.

Chapter 30 • Section 2   1007

ACTIVITY
Connecting with Culture

Cultural pride and education are very important tools for gaining self-determination. To help students understand the importance of cultural heritage and the ways in which it is taught, have them list as many aspects as possible of their own cultural heritage and recall briefly how they learned about them. **(Verbal/Linguistic)**

BACKGROUND
Biography

During the turbulent decade of the 1960s, Ben Nighthorse Campbell (b. 1933), a Northern Cheyenne, channeled an angry adolescence into the study of martial arts. It eventually earned him the captaincy of the 1964 United States Olympic Judo Team at the Tokyo games. In 1982, Campbell became the first Native American to serve in Congress since the 1930s. In 1992, he was elected to represent Colorado in the United States Senate.

READING CHECK
The Broken Treaties Caravan arrived in Washington, D.C., in 1972 and took over the offices of the Bureau of Indian Affairs. Violence erupted during the 1973 confrontation between American Indian Movement members and federal agents at Wounded Knee.

CUSTOMIZE FOR ...
Less Proficient Readers

Ask students to correct the following incorrect statements.

- Native Americans have rates of unemployment and alcoholism roughly equal to those of whites.
- The Seneca protest against the building of the Kinzua Dam succeeded in halting its construction.
- AIM's main goal was to secure more government handouts for Native Americans.

☑ TEST PREPARATION
Have students reread the section "The American Indian Movement" on this page and then answer the question below.

One of the legal rights sought for Native Americans was *autonomy*. Which of the following is the best definition for autonomy?

A Independence.

B Freedom.

Ⓒ Self-government.

D Legal authority.

CAPTION ANSWERS
Viewing History It is a famous symbol of national pride for white Americans and so would attract attention. Also, symbolically, Banks is bringing his grievances to the "attention" of the most honored of American leaders.

Chapter 30 Section 2 • **1007**

Reading Comprehension

1. Latinos are from Spanish-speaking Latin America, and Chicanos are Mexican Americans.

2. The UFW pressed for improved working conditions and higher wages for migrant farm workers. They orchestrated consumer boycotts to force recalcitrant farm owners to grant concessions to migrant laborers.

3. It organized Japanese Americans in an attempt to gain compensation for property losses sustained by Japanese Americans who were interned during World War II.

4. The American Indian Movement (AIM).

Critical Thinking and Writing

5. Native Americans used the aggressive tactics of militant black groups, such as taking over government buildings and creating standoffs with federal authorities. Native Americans wanted to protect what was left of Native American tribal lands and customs, and to gain autonomy. Latinos and Asian Americans, on the other hand, did not seek autonomy.

6. Answers will vary, but should be supported with facts from the section.

Take It to the NET

Encourage students to include both personal history and professional accomplishments in their biographical research.

---

refused to leave until the United States government agreed to investigate the treatment of Indians and the poor conditions on the reservation, and to review more than 300 treaties. Other Native American leaders supported the occupation. Onondaga Chief Oren Lyons, speaking for the Iroquois, said:

> 66 We support the Oglala Sioux Nation or any Indian Nation that will fight for its sovereignty. . . . The issue here at Wounded Knee is the recognition of the treaties between the United States Government and the sovereign nations that were here before. 99
>
> —Onondaga Chief Oren Lyons

VIEWING HISTORY Echoes of history surrounded the Sioux village of Wounded Knee during the AIM protest there. **Identifying Alternatives** (a) Why did some people who sympathized with AIM's goals object to the organization's tactics? (b) What other tactics might AIM have used? Do you think they would have been as effective?

Federal marshals and FBI agents put the village under siege, and agents arrested some 300 people, including news reporters and outside supporters. The standoff finally ended in May, when protesters agreed to surrender their weapons and to leave the reservation. In exchange, the government consented to reexamine Indian treaty rights. But during the siege, two AIM members had been killed and about a dozen people hurt, including two federal marshals.

Government Response Native American activism brought some positive government action. The Kennedy and Johnson administrations tried to bring jobs and income to some reservations by encouraging industries to locate there and by leasing reservation lands to energy and development corporations. But many Native Americans worried about the effects that these projects would have on the land, and later sought to renegotiate or cancel many of the leases.

A number of laws passed in the 1970s favored Native American rights. The Indian Education Act of 1972 gave parents and tribal councils more control over schools and school programs. The Indian Self-Determination and Education Assistance Act of 1975 upheld Native American autonomy and let local leaders administer federally supported social programs for housing and education. Native Americans also continued to win legal battles to regain land, mineral, and water rights.

Section 2 Assessment

READING COMPREHENSION

1. What are the family origins of **Latinos** and of Chicanos?

2. How did the **UFW** help **migrant farm workers**?

3. What was the purpose of the **Japanese American Citizens League**?

4. Which Native American group led the protest at Wounded Knee?

CRITICAL THINKING AND WRITING

5. **Making Comparisons** How and why was the Native Americans' struggle for equality different from that of Latinos and Asian Americans?

6. **Writing to Inform** Write a paragraph about one protest covered in this section. Include its purpose and its effect.

Take It to the NET

Activity: Writing a Biography Use both primary and secondary sources to write a biography of the United Farm Workers' founder César Chávez. Include quotes and important dates in his life. Use the links provided in the *America: Pathways to the Present* area of the following Web site for help in completing this activity.

www.phschool.com

1008   Chapter 30 • *An Era of Activism*

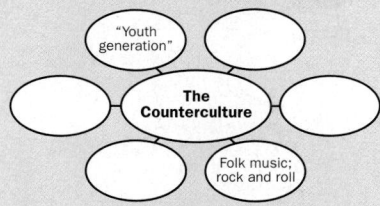
Setting the Scene If the man in the gray flannel suit was the symbol of the 1950s, then the long-haired hippie dressed as outrageously as possible in bright colors, beads, and flowers was the symbol of the 1960s. The former looked adult and responsible, and was clearly dressed for nine-to-five success. He was the organization man, and conformed to the culture of his time. The latter, the hippie, rejected the gray flannel suit and the regimented life it represented. The hippie generation favored "flower power" over corporate and military power, and eventually influenced the dominant culture.

A Time of Change

In the 1960s, many young people adopted values that ran counter to, or against, the mainstream culture that they saw around them. Members of this **counterculture** valued youth, spontaneity, and individuality. Also called hippies, these young people promoted peace, love, and freedom. And they experimented with new styles of dress and music, freer attitudes toward sexual relationships, and the recreational use of drugs. The result was often a "generation gap," or a lack of understanding and communication between the older and younger generations.

The so-called youth generation had an enormous influence on American society. First of all, it was the largest generation in American history. The "baby boom" that followed World War II resulted in a huge student population in the 1960s. By sheer numbers, the baby boomers became a force for change. The music industry rushed to produce the music they liked; clothing designers copied the styles they

The hippie (seated below) is doing his best *not* to look like the man of the fifties (at left).

Focus Explain that in the 1960s, a youth culture rejected conventional norms and values. Ask what norms and values were embraced by the counterculture. How did the counterculture affect American life?

Instruct Discuss the aspects of American life that hippies rejected. What sort of life did hippies want to build for themselves? Discuss the reactions of other Americans to hippies and would-be hippies. Why did hippies attract so much attention? Why did some more conservative Americans feel threatened by the hippie lifestyle? Ask students which aspects of the counterculture some people considered dangerous.

Assess/Reteach Have students list the aspects of American society that were affected by the counterculture. Then have them analyze each aspect to see whether the impact of the counterculture endured beyond the era to this day.

VIEWING HISTORY The Andy Warhol painting (above) and the Op Art poster (at right) show the irreverance of 1960s artists. **Making Comparisons** *What do the two art works have in common? How are they different?*

introduced; universities changed college courses and rules to accommodate them. Politicians, too, found that they could not ignore the voice of the baby boom generation.

Sixties Style The look of the 1960s was distinctive, frivolous, and free. But it was also a signal of changing attitudes. The counterculture rejected restrictions and challenged authority. Many young women gave up the structured hairstyles of the 1950s and began wearing their hair long and free. They also chose freer fashions, such as loose-fitting dresses. Men, too, let their hair grow long and wore beards. Their clothing was as different from a gray flannel suit as they could make it—and that was the point. These styles announced a rejection of the corporate world and its uniform. Of course, hippie dress itself became a kind of uniform for the youth generation.

Many members of the counterculture identified with the poor and downtrodden around the world and at home. They fought for the civil rights of minority groups in the United States, and sided with those they believed were oppressed abroad. Hippies often adopted the dress of working people, including blue jeans, plain cotton shirts, peasant blouses, and other simple garments. They also sought out apparel of indigenous peoples, such as ponchos from South America, dashikis from Africa, jewelry made by Native Americans, and other hand-made items.

The colorful look of the sixties was not confined to clothing. Hippies painted their cars—and their bodies. And this spirit of fun and irreverence also invaded the art world. The Pop Art of the 1960s, such as paintings by Andy Warhol and Roy Lichtenstein, featured realistic depictions of the artifacts of modern life. Scorned at the time, these satirical paintings of soup cans and comic books now hang in art museums. Another style, Op Art, captured the spirit of the sixties with its fluorescent colors and dizzying optical illusions. Many of the images were—or looked as though they were—created under the influence of psychedelic drugs. Op Art was especially popular for posters and album covers showcasing popular rock groups.

The Sexual Revolution Just as participants in the counterculture demanded more freedom to make personal choices in how they dressed, they also demanded more freedom to choose how they lived. Their new views of sexual conduct, which rejected many traditional restrictions on behavior, were labeled "the sexual revolution." Some of those who led this revolution argued that sex should be separated from its traditional ties to family life. Many of them also experimented with new living patterns. Some hippies rejected traditional relationships and lived together in communal groups, where they often shared property and chores. Others simply lived together as couples, without getting married.

The sexual revolution in the counterculture led to more open discussion of sexual subjects in the mainstream media. Newspapers, magazines, and books published articles that might not have been printed just a few years earlier. The 1962 book by Helen Gurley Brown, *Sex and the Single Girl*, became a bestseller. In 1966, William H. Masters and Virginia E. Johnson shocked many people

1010   Chapter 30 • *An Era of Activism*

CAPTION ANSWERS

Viewing History They are alike in that both rebel against mainstream formal artistic tradition and middle class culture. The Warhol pokes fun at American consumer conformist culture; the poster makes visual reference to psychedelic drugs. They differ in that Warhol's work represents a type of realism while the Op Art design represents a drug-induced hallucination.

RESOURCE DIRECTORY
Technology

RESOURCE PRO® **Literature Activity** *The Flower Children,* found on Resource Pro, uses lyrics from the song "San Francisco (Be Sure to Wear Flowers in Your Hair)" to describe the group of young people who called themselves "flower children."

RESOURCE PRO® **Visual Learning Activity** *Reflections of the Counterculture,* found on Resource Pro, displays popular buttons that were worn in the 1960s to express views on contemporary issues.

when they published *Human Sexual Response*, a report on their scientific studies of sexuality.

The Drug Scene   Some members of the 1960s counterculture also turned to psychedelic drugs. These powerful chemicals cause the brain to behave abnormally. Users of psychedelic drugs experience hallucinations and other altered perceptions of reality. The beatniks of the 1950s, who were an inspiration to the 1960s counterculture, had experimented with drugs, but the beatniks had been relatively few in number. In the 1960s, the use of drugs, especially marijuana, became much more widespread among the nation's youth.

One early proponent of psychedelic drug use was researcher Timothy Leary. Leary worked at Harvard University with Richard Alpert on the chemical compound lysergic acid diethylamide, commonly known as LSD. The two men were fired from their research posts in 1963 for involving undergraduates in experiments with the drug. Leary then began to preach that drugs could help free the mind. He advised listeners, "Tune in, turn on, drop out."

Leary's view presented just one side of the drug scene. On the other side lay serious danger. The possibility of death from an overdose or from an accident while under the influence of drugs was very real. Three leading musicians of the 1960s—Janis Joplin, Jim Morrison, and Jimi Hendrix—died of complications from drug overdoses. And they were not the only ones. Their deaths represented the tragic excesses to which some people were driven by their reliance on drugs to enhance or to escape from reality.

The Music World

Music both reflected and contributed to the cultural changes of the 1960s. The rock and roll of the 1950s had begun a musical revolution, giving young people a music of their own that scandalized many adults. The early 1960s saw a new interest in folk music. Members of the counterculture turned to traditional songs that had been passed down from generation to generation of "folk," or ordinary people around the world. They also favored songs of protest against oppression; songs of laborers, such as sailors and railroadmen, and songs that originated under slavery.

The year 1964 marked a revolution in rock music that some called the British Invasion. It was the year that the Beatles first toured America. The "Fab Four" had already taken their native England by storm. They became a sensation in the United States as well, not only for their music but also for their irreverent sense of humor and their "mop top" long hair. The Beatles heavily influenced the music of the period, as did another British group, the Rolling Stones. Mick Jagger of the Stones was a dramatic and electrifying showman. Another exciting performer was Texan Janis Joplin, a hard-drinking singer whose powerful interpretations of classic blues songs catapulted her to superstardom.

Woodstock   The diverse strands of the counterculture all came together at the Woodstock Music and Art Fair in August 1969. About 400,000 people gathered for several days in a large pasture in Bethel, New York, to listen to the major bands of the rock world. Despite brutal heat and rain, those who attended the **Woodstock festival** recalled the event with something of a sense of awe for the fellowship they experienced there. Police avoided confrontations with those

STUDENTS OF NORWALK
BEAUTIFY AMERICA
get a haircut

READING CHECK
Describe some influences on American music of the sixties.

Reading Comprehension

1. The group that rejected mainstream American culture, holding different values and experimenting with different lifestyles. It drew its adherents mainly from the vast population of college students resulting from the postwar baby boom.

2. Pop Art is the realistic depiction of items from everyday life in American culture. Op Art used fluorescent colors and strange imagery, reminiscent of psychedelic drugs, in its images.

3. Many young Americans rejected the idea of sex being tied to marriage and experimented with different lifestyles. The counterculture also encouraged experimentation with drugs, especially the psychedelic drugs that some believed would expand the user's imagination.

4. Woodstock had been peaceful.

Critical Thinking and Writing

5. (a) That it was repressed sexually and overly conservative in dress and politics; that middle-aged corporate types were insensitive to the needs of the poor; that mainstream traditional marriages suppressed individuality. (b) Answers will vary, but students should offer evidence to support their respective viewpoints.

6. Letters will vary but should be supported with facts from the section.

Posters should demonstrate knowledge of the performers' work and be visually attractive.

VIEWING HISTORY This group of hippies lived together in a commune and traveled around in their outrageously painted bus. **Drawing Inferences** *How are they showing their rejection of traditional social customs?*

attending by choosing not to enforce drug laws. The crowd remained under control. Tom Law was at Woodstock:

  ❝ *The event was so much bigger than the music. It was a phenomenon. It was absolutely a phenomenon. And it was also the most peaceful, civilized gathering that was probably happening on the planet at the time.* ❞

                      —Tom Law

Other Americans, however, viewed both the festival and the mood it reflected with disgust. Even as some of the older generation began growing their hair longer and wearing "hipper" clothing, they were alarmed at the changes they saw around them. These changes also disturbed many in the younger generation. In particular, some in the mainstream culture deplored the drugs, sex, and nudity they saw at the Woodstock festival and around the country. To them, the counterculture represented a rejection of morals and honored values, and seemed a childish reaction to the problems of the era.

Altamont The fears of those who criticized Woodstock came true at another rock festival held at the Altamont Speedway in California in December 1969. There, 300,000 people gathered for a concert by the Rolling Stones. When promoters of the concert failed to provide adequate security, the Stones hired a band of Hell's Angels, an infamous and lawless motorcycle gang, to keep order. The cyclists ended up beating one man to death when he approached the stage with a gun. This ugly violence contradicted the values preached by the counterculture. It also signaled that the era of "peace and love" would not last forever.

Despite their celebration of simple lifestyles, most hippies were children of the comfortable middle class. American corporations marketed such items as bell-bottom blue jeans and stereo equipment to them, and they eagerly bought the products. When the counterculture fell apart, the hippies melted right back into the mainstream. By the 1980s, many baby boomers who had protested the values of 1950s and 1960s mainstream America would hold executive positions in the same corporations they had once denounced.

Section 3 Assessment

READING COMPREHENSION

1. What was the **counterculture?**

2. What are Pop Art and Op Art?

3. What new attitudes toward sexual activity and drugs were promoted by the counterculture?

4. How was the Altamont concert different from the **Woodstock festival?**

CRITICAL THINKING AND WRITING

5. **Identifying Assumptions** (a) What assumptions about mainstream culture were made by the counterculture? (b) Were they fair? Explain.

6. **Writing a Letter to the Editor** It is 1967, and you are the parent of a teenager. Write a letter to the editor either for or against a rule banning "hippie dress" at your child's school.

Take It to the NET

Activity: Creating an Ad Learn more about sixties folk music and create an ad for a concert featuring several folk performers. Use the links provided in the *America: Pathways to the Present* area of the following Web site for help in completing this activity.
www.phschool.com

CAPTION ANSWERS

Viewing History By living communally, dressing in "hippie" styles, and riding on—as well as in—a bus painted in a wild color scheme.

READING FOCUS

- What efforts were begun in the 1960s to protect the environment?
- How did the government try to balance jobs and environmental protection?
- How did the consumer movement begin, and what did it try to accomplish?

MAIN IDEA

Conditions that came to light in the 1960s as well as the activist mood of the period helped to create movements for preserving the environment and for ensuring the safety of consumer products.

KEY TERMS

Nuclear Regulatory Commission (NRC)
Environmental Protection Agency (EPA)
Clean Air Act
Clean Water Act

TAKING NOTES

Copy the diagram below. As you read, fill in the two circles with the goals and accomplishments of each movement. Place items that apply to both where the circles overlap.

Environmental Movement — Consumer Movement

SECTION OBJECTIVES

1. Read about efforts begun in the 1960s to protect the environment.
2. Understand how the government tried to balance jobs and environmental protection.
3. Find out how the consumer movement began, and what it tried to accomplish.

BELLRINGER

Warm-Up Activity Ask students to recall how many decisions they made on each day of the past week that affected the environment. Discuss how and why they made these decisions. How many of their decisions were good for the environment?

Activating Prior Knowledge Are students aware of the types of concerns that gave rise to the environmental movement of the late 1960s? Can they list some situations that have improved as a result of this movement?

READING STRATEGY

The text states that "the environmental movement and the consumer movement demanded honesty and accountability from industry and government." As students read the section, have them look for evidence to support this statement.

ACTIVITY

Connecting with Government

Have students research the major pieces of environmental legislation that have been passed since 1970. Then, have them make a table that lists the legislation down one column and the categories *Restore Natural Resources, Eliminate Toxic Dumps, Cleaner Industries,* and *Eliminate Sources of Pollution.* Have students note which pieces of legislation impacted which areas of the environment. Which categories have been most affected by environmental legislation? **(Logical/Mathematical)**

Setting the Scene In 1958, a woman in Massachusetts wrote a letter to a friend—and set off a revolution. The letter writer was Olga Owens Huckins, and the friend was Rachel Carson. An airplane had sprayed Huckins's neighborhood with DDT to control mosquitoes, and the next day she had found dead birds in her yard. She asked Carson, a biologist, to look into the connection. The result was *Silent Spring*, the 1962 book that started the environmental movement.

Carson begins *Silent Spring* with "A Fable for Tomorrow." In the fable, she describes a lovely country town surrounded by farms and wilderness, by beauty and the sounds of wildlife. She continues:

> 66 *Then a strange blight crept over the area and everything began to change. Some evil spell had settled on the community: mysterious maladies swept the flocks of chickens; the cattle and sheep sickened and died. Everywhere was a shadow of death. The farmers spoke of much illness among their families. . . . There was a strange stillness. The birds, for example—where had they gone? . . . [T]here was now no sound; only silence lay over the fields and woods and marsh. . . . No witchcraft, no enemy action had silenced the rebirth of new life in this stricken world. The people had done it themselves.* 99
>
> —Rachel Carson in *Silent Spring*

Protecting the Environment

Carson's fable links two protest movements of the 1960s and 1970s. Both the environmental movement and the consumer movement demanded honesty and accountability from industry and government. Consumer advocates insisted upon safety for customers and workers. Environmentalists went further: they called for actions that would preserve and restore the earth's environment and resources. According to environmental activists, the very products that people used in an effort to improve their world and their lives—to control mosquitoes, for example—were damaging not only the health of the environment but the health of the people as well.

Like the women's movement, the environmental movement of the 1960s had roots in the American past. In the late 1890s and early 1900s,

Rachel Carson was already recognized as a distinguished naturalist when she wrote *Silent Spring*.

RESOURCE DIRECTORY

Teaching Resources
Learning Styles Lesson Plans booklet, p. 63
Guided Reading and Review booklet, p. 123

Technology
Section Reading Support Transparencies
Guided Reading Audiotapes (English/Spanish), Ch. 30
Student Edition on Audio CD, Ch. 30
Prentice Hall Presentation Pro CD-ROM, Ch. 30
Companion Web site, www.phschool.com

Focus Inspired by other protest movements, environmentalists and consumer advocates demanded action to preserve the environment and to protect the buyers and users of products in America. Ask students what triggered these movements. How successful were they?

Instruct Explain that many environmental problems grew out of the rapid development of technology, industry, and transportation after World War II. Have students list some voluntary measures that people undertake to preserve the environment. What role should the federal government play in regulating the environment? Should it determine how communities dispose of trash or how manufacturers package items?

Assess/Reteach Have students analyze the progress that has been made in cleaning up the environment over the past thirty years. What areas still need improvement?

BACKGROUND

Then and Now

Despite the truth of Rachel Carson's assertions about the hazards of the chemical DDT, there is another side to DDT. Before its widespread agricultural use, DDT was used to kill malaria-carrying mosquitoes. DDT drastically lowered the spread of malaria, a disease that in India alone claimed about 800,000 lives every year. DDT, now banned, was once the means to the survival of millions.

READING CHECK

That chemical insecticides such as DDT were destroying the environment by killing animals and plants. She pointed out that these chemicals moved through nature's food chain to affect many different types of animal and plant species.

CAPTION ANSWERS

Fast Forward to Today It suggests that if pollution is reduced and habitat is restored, animal species on the brink of extinction can be restored to healthy, self-sustaining population levels.

The Return of the Bald Eagle

In 1963, a year after *Silent Spring* was published, bald eagles were near extinction, with only 417 breeding pairs in the lower 48 states. They were declared an endangered species in 1967. In 1972, DDT was banned, and a year later the Endangered Species Act was passed. The eagles were put under the protection of this act in 1978. Efforts to save the bald eagle included bringing young eaglets from Canada and Alaska and then releasing them in the continental United States, and breeding eagles in captivity and then releasing their offspring into the wild. By 1999, the eagles had made a strong recovery; there were more than 5,000 breeding pairs, and the species was removed from the endangered list. Posing with an eagle named Challenger at an Independence Day ceremony, President Bill Clinton said, "It's hard to think of a better way to celebrate the birth of a nation than to celebrate the rebirth of our national symbol."

? **What does the return of the bald eagle suggest about saving other endangered species? Explain your answer.**

READING CHECK
What was Rachel Carson's main argument in *Silent Spring?*

Progressives had worked to make public lands and parks available for the enjoyment of the population. New Deal programs of the 1930s included tree-planting projects in an effort to put people back to work—and to conserve forests and farmlands. The modern environmental movement, however, would not have started without Rachel Carson.

Rachel Carson Marine biologist Rachel Carson grew up wanting to become a writer. Her mother taught her to appreciate nature and encouraged Carson's growing interest in zoology. In the 1930s and 1940s, Carson combined her talents and began to write about scientific subjects for general audiences. In 1951, she published *The Sea Around Us*, which was an immediate bestseller and won the National Book Award. This book, and her next, *The Edge of the Sea*, made her famous as a naturalist. One of Carson's main themes was that human beings are part of nature, and that all parts of nature interact. She also believed that people carry a great responsibility for the health of nature because they have the power to change the environment. *Silent Spring*, her most influential book, warned against the abuse of that power.

In *Silent Spring*, Carson spoke out against the use of chemical pesticides, particularly DDT. She argued that DDT had increased agricultural productivity but killed various other plants and animals along with the insect pests that were its target. She stated:

> 66 The most alarming of all man's assaults upon the environment is the contamination of air, earth, rivers, and sea with dangerous and even lethal materials. This pollution is for the most part irrecoverable. . . . In this now universal contamination of the environment, chemicals are the sinister and little-recognized partners of radiation in changing the very nature of the world. 99
>
> —Rachel Carson in *Silent Spring*

As Carson explained, chemicals sprayed on crops enter into living organisms and move from one to another in a chain of poisoning and death. Specifically, in the 1960s, the lingering effects of DDT threatened to destroy many species of birds and fish, including the national symbol, the bald eagle.

Silent Spring caused a sensation. The chemical industry fought back vigorously, arguing that Carson confused the issues and left readers "unable to sort fact from fancy." The public, however, was not persuaded by this attack on Carson. So great was national concern that a special presidential advisory committee was appointed. It called for continued research and warned against the widespread use of pesticides. Eventually DDT was banned in the United States, and other chemicals came under stricter control. (For more on the impact of *Silent Spring*, see the "Geography and History" feature that follows this section.)

It was not only DDT that worried people. They became more conscious of poisonous fumes in the air, oil spills on beaches, and toxic wastes buried in the ground. In the mid-1960s, President Lyndon Johnson addressed environmental concerns in his plans for the Great Society:

RESOURCE DIRECTORY

Teaching Resources
Learning with Documents booklet (Visual Learning Activity) *Preserving the Environment,* p. 69

Technology
Color Transparencies *The Way It Works,* H20
Sounds of an Era Audio CD *Rachel Carson on Silent Spring,* 1963 recording (time: 50 seconds)

> *The water we drink, the food we eat, the very air that we breathe, are threatened with pollution. Our parks are overcrowded, our seashores overburdened. Green fields and dense forests are disappearing.*
>
> —Lyndon Johnson

Johnson promised that environmental legislation would be part of his broader reform program.

Nuclear Power   During the 1960s, concern about the overuse of nonrenewable resources, such as oil and gas, encouraged the development of nuclear power plants to generate electricity. Many people considered nuclear power plants to be better than coal-burning plants because they caused less air pollution. Nuclear plants, however, discharged water used to cool the reactor into local waterways. This discharge raised water temperatures, killing fish and plant life. As time went on, objections to nuclear power plants began to develop.

These objections were also fueled by a growing concern about the possibility of nuclear plant accidents. The fear was that in the event of an accident, radioactivity would be released into the air, causing serious damage—or even death—to all plant and animal life in the surrounding area. The **Nuclear Regulatory Commission (NRC),** created in 1974, tried to address these fears as it oversaw the use of nuclear materials in civilian life. Its chief goal was to ensure that nuclear power plants and facilities were operated safely.

Public Response   People from all walks of life were becoming alarmed by environmental problems. Biologist Barry Commoner, for example, warned about rapid increases in pollution in his 1971 book *The Closing Circle.* Meanwhile, the Sierra Club, an organization founded in 1892 to further nature conservation, became active in opposing power projects that the group thought would harm the environment. But it was an environmental catastrophe off the coast of California in 1969 that captured the public's attention. The result of an oil platform blowout, the Santa Barbara oil spill fouled beaches and killed thousands of birds and other wildlife. President Richard Nixon visited the site, and declared, "The Santa Barbara incident has frankly touched the conscience of the American people." And the American people were ready to respond.

Grassroots environmental movements began springing up around the country. Groups supporting conservation efforts and opposing such actions as the building of dams and nuclear plants gained attention. In 1969, Senator Gaylord Nelson of Wisconsin announced plans to hold a national day of discussion and teaching about the environment. The following year, on April 22, 1970, Americans celebrated the first Earth Day. Organizers stressed the important role that Americans could play in improving awareness of environmental issues and in bringing an end to environmental damage. Earth Day would become a yearly observance. Its aim was to heighten concern for the environment, to increase awareness about environmental issues, and to clean up pollution and litter.

VIEWING HISTORY Concern about Earth and its resources prompted Earth Day rallies, mass cleanup activities, and protests against nuclear power plants. **Expressing Problems Clearly** (a) What is the sign carried by the protester really asking people to do? (b) According to environmental activists, why is this action necessary?

ACTIVITY
Connecting with Citizenship

Have each student write a letter to the President of the United States explaining why he or she supports or opposes the opening of new nuclear power plants; the expansion of oil drilling offshore or in the Alaskan wilderness; or the growing of food crops that have been genetically altered to make them resistant to insects without the use of pesticides. In their letters, have students analyze the impact of these technological innovations and projects on the nature of work, the American labor movement, and businesses. Call on students to read their letters to the class. **(Verbal/Linguistic)**

BACKGROUND
Geography in History

Fishermen in the northeastern United States and Quebec were shocked when fish began disappearing from many local streams and lakes in the 1970s. The culprit was acid precipitation, rain and snow made as acidic as vinegar or lemon juice by pollutants from coal- and oil-burning power plants in the Ohio Valley. Ironically, the Clean Air Act had worsened the problem when it tried to disperse local pollution by ordering smokestacks to be built over 500 feet tall. Pollutants were not reduced, but blown far from the source by high-altitude westerly winds.

CUSTOMIZE FOR ...
Less Proficient Writers

Ask students to study the section photos and read the captions. Have them use the photos to write sentences that explain the section's main ideas.

☑ **TEST PREPARATION**

Have students read the section "Rachel Carson" on these pages and then answer the question below.

What was the name of the program proposed by Lyndon Johnson to address what he felt were the American people's most important concerns?

A The New Deal

B A Challenge to Americans

C Let Freedom Ring

Ⓓ The Great Society

CAPTION **A**NSWERS

Viewing History (a) The sign is really asking people to take care of their planet if they want to preserve it as a safe place to live. (b) This is essential because the Earth is being poisoned by pesticides and other pollutants and is in danger of being made uninhabitable by pollution and the potential for accidents at nuclear power plants.

Major Environmental Landmarks, 1964–1976

Legislation	Description
Wilderness Act, 1964	Designated lands to be maintained and preserved for public enjoyment.
Rare and Endangered Species Act, 1966	Established protection for rare, endangered, and threatened plants and animals.
Environmental Protection Agency, 1970	Created as an independent federal agency to administer the laws that affect the environment.
Clean Air Act, 1970	Instituted a research and development program to prevent and control air pollution.
Clean Water Act, 1972	Established regulations for preventing urban and industrial water pollution.
Resource Conservation and Recovery Act, 1974	Established guidelines for storage and/or disposal of existing hazardous waste.
Safe Drinking Water Act, 1974	Established guidelines for safe drinking water.
Toxic Substance Control Act, 1976	Enacted to regulate the commercial manufacture, processing, and distribution of chemical substances.

INTERPRETING CHARTS
The government responded to environmental activism by enacting laws and creating federal agencies. **Analyzing Information** *Which of these laws directly affect human health and safety?*

READING CHECK
How did the government try to balance jobs and environmental protection in Alaska?

Government Actions The efforts of environmental activists and the concern of the public at large helped spur the federal government to create a new agency that would set and enforce national pollution-control standards. In 1970, President Nixon established the **Environmental Protection Agency (EPA)** by combining existing federal agencies concerned with air and water pollution.

One of the EPA's early responsibilities was to enforce the **Clean Air Act.** Passed by Congress in 1970 in response to public concerns about air pollution, the Clean Air Act was designed to control the pollution caused by industries and car emissions. The EPA forged an agreement with car manufacturers to install catalytic converters (devices that convert tailpipe pollutants into less dangerous substances) in cars to reduce harmful emissions.

In 1972, the EPA gained further responsibilities when Congress enacted the **Clean Water Act** to regulate the discharge of industrial and municipal wastewater. The act also provided for grants to build better sewage-treatment facilities. As the nation's watchdog against polluters, the EPA continues to monitor and reduce air and water pollution. It regulates the disposal of solid waste and the use of pesticides and toxic substances.

Balancing Jobs and the Environment

Efforts to clean up and preserve the environment did not come without a cost. Many industry leaders worried that the new regulations would be confusing to follow and overly costly to businesses. They raised concerns that the increased costs associated with cleaning up the air and water would result in the loss of jobs. Government and industry worked to balance the demands of economic development and environmental protection.

The development of oil fields in Alaska provides an example of how the government tried to achieve this balance. Construction began in 1974 on an 800-mile pipeline designed to carry oil across the frozen landscape to ice-free ports in the southern part of Alaska. This development of the oil industry created new jobs and expanded revenues for the state. At the same time, it brought increased concern over the welfare of the Alaskan wilderness and the rights of native Alaskans. The Alaska Native Claims Settlement Act of 1971 had set aside millions of acres of land for the state's native groups, to be used partly for conservation purposes. In 1978, and again in 1980, additional land was added to the state's protected conservation areas.

The Consumer Movement

Just as the birth of the environmental movement was credited to Rachel Carson, the consumer movement of the 1960s was also associated with one individual. Ralph Nader was this era's most important and visible champion of consumer rights. However, the consumer movement, too, had earlier roots. The Pure Food and Drug Act of 1906, for example, had been one early effort to maintain safety standards and protect the public. In the 1960s and early 1970s, though, the consumer movement grew far larger and stronger and had more far-reaching effects.

Attorney Ralph Nader spearheaded the new consumer effort. Nader had been a serious activist all his life. While a student at Princeton University in the early 1950s, Nader protested the spraying of campus trees with DDT. His interest in automobile safety began while he was attending Harvard Law School. In 1964, Daniel Patrick Moynihan, then Assistant Secretary of Labor, hired Nader as a consultant on the issue of automobile safety regulations. The government report Nader wrote developed into a book, *Unsafe at Any Speed: The Designed-in Dangers of the American Automobile,* published the next year. It began:

> **❝** *For over half a century the automobile has brought death, injury, and the most inestimable sorrow and deprivation to millions of people. . . . [T]his mass trauma began rising sharply four years ago reflecting new and unexpected ravages by the motor vehicle. A 1959 Department of Commerce report projected that 51,000 persons would be killed by automobiles in 1975. That figure will probably be reached in 1965, a decade ahead of schedule.* **❞**
>
> —Ralph Nader in *Unsafe at Any Speed*

Like the muckrakers of the Progressive Era, Nader drew attention to the facts with passionate arguments. He called many cars "coffins on wheels," pointing to dangers such as a tendency of some models to flip over. The automobile industry, he charged, knew about these problems but continued to build over one million cars before confronting the safety problems.

Nader's book was a sensation. In 1966, he testified before Congress about automobile hazards. That year, Congress passed the National Traffic and Motor Vehicle Safety Act. The *Washington Post* noted, "Most of the credit for making possible this important legislation belongs to one man—Ralph Nader. . . . A one-man lobby for the public prevailed over the nation's most powerful industry."

Nader broadened his efforts and investigated the meatpacking business, helping to secure support for the Wholesome Meat Act of 1967. He next looked into problems in other industries. Scores of volunteers, called "Nader's Raiders," signed on to help. They turned out report after report on the safety of such products as baby food and insecticides, and they inspired consumer activism. As ordinary Americans began to stand up for their rights, consumer protection offices began to respond to their many complaints.

VIEWING HISTORY Ralph Nader was a "one-man lobby" for consumer safety. **Making Comparisons** *How were the tactics of Ralph Nader and his "raiders" different from those of other activists of the 1960s?*

Reading Comprehension

1. A yearly celebration begun in 1970 to increase public awareness of environmental issues and concerns.
2. The EPA was formed in 1970 to monitor pollution and enforce environmental regulations.
3. The Clean Air Act was designed to regulate air pollution from industries and cars, while the Clean Water Act regulates wastewater disposal and finances the construction of sewage treatment facilities.
4. Ralph Nader's book used colorful language and passionate arguments to raise public awareness of the dangers of automobiles. It demonstrated the impact one person could have on as powerful an entity as the auto industry.

Critical Thinking and Writing

5. Carson's concerns over DDT led her to write the book *Silent Spring.* The book's awakening of public concern over harmful pesticides led people to consider a host of other environmental concerns and to act on them.
6. Answers will vary but should be supported with facts from the section.

Section 4 Assessment

READING COMPREHENSION

1. What is Earth Day?
2. When was the **Environmental Protection Agency** formed and what is its purpose?
3. Describe the **Clean Air Act** and the **Clean Water Act.**
4. Explain the importance of *Unsafe at Any Speed.*

CRITICAL THINKING AND WRITING

5. **Recognizing Cause and Effect** Explain how Rachel Carson's concern with DDT initiated the environmental movement.
6. **Writing an Opinion** Do you think the United States should rely more on nuclear power plants? Write a paragraph that supports your opinion.

Activity: Preparing Testimony Research the EPA or the NRC. Write out testimony you might give in congressional hearings about funding the agency. Use the links provided in the *America: Pathways to the Present* area of the following Web site for help in completing this activity. **www.phschool.com**

Students should incorporate their opinions with facts and data to create a persuasive testimony, and may choose to include an examination of other government-funded agencies.

CAPTION ANSWERS

Viewing History Nader and his raiders worked within the system, lobbying Congress directly and turning out reports to influence public opinion and policy-makers. This approach was very different from, for example, the confrontational activities engaged in by AIM.

REVIEWING KEY TERMS

Students should refer to the definitions of key terms in the chapter to write sentences that show an understanding of the many different social movements that grew out of the civil rights movement of the 1960s.

REVIEWING MAIN IDEAS

11. Fair pay, equal job opportunities, overcoming sexism in the media, sharing domestic responsibilities with men.

12. The ERA was initially approved by Congress in 1972 and sent to the states for ratification. To become law, 38 states needed to ratify it. By 1977, 35 states had ratified the amendment. However, as opposition grew, the deadline for ratification passed without the required number of states on board.

13. Opposition from both men and women. Some women enjoyed being housewives and did not want to work outside of the home, while other women felt that the ERA would hurt the rights women already had.

14. He organized the UFW and led the movement. Chávez was successful in bringing about consumer boycotts of farm products produced by nonunion farms.

15. The JACL persuaded Congress to pass the Japanese American Claims Act in 1948, providing some reparation for treatment of Japanese Americans during World War II.

16. To obtain better treatment for Native Americans; to fight for the observance of treaties made by the U.S. government with Native American nations; and to gain autonomy.

17. The youth culture favored colorful and casual clothing, nontraditional views about sex and relationships, and a willingness to experiment with drugs.

18. The Rolling Stones were giving a concert. They hired a group of Hell's Angels for security. During the show the bikers killed a man who was carrying a gun.

19. Carson wrote the popular book *Silent Spring*, which examined the effect of DDT and other pesticides on the environment. The popularity of the

creating a CHAPTER SUMMARY

Copy the chart (right) on a piece of paper. Use it to organize information about some of the groups that challenged the status quo in the 1960s and 1970s.

For additional review and enrichment activities, see the interactive version of *America: Pathways to the Present*, available on the Web and on CD-ROM.

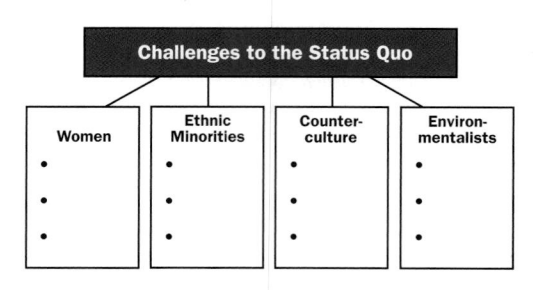

Challenges to the Status Quo

Women	Ethnic Minorities	Counter-culture	Environ-mentalists
•	•	•	•
•	•	•	•
•	•	•	•

★ Reviewing Key Terms

For each of the terms below, write a sentence explaining how it relates to the activism of the 1960s and 1970s.

1. feminism
2. *Roe v. Wade*
3. Latino
4. migrant farm worker
5. United Farm Workers (UFW)
6. autonomy
7. counterculture
8. Woodstock festival
9. Nuclear Regulatory Commission (NRC)
10. Environmental Protection Agency (EPA)

★ Reviewing Main Ideas

11. What were the goals of NOW? (Section 1)
12. Describe the effort to ratify the ERA. (Section 1)
13. What opposition did the women's movement encounter? (Section 1)
14. What role did César Chávez play in the Chicano struggle for equal rights? (Section 2)
15. What did the JACL accomplish? (Section 2)
16. What were the goals of the American Indian Movement? (Section 2)
17. Describe three new attitudes of the youth culture of the 1960s and 1970s. (Section 3)
18. What happened at the Altamont festival? (Section 3)
19. Describe how Rachel Carson influenced the environmental movement. (Section 4)

20. What were two of the targets of Ralph Nader's consumer movement? (Section 4)

★ Critical Thinking

21. **Determining Relevance** (a) How did the civil rights movement affect groups as diverse as women, Native Americans, and environmentalists? (b) Do you think that these groups would have been as successful without the example of the civil rights activists? Explain your answer.

22. **Identifying Central Issues** (a) What underlying problem in American society did the women's movement, the Chicano movement, and the American Indian Movement try to address? (b) What kinds of changes were all three groups fighting for?

23. **Making Comparisons** What was the attitude of the counterculture toward "the establishment" (institutions such as government and big business) and how did they show it? Compare their attitudes and actions to those of the environmental and consumer movements.

24. **Demonstrating Reasoned Judgment** Balancing the demands of economic development and environmental protection often involves making tradeoffs. Choose a current environmental issue or use one that was discussed in the chapter, and write a paragraph suggesting how to balance those demands.

CREATING A CHAPTER SUMMARY

Challenges to the Status Quo

Women	Ethnic Minorities	Counterculture	Environmentalists
• After WW II, women were better educated, sought more opportunities • Civil rights movement gave women new tools to fight discrimination. • Gradual shift in attitudes and laws	• Heightened sense of cultural identity • Greater organization in fight against discrimination • Many different ethnic groups worked to secure their rights.	• Birth of "baby boom" generation after WW II • New styles of parenting, influenced by Dr. Spock and others • Identification by many members of the generation with certain lifestyles and trends in music and culture	• Landmark books *Silent Spring* and *Unsafe at Any Speed* • Earth Day protests attract many. • Beginning with The Great Society, government programs begin to favor restoration and protection of environment.

★ Skills Assessment

Analyzing Political Cartoons ▶

25. Examine the images in the cartoon. What do the ships represent?

26. Who are the people standing on the shore, and what do they represent?

27. Explain the humor in the dialogue, as well as the serious point it is making.

Analyzing Primary Sources

Dennis Banks restated the goals of the American Indian Movement in a speech marking the group's second anniversary. Read the following excerpt from his speech, and answer the questions that follow.

SOME DAY, SON... NONE OF THIS WILL BE YOURS.

> 66 *The government and churches have demoralized, dehumanized, massacred, robbed, raped, promised, made treaty after treaty, and lied to us. . . . We must now destroy this political machine that man has built to prevent us from self-determination.* 99
>
> —Dennis Banks

28. Which of the following was one of AIM's goals as expressed by Dennis Banks?

 A to join the government

 B to make no changes to Native American lifestyles

 C to make radical changes in order to gain self-determination

 D to enter into a new treaty with the government

29. How did Banks suggest that AIM achieve its goals?

 F through peaceful demonstration

 G by destroying the political machine built by the government and churches

 H by joining churches

 J by ignoring the problem

Applying the Chapter Skill: *Recognizing Bias*

30. Look back at the Skills for Life page. Then choose a quoted passage in this chapter, and use the steps for recognizing bias to evaluate that passage.

ACTIVITIES

Writing to LEARN

Writing an Explanation
During the 1960s and 1970s, César Chávez's United Farm Workers organized successful consumer boycotts of grapes, lettuce, and other produce. Explain how boycotts such as these achieve their goals. You may wish to do more reading about the UFW boycotts.

Primary Source CD-ROM

Working With Primary Sources Find additional information on the activism of the 1960s and 1970s on the *Exploring Primary Sources in U.S. History CD-ROM* and use the selection(s) provided to complete the Chapter 30 primary source activity located in the *America: Pathways to the Present* area of the following Web site.
www.phschool.com

Take It to the NET

Chapter Self-Test As a review activity, take the Chapter 30 Self-Test in the *America: Pathways to the Present* area at the Web site listed below. The questions are designed to test your understanding of the chapter content.
www.phschool.com

Chapter 30 Assessment **1019**

---

book helped start the environmental movement of the 1960s.

20. He targeted both the automobile and meatpacking industries.

CRITICAL THINKING

21. (a) It demonstrated nonviolent methods that would be used by later social movements. (b) Other groups probably would not have been as successful without the roadmap that the civil rights movement provided them.

22. (a) They addressed the unfair and unequal treatment received by a large group within American society. (b) To be treated the same as white males, with the same career opportunities, the same protections under law, and the same respect within society.

23. They viewed themselves collectively as the polar opposite of the traditional "establishment." They demonstrated their views by listening to rock music, spurning the traditional hair and clothing styles of their parents, and by other alternative actions—such as sometimes living in communes. The environmental and consumer movements were different in that they did not reject all of mainstream American culture but focused on one aspect of society or government and tried to effect change on that issue.

24. Answers will vary but should be supported with specific examples and should address themes introduced in the chapter.

SKILLS ASSESSMENT

25. The arrival of Europeans in the Americas.

26. They are Native Americans, representing the original inhabitants of the Americas.

27. The words are a play on the sentiment that one generation hands down all that it has achieved to the next generation. The cartoonist is saying that Native Americans quickly lost everything they had when the Europeans arrived.

28. C

29. G

30. Sample response: César Chávez assumes that the arguments of labor movements are correct by stating that the labor movements probably cannot be stopped from achieving their goals.

ANSWERS TO ACTIVITIES

Writing to LEARN

Sample answer: Boycotts have direct economic effects in that they draw upon consumers to stop buying certain products or using certain services.

Primary Source CD-ROM

Direct students to the additional primary sources that can be found on the *Exploring Primary Sources in U.S. History CD-ROM.*

 Take It to the NET

Additional support materials and activities for Chapter 30 of *America: Pathways to the Present* can be found in the Social Studies area at the Prentice Hall School Web site. **www.phschool.com**

Chapter 30 • **1019**

THE ENVIRONMENTAL MOVEMENT

Focus Tell students that when *Silent Spring* appeared in 1962, *ecology* was not a familiar word to most Americans. There was virtually no way for Americans to recycle glass, paper, metal, or plastic. The Environmental Protection Agency did not exist. Most Americans did not know about the ozone layer, and store clerks would have cast strange looks at a shopper who wanted to reuse grocery bags. The publication of *Silent Spring* marks the moment when the American public began to learn about the choices required to safeguard life on Earth.

Instruct Discuss with students the costs and benefits of environmental legislation. Bring up scenarios in which citizens might be angered by the costs and inconvenience of environmental regulations (i.e., consumers facing increasing water bills due to laws mandating cleaner drinking water, or land owners restricted from certain building practices in order to protect the environment). Do they think that environmental legislation is too costly or infringes on their right to live the way they want to? Can the students think of any examples in which environmental restrictions have improved quality of life? What benefits do they bring to society? Have students discuss if the benefits of environmental restrictions outweigh the costs.

Extend Ask students to monitor the local news for reports on environmental issues in your community. Have students outline the persons or groups involved, the environmental problems, and the potential costs to individuals. Students may present this information in a chart.

The Environmental Movement

The publication of Rachel Carson's book *Silent Spring* in 1962 helped spark an awareness of environmental problems during the 1960s. A growing environmental movement led to the first Earth Day in 1970—which featured demonstrations like the one shown here—to raise public awareness of environmental problems.

Environmental Legislation

Concerned citizens pressed the federal government to protect the environment. The 1963 Clean Air Act was followed by the tougher Clean Air Acts of 1970 and 1990, which required states to reduce high levels of pollution. In response to air quality concerns, carmakers and other industries acted to produce more fuel-efficient cars and to reduce harmful emissions. A 1980 law established a trust fund (known as the Superfund) to clean up hazardous waste sites.

Geographic Connection In the image to the left, areas shaded in blue have below-normal ozone levels. Based on this image, what areas suffer from ozone loss?

Growing Concerns

While they continued to fight pollution in the 1980s and 1990s, scientists also addressed the thinning ozone layer and a growing "ozone hole" over Antarctica, shown in the remote sensing image on the right. Certain chemicals cause ozone in the atmosphere to break down, exposing Earth to higher levels of harmful ultraviolet radiation from the sun. An international accord in 1987 committed the world's nations to reducing gases that harm the ozone layer. Another concern was the accumulation of "greenhouse gases" released by industry and motor vehicles (right), which could raise temperatures globally.

1020

RESOURCE DIRECTORY

Teaching Resources
Geography and History booklet, pp. 18–19

Other Print Resources
Nystrom *Atlas of Our Country* Land Use, Population, and Ethnicity, pp. 46–47

Technology
Prentice Hall United States History Video Collection™ Volume 20, *Post-War USA*

Protecting the Mojave

Environmental scientists have worked to protect open space and to preserve wildlife diversity and habitat. In 1994, Congress created the Mojave National Preserve, which protects part of the Mojave Desert from development.

One State's Example

This map of California shows just a few of that state's environmental achievements. The Sacramento and San Joaquin rivers feed canals and aqueducts that provide water to California's farms and cities as well as the Sacramento–San Joaquin Delta—a network of wetlands and inland waterways that flow into San Francisco Bay. Environmental organizations and the government have acted to ensure that enough fresh water flows into the delta and bay to protect fish and other species in danger of extinction. Meanwhile, air quality districts covering the state's largest cities have imposed strict air pollution standards.

Geographic Connection

Why might tougher air quality standards be needed in urban areas?

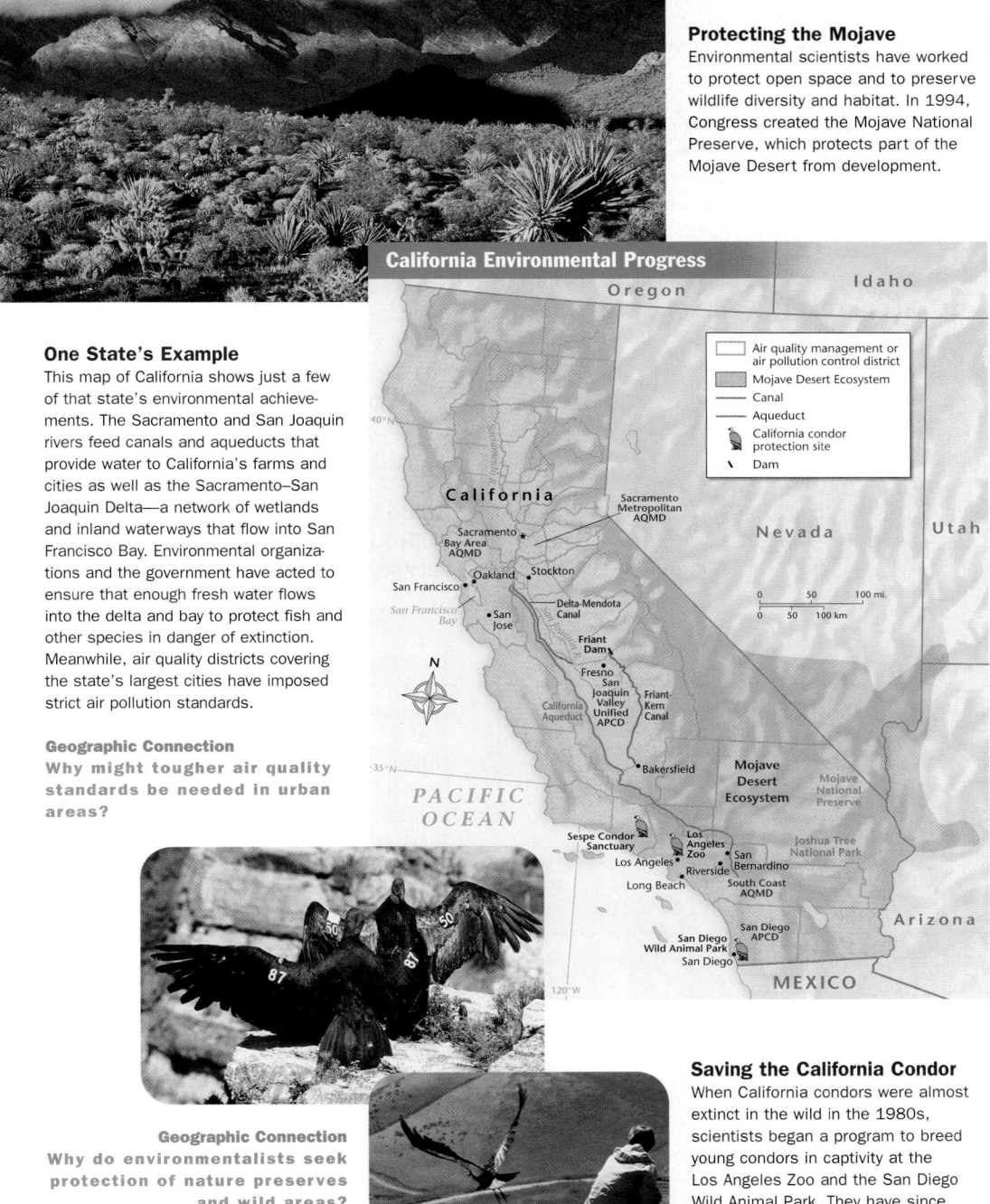

California Environmental Progress

Geographic Connection

Why do environmentalists seek protection of nature preserves and wild areas?

Saving the California Condor

When California condors were almost extinct in the wild in the 1980s, scientists began a program to breed young condors in captivity at the Los Angeles Zoo and the San Diego Wild Animal Park. They have since released these birds in protected areas such as the Sespe Condor Sanctuary.

1021

Chapter 31 Planning Guide
Resource Manager

	CORE INSTRUCTION	READING/SKILLS
Chapter-Level Resources	**Teaching Resources** • Pacing Charts booklet • Block Scheduling booklet **Resource Pro® CD-ROM**, Ch. 31 **Prentice Hall Presentation Pro CD-ROM**, Ch. 31 **www.phschool.com** • eTeach	**Guided Reading Audiotapes (English/Spanish)** **Student Edition on Audio CD**, Ch. 31 **Social Studies Skills Tutor CD-ROM** **Color Transparencies**, A50, A51, C8
1 The War Unfolds 1. Learn about the events that led to the war between North Vietnam and South Vietnam. 2. Become familiar with the Vietnam policies of President Kennedy and Robert McNamara. 3. See how President Johnson changed the course of the war.	**Teaching Resources** **Units 9/10 booklet** • Section 1 Quiz, p. 37 **Learning Styles Lesson Plans booklet**, p. 64	**Guided Reading and Review booklet**, p. 124 **Guide to the Essentials**, p. 156 **Skills for Life booklet**, p. 33 **Section Reading Support Transparencies**
2 Fighting the War 1. Learn how battlefield conditions in Vietnam affected American soldiers. 2. Be able to describe the course of the war between 1965 and 1968. 3. List reasons why the Tet Offensive was a turning point in the war.	**Teaching Resources** **Units 9/10 booklet** • Section 2 Quiz, p. 38	**Guided Reading and Review booklet**, p. 125 **Guide to the Essentials**, p. 157 **Learning with Documents booklet**, p. 36 **Section Reading Support Transparencies**
3 Political Divisions 1. Find out about the role played by students in the protest movements of the 1960s. 2. Learn why President Johnson decided not to seek reelection. 3. Discover how the Vietnam War affected the election of 1968.	**Teaching Resources** **Units 9/10 booklet** • Section 3 Quiz, p. 39 **Learning Styles Lesson Plans booklet**, p. 65	**Guided Reading and Review booklet**, p. 126 **Guide to the Essentials**, p. 158 **Learning with Documents booklet**, p. 24 **Section Reading Support Transparencies**
4 The End of the War 1. Learn how President Nixon's policies led to American withdrawal from Vietnam. 2. Discover why President Nixon campaigned promising to restore law and order. 3. See what happened in Vietnam after the withdrawal of American forces. 4. Determine the legacy of the Vietnam War.	**Teaching Resources** **Units 9/10 booklet** • Section 4 Quiz, p. 40	**Guided Reading and Review booklet**, p. 127 **Guide to the Essentials**, p. 159 **Section Reading Support Transparencies**

ENRICHMENT/PRE-AP

Prentice Hall United States History Video Collection™
www.phschool.com
• Section Activities, Virtual Field Trip, Chapter Activities, Current Events Online

American History Block Scheduling Support
Historical Outline Map Book, p. 70
Sounds of an Era Audio CD

Biography, Literature, and Comparing Primary Sources booklet, pp. 36, 83
Sounds of an Era Audio CD

Great Debates booklet, p. 24
American History Block Scheduling Support
Sounds of an Era Audio CD

Biography, Literature, and Comparing Primary Sources booklet, p. 157
Great Debates booklet, p. 44
Sounds of an Era Audio CD
Exploring Primary Sources in U.S. History CD-ROM
American Pathways Thematic Posters

ASSESSMENT

PRENTICE HALL
ASSESSMENT SYSTEM

Core Assessment
ExamView® Test Bank, Ch. 31
ExamView® Test Bank CD-ROM, Ch. 31

Standardized Test Preparation
Diagnose and Prescribe
Diagnostic Tests for High School Social Studies Skills

Review and Reteach
Review Book for U.S. History

Practice and Assess
Test-taking Strategies With Transparencies
Test-taking Strategies Posters
Test Prep Book for U.S. History
Alternative Assessment Handbook
Document-Based Assessment

Teaching Resources
Units 9/10 booklet
• Section Quizzes, pp. 37–40
• Chapter Tests, pp. 41, 44
www.phschool.com Ch. 31 Self-Test

AmericanHeritage RESOURCES

From the Archives of American Heritage®, p. 1039
AmericanHeritage® My Brush with History™ Videotapes
www.americanheritage.com

iTEXT

Don't miss the exclusive interactive version of this textbook on the Web and on CD-ROM.

Chapter 31 Planning Guide
In Your Classroom

CUSTOMIZE FOR INDIVIDUAL NEEDS

Gifted and Talented

Teacher's Edition
- Customize for Gifted and Talented, pp. 1027, 1031

Teaching Resources
- Biography, Literature, and Comparing Primary Sources booklet, pp. 36, 83, 157

Technology
- Exploring Primary Sources in U.S. History CD-ROM *The Vietnam Veterans Memorial*

ESL

Teacher's Edition
- Customize for ESL, pp. 1039, 1045

Teaching Resources
- Guided Reading and Review booklet, pp. 124–127
- Guide to the Essentials (English/Spanish), Chapter 31

Technology
- Student Edition on Audio CD, Chapter 31
- Guided Reading Audiotapes (English/Spanish), Chapter 31
- Section Reading Support Transparencies

Less Proficient Readers

Teacher's Edition
- Customize for Less Proficient Readers, pp. 1025, 1035

Teaching Resources
- Guided Reading and Review booklet, pp. 124–127
- Guide to the Essentials (English/Spanish), Chapter 31

Technology
- Student Edition on Audio CD, Chapter 31
- Guided Reading Audiotapes (English/Spanish), Chapter 31
- Section Reading Support Transparencies

Less Proficient Writers

Teacher's Edition
- Customize for Less Proficient Writers, p. 1047

Teaching Resources
- Guided Reading and Review booklet, pp. 124–127
- Guide to the Essentials (English/Spanish), Chapter 31

Technology
- Student Edition on Audio CD, Chapter 31
- Guided Reading Audiotapes (English/Spanish), Chapter 31
- Section Reading Support Transparencies

TEACHER'S EDITION INDEX

CHAPTER 31 – PACING SUGGESTIONS

For 90-minute Blocks

- Teach sections 1, 2, and 4 using Transparencies A50, A51, and C8, and the Recent Scholarship note on page 1039 for class discussions.

Running Out of Time?

If you are running short on time to cover this chapter, consider the following options:

- Use Prentice Hall Presentation Pro CD-ROM to create an outline for this chapter.

- Use the Section Summaries for Chapter 31, from **Guide to the Essentials (English/Spanish).**

ADDITIONAL ACTIVITIES

1 The War Unfolds

Connecting with Government
Have students research the Gulf of Tonkin Resolution, including contemporary analyses of its implications. Then have pairs of students role-play a television journalist interviewing Secretary of Defense Robert McNamara. The topic of the interview is the Vietnam War in general and the Resolution in particular. Though it represents an after-the-fact change of thinking, students might find helpful insights in McNamara's account of the policy failures of the Vietnam War, *In Retrospect* (1995), in which he says that he and his administration colleagues "were wrong, terribly wrong." **(Bodily/Kinesthetic)**

2 Fighting the War

Connecting with History and Conflict
For many people, television coverage of the Tet Offensive was a turning point in their feelings about the war in Vietnam. Have students research the impact of television on public support for the war before and after this battle (which began on January 30, 1968). If possible, they should interview adults with whom they are acquainted for their recollections and make audio tapes as a form of oral history. **(Verbal/Linguistic)**

3 Political Divisions

Connecting with Culture
Point out that there have always been protest songs in this country and elsewhere. Have students refer to anthologies of traditional songs to find out how various groups through the years have proclaimed their views through music. If possible, students can play, sing, or recite the lyrics of some of these songs after setting the scene with historical background. One useful source is *Rise Up Singing,* in which songs are organized by topic. **(Rhythmic/Musical)**

4 The End of the War

Connecting with History and Conflict
Remind students that in the 1968 presidential campaign, Richard Nixon said he had a plan for extracting the United States from the Vietnam conflict. Have students research the steps he took from the time of his inauguration onward in regard to the war. Then have them each create a document that compares what he actually did with his original plan as he may earlier have envisioned it. Encourage a class discussion on the effectiveness and morality of the plan as it actually unfolded. **(Verbal/Linguistic)**

INTRODUCING THE CHAPTER

The 1960s and 1970s were decades of deep division and turmoil in the United States. Under Presidents Kennedy and Johnson, the country became increasingly involved in trying to stop a Communist takeover in Vietnam. As the war continued to cost more and more lives and money while achieving little apparent success, many Americans began to question their government's role there. At the same time, a youthful counterculture arose that was critical of the traditional values of many Americans.

TIME LINE ACTIVITY

To provide students with practice in using the time line, ask questions such as these:

1. Which President first applied the domino theory to the situation in Southeast Asia? *(President Eisenhower)*

2. What power did President Johnson gain by virtue of the Gulf of Tonkin Resolution? *(The authority to escalate the war in Vietnam)*

3. In what way was the passage of the Twenty-sixth Amendment related to the Vietnam War? *(It was argued that if 18-year-olds could be drafted to fight in the war, they should be able to vote.)*

eTeach

Be sure to check out this month's online discussion with a Master Teacher. Go to **www.phschool.com**.

Chapter 31

The Vietnam War
(1954–1975)

SECTION 1   The War Unfolds
SECTION 2   Fighting the War
SECTION 3   Political Divisions
SECTION 4   The End of the War

President Kennedy (left) and Vice President Johnson at the 1961 inauguration.

1954
After the French defeat in Vietnam, the United States starts to support the newly established nation of South Vietnam with military advisors and aid.

American Events

1963
U.S. involvement in Vietnam increases. President Kennedy is assassinated.

1964
The Gulf of Tonkin Resolution gives President Johnson complete authority to escalate the war in Vietnam.

1968
A year of crises unfolds with the assassinations of Martin Luther King, Jr., and Robert Kennedy. Violence erupts at the Democratic National Convention in Chicago.

Presidential Terms: Dwight D. Eisenhower 1953–1961   John F. Kennedy 1961–1963   Lyndon B. Johnson 1963–1969

1954   **1960**   **1966**

World Events

The Berlin Wall is built.
1961

The Six-Day War takes place in the Middle East.
1967

The Tet Offensive begins.
1968

RESOURCE DIRECTORY

Teaching Resources
Pacing Charts booklet
Block Scheduling booklet, p. 29
Units 9/10 booklet
• Chapter Summary, p. 36

Technology
Guided Reading Audiotapes (English/Spanish), Ch. 31
Student Edition on Audio CD, Ch. 31
Prentice Hall United States History Video Collection™ Volume 20, *Post-War USA*
Prentice Hall Presentation Pro CD-ROM, Ch. 31
Resource Pro® CD-ROM
Social Studies Skills Tutor CD-ROM
Companion Web site, www.phschool.com

Major Players in the Vietnam Conflict

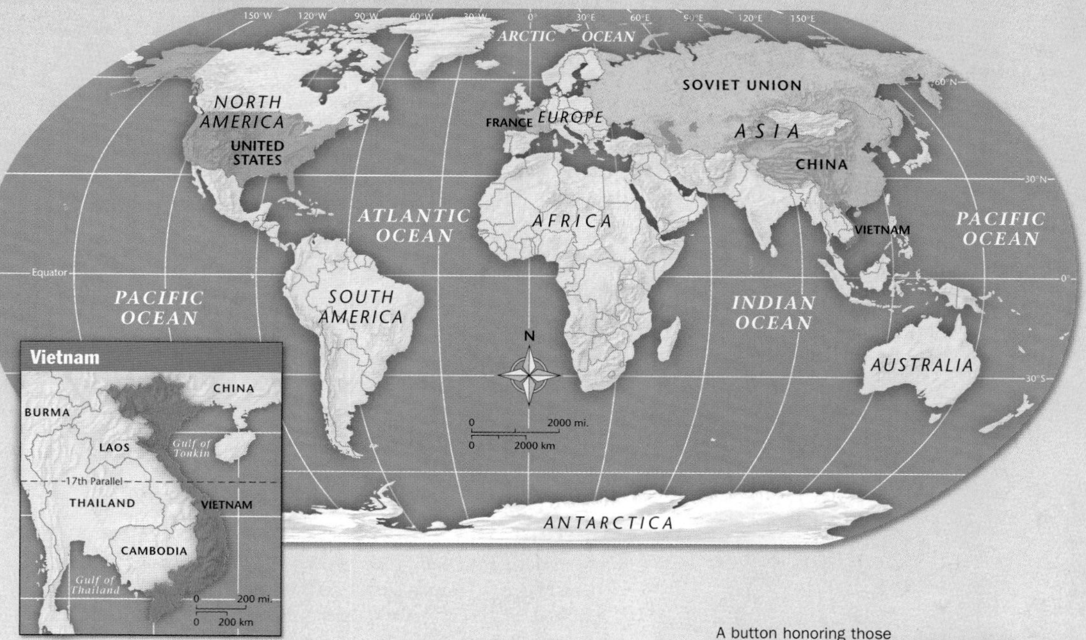

Activating Prior Knowledge
Which countries were the major players in the Vietnam War? *(China, France, the Soviet Union, and the United States)*

Previewing What did the United States fear would happen if there was a Communist takeover of Vietnam? *(The U.S. feared that if Vietnam fell to the Communists, Laos, Cambodia, Burma, and Thailand would fall as well.)*

About the Pictures

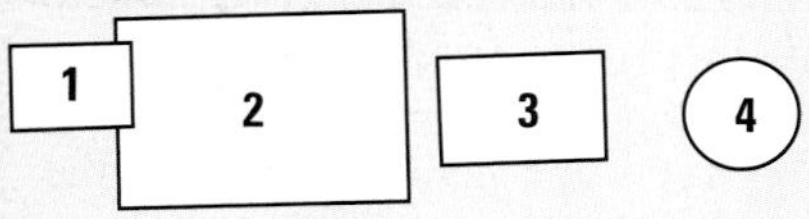

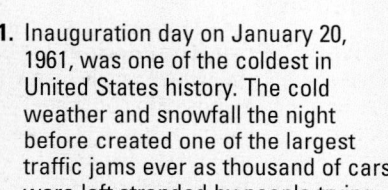

1. Inauguration day on January 20, 1961, was one of the coldest in United States history. The cold weather and snowfall the night before created one of the largest traffic jams ever as thousand of cars were left stranded by people trying to get to the ceremonies.

2. The terrain of Vietnam caused many problems for American soldiers as both their training and equipment proved unsuitable for the jungle climate.

3. Antiwar protests became common as more and more American soldiers were killed in Vietnam. Like the soldiers fighting, the majority of the antiwar protesters were young people.

4. Buttons such as this one were used to commemorate soldiers missing in action in Vietnam. Even today, many American soldiers remain unaccounted for.

Vietnam (inset map)

A button honoring those missing in action in Vietnam.

Antiwar protests sweep the nation.

1970
Four students protesting the Vietnam War are killed by National Guardsmen at Kent State. A similar incident at Jackson State results in two student deaths.

1971
The Twenty-sixth Amendment lowers the voting age to 18. Proponents argue that if 18-year-olds can fight in Vietnam, they should be able to vote.

1973
American troops withdraw from Vietnam, but returning veterans received a mixed welcome at home.

Richard M. Nixon 1969–1974   Gerald R. Ford 1974–1977   Jimmy Carter 1977–1981

1972   **1978**

India and Pakistan go to war.
1971

The Vietnam War ends with the signing of a formal peace agreement in Paris.
1973

Communists take over South Vietnam, Cambodia, and Laos.
1975

Chapter 31   **1023**

BIBLIOGRAPHY

For the Teacher

Fitzgerald, Frances. *Fire in the Lake: The Vietnamese and the Americans in Vietnam.* Random House, 1989 edition. (Considered the classic history of the war.)

Sheehan, Neil. *A Bright Shining Lie: John Paul Vann and America in Vietnam.* Random House, 1989. (The war seen through the story of one American officer.)

For the Student

Kovic, Ron. *Born on the Fourth of July.* Pocket Books, 1996. (A personal account by a disillusioned Vietnam veteran; later made into an Academy Award–winning film.)

O'Brien, Tim. *The Things They Carried.* Broadway Books, 1999. (A blending of fact and fiction on coming to terms with Vietnam.)

Vietnam: A Television History. PBS Video. (Award-winning 13-hour history of the War.)

TEXT

Don't miss the exclusive interactive version of this textbook on the Web and on CD-ROM.

The War Unfolds

SECTION OBJECTIVES

1. Learn about the events that led to the war between North Vietnam and South Vietnam.
2. Become familiar with the Vietnam policies of President Kennedy and Robert McNamara.
3. See how President Johnson changed the course of the war.

BELLRINGER

Warm-Up Activity Ask students to brainstorm words, phrases, and images that come to mind when they hear the word *Vietnam.*

Activating Prior Knowledge
Some students may have family members or family friends who had a connection to the Vietnam War. Ask those students who are aware of such a connection to describe what it is.

READING STRATEGY

Ask students to write the following column headings: *Background of the War, Kennedy's Vietnam Policy, Johnson Commits to Containment.* As students read the section, have them take notes in each column and reflect on the domestic and international effects of the conflict.

ACTIVITY
Connecting with History and Conflict

Ask each student to create a chart to illustrate the buildup of American forces in Vietnam, starting with the 675 military advisers provided before 1960. Have students continue to add to the chart to reflect the progress of the war. As they create the chart, have them contemplate the challenges of changing relationships among nations that caused the United States to enter the Vietnam conflict. **(Visual/Spatial)**

READING FOCUS

- What events led to the war between North Vietnam and South Vietnam?
- What were the Vietnam policies of President Kennedy and Robert McNamara?
- How did President Johnson change the course of the war?

MAIN IDEA

The United States entered the Vietnam War to defeat Communist forces threatening South Vietnam.

KEY TERMS

domino theory
Vietminh
Geneva Accords
Viet Cong
National Liberation Front
Gulf of Tonkin Resolution

TAKING NOTES

Copy the chart below. As you read, fill in some of the causes of the Vietnam War and its early effects on the United States.

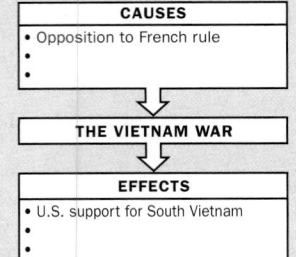

CAUSES
• Opposition to French rule
•
•

↓

THE VIETNAM WAR

↓

EFFECTS
• U.S. support for South Vietnam
•
•

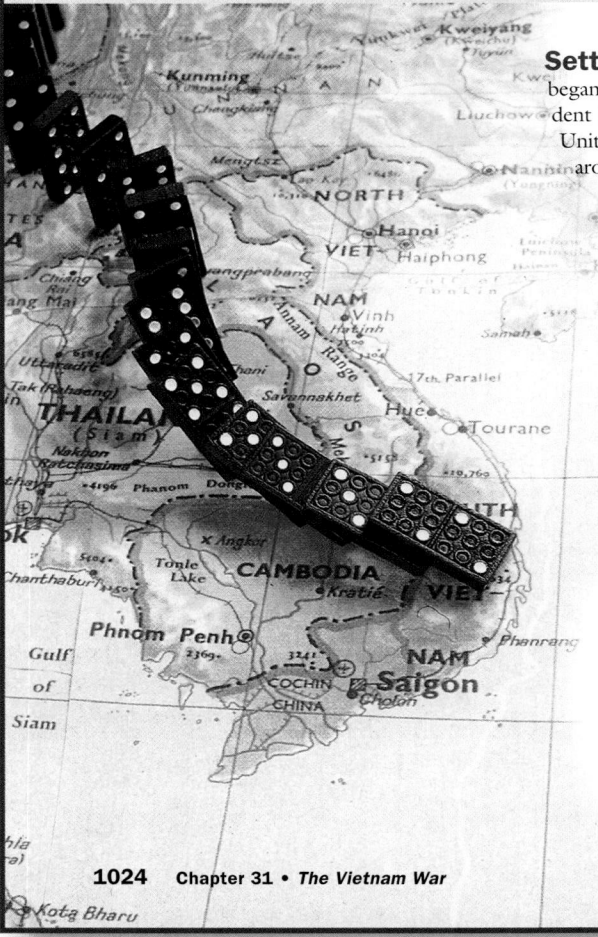

1024   Chapter 31 • *The Vietnam War*

Setting the Scene American involvement in Vietnam began during the early years of the Cold War. It was based on President Harry S Truman's policy of containment which called for the United States to resist Soviet attempts to spread communism around the world. At a news conference in 1954, President Dwight D. Eisenhower described the principle that became associated with American involvement in Southeast Asia:

> *You have a row of dominoes set up, you knock over the first one, and what will happen to the last one is the certainty that it will go over very quickly.*
> —Dwight D. Eisenhower

The **domino theory,** described above, refers to the fear that if one Southeast Asian nation fell to the Communists, the others would also fall. A Communist takeover of Vietnam, because of its geographic location, posed a threat to Cambodia, Laos, Burma, and Thailand.

Background of the War

Vietnam had a history of nationalism that extended back nearly 2,000 years. The Vietnamese spent much of that time resisting attempts by neighboring China to swallow their small country. In the 1800s, France established itself as a new colonial power in Vietnam, and the French met similar resistance from the Vietnamese.

Ho Chi Minh, who sympathized with Communist ideas, fought for independence before, during, and after World War II. He was head of the League for the Independence of Vietnam, commonly called the **Vietminh.**

RESOURCE DIRECTORY

Teaching Resources
Learning Styles Lesson Plans booklet, p. 64
Guided Reading and Review booklet, p. 124

Other Print Resources
Historical Outline Map Book *War in Southeast Asia*, p. 70

Technology
Section Reading Support Transparencies
Guided Reading Audiotapes (English/Spanish), Ch. 31
Student Edition on Audio CD, Ch. 31
Color Transparencies *Time Lines,* C8
Prentice Hall Presentation Pro CD-ROM, Ch. 31
Companion Web site, www.phschool.com

Ho Chi Minh aroused his people's feelings of nationalism against French control. The French opposed the Vietminh by forming the Republic of Vietnam, headed by the emperor Bao Dai. War between these opposing forces continued until May 1954, when the Vietminh defeated the French after a long siege at a fortress in Dien Bien Phu.

A Divided Vietnam In April 1954, an international conference met in Geneva, Switzerland. After the French defeat in Vietnam, representatives of Ho Chi Minh, Bao Dai, Cambodia, Laos, France, the United States, the Soviet Union, China, and Britain arranged a peace settlement. As a result of the **Geneva Accords,** Vietnam was divided into two separate nations in July 1954. Although the border between the two nations was often referred to as the 17th parallel, the demarcation line set in Geneva was actually a few miles south of the parallel.

Ho Chi Minh became president of the new Communist-dominated North Vietnam, with its capital in Hanoi. Ngo Dinh Diem, a former Vietnamese official who had been living in exile in the United States, became president of anti-Communist South Vietnam, with its capital in Saigon. The Geneva agreements called for elections to be held in 1956 to unify the country. South Vietnam refused to support this part of the agreement, claiming that the Communists would not hold fair elections. As a result, Vietnam remained divided.

United States Involvement After World War II, President Truman had pledged American aid to any nation threatened by Communists. Beginning in 1950, the United States provided economic aid to the French effort in Vietnam as a way of gaining French support for the policy of containment in Europe. After the French defeat, the United States began to support anti-Communist South Vietnam.

President Eisenhower pledged his support to South Vietnam's Diem. In 1960, Eisenhower provided about 675 United States military advisors to assist in South Vietnam's struggle against the North. Thus the United States became involved in the Vietnam War.

Kennedy's Vietnam Policy

When President John F. Kennedy took office in 1961, he was determined to prevent the spread of communism at all costs. This meant strengthening

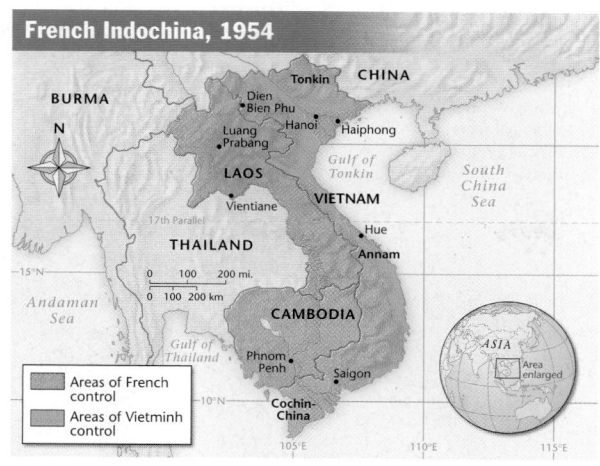

French Indochina, 1954

MAP SKILLS After World War II, France struggled to keep control of its colonies in Southeast Asia. The Vietminh was fighting for Vietnamese independence. **Regions** *In early 1954, where was the largest region of Vietminh (Ho Chi Minh's) control?*

"Personally, I find it a rather unrewarding job."

INTERPRETING POLITICAL CARTOONS This cartoon uses an open sedan chair, similar to a kind of personal transportation popular in Southeast Asia, to make a political point. **Drawing Inferences** *(a) Who are the two men "carrying" President Diem of South Vietnam? (b) What has brought Diem's progress to a halt? (c) Why is the man in front complaining? (d) Explain the point the cartoonist is making.*

Chapter 31 • Section 1 **1025**

LESSON PLAN

Focus Explain that in the 1960s, Presidents Kennedy and Johnson were determined to maintain South Vietnam under an anti-Communist government. Ask how the United States became involved in Vietnam. How did the American presence in Vietnam escalate?

Instruct Discuss Eisenhower's decision to support Diem and Kennedy's decision to increase United States support for the Diem regime. What other decisions might those Presidents have made? Ask students to list the most probable results of those other decisions. Could the nation accept those results today? Why would the results have been unacceptable in the late 1950s and early 1960s?

Assess/Reteach Ask students to state the original rationale for the involvement of the United States in the war in Vietnam. Can they describe ways in which this initial involvement could be linked to other world affairs, especially the Cold War?

CUSTOMIZE FOR ...

Less Proficient Readers

Have students reread the section "A Divided Vietnam." Then have students write down the following dates: April 1954, July 1954, and 1956. Have students list the event that took place during each of these dates, including what countries were involved.

CAPTION ANSWERS

Map Skills The Tonkin region.

Interpreting Political Cartoons President Kennedy and a Vietnamese peasant. The peasant has sat down. He finds supporting Diem "unrewarding." The cartoonist is saying that the United States cannot "carry" the Diem government if the Vietnamese people do not support it.

VIEWING HISTORY Buddhist monks protested Ngo Dinh Diem's government by burning themselves to death on the streets of Saigon. **Identifying Central Issues** *How does this photograph symbolize the difficult problems Johnson inherited in Vietnam?*

and protecting the government that the United States had helped create in South Vietnam.

Kennedy sent Vice President Lyndon Johnson to Vietnam to assess the situation there. Diem told Johnson that South Vietnam would need even more aid if it was to survive. In response, Kennedy increased the number of American military advisors to Vietnam. By the end of 1963, that number had grown to more than 16,000.

Military aid by itself could not ensure success. Diem lacked support in his own country. He imprisoned people who criticized his government and filled many government positions with members of his own family. United States aid earmarked for economic reforms went instead to the military and into the pockets of corrupt officials.

Diem's Downfall Diem launched an unpopular program which relocated peasants from their ancestral lands to "strategic hamlets." These government-run farming communities were intended to isolate the peasants from Communist influences seeping into South Vietnam.

In addition, Diem was a Catholic in a largely Buddhist country. When Diem insisted that Buddhists obey Catholic religious laws, serious opposition developed. In June 1963, a Buddhist monk burned himself to death on the streets of Saigon. Photographs showing his silent, grisly protest appeared on the front pages of newspapers around the world. Other monks followed the example, but their martyrdom did not budge Diem.

Kennedy finally realized that the struggle against communism in Vietnam could not be won under Diem's rule. United States officials told South Vietnamese military leaders that the United States would not object to Diem's overthrow. With that encouragement, military leaders staged a coup in November 1963. They seized control of the government and assassinated Diem as he tried to flee.

McNamara's Role One of the American officials who helped create the Kennedy administration's Vietnam policy was Robert McNamara, President Kennedy's Secretary of Defense. A Republican with a strong business background, McNamara became one of Kennedy's closest

BIOGRAPHY

Robert McNamara was born in San Francisco, California, and grew up across the bay in Oakland. He attended the University of California at Berkeley and went on to earn a graduate degree at Harvard Business School in 1939. McNamara served in the air force during World War II. After the war, he took a job at the Ford Motor Company. Through hard work and solid business decisions, McNamara moved quickly up the corporate ladder. He took over the presidency of Ford Motors in November 1960. This rising star caught the eye of President Kennedy, who offered him a position in his Cabinet just one month later.

Robert McNamara b. 1916

1026   Chapter 31 • *The Vietnam War*

advisors on Vietnam. Later he helped shape the policies that drew the United States deeper into the war.

As Secretary of Defense, McNamara applied his business knowledge, managing to cut costs while modernizing the armed forces. He turned the Pentagon's thinking away from reliance on the threat of nuclear bombs toward the development of a "flexible response" to military crises. He also began to focus his attention on how to handle the conflict in Vietnam.

Later, under Lyndon Johnson, McNamara pushed for direct American involvement in the war. In 1963, however, he still questioned whether a complete withdrawal was not the better alternative. Looking back on that period later, McNamara revealed his feelings:

> 66 I believed that we had done all the training we could. Whether the South Vietnamese were qualified or not to turn back the North Vietnamese, I was certain that if they weren't, it wasn't for lack of our training. More training wouldn't strengthen them; therefore we should get out. The President (Kennedy) agreed. 99
>
> —Robert McNamara

As you will read later in this chapter, the United States did not withdraw. It continued to back South Vietnam and the military leaders who took over the government.

Johnson Commits to Containment

Three weeks after Diem's assassination, President Kennedy himself fell to an assassin's bullet in Dallas, Texas. Lyndon Johnson assumed the presidency and faced an escalating crisis in Vietnam. Johnson believed strongly in the need for containment:

> 66 The Communists' desire to dominate the world is just like the lawyer's desire to be the ultimate judge on the Supreme Court. . . . You see, the Communists want to rule the world, and if we don't stand up to them, they will do it. And we'll be slaves. Now I'm not one of those folks seeing Communists under every bed. But I do know about the principles of power, and when one side is weak, the other steps in. 99
>
> —Lyndon Johnson

Communist Advances Diem's successors established a new military government in South Vietnam that proved to be both unsuccessful and unpopular. The ruling generals bickered among themselves and failed to direct the South Vietnamese army effectively. Communist guerrillas in the south, known as **Viet Cong,** and their political arm, called the **National Liberation Front,** gained control of more territory and earned the loyalty of an increasing number of the South Vietnamese people. Ho Chi Minh and the North Vietnamese aided the Viet Cong throughout the struggle.

Just after Johnson assumed office, he met with Henry Cabot Lodge, who was the United States ambassador to South Vietnam. Lodge told the new President that he faced some tough choices if he wanted to save Vietnam.

Focus on GOVERNMENT

The Powers of the President The United States Constitution divides military power between the executive and legislative branches. It makes the President commander in chief of the army and navy, but gives Congress the power to declare war and the power to raise an army and navy.

Throughout American history, Presidents have used their extensive authority as commander in chief to order military operations without a formal declaration of war. The Gulf of Tonkin Resolution, passed by Congress in 1964, was not a declaration of war, but it gave the President expanded powers to conduct the war in Vietnam.

The nation's anguish over the Vietnam War led Congress to pass the War Powers Act in 1973. The act places close limits on the President's war-making powers: If there is no declaration of war by Congress, it requires the President to

1. notify Congress within 48 hours of committing American troops to combat, and
2. end the combat within 60 days unless Congress authorizes a longer period.

In addition, the act gives Congress the power to end the combat at any time by passing a resolution to that effect.

READING CHECK
Describe the new military government in South Vietnam.

ACTIVITY
Connecting with Government

Refer students to the Constitution and have them identify and study the sections that specify the war-making powers of the President and the Congress. Then have students consider both the Gulf of Tonkin Resolution and the War Powers Act in light of constitutional provisions. Students should then write paragraphs arguing that either the Gulf of Tonkin Resolution or the War Powers Act is closer to the intentions of the Framers. (**Verbal/Linguistic**)

BACKGROUND
Interdisciplinary

The term "Viet Cong" comes from the Vietnamese term *Viet Nam Cong San,* which means "Vietnamese Communists." The term was first used by officials in Diem's regime—and perhaps originally by Diem himself—as a disparaging name for the Communists. The Communists themselves did not use or like the term. They called themselves such things as the People's Liberation Armed Forces or the National Front for the Liberation of Vietnam.

READING CHECK
Corrupt, incompetent, and unpopular.

CUSTOMIZE FOR ...
Gifted and Talented

Ask students to write one or two sentences describing the level of United States involvement in the Vietnam War under Presidents Eisenhower, Kennedy, and Johnson.

✓ TEST PREPARATION

Have students read the quote on this page by Lyndon Johnson and then answer the question below.

Who is Johnson referring to when he talks about the "weak" side?

A The Communists
Ⓑ Vietnam
C The United States
D China

Reading Comprehension

1. It demonstrated the fear on the part of the American government that if one Southeast Asian country fell to communism, others would follow; defying the U.S. policy of containment.

2. (a) The League for the Independence of Vietnam; (b) Communist guerrillas in the South; (c) the political wing of the Viet Cong.

3. Vietnam was divided into two separate nations. Unification and nation-wide elections set for 1956 were prevented by South Vietnam.

4. Diem's policies of relocating peasants and persecuting Buddhists made him unpopular in his own country. Kennedy realized that the struggle against communism could not be won under Diem's rule.

Critical Thinking and Writing

5. Students should include the fact that the resolution gave the President almost complete control over U.S. actions in Vietnam. This usurped the constitutional right of Congress to declare war.

6. Essays will vary but should be supported with facts from the section.

Answers will vary. Students should demonstrate knowledge of the early events of the Vietnam conflict.

GULF OF TONKIN RESOLUTION
Joint Resolution of Congress
H.J. RES 1145 • August 7, 1964
Public Law 88-408; 78 Stat. 384 • August 10, 1964

Resolved by the Senate and House of Representatives of the United States of America in Congress assembled,

That the Congress approves and supports the determination of the President, as Commander in Chief, to take all necessary measures to repel any armed attack against the forces of the United States and to prevent further aggression.

Section 2. The United States regards as vital to its national interest and to world peace the maintenance of international peace and security in southeast Asia. Consonant with the Constitution of the United States and the Charter of the United Nations and in accordance with its obligations under the Southeast Asia Collective Defense Treaty, the United States is, therefore, prepared, as the President determines, to take all necessary steps, including the use of armed force, to assist any member or protocol state of the Southeast Asia Collective Defense Treaty requesting assistance in defense of its freedom.

Section 3. This resolution shall expire when the President shall determine that the peace and security of the area is reasonably assured by international conditions created by action of the United Nations or otherwise, except that it may be terminated earlier by concurrent resolution of the Congress.

The Gulf of Tonkin Resolution tipped the balance of power between Congress (upper photo) and the White House (lower photo).

Johnson was determined to do whatever was needed to win the war. "I am not going to lose Vietnam," he said. Johnson recalled the Communist takeover of China in 1949. Referring to the fact that many Americans had blamed the "loss of China" on the Truman administration, Johnson went on: "I am not going to be the President who saw Southeast Asia go the way China went." Johnson did not want the Southeast Asian "dominoes" to be set in motion by the fall of Vietnam.

Expanding Presidential Power In August 1964, Johnson made a dramatic announcement: North Vietnamese torpedo boats had attacked United States destroyers in the international waters of the Gulf of Tonkin, 30 miles from North Vietnam. Those attacks would change the course of the war.

Details about the attacks were sketchy, and some people doubted that they had even taken place. In any case, Johnson used the Gulf of Tonkin incident to deepen American involvement in Vietnam. The President asked Congress for and obtained a resolution giving him authority to "take all necessary measures to repel any armed attack against the forces of the United States and to prevent further aggression."

Congress passed this **Gulf of Tonkin Resolution** on August 7 by a vote of 416 to 0 in the House of Representatives and 88 to 2 in the Senate. Johnson had been waiting for some time for an opportunity to propose the resolution, which, he noted, "covered everything." The President now had nearly complete control over what the United States did in Vietnam, even without an official declaration of war from Congress.

Section **1** Assessment

READING COMPREHENSION

1. How did the **domino theory** explain American involvement in Southeast Asia?

2. What were (a) the **Vietminh,** (b) the **Viet Cong,** and (c) the **National Liberation Front?**

3. What were the results of the **Geneva Accords?**

4. Why did American officials support the overthrow of Diem's government?

CRITICAL THINKING AND WRITING

5. **Drawing Conclusions** Write a paragraph explaining how the Gulf of Tonkin Resolution affected the balance of power between the President and Congress.

6. **Writing an Outline** Write an outline for an essay from the perspective of Robert McNamara in 1963 in which you present President Kennedy with two options—withdraw from Vietnam or fully support Diem.

Activity: Writing an Editorial
Research events and media coverage from the early years of the Vietnam conflict. Then write an editorial as if it were 1965, and you do not know the eventual outcome of the war. Use the links provided in the *America: Pathways to the Present* area of the following Web site for help in completing this activity.
www.phschool.com

1028 Chapter 31 • *The Vietnam War*

RESOURCE DIRECTORY

Teaching Resources
Units 9/10 booklet
• Section 1 Quiz, p. 37
Guide to the Essentials
• Section 1 Summary, p. 156

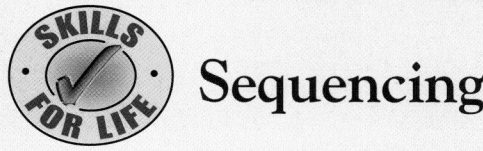

Sequencing

The order in which events occur is called sequence. When you are using several sources to gather information, each source may tell only part of the story. You will need to use sequencing to understand the order in which events took place. And when you are preparing your own report, presenting facts in sequence will help your audience understand your message.

These passages describe events in the 1950s and early 1960s that led to increased American involvement in Vietnam.

LEARN THE SKILL
Use the following steps to present information in sequence:

1. **Identify the order in which events happened.** Look for time-order words such as *later, earlier, now, then, finally, before,* and *after.* Also note any dates, including specific days, months, or parts of the year.

2. **Use visual aids to organize the information.** Make a list of events from all your sources, and the dates the events occurred. Then sort the events by date, and write them in a flowchart or a time line. Now you can add the events that don't have specific dates by inserting them according to clues given by time-order words.

3. **Explain how events are connected.** Present the information in your own words, using dates and time-order words to help your audience understand the sequence of events.

PRACTICE THE SKILL
Answer the following questions:

1. **(a)** Which years are identified in Source A, and what events occurred during those years? **(b)** Which years are identified in Source B, and what events occurred during those years? **(c)** Which time-order words in the sources help you understand the order of events?

2. **(a)** According to both sources, what events occurred in 1961? **(b)** What other event is described in both sources? **(c)** What information not given in Source A is provided by Source B?

3. Create a flowchart or a time line that shows all the events that are described in both sources. Include dates.

APPLY THE SKILL
See the Chapter Review and Assessment for another opportunity to apply this skill.

A

"When Kennedy took office in early 1961 he continued the policies of Truman and Eisenhower in Southeast Asia. . . .

One day in June 1963, a Buddhist monk sat down in the public square in Saigon and set himself afire. More Buddhist monks began committing suicide by fire to dramatize their opposition to the Diem regime. Diem's police raided the Buddhist pagodas and temples, wounded thirty monks, arrested 1,400 people, and closed down the pagodas. . . .

Earlier in 1963, Kennedy's Undersecretary of State, U. Alexis Johnson, was speaking before the Economic Club of Detroit: '. . . Why is [Southeast Asia] desirable, and why is it important? First, it provides a lush climate, fertile soil, rich natural resources, a relatively sparse population in most areas, and room to expand. . . .'

This is not the language that was used by President Kennedy in his explanations to the American public. He talked of Communism and freedom. In a news conference February 14, 1962 he said: 'Yes, as you know, the U.S. for more than a decade has been assisting the government, the people of Vietnam, to maintain their independence.'"

—Howard Zinn,
A People's History of the United States

B

"In 1961, Diem asked for more U.S. assistance, saying, 'The level of their [the Communists] attacks is already such that our forces are stretched to their utmost.'

Kennedy was willing to help, but he was wary of sending in combat troops. Instead, he took measures to enhance the fighting ability of the [South Vietnamese]. . . .

In late August [1963], disapproval of Diem intensified when he declared martial law in South Vietnam and ordered a military crackdown on Communist activists. Once again his troops also targeted Buddhists. . . .

Though the raids momentarily halted the Buddhist uprisings, they infuriated many South Vietnamese and millions of Americans. Kennedy, in response to mounting public outrage over the crackdown, temporarily halted all economic and military aid to South Vietnam on October 2, 1963."

—John M. Dunn,
The Vietnam War: A History of U.S. Involvement

Chapter 31 1029

SEQUENCING

Focus Students learn to construct a sequence of historical events by reviewing documents that describe different portions of the sequence.

Instruct As students sequence the statements in passage A, they may notice a discrepancy. The Undersecretary of State and the President appear to emphasize different approaches to selling the "benefits" of United States involvement in Vietnam. Kennedy speaks of fighting communism and helping the Vietnamese people stay free. The Undersecretary speaks about the benefits to America of exploiting the natural resources of Vietnam. Do students think that both points of view reflect American policies? What might be the importance of the fact that one statement was made a year later than the other? Why might it be significant that President Kennedy made his remarks at a press conference, while the Undersecretary spoke to a group of business leaders?

Extend See the Skills for Life activity in the Resource Directory below.

ANSWERS
PRACTICE THE SKILL

1. **(a)** Early 1961: Kennedy takes office; February 14, 1962: Kennedy talks about helping the people of Vietnam defend their freedom; 1963: Johnson speaks of the benefits of exploiting Vietnam's natural resources; June 1963: Buddhist monks self-immolate to protest the Diem regime and Diem cracks down. **(b)** 1961: Diem asks for more assistance; late August 1963: Diem declares martial law and a crackdown on Communists and Buddhists; October 2, 1963: Kennedy rescinds economic and military aid to South Vietnam. **(c)** A: early, earlier. B: late.

2. **(a)** Kennedy sends aid to South Vietnam. **(b)** Buddhist uprisings. **(c)** Diem's declaration of martial law; U.S. withdrawal of economic and military aid.

3. The flowchart or time line should include all the dates and events from **1. (a)** and **(b)**.

Section 2

Fighting the War

SECTION OBJECTIVES

1. Learn how battlefield conditions in Vietnam affected American soldiers.
2. Be able to describe the course of the war between 1965 and 1968.
3. List reasons why the Tet Offensive was a turning point in the war.

BELLRINGER

Warm-Up Activity Ask students to consider how they would define a "just" war. Is any war just? Does the way the war is waged, including the types of weapons and damage inflicted, determine whether or not it is just?

Activating Prior Knowledge Ask students if they are familiar with the phrases "My Lai massacre" and "the Tet Offensive." Can anyone describe what each of those phrases refers to?

READING STRATEGY

Read the section that summarizes the effects of the war on American soldiers and Vietnamese civilians. As you read, list the different ways in which the soldiers and the civilians suffered.

ACTIVITY
Connecting with History and Conflict

Write the word *morale* on the board, and challenge students to define it in the context of soldiers at war. Ask students what factors might have increased the morale of American troops in Vietnam, and what factors might have decreased it. Record salient responses on the board in the form of a web graphic organizer. Then have students assess the importance of morale in Vietnam, and in any armed conflict. How important is morale to achieving victory? **(Verbal/Linguistic)**

READING FOCUS

- How did battlefield conditions in Vietnam affect American soldiers?
- How would you describe the course of the war between 1965 and 1968?
- Why was the Tet Offensive a turning point in the war?

MAIN IDEA

The violence and brutality of the Vietnam War affected civilians as well as soldiers.

KEY TERMS

land mine
saturation bombing
fragmentation bombs
Agent Orange
napalm
escalation
Ho Chi Minh Trail
hawks
doves
Tet Offensive

TAKING NOTES

As you read, prepare an outline of this section. Use Roman numerals for the major headings of the section, capital letters for the subheadings, and numbers for the supporting details. The sample below will help you get started.

I. Battlefield Conditions
  A. One Soldier's Story
    1. _____
    2. _____
  B. The Ground War
    1. _____
    2. _____

Setting the Scene Nearly 3 million Americans served in the Vietnam War. These soldiers found themselves thousands of miles from home, fighting under conditions that were far different from those they had seen in films. Marine Corps officer James Webb served as rifle platoon and company commander in the An Hoa Basin near Da Nang:

> ❝ We moved through the boiling heat with 60 pounds of weapons and gear, causing a typical Marine to drop 20 percent of his body weight while in the bush. When we stopped we dug chest-deep fighting holes and slit trenches for toilets. We slept on the ground under makeshift poncho [tents]. . . . Sleep itself was fitful, never more than an hour or two at a stretch for months at a time as we mixed daytime patrolling with night-time ambushes, listening posts, foxhole duty, and radio watches. Ringworm, hookworm, malaria, and dysentery were common, as was trench foot when the monsoons came. ❞
>
> —James Webb

American soldiers encountered unfamiliar terrain and conditions when they landed in Vietnam.

RESOURCE DIRECTORY

Teaching Resources
Guided Reading and Review booklet, p. 125
Biography, Literature, and Comparing Primary Sources booklet (Literature) *Experiences of a Young Soldier in Vietnam,* p. 83

Technology
Section Reading Support Transparencies
Guided Reading Audiotapes (English/Spanish), Ch. 31
Student Edition on Audio CD, Ch. 31
Prentice Hall Presentation Pro CD-ROM, Ch. 31
Companion Web site, www.phschool.com

Battlefield Conditions

When Americans first started arriving in Vietnam in large numbers, they encountered all the frustrations of guerrilla warfare. American forces had superior arms and supplies. The Viet Cong, however, had some advantages of their own. For one thing, they were familiar with the swamps and jungles of Vietnam. In addition, they could find protection across the border in Cambodia and Laos. Finally, the Viet Cong could often count on the support of the local population.

American soldiers found the war confusing and disturbing. They were trying to defend the freedom of the South Vietnamese, but the people seemed indifferent to the Americans' effort. The dishonest and inept government in Saigon may have caused that indifference. "We are the unwilling working for the unqualified to do the unnecessary for the ungrateful," Kit Bowen of the First Infantry Division wrote to his father in Oregon.

American troops never knew what to expect next, and they never could be sure who was a friend and who was an enemy. The Vietnamese woman selling soft drinks by the roadside might be a Viet Cong ally, counting government soldiers as they passed. A child peddling candy might be concealing a live grenade.

In the face of this uncertain situation, one GI wrote home:

> ❝ The VC [Viet Cong] are getting much stronger, so I think this war is going to get worse before it gets better. . . . I try and take great pride in my unit and the men I work with. A lot of the men have been in a lot of trouble and have no education or money. But I feel honored to have them call me a friend. ❞
>
> —Letter home from an American soldier

One Soldier's Story Many American soldiers went to war enthusiastic about the job they were being asked to do for their country. Some, like Ron Kovic of Long Island, worried about the Communist threat. Kovic was afraid that Communists "were infiltrating our schools, trying to take over our classes and control our minds." After high school, he joined the marines to do his part to defend his country. He proudly served a tour in Vietnam and signed up for a second tour. This second tour of duty would take a terrible toll on Kovic's body and mind.

Ron Kovic confronted his fears by making an aggressive effort to be a good soldier. But the horrors of war came to haunt him after he accidentally killed a

READING CHECK
What were battlefield conditions like for American soldiers?

LESSON PLAN

Focus American soldiers were not prepared for the brutality of the fighting in Vietnam, and Americans at home were shocked by the violence they witnessed on their television screens. Ask why American forces had little success in Vietnam. How did the war affect Vietnamese civilians?

Instruct Ask students to explain how a guerrilla war differs from a conventional war. Discuss why the superior firepower of the American forces was not more successful against the Viet Cong. Ask students whether the Vietnam War meets the definition of "total war," one in which destruction of property and civilian life is carried out to persuade the enemy that continuing the conflict is not worth the cost.

Assess/Reteach Conditions in Vietnam were uncomfortable and often terrifying for American soldiers. Yet their equipment and technology were superior. The Viet Cong were skillful and wily adversaries, whose intimate knowledge of their surroundings far outweighed their lack of supplies and weapons. Have students compare and contrast the advantages and disadvantages of the two sides.

READING CHECK
Conditions were very difficult. American soldiers discovered that superior firepower had a sharply limited effect on an enemy that used guerrilla tactics and was often assisted by South Vietnamese civilians.

CUSTOMIZE FOR ...

Gifted and Talented

As students read this section, have them create two lists. In the first, they should name the strengths the United States brought to the war. In the second, they should list the factors that might have undercut those strengths in the actual war effort.

ACTIVITY
Student Portfolio

You may wish to have students add the following to their portfolios: Present the following quotation by an American army officer after the total destruction of the village of Ben Tre in January 1968: "It became necessary to destroy the town in order to save it." Then ask students to write a brief explanation of why those opposed to the war frequently quoted this statement. **(Verbal/Linguistic)**

BACKGROUND
Biography

By the early 1990s, Brigadier General Sherian Grace Cadoria, born in 1940 in Marksville, Louisiana, was the highest-ranking African American woman in the United States armed forces. She served in Vietnam from January 1967 to October 1969. She remembers her arrival: "I interviewed for a protocol job. When I got there, the colonel told me I couldn't do the job. He said, 'You can't travel, you can't carry luggage, it's too heavy. Women can't do this.' And I said, 'Nobody said I couldn't carry those hundred-pound bags of cotton when I was just a child.'"

American soldiers like this one endured extremely difficult battle-field conditions in Vietnam.

INTERPRETING DIAGRAMS
Some components of the Viet Cong tunnel system are shown below. **Drawing Conclusions** *How did these tunnels help the Viet Cong hold out against superior firepower?*

United States corporal. Later he shot at shadowy figures in a village hut, only to learn that his unit had killed and wounded innocent children.

The final blow for Ron Kovic came when a sniper's bullet entered his spine. As his spinal column was severed and he lost the feeling in his legs, all he could think of was "the worthlessness of dying right here in this place at this moment for nothing." Kovic survived the bullet wound but was paralyzed from the chest down. The injury caused him to feel, in his words, "like a big clumsy puppet with all his strings cut." Kovic later wrote about his experiences in the book *Born on the Fourth of July.*

The Ground War   The Viet Cong lacked the sophisticated equipment of the United States troops, so they avoided head-on clashes. Instead they used guerrilla warfare tactics, working in small groups to launch sneak attacks and practice sabotage. They often frustrated American search parties by hiding themselves in elaborate underground tunnels. Some of these were equipped with running water and electricity. The largest contained hospitals, stores, and weapons storage facilities.

The various booby traps set by the guerrilla fighters posed constant hazards to the Americans. A soldier might step into a punji trap—a camouflaged pit filled with razor-sharp stakes that were sometimes poisoned. The pressure of a footstep could set off a **land mine**—an explosive device planted in the ground. Many soldiers were wounded or killed by grenades, which were triggered by concealed trip wires. GIs could go weeks without making contact with the enemy—in fact, most never did—but there was always the possibility of sudden danger.

The war was also devastating for Vietnamese civilians. Because American soldiers were never sure who might be sympathetic to the Viet Cong, civilians

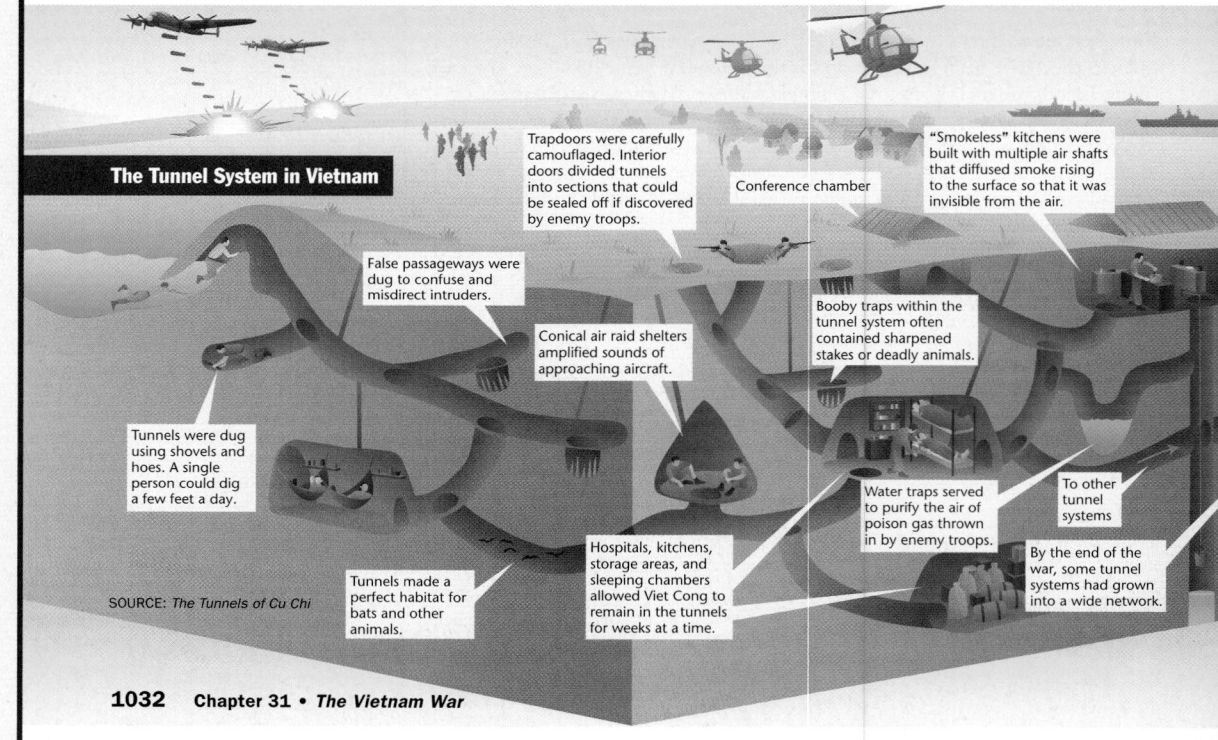

The Tunnel System in Vietnam

Trapdoors were carefully camouflaged. Interior doors divided tunnels into sections that could be sealed off if discovered by enemy troops.

Conference chamber

"Smokeless" kitchens were built with multiple air shafts that diffused smoke rising to the surface so that it was invisible from the air.

False passageways were dug to confuse and misdirect intruders.

Conical air raid shelters amplified sounds of approaching aircraft.

Booby traps within the tunnel system often contained sharpened stakes or deadly animals.

Tunnels were dug using shovels and hoes. A single person could dig a few feet a day.

Water traps served to purify the air of poison gas thrown in by enemy troops.

To other tunnel systems

Tunnels made a perfect habitat for bats and other animals.

Hospitals, kitchens, storage areas, and sleeping chambers allowed Viet Cong to remain in the tunnels for weeks at a time.

By the end of the war, some tunnel systems had grown into a wide network.

SOURCE: *The Tunnels of Cu Chi*

1032   Chapter 31 • *The Vietnam War*

CAPTION ANSWERS

Viewing History Answers will vary but may include fear, confusion, and frustration.

RESOURCE DIRECTORY
Teaching Resources
Biography, Literature, and Comparing Primary Sources booklet (Biography) *John McCain III,* p. 36
Learning with Documents booklet (Primary Source Activity) *An Army Nurse Remembers,* p. 36

Technology
Color Transparencies *Historical Maps,* A50

suffered as much as soldiers. As the struggle intensified, the destruction worsened. The war affected everyone in Vietnam. Le Thanh, a North Vietnamese, recalled the horrors he had witnessed as a child in the 1960s:

> 66 Nobody could get away from the war. It didn't matter if you were in the countryside or the city. While I was living in the country I saw terrible things. . . . I saw children who had been killed, pagodas and churches that had been destroyed, monks and priests dead in the ruins, schoolboys who were killed when schools were bombed. 99

—Le Thanh

The Air War In April 1966, the Americans introduced the huge B-52 bomber into the war to smash roads and heavy bridges in North Vietnam. During air raids, these planes could drop thousands of tons of explosives over large areas. This **saturation bombing** tore North Vietnam apart.

Many of the bombs used in these raids threw pieces of their thick metal casings in all directions when they exploded. These **fragmentation bombs** were not confined to the north alone. They were also used in the south, where they killed and maimed countless civilians. Near the village of My Thuy Phuong, the war suddenly intruded on the life of a peasant who later described the frightening incident:

> 66 One day I was walking back home from the ricefield, carrying tools on my shoulder. Then behind me I heard a large, loud noise. A very bad noise. I looked back and saw an American helicopter following me, shooting down the path toward me. I was very scared, so [I] jumped into the water by the side. Just one moment later, the bullets went right by. So scary. 99

—Vietnamese peasant

United States forces also used chemical weapons against the Vietnamese. Pilots dropped an herbicide known as **Agent Orange** on dense jungle landscapes. By killing the leaves and thick undergrowth, the herbicide exposed Viet Cong hiding places. Agent Orange also killed crops. Later it was discovered that Agent Orange caused health problems in livestock and in humans, including Vietnamese civilians and American soldiers.

Another destructive chemical used in Vietnam was called **napalm.** When dropped from airplanes, this jellylike substance splattered and burned uncontrollably. It also stuck to people's bodies and seared off their flesh.

The Course of the War, 1965–1968

After winning the election in 1964, President Johnson started a gradual military **escalation,** or expansion, of the war. Enemy gains in South Vietnam led Johnson to devote ever more American money and personnel to the conflict. Initially, United States soldiers had gone to Vietnam to advise the South Vietnamese. Now they took on the task of propping up the South Vietnamese government, which was led by military officer Nguyen Cao Ky.

VIEWING HISTORY In addition to killing and injuring many civilians, the war also forced many Vietnamese to flee their homes. **Recognizing Cause and Effect** *What impact do you think the war had on Vietnamese culture? Explain your answer.*

Focus on CULTURE

The Ballad of the Green Berets
For several weeks in 1966, the number one song in the United States was "The Ballad of the Green Berets." This song, written by Staff Sergeant Barry Sadler, popularized American patriotism and honored the United States Army Special Forces, known as the Green Berets:

*"Put silver wings on my son's chest
Make him one of America's best,
He'll be a man they'll test one day,
Have him win the Green Beret."*
—Barry Sadler, medic in Vietnam War

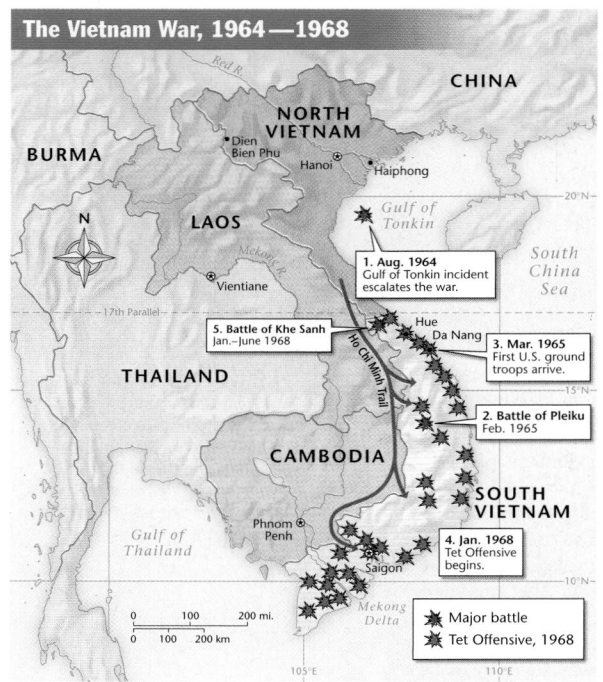

MAP SKILLS The Ho Chi Minh Trail, shown in the map above, was an important supply route for the Viet Cong and North Vietnamese troops. **Movement** (a) Why do you think the Ho Chi Minh Trail was located exactly where it was? (b) How did it contribute to the Tet Offensive?

Intensifying the War

By 1965, the Viet Cong were steadily expanding within South Vietnam. North Vietnamese troops and supplies poured into the south via the **Ho Chi Minh Trail**, a supply route that passed through Laos and Cambodia. In February, a Viet Cong attack at Pleiku within South Vietnam killed 8 Americans and wounded 126. President Johnson responded by authorizing the bombing of North Vietnam.

Two weeks after the Pleiku attack, General William Westmoreland, the commander of United States forces in Vietnam, requested more soldiers. He asked Johnson for two battalions of marines to protect the American airfield at Da Nang. Johnson heeded the request, beginning a rapid buildup of American combat troops. At the start of 1965, some 25,000 American soldiers were stationed in Vietnam. By the end of the year, the number had risen to 184,000.

Despite this large buildup of American troops, between 1965 and 1967 the war was at a stalemate. The American objective was not to conquer North Vietnam but rather to force the enemy to stop fighting. In 1965, President Johnson authorized Operation Rolling Thunder—the relentless bombing campaign that continued for almost three years. Although the bombing produced heavy damage, it failed to stop the Viet Cong. The enemy dug thousands of miles of tunnels through which troops and supplies moved south from North Vietnam.

United States forces launched search and destroy missions, but their victories failed to have a significant effect on the course of the war. Nothing seemed to diminish the enemy's willingness or ability to continue fighting. When the Viet Cong suffered heavy losses, North Vietnam sent new troops.

Hawks and Doves As the war unfolded, it came under increasing criticism at home from both **hawks**—those who supported the war—and **doves**—those who opposed the war. Senator J. William Fulbright, a Democrat and a leading dove, raised questions about the expansion of the war. As head of the Senate Foreign Relations Committee, Fulbright held televised hearings to examine U.S. policy in 1966.

At the hearings, Secretary of State Dean Rusk defended American involvement in Vietnam. George Kennan, who had helped draft U.S. foreign policy after World War II, opposed involvement in Vietnam. He argued that Vietnam was not strategically important to the United States and that Americans should not be called upon to solve the problems of that nation. Although both sides gave voice to their opinions, the war continued in Vietnam.

The Tet Offensive: A Turning Point

In 1967, Nguyen Van Thieu succeeded Ky as president of South Vietnam. Ky and Thieu were more effective leaders than Diem had been, but they remained

---

CAPTION ANSWERS

Map Skills (a) It allowed Viet Cong and North Vietnamese troops to travel in neighboring countries where they thought the United States would not attack them. (b) It allowed the North Vietnamese government to provide the Viet Cong with ammunition and other supplies for the Tet Offensive.

RESOURCE DIRECTORY

Technology
Sounds of an Era Audio CD *Walter Cronkite,* 1968 recording (time: one minute, 20 seconds)

authoritarian. Neither was able to put together an army that could successfully defend the country. The Americans brought with them advanced weaponry and new tactics that achieved some success. However, the American forces failed to drive out the Viet Cong, who were masters at jungle warfare. Month after month the fighting continued. United States planes bombed North Vietnam, and the flow of American soldiers into the south increased. Their number climbed to 385,000 by the end of 1966; to 485,000 by the end of 1967; and to 536,000 by the end of 1968. Despite the large United States presence in South Vietnam, the Communist forces intensified their efforts.

Those efforts reached a climax early in 1968, during Tet, the Vietnamese New Year. On January 30, the Viet Cong and North Vietnamese launched a major offensive. The **Tet Offensive,** shown on the map on the previous page, included surprise attacks on major cities and towns and American military bases throughout South Vietnam. In Saigon, the South Vietnamese capital, the Viet Cong attacked the American embassy and the presidential palace. Fierce fighting continued in Saigon for several weeks.

Communist Brutality   During the Tet Offensive, Communists were uncommonly brutal, slaughtering anyone they labeled an enemy, including minor officials, teachers, and doctors. While the Communists had control of Hue, they ordered all civil servants, military personnel, and those who had worked for the Americans to report to special locations. Of those who obeyed, some 3,000 to 5,000 were killed. Their bodies were found in mass graves after American and South Vietnamese forces retook the city.

Massacre at My Lai   Surrounded by brutality and under extreme distress, American soldiers also sometimes committed atrocities. Such brutality came into sharp focus at My Lai, a small village in South Vietnam. In response to word that My Lai was sheltering 250 members of the Viet Cong, a United States infantry company moved in to clear out the village in March 1968. Rather than enemy soldiers, the company found women, children, and old men. Lieutenant William L. Calley, Jr., was in charge. First he ordered, "Round everybody up." Then he gave the command for the prisoners to be killed. Private Paul Meadlo later described what happened to one group of Vietnamese:

66 We huddled them up. We made them squat down. . . . I poured about four clips [about 68 shots] into the group. . . . Well, we kept right on firing. . . . I still dream about it. . . . Some nights, I can't even sleep. I just lay there thinking about it. 99

—Private Paul Meadlo

Probably more than 400 Vietnamese died in the My Lai massacre. Even more would have perished without the heroic actions of a helicopter crew which stepped in to halt the slaughter. At great risk to himself and his crew, pilot Hugh Thompson landed the helicopter between the soldiers and the fleeing Vietnamese. He ordered his door gunner, 18-year-old Lawrence Colburn, to fire his machine gun at the American troops if they began shooting the villagers. Thompson got out, confronted the leader of the soldiers, and then arranged to evacuate the civilians. Thompson's crew chief, Glenn Andreotta, pulled a child from a ditch full of dead bodies.

The War in Vietnam Escalates	
Year	**Event**
1964	Gulf of Tonkin Resolution passes. Gradual military escalation begins.
1965	President Johnson responds to attacks against American troops by authorizing the bombing of North Vietnam and by rapidly increasing the number of American combat troops in South Vietnam.
1966–1967	The number of American soldiers in South Vietnam continues to increase.
1968	The Viet Cong and North Vietnamese launch the Tet Offensive.

INTERPRETING CHARTS
This chart shows several examples of the escalation of the Vietnam War beginning in 1964. **Determining Relevance** *How did the Gulf of Tonkin Resolution contribute to this escalation?*

 Sounds of an Era

Listen to television journalist Walter Cronkite's editorial about the Tet Offensive and other sounds from the Vietnam era.

Reading Comprehension

1. Land mines planted in the ground were intended to stop advancing soldiers, but could be set off by the footstep of anyone, soldier or civilian. The casings of fragmentation bombs flew in all directions after exploding, killing many.

2. Despite a buildup in American troops, the relentlessness of the Viet Cong kept the war at a stalemate; the U.S. goal was not to conquer North Vietnam, but to force North Vietnam and the Viet Cong to stop fighting.

3. Agent Orange: herbicide that killed leaves and thick undergrowth, exposing Viet Cong positions. Napalm: flammable jelly that splattered and burned uncontrollably, sticking to bodies and burning people to death. Both substances were dropped from aircraft.

4. A supply route from North Vietnam, passing through Laos and Cambodia, which allowed supplies and troops from the North for the Viet Cong to be moved into South Vietnam.

Critical Thinking and Writing

5. Answers should expand on the theme that the Viet Cong won a psychological victory, even though the Americans won a military victory.

6. Letters will vary but should be supported with facts from the section.

Take It to the NET

Answers will vary. Students should demonstrate knowledge of the difficult terrain and climate conditions in Vietnam and the chaotic nature of the fighting itself.

CAPTION ANSWERS

Interpreting Political Cartoons The cartoonist does not think Johnson will be reelected. In the cartoon, Johnson is about to be ground up by the convergence of the Vietnam War and the upcoming election.

Such breaches of the rules of military combat did not go unpunished. Pilot Thompson testified about Calley's conduct at My Lai. Although at first his testimony was covered up, eventually, in 1971, Lieutenant Calley began serving a sentence of life in prison with hard labor for his role in the massacre. Many Americans saw him as a scapegoat, however, and public outcry was such that President Nixon reduced his life sentence to 20 years. Calley was released on good behavior three years later. The heroics of the helicopter crew also did not go unnoticed. In 1998, the United States honored all three men with the Soldier's Medal, the highest award for bravery unrelated to fighting an enemy.

The Tet Offensive became a turning point in the war. Even though the Viet Cong were turned back with heavy losses, they had won a psychological victory. Secretary of State Dean Rusk commented on the American public's reaction to Tet:

INTERPRETING POLITICAL CARTOONS This British cartoon appeared in 1967. **Drawing Inferences** (a) What does the cartoonist think of President Johnson's chances for reelection? (b) How does the cartoon convey this opinion?

66 [E]ven though it was a considerable military set-back for the North Vietnamese and Vietcong out there on the ground, it was, in effect, a brilliant political victory for them here in the United States. I'm not sure I fully understand the reasons why that should have occurred, but it became very clear after the Tet offensive that many people at the grass roots, . . . finally came to the conclusion that if we could not tell them when this was going to end, and we couldn't in any good faith, that we might as well chuck it. 99

—Dean Rusk

The Tet Offensive demonstrated that the Viet Cong could launch a massive attack on targets throughout South Vietnam. Furthermore, as images of the fighting flooded American television, many people at home began to express reservations about American involvement in Vietnam. Many Americans were discouraged, believing that U.S. troops had not been allowed to win the war. In spite of the vocal antiwar protesters, a majority of Americans supported a policy tougher than the one pursued by the administration. President Johnson, caught in the middle, saw his popularity plunge.

Section 2 Assessment

READING COMPREHENSION

1. How did the use of **land mines** and **fragmentation bombs** make the war especially brutal for soldiers and civilians?

2. Why did the early military action result in a stalemate?

3. How were **Agent Orange** and **napalm** used during the war?

4. What was the **Ho Chi Minh Trail?**

CRITICAL THINKING AND WRITING

5. **Analyzing Information** Why was the Tet Offensive a turning point in the Vietnam War? Support your answer with examples.

6. **Writing a Letter to the Editor** Write a letter to the editor of a newspaper. The year is 1968. Write your letter from the point of view of a hawk in support of the war or a dove opposed to the war.

Take It to the NET

Activity: Creating a Diary Entry Investigate battlefield conditions during the Vietnam War. Use your research to write a diary entry from the viewpoint of an American soldier in Vietnam. Use the links provided in the *America: Pathways to the Present* area of the following Web site for help in completing this activity.
www.phschool.com

RESOURCE DIRECTORY

Teaching Resources
Units 9/10 booklet
• Section 2 Quiz, p. 38
Guide to the Essentials
• Section 2 Summary, p. 157

READING FOCUS

- What role did students play in the protest movements of the 1960s?
- Why did President Johnson decide not to seek reelection?
- How did the Vietnam War affect the election of 1968?

MAIN IDEA

The Vietnam War created deep divisions in the Democratic Party and in the nation as a whole.

KEY TERMS

generation gap
New Left
teach-in
conscientious objector
deferment
Middle America

TAKING NOTES

Copy the chart below. As you read, fill in each box with examples and events that reflected the growing divisions among the American people.

```
           Political Divisions
    ┌──────────┬──────────────┬──────────────┐
  Student       Johnson Decides   The Election
  Activism      Not to Run        of 1968
   •              •                •
   •              •                •
   •              •                •
```

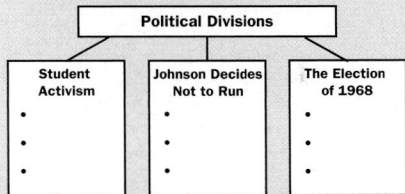

Political Divisions

SECTION OBJECTIVES

1. Find out about the role played by students in the protest movements of the 1960s.
2. Learn why President Johnson decided not to seek reelection.
3. Discover how the Vietnam War affected the election of 1968.

BELLRINGER

Warm-Up Activity Ask students whether the decade in which they are living seems to have a particular theme or identity. Ask them to suggest adjectives that might describe its general tone and compare these adjectives to descriptions of the 1960s and early 1970s.

Activating Prior Knowledge What do students today know about the activities and lifestyles of students of the early 1960s and 1970s? What type of music was popular then? What type of clothing?

READING STRATEGY

Have students write the main headings *Student Activism* and *Resistance to War* on a sheet of paper. As you read the section, write important details in the column under each heading.

ACTIVITY
Connecting with History and Conflict

Ask students to find illustrated books and magazines about the Vietnam War and to select one image that they think best represents the entire war. Students may present their chosen image to the class with a description and explanation of why they chose it. **(Visual/Spatial)**

Setting the Scene As the war in Vietnam unfolded, many loyal and patriotic Americans favored increasing the war effort in order to bring about military victory. Others believed that the war was morally wrong and urged immediate withdrawal of U.S. troops. Opposing viewpoints created deep divisions within the United States:

> ❝ A feeling is widely and strongly held that . . . we are trying to impose some U.S. image on distant peoples we cannot understand, and that we are carrying the thing to absurd lengths. Related to this feeling is the increased polarization that is taking place in the United States, with seeds of the worst split in our people in more than a century. ❞
>
> —John McNaughton, aide to Robert McNamara

Student Activism

In the early 1960s, members of the baby-boom generation began to graduate from high school. Postwar prosperity gave many of these students opportunities

Students were in the forefront of protests against the Vietnam War.

RESOURCE DIRECTORY

Teaching Resources
Learning Styles Lesson Plans booklet, p. 65
Guided Reading and Review booklet, p. 125
Learning with Documents booklet (Key Documents) *The Port Huron Statement,* p. 95

Technology
Section Reading Support Transparencies
Guided Reading Audiotapes (English/Spanish), Ch. 24
Student Edition on Audio CD, Ch. 24
Prentice Hall Presentation Pro CD-ROM, Ch. 24
Companion Web site, www.phschool.com

Focus Explain that during the 1960s, college campuses erupted in student protests. The most dramatic, and perhaps the most effective, protests were against the war in Vietnam. Ask why college students became activists.

Instruct Note that the Port Huron Statement on this page begins with a generational identification: "We are people of this generation." Ask students why they think Hayden began the statement with those words. Discuss how the civil rights movement strengthened students' belief in their ability to bring about change. Ask why student activists, trained in the civil rights movement, worked to change their schools and to stop the Vietnam War. Also, ask why some SDS members transformed themselves into the weathermen, a group that engaged in violence and terrorism.

Assess/Reteach Ask students to discuss their opinion concerning a national army draft. Are they in favor of a draft or opposed to it? Under what circumstances do they think individuals should be exempted from the draft? Are they in favor of the types of deferments and exemptions that were available during the Vietnam War?

BACKGROUND
Military Service

In percentage terms, there were very few conscientious objectors during the Vietnam era. By 1970, a total of about 22,000 men had been approved as conscientious objectors. This number represents about one tenth of one percent of the total number of men who had been registered for military service. Interestingly, a higher percentage of men were classified as conscientious objectors during World War II (about one third of one percent), which enjoyed much wider support. This highlights the fact that conscientious objectors, as a rule, choose this course of action because of their beliefs about war in general, and not based on a value judgment about any particular conflict.

Focus on CITIZENSHIP

Twenty-sixth Amendment Before 1971, nearly all states required voters to be at least 21 years old. (Georgia had allowed 18-year-olds to vote since 1943.) A movement to lower the voting age to 18 nationwide sparked controversy in the 1960s.

Opponents of the effort to lower the voting age pointed to radical student activists and asked, "Do you want people like that to take part in a national election?" Those who favored a lower voting age argued that if 18-year-olds were old enough to fight for their country in Vietnam, they were old enough to vote.

The Twenty-sixth Amendment, ratified in 1971, states: "The right of citizens of the United States, who are eighteen years of age or older, to vote shall not be abridged by any state on account of age."

---

unknown to previous generations. Instead of going directly into the working world after high school, many young men and women could afford to continue their education. College enrollments swelled with more students than ever before.

Change was in the air. It had been building for a while, even through the conformist years of the 1950s. The popular culture of that decade, including rock-and-roll music and rebellious youths on the movie screen, indicated that many young Americans were not satisfied with the values of their parents. The early 1960s saw a widening of this **generation gap.**

Students for a Democratic Society The civil rights movement, discussed in an earlier chapter, also became a steppingstone to other movements for change. Civil rights activists were among those who helped organize Students for a Democratic Society (SDS) in 1960. The organization's declaration of principles and goals, called the Port Huron Statement, appeared in 1962. Written largely by Tom Hayden, a student at the University of Michigan, the statement explained some of the feelings behind a student movement that was gaining strength in the United States:

> 66 *We are people of this generation, bred in at least modest comfort, housed now in universities, looking uncomfortably at the world we inherit. When we were kids the United States was the wealthiest and strongest country in the world. . . . As we grew, however, our comfort was penetrated by events too troubling to dismiss. . . . We would replace power rooted in possession, privilege, or circumstance by power and uniqueness rooted in love, reflectiveness, reason, and creativity. As a social system we seek the establishment of a democracy of individual participation.* 99
>
> —Port Huron Statement

SDS was a tiny organization at the start. Still, it had a major influence on the development of a new political movement that came to be called the **New Left.** Members of the New Left believed that problems such as poverty and racism called for radical changes.

The Free Speech Movement Student activism led to confrontation at the University of California at Berkeley in September 1964. Students became angry when the university administration refused to allow them to distribute civil rights leaflets outside the main gate of the campus.

The students, who had fought for equal rights in the South, argued that their right to free speech was being challenged. They resisted the university's effort to restrict their political activity. When police came to arrest one of their leaders, students surrounded the police car and prevented it from moving. The free speech movement was underway.

The university administration tried to find a compromise, but then its governing board stepped in. The board had the final word over university policy. It decided to hold student leaders responsible for their actions and filed charges against some of them.

On December 2, 1964, thousands of irate students took over the university administration building. That night police moved in. They arrested more than 700 students. Other students, supported by some faculty members, went on strike. They stopped attending classes to show their support for the free speech demonstrators.

Berkeley remained the most radical campus, but student activism spread to other colleges and universities across the United States. In the spring of 1965, activists at several schools launched protests against regulations they thought curbed their freedom. Students at Michigan State University and elsewhere challenged social restrictions, such as the hours when women and men could visit each other's dormitories. Students also sought greater involvement in college policy-making. Others left their campuses to work in campaigns to improve conditions in the inner cities.

The Teach-in Movement Students were among the first to protest the Vietnam War. Some opposed what they regarded as American imperialism. Others viewed the conflict as a civil war that should be resolved by the Vietnamese alone.

As escalation began, antiwar activists used new methods to protest the war. The first **teach-in** took place at the University of Michigan in March 1965 when a group of faculty members decided to make a public statement against the war. Some 50 or 60 professors taught a special night session in which issues concerning the war could be aired.

To their surprise, several thousand people showed up and made the evening a monumental success. Soon other teach-ins followed at colleges around the country. Supporters as well as opponents of the war appeared at the early teach-ins, but soon antiwar voices dominated the sessions.

Draft Resistance A Selective Service Act allowing the government to draft men between the ages of 18 and 26 had been in place since 1951. Relatively few people refused to be drafted in the first half of the 1960s. Most who did were **conscientious objectors** who opposed fighting in the war on moral or religious grounds.

Draft Registration

Since the Civil War, the United States has used a draft in wartime to meet its military needs. During the Vietnam War, about 1.8 million men were drafted between 1964 and 1973. Because college students could receive draft deferments, a large proportion of draftees were young men from minority communities who were too poor to afford college. Reacting to complaints about the system, Congress eliminated the deferment in 1971.

Another effort to make the draft more evenhanded was the lottery system instituted in 1969. This random drawing determined how likely a young man was to be called for military service. Despite these changes, opposition to the draft continued. Some young men burned their draft cards in protest. Thousands even left the country to avoid the draft. In 1973, Congress ended the draft, and the United States converted to an all-volunteer military force.

Today male citizens ages 18 through 25 are required by law to register with the Selective Service System. In a national crisis, if the country needs more soldiers than an all-volunteer service can provide, the draft can be resumed.

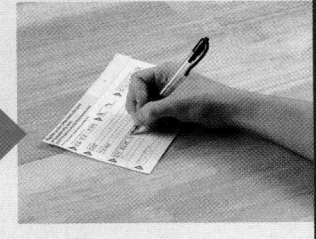

? Why do you think the government requires draft registration?

From the Archives of
AmericanHeritage®

Dr. King Decries the War

April 1967 brought proclamations, draft-card burnings, and mass demonstrations against the United States' continuing grim entanglement in Vietnam. In New York City's Riverside Church on April 4, the Reverend Dr. Martin Luther King, Jr., encouraged conscientious objection to the draft on a nation-wide scale, called the U.S. government the "greatest purveyor of violence in the world today," and offered a five-point plan for a peaceful American withdrawal. It was Dr. King's strongest statement yet on the war, in which "twice as many Negroes as whites" were serving (this view has been challenged in recent years). "If America's soul becomes totally poisoned," he warned, "part of the autopsy must read Vietnam." Source: Nathan Ward, "The Time Machine." *American Heritage®* magazine, April 1992.

CAPTION ANSWERS

Fast Forward to Today To enhance military preparedness.

Have students write journal entries in which they express their thoughts and feelings about the student protesters of the late 1960s. Journal entries might address such questions as: Are the protesters admirable figures? Were the protesters "anti-American"? Were their methods appropriate or inappropriate? **(Verbal/Linguistic)**

BACKGROUND
Global Connections

Immediately after the Tet Offensive, polls showed that most Americans had come to oppose America's involvement in Vietnam. Most historians view this as the turning point in the war. One wrote, "it hardly mattered whether [the North Vietnamese] won their battles . . . or lost . . . . The point was that by engaging the Americans in fierce combat—even accepting loss ratios of as much as ten-to-one [i.e., ten of their soldiers injured or killed for every one American soldier injured or killed], which was an inevitable consequence of the vastly superior American firepower—the North Vietnamese could exact the steady and large toll of American casualties that would destroy the American public's will to continue. It worked precisely as Hanoi had calculated . . . . After Tet, the Americans stopped looking for a fight and started looking for a way out . . . ."

In July 1965, President Johnson doubled the number of men who could be drafted into the armed forces. By the end of the year he had doubled the number again. These actions led to the rise of a draft-resistance movement that urged young men not to cooperate with their local draft boards.

As more and more young men were called into service and sent to fight in Vietnam, Americans began to question the morality and fairness of the draft. College students could receive a **deferment**, or official postponement of their call to serve. Usually this meant they would not have to go to war. Those who could not afford college did not have this avenue open to them. In 1966, the Selective Service System announced that college students who ranked low academically could be drafted.

In 1967, resistance to the military draft began to sweep the country. Many young men tried to avoid the draft by claiming that they had physical disabilities. Others applied for conscientious-objector status. Still others left the country. By the end of the war an estimated 100,000 draft resisters were believed to have gone to countries such as Canada.

Continued Protests In the first six months of 1968, more than 200 major demonstrations erupted at colleges and universities around the country. One of the most dramatic incidents took place in April of 1968 at Columbia University in New York City. Students there linked the issues of civil rights and the war. An SDS chapter sought to get the university to cut its ties with a research institute that did work for the military. At the same time, an African American student organization tried to halt construction of a gymnasium that would encroach upon a nearby minority neighborhood in Harlem.

Together these two groups took over the president's office. Finally the president of Columbia called the police, and hundreds of students were arrested. A student sympathy strike followed, and the university closed early that spring.

Johnson Decides Not to Run

Continuing protests and a growing list of American casualties had steadily increased public opposition to Johnson's handling of the war. By 1967, Secretary of Defense Robert McNamara had lost faith in the war effort. Privately, he urged the President to turn more of the fighting over to the South Vietnamese and to stop the bombing of North Vietnam. Johnson, fearful of risking defeat on the battlefield, ignored the proposal.

As a result of the Tet Offensive, polls showed for the first time that a majority of Americans opposed the war. Television news coverage of Tet increased the impact that the attack had on the public. Millions watched as news anchor Walter Cronkite, known for his objectivity and trustworthiness, said in February of 1968, "It now seems more certain than ever that the bloody experience in Vietnam is to end in stalemate." President Johnson

VIEWING HISTORY New York City Transportation Union members demonstrate in favor of the Vietnam War in 1967. **Drawing Inferences** *Why do you think those in favor of the war felt it necessary to hold demonstrations like this one?*

1040   Chapter 31 • *The Vietnam War*

heard Cronkite's assessment of the war and reacted with dismay. Reportedly he said, "If I've lost Cronkite, I've lost Middle America."

After the Tet Offensive, Johnson rarely left the White House for fear of being assaulted by angry crowds of protesters. He said he felt like "a jackrabbit in a hailstorm, hunkering up and taking it." In early 1968, Johnson watched the campaign of antiwar candidate Eugene McCarthy gain momentum. On March 12, McCarthy almost beat the President in the New Hampshire Democratic primary.

Four days later, another critic of the war, Robert Kennedy, joined the race for the Democratic nomination. Kennedy, the younger brother of President John Kennedy and a senator from New York, had been speaking out against the war in Congress. In March 1967, a year before he announced his candidacy, Kennedy had said this in a speech in the Senate:

> 66 All we say and all we do must be informed by our awareness that this horror is partly our responsibility; not just a nation's responsibility but yours and mine. It is we who live in abundance and send our young men out to die. It is our chemicals that scorch the children and our bombs that level the villages. We are all participants. To know this and feel the burden of this responsibility is not to ignore important interests, not to forget that freedom and security must, at times, be paid for in blood. Still, even though we must know as a nation what it is necessary to do, we must also feel as men the anguish of what we are doing. 99
>
> —Robert Kennedy

Now Kennedy was running against Johnson for the Democratic nomination for President.

On March 31, 1968, President Johnson declared dramatically in a nationally televised speech that he would not run for another term as President:

> 66 I do not believe that I should devote an hour or a day of my time to any personal partisan causes or to any duties other than the awesome duties of this office—the presidency of your country. Accordingly, I shall not seek, and I will not accept, the nomination of my party for another term. 99
>
> —Lyndon Johnson

The Election of 1968

Even before Johnson's announcement, the same issues that were dividing the American public had led to a split in the Democratic Party.

The Democratic Convention Delegates to the Democratic convention met in Chicago that summer to nominate candidates for President and Vice President. By the time the Democrats convened, their party was in shreds. Robert Kennedy had been assassinated in June, and party regulars thought McCarthy was too far out of the mainstream. Instead they supported Vice President Hubert Humphrey, longtime advocate of social justice and civil rights. Humphrey, however, was hurt by his defense of Johnson's policies on Vietnam. In the face of growing antiwar protest, he hardly seemed the one to bring the party together.

VIEWING HISTORY Robert Kennedy announced his candidacy in March 1968. Here, he is campaigning in Nebraska. **Determining Relevance** How much do you think Robert Kennedy's entrance into the race affected Johnson's decision not to seek reelection? Explain your answer.

VIEWING HISTORY As the Democrats gathered in Chicago for their 1968 convention, antiwar protesters gathered too. Chicago police (under the direction of Democratic Mayor Richard Daley) and National Guardsmen used nightsticks, tear gas, and rifles against the demonstrators and others caught up in the protests. **Determining Relevance** *How do you think television broadcasts of scenes like the one at right affected the election? Explain.*

The climax came when the convention delegates voted down a peace resolution and seemed ready to nominate Humphrey for President. As thousands of protesters gathered for a rally near the convention hotel, the police moved in, using their nightsticks to club anyone on the street, including bystanders, hotel guests, and reporters. Historian Theodore H. White vividly recorded the scene that took place in Chicago during the Democratic convention in August 1968:

> 66 *Slam! Like a fist jolting, like a piston exploding from its chamber, comes a hurtling column of police . . . into the intersection, and all things happen too fast: first the charge as the police wedge cleaves through the mob; then screams, whistles, confusion. . . . And as the scene clears, there are little knots in the open clearing—police clubbing youngsters, police dragging youngsters, police rushing them by the elbows, their heels dragging, to patrol wagons. . . .* 99
>
> —Theodore H. White

Much of the violence took place in front of television cameras, while crowds chanted "The whole world is watching." As the convention delegates voted, Senator Abraham Ribicoff of Connecticut denounced the "Gestapo tactics on the streets of Chicago," provoking an angry scene with Chicago mayor Daley. In the end, Humphrey was nominated, but the Democratic Party had been further torn apart.

READING CHECK

Describe what happened at the Democratic National Convention.

The Republicans and the Nation Choose Nixon The Republicans had already held their convention in early August. They had chosen Richard M. Nixon, who had narrowly lost the presidential election of 1960 to John Kennedy. During his campaign, Nixon backed law and order and boasted of a secret plan to end the war in Vietnam.

Nixon was determined to stay "above the fray" and act presidential during the campaign. Therefore he let his running mate, Governor Spiro Agnew of Maryland, make harsh accusations, such as calling Humphrey "squishy soft" on communism. With a well-run and well-financed campaign, Nixon quickly took the lead in public-opinion polls.

Adding to the Democrats' problems was a third-party candidate for President. Alabama governor George C. Wallace, who had been a lifelong Democrat, had gained national fame for playing on racial tensions among southerners. In 1968, representing the American Independent Party, he appealed to blue-collar voters in the North who resented campus radicals and antiwar activists. Wallace won support by attacking those he called "left-wing theoreticians, briefcase-totin' bureaucrats, ivory-tower guideline writers, bearded anarchists, smart-aleck editorial writers, and pointy-headed professors."

Late in the campaign, Humphrey began to catch up to Nixon in the public-opinion polls. But even though President Johnson stopped the bombing of North Vietnam on October 31, it was too late. Many disillusioned Democrats stayed home on election day, voting for no one.

The election, held on November 5, was close. Nixon won 43.4 percent of the popular vote—less than one percentage point more than Humphrey's 42.7 percent. Even so, Nixon gained 302 electoral votes to 191 for Humphrey and 45 for Wallace. Although Democrats kept control of both houses of Congress, the Republicans had regained the White House.

The war significantly influenced the election of 1968. Nixon's win marked the start of a Republican hold on the presidency that would last, with one interruption, for more than 20 years. This political shift reflected how unsettling the 1960s had become for mainstream Americans, a group sometimes called **Middle America.** In an era of chaos and confrontation, Middle America turned to the Republican Party for stability.

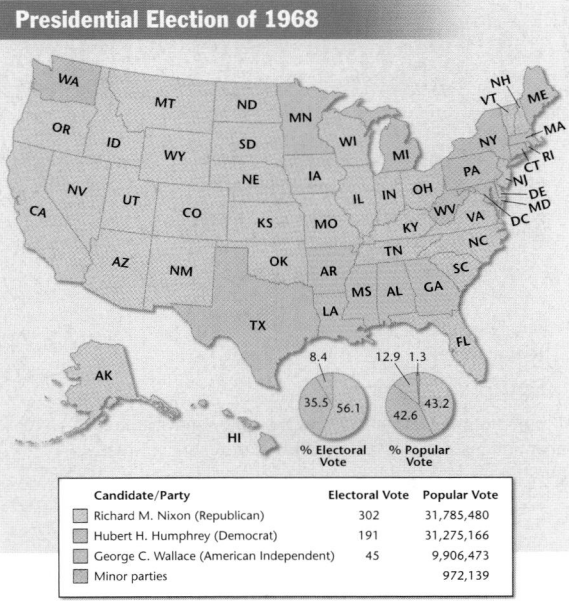

Presidential Election of 1968

Candidate/Party	Electoral Vote	Popular Vote
Richard M. Nixon (Republican)	302	31,785,480
Hubert H. Humphrey (Democrat)	191	31,275,166
George C. Wallace (American Independent)	45	9,906,473
Minor parties		972,139

MAP SKILLS This map shows the results of the election of 1968. **Regions** *(a) Where did Humphrey draw most of his support? (b) Where was Wallace's support? (c) What do you think might have happened if Wallace had given up his candidacy and returned to the Democratic Party?*

Section 3 Assessment

READING COMPREHENSION

1. What was the **generation gap?**
2. Who participated in **teach-ins?**
3. What is a **conscientious objector?**
4. Why did some Americans oppose the practice of **deferment?**
5. Describe the group sometimes referred to as **Middle America.**

CRITICAL THINKING AND WRITING

6. **Making Comparisons** Write a brief summary comparing the different viewpoints that Americans held regarding the Vietnam War.

7. **Writing a List** List several reasons why students played a major role in the protest movements of the 1960s.

Take It to the NET

Activity: Analyzing Primary Sources Select a primary source associated with student activism. Prepare a brief analysis of this source, including point of view, bias, and audience. Use the links provided in the *America: Pathways to the Present* area of the following Web site for help in completing this activity.
www.phschool.com

Chapter 31 • Section 3   1043

Section 3 Assessment

Reading Comprehension

1. Many young Americans rejected the conservative values of their parents.

2. Professors and students; at first both supporters and opponents of the war attended, but soon antiwar voices prevailed.

3. People who opposed fighting in wars on moral and religious grounds.

4. They felt it was unfair to excuse college students from the draft, but not those who could not afford to go to college. The latter group included many members of minority groups. Thus, deferments were seen as discriminatory.

5. Mainstream Americans who turned to the Republican Party for stability during the 1960s.

Critical Thinking and Writing

6. Answers will vary but should be supported with facts from the section.

7. Lists will vary but may include: discontent with current society; the draft impacted them directly; and a desire to end the war.

Take It to the NET

Answers will vary. Students should prepare a clear, detailed analysis of the student activism primary source.

CAPTION ANSWERS

Map Skills (a) The Northeast. (b) The South. (c) Answers will vary, but students should note that much of Wallace's support was from traditional Democrats and might have gone to Humphrey, thus making the election much closer.

Section 4

The End of the War

The End of the War

SECTION OBJECTIVES

1. Learn how President Nixon's policies led to American withdrawal from Vietnam.
2. Discover why President Nixon campaigned promising to restore law and order.
3. See what happened in Vietnam after the withdrawal of American forces.
4. Determine the legacy of the Vietnam War.

BELLRINGER

Warm-Up Activity Ask students whether it is possible for a United States President to continue a course of action strongly opposed by most of the American people. In what ways can the people make their opinions known to the President?

Activating Prior Knowledge Do your students think Lyndon Johnson would have been reelected if he had not withdrawn in 1968? Do they think Robert Kennedy would have become President if he had not been assassinated? How would either of these outcomes have affected the war in Vietnam?

READING STRATEGY

Have students skim the section, reading headings and the first sentence of each paragraph. Then have them list the main headings on a sheet of paper. Under each heading, have them write a sentence or phrase predicting the content of that part of the section. When students have finished reading, have them compare their predictions with the actual content.

READING FOCUS
- How did President Nixon's policies lead to American withdrawal from Vietnam?
- Why did President Nixon campaign promising to restore law and order?
- What happened in Vietnam after the withdrawal of American forces?
- What was the legacy of the Vietnam War?

MAIN IDEA

The end of the Vietnam War involved slow-moving peace negotiations, the gradual withdrawal of American troops, and the fall of South Vietnam.

KEY TERMS

Paris peace talks
Vietnamization
silent majority
POW
MIA

TAKING NOTES

As you read, complete a time line of events leading up to the end of war in Vietnam.

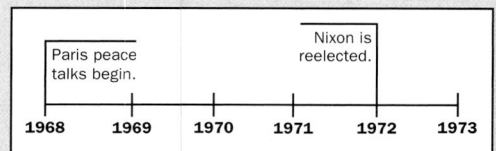

Paris peace talks begin.

Nixon is reelected.

1968   1969   1970   1971   1972   1973

Setting the Scene A year after his election, President Nixon was still seeking—and receiving—the support of Middle America. But he was also well aware of increasing opposition to the Vietnam War. On November 3, 1969, Nixon gave a speech about Vietnam. Sometimes called the "silent majority speech" because of the President's appeal to those he felt quietly supported his policies, the address reviewed the history of America's participation in the Vietnam conflict. Nixon noted that under his administration, "United States casualties have declined" and that "we are finally bringing American men home." He also acknowledged, however, that the war was far from over, and posed the question, "[W]hat is the best way to end it?"

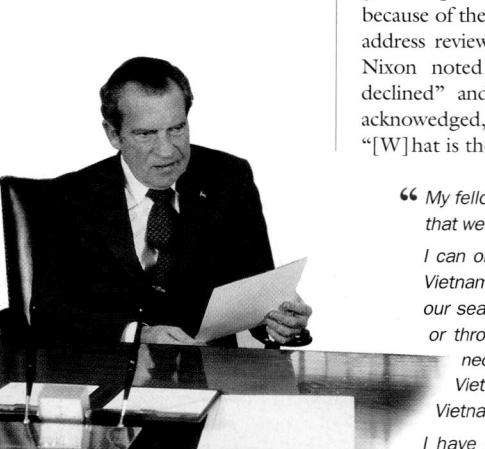

President Richard Nixon in the White House

> 66 My fellow Americans, I am sure you can recognize from what I have said that we really only have two choices open to us if we want to end this war.
>
> I can order an immediate, precipitate withdrawal of all Americans from Vietnam without regard to the effects of that action. Or we can persist in our search for a just peace through a negotiated settlement if possible, or through continued implementation of our plan for Vietnamization if necessary, a plan in which we will withdraw all of our forces from Vietnam on a schedule in accordance with our program, as the South Vietnamese become strong enough to defend their own freedom.
>
> I have chosen this second course. It is not the easy way. It is the right way. . . .
>
> And so tonight—to you, the great silent majority of my fellow Americans—I ask for your support. 99
>
> —Richard Nixon

Nixon's Vietnam Policy

As President Johnson's term drew to a close, he cut back on the bombing of North Vietnam and called for peace negotiations. The **Paris peace talks** began

1044   Chapter 31 • *The Vietnam War*

RESOURCE DIRECTORY

Teaching Resources
Guided Reading and Review booklet, p. 127

Technology
Section Reading Support Transparencies
Guided Reading Audiotapes (English/Spanish), Ch. 31
Student Edition on Audio CD, Ch. 31
Color Transparencies *Historical Maps,* A51
Prentice Hall Presentation Pro CD-ROM, Ch. 31
Companion Web site, www.phschool.com

in May 1968, but failed to produce an agreement. Richard Nixon's claim that he had a secret plan to end the war in Vietnam helped him win the presidency in November.

Withdrawing Troops In June 1969, President Nixon announced a new policy known as **Vietnamization.** This involved removing American forces and replacing them with South Vietnamese soldiers. By 1972, American troop strength dropped to 24,000. As much as Nixon wanted to defuse antiwar sentiment at home, he was determined not to lose the war. Therefore, as he withdrew American troops, he ordered secret bombing raids on the major targets shown on the map at right.

The War Spreads to Cambodia President Nixon also widened the war beyond the borders of Vietnam. In April 1970, Nixon publicly announced that United States and South Vietnamese ground forces were moving into neighboring Cambodia. Their goal was to clear out Communist camps there, from which the enemy was mounting attacks on South Vietnam. The United States, he asserted, would not stand by like "a pitiful helpless giant" while the Viet Cong attacked from Cambodia:

> ❝ We take this action not for the purpose of expanding the war into Cambodia but for the purpose of ending the war in Vietnam and winning the just peace we all desire. We have made and we will continue to make every possible effort to end this war through negotiation at the conference table rather than through more fighting on the battlefield. ❞
> —Richard Nixon

Nixon knew that the invasion of Cambodia would not win the war, but he thought it would help at the bargaining table. He was willing to intensify the war in order to strengthen the American position at the peace talks. Nixon's actions, however, brought chaos and civil war in Cambodia and a fresh wave of protests at home.

Nixon Calls for Law and Order

One of Nixon's campaign pledges had been to restore law and order in the country. This need seemed particularly apparent to Americans in October 1969 when one SDS faction turned to violence. This group called their organization the Weathermen, after a line in a Bob Dylan song—"You don't need a weatherman to know which way the wind blows." They were determined to bring about a revolution immediately. In October, the group converged on Chicago. Dressed in hard hats, boots, and work gloves, members of the Weathermen rampaged through the streets wielding pipes, clubs, rocks, and chains. They tangled with police (as they had planned), regrouped, and came back for still another confrontation. This kind of violence alarmed Americans and turned some against the antiwar movement.

The Silent Majority President Nixon recognized that student radicals, antiwar protesters, and the counterculture in general had never appealed to many Americans. Despite widespread discontent on college

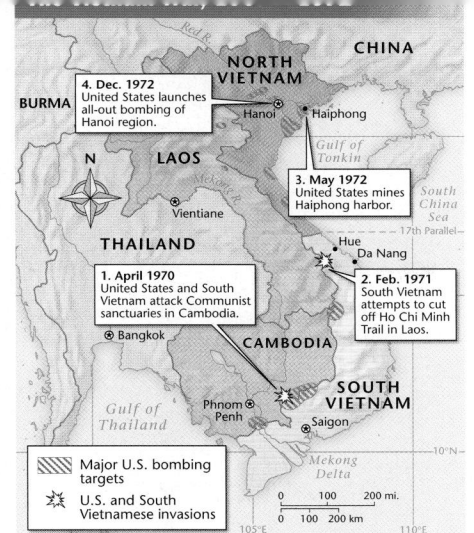

MAP SKILLS Although Nixon began withdrawing troops from Vietnam in 1968, he stepped up bombing raids. **Location** According to this map, in what areas were United States bombing raids concentrated during the later years of the war?

Focus on
GOVERNMENT

The Pentagon Papers In June 1971, *The New York Times* began publishing articles based on a classified government study of American involvement in the Vietnam War. The study, which came to be called the Pentagon Papers, revealed that government officials had lied to Congress and the American people about the war. Presidents had made secret policy decisions, such as giving military aid to France and waging an undercover war against North Vietnam in the early 1960s. Such revelations shocked the public and led to a growing distrust of government that would be reinforced by the events of the 1970s.

Chapter 31 • Section 4 **1045**

COMPARING PRIMARY SOURCES
The Tragedy of Kent State

In May 1970, the National Guard opened fire on a crowd of antiwar protesters at Kent State University in Ohio and killed four students. Reaction to the incident was strong but mixed.

Analyzing Viewpoints Compare the main arguments made by these two women.

In Support of the National Guard's Actions

"He told me they didn't fire those shots to scare the students off. He told me they fired those shots because they knew the students were coming after them, coming for their guns. People are calling my husband a murderer; my husband is not a murderer. He was afraid."

—*Wife of a member of the National Guard, quoted in* Newsweek *magazine, May 18, 1970*

Opposed to the National Guard's Actions

"Nixon acts as if the kids had it coming. But shooting into a crowd of students, that is violence. They say it could happen again if the Guard is threatened. They consider stones threat enough to kill children. I think the violence comes from the government."

—*Mother of Jeffrey Glenn Miller, a student killed at Kent State, quoted in* Life *magazine, May 15, 1970*

This famous photograph of the shooting of a student at Kent State University horrified the nation.

campuses, not all students agreed with the antiwar protesters. Some firmly supported American involvement in Vietnam. Others questioned the war but were troubled by the lawlessness and radicalism of many antiwar protests. These students did not receive the press coverage of their more outspoken classmates. But they did make their opinions known by writing letters to campus newspapers or by challenging the actions of antiwar groups in court.

Likewise, many adults held student protesters responsible for rising crime, growing drug use, and permissive attitudes toward sex. Some of these Americans expressed their patriotism by putting flag decals on their car windows or by attaching bumper stickers that read "My Country, Right or Wrong" and "Love It or Leave It." In the 1969 speech quoted at the beginning of this section, Nixon referred to this large group of Americans as the **silent majority.** To strengthen his position on law and order, Nixon aimed to discourage protest, especially against the war. In his "silent majority speech" he declared, "If a vocal minority, however fervent its cause, prevails over reason and the will of the majority, this nation has no future as a free society."

Kent State and Jackson State Tensions between antiwar activists and law-and-order supporters reached a peak in 1970. The U.S. invasion of Cambodia in 1970 fueled the protest movement on college campuses in the United States. At Kent State University in Ohio, students reacted angrily to the President's actions. They broke windows in the business district downtown. They also burned the army ROTC building, which had become a hated symbol of the war.

In response, the governor of Ohio ordered the National Guard to Kent State. Tension mounted. When students threw rocks at them, the guardsmen loaded their guns and donned gas masks. They hurled tear gas at the students, ordering them to disperse. Then the guardsmen retreated to another position. At the top of a hill, they suddenly turned and began firing on the students below.

Seconds later, four students lay dead, with nine others wounded. Two of the dead had been demonstrators 250 feet away from the guardsmen. The other two were bystanders, almost 400 feet away.

Similar violence flared at Jackson State, a nearly all-black college in Mississippi. A confrontation between students and police left two students dead and eleven wounded.

These attacks horrified Americans. In a sign of the deep divisions in the nation, 100,000 construction workers marched in an angry demonstration in New York City in support of the President.

American Withdrawal

The war dragged on, as did the Paris peace talks. In January 1972, while running for a second term as President, Nixon announced that North Vietnam had refused to accept a proposed settlement. At the end of March, the North Vietnamese began a major assault

on South Vietnam. This led Nixon to order the most intensive bombing campaign of the war. The United States bombed the North Vietnamese capital of Hanoi and mined North Vietnamese harbors.

Just days before the 1972 election, National Security Advisor Henry Kissinger announced, "Peace is at hand." As it turned out, the settlement was not actually final. After Nixon's reelection in November and another round of B-52 bombings of North Vietnam in December, peace finally arrived. In January 1973, the United States, South Vietnam, North Vietnam, and the Viet Cong signed a formal agreement in Paris. Among the provisions in the agreement were these:

1. The United States would withdraw all its forces from South Vietnam within 60 days.
2. All prisoners of war would be released.
3. All parties to the agreement would end military activities in Laos and Cambodia.
4. The 17th parallel would continue to divide North and South Vietnam until the country could be reunited.

Aftermath of the War in Asia

American involvement in the war came to an end in 1973, but the fighting between North and South Vietnam continued for another two years. Americans had believed that they could defend the world from communism anywhere, at any time. American technology and money, they assumed, could always bring victory. Vietnam proved that assumption to be false.

South Vietnam Falls After the withdrawal of American forces, South Vietnamese soldiers steadily lost ground to their North Vietnamese enemies. In the spring of 1975, the North Vietnamese launched a campaign of strikes against strategic cities throughout South Vietnam, the final objective being the seat of government in Saigon.

South Vietnamese forces crumpled in the face of this campaign. On April 29, 1975, with Communist forces surrounding Saigon, the United States carried out a dramatic last-minute evacuation. American helicopters airlifted more than 1,000 Americans and nearly 6,000 Vietnamese from the city to aircraft carriers waiting offshore. On April 30, North Vietnam completed its conquest of South Vietnam, and the Saigon government officially surrendered. After decades of fighting, Vietnam was a single nation under a Communist government.

READING CHECK

How did peace finally arrive?

ACTIVITY
Connecting with History and Conflict

Invite student groups to conduct research on various aspects of the Paris peace talks and provide a brief presentation to the rest of the class. Different presentations could include the settings of the talks, the major issues that were discussed, the attitudes of the participants, or the general mood or atmosphere that prevailed. **(Verbal/Linguistic)**

BACKGROUND
Connections to Today

One of the lasting images of the war in Vietnam for Americans is the scene of the final hours of the United States presence in Saigon (now Ho Chi Minh City). Helicopters that swooped down to the roof of the U.S. embassy were immediately filled with diplomatic and military personnel, then jammed to overflowing with frantic refugees before flying off to safety. For nearly 25 years afterward, the massive building was a reminder of the war, but no longer. The State Department decided in 1997 to demolish the old building and replace it with a sleek new consulate, designed to foster commercial ties. Many people in the city see the change as symbolic of a new era. As one Vietnamese said, "The relationship between the United States and Vietnam is different now. We are doing trade, not fighting a war."

READING CHECK
The Paris Peace Treaty was signed in January 1973 in the wake of a North Vietnamese offensive the previous spring and two final, massive American bombing campaigns.

CUSTOMIZE FOR ...
Less Proficient Writers
Ask students to restate, in their own words, the four conditions for American withdrawal from Vietnam agreed upon when the formal peace agreement was signed in Paris in January 1973.

CAPTION ANSWERS

Viewing History It looks like a hasty, desperate, disorganized retreat that left many would-be refugees behind.

ACTIVITY

Connecting with History and Conflict

Organize students into groups, and have each group create a project entitled "The Legacy of the Vietnam War." Student projects may honor veterans, express concerns, identify postwar policy implications, or convey anything else students feel is the true legacy of America's experience in Vietnam. Projects may take any suitable form, including reports, artwork, bulletin-board displays, songs, and so on. Have groups present their projects to the rest of the class. **(Verbal/Linguistic; Visual/Spatial)**

BACKGROUND

Connections to Today

Some analysts estimate that as many as one million South Vietnamese civilians were forced into "re-education" camps by the new Communist rulers of the country. That amounts to one out of every 20 people. Some were held in the camps for more than ten years. The camps varied widely in terms of how they treated prisoners, but some were horrid. One account tells of a cell built to hold 20 people housing 80, forcing prisoners to take turns breathing through the cell's single air hole. Countless prisoners were tortured, starved, forced into hard labor, and killed outright. Many South Vietnamese who avoided the camps were still forced to endure "re-education" on a smaller scale (say, for weeks at a local prison). That so many Vietnamese fled their home country by boat, risking drowning and pirate attacks, is testament to the brutality of the victorious Communist rule in the former South Vietnam.

Southeast Asia After the War One reason for American involvement in Vietnam was the belief in the domino theory. As you recall, this was the assumption that the entire region would collapse if the Communists won in Vietnam. With the North Vietnamese victory, two additional dominoes did topple—Laos and Cambodia. The rest of the region, however, did not fall.

The suffering of the Cambodian people was one of the most tragic effects of the war in Vietnam. In April 1975, Cambodia fell to the Khmer Rouge, a force of Communists led by the fanatical Pol Pot. In five years of fighting, Cambodia had already suffered as many as a half million civilian casualties, mostly by American bombs. Worse was to come. The Khmer Rouge in effect declared war on anyone "tainted" with Western ways, and they killed as many as 1.5 million Cambodians—a quarter of the population. Many were shot, while the rest died of starvation, from disease, from mistreatment in labor camps, or on forced marches.

Although not so extreme, Vietnam's new leaders also forced hundreds of thousands of South Vietnamese soldiers, civil servants, and other professionals into "re-education camps." Meanwhile, more than 1.5 million Vietnamese fled their country by boat, leaving behind all personal possessions in their determination to escape. In addition to these refugees, hundreds of thousands of Cambodians and Laotians also fled their homelands, many making their way to the United States.

The Legacy of the War

The Vietnam War resulted in more than 58,000 Americans dead and 300,000 wounded. In addition, more than 2,500 Americans were listed as **POWs** (prisoners of war) and **MIAs** (missing in action) at the end of the war. Many of them remain unaccounted for. After Vietnam, soldiers came home to a reception that was quite different than the ones their fathers and grandfathers had received following the World Wars. There were no welcoming ticker-tape parades. Many veterans complained that Americans did not appreciate the sacrifices they had made for their country.

Counting the Costs The Vietnam War was the longest and the least successful war in American history. The costs of the war were enormous. The United States spent at least $150 billion on the war. This expense resulted in growing inflation and economic instability.

The costs of the war were high for Vietnam as well. More bombs rained down on Vietnam than had fallen on all the Axis powers during World War II. The number of dead and wounded Vietnamese soldiers ran into the millions, with countless civilian casualties. The landscape itself would long bear the scars of war. In 1994, the United States announced an end to the long-standing American trade embargo against Vietnam. The next year the United States agreed to restore full diplomatic relations with its former enemy.

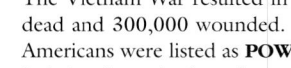

U.S. Forces in Vietnam, 1965–1972

Military forces (in thousands), Year (1965–1972)

SOURCE: *National Archives and Records Administration*

INTERPRETING GRAPHS
United States involvement in Vietnam peaked in 1968. **Analyzing Information** (a) How many United States soldiers were in Vietnam in 1968? (b) When did American casualties begin to decrease? (c) Judging from the two graphs, what is one reason for this decrease?

U.S. Deaths in Vietnam, 1965–1972

U.S. combat deaths (in thousands), Year (1965–1972)

SOURCE: *National Archives and Records Administration*

CAPTION ANSWERS

Interpreting Graphs Over 500,000. 1969. Casualties began to decrease when the United States began withdrawing troops.

RESOURCE DIRECTORY

Teaching Resources
Units 9/10 booklet
- Section 4 Quiz, p. 40
- Chapter 31 Test, p. 41, 44

Guide to the Essentials
- Section 4 Summary, p. 159
- Chapter 31 Test, p. 160

Other Print Resources
Chapter Tests with ExamView® Test Bank CD-ROM, Ch. 31

Technology
Sounds of an Era Audio CD *John Kerry's "Winter Soldier" speech,* 1971 recording (time: 50 seconds)
Exploring Primary Sources in U.S. History CD-ROM: *The Vietnam Veterans Memorial*
ExamView® Test Bank CD-ROM, Ch. 31
Social Studies Skills Tutor CD-ROM

The Vietnam Veterans Memorial Aside from the Civil War, the Vietnam War divided the nation more than any other conflict in American history. The issues were so difficult and emotional that for many years something was forgotten—that the Americans who died in Vietnam should be honored with a national monument.

In 1979, a group of veterans began making plans for a Vietnam Veterans Memorial. They wanted to recognize the courage of American GIs during the Vietnam ordeal and to help heal the wounds the war had caused. A Vietnam veteran named Jan Scruggs started a fund for the memorial. Eventually, he won support from Congress to build a monument in Washington, D.C., near the Lincoln Memorial. The question quickly arose: How could the memorial honor the people who gave their lives, while avoiding the hard political issues surrounding the war?

Scruggs's committee held a contest. Famous architects and artists submitted their ideas. Many were surprised when the winner was a 21-year-old college student named Maya Ying Lin. Her idea was to build a long wall of black granite, cut down into the ground. This wall would display the names of every American man and woman who died in the Vietnam War.

Lin had a reason for each element of the memorial. She chose black granite because it reflects light like a mirror, allowing visitors to see reflections of themselves and the nature around them. She put the memorial on a slope that led below ground level to create a quiet place where visitors could think about life and death and sorrow. She placed the names in the order people died, rather than in alphabetical order, so that the individual passing of each life would be emphasized. The memorial was to be long, but not tall, so that visitors could easily see and touch every name.

Lin's concept suited the needs of a nation that needed to heal. Her simple, abstract design would allow visitors to carry their own beliefs to the memorial, without creating images that might disturb or distract them. The Vietnam Veterans Memorial was completed in 1982, and ever since, people have added to it by leaving personal tokens at the wall in memory of their loved ones.

VIEWING HISTORY A Vietnam veteran holds a flower as he points to a name on the Memorial, which was designed by Maya Lin (lower photo). **Determining Relevance** *How do you think listing the names on the wall has contributed to the Memorial's popularity?*

Reading Comprehension

1. U.S. to withdraw all forces from South Vietnam within 60 days; all POWs to be released; all parties would end military activities in Laos and Cambodia; the 17th parallel would continue to divide North and South Vietnam until the country could be reunited.

2. The signing of the peace agreement in Paris in January 1973.

3. Because American troops were replaced with South Vietnamese soldiers.

4. POWs: prisoners of war; MIAs: missing in action.

Critical Thinking and Writing

5. This violence horrified Americans and displayed the sharp divisions the war had caused in American society.

6. Answers will vary, but might consider such topics as whether President Nixon had a realistic plan for ending the war, or the impact that antiwar demonstrators had on Nixon's actions.

Section **4** Assessment

READING COMPREHENSION

1. What terms were finally agreed to at the **Paris peace talks?**

2. What event led to American withdrawal from Vietnam?

3. Why was President Nixon's policy known as **Vietnamization?**

4. Who are **POWs** and **MIAs?**

CRITICAL THINKING AND WRITING

5. **Determining Relevance** How did violence at Kent State and Jackson State affect American public opinion? Explain your answer.

6. **Making a List** Do you think the United States made every effort to win the war in Vietnam? List reasons why or why not.

Take It to the NET

Activity: Creating a Time Line Much has happened in Vietnam since the end of the war. Create a time line of important events in Vietnam from 1974 to the present. Use the links provided in the *America: Pathways to the Present* area of the following Web site for help in completing this activity.
www.phschool.com

Take It to the NET

Student time lines should indicate events in Vietnam from 1974 to the present. Examples may include: uniting of North and South Vietnam as Socialist Republic of Vietnam; admission to United Nations; overthrow of Pol Pot's government in Cambodia; reestablishing diplomatic relations with the United States.

TEST PREPARATION

Have students read the paragraph on the previous page titled "Southeast Asia After the War" and then answer the question below.

Who were the Khmer Rouge?

A A group of French student activists.

B A group of South Vietnamese who continued to fight after the U.S. left.

C A North Vietnamese religious group.

(D) A group of Communists in Cambodia.

CAPTION ANSWERS

Viewing History Answers will vary. Many students may note that the list draws visitors because they can find and touch the names of their loved ones, and leave mementos in their honor.

Chapter 24

Chapter 31 — Review and Assessment

REVIEWING KEY TERMS

Students should refer to the definitions of key terms in the chapter to write sentences that show an understanding of the Vietnam War.

REVIEWING MAIN IDEAS

11. Johnson used the Gulf of Tonkin Resolution to justify devoting ever-increasing American resources to the war. In 1965, this included a massive influx of American troops and the beginning of Operation Rolling Thunder.

12. It gave the President almost complete control over U.S. actions in Vietnam, even without an official declaration of war from Congress.

13. The doubts of Americans at home increased since the Viet Cong had achieved a psychological victory even though they had suffered a devastating military defeat.

14. The guerrilla warfare in the jungle was confusing and frightening, and soldiers never knew who their friends or enemies were.

15. Guerrilla warfare tactics. Also, they were familiar with the swamps and jungles; they could find protection across the border in Cambodia and Laos; and they could often count on the support of the local population.

16. They participated in various activities, such as violent and nonviolent antiwar protests, teach-ins, draft resistance, and the free-speech movement.

17. Nixon gained support by claiming to have a secret plan to end the war; many Democrats abstained from voting because their party was split; Humphrey was hurt by his support of Johnson's policies.

18. To destroy Viet Cong and North Vietnamese bases there.

19. North Vietnam took over South Vietnam. Communist regimes also took over in Laos and Cambodia, but the rest of the region did not fall to communism.

creating a CHAPTER SUMMARY

Copy this chart (right) on a piece of paper and complete it by adding information about U.S. involvement in Vietnam under each President from Truman through Nixon.

 iTEXT

For additional review and enrichment activities, see the interactive version of *America: Pathways to the Present*, available on the Web and on CD-ROM.

U.S. Involvement in Vietnam		
President	**Action (date)**	**Result**
Truman	Sent economic aid to French in Vietnam (1950)	U.S. began to fight the spread of communism.
Eisenhower	Provided military advisors to South Vietnam (1960)	U.S. became involved in the Vietnam War.
Kennedy	• Increased military aid • Supported overthrow of Diem (1963)	
Johnson		
Nixon		

★ Reviewing Key Terms

For each of the terms below, write a sentence explaining how it relates to the Vietnam War.

1. domino theory
2. Viet Cong
3. Gulf of Tonkin Resolution
4. land mine
5. Agent Orange
6. escalation
7. Ho Chi Minh Trail
8. conscientious objector
9. Middle America
10. Vietnamization

★ Reviewing Main Ideas

11. How did the Vietnam War escalate under President Johnson? (Section 1)
12. How did the Gulf of Tonkin Resolution expand presidential power? (Section 1)
13. Why was the Tet Offensive a turning point in the war? (Section 2)
14. Why was the war so hard on American soldiers fighting in Vietnam? (Section 2)
15. What advantages did the Viet Cong have in the war? (Section 2)
16. What methods did student activists use during the 1960s to oppose the war in Vietnam? (Section 3)
17. How did the war influence the election of 1968? (Section 3)

18. Why did Richard Nixon authorize the invasion of Cambodia in 1970? (Section 4)
19. What happened in Southeast Asia after American withdrawal from Vietnam? (Section 4)

★ Critical Thinking

20. **Comparing Points of View**   Evaluate American involvement in Vietnam from the point of view of the following: a hawk, a dove, a conscientious objector, and a soldier.

21. **Drawing Conclusions**   If you had been a student during the Vietnam War, do you think your views of the conflict would have changed or remained the same throughout the course of the war? What factors might have influenced your views?

22. **Checking Consistency**   President Nixon promised to end the war in Vietnam. Yet he authorized the heaviest bombing raids of the war, and he expanded the war into Cambodia. Were these actions consistent with his promise? Explain.

23. **Drawing Inferences**   Why do you think Vietnam veterans came home to a different reception than the ones veterans of the two World Wars received?

24. **Predicting Consequences**   Since the end of the Vietnam War, government officials have advised caution in global affairs. How do you think Americans would react to United States involvement in "another Vietnam"? Explain your answer.

CREATING A CHAPTER SUMMARY

U.S. Involvement in Vietnam		
President	**Action (date)**	**Result**
Truman	Sent economic aid to French in Vietnam (1950)	U.S. began to fight the spread of communism.
Eisenhower	Provided military advisers to South Vietnam (1960)	U.S. became involved in the Vietnam War.
Kennedy	• Increased military aid (1961) • Supported overthrow of Diem (1963) • McNamara encouraged withdrawal (1963). • Kennedy assassinated (1963)	U.S. became more involved in Vietnam War.
Johnson	• Creates a policy of escalation (1965) • Congress passes Gulf of Tonkin Resolution (1964). • Tet Offensive (1968) • Massacre at My Lai (1968) • Johnson decides not to run for reelection (1968).	• War begins to escalate. • Johnson gains much broader powers. • Viet Cong gain advantage. • Americans become more vocal against the war.
Nixon	• Nixon promises he has "secret plan" to end the war (1968). • Nixon announces plan for "Vietnamization" (1969). • Nixon calls for law and order (1969). • Peace talks begin (1968). • Nixon launches saturation bombing and attacks on Cambodia (1969–1970). • Peace treaty is signed (1973).	• Student protests continue. • Student protesters are killed at Kent State and Jackson State.

© 1972 HERBLOCK

★ Skills Assessment

Analyzing Political Cartoons ▶

25. Examine the images in the cartoon. (a) Who are the two men? (b) What is the occasion shown in the cartoon?

26. (a) What is the significance of the documents held by the man on the right? (b) What does the gravestone refer to?

27. What is the message of the cartoon?

Analyzing Primary Sources

Read this excerpt, and then answer the questions that follow.

> ❝ You have a row of dominoes set up, you knock over the first one, and what will happen to the last one is the certainty that it will go over very quickly. ❞
>
> —Dwight D. Eisenhower

28. Which statement best represents the meaning of the quotation?

   A Southeast Asian nations will support one another in the fight against communism.

   B If one Southeast Asian nation falls to communism, others will also fall.

   C The strongest Southeast Asian nation will remain standing after the others fall to communism.

   D No one can predict what will happen if communism spreads in Southeast Asia.

29. Which of the following events supports the idea expressed in the quotation?

   F American forces could not bring about victory in Vietnam.

   G After decades of fighting, Vietnam became a single nation under a Communist government.

   H Laos and Cambodia became Communist nations.

   J The Vietnam War divided the American people.

Applying the Chapter Skill: *Sequencing*

30. Look back at the Skills for Life page. Write a paragraph telling, in sequence, the events described in the sources.

ACTIVITIES

Writing to LEARN

Writing a Conclusion
Why do you think that what began as a distant war in a small country that very few Americans had ever heard of ended up causing such a crisis in American society? In examining this question, consider the original causes of the war in Vietnam, the causes of American involvement and escalation, and the actions of both the U.S. government and ordinary citizens at home.

Primary Source CD-ROM

Working With Primary Sources Find additional information on the Vietnam War on the *Exploring Primary Sources in U.S. History CD-ROM* and use the selection(s) provided to complete the Chapter 31 primary source activity located in the *America: Pathways to the Present* area of the following Web site.
www.phschool.com

Take It to the NET

Chapter Self-Test As a review activity, take the Chapter 31 Self-Test in the *America: Pathways to the Present* area of the Web site listed below. The questions are designed to test your understanding of chapter content.
www.phschool.com

Chapter 31 Assessment **1051**

TEST PREPARATION

TIPS FOR TEST TAKING

You might want to remind your students of the following:

1. Read the directions carefully.
2. Read each question carefully.
3. For multiple choice questions, try to answer the question before you look at the choices. Read all the choices. Then, eliminate those that are absolutely incorrect.
4. For short answer questions, be sure to answer the question completely if there is more than one part.
5. Answer the easy questions first. Then, go back to the ones that will take more time.
6. Pace yourself. Be sure to set aside enough time for the writing questions.

Write your answers on a separate sheet of paper.

1. The United States Supreme Court, in *Brown* v. *Board of Education* (1954), ended

   A mandatory poll taxes and literacy tests.

   B racial segregation in public schools.

   C discrimination in employment and housing.

   D separation of the races in buses and trains.

2. Which one of the following African Americans became known nationally as a result of the Montgomery, Alabama, bus boycott?

   A Martin Luther King, Jr.

   B James Meredith

   C Malcolm X

   D Barbara Jordan

3. Which one of the following issues was addressed by the Civil Rights Act of 1964?

   A Racial discrimination in public colleges and universities

   B Racial discrimination in voter registration standards

   C Racial segregation in public schools

   D Racial segregation in buses and taxis

4. Which decision of the United States Supreme Court requires police officials to inform suspects of their constitutional rights before questioning them?

   A *Mapp* v. *Ohio* (1961)

   B *Baker* v. *Carr* (1962)

   C *Engel* v. *Vitale* (1962)

   D *Miranda* v. *Arizona* (1966)

Use the table and your knowledge of social studies to answer the following question.

African American Elected Officials*	
Year	Number
1970	1,469
1980	4,890
1985	6,016
1990	7,335

*National, state, and local governments
SOURCE: *Statistical Abstract of the United States, 1995*

5. Which one of the following was the primary cause of the trend shown in the table?

   A *Brown* v. *Board of Education*, 1954

   B Southern Manifesto, 1956

   C Civil Rights Act, 1964

   D Voting Rights Act, 1965

6. Which one of the following events during the Cold War almost led to war between the United States and the Soviet Union?

   A The Bay of Pigs invasion

   B The Cuban Missile Crisis

   C The Gulf of Tonkin incident

   D The Tet Offensive

7. Which one of the following helped to further the women's movement of the 1960s and 1970s?

   A The failed social welfare policies of President Lyndon Johnson

   B The perceived threat to the suffrage movement

   C The high rate of inflation throughout the 1960s

   D The publication of *The Feminine Mystique* by Betty Friedan

Diagnose and Prescribe
- Profile student skills with Diagnostic Tests A&B.
- Address student needs with program materials correlated to test questions.

Review and Reteach
- Provide cumulative content review with the Review Book.

Practice and Assess
- Build test-taking skills with Test-taking Strategies With Transparencies.

Use the graph and your knowledge of social studies to answer the following question.

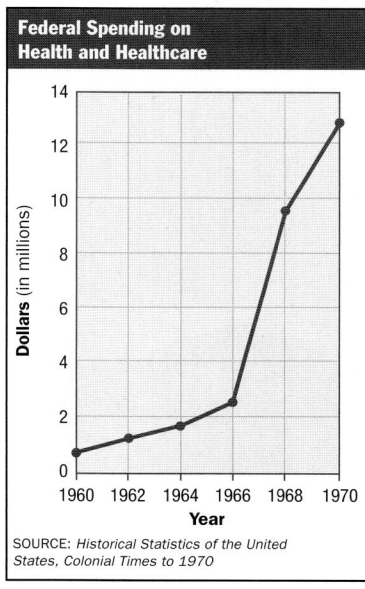

Federal Spending on Health and Healthcare

Dollars (in millions)

Year

SOURCE: *Historical Statistics of the United States, Colonial Times to 1970*

8. Which one of the following caused the trend shown in the line graph?

A Policies of the New Frontier

B Demands of the civil rights movement

C Programs of the Great Society

D The war in Vietnam

9. United States public opinion shifted against the Vietnam War following

A the battle of Dien Bien Phu.

B the assassination of President Ngo Dinh Diem.

C Operation Rolling Thunder.

D the Tet Offensive.

10. Which President established the Environmental Protection Agency (EPA), the federal agency designed to set and enforce national pollution-control standards?

A John Kennedy

B Lyndon Johnson

C Richard Nixon

D Jimmy Carter

11. Which one of the following was the legal basis for the involvement of the United States in Vietnam?

A A declaration of war by Congress

B The Geneva Accords

C The Gulf of Tonkin Resolution

D The Paris agreement

12. President Nixon's policy of Vietnamization was designed to

A replace Americans in Vietnam with South Vietnamese soldiers.

B bomb North Vietnam until it surrendered.

C stop the use of the Ho Chi Minh Trail.

D extend the fighting into Laos and Cambodia.

Writing Practice

13. Describe the major social programs of President Johnson's "Great Society."

14. Describe the role of César Chávez in the fight against discrimination.

15. How did Rachel Carson affect the movement for a cleaner environment?

1. B
2. A
3. B
4. D
5. D
6. B
7. D
8. C
9. D
10. C
11. C
12. A
13. Answers should mention the Economic Opportunity Act (including the Head Start and VISTA programs), the Elementary and Secondary Education Act of 1965, Medicare and Medicaid, and the Immigration Act of 1965.
14. Answers should mention that César Chávez organized migrant Latino farmworkers in an effort to provide better working conditions for them. He founded the United Farm Workers union and organized a successful national boycott of crops grown on nonunion farms.
15. Rachel Carson, a marine biologist and author, wrote *Silent Spring,* a book in which she explained the dangers of the use of chemical pesticides, particularly DDT. The book was a sensation and led to the eventual illegalization of DDT and control of other chemicals in the United States.

1053

Unit 10

Continuity and Change
(1969 to the Present)

INTRODUCING THE UNIT

Continuity and Change (1969 to the Present) The presidencies of Nixon, Ford, and Carter were marked, in succession, by tumult and recovery in government and by a deepening economic crisis. Seeking to re-ignite America's economy, citizens elected conservative Ronald Reagan by a landslide in 1981. He was followed by George H.W. Bush, who led Americans into war in the Persian Gulf in 1991. Bill Clinton presided over a dramatic phase of economic growth in the United States, but his tenure was marred by friction with Congress and scandal. The first President of the twenty-first century, George W. Bush, wants to minimize government's influence in everyday life and to limit United States involvement abroad.

USING HISTORICAL EVIDENCE

Direct students' attention to the picture on these pages. Discuss with students their memories of the transition from one century to another. How do they think the twenty-first century will differ from the twentieth? What types of improvements do they hope for in society and in technology?

Discuss the condition of the world as the twentieth century ended. What situations do students think were most important in the last years of the century? How do they imagine those situations will change, now and in the future?

eTeach

Be sure to check out this month's online discussion with a Master Teacher. Go to **www.phschool.com**.

> **"**The challenge . . . is to make and keep our communities places where we can tolerate, even celebrate, our differences, while pulling together for the common good. 'Of many, one' is the main challenge, I believe; it is my hope for our country and the world.**"**
>
> Ruth Bader Ginsburg,
> Supreme Court Justice, 1998

Americans across the nation celebrated the arrival of the new century with fireworks and festivities, like this celebration in San Francisco, California. ▶

1054

RESOURCE DIRECTORY

Teaching Resources
Units 9/10 booklet
- American Pathways Activity, pp. 84–85
- History's Lasting Impact, pp. 86–87

Geography and History booklet, pp. 20–21

Other Print Resources
Prentice Hall Assessment System
- Document-Based Assessment

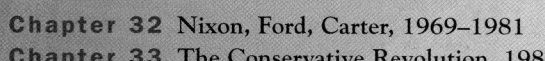

1055

TECHNOLOGY CENTER

 **Take It to the NET**

Prentice Hall School Web site offers student-appropriate Internet activities and links that extend core content. Visit us at the Social Studies area. www.phschool.com

AmericanHeritage®

My Brush with History™ Video Program This new video series lets your students learn history from the people who lived it.

RESOURCE◎PRO®

Teaching Resources on CD-ROM offer lesson-planning flexibility, test-generation capability, and resource manageability.

PRESENTATION PRO CD-ROM Provides you with multimedia lecture notes for each chapter.

SOCIAL STUDIES SKILLS TUTOR CD-ROM Provides interactive practice in Geographic Literacy, Critical Thinking and Reading, Visual Analysis, and Communications.

INTERACTIVE CONSTITUTION CD-ROM Exploring active citizenship and civic responsibilities, this CD-ROM shows students how the Constitution affects their lives today.

EXPLORING PRIMARY SOURCES IN U.S. HISTORY CD-ROM This interactive exploration of primary sources allows students to analyze and evaluate writing and images from American history.

GUIDED READING AUDIOTAPES

STUDENT EDITION ON AUDIO CD

SOUNDS OF AN ERA AUDIO CD Bring the sounds of American history to life in the classroom with music, speeches, poetry, interviews, and news reports.

 **TEXT**

Don't miss the exclusive interactive version of this textbook on the Web and on CD-ROM.

Chapter 32 Planning Guide
Resource Manager

	CORE INSTRUCTION	READING/SKILLS
Chapter-Level Resources	**Teaching Resources** • Pacing Charts booklet • Block Scheduling booklet **Resource Pro® CD-ROM**, Ch. 32 **Prentice Hall Presentation Pro CD-ROM**, Ch. 32 **www.phschool.com** • eTeach	**Guided Reading Audiotapes (English/Spanish)** **Student Edition on Audio CD**, Ch. 32 **Social Studies Skills Tutor CD-ROM** **Color Transparencies**, A57, B18, C9, H20
1 Nixon's Domestic Policy 1. Find out how Richard Nixon's personality affected his relationship with his staff. 2. See how Nixon's domestic policies differed from those of his predecessors. 3. Learn how Nixon applied his "southern strategy." 4. Describe the first moon landing.	**Teaching Resources** **Units 9/10 booklet** • Section 1 Quiz, p. 52	**Guided Reading and Review booklet,** p. 128 **Guide to the Essentials,** p. 161 **Section Reading Support Transparencies**
2 Nixon's Foreign Policy 1. Learn how Henry Kissinger relaxed tensions between the U.S. and the Communist powers. 2. Find out about Nixon's policy toward the People's Republic of China. 3. Discover how Nixon reached an agreement with the Soviet Union on limiting nuclear arms.	**Teaching Resources** **Units 9/10 booklet** • Section 2 Quiz, p. 53 **Learning Styles Lesson Plans booklet,** p. 66	**Guided Reading and Review booklet,** p. 129 **Guide to the Essentials,** p. 162 **Section Reading Support Transparencies**
3 The Watergate Scandal 1. See how the Nixon White House battled its political enemies. 2. Find out about Nixon's reelection campaign. 3. Learn about the Watergate break-in, and see how the story of the scandal unfolded. 4. Discover the events that led directly to Nixon's resignation.	**Teaching Resources** **Units 9/10 booklet** • Section 3 Quiz, p. 54	**Guided Reading and Review booklet,** p. 130 **Guide to the Essentials,** p. 163 **Learning with Documents booklet,** p. 71 **Skills for Life booklet,** p. 34 **Section Reading Support Transparencies**
4 The Ford Administration 1. Find out how Gerald Ford became President. 2. See the types of economic problems the Ford administration faced. 3. Learn about the foreign policy actions Ford took. 4. See how Americans celebrated the nation's bicentennial.	**Teaching Resources** **Units 9/10 booklet** • Section 4 Quiz, p. 55	**Guided Reading and Review booklet,** p. 131 **Guide to the Essentials,** p. 164 **Learning with Documents booklet,** p. 37 **Section Reading Support Transparencies**
5 The Carter Administration 1. Discover some changes Jimmy Carter brought to the presidency. 2. Learn how Carter dealt with domestic issues. 3. Find out about Carter's foreign policies. 4. Discover some factors that influenced the outcome of the 1980 election.	**Teaching Resources** **Units 9/10 booklet** • Section 5 Quiz, p. 56 **Learning Styles Lesson Plans booklet,** p. 67	**Guided Reading and Review booklet,** p. 132 **Guide to the Essentials,** p. 165 **Learning with Documents booklet,** p. 96 **Section Reading Support Transparencies**

ENRICHMENT/PRE-AP

Prentice Hall United States History Video Collection™
www.phschool.com
- Section Activities, Virtual Field Trip, Chapter Activities, Current Events Online

American History Block Scheduling Support

Sounds of an Era Audio CD

Biography, Literature, and Comparing Primary Sources booklet, pp. 85, 159
Sounds of an Era Audio CD
Exploring Primary Sources in U.S. History CD-ROM

American History Block Scheduling Support

Biography, Literature, and Comparing Primary Sources booklet, p. 37
Great Debates booklet, p. 26
Sounds of an Era Audio CD
American Pathways Thematic Posters

ASSESSMENT

Core Assessment
    ExamView® Test Bank, Ch. 32
    ExamView® Test Bank CD-ROM, Ch. 32

Standardized Test Preparation
Diagnose and Prescribe
    Diagnostic Tests for High School Social Studies Skills

Review and Reteach
    Review Book for U.S. History

Practice and Assess
    Test-taking Strategies With Transparencies
    Test-taking Strategies Posters
    Test Prep Book for U.S. History
    Alternative Assessment Handbook
    Document-Based Assessment

Teaching Resources
Units 9/10 booklet
- Section Quizzes, pp. 52–56
- Chapter Tests, pp. 57, 60
www.phschool.com Ch. 32 Self-Test

AmericanHeritage RESOURCES

From the Archives of American Heritage®, pp. 1073, 1080
AmericanHeritage® My Brush with History™ Videotapes
www.americanheritage.com

Don't miss the exclusive interactive version of this textbook on the Web and on CD-ROM.

Chapter 32 Planning Guide
In Your Classroom

CUSTOMIZE FOR INDIVIDUAL NEEDS

Gifted and Talented

Teacher's Edition
- Customize for Gifted and Talented, pp. 1075, 1087

Teaching Resources
- Biography, Literature, and Comparing Primary Sources booklet, pp. 37, 85, 159

Technology
- Exploring Primary Sources in U.S. History CD-ROM *Bugging at Watergate*

ESL

Teacher's Edition
- Customize for ESL, p. 1059

Teaching Resources
- Guided Reading and Review booklet, pp. 128–132
- Guide to the Essentials (English/Spanish), Chapter 32

Technology
- Student Edition on Audio CD, Chapter 32
- Guided Reading Audiotapes (English/Spanish), Chapter 32
- Section Reading Support Transparencies

Less Proficient Readers

Teacher's Edition
- Customize for Less Proficient Readers, p. 1079

Teaching Resources
- Guided Reading and Review booklet, pp. 128–132
- Guide to the Essentials (English/Spanish), Chapter 32

Technology
- Student Edition on Audio CD, Chapter 32
- Guided Reading Audiotapes (English/Spanish), Chapter 32
- Section Reading Support Transparencies

Less Proficient Writers

Teaching Resources
- Guided Reading and Review booklet, pp. 128–132
- Guide to the Essentials (English/Spanish), Chapter 32

Technology
- Student Edition on Audio CD, Chapter 32
- Guided Reading Audiotapes (English/Spanish), Chapter 32
- Section Reading Support Transparencies

TEACHER'S EDITION INDEX

CHAPTER 32 – PACING SUGGESTIONS

For 90-minute Blocks

- Teach sections 1, 2, 3, 4, and 5 using Transparencies A57, B18, C9, and H20, and the Recent Scholarship notes on pages 1072 and 1081 for class discussions.

Running Out of Time?

If you are running short on time to cover this chapter, consider the following options:

- Use the Prentice Hall Presentation Pro CD-ROM to create an outline for this chapter.
- Use the Section Summaries for Chapter 32, from **Guide to the Essentials (English/Spanish)**.

ADDITIONAL ACTIVITIES

1 Nixon's Domestic Policy

Connecting with Government
Tell students that many Presidents have had speechwriters. Among those who wrote for Richard Nixon were William Safire, David Gergen, and Pat Buchanan, all of whom also had careers in politics and the media. Have students research the public life of each of these men, then use that information as the basis of a discussion of what talents speechwriters bring to their jobs and how they use their skills to voice the chief executive's positions. **(Verbal/Linguistic)**

2 Nixon's Foreign Policy

Connecting with Government
Explain that Presidents often require briefing, or background, papers to inform them about events. Because so many topics require the President's attention, the paper must be succinct yet complete in terms of important details. Ask students to prepare such a briefing paper on one of the topics that might have required President Nixon's attention, such as the People's Republic of China, Taiwan, or nuclear arms. Have students share their papers with the class. **(Verbal/Linguistic)**

3 The Watergate Scandal

Connecting with History and Conflict
Have students research archival materials about President Nixon's resignation speech. After the students have watched the speech on videotape (or read the text), encourage a discussion about the emotions such an announcement might have stirred among the American people at the time the speech was delivered. **(Bodily/Kinesthetic)**

4 The Ford Administration

Connecting with Citizenship
Ask students to imagine how the Founding Fathers of the United States might have commented on the bicentennial. Students can role-play various founders as they remark on how their experiment has worked out and how true it has been to its originators' visions. Encourage students to incorporate into their presentations some of the important events they have read about in *America: Pathways to the Present*. **(Bodily/Kinesthetic)**

5 The Carter Administration

Connecting with History and Conflict
Explain to students that John C. Calhoun, Andrew Jackson's first Vice President, was the only other Vice President to resign. Have students research his biography and write a report on the circumstances behind his actions. Especially call students' attention to how Calhoun's differences with Jackson reflected regional differences within the country and foreshadowed the Civil War. Relate the situation to current politics by having students note how often the presidential and vice-presidential choices of major parties have demonstrated an effort by each party to represent various regions of the country. **(Verbal/Linguistic)**

Chapter 32

Nixon, Ford, Carter

(1969–1981)

SECTION 1 Nixon's Domestic Policy

SECTION 2 Nixon's Foreign Policy

SECTION 3 The Watergate Scandal

SECTION 4 The Ford Administration

SECTION 5 The Carter Administration

INTRODUCING THE CHAPTER

The election of President Nixon in 1968 led to a 24-year period of almost uninterrupted Republican control of the White House. The new President's domestic and foreign policies marked a shift in national politics. But Nixon's leadership style led to scandal and his own eventual downfall. Gerald Ford tried to heal the nation after the scandal, but the country's trust in its highest office was severely shaken. It was no surprise, then, when a Washington outsider, Jimmy Carter, was elected to the White House in 1976.

TIME LINE ACTIVITY

To provide students with practice in using the time line, ask questions such as these:

1. What 1973 event in the Middle East would have severe economic implications in the United States? *(The embargo on oil shipments imposed by the Arab members of OPEC)*

2. What 1978 event has had lasting international repercussions, even though it did not fully resolve a conflict? *(The Camp David Accords)*

3. What action taken by the Soviet Union in 1979 resulted in a 1980 U.S. Olympic boycott? *(The Soviet Union invaded Afghanistan.)*

An intercontinental ballistic missile (ICBM)

Apollo 11 astronaut Buzz Aldrin

American Events

1969
The United States achieves the first moon landing.

1972
Nixon travels to China and the Soviet Union to pursue détente. The United States and the Soviet Union sign the SALT I treaty.

1973
Senate investigation of the Watergate scandal reveals White House involvement.

1974
Nixon becomes the first U.S. President to resign. Ford becomes the first nonelected Vice President to assume office as President.

Presidential Terms: Richard M. Nixon 1969–1974

| 1968 | • | 1970 | • | 1972 | • | 1974 |

World Events

China joins the United Nations.
1971

OPEC imposes an embargo on oil shipments.
1973

1056   Chapter 32 • *Nixon, Ford, Carter*

eTeach

Be sure to check out this month's online discussion with a Master Teacher. Go to **www.phschool.com**.

RESOURCE DIRECTORY

Teaching Resources
Pacing Charts booklet
Block Scheduling booklet, p. 29
Units 9/10 booklet
 • Chapter Summary, p. 51

Technology
Guided Reading Audiotapes (English/Spanish),
 Ch. 32
Student Edition on Audio CD, Ch. 32
Prentice Hall United States History Video
 Collection™ Volume 20, *Post-War USA*
Prentice Hall Presentation Pro CD-ROM, Ch. 32
Resource Pro® CD-ROM

Social Studies Skills Tutor CD-ROM
Companion Web site, www.phschool.com

OPEC Nations, 1975

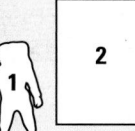

*Organization of Petroleum Exporting Countries

Legend: ▢ OPEC* member

A 1976 bicentennial quarter

Jimmy Carter's less aggressive leadership style challenged the idea of an "imperial presidency."

1975
Ford signs the Helsinki Accords on European security.

1976
The United States celebrates the bicentennial of the signing of the Declaration of Independence.

1978
President Carter negotiates the Camp David Accords to promote peace in the Middle East.

1980
The United States leads a boycott of the Moscow summer Olympics.

1981
American hostages held in Iran are returned to the United States.

Gerald R. Ford 1974–1977   Jimmy Carter 1977–1981   Ronald Reagan 1981–1989

1976   1978   1980   1982

Cambodia captures the *Mayaguez*, an American merchant ship.
1975

The Soviet Union invades Afghanistan.
1979

A rescue attempt fails to free American hostages in Iran.
1980

Chapter 32   **1057**

BIBLIOGRAPHY

For the Teacher

Lukas, J. Anthony. ***Common Ground: A Turbulent Decade in the Lives of Three American Families.*** Vintage, 1986. (A study of the impact of school busing on three economically diverse families.)

Wills, Garry. ***Nixon Agonistes: The Crisis of the Self-Made Man.*** Cherokee Publishing Company, 1990. (A critical and probing analysis of Richard Nixon and his most famous crisis.)

For the Student

The Right Stuff. Bantam, 1983. (Award-winning look at astronauts, based on Tom Wolfe's best-seller.)

All the President's Men. Warner Home Video, 1976. Video. (Fast-paced depiction of *Washington Post* reporters Bob Woodward and Carl Bernstein and the story they uncovered about the Watergate break-in.)

OPEC Nations, 1975

Activating Prior Knowledge
Which countries were Arab members of the Organization of Petroleum Exporting Countries (OPEC)? *(Kuwait, Iran, Iraq, Qatar, United Arab Emirates, and Saudi Arabia)*

Previewing How did these countries react when the United States backed Israel in its war with the Arab nations of Egypt and Syria in 1973? *(They stopped shipping oil to the United States, and OPEC greatly increased its prices to other countries.)*

BACKGROUND
About the Pictures

1. Buzz Aldrin was part of the *Apollo 11* crew, along with Neil Armstrong and Michael Collins. He was the second person to walk on the moon.

2. Some of the first U.S. ICBMs to go operational were the *Atlantis* and the *Titan I,* capable of travelling 7,500 miles and 6,300 miles, respectively.

3. After the Watergate scandal, Nixon resigned, saying he "no longer had a strong enough political base" to stay in office.

4. In 1976 thousands of communities across the United States held various festivals and celebrations in honor of the Declaration of Independence and the events that led to its creation.

5. Before leaving office, Carter was able to create an environmental "superfund" to go toward any disasters that might occur, and he set aside 100 million acres of Alaskan land for preservation.

iTEXT

Don't miss the exclusive interactive version of this textbook on the Web and on CD-ROM.

SECTION OBJECTIVES

1. Find out how Richard Nixon's personality affected his relationship with his staff.
2. See how Nixon's domestic policies differed from those of his predecessors.
3. Learn how Nixon applied his "southern strategy" to the issue of civil rights and to the selection of Supreme Court justices.
4. Describe the first moon landing.

BELLRINGER

Warm-Up Activity Write the word *leadership* on the chalkboard. Ask students to list ideas they associate with this term. Explain that Nixon, upon taking office, exercised a new type of leadership.

Activating Prior Knowledge Ask students to state what they already know about Nixon's presidency. What were important national issues at the time of his election? What did his successful election indicate about the mood of the country?

READING STRATEGY

Have students list the section headings, and as they read, have them add supporting information so that after reading the section, they can outline its main points.

BACKGROUND
Connections to Today

When Richard Milhous Nixon died on April 22, 1994, at age eighty-one, biographer Garry Wills wrote of him: "In some areas of politics, he seemed to know almost everything about anything —except about himself. His strengths and weaknesses fed upon each other. He was a small bitter man and a very grand diplomat. Who can read that riddle? Some of us have spent much of our lives trying to read it, with little better success than his own."

Nixon's Domestic Policy

READING FOCUS

- How did Richard Nixon's personality affect his relationship with his staff?
- How did Nixon's domestic policies differ from those of his predecessors?
- How did Nixon apply his "southern strategy" to the issue of civil rights and to his choice of Supreme Court justices?
- Describe the first manned moon landing.

KEY TERMS

deficit spending
Organization of Petroleum Exporting Countries (OPEC)
embargo
New Federalism

TAKING NOTES

Copy the chart below. As you read, fill in details about the Nixon administration. Add more boxes as needed.

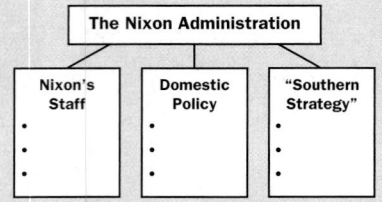

The Nixon Administration

Nixon's Staff	Domestic Policy	"Southern Strategy"
•	•	•
•	•	•
•	•	•

MAIN IDEA

President Richard Nixon relied on several close advisors to help him move the country in a new direction.

Although he was a private man, Nixon loved the applause of a crowd.

Setting the Scene Richard Nixon's victory in 1968 was, for him, particularly sweet. His earlier bid for the presidency, in 1960, had failed. Two years later he had lost another election, for governor of California. Deeply unhappy, Nixon had vowed to retire from politics. Instead, he came back from those bitter defeats to win the nation's highest office at a time when the country sorely needed strong leadership.

Nixon grew up in a low-income family in Whittier, California. He never got over his sense of being an outsider. In 1963, he described how that feeling drove him to achieve:

“ *What starts the process really are laughs and slights and snubs when you are a kid. Sometimes it's because you're poor or Irish or Jewish or Catholic or ugly or simply that you are skinny. But if you are reasonably intelligent and if your anger is deep enough and strong enough, you learn that you can change those attitudes by excellence, personal gut performance. . . .* ”

—Richard Nixon, 1963

Nixon in Person

Unlike most politicians, Richard Nixon was a reserved and remote man. Uncomfortable with people, he often seemed stiff and lacking in humor and charm. He overcame these drawbacks by using modern campaign techniques to get his message across.

Many Americans looked beyond Nixon's personality traits. They respected him for his experience and his service as Vice President under Eisenhower. Many others, though, neither trusted nor liked him.

According to Patrick Buchanan, then a Nixon speech writer, there was "a mean side to his nature." He was willing to say or do anything to defeat his

---

RESOURCE DIRECTORY

Teaching Resources
Guided Reading and Review booklet, p. 128

Technology
Section Reading Support Transparencies
Guided Reading Audiotapes (English/Spanish), Ch. 32
Student Edition on Audio CD, Ch. 32
RESOURCE PRO® Visual Learning Activity
The Imperial President, found on Resource Pro, depicts what some people termed Nixon's "imperial presidency" in two humorous posters from the early 1970s.

Prentice Hall Presentation Pro CD-ROM, Ch. 32
Companion Web site, www.phschool.com

enemies. Those enemies included his political opponents, the government bureaucracy, the press corps, and leaders of the antiwar movement.

Nixon was fully prepared to confront these forces. He wrote, "I believe in the battle, whether it's the battle of the campaign or the battle of this office, which is a continuing battle. It's always there wherever you go."

Insulating himself from people and the press, Nixon had few close friends. He found support and security in his family: his wife Pat and their two daughters. He also established lasting associations with several activists in his political campaigns. Away from the White House, he stayed far from crowds by spending time at his estates in Florida and California.

Nixon believed the executive branch of government had to be strong to be successful. When he took office, he gathered a close circle of trusted advisors around him to pursue that goal.

Nixon's Staff

Cabinet members, representatives of the executive branch departments, have historically been a President's top advisors. Many have been independent-minded people. More than most other post–World War II Presidents, Nixon avoided his Cabinet and preferred to rely on his White House staff to develop his policies. Staff members were team players. They gave him unwavering loyalty.

Two key appointees had direct access to Nixon. They shielded him from the outside world and carried out his orders. One was H. R. Haldeman, an advertising executive who had campaigned tirelessly for Nixon. He became chief of staff. Haldeman once summarized how he served the President: "I get done what he wants done and I take the heat instead of him." The other key staffer was lawyer John Ehrlichman. Ehrlichman served as Nixon's personal lawyer and rose to the post of chief domestic advisor.

Haldeman and Ehrlichman framed issues and narrowed options for the President. They also stood between the President and anybody else who wanted to speak to him. Together they became known as the "Berlin Wall" for the way they protected Nixon's privacy.

A third trusted advisor was John Mitchell, a lawyer. Mitchell had worked with Nixon in New York and had managed his presidential campaign. Nixon asked him to be Attorney General just after the 1968 election. Mitchell had great influence with the President, often speaking with him several times a day.

Another of Nixon's closest advisors did not fit the mold of Haldeman, Ehrlichman, and Mitchell. Henry Kissinger, a Harvard government professor, had no previous ties to Nixon. Still, he acquired tremendous power in the Nixon White House. Nixon first appointed Kissinger to be his national security advisor, and then, in 1973, to be Secretary of State. Kissinger played a major role in shaping foreign policy, both as an advisor to the President and in behind-the-scenes diplomacy.

Domestic Policy

The Vietnam War and domestic policy had both been important in the 1968 political campaign. As you have read, restoring law and order was one element of Nixon's domestic policy. Other domestic issues also required attention, and on these, Nixon broke with many of the policies of Presidents Kennedy and Johnson.

VIEWING HISTORY The Oval Office in the White House saw many meetings of Nixon and his inner circle of advisors. Left to right in this photo are Kissinger, Ehrlichman, the President, and Haldeman. **Synthesizing Information** *What role did Nixon's advisors play in his presidency?*

LESSON PLAN

Focus Explain that as President, Nixon displayed a penchant for secrecy that would develop into an obsession. Point out that this trait would have an important impact on Nixon's presidency.

Instruct Explain that domestically, Nixon hoped to steer the nation in a more conservative direction than had his Democratic predecessors. This proved difficult in the realm of economics, where inflation caused by war spending forced Nixon to act contrary to his stated goals. Explain that the oil crisis further aggravated the nation's economic problems. Discuss the nation's dependence on petroleum. Ask students what might happen if fuel prices rose suddenly today. Point out Nixon's greater success in instituting conservative policies in the area of social programs and law and order.

Assess/Reteach Ask students how Nixon's domestic advisers helped implement his plans. Can students describe how important it is for a President to select a cabinet that represents his views?

CUSTOMIZE FOR ...

ESL

Ask students to read the quotation by Richard Nixon on the previous page. Ask how Nixon's personal characteristics and the qualities he valued in his aides are reflected in this quote. In the discussion, have students choose specific words or phrases from the quotation that best reveal Nixon's sensibility.

✓ TEST PREPARATION

Have students read the quotation by Nixon in the second paragraph on this page and then complete the sentence below.

From the quote, you can infer that Nixon—

A believed the three branches of government should work together.

B was prepared to take a passive role in government.

C thought that he could trust most people in the government.

Ⓓ was suspicious of people and took an aggressive stance as President.

CAPTION ANSWERS

Viewing History They analyzed information for him, provided advice, carried out his orders, protected him from criticism, and guarded his privacy.

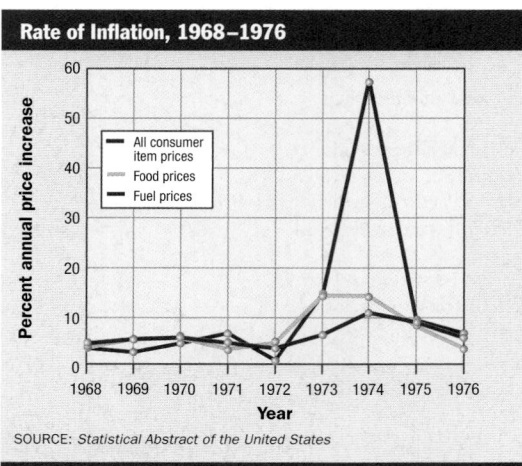

Rate of Inflation, 1968–1976

Percent annual price increase

Legend:
- All consumer item prices
- Food prices
- Fuel prices

Year: 1968 1969 1970 1971 1972 1973 1974 1975 1976

SOURCE: *Statistical Abstract of the United States*

INTERPRETING GRAPHS
Rising oil prices in the 1970s had a strong impact on all parts of the American economy. **Analyzing Information** *When did fuel prices reach their peak? What caused fuel prices to rise so dramatically?*

READING CHECK
What was the state of the nation's fuel supply before the oil embargo?

Inflation The economy was shaky when Nixon took office. Largely because of rising spending for the Vietnam War, inflation had doubled between 1965 and 1968. In addition, the government was spending more than it was taking in from taxes, so the budget deficit was growing. Unemployment was also growing.

Nixon's first priority was to halt inflation. He wanted to bring federal spending under control, even if it led to further unemployment. He was determined, though, to avoid imposing government controls on wages and prices. He had seen such controls in action while working for the Office of Price Administration during World War II. "I will not take the nation down the road of wage and price controls, however politically expedient [helpful] they may seem," he said in 1970.

During Nixon's first few years in office, however, federal spending proved difficult to control. Unemployment and inflation both continued to rise. Although Republicans traditionally aimed for a balanced budget, Nixon began to consider **deficit spending**, or spending more money in a year than the government receives in revenues. In this way he hoped to stimulate the economy. Proposed by British economist John Maynard Keynes during the Great Depression, deficit spending had restored prosperity during World War II. "I am now a Keynesian in economics," Nixon announced in 1971, to many people's surprise.

Finally, in an attempt to slow the high rate of inflation, the President imposed a 90-day freeze on wages, prices, and rents in August 1971, and a 60-day general price freeze in June 1973. Pressure from business and labor, however, led him to lift these controls, and inflation again soared.

Oil Crisis In some ways, the United States had been heading toward an energy crisis long before Nixon took office. The nation's growing population and economy used more energy each year. Coal was plentiful, but environmental concerns discouraged its use. Federal regulations imposed in the mid-1950s kept the price of natural gas low, which meant producers had little incentive to raise their output. Furthermore, the nation's oil production began to decline in 1972. Americans depended on cheap, imported oil for about a third of their energy needs.

Nixon's oil price controls served to aggravate the energy problem. Refineries let supplies run so low during the price freezes that demand could not be met after the controls were lifted.

Unrest in the Middle East turned the energy problem into a crisis. In 1973, Israel and the Arab nations of Egypt and Syria went to war. The United States backed its ally Israel. In response, the Arab members of the **Organization of Petroleum Exporting Countries (OPEC)** imposed an **embargo**, or ban, on the shipping of oil to the United States. OPEC, a group of nations that cooperates to set oil prices and production levels, also quadrupled its prices. The cost of foreign oil skyrocketed.

Higher oil prices, in turn, worsened inflation. A loaf of bread that had cost 28 cents earlier in the 1970s now cost 89 cents. Americans had paid 25 cents a gallon for gas but now paid 65 cents. Consumers reacted to the higher prices by cutting back on spending. The result was a recession.

Social Programs   President Nixon hoped to halt the growth of government spending by cutting back or shutting down some of the social programs that had mushroomed under Johnson's Great Society. Critics claimed that these programs were wasteful, encouraged "welfare cheaters," and discouraged people from seeking work.

Nixon had voiced similar complaints in his campaign, but he now faced a dilemma. On the one hand, he wanted to please conservative voters who demanded cutbacks. On the other hand, he hoped to appeal to traditionally Democratic blue-collar voters and others who favored social programs.

Nixon called for a new partnership between the federal government and the state governments known as the **New Federalism.** Under this policy, states would assume greater responsibility for the well-being of their own citizens. Congress passed a series of "revenue-sharing" bills that granted federal funds to state and local governments to use as they wished.

The "Southern Strategy"

Nixon believed he had little to gain by supporting advances in civil rights. Few African Americans had voted for him in the 1960 race against John Kennedy, and in 1968, he had won just 12 percent of the black vote. Besides, he reasoned, any attempt to appeal to black voters might cost him the support of many white southern voters.

Explaining his position, Nixon once observed that "there are those who want instant integration and those who want segregation forever. I believe that we need to have a middle course between those two extremes." In effect, this meant a slowdown in desegregation.

Nixon's aim was to find the proper "southern strategy" to win over white southern Democrats. Republican Senator Strom Thurmond of South Carolina, who had left the Democratic Party in 1948, became Nixon's strongest southern

to Today

Energy Shortages

Oil shortages caused enormous frustration in the United States during the 1970s. As shown in the photo left, lines at gas stations were long, often extending for blocks. Many people began to buy energy-efficient foreign cars instead of the "gas-guzzling" American models. Midwestern farmers had difficulty finding fuel to dry out their crops before they spoiled. Winter heating-oil shortages led to school closings in Colorado.

Electricity shortages can also cause hardships. When disruption is minor, an area may experience a brownout, a temporary reduction in electrical power.

Blackouts, complete cuts to power, are more serious. Recently, electricity shortages forced "rolling blackouts" in California, shutting off power to selected areas at hours of peak usage. Homes and businesses without alternative energy sources, such as gas-powered generators or solar energy, could not operate computers or other electrical machines and appliances. Low supplies also meant higher prices, which demonstrators (above) in California protested by burning their electricity bills. In any state, energy shortages can have serious negative effects on the economy.

? How are oil shortages of the 1970s similar to more recent energy shortages?

Connecting with Citizenship

Organize students in pairs to develop a "southern strategy" for the Democratic Party to help presidential candidate George McGovern win the South in the 1972 election. Have them present their strategy in a memo to the Democratic National Committee. Then call on pairs to explain their strategy and the reasoning behind it to the class. **(Verbal/ Linguistic)**

BACKGROUND
Presidential Power

One way Nixon cut government programs he did not like was through impoundment, a practice whereby a President refuses to spend money allocated by Congress. The Constitution is silent on whether the President must spend all the funds Congress appropriates, and Presidents dating back to Jefferson had practiced impoundment. But Nixon's use was unprecedented in both its scope and intent. By 1973 he had impounded more than $20 billion, much of which Congress had earmarked for construction of low-rent housing, mass transit, food stamps, and medical research. In 1974 Congress retaliated by passing the Congressional Budget and Impoundment Control Act, which limited a President's ability to impound appropriated funds and established the budget process the federal government uses today.

CAPTION **A**NSWERS

Fast Forward to Today The United States is still heavily dependent upon oil for the nation's energy needs. Much of this oil is still obtained from overseas suppliers. Domestic production of oil in the United States continues to be inadequate for the nation's needs.

VIEWING HISTORY In 1974, police escorts help Boston schools to comply with court-ordered busing. **Drawing Conclusions** *Why did Nixon oppose busing?*

supporter. To keep Thurmond and his colleagues happy, Nixon sought to cut funding for the enforcement of fair housing laws. He also made it easier to meet desegregation requirements.

The Justice Department, headed by John Mitchell, tried to prevent the extension of certain provisions of the Voting Rights Act of 1965 that were due to expire in 1970. This law had greatly increased the number of African Americans who could vote in the South. Congress went ahead with the extension, but through the efforts of his Attorney General, Nixon had made his point to white southern voters.

Another controversial racial issue was the use of busing to end school segregation. In several cities, federal courts ordered school systems to bus students to other schools in order to end the pattern of all-black or all-white schools. Particularly in northern cities, such as Detroit and Boston, some white students and their parents responded to busing with boycotts or violent protests.

In 1971, the Supreme Court issued guidelines for busing that went against Nixon's views. A federal judge in North Carolina had ruled that voluntary integration was not working. In *Swann* v. *Charlotte-Mecklenburg Board of Education,* the Court agreed, saying that busing was one possible option for ending school segregation.

Nixon, who had long opposed busing, then went on television to say he would ask Congress to halt it. He also allowed the Department of Health, Education, and Welfare to restore federal funding to school districts that were still segregated. Nixon's refusal to enforce the Court ruling did not halt busing in the country, but his opposition did limit it.

Nixon's Supreme Court

During the election campaign, Nixon had criticized the Supreme Court for being too liberal and easy on criminals. In his first term, four of the nine justices either died, resigned, or retired. This gave him the extraordinary opportunity to name four new justices and thus reshape the Court. Nixon first named Warren Burger as Chief Justice, replacing Earl Warren. Burger, a moderate, was easily confirmed by the Senate in 1969.

Focus on
GOVERNMENT

The Imperial Presidency Nixon took a broad view of his powers as President of the United States and is counted among several Presidents, including Andrew Jackson and Theodore Roosevelt, who sought to expand the powers of the office. Nixon worked to extend executive privileges to include rights historically reserved for kings and emperors, such as the right to use public funds at his discretion and the right to shield himself from prosecution. Because of these efforts, Nixon contributed to what came to be called the "imperial presidency." The term is sometimes used by critics who think the powers of the presidency have become too strong.

Later nominations reflected Nixon's southern strategy and conservative views. The Senate rejected his first two nominees from the South, with opponents charging the men showed racial bias. Nixon successfully appointed Harry A. Blackmun (1970); Lewis F. Powell, Jr. (1972); and William H. Rehnquist (1972). All three were respected jurists who generally tilted the Court in a more conservative direction. As Justice Blackmun's tenure continued, however, he became increasingly liberal in his decisions.

The First Moon Landing

The Nixon years witnessed the fulfillment of President Kennedy's commitment in 1961 to achieve the goal, "before this decade is out, of landing a man on the moon." That man was *Apollo 11* astronaut Neil A. Armstrong.

On July 20, 1969, at 10:56 P.M. Eastern Daylight Time, Armstrong descended from the *Eagle* lunar landing craft and set foot on the moon's surface. Armstrong radioed back the famous message: "That's one small step for man, one giant leap for mankind."

Television viewers around the world witnessed this triumph of the *Apollo* program, carried out by the National Aeronautics and Space Administration (NASA). The *Apollo 11* crew included Edwin E. "Buzz" Aldrin, Jr., who landed with Armstrong in the *Eagle,* and Michael Collins, who remained in the *Apollo 11* command module circling the moon.

Aldrin joined Armstrong in the two-hour moon walk, during which they collected rock and soil samples and set up scientific instruments to monitor conditions on the moon. They also photographed the landing site, a dusty plain in an area called the Sea of Tranquillity.

The *Eagle* and its crew stayed on the moon for 21 hours and 36 minutes before lifting off to rejoin Collins for the return trip. After a safe splashdown, the astronauts were quarantined for 18 days to ensure that they had not picked up any unknown lunar microbes. They emerged to a hero's welcome.

VIEWING HISTORY Astronaut Buzz Aldrin takes a walk on the moon. **Drawing Inferences** *Why was the government so committed to the space program?*

Section 1 Assessment

READING COMPREHENSION

1. What is **deficit spending?** How did Nixon attempt to control inflation?

2. Why was the United States vulnerable to **OPEC?**

3. How did the 1973 oil **embargo** affect the United States?

4. What was the **New Federalism?**

5. Describe the busing issues and events of the 1970s.

CRITICAL THINKING AND WRITING

6. **Recognizing Bias** How was Nixon's image of himself as an outsider reflected in the way he ran the White House? Use specific examples in your explanation.

7. **Writing to Persuade** Write an outline for a persuasive essay either supporting or opposing Nixon's domestic policies.

 Take It to the NET

Activity: Writing a Newspaper Article Research an area of President Nixon's domestic policy, and write a newspaper article on the topic you selected. Use the links provided in the *America: Pathways to the Present* area of the following Web site for help in completing this activity.
www.phschool.com

Chapter 32 • Section 1 **1063**

Section 1 Assessment

Reading Comprehension

1. Spending more money in a year than the government receives in revenues.

2. The United States depended on cheap, imported oil for about one-third of its energy needs.

3. Foreign oil prices skyrocketed; inflation worsened; and higher prices caused people to cut back on spending, which resulted in a recession.

4. A partnership between the federal government and the state governments granting the states greater responsibility for the well-being of their own citizens. This included the introduction of block grants of federal money to states. The individual states then decided how to spend their respective federal grants.

5. Federal courts in several cities ordered school systems to desegregate immediately by busing African American students to formerly all-white schools and vice versa. Boycotts and violent protests resulted in some (mostly northern) cities. The Supreme Court ruled in favor of busing, but Nixon impeded the process. He asked Congress, unsuccessfully, to halt busing, and he restored federal funding to segregated school districts.

Critical Thinking and Writing

6. Sample answer: His penchant for secrecy, and the fact that Nixon essentially ignored his Cabinet and relied instead on a very small circle of advisors.

7. Outlines will vary but should persuade the reader by using facts from the section.

 **Take It to the NET**

Articles will vary, but should demonstrate an understanding of Nixon's domestic policies overall, with a focus on one particular issue.

CAPTION ANSWERS

Viewing History Sample answer: To win the "space race" that had been going on for a decade between the United States and the Soviet Union.

SECTION OBJECTIVES

1. Learn about the role Henry Kissinger played in relaxing tensions between the United States and the major Communist powers.

2. Find out about Nixon's policy toward the People's Republic of China.

3. Discover how Nixon reached an agreement with the Soviet Union on limiting nuclear arms.

BELLRINGER

Warm-Up Activity Present students with the following situation: The United States is locked in a costly competition with powerful enemies for influence around the world, and no one is winning. How should the United States break the stalemate? Explain that Nixon faced a similar predicament during his presidency.

Activating Prior Knowledge Ask students to state what they know about relations between the United States and China in the years following World War II, leading up to the 1970s. Was there open dialogue and freedom of movement between the two countries at that time?

READING STRATEGY

As students read the section, have them take notes on the following topics: (a) Henry Kissinger and American foreign policy; (b) United States relations with China; and (c) United States relations with the Soviet Union. Have students consider the challenges of changing relationships among nations.

CAPTION ANSWERS

Viewing History Kissinger was a foreign affairs expert, and he knew how to persuade Nixon. The two men had much in common. For instance, both were by nature intensely suspicious. Nixon and Kissinger also both liked to operate under a cloak of secrecy.

1064 • Chapter 32 Section 2

READING FOCUS

- What role did Henry Kissinger play in relaxing tensions between the United States and the major Communist powers?
- What was Nixon's policy toward the People's Republic of China?
- How did Nixon reach an agreement with the Soviet Union on limiting nuclear arms?

MAIN IDEA

President Nixon's foreign policy led to more positive relationships with China and the Soviet Union.

KEY TERMS

realpolitik
détente
SALT I

TAKING NOTES

Copy the web diagram below. Include three or four blank circles. As you read, fill in each blank circle with important facts about U.S. relations with China and the Soviet Union during Nixon's presidency.

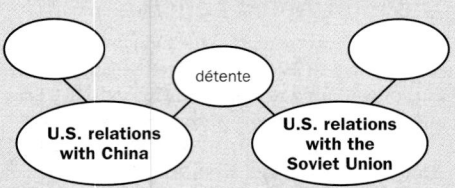

détente

U.S. relations with China

U.S. relations with the Soviet Union

Setting the Scene As President, Richard Nixon's greatest achievements came in the field of foreign policy. "I've always thought this country could run itself domestically without a President," he observed. In his first Inaugural Address, Nixon set the stage for a new direction in foreign relations:

VIEWING HISTORY President Nixon owed the success of much of his foreign policy to his national security advisor, and later, Secretary of State, Henry Kissinger. **Demonstrating Reasoned Judgment** Why did Nixon rely so heavily on Kissinger's advice?

> **66** *After a period of confrontation, we are entering an era of negotiation. Let all nations know that during this administration our lines of communication will be open. We seek an open world. Open to ideas, open to the exchange of goods and people. A world in which no people, great or small, will live in angry isolation. We cannot expect to make everyone our friend, but we can try to make no one our enemy.* **99**
> —Nixon's First Inaugural Address, January 20, 1969

Nixon's creative approach to foreign affairs helped ease Cold War tensions. Aided by the skillful diplomacy of Henry Kissinger, Nixon helped establish ties with China and crafted stronger relations with the Soviet Union.

Henry Kissinger

While Nixon had a keen understanding of foreign policy, he relied heavily on Henry Kissinger in charting his course. Kissinger quickly gained the President's confidence. By the time Nixon appointed Kissinger Secretary of State in 1973, he was a dominant figure in the administration.

Practical Politics Kissinger had written his doctoral dissertation on Klemens von Metternich, an Austrian statesman and diplomat in the nineteenth century who had helped maintain stability in Europe amid liberal change. Kissinger's studies in European history gave him an admiration for ***realpolitik***, a German term meaning "practical politics." Nations that follow this policy make decisions based on maintaining their own strength rather than following moral principles. Kissinger would later apply this approach to his dealings with China and the Soviet Union.

RESOURCE DIRECTORY

Teaching Resources
Learning Styles Lesson Plans booklet, p. 66
Guided Reading and Review booklet, p. 129

Technology
Section Reading Support Transparencies
Guided Reading Audiotapes (English/Spanish), Ch. 32
Student Edition on Audio CD, Ch. 32
Color Transparencies *Time Lines,* C9
Prentice Hall Presentation Pro CD-ROM, Ch. 32
Companion Web site, www.phschool.com

Nixon liked to be flattered, and he liked people who could talk tough. Kissinger, who understood what Nixon wanted from an advisor, soon became the man Nixon talked to most. "Henry, of course, was not a personal friend," Nixon later said, but the two spoke five or six times a day, sometimes in person, sometimes by phone, and often for hours at a time.

Both men were suspicious and secretive. They tended not to seek consensus, or general agreement with others, but to keep information to themselves. "They tried not to let anyone else have a full picture, even if it meant deceiving them," noted Lawrence Eagleburger, a State Department official.

Kissinger's actual influence in shaping American foreign policy was broader than his official role as Secretary of State. He knew how to frame questions in ways the President wanted. He could condense complex foreign policy issues into briefing papers that gave Nixon clear options for making decisions. In his memoirs, Kissinger wrote:

> ❝ Nixon could be very decisive. Almost invariably during his Presidency, his decisions were courageous and strong and often taken in loneliness against all expert advice. But wherever possible Nixon made these decisions in solitude on the basis of memoranda or with a few very intimate aides. ❞
>
> —Henry Kissinger, *The White House Years*

Public Opinion Kissinger also understood the power of the press. He had a remarkable ability to use the media to shape public opinion. Journalists depended on him for stories, so they were afraid to anger him. "You know you are being played like a violin," a *Time* magazine reporter observed, "but it's still extremely seductive."

Kissinger's efforts in ending the Vietnam War and easing Cold War tensions made him a celebrity. He shared the 1973 Nobel peace prize with North Vietnam's Le Duc Tho (who refused it); he appeared on 21 *Time* magazine covers; and in a 1973 Gallup poll, he led the list of the most-admired Americans. Kissinger's efforts in the Nixon administration left a lasting mark on American foreign policy.

Relaxing Tensions

Nixon and Kissinger's greatest accomplishment was in bringing about **détente**, or a relaxation in tensions, between the United States and the world's two Communist giants. China and the Soviet Union were sworn enemies of the United States. Nixon's willingness to conduct talks with them stunned many observers. In the 1950s, Nixon had been one of the most bitter and active anti-Communists in government. He had made his reputation by demanding that the United States stand firm against the Communist threat.

As President, however, Nixon dealt imaginatively with both China and the Soviet Union. Nixon distrusted government bureaucracy, so he kept much of his diplomacy secret. Bypassing Congress, and often bypassing his own advisors, he and Kissinger reversed the direction of postwar American foreign policy.

Nixon drew on Kissinger's understanding that foreign affairs were more complex than a simple standoff between the United States and communism.

BIOGRAPHY

Henry Kissinger
b. 1923

Like a number of other German Jews, 15-year-old Henry Kissinger and his family fled Nazi Germany in 1938 and settled in New York City. During the day, the young immigrant worked at a shaving brush company. At night he completed high school courses. Kissinger became a naturalized citizen in 1943, and served in the United States Army during World War II. Kissinger had attended City College of New York before the war and later transferred to Harvard. There he completed both undergraduate and graduate degrees. As a Harvard professor, Kissinger became a recognized expert on foreign relations. Nixon lured him away from Harvard in 1969 by offering him a job as his national security advisor.

After his years in Washington, D.C., Kissinger went on to become a foreign policy consultant and lecturer. He has written several books, including the first volume of his memoirs, *The White House Years* (1979).

READING CHECK
What were some obstacles to achieving détente?

VIEWING HISTORY Chinese premier Zhou Enlai and President Richard Nixon congratulate each other on the new ties between their nations. **Determining Relevance** *Why was it important for the press to capture such moments?*

The President and First Lady Pat Nixon head a group touring the Great Wall of China.

The Soviet Union and China, once allies, had become bitter enemies. This stunning development had the potential to reshape global politics. "The deepest international conflict in the world today," Kissinger noted, "is not between us and the Soviet Union but between the Soviet Union and Communist China."

A New Approach to China

The most surprising policy shift was toward China. In 1949, the Communists had taken power and established the People's Republic of China. Many Americans saw all Communists as part of a united plot to dominate the world. As a result, the United States did not formally recognize the new Chinese government. In effect, the United States officially pretended that it did not exist.

Even when the Chinese-Soviet alliance crumbled, the United States clung to its position. It insisted that the government of Jiang Jieshi, which was set up on the island of Taiwan when the Nationalists fled the Chinese mainland, was the rightful government of all China.

Opportunity for Change Quietly, Nixon began to prepare the way for a new policy of *realpolitik*. His first foreign policy report to Congress in 1970 began:

> 66 The Chinese are a great and vital people who should not remain isolated from the international community. . . . United States policy is not likely soon to have much impact on China's behavior, let alone its ideological outlook. But it is certainly in our interest, and in the interest of peace and stability in Asia and the world, that we take what steps we can toward improved practical relations with Peking [Beijing]. 99

—Richard Nixon, report to Congress, 1970

The administration undertook a series of moves designed to improve the relationship between the United States and China:

1. In January and February 1970, American and Chinese ambassadors met in Warsaw, Poland.
2. In October 1970, in a first for an American President, Nixon referred to China by its official title, the People's Republic of China.
3. In March 1971, the United States government lifted restrictions on travel to China.
4. In April 1971, an American table-tennis team accepted a Chinese invitation to visit the mainland, beginning what was called "ping-pong diplomacy."
5. In June 1971, the United States ended its 21-year embargo on trade with the People's Republic of China.

In July 1971, after extensive secret diplomacy by Kissinger, Nixon made the dramatic announcement that he planned to visit China the following year. He would be the first United States President ever to travel to that country.

Nixon understood that the People's Republic was an established government that would not simply disappear. Other nations had recognized the government, and it was time for the United States to do the same. Similarly, other countries wanted to give China's seat in the United Nations to the People's Republic. The United States could no longer

1066   Chapter 32 • *Nixon, Ford, Carter*

convince the world to oppose this change. In October 1971, Taiwan lost its seat in the United Nations to the People's Republic of China.

Benefiting From Friendship Nixon had other motives as well. He recognized that he could use Chinese friendship as a bargaining chip in his negotiations with the Soviet Union. (In other words, the Soviet Union might compromise with the United States in order to keep the United States and China from developing too close a relationship.) Press coverage of the trip would give Nixon a boost at home. Also, he believed that he could take this action without suffering political damage, because of his reputation as a strong anti-Communist.

Nixon traveled to China in February 1972. He met with Mao Zedong, the Chinese leader who had led the revolution in 1949. He spoke with Premier Zhou Enlai about international problems and ways of dealing with them. He and his wife Pat toured the Great Wall and other Chinese sights, all in front of television cameras that sent the historic pictures home.

When he returned to the United States, Nixon waited in his plane until prime time so that his return would be seen by as many television viewers as possible. Formal relations were not yet restored—that would take a few more years—but the basis for diplomatic ties had been established. While some members of Congress remained outspoken in their opposition to Communist China, most members—and most Americans—applauded Nixon for taking a more realistic approach to Asia.

NOTABLE PRESIDENTS
Richard M. Nixon

*37th President
1969–1974*

"In trusting too much in government, we have asked of it more than it can deliver."
—**Second Inaugural Address, 1973**

Born in Yorba Linda, California, in 1913, Richard Milhous Nixon spent his early years in southern California. He worked at his family's gas station and grocery store while attending Whittier College, and then moved to North Carolina, where he graduated from the Duke University School of Law.

Nixon returned to California to practice law. A few years later, in 1940, he married Patricia Ryan. Nixon served as a naval officer during World War II. When the war was over, Nixon began his political career, winning a seat as a Republican in the U.S. House of Representatives. During this time, Nixon gained national prominence for his lead role within the House Un-American Activities Committee (HUAC) in 1948. While serving on HUAC, Nixon showed himself to be an aggressive politician, while gaining many admirers, as well as critics, for his anti-Communist zeal.

After two terms in the House, Nixon was elected to the United States Senate, and then served as Vice President during the Eisenhower administration, from 1953 to 1961.

Many believe Nixon's greatest successes while President were in the field of foreign relations. However, his foreign policy achievements are often overshadowed by the Watergate scandal, and what many saw as Nixon's failure to preserve the trust of the American people. The scandal forced Nixon to resign from office in 1974, the only President in United States history to do so.

After leaving office, Nixon wrote several books and traveled to many countries, including China and the Soviet Union, where he continued his work on foreign relations. He died in 1994.

Connecting to Today
Examine recent U.S. foreign policy decisions. How do they compare to Nixon's approach to foreign relations?

 **Take It to the NET Biography** To read more about Richard Nixon, visit the links provided in the *America: Pathways to the Present* area of the following Web site. **www.phschool.com**

Connecting with History and Conflict

The SALT I treaty negotiated between the Soviet Union and the United States marked a major step forward in relations between the two countries. Have students create an illustrated time line of the history of arms control negotiations between the Soviet Union (and the independent post-Soviet republics) and the United States. The time line should highlight the important successes and failures of these negotiations. **(Visual/Spatial)**

BACKGROUND
Connections to Today

Though Richard Nixon reestablished diplomatic relations with China, he remained watchful and somewhat wary of that vast country. At the time, he told his speechwriter William Safire, "We may have created a Frankenstein." In his last book, *Beyond Peace,* written shortly before his death, Nixon noted: "The giant is awake and is beginning to move the world." Nixon felt certain that economic freedom in China would ultimately lead to political freedom, ". . . but only," he wrote, "if economic freedom is not suppressed by frightened political dictators or sabotaged by shortsighted U.S. policies cutting back on trade with China because of its human rights abuses."

SLBM Submarine-Launched Ballistic Missile

ICBM Intercontinental Ballistic Missile

ABM Anti-Ballistic Missile

Average range: 600–3,500 miles. These missiles, launched by submarines beneath the surface, are a type of IRBM (Intermediate-Range Ballistic Missile) with smaller warheads and a shorter range than ICBMs. The advantage of submarine-launched missiles is that they are difficult for the enemy to locate and destroy.

Poseidon C-3 Introduced in 1971, the Poseidon had a range of about 2,800 miles and could carry multiple warheads.

Range: Up to 8,000 miles. These are missiles fired from underground silos. After an initial burst of power, they travel most of the distance to their target by momentum.

Minuteman III This missile was the most widely deployed ICBM around the time of the SALT talks. It was the first missile to carry Multiple Independent Re-entry Vehicles (MIRVs), meaning that a single Minuteman missile can send warheads to several targets.

In the late 1960s, both the United States and the Soviet Union deployed interceptor missile systems meant to destroy incoming ballistic missiles. The United States built these missiles mainly to protect ICBM launch sites. Safeguard, the ABM program created under Nixon, was shut down in 1975 because it was judged to be unreliable.

Spartan The Spartan missile had a range of 465 miles.

Sprint This smaller missile had a 25-mile range.

INTERPRETING DIAGRAMS
The SALT I Treaty limited the stockpiling of missiles in various categories. **Synthesizing Information** *Which type of missile is used to ward off other missiles?*

Limiting Nuclear Arms

Several months after his 1972 China trip, Nixon visited the Soviet Union. He received as warm a welcome in Moscow as he had in Beijing. In a series of friendly meetings between Nixon and Premier Leonid I. Brezhnev, the two nations reached several decisions. They agreed to work together to explore space, eased longstanding trade limits, and completed negotiations on a weapons pact.

Balancing the Superpowers Nixon viewed arms control as a vital part of his foreign policy. Like many Americans, he was worried about the superpowers' growing stockpiles of nuclear weapons. The Limited Test Ban Treaty of 1963 had ended testing of new bombs in the atmosphere, but underground testing continued. The two superpowers were making bigger and more powerful bombs all the time. Some people feared that the world might be destroyed unless these weapons were brought under control.

Nixon was determined to address the nuclear threat and to deal creatively with the Soviet Union at the same time. He had taken office with the intention of building more nuclear weapons to keep ahead of the Soviet Union, but he came to believe that this kind of arms race made little sense. Each nation already had more than enough weapons to destroy its enemy many times over. The nuclear age demanded balance between the superpowers.

Weapons Talks To address the issue, the United States and the Soviet Union had begun the Strategic Arms Limitation Talks in 1969. In 1972, the talks produced a treaty that would limit offensive nuclear weapons. This treaty was ready for Nixon to sign during his visit to Moscow.

The first Strategic Arms Limitation Treaty, known as **SALT I,** included a five-year agreement that froze the number of intercontinental ballistic missiles (ICBMs) and submarine-launched ballistic missiles (SLBMs) at 1972 levels. The treaty also included an agreement restricting the development and deployment of antiballistic missile defense systems (ABMs), which were designed to shoot down attacking missiles.

ACTIVITY

Connecting with History and Conflict

Organize students into groups to analyze SALT I and develop a theory to explain why it banned ABM systems in addition to limiting offensive missiles. Tell groups to also see if they can agree as a group whether or not SALT I would have reduced their fears of nuclear war had they been old enough to vote at the time the treaty was signed. Have representatives of each group explain its conclusions and reasoning to the class. **(Logical/Mathematical)**

BACKGROUND

Global Connections

In the 1970s the Soviet Union's rise as a nuclear superpower intensified the Cold War. In 1971, for the first time, the Soviet Union surpassed the United States in total number of land- and submarine-based nuclear missiles. A confident Foreign Minister Andrei Gromyko boasted that in world affairs, "No question of any significance . . . can now be decided without the Soviet Union or in opposition to it."

CAPTION ANSWERS

Interpreting Diagrams Anti-Ballistic Missile (ABM).

RESOURCE DIRECTORY

Teaching Resources
Units 9/10 booklet
• Section 2 Quiz, p. 53
Guide to the Essentials
• Section 2 Summary, p. 162

While Congress approved SALT I and the treaty went into effect, some government officials were troubled by the agreement. They worried that the treaty's limitation on missiles might leave the United States unprepared to defend itself in an emergency. One solution was to improve conventional weapons, which were not limited by the treaty. Therefore, Secretary of Defense Melvin Laird made the Pentagon's approval contingent on a commitment to move ahead with plans to build a better bomber and a larger submarine. At the same time, both the United States and the Soviet Union began to develop a new technology that used multiple nuclear warheads on a single missile, and was correspondingly more destructive.

SALT I was a triumph for the Nixon administration and an important step forward. Yet it did not reduce the number of warheads the two nations possessed. Nor did it stop them from improving nuclear weapons in other ways. Still, it helped to ease what had been growing concerns about the arms race, and it demonstrated the willingness of the United States and the Soviet Union to work together toward a common goal. In showing that arms control agreements between the superpowers were possible, SALT I paved the way for more progress in the future.

About a year before the signing of SALT I, Nixon pointed out that the potential benefits of negotiating with the Soviet Union went beyond the issue of limiting nuclear arms:

> 66 *Perhaps for the first time, the evolving strategic balance allows a Soviet-American agreement which yields no unilateral [one-sided] advantages. The fact [that] we have begun to discuss strategic arms with the USSR is in itself important. Agreement in such a vital area could create a new commitment to stability, and influence attitudes toward other issues.* 99

—Richard Nixon

Focus on GOVERNMENT

Shuttle Diplomacy After the Arab-Israeli War in 1973, Kissinger undertook what came to be known as shuttle diplomacy, traveling back and forth between Middle Eastern capitals to arrange peace. In April 1974, he secured a cease-fire agreement between Israel and Syria, whose forces had been fighting on the Golan Heights. In June, President Nixon visited the Middle East to recognize the success of Kissinger's efforts to reduce tensions in the region. Others holding the office of Secretary of State since Kissinger have followed his lead, using shuttle diplomacy to further U.S. foreign policy goals.

Section 2 — Assessment

READING COMPREHENSION

1. How did Kissinger use *realpolitik* to carry out Nixon's foreign policy?

2. What is the meaning of **détente?** Why was it difficult to achieve détente with Communist nations?

3. What did the term "ping-pong diplomacy" refer to in the Nixon administration? What steps were taken to improve the relationship between the United States and China?

4. What were Nixon's concerns about nuclear weapons?

5. What was **SALT I?**

CRITICAL THINKING AND WRITING

6. **Identifying Central Issues** What were Nixon's policies toward China and the Soviet Union? Why were they so surprising at the time?

7. **Drawing Conclusions** Why did Nixon and Kissinger believe it was important to relax the tensions between the United States and both China and the Soviet Union?

8. **Writing an Opinion** Considering the limitations of SALT I, do you think it was an important treaty? Make a list of reasons to support your opinion.

Take It to the NET

Activity: Writing an Editorial
Research an aspect of President Nixon's foreign policy that interests you. Write an editorial for your local newspaper reacting to the events or policies you have studied. Use the links provided in the *America: Pathways to the Present* area of the following Web site for help in completing this activity.
www.phschool.com

Chapter 32 • Section 2   1069

Section 2 — Assessment

Reading Comprehension

1. He used the policy of making decisions based on maintaining the strength of one's nation rather than following moral principles in his dealings with China and the Soviet Union.

2. A relaxation in tensions. China and the Soviet Union were sworn enemies of the U.S.

3. The U.S. National Table Tennis team traveled to mainland China in order to play against the Chinese National team in April 1971. This was part of the Nixon era warming of relations between the two countries. This effort included other measures, such as the U.S. government lifting restrictions on travel to China.

4. He was worried about the superpowers' growing stockpiles of nuclear weapons, and he shared the concern of the American people that the growing arsenal posed a threat to the world if weapons went uncontrolled.

5. The Strategic Arms Limitation Treaty signed by the United States and the Soviet Union in 1972. This was the culmination of arms control talks that had begun in 1969 with the goal of limiting offensive nuclear weapons.

Critical Thinking and Writing

6. His policies involved working to improve American relations with both Communist China and the Soviet Union. This plan was surprising because in the past, Nixon had insisted on a firm stand against Communist countries.

7. Former allies, China and the Soviet Union had become enemies. This new relationship had the potential to reshape global politics.

8. Possible answer: It was the first step toward limiting arms on the part of the United States and the Soviet Union, and it opened the door to further discussions between the two superpowers.

Take It to the NET

Editorials will vary, but should thoroughly examine one of Nixon's foreign policies, presenting facts as well as opinion.

SECTION OBJECTIVES

1. See how the Nixon White House battled its political enemies.
2. Find out how the Committee to Re-elect the President conducted itself during Nixon's reelection campaign.
3. Learn about the Watergate break-in, and see how the story of the scandal unfolded.
4. Discover the events that led directly to Nixon's resignation.

BELLRINGER

Warm-Up Activity Ask students how they would feel if they discovered that the President might have broken the law. Ask them to discuss the impact of such news and its effect on the perception of the symbolic role of the President.

Activating Prior Knowledge Can students list other Presidents who were subjected to Congressional investigations? What were the outcomes of those investigations?

READING STRATEGY

As students read, have them take notes on the various events related to the Watergate scandal. Have them use the terms *Who, What, When, Where,* and *Why* to help them organize each piece of information.

CAPTION ANSWERS

Interpreting Political Cartoons Sample answer: Nixon has more enemies than he has friends.

The Watergate Scandal

READING FOCUS

- How did the Nixon White House battle its political enemies?
- How did the Committee to Reelect the President conduct itself during Nixon's reelection campaign?
- What was the Watergate break-in, and how did the story of the scandal unfold?
- What events led directly to Nixon's resignation?

MAIN IDEA

The break-in at the Watergate apartment complex started a scandal that led to President Nixon's resignation.

KEY TERMS

wiretap
Watergate scandal
special prosecutor
impeach

TAKING NOTES

Copy the cause-and-effect diagram below. As you read, add information about the Watergate scandal and Nixon's resignation.

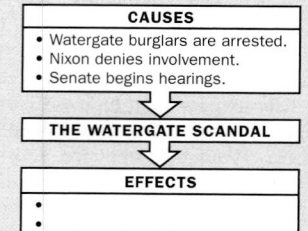

CAUSES
• Watergate burglars are arrested.
• Nixon denies involvement.
• Senate begins hearings.

THE WATERGATE SCANDAL

EFFECTS
•
•

Setting the Scene President Nixon was determined to win an overwhelming victory in the 1972 election. With such a mandate, he would be in a strong position to move his programs through Congress. Fiercely loyal aides carried out schemes to help ensure that the President would win, some of them committing crimes in the process. When Nixon tried to hide their illegal actions, he involved himself in a scandal that ended his presidency and shook the foundations of American government.

In a detailed chronicle of the events surrounding the fall of Richard Nixon, author Theodore H. White observed:

INTERPRETING POLITICAL CARTOONS This 1973 cartoon pokes fun at Nixon for compiling an "enemies list." **Drawing Inferences** *What message is conveyed by the two lists in the cartoon?*

"YOU THOUGHT OF ANOTHER NAME? OH, GOOD, SIR... FOR WHICH LIST?"

66 *The true crime of Richard Nixon was simple: he destroyed the myth that binds America together, and for this he was driven from power.*

The myth he broke was critical—that somewhere in American life there is at least one man who stands for law, the President. . . . It was that faith that Richard Nixon broke, betraying those who voted for him even more than those who voted against him. 99

—Theodore H. White, *Breach of Faith*

Battling Political Enemies

The President's suspicious and secretive nature caused the White House to operate as if it were surrounded by political enemies. Nixon's staff tried to protect him at all costs from anything that might weaken his political position.

The Enemies List One result of this mind-set was what became known as the "enemies list." Special counsel Charles W. Colson helped develop a list of prominent people who were seen as unsympathetic to the administration. It included politicians such as Senator Edward Kennedy, reporters such as Daniel

---

RESOURCE DIRECTORY

Teaching Resources
Guided Reading and Review booklet, p. 130

Technology
Section Reading Support Transparencies
Guided Reading Audiotapes (English/Spanish), Ch. 32
Student Edition on Audio CD, Ch. 32
Prentice Hall Presentation Pro CD-ROM, Ch. 32
Companion Web site, www.phschool.com

Schorr, and a number of outspoken performers such as comedian Dick Gregory and actors Jane Fonda and Steve McQueen. Aides then considered how to harass these White House "enemies." One idea, for example, was to arrange income tax investigations of people on the list.

Wiretaps In 1968, Nixon had campaigned as a man who believed in law and order. Sometimes, however, he was willing to take illegal actions. In 1969, someone in the National Security Council appeared to have leaked secret information to the *New York Times*. In response, Nixon ordered Henry Kissinger to install **wiretaps,** or listening devices, on the telephones of several members of his own staff. He also ordered wiretaps on some news reporters' phones. These wiretaps, installed for national security reasons, were legal at the time. Yet they would lead to other, illegal wiretaps, many of them for political purposes.

The Plumbers In the spring of 1971, Daniel Ellsberg, a former Defense Department official, handed the *New York Times* a huge, secret Pentagon study of the Vietnam War. In June 1971, as you have read, the *New York Times* began to publish this study, which became known as the Pentagon Papers. The documents showed that previous Presidents had deceived Congress and the American people about the real situation in Vietnam.

Nixon was furious that Ellsberg could get away with leaking secret government information. He was even more furious when leaks to the press continued. He and Kissinger were in the midst of secret discussions with China and the Soviet Union, and he did not want those talks to become public.

Nixon approved a plan to organize a special White House unit to stop government leaks. The group, nicknamed the Plumbers, included E. Howard Hunt, a spy novelist and former CIA agent, and G. Gordon Liddy, a former FBI agent. In September 1971, with approval from White House chief domestic advisor John Ehrlichman, the undercover unit broke into the office of Ellsberg's psychiatrist. The Plumbers hoped to find and disclose damaging information about Ellsberg's private life. Their goal was to punish Ellsburg for leaking the Pentagon Papers.

Nixon's Reelection Campaign

Determined to ensure Nixon's victory in 1972, the Committee to Reelect the President used similarly questionable tactics. Headed by John Mitchell, who resigned as Attorney General to assume command, the Committee launched a special fund-raising campaign. It wanted to collect as much money as possible before a new law made it necessary to report such contributions. The money would fund both routine campaign activities and unethical actions hidden from the public.

Though a few of the Committee's actions might have been considered annoying pranks, others were damaging. In 1972, people on the Committee payroll made up a letter attempting to discredit Edmund Muskie, a Democratic senator from Maine and a leading presidential contender. Then they leaked the letter to a conservative New Hampshire newspaper.

Charging Muskie with making insulting remarks about French Canadians living in the state, the letter was timed to arrive two weeks before the New Hampshire primary. The letter also claimed that Muskie's wife was an alcoholic. The normally composed Muskie broke down in tears in front of TV cameras, seriously hurting his candidacy.

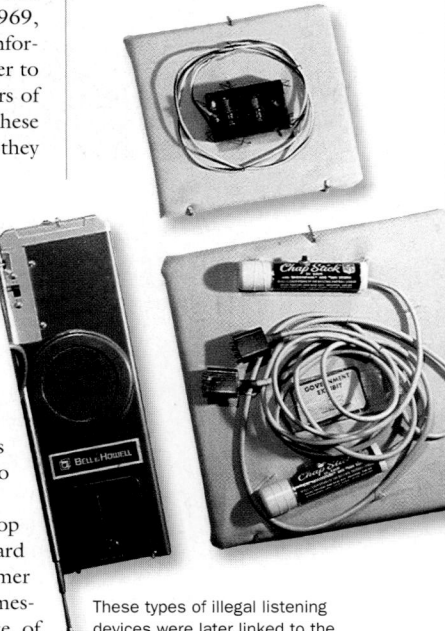

These types of illegal listening devices were later linked to the Nixon administration.

READING CHECK
Why did the press leaks infuriate Nixon?

Focus Tell students that Nixon's suspicious nature and his willingness to use his presidential power for partisan political ends set in motion a series of events that compromised the presidency itself. Ask students how the people of the United States reacted to presidential wrongdoing.

Instruct Discuss the atmosphere in the White House as described in this section. What does the existence of the "enemies list" reveal about Nixon's view of the world? Ask students to consider the fact that Nixon harassed those he perceived as hostile by arranging income tax investigations of them. Are such actions an abuse of power? Why or why not?

Assess/Reteach Ask students to list Nixon's attributes as President, both positive and negative. Do they think that, in the end, the value of his accomplishments outweighs the impact of his illegal actions?

ACTIVITY
Connecting with Government

Ask students to create a poem or a rap that expresses their evaluation of Richard Nixon as President. Remind students to consider Nixon's strengths and successes as well as his flaws and failures before forming an opinion about him. Invite students to present their creations to the class. **(Musical/Rhythmic)**

READING CHECK
Nixon was a deeply suspicious and insecure person. Also, leaks might disturb the secret talks he and Kissinger were having with China and the Soviet Union.

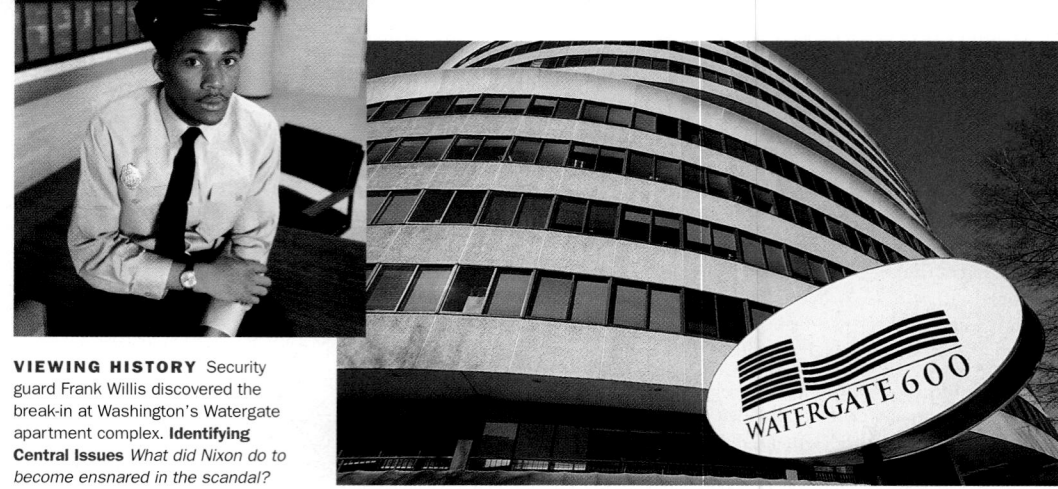

VIEWING HISTORY Security guard Frank Willis discovered the break-in at Washington's Watergate apartment complex. **Identifying Central Issues** What did Nixon do to become ensnared in the scandal?

A May 1973 *Time* magazine cover shows some players in the Watergate scandal, from left, John Ehrlichman; John W. Dean III; H. R. Haldeman; James McCord, Jr.; E. Howard Hunt; and G. Gordon Liddy.

Attempts such as this to sabotage Nixon's political opponents came to be known as "dirty tricks." They included sending hecklers to disrupt Democratic campaign meetings and assigning spies to join the campaigns of major candidates.

The Watergate Break-In

Within the Committee to Reelect the President, a group formed to gather intelligence. The group, which included "Plumbers" Liddy and Hunt, masterminded several outlandish plans.

One scheme called for wiretapping top Democrats to try to find damaging information about delegates at their convention. Twice, Committee leader John Mitchell refused to go along—not because the plan was illegal, but because it was too expensive. Finally, in March 1972, he approved a different idea. Liddy would oversee the wiretapping of phones at Democratic National Committee headquarters in the Watergate apartment complex in Washington, D.C.

The first break-in to install illegal listening devices failed. A second attempt early on the morning of June 17, 1972, ended with the arrest of the five men involved. One suspect was James McCord, a former CIA employee working as a security officer for the Committee to Reelect the President. The Watergate burglars carried money that could be linked to the Committee, thus tying the break-in directly to Nixon's reelection campaign.

When the FBI traced the money carried by the Watergate burglars to the reelection committee, Nixon contacted the CIA. He authorized that organization to try to persuade the FBI to stop its investigation on the grounds that the matter involved "national security."

This action would come back to haunt the President. Although he had not been involved in planning the break-in, Nixon was now part of the illegal coverup. The break-in and the coverup became known as the **Watergate scandal.**

In the months following the Watergate break-in, the incident barely reached the public's notice. Behind the scenes in the White House, some of the President's closest aides worked feverishly to keep the truth hidden.

1072 Chapter 32 • *Nixon, Ford, Carter*

In the summer of 1972, Nixon advisors H. R. Haldeman, John Ehrlichman, John Mitchell, and others launched a scheme to bribe the Watergate defendants. They distributed hundreds of thousands of dollars in illegal "hush money" to buy their silence. Also, to shield the President, Mitchell and other top officials coached the defendants about how to commit perjury by lying under oath in court.

Their efforts paid off in the November presidential election. Nixon trounced Senator George McGovern of South Dakota, a liberal Democrat, by 520 to 17 electoral votes and a sizable majority of the popular vote. Nixon had the mandate he wanted, though he did not get a Republican majority in either house of Congress.

The Scandal Unfolds

Despite Nixon's victory in the election, the Watergate story refused to go away. Newspapers such as the *Washington Post* continued to ask probing questions of administration officials. Nixon himself had proclaimed publicly that "no one in the White House staff, no one in this administration, presently employed, was involved in this very bizarre incident." Not everyone believed him.

The Watergate Trial The trial of the Watergate burglars began in January 1973 before Judge John J. Sirica. All the defendants either pleaded guilty or were found guilty. Meanwhile, the White House and the President himself were becoming more deeply involved. In March 1973, just before the judge handed down the sentences, Nixon personally approved the payment of "hush money" to defendant E. Howard Hunt.

At sentencing time, Judge Sirica was not convinced that the full story had yet been told. Criticizing the prosecution, he said:

> 66 I have not been satisfied, and I am still not satisfied that all the pertinent facts that might be available—I say might be available—have been produced before an American jury. . . . I would hope that the Senate committee is granted the power by Congress . . . to try to get to the bottom of what happened in this case. 99
>
> —Judge John J. Sirica

To prompt the burglars to talk, Sirica sentenced them to long prison terms, up to 40 years. Their sentences could be reduced, he suggested, if they cooperated with the upcoming Senate hearings on Watergate.

Watergate Chronology

1972

June: Five men linked to Nixon's reelection campaign are arrested for breaking into the Democratic National Committee headquarters.

1973

April: Nixon denies knowledge of the break-in.

May: The Senate Select Committee on Presidential Campaign Activities begins hearings (right).

June: Former Nixon counsel John Dean tells the committee that Nixon authorized a coverup.

July: The committee discovers that Nixon had been secretly recording presidential conversations since 1971 and orders Nixon to release certain tapes. Nixon refuses.

August: Special Prosecutor Archibald Cox sues Nixon for the tapes.

October: Nixon offers summaries of the tapes, which Cox rejects. Nixon fires Cox, setting off a series of firings known as the "Saturday Night Massacre." The House takes steps to impeach Nixon. Nixon releases all but two of the requested tapes.

November: An 18½-minute gap is found on one of the tapes.

1974

January: Nixon claims "executive privilege."

April: Nixon is ordered to surrender more tapes and related documents. Nixon supplies 1,254 pages of edited transcripts. Special Prosecutor Leon Jaworski sues Nixon for the originals.

July: The Supreme Court orders Nixon to surrender the tapes and documents. The House Judiciary Committee recommends impeachment.

August: Nixon releases transcripts that prove he learned of the break-in as early as June 23, 1972, and ordered the coverup. Nixon resigns August 9. His resignation speech is televised (right).

INTERPRETING TIME LINES
As the investigation unfolded, it became increasingly clear that Nixon had something to hide.
Analyzing Information *How was the investigation an example of the federal system of checks and balances?*

ACTIVITY
Connecting with Government

This activity might take place over several class periods. Divide the class into groups of four. Have students explore the Constitution's guidelines for impeachment, as well as the charges and evidence against President Nixon. Then ask students to debate whether or not Nixon should have been impeached for his involvement in Watergate. **(Logical/Mathematical; Verbal/Linguistic)**

From the Archives of
American Heritage®

About the Presidents

The presidency of Richard Nixon (1969–1974) defies simple assessments. While his presidency was scandal-ridden, and Nixon stands as the only President ever forced to resign from office, his historic legacy is complex. Nixon had acute political intelligence and a knack for innovative policy making. In domestic policy he oversaw the creation of the Occupational Safety and Health Administration and the Environmental Protection Agency. In foreign policy he pursued détente with the Soviet Union and opened relations with the People's Republic of China. In doing so, Nixon laid the foundation for stable relations between the United States and the world's dominant Communist powers. Source: Adapted from Henry F. Graff's *The Presidents*, Scribner's, 1984, by the editors of *American Heritage®* magazine.

CAPTION ANSWERS

Interpreting Time Lines Congress and the Supreme Court checked the abuses of the executive branch of the federal government.

Woodward and Bernstein Meanwhile, two *Washington Post* reporters were following a trail of leads. Bob Woodward and Carl Bernstein, both young and eager, sensed that the trail would lead to the White House.

Even before the election, Woodward and Bernstein had learned about the secret funds of the Committee to Reelect the President. They had written about the political spying and sabotage. As they began to realize who was involved, they called John Mitchell and asked him to verify their story. He denied it angrily.

The Senate Investigates In February 1973, a Senate Select Committee on Presidential Campaign Activities had begun to investigate the Watergate affair. James McCord, one of the convicted Watergate burglars, responded to his lengthy prison sentence by testifying before the committee in secret session. He gave members a vague sense of what had gone on, and he suggested that Nixon staffers were involved. The stories by Woodward and Bernstein helped the probe. In turn, leaks from the Senate committee aided these and other reporters.

As rumors of White House involvement grew, Nixon tried to protect himself. In April 1973, he forced Haldeman and Ehrlichman, his two closest aides, to resign. On national television he proclaimed that he would take final responsibility for the mistakes of others, for "there can be no whitewash at the White House."

The investigation ground on. In May 1973, the Senate committee, chaired by Senator Sam Ervin of North Carolina, began televised public hearings on Watergate. Millions of Americans watched, fascinated, as the story unfolded like a mystery thriller. John Dean, the President's personal legal counsel, sought to save himself by testifying that Nixon knew about the coverup. Other staffers described illegal activities at the White House.

VIEWING HISTORY Reporters Carl Bernstein (left) and Bob Woodward of the *Washington Post* persisted in tracking down information to uncover the Watergate story. **Recognizing Cause and Effect** *How did their reporting affect the official investigation?*

COMPARING PRIMARY SOURCES
Should Nixon Be Impeached?

In July 1974, the House Judiciary Committee debated the possible impeachment of President Richard Nixon. **Analyzing Viewpoints** Compare the main arguments made by the two speakers.

In Favor of Impeachment

"My faith in the Constitution is whole, it is complete, it is total, and I am not going to sit here and be an idle spectator to the diminution [lessening], the subversion [undermining], the destruction of the Constitution. . . . The Framers confided in the Congress the power if need be to remove . . . a President swollen with power and grown tyrannical."

—Texas Representative
Barbara Jordan, Democrat

Opposed to Impeachment

"As the trust is placed in Congress to safeguard the liberties of the people through the . . . powers to remove a President, so must Congress's vigilance be fierce in seeing that the trust is not abused. . . . Not only do I not believe that any crimes by the President have been proved beyond a reasonable doubt, but I do not think the proof even approaches the lesser standards of proof which some of my colleagues . . . suggested we apply."

—Michigan Representative
Edward Hutchinson, Republican

The most dramatic moment came when Alexander Butterfield, a former presidential assistant, revealed the existence of a secret taping system in the President's office that recorded all meetings and telephone conversations. The system had been set up to provide a historical record of Nixon's presidency. Now those audiotapes could show whether or not Nixon had been involved in the coverup.

The "Saturday Night Massacre"　In an effort to demonstrate honesty, Nixon agreed in May 1973 to the appointment of a special Watergate prosecutor. A **special prosecutor** works for the Justice Department but conducts an independent investigation of claims of wrongdoing by government officials. Archibald Cox, a Harvard law professor, took the post and immediately asked for the tapes. Nixon refused to release them. When Cox persisted, Nixon ordered him fired on Saturday, October 20, 1973. This action triggered a series of resignations and firings that became known as the "Saturday Night Massacre."

An Administration in Jeopardy　By that time, Nixon was in serious trouble. His public approval rating plummeted. After Cox's firing, *Time* magazine declared, "The President Should Resign."

Leon Jaworski of Texas, Cox's replacement as special prosecutor, also asked for the tapes. Nixon then tried to demonstrate innocence by releasing edited transcripts of some of his White House conversations. He carefully cut out the most damaging evidence. Still, many people were angry and disillusioned when they read even the edited comments of some of the conversations in the Oval Office.

Meanwhile, a subplot had emerged in the troubled White House. Vice President Spiro Agnew stood accused of evading income taxes and taking bribes. Early in October 1973, just ten days before the "Saturday Night Massacre," he resigned in disgrace. To succeed Agnew, Nixon named Gerald R. Ford, the House Minority Leader. For nearly two months, until the Senate confirmed Ford, the nation had a President in big trouble—and no Vice President.

Hearings Begin　Nixon had to make another move. After the "Saturday Night Massacre," Congress had begun the process to help them determine if they should **impeach** the President—to charge him with misconduct while in office.

In July 1974, the House Judiciary Committee, which included 21 Democrats and 17 Republicans, began to hold hearings to determine if there were adequate grounds for impeachment. This debate, like the earlier hearings, was broadcast on national television. The country watched anxiously as even Republicans deserted the President. Representative M. Caldwell Butler of Virginia spoke for many of them when he said:

> 66 For years we Republicans have campaigned against corruption and misconduct. . . . But Watergate is our shame. Those things have happened in our house and it is our responsibility to do what we can to clear it up. . . . In short, power appears to have corrupted. It is a sad chapter in American history, but I cannot condone what I have heard; I cannot excuse it; and I cannot and will not stand for it. 99
> —Representative M. Caldwell Butler, 1974

BIOGRAPHY

Barbara Jordan 1936–1996

Born in Houston, Texas, Barbara Jordan grew up in a segregated society. She graduated from Texas Southern University, and then earned a law degree from Boston University.

Barbara Jordan's political career included many "firsts." In 1966, she became the first African American in the Texas state senate since Reconstruction. In 1972, Jordan became the first African American woman from Texas elected to the House of Representatives.

As a member of the House Judiciary Committee, Jordan took part in the Watergate hearings in July 1974. Her strong opinions were based on her belief that Nixon's actions threatened the Constitution.

Jordan was reelected to the House in 1974 and 1976. Retiring from politics in 1978, she taught political ethics at the Lyndon B. Johnson School of Public Affairs (University of Texas). Jordan was the keynote speaker at the Democratic conventions in 1976 and 1992.

Chapter 32 • Section 3　**1075**

ACTIVITY
Connecting with History and Conflict

Invite students to research library and other resources for primary or secondary sources regarding one of the following topics: the Saturday Night Massacre, Nixon's release of the tapes following the Supreme Court's ruling, or Nixon's last day as President. Then have them use the information they gather to write a news story of the event that might have appeared in the newspaper the next day. (**Verbal/Linguistic**)

BACKGROUND
A Vice President Resigns

Calls for Nixon's resignation or impeachment after the Saturday Night Massacre were also linked to Spiro Agnew's resignation as Vice President. Agnew's verbal attacks on opponents of the Vietnam War and the network news media during Nixon's first term had made him a hero of political conservatives. But they also earned him the disdain of majority Democrats in the House and Senate. On the day he left office, Agnew pleaded *nolo contendere,* or "no contest," to tax evasion, for which he was fined $10,000 and placed on three years' unsupervised probation.

CUSTOMIZE FOR ...
Gifted and Talented

Have students research and report on the process of impeachment, including who is responsible for initiating the process.

✓ TEST PREPARATION

Have students reread the section under the heading "The Saturday Night Massacre" and then answer the question below.

Who supervises the activities of a special prosecutor?

A　The Supreme Court

B　Congress

C　The President

Ⓓ　The Justice Department

Section 3 Assessment

Reading Comprehension

1. His suspicious and secretive nature and his staff's attempt to protect him at all costs. To formulate plans to harass White House enemies through such methods as income tax investigations.

2. Nixon ordered Kissinger to install the wiretaps on the telephones of several members of President Nixon's staff and on some news reporters' phones to monitor the flow of information out of, and in regard to, the White House.

3. Through articles in the *Washington Post* investigated and written by Woodward and Bernstein, and through the Senate investigation that began in February 1973.

4. Archibald Cox asked for the tapes in his capacity as an independent investigator working on behalf of the Justice Department. Nixon refused and eventually ordered Cox to be fired, which triggered the "Saturday Night Massacre."

5. A series of resignations and firings.

6. To charge the President with misconduct while in office.

Critical Thinking and Writing

7. Answers will vary.

8. Outlines will vary but should be supported with facts from the section.

Take It to the NET

Students should consider the charges and evidence against President Nixon and explore the Constitution's guidelines for impeachment.

By sizable tallies, the House Judiciary Committee voted to impeach the President on charges of obstruction of justice, abuse of power, and refusal to obey a congressional order to turn over his tapes. To remove him from office, a majority of the full House of Representatives would have to vote for impeachment, and the Senate would then have to hold a trial, with two thirds of the senators present voting to convict. The outcome seemed obvious.

Nixon Resigns

On August 5, after a brief delay, Nixon finally obeyed a Supreme Court ruling and released the tapes. They contained a disturbing gap of $18\frac{1}{2}$ minutes, during which the conversation had been mysteriously erased. Still, the tapes gave clear evidence of Nixon's involvement in the coverup.

Three days later, Nixon appeared on television and painfully announced that he would leave the office of President the next day. On August 9, 1974, Nixon resigned, the first President ever to do so. That same day, in a smooth constitutional transition, Vice President Gerald Ford was sworn in. "Our long national nightmare is over," he said.

The Watergate scandal still stands as a low point in American political history. Government officials abused the powers granted to them by the people. A President was forced to resign in disgrace. Many Americans lost a great deal of faith and trust in their government.

However, the scandal also proved the strength of the nation's constitutional system, especially its balance of powers. When members of the executive branch violated the law instead of enforcing it, the judicial and legislative branches of government stepped in and stopped them. As President Ford said upon taking office, "Our constitution works. Our great republic is a government of laws, not of men."

VIEWING HISTORY In this famous photograph, former President Richard Nixon offers the crowd his familiar salute as he leaves Washington, D.C., following his resignation. **Drawing Conclusions** *Why is the Watergate scandal an important part of American political history?*

Section 3 Assessment

READING COMPREHENSION

1. Why did Nixon keep an "enemies list"? How was the list used?

2. Describe the use of **wiretaps** within the Nixon White House.

3. How did the public learn about Nixon's role in the **Watergate scandal?**

4. What role did the **special prosecutor** play in the Watergate investigation?

5. Describe what became known as the "Saturday Night Massacre."

6. What does it mean to **impeach?**

CRITICAL THINKING AND WRITING

7. **Posing Questions** Write three questions you would want to ask President Richard Nixon if you were a member of the House Judiciary Committee preparing for impeachment hearings.

8. **Writing an Opinion** Write an outline for an essay in which you evaluate Nixon's role in the Watergate scandal, and state your opinion as to whether or not he should have resigned.

Take It to the NET

Activity: Organizing a Debate Investigate events leading up to the Watergate scandal. Participate in a classroom debate on whether to impeach President Nixon. Use the links provided in the *America: Pathways to the Present* area of the following Web site for help in completing this activity.
www.phschool.com

CAPTION ANSWERS

Viewing History The contempt for law demonstrated by the Watergate conspirators; Nixon was the first President to resign; Americans became cynical in their views of government. One positive aspect is that the structure of government proved to be strong and resilient.

RESOURCE DIRECTORY

Teaching Resources
Units 9/10 booklet
• Section 3 Quiz, p. 54
Guide to the Essentials
• Section 3 Summary, p. 163

Creating a Multimedia Presentation

The Space Age helped launch new technologies as well as put men on the moon. Today, "reports" are no longer limited to handwritten or typewritten papers. With the help of computers, audio recorders, scanners, VCRs, and more, you can add graphics, photos, and maps; intersperse a written report with audio segments and video clips; and even make your own Web site with quizzes and links.

LEARN THE SKILL
Use the following steps to create a multimedia presentation:

1. **Define your topic.** Multimedia presentations are best suited to topics that have a variety of aspects or subtopics and that lend themselves to visual or audio segments. But your topic should not be so broad that you cannot cover it thoroughly.

2. **Make a "blueprint"—a written plan—for your project.** Find out what media are available to you. Brainstorm! List main subtopics, key sources of information, and the sequence and description of segments. If you are working with a team, assign roles to all team members.

3. **Develop your presentation.** Set deadlines for each main task. Do research, write scripts, and gather materials. Collecting more material than you need will give you flexibility in editing and assembling your work. As in a written report, make sure your ideas flow logically.

4. **Present your work.** The best presentations are interactive, so try to involve your audience in the presentation.

PRACTICE THE SKILL
Answer the following questions:

1. **(a)** Do you think the history of space flight would be too broad or too narrow a topic, or would it be manageable? Explain. **(b)** Evaluate the first moon landing as a topic. **(c)** What audio or video segments might you use for each of these topics?

2. **(a)** Suppose your topic is the first moon landing. What might your subtopics be? **(b)** Besides NASA's Web site (www.nasa.gov), what other sources might be helpful? (Don't forget "stills," such as magazine photographs, newspaper headlines, or diagrams. You might also do your own research by taping interviews with people who watched the moon landing on television as it happened.) **(c)** Create a blueprint for your presentation.

3. **(a)** How much time will you need to gather or create materials? **(b)** How much time will you need to write a script? **(c)** Create a schedule and assign tasks.

4. **(a)** Who is your audience? It might be your classmates, a community group, or younger students. **(b)** How will you involve your audience in the presentation?

APPLY THE SKILL
See the Chapter Review and Assessment for another opportunity to apply this skill.

CREATING A MULTIMEDIA PRESENTATION

Focus Students will learn how to gather together and organize material to create a multimedia presentation.

Instruct Talk with students about the types of topics that are appropriate for multimedia presentations. Topics should be focused and should suggest both visual and audio components. Ask students if they think a multimedia presentation has the potential to be more engaging than a written presentation. What elements do they think will help make a presentation interesting? Brainstorm with students to generate a list of subjects that would naturally lead to a multimedia treatment.

Extend See the Skills for Life activity in the Resource Directory below.

ANSWERS
PRACTICE THE SKILL

1. **(a)** Too broad; it is more than fifty years long, and would require detailed explanation of many different events. **(b)** The first moon landing is a good topic: it can be described in relatively brief terms; there are many examples of photographs and audio clips that would make an effective presentation. **(c)** The history of space flight: stills and video of rocket launches and spaceship recoveries, audio tapes of astronauts in space, photos and video of returning astronauts, photos and videos of Earth and outer space as seen from spacecraft, and the *Challenger* disaster. The first moon landing: flight video and interviews with those astronauts.

2. **(a)** Possible answers: the astronauts, the flight, the moonwalk, the public reaction. **(b)** Possible answers: the National Air and Space Museum, which maintains an online gallery with many images of *Apollo* artifacts. **(c)** Answers will vary.

3. **(a)** Answers will vary, but should be realistic. **(b)** Answers will vary. **(c)** Answers will vary.

4. **(a)** Answers will vary. **(b)** Answers will vary.

Section 4
The Ford Administration

The Ford Administration

READING FOCUS

- How did Gerald Ford become President, and why did he pardon Richard Nixon?
- What economic problems did the Ford administration face?
- What actions in foreign policy did President Ford take during his term?
- How did Americans celebrate the nation's bicentennial?

MAIN IDEA

After becoming President, Gerald Ford worked to reunite the country while facing economic problems at home and challenges abroad.

KEY TERMS

stagflation
War Powers Act
Helsinki Accords
bicentennial

TAKING NOTES

As you read, prepare an outline of this section. Use Roman numerals to indicate the major headings, capital letters for the subheadings, and numbers for the supporting details.

> **The Ford Administration**
> I. Ford Becomes President
>   A. Background
>   1. Served in House of Representatives
>   2. _____

Setting the Scene The new President, Gerald R. Ford, faced a difficult job. In his autobiography he recalled the situation he faced when he took office in August 1974:

> 66 *The years of suspicion and scandal that had culminated in Nixon's resignation had demoralized our people. They had lost faith in their elected leaders and in their institutions. I knew that unless I did something to restore their trust, I couldn't win their consent [approval] to do anything else. . . . The New Frontier and Great Society promises of the 1960s had been partly responsible for the national disillusionment. The country didn't need more promises. It yearned for performance instead.* 99

> —Gerald R. Ford, *A Time to Heal*

President Gerald Ford is shown with his wife Betty Ford, the new First Lady, after taking the oath of office.

Ford had to help the United States emerge from its worst political scandal. At the same time, the economy was in trouble, and the divisions over the Vietnam War had hardly begun to heal.

Ford Becomes President

"Jerry" Ford was one of the most popular politicians in Washington when he was appointed Vice President in October 1973, following Spiro Agnew's resignation. A football star at the University of Michigan, Ford had played on the national championship teams of 1932 and 1933, and had been a college all-star. After earning a law degree and serving in the navy during World War II, he entered politics. In 1948, he won election to the House of Representatives, where he rose to become Minority Leader in 1965. He was an unassuming man who believed in hard work and self-reliance.

Ford described himself as "conservative in fiscal affairs, moderate in domestic affairs, internationalist in foreign affairs." Over the years, he had opposed much government spending—federal aid to education, the antipoverty program, and spending for mass transit. He had supported defense spending and measures for law and order.

Nixon saw Ford as a noncontroversial figure who might bolster his own support in Congress. When Ford was confirmed as Vice President, Congress and the public were interested mainly in his reputation for honesty, integrity, and stability. Some, however, questioned whether he was qualified to take over the presidency if that became necessary. Despite Ford's long experience in Congress, he had little experience as an administrator or in foreign affairs. Ford acknowledged his own limitations when he was sworn in, saying, "I am a Ford, not a Lincoln."

When Nixon resigned in August 1974, Ford became the first nonelected President. Other Vice Presidents who had moved into the White House had been elected to the vice presidency as part of the national ticket. To fill the vice-presidential vacancy, Ford named former New York Governor Nelson Rockefeller. This created the unique situation of having both a President and a Vice President who had been appointed, not elected.

The Nixon Pardon

Ford became President at the end of a turbulent time in the country's history. The nation was disillusioned by Watergate. During the scandal, many Americans had wondered whether the Constitution would survive Nixon's actions. Few people looked forward to the prospect of an impeachment trial. It would have been only the second in United States history; the first was that of Andrew Johnson in 1868. When Ford assumed the presidency, the nation needed a leader who could take it beyond the ugliness of Watergate.

In response to this public mood, President Ford declared that it was a time for "communication, conciliation, compromise and cooperation." Americans were on his side. *Time* magazine noted "a mood of good feeling and even exhilaration in Washington that the city had not experienced for many years."

All too quickly, Ford lost some popular support. Barely a month after Nixon had resigned, Ford pardoned the former President for "all offenses" he might have committed, avoiding further prosecution. On national television, Ford explained that he had looked to God and his own conscience in deciding "the right thing" to do about Nixon and "his loyal wife and family":

> 66 *Theirs is an American tragedy in which we have all played a part. It could go on and on and on, or someone must write the end to it. I have concluded that only I can do that, and if I can I must. . . . My conscience tells me that only I, as President, have the constitutional power to firmly shut and seal this book. My conscience tells me that it is my duty not merely to proclaim domestic tranquility but to use every means that I have to ensure it.* 99
>
> —Gerald R. Ford, September 8, 1974

Ford expected criticism of the pardon, but he underestimated the widespread negative reaction. Many of Nixon's loyalists were facing prison for their role in Watergate. The former President, however, walked away without a penalty. Although some people supported Ford's action, his generous gesture

The New York Times
FORD GIVES PARDON TO NIXON, WHO REGRETS 'MY MISTAKES'

VIEWING HISTORY Betty Ford described her husband as "an accidental Vice President, and an accidental President, and in both jobs he replaced disgraced leaders." **Predicting Consequences** *What political risks did President Ford take when he pardoned Richard Nixon?*

READING CHECK
Describe the public mood during the Watergate scandal. How did Ford respond to this mood?

Focus on GOVERNMENT

Granting Pardons The President's power to "grant reprieves and pardons for offenses against the United States, except in cases of impeachment," is provided by Article II, Section 2 of the Constitution. Most often, pardons are given to individuals who have been convicted in court. President Ford's pardon of Nixon was unusual in that it was awarded before a trial ever took place. Whoever is granted a pardon must, in turn, accept it in order for that pardon to be carried out. Though Nixon was never convicted of his alleged crimes, he was seen to have admitted guilt when he accepted his pardon.

INTERPRETING GRAPHS
Ford's administration saw the worst economic slump in the United States since the Great Depression. **Analyzing Information** *In what year were consumer prices highest in the 1970s? When did unemployment peak in this decade?*

backfired. Some people suggested that a bargain had been made when Nixon resigned. Many also criticized the new President's judgment. Ford was occasionally booed when he made public speeches, just as Johnson and Nixon had been for their stands on the Vietnam war. To counter the reactions, he went before a House committee in October to explain his reasons. The public, angry both at Watergate and the pardon, voted a number of Republicans out of office in the 1974 congressional elections.

Economic Problems

While focusing on the Watergate scandal, the nation had paid less attention to other issues. In the meantime, some conditions had grown worse. Now, facing a hostile Congress, the new administration found it hard to provide direction.

The Economy Stalls Months of preoccupation with Watergate had kept Nixon from dealing with the economy. By 1974, inflation was at about 11 percent, much higher than it had been in the past. Unemployment climbed from about 5 percent in January 1974 to just over 7 percent by the year's end. Home building, usually a sign of a healthy economy, slowed as interest rates rose. The fears of investors brought a drop in stock prices.

Usually, federal policymakers had to deal with either inflation (the result of a rapidly growing economy) or unemployment (the result of a slow economy). Most economists believed that each of those trends could balance out the other. For example, a moderate rise in inflation would help lower the rate of unemployment. Now, however, inflation and unemployment both rose, while the economy remained stalled and stagnant. Economists named this new situation **stagflation.**

By the time Ford assumed the presidency, the country was in a recession, a period in which the economy is shrinking. Not since Franklin Roosevelt took office during the Great Depression had a new President faced such harsh economic troubles.

Ford's approach—like Herbert Hoover's in the early 1930s—was to try to restore public confidence. Early in October 1974, he sent Congress an economic program called "WIN," or "Whip Inflation Now." The President asked Americans to wear red and white "WIN" buttons; to save money, not spend it; to conserve fuel; and to plant vegetable gardens to counter high grocery store prices. The WIN campaign

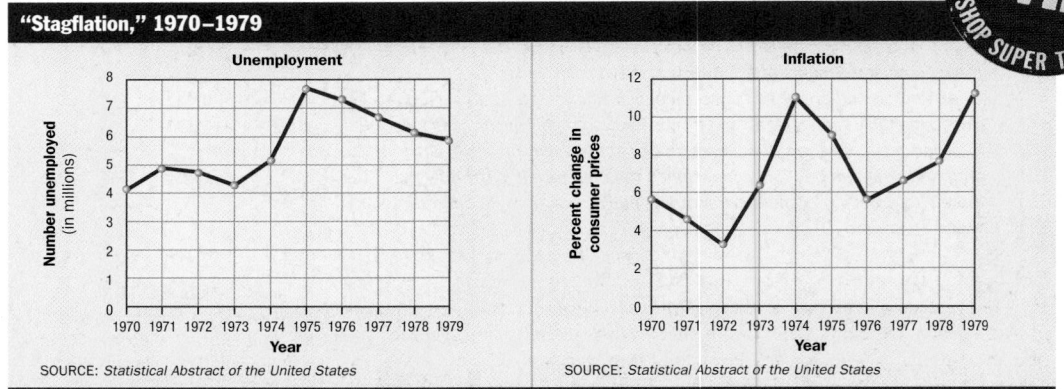

"Stagflation," 1970–1979

Unemployment

Inflation

SOURCE: *Statistical Abstract of the United States*

SOURCE: *Statistical Abstract of the United States*

depended on people voluntarily changing their everyday actions, but it had no real incentives. It soon faded away.

Eventually, Ford recognized the need for more direct action. The Federal Reserve tightened the money supply to control inflation, but the recession only worsened. Job layoffs were widespread. Unemployment soared to over 8 percent in 1975. Congress then backed an antirecession spending program. Despite his belief in less government spending, Ford backed an increase in unemployment benefits; he also supported a multibillion-dollar tax cut. While the economy did recover slightly, inflation and unemployment remained high.

Conflicts With Congress   In spite of his long experience as a congressional leader, President Ford was often at odds with the Democratic-controlled Congress. He basically believed in limited government, while Congress wanted the government to take a more active role in the economy. Jerold F. terHorst, Ford's first press secretary, noted how Ford's own sense of decency came into conflict with his view of government:

> 66 If he saw a schoolkid in front of the White House who needed clothing, he'd give him the shirt off his back, literally. Then he'd go right in the White House and veto a school-lunch bill. 99
>
> —Jerold F. terHorst

Ford vetoed bills to create a consumer protection agency and to fund programs for education, housing, and health care. Congress responded by creating its highest percentage of veto overrides since the presidency of Franklin Pierce in the 1850s.

Foreign Policy Actions

In foreign policy, Ford generally followed Nixon's approach and worked for détente. He kept Henry Kissinger on as Secretary of State. In 1974 and 1975, Ford made a series of trips abroad. He met with European leaders and was the first American President to visit Japan. Ford also visited China in order to continue improving the political and trade ties that Nixon had initiated. In Africa and elsewhere, the administration acted to develop relationships with countries that had recently gained independence after many years of colonial rule.

Southeast Asia   In his policy toward Southeast Asia, Ford paid the price for Nixon's poor relationship with Congress. In 1973, Congress, angry at the growth of the "imperial presidency," had passed the **War Powers Act** over Nixon's veto. This law was designed to limit a President's ability to involve the United States in foreign conflicts without receiving a formal declaration of war from Congress. It stated that:

1. Within 48 hours of committing troops to overseas combat, the President must notify Congress of the reasons for this decision and the expected length of the mission.
2. The troops may not stay overseas for more than 60 days without congressional approval.
3. Congress can demand that the President bring the troops home.

In the spring of 1975, North Vietnam began a new offensive against the South. Ford asked for military aid to help South Vietnam meet the attack, but Congress rejected his request. Most Americans had no wish to become involved in Vietnam again, and Congress was willing to do anything—including using the War Powers Act if necessary—to make sure the United States stayed out of the war.

VIEWING HISTORY Continuing Nixon's policy of détente, President Ford (right) met with Soviet General Secretary Leonid Brezhnev (left) and other leaders at a 1975 summit in Finland. **Drawing Conclusions** *In what ways did Ford follow Nixon's policy of détente?*

Reading Comprehension

1. Inflation and unemployment were high as the economy continued to shrink.
2. It was designed to limit a President's ability to involve the United States in foreign conflicts without receiving a formal declaration of war from Congress.
3. The United States, Canada, the Soviet Union, and about 30 European countries pledged economic cooperation, respect for existing national boundaries, and promised to promote human rights.
4. The 200th anniversary of the signing of the Declaration of Independence.

Critical Thinking and Writing

5. Answers should reflect an understanding of Ford's wish to bring an end to Watergate and of the widespread, negative public reaction to his decision.
6. Articles will vary, but should be supported with facts from the section.

Take It to the NET

Time lines should chronicle the Ford presidency and may include some of the following events: Nixon's resignation, Ford's inauguration, the Nixon pardon, stagflation, "WIN," the War Powers Act, the Helsinki Accords.

VIEWING HISTORY Majestic tall ships sail past the Statue of Liberty in celebration of the bicentennial. **Drawing Inferences** *What images of the nation's past do these ships bring to mind?*

By late April, the South Vietnamese capital, Saigon, was about to fall. Ford agreed to an American airlift that helped evacuate thousands of Americans and Vietnamese.

Southeast Asia remained a foreign policy problem even after the fall of South Vietnam. In May 1975, soldiers from Communist Cambodia (which had fallen to the Khmer Rouge) captured the *Mayaguez*, an American merchant ship cruising in Cambodian waters. When protests by the United States went unanswered, Ford sent the marines to recapture the ship. The crew was retrieved, but at a high cost: 41 Americans were killed. Later investigations showed that the Cambodian government apparently had been preparing to return both ship and crew. For the administration, however, the incident was a chance to dispel the impression of American weakness in the region.

Europe and the Soviet Union On another foreign policy front, President Ford signed the **Helsinki Accords,** a series of agreements on European security made at a 1975 summit meeting in Finland. The United States, Canada, the Soviet Union, and about 30 European countries pledged to cooperate economically, respect existing national boundaries, and promote human rights. Ford also continued Strategic Arms Limitation Talks (SALT) with the Soviet Union, holding out hope for further limits on nuclear weapons.

The Nation's Birthday

Americans held a nationwide birthday party to mark July 4, 1976, the **bicentennial,** the 200th anniversary of the signing of the Declaration of Independence. Throughout the summer, people in small towns and big cities across the country celebrated with parades, concerts, air shows, political speeches, and fireworks. With so many Americans discouraged by Watergate, Vietnam, and the recession, the celebrations could not have been better timed.

On the Fourth of July, more than 200 sailing ships paraded into New York City's harbor while millions watched from many countries. Cities across the nation staged spectacular fireworks shows and long parades. Many observers saw in the bicentennial celebrations a revival of optimism after years of gloom.

Section 4 Assessment

READING COMPREHENSION

1. How did **stagflation** and recession harm the economy in the 1970s?

2. What was the purpose of the **War Powers Act?**

3. Who participated in the **Helsinki Accords,** and what were the agreements?

4. What did the **bicentennial** commemorate?

CRITICAL THINKING AND WRITING

5. **Predicting Consequences** What might have happened if Ford had not pardoned Nixon?

6. **Writing a News Story** Write the lead article for a local newspaper on July 4, 1976. Describe the significance of the nationwide celebrations on that day in the context of recent events.

Take It to the NET

Activity: Creating a Time Line Investigate the key events of the Ford presidency, from his inauguration to his defeat in the 1976 election. Create a time line of Ford's term in office using pictures and quotations. Use the links provided in the *America: Pathways to the Present* area of the following Web site for help in completing this activity. **www.phschool.com**

CAPTION ANSWERS

Viewing History Sample answer: Dignity, joy, pride, and strength.

RESOURCE DIRECTORY

Teaching Resources
Units 9/10 booklet
• Section 4 Quiz, p. 55
Guide to the Essentials
• Section 4 Summary, p. 164
Learning with Documents booklet (Primary Source Activity) *1976: The Bicentennial Year,* p. 37

READING FOCUS

- What changes did Jimmy Carter bring to the presidency?

- How did Carter deal with domestic issues?

- What ideals guided Carter's foreign policy?

- What factors influenced the outcome of the 1980 election?

MAIN IDEA

Jimmy Carter's human rights diplomacy brought notable accomplishments in foreign policy, but his inability to work effectively with Congress blocked the success of his domestic programs.

KEY TERMS

incumbent
deregulation
amnesty
affirmative action
Camp David Accords
dissident

TAKING NOTES

Copy the chart below. As you read, fill in the major initiatives President Carter took and the results of each action.

The Carter Administration		
Policy	**Action**	**Result**
Economy	Cut government spending	Increased unemployment and business failures
Energy		
Civil Rights		
Foreign Relations		

Setting the Scene The 1976 presidential campaign brought surprises for both political parties. Gerald Ford, who said at first that he would not be a candidate for President, later changed his mind. Even though Ford was the **incumbent**—the current office holder—he faced strong opposition from conservative fellow Republicans inside his own party. The Democrats nominated a candidate few Americans had even heard of at the start of the campaign: James Earl ("Jimmy") Carter, Jr., a former governor of Georgia. Carter went on to defeat Ford by a narrow margin.

In his Inaugural Address, President Carter outlined his beliefs:

66 *The American dream endures. We must once again have full faith in our country—and in one another. . . . Our commitment to human rights must be absolute, our laws fair, our natural beauty preserved; the powerful must not persecute the weak, and human dignity must be enhanced.* 99
—Jimmy Carter, Inaugural Address, January 20, 1977

Carter's Presidency

Jimmy Carter, a southerner with no national political experience, was different from his recent predecessors in the White House. His family had lived for generations in the rural South. A 1946 graduate of the United States Naval Academy, Carter served as an engineering officer on nuclear submarines. When his father died, he took over management of the family's peanut farm and warehouse. He entered politics in 1962 and was elected governor of Georgia in 1970.

Carter was a born-again Baptist whose deeply felt religious faith was central to his view of the world. While holding his own strong religious beliefs, though, Carter respected those of others.

At first, people responded warmly to Carter's "down home" approach. They loved it when he and his wife Rosalynn dismissed their limousine after the inauguration and strolled

Abandoning the traditional limousine ride, President Jimmy Carter takes an inaugural stroll with his wife Rosalynn and daughter Amy.

Chapter 32 • Section 5 **1083**

RESOURCE DIRECTORY

Teaching Resources
Learning Styles Lesson Plans booklet, p. 67
Guided Reading and Review booklet, p. 132

Technology
Section Reading Support Transparencies
Guided Reading Audiotapes (English/Spanish), Ch. 32
Student Edition on Audio CD, Ch. 32
Prentice Hall Presentation Pro CD-ROM, Ch. 32
Companion Web site, www.phschool.com

Section **5**

The Carter Administration

SECTION OBJECTIVES

1. Discover some changes Jimmy Carter brought to the presidency.

2. Learn how Carter dealt with domestic issues.

3. Find out about the ideals that guided Carter's foreign policy.

4. Discover some factors that influenced the outcome of the 1980 election.

BELLRINGER

Warm-Up Activity Ask students how they would rate the honesty of the current President and administration. Ask if they can envision any situation in which a President should be less than completely open and honest with the public.

Activating Prior Knowledge Jimmy Carter was celebrated for his honesty, his righteousness, and his moral certainty, qualities that have served him well in the years since his presidency. Can students name some of the types of activities in which Carter has been engaged since his presidency?

READING STRATEGY

Have students write the words *Jimmy Carter* in the center of a web diagram. Then as they read the section, have them note major details about Carter in surrounding circles.

ACTIVITY

Connecting with Government

Ask students to create political cartoons that express an opinion on the election of Jimmy Carter as President. Suggest to students that their cartoons could focus on some aspect of Carter's personal background, his level of political experience, or his status as a Washington "outsider" in presenting a viewpoint on what his presidency might be like. **(Visual/Spatial)**

Focus Explain that in 1976, Jimmy Carter, former governor of Georgia, was elected President. Ask what promises Carter made to the American people.

Instruct Discuss how Ford's failure to convey a "presidential" image on television affected the election of 1976. Ask students which recent President they think has had the strongest "presidential" image, and whether that President was also a good leader.

Discuss how Carter's outsider status and his choice of other outsiders as his key advisers hampered his ability to work with Congress.

Assess/Reteach Ask students to analyze the degree to which Carter's essential human decency, as perceived by the electorate, influenced his election. Why was this quality so important to voters in the election of 1976?

READING CHECK

Sample answer: He had a "down-home" approach; he eliminated many of the ceremonial details of White House life; he appointed many more women and minorities to his staff than previous administrations had. He came to office as an untarnished "Washington outsider."

VIEWING HISTORY The Carters brought an informal style to the presidency. In spite of the President's low-key image, he was known among friends as a "super-achiever." **Identifying Central Issues** Why do you think Carter's style appealed to many people?

READING CHECK
How did Carter attempt to become a different kind of President?

down Pennsylvania Avenue with their young daughter. He spoke to the nation on television wearing a cardigan sweater instead of a business suit. He eliminated many of the ceremonial details of White House life, such as trumpets to announce his entrance at official receptions. Some critics, however, began to complain about a lack of dignity and ceremony in the presidency.

The new President appointed many more women and minorities to his staff than previous administrations had done. Of about 1,200 full-time appointees, 12 percent were women, 12 percent were African American, and another 4 percent were Hispanic. In nominating federal judges, he chose four times as many women as had all previous Presidents combined.

Carter's lack of connections to Washington had helped him in the election campaign, since he had not been tarnished by failure or scandal. Once he became President, though, the "Washington outsider" role had disadvantages. The White House staff and other close advisors were also southerners, mostly Georgians. They had little sense of how crucial it was for the President to work with Congress. Carter himself was uneasy with Congress's demands and found it difficult to get legislation passed. He had no congressional experience and no former colleagues in Congress. He lacked Lyndon Johnson's ability to win over reluctant politicians.

Carter's Domestic Policies

Jimmy Carter had little success in promoting his domestic programs. Looking back, he wrote, "I quickly learned that it is a lot easier to hold a meeting, reach a tentative agreement, or make a speech than to get a controversial program through Congress."

That was not the only problem. As the *New York Times* columnist Tom Wicker observed, Carter "never established a politically coherent administration." His strategies were not clearly defined. Public support faded as his programs floundered.

Economic Issues Carter inherited an unstable economy. Like his predecessors, he had trouble controlling inflation without hurting economic growth. To prevent another recession, Carter tried to stimulate the economy with government deficit spending. As deficits grew, the Federal Reserve Board increased the money supply. However, inflation then rose to about 10 percent.

In an attempt to stop inflation, slow the economy, and reduce the deficit, Carter then cut federal spending. The cuts fell mostly on social programs,

CAPTION ANSWERS

Viewing History Sample answer: His down-to-earth style was a refreshing contrast to Nixon's imperial and dishonest administration.

RESOURCE DIRECTORY

Teaching Resources

Learning with Documents booklet (Key Documents) *Barbara Jordan, Keynote Address to the Democratic National Convention*, p. 96

Biography, Literature, and Comparing Primary Sources booklet (Biography) *Patricia Roberts Harris*, p. 37

Technology

RESOURCE **PRO**® **Primary Source Activity**
A Crisis of Confidence, found on Resource Pro, presents an excerpt from a televised address in which President Carter talks about factors he sees "threatening to destroy the social and political fabric of America."

angering liberal Democrats. At the same time, the slowdown in the economy increased unemployment and the number of business failures. The situation became worse in 1980, when the new federal budget called for increased government spending. In reaction, bond prices fell and interest rates soared. Americans lost confidence in Carter and his economic advisors.

Deregulation   Carter had more success in the area of **deregulation**—the reduction or removal of government controls in several industries. In the late 1800s and early 1900s, agencies such as the Interstate Commerce Commission had been established to regulate rates and business practices. Over time, government regulations had multiplied. Carter argued that they hurt competition and increased consumer costs.

To encourage greater energy production, Carter proposed removing controls on prices for oil and natural gas. He also took steps to deregulate the railroad, trucking, and airline industries. While consumer groups and many liberal Democrats opposed deregulation, it continued during the next two administrations, both of which were Republican.

Energy Issues   In the late 1970s, more than 40 percent of the oil used in the United States came from other countries. OPEC, the Organization of Petroleum Exporting Countries, had been raising oil prices steadily since 1973. In April 1977, Carter presented his energy program to Congress and the public. He asked people to save fuel by driving less and using less heat and air conditioning in their homes and offices. He also created a new Cabinet department, the Department of Energy, to coordinate the federal programs promoting conservation and researching new energy sources. Carter called the need for energy conservation the "moral equivalent of war."

Representatives from states that produced oil and gas fiercely opposed Carter's energy plan. Many proposals were stalled in Congress for months. In 1978, though, the National Energy Act finally passed. It included these directives:

1. Tax sales of inefficient, "gas-guzzling," cars.
2. Convert new utilities to fuels other than oil or natural gas.
3. Deregulate prices for domestic oil and natural gas.
4. Provide tax credits or loans to homeowners for using solar energy and improving the insulation in their homes.
5. Fund research for alternative energy sources such as solar energy and synthetic fuels.

Nuclear power seemed to be a promising alternative energy source. Serious questions remained about its cost and safety, however. In March 1979, people's doubts appeared to be confirmed by an accident at the nuclear power plant at Three Mile Island, near Harrisburg, Pennsylvania. A partial meltdown of the reactor core occurred, releasing some radiation. About 140,000 people who lived near the plant fled their homes, terrified by the idea of a radioactive leak. The story made headlines around the world.

COMPARING PRIMARY SOURCES
On Nuclear Energy

The need to reduce the dependence on foreign oil prompted viewpoints strongly for and against nuclear power.

Analyzing Viewpoints What are the main concerns of each of the speakers below?

In Favor of Nuclear Energy

"When you debate the issue of nuclear energy, you are actually debating the issue of growth. Growth will be the key issue for the remainder of this century, and it is the resolution of that issue which will determine the lifestyles of most Americans for generations. . . . Economic growth has been inextricably linked to the growth of the supply of energy throughout history."

—Senator James A. McClure (Idaho), addressing the National Conference on Energy Advocacy, February 2, 1979

Opposed to Nuclear Energy

"If this country . . . continues to rely more and more on nuclear power a meltdown disaster is almost predictable. . . . For years now, the utilities and nuclear power industry have refused to listen to scientific logic and reasoning concerning the dangers of this technology. . . . Perhaps it is time for emotion and for passion and for commitment to stir our souls and our hearts and our minds once again into action."

—Dr. Helen Caldicott, in Nuclear Madness, What You Can Do!, 1980

ACTIVITY
Connecting with Economics

Pair students to determine how each of the provisions of the National Energy Act of 1978 could be expected to contribute to energy conservation. Call on pairs to report their conclusions to the class. **(Logical/Mathematical)**

BACKGROUND
Connections to Today

The election of born-again Baptist Jimmy Carter encouraged evangelical Christians to again become involved with politics and government. This group was not very active in politics after losing the battle over teaching evolution in public schools in the 1920s. Until the 1970s they were less politically active than other Americans and less likely than other Christians to support their churches' involvement in political issues. However, Carter's campaign, which stressed the need for a return of morality to government, was one of the events that gave many evangelical Christians a new sense of entitlement and political legitimacy. They responded by becoming more involved in politics than most other Christians. From this transformation, the conservative political movement known today as the "religious right" was born.

1086

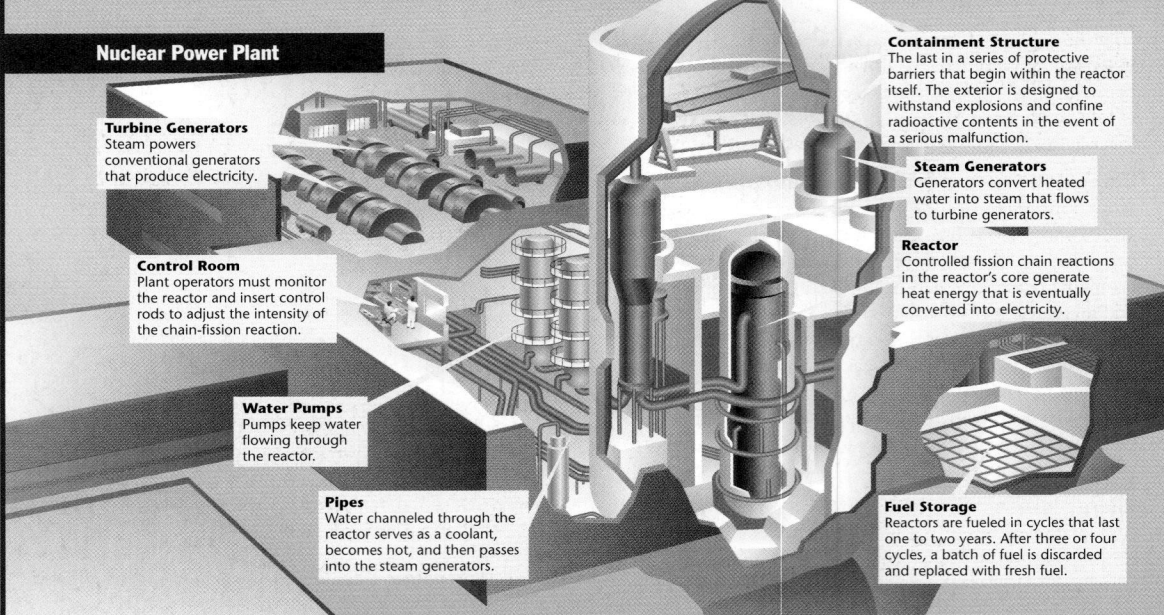

Nuclear Power Plant

Containment Structure
The last in a series of protective barriers that begin within the reactor itself. The exterior is designed to withstand explosions and confine radioactive contents in the event of a serious malfunction.

Steam Generators
Generators convert heated water into steam that flows to turbine generators.

Reactor
Controlled fission chain reactions in the reactor's core generate heat energy that is eventually converted into electricity.

Turbine Generators
Steam powers conventional generators that produce electricity.

Control Room
Plant operators must monitor the reactor and insert control rods to adjust the intensity of the chain-fission reaction.

Water Pumps
Pumps keep water flowing through the reactor.

Pipes
Water channeled through the reactor serves as a coolant, becomes hot, and then passes into the steam generators.

Fuel Storage
Reactors are fueled in cycles that last one to two years. After three or four cycles, a batch of fuel is discarded and replaced with fresh fuel.

ACTIVITY
Connecting with Citizenship

Invite students to imagine that they are living in the late 1970s. Have them write letters to the editor explaining why they support or oppose President Carter's pardon of Vietnam draft evaders or the Supreme Court's ruling in the *Bakke* decision. Select letters representing each side of each issue to share with the class. **(Verbal/Linguistic)**

BACKGROUND
Art History

In an amazing coincidence, just nine days before the partial meltdown at Three Mile Island, Columbia Pictures released a movie entitled *The China Syndrome,* a nuclear industry term for a theoretical scenario in which a reactor meltdown bores a hole in the earth all the way to China. The movie, starring Michael Douglas, Jane Fonda, and Jack Lemmon, is about a serious accident at a fictional nuclear power plant. Its story line magnified public concern over the TMI accident. Also unsettling was that the movie had been based on a real event in Alabama in 1975, when a failed system nearly caused a meltdown of a reactor's nuclear fuel and threatened a possible real "China syndrome."

INTERPRETING DIAGRAMS
Inside a nuclear power plant, a series of steps lead to the production of electricity. **Synthesizing Information** *What element is used to cool the reactor?*

Carter named a commission to investigate the accident at Three Mile Island. The commission's report identified operator errors that had made the initial problem worse. In his response to the report, Carter noted "very serious shortcomings in the way that both the government and the utility industry regulate and manage nuclear power." He proposed reorganizing the Nuclear Regulatory Commission, the agency in charge of nuclear power. He also called on utility companies to improve standards.

Civil Rights Issues   Carter's concern for moral values influenced his approach to domestic questions. Soon after taking office, he carried out his promise to grant **amnesty**—a general pardon—to those who had evaded the draft during the Vietnam War. Because that war still divided Americans, reactions were mixed.

As governor of Georgia, Carter had had a good civil rights record. As President, Carter tried to move beyond the civil rights battles of the 1950s and 1960s. Many of Carter's staff appointments, such as the United Nations ambassadorship for Andrew Young, won the approval of African Americans. On the other hand, many African Americans were disappointed by the President's weak support for social programs.

In 1978, the Supreme Court ruled on a civil rights case that would have important effects on **affirmative action** policies. First enacted during Lyndon Johnson's presidency, such policies aim to make up for past discrimination against women and members of minority groups by increasing their opportunities in areas such as employment and education. Allan Bakke, a white applicant, was refused admission to the medical school at the University of California (Davis) in 1973 and 1974. He sued the school, saying that its affirmative action policy amounted to "reverse discrimination." Specifically, Bakke charged that the policy of reserving 16 of 100 class spaces for minority group applicants violated both the Civil Rights Act of 1964 and the Constitution.

CAPTION ANSWERS

Interpreting Diagrams Water.

RESOURCE DIRECTORY

Teaching Resources
Great Debates booklet (Great Debates) *What Should Be the Rights of the Accused?* p. 26

Technology
Color Transparencies *The Way It Works,* H20

In a complex ruling in *Regents of the University of California* v. *Bakke*, the Court ordered that Bakke be admitted to the California medical school. It also upheld the school's right to consider race as one factor in admission decisions, but it did not allow the use of numerical quotas. While the Court decision supported the concept of affirmative action, the case signaled the start of a backlash against the policy.

Carter's Foreign Policy

Although Jimmy Carter had little diplomatic experience when he took office, his personal beliefs greatly influenced his decisions on foreign affairs. Support for human rights was the cornerstone of Carter's foreign policy.

Camp David Accords   Carter's commitment to finding ethical solutions to complicated problems was most visible in the Middle East. In that unstable region, Israel and the Arab nations had fought several wars, most recently in 1967 and 1973. In 1977, though, Egypt's President Anwar el-Sadat made a historic visit to Israel to begin negotiations with Prime Minister Menachem Begin. The two men had such different personalities, however, that they had trouble compromising. Carter intervened, sending Secretary of State Cyrus Vance to invite them to Camp David, the presidential retreat in the Maryland hills.

At Camp David in September 1978, Carter assumed the role of peacemaker. He practiced highly effective personal diplomacy to bridge the gap between Sadat and Begin. They finally agreed on a framework for peace that became known as the **Camp David Accords.** Under the resulting peace treaty, Israel would withdraw from the Sinai peninsula, which it had occupied since 1967. Egypt, in return, became the first Arab country to recognize Israel's existence as a nation.

The Camp David Accords, of course, did not solve all the problems in the Middle East. Among the remaining problems were issues concerning the Palestinians. Many had fled their homes when Arab nations declared war on Israel immediately after that country was established in 1948. Still, as Secretary of State Vance noted:

VIEWING HISTORY President Carter congratulates Egypt's President Sadat (left) and Israel's Prime Minister Begin (right) on the signing of the Camp David Accords. **Drawing Conclusions** *What were the major achievements of the accords?*

> 66 The Camp David Accords rank as one of the most important achievements of the Carter administration. First, they opened the way to peace between Egypt and Israel, which transformed the entire political, military, and strategic character of the Middle East dispute. Genuine peace between Egypt and Israel meant there would be no major Arab-Israeli war, whatever the positions of [other Arab groups]. 99
>
> —Cyrus Vance, *Hard Choices*

Soviet-American Relations   Several issues complicated the relationship between the United States and the Soviet Union. Détente was at a high point when Carter took office. However, Carter's stand on human rights angered Soviet leaders, undermining the efforts of the two nations to work together. The Soviets were especially annoyed when the President spoke in support of Soviet **dissidents**—writers and other activists who criticized the actions of their government. Soviet citizens were denied the right to speak freely or to criticize their political leaders. Carter believed that such rights were essential

Focus on WORLD EVENTS

The Panama Canal In the early 1900s, President Theodore Roosevelt had been proud of the way the United States had gained control of land for the Panama Canal. Many Latin Americans, though, resented the continuing United States presence in Panama.

In spite of bitter debate in Congress, in 1978 President Carter convinced the Senate to ratify two treaties dealing with the canal. One treaty was an agreement to return the canal to Panama by the year 2000. The other gave the United States the right to take military action to keep the canal open. The pacts protected American interests while improving relations with Latin America.

and was outspoken in defending them, even when such a defense caused international friction.

In spite of the discord, a second round of Strategic Arms Limitation Talks (SALT II) led Carter and Soviet leader Leonid Brezhnev to sign a new treaty in June 1979. More complicated than SALT I, this agreement limited the number of nuclear warheads and missiles held by each superpower.

Late in 1979, before the Senate could ratify SALT II, the Soviet Union invaded Afghanistan, a country on its southern border, to bolster a Soviet-supported government there. Carter telephoned Brezhnev and told him that the invasion was "a clear threat to the peace." He added, "Unless you draw back from your present course of action, this will inevitably jeopardize the course of United States–Soviet relations throughout the world." A United Nations resolution also called for Soviet withdrawal.

Carter halted American grain shipments to the Soviet Union and took other steps to show United States disapproval of Soviet aggression. Realizing that SALT II surely would be turned down, he removed the treaty from Senate consideration. (Although SALT II was never ratified, both countries followed the terms of the treaty based on its signing.) Carter also imposed a boycott on the 1980 summer Olympic Games to be held in Moscow. Eventually, some 60 other nations joined the Olympic boycott. Détente was effectively dead.

The Iran Hostage Crisis Iran, Afghanistan's neighbor to the west, was the scene of the worst foreign policy crisis of the Carter administration. For years the United States had supported the shah (or king) of Iran, Mohammad Reza Shah Pahlavi. The shah had taken many steps to modernize Iran. He was also a reliable supplier of oil and a pro-Western force in the region. For these reasons, Americans overlooked the corruption and harsh repression of the shah's government.

In January 1979, revolution broke out in Iran. It was led by Muslim fundamentalists, who wanted to bring back traditional ways, and by liberal critics of the shah, who wanted more political and economic reforms. As the revolution spread, the shah fled the country. He was replaced by an elderly Islamic leader, the Ayatollah Ruholla Khomeini, who had been in exile. Khomeini and his followers were aggressively anti-Western and planned to make Iran a strict Islamic state.

In October, out of concern for the shah's health, Carter let him enter the United States for medical treatment. Many Iranians were outraged. On November 4, 1979, angry followers of Khomeini seized the American embassy in Tehran and took Americans, mostly embassy workers, hostage.

VIEWING HISTORY Iranian protestors express anti-American sentiment in Tehran, where the American embassy was seized. **Identifying Central Issues** *What events led to the hostage crisis?*

For 444 days, revolutionaries imprisoned 52 hostages in different locations. The prisoners were blindfolded and moved from place to place. Some were tied up and beaten. Others spent time in solitary confinement and faced mock executions intended to terrorize them. One of the hostages, Kathryn Koob, described part of her experiences:

❝ [T]he sounds outside the embassy were nerve-wracking. . . . There seemed to be a continuous crowd of people shouting anti-American slogans, listening to the exhortations [cries] of the students and mullahs [clergymen] who were always on hand. In addition to the crowd noises, there were three or four loudspeakers blaring newscasts. . . . As I sat confined in my chair I thought . . . I just can't take this. ❞

—Kathryn Koob, *Guest of the Revolution*

Meanwhile, the American public became more impatient for the hostages' release. President Carter tried many approaches to secure the hostages' freedom. He broke diplomatic relations with Iran and froze all Iranian assets in the United States. Khomeini held out, insisting that the shah be sent back for trial. In April 1980, Carter authorized a risky commando rescue mission. It ended in disaster when several helicopters broke down in the desert, and eight American soldiers were killed. The government was humiliated, and Carter's popularity dropped further. Even after the shah died in July, the standoff continued. Carter's chances for reelection appeared dim.

The 1980 Election

Despite Carter's achievements in the Middle East and his commitment to serious goals, his administration had lost the confidence of many Americans. Rising inflation in early 1980 dropped his approval rating to 21 percent in public opinion polls. Unemployment was still over 7 percent. At times Carter himself seemed to have lost confidence. In two speeches in July, he spoke of a national "crisis of confidence" and a "national malaise."

In the Democratic primaries leading up to the 1980 elections, Massachusetts Senator Edward M. Kennedy won a large number of delegate votes. Kennedy withdrew just as the Democratic National Convention began, however, and Carter was nominated again. Nonetheless, many people were ready for the optimism of the Republican candidate, Ronald Reagan. A leading conservative, Reagan had failed to win his party's nomination in 1976. In 1980, however, Reagan won the nomination, and went on to win the election by a landslide.

After months of secret talks, the Iranians agreed to release the 52 hostages in early 1981. Not until the day Carter left office, however, were they allowed to come home. Newly elected President Reagan sent Carter, as a private citizen, to greet the hostages as they arrived at a U.S. military base in West Germany.

VIEWING HISTORY Jubilant Americans returned home after being held hostage by Iranians. **Drawing Conclusions** How did Carter's handling of the hostage crisis affect his career?

Section 5 Assessment

READING COMPREHENSION

1. What is an **incumbent?**

2. What issues concerning **deregulation, amnesty,** and **affirmative action** came up during Carter's presidency?

3. What were the **Camp David Accords?**

4. Why did the United States and the Soviet Union clash over Soviet **dissidents?**

CRITICAL THINKING AND WRITING

5. **Making Comparisons** List examples of the positive and negative results of Carter's approach to foreign policy.

6. **Writing a Letter to the Editor** Write a letter in which you support or oppose Carter's program to conserve energy.

 Take It to the NET

Activity: Brainstorming
Research the Iran Hostage Crisis. With your class, explore alternative ways that could have been used to approach the crisis. Use the links provided in the *America: Pathways to the Present* area of the following Web site for help in completing this activity.
www.phschool.com

Section 5 Assessment

Reading Comprehension

1. The current office holder.

2. President Carter removed price controls on oil and natural gas in the hope of increasing energy production. He also began to deregulate the railroad, trucking and airline industries. He granted amnesty to those who had evaded the draft during the Vietnam War; the 1978 Supreme Court ruling in *Regents of the University of California* v. *Bakke* started a backlash against affirmative action.

3. A framework for peace between Egypt and Israel, which was brokered by President Carter.

4. Carter believed that it was wrong for Russian leaders to deny Soviet citizens the right to speak freely and to criticize their political leaders.

Critical Thinking and Writing

5. Positive: Camp David Accords initiated Middle East peace talks; the Panama Canal treaties showed U.S. willingness to deal fairly with other nations. Negative: Carter had very little success in dealing with the Soviet Union; his response to the Iran hostage crisis was clumsy and ineffective.

6. Letters will vary but should be supported with facts from the section.

 **Take It to the NET**

Students should evaluate the effectiveness of President Carter's decisions in regard to the hostage crisis and should also consider alternative courses of action.

CAPTION ANSWERS

Viewing History It caused his popularity to plunge and damaged his chances for reelection.

REVIEWING KEY TERMS

Students should refer to the definitions of key terms in the chapter to write sentences that show an understanding of the respective administrations of Nixon, Ford, and Carter.

REVIEWING MAIN IDEAS

13. The bills would satisfy conservatives who wanted a smaller government. This technique also reassured those who favored social programs that they would continue with greater discretion to state governments.

14. Nixon made little attempt to appeal to African Americans or press for civil rights. He preferred to court the votes of southern white Democrats.

15. Kissinger practiced *realpolitik*, or acting in the nation's best interests rather than upon moral principles. Kissinger gained Nixon's trust in regard to foreign affairs and supported Nixon's use of secret negotiations.

16. Nixon was convinced that Communist China could no longer be ignored by the United States. He lifted travel restrictions for Americans who wished to visit China, arranged for the American Ambassador in Warsaw to meet with his Chinese counterpart, welcomed the initiation of "ping-pong diplomacy," and allowed trade to resume between the two nations. Nixon visited the People's Republic of China in 1972.

17. The committee adopted a no-holds-barred approach to winning, using "dirty tricks" against political opponents. These included a vicious criticism of Senator Edmund Muskie and his wife, and spies in an opponent's campaign staff.

18. Nixon attempted to indirectly pressure the FBI into dropping its Watergate investigation. He was also fully aware beforehand that one of the burglars had been paid to keep quiet.

19. He wanted to put an end to a very unpleasant episode and get on with the nation's real business. The public reaction was extremely negative. Many people felt that Nixon should share the fate of the Watergate conspirators who were going to jail.

20. Ford confronted the faltering economy by federal funding for unemployment compensation, the voluntary

---

creating a CHAPTER SUMMARY

Copy this chart (right) on a piece of paper and complete it by adding information about the issues and policies under each President's administration. Some entries have been completed for you as examples.

For additional review and enrichment activities, see the interactive version of *America: Pathways to the Present*, available on the Web and on CD-ROM.

Presidents and Issues, 1969–1981

President	Economic Issues	Foreign Policy	Civil Rights	Energy Issues
Nixon				Oil crisis
Ford	Stagflation			
Carter		Camp David Accords		

★ Reviewing Key Terms

For each of the terms below, write a sentence explaining how it relates to the Nixon, Ford, or Carter administration.

1. deficit spending
2. embargo
3. *realpolitik*
4. détente
5. special prosecutor
6. impeach
7. Helsinki Accords
8. incumbent
9. deregulation
10. amnesty
11. affirmative action
12. Camp David Accords

★ Reviewing Main Ideas

13. How did the New Federalism fit into Nixon's approach to domestic policy? (Section 1)
14. What was Nixon's "southern strategy"? (Section 1)
15. How did Henry Kissinger affect American foreign policy under President Nixon? (Section 2)
16. How did the Nixon administration change United States policy toward China? (Section 2)
17. What measures did the Committee to Reelect the President take to win the 1972 election? (Section 3)
18. What illegal actions did Nixon take in attempting to cover up the Watergate break-in? (Section 3)
19. Why did Ford grant Nixon a pardon? (Section 4)

20. What programs did Ford propose to solve the nation's economic problems? (Section 4)
21. How did Carter's lack of Washington experience affect his administration? (Section 5)
22. Evaluate the impact of the Iran hostage crisis on the 1980 presidential election. (Section 5)

★ Critical Thinking

23. **Synthesizing Information** How did the Watergate scandal shape politics in the 1970s?
24. **Drawing Conclusions** In 1975, Congress refused President Ford's request to send military aid to South Vietnam. Which do you think played a larger role in Congress's decision—the War Powers Act or public opinion? Why?
25. **Checking Consistency** Although Americans complained about fuel shortages during the 1970s, many did not support Carter's energy program or try to conserve oil and gas. How do you explain this inconsistent behavior?
26. **Identifying Central Issues** How did the relationship between the United States and the Soviet Union evolve during the 1970s?
27. **Making Comparisons** In what ways was "Nixon the President" different from "Nixon the Congressman"? How can you account for this change?

CREATING A CHAPTER SUMMARY

Presidents and Issues, 1969–1981

President	Economic Issues	Foreign Policy	Civil Rights	Energy Issues
Nixon	Deficit spending	Détente; reestablishment of diplomatic relations with China	Slowdown in desegregation	Oil crisis
Ford	Stagflation	Helsinki Accords	Congress overrides vetoes to establish Consumer Protection Agency and to fund programs for education, housing, and health care.	Encouraging people to conserve fuel
Carter	Deregulation	Camp David Accords	Amnesty; affirmative action	Safety of nuclear power; establishment of Department of Energy

★ Skills Assessment

Analyzing Political Cartoons ▶

28. This cartoon appeared during the Watergate scandal. What is Nixon doing?

29. What symbolism is used? What is the meaning behind the symbolism?

30. What is the cartoon's message? Write a caption that could be used with the cartoon.

Interpreting Data

Turn to the line graph on page 1060 titled "Rate of Inflation, 1968–1976," in Section 1.

31. When did overall consumer prices reach their peak?

   A 1968
   B 1971
   C 1974
   D 1976

32. What is the best description of the rate of inflation during the period from 1968 to 1972?

   F stayed about the same
   G rose steadily
   H dropped steadily
   J rose and dropped wildly from year to year

33. Using this graph and the information in this chapter, examine the relationship between food and fuel prices. Write a paragraph that explains how food prices might be affected by changes in fuel prices.

Applying the Chapter Skill: *Creating a Multimedia Presentation*

34. Review the major topics discussed in this chapter. Develop a blueprint for a mulitmedia presentation on a topic you have not yet explored. Consider using information from previous chapters to provide a background for your topic.

ACTIVITIES

Writing to LEARN

Writing an Opinion
Partly due to the Watergate scandal, Congress and the press keep a watchful eye on top government officials. They probe any questionable activity — past or present, public or private. Is this level of watchfulness good or bad for the country? Support your opinion in an essay.

Primary Source CD-ROM

Working With Primary Sources Find additional information on the Nixon, Ford, and Carter administrations on the *Exploring Primary Sources in U.S. History CD-ROM* and use the selection(s) provided to complete the Chapter 32 primary source activity located in the *America: Pathways to the Present* area of the following Web site.
www.phschool.com

Take It to the NET

Chapter Self-Test As a review activity, take the Chapter 32 Self-Test in the *America: Pathways to the Present* area at the Web site listed below. The questions are designed to test your understanding of the chapter content.
www.phschool.com

and unsuccessful "WIN" program, and proposing a large tax cut.

21. Carter's "outsider" status helped to get him elected. However, neither he nor his staff were ever able to master the art of working effectively with members of Congress.

22. Carter's inability to resolve the hostage crisis hurt him considerably in the 1980 election.

CRITICAL THINKING

23. Many Americans lost a great deal of faith in their government. However, the scandal also proved the strength of the constitutional system.

24. The Vietnam War had become highly unpopular in the United States by the early 1970s. Therefore, public opinion was probably the most important factor in the decision by Congress to deny further military aid to South Vietnam.

25. Possible answer: It is often very difficult to get people to make significant changes in the way they behave.

26. During Nixon's presidency, through détente and SALT I, relations improved. During Carter's presidency, relations soured due to strife over dissidents and the Soviet Union's invasion of Afghanistan. The latter interfered with the passing of SALT II, disrupted American grain shipments to Russia, and caused an American boycott of the Moscow Olympics.

27. The most evident change was in his attitudes toward communism. As a member of Congress, Nixon was staunchly anti-Communist. However, as President, he sought to improve relations with Communist countries. This change was due primarily to changing times and to the differences between the job of Congressman and that of being the President.

SKILLS ASSESSMENT

28. He is trapped in a web.

29. The symbolism of a spider's web. Spools of recording tape are also caught in the web, a reference to the White House tapes, central to the Watergate scandal. The symbolism is that Nixon and the tapes are inextricably linked in the scandal.

30. Nixon has trapped himself in a web of lies. Sample caption: "Caught in his own web."

31. C

32. F

33. Answers will vary, but blueprints should include subtopics, key sources of information, and the sequence and description of segments.

A COLD WAR TEST

Focus Have students find the meaning of each of these words in a dictionary before they begin to read: *mecca, familiarity, anachronistic, vernacular, apocalyptic, admonishment, tranquility, indelibly.* Ask them to consider, as they read, the positive and negative effects of high defense spending on a nation's economy.

Instruct Ask students to review the selection and find evidence that Greenfield's direct exposure to the Cold War both scared and thrilled him. *(Greenfield indicates his discomfort at the thunderous noise that preceded the launching and describes his awe at the rocketing missile.)* How is Greenfield's ambivalence a metaphor for the feelings of the nation as a whole? *(Many Americans were impressed by U.S. power yet afraid that it could destroy the world.)* Have students find examples in the selection of routine American and Soviet practices during the Cold War. *(Security checks, other preliminaries to boarding Navy ships)*

Analyzing the Document Use this additional question to generate class discussion:

Critical Thinking: Determining Relevance What purpose do specific details—such as the names of TV programs that Greenfield watched, types of clothing that he wore, and things that he did in his free time—serve in Greenfield's story? *(Such details strengthen the story by creating in the reader's mind images of "an average 12-year-old in 1974.")*

AmericanHeritage®
MY BRUSH WITH **HISTORY**™
by CRAIG B. GREENFIELD

A Poseidon missile is launched from a submarine.

A Cold War Test

The Cold War decades were a boom time for the American defense industry. The billions spent each year to develop and produce modern weapons not only helped protect the nation, but also boosted its economy. In the passage below, Craig B. Greenfield, whose father worked for a defense contractor, describes a visit to see his father's handiwork in action.

IT WAS 1974. As your average twelve-year-old, my world was one of mischievous after-school activities, mixed with the usual sandlot sports, awkward encounters with girls, and homework. With the exception of the trendy peace-sign belt buckle and fingers-gesturing peace-sign T-shirt that I owned, I had only a faint familiarity with the politics of peace and war in faraway Vietnam. In fact, my only real exposure to those events came from those television voices that came between "Gilligan's Island" and "Adam 12," who spoke of the specter of nuclear holocaust that losing to communism in Asia might invite.

All that changed one winter with a brief but profound encounter with the inner workings and realities of the Cold War.

My family had taken a vacation that December. With my father employed as an electrical engineer by the Sperry Corporation, a leading Long Island defense contractor, and my mother keeping busy with her family at home, we set out for Fort Lauderdale to combine some sunshine with the duty of visiting all our recently retired relatives. A much-anticipated highlight of this trip for me was to be a visit to the newly opened Disney World. But compared with the show I was to see, that children's mecca turned out to be just a roadside attraction.

We were relaxing in the cool comfort of my uncle's condominium when my father proudly announced that he had arranged for a side trip to Cape Canaveral for what he called, in the acronymistic vernacular of the defense industry, a DASO, or "daytime at sea operation," wherein a Poseidon missile would be launched from an actual submarine. Although I viewed this devel-

The nuclear-powered strategic missile submarine USS Lafayette underway

1092

RESOURCE DIRECTORY

Technology
AmericanHeritage® **My Brush with History**™
 Videotapes *A Cold War Test*

☑ **TEST PREPARATION**

Have students use the excerpt on these pages to answer the following question.

Which statement best describes the speaker's feelings about Cold War weapons development and production?

Ⓐ He feels that U.S. military preparedness helped end the Cold War and is grateful.

B He feels proud of his father's achievement.

C He feels that high defense spending prevented the United States from adequately addressing problems such as poverty.

D He feels that the nation should have done more to prepare militarily.

opment as one more dreaded lengthy car ride full of slap fighting with my brother, to my father, who had worked hard on developing submarine navigation systems, it was a rare and valuable chance to see his engineering achievement at work—a demonstration otherwise possible only in an apocalyptic armed launch situation.

With a quick good-bye we set off on our three-hour journey to Port Canaveral, neighboring the cape, where so many televised space shots originated, my father's excitement manifesting itself in driving at a clip that ultimately got him ticketed.

THE MISSILE LAUNCH We arrived at Cape Canaveral and were processed in true Cold War fashion: security clearance, identification cards, and a short, sharp admonishment to stay only in certain areas of the host Navy ship during our day at sea. Then we proceeded up the gangplank and onto the huge auxiliary ship *Compass Island* (EAG 153), which had seen action over the years as a part of the U.S. Military Sealift Command.

I spent the hours-long voyage out to sea exploring the ship and listening to a succession of lectures about this and that capability, guidance system, and the like on both the *Compass Island* and the day's feature attraction, the five-hundred-foot long Poseidon submarine USS *Lafayette* (SSBN 616), which rode regally beside us until it majestically submerged into the sparkling Atlantic water, trailed only by its perfect wake and the indiscreet presence of an antenna-laden Soviet "fishing trawler."

At dusk, with the Florida sun low on the horizon, everyone aboard became aware of the countdown that had actually been going on all day. With fifteen seconds left and our formidable companion well hidden under the sea, the boat buzzed with anticipation and excitement.

At about five seconds to launch, our immense host ship began to rock to and fro, despite the relative tranquillity of the Atlantic shortly before. At four seconds to launch the boat was heaving so violently that all of us had to brace ourselves. At three seconds to launch the rumbling became so loud that I imagined myself being in the center of a thunderclap. At two seconds to launch, with the blocks-long ship in its turbulent pitch and roll and the noise of eruption becoming ever

louder, the inside missile hatch of the submarine blew open explosively far below. Finally, rising on a column of fire, the thirty-four-foot body of the C-3 Poseidon missile emerged from the boiling sea and, with a zig right and a zag left, rocketed skyward and headed toward its destination in the Indian Ocean, nearly three thousand miles away. As I gazed awestruck, my jaw opened wide, that image implanted itself indelibly in my memory.

Today, more than twenty years later, with the disintegration of Soviet communism receding into history, what occurred on that winter day at sea seems almost to have been staged for a movie rather than the profound and scary reality that it was.

However, that vivid childhood memory allows me as an adult to appreciate fully the magnitude of the resources involved in that endeavor called the Cold War. Having personally lived with the practical realities of the Cold War—and having been fed, clothed, and educated with the money that the employment of thousands like my father in the defense industry brought—I greet these new historical developments with both a sense of hope for a peaceful future and a sense of what brought them about.

Source: *American Heritage* magazine, July 1995.

Understanding Primary Sources

1. What was the Soviet "fishing trawler" carrying?
2. How would these items be used?

American Heritage®
MY BRUSH WITH **HISTORY**™

 Videotapes

For more information about the Cold War, view "A Cold War Test."

1093

Chapter 33 Planning Guide
Resource Manager

	CORE INSTRUCTION	READING/SKILLS
Chapter-Level Resources	**Teaching Resources** • Pacing Charts booklet • Block Scheduling booklet **Resource Pro® CD-ROM**, Ch. 33 **Prentice Hall Presentation Pro CD-ROM**, Ch. 33 **www.phschool.com** • eTeach	**Guided Reading Audiotapes (English/Spanish)** **Student Edition on Audio CD**, Ch. 33 **Social Studies Skills Tutor CD-ROM** **Color Transparencies**, F10, G13, G14
1 Roots of the New Conservatism 1. Find out about the major events in Ronald Reagan's political career. 2. Learn how conservatism evolved in the years between the 1930s and the 1970s. 3. Discover why the 1980 election marked a turning point in United States history.	**Teaching Resources** **Units 9/10 booklet** • Section 1 Quiz, p. 64 **Learning Styles Lesson Plans booklet**, p. 68	**Guided Reading and Review booklet,** p. 133 **Guide to the Essentials**, p. 167 **Learning with Documents booklet,** p. 98 **Skills for Life booklet**, p. 35 **Section Reading Support Transparencies**
2 The Reagan Revolution 1. Read to find out how President Reagan attempted to change the economy. 2. Find out how Reagan changed the federal government. 3. Reflect on major initiatives and key foreign policy crises of Reagan's first term. 4. Explore the ways in which the economy moved from recession to recovery in the early 1980s.	**Teaching Resources** **Units 9/10 booklet** • Section 2 Quiz, p. 65	**Guided Reading and Review booklet,** p. 134 **Guide to the Essentials**, p. 168 **Learning with Documents booklet,** p. 97 **Section Reading Support Transparencies**
3 Reagan's Second Term 1. Observe the ways in which the United States experienced a renewal of patriotism in the 1980s. 2. Find out about some important social debates that continued through Reagan's term in office. 3. See how the economy evolved during the 1980s. 4. Discover how Reagan's hands-off style of governing led to problems. 5. Consider the legacy of Reagan's presidency.	**Teaching Resources** **Units 9/10 booklet** • Section 3 Quiz, p. 66	**Guided Reading and Review booklet,** p. 135 **Guide to the Essentials**, p. 169 **Learning with Documents booklet,** p. 72 **Section Reading Support Transparencies**
4 The George H. W. Bush Presidency 1. See what challenges George H.W. Bush faced during the 1988 presidential election. 2. Find out how the Cold War came to an end. 3. Learn about the ways in which the United States played a new international role after the Cold War. 4. Observe the effect domestic issues had on Bush's presidency.	**Teaching Resources** **Units 9/10 booklet** • Section 4 Quiz, p. 67 **Learning Styles Lesson Plans booklet**, p. 69	**Guided Reading and Review booklet,** p. 136 **Guide to the Essentials**, p. 170 **Section Reading Support Transparencies**

ENRICHMENT/PRE-AP

Prentice Hall United States History Video Collection™
www.phschool.com
- Section Activities, Virtual Field Trip, Chapter Activities, Current Events Online

Sounds of an Era Audio CD

Great Debates booklet, p. 28
American History Block Scheduling Support
Exploring Primary Sources in U.S. History CD-ROM

Biography, Literature, and Comparing Primary Sources booklet, pp. 88, 161

Biography, Literature, and Comparing Primary Sources booklet, p. 38
American History Block Scheduling Support
Nystrom *Atlas of Our Country,* pp. 34–35
Sounds of an Era Audio CD
American Pathways Thematic Posters

ASSESSMENT

PRENTICE HALL
ASSESSMENT SYSTEM

Core Assessment
ExamView® Test Bank, Ch. 33
ExamView® Test Bank CD-ROM, Ch. 33

Standardized Test Preparation
Diagnose and Prescribe
Diagnostic Tests for High School Social Studies Skills

Review and Reteach
Review Book for U.S. History

Practice and Assess
Test-taking Strategies With Transparencies
Test-taking Strategies Posters
Test Prep Book for U.S. History
Alternative Assessment Handbook
Document-Based Assessment

Teaching Resources
Units 9/10 booklet
- Section Quizzes, pp. 64–67
- Chapter Tests, pp. 68, 71

www.phschool.com Ch. 33 Self-Test

AmericanHeritage RESOURCES

From the Archives of American Heritage®, pp. 1110, 1116
AmericanHeritage® My Brush with History™ Videotapes
www.americanheritage.com

Don't miss the exclusive interactive version of this textbook on the Web and on CD-ROM.

Chapter 33 Planning Guide
In Your Classroom

CHAPTER 33 – PACING SUGGESTIONS

 ### For 90-minute Blocks
- Teach section 1 using Transparencies F10, G13, and G14, and the Recent Scholarship note on page 1104 for class discussions.

 ### Running Out of Time?
If you are running short on time to cover this chapter, consider the following options:
- Use the Prentice Hall Presentation Pro CD-ROM to create an outline for this chapter.
- Use the Section Summaries for Chapter 33, from **Guide to the Essentials (English/Spanish).**

ADDITIONAL ACTIVITIES

1 Roots of the New Conservatism

Connecting with Government
Explain that President Carter reorganized the cabinet. In 1979 he split the responsibilities of the Secretary of Health, Education, and Welfare so that there was a separate Secretary of Education. (The former's domain was then renamed the Department of Health and Human Services.) Though a number of conservative Republicans over the years called for the elimination of the Department of Education, that never happened—even under Republican administrations. Have students research and report on the basis of the dispute over this department. **(Verbal/Linguistic)**

2 The Reagan Revolution

Connecting with Economics
Have students track and present data on the budgets of any five presidential administrations in U.S. history, indicating whether or not the respective budgets were or were not balanced. Then have them research historical events that occurred during the periods in which the budgets they chose mostly showed a deficit. From this information, have them develop a theory on why it is sometimes very difficult to balance the budget. **(Logical/Mathematical)**

3 Reagan's Second Term

Connecting with Government
Have students research (and then use a graphic to show) how the confirmation process for a Justice of the U.S. Supreme Court has worked throughout U.S. history. Suggest that students include what they can learn through examining the respective experiences of Robert Bork and Clarence Thomas, and about what opportunities exist for public input in this procedure. **(Visual/Spatial)**

4 The George H. W. Bush Presidency

Connecting with History and Conflict
Have students research the period after the reunification of Germany, then compose an outline for a report on how the euphoria over the fall of the Berlin Wall in 1989 was cooled by the realities of bringing together two states that had developed under radically different philosophies. The outline should include such issues as economic development, politics, education, and the treatment of foreign-born workers. **(Verbal/Linguistic)**

Chapter 33
The Conservative Revolution
(1980–1992)

INTRODUCING THE CHAPTER

After the political, social, and cultural upheavals of the 1960s and 1970s, many Americans felt change had gone too far and wanted to return to smaller government and more conservative ideas. The policies of Ronald Reagan and his successor, George H.W. Bush, carried out the social and economic goals of "New Right" conservatives.

TIME LINE ACTIVITY

To provide students with practice in using the time line, ask questions such as these:

1. In what year did unemployment reach a 40-year high? *(1982)*

2. What definitive anti-apartheid action was made by the United States and Great Britain in 1986? *(Both governments banned most trade with South Africa, seeking a change in that country's laws.)*

3. What action did George H.W. Bush take in 1990 that went against one of his campaign pledges? *(He raised taxes.)*

eTeach

Be sure to check out this month's online discussion with a Master Teacher. Go to **www.phschool.com**.

Chapter 33 — The Conservative Revolution (1980–1992)

SECTION 1 Roots of the New Conservatism
SECTION 2 The Reagan Revolution
SECTION 3 Reagan's Second Term
SECTION 4 The George H. W. Bush Presidency

Nancy Reagan and Ronald Reagan

Space Shuttle *Columbia*

1980
Conservatives sweep the 1980 federal elections. Ronald Reagan is elected President, and Republicans win control of the Senate.

American Events

1981
President Reagan cuts income tax rates and announces plans to curb government spending.

1982
Unemployment reaches a 40-year high of 10.8 percent during a sharp recession.

1984
Reagan wins a second term in office aided by an economic boom.

Presidential Terms:
Jimmy Carter 1977–1981

Ronald Reagan 1981–1989

1980 · 1982 1984

World Events

Argentina and Great Britain battle for control of the Falkland Islands.
1982

Indira Gandhi, prime minister of India, is assassinated.
1984

1094 Chapter 33 • *The Conservative Revolution*

RESOURCE DIRECTORY

Teaching Resources
Pacing Charts booklet
Block Scheduling booklet, p. 28
Units 9/10 booklet
 • Chapter Summary, p. 63

Technology
Guided Reading Audiotapes (English/Spanish), Ch. 33
Student Edition on Audio CD, Ch. 33
Sounds of an Era Audio CD *Barry Goldwater,* 1964 recording (time: 10 seconds); *Ronald Reagan,* 1981 recording (time: 20 seconds)
Prentice Hall United States History Video Collection™ Volume 20, *Post-War USA*
Prentice Hall Presentation Pro CD-ROM, Ch. 33
Resource Pro® CD-ROM
Social Studies Skills Tutor CD-ROM
Companion Web site, www.phschool.com

Cold War Events, 1980–1989

Map Labels:
- Los Angeles Olympic Games, 1984 — UNITED STATES
- Grenada Invasion, 1983 — GRENADA
- Contra Rebellion, 1983–1990 — NICARAGUA
- Fall of Berlin Wall, 1989 — GERMANY
- Collapse of Soviet Union, 1991 — SOVIET UNION
- Chernobyl Disaster, 1986
- Tiananmen Square, 1989 — CHINA
- ARCTIC OCEAN
- ATLANTIC OCEAN
- PACIFIC OCEAN
- PACIFIC OCEAN
- INDIAN OCEAN
- Equator

Legend:
- USA and allies
- American military aid
- Other Western military aid
- Communist countries
- Soviet military aid
- Western and Soviet aid

0   2000 mi.
0   2000 km

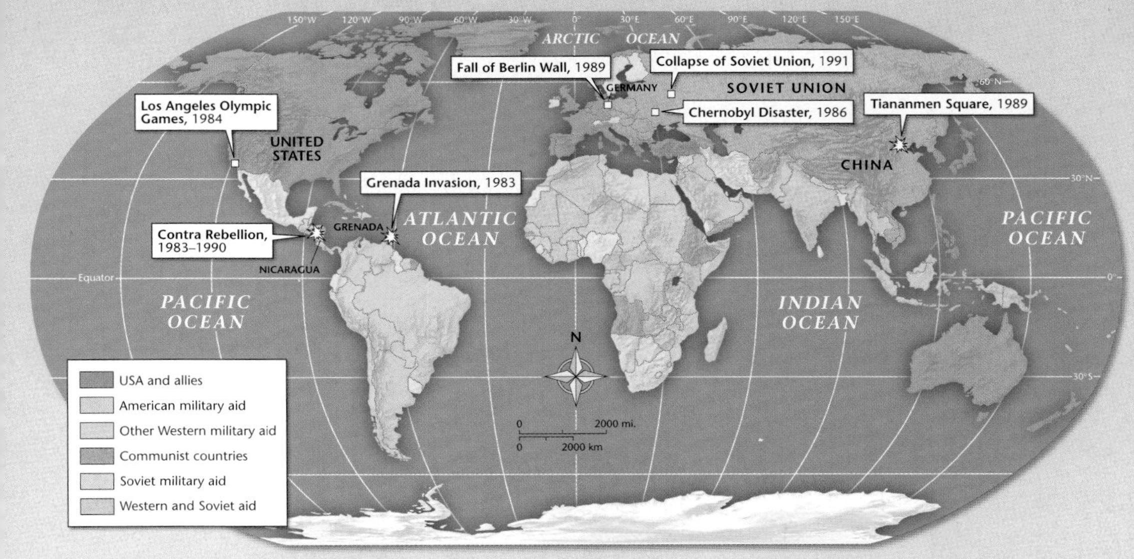

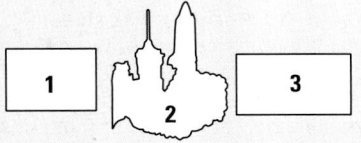

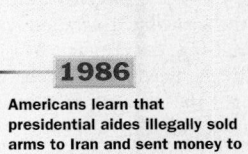

1986
Americans learn that presidential aides illegally sold arms to Iran and sent money to support anti-Communist rebels in Nicaragua.

1990
President Bush agrees to raise taxes to fight budget deficits.

1991
American troops lead an international force to liberate Kuwait and defeat Iraq in Operation Desert Storm.

George H. W. Bush 1989–1993

Timeline: 1986 • 1988 • 1990 • 1992

1985 Britain and the United States ban most trade with South Africa over apartheid.

1987 Palestinians rebel against Israel.

1989 China crushes Beijing protests.

1990 Germany is reunified.

1991 Gorbachev resigns, and the Soviet Union dissolves into 15 republics.

Chapter 33   **1095**

BIBLIOGRAPHY

For the Teacher

Atkinson, Rick. *Crusade: The Untold Story of the Persian Gulf War.* Houghton Mifflin, 1993. (A *Washington Post* reporter looks at the war three years later.)

Hunter-Gault, Charlayne. *In My Place.* Vintage, 1993. (A successful journalist remembers her youth as one of the first two African American students at the University of Georgia.)

For the Student

Ashe, Arthur, and Arnold Rampersad. *Days of Grace: A Memoir.* Ballantine, 1994. (Reflections by the African American tennis champion and activist who died of AIDS.)

Erdrich, Louise. *Love Medicine: New and Expanded Version.* HarperCollins, 1993. (Updated version of the author's first novel of Native American life.)

Cold War Events, 1980–1989

Activating Prior Knowledge Which of the Cold War events displayed on this map took place in Communist countries? *(The collapse of the Soviet Union, the Chernobyl disaster, Tiananmen Square, and the fall of the Berlin Wall)*

Previewing Ask students what effect they think the Cold War events had on the 1984 Olympics. *(Because the Olympics were held in the United States, they were very pro-American, and some Communist countries boycotted the games.)*

BACKGROUND
About the Pictures

1. President Reagan's wife, Nancy, was his closest adviser and confidante.
2. The explosion of the *Challenger* space shuttle in 1987 was one of the greatest domestic tragedies that occurred during Reagan's presidency.
3. The stated goal of Operation Desert Storm was the liberation of oil-rich Kuwait from invading Iraqi forces.

iTEXT

Don't miss the exclusive interactive version of this textbook on the Web and on CD-ROM.

Section 1
Roots of the New Conservatism

SECTION OBJECTIVES

1. Find out about the major events in Ronald Reagan's political career.
2. Learn how conservatism evolved in the years between the 1930s and the 1970s.
3. Discover why the 1980 election marked a turning point in United States history.

BELLRINGER

Warm-Up Activity Ask students what the terms *conservative* and *conservatism* mean to them. Ask them to identify two contemporary issues that would fit their definitions of the terms.

Activating Prior Knowledge Ask students if they can answer the following question: What aspect of American society in 1980 most likely led to the election of Ronald Reagan? *(The condition of the United States economy)*

READING STRATEGY

As students read the section, have them list significant events and individuals in the growth of the conservative movement. Then ask students to write a sentence that evaluates the impact of each event and individual on American society.

ACTIVITY
Connecting with Citizenship

Invite students to imagine that they are media consultants for presidential candidate Ronald Reagan in 1980. In this role, each student is to prepare a 15-second "sound bite" for the candidate to use in explaining to interviewers why Reagan switched political parties. Select students to deliver their sound bites to the class. **(Verbal/Linguistic)**

READING FOCUS

- What were the major events in Ronald Reagan's political career?
- How did conservatism evolve in the years between the 1930s and the 1970s?
- Why did the 1980 election mark a turning point in United States history?

MAIN IDEA

After decades of federal government expansion and social and cultural change, a conservative movement gained strength during the 1970s. In 1980, it brought Ronald Reagan to power.

KEY TERMS

Reagan Democrat
New Right
televangelism

TAKING NOTES

Copy this flowchart. As you read, fill in the boxes with some of the major events in the history of the conservative movement. The first box has been completed to help you get started.

Conservatives reject high costs and spending of the New Deal.	→		→		→	

Setting the Scene Two weeks after Ronald Reagan won the presidency in 1980, Richard Nixon wrote to the president-elect to recommend advisors for top positions:

> 66 *Washington needs new men and new ideas. By your appointments, you can give the country a sense of excitement, hope and drive to government which we have not seen since FDR.* 99
> —Richard Nixon

By most accounts, Reagan succeeded. Six years after the Watergate scandal drove Nixon from the White House, Reagan arrived in Washington at the head of a more conservative and powerful Republican Party. Reagan achieved many of his goals through the strength of his administration and the appeal of his warm personality and firm beliefs.

Although the 1980 election appeared to mark a sudden shift in American politics, the roots of change lay deep in the past. The new President voiced the growing frustrations of voters around the country who believed that government had grown too large and had lost touch with the needs of the people. Reagan's own political journey reflected the growing conservatism of millions of Americans.

Reagan's Political Career

Reagan was originally a Democrat who considered Franklin D. Roosevelt, architect of the New Deal, his political hero. When Reagan began his career as a movie actor in Hollywood, he became actively involved in the political affairs of the actors' union.

After World War II, Reagan found himself less comfortable with the Democratic Party, and he joined the Republican Party in the 1950s. He served as a spokesman for General Electric, making speeches that praised capitalism and attacked government regulation. He also spoke out strongly against

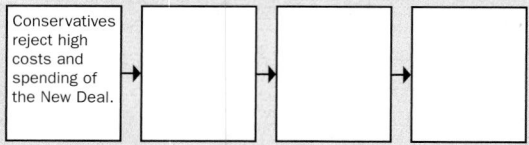

With this 1980 campaign poster, Ronald Reagan appealed to voters' patriotism and their unhappiness with the direction of the country.

RESOURCE DIRECTORY

Teaching Resources
Learning Styles Lesson Plans booklet, p. 68
Guided Reading and Review booklet, p. 133

Technology
Section Reading Support Transparencies
Guided Reading Audiotapes (English/Spanish), Ch. 33
Student Edition on Audio CD, Ch. 33
Color Transparencies *American Photo,* F10
Prentice Hall Presentation Pro CD-ROM, Ch. 33
Companion Web site, www.phschool.com

Communists in the United States. Ronald Reagan was now clearly in the conservative camp.

Reagan gained national attention in 1966, when he was elected governor of California. Likable, photogenic, and committed to conservative values, he gained support for cutbacks in social programs in his state. During his eight years as governor, Reagan eliminated California's budget deficit by modestly increasing taxes and reforming state spending. He called for similar reforms of social programs run by the federal government.

The Evolution of Conservatism

Reagan's political transition took place against the backdrop of a national debate over the proper size and scope of government. During the prosperous 1920s, conservative Republicans had won national elections by promising to keep taxes low and minimize spending. The Great Depression reshaped the debate with Franklin Roosevelt's introduction of New Deal programs that greatly enlarged the size and cost of the federal government.

New Deal Opponents New Deal agencies, which provided banking regulation, assistance to farmers, aid for the unemployed, and a great deal more, changed the role of the President and the federal government. Critics argued that in a capitalist country, government should not undertake these tasks. They said that the nation could not afford the high federal spending and substantial budget deficits that resulted.

Some of these critics joined to form the American Liberty League. Established in 1934, this organization included both industrialists and politicians. The Liberty League sought to teach respect for the rights of individuals and property and to underscore the importance of individual enterprise. All of these values, members claimed, were being undermined by FDR's large government programs.

In 1937, an attempt by Roosevelt to "pack" the Supreme Court by adding new justices caused a backlash. Conservatives in both major political parties formed a coalition that opposed further New Deal legislation. Nevertheless, Republicans struggled to overcome Roosevelt's enduring popularity as President. Led by Roosevelt and later by Harry S Truman, the Democrats kept control of the White House for twenty years.

From Eisenhower to Goldwater The election of Dwight D. Eisenhower as President in 1952 began eight years of Republican rule. Eisenhower called his approach to government "modern Republicanism." He accepted the basic outlines of the New Deal and never attempted to dismantle the federal bureaucracy. The federal bureaucracy even expanded, as it did in 1953 with the creation of a Department of Health, Education, and Welfare, headed by Oveta Culp Hobby.

In 1964, the Republican candidate for President, Senator Barry Goldwater of Arizona, ran on a staunchly conservative platform. Facing Democrat Lyndon B. Johnson, Goldwater opposed government activism, including social security, federal civil rights

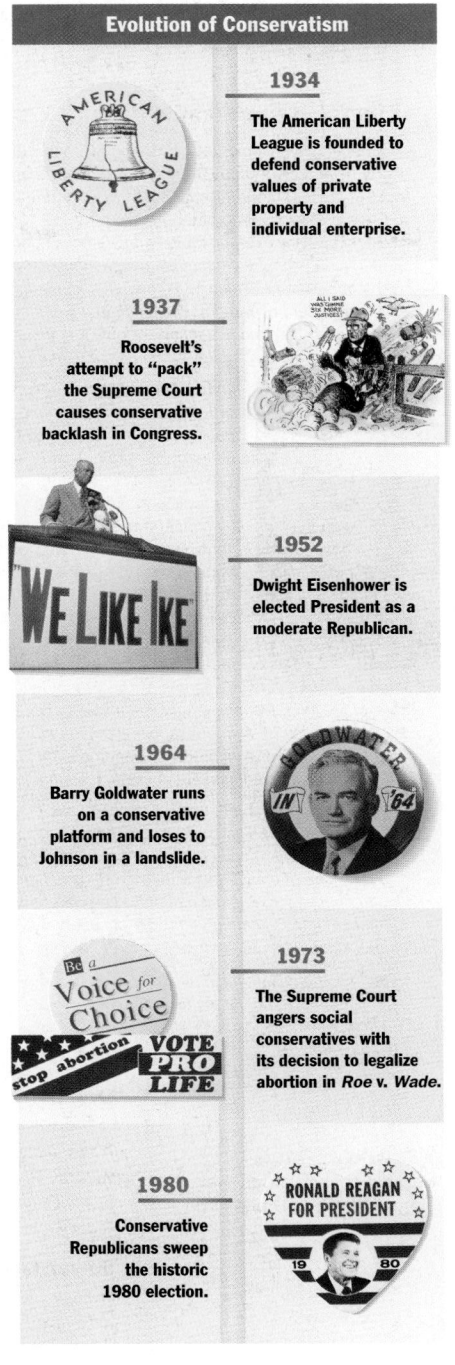

Evolution of Conservatism

1934
The American Liberty League is founded to defend conservative values of private property and individual enterprise.

1937
Roosevelt's attempt to "pack" the Supreme Court causes conservative backlash in Congress.

1952
Dwight Eisenhower is elected President as a moderate Republican.

1964
Barry Goldwater runs on a conservative platform and loses to Johnson in a landslide.

1973
The Supreme Court angers social conservatives with its decision to legalize abortion in *Roe* v. *Wade*.

1980
Conservative Republicans sweep the historic 1980 election.

Fast Forward to Today

Liberal Republicans

Historically, the Democratic Party and Republican Party have included coalitions of both liberals and conservatives. Liberal Republicans dominated their party's presidential nominations from the 1930s to the 1960s. However, Goldwater defeated a liberal Republican in the primaries to win the nomination with conservative support. At the 1964 convention, Goldwater denounced "moderation" in a fiery speech that inspired his followers but upset many liberals and moderates in the GOP.

Today Old coalitions have broken up, and the two major parties are clearly divided by philosophy on a national level. The conservative wing of the Republican Party, strengthened by conservative ex-Democrats, controls most leadership positions in the GOP. Some liberal Republicans and conservative Democrats still flourish at state and local levels, but they face difficulties running for Congress or the presidency. One of the few liberal Republicans in the Senate, James Jeffords of Vermont (above), broke his life-long ties to his party in 2001 to become an Independent aligned with Democrats. He said,

"Looking ahead, I can see more and more instances where I will disagree with [President George W. Bush] on very fundamental issues: the issues of choice [abortion rights], the direction of the judiciary, tax and spending decisions, missile defense, energy and the environment, and a host of other issues, large and small."

 How did Goldwater's 1964 campaign lay the foundation for later Republican victories?

READING CHECK
How did conservatives feel about Johnson's Great Society?

laws and antipoverty programs. He also demanded a military buildup against a possible Soviet attack.

Many members of the Republican Party, particularly in the Northeast, felt Goldwater was too conservative to lead their party. Johnson portrayed Goldwater as a dangerous extremist and crushed him in the 1964 election. Goldwater only won his home state of Arizona and several southern states that were unhappy with federal desegregation initiatives. Some analysts concluded that Goldwater's conservatism would never gain wide support. His victory in the South, however, showed that southern conservatives might break their historic ties to the Democrats if a Republican candidate better represented their conservative views.

The Great Society Conservatives found themselves silenced for a time following Goldwater's decisive defeat in 1964. The Democratic landslide in the election gave liberals the political upper hand in the mid-1960s. Congress cooperated as President Johnson pushed ahead with his Great Society program, an extension of the New Deal, starting in 1965.

"Is a new world coming?" Johnson asked. "We welcome it, and we will bend it to the hopes of man."

The Great Society promised something for everyone. The Office of Economic Opportunity helped the poor and gave them a voice in handling their own affairs. Medicare provided medical care for the elderly, while Medicaid gave similar aid to the poor. The Great Society included the most far-reaching school support program in American history. In 1965, a new Department of Housing and Urban Development gave Cabinet-level visibility to the effort to revive the nation's cities and provide good housing for all Americans. However, the Great Society cost billions of dollars annually and raised expectations beyond what the government could meet.

Nixon and the Welfare State In 1968, Richard Nixon won the presidency, bringing Republicans back to power. Nixon wanted to trim social welfare programs, which he believed encouraged people not to work, and to bring the budget under control.

Yet in fact, the federal government continued to grow during Nixon's presidency. The Occupational Safety and Health Act (OSHA) of 1970 provided for employee rights in the workplace and demanded that safety standards be maintained with federal enforcement regulation. Also in 1970, the Environmental Protection Agency (EPA) was created to oversee federal antipollution laws. Opponents of government growth criticized these efforts for interfering with private enterprise.

Social Issues Many conservatives were deeply troubled by rapid cultural changes of the period. Rock music was becoming increasingly shocking, its lyrics more openly sexual and drug-oriented. The use of illegal drugs became widespread, and a wave of radical and often violent student protests swept college campuses. Reagan's strong opposition to riots at the University of California at Berkeley encouraged many voters to support him in his successful 1966 run for governor of California. One of his first acts as governor was to dismiss that university's president for being too soft on student protests.

The sexual revolution was another source of conservative concern. The use of the new birth control pill encouraged promiscuity, critics said. Also, after the 1973 Supreme Court ruling in *Roe* v. *Wade* legalized abortion, anti-abortion forces launched a campaign to overturn that decision. The movement for gay and lesbian rights further angered many conservative Americans.

The women's movement caused still another rift. As women worked for equal rights and began to gain new opportunities, some conservatives reacted vigorously. A woman's place was at home, they argued. Phyllis Schlafly, who campaigned against ratification of the Equal Rights Amendment, echoed the desire to retain women's traditional roles.

Civil Rights Some government programs that were aimed at ending racial segregation and discrimination also disturbed conservatives. Most people supported the desegregation of public schools following *Brown* v. *Board of Education* in 1954. However, many questioned why their children had to be bused to distant schools each day for diversity's sake when neighborhood schools were much closer.

Another controversy involved affirmative action programs. These programs committed the government and private companies to give special consideration to groups discriminated against in the past, both women and members of minority groups. Some critics called affirmative action programs "reverse discrimination." This issue attracted some Democratic blue-collar workers to the Republican ranks, where they would help elect Ronald Reagan to the presidency. The **Reagan Democrats,** as they were known, would help Republicans win many victories in the 1980s.

Turning Point: The Election of 1980

In 1976, Ronald Reagan had challenged President Gerald Ford for the Republican nomination. He lost this contest by a narrow margin. In 1980, Reagan again sought the nomination. Republican moderates claimed that he, like Goldwater in 1964, was too conservative to defeat the Democratic President, Jimmy Carter. However, social changes were underway that would prove this prediction wrong.

The New Right Coalition By 1980, conservative groups had formed a powerful political coalition known as the **New Right.** A key concern of many conservatives in the New Right was the size of government and its role in the economy. They proposed cutting government-funded social programs.

Other groups in the New Right wanted to restore what they considered Christian values to society. Members of the Moral Majority, led by the Reverend Jerry Falwell of Virginia,

VIEWING HISTORY Richard Nixon, shown here at Grand Teton National Park, signed legislation to extend federal oversight of the environment. **Recognizing Ideologies** *Why were some conservatives unhappy with Richard Nixon's acts as President?*

Focus on
WORLD EVENTS

Margaret Thatcher Ronald Reagan found a strong ally in Margaret Thatcher, Britain's first woman prime minister. Thatcher governed from 1979 to 1990 and shared Reagan's support for free enterprise and his hostility toward communism. Like Reagan, Thatcher won office in difficult economic times by promising to cut taxes and reduce the size of government. Although her tough economic policies forced many inefficient factories and mines to close, she succeeded in curbing labor strife and in invigorating other sectors of the economy.

Reading Comprehension

1. They felt that it undermined the rights of individuals, property, and individual enterprise; and that the nation could not afford the high federal spending and resulting deficits.

2. Primarily because the government continued to grow larger under both Eisenhower and Nixon.

3. By offering the hope of ending forced busing and affirmative action.

4. Moral Majority televangelists and those who wanted to reduce both the size of the government and its social programs.

Critical Thinking and Writing

5. Reagan was very effective in televised debates and speeches due to his talent as a witty and optimistic public speaker. The New Right also used television to propagate conservative views that Reagan shared.

6. Answers will vary but should be supported with facts from the section.

Take It to the NET

President Reagan voiced the growing frustrations of voters who believed the government was too large. He proposed that decreasing the size of the bureaucracy and limiting government intervention in people's lives would solve the economic problems facing America.

VIEWING HISTORY Jerry Falwell and other televangelists helped change the way political candidates portrayed themselves and their opponents in the media. **Identifying Assumptions** What were some of the issues addressed by the New Right?

wanted to follow the dictates of the Bible and revive the traditional values they believed had strengthened the country in the past.

Falwell and other evangelists used the power of television to reach millions of people. In a format that became known as **televangelism,** they appealed to viewers to contribute money to their campaign. They delivered fervent sermons on specific political issues and used the money they raised to back conservative politicians.

A Reagan Landslide The growing strength of conservatives in the Republican Party gave Ronald Reagan the GOP presidential nomination in 1980. During the campaign, Reagan seized on growing discontent. His attacks on incumbent Jimmy Carter's handling of the economy were particularly effective. Criticizing Carter's economic record, he poked fun at the President's use of technical language:

   ❝ I'm talking in human terms and he is hiding behind a dictionary. If he wants a definition, I'll give him one. A recession is when your neighbor loses his job. A depression is when you lose yours. A recovery is when Jimmy Carter loses his. ❞

—Ronald Reagan, 1980

The continuing hostage crisis in Iran, as well as other issues, hurt Carter, and Reagan won in a landslide. He gained 51 percent of the popular vote to Carter's 41 percent. (Illinois Representative John Anderson, a Republican, ran as a moderate third-party candidate.) Carter carried but six states and the District of Columbia, including his home state of Georgia. Carter won only 49 electoral votes while Reagan picked up 489.

Swept along by Reagan's popularity, the Republicans gained control of the Senate for the first time since Eisenhower's first term. Several noted Democratic senators, including Frank Church of Idaho and Birch Bayh of Indiana, lost their seats to underdog Republican challengers. Conservatives now controlled the nation's agenda.

Section 1 Assessment

READING COMPREHENSION

1. Why did conservatives oppose Franklin Roosevelt's New Deal?

2. Why were some conservatives dissatisfied with Republican Presidents like Eisenhower and Nixon?

3. How did Reagan appeal to the voters who became known as **Reagan Democrats?**

4. What groups were part of the **New Right?**

CRITICAL THINKING AND WRITING

5. **Recognizing Cause and Effect** How did Reagan use modern technology and new political techniques to increase his popularity?

6. **Writing an Outline** Create an outline describing the goals of conservative politicians in 1980 and how they worked to accomplish these goals.

Take It to the NET

Activity: Analyzing Primary Sources Study Ronald Reagan's first inaugural address online. How does this address reflect the evolution of conservatism in America? Use the links provided in the *America: Pathways to the Present* area of the following Web site for help in completing this activity.
www.phschool.com

1100 Chapter 33 • *The Conservative Revolution*

CAPTION ANSWERS

Viewing History The size and role of government; following dictates of the Bible; reviving traditional values.

RESOURCE DIRECTORY

Teaching Resources
Units 9/10 booklet
• Section 1 Quiz, p. 64
Guide to the Essentials
• Section 1 Summary, p. 167

Technology
Sounds of an Era Audio CD *Ronald Reagan*
(time: 5 seconds)

Analyzing Trends in Electoral College Maps

As you recall, votes in a presidential election are not cast directly for a presidential candidate but rather for presidential electors—the members of the electoral college. Each state has as many electoral votes as it has members of Congress: two for its two Senate seats, plus at least one more based on its representation in the House, which is in turn determined by the state's population. In all states but Maine and Nebraska, it's "winner take all": The candidate with the most popular votes gets *all* of a state's electoral votes. Therefore, it's not surprising that states and regions with the largest population—and most electoral votes—get the most attention from presidential candidates.

Electoral college maps show shifts in population—and political clout. Maps that also show election results reveal where the strength of a candidate or a party lies.

LEARN THE SKILL

Use the following steps to analyze trends shown in electoral college maps:

1. **Determine what information the maps provide.** In some electoral college maps, population size determines the size of each state on the map. Other maps just use the number of electoral votes. Still others show election results.

2. **Look for differences between the maps.** Note differences in population and electoral votes for particular states and for regions over time.

3. **Draw conclusions about population shifts and party strengths.** Relate what you know from other sources to what you see on the maps.

PRACTICE THE SKILL

Answer the following questions:

1. **(a)** What kind of information does Map A provide? How does the map present the information? **(b)** Does Map B provide more, less, or the same kind of information as Map A? Explain. **(c)** How is Map C different from Map A?

2. Between 1948 and 1980: **(a)** Which two states gained the most population? **(b)** Which two states lost the most population? **(c)** Which region(s) gained political clout?

3. **(a)** If you had been a candidate in 1948, where would you have concentrated your resources? **(b)** In 1980, what regions would you have concentrated on? **(c)** What conclusions can you draw about the changes in the political landscape between 1948 and 1980?

APPLY THE SKILL

See the Chapter Review and Assessment for another opportunity to apply this skill.

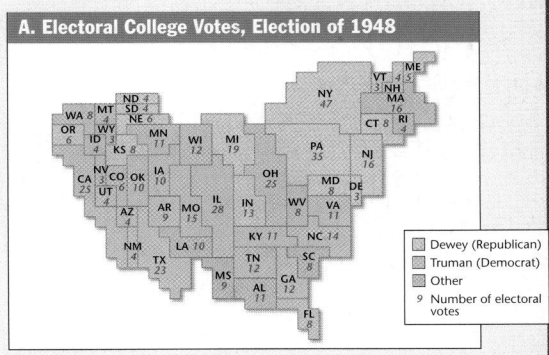

A. Electoral College Votes, Election of 1948

Dewey (Republican)
Truman (Democrat)
Other
9 Number of electoral votes

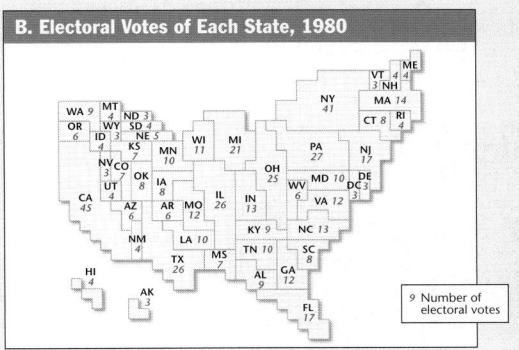

B. Electoral Votes of Each State, 1980

9 Number of electoral votes

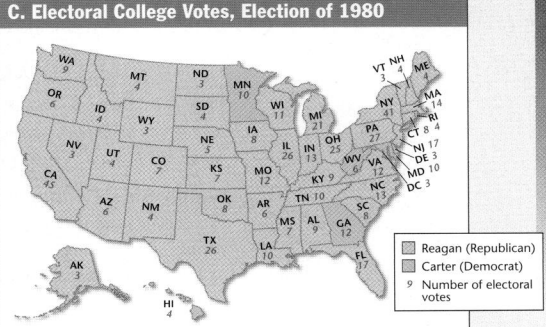

C. Electoral College Votes, Election of 1980

Reagan (Republican)
Carter (Democrat)
9 Number of electoral votes

Chapter 33 **1101**

ANALYZING TRENDS IN ELECTORAL COLLEGE MAPS

Focus Students learn to analyze trends in population and regional political influence by comparing electoral college maps.

Instruct Discuss with students how the electoral college system may influence campaigns and issues. States that don't traditionally vote Democratic or Republican and/or that have many electoral votes receive the most attention from candidates. Issues that are important to these key "swing" states could dominate politics to the exclusion of other issues. Discuss recent election campaigns in view of the electoral votes in each state.

Extend See the Skills for Life activity in the Resource Directory below.

ANSWERS
PRACTICE THE SKILL

1. **(a)** Map A shows the number of electoral votes of each state, the relative population of each state, and which candidate won the electoral votes of each state in the election of 1948. The number of electoral votes is included in an outline of the state, sized to reflect its population compared to that of other states, and the states won by each candidate are color-coded. **(b)** Map B provides less information than Map A. It doesn't show the election results for a given year. **(c)** Map C shows the states with geographical boundaries and doesn't represent each state sized to reflect its population; it shows the results of a different election.

2. **(a)** California and Florida. **(b)** New York and Pennsylvania. **(c)** The South and the West.

3. **(a)** In the Northeast, particularly New York and Pennsylvania. **(b)** The West, the Southwest, and the Middle Atlantic States. **(c)** From 1948 to 1980, some of the political clout has shifted out of the Northeast into the West and the Southwest.

SECTION OBJECTIVES

1. Read to find out how President Reagan attempted to change the economy.
2. Find out how Reagan changed the federal government.
3. Reflect on major initiatives and key foreign policy crises of Reagan's first term.
4. Explore the ways in which the economy moved from recession to recovery in the early 1980s.

BELLRINGER

Warm-Up Activity Ask students to suggest their own ideas for a fair method of taxing people to pay for government services. What kinds of income or purchases would they tax? How would they make sure the tax was fair?

Activating Prior Knowledge Did everyone in the United States agree with the principles of the Conservative Revolution? What percentage of voters favored Ronald Reagan in the 1980 election? Which leaders represented other viewpoints?

READING STRATEGY

Have students skim the section and write down main headings, then rewrite each heading as a question. As they read, have students answer their questions and reflect on actions of government and the private sector to expand economic opportunities to all citizens.

ACTIVITY
Connecting with Economics

Pair students and have each pair develop two diagrams: one illustrating how business growth is stimulated according to Keynesian theory and the other showing how supply-side economics creates business growth. Select pairs to explain and interpret their diagrams for the class. **(Visual/Spatial; Logical/Mathematical)**

The Reagan Revolution

READING FOCUS

- How did President Reagan attempt to change the economy?
- In what ways did Reagan change the federal government?
- What were the major initiatives and key foreign policy crises of Reagan's first term?
- How did the economy move from recession to recovery in the early 1980s?

MAIN IDEA

Ronald Reagan worked to boost the nation's pride and prosperity by cutting taxes, shrinking the federal government, and increasing defense spending.

KEY TERMS

supply-side economics
New Federalism
Strategic Defense Initiative (SDI)

TAKING NOTES

As you read, prepare an outline of this section. Use Roman numerals to indicate the major headings of the section, capital letters for the subheadings, and numbers for the supporting details. The sample below will help you get started.

> I. Changing the Economy
>   A. Supply-Side Economics
>   1. "Reaganomics" reverses earlier theories of high spending and debt.
>   2. _____
>   B. Cutting Taxes
>   1. _____
>   2. _____
> II. Changing the Government

Setting the Scene During the 1980 campaign, Ronald Reagan stressed three broad policies that he would pursue if elected President: slashing taxes, eliminating unnecessary government programs, and bolstering the defense capability of the United States. His goals were to reshape the federal government and restore the country's strength and prosperity. As he addressed the United States for the first time as President, he reaffirmed his promises to the American people:

Ronald Reagan takes the oath of office with his wife, Nancy, at his side.

66 In the days ahead I will propose removing the roadblocks that have slowed our economy and reduced productivity. Steps will be taken aimed at restoring the balance between various levels of government. Progress may be slow, measured in inches and feet, not miles, but we will progress. It is time to reawaken this industrial giant, to get government back within its means, and to lighten our punitive tax burden. And these will be our first priorities, and on these principles there will be no compromise. 99

—Ronald Reagan,
First Inaugural Address, 1981

In his first term, Reagan moved aggressively to put his principles into action.

Changing the Economy

President Reagan brought to Washington a plan for economic change that conservatives had long sought to implement. In simple terms, he wanted to put more money back into people's pockets, instead of into tax coffers.

Supply-Side Economics Reagan's main goal was to spur business growth. His economic program, dubbed "Reaganomics," rested on the theory of supply-side economics. This theory reversed earlier policies based on the ideas of English economist John Maynard Keynes.

RESOURCE DIRECTORY

Teaching Resources
Guided Reading and Review booklet, p. 134

Technology
Section Reading Support Transparencies
Guided Reading Audiotapes (English/Spanish), Ch. 33
Student Edition on Audio CD, Ch. 33
Exploring Primary Sources in U.S. History CD-ROM *A Time for Choosing, Ronald Reagan*
Prentice Hall Presentation Pro CD-ROM, Ch. 33
Companion Web site, www.phschool.com

In the 1920s and 1930s, Keynes had argued that the government could best improve the economy by increasing consumers' demand for goods. This meant giving people more money—either directly, through government payments and programs, or indirectly, by creating jobs. Once people had more money to spend, Keynes argued, they would purchase more goods and services, which would cause the economy to grow.

Keynesian theory had helped explain the Great Depression and the recovery that took place as the United States began a massive military spending program during World War II. In the postwar years, most economists accepted Keynesian arguments. Federal spending was seen as an essential tool for keeping the economy healthy.

In contrast to Keynesian theory, **supply-side economics** focused not on the demand for goods but on the supply of goods. It predicted that cutting taxes would put more money into the hands of businesses and investors—those who supplied the goods for consumers to buy.

The theory assumed that businesses would then hire more people and produce more goods and services, making the economy grow faster. The real key, therefore, was encouraging business leaders to invest in their companies. Their individual actions would create and promote greater national economic abundance. But without tax cuts, high taxes would discourage entrepreneurs from investing, and drain needed capital from the economy.

Cutting Taxes Reagan's first priority was a tax cut. In October 1981, a 5 percent cut went into effect, followed by 10 percent cuts in 1982 and 1983. In 1986, during Reagan's second term, Congress passed the most sweeping tax reform in history. The law closed loopholes that had allowed some people to avoid paying their fair share of taxes. It simplified the tax system by reducing the number of income brackets that determined how much tax a person paid. While all taxpayers benefited from these measures, wealthy Americans benefited most. The tax rate on the highest incomes dropped from 70 percent before Reagan took office to 50 percent in 1984, and to 28 percent after the 1986 tax reform.

Changing the Government

As you read in the previous section, for generations, conservatives had criticized government growth. Now, however, they had a Chief Executive committed to limiting both the size and the role of the federal government.

Cutting Regulations Reagan embarked on a major program of deregulation. Like President Carter before him, Reagan wanted to eliminate government regulations that he believed stifled free market competition.

By the time of Reagan's presidency, regulation had been expanding for nearly a century. The Interstate Commerce Commission, established in 1887, was the first step. Government regulations grew during the Progressive Era of the early 1900s and in the New Deal years of the 1930s. Regulation was intended to protect

Focus on ECONOMICS

Tax Reform Before the 1986 tax reform, taxpayers were able to exclude money spent on many different types of expenses from taxation, including money spent on child care, medical bills, and political contributions. Over time, these categories of expenses, known as deductibles, multiplied, making it easier for many people to find new and innovative ways to lower their taxes. By using their deductions creatively, taxpayers could effectively choose how much to pay in taxes. The elimination of so many loopholes in 1986 meant that the top tax rate could drop from 50 percent to 28 percent without a serious loss of revenue.

INTERPRETING GRAPHS
Reagan reduced the top income tax rate from 70 percent to 28 percent.
Analyzing Information *What was the top income tax rate when Reagan ran for reelection in 1984?*

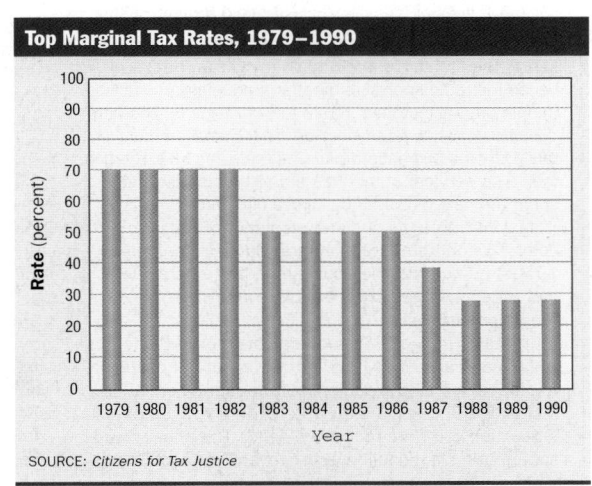

Top Marginal Tax Rates, 1979–1990

SOURCE: *Citizens for Tax Justice*

Chapter 33 • Section 2   **1103**

Chapter 33 Section 2 • **1103**

companies from unfair competition, workers from unsafe working conditions, and consumers from ineffective or unsafe products.

Reagan continued and expanded the deregulation of the energy, transportation, and banking industries begun under the Carter administration. He cut the number and size of regulatory agencies like the Environmental Protection Agency, which had its budget, and therefore its functions, reduced. Reagan argued that regulations made life difficult for producers, which meant fewer jobs for workers and higher prices for consumers. The more that businesses spent to comply with government rules, he charged, the less they could spend on new factories and equipment.

Reagan also challenged the powers of labor unions. In August 1981, the Professional Air Traffic Controllers Organization (PATCO) called a strike to win higher pay and improved working conditions. The move threatened to interrupt air travel across the country because air traffic controllers determine how and where the nation's commercial aircraft fly between airports. Reagan gave the 13,000 strikers two days to return to work, and when most chose to stay out on strike, he fired them. His decisive move caused short-term problems in the air traffic control system, but Reagan savored a victory that "convinced people who might have thought otherwise that I meant what I said."

Slowing Federal Growth Reagan also attempted to cut the size of the federal government. The President believed that any American could succeed through individual effort. This belief ran counter to the argument on which welfare was based: that government should help people who could not help themselves. Reagan charged that the government had become too intrusive in people's lives:

NOTABLE PRESIDENTS
Ronald Reagan

"I find no national malaise. I find nothing wrong with the American people."

—**Ronald Reagan, 1980**

Ronald Reagan was born in rural Tampico, Illinois, in 1911. The first in his family to go to college, Reagan became a radio sportscaster after graduating. His ability to spin dramatic stories from a few dry facts helped him become known in later years as the "Great Communicator." During a business trip to California in 1937, Reagan took a screen test at the Warner Brothers studio. He spent the next ten years building a film career.

In 1947, Reagan became president of the film actors' union, the Screen Actors' Guild. In the mid-1950s, he became the spokesman for General Electric. He spoke against communism and the "containment" policy.

In 1966, Reagan was elected governor of California. Likable and articulate, Reagan was a natural politician who appealed to any audience. In the presidential election of 1980, he asked the voters, "Are you better off today than you were four years ago?" The answer was apparent in his landslide victory over President Carter.

40th President 1981–1989

In 1984, Reagan was reelected, becoming the third Republican President to win reelection since the Depression. Americans remember Reagan for his presidential style—unassuming, personable, candid, and optimistic. A later President, Bill Clinton, summed it up: "[Reagan's] unwavering hopefulness reminded us that optimism is one of our most fundamental virtues."

Connecting to Today
Ronald Reagan reminded Americans how important the role of the President is in helping overcome national self-doubt. How has the self-confidence of the United States changed since 1980? Explain.

Take It to the NET Biography To read more about Ronald Reagan, visit the links provided in the *America: Pathways to the Present* area of the following Web site. **www.phschool.com**

> **"** It is . . . my intention . . . to make [government] work—work with us, not over us; to stand by our side, not ride on our back. Government can and must provide opportunity, not smother it; foster productivity, not stifle it. **"**
>
> —Ronald Reagan, First Inaugural Address, 1981

Drawing support from opponents of the programs created by Lyndon Johnson's Great Society, Reagan attacked these issues head-on. The administration eliminated public service jobs that were part of an employment training program. It reduced unemployment compensation. It lowered welfare benefits and reduced spending on food stamps. It raised fees for Medicare patients. Despite cuts in these specific programs, total federal spending on social welfare rose between 1980 and 1982, although more slowly than it might have risen without cuts.

While he cut back the role of the federal government, Reagan sought to give more responsibility to state and local governments. Borrowing a term from the Nixon administration, he called his plan the **New Federalism.** Under this plan, the federal government would no longer tell states exactly how federal aid had to be used. Rather, it would let states create and pay for programs as they saw fit.

The New Federalism program never worked as planned. A recession early in Reagan's presidency left a number of cities and states nearly bankrupt. They now had more responsibility, but not enough money for the programs formerly funded directly by the federal government.

Reagan's Foreign Policy

While taking decisive measures to change the direction of domestic policy, Reagan was equally determined to defend American interests in the Cold War. He believed in a tough approach toward the Soviet Union, which he called an "evil empire." He favored large defense budgets to strengthen both conventional military forces and the nuclear arsenal.

Military Buildup The costs of the buildup were enormous. Over a five-year period, the United States spent an unprecedented $1.1 trillion on defense. These expenditures contributed to the growing budget deficits. Conservatives considered this the cost of fighting the Cold War.

Much of this money went into new weapons and new technology. The United States continued to develop new missiles, such as the intercontinental MX, as well as new bombers and submarines that could carry nuclear weapons. Reagan also explored ways to protect American territory against nuclear attack. In 1983, Reagan announced the **Strategic Defense Initiative (SDI),** popularly known as "Star Wars" after the 1977 film. SDI proposed the creation of a massive satellite shield in space to intercept and destroy incoming Soviet missiles.

Trouble Spots Abroad Relations with the Soviet Union remained frosty during Reagan's first term. The Soviets criticized the American defense buildup. They also complained when the United States stationed new intermediate-range nuclear missiles in Western Europe.

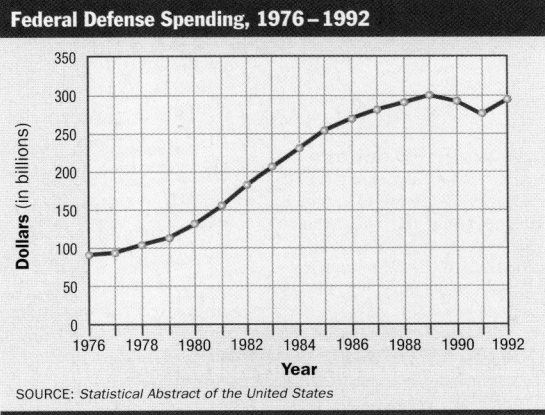

Federal Defense Spending, 1976–1992

Dollars (in billions), by Year

SOURCE: *Statistical Abstract of the United States*

INTERPRETING GRAPHS
Notice the change in defense spending in the early 1980s.
Analyzing Information *By how much did the defense budget increase during President Reagan's two terms in office?*

Reagan salutes an honor guard of American soldiers with Secretary of Defense Caspar Weinberger (right).

The United States encountered difficulties in the Middle East as well. The country of Lebanon had become a battleground for a variety of armed political groups, some backed by neighboring countries. In 1982, Reagan sent several thousand marines to Beirut, the Lebanese capital, as part of a peacekeeping force. In October 1983, a terrorist truck loaded with explosives crashed through the gates of a marine barracks, killing 241 Americans.

The attack horrified the nation. Many Americans demanded an immediate withdrawal from Lebanon, and by the following February, all the troops had left.

The North African nation of Libya, under General Qaddafi, sponsored terrorist attacks on American and Israeli targets in Europe. Responding to one such incident, a bombing in West Berlin in which an American serviceman was killed, Reagan ordered air attacks on Libya on April 14, 1986.

Fighting Communism in the Americas Reagan feared that Communist forces would gain power and threaten American interests in the Western Hemisphere. In El Salvador, the United States supported a repressive military regime in its efforts to resist guerrillas, some of whom were Marxists. Reagan increased military aid to El Salvador to the level of about $1 million a day. In Nicaragua, as you will read in the next section, the United States helped guerrillas who were fighting to overthrow that nation's leftist government.

Reagan claimed a victory over communism on the tiny Caribbean island of Grenada. He ordered United States military forces to Grenada in October 1983, after a military group staged a coup and installed a government sympathetic to Communist Cuba. The official aim of the invasion was to safeguard several hundred American medical students on the island. However, United States forces also overthrew the Grenadian government and remained in Grenada to oversee free elections.

Recession and Recovery

During Reagan's first two years in office, the United States experienced the worst economic downturn since the Great Depression. The Federal Reserve Bank raised interest rates to reduce inflation. However, high interest rates hurt businesses and discouraged Americans from borrowing to purchase goods or invest in new equipment. Foreign competition also cost thousands of American jobs. By 1982, unemployment had

INTERPRETING GRAPHS
Examine the graph below showing the federal deficit from 1980 to 1992. **Synthesizing Information** *What happened to the federal deficit during Reagan's years in office? How did Reagan's policies contribute to that trend?*

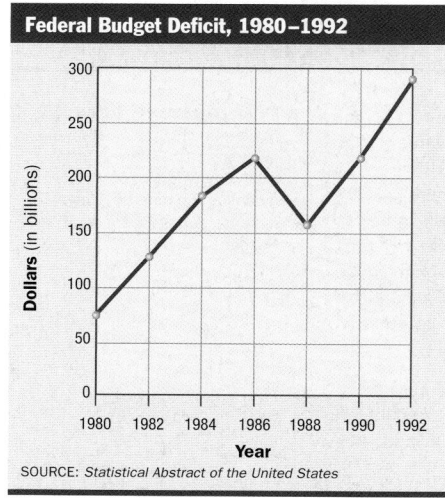

Federal Budget Deficit, 1980–1992

SOURCE: *Statistical Abstract of the United States*

reached a postwar high of 10.8 percent and several hundred businesses were going bankrupt each week.

The 1981–1982 recession did, however, pave the way for a healthier economy. The high interest rates cooled down inflation, and as Reagan's tax cuts took effect, consumer spending began to rise. By 1983, both inflation and unemployment had already dropped below 10 percent. Business leaders gained new confidence, and increased their investments. The stock market pushed upward. Republicans claimed that the recovery demonstrated the wisdom of supply-side economics.

An important prediction of the supply-side theorists had not come true, however. Cuts in tax rates were supposed to generate so much economic growth that the government's tax revenues would actually increase. As a result, the federal deficit, or the amount by which the government's spending exceeds its income in a given year, was supposed to decrease.

During the 1980 campaign, Reagan had vowed to balance the federal budget if elected. But, the combination of tax cuts and defense spending pushed the deficit up, not down. The deficit ballooned from nearly $80 billion in 1980 to a peak of $221 billion in 1986.

While the rising deficits did help the government cut back on domestic spending, they drove the nation as a whole deeper into debt. The national debt, the total amount of money owed by the government, rose from $909 billion in 1980 to $3.2 trillion in 1990. Future generations would have to bear the burden of interest payments on this monumental debt.

In spite of these challenges, many Americans supported President Reagan. They shared his values and principles. In 1981, the nation reacted with horror when Reagan was wounded in an assassination attempt. The courage and humor with which he faced the situation only reinforced Americans' respect for their President.

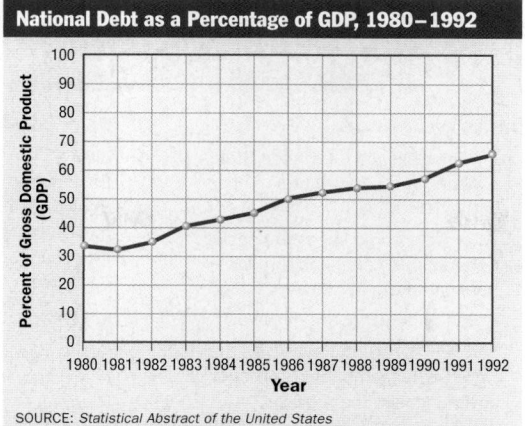

National Debt as a Percentage of GDP, 1980–1992

Percent of Gross Domestic Product (GDP) vs *Year*

SOURCE: *Statistical Abstract of the United States*

INTERPRETING GRAPHS As the federal government continued to spend more money than it received in taxes, the federal debt rose as a percentage of Gross Domestic Product (GDP). **Analyzing Information** *Review the definitions of national debt and Gross Domestic Product in the glossary and explain in your own words what it means if the national debt represents 60 percent of GDP.*

Section 2 Assessment

READING COMPREHENSION

1. How was **supply-side economics** expected to change the role of the federal government in the economy?

2. (a) What were Reagan's foreign policy goals? (b) How did the **Strategic Defense Initiative** support these goals?

3. Describe the course of the United States economy in the early 1980s.

CRITICAL THINKING AND WRITING

4. **Identifying Central Issues** What major shifts in philosophy and policies did Reagan bring to the federal government?

5. **Drawing Conclusions** What consequences could result from cutting regulations enforced by the federal government?

6. **Writing to Persuade** Write a short paragraph defending or opposing American intervention in Grenada in 1983.

 Take It to the NET

Activity: Analyzing Primary Sources Select a speech from Ronald Reagan's first term as President. What does this speech reveal about President Reagan and his policies? Use the links provided in the *America: Pathways to the Present* area of the following Web site for help in completing this activity. www.phschool.com

Chapter 33 • Section 2   **1107**

Reading Comprehension

1. Government would put more money in the hands of the businesses, rather than individuals, by cutting taxes, encouraging investment, and through deregulation.

2. (a) To inaugurate a major military buildup and to take a hard line against the Soviet Union. (b) It seemed to offer a sophisticated new defense against the Soviet Union's nuclear weapons.

3. A sharp recession followed by an economic recovery during which time both inflation and unemployment dropped.

Critical Thinking and Writing

4. An emphasis on limiting the size and role of the federal government domestically, and a foreign policy of strengthening the military.

5. Health and pollution problems could increase; consumers' rights and worker safety might be compromised.

6. Paragraphs will vary, but should persuade the reader with facts from the section.

 **Take It to the NET**

Answers will vary but might focus on Reagan's foreign policy concerns and his goals of reducing government size and maintaining adequate levels of defense spending.

CAPTION ANSWERS

Interpreting Graphs Sample answer: The federal government had borrowed, and needed to repay, a sum of money equal to 60 percent of the total value of goods and services produced in the United States in a year.

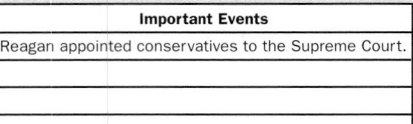

Reagan's Second Term

SECTION OBJECTIVES

1. Observe the ways in which the United States experienced a renewal of patriotism in the 1980s.

2. Find out about some important social debates that continued through Reagan's term in office.

3. See how the economy evolved during the 1980s.

4. Discover how Reagan's hands-off style of governing led to problems.

5. Consider the legacy of Reagan's presidency.

BELLRINGER

Warm-Up Activity Ask students to think about the American belief that all people are "created equal." In what ways is this belief reflected in social and economic policies?

Activating Prior Knowledge Ask students to state what patriotism means to them. Can they list some concrete symbols of patriotism or some specific acts that they would define as patriotic?

READING STRATEGY

As students read the section, have them list the key events and crises described. Then, for each event, have them summarize the significance of its outcome.

CAPTION ANSWERS

Viewing History The economy was booming, and many Americans were satisfied with Reagan's leadership.

READING FOCUS

- In what ways did the United States experience a renewal of patriotism in the 1980s?

- What were some important social debates that continued through Reagan's term in office?

- How did the economy evolve during the 1980s?

- How did Reagan's hands-off style of governing lead to problems?

- What was the legacy of Reagan's presidency?

KEY TERMS

AIDS
Sandinista
Contra
Iran-Contra affair
INF Treaty
entitlement

MAIN IDEA

After a decisive reelection victory in 1984, Reagan continued his conservative policies on economic and social issues. In domestic and foreign affairs, the administration had key successes but also some serious missteps.

TAKING NOTES

As you read, complete the chart below to show some of the accomplishments and important events of Reagan's presidency.

Important Events
Reagan appointed conservatives to the Supreme Court.

Setting the Scene Campaigning for reelection in 1984, Ronald Reagan asked voters if they were better off than they had been four years before. As they roared their approval, he told them, "You ain't seen nothing yet." His campaign advertisements, such as one depicting "Morning in America," heralded a new day of optimism.

Reagan faced Democrat Walter Mondale, former Vice President under Carter. Mondale's running mate was New York Representative Geraldine Ferraro, the first woman ever on a major party's presidential ticket.

The relative strength of the economy and Reagan's popularity gave the President a landslide victory over Mondale. Reagan took 59 percent of the popular vote and all the electoral votes except those of the District of Columbia and Mondale's home state of Minnesota. It was the second largest electoral-vote margin in history.

VIEWING HISTORY Geraldine Ferraro (right) made history when Walter Mondale (left) asked her to be the first woman to run for Vice President on a major-party ticket. **Drawing Conclusions** Why did Reagan defeat Walter Mondale easily?

Patriotic Renewal

Reagan wanted to recreate the sense of community he had known in his youth and to help revive the virtues that had made America strong. The nation had endured turbulence in the years following the Vietnam War. The 1980s offered several occasions to celebrate patriotic renewal.

The 1984 Olympic Games were held in Los Angeles, the first time the Summer Games had come to the United States in half a century. The opening ceremonies, televised worldwide to hundreds of millions of viewers, were festive, patriotic affairs.

Some Communist countries, including the Soviet Union and East Germany, boycotted the games. The move was in retaliation to an American-led boycott of the 1980 Moscow games to protest the Soviet invasion of Afghanistan in 1979. As a result of the 1984 boycott, the United States won an unusually high number of medals.

Two years later, in 1986, the nation celebrated the centennial of the Statue of Liberty in New York harbor. This monument, a welcoming sight to many

---

RESOURCE DIRECTORY

Teaching Resources
Guided Reading and Review booklet, p. 135
Biography, Literature, and Comparing Primary Sources booklet (Comparing Primary Sources) *On the Legacy of the Civil Rights Movement,* p. 161
Biography, Literature, and Comparing Primary Sources booklet (Literature) *Masters of the Universe,* p. 88

Technology
Section Reading Support Transparencies
Guided Reading Audiotapes (English/Spanish), Ch. 33
Student Edition on Audio CD, Ch. 33
Sounds of an Era Audio CD *Ronald Reagan,* 1984 campaign speech (time: 20 seconds)
Prentice Hall Presentation Pro CD-ROM, Ch. 33
Companion Web site, www.phschool.com

immigrants as they entered the United States, was a symbol of freedom around the world. But the copper lady in flowing robes had deteriorated over the course of a century. Now, after a massive campaign to refurbish the statue, the nation held a spectacular centennial celebration.

The following year, the United States celebrated the 200th anniversary of the Constitution, drafted in 1787. Government and private groups sponsored lectures, workshops, and meetings focusing on the features of the Constitution that had made the nation strong. This observance helped renew the public's appreciation of such enduring ideas as balanced government and separation of powers.

Continuing Social Debates

In the years leading to Reagan's election, conservatives gained public support with their stands on social issues as well as economic issues. In the 1980s, conservative policies on social issues made these "hot" issues even hotter.

Civil Rights The federal government's commitment to extend voting rights had given the vote to millions of African Americans who had been denied it for decades. These new voters helped elect an increasing number of African American candidates to local, state, and national offices. In 1983, the cities of Charlotte, North Carolina, Philadelphia, and Chicago elected their first black mayors: Harvey Gantt, Wilson Goode, and Harold Washington, respectively. These cities joined Cleveland, Los Angeles, Detroit, and Atlanta, which had voted African Americans to the mayor's office for the first time in the 1960s and 1970s. In 1989, New York City voters chose African American David Dinkins to be mayor of the nation's most populous city.

Altogether, the number of African American elected officials rose from 4,890 in 1980 to 7,335 ten years later. The vast majority of these officeholders hailed from the Southeast.

In 1983, Reagan signed a bill making the birthday of Martin Luther King, Jr., a national holiday. Despite this symbolic victory, resistance to civil rights initiatives was growing, as critics complained that many policies trampled on the rights of state and local governments. Reagan tried to prevent the extension of the

Mary Lou Retton became the star of the Los Angeles Olympics at age 16. The American gymnast won five medals, the most medals won by any United States athlete that year.

COMPARING PRIMARY SOURCES

The Legacy of the Civil Rights Movement

Decades after the civil rights movement, Americans disagreed on how much progress had been made.

Analyzing Viewpoints Compare the main arguments in the two quotations below.

Substantial Progress

"Before the civil rights movement, there was a very wide separation between blacks and whites. I don't think the separation is as great today. There has been more speaking out. Blacks now let themselves open up and say how they feel in no uncertain terms. I think there are friendships between blacks and whites that didn't exist before. In spite of everything, I think the racial situation is healthier than it was before. Blacks are no longer invisible."

—Eileen Barth, retired social worker, quoted in Race by Studs Terkel, 1992

Little or No Progress

"The country is more segregated today than it was when [Martin Luther] King and [Robert] Kennedy were alive. What Dr. King and Bobby were fighting was segregation and discrimination imposed by law, by the state. . . . All of that has changed. . . . But in the North, everybody knows what's happened in the cities. At universities, there's much more black withdrawal into separate communities. I grew up thinking we were going to have an integrated society, not just an end to official racism."

—Anthony Lewis, New York Times, April 1993

LESSON PLAN

Focus Explain that the personable Ronald Reagan was popular with the majority of Americans in large part because he made Americans feel good about themselves and their country. What difficulties became apparent during his second term?

Instruct Discuss the economic, social, and judicial issues that developed during the Reagan era, such as the growing gap between rich and poor, the recession, the defeat of the Equal Rights Amendment, conservative appointments to the Supreme Court, and the extension of the Voting Rights Act of 1965. Did these events help or hurt the conservative cause?

Explain the rapid changes going on in the Soviet Union during this period. Discuss the effects of these changes on Reagan's relationship with Mikhail Gorbachev.

Assess/Reteach How did the problems that emerged during Ronald Reagan's second term affect his standing with the American people? How did those problems affect his legacy?

ACTIVITY
Connecting with Culture

Have students work in pairs or individually to compose a poem, song, or rap that celebrates the bicentennial of the Statue of Liberty or the U.S. Constitution, or the advances in civil rights in the 1980s. Invite students to perform their compositions. **(Musical/Rhythmic)**

CUSTOMIZE FOR ...
Less Proficient Writers

Have students reread the section "Continuing Social Debates" and then make a list of the subheads in the section. After each subhead they should list the conservative response to each issue.

Connecting with Government

A President's ability to choose Supreme Court Justices can have long-term effects. Have students research the biographies and judicial histories of the Justices named by Reagan, tracing their votes and influence from the date of their appointments to today. Ask them to evaluate the impact of Reagan's judicial appointments on major decisions made by the Supreme Court. Have students share their findings with the class in an oral presentation or in a poster. **(Verbal/Linguistic; Visual/Spatial)**

From the Archives of
American Heritage®

About the Presidents

With his political identity forged in Barry Goldwater's presidential campaign of 1964, Ronald Reagan (1981–1989) was thought to be far too conservative to be a viable candidate for the presidency. But Reagan's call for a reduced federal role in domestic affairs and his projection of American ideals abroad won him a handy victory in the campaign of 1980. Despite a sharp recession in his first term, Reagan's popularity soared as he won his race for a second term in a landslide. Reagan was widely admired for his optimistic temperament and unwavering patriotism. Yet the true legacy of his presidency was to oversee a substantial shift in public opinion toward the conservative end of the spectrum. Source: Adapted from Henry F. Graff's *The Presidents,* Scribner's, 1996, by the editors of *American Heritage®* magazine.

VIEWING HISTORY Pro-choice and anti-abortion activists gathered at this rally. **Determining Relevance** *How did Reagan advance the anti-abortion cause as President?*

Voting Rights Act of 1965, backing off only after intense criticism. He appointed federal judges who were less sympathetic to civil rights goals. The administration also worked to end some affirmative action programs.

The Women's Movement As women gained access to jobs and other opportunities previously denied to them, the women's movement met with a backlash. One sign of this backlash was the defeat in 1982 of the proposed Equal Rights Amendment, which failed to gain the approval of enough state legislatures to be ratified.

Anti-abortion groups took aim at the right to abortion granted in the 1973 *Roe* v. *Wade* Supreme Court decision. Opponents lobbied to halt federal funding of abortions for the poor.

Sexual Orientation The campaign for homosexual rights caused similar polarization. Contributing to the backlash was the spread of acquired immunodeficiency syndrome, known simply as **AIDS.** Most victims of the virus were intravenous drug users and homosexual men. Some people contracted the virus through contaminated blood transfusions. By the late 1980s, the rising costs associated with researching a cure and treating and caring for AIDS patients caused alarm among some Americans. Many people believed the government should promote abstinence as the best way to prevent AIDS, rather than providing controversial information on alternative forms of prevention. Even as AIDS spread into the larger community, the resistance to gay rights grew more vocal.

Conservatives on the Supreme Court Many of these social concerns wound up in the judicial system, just as the courts' temperament began to shift. Reagan's appointees to the federal courts were fairly conservative. In 1981, he selected Arizona judge Sandra Day O'Connor as the nation's first woman Supreme Court justice. In 1986, Reagan chose another conservative, Antonin Scalia, for the Supreme Court and raised conservative Justice William Rehnquist to the post of Chief Justice.

While O'Connor, Scalia, and Rehnquist won Senate confirmation, Reagan's next Supreme Court appointment, conservative judge and former law professor Robert Bork, did not. The Democratic Party had won control of the Senate in the 1986 elections and most Democratic senators did not share Reagan's goal of appointing conservative judges. Liberal groups joined together in 1987 to lobby the Senate to reject Bork's nomination. The nominee whom the Senate finally approved, Anthony Kennedy, was known as a moderate conservative. He joined the Court in 1988.

An Evolving Economy

While many parts of the economy boomed after the recession of 1982, other industries grew slowly or not at all. As a result, prosperity was felt unevenly across the country.

The Farm Crisis America's farmers, who grew more than enough grain to feed Americans and sell excess crops abroad, faced oversupply and falling prices in the 1980s. For a variety of reasons, foreign demand fell and supplies of grain outpaced demand. The price of a bushel of wheat fell from $3.91 in 1980 to $3.39 in 1984, and to $2.42 in 1986;

BIOGRAPHY

Sandra Day O'Connor
b. 1930

Born in El Paso, Texas, Sandra Day entered Stanford University in California at age 16 and went on to graduate third in her class at Stanford Law School in 1952. Despite her outstanding record, as a woman she was unable to get a job in a private law firm. She found work as an attorney in a county government office, married, and later opened a private practice in Arizona.

After taking time off to raise her children, she returned to full-time work in 1965, serving in a variety of roles: assistant attorney general, state senator (and the first woman majority leader), and superior court judge. In 1979, Arizona Governor Bruce Babbitt appointed O'Connor to the state appeals court. Reagan elevated her to the Supreme Court two years later.

Viewing History He appointed conservatives to the judiciary.

RESOURCE DIRECTORY

Teaching Resources
Learning with Documents booklet (Visual Learning Activity) *Short-Lived Approval,* p. 72

Technology
(RESOURCE PRO®) **Biography** *Sandra Day O'Connor,* found on Resource Pro, profiles the first woman appointed to serve on the United States Supreme Court.
(RESOURCE PRO®) **Critical Thinking Activity** *Recognizing Ideologies: The Bork Nomination,* found on Resource Pro, helps students apply

this skill by analyzing the Senate debate about one of Reagan's nominees to the Supreme Court, Robert H. Bork.

a bushel of corn that earned farmers $3.11 in 1980 brought in less than half that much money six years later.

Falling prices hit farmers hard because so many had gone into debt to buy machinery and land when grain prices were high. Only a few years earlier, President Carter's Agriculture Secretary Earl Butz had told them to fill their fields with grain by planting "fencerow to fencerow." Farmers who could not pay their debts risked losing their farms to bankruptcy.

The plight of the family farmer won a lot of sympathy from the public, and members of Congress representing agricultural states sought relief in Washington. The federal government intervened to increase farm income with continued price supports and credit. By 1987, federal spending on agriculture consumed more than $20 billion yearly and supplied 30 percent of America's farm income. Government aid may have protected many farmers from bankruptcy in the 1980s, but it was an expensive and temporary solution that did not address fundamental problems in American agriculture.

Shifts in Manufacturing Several industries with deep roots in the United States lost ground in the 1980s to foreign competition. The recession of 1981–1982 accelerated job losses and factory closings, and many people who lost high-paying manufacturing jobs during the recession were unable to find similar work when the economy picked up. The number of workers in the metal industry, including steel mills, declined from 1,140,000 in December 1980 to 814,000 two years later. While the economy expanded quickly after 1982, the number of metalworking jobs fell further to 728,000 in December 1986. The textile industry also suffered continual job losses.

These losses were part of a historic shift in the United States economy away from manufacturing. In most cases, workers found new jobs in different industries and the parent companies emerged stronger and better able to compete with foreign companies. However, the volume of layoffs and factory closings required difficult adjustments for the workers and cities that were hit hardest, particularly in the Northeast and the Upper Midwest.

Unequal Wealth Wealthy Americans, more than anyone else, flourished under Reagan. The net worth of *Forbes* magazine's 400 richest Americans nearly tripled in the Reagan years. Political analyst Kevin Phillips described this new class:

> 66 The truth is that the critical concentration of wealth in the United States was developing at higher levels—decamillionaires, centimillionaires, half-billionaires and billionaires. Garden variety millionaires had become so common that there were about 1.5 million of them by 1989. 99
> —Political analyst Kevin Phillips,
> *New York Times Magazine*, June 24, 1990

By the late 1980s, wealth was more unevenly distributed than at any time since the end of World War II. In terms of current dollars, the average income earned by the top fifth of American households rose 23 percent, from $93,225 in 1980 to $114,912 in 1989. Among the bottom fifth, average household income rose only 4 percent, from $9,075 to $9,433 in the same time period. Many families increased their total income by having both husband and wife

Focus on TECHNOLOGY

The Space Shuttle The first of a new breed of spacecraft took to the sky on April 21, 1981. Unlike the Apollo program rockets that fell to the earth after use, the space shuttle *Columbia* looked and landed like an airplane and could take off again and again to complete multiple missions.

The promising space shuttle program suffered a disastrous setback on January 28, 1986, when the *Challenger* exploded in midair less than two minutes after takeoff. *Challenger*'s crew included Christa McAuliffe, a New Hampshire teacher chosen to teach a class from space. The explosion halted NASA's shuttle program for two years while scientists worked to eliminate future technical problems.

READING CHECK
What changes did the American economy undergo in the 1980s?

ACTIVITY
Connecting with Citizenship

The 1984 presidential election was historic: it included the first woman candidate for a major party and the greatest electoral-vote margin for the victor. Have students discuss and "replay" the election in light of the events of Reagan's second term. Have one group represent the Reagan-Bush campaign team; the other, Mondale-Ferraro. Each group should decide what issues it will emphasize and why. **(Verbal/Linguistic)**

BACKGROUND
Connections to Today

One way the federal government continues to support agriculture is by purchasing farm products and giving them away to feed needy Americans. This practice helps farmers as well as many others in society. For example, through the National School Lunch Program, the government donates beef, chicken, eggs, fruits, vegetables, nuts, and other agricultural produce to some 96,000 schools nationwide. About 15 to 20 percent of the food served in school cafeterias comes from this program. To receive this free food, schools must offer free and reduced-price lunches to children from low-income families. Other programs distribute similar foods to ensure that the elderly, preschool children, pregnant women, and low-income Americans receive adequate nourishment. The government also provides the farm products it buys to community food banks and to the Red Cross for distribution during disasters.

READING CHECK
Farm income declined sharply. Foreign manufacturers became dominant in many traditional industries. American firms endured layoffs and factory closings, but they emerged leaner and more competitive. A wide gap opened between rich and poor.

CUSTOMIZE FOR ...
ESL

Ask students to write the heading *The Farm Crisis* on a piece of paper. Then have them make two columns. One column should be headed *Problems*. There students might list such causes as oversupply, falling prices, and decline in foreign demand. The second column should be headed *Solutions.* There students could list such actions as increased price supports and credit, and increased federal spending on agriculture.

✓ TEST PREPARATION

Have students review the material on this page about shifts in manufacturing and then answer the following question.

Which of the following industries never recovered the jobs it lost during the recession of 1981–1982?

A Financial services

B Steel

C Auto manufacturing

D Entertainment

Connecting with History and Conflict

Organize students into two pairs of groups for a class debate on Nicaragua and the Iran-Contra affair. One group should support the Reagan administration's Nicaragua policies, and a second group should oppose them. The third and fourth groups should do the same for the Iran-Contra affair. Allow groups time to prepare a one-sentence statement in support of its position for each group member. Then ask students in each pair of groups to alternately present their statements, pro and con, as you list them on the chalkboard. At the end of the debate, poll the class to determine which pair of groups had the most compelling arguments. **(Verbal/ Linguistic)**

BACKGROUND
Global Connections

Nicaragua had been controlled by the wealthy Somoza family for 40 years when the Sandinista National Liberation Front led the overthrow of the government in 1979. The Sandinistas nationalized industry and took land from the rich to give to the peasants. Nicaraguans who were unhappy with some of these reforms and the Sandinistan dictatorship joined with Somoza supporters to fight the Sandinista government. These guerrillas—known as Contras, which means "against"—attacked from bases across the border in Honduras and Costa Rica. Thousands in Nicaragua and neighboring countries died as fighting raged through the 1980s. A negotiated cease-fire in 1990 let Nicaraguans choose their first democratically-elected government.

INTERPRETING CHARTS
Soviet leader Mikhail Gorbachev's policy of *glasnost* helped slow the arms race between the United States and the Soviet Union. **Drawing Conclusions** Why do you think arms control agreements were still necessary in the post-Soviet era?

Arms Control Agreements, 1979–1993	
Legislation	**Purpose**
SALT II (Strategic Arms Limitation Treaty) 1979	Reduced strategic offensive weapons systems, specifically nuclear arms. Set limits on the types and numbers of weapons each nation could build.
INF (Intermediate-Range Nuclear Forces Treaty) 1987	Required both nations to destroy ground-launched and ballistic cruise missiles and their launchers within three years.
START II (Strategic Arms Reduction Treaty) 1993	Signed by the United States and former Soviet republics. Nations reserved the right to inspect former INF missile sites to ensure that no missiles were being manufactured.

work outside the home. The wages of individuals, however, declined. The growth in income inequality continued long after Reagan left office and also occurred in other countries over the same period of time.

Reagan's Hands-off Style

Ronald Reagan favored less government regulation of the economy. A decade later, neither party—the Republicans nor the Democrats—would argue with that. Reagan also followed a hands-off style in running the government. He delegated authority to those who worked for him, rather than becoming involved in every decision. Several times this approach led to problems.

The S & L Scandal "Thrift institutions," or savings and loan banks (often called S & Ls) made home mortgage loans to individuals. The Reagan administration, with the help of Democrats in Congress, pressed for the deregulation of S & Ls to permit them to make riskier but more profitable investments.

Officials at some deregulated S & Ls took advantage of the new laws to make huge fortunes for themselves. Many made risky investments in an overheated real estate market. When the market cooled down in the late 1980s, many S & Ls collapsed, taking with them about $2.6 billion in depositors' savings.

Because bank accounts are insured by the federal government, taxpayers had to make up the billions of dollars lost when hundreds of S & Ls failed. A number of banking officials were prosecuted for their role in the scandal and for their efforts to cover it up.

The Iran-Contra Affair In Nicaragua, the Reagan administration sought to undermine the Marxist government that had seized power in 1979. The ruling group, the **Sandinistas**, was named after a Nicaraguan freedom fighter from the 1920s. Reagan feared that the Sandinistas' revolution would spread Marxist upheaval to other Latin American countries.

Working through the Central Intelligence Agency, the United States trained and armed Nicaraguan guerrillas known as **Contras**, from the Spanish word for "counterrevolutionaries." This policy violated laws on American intervention in the affairs of other nations.

Congress discovered these secret missions and in 1984 cut off military aid to the Contras. Some members of the Reagan administration still believed that aid to the Contras was justified. These officials took the profits from secret arms sales to Iran and then sent the profits to the Contras. The arms sales were meant to encourage the release of American hostages held in Lebanon by pro-Iranian terrorists.

When the secret actions became public in the fall of 1986, Oliver North, the marine lieutenant colonel who had made the arrangements, took the blame. The **Iran-Contra affair**, as this scandal came to be called, caused the most serious criticism that the Reagan administration ever faced. The President himself claimed no knowledge of North's operations.

The Reagan Legacy

The Iran-Contra affair did not damage Ronald Reagan's personal approval ratings. When he left office in 1989, polls showed that more than 60 percent of the American people gave him high marks for his overall performance.

Foreign Policy Success One reason for the President's continued popularity was the improvement in relations between the United States and the Soviet

CAPTION ANSWERS

Interpreting Charts Sample answer: Because a great many missiles still existed.

RESOURCE DIRECTORY

Teaching Resources
Units 9/10 booklet
• Section 3 Quiz, p. 66
Guide to the Essentials
• Section 3 Summary, p. 169

Technology
RESOURCE **PRO**® **Primary Source Activity**
An Explanation of Iran-Contra, found on Resource Pro, uses an excerpt from President Reagan's televised address to demonstrate how he defended his involvement in the scandal.

Union during Reagan's second term. Despite his fierce anti-Communist stance, Reagan developed a close relationship with Mikhail Gorbachev, who became the Soviet leader in 1985.

To reform the ailing Soviet system, Gorbachev proposed a program of *glasnost,* a Russian word meaning "political openness." He also initiated *perestroika,* or "restructuring," an economic policy to allow limited free enterprise.

These moves paved the way toward better relations between the United States and the Soviet Union. Reagan and Gorbachev signed the Intermediate-Range Nuclear Forces (INF) Treaty in 1987. The **INF Treaty** provided for the destruction of about 2,500 Soviet and American missiles in Europe.

Domestic Policy Initiatives   Another reason for Reagan's popularity was his stated commitment to reducing the size of government. Reagan's policies, however, did not dramatically reduce the Washington bureaucracy. Payments for **entitlements**—programs such as Social Security, Medicare, and Medicaid, which guarantee payments to a particular group of recipients—grew faster than policymakers had expected. Social Security expenditures, for example, skyrocketed as the nation's elderly population continued to rise. The Reagan administration could not restrain the growth of these programs.

Economic turmoil erupted near the end of Reagan's presidency. Investor fears about the huge budget deficits and rising national debt prompted a stock market crash in 1987. Following six weeks of falling prices, the market suffered a huge 22.6 percent drop on October 19. The speculative bubble of the 1980s had burst.

Although the stock market did recover, Reagan's successor, George H. W. Bush, inherited many economic problems. By the end of the decade, the nation found itself in the midst of another recession.

For most Americans, Ronald Reagan's two-term presidency was marked by his vigorous emphasis on restoring national pride, and the force of his own optimistic personality. Reagan's presidency made many Americans feel confident for the first time since the Kennedy years.

VIEWING HISTORY Relations between the United States and the Soviet Union warmed during Reagan's second term. Here, Reagan and Gorbachev meet outside St. Basil's Cathedral in Moscow. **Recognizing Cause and Effect** *Why do you think* glasnost *and* perestroika *helped smooth relations between the two countries?*

Section 3 — Assessment

READING COMPREHENSION

1. How did Americans celebrate their patriotism in the 1980s?

2. In what ways did the Reagan administration address ongoing debates on race?

3. How did Reagan's style of governing contribute to the **Iran-Contra affair?**

4. Why did **entitlement** spending have a negative effect on President Reagan's legacy?

CRITICAL THINKING AND WRITING

5. Analyzing Cause and Effect Despite some failures, Reagan was a highly popular President. How did Reagan's economic successes and his patriotism affect public opinion?

6. Defending a Position In a short essay, explain how the influence of conservatives was felt during the Reagan years, both in social issues and in changes to the Supreme Court.

Activity: Writing a Biography
Choose one Supreme Court justice appointed by Reagan and write a biography, being sure to include the person's educational background and how he or she changed the Court. Use the links provided in the *America: Pathways to the Present* area of the following Web site for help in completing this activity.
www.phschool.com

Section 3 — Assessment

Reading Comprehension

1. 1984 Olympic Games; celebrations of the centennial of the Statue of Liberty and the 200th anniversary of the Constitution.

2. Birthday of Martin Luther King, Jr., was established as a national holiday; tried to prevent the extension of the Voting Rights Act; appointed federal judges who were less sympathetic to civil rights goals; worked to end some affirmative action programs.

3. Reagan's hands-off style enabled other government officials to violate American neutrality laws, acting without the President's knowledge.

4. It contradicted his commitment to reducing the size of the federal government.

Critical Thinking and Writing

5. Sample answer: His ability to arouse patriotism and national confidence secured high opinion ratings even in times of scandal.

6. Essays will vary, but might mention the rise in popularity of televangelists or the promotion of William Rehnquist, a conservative, to the position of Chief Justice of the U.S. Supreme Court.

Take It to the NET

Answers will vary. Encourage students to include both personal history and professional accomplishments in their biographical research.

CAPTION ANSWERS

Viewing History Because these programs meant the Soviet Union was moving away from communism and toward democracy.

Section **4** The George H. W. Bush Presidency

SECTION OBJECTIVES

1. See what challenges George H.W. Bush faced in the 1988 presidential election.

2. Find out how the Cold War came to an end.

3. Learn about the ways in which the United States played a new international role after the Cold War.

4. Observe the effect domestic issues had on Bush's presidency.

BELLRINGER

Warm-Up Activity Ask students when, in their opinion, the Cold War really ended. What actions and attitudes have changed with the end of the Cold War?

Activating Prior Knowledge Ask students to name some of the causes of the Cold War. Which of these causes are still in dispute today? Which of these causes have been resolved?

READING STRATEGY

As students read, have them identify as many cause-and-effect relationships as they can. Have students list these relationships in a chart.

ACTIVITY
Connecting with Citizenship

Ask students to design placards or bumper stickers that reflect the spirit and issues of the presidential election campaign of 1988. Tell them that their creations can either promote or attack a candidate and should include a graphic and a catch phrase or slogan that is appropriate to the position taken. You may wish to provide the class with the supplies to create their work full-size and in color. **(Visual/Spatial)**

The George H. W. Bush Presidency

READING FOCUS

- What challenges did George Bush face in the 1988 presidential election?
- How did the Cold War come to an end?
- In what ways did the United States play a new international role after the end of the Cold War?
- What effect did domestic issues have on Bush's presidency?

MAIN IDEA

George H. W. Bush achieved notable foreign policy successes, but domestic crises eroded his public support.

KEY TERMS

Strategic Arms Reduction Treaty
Persian Gulf War
downsizing

TAKING NOTES

Copy the web diagram below. As you read, fill in each blank circle with important events that affected George Bush's domestic and foreign policy.

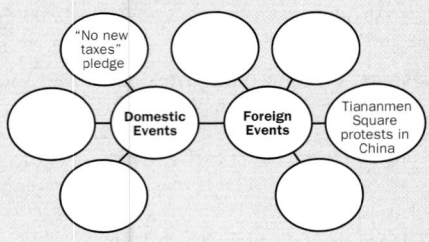

Setting the Scene It is not easy to follow a legendary President. George Bush had the same problem as William Howard Taft, who succeeded Theodore Roosevelt in 1909. So did Harry Truman, who inherited the presidency upon the death of Franklin D. Roosevelt in 1945. Ronald Reagan remained enormously popular as he left office in 1989, and Bush sought to continue the revolution his predecessor had begun. But he lacked Reagan's charismatic appeal and found that it was not always easy to measure up.

George Bush won a solid victory in the 1988 election.

The 1988 Election

The son of a well-to-do Connecticut senator, Bush served in World War II as a bomber pilot in the Pacific and was awarded the Distinguished Flying Cross. After the war, he had a profitable career in the Texas oil industry.

In 1966, he began a long and distinguished political career, serving in many roles: member of Congress from Texas; ambassador to the United Nations under Nixon; chairperson of the Republican National Committee; American envoy to China under President Ford; and head of the Central Intelligence Agency (CIA) until 1977. He was well connected and earned a reputation as a moderate and loyal Republican.

Despite these impressive credentials, Bush lacked the support of conservatives in the Republican Party. Some Republicans, whose hero was Ronald Reagan, questioned Bush's commitment to their cause. They were concerned about his apparent early sympathy for abortion rights, and they never truly forgave him for calling Reagan's economic plans "voodoo economics" during the 1980 primary election campaign. Bush's loyal service as Reagan's Vice President for eight years had failed to ease their fears.

Bush began the 1988 campaign far behind his Democratic opponent, Governor Michael Dukakis of Massachusetts. Dukakis had revived

RESOURCE DIRECTORY

Teaching Resources
Learning Styles Lesson Plans booklet, p. 69
Guided Reading and Review booklet, p. 136

Technology
Section Reading Support Transparencies
Guided Reading Audiotapes (English/Spanish), Ch. 33
Student Edition on Audio CD, Ch. 33
Prentice Hall Presentation Pro CD-ROM, Ch. 33
Companion Web site, www.phschool.com

his state after years of economic distress and promised to bring the "Massachusetts Miracle" to the rest of the nation.

Bush took the offensive in what soon became a nasty contest. One part of his campaign was a pledge that there would be "no new taxes" if he became President. Reagan's popular tax cuts had contributed to the huge budget deficit and national debt. Reagan's successor would be under great pressure to raise taxes in order to reduce the deficit. Yet Bush publicly committed himself to holding the line on taxes.

Bush attacked Dukakis on many issues. He aired ads describing Dukakis as soft on crime and questioning the accuracy of the "Massachusetts Miracle." His campaign challenged Dukakis's environmental record by airing pictures of garbage in the polluted Boston harbor. Bush's attack ads successfully damaged Dukakis, although they apparently alienated some voters. Americans complained that neither candidate addressed the major issues facing the country. Nearly half of all eligible voters stayed home.

Bush won a solid 54 percent of the popular vote and carried 40 states in a 426–111 electoral vote win. But he failed to gain the mandate Reagan had enjoyed, as Democrats still controlled both houses of Congress.

The Cold War Ends

Bush's major triumphs came in foreign policy. Even more than Reagan, Bush benefited from the historic changes in the Communist world that were unleashed by Mikhail Gorbachev.

The Soviet leader started a chain reaction that would eventually bring down Europe's "Iron Curtain" and dissolve the Soviet Union. It began with Gorbachev's public statements encouraging Eastern European leaders to adopt *perestroika* and *glasnost*. The suggestion was unthinkable in a region where police states efficiently smothered all opposition. Yet it was enough to give hope and inspiration to anti-Communist movements throughout

READING CHECK
What strategies did George Bush use in the 1988 presidential election?

MAP SKILLS In the late 1980s the Eastern bloc shattered into a jigsaw puzzle of diverse countries. **Regions** What kinds of problems do you think might follow the breakup of such a large nation as the Soviet Union?

Europe and Western Asia After the Cold War, 1994

Chapter 33 • Section 4   **1115**

✓ TEST PREPARATION

Have students reread the two paragraphs under the subheading "The Cold War Ends" and then answer the question below.

What gave hope to anti-Communist movements in Eastern Europe?

A The election of George Bush as President.

B Concessions by many Communist leaders.

C Gorbachev's assumption of leadership of the Soviet Union in 1985.

Ⓓ Gorbachev's public statements about his policies and his encouragement of Eastern European nations to adopt them.

LESSON PLAN

Focus Emphasize that it is very difficult to follow a popular President. What challenges did George Bush face in this respect? Explain that Bush found his greatest strength in foreign policy. What major world events took place during the Bush administration?

Instruct Explain that as President, Bush inherited a varied assortment of policies from his popular predecessor. Bush concentrated on foreign policy—where his own background and strengths lay—but also had to deal with economic problems inherited from the Reagan administration. How successful was he domestically and in the sphere of foreign affairs?

Assess/Reteach Ask students to discuss their perception of the legacy of a presidency that is judged to be strong on international affairs, yet weak on domestic affairs.

READING CHECK
Attack advertisements criticizing the record of Governor Michael Dukakis. Bush also promised not to raise taxes.

CAPTION ANSWERS

Map Skills Sample answer: Ethnic conflicts might arise between groups vying for power in the new governments; groups might fight over economic resources.

Eastern Europe that had worked for decades, at great risk, to keep a democratic spirit alive.

Poland In Poland, the stage was set for the downfall of Soviet communism. The story had begun in 1970, when severe food shortages provoked riots in the city of Gdansk. A witness to those riots was a young electrician named Lech Walesa, who worked in the huge Lenin Shipyard at Gdansk. Walesa became involved in anti-Communist union organizing and lost his job after helping to lead a protest in 1976.

When shipyard workers at Gdansk launched a strike in 1980, Walesa climbed over the fence of the facility and joined them, becoming head of a movement that grew with great speed. After two tense weeks, the government gave in to workers' demands for the right to form a free and independent trade union.

Union activity spread throughout Poland, forming an alliance called Solidarity. The Communist government launched a crackdown in 1981, banning Solidarity and jailing its leaders, including Walesa. But support for Solidarity remained alive. In 1983, Walesa, a plain-speaking man with little education, won the Nobel peace prize for his acts of courage.

In 1988, further economic collapse in Poland sparked a new round of protests and strikes. The Communist-led government agreed to meet with Solidarity and together they scheduled free elections for June 1989. In Poland's first free elections in half a century, voters chose as president the electrician from Gdansk, Lech Walesa.

VIEWING HISTORY Berliners from both sides of the city celebrated the fall of the Berlin Wall with joyous, all-night celebrations. **Making Comparisons** *Compare and contrast the roles played by ordinary people in the fall of communism in East Germany and in the Soviet Union.*

The Berlin Wall Falls Throughout Eastern Europe, anti-Communist revolts broke out. Each country had its own stories of courage and its own heroes. In Czechoslovakia, a poet and playwright once persecuted by the Communists, Vaclav Havel, was elected president. Eventually, new regimes took charge in Bulgaria, Hungary, Romania, and Albania. But the most dramatic events of 1989 took place in East Germany.

East Germany's hardline Communist rulers maintained a strong grip on the state, symbolized by the Berlin Wall that divided East Germans from the democratic West. In the summer of 1989, East German tourists visiting Hungary took advantage of newly opened borders there to escape to Austria and West Germany. Their flight embarrassed East German leaders. In East German cities, nonviolent protests pressured the country's dictator, Erich Honecker, to institute reforms and open border crossings. On November 9, the government announced that East Germans could travel freely to West Germany.

East Germans flooded around and over the hated Berlin Wall. Germans scaled it from both sides and stood atop the structure, cheering and chanting and waving signs. They came with sledgehammers and smashed it with glee. The wall, the most potent symbol of the Cold War, had been breached. Within a month, the Communist Party had begun to collapse. A year later, East and West Germany reunified.

The Soviet Union Gorbachev hoped to reform the Soviet system while keeping the Communist Party in power, but events slipped beyond his control. In August 1991, conservative Communists in the Soviet Union staged a coup and held Gorbachev captive, hoping to pressure him to resign. The coup quickly collapsed, but the Soviet Union's 15 republics sensed weakness in the central government and began to move toward independence.

Gorbachev resigned the presidency of the Soviet Union on December 25, 1991. One week later the Soviet Union no longer existed. It had been replaced by a loose alliance of former Soviet republics called the Commonwealth of Independent States. Russia's new president, Boris Yeltsin, emerged as the dominant leader in this fragmented land.

As the Soviet Union disintegrated, Bush continued arms-control talks with Gorbachev. The Soviets and Americans signed a number of pacts that signaled the end of the Cold War. Agreements in 1989 and 1990 limited the buildup of nuclear and chemical weapons. The first **Strategic Arms Reduction Treaty,** known as START I, called for dramatic reductions in the two nations' supplies of long-range nuclear weapons. It was signed in 1991. After the Soviet Union collapsed, Bush continued to negotiate with President Boris Yeltsin of Russia.

"The Cold War is now behind us," Gorbachev had declared. "Let us not wrangle over who won it." But clearly the United States was now the world's lone superpower.

A New International Role

President Bush hoped the world would move smoothly from the hostility of the Cold War to a peaceful "New World Order" under the leadership of the United States and its allies. Instead, conflicts in different regions of the world became the focus of American foreign policy. As the world's sole superpower, the United States needed to respond to crises abroad in a new way.

Tiananmen Square The People's Republic of China occupied much of America's attention in 1989. As Communist governments tottered in Eastern Europe, Chinese students gathered in the capital, Beijing, to march for democracy and reform. In May, protesters occupied Tiananmen Square in the heart of the city, despite official orders to leave. Their numbers soon swelled to more than one million across the city. In Tiananmen Square, they built a "Goddess of Democracy" modeled on the Statue of Liberty.

On June 3, China's leaders ordered the army to attack the protester camps. Hundreds, possibly thousands, of demonstrators died and others quickly scattered in the face of overwhelming military force. The government cracked down on the democracy movement after the attack and many more people were imprisoned and executed.

Bush valued the relationship the United States had with China. Rather than attack China's leaders and risk an international crisis, Bush preferred to negotiate quietly and encourage trade between China and the United States. His nonconfrontational stance upset many people who believed he was indifferent to human rights in China.

Statues of Communist heroes such as Vladimir Lenin (shown above) and Karl Marx were removed from cities across Eastern Europe in the 1990s.

Focus on ECONOMICS

China's Transformation Although China's Communist Party held onto power in the 1980s and 1990s, it had long before begun to abandon some of its Communist principles. Under Deng Xiaoping, China moved toward a market-oriented economy based on capitalism and foreign trade. Exports to the United States increased from $4 billion in 1985 to nearly $26 billion in 1992.

ACTIVITY
Connecting with Science and Technology

Ask students to research the size and status of the missile arsenals of the United States and former Soviet Union today. The central question to be addressed is: How many nuclear warheads does each nation now possess, and how has the size of its arsenal changed due to the START initiatives? Have students present their findings in the form of a graph. Ask the class to assess the impact of the Cold War's end on each side's nuclear capability. **(Logical/Mathematical)**

BACKGROUND
Global Connections

The attack on the Tiananmen Square protesters dramatically impacted events in Eastern Europe. For weeks after the massacre, democratic reformers in the satellite nations moved more cautiously, fearing that the Soviet Union might pressure their governments to adopt a "Tiananmen solution." In July 1989, however, Gorbachev advised the Eastern European nations to pursue their own independent solutions to their problems. Emboldened by this statement, hundreds of thousands of Hungarians, East Germans, and Czechs rose up in nonviolent protests against their Communist governments. An estimated one million Latvians, Lithuanians, and Estonians demanded freedom by forming a human chain that linked their capitals. By year's end, all of the Eastern European satellite nations were free of Communist rule.

CUSTOMIZE FOR ...
Gifted and Talented

Ask students to look at the Bush administration and several previous administrations and analyze what makes a President choose to emphasize either foreign or domestic policies. Is the main reason the course of world events? Or are some leaders naturally more interested in either one or the other? Have students illustrate their answers with solid biographical and historical details.

The Invasion of Panama Bush enjoyed more support later that year when he acted against the Central American nation of Panama. Bush suspected General Manuel Noriega, Panama's dictator, of smuggling cocaine into the United States. After Noriega declared war on the United States, Bush launched a lightning attack against Panama in December 1989 and quickly won control of the country. Noriega surrendered to American forces on January 3, 1990, and two years later a federal jury in Florida convicted him of drug smuggling. The invasion demonstrated Bush's willingness to act boldly to stop the flow of drugs into the United States.

The Persian Gulf War In August 1990, the Arab nation of Iraq, headed by a brutal dictator, Saddam Hussein, launched a sudden invasion of neighboring Kuwait. Saddam justified the assault by citing centuries-old territorial claims. But in fact he had his sights on Kuwait's substantial oil wealth.

Of concern to the Bush administration was the flow of Kuwaiti oil to the West. Bush viewed the protection of those oil reserves as an issue of national security. The administration was also concerned about the security of Saudi Arabia, a key Arab ally in the region, and Saddam's investment in destructive weapons. Bush responded strongly:

Sounds of an Era
Listen to George Bush's speech and other sounds from the Reagan-Bush era.

> 66 There is much in the modern world that is subject to doubts or questions—washed in shades of gray. But not the brutal aggression of Saddam Hussein against a peaceful, sovereign nation and its people. It's black and white. The facts are clear. The choice is unambiguous—right versus wrong. 99
>
> —George Bush, 1990

Americans at first seemed reluctant to get involved in a territorial matter between Arab nations. As the weeks passed, however, rising oil prices and reports of Iraqi atrocities against Kuwaiti civilians drew increasing concern.

Months of diplomatic efforts failed to persuade Saddam to withdraw. Finally, the United States, working through the United Nations, mobilized an alliance of 28 countries to launch the **Persian Gulf War.** It was a limited military operation to drive Iraqi forces out of Kuwait.

To organize military operations, President Bush turned to General Colin Powell. Powell had risen quickly through the ranks of the military. In 1979, at age 42, he had become the Army's youngest brigadier general. He was the first African American to serve as national security advisor. By 1989, he had been named the nation's youngest ever Chairman of the Joint Chiefs of Staff, the top military officer in the nation.

VIEWING HISTORY American soldiers fought a brief, victorious war, aided by the open terrain that provided no shelter for Iraq's armies. **Determining Relevance** *Why did the Bush administration decide to intervene militarily in this regional conflict?*

Powell's battle plan was simple. He would use airpower to destroy Iraq's ability to wage war, and then smash the Iraqi forces occupying Kuwait. A series of massive air strikes, known as "Operation Desert Storm," was launched on January 16–17, 1991. UN forces, directed by General Powell and led by Norman Schwarzkopf, liberated Kuwait in just six weeks of war. The allies had lost fewer than 300 soldiers, while tens of thousands of Iraqi troops had died.

Bush opted not to send troops deep into Iraq to oust Saddam, expecting that Saddam's opponents would soon overthrow him. Yet Saddam's opposition

1118   Chapter 33 • *The Conservative Revolution*

proved weaker than Bush's advisors had thought, and he remained in power.

Domestic Issues

Bush's leadership during the Persian Gulf War drove his approval rating up to an astounding 89 percent. Yet while his foreign policy generally won him praise, Americans began to believe that Bush did not have a clear plan for handling domestic problems. In the end, this perception helped usher him out of office.

Bush angered many moderates and liberals with his nomination of Clarence Thomas, a conservative black judge, to the Supreme Court in 1991. Thomas faced grilling about his views on civil rights and about charges of past sexual harassment. Thomas won confirmation after stormy televised Senate hearings that ignited public debate on the issue of sexual harassment.

Budget deficits continued to swell during Bush's presidency. Bush countered by slowing spending for social programs. Finally, he agreed to a deficit reduction plan that included new taxes. The tax hike broke Bush's 1988 campaign promise and generated public anger.

Bush's real undoing was a recession that began in the early 1990s. Turmoil in the Persian Gulf led gasoline prices to rise rapidly, creating unexpected costs for businesses and consumers alike. The end of the Cold War enabled the United States to spend less on defense. As a result, firms that supplied planes, ships, and military hardware laid off workers. Companies in several other industries also laid off workers to cut costs in a process called **downsizing.** By 1991, the jobless rate reached 7 percent, the highest level in nearly five years. The recession was felt unevenly across the country. States that relied heavily on defense spending, including California and Connecticut, were hit much harder than others.

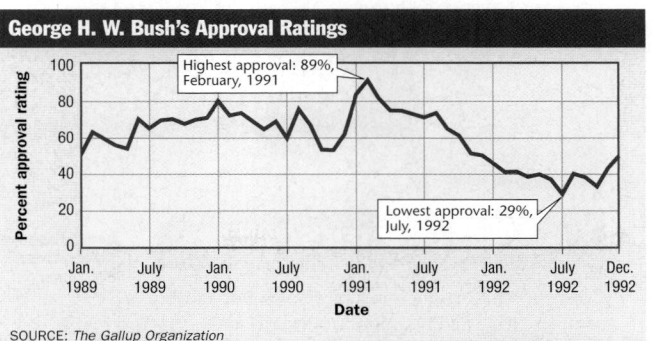

George H. W. Bush's Approval Ratings

Highest approval: 89%, February, 1991

Lowest approval: 29%, July, 1992

SOURCE: *The Gallup Organization*

INTERPRETING GRAPHS
The percentage of Americans who believed Bush was doing a good job plunged from a high of 89 percent during the Gulf War to only 29 percent 17 months later. **Analyzing Information** *What were Bush's approval ratings in early 1990, before the Gulf War and the recession?*

Section 4 — Assessment

READING COMPREHENSION

1. What factors helped George Bush win the 1988 presidential election?

2. List two reasons why Communist regimes in Eastern Europe collapsed in 1989.

3. How did China's Communist government react to democracy protests in 1989?

4. What domestic issues damaged Bush's popularity?

CRITICAL THINKING AND WRITING

5. **Making Comparisons** How was the Persian Gulf War fought differently from the Vietnam War?

6. **Demonstrating Reasoned Judgment** Was it reasonable for Americans to believe that the Cold War would be followed by international peace and cooperation? Why or why not?

7. **Defending a Position** Some people describe George Bush's presidency as Reagan's third term. Explain whether you agree or disagree.

 Take It to the NET

Activity: Making a Flowchart
What have been the lasting effects of the Persian Gulf War? Research this conflict and create a flowchart of key events in the region before, during, and after the war. Use the links provided in the *America: Pathways to the Present* area at the following Web site for help in completing this activity.
www.phschool.com

Chapter 33 • Section 4   **1119**

Section 4 — Assessment

Reading Comprehension

1. His commitment to no new taxes; his attack ads targeting Dukakis's campaign.

2. Sample answer: Gorbachev's leadership; popular protest against the regimes.

3. Cracked down on democracy movement, executing and imprisoning protesters.

4. Nomination of Clarence Thomas; recession; tax hike.

Critical Thinking and Writing

5. Persian Gulf War was fought quickly, with defined goals and a minimum of U.S. casualties.

6. Answers will vary but should be supported with facts from the section.

7. Answers will vary but should include references to the economic and foreign policy goals of the two men.

 Take It to the NET

Flowcharts may include the Iraqi military buildup and the invasion of Kuwait, international trade embargoes against Iraq, Iraqi reaction to the initiation of Operation Desert Storm, and "Gulf War Syndrome."

CUSTOMIZE FOR ...

Less Proficient Writers
Ask students to write two headings: *World* and *United States.* Under each heading have them list the major events that took place in each region during the Bush administration.

CAPTION ANSWERS

Interpreting Graphs His approval ratings were between 60 percent and 80 percent.

REVIEWING KEY TERMS

Students should refer to the definitions of key terms in the chapter to write sentences that show an understanding of the conservative revolution.

REVIEWING MAIN IDEAS

16. Sample answer: women's movement; sexual revolution; government spending.

17. They were an active and powerful conservative coalition whose views aligned with Reagan's. They used the technology of television to spread their message and gain support and contributions for their campaign.

18. Taxes were cut.

19. While the tax cuts did contribute to economic recovery, the budget was not balanced during his term.

20. Reagan wanted to confront Communist governments and prevent the spread of communism.

21. Supply-side economics was the antithesis of Keynesian theory; tax cuts were supposed to help business; wealth was unevenly distributed; crisis in some farm and manufacturing industries.

22. Reagan lacked enthusiasm for civil rights and affirmative action. His nomination of conservative justices to the Supreme Court was a reflection of his position on these issues.

23. It encouraged anti-Communist movements throughout Eastern Europe to pursue democracy.

24. He muted official American criticism of the brutal crackdown in Tiananmen Square by the Chinese Communist government. He perhaps felt less obliged to criticize Communist regimes than Reagan had since the Cold War was ending.

CRITICAL THINKING

25. Possible answers: (a) Reagan pressured Communist governments while failing to promote civil rights and affirmative action at home. (b) Bush projected American military force into regional conflicts in Panama and Kuwait. Bush appointed a staunch conservative, Clarence Thomas, to the Supreme Court.

creating a CHAPTER SUMMARY

Copy this chart (right) on a piece of paper and complete it by adding important events and issues that fit each heading. Some entries have been completed for you as examples.

For additional review and enrichment activities, see the interactive version of *America: Pathways to the Present*, available on the Web and on CD-ROM.

Time Period	Important Events
Evolution of Conservatism (1934–1981)	• American Liberty League is founded to oppose the New Deal. • Barry Goldwater runs for President as a staunch conservative. •
Ronald Reagan's First Term (1981–1985)	
Ronald Reagan's Second Term (1985–1989)	
George H. W. Bush's Administration (1989–1993)	

★ Reviewing Key Terms

For each of the terms below, write a sentence explaining how it relates to the presidencies of Ronald Reagan and George Bush.

1. Reagan Democrat
2. New Right
3. televangelism
4. supply-side economics
5. New Federalism
6. Strategic Defense Initiative (SDI)
7. AIDS
8. Sandinista
9. Contra
10. Iran-Contra affair
11. INF Treaty
12. entitlement
13. Strategic Arms Reduction Treaty
14. Persian Gulf War
15. downsizing

★ Reviewing Main Ideas

16. List three conservative criticisms of society in the 1960s and 1970s. (Section 1)

17. How did the New Right help Ronald Reagan win the 1980 presidential election? (Section 1)

18. How did supply-side economics change the federal government's tax policy? (Section 2)

19. Did Reagan's tax cuts achieve all of his economic and budgetary goals? (Section 2)

20. How did Reagan view Communist governments in other countries? (Section 2)

21. What role did Supreme Court appointments have in Reagan's conservative strategy? (Section 3)

22. Describe four economic trends of the 1980s. (Section 3)

23. What was the impact on Eastern Europe of Gorbachev's call for *perestroika* and *glasnost*? (Section 4)

24. How did President Bush change America's foreign policy at the end of the Cold War? (Section 4)

★ Critical Thinking

25. **Recognizing Ideologies** (a) How did conservative beliefs affect Reagan's policies? (b) How did they affect Bush's policies?

26. **Identifying Assumptions** Read the selection from Ronald Reagan's first inaugural speech in Section 2. (a) What words does Reagan use to describe government regulations and taxes? (b) What does his choice of words say about his view of government?

27. **Synthesizing Information** During his first term, Reagan called the Soviet Union an "evil empire." In his second term, he developed a working relationship with Gorbachev. What do you think accounts for this change in strategy?

28. **Understanding Cause and Effect** Was Reagan responsible for all the changes in the American economy in the 1980s? Explain your answer.

29. **Drawing Conclusions** Why did President Bush respond differently to the crisis in Panama than he did to the crisis in China?

CREATING A CHAPTER SUMMARY	
Time Period	**Important Events**
Evolution of Conservatism (1934–1981)	• American Liberty League is founded to oppose the New Deal. • Barry Goldwater runs for President as a staunch conservative. • Formation of the New Right Coalition
Ronald Reagan's First Term (1981–1985)	• Unemployment reaches 40-year high. • Reagan reduces top income tax rate. • United States attacks Libya following terrorist bombing. • Economy recovers from recession.
Ronald Reagan's Second Term (1985–1989)	• Resurgence of patriotism • Farm crisis • Shifts in manufacturing • S & L scandal • Iran-Contra affair
George H.W. Bush's Administration (1989–1993)	• End of the Cold War • Fall of Berlin Wall • Tiananmen Square protests • Defeat of communism in many Eastern European countries • Invasion of Panama • Persian Gulf War

★ Skills Assessment

Analyzing Political Cartoons ▶

30. Analyze the images in the cartoon. (a) Who is the man? (b) What does the ship symbolize? (c) How do you know?

31. (a) Where is the ship headed? (b) What is the man's attitude about the ship's course?

32. Summarize the cartoonist's message.

Interpreting Data

Turn to the Federal Budget Deficit graph in Section 2.

33. During the Reagan years, what happened to the overall course of the budget deficit?

    A It rose steadily.
    B It fell.
    C It increased by about $210 billion.
    D It increased, and then fell back to its original level.

34. What was the major cause of deficit increases during the period shown in the graph?

    F the cost of the Persian Gulf War
    G the Strategic Defense Initiative
    H increased defense spending and tax cuts under Reagan
    J Bush's pledge not to raise taxes

35. **Writing** Do you think the government should be allowed to spend more money in any given year than it earns in revenues from taxes and other sources? Why or why not?

Applying the Chapter Skill: *Analyzing Trends in the Electoral College Map*

36. Review the information on the Skills for Life page. (a) Which regions of the country lost political clout between 1948 and 1980? (b) Did this change affect the outcome of the 1980 presidential election? Explain your answer.

ACTIVITIES

Writing to LEARN

Writing to Compare and Contrast
Is the conservative revolution alive and well today? Write an essay to explain your answer. Include examples of issues from the presidencies of Ronald Reagan and George H. W. Bush that either continue to be debated today or else have faded in significance.

Primary Source CD-ROM

Working With Primary Sources Find additional information on the conservative revolution on the *Exploring Primary Sources in U.S. History CD-ROM* and use the selection(s) provided to complete the Chapter 33 primary source activity located in the *America: Pathways to the Present* area of the following Web site. **www.phschool.com**

Take It to the NET

Chapter Self-Test As a review activity, take the Chapter 33 Self-Test in the *America: Pathways to the Present* area at the Web site listed below. The questions are designed to test your understanding of the chapter content. **www.phschool.com**

Chapter 33 Assessment **1121**

---

27. Answers will vary, but will probably focus on the fact that Reagan and Gorbachev got along well together personally, and that Gorbachev was an entirely different kind of Soviet leader, one with whom it was possible to reach meaningful agreements.

28. Possible answer: No. Manufacturing industries would have been hit hard by foreign competition with or without Reagan.

29. Panama was a much weaker nation, and much less valuable as a trading partner, than China. Thus, a strong response by Bush in Panama was not as likely to escalate into a major crisis.

SKILLS ASSESSMENT

30. (a) Ronald Reagan. (b) The U.S. economy. (c) The name "*S.S. Reagonomics*" is printed on the life preserver.

31. (a) Toward an iceberg. (b) He is oblivious to the disaster ahead.

32. Reagan's economic policies are leading the nation toward disaster.

33. C

34. H

35. Answers will vary, but might take into account the long-term burden that paying a deficit places upon a nation.

36. (a) The Northeast lost political clout from 1948 to 1980. (b) This change had no effect on the outcome of the 1980 presidential election because the number of electoral votes remained the same for the states that Carter won.

THE RISE OF THE SUNBELT

Focus Point out that until the mid-twentieth century, the South was mainly agricultural. The cities of the Northeast and North Central regions dominated business, banking, and manufacturing.

Instruct Ask students to describe economic and political changes they have observed in their own communities. They may consider:

- **Population** Has the population of the community grown or declined since the 1970s? What factors have caused the change? What effects have population changes had on services such as schools and libraries?

- **Business and industry** Have new firms and factories located in the area? Or have businesses closed or downsized? Has the number of jobs increased? What about service businesses such as supermarkets or video rental stores?

- **Politics** Is the community traditionally Democratic or Republican? What political issues are important in the community?

- **Environment** Have air and water quality improved or declined? Do growing populations put pressure on water supplies and other resources?

Extend The rise of the Sunbelt has had far-reaching ramifications. Have small groups research the growth of recreational attractions in the Sunbelt—e.g., Disney World, new sports franchises—as well as increased sales of sportswear and recreational equipment. What other effects on popular culture or consumer buying habits can they identify?

ANSWERS

1. Jobs were disappearing in the Northeast and Midwest at the same time that employment opportunity was growing in the Sunbelt. Also, people sought warmer weather and opportunities for outdoor recreation in the Sunbelt.

The Rise of the Sunbelt

During the second half of the twentieth century, people and jobs moved on a massive scale from northern portions of the United States to the Sunbelt, a region encompassing states in the South and the Southwest.

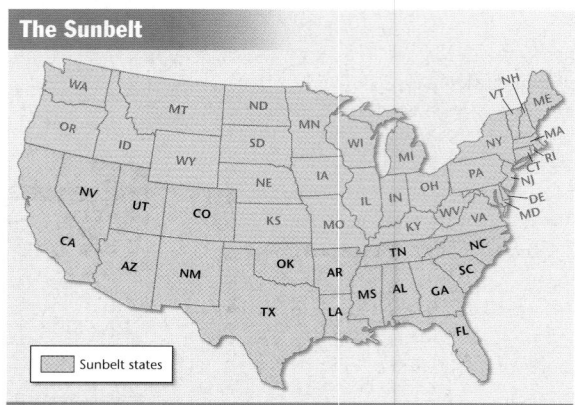
The Sunbelt

Sunbelt states

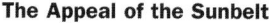

Why People Left
Cold, snowy winters, and older, declining industries made life challenging in the Midwest and the Northeast. In the 1970s and 1980s, many factories in these regions shut down, and jobs moved south or overseas.

The Appeal of the Sunbelt
Many new jobs became available in the Sunbelt. Employers chose to locate in this region because of lower labor and energy costs. Also, some Sunbelt states had lower business taxes. Families and individuals were drawn to the Sunbelt both by abundant jobs and by its warmer climate and opportunities for year-round outdoor recreation.

Geographic Connection
Why did many Americans move from the Northeast and the Midwest to the Sunbelt?

1122

RESOURCE DIRECTORY

Teaching Resources
Geography and History booklet, pp. 20–21

Other Print Resources
Nystrom _Atlas of Our Country_ Regions of Our Country, pp. 48–67

Technology
Prentice Hall United States History Video Collection™ Volume 20, _Post-War USA_

Sunbelt Development

The Sunbelt offers abundant land for new construction. This mixed office and residential development in southern California illustrates the combination of new employment, housing, and opportunities for outdoor activities that draw people to the Sunbelt.

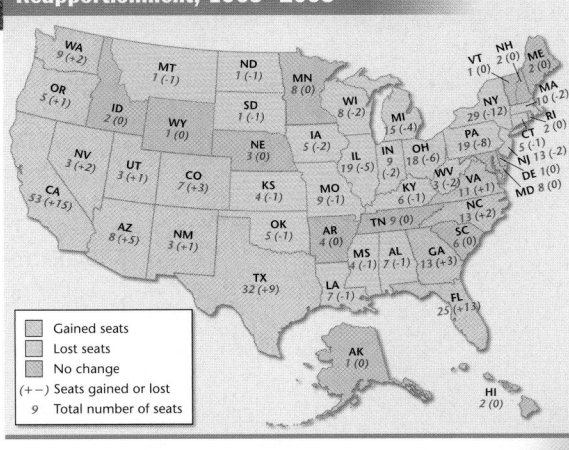

Reapportionment, 1963–2003

WA 9 (+2)
MT 1 (-1)
ND 1 (-1)
MN 8 (0)
VT 1 (0)
NH 2 (0)
ME 2 (0)
OR 5 (+1)
ID 2 (0)
WY 1 (0)
SD 1 (-1)
WI 8 (-2)
MI 15 (-4)
NY 29 (-12)
MA 10 (-2)
NV 3 (+2)
UT 3 (+1)
CO 7 (+3)
NE 3 (0)
IA 5 (-2)
IL 19 (-5)
IN 9 (-2)
OH 18 (-6)
PA 19 (-8)
RI 2 (0)
CT 5 (-1)
NJ 13 (-2)
CA 53 (+15)
KS 4 (-1)
MO 9 (-1)
KY 6 (-1)
WV 3 (-2)
VA 11 (+1)
DE 1 (0)
MD 8 (0)
AZ 8 (+5)
NM 3 (+1)
OK 5 (-1)
AR 4 (0)
TN 9 (0)
NC 13 (+2)
SC 6 (0)
TX 32 (+9)
LA 7 (-1)
MS 4 (-1)
AL 7 (-1)
GA 13 (+3)
FL 25 (+13)
AK 1 (0)
HI 2 (0)

Gained seats
Lost seats
No change
(+ −) Seats gained or lost
9 Total number of seats

New Political Influence

This map shows changes in congressional representation between 1963 and 2003. States that grew faster than the national average gained seats, while those that grew more slowly or lost population also lost seats. Except in a few older southern states, rapid growth in most of the Sunbelt brought dramatic increases in congressional representation and national political influence. Since 1964, a candidate from the Sunbelt has won every presidential election.

Geographic Connection

How have shifts in population affected political power at the national level? Which states gained the most seats? Which states lost the most seats?

Joining the Major Leagues

Sunbelt cities that once had only minor-league teams have grown so much that they now attract major-league teams, such as the Jacksonville Jaguars.

Chapter 34 Planning Guide
Resource Manager

Chapter-Level Resources	CORE INSTRUCTION	READING/SKILLS
	Teaching Resources • Pacing Charts booklet • Block Scheduling booklet **Resource Pro® CD-ROM**, Ch. 34 **Prentice Hall Presentation Pro CD-ROM**, Ch. 34 **www.phschool.com** • eTeach	**Guided Reading Audiotapes (English/Spanish)** **Student Edition on Audio CD**, Ch. 34 **Social Studies Skills Tutor CD-ROM** **Color Transparencies**, A52, A53, A59, B19, B20, C10, E19, E20, G12, G115
1 Politics in Recent Years 1. Find out what led to Bill Clinton's election in 1992 and what issues he tackled in his first term. 2. See why Republicans issued a Contract with America. 3. Read about the scandals that were debated during Clinton's second term. 4. Think about the results of the 2000 election and the goals the new President set. 5. Learn how Americans responded to terrorist attacks in 2001.	**Teaching Resources** **Units 9/10 booklet** • Section 1 Quiz, p. 75	**Guided Reading and Review booklet,** p. 137 **Guide to the Essentials,** p. 174 **Learning with Documents booklet,** pp. 73, 98 **Skills for Life booklet,** p. 36 **Section Reading Support Transparencies**
2 The United States in a New World 1. Read about political changes that took place in the world in the 1990s. 2. Find out how the Clinton administration promoted peace abroad. 3. Describe U.S. relations with China. 4. Discover the impact of an expanding global economy.	**Teaching Resources** **Units 9/10 booklet** • Section 2 Quiz, p. 76 **Learning Styles Lesson Plans booklet,** p. 70	**Guided Reading and Review booklet,** p. 138 **Guide to the Essentials,** p. 175 **Section Reading Support Transparencies**
3 Americans in the New Millennium 1. Learn about factors that contributed to the growing diversity of the nation's population. 2. Find out how Americans disagreed about how to make diversity work. 3. Discover the economic and political impact of the nation's aging population. 4. Read to find out how the technological revolution at the end of the twentieth century affected American life.	**Teaching Resources** **Units 9/10 booklet** • Section 3 Quiz, p. 77 **Learning Styles Lesson Plans booklet,** p. 71	**Guided Reading and Review booklet,** p. 139 **Guide to the Essentials,** p. 176 **Learning with Documents booklet,** p. 39 **Section Reading Support Transparencies**

ENRICHMENT/PRE-AP

Prentice Hall United States History Video Collection™
www.phschool.com
  • Section Activities, Virtual Field Trip, Chapter Activities, Current Events Online

Biography, Literature, and Comparing Primary Sources booklet, p. 89
American History Block Scheduling Support
Nystrom *Atlas of Our Country,* pp. 34–35
Sounds of an Era Audio CD
Exploring Primary Sources in U.S. History CD-ROM

Biography, Literature, and Comparing Primary Sources booklet, p. 39
Great Debates booklet, p. 48
American History Block Scheduling Support
Historical Outline Map Book, pp. 72, 74, 75, 76, 78, 79

Biography, Literature, and Comparing Primary Sources booklet, p. 163
American History Block Scheduling Support
Nystrom *Atlas of Our Country,* pp. 36–37
Historical Outline Map Book, p. 82
Exploring Primary Sources in U.S. History CD-ROM
American Pathways Thematic Posters

ASSESSMENT

PRENTICE HALL ASSESSMENT SYSTEM

Core Assessment
  ExamView® Test Bank, Ch. 34
  ExamView® Test Bank CD-ROM, Ch. 34

Standardized Test Preparation
Diagnose and Prescribe
  Diagnostic Tests for High School Social Studies Skills

Review and Reteach
  Review Book for U.S. History

Practice and Assess
  Test-taking Strategies With Transparencies
  Test-taking Strategies Posters
  Test Prep Book for U.S. History
  Alternative Assessment Handbook
  Document-Based Assessment

Teaching Resources
Units 9/10 booklet
  • Section Quizzes, pp. 75–77
  • Chapter Tests, pp. 78, 81
www.phschool.com Ch. 34 Self-Test

AmericanHeritage RESOURCES

From the Archives of American Heritage®, p. 1128
AmericanHeritage® My Brush with History™ Videotapes
www.americanheritage.com

Don't miss the exclusive interactive version of this textbook on the Web and on CD-ROM.

Chapter 34 Planning Guide
In Your Classroom

CUSTOMIZE FOR INDIVIDUAL NEEDS

Gifted and Talented

Teacher's Edition
- Customize for Gifted and Talented, p. 1127

Teaching Resources
- Biography, Literature, and Comparing Primary Sources booklet, pp. 39, 89, 163

Technology
- Exploring Primary Sources in U.S. History CD-ROM *On the Pulse of the Morning, Maya Angelou; Inaugural Address, President George W. Bush*

ESL

Teacher's Edition
- Customize for ESL, p. 1139

Teaching Resources
- Guided Reading and Review booklet, pp. 137–139
- Guide to the Essentials (English/Spanish), Chapter 34

Technology
- Student Edition on Audio CD, Chapter 34
- Guided Reading Audiotapes (English/Spanish), Chapter 34
- Section Reading Support Transparencies

Less Proficient Readers

Teacher's Edition
- Customize for Less Proficient Readers, pp. 1131, 1145

Teaching Resources
- Guided Reading and Review booklet, pp. 137–139
- Guide to the Essentials (English/Spanish), Chapter 34

Technology
- Student Edition on Audio CD, Chapter 34
- Guided Reading Audiotapes (English/Spanish), Chapter 34
- Section Reading Support Transparencies

Less Proficient Writers

Teacher's Edition
- Customize for Less Proficient Writers, pp. 1131, 1147

Teaching Resources
- Guided Reading and Review booklet, pp. 137–139
- Guide to the Essentials (English/Spanish), Chapter 34

Technology
- Student Edition on Audio CD, Chapter 34
- Guided Reading Audiotapes (English/Spanish), Chapter 34
- Section Reading Support Transparencies

TEACHER'S EDITION INDEX

CHAPTER 34 – PACING SUGGESTIONS

For 90-minute Blocks

- Teach sections 1, 2, and 3 using Transparencies A52, A53, A59, B19, B20, C10, E19, E20, G12, and G115, and the Recent Scholarship notes on pages 1139 and 1153 for class discussions.

Running Out of Time?

If you are running short on time to cover this chapter, consider the following options:

- Use the Prentice Hall Presentation Pro CD-ROM to create an outline for this chapter.

- Use the Section Summaries for Chapter 34, from **Guide to the Essentials (English/Spanish)**.

ADDITIONAL ACTIVITIES

1 Politics in Recent Years

Connecting with Citizenship
Explain that in recent years the outcome of presidential races has been more difficult to predict because there is currently less party loyalty than ever before. Fewer voters take steps to register themselves as Democrat or Republican, while many consider themselves Independents. That means that their votes can go either way, depending on the candidates' appeal. Have students work in small groups to research the recent surge in Independent voters and develop a list of the effects this shift has had on presidential politics. Discuss the lists with the class. **(Verbal/Linguistic)**

2 The United States in a New World

Connecting with Economics
Explain to students that one of the recent controversies about U.S. relations with China was the issue of normalizing trade. The issue was whether to grant China most-favored-nation status. Have students research the internal and external factors that made this an issue, then present an oral or written report on how it evolved during the Clinton administration. **(Verbal/Linguistic)**

3 Americans in the New Millennium

Connecting with Science and Technology
To demonstrate how the Information Age can be utilized to keep voters informed about important topics, suggest that small groups of students each create a mock-up (on paper) of a new Web site about any topic they have studied. Examples might include education funding, immigration, the global economy, affirmative action, health care, or availability of technology to all segments of the population. Once students have developed a broad design for the site, they should invite input from other students and incorporate those suggestions for the next level of development. **(Visual/Spatial)**

Chapter 34

Entering a New Era

(1992 to the Present)

INTRODUCING THE CHAPTER

Sweeping changes in world affairs in the early 1990s changed the face of world politics. Although the Cold War was over, these developments offered new challenges to the United States, now the only superpower, and to the President. The United States also faced challenging issues at home, as immigration and an aging population changed the demographics of American society.

TIME LINE ACTIVITY

To provide students with practice in using the time line, ask questions such as these:

1. What organization designed to regulate international commerce was established in 1995? *(The World Trade Organization)*

2. What 1996 act changed the way the government responds to families in need? *(The Welfare Reform Act)*

3. What did NATO do in 1999 in an attempt to keep peace in Kosovo? *(NATO launched airstrikes.)*

eTeach

Be sure to check out this month's online discussion with a Master Teacher. Go to **www.phschool.com**.

Chapter 34 Entering a New Era

(1992 to the Present)

SECTION 1 Politics in Recent Years
SECTION 2 The United States in a New World
SECTION 3 Americans in the New Millennium

SPECIAL ISSUE
TIME
Take a good look at this woman. She was created by a computer from a mix of several races. What you see is a remarkable preview of…

THE NEW FACE OF AMERICA
How Immigrants Are Shaping the World's First Multicultural Society

This computer-generated portrait combined the characteristics of all the races present in the United States.

American Events

1992
Bill Clinton is elected President.

1994
The Republicans, running on their "Contract with America," win the 1994 congressional elections.

1996
Congress passes the Welfare Reform Act.

Presidential Terms:
George H. W. Bush 1989–1993

William J. Clinton 1993–2001

| 1992 | 1994 | • | 1996 |

World Events

Nelson Mandela is elected president of South Africa.
1994

The World Trade Organization is established.
1995

RESOURCE DIRECTORY

Teaching Resources
Pacing Charts booklet
Block Scheduling booklet, p. 30
Units 9/10 booklet
• Chapter Summary, p. 74

Technology
Guided Reading Audiotapes (English/Spanish), Ch. 34
Student Edition on Audio CD, Ch. 34
Prentice Hall United States History Video Collection™ Volume 20, *Post-War USA*
Prentice Hall Presentation Pro CD-ROM, Ch. 34
Resource Pro® CD-ROM
Social Studies Skills Tutor CD-ROM
Companion Web site, www.phschool.com

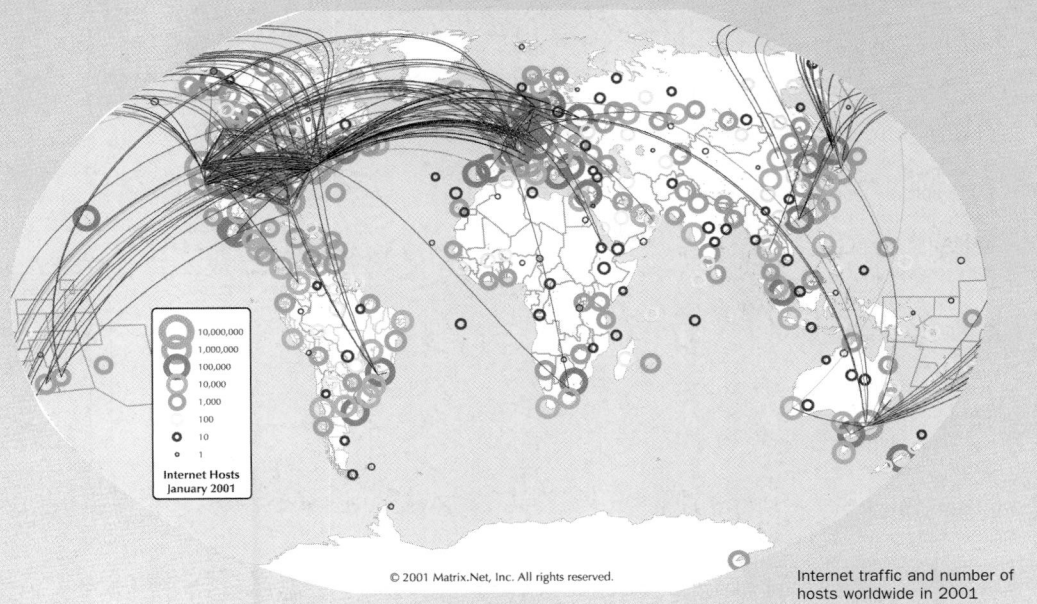

Internet Hosts
January 2001

10,000,000
1,000,000
100,000
10,000
1,000
100
10
1

© 2001 Matrix.Net, Inc. All rights reserved.

Internet traffic and number of hosts worldwide in 2001

Activating Prior Knowledge Which areas of the world have the most Internet traffic? *(The United States and Europe)*

Previewing What role do you think the Internet has played in international affairs? *(The Internet has made information accessible on a worldwide basis. People have greater access to education, business, and entertainment right from their homes and places of work.)*

BACKGROUND
About the Pictures

1 2 3 4

1. The 1992 presidential race included three major candidates for the first time since 1912: George Bush, Bill Clinton, and Ross Perot.

2. In the 1990s the United States became more diverse than it had ever been in its history.

3. The results of the 2000 presidential election took 36 days and several court battles to decide.

4. In a spontaneous outburst of patriotism, the Congressional members sang "God Bless America." The event was broadcast on live television.

A display of national unity by the United States Congress following the terrorist attacks

1998
The House of Representatives votes to impeach President Clinton.

2000
The Supreme Court's ruling in *Bush* v. *Gore* ends recounts in Florida, leading to George W. Bush's victory in the 2000 presidential election.

2001
Terrorists attack the United States, crashing hijacked planes into the World Trade Center in New York City and the Pentagon in Washington, D.C.

George W. Bush 2001–

1998   **2000**   **2002**

Voters in Northern Ireland and Ireland approve the Good Friday Accords.
1998

NATO launches airstrikes against Serbia to keep peace in Kosovo.
1999

Chapter 34 **1125**

BIBLIOGRAPHY

For the Teacher

Bell, Derrick. *Faces at the Bottom of the Well: The Permanence of Racism.* Basic, 1993. (Attitudes toward race revealed through dialogues and myths.)

Glickman, Rose L. *Daughters of Feminists.* St. Martin's Press, 1993. (Reports on 50 women raised by feminist mothers.)

Takaki, Ronald. *A Different Mirror: A History of Multicultural America.* Little, Brown, 1993. (An attempt to view all American history from a multicultural perspective.)

For the Student

Ashabraner, Brent. *An Ancient Heritage: The Arab American Minority.* HarperCollins, 1993. (Personal reflections on the experience of being Arab American.)

Cisneros, Sandra. *The House on Mango Street.* Arte Publico, 1989. (A short story collection by a Mexican American writer.)

Santiago, Esmeralda. *When I Was Puerto Rican.* Addison-Wesley, 1993.

Smith, Jessie Carney. *Black Firsts: 2,000 Years of Extraordinary Achievement.* Visible Ink Press, 1994. (Chronicles the "firsts" among people of color.)

TEXT

Don't miss the exclusive interactive version of this textbook on the Web and on CD-ROM.

Politics in Recent Years

SECTION OBJECTIVES

1. Find out what led to Bill Clinton's election in 1992 and what issues he tackled in his first term.
2. See why Republicans issued a Contract with America.
3. Read about the scandals that were debated during Clinton's second term.
4. Think about the results of the 2000 election and the goals the new President set.
5. Learn how Americans responded to the terrorist attacks in 2001.

BELLRINGER

Warm-Up Activity Ask students to suppose that they are making a decision about how to vote in the 2000 presidential election. What factors and issues would influence their decision? How would they have voted?

Activating Prior Knowledge Have students list four or five major events they can recall taking place during Bill Clinton's presidency.

READING STRATEGY

As students read the section, have them list the actions of government and the private sector to expand economic opportunities to all citizens during the 1990s.

READING FOCUS

- What led to Bill Clinton's election in 1992 and what issues did he tackle during his first term?
- Why did Republicans issue a Contract with America?
- What scandals were debated during Clinton's second term?
- What were the results of the 2000 election, and what goals did the new President set?
- How did Americans respond to the terrorist attacks in 2001?

MAIN IDEA

Bill Clinton's presidency included many low points but it was also marked by great successes. The highs and lows of the Clinton years were followed by the close election of 2000.

KEY TERMS

Contract with America
Whitewater affair

TAKING NOTES

As you read, complete the chart below to show the major political issues of the 1990s.

Politics and Elections

1992 Election	1996 Election	2000 Election
• Bush (R.) vs. Clinton (D.) vs. Perot (I.)	• Dole (R.) vs. Clinton (D.) vs. Perot (Reform)	• George W. Bush (R.) vs. Gore (D.)
• Pro-Bush: won Gulf War...	• Pro-Dole:	• Pro-Bush:
• Pro-Clinton: control of political center...	• Pro-Clinton:	• Pro-Gore:
• Result: Clinton wins.	• Result:	• Result:

Setting the Scene

An earnest young man named Bill Clinton reached out and firmly grasped President John F. Kennedy's hand. At just 17, this high school student from a small town in Arkansas was actually shaking hands with the President! Later, the experience contributed to Clinton's decision to pursue a career in politics. In 1993, some three decades after this meeting, Clinton was back in the White House. This time he stayed for eight years, for he had become the forty-second President of the United States.

The 1992 Election

The 1992 presidential campaign was a three-way race. Not since 1912, when President Taft faced both Woodrow Wilson and former President Theodore Roosevelt, had a third candidate played such a major role in a presidential election.

The Candidates On the Republican side, President George Bush sought a second term. The Republicans argued that they could best deal with what they charged was a continuing decline in family values. In addition, they hailed President Bush for his role in ending the Cold War and winning the Gulf War. However, the recession of the early 1990s continued, and economic issues dominated the campaign.

Independent candidate H. Ross Perot, a billionaire Texas businessman, entered the race out of frustration over government policies dealing with the budget and the economy. Perot ran as a Washington "outsider." He said that he had no ties to special interest groups and pledged that he would consider the needs of the country as a whole.

The Democrats nominated Arkansas governor Bill Clinton as their candidate. Clinton promised to end the recession and to deal with the nation's other

After meeting President Kennedy at age 17, Bill Clinton decided to pursue a career in politics. Like JFK, Clinton benefited from a media age campaign.

RESOURCE DIRECTORY

Teaching Resources
Guided Reading and Review booklet, p. 137

Technology
Section Reading Support Transparencies
Guided Reading Audiotapes (English/Spanish), Ch. 34
Student Edition on Audio CD, Ch. 34
Color Transparencies *Historical Maps,* A54
Prentice Hall Presentation Pro CD-ROM, Ch. 34
Companion Web site, www.phschool.com

nagging economic problems. He also pledged to address the federal budget deficit and the problems in the healthcare system.

Campaign Issues Like his hero, President Kennedy, Clinton believed that government was necessary "to make America work again." At the same time, he believed in the need to reduce the size of government to make it more efficient and responsive. Clinton believed he could reconcile both conservative and liberal views. He called himself a "New Democrat," in an effort to shed the traditional stereotype of the "tax-and-spend," big-government Democrat. Clinton's message appealed to Americans who were frustrated at the seemingly endless bickering between Democrats and Republicans in Congress.

Some critics charged that Clinton would say whatever was necessary—regardless of the truth—to win the election. When a woman claimed to have had an affair with Clinton, and produced evidence that seemed to support her story, Clinton denied her charges. In addition, Clinton's statements about how and why he had avoided the draft during the Vietnam War seemed untruthful to some.

Yet these issues of personal character were not strong enough to defeat the hard-working Clinton. His supporters praised his refusal to quit and began calling him the "comeback kid." That nickname also reminded voters that Clinton, at 46, was a full generation younger than the 68-year-old Bush.

On election day, Clinton received 43 percent of the votes, while Bush polled nearly 38 percent. Perot's strong showing of about 19 percent meant that Clinton became President with less than a majority of the popular vote. In the electoral college, Clinton won 370 votes versus 168 for Bush. Perot won no electoral votes.

VIEWING HISTORY Even before he ran for President, Bill Clinton had a reputation as a brilliant campaigner. Here, he greets a crowd of supporters during his successful 1992 presidential campaign. **Analyzing Visual Information** *How does this photo illustrate some of the challenges of campaigning for President?*

Clinton's First Term

Bill Clinton began his first term as President in January 1993. He recognized that the voters wanted a change from the politics of the recent past:

    ❝ *Thomas Jefferson believed that to preserve the very foundations of the nation we would need dramatic change from time to time. Well, my fellow Americans, this is our time. Let us embrace it. . . . Today we pledge an end to the era of deadlock and drift, and a new season of American renewal has begun.* ❞

           —Bill Clinton, First Inaugural Address

Clinton was buoyed by the fact that Democratic majorities existed in both the House and the Senate. For the first time in more than a decade, the executive and legislative branches would be in the hands of the same political party.

Economic Reform In dealing with the economy, Clinton tried to follow a middle course. He wanted to end the lingering recession by raising spending or cutting taxes. At the same time, he needed to reduce the budget deficit, which meant cutting spending or raising taxes.

Following this course proved more challenging than Clinton had anticipated. Congress did approve Clinton's first budget, but just barely. The House

Clinton's charisma and connection to popular culture broadened his appeal as a presidential candidate in 1992. During the campaign, Clinton used the slogan "It's the economy, stupid!" to suggest that he could address the nation's economic issues.

Sounds of an Era

Listen to a campaign speech by Bill Clinton emphasizing the economy and other sounds from recent years.

passed the measure by only two votes, and in the Senate, Vice President Gore had to break a 50-50 tie. To reduce the deficit, the budget included both spending cuts and tax increases. Neither action was well received by the public.

The Battle Over Healthcare When Clinton took office, an estimated 37 million Americans had no health insurance. For years, this number had been rising, as were the costs of healthcare. Many Americans were finding it increasingly difficult to afford medical care. Soon after taking office, Clinton appointed his wife Hillary to head a task force to analyze healthcare and propose reforms.

"This healthcare system of ours is badly broken, and it is time to fix it," Clinton declared to a national TV audience in September 1993. "We must make this our most urgent priority." The proposal he presented to Congress called for the creation of a government-supervised health insurance program that would guarantee affordable coverage to every American.

Although the public at first seemed to favor healthcare reform, Clinton's plea was vigorously opposed by a number of insurance, professional, and small-business groups. Congressional Republicans charged that the program would be expensive for taxpayers, and they attacked it as an example of big government. Democrats too disagreed on how far the program should go. The debate continued for about a year. In the end, Clinton's plan for healthcare reform failed to gain the necessary support in Congress.

The Republicans' Contract With America

The failure of his healthcare plan signaled trouble for the President. During the 1994 midterm elections, Georgia Representative Newt Gingrich called on Republican candidates to endorse what he called a **Contract with America.** This contract was a pledge to scale back the role of the federal government, eliminate some regulations, cut taxes, and balance the budget.

Many voters, feeling that the Democratic-controlled Congress had lost touch with their concerns, responded enthusiastically. In November 1994, voters

---

ACTIVITY
Student Portfolio

You may wish to have students add the following to their portfolios: Maya Angelou wrote and presented the poem "On the Pulse of Morning" at Bill Clinton's inauguration in 1993. Many people were reminded of Robert Frost's reading of his inaugural poem "The Gift Outright" 32 years before at the inauguration of John F. Kennedy. Help students find copies of both poems and ask them to write a brief essay that compares and contrasts them. What differences in attitude or philosophy between the two poets can they identify? How do they differ in their definitions of who is an American? How does each transcend American culture and convey universal themes?

From the Archives of
AmericanHeritage®

About the Presidents

For most of his career Bill Clinton (1992–2001) has been a remarkably successful politician. He successfully campaigned for the Arkansas governor's seat in 1978, becoming the nation's youngest governor in decades. Through much of the 1980s and early 1990s, he won repeated reelection to the office and became a national leader of the Democratic Party. He was elected twice to the presidency, breaking a 12-year Republican run in the office. Yet Clinton's career must also be seen in light of his losses. As a political apprentice, he fought on a number of failed campaigns, most notably that of George McGovern in 1972, and Clinton himself also suffered a stinging loss running for reelection after his first term as governor. In the second term of his presidency scandal engulfed Clinton and the White House, leaving his ultimate legacy in doubt. Source: Adapted from Henry F. Graff's *The Presidents,* Scribner's, 1996, by the editors of *American Heritage®* magazine.

COMPARING PRIMARY SOURCES
Regulating Health Maintenance Organizations (HMOs)

During the 1990s, many people debated whether stricter regulations should be placed on HMOs.
Analyzing Viewpoints What concerns do these two editorials raise regarding the regulation of HMOs?

Opposed to Stricter HMO Regulations
"Proponents of [greater regulation of HMOs] say their intention is only to improve a managed care system that's put too much emphasis on finances and not enough emphasis on patient care. . . . However, . . . HMOs have brought revolutionary changes to a health care system that had the exact opposite problem only a few decades ago—too little attention to finances and too much wasteful spending in order to pay for new buildings, equipment, and other dubious expenditures that led to double-digit cost increases."
—*Editorial,* Boston Business Journal, *April 10–16, 1998*

In Favor of Stricter HMO Regulations
"Market discipline of [HMOs] must include legal constraints that enforce remedies for broken contracts and civil injuries. Without the sanction of having to compensate the victims of their wrongdoing, HMOs will continue to cut their expenditures by withholding deserved treatment and paying their managers bonuses for actions that drive down the quality of care. Horror stories . . . will continue, and managed care will never achieve its fundamental purpose—to reduce cost without impairing the quality of care."
—*Editorial by Ronald F. Hoffman and Mark O. Heipler,* The Washington Post, *April 4, 1998*

1128 Chapter 34 • *Entering a New Era*

RESOURCE DIRECTORY

Teaching Resources
Biography, Literature, and Comparing Primary Sources booklet (Literature) *The Republican Revolution,* p. 89

Other Print Resources
Nystrom *Atlas of Our Country* *People on the Move,* pp. 34–35

■ **American History Block Scheduling Support** *Presidential Power: Changes in the Twentieth Century,* found in The Nation After World War II folder, includes interdisci-

plinary lesson suggestions and activities for Geography and History, Primary Sources, Biography, and Literature.

Technology
Sounds of an Era Audio CD *Bill Clinton's Democratic Nomination Acceptance Speech,* 1992 recording; *Anti-National Health Care Television Ad*
Exploring Primary Sources in U.S. History CD-ROM *On the Pulse of the Morning, Maya Angelou*

elected Republicans in large numbers, giving them majorities in both houses of Congress for the first time in more than four decades.

Congress Versus the President   The first-term Republicans quickly became a potent force in the House. For leadership they looked to Newt Gingrich, who was elected Speaker of the House. There was talk of a new era in American politics in which Congress, not the President, would set the nation's course.

The Republicans in Congress moved swiftly to keep the pledges they had made during the campaign. They demanded that the budget be balanced in seven years and proposed cuts in many social services. Recalling the achievements of the first 100 days of the New Deal in 1933, Gingrich demanded action on these items within the session's first 100 days. In most cases, approval was given.

Many of the bills approved by the House never became law, however. Some were rejected by the Senate, while others were vetoed by Clinton. Even so, Gingrich claimed that he had "changed the whole debate in American politics." That is, Americans were no longer debating whether to cut government and balance the budget, but rather how to do so.

The Government Is Shut Down   At the end of 1995, Clinton and Gingrich clashed over the size of budget cuts and the timetable for balancing the budget. When they were unable to compromise, budget allocations expired without reauthorization, leading to the temporary closure of government offices and the disruption of services to millions of Americans. Not until the spring of 1996 did Congress and the President come to an agreement on the budget.

The battle over the budget marked the start of yet another Clinton comeback. Many Americans blamed congressional Republicans for the government shutdown and began to regard them as uncompromising and extreme. By labeling proposed Republican spending cuts as mean-spirited and by presenting himself as one who could make needed reforms, Clinton raised his approval rating in national polls.

Welfare Reform   In August 1996, Congress and Clinton agreed on a sweeping reform of the nation's welfare system. Affected were 12.8 million people receiving Aid to Families with Dependent Children (AFDC). The new law eliminated federal guarantees of cash assistance and gave states authority to run their own welfare programs with block grants of federal money. It also established a lifetime limit of five years of aid per family and required most adults to work within two years of receiving aid. The historic policy change reversed six decades of social welfare legislation.

Clinton's Second Term

When the Republicans took control of Congress in 1995, Clinton's chances for reelection seemed slim. The Republican message appeared to have great appeal to voters. In the months that followed, Clinton worked hard to counter that message and to show that he was not a "tax-and-spend liberal."

The 1996 Election   The Republican nominee for President in 1996 was Bob Dole, Senate Majority Leader and a respected member of Congress for 35 years. Ross Perot again entered the race, this time as the nominee of the newly created Reform Party.

As the election approached, Clinton successfully maneuvered several popular bills through Congress, including one raising the minimum wage. In addition,

VIEWING HISTORY In an outdoor press conference, Newt Gingrich outlines the accomplishments of the Republicans' Contract with America. **Identifying Central Issues** *How did the Contract change the debate on cutting government spending?*

READING CHECK
What factors led to Clinton's reelection in 1996?

Focus on CULTURE

The Oklahoma City Bombing Just after 9 A.M., on April 19, 1995, a bomb exploded outside the Murrah Federal Building in Oklahoma City.

The wreckage from the 9-story building left mounds of rubble and debris. For nearly two weeks, rescue workers searched for trapped bodies. A horrified nation watched with sympathy and waited for some explanation. After the dust had settled, 168 people, 19 of them children from the building's day care center, were dead.

At first, many people suspected that the attack was carried out by a foreign terrorist, but soon investigators discovered that the terrorist came from the United States. The federal government charged Gulf War veteran Timothy McVeigh with the bombing. In 1997, McVeigh was found guilty and sentenced to die. His execution took place in June 2001. McVeigh's execution, however, was only a small part of the healing process for the families and friends of the victims, whose lives were forever changed after the explosion. The Oklahoma City National Memorial now stands as a lasting tribute to the victims and the memory of this devastating act of terrorism.

The Senate issued tickets for Bill Clinton's impeachment trial.

the economy, which had been an important factor in the 1992 campaign, had become strong. Again, the economy worked in Clinton's favor.

On election day, voters returned Clinton to office with 49 percent of the popular vote. Dole received 41 percent, while Perot dropped off to 8 percent. In the electoral college, Clinton gathered 379 votes to 159 for Dole.

Scandal and the Second Term Charges of scandal in Clinton's first term, which Bob Dole had emphasized in the 1996 campaign, continued into the new administration. In what came to be known as the **Whitewater affair,** Clinton was accused of having taken part in fraudulent loans and land deals in Arkansas years earlier and of having used his influence as then-governor to block an investigation of his business partners. Attorney General Janet Reno appointed a special prosecutor to look into these charges. As a result, some of Clinton's friends and former associates were convicted of various crimes and sentenced to prison. Yet no evidence was found to link the President to any wrongdoing.

Another charge made against Clinton, shortly after his reelection, was that he had accepted illegal campaign donations in return for political favors. A Senate committee found violations of campaign finance laws by members of both political parties, but Clinton was not directly linked to these violations.

Clinton Is Impeached Clinton's sixth year in office, 1998, began with good news: the government had achieved its first budget surplus since 1969. This bright moment was short-lived, however. Later that year, a scandal erupted that engulfed Clinton, leading to only the second impeachment of a President in the nation's history.

The crisis arose when the special prosecutor, Kenneth Starr, who had been looking into the Whitewater affair, began to investigate the relationship between Clinton and a young White House intern, Monica Lewinsky. Under oath in a separate sexual harassment lawsuit, Clinton had denied having sexual relations with the intern. He repeated this denial again to a grand jury convened by Starr in August. Eventually, Clinton admitted to having had an "inappropriate relationship" and to having "misled" his family and the country.

In September, Starr sent a report listing numerous grounds for impeachment to the House of Representatives. This report led to a bitterly partisan debate in the House and throughout the country. Polls showed that while most Americans criticized Clinton's actions, a majority believed that he was doing a good job as President and should not be impeached. On December 19, 1998, however, the full House voted to impeach Clinton on charges of perjury and obstruction of justice. Most Republicans voted yes; most Democrats voted no.

The Senate trial that followed opened on January 7, 1999. Many senators believed that Clinton had committed offenses, but debate centered on whether these offenses qualified as "high crimes and misdemeanors," the constitutional requirement for conviction of a President. On February 12, 1999, the Senate voted to acquit the President.

Support for Clinton throughout the process may have been bolstered by an unprecedented economic boom. The Clinton presidency marked the longest period of economic expansion in American history. As the economy continued to grow, the nation maintained low levels of unemployment and inflation.

The 2000 Election

The mixture of a strong economy and a scandal-ridden presidency promised a close presidential election in 2000. The nation's prosperity suggested that Vice President Gore, the Democrats' candidate, had a good chance of winning the election. However, some critics believed that he lacked the kind of strong personality that allowed Bill Clinton to rise above scandals and dominate the political center.

During the campaign, Republicans spoke of returning morality and respect to the White House. Leading up to the election, national polls showed that the Republican candidate, Texas Governor George W. Bush (son of former President Bush), was virtually tied with Vice President Gore. Polls also showed that many Americans were not enthusiastic about either candidate.

Much of the campaign debate focused on what the government should do with the federal budget surplus. Bush and the Republicans wanted to give much of this money back to the public in the form of a tax cut. Democrats argued that most of Bush's tax cut would only benefit the wealthiest portion of Americans, and that the surplus should instead be used to protect Social Security and pay down the national debt.

On election night, the votes in several states were too close to call; neither candidate had captured the 270 electoral votes needed to win the presidency. One undecided state, Florida, could give either candidate enough electoral votes to win the presidency. By state law a recount of the votes was required, due to the close results. Florida became a battleground for the presidency as lawyers, politicians, and the media swarmed there to monitor the recount.

Democrats and Republicans argued bitterly over how the recount should proceed. Charges were made on both sides that the recounts were not fair or accurate. For 36 days, the nation watched, waited, and argued as the two parties engaged in a variety of court battles.

Eventually, matters reached the U.S. Supreme Court in the case of *Bush v. Gore*. Like the nation, the nine justices were sharply divided about how to remedy the election crisis. By a majority of five to four, they issued a ruling that discontinued all recounts in Florida. This ruling effectively secured the presidency for George W. Bush. Although Gore won the national popular vote, Bush won 271 electoral votes to Gore's 266.

The George W. Bush Administration

After being sworn in as President in January 2001, George W. Bush faced many challenges. From the outset, he conducted the presidency in a much different style than that of his predecessor.

Change in Presidential Style Analysts described Bush's approach to the presidency as corporate in contrast to Clinton's more laid-back style. Unlike

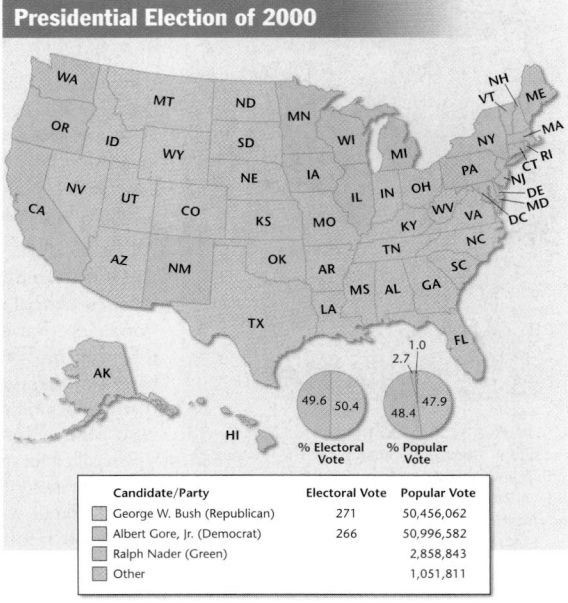

Presidential Election of 2000

Candidate/Party	Electoral Vote	Popular Vote
George W. Bush (Republican)	271	50,456,062
Albert Gore, Jr. (Democrat)	266	50,996,582
Ralph Nader (Green)		2,858,843
Other		1,051,811

MAP SKILLS The 2000 election was the fourth time in history that the person winning the popular vote failed to win the presidency. **Regions** Which region(s) in the United States generally supported the Vice President?

VIEWING HISTORY Election workers in Florida examined ballots to determine voter intentions during the recount that followed the close 2000 election. **Predicting Consequences** How might the election disputes affect voting practices in the future?

Chapter 34 • Section 1   **1131**

VIEWING HISTORY The new President, George W. Bush, walks with his wife Laura on Inauguration Day in 2001. **Synthesizing Information** *(a) What challenges did Bush face upon entering office? (b) What was his approach to these challenges?*

Clinton, Bush was a stickler about being on time to meetings and wearing business clothing in the White House. He kept a strict schedule and preferred to wake up early and leave the office at the end of the workday. Clinton, on the other hand, had often worked long into the night but kept a more casual atmosphere in the White House.

Bush also delegated more responsibility to advisors and staff members. Rather than focus on the tiny details of his administration's policies, Bush preferred to take a broader view, acting as a manager for his Cabinet. In addition, he gave his Vice President, Dick Cheney of Wyoming, an unprecedented role in setting policy.

Bush on Domestic Policy Early in his presidency, Bush focused on a few central issues. In particular, he succeeded in gaining congressional approval of a tax cut based on his campaign proposal. Under this plan, most taxpayers received rebates of $300. Bush argued that by returning money to the taxpayers, he would jumpstart an economy that was beginning to falter.

Bush also pushed for the passage of a major education reform bill. The President's plan called for increased accountability for student performance, flexible funding at the state and local levels, and targeted funds for improving schools and teacher quality through research-based programs and practices. It also proposed to give parents more information about the quality of their children's schools.

Attack on America

On September 11, 2001, Americans reacted with horror when terrorists struck at targets in New York City and Washington, D.C. Using hijacked commercial airplanes as their weapons, the terrorists crashed into both towers of New York's World Trade Center and plowed into part of the Pentagon. A fourth plane crashed in a field near Pittsburgh, Pennsylvania. A total of 266 passengers and crew on the four planes lost their lives.

The attack on the Pentagon took place less than an hour after the first plane hit New York. Damage was contained to a recently renovated section of the building, but fires raged for hours, preventing emergency workers from entering the wreckage. More than 100 people working in the Pentagon were killed.

In New York, the impact of the fully fueled jets caused both towers to burst into flames. Debris rained down on employees evacuating the buildings and on emergency workers rushing to respond to the scene. The fires led to the catastrophic collapse of both 110-story buildings. The fallen structures in turn caused serious damage to other buildings in the World Trade Center complex and the surrounding area. More than 5,000 people were missing after the assault and were presumed dead.

Following the attacks, the Federal Aviation Administration ordered a nationwide "ground stop." This action halted all takeoffs and required airborne planes to land as quickly as possible. Many incoming international flights were diverted to Canada.

On the ground in New York, emergency workers battled fires and began a search-and-rescue operation. Tragically, the speedy response to the disaster had led to the deaths of hundreds of firefighters and police officers who were in and around the buildings when they collapsed.

While no groups or individuals claimed responsibility for the attacks, law-enforcement officials immediately began an investigation into those suspected of carrying out the assaults and the network that supported them. Countries around the world pledged their support in the efforts to hunt down the criminals.

In a speech to the nation, President Bush declared, "Whether we bring our enemies to justice or bring justice to our enemies, justice will be done." Bush also named a new Cabinet-level Office of Homeland Security, to be headed by Pennsylvania Governor Tom Ridge.

Within days of the attack, government officials named Saudi dissident Osama bin Laden as "a prime suspect" for masterminding the plot. Bin Laden had been implicated in a series of earlier attacks on U.S. targets, including the U.S. embassies in Kenya and Tanzania and the American ship the USS *Cole*. Bin Laden was believed to be hiding in Afghanistan under the protection of the Taliban, a religious fundamentalist group that ruled Afghanistan. The United States demanded that the Taliban shut down terrorist training camps and turn over bin Laden and other terrorist leaders. The Taliban refused to meet these demands, and as a result, President Bush vowed that they would "pay a price."

On October 7, the United States, along with Great Britain, launched a bombing campaign known as "Operation Enduring Freedom" on Taliban military and communications bases. At the same time, U.S. planes also dropped humanitarian packages of food and supplies for starving Afghan civilians. President Bush made it clear that these bombings were only the beginning of a relentless pursuit to rid the world of terrorism and those who support it.

On the homefront, Americans responded to the tragedy with an outpouring of support for the victims, their families, and the rescue workers at all three sites. Many gave blood or donated money and supplies to relief agencies. The country stood united in its grief, with millions attending vigils and services for the victims. As American citizens struggled to make sense of the terrible events and mourned the losses, a new sense of patriotism and unity swept the nation. Suddenly, American flags appeared on homes, cars, businesses, and public spaces—a symbol of the nation's determination to seek justice, uphold American values, and emerge from adversity strengthened and whole.

Rescue workers proudly raise the American flag amidst the rubble of the fallen World Trade Center towers.

Reading Comprehension

1. He promised to end the recession and deal with other economic problems, including the federal budget deficit and a health care system in disarray. Campaigning as a "New Democrat," Clinton appealed to Americans who were frustrated by partisan disagreements in Congress. His youth and energy appealed to voters.

2. A pledge to reduce the role of the federal government, eliminate some regulations, cut taxes, and balance the budget.

3. These scandals did not seem to deter Clinton. His popularity remained high, possibly due in part to the economic boom.

4. Bush's style was more formal and "by the books" than Clinton's laid-back manner. Bush delegated more responsibility to advisors and staff members than Clinton had. Bush also gave his Vice President an unprecedented role in setting policy.

5. He appointed Governor Tom Ridge to head a new Cabinet-level Office of Homeland Security. After giving Taliban leaders the chance to shut down terrorist training camps and turn over terrorists leaders, including bin Laden, to no avail, Bush launched Operation Enduring Freedom.

Critical Thinking and Writing

6. The two parties generally differed on economic issues: balancing the budget, where to cut spending, and the size of government, as well as on the issue of impeachment. Answers describing reasons for the existing bitterness will vary, but should refer to the parties' respective histories, as well as the events of the 1990s.

7. Answers will vary, but should be supported by facts from the section.

Section 1   Assessment

READING COMPREHENSION

1. Why did many American voters support Clinton in 1992?

2. What was the Republicans' **Contract with America?**

3. How did scandals such as the **Whitewater affair** and impeachment affect Clinton's presidency?

4. How did the presidential styles of Bill Clinton and George W. Bush differ?

5. What actions did President Bush take following a terrorist attack on America?

CRITICAL THINKING AND WRITING

6. **Recognizing Ideologies** Democrats and Republicans had many bitter confrontations and much partisan debate throughout the 1990s. On what issues did they differ? Why do you think there was a high level of bitterness between the two parties?

7. **Writing a Letter to the Editor** Write a letter to your local newspaper explaining why you think the results of the 2000 election were controversial. Suggest ideas about how to avoid this situation in the future.

 Take It to the NET

Activity: Creating a Bar Graph
The economy played a key role in American politics during the 1990s. Research an economic variable, such as the unemployment rate, and plot its performance over the past five years. Use the links provided in the *America: Pathways to the Present* area of the following Web site for help in completing this activity.
www.phschool.com

Chapter 34 • Section 1   1133

 **Take It to the NET**

Answers will vary, but should effectively use either a bar graph or a line graph to track the changes in an economic variable such as unemployment, national income, or government budget.

Predicting Consequences

Predicting consequences means studying what has happened in the past, and using this knowledge to try to forecast what might happen in the future. Social
scientists use this skill to predict trends. They study data from the census and other statistical sources and then relate patterns in the data to historical events. For example, what has the rate of population growth been over recent decades? What does this suggest about the rate of population growth in the next few years? What events have affected this growth? Which groups are likely to grow faster and which groups are likely to grow more slowly? The table at right answers some of these questions.

Change in Number of Families and Median Income,* by Selected Ethnic Groups, 1980–1995

	Year	Number of Families (in thousands)	Percent Change (from preceding census)	Median Income (in dollars)	Percent Change (from preceding census)
White Families	1980	52,710	—	40,561	—
	1990	56,803	+7.8	43,044	+6.1
	1995	58,872	+3.6	42,646	−1.0
African American Families	1980	6,317	—	23,469	—
	1990	7,471	+18.3	24,980	+6.4
	1995	8,055	+7.8	25,970	+4.0
Latino Families	1980	3,235	—	27,251	—
	1990	4,981	+54.0	27,321	+0.3
	1995	6,287	+26.2	24,570	−10.0

* In 1995 dollars. Median income represents the center of the income distribution—exactly half of the families in the group earn more and half earn less than the median income.

SOURCE: *Statistical Abstract of the United States*

LEARN THE SKILL

Use the following steps to predict consequences from a table:

1. **Identify the kinds of information in the table.** Determine what is being measured by the data in the table. Note the time span of the table and the time intervals it shows.

2. **Analyze the rate of change.** Compare the rate, or percent, of change of different ethnic groups at different time periods.

3. **Use your knowledge of history and the trends you have noted in the data to predict future trends.** Determine whether some of the changes and trends you have found in the data were the consequences of particular historical events. In this case, consider the Immigration Act of 1965, which allowed more people from places other than Europe to immigrate to the United States, and the Immigration Act of 1990, which further increased immigration quotas by 40 percent.

APPLY THE SKILL

See the Chapter Review and Assessment for another opportunity to apply this skill.

PRACTICE THE SKILL

Answer the following questions:

1. **(a)** What does this table tell you about the number of families in various ethnic groups in the United States? **(b)** What periods of time does the table cover? **(c)** By what percentage did the number of Latino families increase between 1990 and 1995? **(d)** What does it mean if one group has a lower median income than another group?

2. **(a)** Which group of families is growing at the fastest rate? **(b)** Which group's median income has grown at the fastest rate? **(c)** Which group seems the most economically vulnerable—that is, which has the least stable median income?

3. **(a)** How might the table illustrate the effects of the 1965 law? **(b)** What consequences might the 1990 law have by the year 2010? **(c)** If an economic recession began early in the twenty-first century, which group's median income would you expect to drop the most? **(d)** What changes in the trends shown on the table would have to take place in order to alter your predictions?

PREDICTING CONSEQUENCES

Focus Students will use the statistics in a table to predict patterns of population growth and median income for three ethnic groups.

Instruct Have students examine the title and headings in the table. Make sure that they understand what the numbers in the Percent Change columns mean. Explain, for example, that the percentage in the 1995 row covers the period from 1990 to 1995. Ask students to compare the percentages for the three ethnic groups and to note any differences among them.

Extend See the Skills for Life Activity in the Resource Directory below.

ANSWERS

PRACTICE THE SKILL

1. **(a)** It tells the changes in population and in income over time. **(b)** 1980–1995. **(c)** 26.2. **(d)** More than half the families in that group earn less than the median income for the other group.

2. **(a)** Latinos. **(b)** African Americans. **(c)** Latinos.

3. **(a)** The rapid increase in the number of Latino families between 1980 and 1995 reflects the continuing rise in the number of immigrants coming from Latin America after 1965. **(b)** The number of Latino families in the United States is likely to grow at a much faster rate than the number of white or African American families. **(c)** Latino families. **(d)** Sample answer: If the number of Latino families dropped significantly or if the Latino median income stabilized.

RESOURCE DIRECTORY

Teaching Resources
Skills for Life booklet, p. 36

Technology
Social Studies Skills Tutor CD-ROM
Interactive Practice in
• Geographic Literacy
• Critical Thinking and Reading
• Visual Analysis
• Communications

Section 2 — The United States in a New World

Section 2 — The United States in a New World

READING FOCUS

- What political changes took place in the world in the 1990s?
- How did the Clinton administration promote peace abroad?
- Describe U.S. relations with China.
- What was the impact of an expanding global economy?

MAIN IDEA

The United States faced new challenges in the post–Cold War world, including the collapse of communism, increased ethnic tensions in several countries, and the expansion of the global economy.

KEY TERMS

apartheid
economic sanctions
North American Free Trade Agreement (NAFTA)
World Trade Organization (WTO)
multinational corporation

TAKING NOTES

As you read, complete this chart showing the role of the United States in events around the world.

Nation or Region	U.S. Role
Iraq	As part of the United Nations, continued attempts to promote peace in the region. Launched air strikes, implemented economic sanctions, sent inspectors to ensure Iraq's dangerous weapons were destroyed.
Israel	
The Balkans	
China	
North America	

Setting the Scene

Witnessing the collapse of communism in the Soviet Union and Eastern Europe, President George H. W. Bush had spoken hopefully of the dawn of a "New World Order" in 1990. By this he had meant a more stable and peaceful world in which "the strong respect the rights of the weak." Many people believed, however, that the world was becoming less stable. While some nations had thrown off repressive governments and become more democratic, others were being torn apart by racial, cultural, or religious tensions. A few observers joked grimly of a "New World Disorder."

Political Changes Worldwide

In the 1980s, communism in the Soviet Union and racial oppression in South Africa had seemed like permanent world problems. For decades they had helped shape American foreign policy. By the late 1990s, however, revolutionary events had changed conditions in these and other nations.

Russia and Eastern Europe As the old Soviet empire crumbled, the United States tried to promote the move toward Western-style democracy in the former Soviet republics. For example, it applauded the election that brought Boris Yeltsin to power as president of Russia.

To help Russia create a free market economy, the international community offered billions in aid, but it was far from enough. Goods remained in short supply and the Russian economy remained unstable. In the fall of 1993, the Russian parliament resisted reforms that Yeltsin argued were necessary. In response, he dissolved the parliament and tightened censorship in a bid to silence his political opponents.

Russian reformers, angry at these curbs on freedom, soon grew angrier. In 1994, Yeltsin ordered troops into Chechnya, a republic that sought independence from Russia. After nearly two years of

VIEWING HISTORY The Russian president, Boris Yeltsin, addresses a crowd in 1993. **Identifying Central Issues** How did Russia change after the Cold War?

SECTION OBJECTIVES

1. Read about political changes that took place in the world in the 1990s.
2. Find out how the Clinton administration promoted peace abroad.
3. Describe U.S. relations with China.
4. Discover the impact of an expanding global economy.

BELLRINGER

Warm-Up Activity Ask students what countries they have heard about in the news in the last few weeks. What problems are making news? Do they involve the United States? What is the responsibility of the United States to those countries?

Activating Prior Knowledge Ask students to state their opinions about the responsibility of the United States to become engaged in international struggles. In their opinion, what constitutes a situation that demands a direct military response from the United States?

READING STRATEGY

Before students read the section, have them sketch a rough outline map of the world. As they read, have them highlight areas of United States involvement and write a brief note explaining the region's connection to the United States. Have them describe the dynamic relationship between U.S. international trade policies and the U.S. free enterprise system.

CAPTION ANSWERS

Viewing History Russia began a move toward Western-style democracy. However, continuing economic problems (despite American aid) created unrest.

RESOURCE DIRECTORY

Teaching Resources
Learning Styles Lesson Plans booklet, p. 70
Guided Reading and Review booklet, p. 138

Other Print Resources
Historical Outline Map Book *The World,* p. 71

Technology
Section Reading Support Transparencies
Guided Reading Audiotapes (English/Spanish), Ch. 34

Student Edition on Audio CD, Ch. 34
Prentice Hall Presentation Pro CD-ROM, Ch. 34
Companion Web site, www.phschool.com

Focus Explain that for 50 years American foreign policy had been based on Cold War philosophy. Now the nation had to find new ways of dealing with many nations around the world. Ask students how this "new world" offered both hopes and challenges.

Instruct Explain that Americans have a long history of ambivalence about involvement in foreign affairs. Ask students if world events have made such a stand impossible today. How does an isolationist stance affect policies and positions on trade? Discuss the position of the United States as the world's remaining superpower. What are the responsibilities of that position?

Assess/Reteach Ask students to consider the kinds of changes that have resulted from political shifts, an increase in ethnic tensions, a rise in worldwide terrorism, and an increasing emphasis on a global economy.

READING CHECK

The war in Chechnya damaged Boris Yeltsin's political standing. However, a renewal of hostilities in the same region increased the popularity of Vladimir Putin (Yeltsin's successor).

---

fierce fighting, a cease-fire was finally reached, and the Russian troops were withdrawn. With an already ailing economy, charges of government corruption, and thousands of people killed in Chechnya, Yeltsin lost much of his public support.

In 1999, the conflict over Chechnya became the source of great public support for Vladimir Putin, whom Yeltsin had appointed Russia's prime minister. A series of Chechen terrorist attacks in Russia that year prompted Putin to order air raids and a full-scale ground invasion against Chechnya. This act was widely popular in Russia, and political parties that were allied with Putin performed well in that year's parliamentary elections. Yeltsin, in poor health, resigned his post at the end of the year, making Putin the acting president of Russia. In the next presidential election, Russian voters officially elected Putin their new president.

Political changes also continued to occur in Eastern Europe. In the early 1990s, Poland, led by Solidarity hero Lech Walesa, had undertaken bold economic reforms to create a free market. Economic progress was initially slow and many people quickly grew concerned. In 1995, Polish voters elected Aleksander Kwasniewski as president. Despite his Communist background, Kwasniewski continued to push for a free market economy. Eventually the economy began to rebound.

In a clear sign that there was no returning to the past, Poland, Hungary, and the Czech Republic all joined NATO in 1999. NATO held out hope of membership to other former Communist nations in the region if they continued to make progress toward democracy.

F. W. de Klerk and Nelson Mandela shared the 1993 Nobel peace prize for their work in ending apartheid.

South Africa As stunning as the collapse of communism was South Africa's rejection of **apartheid,** the systematic separation of people of different racial backgrounds. South Africa's white minority, which made up only about 15 percent of the population, had long denied equal rights to the black majority. To encourage reform, the United States and other nations had used **economic sanctions,** or trade restrictions and economic measures intended to punish another nation. Finally, in 1990, Prime Minister F. W. de Klerk released anti-apartheid leader Nelson Mandela from jail. Mandela had been held prisoner for 27 years.

Former rivals de Klerk and Mandela worked together to end apartheid. In 1994, South Africa held its first elections in which blacks as well as whites voted. These elections produced a new government, led by a new president, Nelson Mandela, and his anti-apartheid organization, the African National Congress (ANC). Despite fears of civil war, South Africa made a peaceful transition to black majority rule.

From 1996 to 1998, a government-appointed Truth and Reconciliation Commission investigated the brutal crimes of the apartheid era. Its final report, published in 1998, won international praise for addressing wrongdoings on both sides and for continuing the nation's move toward peace.

The Difficult Search for Peace

For the United States, promoting the spread of democracy to new areas was a satisfying challenge. Far less satisfying was the task of trying to stop the terrifying violence that erupted in several different regions of the world. President Clinton had to balance Americans' desire to promote peace with their fear of costly commitments—a fear magnified by memories of the Vietnam War.

One conflict in Africa demonstrated how hard it was to maintain this balance. In the early 1990s, the East African nation of Somalia suffered from a devastating famine, made worse by a civil war. President Bush sent American

---

RESOURCE DIRECTORY

Other Print Resources

■ **American History Block Scheduling Support** *The End of the Cold War,* found in The Nation After World War II folder, includes interdisciplinary lesson suggestions and activities for Geography and History, Primary Sources, Biography, and Literature.

Historical Outline Map Book *Africa,* p. 74; *Europe,* p. 77; *The Middle East,* p. 78

troops to Somalia in 1992 to assist a United Nations (UN) relief effort. The food crisis eased, but Somalia's government remained unable to control the armed groups that ruled the countryside. The following year, after more than a dozen United States soldiers were killed in a battle with Somali rebels, President Clinton recalled the troops without having restored order.

Israel   In September 1993, Palestine Liberation Organization (PLO) leader Yasir Arafat and Israeli Prime Minister Yitzhak Rabin signed a historic peace agreement in Washington, D.C. It was an extremely difficult step for both sides. However, as Rabin noted, "Peace is not made with friends. Peace is made with enemies."

The pact provided for Palestinian self-rule in the Gaza Strip (between Israel and the Sinai Peninsula) and in the town of Jericho on the West Bank of the Jordan River. The agreement also set the stage for talks on the status of the rest of the West Bank. Israel had seized these areas in the Six-Day War of 1967. Also in the agreement, the PLO formally recognized Israel's right to exist.

The Middle East peace process had other successes. In 1994, Israel and Jordan signed a treaty ending the state of war that had existed between them. Israel and Syria began talks as well.

Extremists on both sides, meanwhile, tried to destroy the prospects for peace by committing terrorist attacks. In 1995, a Jewish extremist assassinated Prime Minister Rabin.

Benjamin Netanyahu, Israel's next elected prime minister, was more reluctant than Rabin to grant concessions to the Palestinians. Progress toward a peace agreement slowed. In 1999, though, Ehud Barak became prime minister and called for a new commitment to peace talks. The following year, President Clinton invited Barak and Arafat to Camp David in an effort to settle the issues that still divided them. While the two sides had made tremendous progress since their 1993 agreement, they were unable to solve all the remaining issues, such as control of the holy city of Jerusalem.

Hopes for peace then faded rapidly. Violence increased, and Ariel Sharon—a fierce critic of the concessions Israel had made in the search for peace—became Israeli prime minister after a landslide victory over Barak. Violence continued in 2001 as the new Bush administration worked on other ways to keep the peace process alive.

The Balkans   The United States played a key role in the peacekeeping process elsewhere as well. One place where peace seemed especially difficult to achieve was Yugoslavia, a nation of several distinct ethnic and religious groups.

Tensions among these groups had remained below the surface for several decades, while a Communist government ruled Yugoslavia. With the collapse of communism, however, these underlying problems erupted, resulting in violent conflict.

Some of the Yugoslav republics, like Bosnia and Croatia, wanted to become independent nations. The republic of Serbia—and its leader, Slobodan Milosevic—wanted to preserve a unified Yugoslavia, dominated by Serbia. A minority of the Bosnians were ethnic Serbs; they, too, opposed independence for Bosnia. Thus, when Bosnia declared its independence in 1991, the Bosnian Serbs took military action. Backed by Serbia, the Bosnian Serbs began a siege of Sarajevo, Bosnia's major city, and carried on a ferocious "ethnic cleansing" campaign to remove

President Clinton presided over the signing of the 1993 peace accord between Israel's Yitzhak Rabin (left) and the PLO's Yasir Arafat (right).

READING CHECK
Why did it seem that peace-keeping in the former Yugoslavia would be especially difficult?

ACTIVITY
Connecting with Geography
Ask students to suppose that they are foreign correspondents for radio or television news. Divide students into groups and assign (or let students choose) one of the regions mentioned in the section. Each group should research recent newspaper and magazine articles about events in its region, then prepare a report to broadcast back to the United States, explaining the situation there. **(Verbal/Linguistic)**

BACKGROUND
A Diverse Nation
"[Africa is] where we came from, it's where civilization started. How can we turn our backs on it?" said George Curry, editor of the African American magazine *Emerge*. He spoke for many African Americans for whom South African history has been painfully relevant. One South African who attracted worldwide admiration was Nelson Mandela (b. 1918). Despite years of imprisonment under apartheid, Mandela emerged as a consummate peacemaker. For working to end apartheid, he shared the 1993 Nobel peace prize with white South African leader F. W. de Klerk. In 1994 Mandela became South Africa's President after a landslide victory in its first democratic, all-race election.

READING CHECK
Ethnic and religious tensions had deep roots. Serbia resisted demands for self-rule in Bosnia, Croatia, and Kosovo. Peacekeeping was further hampered by the vicious nature of the fighting.

☑ **TEST PREPARATION**
Have students read the section "South Africa" and then answer the question below.

What was one of the results of South Africa's rejection of apartheid?

A   Civil war broke out.

B   A dictator was installed.

C   Riots broke out, spreading to all major cities.

D   There was a peaceful transition of power.

MAP SKILLS This map shows the regions of Bosnia and Herzegovina controlled by various groups. At right, U.S. soldiers patrol the village of Curenica in Kosovo, as part of a NATO peacekeeping operation. **Regions** *How does the map demonstrate the problems facing the former Yugoslavia?*

non-Serbs from the republic. Millions were forced to flee their homes, and more than 200,000 people were killed in the most brutal violence seen in Europe since World War II.

When Clinton campaigned for President in 1992, he had promised to take strong action in Bosnia. Once in office, however, he hesitated, partly because America's European allies resisted the use of force. Finally, in mid-1995, an American-led NATO bombing campaign pushed the Bosnian Serbs into peace talks. These talks, held in Dayton, Ohio, produced a cease-fire and the commitment to allow foreign peacekeeping troops, including thousands of U.S. troops.

Although these steps toward peace had been taken, none of the underlying problems had gone away. New troubles began in Kosovo, another part of the former Yugoslavia. As in Bosnia, the majority population of Kosovo was not Serbian. Most people living there were ethnic Albanians, and they wanted more self-rule. That demand led to another brutal round of violence, this time between Serbs and ethnic Albanians.

Thousands of ethnic Albanian refugees fled Kosovo in 1998 as the fighting spread. For a time the Kosovo Liberation Army managed to occupy nearly half of Kosovo. The Serbs then took control and began a violent campaign closely resembling their actions in Bosnia.

In 1999, the United States and NATO threatened airstrikes if both sides would not commit to a peace conference. The Kosovar Albanians agreed but the Serbs did not. Acting on its threat, NATO launched a series of airstrikes against Serbia, which forced Serbian leader Milosevic to allow an international peacekeeping force to enter Kosovo. The Albanian refugees were able to return home.

Meanwhile, Serbian opposition to Milosevic was growing. In 2000, voters overwhelmingly rejected Milosevic and declared Vojislav Kostunica their new leader. When Milosevic refused to accept the election results, many Serbs organized a revolt and forced him from power. Reaction around the world was generally positive. Not only Western nations, but also Russia (which had backed Milosevic) welcomed Kostunica as Yugoslavia's new leader. The next year, Milosevic was indicted by an international tribunal for war crimes and taken to the Netherlands to stand trial.

Northern Ireland In Northern Ireland, the United States encouraged renewed efforts in the 1990s to end decades of violence between Protestants and Catholics. In 1996, President Clinton asked former U.S. Senator George Mitchell to lead talks that included representatives of the warring factions and the British and Irish governments.

After months of tense negotiations, Mitchell's efforts paid off. In 1998, all major parties to the peace process signed the Good Friday Accords, agreeing to major reforms in the government of the British province. By large majorities, voters in both Northern Ireland and Ireland later approved the agreement. It stopped short of unifying the two Irelands, which Catholics had desired. Still, it offered the best hope yet for ending the violence.

Iraq After the Gulf War   Despite Iraq's defeat in the Persian Gulf War, Iraqi leader Sadaam Hussein continued to oppress opposition groups within the country. He also refused to cooperate fully with UN inspectors sent to Iraq to ensure that the nation destroyed its most dangerous weapons.

President Clinton called for a new government in Iraq, one "committed to peace." UN forces launched several missile and aircraft attacks on Iraq in the 1990s. The United Nations also maintained the economic sanctions it had imposed on Iraq after Iraq's invasion of Kuwait. Over time, however, support for these sanctions began to weaken. By cutting off most of Iraq's trade, it was feared, the sanctions hurt the Iraqi people far more than the Iraqi government. To help deal with this problem, the United Nations set up an "oil-for-food" program, in which Iraq could export small amounts of oil in exchange for food and materials that would help them to grow food. Still, a decade after the Persian Gulf War, UN and U.S. officials were not convinced that any real progress had been made toward a free and peaceful Iraq.

Afghanistan   Afghanistan became a focal point for the United States after the Soviet invasion of that nation in 1979. The Soviets, located on the Afghan border, considered internal agitation there a threat to their own security. The United States responded by boycotting the 1980 Olympic Games in Moscow and withdrawing the SALT II arms control treaty from the American Senate. The campaign proved unsuccessful, and eventually the Soviet Union withdrew. In 1996, a group of Muslim fundamentalists, called the Taliban, seized the Afghan capital of Kabul from the ruling pro-Soviet government. The Taliban sought to set up what their leaders considered a pure Islamic state, banning such things as television and music. The Taliban also provided sanctuary for Osama bin Laden, the wealthy Saudi Arabian businessman exiled from his own country and implicated in the terrorist bombings of September 11, 2001.

Relations With China

While the United States attempted to help the peace process within other nations, it also sought to remain on peaceful terms with China. China's economic growth, combined with its size, made it an increasingly important power in the 1990s. As a result, the United States began working more closely with China on various issues, including trade and regional security. However, underlying tensions between the two nations remained just below the surface.

Probably the greatest source of tension was the issue of Taiwan. China viewed Taiwan as part of China and refused to rule out the use of force to gain control of the island. In particular, China warned Taiwan not to declare its independence from the mainland. The United States, on the other hand, was a major supplier of weapons to Taiwan and opposed any military action by China against Taiwan.

In 1996, as Taiwan was preparing for elections, China held missile tests and military exercises in an effort to frighten Taiwanese voters away from supporting a pro-independence candidate. President Clinton responded by sending warships to the area to show the commitment of the United States to Taiwan. Relations continued to sour in 1999 when NATO warplanes mistakenly bombed the Chinese embassy in Belgrade during its airstrikes on Yugoslavia.

Relations improved later that year, when the United States and China worked on ways to expand China's trade

VIEWING HISTORY In April 1999, the United States and China agreed to expand commercial air service between the two nations. Here, Secretary of State Madeleine Albright shakes hands with Chinese Foreign Minister Tang Jiaxuan after signing the agreement. **Drawing Conclusions** *Why was the United States interested in expanding trade with China?*

Connecting with Economics

Have students learn more about the eurodollar. Tell students to find newspaper and magazine articles describing European reaction to the euro. Which countries easily accepted the euro and which resisted it? What does a country's response to the eurodollar say about its self-image, its economy, and its willingness to join the European Union? **(Logical/Mathematical)**

BACKGROUND

Trade Blocs

NAFTA is not the only trade bloc in the Western Hemisphere. The Caribbean region has the Association of Caribbean States (ACS), while Argentina's Carlos Menem has worked to create Mercosur, the Southern Common Market, with Argentina's neighbors Brazil, Paraguay, and Uruguay. In the Pacific, ASEAN (Association of Southeast Asian Nations) is emerging as an economic bloc.

READING CHECK

The EEC was established in 1957 to foster trade and economic development. The evolution of this entity into the European Union was an effort to create a European system to coordinate political, monetary, and economic issues.

President George W. Bush consults with National Security Advisor Condoleezza Rice in the Oval Office of the White House.

READING CHECK

Why did some European nations want to form the European Union?

with other nations. In 2000, President Clinton signed the U.S.-China Relations Act. This act was designed to encourage trade between the two nations by keeping U.S. tariffs on Chinese imports low.

Tensions grew again, however, in April 2001 when a U.S. spy plane and a Chinese fighter plane collided off the coast of China. The incident led to a standoff between the two governments, leaving relations between them strained. The new Bush administration stated, moreover, that the United States would defend Taiwan from military attacks by China, a policy that previous Presidents had not declared openly. China, in turn, warned the United States against sales of advanced weapons to Taiwan.

Trade and the Global Economy

Despite the many political developments of the mid- and late 1990s, the most important development in global terms may have been economic: the continuing growth of world trade. The United States was active in promoting this trend.

The European Union In 1957, six European nations had set up the European Economic Community (EEC) to coordinate their economic and trade policies. Over time, other nations had joined them. Meanwhile, member nations agreed to move toward dismantling the tariffs on one another's exports, thereby creating a single market.

In 1993, the EEC nations formed the European Union (EU) to begin coordinating their political and monetary policies as well. The EU, now with more than a dozen members, has a parliament and a council in which all member nations are represented. In the late 1990s, member nations agreed to replace their individual monetary systems gradually with a single new currency called the eurodollar, or euro.

The EU's goal is to create a European economic unit that rivals the size and strength of the American economy. The United States has generally supported Europe's progress toward economic cooperation. As a Clinton administration official stated, "Close partnership between the United States and the European Union is essential to our common agenda of democratic renewal." Today, the EU's largest trading partner is the United States.

NAFTA Meanwhile, the United States sought to encourage greater economic cooperation within the Western Hemisphere. Many economists believed that free

RESOURCE DIRECTORY

Teaching Resources
Biography, Literature, and Comparing Primary Sources booklet (Biography) *Ron Brown*, p. 39
Great Debates booklet (Great Debates) *Building an International Manned Space Station*, p. 48

Other Print Resources
Historical Outline Map Book *Western Hemisphere*, p. 72; *North America*, p. 79

trade would benefit the economy by encouraging foreign investment, reducing prices, raising exports, and improving living standards. In 1992, the United States, Canada, and Mexico signed the **North American Free Trade Agreement (NAFTA),** which called for a gradual removal of trade restrictions among the three nations. NAFTA's main purpose was to stimulate economic growth. The resulting free trade zone created a single market similar to the market of the European Union.

NAFTA aroused tremendous controversy in the United States. Its opponents worried that American factories would move to Mexico, where wages were lower and government regulations (such as environmental controls) were less strict. Its supporters claimed that it would instead create more American jobs by increasing exports to Mexico and Canada.

The U.S. Senate ratified NAFTA, but only after a bruising battle. After NAFTA had been in effect for several years, the government's first study of the agreement revealed it to be only a limited success. The report cited a "modest" increase in United States exports to Mexico and estimated that perhaps 90,000 to 160,000 new, NAFTA-related jobs had been created. Some 128,000 American jobs had disappeared, however. Even with these mixed results, President Clinton and others continued their efforts to expand NAFTA to include other countries in the Western Hemisphere.

GATT and the WTO Clinton's support for NAFTA reflected his foreign policy goal of expanding United States trade throughout the world. As part of this effort, the United States joined many other countries in adopting a revised version of the General Agreement on Tariffs and Trade (GATT) in 1994. The goal of GATT, originally established in 1948, was to reduce tariffs and expand world trade. In 1995, the **World Trade Organization (WTO)** was established to ensure that countries complied with GATT, as well as to negotiate new trade agreements and resolve trade disputes.

The reaction to the WTO was similar to the reaction to NAFTA. Many people supported these efforts to expand world trade, but resistance to these efforts was growing. In late 1999, anti-WTO demonstrators gathered from around the world in Seattle, where the WTO was meeting to plan a new round

Focus on ECONOMICS

Tariffs *Taxes on foreign goods imported into a country.*

The Historical Context In the 1980s and 1990s, a number of governments worked together to reduce tariffs in the hope that expanded trade would stimulate economic growth. These efforts resulted in regional trade agreements, such as NAFTA, and the formation of the World Trade Organization to resolve trade disputes.

The Concept Today Tariffs remain a controversial issue. Some Americans worry that as American tariffs are lowered, jobs will shift from the United States to less-developed nations. Other Americans, in contrast, argue that lower tariffs worldwide will boost American exports and create new jobs.

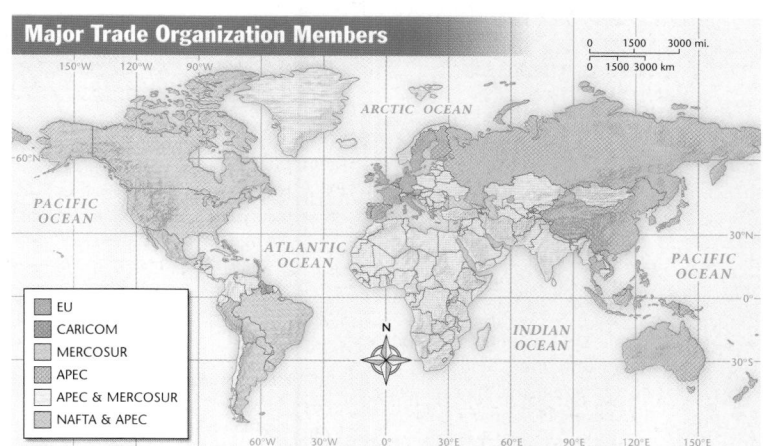

Major Trade Organization Members

- EU
- CARICOM
- MERCOSUR
- APEC
- APEC & MERCOSUR
- NAFTA & APEC

MAP SKILLS Many countries are members of major regional trade organizations including the Caribbean Community and Common Market (CARICOM), the Southern Common Market (MERCOSUR), and the Asia Pacific Economic Cooperation (APEC). **Regions** *(a) How are trade organizations divided geographically? (b) What is the purpose of these organizations?*

Chapter 34 • Section 2   1141

VIEWING HISTORY Anti–World Trade Organization protesters wave signs as they sit on a street in downtown Seattle. **Recognizing Ideologies** *What beliefs led protesters to rally against the WTO?*

of international trade agreements. Made up of different groups, including environmentalists and labor union members, protesters attacked the growing power and influence of giant worldwide corporations. They feared that organizations such as the WTO gave big business too much influence over governments. Speaking out against corporate influence, the protesters called for greater attention to the rights of workers, the welfare of poorer nations, and the global environment.

WTO officials and supporters of free trade believed that the demonstrators were mistaken. Australia's trade minister said that "on both the labor standards and the environment there are very clear and demonstrable benefits that can flow from improved trade and trade liberalization across the world to those sectors—particularly in the developing world."

Rise of Multinationals The debate over the WTO stemmed in part from the growing importance of **multinational corporations,** businesses that operate in more than one country. In the late 1990s, an estimated 37,000 multinational firms operated about 200,000 foreign branches. They accounted for more than $3 trillion in worldwide assets.

Multinationals benefit consumers and workers by providing jobs and products around the world. They also spread advanced technologies and production methods to new countries. Often the jobs they provide help poorer nations obtain better living standards for their people.

On the other hand, multinational firms can greatly influence—not always positively—the culture and politics in the countries in which they operate. Critics complain that the employees of multinationals in poorer countries often receive low wages and endure harsh working conditions. Whatever their advantages and disadvantages, trends suggest that multinationals will become increasingly visible and important in the world economy in the years ahead.

Section 2 Assessment

READING COMPREHENSION

1. Why did the United States impose **economic sanctions** on South Africa during **apartheid?**
2. What steps did the United States take to promote peace around the world?
3. What has been the greatest source of tension between China and the United States?
4. What were the goals of the European Union, **NAFTA,** and the **WTO?**

CRITICAL THINKING AND WRITING

5. **Identifying Central Issues** Why have efforts to reduce tariffs and expand free trade been controversial in the United States?
6. **Drawing Conclusions** What questions did Americans raise about their nation's political and economic role in the post–Cold War era?
7. **Writing to Persuade** Write a brief essay to your senator either in support of or against the expansion of NAFTA to include other countries in the Western Hemisphere.

Take It to the NET

Activity: Writing a Summary
The United States is a member of many global organizations. Select one of these organizations and research its goals and the role the United States plays as a member. Then, prepare a brief "executive summary" on what you've learned. Use the links provided in the *America: Pathways to the Present* area of the following Web site for help in completing this activity.
www.phschool.com

Section 2 Assessment

Reading Comprehension

1. They hoped that economic sanctions might encourage reform.
2. Possible answers: Participating in UN relief efforts in Somalia; U.S. activity in support of resolving the conflict in Kosovo; sponsoring George Mitchell's activities in regard to seeking peace in Northern Ireland.
3. Taiwan: China viewed Taiwan as part of China. On the other hand, the United States was a major supplier of weapons to Taiwan and opposed any military action by China against Taiwan.
4. European Union: To create a European economic unit that rivals that of the American economy. NAFTA: To stimulate economic growth within the Western Hemisphere through the gradual removal of trade restrictions between the United States, Canada, and Mexico. WTO: To ensure that countries complied with GATT and to negotiate new trade agreements and resolve trade disputes.

Critical Thinking and Writing

5. Many Americans believe that these efforts lead to the loss of jobs in the United States as businesses relocate their factories to nations where operating costs are far lower. Some Americans also feel that international trade expansion makes business too powerful, at the expense of workers' rights and the environment.
6. The role of the United States as peacekeeper in nations around the world and the costs involved, and how best to foster economic ties with other nations without harming American interests.
7. Essays will vary, but should be supported with facts from the section.

Take It to the NET

Summaries will vary but should present information clearly and accurately and should include quotes and specific facts.

Caption Answers

Viewing History The belief that organizations such as the WTO give big businesses too much control and/or influence over government policies, and that more attention needs to be paid to workers' rights, the environment, and the welfare of developing nations.

RESOURCE DIRECTORY

Teaching Resources
Units 9/10 booklet
- Section 2 Quiz, p. 76

Guide to the Essentials
- Section 2 Summary, p. 173

Technology
Color Transparencies *American Diversity,* G115

Americans in the New Millennium

READING FOCUS

- What factors contributed to the growing diversity of the nation's population?
- In what ways did Americans disagree over how to make diversity work?
- What is the economic and political impact of the nation's aging population?
- How did the technological revolution at the end of the twentieth century affect American life?

MAIN IDEA

In the 1990s, the United States sought new ways to create unity out of its ethnic and cultural diversity and to deal with the consequences of an aging population and a technological revolution.

KEY TERMS

bilingual education
multiculturalism
Internet

TAKING NOTES

As you read, complete the flowchart below to show the many changes occurring the United States.

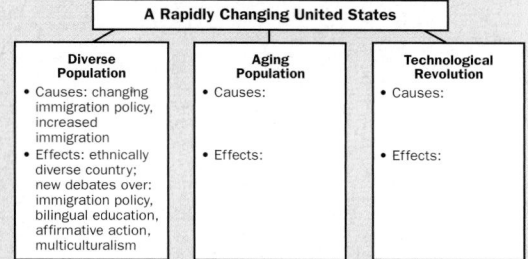

A Rapidly Changing United States

Diverse Population	Aging Population	Technological Revolution
• Causes: changing immigration policy, increased immigration • Effects: ethnically diverse country; new debates over: immigration policy, bilingual education, affirmative action, multiculturalism	• Causes: • Effects:	• Causes: • Effects:

Setting the Scene The Latin motto of the United States, found on American coins, is *e pluribus unum*, meaning "from many, one." This brief phrase reflects the patterns of the nation's past and the possibilities for its future. The United States was created when 13 separate colonies agreed to form a single union. Since then, people from an astonishing variety of lands have come to the United States and have enriched this nation's culture. That process continues today. Creating unity out of diversity remains one of the nation's greatest challenges and a key to its future.

A Nation of Diversity

In the 1990s, as a result of another wave of immigration, the United States became more diverse than at any time in its history. Close to 80 percent of all legal immigrants during this time came from Asia and Latin America. Earlier in the century, most immigrants had come from various places in Europe. As points of origin shifted away from Europe, Los Angeles began to attract about the same number of immigrants as New York City, which had been the major port of entry a century before.

At the beginning of the twenty-first century, some 30 percent of the nation's people were either African American, Latino, Asian American, or Native American. This expanding diversity meant that the United States was becoming, in the words of writer Ben J. Wattenberg, "the first universal nation."

Changing Immigration Policies Changing immigration policies contributed to the nation's growing diversity. Laws passed in the 1920s had strictly limited immigration and had given preference to immigrants from northern and western Europe. The Immigration Act of 1965, though, eliminated this bias of favoring European immigrants. In 1986, the Immigration Reform and Control Act sought to reduce illegal immigration, in part by forbidding employers to hire illegal aliens. At the same time, however, it permitted illegal aliens who had lived in the United States since 1982 to register to become citizens. The Immigration

This California road sign warns drivers to be on the lookout for undocumented aliens who might have crossed the border from Mexico.

RESOURCE DIRECTORY

Teaching Resources
Learning Styles Lesson Plans booklet, p. 71
Guided Reading and Review booklet, p. 139
Learning with Documents booklet (Primary Source Activity) *Trying to Break the Cycle of Crime,* p. 39

Technology
Section Reading Support Transparencies
Guided Reading Audiotapes (English/Spanish), Ch. 34
Student Edition on Audio CD, Ch. 34
Color Transparencies *American Diversity,* G12
Prentice Hall Presentation Pro CD-ROM, Ch. 34
Companion Web site, www.phschool.com

SECTION OBJECTIVES

1. Learn about factors that contributed to the growing diversity of the nation's population.
2. Find out how Americans disagreed about how to make diversity work.
3. Discover the economic and political impact of the nation's aging population.
4. Read to find out how the technological revolution at the end of the twentieth century affected American life.

BELLRINGER

Warm-Up Activity Ask students to take a poll of their classroom. What ethnic and national groups are represented?

Activating Prior Knowledge Ask students what they know about immigration in the United States over the past 150 years. From which countries did most immigrants come in the late nineteenth century? In the early twentieth century? At mid-century? Today?

READING STRATEGY

Before students read the section, have them write down the major headings. Then have them make notes under each heading of the main points raised there.

ACTIVITY
Connecting with Citizenship

Tell students to write a short essay reflecting on the increasing diversity of the United States. Have students consider the nation's origin as they think about the many different groups who now live here together. Is the current complexion of the United States a reflection of the ideas expressed by the Framers of the Constitution? Is it possible for citizens with different ethnic and religious backgrounds to live together in relative harmony? What are the challenges and the benefits of a diverse population? **(Verbal/Linguistic)**

Focus The face of America was changing in the late 1990s. More Americans were immigrating from places outside Europe, especially from Asia and Latin America. Americans were also growing older. Ask what challenges these changes pose for the United States in the early years of the twenty-first century.

Instruct Explain that, while nearly all Americans are immigrants or descendants of immigrants, it has often been difficult for the newest group to be accepted. Discuss the various ways in which Americans have tried to make diversity work.

Have students discuss their views of the coming decades. For example, how might the "aging of America" affect family relationships?

Assess/Reteach Ask students to consider the ways in which the United States, part of a changing world, is itself changing as it faces the challenges of immigration, an aging population, and new technologies.

ACTIVITY
Connecting with Geography

Divide the class into pairs. Assign each pair of students one of the 50 states. Then direct them to the United States Census Bureau link in the *America: Pathways to the Present* area at the Prentice Hall School Web site, www.phschool.com. Have students pose and answer questions about geographic distributions and patterns of their chosen state as shown on the map database.

INTERPRETING GRAPHS
These graphs show the recent and projected ethnic makeup of the United States. **Analyzing Information** *According to the graphs, which group in the United States will experience the most dramatic rate of growth between 2000 and 2050?*

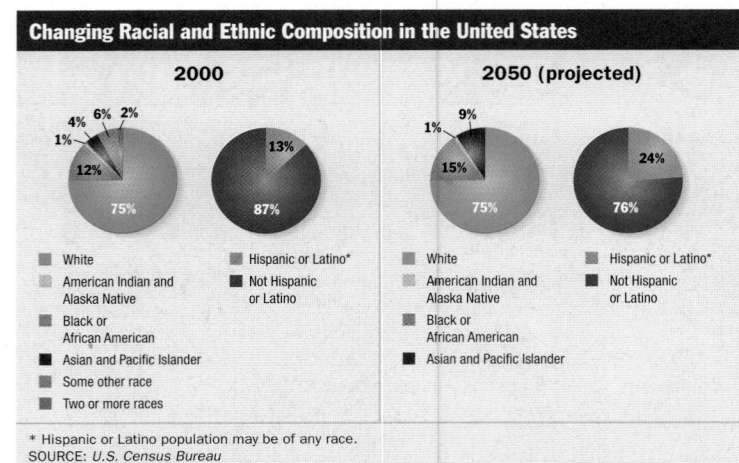

Changing Racial and Ethnic Composition in the United States

2000
- 1%
- 4%
- 6%
- 2%
- 12%
- 75%
- 13%
- 87%

2050 (projected)
- 1%
- 9%
- 15%
- 75%
- 24%
- 76%

White
American Indian and Alaska Native
Black or African American
Asian and Pacific Islander
Some other race
Two or more races

Hispanic or Latino*
Not Hispanic or Latino

* Hispanic or Latino population may be of any race.
SOURCE: U.S. Census Bureau

Act of 1990 increased immigration quotas by 40 percent. It also erased restrictions that had denied entrance to many people in the past.

Changing Population Patterns Changes in immigration affected the nation's demographics, or population patterns. While earlier immigrants had settled mainly on the East Coast, many of the new arrivals chose the Sun Belt. (The Sun Belt is the group of states stretching from Florida to California.) Like earlier immigrants, most immigrants of the 1990s settled in urban areas.

In the nation's 100 largest cities in 2000, minorities accounted for 56 percent of the total population, and made up at least half the population in 48 of those cities. African Americans formed a majority of the residents in Detroit, Baltimore, Memphis, and Washington, D.C. Latinos were most heavily concentrated in El Paso, Santa Ana, and Miami. Large numbers of Asian Americans settled in San Francisco.

The most diverse population of all could be found in Los Angeles. Korean, Vietnamese, Cambodian, and Taiwanese newcomers joined established groups of Mexican Americans, African Americans, and European Americans. Like the many nationalities that had crowded into New York City a century earlier, these groups competed for jobs and housing. Similar competition occurred in other cities with large immigrant populations.

Minorities in Politics As minority groups grew in size, they also gained new political power. In 1992, Carol Moseley-Braun, an Illinois Democrat, became the first African American woman to win election to the United States Senate. Also in 1992, Ben Nighthorse Campbell, a Republican from Colorado, became the first Native American to be elected to the United States Senate. Thirty-seven African Americans, 19 Latinos, and 4 Asian Americans took office in the United States House at the start of George W. Bush's presidency.

Making Diversity Work

As American society became more diverse, government, private organizations, and individual citizens all undertook efforts to make diversity work. Some of these efforts aroused controversy.

Focus on CULTURE

Understanding the New Census Data The 2000 Census began a new system for reporting race in the United States. In the 1990 census, respondents could identify their race by choosing one of four racial categories. The 2000 Census expanded these categories to six. The most significant change in 2000, however, was a new set of directions, which allowed respondents to choose more than one racial category by which to identify themselves. In the chart above, the "Two or more races" category represents those respondents who chose to identify themselves in such a way.

Analysts point out that the American system of racial classification has undergone considerable changes in the past. Asian Indians, for example, were included in the white race in 1970, but beginning in 1980, became a part of the Asian and Pacific Islander race. As the nation's racial makeup continues to change, the Census will continue to work to find new and better ways of reporting race.

1144   Chapter 34 • *Entering a New Era*

Interpreting Graphs Hispanic or Latino.

RESOURCE DIRECTORY

Teaching Resources
Biography, Literature, and Comparing Primary Sources booklet (Comparing Primary Sources) *On Immigration Policy,* p. 163

Other Print Resources
Nystrom *Atlas of Our Country* The Fourth Wave of Immigration, pp. 36–37
Historical Outline Map Book *Political United States,* p. 82

Technology
Color Transparencies *Historical Maps,* A53, A59; *Fine Art,* E19, E20
Exploring Primary Sources in U.S. History CD-ROM *Texas State Constitution*
RESOURCE PRO Biography *Amy Tan,* found on Resource Pro, profiles the author of the best-selling novel *The Joy Luck Club,* which depicts life in America from the perspective of a group of Chinese American women.

The Debate Over Immigration In the 1990s, as in earlier periods of increased immigration, Americans disagreed over how immigration would affect the nation. Some people warned that immigration would cause the breakdown of American society. Others called immigration the nation's best hope for a prosperous future. In between these two extremes were several other arguments for either restricting or expanding immigration.

People who favored restricting immigration offered these arguments:

1. Immigrants hurt the economy. Because immigrants are willing to work for low wages, some Americans fear they will take jobs away from native-born Americans and drive down the pay of other workers.

2. Immigration services are costly. Some people who favor restricting immigration point to the fact that the federal government sets immigration policy but does not pay for all the services immigrants require. This problem is particularly costly in California, which has more immigrants than any other state.

3. Immigrant groups fragment American society. Some opponents of immigration believe that newer immigrant groups are dividing the United States by staying within their separate ethnic groups rather than adapting to American culture, as previous immigrants did. They fear, for example, that new immigrants will not learn English. **Bilingual education,** in which students are taught in their native language as well as English while their English skills improve, has come under attack. Opponents of bilingual education believe that these programs encourage immigrants to continue using their native language rather than assimilate into the American mainstream.

Those who supported expanded immigration offered their own arguments:

1. Immigrants help, not hurt, the economy. Supporters of immigration point out that immigrants contribute to the economy as consumers, small-business owners, and taxpayers. Immigrants also take jobs few native-born Americans want. They often arrive highly motivated to work, with strong family bonds that promote discipline and high standards.

2. Most immigrants do not receive public assistance. For example, a study in 1997 showed that only 5.7 percent of immigrants received aid to families with dependent children (AFDC), in contrast to 3.9 percent of the native-born population. In addition, most legal immigrants must wait five years before becoming eligible for welfare.

3. Immigration is a good investment for the future. Supporters of immigration claim that it will pay off in future years by expanding both the size of the work force and the number of taxpayers.

Affirmative Action Another heated debate concerned affirmative action. The goal of the first affirmative action policies, introduced by President Johnson in the 1960s, was to improve employment and educational opportunities by giving preference to African Americans and to other minorities and women who had been discriminated against in the past. Some people argued, however, that giving special treatment to some groups was unfair to everyone else.

In 1996, California voters passed Proposition 209, ending affirmative action in state hiring and education. That same year, a federal court struck down an affirmative action admissions program at the University of Texas. The state's attorney general decided not to appeal the ruling to the Supreme Court. His decision reflected growing public doubts about affirmative action across the nation. Among the critics of the policy were some well-known African Americans, including Supreme Court Justice Clarence Thomas.

The courts in recent years have heard a variety of affirmative action cases. The issue remains complex and difficult to decide. Can race be the deciding

Despite some opposition to Proposition 209, California residents voted to pass the measure that ended affirmative action in government and education.

factor in a hiring decision, or just one of many factors? Is it proper for an organization to set numerical targets for selecting minorities or women? Should a less-qualified applicant ever be selected over a more-qualified one, simply because he or she belonged to a group that experienced discrimination in the past? While both supporters and opponents of affirmative action agree on the idea of fairness, the concept of fairness is not always easy to define.

Multiculturalism Another effort to make diversity work was **multiculturalism,** a movement that called for greater attention to non-European cultures in such areas as education. For example, advocates of multicultural education argued that school textbooks should include more information on the contributions of people from all groups.

Others disapproved of this approach. Professor Arthur M. Schlesinger, Jr., referred to multiculturalism as "ethnic cheerleading." He criticized the use of history to make people feel good about themselves rather than to discover the truth about the past. Other critics worried that extreme versions of multiculturalism could damage the unity of society. They argued that the approach emphasized differences between groups rather than the shared values and experiences of all Americans.

America's Aging Population

As the United States approached the turn of the millennium, its population was older than ever before. Elderly people made up the fastest-growing age group in the country. The number of people 65 years old and over increased nearly elevenfold between 1900 and 1999, while the nation's total population only tripled. In 1999, nearly 13 percent of all Americans were 65 or older, compared to 4 percent in 1900. Advances in medical care increased the average life expectancy of newborns from 47 to 77 years during the 1900s. Clearly, an "aging revolution" was under way.

The "graying of America" had important political and economic effects. Many older Americans advocated passing legislation that prohibited forced retirement at a specific age. In addition, because older Americans were growing in number and living longer, the cost of government programs that served them increased greatly. The Social Security system, for example, faced difficulties because the number of retirees receiving benefits from the program was rising faster than the number of workers paying taxes into it. In 1983, Congress tried to deal with the problem by raising taxes for workers and setting a later age for retirement benefits to begin. Experts warned, however, that more radical steps would have to be taken before the huge baby boom generation begins retiring in the twenty-first century.

In fact, polls showed that many young Americans doubted that the Social Security system would even exist when they reached retirement age. Some of those polled also indicated that they resented paying high taxes to provide benefits for retired persons. Observers suggested that conflict between generations could become another source of tension in American society. Ensuring the long-term health of Social Security remains a difficult but important challenge for the federal government.

There was similar pressure on the nation's medical system. Medicare, a federal program established during the Great Society of the 1960s, paid for many of the medical expenses of older Americans. As the number of recipients and the price of healthcare rose, however, Medicare costs exploded from $7.5 billion in 1970 to more than $200 billion in the 1990s. As with Social Security, federal

VIEWING HISTORY The elderly population of the United States is the fastest-growing segment of American society. Almost all Americans aged 65 and over are insured by Medicare. **Expressing Problems Clearly** *What challenges does the Medicare system face?*

lawmakers agreed that long-term changes were needed but disagreed on what those changes should be.

A Technological Revolution

The modern communications revolution began more than a century ago when Samuel Morse developed the telegraph. Since then, communications technology has made major advances with the invention of the telephone, radio, television, and the computer. In the last several decades, the invention of many more ways to store, retrieve, and transmit information has created a new era in communications known as the Information Age.

Communication and Information The centerpiece of the Information Age, of course, is the computer. Between 1984 and 2000, the percentage of American households with a computer jumped from 8 percent to 51 percent.

Originally the size of a room, computers have decreased in size as they have grown in their ability to store and retrieve information. Computers now steer spacecraft, route telephone calls, and assist in all kinds of scientific research.

The **Internet,** a computer network that links millions of people around the world, has revolutionized many areas of American life, from entertainment to education to business. Access to the Internet has spread to schools, businesses, libraries, homes, and even some cafés, where "net-surfing" allows customers to work at computers and drink coffee at the same time. Businesses, seeing the Internet as a way to reach a global audience of millions, have scrambled to set up their own Web sites.

The "New Economy" The United States enjoyed the greatest period of economic expansion in its history during the 1990s, thanks in large part to the technological boom. Investors and entrepreneurs, excited about the opportunities offered by the Internet and other new technologies, created many new businesses and worked on ways to improve old ones. Waves of what came to be called "dot com" companies appeared, each trying to corner a unique market of online business.

The face of business also began to change. New entrepreneurs sported jeans and T-shirts and maintained more casual workplaces. This relaxed style even spread to some older businesses, where workers could enjoy greater benefits, such as more flexible schedules.

How will these changes affect employment? While computers have replaced some human workers, the growth of high-tech industries has created thousands of new jobs. These jobs demand a high level of education and skills. One feature of the new economy is the lack of stable, well-paying jobs for unskilled workers. Education, therefore, has never been as important to economic success as it is now.

Impact on Education Computers and the Internet have become essential parts of American society, but their place in schools is still being determined. An important task for schools will be to find the right balance between traditional teaching and the use of new technology. For many schools, an even bigger challenge will be to find enough money to fund the new and ever-changing technology.

In addition, as the Internet becomes more important as a research tool, students will have to learn how to evaluate the information that is available online. While some of this information is of very high quality, not all of it is reliable.

American BIOGRAPHY

Bill Gates
b. 1955

In 1975, Bill Gates envisioned the future of computers and set to work turning that vision into reality. That year, at the age of 19, Gates dropped out of Harvard University to join his high school friend Paul Allen in establishing a new company. During high school, Bill had used his computer knowledge to help create a company that sold traffic data to local governments. In 1975, the two friends first read about a kit computer in *Popular Electronics* magazine. "Paul and I didn't know exactly how it would be used, but we were sure it would change us and the world of computing."

At first, people couldn't make the kit computer do much. Gates and Allen changed that by writing software, or the coded instructions for performing specific tasks, to run on the computer. Their efforts transformed it from a device with limited uses into a general-purpose computer that was similar to (though much less powerful than) those we use today. The company that the two friends started for marketing their software, later named Microsoft, grew to become a giant in the computer industry. Located near Seattle, Washington, where Gates was born, its success made Gates a billionaire by the age of 31.

Chapter 34 • Section 3   **1147**

ACTIVITY
Connecting with Geography

Have students find out about Internet access around the world. For example, how many people in Asian or African nations now have Internet access? How does the lack of Internet access affect these people? Then have students make a map of the area they have focused on. Tell students to indicate the countries that have Internet access and those that do not. **(Visual/Spatial)**

BACKGROUND
Interdisciplinary

High-tech wizards have created the Internet and, along with it, the ability to disseminate information quickly. However, even the smartest programmers seem unable to stem the spread of computer viruses. A virus is a code that attaches itself to another code in a computer with the express aim of reproducing itself. Some viruses are created to erase files or lock up the operating system of another computer. Other viruses are less destructive; they can be formed when an infected program is run that was received via e-mail or the Internet. For this reason, it's important to scan for viruses.

READING CHECK

The government has tried to protect the rights of businesses (such as record companies) threatened by new technologies. On the other hand, the government has tried to protect consumers from communications entities deemed to be monopolies (such as Microsoft).

What Comes Next?

Of course, no one knows for sure what the future holds, but everyone from scientists and politicians to sociologists and historians is talking about what comes next. Surely, the world is bound for another makeover. Think about how much the world has changed since 1900. Who in 1900 could have dreamed of such a thing as the Internet?

Think about the speed of change. The Internet is already evolving as people begin to access it from wireless devices. Experts see a future in which our lives are filled with Internet-enabled appliances, cars, airplanes, and houses.

What exists now that will soon become obsolete? Will we still have a need for books? Most people expect that books aren't going anywhere, but that they will surely change. Businesses are already working on new types of books, into which content can be loaded in the form of digital ink. The covers of such an adaptable book can be customized to fit your hands. Politics will change as well. Experts see world conflicts being resolved through mini-wars, in which powerful peace-oriented nations plan targeted attacks on smaller rogue enemies. The presence of nuclear weapons means that most nations will want to avoid a world war at all costs.

Many Americans contemplate the possibility of time-travel, alternate universes, genetically-engineered people, or replaceable bodies and brains. While many of these ideas are both exciting and frightening, Americans will adapt as they always have to whatever comes next.

? **Why do you think the prospect of change is both frightening and exciting for Americans? Explain.**

READING CHECK
How has the government reacted to developments in communications technology?

Impact on Foreign Affairs New technologies created both opportunities and challenges for governments around the world. President Clinton claimed that "in the new century, liberty will spread [around the world] by cell phone and cable modem." New communications and information technology encouraged greater ties among people in different nations. Through the Internet, for example, more people around the world than ever before could gain access to the same pools of information.

However, countries in several regions lacked the wealth or infrastructure to become active participants in this global network. In 2001, only about 8 percent of the world population had access to the Internet. By contrast, in the United States nearly 60 percent of the people could go online. As technology changed ever more quickly, fears rose that much of the developing world would be left further and further behind.

Impact on Government The federal government also had to confront domestic issues raised by the Internet and other new technologies. The issue of maintaining privacy was an important concern. Many people worried that the privacy of e-mail conversations or online purchases was not being sufficiently protected.

Another controversial issue concerned ownership rights. One company, Napster, had grown widely popular because its software allowed users to trade song files over the Internet for free. Many record companies and some musicians believed that such sharing of music was illegal because the owners of this music (the record companies and artists) did not make any money when these song files were shared. Not all artists opposed Napster, however. Networks like Napster, some believed, gave consumers access to new music and to little-known musicians who otherwise would have trouble breaking into the industry.

Record companies sued Napster in an effort to halt the trading of copyrighted material on the Internet. A federal judge ruled in favor of the record companies and ordered Napster to stop trading copyrighted material. Other networks not affected by the judge's ruling, though, soon took Napster's place. The debate over whether Napster promoted stealing or sharing was certain to continue.

The government also faced a problem with the giant software company Microsoft. By 1998, Microsoft had become the world's second most valuable company, worth some $200 billion. However, Microsoft's size and success helped make the company controversial. Several competitors argued that Microsoft was trying to drive them out of business.

In 1998, the federal government sued Microsoft for violating the Sherman Antitrust Act of 1890. The government accused Microsoft of using its power to gain a monopoly over the market for software needed to browse the Internet. In 2000, a federal judge ruled that Microsoft was indeed a monopoly and had used unfair business practices, and he ordered that the company be split apart. The following year, an appeals court reversed this order but upheld the judgment that Microsoft had acted improperly. The Justice Department announced later that year that it would abandon its efforts to break up Microsoft.

Impact on Daily Life   The new technologies of the late twentieth century left their mark on Americans' daily lives. Many people kept in touch with friends and family through e-mail as well as (or instead of) through letters or telephone calls. They brought cell phones or hand-held computers along with them on daily errands and vacations. They used the Internet to shop, look for jobs, or to check the weather forecast or sports results. Everything they needed to know about the products they bought, the restaurants where they ate, and the companies in which they invested was only a few "clicks" away.

Some Americans, though, began to wonder whether all of these changes were good. Did people have access to more information than they could use? Had the pace of life grown too fast? Would the United States, like the world as a whole, become divided into two groups: one with access to the new technology and the other too poor to afford it? While modern technology appeared to provide people with greater freedom, could it also be misused to restrict freedom?

Facing the Future

Near the end of his life, Thomas Jefferson wrote, "If a nation expects to be ignorant and free . . . it expects what never was and never will be." Freedom, in other words, does not maintain itself. We must all commit ourselves to its preservation by working to understand and participate in the events around us.

The wealth and power our nation now enjoys might cause some of us to lose sight of this lesson. Yet as changes occur increasingly quickly in the years ahead, bringing advances—and challenges—we can hardly imagine, Jefferson's words could become more true than ever before.

VIEWING HISTORY This satellite image shows North America at night. **Drawing Inferences** *Study the photograph. What can you infer about population density patterns in the United States?*

Section 3   Assessment

READING COMPREHENSION

1. What effects did increasing immigration have on the United States?

2. Explain the debate over **bilingual education** and **multiculturalism.**

3. How has the increase in the number of older Americans caused difficulties for the Social Security system?

4. What challenges did the **Internet** pose for the federal government?

CRITICAL THINKING AND WRITING

5. **Drawing Inferences** How can the country's immigration policies affect its economy?

6. **Predicting Consequences** Why is it important for Americans to create unity out of diversity?

7. **Writing to Persuade** Explain how you think schools can best prepare students to take advantage of modern technological innovations like the Internet.

 Take It to the NET

Activity: Writing an Editorial
Review current themes and issues regarding bilingual education in the United States. Gather data about existing programs and write an editorial stating whether or not you believe bilingual education is headed in the right direction in America. Use the links provided in the *America: Pathways to the Present* area of the following Web site for help in completing this activity.
www.phschool.com

Chapter 34 • Section 3   1149

Section 3   Assessment

Reading Comprehension

1. Minorities made up a much larger part of the population and gained political power; development of bilingual education; it led to debate on how to handle a diverse society.

2. Bilingual education: Supporters believe students should be taught in both their native language and English. Opponents believe this approach prevents these students from learning English and assimilating into American culture. Multiculturalism: Supporters feel that education should fully encompass non-European cultures. Opponents fear that this approach masks the truth about the past, and that extreme multiculturalism could damage the unity of society.

3. The number of retirees receiving benefits from the program was rising faster than the number of workers paying taxes into it.

4. Challenges: maintaining privacy; ownership rights; monopolies.

Critical Thinking and Writing

5. Opponents of expanded immigration claim that large numbers of immigrants require entitlements and compete with native-born workers for jobs. Supporters feel that immigrants benefit society and do not draw off resources.

6. Possible answer: If Americans do not unite, opposing groups could develop hostility toward one another, resulting in political battles or other conflicts.

7. Answers will vary, but should include a discussion of issues of funding, how to teach students to evaluate the validity of Internet sources, and the costs and benefits of other new technologies.

 **Take It to the NET**

Editorials will vary, but should persuade readers with facts gathered about existing programs and predictions about the future of bilingual education in America.

CAPTION ANSWERS

Viewing History The United States is most densely populated along the East and West coasts, and most populated in the northeast section.

REVIEWING KEY TERMS

Students should refer to the definitions of key terms in the chapter to write sentences about the important controversies and conflicts facing America and the world during the 1990s and today.

REVIEWING MAIN IDEAS

10. Successes: economic reform, balancing the budget, welfare reform. Failures: health care reform, impeachment.

11. Republicans had won a majority in both houses of Congress in the midterm elections, and many backed Gingrich's Contract with America, a conservative plan for cutting the size of government.

12. It took part in the NATO bombing campaigns and committed troops to NATO peacekeeping forces stationed in the area.

13. Supporters said that NAFTA would create new jobs by increasing exports to Canada and Mexico. Opponents argued that manufacturers would move factories to Mexico, resulting in a loss of American jobs.

14. The Immigration Act of 1965 eliminated bias in favor of European immigration, increasing the number of immigrants from Asia, Africa, and Latin America. The 1986 Immigration Reform and Control Act allowed immigrants who had been living in the United States since 1982 to become citizens, and the Immigration Act of 1990 increased immigration quotas.

15. Business: While computers have replaced some human workers, high-tech industries have created a wealth of new jobs and allowed the United States to enjoy a period of vast economic expansion. Stable, well-paying jobs for unskilled workers are in short supply due to the expansion of technology in the workplace. Education: Education is critical for acquiring jobs in an increasingly technological society. In the classroom, the right balance between traditional teaching and the use of technology is still being examined, as is funding and evaluating the information gleaned from the Internet as a research tool. Daily life: facilitating rapid communication between people; shaping

creating a CHAPTER SUMMARY

Copy the web diagram (right) on a separate sheet of paper to summarize international events in recent years.

For additional review and enrichment activities, see the interactive version of *America: Pathways to the Present*, available on the Web and on CD-ROM.

Recent International Events
- Trade Organizations: WTO, EU, NAFTA
- Wars and Conflicts: The Balkans, Israel, Iraq
- Peace Initiatives: Russia/Eastern Europe, Northern Ireland, South Africa

★ Reviewing Key Terms

For each of the terms below, write a sentence explaining how it related to the United States at the end of the twentieth century.

1. Contract with America
2. Whitewater affair
3. apartheid
4. economic sanctions
5. North American Free Trade Agreement
6. World Trade Organization
7. multinational corporation
8. multiculturalism
9. Internet

★ Reviewing Main Ideas

10. What were some domestic successes and failures for Bill Clinton in the 1990s? (Section 1)

11. After the 1994 elections, why did Republicans believe that they had a mandate to reduce the size of the federal government? (Section 1)

12. What role did the United States play in producing cease-fires in Bosnia and Kosovo? (Section 2)

13. Give reasons why some people supported NAFTA and others opposed it. (Section 2)

14. How did government policy contribute to the diversity of the United States? (Section 3)

15. Analyze the impact of recent technological innovations on business, education, and daily life. (Section 3)

★ Critical Thinking

16. Demonstrating Reasoned Judgment The United States intervened in some foreign conflicts during the 1990s and launched a war on terrorism in 2001. What do you think should be the role of the United States in future overseas conflicts?

17. Identifying Assumptions What arguments might supporters and opponents of affirmative action give in defense of their different positions?

18. Drawing Inferences President Clinton gave his speech regarding the need for healthcare reform to a national TV audience in 1993 as a way of rallying public support for reform. What benefits and drawbacks does television offer to Presidents?

19. Predicting Consequences Think about how technology affects our daily lives. What changes might take place as a result of technological advances in the next five to ten years?

20. Synthesizing Information What various factors and events in the late 1990s helped cause the election of 2000 to be so close?

CREATING A CHAPTER SUMMARY

WTO: An organization to help negotiate trade agreements and resolve trade disputes worldwide
EU: An organization of European countries working to create a single European market
NAFTA: An agreement signed by the United States, Canada, and Mexico removing trade restrictions

The Balkans: With the collapse of communism, ethnic violence erupts.
Israel: Israel and the PLO sign a peace agreement, but hostilities increase again.
Iraq: Iraq still refuses to cooperate with UN inspectors, and some sanctions are still in place.

Russia/Eastern Europe: Elections are held in Russia as it moves toward democracy; in Eastern Europe, countries move toward a free market economy, some joining NATO.
Northern Ireland: The Good Friday peace accords were signed to help halt violence between Protestants and Catholics.
South Africa: The country ends apartheid, and first elections are held.

★ Skills Assessment

Analyzing Political Cartoons ▶

21. Read the title of the cartoon. Why do people go on vacations?

22. Examine the scene. (a) What activities do you traditionally associate with a trip to the beach? (b) How is this scene different?

23. What comment is the cartoonist making about 1990s lifestyle?

Interpreting Data

Turn to the racial and ethnic composition graphs in Section 3.

24. Which of the following groups made up 12 percent of the United States population in 2000?

   A White
   B Black or African American
   C American Indian and Alaskan Native
   D Asian and Pacific Islander

25. Which of the following groups will more than double its percentage of the United States population by 2050?

   F White
   G Black or African American
   H Asian and Pacific Islander
   J Hispanic or Latino Origin

26. What percentage of the United States population reported that they belonged to one racial category in 2000?

   A 98 percent
   B 6 percent
   C 94 percent
   D 13 percent

Applying the Chapter Skill:
Predicting Consequences

27. Review the steps needed to predict consequences on page 1134. Then describe the consequences of the nation's aging population.

A 90s VACATION.

ACTIVITIES

Writing to LEARN

Writing a Conclusion
Reread the statement by Thomas Jefferson at the end of Section 3. Describe in your own words how education and freedom are related. Why will education be so important to workers of the twenty-first century?

Primary Source CD-ROM

Working With Primary Sources Find additional information on the United States in recent years on the *Exploring Primary Sources in U.S. History CD-ROM* and use the selection(s) provided to complete the Chapter 34 primary source activity located in the *America: Pathways to the Present* area of the following Web site. **www.phschool.com**

Take It to the NET

Chapter Self-Test As a review activity, take the Chapter 34 Self-Test in the *America: Pathways to the Present* area at the Web site listed below. The questions are designed to test your understanding of the chapter content. **www.phschool.com**

Chapter 34 Assessment   1151

---

the way we shop, hunt for jobs, and acquire information.

CRITICAL THINKING

16. Sample answers: The United States, as the world's lone superpower, has an obligation to take on the role of peacekeeper. Or, becoming involved in dangerous situations such as Bosnia or Somalia may be too costly in money and lives.

17. Opponents: Preferential treatment for certain people robs those people of their dignity and self-worth; it is unfair to other groups. Supporters: Gives those who faced discrimination in the past improved employment and educational opportunities.

18. Answers will vary. Benefits might include reaching out to all people. Drawbacks might include appearing unpersuasive if the individual lacks "television appeal."

19. Answers will vary, but should use current technological advancements as a base for speculation and prediction.

20. Possible answers: Clinton's impeachment, the booming economy, political tensions between Democrats and Republicans.

SKILLS ASSESSMENT

21. Relaxation; freedom from work or school.

22. (a) Blankets and towels; coolers; swimming; looking for seashells; sunbathing; making sand castles. (b) Instead of engaging in these activities, the family shown is surrounded by portable, mostly business-related, technology, which they are using.

23. Americans no longer know how to relax. The array of communications technology we have created does not free us from work, but enables us to do more of it.

24. B

25. H

26. A

27. Answers will vary, but might involve such predictions as the percentage of Americans who will be 65 or older in 2050.

American Pathways
ECONOMICS

Free Enterprise and the American Economy

In 1776, Scottish economist Adam Smith published *The Wealth of Nations,* a book that promoted capitalism, an economic system based on free enterprise and little government interference. Capitalism has suited independent, industrious, and competitive Americans, who have enjoyed the fruits of a productive economy for two centuries.

1 The Market Revolution
1793–1824 The new nation's abundant natural resources and its political and legal systems, which protected patent and property rights, allowed hard-working Americans to bring about a "market revolution." New, profitable manufacturing enterprises sprang up throughout the Northeast and the Ohio Valley.

Title page of Adam Smith's *The Wealth of Nations* (above right)

2 Nationalism and Sectionalism
1816–1865 In the ongoing power struggle between the federal government and the states, Congress and the Supreme Court worked to strengthen nationalism. The economy, especially the northern industrial economy, expanded. At the same time, slavery was becoming the economic cornerstone of the agricultural South. This issue and other sectional tensions eventually sparked the Civil War.

Currency issued by state-chartered banks and individual companies from the Free Banking Era, 1837–1863 (above)

3 Industrial Expansion and Progressive Reforms
1865–1914 After the Civil War, industry thrived in a free market, with little interference from the government. During the Progressive Era, reformers concerned about low pay and harsh working conditions in the nation's factories pressed government officials to regulate corporations more closely.

An early Ford Motor Company assembly line (above)

1152

 A Consumer Economy

1919–1929 During the 1920s, new products and Americans' power to purchase them grew rapidly, producing a decade of enormous business growth.

 The Great Depression and the New Deal

1929–1941 Overproduction and risky investment practices set the stage for economic disaster. On October 29, 1929, stock prices tumbled in what is known as the Great Crash. Investors lost millions of dollars and the economy sank into a devastating Depression. President Franklin D. Roosevelt developed government programs to help American businesses and families recover.

A soup kitchen during the Depression (above)

 Postwar Ups and Downs

1944–1987 The national economy finally rebounded with the advent of World War II. Pent-up consumer demand, the GI Bill, and the business shift to peacetime manufacturing helped create a postwar economic boom. In the 1970s and early 1980s, however, the economy sagged.

A 1950s automobile (above)

 The Information Age and the Global Economy

1974–Present The personal computer ushered in the Information Age, which, along with increased world trade and corporate multinationalism, created new opportunities and challenges for the American economy.

The New York Stock Exchange located on Wall Street in New York City's financial district (left)

Continuity and Change

1. How does the United States' system of government support free enterprise?
2. What evidence of a typical business cycle can you find in the history of the American economy?

Take It to the NET: Creating a Study Guide
Print and complete the study guide for this topic found in the *America: Pathways to the Present* area of the following Web site. **www.phschool.com**

1153

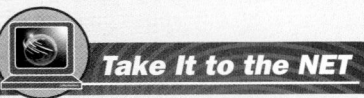

Take It to the NET

Students can print the American Pathways thematic study guide for this topic at the Prentice Hall School Web site, or you can provide students with copies of the study guide, which is found in the Units 9/10 booklet, the American Pathways Activity, pages 84–85. Students should use their texts to fill in a one-sentence description for each event on the study guide. When completed for each of the American Pathways topics, the thematic study guides will aid students in preparing for an end-of-course exam.

ANSWERS

1. The United States' system of government supports free enterprise in many ways. The government enforces a system of laws that upholds the rights of private property owners. The government also issues and protects patents and enforces legal contracts.

2. Possible answers: The panics of 1837 and 1839, which had followed a boom in the economy; the Depression of 1893–1897 after the industrial expansion of the Gilded Age; the Great Depression following the boom of the 1920s; the stagflation and recession after the post–World War II boom ended in the 1970s; the 1987 stock market collapse that broke the speculative bubble of the 1980s.

TEST PREPARATION

Write your answers on a separate sheet of paper.

1. Which one of the following did President Richard Nixon use to try to stop inflation in the United States economy?

   A Veto power over congressional spending

   B Federal Reserve interest rates

   C Federal price, wage, and rent controls

   D Balancing the federal budget

2. What was the purpose of the "southern strategy" of President Richard Nixon?

   A To gain votes from whites opposed to changes in civil rights

   B To allow the Vietnamese to fight the war on their own

   C To control the expansion of suburbs into farmlands

   D To limit the power of Republicans in the eastern states

3. How is President Gerald Ford unique among all of the United States Presidents?

   A He changed political parties as President.

   B He was the only President who also was an athlete.

   C He served as Vice President for two different Presidents.

   D He was the only unelected President.

> "Our Constitution works. Our great republic is a government of laws, not men."
>
> —President Gerald Ford, August 9, 1974

4. President Ford was speaking about the

   A failure of United States military policy in Vietnam.

   B investigation and resignation of Nixon following the Watergate scandal.

   C need for a comprehensive national energy policy.

   D use of presidential veto power.

5. Which one of the following is a correct statement about the Supreme Court decision in *Regents of the University of California* v. *Bakke*?

   A It extended the scope of the *Brown* v. *Board of Education* decision.

   B It required busing to achieve integration in public schools.

   C It limited the power of the President to spend money on education.

   D It was the first limit on affirmative action programs.

6. Which President was responsible for the Strategic Defense Initiative (SDI)?

   A Gerald Ford

   B Ronald Reagan

   C George H. W. Bush

   D Bill Clinton

1154

TIPS FOR TEST TAKING

Use this sample exam to help your students prepare for standardized tests.

You might want to remind your students of the following:

1. Read the directions carefully.

2. Read each question carefully.

3. For multiple choice questions, try to answer the question before you look at the choices. Read all the choices. Then, eliminate those that are absolutely incorrect.

4. For short answer questions, be sure to answer the question completely if there is more than one part.

5. Answer the easy questions first. Then, go back to the ones that will take more time.

6. Pace yourself. Be sure to set aside enough time for the writing questions.

PRENTICE HALL
ASSESSMENT
SYSTEM

Diagnose and Prescribe
- Profile student skills with Diagnostic Tests A&B.
- Address student needs with program materials correlated to test questions.

Review and Reteach
- Provide cumulative content review with the Review Book.

Practice and Assess
- Build test-taking skills with Test-taking Strategies With Transparencies.

Use the chart and your knowledge of social studies to answer the following questions.

Year	U.S. Deficit (millions of dollars)
1980	$ 73,835
1982	127,989
1984	185,388
1986	221,245

SOURCE: *Statistical Abstract of the United States, 1995*

7. The growing deficit during the 1980s was a result of the

   A anti-inflationary policies of President Jimmy Carter.

   B supply-side economic policies of President Ronald Reagan.

   C overseas military activities of President George H. W. Bush.

   D limited popularity of President Bill Clinton.

8. President George H. W. Bush used military power to

   A break down the Berlin Wall.

   B stop a revolution in Grenada.

   C force Iraq out of Kuwait.

   D end the Communist threat in Vietnam.

9. Which one of the following was a major goal of President Bill Clinton when he was elected in 1992?

   A To solve healthcare problems in the United States

   B To limit the spending excesses of Congress

   C To limit the power of the Republican majority in Congress

   D To end United States military involvement overseas

10. Newt Gingrich and the Republican majority in Congress were blamed for which one of the following?

    A United States military failure in Somalia

    B The negative effects of the NAFTA treaty

    C The government shutdown at the end of 1995

    D Rising inflation rates in 1997

11. Under President Bill Clinton, the United States experienced the

    A highest rate of inflation in the world.

    B highest level of unemployment in its history.

    C longest period of economic expansion in its history.

    D longest period of economic recession in its history.

Writing Practice

12. Describe President Nixon's policies for dealing with the Soviet Union and China.

13. How did the Camp David Accords change the Middle East?

14. Describe two problems the United States faces with the "graying of America."

1. C
2. A
3. D
4. B
5. D
6. B
7. B
8. C
9. A
10. C
11. C
12. Nixon followed a policy of *realpolitik,* or "practical politics," with China, which included laying the groundwork for establishing diplomatic ties, lifting restrictions on travel, and removing an embargo on trade. With the Soviet Union, Nixon agreed to cooperate on space exploration, ease trade limits, and negotiate a weapons pact.
13. Under the Camp David Accords, Israel withdrew from the Sinai Peninsula, and Egypt recognized Israel's existence as a nation. The peace between Egypt and Israel helped to make the Middle East more stable.
14. Problems include the increased cost of government programs that serve the elderly, such as Social Security and Medicare. There are also concerns about potential intergenerational conflict.

OF PLYMOUTH PLANTATION 1620–1647
BY WILLIAM BRADFORD

Focus Have students read the introduction and look up the meanings of the vocabulary words. Then explain that the excerpt offers an eyewitness account of the dramatic events surrounding the Pilgrims' establishment of relations with the Native Americans on Cape Cod.

Instruct Ask your students to review the events that Bradford describes. Why do they think the Pilgrims were first confronted by Native Americans' arrows, and then received peaceful overtures? Ask students to speculate on what might have been going on among the Native Americans that caused this change of attitude. What role did Squanto play in establishing peaceful relations? What role did Massasoit play?

Extend Ask students to research the history of one of the various Native American groups that lived on Cape Cod and in southern New England at the time of the Pilgrims' arrival. For the group they select, ask students to find out about the relationship between that group and European settlers, the background of any key individuals, and the status of that group today—where it is located, how many members it has, how much land it holds, and the group's current economic status.

American Literature
Unit 1

Of Plymouth Plantation
1620–1647
BY WILLIAM BRADFORD

William Bradford sailed on the Mayflower *to North America in 1620. One of approximately 100 religious pilgrims to land on present-day Cape Cod in November, he helped establish a colony at Plymouth and served as its governor. Full of adventure, passion, wisdom, and even humor, Bradford's remarkable narrative about this exploration has been called one of the greatest books of the seventeenth century. The following excerpts describe two early encounters with Native Americans. The first occurred less than one month after the* Mayflower's *landfall, in early December, when an exploring party was camped around present-day Eastham, Massachusetts; the second occurred in the early spring near Plymouth.*

VOCABULARY Before you read the selection, find the meaning of these words in a dictionary:
providence
shallop
skulk

So they rested till about five of the clock in the morning; for the tide, and their purpose to go from thence, made them be stirring betimes. So after prayer they prepared for breakfast, and it being day dawning it was thought best to be carrying things down to the boat. But some said it was not best to carry the arms down, others said they would be the readier, for they had lapped them up in their coats from the dew; but some three or four would not carry theirs till they went themselves. Yet as it fell out, the water being not high enough, they laid them down on the bank side and came up to breakfast.

But presently, all on the sudden, they heard a great and strange cry, which they knew to be the same voices they heard in the night, though they varied their notes; and one of their company being abroad came running in and cried, "Men, Indians! Indians!" And withal, their arrows came flying amongst them. Their men ran with all speed to recover their arms, as by the good providence of God they did. In the meantime, of those that were there ready, two muskets were discharged at them, and two more stood ready in the entrance of their rendezvous but were commanded not to shoot till they could take full aim at them. And the other two charged again with all speed, for there were only four had arms there, and defended the barricado, which was first assaulted. The cry of the Indians was dreadful, especially when they saw their men run out of the rendezvous toward the shallop to recover their arms, the Indians wheeling about upon them. But some running out with coats of mail on, and cutlasses in their hands, they soon got their arms and let fly amongst them and quickly stopped their violence. Yet there was a lusty man, and no less valiant, stood behind a tree within half a musket shot, and let his arrows fly at them; he was seen [to] shoot three arrows, which were all avoided. He stood three shots of a musket, till one taking full aim at him and made the bark or splinters of the tree fly about his ears, after which he gave an extraordinary shriek and away they went, all of them. . . .

Painting of the Pilgrims landing at Plymouth

Thus it pleased God to vanquish their enemies and give them deliverance; and by His special providence so to dispose that not any one of them were either hurt or hit, though their arrows came close by them and on every side [of] them; and sundry of their coats, which hung up in the barricado, were shot through and through. Afterwards they gave God solemn thanks and praise for their deliverance, and gathered up a bundle of their arrows and sent them to England afterward by the master of the ship, and called that place the First Encounter. . . .

Indian Relations

All this while the Indians came skulking about them, and would sometimes show themselves aloof off, but when any approached near them, they would run away; and once they stole away their tools where they had been at work and were gone to dinner. But about the 16th of March, a certain Indian came boldly amongst them and spoke to them in broken English, which they could well understand but marveled at it. At length they understood by discourse with him, that he was not of these parts, but belonged to the eastern parts where some English ships came to fish, with whom he was acquainted and could name sundry of them by their names, amongst whom he had got his language. He became profitable to them in acquainting them with many things concerning the state of the country in the east parts where he lived, which was afterwards profitable unto them; as also of the people here, of their names, number and strength, of their situation and distance from this place, and who was chief amongst them. His name was Samoset. He told them also of another Indian whose name was Squanto, a native of this place, who had been in England and could speak better English than himself.

Being, after some time of entertainment and gifts dismissed, a while after he came again, and five more with him, and they brought again all the tools that were stolen away before, and made way for the coming of their great Sachem, called Massasoit. Who, about four or five days after, came with the chief of his friends and other attendance, with the aforesaid Squanto. With whom, after friendly entertainment and some gifts given him, they made a peace with him (which hath now continued this 24 years) in these terms:

1. That neither he nor any of his should injure or do hurt to any of their people.

2. That if any of his did hurt to any of theirs, he should send the offender, that they might punish him.

3. That if anything were taken away from any of theirs, he should cause it to be restored; and they should do the like to his.

4. If any did unjustly war against him, they would aid him; if any did war against them, he should aid them.

5. He should send to his neighbours confederates to certify them of this, that they might not wrong them, but might be likewise comprised in the conditions of peace.

6. That when their men came to them, they should leave their bows and arrows behind them.

After these things he returned to his place called Sowams, some 40 miles from this place, but Squanto continued with them and was their interpreter and was a special instrument sent of God for their good beyond their expectation. He directed them how to set their corn, where to take fish, and to procure other commodities, and was also their pilot to bring them to unknown places for their profit, and never left them till he died.

Analyzing the Document Use this additional question to generate class discussion:

Critical Thinking: Making Comparisons What were the prospects of survival for the Pilgrim settlers before and after they met Squanto? *(Before they met Squanto, they were not likely to survive, because they were in an unfriendly territory, constantly at risk of attack, and unfamiliar with their surroundings. After they met Squanto, their prospects for survival increased dramatically because he brought them peace, and showed them the best ways to raise and gather food in the area.)*

Analyzing Literature

Use the passage on these pages to answer the following questions.

1. Whom do the colonists credit and thank for rescuing them from the first Indian attack?
   A Squanto
   B God
   C Sachem
   D Bradford

2. What does this tell you about the *Mayflower* explorers?
   A They have faith in their governor.
   B They are able to rely on all of the natives for support.
   C They trust no one and nothing.
   D They have strong religious faith.

3. **Critical Thinking: Identifying Assumptions** From these two brief excerpts, how would you describe the Native Americans' initial feelings about the new settlers? Why do you suppose the natives feel this way?

✓ TEST PREPARATION

Have students use the excerpt on these pages to answer the question below.

What was one of the results of the meeting between the Native Americans and the Pilgrims?

A Hostilities broke out.

(B) Terms for peaceful coexistence were negotiated.

C The Native Americans brought the Pilgrims to their village.

D Future European settlements had to be made in another area.

ANSWERS

1. B
2. D

3. Answers might include hostility, fear, and curiosity. Reasons might include the Pilgrims' weapons, different appearance and customs, etc.

American Literature
Unit 2

APRIL MORNING
BY HOWARD FAST

Focus Have students read the introduction and look up the meanings of the vocabulary words. Then explain that the excerpt from Howard Fast's *April Morning* dramatizes the tension of the American Revolution by portraying the war's first battle through the eyes of a fictional young observer.

Instruct Ask students to recall facts about the Battles at Lexington and Concord based on their reading. Then ask them to write a brief summary of the battles, labeled "historical writing." After students have read the selection, ask them to write another brief summary based on their reading, labeled "literary writing." Ask volunteers to read their summaries aloud. Discuss the differences between the two kinds of writing.

Extend Ask students to write the next chapter of *April Morning,* supposing that they are the boy in Fast's book. They should focus on the aftermath of the Battle at Lexington and draw on their knowledge of the events described in the chapter. Have volunteers read their chapters aloud to the class.

April Morning
BY HOWARD FAST

The fighting at Lexington and Concord, Massachusetts, on April 19, 1775, marked the beginning of the American Revolution. In the following excerpt from his historical novel April Morning, *Howard Fast captures the sights and sounds of the skirmish at Lexington Green.*

VOCABULARY Before you read the selection, find the meaning of these words in a dictionary:
dissipate
jubilation

Minuteman statue, Concord, Massachusetts

When the British saw us, they were on the road past Buckman's [Tavern]. First, there were three officers on horseback. Then two flag-bearers, one carrying the regimental flag and the other bearing the British colors. Then a corps of eight drums. Then rank after rank of the redcoats, stretching back on the road and into the curtain of mist, and emerging from the mist constantly, so that they appeared to be an endless force and an endless number. It was dreamlike and not very believable, and it caused me to turn and look at the houses around the common, to see whether all the rest of what we were, our mothers and sisters and brothers and grandparents, were watching the same thing we watched. My impression was that the houses had appeared by magic, for I could only remember looking around in the darkness and seeing nothing where now all the houses stood—and the houses were dead and silent, every shutter closed and bolted, every door and storm door closed and barred. Never before had I seen the houses like that, not in the worst cold or the worst storms.

And the redcoats did not quicken their pace or slow it, but marched up the road with the same even pace, up to the edge of the common; and when they were there, one of the officers held up his arm—and the drums stopped and the soldiers stopped, the line of soldiers stretching all the way down the road and into the dissipating mist. They were about one hundred and fifty paces from us.

The three officers sat on their horses, studying us. The morning air was cold and clean and sharp, and I could see their faces and the faces of the red-coat soldiers behind them, the black bands of their knapsacks, the glitter of their buckles. Their coats were red as fire, but their light trousers were stained and dirty from the march.

Then, one of the officers sang out to them, "Fix bayonets!" and all down the line, the bayonets sparkled in the morning sun, and we heard the ring of metal against metal as they were clamped onto the guns. . . .

Then another British officer—I discovered afterward that he was Major Pitcairn—called out orders: "Columns right!" and then, "By the left flank," and, "Drums to the rear!" The drummers stood still and beat their drums, and the redcoats marched past them smartly, wheeling and parading across the common, while the three mounted officers spurred over the grass at a sharp canter, straight across our front and then back, reining in their prancing horses to face us. Meanwhile, the redcoats marched onto the common, the first company

1158 American Literature

wheeling to face us when it was past our front of thirty-three men, the second company repeating the exercise, until they made a wall of red coats across the common, with no more than thirty or forty paces separating us. Even so close, they were unreal; only their guns were real, and their glittering bayonets too—and suddenly, I realized, and I believed that everyone else around me realized, that this was not to be an exercise or a parade or an argument, but something undreamed of and unimagined.

I think the Reverend was beginning to speak when Major Pitcairn drove down on him so that he had to leap aside. My father clutched the Reverend's arm to keep him from falling, and wheeling his horse, Major Pitcairn checked the beast so that it pawed at the air and neighed shrilly. The Reverend was speaking again, but no one heard his words or remembered them. The redcoats were grinning; small, pinched faces under the white wigs—they grinned at us. Leaning over his horse, Major Pitcairn screamed at us:

"Lay down your arms . . . Disperse, do you hear me! Disperse, you lousy peasant scum! Clear the way, do you hear me! Get off the King's green!"

At least, those were the words that I seem to remember. Others remembered differently; but the way he screamed, in his strange London accent, with all the motion and excitement, with his horse rearing and kicking at the Reverend and Father, with the drums beating again and the fixed bayonets glittering in the sunshine, it's a wonder that any of his words remained with us.

Yet for all that, this was a point where everything appeared to happen slowly. Abel Loring clutched my arm and said dryly, "Adam, Adam, Adam." He let go of his gun and it fell to the ground. "Pick it up," I said to him, watching Father, who pulled the Reverend into the protection of his body. Jonas Parker turned to us and cried at us:

"Steady! Steady! Now just hold steady!"

We still stood in our two lines, our guns butt end on the ground or held loosely in our hands. Major Pitcairn spurred his horse and raced between the lines. Somewhere, away from us, a shot sounded. A redcoat soldier raised his musket, leveled it at Father, and fired. My father clutched at his breast, then crumpled to the ground like an empty sack and lay with his face in the grass. I screamed. I was two [persons]. One part of me was screaming; another part of me looked at Father and grasped my gun in aching hands. Then the whole British front burst into a roar of sound and flame and smoke, and our whole world crashed at us, and broke into little pieces that fell around our ears, and came to an end; and the roaring, screaming noise was like the jubilation of the damned.

I ran. I was filled with fear, saturated with it, sick with it. Everyone else was running. The boys were running and the men were running. Our two lines were gone, and now it was only men and boys running in every direction that was away from the British, across the common and away from the British.

British uniform jacket like those worn at Lexington

Analyzing the Document Use this additional question to generate class discussion:

Critical Thinking: Demonstrating Reasoned Judgment Do you think that the shooting and resulting death that occurred in Lexington were inevitable? *(Answers will vary. Students should point out that the British were provoking the colonists with their show of force and bravado.)*

Analyzing Literature

Use the passage on these pages to answer the following questions.
1. How does the British force at Lexington compare with the colonists' force?
   A The two forces are roughly equal.
   B The colonists' force is much larger.
   C The British force is much larger.
   D The mist makes it impossible to compare the two forces.
2. What does the narrator mean by the use of such words as "dreamlike" and "unreal" to describe the events of that morning?
   A He has not witnessed the events and is only imagining how they must have looked.
   B He has arrived on the scene too late to understand what is happening.
   C He is too young to understand what is happening.
   D He has difficulty believing what is happening.
3. **Critical Thinking: Drawing Conclusions** Based on this account, what do you think caused the fighting at Lexington? Explain your answer.

TEST PREPARATION

Have students use the excerpt on these pages to answer the question below.

On what date did the American Revolution begin?
   A April 17, 1775
   B April 18, 1775
   C April 19, 1775
   D April 17, 1776

ANSWERS

1. C
2. D
3. The British taunted the colonists; a colonist fired a single shot, and the British retaliated.

American Literature

INCIDENTS IN THE LIFE OF A SLAVE GIRL
BY HARRIET ANN JACOBS

Focus Have students read the introduction and look up the meanings of the vocabulary words. Point out that the autobiography of Harriet Ann Jacobs reveals both the subtle and the blatant abuses that even the kindest slave owners dealt the enslaved.

Instruct Divide the class into two groups and have each group make a list of the hardships described by Harriet Ann Jacobs. Then reconvene as a class and have the groups compare their lists. Use the lists as a basis for discussing the various challenges that African Americans faced in the mid-1800s.

Extend Have students research the daily life of an enslaved person on a southern plantation. Students might use such sources as *Six Women's Slave Narratives* by William Andrews. Then ask pairs of students to prepare a skit that demonstrates the daily life of the person chosen. Discuss with the class what the skit revealed about that person and the history of the times.

American Literature
Unit 3

Incidents in the Life of a Slave Girl

By HARRIET ANN JACOBS

Harriet Ann Jacobs was born into slavery in Edenton, North Carolina, in 1813. Her long and remarkable road to freedom began in 1835, when she and her two young children went into hiding in her hometown. In 1842, Jacobs escaped to New York with her son and daughter. There she made a home for her children and was eventually bought by the Colonization Society and freed in 1852. Shortly afterward she wrote her autobiography, which provides a personal account of what it was like to be enslaved in the 1800s.

VOCABULARY Before you read the selection, find the meaning of these words in a dictionary:
toilsome
bequeath
chattel
defraud

Antislavery logo linking the women's rights and abolitionist movements

I was born a slave; but I never knew it till six years of happy childhood had passed away. My father was a carpenter, and considered so intelligent and skillful in his trade, that, when buildings out of the common line were to be erected, he was sent for from long distances, to be head workman. On condition of paying his mistress two hundred dollars a year, and supporting himself, he was allowed to work at his trade, and manage his own affairs. His strongest wish was to purchase his children; but, though he several times offered his hard earnings for that purpose, he never succeeded.

I was so fondly shielded that I never dreamed I was a piece of merchandise, trusted to them for safe keeping, and liable to be demanded of them at any moment. . . .

Such were the unusually fortunate circumstances of my early childhood. When I was six years old, my mother died; and then, for the first time, I learned, by the talk around me, that I was a slave. My mother's mistress was the daughter of my grandmother's mistress. She was the foster sister of my mother; they were both nourished at my grandmother's breast. In fact, my mother had been weaned at three months old, that the babe of the mistress might obtain sufficient food. They played together as children; and, when they became women, my mother was a most faithful servant to her white foster sister. On her death-bed her mistress promised that her children should never suffer for any thing; and during her lifetime she kept her word. They all spoke kindly of my dead mother, who had been a slave merely in name, but in nature was noble and womanly. I grieved for her, and my young mind was troubled with the thought who would now take care of me and my little brother. I was told that my home was now to be with her mistress; and I found it a happy one. No toilsome or disagreeable duties were imposed upon me. My mistress was so kind to me that I was always glad to do her bidding, and proud to labor for her as much as my young years would permit. . . .

1160 American Literature

When I was nearly twelve years old, my kind mistress sickened and died. As I saw the cheek grow paler, and the eye more glassy, how earnestly I prayed in my heart that she might live! I loved her; for she had been almost like a mother to me. My prayers were not answered. She died, and they buried her in the little churchyard, where, day after day, my tears fell upon her grave.

I was sent to spend a week with my grandmother. I was now old enough to begin to think of the future; and again and again I asked myself what they would do with me. I felt sure I should never find another mistress so kind as the one who was gone. She had promised my dying mother that her children should never suffer for any thing; and when I remembered that, and recalled her many proofs of attachment to me, I could not help having some hopes that she had left me free. . . .

After a brief period of suspense . . . we learned that she had bequeathed me to her sister's daughter, a child of five years old. So vanished our hopes. My mistress had taught me the precepts of God's Word: "Thou shalt love thy neighbor as thyself." "What-soever ye would that men should do unto you, do ye even so unto them." But I was her slave, and I suppose she did not recognize me as her neighbor. I would give much to blot out from my memory that one great wrong. As a child, I loved my mistress; and, looking back on the happy days I spent with her, I try to think with less bitterness of this act of injustice. While I was with her, she taught me to read and spell; and for this privilege, which so rarely falls to the lot of a slave, I bless her memory. . . .

My grandmother's mistress had always promised her that, at her death, she should be free; and it was said that in her will she made good the promise. But when the estate was settled, Dr. Flint told the faithful old servant that, under existing circumstances, it was necessary she should be sold.

On the appointed day, the customary advertisement was posted up, proclaiming that there would be a "public sale of negroes, horses, &c." Dr. Flint called to tell my grandmother that he was unwilling to wound her feelings by putting her up at auction, and that he would prefer to dispose of her at private sale. My grandmother saw through his hypocrisy; she understood very well that he was ashamed of the job. She was a very spirited woman, and if he was base enough to sell her, when her mistress intended she should be free, she was determined the public should know it. She had for a long time supplied many families with crackers and preserves; consequently, "Aunt Marthy," as she was called, was generally known, and every body who knew her respected her intelligence and good character. Her long and faithful service in the family was also well known, and the intention of her mistress to leave her free. When the day of sale came, she took her place among the chattels, and at the first call she sprang upon the auction-block. Many voices called out, "Shame! Shame! Who is going to sell *you*, Aunt Marthy? Don't stand there! That is no place for *you*." Without saying a word, she quietly awaited her fate. No one bid for her. At last, a feeble voice said, "Fifty dollars." It came from a maiden lady, seventy years old, the sister of my grandmother's deceased mistress. She had lived forty years under the same roof with my grandmother; she knew how faithfully she had served her owners, and how cruelly she had been defrauded of her rights; and she resolved to protect her.

TO BE SOLD on board the Ship *Bance-Island*, on tueſday the 6th of *May* next, at *Aſhley-Ferry*; a choice cargo of about 250 fine healthy NEGROES, juſt arrived from the Windward & Rice Coaſt. —The utmoſt care has already been taken, and ſhall be continued, to keep them free from the leaſt danger of being infected with the SMALL-POX, no boat having been on board, and all other communication with people from *Charles-Town* prevented.
Auſtin, Laurens, & Appleby.

N. B. Full one Half of the above Negroes have had the SMALL-POX in their own Country.

Slave sale advertisment

SLAVERY IN MASSACHUSETTS
BY HENRY DAVID THOREAU

Focus Have students read the intro-duction and look up the meanings of the vocabulary words. Then explain that the excerpt is a speech written to protest the return of two escaped slaves to slavery in the South under terms of the Fugitive Slave Law.

Instruct Ask your students to review the many contrasts Thoreau presents between the intentions of the Founding Fathers—to secure "Liberty and Justice for All" and justifications made in support of slaveholding. Have stu-dents list these contrasts. Do they believe Thoreau builds a convincing argument? What points would they add to the list to further demonstrate the contradiction inherent in a country established to preserve freedom that nonetheless sanctions slavery?

Extend Ask students to research the writings and speeches of a prominent abolitionist of the mid-nineteenth cen-tury. How did this individual seek to persuade others to support his or her cause? As a class, create a time line that demonstrates major events and major legislation passed in the years 1850–1861 to underscore the growing rift between the North and South.

American Literature
Unit 4

Slavery in Massachusetts
BY HENRY DAVID THOREAU

Henry David Thoreau, remembered most widely today for his nature writings such as Walden, *also had a considerable reputation as an abolitionist speaker. He delivered a version of the speech containing the following excerpt at an "Anti-Slavery Celebration" in Framingham, Massachusetts, on July 4, 1854. The event was a protest against official Independence Day observances.*

Behind Thoreau's anger lay two recent events, both triggered by the Fugitive Slave Law (part of the Compromise of 1850). On April 12, 1851, the Massachusetts state government had returned a fugitive slave named Thomas Sims to his Georgia master. Tensions surrounding the case ran so high that the government had employed 300 armed guards to escort Sims to a ship that sailed before dawn. In the second incident, nine men had been arrested for attempting to rescue another slave, Anthony Burns, from the Boston courthouse where he was held before being returned to his Virginia master.

VOCABULARY Before you read the selection, find the meaning of these words in a dictionary:
humane
incapacity
tribunal
precedent
docket

Henry David Thoreau

Three years ago, also, just a week after the authorities of Boston assembled to carry back a perfectly innocent man, and one whom they knew to be innocent, into slavery, the inhabitants of Concord caused the bells to be rung and the cannons to be fired, to cele-brate their liberty—and the courage and love of liberty of their ancestors who fought at the bridge. As if *those* three millions had fought for the right to be free themselves, but to hold in slavery three millions others. Now-a-days, men wear a fool's cap, and call it a liberty cap. I do not know but there are some, who, if they were tied to a whipping-post, and could get but one hand free, would use it to ring the bells and fire the cannons, to celebrate *their* liberty. So some of my townsmen took the liberty to ring and fire; that was the extent of their freedom; and when the sound of the bells died away, their liberty died away also; when the powder was all expended, their liberty went off with the smoke.

The joke could be no broader, if the inmates of the prisons were to sub-scribe for [agree to purchase] all the powder to be used in such salutes, and hire the jailors to do the firing and ringing for them, while they enjoyed it through the grating.

This is what I thought about my neighbors.

Every humane and intelligent inhabitant of Concord, when he or she heard those bells and those cannons, thought not with pride of the events of the 19th of April, 1775, but with shame of the events of the 12th of April, 1851. But now we have half buried that old shame under a new one. . . .

I wish my countrymen to consider, that whatever the human law may be, neither an individual nor a nation can ever commit the least act of injustice against the obscurest individual, without having to pay the penalty for it. A government which deliberately enacts injustice, and persists in it, will at length ever become the laughing-stock of the world.

Much has been said about American slavery, but I think that we do not even yet realize what slavery is. If I were seriously to propose to Congress to make mankind into sausages, I have no doubt that most of the members would smile at my proposition, and if any believed me to be in earnest, they would think that I proposed something much worse than Congress had ever done. But if any of them will tell me that to make a man into a sausage would be much worse,—would be any worse, than to make him into a slave,—than it was to enact the Fugitive Slave law, I will accuse him of foolishness, of intellectual incapacity, of making a distinction without a difference. The one is just as reasonable a proposition as the other. . . .

Recent events will be valuable as a criticism on the administration of justice in our midst, or, rather, as showing what are the true resources of justice in any community. It has come to this, that the friends of liberty, the friends of the slave, have shuddered when they have understood that his fate was left to the legal tribunals of the country to be decided. Free men have no faith that justice will be awarded in such a case; the judge may decide this way or that; it is a kind of accident, at best. It is evident that he is not a competent authority in so important a case. It is no time, then, to be judging according to his precedents but to establish a precedent for the future. . . .

It is to some extent fatal to the courts, when the people are compelled to go behind them. I do not wish to believe that the courts were made for fair weather, and for very civil cases merely,—but think of leaving it to any court in the land to decide whether more than three millions of people, in this case, a sixth part of a nation, have a right to be freemen or not! But it has been left to the courts of *justice*, so-called—to the Supreme Court of the land—and, as you all know, recognizing no authority but the Constitution, it has decided that the three millions are, and shall continue to be, slaves. Such judges as these are merely the inspectors of a pick-lock and murderer's tools, to tell him whether they are in working order or not, and there they think that their responsibility ends. There was a prior case on the docket, which they, as judges appointed by God, had no right to skip; which having been justly settled, they would have been saved from this humiliation. It was the case of the murderer himself.

The law will never make men free; it is men who have got to make the law free. They are the lovers of law and order, who observe the law when the government breaks it.

William Lloyd Garrison published Thoreau's speech in his famous antislavery newspaper *The Liberator*.

American Literature

Analyzing the Document Use this additional question to generate class discussion:

Critical Thinking: Identifying Assumptions What does Thoreau assume when he encourages his listeners to "observe the law when the government breaks it"? *(He assumes that by establishing the Fugitive Slave Law, the government was in effect breaking the law, since the United States was established on principles of freedom for all.)*

Analyzing Literature

Use the passage on these pages to answer the following questions.
1. To whom does Thoreau compare his neighbors as they celebrated Independence Day?
   A Supreme Court Justices
   B prison inmates
   C murderers
   D sausage makers
2. Why does he think they are imprisoned—or slaves—themselves?
   A because he believes no one can truly be free while also supporting slavery
   B because the state government has banned all protests against slavery
   C because many of his neighbors have served jail terms
   D because the U.S. Supreme Court has issued a warrant for their arrest
3. **Critical Thinking: Making Comparisons** At the end of this excerpt, Thoreau encourages people to observe a higher law when the government's law is unjust. At what other times in our nation's history have civic leaders encouraged this philosophy? In your opinion, is this philosophy always justified? Why or why not?

✓ TEST PREPARATION

Have students use the excerpt on these pages to answer the question below.

When Thoreau speaks of the events of April 19, 1775, to what is he referring?

A Paul Revere's ride.

Ⓑ The Battles of Lexington and Concord.

C The signing of the Declaration of Independence.

D The end of the War for Independence.

ANSWERS

1. B
2. A
3. Answers will vary, but might mention the 1960s' civil rights movement, labor protests, and others.

American Literature
Unit 5

HUNGRY HEARTS
BY ANZIA YEZIERSKA

Focus Have students read the introduction and look up the meanings of
the vocabulary words. Explain that
throughout American history, a vast difference has existed between the idealized, popular view of the United States
and the reality that greets immigrants.
Ask students to think about whether the
people who painted such glorified pictures of the United States were lying or
simply focusing only on some aspects
of society and not on others.

Instruct Ask students whether they
have undertaken a new experience,
such as trying out for a part in a play,
attending a new school, or going to a
party where they know few people.
Ask students to compare their expectations of the experience to the reality.
Then ask them to compare those
feelings to those described by Anzia
Yezierska. How are they similar? How
are they different?

Extend Ask students to conduct further
research on the immigrant experience,
either for Europeans coming through
Ellis Island or for Asians coming through
Angel Island. Students may choose to
concentrate on a period different from
that of the selection, such as the present. Have students present the results of
their research to the class. Discuss how
the experiences described are both similar to and different from those in the
selection.

VOCABULARY Before
you read the selection,
find the meaning of these
words in a dictionary:
steerage
Cossack
dilapidated
maw

**Young girl working at a
spinning machine,** *circa*
early 1900s

Hungry Hearts
BY ANZIA YEZIERSKA

*Like many other immigrants who flooded into the nation's cities during the late
1800s, Anzia Yezierska and her family came to New York to escape ethnic persecution in their homeland. In her autobiography,* Hungry Hearts, *Yezierska
describes what it was like to leave her Russian village and begin a new life in the
United States.*

Steerage—dirty bundles—foul odors—seasick humanity—but I saw
and heard nothing of the foulness and ugliness around me. I floated
in showers of sunshine; visions upon visions of the new world
opened before me.

From lips flowed the golden legend of the golden country:

"In America you can say what you feel—you can voice your thoughts in the
open streets without fear of a Cossack."

"In America is a home for everybody. The land is your land. Not like in
Russia where you feel yourself a stranger in the village where you were born
and raised—the village in which your father and grandfather lie buried." . . .

" . . . Everybody can do what he wants with his life in America."

"There are no high or low in America. Even the President holds hands with
Gedalyeh Mindel."

"Plenty for all. Learning flows free like milk and honey."

"Learning flows free."

The words painted pictures in my mind. I saw before me free schools, free
colleges, free libraries, where I could learn and learn and keep on learning. . . .

"Land! Land!" came the joyous shout.

"America! We're in America!" cried my mother, almost smothering us in
her rapture.

All crowded and pushed on deck. They strained and stretched to get the
first glimpse of the "golden country," lifting their children on their shoulders
that they might see beyond them.

Men fell on their knees to pray. Women hugged their babies and wept.
Children danced. Strangers embraced and kissed like old friends. Old men and
women had in their eyes a look of young people in love.

Age-old visions sang themselves in me—songs of freedom of an
oppressed people.

America!—America! . . .

Between buildings that loomed like mountains, we struggled with our
bundles, spreading around us the smell of the steerage. Up Broadway, under
the bridge, and through the swarming streets of the ghetto, we followed
Gedalyeh Mindel.

I looked about the narrow streets of squeezed-in stores and houses, ragged clothes, dirty bedding oozing out of the windows, ash-cans and garbage-cans cluttering the side-walks. A vague sadness pressed down my heart—the first doubt of America.

"Where are the green fields and open spaces in America?" cried my heart. "Where is the golden country of my dreams?"

A loneliness for the fragrant silence of the woods that lay beyond our mud hut welled up in my heart, a longing for the soft, responsive earth of our village streets. All about me was the hardness of brick and stone, the stinking smells of crowded poverty.

"Here's your house with separate rooms like in a palace." Gedalyeh Mindel flung open the door of a dingy, airless flat.

"Oi weh!" my mother cried in dismay. "Where's the sunshine in America?"

She went to the window and looked out at the blank wall of the next house. "Gottuniu! Like in a grave so dark . . ."

"It ain't so dark, it's only a little shady." Gedalyeh Mindel lighted the gas. "Look only"—he pointed with pride to the dim gaslight. "No candles, no kerosene lamps in America, you turn on a screw and put to it a match and you got it light like with sunshine."

Again the shadow fell over me, again the doubt of America!

In America were rooms without sunlight, rooms to sleep in, to eat in, to cook in, but without sunshine. And Gedalyeh Mindel was happy. Could I be satisfied with just a place to sleep and eat in, and a door to shut people out—to take the place of sunlight? Or would I always need the sunlight to be happy?

And where was there a place in America for me to play? I looked out into the alley below and saw pale-faced children scrambling in the gutter. "Where is America?" cried my heart. . . .

"Heart of mine!" my mother's voice moaned above me. "Father is already gone an hour. You know how they'll squeeze from you a nickel for every minute you're late. Quick only!"

I seized my bread and herring and tumbled down the stairs and out into the street. I ate running, blindly pressing through the hurrying throngs of workers—my haste and fear choking each mouthful.

I felt a strangling in my throat as I neared the sweatshop prison [factory where she worked]; all my nerves screwed together into iron hardness to endure the day's torture.

For an instant I hesitated as I faced the grated window of the old dilapidated building—dirt and decay cried out from every crumbling brick.

In the maw of the shop, raging around me the roar and the clatter, the clatter and the roar, the merciless grind of the pounding machines. Half maddened, half deadened, I struggled to think, to feel, to remember—what am I—who am I—why was I here?

I struggled in vain—bewildered and lost in a whirlpool of noise.

"America—America—where was America? . . ."

Analyzing the Document Use this additional question to generate class discussion:

Critical Thinking: Making Comparisons Although Yezierska highlights the differences between her homeland and the United States, were there any similarities? *(Answers will vary, but students may suggest that Yezierska feared for her safety in both places. Also, her life in the United States was restricted by the number of hours she had to work; she points to restrictions in her homeland as well.)*

Analyzing Literature

Use the passage on these pages to answer the following questions.

1. Which statement best describes Anzia Yezierska's image of the United States before she arrives?
   A It is her homeland.
   B It is a land of freedom for all.
   C It is a crowded and dark country.
   D It is not a place of safety.
2. What is her biggest disappointment about the United States?
   A It reminds her too much of her former home.
   B It has too much open space.
   C It has no jobs.
   D It seems to want her only as a laborer, not as a complete person.
3. **Critical Thinking: Predicting Consequences** In what different ways might immigrants have reacted to disappointments in the United States?

✓ TEST PREPARATION

Have students use the excerpt on these pages to answer the question below.

Where did Anzia Yezierska work after she came to America?

A On a farm.

B In a tenement.

C She was unable to find work.

D In a sweatshop, or factory.

ANSWERS

1. B
2. D
3. Answers will vary, but students may respond that because they had to work so hard in such dingy surroundings, some immigrants may have been depressed about their lives in the United States; others may have thought it worthwhile to remain in America because there were still more opportunities available here than in Europe.

American Literature
Unit 6

A FAREWELL TO ARMS
BY ERNEST HEMINGWAY

Focus Have students read the introduction and look up the meanings of the vocabulary words. Then explain that in this passage, two World War I ambulance drivers, one American and one Italian, discuss the war. The passage clearly conveys the banality and horror of war.

Instruct Ask students to find words and phrases that convey Frederick Henry's attitude toward the war and his work. In their opinion, is he motivated and energetic, or depressed and apathetic? What might have caused him to arrive at the state of mind demonstrated in the passage? Have students focus on the portion of the text that describes the narrator's perception of the bombardment that takes place in the night. As he describes it, does it seem immediate, or remote? What is his response to the wounded arriving in camp? Is he emotionally engaged with them, or is he detached?

Extend Have students research the history of World War I to learn more about conditions at the time this passage takes place. What battles actually took place in this mountainous region?

Trench warfare in World War I

A Farewell to Arms
BY ERNEST HEMINGWAY

Ernest Hemingway's second novel, A Farewell to Arms, *is set during World War I and focuses on the war efforts in the mountainous region along Italy's northeastern border with present-day Austria and Slovenia, an area referred to in the book as the "Bainsizza." In the excerpt that follows, the main character, American army officer Frederick Henry, an ambulance driver, discusses the war with Gino, a native Italian and fellow driver.*

VOCABULARY Before you read the selection, find the meaning of these words in a dictionary:
quadrilateral
hallow

I did not believe in a war in the mountains. I had thought about it a lot, I said. You pinched off one mountain and they pinched off another but when something really started every one had to get down off the mountains.

What were you going to do if you had a mountain frontier? he asked.

I had not worked that out yet, I said, and we both laughed. "But," I said, "in the old days the Austrians were always whipped in the quadrilateral around Verona. They let them come down onto the plain and whipped them there."

"Yes," said Gino. "But those were Frenchmen and you can work out military problems clearly when you are fighting in somebody else's country."

"Yes," I agreed, "when it is your own country you cannot use it so scientifically."

"The Russians did, to trap Napoleon."

"Yes, but they had plenty of country. If you tried to retreat to trap Napoleon in Italy you would find yourself in Brindisi."

"A terrible place," said Gino. "Have you ever been there?"

"Not to stay."

"I am a patriot," Gino said. "But I cannot love Brindisi or Taranto."

"Do you love the Bainsizza?" I asked.

"The soil is sacred," he said. "But I wish it grew more potatoes. You know when we came here we found fields of potatoes the Austrians had planted."

"Has the food really been short?"

"I myself have never had enough to eat but I am a big eater and have not starved. The mess is average. The regiments in the line get pretty good food but those in support don't get so much. Something is wrong somewhere. There should be plenty of food."

"The dogfish are selling it somewhere else."

"Yes, they give the battalions in the front line as much as they can but the ones in back are very short. They have eaten all the Austrians' potatoes and chestnuts from the woods. They ought to feed them better. We are big eaters. I am sure there is plenty of food. It is very bad for the soldiers to be short of food. Have you ever noticed the difference it makes in the way you think?"

"Yes," I said. "It can't win a war but it can lose one."

"We won't talk about losing. There is enough talk about losing. What has been done this summer cannot have been done in vain."

I did not say anything. I was always embarrassed by the words sacred, glorious, and sacrifice and the expression in vain. We had heard them, sometimes standing in the rain almost out of earshot, so that only the shouted words came through, and had read them, on proclamations that were slapped up by billposters over other proclamations, now for a long time, and I had seen nothing sacred, and the things that were glorious had no glory and the sacrifices were like the stockyards at Chicago if nothing was done with the meat except to bury it. There were many words that you could not stand to hear and finally only the names of places had dignity. Certain numbers were the same way and certain dates and these with the names of the places were all you could say and have them mean anything. Abstract words such as glory, honor, courage, or hallow were obscene beside the concrete names of villages, the numbers of roads, the names of rivers, the numbers of regiments and the dates. Gino was a patriot, so he said things that separated us sometimes, but he was also a fine boy and I understood his being a patriot. He was born one. He left with Peduzzi in the car to go back to Gorizia.

It stormed all that day. The wind drove down the rain and everywhere there was standing water and mud. The plaster of the broken houses was gray and wet. Late in the afternoon the rain stopped and from out number two post I saw the bare wet autumn country with clouds over the tops of the hills and the straw screening over the roads wet and dripping. The sun came out once before it went down and shone on the bare woods beyond the ridge. There were many Austrian guns in the woods on that ridge but only a few fired. I watched the sudden round puffs of shrapnel smoke in the sky above a broken farmhouse near where the line was; soft puffs with a yellow white flash in the centre. You saw the flash, then heard the crack, then saw the smoke ball distort and thin in the wind. There were many iron shrapnel balls in the rubble of the houses and on the road beside the broken house where the post was, but they did not shell near the post that afternoon. We loaded two cars and drove down the road that was screened with wet mats and the last of the sun came through in the breaks between the strips of mattings. Before we were out on the clear road behind the hill the sun was down. We went on down the clear road and as it turned a corner into the open and went into the square arched tunnel of matting the rain started again.

The wind rose in the night and at three o'clock in the morning with the rain coming in sheets there was a bombardment and the Croatians came over across the mountain meadows and through patches of woods and into the front line. They fought in the dark in the rain and a counter-attack of scared men from the second line drove them back. There was much shelling and many rockets in the rain and machine-gun and rifle fire all along the line. They did not come again and it was quieter and between the gusts of wind and rain we could hear the sound of a great bombardment far to the north.

The wounded were coming into the post, some were carried on stretchers, some walking and some were brought on the backs of men that came across the field. They were wet to the skin and all were scared. We filled two cars with stretcher cases as they came up from the cellar of the post and as I shut the door of the second car and fastened it I felt the rain on my face turn to snow. The flakes were coming heavy and fast in the rain.

Analyzing Literature

Use the passage on these pages to answer the following questions.

1. What is the narrator's attitude about the war?
   A He is a patriot and defender of his homeland.
   B He is tired and does not believe in the part of the war in which he is fighting.
   C He wants to motivate others to get involved in the war.
   D He is fiercely determined to defeat the enemy.

2. Why might the narrator be embarrassed by Gino's patriotism?
   A He is a shy man who is easily embarrassed by things.
   B Gino is trying to convince him to stay in Italy after the war, and he doesn't want to.
   C His job of handling dead and injured men makes it hard for him to sympathize with Gino.
   D He knows too much about Gino's past to believe him fully.

3. **Critical Thinking: Determining Relevance** Hemingway is known for using simple words and short, descriptive sentences. Do you think this style effectively conveys the feeling of being in a war? Why or why not?

American Literature 1167

✓ TEST PREPARATION

Have students use the excerpt on these pages to answer the question below.

Which word best describes Frederick Henry's attitude toward war in general?

A Excited
Ⓑ Disillusioned
C Angry
D Frightened

ANSWERS

1. B
2. C
3. Answers will vary, but might mention a certain starkness, which is a kind of symbolism through which Hemingway conveys his own emotions about war.

Growing Up
By Russell Baker

Focus Have students read the introduction and look up the meanings of the vocabulary words. Then explain that "going on relief" (what today would be called "going on welfare") has often been viewed as shameful in the United States. That is why President Franklin Roosevelt tried so hard to find work for the nation's unemployed, instead of giving them handouts. Some people were not eligible for any of Roosevelt's programs, however, and, like Baker's family, ended up on relief anyway, despite their best efforts.

Instruct Ask students to find evidence of how the Depression affected Baker and his family. What was Baker's attitude toward people who accepted government relief? How might his attitude toward accepting relief have been changed by his experience?

Extend Have students suppose that they are Baker or his mother. Ask them to write a letter to President or Mrs. Roosevelt that Baker or his mother could have written explaining their plight.

American Literature Unit 7

Growing Up

By RUSSELL BAKER

Single parents rarely have an easy life, and during the Depression their families' very survival was threatened. Because they were the sole caregivers for their children, they could not travel to look for work. Many had no choice but to accept aid from the government. In the following excerpt from his 1982 autobiography, Growing Up, *Russell Baker, a* New York Times *columnist, remembers those difficult days and one trying day in particular.*

VOCABULARY Before you read the selection, find the meaning of these words in a dictionary:
dilapidation
appetizing
edible
incriminating
ostentatious

The paper route earned me three dollars a week, sometimes four, and my mother, in addition to her commissions on magazine sales, also had her monthly check coming from Uncle Willie, but we'd been in Baltimore a year before I knew how desperate things were for her. One Saturday morning she told me she'd need Doris and me to go with her to pick up some food. I had a small wagon she'd bought me to make it easier to move the Sunday papers, and she said I'd better bring it along. The three of us set off eastward, passing the grocery stores we usually shopped at, and kept walking until we came to Fremont Avenue, a grim street of dilapidation and poverty in the heart of East Baltimore.

"This is where we go," she said when we reached the corner of Fremont and Fayette Street. It looked like a grocery, with big plate-glass windows and people lugging out cardboard cartons and bulging bags, but it wasn't. I knew very well what it was.

"Are we going on relief?" I asked her.

"Don't ask questions about things you don't know anything about," she said. "Bring that wagon inside."

I did, and watched with a mixture of shame and greed while men filled it with food. None of it was food I liked. There were huge cans of grapefruit juice, big paper sacks of cornmeal, cellophane bags of rice and prunes. It was hard to believe all this was ours for no money at all, even though none of it was very appetizing. My wonder at this free bounty quickly changed to embarrassment as we headed home with it. Being on relief was a shameful thing. People who accepted the government's handouts were scorned by everyone I knew as idle no-accounts without enough self-respect to pay their own way in the world. I'd often heard my mother say the same thing of families in the neighborhood suspected of being on relief. These, I'd been taught to believe, were people beyond hope. Now we were as low as they were.

Pulling the wagon back toward Lombard Street, with Doris following behind to keep the edible proof of our disgrace from falling off, I knew my mother was far worse off than I'd suspected. She'd never have accepted such shame otherwise. I studied her as she walked along beside me, head high as always, not a bit bowed in disgrace, moving at her usual quick, hurry-up pace. If she'd given up on life, she didn't show it, but on the other hand she was

WORLD'S HIGHEST STANDARD OF LIVING

There's no way like the American Way

Citizens in a Kentucky relief line stand before a billboard promoting the country's high standard of living.

Critical Thinking: Identifying Assumptions What did Russell Baker assume about people who accepted relief? *(Baker assumed that people on relief were shamefully lazy and didn't want to work to pay their own way. He also assumed that they had given up hope for their lives.)*

unhappy about something. I dared to mention the dreaded words only once on that trip home.

"Are we on relief now, Mom?"

"Let me worry about that," she said.

What worried me most as we neared home was the possibility we'd be seen with the incriminating food by somebody we knew. There was no mistaking government-surplus food. The grapefruit-juice cans, the prunes and rice, the cornmeal—all were ostentatiously unlabeled, thus advertising themselves as "government handouts." Everybody in the neighborhood could read them easily enough, and our humiliation would be gossiped through every parlor by sundown. I had an inspiration.

"It's hot pulling this wagon," I said. "I'm going to take my sweater off."

It wasn't hot, it was on the cool side, but after removing the sweater I laid it across the groceries in the wagon. It wasn't a very effective cover, but my mother was suddenly affected by the heat too.

"It is warm, isn't it, Buddy?" she said. Removing her topcoat, she draped it over the groceries, providing total concealment.

"You want to take your coat off, Doris?" asked my mother.

"I'm not hot, I'm chilly," Doris said.

It didn't matter. My mother's coat was enough to get us home without being exposed as three of life's failures.

Analyzing Literature

Use the passage on these pages to answer the following questions.

1. What conclusion does Baker draw from his mother's decision to accept government relief?

 A His mother has given up on life.

 B His mother no longer cares what others think of her.

 C His mother wants him to quit his paper route.

 D His mother is desperately poor.

2. Baker places his sweater in the wagon because he is

 A hot.

 B ashamed of the government-surplus food.

 C ashamed of his mother.

 D ashamed of the wagon.

3. **Critical Thinking: Recognizing Ideologies** How might this experience have changed Baker's image of those who accepted government help?

✓ TEST PREPARATION

Have students use the excerpt on these pages to answer the question below.

How would the neighbors know that the Bakers were on relief?

 A The food had official government labels on it.

 Ⓑ The food was not labeled.

 C They would have seen them at the store.

 D No one would want to buy grapefruit juice, cornmeal, prunes, and rice.

ANSWERS

1. D

2. B

3. Answers should indicate that he probably realized many people who accepted government relief were as hardworking and honest as his own family.

American Literature

American Literature
Unit 8

Night
BY ELIE WIESEL

*Elie Wiesel, a Hungarian Jew, lost his parents and a sister in the Holocaust.
Released from the Buchenwald concentration camp in 1945, he waited ten years
before writing of his experiences.* Night, *the book he eventually wrote, is one of the
most powerful memoirs written by survivors of the Nazi camps. The excerpt
below recalls Wiesel's first night in the camp.*

VOCABULARY Before
you read the selection,
find the meaning of these
words in a dictionary:
nocturnal
antechamber
bestial
truncheon
crematory
lucidity
redemption
Talmud

Never shall I forget that night, the first night in camp, which has
turned my life into one long night, seven times cursed and
seven times sealed. Never shall I forget that smoke. Never shall
I forget the little faces of the children, whose bodies I saw
turned into wreaths of smoke beneath a silent blue sky.

Never shall I forget those flames which consumed my faith forever.

Never shall I forget that nocturnal silence which deprived me, for all eternity, of the desire to live. Never shall I forget those moments which murdered
my God and my soul and turned my dreams to dust. Never shall I forget these
things, even if I am condemned to live as long as God Himself. Never.

The barracks we had been made to go into was very long. In the roof were
some blue-tinged skylights. The antechamber of Hell must look like this. So
many crazed men, so many cries, so much bestial brutality!

There were dozens of prisoners to receive us, truncheons in their hands,
striking out anywhere, at anyone, without reason. Orders:

"Strip! Fast! *Los!* Keep only your belts and shoes in your hands. . . ."

We had to throw our clothes at one end of the barracks. There was already
a great heap there. New suits and old, torn coats, rags. For us, this was the
true equality: nakedness. Shivering with the cold.

Some SS officers moved about in the room, looking for strong men. If
they were so keen on strength, perhaps one should try and pass oneself off as
sturdy? My father thought the reverse. It was better not to draw attention to
oneself. Our fate would then be the same as the others. (Later, we were to
learn that he was right. Those who were selected that day were enlisted in the
Sonder-Kommando, the unit which worked in the crematories. Bela Katz—son
of a big tradesman from our town—had arrived at Birkenau with the first
transport, a week before us. When he heard of our arrival, he managed to get
word to us that, having been chosen for his strength, he had himself put his
father's body into the crematory oven.)

Blows continued to rain down.

"To the barber!"

Belt and shoes in hand, I let myself be dragged off to the barbers. They took
our hair off with clippers, and shaved off all the hair on our bodies. The same
thought buzzed all the time in my head—not to be separated from my father.

**Survivors of a Nazi
concentration camp**

Freed from the hands of the barbers, we began to wander in the crowd, meeting friends and acquaintances. These meetings filled us with joy—yes, joy—"Thank God! You're still alive!"

But others were crying. They used all their remaining strength in weeping. Why had they let themselves be brought here? Why couldn't they have died in their beds? Sobs choked their voices.

Suddenly, someone threw his arms round my neck in an embrace: Yechiel, brother of the rabbi of Sighet. He was sobbing bitterly. I thought he was weeping with joy at still being alive.

"Don't cry, Yechiel," I said. "Don't waste your tears. . . ."

"Not cry? We're on the threshold of death. . . . Soon we shall have crossed over. . . . Don't you understand? How could I not cry?"

Through the blue-tinged skylights I could see the darkness gradually fading. I had ceased to feel fear. And then I was overcome by an inhuman weariness.

Those absent no longer touched even the surface of our memories. We still spoke of them—"Who knows what may have become of them?"—but we had little concern for their fate. We were incapable of thinking of anything at all. Our senses were blunted; everything was blurred as in a fog. It was no longer possible to grasp anything. The instincts of self-preservation, of self-defense, of pride, had all deserted us. In one ultimate moment of lucidity it seemed to me that we were damned souls wandering in the half-world, souls condemned to wander through space till the generations of man came to an end, seeking their redemption, seeking oblivion—without hope of finding it.

Toward five o'clock in the morning, we were driven out of the barracks. The Kapos beat us once more, but I had ceased to feel any pain from their blows. An icy wind enveloped us. We were naked, our shoes and belts in our hands. The command: "Run!" And we ran. After a few minutes of racing, a new barracks.

A barrel of petrol at the entrance. Disinfection. Everyone was soaked in it. Then a hot shower. At high speed. As we came out from the water, we were driven outside. More running. Another barracks, the store. Very long tables. Mountains of prison clothes. On we ran. As we passed, trousers, tunic, shirt, and socks were thrown to us.

Within a few seconds, we had ceased to be men. If the situation had not been tragic, we should have roared with laughter. Such outfits! Meir Katz, a giant, had a child's trousers, and Stern, a thin little chap, a tunic which completely swamped him. We immediately began the necessary exchanges.

I glanced at my father. How he had changed! His eyes had grown dim. I would have liked to speak to him, but I did not know what to say.

The night was gone. The morning star was shining in the sky. I too had become a completely different person. The student of the Talmud, the child that I was, had been consumed in the flames. There remained only a shape that looked like me. A dark flame had entered into my soul and devoured it.

So much had happened within such a few hours that I had lost all sense of time. When had we left our houses? And the ghetto? And the train? Was it only a week? One night—*one single night*?

How long had we been standing like this in the icy wind? An hour? Simply an hour? Sixty minutes?

Surely it was a dream.

Analyzing Literature

Use the passage on these pages to answer the following questions.
1. Prisoners who appear stronger than others are
   A killed immediately.
   B given special privileges.
   C assigned to work in crematories.
   D beaten more severely.
2. The reference to fog on the first night describes the
   A mental confusion of the prisoners.
   B mental confusion of the guards.
   C atmosphere surrounding the camp.
   D atmosphere within the crowded barracks.
3. **Critical Thinking: Drawing Conclusions** Explain what Wiesel means by the sentence, "Surely it was a dream."

Analyzing the Document Use this additional question to generate class discussion:

Critical Thinking: Formulating Questions What questions might you ask of Elie Wiesel to learn more about his life? *(Questions might include: What sort of work were you forced to do at the concentration camp? How did you survive? Why did you wait ten years to write about your experiences? Do you think that the Holocaust could be repeated today?)*

✓ TEST PREPARATION

Have students use the excerpt on these pages to complete the following sentence.

Elie Wiesel's friend Yechiel was weeping after they left the barber because—

A he no longer had any hair.

B he was still alive.

C he was exhausted.

D he knew how close they were to death.

ANSWERS

1. C

2. A

3. Wiesel was probably wondering how this nightmare could really be happening. He had lost all sense of time and everything felt foggy. He might have been asking himself how it was possible that this atrocity was not a dream.

American Literature

"LETTER FROM BIRMINGHAM JAIL"
BY MARTIN LUTHER KING, JR.

Focus Have students read the introduction and look up the meanings of the vocabulary words. Then remind students that before the civil rights movement, segregation was widely practiced in the United States, particularly in the South. Ask students to what extent they think racial tension is still evident in our society today, despite the gains made by the civil rights movement.

Instruct Discuss the various peaceful channels for effecting change in American society (e.g., letters to elected officials, petition drives, letters to the editor). What methods for effecting change can Americans turn to if these methods fail? Discuss the various ways that Martin Luther King, Jr., tried to bring about change (speeches, marches, mass protests). Ask students to list Dr. King's justifications for staging the mass protest that resulted in his being jailed.

Extend Ask students to look up articles on Martin Luther King, Jr., and the civil rights movement in issues of *Time, Newsweek,* or other news and popular magazines from the 1960s in the library or on the Internet. What can they learn from these sources about the civil rights movement and about what it was like for both white and African Americans to live during that time? You may wish to have students make photocopies of headlines, photos, and articles for a bulletin board display on civil rights.

American Literature
Unit 9

"Letter from Birmingham Jail"
BY MARTIN LUTHER KING, JR.

In 1963, the Reverend Martin Luther King, Jr., and the Southern Christian Leadership Conference staged a mass protest in Birmingham, Alabama. King was arrested for his participation in the protest, and from his jail cell he wrote a letter, which is excerpted below. The letter was his answer to eight Birmingham clergymen who had condemned the civil rights demonstration and criticized King as an "outside agitator" coming to stir up trouble in Birmingham.

VOCABULARY Before you read the selection, find the meaning of these words in a dictionary:
deplore
unduly
ominous
complacency
manifest

My Dear Fellow Clergymen:
You deplore the demonstrations taking place in Birmingham. But your statement, I am sorry to say, fails to express a similar concern for the conditions that brought about the demonstrations. . . .
We know through painful experience that freedom is never voluntarily given by the oppressor; it must be demanded by the oppressed. Frankly, I have yet to engage in a direct-action campaign that was "well timed" in the view of those who have not suffered unduly from the disease of segregation. For years now I have heard the word "Wait!" It rings in the ear of every Negro with piercing familiarity. This "Wait!" has almost always meant "Never." We must come to see, with one of our distinguished jurists, that "justice too long delayed is justice denied."
. . . Perhaps it is easy for those who have never felt the stinging darts of segregation to say, "Wait." But when you have seen vicious mobs lynch your mothers and fathers at will and drown your sisters and brothers at whim; when you have seen hate-filled policemen curse, kick, and even kill your black brothers and sisters; when you see the vast majority of your twenty million Negro brothers smothering in an airtight cage of poverty in the midst of an affluent society; when you suddenly find your tongue twisted and your speech stammering as you seek to explain to your six-year-old daughter why she can't go to the public amusement park that has just been advertised on television, and see tears welling up in her eyes when she is told that Funtown is closed to colored children, and see ominous clouds of inferiority beginning to form in her little mental sky, and see her beginning to distort her personality by developing an unconscious bitterness toward white people; . . . then you will understand why we find it difficult to wait. . . .
You speak of our activity in Birmingham as extreme. At first I was rather disappointed that fellow clergymen would see my nonviolent efforts as those of an extremist. I began thinking about the fact that I stand in the middle of two opposing forces in the Negro community. One is a force of

Protester picketing a restaurant in the South

As his son looks on, Martin Luther King, Jr., removes a cross that had been burned in front of his home in Atlanta, Georgia, in 1960.

American Literature

Analyzing the Document Use this additional question to generate class discussion:

Critical Thinking: Recognizing Cause and Effect What effect did King see in his daughter after he explained that the amusement park was only for white families? *(King saw the first feelings of inferiority and resentment.)*

complacency, made up in part of Negroes who, as a result of long years of oppression, are so drained of self-respect and a sense of "somebodiness" that they have adjusted to segregation; and in part of a few middle-class Negroes who, because of a degree of academic and economic security and because in some ways they profit by segregation, have become insensitive to the problems of the masses. The other force is one of bitterness and hatred, and it comes perilously close to advocating violence. It is expressed in the various black nationalist groups that are springing up across the nation, the largest and best-known being Elijah Muhammad's Muslim movement. . . .

I have tried to stand between these two forces, saying that we need emulate neither the "do-nothingism" of the complacent nor the hatred and despair of the black nationalist. For there is the more excellent way of love and nonviolent protest. I am grateful to God that, through the influence of the Negro church, the way of nonviolence became an integral part of our struggle. . . .

Oppressed people cannot remain oppressed forever. The yearning for freedom eventually manifests itself, and that is what has happened to the American Negro. Something within has reminded him of his birthright of freedom, and something without has reminded him that it can be gained.

Analyzing Literature

Use the passage on these pages to answer the following questions.
1. Why, according to King, could African Americans not expect whites to grant them freedom?
   A Those in power never give up power without a struggle.
   B African Americans do not yet deserve full freedom.
   C African Americans are too divided on the issue of segregation.
   D "Do-nothingism" is too common among African Americans.
2. Between which two groups does King see himself as standing?
   A blacks and whites
   B black clergymen and white clergymen
   C blacks who favor him and blacks who favor his enemies
   D blacks who accept segregation and blacks who advocate hatred
3. **Critical Thinking: Expressing Problems Clearly** Restate in your own words the message that "justice too long delayed is justice denied."

American Literature **1173**

✓ TEST PREPARATION

Have students use the excerpt on these pages to complete the following sentence.

King criticizes the Birmingham clergy because they—
   A advocate the black nationalist movement.
   B support direct-action campaigns.
   Ⓒ are more concerned with the protests than their underlying causes.
   D do not think that African Americans are oppressed.

ANSWERS

1. A
2. D
3. Sample answer: If people have to wait too long to be treated fairly, they are not truly receiving justice.

American Literature
Unit 10

"Straw into Gold:
The Metamorphosis of
the Everyday"

BY SANDRA CISNEROS

*Recent years have witnessed an explosive growth in the diversity of American
literature. Works by women, African Americans, Hispanic Americans, and Asian
Americans have been both critical and sales successes, and these works reflect
themes as diverse as their authors. One member of the new generation of writers
is Sandra Cisneros, who was born in Chicago in 1954. The following selection is
taken from her essay "Straw into Gold: The Metamorphosis of the Everyday."*

VOCABULARY Before
you read the selection,
find the meaning of these
words in a dictionary:
threshold
taboo
vagabonding
sappy

Sandra Cisneros

I've managed to do a lot of things in my life I didn't think I was capable of and which many others didn't think me capable of either.

Especially because I am a woman, a Latina, an only daughter in a
family of six men. My family would've liked to have seen me married
long ago. In our culture, men and women don't leave their father's
house except by way of marriage. I crossed my father's threshold with nothing
carrying me but my own two feet. A woman whom no one came for and no
one chased away.

To make matters worse, I had left before any of my six brothers had ventured
away from home. I had broken a terrible taboo. Somehow, looking back at
photos of myself as a child, I wonder if I was aware of having begun already my
own quiet war.

I like to think that somehow my family, my Mexicanness, my poverty all had
something to do with shaping me into a writer. I like to think my parents were
preparing me all along for my life as an artist even though they didn't know it.
From my father I inherited a love of wandering. He was born in Mexico City but
as a young man he traveled into the U.S. vagabonding. He eventually was drafted
and thus became a citizen. Some of the stories he has told about his first months
in the U.S. with little or no English surface in my stories in *The House on Mango
Street* as well as others I have in mind to write in the future. From him I inherited
a sappy heart. (He still cries when he watches the Mexican soaps [soap operas]—
especially if they deal with children who have foresaken their parents.)

My mother was born like me—in Chicago, but of Mexican descent. It would
be her tough, streetwise voice that would haunt all my stories and poems. An
amazing woman who loves to draw and read books and can sing an opera. A
smart cookie. . . .

What would my teachers say if they knew I was a writer? Who would've
guessed it? I wasn't a very bright student. I didn't much like school because we
moved so much and I was always new and funny-looking. In my fifth-grade report

1174   American Literature

card, I have nothing but an avalanche of C's and D's, but I don't remember being that stupid. I was good at art and I read plenty of library books and Kiki [her brother] laughed at all my jokes. At home I was fine, but at school I never opened my mouth except when the teacher called on me, the first time I'd speak all day.

When I think how I see myself, it would have to be at age eleven. I know I'm thirty-two on the outside, but inside I'm eleven. I'm the girl in the picture with skinny arms and a crumpled shirt and crooked hair. I didn't like school because all they saw was the outside me. School was lots of rules and sitting with your hands folded and being very afraid all the time. I liked looking out the window and thinking. I liked staring at the girl across the way writing her name over and over again in red ink. I wondered why the boy with the dirty collar in front of me didn't have a mama who took better care of him.

I think my mama and papa did the best they could to keep us warm and clean and never hungry. We had birthday and graduation parties and things like that, but there was another hunger that had to be fed. There was a hunger I didn't even have a name for. Was this when I began writing?

In 1966 we moved into a house, a real one, our first real home. This meant we didn't have to change schools and be the new kids on the block every couple of years. We could make friends and not be afraid we'd have to say goodbye to them and start all over. My brothers and the flock of boys they brought home would become important characters eventually for my stories—Louie and his cousins, Meme Ortiz and his dog with two names, one in English and one in Spanish. . . .

This was the period in my life, that slippery age when you are both child and woman and neither, I was to record in *The House on Mango Street*. I was still shy. I was a girl who couldn't come out of her shell.

How was I to know I would be recording and documenting the women who sat their sadness on an elbow and stared out a window? It would be the streets of Chicago I would later record, but from a child's eyes.

I've done all kinds of things I didn't think I could do since then. I've gone to a prestigious university, studied with famous writers, and taken away an MFA [Master of Fine Arts] degree. I've taught poetry in the schools in Illinois and Texas. I've gotten an NEA [National Endowment for the Arts] grant and run away with it as far as my courage would take me. I've seen the bleached and bitter mountains of the Peloponnesus. I've lived on a Greek island. I've been to Venice twice. In Rapallo, I met Ilona once and forever and took her sad heart with me across the south of France and into Spain. . . .

I've moved since Europe to the strange and wonderful country of Texas, land of polaroid-blue skies and big bugs. I met a mayor with my last name. I met famous Chicana/o artists and writers and *politicos* [politicians].

Texas is another chapter in my life. It brought with it the Dobie-Paisano Fellowship, a six-month residency on a 265-acre ranch. But most important Texas brought Mexico back to me.

Sitting at my favorite people-watching spot, the snaky Woolworth's counter across the street from the Alamo, I can't think of anything else I'd rather be than a writer. I've traveled and lectured from Cape Cod to San Francisco, to Spain, Yugoslavia, Greece, Mexico, France, Italy, and finally today to Seguin, Texas. Along the way there is straw for the taking. With a little imagination, it can be spun into gold.

Analyzing Literature

Use the passage on these pages to answer the following questions.
1. How does Cisneros think her family and background affected her as a writer?
   A They shaped the kind of writer she became.
   B She became a writer in order to escape them.
   C They prevented her from becoming a serious writer.
   D They played no role in her career as a writer.
2. Cisneros's teachers would be surprised at her choice of occupation because she
   A always hated writing.
   B was not curious about the world around her.
   C got poor grades and participated little in class.
   D was constantly changing schools.
3. **Critical Thinking: Formulating Questions** In this excerpt, Cisneros refers to accomplishing things she did not expect to accomplish. If you were interviewing Cisneros for a newspaper story on this topic, what questions might you ask her?

Analyzing the Document Use this additional question to generate class discussion:

Critical Thinking: Making Comparisons How is Sandra Cisneros's adult life different from her childhood? *(Answers will vary, but students may point out that she is no longer poor, has traveled the world, has taught classes, and has accomplished more than she ever dreamed she would.)*

ANSWERS

1. A
2. C
3. Questions may include: How did your culture affect what you expected to accomplish? How did you accomplish these things despite your expectations? What else would you like to accomplish?

✓ **TEST PREPARATION**

Have students use the excerpt on these pages to answer the question below.

For what reason was Cisneros, as a Latina, expected to leave her father's house?

A She was expected to stay and take care of the family.

(B) She was expected to leave when she was married.

C She was expected to leave when she had a profession.

D She was expected to leave when her brothers needed her help outside the home.

THE PLEDGE OF ALLEGIANCE AND THE IROQUOIS CONSTITUTION

Focus Have students read the introductions and look up the meanings of the vocabulary words. Students may be surprised to learn the origin of the Pledge of Allegiance. Point out that the Iroquois Constitution, credited to Native American leader Dekanawidah, existed in oral form until it was finally written down for posterity in the early twentieth century.

Instruct Talk with students about the fact that the Five Nations remained united and strong (even incorporating an additional group in the 1720s) for more than 100 years after the arrival of European settlers. How do students think the Iroquois Constitution helped make this possible? In what ways does the Pledge of Allegiance serve the same function for the people of the United States today?

Eventually, the Six Nation Confederacy fell apart as the Native American groups were overcome. Ask students to apply the adage "United we stand—divided we fall" to that situation.

Assign sections of the Iroquois document to different groups of students. Have them read and discuss their section, then present a summary of it to classmates.

Extend As a class, generate a list that summarizes the proper procedure for conducting Council meetings according to the Iroquois Constitution. Have students research the current method of conducting committee meetings in the U.S. Congress. Then compare the procedures of the Iroquois Council meetings with the procedures used by the U.S. congressional committees.

Pledge of Allegiance
By FRANCIS BELLAMY

The Pledge of Allegiance first appeared in 1892 in a magazine called The Youth's Companion. *The original Pledge, attributed to Francis Bellamy, stated: "I pledge allegiance to my Flag and the Republic for which it stands; one Nation indivisible with liberty and justice for all." In 1924, "my Flag" was changed to "the Flag of the United States of America." Congress officially recognized the Pledge in 1942 and added the words "under God" in 1954.*

I pledge allegiance to the Flag of the United States of America, and to the Republic for which it stands, one nation under God, indivisible, with liberty and justice for all.

The Iroquois Constitution
By DEKANAWIDAH

VOCABULARY Before you read the selection, find the meaning of these words in a dictionary:
transact
dispatch

The Five (and later Six) Nations Confederacy, which originated sometime between 1390 and 1500, was an alliance of Native American tribes (the Mohawk, Onondaga, Seneca, Oneida, Cayuga, and eventually the Tuscarora) located in present-day upstate New York.

The Iroquois Constitution, generally attributed to a leader named Dekanawidah, lists the decision-making methods and governing principles of this alliance. It contains detailed descriptions of council meeting procedure, war conduct, foreign policy, and trade policy. It also describes many aspects of daily tribal life including ceremonies and rituals connected with religion, birth, adoption, and death. The unity inspired by these laws enabled the Iroquois Confederacy to remain a powerful force in the New World for at least 250 years, until factionalism and war with British and French colonists caused its council fires to be extinguished and its tribes to be dispersed in the late 1700s.

Over time, parts of the Iroquois Constitution's teachings became familiar to scholars of Native American history. But the Constitution itself continued to exist—as it had for hundreds of years—only in oral form. Its knowledge was transmitted from generation to generation, assisted by a collection of wampum belts and strings that helped tribal lords (or "sachems") remember the laws. In the late 1800s, when these belts and strings started to become lost or destroyed, the Six Nations leaders turned to the University of the State of New York and the New York State Museum for help in preserving them. They also began efforts to put their Constitution into written form.

The following excerpts from the beginning of the Iroquois Constitution were first published in 1916 in the New York State Museum Bulletin *by Arthur Caswell Parker, an expert in Native American affairs and an archaeologist at the Peabody Museum (Harvard University) and the New York State Museum. The manuscripts he used originated at the Six Nations Reservation in Ontario, Canada, in 1910. They were compiled and translated by Seth Newhouse, a Mohawk, and corrected by Albert Cusick, a New York Onondaga-Tuscarora.*

The Great Binding Law, Gayanashagowa

1. I am Dekanawidah and with the Five Nations' Confederate Lords I plant the Tree of Great Peace. I plant it in your territory, Adodarhoh, and the Onondaga Nation, in the territory of you who are Firekeepers. I name the tree the Tree of the Great Long Leaves. Under the shade of this Tree of the Great Peace we spread the soft white feathery

down of the globe thistle as seats for you, Adodarhoh, and your cousin Lords. We place you upon those seats, spread soft with the feathery down of the globe thistle, there beneath the shade of the spreading branches of the Tree of Peace. There shall you sit and watch the Council Fire of the Confederacy of the Five Nations, and all the affairs of the Five Nations shall be transacted at this place before you, Adodarhoh, and your cousin Lords, by the Confederate Lords of the Five Nations.

2. Roots have spread out from the Tree of the Great Peace, one to the north, one to the east, one to the south and one to the west. The name of these roots is The Great White Roots and their nature is Peace and Strength. If any man or any nation outside the Five Nations shall obey the laws of the Great Peace and make known their disposition to the Lords of the Confederacy, they may trace the Roots to the Tree and if their minds are clean and they are obedient and promise to obey the wishes of the Confederate Council, they shall be welcomed to take shelter beneath the Tree of the Long Leaves. We place at the top of the Tree of the Long Leaves an Eagle who is able to see afar. If he sees in the distance any evil approaching or any danger threatening he will at once warn the people of the Confederacy.

3. To you Adodarhoh, the Onondaga cousin Lords, I and the other Confederate Lords have entrusted the caretaking and the watching of the Five Nations Council Fire. When there is any business to be transacted and the Confederate Council is not in session, a messenger shall be dispatched either to Adodarhoh, Hononwirehtonh or Skanawatih, Fire Keepers, or to their War Chiefs with a full statement of the case desired to be considered. Then shall Adodarhoh call his cousin (associate) Lords together and consider whether or not the case is of sufficient importance to demand the attention of the Confederate Council. If so, Adodarhoh shall dispatch messengers to summon all the Confederate Lords to assemble beneath the Tree of the Long Leaves. When the Lords are assembled the Council Fire shall be kindled, but not with chestnut wood, and Adodarhoh shall formally open the Council. Then shall Adodarhoh and his cousin Lords, the Fire Keepers, announce the subject for discussion. The Smoke of the Confederate Council Fire shall ever ascend and pierce the sky so that other nations who may be allies may see the Council Fire of the Great Peace. Adodarhoh and his cousin Lords are entrusted with the Keeping of the Council Fire. . . .

More than just items of trade, wampum belts helped Iroquois leaders remember important laws and events.

5. The Council of the Mohawk shall be divided into three parties as follows: Tekarihoken, Ayonhwhathah and Shadekariwade are the first party; Sharenhowaneh, Deyoenhegwenh and Oghrenghrehgowah are the second party, and Dehennakrineh, Aghstawenserenthah and Shoskoharowaneh are the third party. The third party is to listen only to the discussion of the first and second parties and if an error is made or the proceeding is irregular they are to call attention to it, and when the case is right and properly decided by the two parties they shall confirm the decision of the two parties and refer the case to the Seneca Lords for their decision. When the Seneca Lords have decided in accord with the Mohawk Lords, the case or question shall be referred to the Cayuga and Oneida Lords on the opposite side of the house. . . .

7. Whenever the Confederate Lords shall assemble for the purpose of holding a council, the Onondaga Lords shall open it by expressing their gratitude to their cousin Lords and greeting them, and they shall make an address and offer thanks to the earth where men dwell, to the streams of water, the pools, the springs and the lakes, to the maize and the fruits, to the medicinal herbs and trees, to the forest trees for their usefulness, to the animals that serve as food and give their pelts for clothing, to the great winds and the lesser winds, to the Thunderers, to the Sun, the mighty warrior, to the moon, to the messengers of the Creator who reveal his wishes and to the Great Creator who dwells in the heavens above, who gives all the things useful to men, and who is the source and the ruler of health and life.

Then shall the Onondaga Lords declare the council open.

Analyzing Documents

Use the passage on these pages to answer the following questions.
1. Into how many parties was the Council of the Mohawk divided?
   A three
   B four
   C five
   D six
2. What was the function of the third party?
   A to keep the tribal council fire burning
   B to declare the council open
   C to express gratitude to and greet the other lords
   D to monitor the other two parties
3. **Critical Thinking: Making Comparisons** What similarities can you see between the structure of the United States government and the interaction among the three parties of the Council of the Mohawk?

Primary Source CD-ROM Find additional American historical documents on the *Exploring Primary Sources in U.S. History* CD-ROM.

Analyzing the Documents Use this additional question to generate class discussion:

Critical Thinking: Recognizing Ideologies Ask students to discuss the respective roles that the Pledge of Allegiance and the excerpt from the Iroquois Constitution were expected to play in maintaining the unity of their respective nations. *(Answers will vary.)*

☑ **TEST PREPARATION**

Have students use the excerpt from the Iroquois Constitution on these pages to answer the following question.

According to the Iroquois Constitution, which of the following leaders was probably the most powerful?
A Geronimo
B Hononwirehtonh
Ⓒ Dekanawidah
D Skanawatih

ANSWERS

1. A
2. D
3. Answers should cite the Supreme Court's function as a check on the other two government branches.

THE MAYFLOWER COMPACT AND AN ACT FOR THE GRADUAL ABOLITION OF SLAVERY

Focus Have students read the introductions and look up the meanings of the vocabulary words. Explain that the first document was created to assert the common vision of the Pilgrims. The second document was created to make Pennsylvania's position on slavery abundantly clear.

Instruct Ask students to recall the reasons the Pilgrims came to America. *(Their primary goal was to secure religious freedom for themselves, in spite of the tremendous odds against them.)* Considering those circumstances, ask students to comment on the importance of a unifying document such as the Mayflower Compact.

As students analyze "An Act for the Gradual Abolition of Slavery," discuss with them the careful way in which its writers formed the analogy between colonists and slaves. Critical to the logic of the document is the strong statement of equality among all people. Ask students to discuss the ways in which this statement echoes the Declaration of Independence.

Extend Have students speculate on what might have happened if the unrest amongst the *Mayflower's* passengers that inspired the Mayflower Compact had degenerated into a full-blown mutiny, and the settlement at Plymouth had not been established. Then have students research the tenets of the Quaker faith and the geographic areas of the colonies in which large numbers of Quakers settled. Ask students to discuss what role Quaker philosophy might have had in inspiring Pennsylvania's Act for the Gradual Abolition of Slavery.

ANSWERS

1. B
2. B
3. Answers might mention the long boat journey, illness, and the danger of being in a new land with winter approaching.

The Mayflower Compact

VOCABULARY Before you read the selection, find the meaning of these words in a dictionary:
sovereign
covenant

The Mayflower landed in present-day Cape Cod in 1620. Before coming ashore, several passengers spoke out mutinously, claiming they would not accept command from the expedition's leaders. Faced with this challenge, the pilgrim fathers drafted the document now known as the Mayflower Compact as a way of reasserting shared interests. It was signed by 41 people.

Analyzing Documents

Use the passage on this page to answer the following questions.
1. Which of the following was a goal of the pilgrims' voyage, according to the document?
   A to bring back wealth to the European patrons of the voyage
   B to advance the Christian faith
   C to conquer the native peoples
   D to seek converts
2. What did the signers of this document promise to do after they had established laws?
   A build shelters
   B submit to and obey the laws
   C notify the king immediately of the laws
   D debate and modify the policies until all present were satisfied
3. **Critical Thinking: Identifying Central Issues** What circumstances of the pilgrims' situation might have made this document necessary? Why do you think some of the passengers were mutinous?

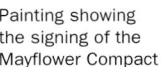   **Primary Source CD-ROM** Find additional American historical documents on the *Exploring Primary Sources in U.S. History* CD-ROM.

"In the name of God, Amen. We, whose names are underwritten, the Loyal Subjects of our dread Sovereign Lord, King James, by the Grace of God, of England, France and Ireland, King, Defender of the Faith, e&.

Having undertaken for the Glory of God, and Advancement of the Christian Faith, and the Honour of our King and Country, a voyage to plant the first colony in the northern parts of Virginia; do by these presents, solemnly and mutually in the Presence of God and one of another, covenant and combine ourselves together into a civil Body Politick, for our better Ordering and Preservation, and Furtherance of the Ends aforesaid; And by Virtue hereof to enact, constitute, and frame, such just and equal Laws, Ordinances, Acts, Constitutions and Offices, from time to time, as shall be thought most meet and convenient for the General good of the Colony; unto which we promise all due submission and obedience.

In Witness whereof we have hereunto subscribed our names at Cape Cod the eleventh of November, in the Reign of our Sovereign Lord, King James of England, France and Ireland, the eighteenth, and of Scotland the fifty-fourth. Anno Domini, 1620."

Painting showing the signing of the Mayflower Compact

An Act for the Gradual Abolition of Slavery
Pennsylvania, 1780

VOCABULARY Before you read the selection, find the meaning of these words in a dictionary:
abhorrence
fortitude
thraldom

During the Revolutionary War, the British had occupied eastern Pennsylvania from 1777 to 1778. Their mistreatment of the revolutionaries helped galvanize sentiment in the state against oppression of all kinds. As a result, the Quakers and other groups who had long opposed slavery intensified their campaigns for its abolishment. Although many compromises eventually were made with slave owners, the act containing the following excerpt was passed in 1780. It did not immediately free any slaves, but instead prevented people from being "born into" servitude, established upper age limits for releasing young slaves, and

✓ TEST PREPARATION

Have students use the text of the Mayflower Compact to complete the following sentence.

According to the Mayflower Compact itself, the document was written to—
   A reinforce loyalty to the King.
   B repress rebellion within the group.
   C reinforce religious beliefs.
   Ⓓ create a common set of laws for the good of the group.

required slave owners to register slaves or free them by default. The act made Pennsylvania the first political entity in the western world to legislate against slavery, and in so doing "to add one more step to universal civilization."

An Act for the gradual abolition of Slavery.

WHEN we contemplate our abhorrence of that condition to which the arms and tyranny of Great Britain were exerted to reduce us; when we look back on the variety of dangers to which we have been exposed, and how miraculously our wants in many instances have been supplied, and our deliverances wrought, when even hope and human fortitude have become unequal to the conflict; we are unavoidably led to a serious and grateful sense of the manifold blessings which we have undeservedly received from the hand of that Being from whom every good and perfect gift cometh. Impressed with these ideas, we conceive that it is our duty, and we rejoice that it is in our power to extend a portion of that freedom to others, which hath been extended to us; and a release from that state of thraldom to which we ourselves were tyrannically doomed, and from which we have now every prospect of being delivered. It is not for us to inquire why, in the creation of mankind, the inhabitants of the several parts of the earth were distinguished by a difference in feature or complexion. It is sufficient to know that all are the work of an Almighty Hand. We find in the distribution of the human species, that the most fertile as well as the most barren parts of the earth are inhabited by men of complexions different from ours, and from each other; from whence we may reasonably, as well as religiously, infer, that He who placed them in their various situations, hath extended equally his care and protection to all, and that it becometh not us to counteract his mercies. We esteem it a peculiar blessing granted to us, that we are enabled this day to add one more step to universal civilization, by removing as much as possible the sorrows of those who have lived in undeserved bondage, and from which, by the assumed authority of the kings of Great Britain, no effectual, legal relief could be obtained. Weaned by a long course of experience from those narrower prejudices and partialities we had imbibed, we find our hearts enlarged with kindness and benevolence towards men of all conditions and nations; and we conceive ourselves at this particular period extraordinarily called upon, by the blessings which we have received, to manifest the sincerity of our profession, and to give a Substantial proof of our gratitude.

And whereas the condition of those persons who have heretofore been denominated Negro and Mulatto slaves, has been attended with circumstances which not only deprived them of the common blessings that they were by nature entitled to, but has cast them into the deepest afflictions, by an unnatural separation and sale of husband and wife from each other and from their children; an injury, the greatness of which can only be conceived by supposing that we were in the same unhappy case. In justice therefore to persons so unhappily circumstanced, and who, having no prospect before them whereon they may rest their sorrows and their hopes, have no reasonable inducement to render their service to society, which they otherwise might; and also, in grateful commemoration of our own happy deliverance from that state of unconditional submission to which we were doomed by the tyranny of Britain.

Be it enacted, and it is hereby enacted, by the representatives of the freemen of the commonwealth of Pennsylvania, in General Assembly met, and by the authority of the same, That all persons, as well Negroes and Mulattoes as others, who shall be born within this state from and after the passing of this act, shall not be deemed and considered as servants for life, or slaves; and that all servitude for life, or slavery of children, in consequence of the slavery of their mothers, in the case of all children born within this state, from and after the passing of this act as aforesaid, shall be, and hereby is utterly taken away, extinguished and for ever abolished. . . .

Analyzing Documents

Use the passage on this page to answer the following questions.

1. Which of the following does this document give as a reason for abolishing slavery in Pennsylvania?
   A Ending slavery would commemorate Pennsylvania's own deliverance from British slavery.
   B Slaves who were separated from their families were a menace to society.
   C Slave owners would profit from abolition because their slaves would become more loyal.
   D Pennsylvania's political leaders were deeply indebted to their slaves.

2. Before the passage of this act, what authority prevented Pennsylvania slaves from obtaining "legal relief"?
   A the United States government
   B the military-industrial state
   C the kings of Britain
   D the British army

3. **Critical Thinking: Identifying Central Issues** If the British had not occupied Pennsylvania and mistreated its residents, do you think this act would have been passed? Choose a passage in the text upon which to base your answer.

 Primary Source CD-ROM Find additional American historical documents on the *Exploring Primary Sources in U.S. History* CD-ROM.

American Documents

Analyzing the Documents Use this additional question to generate class discussion:

Critical Thinking: Making Comparisons In what fundamental way did the Pilgrims at Plymouth differ in their beliefs from those who wrote Pennsylvania's Act for the Gradual Abolition of Slavery? *(The Pilgrims considered themselves to be loyal subjects of the King of England.)*

✔ TEST PREPARATION

Have students use the excerpt from *An Act for the Gradual Abolition of Slavery* to answer the following question.

What is meant by the document's phrase "tyrannically doomed"?

A Frightened of unjust leaders.

Ⓑ Subjected to oppression by brutal, unjust leadership.

C Fated to be oppressed.

D Doomed to be dominated.

ANSWERS

1. A
2. C
3. No. Answers should mention the first two sentences of the document, which clearly connect the institution of slavery with the Pennsylvanians' own mistreatment at the hands of the British.

PRESIDENT WILSON'S ADDRESS TO CONGRESS

Focus Remind students that for more than two years prior to this address, the United States had refrained from active military involvement in the Great War. There was considerable isolationist sentiment in the country. However, America's people, as well as its policymakers, had far more sympathy for the Allies (particularly Great Britain) than for Germany. Thus, when the German Navy resumed unrestricted submarine warfare, it was clear that the time for American passivity had ended.

Instruct Ask students to review the document in search of words and phrases that indicate Wilson's determination, in spite of personal reluctance, to take the step of declaring war on Germany. *(For example: "extraordinary session . . . there are serious, very serious, choices of policy to be made. . . . We must put excited feeling away. Our motive will . . . be . . . the vindication . . . of human right . . . .")* There are many other powerful statements in the document as well. Have students seek them out and read them to the class.

Extend Have students conduct library or Internet research to learn about Wilson's position toward the Great War prior to this speech of April 2, 1917.

VOCABULARY Before you read the selection, find the meaning of these words in a dictionary:
belligerent
proscribe
autocratic
nullify
indemnity
dominion

President Wilson's Address to Congress

April 2, 1917

In a special session of Congress held on April 2, 1917, President Woodrow Wilson delivered this "war message." Four days later, Congress overwhelmingly passed the resolution that brought the United States into World War I.

Gentlemen of the Congress:

I have called the Congress into extraordinary session because there are serious, very serious, choices of policy to be made, and made immediately, which it was neither right nor constitutionally permissible that I should assume the responsibility of making.

On the 3rd of February last I officially laid before you the extraordinary announcement of the Imperial German Government that on and after the 1st day of February it was its purpose to put aside all restraints of law or of humanity and use its submarines to sink every vessel that sought to approach either the ports of Great Britain and Ireland or the western coasts of Europe or any of the ports controlled by the enemies of Germany within the Mediterranean. . . . The new policy has swept every restriction aside. Vessels of every kind, whatever their flag, their character, their cargo, their destination, their errand, have been ruthlessly sent to the bottom without warning and without thought of help or mercy for those on board, the vessels of friendly neutrals along with those of belligerents. Even hospital ships and ships carrying relief to the sorely bereaved and stricken people of Belgium, though the latter were provided with safe-conduct through the proscribed areas by the German Government itself and were distinguished by unmistakable marks of identity, have been sunk with the same reckless lack of compassion or of principle.

I was for a little while unable to believe that such things would in fact be done by any government that had hitherto subscribed to the humane practices of civilized nations. . . . I am not now thinking of the loss of property involved, immense and serious as that is, but only of the wanton and wholesale destruction of the lives of noncombatants, men, women, and children, engaged in pursuits which have always, even in the darkest periods of modern history, been deemed innocent and legitimate. Property can be paid for; the lives of peaceful and innocent people can not be. The present German submarine warfare against commerce is a warfare against mankind.

It is a war against all nations. American ships have been sunk, American lives taken, in ways which it has stirred us very deeply to learn of, but the ships and people of other neutral and friendly nations have been sunk and overwhelmed in the waters in the same way. There has been no discrimination. The challenge is to all mankind. Each nation must decide for itself how it will meet it. The choice we make for ourselves must be made with a moderation of counsel and a temperateness of judgment befitting our character and our motives as a nation. We must put excited feeling away. Our motive will not be revenge or the victorious assertion of the physical might of the nation, but only the

Lifeboat containing survivors from a German submarine attack (above); German submarine off the United States coast (right)

vindication of right, of human right, of which we are only a single champion. . . .

With a profound sense of the solemn and even tragical character of the step I am taking and of the grave responsibilities which it involves, but in unhesitating obedience to what I deem my constitutional duty, I advise that the Congress declare the recent course of the Imperial German Government to be in fact nothing less than war against the Government and people of the United States; that it formally accept the status of belligerent which has thus been thrust upon it, and that it take immediate steps not only to put the country in a more thorough state of defense but also to exert all its power and employ all its resources to bring the Government of the German Empire to terms and end the war. . . .

While we do these things, these deeply momentous things, let us be very clear, and make very clear to all the world what our motives and our objects are. . . . Our object . . . is to vindicate the principles of peace and justice in the life of the world as against selfish and autocratic power and to set up amongst the really free and self-governed peoples of the world such a concert of purpose and of action as will henceforth ensure the observance of those principles. . . .

We have no quarrel with the German people. We have no feeling towards them but one of sympathy and friendship. It was not upon their impulse that their Government acted in entering this war. It was not with their previous knowledge or approval. It was a war determined upon as wars used to be determined upon in the old, unhappy days when peoples were nowhere consulted by their rulers and wars were provoked and waged in the interest of dynasties or of little groups of ambitious men who were accustomed to use their fellow men as pawns and tools. . . .

We are accepting this challenge of hostile purpose because we know that in such a government, following such methods, we can never have a friend; and that in the presence of its organized power, always lying in wait to accomplish we know not what purpose, there can be no assured security for the democratic governments of the world. We are now about to accept gage of battle with this natural foe to liberty and shall, if necessary, spend the whole force of the nation to check and nullify its pretensions and its power. We are glad, now that we see the facts with no veil of false pretence about them, to fight thus for the ultimate peace of the world and for the liberation of its peoples, the German peoples included: for the rights of nations great and small and the privilege of men everywhere to choose their way of life and of obedience. The world must be made safe for democracy. Its peace must be planted upon the tested foundations of political liberty. We have no selfish ends to serve. We desire no conquest, no dominion. We seek no indemnities for ourselves, no material compensation for the sacrifices we shall freely make. We are but one of the champions of the rights of mankind. We shall be satisfied when those rights have been made as secure as the faith and the freedom of nations can make them. . . .

It is a distressing and oppressive duty, gentlemen of the Congress, which I have performed in thus addressing you. There are, it may be, many months of fiery trial and sacrifice ahead of us. It is a fearful thing to lead this great peaceful people into war, into the most terrible and disastrous of all wars, civilization itself seeming to be in the balance. But the right is more precious than peace, and we shall fight for the things which we have always carried nearest our hearts—for democracy, for the right of those who submit to authority to have a voice in their own governments, for the rights and liberties of small nations, for a universal dominion of right by such a concert of free peoples as shall bring peace and safety to all nations and make the world itself at last free. To such a task we can dedicate our lives and our fortunes, everything that we are and everything that we have, with the pride of those who know that the day has come when America is privileged to spend her blood and her might for the principles that gave her birth and happiness and the peace which she has treasured. God helping her, she can do no other.

Analyzing Documents

Use the passage on these pages to answer the following questions.

1. What action by the German government prompted Wilson's speech?
   - **A** It sent Wilson a hostile telegram, threatening war.
   - **B** It declared war on an ally of the United States.
   - **C** It began to sink neutral passenger and medical ships in European waters.
   - **D** It sent troops across its border with Austria.

2. Which of the following best expresses Wilson's attitude toward the German people?
   - **A** They were at fault for their government's actions.
   - **B** They were not to blame for their government's actions.
   - **C** They were to be thanked for saving lives with their medical ships.
   - **D** They were obligated to help the United States make the world safe for democracy.

3. **Critical Thinking: Recognizing Ideologies** Wilson was acting out of what he believed to be his "constitutional duty." Do you agree with him that part of our United States constitutional duty is to "make the world safe for democracy"?

 Primary Source CD-ROM Find additional American historical documents on the *Exploring Primary Sources in U.S. History* CD-ROM.

Analyzing the Document Use this additional question to generate class discussion:

Critical Thinking: Identifying Central Issues What did Wilson mean by the phrase "right is more precious than peace"? *(Answers will vary.)*

✓ TEST PREPARATION

Have students use the document on these pages to answer the following question.

Why does Wilson refer to the step he is taking as "tragical"?

A Because its outcome is uncertain.

B Because he was a fighter by nature.

Ⓒ Because he opposes war in principle, and he envisions American casualties and American hardships as a result of his own action.

D Because he is not angry with the German people.

ANSWERS

1. C

2. B

3. Answers will vary.

THE UNIVERSAL DECLARATION OF HUMAN RIGHTS

Focus Have students read the introduction and look up the meanings of the vocabulary words.

Explain to students that this declaration was written soon after the establishment of the United Nations, following the end of World War II.

Instruct This important document has served to assist the United Nations in fulfilling its responsibilities for more than 50 years. Divide the class into small groups. Ask each group to study and discuss one of the articles of the document. Have each group rewrite the article in their own words and be able to state its importance. Hold a classroom discussion in which students compare this document to the Bill of Rights and the Reconstruction Amendments of the U.S. Constitution.

Extend Interested students may continue their examination of this document by seeking out examples in world history over the last 50 years in which the United Nations has intervened in a conflict in order to uphold the tenets of this document.

VOCABULARY Before you read the selection, find the meaning of these words in a dictionary:
inalienable
barbarous
advent
aspiration
dignity
sovereignty
incitement
exile

Official emblem of the United Nations, showing a world map centered on the North Pole and surrounded by two olive branches

The Universal Declaration of Human Rights

December 10, 1948
THE UNITED NATIONS

On December 10, 1948, the General Assembly of the United Nations adopted and proclaimed the Universal Declaration of Human Rights. Following this historic act, the Assembly called upon all member countries to publicize the text of the Declaration and "to cause it to be disseminated, displayed, read and expounded principally in schools and other educational institutions, without distinction based on the political status of countries or territories."

The Universal Declaration of Human Rights

PREAMBLE

Whereas recognition of the inherent dignity and of the equal and inalienable rights of all members of the human family is the foundation of freedom, justice and peace in the world,

Whereas disregard and contempt for human rights have resulted in barbarous acts which have outraged the conscience of mankind, and the advent of a world in which human beings shall enjoy freedom of speech and belief and freedom from fear and want has been proclaimed as the highest aspiration of the common people,

Whereas it is essential, if man is not to be compelled to have recourse, as a last resort, to rebellion against tyranny and oppression, that human rights should be protected by the rule of law,

Whereas it is essential to promote the development of friendly relations between nations,

Whereas the peoples of the United Nations have in the Charter reaffirmed their faith in fundamental human rights, in the dignity and worth of the human person and in the equal rights of men and women and have determined to promote social progress and better standards of life in larger freedom,

Whereas Member States have pledged themselves to achieve, in co-operation with the United Nations, the promotion of universal respect for and observance of human rights and fundamental freedoms,

Whereas a common understanding of these rights and freedoms is of the greatest importance for the full realization of this pledge,

Now, Therefore THE GENERAL ASSEMBLY proclaims THIS UNIVERSAL DECLARATION OF HUMAN RIGHTS as a common standard of achievement for all peoples and all nations, to the end that every individual and every organ of society, keeping this Declaration constantly in mind, shall strive by teaching and education to promote respect for these rights and freedoms and by progressive measures, national and international, to secure their universal and effective recognition and observance, both among the peoples of Member States themselves and among the peoples of territories under their jurisdiction.

Article 1. All human beings are born free and equal in dignity and rights. They are endowed with reason and conscience and should act towards one another in a spirit of brotherhood.

The United Nations building in New York City (above) and the Peace Palace in The Hague, The Netherlands (right), home of the International Court of Justice

Analyzing the Document Use this additional question to generate class discussion:

Critical Thinking: Making Comparisons Ask students to find portions of the Universal Declaration of Human Rights that echo the Declaration of Independence. *(Answers will vary, but should include Articles 1 and 3.)*

Article 2. Everyone is entitled to all the rights and freedoms set forth in this Declaration, without distinction of any kind, such as race, colour, sex, language, religion, political or other opinion, national or social origin, property, birth or other status. Furthermore, no distinction shall be made on the basis of the political, jurisdictional or international status of the country or territory to which a person belongs, whether it be independent, trust, non-self-governing or under any other limitation of sovereignty.

Article 3. Everyone has the right to life, liberty and security of person.

Article 4. No one shall be held in slavery or servitude; slavery and the slave trade shall be prohibited in all their forms.

Article 5. No one shall be subjected to torture or to cruel, inhuman or degrading treatment or punishment.

Article 6. Everyone has the right to recognition everywhere as a person before the law.

Article 7. All are equal before the law and are entitled without any discrimination to equal protection of the law. All are entitled to equal protection against any discrimination in violation of this Declaration and against any incitement to such discrimination.

Article 8. Everyone has the right to an effective remedy by the competent national tribunals for acts violating the fundamental rights granted him by the constitution or by law.

Article 9. No one shall be subjected to arbitrary arrest, detention or exile.

Article 10. Everyone is entitled in full equality to a fair and public hearing by an independent and impartial tribunal, in the determination of his rights and obligations and of any criminal charge against him. . . .

Analyzing Documents

Use the passage on these pages to answer the following questions.
1. According to the document, all humans are born "free and equal" in
   A dignity and rights.
   B religion and political opinion.
   C financial status.
   D national origin.
2. What right does the document provide to individuals for addressing criminal charges against them?
   A They may write a letter to a regional authority in response to the charge.
   B They may take the matter up with a member of their congress.
   C They have the right to remain silent.
   D They are entitled to a fair public hearing by an impartial tribunal.
3. **Critical Thinking: Identifying Assumptions** This document assumes that individuals or nations in conflict should be given impartial hearings. What type of organization is needed to ensure that this occurs? Where is this tribunal conducted?

 Primary Source CD-ROM Find additional American historical documents on the *Exploring Primary Sources in U.S. History* CD-ROM.

✓ TEST PREPARATION

Have students use the document on these pages to answer the following question.

What is meant by the word "contempt" in the preamble of this document?

Ⓐ Disdain
B Disregard
C Disinclination
D Destruction

ANSWERS

1. A
2. D
3. Answers should mention some sort of world court or tribunal. This court is conducted in The Hague, Netherlands.

Eisenhower's Farewell Address to the Nation

January 17, 1961

EISENHOWER'S FAREWELL ADDRESS TO THE NATION

Focus Have students read the introduction and look up the meanings of the vocabulary words.

Explain that President Eisenhower chose to focus his statement on what he viewed as the greatest threat to the world in the years of his presidency: the unbridled growth of communism.

Instruct Eisenhower's speech reflects his position that the threat of communism, though in his opinion insidious and widespread, required a very careful response, one that emphasized negotiation and communication as well as the maintenance of American military strength. Have students isolate portions of the document that present this viewpoint. Eisenhower's speech uses many strong words and phrases to emphasize his points. Have students seek out and discuss some of the most powerful of those statements.

Extend Did subsequent Presidents heed Eisenhower's request for dialogue and negotiation with enemies while maintaining national strength? What Communist nations brought the United States into crisis less than two years after Eisenhower spoke? *(The Soviet Union and Cuba)* In what ways did President Kennedy follow Eisenhower's advice, as given in this speech, following this crisis? *(By negotiating a peaceful solution to the Cuban Missile Crisis while preparing for military action)*

VOCABULARY Before you read the selection, find the meaning of these words in a dictionary:
ideology
atheistic
insidious
indefinite
transitory
provocation

President Dwight D. Eisenhower

Dwight D. Eisenhower served as President of the United States from 1953 to 1961. Previously, he had served as an officer in two world wars, earned the title of "Supreme Commander, Allied Expeditionary Forces" during the invasion of Normandy on D-Day in 1944, and held the presidency of New York's Columbia University for two years. His farewell speech to the nation, given at the height of the Cold War weapons race, contained a famous warning against the buildup of undue power in an American "military-industrial complex" of armed forces leaders and armaments manufacturers. The following excerpts from the speech reveal that this former general also had strong opinions about the proper uses of such military power in the world.

. . . We now stand ten years past the midpoint of a century that has witnessed four major wars among great nations. Three of these involved our own country. Despite these holocausts America is today the strongest, the most influential and most productive nation in the world. Understandably proud of this pre-eminence, we yet realize that America's leadership and prestige depend, not merely upon our unmatched material progress, riches and military strength, but on how we use our power in the interests of world peace and human betterment.

Throughout America's adventure in free government, such basic purposes have been to keep the peace; to foster progress in human achievement, and to enhance liberty, dignity and integrity among peoples and among nations.

To strive for less would be unworthy of a free and religious people.

Any failure traceable to arrogance or our lack of comprehension or readiness to sacrifice would inflict upon us a grievous hurt, both at home and abroad.

Progress toward these noble goals is persistently threatened by the conflict now engulfing the world. It commands our whole attention, absorbs our very beings. We face a hostile ideology global in scope, atheistic in character, ruthless in purpose, and insidious in method. Unhappily the danger it poses promises to be of indefinite duration. To meet it successfully, there is called for, not so much the emotional and transitory sacrifices of crisis, but rather those which enable us to carry forward steadily, surely, and without complaint the burdens of a prolonged and complex struggle—with liberty the stake. Only thus shall we remain, despite every provocation, on our charted course toward permanent peace and human betterment.

Crises there will continue to be. In meeting them, whether foreign or domestic, great or small, there is a recurring temptation to feel that some spectacular and costly action could become the miraculous solution to all current difficulties. A huge increase in the newer elements of our defenses; development of unrealistic programs to cure every ill in agriculture; a dramatic expansion in basic and applied research—these and many other possibilities, each possibly promising in itself, may be suggested as the only way to the road we wish to travel.

But each proposal must be weighed in light of a broader consideration; the need to maintain balance in and among national programs—balance between the private and the public economy, balance between the cost and hoped for advantages—balance between the clearly necessary and the comfortably desirable; balance between our essential requirements as a nation and the duties imposed by the nation upon the individual; balance between the actions of the moment and the national welfare of the future. Good judgment seeks balance and progress; lack of it eventually finds imbalance and frustration.

The record of many decades stands as proof that our people and their Government have, in the main, understood these truths and have responded to them well in the face of threat and stress. . . .

Until the latest of our world conflicts, the United States had no armaments industry. American makers of plowshares could, with time and as required, make swords as well. But now we can no longer risk emergency improvisation of national defense; we have been compelled to create a permanent armaments industry of vast proportions. Added to this, three and a half million men and women are directly engaged in the defense establishment. We annually spend on military security more than the net income of all United States corporations.

This conjunction of an immense military establishment and a large arms industry is new in the American experience. The total influence—economic, political, even spiritual—is felt in every city, every Statehouse, every office of the Federal government. We recognize the imperative need for this development. Yet we must not fail to comprehend its grave implications. Our toil, resources and livelihood are all involved; so is the very structure of our society.

In the councils of government, we must guard against the acquisition of unwarranted influence, whether sought or unsought, by the military-industrial complex. The potential for the disastrous rise of misplaced power exists and will persist.

We must never let the weight of this combination endanger our liberties or democratic processes. We should take nothing for granted. Only an alert and knowledgeable citizenry can compel the proper meshing of the huge industrial and military machinery of defense with our peaceful methods and goals, so that security and liberty may prosper together. . . .

Down the long lane of the history yet to be written America knows that this world of ours, ever growing smaller, must avoid becoming a community of dreadful fear and hate, and be, instead, a proud confederation of mutual trust and respect.

Such a confederation must be one of equals. The weakest must come to the conference table with the same confidence as do we, protected as we are by our moral, economic, and military strength. That table, though scarred by many past frustrations, cannot be abandoned for the certain agony of the battlefield.

Disarmament, with mutual honor and confidence, is a continuing imperative. Together we must learn how to compose differences, not with arms, but with intellect and decent purpose. Because this need is so sharp and apparent I confess that I lay down my official responsibilities in this field with a definite sense of disappointment. As one who has witnessed the horror and the lingering sadness of war—as one who knows that another war could utterly destroy this civilization which has been so slowly and painfully built over thousands of years—I wish I could say tonight that a lasting peace is in sight. . . .

You and I—my fellow citizens—need to be strong in our faith that all nations, under God, will reach the goal of peace with justice. May we be ever unswerving in devotion to principle, confident but humble with power, diligent in pursuit of the Nations' great goals.

To all the peoples of the world, I once more give expression to America's prayerful and continuing aspiration:

We pray that peoples of all faiths, all races, all nations, may have their great human needs satisfied; that those now denied opportunity shall come to enjoy it to the full; that all who yearn for freedom may experience its spiritual blessings; that those who have freedom will understand, also, its heavy responsibilities; that all who are insensitive to the needs of others will learn charity; that the scourges of poverty, disease and ignorance will be made to disappear from the earth, and that, in the goodness of time, all peoples will come to live together in a peace guaranteed by the binding force of mutual respect and love.

Now, on Friday noon, I am to become a private citizen. I am proud to do so. I look forward to it.

Thank you, and good night.

Analyzing Documents

Use the passage on these pages to answer the following questions.

1. For what ends, according to Eisenhower, should the United States use its economic and military strength?
   A fighting terrorism and fascism
   B promoting world peace and human betterment
   C increasing arts and sciences education
   D promoting balance and proper posture
2. To what specific "hostile ideology global in scope, atheistic in character, ruthless in purpose, and insidious in method" was Eisenhower referring in his speech?
   A terrorism
   B secular humanism
   C communism
   D religious fundamentalism
3. **Critical Thinking: Making Comparisons** Does America face any global "hostile ideologies" today? What are they? How are we responding to them?

 Primary Source CD-ROM Find additional American historical documents on the *Exploring Primary Sources in U.S. History* CD-ROM.

Analyzing the Document Use this additional question to generate class discussion:

Critical Thinking: Recognizing Ideologies Ask students to summarize Eisenhower's position on disarmament. *(He described disarmament as "a continuing imperative.")*

✔ TEST PREPARATION

Have students use the excerpt on these pages to answer the following question.

How did Eisenhower, former Supreme Commander of the Allied Expeditionary Forces in World War II, feel about armed conflict as he left the presidency?

A He recognized it as an inevitable necessity.

B He urged against it.

C He was opposed to war in any form.

Ⓓ He felt that it was necessary to maintain a strong military, while also pursuing diplomatic solutions to crises.

ANSWERS

1. B
2. C
3. Answers will vary, but might mention terrorism and our war against it.

Address to the Forty-Third UN General Assembly Session

December 7, 1988

By MIKHAIL GORBACHEV

ADDRESS TO THE FORTY-THIRD UN GENERAL ASSEMBLY SESSION

Focus Have students read the introduction and look up the meanings of the vocabulary words.

Explain to students that Gorbachev's extraordinary speech and other actions he took as Soviet General Secretary ultimately led to the "new world order" he envisioned.

Instruct Remind students that when Gorbachev made his speech, the Soviet Union was still united as an enormous nation-state. However, Soviet-bloc nations, such as Poland, Czechoslovakia and others, were very soon to achieve freedom.

In Gorbachev's speech, there are many references to changes in the world itself that he believed reflected changes in the way leaders should manage relations between nations. Ask students if they feel that with this speech, Gorbachev was primarily making observations, or was he seeking to stir the world to action? Was he doing both? Would students consider him an observer, a prophet, an instigator, or all three?

Extend Ask students to compare and contrast Gorbachev's observations about the pervasiveness of global conflict and the emergence "of a mutually connected and integral world." Remind students that when Gorbachev made this speech, the Internet was not available to the general public, and e-mail was not yet widely used. In what ways is Gorbachev's observation even more accurate today than it was when he made it?

American Documents

VOCABULARY Before you read the selection, find the meaning of these words in a dictionary:
ubiquitous
ideological
immutable
prerequisites
infringing
inertia
tenet

On December 7, 1988, Soviet General Secretary Mikhail Gorbachev addressed the United Nations General Assembly. After speaking about the recent changes in the Soviet Union, Gorbachev announced drastic cuts in the Soviet military presence in Eastern Europe and along the Chinese border—a move that ultimately allowed Soviet satellite nations to choose their own paths. In the following excerpts from that speech, Gorbachev reflects on a "new world order" and United States–Soviet relations.

. . . Today we have entered an era when progress will be based on the interests of all mankind. Consciousness of this requires that world policy, too, should be determined by the priority of the values of all mankind.

The history of the past centuries and millennia has been a history of almost ubiquitous wars, and sometimes desperate battles, leading to mutual destruction. They occurred in the clash of social and political interests and national hostility, be it from ideological or religious incompatibility. All that was the case, and even now many still claim that this past—which has not been overcome—is an immutable pattern. However, parallel with the process of wars, hostility, and alienation of peoples and countries, another process, just as objectively conditioned, was in motion and gaining force: The process of the emergence of a mutually connected and integral world.

Further world progress is now possible only through the search for a consensus of all mankind, in movement toward a new world order. We have arrived at a frontier at which controlled spontaneity leads to a dead end. The world community must learn to shape and direct the process in such a way as to preserve civilization, to make it safe for all and more pleasant for normal life. It is a question of cooperation that could be more accurately called "co-creation" and "co-development." The formula of development "at another's expense" is becoming outdated. In light of present realities, genuine progress by infringing upon the rights and liberties of man and peoples, or at the expense of nature, is impossible. . . .

Gorbachev addresses the United Nations.

. . . Behind differences in social structure, in the way of life, and in the preference for certain values, stand interests. There is no getting away from that, but neither is there any getting away from the need to find a balance of interests within an international framework, which has become a condition for survival and progress. As you ponder all this, you come to the conclusion that if we wish to take account of the lessons of the past and the realities of the present, if we must reckon with the objective logic of world development, it is necessary to seek—and to seek jointly—an approach toward improving the international situation and building a new world. If that is so, then it is also worth agreeing on the fundamental and truly universal prerequisites and principles for such activities. It is evident, for example, that force and the threat of force can no longer be, and should not be instruments of foreign policy. . . .

The compelling necessity of the principle of freedom of choice is also clear to us. The failure to recognize this . . . is fraught with very dire consequences, consequences for world peace. Denying that right to the peoples, no matter what the pretext, no matter what the words are used to conceal it, means infringing upon even the unstable balance that is, has been possible to achieve.

Freedom of choice is a universal principle to which there should be no exceptions. We have not come to the conclusion of the immutability of this principle simply through good motives. We have been led to it through impartial analysis of the objective processes of our time. The increasing varieties of social development in different countries are becoming an ever more perceptible feature of these processes. This relates to both the capitalist and socialist systems. The variety of sociopolitical structures which has grown over the last decades from national liberation movements also demonstrates this. This objective fact presupposes respect for other people's views and stands, tolerance, a preparedness to see phenomena that are different as not necessarily bad or hostile, and an ability to learn to live side by side while remaining different and not agreeing with one another on every issue.

. . . We are not giving up our convictions, philosophy, or traditions. Neither are we calling on anyone else to give up theirs. Yet we are not going to shut ourselves up within the range of our values. That would lead to spiritual impoverishment, for it would mean renouncing so powerful a source of development as sharing all the original things created independently by each nation. In the course of such sharing, each should prove the advantages of his own system, his own way of life and values, but not through words or propaganda alone, but through real deeds as well. That is, indeed, an honest struggle of ideology . . .

Finally, being on U.S. soil, but also for other, understandable reasons, I cannot but turn to the subject of our relations with this great country. . . . Relations between the Soviet Union and the United States of America span $5\frac{1}{2}$ decades. The world has changed, and so have the nature, role, and place of these relations in world politics. For too long they were built under the banner of confrontation, and sometimes of hostility, either open or concealed. But in the last few years, throughout the world people were able to heave a sigh of relief, thanks to the changes for the better in the substance and atmosphere of the relations between Moscow and Washington.

No one intends to underestimate the serious nature of the disagreements, and the difficulties of the problems which have not been settled. However, we have already graduated from the primary school of instruction in mutual understanding and in searching for solutions in our and in the common interests. The U.S.S.R. and the United States created the biggest nuclear missile arsenals, but after objectively recognizing their responsibility, they were able to be the first to conclude an agreement on the reduction and physical destruction of a proportion of these weapons, which threatened both themselves and everyone else. . . .

We are not inclined to oversimplify the situation in the world. Yes, the tendency toward disarmament has received a strong impetus, and this process is gaining its own momentum, but it has not become irreversible. Yes, the striving to give up confrontation in favor of dialogue and cooperation has made itself strongly felt, but it has by no means secured its position forever in the practice of international relations. Yes, the movement toward a nuclear-free and nonviolent world is capable of fundamentally transforming the political and spiritual face of the planet, but only the very first steps have been taken. Moreover, in certain influential circles, they have been greeted with mistrust, and they are meeting resistance.

The inheritance of inertia of the past are continuing to operate. Profound contradictions and the roots of many conflicts have not disappeared. The fundamental fact remains that the formation of the peaceful period will take place in conditions of the existence and rivalry of various socioeconomic and political systems. However, the meaning of our international efforts, and one of the key tenets of the new thinking, is precisely to impart to this rivalry the quality of sensible competition in conditions of respect for freedom of choice and a balance of interests. In this case it will even become useful and productive from the viewpoint of general world development; otherwise, if the main component remains the arms race, as it has been till now, rivalry will be fatal. Indeed, an ever greater number of people throughout the world, from the man in the street to leaders, are beginning to understand this. . . .

Analyzing Documents

Use the passage on these pages to answer the following questions.

1. Gorbachev did not call for nations to give up their own traditions, but issued a reminder that remaining isolated "within the range" of one's own values would lead to
   A world war.
   B unilateral disarmament.
   C spiritual impoverishment.
   D economic rivalry.
2. According to the speech, what quality should the rivalry between conflicting nations and interests have?
   A fierce and punishing aggression
   B a friendly playfulness
   C sensible competition and respect for freedom of choice
   D the underlying threat of military force
3. **Critical Thinking: Making Comparisons** To what extent have the nations of the world lived up to Gorbachev's ideals since his 1988 speech? Support your claim with historical events from the text.

 Primary Source CD-ROM Find additional American historical documents on the *Exploring Primary Sources in U.S. History* CD-ROM.

American Documents

Analyzing the Document Use this additional question to generate class discussion:

Critical Thinking: Identifying Assumptions In his speech, Gorbachev suggested that "Freedom of choice is a universal principle to which there should be no exceptions." Ask students to reflect on how that statement relates to the dissolution of the Soviet bloc that took place under his leadership and in subsequent years? *(Answers will vary.)*

✓ TEST PREPARATION

Have students use the excerpt on these pages to answer the following question.

What is meant by Gorbachev's phrase "controlled spontaneity"?

Ⓐ People should be able to exercise freedom of choice, within limits. Most importantly, the world should be a civilized place.

B People should have fun, and then they should get to work.

C The world should be a place with lots of opportunity for recreation.

D Everyone should be able to enjoy freedom.

ANSWERS

1. C
2. C
3. Answers will vary.

Illustrated Databank

United States: Political

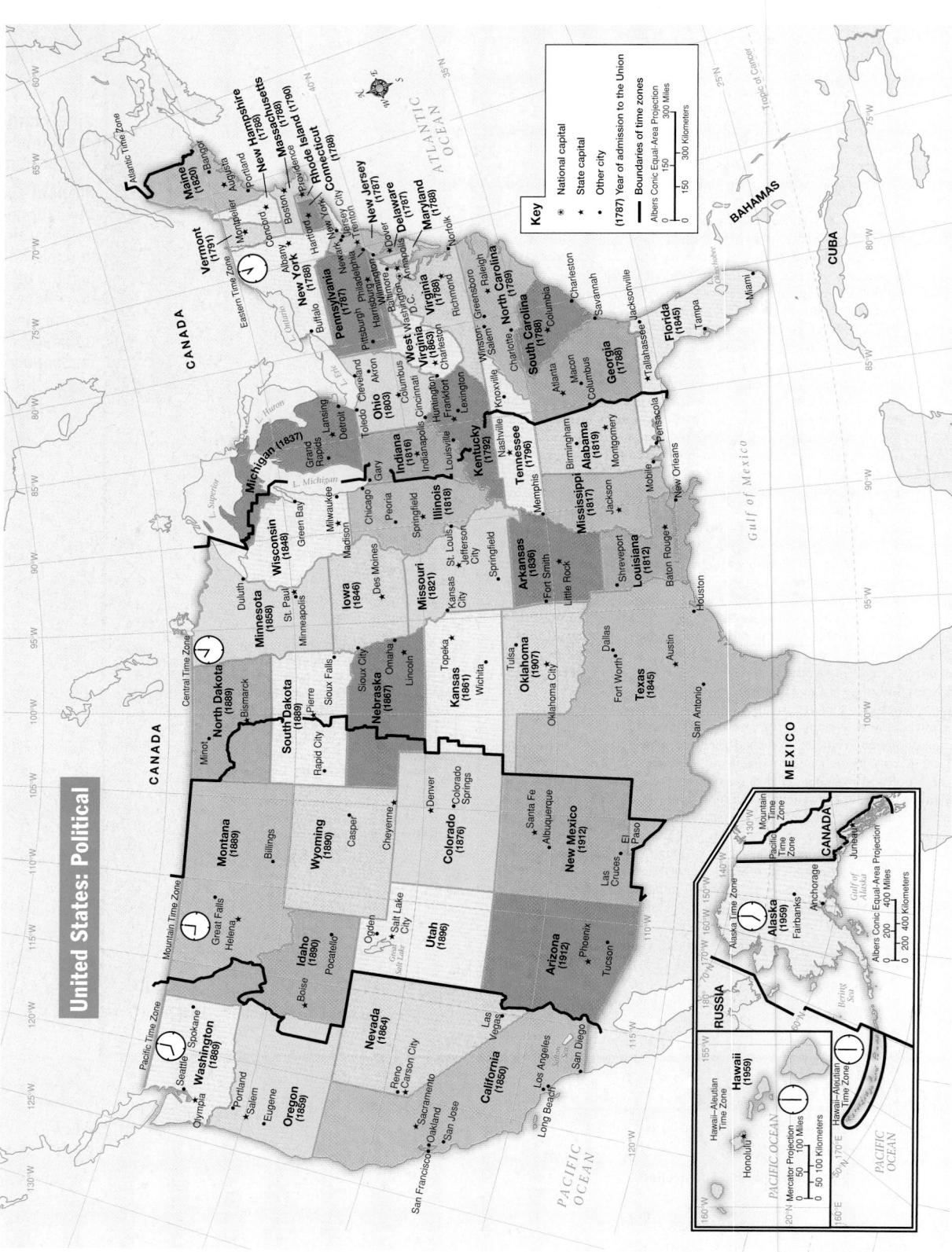

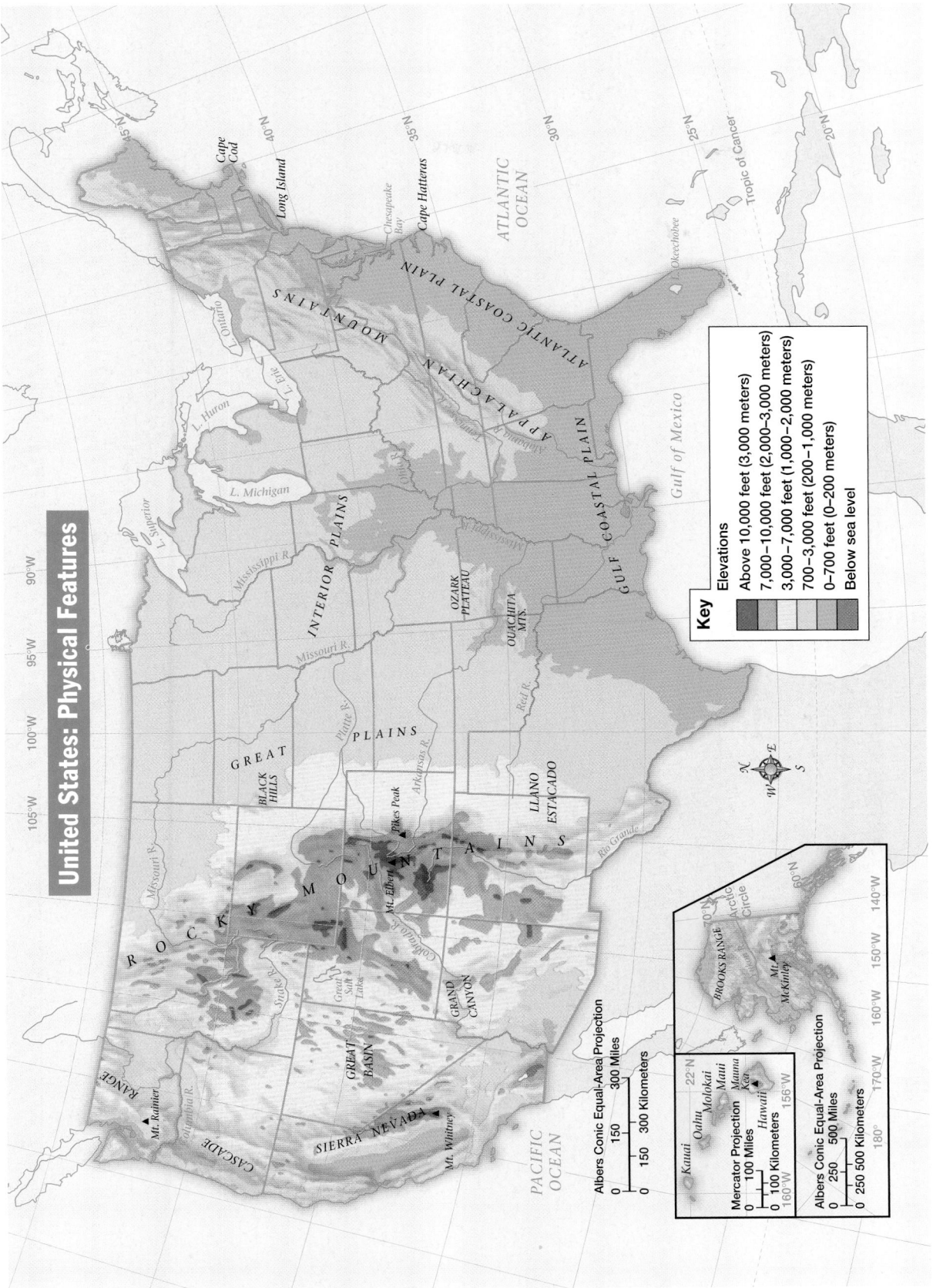

United States: Physical Features

Long Island
Cape Cod

ATLANTIC OCEAN

Chesapeake Bay
Cape Hatteras

APPALACHIAN MOUNTAINS

ATLANTIC COASTAL PLAIN

Tropic of Cancer

Okeechobee

L. Ontario
L. Erie
L. Huron
L. Superior
L. Michigan

GULF COASTAL PLAIN

Gulf of Mexico

Ohio R.

Mississippi R.

INTERIOR PLAINS

OZARK PLATEAU

OUACHITA MTS.

Mississippi R.

Missouri R.

Red R.

GREAT PLAINS

BLACK HILLS

Platte R.

Arkansas R.

LLANO ESTACADO

Rio Grande

Pikes Peak

Mt. Elbert

ROCKY MOUNTAINS

Colorado R.

Great Salt Lake

Snake R.

Columbia R.

GREAT BASIN

GRAND CANYON

SIERRA NEVADA

Mt. Whitney

CASCADE RANGE

Mt. Rainier

PACIFIC OCEAN

Key

Elevations

Above 10,000 feet (3,000 meters)
7,000–10,000 feet (2,000–3,000 meters)
3,000–7,000 feet (1,000–2,000 meters)
700–3,000 feet (200–1,000 meters)
0–700 feet (0–200 meters)
Below sea level

Albers Conic Equal-Area Projection

300 Miles
0   150   300
0   150   300 Kilometers

BROOKS RANGE

Mt. McKinley

Arctic Circle

Albers Conic Equal-Area Projection
500 Miles
0   250   500
0   250   500 Kilometers

Kauai
Oahu
Molokai
Maui
Mauna Kea
Hawaii

Mercator Projection
100 Miles
0   100
0   100 Kilometers

United States: Natural Resources

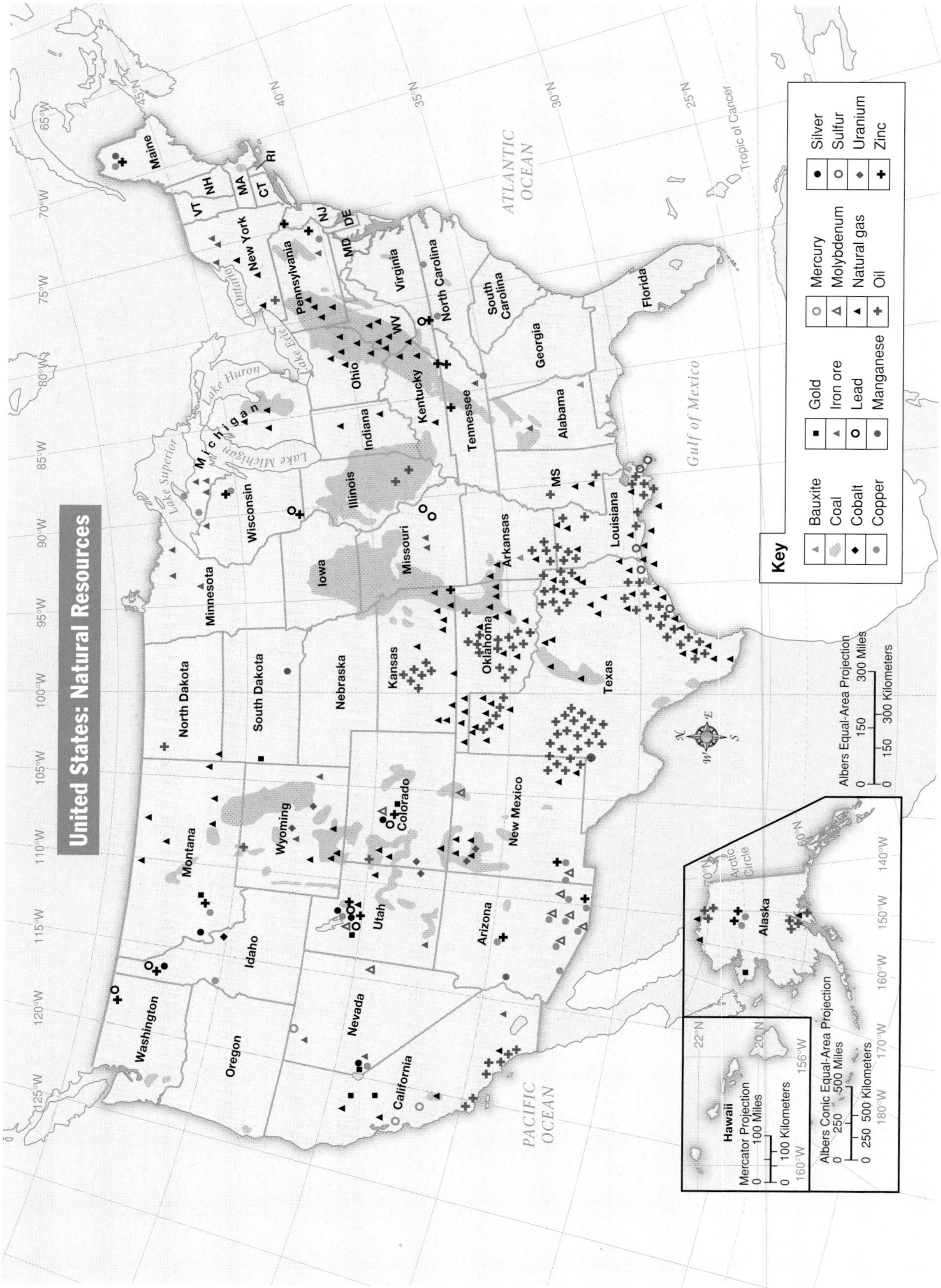

Key

Bauxite		Gold		Mercury		Silver	
Coal		Iron ore		Molybdenum		Sulfur	
Cobalt		Lead		Natural gas		Uranium	
Copper		Manganese		Oil		Zinc	

ATLANTIC OCEAN

PACIFIC OCEAN

Gulf of Mexico

Tropic of Cancer

Albers Equal-Area Projection
0   150   300 Miles
0   150   300 Kilometers

Alaska
Arctic Circle

Hawaii
Mercator Projection
0   100 Miles
0   100 Kilometers

Albers Conic Equal-Area Projection
0   250   500 Miles
0   250   500 Kilometers

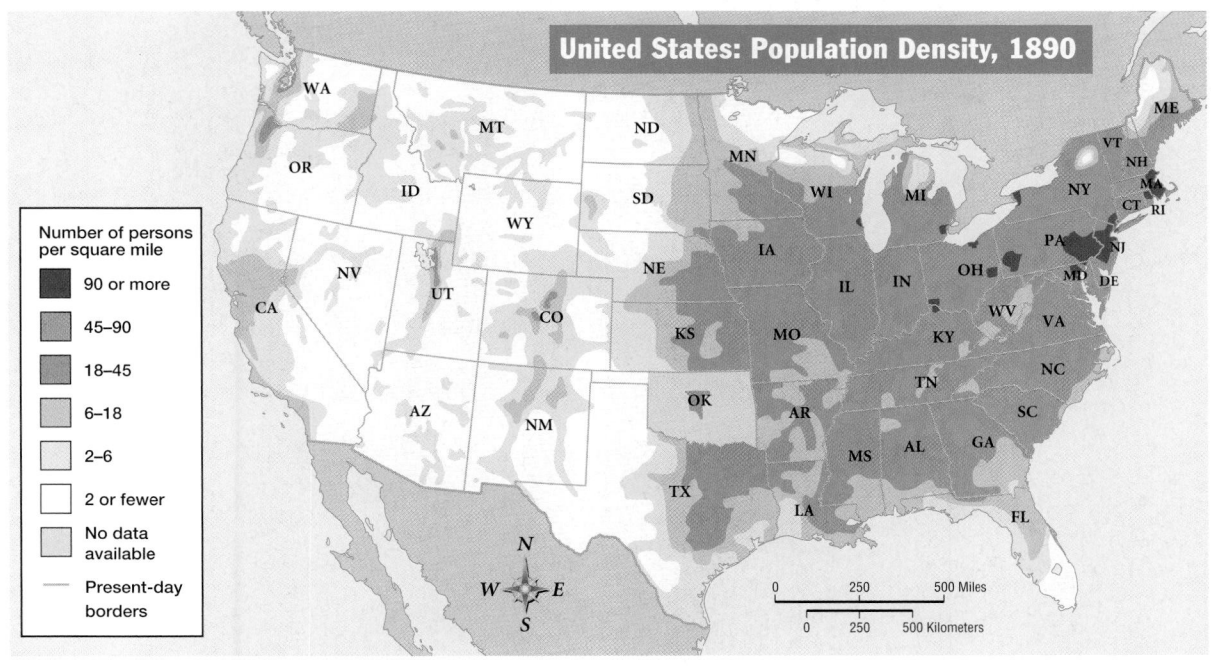

United States: Population Density, 1890

Number of persons per square mile

- 90 or more
- 45–90
- 18–45
- 6–18
- 2–6
- 2 or fewer
- No data available
- Present-day borders

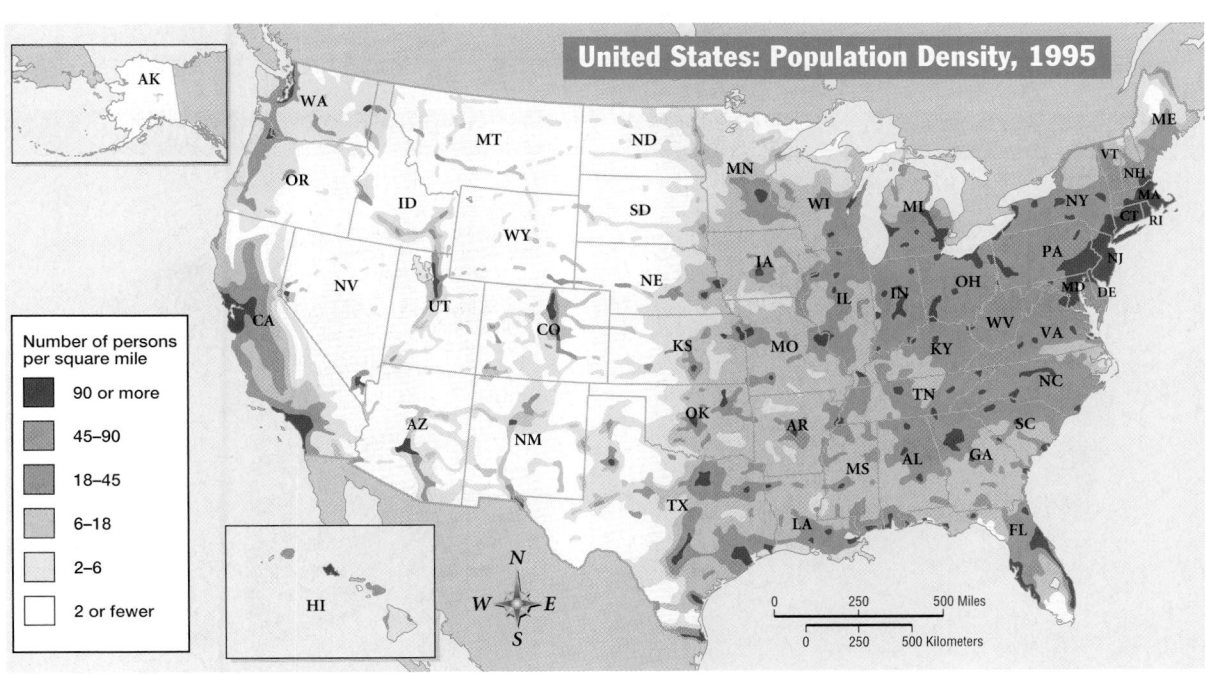

United States: Population Density, 1995

Number of persons per square mile

- 90 or more
- 45–90
- 18–45
- 6–18
- 2–6
- 2 or fewer

Territorial Expansion From 1763

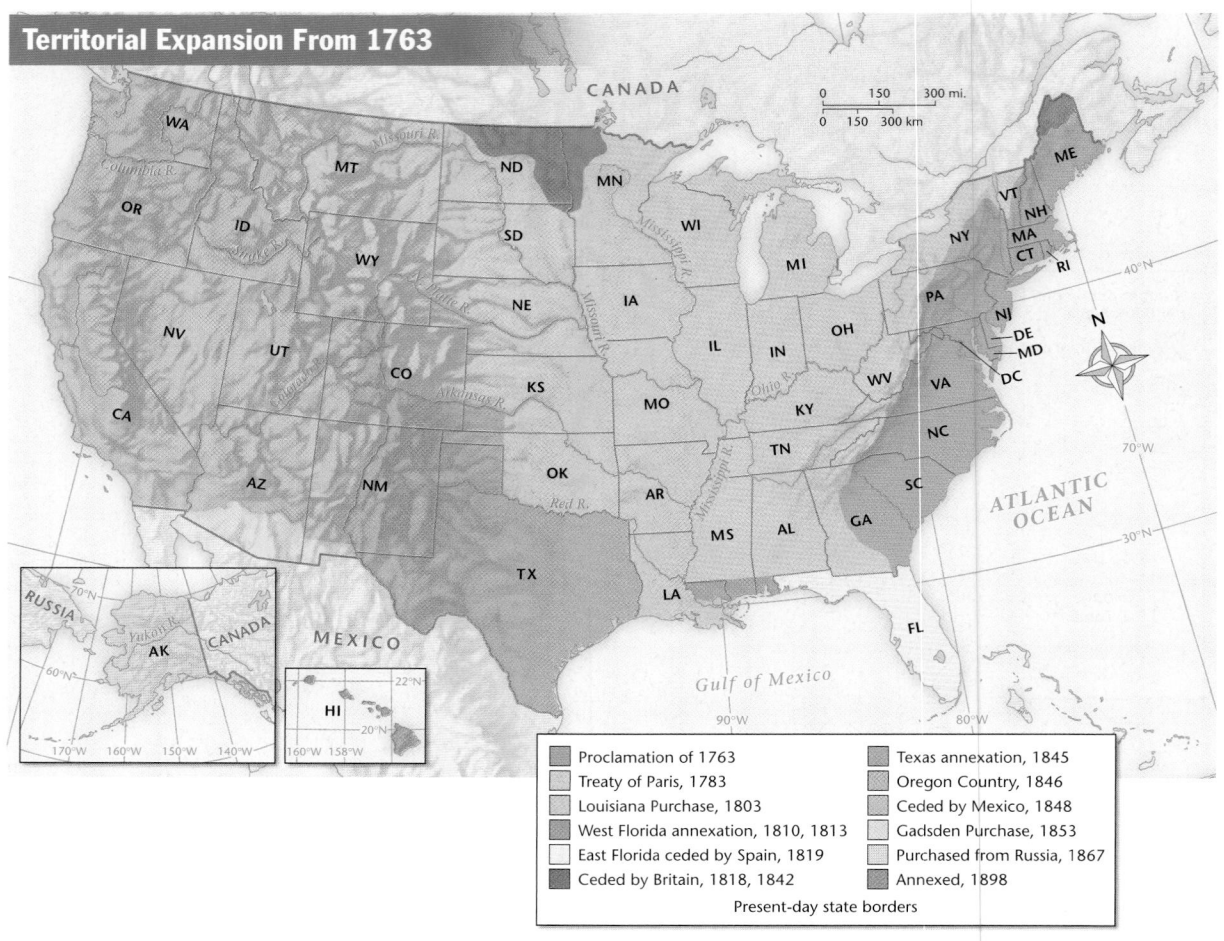

Proclamation of 1763
Treaty of Paris, 1783
Louisiana Purchase, 1803
West Florida annexation, 1810, 1813
East Florida ceded by Spain, 1819
Ceded by Britain, 1818, 1842
Texas annexation, 1845
Oregon Country, 1846
Ceded by Mexico, 1848
Gadsden Purchase, 1853
Purchased from Russia, 1867
Annexed, 1898

Present-day state borders

United States Ethnic Groups, 1790

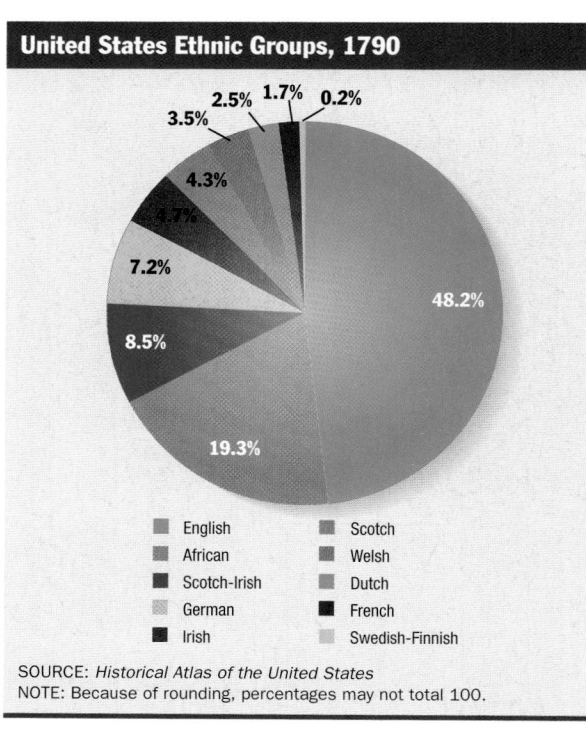

48.2%
19.3%
8.5%
7.2%
4.7%
4.3%
3.5%
2.5%
1.7%
0.2%

English
African
Scotch-Irish
German
Irish
Scotch
Welsh
Dutch
French
Swedish-Finnish

SOURCE: *Historical Atlas of the United States*
NOTE: Because of rounding, percentages may not total 100.

United States Ancestry (Self-Reported), 2000

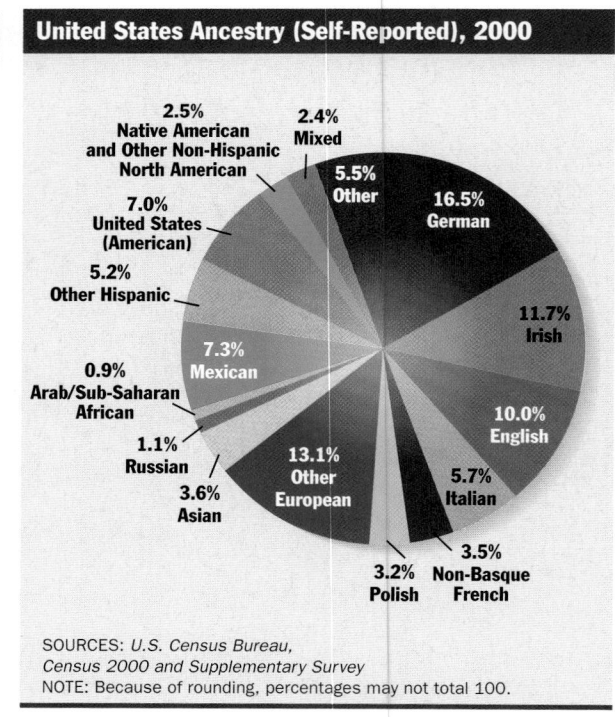

2.5% Native American and Other Non-Hispanic North American
2.4% Mixed
5.5% Other
16.5% German
7.0% United States (American)
5.2% Other Hispanic
11.7% Irish
7.3% Mexican
10.0% English
0.9% Arab/Sub-Saharan African
5.7% Italian
1.1% Russian
13.1% Other European
3.6% Asian
3.5% Non-Basque French
3.2% Polish

SOURCES: *U.S. Census Bureau, Census 2000 and Supplementary Survey*
NOTE: Because of rounding, percentages may not total 100.

United States Population, 1800–2000

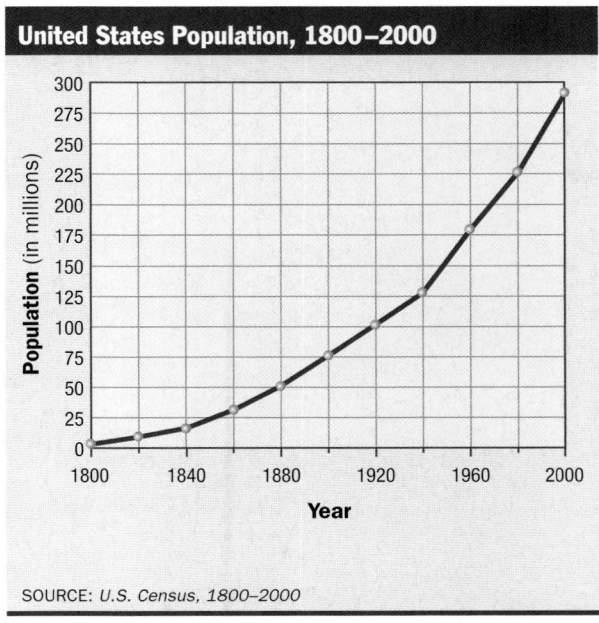

Population (in millions)

Year

SOURCE: U.S. Census, 1800–2000

United States Median Age, 1840–2040

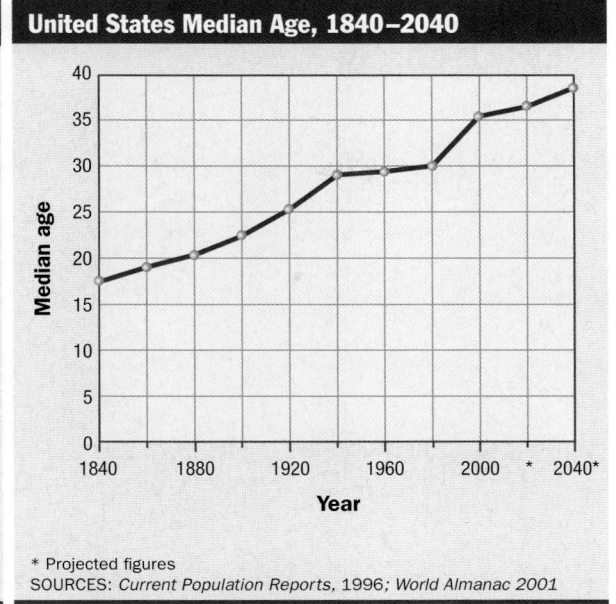

Median age

Year

* Projected figures
SOURCES: *Current Population Reports*, 1996; *World Almanac 2001*

United States Birthrate, 1910–2000

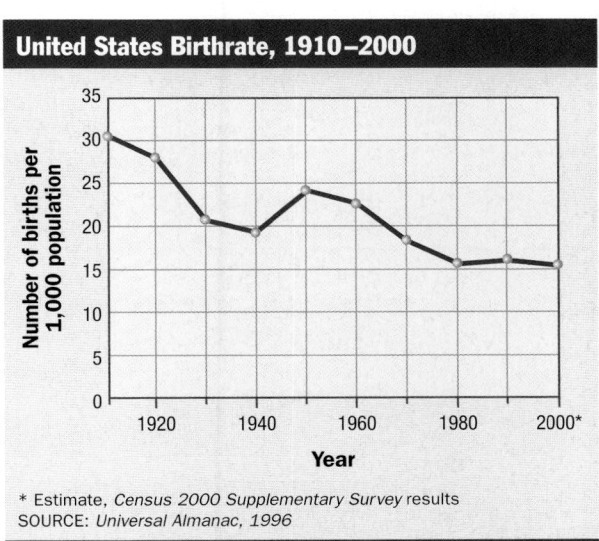

Number of births per 1,000 population

Year

* Estimate, *Census 2000 Supplementary Survey* results
SOURCE: *Universal Almanac, 1996*

United States Population by Race, 2000

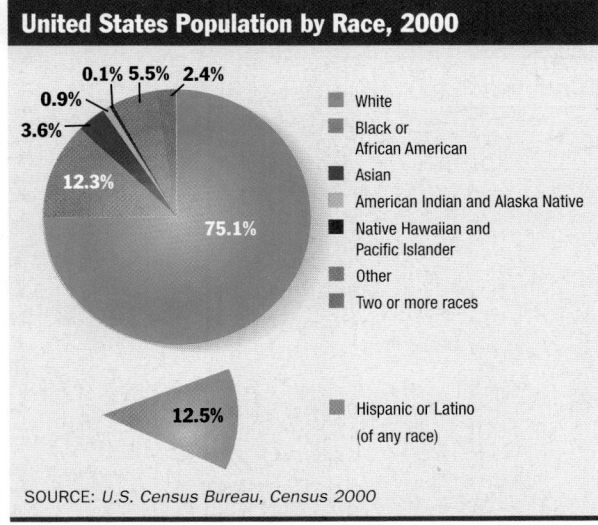

- 0.1%
- 5.5%
- 2.4%
- 0.9%
- 3.6%
- 12.3%
- 75.1%
- 12.5%

- White
- Black or African American
- Asian
- American Indian and Alaska Native
- Native Hawaiian and Pacific Islander
- Other
- Two or more races
- Hispanic or Latino (of any race)

SOURCE: *U.S. Census Bureau, Census 2000*

United States Hispanic or Latino Population, 2000

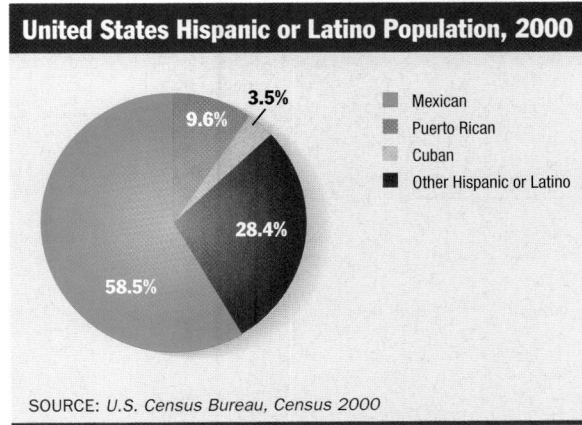

- 3.5%
- 9.6%
- 28.4%
- 58.5%

- Mexican
- Puerto Rican
- Cuban
- Other Hispanic or Latino

SOURCE: *U.S. Census Bureau, Census 2000*

United States Asian Population, 2000

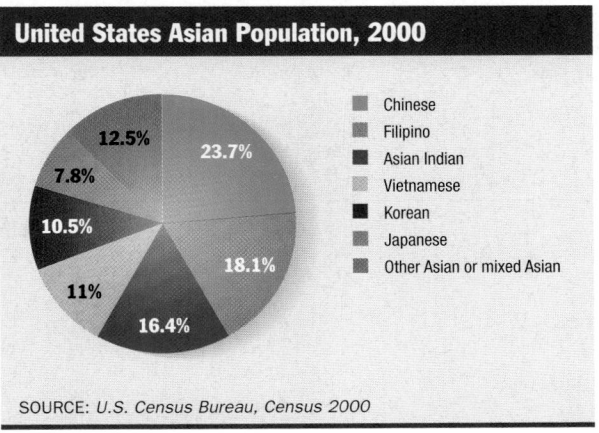

- 12.5%
- 23.7%
- 7.8%
- 18.1%
- 10.5%
- 11%
- 16.4%

- Chinese
- Filipino
- Asian Indian
- Vietnamese
- Korean
- Japanese
- Other Asian or mixed Asian

SOURCE: *U.S. Census Bureau, Census 2000*

Illustrated Databank

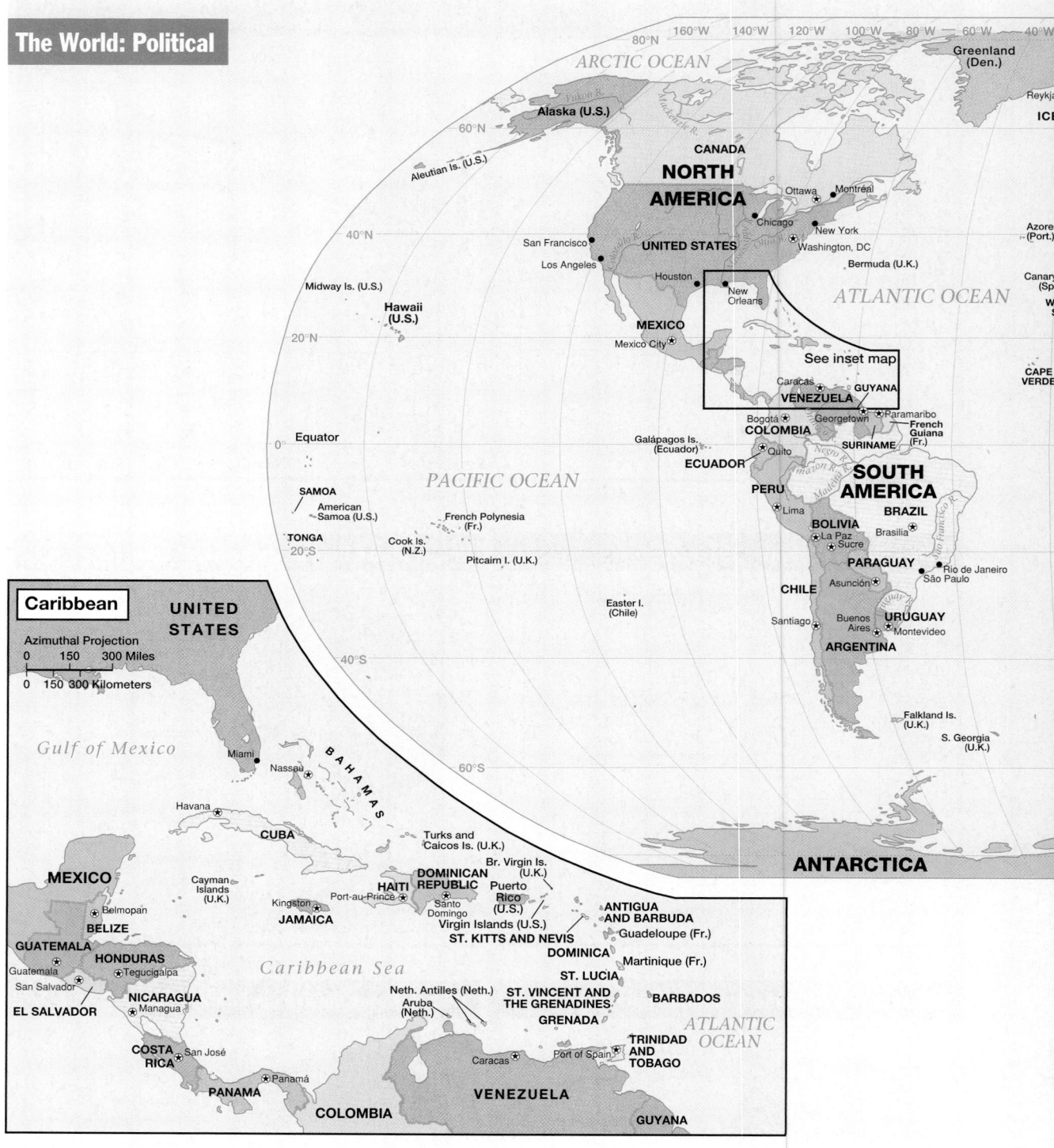

Caribbean

Azimuthal Projection

0   150   300 Miles

0   150 300 Kilometers

Illustrated Databank

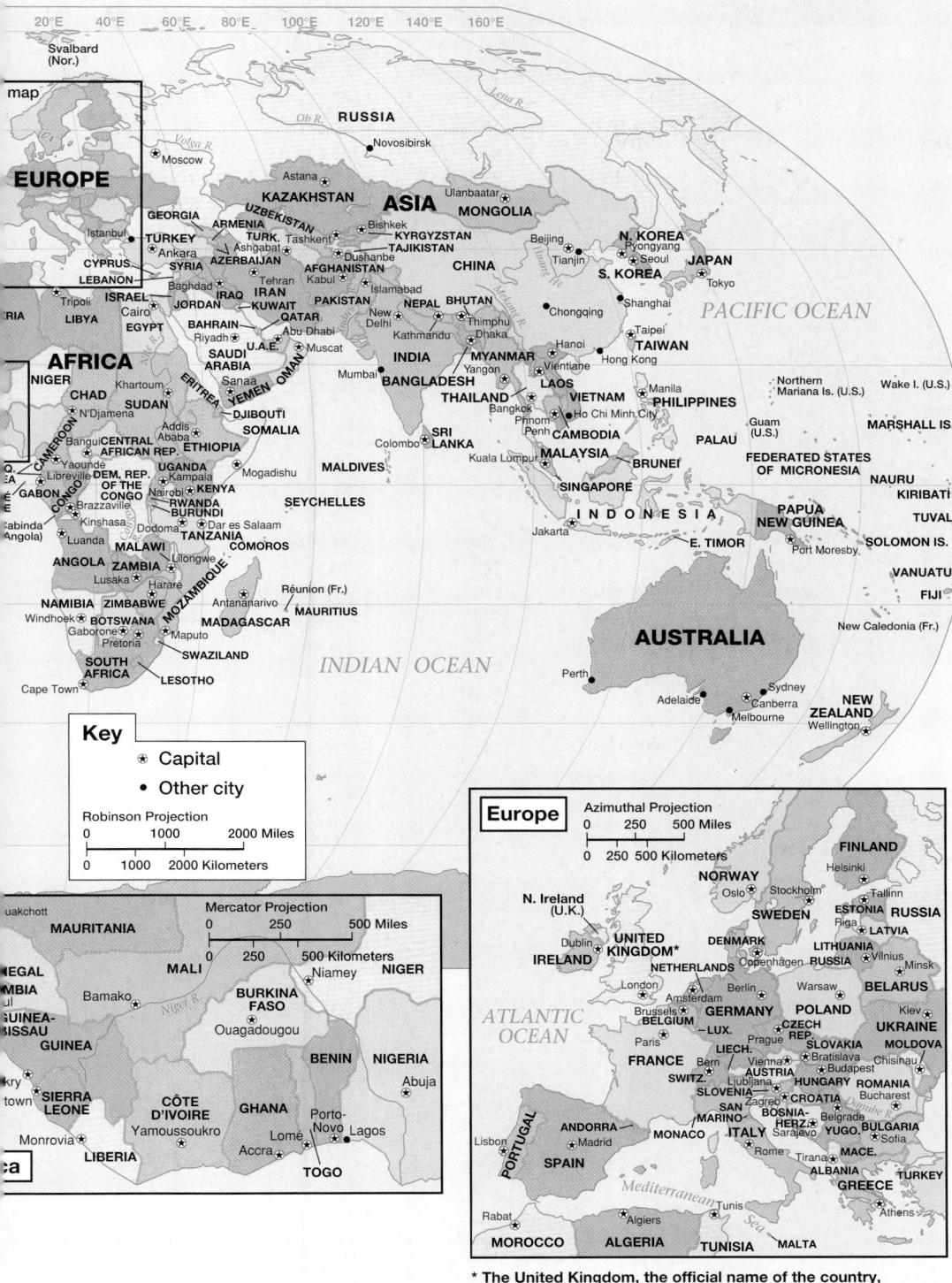

Key

⊛ Capital

● Other city

Robinson Projection

| 0 | 1000 | 2000 Miles |

| 0 | 1000 | 2000 Kilometers |

20°E 40°E 60°E 80°E 100°E 120°E 140°E 160°E

Svalbard
(Nor.)

map

EUROPE

RUSSIA

Ob R.
Novosibirsk

Moscow

Astana

KAZAKHSTAN **ASIA**
Ulanbaatar
MONGOLIA

GEORGIA
ARMENIA UZBEKISTAN
TURKEY Bishkek KYRGYZSTAN
Istanbul TURK. Tashkent
Ankara Ashgabat TAJIKISTAN Beijing
CYPRUS AZERBAIJAN Dushanbe
SYRIA AFGHANISTAN CHINA Tianjin
LEBANON Tehran Kabul Islamabad
Baghdad IRAN PAKISTAN New
ISRAEL IRAQ KUWAIT Delhi
Cairo JORDAN QATAR NEPAL BHUTAN
LIBYA BAHRAIN Riyadh Abu Dhabi Kathmandu Thimphu Dhaka
EGYPT U.A.E. Muscat
SAUDI OMAN INDIA
ARABIA Sanaa Mumbai BANGLADESH MYANMAR
NIGER Khartoum ERITREA YEMEN THAILAND LAOS
CHAD SUDAN DJIBOUTI Yangon
N'Djamena Addis SOMALIA Bangkok
CAMEROON Ababa Colombo SRI CAMBODIA
Bangui CENTRAL ETHIOPIA LANKA Phnom
AFRICAN REP. Kuala Lumpur Penh
Yaounde UGANDA MALDIVES MALAYSIA
GABON DEM. REP. Kampala KENYA
OF THE Nairobi SINGAPORE
CONGO RWANDA Dodoma SEYCHELLES
Brazzaville BURUNDI Dar es Salaam
Cabinda Kinshasa TANZANIA COMOROS
(Angola) Luanda MALAWI Lilongwe
ANGOLA ZAMBIA Réunion (Fr.)
Lusaka Harare MAURITIUS
NAMIBIA ZIMBABWE Antananarivo
Windhoek BOTSWANA MADAGASCAR
Gaborone Pretoria Maputo
SOUTH SWAZILAND
Cape Town AFRICA LESOTHO

PYONGYANG
N. KOREA
Pyongyang
S. KOREA JAPAN
Seoul Tokyo
Chongqing Shanghai

PACIFIC OCEAN

Taipei
Hong Kong TAIWAN
Hanoi
Vientiane
VIETNAM Manila
Ho Chi Minh City PHILIPPINES
Northern Wake I. (U.S.)
Mariana Is. (U.S.)
Guam MARSHALL IS.
(U.S.)
PALAU
FEDERATED STATES NAURU
OF MICRONESIA KIRIBATI
TUVALU
PAPUA
NEW GUINEA
Jakarta I N D O N E S I A Port Moresby SOLOMON IS. VANUATU
E. TIMOR FIJI
New Caledonia (Fr.)

INDIAN OCEAN

AUSTRALIA

Perth Sydney
Adelaide Canberra
Melbourne **NEW
ZEALAND**
Wellington

Africa

Mercator Projection

| 0 | 250 | 500 Miles |

| 0 | 250 | 500 Kilometers |

uakchott
MAURITANIA
SENEGAL MALI Niamey NIGER
AMBIA Bamako Niger R.
kry GUINEA- BURKINA
BISSAU FASO
GUINEA Ouagadougou
SIERRA CÔTE BENIN NIGERIA
LEONE D'IVOIRE GHANA Abuja
Monrovia Yamoussoukro Porto-
LIBERIA Lomé Novo Lagos
Accra
TOGO

Europe

Azimuthal Projection

| 0 | 250 | 500 Miles |

| 0 | 250 500 Kilometers |

FINLAND
Helsinki
NORWAY
Oslo Stockholm Tallinn
N. Ireland SWEDEN ESTONIA RUSSIA
(U.K.) Riga LATVIA
Dublin UNITED DENMARK LITHUANIA
IRELAND KINGDOM* Copenhagen RUSSIA Vilnius Minsk
ATLANTIC NETHERLANDS Berlin Warsaw BELARUS
OCEAN London Amsterdam Kiev
Brussels GERMANY POLAND UKRAINE
BELGIUM CZECH Prague MOLDOVA
Paris LUX. REP. SLOVAKIA Chisinau
LIECH. Vienna Bratislava
FRANCE Bern AUSTRIA Budapest ROMANIA
SWITZ. Ljubljana HUNGARY Bucharest
SLOVENIA Zagreb CROATIA
SAN Belgrade BULGARIA
PORTUGAL ANDORRA MARINO BOSNIA- YUGO. Sofia
Madrid MONACO HERZ. Sarajevo
Lisbon ITALY Rome Tirana MACE.
SPAIN ALBANIA TURKEY
GREECE Athens
Rabat Algiers Tunis
Mediterranean
Sea
MOROCCO ALGERIA TUNISIA MALTA

* The United Kingdom, the official name of the country,
is more often referred to as Great Britain.

Profile of the Fifty States

State	Capital	Entered Union	Population (2000)	Population Rank	Land Area (Sq. Mi.)	Land Area Rank
Alabama	Montgomery	1819	4,447,100	23rd	50,744	28th
Alaska	Juneau	1959	626,932	48th	571,951	1st
Arizona	Phoenix	1912	5,130,632	20th	113,635	6th
Arkansas	Little Rock	1836	2,673,400	33rd	52,068	27th
California	Sacramento	1850	33,871,648	1st	155,959	3rd
Colorado	Denver	1876	4,301,261	24th	103,718	8th
Connecticut	Hartford	1788	3,405,565	29th	4,845	48th
Delaware	Dover	1787	783,600	45th	1,954	49th
Florida	Tallahassee	1845	15,982,378	4th	53,927	26th
Georgia	Atlanta	1788	8,186,453	10th	57,906	21st
Hawaii	Honolulu	1959	1,211,537	42nd	6,423	47th
Idaho	Boise	1890	1,293,953	39th	82,747	11th
Illinois	Springfield	1818	12,419,293	5th	55,584	24th
Indiana	Indianapolis	1816	6,080,485	14th	35,867	38th
Iowa	Des Moines	1846	2,926,324	30th	55,869	23rd
Kansas	Topeka	1861	2,688,418	32nd	81,815	13th
Kentucky	Frankfort	1792	4,041,769	25th	39,728	36th
Louisiana	Baton Rouge	1812	4,468,976	22nd	43,562	33rd
Maine	Augusta	1820	1,274,923	40th	30,862	39th
Maryland	Annapolis	1788	5,296,486	19th	9,774	42nd
Massachusetts	Boston	1788	6,349,097	13th	7,840	45th
Michigan	Lansing	1837	9,938,444	8th	56,804	22nd
Minnesota	St. Paul	1858	4,919,479	21st	79,610	14th
Mississippi	Jackson	1817	2,844,658	31st	46,907	31st
Missouri	Jefferson City	1821	5,595,211	17th	68,886	18th
Montana	Helena	1889	902,195	44th	145,552	4th
Nebraska	Lincoln	1867	1,711,263	38th	76,872	15th
Nevada	Carson City	1864	1,998,257	35th	109,826	7th
New Hampshire	Concord	1788	1,235,786	41st	8,968	44th
New Jersey	Trenton	1787	8,414,350	9th	7,417	46th
New Mexico	Santa Fe	1912	1,819,046	36th	121,356	5th
New York	Albany	1788	18,976,457	3rd	47,214	30th
North Carolina	Raleigh	1789	8,049,313	11th	48,711	29th
North Dakota	Bismarck	1889	642,200	47th	68,976	17th
Ohio	Columbus	1803	11,353,140	7th	40,948	35th
Oklahoma	Oklahoma City	1907	3,450,654	27th	68,667	19th
Oregon	Salem	1859	3,421,399	28th	95,997	10th
Pennsylvania	Harrisburg	1787	12,281,054	6th	44,817	32nd
Rhode Island	Providence	1790	1,048,319	43rd	1,045	50th
South Carolina	Columbia	1788	4,012,012	26th	30,110	40th
South Dakota	Pierre	1889	754,844	46th	75,885	16th
Tennessee	Nashville	1796	5,689,283	16th	41,217	34th
Texas	Austin	1845	20,851,820	2nd	261,797	2nd
Utah	Salt Lake City	1896	2,233,169	34th	82,144	12th
Vermont	Montpelier	1791	608,827	49th	9,250	43rd
Virginia	Richmond	1788	7,078,515	12th	39,594	37th
Washington	Olympia	1889	5,894,121	15th	66,544	20th
West Virginia	Charleston	1863	1,808,344	37th	24,078	41st
Wisconsin	Madison	1848	5,363,675	18th	54,310	25th
Wyoming	Cheyenne	1890	493,782	50th	97,100	9th

SOURCE: *World Almanac, Census 2000*

Illustrated Databank

Presidents of the United States

George Washington
(1732–1799)
Years in Office: 1789–1797
No political party
Elected from: Virginia
Vice President: John Adams

John Adams
(1735–1826)
Years in Office: 1797–1801
Federalist
Elected from: Massachusetts
Vice President: Thomas Jefferson

Thomas Jefferson
(1743–1826)
Years in Office: 1801–1809
Democratic Republican
Elected from: Virginia
Vice Presidents: Aaron Burr,
  George Clinton

James Madison
(1751–1836)
Years in Office: 1809–1817
Democratic Republican
Elected from: Virginia
Vice Presidents: George Clinton,
  Elbridge Gerry

James Monroe
(1758–1831)
Years in Office: 1817–1825
National Republican
Elected from: Virginia
Vice President: Daniel Tompkins

John Quincy Adams
(1767–1848)
Years in Office: 1825–1829
National Republican
Elected from: Massachusetts
Vice President: John Calhoun

Andrew Jackson
(1767–1845)
Years in Office: 1829–1837
Democrat
Elected from: Tennessee
Vice Presidents: John Calhoun, Martin
  Van Buren

Martin Van Buren
(1782–1862)
Years in Office: 1837–1841
Democrat
Elected from: New York
Vice President: Richard Johnson

William Henry Harrison*
(1773–1841)
Year in Office: 1841
Whig
Elected from: Ohio
Vice President: John Tyler

John Tyler
(1790–1862)
Years in Office: 1841–1845
Whig
Elected from: Virginia
Vice President: none

James K. Polk
(1795–1849)
Years in Office: 1845–1849
Democrat
Elected from: Tennessee
Vice President: George Dallas

Zachary Taylor*
(1784–1850)
Years in Office: 1849–1850
Whig
Elected from: Louisiana
Vice President: Millard Fillmore

Millard Fillmore
(1800–1874)
Years in Office: 1850–1853
Whig
Elected from: New York
Vice President: none

Franklin Pierce
(1804–1869)
Years in Office: 1853–1857
Democrat
Elected from: New Hampshire
Vice President: William King

James Buchanan
(1791–1868)
Years in Office: 1857–1861
Democrat
Elected from: Pennsylvania
Vice President: John Breckinridge

Abraham Lincoln**
(1809–1865)
Years in Office: 1861–1865
Republican
Elected from: Illinois
Vice Presidents: Hannibal Hamlin,
  Andrew Johnson

Andrew Johnson
(1808–1875)
Years in Office: 1865–1869
Democrat†
Elected from: Tennessee
Vice President: none

Ulysses S. Grant
(1822–1885)
Years in Office: 1869–1877
Republican
Elected from: Illinois
Vice Presidents: Schuyler Colfax,
    Henry Wilson

Rutherford B. Hayes
(1822–1893)
Years in Office: 1877–1881
Republican
Elected from: Ohio
Vice President: William Wheeler

James A. Garfield**
(1831–1881)
Year in Office: 1881
Republican
Elected from: Ohio
Vice President: Chester A. Arthur

Chester A. Arthur
(1830–1886)
Years in Office: 1881–1885
Republican
Elected from: New York
Vice President: none

Grover Cleveland
(1837–1908)
Years in Office: 1885–1889
Democrat
Elected from: New York
Vice President: Thomas Hendricks

Benjamin Harrison
(1833–1901)
Years in Office: 1889–1893
Republican
Elected from: Indiana
Vice President: Levi Morton

Grover Cleveland
(1837–1908)
Years in Office: 1893–1897
Democrat
Elected from: New York
Vice President: Adlai Stevenson

William McKinley**
(1843–1901)
Years in Office: 1897–1901
Republican
Elected from: Ohio
Vice Presidents: Garret Hobart,
    Theodore Roosevelt

Theodore Roosevelt
(1858–1919)
Years in Office: 1901–1909
Republican
Elected from: New York
Vice President: Charles Fairbanks

William Howard Taft
(1857–1930)
Years in Office: 1909–1913
Republican
Elected from: Ohio
Vice President: James Sherman

Woodrow Wilson
(1856–1924)
Years in Office: 1913–1921
Democrat
Elected from: New Jersey
Vice President: Thomas Marshall

Warren G. Harding*
(1865–1923)
Years in Office: 1921–1923
Republican
Elected from: Ohio
Vice President: Calvin Coolidge

Calvin Coolidge
(1872–1933)
Years in Office: 1923–1929
Republican
Elected from: Massachusetts
Vice President: Charles Dawes

Herbert C. Hoover
(1874–1964)
Years in Office: 1929–1933
Republican
Elected from: New York
Vice President: Charles Curtis

Franklin D. Roosevelt*
(1882–1945)
Years in Office: 1933–1945
Democrat
Elected from: New York
Vice Presidents: John Garner,
    Henry Wallace, Harry S Truman

Harry S Truman
(1884–1972)
Years in Office: 1945–1953
Democrat
Elected from: Missouri
Vice President: Alben Barkley

Dwight D. Eisenhower
(1890-1969)
Years in Office: 1953–1961
Republican
Elected from: New York
Vice President: Richard M. Nixon

John F. Kennedy**
(1917-1963)
Years in Office: 1961–1963
Democrat
Elected from: Massachusetts
Vice President: Lyndon B. Johnson

Lyndon B. Johnson
(1908-1973)
Years in Office: 1963–1969
Democrat
Elected from: Texas
Vice President: Hubert Humphrey

Richard M. Nixon***
(1913-1994)
Years in Office: 1969–1974
Republican
Elected from: New York
Vice Presidents: Spiro Agnew,
  Gerald R. Ford

Gerald R. Ford
(1913-)
Years in Office: 1974–1977
Republican
Elected from: Michigan
Vice President: Nelson Rockefeller

James E. Carter
(1924-)
Years in Office: 1977–1981
Democrat
Elected from: Georgia
Vice President: Walter F. Mondale

Ronald W. Reagan
(1911-)
Years in Office: 1981–1989
Republican
Elected from: California
Vice President: George H. W. Bush

George H. W. Bush
(1924-)
Years in Office: 1989–1993
Republican
Elected from: Texas
Vice President: J. Danforth Quayle

William J. Clinton
(1946-)
Years in Office: 1993–2001
Democrat
Elected from: Arkansas
Vice President: Albert Gore Jr.

George W. Bush
(1946-)
Years in Office: 2001–
Republican
Elected from: Texas
Vice President: Richard Cheney

* Died in office
** Assassinated
*** Resigned
† Elected Vice President on the coalition
  Union Party ticket

Key Supreme Court Cases

These pages provide summaries of key Supreme Court rulings over the course of the nation's history. For additional material and links to Supreme Court cases, see the America: Pathways to the Present *companion Web site at* **www.phschool.com**

Baker v. Carr, 1962

(14th Amendment) Rapid population growth in Nashville and reluctance of the rural-dominated Tennessee legislature to redraw state legislature districts led Mayor Baker of Nashville to ask for federal court help. The federal district court refused to enter the "political thicket" of redistricting, and the case was appealed. The Court directed a trial to be held in a Tennessee federal court. The case led to the 1964 *Westberry* decision, which created the "one man, one vote" equal representation concept.

Bethel School District #403 v. Fraser, 1986

(1st Amendment, freedom of speech) A high school student gave a sexually suggestive political speech at a high school assembly to elect student officers. The school administration strongly disciplined the student, Fraser, who argued that school rules unfairly limited his freedom of political speech. Fraser's view was upheld in Washington State court. The Supreme Court, however, found that "it does not follow . . . that simply because the use of an offensive form of expression [is permitted by] adults making . . . a political point, the same latitude must be permitted to children in a public school."

Bob Jones University v. United States, 1983

(14th and 1st amendments) Bob Jones University, a private school, denied admission to applicants in an interracial marriage or who "espouse" interracial marriage or dating. The Internal Revenue Service then denied tax-exempt status to the school because of racial discrimination. The university appealed, claiming that its policy was based on the Bible. The Court upheld the IRS ruling, stating that "Government has a fundamental overriding interest" in ending racial discrimination in education.

Brown v. Board of Education of Topeka, 1954

(14th Amendment) Probably no twentieth-century Supreme Court decision so deeply stirred and changed life in the United States as *Brown*. A 10-year-old girl from Topeka, Kansas, was not permitted to attend her neighborhood school because she was an African American. The Court found that segregation itself was a violation of the Equal Protection Clause, commenting that "in the field of public education the doctrine of 'separate but equal' has no place. . . . Segregation is a denial of the equal protection of the laws." The decision overturned *Plessy*, 1896.

City of Philadelphia v. New Jersey, 1978

The Court decided that New Jersey may not restrict the importation of solid or liquid waste that originated outside the State. The Commerce Clause protects all objects of interstate trade, including waste. A State may not discriminate against items that are identical except for their origin, and thus may not prohibit out-of-state waste that is no different from domestically produced waste. Although waste disposal is a problem in many locations, States may not constitutionally deal with the problem by erecting a barrier against the movement of interstate trade.

The Civil Rights Cases, 1883

(14th Amendment) The Civil Rights Acts of 1875 included punishments for businesses that practiced discrimination. The Court ruled on a number of cases involving the Acts in 1883, finding that the Constitution, "while prohibiting discrimination by governments, made no provisions . . . for acts of racial discrimination by private individuals." The decision limited the impact of the Equal Protection Clause, giving tacit approval to segregation in the private sector.

Cruzan v. Director, Missouri Dept. of Health, 1990

(9th Amendment, right to die) A Missouri woman was in a coma from an automobile accident in 1983. Her family, facing astronomical medical bills and deciding that "her life had ended in 1987," directed the health-care providers to end intravenous feeding. The State of Missouri opposed the family's decision, and the family went to court. The Court ruled that states could require "clear and convincing" evidence that Cruzan would have wanted to die. However, the Court did not require other states to meet the Missouri standard. At a subsequent hearing, "clear and convincing evidence" was presented. The intravenous feeding was ended, and Cruzan died on December 26, 1990.

Dennis v. United States, 1951

(1st Amendment) The Smith Act of 1940 made it a crime for any person to work for the violent overthrow of the United States in peacetime or war. Eleven Communist party leaders, including Dennis, had been convicted of violating the Smith Act, and they appealed. The Court upheld the Act. Much modified by later decisions, the Dennis case focused on anti-government speech as an area of controversy.

Dred Scott v. Sandford, 1857

(6th Amendment) This decision upheld property rights over human rights by saying that Dred Scott, a slave, could not become a free man just because he had traveled in "free soil" states with his master. A badly divided nation was further fragmented by the decision. "Free soil" federal laws and the Missouri Compromise line of 1820 were held unconstitutional because they deprived a slave owner of the right to his "property" without just compensation. This narrow reading of the Constitution, a landmark case of the Court, was most clearly stated by Chief Justice Roger B. Taney, a states' rights advocate.

Edwards v. South Carolina, 1963

(1st Amendment, freedom of speech and assembly) A group of mostly African American civil rights activists held a rally at the South Carolina State Capitol, protesting segregation. A hostile crowd gathered, and the rally leaders were arrested and convicted of "breach of the peace." The Court overturned the convictions, saying, "The Fourteenth Amendment does not permit a State to make criminal the peaceful expression of unpopular views."

Engel v. Vitale, 1962

(1st Amendment) The state Board of Regents of New York required the recitation of a 22-word nonsectarian prayer at the beginning of each school day. A group of parents filed suit against the required prayer, claiming it violated their 1st Amendment rights. The Court ruled New York's action unconstitutional, observing, "There can be no doubt that . . . religious beliefs [are] embodied in the Regents' prayer."

Escobedo v. Illinois, 1964

(6th Amendment) A person known to Chicago-area police confessed to a murder but had not been provided with a lawyer while under interrogation. The Court's decision in the case extended the "exclusionary rule" to illegal confessions in state court proceedings. Carefully defining an "Escobedo Rule," the Court said, "where . . . the investigation is no longer a general inquiry . . . but has begun to focus on a particular suspect . . . (and where) the suspect has been taken into custody . . . the suspect has requested . . . his lawyer, and the police have not . . . warned him of his right to remain silent, the accused has been denied . . . counsel in violation of the Sixth Amendment."

Everson v. Board of Education, 1947

(1st Amendment) In a case known as "the New Jersey School Bus Case," the Court considered New Jersey's use of public funds to operate school buses that carried some students to parochial schools. The Court permitted New Jersey to continue the payments, saying that the aid to children was not governmental support for religion. The decision, however, strongly stated that the wall separating church and state must be kept "high and impregnable." This was a clear incorporation of 1st Amendment limits on states.

Ex parte Milligan, 1866

(Article II) An Indiana man was arrested, treated as a prisoner of war, and imprisoned by a military court during the Civil War under presidential order. He claimed that his right to a fair trial was interfered with and that military courts had no authority outside of "conquered territory." The Court ordered him to be released on the grounds that the Constitution "is a law for rulers and people, equally in war and peace" and covers all people "at all times, and under all circumstances." The Court held that presidential powers in time of war did not extend to creating another court system run by the military.

Furman v. Georgia, 1972

(8th Amendment) Three death penalty cases, including *Furman*, raised the issue of racial imbalances in the use of death sentences by state courts. Furman had been sentenced to death in Georgia. Overturning state death penalty laws, the Court noted an "apparent arbitrariness of the use of the sentence." Many states rewrote their death penalty statutes, and these were generally upheld in *Gregg*, 1976.

Gibbons v. Ogden, 1824

(Article I, Section 8) This case examined the power of Congress to regulate interstate commerce. Ogden's exclusive New York ferry license gave him the right to operate steamboats to and from New York. Ogden claimed that Gibbons's federal license did not give him landing rights in New York City. Federal and state regulation of commerce conflicted. The Court strengthened the power of the United States to regulate interstate business. Federal controls on television, pipelines, and banking are based on *Gibbons*.

Gideon v. Wainwright, 1963

(14th Amendment) Gideon was charged with breaking into a poolroom. He could not afford a lawyer, and Florida refused to provide counsel for trials not involving the death penalty. Gideon defended himself poorly and was sentenced to five years in prison. The Court called for a new trial, arguing that the Due Process Clause of the 14th Amendment applied to the 6th Amendment's guarantee of counsel for all poor persons facing a felony charge. Gideon later was found not guilty with the help of a court-appointed attorney.

Gitlow v. New York, 1925

(1st and 14th amendments) For the first time, the Court considered whether the 1st and 14th amendments had influence on state laws. The case, involving "criminal anarchy" under New York law, was the first consideration of what came to be known as the "incorporation" doctrine, under which, it was argued, the provisions of the 1st Amendment were "incorporated" by the 14th Amendment. Although New York law was not overruled in the case, the decision clearly indicated that the Court could make such a ruling. Another important incorporation case is *Powell*, 1932.

Goss v. Lopez, 1975

(14th Amendment, Due Process Clause) Ten Ohio students were suspended from their schools without hearings. The students challenged the suspensions, claiming that the absence of a preliminary hearing violated their 14th Amendment right to due process. The Court agreed with the students, holding that "having chosen to extend the right to an education . . . Ohio may not withdraw that right on grounds of misconduct, absent fundamentally fair procedures to determine whether the misconduct has occurred, and must recognize a student's legitimate entitlement to a public education as a property interest that is protected by the Due Process Clause."

Gregg v. Georgia, 1976

(8th Amendment) In the 1970s, activists tried to get the death penalty reinstated. Several test cases failed when the Court found the sentence had been motivated by racism, issued arbitrarily, or handed down without due process. The case of Gregg, convicted of murdering two men, was considered to be free from such problems. Finding that his conviction and death sentence were fair and consistent with state law, the Court ruled that Georgia's death penalty did not violate the "cruel and unusual punishment" clause of the 8th Amendment. For the first time, the Court clearly affirmed that "punishment of death does not invariably violate the Constitution."

Griswold v. Connecticut, 1965

(14th Amendment) A Connecticut law forbade the use of "any drug, medicinal article, or instrument for the purpose of preventing conception." Griswold, director of Planned Parenthood in New Haven, was arrested for counseling married couples. After conviction, he appealed. The Court overturned the Connecticut law, saying that "various guarantees (of the Constitution) create zones of privacy" and asking, "would we allow the police to search the sacred precincts of marital bedrooms . . . ?" The decision is significant for examining the concept of "unenumerated rights" in the 9th Amendment, later central to *Roe*, 1973.

Hazelwood School District v. Kuhlmeier, 1988

(1st Amendment, freedom of speech) In 1983, the principal of Hazelwood East High School in Missouri removed two articles from the upcoming issue of the student newspaper, deeming their content "inappropriate, personal, sensitive, and unsuitable for student readers." Several students sued the school district, claiming that their 1st Amendment right to freedom of expression had been violated. The Court upheld the principal's action, stating that "a school need not tolerate student speech that is inconsistent with its basic educational mission, even though the government could not censor similar speech outside the school." School officials had full control over school-sponsored activities "so long as their actions are reasonably related to legitimate pedagogical concerns. . . ."

Heart of Atlanta Motel, Inc. v. United States, 1964

(Article I, Section 8) The Civil Rights Act of 1964 outlawed race discrimination in "public accommodations," including motels that refused rooms to blacks. Although local desegregation appeared to fall outside federal authority, the government argued that it was regulating interstate commerce. The Court agreed, declaring, "The power of Congress to promote interstate commerce also includes the power to regulate the local incidents thereof, including local activities . . . which have a substantial and harmful effect upon that commerce." Racial segregation of private facilities engaged in interstate commerce was found unconstitutional.

In re Gault, 1966

(14th Amendment) Before *Gault*, proceedings against juveniles were generally handled as "family law," not "criminal law," and offenders received few due process rights. Gault was sentenced to six years in state juvenile detention for an alleged obscene phone call. He was not provided counsel and not permitted to confront or cross-examine the key witness. The Court overturned the juvenile proceedings and required that states provide juveniles "some of the due process guarantees of adults," including a right to a phone call, to counsel, to cross-examine, to confront the accuser, and to be advised of the right to silence.

Ingraham v. Wright, 1977

(8th Amendment) A majority of the Supreme Court concluded that the 8th Amendment historically protected people convicted of crimes, and does not apply to public school students. If authorized by local law or custom, public schools have the right to administer reasonable discipline, and students do not have a due process right to notice or a hearing before punishment administered in accordance with law or custom.

Johnson v. Santa Clara Transportation Agency, 1987

(Discrimination) Under its affirmative action plan, the Transportation Agency in Santa Clara, California, was authorized to "consider as one factor the sex of a qualified applicant" in an effort to combat the significant underrepresentation of women in certain job classifications. When the Agency promoted Diane Joyce, a qualified woman, over Paul Johnson, a qualified man, for the job of road dispatcher, Johnson sued, claiming that the Agency's consideration of the sex of the applicants violated Title VII of the Civil Rights Act of 1964. The Court upheld the Agency's promotion policy, arguing that the affirmative action plan created no "absolute bar" to the advancement of men but rather represented "a moderate, flexible, case-by-case approach to effecting a gradual improvement in the representation of minorities and women . . . in the Agency's work force, and [was] fully consistent with Title VII."

Key Supreme Court Cases

Korematsu v. United States, 1944

(5th Amendment) Two months after Japan attacked Pearl Harbor, President Roosevelt ordered the internment of more than 110,000 Japanese Americans living on the West Coast. Although many Japanese Americans were United States citizens, they had to abandon their property and live in primitive camps far from the coast. Korematsu refused to report to an assembly center and was arrested. The Court rejected his appeal, noting that "pressing public necessity [World War II] may sometimes justify the existence of restrictions which curtail the civil rights of a single racial group" but added that "racial antagonism" never can justify such restrictions. The *Korematsu* decision has been widely criticized, particularly since few Americans of German or Italian descent were interned.

Lemon v. Kurzman, 1971

(1st Amendment, Establishment Clause) In overturning state laws regarding aid to church-supported schools in this and a similar Rhode Island case, the Court created the *Lemon* test, limiting "excessive government entanglement with religion." The Court noted that any state law about aid to religion must meet three criteria: (1) the purpose of the aid must be clearly secular, not religious; (2) its primary effect must neither advance nor inhibit religion; and (3) it must avoid "excessive entanglement of government with religion."

Mapp v. Ohio, 1961

(4th and 14th amendments) Before *Mapp*, the admission of evidence gained by illegal searches was permitted by some state constitutions. Cleveland police raided Mapp's home without a warrant and found obscene materials. She appealed her conviction, saying that the 4th and 14th amendments protected her against improper police behavior. The Court agreed, extending "exclusionary rule" protections to citizens in state courts. The Court said that the prohibition against unreasonable searches would be "meaningless" unless evidence gained in such searches was excluded. The case developed the concept of "incorporation" begun in *Gitlow*, 1925.

Marbury v. Madison, 1803

(Article III) Chief Justice Marshall established "judicial review" as a power of the Supreme Court. After his defeat in the 1800 election, President Adams appointed many Federalists to the federal courts, but the commissions were not delivered. New Secretary of State James Madison refused to deliver them. Marbury sued in the Supreme Court. The Court declared a portion of the Judiciary Act of 1789 unconstitutional, thereby establishing the Court's power to find acts of Congress unconstitutional.

Massachusetts v. Sheppard, 1984

(4th Amendment) A search in Massachusetts was based on a warrant issued on an improper form. Sheppard argued that the search was illegal and the evidence was inadmissible under *Mapp*, 1961. Massachusetts argued that the police acted in "good faith," believing that the warrant was correct. The Court agreed with Massachusetts, noting that the exclusionary rule should not be applied when the officer conducting the search had acted with the reasonable belief that he was following proper procedures.

McCulloch v. Maryland, 1819

(Article I, Section 8) Called the "Bank of the United States" case. A Maryland law required federally chartered banks to use only a special paper to print money, which amounted to a tax. McCulloch, the cashier of the Baltimore branch of the bank, refused to use the paper, claiming that states could not tax the federal government. The Court declared the Maryland law unconstitutional, commenting ". . . the power to tax implies the power to destroy."

Miller v. California, 1973

(1st Amendment) In *Miller*, the Court upheld a stringent application of California obscenity law by Newport Beach, California, and attempted to define what is obscene. The "Miller Rule" included three criteria: (1) that the average person would, applying contemporary community standards, find that the work appealed to the prurient interest; (2) that the work depicts or describes, in an offensive way, sexual conduct defined by state law; and (3) that "the work, taken as a whole, lacks serious literary, artistic, political or scientific value. . . ."

Miranda v. Arizona, 1966

(5th, 6th, and 14th amendments) Arrested for kidnapping and sexual assault, Miranda signed a confession including a statement that he had "full knowledge" of his legal rights. After conviction, he appealed, claiming that without counsel and without warnings, the confession was illegally obtained. The Court agreed with Miranda that "he must be warned prior to any questioning that he has the right to remain silent, that anything he says can be used against him in a court of law, that he has a right to . . . an attorney and that if he cannot afford an attorney one will be appointed for him. . . ." Although later modified, *Miranda* firmly upheld citizens' rights to a fair trial in state courts.

Mueller v. Allen, 1983

(1st and 14th amendments) Minnesota law allowed taxpayers to deduct the costs of tuition, textbooks, and transportation for children in elementary and secondary schools. Several taxpayers sued to prevent parents with children in religious schools from claiming this deduction, arguing that this would constitute state sponsorship of religion. The Court disagreed, ruling that the deduction was not intended to promote religion and was available to all parents with school-age children. The Court argued that a law must have the advancement of religion as its primary purpose to be found unconstitutional.

New Jersey v. T.L.O., 1985

(4th and 14th amendments) After T.L.O., a New Jersey high school student, denied an accusation that she had been smoking in the school lavatory, a vice-principal searched her purse and found cigarettes, marijuana, and evidence that T.L.O. had been involved in marijuana dealing at the school. T.L.O. was then sentenced to probation by a juvenile court, but appealed on the grounds that the evidence against her had been obtained by an "unreasonable" search. The Court rejected T.L.O.'s arguments, stating that the school had a "legitimate need to maintain an environment in which learning can take place," and that to do this "requires some easing of the restrictions to which searches by public authorities are ordinarily subject." The Court thus created a "reasonable suspicion" rule for school searches, a change from the "probable cause" requirement in the wider society.

New York Times v. United States, 1971

(1st Amendment) In June 1971, the *New York Times* published the first in a series of secret government documents known as the "Pentagon Papers," which detailed how the United States became involved in the Vietnam War. The Justice Department obtained a court order forbidding the newspaper from printing more documents. The *New York Times* and other newspapers challenged the order. The Court cited the 1st Amendment guarantee of a free press and refused to uphold the ban, noting that the government must prove that publication would harm the nation's security. The decision limited "prior restraint" of the press.

Nix v. Williams, 1984

(4th Amendment, illegal evidence) A man was convicted of murdering a 10-year-old girl after he led officers to the body. He had been arrested, but not advised of his rights, in a distant city. During a conversation with a police officer while in transit, Williams agreed that the child should have a proper burial and directed the officer to the body. Later, on appeal, Williams's attorneys argued that the body should not be admitted as evidence because the questioning was illegal. The Court disagreed, observing that search parties were within 2.5 miles of the body. "Evidence otherwise excluded may be admissible when it would have been discovered anyway." The decision was one of several "exceptions to the exclusionary rule" handed down by the Court in the 1980s.

Nixon v. Fitzgerald, 1982

In 1968, A. Ernest Fitzgerald, an Air Force management analyst, testified against the government before a congressional subcommittee about cost overruns and problems with the development of an airplane. In 1970, he lost his job in a "reorganization," but he blamed President Nixon's office for firing him in retaliation for his testimony. A long series of official complaints and investigations turned up incriminating evidence against Nixon and two of his aides, including a memo about Fitzgerald recommending that Nixon "let him bleed." Nixon initially took responsibility for the firing at a press conference, but he retracted his admission the next day. Eventually, he offered to settle out of court for a large sum. Fitzgerald persisted, and a final Nixon appeal on the grounds of presidential immunity from prosecution was dismissed by a Federal District Court.

Just as the case seemed about to go to trial, more than ten years after the fact, the Supreme Court intervened. It ruled that a President or former President is entitled to absolute immunity from liability based on his official acts. The President must be able to act forcefully and independently, without fear of liability. Diverting the President's energies with concerns about private lawsuits could impair the effective functioning of government. The President's absolute immunity extends to all acts within the "outer perimeter" of his duties of office, since otherwise he would be required to litigate over the nature of the acts and the scope of his duties in each case. The remedy of impeachment, the vigilant scrutiny of the press, the Congress, and the public, and presidential desire to earn reelection and concern with historical legacy all protect against presidential wrongdoing.

Nixon v. Shrink Missouri Government PAC, 2000

In *Buckley v. Valeo,* 1976, the Supreme Court had upheld a $1000 limit on contributions by individuals to candidates for federal office. In *Nixon v. Shrink Missouri Government PAC,* the Court concluded that large contributions will sometimes create actual corruption, and that voters will inevitably be suspicious of the fairness of a political process that allows wealthy donors to contribute large amounts. The Court concluded that the Missouri contribution limits were appropriate to correct this problem and did not impair the ability of candidates to communicate their messages to the voters and to mount an effective campaign.

Plessy v. Ferguson, 1896

(14th Amendment, Equal Protection Clause) A Louisiana law required separate seating for white passengers and black passengers on public railroads. Plessy argued that the policy violated his right to "equal protection of the laws." The Court disagreed, saying that segregation was permissible if facilities were equal. It ruled that the 14th Amendment was "not intended to give Negroes social equality but only political and civil equality. . . ." The Louisiana law was seen as a "reasonable exercise of (state) police power. . . ." This "separate but equal" ruling allowed the segregation of public facilities throughout the South until *Plessy* was overturned by the *Brown v. Board of Education* case of 1954.

Powell v. Alabama, 1932

(6th Amendment, right to counsel) The case involved the "Scottsboro Boys," seven black men accused of rape. The men were quickly prosecuted without counsel and sentenced to death. The Court overturned the decision, stating that poor people facing the death penalty in state courts must be provided counsel, saying that "there are certain principles of Justice which . . . no [state] may disregard." The case was a step toward incorporating the Bill of Rights into state constitutions.

Printz v. United States, 1997

The Supreme Court ruled that the Brady Act's interim provision requiring certain State or local law enforcement agents to perform background checks on prospective handgun purchasers was unconstitutional. Although no provision of the Constitution deals explicitly with federal authority to compel State officials to execute federal law, a review of the Constitution's structure and of prior Supreme Court decisions leads to the conclusion that Congress does not have this power.

Regents of the University of California v. Bakke, 1978

(14th Amendment) Under an affirmative action program, the medical school of the University of California at Davis reserved 16 of 100 slots in each class for "disadvantaged citizens." When Bakke, who is white, was not accepted by the school, he claimed racial discrimination in violation of the 14th Amendment. The Court ruled narrowly, requiring Bakke's admission but not overturning affirmative action, preferring to review such questions on a case-by-case basis.

Reno v. ACLU, 1997

The Supreme Court ruled that the "indecent transmission" provision and the "patently offensive display" provision of the Communications Decency Act violated the 1st Amendment's freedom of speech. The Internet does not have the special features (such as historical governmental oversight, limited frequencies, and "invasiveness") that have justified allowing greater regulation of content in radio and television.

Reno v. Condon, 2000

The Court upheld the federal law that forbids States from selling addresses, telephone numbers, and other information that drivers put on license applications. They agreed with the Federal Government that information, including motor vehicle license information, is an "article of commerce" in the interstate stream of business and therefore is subject to regulation by Congress. The Court emphasized that the statute did not impose on the States any obligation to pass particular laws or policies and thus did not interfere with the States' sovereign functions.

Reynolds v. Sims, 1964

Most states have constitutional provisions to reapportion representation in their state legislatures every ten years, based on the U.S. Census. By the 1950s, however, it had become clear that some states were ignoring these laws. The United States was becoming more urban, and one-time rural majorities—now minorities—were holding on to political power at the state level by refusing to reapportion. A complaint was filed by a group of residents, taxpayers, and voters of Jefferson County, Alabama, challenging the apportionment of the Alabama legislature, which was still based on the 1900 federal census. The Court supported the "one person, one vote" formula, and applied it to this case, calling for reapportionment based on current census data.

Roe v. Wade, 1973

(9th Amendment) A Texas woman challenged a state law forbidding the artificial termination of a pregnancy, saying that she "had a fundamental right to privacy." The Court upheld a woman's right to choose, noting that the state's "important and legitimate interest in protecting the potentiality of human life" became "compelling" at the end of the first trimester, but that before then "the attending physician, in consultation with his patient, is free to determine, without regulation by the state, that . . . the patient's pregnancy should be terminated." The decision struck down state regulation of abortion in the first three months of pregnancy and was later modified by *Webster*, 1989.

Rostker v. Goldberg, 1981

(5th Amendment) In 1980, President Carter reinstated draft registration. For the first time, both sexes were ordered to register. When Congress refused to fund the registration of women, several men sued, arguing that a selective draft violated their due process rights. The Court disagreed, noting that "the purpose of registration was to prepare for draft of combat troops" and that "Congress and the Executive have decided that women should not serve in combat."

Roth v. United States, 1957

(1st Amendment) A New York man named Roth operated a business that used the mail to invite people to buy materials considered obscene by postal inspectors. The Court, in its first consideration of censorship of obscenity, created the "prevailing community standards" rule, which required a consideration of the work as a whole. In its decision, the Court defined as obscene that which offends "the average person, applying contemporary community standards."

Schenck v. United States, 1919

(1st Amendment) Schenck, a member of an antiwar group, had urged men who were drafted into military service in World War I to resist and to avoid induction. He was charged with violating the Espionage Act of 1917, which outlawed active opposition to the war. The Court limited free speech in time of war, stating that Schenck's words presented a "clear and present danger. . . ." Although later decisions modified this one, the *Schenck* case created a precedent that 1st Amendment rights are not absolute.

School District of Abington Township, Pennsylvania v. Schempp, 1963

(1st Amendment) Some Pennsylvania parents challenged a state law that required Bible readings each day at school. The Court agreed with the parents, saying that the Establishment Clause and Free Exercise Clause forbade states from engaging in religious activity. The Court ruled that if the purpose and effect of a law "is the advancement or inhibition of religion," it "exceeds the scope of legislative power."

Sheppard v. Maxwell, 1966

(14th Amendment) Sam Sheppard was convicted of murdering his wife in a trial sensationalized by the national media. Sheppard appealed, claiming that the pretrial publicity had made it impossible for him to get a fair trial. Rejecting arguments about freedom of the press, the Court overturned the conviction and ordered a new trial. Because of *Sheppard*, judges have issued "gag" orders limiting pretrial publicity.

South Dakota v. Dole, 1986

In 1984, Congress voted to withhold five percent of federal highway funds from any state that did not set a minimum drinking age at 21. South Dakota, which would lose money under the new law, challenged the government's right to coerce states to adopt specific policies through funding cuts. The Court ruled that highway funding was not an entitlement, and the national government could impose reasonable conditions upon the states in the interest of the "general welfare." All states that wished to continue to receive full federal highway aid were required to raise the legal age to purchase and consume alcohol to 21 years. In recent years, the threat of spending cuts has become a powerful tool of federal policy.

Tennessee Valley Authority v. Hiram G. Hill, Jr., et al., 1978

The Tellico Dam was nearly completed—and $100 million had been spent on it—when local residents succeeded in halting construction to save a tiny, nearly extinct fish called the snail darter. The fish's only habitat would have been flooded by the dam. The Court found the injunction against the TVA's completion of the nearly finished dam to be proper to prevent violation of the Endangered Species Act. Congress had declared the value of endangered species "incalculable." The Court refused to overrule Congress's judgment. The ruling affirmed the Environmental Protection Agency's power to protect the environment.

Texas v. Johnson, 1989

(1st Amendment) To protest national policies, Johnson doused a United States flag with kerosene and burned it outside the 1984 Republican National Convention in Dallas. He was arrested and convicted under a Texas law prohibiting the desecration of the Texas and United States flags. The Court ruled that the Texas law placed an unconstitutional limit on "freedom of expression," noting that ". . . nothing in our precedents suggests that a state may foster its own view of the flag by prohibiting expressive conduct relating to it."

Thompson v. Oklahoma, 1988

(8th Amendment, capital punishment) A 15-year-old from Oklahoma was convicted of murder and was sentenced to death at age 16. The Court overturned the death sentence, holding that "[t]he Eighth and Fourteenth Amendments prohibit the execution of a person who was under 16 years of age at the time of his or her offense." A death penalty was deemed cruel and unusual punishment for someone so young.

Tinker v. Des Moines School District, 1969

The Court upheld school students' 1st Amendment rights. Because students do not "shed their constitutional rights to freedom of speech or expression at the schoolhouse gate," schools must show a possibility of "substantial disruption" before free speech can be limited at school. Students may express personal opinions as long as they do not materially disrupt classwork, create substantial disorder, or interfere with the rights of others. In this case, the wearing of black armbands was a "silent, passive expression of opinion" without these side effects, and thus constitutionally could not be prohibited by the school.

United States v. Eichman, 1990

The Court agreed with the trial courts' rulings that the Flag Protection Act violated the 1st Amendment. Flag-burning constitutes expressive conduct, and thus is entitled to constitutional protection. The Act prevents protesters from using the flag to express their opposition to governmental policies and activities. Although the protesters' ideas may be offensive or disagreeable to many people, the government may not prohibit them from expressing those ideas.

United States v. Lopez, 1990

(Article I, Section 8, Commerce Clause) Alfonzo Lopez, a Texas high school student, was convicted of carrying a weapon in a school zone under the Gun-Free School Zones Act of 1990. He appealed his conviction on the basis that the Act, which forbids "any individual knowingly to possess a firearm at a place that [he] knows . . . is a school zone," exceeded Congress's legislative power under the Commerce Clause. The Court agreed that the Act was unconstitutional, stating that to uphold the legislation would "bid fair to convert congressional Commerce Clause authority to a general police power of the sort held only by the States."

United States v. Nixon, 1974

President Nixon was widely suspected of participating in the coverup of the Watergate break-in. After journalists discovered that he had recorded all of his conversations in the White House, Congress demanded that Nixon hand over the tapes. The President cited executive privilege, arguing that his office placed him above the law. The Court overruled Nixon and ordered him to surrender the tapes. Limiting executive privilege, it ruled that the President's "generalized interest in confidentiality" was subordinate to "the fundamental demands of due process of law in the fair administration of criminal justice." The tapes implicated Nixon in the coverup and led to his resignation.

Wallace v. Jaffree, 1985

(1st Amendment, Establishment Clause) An Alabama law authorized a one-minute period of silence in all public schools "for meditation or voluntary prayer." A group of parents, including Jaffree, challenged the constitutionality of the statute, claiming it violated the Establishment Clause of the 1st Amendment. The Court agreed with Jaffree and struck down the Alabama law, determining that "the State's endorsement . . . of prayer activities at the beginning of each schoolday is not consistent with the established principle that the government must pursue a course of complete neutrality toward religion."

Walz v. Tax Commission of the City of New York, 1970

(1st Amendment, Establishment Clause) State and local governments routinely exempt church property from taxes. Walz claimed that such exemptions were a "support of religion." The Court disagreed, noting that such exemptions constituted a "benevolent neutrality" between government and churches, not a support of religion. Governments must avoid taxing churches, because taxation would give government a "control" over religion prohibited by the "wall of separation of church and state" noted in *Everson*, 1947.

Webster v. Reproductive Health Services, 1989

(9th Amendment) A 1986 Missouri law stated that (1) life begins at conception; (2) unborn children have rights; (3) public funds could not be used for abortions not necessary to save the life of the mother; and (4) public funds could not be used for abortion counseling. Healthcare providers in Missouri filed suit, challenging the law, claiming that it was in conflict with *Roe*, 1973, and that it intruded into "privacy questions." A 5–4 Court upheld the Missouri law, stating that the people of Missouri, through their legislature, could put limits on the use of public funds. The *Webster* decision narrowed the *Roe* decision.

Weeks v. United States, 1914

(4th Amendment) A search without proper warrant was conducted in San Francisco, and the evidence collected was used by a postal inspector to prosecute Weeks. Weeks claimed that the evidence was gained by an illegal search, and thus was inadmissible. The Court agreed, applying for the first time an "exclusionary rule" for illegally gained evidence in federal courts.

The decision stated ". . . if letters and private documents can thus be seized and used as evidence . . . his right to be secure against such searches . . . is of no value, and . . . might as well be stricken from the Constitution." See also *Mapp* v. *Ohio*, 1961; *Massachusetts* v. *Sheppard*, 1984; and *Nix* v. *Williams*, 1984.

West Virginia Board of Education v. Barnette, 1943

The beliefs of Jehovah's Witnesses forbid them to salute the United States flag. In the patriotic climate of World War II, thousands of children who refused to salute were expelled from public schools. The Court ruled that a compulsory flag salute violated the 1st Amendment's exercise of the religion clause and was therefore unconstitutional. "No official, high or petty, can prescribe what shall be orthodox in politics, nationalism, religion, or other matters of opinion."

Westside Community Schools v. Mergens, 1990

(1st Amendment, Establishment Clause) A request by Mergens to form a student Christian religious group at school was denied by an Omaha high school principal. Mergens took legal action, claiming that a 1984 federal law required "equal access" for student religious groups. The Court ordered the school to permit the formation of the club, stating, "a high school does not have to permit any extracurricular activities, but when it does, the school is bound by the Act of 1984. Allowing students to meet on campus and discuss religion is constitutional because it does not amount to a 'State sponsorship of a religion.' "

Wisconsin v. Yoder, 1972

(1st Amendment, Free Exercise Clause) Members of the Amish religious sect in Wisconsin objected to sending their children to public schools after the eighth grade, claiming that such exposure of the children to another culture would endanger the group's self-sufficient agrarian lifestyle essential to their religious faith. The Court agreed with the Amish, while noting that the Court must move carefully to weigh the State's "legitimate social concern when faced with religious claim for exemption from generally applicable educational requirements."

Glossary

A

abolitionist movement Movement to end slavery (p. 318)

abstinence Refraining from some activity, such as drinking (p. 313)

Adams-Onís Treaty 1819 treaty between the United States and Spain, in which Spain ceded Florida to the United States; also called the Transcontinental Treaty (p. 252)

administration Term of office; also the members and agencies of the executive branch as a whole (p. 167)

affirmative action Policy that gives special consideration to women and members of minorities to make up for past discrimination (p. 1086)

agenda List of items to accomplish (p. 213)

Agent Orange An herbicide used as a chemical weapon during the Vietnam War to kill vegetation and expose enemy hiding places (p. 1033)

Agricultural Adjustment Administration (AAA) Established in 1933 to raise farm prices through government financial assistance (p. 772)

AIDS Acquired immune deficiency syndrome, a virus that began spreading in the early 1980s and has killed many people (p. 1110)

Albany Plan of Union 1754 proposal by Benjamin Franklin for the creation of a grand council of representatives from Britain's American colonies (p. 105)

alien A noncitizen (p. 532)

Alien and Sedition Acts Laws passed by Congress in 1798 that enabled the government to imprison or deport aliens and to prosecute critics of the government (p. 208)

Alliance for Progress President Kennedy's proposal for cooperation among nations of the Western Hemisphere to meet the basic needs of their people (p. 989)

Allies In World War I, Russia, France, Serbia, and Great Britain; in World War II, the alliance of Great Britain, the United States, the Soviet Union, and other nations (pp. 649, 810)

almanac Book containing information such as calendars and weather predictions (p. 79)

amend To revise (p. 151)

America First Committee Group formed in 1940 by isolationists to block further aid to Britain (p. 819)

American Expeditionary Force (AEF) Name given to American troops in Europe in World War I (p. 657)

American Indian Movement (AIM) Organization formed in 1968 to help Native Americans (p. 1007)

American Liberty League Organization founded in 1934 in opposition to the New Deal (p. 779)

American System A combination of government-backed economic development and protective tariffs aimed at encouraging business growth (p. 294)

amnesty A general pardon for certain crimes (p. 1086)

anarchist A radical who opposes all government (p. 481)

annex To join or attach, as in the joining of a new territory to an existing country (pp. 351, 585)

anti-Federalists Opponents of the Constitution during the debate over its ratification; opposed the concept of a strong central government (p. 159)

anti-Semitism Hostility or discrimination toward Jews (p. 841)

apartheid (uh PAHR tayt) The systematic segregation of people of different racial backgrounds (p. 1136)

appeasement Policy of giving in to a competitor's demands in order to preserve the peace (p. 805)

apportionment Distribution of seats in a legislative body (p. 980)

apprentice Person placed under a legal contract to work for another person in exchange for learning a trade (p. 79)

arbitration Settlement of a dispute by a person or panel chosen to listen to both sides and come to a decision (p. 590)

armistice A cease-fire or truce (p. 662)

arms race The struggle to gain weapons' superiority (p. 892)

arsenal Place where weapons are made or stored (p. 368)

Articles of Confederation Plan that established, in 1781, a limited national government in the United States, later replaced by the Constitution of the United States (p. 145)

assembly line Manufacturing process in which each worker does one specialized task in the construction of the final product (p. 726)

assimilation Process by which people of one culture merge into and become part of another culture (pp. 222, 553)

Atlantic Charter Agreement signed by President Franklin Roosevelt and Prime Minister Winston Churchill in 1941 outlining the two nations' war aims (p. 832)

autocrat Ruler with unlimited power (p. 650)

autonomy Self-government, with respect to local matters (p. 1007)

Axis Powers In World War II, Germany, Italy, and Japan (p. 805)

B

baby boom Dramatic increase in birthrate, especially in the years following World War II (p. 904)

Bacon's Rebellion Revolt in 1676 by Virginia colonists against the royal governor (p. 48)

balance of trade Difference in value between imports and exports (p. 71)

banana republic Term used to describe a Central American nation dominated by United States business interests (p. 587)

bank note Piece of paper that a bank issues to its customers and that can be exchanged for gold or silver coin (p. 279)

barrio A Spanish-speaking neighborhood (pp. 687, 857)

barter To trade goods or services without money (p. 9)

Bataan Death March Brutal march of American and Filipino prisoners by Japanese soldiers in 1942 (p. 847)

Battle of the Alamo Capture by Mexican troops of a Texas-held mission in San Antonio in 1836 (p. 264)

Battle of Antietam Civil War battle in Maryland in 1862 (p. 389)

Battle of the Bulge World War II battle in which German forces launched a final counterattack in the west (p. 846)

Battle of Bunker Hill Revolutionary War battle in 1775 north of Boston (p. 128)

Battle of Chancellorsville Civil War battle in 1863 in Virginia, won by the Confederacy (p. 403)

Battle of Cold Harbor Civil War battle in 1864 in Virginia (p. 411)

Battle of the Coral Sea 1942 World War II battle between American and Japanese aircraft (p. 848)

Battle of Fallen Timbers Battle between American and Native American forces in 1794 over Ohio Territory that led to the defeat of the Native Americans (p. 221)

Battle of Fredericksburg Civil War battle in 1862 in Virginia, won by the Confederacy (p. 403)

Battle of Gettysburg Civil War battle in 1863 in Pennsylvania, won by the Union and a turning point in the war (p. 404)

Battle of Guadalcanal (gwahd ul kuh NAL) 1942–1943 World War II battle between the United States and Japan (p. 849)

Battle of Iwo Jima 1945 World War II battle between the United States and Japan (p. 851)

Battle of Leyte Gulf 1944 World War II naval battle between the United States and Japan (p. 850)

Battle of Little Bighorn 1876 Sioux victory over army troops led by George Custer (p. 495)

Battle of Midway 1942 World War II battle between the United States and Japan, a turning point in the war in the Pacific (p. 849)

Battle of New Orleans Battle in 1815 between American and British troops for control of New Orleans, ending in an American victory (p. 228)

Battle of Okinawa 1945 World War II battle between the United States and Japan (p. 851)

Battle of Saratoga Revolutionary War battle in 1777 in New York, a turning point in the war (p. 132)

Battle of Shiloh Civil War battle in Tennessee in 1862 (p. 386)

Battle of Spotsylvania Civil War battle in 1864 in Virginia (p. 411)

Battle of Tippecanoe Battle in the Indiana Territory in 1811 between U.S. and Native American forces that led to the defeat of the Native Americans (p. 222)

Battle of Trenton Revolutionary War battle in 1776 in New Jersey (p. 131)

Battle of the Wilderness Civil War battle in 1864 in Virginia, won by the Confederacy (p. 411)

Battle of Yorktown Revolutionary War battle in 1781 in Virginia that ended in a decisive American victory (p. 135)

Battles of Lexington and Concord First battles of the Revolutionary War, on April 19, 1775 (p. 116)

Bay of Pigs invasion Failed invasion of Cuba by a group of anti-Castro forces in 1961 (p. 984)

beatnik In the 1950s, a person who criticized American society as apathetic and conformist (p. 911)

Berlin airlift Moving supplies into West Berlin by American and British planes during a Soviet blockade in 1948–1949 (p. 879)

Berlin Wall Barrier built by the East German government to separate Communist and non-Communist Berlin (p. 986)

Bessemer process A process for making steel more efficiently, patented in 1856 (p. 463)

bicentennial 200th anniversary (p. 1082)

bilingual education The teaching of students in their native language as well as in English (p. 1145)

Bill of Rights First ten amendments to the Constitution (p. 162)

bimetallic standard Currency of the United States, prior to 1873, which consisted of gold or silver coins as well as U.S. treasury notes that could be traded in for gold or silver (p. 508)

black codes Laws that restricted freedmen's rights (p. 430)

Black Hawk War Uprising led by a warrior named Black Hawk in which Native Americans tried to reclaim their land in the Illinois Territory (p. 302)

blacklist List that circulated among employers, beginning in 1947, containing the names of persons who should not be hired (p. 882)

black nationalism A belief in the separate identity and racial unity of the African American community (p. 955)

black power African American movement seeking unity and self-reliance (p. 956)

Black Tuesday October 29, 1929, the day on which the Great Crash of the stock market began (p. 741)

Bland-Allison Act 1878 law that required the federal government to purchase and coin more silver, increasing the money supply and causing inflation (p. 509)

blitzkrieg (BLITS kreeg) Kind of warfare emphasizing rapid and mechanized movement; used by Germany during World War II (p. 808)

blockade To isolate, or close off, a place from outside contact (p. 134)

blue law Regulation that prohibited certain private activities people considered immoral, such as drinking alcohol on Sundays (p. 522)

bonanza farm Farm controlled by large businesses, managed by professionals, and raising massive quantities of single cash crops (p. 504)

Bonus Army A group of World War I veterans and their families who protested in Washington, D.C., in 1932, demanding immediate payment of a pension bonus that had been promised for 1945 (p. 758)

boomers Settlers who ran in land races to claim land upon the 1889 opening of Indian Territory for settlement (p. 497)

bootlegger Term used to describe a supplier of illegal alcohol during Prohibition (p. 700)

Border States In the Civil War, the states between the North and South: Delaware, Maryland, Kentucky, and Missouri (p. 369)

Boston Massacre Incident on March 5, 1770, in which British soldiers in Boston killed five colonists (p. 114)

boycott Refusal to buy a certain product or to use a service (p. 112)

bracero A term used in 1942 to describe a Mexican farm laborer brought to the United States (p. 857)

brinkmanship A 1956 term used by Secretary of State John Dulles to describe a policy of risking war in order to protect national interests (p. 892)

Brown v. Board of Education of Topeka, Kansas 1954 Supreme Court case in which racial segregation in public schools was outlawed (p. 931)

Bull Moose Party Nickname of the Progressive Party (p. 630)

bureaucracy Departments that make up a large organization, such as a government (p. 213)

Burma Road A 700-mile-long highway linking Burma (present-day Myanmar) to China (p. 816)

business cycle Periods in which a nation's economy grows, then contracts (p. 741)

buying on margin An option that allowed investors to purchase a stock for only a fraction of its price and borrow the rest (p. 732)

C

Cabinet Leaders of the executive departments of the federal government (p. 166)

California Gold Rush Mass migration to California following the discovery of gold in 1848 (p. 255)

Camp David Accords 1978 agreement between Israel and Egypt that made a peace treaty between the two nations possible (p. 1087)

canister A special type of shell filled with bullets (p. 384)

carpetbagger Negative nickname for a northern Republican who moved to the South after the Civil War (p. 435)

carpet bombing Method of aerial bombing in which large numbers of bombs are dropped over a wide area (p. 837)

cartel Loose association of businesses that make the same product (p. 470)

cash and carry World War II policy requiring nations at war to pay cash for all nonmilitary goods and to be responsible for transporting the goods from the United States (p. 818)

cash crop Crop that is grown for sale (p. 27)

casualty Military term for a person killed, wounded, captured, or missing in action (pp. 128, 382)

cede To surrender officially or informally (p. 252)

centralized Concentrated in one place (p. 277)

Central Powers In World War I, Germany and Austria-Hungary (p. 649)

charter Certificate of permission given by a government (p. 44)

checks and balances System in which each of the branches of the federal government can check the actions of the other branches (p. 155)

Chinese Exclusion Act Law passed in 1882 that prohibited Chinese laborers from entering the country, but did not prevent entry of those who had previously established U.S. residence (p. 532)

civil disobedience Nonviolent refusal to obey a law in an effort to change that law (p. 636)

Civilian Conservation Corps (CCC) Established by Congress in 1933, this program put more than 2.5 million young men to work restoring and maintaining forests, beaches, and parks (p. 771)

civil rights Citizens' personal liberties guaranteed by law, such as voting rights and equal treatment (p. 431)

Civil Rights Act of 1964 Law that made discrimination illegal in a number of areas, including voting, schools, and jobs (p. 951)

civil service The government's nonelected workers (p. 522)

Civil War War between the Union states of the North and the Confederate states of the South; fought from 1861 to 1865 (p. 380)

clan Groups of families who are all descended from a common ancestor (p. 8)

Clayton Antitrust Act Law passed in 1914 to strengthen the Sherman Antitrust Act of 1890; specified big businesses activities that were forbidden (p. 632)

Clean Air Act Law passed in 1970 that aimed to control pollution caused by industrial and auto emissions (p. 1016)

Clean Water Act Law passed in 1972 that aimed to control pollution caused by the discharge of industrial and municipal wastewater, and provided for grants to build better sewage-treatment facilities (p. 1016)

closed shop Workplace open only to union members (p. 775)

cloture (KLOH chur) In the Senate, a three-fifths vote to limit debate and call for a vote on an issue (p. 951)

coalition Alliance of groups with similar goals (p. 786)

Cold War The competition that developed after World War II between the United States and the Soviet Union for power and influence in the world, lasting until the collapse of the Soviet Union (p. 872)

collaboration Close cooperation (p. 810)

collective bargaining Process in which workers negotiate as a group with employers (p. 479)

collective security The principle of mutual military assistance among nations (p. 879)

colony An area of land settled by immigrants who continue to be ruled by their parent country (p. 36)

Columbian Exchange The transatlantic trade of crops, technology, and culture between the Americas and Europe, Africa, and Asia that began in 1492 with Columbus's first voyage to the Americas (p. 26)

Common Sense Pamphlet written by Thomas Paine and published in January 1776, which called for American independence from Britain (p. 118)

communism Official ideology of the Soviet Union, characterized there by complete government ownership of land and property, single-party control of the government, the lack of individual rights, and the call for worldwide revolution (p. 713)

Compromise of 1850 Agreement designed to ease tensions caused by the expansion of slavery into western territories (p. 356)

Compromise of 1877 Agreement in which Democrats agreed to give Rutherford B. Hayes the victory in the presidential election of 1876, and Hayes, in return, agreed to remove the remaining federal troops from southern states (p. 445)

compulsory Required (p. 606)

concentration camp A place where political prisoners are confined, usually under harsh conditions (p. 842)

concession A grant for a piece of land in exchange for a promise to use the land for a specific purpose (p. 598)

Confederate States of America Association of seven seceding Southern states, formed in 1861 (p. 371)

conglomerate Corporation made up of three or more unrelated businesses (p. 901)

congregación A village in which Native Americans settled, when forced to do so by Spaniards; settlers farmed and worshiped like Catholic Europeans (p. 41)

congregation The people of a church; a religious gathering (p. 245)

Congressional Union (CU) Radical organization formed in 1913 and led by Alice Paul that campaigned for a constitutional amendment guaranteeing women's suffrage (p. 638)

Congress of Racial Equality (CORE) Organization founded by pacifists in 1942 to promote racial equality through peaceful means (pp. 857, 937)

conquistador A Spanish conqueror (p. 38)

conscientious objector A person who opposes war on moral or religious grounds (p. 1039)

conservationist A person who favors the protection of natural resources (p. 629)

constitution Plan of government that describes the different parts of the government and their duties and powers (p. 145)

Constitutional Convention Convention that met in Philadelphia in 1787 to draft the Constitution of the United States (p. 150)

consumer economy An economy that depends on a large amount of spending by consumers (p. 723)

containment American policy of resisting further expansion of communism around the world (p. 873)

Contra Spanish word for "counterrevolutionary," a rebel opposed to Nicaragua's Communist government in the 1980s (p. 1112)

contraband Items seized from the enemy during wartime (p. 396)

Contract with America Pledge, made by Republican candidates in the 1994 election campaign, to scale back government, eliminate some regulations, cut taxes, and balance the budget (p. 1128)

convoy Group of unarmed ships surrounded by a ring of armed naval vessels (p. 658)

Copperhead During the Civil War, an antiwar Northern Democrat (p. 393)

cotton belt Common 1850s nickname for the band of states from South Carolina to Texas whose economies relied almost completely on cotton production (p. 285)

cotton gin Machine that separates the seeds from raw cotton fiber (p. 274)

counterculture Group of young Americans in the 1960s who rejected conventional customs and mainstream culture (p. 1009)

craft union A union for laborers devoted to a specific craft (p. 479)

Cross of Gold Speech William Jennings Bryan's 1896 address at the Democratic Convention; one of the most famous speeches in American history (p. 512)

Crusades Series of military campaigns by European Christians from 1096 to 1291 to win Jerusalem from the Turks (p. 11)

Cuban Missile Crisis 1962 crisis that arose between the United States and the Soviet Union over a Soviet attempt to deploy nuclear missiles in Cuba (p. 986)

D

Dartmouth College v. *Woodward* 1819 case in which the Supreme Court ruled that states could not interfere with private contracts (p. 291)

Dawes Act 1887 law that divided reservation land into private family plots (p. 496)

daylight savings time Turning clocks ahead by one hour for summer (p. 666)

D-Day Code name for the Allied invasion of France on June 6, 1944 (p. 838)

death camp In World War II, a German camp created solely for the purpose of mass murder (p. 843)

Declaration of Independence 1776 statement, issued by the Second Continental Congress, explaining why the colonies wanted independence from Britain (p. 119)

de facto **segregation** Separation caused by social conditions such as poverty (p. 957)

deferment Official postponement, as in a postponement of compulsory military service (p. 1040)

deficit spending Paying out more money from the annual federal budget than the government receives in revenues (pp. 782, 1060)

deflation A drop in the prices of goods (p. 508)

de jure **segregation** Racial segregation created by law (p. 957)

demagogue (DEHM uh gawg) A leader who manipulates people with half-truths, deceptive promises, and scare tactics (p. 780)

democracy Government by the people (p. 146)

demographics The statistics that describe a population, such as data on race or income (p. 686)

denomination A religious subgroup (p. 246)

department store Large retail establishment that carries a wide variety of goods and sells in large quantities (p. 570)

depression A severe economic downturn marked by a decrease in business activity, widespread unemployment, and falling prices and wages (p. 228)

deregulation The reduction or removal of government controls (p. 1085)

détente A relaxation in political tensions between nations (p. 1065)

deterrence The policy of making the military power of the United States and its allies so strong that no enemy would attack for fear of retaliation (p. 892)

direct primary Election in which all citizens vote to select nominees for upcoming elections (p. 624)

disarmament Program in which the nations of the world voluntarily give up their weapons (p. 718)

discrimination Unequal treatment of a group of people because of their nationality, race, sex, or religion (p. 333)

dissent Difference of opinion or belief (p. 93)

dissident A person who criticizes the actions of his or her government (p. 1087)

diversity Variety (p. 59)

division of labor Way of producing in which different tasks are performed by different persons (p. 475)

dollar diplomacy President Taft's policy of encouraging American investment in foreign economies (p. 602)

domestic affairs Issues relating to a country's internal matters (p. 166)

domino theory Belief that if one country falls to communism, neighboring countries will likewise fall (p. 1024)

dove Nickname for a person who opposes war, as in the Vietnam War (p. 1034)

Dow Jones Industrial Average Measure of average of stock prices of major industries (p. 740)

downsizing Laying off of workers to cut costs (p. 1119)

draft Required military service (p. 391)

Dred Scott v. *Sandford* 1857 Supreme Court decision that stated that slaves were not citizens; that living in a free state or territory, even for many years, did not free slaves; and declared the Missouri Compromise unconstitutional (p. 365)

dry farming Techniques used to raise crops in areas that receive little rain; water conservation techniques (p. 504)

dumbbell tenement A tenement building that narrowed in the middle, forming air shafts on either side, and allowed light and air into the rooms (p. 537)

Dust Bowl Term used to describe the central and southern Great Plains in the 1930s when the region sustained a period of drought and dust storms (p. 746)

duty A tax on imports (p. 72)

E

economic sanctions Trade restrictions and other economic measures intended to punish another nation (p. 1136)

economies of scale Phenomenon that as production increases, the cost of each item produced is often lowered (p. 471)

electoral college Group of electors, chosen by the voters, who vote for President (p. 156)

emancipation Freeing of enslaved people (p. 319)

Emancipation Proclamation A presidential decree, by President Lincoln, effective January 1, 1863, that freed slaves in Confederate-held territory (p. 395)

embargo A ban or a restriction on trade (pp. 218, 1060)

encomienda **system** A system in which Native Americans were required to farm, ranch, or mine for the profit of an individual Spaniard; in return, the Spaniard was supposed to ensure the worker's well-being (p. 39)

Enforcement Act of 1870 Passed by Congress to ban the use of terror, force, or bribery to prevent people from voting because of their race (p. 443)

Enlightenment Eighteenth-century movement that emphasized science and reason to improve society (p. 119)

entitlement Government program that guarantees payments to a particular group, such as the elderly (p. 1113)

Environmental Protection Agency (EPA) Government organization formed in 1970 to set and enforce national pollution-control standards (p. 1016)

Equal Rights Amendment Proposed constitutional amendment, never ratified, to prohibit discrimination on account of sex (p. 1000)

escalation Expansion by stages, as from a local to a national conflict (p. 1033)

evangelical (ee van JEHL ih cuhl) Focusing on emotionally powerful preaching, rather than formal ceremonies, and on the teachings of the Bible (p. 245)

executive branch Branch of government, headed by the President, that enforces the laws (p. 145)

Exoduster An African American who migrated to the West after the Civil War (p. 490)

F

facism Political philosophy that emphasizes the importance of the nation or an ethnic group, and the supreme authority of the leader over that of the individual (p. 800)

faction Group organized around a common interest and concerned only with furthering that interest (p. 159)

Federal Reserve System Nation's central banking system, established in 1913 (p. 632)

Federalists Supporters of the Constitution during the debate over its ratification; favored a strong national government (p. 158)

federal system of government A system in which power is shared among state and national authorities (p. 154)

Federal Trade Commission (FTC) 1914 Commission established by Wilson and Congress to enforce the Clayton Act and set up fair-trade laws (p. 632)

feminism Theory favoring the political, economic, and social equality of men and women (p. 996)

feudalism Political and economic system in medieval Europe, in which lesser lords received lands from powerful nobles in exchange for service (p. 11)

Fifteenth Amendment Constitutional amendment, ratified in 1870, that guaranteed voting rights to all citizens (p. 434)

filibuster A tactic in which senators prevent a vote on a measure by taking the floor and refusing to stop talking (p. 951)

First Battle of Bull Run First major battle of the Civil War, won by the Confederates in July 1861 (p. 382)

First Continental Congress Assembly of representatives from the colonies that first met in Philadelphia in September 1774 (p. 115)

flapper A 1920s term used to describe a new type of young woman; rebellious, energetic, and bold (p. 684)

Fort Sumter Federal fort in the harbor of Charleston, South Carolina; the Confederate attack on the fort marked the start of the Civil War (p. 372)

Fourteen Points President Wilson's proposal in 1918 for a postwar European peace (p. 669)

Fourteenth Amendment Constitutional amendment, ratified in 1868, to guarantee citizens equal protection under the law (p. 431)

fragmentation bomb A type of bomb that, upon explosion, causes pieces of its thick metal casings to be thrown in all directions (p. 1033)

franchise A business that contracts with a large parent company to offer certain goods and services (p. 901)

free enterprise system Economic system characterized by private or corporate ownership of capital goods (p. 278)

free silver The unlimited coining of silver dollars (p. 509)

free soiler Person dedicated to preventing the expansion of slavery into the western territories (p. 363)

Freedmen's Bureau Created by Congress in 1865, the first major federal relief agency in the United States (p. 429)

Freedom Ride 1961 event organized by CORE and SNCC in which an interracial group of civil rights activists tested southern states' compliance to the Supreme Court ban of segregation on interstate buses (p. 942)

French and Indian War War from 1754 to 1763 between France (with allied Indian nations) and Britain and its colonists, for control of eastern North America (p. 104)

Fugitive Slave Act Part of the Compromise of 1850, a law ordering all citizens of the United States to assist in the return of slaves (p. 357)

fundamentalism Set of religious beliefs including traditional Christian ideas about Jesus Christ; the belief that the Bible was inspired by God and does not contain contradictions or errors, and is literally true (p. 702)

G

Gadsden Purchase 1853 purchase by the United States of southwestern lands from Mexico (p. 353)

gag rule Rule passed by the House of Representatives in 1836 prohibiting antislavery petitions from being read or acted upon (p. 325)

generation gap A term used to describe the widening difference in values between a younger generation and their parents (p. 1038)

Geneva Accords A 1954 international conference in which Vietnam was divided into two nations (p. 1025)

Geneva Convention A set of international standards of conduct for treating prisoners of war, established in 1929 (p. 847)

genocide Organized killing of an entire people (p. 663)

Gentlemen's Agreement 1907 agreement between the United States and Japan that restricted Japanese immigration (p. 532)

gentry In colonial America, men and women wealthy enough to hire others to work for them (p. 78)

Gettysburg Address A famous speech by President Lincoln on the meaning of the Civil War, given in November 1863 at the dedication of a national cemetery on the site of the Battle of Gettysburg (p. 409)

ghetto Area in which one ethnic or racial group dominates (p. 530)

Ghost Dance A Native American purification ritual (p. 495)

ghost town Town that has been abandoned due to lack of economic activity (p. 256)

GI Term used for American soldiers in World War II, derived from the term "Government Issue" (p. 827)

Gibbons* v. *Ogden 1824 case in which the Supreme Court ruled that states could not regulate commerce on interstate waterways (p. 292)

GI Bill of Rights Law passed in 1944 to help returning veterans buy homes and pay for higher education (p. 904)

Gilded Age Term coined by Mark Twain to describe the post-Reconstruction era (p. 520)

graft Use of one's job to gain profit; a major source of income for political machines (p. 539)

grandfather clause Passage in a law that exempts a group of people from obeying the law if they had met certain conditions before the law was passed (p. 565)

Grange, the Established in 1867 and also known as the Patrons of Husbandry, this organization helped farmers form cooperatives and pressured state legislators to regulate businesses on which farmers depended (p. 510)

Great Awakening Religious revival in the American colonies during the 1730s and 1740s (p. 92)

Great Compromise Compromise at the Constitutional Convention calling for a two-house legislature, with one house elected on the basis of population and the other representing each state equally (p. 153)

Great Crash The collapse of the American stock market in 1929 (p. 741)

Great Depression The most severe economic downturn in the nation's history, which lasted from 1929 to 1941 (p. 743)

Greater East Asia Co-Prosperity Sphere As announced in 1940 by Japan's prime minister, the area extending from Manchuria to the Dutch East Indies in which Japan would expand its influence (p. 816)

Great Migration Migration of English settlers to Massachusetts Bay Colony beginning in the 1630s (p. 52)

Great Plains Vast grassland between the Mississippi River and the Rocky Mountains (pp. 258, 491)

Great Society President Lyndon Johnson's proposals for aid to public education, voting rights, conservation and beautification projects, medical care for the elderly, and elimination of poverty (p. 976)

Great White Fleet A force of United States Navy ships that undertook a world cruise in 1907 (p. 607)

greenback Name given to the national paper currency created in 1862 (p. 393)

Gross National Product (GNP) Total annual value of goods and services a country produces (p. 725)

guerrilla (guh RIL uh) A soldier who uses surprise raids and hit-and-run tactics (p. 416)

Gulf of Tonkin Resolution 1964 Congressional resolution authorizing President Johnson to take military action in Vietnam (p. 1028)

H

Harlem Renaissance African American literary awakening of the 1920s, centered in Harlem (p. 696)

haven A safe place (p. 62)

hawk Nickname for a supporter of war, as in the Vietnam War (p. 1034)

Hawley-Smoot tariff The highest import tax in history, passed by Congress in 1930 (p. 757)

Haymarket Riot 1886 labor-related violence in Chicago (p. 482)

Head Start A preschool program for children from low-income families that also provides healthcare, nutrition services, and social services (p. 978)

Helsinki Accords Series of agreements on European security made in 1975 (p. 1082)

hidalgo (hih DAL goh) A Spanish noble (p. 37)

Ho Chi Minh Trail A supply route used to carry troops and supplies from North Vietnam to South Vietnam (p. 1034)

holding company Firm that buys up stocks and bonds of smaller companies (p. 626)

Hollywood Ten Group of people in the film industry who were jailed for refusing to answer congressional questions regarding Communist influence in Hollywood (p. 882)

Holocaust Nazi Germany's systematic attempt to murder all European Jews (p. 841)

home rule System that gives cities a limited degree of self-rule (p. 622)

Homestead Act 1862 law that gave 160 acres of land to citizens who met certain conditions (p. 489)

homesteader One who farmed claims under the Homestead Act (p. 502)

Homestead Strike 1892 strike in Pennsylvania against Carnegie steel (p. 482)

Hooverville Term used to describe a makeshift homeless shelter during the early years of the Great Depression (p. 746)

horizontal consolidation The process of bringing together many firms in the same business to form one large company (p. 471)

House of Burgesses Virginia legislature formed in 1619 (p. 46)

House Un-American Activities Committee (HUAC) Established in 1938 to investigate disloyalty in the United States (p. 882)

hundred days Period at the start of Franklin Roosevelt's presidency in 1933, when many New Deal programs were passed by Congress (p. 769)

I

ICBM Intercontinental ballistic missile (p. 893)

immigrant Person who enters a new country to settle (p. 89)

Immigration Act of 1965 Law that ended quotas for individual countries and replaced them with more flexible limits (p. 979)

impeach To charge a public official with wrongdoing in office (pp. 433, 1075)

imperialism Policy by a stronger nation to attempt to create an empire by dominating weaker nations economically, politically, culturally, or militarily (p. 584)

impressment Policy of forcing people into military or public service (p. 224)

inauguration Official swearing-in ceremony (p. 165)

incumbent Person currently in office (p. 1083)

indentured servant Person who agrees to work for another person for a specified period of time, usually seven years, under a contract, in return for transportation, food, and shelter (p. 47)

Indian Removal Act 1830 law calling for the President to give Native Americans land in parts of the Louisiana Purchase in exchange for land taken from them in the East (p. 301)

indigo Type of plant used in making a blue dye for cloth (p. 81)

industrialization The growth of industry (p. 281)

Industrial Revolution Effort, beginning in Britain in the late 1700s, to increase production by using machines powered by sources other than humans or animals (p. 272)

industrial union Union that organizes workers from all crafts in a given industry (p. 481)

inflation A steady increase in prices over time, reducing the ability to buy (p. 134)

infrastructure The public property and services that a society uses (p. 439)

INF Treaty Intermediate-Range Nuclear Forces, an agreement signed in 1987 by Ronald Reagan and Mikhail Gorbachev that provided for the destruction of about 2,500 Soviet and American missiles in Europe (p. 1113)

initiative A process in which citizens can put a proposed new law directly on the ballot in the next election by collecting voters' signatures on a petition (p. 624)

injunction Court order prohibiting a certain activity (p. 617)

installment plan A payment plan that allows customers to make payments at set intervals over a period of time until the total debt is paid (p. 724)

integration Process of bringing people of different races together (p. 934)

interchangeable parts A system of manufacturing in which all parts are made to an exact standard for easy mass-assembly (p. 274)

interest An extra sum of money that borrowers have to repay creditors in return for the loan (p. 201)

interned Confined (p. 858)

Internet A computer network that links millions of people (p. 1147)

interracial Between, among, or involving people of different races (p. 937)

Interstate Commerce Act 1887 law passed to regulate railroad and other interstate businesses (p. 511)

investment capital Money that a business spends in hopes of future gains (p. 278)

Iran-Contra affair Scandal in the Reagan administration involving the use of money from secret Iranian arms sales to support the Nicaraguan Contras (p. 1112)

Irish Potato Famine Famine in Ireland in the 1840s that led to a surge in immigration to the United States (p. 332)

iron curtain Term coined by Winston Churchill to describe the division between Communist and non-Communist life (p. 872)

island-hopping A military strategy used during World War II that involved selectively attacking specific enemy-held islands and bypassing others (p. 850)

isolationism Policy of avoiding political or economic alliances with foreign countries (p. 718)

isthmus A narrow strip of land that joins two larger land areas (p. 37)

itinerant (i TIHN uhr uhnt) Traveling from place to place, or on a circuit (p. 92)

J

Japanese American Citizens League (JACL) Organization of Japanese Americans working to promote the rights of Asian Americans (p. 1006)

Jay's Treaty Treaty signed in 1794 between the United States and Britain in which Britain sought to improve trade relations and agreed to withdraw from forts in the Northwest Territory (p. 204)

Jazz Age Term used to describe the 1920s (p. 694)

Jim Crow Statutes, beginning in the 1890s, that required segregation of public services by race (p. 565)

jingoism A feeling of strong national pride and a desire for an aggressive foreign policy (p. 591)

joint-stock company Company funded and run by a group of investors who share the company's profits and losses (p. 44)

judicial branch Branch of government, made up of courts and judges, that interprets and applies the laws (p. 145)

judicial review Power of federal courts to review state laws and state court decisions to determine if they are constitutional (p. 214)

K

kamikaze (kah mih KAH zee) In World War II, a Japanese suicide plane (p. 850)

Kansas-Nebraska Act 1854 law that called for the creation of these two new territories, and stated that the citizens in each territory should decide whether slavery would be allowed there (p. 360)

Kellogg-Briand Pact Agreement signed in 1928 in which nations agreed not to pose the threat of war against one another (p. 721)

King Philip's War War, beginning in 1675, between English colonists and Native Americans (p. 57)

kinship Family relationships (p. 8)

Korean War Conflict over the future of the Korean peninsula, fought between 1950 and 1953 and ending in a stalemate (p. 886)

Kristallnacht The name given to the night of violence on November 9, 1938, when Nazi storm troopers looted and destroyed Jewish homes, businesses, and synagogues and arrested thousands of Jews in Germany and Austria (p. 842)

L

labor union Organization of workers formed to protect the interest of its members (p. 283)

laissez-faire (LES ay FAYR) Doctrine stating that government generally should not interfere in private business (p. 521)

land mine An explosive device planted in the ground (p. 1032)

land speculator Person who buys up large areas of land in the hope of selling them later for a profit (p. 489)

Latino Person whose family origins are in Spanish-speaking Latin America (p. 1003)

League of Nations International organization formed after World War I that aimed to ensure the security and peace for all its members (p. 670)

legislative branch Branch of government that makes the laws; Congress (p. 145)

legislature A lawmaking assembly (p. 46)

Lend-Lease Act 1941 law that authorized the President to aid any nation whose defense he believed was vital to American security (p. 819)

Lewis and Clark expedition Journey by Meriwether Lewis and William Clark through the Louisiana Territory from 1804–1806 (p. 216)

Liberty Bond Special war bond sold by the government to support the Allied cause during World War I (p. 664)

Liberty ship A type of large, sturdy merchant ship built in World War II (p. 828)

Limited Test Ban Treaty 1963 treaty in which the United States and the Soviet Union agreed not to test nuclear weapons above the ground (p. 989)

Lincoln-Douglas Debates A series of seven debates between Abraham Lincoln and Stephen A. Douglas on the issue of slavery in the territories (p. 366)

lineage Kinship groups that trace their origin to a common ancestor (p. 18)

literacy The ability to read and write (p. 553)

long drive Moving of cattle from distant ranges to busy railroad centers that shipped the cattle to market (p. 501)

loose construction Belief that the government can do anything that the Constitution does not prohibit (p. 202)

Lost Generation Group of American writers in the 1920s who shared the belief that they were lost in a greedy, materialistic world that lacked moral values, and who often chose to flee to Europe (p. 696)

Louisiana Purchase Purchase by the United States of the Louisiana Territory from France in 1803 (p. 215)

Lower South States of Texas, Louisiana, Mississippi, Alabama, Florida, Georgia, and South Carolina (p. 370)

Loyalist Person who remained loyal to Great Britain during the Revolution (p. 128)

lynching Murder of an accused person by a mob without a lawful trial (p. 566)

M

Magna Carta A "great charter" signed by King John in 1215 that granted certain rights to English nobles and became the foundation for future American ideals of liberty and justice (p. 12)

mail-order catalog Printed material advertising a wide range of goods that can be purchased by mail (p. 571)

Manchurian incident Situation in 1931 when Japanese troops, claiming that Chinese soldiers had tried to blow up a railway line, took matters in their own hands by capturing several southern Manchurian cities, and by continuing to take over the country even after Chinese troops had withdrawn (p. 814)

mandate A public endorsement, expressed to a candidate by voters (p. 969)

Manhattan Project Secret American program during World War II to develop an atomic bomb (p. 852)

manifest destiny Argument that it was the undeniable fate of the United States to expand across North America (pp. 253, 351)

manufacturing Making of goods by machinery (p. 276)

Marbury v. *Madison* 1803 Supreme Court case that established the principle of judicial review (p. 214)

March on Washington 1963 civil rights demonstration in Washington, D.C., in which protesters called for "jobs and freedom" (p. 949)

Market Revolution Shift from a home-based, often agricultural, economy to one based on money and the buying and selling of goods (p. 276)

Marshall Plan Program of American economic assistance to Western Europe, announced in 1947 (p. 877)

martial law Emergency rule by military authorities, during which some Bill of Rights guarantees are suspended (p. 394)

Massacre at Wounded Knee 1890 shooting of a group of unarmed Sioux by army troops (p. 495)

mass media Print and broadcast methods of communicating information to large numbers of people (p. 692)

mass production Production of goods in great amounts (p. 464)

Mayflower Compact Agreement in which settlers of Plymouth Colony agreed to obey their government's laws (p. 51)

McCarran-Walter Act Passed by Congress in 1952, this law reaffirmed the quota system that had been established for each country in 1924 (p. 883)

McCarthyism Term used to describe McCarthy's anti-Communist smear tactics (p. 889)

McCulloch v. *Maryland* 1819 case in which the Supreme Court ruled that Congress has the authority to take actions necessary to fulfill its constitutional duties (p. 291)

Medicaid Federal program that provides low-cost health insurance to poor Americans of any age (p. 978)

Medicare Federal program that provides hospital and low-cost medical insurance to most Americans age 65 and older (p. 978)

mercantilism Economic theory that a country should acquire as much bullion, or gold and silver, as possible by exporting more goods than it imports (p. 71)

mercenary A foreign soldier who fights for pay (p. 129)

mestizo (mehs TEE zoh) A person of mixed Spanish and Native American heritage (p. 39)

Mexican War Conflict between the United States and Mexico from 1846 to 1848, ending with a United States victory (p. 352)

MIA Missing in action (p. 1048)

Middle Ages Era in European history from about A.D. 500 to 1300 (p. 10)

Middle America Term sometimes used to describe mainstream Americans (p. 1043)

middle class A new class of merchants, traders, and artisans that arose in Europe in the late Middle Ages; in modern times, the social class between the very wealthy and the lower working class (p. 12)

Middle Colonies English colonies of New York, New Jersey, Pennsylvania, and Delaware (p. 59)

Middle Passage One leg of the triangular trade; term also used to refer to the forced transport of slaves from Africa to the Americas (p. 84)

midnight judge Last-minute judicial appointments of judges with Federalist beliefs that were made by President Adams just before Thomas Jefferson took office (p. 214)

migrant farm worker Person who works long hours for low wages, moving from farm to farm, often from state to state, to provide the labor needed to plant, cultivate, and harvest crops (p. 1004)

migration Movement of people for the purpose of settling in a new place (pp. 4, 90)

militarism Policy of aggressively building up a nations' armed forces in preparation for war, as well as giving the military more authority over the government and foreign policy (p. 647)

military-industrial complex The military establishment as it developed links to the corporate and scientific communities, employing 3.5 million Americans by 1960 (p. 888)

militia Armed citizens who serve as soldiers during an emergency (p. 105)

Miranda rule Rule that police officers must inform persons accused of a crime of their legal rights (p. 980)

mission Headquarters from which people from another country seek to spread their religion (p. 40)

Missouri Compromise 1820 agreement calling for the admission of Missouri as a slave state and Maine as a free state, and outlawing slavery in future states to be created north of 36° 30' N latitude (p. 229)

mobile society A society in which people are constantly moving about (p. 243)

mobilization The readying of troops for war (p. 648)

Modern Republicanism President Eisenhower's approach to government, described as "conservative when it comes to money, liberal when it comes to human beings" (p. 917)

monarch One who rules over a territory, state, or kingdom (p. 12)

monetary policy The federal government's plan for the makeup and quantity of the nation's money supply (p. 508)

money supply The amount of money in the national economy (p. 508)

monopoly Complete control of a product or service (p. 470)

Monroe Doctrine Declaration by President Monroe in 1823 that the United States would oppose efforts by any outside power to control a nation in the Western Hemisphere (p. 292)

Montgomery bus boycott Protest in 1955–1956 by African Americans against racial segregation in the bus system of Montgomery, Alabama (p. 933)

Morrill Land-Grant Act Passed by Congress in 1862, this law distributed millions of acres of western lands to state governments in order to fund state agricultural colleges (p. 489)

mountain man An American fur trader who explored the Rocky Mountains and regions farther west in the early 1800s (p. 253)

muckraker Journalist who uncovers wrongdoing in politics or business (p. 616)

multiculturalism Movement calling for greater attention to non-European cultures in such areas as education (p. 1146)

multinational corporation A corporation that operates in more than one country (p. 1142)

municipal Relating to a city, as in municipal government (p. 622)

Munn **v.** *Illinois* 1877 Supreme Court decision that allowed states to regulate certain businesses within their borders (p. 524)

mutiny Revolt against a superior authority (p. 84)

N

napalm (NAY pahm) Highly flammable chemical dropped from U.S. planes in firebombing attacks during the Vietnam War (p. 1033)

National Aeronautics and Space Administration (NASA) Created in 1958 by the United States government as an independent agency for space exploration (p. 918)

National American Woman Suffrage Association (NAWSA) Organization formed in 1890 to continue the pursuit of women's rights, especially the right to vote (p. 637)

National Association for the Advancement of Colored People (NAACP) Organization founded in 1909 to abolish segregation and discrimination, to oppose racism, and to gain civil rights for African Americans (p. 567)

national debt Total amount of money that the federal government borrows and has to pay back (p. 786)

National Defense Education Act 1958 measure designed to improve science and mathematics instruction in schools (p. 918)

nationalism Devotion to one's nation (p. 585)

nationalization Government takeover and ownership of banks, and the redistribution of their wealth (p. 780)

National Liberation Front Political arm of the Viet Cong (p. 1027)

National Organization for Women (NOW) Organization formed in 1966 to promote the full participation of women in American society (p. 998)

Nation of Islam Organization, also called the Black Muslims, dedicated to black separation and self-help (p. 954)

nativism A policy of favoring native-born Americans over immigrants (pp. 359, 544)

naturalize To apply for and be granted American citizenship (p. 333)

natural rights Rights that belong to people simply because they are human (p. 121)

Nazism An extreme form of facism shaped by Hitler's fanatical ideas about German nationalism and racial superiority (p. 803)

neutral Not taking sides in a conflict or dispute (p. 203)

Neutrality Acts 1939 laws designed to keep the United States out of future wars (p. 818)

New Deal Term used to describe President Franklin Roosevelt's relief, recovery, and reform programs designed to combat the Great Depression (p. 769)

New England Colonies English colonies that became the states of Connecticut, Rhode Island, Massachusetts, Vermont, New Hampshire, and Maine (p. 50)

New Federalism President Nixon's call for a new partnership between the federal government and state governments; President Reagan's plan to cut back the role of the federal government while giving more responsibility to state and local governments (pp. 1061, 1105)

New Frontier President Kennedy's proposals to improve the economy, assist the poor, and advance the space program (p. 970)

New Left New political movement of the late 1960s that called for radical changes to fight poverty and racism (p. 1038)

New Nationalism Theodore Roosevelt's plan for greater federal regulation of business and workplaces, income and inheritance taxes, and electoral reforms (p. 630)

New Right A political coalition formed by conservative groups by 1980 (p. 1099)

Niagara Movement Founded in 1905, a group of African Americans that called for full civil liberties, an end to racial discrimination, and recognition of human brotherhood (p. 557)

Nisei (nee SAY) A Japanese American whose parents were born in Japan (p. 627)

nomadic People who move their homes regularly, usually in search of available food sources (pp. 259, 491)

nonviolent protest A peaceful way of protesting against restrictive policies (p. 938)

North American Free Trade Agreement (NAFTA) Agreement calling for the removal of trade restrictions among the United States, Canada, and Mexico (p. 1141)

North Atlantic Treaty Organization (NATO) 1949 alliance of nations that agreed to band together in the event of war and to support and protect each nation involved (p. 879)

Nuclear Regulatory Commission (NRC) Government organization formed in 1974 to oversee the civilian uses of nuclear materials (p. 1015)

nullify To reject, as in when a state judges a federal law to be unconstitutional (pp. 208, 299)

Nuremberg Trials Series of trials in 1945 conducted by an International Military Tribunal in which former Nazi leaders were charged with crimes against peace, crimes against humanity, and war crimes (p. 845)

O

obsolete Outdated (p. 349)

Office of War Mobilization Federal agency formed to coordinate issues related to war production during World War II (p. 828)

oligopoly A market structure dominated by only a few large, profitable firms (p. 470)

Olive Branch Petition Plea by the American colonists to King George III in 1775 that he halt the fighting (p. 119)

Open Door Policy American approach to China around 1900, favoring open trade relations between China and other nations (p. 596)

oral history The traditions passed from generation to generation by word of mouth (p. 8)

Oregon Trail Trail from Independence, Missouri, to Oregon, used by many pioneers during the 1840s (p. 254)

Organization of Petroleum Exporting Countries (OPEC) Group of nations that work together to regulate the price and supply of oil (p. 1060)

P

Pacific Railway Acts Laws passed in 1862 and 1864 giving large land grants to the Union Pacific and Central Pacific railroads (p. 489)

pardon An official forgiveness of a crime (p. 426)

Paris peace talks Negotiations between the United States and North Vietnam, beginning in 1968 (p. 1044)

pass A low place in a mountain range that allows travelers to cross over to the other side (p. 254)

patent A license that gives an inventor the exclusive right to make, use, or sell an invention for a set period of time (pp. 274, 457)

patriotism Love of one's country; the passion that aims to serve one's country, either in defending it from invasion, or in protecting its rights and maintaining its laws and institutions in vigor and purity (p. 136)

patronage Practice of hiring political supporters for government jobs (p. 298)

Peace Corps Federal program established to send volunteers to help developing nations around the world (p. 990)

Pendleton Civil Service Act 1883 law that created a Civil Service Commission and stated that federal employees could not be required to contribute to campaign funds nor be fired for political reasons (p. 523)

penny auction Farm auctions during the Great Depression at which neighbors saved each other's property from foreclosure by bidding low (p. 753)

Pequot War War between English settlers and Pequot Indians in 1637 (p. 55)

per capita income Average annual income per person (p. 900)

persecute To oppress someone because of his or her beliefs (p. 51)

Persian Gulf War In 1991, a limited military operation to drive Iraqi forces out of Kuwait (p. 1118)

philanthropist A person who gives donations to worthy causes (p. 323)

Pickett's Charge Unsuccessful charge by Confederate infantry during the Battle of Gettysburg (p. 406)

piecework System in which workers are paid not by the amount of time worked but by the number of items they produce (p. 474)

Pilgrim One of the group of English Separatists who established Plymouth Colony in 1620 (p. 51)

placer mining A mining technique in which miners shovel loose dirt into boxes and then run water over the dirt to separate it from gold or silver particles (p. 499)

plantation Large farm on which crops are raised mainly for sale (p. 27)

Platt Amendment An addition to the 1900 Cuban constitution by the American government that gave the United States the right to establish naval bases in Cuba and to intervene in Cuban affairs whenever necessary (p. 594)

Plessy* v. *Ferguson 1896 Supreme Court decision that held that segregation was legal as long as the separate facilities provided for blacks were equal to those provided to whites (p. 566)

pocket veto Type of veto a chief executive may use after a legislature has adjourned; it is applied when the chief executive does not formally sign or reject a bill within the time period allowed to do so (p. 427)

pogrom Violent massacre of Jews (p. 528)

political machine An unofficial city organization designed to keep a particular party or group in power and usually headed by a single, powerful boss (p. 538)

political party Group of people who seek to win elections and hold public office in order to control government policies and programs (p. 205)

poll tax A special fee that must be paid before a person can vote (p. 565)

Pontiac's Rebellion 1763 rebellion by Native Americans in the Great Lakes region (p. 110)

popular sovereignty Policy of letting the people in a territory decide whether slavery would be allowed there (p. 360)

Populist Follower of the People's Party (or Populist party) formed in 1891 to advocate a larger money supply and other economic reforms (p. 511)

POW Prisoner of war (p. 1048)

preamble An introduction (p. 120)

precedent (PREHS ih dehnt) An act or a statement that becomes an example, rule, or tradition to be followed (p. 167)

prejudice An unreasonable, usually unfavorable opinion of another group (p. 347)

presidio (prih SEE dee oh) Fort built in Southwest by Spanish (pp. 40, 261)

price controls System of pricing determined by the government (p. 665)

prime minister Highest official in a parliamentary government (p. 106)

privateer Privately owned ship hired by a government to attack enemy ships (p. 43)

Proclamation of 1763 Order by the British king that closed the region west of the Appalachian Mountains to all settlement by colonists (p. 110)

productivity The amount of goods and services created in a given period of time (p. 457)

profiteering Selling scarce items at unreasonably high prices (p. 134)

Progressive Era The period from about 1890 to 1920, during which a variety of reforms were enacted at the local, state, and federal levels (p. 615)

prohibition A ban on the manufacture and sale of alcoholic beverages (p. 544)

propaganda Information intended to sway public opinion (p. 650)

proprietary colony A colony granted by a king or queen to an individual or a group that has full governing rights (p. 60)

public works program Government-funded projects to build public facilities (p. 770)

Pueblo Revolt of 1680 Revolt by Pueblo people in New Mexico against Spain (p. 41)

Pullman Strike 1894 railway workers' strike that spread nationwide (p. 483)

puppet state A supposedly independent country under the control of a powerful neighbor (p. 814)

purge In political terms, the process of removing enemies and undesirable individuals from power (p. 801)

Puritans People who favored the purification of England's Anglican Church (p. 51)

push-pull factors Events and conditions that either force (push) people to move elsewhere or strongly attract (pull) them to do so (p. 488)

Q

Quaker Member of a Protestant group that emphasizes equality (p. 60)

quarantine A time of isolation to prevent the spread of a disease (p. 529)

quota A numerical limit (p. 719)

R

racism Belief that differences in character or intelligence are due to one's race; asserting the superiority of one race over another or others (p. 605)

Radical Republicans Group of congressmen from within the Republican Party who believed that the Civil War had been fought over the moral issue of slavery, and insisted that the main goal of Reconstruction should be a total restructuring of society to guarantee blacks true equality (p. 427)

ragtime A type of music featuring melodies with shifting accents over a steady, marching-band beat; originated among black musicians in the South and Midwest in the 1880s (p. 563)

ratify Approve or sanction (p. 158)

rationing Distribution of goods to consumers in a fixed amount (p. 666)

Reagan Democrat Democratic, blue-collar workers who tended to vote Republican during the 1980s (p. 1099)

realpolitik (ray AHL poh lih teek) A German term meaning "practical politics," or foreign policy based on interests rather than moral principles (p. 1064)

rebate A partial refund (p. 524)

recall Procedure that permits voters to remove public officials from office before the next election (p. 624)

recession A period of slow business activity (p. 786)

recognition Official acceptance as an independent nation (p. 392)

Reconstruction Program implemented by the federal government between 1865 and 1877 to repair the damage to the South caused by the Civil War and restore the southern states to the Union (p. 424)

Reconstruction Finance Corporation (RFC) Corporation set up by President Hoover in 1932 to give government credit to a number of institutions, such as large industries, railroads, and insurance companies (p. 757)

reconversion The social and economic transition from wartime to peacetime (p. 912)

Red Scare Intense fear of communism and other politically radical ideas (p. 714)

referendum Process that allows citizens to approve or reject a law passed by their legislature (p. 624)

Reformation Revolt against the Catholic Church that began in 1517 (p. 15)

religious tolerance Idea that people of different religions should live in peace together (p. 52)

Renaissance Era of European history extending from the 1300s to the 1500s (p. 13)

reparations Payment from an enemy for economic injury suffered during a war (p. 671)

republic Government run by the people through their elected representatives (p. 146)

republican virtues Virtues the American people would need to govern themselves, such as self-reliance, industry, frugality, harmony, and the ability to sacrifice individual needs for the good of the community (p. 242)

reservation Federal land set aside for Native Americans (pp. 221, 492)

Resistance Movement in France that opposed German occupation during World War II (p. 810)

restrictive covenant Agreement among homeowners not to sell real estate to certain groups of people, such as Jews or African Americans (p. 531)

revenue Income (p. 786)

revival A gathering where people are "revived," or brought back to a religious life (p. 245)

Revolutionary War American colonists' war of independence from Britain, fought from 1775 to 1783 (p. 116)

rock-and-roll Music, popular in the 1950s, that grew out of rhythm and blues (p. 910)

Roe v. Wade 1973 Supreme Court decision that legalized abortion (p. 1000)

Roosevelt Corollary President Theodore Roosevelt's 1904 extension of the Monroe Doctrine in which he asserted the right of the United States to intervene in the affairs of Latin American nations (p. 600)

royal colony Colony with a governor appointed by the king (p. 46)

rule of law A type of government in which decisions must be based on the law, not on personal wishes (p. 121)

rural Pertaining to the countryside (p. 281)

rural free delivery (RFD) Beginning in 1896, free delivery offered by the U.S. Post Office to farm families in the rural Midwest (p. 571)

Russian Revolution Collapse of the czar's government in Russia in 1917, after which the Russian monarchy was replaced with a republican government (p. 656)

S

sachem A Native American leader (p. 55)

Salem witch trials The prosecution and execution of 20 women and men for witchcraft in Massachusetts in 1692 (p. 54)

SALT I Strategic Arms Limitation Treaty, a 1972 agreement between the United States and the Soviet Union on limiting nuclear weapons (p. 1068)

salutary neglect Great Britain's policy in the early 1700s of not interfering in the American colonies' politics and economy as long as such neglect served British economic interests (p. 73)

Sandinista In the 1980s, a member of the ruling Marxist group in Nicaragua (p. 1112)

Santa Fe Trail Trail from Independence, Missouri, to Santa Fe, New Mexico, in the mid-1800s (p. 255)

satellite nation A country dominated politically and economically by another nation, especially by the Soviet Union during the Cold War (p. 871)

saturation bombing The dropping of a large concentration of bombs over a certain area (p. 1033)

savanna Region near the equator with tropical grasslands and scattered trees (p. 18)

scab Negative term for a worker called in by an employer to replace striking laborers (p. 481)

scalawag Negative nickname for a white southern Republican after the Civil War (p. 435)

scarce In short supply (p. 21)

Scopes trial 1925 court case in which Clarence Darrow and William Jennings Bryan debated the issue of teaching evolution in public schools (p. 702)

secede To withdraw formally from a membership in a group or organization (p. 299)

secessionist Person who wanted the South to secede (p. 371)

Second Continental Congress Assembly of representatives from the colonies that first met in May 1775 in Philadelphia (p. 119)

Second Great Awakening Religious movement of the early 1800s (p. 245)

Second New Deal Period of legislative activity launched by President Franklin Roosevelt in 1935 (p. 774)

Second Seminole War 1835 war in which the Seminoles tried to retain their land in Florida (p. 302)

section A geographic region (p. 280)

sedition Speech or action that encourages rebellion (p. 667)

segregation Forced separation, oftentimes by race (pp. 315, 565)

Selective Service Law passed in 1917 authorizing a draft of young men for military service in World War I (p. 657)

Selective Training and Service Act 1940 law requiring all males aged 21 to 36 to register for military service (p. 826)

self-determination The power to make decisions about one's own future (p. 669)

self-sufficient Having the necessary resources to get along without outside help (p. 82)

Seneca Falls Convention The first women's rights convention in United States history, held in 1848 (p. 329)

separation of powers The Constitutional allotting of powers within the federal government among the legislative, executive, and judicial branches (p. 155)

settlement house Community center organized to provide various services to the urban poor (p. 542)

sharecropping System of farming in which a farmer tends some portion of a planter's land and receives a share of the crop at harvest time as payment (p. 437)

Shays' Rebellion An uprising against taxes in Massachusetts in 1786 and 1787 (p. 148)

shell Device that explodes in the air, or when it hits a solid target (p. 384)

Sherman Antitrust Act Law passed by Congress in 1890 that outlawed any combination of companies that restrained interstate trade or commerce (p. 472)

Sherman Silver Purchase Act Law passed by Congress in 1890 to increase the amount of silver the government was required to purchase every month (p. 509)

siege Tactic in which an enemy is surrounded and starved in order to make it surrender (pp. 107, 408)

silent majority Term used by President Nixon to describe Americans who opposed the counterculture (p. 1046)

sit-down strike Labor protest in which laborers stop working but refuse to leave the workplace (p. 787)

sit-in Form of protest in which protesters seat themselves and refuse to move (p. 941)

social Darwinism Derived from Darwin's theory of natural selection, the belief that society should do as little as possible to interfere with people's pursuit of success (p. 469)

social gospel movement A social reform movement that developed within religious institutions and sought to apply the teachings of Jesus directly to society (p. 542)

socialism An economic and political philosophy that favors public (or social) instead of private control of property and income (p. 477)

Social Security System System established by the 1935 Social Security Act to provide financial security, in the form of regular payments, to people who cannot support themselves (p. 776)

social welfare program Program designed to ensure a basic standard of living for all citizens (p. 622)

sociology Term coined by philosopher Auguste Comte to

describe the study of how people interact with one another in a society (p. 543)

soddie A sod home with walls and roof made from blocks of sod—strips of grass with the thick roots and earth attached (p. 503)

solid South Term used to describe the domination of post–Civil War southern politics by the Democratic Party (p. 444)

sooners In 1889, people who illegally claimed land by sneaking past government officials before the land races began (p. 497)

Southern Christian Leadership Conference (SCLC) Civil rights organization that advocated nonviolent protest; formed in 1957 by Dr. Martin Luther King, Jr., and other leaders (p. 938)

Southern Colonies The English colonies of Virginia, Maryland, the Carolinas, and Georgia (p. 62)

speakeasies Bars that operated illegally during the time of Prohibition (p. 700)

specialization In production, a system in which each worker performs a single part of an entire process (p. 278)

special prosecutor An attorney appointed by the Justice Department to investigate wrongdoing by government officials (p. 1075)

specie gold or silver coin (p. 148)

speculation The practice of making high-risk investments in hopes of getting a huge return (p. 732)

sphere of influence Area of economic and political control exerted by one nation over another nation or other nations (p. 596)

spoils Rewards gained through military victory (p. 670)

spoils system System or practice of giving appointed offices as rewards from the successful party in an election; name for the patronage system under President Jackson (p. 298)

Sputnik The first artificial satellite to orbit Earth, launched by the Soviets in 1957 (p. 893)

stagflation Combination of high inflation and high unemployment, with no economic growth (p. 1080)

stalemate Situation in which neither side in a conflict is able to gain the advantage (p. 649)

Stamp Act 1765 law passed by the British Parliament that taxed newspapers, legal documents, and other printed materials in the colonies (p. 111)

staple crop A crop that is in constant demand, such as cotton, wheat, or rice (p. 74)

states' rights The powers that the Constitution neither gives to the federal government nor denies to the states (p. 299)

steerage A large open area beneath a ship's deck, often used to house traveling immigrants (p. 528)

stereotype An exaggerated or oversimplified description of reality held by a number of people (p. 505)

Stono Rebellion Slave revolt in South Carolina in 1739 (p. 88)

Strategic Arms Reduction Treaty Agreement signed in 1991 and known as START, which called for the reduction in the supplies of long-range nuclear weapons in Russia and the United States (p. 1117)

Strategic Defense Initiative (SDI) President Reagan's proposed defense system against a Soviet missile attack, popularly known as "Star Wars" (p. 1105)

strict construction Belief that the government should not do anything that the Constitution does not specifically say it can do (p. 202)

strike A work stoppage intended to force an employer to meet certain demands, as in the demand for higher wages (p. 283)

Student Nonviolent Coordinating Committee (SNCC) An offshoot of SCLC, a student civil rights organization founded in 1960 (p. 939)

subsidy A payment made by the government to encourage the development of certain key industries (p. 521)

suburb Residential community surrounding a city (p. 535)

suffrage The right to vote (p. 330)

supply-side economics Theory that tax reductions will increase investment and thereby encourage business growth (p. 1103)

Sussex pledge Pledge by the German government in 1916 that its submarines would warn ships before attacking (p. 655)

sweatshop Factory where employees work long hours at low wages and under poor working conditions (p. 474)

synagogue Jewish house of worship (p. 60)

T

Taft-Hartley Act Law passed by Congress in 1947 that allowed the President to declare an 80-day cooling-off period when strikes affected industries that in turn affected the national interest, and required strikers to return to work while the government conducted a study of the situation (p. 913)

tariff Tax on foreign goods imported into a country (p. 201)

Tariff of 1828 A high tariff on imports that benefited the industrial North while forcing Southerners to pay higher prices on manufactured goods; called the "Tariff of Abominations" by Southerners (p. 298)

teach-in Special session of lecture and discussion on a controversial topic that often occurred during the Vietnam War era (p. 1039)

Teapot Dome scandal Scandal during the Harding administration involving the granting of oil-drilling rights on government land in return for money (p. 720)

televangelism The use of television by evangelists to reach millions of people, especially for fund-raising (p. 1100)

temperance movement An organized campaign to eliminate alcohol consumption (pp. 312, 544)

tenant farming System of farming in which a person rents land to farm from a planter (p. 438)

tenement A low-cost apartment building that often has poor standards of sanitation, safety, and comfort and is designed to house as many families as possible (pp. 283, 536)

Tennessee Valley Authority (TVA) Federal project to provide inexpensive electric power, flood control, and recreational opportunities to the Tennessee River valley (p. 772)

Tet Offensive 1968 attack by Viet Cong and North Vietnamese forces throughout South Vietnam (p. 1035)

Texas War for Independence Successful revolt by Texans against Mexican rule in 1835–1836 (p. 264)

Thirteenth Amendment Constitutional amendment, ratified in 1865, abolishing slavery (p. 414)

38th parallel Latitudinal line that divided North and South Korea at approximately the midpoint of the peninsula (p. 885)

Three-Fifths Compromise Compromise at the Constitutional Convention calling for three fifths of a state's slave population to be counted for the purposes of legislative representation (p. 153)

totalitarian A government that exerts total control over the nation and citizens' lives (p. 800)

Trail of Tears The forced movement of Cherokees in 1838 to land west of the Mississippi River (p. 301)

trans-Appalachia Area west of the Appalachian mountains (p. 249)

transcendentalism Philosophical movement of the mid-1800s that emphasized spiritual discovery and insight rather than reason (p. 311)

transcontinental railroad Railway extending from coast to coast (p. 460)

transistor A tiny circuit device invented in 1947 that amplifies, controls, and generates electrical signals (p. 902)

Treaty of Ghent Agreement, signed in 1814, that ended the War of 1812 (p. 227)

Treaty of Greenville Treaty signed in 1795 by the United States and several Native American peoples in which the Native Americans gave up control of most of Ohio (p. 221)

Treaty of Guadalupe Hidalgo Treaty signed in 1848 by the United States and Mexico, ending the Mexican War (p. 353)

Treaty of Paris (1763) Treaty that ended the French and Indian War and in which France gave up its land claims in North America to Britain (p. 108)

Treaty of Paris (1783) Treaty that ended the Revolutionary War and in which Britain acknowledged American independence (p. 136)

Treaty of Tordesillas 1494 treaty in which Portugal and Spain divided the non-Christian world (p. 27)

triangular trade Trade between the Americas, Europe, and Africa (p. 75)

Truman Doctrine Harry Truman's 1947 speech before a joint session of Congress, calling the United States to take a leadership role in the world, and declaring that the United States would support nations threatened by communism (p. 874)

trust A group of separate companies that are placed under the control of a single managing board (p. 472)

trustee Someone entrusted to look after a business (p. 63)

Turner's Rebellion Unsuccessful slave revolt led by Nat Turner in 1831 (p. 289)

Turner thesis 1893 theory of Frederick Jackson Turner that claimed that the frontier had played a key role in forming the American character (p. 505)

Twenty-first Amendment Constitutional amendment ratified in 1933 to repeal Prohibition (p. 754)

Twenty-fourth Amendment Constitutional amendment ratified in 1964 to outlaw the poll tax (p. 953)

U

U-boat A German submarine (p. 653)

Underground Railroad A network of escape routes that provided protection and transportation for slaves fleeing north to freedom (p. 322)

Union The United States as a national unit; or, during the Civil War, the North (p. 346)

United Farm Workers (UFW) Union created by César Chávez to organize Mexican field hands in the West (p. 1005)

United States Constitution Plan of government that describes the different parts of the government and their duties and powers, established in 1787 (p. 150)

Upper South Designation used in the Civil War encompassing the states of Virginia, North Carolina, Tennessee, and Arkansas (p. 373)

urban Relating to a city (p. 281)

utopian community A small society dedicated to perfection in social and political conditions (p. 315)

U-2 incident A 1960 incident in which the Soviet military used a guided missile to shoot down an American U-2 spy plane over Soviet territory (p. 893)

V

vaudeville A type of inexpensive variety show that first appeared in the 1870s, often consisting of comic sketches, song-and-dance routines, and magic acts (p. 559)

Versailles Treaty 1919 treaty that ended World War I (p. 671)

vertical consolidation Process of gaining control of the many different businesses that make up all phases of a product's development (p. 471)

veto To prevent from becoming a law (p. 152)

vice Immoral or corrupt behavior (p. 545)

victory garden A home vegetable garden created to boost food production during World War II (p. 831)

Viet Cong Communist guerrillas in South Vietnam (p. 1027)

Vietminh Common name for the League for Independence of Vietnam (p. 1024)

Vietnamization President Nixon's policy of replacing American military forces with those of South Vietnam (p. 1045)

vigilante A citizen who takes the law into his or her own hands (p. 667)

Virginia and Kentucky Resolutions Resolutions passed in 1798 that attacked the Alien and Sedition Acts as being unconstitutional (p. 208)

Volunteers in Service to America (VISTA) Federal program that sends volunteers to help people in poor communities (p. 978)

Voting Rights Act of 1965 Law aimed at reducing the barriers that prevented African Americans from voting, in part by increasing the federal government's authority to register voters (p. 953)

W

Wagner Act Law passed in 1935 that aided unions by legalizing collective bargaining and closed shops, and by establishing the National Labor Relations Board (p. 775)

Wannsee Conference 1942 conference in Germany concerning the plan to murder European Jews (p. 843)

war of attrition A type of war in which one side inflicts continuous losses on the other in order to wear down its strength (p. 383)

War of 1812 War between the United States and Great Britain (p. 225)

War Powers Act 1973 law limiting a President's ability to involve the United States in foreign conflicts without receiving a formal declaration of war from Congress (p. 1081)

War Refugee Board (WRB) Federal agency created in 1944 to try to help people threatened with murder by the Nazis (p. 844)

Warren Commission Commission, headed by Chief Justice Earl Warren, that investigated the assassination of President Kennedy (p. 973)

Warsaw ghetto An area of Warsaw sealed off by the Nazis to confine the Jewish population, forcing them into poor, unsanitary conditions (p. 843)

Warsaw Pact Military alliance between the Soviet Union and the nations of Eastern Europe, formed in 1955 (p. 880)

Watergate scandal Scandal involving illegal activities that led ultimately to the resignation of President Nixon in 1974 (p. 1072)

welfare capitalism An approach to labor relations in which companies meet some of their workers' needs without prompting by unions, thus preventing strikes and keeping productivity high (p. 731)

Whiskey Rebellion Unrest in 1794 caused by opposition to a tax on whiskey (p. 204)

Whitewater affair Charges that President Clinton had engaged in improper business transactions before becoming President (p. 1130)

Wilmot Proviso Amendment to an 1846 bill stating that slavery would not be permitted in any of the territory acquired from Mexico; though it never became law, Northerners continued to attach it to bills related to new territories (p. 354)

wiretap A listening device used to intercept telephone information (p. 1071)

Woodstock festival 1969 music festival in upstate New York (p. 1012)

World Trade Organization (WTO) International organization formed in 1995 to encourage the expansion of world trade (p. 1141)

writ of *habeas corpus* Legal protection requiring that a court determine whether a person is lawfully imprisoned (p. 395)

X

XYZ affair Controversy in 1798 over French demands for bribes from American negotiators (p. 207)

Y

yellow journalism Sensational news coverage, emphasizing crime and scandal (p. 563)

Z

zeppelin A German floating airship (p. 661)

Zimmermann note A telegram sent by Germany's foreign secretary in 1917 to Mexican officials proposing an alliance with Mexico and promising the United States territory if Mexico declared war on the United States (p. 656)

Spanish Glossary

A

abolitionist movement/movimiento abolicionista
Movimiento para acabar con la esclavitud (pág. 318)

abstinence/abstinencia Acción de abstenerse de alguna actividad, como consumir bebidas alcohólicas (pág. 313)

Adams-Onís Treaty/Tratado Adams-Onís Tratado firmado en 1819 entre los Estados Unidos y España en el que España le cedió la Florida a los Estados Unidos; también se conoce como Tratado Transcontinental (pág. 252)

administration/administración Plazo para ejercer un cargo; también se refiere al conjunto de miembros y entidades de la rama ejecutiva (pág. 167)

affirmative action/discriminación positiva Política que concede consideración especial a las mujeres y a los miembros de grupos minoritarios para compensarlos por discriminaciones pasadas (pág. 1086)

agenda/agenda Lista de asuntos para llevar a cabo (pág. 213)

Agent Orange/agente naranja Herbicida que se utilizó como arma química durante la Guerra de Vietnam para exterminar la vegetación y poner al descubierto zonas enemigas ocultas (pág. 1033)

Agricultural Adjustment Administration (AAA)/Administración de Ajuste Agrícola (AAA) Se estableció en 1933 para elevar los precios de los productos agrícolas a través de subsidios o apoyo económico del gobierno (pág. 772)

AIDS/SIDA Síndrome de inmunodeficiencia adquirida; causado por un virus que ha matado a muchas personas desde principios de la década de 1980 (pág. 1110)

Albany Plan of Union/Plan de la Unión Albany Propuesta realizada en 1754 por Benjamín Franklin para la creación de un gran consejo de representantes de las colonias de Gran Bretaña en América (pág. 105)

Alien and Sedition Acts/Leyes sobre Extranjeros y Sedición Leyes aprobadas por el Congreso en 1798 que facultaban al gobierno para encarcelar o deportar extranjeros y enjuiciar a quienes se opusieran al gobierno (pág. 208)

alien/extranjero Alguien que no es ciudadano (pág. 105)

Alliance for Progress/Alianza para el Progreso Propuesta del presidente Kennedy para la cooperación entre las naciones del hemisferio occidental con el fin de satisfacer las necesidades básicas de sus habitantes (pág. 989)

Allies/aliados En la Primera Guerra Mundial: Rusia, Francia, Serbia y Gran Bretaña; en la Segunda Guerra Mundial: la alianza de Gran Bretaña, los Estados Unidos de América, la Unión Soviética y otras naciones (págs. 649, 810)

almanac/almanaque Libro que contiene información como calendarios y predicciones climatológicas (pág. 79)

amend/enmendar Corregir (pág. 151)

America First Committee/Primer Comité Estadounidense Grupo formado en 1940 por aislacionistas para bloquear la ayuda a Gran Bretaña (pág. 819)

American Expeditionary Force (AEF)/Cuerpo Expedicionario Estadounidense (AEF) Nombre que se le dio a las tropas estadounidenses en Europa durante la Primera Guerra Mundial (pág. 657)

American Indian Movement (AIM)/Movimiento Indio Estadounidense (AIM) Organización formada en 1968 para ayudar a los indígenas (pág. 1007)

American Liberty League/Asociación para la Libertad de los Estados Unidos Organización fundada en 1934 en oposición al Nuevo Trato (pág. 779)

American System/sistema estadounidense Combinación de un desarrollo económico respaldado por el gobierno y tarifas proteccionistas orientados al crecimiento comercial (pág. 294)

amnesty/amnistía Perdón general para ciertos crímenes (pág. 1086)

anarchist/anarquista Persona radical que se opone a todo tipo de gobierno (pág. 481)

annex/anexar Incorporar o unir, refiriéndose al caso de la unión de un territorio nuevo a un país determinado (págs. 351, 585)

anti-Federalist/antifederalista Persona que se oponía a la Constitución durante el debate sobre la ratificación; en contra del concepto de un gobierno nacional sólido (pág. 159)

anti-Semitism/antisemitismo Hostilidad o discriminación hacia los judíos (pág. 841)

apartheid/*apartheid* La discriminación sistemática de personas con diferentes antecedentes raciales (pág. 1136)

appeasement/pacificación Política de aceptación de las demandas de un competidor con el fin de preservar la paz (pág. 805)

apportionment/distribución de las asignaciones Distribución de escaños en un cuerpo legislativo (pág. 979)

apprentice/aprendiz Persona que trabaja bajo un contrato legal para otra persona con el fin de aprender un oficio (pág. 79)

arbitration/arbitraje Conciliación de una disputa a través de una persona o grupo de expertos que escuchan a ambas partes y toman una decisión (pág. 590)

armistice/armisticio Cese al fuego o tregua (pág. 662)

arms race/carrera armamentista Competencia entre naciones para obtener la superioridad de armamento (pág. 892)

arsenal/arsenal Lugar en el que se fabrican o almacenan armas (pág. 368)

Articles of Confederation/Artículos de la Confederación Plan que estableció en 1781 un gobierno nacional limitado en los Estados Unidos; más tarde fue reemplazado por la Constitución de los Estados Unidos (pág. 145)

assembly line/línea de montaje Proceso de fabricación en el cual cada trabajador realiza una tarea determinada en la construcción del producto final (pág. 762)

assimilation/asimilación Proceso por el cual las personas de una cultura se incorporan y se vuelven parte de otra (págs. 222, 553)

Atlantic Charter/Carta del Atlántico Acuerdo firmado en 1941 por el presidente Franklin Roosevelt y el primer ministro Winston Churchill en el que se resumen los objetivos de guerra de las dos naciones (pág. 832)

autocrat/autócrata Mandatario con poder ilimitado (pág. 650)

autonomy/autonomía Capacidad de un pueblo de gobernarse a sí mismo con respecto a asuntos locales (pág. 1007)

Axis Powers/Potencias del Eje En la Segunda Guerra Mundial: Alemania, Italia y Japón (pág. 805)

B

baby boom/*baby boom* Aumento dramático en la tasa de natalidad, sobre todo en los años que siguieron a la Segunda Guerra Mundial (pág. 904)

Bacon's Rebellion/Rebelión de Bacon Revuelta organizada en 1676 por los colonizadores de Virginia contra el gobernador nombrado por el rey (pág. 48)

balance of trade/balanza comercial Diferencia del valor entre las importaciones y las exportaciones (pág. 71)

banana republic/república bananera Término utilizado para describir a una nación centroamericana que esté dominada por los intereses financieros de los Estados Unidos (pág. 587)

bank note/billete bancario Pedazo de papel que un banco emite a sus clientes y que puede ser canjeado por monedas de oro o plata (pág. 279)

***barrio*/barrio** Un vecindario de hispanohablantes (págs. 687, 857)

barter/canjear Comerciar con productos o servicios sin utilizar dinero (pág. 9)

Bataan Death March/Marcha de la muerte de Bataán Marcha brutal de prisioneros norteamericanos y filipinos dirigida por soldados japoneses en 1942 (pág. 847)

Battle of the Alamo/Batalla del Álamo Toma de tropas mexicanas de una misión liderada por tropas texanas en San Antonio en 1836 (pág. 264)

Battle of Antietam/Batalla de Antietam Batalla de la Guerra Civil; ocurrió en Maryland en 1862 (pág. 389)

Battle of the Bulge/Batalla de las Ardenas Batalla de la Segunda Guerra Mundial en la que fuerzas alemanas lanzaron un contraataque final en el oeste (pág. 846)

Battle of Bunker Hill/Batalla de Bunker Hill Batalla de la Guerra Revolucionaria que tuvo lugar en 1775 al norte de Boston (pág. 128)

Battle of Chancellorsville/Batalla de Chancellorsville Batalla de la Guerra Civil; tuvo lugar en Virginia, en 1863, y la ganó la Confederación (pág. 403)

Battle of Cold Harbor/Batalla de Cold Harbor Batalla de la Guerra Civil; ocurrió en 1864 en Virginia (pág. 411)

Battle of the Coral Sea/Batalla del Mar del Coral Batalla de la Segunda Guerra Mundial entre aviones norteamericanos y japoneses; tuvo lugar en 1942 (pág. 848)

Battle of Fallen Timbers/Batalla de Fallen Timbers Batalla entre las fuerzas estadounidenses e indígenas en 1794 sobre el territorio de Ohio, que trajo consigo la derrota de los indígenas (pág. 221)

Battle of Fredericksburg/Batalla de Fredericksburg Batalla de la Guerra Civil; ocurrió en Virginia, en 1862, y la ganó la Confederación (pág. 403)

Battle of Gettysburg/Batalla de Gettysburg Batalla de la Guerra Civil; tuvo lugar en Pennsylvania, en 1863, y la ganó la Unión; representó un momento crucial en la guerra (pág. 404)

Battle of Guadalcanal/Batalla de Guadalcanal Batalla de la Segunda Guerra Mundial que fue librada de 1942 a 1943 entre los Estados Unidos y Japón (pág. 849)

Battle of Iwo Jima/Batalla de Iwo Jima Batalla de la Segunda Guerra Mundial que ocurrió en 1945 entre los Estados Unidos y Japón (pág. 851)

Battle of Leyte Gulf/Batalla del Golfo Leyte Batalla naval de la Segunda Guerra Mundial librada en 1944 entre los Estados Unidos y Japón (pág. 851)

Battle of Little Bighorn/Batalla de Little Bighorn Victoria de la tribu Sioux sobre las tropas armadas dirigidas por George Custer; ocurrió en 1876 (pág. 495)

Battle of Midway/Batalla de Midway Batalla de la Segunda Guerra Mundial librada en 1942 entre los Estados Unidos y Japón; fue un momento crucial en la guerra en el Pacífico (pág. 849)

Battle of New Orleans/Batalla de Nueva Orleáns Batalla que tuvo lugar en 1815 entre tropas estadounidenses y tropas británicas para obtener el control de Nueva Orleáns, cuya victoria fue para los estadounidenses (pág. 228)

Battle of Okinawa/Batalla de Okinawa Batalla de la Segunda Guerra Mundial librada en 1945 entre los Estados Unidos y Japón (pág. 852)

Battle of Saratoga/Batalla de Saratoga Batalla de la Guerra Revolucionaria que ocurrió en 1777 en Nueva York, considerada como un momento crucial en la guerra (pág. 132)

Battle of Shiloh/Batalla de Shiloh Batalla de la Guerra Civil; tuvo lugar en Tennessee en 1862 (pág. 386)

Battle of Spotsylvania/Batalla de Spotsylvania Batalla de la Guerra Civil; ocurrió en 1864, en Virginia (pág. 411)

Battle of Tippecanoe/Batalla de Tippecanoe Batalla que tuvo lugar en el territorio de Indiana en 1811 entre fuerzas estadounidenses y tropas indígenas; terminó con la derrota de los indígenas (pág. 222)

Battle of Trenton/Batalla de Trenton Batalla de la Guerra Revolucionaria que ocurrió en 1776 en Nueva Jersey (pág. 131)

Battle of the Wilderness/Batalla de Wilderness Batalla de la Guerra Civil; tuvo lugar en Virginia, en 1864, y la ganó la Confederación (pág. 411)

Battle of Yorktown/Batalla de Yorktown Batalla de la Guerra Revolucionaria; tuvo lugar en 1781 en Virginia y finalizó con una victoria decisiva para los estadounidenses (pág. 135)

Battles of Lexington and Concord/Batallas de Lexington y Concord Primeras batallas de la Guerra Revolucionaria que tuvieron lugar el 19 de abril de 1775 (pág. 116)

Bay of Pigs invasion/Invasión a la Bahía de Cochinos Invasión fallida a Cuba realizada por un grupo de fuerzas anticastristas en 1961 (pág. 984)

beatnik/*beatnik* Persona que, en la década de 1950 criticaba y consideraba a la sociedad estadounidense como indiferente y conformista (pág. 911)

Berlin airlift/puente aéreo de Berlín Operación en la que aviones norteamericanos e ingleses transportaron provisiones a Berlín Occidental durante un bloqueo soviético de 1948 a 1949 (pág. 879)

Berlin Wall/Muro de Berlín Barrera construida por el gobierno de Alemania Oriental para separar la zona comunista de Berlín de la no comunista (pág. 986)

Bessemer process/proceso Bessemer Proceso patentado en 1856 para elaborar acero de manera más eficiente (pág. 463)

bicentennial/bicentenario Fecha en que se cumplen 200 años de un acontecimiento (pág. 1082)

bilingual education/educación bilingüe La enseñanza a los estudiantes en su lengua materna y en inglés (pág. 1145)

Bill of Rights/Declaración de Derechos Las primeras diez enmiendas a la Constitución (pág. 162)

bimetallic standard/patrón bimetálico Moneda de los Estados Unidos, antes de 1873, que constaba de monedas de oro o de plata, así como de bonos fiscales que podían ser intercambiados por oro o plata (pág. 508)

black codes/*black codes* o códigos negros Leyes que restringían los derechos de los libertos (pág. 430)

Black Hawk War/Guerra del Halcón Negro Levantamiento dirigido por un guerrero llamado Halcón Negro en el que los indígenas trataron de reclamar su tierra en el territorio de Illinois (pág. 302)

blacklist/lista negra Lista que a principios de 1947 circulaba entre los empleadores y que contenía los nombres de las personas que no debían ser contratadas (pág. 882)

black nationalism/nacionalismo negro Creencia en la identidad propia y la unidad racial de la comunidad estadounidense de raza negra (pág. 955)

black power/poder negro Movimiento estadounidense de raza negra que busca la unión y la independencia (pág. 956)

Black Tuesday/Martes Negro El 29 de octubre de 1929, día en que empezó la gran caída de la bolsa de valores (pág. 741)

Bland-Allison Act/Ley de Bland-Allison Ley promulgada en 1878 que exigía al gobierno federal comprar y acuñar más plata, lo que aumentó la oferta monetaria y causó inflación (pág. 509)

blitzkrieg/*blitzkrieg* o Guerra Relámpago Tipo de guerra que enfatiza el movimiento rápido y mecanizado; utilizada por Alemania durante la Segunda Guerra Mundial (pág. 808)

blockade/bloquear Cerrar o aislar un lugar de todo contacto exterior (pág. 134)

blue law/leyes azules Reglamentos que prohibían ciertas actividades privadas que se consideraban inmorales, como ingerir bebidas alcohólicas los domingos (pág. 134)

bonanza farm/granja "la bonanza" Granja controlada por empresas grandes y manejada por profesionales, en la que se cultivan inmensas cantidades de cosechas que se venden al contado (pág. 522)

Bonus Army/Armados para la Bonificación Un grupo de veteranos de la Primera Guerra Mundial y sus familias que protestaron en Washington, D.C., en 1932, exigiendo el pago inmediato de la bonificación de retiro prometida en 1945 (pág. 758)

boomers/pioneros Colonos que corrían para ganar un pedazo de tierra cuando el territorio indio se abrió para la colonización, en 1889 (pág. 497)

bootlegger/contrabandista de licores Término para describir a un vendedor de alcohol ilegal durante el período de Prohibición (pág. 700)

Border States/Estados fronterizos En la Guerra Civil, los estados entre el norte y el sur: Delaware, Maryland, Kentucky y Missouri (pág. 369)

Boston Massacre/Masacre de Boston Incidente ocurrido el 5 de marzo de 1770 en el que los soldados británicos mataron a cinco colonos (pág. 114)

boycott/boicot Rechazo a comprar un producto determinado o utilizar un servicio determinado (pág. 112)

bracero/bracero Término utilizado en 1942 para describir a los campesinos mexicanos traídos a los Estados Unidos (pág. 857)

brinkmanship/*brinkmanship* Término utilizado en 1956 por el secretario de estado John Dulles para describir la habilidad de llegar al borde de una guerra sin participar en ella, con el fin de proteger los intereses nacionales (pág. 892)

***Brown v. Board of Education of Topeka, Kansas*/Brown vs. la Junta de Educación de Topeka, Kansas** Caso de la Suprema Corte ocurrido en 1954 en el que se prohibió la discriminación racial en las escuelas públicas (pág. 931)

Bull Moose Party/Partido Bull Moose Sobrenombre del Partido Progresista (pág. 630)

bureaucracy/burocracia Departamentos que conforman una gran organización, como en el caso de un gobierno (pág. 213)

Burma Road/Carretera Birmania Autopista de 700 millas de largo que une Birmania (hoy en día Myanmar) con China (pág. 816)

business cycle/ciclo comercial Períodos en los que la economía de una nación crece y luego disminuye (pág. 741)

buying on margin/compra de valores a crédito Opción que permite a los inversionistas adquirir al contado valores por tan sólo una parte de su precio y pedir un préstamo para el resto (pág. 732)

C

Cabinet/Gabinete Líderes de los departamentos ejecutivos del gobierno federal (pág. 166)

California Gold Rush/fiebre de oro de California Migración en masa a California en busca de oro en 1848 (pág. 255)

Camp David Accords/Acuerdos de Camp David Convenio firmado en 1978 entre Israel y Egipto que hizo posible un tratado de paz entre las dos naciones (pág. 1057)

canister/bote de metralla Tipo especial de recipiente lleno de balas (pág. 384)

carpetbagger/norteño en busca de dinero fácil Sobrenombre negativo para referirse a un republicano del norte que se iba al sur después de la Guerra Civil (pág. 435)

carpet bombing/bombardeo masivo Método de bombardeo aéreo en el que se arrojan muchas bombas sobre un área extensa (pág. 837)

cartel/cartel Asociación eventual de empresas que elaboran el mismo producto (pág. 470)

cash and carry/pago al contado y transporte propio Política de la Segunda Guerra Mundial que exigía a las naciones en guerra pagar en efectivo todos aquellos productos que no fueran militares y encargarse de su transporte desde los Estados Unidos (pág. 818)

cash crop/cultivo en efectivo Cosecha que se cultivaba para la venta (pág. 27)

casualty/baja Término militar para una persona asesinada, herida, capturada o perdida en el campo de batalla (págs. 128, 382)

cede/ceder Rendirse oficialmente o de manera informal (pág. 252)

centralized/centralizado Concentrado en un lugar (pág. 277)

Central Powers/potencias centrales En la Primera Guerra Mundial: Alemania y Austria-Hungría (pág. 649)

checks and balances/pesos y contrapesos Sistema en el que cada rama del gobierno federal revisa las acciones de las otras ramas (pág. 155)

Chinese Exclusion Act/Ley de Exclusión de los Chinos Ley aprobada en 1882 que prohibía a los trabajadores chinos entrar al país; sin embargo, no impedía la entrada a aquellos que habían establecido con anterioridad su residencia en los Estados Unidos (pág. 532)

civil disobedience/desobediencia civil Rechazo pacífico a obedecer una ley en un esfuerzo por cambiarla (pág. 636)

Civilian Conservation Corps (CCC)/Asociación para la Conservación Civil (CCC) Este programa, establecido por el Congreso en 1933, puso a más de 2.5 millones de jóvenes a trabajar en la restauración y el mantenimiento de bosques, playas y parques (pág. 771)

Civil Rights Act of 1964/Ley de los Derechos Civiles de 1964 Ley que declaró ilegal la discriminación en un gran número de asuntos, tales como el voto, las escuelas y los empleos (pág. 951)

civil rights/derechos civiles Libertades individuales de los ciudadanos garantizadas por la ley, como el derecho al voto y el mismo trato a todos los habitantes (pág. 431)

civil service/administración pública Los trabajadores del gobierno no elegidos (pág. 522)

Civil War/Guerra Civil Guerra entre los estados de la Unión del norte y los estados Confederados del sur que tuvo lugar de 1861 a 1865 (pág. 380)

clan/clan Grupos de familias que descienden de un antepasado común (pág. 8)

Clayton Antitrust Act/Ley Antimonopolista Clayton Ley aprobada en 1914 para fortalecer la Ley Antimonopolista Sherman de 1890; especificaba las actividades que estaban prohibidas en las grandes empresas (pág. 632)

Clean Air Act/Ley de Protección de la Calidad del Aire Ley aprobada en 1970 con el fin de controlar la contaminación causada por la emisión de gases de las industrias y los automóviles (pág. 1016)

Clean Water Act/Ley de Protección de la Calidad del Agua Ley aprobada en 1972 con el fin de controlar la contaminación causada por la eliminación de aguas de desecho industriales y municipales, y de otorgar concesiones para construir mejores instalaciones para el tratamiento de aguas negras (pág. 1016)

closed shop/obligación de reclutar trabajadores sindicados Lugar de trabajo abierto sólo a miembros del sindicato (pág. 775)

cloture/votación calificada para cerrar el debate En el Senado, el voto de las tres quintas partes para limitar el debate y pedir un voto para un asunto determinado (pág. 951)

coalition/coalición Alianza de grupos con metas similares (pág. 786)

Cold War/Guerra Fría La competencia que se desarrolló después de la Segunda Guerra Mundial entre los Estados Unidos y la Unión Soviética por el poder y la influencia en el mundo; duró hasta la caída de la Unión Soviética en 1991 (pág. 872)

collaboration/colaboración Cooperación cercana (pág. 810)

collective bargaining/acuerdo colectivo Procedimiento en el cual los trabajadores negocian como grupo con los patrones (pág. 479)

collective security/seguridad colectiva El principio de apoyo militar mutuo entre las naciones (pág. 879)

colony/colonia Un área de tierra poblada por inmigrantes que siguen siendo regidos por su país natal (pág. 36)

Columbian Exchange/intercambio colombino El comercio trasatlántico de cosechas, tecnología y cultura entre América y Europa, África y Asia; comenzó en 1492 con el primer viaje de Cristóbal Colón a América (pág. 26)

Common Sense/El sentido común Panfleto escrito por Thomas Paine y publicado en enero de 1776, que hacía un llamado para la independencia estadounidense de Gran Bretaña (pág. 118)

communism/comunismo Ideología oficial de la Unión Soviética, caracterizada por la posesión total de la tierra y las propiedades por parte del gobierno, el control del gobierno a través de un solo partido, la falta de derechos individuales y la exigencia de una revolución mundial (pág. 713)

Compromise of 1850/Acuerdo de 1850 Acuerdo diseñado para disminuir las tensiones de la expansión de la esclavitud en territorios occidentales (pág. 356)

Compromise of 1877/Acuerdo de 1877 Acuerdo en el que los demócratas acordaron otorgar a Rutherford B. Hayes la victoria en la elección presidencial de 1876, y en el que Hayes acordó, a su vez, retirar las tropas federales de los estados del sur (pág. 445)

compulsory/obligatorio Requerido, como en el caso del servicio militar (pág. 606)

concentration camp/campo de concentración Lugar donde se confinan prisioneros políticos, por lo general bajo condiciones muy severas (pág. 842)

concession/concesión La cesión de un pedazo de tierra a cambio de la promesa de utilizarla para un fin específico (pág. 598)

Confederate States of America/Estados Confederados de América Asociación de siete estados del sur formada en 1861 (pág. 371)

conglomerate/conglomerado Corporación formada por tres o más empresas que no se relacionan entre sí (pág. 901)

congregación/congregación Pueblo en el que se establecían los indígenas, obligados por los españoles; allí cultivaban la tierra y tenían prácticas religiosas similares a los de los católicos europeos (pág. 41)

congregation/congregación Integrantes de una iglesia; asamblea religiosa (pág. 245)

Congressional Union (CU)/Unión Congresional (CU) Organización radical formada en 1915 y dirigida por Alice Paul, cuya campaña era en favor de una enmienda constitucional que garantizara el sufragio de las mujeres (pág. 638)

Congress of Racial Equality (CORE)/Congreso para la Igualdad Racial (CORE) Organización fundada por pacifistas en 1942 para promover la igualdad racial por medios pacíficos (págs. 857, 937)

conquistador/conquistador Conquistador español (pág. 38)

conscientious objector/objetor de conciencia Persona que se opone a la guerra por motivos morales o religiosos (pág. 1039)

conservationist/conservacionista Persona que apoya la protección de los recursos naturales (pág. 629)

Constitutional Convention/Convención Constitucional Convención que tuvo lugar en Filadelfia en 1787 para redactar la Constitución de los Estados Unidos (pág. 150)

constitution/constitución Plan gubernamental que describe las diferentes partes del gobierno, sus deberes y poderes (pág. 145)

consumer economy/economía de consumo Economía que depende de una gran cantidad de gastos por parte de los consumidores (pág. 723)

containment/contención Política estadounidense que se opone a una mayor expansión del comunismo en el mundo (pág. 873)

contraband/contrabando Artículos confiscados al enemigo durante el período de guerra (pág. 396)

Contra/contra Término utilizado en español para referirse a un "contrarrevolucionario", o sea, un rebelde que se oponía al gobierno comunista de Nicaragua en la década de 1980 (pág. 1112)

Contract with America/Contrato con América Garantía ofrecida por los candidatos republicanos en la campaña electoral de 1994 de limitar el gobierno, eliminar algunas leyes, reducir impuestos y equilibrar el presupuesto (pág. 1128)

convoy/convoy Grupo de barcos sin armas rodeados por un anillo de buques navales armados (pág. 658)

Copperhead/"cabeza de cobre" Apodo que se les daba durante la Guerra Civil a los demócratas pacifistas del norte (pág. 393)

cotton belt/región algodonera o cinturón algodonero Sobrenombre utilizado en la década de 1850 para denominar la franja de estados que se extendía de Carolina del Sur a Texas, cuyas economías se basaban casi por completo en la producción de algodón (pág. 285)

cotton gin/despepitadora de algodón Máquina para separar las semillas de la fibra de algodón en bruto (pág. 274)

counterculture/contracultura Grupo de jóvenes estadounidenses que en la década de 1960 rechazaban las costumbres convencionales y la cultura tradicional (pág. 1009)

craft union/gremio de artesanos Sindicato formado por trabajadores dedicados a un oficio específico (pág. 479)

Cross of Gold Speech/Discurso de la Cruz de Oro Discurso pronunciado en 1896 por William Jennings Bryan en la Asamblea Demócrata; uno de los discursos más famosos de la historia de los Estados Unidos (pág. 512)

Crusades/Cruzadas Serie de campañas militares dirigidas por cristianos europeos en contra de los turcos, que tuvo lugar de 1096 a 1291 para apoderarse de Jerusalén (pág. 11)

Cuban Missile Crisis/ crisis de los misiles cubanos Crisis que surgió en 1962 entre los Estados Unidos y la Unión Soviética a raíz de un intento soviético por desplegar misiles nucleares en Cuba (pág. 986)

D

Dartmouth College v. Woodward/Dartmouth College vs. Woodward Caso presentado en 1819 en el que la Suprema Corte establecía que los estados no podían interferir en los contratos privados (pág. 291)

Dawes Act/Ley de Dawes Ley promulgada en 1887 que dividió las reservaciones en lotes familiares privados (pág. 496)

daylight savings time/horario de verano Horario en el que se adelantan los relojes una hora durante el verano (pág. 666)

D-Day/Día D Nombre en clave para referirse a la invasión de los aliados a Francia el 6 de junio de 1944 (pág. 838)

death camp/campo de la muerte Campo alemán creado durante la Segunda Guerra Mundial con el único propósito del asesinato en masa (pág. 843)

Declaration of Independence/Declaración de la Independencia Declaración promulgada en 1776 por el Segundo Congreso Continental, que explica por qué las colonias querían independizarse de Gran Bretaña (pág. 119)

de facto **segregation/segregación** *de facto* **o de hecho** Separación causada por condiciones sociales como la pobreza (pág. 957)

deferment/postergación Aplazamiento oficial de un evento, como el servicio militar (pág. 1040)

deficit spending/gastos en exceso de los ingresos Cuando se gasta más dinero del presupuesto federal anual en comparación con los ingresos que recibe el gobierno (págs. 782, 1060)

deflation/deflación Caída de los precios de los productos (pág. 508)

de jure **segregation/segregación** *de jure* **o de ley** Segregación racial creada por ley (pág. 957)

demagogue/demagogo Líder que manipula a las personas con verdades a medias, falsas promesas y tácticas de intimidación (pág. 780)

democracy/democracia Forma de gobierno en que la autoridad reside en el pueblo (pág. 146)

demographics/estadísticas demográficas Estadísticas que describen una población, como los datos sobre la raza o los ingresos (pág. 686)

denomination/grupo religioso Un subgrupo religioso generalmente mayor que una secta (pág. 246)

department store/tienda por departamentos Establecimiento grande que vende al menudeo, ofrece una amplia variedad de productos y vende en grandes cantidades (pág. 570)

depression/depresión Una baja severa en la economía marcada por la disminución en la actividad empresarial, el desempleo general y la caída de precios y salarios (pág. 228)

deregulation/desregulación La reducción o revocación del control del gobierno (pág. 1085)

détente/distensión Moderación de las tensiones políticas entre las naciones (pág. 1065)

deterrence/disuasión Política de fortalecer el poder militar de los Estados Unidos y de sus aliados a tal grado que el enemigo desista por temor a las represalias (pág. 892)

direct primary/elección primaria directa Elección en la que todos los ciudadanos votan para elegir a los candidatos para las próximas elecciones (pág. 624)

disarmament/desarme Programa en el que las naciones del mundo entregan voluntariamente sus armas (pág. 718)

discrimination/discriminación Trato desigual a un grupo de personas debido a su nacionalidad, raza, sexo o religión (pág. 333)

dissent/disentimiento Diferencia de opiniones o creencias (pág. 93)

dissident/disidente Persona que critica las acciones del gobierno (pág. 1087)

diversity/diversidad Variedad (pág. 59)

division of labor/distribución del trabajo Forma de producción en la que diferentes personas realizan diferentes tareas (pág. 475)

dollar diplomacy/diplomacia del dólar Política establecida por el presidente Taft que consiste en estimular la inversión estadounidense en economías extranjeras (pág. 602)

domestic affairs/asuntos nacionales Aspectos relacionados con los asuntos internos de un país (pág. 166)

domino theory/teoría del dominó Creencia de que si un país cae en manos del comunismo, los países vecinos también lo hacen (pág. 1024)

dove/paloma Sobrenombre para una persona que se opone a la guerra, como en el caso de quienes se oponían a la Guerra de Vietnam (pág. 1028)

Dow Jones Industrial Average/promedio industrial Dow Jones Medida promedio de los precios de las acciones de las principales industrias (pág. 740)

downsizing/reducción de personal Despido de empleados para reducir costos (pág. 1119)

draft/reclutamiento Servicio militar obligatorio (pág. 391)

Dred Scott **v.** *Sandford/Dred Scott* **vs.** *Sandford* Decisión tomada por la Suprema Corte en 1857 que establecía que los esclavos no eran ciudadanos; que el hecho de vivir en un estado o territorio libre, aun durante muchos años, no liberaba a los esclavos; declaraba inconstitucional la Concesión de Missouri (pág. 365)

dry farming/cultivo seco Técnicas utilizadas para cultivar productos en áreas con poca lluvia; técnicas de conservación del agua (pág. 504)

dumbbell tenement/*dumbbell tenement* Construcción formada por dos edificios cuya separación es muy angosta, lo que produce corrientes de aire en cada lado y permite que entre luz y aire en las habitaciones (pág. 537)

Dust Bowl/tazón de polvo, el Término que describía las grandes praderas del centro y del sur de los Estados Unidos en la década de 1930, cuando la región sufrió un período de sequía y tolvaneras (pág. 746)

duty/arancel Impuesto sobre las importaciones (pág. 72)

E

economic sanctions/sanciones económicas Restricciones comerciales y otras medidas económicas planeadas para castigar a otra nación (pág. 1136)

economies of scale/economías de escala Fenómeno en que a medida que aumenta la producción, el costo de cada artículo producido generalmente disminuye (pág. 471)

electoral college/colegio electoral Grupo de electores, seleccionados por los votantes, que votan para elegir al Presidente (pág. 156)

emancipation/emancipación Liberación de esclavos (pág. 319)

Emancipation Proclamation/Proclamación de la Emancipación Decreto presidencial del presidente Lincoln que empezó a regir el 1 de enero de 1863, en el que se liberaba a los esclavos del territorio que estaba bajo el poder de los confederados (pág. 395)

embargo/embargo Prohibición o restricción en el comercio (págs. 218, 1060)

encomienda **system/sistema de encomiendas** Sistema en el que los indígenas debían trabajar en ranchos, minas o granjas en beneficio de un español, a cambio de su bienestar (pág. 39)

Enforcement Act of 1870/Ley Contra la Coacción de 1870 Ley aprobada por el Congreso en la que se prohíbe el uso del terror, la fuerza o el soborno para impedir que las personas voten debido a su raza (pág. 443)

Enlightenment/Ilustración, la Movimiento del siglo XVIII que enfatizaba la necesidad de la ciencia y la razón para mejorar la sociedad (pág. 119)

entitlement/programa de ayuda social Programa gubernamental que garantiza un pago a un grupo social determinado, por ejemplo, a las personas de la tercera edad (pág. 1113)

Environmental Protection Agency (EPA)/Agencia para la Protección Ambiental (EPA) Organización gubernamental formada en 1970 para establecer y hacer cumplir los estándares nacionales de control de contaminantes (pág. 1016)

Equal Rights Amendment/Enmienda para la Igualdad de Derechos Enmienda constitucional propuesta, que nunca se ratificó, en la que se prohíbe la discriminación de las personas a causa de su sexo (pág. 1000)

escalation/escalamiento Expansión por etapas, por ejemplo, de un conflicto local a uno nacional (pág. 1033)

evangelical/evangélico Que se centra en la predicación emocionalmente poderosa, en lugar de las ceremonias formales, así como en las enseñanzas de la Biblia (pág. 245)

executive branch/rama ejecutiva Rama del gobierno, encabezada por el Presidente, que hace cumplir las leyes (pág. 145)

Exoduster/*exoduster* Estadounidense de raza negra que emigró al Oeste después de la Guerra Civil (pág. 490)

F

facism/fascismo Filosofía política que enfatiza la importancia de una nación o grupo étnico, así como la autoridad suprema del líder sobre la del individuo (pág. 800)

faction/facción Grupo organizado en torno a un interés común y preocupado únicamente en apoyar ese interés (pág. 159)

Federalists/federalistas Partidarios de la Constitución durante el debate sobre su ratificación; en favor de un gobierno nacional sólido (pág. 158)

Federal Reserve System/sistema de la reserva federal El sistema bancario central de la nación, establecido en 1913 (pág. 632)

federal system of government/sistema federal de gobierno Sistema en el que las autoridades nacionales y estatales comparten el poder (pág. 154)

Federal Trade Commission (FTC)/Comisión Federal de Comercio (FTC) Comisión establecida en 1914 por el presidente Wilson y el Congreso para hacer cumplir el Ley Clayton y establecer leyes para un comercio recíproco (pág. 632)

feminism/feminismo Teoría que apoya la igualdad política, económica y social entre hombres y mujeres (pág. 996)

feudalism/feudalismo Sistema político y económico de la Europa medieval, en el que los señores feudales recibían tierras de los nobles poderosos a cambio de su servicio (pág. 11)

Fifteenth Amendment/Decimoquinta enmienda Enmienda constitucional, ratificada en 1870, que garantiza a todos los ciudadanos el derecho al voto (pág. 434)

filibuster/obstruccionismo Táctica en la que los senadores obstruyen un voto al tomar la palabra y prolongar excesivamente su discurso (pág. 951)

First Battle of Bull Run/Primera Batalla de Bull Run Primera batalla de la Guerra Civil, en la que triunfaron los Confederados en julio de 1861 (pág. 382)

First Continental Congress/Primer Congreso Continental Asamblea de representantes de las colonias que se reunieron por primera vez en Filadelfia en septiembre de 1774 (pág. 115)

flapper/*flapper* Término utilizado en la década de 1920 para describir a un nuevo tipo de jovencita; rebelde, llena de energía, amante de las diversiones y atrevida (pág. 684)

Fort Sumter/Fuerte Sumter Fuerte federal ubicado en el puerto de Charleston, Carolina del Sur; el ataque de los Confederados al fuerte marcó el inicio de la Guerra Civil (pág. 372)

Fourteen Points/Propuesta de los Catorce Puntos Propuesta del presidente Wilson en 1918 para lograr la paz europea durante la posguerra (pág. 669)

Fourteenth Amendment/Decimocuarta enmienda Enmienda constitucional, ratificada en 1868, para garantizar a los ciudadanos igualdad en la protección otorgada por la ley (pág. 431)

fragmentation bomb/bomba de fragmentación Un tipo de bomba que al explotar lanza en todas direcciones los fragmentos de su gruesa cubierta metálica (pág. 1033)

franchise/franquicia Empresa que firma un contrato con una compañía más grande para ofrecer algunos bienes y servicios (pág. 901)

Freedmen's Bureau/Agencia de libertos Primera organización principal de auxilio federal de los Estados Unidos, creada por el Congreso en 1865 (pág. 429)

Freedom Ride/Paseo de la Libertad Evento organizado en 1961 por el CORE y el SNCC, en el que un grupo interracial de activistas de los derechos civiles puso a prueba el acatamiento de los estados del sur a la prohibición de la segregación racial en autobuses interestatales, dictada por la Corte Suprema (pág. 942)

free enterprise system/sistema de libre empresa Sistema económico caracterizado por la propiedad privada o empresarial de los elementos utilizados en la producción (pág. 278)

free silver/acuñación libre de plata Acuñación ilimitada de dólares de plata (pág. 509)

free soiler/*free soiler* Persona dedicada a impedir la expansión de la esclavitud en los territorios occidentales (pág. 363)

French and Indian War/Guerra francesa e indígena Guerra que tuvo lugar de 1754 a 1763 entre Francia, las naciones indígenas aliadas, y Gran Bretaña y sus colonizadores, por el control del este de Norteamérica (pág. 104)

Fugitive Slave Act/Ley del Esclavo Fugitivo Esta ley, parte del Acuerdo de 1850, ordenaba a todos los ciudadanos de los Estados Unidos a tomar parte en la devolución de esclavos (pág. 357)

fundamentalism/fundamentalismo Conjunto de creencias religiosas, entre ellas, las ideas cristianas tradicionales sobre Jesucristo, la creencia de que la Biblia fue inspirada por Dios y carece de contradicciones o errores y es literalmente verdadera (pág. 702)

G

Gadsden Purchase/la compra de Gadsden Compra de Estados Unidos a Mexico de territorios del sudoeste realizada en 1853 (pág. 353)

gag rule/ley de la mordaza Ley aprobada por la Cámara de Representantes en 1836 que prohibía la lectura o la realización de peticiones antiesclavistas (pág. 325)

generation gap/brecha generacional Término que describe la gran diferencia entre los valores de una generación más joven y la de sus padres (pág. 1038)

Geneva Accords/Acuerdos de Ginebra Conferencia internacional que tuvo lugar en 1954 y en la que se dividió a Vietnam en dos naciones (pág. 1025)

Geneva Convention/Convención de Ginebra Conjunto de normas de conducta internacionales para el trato de los prisioneros de guerra, establecidas en 1929 (pág. 847)

genocide/genocidio Matanza organizada de un pueblo entero (pág. 663)

Gentlemen's Agreement/Pacto de los caballeros Acuerdo firmado en 1907 entre los Estados Unidos y Japón para resstringir la inmigración japonesa (pág. 532)

gentry/alta burguesía Hombres y mujeres de la época colonial de los Estados Unidos, que eran lo sufientemente acaudalados para contratar a gente a su servicio (pág. 78)

Gettysburg Address/Discurso de Gettysburg Un discurso famoso que dio el presidente Lincoln en noviembre de 1863 sobre el significado de la Guerra Civil, durante la dedicatoria de un cementerio nacional en la zona donde se libró la Batalla de Gettysburg (pág. 409)

ghetto/*ghetto* Área en la que domina un grupo étnico o racial (pág. 530)

Ghost Dance/Danza de los espíritus Un ritual de purificación realizado por los indígenas estadounidenses (pág. 495)

ghost town/pueblo fantasma Pueblo abandonado debido a la falta de actividad económica (pág. 256)

Gibbons* v. *Ogden*/*Gibbons* vs. *Ogden Caso presentado en 1824 en el que la Suprema Corte establecía que los estados no podían regular el comercio sobre canales navegables interestatales (pág. 292)

GI Bill of Rights/Declaración de los Derechos de los Soldados de Infantería Ley aprobada en 1944 que ayudaba a los veteranos que regresaban a adquirir una casa y costear su educación superior (pág. 904)

Gilded Age/Edad Dorada Término acuñado por Mark Twain para describir la era posterior a la reconstrucción (pág. 520)

GI/soldado de infantería Término utilizado para describir a los soldados estadounidenses en la Segunda Guerra Mundial, se deriva del término "Asunto gubernamental" (pág. 827)

graft/corrupción Utilizar el empleo para obtener una ganancia; una de las principales fuentes de ingreso para los aparatos políticos (pág. 539)

grandfather clause/cláusula del abuelo Pasaje que exime a un grupo de personas de obedecer una ley si reunen ciertas condiciones antes de la aprobación de la misma (pág. 565)

Grange, the/ Granja, la Organización establecida en 1867 y también conocida como los Mecenas de la Agricultura; ayudaba a los granjeros a formar cooperativas y presionaba a los legisladores del estado para que regularan las empresas de las que dependían estos campesinos (pág. 510)

Great Awakening/Gran Despertar, el Renacimiento religioso de las colonias norteamericanas durante la década de 1730 y 1740 (pág. 92)

Great Compromise/Gran Acuerdo, el Acuerdo celebrado en la Convención Constitucional que exigía una legislatura con dos cámaras, una elegida con base en la población y la otra que representara cada estado de manera equitativa (pág. 153)

Great Crash/Gran Crash, el El derrumbe de la bolsa de valores estadounidense que tuvo lugar en 1929 (pág. 741)

Great Depression/Gran Depresión, la La baja económica más severa en la historia de la nación; duró de 1929 a 1941 (pág. 743)

Greater East Asia Co-Prosperity Sphere/esfera de prosperidad de Asia Oriental Proclamada en 1940 por el ministro de Japón; área que se extendía de Manchuria a las Indias Orientales Holandesas en las que Japón extendería su influencia (pág. 816)

Great Migration/Gran Migración, la Migración de colonizadores ingleses hacia la colonia de la bahía de Massachusetts a principios de la década de 1630 (pág. 52)

Great Plains/Grandes Llanuras, las Llanura de gran tamaño entre el río Mississippi y las montañas Rocosas (págs. 258, 491)

Great Society/Gran Sociedad, la Propuestas del presidente Lyndon Johnson para el apoyo a la educación, el derecho al voto, los proyectos de conservación y embellecimiento, la atención médica para las personas de la tercera edad y la eliminación de la pobreza (pág. 976)

Great White Fleet/Gran Flota Blanca, la Un grupo de barcos de la Marina de los Estados Unidos que realizó una excursión por todo el mundo en 1907 (pág. 607)

greenback/papel moneda Nombre que se le da al dinero en forma de billetes creado en 1862 (pág. 393)

Gross National Product (GNP)/Producto Nacional Bruto (GNP) Valor anual total de los bienes y servicios que produce un país (pág. 725)

guerrilla/guerrillero Soldado que utiliza ataques sorpresivos y tácticas que consisten en atacar y huir (pág. 416)

Gulf of Tonkin Resolution/Acuerdo del golfo de Tonkín Resolución del Congreso autorizada en 1964 por el presidente Johnson para emprender una acción militar en Vietnam (pág. 1028)

H

Harlem Renaissance/Renacimiento de Harlem Despertar literario estadounidense de raza negra durante la década de 1920, centrado en Harlem (pág. 696)

haven/refugio Lugar seguro (pág. 62)

hawk/halcón Sobrenombre para un partidario de la guerra, como en el caso de los partidarios de la Guerra de Vietnam (pág. 1034)

Hawley-Smoot tariff/tarifa Hawley-Smoot El impuesto de importación más alto de la historia, aprobado por el Congreso en 1930 (pág. 757)

Haymarket Riot/disturbios de Haymarket Trifulca laboral violenta que ocurrió en Chicago en 1886 (pág. 482)

Head Start/*Head Start* Un programa preescolar para niños de familias de escasos recursos que también proporciona servicios sociales, de salud y de nutrición (pág. 978)

Helsinki Accords/Acuerdos de Helsinki Serie de acuerdos sobre la seguridad europea firmados en 1975 (pág. 1082)

hidalgo/hidalgo Noble español (pág. 37)

Ho Chi Minh Trail/Sendero de Ho Chi Minh Ruta de abastecimiento que transportaba tropas y provisiones de Vietnam del Norte a Vietnam del Sur (pág. 1034)

holding company/compañía tenedora Empresa que compra acciones y títulos de compañías más pequeñas (pág. 626)

Hollywood Ten/el grupo de los diez de Hollywood Grupo de personas de la industria del cine que fueron encarceladas por negarse a responder preguntas del Congreso relacionadas con la influencia comunista en Hollywood (pág. 882)

Holocaust/Holocausto Intento sistemático de la Alemania Nazi de asesinar a todos los judíos europeos (pág. 841)

home rule/autonomía Sistema que le da a las ciudades un grado limitado de gobierno autónomo (pág. 622)

Homestead Act/Ley de Posesión de Tierras Ley promulgada en 1862 que otorgaba 160 acres de tierra a los ciudadanos que reunían ciertas condiciones (pág. 489)

homesteader/colono Persona que tramitaba los títulos bajo la ley de posesión de tierras (pág. 502)

Homestead Strike/Huelga por la Posesión de Tierras Huelga que tuvo lugar en 1892 en Pennsylvania en contra de Carnegie Steel (pág. 482)

Hooverville/*Hooverville* Término que describía un albergue temporal para personas sin hogar durante los primeros años de la Gran Depresión (pág. 746)

horizontal consolidation/integración horizontal El proceso de reunir muchas compañías dentro de la misma empresa para formar una compañía más grande (pág. 471)

House of Burgesses/Cámara de los Burgueses, la Cuerpo legislativo de Virginia formado en 1619 (pág. 46)

House Un-American Activities Committee (HUAC)/ Comité del Congreso para la Investigación de Actividades Antiestadounidenses (HUAC) Establecido en 1938 para investigar acciones desleales en los Estados Unidos (pág. 882)

hundred days/Cien Días, los Período inicial de la presidencia de Franklin Roosevelt, en 1933, cuando el Congreso aprobó muchos programas del Nuevo Trato (pág. 769)

I

ICBM/ICBM Misil balístico intercontinental (pág. 893)

immigrant/inmigrante Persona que ingresa a un nuevo país para establecerse (pág. 89)

Immigration Act of 1965/Ley de Inmigración de 1965 Ley que eliminó el número fijo de inmigrantes que se podían admitir en los Estados Unidos, provenientes de diferentes países, y los reemplazó con límites más flexibles (pág. 979)

impeach/incapacitación (presidencial) Someter a un funcionario público (generalmente el presidente) a un proceso de incapacitación por un mal desempeño de sus funciones (págs. 433, 1075)

imperialism/imperialismo Política practicada por una nación más fuerte en un intento de crear un imperio mediante el dominio económico, político, cultural o militar de las naciones más débiles (pág. 584)

impressment/leva Política que obliga a la población a ingresar al servicio militar o al servicio público (pág. 224)

inauguration/toma de posesión Ceremonia oficial en la que un funcionario pronuncia un juramento (pág. 165)

incumbent/titular Funcionario público actual (pág. 1083)

indentured servant/siervo obligado por contrato Alguien que trabaja para otra persona por contrato durante un período de tiempo específico, por lo general siete años, a cambio de transporte, alimento y un lugar donde vivir (pág. 47)

Indian Removal Act/Ley de transferencia indígena Ley promulgada en 1830 que demandaba al Presidente otorgar a los indígenas estadounidenses tierras en parte del territorio adquirido en la compra de Luisiana a cambio del territorio que se les había quitado en el Este (pág. 301)

indigo/índigo Tipo de planta que se utiliza para hacer un tinte azul con el que se tiñe tela (pág. 81)

industrialization/industrialización Crecimiento de la industria (pág. 281)

Industrial Revolution/Revolución Industrial Esfuerzo que se inició en Gran Bretaña a finales de la década de 1700 para aumentar la producción utilizando máquinas que funcionaban por medios distintos a la fuerza humana o animal (pág. 272)

industrial union/sindicato industrial Sindicato que organiza a los trabajadores de todos los oficios en una industria determinada (pág. 481)

inflation/inflación Aumento continuo en los precios con el paso del tiempo que reduce la capacidad de compra (pág. 134)

infrastructure/infraestructura La propiedad pública y los servicios que utiliza una sociedad (pág. 439)

INF Treaty (Intermediate-Range Nuclear Forces)/ Tratado INF (Fuerzas Nucleares de Alcance Medio) Acuerdo firmado en 1987 por Ronald Reagan y Mikhail Gorbachev que tenía como objetivo la destrucción de aproximadamente 2,500 misiles soviéticos y estadounidenses en Europa (pág. 1113)

initiative/iniciativa Procedimiento por el cual los ciudadanos pueden someter un ley directamente a votaciòn por elevar una petición pública (pág. 624)

injunction/interdicción Orden judicial que prohíbe la realización de una actividad determinada (pág. 617)

installment plan/pago a plazos Plan de pago a plazos que permite a los clientes realizar pagos en intervalos establecidos durante un período de tiempo hasta cubrir la deuda total (pág. 724)

integration/integración Proceso que reúne a personas de diferentes razas (pág. 934)

interchangeable parts/sistema de partes intercambiables Un sistema de fabricación en el que todas las partes están hechas de acuerdo con un patrón para facilitar el montaje en masa. (pág. 274)

interest/interés Cantidad extra de dinero que tienen que pagar los deudores a los acreedores (pág. 201)

interned/confinado Encerrado (pág. 858)

Internet/Internet Red de computadoras que une a millones de personas alrededor del mundo (pág. 1147)

interracial/interracial Que comprende personas de diferentes razas o su participación (pág. 937)

Interstate Commerce Act/Ley de Comercio Interestatal Ley aprobada en 1887 para regular la empresa ferroviaria y otras empresas interestatales (pág. 511)

investment capital/capital de inversión Dinero que una empresa invierte para obtener futuras ganancias (pág. 278)

Iran-Contra affair/caso Irán-contras Escándalo durante la administración de Reagan por el uso de dinero obtenido de la venta secreta de armas iraníes para apoyar a los contras nicaragüenses (pág. 1112)

Irish Potato Famine/hambruna irlandesa, la Hambruna en Irlanda en la década de 1840, que trajo consigo una oleada de inmigración a los Estados Unidos (pág. 332)

iron curtain/cortina de hierro Término acuñado por Winston Churchill para describir la división entre la vida comunista y la no comunista (pág. 872)

island-hopping/estrategia de isla a isla Estrategia militar utilizada durante la Segunda Guerra Mundial que consistía en atacar selectivamente ciertas islas bajo el dominio del enemigo y pasar por alto las demás (pág. 850)

isolationism/aislacionismo Política que consiste en evitar alianzas políticas o económicas con otros países (pág. 718)

isthmus/istmo Franja estrecha de tierra que une dos áreas de tierra más grandes (pág. 37)

itinerant/errante Que viaja de un lugar a otro o en un área determinada (pág. 92)

J

Japanese American Citizens League (JACL)/Asociación de Ciudadanos Estadounidenses de Origen Japonés (JACL) Organización de estadounidenses de origen japonés que trabajan para promover los derechos de los estadounidenses de origen asiático (pág. 1006)

Jay's Treaty/Tratado de Jay Tratado firmado en 1794 entre los Estados Unidos y Gran Bretaña en el que Gran Bretaña buscaba mejorar las relaciones comerciales y acordó retirarse de los fuertes ubicados en el territorio noroeste (pág. 204)

Jazz Age/Época del *jazz* Término para describir la década de 1920 (pág. 694)

Jim Crow/Jim Crow Estatutos que, a principios de la década de 1890, exigían la segregación racial en la prestación de los servicios públicos (pág. 565)

jingoism/jingoísmo Sentimiento de orgullo nacional arraigado y deseo de tener una política exterior agresiva (pág. 591)

joint-stock company/sociedad de capitales Compañía fundada y manejada por un grupo de inversionistas que comparten las ganancias y las pérdidas de la compañía (pág. 44)

judicial branch/rama judicial Rama del gobierno, formada por tribunales y jueces, que interpreta y aplica las leyes (pág. 145)

judicial review/revisión judicial Poder de las cortes federales para revisar las leyes estatales y las decisiones de la corte federal con el fin de determinar si son constitucionales (pág. 214)

K

kamikaze/kamikaze Avión suicida japonés en la Segunda Guerra Mundial (pág. 850)

Kansas-Nebraska Act/Ley Kansas-Nebraska Ley promulgada en 1854 que exigía la creación de estos dos territorios nuevos y les pedía a los ciudadanos que decidieran sobre la esclavitud en su territorio (pág. 360)

Kellogg-Briand Pact/Pacto Kellogg-Briand Acuerdo firmado en 1928 en el que las naciones acordaron no representar una amenaza de guerra entre ellas (pág. 721)

King Philip's War/Guerra del Rey Felipe Guerra que comenzó en 1675 entre los colonizadores ingleses y los indígenas norteamericanos (pág. 57)

kinship/parentesco Relación entre los miembros de una familia (pág. 8)

Korean War/Guerra Coreana Conflicto sobre el futuro de la península coreana, luchado entre 1950 y 1953, que llegó a punto muerto (pág. 886)

Kristallnacht/Kristallnacht Nombre que se le da a la noche violenta del 9 de noviembre de 1938 en Alemania y Austria, cuando milicianos nazis saquearon y atacaron hogares, negocios y sinagogas judías, además de arrestar a miles de judíos (pág. 842)

L

labor union/sindicato laboral Organización de trabajadores formada para proteger los intereses de sus miembros (pág. 283)

laissez-faire/laissez-faire Doctrina que establece que, por lo general, el gobierno no debe interferir en las empresas privadas (pág. 521)

land mine/mina terrestre Dispositivo explosivo enterrado en el suelo (pág. 1032)

land speculator/especulador de tierras Persona que compra grandes áreas de tierra con la esperanza de venderlas después para obtener una ganancia (pág. 489)

Latino/latino Persona cuyo origen familiar está en la América Latina hispanohablante (pág. 1003)

League of Nations/Liga de las Naciones Organización internacional formada después de la Primera Guerra Mundial, cuyo objetivo es asegurar la seguridad y la paz de todos sus miembros (pág. 670)

legislative branch/rama legislativa Rama de gobierno que dicta las leyes; Congreso (pág. 145)

legislature/cuerpo legislativo Asamblea que dicta las leyes (pág. 46)

Lend-Lease Act/Ley de Préstamos y Arriendos Ley promulgada en 1941 que autorizó al Presidente a apoyar a cualquier nación cuya defensa considerara vital para la seguridad de los Estados Unidos (pág. 819)

Lewis and Clark expedition/expedición de Lewis y Clark Viaje realizado por Meriwether Lewis y William Clark por el territorio de Luisiana de 1804 a 1806 (pág. 216)

Liberty Bond/Garantía de libertad Garantía especial de guerra concedida por el gobierno para apoyar la causa de los aliados durante la Primera Guerra Mundial (pág. 664)

Liberty ship/buque "Liberty" Un tipo de barco mercante, grande y fuerte, construido en la Segunda Guerra Mundial (pág. 828)

Limited Test Ban Treaty/Tratado de Prohibición Limitada de Pruebas Nucleares Tratado firmado en 1963, en el que los Estados Unidos y la Unión Soviética acordaron abstenerse de realizar pruebas con armas nucleares en tierra (pág. 989)

Lincoln-Douglas Debates/Debates entre Lincoln y Douglas Serie de siete debates entre Abraham Lincoln y Stephen A. Douglas sobre el tema de la esclavitud en los territorios del país (pág. 366)

lineage/linaje Grupos de parentesco que delimitan su origen por un antepasado común (pág. 18)

literacy/alfabetismo La capacidad de una persona de leer y escribir (pág. 553)

long drive/paseo largo Desplazamiento del ganado de praderas distantes a centros ferroviarios activos que lo transportaban para venderlo (pág. 501)

loose construction/interpretación libre Creencia de que el gobierno puede hacer todo lo que la Constitución no prohíbe (pág. 202)

Lost Generation/Generación Perdida, la Grupo de escritores de la década de 1920 que compartían la idea de que estaban perdidos en un mundo codicioso, materialista y sin valores morales; a menudo decidían huir a Europa (pág. 696)

Louisiana Purchase/Compra de Luisiana Compra del territorio de Louisiana que los Estados Unidos le hicieron a Francia en 1803 (pág. 215)

Lower South/Bajo Sur, el Estados de Texas, Luisiana, Mississippi, Alabama, Florida, Georgia y Carolina del Sur (pág. 370)

Loyalist/colono leal Persona que era leal a Gran Bretaña durante la Revolución (pág. 128)

lynching/linchamiento Asesinato de un acusado, efectuado por una multitud sin que se realice un juicio legal (pág. 566)

M

Magna Carta/Carta Magna Una "gran carta" firmada por el rey Juan en 1215 que concedía algunos derechos a los nobles ingleses y que se convirtió en la base para futuros ideales de libertad y justicia en los Estados Unidos (pág. 12)

mail-order catalog/catálogo de ventas por correo Material impreso que muestra una gran variedad de productos que se pueden ser adquirir por correo (pág. 571)

Manchurian Incident/incidente de Manchuria En 1931, las tropas japonesas, que alegaban que los soldados chinos habían tratado de hacer explotar una vía férrea, se hicieron cargo del problema al tomar varias ciudades de Manchuria del sur para después apoderarse del país, incluso después de que las tropas chinas se habían retirado (pág. 814)

mandate/delegación Declaración pública de apoyo que los votantes expresan a un candidato (pág. 969)

Manhattan Project/Proyecto Manhattan Programa estadounidense secreto durante la Segunda Guerra Mundial para desarrollar una bomba atómica (pág. 852)

manifest destiny/destino manifiesto Argumento que establece que los Estados Unidos estaban destinados a expandirse a lo largo de América del Norte (págs. 253, 351)

manufacturing/manufactura La fabricación de productos mediante maquinaria (pág. 276)

Marbury* v. *Madison/Marbury* vs. *Madison Caso de la Suprema Corte presentado en 1803 que establecía el principio de la revisión judicial (pág. 214)

March on Washington/Marcha en Washington Manifestación por los derechos civiles realizada en 1963 en Washington, D.C., en la cual los inconformes exigían empleos y libertad (pág. 949)

Market Revolution/revolución del mercado Cambio de una economía basada en el hogar y por lo general agrícola a una economía basada en el dinero, y en la compra y venta de productos (pág. 276)

Marshall Plan/Plan Marshall Programa de apoyo económico estadounidense a Europa Occidental, anunciado en 1947 (pág. 877)

martial law/ley marcial Ley de emergencia dictada por autoridades militares, durante la cual se suspenden algunas garantías de la Declaración de Derechos (pág. 394)

Massacre at Wounded Knee/masacre en Wounded Knee Tiroteo realizado en 1890 por tropas militares contra un grupo de indígenas Sioux desarmados (pág. 495)

mass media/medios masivos de comunicación Métodos, impresos y transmitidos para difundir información a un gran número de personas (pág. 692)

mass production/producción en masa Fabricación de productos en grandes cantidades (pág. 464)

Mayflower Compact/Acuerdo Mayflower Convenio en el que los colonos de Plymouth acordaron acatar las leyes de su gobierno (pág. 51)

McCarran-Walter Act/Ley McCarran-Walter Ley aprobada por el Congreso en 1952 que reafirmó el sistema de cupos que había sido establecido para cada país en 1924 (pág. 883)

McCarthyism/macartismo Término para describir las tácticas de difamación anticomunista del senador Joseph McCarthy (pág. 889)

McCulloch* v. *Maryland/McCulloch* vs. *Maryland Caso presentado en 1819 en el que la Suprema Corte estableció que el Congreso tenía la autoridad de emprender las acciones necesarias para cumplir sus deberes constitucionales (pág. 291)

Medicaid/*Medicaid* Programa federal que proporciona seguro médico a muy bajo costo a estadounidenses de escasos recursos y de cualquier edad (pág. 978)

Medicare/*Medicare* Programa federal que proporciona atención hospitalaria y seguro médico a muy bajo costo a la mayoría de los estadounidenses de 65 años en adelante (pág. 978)

mercantilism/mercantilismo Teoría económica que sostiene que un país debe tratar de adquirir y conservar el mayor número posible de lingotes de oro y plata mediante el aumento de exportaciones en comparación con las importaciones (pág. 71)

mercenary/mercenario Soldado extranjero que pelea por dinero (pág. 129)

mestizo/mestizo Descendiente de españoles e indígenas (pág. 39)

Mexican War/Guerra entre México y los Estados Unidos Conflicto entre los Estados Unidos y México que ocurrió de 1846 a 1848 y que terminó con la victoria de los Estados Unidos (pág. 352)

MIA/desaparecido en combate Perdido en el campo de acción (pág. 1048)

Middle Ages/Edad Media Período en la historia europea que tuvo lugar aproximadamente de los años 500 a 1300 d.C. (pág. 10)

Middle America/estadounidense promedio Término utilizado a veces para describir la persona estadounidense típica de clase media (pág. 1043)

middle class/clase media Una clase nueva de mercaderes, comerciantes y artesanos que surgió a finales de la Edad Media; en nuestros días, la clase social ubicada entre la clase muy acaudalada y la clase obrera (pág. 12)

Middle Colonies/colonias medias Colonias inglesas de Nueva York, Nueva Jersey, Pennsylvania y Delaware (pág. 59)

Middle Passage/el cruce del Atlántico Una parte del comercio triangular; término que también se refiere al transporte forzado de esclavos de África a América (pág. 84)

midnight judge/juez de medianoche Nombramientos judiciales de última hora de jueces con ideas federalistas realizados por el presidente Adams, justo antes de que Thomas Jefferson asumiera el poder (pág. 214)

migrant farm worker/campesino migratorio Persona que trabaja muchas horas a cambio de un salario muy bajo y que va de una granja a otra, generalmente de un estado a otro, para trabajar en las plantaciones (pág. 1004)

migration/migración Desplazamiento de personas con el fin de establecerse en otro lugar (págs. 4, 90)

militarism/militarismo Política que consiste en la acumulación agresiva de las fuerzas militares de una nación como preparativo para una guerra, así como en otorgar a los militares más autoridad sobre el gobierno y las políticas extranjeras (pág. 647)

military-industrial complex/complejo militar-industrial El establecimiento militar de 1960 en el que se desarrollaron vínculos con las comunidades empresariales y científicas, y se emplearon 3.5 millones de estadounidenses (pág. 888)

militia/milicia Civiles armados que sirven como soldados durante una emergencia (pág. 105)

Miranda rule/regla Miranda Regla que establece que la policía debe informar a las personas acusadas de un crimen sobre sus derechos constitucionales (pág. 980)

mission/misión Sede desde la cual personas de otro país tratan de difundir su religión (pág. 40)

Missouri Compromise/Concesión de Missouri Acuerdo firmado en 1820 que demanda el reconocimiento de Missouri como un estado esclavista y de Maine como un estado libre, así como la prohibición de la esclavitud en futuros estados que se crearían al norte de la latitud de 36° 30'N (pág. 229)

mobile society/sociedad móvil Sociedad en la que sus miembros se trasladan constantemente (pág. 243)

mobilization/movilización El alistamiento de las tropas para una guerra (pág. 648)

Modern Republicanism/republicanismo moderno Propuesta del presidente Eisenhower al gobierno, descrita como "conservadora cuando se trata de dinero y liberal cuando se trata de seres humanos" (pág. 917)

monarch/monarca Quien gobierna un territorio, estado o reino (pág. 12)

monetary policy /política monetaria Plan del gobierno federal de la composición y la cantidad del suministro nacional de dinero (pág. 508)

money supply/masa monetaria La cantidad de dinero con la que cuenta la economía nacional (pág. 508)

monopoly/monopolio Control total de un producto o servicio (pág. 470)

Monroe Doctrine/Doctrina Monroe Declaración realizada en 1823 por el presidente Monroe que establecía que los Estados Unidos se opondrían a los esfuerzos de cualquier potencia externa por controlar una nación en el hemisferio occidental (pág. 292)

Montgomery bus boycott/boicot a los autobuses Montgomery Protesta realizada por estadounidenses de raza negra de 1955 a 1956 en contra de la segregación racial en el sistema de transporte de Montgomery, Alabama (pág. 933)

Morrill Land-Grant Act/Ley Morill para la Concesión de Tierras Ley aprobada por el Congreso en 1862 que distribuía millones de acres de tierras del occidente del país a los gobiernos estatales para financiar corporaciones agrícolas estatales (pág. 489)

mountain man/montañés Comerciante estadounidense de pieles que exploraba las montañas Rocosas y las regiones del oeste a principios del siglo XIX (pág. 253)

muckraker/descubridor de escándalos Periodista que descubre actos ilícitos en la política o en las empresas (pág. 616)

multiculturalism/multiculturalismo Movimiento que demanda mayor atención a las culturas no europeas en áreas como la educación (pág. 1146)

multinational corporation/corporación multinacional Corporación que opera en más de un país (pág. 1142)

municipal/municipal Que pertenece a una ciudad, por ejemplo, el gobierno municipal (pág. 622)

Munn **v.** *Illinois/Munn* **vs.** *Illinois* Decisión de la Suprema Corte tomada en 1877 que permitía a los estados regular algunas empresas dentro sus límites fronterizos (pág. 524)

mutiny/motín Rebelión contra una autoridad superior (pág. 84)

N

napalm/*napalm* Substancia química altamente inflamable lanzada por aviones estadounidenses en bombardeos durante la Guerra de Vietnam (pág. 1033)

National Aeronautics and Space Administration (NASA)/ Administración Nacional de la Aeronáutica y el Espacio (NASA) Creada en 1958 por el gobierno de los Estados Unidos como una agencia independiente para la exploración del espacio (pág. 918)

National American Woman Suffrage Association (NAWSA)/Asociación Estadounidense para el Sufragio de la Mujer (NAWSA) Organización formada en 1890 para continuar la obtención de los derechos de las mujeres, especialmente el de votar (pág. 637)

National Association for the Advancement of Colored People (NAACP)/Asociación Nacional para el Progreso de las Personas de Color (NAACP) Organización fundada en 1909 para abolir la segregación y discriminación, luchar contra el racismo y lograr que los estadounidenses de raza negra gozaran de derechos civiles (pág. 567)

national debt/deuda nacional Cantidad total de dinero que debe el gobierno federal y que tiene que pagar (pág. 768)

National Defense Education Act/Ley para la Mejoría de la Educación en Defensa de la Nación Medida tomada en 1958 para mejorar la enseñanza de las ciencias y matemáticas en las escuelas (pág. 918)

nationalism/nacionalismo Devoción por la nación a la que uno pertenece (pág. 585)

nationalization/nacionalización Adquisición por parte del gobierno de instituciones como bancos, con redistribución de sus recursos económicos (pág. 780)

National Liberation Front/Frente de Liberación Nacional Arma política del Viet Cong (pág. 1027)

National Organization for Women (NOW)/Organización Nacional para las Mujeres (NOW) Organización formada en 1966 para fomentar la participación total de las mujeres en la sociedad estadounidense (pág. 998)

Nation of Islam/Nación del Islam Organización dedicada a la lucha por la separación de la raza negra y el esfuerzo propio; también llamada los Musulmanes Negros (pág. 954)

nativism/nativismo Una política que favorece a los nativos de los Estados Unidos frente a los inmigrantes (págs. 359, 544)

naturalize/naturalizarse Solicitar y recibir la ciudadanía estadounidense (pág. 333)

natural rights/derechos naturales Derechos que se tienen simplemente por el hecho de ser seres humanos (pág. 121)

Nazism/nazismo Una especie extrema de fascismo delineada por las ideas fanáticas de Adolfo Hitler sobre el nacionalismo alemán y la superioridad racial (pág. 803)

Neutrality Acts/Leyes de Neutralidad Leyes promulgadas en 1939 diseñadas para mantener a los Estados Unidos fuera de futuras guerras (pág. 818)

neutral/neutral Que no toma partido en un conflicto o disputa (pág. 203)

New Deal/Nuevo Trato Término que describe los programas de apoyo, recuperación y reforma diseñados por el presidente Franklin Roosevelt para combatir la Gran Depresión (pág. 769)

New England Colonies/colonias de Nueva Inglaterra Colonias inglesas que se convirtieron en los estados de Connecticut, Rhode Island, Massachusetts, Vermont, New Hampshire y Maine (pág. 50)

New Federalism/nuevo federalismo Llamado del Presidente Nixon a una asociación nueva entre el gobierno federal y los gobiernos de los estados; plan del presidente Reagan para reducir el papel del gobierno federal y otorgar más responsabilidad a los gobiernos estatales y locales (págs. 1061, 1105)

New Frontier/nueva frontera Propuestas del presidente Kennedy para mejorar la economía, ayudar a los pobres y desarrollar el programa de exploración espacial (pág. 970)

New Left/nueva izquierda Nuevo movimiento político que tuvo lugar a finales de la década de 1960 y que demandaba cambios radicales para combatir la pobreza y el racismo (pág. 1038)

New Nationalism/nuevo nacionalismo Plan de Theodore Roosevelt para lograr una mayor regulación federal de las empresas y lugares de trabajo, de los impuestos a las utilidades e impuestos de sucesión, y de las reformas electorales (pág. 630)

New Right/nueva derecha Una coalición política de grupos conservadores formada en 1980 (pág. 1099)

Niagara Movement/movimiento Niágara Grupo de estadounidenses de raza negra fundado en 1905, que demandaba libertad civil, eliminación de la discriminación racial y reconocimiento de la hermandad (pág. 557)

Nisei/*Nisei* Estadounidense de origen japonés cuyos padres nacieron en Japón (pág. 627)

nomadic/nómadas Personas que cambian de hogar con regularidad, generalmente en busca de fuentes de alimento disponibles (págs. 259, 491)

nonviolent protest/protesta pacífica Una forma pacífica de protestar en contra de las políticas restrictivas (pág. 938)

North American Free Trade Agreement (NAFTA)/Tratado de Libre Comercio de Norteamérica (TLCN) Acuerdo que demanda la eliminación de las restricciones comerciales entre los Estados Unidos, Canadá y México (pág. 1141)

North Atlantic Treaty Organization (NATO)/Organización del Tratado del Atlántico Norte (OTAN) Alianza de naciones que en 1949 acordaron agruparse en caso de guerra, además de apoyar y proteger a cada nación participante (pág. 879)

Nuclear Regulatory Commission (NRC)/Comisión Nuclear Reguladora (NRC) Organización gubernamental formada en 1974 para examinar el uso civil de los materiales nucleares (pág. 1015)

nullify/anular Rechazar, como cuando un estado juzga que una ley federal es inconstitucional (págs. 208, 299)

Nuremberg Trials/Juicios de Nuremberg Serie de juicios realizados en 1945 por un Tribunal Militar Internacional en los que antiguos líderes nazis fueron acusados de crímenes de guerra y crímenes contra la paz y la humanidad (pág. 845)

O

obsolete/obsoleto Anticuado (pág. 349)

Office of War Mobilization/Oficina de Movilización de Guerra Agencia federal formada para coordinar cuestiones relacionadas con la producción de la guerra durante la Segunda Guerra Mundial (pág. 828)

oligopoly/oligopolio Una estructura de mercado dominada sólo por unas cuantas compañías grandes y lucrativas (pág. 470)

Olive Branch Petition/Petición de la rama de olivo Petición de los colonizadores estadounidenses al Rey Jorge III en 1775 para que diera fin a la lucha (pág. 119)

Open Door Policy/política de libre acceso Propuesta que realizó Estados Unidos a China alrededor de 1900 y que apoya las relaciones de libre comercio entre China y otras naciones (pág. 596)

oral history/historia oral Las tradiciones transmitidas de generación a generación a través de relatos orales (pág. 8)

Oregon Trail/Ruta de Oregon Ruta que unía a Independencia, Missouri y Oregon, utilizada por muchos pioneros durante la década de 1840 (pág. 254)

Organization of Petroleum Exporting Countries (OPEC)/Organización de Países Exportadores de Petróleo (OPEP) Grupo de naciones que trabajaron de manera conjunta para regular el precio y el suministro del petróleo (pág. 1060)

P

Pacific Railway Acts/Leyes para el Ferrocarril del Pacífico Leyes aprobadas en 1862 y 1864 que otorgaron grandes concesiones de tierra para la construcción de las vías férreas Union Pacific y Central Pacific (pág. 489)

pardon/perdón Exoneración oficial de un crimen (pág. 426)

Paris peace talks/diálogos de paz de París Negociaciones entre los Estados Unidos y Vietnam del Norte que se iniciaron en 1968 (pág. 1044)

pass/desfiladero Área baja de una cordillera que permite a los viajeros cruzar al otro lado (pág. 254)

patent/patente Licencia expedida a un inventor que le da el derecho exclusivo de fabricar, utilizar, o vender su invento durante un período de tiempo establecido (págs. 274, 457)

patriotism/patriotismo Amor por el país al que uno pertenece; pasión que tiene como objetivo servir al propio país, ya sea defendiéndolo de una invasión o protegiendo sus derechos y manteniendo sus leyes e instituciones en vigor y transparencia (pág. 136)

patronage/clientelismo La práctica de contratar partidarios políticos para empleos públicos (pág. 298)

Peace Corps/Cuerpo de Paz Programa federal establecido para enviar voluntarios a auxiliar países en vías de desarrollo (pág. 990)

Pendleton Civil Service Act/Ley Pendleton del Servicio Civil Ley promulgada en 1883 que creó una Comisión de Servicio Civil y estableció que los empleados federales no estaban obligados a contribuir al financiamiento de las campañas ni podían ser despedidos por razones políticas (pág. 523)

penny auction/subasta de a centavo Subastas de granjas durante la Gran Depresión en las que los vecinos salvaban a los demás de perder su propiedad a través de ofertas muy bajas (pág. 753)

Pequot War/guerra de Pequot, la Guerra entre los colonizadores ingleses y los indígenas Pequot en 1637 (pág. 55)

per capita income/ingreso per capita Ingreso anual promedio por persona (pág. 900)

persecute/hostigar, perseguir Oprimir a alguien por sus ideas (pág. 51)

Persian Gulf War/Guerra del Golfo Pérsico Operación militar limitada que tuvo lugar en 1991 y cuyo objetivo era sacar a las fuerzas iraquíes de Kuwait (pág. 1118)

philanthropist/filántropo Persona que hace donaciones para buenas causas (pág. 323)

Pickett's Charge/ataque de Pickett Ataque fallido de la infantería de los confederados durante la Batalla de Gettysburg (pág. 406)

piecework/trabajo por pieza Sistema en el que el pago de los trabajadores no se basa en el tiempo trabajado sino en el número de artículos que producen (pág. 474)

Pilgrim/peregrino Miembros del grupo de separatistas ingleses que fundaron la colonia de Plymouth en 1620 (pág. 51)

placer mining/explotación de placeres Técnica minera en la que los mineros echaban en cajas tierra de los placeres y luego le vertían agua para separarla de las partículas de oro o plata (pág. 499)

plantation/plantación Granja de gran extensión en la que se cultivan cosechas principalmente para la venta (pág. 27)

Platt Amendment/enmienda Platt Anexo a la constitución cubana de 1900 realizado por el gobierno estadounidense que le dio a los Estados Unidos el derecho de establecer bases navales en Cuba e intervenir en los asuntos de Cuba cuando fuera necesario (pág. 594)

Plessy v. *Ferguson/Plessy* vs. *Ferguson* Decisión tomada en 1896 por la Suprema Corte que consistía en la legalidad de la segregación siempre y cuando las instalaciones asignadas a la gente de color fueran iguales a las asignadas a los de raza blanca (pág. 566)

pocket veto/veto indirecto Tipo de veto que puede utilizar un presidente después de que se haya suspendido una legislatura; se aplica cuando el presidente no firma o rechaza formalmente una propuesta dentro del tiempo permitido (pág. 427)

pogrom/pogrom Masacre de judíos (pág. 528)

political machine/aparato político Organización urbana extraoficial diseñada para mantener un partido o grupo particular en el poder y bajo la dirección de un solo jefe poderoso (pág. 538)

political party/partido político Grupo de personas que buscan ganar las elecciones y tener un puesto público con el fin de controlar la política y los programas del gobierno (pág. 205)

poll tax/impuesto sobre el padrón electoral Un gravamen especial que debe ser pagado para que una persona pueda votar (pág. 565)

Pontiac's Rebellion/rebelión de Pontiac Rebelión de los indígenas norteamericanos en 1763 en la región de los Grandes Lagos (pág. 110)

popular sovereignty/soberanía popular Política que consistía en dejar que los habitantes de un territorio decidieran si debían o no permitir la esclavitud en ese lugar (pág. 360)

Populist/populista Seguidor del Partido del Pueblo (o Partido Populista) formado en 1891 para apoyar una oferta monetaria más grande y otras reformas económicas (pág. 511)

POW/prisionero de guerra Prisionero capturado durante una guerra (pág. 1048)

preamble/preámbulo Introducción (pág. 120)

precedent/precedente Ley o declaración que se vuelve un ejemplo, norma o tradición que se debe seguir (pág. 167)

prejudice/prejuicio Una opinión irracional y sin fundamentos, por lo general desfavorable, acerca de otro grupo (pág. 347)

presidio/fortaleza Fuerte construido en la región del suroeste por los españoles (págs. 40, 261)

price controls/control de precios Sistema determinado por el gobierno para el establecimiento de precios (pág. 665)

prime minister/primer ministro Funcionario de mayor rango en un gobierno parlamentario (pág. 106)

privateer/corsario Barco particular contratado por un gobierno para atacar barcos enemigos (pág. 43)

Proclamation of 1763/Proclamación de 1763 Orden dictada por el rey británico que cerraba la región oeste de los montes Apalaches a todo establecimiento por parte de colonizadores (pág. 110)

productivity/productividad Cantidad de bienes y servicios creada en un período de tiempo determinado (pág. 457)

profiteering/acaparamiento La venta de escasos productos a precios irrazonablemente altos (pág. 134)

Progressive Era/período progresista El período entre 1890 y 1920 durante el cual se aprobaron diversas reformas a nivel local, estatal y federal (pág. 615)

prohibition/prohibición Una restricción en la producción y venta de bebidas alcohólicas (pág. 544)

propaganda/propaganda Información orientada a influir en la opinión pública (pág. 650)

proprietary colony/colonia propietaria una colonia en que el rey o reina le da a un individuo o grupo con plenos derechos de gobierno (pág. 60)

public works program/programa de obras públicas Proyectos financiados por el gobierno para construir instalaciones públicas (pág. 770)

Pueblo Revolt of 1680/revuelta de Pueblo de 1860 Revuelta de los habitantes de Pueblo en Nuevo México en contra de los españoles (pág. 41)

Pullman Strike/huelga Pullman Huelga de los trabajadores ferroviarios que tuvo lugar en 1894 y que se extendió por toda la nación (pág. 483)

puppet state/estado títere Un país supuestamente independiente que se encuentra bajo el control de un vecino poderoso (pág. 814)

purge/purga En términos políticos, el proceso de sacar del poder a los enemigos e individuos indeseables (pág. 801)

Puritans/puritanos personas a favor de la purificación de la Iglesia Anglicana de Inglaterra (pág. 51)

push-pull factors/factores de expulsión del país de origen y de atracción por otro país Sucesos y condiciones que fuerzan a las personas a irse a otra parte o las atraen fuertemente a hacerlo (pág. 488)

Q

Quaker/Cuáquero Miembro de un grupo protestante que enfatiza la igualdad (pág. 60)

quarantine/cuarentena Período de aislamiento para prevenir la propagación de una enfermedad (pág. 529)

quota/cuota Límite numérico (pág. 719)

R

racism/racismo Creencia en que la raza determina las diferencias de carácter o inteligencia; afirmar la superioridad de una raza sobre otra u otras (pág. 605)

Radical Republicans/republicanos radicales Grupo de congresistas miembros del Partido Republicano que creían que en la Guerra Civil se había luchado por el problema moral de la esclavitud; insistía en que la principal meta de la Reconstrucción debía ser una reestructuración total de la sociedad para garantizar a la gente de color la verdadera igualdad (pág. 427)

ragtime/*ragtime* Tipo de música que se califica de melodias con acentos que cambian contra un ritmo constante, que tuvo su orígen entre los músicos negros en la región central y el sur en el década de 1880 (pág. 563)

ratify/ratificar Aprobar o autorizar (pág. 158)

rationing/racionamiento Distribución de una cantidad fija de productos a los consumidores (pág. 666)

Reagan Democrat/demócratas Reagan Obreros demócratas que tendían a votar por el partido Republicano durante la década de 1980 (pág. 1099)

realpolitik/realpolitik Término alemán que significa "política práctica" o política extranjera basada en los intereses más que en los principios morales (pág. 1064)

rebate/reembolso Devolución parcial (pág. 524)

recall/revocación Procedimiento que permite a los votantes destituir a funcionarios públicos de su puesto antes de la siguiente elección (pág. 624)

recession/recesión Período de poco movimiento en el negocio (pág. 786)

recognition/reconocimiento Aceptación oficial como nación independiente (pág. 392)

Reconstruction Finance Corporation (RFC)/Corporación Financiera para la Reconstrucción (RFC) Corporación establecida por el presidente Hoover en 1932, que otorgó crédito público a varias instituciones, entre ellas, industrias grandes, compañías ferroviarias y compañías de seguros (pág. 757)

Reconstruction/Reconstrucción Programa puesto en práctica por el gobierno federal entre 1865 y 1877 para reparar el daño al sur causado por la Guerra Civil y restituir los estados del sur a la Unión (pág. 424)

reconversion/reconversión Transición social y económica de los tiempos de guerra a los tiempos de paz (pág. 912)

Red Scare/amenaza roja Miedo intenso al comunismo y a otras ideas políticamente radicales (pág. 714)

referendum/referéndum Proceso que permite a los ciudadanos aprobar o rechazar una ley aprobada por su legislatura (pág. 624)

Reformation/Reforma, la Revuelta en contra de la Iglesia Católica que empezó en 1517 (pág. 15)

religious tolerance/tolerancia religiosa Idea de que las personas de diferentes religiones deben convivir en paz (pág. 52)

Renaissance/Renacimiento Período de la historia europea que se extiende del siglo XIV al XVI (pág. 13)

reparations/compensaciones Pagos que realiza un enemigo por el daño económico ocasionado durante la guerra (pág. 671)

republic/república Gobierno manejado por el pueblo a través de los representantes elegidos (pág. 146)

republican virtues/virtudes republicanas Virtudes que el pueblo estadounidense necesitaría para gobernarse a sí mismo, tales como confianza en uno mismo, destreza, sobriedad, armonía y capacidad para sacrificar las necesidades individuales por el bien de la comunidad (pág. 242)

reservation/reservación Territorio federal reservado para las tribus de indígenas (págs. 221, 492)

Resistance/Resistencia Movimiento en Francia que se opuso a la ocupación alemana durante la Segunda Guerra Mundial (pág. 810)

restrictive covenant/cláusula de prohibición de competencia Acuerdo entre los dueños de fincas para no vender sus propiedades a ciertos grupos de personas, como judíos o estadounidenses de raza negra (pág. 531)

revenue/ingreso Entrada económica (pág. 786)

revival/resucitación Reunión en la que los asistentes son "resucitados" o reincorporados a la vida religiosa (pág. 245)

Revolutionary War/guerra revolucionaria Guerra de los colonos norteamericanos para independizarse de la Gran Bretaña; tuvo lugar de 1775 a 1783 (pág. 116)

rock-and-roll/*rock-and-roll* Música que surgió del rhythm and blues y que se volvió popular en la década de 1950 (pág. 910)

Roe* v. *Wade*/*Roe* vs. *Wade Decisión tomada en 1973 por la Suprema Corte para legalizar el aborto (pág. 1000)

Roosevelt Corollary/Corolario Roosevelt Extensión de la Doctrina Monroe realizada por el presidente Theodore Roosevelt en 1904, en la que hacía valer el derecho de los Estados Unidos de intervenir en las naciones de América Latina (pág. 600)

royal colony/colonia real Colonia con un gobernador designado por el rey (pág. 46)

rule of law/imperio de la ley, el Tipo de gobierno en el que las decisiones deben basarse en la ley y no en deseos personales (pág. 121)

rural free delivery (RFD)/entrega postal rural gratuita (RFD) En 1896, el Sistema Postal de los Estados Unidos ofreció entregar el correo de manera gratuita a las familias campesinas en los estados rurales centrales (pág. 571)

rural/rural Perteneciente al campo (pág. 281)

Russian Revolution/revolución rusa Colapso del gobierno zarista de Rusia en 1917, después del cual la monarquía rusa fue reemplazada por un gobierno republicano (pág. 656)

S

sachem/*sachem* Líder indígena (pág. 55)

Salem witch trials/juicios de las brujas de Salem La persecución y ejecución de 20 mujeres y hombres acusados de realizar brujería en Massachusetts en 1692 (pág. 54)

SALT I/Primer Tratado sobre Limitación de Armas Estratégicas *(SALT I)* Tratado firmado en 1972 entre los Estados Unidos y la Unión Soviética para restringir las armas nucleares (pág. 1068)

salutary neglect/negligencia útil Política de Gran Bretaña a principios del siglo XVIII que consistía en no interferir en la política y economía de las colonias americanas, siempre y cuando dicha negligencia sirviera a los intereses económicos de Gran Bretaña (pág. 73)

Sandinista/sandinista En la década de 1980, un miembro del grupo marxista prevaleciente en Nicaragua (pág. 1112)

Santa Fe Trail/Ruta de Santa Fe Ruta que unía a Independencia, Missouri y Santa Fe, Nuevo México a mediados del siglo XIX (pág. 255)

satellite nation/nación satélite Un país dominado política y económicamente por otra nación, sobre todo por la Unión Soviética durante la Guerra Fría (pág. 871)

saturation bombing/bombardeo de saturación El lanzamiento de una gran concentración de bombas sobre un área determinada (pág. 1033)

savanna/sabana Región ubicada cerca del ecuador con prados tropicales y árboles dispersos (pág. 18)

scab/rompehuelgas Término negativo para un obrero que ha sido llamado por un empleador para que reemplace a los trabajadores que están en huelga (pág. 481)

scalawag/caballo piojoso o sureño pro-yanqui Sobrenombre ofensivo utilizado para referirse a un republicano blanco del sur después de la Guerra Civil (pág. 435)

scarce/escaso En poca cantidad (pág. 21)

Scopes trial/juicio de Scopes Caso presentado ante los tribunales en 1925 por Clarence Darrow y William Jennings Bryan, en el que se debatía la enseñanza de la evolución en las escuelas públicas (pág. 702)

secede/separarse Dejar de ser miembro formalmente de un grupo u organización (pág. 299)

secessionist/secesionista Persona que quería la separación del Sur (pág. 371)

Second Continental Congress/Segundo Congreso Continental Asamblea de representantes de las colonias que se reunieron por primera vez en Filadelfia en mayo de 1775 (pág. 119)

Second Great Awakening/el Segundo Gran Despertar Movimiento religioso que tuvo lugar a principios del siglo XIX (pág. 245)

Second New Deal/segundo Nuevo Trato Período de actividad legislativa iniciado por el presidente Franklin Roosevelt en 1935 (pág. 774)

Second Seminole War/Segunda Guerra Seminole Guerra que tuvo lugar en 1835 en la que los Seminoles trataron de conservar sus tierras en la Florida (pág. 302)

section/sección Región geográfica (pág. 280)

sedition/sedición Cualquier discurso o acción que fomente la rebelión (pág. 667)

segregation/segregación Separación forzada, frecuentemente por las diferencias de raza (págs. 315, 565)

Selective Service Act/Ley del Servicio Militar Obligatorio Ley aprobada en 1917 que autoriza el reclutamiento de jóvenes para el servicio militar en la Primera Guerra Mundial (pág. 657)

Selective Training and Service Act/Ley del Servicio y Capacitación Militar Obligatorios Ley promulgada en 1940 que exige que todos los hombres de 21 a 36 años deben realizar el servicio militar (pág. 826)

self-determination/autodeterminación El poder de tomar decisiones sobre el futuro de uno mismo (pág. 669)

self-sufficient/autosuficiente Que tiene los recursos necesarios para progresar sin ayuda externa (pág. 82)

Seneca Falls Convention/Convención Seneca Falls La primera convención sobre los derechos de las mujeres en la historia de los Estados Unidos, presidida en 1848 (pág. 329)

separation of powers/división de poderes El reparto constitucional de poderes dentro del gobierno federal entre las ramas legislativa, ejecutiva y judicial (pág. 155)

settlement house/casa del pueblo Centro comunitario organizado para proporcionar varios servicios a las personas de escasos recursos que viven en zonas urbanas (pág. 542)

sharecropping/aparcería Sistema practicado en la agricultura en el que un campesino trabaja un pedazo de tierra del propietario y recibe como pago una parte de la cosecha (pág. 437)

Shays' Rebellion/rebelión de Shays Levantamiento contra los impuestos en Massachusetts en 1786 y 1787 (pág. 148)

shell/granada Aparato que explota en el aire o cuando golpea un objetivo sólido (pág. 384)

Sherman Antitrust Act/Ley Antimonopolista Sherman Ley aprobada por el Congreso en 1890 que prohibía cualquier combinación de empresas que limitara el intercambio o comercio interestatal (pág. 472)

Sherman Silver Purchase Act/Ley Sherman para la Adquisición de Plata Ley aprobada por el Congreso en 1890 para aumentar la cantidad de plata que el gobierno debía comprar cada mes (pág. 509)

siege/sitio Táctica que consiste en cercar a un enemigo y dejarlo sin alimentos para que se rinda (págs. 107, 408)

silent majority/mayoría silenciosa Término utilizado por el presidente Nixon para describir a los estadounidenses que se oponían a la contracultura (pág. 1046)

sit-down strike/huelga de brazos caídos Protesta laboral en la que los trabajadores dejan de trabajar pero se niegan a abandonar el lugar de trabajo (p. 787)

sit-in/sentada Forma de protesta en la que los inconformes se sientan y se niegan a irse (pág. 941)

social Darwinism/darwinismo social Idea que se deriva de la teoría de Darwin de la selección natural; consiste en que la sociedad debe interferir lo menos posible en la búsqueda del éxito de las personas (pág. 469)

social gospel movement/movimiento evangélico social Una reforma social que se desarrolló en las instituciones religiosas y buscó aplicar las enseñanzas de Jesús directamente a la sociedad (pág. 542)

socialism/socialismo Filosofía económica y política que apoya el control público (o social), en lugar del control privado, de la propiedad y los ingresos (pág. 477)

Social Security System/sistema de seguridad social Sistema establecido por el Ley de Seguridad Social de 1935 para proporcionar seguridad económica, a manera de pagos regulares, a quienes no pueden mantenerse por sí mismos (pág. 776)

social welfare program/programa de bienestar social Programa diseñado para asegurar una norma de vida o de subsistencia básica a todos los ciudadanos (pág. 622)

sociology/sociología Término acuñado por el filósofo Auguste Comte para describir el estudio de la forma en que las personas interactúan en una sociedad (pág. 543)

soddie/casa de tepes Casa cuyas paredes y techo están hechas de bloques de pasto compuesto por gruesas raíces y tierra (pág. 503)

solid South/sur sólido Término que describe el dominio del Partido Demócrata sobre las políticas del sur posteriores a la Guerra Civil (pág. 444)

sooners/*sooners* En 1889, las personas que exigían ilegalmente un pedazo de tierra escabulléndose de las autoridades antes de que empezaran las carreras por la tierra (pág. 497)

Southern Christian Leadership Conference (SCLC)/Conferencia del Liderazgo Cristiano del Sur (SCLC) Organización de los derechos civiles que apoyaba las protestas pacíficas; formada en 1957 por el Dr. Martin Luther King Jr. y otros líderes (pág. 938)

Southern Colonies/colonias del sur Las colonias inglesas de Virginia, Maryland, las Carolinas y Georgia (pág. 62)

speakeasies/tabernas clandestinas Bar que operaba ilegalmente durante el período de la Prohibición (pág. 700)

specialization/especialización Sistema de producción en el que cada trabajador realiza una parte específica de un proceso (pág. 278)

special prosecutor/fiscal especial Un abogado designado por el Departamento de Justicia para investigar actos ilegales de funcionarios públicos (pág. 1075)

specie/metálico moneda de oro o plata (pág. 148)

speculation/especulación Práctica que consiste en hacer inversiones de alto riesgo con la esperanza de obtener una enorme ganancia (pág. 732)

sphere of influence/esfera de influencia Área de control económico y político ejercido por una nación sobre otra u otras (pág. 596)

spoils/botín Ganancias obtenidas en una victoria militar (pág. 670)

spoils system/sistema de repartirse empleos entre los del partido victorioso Sistema o práctica electoral que consistía en la asignación de cargos como recompensa por parte del partido político ganador; nombre para designar el sistema de clientelismo bajo el mandato del presidente Jackson (pág. 298)

Sputnik/*Sputnik* El primer satélite artificial en entrar en la órbita de la Tierra, lanzado por los soviéticos en 1957 (pág. 893)

stagflation/estanflación Combinación de un alto nivel de inflación y desempleo sin ningún crecimiento económico (pág. 1080)

stalemate/estancamiento Situación en la que ninguna de las partes del conflicto logra obtener ventaja (pág. 649)

Stamp Act/Ley de la Estampilla Ley aprobada en 1765 por el Parlamento británico que imponía impuestos a los periódicos, documentos legales y otros materiales impresos en las colonias (pág. 111)

staple crop/cultivo básico Cultivo que está en constante demanda, como algodón, trigo o arroz (pág. 74)

states' rights/derechos de los estados Los poderes que la Constitución le niega al gobierno y les confiere a los estados (pág. 299)

steerage/entrecubierta Un área abierta muy grande debajo de la cubierta de un barco, por lo general utilizada para alojar inmigrantes (pág. 528)

stereotype/estereotipo Descripción exagerada o demasiado simplificada de la realidad arraigada en ciertas personas (pág. 505)

Stono Rebellion/rebelión Stono Revuelta de esclavos en Carolina del Sur en 1739 (pág. 88)

Strategic Arms Reduction Treaty/Tratado para la Reducción de Armas Estratégicas Acuerdo firmado en 1991 y conocido como START, que demandaba la reducción del suministro de armas nucleares de largo alcance en Rusia y los Estados Unidos (pág. 1117)

Strategic Defense Initiative (SDI)/Iniciativa de Defensa Estratégica (SDI) Sistema de defensa propuesto por el presidente Reagan en contra de ataques soviéticos con misiles, popularmente conocido como la "Guerra de las Galaxias" (pág. 1105)

strict construction/interpretación estricta Idea de que el gobierno no debe hacer nada que la Constitución no especifique que pueda hacer (pág. 202)

strike/huelga Un paro laboral con el propósito de forzar a los empleadores a cumplir algunas demandas, por ejemplo, un aumento en los salarios (pág. 283)

Student Nonviolent Coordinating Committee (SNCC)/Comité Coordinador Estudiantil Pacifista (SNCC) Organización de los derechos civiles de los estudiantes fundada en 1960, como rama del SCLC (pág. 939)

subsidy/subsidio Un pago realizado por el gobierno para fomentar el desarrollo de ciertas industrias clave (pág. 521)

suburb/área suburbana Comunidad residencial que rodea una ciudad (pág. 535)

suffrage/sufragio El derecho al voto (pág. 330)

supply-side economics/economía de oferta Teoría que establece que la reducción de impuestos aumentará la inversión y, por lo tanto, estimulará el crecimiento de las empresas (pág. 1103)

Sussex pledge/promesa Sussex Compromiso adquirido por el gobierno alemán en 1916 de que sus submarinos advertirían a los barcos antes de atacarlos (pág. 655)

sweatshop/fábrica explotadora Fábrica donde los empleados trabajan muchas horas a cambio de salarios muy bajos y en malas condiciones de trabajo (pág. 474)

synagogue/sinagoga Templo judío (pág. 60)

T

Taft-Hartley Act/Ley Taft-Hartley Ley aprobada por el Congreso en 1947 que permitió al Presidente declarar un período de calma de 80 días cuando las huelgas golpearon las industrias y afectaron los intereses nacionales; asimismo, pedía a los huelguistas que volvieran a su trabajo mientras el gobierno estudiaba la situación (pág. 913)

Tariff of 1828/tarifa de 1828 Impuesto muy alto sobre las importaciones que beneficiaba a la región industrial del Norte y forzaba a los del Sur a pagar precios más altos por productos fabricados; los del Sur la llamaban la "tarifa abominable" (pág. 298)

tariff/tarifa Impuesto asignado a los productos extranjeros que se importan a un país (pág. 201)

teach-in/asamblea especial Sesión especial de disertación y discusión sobre un tema controversial utilizada durante la época de la Guerra de Vietnam (pág. 1039)

Teapot Dome scandal/escándalo Teapot Dome Escándalo durante la administración de Harding que involucraba la concesión de los derechos de explotación petrolera en el territorio público a cambio de dinero (pág. 720)

televangelism/televangelismo El uso de la televisión por los predicadores para ganarse a millones de personas, especialmente para recaudar dinero (pág. 1100)

temperance movement/movimiento de moderación Una campaña organizada para eliminar el consumo de bebidas alcohólicas (págs. 312, 544)

tenant farming/agricultura por arrendamiento Sistema agrícola en el que el propietario de una plantación le arrienda la tierra a un agricultor paraque la trabaje (pág. 438)

tenement/casa de vecindad Edificio de apartamentos de bajo costo y por lo regular con normas de sanidad, seguridad y comodidad deficientes; diseñado para alojar el mayor número posible de familias (págs. 283, 536)

Tennessee Valley Authority (TVA)/Autoridad del valle de Tennessee (TVA) Proyecto federal para proporcionar energía eléctrica, control de inundaciones y oportunidades recreativas, a muy bajo precio, al valle del río Tennessee (pág. 772)

Tet Offensive/Ofensiva Tet Ataque realizado en 1968 por el Viet Cong y las fuerzas vietnamitas del Norte a través de Vietnam del Sur (pág. 1035)

Texas War for Independence/Guerra de Texas por la Independencia Revuelta exitosa realizada por Texas en contra del gobierno mexicano de 1835–1836 (pág. 264)

Thirteenth Amendment/Decimotercera enmienda Enmienda constitucional ratificada en 1865 para abolir la esclavitud (pág. 414)

38th parallel/paralelo 38 Línea de latitud que dividía Corea del Norte y Corea del Sur aproximadamente en el punto céntrico de la península (pág. 885)

Three-Fifths Compromise/Acuerdo de la tres quintas partes Acuerdo dictado en la Convención Constitucional que demandaba que se contaran las tres quintas partes de la población de esclavos de un estado para fines de representación (pág. 153)

totalitarian/totalitario Término para describir a un gobierno que ejerce un control total sobre la nación y la vida de los ciudadanos (pág. 800)

Trail of Tears/ruta de las lágrimas El traslado forzado de la tribu Cherokee en 1838 hacia el territorio oeste del río Mississippi (pág. 301)

trans-Appalachia/transapalache Área oeste de los montes Apalaches (pág. 249)

transcendentalism/trascendentalismo Movimiento filosófico de mediados del siglo XIX que enfatizaba el descubrimiento espiritual y la perspicacia por encima de la razón (pág. 311)

transcontinental railroad/ferrocarril transcontinental Vía férrea que se extiende de costa a costa (pág. 460)

transistor/transistor Circuito diminuto inventado en 1947 que amplifica, controla y genera señales eléctricas (pág. 902)

Treaty of Ghent/Tratado de Ghent Acuerdo firmado en 1814 que puso fin a la guerra de 1812 (pág. 227)

Treaty of Greenville/Tratado de Greenville Tratado firmado en 1795 por los Estados Unidos y varios pueblos indígenas en el que los indígenas cedieron el control de la mayor parte de Ohio (pág. 221)

Treaty of Guadalupe Hidalgo/Tratado de Guadalupe Hidalgo Tratado firmado en 1848 por los Estados Unidos y México, que puso fin a la Guerra entre México y los Estados Unidos (pág. 353)

Treaty of Paris (1763)/Tratado de París (1763) Tratado que terminó con la Guerra francesa e indígena en el que Francia cedía sus tierras en Norteamérica a Gran Bretaña (pág. 108)

Treaty of Paris (1783)/Tratado de París (1783) Tratado que puso fin a la Guerra Revolucionaria y en el que Gran Bretaña reconocía la independencia estadounidense (pág. 136)

Treaty of Tordesillas/Tratado de Tordesillas Tratado firmado en 1494 en el que Portugal y España dividieron el mundo no cristiano (pág. 27)

triangular trade/comercio triangular Comercio entre América, Europa y África (pág. 75)

Truman Doctrine/Doctrina Truman Discurso emitido por Harry Truman en 1947 antes de una sesión conjunta del Congreso, en el que pedía que los Estados Unidos asumieran un papel de liderazgo en el mundo y declaraba que apoyarían a las naciones amenazadas por el comunismo (pág. 847)

trust/consorcio Un grupo de empresas distintas que están bajo el control de un solo consejo administrativo (pág. 472)

trustee/fiduciario Alguien encargado de ocuparse de una empresa (pág. 63)

Turner's Rebellion/rebelión de Turner Revuelta infructuosa de esclavos dirigida por Nat Turner en 1831 (pág. 289)

Turner thesis/tesis Turner Teoría desarrollada en 1893 por Frederick Jackson Turner, que afirmaba que la región fronteriza había jugado un papel clave en la formación del carácter de los estadounidenses (pág. 505)

Twenty-first Amendment/Vigésima primera enmienda Enmienda constitucional ratificada en 1933 para anular el período de la Prohibición (pág. 754)

Twenty-fourth Amendment/Vigésima cuarta enmienda Enmienda constitucional ratificada en 1964 para prohibir el impuesto sobre el padrón electoral (pág. 953)

U

U-boat/*U-boat* Submarino alemán (pág. 653)

U-2 incident/incidente U-2 Incidente ocurrido en 1960 en el que las fuerzas armadas soviéticas utilizaron un misil guiado para derribar un avión espía U-2 estadounidense que volaba en territorio soviético (pág. 893)

Underground Railroad/vía férrea subterránea Una red de rutas de escape que protegían y transportaban a los esclavos que huían al norte en busca de la libertad (pág. 322)

Union/Unión, la Los Estados Unidos como unidad nacional; o, durante la Guerra Civil, el Norte (pág. 346)

United Farm Workers (UFW)/Agricultores Unidos (UFW) Sindicato creado por César Chávez para organizar a los agricultores mexicanos en el Oeste (pág. 1005)

United States Constitution/Constitución de los Estados Unidos Plan de gobierno, aprobado por la Convención Constitucional en septiembre de 1787, que describe las diferentes partes del gobierno, sus deberes y poderes (pág. 150)

Upper South/Alto Sur, el Designación durante la Guerra Civil de los estados de Virginia, Carolina del Norte, Tennessee y Arkansas (pág. 373)

urban/urbano Perteneciente a una ciudad (pág. 281)

utopian community/comunidad utópica Pequeña sociedad que busca la perfección en el ámbito social y político (pág. 315)

V

vaudeville/*vaudeville* Un tipo de teatro de variedades que apareció por primera vez en la década de 1870; generalmente consta de diálogos cómicos, números de música y baile, y actos de magia (pág. 559)

Versailles Treaty/Tratado de Versalles Tratado firmado en 1919 que dio fin a la Primera Guerra Mundial (pág. 671)

vertical consolidation/consolidación vertical Proceso para obtener el control de las diferentes empresas que componen todas las fases del desarrollo de un producto (pág. 471)

veto/vetar Impedir la aprobación de una ley (pág. 152)

vice/vicio Comportamiento inmoral o corrupto (pág. 545)

victory garden/jardín de la victoria Un jardín doméstico de hortalizas creado para apoyar la producción de alimentos durante la Segunda Guerra Mundial (pág. 831)

Viet Cong/Viet Cong Guerrillas comunistas de Vietnam del Sur (pág. 1027)

Vietminh/Vietminh Nombre común de la Liga para la Independencia de Vietnam (pág. 1024)

Vietnamization/vietnamización Política del presidente Nixon para reemplazar las fuerzas militares estadounidenses por las de Vietnam del Sur (pág. 1045)

vigilante/miembro de un grupo de autodefensa Ciudadano que hace justicia por su propia cuenta (pág. 667)

Virginia and Kentucky Resolutions/Resoluciones de Virginia y Kentucky Resoluciones aprobadas en 1798 que declaraban inconstitucionales las Leyes sobre Extranjeros y Sedición (pág. 208)

Volunteers in Service to America (VISTA)/Voluntarios al Servicio de Norteamérica (VISTA) Programa federal que envía voluntarios a las comunidades pobres para brindarles ayuda (pág. 978)

Voting Rights Act of 1965/Ley de Derecho al Voto de 1965 Ley cuyo objetivo era reducir los obstáculos que tenían los estadounidenses de raza negra para votar, mediante el aumento de la autoridad federal para registrar a los votantes (pág. 953)

W

Wagner Act/Ley Wagner Ley aprobada en 1935 para apoyar a los sindicatos mediante la legalización de acuerdos colectivos y el establecimiento del Consejo Nacional para las Relaciones Laborales (pág. 775)

Wannsee Conference/Conferencia Wannsee Conferencia celebrada en 1942 en Alemania, cuyo tema principal era la elaboración del plan para asesinar a los judíos europeos (pág. 843)

War of 1812/guerra de 1812 Guerra entre los Estados Unidos y Gran Bretaña (pág. 225)

war of attrition/guerra por desgaste Tipo de guerra en el que una de las partes causa a la otra continuas pérdidas para mermar su fuerza (pág. 383)

War Powers Act/Ley de Poderes de Guerra Ley promulgada en 1973 que limita la capacidad de un presidente para involucrar a los Estados Unidos en conflictos externos sin recibir una declaración de guerra formal expedida por el Congreso (pág. 1081)

War Refugee Board (WRB)/Consejo para los Refugiados de Guerra (WRB) Agencia federal creada en 1944 para ayudar a las personas amenazadas de muerte por los nazis (pág. 844)

Warren Commission/Comisión Warren Comisión encabezada por el presidente de la Corte Suprema, Earl Warren, que investigaba el asesinato del presidente Kennedy (pág. 973)

Warsaw ghetto/ghetto de Varsovia Área de Varsovia cerrada por los nazis para confinar a los judíos y obligarlos a vivir en condiciones malas e insalubres (pág. 843)

Warsaw Pact/Pacto de Varsovia Alianza militar formada en 1955 entre la Unión Soviética y las naciones de Europa Oriental (pág. 880)

Watergate scandal/escándalo de Watergate Escándalo que involucró actividades ilegales que llevaron finalmente a la renuncia del presidente Nixon en 1974 (pág. 1072)

welfare capitalism/capitalismo benefactor Una propuesta de relaciones laborales en la cual las empresas cubrían algunas de las necesidades de sus trabajadores sin la presión de los sindicatos, y así prevenían huelgas y mantenían una productividad elevada (p. 731)

Whiskey Rebellion/rebelión del whisky Disturbios de 1794 causados por la oposición a un impuesto en el whisky (pág. 204)

Whitewater affair/caso Whitewater Cargos que se le imputaron al presidente Clinton por realizar transacciones empresariales inadecuadas antes de subir a la presidencia (pág. 1130)

Wilmot Proviso/Cláusula Wilmot Enmienda a un documento escrito en 1846 que establecía que no se permitiría la esclavitud en ningún territorio adquirido de México; aunque nunca se volvió ley, los habitantes del norte continuaron aplicándola a los documentos relacionados con los territorios nuevos (pág. 354)

wiretap/conectador para interceptar líneas telefónicas Un aparato auditivo que se utiliza para interceptar las llamadas telefónicas (pág. 1071)

Woodstock festival/festival de Woodstock Festival de música que tuvo lugar en 1969 en la región norte del estado de Nueva York (pág. 1012)

World Trade Organization (WTO)/Organización Mundial de Comercio (OMC) Organización internacional formada en 1995 para fomentar la expansión del comercio mundial (pág. 1141)

writ of *habeas corpus*/auto de *habeas corpus* Protección legal que exige que una corte determine si una persona debe ser encarcelada o no (pág. 395)

X

XYZ affair/caso XYZ Controversia de 1798 sobre las demandas francesas por sobornos que realizaron negociadores estadounidenses (pág. 207)

Y

yellow journalism/amarillismo Cobertura de noticias sensacionalistas, centradas en crímenes y escándalos (pág. 563)

Z

zeppelin/zepelín Globo dirigible alemán (pág. 661)

Zimmermann note/nota Zimmermann Telegrama del ministro de Relaciones Exteriores alemán a funcionarios mexicanos, enviado en 1917, que proponía una alianza con México y prometía ceder territorio estadounidense a cambio de una declaración de guerra a los Estados Unidos (pág. 656)

Biographical Dictionary

A

Adams, Abigail First Lady, 1797–1801; as the wife of Patriot John Adams, she urged him to promote women's rights at the beginning of the American Revolution (p. 121)

Adams, John Second President of the United States, 1797–1801; worked to relieve increasing tensions with France; lost reelection bid to Jefferson in 1800 as the country moved away from Federalist policies (p. 207)

Adams, John Quincy Sixth President of the United States, 1825–1829; proposed greater federal involvement in the economy through tariffs and improvements such as roads, bridges, and canals (p. 293)

Addams, Jane Cofounder of Hull House, the first settlement house, in 1889; remained active in social causes through the early 1900s (p. 542)

Agnew, Spiro Vice President under President Richard Nixon until forced to resign in 1973 for crimes committed before taking office; known for his harsh campaign attacks (p. 1042)

Allen, Richard African American religious leader; helped found the African Methodist Episcopal Church (AME) in 1816 (p. 248)

Anthony, Susan B. Political activist and women's rights leader in the late 1800s (p. 636)

Armstrong, Louis Jazz musician famous for his long trumpet solos and "scat" singing (p. 695)

Arthur, Chester A. Twenty-first President of the United States, 1881–1885; signed 1883 Pendleton Act, which instituted the Civil Service (p. 523)

Askia, Muhammad Ruler of the African empire of Songhai, 1493–1528; promoted Islamic culture (p. 20)

Austin, Stephen Leader of first American group of Texas settlers in 1822 (p. 263)

B

Bakke, Allan Student who won a suit against the University of California in 1978 on the grounds that the affirmative action program had denied him admission (p. 1086)

Baldwin, James African American author and spokesperson for the civil rights movement during the 1960s (p. 954)

Banks, Dennis Native American leader in 1960s and 1970s; helped organize American Indian Movement (AIM) and the 1973 Wounded Knee occupation (p. 1007)

Barton, Clara Volunteer known as the "angel of the battlefield" during the Civil War; founded the American Red Cross (p. 399)

Beecher, Catharine Author whose 1841 book *A Treatise on Domestic Economy* argued that women should support reform from the home (p. 327)

Beecher, Lyman Revivalist during the Second Great Awakening; feared the rise of selfishness in the United States (p. 311)

Begin, Menachem Israeli leader during the 1970s; began the Middle East peace process by signing the 1978 Camp David Accords with Egypt (p. 1087)

Bell, Alexander Graham Inventor; developed the telephone in 1876; one of the founders of American Telephone & Telegraph (AT&T) (p. 460)

Bellamy, Edward Author of the novel *Looking Backward* (1888), which proposed nationalizing trusts to eliminate social problems (p. 616)

Bethune, Mary McLeod African American educator, New Deal worker; founded Bethune Cookman College in the 1920s; advised the National Youth Administration (p. 773)

Beveridge, Albert J. Indiana senator in the early 1900s; saw United States imperialism as a duty owed to "primitive" societies (p. 588)

Booth, John Wilkes Southern actor who assassinated President Abraham Lincoln in 1865 (p. 417)

Breckinridge, John C. Presidential candidate of the southern wing of the Democratic Party in 1860 (p. 369)

Brown, John Abolitionist crusader who massacred proslavery settlers in Kansas before the Civil War; hoped to inspire slave revolt with 1859 attack on Virginia arsenal; executed for treason against the state of Virginia (p. 368)

Bruce, Blanche African American senator from Mississippi during Reconstruction (p. 434)

Bryan, William Jennings Advocate of silver standard and proponent of Democratic and Populist views from the 1890s through the 1910s; Democratic candidate for President in 1896, 1900, and 1908 (p. 512)

Buchanan, James Fifteenth President of the United States, 1857–1861; supported by the South; attempted to moderate fierce disagreement over expansion of slavery (p. 365)

Bush, George H. W. Forty-first President of the United States, 1989–1993; continued Reagan's conservative policies; brought together United Nations coalition to fight the Persian Gulf War (p. 1114)

Bush, George W. Forty-third President of the United States; took office in 2001; led efforts to unite world against terrorism (p. 1131)

Byrd, William Wealthy plantation owner in colonial Virginia whose diary gives a vivid picture of colonial life (p. 79)

C

Calhoun, John C. Statesman from South Carolina who held many offices in the federal government; supported slavery, cotton exports, states' rights; in 1850 foresaw future conflicts over slavery (p. 294)

Carnegie, Andrew Industrialist who made a fortune in steel in the late 1800s through vertical consolidation; as a philanthropist, he gave away some $350 million (p. 468)

Carson, Rachel Marine biologist, author of *Silent Spring* (1962), which exposed harmful effects of pesticides and inspired concern for the environment (p. 1013)

Carter, James Earl, Jr. Thirty-ninth President of the United States, 1977–1981; advocated concern for human rights in foreign policy; assisted in mediating the Camp David Accords (p. 1087)

Castro, Fidel Revolutionary leader who took control of Cuba in 1959; ally of Soviet Union through the 1980s (p. 983)

Catt, Carrie Chapman Women's suffrage leader in the early 1900s; helped secure passage of Nineteenth Amendment in 1920; headed National American Woman Suffrage Association (p. 638)

Champlain, Samuel de French explorer who founded the city of Quebec in 1608 (p. 49)

Chávez, César Latino leader from 1962 to his death in 1993; organized the United Farm Workers (UFW) to help migratory farm workers gain better pay and working conditions (p. 1004)

Cheney, Richard Vice President under George W. Bush (p. 1132)

Chisholm, Shirley New York Representative from 1969–1983; a founder of the National Women's Political Caucus (p. 999)

Churchill, Winston Leader of Great Britain before and during World War II; powerful speechmaker who rallied Allied morale during the war (p. 807)

Clark, William Leader, with Meriwether Lewis, of expedition through the West beginning in 1804; brought back scientific samples, maps, and information on Native Americans (p. 216)

Clay, Henry Statesman from Kentucky; accused by Jackson of giving votes to John Q. Adams in return for post as Secretary of State; endorsed government promotion of economic growth; advocate of Compromise of 1850 (p. 294)

Cleveland, Grover Twenty-second and twenty-fourth President of the United States, 1885–1889, 1893–1897; supported railroad regulation and a return to the gold standard (p. 524)

Clinton, William J. Forty-second President of the United States, 1993–2001; advocated economic and healthcare reform; second President to be impeached (p. 1126)

Columbus, Christopher Explorer whose voyage for Spain to North America in 1492 opened the Atlantic World (p. 22)

Coolidge, Calvin Thirtieth President of the United States, 1923–1929; promoted big business and opposed social aid (p. 720)

Coughlin, Father Charles E. "Radio Priest" who supported and then attacked President Franklin Roosevelt's New Deal; prevented by the Catholic Church from broadcasting after he praised Hitler (p. 778)

Coxey, Jacob S. Populist who led Coxey's Army in a march on Washington, D.C., in 1894 to seek government jobs for the unemployed (p. 525)

Custer, George Armstrong General who directed army attacks against Native Americans in the 1870s; killed in 1876 at Little Bighorn in Montana (p. 495)

D

Davis, Jefferson President of the Confederate States of America; ordered attack on Fort Sumter, the first battle of the Civil War (p. 371)

de Tocqueville, Alexis French writer; wrote *Democracy in America* following a visit to the United States in the 1830s (p. 295)

Dewey, George Officer in United States Navy, 1861–1917; led a surprise attack in the Philippines during the Spanish-American War that destroyed the entire Spanish fleet (p. 592)

Diem, Ngo Dinh Leader of South Vietnam, 1954–1963; supported by United States, but not by Vietnamese Buddhist majority; assassinated in 1963 (p. 1025)

Dix, Dorothea Advocate of prison reform and of special institutions for the mentally ill in Massachusetts before the Civil War (p. 315)

Dole, Robert Senator from Kansas, 1969–1996; challenged Bill Clinton for the presidency in 1996 (p. 1129)

Douglas, Stephen Illinois senator who introduced the Kansas-Nebraska Act, which allowed new territories to choose their own position on slavery; debated Abraham Lincoln on slavery issues in 1858 (pp. 360, 366)

Douglass, Frederick African American abolitionist leader who spoke eloquently for abolition in the United States and Britain before the Civil War (p. 320)

Du Bois, W.E.B. African American scholar and leader in early 1900s; encouraged African Americans to attend colleges to develop leadership skills (p. 557)

E

Edison, Thomas A. Inventor; developed the light bulb, the phonograph, and hundreds of other inventions in the late 1800s and early 1900s (p. 458)

Ehrlichman, John Advisor on domestic policy to President Richard Nixon; deeply involved in Watergate (p. 1059)

Einstein, Albert Physicist who fled Nazi persecution and later encouraged President Roosevelt to develop the atomic bomb (p. 852)

Eisenhower, Dwight D. Thirty-fourth President of the United States, 1953–1961; leader of Allied forces in World War II; as President, he promoted business and continued social programs (p. 916)

Albert Einstein

Ellington, Duke African American musician, bandleader, and composer of the 1920s and 1930s (p. 694)

Ellsberg, Daniel Defense Department official; leaked Pentagon Papers to the *New York Times* in 1971, revealing government lies to the public about Vietnam (p. 1071)

Emerson, Ralph Waldo Leader in the Transcendental movement; lecturer and writer (p. 311)

Equiano, Olaudah Antislavery activist who wrote an account of his enslavement (p. 84)

F

Father Divine African American minister; his Harlem soup kitchens fed the hungry during the Great Depression (p. 749)

Fillmore, Millard Thirteenth President of the United States, 1850–1853; promoted the Compromise of

1850 to smooth over disagreements about slavery in new territories (p. 358)

Finney, Charles Grandison Revivalist during the Second Great Awakening; emphasized religious conversion and personal choice (p. 310)

Fitzgerald, F. Scott Novelist who depicted the United States and the world during the 1920s in novels such as *The Great Gatsby* (p. 696)

Fitzhugh, George Southern author who criticized northern industrialists for exploiting workers in his 1857 book *Cannibals All!* (p. 348)

Ford, Gerald R. Thirty-eighth President of the United States, 1974–1977; succeeded and pardoned Nixon; failed to establish strong leadership (p. 1078)

Ford, Henry Pioneering auto manufacturer in the early 1900s; made affordable cars for the masses using assembly line and other production techniques (p. 725)

Franklin, Benjamin Colonial inventor, printer, writer, statesman; contributed to the Declaration of Independence and the Constitution (p. 79)

Frémont, John C. Explorer, military officer, and politician; led United States troops in 1846 Bear Flag Revolt when the United States took California from Mexico; ran for President as a Republican in 1856 (p. 352)

Friedan, Betty Feminist author; criticized limited roles for women in her 1963 book *The Feminine Mystique* (p. 998)

G

Garfield, James A. Twentieth President of the United States, 1881; his assassination by a disappointed office seeker led to the reform of the spoils system (p. 523)

Garrison, William Lloyd White leader of radical abolition movement based in Boston; founded *The Liberator* in 1831 to work for an immediate end to slavery (p. 320)

Garvey, Marcus African American leader from 1919 to 1926 who urged African Americans to return to their "motherland" of Africa; provided early inspiration for "black pride" movements (p. 704)

Gates, Bill Founder of Microsoft; revolutionized personal computing; investigated for questionable business practices (p. 1147)

George III King of England during the American Revolution (p. 109)

George, Henry Author of *Progress and Poverty* (1879), linking land speculation and poverty; proposed a single tax based on land value (p. 616)

Gingrich, Newt Representative from Georgia, 1979–1998; called on Republican congressional candidates in 1994 elections to endorse "Contract with America" (p. 1128)

Goodnight, Charles Texas cattle baron who helped blaze the Goodnight-Loving Trail through the Southwest (p. 502)

Gorbachev, Mikhail Soviet leader whose bold reforms led to the breakup of the Soviet Union in the late 1980s (p. 1113)

Gore, Albert A. Senator from Tennessee; Vice President under President William Clinton, 1993–2001 (p. 1131)

Graham, Billy Evangelist and presidential advisor; known for leading large-scale crusades, or religious rallies (p. 908)

Grant, Ulysses S. Eighteenth President of the United States, 1869–1877; commander of Union forces who accepted Lee's surrender in 1865 (p. 384)

H

Haldeman, H. R. Chief of Staff under President Richard Nixon; deeply involved in Watergate (p. 1059)

Hamilton, Alexander Officer in the War for Independence; delegate to the Constitutional Convention; Federalist and first Secretary of the Treasury (p. 166)

Handsome Lake Leader of the Seneca in late 1700s; encouraged blending of Native American and white American cultures (p. 221)

Harding, Warren G. Twenty-ninth President of the United States, 1921–1923; presided over a short administration marked by corruption (p. 712)

Harrington, Michael Author; wrote *The Other America* in 1962, which described areas of poverty in the otherwise prosperous United States (p. 971)

Harrison, Benjamin Twenty-third President of the United States, 1889–1893; signed 1890 Sherman Antitrust Act later used to regulate big business (p. 525)

Harrison, William Henry Ninth President of the United States, 1841; died of pneumonia after only a month in office (p. 303)

Hayes, Rutherford B. Nineteenth President of the United States, 1877–1881; promised to withdraw Union troops from the South in order to end dispute over his election; attacked spoils system (p. 444)

Hearst, William Randolph Newspaper publisher from 1887 until his death in 1951; used "yellow journalism" in the 1890s to stir up sentiment in favor of the Spanish-American War (p. 591)

Hiss, Alger Former State Department official investigated as a possible Communist spy by House Un-American Activities Committee after World War II; convicted of perjury in 1950 (p. 883)

Hitler, Adolf German leader of National Socialist (Nazi) Party, 1933–1945; rose to power by promoting racist and nationalist views (p. 802)

Ho Chi Minh Leader of the Communist Party in Indochina after World War II; led Vietnamese against the French, then North Vietnamese against the United States in the Vietnam War (p. 1024)

Hoover, Herbert Thirty-first President of the United States, 1929–1933; worked to aid Europeans during World War I; responded ineffectively to 1929 stock market crash and Great Depression (p. 730)

Houston, Sam Leader of Texas troops in war for independence from Mexico in 1836; elected first president of independent Texas (p. 265)

Hughes, Langston Writer active during the Harlem Renaissance (p. 697)

Humphrey, Hubert Democratic presidential candidate in 1968; lost narrowly to Nixon in an election bid hurt by his support for the Vietnam War and by third-party candidate George Wallace (p. 1041)

Hutchinson, Anne Critic of Puritan leadership of Massachusetts Bay Colony; banished for her religious beliefs (p. 55)

I

Isabella Ruler of Spanish Christian kingdoms with Ferdinand in late 1400s; sponsored Columbus's voyage to North America (p. 16)

J

Jackson, Andrew Seventh President of the United States, 1829–1837; supported minimal government and the spoils system; vetoed rechartering of the national bank; pursued harsh policy toward Native Americans (p. 299)

Jackson, Stonewall Confederate general known for his swift strikes against Union forces; earned nickname "Stonewall" by holding his forces steady under extreme pressure at the First Battle of Manassas (p. 381)

Jefferson, Thomas Third President of the United States, 1801–1809; main author of the Declaration of Independence; a firm believer in the people and decentralized power; reduced the federal government (p. 210)

Johnson, Andrew Seventeenth President of the United States, 1865–1869; clashed with Radical Republicans on Reconstruction programs; was impeached, then acquitted, in 1868 (p. 427)

Johnson, Lyndon B. Thirty-sixth President of the United States, 1963–1969; expanded social assistance with his Great Society program; increased United States commitment during Vietnam War (p. 976)

Jordan, Barbara Member of Congress from Texas; first African American and woman to represent her state in Congress; gave keynote addresses at 1976 and 1992 Democratic National Conventions (p. 1075)

Joseph, Chief Leader of Nez Percé; forced to give up his home by United States army, fled toward Canada; captured in 1877 (p. 493)

K

Kelley, Florence Progressive reformer active from 1886 to 1920; worked in state and federal government for laws on child labor, workplace safety, and consumer protection (p. 618)

Kennedy, John F. Thirty-fifth President of the United States, 1961–1963; seen as youthful and inspiring; known for his firm handling of the Cuban Missile Crisis; assassinated in 1963 (p. 972)

Kennedy, Robert F. Attorney General under his brother, President John Kennedy, in the early 1960s; supported civil rights; assassinated while running for President in 1968 (p. 1041)

Keynes, John Maynard British economist who believed that government spending could help a faltering economy; his theories helped shape New Deal legislation (p. 758)

Khomeini, Ayatollah Ruholla Islamic fundamentalist leader of Iran after the 1979 overthrow of the Shah; approved holding of American hostages (p. 1088)

Khrushchev, Nikita Soviet leader from 1953 to 1964; opposed President Kennedy in the Cuban Missile Crisis (p. 985)

King, Martin Luther, Jr. African American civil rights leader from the mid-1950s until his assassination in 1968; used nonviolent means such as marches, boycotts, and legal challenges to win civil rights (p. 938)

Kissinger, Henry Secretary of State under Presidents Richard Nixon and Gerald Ford; used *realpolitik* to open relations with China, to end the Vietnam War, and to moderate Middle East conflict (p. 1065)

L

Lafayette, Marquis de French officer who assisted American forces in the War for Independence (p. 132)

Lange, Dorothea Photographed migrant farm workers during the Great Depression; inspired government aid programs and Steinbeck's *The Grapes of Wrath* (p. 749)

Dorothea Lange

Lee, Jason First Methodist missionary to Oregon Country in 1834; built a mission school in Willamette Valley (p. 253)

Lee, Robert E. General of Confederate forces during the Civil War (p. 388)

Lenin, Vladimir I. Revolutionary leader in Russia; established a Communist government in 1917 (p. 659)

Levitt, William J. Built new communities in the suburbs after World War II, using mass-production techniques (p. 904)

Lewis, John L. Head of United Mine Workers through World War II; used strikes during the war to win pay raises (p. 829)

Lewis, Meriwether Leader with William Clark of expedition through the West beginning in 1804; brought back scientific samples, maps, and information on Native Americans (p. 216)

Lincoln, Abraham Sixteenth President of the United States, 1861–1865; known for his effective leadership during the Civil War and his Emancipation Proclamation declaring the end of slavery in Confederate-held territory (p. 394)

Lindbergh, Charles A. Aviator who became an international hero when he made the first solo flight across the Atlantic Ocean in 1927 (p. 688)

Little Turtle Native American leader of the late 1700s; adopted policy of accommodation (p. 221)

Lodge, Henry Cabot Massachusetts senator of early 1900s; supported United States imperialism (p. 588)

Long, Huey Louisiana politician in 1930s; suggested redistributing large fortunes by means of grants to families; assassinated in 1935 (p. 781)

M

MacArthur, Douglas United States general during the Great Depression, World War II, and Korean War; forced by Truman to resign in 1951 (p. 887)

Madison, James Fourth President of the United States, 1809–1817; called the Father of the Constitution for his leadership at the Constitutional Convention (p. 151)

Mahan, Alfred T. Author who argued in 1890 that the economic future of the United States rested on new overseas markets protected by a larger navy (p. 587)

Malcolm X African American leader during the 1950s and 1960s; eloquent spokesperson for African American self-sufficiency; assassinated in 1965 (p. 954)

Mann, Horace School reformer and supporter of public education before the Civil War; devised an educational system in Massachusetts later copied by many states (p. 314)

Mao Zedong Leader of Communists who took over China in 1949; remained in power until his death in 1976 (p. 885)

Marshall, George C. Army Chief of Staff during World War II and Secretary of State under President Harry Truman; assisted economic recovery in Europe after World War II and established strong allies for the United States through his Marshall Plan (p. 877)

Marshall, John Chief Justice of the Supreme Court appointed by John Adams; set precedents that established vital powers of the federal courts (p. 214)

Marshall, Thurgood First African American Supreme Court Justice; as a lawyer, won landmark school desegregation case *Brown* v. *Board of Education* in 1954 (p. 931)

McCarthy, Eugene Candidate in the 1968 Democratic presidential race who opposed the Vietnam War; convinced President Lyndon Johnson not to run again through his strong showing in the primaries (p. 1041)

McCarthy, Joseph R. Republican senator from Wisconsin in the late 1940s and early 1950s; led a crusade to investigate officials he claimed were Communists; discredited in 1954 (p. 889)

McClellan, George Early Union army leader in the Civil War; careful organizer and planner who moved too slowly for northern politicians; ran against President Abraham Lincoln in the election of 1864 (p. 384)

McKinley, William Twenty-fifth President of the United States, 1897–1901; supported tariffs and a gold standard; expanded the United States by waging the Spanish-American War (p. 526)

McNamara, Robert Secretary of Defense under Presidents Kennedy and Lyndon Johnson; expanded American involvement in Vietnam War (p. 1026)

Meade, George G. Union commander at Battle of Gettysburg in 1863; defended the high ground and forced the Confederate army to attack, causing great casualties (p. 405)

Metacom Leader of Pokanokets in Massachusetts; also known by his English name, King Philip; led Native Americans in King Philip's War, 1675–1676 (p. 56)

Mitchell, John Attorney General under President Richard Nixon; deeply involved in Watergate scandal (p. 1059)

Monroe, James Fifth President of the United States, 1817–1825; acquired Florida from Spain; declared Monroe Doctrine to keep foreign powers out of the Americas (p. 228)

Morse, Samuel F. B. Artist and inventor; developed telegraph and Morse code in 1844 (p. 350)

Mott, Lucretia Women's rights leader; helped organize first women's convention in Seneca Falls, New York, in 1848 (p. 329)

Mussolini, Benito Italian fascist leader who took power in the 1920s; called *Il Duce* ("the leader"); known for his brutal policies (p. 802)

N

Nader, Ralph Consumer advocate; published *Unsafe at Any Speed* in 1965, criticizing auto safety and inspiring new safety laws; Green Party candidate for president in the 2000 election (p. 1016)

Nimitz, Chester Leader of American naval forces in World War II Battle of Midway, during which several Japanese aircraft carriers were destroyed (p. 849)

Nixon, Richard M. Thirty-seventh President, 1969–1974; known for his foreign policy toward the Soviet Union and China and for illegal acts he committed in the Watergate affair that forced his resignation (p. 1067)

O

O'Connor, Sandra Day First woman Supreme Court Justice; appointed by President Reagan in 1981 (p. 1110)

Oppenheimer, J. Robert Physicist who led American effort in World War II to develop first atomic bomb (p. 852)

P

Pahlavi, Muhammed Reza Shah, Leader of Iran, from 1941 until his overthrow in 1979; supported by the United States; brought modernization to his country along with repression and corruption (p. 1088)

Paine, Thomas Author of political pamphlets during 1770s and 1780s; wrote *Common Sense* in 1776 (p. 118)

Parks, Rosa Civil rights worker whose arrest in 1955 touched off the Montgomery bus boycott (p. 933)

Paul, Alice Women's suffrage leader of early 1900s; her Congressional Union used aggressive tactics to push the Nineteenth Amendment (p. 638)

Penn, William English Quaker who founded the colony of Pennsylvania in 1681 (p. 60)

Perkins, Frances Secretary of Labor 1933–1945 under President Franklin Delano Roosevelt; first woman Cabinet member (p. 773)

Perot, H. Ross Billionaire businessman who challenged Bill Clinton and George H. W. Bush for the presidency in 1992; strong opponent of NAFTA (p. 1126)

Pershing, John Leader of the American Expeditionary Forces during World War I (p. 657)

Pierce, Franklin Fourteenth President of the United States, 1853–1857; signed the Kansas-Nebraska Act, which renewed conflicts over slavery in the territories (p. 359)

Pinckney, Eliza Lucas South Carolina plantation manager in the 1740s; promoted indigo as a staple crop (p. 81)

Polk, James K. Eleventh President of the United States, 1845–1849; led expansion of United States to southwest through war against Mexico (p. 351)

Polo, Marco Venetian traveler to China in the late 1200s; his book about the journey helped make Europeans aware of trade opportunities in eastern Asia (p. 12)

Popé Medicine man who led Pueblos and Apaches against Spanish rule in the Pueblo Revolt of 1680 (p. 41)

Prosser, Gabriel Planned a slave revolt in Virginia in 1800 that failed before it could get underway; captured and executed (p. 209)

Pulitzer, Joseph Early 1900s newspaper publisher; used "yellow journalism" to stir up public sentiment in favor of the Spanish-American War (p. 561)

R

Randolph, A. Philip Civil rights activist from the 1930s to the 1950s; planned the Washington march that pressured President Franklin D. Roosevelt into opening World War II defense jobs to African Americans (p. 856)

Reagan, Ronald Fortieth President of the United States, 1981–1989; popular conservative leader who promoted supply-side economics and created huge budget deficits (p. 1102)

Riis, Jacob Reformer who wrote *How the Other Half Lives,* describing the lives of poor immigrants in New York City in the late 1800s (p. 538)

Robinson, Jackie Athlete who in 1947 became the first African American to play baseball in the major leagues (p. 930)

Rockefeller, Nelson Vice President appointed by President Gerald Ford in 1974; the nation's only non-elected Vice President to serve with a nonelected President (p. 1079)

Roosevelt, Eleanor First Lady 1933–1945; tireless worker for social causes, including women's rights and civil rights for African Americans and other groups (p. 773)

Roosevelt, Franklin D. Thirty-second President of the United States, 1933–1945; fought the Great Depression through his New Deal social programs; battled Congress over Supreme Court control; proved a strong leader during World War II (p. 771)

Roosevelt, Theodore Twenty-sixth President of the United States, 1901–1909; fought trusts, aided Progressive reforms, built Panama Canal, and increased United States influence overseas (p. 601)

Rosenberg, Julius and Ethel Husband and wife convicted and executed in 1953 for passing atomic secrets to the Soviet Union; records opened after the end of the Cold War suggest Julius was guilty, but that Ethel did not take part in espionage (p. 883)

Rowson, Susanna Haswell Author of *Charlotte Temple* (1794), a popular moralizing novel that encouraged women to look beyond appearances when choosing a husband (p. 243)

S

Sacajawea Shoshone woman who served as guide and translator for Lewis and Clark on their exploratory journey through the West in the early 1800s (p. 216)

Sacco, Nicola Immigrant and anarchist tried and sentenced to death, in a highly controversial case, for a 1920 murder at a Massachusetts factory (p. 715)

Sadat, Anwar el- Egyptian leader in the 1970s; began the Middle East peace process by signing the 1978 Camp David Accords with Israel (p. 1087)

Salinger, J. D. Author of 1951 novel *The Catcher in the Rye,* which criticized 1950s pressure to conform (p. 910)

Santa Anna, Antonio López de Mexican dictator who led government and troops in war against Texas; won the battle of the Alamo (p. 264)

Schlafly, Phyllis Conservative activist; led campaign during the 1970s and 1980s to block the Equal Rights Amendment (p. 1001)

Seward, William Henry Republican antislavery leader during the 1860s; acquired Alaska in 1867 as Secretary of State (p. 443)

Sherman, William Tecumseh Union general in the Civil War; known for his destructive march from Atlanta to Savannah in 1864 (p. 413)

Sirica, John J. Washington judge who presided over the Watergate investigation in the 1970s; gave tough sentences to convicted participants and ordered President Richard Nixon to release secret tapes (p. 1073)

Sitting Bull, Chief Leader of Sioux in clashes with United States Army in Black Hills in 1870s (p. 494)

Slater, Samuel English textile worker who brought the Industrial Revolution to the United States by duplicating British textile machinery from memory (p. 273)

Smith, John Leader of the Jamestown, Virginia, colony in the early 1600s (p. 45)

Smith, Joseph Founder of Church of Jesus Christ of Latter-day Saints, or Mormons, in New York in 1830; killed by a mob in Illinois in 1844 (p. 247)

Spock, Benjamin Pediatrician and author of *The Common Sense Book of Baby and Child Care* (1946), which encouraged mothers to stay home with their children rather than work (p. 909)

Stalin, Joseph Leader of the Soviet Union from 1924–1953; worked with Roosevelt and Churchill during World War II but afterwards became an aggressive participant in the Cold War (p. 801)

Stanton, Elizabeth Cady Women's rights leader in the 1800s; helped organize first women's convention; wrote the Declaration of Sentiments on women's rights in 1848 (p. 330)

Starr, Ellen Gates Cofounder of Chicago's Hull House, the first settlement house, in 1889 (p. 542)

Steinem, Gloria Journalist, women's rights leader since 1960s; founded *Ms.* magazine in 1972 to cover women's issues (p. 999)

Stevenson, Adlai Senator from Illinois and Democratic candidate for President in 1952 and 1956 against Eisenhower (p. 916)

Stilwell, Joseph World War II general active in the campaign against Japan in Southeast Asia (p. 847)

Stowe, Harriet Beecher Author of the novel *Uncle Tom's Cabin* (1852), which contributed significantly to antisouthern feelings among Northerners before the Civil War (p. 348)

Sumner, Charles Abolitionist and senator from Massachusetts; beaten badly with a cane in the Senate by a southern congressman after making an antislavery speech (p. 364)

Charles Sumner

T

Taft, William Howard Twenty-seventh President of the United States, 1909–1913; continued Progressive reforms of President Theodore Roosevelt; promoted "dollar diplomacy" to expand foreign investments (p. 602)

Taney, Roger Chief Justice of the Supreme Court who wrote an opinion in the 1857 *Dred Scott* case that declared the Missouri Compromise unconstitutional (p. 365)

Taylor, Zachary Twelfth President of the United States, 1849–1850; Mexican War officer (p. 356)

Tecumseh Native American leader in the late 1700s and early 1800s; led a pan-Indian movement that tried to unite several groups despite their differences (p. 222)

Tenskwatawa Native American leader of the early 1800s known as the Prophet; he called for a return to traditional ways and rejection of white values (p. 222)

Thoreau, Henry David Transcendentalist author known for his work *Walden* (1854) and other writings (p. 312)

Travis, William Leader in Texas's bid for independence from Mexico in 1836; died at the Alamo after appealing to the United States for help (p. 264)

Truman, Harry S Thirty-third President of the United States, 1945–1953; authorized use of atomic bomb; signed Marshall Plan to rebuild Europe (p. 870)

Truth, Sojourner Abolitionist and women's rights advocate before the Civil War; as a former slave, she spoke effectively to white audiences on abolition issues (pp. 322, 331)

Tubman, Harriet "Conductor" on the Underground Railroad, which helped slaves escape to freedom before the Civil War (p. 323)

Turner, Frederick Jackson Historian who wrote an essay in 1893 emphasizing the western frontier as a powerful force in the formation of the American character (p. 505)

Turner, Nat African American preacher who led a slave revolt in 1831; captured and hanged after the revolt failed (p. 289)

Tweed, William Marcy Boss of the Tammany Hall political machine in New York City; convicted of forgery and larceny in 1873 and died in jail in 1878 (p. 539)

Tyler, John Tenth President of the United States, 1841–1845; accomplished little due to quarrels between Whigs and Jacksonian Democrats (p. 303)

V

Van Buren, Martin Eighth President of the United States, 1837–1841; Jacksonian Democrat; was voted out of office after the Panic of 1837 brought widespread unemployment and poverty (p. 303)

Vance, Cyrus Secretary of State under President Jimmy Carter; invited Israelis and Egyptians to Camp David in 1978 to begin Middle East peace process (p. 1087)

Vanzetti, Bartolomeo Immigrant and anarchist tried and sentenced to death in a highly controversial case, for a 1920 murder at a Massachusetts factory (p. 715)

Vesey, Denmark African American who planned 1822 South Carolina slave revolt; captured and hanged after revolt failed (p. 288)

von Steuben, Friedrich Prussian officer who trained Washington's troops at Valley Forge (p. 132)

W

Walker, David African American author of *Appeal to the Colored Citizens of the World* (1829), which called for an immediate end to slavery (p. 318)

Walker, Madam C. J. African American leader and businesswoman in the early 1900s; she spoke out against lynching (p. 568)

Wallace, George C. Third-party candidate for President in 1968; focused his campaign on issues of blue-collar anger in the North and racial tension (p. 1043)

Warren, Earl Chief Justice of United States Supreme Court 1953–1968; investigated President Kennedy's assassination; led in many decisions that protected civil rights, rights of the accused, and right to privacy (p. 981)

Washington, Booker T. African American leader from the late 1800s until his death in 1915; founded Tuskegee Institute in Alabama; encouraged African Americans to learn trades (p. 556)

Washington, George First President of the United States, 1789–1797; led American forces in the War for Independence; set several federal precedents, including the two-term maximum for presidential office (p. 167)

Webster, Noah Author of the best-known American dictionary in the early 1800s; promoted a standard national language and public support for education (p. 240)

Whitman, Narcissa Prentiss Missionary; one of the first white women to cross the Rocky Mountains to Oregon in 1836 (p. 253)

Whitney, Eli Inventor; developed the cotton gin in 1793, which rapidly increased cotton production in the South and led to a greater demand for slave labor (p. 273)

Wilhelm, Kaiser Emperor of Germany during World War I; symbol to the United States of German militarism and severe efficiency (p. 650)

Wilson, Woodrow Twenty-eighth President of the United States, 1913–1921; tried to keep the United States out of World War I; proposed League of Nations (p. 631)

Y

Yeltsin, Boris Leader of Russia in late 1980s and 1990s; took over from Mikhail Gorbachev as reforms continued and Communist Party control ended (p. 1135)

York, Alvin American soldier who was awarded the Congressional Medal of Honor for bravery during World War I (p. 663)

Young, Brigham Mormon leader who supervised migration to Utah beginning in the 1840s; first governor when Utah became a United States territory (p. 255)

Z

Zenger, Peter Colonial printer arrested for libel; his landmark trial established truth as a defense against libel (p. 79)

Biographical Dictionary

Index

Note: Entries with a page number followed by a *c* indicate a chart or graph on that page; *go* indicates a graphic organizer; *m* indicates a map; and *p* indicates a picture.

Index

Index

Index

thirteen, *circa* 1750, 35*m*
trades and occupations, 79–80
trends relating to emerging tensions in, 89*go*
women in, 80–81, 80*p*
colonization
by England, 43–44, 74, 104–105
by France, 74, 104–105
by Spain, 36, 37–41
Colorado, 1188*m*, 1196
in Dust Bowl, 739*m*
gains statehood, 487
gold strikes in, 256
Mexican Americans in, 1004
mining in, 498, 499*m*
Native Americans in, 493, 494*m*
Columbia, 1094*p*, 1111
Columbian Exchange, 26*c*
devastation of Native Americans, due to, 26
Columbus, Christopher, 22–25, 22*p*, 29, xlvi*q*
early life of, 22–23
excerpt from letter to Queen Isabella and King Ferdinand, 25*q*
impact of findings of, 26–27
meets first Native Americans, 24–25
return trip of, 25
voyages of, 23–24, 36
Comanche, 259, 260, 261
Commentaries on the Laws of England (Blackstone), 80*q*
commercials, 902. *See also* advertising
Committee for Industrial Organization. *See* Congress of Industrial Organizations (CIO)
Committee on Civil Rights, 914
Committees of Correspondence, 114, 115. *See also* First Continental Congress
Commodity Credit Corporation, 915
Commoner, Barry, 1015
Common Sense (Paine), 118, 118*p*, 118*q*, 119
many colonists support separation from England after reading, 118
Commonwealth of Independent States, 1117
communication, 276, 457, 584, 459–460
communism, 643. *See also* Vietnam War
American fears about, 713–714
collapse of, 1135
desire of Soviet Union to spread, 871
disillusionment with, 881
expansion in Asia of, 885–886
fighting, in the Americas, 1106
origins of, 713
spreads in Eastern Europe, 871–872
Communist Manifesto (Marx), 478
Communist Party, 713
in China, Mao Zedong's leadership of, 885
collapse of, 1116
during Great Depression, 754, 881
Communists. *See also* containment; Vietnam; Vietnam War
brutality of, during Tet Offensive, 1035
hysteria related to, and McCarthyism, 889. *See also* McCarthy, Joseph

perception of U.S. threat regarding, 883
as spies, in America, 881
take control of China, 880
Community Service Organization, 935
Compromise of 1850, 356–359, 356*m*, 362. *See also* Calhoun, John C.; Clay, Henry; Webster, Daniel
important elements of, 355*go*
Compromise of 1877, 444–445
computers, 901, 902–903, 1147
Comstock, Anthony, 545
Comstock Law, 545
Comstock Lode, 498
concentration camps, 842, 843
Coney Island, 560
Confederate States of America, 371
currency of, 399*g*
fall of, 425
lack of recognition for, 392
open rebellion of. *See also* Sumter, Fort
conformity, 907, 908, 909, 1009*p*
conglomerates, 901
Congressional Union (CU), 638, 639
Congress of Industrial Organizations (CIO), 786
merges with AFL, 904. *See also* American Federation of Labor (AFL)
Congress of Racial Equality (CORE), 857, 937–938
creates the sit-in, 857, 941
Congress, United States. *See also* U.S. House of Representatives; U.S. Senate
80th, 914, 915
84th, 933*q*
African Americans elected to, 439*p*, 443*g*
amends Constitution, 431
anti-Klan laws and, 443. *See also* Enforcement Act of 1870
Articles of Confederation and, 145
Bank of the United States and, 201, 302
Compromise of 1850 and, 358. *See also* Compromise of 1850
creation of, 155–156
display of national unity by, 1125*p*
Gulf of Tonkin Resolution and, 1027
Hamilton debt plan and, 201
increases taxes during World War I, 651
is pressed to expand navy, 587–588
Marshall Plan and, 877
Neutrality Acts, 815–816
ratifies separate World War I peace treaties, 672
reaches Missouri Compromise, 229
Reconstruction plan and, 426
regulation of railroads by, 511
Theodore Roosevelt and, 600
war resolution against Japan, 821
Conkling, Roscoe, 523
Connally, John, 972–973
Connecticut, 50, 61*c*, 82, 119, 227, 1188*m*, 1196
early government in, 54
Eli Whitney builds musket factory in, 281. *See also* Whitney, Eli

Puritans burn Pequot fort in, 55. *See also* Pequot War
Yale established in colonial, 82
Connor, Eugene "Bull," 945, 946
conquistadors, 38
Conrad, Frank, 693
conscientious objectors, 658, 1039, 1040
conservation movement, 601, 627, 1015, 1016
"Conservative Critique, A" (Taft, Robert A.), 781
conservative movement, 1096*go*. *See also* conservatism
controls U.S. agenda, 1100
evolution of, 1097–1099, 1097*c*, 1119*go*
major events in history of, 1096*go*
social concerns of, 1098–1099
Constitution. *See* U.S. Constitution
Constitutional Convention, 142*p*, 150–154, 150*go*, 232
divisions at, 151–152
George Washington presiding over, 100–101*p*
ideas discussed at, 157
Constitutional Union Party, 370
constitutions, state, 145–146
Constitution, USS ("Old Ironsides"), 224*p*, 225–226
consumer economy, 723, 1153. *See also* economy
of 1920s, 725
thriving, postwar, 900–901
consumer movement, 1013*go*, 1016–1017
containment, 873, 881, 991
as important part of foreign policy, 891
Johnson commits to, 1027–1028
Truman applies policy of, 873–874, 1024, 1025
Continental Army, 131, 132
driven from New York, 130
transformed into effective fighting force, 132
Washington leads, 128
Continental Congress, 133–134
currency, 134*p*
Great Seal of the United States, adopted by, 147*p*
Continental Divide, 610
contraband, 396. *See also* slaves
Contract Labor Act (1864), 473. *See also* immigration
repeal of, 544
Contract with America, 1128–1129
Contras, aid to, 1112
Convention of 1818, 253
convoy system, in World War I, 658
Conyngham, David, 420–421
Coolidge, Calvin, 717, 721*p*, 1198
death of, 755
laissez-faire policy of, 720
policies of, 720–721
Cooper, Anna Julia, 556, 568
Coos, 6
Copperheads, 393–394
Coral Sea, Battle of the, 848–849
Coram, Thomas, 74
Corbin, Margaret, 129
Córdoba, Treaty of, 262

Index

Index

Gulf of Tonkin Resolution, 594, 1027, 1028. *See also* Vietnam War
Gullah language, 85
Gutenberg, Johann, 14–15
Gutiérrez, José, 1005

H

habeas corpus, suspension of writ of, 395
Hague Draft Rules of Air Warfare, 810
Haldeman, H. R., 1059, 1059*p*, 1073, 1074
Hale, Nathan, 130, 130*p*
Hale, Sarah Joseph, 331
Half-Breeds, 523
Half Slave and Half Free (Levine), 370
Hall, James, 249, 249*q*, 250
Halsey, William, 850, 864*p*
Hamer, Fannie Lou, 952, 952*q*
Hamilton, Alexander, 147, 157, 158–159, 158*p*, 166*p*, 201*p*, 205*q*, 210*q*
  background of, 166–167
  and common characteristics with Thomas Jefferson, 200*go*
  duel of Burr and, 217
  economic program of, 200–201
  as head of Department of the Treasury, 166–167, 200–202
  opposition to, 202–203
  view of Bank of the United States of, 302
Hancock, John, 116, 119
Hancock, Winfield S., 523
Handsome Lake, 221–222, 222*q*. *See also* Seneca
Harding, Warren G., 672, 699, 712, 712*p*, 712*q*, 718*p*, 719*q*, 1198
  Cabinet appointments of, 718
  death of, 720
  foreign policy of, 718
  presidency of, 717–720
Harlem, 694, 705, 914. *See also* Harlem Renaissance
Harlem Hell Fighters (369th Infantry Regiment), 659
Harlem Renaissance, 696–697
Harrington, Michael, 971, 982
Harrison, Benjamin, 525, 1198
  approves Sherman Antitrust Act, 511
Harrison, William Henry, 220, 222, 225, 303, 1197
  campaign poster, 303*p*
Hartford Convention, 227
Hartford Female Seminary, 327
Harvard College, 81, 81*p*
Havel, Vaclav, 1116
Hawaii, 97*p*, 1188*m*, 1196
  annexation of, 595
  U.S. treaty signed with, 586
Hawley-Smoot Tariff, 757, 818
Hawthorne, Nathaniel, 272*q*, 316, 474
Hay-Bunau-Varilla Treaty, 599
Hayden, Tom, 1038
Hayes, Rutherford B., 444–445, 480
  fights spoils system, 522–523
  installs telephone in White House, 460

"plowing under" Reconstruction, 445*p*
  vetoes Bland-Allison Act, 509
Hay, John, 537, 596, 599*q*. *See also* China
Haymarket Riot, 481–482
Hayne, Robert, 299
Hays, Mary, 129
headright system, 46. *See also* land ownership
Head Start, 967*p*, 978, 982*p*
health maintenance organizations (HMOs), opposing viewpoints on regulating, 1128
Hearst, William Randolph, 562, 591, 591*p*, 599, 693
Helsinki Accords, 1082
Hemingway, Ernest, 696
Hendrick, 91, 91*q*
Henry, Fort, 385
Henry, Joseph, 275*c*
Henry, Patrick, 115, 116, 116*q*, 119, 159
Henry VIII, King (of England), 50
Hepburn Act, 626, 626*c*
heroes, 688–690
Hessians, 129, 131
Hickory Point, Battle of, 363*p*
Hidalgo, Miguel, 262–263
Higher Education Act, 999
highways, 906
  business development along, 737*p*, 922*p*, 923*p*
  changes in daily life, due to, 737
  principal U.S. (1926), 736*m*
  projected interstate highway system (1957), 905*m*
Hill, James J., 461, 468, 483
hippies, 1009, 1009*p*, 1010, 1012, 1012*p*
Hiroshima, 852*p*, 853. *See also* atomic bomb
Hispanic Americans. *See* Chicano movement; Latinos; Mexican Americans
Hispaniola, 25. *See also* Columbus, Christopher
Hiss, Alger, 883
History and Description of Africa, The (Africanus), 20*q*
History of Plymouth Plantation (Bradford), 51
History of the American Revolution (Warren), 240
Hitler, Adolf, 798*p*, 800*p*, 803*p*, 808*p*, 810*p*
  appeasement of, 805
  Aryan superiority theory of, 803, 841*q*
  becomes chancellor of Germany, 803–804
  breaks nonagression pact with Stalin, 835
  control of Europe by (1942), 825*m*
  Europe of (1942), 825*m*
  signs nonagression pact with Stalin, 808, 868
  suicide of, 840
Hobbes, Thomas, 120
hobos, 746, 753. *See also* Great Depression
Ho Chi Minh, 1024–1025, 1027

Ho Chi Minh Trail, 1034, 1034*m*. *See also* Vietnam War
holding companies, 626
Holland, 59
Hollywood, 691*p*, 1096
  during the Depression, 788–789
  growth of film industry in, 691
  House Un-American Activities Committee (HUAC) investigates, 882
Hollywood Ten, 882
Holmes, Oliver Wendell, Jr., 714
Holocaust, 843–845, 891
  estimated Jewish losses in, 844*m*
homeless people, during Great Depression, 746
Homer, Winslow, 436
Homestead Act, 393, 438, 489, 502, 528
homesteaders, 502–504, 503*p*, 506
Homestead Strike, 482, 511
Honecker, Erich, 1116
Hood, James, 413
Hooker, Joseph "Fighting Joe," 403–404
Hooker, Thomas, 54
Hoover Dam, 757. *See also* Boulder Dam
Hoover, Herbert, 666*q*, 717, 718, 720, 721, 730*p*, 730*q*, 740, 741, 760*q*. *See also* Great Depression
  Bonus Army and, 758–759
  campaign theme song of, 756
  criticizes New Deal, 784*q*
  holds to principle of voluntary action, 757
  insists on confidence, 756–757
  unpopularity of, 758–759
  during World War I, 665–666
Hoover, J. Edgar, 701
Hoovervilles, 746, 746*p*, 754
Hopewell, 8
Hopi, 7
Hopkins, Harry, 770, 770*q*, 772, 786
Hopper, Edward, 695
horizontal consolidation, 471*p*
horse, impact of, 260*p*, 491–492
  on Plains Indians, 259
House Judiciary Committee, 1073, 1075–1076
Houseman, John, 790
House of Burgesses, 46, 73*p*. *See also* Virginia
House Un-American Activities Committee (HUAC), 882, 1067
  investigations of, 790, 883
Houston, Sam, 264–265, 265*p*
  background of, 265
Howe, William, 128, 130, 131
Hudson, Henry, 43
Hughes, Charles Evans, 633, 655, 718
Hughes, Langston, 697, 697*p*
Hughes, Sarah T., 975, 975*p*
Hull House, 542–543, 618. *See also* Addams, Jane
humanism, 14
Humphrey, Hubert, 1041, 1042–1043
Hungary, 871–872
Huns. *See* World War I, hostility to Germans during
Hunt, E. Howard, 1071, 1072, 1073
Huntington, Collis P., 521
Huron, 90, 110

Hurston, Zora Neale, 696*p*, 697, 788
Hussein, Saddam, 1118
Hutchinson, Anne, 55
Hutchinson, Thomas, 112
Hutchinson, William, 55
hydrogen bomb, 880, 892, 989
hydrophones, 654, 658. *See also* U-
    boats

I

Ickes, Harold L., 772, 829
Idaho, 1188*m*, 1196
    gains statehood, 487*m*
    gold strikes in, 256
    mining in, 499
    national parks in, 505, 623*m*
    Native Americans in, 494*m*
Ide, William B., 352
"I Have a Dream" speech, 856, 950,
    950*q*
Illinois, 280–281, 1188*m*, 1196
    abolitionist movement in, 323, 325
    Cahokia, early history of, 8
    civil rights movement in, 937
    election of 1960, 969, 969*m*
    gains statehood, 250
    growth of Chicago, due to railroads,
    349
    Haymarket Riot, 481–482, 482*p*
    land division in, 196*c*, 197*p*
    Mormon migration to, 255
    strikes in, 480, 482–483
illiteracy, in the United States
    (1870–1920), 554*g*
immigrants, 332*p*, 527*p*, 549*p*. *See also*
    immigration
    aboard ship, 528*p*
    American worries about, 714
    arrival in America of, 529
    from Asia, 531–532, 548*p*
    in colonies, 89–90
    from Cuba, 1004
    difficult journey for, 528
    discrimination against potential, 883.
    See also McCarran-Walter Act
    distribution of, in the U.S.
    (1899–1910), 519*m*
    education for, 553–554. *See also*
    assimilation
    estimated number of, to the United
    States, by region (1871–1920),
    540*c*
    from Europe, 529–531
    fear of, 359*p*, 666–667
    German, 90, 333, 349, 548
    hopes and dreams of, 528
    hostility toward, 333–334
    Irish, 90, 332–334, 349, 548. *See also*
    Irish Potato Famine
    Japanese, 532, 601
    as laborers, 333, 473
    literacy tests for, 666–667
    physical exams for, 529–530
    "picture brides," 532
    post–World War I fears related to,
    719
    reaction of, to World War I, 650
    reasons of, for coming to America,
    527*go*
    reformers try to help, 542*p*

settlement of, in Sun Belt, 1144
settling of, 490, 530
working in factories, 459
working on transcontinental railroad,
    461
World War I posters with appeals to,
    666*p*
immigration. *See also* immigrants
    to Argentina, 530
    Asian (1951–1978), 1006*g*
    Chinese, 531*p*, 548*p*
    Congress acts to limit, 687
    debate over, 1145
    in the early 1990s, 549
    European (1870–1920), 529*g*
    European (1919–1929), 719*g*
    growing turmoil over, 360–361
    halt of, during World War I, 668
    from Italy, 579*c*
    from Japan, 532, 585*m*
    of Jews, in the 1840s, 247
    Mexican policy of, in Texas, 264
    from Mexico, 532–533, 533*p*, 549,
    1004
    policies, changing, 1143–1144
    quotas, 719, 979
    reform, 979
    rising, 332–333
    surge in, 359–360, 549. *See also*
    nativism
    to the United States (1840s–1850s),
    332*go*
    wave of 1990s, 1143
Immigration Act of 1965, 549, 979,
    1143
Immigration Act of 1990, 1143–1144
Immigration Reform and Control
    Act, 1143
Immigration Restriction Act, 533
impeachment, 232, 1073
    of Clinton, 1130
    of Andrew Johnson, 233. *See also*
    Johnson, Andrew
    hearings for Nixon, 1075–1076
    opposing viewpoints on, 1074
Impending Crisis 1848–1861, The
    (Potter), 370
imperialism, 647
    American, in Western Hemisphere,
    586
    appeal of, 606–607
    arguments for and against, 604*go*
    growth of, 584–585
    of Japan, 815–816
    motivation behind, 586
    opposition to, 593, 604
    viewed from abroad, 607
    world (*circa* 1900), 583*m*
impressment, 217, 224–225, 227
Incas, 261
    resistance of, 38
indentured servants, 46–47, 75, 80
    used for tobacco processing, 46*p*
Independents, 523, 1098
Indiana, 280, 316, 1188*m*, 1196
    allows white adult men to vote, 298
    gains statehood, 250
    land division in, 196*c*, 197*p*
    Native Americans fight American
    expansion into, 220
    New Harmony, 308*p*
    Prophetstown, established by

Tenskwatawa, 222
    Revolutionary War in, 134
    Territory, 222
Indian Country, 251
Indian Education Act of 1972, 1008
Indian Removal Act, 301
Indian Reorganization Act, 771
Indian Self-Determination and Edu-
    cation Assistance Act of 1975,
    1008
Indian Territory, 301, 497. *See also*
    Oklahoma
Indian wars, 492–495, 493*p*, 497. *See
    also* Native Americans; specific bat-
    tles
industrialists, 470, 472
    convert to civilian production, 901
    golden period for, 520
    opposition to expansion by, 606
industrialization, 438–439, 456, 467
    changes in daily life due to, 584
    contributors to, 484*go*
    effect of, on workers, 473*go*
    harsh side of, 469
    rapid increase in Northeast of,
    281–282
    women feel impact of, 326
    workers of, 473*p*
Industrial Revolution, 272–274, 896
industrial unions, 481
Industrial Workers of the World
    (IWW), 479, 667
industries
    birth of U.S. textile, 273–274. *See also*
    textile mills, centralized
    condition of, after World War I, 729
    decline of, 733
    foreign competition to, 1111
    growth of, 459, 468*p*, 728
    importance of railroads to, 462–463
    move into war production, 827–828
    protectors of, 470*p*
    switch production in World War I,
    665
inflation, 134, 508, 509, 1106, 1107.
    See also economy
    under Carter, 1084, 1089
    controlling, during World War II, 830
    fear of, 913
    low, under Clinton, 1130
    under Nixon, 1060, 1080–1081
    rate of (1968–1976), 1060*g*
    during Revolutionary War, 134
    in South, 398, 399*g*
    in Spain, during 1500s, 40
*Influence of Sea Power Upon History,
    The, 1660–1783* (Mahan), 587
influenza epidemic, 662
Information Age, 896, 1147–1149,
    1153
infrastructure, 439
Ingalik, 5
Inglis, Charles, 119
initiative, institution of, 624
Inquisition, 16
installment plans, 726, 732. *See also*
    credit
integration, 962–963, 962*p*. *See also*
    civil rights; civil rights movement
    black opposition to, 955. *See also*
    black nationalism

victory of, 211, 212
view of Bank of the United States of, 302

Jeffersonian Republicans, 204–205, 207, 210–211, 291. *See also* Jefferson, Thomas
  conflict among, 293
  tensions between Federalists and, 208
  vs. Federalists, 202*c*

Jews
  Denmark's rescue of, 843
  Holocaust and, 843–845, 844*m*
  identification for, 843*p*
  immigration of, in the 1840s, 247
  Nazi persecution of, 841*p*, 842–843
  in New Amsterdam, 60
  resistance of, 844
  seek safety in Palestine, 891

Jiang Jieshi, 815–816, 847, 880, 885
  on Taiwan, 887

Jim Crow laws, 306, 565–566, 576–577, 577*p*, 634, 704, 773, 855

jingoism, 591

John, King (of England), 12–13

Johnson, Andrew, 414, 422*p*, 428, 1079, 1198
  Congress and, 432
  impeachment of, 233, 433
  opposition to Reconstruction policies of, 431
  Reconstruction plan of, 427, 430
  ticket for impeachment trial of, 233*p*

Johnson, Claudia "Lady Bird" (Mrs. Lyndon B.), 975*p*, 976

Johnson, James Weldon, 696–697

Johnson, Lyndon B., 615, 758, 966*p*, 975*q*, 976*p*, 976*q*, 977*q*, 1014, 1015*q*, 1022*p*, 1027*p*, 1027*q*, 1041*q*, 1097–1098, 1199. *See also* Great Society programs
  affirmative action and, 1145
  assumes presidency, 1027
  background of, 976–977
  becomes President, 973
  civil rights and, 950–951, 952–953
  "daisy" campaign commercial, 977, 977*p*
  Dominican Republic and, 991
  goes to South Vietnam, 1026
  Great Society programs, 976, 977–979
  as Kennedy running mate, 969
  opposition to, 1040–1041
  refuses to run for second term, 958
  takes oath of office, 975, 975*p*
  Vietnam War and, 991, 1036, 1040–1041
  war on poverty, 978

Johnston, Joseph, 388, 413

joint-stock company, 44

Joliet, Louis, 49*p*, 50, 50*p*

Jolson, Al, 692

Jones Act, 595. *See also* Puerto Rico

Jones, Mary Harris "Mother," 619, 619*p*

Joplin, Janis, 1011

Joplin, Scott, 563

Jordan, Barbara, 959, 959*q*, 1074*q*, 1075, 1075*p*

Joseph, Chief, 493*p*

Journal of the Federal Convention (Madison), 150

Journey in the Seaboard Slave States, A (Olmsted), 334

judicial review, 214–215, 232, 307. *See also* Supreme Court

Judiciary Act of 1789, 214, 232

Judiciary Act of 1801, 214, 232

judiciary, federal, 157
  Jefferson and, 214

Jungle, The (Sinclair), 613*p*, 614, 617

Jutland, Battle of, 654

K

Kaiser, Henry J., 828

Kalakaua, King (of Hawaii), 595

kamikazes, 850, 851, 852*p*

Kansas, 360–361, 365–366, 498–499, 1188*m*, 1196
  "Bleeding Kansas," 364, 364*m*
  Brown v. *Board of Education,* 931–932, 944*c*, 1099
  cattle industry in, 500
  Coronado reaches, 40
  Dust Bowl migrants leave, 747
  gains statehood, 487*m*
  Territory, 363
  two competing capitals in, 363–364

Kansas-Nebraska Act, 360–361. *See also* Kansas; Nebraska
  demands for repeal of, 361
  meetings to protest, 361
  proslavery forces win passage of, 363
  supports practice of popular sovereignty, 360

Karisefni, Thorfinn, 23

Kearny, Stephen, 352

Kearsarge, U.S.S., 392*p*

Keith, Minor C., 587, 607

Kelley, Florence, 618–619, 619*p*, 625

Kellogg-Briand Pact, 721, 813, 814

Kennan, George, 873

Kennedy, Anthony, 1110

Kennedy, Caroline, 970*p*, 972, 973*p*

Kennedy, Edward M., 973*p*, 1070, 1089

Kennedy, Jacqueline Bouvier (Mrs. John F.), 966*p*, 972–973, 972*p*, 973*p*, 975*p*

Kennedy, John F., 233*p*, 945*q*, 948*p*, 949*q*, 966*p*, 969*p*, 970*p*, 970*q*, 972*p*, 972*q*, 987*p*, 988*q*, 1007, 1022*p*, 1126*p*, 1199
  African Americans and, 948–949
  assassination of, 950, 972–973, 974, 1027
  Bay of Pigs invasion, 983–985
  Berlin crisis and, 985–986
  civil rights and, 948–949
  Cold War and, 983, 985–986
  Executive Orders of, 952*c*, 971
  Khrushchev and, 985, 986. *See also* Cuban Missile Crisis
  New Frontier, 968*go*
  space program of, 972
  televised debate of Richard M. Nixon and, 968, 968*p*
  Vietnam policy of, 1025–1027
  Vietnam War and, 1026–1027

Kennedy, John F., Jr., 970*p*, 972, 973*p*

Kennedy, Robert F., 948*p*, 973*p*, 976, 987, 989, 1041, 1041*p*, 1041*q*
  assassination of, 958–959, 958*p*, 1041
  sends federal marshals to protect Freedom Riders, 944

Kennesaw Mountain, Battle of, 342–343*p*

Kent, Rockwell, 695

Kent State University, 1046, 1046*p*

Kentucky, 243, 285, 1188*m*, 1196
  birth of Lincoln in, 366
  frontier, Daniel Boone explores, 106
  gains statehood, 250
  Jackson vetoes road bill for, 298
  Second Great Awakening and, 245

Kerner Commission, 957

Kerouac, Jack, 737, 911, 911*p*

Key, Francis Scott, 226–227

Keynesian theory, 1103

Keynes, John Maynard, 758, 829, 1060, 1102–1103

Khmer Rouge, 1048, 1082

Khomeini, Ayatollah Ruholla, 1088, 1089

Khrushchev, Nikita, 233*p*, 893*p*, 949, 983*p*, 989
  Kennedy and, 985, 986, 989. *See also* Cuban Missile Crisis

Killebrew, Bruce, 962–963, 962*p*

King, Coretta Scott, 953*p*

King, Martin Luther, Jr., 856, 933, 933*q*, 938–939, 938*p*, 950*p*, 953*p*, 958*q*, 965*p*
  arrest of, in Birmingham, 945–946. *See also* "Letter from Birmingham Jail"
  birthday of, becomes national holiday, 1109
  "I Have a Dream" speech, 950, 950*q*
  Montgomery bus boycott and, 933–934
  Selma March, 944*c*, 953, 953*p*, 965*p*
  supports sit-ins, 942

King Philip's War, 55–57, 56*p*. *See also* Metacom
  1675–1676, 56*m*
  economic effects of, 57
  economy after, 57

Kings Mountain, Battle of, 135

kinship, 8, 86

Kissinger, Henry, 1047, 1059, 1059*p*, 1064–1065, 1064*p*, 1065*p*, 1065, 1069*q*, 1071, 1081

Knights of Labor, 478–479, 619

Know-Nothing Party, 544, 548
  nominates Millard Fillmore, 364
  rise of, 359
  whips up fears against immigrants, 359*p*

Knox, Henry, 128, 166, 166*p*

Koob, Kathryn, 1088, 1088*q*

Korea
  conflict between China and Japan over, 585
  division of, 885
  Japanese rule of, 813, 885
  Japan gains control over, 601

Korean War, 594, 884–888 (1950–1953), 886*m*
  American soldiers during, 884*p*
  causes and effects of, 884*go*

Pequot War, 55
per capita income, increase of postwar, 900
perestroika, 1113, 1115
Perkins, Frances, 773
Perot, H. Ross, 1126–1127, 1129–1130
Perry, Matthew C., 586, 813
Perry, Oliver Hazard, 226
Pershing, John J., 603, 657, 658, 659*p*
Persian Gulf War, 406, 594, 1118–1119, 1118*p*, 1126, 1139
Peru, 38
Petersburg, siege of, 411–412
Petition of Right, 120*c*
Petrarch, 14
petroglyphs, Native North American, 4*p*
Philadelphia
in the 1730s, 77*p*
abolitionist problems in, 325
British occupation of, 131
colonial, 74–75
Constitutional Convention meets in, 150. See also Constitutional Convention
First Continental Congress meets in, 115
Independence Hall, 150*p*, 232*p*
members of Continental Congress flee, 130
riots, in Irish districts of, 334
Second Continental Congress meets in, 119
philanthropists, 468, 554, 555
Philip II, King (of Spain), 36
Philip, King. See Metacom
Philippine Islands, 605
American and Filipino prisoners in, 847*p*
campaign to liberate, 850
dilemma in, 593–594
fall of, 847
Japan attacks, 846
opposition to occupation of, 604
Spanish-American War and, 592
phonograph, 458*p*, 563
photography, 538, 560
Picasso, Pablo, 806
Pickering, William, 918*p*
Pickett's Charge, 406–407
piecework, 474
Pierce, Franklin, 358*p*, 359, 1197
Pietà, 14
Pike, Zebulon, 216
Pilgrims, 51–52, 51*p*
Pilgrim's Progress (Bunyan), 616
Pinchback, P.B.S., 434, 435
Pinchot, Gifford, 627, 629
Pinckney, Eliza Lucas, 80–81, 81*q*
Pinckney, Thomas, 205, 211, 217–218, 251
Pinckney Treaty
Adams accuses Spain of breaking, 252
components of, 251
Pinkertons, 482, 511
Pinta, 24
pioneers
benefits of log cabins to, 250
cross Great Plains, 258
use Oregon Trail as westward route, 254

Pitcairn, John, 131
Pitcher, Molly. *See* Hays, Mary
Pitt, William, 106
and Napoleon Bonaparte (cartoon), 203*p*
Pizarro, Francisco, 38
placer mining, 499. *See also* mining
Plains Indians, 259, 260*p*
plantation system, 27–28, 74*p*, 85, 286, 287–288, 335, 335*p*, 392, 397–398, 437. *See also* cotton
Platt Amendment, 594–595. *See also* Cuba
Pledge of Allegiance, 908, 962–963, 1176
Plessy v. Ferguson, 306, 566, 931
Plimoth Plantation, 67*p*. *See also* Plymouth Colony
Plumbers, 1071, 1072. *See also* Watergate scandal
Plymouth Colony, 51–52
becomes part of Massachusetts, 54
hardships of, 52
Pocahontas, 47, 47*p*
pocket veto, 427
Poems on Various Subjects, Religious and Moral (Wheatley), 241
pogroms, 528
Pokanoket, 56
Poland, economic reforms in, 1136
free elections in, 1116
Hitler's invasion of, 808
issue of, at Yalta, 869
revolt in, 891
tensions over, 870–871
polio vaccine, 903
political machines, 538–539, 622–623
political parties, 204–205. *See also* specific parties
changes in, 359–360
presidential electors and, 211. *See also* Twelfth Amendment
rise of opposition, 295
role played by, 209
and third party challenges, 209
Polk, James K., 322, 351–352, 352*p*, 1197
polls, election, in 1948, 915
poll tax, 565. *See also* voting restrictions
outlawing of, 953
pollution, 615, 1015
Polo, Marco, 12
Ponce de León, Juan, 37
Pontiac's Rebellion, 110
Poor Richard's Almanac (Franklin), 79
pope, 11, 13, 333
Popé, 41. *See also* Pueblo; Pueblo Revolt
Pope, John, 388–389
popular culture
birth of, during 1920s, 723
the highway in, 737*p*
Hopalong Cassidy lunch box, 901*p*
mass media and, 693
plastic flamingo of 1950s, 898*p*
Wild West, fixed in, 505–506
during World War II, 830
popular sovereignty, 360, 369
Stephen Douglas and, 361*p*, 369
population, 1134*c*. *See also* immigration; migration
density, 257*m*

diverse, of California, 269*p*
explosive increase in, 242–243
free and enslaved black (1820–1860), 320*g*
growth of, in cities, 535–536, 570
of Massachusetts Colony, 99*c*
shifts in, 473, 474*g*
United States (1780–1830), 242*g*
Populists, 511, 512, 526, 651
Port Huron Statement, 1038, 1038*q*
Portugal, 27–28
competition between Spain and, 24
explorations of, 24
Potawatomi, 110
Potsdam Conference, 866*p*, 870
Potter, David M., 370
Powell, Colin, 1118
Powell, John Wesley, 627
Powell, Lewis F., Jr., 1063
Powhatan, 44–45, 47
prairie, 280–281, 301. *See also* Great Plains
preachers, itinerant, 92–93. *See also* Great Awakening
Prentiss, Narcissa, 253
preparedness movement, 651, 655, 657
Presbyterians, 62
Prescott, Samuel, 116
President. *See also* U.S. Constitution
powers of, 157, 1027
term of, 156, 233. *See also* Twenty-second Amendment
Presidential Reconstruction, 427. *See also* Johnson, Andrew; Reconstruction
presidios, 40, 261
Presley, Elvis, 910, 910*p*
press, freedom of, 79. *See also* newspapers; yellow journalism
price controls, World War I, 665–666
price index, 134*g*. *See also* economy
Prince Henry the Navigator. *See* Henry, Prince (of Portugal)
Princeton, Battle of, 131
Princip, Gavrilo, 646
Principles of Scientific Management, The (Taylor), 474
printing press, 14–15
prison camps, 399
prison reform. *See* reform, prison
privateers, 43, 226
Proclamation of 1763, 110
productivity, 457, 459
increase of worker, 474–475
problem of rising, 732–733
profiteering, during Revolutionary War, 134
Progressive Era, 1017, 1103, 1152
background of, 615
factors relating to, 614*go*
legislation, 626*c*
limits of, 633–634
organizations, 617–618, 617*p*
political reforms, 624*c*
reforms, 640*go*
Progressive Party, 622, 630*p*, 914. *See also* Progressives
Progressives, 512, 651, 779, 1014
goals and beliefs of, 615, 618
reforms of, 621*go*, 622–623
resistance to, 619

Index

Japan and, as allies and trade partners, 816
life in the new, 240*go*
Louisiana Purchase increases size of, 215
-Mexico border region, 263
as nation of immigrants, 548–549. See also immigrants; immigration
neutrality of, 651
new mobility of early, 243
opposing viewpoints on survival of early, 148
overseas possessions, 1900, 678*m*
population (1780–1830), 242*g*
rapidly changing, 1143*go*
relations with China, 1139–1140
role of, in events around world, 1135*go*
secession divides, 370–372. See also Civil War
signs treaty of alliance with France in 1778, 132
and Soviet Union struggle for world leadership, 892
terrorist attacks strike, 1132–1133
United States Army Special Forces. See Green Berets
United States Department of Agriculture (USDA), 504
United States Department of Justice, 317
United States Post Office, 571
United States Sanitary Commission, 400
United States v. Cruikshank, 444
United States v. Reese, 444
Universal Negro Improvement Association (UNIA), 704–705
universities, rise of, 13
Up From Slavery **(Washington),** 556
Upper South, secession of, 373
urbanization, 282–283, 536–538, 570, 683*m*, 686–687
problems associated with, 310. See also cities, problems of
urban and rural populations (1800–1850), 282*g*
women feel impact of, 326
U.S.-China Relations Act, 1140
U.S. Civil Service Commission, 601
U.S. Congress. See Congress
U.S. Constitution, 154–157, 391, 395. See also Bill of Rights; specific amendments
arguments for and against, 170*go*
Article II, 211
Article II, Section 2, 925*q*
Article I, Section 8, Clause 18, 156*q*
cartoon pertaining to, 159*p*
checks and balances established by, 155, 432, 1027. See also checks and balances
Elastic Clause, 156
Framers of, and slavery, 153, 349
loose construction of, 202, 291–292. See also Bank of the United States
opponents of, 159–160. See also anti-Federalists
original states and ratification of, 143*m*
powers of the President, 1027
Preamble, 153*p*, 154*q*

proponents of, 158–159. See also Federalists; Nationalists
proposed, debate over, 159
ratification of, 160–161
separation of powers, 155, 1027. See also separation of powers
strict construction of, 202, 291–292
two hundredth anniversary of, 1109
"We the People" most important words of, 153, 153*p*
U.S. Forest Service, 626*c*, 627, 629
U.S. House of Representatives, 155–156
chooses Jefferson as President, 211
impeaches Andrew Johnson, 233. See also Johnson, Andrew
votes to impeach Clinton, 1130
U.S. Route 40. See Cumberland Road
U.S. Senate, 155–156
investigates Watergate affair, 1074–1075
rejects Versailles Treaty, 673
votes to acquit Clinton, 1130
U.S. Signal Corps, members of, 381*p*
U.S. Steel Corporation, 716, 728, 970
U.S. Supreme Court. See Supreme Court
Utah, 1188*m*, 1196
attack at Mountain Meadows, 255
Compromise of 1850 and, 356–359, 356*m*
farming in, 504
gains statehood, 487*m*
Mormon migration to, 255
Newspaper Rock State Historical Monument, 4*p*
national parks in, 613*m*
railroad in, 461, 461*m*
Territory, 255
Ute, 7
utopian communities, 308*p*, 315–316
Brook Farm, 316, 316*p*

V

vacuum tube, 902, 903*p*
Valley Forge, 133–134,
harsh winter conditions at, 133*p*
Van Buren, Martin, 302–303
Vance, Cyrus, 1087, 1087*q*
Vanderbilt, Cornelius, 468, 520
Van der Donck, Adriaen, 59, 59*q*
Vanzetti, Bartolomeo, 710*p*, 715
vaudeville, 559–560
V-E Day (Victory in Europe Day), 840
Velasco, Treaty of, 265
Vermont, 50, 1188*m*, 1196
colonists spread into, 90
election of 1936, 776
many rebels head for, after Shays' Rebellion, 149
militia, 127
Versailles Treaty, 671–672, 804–805, 672, 673, 712
vertical consolidation, 471*p*, 727
Vesey, Denmark, 288–289
Vespucci, Amerigo, 3*p*, 26
veto
overrides of, under Ford, 1081
presidential, 157, 232, 298, 302, 427

Truman uses, against McCarran-Walter Act, 883
in UN, 869
use of, by Coolidge, 733
use of by Soviet Union, in Security Council, 879
Vichy France, 810
Vicksburg, 407
siege of, 407*m*, 408
victory gardens, 831, 831*p*
Viet Cong, 1027, 1031–1033, 1032*c*, 1034, 1035, 1036, 1045
Vietminh, 1024. See also Ho Chi Minh
Vietnam, 976. See also Vietnam War
becomes single nation, 1047
evacuees from conflict in, 1047*p*
French defeat in, 1025
increased American involvement in, 1029
international conference divides, 891
Johnson and, 991
U.S. deaths in (1965–1972), 1048*g*
U.S. forces in (1965–1972), 1048*g*
U.S. involvement in, 1050*go*
Vietnamization, 1044, 1045
Vietnam Veterans Memorial, 1049, 1049*p*
Vietnam War, 406, 594, 1033*p*, 1034*m*, 1036*p*, 1045*m*
aftermath of, 1047
Agent Orange, 1033
air war, 1033, 1034
American soldiers in, 1030*p*, 1032*p*
amnesty granted to draft evaders during, 1086
background of, 1024–1025
battlefield conditions of, 1031–1033
Cambodia and, 1045
causes and effects of, 1024*go*
costs of, 1048
demonstration in favor of, 1040*p*
divisions created by, 1037, 1037*go*
effects of, 1030*go*
Eisenhower and, 1025
end of, 1044*go*
escalation of, 1033–1034, 1035*c*
fragmentation bombs, 1033
ground war, 1032–1033
hawks and doves of, 1034
Johnson and, 1027–1028, 1033–1034, 1036. See also Gulf of Tonkin Resolution
Kennedy and, 1025–1027
land mines, 1032
legacy of, 1048–1049
major players in, 1023*m*
MIAs (missing in action), 1048
My Lai Massacre, 1035–1036
napalm, 1033
Nixon and, 1044–1045
Pentagon Papers and, 1071
POWs (prisoners of war), 1048
protests against, 1036, 1037*p*, 1039–1040, 1042*p*
saturation bombing, 1033
Tet Offensive, 1034–1037, 1034*m*
U.S. withdrawal from, 1045
Vigilancia, 656
vigilantes, 667
Villa, Francisco "Pancho," 603
Virginia, 61*c*, 90, 119, 135, 1188*m*, 1196

comes of age, 998–1000
conditions that led to, 996*go*
issues of, 998, 1000
opposition to, 1001
shift in attitudes, due to, 999
Women's Political Council (WPC), 933
Women's Trade Union League, 668, 774
Wood, Leonard, 594, 658
Woodstock festival, 1011–1012
Woodward, Bob, 1074*p*
Worcester, Samuel Austin, 301
Worcester v. *Georgia,* 301
work force. *See also* labor unions
African American women in, 860–861
American (1940 and 1960), 904*g*
changes in, 903–904
desire of foreign markets by, 587
in World War II, 828–829
working mothers, opposing viewpoints on, 999
Works Progress Administration (WPA), 774, 775*c*
the arts and, 789–790, 790*p*
expansion of, 786
World Anti-Slavery Convention, 329
World's Columbian Exposition (1893), 459*p*
World Trade Center
rescue workers raise American flag at, 1133*p*
terrorist attacks strike, 1132–1133
World Trade Organization (WTO), 1141–1142
protests, 1141–1142, 1142*p*
World War I, 594, 643*p*
airplane, 676*p*, 677*p*
Allied losses in, 662–663
Americans help save Paris during, 659–660
antiwar sentiment during, 667
armistice, 662
Big Four of, 671
bombing raids, 661
causes and effects, 646*go*
causes of, 647–648
diary of pilot in, 676–677
division of land after, 671
domestic problems in America after, 673
in Europe (1914–1918), 647*m*
Europe after, 672*m*
events, 674*go*
financing, 664–665
the German Advance (1914), 648*m*
hostility to Germans during, 667
impact on suffrage movement, 639
mobilization before, 648
modern warfare of, 649–650
need for laborers during, 533
preparedness movement, 651
problems on the home front, 664*go*
severe problems in Europe after, 876–877
social changes during, 668
societal changes after, 684
training camp, 658*p*
war in the air, 660–661
the Western Front (1914–1916), 648*m*

World War II, 594, 643*p*, 709, 807*go*, 840*p*
African Americans and, 827, 931
aircraft carriers, 848
Allied air war, 837
American troops in the South Pacific, 824*p*
in the Atlantic, 833
battles in the Pacific, 848–852. *See also* specific battles
blitzkrieg, 808, 809
deaths, estimated, 850*c*
Dunkirk, 809–810
end of, 853
ends in Europe, 839–840
events, 862*go*
events in Europe and North Africa, 832*go*
fall of France, 810
as GI war, 827
on the home front, 830–831
ideological impact of, 931
invasion of Western Europe, 837–839
island-hopping, 850
Normandy invasion, 838–839, 838*m*
North Africa campaign, 833–834
in the Pacific, 846*go*
political regimes in Europe before, 799*m*
in Soviet Union, 835–837
support for/opposition to, 817*go*
U.S. Navy radiomen, 864*p*
war crimes, 847
in the West, 808–810
women and, 860, 860*p*
World Wide Web, 317, 460. *See also* Internet
Worthington, Thomas, 221
Wounded Knee, Battle of, 495
Wounded Knee Massacre, 495, 1007
Wright, Orville, 689
Wright, Richard, 789
Wright, Wilbur, 689
writers, 695–697
expatriate, 696
Harlem Renaissance, 696–697
Lost Generation, 695–696
Wyoming, 503, 1188*m*, 1196
cattle industry in, 500, 502
Cheyenne, 493, 502
gains statehood, 487*m*
national parks in, 505, 613*m*
Native Americans in, 494, 494*m*
railroads in, 462*p*
suffrage in, 329
Teapot Dome Scandal, 720, 720*p*

X

Xiaoping, Deng, 1117
XYZ Affair, 207–208, 208*p*

Y

Yalta, 840, 868*p*, 869
Yates, Robert, 160
"yellow dog" contracts, 479
yellow fever, 594, 598, 611
yellow journalism, 561–562, 591, 607.
See also newspapers
Yellowstone National Park, 486*p*, 505, 627
Yeltsin, Boris, 1117, 1135–1136, 1135*p*
York, Alvin, 663, 663*p*
York, Duke of
captures Delaware from Dutch, 62
charter of, 60
sends troops to New Amsterdam, 60
Yorktown, Battle of, 135
Yosemite National Park, 627, 627*p*
Young, Brigham, 255
Young Men's and Young Women's Christian Associations, 568
youth culture, 908
Yugoslavia, 1137–1138
creation of, 672
former, 1998, 1138*m*
Yurok, 6

Z

Zenger, John Peter, trial of, 79
zeppelins, 661
Zimmermann, Arthur, 655
Zimmermann note, 655–656, 655*p*
zoot suit riots, 858
Zuñi, 7
Pueblo, Archangel St. Michael, at, 40*p*

Acknowledgments

STAFF CREDITS

The people who made up the *America: Pathways to the Present* team—representing editorial, editorial services, design services, market research, online services/multimedia development, product marketing, production services, and publishing processes—are listed below. Bold type denotes core team members.

Leann Davis Alspaugh, Mary Ann Barton, Suzanne Biron, Margaret Broucek, Sarah M. Carroll, Siobhan Costello, Alex Crumbley, Anne Drowns, Deborah Dukeshire, Deborah Feldheim, **Thomas Ferreira, Gabriela Perez Fiato, Mary Ann Gundersen,** Lance Hatch, Kerri Hoar, Kate House, Katharine Ingram, Nancy Jones, Kevin Keane, Suzanne Klein, Michael Locker, Meredith Mascola, **Constance McCarty,** Anne McLaughlin, Terri Mitchell, Mark O'Malley, Jen Paley, Elizabeth Pearson, Jill Ratzan, Lynn Robbins, **Luess Sampson-Lizotte,** Hope Schuessler, Mark Staloff, Susan Swan, Jerry Thorne, Stacy Tibbetts, Bernadette Walsh, Roberta Warshaw, **Merce Wilczek,** Matthew Wilson, Amy Winchester, Helen Young

COVER IMAGE

Front Cover Lincoln Memorial: Joseph Sohm/PictureQuest; Flag background: Jim Barber/The StockRep, Inc. **Back Cover** Stone

MAPS

Mapping Specialists Limited: 1188, 1189, 1190, 1194–1195; **XNR Productions Inc.:** 3, 8, 15, 19, 25, 35, 37, 39, 43, 54, 56, 66, 67, 69, 75, 79, 90, 93, 97, 103, 106, 110, 129, 135, 143, 196, 197, 199, 212, 216, 225, 229, 239, 251, 252, 254, 257, 264, 268, 269, 271, 286, 300, 309, 345, 353, 356, 364, 369, 373, 377, 379, 385, 386, 395, 403, 404, 407, 412, 423, 432, 441, 444, 455, 466, 487, 494, 499, 501, 511, 516, 519, 526, 530, 551, 583, 585, 592, 595, 597, 599, 602, 610, 613, 623, 631, 632, 639, 645, 646, 647, 648, 659, 672, 678, 683, 687, 688, 689, 711, 736–737, 739, 747, 761, 767, 772, 773, 799, 801, 804, 809, 815, 820, 825, 833, 835, 838, 844, 848, 867, 873, 878, 886, 891, 899, 905, 923, 925, 929, 932, 943, 967, 969, 984, 986, 995, 1021, 1023, 1025, 1034, 1043, 1045, 1057, 1095, 1101, 1115, 1122, 1123, 1131, 1138, 1141, 1192

ILLUSTRATION

Leann Davis Alspaugh: 160, 1097; **argosypublishing.com:** 383, 471, 474, 522, 523, 537, 565, 624, 693, 717, 719, 724, 732, 1048, 1103, 1105, 1106, 1107, 1112; **Kenneth Batelman:** 6, 26, 155, 274, 277, 464, 660–661, 726–727, 742, 985, 988, 1032, 1068, 1086; **Matt Mayerchak & Laura Glassman:** 2–3, 34–35, 68–69, 102–103, 142–143, 198–199, 238–239, 270–271, 308–309, 344–345, 378–379, 380, 390, 399, 402, 410, 416, 418, 422–423, 424, 430, 436, 442, 445, 446, 454–455, 486–487, 488, 491, 496, 498, 502, 507, 514, 518–519, 550–551, 552, 554, 559, 564, 566, 569, 574, 582–583, 612–613, 614, 621, 628, 635, 644–645, 646, 653, 657, 664, 669, 670, 682–683, 710–711, 738–739, 766–767, 798–799, 824–825, 866–867, 898–899, 904, 928–929, 966–967, 994–995, 1022–1023, 1056–1057, 1094–1095, 1124–1125; **Jen Paley:** 4, 10, 17, 22, 29, 30, 36, 42, 46, 49, 58, 59, 61, 64, 70, 77, 83, 86, 89, 94, 98, 99, 104, 109, 113, 114, 118, 120, 127, 133, 134, 138, 144, 146, 150, 152, 154, 158, 161, 164, 165, 170, 200, 202, 207, 213, 218, 220, 224, 230, 234, 235, 240, 242, 249, 258, 266, 272, 275, 280, 282, 285, 288, 290, 291, 295, 296, 297, 304, 310, 313, 318, 320, 326, 332, 336, 340, 346, 350, 351, 354, 355, 363, 365, 369, 374, 437, 438, 443, 451, 456, 467, 473, 477, 484, 504, 520, 527, 529, 534, 540, 541, 546, 554, 578, 579, 584, 587, 589, 591, 598, 604, 608, 620, 626, 640, 674, 679, 684, 685, 691, 699, 706, 712, 723, 730, 734, 740, 741, 743, 745, 752, 756, 762, 768, 772, 775, 777, 785, 786, 792, 794, 795, 800, 807, 813, 817, 822, 826, 829, 832, 841, 846, 850, 855, 862, 868, 875, 876, 877, 880, 884, 888, 889, 894, 900, 902, 904, 907, 909, 912, 920, 924, 925, 930, 936, 941, 944, 948, 952, 954, 960, 968, 971, 975, 978, 979, 983, 992, 996, 997, 1003, 1006, 1009, 1013, 1016, 1018, 1024, 1028, 1030, 1035, 1037, 1044, 1050, 1052, 1053, 1058, 1060, 1064, 1070, 1078, 1080, 1083, 1090, 1096, 1102, 1108, 1114, 1119, 1120, 1126, 1134, 1135, 1143, 1144, 1150, 1154, 1155, 1192, 1193, 1196; **Hope Schuessler:** 13, 1073

PHOTOGRAPHY

Front Matter i, Jim Barber/The StockRep, Inc.; **ii T,** Courtesy, Andrew Cayton, Ph.D.; **ii TM,** Courtesy, Elisabeth Israels Perry, Ph.D.; **ii BM,** Courtesy, Linda Reed, Ph.D.; **ii B,** Courtesy, Allan M. Winkler, Ph.D.; **iii T,** Amon Carter Museum of Western Art; **iii B,** Shelburne Museum; **iv,** The Granger Collection, NY; **ix,** The Granger Collection, NY

Table of Contents x ML, Library of Congress; **x MR,** The Granger Collection, NY; **x B,** National Archives; **xi BL,** Franklin D. Roosevelt Library; **xi TR,** Corbis; **xi MR,** FDR Library; **xi BR,** Gary Waltz/The Image Works; **xii TL,** The Granger Collection, NY; **xii ML,** Harry S. Truman Presidential Library; **xii BL,** J.R. Eyerman/TimePix; **xii BM,** Corbis; **xii BR,** © 1959 Newsweek Inc. All rights reserved. Reprinted by permission.; **xiii BL,** Guido Rossi/Hulton/Archive/Getty Images; **xiii TR,** Don Uhrbrock *LIFE* Magazine © Time Warner; **xiii TM,** Al Freni/*LIFE* Magazine © Time Warner; **xiii BM,** David J. Frent; **xiii BR,** Lambert/Hulton/Archive/Getty Images; **xiv T,** Steve Northup, ©Time Inc. *Time* Magazine; **xiv M,** David J. Frent; **xiv B,** Library of Congress; **xv TL,** New Holland Machine Company; **xv BL,** Thomas E. Franklin/Bergen Record/Corbis SABA; **xv TR,** Hulton/Liaison/Getty Images; **xviii T,** Matt Heron/Take Stock; **xviii B,** The Granger Collection, NY; **xix T,** Art Resource, NY; **xix B,** UPI/Bettmann Archives/Corbis; **xx,** The Pilgrim Society; **xxi,** National Portrait Gallery, Smithsonian Institution, Washington, DC. Art Resource, NY; **xxii,** Theodore Roosevelt Collection Harvard College Library; **xxiii,** Magnum Photos, Inc.; **xxix T,** American Textile History Museum; **xxix M,** Library of Congress; **xxix B,** Jewish Hospital/University of Louisville; **xxvi L,** Library of Congress; **xxvi TR,** Greg E. Mathieson/MAI Photo News Agency, Inc.; **xxvi BR,** Library of Congress; **xxvii T,** all Courtesy of the Federal Reserve Bank of San Francisco; **xxvii M,** AP/Wide World Photos; **xxvii B,** Brown Brothers; **xxviii TL,** Bob Adelman/Magnum Photos, Inc.; **xxviii TR,** Hulton/Liaison/Getty Images; **xxviii B,** inset Hulton/Archive/Getty Images; **xxviii BR,** Time Life Books; **xxx,** Corel Corp.; **xxxi T,** Corel Corp.; **xxxi M,** Corel Corp.; **xxxi B,** Corel Corp.

Unit Openers xlvi–1, Giraudon/Art Resource, NY; **100–101,** Architect of the Capitol; **236–237,** New York Public Library; **340–341,** The Granger Collection, NY; **452–453,** National Cowboy Hall of Fame; **580–581,** Museum of the City of New York; **680–681,** New York Historical Society/Bridgeman Art Library; **796–797,** Corbis; **926–927,** Corbis; **1054–1055,** Brad Perks

American Heritage 32, Art Archive; **33,** Corbis; **140,** Francis G. Mayer/Corbis; **141,** Visions of America; **338 L,** Photograph from *The Underground Railroad* by Raymond Bial. Copyright © 1995 by Raymond Bial. Reprinted by permission of Houghton Mifflin Company. All rights reserved.; **338 R,** Louis Pshoyos/Contact Press; **339,** The Charleston Museum; **420 TL,** Museum of the Confederacy; **420 BL,** Confederate Memorial Hall, New Orleans. From *Echoes of Glory: Arms & Equipment of the Confederacy*. Photo by Larry Sherer © 1991 Time-Life Books.; **420 TR,** Smithsonian Institution. Photo taken by Larry Sherer ©1985 Time-Life Books.; **420 BR,** C. Paul Loane Collection. Photo by Larry Sherer © 1991 Time-Life Books, Inc.; **421,** National Archives; **576,** Kansas State Historical Society; **576,** Hulton/Archive/Getty Images; **676,** Hulton/Liaison Agency/Getty Images; **677 T,** Hulton/Liaison Agency/Getty Images; **677 B,** Corbis; **764,** AP/Wide World Photos; **765,** National Baseball Hall of Fame and Museum; **864 T,** U.S. Naval Historical Foundation; **864 B,** U.S. Naval Historical Foundation; **865,** Hulton/Archive/Getty Images; **962 T,** Library of Congress; **962 B,** Corbis; **963,** Corbis; **1092 T,** AP/Wide World Photos; **1092 B,** Corbis; **1093,** Prentice Hall

American Pathways 96 L, New Holland Machine Company; **96 TR,** Shelburne Museum; **96 BR,** Library of Congress; **97,** Terry Donnelly/Stone; **232 L,** Library of Congress; **232 R,** David Ball/Corbis Stock Market; **233 TL,** Russ Lappa; **233 BL,** Corbis; **233 TR,** Hulton/Archive/ Getty Images; **233 BR,** Mark Godfrey/The Image Works; **306 T,** Robert Shafer/Stone; **306 B,** The Western Reserve Historical Society; **307 T,** Supreme Court Historical Society; **307 BL,** Bob Daemmrich Photography, Inc.; **307 BR,** Monkmeyer Press; **448 T,** The Granger Collection, NY; **448 M,** The Granger Collection, NY; **448 B,** Archives of Atlanta Historical Society; **449 L,** AP/Wide World Photos; **449 R,** Brown Brothers; **548 T,** Hulton Getty/Liaison Agency, Inc.; **548 M,** Library of Congress; **548 B,** Culver Pictures; **549 L,** Library of Congress; **549 R,** Ken Fisher/Stone; **642 T,** Emanuel Gottlieb Leutze, The Metropolitan Museum of Art, Gift of John S. Kennedy, 1897. (97.34); **642 B,** Greg E. Mathieson/MAI Photo News Agency, Inc.; **643 TL,** Corbis; **643 BL,** Thomas E. Franklin/*Bergen Record*/Corbis SABA; **643 R,** Hulton/ Liaison/Getty Images; **708 T,** Yale University Art Gallery, Mabel Brady Garven Collection; **708 ML,** The Granger Collection, NY; **708 MR,** Library of Congress; **708 B,** The Kobal Collection; **709 T,** Time Life Books; **709 ML,** Hulton/Archive/Getty Images; **709 MR,** Corbis; **709 B,** Hulton/Archive/Getty Images; **896 TL,** American Textile History Museum; **896 BL,** The Granger Collection, NY; **896 R,** AT&T Archives; **897 T,** Library of Congress; **897 M,** Intel Corporation Museum Archives & Collection; **897 B,** Jewish Hospital/University of Louisville; **964 T,** The Granger Collection, NY; **964 M,** The Granger Collection, NY; **964 B,** Hulton/Liaison/Getty Images; **965 T,** Bob Adelman/Magnum Photos; **965 B,** Bob Daemmrich Photography, Inc.; **1152 TR,** Prentice Hall; **1152 L,** Courtesy of the Federal Reserve Bank of San Francisco; **1152 L,** Courtesy of the Federal Reserve Bank of San Francisco; **1152 L,** Courtesy of the Federal Reserve Bank of San Francisco; **1152 L,** Courtesy of the Federal Reserve Bank of San Francisco; **1152 BR,** Ford Motor Company; **1153 T,** FPG International; **1153 B,** AP/Wide World Photos; **1153 M,** Picture Research Consultants

Skills 317, Brian Smith; **558,** John McCutcheon; **722,** *Saturday Evening Post,* June 30, 1928, Curtis Archives; **812,** AP/Wide World Photos; **1077 T,** NASA; **1077 B,** NASA

Geography & History 66 L, Skyscan; **66 R,** Pilgrim Hall Museum; **67 T,** Corbis; **67 B,** Curtis B. Johnson; **67 inset,** American Antiquarian Society; **196 T,** Raymond Bial; **196 B,** Culver Pictures, Inc.; **197 T,** The Granger Collection; **197 B,** Richard Hamilton Smith/Corbis; **268 L,** Western History Division, Denver Public Library, photo by L.C. McClure; **268 R,** Color-Pic, Inc.; **269 L,** Culver Pictures, Inc.; **269 R,** Culver Pictures, Inc.; **376 TL,** The Granger Collection, NY; **376 BL,** Culver Pictures, Inc.; **376 TR,** Museum of American Textile History; **376 BR,** Culver Pictures, Inc.; **377,** The New York Historical Society; **516–517 B,** Brown Brothers; **517 T,** Corbis; **517 M,** Corbis; **517 B inset,** Kansas State Historical Society; **610 T,** Corbis; **610–611 B,** LHSIM/Stone; **611 T,** Corbis; **611 M,** Archive Photos; **611 B,** The Metropolitan Museum of Art; **736,** Brown Brothers; **737 TL,** Harold Kramer, mapsofpa.com; **737 BL,** Walts Postcards; **737 BM,** Walts Postcards; **737 TR,** Library of Congress; **737 BR,** Corbis; **922 T,** SuperStock; **922 M,** Josef Scaylea/Corbis; **922 B,** Donovan Marks Photography; **923 T,** Michael Dwyer/Stock Boston; **923 B,** Robert Brenner/PhotoEdit; **1020 T,** Ken Regan/Camera 5; **1020 M,** NASA/Science Photo Library/Photo Researchers, Inc.; **1020 B,** Mark Richards/PhotoEdit; **1021 T,** Tom Bean; **1021 M,** Tom Brownold; **1021 B,** Isaac Hernandez/Mercury Press International; **1122 T,** Frank Frisk/GreatLakesPhotos.com; **1122 B,** Spencer Grant/PhotoEdit; **1123 T,** Rancho Santa Margarita; **1123 BL,** Corbis; **1123 BR,** PhotoDisc, Inc

Chapter 1 2 L, Tony Linck; **2 R,** Art Resource; **3 L,** Corbis Sygma; **3 R,** Art Resource, NY; **4,** Omni-Photo Communications, Inc.; **5,** Courtesy The Edward E. Ayer Collection, The Newberry Library; **7,** Bob Daemmrich/Stock Boston; **8,** Tony Linck; **9,** Etowah Indian Mounds Historic

Site; **10,** The Granger Collection, NY; **11,** Giraudon/Art Resource, NY; **12,** Michael Holford; **13 T,** The Granger Collection, NY; **13 B,** The Granger Collection, NY; **14 T,** Louvre, Paris, France/Art Resource, NY; **14 B,** The Granger Collection, NY; **16 T,** London Science Museum. Photo © Michael Holford; **16 B,** The Granger Collection, NY; **17,** Photograph by Jeffrey Ploskonka, National Museum of African Art, Eliot Elisofon Archive, Smithsonian Institution; **18 T,** SuperStock; **18–19 B,** Panoramic Images; **20,** Barth, Heinrich, *Travels and Discoveries in North and Central Africa,* London,1857. General Research Division. The New York Public Library, Astor, Lenox and Tilden Foundations.; **21,** Photograph by Jeffrey Ploskonka, National Museum of African Art, Eliot Elisofon Archive, Smithsonian Institution; **22,** The Metropolitan Museum of Art, Gift of J. Pierpont Morgan, 1900 (10.18.2); **23,** Library of Congress; **24,** SuperStock; **27,** London Science Museum. Photographed by Michael Holford; **28,** The Granger Collection, NY; **31,** Steve Kelley/Copley News Service

Chapter 2 34 L, The Granger Collection, NY; **34 R,** The Pilgrim Society; **35,** Laurie Minor-Penland, Smithsonian Institution; **36,** The Granger Collection, NY; **38,** The Bridgeman Art Library; **40,** Diane Nordeck, Smithsonian Institution; **41,** Texas Memorial Museum, Austin; **42,** The Granger Collection, NY; **43,** National Maritime Museum; **44,** Colonial National Historical Park; **46,** Fairholt, F.W, *Tobacco: Its history,...London.* 1859 (detail) Arents Collection, The New York Public Library, Astor, Lenox and Tilden Foundations; **47,** Architect of the Capitol; **48,** Library of Congress; **49,** Hulton/Liaison/Getty Images; **50 T,** Chicago Historical Society; **50 B,** Peabody & Essex Museum. Photo by Mark Sexton; **51,** Vose Galleries of Boston, Inc.; **53,** Folger Shakespeare Library; **55,** Culver Pictures, Inc.; **56,** Library of Congress; **59,** Chicago Historical Society; **60,** AP/Wide World Photos; **62,** NC Division of Archives and History; **63,** Methodist Collection of Drew University, Madison, New Jersey; **65,** From *Divine Examples of God's Severe Judgments upon Sabbath-Breakers* (London, 1671)

Chapter 3 68 L, The Granger Collection, NY; **68 R,** The Granger Collection, NY; **69 L,** The Granger Collection, NY; **69 R,** Library of Congress; **70,** Hargrett Rare Book and Manuscript Library, University of Georgia Libraries; **72,** Library of Congress; **73,** Library of Congress; **74,** Carolina Art Association, Gibbes Art Museum; **77 T,** Corbis; **77 B,** The Library Company of Philadelphia; **78 T,** Pilgrim Hall Museum; **78 B,** The Bridgeman Art Library; **79 T,** The Granger Collection, NY; **79 B,** Museum of Early Southern Decorative Arts; **80 T,** Wethersfield Historical Society; **80 B,** Breton Littlehales © National Geographic Society; **81 L,** Massachusetts Historical Society; **81 M,** Mark Gamba/Corbis Stock Market; **81 R,** Russ Lappa; **82 T,** Harvard University; **82 M,** The College of William and Mary; **82 B,** Yale University; **83,** Victor Englebert; **84 T,** National Maritime Museum; **84 B,** Royal Albert Memorial Museum, Exeter/Bridgeman Art Library, London/New York; **85,** Courtesy Linda O. King/Coastal Islands Historical Society; **86,** Abby Aldrich Rockefeller Foundation, Colonial Williamsburg; **87,** Florida Natural History Museum; **88,** Massachusetts Historical Society; **89,** The New York Historical Society; **92 T,** Library of Congress; **92 B,** Library of Congress; **95,** From *Divine Examples of God's Severe Judgments upon Sabbath-Breakers* (London, 1671)

Chapter 4 102 L, SuperStock; **102 R,** Colonial Williamsburg Foundation; **103 L,** Emanuel Gottlieb Leutze, The Metropolitan Museum of Art, Gift of John S. Kennedy, 1897; **103 R,** Hulton/Liaison/Getty Images; **104,** Library of Congress; **105,** Library of Congress; **107 T,** National Gallery of Canada, Ottawa; **107 B,** The Bridgeman Art Library; **108,** Northwind Pictures; **109,** Scottish National Portrait Gallery; **111,** The Granger Collection, NY; **112 T,** Library of Congress; **112 B,** Corbis-Bettmann; **113,** Colonial Williamsburg Foundation; **114,** The Granger Collection, NY; **115,** Library of Congress; **116,** Corbis; **118 T,** Library of Congress; **118 B,** Library of Congress; **119,** Library of Congress; **121,** Massachusetts Historical Society; **122,** The Granger Collection, NY; **127,** The Granger Collection, NY; **128,** Gift of Edgar William and Bernice Chrysler Garbisch, © 1994 National Gallery of Art, Washington, D.C. ; **130 T,** Corbis; **130 B,** Emanuel Gottlieb Leutze, The Metropolitan Museum of Art, Gift of John S. Kennedy, 1897; **131,** Lexington Historical Society/photo by Rob Huntley/Lightstream; **132,** The Granger Collection, NY; **133,** Library of Congress; **134,** The Granger Collection, NY; **135,** Private Collection; **137,** Abbot Hall, Marblehead, MA; **139,** Prentice Hall

Chapter 5 142 L, Shelburne Museum; **142 R,** "Signing of the Constitution" by Thomas Prichard Rossiter, 1872. Independence National Historic Park, Philadelphia.; **143,** "Washington at Verplancke's Point" by John Trumball, 1790. Courtesy of Winterthur Museum; **144,** SuperStock; **145,** The National Archives of the United States by Herman Viola. Publisher Harry N. Abrams, Inc. Photograph by Jonathan Wallen.; **146,** Eric P. Newman Numismatic Education Society. Rob Huntley/Lightstream; **147,** The Granger Collection, NY; **148,** Culver Pictures, Inc.; **149,** Library of Congress; **150,** Free Library of Philadelphia; **151,** Library of Congress; **153 T,** National Portrait Gallery, Smithsonian Institution/Art Resource, NY; **153 B,** Library of Congress; **157,** Independence National Historic Park; **158 T,** Library of Congress; **158 M,** The Library Company of Philadelphia; **158 B,** Art Resource, NY; **159,** Courtesy, American Antiquarian Society; **160,** Shelburne Museum; **162,** SuperStock; **163,** The Granger Collection, NY; **165,** Museum of American Political Life. Photo by Sally Anderson-Bruce; **166,** Hulton Getty/Liaison Agency, Inc.; **167,** Art Resource, NY; **168,** White House Historical Association; **169,** The Granger Collection, NY; **171,** Library of Congress

Chapter 6 198 L, Atwater Kent Museum; **198 R,** The Granger Collection, NY; **199,** The Granger Collection, NY; **200,** North Wind Picture Archives; **201,** Art Resource, NY; **203,** Corbis; **204,** Atwater Kent Museum; **205 T,** Library of Congress; **205 B,** The Old Print Shop; **206,** Courtesy, Winterthur Museum; **207,** White House Historical Association; **208,** Corbis; **209,** Corbis; **210,** ©White House Historical Association/Photo by National Geographic Society; **213,** Picture Research Consultants & Archives; **214,** United States Signal Corps; **215,** Corbis; **215 inset,** Corbis; **217,** Courtesy Malcolm Rutherford; **220,** Corbis; **221 T,** Chicago Historical Society; **221 B,** Ohio Historical Society; **222,** National Portrait Gallery, Smithsonian Institution, Washington, DC #83-7221; **223,** Corbis; **224,** The Granger Collection, NY; **226,** Brown University Library; **228,** "Andrew Jackson at the Battle of New Orleans" by Dennis M. Carter. The Historic New Orleans Collection; **231,** The New York Historical Society

Chapter 7 238 L, The National Portrait Gallery; **238 M,** Pennsylvania Academy of the Fine Arts; **238 R,** The New York Historical Society; **239 L,** Courtesy of the Texas Memorial Museum, The University of Texas at Austin; **239 R,** Color-Pic, Inc.; **240,** The Bridgeman Art Library; **241 T,** Pennsylvania Hospital; **241 B,** National Archives; **243,** Library of Congress; **244 T,** Pennsylvania

Academy of the Fine Arts, Gift of Paul Beck; **244 B,** Pocumtuck Valley Memorial Association; **245 T,** Dukes County Historical Society/photo by Robert Schellhammer ©1994; **245 B,** New Bedford Whaling Museum; **246 T,** New Wave Photography; **246 B,** North Wind Pictures; **247,** Library of Congress; **248,** Library of Congress; **249,** Panoramic Images; **253,** Utah State Historical Society; **255,** Amon Carter Museum Fort Worth, Texas; **256,** The Granger Collection, NY; **258–259,** Panoramic Images; **260 T,** Collection of Western Americana, Beinecke Rare Book and Manuscript Library, Yale University; **260 B,** © Jerry Jacka; **262,** Fine Arts Museums of San Francisco. Gift of Mrs. Eleanor Martin, 37566; **263 T,** AP/Wide World Photos; **263 B,** Library of Congress; **265,** The R.W. Norton Art Gallery, Shreveport, La. Used by permission.; **267,** Library of Congress

Chapter 8 270 L, SuperStock; **270 R,** The Granger Collection, NY; **271,** Woolaroc Museum, Bartlesville, OK; **272,** Smithsonian Institution; **273,** Culver Pictures; **275,** The New York Historical Society; **276,** Corbis; **278,** Library of Congress; **279,** Lowell Historical Society; **280,** Museum of American Textile History. Photo © Rob Huntley/Lightstream; **281,** Library of Congress; **283,** Culver Pictures, Inc.; **284,** Culver Pictures, Inc.; **285,** Rauner Special Collections, Dartmouth College Library; **286 T,** U.S. Department of Agriculture; **286 B,** Library of Congress; **289,** Library of Congress; **290,** National Portrait Gallery, Smithsonian Institution/Art Resource, NY; **291,** Duke University Archives; **293 T,** The Metropolitan Museum of Art; **293 B,** Collection of the New York Historical Society; **294,** Library of Congress; **297,** Museum of the City of New York; **298,** The Granger Collection, NY; **299,** White House Historical Association; **300,** Woolaroc Museum, Bartlesville, OK; **301,** Library of Congress; **303,** Library of Congress; **305,** The New York Historical Society

Chapter 9 308 L, The Granger Collection, NY; **308 R,** Collection of Sue and Lars Hotham. Photo © Rob Huntley/Lightstream; **310,** The Granger Collection, NY; **312 T,** The Granger Collection, NY; **312–313 B,** Corbis; **314 T,** The Metropolitan Museum of Art Gift of I.N.Phelps Stokes, Edward S. Hawes, Alice Mary Hawes, Marion Augusta Hawes, 1937 (37.14.22); **314 B,** Collection of Sue and Lars Hotham. Photo © Rob Huntley/Lightstream; **315,** Boston Athenaeum; **316 T,** Massachusetts Historical Society; **316 B,** Eileen P. Keane; **318,** Library of Congress; **319,** Corbis; **320,** Library of Congress; **321,** The Granger Collection, NY; **322,** The Granger Collection, NY; **323,** Sophia Smith Collection, Smith College; **324,** New York Public Library; **325,** The Granger Collection, NY; **326,** The Granger Collection, NY; **327,** The Schlesinger Library; **328 T,** Courtesy, American Antiquarian Society; **328 B,** The Granger Collection, NY; **329 L,** AP Photo/Joe Marquette; **329 R,** The Granger Collection, NY; **330 L,** The Granger Collection, NY; **330 R,** Seneca Falls Historical Society; **331,** Women's Rights Collection, Sophia Smith Archives; **332,** *Harper's Weekly*; **333,** USDA; **335,** "Colonel and Mrs. James A. Whiteside, Son Charles and Servants" by James Cameron. Hunter Museum of Art, Chattanooga, Tenn. Gift of Mr. and Mrs. Thomas B. Whiteside; **337,** Library of Congress

Chapter 10 344 L, Courtesy of the Texas Memorial Museum, The University of Texas at Austin; **344 M,** The Bridgeman Art Library; **344 R,** Library of Congress; **345 L,** Missouri Historical Society; **345 R,** Library of Congress; **346 L,** Museum of American Textile History; **346 R,** Grant Heilman; **347 T,** Library of Congress; **347 B,** Corbis; **348,** Radcliffe College Archives, Schlesinger Library; **349 L,** Chicago Historical Society; **349 R,** Chicago Historical Society; **351,** Courtesy of Texas Memorial Museum, The University of Texas at Austin; **352 T,** Library of Congress; **352 B,** Russ Lappa; **355,** The Huntington Library, Art Collections, and Botanical Gardens, San Marino, California/SuperStock; **356,** The Bridgeman Art Library; **357,** Library of Congress; **358 T,** National Portrait Gallery, Smithsonian Institution, Washington, DC. Art Resource, NY; **358 B,** The Bridgeman Art Library; **359 T,** SuperStock; **359 B,** Milwaukee County Historical Society; **361,** Chicago Historical Society; **363,** Anne S. K. Brown Military Collection, Providence, RI; **365,** Missouri Historical Society; **366,** Library of Congress; **367,** Illinois State Historical Library; **368,** Boston Athenaeum; **371 T,** Chicago Historical Society; **371 B,** The New York Public Library Prints Division; **372 L,** National Geographic Society; **372 R,** The Granger Collection, NY; **375,** Library of Congress

Chapter 11 378 L, Artist: Douglas Volk, Minnesota Historical Society; **378 R,** Greg E. Mathieson/MAI Photo News Agency, Inc.; **379,** Brown University Library; **380,** Culver Pictures, Inc.; **381,** Culver Pictures, Inc.; **384 L,** Rick Vargas and Richard Strauss, Smithsonian Institution; **384 R,** Collection of David & Kevin Kyle; **385,** Collection of Michael J. McAfee. Courtesy William Gladstone. Photo © Seth Goltzer; **387,** The Collection of Jay P. Altmayer; **388,** Museum of the Confederacy; **389,** Museum of the Confederacy; **390,** Rick Vargas and Richard Strauss, Smithsonian Institution; **392,** John G. Johnson Collection, Philadelphia Museum of Art; **394,** McLellan Lincoln Collection, John Hay Library, Brown University; **396,** Corbis; **397,** Chicago Historical Society; **398,** Culver Pictures, Inc.; **400,** Corbis; **400 inset,** American Antiquarian Society; **402,** Courtesy of Museum of the Confederacy, Richmond, Virginia, Confederate Veteran, 1904; **405,** The Granger Collection, NY; **406 TR,** National Archives; **406 BR,** John Bernard Shaw/Corbis Sygma; **406 L,** Philip Jones Griffiths/MP, Zenith Electronics Corporation; **407,** The Beverly R. Robinson Collection, U.S. Naval Academy Museum; **409,** Brown University Library; **410,** The Granger Collection, NY; **413,** The Granger Collection, NY; **414,** The Granger Collection, NY; **415,** Rob Crandall/Folio, Inc.; **416,** Virginia Historical Society; **417,** Anne S.K. Brown Military Collection, Brown University Library, Providence, RI; **419,** Culver Pictures, Inc.

Chapter 12 422 L, The Granger Collection, NY; **422 R,** Library of Congress; **424,** Brown Brothers; **425,** The Granger Collection, NY; **426 T,** Courtesy of the Museum of the Confederacy/Library of Congress; **426 B,** Library of Congress; **428 L,** Collection of William Gladstone; **428 R,** Collection of William Gladstone; **429,** The Granger Collection, NY; **430,** The Granger Collection, NY; **432 T,** The Granger Collection, NY; **432 B,** Corbis; **433,** Russ Lappa; **434,** Library of Congress; **435,** Collection of Nancy Gewirz, Antique Textile Resource, Bethesda, Maryland; **436,** Los Angelos County Museum of Art: Acquisition made possible through museum trustees; **437,** The New York Historical Society; **439 T,** Courtesy of the Witte Museum; **439 B,** Library of Congress; **440,** Prentice Hall; **442 inset,** Collection of State Historical Museum/Mississippi Department of Archives and History; **442,** Rutherford B. Hayes Presidential Center; **445,** The Granger Collection, NY; **447,** Library of Congress

Chapter 13 454 L, Library of Congress; **454 R,** Light-Foot Collection; **455,** The Granger Collection, NY; **456 T,** The Granger Collection, NY; **456 B,** The Granger Collection, NY; **457 T,**

Courtesy of the Federal Reserve Bank of San Francisco; **457 B,** Archive Photos; **458 T,** Library of Congress; **458 B,** National Geographic Society; **459,** Hulton/Archive/Getty Images; **461,** Index Stock Imagery, Inc.; **461 inset,** The Granger Collection, NY; **462,** The Oakland Museum History Department; **463,** Hulton/Archive/Getty Images; **464,** Chicago Historical Society; **465,** Museum of the City of New York; **467,** Corbis; **468,** Museum of American Textile History; **469,** Library of Congress; **470,** Library of Congress; **473,** Brown Brothers; **474,** Putman County Historical Society, Cold Spring, N.Y.; **476 L,** Library of Congress; **476 R,** Library of Congress; **477 L,** Library of Congress; **477 R,** Picture Research Consultants, Inc.; **478 L,** The Granger Collection, NY; **478 R,** Collection of Ralph J. Brunke; **481,** Brown Brothers; **482,** Corbis; **483,** Brown Brothers; **485,** Library of Congress

Chapter 14 486 L, National Anthropological Archives/Smithsonian Institution; **486 R,** Thomas Moran, *Grand Canyon of the Yellowstone,* 1872, oil on canvas, The U.S. Department of the Interior Museum, Washington, D.C.; **486 M,** Corbis; **488–489,** Jake Rajs/Stone; **490,** Corbis; **491,** National Museum of American Art, Smithsonian Institution, Washington, D.C. Gift of Mrs. Joseph Harrison, Jr. Art Resource, NY; **493 T,** Library of Congress; **493 B,** Colorado Historical Society; **494–495,** National Anthropological Archives/Smithsonian Institution; **495 T,** SuperStock; **497 T,** Cumberland County Historical Society; **497 B,** Cumberland County Historical Society; **498,** California State Library; **500,** Library of Congress; **502,** Amon Carter Museum of Western Art; **503,** Denver Public Library; **505 T,** Buffalo Bill Historical Center, Cody, WY; **505 B,** Library of Congress; **506,** Photofest; **509 both,** American Gold Exchange, Austin, TX; **510 T,** Kansas State Historical Society; **510 B,** East Carolina Manuscript Collection, J.Y. Joyner Library, East Carolina University; **512,** Library of Congress; **515,** Library of Congress

Chapter 15 518 L, The Granger Collection, NY; **518 M,** Division of Political History, Smithsonian Institution; **518 R,** Visions of America; **520,** The Granger Collection, NY; **521,** *Puck,* March 10, 1897; **523 T,** Library of Congress; **523 B,** Library of Congress; **525 L,** Collection of David J. Frent and Janice L. Frent; **525 R,** Collection of David J. Frent and Janice L. Frent; **527,** Courtesy George Eastman House; **528 T,** The Museum of the City of New York; **528 BL,** National Park Service Collection, Gift of Angelo Forgione; **528 BR,** Chermayeff & Geisma; **531,** Library of Congress; **532,** California Department of Parks and Recreation, courtesy Fred Wasserman; **533,** El Paso Border Heritage Center; **534,** Brown Brothers; **535 T,** Library of Congress; **535 B,** Library of Congress; **536,** Library of Congress; **538,** Museum of the City of New York, Gift of Joseph Varner Reed; **539,** Thomas Nast; **541,** Library of Congress; **542,** Library of Congress; **543,** California Museum of Photography; **544,** Chermayeff & Geisma; **545,** Corbis; **547,** *Puck,* 1909

Chapter 16 550, Culver Pictures, Inc.; **551 L,** The Kobal Collection; **551 M, TR,** Wood River Gallery, Mill Valley, California; **551 BR,** Wood; **551 R,** Chicago Historical Society; **552,** Kansas State Historical Society; **553,** The McGuffy Museum; **554,** Oldest Wooden School House, St. Augustine, Florida; **555,** Sophia Smith Collection; **556,** Brown Brothers; **557,** The New York Public Library; **558,** John McCutcheon; **559 L,** Rick Vargas, Smithsonian Institution; **559 R,** National Baseball Library and Archive, Cooperstown, NY; **560,** Barbara Puorro Galasso/ George Eastman House; **561,** Brooklyn Museum; **562,** Corbis; **563,** Fisk University Special Collections; **564,** Corbis; **565,** Mauldin/© 1962 *St. Louis Post-Dispatch;* **567,** The Granger Collection; **568,** Corbis; **569,** Corbis; **570,** Courtesy of The Maytag Company; **571 L,** The Granger Collection, NY; **571 M,** Tony Freeman/PhotoEdit; **571 R,** Bob Daemmrich Photography; **572,** Kansas State Historical Society; **573,** Charles Dana Gibson; **575,** Library of Congress

Chapter 17 582 L, National Portrait Gallery, Smithsonian Institution/Art Resource, NY; **582 TR,** New York Historical Society; **582 BR,** Chicago Historical Society; **583 L,** Courtesy of the U.S. Naval Academy Museum; **583 R,** Schalkwijk/New York Historical Society; **584,** Library of Congress; **587,** The Oakland Museum of California; **588,** Library of Congress; **589,** The Granger Collection, NY; **591,** Corbis; **593,** *Puck* magazine 1898; **594 L,** Library of Congress; **594 M,** National Archives; **594 R,** AP/Wide World Photos; **596,** Culver Pictures, Inc.; **598,** Corbis; **599 T,** Panama Canal Museum; **599 BL,** Panama Canal Museum; **599 BR,** Panama Canal Museum; **600,** Library of Congress; **601,** Theodore Roosevelt Collection Harvard College Library; **604,** The Granger Collection, NY; **606,** Courtesy of the U.S. Naval Academy Museum; **607,** Prentice Hall; **609,** *Puck,* June 29, 1904

Chapter 18 612 L, Sophia Smith College Archives; **612 R,** Texas State Library & Archives Commission; **613,** Dartmouth College College Library, Special Collection; **614,** Brown Brothers; **614 inset,** Courtesy of the Decorative & Industrial Arts Collection of the Chicago Historical Society; **615,** Corbis Sygma; **616,** Culver Pictures, Inc.; **617,** Brown Brothers; **617 inset,** Library of Congress; **618,** Labor Management Documentation Center, Cornell University; **619 T,** Corbis; **619 B,** Corbis; **621,** Corbis; **622–623,** Texas State Library & Archives Commission; **625,** State Historical Society of Wisconsin; **627,** Hulton/Archive/Getty Images; **628,** White House Historical Association; **629,** The Granger Collection, NY; **630 T,** Museum of American Political Life; **630 B,** Theodore Roosevelt Collection Harvard College Library; **633 T,** Bettmann/Corbis; **633 B,** David J.Frent; **634 T,** National Association for the Advancement of Colored People; **634 B,** Schomburg Center for Research in Black Culture; **635,** Courtesy of the Women's Voters of the United States; **636,** Meserve-Kunhardt Collection; **638 T,** Library of Congress; **638 B,** "Vote Yes" suffrage poster/Smithsonian Institution; **641,** Library of Congress

Chapter 19 644 L, Culver Pictures, Inc.; **644 R,** The Granger Collection, NY; **645 L,** Hulton/Archive/Archive Photos; **645 M,** Corbis; **645 R,** Library of Congress; **646,** Hulton/Archive/Archive Photos; **648,** Museum of the City of New York; **649 T,** Collection of Stuart S. Corning, Jr. Photo © Rob Huntley/Lightstream; **649 B,** Bayerisches Haupstaatsarchiv; **651,** Culver Pictures, Inc.; **653,** The Granger Collection, NY; **654 TL,** Library of Congress; **654 BL,** From the publication "My Four Years in Germany"; **654 R,** The Granger Collection, NY; **655,** National Archives; **656,** Library of Congress; **657,** Library of Congress; **658,** Hulton/Archive/Archive Photos; **659,** Hulton/Archive/Archive Photos; **661,** Russ Lappa; **662 T,** Culver Pictures, Inc.; **662 B,** Corbis; **663,** Brown Brothers; **664,** Library of Congress; **665,** National Archives ; **666 T,** Museum of the City of New York; **666 B,** Museum of the City of New York; **667,** Wayne State University, Archives of Labor and Urban Affairs; **668,** Museum of the City of New York; **669,** SuperStock; **670,** Hulton/Archive/Archive Photos; **675,** Stock Montage

Chapter 20 682 L, *Chicago Daily Tribune;* **682 M,** Corbis; **682 R,** Corbis; **683 L,** John Sloan, *Sixth Avenue Elevated at Third Street,* 1928 (detail). Collection of Whitney Museum of American Art, Purchase 36. 154. Photograph 1998: Whitney Museum of American Art, NY; **683 R,** Superstock; **684,** Corbis; **686,** Brown Brothers; **688,** Culver Pictures, Inc.; **689,** Corbis; **690,** Corbis; **691,** SuperStock; **692,** Culver Pictures, Inc.; **694 T,** Corbis; **694 B,** SuperStock; **695,** Purchased with funds from the Edmunson Art Foundation. Inc., Des Moines Art Center Permanent Collections, 1958.2; **696 L,** Corbis; **696 M,** Brown Brothers; **696 R,** Beinecke Library, Yale University; **697,** Cartier Bresson/Magnum Photos; **699,** The Michael Barson Collection/ Past Perfect. RH/LS; **700,** Library of Congress; **701,** Chicago Historical Society; **702 T,** Corbis; **702 B,** Brown Brothers; **703,** *Chicago Daily Tribune;* **704,** Chermayeff & Geisma; **705 T,** Schomburg Center for Black Research; **705 B,** Brown Brothers; **707,** Historical Society of Wisconsin

Chapter 21 710 L, UPI/Bettmann Archives/Corbis; **710 R,** Calvin Coolidge Memorial Foundation; **711 L,** Gary Waltz/The Image Works; **711 R,** Corbis; **712,** Hulton/Archive/Getty Images; **713,** Hulton/Archive/Getty Images; **714,** The Granger Collection, NY; **716,** Corbis; **718,** Ohio Historical Society; **720,** David J. Frent; **721,** *LIFE* Magazine December 10,1925; **723,** Western Historical Manuscript Collection, Kansas City; **724,** Courtesy of Speigel; **725,** The Granger Collection, NY; **726,** Henry Ford Museum; **727,** The Granger Collection, NY; **728 T,** Hulton/Liaison/Getty Images; **728 B,** Schenectady Mueseum; **729,** Culver Pictures Inc./PictureQuest; **730,** Culver Pictures Inc.; **731,** Boston Athenaeum; **733,** Corbis; **735,** The Granger Collection, NY

Chapter 22 738 L, Library of Congress; **738 R,** Museum of the City of New York/Hulton/Archive/Getty Images; **739,** Hulton/Archive/Getty Images; **740,** Hulton/Archive/Getty Images; **744,** The Granger Collection, NY; **745,** *Detroit News;* **746,** Museum of the City of New York. Photograph by Bernice Abbott, Federal Arts Project; **748 L,** Library of Congress; **748 R,** Library of Congress; **749,** Library of Congress; **750,** FPG International; **753,** Collection of Ryan Brown; **754,** Culver Pictures, Inc.; **755,** Corbis/Bettmann; **756,** FDR Library; **757,** Corbis; **758 L,** Corbis; **758 M,** The White House Photo Office; **758 R,** Karl Gehring/Liaison/Getty Images; **759,** Corbis; **763,** Reprinted from the *Albany Evening News,* 6/7/31, with permission of the *Times Union,* Albany, NY

Chapter 23 766 L, Library of Congress; **766 R,** The Granger Collection, NY; **767 L,** Richard Berenholtz/Corbis Stock Market; **767 R,** The Kobal Collection; **768,** Hoover Presidential Library; **769,** FDR Library; **770 L,** Library of Congress; **770 R,** U.S. Forest Service; **771 T,** Corbis; **771 B,** Corbis; **773,** FDR Library; **774,** Hulton/Archive/Getty Images; **776,** Library of Congress; **777,** *The New Yorker* Collection, 1963, Peter Arno from www.cartoonbank.com. All rights reserved.; **778,** Margaret Bourke-White, *LIFE* Magazine© Time Warner; **779,** Corbis; **780,** ©1935,1963 by the Conde Nast Publications Inc.; **781 T,** Corbis; **781 B,** UPI/Bettman Archives/Corbis; **783,** The Granger Collection, NY; **785,** Corbis; **786,** Corbis; **787,** Library of Congress; **788,** Corbis; **789 L,** Corbis; **789 R,** Corbis; **790,** James Prigoff; **791,** Picture Research Consultants; **793,** Franklin D. Roosevelt Library

Chapter 24 798 L, A.K.G., Berlin/SuperStock; **798 R,** Hulton /Archive/Getty Images; **799,** Sovfoto/Eastfoto; **800,** U.S. Holocaust Memorial Museum; **802,** Moro Roma; **803 T,** AP/Wide World Photos; **803 M,** Collection of Chester Stott, ©Rob Huntley/Lightstream; **803 B,** Corbis; **804,** Liaison/Getty Images; **805 T,** Corbis; **805 B,** Corbis; **806,** Estate of Pablo Picasso/Artists Rights Society (ARS), New York/Art Resource, N.Y.; **807,** Corbis; **808,** The Granger Collection, NY; **809,** The Granger Collection, NY; **810 T,** Corbis; **810 B,** Library of Congress; **811,** Corbis; **812,** AP/Wide World Photos; **813,** Admiral Nimitz Museum; **814 T,** Paul Dorsey/TimePix; **814 B,** Corbis; **817,** Corbis; **818,** Brown Brothers; **819,** Corbis; **821,** Bettman/Corbis; **823,** Dr. Seuss

Chapter 25 824 L, Jeff Tinsley, Smithsonian Instituion; **824 R,** The Granger Collection, NY; **825 L,** Liaison/Getty Images; **825 R,** Library of Congress; **826,** Collection of Chester H. Stott, ©Rob Huntley/Lightstream; **827 T,** National Archives; **827 B,** Bill Mauldin; **828,** The Bancroft Library, Kaiser Pictorial Collection; **828 inset,** Jeff Tinsley, Smithsonian Institution; **829,** Lawrence Thornton/Hulton/Archive/Getty Images; **830 inset,** National Museum of American History, Smithsonian Institution, Washington D.C.; **830,** H. Armstrong Roberts; **831,** Pearson Education/PH College; **832,** The Granger Collection, NY; **833,** National Archives; **834 T,** U.S. Army; **834 B,** Imperial War Museum; **836,** Liaison/Getty Images; **837,** National Portrait Gallery, Smithsonian Institution, Washington D.C., Art Resource, NY; **839,** Corbis; **840,** U.S. Army; **841,** Hulton/Archive/Getty Images; **842 T,** Courtesy of U.S. Holocaust Memorial Museum Archives; **842 B,** Rijksinstituut voor Oorlogsdocumentatie, courtesy of U.S. Holocaust Memorial Museum Archives; **843 T,** U.S. Holocaust Memorial Museum; **843 M,** U.S. Holocaust Memorial Museum; **843 B,** U.S. Holocaust Memorial Museum; **844,** U.S. Holocaust Memorial Museum; **845,** U.S. Holocaust Memorial Museum; **846,** Liaison/Getty Images; **847,** Liaison/Getty Images; **849,** Keystone/Hulton/Archive/Getty Images; **851,** AP Photo/Joe Rosenthal; **852 T,** Hulton/Archive /Getty Images; **852 B,** The Art Archive; **853,** SuperStock; **855,** Hulton/Archive/Getty Images; **856,** National Portrait Gallery, Gift of the Harmon Foundation/Art Resource, NY; **857 inset,** Collection of Jeff Ikler/© Huntley/Lightstream; **857,** Library of Congress; **858,** National Archives; **859,** Photri Inc.; **860 T,** Collection of Col. Stuart S. Corning, Jr., © Rob Huntley/Lightstream; **860 B,** Library of Congress; **861,** Ellen Kaiper Collection, Oakland; **863,** *Des Moines Register*

Chapter 26 866 L, Corbis; **866 R,** Hulton /Archive/Getty Images; **868,** U.S. Army; **869,** Harry S Truman Presidential Library; **870,** Harry S Truman Presidential Library; **872 T,** The Michael Barson Collection/Past Perfect; **872 B,** UPI/Bettman Archives/Corbis; **873,** Courtesy of the J.N. Ding Darling Foundation; **874,** © 1949 Time, Inc. Reprinted with permission; **876,** American Stock/Hulton/Archive/Getty Images; **877,** AP/Wide World Photos; **878,** Corbis; **879,** AP/Wide World Photos; **881,** GP Putnam's Sons; **882 T,** The Michael Barson Collection/Past Perfect, ©Rob Huntley/Lightstream; **882 B,** The Michael Barson Collection/Past Perfect, ©Rob Huntley/Lightstream; **883,** Brown Brothers; **884,** Corbis; **885,** Eastfoto; **887,** Culver Pictures; **889,** Herblock/*Washington Post;* **890 T,** Corbis; **890 B,** The Granger Collection, NY; **892,** Corbis; **893,** © 1959 Newsweek Inc. All rights reserved. Reprinted by permission.; **895,** From *Herblock: A Cartoonist's Life* (Macmillan Publishing, 1993)

PRIMARY SOURCES BIBLIOGRAPHY

Chapter 1 Leo Africanus: Bennett, Jr., Lerone. Before the Mayflower: A History of the Negro in America. Johnson Publishing Company, 1966, p. 18; Christopher Columbus: Morison, Samuel Eliot. Admiral of the Ocean Sea: A Life of Christopher Columbus. Little Brown, 1942, p. 231; Garcilaso de la Vega: Garcilaso de la Vega, El Inca. The Royal Commentaries of Peru, La Florida Del Inca. Fondo de Cultura Económica, 1956, pp. 220, 229.

Chapter 2 Fray Alonso de Benavides: Kupperman, Karen Ordahl, ed. Major Problems in American Colonial History: Documents and Essays. D.C. Heath, 1993, p. 43; John White: Hakluyt, Richard. The Principal Navigations, Voyages, Traffiques, and Discoveries of the English Nation, Edinburgh, 1889, quoted in Berger, Josef and Dorothy Berger, eds. Diary of America. Simon & Schuster, 1957, quoted in Colbert, David, ed. Eyewitness to America: 500 Years of America in the Words of Those Who Saw it Happen. Pantheon Books, 1997, pp. 13–15; John Smith: Lankford, John, ed. Captain John Smith's America: Selections from His Writings. Harper Torchbooks, Harper and Row, 1967, p. 105; Mayflower Compact: Caffrey, Kate. The Mayflower. Stein and Day, 1974, p. 340; John Winthrop: "A Modell of Christian Charity." Collections of the Massachusetts Historical Society, 3rd series, vol. 7, 1838, pp. 33–34, 44–48; Miantonomo: Cronon, William. Changes in the Land: Indians, Colonists, and the Ecology of New England. Hill and Wang, 1983, p. 162; Metacom: Bourne, Russell. The Red King's Rebellion. Atheneum, 1990, p. 107; Adriaen Van der Donck: Jennings, Francis. The Ambiguous Iroquois Empire. W.W. Norton & Company, 1984, p. 47.

Chapter 3 Anonymous: Hawke, David Freeman. Everyday Life in Early America. Harper & Row, 1988, p. 22; William Blackstone: Ulrich, Laurel Thatcher. Good Wives. Oxford University Press, 1982, p. 7; Eliza Pinckney: Ravenel, Harriott Horry. Eliza Pinckney. Charles Scribner's Sons, 1896, p. 6; Olaudah Equiano: Edwards, Paul, ed. Equiano's Travels. Heinemann Educational Books, 1967, p. 25; Equiano: Edwards, p. 32; Charles Ball: Bayliss, John F., ed. Black Slave Narratives. Macmillan, 1970, p. 52; Peter Kalm: Middleton, Richard. Colonial America: A History, 1585–1776. Blackwell, 1996, p. 249; Chief Hendrick: The American Heritage History of the Thirteen Colonies. The American Heritage Publishing Company, 1967, p. 258; Jonathan Edwards: Kupperman, Karen Ordahl, ed. Major Problems in American Colonial History: Documents and Essays. D.C. Heath, 1993, p. 369; George Whitefield: Gaustad, Edwin Scott. The Great Awakening in New England. Quadrangle Books, 1957, p. 27.

Chapter 4 George Washington: Letter from Washington to his brother. Fort Necessity National Battlefield, Jumonville Glen, at www. nps.gov; Alexander Spotswood: R. A. Brock, ed. The Official Letters of Alexander Spotswood. Richmond, VA: Virginia Historical Society, 1882, vol. II, p. 296; Massachusetts militiaman: Monk, Linda, ed. Ordinary Americans: U.S. History Through the Eyes of Everyday People. Close Up Publishing, 1994, p. 24; John Dickinson: Current, Richard N., et al., eds. Words That Made American History: Colonial Times to the 1870's. Little Brown, 1972, Third Edition, Vol. One, p. 69; Declaration of Rights and Grievances: Morgan, Edmund S., ed. Prologue to Revolution: Sources and Documents on the Stamp Act Crisis, 1764–1766. University of North Carolina Press, 1959, pp. 62–63; Declaration and Resolves of the First Continental Congress: Commager, Henry Steele, ed. Documents of American History, 8th ed. Appleton-Century-Crofts, 1968, p. 83; Patrick Henry:

Commager, Henry Steele, and Richard B. Morris, eds. *The Spirit of 'Seventy-Six: The Story of the American Revolution as Told by Participants.* New York: Bonanza Books, 1983, pp. 108–109; **Thomas Paine, *Common Sense:*** Curti, Merle, et al., eds., *American Issues: The Social Record,* 4th ed. rev. New York: J. B. Lippincott, 1971, vol. 1, pp. 82, 84; **John Locke:** *Two Treatises of Government,* Mark Goldie, ed. London, Orion Publishing Group, 1993, pp. 223–224; **Abigail Adams:** Gelles, Edith B. *First Thoughts: Life and Letters of Abigail Adams.* Twayne Publishers, Simon & Schuster Macmillan, 1998, pp. 14–15; **Ralph Waldo Emerson, "Concord Hymn":** Allison, Alexander W., et al., eds. *The Norton Anthology of Poetry,* 3rd ed. W. W. Norton & Company, 1983, p. 665; **Thomas Paine, *The Crisis:*** Foot, Michael, and Isaac Kramnick, eds. Thomas Paine Reader. Penguin Books, 1987, p. 116; **Soldier at the Battle of Princeton:** Commager and Morris, p. 519; **George Washington at Valley Forge:** Letter to the Continental Congress. James Madison Center, James Madison University, at www.jmu.edu

Chapter 5 George Washington: Resignation Address to the Continental Congress, Annapolis, MD, Dec. 23, 1783. *The Papers of George Washington,* at www.virginia.edu; **Art. III, Articles of Confederation:** Commager, Henry Steele, ed. *Documents of American History,* 8th ed. Appleton-Century-Crofts, 1968, p. 111; **Fisher Ames:** Wood, Gordon S. *The Creation of the American Republic, 1776–1787.* W. W. Norton & Company, 1969, p. 411; **Richard Price:** Wood, p. 396; **James Madison:** Scott, E.H., ed. *Journal of the Federal Convention.* Albert, Scott & Co., 1893, p. 3; **Thomas Jefferson:** Letter to James Madison, December 20, 1787, "In Congress Assembled: Continuity and Change in the Governing of the United States," *American Memory,* Library of Congress, at http://memory.loc.gov; ***The Federalist,* No. 10:** *The Annals of America.* Vol. 3, 1784–1796: *Organizing the New Nation.* Encyclopaedia Britannica, 1968, p. 219; **Robert Yates and John Lansing:** Commager, p. 149; **The Virginia Declaration of Rights, Sec. 8:** National Archives and Records Administration, at www. nara.gov; **Virginia Statute for Religious Liberty:** Commager, p. 126; **Le Comte de Moustier:** Harwell, Richard. *Washington.* Charles Scribner's Sons, 1968, p. 567; **George Washington, First Inaugural Address:** Inaugural Addresses of the Presidents of the United States. Washington, D.C.: U.S. G.P.O.: for sale by the Supt. of Docs., U.S. G.P.O., 1989; Bartleby.com, 2001. www. bartleby.com/124. [May 17, 2001]

Chapter 6 George Washington: Fitzpatrick, John C., ed., *The Writings of George Washington.* Washington, 1931–1941, quoted in Elkins, Stanley and Eric McKitrick. *The Age of Federalism.* Oxford University Press, 1993, p. 75; **Alexander Hamilton:** Miller, John C. *The Federalist Era,* 1789–1801. Harper and Row, 1960, p. 81; **George Washington's Farewell Address:** Commager, Henry Steele, ed. *Documents of American History,* vol. 1, 8th ed. Appleton-Century-Crofts, 1968, pp. 172–174; **John Adams's Inaugural Address:** Hunt, John Gabriel, ed. *The Inaugural Addresses of the Presidents.* Grammercy Books, 1997, p. 17; **Alexander Hamilton:** *The Public Conduct and Character of John Adams, Esq., President of the United States.* Private pamphlet, New York, October 24, 1800, quoted in Cornog, Evan, and Richard Whelan. *Hats in the Ring: An Illustrated History of American Presidential Campaigns.* Random House, 2000, p. 21; **Thomas Jefferson's First Inaugural Address:** Ravitch, Diane, ed. *The Democracy Reader.* HarperPerennial, 1992, p. 140; **Thomas Jefferson:** Peterson, Merrill D., ed. *Thomas Jefferson.* Library of America, 1984, p. 494; **Tecumseh:** Bryan, William Jennings, ed. *The World's Famous Orations,* vol. 3. Funk and Wagnalls, 1906, pp. 14–15; **Handsome Lake:** Wallace, Anthony F. C. *The Death and Rebirth of the Seneca.* Vintage Books, 1972, p. 268; **Tecumseh:** Edmunds, David R. *Tecumseh and the Quest for Indian Leadership.* Little, Brown and Company, 1984, p. 205; **James Madison:** "To The Senate and House of Representatives of the United States, June 1, 1812," quoted in Richardson, James D. *A Compilation of the Messages and Papers of the Presidents, 1798–1908,* vol. 1. Bureau of National Literature and Art, 1909, pp. 500–505.

Chapter 7 Noah Webster: Wood, Gordon S. *The Rising Glory of America, 1760–1820.* Northeastern University Press, 1990, p. 169; **Zadoc Long:** Rothman, Ellen K. *Hands and Hearts: A History of Courtship in America.* Harvard University Press, 1984; **William Thacher:** Gorn, Elliot J., et al. *Constructing the American Past: A Source Book of a People's History.* HarperCollins, 1991, p. 185; **Richard Allen:** Hatch, Nathan O. *The Democratization of American Christianity.* Yale University Press, 1989, p. 107; **James Hall:** *Letters from the West.* Scholars' Facsimiles and Reprints, 1967, p. 171; **Account of an Expedition from Pittsburgh to the Rocky Mountains:** *Account of an Expedition from Pittsburgh to the Rocky Mountains,* Vol. 2. Carey & Lea, 1823, p. 351; **James R. Walker:** *Lakota Society.* University of Nebraska Press, 1982, p. 74; **William Travis:** Ramsdell, Charles. "The Storming of the Alamo," *American Heritage,* Vol. XII, No. 2, February 1961, p. 91.

Chapter 8 Nathaniel Hawthorne: Randall Stewart, ed. Yale University Press, 1932. Cited in Marx, Leo. *The Machine in the Garden.* Oxford University Press, 1964; **Alexis de Tocqueville:** Pierson, George Wilson. *Tocqueville in America.* Johns Hopkins University Press, 1996, p. 496; **millworker:** Larcom, Lucy. *A New England Girlhood.* Corinth Books, 1961, pp. 145–156; **Harriet Robinson:** Davis, David Byron. *Antebellum American Culture: An Interpretive Anthology.* D. C. Heath, 1979, pp. 87–88; **David Christy:** Christy, David. *Cotton Is King.* Moore, Wilstach, Keys and Co., 1855, p. 11; **Moses Grandy:** Grandy, Moses. *Narrative of the Life of Moses Grandy Late a Slave in the United States of America.* Oliver Johnson Publishing Company, 1844, p. 11, quoted in Lerner, Gerda. *Black Women in White America, A Documentary History.* Vintage Books, 1973, p. 9; **James Monroe, 1817:** Monroe, James. *A Narrative of a Tour of Observation, Made during the Summer of 1817.* Cited in Waldstreicher, David. *In the Midst of Perpetual Fetes.* University of North Carolina Press, 1997, p. 302; **James Monroe:** Commager, Henry Steele, ed. *Documents of American History,* 8th ed. Appleton-Century-Crofts, 1968, pp. 236–237; **John Quincy Adams:** Wilentz, Sean, ed. *Major Problems in the Early Republic, 1778–1848.* D. C. Heath, 1992, p. 341; **Daniel Webster:** Webster, Daniel, and Charles M. Wiltse and Harold D. Moser, eds. *The Papers of Daniel Webster: Correspondence,* Daniel Webster to Ezekiel Webster, January 17, 1829. University Press of New England, 1986. Cited in Cole, Daniel B. *The Presidency of Andrew Jackson.* University Press of Kansas, 1993, pp. 6–7; **Cherokee public appeal:** Van Every, Dale. *Disinherited: The Lost Birthright of the American Indian.* William Morrow and Company, 1966, pp. 135–136; **President Jackson:** Commager, p. 260; **President Jackson:** Wilentz, p. 388.

Chapter 9 Henry David Thoreau: *Walden.* Princeton University Press, 1971, p. 326; **Horace Mann:** "Horace Mann." Encyclopaedia Britannica, vol. 11, 1983, p. 455; Germantown Mennonites: Commager, Henry Steele, ed. *Documents of American History,* 8th ed. Appleton-Century-Crofts, 1968, p. 37; **William Lloyd Garrison:** Wilentz, Sean, ed. *Major Problems in the Early Republic,* 1787–1848. D. C. Heath, 1992, p. 477; **Frederick Douglass:** speech in Rochester, N.Y., August 4, 1857; **Martin Delany:** Wilentz, p. 514; **Catharine Beecher:** *A Treatise on Domestic Economy.* T. H. Webb, 1842, pp. 26–34, 36–38; **Elizabeth Cady Stanton:** Stanton, Elizabeth Cady, et al. *History of Woman Suffrage,* Vol. 1. Fowler and Wells, 1889, pp. 58–59; **Sojourner Truth:** *Anti-Slavery Bugle,* Salem, Ohio, June 21, 1851, 4: p. 81–82.

Chapter 10 Harriet Beecher Stowe: *Uncle Tom's Cabin.* New American Library, 1981, p. 32; **Harriet Beecher Stowe:** p. 93; **George Fitzhugh:** Gorn, Elliot J., et al. *Constructing the American Past: A Source Book of a People's History,* Vol. 1. HarperCollins, 1991, p. 259; **John C. Calhoun:** Wiltse, Charles M. *John C. Calhoun: Sectionalist,* 1840–1850. The Bobbs-Merrill Company, 1951, p. 461; **Daniel Webster:** Morris, Richard B., and Jeffrey B. Morris, eds. *Encyclopedia of American History.* Harper and Row, 1976, p. 1179. **The American Party:** Holt, Michael F. *The Political Crises of the 1850's.* John Wiley and Sons, 1978, p. 163; **Stephen Douglas:** Holt, p. 145; **William H. Seward:** McPherson, James. *Battle Cry of Freedom.* Oxford University Press, 1988, p. 145; **Roger Taney:** Heffner, Richard D. *A Documentary History of the United States.* New American Library, 1976, p. 141; **Abraham Lincoln:** Angle, Paul M. *Created Equal? The Complete Lincoln-Douglas Debates of 1858.* The University of Chicago Press, 1958, p. 42; **Abraham Lincoln:** *Selected Speeches and Writings.* The Library of America, 1992, p. 131; **John Brown:** Oates, Stephen B. *To Purge This Land with Blood: A Biography of John Brown.* HarperTorchbooks, 1970, p. 351; **Augusta, Georgia, newspaper editor:** Holt, Michael F. *The Political Crisis of the 1850's.* John Wiley and Sons, 1978, p. 241; **Abraham Lincoln (First Inaugural Address):** Ravitch, Diane, ed. *The Democracy Reader.* HarperPerennial, 1992, p. 165.

Chapter 11 Sallie Hunt: B. A. Botkin, ed. *A Civil War Treasury of Tales, Legends and Folklore.* Random House, 1960, p. 21; **Abraham Lincoln:** Ward, Geoffrey C. *The Civil War: An Illustrated History.* Alfred A. Knopf, 1990, p. 110; **Elisha Stockwell:** Murphy, Jim. *The Boys' War.* Clarion Books, 1990, p. 33; **Louis Wigfall:** McPherson, James M. *Battle Cry of Freedom.* Oxford University Press, 1998, p. 430; **Abraham Lincoln:** McPherson, p. 510; **Emancipation Proclamation:** Boorstin, Daniel, ed. *An American Primer.* University of Chicago Press, 1968, p. 431; **Lewis Douglass:** Chang, Ina. *A Separate Battle: Women and the Civil War.* Lodestar Books, 1991, p. 65; **Frederick Douglass:** Douglass' Monthly, August, 1863; **Cornelia Hancock:** *South After Gettysburg.* University of Nebraska Press, 1998; **Civil War drummer boy:** Murphy, p. 43; **soldier at Gettysburg:** E. B. Long. *The Civil War Day by Day.* Da Capo Press, 1971, p. 377; **Mary Ann Loughborough:** Gragg, Rod, *The Illustrated Confederate Reader.* Harper and Row, 1989, p.82; **Abraham Lincoln:** *Selected Speeches and Writings.* First Vintage Books, Library of America, p. 450; **R.B. Prescott:** Meltzer, Milton, ed. *Voices from the Civil War.* Thomas Y. Crowell, 1989, pp. 179–181; **Henrietta Lee:** Gragg, p. 88; **Abraham Lincoln:** Lincoln, p. 450.

Chapter 12 Val C. Giles: Lasswell, Mary, and ed., *Rags and Hope: The Memoirs of Val C. Giles,* New York: Coward-McCann, 1961. **Abraham Lincoln:** *Selected Speeches and Writings.* First Vintage Books, Library of America, p. 450; **Charlotte Forten:** "Life on the Sea Islands," Atlantic Monthly, Vol. 13 (May and June) 1864, pp. 588–589, 591–594, 666–667; **Black Union Soldier:** Litwack, Leon F. *Been in the Storm So Long, The Aftermath of Slavery.* Vintage Books, 1979, Chapter 7.

Chapter 13 Samuel F.B. Morse: Morse, Edward Lind, ed., *Samuel F.B. Morse, His Letters and Journals,* 2 vols., Houghton Mifflin, 1914, quoted in Ambrose, Stephen and Douglas Brinkley. *Witness to America: An Illustrated Documentary History of the United States from the Revolution to Today.* Harper Collins, 1999, p. 96; **Abram Stevens Hewitt:** *Address Delivered on the Occasion of the Opening of the New York and Brooklyn Bridge, May 24th, 1883,* John Polemus, 1883, quoted in Graebner, William and Leonard Richards, eds., *The American Record: Images of the Nation's Past,* Vol. 2, Alfred Knopf, 1982, p. 50; **Andrew Carnegie:** "How I Served My Apprenticeship." *Youth's Companion,* April 23, 1896, quoted in Ambrose, pp. 301–305; **Andrew Carnegie:** *The Empire of Business.* Doubleday, 1902, pp. 138–140, quoted in Kirkland, Edward Chase. *Dream and Thought in the Business Community, 1860–1900.* Cornell, 1956, pp. 156–157; **Sadie Frowne:** "The Story of a Sweatshop Girl," *The Independent 54,* September 25, 1902, pp. 2279–2282, quoted in Bailey, Thomas A. and David M. Kennedy. *The American Spirit: United States History as Seen by Contemporaries,* Vol. 2, 8th ed. D.C. Heath and Company, 1994, pp. 80–85; **Frederick Winslow Taylor:** *The Principles of Scientific Management.* W.W. Norton and Company, 1911, p. 39; **Samuel Gompers:** *Letter from American Federationist,* Vol. 1, September 1894, pp. 150–152, quoted in Hofstadter, Richard, ed., *Great Issues in American History From Reconstruction to the Present Day, 1864–1969,* Vintage Books, 1969, pp. 187–191; **Eugene V. Debs:** *Declaration of Principles, American Railway Union, 1893,* quoted in Salvatore, Nick; **Eugene V. Debs:** *Citizen and Socialist.* University of Illinois Press, 1982, p. 116; **August Spies:** Kogan, B. R. "The Chicago Haymarket Riot," 1959 (a reproduction of the circular in the Chicago Historical Society collection).

Chapter 14 Mary Clark: Nelson, Paula M. *After the West Was Won: Homesteaders and Town-Builders in Western South Dakota, 1900–1917.* University of Iowa Press, 1986, quoted in Jones, Mary Ellen. *Daily Life on the 19th-Century Frontier.* The Greenwood Press, 1998, p. 187; **death song sung by a Cherokee:** Thomas, David hurst, et al. *The Native Americans: An Illustrated History.* Turner Publising, 1993, p. 332; **newspaper reporter:** Fite, Gilbert. *The Farmer's Frontier, 1865–1900.* University of New Mexico Press, 1974, p. 205; **diary of a Union Pacific engineer:** Ward, Geoffrey C. *The West: An Illustrated History.* Little, Brown and Company (The West Book Project), 1996, p. 222; **cowboy Charles A. Siringo:** Jones, Mary Ellen. *Daily Life on the 19th-Century Frontier.* The Greenwood Press, 1998, p. 167; **"The Old Chisholm Trail":** Forbis, William H. *The Old West: The Cowboys.* Time-Life Books, 1973, p. 154; **"Commercial and Financial Chronicle," September 21, 1879:** quoted in Fite, p. 82; **Washington Gladden:** *The Annals of America.* Vol. 11, 1884–1894: *Agrarianism and Urbanization.* Encyclopaedia Britannica, 1968, p. 356.

Acknowledgments

1294 Acknowledgments

Chapter 15 Peter Mossini: Coan, Peter M. *Ellis Island Interviews: In Their Own Words.* Facts on File, 1997, p. 45; **Fiorello LaGuardia:** *The Making of an Insurgent.* J. B. Lippincott Co., 1948, pp. 64-65; **Emily Dinwiddie:** "Some Aspects of Italian Housing and Social Conditions in Philadelphia," Charities and the Commons, Vol. 12, 1904, p. 490; **Pedro Martínez:** Hoobler, Dorothy and Thomas Hoobler. *The Mexican American Family Album.* Oxford University Press, 1994, p. 34; **Council of Hygiene and Public Health:** Dolkart, Andrew S. and Ruth Limmer. "The Tenement As History And Housing." Lower East Side Tenement Museum, New York; **Ellen Swallow Richards:** *Conservation by Sanitation; Air and Water Supply; Disposal of Waste.* Wiley, 1911; **Jacob Riis:** *How the Other Half Lives.* Penguin, 1997, p. 6; **Frances Willard:** *Glimpses of Fifty Years: The Autobiography of an American Woman.* H.J. Smith & Co., 1889, pp. 339-341.

Chapter 16 Mary Antin: Levinson, Nancy Smiler. *Turn of the Century: Our Nation One Hundred Years Ago.* Lodestar Books, 1994, pp. 54-55. **Tony Longo:** Loeper, John J. *Going to School in 1876.* Atheneum, 1984, pp. 64-65; **Pauli Murray:** *Proud Shoes.* Harper and Row, 1956, pp. 269-270; **Booker T. Washington:** *Address of Booker T. Washington, principal of the Tuskegee Normal and Industrial Institute, Tuskegee, Alabama, delivered at the opening of the Cotton States and International Exposition, at Atlanta, Ga., September 18, 1895.* Daniel A. P. Murray Pamphlet Collection, Library of Congress, 1894, pp. 7-9; **W.E.B. Du Bois:** Du Bois, W.E.B. *The Negro Problem: A Series of Articles by Representative American Negroes of Today.* J. Pott and Company, 1903, pp. 33-75; **Jack Norworth:** "Take Me Out to the Ball Game." Words by Jack Norworth, music by Albert Von Tilzer. www.geocities.com; **Albon Holsey:** Litwack, Leon F. *Trouble in Mind: Black Southerners in the Age of Jim Crow.* Alfred A. Knopf, 1998; p. 16; **Frederick Howe:** Levinson, p. 95.

Chapter 17 Henry Cabot Lodge: "Our Blundering Foreign Policy," *The Forum,* Vol. 19, March 1895, pp. 14-17, quoted in Hofstadter, Richard, ed., *Great Issues in American History from Reconstruction to the Present Day, 1864-1969,* Vintage Books, 1969, pp. 187-191; *New York Journal* Headline: *New York Journal,* October 10, 1897, quoted in Bailey, Thomas A. and David M. Kennedy. *The American Spirit: United States History as Seen by Contemporaries,* Vol. 2, 8th ed. D.C. Heath and Company, 1994, pp. 171-172; **William McKinley:** Interview at the White House, November 21, 1899, *Christian Advocate,* January 22, 1903, quoted in Olcott, C.S. *The Life of William McKinley,* Vol. 2, 1916, pp. 110-111, quoted in Bailey, pp. 179-180; **John Hay:** Telegram to U.S. minister in Bogotá. *Foreign Relations of the United States, 1903.* Washington D.C.: Government Printing Office, 1904, p. 146, quoted in Bailey, pp. 190-191; **Theodore Roosevelt:** Hart, Albert Bushnell, and Herbert Ronald Ferleger, eds. *Theodore Roosevelt Cyclopedia.* Roosevelt Memorial Association, 1941, p. 407; **Theodore Roosevelt's Corollary to the Monroe Doctrine:** "Roosevelt's Annual Message, December 5, 1905," quoted in Commager, Henry Steele, ed. *Documents of American History,* vol. 2, 8th ed. Appleton-Century-Crofts, 1968, p. 34; **Theodore Roosevelt:** Letter to Henry Cabot Lodge, from Morison, Elting E., ed. *The Letters of Theodore Roosevelt,* Vol. 2, Harvard University Press, 1951, quoted in Bailey, pp. 197-198; **Carl Schurz Platform of the Anti-Imperialist League:** "The Policy of Imperialism," Liberty Tracts No. 4, Address by Carl Schurz to Anti-Imperialist Conference in Chicago, October 17, 1899, quoted in Hofstadter, pp. 202-204; **Carl Schurz:** Ibid.; **Bishop Alexander Walters:** "Wisconsin Weekly Advocate," August 17, 1899, quoted in Gatewood, Willard B., Jr. *Black Americans and the White Man's Burden, 1898-1903.* University of Illinois Press, 1975, p. 200; **Walter Hines Page:** "The War With Spain And After," *Atlantic Monthly,* Vol. 81, June 1898, pp. 725-727, quoted in Hofstadter, p. 201.

Chapter 18 Upton Sinclair: *The Jungle.* Doubleday, 1906, pp. 96-97; **Edward Bellamy:** Bellamy, Edward. *Looking Backward.* River City Press, 1888, p. 56; **Jane Addams:** Addams, Jane. "Why Women Should Vote." *Ladies Home Journal,* Vol. XXVII, January 1910, pp. 21-22; **Rose Schneiderman:** Mitelman, Bonnie. "Rose Schneiderman and the Triangle Shirtwaist Fire." American History Illustrated, July 1981; **Robert M. La Follette:** La Follette, Robert M. *A Personal Narrative of Political Experiences,* 1913, published online at the Library of Congress's American Memory Web site www.lcweb2.loc.gov; **Woodrow Wilson campaign speech:** Wilson, Woodrow. *The New Freedom: A Call for the Emancipation of the Generous Energies of a People.* Double Day, Page and Company, 1913, pp. 163-191, published online at www.1912.history.ohio-state.edu; **Lyman Abbott:** Abbott, Lyman. "Why Women DO Not Wish the Suffrage." *The Atlantic Monthly,* September 1903, published online at www.theatlantic.com; **Susan B. Anthony:** Sherr, Lynn. *Failure Is Impossible: Susan B. Anthony in Her Own Words.* Times Books, 1995, pp. 110-112.

Chapter 19 Borijove Jevtic: Carey, John. *Eyewitness to History.* Faber and Faber, 1987, p. 443; **The New York Times:** "He Kept Us Out of War." October 21, 1916; **Arthur Zimmermann:** Leckie, Robert. *The Wars of America.* Harper and Row, 1968, p. 628; **Woodrow Wilson:** Cooper, John Milton, Jr. *Pivotal Decades: The United States, 1900-1920.* W. W. Norton and Company, 1990, p. 265; **Anonymous:** Grist, N R. "A Letter from Camp Devens 1918," *British Medical Journal,* December 22-29, 1979; **Corporal Elmer Sherwood:** Berger, Dorothy and Josef, eds. *Diary of America.* Simon and Schuster, 1957, p. 536; **Henry Ford:** Conot, Robert. *American Odyssey.* William Morrow and Co., 1974, p. 181; Herbert Hoover: "Gospel of the Clean Plate." *Ladies Home Journal,* August 1917, p. 25; **Woodrow Wilson:** Commager, Henry Steele, ed. *Documents of American History,* vol. II, 8th ed. Appleton-Century-Crofts, 1968, p. 138; **Alice Lord O'Brian:** *No Glory: Letters from France, 1917-1919.* Airport Publishers, 1936, pp. 8, 141, 152-153.

Chapter 20 Preston Slosson: *The Great Crusade and After, 1914-1928.* Macmillan, 1930, p. 157; **George Gershwin:** Colbert, David, ed. *Eyewitness to America.* Pantheon, 1997, p. 347; **Sinclair Lewis:** *Main Street.* Harcourt, Brace and Company, 1920, p. 265; **Edna St. Vincent Millay:** Allison, Alexander W., et al., eds. *The Norton Anthology of Poetry,* Third Edition. W. W. Norton & Company, 1983, p. 1032; **Langston Hughes:** *I, Too* from SELECTED POEMS OF LANGSTON HUGHES by Langston Hughes. Copyright © 1926 Alfred A. Knopf, Inc. Renewed 1954 Estate of Langston Hughes. Reprinted by permission of Alfred A. Knopf, Inc. **Alice Longworth:** *Crowded Hours: Reminiscences of Alice Roosevelt Longworth.* Charles Scribner's Sons, 1933, p. 324; **Paul Morand:** Colbert, p. 364; **Klansman's Manual:** Marcus, Robert D., and David Burner. *America Firsthand,* Vol. II. St. Martin's Press, 1989, p. 238.

Chapter 21 Warren G. Harding, Boston, May 14, 1920: Schortemeier, Frederick E. *Rededicating America: Life and Recent Speeches of Warren G. Harding.* Bobbs-Merrill, 1920, p. 223; **Warren G. Harding, October 26, 1929:** Russell, Francis. *President Harding: His Life and Times, 1865-1923.* Eyre & Spottiswoode, 1969, pp. 471-472. **Earnest Elmo Calkins:** *Business the Civilizer.* Little, Brown, and Company, 1928, quoted in Marcus, Robert D. and David Burner. *America Firsthand,* Vol. II. St. Martin's Press, 1989, p. 225; **Herbert Hoover, New York City, October 1928:** Birley, Robert, ed. *Speeches and Documents in American History,* Vol. IV. Oxford University Press, p. 89, first published in *The World's Classics, 1942.*

Chapter 22 Gordon Thomas and Max Morgan-Witts: *The Day the Bubble Burst.* Doubleday & Company, 1979, quoted in Cary, John H. and Julius Weinberg, eds. *The Social Fabric: American Life from the Civil War to the Present.* 4th ed. Little, Brown and Company, 1984, p. 299; **Ann Rivington:** "We Live on Relief." *Scribner's Magazine* 95, April 1934, pp. 282-285, quoted in Kutler, Stanley I. *Looking for America: The People's History.* 2nd ed., Vol. 2. W.W. Norton and Company, 1979, pp. 360-361; **Robert Conot:** *American Odyssey.* William Morrow and Company, 1974, p. 283; **Gordon Parks:** *Voices in the Mirror: An Autobiography.* Doubleday, 1990; **Wilson Ledford:** "How I Lived During the Depression." Interview taped and transcribed by Reuben Hiatt, November 7, 1982, quoted in Snell, William R. ed. *Hard Times Remembered: Bradley County and the Great Depression.* Bradley County Historical Society, 1983, pp. 117-121; **Gerald W. Johnson:** "The Average American and the Depression." *Current History,* February 1932; **Kitty McCulloch:** Terkel, Studs. *Hard Times: An Oral History of the Great Depression.* Pantheon Books, 1970; **Harry Haugland:** "The Right to Live." Unpublished, quoted in Kutler, pp. 373-374; **Clarence Lee:** Quoted in *Riding the Rails.* Dirs. Michael Uys and Lexy Lovell, WGBH Educational Foundation, 1998, Transcript; **William Saroyan:** *Inhale and Exhale.* Random House, 1936, p. 81; **"Brother Can You Spare a Dime?":** *Brother, Can You Spare A Dime?* Words by E.Y. Harburg, Music by Jay Gorney. Copyright © 1932 (Renewed) Glocca Morra Music Corp. and Gorney Music Publishing c/o Next Decade Music (ASCAP); **"Happy Days Are Here Again":** *Happy Days Are Here Again* by Milton Ager & Jack Yellin. Copyright © 1929 (Renewed) EMI Robbins Catalog, Inc. c/o EMI Music Publishing, Inc. (ASCAP); **Herbert Hoover:** Myers, William S., ed. *The State Papers and Other Public Writings of Herbert Hoover.* Doubleday, Doran and Company, Inc., Vol. II, 1934, pp. 408-413; **Franklin D. Roosevelt:** *The New York Times,* September 24, 1932; **Roosevelt's First Inaugural Address:** Commager, Henry Steele, ed. *Documents of American History,* vol. 2, 8th ed. Appleton-Century-Crofts, 1968, p. 240.

Chapter 23 Harry Hopkins: Dawley, Alan. *Struggles for Justice: Social Responsibility and the Liberal State.* Harvard University Press, 1991, p. 367; **George Dobbin:** Federal Writers' Project. *These Are Our Lives.* University of North Carolina Press, 1939; **Roosevelt administration official:** Markowitz, Gerald, and David Rosner, eds. "Slaves of the Depression." Workers' Letters About Life on the Job. Cornell, 1987, p. 154; **Sam T. Mayhew:** Terrill, Tom E., and Jerrold Hirsch, eds. *Such As Us: Southern Voices of the Thirties.* University of North Carolina Press, 1978; **Franklin Roosevelt:** White, Walter. *A Man Called White: The Autobiography of Walter White.* Viking Press, 1948, pp. 179-180; **James Agee:** Agee, James, and Walker Evans. *Let Us Now Praise Famous Men.* Boston: Houghton Mifflin Company, 1941, pp. 118-120; **Walter Reuther:** Madison, Charles A. *American Labor Leaders, Personalities and Forces in the Labor Movement.* Ungar, 1950, p. 382.

Chapter 24 The Party Rally of Honor: *Der Parteitag der Ehre vom 8. bis 14. September 1936.* Zentralverlag der NSDAP, 1936, pp. 170-177; **Nazi Poster:** Hitler, Adolf. *Mein Kampf.* Reynal & Hitchcock, 1940, p. 527; **Alfred Duff Cooper:** Churchill, Winston. *The Gathering Storm.* Vol. 1 of *The Second World War.* Houghton Mifflin, 1948, pp. 291-292. **Winston Churchill:** Baldwin, Hanson W. *The Crucial Years: 1939-1941.* Harper and Row, 1976, p. 127; **Hirota Koki:** Brendon, Piers. *The Dark Valley.* Alfred A. Knopf, 2000, p. 455; **Franklin D. Roosevelt:** Davis, Kenneth S. *FDR: The New Deal Years, 1933-1937.* Random House, 1986, p. 640; **Franklin D. Roosevelt:** Commager, Henry Steele, ed. *Documents of American History,* vol. II, 8th ed. Appleton-Century-Crofts, 1968, p. 452.

Chapter 25 Franklin D. Roosevelt: Rosenman, Samuel I., comp. *The Public Papers and Addresses of Franklin D. Roosevelt, 1940 Volume: War—And Aid to Democracies.* MacMillan, 1941, p. 643; **Franklin D. Roosevelt:** Commager, Henry Steele, ed. *Documents of American History,* vol. II, 8th ed. Appleton-Century-Crofts, 1968, p. 449; **Franklin D. Roosevelt and Winston S. Churchill:** Curti, Merle, Isidore Starr, and Lewis Paul Todd, eds. *Living American Documents.* Harcourt, 1961, p. 304; **German infantryman:** Carey, John, ed. *Eyewitness to History.* Harvard University Press, 1987, p. 576; **Lieutenant Robert Edlin:** Colbert, Robert, ed. *Eyewitness to America.* Pantheon, 1997, p. 420; **Adolf Hitler:** *Mein Kampf.* Reynal & Hitchcock, 1940, p. 826; **Leon Bass:** *Holocaust and Human Behavior.* Facing History and Ourselves National Foundation, p. 414; **Hiroshima survivor:** Cook, Haruko Taya, and Theodore Cook. *Japan at War: An Oral History.* The New Press, 1992, p. 397; **A. Philip Randolph:** Anderson, Jervis. *A. Philip Randolph.* Harcourt, 1973, p. 249; **Lloyd Brown:** Blum, John Morton. *V Was for Victory: Politics and American Culture During World War II.* Harcourt Brace Jovanovich, 1976, p. 191; **Henry Murakami:** Harris, Mark Jonathan, et al. *The Homefront: America During World War II.* G. P. Putnam's Sons, 1984, p. 113.

Chapter 26 Winston Churchill: *The Annals of America,* vol. 16, 1940-1949: *The Second World War and After.* Encyclopaedia Britannica, 1968, p. 367; **Harry Truman:** Commager, Henry Steele, ed. *Documents of American History,* vol. II, 8th ed. Appleton-Century-Crofts, 1968, p. 525; **Harry Truman:** "Race for the Superbomb," *The American Experience.* www.pbs.org; **George C. Marshall:** Commager, Henry Steele, ed. *Documents of American History,* vol. II, 8th ed. Appleton-Century-Crofts, 1968, p. 532; **Arnold Winter:** Tomedi, Rudy. *No Bugles, No Drums: An Oral History of the Korean War.* John Wiley and Sons, 1993, p. 26; **Tom Clawson:** Tomedi, pp. 147-148; **Douglas MacArthur:** Phillips, Cabell. *The Truman Presidency: The History of a Triumphant Succession.* The Macmillan Company, 1966, p. 348; **Edward R. Murrow:** *See It Now* broadcast, March 29, 1954, published online at www.indiana.edu; **Margaret Chase Smith:** "Declaration of Conscience," Margaret Chase Smith Library, published online at www.mcslibrary.org; **Dwight D. Eisenhower:** Commager, Henry Steele, ed. *Documents of American History,* vol. II, 8th ed. Appleton-Century-Crofts, 1968, p. 667.

Chapter 27 Harry Henderson: "The Mass-Produced Suburbs, Part I: How People Live in America's Newest Towns," *Harper's Magazine,* November 1953, Vol. 207, No. 1242, p. 26; **Malvina Reynolds:** *Little Boxes* by Malvina Reynolds. Copyright © 1962 (Renewed) Schroder Music Company (ASCAP); **Geoffrey Perrett:** *A Dream of Greatness: The American People, 1945–1963.* Coward, McCann & Geoghegan, 1979, p. 307; **Betty Friedan:** *The Feminine Mystique.* W.W. Norton & Company, 1963; **Allen Ginsberg:** *Howl* from HOWL & OTHER POEMS by Allen Ginsberg. Copyright © 1956, 1959 by Allen Ginsberg. Reprinted by permission of City Lights Books; **Richard Nixon:** Wicker, Tom. *One of Us: Richard Nixon and the American Dream.* Random House, 1991, p. 98; **Dwight Eisenhower:** Holbo, Paul S., and Robert W. Sellen, eds. *The Eisenhower Era.* Dryden Press, 1974, p. 113.

Chapter 28 Chief Justice Warren: Opinion of the Court in *Brown* v. *Board of Education of Topeka,* quoted in Commager, Henry Steele, ed. *Documents of American History,* vol. 2, 8th ed. Appleton-Century-Crofts, 1968, pp. 607–608; **84th Congress's Southern Manifesto:** from *Congressional Record,* 84th Congress, 2nd session, March 12, 1956, pp. 4515–4516, quoted in Bailey, Thomas A. and David M. Kennedy. *The American Spirit: United States History as Seen by Contemporaries,* Vol. 2, 8th ed. D.C. Heath and Company, 1994, pp. 463–464; **Martin Luther King, Jr.:** Sitkoff, Harvard. *The Struggle for Black Equality: 1954–1980.* Hill and Wang, 1981, p. 50; **Martin Luther King, Jr.:** *Stride Toward Freedom: The Montgomery Story.* Harper and Row, 1958, pp. 53–55; **Elizabeth Eckford:** Bates, Daisy. *The Long Shadow of Little Rock.* David McKay, 1962, quoted in Raskin, Jamin B. We the Students: *Supreme Court Decisions for and about Students.* Congressional Quarterly Press, 2000, p. 178; **Dwight D. Eisenhower:** Address of September 24, 1957 from *Vital Speeches,* vol. 24, October 15, 1957, pp. 11–12, quoted in Bailey, pp. 465–466; **John Lewis:** Morrison, Joan and Robert K. Morrison. *From Camelot to Kent State: The Sixties Experience in the Words of Those Who Lived It.* Times Books, 1987, pp. 25–26; **W.E.B. DuBois:** Aptheker, Herbert, ed. *Pamphlets and Leaflets* by W.E.B. DuBois. Kraus-Thomason Organization Limited, 1986, p. 116; **Southern Christian Leadership Conference:** Sitkoff, p. 65; **SCLC leaflet:** Sitkoff, p. 59; **Todd Gitlin:** *The Sixties: Years of Hope, Days of Rage.* Bantam Books, 1987, pp. 148–149; **John Lewis:** Hampton, Henry, et al. *Voices of Freedom: An Oral History of the Civil Rights Movement from the 1950's Through the 1980's.* Bantam Books, 1990, p. 58; **James Farmer:** Hampton, p. 78; **James Meredith:** "I'll Know Victory or Defeat," *The Saturday Evening Post,* November 10, 1962, p. 17, quoted in Katz, William Loren. *Eyewitness: The Negro in American History,* 3rd ed. David S. Lake Publishers, 1974, pp. 496–497; **Martin Luther King, Jr.:** "Letter From Birmingham Jail." *Essay Series.* A. J. Muste Memorial Institute, p. 18; **John F. Kennedy:** *Radio and Television Report to the American People on Civil Rights,* June 11, 1963; **Bob Dylan:** *Blowin' In The Wind* by Bob Dylan. Copyright © 1962 (Renewed 1990) Special Rider Music (SESAC); **Martin Luther King, Jr.:** "I Have a Dream." Speech in Washington, D.C., August 1963, quoted in Winkler, Allan M. *The Recent Past: Readings on America Since World War II.* Harper and Row, 1989, p. 275; **Fannie Lou Hamer:** Harley, Sharon, et al. *The African American Experience: A History. Globe Book Company,* 1992, p. 336; **Malcolm X:** *The Autobiography of Malcolm X.* Ballantine Books, 1990, pp. 245–246; **Stokely Carmichael:** Nash, Gary B., et al., eds. *The American People.* Harper and Row, 1986, p. 1001; **Martin Luther King, Jr.:** Kaiser, Charles. *1968 in America: Music, Politics, Chaos, Counterculture, and the Shaping of a Generation.* Weidenfeld and Nicolson, 1988, p. 144; **Barbara Jordan:** Harley, et al., p. 343.

Chapter 29 John F. Kennedy's Inaugural Address: Commager, Henry Steele, ed. *Documents of American History,* 8th ed. Appleton-Century-Crofts, 1968, pp. 668–670; **Kennedy speech at Rice University:** Swenson, Lloyd S., James M. Grimwood, and Charles C. Alexander. *This New Ocean, A History of Project Mercury.* NASA, 1966, frontispiece and p. 470; **Lyndon Johnson:** "Address Before a Joint Session of Congress, November 27, 1963." National Archives and Records Administration, The Lyndon B. Johnson Library and Museum, published online at www.lbjlib.utexas.edu; **John F. Kennedy's Inaugural Address:** Commager, pp. 668–670; **Senator J. William Fulbright:** Schlesinger, Arthur M. *A Thousand Days: John F. Kennedy in the White House.* Houghton Mifflin, 1965, p. 251; **Kennedy:** "Radio and Television Report to the American People on the Soviet Arms Buildup in Cuba, October 22, 1962." John Fitzgerald Kennedy Library, published online at www.jfklibrary.org.

Chapter 30 Helen Reddy: *I Am Woman* by Helen Reddy & Ray Burton. Copyright © 1971 Buggerlugs Music c/o Irving Music (BMI) and Irving Music (BMI).; **Phyllis Schlafly:** Nash, Gary B. *The American People: Creating a Nation and a Society.* Harper and Row, 1986, p. 1008; **César Chávez:** *Autobiography of La Causa.* W. W. Norton, 1975, p. 293; **Onondaga Chief Oren Lyons:** *Voices from Wounded Knee: The People Are Standing Up.* Akwesasne Notes, 1974, p. 96; **Tom Law:** Makower, Joel. *Woodstock: The Oral History.* Doubleday, 1989, p. 333; **Rachel Carson:** *Silent Spring.* Houghton Mifflin, 1962, pp. 2–3; **Rachel Carson:** *Silent Spring.* p. 6; **Lyndon Johnson:** Archer, Jules, *The Incredible Sixties: The Stormy Years That Changed America.* Harcourt Brace Jovanovich, 1986, p. 172; **Ralph Nader:** *Unsafe at Any Speed: The Designed-in Dangers of the American Automobile.* Grossman Publishers, 1972, preface.

Chapter 31 Dwight Eisenhower: Press conference of April 7, 1954. *The Columbia World of Quotations.* Columbia University Press, 1996, no. 18606. **Robert McNamara:** Shapley, Deborah. *Promise and Power: The Life and Times of Robert McNamara.* Little, Brown and Company, 1993, p. 263; **Lyndon B. Johnson:** Kearns, Doris. *Lyndon Johnson and the American Dream.* Harper and Row, 1976, p. 316; **James Webb:** "Heroes of the Vietnam Generation," *The American Enterprise,* September 2000, p. 22; **Letter home from an American soldier:** Edelman, Bernard, ed. *Dear America: Letters Home from Vietnam.* New York Veterans Memorial Commission; **Le Thanh:** Chanoff, David, and Van Toai Doan. *Portrait of the Enemy.* Random House, 1986, pp. 62–63; **Vietnamese peasant:** Trullinger, James Walker, Jr. *Village at War: An Account of Revolution in Vietnam.* Longman, 1980, p. 118. **Private Paul Meadlo:** *The New York Times,* November 25, 1969, p. 16; **Dean Rusk:** *Vietnam: A Television History: The Tet Offensive (1968),* transcript. www.pbs. org; **John McNaughton:** Karnow, Stanley, *Vietnam: A History.* Viking, 1983, p. 479; **Port Huron Statement:** Hayden, Tom. *Students for a Democratic Society.* Quoted in Winkler, Allan. *The Recent Past: Readings on America Since World War II.* Harper and Row, 1989, pp. 218–219; **Robert F. Kennedy:** Holland, Gini, *A Cultural History of the United States Through the Decades: The 1960s.* Lucent Books, 1999, p. 54; **Lyndon Johnson:** King, Larry L. "LBJ and Vietnam" from *A Sense of History: The Best Writing from the Pages of American Heritage.* American Heritage/Houghton Mifflin Company, 1985, p. 801; **Theodore H. White:** *The Making of the President 1968.* Atheneum, 1969, p. 298; **Richard Nixon:** "Nixon's 'Silent Majority' speech," *Vietnam War History, Speeches, Commentary.* www.geocities.com; **Richard Nixon:** Address to the Nation on the Situation in Southeast Asia. April 30, 1970.

Chapter 32 Richard Nixon: Wicker, Tom. *One of Us: Richard Nixon and the American Dream.* Random House, 1991, p. 9; **Richard Nixon's First Inaugural Address:** *Inaugural Addresses of the Presidents of the United States.* Washington, D.C.: U.S. G.P.O.: for sale by the Supt. of Docs., U.S. G.P.O., 1989; Bartleby.com, 2001. www.bartleby.com/124/. [November 6, 2001]; **Henry Kissinger:** *The White House Years.* Little, Brown and Company, 1979, p. 45; **Richard Nixon, report to Congress, 1970:** *The Memoirs of Richard Nixon.* Grosset & Dunlap, 1978, p. 545; **Richard Nixon:** *Public Papers of the Presidents of the United States: Richard Nixon,* p. 320; **Theodore H. White:** *Breach of Faith.* Atheneum Publishers, Reader's Digest Press, 1975, p. 322; **John J. Sirica:** Bernstein, Carl, and Bob Woodward. *All the President's Men.* Warner Paperback Books, 1975, p. 268; **M. Caldwell Butler:** Burns, James MacGregor. *The Crosswinds of Freedom.* Alfred A. Knopf, 1989, p. 507; **Gerald R. Ford:** *A Time to Heal.* Harper and Row, 1979, pp. 124–125; **Gerald R. Ford:** *A Time to Heal,* pp. 177–178; **Jerald F. terHorst:** P. Goldman, et al. "How Good a President?" October 18, 1976, p. 31; **Jimmy Carter's Inaugural Address:** *Inaugural Addresses of the Presidents of the United States.* Washington, D.C.: U.S. G.P.O.: for sale by the Supt. of Docs., U.S. G.P.O., 1989; Bartleby.com, 2001. www.bartleby.com/124/. [November 6, 2002]; **Cyrus Vance:** *Hard Choices: Critical Years in America's Foreign Policy.* Simon and Schuster, 1983, pp. 228–229; **Kathryn Koob:** *Guest of the Revolution.* Thomas Nelson Publishers, 1982, p. 73.

Chapter 33 Richard Nixon: Cannon, Lou. *Role of a Lifetime.* Simon & Schuster, 1991, p. 71; **Ronald Reagan:** Willis, Henry. "Reagan Rejects Debate With Carter." *Eugene Register-Guard,* September 26, 1980, p. 7; **Ronald Reagan:** *Speaking My Mind.* Simon & Schuster, 1989. p. 64; **Ronald Reagan:** "Putting America Back to Work," January 20, 1981. *Vital Speeches of the Day,* Vol. XLVII, No. 9, February 15, 1981; **Kevin Phillips:** "Reagan's America: A Capital Offense." *The New York Times Magazine,* June 24, 1990; **George Bush:** "Open Letter to College Students on the Persian Gulf Crisis," January 9, 1991.

Chapter 34 Bill Clinton's First Inaugural Address: *The New York Times,* January 22, 1993, p. A13.

SOURCE READINGS ACKNOWLEDGMENTS/LITERATURE

Unit 1 Of Plymouth Plantation, 1640–1647: From *Of Plymouth Plantation,*1640–1647 by William Bradford. Ed. Samuel Eliot Morison. New York: Knopf, 1952. **Unit 2 April Morning:** From *April Morning* by Howard Fast. Copyright ©1961 by Howard Fast. Copyright renewed 1989. **Unit 3 Incidents in the Life of a Slave Girl:** Hariet Ann Jacobs, *Incidents in the Live of a Slave Girl: Written by Herself.* (Cambridge, MA: Harvard University Press, 1987). **Unit 4 Slavery in Massachusetts:** Henry David Thoreau. From *The Norton Anthology of American Literature,* Second Edition, Vol. 1. Ed. Nina Baym, et al. New York: W.W. Norton and Company, 1985. **Unit 5 Hungry Hearts:** Anzia Yezierska. Permission granted by Ayer Company Publishers. **Unit 6 A Farewell to Arms:** Ernest Hemingway. New York: Charles Scribner's Sons, 1957. **Unit 7 Growing Up:** From *Growing Up,* by Russell Baker. Copyright © 1982 by Russell Baker. **Unit 8 Night:** Excerpt from NIGHT by Eli Wiesel, translated by Stella Rodway. Copyright © by MacGibbon & Kee. Copyright renewed © 1988 by the Collins Publishers Group. **Unit 9 "Letter from Birmingham Jail":** Excerpt from *Letter from Birmingham Jail* from WHY WE CAN'T WAIT by Martin Luther King, Jr. Copyright © 1963 Martin Luther King, Jr. Copyright renewed 1991 by Coretta Scott King. Reprinted by arrangement with The Heirs to the Estate of Martin Luther King, Jr. c/o Writer's House, Inc. as agent for the proprietor. **Unit 10 "Straw Into Gold: The Metamorphosis of the Everyday":** Excerpt from *Straw Into Gold: The Metamorphosis of the Everyday* by Sandra Cisneros. Copyright © 1987 by Sandra Cisneros. Reprinted by permission of Susan Bergholz Literary Services, New York. All rights reserved.

SOURCE READINGS ACKNOWLEDGMENTS/DOCUMENTS

The Iroquois Constitution: by Dekanawidah. Published online at The University of Oklahoma Law Center www.law.ou.edu/hist/iroquois.html; **The Mayflower Compact:** Published online at The University of Oklahoma Law Center www.law.ou.edu/hist/mayflow.html; **An Act for the Gradual Abolition of Slavery:** Pennsylvania,1780. Published online at The Avalon Project at the Yale Law School www.yale.edu/lawweb/avalon/states/statutes/pennst01.htm. Spelling updated.; **President Wilson's Address to Congress:** April 2, 1917. Published online at The World War I Document Archive www.lib.byu.edu/~rdh/wwi/1917/wilswarm.html; **The Universal Declaration of Human Rights:** The United Nations. Published online at The United Nations www.un.org/Overview/rights.html; **President Eisenhower's Farewell Address to the Nation:** January 17, 1961. Published online at University of Houston History Department http://vi.uh.edu/pages/buzzmat/ikefarewell.htm; **Mikhail Gorbachev's Address to the Forty-Third UN General Assembly Session:** December 7, 1988. Published online at CNN Interactive www.cnn.com/SPECIALS/cold.war/episodes/23/documents/gorbachev/

Note: Every effort has been made to locate the copyright owner of material used in this textbook. Omissions brought to our attention will be corrected in subsequent editions.